The Red Book
2014-15

Consultant Editors

Bill Dodwell LLB, LLM, CTA (Fellow), ACA
Kevin Prosser QC

Wolters Kluwer (UK) Limited
145 London Road
Kingston-upon-Thames
Surrey
KT2 6SR
Telephone: +44 (0) 844 561 8166
Fax: +44 (0) 208 547 2638
Email: cch@wolterskluwer.co.uk
Website: www.cch.co.uk

Disclaimer

This publication is sold with the understanding that neither the publisher nor the authors, with regard to this publication, are engaged in rendering legal or professional services. The material contained in this publication neither purports, nor is intended to be, advice on any particular matter.

Although this publication incorporates a considerable degree of standardisation, subjective judgment by the user, based on individual circumstances, is indispensable. This publication is an "aid" and cannot be expected to replace such judgment.

Neither the publisher nor the authors can accept any responsibility or liability to any person, whether a purchaser of this publication or not, in respect of anything done or omitted to be done by any such person in reliance, whether sole or partial, upon the whole or any part of the contents of this publication.

Legislative and other material

While copyright in all statutory and other materials resides in the Crown or other relevant body, copyright in the remaining material in this publication is vested in the publisher.

The publisher advises that any statutory or other materials issued by the Crown or other relevant bodies and reproduced and quoted in this publication are not the authorised official versions of those statutory or other materials. In the preparation, however, the greatest care has been taken to ensure exact conformity with the law as enacted or other material as issued.

Crown copyright legislation is reproduced under the terms of Crown Copyright Policy Guidance issued by HMSO. Other Crown copyright material is reproduced with the permission of the controller of HMSO. European Communities Copyright material is reproduced with permission.

Telephone Helpline Disclaimer Notice

Where purchasers of this publication also have access to any Telephone Helpline Service operated by Wolters Kluwer (UK), then Wolters Kluwer's total liability to contract, tort (including negligence, or breach of statutory duty) misrepresentation, restitution or otherwise with respect to any claim arising out of its acts or alleged omissions in the provision of the Helpline Service shall be limited to the yearly subscription fee paid by the Claimant.

British Library Cataloguing-in-Publication Data.

A catalogue record for this book is available from the British Library.

Typeset by Innodata Inc., India

Printed and bound in Spain by Rotabook, S.L.

v

The Red Book

Senior Technical Editor

PAUL ROBBINS BA(Hons), ACA, CTA

Technical Editors

SARAH ARNOLD ACA, CTA
STEPHEN KESBY FCA, CTA, AIIT

Foreword

We wrote last year about the phenomenon of taxation in the news – at a level that none of us can recall in earlier decades. 2014 is the year when governments globally start to deliver changes to the international tax system to restore credibility in some aspects.

In October 2014, 44 countries are set to ratify the Common Reporting Standard, which is intended to provide for the automatic exchange of information globally. The standard has been designed by the OECD and builds on concepts developed by the United States' FATCA regime. The aim of the standard is to limit the scope for tax evasion by individuals, by requiring that financial institutions pass information about the assets and income of individual account holders to their national tax authority, which will then pass the information to the national tax authority of the country where the individual is resident. The Common Reporting Standard takes effect in 2016 and the first information will be delivered in 2017. A number of well-known jurisdictions used by international investors have indicated they will sign up – including Switzerland, Singapore and the UK's Crown Dependencies.

The pioneer in automatic information exchange was the EU's Savings Directive but it was of limited effect and efforts to widen its impact were blocked for several years by Luxembourg and Austria. Just as a new Directive is finally agreed to take effect from 2016, the EU's home-grown plan looks to be superseded by the new global standard. The impetus for change came from the United States, which had the economic muscle to force global financial institutions to sign up for its FATCA regime, which requires that information be provided to the US Internal Revenue Service about assets owned and income earned by US citizens. The penalty for failing to sign up is that a 30 per cent withholding tax would be applied by the US to income earned by funds invested in the US. US FATCA was in turn picked up by the UK which requested that its Crown Dependencies make similar disclosures to the UK – and in due course to other countries. The UK has worked with France, Germany, Italy and Spain to extend the FATCA-based principles into Europe and the OECD. The global standard has similar reporting requirements to the US standard, making it easier for financial institutions to adopt.

The era when individuals could invest overseas secure in the knowledge that their government and tax authority would not find out about it is coming to an end.

Alongside the Common Reporting Standard sits the OECD's Mutual Assistance Convention – now signed by 65 countries.

The first output of the OECD's Base Erosion and Profit Shifting project will arrive in September 2014, with seven papers to be delivered to the G20 Finance Ministers at their meeting. The output from the project is scheduled to be delivered in three instalments – and it's becoming clear that there are considerable inter-dependencies between the individual actions. Given that the effectiveness of the changes will depend on political negotiation and ultimate agreement, potentially the outcome may need to await the end of the project. Final papers this year will cover Treaty Abuse; Hybrid Mismatches and Transfer Pricing Documentation, including the country-by-country reporting template. Additionally the report from the Digital Taskforce will be presented to the G20. At the time of writing, drafts are available which suggest that there is no appetite amongst the G20 and OECD to devise a wholly new taxation regime for digital services. Instead, the short-term focus will be on making changes to the definition of taxable presence by lowering the threshold and also by revising the rules for allocating profits from intangible assets. Whether these measures alone will be sufficient to satisfy political demand for more effective taxation of digital services will no doubt be assessed in several years' time.

Additionally three interim papers will be presented to the G20. One will cover Intangibles and will form part of a new chapter 6 to be added to the OECD's Transfer Pricing guidelines. This is a first instalment, with further work due to be delivered by September 2015. The direction of travel is to enhance the link between people-based activities and profits. Legal rights are vital, but there is concern that too much weight has historically been given to the legal ownership of inherently mobile assets – which can lead to substantial profits being allocated to locations with little substance in the form of people.

The second interim report will cover the area of harmful tax practices. The OECD produced in 1998 a definition of harmful practices and will report on its review of member country regimes. This is an issue currently being hotly debated within the European Union, in relation to incentive regimes for intangible assets, including patent boxes. A harmful regime is typically something that aims to attract income without people-based activities, or is one which is targeted at non-residents. There is a dispute over how to measure the income and activities in relation to IP or patent boxes. Some countries argue that this should be determined by transfer pricing principles; others are keener on a so-called nexus approach which seeks to identify the activities carried on by the company. The main difference between the two is that the transfer pricing method allows for sub-contracting of research and development, which is very common within a group as well as to third parties. Few multinationals locate all their R&D activities in a single location. This is a debate where a resolution may be hard to achieve.

The third report will look at the feasibility of a multilateral instrument to implement BEPS measures. It is clear that changes to the world's 3,000 double taxation treaties will require something better than bilateral negotiation. It is also likely that implementing coordinated domestic measures will need a binding international agreement.

Back in the UK, the past year has seen considerable focus on tax avoidance. A number of cases have been decided by the Court of Appeal and lower Tribunals, typically in relation to marketed schemes undertaken by many individuals, or occasionally by several groups of companies. HM Revenue & Customs have a very high success rate; in fact it's hard to think of a single case where the taxpayer has had an outright victory, except for *UBS AG v R & C Commrs* [2013] BTC 1,525 which concerned a scheme to pay bankers' bonuses by means of shares in a SPV structured to fall within the concept of restricted securities. In some cases, the outcome has been an *increase* in taxation payable by a group of companies, or an individual, compared to the amount that would have been paid in the absence of undertaking the scheme. Many will be shocked that such an outcome could be possible – not least because the principle embedded in the General Anti-Abuse Rule is that a disallowed scheme should be neutralised rather than made penal.

HMRC are under considerable pressure to bring the tens of thousands of open cases to resolution and this has led to some controversial plans for accelerated payments of tax included in *Finance Act* 2014. HMRC say that they are faced with large numbers of taxpayers who simply fail to settle cases even though HMRC have won an equivalent case before the First-tier, or higher, Tribunal. Accordingly "follower" penalties have been introduced which impose a penalty on a taxpayer who does not amend his return in line with a judgment in an equivalent case. The controversy concerns whether or not a case is indeed identical to one already decided and the lack of an obvious appeal right. Late amendments provided an appeal right (to the First Tier Tribunal) but importantly provided a reasonableness test. This should mean that in practice follower notices are more likely to be limited to those undertaking identical schemes to ones which have been the subject of a Tribunal decision.

The related – but much more financially significant – change is that HMRC may start issuing accelerated payment notices to pay tax in cases where a follower notice has been issued, or where a taxpayer has undertaken arrangements where a scheme reference number has been issued under the tax disclosure rules. Exchequer Secretary David Gauke said that the government's intention is to remove the cash-flow advantage of undertaking a tax scheme. If the taxpayer ultimately wins the case, either by agreement with HMRC or following litigation, then naturally the tax payment would be refunded with the usual interest. This power to require payment does not carry an appeal right, which seems unjust in principle. HMRC have naturally declared that they will operate the power carefully and take account of representations on the calculations. It may be that some will seek to challenge HMRC's judgments through judicial review.

The final part of the package is a new right for HMRC to take money from a taxpayer's bank account without consent and without a court order. The Treasury Select Committee challenged this new power, noting in their Budget 2014 Report "The proposal to grant HMRC the power to recover money directly from taxpayers' bank accounts is of considerable concern to the Committee." The power requires that HMRC leave at least £5,000 in the taxpayer's bank account and that it has tried on a number of occasions to contact the taxpayer to request payment. The controversy perhaps ensures that great care will be used in administering this power but it remains a matter of concern that there should be no judicial oversight.

Yet again the Finance Act is a substantial piece of legislation, adding 600 pages to the UK's already over-long legislation. This one contains considerable anti-avoidance measures, including wide-ranging new rules which seek to impose PAYE where employees are provided through employment intermediaries – both offshore and onshore. The measures originally announced have been improved by consultation but remain complex to administer. The measures are estimated to bring in hundreds of millions of pounds in additional tax, no doubt through countering failure to report income.

Partnerships come in for some heavily criticised changes. The House of Lords Economic Affairs Finance Bill sub-committee heard from a wide range of witnesses and urged the government to defer the changes. Unfortunately the revenue had already been built into the Red Book and so the plans proceeded regardless. There are two targets: salaried partners in LLPs who until April 2014 could be treated as self-employed, thus benefitting from a deferral in paying income tax and the absence of employer's National Insurance contributions. The Act provides for the three factors drawn from case law to be used to determine whether or not an individual should be treated as an equity partner, or as an employee. The factors are guaranteed income; significant influence over the partnership and partnership capital. The difficulty is that the law now provides for a bright-line statutory formula, instead of the application of judgment. The result has proved to be that too many salaried partners (and some true equity partners whose remuneration model does not meet the statutory scheme) have been forced to raise unnecessary partnership capital, to make sure that they passed at least one of the three tests. Of course a bright line test is easier to apply, as we see for example with the new test of statutory residence. However, this test does not work well. The second aspect of the rules is intended to counter the use of a company in a partnership to allow some part of partnership profit to be taxed at the lower corporate rate.

However, alongside the revenue raisers are some important new policy measures. The Act introduces from 2015 the married couples' transferable allowance. The allowance offers a married couple a tax saving of up to £200 per annum. The allowance is only given where neither of the couple is a higher or additional rate taxpayer. It does come with a cliff edge: the theoretical extra pound of income that tips an individual into the higher rate means that no part of the transferable allowance may be claimed. Interestingly, analysis from the OECD shows that the most disadvantaged group of taxpayers in the UK is the married couple, with a single earner. This new allowance slightly redresses that balance.

The biggest surprise in the Finance Act is the new approach to defined contribution pensions. As the Treasury Committee noted, Budget secrecy was vital as the announcement that from 2015 pensioners will no longer need to use their pension fund to purchase an annuity was market sensitive. The share prices of annuity providers dropped, when investors appreciated that the move could reduce overall profitability of the companies. The move applies only to defined contribution schemes, since it is thought too complex to hand over a fund to a potential pensioner from a defined benefit fund. Alongside the new freedom will be a lower tax rate on monies withdrawn from a pension fund; it drops to 40 per cent from the previously penal 55 per cent. *Finance Act* 2014 contains measures allowing potential pensioners to defer taking an annuity until the full reforms are introduced in 2015. It also allows those with low-value pension rights to take the fund as a lump sum.

Another rabbit from the Chancellor's proverbial hat turned out to be a short-term extension of the annual investment allowance. The annual allowance increases to £250,000 per group of companies until December 2015 – at the huge cost of £1.8 billion. The actual number of businesses which are expected to have annual expenditure on plant and machinery of between £100–£250,000 is relatively small but the total cost of the measure is high since it applies to most businesses. Yet again there is a trap for those spending their money at the end of the period, where badly drafted rules can mean that the actual allowance is much lower than the £250,000 expected. It's worth consulting CCH commentaries and the websites of professional bodies for more details of the trap.

There's also a new relief for individuals who invest money in qualifying social enterprises. The new scheme is based on the over-technical conditions of the enterprise investment scheme, where there have been too many cases of investors and companies meeting the spirit of the relief but being caught out by its technicality. A social investor can get 30 per cent tax relief on a qualifying investment, which may be shares or loans to the enterprise. It remains to be seen whether small, relatively unsophisticated social enterprises can manage to navigate their way through the law.

The consulting editors would, as usual, like to thank the CCH team for their hard work in putting together this ever more complex publication in such a short time. We anticipate a different approach next year, when the General Election will no doubt mean that we have two, shorter, Finance Acts.

Bill Dodwell LLB, LLM, CTA (Fellow), ACA
Kevin Prosser QC

July 2014

July 2014

Publisher's Note

Volume 1A contains the text of the *Taxes Management Act* 1970, the *Income and Corporation Taxes Act* 1988, the *Taxation of Chargeable Gains Act* 1992 and the *Capital Allowances Act* 2001. It also contains all other significant Acts affecting the imposition and collection of income tax, corporation tax and capital gains tax, up to and including the *Transport Act* 2000. Enactments are presented in chronological order.

Volume 1B includes the *Income Tax (Earnings and Pensions) Act* 2003, the *Income Tax (Trading and Other Income) Act* 2005, the *Commissioners for Revenue and Customs Act* 2005 and the *Income Tax Act* 2007. It also contains all other significant Acts relating to income tax, corporation tax and capital gains tax up to and including the *Income Tax Act* 2007, presented in chronological order.

Volume 1C includes the *Tribunals, Courts and Enforcement Act* 2007, the *Corporation Tax Act* 2009, the *Corporation Tax Act* 2010 and the *Taxation (International and Other Provisions) Act* 2010. It also contains all other significant Acts relating to income tax, corporation tax and capital gains tax up to and including the *Taxation (International and Other Provisions) Act* 2010, presented in chronological order.

Volume 1D includes contains all significant Acts relating to income tax, corporation tax and capital gains tax from the *Finance Act* 2010 to the *Finance Act* 2014, presented in chronological order.

Volume 1E includes statutory instruments relevant to the taxes covered in Volumes 1A, 1B, 1C and 1D.

Volume 1F includes EC directives, HMRC directions, extra-statutory concessions, statements of practice, HMRC Briefs and extensive *Tax Bulletin* extracts relevant to the taxes covered in Volumes 1A, 1B, 1C and 1D.

Also in Volume 1F, there is a selection of important HMRC press releases as well as selected extracts from ICAEW technical releases and selected releases from the Chartered Institute of Taxation. The volume also includes extracts from the Treasury General Consents, the Series 7 Prospectus for Certificates of Tax Deposit and other such documents, and lists of clearance procedures. Selected Accounting Standards are also included.

The Index volume covers material in Volumes 1A, 1B, 1C, 1D, 1E and 1F. It contains the comprehensive topic index, lists of definitions and meanings and a consolidated destination table where pre-consolidation enactments can now be traced in the *Income and Corporation Taxes Act* 1988, the *Taxation of Chargeable Gains Act* 1992, the *Capital Allowances Act* 2001, the *Income Tax (Earnings and Pensions) Act* 2003, the *Income Tax (Trading and Other Income) Act* 2005, the *Income Tax Act* 2007, the *Corporation Tax Act* 2009, the *Corporation Tax Act* 2010 and the *Taxation (International and Other Provisions) Act* 2010. The table also includes destinations for PAYE and sub-contractor regulations following the consolidations in the *Income Tax (Sub-contractors in the Construction Industry) Regulations* 1993 (SI 1993/743) and the *Income Tax (Employments) Regulations* 2003 (SI 2003/2682).

The Index volume also includes the "Stop Press" section which contains material that was issued too late to go in its normal location. In the main, the items normally included here are statutory instruments, some of which have been formally laid, but some of which may be the latest draft available at the time of going to press. These drafts have been included because, when laid, they will form an important part of the 2014–15 legislative picture. Readers should, however, be aware that they are potentially subject to amendment.

Volume 1G includes all relevant material on National Insurance contributions, tax credits, inheritance tax and petroleum revenue tax.

Volume 1H includes all relevant material on stamp taxes.

Volume 2 includes all relevant material on value added tax.

The legislation is reproduced so as to show those provisions which are in force in 2014–15. The Acts have been abridged by the omission of the full text of provisions which either amend earlier enactments (unless the amendment is prospective) or have been repealed. However, the *Finance Act* 2014 appears in full text in Volume 1D, in so far as it relates to income tax, corporation tax and capital gains tax, and in the relevant parts of Volume 1G and in Volumes 1H and 2 for the taxes dealt with in those volumes.

Prospective changes for which no effective date in 2014–15 has been announced at the time of going to press, or where the effective date has been announced but is after 2014–15, are noted under the provisions to be amended or in the case of, for example, entirely new sections, at the place where they will appear when they enter into force, with reference made to the place where the text of the changes can be found. Prospective changes which enter into force during 2014–15 are made to the provisions amended, substituted, etc. with a "History" note setting out the "former" provisions in smaller type beneath. Where prospective legislation is amended before it takes effect it is shown in amended form at the place where it is introduced, but the "target" legislation to be amended carries only a brief description of the amendment.

Where, because of subsequent amendments, provisions do not appear as originally enacted, the former wording is reproduced only where it is either in force in 2014–15 or likely to be of practical relevance to 2014–15 liabilities. Details of such amendments and, where appropriate, former wording in smaller type appear as "History" notes beneath the amended provisions. In some cases whole sections are involved and these appear in smaller type in their entirety.

Derivation notes under provisions of the *Income and Corporation Taxes Act* 1988, the *Taxation of Chargeable Gains Act* 1992, the *Capital Allowances Act* 2001, the *Income Tax (Earnings and Pensions) Act* 2003, the *Income Tax (Trading and Other Income) Act* 2005, the *Income Tax Act* 2007, the *Corporation Tax Act* 2009, the *Corporation Tax Act* 2010, and the *Taxation (International and Other Provisions) Act* 2010 indicate the former enactments.

Extensive cross references appear throughout, at the end of each section or paragraph, both to other provisions of the Taxes Acts and to extraneous legislation. Cross references under a section, paragraph, etc. mainly refer to provisions which explicitly mention that section, paragraph, etc. The order of cross references is first to list those involving the Act in point, then those involving the *Income and Corporation Taxes Act* 1988, then those involving other Taxes Acts in chronological order, and then those involving extraneous Acts, again in chronological order. Effective, or implicit, cross references are mentioned by way of editorial note (see below).

Relevant statutory instruments, extra-statutory concessions, statements of practice, *Tax Bulletin* decisions and interpretations (these are all reproduced) are noted. Other related materials (*Tax Bulletin* articles and special editions, HMRC press releases and booklets, releases from accountancy bodies and the Law Society, etc.) which affect particular provisions are also noted even if they are not reproduced. European material related to the provision in question is also noted, and editorial notes are inserted where additional comment is appropriate.

While Parliamentary materials or their equivalent had in other jurisdictions long been used as an aid to the interpretation of legislative acts, the decision of the House of Lords in *Pepper (HMIT) v Hart and related appeals* [1992] BTC 591 that ministerial statements may be so used in limited circumstances was an innovation in the UK. The cases in which such use can be made of Parliamentary material are at present limited to circumstances where: legislation is ambiguous, obscure or leads to an absurdity, the material relied upon consists of statements by a minister or other promoter of the Bill, and the statements relied upon are clear. A range of annotations covering Parliamentary material are grouped together under the generic heading of "**Hansard Extracts**" in the "Other materials" division. Editorial judgment has been used in selecting some of the more significant of such references, or those with the most widespread application; the coverage of Parliamentary material in the footnotes is by no means exhaustive.

As part of HMRC's response to the Government's code of practice on access to Government information, the HMRC guidance manuals have been made available to the public. The manuals provide HMRC staff with guidance on the interpretation of tax law and the operation of the tax system. References to useful material contained in the manuals appear under the heading "**HMRC manuals**". Editorial judgment has been used in selecting the references.

The publisher advises that the Acts, Regulations and other official material in this publication are not the authorised official versions. However, the greatest care has been taken to ensure exact conformity with the law as enacted and with the text of extra-statutory material. Some changes in printing style have been adopted for convenience and to improve readability. For example, marginal notes appearing in the official statutes have been reproduced in bold type in the first line of the section to which they relate. Many words and phrases have also been reproduced in bold where they are defined in the legislation so that the definitions can be located more easily.

Our role as publisher is not to guess which parts will be of greatest practical interest but rather to present all the legislation and related material accurately and to annotate it helpfully. We always welcome comments and suggestions from our readers and we thank those who have offered constructive thoughts over the past year.

ABBREVIATIONS

The following abbreviations are commonly used throughout this publication.

ACT	advance corporation tax
AEA 1925	Administration of Estates Act 1925
AIM	Alternative Investment Market
AIS	accrued income scheme
AL	aggregates levy
App.	appendix
APR	annual percentage rate
APRT	advance petroleum revenue tax
ARPA 2004	Age-Related Payments Act 2004
art.	article(s)
ATCSA 2001	Anti-Terrorism, Crime and Security Act 2001
ATED	Annual tax on enveloped dwellings
BB	Customs and Excise Business Briefs
BEN	business economic note
BES	business expansion scheme
BN	Budget Notes
BRNAA 2011	Budget Responsibility and National Audit Act 2011
BSA 1986	Building Societies Act 1986
B(S)A 1985	Bankruptcy (Scotland) Act 1985
BTC	British Tax Cases, 1982–current (CCH)
CA 1985	Companies Act 1985
CA 2006	Companies Act 2006
CHA 2011	Charities Act 2011
CAA 1968	Capital Allowances Act 1968
CAA 1990	Capital Allowances Act 1990
CAA 2001	Capital Allowances Act 2001
CCH	CCH Information, a division of Wolters Kluwer (UK) Ltd
CCL	climate change levy
C & E Commrs	Commissioners of Customs and Excise
CED(GR)A 1979	Customs and Excise Duties (General Reliefs) Act 1979
CEMA 1979	Customs and Excise Management Act 1979
CFC	controlled foreign company
CGT	capital gains tax
CGTA 1979	Capital Gains Tax Act 1979
Ch.	Chapter(s) (of a statute/SI etc.)
CIC	close investment-holding company
CIOT	Chartered Institute of Taxation
CJPA 2001	Criminal Justice and Police Act 2001
cl.	clause(s)
col.	column(s)
Commr; Commrs	commissioner; commissioners
Conv.	convention
CPA 1947	Crown Proceedings Act 1947
CRCA 2005	Commissioners for Revenue and Customs Act 2005
CRGA 2010	Constitutional Reform and Governance Act 2010
CRT	composite rate tax
CSPSSA 2000	Child Support, Pensions and Social Security Act 2000
CT	corporation tax
CTA 2009	Corporation Tax Act 2009
CTA 2010	Corporation Tax Act 2010
CTD	certificates of tax deposits
CTFA 2004	Child Trust Funds Act 2004
CTT	capital transfer tax

CTTA 1984	Capital Transfer Tax Act 1984
DDA(S)A 2002	Debt Arrangement and Attachment (Scotland) Act 2002
Dir.	EC directives
DLT	development land tax
DLTA 1976	Development Land Tax Act 1976
DPA 1998	Data Protection Act 1998
DSS	Department of Social Security
DTI	Department of Trade and Industry
EA 2002	Employment Act 2002
EA 2004	Energy Act 2004
EC	European Community/Communities
edn.	edition
EEC	European Economic Community
EEIG	European Economic Interest Grouping
e.g.	(exempli gratia) for example
EIS	enterprise investment scheme
ELPA 2010	Equitable Life (Payments) Act 2010
EMPA 2003	Electricity (Miscellaneous Provisions) Act 2003
ERA 1996	Employee Rights Act 1996
ESC	extra-statutory concession
ESOP	employee stock ownership plan
ESOT	employee share ownership trust
etc.	(et cetera) and so on
et seq.	(et sequens) and the following
EU	European Union
FA	Finance Act
FA 2014	Finance Act 2014
FI 1985	Films Act 1985
FIA 2000	Freedom of Information Act 2000
FII	franked investment income
F(No. 2)A	Finance (No. 2) Act
F(No. 2)A 2010	Finance (No. 2) Act 2010
F(No. 3)A	Finance (No. 3) Act
F(No. 3)A 2010	Finance (No. 3) Act 2010
FSMA 2000	Financial Services and Markets Act 2000
FYA	first-year allowance
GAAP	generally accepted accounting practice
Grp.	Group (VAT legislation)
HA 1988	Housing Act 1988
HM	Her Majesty
HMIT	Her Majesty's Inspector of Taxes
HMRC	HM Revenue & Customs
HMSO	Her Majesty's Stationery Office
HRA 1998	Human Rights Act 1998
IA	initial allowance
IA 1986	Insolvency Act 1986
ICAEW	Institute of Chartered Accountants in England and Wales
ICAS	Institute of Chartered Accountants of Scotland
ICTA 1970	Income and Corporation Taxes Act 1970
ICTA 1988	Income and Corporation Taxes Act 1988
i.e.	(id est) that is
IHT	inheritance tax
IHTA 1984	Inheritance and Trustee's Power's Act 2014
IHTPA 2014	Inheritance Tax Act 1984
INA 1978	Interpretation Act 1978
IoT	Institute of Taxation
IPT	insurance premium tax
IR Commrs	Commissioners of Inland Revenue

IRDec.	Inland Revenue decision
IRInt.	Inland Revenue interpretation
IRRA 1890	Inland Revenue Regulation Act 1890
IT	income tax
ITA 2007	Income Tax Act 2007
ITEPA 2003	Income Tax (Earnings and Pensions) Act 2003
ITTOIA 2005	Income Tax (Trading and Other Income) Act 2005
LA 2011	Localism Act 2011
LAUTRO	Life Assurance and Unit Trust Regulatory Organisation
LBTTSA 2013	Land and Buildings Transaction Tax (Scotland) Act 2013
LFT	landfill tax
LIFFE	London International Financial Futures and Options Exchange
LLPA 2000	Limited Liability Partnerships Act 2000
LPA 1907	Limited Partnerships Act 1907
LPA 1925	Law of Property Act 1925
LRRA 2006	Legislative and Regulatory Reform Act 2006
LSG	Law Society Gazette
MCT	mainstream corporation tax
MIRAS	mortgage interest relief at source
Misc.	miscellaneous items (denoted by number)
NB	(nota bene) note well
NHA 1980	National Heritage Act 1980
NI	Northern Ireland
NIC	National Insurance contributions
NICA 2002	National Insurance Contributions Act 2002
NICA 2004	National Insurance Contributions and Statutory Payments Act 2004
NICA 2006	National Insurance Contributions Act 2006
NICA 2008	National Insurance Contributions Act 2008
NICA 2014	National Insurance Contributions Act 2014
NICSPA 2004	National Insurance Contributions and Statutory Payments Act 2004
NR	Customs and Excise News Releases
O.	Order(s)
OJ	Official Journal of the European Communities
OJ "L" series	Official Journal of the European Communities, Legislation Series (cited by year, issue number and page, for example OJ 1989 L1/1 is the first page of the first issue of the legislation series of the Official Journal for 1989)
OPB	Occupational Pensions Board
Ors	others
OTA 1975	Oil Taxation Act 1975
OTA 1983	Oil Taxation Act 1983
p.; pp.	page; pages
PA 2004	Pensions Act 2004
PA 2007	Pensions Act 2007
PA 2011	Pensions Act 2011
PA 2014	Pensions Act 2014
PAA 2009	Perpetuities and Accumulations Act 2009
p.a.	per annum (each year)
PACE 1994	Police and Criminal Evidence Act 1994
para.	paragraph(s)
PAYE	pay as you earn
PCA 2002	Proceeds of Crime Act 2002
PCTA 1968	Provisional Collection of Taxes Act 1968
PEP	personal equity plan
PET	potentially exempt transfer
PLDA 1808	Probate and Legacy Duties Act 1808
PN	Customs and Excise Press Notices
PPS	personal pension scheme

PR	press release(s)
PRP	profit-related pay
PRT	petroleum revenue tax
PRTA 1980	Petroleum Revenue Tax Act 1980
PSA 1993	Pension Schemes Act 1993
PSA 2011	Postal Services Act 2011
PSO	Pensions Schemes Office
Pt.	Part(s)
QCB	qualifying corporate bond
r.	rule(s)
RA 1898	Revenue Act 1898 and similarly coded for appropriate subsequent years
RA 2005	Railways Act 2005
R&C Commrs	Revenue and Customs Commissioners
RDDA 1998	Regional Development Agencies Act 1998
reg.	regulations
Regulations	EC Regulations
RPI	retail prices index
RSC	Rules of the Supreme Court 1965
s.	section(s)
SA 1891	Stamp Act 1891
SAYE	save as you earn
SCA 1998	Scotland Act 1998
SCA 2012	Scotland Act 2012
SCA 1981	Supreme Court Act 1981
SCDA 2012	Small Charitable Donations Act 2012
Sch.	Schedule(s)
SDMA 1891	Stamp Duty Management Act 1891
SDLT	stamp duty land tax
SDLTCN	Stamp Duty Land Tax Customer Newsletter
SDRT	stamp duty reserve tax
SD(TP)A 1992	Stamp Duty (Temporary Provisions) Act 1992
SERPS	state earnings-related pension scheme
SFO	Superannuation Funds Office
SI	statutory instrument
SMP	statutory maternity pay
SOCN	Stamp Office Customer Newsletter
SOCPA 2005	Serious Organised Crime and Police Act 2005
SP	Statement of practice
SPCA 2002	State Pension Credit Act 2002
SRO	self-regulating organisation
SR & O	statutory rules and orders
SSA 1975	Social Security Act 1975
SSA 1980	Social Security Act 1980
SSA 1986	Social Security Act 1986
SSA 1989	Social Security Act 1989
SSA 1998	Social Security Act 1998
SSAA 1992	Social Security Administration Act 1992
SSAP	Statement of Standard Accounting Practice
SSCBA 1992	Social Security Contributions and Benefits Act 1992
SS(CP)A 1992	Social Security (Consequential Provisions) Act 1992
SS(TF)A 1999	Social Security Contributions (Transfer of Functions, etc.) Act 1999
SSFA 2001	Social Security Fraud Act 2001
SSHBA 1982	Social Security Housing Benefits Act 1982
SS(MP)A 1977	Social Security (Miscellaneous Provisions) Act 1977
SSP	statutory sick pay
SSPA 1975	Social Security Pensions Act 1975
SSPA 1994	Statutory Sick Pay Act 1994
STA 1963	Stock Transfer Act 1963

STB	Stamp Taxes Bulletin
subcl.	subclause(s)
subpara.	subparagraph(s)
subs.	subsection(s)
TA 2000	Transport Act 2000
TAURUS	Transfer and Automated Registration of Uncertified Stock
TB	Tax Bulletin article
TBSE	Tax Bulletin special edition
TCA 2002	Tax Credits Act 2002
TCIA 2013	Trusts (Capital and Income) Act 2013
TCEA 2007	Tribunals, Courts and Enforcement Act 2007
TCGA 1992	Taxation of Chargeable Gains Act 1992
TERA 2000	Terrorism Act 2000
TESSA	tax-exempt special savings account
TIOPA 2010	Taxation (International and Other Provisions) Act 2010
TMA 1970	Taxes Management Act 1970
TR	technical release
TSA 2014	Tribunals (Scotland) Act 2014
TSBA 1985	Trustee Savings Bank Act 1985
TULR(C)A 1992	Trade Union and Labour Relations (Consolidation) Act 1992
TWDV	tax written-down value
UCITS	Undertakings for Collective Investment in Transferable Securities
UK	United Kingdom
USM	Unlisted Securities Market
VAT	value added tax
VATA 1983	Value Added Tax Act 1983
VATA 1994	Value Added Tax Act 1994
VCT	Venture Capital Trust
vol.	volume(s)
WDA	writing down allowance
WDV	written-down value
WFT	windfall tax
WRA 2012	Welfare Reform Act 2012
WRPA 1999	Welfare Reform and Pensions Act 1999
¶	CCH paragraph

TMA 1970	Taxes Management Act 1970
TR	technical release
TSA 2014	Tribunals (Scotland) Act 2014
TSBA 1985	Trustee Savings Bank Act 1985
TU(LR)(C)A 1992	Trade Union and Labour Relations (Consolidation) Act 1992
TWDV	tax written-down value
UCITS	Undertakings for Collective Investment in Transferable Securities
UK	United Kingdom
USM	Unlisted Securities Market
VAT	value added tax
VATA 1983	Value Added Tax Act 1983
VATA 1994	Value Added Tax Act 1994
VCT	Venture Capital Trust
vol.	volume(s)
WDA	writing down allowance
WDV	writing-down value
WFT	windfall tax
WRA 2012	Welfare Reform Act 2012
WRPA 1999	Welfare Reform and Pensions Act 1999
¶	CCH paragraph

About the Publisher

Wolters Kluwer (UK) Limited is part of the international Wolters Kluwer Group. Wolters Kluwer is the leading publisher specialising in tax, business and law publishing throughout Europe, the US and the Asia Pacific region. The group produces a wide range of information services in different media for the accounting and legal professions and for business.

All Wolters Kluwer (UK) Limited publications are designed to be practical and authoritative reference works and guides and are written by our own highly qualified and experienced editorial team and specialist outside authors.

Wolters Kluwer (UK) Limited publishes information packages including electronic products, loose-leaf reporting services, newsletters and books on UK and European legal topics for distribution world-wide. The UK operation also acts as distributor of the publications of the overseas affiliates.

Wolters Kluwer (UK) Limited

145 London Road

Kingston-upon-Thames

Surrey

KT2 6SR

Telephone: 0844 561 8166

Facsimile: 0208 547 2638

Email: cch@wolterskluwer.co.uk

Website: www.cch.co.uk

About the Consultant Editors

Bill Dodwell graduated from King's College, London, and Queens' College, Cambridge with LL.B and LL.M degrees in law. He became a partner in Deloitte in 2002, after 24 years with Arthur Andersen. He is a Fellow of the Chartered Institute of Taxation and a member of the ICAEW. Bill is Vice President of the CIOT and Chairman of their Technical Committee. He is also a member of the Tax Law Review Committee. Bill leads Deloitte's Tax Policy Group, which is responsible for knowledge, tax training and tax-specific IT applications. The group is responsible for making representations to the OECD, the UK Treasury and tax authorities. He speaks regularly to the media on tax matters. His current and former clients include some of Deloitte's larger clients, both UK companies investing overseas and other multinationals investing into the UK.

Kevin Prosser QC read law at University College, London and St Edmund Hall, Oxford. He was called to the Bar in 1982, and since 1983 has been a member of Pump Court Tax Chambers, specialising in all forms of tax advice and litigation. He has been a QC since 1996, a Recorder since 2000, a Deputy High Court Judge since 2008, and is the current Chairman of the Revenue Bar Association.

Acknowledgement

CCH gratefully acknowledges the endorsement of this publication by the Chartered Institute of Taxation.

THE
CHARTERED
INSTITUTE OF
TAXATION

Acknowledgement

CCH gratefully acknowledges the endorsement of this publication by the Chartered Institute of Taxation.

THE
CHARTERED
INSTITUTE OF
TAXATION

Table of Contents

STATUTORY INSTRUMENTS

Table of Content

> **Note:** For statutory instruments relating to taxes other than income, corporation and capital gains taxes, see the relevant divisions.
>
> Those statutory instruments listed below which contain substantive provisions are reproduced in this division. Statutory instruments which do no more than amend other instruments are not reproduced; the amendments made by them have been consolidated in the relevant amended regulations or orders. They are, however, listed below for information.

CHRONOLOGICAL LISTING

continued over

STATUTORY INSTRUMENTS

Page

continued over

STATUTORY INSTRUMENTS

continued over

STATUTORY INSTRUMENTS   Page

continued over

STATUTORY INSTRUMENTS Page

continued over

STATUTORY INSTRUMENTS Page

continued over

STATUTORY INSTRUMENTS

continued over

STATUTORY INSTRUMENTS

Page

continued over

STATUTORY INSTRUMENTS STATUTORY INSTRUMENTS Page

continued over

STATUTORY INSTRUMENTS

continued over

STATUTORY INSTRUMENTS Page

continued over

STATUTORY INSTRUMENTS

continued over

STATUTORY INSTRUMENTS Page

continued over

STATUTORY INSTRUMENTS   Page

Statutory Instruments

continued over

STATUTORY INSTRUMENTS

continued over

STATUTORY INSTRUMENTS STATUTORY INSTRUMENTS Page

continued over

STATUTORY INSTRUMENTS

continued over

STATUTORY INSTRUMENTS

continued over

STATUTORY INSTRUMENTS

continued over

STATUTORY INSTRUMENTS Page

continued over

STATUTORY INSTRUMENTS

continued over

STATUTORY INSTRUMENTS TUTORY INSTRUMENTS **Page**

continued over

STATUTORY INSTRUMENTS

continued over

13,025

CRITICAL INSTRUMENTS

continued over

STATUTORY INSTRUMENTS Page

continued over

STATUTORY INSTRUMENTS Page

continued over

STATUTORY INSTRUMENTS   Page

continued over

continued over

STATUTORY INSTRUMENTS

continued over

STATUTORY INSTRUMENTS

Page

continued over

STATUTORY INSTRUMENTS

continued over

continued over

STATUTORY INSTRUMENTS

continued over

STATUTORY INSTRUMENTS   Page

continued over

STATUTORY INSTRUMENTS   Page

continued over

STATUTORY INSTRUMENTS   Page

continued over

STATUTORY INSTRUMENTS
Page

continued over

13,039

continued over

STATUTORY INSTRUMENTS   Page

continued over

STATUTORY INSTRUMENTS   Page

continued over

STATUTORY INSTRUMENTS   Page

continued over

STATUTORY INSTRUMENTS

continued over

continued over

STATUTORY INSTRUMENTS Page

continued over

STATUTORY INSTRUMENTS   Page

continued over

STATUTORY INSTRUMENTS   Page

STATUTORY INSTRUMENTS

continued over

STATUTORY INSTRUMENTS Page

continued over

STATUTORY INSTRUMENTS   Page

continued over

STATUTORY INSTRUMENTS

continued over

STATUTORY INSTRUMENTS   Page

continued over

STATUTORY INSTRUMENTS

continued over

STATUTORY INSTRUMENTS

continued over

STATUTORY INSTRUMENTS

Page

continued over

STATUTORY INSTRUMENTS   Page

continued over

13,057

continued over

STATUTORY INSTRUMENTS

continued over

STATUTORY INSTRUMENTS

continued over

STATUTORY INSTRUMENTS   Page

continued over

STATUTORY INSTRUMENTS

continued over

STATUTORY INSTRUMENTS   Page

continued over

STATUTORY INSTRUMENTS

Statutory Instruments

continued over

STATUTORY INSTRUMENTS   Page

continued over

13,065

STATUTORY INSTRUMENTS

Page

continued over

STATUTORY INSTRUMENTS

continued over

STATUTORY INSTRUMENTS

Page

2014/600   Tribunals, Courts and Enforcement Act 2007 (Consequential, Transitional and Saving Provision) Order 2014 (revokes SI 1994/236) 15,244

2014/649   Child Trust Funds (Amendment) Regulations 2014 (amends SI 2004/1450). Not reproduced.

2014/654   Individual Savings Account (Amendment) Regulations 2014 (amends SI 1998/1870). Not reproduced.

2014/685   Investment Transactions (Tax) Regulations 2014 (amends SI 2006/964, SI 2009/3001, SI 2011/2999 and SI 2013/2819) 15,249

2014/768   Tribunals, Courts and Enforcement Act 2007 (Commencement No. 11) Order 2014 (sets 6 April 2014 as the commencement date for the coming into force of specified provisions). Not reproduced.

2014/854   Annual Tax on Enveloped Dwellings (Indexation of Annual Chargeable Amounts) Order 2014 (sets amounts for 2014–15). 15,252

2014/859   Income Tax (Professional Fees) Order 2014 (amends ITEPA 2003, s. 343(2)). Not reproduced.

2014/906   Finance Act 2008, s. 127 and Pt. 1 of Sch. 43 (Appointed Day) Order 2014 (sets 6 April 2014 as the appointed day). Not reproduced.

2014/992   Finance Act 2009, Sections 101 and 102 (Interest on Late Payments and Repayments), Appointed Days and Consequential Provisions Order 2014 (sets 6 May 2014 as the appointed day for specified taxes). Not reproduced.

2014/1017   Income Tax (Pay As You Earn) (Amendment No. 2) Regulations 2014 (amends SI 2003/2682). Not reproduced.

2014/1120   Taxation of Chargeable Gains (Gilt-edged Securities) Order 2014 (specifies securities for the purposes of TCGA 1992, Sch. 9). Not reproduced.

2014/1230   Universal Credit (Transitional Provisions) Regulations 2014 (revokes SI 2013/386). Not reproduced.

2014/1264   Revenue and Customs (Amendment of Appeal Provisions for Out of Time Reviews) Order 2014 (amends SI 2007/2157, reg. 43F). Not reproduced.

2014/1283   Finance Act 2009, Sections 101 and 102 (Interest on Late Payments and Repayments) (Consequential Amendments) Order 2014 (amends ITTOIA 2005, s. 54(2) and CTA 2009, s. 1303(2)). Not reproduced.

2014/1327   Government Alternative Finance Arrangements Regulations 2014. Not reproduced as not tax provisions.

2014/1449   Registered Pension Schemes (Transfer of Sums and Assets) (Amendment) Regulations 2014 (amends SI 2006/499). Not reproduced.

2014/1450   Individual Savings Account (Amendment No. 2) Regulations 2014 (amends SI 1998/1870). Not reproduced.

2014/1453   Child Trust Funds (Amendment No. 2) Regulations 2014 (amends SI 2004/1450). Not reproduced.

continued over

STATUTORY INSTRUMENTS

Page

STATUTORY INSTRUMENTS   Page

continued over

STATUTORY INSTRUMENTS

continued over

STATUTORY INSTRUMENTS   Page

continued over

STATUTORY INSTRUMENTS

continued over

STATUTORY INSTRUMENTS UTORY INSTRUMENTS **Page**

continued over

STATUTORY INSTRUMENTS   Page

continued over

STATUTORY INSTRUMENTS   Page

continued over

STATUTORY INSTRUMENTS

continued over

STATUTORY INSTRUMENTS · Page

continued over

STATUTORY INSTRUMENTS

STATUTORY INSTRUMENTS

Page

continued over

STATUTORY INSTRUMENTS

continued over

STATUTORY INSTRUMENTS

Page

continued over

STATUTORY INSTRUMENTS   Page

continued over

13,083

STATUTORY INSTRUMENTS

continued over

STATUTORY INSTRUMENTS   Page

continued over

13,085

STATUTORY INSTRUMENTS

Page

continued over

STATUTORY INSTRUMENTS

continued over

13,087

continued over

Statutory Instruments

STATUTORY INSTRUMENTS   Page

continued over

STATUTORY INSTRUMENTS

Statutory Instruments

continued over

STATUTORY INSTRUMENTS   Page

13,091

STATUTORY INSTRUMENTS   Page

continued over

STATUTORY INSTRUMENTS

continued over

STATUTORY INSTRUMENTS

continued over

STATUTORY INSTRUMENTS Page

continued over

STATUTORY INSTRUMENTS

STATUTORY INSTRUMENTS

Page

continued over

continued over

Statutory Instruments

continued over

STATUTORY INSTRUMENTS

continued over

STATUTORY INSTRUMENTS

continued over

STATUTORY INSTRUMENTS

continued over

continued over

STATUTORY INSTRUMENTS   Page

continued over

STATUTORY INSTRUMENTS   Page

continued over

Statutory Instruments

STATUTORY INSTRUMENTS   Page

continued over

STATUTORY INSTRUMENTS

continued over

STATUTORY INSTRUMENTS

continued over

STATUTORY INSTRUMENTS

Page

continued over

STATUTORY INSTRUMENTS

continued over

STATUTORY INSTRUMENTS | Page

continued over

STATUTORY INSTRUMENTS

STATUTORY INSTRUMENTS

continued over

STATUTORY INSTRUMENTS Page

continued over

STATUTORY INSTRUMENTS

continued over

STATUTORY INSTRUMENTS Page

continued over

STATUTORY INSTRUMENTS   Page

continued over

Statutory Instruments

STATUTORY INSTRUMENTS

continued over

STATUTORY INSTRUMENTS

continued over

STATUTORY INSTRUMENTS

continued over

STATUTORY INSTRUMENTS   Page

continued over

STATUTORY INSTRUMENTS

continued over

STATUTORY INSTRUMENTS | Page

continued over

STATUTORY INSTRUMENTS

continued over

STATUTORY INSTRUMENTS

continued over

STATUTORY INSTRUMENTS

continued over

STATUTORY INSTRUMENTS

continued over

STATUTORY INSTRUMENTS

STATUTORY INSTRUMENTS

Page

continued over

STATUTORY INSTRUMENTS

continued over

STATUTORY INSTRUMENTS

continued over

STATUTORY INSTRUMENTS Page

continued over

STATUTORY INSTRUMENTS

continued over

continued over

STATUTORY INSTRUMENTS

continued over

STATUTORY INSTRUMENTS

continued over

STATUTORY INSTRUMENTS

continued over

Statutory Instruments

VISITING FORCES (INCOME TAX AND DEATH DUTIES) (DESIGNATION) ORDER 1964

(SI 1964/924)

Order in Council made on 23 June 1964 under s. 73 of the Finance Act 1960 [ICTA 1988, s. 323].

1 The Federal Republic of Germany is hereby designated for the purposes of section 73 of the Finance Act 1960 [ICTA 1988, s. 323].

2 This Order may be cited as the Visiting Forces (Income Tax and Death Duties) (Designation) Order 1964, and shall come into operation on the 30th June 1964.

CAPITAL GAINS TAX REGULATIONS 1967

(1967/149, as amended by SI 1994/1813, SI 2009/56 and SI 2013/557)

Made on 9 February 1967 by the Commissioners of Inland Revenue under para. 2 of Sch. 10 to the Finance Act 1965 [now TMA 1970, s. 57] and s. 8 of the Tribunals and Inquiries Act 1958 as amended by s. 3 of the Tribunals and Inquiries Act 1966 [now Tribunals and Inquiries Act 1971, s. 10 and Sch. 1, para. 29].

CITATION AND COMMENCEMENT

1   These Regulations may be cited as the Capital Gains Tax Regulations 1967, and shall come into operation on 16th February 1967.

INTERPRETATION

2(1)   In these Regulations, unless the context otherwise requires–

"appeal" means an appeal against an assessment to capital gains tax or against a decision on a claim relating to capital gains tax;

"the Board" means the Commissioners of Inland Revenue;

"third party" means a third or subsequent party joined under Regulation 8;

references to Part III of the Finance Act 1965 [TCGA 1992] include Schedules 6 to 10 to that Act [the Schedules to TCGA 1992, TMA 1970] and any other enactment to be construed as one with the said Part III;

subject to Regulation 15, other expressions have the same meaning as in Part III of the Finance Act 1965 [in TCGA 1992].

The Interpretation Act 1889 shall apply to these Regulations as it applies to an Act of Parliament.

History – In reg. 2(1), definition of "Commissioners" omitted by SI 2009/56, art. 3(2) and Sch. 2, para. 2(2), operative from 1 April 2009 subject to transitional and saving provisions in SI 2009/56, Sch. 3. Former definition read as follows:
    "**"Commissioners"** means (subject to Regulation 17) General Commissioners or Special Commissioners;".
In reg. 2(1), definition of "references to the Income Tax Management Act 1964" omitted by SI 2009/56, art. 3(2) and Sch. 2, para. 2(3), operative from 1 April 2009 subject to transitional and saving provisions in SI 2009/56, Sch. 3. Former definition read as follows:
    "references to the Income Tax Management Act 1964 [TMA 1970] are references to that Act as applied in relation to capital gains tax by paragraph 1 of Schedule 10 to the Finance Act 1965;".
Notes – TCGA 1992, s. 1, 291: provisions to be construed as one with that Act.
Interpretation Act 1889 now repealed and re-enacted as Interpretation Act 1978.

REPRESENTATIONS IN WRITING

6   [Omitted by SI 1994/1813, reg. 2(1) and Sch. 1, para. 27, Sch. 2, Pt. II.]

History – Reg. 6 omitted by SI 1994/1813, reg. 2(1) and Sch. 1, para. 27, Sch. 2, Pt. II with effect from 1 September 1994.

REPRESENTATION OF THE INSPECTOR

7   [Omitted by SI 1994/1813, reg. 2(1) and Sch. 1, para. 27, Sch. 2, Pt. II.]

History – Reg. 7 omitted by SI 1994/1813, reg. 2(1) and Sch. 1, para. 27, Sch. 2, Pt. II, with effect from 1 September 1994.

JOINDER OF THIRD PARTIES IN APPEALS

8(1)   Where the market value of an asset on a particular date or the apportionment of any amount or value is a material question in an appeal any person whose liability to capital gains tax for any period may be affected by that market value or by the manner in which that amount or value is apportioned may apply under this Regulation to be joined as a party in the appeal.

8(2)   An application under this Regulation to be joined as a party in an appeal shall be made in writing to an officer of Revenue and Customs stating–

(a)   the name and address of the applicant;

(b)   the question which may affect his liability to capital gains tax;

(c)   how his liability may be affected; and

(d)   his contention with regard to that question.

8(3)   The officer shall send a copy of the application to the appellant and to any other party to the appeal.

8(4)   If the application is received by the officer before the appeal has been notified to the tribunal, the officer shall, if satisfied that it is proper to join the applicant as a party in the appeal, join the applicant as a third party and give notice of the joinder to the appellant and any other party to the appeal.

8(5)   If the application is received by the officer after the appeal has been notified to the tribunal, or the officer is not satisfied that it is proper to join the applicant as a party in the appeal, the officer shall refer the application to the tribunal, which may at its discretion allow or refuse the application.

8(6)   [Omitted by SI 1994/1813, reg. 2(1) and Sch. 1, para. 27, Sch. 2, Pt. II.]

8(7)   At the hearing and on the determination of the appeal or of any question in the appeal a third party shall, so far as relates to the question in which he is interested, have the same rights as an appellant, including any right to require the statement of a case for the opinion of any Court.

8(8)   [Omitted by SI 1994/1813, reg. 2(1) and Sch. 1, para. 27, Sch. 2, Pt. II.]

8(9)   A person entitled under section 26(5) of the Finance Act 1965 (proceedings consequent on death) to be a party to an appeal shall, if he wishes to be made a party, apply to be joined under this Regulation.

History – In reg. 8(2), the words "an officer of Revenue and Customs" substituted for the words "the inspector" by SI 2009/56, art. 3(2) and Sch. 2, para. 3(2), operative from 1 April 2009 subject to transitional and saving provisions in SI 2009/56, Sch. 3. In reg. 8(3), the word "officer" substituted for the word "inspector" by SI 2009/56, art. 3(2) and Sch. 2, para. 3(3), operative from 1 April 2009 subject to transitional and saving provisions in SI 2009/56, Sch. 3.
Reg. 8(4) substituted by SI 2009/56, art. 3(2) and Sch. 2, para. 3(4), operative from 1 April 2009 subject to transitional and saving provisions in SI 2009/56, Sch. 3. Former reg. 8(4) read as follows:

> "**8(4)**   If the application is received by the inspector not later than thirty days before the date fixed for the hearing of the appeal (or of the question), or if when he receives the application no date has been fixed, he shall, if he is satisfied that it is proper to join the applicant as a party in the appeal, join him as a third party and give notice of the joinder to the appellant and any other party to the appeal.".

Reg. 8(5) substituted by SI 2009/56, art. 3(2) and Sch. 2, para. 3(4), operative from 1 April 2009 subject to transitional and saving provisions in SI 2009/56, Sch. 3. Former reg. 8(5) read as follows:

> "**8(5)**   If the application is received by the inspector later than thirty days before the date fixed for the hearing of the appeal (or of the question) but before it has been determined, or if he is not satisfied that it is proper to join the applicant as a party in the appeal, he shall refer the application to the Commissioners before whom the appeal is brought, and those Commissioners may in their discretion allow or refuse the application.".

Reg. 8(6) and 8(8) omitted by SI 1994/1813, reg. 2(1) and Sch. 1, para. 27, Sch. 2, Pt. II, with effect from 1 September 1994.

APPLICATIONS FOR DETERMINATION OF MARKET VALUE

9(1)   Where the market value of an asset on a particular date or the apportionment of any amount or value may affect the liability to capital gains tax for any period (and whether for the same or different periods) of two or more persons and is not (and has not been) a material question in an appeal already brought by any of them, any of those persons may apply to the tribunal to determine that market value or the manner in which that amount or value should be apportioned.

9(2)   An application under this Regulation shall be made by notice in writing sent to an officer of Revenue and Customs stating the question for determination and (to the best of the applicant's knowledge) the names and addresses of the other persons whose liability to capital gains tax may be affected by the question.

9(3)   [Omitted by SI 2009/56, art. 3(2) and Sch. 2, para. 4(4).]

9(4)   The officer shall be a party to proceedings under this Regulation.

9(5)   [Omitted by SI 2009/56, art. 3(2) and Sch. 2, para. 4(6).]

9(6)   Subject to paragraphs (1) to (4) above, these Regulations, Part III of the Finance Act 1965 [TMA 1970, s. 47], and any enactment directly or indirectly applied by the said Part III shall, so far as they are applicable and with any necessary modifications, apply in relation to proceedings under this Regulation as they apply in relation to an appeal against an assessment to capital gains tax.

History – In reg. 9(1), the word "tribunal" substituted for the word "Commissioners" by SI 2009/56, art. 3(2) and Sch. 2, para. 4(2), operative from 1 April 2009 subject to transitional and saving provisions in SI 2009/56, Sch. 3.
In reg. 9(2), the words "an officer of Revenue and Customs" substituted for the words "the inspector" by SI 2009/56, art. 3(2) and Sch. 2, para. 4(3), operative from 1 April 2009 subject to transitional and saving provisions in SI 2009/56, Sch. 3.
Reg. 9(3) omitted by SI 2009/56, art. 3(2) and Sch. 2, para. 4(4), operative from 1 April 2009 subject to transitional and saving provisions in SI 2009/56, Sch. 3. Former reg. 9(3) read as follows:

> "**9(3)**   In relation to proceedings under this Regulation references in Schedule 3 to the Income Tax Management Act 1964 [TMA 1970, Sch. 3] (rules for assigning proceedings to Commissioners) to the place where the appellant ordinarily resided in the year of assessment to which the proceedings relate shall, in cases where the application does not relate to any ascertained year of assessment, be construed as references to the place where the applicant ordinarily resides at the time of making the application.".

In reg. 9(4), the word "officer" substituted for the word "inspector" by SI 2009/56, art. 3(2) and Sch. 2, para. 4(5), operative from 1 April 2009 subject to transitional and saving provisions in SI 2009/56, Sch. 3.
Reg. 9(5) omitted by SI 2009/56, art. 3(2) and Sch. 2, para. 4(6), operative from 1 April 2009 subject to transitional and saving provisions in SI 2009/56, Sch. 3. Former reg. 9(5) read as follows:

"**9(5)** An election to bring proceedings under this Regulation before the Special Commissioners instead of before the General Commissioners (or, if the proceedings are in Northern Ireland, before a county court instead of before the Special Commissioners) shall, if not made in the notice of application, be made by notice in writing to the inspector within thirty days thereafter.".

In reg. 9(6), "(4)" substituted for "(5)" by SI 2009/56, art. 3(2) and Sch. 2, para. 4(7), operative from 1 April 2009 subject to transitional and saving provisions in SI 2009/56, Sch. 3.

REFERENCES OF QUESTIONS OF VALUE TO OTHER TRIBUNALS

10(1) [Omitted by SI 1994/1813, reg. 2(1) and Sch. 1, para. 27, Sch. 2, Pt. II.]

10(2) [Repealed by FA 1969, Sch. 21, Pt. VIII.]

10(3) [Omitted by SI 1994/1813, reg. 2(1) and Sch. 1, para. 27, Sch. 2, Pt. II.]

History – Reg. 10(1) and 10(3) omitted by SI 1994/1813, reg. 2(1) and Sch. 1, para. 27, Sch. 2, Pt. II, with effect from 1 September 1994.

CONCLUSIVE EFFECT OF A DETERMINATION ON APPEAL

11(1) Where the market value of an asset on a particular date or the apportionment of any amount or value (being a market value or apportionment affecting or which may affect the liability to capital gains tax of two or more persons) is finally determined on an appeal that determination shall, subject to Regulation 14, be in all proceedings relating to capital gains tax conclusive between the Board or any officer of the Board and the following persons–

(a)   parties to the appeal; and

(b)   any person who was entitled to apply to be joined as a third party in the appeal, and had notice, in reasonable time for making such application, of the appeal and of the question in the appeal entitling him so to apply, not being a person who did so apply without undue delay and whose application was not allowed.

11(2) For the purposes of these Regulations–

(a)   the determination of an appeal or a question in an appeal shall be treated as final when the determination can no longer be varied by the tribunal making it or by the order of any court;

(b)   the market value of an asset on a particular date or the apportionment of any amount or value shall be deemed to have been finally determined on an appeal notwithstanding that there was no dispute concerning that market value or apportionment if the market value or apportionment was a material question in the appeal and the appeal has been finally determined.

11(3) [Omitted by SI 1994/1813, reg. 2(1) and Sch. 1, para. 27, Sch. 2, Pt. II.]

11(4) [Omitted by SI 1994/1813, reg. 2(1) and Sch. 1, para. 27, Sch. 2, Pt. II.]

History – Reg. 11(3) and 11(4) omitted by SI 1994/1813, reg. 2(1) and Sch. 1, para. 27, Sch. 2, Pt. II, with effect from 1 September 1994.

AGREEMENTS IN WRITING OF MARKET VALUE OR APPORTIONMENT

12(1) An agreement or notification which apart from this Regulation would have effect under section 54 of the Taxes Management Act 1970 (settlement of appeals by agreement or withdrawal) as if an appeal had been determined by the tribunal shall not have that effect in relation to any appeal in which a third party has been joined unless, at the time when such agreement is made or notification is given, the question in which the third party is interested had been finally determined on the appeal or disposed of by an agreement made in accordance with paragraph (2) below.

12(2) Where the market value of an asset on a particular date or the apportionment of any amount or value may affect the liability to capital gains tax of two or more persons and is a material question in an appeal, then if the market value or apportionment is agreed in writing between an officer of the Board and all the parties to the appeal whose liability may be affected by it the agreement shall in all proceedings relating to the capital gains tax be conclusive between the Board or any officer of the Board and the following persons–

(a)   parties to the agreement; and

(b)   any person who was entitled, in respect of the question in the appeal to which the agreement relates, to apply to be joined as a third party in the appeal, and had notice of the appeal and of the question in the appeal not less than thirty days before the agreement was made, not being a person who did so apply before the agreement was made.

12(3) A document purporting to be an agreement made in accordance with paragraph (2) above and produced from proper custody may be received in evidence in any proceedings relating to capital gains tax without further proof as such an agreement made by the persons by whom it purports to be signed.

History – In reg. 12(1), the words "54 of the Taxes Management Act 1970" substituted for the words "510 of the Income Tax Act 1952" by SI 2009/56, art. 3(2) and Sch. 2, para. 5(2)(a), operative from 1 April 2009 subject to transitional and saving provisions in SI 2009/56, Sch. 3.
In reg. 12(1), the words "the tribunal" substituted for the word "Commissioners" by SI 2009/56, art. 3(2) and Sch. 2, para. 5(2)(b), operative from 1 April 2009 subject to transitional and saving provisions in SI 2009/56, Sch. 3.
In reg. 12(2), the word "an" substituted for the words "the inspector or any other" by SI 2009/56, art. 3(2) and Sch. 2, para. 5(3), operative from 1 April 2009 subject to transitional and saving provisions in SI 2009/56, Sch. 3.

PERSONS AFFECTED BY A DETERMINATION OR AGREEMENT IN WRITING

13(1) A determination or agreement which is by virtue of these Regulations conclusive against or in favour of any person shall to the same extent be conclusive against or in favour of his personal representatives and his trustee or assignee in bankruptcy or under a deed of arrangement.

13(2) A determination or agreement relating to any settled property which is by virtue of these Regulations conclusive against or in favour of the trustees of the settlement shall to the same extent be conclusive against or in favour of any person becoming absolutely entitled to that property as against the trustees.

13(3) A determination or agreement relating to an asset comprised in the estate of a deceased person, or in a testamentary disposition made by him, which is by virtue of these Regulations conclusive against or in favour of his personal representatives shall to the same extent be conclusive against or in favour of any person acquiring the asset as legatee.

13(4) Where paragraph 20 of Schedule 7 to the Finance Act 1965 [TCGA 1992, s. 58] (disposals between husband and wife) or section 31(4) of that Act [TCGA 1992, s. 258] (disposals of certain works of art, etc.) applies in respect of the disposal of an asset, a determination or agreement relating to the asset which is by virtue of these Regulations conclusive against or in favour of the person making the disposal shall to the same extent be conclusive against or in favour of the person acquiring the asset.

FRAUD OR WILFUL DEFAULT

14 A determination or agreement shall not by virtue of these Regulations be conclusive in favour of any person if it is shown that any form of fraud or wilful default committed by or on behalf of that person procured or contributed to procure the determination or agreement.

INTERPRETATION OF CERTAIN EXPRESSIONS

15 For the purposes of these Regulations–

(a)   The market value of an asset or the apportionment of any amount or value is a material question in an appeal notwithstanding that there is no dispute thereon between the appellant and the inspector if the adoption of a different market value or of a different apportionment might produce a different determination on the appeal.

(b)   A person shall not be treated as being at any date a person whose liability to capital gains tax may be affected by the market value of an asset or by the apportionment of any amount or value paid, payable or ascertained in connection with an asset unless on or before that date, but since 6th April 1965, there has been (or is deemed to have been) a disposal or acquisition of the asset by that person, or by personal representatives from whom they may acquire the asset as legatee, or by a company or trustees whose chargeable gains may to any extent be treated as accruing to that person under section 13 (attribution of gains to members of nonresident companies), 86 (attribution of gains to settlors with interest in nonresident or dual resident settlements) or 87 (non-UK resident settlements: attribution of gains to beneficiaries) of the Taxation of Chargeable Gains Act 1992.

(c)   Personal representatives or trustees who are for the purposes of Part III of the Finance Act 1965 [TCGA 1992] treated as a single and continuing body of persons shall be treated as a single person distinct from the persons who may from time to time be the personal representatives or trustees, and if the same persons are personal representatives or trustees in respect of more than one estate or settlement they shall be treated as a separate person in respect of each estate or settlement.

History – Reg. 15(b) substituted by SI 2013/557, reg. 2(2), with effect from 6 April 2013. Former reg. 15(b) read as follows:
"(b)   A person shall not be treated as being at any date a person whose liability to capital gains tax may be affected by the market value of an asset or by the apportionment of any amount or value paid, payable or ascertained in connection with an asset unless–
      (i)   on or before that date, but since 6th April 1965, there has been (or is deemed to have been) a disposal or acquisition of the asset by him, or by personal representatives from whom he may acquire the asset as legatee, or by a company or trustees whose chargeable gains may to any extent be treated as having accrued to him under section 41 or 42 of the Finance Act 1965 [TCGA 1992, s. 13 or CGTA 1979, s. 17, as applied by TCGA 1992, Sch. 11, para. 18] (non-resident companies and trusts); and

(ii) he is at that date, or was during the year of assessment in which any such disposal or acquisition was made, resident or ordinarily resident in the United Kingdom or carrying on a trade in the United Kingdom:

Provided that section 10(3) of the Finance Act 1956 [ICTA 1988, s. 207, as applied by TCGA 1992, s. 9(2)] (determination of questions of ordinary residence) shall not apply to a question arising under this paragraph.".

NOTIFICATION OF THIRD PARTIES

16 Where it appears to the inspector that a person is entitled to apply to be joined as a third party in an appeal the inspector may, and at that person's request shall, notify him of the appeal and disclose to him (so far as relevant to his interest in that appeal) the market value of any asset or the apportionment of any amount or value used in making the assessment or decision from which the appeal is brought.

PROCEEDINGS IN NORTHERN IRELAND

17 [Omitted by SI 2009/56, art. 3(2) and Sch. 2, para. 6.]

Notes – Reg. 17 omitted by SI 2009/56, art. 3(2) and Sch. 2, para. 6, operative from 1 April 2009. Former reg. 17, which was already spent, related to the meaning of "general commissioners" in relation to proceedings in Northern Ireland: from 3 April 1989, general commissioners were appointed in the same way as for England and Wales.

SERVICE BY POST

18 Any notice or other document to be given, served, sent or delivered under these Regulations may be served by post.

Notes – Interpretation Act 1978, s. 7, 23 and Sch. 2, para. 3: service by post deemed effected by properly addressing, pre-paying and posting a letter containing the document etc.

DOUBLE TAXATION RELIEF (TAXES ON INCOME) (GENERAL) REGULATIONS 1970

(SI 1970/488 as amended by SI 1973/317 and SI 1996/783)

Made on 24 March 1970 by the Commissioners of Inland Revenue under s. 351 of the Income Tax Act 1952 and s. 64 of the Finance Act 1965 [ICTA 1988, s. 791].

1(1)   These Regulations may be cited as the Double Taxation Relief (Taxes on Income) (General) Regulations 1970 and shall come into operation on 6 April 1970.

1(2)   The Interpretation Act 1889 shall apply to these regulations as it applies to an Act of Parliament.

1(3)   In these Regulations **"the Board"** means the Commissioners of Inland Revenue; **"year"** means year of assessment.

1(4)   Except in relation to payments which are income of the year 1969–70 or an earlier year the Double Taxation Relief (Taxes on Income) (General) Regulations 1966 shall cease to have effect from 6 April 1970:

Provided that any notice, direction or claim given or made under Regulation 2, 9 or 11 of the said Regulations of 1966 (including any notice, direction or claim having effect as if so given or made) which was in force immediately before the coming into operation of these Regulations shall continue in force as if given or made under the corresponding provision of these Regulations and the following provisions of these Regulations shall apply accordingly.

Notes – Interpretation Act 1889 now repealed and re-enacted as Interpretation Act 1978.

2(1)   The following provisions of these Regulations shall have effect where, under arrangements having effect under section 497 of the Income and Corporation Taxes Act 1970 [ICTA 1988, s. 788], persons resident in the territory with the government of which the arrangements are made are entitled to exemption or partial relief from United Kingdom income tax in respect of any income from which deduction of tax is authorised or required by the Income Tax Acts.

2(2)   Any person who pays any such income (referred to in these Regulations as **"the United Kingdom payer"**) to a person in the said territory who is beneficially entitled to the income (such person being referred to in these Regulations as **"the non-resident"**) may be directed by a notice in writing given by or on behalf of the Board that in paying any such income specified in the notice to the non-resident he shall–

(a)   not deduct tax, or

(b)   not deduct tax at a higher rate than is specified in the notice, or

(c)   deduct tax at a rate specified in the notice instead of at the lower or basic rate otherwise appropriate;

and where such notice is given, any income to which the notice refers, being income for a year for which the arrangements have effect, which the United Kingdom payer pays after the date of the notice to the non-resident named therein shall, subject to the following provisions of these Regulations, be paid as directed in the notice:

Provided that income specified in a notice given under this paragraph shall not include distributions in respect of which income tax is chargeable under Schedule F.

History – In reg. 2(2)(c), words "lower or basic" substituted by SI 1996/783, reg. 2, operative from 6 April 1996.

3   Where a notice given under Regulation 2(2) directs the United Kingdom payer to deduct tax at a rate specified in the notice, the provisions of the Income Tax Acts under which he would, but for the notice, have been chargeable with or liable to account for all or part of any tax deducted at the lower or basic rate shall apply as if those Acts required him to deduct tax at the rate so specified.

History – In reg. 3, words "lower or basic" substituted by SI 1996/783, reg. 2, operative from 6 April 1996.

4(1)   Where but for a notice given under Regulation 2(2) the United Kingdom payer would have been entitled to retain any income tax deductible on making any payment, there shall be made to him again the income tax otherwise payable by him for the relevant year an allowance equal to the amount of tax which, but for the notice, he would have been entitled to retain on making the payment but in compliance with the notice has not deducted.

4(2)   **"The relevant year"** means the year the lower or basic rate for which would (but for the notice) have determined the amount of the deduction authorised.

History – In reg. 4(2), words "lower or basic" substituted by SI 1996/783, reg. 2, operative from 6 April 1996.

5 The United Kingdom payer shall not, in respect of any payment, be charged with or liable to account for any tax which, but for a notice given under Regulation 2(2), he would have been required by the Income Tax Acts to deduct and account for on making the payment but in compliance with the notice has not deducted.

6 Where in compliance with a notice given under Regulation 2(2) a company makes the payment without deducting tax which, but for the notice, it would have been required to deduct in accordance with section 53 or 54 of the Income and Corporation Taxes Act 1970 [ICTA 1988, s. 349], the payment shall be treated for the purposes of section 248(4) of that Act [s. 338(4)] (which prohibits certain payments from being treated as charges on income for corporation tax) as if the company had deducted that tax in accordance with the said section 53 or 54 [s. 349] and had accounted for it under Part XI of that Act [ICTA 1988, Pt. VIII].

7 Where, but for a notice given under Regulation 2(2), a person would have been chargeable with tax under section 53 of the Income and Corporation Taxes Act 1970 [ICTA 1988, s. 349] in respect of any such payment as is mentioned in subsection (1) thereof, the provisions of the Income Tax Acts relating to relief for losses shall apply as if the tax which he would have been so chargeable but in accordance with Regulation 5 is not so chargeable had been paid by him under an assessment under the said section 53 [s. 349].

8 Any notice given under Regulation 2(2) may be expressed to become ineffective if certain specified events happen, or, whether so expressed or not, may be cancelled by a notice of cancellation given by or on behalf of the Board, and if to the knowledge of the United Kingdom payer any of those events happens or if such notice of cancellation is given, any payment made to the non-resident by the United Kingdom payer after the happening of that event becomes known to the United Kingdom payer or after the receipt of that notice, as the case may be, shall be subject to deduction of tax in accordance with the Income Tax Acts.

9 If it is discovered after a notice has been given under Regulation 2(2) that the non-resident is not entitled to exemption or partial relief from tax in respect of income referred to in the notice, any tax which, but for the notice, would have been deductible from any payment made to the non-resident by the United Kingdom payer but in compliance with the notice has not been so deducted—

(a)   may be assessed on the non-resident under Case VI of Schedule D by an Inspector, or

(b)   shall, if a direction to that effect is given by or on behalf of the Board, be deducted by the United Kingdom payer out of so much of the first payment made to the non-resident after the date of the direction as remains after the deduction of any tax deductible therefrom under the Income Tax Acts, and any balance which cannot be deducted out of the first such payment shall be deducted, subject to the same limitation, out of the next such payment, and so on until the whole of the tax (the amount of which shall be specified in the direction) has been deducted.

Any tax which the United Kingdom payer is required to deduct under paragraph (b) of this Regulation shall be accounted for as if it was tax deductible under section 53 of the Income and Corporation Taxes Act 1970 [ICTA 1988, s. 349] in respect of the payment from which it is deducted.

10 A notice may be given under Regulation 2(2) where income is paid to a person authorised to receive that income on behalf of the non-resident, and in such a case the references in these Regulations to payment to the non-resident shall be treated as including references to payment to that person.

11 Regulations 2(2) and 8 shall not apply to payments in respect of coupons for any interest, but any such payments may, under arrangements approved by the Board, be made without deduction of tax or with tax deducted at a rate specified in the arrangements, if the non-resident or any person acting on his behalf makes a claim to the United Kingdom payer to that effect in such form as may be prescribed by the Board, and in the case of any payments so made Regulations 3 to 7 inclusive and Regulation 9 shall, with any necessary modifications, apply as if the claim were a notice given under Regulation 2(2).

MINERAL ROYALTIES (TAX) REGULATIONS 1971
(SI 1971/1035)

Made on 23 June 1971 by the Inland Revenue Commissioners under s. 29(6) of the Finance Act 1970 [ICTA 1988, s. 122(5)].

1(1) These Regulations may be cited as the Mineral Royalties (Tax) Regulations 1971, and shall come into operation on 1st July 1971.

1(2) The Interpretation Act 1889 shall apply for the interpretation of these Regulations as it applies for the interpretation of an Act of Parliament.

1(3) In these Regulations:–

"**the "principal section"**" means section 29 of the Finance Act 1970 [ICTA 1988, s. 122];

"**agreement**" means a mineral lease or agreement, as defined in the principal section;

"**specified operations**" means the winning and working, grading, washing, grinding and crushing of minerals, but in relation to any particular agreement, includes only such of those operations as are in fact authorised by the agreement;

"**rights**" includes liberties.

Notes – See now Interpretation Act 1978.

2 Subject to Regulation 3 below, where a payment is made on or after 6th April 1970 in respect of a sum receivable on or after that date under an agreement which relates both to the winning and working of minerals and to other matters, then, notwithstanding any allocation of the payment under the terms of the agreement, so much but no more of the payment is to be treated for the purposes of the principal section as mineral royalties as might reasonably have been expected to be provided for by the agreement if–

(a)   it conferred only the right to carry out specified operations in relation to minerals in or under the land to which the agreement relates; and

(b)   any buildings, structures, roads, shafts, adits or other works existing on the land at the time when the agreement was granted or made were not in existence.

Provided that no such payments are to be treated as mineral royalties unless minerals in or under the land are being or have been won and worked pursuant to rights conferred by or under the agreement, or there is reasonable prospect of their being so won and worked.

3 The whole of a payment under an agreement shall for the purposes of the principal section be treated as a mineral royalty if under Regulation 2 above nine-tenths or more of it would be so treated.

4 Nothing in these Regulations applies to any periodical payments such as are referred to in subsection (9)(b) of the principal section [ICTA 1988, s. 122(2)(b)] (payments made under certain statutes in Northern Ireland).

FRIENDLY SOCIETIES (LIFE ASSURANCE PREMIUM RELIEF) REGULATIONS 1977

(SI 1977/1143, as amended by SI 1978/1160 and SI 1984/323)

Made on 7 July 1977 by the Chief Registrar of Friendly Societies under para. 13 of Sch. 4 to the Finance Act 1976 [ICTA 1988, Sch. 14, para. 3].

Cross references – FA 2012, Sch. 39, para. 26: modified application of SI 1977/1143.

CITATION AND COMMENCEMENT

1 These Regulations may be cited as the Friendly Societies (Life Assurance Premium Relief) Regulations 1977, and shall come into operation on 18th August 1977.

INTERPRETATION

2(1) In these Regulations–

"**friendly society**", subject to paragraph (1A) of this regulation, means a friendly society, not being a collecting society, registered under the Friendly Societies Act 1974 and includes a Northern Ireland Friendly Society.

"**collecting society**" has the meaning assigned by section 1 of the Industrial Assurance Act 1923 (c. 8) as amended by Schedule 6 to the Companies Act 1967 (c. 81);

"**Northern Ireland Friendly Society**" means a friendly society, not being a collecting society, which is registered in Northern Ireland for purposes corresponding to the Friendly Societies Act 1974.

"**friendly society contract**" means a contract made by a friendly society with a member of the society in the course of its business in Great Britain, whether contained in the rules of the society or not;

"**the prescribed scheme**" means the scheme prescribed in Schedule 1 to these Regulations;

"**an approved scheme**" means a special scheme approved by the Chief Registrar of Friendly Societies in the circumstances provided for in Regulation 7 of these Regulations;

"**actuary**" means an actuary having the qualifications which are prescribed by the Friendly Societies (Qualifications of Actuaries) Regulations 1968 (SI 1968/1481);

"**net contribution**" has the meaning assigned in paragraph 3 of Schedule 1 to these Regulations;

"**gross contribution**" means the contribution of the amount payable under the contract;

"**parent**" includes a stepfather or stepmother.

2(1A) References in these Regulations to a friendly society shall include references to a branch thereof registered under the Friendly Societies Act 1974.

2(2) The rules for the construction of Acts of Parliament contained in the Interpretation Act 1889 shall apply for the purposes of the interpretation of these Regulations.

History – In reg. 2(1), the definition of "friendly society" substituted and the definition of "Northern Ireland Friendly Society" inserted by SI 1978/1160, reg. 2, with effect from 4 September 1978.
Reg. 2(1A) inserted by SI 1978/1160, reg. 2, with effect from 4 September 1978.
Notes – See now Interpretation Act 1978.

ADOPTION OF A SCHEME

3(1) A friendly society may by resolution of its committee of management passed before 1st October 1978 adopt–

(a)   the prescribed scheme, or

(b)   an approved scheme

for the purpose of securing that in the case of friendly society contracts to which the scheme so adopted applies amounts equal to 17½ per cent of the contributions payable are retained by or refunded to the persons paying the contributions.

3(2) Where a friendly society has adopted any such scheme amounts equal to 17½ per cent of the contributions payable under contracts made before 14th March 1984 to which the scheme applies shall be retained by or refunded to the persons paying the contributions as provided in the scheme so adopted.

3(3) Written notice of a resolution adopting the prescribed or an approved scheme shall within fourteen days of the passing thereof be sent by the society to the Chief Registrar of Friendly Societies.

3(4) Where a friendly society has resolved to adopt the prescribed or an approved scheme any right conferred by section 21 of the Friendly Societies Act 1974 on any person to receive a copy of the rules of the society shall be extended so as to include the right to receive a copy of the resolution and of the scheme adopted by the resolution.

History – In reg. 3(2) the words "made before 14th March 1984" inserted by SI 1984/323, reg. 3, with effect from 14 March 1984.

Cross references – SI 1984/323, reg. 2: scheme not to authorise deductions in respect of contracts made after 13 March 1984 (see reg. 3(1)).

SI 1984/323, reg. 3: modification of reg. 3(2), inserting the words "made before 14th March 1984" after "payable under contracts", operative from 14 March 1984.

INCREASE IN CONTRIBUTION

4(1) A resolution adopting the prescribed scheme may provide that in respect of any specified class of contract made by the society before 6th April 1979 to which the scheme applies under which the contribution does not exceed £4 every four weeks the contribution shall be increased with effect from that date to such sum as after deduction of 17½ per cent thereof equals the amount expressed in the contract to be the contribution.

4(2) Where such provision is made the resolution shall operate so as to effect the above mentioned increase in the contribution payable under every contract of a class to which the provision relates, and the prescribed scheme shall take effect accordingly.

CORRESPONDING INCREASE IN SUM ASSURED

5(1) Where an increase in contribution has been effected under Regulation 4 the sum assured or guaranteed by the contract under which the increased contribution is payable shall be increased by an amount determined in accordance with rules which have been certified by an actuary to be fair in relation to the increased contribution payable and have been approved by the Chief Registrar of Friendly Societies.

5(2) Where the sum assured or guaranteed by a contract is increased by virtue of the preceding paragraph the society shall on being requested in writing to do so by the person by whom the increased contribution is payable notify him in writing of the amount of the increase in the sum assured or guaranteed.

6(1) Where a friendly society has adopted the prescribed scheme by a resolution making such provision as is referred to in Regulation 4(1) the member insured under a contract of a class specified in the provision which was made before 6th April 1979 and under which the contribution exceeds £4 every four weeks may before that date irrevocably elect, in the form set out in Schedule 2 to these Regulations or in a form to the like effect, that the contribution payable under the contract under which he is insured shall be increased with effect from 6th April 1970 to such sum as is mentioned in Regulation 4(1).

6(2) Where such election has been made the increase in contribution shall be effective as from 6th April 1979 as if it had been effected under Regulation 4(2), and Regulation 5 shall apply in respect of an increase in contribution under this regulation as it applies in relation to an increase under Regulation 4.

APPROVED SCHEMES

7 The Chief Registrar of Friendly Societies may before 1st October 1978 approve a special scheme intended to be adopted by a friendly society for the purposes mentioned in Regulation 3 if in his opinion in view of the manner in which the business of the society is conducted, or any other relevant matter, it is expedient that the special scheme should be adopted.

NOTICE TO CONTRIBUTION PAYERS

8 Every friendly society which carries on life or endowment business shall take all reasonable steps to ensure that every person who on 31st December 1978 is paying contributions under a friendly society contract which forms part of such business receives a notice in a form approved by the Chief Registrar of Friendly Societies setting out–

(a)   the effect of these Regulations,

(b)   whether the society has adopted the prescribed or an approved scheme, and

(c)   the effect of the scheme which has been adopted;

and, as regards contracts made between 1st January 1979 and 5th April 1979, that such notice is received by the prospective contribution payer before the contract is made.

AMENDMENTS OF RULES

9 Notwithstanding anything contained in the rules of a friendly society which has adopted the prescribed scheme or an approved scheme, the committee of management of the society may by resolution passed before 6th April 1979 make amendments to the rules of the society in connection with the adoption by the society of any such scheme.

MODIFICATION OF ENACTMENTS

10 The enactments mentioned in Schedule 3 to these Regulations shall have effect subject to the adaptations and modifications set out in that Schedule.

SCHEDULE 1 – PRESCRIBED SCHEME

Regulation 2(1)

1 The scheme applies to every friendly society contract made before 14th March 1984 assuring life or endowment benefits under which contributions are payable to a friendly society which has adopted the scheme in accordance with Regulation 3.

History – In para. 1, the words "made before 14th March 1984" inserted by SI 1984/323, reg. 3, with effect from 14 March 1984.

2 Where the member is resident in the United Kingdom and entitled to relief under section 19 of the Income and Corporation Taxes Act 1970 [ICTA 1988, s. 266], the liability of the member in respect of any contribution due and payable after 5th April 1979 under a contract to which the scheme relates shall be discharged by payment of the net contribution; and any payment made on account of such a contribution shall be deemed to have been made after deducting 17½ per cent from an amount payable in respect of the gross contribution.

History – In para. 2, the words "due and payable after 5th April 1979" substituted by SI 1978/1160, reg. 2, with effect from 4 September 1978.

3 The net contribution shall be a sum equal to 82½ per cent of the gross contribution, except that–

(a) where the gross contribution does not exceed £4 every four weeks and the said sum is not a multiple of one halfpenny, the said sum shall be rounded off to the nearer halfpenny, or, if the said sum is a multiple of one half of one halfpenny, to the nearer penny, and

(b) where the gross contribution exceeds £4 every four weeks and the said sum is not a multiple of one penny, the said sum shall be rounded off to the nearer penny, or, if the said sum is a multiple of one halfpenny, to the nearer even penny.

SCHEDULE 2 – LIFE ASSURANCE PREMIUM RELIEF

Regulation 6(1)

FORM OF ELECTION BY MEMBER

To: (Name of friendly society) . . . .

I (Name) . . . . of (Address) . . . . irrevocably choose that as from 6th April 1979 the tax relief to which I shall be entitled in respect of the contract particulars of which are set out below shall take the form of an increase in the sum assured of an amount determined in accordance with rules approved by the Chief Registrar of Friendly Societies.

I understand that if I do not sign this form I shall be entitled to deduct and retain 17½ per cent of the contributions at present payable under the contract.

Signature of member . . . .

Date:

Particulars of Contract

Number, if any, and date of contract

Amount of contribution and interval at which payable

SCHEDULE 3 – ADAPTATIONS AND MODIFICATIONS OF ENACTMENTS

Regulation 10

[Amending provisions, not reproduced here.]

Statutory Instruments

INDUSTRIAL ASSURANCE (LIFE ASSURANCE PREMIUM RELIEF) REGULATIONS 1977

(SI 1977/1144, as amended by SI 1978/1161 and SI 1984/322)

Made on 7 July by the Industrial Assurance Commissioner under para. 13 of Sch. 4 to the Finance Act 1976 [ICTA 1988, Sch. 14, para. 3].

Cross references – FA 2012, Sch. 39, para. 27: modified application of SI 1977/1144.

CITATION AND COMMENCEMENT

1 These Regulations may be cited as the Industrial Assurance (Life Assurance Premium Relief) Regulations 1977, and shall come into operation on 18th August 1977.

INTERPRETATION

2(1) In these Regulations–

"industrial assurance company" and **"collecting society"** have the meanings assigned by section 1 of the Industrial Assurance Act 1923 (c 8) as amended by Schedule 6 to the Companies Act 1967 (c 81);

"industrial assurance contract" means a contract of assurance made by an industrial assurance company in the course of its industrial assurance business in Great Britain or a contract made by a collecting society with a member of the society in the course of its industrial assurance business in Great Britain, whether contained in the rules of the society or not;

"collecting society contract" means a contract, other than an industrial assurance contract, made by a collecting society with a member of the society in the course of business in Great Britain, whether contained in the rules of the society or not;

"the prescribed scheme" means the scheme prescribed in Schedule 1 to these Regulations;

"an approved scheme" means a special scheme approved by the Industrial Assurance Commissioner in the circumstances provided for in Regulation 7 of these Regulations;

"actuary" means an actuary having the qualifications which are prescribed by the Friendly Societies (Qualifications of Actuaries) Regulations 1968 (SI 1968/1481);

"net premium" has the meaning assigned in paragraph 3 of Schedule 1 to these Regulations;

"gross premium" means the premium of the amount payable under the policy or contract;

"parent" includes a stepfather and a stepmother.

2(2) The rules for the construction of Acts of Parliament contained in the Interpretation Act 1889 shall apply for the purposes of the interpretation of these Regulations.

Notes – See now Interpretation Act 1978.

ADOPTION OF A SCHEME

3(1) An industrial assurance company or collecting society may by resolution of its board of directors or, as the case may be, of its committee of management passed before 1st October 1978, adopt–

(a)   the prescribed scheme, or

(b)   an approved scheme

for the purpose of securing that in the case of policies or contracts to which the scheme so adopted applies amounts equal to 17½ per cent of the premiums payable are retained by or refunded to the person paying the premiums.

3(2) Where an industrial assurance company or collecting society has adopted any such scheme amounts equal to 17½ per cent of the premiums payable under–

(a)   policies in respect of assurances made before 14th March 1984, or

(b)   contracts made before that date, to which

the scheme applies shall be retained by or refunded to the persons paying the premiums as provided in the scheme so adopted.

3(3) Written notice of a resolution adopting the prescribed or an approved scheme shall within fourteen days of the passing thereof be sent by the industrial assurance company or collecting society to the Industrial Assurance Commissioner.

3(4) Where a collecting society has resolved to adopt the prescribed or an approved scheme any right conferred by section 21 of the Friendly Societies Act 1974 (c 46) or section 10(1) of the Industrial Assurance and Friendly Societies Act 1948 (c 39) on any person to receive a copy of the rules of the society or of an amendment thereof shall be extended so as to include the right to receive a copy of the resolution and of the scheme adopted by the resolution.

History – In reg. 3(2) para. (a) and (b) substituted by SI 1984/322, reg. 3, with effect from 14 March 1984.

INCREASE IN PREMIUM

4(1) A resolution adopting the prescribed scheme may provide that in respect of any specified class of policy or contract issued or made by the company or society before 6th April 1979 to which the scheme applies under which the premium does not exceed £4 every four weeks the premium shall be increased with effect from that date to such sum as after deduction of 17½ per cent thereof equals the amount expressed in the policy or contract to be the premium.

4(2) Where such provision is made the resolution shall operate so as to effect the above mentioned increase in the premium payable under every policy or contract of a class to which the provision relates, and the prescribed scheme shall take effect accordingly.

CORRESPONDING INCREASE IN SUM ASSURED

5(1) Where an increase in premium has been effected under Regulation 4 the sum assured or guaranteed by the policy or contract under which the increased premium is payable shall be increased by an amount determined in accordance with rules which have been certified by an actuary to be fair in relation to the increased premium and have been approved by the Industrial Assurance Commissioner.

5(2) Where the sum assured or guaranteed by a policy or contract is increased by virtue of the preceding paragraph the company or society shall on being requested in writing to do so by the person by whom the increased premium is payable notify him in writing of the amount of the increase in the sum assured or guaranteed.

6(1) Where an industrial assurance company or collecting society has adopted the prescribed scheme by a resolution making such provision as is referred to in Regulation 4(1), the person insured under a policy or contract of a class specified in the provision which was issued or made before 6th April 1979 and under which the premium exceeds £4 every four weeks may before that date irrevocably elect, in the form set out in Schedule 2 to these Regulations or in a form to the like effect, that the premium under the contract under which he is insured shall be increased with effect from 6th April 1979 to such sum as is mentioned in Regulation 4(1).

6(2) Where such election has been made the increase in premium shall be effective as from 6th April 1979 as if it had been effected under Regulation 4(2), and Regulation 5 shall apply in respect of an increase in premium under this Regulation as it applies in relation to an increase under Regulation 4.

APPROVED SCHEMES

7 The Industrial Assurance Commissioner may before 1st October 1978 approve a special scheme intended to be adopted by an industrial assurance company or collecting society for the purposes mentioned in Regulation 3 if in his opinion, in view of the manner in which the business of the company or society is conducted, or any other relevant matter, it is expedient that the special scheme should be adopted.

NOTICE TO PREMIUM PAYERS

8 Every industrial assurance company and collecting society shall take all reasonable steps to ensure that every person who on 31st December 1978 is paying premiums under an industrial assurance or collecting society contract made by it receives a notice in a form approved by the Industrial Assurance Commissioner setting out–

(a)   the effect of these Regulations,

(b)   whether the company or society has adopted the prescribed or an approved scheme, and

(c)   the effect of the scheme which has been adopted;

and as regards contracts made between 1st January 1979 and 5th April 1979, that such notice is received by the prospective premium payer before the contract is made.

AMENDMENT OF RULES

9 Notwithstanding anything contained in the rules of a collecting society which has adopted the prescribed scheme or an approved scheme, the committee of management of the society may by resolution passed before 6th April 1979 make amendments to the rules of the society in connection with the adoption by the society of any such scheme.

MODIFICATION OF ENACTMENTS

10 The enactments mentioned in Schedule 3 to these Regulations shall have effect subject to the adaptations and modifications set out in that Schedule.

SCHEDULE 1 – PRESCRIBED SCHEME

Regulation 2(1)

1 The scheme applies to every industrial assurance or collecting society contract made before 14th March 1984 under which premiums are payable to an industrial assurance company or collecting society which has adopted the scheme in accordance with Regulation 3.

History – In para. 1, the words "made before 14th March 1984" inserted by SI 1984/322, reg. 3, with effect from 14 March 1984.

2 Where the person assured or member, as the case may be, is resident in the United Kingdom and entitled to relief under section 19 of the Income and Corporation Taxes Act 1970 [ICTA 1988, s. 266], the liability of that person or member in respect of any premium due and payable after 5th April 1979 under a contract to which the scheme relates shall be discharged by payment of the net premium; and any payment made on account of such a premium shall be deemed to have been made after deducting 17½ per cent from an amount payable in respect of the gross premium.

History – In para. 2, the words "due and payable after 5th April 1979" substituted by SI 1978/1161, reg. 2, with effect from 4 September 1978.

3 The net premium shall be a sum equal to 82½ per cent of the gross premium, except that–

(a)   in relation to an industrial assurance contract, where the said sum is not a multiple of one halfpenny, it shall be rounded off to the nearer halfpenny, or, if the said sum is a multiple of one half of one halfpenny, the nearer penny; and

(b)   in relation to a collecting society contract, where the said sum is not a multiple of one penny, it shall be rounded off to the nearer penny, or, if the said sum is a multiple of one halfpenny, to the nearer even penny.

SCHEDULE 2 – LIFE ASSURANCE PREMIUM RELIEF

Regulation 6(1)

FORM OF ELECTION BY POLICYHOLDER

To: (Name of industrial assurance company or collecting society) ....

I (Name) .... of (Address) ....

irrevocably choose that as from 6th April 1979 the tax relief to which I shall be entitled in respect of the premiums paid by me in respect of the policy particulars of which are set out below shall take the form of an increase in the sum assured of an amount determined in accordance with rules approved by the Industrial Assurance Commissioner.

I understand that if I do not sign this form I shall be entitled to deduct and retain 17½ per cent of the premium at payable under the policy.

Date: ....   Signature ....

Particulars of Policy

Number (if any) and   Amount of premium
date of policy ....   and interval at which
                                                       payable ....

SCHEDULE 3 – ADAPTATIONS AND MODIFICATIONS OF ENACTMENTS

Regulation 10

THE INDUSTRIAL ASSURANCE ACT 1923

1 Subsection (1) of section 23 of the Industrial Assurance Act 1923, as it applies to an industrial assurance contract to which the prescribed scheme, or an approved scheme which provides for payment of net premiums, applies, shall have effect as if for the words "the amount due" there were substituted the words "the amount of the net premiums, as defined in the Industrial Assurance (Life Assurance Premium Relief) Regulations 1977, due".

2 In its application to the valuation of a policy of which the sum assured or guaranteed has been increased under regulations 5 or 6, Schedule 4 to the Industrial Assurance Act 1923 shall have effect subject to the following modifications–

(a) The value of the policy shall be the aggregate of the value of the sum assured or guaranteed by the policy immediately before the increase and of the value of the increase in the sum assured or guaranteed.

(b) For the purpose of the valuation of the increase in the sum assured or guaranteed, paragraphs 1 and 2 of Schedule 4 shall have effect as if the increase had been assured by a policy effected on the next anniversary date of the policy after 6th April 1979 for the then unexpired term of the policy.

THE INDUSTRIAL ASSURANCE AND FRIENDLY SOCIETIES ACT 1929 (C 28)

3 In the Schedule to the Industrial Assurance and Friendly Societies Act 1929 the words "premiums actually paid", in their application to a policy in respect of which under the prescribed scheme or an approved scheme payment of any premium due has been discharged by payment of 82½ per cent of that premium, shall include premiums in respect of which such payment has been made.

4 In its application to a policy of which the sum assured or guaranteed has been increased under Regulation 5 or 6, paragraph 1 of the said Schedule shall have effect subject to the following modifications–

(a) for the purpose of calculating the amount assured by the free paid up policy the sum assured by the surrendered policy shall be divided into the original sum assured and the increase in the sum assured, any addition to the sum assured by the surrendered policy by way of bonus on or after 6th April 1979 to be allocated proportionately between and to be treated as comprised in the original sum assured and the increase in the sum assured respectively;

(b) the amount assured by the free policy shall consist of the aggregate of proportions of the original sum assured and of the increase in the sum assured calculated as follows:–

(i) the proportion of the original sum assured shall be the same proportion as the amount of the original premiums actually paid bears to the amount of the original premiums which would have been payable under the surrendered policy had the full number of original premiums become payable thereunder;

(ii) the proportion of the increase in the sum assured shall be the same proportion as the amount of the increase in premiums actually paid bears to the amount of the increase in premiums which would have been payable under the surrendered policy had the full number of increases in premium become payable thereunder.

5 For the purposes of sub-paragraph (b)(i) of the preceding paragraph and this paragraph–

"the original premiums" means the premiums of the amount payable under the policy before the increase in premium was effected under Regulation 4(1) or 6(2), including, in respect of premiums paid, or which would have been payable, after 6th April 1979, payments of that amount included in premiums paid, or which would have been payable, after that date;

"the original sum assured" means the sum (including any addition by way of bonus) assured or guaranteed under the surrendered policy on 6th April 1979 before the increase under Regulation 5 or 6 takes effect, together with any addition made thereto in respect of the due proportion of any bonus added on or after 6th April 1979;

"the amount of the increase in the sum assured" means the sum assured by the surrendered policy in so far as it exceeds the original sum assured as at 6th April 1979, together with any addition made thereto in respect of the due proportion of any bonus added on or after 6th April 1979.

Statutory Instruments

THE INDUSTRIAL ASSURANCE AND FRIENDLY SOCIETIES ACT 1948

6 For the purpose of subsection (2) of section 2 of the Industrial Assurance and Friendly Societies Act 1948 (power to insure life of parent or grandparent for not more than £30) there shall be excluded so much of any sum insured to be paid, or paid, on the death of any one of a person's parents or grandparents as represents any increase in any sum assured or guaranteed effected under Regulation 5 or 6.

THE RESERVE AND AUXILIARY FORCES (PROTECTION OF CIVIL INTERESTS) ACT 1951 (C 65)

7 Subsection (3) of section 56 of the Reserve and Auxiliary Forces (Protection of Civil Interests) Act 1951, as it applies to an industrial assurance contract or a collecting society contract of which the sum assured or guaranteed has been increased under Regulation 5 or 6 and which is a contract for the whole term of life, shall have effect as if it provided that the terms of the contract shall be varied in accordance with the following provisions–

(a) the relevant arrears shall be extinguished by a reduction of the sum assured or guaranteed under the policy, the amount of the reduction to be such an amount as shall be determined by an actuary;

(b) the industrial assurance company or collecting society shall at the time for writing off give written notice to the owner of the policy of the amount of the reduction so determined;

(c) the owner of the policy may, within six months of receiving such notice, appeal to the Industrial Assurance Commissioner on the ground that such reduction is not fair in relation to the amount of the extinguished relevant arrears;

(d) if on such appeal, and after giving the owner of the policy and the company or society an opportunity of being heard, the Industrial Assurance Commissioner is satisfied that the reduction is not fair, he may direct the company or society to make such increase as he may consider appropriate in the sum assured or guaranteed to which the appeal relates.

FRIENDLY SOCIETIES ACT 1974

8 In applying the limits imposed by section 64 of the Friendly Societies Act 1974 (limits on amounts which a member, or person claiming through a member, of a registered friendly society is entitled to receive from one or more such societies) there shall be disregarded any increase in any sum assured or guaranteed which is effected under Regulation 5 or 6.

9 For the purposes of section 72 of the Friendly Societies Act 1974 (power of registered friendly societies to insure life of parent or grandparent for not more than £30) there shall be excluded so much of any sum insured to be paid, or paid, on the death of any one of a person's parents or grandparents as represents any increase in any sum assured or guaranteed which is effected under Regulation 5 or 6.

INCOME TAX (LIFE ASSURANCE PREMIUM RELIEF) REGULATIONS 1978

(SI 1978/1159, as amended by SI 1979/346, SI 1979/1576, SI 2001/3629 and SI 2009/56)

Made on 4 August 1978 by the Commissioners of Inland Revenue under para. 16 of Sch. 4 to the Finance Act 1976 (as amended by para. 10 of Sch. 3 to the Finance Act 1978) [ICTA 1988, Sch. 14, para. 7].

Cross references – FA 2012, Sch. 39, para. 25: modified application of SI 1978/1159.

CITATION AND COMMENCEMENT

1 These Regulations may be cited as the Income Tax (Life Assurance Premium Relief) Regulations 1978, and shall come into operation on 6th April 1979.

INTERPRETATION

2(1) In these Regulations unless the context otherwise requires:–

"**the Board**" means the Commissioners of Inland Revenue;

"**authorised officer**" in relation to a life office means an official authorised for the purposes of these Regulations by resolution of the life office's Board, except that–

(a) in relation to a registered friendly society, it means an official so authorised by resolution of the society's committee of management, and

(b) in relation to underwriters falling within subsection (2)(a)(ii) of section 19 of the Income and Corporation Taxes Act 1970 [ICTA 1988, s. 266(2)(a)(ii)], it means the underwriting agent through whom their business is carried on;

"**deficiency**" means a deficiency recoverable under paragraph 5(b) of Schedule 4 [ICTA 1988, s. 266(5)(b)];

"**financial year**" in relation to a life office means a period for which the office makes up its accounts;

"**four-weekly accounting period**" means the period of 28 days commencing on 1st January in a calendar year, and each succeeding period throughout the year being a period of 28 days, except that a period including 29th February and the period commencing on 3rd December shall be extended to 29 days;

"**income tax month**" means the period beginning on the 6th day of any calendar month and ending on the 5th day of the following calendar month; and in Regulations 6 and 7 below, in relation to an income tax month–

"**relevant calendar month**" means a calendar month falling partly in the income tax month, and

"**component part**" means the part falling within it of a relevant calendar month;

"**industrial branch business**" means any such business carried on before 1st December 2001 as was industrial assurance business as defined in section 1(2) of the Industrial Assurance Act 1923 or Article 3(1) of The Industrial Assurance (Northern Ireland) Order 1979;

"**insurance**" includes a contract for a deferred annuity;

"**life office**" means any such body as is mentioned in section 19(2)(a) of the Income and Corporation Taxes Act 1970 as amended by paragraph 3 of Schedule 4 [ICTA 1988, s. 266(2)(a)];

"**net of deduction**" means net of the deduction authorised by paragraph 5 of Schedule 4 [ICTA 1988, s. 266(5)] (or by that paragraph as modified by Regulation 4 below);

"**ordinary branch business**" means life assurance business other than industrial branch business;

"**Schedule**" means Schedule 4 to the Finance Act 1976.

2(2) The Interpretation Act 1889 shall apply for the interpretation of these Regulations as it applies for the interpretation of an Act of Parliament.

History – In reg. 2(1) at the definition for "industrial branch business" the words "any such business carried on before 1st December 2001 as was" inserted at the beginning by SI 2001/3629, art. 110; with effect from 1 December 2001.
In reg. 2(1) definition of "industrial branch business" amended by SI 1979/1576, operative from 3 January 1980.

Notes – In reg. 2(2) reference to Interpretation Act 1889 should be construed as a reference to Interpretation Act 1978.

INFORMATION TO BE GIVEN TO THE LIFE OFFICE

3(1)   A life office may at any time by notice in writing require an individual who pays or proposes to pay premiums net of deduction to furnish to the life office a statement under this Regulation.

3(2)   A statement under this Regulation shall be in such form and contain such particulars as the Board prescribe, and the particulars prescribed shall be such as are necessary for determining whether the person paying the premiums is or will be entitled to pay them net of deduction.

3(3)   Where an individual has been required to furnish a statement under this Regulation in relation to any insurance and has not furnished it then (until he does so)–

(a)   if the statement was required before the first premium in respect of that insurance became due, he shall not be entitled to pay any premiums in respect of that insurance net of deduction, and

(b)   in any other case, he shall not be entitled to pay net of deduction any premiums in respect of that insurance falling due more than 60 days after the date on which the notice requiring the statement was issued.

3(4)   If notwithstanding the furnishing of a statement under this Regulation in relation to any insurance the life office concerned is not satisfied that the premiums are properly payable net of deduction, and the person paying them does not agree to pay them without deduction, the life office shall notify the Board forthwith.

3(5)   Without prejudice to the generality of paragraph (1) above–

(a)   a life office shall not accept payment of premiums net of deduction in respect of any insurance without first obtaining a statement under this Regulation in relation to that insurance, unless the particulars required in the statement are already in the possession of the life office, or the Board have by notice in writing to the life office dispensed with the requirement of this sub-paragraph in relation to that insurance, and

(b)   where premiums in respect of any insurance are being paid net of deduction and it appears to the life office that they are no longer properly so payable, the life office shall require a statement under this Regulation unless the person paying the premiums agrees to pay them without deduction.

3(6)   Paragraph (5)(a) above shall not apply to insurances made before 1st September 1978 if the life office concerned has established to the satisfaction of the Board that on the basis of the information in the hands of the life office there is not a probability of more than one in ten that the amount claimed to be recoverable for any period under paragraph 5(b) of Schedule 4 in respect of such insurances will exceed by more than 0.5 per cent the amount properly recoverable.

3(7)   Paragraphs (5)(a) and (6) above shall not apply to an insurance made before 6th April 1979 to which paragraph 11 of Schedule 4 [ICTA 1988, Sch. 14, para. 2] applies.

History – In reg. 3(5)(a) the words "or the Board ...that insurance" inserted by SI 1979/346, reg. 2, operative from 6 April 1979.

ROUNDING OF SUMS PAYABLE BY WAY OF NET PREMIUM

4(1)   This Regulation has effect for adjusting in certain cases the net amount payable by way of premium after the deduction authorised under paragraph 5 of Schedule 4 [ICTA 1988, s. 266(5)], and in those cases the amount treated as deducted and retained under that paragraph shall also be adjusted accordingly.

4(2)   In the case of–

(a)   an industrial assurance contract, as defined in any Regulations made under paragraph 13 of Schedule 4 [ICTA 1988, Sch. 14, para. 3], or

(b)   a friendly society contract, as defined in any such Regulations, in respect of which the premiums do not (before any deduction under paragraph 5 of Schedule 4 [ICTA 1988, s. 266(5)]) exceed £4 every four weeks,

if the net amount payable is otherwise not a multiple of one new halfpenny it shall be adjusted and shall–

(i)   where the premium is one to which a scheme adopted under Regulations made under paragraph 13 of Schedule 4 [ICTA 1988, Sch. 14, para. 3] applies, be the amount payable in accordance with the scheme, and

(ii)   in any other case be rounded to the nearer new halfpenny or, if it is a multiple of one half of one new halfpenny, to the nearer new penny.

4(3)   In the case of any insurance not included in paragraph (2)(a) or (b) above, if the net amount payable is otherwise not a multiple of one new penny it shall be rounded to the nearer new penny or, if it is a multiple of one new halfpenny, to the nearer even new penny.

DEFICIENCY CLAIMS: INTRODUCTORY

5(1)   Sums recoverable by a life office under paragraph 5(b) of Schedule 4 [ICTA 1988, s. 266(5)(b)] shall be recovered on a claim made to the Board for the purpose under these Regulations.

5(2)   A claim for any period allowed by these Regulations shall be a claim relating to the deficiency arising in respect of premiums received in that period, and accordingly references to premiums "for" a period are to premiums received in that period.

5(3)   Subject to paragraph (4) below a claim shall be for the claimant's financial year, and is referred to in these Regulations as an **"annual claim"**.

5(4)   A claim may also be made in accordance with Regulation 6 or 8 below for a period shorter than the claimant's financial year, and is referred to in these Regulations as an **"interim claim"**.

5(5)   A life office which carries on both industrial branch business and ordinary branch business may make annual and interim claims separately for business of each branch.

INTERIM CLAIMS IN ADVANCE

6(1)   An interim claim for a period allowed by paragraphs (2) and (3) below may be made at any time within one month before the period for which it is made, and is referred to in these Regulations as an **"interim claim in advance"**

6(2)   The three kinds of period for which an interim claim in advance may be made are–

(a)   a calendar month, or

(b)   an income tax month, or

(c)   in the case of a claim relating to industrial branch business only, a four-weekly accounting period.

6(3)   Interim claims in advance made by one life office may not (except where a change is authorised by prior approval of the Board) be made for periods of different kinds:

Provided that if the first claim made for industrial branch business (or the first such claim made after an authorised change) is a separate claim made for a four-weekly accounting period, this paragraph shall then apply separately in relation to industrial branch business and ordinary branch business.

6(4)   An interim claim in advance for a period shall be based on an estimate of the deficiency that will arise in respect of premiums for that period, and the estimate shall be certified by an authorised officer of the claimant as being the best estimate that can reasonably be made of the deficiency; and if the claim is for an income tax month the estimate shall show the part of the deficiency attributed to each component part of the month.

6(5)   If the Board are satisfied with the estimate they shall pay the estimated amount of the deficiency to the claimant before the end of the period for which the claim is made; if they are not so satisfied, they shall pay to the claimant before the end of the period such lesser amount if any as in their estimation will approximate to the deficiency.

SUPPLEMENTARY STATEMENTS

7(1)   When a payment has been made to a life office under Regulation 6(5) above on an interim claim in advance, the life office shall deliver to the Board a supplementary statement under this Regulation, and (except where paragraph (5)(b) below applies) shall deliver the statement within two months after the end of the period for which the claim was made.

7(2)   The supplementary statement shall be a statement correcting (or confirming) the estimate of the deficiency given in accordance with Regulation 6(4) above, and shall–

(a)   be based as far as possible on the amount of the premiums actually received in the period covered by the statement, and only as far as may be necessary on a revised estimate, and

(b)   (subject to paragraph (5) below) be for the same period as the interim claim in advance;

and any estimate contained in the supplementary statement shall be certified by an authorised officer of the life office as the best estimate that can reasonably be made.

7(3)   If the supplementary statement shows a deficiency greater than the payment made under Regulation 6(5), the Board shall if satisfied with the statement pay the amount of the difference to the life office forthwith by way of supplementary payment on the claim; if the supplementary statement shows a deficiency less than the payment made under Regulation 6(5), the life office shall repay the amount of the difference to the Board with the statement.

7(4)　If in respect of an interim claim on which a payment has been made under Regulation 6(5) above a life office fails to deliver a supplementary statement within the time required by this Regulation, the amount of the payment shall immediately be recoverable by the Board in the same manner as tax charged by an assessment which has become final and conclusive.

7(5)　Where the interim claim in advance was for an income tax month the life office shall (instead of delivering a statement for that month) deliver a supplementary statement for each of the relevant calendar months, and the supplementary statement for a relevant calendar month shall–

(a)　provide the information required by paragraph (2) above in respect of that month, and

(b)　be delivered within two months and five days after the end of that month.

INTERIM CLAIMS IN ARREAR

8(1)　An interim claim for a period allowed by paragraph (2) below may be made at any time within six months after the end of the period for which it is made.

8(2)　The period for which a claim may be made under this Regulation shall be one which–

(a)　is not shorter than one calendar month, and

(b)　falls wholly within the claimant's same financial year, and

(c)　does not include any part of a period in respect of which a payment was made under Regulation 6(5) above (unless the payment in respect of that period or that part was recovered under Regulation 7(4) above).

8(3)　A claim under this Regulation may only be made to recover the deficiency arising in respect of premiums actually received and may not be based on an estimate.

8(4)　If the deficiency claimed is established to the Board's satisfaction, they shall pay the amount of the deficiency to the claimant; if they are not so satisfied they shall pay to the claimant any lesser amount established to their satisfaction.

ANNUAL CLAIMS

9(1)　An annual claim for the claimant's financial year may, subject to paragraph (2) below, be made at any time within six years after the end of the financial year.

9(2)　Where in relation to any financial year a life office has received and not repaid any payment on a relevant interim claim, it shall within one year after the end of the financial year make an annual claim to establish the deficiency for that year.

In this Regulation **"relevant interim claim"** means, in relation to a financial year, an interim claim for a period falling wholly or partly within that year.

9(3)　An annual claim shall be a claim to establish and, so far as not already recovered, to recover the deficiency arising in respect of premiums actually received in the year and may not be based on an estimate.

9(4)　An annual claim required under paragraph (2) above shall bring into account payments made on relevant interim claims, and shall apportion as may be necessary any payment made on a relevant interim claim for any period falling partly in a different year; and for the purpose of this Regulation the **"aggregate of the relevant interim payments"** means the aggregate of the payments made (and not repaid) on relevant interim claims but excluding any part of a payment apportioned to a different year.

9(5)　Where the aggregate of the relevant interim payments shown by a claim exceeds the deficiency for the year shown by the claim, the life office shall repay the amount of the excess to the Board with the claim.

9(6)　If a life office fails to make an annual claim required under paragraph (2) above within the time limited by that paragraph, the Board may issue a notice to the life office showing the aggregate of the relevant interim payments for the year, and stating that the Board are not satisfied that the deficiency for the year exceeds a lower amount stated in the notice.

9(7)　If an annual claim is not delivered to the Board within two weeks after the issue of a notice under paragraph (6) above the amount of the difference between the aggregate and the lower amount stated in the notice shall immediately be recoverable by the Board in the same manner as tax charged by an assessment which has become final and conclusive.

9(8) Where an annual claim has been made and the claimant subsequently discovers that an error or mistake has been made in the claim, the claimant may make a supplementary claim within the time allowed by paragraph (1) above.

Cross references – FA 2012, Sch. 39, para. 25: modified application of annual claims rules.

DEFICIENCY CLAIMS: SUPPLEMENTARY PROVISIONS

10(1) Section 42 of the Taxes Management Act 1970 shall not apply to claims under these Regulations.

10(2) No appeal shall lie from the Board's decision on an interim claim.

10(3) An appeal may be made against the Board's decision on an annual claim, and the appeal shall be brought by giving written notice to the Board within 30 days of receipt of written notice of the decision.

10(4) No payment or repayment made or other thing done on or in relation to an interim claim or a notice under Regulation 9(6) above shall prejudice the decision on an annual claim.

10(5) Part V of the Taxes Management Act 1970 (appeals and other proceedings) shall apply to an appeal under paragraph (3) above, and on an appeal that is notified to the tribunal, the tribunal may vary the decision appealed against whether or not the variation is to the advantage of the appellant.

10(6) All such payments and repayments shall be made as are necessary to give effect to the Board's decision on an annual claim, or to any variation of that decision on appeal.

10(7) Claims and supplementary statements under these Regulations shall be in such form and contain such particulars as the Board prescribe and shall be signed by an authorised officer of the life office; and forms prescribed for annual claims may require a report to be given by the life office's auditor.

10(8) Where for the purposes of an annual claim for a financial year it is necessary to apportion any payment made on an interim claim for a period falling partly within and partly outside that year, the apportionment shall be made in such manner as the Board prescribe.

History – In reg. 10(3), the words "may be made against" substituted for the words "shall lie to the Special Commissioners from" by SI 2009/56, art. 3(2) and Sch. 2, para. 7(2), operative from 1 April 2009 subject to transitional and saving provisions in SI 2009/56, Sch. 3.

In reg. 10(5), the words "that is notified to the tribunal, the tribunal" substituted for the words "the Special Commissioners" by SI 2009/56, art. 3(2) and Sch. 2, para. 7(3), operative from 1 April 2009 subject to transitional and saving provisions in SI 2009/56, Sch. 3.

INFORMATION FROM POLICYHOLDERS

11 The Board may by notice in writing require any person who has or had a policy of life insurance or contract for a deferred annuity with a life office or who pays or paid premiums under such a policy or contract to furnish them within such time as they may direct with such information (including copies of relevant documents) as they require for the purposes of section 19 of the Income and Corporation Taxes Act 1970 or of Schedule 4 [ICTA 1988, s. 266 and Sch. 14].

INSPECTION OF RECORDS

12(1) Every person to whom premiums are paid in respect of which a claim is made under these Regulations shall, whenever required to do so, make available for inspection by an authorised officer of the Board all such books, documents and other records in his possession or under his control containing information relating to—

(a) such premiums and the policies or contracts under which such premiums are paid, or

(b) the persons holding such policies or contracts or paying such premiums,

as may reasonably be required for determining whether the deficiency for which any claim is made under these Regulations is properly recoverable.

12(2) Where records are maintained by computer the person required to make them available for inspection shall provide the officer making the inspection with all facilities necessary for obtaining information from them.

12(3) Every statement made under Regulation 3 above shall be preserved by the life office to which it is made (or which is the insurer for the time being), in such manner as may be approved by the Board so as to be available for inspection under this Regulation, until three years after the termination of the insurance or contract to which it relates.

Cross references – FA 1988, s. 127(1): computer records – in reg. 12 references to a document or copy of a document to be construed in accordance with Civil Evidence Act 1968, Pt. I. This has the effect of giving the Revenue access under reg. 12 to computer records. See FA 1988, s. 127(2)–(4) for ancillary rights of access to computer hardware. For application to Scotland and Northern Ireland, see FA 1988, s. 127(5).

FRIENDLY SOCIETIES (LIFE ASSURANCE PREMIUM RELIEF) (CHANGE OF RATE) REGULATIONS 1980

(SI 1980/1947, as amended by SI 2001/3629 and FA 2012)

Made on 15 December 1980 by the Chief Registrar of Friendly Societies under para. 13 of Sch. 4 to the Finance Act 1976 [ICTA 1988, Sch. 14, para. 3]

Cross references – FA 2012, Sch. 39, para. 26: modified application of SI 1980/1947.

CITATION AND COMMENCEMENT

1 These Regulations may be cited as the Friendly Societies (Life Assurance Premium Relief) (Change of Rate) Regulations 1980, and shall come into operation on 20th January 1981.

INTERPRETATION

2 In these Regulations–

"**the 1977 Regulations**" means the Friendly Societies (Life Assurance Premium Relief Regulations 1977;

"**friendly society**" means a friendly society, not being a collective society, registered under the Friendly Societies Act 1974 or a branch so registered under that Act of a friendly society so registered;

"**collecting society**" means a society which before 1st December 2001 was a collecting society within the meaning assigned by section 1 of the Industrial Assurance Act 1923 as amended by Schedule 6 to the Companies Act 1967;

"**the prescribed scheme**" means the scheme prescribed in Schedule 1 to the Friendly Societies (Life Assurance Premium Relief) Regulations 1977;

"**an approved scheme**" means a special scheme approved by the Chief Registrar of Friendly Societies in the circumstances provided for in regulation 7 of the Friendly Societies (Life Assurance Premium Relief) Regulations 1977;

"**gross contribution**" means the contribution of the amount payable under the contract;

"**actuary**" means an actuary having the qualifications which are prescribed by the Friendly Societies (Qualifications of Actuaries) Regulations 1968;

"**the authorised percentage**" means the percentage for the time being in force under paragraph 5(a) of Schedule 4 to the Finance Act 1976;

"**the effective date**" means the date on which a change in the authorised percentage takes effect;

"**parent**" includes a stepfather and a stepmother.

History – In reg. 2, at the beginning of definition for "collecting society" the words "means a society which before 1st December 2001 was a collecting society within" substituted for the word "has", by SI 2001/3629, art. 111; with effect from 1 December 2001.

AMENDMENT OF A SCHEME

3(1) Where a friendly society has adopted the prescribed scheme or an approved scheme in accordance with the provisions of the 1977 Regulations the society may by resolution of its committee of management passed within eight months of the passing of any Act making a change in the authorised percentage, amend any such scheme so that amounts equal to the authorised percentage of the gross contributions due and payable on or after the effective date under the contracts to which the scheme applies shall be retained by or refunded to the persons paying the contributions.

3(2) Where a friendly society has amended any such scheme, amounts equal to the authorised percentage of the gross contributions payable under contracts to which the scheme applies shall be retained by or refunded to the persons paying the contributions as provided in the scheme so amended.

3(3) Written notice of a resolution amending the prescribed scheme or an approved scheme shall within fourteen days of the passing thereof be sent by the society to the Chief Registrar of Friendly Societies.

3(4) Where a friendly society has resolved to amend the prescribed scheme or an approved scheme any right conferred by section 21 of the Friendly Societies Act 1974 on any person to receive a copy of the rules of the society shall be extended so as to include the right to receive a copy of the resolution and of the amended scheme adopted by the resolution.

AMENDMENT OF GROSS CONTRIBUTION

4(1)   Where, by virtue of regulation 4 of the 1977 Regulations, a resolution adopting the prescribed scheme provided that the gross contribution was to be increased with effect from 6th April 1979 in respect of any specified class of contract, a resolution amending the prescribed scheme may also amend the gross contribution so that with effect from the effective date the gross contributions shall be amended to such sum as after deduction of the authorised percentage thereof equals the amount expressed in the contract to be the contribution.

4(2)   Where such an amendment is made, the resolution shall operate so as to effect the above mentioned amendment in the gross contribution payable under every contract of a class to which the provision relates, and the prescribed scheme as amended shall take effect accordingly.

CORRESPONDING AMENDMENT TO SUM ASSURED

5   Where a gross contribution has been amended under regulation 4, the sum assured or guaranteed by the contract may be amended by an amount determined in accordance with rules which have been certified by an actuary to be fair in relation to the gross contribution payable and have been approved by the Chief Registrar of Friendly Societies.

Prospective amendments – Reg. 5 substituted by FA 2012, Sch. 39, para. 26(5) from a date to be appointed.

6   Where the gross contribution is amended in accordance with these Regulations, the society shall, on being requested in writing after 5th April 1981 to do so by the person by whom the contribution is payable, notify him in writing of the amount of the effect of the amendment on the sum assured or guaranteed or of any other effect.

7   Where by virtue of regulation 6 of the 1977 Regulations a person insured under a contract irrevocably elected that the contribution under the contract under which he was insured should be increased with effect from 6th April 1979, the amendment to the gross contribution shall apply as from the effective date as if it had been effected under regulation 4(2), and regulations 5 and 6 shall apply in respect of an amended contribution under this regulation as they apply in relation to an amendment under regulation 4.

AMENDMENT OF APPROVED SCHEME

8   Where a friendly society adopted an approved scheme under regulation 7 of the 1977 Regulations the Chief Registrar of Friendly Societies may, within eight months of the passing of any Act making a change in the authorised percentage, approve any amendment to the scheme which in his view is expedient or necessary to give effect to the change in the authorised percentage.

Prospective amendments – Reg. 8 substituted by FA 2012, Sch. 39, para. 26(6) from a date to be appointed.

NOTICE OR ADVERTISEMENT

9   Where a friendly society has, in accordance with the provisions of these Regulations, amended the prescribed scheme or an approved scheme adopted by it, as soon as is reasonably practicable it shall either:

(a)   serve upon every person paying contributions to the society who is affected by the amendment a notice containing a statement setting out the effects thereof; or

(b)   publish or cause to be published such notice by advertisement in one or more newspapers in general circulation in the area where the society carries on business.

AMENDMENT OF RULES

10   Notwithstanding anything contained in the rules of a friendly society which has amended the prescribed scheme or an approved scheme, the committee of management of the society may, by resolution passed before the effective date, make amendments to the rules of the society in connection with the amendment by the society of any such scheme.

MODIFICATION OF ENACTMENTS

11   The enactments mentioned in the Schedule to these Regulations shall have effect subject to the adaptations and modifications set out in that Schedule.

SCHEDULE – ADAPTATIONS AND MODIFICATIONS OF ENACTMENTS

Regulation 11

[Amending provisions, not reproduced here.]

INDUSTRIAL ASSURANCE (LIFE ASSURANCE PREMIUM RELIEF) (CHANGE OF RATE) REGULATIONS 1980

(SI 1980/1948, as amended by FA 2012)

Made on 15 December 1980 by the Industrial Assurance Commissioner under para. 13 of Sch. 4 to the Finance Act 1976 [ICTA 1988, Sch. 14, para. 3].

Cross references – FA 2012, Sch. 39, para. 27: modified application of SI 1980/1948.

CITATION AND COMMENCEMENT

1 These Regulations may be cited as the Industrial Assurance (Life Assurance Premium Relief) (Change of Rate) Regulations 1980, and shall come into operation on 20th January 1981.

INTERPRETATION

2 In these Regulations–

"**the 1977 Regulations**" means the Industrial Assurance (Life Assurance Premium Relief) Regulations 1977;

"**industrial assurance company**" and "**collecting society**" have the meanings assigned by section 1 of the Industrial Assurance Act 1923 as amended by Schedule 6 to the Companies Act 1967;

"**the prescribed scheme**" means the scheme prescribed in Schedule 1 to the Industrial Assurance (Life Assurance Premium Relief) Regulations 1977;

"**an approved scheme**" means a special scheme approved by the Industrial Assurance Commissioner in the circumstances provided for in regulation 7 of the Industrial Assurance (Life Assurance Premium Relief) Regulations 1977;

"**actuary**" means an actuary having the qualifications which are prescribed by the Friendly Societies (Qualifications of Actuaries) Regulations 1968;

"**net premium**" has the meaning assigned in paragraph 3 of Schedule 1 to the Industrial Assurance (Life Assurance Premium Relief) Regulations 1977;

"**gross premium**" means the premium of the amount payable under the policy or contract;

"**the authorised percentage**" means the percentage for the time being in force under paragraph 5(a) of Schedule 4 to the Finance Act 1976;

"**the effective date**" means the date on which a change in the authorised percentage takes effect;

"**amended net premium**" shall be a sum equal to the gross premium less the authorised percentage, such sum to be rounded off in accordance with the principles set out in Schedule 1 of the 1977 Regulations;

"**parent**" includes a stepfather and a stepmother.

AMENDMENT OF A SCHEME

3(1) Where an industrial assurance company or collecting society has adopted the prescribed scheme or an approved scheme in accordance with the provisions of the 1977 Regulations the company or society may, by resolution of its board of directors or, as the case may be, of its committee of management, passed within eight months of the passing of any Act making a change in the authorised percentage, amend any such scheme so that amounts equal to the authorised percentage of the gross premiums due and payable on or after the effective date under policies or contracts to which the scheme applies shall be retained by or refunded to the persons paying the premiums.

3(2) Where an industrial assurance company or collecting society has amended any such scheme, amounts equal to the authorised percentage of the gross premiums payable under policies or contracts to which the scheme applies shall be retained by or refunded to the persons paying the premiums as provided in the scheme so amended.

3(3) Written notice of a resolution amending the prescribed scheme or an approved scheme shall within fourteen days of the passing thereof be sent by the industrial assurance company or collecting society to the Industrial Assurance Commissioner.

3(4)   Where a collecting society has resolved to amend the prescribed scheme or an approved scheme any right conferred by section 21 of the Friendly Societies Act 1974 or section 10(1) of the Industrial Assurance and Friendly Societies Act 1948 on any person to receive a copy of the rules of the society or of an amendment therof shall be extended so as to include the right to receive a copy of the resolution and of the amended scheme adopted by the resolution.

AMENDMENT OF GROSS PREMIUM

4(1)   Where, by virtue of regulation 4 of the 1977 Regulations, a resolution adopting the prescribed scheme provided that the gross premium was to be increased with effect from 6th April 1979 in respect of any specified class of policy or contract, a resolution amending the prescribed scheme may also amend the gross premium so that with effect from the effective date the gross premium shall be amended to such sum as after deduction of the authorised percentage thereof equals the amount expressed in the policy or contract to be the premium.

4(2)   Where such an amendment is made, the resolution shall operate so as to effect the above mentioned amendment in the gross premium payable under every policy or contract of a class to which the provision relates, and the prescribed scheme as amended shall take effect accordingly.

CORRESPONDING AMENDMENT TO SUM ASSURED

5   Where a gross premium has been amended under regulation 4, the sum assured or guaranteed by the policy or contract may be amended by an amount determined in accordance with rules which have been certified by an actuary to be fair in relation to the gross premium payable and have been approved by the Industrial Assurance Commissioner.

Prospective amendments – Reg. 5 substituted by FA 2012, Sch. 39, para. 27(5) from a date to be appointed.

6   Where the gross premium is amended in accordance with these Regulations, the industrial assurance company or collecting society shall, on being requested in writing after 5th April 1981 to do so by the person by whom the premium is payable, notify him in writing of the effect of the amendment on the sum assured or guaranteed or of any other effect.

7   Where by virtue of regulation 6 of the 1977 Regulations a person insured under a policy or contract irrevocably elected that the premium under the contract under which he was insured should be increased with effect from 6th April 1979, the amendment to the gross premium shall apply as from the effective date as if it had been effected under regulation 4(2), and regulations 5 and 6 shall apply in respect of an amended premium under this regulation as they apply in relation to an amendment under regulation 4.

AMENDMENT OF APPROVED SCHEMES

8   Where an industrial assurance company or a collecting society adopted an approved scheme under regulation 7 of the 1977 Regulations, the Industrial Assurance Commissioner may, within eight months of the passing of any Act making a change in the authorised percentage, approve any amendment to the scheme which in his view is expedient or necessary to give effect to the change in the authorised percentage.

Prospective amendments – Reg. 8 substituted by FA 2012, Sch. 39, para. 27(6) from a date to be appointed.

NOTICE OR ADVERTISEMENT

9   Where an industrial assurance company or collecting society has, in accordance with the provisions of these regulations, amended the prescribed scheme or an approved scheme adopted by it, as soon as is reasonably practicable it shall either:

(a)   serve upon every person paying premiums to the company or society who is affected by the amendment a notice containing a statement setting out the effects thereof; or

(b)   publish or cause to be published such notice by advertisement in one or more newspapers in general circulation in the area where the company or society carries on business.

AMENDMENT OF RULES

10   Notwithstanding anything contained in the rules of a collecting society which has amended the prescribed scheme, the committee of management of the society may, by resolution passed before the effective date, make amendments to the rules of the society in connection with the amendment by the society of any such scheme.

MODIFICATIONS OF ENACTMENTS

11   The enactments mentioned in the Schedule to these Regulations shall have effect subject to the adaptations and modifications set out in that Schedule.

SCHEDULE – ADAPTATIONS AND MODIFICATIONS OF ENACTMENTS

Regulation 11

[Amending provisions, not reproduced here.]

INCOME TAX (INTEREST RELIEF) REGULATIONS 1982

(SI 1982/1236, as amended by SI 1983/311, SI 1985/1252, SI 1988/1347, SI 1995/1213, SI 1996/1184 and SI 2009/56)

Made on 31 August 1982 and laid before the House of Commons on 1 September 1982, in exercise of the powers conferred on the Commissioners of Inland Revenue by s. 29(3) of the Finance Act 1982 [ICTA 1988, s. 378(3)].

CITATION AND COMMENCEMENT

1 These Regulations may be cited as the Income Tax (Interest Relief) Regulations 1982, and shall come into operation on 1st October 1982.

INTERPRETATION

2(1) In these Regulations unless the context otherwise requires:–

"**authorised officer**" means the official registered by the Board as being authorised for the purposes of these Regulations by the lender;

"**the Board**" means the Commissioners of Inland Revenue;

"**financial year**" in relation to a lender means a period of 12 months or the period (not necessarily a period of 12 months) for which the lender makes up its accounts;

"**lender**" means a qualifying lender for the purposes of section 26;

"**limited loan**" means a loan to which either paragraph 5(1) or (2) or paragraph 24(3) of Schedule 1 to the Finance Act 1974 [ICTA 1988, s. 357(1) or 365(3)] applies;

"**a qualifying borrower**" has the meaning given by Part III of Schedule 7 [ICTA 1988, s. 376], which shall be deemed to include, for the application to them of sections 26 and 28 and Schedule 7 [ICTA 1988, s. 369 to 377] and these regulations those personal representatives and trustees to whom reference is made in Regulation 7A below, so long as they are all resident in the United Kingdom and in Regulation 7B below, so long as the conditions in that Regulation are fulfilled;

"**relevant loan interest**" has the meaning given by Part I of Schedule 7 [ICTA 1988, s. 370–373];

"**Schedule 7**" means Schedule 7 to the Finance Act 1982 [ICTA 1988, s. 370–376];

"**section 26**" means section 26 of the Finance Act 1982 [ICTA 1988, s. 369];

"**section 28**" means section 28 of the Finance Act 1982 [ICTA 1988, s. 377];

"**tax year**" means a period of 12 months ending on 5th April.

2(2) In the application of these Regulations to Scotland–

(a) "**a freehold or leasehold estate**" means any interest in land; and

(b) any reference to **a loan on the security of such an estate** is a reference to a loan upon a heritable security within the meaning of section 9(8)(a) of the Conveyancing and Feudal Reform (Scotland) Act 1970.

History – In the definition of "a qualifying borrower" in reg. 2(1) words "which shall be ... fulfilled" inserted by SI 1983/311, operative from 15 March 1983.

LOANS WHICH THE BORROWER MAY BRING WITHIN THE TAX DEDUCTION SCHEME

3(1) Loans the interest on which paid by a qualifying borrower is relevant loan interest are loans specified for the purposes of paragraph 7(1)(a) of Schedule 7 [ICTA 1988, s. 374(1)(a)] except–

(a) loans in respect of property which is used as the only or main residence of a dependent relative or former or separated spouse of his;

(b) loans the interest on which is eligible for relief under paragraph 4A of Schedule 1 to the Finance Act 1974 [ICTA 1988, s. 356]; or

(c) loans to which the provisions of sub-paragraphs (b), (c) or (d) of the said paragraph 7(1) [ICTA 1988, s. 374(1)(b)–(d)] apply.

3(2) [Omitted by SI 1995/1213, reg. 3.]

3(3) Where the borrower is unable to provide the lender with the notice to which the said paragraph 7(1)(a) [ICTA 1988, s. 374(1)(a)] refers he may, if he considers that the interest payable on his loan is or will be relevant loan interest, apply to the Board for a notice under paragraph 7(1)(b) of Schedule 7 [ICTA 1988, s. 374(1)(b)] and the Board shall notify him of their decision on his application.

History – Reg. 3(1)(b) substituted by SI 1983/311, operative from 15 March 1983.
Reg. 3(2) omitted by SI 1995/1213, reg. 3, operative from 4 May 1995.

Cross references – SI 1988/1347, reg. 8: housing associations.

LOANS MADE BEFORE TAX YEAR 1983–84 WHICH THE LENDER MAY BRING WITHIN THE TAX DEDUCTION SCHEME

4 Loans of the following descriptions, not being loans to which the interest on which paragraph 2(3) of Schedule 7 [ICTA 1988, s. 370(3)] applies, are specified for the purposes of paragraph 7(1)(d) of Schedule 7 [ICTA 1988, s. 374(1)(d)]–

(a)   a loan secured on a freehold or leasehold estate in respect of property in relation to which the loan was granted in which the borrower (and in the case of joint borrowers each of them), or a dependent relative, or former or separated spouse of his, is residing at the time when the loan is made, or will so reside within 12 months of that time; being a loan–

    (i)   which is not a limited loan (unless it is a limited loan in respect of which notice has been given to the Board under Regulation 7(1) before 1st December 1982);

    (ii)   in respect of which the lender has undertaken:

        (a)   to inform the Board that it is a loan to which this Regulation applies together with the name and address of each borrower, and where known the Tax District to which he makes his return together with his tax reference; and

        (b)   to notify the borrower, not later than 30 days before the first payment of relevant loan interest falls due, that interest payable on the loan appears to be relevant loan interest; and

    (iii)   in respect of which the lender has not been notified that the interest is not relevant loan interest;

(b)   a loan which is not a limited loan but otherwise qualifies for relief under the provisions of paragraph 24 of Schedule 1 to the Finance Act 1974 [ICTA 1988, s. 365].

Cross references – SI 1988/1347, reg. 9: reg. 4 to have effect in relation to housing associations.

COMMENCEMENT OF TAX DEDUCTION SCHEME BEFORE TAX YEAR 1983–84 IN CERTAIN CASES

5 Where the Board is satisfied that it is the practice for borrowers to have been given relief under section 75 of the Finance Act 1972 on the basis of amounts of interest paid to a lender in a period of 12 months ending after February but before 6th April and the lender, not being a lender within the provisions of paragraph 2(4) of Schedule 7, notifies the Board that it wishes the tax deduction scheme to begin to apply on a date before 6th April 1983 but not before 1st March 1983, the Board shall notify it of the date on which the scheme may begin to apply accordingly.

APPLICATION OF TAX DEDUCTION SCHEME TO HOME IMPROVEMENT LOANS

6 Where before 1st December in any year a lender notifies the Board that it wishes home improvement loans which it has made to which paragraph 4(1)(b) of Schedule 7 [ICTA 1988, s. 372(1)(b)] applies to be brought within the tax deduction scheme, the scheme shall begin to apply to relevant loan interest payable on such loans in the tax year beginning in the next following year; but in the case of home improvement loans to be made on or after the date of the lender's notice to the Board it shall begin to apply from the date specified in the notice.

APPLICATION OF TAX DEDUCTION SCHEME TO LIMITED LOANS

7(1)

(a)   Subject to the provisions of sub-paragraph (b)–

    (i)   where before 1st October in any year a lender notifies the Board that it wishes limited loans which it has made to be brought within the tax deduction scheme, the scheme shall begin to apply in the tax year beginning in the next following year to the relevant loan interest payable on those loans in respect of which the Board has given notice as provided by paragraph 7(1)(b) of Schedule 7 [ICTA 1988, s. 374(1)(b)]; but in the case of limited loans which the lender makes on or after the date of the lender's notice the scheme shall begin to apply to the relevant loan interest payable on those loans after the date specified in the notice, not being a date earlier than 30 days after the date of that notice;

(ii)   where at any time a lender notifies the Board of its wish to bring within the tax deduction scheme only those limited loans which it will make on or after the date of the lender's notice to the Board the scheme shall begin to apply to the relevant loan interest payable on those loans after the date specified in the notice, not being a date earlier than 30 days after the date of that notice.

(b)   within 30 days of the lender's giving such notice the Board may notify the lender that the scheme shall not begin to apply in accordance with its notice and, where the Board so notifies the lender, the scheme shall begin to apply only on the date and to the loans which the Board has in writing authorised.

7(2)   Where a lender has not so notified the Board under paragraph (1)(a) the tax deduction scheme shall not begin to apply in the following circumstances:–

(a)   for the tax year 1983–84, in respect of interest on a loan which was a limited loan,

    (i)   when the interest was last charged by the lender to the borrower's account in its records before February 1983, or

    (ii)   in the case of a loan made after January 1983, when the loan was made;

(b)   for any tax year after 5th April 1984 in respect of interest on a loan which was a limited loan

    (i)   when the interest was last charged by the lender to the borrower's account in its records at any time before March in the previous tax year, or

    (ii)   in the case of a loan made after the date when the qualifying lender last charged interest to borrowers' accounts in its records at any time before March in the previous tax year, when the loan was made.

History – Reg. 7(1)(a) substituted by SI 1985/1252, operative from 1 September 1985. Reg. 7(2)(b) substituted by SI 1983/311, operative from 15 March 1983.

APPLICATION OF TAX DEDUCTION SCHEME TO CERTAIN PERSONAL REPRESENTATIVES AND TRUSTEES

7A   Interest which is paid and payable in the United Kingdom by persons as personal representatives of a deceased person or as trustees of a settlement made by his will the whole of which would have been eligible for relief under section 75 of the Finance Act 1972 [ICTA 1988, s. 353] (by virtue of paragraph 8 of Schedule 1 to the Finance Act 1974) [ICTA 1988, s. 358], apart from section 26(1) [ICTA 1988, s. 369(1)] and paragraph 5 of Schedule 1 to the Finance Act 1974 [ICTA 1988, s. 357], is relevant loan interest within the meaning of Part I of Schedule 7 [ICTA 1988, s. 370 to 373] (but as if sub-paragraph (3) of paragraph 2 of that Schedule [ICTA 1988, s. 370(3)] were omitted) to which section 26(1) [ICTA 1988, s. 369(1)] applies.

History – Reg. 7A added by SI 1983/311, reg. 6.

7B   In determining whether loan interest paid and payable by trustees to whom reference is made in section 24(4) of the Housing Subsidies Act 1967 (option mortgages) or Article 143(6) of the Housing (Northern Ireland) Order 1981 (option mortgages in Northern Ireland) is relevant loan interest, Schedule 7 [ICTA 1988, s. 370 to 376] shall have effect as if for sub-paragraph (3) of paragraph 2 there were substituted the words–

    "(3)   This sub-paragraph applies to interest payable by trustees which becomes due on or after 1st April 1983 and is payable on a loan–

        (a)   in respect of which there is in force on 31st March 1983 an option notice given under section 24(2) of the 1967 Act (option mortgages) or under Article 142(2) of the 1981 Order which has effect by virtue of section 24(4) of that Act or, as the case may be, by virtue of Article 143(6) of that Order; and

        (b)   which relates to a dwelling in respect of which, at the time the interest is paid and on the assumption that one of those provisions continues to be applicable, the conditions in section 24(4) of the 1967 Act or, as the case may be, Article 143(6) of the 1981 Order are fulfilled."

History – Reg. 7B inserted by SI 1983/311, reg. 6.

VARIATION OF REPAYMENT TERMS OF CERTAIN LOANS

8(1)   Expressions used in this Regulation have the same meaning as in section 28 [ICTA 1988, s. 377].

8(2)   Subject to the provisions of this Regulation the amount of each combined payment and the date on which it becomes due from a borrower, to whom a specified lender has given a notice under section 28(2)(a) [ICTA 1988, s. 377(2)(a)] to vary the terms of repayment of the loan, shall be notified to the borrower by the lender.

8(3)   The notice under section 28(2)(a) [ICTA 1988, s. 377(2)(a)] shall be in a form prescribed or authorised by the Board but shall not have effect unless–

(a)   it contains a statement of the borrower's right under section 28(2)(b) [ICTA 1988, s. 377(2)(b)] to give a counter notice; and

(b)   there is a period of not less than 30 days between the giving of the notice and the due date for the first of the combined payments to which the notice relates.

8(4)   A borrower shall be entitled to give a counter notice under section 28(2)(b) [ICTA 1988, s. 377(2)(b)] not later than 3 months after the due date for the first combined payment to which paragraph (2) above refers.

8(5)   In receipt of the borrower's counter notice under section 28(2)(b) [ICTA 1988, s. 377(2)(b)] the lender shall give notice to the borrower of–

(a)   the amount of the combined payments which will be due from him after taking account of the requirements of section 28(4) [ICTA 1988, s. 377(4)];

(b)   the due date for the first such combined payment which shall be–

(i)   where the borrower gives a counter notice under section 28(2)(b) [ICTA 1988, s. 377(2)(b)] within 30 days of the lender's notice under section 28(2)(a) [ICTA 1988, s. 377(2)(a)], the date for the first combined payment to which paragraph (2) above refers; or

(ii)   in any other case, a date not later than what apart from the borrower's counter notice, would have been the date of the second of his combined payments falling due after the date of that counter notice;

(c)   an estimate of the total period which, assuming there is no change in the amount of the borrower's combined payments, will be required to satisfy the principal and the interest on the loan by means of those payments; and

(d)   a statement of the borrower's right under section 28(4) [ICTA 1988, s. 377(4)] to make additional repayments of capital.

REPAYMENT CLAIMS BY CERTAIN BORROWERS

8A(1)   Where in a tax year a borrower has not been able to deduct the full amount of the sums deductible under the provisions of section 26(1) [ICTA 1988, s. 369(1)] from payments of relevant loan interest by reason of the circumstances described in paragraph 11 of Schedule 7 [ICTA 1988, s. 375(8)], he may make a claim to the Board for payment of a sum equal to the amount which he has not been able to deduct.

8A(2)   Section 42 of the Taxes Management Act 1970 shall not apply to such a claim.

8A(3)   The Board shall notify the borrower of its decision on the claim.

History – Reg. 8A inserted by SI 1983/311, reg. 7, operative from 15 March 1983.

8B(1)   This regulation applies in any case where an amount to which a borrower is not entitled is paid to him by the Board pursuant to a claim under regulation 8A.

8B(2)   An officer of the Board may make such assessments as may in his judgment be required for recovering that amount from the borrower.

8B(3)   The Taxes Management Act 1970 shall apply to an assessment under paragraph (2) as if it were an assessment to income tax for the year of assessment for which the payment was made.

8B(4)   If in a case to which paragraph (1) applies, the borrower fraudulently or negligently makes any false statement or representation in connection with the making of a claim under regulation 8A, he shall be liable to a penalty not exceeding the amount referred to in that paragraph.

8B(5)   If in a case to which paragraph (1) applies, the borrower is required to give notice under subsection (1) of section 375 of the Income and Corporation Taxes Act 1988, and there is any unreasonable delay in the giving of the notice, he shall be liable to a penalty not exceeding so much of the amount referred to in that paragraph as is attributable to that delay.

History – Reg. 8B(3) substituted by SI 1996/1184, reg. 3, with effect in any case where an assessment is made on or after 20 May 1996, and is for the year 1996–97 or any subsequent year of assessment.
Reg. 8B inserted by SI 1995/1213, reg. 4, operative from 4 May 1995.

Cross references – SI 1996/1184, reg. 4: where an assessment is made on or after 6 April 1988 and is for the year 1995–96 or any earlier year of assessment reg. 8B(3) is substituted so as to read as follows:

> "**8B(3)**   The Taxes Management Act 1970 shall apply to an assessment under paragraph (2) as if it were an assessment to income tax for the year of assessment for which the payment was made and as if the assessment were among those specified in section 55(1) of that Act (recovery of tax not postponed).".

REPAYMENT CLAIMS BY LENDERS: INTRODUCTORY

9(1)   Sums recoverable by a lender under section 26(7) [ICTA 1988, s. 369(6)] shall be recovered on a claim to the Board for the purpose under these Regulations.

9(2)   Subject to paragraph (3) a claim shall be for the lender's financial year, and is referred to in these Regulations as an **"annual claim"**.

9(3)   A claim may also be made in accordance with Regulations 10 or 12 for a period shorter than the claimant's financial year and is referred to in these Regulations as an **"interim claim"**.

9(4)   No payment in respect of sums recoverable on such a claim shall be made to a lender before 1st April 1983.

INTERIM CLAIMS IN ADVANCE

10(1)   An interim claim for a period allowed by paragraphs (2) and (3) may be made not later than 1 month, or such shorter period as the Board may allow, before the date to which paragraph (5) refers, and is referred to in these Regulations as an **"interim claim in advance"**.

10(2)   The periods for which an interim claim in advance may be made are:–

(a)   1 calendar month; or

(b)   3 calendar months.

10(3)   Interim claims in advance made by a lender may not (except where authorised by prior written approval of the Board) be made for different periods.

10(4)   An interim claim in advance for a period shall be based on an estimate of the amount deductible by borrowers in respect of payments of relevant loan interest to the lender falling due in that period, and the estimate shall be certified by an authorised officer of the lender as being the best estimate that can reasonably be made of the amount deductible.

10(5)   If the Board are satisfied with the estimate they shall pay a sum equal to the estimated amount deductible on the date prescribed in paragraph (6) or where it is not a working day the next following working day; if they are not so satisfied they shall pay the lender such lesser sum, if any, as in their estimation will approximate to the amount deductible.

10(6)   Subject to paragraph (7), the date referred to in paragraph (5) is–

(a)   in the case of a claim for 1 calendar month the 23rd of the month;

(b)   in the case of a claim for 3 calendar months the 15th of the second of those months.

10(7)   In the case of a claim for 1 calendar month, if the lender so claims and satisfies the condition in paragraph (8), the date referred to in paragraph (5) above is the 2nd, 9th or 15th instead of the 23rd of the month.

10(8)   The condition mentioned in paragraph (7) is that the lender's mean repayment date is closer to the date on which repayment is claimed than each of the other 3 dates and the lender's **"mean repayment date"** means–

(a)   the date which is found by multiplying the date of each day of the months of April to September in the previous year by the payments of interest due on that day, adding together the products so calculated for all the days of those 6 months, and dividing the total of those products by the total of all payments of interest due in those months; or

(b)   a date arrived at on some other basis which is authorised by the Board.

SUPPLEMENTARY STATEMENTS

11(1)   When a payment has been made to a lender under Regulation 10(5) on an interim claim in advance, the lender shall deliver to the Board a supplementary statement under this Regulation and (except when paragraph (5) below applies) shall deliver the statement within 4 months after the end of the period for which the claim was made.

11(2)   The supplementary statement shall be a statement correcting (or confirming) the estimate of the amount deductible given in accordance with Regulation 10(4) above, and shall–

(a)   be based as far as possible on the amount of relevant loan interest which actually fell due in the period covered by the statement, and only as far as may be necessary on a revised estimate; and

(b)   be for the same period as the interim claim in advance;

and any estimate contained in the supplementary statement shall be certified by an authorised officer of the lender as the best estimate that can reasonably be made.

11(3)   If the supplementary statement shows that the amount deductible was greater than the payment made under Regulation 10(5) the Board shall, if satisfied with the statement, pay the amount of the difference to the lender by way of supplementary payment on the claim, but if the supplementary statement shows that the amount deductible was less than the payment made under Regulation 10(5) the lender shall repay the amount of the difference to the Board with the statement.

11(4)   If in respect of an interim claim on which a payment has been made under Regulation 10(5) a lender fails to deliver a supplementary statement within the time required by this Regulation, the amount of the payment shall immediately be recoverable by the Board in the same manner as tax charged by an assessment on the lender which has become final and conclusive.

11(5)   Where the lender debits interest in arrear to a borrower's account in its records and at intervals of more than a month the supplementary statement shall, if this date is later than the date in paragraph (1) above, be delivered not later than 5 months after the end of the month in which interest is so debited.

INTERIM CLAIMS IN ARREAR

12(1)   An interim claim for a period allowed by paragraph (2) may be made by a lender within 6 months after the end of the period for which it is made.

12(2)   The period for which a claim may be made under this Regulation shall be one which:–

(a)   is not shorter than 1 calendar month;

(b)   falls within the lender's same financial year; and

(c)   does not include any part of a period in respect of which a payment was made under Regulation 10(5) (unless the payment in respect of the period or that part was recovered under Regulation 11(4)).

12(3)   A claim under this Regulation may not be based on an estimate but may only be made to recover the amount deductible in respect of interest which fell due in the period.

12(4)   If the amount claimed is established to the Board's satisfaction they shall pay the amount to the claimant; if they are not so satisfied they shall pay to the claimant any lesser amount established to their satisfaction.

ANNUAL CLAIMS

13(1)   An annual claim for the lender's financial year may not be made at any time more than 6 years after the end of the financial year.

13(2)   Except where in relation to any financial year a lender repays all the payments made to it on relevant interim claims, it shall within 1 year after the end of the financial year make an annual claim to establish the amount deductible for that financial year.

In this Regulation **"relevant interim claim"** means, in relation to a financial year, an interim claim for a period falling wholly or partly within that financial year.

13(3)   The annual claim may not be based on an estimate and shall, unless the lender makes an election under paragraph (4), include only the tax deducted from interest payments due from borrowers during the financial year to which the claim relates and paid not later than 4 months after the end of that year.

13(4)   Where however a loan is secured on a freehold or leasehold estate in respect of property in relation to which the loan is made, the lender may in respect of any such loan elect to include in an annual claim the amount of tax deductible in respect of interest payments due from the borrower in the year, but always excluding amounts of tax deductible in respect of interest written off as a bad debt in the accounts of the lender for the financial year to which the claim relates.

13(5)

(a)   Where in a tax year before the passing of the Act imposing tax for that year any deduction has been made in accordance with section 26 [ICTA 1988, s. 369] from a payment of interest at a rate in excess of the rate of tax ultimately so imposed, the lender may include in his annual claim the amount of the excess not recovered where—

    (i)   the loan has been repaid before the passing of the said Act, and

    (ii)   the lender has not been able to recover from the borrower the excess so deducted by the end of its financial year or within 6 months of the deduction whichever is the later.

(b)   The amount included in respect of the excess shall be repaid to the lender by the Board as if it were an amount deductible from relevant loan interest in accordance with section 26 [ICTA 1988, s. 369] and the Board shall be entitled to recover from the borrower the amount so repaid in the same manner as tax charged by an assessment on the borrower which has become final and conclusive.

13(6)   An annual claim shall bring into account payments made on relevant interim claims, and shall apportion as may be necessary any payment made on such claim for any period falling partly in a different financial year; and for the purpose of this Regulation the **"aggregate of the relevant interim payments"** means the aggregate of the payments made (and not repaid) on relevant interim claims but excluding any part of a payment relating to a different financial year.

13(7)   Where the aggregate of the relevant interim payments shown by an annual claim exceeds the amount deductible for the financial year shown on the claim, the lender shall repay the amount of the excess to the Board with the claim.

13(8)   If a lender fails to make an annual claim required under paragraph (2) within the time limited by that paragraph, the Board may issue a notice to the lender showing the aggregate of the relevant interim payments for the year, and stating that the Board are not satisfied that the amount due to the lender for the year exceeds the lower amount stated in the notice.

13(9)   If an annual claim is not delivered to the Board with 14 days after the issue of such a notice under paragraph (8) the amount of the difference between the aggregate and the lower amount stated in the notice shall immediately be recoverable by the Board in the same manner as tax charged by an assessment on the lender which has become final and conclusive.

13(10)   Where an annual claim has been made and the lender subsequently discovers that an error or mistake has been made in the claim the lender may make a supplementary annual claim within the time allowed in paragraph (1).

History – Reg. 13(3) substituted by SI 1983/311, operative from 15 March 1983.

LENDERS' CLAIMS: SUPPLEMENTARY PROVISIONS

14(1)   Section 42 of the Taxes Management Act 1970 shall not apply to claims under these Regulations.

14(2)   No appeal shall lie from the Board's decision on an interim claim.

14(3)   An appeal may be made against the Board's decision on an annual claim, and the appeal shall be brought by giving written notice to the Board within 30 days of receipt of written notice of the decision.

14(4)   No payment or repayment made or other thing done on or in relation to an interim claim or a notice under Regulation 13(8) shall prejudice the decision on an annual claim.

14(5)   Part V of the Taxes Management Act 1970 (appeals and other proceedings) shall apply to an appeal under paragraph (3) above, and on an appeal that is notified to the tribunal, the tribunal may vary the decision appealed against whether or not the variation is to the advantage of the appellant.

14(6)   All such assessments, payments and repayments shall be made as are necessary to give effect to the Board's decision on an annual claim, or to any variation of that decision on appeal.

14(7)   Claims and supplementary statements under these Regulations shall be in such form and contain such particulars as the Board prescribe and shall be signed by an authorised officer of the lender; and forms prescribed for annual claims may require a report to be given by the lender's auditor.

14(8)   Where for the purposes of an annual claim for a financial year it is necessary to apportion any amount included in an interim claim for a period falling partly within and partly outside that financial year, the apportionment shall be made in such manner as the Board may prescribe.

History – In reg. 14(3), the words "may be made against" substituted for the words "shall lie to the Special Commissioners from" by SI 2009/56, art. 3(2) and Sch. 2, para. 10(2), operative from 1 April 2009 subject to transitional and saving provisions in SI 2009/56, Sch. 3.
In reg. 14(5), the words "that is notified to the tribunal, the tribunal" substituted for the words "the Special Commissioners" by SI 2009/56, art. 3(2) and Sch. 2, para. 10(3), operative from 1 April 2009 subject to transitional and saving provisions in SI 2009/56, Sch. 3.

INFORMATION TO BE PROVIDED TO BORROWERS BY LENDERS

15 A lender shall, at his request, provide the borrower with a certificate showing in respect of a tax year the amount of relevant loan interest due from and paid by the borrower and the amount of tax deducted from that interest.

INFORMATION TO BE PROVIDED TO THE BOARD

16 The Board may by notice in writing require any person who is a party to a loan agreement to which sections 369 to 376 of the Income and Corporation Taxes Act 1988 apply, or could in the opinion of the Board apply, or a member or tenant of a housing association which is a party to such a loan agreement, to furnish them, within such time (not being less than 14 days) as may be provided by the notice, such information (including copies of any relevant documents or records) as they may reasonably require for the purposes of those sections including, in the case of a loan to a housing association, a certificate that all or any specified conditions of the tax deduction scheme are satisfied.

History – Reg. 16 substituted by SI 1988/1347, reg. 10, operative from 1 August 1988 and previously substituted by SI 1983/368, reg. 8.

INSPECTION OF RECORDS

17(1) Every person to whom payments of interest are made in respect of which a repayment claim is made by a lender under these Regulations shall, whenever required to do so, make available for inspection by an officer of the Board authorised for that purpose all such books, documents and other records in his possession or under his control containing information relating to:–

(a) such interest and the terms of the loans (including relevant contracts or deeds) under which such interest is paid or,

(b) the persons holding such contracts or deeds or paying such interest

as may reasonably be required for determining whether the amount for which any such claim is made is properly recoverable.

17(2) Where records are maintained by computer the person required to make them available for inspection shall provide the officer making the inspection with all facilities necessary for obtaining information from them.

17(3)

(a) Every notice given to it by the borrower under paragraph 7(1)(a) of Schedule 7 [ICTA 1988, s. 374(1)(a)] shall be preserved by the lender to whom it is given and in such manner as may be approved by the Board, so as to be available for inspection under this Regulation, until two years after the termination of the loan or, if earlier, the date from which the interest ceases to be relevant loan interest;

(b) a copy of the notice shall on its written request be made available to the Board.

Cross references – FA 1988, s. 127(1): construction of references in Taxes Acts to "document" and "copy of a document". See FA 1988, s. 127(2)–(4) for ancillary rights of access to computer hardware.

APPLICATION OF PENALTY PROVISIONS OF THE TAXES MANAGEMENT ACT 1970

18 [Amends the Table at TMA 1970, s. 98.]

BORROWERS' APPEALS: SUPPLEMENTARY PROVISIONS

19(1) [Omitted by SI 2009/56, art. 3(2) and Sch. 2, para. 11(2).]

19(2) An appeal shall be brought by giving written notice to the Board within 30 days of the receipt by the borrower of the Board's decision or the notice as the case may be.

19(3) Part V of the Taxes Management Act 1970 (appeals and other proceedings) shall apply to an appeal under this Regulation, and on an appeal that is notified to the tribunal, the tribunal may vary the decision or notice appealed from whether or not the variation is to the advantage of the appellant.

19(4) All such payments or repayments shall be made by the inspector as are necessary to give effect to the Board's decision or notice or to any variation of that decision or notice on appeal.

19(5)–(6) [Omitted by SI 1995/1213, reg. 5.]

History – Reg. 19(1) omitted by SI 2009/56, art. 3(2) and Sch. 2, para. 11(2), operative from 1 April 2009 subject to transitional and saving provisions in SI 2009/56, Sch. 3. Former reg. 19(1) read as follows:

"**19(1)**   An appeal by a borrower shall lie to the General Commissioners except that the borrower may elect (in accordance with section 46(1) of the Taxes Management Act 1970) to bring his appeal before the Special Commissioners–

(a)   from the Board's decision on his application under Regulation 3(3);

(b)   from a notice issued to him by the Board under paragraph 7(1)(b) of Schedule 7 [ICTA 1988, s. 374(1)(b)] (notice that interest may be paid under deduction of tax);

(c)   from a notice issued to him by the Board under paragraph 10 of Schedule 7 [ICTA 1988, s. 375(6) and (7)] (notice that interest is not relevant loan interest); and

(d)   from a decision on his claim under Regulation 8A.".

Former reg. 19(1)(d) inserted by SI 1983/311, reg. 9, operative from 15 March 1983.

In reg. 19(3), the words "that is notified to the tribunal, the tribunal" substituted for the words "the General or Special Commissioners" by SI 2009/56, art. 3(2) and Sch. 2, para. 11(3), operative from 1 April 2009 subject to transitional and saving provisions in SI 2009/56, Sch. 3.

In reg. 19(4), the word "assessments" which preceded the word "payment" omitted by SI 1995/1213, reg. 5, operative from 4 May 1995.

Reg. 19(5), (6) omitted by SI 1995/1213. reg. 5, operative from 4 May 1995.

CAPITAL ALLOWANCES (VEHICLES FOR THE DISABLED) (SIMILAR PAYMENTS) ORDER 1984

(SI 1984/2060)

Made on 19 December 1984 by the Treasury under s. 43(3) of the Finance Act 1971 and s. 64(12) of the Finance Act 1980 [CAA 2001, s. 82(4), and Sch. 3, para. 47(6)].

1 This Order may be cited as the Capital Allowances (Vehicles for the Disabled) (Similar Payments) Order 1984 and shall come into operation on 1st February 1985.

2 In this Order–

> **"army inter-war pensioners"** means former members of Her Majesty's military forces in receipt of a disability pension paid by the Secretary of State for Defence on account of disability attributable to injury sustained after 30th September 1921 but before 3rd September 1939.

3 The following payments are hereby specified as appearing to be of a similar kind to payments within paragraphs (a), (b) and (c) of subsection (3) of the said section 43 and of subsection (12) of the said section 64 for the purposes of the making of first-year allowances in respect of capital expenditure on the provision of mechanically propelled road vehicles, that is to say–

(1)   mobility supplement paid under the Naval and Marine Pay and Pensions (Disablement Awards) Order 1984 or under the Naval and Marine Pay and Pensions (Disablement Awards) (No. 2) Order 1984;

(2)   mobility supplement paid under Queen's Regulations for the Royal Air Force; and

(3)   supplementary allowance paid under Royal Warrant dated 30th December 1949 to army inter-war pensioners equivalent to the mobility supplement provided for by Article 26A of the Naval Military and Air Forces etc. (Disablement and Death) Service Pensions Order 1983.

(4)   This Order has effect in relation to expenditure incurred on or after 21st November 1983.

FILMS CO-PRODUCTION AGREEMENTS ORDER 1985

(SI 1985/960, as amended by SI 2008/1783)

Made on 25 June 1985

1 This Order may be cited as the Films Co-Production Agreements Order 1985 and shall come into operation on 22nd July 1985.

2 A film with respect to which the requirements of Schedule 1 to the Films Act 1985 as to the eligibility of a film for certification as a British film are not fulfilled shall be treated as a film with respect to which those requirements are fulfilled if the film was made in accordance with the respective agreements made between the Government of the United Kingdom and the Governments of the countries set out in the Schedule to this Order.

SCHEDULE

Country	Date of Agreement	Command Paper
Australia	12th June 1990	Cm. 1758
Canada	12th September 1975	Cmnd. 6380
	9th July 1985	Cmnd. 9887
	5th July 1991	Cm. 1807
France	8th November 1994	Cm. 2992
India	5th December 2005	Cm. 7432
Jamaica	23rd April 2007	Cm. 7168
New Zealand	14th April 1993	Cm. 2638
South Africa	24th May 2006	Cm. 6866

History – Schedule substituted by SI 2008/1783, reg. 2, with effect from 1 August 2008.

CAPITAL GAINS TAX (PARALLEL POOLING) REGULATIONS 1986

(SI 1986/387)

Made on 3 March 1986 by the Treasury in exercise of the powers conferred on them by para. 21 of Sch. 19 to the Finance Act 1985 [for continued effect, see TCGA 1992, s. 112].

1 These Regulations may be cited as the Capital Gains Tax (Parallel Pooling) Regulations 1986 and shall come into operation on 1st April 1986.

2 In these Regulations unless the context otherwise requires;—

"**new holding**" has the meaning given to it by paragraph 9(3) of Schedule 19 with the omission therefrom of the words "or sub-paragraph (2)";

"**qualifying securities**" are securities to which Regulation 3 applies;

"**relevant securities**" has the meaning given to it by section 88(9) of the Finance Act 1982 [TCGA 1992, s. 108];

"**Schedule 6**" means Schedule 6 to the Finance Act 1983;

"**Schedule 19**" means Schedule 19 to the Finance Act 1985;

"**1982 holding**" has the meaning given to it by paragraph 6 of Schedule 19 [TCGA 1992, s. 109(1)];

"**1983 holding**" is a holding within the meaning of paragraph 3(3) of Schedule 6.

Notes – FA 1983, Sch. 6 gave details of the election for parallel pooling.
FA 1985, s. 68 and Sch. 19 provided for the notification of indexation allowance so as to remove the 12-month qualifying holding period and to enable the allowance to create or augment a loss, with special rules for certain shares, consequently restricting the application of parallel pooling to disposals before 1 April 1985 (for the rules mentioned above, see now TCGA 1992, s. 55 and 104–114).

3 These Regulations shall have effect in relation to a disposal on or after 1st April 1985 of qualifying securities, within the meaning of Schedule 6,–

(a)   in respect of which an election under that Schedule had been made by a company and not revoked on or before 31st March 1987 or such further time as may be allowed by the Board under paragraph 20(1) of Schedule 19 [TCGA 1992, Sch. 6]; and

(b)   which, immediately before 1st April 1985, were regarded as indistinguishable parts of a single asset by virtue of paragraph 3 of Schedule 6;

and are designed to enable section 68 of, and Parts I to V of Schedule 19 to, the Finance Act 1985 [TCGA 1992, s. 55] to have full effect in relation to the qualifying securities concerned.

4 Of qualifying securities in each 1983 holding which is held by a company immediately before 1st April 1985 there shall be identified as at that time for the purposes of these Regulations–

(a)   by reference to the provisions of Regulations 5, 6, 7 and 8, the 1982 holding and the new holding of such of those securities as are not relevant securities; and

(b)   by reference to the provisions of Regulations 5, 6 and 9, the 1982 holding (and the securities not in the 1982 holding) of such of those securities as are relevant securities;

and, as modified by these Regulations, the relevant provisions of the said section 68 and Schedule 19 shall apply in relation to the 1982 holdings, the new holdings and the holdings of relevant securities.

Notes – See note to reg. 2 above.

5 For the purposes of these Regulations or, as the case may be, the Schedule hereto, "A" to "H" shall be identified by reference to the circumstances obtaining in relation to each 1983 holding held by a company immediately before 1st April 1985 as follows–

(a)   A is the number of qualifying securities in the 1983 holding.

(b)   B is the amount of the unindexed pool of expenditure (within the meaning of paragraph 6 of Schedule 6) attributable to the 1983 holding.

(c)   C is the amount of the indexed pool of expenditure attributable to the 1983 holding, computed on the assumption that an operative event within the meaning of paragraph 7(3) of Schedule 6 occurred immediately before 1st April 1985.

(d)   D is the aggregate of–

(i)   A; and

   (ii)   the number of securities which are of the same class as those to which paragraph (a) above refers, but which, because the conditions of paragraph 3(3)(b) of Schedule 6 are not fulfilled, do not form part of the 1983 holding.

(e)   E is the aggregate of–

   (i)   B; and

   (ii)   the relevant allowable expenditure in relation to a disposal immediately before 1st April 1985 of the whole of the securities to which paragraph (d)(ii) above refers.

(f)   F is the aggregate of the relevant allowable expenditure in relation to all disposals by the company made after March 1982 and before April 1985 of securities which are of the same class as those to which paragraph (a) above refers and which were acquired after 6th April 1965.

(g)   G is–

   (i)   the number of securities of that same class which were held by the company immediately before 1st April 1982 and which comprise a holding within the meaning of Part II of Schedule 13 to the Finance Act 1982; or

   (ii)   where on or after 1st April 1982 there has been a reorganisation of share capital within the meaning of section 77(1) of the Capital Gains Tax Act 1979, the number of shares which (on the assumption that there had been no part disposal of original shares within the meaning of the provisions of that subsection) would comprise a new holding within the meaning of that section.

(h)   H is the amount which would be the aggregate of the relevant allowable expenditure in relation to a disposal by the company immediately before 1st April 1985 of the whole of the securities to which paragraph (g) above refers.

6(1)   J is the number of qualifying securities in the 1982 holding, rounded to the nearest whole number and is given by the formula–

$$G \times \frac{E}{E+F}$$

6(2)   In relation to a disposal by the company of the whole of the 1982 holding on or after 1st April 1985, K is the relevant allowable expenditure, given by the formula–

$$H \times \frac{E}{E+F}$$

7   In respect of qualifying securities (**"the securities"**)–

(a)   the number of the securities which fall to be included in the new holding is given by the formula $A - J$;

(b)   the relevant allowable expenditure in relation to a disposal by the company of all the securities referred to in paragraph (a) above immediately before 1st April 1985 is given by the formula $B - K$;

(c)   the indexed pool of expenditure in relation to the securities referred to in paragraph (a) above for the purposes of paragraph 13(2) of Schedule 19 is given by the formula–

$$(B - K)\left(\frac{C}{B} + 0.05\right).$$

8   In respect of the new holding (**"the holding"**)–

(a)   the number of securities in the holding is given by the formula $D - J$;

(b)   the qualifying expenditure in relation to the holding is given by the formula $E - K$;

(c)   the indexed pool of expenditure in relation to the holding is given by the aggregate of–

   (i)   the amount given by the formula

$$(B - K)\left(\frac{C}{B} + 0.05\right);$$

   (ii)   the relevant allowable expenditure in relation to a disposal by the company immediately before 1st April 1985 of the whole of the securities to which Regulation 5(d)(ii) refers; and

   (iii)   any indexation allowance applicable to such a disposal on the assumption that the amendment of the Finance Act 1982 made by paragraphs 1 and 2 of Schedule 19 had always had effect.

9(1) This Regulation applies to a holding of relevant securities (**"relevant securities holding"**) which are qualifying securities comprised in a 1983 holding held by the company immediately before 1st April 1985 and, for the purposes of this Regulation, references to qualifying securities in Regulations 5 and 6 shall be treated as references to the relevant securities holding.

9(2) In respect of the relevant securities holding–

(a) the number of relevant securities in the holding, not being relevant securities in the 1982 holding, is given by the formula $A - J$;

(b) the relevant securities in the holding to which paragraph (a) above refers shall be treated for the purposes of the Capital Gains Tax Act 1979 as having been acquired on 31st March 1984;

(c) the amount of the relevant allowable expenditure in relation to a disposal on or after 1st April 1985 of all the relevant securities in the holding to which paragraph (a) above refers is given by the formula

$$(B - K) \times \frac{C}{B}$$

and shall be apportioned rateably to the relevant securities.

10 The Schedule to these Regulations shall have effect only for providing an example of the operation of the Regulations and, in the event of any conflict between the provisions of the Schedule and the Regulations, the Regulations shall prevail.

SCHEDULE

Regulation 10

INTRODUCTORY

In this Schedule–

Part I is a statement of facts which are to be assumed;

Part II is an application of the Regulations to qualifying securities which are not relevant securities;

Part III is an application of the Regulations to qualifying securities which are relevant securities.

Part I – Qualifying Securities And Expenditure

PG plc held, acquired or disposed of qualifying securities as follows:–

Date		Number of securities	Expenditure/ proceeds
31st March 1982	holding	1,000	6,000
1st September 1982	purchased	2,000	12,000
1st March 1983	purchased	3,000	10,000
1st September 1983	rights	6,000	12,000
1st January 1985	sold	3,000	12,000
31st January 1985	purchased	3,000	10,000

2. RETAIL PRICES INDEX

The Retail Prices Index is assumed to be:–

March 1982	100	September 1984	112
September 1983	107	January 1985	114
March 1984	110	March 1985	116

3. CALCULATION OF INDEXED POOL OF EXPENDITURE IN ACCORDANCE WITH SCHEDULE 6

	Securities	Excluded from pools £	Unindexed pool £	Indexed pool £
			Expenditure	
31st March 1982	1,000		6,000	6,000
1st September 1983 indexed rise: £6,000 × $\frac{107-100}{100}$ = £6,000 × .070				420
Additions to 1983 holding	2,000 *(Acquired 1st September 1982)*		12,000	12,000
Rights taken up	3,000	6,000		
	6,000	6,000	18,000	18,420
1st March 1984 indexed rise: £18,420 × $\frac{110-107}{107}$ = £18,420 × .028				516
Additions (including rights) to 1983 holding	6,000	6,000	10,000	10,000
	12,000	12,000	28,000	28,936
1st September 1984 indexed rise: £28,936 × $\frac{112-110}{110}$ = £28,936 × .018				521
Expiry of 12 months following rights issue; expenditure no longer excluded		(12,000)	12,000	12,000
	12,000		40,000	41,457
1st January 1985 indexed rise: £41,457 × $\frac{114-112}{112}$ = £41,457 × .018				746
	12,000		40,000	42,203
Disposal	3,000		10,000	10,551
	9,000		30,000	31,652

4. SECURITIES HELD LESS THAN ONE YEAR AT 31ST MARCH 1985

The 3,000 securities acquired on 31st January 1985 for £10,000 do not qualify for inclusion in the 1983 holding on 31 March 1985.

Part II – Qualifying Securities which are not Relevant Securities

STEP 1 – Regulation 5(a)–(c)

Index the indexed pool as if an operative event had occurred immediately before 1st April 1985

Indexed pool (see Part I. 3, above) £31,652

$£31,652 \times \dfrac{116 - 114}{114} = £31,652 \times .018$ 570

£32,222

Therefore–

A = 9,000

B = 30,000

C = 32,222.

STEP 2 – Regulation 5(d) and (e)

Number of securities not within 1983 holding

(see Part I.4, above) 3,000

Relevant allowable expenditure £10,000

Therefore–

D = 9,000 + 3,000 = 12,000

E = 30,000 + 10,000 = 40,000.

STEP 3 – Regulation 5(f)

F = 10,000.

STEP 4 – Regulation 5(g) and (h)

Number of securities held on 31st March 1982 1,000

Rights issue 1 for 1 1,000

G = 2,000

Relevant allowable expenditure on securities = £6,000

Relevant allowable expenditure on rights

1,000 @ £2 per share = £2,000

H = £8,000.

STEP 5 – Regulation 6

$J = 2,000 \times \dfrac{40,000}{40,000 + 10,000}$ = 1,600

$K = £8,000 \times \dfrac{40,000}{40,000 + 10,000}$ = £6,400

Therefore the 1982 holding comprises:

1,600 shares – relevant allowable expenditure £6,400.

Note: applying the above fraction to the separate components of H (step 4) £4,800 will qualify for indexation from March 1982 and £1,600 from September 1983 for the purposes of section 87 of, and paragraph 5 of Schedule 13 to, the Finance Act 1982.

STEP 6 – Regulation 7

Number of securities in the 1983
holding forming part of new holding = 9,000 – 1,600　　=　7,400

Relevant allowable expenditure
on these securities = £30,000 – £6,400　　=　£23,600

Aggregate of relevant allowable expenditure and indexation
allowance for the purposes of paragraph 13(2), Schedule 19

$$= (30,000 - 6,400) \left(\frac{32,222}{30,000} + 0.05 \right) \qquad £26,528$$

STEP 7 – Regulation 8

Number of securities in new holding = 12,000 – 1,600　　=　10,400

Qualifying expenditure = £40,000 – £6,400　　=　£33,600

Relevant allowable expenditure in relation
to securities not included in 1983 holding　　=　£10,000

Indexation allowance　　=　£180

Indexed pool in relation to the new holding
= £26,528 + £10,000 + £180　　=　£36,708.

SUMMARY

1982 holding: 1,600 securities – relevant allowable expenditure £6,400 (of which £4,800 qualifies for indexation from March 1982 and £1,600 from September 1983).
New holding: 10,400 securities – qualifying expenditure £33,600 and indexed pool of expenditure £36,708.

Part III – Qualifying Securities which are Relevant Securities

STEPS 1–5 as in Part II above.

STEP 6 – Regulation 9

Number of relevant securities in 1983 holding
not forming part of 1982 holding = 9,000 – 1,600　　=　7,400

Relevant allowable expenditure

$$= (30,000 - 6,400) \times \frac{32,222}{30,000} \qquad £25,348$$

Expenditure apportioned to securities

$$\frac{£25,348}{7,400} \qquad £3.4254$$

Deemed date of acquisition of those securities – 31st March 1984.

SUMMARY

1982 holding: 1,600 securities – relevant allowable expenditure £6,400 (of which £4,800 qualifies for indexation from March 1982 and £1,600 from September 1983).
Other relevant securities: 7,400 securities treated as acquired on 31st March 1984 – relevant allowable expenditure £25,348.
3,000 securities treated as acquired on 31st January 1986 – relevant allowable expenditure £10,000.

CHARITABLE DEDUCTIONS (APPROVED SCHEMES) REGULATIONS 1986

(SI 1986/2211 as amended by SI 2000/759, SI 2000/2083, SI 2003/1745, SI 2009/56, Statute Law (Repeals) Act 2013 and SI 2014/584)

Made by the Treasury, in exercise of the powers conferred on them by s. 28 of the Finance Act 1986 [ITEPA 2003, s. 715(1)–(5)].

CITATION AND COMMENCEMENT

1 These Regulations may be cited as the Charitable Deductions (Approved Schemes) Regulations 1986, and shall come into operation on 8th January 1987.

INTERPRETATION

2 In these Regulations unless the context otherwise requires:–

"**approved agency**" means a body approved as agent in accordance with Regulation 5;

"**approved scheme**" means a scheme approved in accordance with Regulation 3;

"**employer**" means a person paying emoluments;

"**employee**" means any person entitled to receive payments of emoluments;

"**emoluments**" means income to be taken into account in assessing liability to income tax under Schedule E, from payments of which income tax falls to be deducted by virtue of section 204 of the Taxes Act [ICTA 1988, s. 203] and regulations under that section;

"**income tax month**" means the period beginning on the 6th day of any calendar month and ending on the 5th day of the following calendar month;

"**scheme**" includes a kind of scheme;

"**year**" means the period beginning on any 6th day of April and ending on the following 5th day of April.

History – In reg. 2, the definition of "supplement" omitted by SI 2014/584, reg. 3, with effect from 6 April 2014.

SI 2003/1745, reg. 3 extends the insertion made by SI 2000/2083, reg. 3 (see below) to supplements payable under section 38 of the Finance Act 2000 in respect of sums withheld by an employer as mentioned in that section on or after 6 April 2003 and before 6 April 2004.

Definition of "supplement" inserted by SI 2000/2083, reg. 3, with effect from 21 August 2000 in relation to supplements payable in respect of sums withheld on or after 6 April 2000 and before 6 April 2003.

APPROVAL OF SCHEMES

3 The Board may grant approval of a scheme for the purposes of section 27 of the Finance Act 1986 [ICTA 1988, s. 202(1)–(7) and (11)] if it is satisfied on an application by an approved agency that the scheme provides:–

(a) for a contract between the approved agency and an employer to give effect to the scheme;

(b) that any employee to whom the employer pays emoluments on or after 6th April 1987 may request the employer, in such form as the Board may approve or prescribe, to withhold from such emoluments such sum as the employee may specify pursuant to the scheme to be paid (subject to the provisions of the scheme) either by way of gift to such charity or charities as the employee may specify or in exchange for vouchers which the employee may surrender by way of gift to the charity or charities of his choice;

(c) that under the scheme the employer is constituted the agent of the approved agency in holding moneys withheld from employees pursuant to the scheme;

(d) for any minimum sum which may be withheld pursuant to the scheme and for any limit which may be imposed on the number of charities which one employee may specify pursuant to the scheme;

(e) [omitted by SI 2000/2083,]

(f) that no sum so withheld shall be due to the specified charity pursuant to a deed of covenant or, where the sum withheld is paid in exchange for vouchers, that the value of those vouchers shall not be due to the charity or charities to which they are surrendered pursuant to a deed of covenant;

Statutory Instruments

(g) that the employer is to be bound to pay over to the approved agency sums withheld from employees pursuant to the scheme in any income tax month within 14 days of the end of that income tax month;

(h) that the approved agency will if so requested give written receipts to the employer in respect of sums paid over to it;

(i) that in no circumstances will sums duly withheld and paid over to the approved agency be returnable to the employer or to any employee;

(j) that the approved agency will, subject to any deduction in respect of its charges, pay sums paid to it by the employer pursuant to the scheme to the charities respectively specified by the employees or provide the employees with vouchers to be surrendered to the charities of their choice;

(ja) that the approved agency will pay to the charities specified by the employees the sums paid to it by the employer pursuant to the scheme before the expiry of the relevant period relating to such sums set out in regulation 4A;

(k) that the approved agency will if so requested by an employee at the end of any year give him a certificate of the amounts which the approved agency has paid to charities specified by him in respect of sums withheld from his emoluments in that year and of the maximum time elapsing in any period specified by the employee between the receipt of such sums from the employer and the payment to the charities of amounts in respect of such sums;

(l) that if for any reason it becomes impossible for the approved agency to pay any amount to a charity specified by an employee the approved agency shall pay that amount to such other charity as it may consider has objects similar to those of the charity specified by the employee, but so that it shall not in any circumstances appropriate that amount to its own funds; and that on so paying that amount to that other charity the approved agency will give notice to the employee that it has done so;

(m) that where an employee has been provided with a voucher by which payment may be made to a charity and that voucher has not been presented to the approved agency by way of payment within a time prescribed by the approved agency the approved agency will pay the amount represented by that voucher to such other charity as it sees fit, but so that it shall not in any circumstances appropriate that amount to its own funds; and that on so paying that amount to that other charity the approved agency will give notice to the employee that it has done so;

(n) for the method by which the approved agency's charges in relation to the operation of the scheme will be met and for the determining of the amount of such charges.

History – In reg. 3(b) the words ", subject to paragraph (e)," omitted by SI 2000/2083, reg. 4(a), operative from 21 August 2000. Reg. 3(e) omitted by SI 2000/2083, reg. 4(b), operative from 21 August 2000.
In reg. 3(ja), the words "before the expiry of the relevant period relating to such sums" substituted for the words "within a period which does not exceed the period" by SI 2014/584, reg. 4, with effect from 6 April 2014.
Reg. 3(ja) inserted by SI 2000/759, reg. 3, operative from 6 April 2000.

4 Applications by an approved agency in accordance with Regulation 3 shall be in such form as the Board may approve or prescribe.

PERIOD FOR PAYMENT BY AGENCIES TO CHARITIES

4A(1) An approved agency shall, notwithstanding anything in the provisions of an approved scheme or in a contract entered into with the employer to give effect to an approved scheme, pay to the charities specified by the employees the sums paid to it by the employer pursuant to the scheme before the expiry of the relevant period in relation to such sums.

4A(2) The relevant period in relation to a sum referred to in paragraph (1), subject to paragraphs (3) and (4), is–

(a) the period of 35 days beginning on the day when the approved agency receives the sum described in paragraph (1) provided the approved agency is notified (on or before that day) of the identity of–

    (i) the employee from whose emoluments the sum was withheld, and

    (ii) the charity or charities specified by that employee;

(b) in any other case, the period of 60 days beginning on the day on which the approved agency receives–

    (i) the sum described in paragraph (1) or, if later,

    (ii) notification of the identity of the charity or charities specified by the employee from whose emoluments the sum was withheld.

4A(3)   The receipt by an approved agency of a voucher provided to an employee by which payment may be made to a charity pursuant to an approved scheme shall be treated as a notification of the identity of a charity for the purposes of paragraph (2).

4A(4)   Where–

(a)   the relevant period in paragraph (2) (a) applies in relation to a sum, and

(b)   the approved agency has made no payment pursuant to a scheme to the charity specified in relation to the sum within the 12 months period ending immediately before the receipt of that sum,

the approved agency may treat the relevant period specified by that paragraph as the period of 60 days beginning on the day when the sum is received.

History – Reg. 4A substituted by SI 2014/584, reg. 5, with effect from 6 April 2014. Former reg. 4A read as follows:

"**4A(1)**   An approved agency shall, notwithstanding anything in the provisions of an approved scheme or in a contract entered into with the employer to give effect to an approved scheme, pay to the charities specified by the employees the sums paid to it by the employer pursuant to the scheme not later than 60 days following either–
(a)   the date on which it receives the sums paid to it from the employer or, if later,
(b)   the date on which it receives notification of the charity or charities specified by an employee.

4A(2)   Where an employee has been provided with a voucher by which payment may be made to a charity, the date on which a charity presents that voucher to the approved agency for payment shall be treated for the purposes of paragraph (1)(b) as the date on which the approved agency receives notification of the specification of that charity by the employee.

4A(3)   The prescribed period for the purposes of section 38(1) of the Finance Act 2000 shall be–
(a)   the period of 7 days following the coming into force of the Charitable Deductions (Approved Schemes) (Amendment) Regulations 2003, or
(b)   if it ends later, the period within which payment of the sums paid to the approved agency by the employer pursuant to the scheme is to be made under this regulation.

History – Reg. 4A(3) substituted by SI 2003/1745, reg. 4, with effect in relation to supplements payable under section 38 of the Finance Act 2000 in respect of sums witheld by an employer as mentioned in that section on or after 6 April 2003 and before 6 April 2004.

Former reg. 4A(3) inserted by SI 2000/2083, with effect from 21 August 2000 in relation to supplements payable in respect of sums withheld on or after 6 April 2000 and before 6 April 2003.

Reg. 4A inserted by SI 2000/759, reg. 4, operative from 6 April 2000."

APPROVAL OF AGENCIES

5   The Board may grant approval as an agent for the purposes of section 27 of the Finance Act 1986 [ICTA 1988, s. 202(1)–(7) and (11)] to any charity which the Board is satisfied is prepared and able to act as an approved agency in relation to approved schemes and to comply with the provisions of these Regulations.

6   Applications by a charity for approval as an agent in accordance with Regulation 5 shall be in such form as the Board may approve or prescribe.

WITHDRAWAL OF APPROVAL OF AGENCIES

7   If at any time the Board is of opinion that an approved agency has ceased to be a charity or has failed to act properly in relation to an approved scheme or has failed to comply with these Regulations, it may give notice of withdrawal of approval to the approved agency and thereupon, from such date as the Board may specify in its notice, the agency shall cease to be approved and all schemes which have been approved on its application shall cease to be approved and all contracts to give effect to such schemes shall determine. When the Board gives such notice it shall inform every employer who has a contract with the approved agency to give effect to an approved scheme that it has so given notice.

APPEALS

8(1)   Any person aggrieved by the Board's refusal to grant him approval as an agent in accordance with Regulation 5 or by the Board's withdrawal of such approval in accordance with Regulation 7 may appeal, by notice in writing given to the Board within 30 days from the date on which he is notified of the Board's refusal or withdrawal of approval.

8(2)   Any approved agency aggrieved by the Board's refusal to grant approval of a scheme in accordance with Regulation 3, may appeal, by notice in writing given to the Board within 30 days from the date on which it is notified of the Board's refusal.

History – In reg. 8(1), the word "appeal" inserted after "may" by SI 2009/56, art. 3(2) and Sch. 2, para. 22(2)(a), operative from 1 April 2009 subject to transitional and saving provisions in SI 2009/56, Sch. 3.

In reg. 8(1), the words ", require the matter to be determined by the Special Commissioners, and the Special Commissioners shall hear and determine the matter in like manner as an appeal", which appeared after "withdrawal of approval", omitted by SI 2009/56, art. 3(2) and Sch. 2, para. 22(2)(b), operative from 1 April 2009 subject to transitional and saving provisions in SI 2009/56, Sch. 3.

In reg. 8(2), the word "appeal" inserted after "may" by SI 2009/56, art. 3(2) and Sch. 2, para. 22(3)(a), operative from 1 April 2009 subject to transitional and saving provisions in SI 2009/56, Sch. 3.

In reg. 8(2), the words ", require the matter to be determined by the Special Commissioners, and the Special Commissioners shall hear and determine the matter in like manner as an appeal", which appeared after "Board's refusal", omitted by SI 2009/56, art. 3(2) and Sch. 2, para. 22(3)(b), operative from 1 April 2009 subject to transitional and saving provisions in SI 2009/56, Sch. 3.

INFORMATION, RETURNS AND RECORDS

9(1)   Every approved agency shall, within 30 days of entering into a contract with an employer giving effect to an approved scheme, inform the Board, in such form as the Board may approve or prescribe, of the date of the contract and of the name and address of the employer.

9(2)   Where a contract giving effect to an approved scheme is terminated the approved agency shall, within 30 days, inform the Board of such termination.

9(3)   An approved agency must inform the Board in writing of its failure to make payment to a charity in accordance with regulation 4A no later than 7 days after the expiry of the relevant period applicable in relation to the sum concerned stating the amount of the sum and the reasons for failure to comply with that regulation.

History – SI 2003/1745, reg. 5 extends the substitution made by SI 2000/2083, reg. 6 (see below) to supplements payable under section 38 of the Finance Act 2000 in respect of sums witheld by an employer as mentioned in that section on or after 6 April 2003 and before 6 April 2004.
Reg. 9(3) substituted by SI 2014/584, reg. 6, with effect from 6 April 2014. Former reg. 9(3) read as follows:
> "**9(3)**   Where an approved agency has not paid to the charities specified by the employees–
> (a)   the sums paid to it by the employer pursuant to the scheme within the period set out in regulation 4A(1) and (2), or
> (b)   any supplements relating to those sums within the period prescribed by regulation 4A(3),
> the approved agency shall, not later than 7 days following the last day on which it should have paid those sums or supplements to the charities, inform the Board by furnishing a statement of those sums or supplements and the reasons why it has not been able to comply with regulation 4A."

Reg. 9(3) substituted by SI 2000/2083 reg. 6, with effect from 21 August 2000 in relation to supplements payable in respect of sums withheld on or after 6 April 2000 and before 6 April 2003.
Former reg. 9(3) substituted by SI 2000/759 reg. 5, operative from 6 April 2000.

10   On the ending of each year every approved agency shall, within 30 days of the end of such year or within such further time as the Board may allow, furnish a return to the Board, in such form as the Board may approve or prescribe, of the sums received from each employer with whom it has at any time within the year had a subsisting contract to give effect to an approved scheme, of the numbers of employees from whose emoluments such sums have been withheld, of the number of vouchers issued pursuant to any contract and the total values of such vouchers, of the amounts paid by it to each charity in relation to such approved schemes, and of its charges in relation to the operation of schemes.

11(1)   Every approved agency shall retain:–

(a)   records of approved schemes,

(b)   records of contracts with employers until 3 years from the termination of each contract, and

(c)   for not less than 3 years, records of sums received from employers, records of amounts paid to all charities specified by employees, and records of vouchers for charities issued by it to employees pursuant to approved schemes

(d)   [Omitted by SI 2014/584, reg. 7(b).]

11(2)   Every approved agency, when so required by notice served on it by the Board, shall within 30 days of such service produce for inspection by an officer of the Board all records required to be retained by it by paragraph (1) of this Regulation.

History – SI 2003/1745, reg. 6 extends the substitution made by SI 2000/2083, reg. 7 (see below) to supplements payable under section 38 of the Finance Act 2000 in respect of sums witheld by an employer as mentioned in that section on or after 6 April 2003 and before 6 April 2004.
In reg. 11(1), the word "and" immediately preceding para. (c) inserted by SI 2014/584, reg. 7(a), with effect from 6 April 2014.
Reg. 11(1)(d) omitted by SI 2014/584, reg. 7(b), with effect from 6 April 2014. Former reg. 11(1)(d) read as follows:
> "(d)   for not less than 3 years, records of all supplements paid to charities specified by employees and records of all amounts received from the Board under section 38 of the Finance Act 2000."

Former reg. 11(1)(d) inserted by SI 2000/2083, reg. 7, with effect from 21 August 2000 in relation to supplements payable in respect of sums withheld on or after 6 April 2000 and before 6 April 2003.

12(1)   Every employer who has entered into a contract with an approved agency pursuant to an approved scheme shall retain:–

(a)   a copy of such contract until 3 years from the termination of the contract,

(b)   all forms of request to deduct given by employees pursuant to the approved scheme until 3 years from the revocation or lapse of such request and,

(c)   for not less than 3 years, records of all sums withheld from such employees pursuant to the approved scheme and evidence of all payments made to the approved agency pursuant to the approved scheme.

12(2) Every employer who has entered into a contract with an approved agency pursuant to an approved scheme, when so required by notice served on him by the Board, shall within 30 days of such service produce for inspection by an officer of the Board all documents and records required to be retained by him pursuant to paragraph (1) of this Regulation.

Notes – FA 1988, s. 127(1): construction of references in Taxes Acts to "document" and "copy of document". See FA 1988, s. 127(2)–(4) for ancillary rights of access to computer hardware.

TERMINATION OF CONTRACTS

13 If at any time an employer who has contracted to give effect to a scheme has without reasonable excuse failed in a significant respect to give effect to the scheme in accordance with his contract the approved agency shall forthwith give notice to the employer of termination of the contract.

EMPLOYEE LEAVING EMPLOYMENT

14 Where an employee who has requested his employer to withhold any sum pursuant to an approved scheme leaves his employment, the employer shall provide the employee with a statement, in such form as the Board may approve or prescribe, of the total amount so withheld from the employee's emoluments from that employment in the year in which the employee so leaves his employment.

SERVICE BY POST

15 Any notice which is authorised or required to be given or served under these regulations may be sent by post.

OVERPAYMENT OF SUPPLEMENT TO BE TREATED AS UNPAID TAX

16 [Repealed by Statute Law (Repeals) Act 2013, s. 1 and Sch. 1, Pt. 10.]

History – Reg. 16 repealed by Statute Law (Repeals) Act 2013, s. 1 and Sch. 1, Pt. 10, with effect from 31 January 2013. Former reg. 16 read as follows:

"**16** Where the Board has made an overpayment under section 38 of the Finance Act 2000 to an approved agent, the amount of that overpayment may be assessed and recovered as if it were an amount of unpaid tax for the purposes of the Taxes Acts.".

SI 2003/1745, reg. 6 extends the insertion made by SI 2000/2083, reg. 8 (see below) to supplements payable under section 38 of the Finance Act 2000 in respect of sums withheld by an employer as mentioned in that section on or after 6 April 2003 and before 6 April 2004.

Former reg. 16 inserted by SI 2000/2083, reg. 8, with effect from 21 August 2000 in relation to supplements payable in respect of sums withheld on or after 6 April 2000 and before 6 April 2003.

INCOME TAX (ENTERTAINERS AND SPORTSMEN) REGULATIONS 1987

(SI 1987/530, as amended by SI 2012/1359 and SI 2013/605)

Made on 26 March 1987 by the Treasury in exercise of the powers conferred on them by Sch. 11 to the Finance Act 1986 [ITA 2007, s. 965–970].

CITATION AND COMMENCEMENT

1 These Regulations may be cited as the Income Tax (Entertainers and Sportsmen) Regulations 1987 and shall come into force on 1st May 1987.

INTERPRETATION

2(1) In these Regulations unless the context otherwise requires–

"**associate**" has the meaning given to it by section 303(3) of the Taxes Act [ITA 2007, s. 253(1)];

"**Board**" means Commissioners of Inland Revenue;

"**control**" shall be construed in accordance with section 302(2) to (6) of the Taxes Act [ICTA 1988, s. 416(2)–(6)];

"**entertainer**" means any description of individuals (and whether performing alone or with others) who give performances in their character as entertainers or sportsmen in any kind of entertainment or sport; and "entertainment or sport" in this definition includes any activity of a physical kind, performed by such an individual, which is or may be made available to the public or any section of the public and whether for payment or not;

"**Management Act**" means the Taxes Management Act 1970;

a payment or transfer to which regulation 3 applies is described as "**connected**";

"**relevant activity**" has the meaning given to it by regulation 6;

"**the relevant amount**" means the amount of the personal allowance in section 35(1) of the Income Tax Act 2007 which applies for the tax year in which the payment or transfer is made;

"**Schedule 11**" means Schedule 11 to the Finance Act 1986 [ITA 2007, s. 965–970];

"**the Taxes Act**" means the Income and Corporation Taxes Act 1970 [ICTA 1988];

"**the Tax Acts**" has the meaning given to it by section 526(2) of the Taxes Act [ICTA 1988, s. 831(2)];

"**tax payment**" has the meaning given to it by regulation 4;

"**tax year**" means year of assessment;

"**value transferred**" in relation to a transfer means the gross amount to which regulation 17(1) refers.

2(2) Section 533 of the Taxes Act [ICTA 1988, s. 839 and ITA 2007, s. 993] (meaning of connected persons) applies for the purposes of these Regulations.

History – In reg. 2(1), definition of "the relevant amount" inserted by SI 2012/1359, reg. 2(2), with effect in relation to a payment or transfer made on or after 1 July 2012.

PAYMENTS OR TRANSFERS WITH PRESCRIBED CONNECTION

3(1) This regulation applies for the purposes of and subject to the provisions of paragraph 2 of Schedule 11 [ITA 2007, s. 966], the other provisions of that Schedule and these Regulations.

3(2) Subject to paragraph (3) a payment or a transfer made for, in respect of, or which in any way derives either directly or indirectly from, the performance of a relevant activity, has a connection of a prescribed kind with the relevant activity.

3(3) The following are descriptions of payments to which paragraph (2) shall not apply–

(a)   a payment out of which a sum representing tax is or falls to be deducted under the Taxes Act apart from Schedule 11 [ITA 2007, s. 965–970] or these Regulations;

(b)   (i)   a payment (to which paragraph (ii) applies) made to a person who is resident in the United Kingdom, not being a person who is connected with or an associate of the entertainer concerned;

       (ii)   a payment to which paragraph (i) refers is a payment–

(a)   which falls to be made for the provision of services ancillary to the performance of a relevant activity, and

(b)   which is of an amount or value which does not exceed what would be reasonable for that provision between persons dealing with each other at arms' length;

(c)   any payment made to an entertainer in respect of the proceeds of sale of records deriving from a sound recording made by the entertainer, being payments calculated by reference to those proceeds or payments on accounts of those proceeds.

History – In reg. 3(b)(i), the words "and ordinarily resident" omitted by SI 2013/605, reg. 3, with effect for the purposes of a person's liability to income tax for the tax year 2013–14 or any subsequent tax years.

TAX PAYMENTS – RULES FOR CALCULATION

4(1)   Each of the sums mentioned in paragraph 2(2) and (3) of Schedule 11 [ITA 2007, s. 966(1), (2), (4) and (7)] (*tax payment*) shall be calculated in accordance with the rules prescribed by this regulation.

4(2)   Except where it is otherwise provided by these Regulations or there is an arrangement to which this regulation refers, the tax payment shall be a proportion of the connected payment or of the value transferred by a connected transfer equal to the basic rate of income tax for the tax year in which the payment or transfer is made.

4(3)

(a)   Subject to sub-paragraph (b), where the connected payments and the value transferred by connected transfers for a tax year made to an entertainer, or to a person who is connected with him or who is an associate of his, do not together exceed the relevant amount the tax payment shall be a nil amount;

(b)   connected payments and the value transferred by connected transfers made by any person who is connected with any other person by whom connected payments or connected transfers are made to the entertainer, or by any associate of such other person, shall together be treated as constituting a single connected payment in determining whether they exceed the relevant amount.

4(4)   An arrangement to which paragraph (2) refers is an arrangement in writing between the Board and the person by whom the connected payment or connected transfer is made, the entertainer, or the recipient of the connected payment or connected transfer, made following a decision by the Board on an application to which regulation 5 refers, under which the tax payment is an amount which, as a proportion of the connected payment or value transferred by the connected transfer, is an amount less than the said basic rate (**"reduced tax payment"**).

4(5)   The reduced tax payment may be arrived at by reference to a percentage of the connected payment or of the value transferred by a connected transfer or as a lump sum calculated without reference to any such percentage.

4(6)   In making an arrangement of the kind to which paragraph (2) refers the Board–

(a)   shall, subject to sub-paragraph (b) and paragraph (7) below, at all times aim at securing that the tax payment shall be, as nearly as may be, the amount of the liability to tax of the entertainer or other person arising in relation to the connected payment or connected transfer under the Tax Acts, Schedule 11 [ITA 2007, s. 965–970] and these Regulations, and

(b)   may take into account the fact that the liability to the Board for tax has, in a manner satisfactory to them, been secured or otherwise provided for, whether by a guarantee (of whatever person) or other means.

4(7)   Where–

(a)   a person makes a connected payment or connected transfer in relation to a relevant activity, and

(b)   in respect of the same relevant activity that person has received a connected payment or connected transfer in respect of which the amount of the tax payment has been paid under these Regulations,

the person concerned shall not be required to deduct out of the connected payment or pay in respect of the connected transfer (to which sub-paragraph (a) refers) any sum to which paragraph 2 of Schedule 11 [ITA 2007, s. 966] applies unless, and to the extent that, the tax payment which then falls to be made exceeds the amount of the tax payment to which sub-paragraph (b) refers.

History – In reg. 4(3)(a) and (b), the words "the relevant amount" substituted for "£1,000" by SI 2012/1359, reg. 2(2), with effect in relation to a payment or transfer made on or after 1 July 2012.

REDUCED TAX PAYMENT – APPLICATION TO BE MADE TO THE BOARD

5(1) Where a connected payment or connected transfer falls to be made subject to a tax payment to which regulation 4(2) refers the person by whom the connected payment or connected transfer is made, the entertainer, or recipient of the connected payment or connected transfer, may make an application in writing to the Board, not later than 30 days before the connected payment or connected transfer falls to be made, that it shall be subject instead to a reduced tax payment (within the meaning of regulation 4).

5(2) Unless and until there is in force an arrangement under which such a reduced tax payment falls to be made regulation 4(2) shall at all times continue to apply to the connected payment or connected transfer.

RELEVANT ACTIVITY

6(1) Subject to this regulation, any activity performed in the United Kingdom by an entertainer (whether alone or involving others) of any of the descriptions in paragraph (2) is an activity of a prescribed description (**"relevant activity"**) for the purposes of paragraph 1 of Schedule 11 [ITA 2007, s. 966(1), (7)], that Schedule and these Regulations.

6(2) A relevant activity to which paragraph (1) refers is an activity performed in the United Kingdom by an entertainer in his character as entertainer on or in connection with a commercial occasion or event and includes–

(a)   any appearance of the entertainer by way of or in connection with the promotion of any such occasion or event;

(b)   any participation by the entertainer in or for sound recording, films, videos, radio, television or other similar transmissions (whether live or recorded).

6(3) A commercial occasion or event to which paragraph (2) refers includes any description of occasion or event–

(a)   for which an entertainer (or other person) might receive or become entitled, for or by virtue of the entertainer's performance of the activity, to receive anything by way of cash or any other form of property; or

(b)   which is designed to promote commercial sales or activity by advertising, the endorsement of goods or services, sponsorship, or other promotional means of any kind.

6(4) For the purpose of this regulation–

     "film" includes any record (with or without sound), however made, of a sequence or series of one or more visual images, which is a record capable of being used as a means of showing part or all of that sequence or series as a moving or still picture, and

     "record" in this definition includes video.

PERSONS OTHER THAN ENTERTAINERS RECEIVING CONNECTED PAYMENTS OR TRANSFERS

7(1) Any description of person in paragraph (2) is a person (not being the entertainer) to whom paragraph 7(1) of Schedule 11 [ICTA 1988, s. 556(2) and ITTOIA 2005, s. 13(5)] refers.

7(2) The descriptions of persons to whom paragraph (1) refers are–

(a)   any person who is under the control of the entertainer;

(b)   any person who is–

     (i)   not resident in the United Kingdom, and

     (ii)   not liable to tax by reason of residence, domicile, place of management or otherwise, in a territory outside the United Kingdom where the rate of tax charged on the profits or income of such a person is a rate exceeding 25 per cent;

(c)   (i)   subject to paragraph (ii), any person in receipt (whether directly or indirectly) of a connected payment or value transferred by a connected transfer which is, is treated as, or falls to be included in the computation of, income arising under a settlement in relation to which the entertainer is a settlor;

     (ii)   for the purposes of paragraph (i)–

     "income arising under a settlement" and **"settlor"** have the meanings given to them by section 454 of the Taxes Act [ICTA 1988, s. 681] and

     "settlement" has the meaning given to it by section 444(2) of the Taxes Act [ICTA 1988, s. 670];

(d)   (i)   any person to whom paragraph (2) of this regulation does not otherwise apply who receives any connected payment or connected transfer (whether directly or indirectly) at or in respect of a time when there is in force between that person and the entertainer concerned a contract or arrangement to which paragraph (ii) applies;

     (ii)   a contract or arrangement to which paragraph (i) refers is a contract or arrangement by or under which it is reasonable to suppose that the entertainer (or other person who is connected with or is an associate of the entertainer) is, will or may become, entitled to receive amounts, whether by way of cash or other value, not substantially less than the appropriate amount of profits or gains arising from the connected payment or connected transfer to which paragraph 8(1) of Schedule 11 [ITTOIA 2005, s. 13(7) and (8)] applies.

COMPUTATION OF PROFITS ARISING FROM CERTAIN PAYMENTS AND TRANSFERS ATTRIBUTED TO ENTERTAINER

8(1) Subject to the provisions of these Regulations, the profits or gains (to which paragraph 7(2) of Schedule 11 [ICTA 1988, s. 556(3)(a)] refers) arising from the connected payment or connected transfer (to which paragraph 7(1) of that Schedule [ICTA 1988, s. 556(2) and ITTOIA 2005, s. 13(5)] refers) shall be computed in accordance with the provisions of the Taxes Act relating to the charging of profits or gains under Case I or II (as the case may be) of Schedule D, so that a just and reasonable amount of such a payment or value transferred by such a transfer is charged to tax as such profits or gains; and

8(2) Notwithstanding any provision of the Taxes Act, in computing the said profits or gains such deductions of expenses incurred by any person (not being the entertainer) in relation to the payment or transfer concerned shall be made as are just and reasonable.

RETURNS OF INFORMATION TO BE FURNISHED BY MAKER OF CONNECTED PAYMENTS OR CONNECTED TRANSFERS

9(1) A person who makes a connected payment or connected transfer shall, in accordance with this regulation, make a return to the Board of the connected payment or connected transfer which he makes and of any tax payment (including a nil amount) for which he is accountable to the Board.

9(2) A return shall be made in the tax year for each successive period ending on 30th June, 30th September, 31st December and 5th April.

9(3) The return for each period shall be made within 14 days after the end of the period.

9(4) The Board may by notice in writing require any person who makes a connected payment or connected transfer, within such time as may be specified in the notice, to furnish to them particulars of such payments or transfers including–

(a)   the dates and the amounts of each payment;

(b)   the dates of and the value transferred by each transfer;

(c)   a sufficient description to enable any asset or money's worth transferred to be identified;

(d)   the business and private name and address of the person to whom each payment or transfer was made;

(e)   the name and address of the entertainer concerned;

(f)   the relevant activity to which the payment or transfers relates, including full particulars of all performances.

9(5) The Management Act shall apply to a return to which this regulation relates as it applies to a return under the Taxes Acts.

TAX PAYMENTS – DUE DATE

10(1) A tax payment (including any reduced tax payment), whether any deduction out of a connected payment or provision in respect of a connected transfer has been made or not, shall be due at the time by which the return under regulation 9(1) is to be made (**"the due date"**) and payment shall be made before, or at the time when, that return is made.

10(2) A payment at any time so due shall be payable by the person who makes the connected payment or connected transfer concerned, without the making of any assessment in respect of it.

10(3) Subject to the provisions of regulation 11, tax which has become due and payable under this regulation (whether or not it has been paid when the assessment is made) may be assessed on the person from whom it is due if that tax, or any part of it, is not paid on or before the due date.

ASSESSMENT OF TAX PAYMENTS

11(1) Assessments in respect of any tax due and payable in respect of any period to which regulation 9(2) refers may be made by the Board in relation to a tax year or to the period in question.

11(2) Notwithstanding that an assessment under paragraph (1) may be said to relate to a period which is not a tax year–

(a) all the provisions of the Income Tax Acts as to the time within which an assessment may be made or the tax year to which an assessment relates shall apply to such an assessment, and

(b) the provisions of sections 36 and 37 of the Management Act as to the circumstances in which an assessment may be made out of time shall apply accordingly, but on the footing that the assessment relates to the tax year in which the period (to which regulation 9(2) refers) ends.

11(3) Any tax which becomes due under an assessment made under paragraph (1)–

(a) shall be payable on or before whichever is earlier of the due date to which regulation 10(1) refers or the 14th day after the date of the notice of the assessment, and

(b) shall be treated for all the purposes of Parts VI and IX of the Management Act (including the purposes of section 69 of that Act) as tax with which the person assessed is charged by an assessment to income tax under Schedule D.

TAX LIABILITIES AND TAX PAYMENTS – SUPPLEMENTARY

12(1) Where under these Regulations there is accounted for and paid to the Board an amount of tax which is–

(a) in respect of a connected payment or connected transfer, or

(b) paid under an assessment made under regulation 11,

that amount shall, subject to this regulation, be treated as a payment of tax on account of the tax liability (of whatever person) in respect of the connected payment or connected transfer concerned.

12(2) Where, in respect of a connected payment or connected transfer, there is a liability to tax under the Tax Acts as well as under Schedule 11 [ICTA 1988, s. 555–558] or these Regulations, the Board shall allocate any payment made to them to which paragraph (1) refers as is just and reasonable in discharge of some or all of those liabilities of the entertainer or other person concerned to whom these Regulations apply.

12(3) Where–

(a) by virtue of paragraph 8 of Schedule 11 [ITTOIA 2005, s. 13 and 14] and these Regulations a connected payment or the value transferred by a connected transfer falls to be included in the amount of profits or gains to which paragraph 8(1)(a) [ICTA 1988, s. 557(1)(a)] refers, and

(b) the amount of the connected payment or the value transferred (or an amount in respect of that value) is charged to tax under Schedule E

the amount charged under Schedule E (to which sub-paragraph (b) refers) shall be treated as expenditure which falls to be deducted in computing the profits or gains to which sub-paragraph (a) refers.

12(4) Where a payment is a connected payment–

(a) which is, is treated as, or falls to be included in a computation of, income of the entertainer chargeable to tax by virtue of the provisions of Part XVI of the Taxes Act [ICTA 1988, Pt. XV], or

(b) which is a receipt of a company which provides the services of the entertainer to perform the relevant activity, being a receipt which falls to be included in the computation of its profits which are chargeable to tax under Schedule D,

the charge under Schedule 11 [ITA 2007, s. 965–970] shall have effect and the charges to which sub-paragraphs (a) and (b) refer shall be disregarded.

12(5) A person making a connected payment or connected transfer in respect of which a tax payment has been made by virtue of these Regulations shall furnish the recipient with a certificate showing the gross amount of the payment or the value transferred, the amount of the tax payment, and the amount actually paid.

CLAIM THAT TAX PAYMENT EXCESSIVE TO BE MADE TO BOARD

13(1) Notwithstanding any other provision of these Regulations, where there has been made to a recipient a connected payment or connected transfer in respect of which a tax payment has been made, the entertainer or any person who, by virtue of Schedule 11 [ITA 2007, s. 965–970] or these Regulations is, or is treated as, the person to whom (in relation to the connected payment or connected transfer) any tax liability arises may, by a claim in writing made to the Board, claim that the amount of the tax payment made is excessive.

13(2) Subject to paragraph (3) the claim shall be treated as a claim made to an inspector to which section 42 of the Management Act applies.

13(3) The claim shall be made not before, but within six years after, the end of the tax year in which the connected payment or connected transfer was made.

ADMINISTRATION OF TAX – SUPPLEMENTARY

14(1) Nothing in these Regulations shall be taken to prejudice any powers conferred by or under the Tax Acts for the recovery of tax, penalties or interest by means of an assessment or otherwise.

14(2) Subject to the provisions of these Regulations, the Management Act shall apply in relation to any tax assessable under these Regulations as if–

(a) an assessment of such tax was an assessment specified in section 55(1) (recovery of tax not postponed); and

(b) section 87 of that Act applies–

  (i) with the insertion of the words "or the Income Tax (Entertainers and Sportsmen) Regulations 1987" after "Finance Act 1972" in subsection (1), and after "Schedule 20" in subsections (2)(b), (5) and (6),

  (ii) with the insertion after "company" in subsection (5) of the words "or individual", and

  (iii) with the insertion after "Schedules" in subsection (7) of the words "or those Regulations".

MODIFICATIONS AND ADAPTATIONS OF ENACTMENTS IN RELATION TO TRADES ETC.

15(1) In this regulation–

(a) **"world-wide trade"** means a trade of an entertainer which is a trade apart from Schedule 11 [ITA 2007, s. 965–970] and these Regulations, and a **"Schedule 11 trade"** means a trade which is a separate trade of an entertainer only by virtue of Schedule 11 [ITA 2007, s. 965–970] and these Regulations;

(b) **"trade"** includes professional or vocation.

15(2) For the purposes of section 171 of the Taxes Act [ITA 2007, s. 83–88] (carry forward of losses) the world-wide trade and the Schedule 11 trade shall be treated as the same trade.

15(3) For the purposes of section 174 of the Taxes Act [ITA 2007, s. 89–94] (carry back of terminal losses) a loss sustained for any relevant period under a Schedule 11 trade (to which otherwise that section would apply) shall not be a terminal loss except where the world-wide trade is permanently discontinued in that period, in which case such a loss in either trade shall be available under that section to be deducted or set off against profits or gains of those trades.

15(4) For the purposes of section 30 of the Finance Act 1978 [ITA 2007, s. 72–74] (losses in early years of trade) the world-wide trade and the Schedule 11 trade shall be treated as the same trade, but that section shall apply to any such loss of an entertainer only in the tax year in which the world-wide trade was first carried on and in the next 3 succeeding tax years.

APPORTIONMENT OF PAYMENTS, TRANSFERS ETC.

16(1) The provisions of paragraph (2) are by way of supplementation of the provisions of section 127 of the Taxes Act [ICTA 1988, s. 72].

16(2) Where, in the case of any payment, value transferred or profits or gains to which Schedule 11 [ITA 2007, s. 965–970] or these Regulations apply, it is necessary, in order to arrive at the appropriate amount of such payment, value or profits or gains for any tax year or other period, to make any apportionment, division or aggregation of any amounts or values, any such apportionment, division or aggregation, shall be made as is just and reasonable.

VALUE OF TRANSFERS – RULES FOR CALCULATION AND GROSSING UP

17(1)

(a)   The actual worth of what is transferred by a transfer to which paragraph 2(3) of Schedule 11 [ITA 2007, s. 966(1), (2), (4) and (7)] applies (**"the net value"**) shall be treated as a net amount corresponding to a gross amount from which income tax at the basic rate has been deducted; and

(b)   the said gross amount shall be treated as the value of what is transferred for the purposes of paragraph 2(4) of Schedule 11 [ITA 2007, s. 967(1)].

17(2)

(a)   The net value to which paragraph (1) refers shall be the cost of what is transferred, and

(b)   the cost of what is transferred to which sub-paragraph (a) refers is the cost in or in connection with its provision (including its provision to the person who makes the transfer) or transfer, less so much of that cost which has been borne by the entertainer.

CAPITAL GAINS TAX (DEFINITION OF UNIT TRUST SCHEME) REGULATIONS 1988

(SI 1988/266, as amended by SI 2000/2550 and SI 2001/3629)

Made on 18 February 1988 by the Treasury in exercise of the powers conferred on them by s. 92 of the Capital Gains Tax Act 1979 [TCGA 1992, s. 99(3)].

CITATION AND COMMENCEMENT

1 These Regulations may be cited as the Capital Gains Tax (Definition of Unit Trust Scheme) Regulations 1988 and shall come into force on 11th March 1988.

INTERPRETATION

2 In these Regulations unless the context otherwise requires–

"**limited partnership**" means a limited partnership registered under the Limited Partnerships Act 1907 and

"**general partner**" and "**limited partner**" have the same meanings as in that Act,

"**limited partnership scheme**" means a unit trust scheme of the description specified in regulation 4;

"**participant**" in relation to a unit trust scheme, shall be construed in accordance with section 235 of the Financial Services and Markets Act 2000;

"**the principal Act**" means the Capital Gains Tax Act 1979 [TCGA 1992];

"**scheme property**" means, in relation to a unit trust scheme, property of any description, including money, which is held on trust for the participants in the scheme;

"**unit trust scheme**" means a scheme which, apart from these Regulations, is a unit trust scheme for the purposes of the principal Act.

History – In reg. 2, the definition of "participant" substituted by SI 2001/3629, art. 116; with effect from 1 December 2001.

EXCEPTION OF CERTAIN UNIT TRUST SCHEMES FROM THE PRINCIPAL ACT

3 A unit trust scheme which is–

(a)   a limited partnership scheme, or

(b)   a profit sharing scheme which has been approved in accordance with Part I of Schedule 9 to the Finance Act 1978 [ICTA 1988, Sch. 9, Pt. I], or

(c)   an employee share ownership plan approved under Schedule 8 to the Finance Act 2000,

shall be treated as not being a unit trust scheme for the purposes of the principal Act.

History – Reg. 3(c) inserted by SI 2000/2550, reg. 2, operative from 11 October 2000.

DESCRIPTION OF A LIMITED PARTNERSHIP SCHEME

4 A unit trust scheme is a limited partnership scheme when the scheme property is held on trust for the general partners and the limited partners in a limited partnership.

INCOME TAX (DEFINITION OF UNIT TRUST SCHEME) REGULATIONS 1988

(SI 1988/267, as amended by SI 1992/571, SI 1992/3133, SI 1994/1479, SI 2000/2551 and SI 2001/3629)

Made on 18 February 1988 by the Treasury in exercise of the powers conferred on them by s. 354A(7) of the Income and Corporation Taxes Act 1970 [ITA 2007, s. 1007(1) and (2)].

CITATION AND COMMENCEMENT

1 These Regulations may be cited as the Income Tax (Definition of Unit Trust Scheme) Regulations 1988 and shall come into force on 11th March 1988 and shall have effect in accordance with regulation 9.

INTERPRETATION

2(1) In these Regulations unless the context otherwise requires—

"**charitable unit trust scheme**" means a unit trust scheme of one of the descriptions specified in regulation 7;

"**enterprise zone**" has the same meaning as in section 74 of the Finance Act 1980 [CAA 2001, s. 298];

"**enterprise zone property scheme**" means a unit trust scheme of the description specified in regulation 4;

"**inspector**" means any inspector of taxes;

"**limited partnership**" means a limited partnership registered under the Limited Partnerships Act 1907 and

"**general partner**" and "**limited partner**" have the same meanings as in that Act;

"**limited partnership scheme**" means a unit trust scheme of the description specified in regulation 8;

"**participant**" in relation to a unit trust scheme, shall be construed in accordance with section 235 of the Financial Services and Markets Act 2000;

"**Schedule A**" means the Schedule referred to as Schedule A in section 67(1) of the Taxes Act [ICTA 1988, s. 15(1)];

"**Schedule D**" means the Schedule referred to as Schedule D in section 108 of the Taxes Act [ICTA 1988, s. 18];

"**scheme property**" means, in relation to a unit trust scheme, property of any description, including money, which is held on trust for the participants in the scheme;

"**section 354A**" means section 354A of the Taxes Act [ICTA 1988, s. 469];

"**tax year**" means a year beginning with 6th April in any year and ending with 5th April in the following year;

"**the Taxes Act**" means the Income and Corporation Taxes Act 1970 [ICTA 1988];

"**trustee**" means, in relation to a unit scheme, the person holding the scheme property on trust for the participants;

"**unit trust scheme**" means a scheme which, apart from these Regulations, is a unit trust scheme for the purposes of section 354A [ICTA 1988, s. 469].

2(2) The provisions of section 56 of the Finance Act 1985 shall have effect to determine when the capital expenditure is to be taken to be incurred for the purposes of these Regulations.

History – In reg. 2, the definition of "participant" substituted by SI 2001/3629, art. 117; with effect from 1 December 2001; the former definition of the term was "in relation to a unit trust scheme, has the meaning given by section 75(2) of the Financial Services Act 1986;".

EXCEPTION OF CERTAIN UNIT TRUST SCHEMES FROM SECTION 354A [ICTA 1988, S. 469]

3 Subject to the provisions of these Regulations, a unit trust scheme which is—

(a) an enterprise zone property scheme, or

(b) a charitable unit trust scheme, or

(c) a limited partnership scheme, or

(d)   a profit sharing scheme which has been approved in accordance with Part I of Schedule 9 to the Finance Act 1978 [ICTA 1988, Sch. 9, Pt. I], or

(e)   an employee share ownership plan approved under Schedule 8 to the Finance Act 2000,

shall be treated as not being a unit trust scheme for the purposes of section 354A [ICTA 1988, s. 469].

History – Reg 3(e) inserted by SI 2000/2551, reg. 2, operative from 11 October 2000.

DESCRIPTION OF AN ENTERPRISE ZONE PROPERTY SCHEME

4(1)   A unit trust scheme is an enterprise zone property scheme when it has the characteristics mentioned in paragraph 4(2) below.

4(2)   Those characteristics are—

(a)   that, except as provided in paragraph 4(3)(a) below, the scheme property consists wholly of land (including any buildings or structures on that land)–

    (i)   the whole or substantially the whole of which, at the time when it became subject to the trusts of the scheme, was situated or formerly situated in one or more enterprise zones, and

    (ii)   any part of which not so situated or formerly situated was contiguous with land forming part of the scheme property which, at that time, was so situated;

(b)   that, except as provided in paragraph 4(3)(b) below, the contributions of the participants are expended on–

    (i)   the construction of, or the purchase of interests in, buildings or structures on that land,

    (ii)   the provision of machinery or plant which is an integral part of such buildings or structures,

as well as on the acquisition of, or of rights in or over, that land;

(c)   that so much of the expenditure referred to in sub-paragraph (b) above as is not–

    (i)   expenditure on the acquisition of, or rights in or over, the land itself, or

    (ii)   expenditure in relation to a building or structure, or to that part of a building or structure, which is not on land situated or formerly situated in an enterprise zone, or

    (iii)   expenditure on the provision of machinery or plant,

is expenditure in relation to which Chapter I of Part I of the Capital Allowances Act 1968 applies with the modifications specified in Schedule 13 to the Finance Act 1980 [see CAA 1990, Pt. I];

(d)   that the terms of the scheme secure that–

    (i)   the contributions of the participants are all to be made within the same tax year and no contributions can be made by participants in any subsequent tax year;

    (ii)   the capital expenditure referred to in sub-paragraph (b) above is to be incurred wholly in the tax year in which the participants make their contributions;

    (iii)   the nature of the rights and interests of all participants in the scheme is the same;

    (iv)   the rights and interests of the participants in the scheme cannot be purchased, or otherwise redeemed or cancelled, by the trustee in whole or in part except by way of distribution to the participants generally;

    (v)   in relation to any arrangements which are entered into after the making of these Regulations, the trustee is irrevocably authorised and obliged to undertake on behalf of the participants the responsibilities specified in regulation 5 and the duty once in every tax year to provide to the inspector in writing the information with respect to the preceding tax year concerning the participants in the scheme which is specified by regulation 6(2).

4(3)   A unit trust scheme is an enterprise zone property scheme notwithstanding that–

(a)   the scheme property at any time consists also of–

    (i)   cash held temporarily by the trustee pending its expenditure as mentioned in paragraph 4(2)(b) above or sub-paragraph (b) below, or its distribution to the participants generally;

    (ii)   cash or other assets held by the trustee in connection with the management of the scheme property; or

(b)   the contributions of the participants are expended for purposes incidental to, or arising out of, the expenditure referred to in paragraph 4(2)(b) above.

4(4)   References in paragraph (2) of this Regulation to land formerly situated in an enterprise zone or in one or more enterprise zones are references to land on which buildings or structures were constructed where the expenditure on such construction was incurred, or was incurred under a contract entered into, at a time when the land was in an enterprise zone, being a time not more than ten years after the land was first included in an enterprise zone.

History – The words "or formerly situated" in reg. 4(2)(a)(i), (ii) and (c)(ii), and reg. 4(4), inserted by SI 1992/571, reg. 3, 4, operative from 31 March 1992.

RESPONSIBILITIES OF TRUSTEE OF AN ENTERPRISE ZONE PROPERTY SCHEME

5(1) The responsibilities of the trustee of an enterprise zone property scheme specified in this regulation are to negotiate and agree with the inspector on behalf of the participants–

(a) the amount of any expenditure referred to in regulation 4(2)(b) which is–

  (i) capital expenditure of each of the participants for a chargeable period in relation to which Chapter I of Part I of the Capital Allowances Act 1968 applies, or applies with the modifications specified in Schedule 13 to the Finance Act 1980 [see CAA 1990, Pt. I], and

  (ii) capital expenditure of each of the participants on the provision of machinery or plant in respect of which a writing-down allowance is to be or may be made in accordance with section 44 of the Finance Act 1971 [CAA 1990, s. 24];

(b) where, in relation to a building or structure which forms part of the scheme property, an event occurs which gives rise or may give rise to a balancing allowance or a balancing charge to or on each of the participants, the amount of any saler, insurance, salvage or compensation moneys within the meaning of section 86(1) of the Capital Allowances Act 1968 [CAA 1990, s. 154(1)] relevant to that event;

(c) the disposal value, calculated in accordance with section 44(6) of the Finance Act 1971 [CAA 2001, s. 61], of any plant and machinery forming part of the scheme property which is or may be required to be brought into account by each of the participants for a chargeable period;

(d) the amount of any profits or gains arising for each accounting period of the scheme in respect of rents or receipts from the scheme property which are chargeable on the participants under Schedule A;

(e) the amount of any interest of money or other annual profits or gains from scheme property which are chargeable on the participants under Schedule D.

5(2) The trustee of an enterprise zone property scheme shall also be responsible for providing within three months after the end of each accounting period of the scheme to each person who was a participant in the scheme at any time during that period, or to his personal representative as the case may be, a certificate showing in relation to that participant–

(a) the parts of amounts of capital expenditure incurred in that period, and agreed with the inspector in accordance with paragraph 5(1)(a)(i) and (ii) above, which are attributable to his interest in the scheme at the time when the expenditure in question was incurred;

(b) the parts of amounts of sale, insurance, salvage or compensation moneys in relation to events occurring in that period, and of the disposal values of plant and machinery agreed with the inspector in accordance with paragraph 5(1)(b) and (c) above, which are attributable to his interest in the scheme at the relevant time;

(c) the parts of amounts agreed with the inspector to be chargeable under Schedule A or Schedule D, as the case may be, in accordance with paragraph 5(1)(d) and (e) above which are attributable to his interest in the scheme for any period in the accounting period in question during which he held that interest.

PROVISION OF INFORMATION BY TRUSTEE OF AN ENTERPRISE ZONE PROPERTY SCHEME

6(1) The information concerning the participants in an enterprise zone property scheme which the trustee of the scheme shall once in every tax year provide to the inspector in writing with respect to the preceding tax year is that specified by paragraph 6(2) below.

6(2) The information specified by this paragraph is–

(a) the name, address and tax office reference, and, if an individual resident in the United Kingdom at any time in the preceding tax year, the national insurance number, of each person who was a participant in the scheme at any time in the tax year;

(b) in respect of each such participant, the interest which he had in the scheme at any such time;

(c)   a copy of any certificate referred to in regulation 5(2) which is supplied to a participant or his personal representative in relation to an accounting period of the scheme ending in, or at the same time as, the preceding tax year.

DESCRIPTIONS OF A CHARITABLE UNIT TRUST SCHEME

7(1) A unit trust scheme is a charitable unit trust scheme if it is one of the descriptions specified in paragraph 7(2) below.

7(2) Those descriptions are–

(a)   a common investment fund established under section 22 of the Charities Act 1960 or section 25 of the Charities Act (Northern Ireland) 1964;

(aa)   a common deposit fund established under section 22A of the Charities Act 1960;

(b)   an investment fund or a deposit fund within the meaning of the Scheme scheduled to the Church Funds Investment Measure 1958 or of the scheme contained in the First Schedule to the Methodist Church Funds Act 1960;

(c)   a fund held by the Church of Scotland Trust under the provisions of section 15 of the Church of Scotland Trust Order 1932 or under the provisions of the Church of Scotland (Properties and Investments) Order 1994;

(ca)   a fund held by the Church of Scotland General Trustees or the Church of Scotland Investors Trust under the provisions of the Church of Scotland (Properties and Investments) Order 1994;

(d)   a unit trust scheme under the terms of which–

   (i)   the scheme property is held by the trustee on trust for charitable purposes only, and

   (ii)   the participants are required to be bodies of persons established for charitable purposes only or trustees of trusts so established;

   and the income of the participants in which is in either case applied to charitable purposes only.

History – Reg. 7(2)(aa) inserted by SI 1992/3133, reg. 2, operative from 1 January 1993.
In reg. 7(2)(c), the words "or under the provisions of the Church of Scotland (Properties and Investments) Order 1994" inserted, and reg. 7(2)(ca) inserted by SI 1994/1479, reg. 2, operative from 27 June 1994.

DESCRIPTION OF A LIMITED PARTNERSHIP SCHEME

8 A unit trust scheme is a limited partnership scheme when the scheme property is held on trust for the general partners and the limited partners in a limited partnership.

EFFECT OF REGULATIONS

9 These Regulations shall have effect in relation to distribution periods (within the meaning of section 354A [ICTA 1988, s. 469]) beginning on or after 11th March 1988.

PERSONAL PENSION SCHEMES (MINIMUM CONTRIBUTIONS UNDER THE SOCIAL SECURITY ACT 1986) REGULATIONS 1988

(SI 1988/1012, as amended by SSCTFA 1999 and SI 1999/671)

Made on 9 June 1988 by the Commissioners of Inland Revenue, in exercise of the powers conferred on them by s. 649(4) of the Income and Corporation Taxes Act 1988.

CITATION AND COMMENCEMENT

1 These Regulations may be cited as the Personal Pension Schemes (Minimum Contributions under the Social Security Act 1986) Regulations 1988 and shall come into force on 1st July 1988.

INTERPRETATION

2 In these Regulations unless the context otherwise requires—

"the Act" means the Income and Corporation Taxes Act 1988;

"the Board" means the Commissioners of Inland Revenue;

"tax week" means one of the successive periods in a tax year beginning with the first day of that year and every 7th day thereafter; the last day of a tax year (or, in the case of a tax year ending in a leap year, the last 2 days) to be treated accordingly as a separate tax week;

"tax year" means the 12 months beginning with 6th April in any year.

RECOVERY OF ANY INCREASE ATTRIBUTABLE TO SECTION 649 OF THE ACT BY THE SECRETARY OF STATE

3 [Revoked by SSCTFA 1999, s. 26(3) and Sch. 10, Pt. II.]

History – Reg. 3 revoked by SSCTFA 1999, s. 26(3) and Sch. 10, Pt. II, with effect from 1 April 1999 (by virtue of SI 1999/527).

INFORMATION

4 [Revoked by SSCTFA 1999, s. 26(3) and Sch. 10, Pt. II.]

History – Reg. 4 revoked by SSCTFA 1999, s. 26(3) and Sch. 10, Pt. II, with effect from 1 April 1999 (by virtue of SI 1999/527).

5 [Revoked by SSCTFA 1999, s. 26(3) and Sch. 10, Pt. II.]

History – Reg. 5 revoked by SSCTFA 1999, s. 26(3) and Sch. 10, Pt. II, with effect from 1 April 1999 (by virtue of SI 1999/527).

RECOVERY OF AMOUNTS REPRESENTING BASIC RATE TAX

6(1) The like provisions as are contained in section 30 of the Taxes Management Act 1970 (recovery of overpayment of tax, etc.) shall apply in relation to the payment by the Secretary of State of an amount by way of minimum contributions which—

(a)   he was not required to pay, or

(b)   he was required to pay but which he paid to other persons than the trustees or managers of the personal pension scheme to whom he should have made the payment

as if an amount representing income tax at the basic rate on the amount paid had been income tax repaid to the person to, or in respect of, whom the amount was paid to which that person was not entitled.

6(2) An assessment made by virtue of this regulation shall be made by the Board and, subject to the provisions of these Regulations, the like provisions as are contained in the Taxes Management Act 1970 shall apply as if the assessment were an assessment to tax for the year of assessment in respect of which the amount was paid.

NORTHERN IRELAND

7 In relation to Northern Ireland, these Regulations shall have effect as if—

(a)   references to the Secretary of State were references to the Department of Health and Social Services for Northern Ireland; and

(b)   [revoked by SI 1999/671, art. 24(3) and Sch. 9, Pt. II.]

History – Reg. 7(b) revoked by SI 1999/671, art. 24(3) and Sch. 9, Pt. II, with effect from 1 April 1999 (by virtue of SR 1999/149, art. 2 and Sch. 2).

PERSONAL PENSION SCHEMES (RELIEF AT SOURCE) REGULATIONS 1988

(SI 1988/1013, as amended by SI 2000/2315)

Made on 9 June 1988 by the Commissioners of Inland Revenue, in exercise of the powers conferred on them by s. 639 of the Income and Corporation Taxes Act 1988.

ARRANGEMENT OF REGULATIONS

CITATION AND COMMENCEMENT

1 These Regulations may be cited as the Personal Pension Schemes (Relief at Source) Regulations 1988 and shall come into force on 1st July 1988.

INTERPRETATION

Notes – Reg. 2(1) amended by SI 2000/2315, operative from 1 October 2000 with effect for personal pension schemes on and after 6 April 2001. See history note.

2(1) In these Regulations unless the context otherwise requires–

"arrangements" means approved personal pension arrangements within the meaning of section 630;

"basis year" shall be construed in accordance with section 646B;

"the Board" means the Commissioners of Inland Revenue;

"earnings threshold" has the meaning given by section 630(1);

"electronic signature" has the meaning given by section 7(2) of the Electronic Communications Act 2000;

"net contribution" means a contribution from which an individual deducts an amount equal to income tax at the basic rate by virtue of section 639(3) and (4);

"net relevant earnings" means relevant earnings computed in accordance with section 646;

"permitted maximum" has the meaning given by section 638(4);

"qualifying post-cessation year" has the meaning given by section 646D(4) and (5);

"relevant earnings" has the meaning given by section 644;

"relevant superannuation scheme" means a scheme or arrangement as defined in section 645(3);

"retirement annuity contract or trust scheme" means a retirement annuity contract or trust scheme approved by the Board under Chapter III of Part XIV of the Act;

"scheme" means an approved personal pension scheme within the meaning of section 630;

"section" means a section of the Income and Corporation Taxes Act 1988;

"tax month" means a period beginning on the 6th day of any month and ending with the 5th day of the following month;

"year of assessment" means a year beginning with 6th April in any year and ending with 5th April in the following year.

2(2) The Table below indexes other definitions in these Regulations–

Term defined	Regulation
annual claim	8
interim claim	8

History – In reg. 2(1) definitions of "basis year", "earnings threshold", and "electronic signature" inserted by SI 2000/2315, reg. 3, operative from 1 October 2000 with effect with respect to personal pension schemes on and after 6 April 2001.
In reg. 2(1) definitions of "net relevant earnings", "permitted maximum", "qualifying post-cessation year" and "relevant earnings" substituted for definitions of "net relevant Schedule E earnings " and "relevant Schedule E earnings" by SI 2000/2315, reg. 3(c), operative from 1 October 2000 with effect with respect to personal pension schemes on and after 6 April 2001. Former definitions read as follows:

> ""**net relevant Schedule E earnings**" means "relevant Schedule E earnings" computed in accordance with section 646;
> "**relevant Schedule E earnings**" means "relevant earnings" within the meaning of section 644 but with the omission of subsection 2(c) and (d) of that section;"

PRESCRIBED CASES AND CONDITIONS: INTRODUCTORY

3 Regulation 4 prescribes the cases in which, and regulations 5 to 7 the conditions subject to which, relief under section 639 shall be given in accordance with subsections (3) and (4) of that section.

PRESCRIBED CASES

Notes – Reg. 4 amended by SI 2000/2315, operative from 1 October 2000 with effect for personal pension schemes on and after 6 April 2001. See history note.

4 The prescribed cases are cases where an individual is eligible, by virtue of satisfying the provisions of section 632A of the Taxes Act, to make contributions for a year of assessment to the approved personal pension scheme concerned.

History – In reg. 4 the words "an individual is eligible, by virtue of satisfying the provisions of section 632A of the Taxes Act, to make contributions for a year of assessment to the approved personal pension scheme concerned" substituted for the words "under arrangements an individual is paying contributions in respect of net relevant Schedule E earnings" by SI 2000/2315, reg. 4, operative from 1 October 2000 with effect with respect to personal pension schemes on and after 6 April 2001.

PRESCRIBED CONDITIONS

Notes – Reg. 5, 6 and 7 amended by SI 2000/2315, operative from 1 October 2000 with effect for personal pension schemes on and after 6 April 2001. See history note for each regulation.

5(1) The condition prescribed in this regulation is that an individual shall furnish to the scheme administrator before the time specified in paragraph (3) the particulars specified in paragraph (2).

5(2) The particulars specified in this paragraph are–

(a) his full name and permanent residential address including, where the address is in the United Kingdom, the postcode;

(b) his date of birth;

(c) his national insurance number, unless aged under 16 or a citizen of a country outside the United Kingdom who is not resident in the United Kingdom;

(d) except where the scheme is an occupational pension scheme within the meaning of section 1 of the Pension Schemes Act 1993 , the category of status specified in paragraph (2A) that is applicable in his case or, if more than one category is applicable, the one that is his principal source of income;

(e) in the circumstances specified in paragraph (2B), the requisite evidence, that is to say–

    (i) a declaration specifying the year of assessment concerned, or an earlier year of assessment not being more than five years preceding that year, as the basis year for the purposes of section 646B (presumption of same level of relevant earnings etc. for 5 years);

    (ii) where the individual is an employee, the full names and addresses of all those employers who have paid, or will pay, net relevant earnings to him; and

    (iii) the particulars specified in paragraph (2C) for the basis year.

5(2A) The categories of status specified in this paragraph for the purposes of paragraph (2)(d) are as follows–

(a) employed, that is, a person chargeable to tax under Schedule E for the year of assessment concerned in respect of emoluments from an office or employment held by him;

(b) a person chargeable to tax under Schedule E for the year of assessment concerned in respect of a pension;

(c) self-employed, that is, a person chargeable to tax under Schedule D for the year of assessment concerned in respect of annual profits or gains arising or accruing from any trade, profession or vocation carried on by him;

(d) a child under the age of 16;

(e) other status not falling within any of sub-paragraphs (a) to (d) and, in relation to that status, specifying which of the following is applicable in his case or, if more than one, the most applicable–

  (i) caring for one or more children aged under 16,

  (ii) caring for a person aged 16 or over,

  (iii) in full time education,

  (iv) unemployed, or

  (v) other.

5(2B) The circumstances specified in this paragraph are where the total contributions to be made by the individual and, where he is an employee, his employer for the year of assessment concerned will exceed the earnings threshold, and the year of assessment either–

(a) is not a year already specified in a declaration under paragraph (2)(e)(i) as the basis year or is not one of the 5 years of assessment following that year, or

(b) is such a year but the total contributions to be made by the individual and, where he is an employee, his employer for that year will exceed the permitted maximum based on the net relevant earnings of the individual in the basis year specified in the declaration.

5(2C) The particulars specified in this paragraph are–

(a) where the individual is an employee, one of the following–

  (i) a copy of his payslip or Inland Revenue Form P60 showing relevant earnings for the basis year;

  (ii) a declaration of his employer, signed by the employer or a person nominated by the employer, stipulating the amount of remuneration paid to the employee for the basis year or, where the basis year is the current year, an estimate of the amount of remuneration to be paid to the employee for that year;

  (iii) a copy of the self-assessment included in the individual's income tax return for the basis year;

  (iv) such other particulars of relevant earnings as may be required by notice in writing given by the Board;

(b) where the individual is self-employed, one of the following–

  (i) a copy of the accounts for the basis year of the individual's trade, profession or vocation;

  (ii) a copy of the income tax return for the basis year of the individual, or of the self-assessment included in that return, showing net relevant earnings of the individual;

  (iii) such other particulars of relevant earnings as may be required by notice in writing given by the Board.

5(2D) The reference in paragraph (2C)(a)(ii) to a declaration includes a declaration produced in electronic form and incorporating an electronic signature of the employer.

5(3) The time specified in this paragraph is–

(a) in relation to the particulars specified in paragraph (2)(a) to (d), the time at which the individual first pays a net contribution;

(b) in relation to the particulars specified in paragraphs (2)(e) and (2C), immediately after the expiry of thirty days following the day on which the individual first pays a net contribution for the year of assessment concerned that, when aggregated with previous contributions made by him for that year, exceeds the earnings threshold or, as the case may be, the permitted maximum based on the net relevant earnings of the individual in the basis year.

Statutory Instruments

History – In reg. 5(1) words "in writing" and ", or within" omitted by SI 2000/2315, reg. 5, operative from 1 October 2000 with effect for personal pension schemes on and after 6 April 2001. Reg. 5(1) formerly read as follows:

"**5(1)** The condition prescribed in this regulation is that an individual shall furnish in writing to the scheme administrator before, or within, the time specified in paragraph (3) the particulars specified in paragraph (2)."

In reg. 5(2) words "permanent residential address including, where the address is in the United Kingdom, the postcode" substituted for "address" by SI 2000/2315, reg. 6, operative from 1 October 2000 with effect for personal pension schemes on and after 6 April 2001.

In reg. 5(2)(c) words ", unless aged under 16 or a citizen of a country outside the United Kingdom who is not resident in the United Kingdom" added by SI 2000/2315, reg. 6, operative from 1 October 2000 with effect for personal pension schemes on and after 6 April 2001.

Reg. 5(2)(d)–(e) substituted for reg. 5(2)(d)–(f) by SI 2000/2315, reg. 6, operative from 1 October 2000 with effect for personal pension schemes on and after 6 April 2001. Reg. 5(2)(d)–(f) originally read as follows:

"(d) the full name and address of his employer who has paid, or will pay, net relevant Schedule E earnings to him;
(e) an estimate of his net relevant Schedule E earnings for the year of assessment in which he will first pay a net contribution;
(f) the full name and address of any employer of his, other than the employer referred to in sub-paragraph (d), who has paid net relevant Schedule E earnings to him."

Reg. 5(2A)–(2D) inserted by SI 2000/2315, reg. 7, operative from 1 October 2000 with effect for personal pension schemes on and after 6 April 2001.

Reg. 5(3) substituted by SI 2000/2315, reg. 8, operative from 1 October 2000 with effect for personal pension schemes on and after 6 April 2001. Reg. 5(3) originally read as follows:

"**5(3)** The time specified in this paragraph is–
(a) in relation to the particulars specified in paragraph (2)(a), (b), (c) and (d), before the time at which the individual first pays a net contribution,
(b) in relation to the particulars specified in paragraph 2(e), within 30 days after the date on which the individual–
(i) first pays a net contribution,
(ii) pays a net contribution of such an amount that, except where section 641 or 642 applies, the total net contributions paid by him in the year of assessment exceeds the maximum amount permitted under section 640 on the assumption that his net relevant Schedule E earnings for that year of assessment are not in excess of the estimate referred to in paragraph 2(e) and last furnished to the scheme administrator under this paragraph; and
(c) in relation to the particulars specified in paragraph 2(f), within 30 days after the date on which the individual first pays a net contribution in respect of net relevant Schedule E earnings paid to him by an employer of his other than the employer referred to in paragraph (2)(d)."

6(1) The condition prescribed in this regulation is that an individual shall furnish to the scheme administrator before the time specified in paragraph (3) the certificates specified in paragraph (2).

6(2) The certificates specified in this paragraph are certificates which show–

(a) that, except where subsection (4) or subsection (5) of section 645 applies, the individual is not participating in a relevant superannuation scheme;

(b) whether or not the individual is paying contributions under other arrangements or under a retirement annuity contract or trust scheme;

(c) that the total contributions which the individual–
(i) is paying under any arrangements or scheme referred to in sub-paragraph (b), and
(ii) will pay under the arrangements to which the certificate relates
do not together exceed the maximum amount permitted under section 640;

(d) that the individual's eligibility to make contributions for the year of assessment concerned arises by virtue of section 632A(4) (actual net relevant earnings), the individual does not fulfil any of the conditions in section 632A(6) to (9), and his net relevant earnings do not fall within section 644(5).

6(3) The time specified in this paragraph is–

(a) in relation to the certificate specified in paragraph (2)(a), (b) or (c)–
(i) the time at which the individual first pays a net contribution;
(ii) the time at which the individual makes a declaration in accordance with regulation 5(2)(e)(i) specifying a year of assessment as the basis year for the purposes of section 646B;

(b) in relation to the certificate specified in paragraph (2)(d), the time at which the individual first pays a net contribution, being a time when his eligibility to do so arises by virtue of section 632A(4) and he does not fulfil any of the conditions in section 632A(6) to (9).

History – In reg. 6(1) words ", or within," omitted by SI 2000/2315, reg. 9, operative from 1 October 2000 with effect for personal pension schemes on and after 6 April 2001. Reg. 6(1) originally read as follows:

"**6(1)** The condition prescribed in this regulation is that an individual shall furnish to the scheme administrator before, or within, the time specified in paragraph (3) the certificates specified in paragraph (2)."

In reg. 6(2)(c) the words "the maximum amount permitted under section 640" substituted for "the total of the maximum amount permitted under section 640 and so much of any relief given under section 639(1) as is given by virtue of section 642" by SI 2000/2315, reg. 10, operative from 1 October 2000 with effect for personal pension schemes on and after 6 April 2001.

Reg. 6(2)(d) substituted by SI 2000/2315, reg. 10, operative from 1 October 2000 with effect for personal pension schemes on and after 6 April 2001. Reg. 6(2)(d) originally read as follows:

"(d) that the relevant Schedule E earnings in respect of which the individual will pay, or has paid, a net contribution do not fall within section 644(5)."

Reg. 6(3) substituted by SI 2000/2315, reg. 11, operative from 1 October 2000 with effect for personal pension schemes on and after 6 April 2001. Reg. 6(3) originally read as follows:

> "**6(3)**   The time specified in this paragraph is—
> (a)   in relation to the certificate specified in paragraph (2)(a)—
>   (i)   before the time specified in regulation 5(3)(a),
>   (ii)   within 60 days after the date specified in regulation 5(3)(c),
>   (iii)   within 30 days after the expiry of a period of five years from the date on which the individual last furnished a certificate under this sub-paragraph;
> (b)   in relation to the certificates specified in paragraph 2(b) and (c), before the time specified in regulation 5(3)(a); and
> (c)   in relation to the certificate specified in paragraph (2)(d)—
>   (i)   before the time specified in regulation 5(3)(a),
>   (ii)   within 60 days after the date specified in regulation 5(3)(c)."

7(1)   The condition prescribed in this regulation is that on every occasion on which an individual furnishes particulars or a certificate (or both) in accordance with regulation 5 or 6 he shall furnish the declarations specified in paragraph (2).

7(2)   The declarations specified in this paragraph are declarations by the individual to the effect that—

(a)   in relation to—

     (i)   the particulars specified in regulation 5(2), they are to the best of the knowledge and belief of the individual correct and complete;

     (ii)   a certificate specified in regulation 6(2), it is to the best of the knowledge and belief of the individual correct;

(b)   the individual will, not later than the date specified in paragraph (3), give notice to the administrator if an event occurs as a result of which the individual, having regard to section 632A(3) to (9), will no longer be eligible to make contributions.

7(3)   The date specified for the purposes of sub-paragraph (b) of paragraph (2) is the 5th April in the year of assessment in which the event referred to in that sub-paragraph occurs or the date that is 30 days following the occurrence of that event, whichever is the later.

7(4)   Certificates furnished under regulation 6, and declarations furnished under this regulation, if in writing, shall be signed by the maker of the certificates or declarations.

7(5)   Where particulars, certificates or declarations furnished by an individual under regulation 5 or 6 or this regulation are not in writing, the scheme administrator may—

(a)   make a declaration in writing on behalf of the individual that the particulars or (as the case may be) the terms of the certificates or declarations so furnished are those recorded in the declaration, and

(b)   send a copy of the declaration to the individual.

7(6)   Subject to any corrections notified by the individual to the scheme administrator within the period of 30 days following the date on which the copy of the declaration referred to in paragraph (5) was sent to the individual, and incorporated in a new declaration made by the scheme administrator, any such declaration shall take effect as from the date on which the copy of it was sent to the individual in accordance with that paragraph.

7(7)   Particulars, certificates or declarations furnished by an individual under regulation 5, 6 or this regulation shall be regarded as furnished in writing for the purposes of this regulation if they are furnished—

(a)   by telephonic facsimile transmission, or

(b)   by electronic communication containing an electronic signature of the individual.

7(8)   Declarations made by the scheme administrator under paragraph (5) of this regulation shall be regarded as made in writing if they are produced by electronic means; and the copy of a declaration to be sent to the individual in accordance with sub-paragraph (b) of that paragraph may be sent by telephonic facsimile transmission or by electronic communication.

History – In reg. 7(2) the word "signed" which followed the word "declarations" omitted by SI 2000/2315, reg. 12, operative from 1 October 2000 with effect for personal pension schemes on and after 6 April 2001.
Reg. 7(2)(b) substituted by SI 2000/2315, reg. 12, operative from 1 October 2000 with effect for personal pension schemes on and after 6 April 2001. Reg. 7(2)(b) originally read as follows:

> "(b)   the individual will within 30 days give notice in writing to the scheme administrator if–
>   (i)   he ceases to be employed by an employer who has paid net relevant Schedule E earnings to him,
>   (ii)   except where subsection (4) or subsection (5) of section 645 applies, he participates in a relevant superannuation scheme."

Reg. 7(3)–(8) inserted by SI 2000/2315, reg. 13, operative from 1 October 2000 with effect for personal pension schemes on and after 6 April 2001.

CLAIMS: INTRODUCTORY

8(1) Amounts recoverable by a scheme administrator under section 639(4)(b) shall be recovered on a claim made to the Board for the purpose of these Regulations.

8(2) Subject to paragraph (3), a claim shall be for a year of assessment (**"annual claim"**).

8(3) A claim may also be made in accordance with regulation 9 for a tax month (**"interim claim"**).

8(3A) No annual claim or interim claim may be made in respect of contributions made by an individual in a year of assessment that exceed the earnings threshold unless that year of assessment is–

(a)   the basis year specified in a declaration under regulation 5(2)(e)(i),

(b)   one of the 5 years of assessment following that year, or

(c)   a qualifying post-cessation year.

8(4) Notwithstanding the provisions of any other enactment, the Board shall not be under an obligation to make any payment under regulation 9 or 10 earlier than the end of the month following the month in which the claim is received.

History – Reg. 8(3A) inserted by SI 2000/2315, reg. 14, operative from 1 October 2000 with effect for personal pension schemes on and after 6 April 2001.

INTERIM CLAIMS

9(1) Subject to paragraph (3), an interim claim for a tax month may be made by a scheme administrator within 6 months after the end of the tax month for which it is made.

9(2) A claim under this regulation may not be based on an estimate but may only be made to recover an amount deducted in respect of contributions paid in the tax month.

9(3) An interim claim may not be made for the tax month ending 5th October or any subsequent month until the annual claim for the preceding year of assessment has been made by the scheme administrator and received by the Board.

9(4) If the amount claimed is established to the Board's satisfaction they shall pay the amount to the claimant; if they are not so satisfied they shall pay to the claimant any lesser amount established to their satisfaction.

9(5) Where a scheme administrator discovers that an amount paid to him under paragraph (4) was excessive he shall bring into account in the interim claim made by him next after the discovery (in this regulation referred to as **"the subsequent claim"**) the amount of the excess; and if that amount exceeds the amount deducted in respect of the tax month for which the subsequent claim is made–

(a)   the scheme administrator shall repay the amount of the excess to the Board with the claim; and

(b)   if he fails so to do that amount shall immediately be recoverable by the Board in the same manner as tax charged by an assessment on the scheme administrator which has become final and conclusive.

ANNUAL CLAIMS

Notes – Reg. 10 amended by SI 2000/2315, operative from 1 October 2000 with effect for personal pension schemes on and after 6 April 2001. See history note.

10(1) An annual claim for a year of assessment may, subject to paragraph (2), be made at any time within 6 years after the end of the year of assessment.

10(2) Where in relation to any year of assessment a scheme administrator has received and not repaid in full any amount on an interim claim he shall within 6 months after the end of the year of assessment make an annual claim.

10(3) A claim under this regulation–

(a)   may not be based on an estimate but may only be made to recover an amount deducted in respect of contributions paid in respect of the year of assessment, and

(b)   shall bring into account payments made in respect of the year of assessment; and for the purpose of this regulation **"aggregate interim payments"** means the aggregate of payments made (and not repaid) on interim claims.

10(4) Where the aggregate of the interim payments shown by an annual claim exceeds the amount deducted for the year of assessment–

(a)   the scheme administrator shall repay the amount of the excess to the Board with the claim; and

(b)   if he fails so to do, that amount shall immediately be recoverable by the Board in the same manner as tax charged by an assessment on the scheme administrator which has become final and conclusive.

10(5) If a scheme administrator fails to make an annual claim under paragraph (2) within the time limited by that paragraph, the Board may issue a notice to the scheme administrator showing the aggregate interim payments for the year, and stating that the Board are not satisfied that the amount due to the scheme administrator for the year of assessment exceeds the lower amount stated in the notice.

10(6) If an annual claim is not delivered to the Board within 14 days after the issue of a notice under paragraph (5), the amount of the difference between the aggregate amount and the amount stated in the notice shall immediately be recoverable by the Board in the same manner as tax charged by an assessment on the scheme administrator which has become final and conclusive.

10(7) Where an annual claim has been made and the scheme administrator subsequently discovers that an error or mistake has been made in the claim the scheme administrator may make a supplementary claim within the time limited by paragraph (1).

History – In reg. 10(3)(a)the words "paid in respect of" substituted for the words "paid in" by SI 2000/2315, reg. 15, operative from 1 October 2000 with effect for personal pension schemes on and after 6 April 2001.

CLAIMS: SUPPLEMENTARY PROVISIONS

11(1) Section 42 of the Taxes Management Act 1970 (procedure for making claims) shall not apply to a claim under these Regulations.

11(2) No appeal shall lie from the Board's decision on an interim claim.

11(3) An appeal shall be to the Special Commissioners from the Board's decision on an annual claim, and the appeal shall be brought by giving written notice to the Board within 30 days of receipt of written notice of the decision.

11(4) No payment made or other thing done on or in relation to an interim claim shall prejudice the decision on an annual claim.

11(5) The like provisions as are contained in Part V of the Taxes Management Act 1970 (appeals and other proceedings) shall apply to an appeal under paragraph (3), and on an appeal the Special Commissioners may vary the decision appealed against whether or not the variation is to the advantage of the appellant.

11(6) All such assessments, payments and repayments shall be made as are necessary to give effect to the Board's decision on an annual claim, or as any variation of that decision on appeal.

11(7) Claims under these Regulations–

(a)   shall contain such information and be in such form as the Board may prescribe (and forms prescribed for annual claims may require a report to be given by the scheme administrator's auditor);

(b)   shall contain declarations to the effect that–

     (i)   sufficient records in respect of the scheme are maintained so as to enable the requirements of these Regulations to be satisfied, and

     (ii)   the information contained in the claim (including the declaration referred to in paragraph (i)) is correct; and

(c)   shall be signed by the scheme administrator or by an authorised representative in the service of the scheme administrator.

RECOVERY ON WITHDRAWAL OF APPROVAL OF SCHEMES OR OF ARRANGEMENTS

12 Where a scheme administrator gives to the Board information in accordance with regulation 14(2) he shall at the time that he gives the information–

(a)   pay to the Board the amount (if any) referred to in regulation 14(3)(d); and

(b)   if he fails so to do, that amount shall immediately be recoverable by the Board in the same manner as tax charged by an assessment on the scheme administrator which has become final and conclusive.

RECOVERY OF AMOUNTS BY ASSESSMENT

13(1) The like provisions as are contained in section 30 of the Taxes Management Act 1970 (recovery of overpayment of tax, etc.) shall apply in relation to the payment by the Board of an amount–

(a)   paid under these Regulations to which a scheme administrator was not entitled, or

(b)   recoverable from a scheme administrator under regulation 9(5), regulation 10(4) or (6) or regulation 12, as if it had been income tax repaid to the scheme administrator to which he was not entitled.

13(2) An assessment made by virtue of this regulation shall be made by the Board and, subject to the provisions of these Regulations, the like provisions as are contained in the Taxes Management Act 1970 shall apply as if the assessment were an assessment to tax for the year of assessment in respect of which the amount was paid or is recoverable.

INFORMATION

14(1) The Board may by notice in writing require any person who is, or who at any time has been,–

(a) a scheme administrator to whom net contributions have been paid, or

(b) an individual who has paid such contributions,

to give to them within such time (not being less than 14 days) as may be provided in the notice such information and in such form as may be prescribed in the notice.

14(2) If the Board by notice under section 650 withdraw their approval of a scheme, or of arrangements made in accordance with it and under which net contributions have been paid, the scheme administrator shall within 30 days give to the Board in relation to that scheme, or to those arrangements, the information prescribed in paragraph (3).

14(3) The information prescribed in this paragraph is–

(a) the full name, address, national insurance number, and where known tax office reference of each individual who has paid net contributions after the date specified in the notice in relation to the scheme, or to the arrangements, as the case may be (in this regulation referred to as **"the relevant contributions"**);

(b) the amount of the relief obtained under section 639(1) by means of the relevant contributions;

(c) the amount of such relief actually due; and

(d) the difference between the relief referred to in sub-paragraph (b) and that referred to in sub-paragraph (c).

14(4) If an individual who has paid net contributions fails to comply with the requirements of regulations 5 to 7, the scheme administrator to whom such contributions have been made shall within 30 days give to the Board the information prescribed in paragraph (5).

14(5) The information prescribed in this paragraph is–

(a) the full name, address, national insurance number, and where known tax office reference of the individual;

(b) the amount of relief obtained by him under section 639(1) by means of such contributions;

(c) the amount of such relief actually due; and

(d) the difference between the relief referred to in sub-paragraph (b) and that referred to in sub-paragraph (c).

INSPECTION OF RECORDS

15(1) Every scheme administrator to whom net contributions have been paid shall, whenever required so to do, make available for inspection by a person authorised by the Board for that purpose all books, documents and other records (including all particulars, certificates and declarations furnished under regulations 5 to 7) in his possession or under his control relating to–

(a) such contributions paid to him,

(b) the scheme and the arrangements made in accordance with it and under which the contributions were paid, and

(c) the individual who paid the contributions.

15(2) Where records are maintained by computer the scheme administrator shall provide the person making the inspection with all facilities necessary to obtain information from them.

15(3) Subject to paragraph (4), all books, documents and records referred to in paragraph (1), shall be preserved by the scheme administrator so as to be available for inspection under this regulation for a period of six years following the termination of the scheme, or of arrangements made in accordance with it, to which they relate.

15(4) All particulars, certificates and declarations furnished under regulations 5 to 7 shall be so preserved for a period of six years following the date on which the individual to whom they relate ceased to make net contributions.

TAXES (INTEREST RATE) REGULATIONS 1989

(SI 1989/1297, as amended by SI 1991/889, SI 1993/2212, SI 1994/1307, SI 1994/1567, SI 1996/2644, SI 1996/3187, SI 1997/1681, SI 1997/2707, SI 1998/310, SI 1998/3176, SI 1999/1928, SI 1999/2538, SI 1999/2637, SI 2000/893, SI 2001/204, SI 2001/254, SI 2005/2462, SI 2007/684, SI 2008/778, SI 2008/3234, SI 2009/199, SI 2009/2032, SI 2010/415, SI 2011/701, SI 2011/702 and SI 2014/496)

Made on 27 July 1989 by the Treasury, in exercise of the powers conferred on them by s. 178 of the Finance Act 1989.

Notes – FA 1989, s. 178(1) has effect for the purposes of the enactments specified in these regulations for periods beginning on or after 18 August 1989 by virtue of SI 1989/1298 (C 44).

CITATION AND COMMENCEMENT

1 These Regulations may be cited as the Taxes (Interest Rate) Regulations 1989 and shall come into force on 18th August 1989.

INTERPRETATION

2(1) In these Regulations unless the context otherwise requires–

"**the 1998 Regulations**" means the Corporation Tax (Instalment Payments) Regulations 1998;

"**established rate**" means–

(a) on the coming into force of these Regulations, 14 per cent per annum; and

(b) in relation to any date after the first reference date after the coming into force of these Regulations, the reference rate found on the immediately preceding reference date;

"**operative date**" means–

(a) the twelfth working day after the reference date, or

(b) where regulation 3ZA or 3BA applies–

(i) where the reference date is the first Tuesday, the day which is the Monday next following the first Tuesday, or

(ii) where the reference date is the second Tuesday, the day which is the Monday next following the second Tuesday;

"**reference date**" means–

(a) the working day following the day on which the most recent meeting of the Monetary Policy Committee of the Bank of England took place, or

(b) where regulation 3ZA or 3BA applies–

(i) the day which is the Tuesday next following the day on which that meeting took place ("the first Tuesday"), and

(ii) the day which is the Tuesday ("the second Tuesday") occurring two weeks after the first Tuesday;

"**section 178**" means section 178 of the Finance Act 1989;

"**working day**" means any day other than a non-business day within the meaning of section 92 of the Bills of Exchange Act 1882.

2(2) In these Regulations the reference rate found on a reference date is the official bank rate determined by the most recent meeting of the Monetary Policy Committee of the Bank of England.

History – In reg. 2(1), in para. (a) of the definition of "operative date", the word "twelfth" substituted for the word "eleventh" by SI 2009/2032, reg. 3(2)(a), with effect from 12 August 2009.

In reg. 2(1), the definition of "operative date" substituted by SI 2008/3234, reg. 2(2)(a), with effect from 7 January 2009. The former definition read as follows–

"'**operative date**' means the sixth day of each month or, where regulation 3ZA or 3BA applies, means the day of each month which is the Monday next following the day referred to in the definition of "reference date" below as "the first Tuesday", and the day of each month which is the Monday next following the day referred to in that definition as "the second Tuesday";".

In reg. 2(1), in para. (a) of the definition of "reference date", the word "second" (which appeared before the word "working") omitted by SI 2009/2032, reg. 3(2)(b), with effect from 12 August 2009.

In reg. 2(1), the definition of "reference date" substituted by SI 2008/3234, reg. 2(2)(b), with effect from 7 January 2009. The former definition read as follows–

"'**reference date**' means the day of each month which is the twelfth working day before the sixth day of the following month or, where regulation 3ZA or 3BA applies, means the day of each month which is the Tuesday next following the day on which the most recent meeting of the Monetary Policy Committee of the Bank of England took place ("the first

Tuesday"), and the day of each month which is the Tuesday ("the second Tuesday") occurring two weeks after the first Tuesday;".

In reg. 2(1), definition of "the 1998 Regulations" inserted, words from "or, where regulation 3ZA" to the end added to each of the definitions of "operative date" and "reference date" by SI 1998/3176, reg. 3, and in reg. 2(2), para. (i), (ii) and (iii) substituted for former wording by SI 1998/3176, reg. 4, operative from 7 January 1999.

Reg. 2(2) substituted by SI 2009/2032, reg. 3(3), with effect from 12 August 2009.

APPLICABLE RATE OF INTEREST EQUAL TO ZERO

2A [Omitted by SI 2009/2032, reg. 4.]

History – Reg. 2A omitted by SI 2009/2032, reg. 4, with effect from 12 August 2009.
Former reg. 2A inserted by SI 2008/3234, reg. 2(2)(c), with effect from 7 January 2009.

APPLICABLE RATES OF INTEREST ON UNPAID TAX, TAX REPAID AND REPAYMENT SUPPLEMENT

3(1)   For the purposes of–

(a)   section 86 (except where regulation 3AA(1)(aa) applies) and section 88 of the Taxes Management Act 1970,

(aa)   [omitted by SI 2011/702, art. 16,]

(ab)   [omitted by SI 2011/701, art. 10,]

(b)   section 118F of and paragraph 6B of Schedule 3 to the Income and Corporation Taxes Act 1988,

(ba)   section 71(8A) of the Social Security Administration Act 1992 and section 69(8A) of the Social Security Administration (Northern Ireland) Act 1992, as they have effect in any case where the amount recoverable referred to in each of those sections is in respect of working families' tax credit or disabled person's tax credit, and paragraph 8 of Schedule 4 to the Tax Credits Act 1999;

(c)   paragraph 6(2)(a) of Schedule 1 to the Social Security Contributions and Benefits Act 1992,

(d)   section 15A of the Stamp Act 1891, and

(e)   sections 87 and 88 of the Finance Act 2003

the rate applicable under section 178 shall, subject to paragraph (2), be 8.5 per cent per annum.

3(2)   Where, on a reference date after 1st January 1997, the reference rate found on that date differs from the established rate, the rate applicable under section 178 for the purposes of the enactments referred to in paragraph (1) shall, on and after the next operative date, be the percentage per annum found by applying the formula specified in paragraph (3).

3(3)   The formula specified in this paragraph is

$$RR + 2.5$$

where RR is the reference rate referred to in paragraph (2).

History – See History note at foot of reg. 3AB.
Reg. 3(1)(a) amended by SI 2001/204, reg. 3, by substituting the words "section 86 (except where regulation 3AA(1)(aa) applies) and section 88" for "sections 86 and 88", operative from 6 March 2001.
Reg. 3(1)(aa) omitted by SI 2011/702, art. 16, with effect from 1 April 2011, but subject to SI 2011/702, art. 20, which provides that the omission does not have effect in relation to a return or other document which is required to be made or delivered to HMRC, or an amount of tax which is payable, in relation to the tax year 2009–10 or any previous tax year. Former reg. 3(1)(aa) read as follows:
    "(aa)   section 59C of the Taxes Management Act 1970, as it applies to any income tax or capital gains tax which has become payable in accordance with–
        (i)   section 55 of that Act, so far as it relates to an amendment or assessment referred to in paragraphs (a) and (b) of sub-section (1) of that section, or
        (ii)   section 59B of that Act, ".
Reg. 3(1)(ab) omitted by SI 2011/701, art. 10, with effect from 31 October 2011. Former reg. 3(1)(ab) read as follows:
    "(ab)   section 103A of the Taxes Management Act 1970, so far as it relates to–
        (i)   any person who may be required by a notice under section 8, 8A or 12AA of that Act (or under any of those sections as extended by section 12 of that Act) to make and deliver a return for a year of assessment or other period, and
        (ii)   income tax or capital gains tax,".
Reg. 3(1)(aa), (ab) inserted by SI 1998/310, operative from 9 March 1998.
Reg. 3(1)(b) amended by SI 1999/2538, reg. 3(a), by omitting the word "and" which appeared at the end of sub-para. (b), operative from 1 October 1999.
Reg. 3(1)(b) amended by SI 1997/2707, reg. 2, by inserting reference to ICTA 1988, s. 118F, operative from 9 December 1997.
Reg. 3(1)(ba) inserted by SI 2001/254, reg. 2, operative from 7 March 2001.
Reg. 3(1)(c) amended by SI 1999/2538, reg. 3(b), by inserting the word "and" after sub-para. (c), operative from 1 October 1999.
Reg. 3(1)(d) inserted by SI 1999/2538, reg. 3(b), operative from 1 October 1999.
Reg. 3(1)(e) inserted, and the word "and" moved from the end of reg 3(1)(c) to the end of reg. 3(1)(d), by SI 2005/2462 reg. 3, operative from 26 September 2005.

3AA(1) For the purposes of–

(a)   sections 86A and 87 of the Taxes Management Act 1970,

(aa)   section 86 of the Taxes Management Act 1970 as it has effect in relation to accounting periods of companies ending before 1st October 1993 (interest on unpaid assessed corporation tax),

(b)   paragraph 3 of Schedule 16A to the Finance Act 1973,

(c)   paragraphs 15 of Schedule 2, and paragraph 8 of Schedule 5, to the Oil Taxation Act 1975,

(d)   [omitted by SI 2009/2032, reg. 5;]

(e)   [omitted by SI 1999/2538;]

(f)   [omitted by SI 2009/2032, reg. 5;]

the rate applicable under section 178 shall, except where regulation 3AC applies and subject to paragraph (2), be–

(i)   where paragraph (aa) above applies, 6.5 per cent per annum;

(ii)   in all other cases, 6.25 per cent per annum.

3AA(2) Where, on a reference date after 1st January 1997, the reference rate found on that date differs from the established rate, the rate applicable under section 178 for the purposes of the enactments referred to in paragraph (1) shall, on and after the next operative date, be the percentage per annum found by applying the formula specified in paragraph (3).

3AA(3) The formula specified in this paragraph is–

$$RR + 2.5,$$

where RR is the reference rate referred to in paragraph (2).

History – In reg. 3AA(1)(c) the words "and 16" and sub-para. (d) and (f) omitted by SI 2009/2032, reg. 5(2), with effect from 12 August 2009.
In reg. 3AA(1) the words
"be–
    (i)   where paragraph (aa) above applies, 6.5 per cent per annum;
    (ii)   in all other cases, 6.25 per cent per annum."
substituted for "be 6.25 per cent per annum" by SI 2001/204, reg. 4, operative from 6 March 2001.
In reg. 3AA(1), words "except where regulation 3AC applies and" inserted by SI 1999/2637, reg. 3, operative from 14 October 1999.
Reg. 3AA(1)(aa) inserted by SI 2001/204, reg. 4, operative from 6 March 2001.
Reg. 3AA(1)(e) omitted by SI 1999/2538, reg. 4, with effect from 1 October 1999.
In reg. 3AA(2) the words "and, if the result is not a multiple of one-quarter, rounding the result down to the nearest amount which is such a multiple" omitted by SI 2009/2032, reg. 5(3), with effect from 12 August 2009.
Reg. 3AA(3) substituted by SI 2009/2032, reg. 5(4), with effect from 12 August 2009.
See History note to reg. 3AB.

3AB(1) For the purposes of–

(a)   section 824 of the Income and Corporation Taxes Act 1988,

(b)   paragraph 6(2)(b) of Schedule 1 to the Social Security Contributions and Benefits Act 1992,

(c)   section 283 of the Taxation of Chargeable Gains Act 1992,

(d)   section 92 of the Finance Act 1986,

(e)   section 110 of the Finance Act 1999; and

(f)   section 89 of the Finance Act 2003

the rate applicable under section 178 shall, subject to paragraph (2), be 4 per cent per annum.

3AB(2) Where, on a reference date after 1st January 1997, the reference rate found on that date differs from the established rate, the rate applicable under section 178 for the purposes of the enactments referred to in paragraph (1) shall, on and after the next operative date, be the higher of–

(a)   0.5% per annum, and

(b)   the percentage per annum found by applying the formula specified in paragraph (3).

3AB(3) The formula specified in this paragraph is–

$$RR - 1,$$

where RR is the reference rate referred to in paragraph (2).

History – Reg. 3AB(1)(b) amended by SI 1999/2538, reg. 5(a), by omitting the word "and" which appeared at the end of sub-para. (b), operative from 1 October 1999.
Reg. 3AB(1)(d), (e) inserted by SI 1999/2538, reg. 5(b), operative from 1 October 1999.
Reg. 3AB(1)(f) inserted, and the word "and" moved from the end of reg 3AB(1)(d) to the end of reg. 3AB(1)(e), by SI 2005/2462 reg. 4, operative from 26 September 2005.
In reg. 3AB(2) the words from "higher" to the end substituted for the words "percentage per annum found by applying the formula specified in paragraph (3) and, if the result is not a multiple of one-quarter, rounding the result down to the nearest amount which is such a multiple; and" by SI 2009/2032, reg. 7(2), with effect from 12 August 2009.
Reg. 3AB(3) substituted by SI 2009/2032, reg. 7(3), with effect from 12 August 2009.

In former reg. 3AB(3) the reference to "BR" substituted for "LR" by SI 2008/778, reg. 2, with effect from 6 April 2008.
In former reg. 3AB(3) the words "BR is the percentage at which income tax at the basic rate" substituted for "LR is the percentage at which income tax at the lower rate" by SI 2008/778, reg. 2, with effect from 6 April 2008.
Reg. 3, 3AA and 3AB substituted for former reg. 3 by SI 1996/3187, reg. 2, operative from 31 January 1997.

3AC(1) For the purposes of section 87 of the Taxes Management Act 1970 in so far as it relates to tax that becomes due and payable on or after 14th October 1999, the rate applicable under section 178 shall, subject to paragraph (2), be 7.5 per cent per annum.

3AC(2) Where on a reference date after 14th October 1999 the reference rate found on that date differs from the established rate, the rate applicable under section 178 for the purposes mentioned in paragraph (1) shall, on and after the next operative date, be the percentage per annum found by applying the formula specified in paragraph (3).

3AC(3) The formula specified in this paragraph is—

$$RR + 2.5$$

where RR is the reference rate referred to in paragraph (2).

History – Reg. 3AC inserted by SI 1999/2637, reg. 4, operative from 14 October 1999.

APPLICABLE RATE OF INTEREST ON OVERDUE CORPORATION TAX

3A(1) For the purposes of section 87A of the Taxes Management Act 1970, the rate applicable under section 178 shall, except where regulation 3ZA or 3ZB applies and subject to paragraph (2), be 6.25 per cent per annum.

3A(2) Where, on a reference date after 1st October 1993, the reference rate found on that date differs from the established rate, the rate applicable under section 178 for the purposes of the enactment referred to in paragraph (1) shall, on and after the next operative date, be the percentage per annum found by applying the formula specified in paragraph (3).

3A(3) The formula specified in this paragraph is—

$$RR + 2.5,$$

where RR is the reference rate referred to in paragraph (2).

History – In reg. 3A(1), words "except where regulation 3ZA or 3ZB applies and" inserted by SI 1998/3176, reg. 5, operative from 7 January 1999.
In reg. 3A(2) the words " and, if the result is not a multiple of one-quarter, rounding the result down to the nearest amount which is such a multiple" omitted by SI 2009/2032, reg. 8(2), with effect from 12 August 2009.
Reg. 3A(3) substituted by SI 2009/2032, reg. 7(3), with effect from 12 August 2009.
Reg. 3A was inserted by SI 1993/2212, reg. 2, operative 1 October 1993.

3AAA(1) For the purposes of—

(a)   paragraph 16 of Schedule 2 to the Oil Taxation Act 1975,

(b)   paragraph 59 of Schedule 8 to the Development Land Tax Act 1976, and

(c)   section 825 of, and paragraph 3 of Schedule 19A to, the Income and Corporation Taxes Act 1988,

the rate applicable under section 178 shall, subject to paragraph (3), be the percentage per annum found by applying the formula specified in paragraph (2), but if the result is not a multiple of one-quarter the result shall be rounded down to the nearest amount which is such a multiple.

3AAA(2) The formula specified for the purposes of paragraph (1) is—

$$\frac{(RR + 2.5) \times 80}{100}$$

where RR is the official bank rate determined at the meeting of the Monetary Policy Committee of the Bank of England which immediately preceded the coming into force of these Regulations.

3AAA(3) Where on a reference date after the coming into force of these Regulations, the reference rate found on that date differs from the established rate, the rate applicable under section 178 for the purposes of the enactments referred to in paragraph (1) shall, on and after the next operative date, be the higher of—

(a)   0.5% per annum, and

(b)   the percentage per annum found by applying the formula specified in paragraph (4).

3AAA(4) The formula specified in this paragraph is—

$$RR - 1,$$

where RR is the reference rate referred to in paragraph (3).

History – Reg. 3AAA inserted by SI 2009/2032, reg. 6, with effect from 12 August 2009.

3ZA(1) For the purposes of section 87A of the Taxes Management Act 1970 in so far as it relates, by virtue of subsection (1A) of that section, to an amount or amounts treated as becoming due and payable in respect of the total liability of a large company for an accounting period ending on or after 1st July 1999 in accordance with regulation 5 of the 1998 Regulations, the rate applicable under section 178 shall, subject to paragraph (2), be 8.25 per cent per annum.

3ZA(2) Where on a reference date after 7th January 1999 the reference rate found on that date differs from the established rate, the rate applicable under section 178 for the purposes mentioned in paragraph (1) shall, on and after the next operative date and as respects the period specified in paragraph (3), be the percentage per annum found by applying the formula specified in paragraph (4).

3ZA(3) The period specified in this paragraph is any period falling between –

(a) the date on which the first instalment payment is treated as becoming due and payable for the accounting period concerned under regulation 5 of the 1998 Regulations, and

(b) the day following the expiry of nine months from the end of that accounting period,

during which any amount treated as becoming due and payable in accordance with regulation 5 of those Regulations for that accounting period remains unpaid.

3ZA(4) The formula specified in this paragraph is–

$$RR + 1$$

Where RR is the reference rate referred to in paragraph (2).

History – In reg. 3ZA(4) "RR + 1" substituted by SI 2000/893 reg. 2, operative from 19 April 2000 and with effect on and after 20 April 2000 in relation to interest running from before that day as well as interest running from, or from after, that day. Reg. 3ZA inserted by SI 1998/3176, reg. 6, operative from 7 January 1999.

3ZB(1) For the purposes of section 87A of the Taxes Management Act 1970 insofar as it relates to an unpaid amount in respect of the total liability of a company for an accounting period ending on or after 1st July 1999, other than an amount to which regulation 3ZA applies, the rate applicable under section 178 shall, subject to paragraph (2), be 8.5 per cent per annum.

3ZB(2) Where on a reference date after 7th January 1999 the reference rate found on that date differs from the established rate, the rate applicable under section 178 for the purposes mentioned in paragraph (1) shall, on and after the next operative date, be the percentage per annum found by applying the formula specified in paragraph (3).

3ZB(3) The formula specified in this paragraph is–

$$RR + 2.5,$$

where RR is the reference rate referred to in paragraph (2).

History – Reg. 3ZB inserted by SI 1998/3176, reg. 6, operative from 7 January 1999.

APPLICABLE RATE OF INTEREST ON TAX OVERPAID

3B(1) For the purposes of section 826 of the Income and Corporation Taxes Act 1988, the rate applicable under section 178 shall, except where regulation 3BA or 3BB applies and subject to paragraph (2), be 3.25 per cent per annum.

3B(2) Where, on a reference date after 1st October 1993, the reference rate found on that date differs from the established rate, the rate applicable under section 178 for the purposes of the enactment referred to in paragraph (1) shall, on and after the next operative date, be the higher of–

(a) 0.5% per annum, and

(b) the percentage per annum found by applying the formula specified in paragraph (3).

3B(3) The formula specified in this paragraph is–

$$RR - 1,$$

where RR is the reference rate referred to in paragraph (2).

History – In reg. 3B(2) the words from "higher" to the end substituted for the words "percentage per annum found by applying the formula specified in paragraph (3) and, if the result is not a multiple of one-quarter, rounding the result down to the nearest amount which is such a multiple" by SI 2009/2032, reg. 9(2), with effect from 12 August 2009.
In reg. 3B(1), words "except where regulation 3ZA or 3ZB applies and" inserted by SI 1998/3176, reg. 5, operative from 7 January 1999.
Reg. 3B(3) substituted by SI 2009/2032, reg. 8(3), with effect from 12 August 2009.
Reg. 3B was inserted by SI 1993/2212, reg. 2, operative 1 October 1993.

3BA(1) For the purposes of section 826 of the Income and Corporation Taxes Act 1988 insofar as it relates to an amount paid by a company in respect of its total liability for an accounting period ending on or after 1st July 1999, being an amount falling within paragraph (d) of subsection (1) of that section (overpayment of instalment by large company under regulation 5 of the 1998 Regulations) or an amount falling within paragraph (e) of that subsection (payment by company other than large company prior to the day following the expiry of nine months from the end of the accounting period concerned), the rate applicable under section 178 shall, subject to paragraph (2), be 6 per cent per annum.

3BA(2) Where on a reference date after 7th January 1999 the reference rate found on that date differs from the established rate, the rate applicable under section 178 for the purposes mentioned in paragraph (1) shall, on and after the next operative date and as respects the period specified in paragraph (3), be the higher of–

(a) 0.5% per annum, and

(b) the percentage per annum found by applying the formula specified in paragraph (4).

3BA(3) The period specified in this paragraph is any period falling between–

(a) the date on which the first instalment payment is treated as becoming due and payable for the accounting period concerned under regulation 5 of the 1998 Regulations or, in the case of a company other than a large company, the date on which the first instalment payment would be so treated if the company were a large company, and

(b) the day following the expiry of nine months from the end of that accounting period,

during which there exists an amount paid by the company in respect of its total liability to which paragraph (1) applies.

3BA(4) The formula specified in this paragraph is–

$$RR - 0.25,$$

where RR is the reference rate referred to in paragraph (2).

History – In reg. 3BA(2) the words from "higher" to the end substituted for the words "percentage per annum found by applying the formula specified in paragraph (4)" by SI 2009/2032, reg. 10(2), with effect from 12 August 2009.
Reg. 3BA inserted by SI 1998/3176, reg. 8, operative from 7 January 1999.

3BB(1) For the purposes of section 826 of the Income and Corporation Taxes Act 1988 insofar as it relates to an amount overpaid by a company in respect of its total liability for an accounting period ending on or after 1st July 1999, being an amount paid, or which remains overpaid, on or after the day following the expiry of nine months from the end of that period, the rate applicable under section 178 shall, subject to paragraph (2) and on and after that day, be 5 per cent per annum.

3BB(2) Where on a reference date after 7th January 1999 the reference rate found on that date differs from the established rate, the rate applicable under section 178 for the purposes mentioned in paragraph (1) shall, on and after the next operative date, be the higher of–

(a) 0.5% per annum, and

(b) the percentage per annum found by applying the formula specified in paragraph (3).

3BB(3) The formula specified in this paragraph is–

$$RR - 1,$$

where RR is the reference rate referred to in paragraph (2).

History – In reg. 3BB(1) the words ", or which remains overpaid," inserted after the words "being an amount paid" by SI 1999/1928, reg. 3, operative from 28 July 1999.
In reg. 3BB(1) the words "and on and after that day" inserted after the words "paragraph (2)" by SI 1999/1928, reg. 3, operative from 28 July 1999.
In reg. 3BB(2) the words from "higher" to the end substituted for the words "percentage per annum found by applying the formula specified in paragraph (3)" by SI 2009/2032, reg. 11(2), with effect from 12 August 2009.
Reg. 3BB inserted by SI 1998/3176, reg. 8, operative from 7 January 1999.

APPLICABLE RATE OF INTEREST ON UNPAID INHERITANCE TAX, CAPITAL TRANSFER TAX AND ESTATE DUTY

4(1) For the purposes of–

(a) section 8(9) of the Finance Act 1894,

(b) section 18 of the Finance Act 1896,

(c) section 61(5) of the Finance Act (1909–10) Act 1910,

(d) section 17(3) of the Law of Property Act 1925,

(e) section 73(6) of the Land Registration Act 1925; and

(f) sections 233 of the Inheritance Tax Act 1984,

(g)   section 236(4) of the Inheritance Tax Act 1984 so far as it relates to tax charged by virtue of section 147(4) of that Act,

the rate applicable under section 178 shall, subject to paragraph (2), be 11 per cent per annum.

4(2) Where, on a reference date after the coming into force of these Regulations, the reference rate found on that date differs from the established rate, the rate applicable under section 178 for the purposes of the enactments referred to in paragraph (1) shall, on and after the next operative date, be the percentage per annum found by applying the formula specified in paragraph (3).

4(3) The formula specified in this paragraph is–

$$RR + 2.5,$$

where RR is the reference rate referred to in paragraph (2).

History – In reg. 4(1) the words "[and] 236(3) and (4)" (the "and" in square brackets not actually specified in the amending provision) omitted and sub-para. (g) inserted by SI 2009/2032, reg. 12(2), with effect from 12 August 2009.
In reg. 4(2) the words "and, if the result is not a whole number, rounding the result down to the nearest such number" omitted by SI 2009/2032, reg. 12(3), with effect from 12 August 2009.
Reg. 4(3) substituted by SI 2009/2032, reg. 12(4), with effect from 12 August 2009.

APPLICABLE RATE ON REPAYMENTS OF INHERITANCE TAX, CAPITAL TRANSFER TAX AND ESTATE DUTY

4A(1) For the purposes of–

(a)   section 48(1) of the Finance Act 1975,

(b)   sections 235(1) of the Inheritance Tax Act 1984,

(c)   section 236(3) of the Inheritance Tax Act, and

(d)   section 236(4) of the Inheritance Tax Act so far as it relates to tax repayable under section 147(2) of that Act,

the rate applicable under section 178 shall, subject to paragraph (3), be the percentage per annum found by applying the formula specified in paragraph (2), but if the result is not a whole number the result shall be rounded down to the nearest such number.

4A(2) The formula specified for the purposes of paragraph (1) is–

$$\frac{(RR + 2) \times 80}{100} - 1,$$

where RR is the official bank rate determined at the meeting of the Monetary Policy Committee of the Bank of England which immediately preceded the coming into force of these Regulations.

4A(3) Where on a reference date after the coming into force of these Regulations, the reference rate found on that date differs from the established rate, the rate applicable under section 178 for the purposes of the enactments referred to in paragraph (1) shall, on and after the next operative date, be the higher of–

(a)   0.5% per annum, and

(b)   the percentage per annum found by applying the formula specified in paragraph (4).

4A(4) The formula specified in this paragraph is–

$$RR - 1,$$

where RR is the reference rate referred to in paragraph (3).

History – Reg. 4A inserted by SI 2009/2032, reg. 13, with effect from 12 August 2009.

APPLICABLE RATE OF OFFICIAL RATE OF INTEREST

5(1) Subject to paragraph (2), the rate applicable under section 178 for the purposes of Chapter 7 of Part 3 of the Income Tax (Earnings and Pensions) Act 2003 ("Chapter 7") shall, on and after 6th April 2014, be 3.25 per cent per annum.

5(2) In relation to a loan outstanding for the whole or part of a year of assessment where–

(a)   the loan was made in the currency of a country or territory specified in the Table below,

(b)   the benefit of the loan is obtained by reason of the employment of a person who normally lives in that country or territory, and

(c)   that person has lived in that country or territory at some time in the period of six years ending with that year, the rate applicable under section 178 for the purposes of Chapter 7 and the date on and after which that rate has effect shall be ascertained from the entries in the Table below relating to the country or territory concerned.

Country or territory	Date on and after which applicable rate has effect	Applicable Rate
Japan	6th June 1994	3.9 per cent per annum.
Switzerland	6th July 1994	5.5 per cent per annum.

History – In reg. 5(1), the words "on and after 6th April 2014, be 3.25 per cent per annum" substituted for "on and after 6th April 2010, be 4.00 per cent per annum" by SI 2014/496, reg. 2, with effect from 6 April 2014.

In reg. 5(1) the words "on and after 6th April 2010, be 4.00 per cent per annum" substituted for the words "on and after 1st March 2009, be 4.75 per cent per annum" by SI 2010/415, reg. 2, with effect from 6 April 2010.

Reg. 5(1) substituted by SI 2009/199, reg. 2(2), with effect from 1 March 2009.

Reg. 5(1) substituted by SI 2007/684, reg. 2, with effect from 6 April 2007.

In reg. 5(1), the words "6th March 1999" and "6.25 per cent per annum" respectively substituted for the words "6th August 1997 " and "7.25 per cent per annum" by SI 1999/419.

In reg. 5(2), "Chapter 7" substituted for "section 181" by SI 2009/199, reg. 2(3), with effect from 1 March 2009.

In reg. 5(2) the reference to s. "181" substituted for "160" by SI 2007/684, reg. 3, with effect from 6 April 2007.

In reg. 5(2), in the entry relating to Switzerland in the table, the words "6 July 1994" and "5.5 per cent per annum" respectively substituted for the words "6 June 1994" and "5.7 per cent per annum" by SI 1994/1567, reg. 2, with effect from 6 July 1994.

Reg. 5 substituted by SI 1994/1307, reg. 2, with effect from 6 June 1994.

HMRC Manuals – EIM 26100: The benefits code: beneficial loans.

EFFECT OF CHANGE IN APPLICABLE RATE

6 Where the rate applicable under section 178 for the purpose of any of the enactments referred to in these Regulations changes on an operative date by virtue of these Regulations, that change shall have effect for periods beginning on or after the operative date in relation to interest running from before that date as well as from or from after that date.

History – In reg. 6 the words "these Regulations" substituted for the words "regulation 3(1) or 4(1)" by SI 2009/2032, reg. 14, with effect from 12 August 2009.

In reg. 6, reference to reg. 5(1) omitted by SI 1991/889, reg. 4, operative from 6 April 1991.

WATER REORGANISATION (CAPITAL ALLOWANCES) ORDER 1989

(SI 1989/2017)

Made on 1 November 1989 by the Secretary of State for Wales, in relation to the successor company nominated by him, and the Secretary of State for the Environment, in relation to the other successor companies, in exercise of the powers conferred on them by s. 95(1) and (2) of the Water Act 1989 and with the consent of the Treasury.

CITATION, COMMENCEMENT AND INTERPRETATION

1(1) This Order may be cited as the Water Reorganisation (Capital Allowances) Order 1989 and shall come into force on 15th November 1989.

1(2) In this Order **"the Act"** means the Water Act 1989.

WRITING-DOWN ALLOWANCES – INDUSTRIAL BUILDINGS AND STRUCTURES

2(1) The amount specified in column (2) of Part I or Part II of Schedule 1 to this Order in relation to a successor company (being a company wholly owned by the Crown) shall be taken, for the purposes of sub-section (3) of section 2 of the Capital Allowances Act 1968 (writing-down allowances) [CAA 2001, s. 311 and Sch. 3, para. 67)], to be the residue on the transfer date of expenditure in relation to which the property vested in that company in accordance with a scheme under Schedule 2 to the Act and described in column (1) of the said Part I or Part II is a relevant interest for the purposes of the said section 2.

2(2) The period specified in column (3) of Part I or Part II of Schedule 1 in relation to a successor company shall be treated, for the purposes of the said section 2, and in relation to the property vested and described as mentioned in paragraph (1), as the part of the period of 25 or, as the case may be, 50 years which is unexpired on the transfer date.

WRITING-DOWN ALLOWANCES – MACHINERY AND PLANT

3 For the purposes of section 95(2) of the Act, each successor company (being a company wholly owned by the Crown) shall be treated as having incurred on the transfer date capital expenditure of the amount specified in relation to that company in column (2) of Schedule 2 to this Order in respect of the deemed acquisition for the purposes for which they are used by that company on and after that date of the motor cars, plant and machinery vested in it in accordance with a scheme under Schedule 2 to the Act and described in column (1) of Schedule 2 to this Order.

SCHEDULE 1 – WRITING-DOWN ALLOWANCES – INDUSTRIAL BUILDINGS AND STRUCTURES

Article 2

[Not reproduced: Sch. 1 specifies the residue of expenditure and unexpired life of industrial buildings and structures vesting in the successor companies at 1 September 1989.]

SCHEDULE 2 – WRITING-DOWN ALLOWANCES – MACHINERY AND PLANT

Article 3

[Not reproduced: Sch. 2 specifies the amount of capital expenditure which the successor companies are deemed to have incurred on 1 September 1989 in respect of machinery and plant vesting in them.]

ATOMIC ENERGY (MUTUAL ASSISTANCE CONVENTION) ORDER 1990

(SI 1990/235)

Made on 14 February 1990; coming into force in accordance with art. 1.

Whereas Her Majesty in pursuance of the Regency Acts 1937 to 1953 was pleased, by Letters Patent dated the 18th Day of January 1990, to delegate to the six Counsellors of State therein or any two or more of them full power and authority during the period of Her Majesty's absence from the United Kingdom to summon and hold on Her Majesty's behalf her Privy Council and to signify thereat Her Majesty's approval for anything for which Her Majesty's approval in Council is required;

Now, therefore, Her Majesty Queen Elizabeth The Queen Mother and His Royal Highness The Prince Charles, Prince of Wales, being authorised thereto by the said Letters Patent, and in pursuance of the powers conferred by section 5(4) of the Atomic Energy Act 1989, and by and with the advice of Her Majesty's Privy Council, do on Her Majesty's behalf order, and it is hereby ordered, as follows:

1 This Order may be cited as the Atomic Energy (Mutual Assistance Convention) Order 1990 and shall come into force on the date on which the Convention on Assistance in the case of a Nuclear Accident or Radiological Emergency opened for signature at Vienna on 26th September 1986 (hereinafter referred to as the Convention) enters into force in respect of the United Kingdom (which date will be notified in the London, Edinburgh and Belfast Gazettes).

2 It is hereby certified that her Majesty's Government in the United Kingdom has, under paragraph 9 of Article 8 of the Convention, made the declaration which is set out in the Schedule to this Order.

SCHEDULE – DECLARATION

Article 2

In pursuance of paragraph 9 of Article 8 of the Convention on Assistance in the Case of a Nuclear Accident or Radiological Emergency, the United Kingdom hereby declares that it considers itself bound by paragraphs 2 and 3 of the said Article 8 to the following extent:

(1) in cases where assistance is provided by the International Atomic Energy Agency, to the extent to which the privileges and immunities provided for in those paragraphs are accorded in the Agreement on the Privileges and Immunities of the International Atomic Energy Agency, approved by the Board of Governors on 1st July 1959;

(2) in cases where assistance is provided by any other international intergovernmental organisation, to the extent to which the United Kingdom has agreed to accord the privileges and immunities provided for in those paragraphs;

(3) in cases where assistance is provided by a State Party to the Convention, to the following extent:

(i)   in relation to the State Party providing assistance to the extent that that State Party is itself bound by those paragraphs in relation to the United Kingdom;

(ii)   the United Kingdom shall only be bound to apply paragraph 2(b) in cases where the State party is providing assistance without cost to the United Kingdom; and

(iii)   the exemption from taxation provided for in paragraph 2(b) shall only extend to an exemption from income tax on the salaries and emoluments of personnel which are paid from the State Party providing assistance and the United Kingdom reserves the right to take those salaries and emoluments into account for the purpose of assessing the amount of taxation to be applied to income from other sources.

Cross references – ITEPA 2003, s. 1(1): imposition of income tax on employment income.

EUROPEAN COMMUNITIES (PRIVILEGES OF THE EUROPEAN SCHOOL) ORDER 1990

(SI 1990/237)

Made on 14 February 1990. Operative from 15 February 1990.

Notes – A Department of Education and Science press release, 14 March 1990 (not reproduced) stated that appropriate tax exemptions for periods before the coming into force of the order (15 February 1990) would, with the approval of Treasury ministers, be given by extra-statutory concession.

Whereas Her Majesty in pursuance of the Regency Acts 1937 to 1953 was pleased, by Letters Patent dated the 18th day of January 1990, to delegate to the six Counsellors of State therein named or any two or more of them full power and authority during the period of Her Majesty's absence from the United Kingdom to summon and hold on Her Majesty's behalf Her Privy Council and to signify thereat Her Majesty's approval for anything for which Her Majesty's approval in Council is required;

And whereas a draft of this Order has been laid before Parliament and has been approved by a resolution of each House of Parliament;

Now, therefore, Her Majesty Queen Elizabeth The Queen Mother and His Royal Highness The Prince Charles, Prince of Wales, being authorised thereto by the said Letters Patent, and in pursuance of the powers conferred by section 2(2) of the European Communities Act 1972, and by and with the advice of Her Majesty's Privy Council, do on Her Majesty's behalf order, and it is hereby ordered, as follows:

PART I – GENERAL

1 This Order may be cited as the European Communities (Privileges of the European School) Order 1990 and shall come into force on the day after the day on which it is made.

2(1) For the purposes of this Order, **"the School"** means the European School established at Culham; **"staff members"** means the headmaster, deputy heads, secondary school teachers, primary school teachers, kindergarten teachers and educational advisers appointed, assigned or seconded to the School in accordance with Article 12(2) and (3) of the Statute of the European School.

2(2) In this Order **"the 1961 Convention Articles"** means the Articles (being certain Articles of the Vienna Convention on Diplomatic Relations signed in 1961) which are set out in Schedule 1 to the Diplomatic Privileges Act 1964.

PART II – THE SCHOOL

3 The School shall have the legal capacities of a body corporate.

4 Within the scope of its official activities, the School shall have exemption from taxes on income and capital gains.

5 The School shall have relief, under arrangements made by the Secretary of State, by way of refund of value added tax paid on the supply of goods or services of substantial value which are necessary for the official activities of the School, such relief to be subject to compliance with such conditions as may be imposed in accordance with the arrangements; provided that no refund shall be made in respect of any claim for goods or services where the value of the goods or services does not amount in the aggregate to £100.

6 The School shall have exemption from duties (whether of customs or excise) and taxes on the importation of goods imported by or on behalf of the School and necessary for the exercise of its official activities, such exemption to be subject to compliance with such conditions as the Commissioners of Customs and Excise may prescribe for the protection of the Revenue.

PART III – STAFF MEMBERS

7 Staff members shall enjoy:

(a) provided that they are seconded to the School by a member State other than the United Kingdom and are subject to its social security legislation, exemptions whereby for the purposes of the enactments relating to social security including enactments in force in Northern Ireland–

      (i)   services rendered for the School by them shall be deemed to be excepted from any class of employment in respect of which contributions or premiums under those enactments are payable, but

      (ii)   no person shall be rendered liable to pay any contribution or premium which he would not be required to pay if those services were not deemed to be so excepted;

(b)   unless they are British citizens, British Dependent Territories citizens or British Overseas citizens or are permanently resident in the United Kingdom, the like exemption from duties and taxes on the importation of furniture and personal effects (including one motor car each) which–

      (i)   at the time when they first enter the United Kingdom to take up their post, are imported for personal use or for that of their families forming part of their households, and

      (ii)   were in their ownership or possession or which they were under contract to purchase immediately before they so entered the United Kingdom,

as in accordance with paragraph 1 of Article 36 of the 1961 Convention Articles is accorded to a diplomatic agent; and

(c)   (i)   in the case of staff members who are seconded to the School by a member State other than the United Kingdom, exemption from income tax in respect of salaries and emoluments paid to them by the School as well as those paid to them by the member State which seconded them;

      (ii)   in the case of staff members who are seconded to the School by the United Kingdom, exemption from income tax in respect of salaries and emoluments paid to them by the School.

Cross references – ITEPA 2003, s. 1(1): imposition of income tax on employment income.

MOVEMENTS OF CAPITAL (REQUIRED INFORMATION) REGULATIONS 1990

(SI 1990/1671)

Made on 10 August 1990 by the Commissioners of Inland Revenue, in exercise of the powers conferred on them by s. 765A(2) of the Income and Corporation Taxes Act 1988.

Statements of practice – SP 2/92; guidance on whether Treasury consent should be sought for a transaction, in accordance with ICTA 1988, s. 765A, and procedure for provision of information.

Other material – IR press release, 9 February 1994: reporting requirements apply from 1 January 1994 to movements of capital between persons resident in member states of the European Economic Area (EC member states, Iceland, Norway and Liechtenstein).

CITATION AND COMMENCEMENT

1   These Regulations may be cited as the Movements of Capital (Required Information) Regulations 1990 and shall come into force on 3rd September 1990.

INTERPRETATION

2   In these Regulations unless the context otherwise requires–

"**the Board**" means the Commissioners of Inland Revenue;

"**control**" has, in relation to a body corporate, the meaning given by section 840 of the Income and Corporation Taxes Act 1988;

"**the Directive**" means the Directive of the Council of the European Communities dated 24th June 1988 No. 88/361/EEC;

"**the non-resident body corporate**" means the body corporate which is not resident in the United Kingdom and created or issued shares or debentures, or the shares or debentures of which were transferred to any person, in the course of a relevant transaction;

"**the principal section**" means section 765A of the Income and Corporation Taxes Act 1988;

"**relevant transaction**" means a movement of capital which would be unlawful under section 765(1) of the Income and Corporation Taxes Act 1988 if Article 1 of the Directive did not apply to it;

"**the resident body corporate**" means the body corporate resident in the United Kingdom which has carried out a relevant transaction;

and any question whether a person is **connected** with another shall be determined in accordance with the like provisions as are contained in section 839(2) to (8) of the Income and Corporation Taxes Act 1988.

INFORMATION REQUIRED FOR THE PURPOSES OF THE PRINCIPAL SECTION

3(1)   This regulation specifies the information relating to a relevant transaction and the persons connected with it (in this regulation referred to as "**the required information**") which, subject to paragraph (5) below, is required to be given to the Board by the resident body corporate within six months of the carrying out of a relevant transaction.

3(2)   The required information so far as it relates to the resident body corporate is–

(a)   its name;

(b)   the nature of its trade or business;

(c)   the tax office to which its accounts are submitted and its reference number there.

3(3)   The required information so far as it relates to the non-resident body corporate is–

(a)   its name;

(b)   the territory from the laws of which it derives its status as a body corporate;

(c)   where the relevant transaction was causing or permitting the non-resident body corporate to issue shares, or to create and issue debentures, the member State in which the non-resident body corporate is claimed to have been resident for the purposes of the Directive at the time of that issue, or of that creation and issue, as the case may be, the grounds on which that claim is made and the facts which support it;

(d)   the nature of its trade or business;

(e)   the extent to which the resident body corporate has control over it and the means by which, or the powers by virtue of which, that control is exercisable–

   (i)   before the relevant transaction was carried out, and

   (ii)   after the relevant transaction was carried out.

3(4)   The required information so far as it relates to the relevant transaction is a full description of the transaction and of all steps taken in the course of the transaction and, without prejudice to the generality of that requirement, includes in particular–

(a)   the date on which the transaction was carried out;

(b)   the name of any person to whom shares or debentures were issued or transferred;

(c)   where that person is a body corporate, the territory from the laws of which it derives that status;

(d)   the member State in which that person is claimed to have been resident for the purposes of the Directive at the time of the issue or transfer, the grounds on which that claim is made and the facts which support it;

(e)   whether, and if so in what way, any such person is connected with the resident body corporate;

(f)   where the relevant transaction was causing or permitting the non-resident body corporate to issue shares–

   (i)   the class or category of those shares,

   (ii)   the dividend rights attaching to them, and

   (iii)   if the terms on which they were issued included provision for their redemption, the circumstances in which they can be redeemed;

(g)   where the relevant transaction was causing or permitting the non-resident body corporate to create and issue debentures–

   (i)   the rate at which interest is payable on the amount secured by them,

   (ii)   any amount by which the issue price was less than the amount payable on their redemption, and

   (iii)   whether any amount payable in respect of the debentures is determined by reference to the movement of an index of prices, earnings or any other indicator of an economic nature published in the United Kingdom or elsewhere;

(h)   where the relevant transaction was transferring shares or debentures, or causing or permitting shares or debentures to be transferred–

   (i)   the name of any body corporate making the transfer if that body corporate was not the resident body corporate,

   (ii)   the territory from the laws of which that body corporate derives that status,

   (iii)   the member State in which it is claimed to have been resident for the purposes of the Directive at the time of the transfer, the grounds on which that claim is made and the facts which support it;

(i)   the consideration given for any issue or transfer of shares or debentures and, if that issue or transfer was not for full consideration in money or money's worth, the reason why full consideration was not given;

(j)   the reason for the transaction and an estimate of the effect of that transaction on the liability to tax in the United Kingdom of the resident body corporate and of any company which would be deemed to be a member of the group of companies which includes the resident body corporate for the purposes of Chapter IV of Part X of the Income and Corporation Taxes Act 1988, if in section 413(3) of that Act the words "51 per cent subsidiary" were substituted for the words "75 per cent subsidiary".

3(5)   Where a resident body corporate has caused or permitted shares or debentures to be created, issued or transferred, or has transferred shares or debentures, and another resident body corporate has already given the required information relating to the creation, issue or transfer in question and the persons connected with it, the first mentioned resident body corporate is not required to give any information relating to those matters or those persons.

NOTICE TO GIVE FURTHER PARTICULARS – PRESCRIBED PERIOD

4   The period prescribed by this regulation within which the resident body corporate shall give to the Board such further particulars as the Board may require in accordance with subsection (2)(b) of the principal section is 60 days from the date of the notice given by the Board under that subsection.

TAX-EXEMPT SPECIAL SAVINGS ACCOUNT REGULATIONS 1990

(SI 1990/2361, as amended by SI 1995/1929, SI 1995/3239, SI 1996/844, SI 2001/3629 and SI 2003/2096)

Made on 28 November 1990 by the Commissioners of Inland Revenue, in exercise of the powers conferred on them by s. 326C(1) of the Income and Corporation Taxes Act 1988 [Repealed].

ARRANGEMENT OF REGULATIONS

CITATION AND COMMENCEMENT

1 These Regulations may be cited as the Tax-exempt Special Savings Account Regulations 1990 and shall come into force on 19th December 1990.

INTERPRETATION

2(1) In these Regulations unless the context otherwise requires—

"account" means a deposit account or share account which is a tax-exempt special savings account for the purposes of section 326A of the Taxes Act;

"account-holder" means the holder of an account;

"the Board" means the Commissioners of Inland Revenue;

"EEA Agreement" means the Agreement on the European Economic Area signed at Oporto on 2nd May 1992 as adjusted by the Protocol signed at Brussels on 17th March 1993;

"EEA State" means a State, other than the United Kingdom, which is a Contracting Party to the EEA Agreement;

"follow-up account" has the same meaning as in section 326BB(1) of the Taxes Act;

"notice" means notice in writing and

"notify" shall be construed accordingly;

"the principal sections" means sections 326A, 326B and 326BB of the Taxes Act;

"relevant European institution" has the meaning given by section 326A(10) of the Taxes Act; a **"society, person or institution"** means a building society or a person falling within section 840A(1)(b) of the Taxes Act or a relevant European institution;

"**the Taxes Act**" means the Income and Corporation Taxes Act 1988;

"**year**" means a year beginning with 6th April in any year and ending with 5th April in the following year.

2(2) For the purposes of these Regulations an account held by an individual matures when a period of five years throughout which the account was a tax-exempt special savings account comes to an end.

History – The definition for "society, person or institution" substituted by SI 2001/3629, art. 130, with effect from 1 December 2001 (the former definition being "society or institution", which meant "a building society or an institution authorised under the Banking Act 1987 or a relevant European institution").
Definitions of "EEA Agreement", "EEA State" and "relevant European institution" inserted, and definition of "society or institution" amended by adding the words "or a relevant European institution", by SI 1995/3239, reg. 8, operative from 2 January 1996.
Former reg. 2 re-numbered reg. 2(1), definition of "follow-up account" inserted, reference in definition of "the principal sections" to s. 326BB added, and reg. 2(2) added, by SI 1995/1929, reg. 3, operative from 11 August 1995.

INTRODUCTORY

3 These Regulations–

(a) prescribe a condition additional to those set out in section 326A of the Taxes Act which must be satisfied if an account is to be or remain a tax-exempt special savings account;

(b) make provision for the giving by the Board to societies, persons and institutions of notices prohibiting them from operating new accounts, including provision about appeals against the giving of notices;

(c) require societies, persons and institutions operating or proposing to operate accounts to give information and send documents to the Board and to make documents available for inspection;

(cc) provide that subsection (2) of section 326BB of the Taxes Act does not apply in relation to a follow-up account unless at the time prescribed by these Regulations the society, person or institution with which the account is held has a document of a prescribed description containing such information as is prescribed by these Regulations;

(cd) require societies, persons and institutions operating accounts which mature to give to the individuals who have held them certificates containing such information as is prescribed by these Regulations;

(d) make provision as to the transfer of accounts from one society, person or institution to another;

(e) generally supplement the provisions of the principal sections.

History – The words ", person" and ", persons" at reg. 3(b), (c), (cc), (cd) and (d) inserted by SI 2001/3629, art. 133, with effect from 1 December 2001.
Reg. 3(cc), (cd) inserted by SI 1995/1929, reg. 4, operative from 11 August 1995.

ADDITIONAL CONDITION AS TO TRANSFERABILITY

4 An account must be transferable from one society, person or institution to another society, person or institution which–

(a) has notified the Board of its intention to operate accounts,

(b) has not ceased, or ceased to be entitled, to operate accounts, and

(c) has not been prohibited from operating new accounts by the giving of a prohibition notice which is in force,

but not otherwise, on such terms as may be agreed between the account-holder and any society, person or institution concerned.

History – The word ", person" inserted (three times) by SI 2001/3629, art. 133(2), with effect from 1 December 2001.

NOTIFICATION BY SOCIETY, PERSON OR INSTITUTION OF INTENTION TO OPERATE ACCOUNTS

5(1) A society, person or institution shall before it begins to operate accounts notify the Board of its intention to do so and as part of that notification shall provide the Board with the information specified in paragraph (2) or, in the case of a relevant European institution, the information specified in paragraph (2A) and a certificate in the terms specified in paragraph (3).

5(2) The information specified in this paragraph is–

(a) the name under which it is incorporated or registered and, if it is not incorporated or registered in the United Kingdom, the State or territory in which it is incorporated or registered;

(b) its principal address in the United Kingdom including postcode;

(c) the tax office to which its accounts are submitted and its reference number there; and

(d)   the date from which it intends to operate accounts.

5(2A)   The information specified in this paragraph is–

(a)   the name under which it is incorporated or registered and the EEA State in which it is incorporated or registered;

(b)   where it has a branch or business establishment in the United Kingdom and intends to operate all accounts opened with it through that branch or establishment–

      (i)   the address of that branch or business establishment including postcode, and

      (ii)   the tax office to which its accounts are submitted and its reference number there;

(c)   where it has a branch or business establishment in the United Kingdom and does not so intend which of the three requirements in regulation 3 of the Tax-exempt Special Savings Account (Relevant European Institutions) Regulations 1995 it proposes to fulfil;

(d)   where it does not have a branch or business establishment in the United Kingdom–

      (i)   whether it proposes to establish such a branch or business establishment through which it will operate all accounts opened with it, and

      (ii)   if not, which of the three requirements mentioned in regulation 3 of the Tax-exempt Special Savings Account (Relevant European Institutions) Regulations 1995 it proposes to fulfil;

(e)   the date from which it proposes to operate accounts.

5(3)   The certificate specified in this paragraph is a certificate that the society, person or institution is a building society or falls within section 840A(1)(b) of the Taxes Act or is a relevant European institution as the case may be.

History – The word ", person" inserted in the heading of reg. 5 and at reg. 5(1) and (3) by SI 2001/3629, art. 133(2), with effect from 1 December 2001.

Reg. 5 amended by SI 1995/3239, operative from 2 January 1996, by inserting in reg. 5(1) the words "or, in the case … in paragraph (2A)", reg. 5(2A), and in reg. 5(3) the words "or is a relevant European institution".

Reg. 5(3) amended by SI 2001/3629, art. 131 substituting the words "falls within section 840A(1)(b) of the Taxes Act" for the former "is authorised under the Banking Act 1987", with effect from 1 December 2001.

CONDITIONS FOR APPLICATION FOR AN ACCOUNT TO BE OPENED

6(1)   An application by an individual for an account to be opened must be made to a society, person or institution in writing and shall contain the information as to the individual specified in paragraph (2), the declaration by the individual specified in paragraph (3) and the statement specified in paragraph (4).

6(2)   The information specified in this paragraph is–

(a)   his full name,

(b)   his permanent address including postcode,

(c)   his date of birth, and

(d)   if he has one, his national insurance number.

6(3)   The declaration by the individual specified in this paragraph is that–

(a)   he is aged 18 or more,

(b)   he does not hold any other account (with the same or any other society, person or institution) which will not have matured or have been closed at the time when the account in respect of which the application is made is opened,

(c)   he has not made and will not make any other application for an account to be opened (with the some or any other society, person or institution) which he will hold simultaneously with the account in respect of which the application is made,

(d)   he will not hold the account on behalf of another person, and

(e)   to the best of his knowledge all information provided in the application is true.

6(4)   The statement specified in this paragraph is that false statements made in connection with the application may result in penalties or prosecution.

6(5)   A society, person or institution may not accept an application from an individual if it has reason to believe that he–

(a)   is not, or might not be entitled to, open an account, or

(b)   has given untrue information in his application.

History – The word ", person" inserted in reg. 6(1),(3)(b),(3)(c) and (5) by SI 2001/3629, art. 133(2), with effect from 1 December 2001.

Reg. 6(3)(b), (c) substituted by SI 1995/1929, reg. 5, operative from 11 August 1995.

TRANSFER OF ACCOUNTS

7(1)   Subject to paragraph (2), where–

(a)   arrangements are made by an account-holder to transfer an account from one society, person or institution (**"the transferor"**) to another society, person or institution (**"the transferee"**), or

(b)   an account is transferred in consequence of the transferor ceasing, or ceasing to be entitled, to operate accounts,

the transfer shall have effect and the account shall not be otherwise affected for the purposes of the principal sections and these Regulations by reason of the transfer.

7(2)   The transferor shall within 30 days after the date of transfer give the transferee a notice containing the information specified in paragraph (3) and the declaration specified in paragraph (4) and shall supply the transferee with the original written application made by the account-holder for the account to be opened or a certified copy of that application.

7(3)   The information specified in this paragraph is–

(a)   as regards the account-holder–

    (i)   his full name,

    (ii)   his permanent address including postcode,

    (iii) his date of birth, and

    (iv)   if he he has one, his national insurance number, and

(b)   as regards the account–

    (i)   the number allocated to that account by the transferor,

    (ii)   the date of transfer,

    (iii) the date on which the account was opened (whether with the transferor or with any other society, person or institution which previously operated the account),

    (iv)   the total of all amounts deposited in, or subscribed for shares in connection with, the account since it was opened,

    (v)   the total of all amounts of interest, dividend and bonus paid or credited to the account since it was opened,

    (vi)   the total of all amounts deposited in, or subscribed for shares in connection with, the account in the period beginning with the last anniversary of the opening of the account before the date of transfer and ending with the date of transfer,

    (vii) the amount of interest, dividend and bonus paid or credited to the account which was not available for withdrawal at the date of transfer, and

    (viii) the amount which was available for withdrawal at that date.

7(4)   The declaration specified in this paragraph is a declaration by the transferor that–

(a)   the total of all amounts withdrawn from the account in the period beginning with the date on which it was opened and ending with the date of transfer, together with any fee payable to the transferor in connection with the transfer which is to be paid out of the account, does not exceed the total of all amounts of interest, dividend and bonus paid or credited to the account in that period after deducting income tax from each such amount at the applicable rate;

(b)   the account-holder has not assigned any rights to the account nor used such rights as security for a loan;

(c)   the information contained in the notice is to the best of its knowledge correct and that it has fulfilled all its obligations to the account-holder.

7(4A)   In paragraph (4)(a) **"the applicable rate"** means–

(a)   in the case of an amount of interest, dividend or bonus paid or credited before 6th April 1996, the basic rate for the year of assessment in which the amount was paid or credited; and

(b)   in any other case, the lower rate for the year of assessment in which it was paid or credited.

7(5)   Where the account being transferred is a follow-up account, the transferor shall, in addition to satisfying the preceding requirements of this regulation, within 30 days after the date of transfer give the transferee–

(a)   any document held by him of the description prescribed by regulation 7B(2), or

(b)   a certified copy of any document of that description previously held by him, or

(c)   a print-out or other copy of any record constituting a document of that description.

History – The word ", person" inserted in reg. 7(1),(3)(b)(iii) by SI 2001/3629, art. 133(2), with effect from 1 December 2001.

In reg 7(4)(a), words "applicable rate" substituted, and reg. 7(4A) inserted, by SI 1996/844, operative from 6 April 1996. Reg. 7(5) added by SI 1995/1929, reg. 6, operative from 11 August 1995.

MATURED ACCOUNTS

7A(1) Subject to paragraph (2), a society, person or institution with which a matured account in respect of which the condition in section 326BB(1)(b) of the Taxes Act is satisfied is or has been held shall, if the account-holder so requires by notice to the society, person or institution, within 30 days after the date of the notice give to the account-holder a certificate containing the information prescribed by paragraph (3) and the declaration prescribed by paragraph (4).

7A(2) A society, person or institution shall not give the certificate referred to in paragraph (1)—

(a)   before the account has matured, or

(b)   after the expiry of a period of 18 months commencing with the date on which the account matured.

7A(3) The information prescribed by this paragraph is—

(a)   as regards the account-holder—

     (i)   his full name,

     (ii)   his permanent address including postcode,

     (iii)   if he has one, his national insurance number, and

(b)   as regards the account—

     (i)   the name of the society, person or institution with which it was held when it matured;

     (ii)   the number allocated to it by that society, person or institution;

     (iii)   the date on which it matured; and

     (iv)   the total amount deposited in, or subscribed for shares in connection with, the account since it was opened.

7A(4) The declaration prescribed by this paragraph is a declaration by the society, person or institution that the account was a tax-exempt special savings account throughout a period of five years and that the information given in the certificate is correct.

History – The word ", person" inserted in reg. 7A(1), (2), (3)(b)(i) and (ii) and (4) by SI 2001/3629, art. 133(2), with effect from 1 December 2001.

Reg. 7A inserted by SI 1995/1929, reg. 7, operative from 11 August 1995.

FOLLOW-UP ACCOUNTS

7B(1) Subsection (2) of section 326BB of the Taxes Act shall not apply to a follow-up account unless, at the time when the total amount deposited in, or subscribed for shares in, the account first exceeds £3,000, the society, person or institution holds a document of the description prescribed by paragraph (2) containing the information prescribed by that paragraph.

7B(2) The description prescribed by this paragraph is that the document is either—

(a)   a certificate given in accordance with regulation 7A(1) and (2) by the society, person or institution with which the account-holder held a matured account, or

(b)   where the account-holder holds a follow-up account with the same society, person or institution with which he held a matured account, a record kept by means of a computer or otherwise which was derived from the records of the society, person or institution and shows—

     (i)   as regards the account-holder, the information prescribed by sub-paragraph (a) of regulation 7A(3), and

     (ii)   as regards the matured account, the information prescribed by paragraphs (ii) to (iv) inclusive of sub-paragraph (b) of paragraph (3) of that regulation.

History – The word ", person" inserted in reg. 7B(1), (2)(a) and (b) by SI 2001/3629, art. 133(2), with effect from 1 December 2001.

Reg. 7B inserted by SI 1995/1929, reg. 7, operative from 11 August 1995.

PROHIBITION NOTICES

8(1) The Board may in the circumstances specified in paragraph (2) give a notice (in this regulation and in regulation 9 referred to as a **"prohibition notice"**) to a society, person or institution prohibiting the society, person or institution to which it is given from operating new accounts.

8(2) The circumstances specified in this paragraph are where the Board have reason to believe that the society, person or institution has failed to comply with any provision of the principal sections or of these Regulations.

8(3) A prohibition notice shall state–

(a) the date from which the society, person or institution is prohibited from operating new accounts; and

(b) the circumstances in which the notice is given.

8(4) A prohibition notice shall remain in force until it is cancelled by a further notice given by the Board to the society, person or institution withdrawing the prohibition from operating new accounts or it is quashed by the Special Commissioners on appeal.

History – The word ", person" inserted in reg. 8(1), (2), (3)(a) and (4) by SI 2001/3629, art. 133(2), with effect from 1 December 2001.

APPEALS AGAINST PROHIBITION NOTICES

9(1) A society, person or institution to whom a prohibition notice has been given under regulation 8 may appeal against the notice by notice given to the Board within 30 days after the date of the notice of prohibition.

9(2) The appeal shall be to the Special Commissioners.

9(3) The like provisions as are contained in Part V of the Taxes Management Act 1970 shall apply to an appeal under this regulation and the Special Commissioners shall on appeal to them confirm the prohibition notice unless they are satisfied that it ought to be quashed.

History – The word ", person" inserted in reg. 9(1) by SI 2001/3629, art. 133(2), with effect from 1 December 2001.

SOCIETY, PERSON OR INSTITUTION CEASING TO ACT

10 A society, person or institution shall give notice to the Board and to the account-holder of its intention to cease to operate an account within a reasonable time before it so ceases so that its obligations in relation to the account (including the transfer of the account to another society, person or institution) can be conveniently discharged at or about the time it ceases to act.

History – The word ", person" inserted in the heading to reg. 10 and twice in the text by SI 2001/3629, art. 133(2), with effect from 1 December 2001.

SOCIETY, PERSON OR INSTITUTION CEASING TO BE ENTITLED TO OPERATE ACCOUNTS

11 A society, person or institution shall cease to be entitled to operate accounts and shall notify the Board forthwith of that fact where–

(a) it ceases to be a building society or to fall within section 840A(1)(b) of the Taxes Act or to be a relevant European institution, as the case may be; or

(b) its directors have made a proposal under Part I of the Insolvency Act 1986 for a composition in satisfaction of its debts or a scheme of arrangement of its affairs; or

(c) it enters administration; or

(d) a receiver or manager of its property has been appointed; or

(e) a resolution has been passed or a petition has been presented to wind it up; or

(f) action has been taken in relation to it under the law of an EEA State corresponding to that described in paragraph (b), (c), (d) or (e).

History – The word ", person" inserted in the heading to reg. 11 and in the text by SI 2001/3629, art. 133(2), with effect from 1 December 2001.
Reg. 11(a) amended by SI 2001/3629, art. 132 substituting the words "fall within section 840A(1)(b) of the Taxes Act" for the former "be authorised under the Banking Act 1987", with effect from 1 December 2001.
In reg. 11(c) the words "it enters administration" substituted for "an administration order is made in relation to it" by SI 2003/2096, art. 5 and Sch., para. 46 with effect from 15 September 2003. Transitional provisions are contained in art. 6.
Reg. 11 amended by SI 1995/3239, reg. 10, operative from 2 January 1996, by adding reference to a relevant European institution in para. (a), and adding para. (f) (word "; or" at end of para. (e) inserted by SI 1996/844).

Transitional – SI 2003/2096, art. 6 contains transitional provisions so that the former rules remain in effect where a petition for an administration order was presented prior to 15 September 2003.

RETURN OF AGGREGATE INFORMATION BY SOCIETY, PERSON OR INSTITUTION

12(1) A society, person or institution shall within 30 days after each of the aggregate reporting dates specified in paragraph (2), and after ceasing to or ceasing to be entitled to operate accounts, deliver to the Board a return signed on behalf of the society, person or institution making it which contains the aggregate information specified in paragraph (3), stated separately in relation to accounts in respect of which a document of the description prescribed by regulation 7B(2), or a certified copy of such a document or a print-out or other copy of the record constituting such a document received in connection with the transfer of the account from another society, person or institution, is held and other accounts.

12(2) The aggregate reporting dates specified in this paragraph are 31st March, 30th June, 30th September and 31st December in each year that the society, person or institution operates accounts.

12(3) The aggregate information specified in this paragraph is information relating to the period beginning with 1st January 1991, or the date on which the society, person or institution first began to operate accounts, and ending with the relevant aggregate reporting date or date of cessation, as to–

(a)   the total number of accounts opened by the society, person or institution in that period (including accounts transferred to other societies, persons or institutions but excluding those transferred from other societies, persons or institutions);

(b)   the total number of accounts closed in that period, whether at the end of the period of five years beginning with the day on which they were opened or on the earlier death of the account-holder;

(c)   the total number of accounts which ceased to be tax-exempt special savings accounts in that period for any of the reasons mentioned in section 326B(1) of the Taxes Act;

(d)   the total number of accounts transferred to other societies , persons or institutions in that period;

(e)   the total amount which in that period was deposited in, or subscribed for shares in connection with, accounts which were being operated by the society, person or institution at the relevant aggregate reporting date or date of cessation;

(f)   the total amount of interest, dividends and bonus which in that period was credited to accounts which were being operated by the society, person or institution at the relevant aggregate reporting date or date of cessation;

(g)   the total amount held in accounts at the relevant aggregate reporting date or date of cessation; and

(h)   the total amount of income tax deducted from interest. dividends and bonus paid or credited to accounts which ceased to be tax-exempt special savings accounts for any of the reasons mentioned in section 326B(1) of the Taxes Act.

History – The word ", persons" inserted at reg. 12(3)(a) and (d) and the word ", person" inserted in the heading to reg. 12 and in 12(1), (2) and (3) by SI 2001/3629, art. 133, with effect from 1 December 2001.
In reg. 12(1), the words ", stated separately" to the end inserted by SI 1995/1929, reg. 8, operative from 11 August 1995.

RETURN OF INDIVIDUAL INFORMATION BY SOCIETY, PERSON OR INSTITUTION

13(1) A society, person or institution shall within three months after each of the individual reporting dates specified in paragraph (2), and after ceasing to or ceasing to be entitled to operate accounts, deliver to the Board a return signed on behalf of the society, person or institution making it (or, where the return is made on magnetic tape, accompanied by a certificate signed on behalf of the, society, person or institution as to the contents of the tape) which contains the individual information specified in paragraph (3).

13(2) The individual reporting dates specified in this paragraph are 31st March 1992 and 31st March in each year thereafter.

13(3) The individual information specified in this paragraph is information relating to each account operated in the period beginning with the date on which the society, person or institution began to operate accounts, or with the day following the previous individual reporting date, whichever is the later, and ending with the relevant individual reporting date or date of cessation, as to–

(a)   as regards the account-holder–

      (i)   his full name,

      (ii)   his permanent address including postcode,

      (iii)   his date of birth, and

      (iv)   if he has one, his national insurance number, and

(b)   as regards the account–

      (i)   the number allocated to that account by the society, person or institution,

      (ii)   the date on which the account was opened (whether with the society, person or institution making the return or with any other society, person or institution which previously operated the account), (iia)   whether the account is one in respect of which a document of the description prescribed by regulation 7B(2), or a certified copy of such a document or a print-out or other copy of the record constituting such a document received in connection with the transfer of the account from another society, person or institution, is held;

(iii)   all amounts deposited in, or subscribed for shares in connection with, the account in the period beginning with the date on which the account was opened and ending with the relevant individual reporting date or date of cessation,

(iv)   the balance at the relevant individual reporting date or date of cessation,

(v)   in the case of an account which has closed or has ceased to be a tax-exempt special savings account, the date on which that happened, and

(vi)   in either of the cases referred to in paragraph (v), whether the account was closed at the end of the period of five years beginning with the day on which the account was opened, or on the earlier death of the account holder, or ceased to be a tax-exempt special savings account for any of the reasons mentioned in section 326B(1) of the Taxes Act, or was transferred to another society, person or institution.

History – The word ", person" inserted in the heading to reg. 13 and in reg. 13(1) and (3) by SI 2001/3629, art. 133(2), with effect from 1 December 2001.
Reg. 13(3)(b)(iia) inserted by SI 1995/1929, reg. 9, operative from 11 August 1995.

RECORDS TO BE KEPT BY SOCIETY, PERSON OR INSTITUTION

14(1)   A society, person or institution shall at all times keep sufficient records in respect of each account that it operates to enable the requirements of the principal sections and of these Regulations to be satisfied.

14(2)   In particular, but without prejudice to the generality of paragraph (1), the society, person or institution shall preserve so as to be available for inspection under regulation 16 for a period of two years after the account was closed or ceased to be a tax-exempt special savings account–

(a)   every application made under regulation 6;

(b)   every document of the description prescribed by regulation 7B(2);

(c)   every certified copy of such a document received in connection with the transfer of the account from another society, person or institution;

(d)   a record of amounts deposited in or subscribed in connection with or withdrawn from the account.

History – The word ", person" inserted in the heading to reg. 14 and in reg. 14(1) and (2) by SI 2001/3629, art. 133(2), with effect from 1 December 2001.
Reg. 14 substituted by SI 1995/1929, reg. 10, operative from 11 August 1995.

INFORMATION TO BE PROVIDED TO THE BOARD

15   The Board may by notice require any society, person or institution which operates or which at any time has operated accounts, or any individual who is or has at any time been an account-holder, within such time (not being less than 14 days) as may be provided by the notice, to furnish them with such information (including copies of or extracts from any relevant books or other records) relating to–

(a)   any account; or

(b)   any account (not being a tax-exempt special savings account) with which they have reason to believe an account is or may be connected within the meaning of section 326A(8) of the Taxes Act;

as they may reasonably require for the purposes of the principal sections or of these Regulations.

History – The word ", person" inserted in the reg. 15 by SI 2001/3629, art. 133(2), with effect from 1 December 2001.

INSPECTION OF RECORDS BY OFFICER OF THE BOARD

16   The Board may by notice require any society, person or institution which operates or which at any time has operated accounts, or any individual who is or has at any time been an account-holder, within such time (not being less than 14 days) as may be provided in the notice, to make available for inspection at a place within the United Kingdom by an officer of the Board authorised for that purpose such documents (including relevant books and other records) as are in that person's possession or under that person's control containing information relating to–

(a)   any account; or

(b)   any account (not being a tax-exempt special savings account) with which they have reason to believe an account is or may be connected within the meaning of section 326A(8) of the Taxes Act:

as they may reasonably require for the purposes of the principal sections or of these Regulations.

History – The word ", person" inserted in the reg. 16 by SI 2001/3629, art. 133(2), with effect from 1 December 2001.
In reg. 16, words "at a place within the United Kingdom" inserted by SI 1996/3239, reg. 11, operative from 2 January 1996.

EUROPEAN BANK FOR RECONSTRUCTION AND DEVELOPMENT (IMMUNITIES AND PRIVILEGES) ORDER 1991

(SI 1991/757, as amended by SI 1999/2034 and OTA 2002)

Made on 20 March 1991; coming into force on a date to be notified.

Whereas a draft of this Order has been laid before Parliament in accordance with section 10 of the International Organisations Act 1968 (hereinafter referred to as the Act) and has been approved by a resolution of each House of Parliament;

Now, therefore, Her Majesty, by virtue and in exercise of the powers conferred on Her by section 1 of the Act or otherwise in Her Majesty vested, is pleased, by and with the advice of Her Privy Council, to order, and it is hereby ordered, as follows:

PART I – GENERAL

CITATION, ENTRY INTO FORCE AND REVOCATION

1(1) This Order may be cited as the European Bank for Reconstruction and Development (Immunities and Privileges) Order 1991 and shall come into force on the date on which the Headquarters Agreement between the Government of the United Kingdom of Great Britain and Northern Ireland and the European Bank for Reconstruction and Development enters into force. That date will be notified in the London, Edinburgh and Belfast Gazettes.

1(2) The European Bank for Reconstruction and Development (Immunities and Privileges) Order 1990 is revoked.

INTERPRETATION

2 In this Order:

(a)   **"the 1961 Convention Articles"** means the Articles (being certain Articles of the Vienna Convention on Diplomatic Relations signed in 1961) which are set out in Schedule 1 to the Diplomatic Privileges Act 1964;

(b)   **"Agreement Establishing the Bank"** means the Agreement Establishing the European Bank for Reconstruction and Development signed in Paris on 29th May 1990, and any amendments thereto;

(c)   **"Bank"** means the European Bank for Reconstruction and Development;

(d)   the terms **"Member"**, **"President"**, **"Vice-President"**, **"Governor"**, **"Alternate Governor"**, **"Temporary Alternate Governor"**, **"Board of Governors"**, **"Director"**, **"Alternate Director"** and **"Temporary Alternate Director"**, **"Board of Directors"**, have the same meaning as in the Agreement Establishing the Bank, its By-laws or Rules of Procedure;

(e)   **"Premises of the Bank"** means the land, buildings and parts of buildings, including access facilities, used for the Official Activities of the Bank;

(f)   **"Representatives of Members"** means heads of delegations of Members participating in meetings convened by the Bank other than meetings of the Board of Governors or the Board of Directors;

(g)   **"Members of Delegations"** means alternates, advisers, technical experts and secretaries of delegations of Representatives of Members;

(h)   **"Officers"** means the President, the Vice-President and other persons appointed by the President to be Officers of the Bank;

(i)   **"Employees of the Bank"** means the staff of the Bank excluding those staff both recruited locally and assigned to hourly rates of pay;

(j)   **"Archives of the Bank"** includes all records, correspondence, documents, manuscripts, still and moving pictures and films, sound recordings, computer programmes and written materials, video tapes or discs, and discs or tapes containing data belonging to, or held by, the Bank;

(k)   **"Official Activities of the Bank"** includes all activities undertaken pursuant to the Agreement Establishing the Bank, and all activities appropriate to fulfil its purpose and functions under

Articles 1 and 2 of that Agreement, or undertaken in exercise of its powers under Article 20 of that Agreement including its administrative activities; and

(l) **"Persons Connected with the Bank"** means Governors, Alternate Governors, Temporary Alternate Governors, Representatives of Members, Members of Delegations, Directors, Alternate Directors, Temporary Alternate Directors, the President, the Vice-Presidents, Officers and Employees of the Bank, and experts performing missions for the Bank.

PART II – THE BANK

3 The Bank is an organisation of which the United Kingdom and other sovereign Powers are members.

4 The Bank shall have the legal capacities of a body corporate.

5(1) Except to the extent that the Board of Directors of the Bank shall have waived immunity, the Bank shall have immunity from suit and legal process –

(a) where the Bank has no office in the United Kingdom, nor has appointed an agent in the United Kingdom for the purpose of accepting service or notice of process, nor has issued or guaranteed securities in the United Kingdom; or

(b) where actions are brought by any member of the Bank or by any person acting for or deriving claims from any member of the Bank; or

(c) in respect of any form of seizure of, or restraint, attachment or execution on, the property or assets of the Bank, wheresoever located or by whomsoever held, before the delivery of final judgment against the Bank; or

(d) in respect of the search, requisition, confiscation or expropriation of, or any other form of interference with, or taking of or foreclosure on, the property or assets of the Bank, wheresoever located and by whomsoever held.

5(2) Without prejudice to paragraph (1), the Bank shall, within the scope of its Official Activities, have immunity from suit and legal process, except that the immunity of the Bank shall not apply–

(a) to the extent that the Bank shall have expressly waived any such immunity in any particular case or in any written document;

(b) in respect of a civil action arising out of the exercise of its powers to borrow money, to guarantee obligations and to buy or sell or underwrite the sale of any securities;

(c) in respect of a civil action by a third party for damage arising from a road traffic accident caused by an Officer or an Employee of the Bank acting on behalf of the Bank;

(d) in respect of a civil action relating to death or personal injury caused by an act or omission in the United Kingdom;

(e) in respect of the enforcement of an arbitration award made against the Bank as a result of an express submission to arbitration by or on behalf of the Bank; or

(f) in respect of any counter-claim directly connected with court proceedings initiated by the Bank.

6(1) The Premises of the Bank and the Archives of the Bank shall have the like inviolability as, in accordance with the 1961 Convention Articles, is accorded in respect of the official archives and premises of a diplomatic mission, except that the Premises of the Bank may be entered with the consent of and under conditions approved by the President; such consent may be assumed in the case of fire or other disasters requiring prompt action.

6(2) The Premises of the Bank may be entered in connection with fire prevention, sanitary regulations or emergencies without the prior consent of the Bank in such circumstances and in such a manner as may have been determined by any agreement for that purpose entered into between the Government and the Bank.

7 Within the scope of its Official Activities the Bank, its property, assets, income and profits shall have exemption from income tax, capital gains tax and corporation tax.

8 The Bank shall have the like relief from rates on the Premises of the Bank as in accordance with Article 23 of the 1961 Convention Articles is accorded in respect of the premises of a diplomatic mission.

9 The Bank shall have exemption from duties (whether of customs or excise) and taxes on the importation by it or on its behalf of goods necessary for the exercise of the Official Activities of the Bank and on the importation of any publications of the Bank imported by it or on its behalf, such

Statutory Instruments

exemption to be subject to compliance with such conditions as the Commissioners of Customs and Excise may prescribe for the protection of the Revenue.

10   The Bank shall have exemption from prohibitions and restrictions on importation or exportation in the case of goods imported or exported by the Bank and necessary for the exercise of its Official Activities and in the case of any publications of the Bank imported or exported by it.

11   The Bank shall have relief, under arrangements made by the Commissioners of Customs and Excise, by way of refund of duty (whether of customs or excise) paid on imported hydrocarbon oil (within the meaning of the Hydrocarbon Oil Duties Act 1979) or value added tax paid on the importation of such oil which is bought in the United Kingdom and is necessary for the exercise of its Official Activities, such relief to be subject to compliance with such conditions as may be imposed in accordance with the arrangements.

12   The Bank shall have relief, under arrangements made by Secretary of State, by way of refund of car tax and value added tax paid on any official vehicle and value added tax paid on the supply of any goods or services which are supplied for the Official Activities of the Bank, such relief to be subject to compliance with such conditions as may be imposed in accordance with the arrangements.

12A   The Bank shall have relief, under arrangements made by Secretary of State, by way of refund of Insurance Premium Tax and Air Passenger Duty paid by the Bank in the exercise of its official activities.

History – Art. 12A inserted by SI 1999/2034, art. 2 and Schedule, with effect from 1 August 1999.

PART III – PERSONS CONNECTED WITH THE BANK

13(1)   A Person Connected with the Bank shall enjoy–

(a)   such immunity from suit and legal process, even after the termination of his mission or service, in respect of acts performed by him in his official capacity including words written or spoken by him, except in respect of civil liability in the case of damage arising from a road traffic accident caused by him;

(b)   such immunity from suit and legal process as is necessary to ensure that all their official papers and documents have the like inviolability as, in accordance with the 1961 Convention Articles, is accorded in respect of official archives of a diplomatic mission.

13(2)   In addition to the immunities set out in paragraph (1), Directors, Alternate Directors, Officers and Employees, and experts performing missions for the Bank under contract longer than 18 months shall, at the time of first taking up their post in the United Kingdom, be exempt from duties (whether of customs or excise) and taxes on the importation of articles (except payments for services) in respect of import of their furniture and personal effects (including one motor car each), and the furniture and personal effects of members of their family forming part of their household, which are in their ownership or possession or already ordered by them and intended for their personal use or for their establishment.

13(3)   In addition to the privileges and immunities set out in paragraph (1), Governors, Alternate Governors, and Representatives of Members shall enjoy–

(i)   the like exemption from duties (whether of customs or excise) and taxes on the importation of their personal baggage, and the like privilege as to the importation of such articles, as in accordance with paragraph 1 of Article 36 of the 1961 Convention Articles is accorded to a diplomatic agent;

(ii)   the like exemption and privileges in respect of their personal baggage as in accordance with paragraph 2 of Article 36 of the 1961 Convention Articles are accorded to a diplomatic agent;

(iii)   such immunity from suit and legal process as is necessary to ensure that their personal baggage cannot be seized;

(iv)   immunity from arrest or detention.

13(4)   In addition to the immunities set out in paragraph (1), the President and five vice-presidents, as nominated by the President, shall enjoy–

(a)   the like immunity from suit and legal process, the like inviolability of residence and the like exemption or relief from taxes (other than income tax in respect of their emoluments and duties and taxes on the importation of goods) as are accorded to or in respect of a diplomatic agent;

(b)   the like exemption or relief from being subject to a community charge, or being liable to pay anything in respect of a community charge or anything by way of contribution in respect of a collective community charge, as is accorded to or in respect of a diplomatic agent;

(c)   the like exemption from duties and taxes on the importation of articles imported for their personal use, including articles intended for their establishment, as in accordance with paragraph 1 of Article 36 of the 1961 Convention Articles is accorded to a diplomatic agent;

(d)   the like exemption and privileges in respect of their personal baggage as in accordance with paragraph 2 of Article 36 of the 1961 Convention Articles are accorded to a diplomatic agent;

(e)   relief, under arrangements made by the Commissioners of Customs and Excise, by way of refund of duty (whether of customs or excise) or value added tax paid on any hydrocarbon oil (within the meaning of the Hydrocarbon Oil Duties Act 1979) which is bought in the United Kingdom by them or on their behalf and which is for their personal use or for that of members of their family forming part of their household, such relief to be subject to compliance with such conditions as may be imposed in accordance with the arrangements.

13(5)   Paragraphs (2), (3) and (4) of this Article shall not apply to any person who is a British citizen, British overseas territories citizen, a British Overseas citizen, or a British National (Overseas), or who is a permanent resident of the United Kingdom.

13(6)   Part IV of Schedule 1 to the Act shall not operate so as to confer any privilege or immunity on the official staff of representatives other than Members of Delegations, nor so as to confer any privilege or immunity on the family of any person to whom this Article applies.

13(7)   Neither the provisions of the preceding paragraphs of this Article, nor those of Part IV of Schedule 1 to the Act, shall operate so as to confer any privilege or immunity on any persons as the representative of the United Kingdom or as a member of the delegation of such a representative.

13(8)   Any privilege or immunity conferred by the preceding paragraphs of this Article may be waived as follows:–

(i)   in the case of any privilege or immunity conferred on any officer or employee of the Bank (other than the President or a Vice-President), or on an expert performing a mission for the Bank, by the President;

(ii)   in the case of any privilege or immunity conferred on the President or a Vice President, by the Board of Directors;

(iii)   in the case of any privilege or immunity conferred on a Representative of a Member or a member of his delegation, by the Member concerned.

History – In art. 13(5) the words "British overseas territories citizen" substituted by OTA 2002, s. 2(3), with effect from 26 February 2002.

14(1)   As from the date on which an internal effective tax for the benefit of the Bank on the salaries and emoluments paid to him by the Bank is applied, any Director, Alternate, Officer and Employee of the Bank shall enjoy exemption from income tax in respect of such salaries and emoluments, provided that nothing in this paragraph shall be interpreted as precluding such salaries and emoluments from being taken into account for the purpose of assessing the amount of taxation to be applied to income from other sources.

14(2)   Paragraph (1) of this Article shall not apply to pensions or annuities paid by the Bank.

15   As from the date on which the Bank establishes or joins a social security scheme, the Directors, Alternate Directors, Officers and Employees of the Bank shall enjoy exemptions whereby for the purposes of the enactments relating to social security, including enactments in force in Northern Ireland –

(i)   services rendered for the Bank by them shall be deemed to be excepted from any class of employment in respect of which contributions or premiums under those enactments are payable, but

(ii)   no person shall be rendered liable to pay any contribution or premium which he would not be required to pay if those services were not deemed to be so excepted.

TAXES (RELIEF FOR GIFTS) (DESIGNATED EDUCATIONAL ESTABLISHMENTS) REGULATIONS 1992

(SI 1992/42, as amended by SI 1993/561 and SI 2010/1172)

Made on 10 January 1992 in exercise of the powers conferred by s. 84 of the Income and Corporation Taxes Act 1988 [and ITTOIA 2005, s. 110] by the Secretary of State for Education and Science, as respects England, the Secretary of State for Scotland, as respects Scotland, and the Secretary of State for Wales, as respects Wales.

1 These Regulations may be cited as the Taxes (Relief for Gifts) (Designated Educational Establishments) Regulations 1992 and shall come into force on 4th February 1992.

2(1) In these Regulations–

"**charity**" has the same meaning as in section 506 of the Income and Corporation Taxes Act 1988, and a charity is an educational charity if the charitable purposes for which it is established are exclusively educational purposes;

"**the 1980 Act**" means the Education (Scotland) Act 1980; and

"**the 1989 Act**" means the Self-Governing Schools etc (Scotland) Act 1989.

2(2) Expressions used in these Regulations in relation to **educational establishments in England and Wales** have the same meaning as in the Education Acts 1944 to 1992.

2(3) Expressions used in these Regulations in relation to **educational establishments in Scotland** have the same meaning as in the 1980 Act or the 1989 Act.

3 The educational establishments and categories of educational establishments specified in the Schedule to these Regulations are hereby designated for the purposes of section 84 of the Income and Corporation Taxes Act 1988.

History – In reg. 2(2), reference to the Education Acts 1944 to 1992 substituted by SI 1993/561, reg. 2(a), operative from 1 April 1993.

SCHEDULE

Regulation 3

PART I – SCHOOLS: ENGLAND AND WALES

1 Any school maintained by a local authority.

2 Any grant-maintained school.

3 Any special school not maintained by a local authority.

4 Any independent school registered pursuant to section 70 of the Education Act 1944 which is conducted by an educational charity.

5 Any school maintained by the Service Children's Education Authority.

6 The European School established under Article 1 of the Statute of the European School, any school designated as a European School under Article 1 of the Protocol to that Statute and the European School established under article 1 of the Supplementary Protocol to that Statute.

7 Any nursery school recognised by the Secretary of State for the purpose of receiving grant under regulation 5 of the Direct Grant Schools Regulations 1959.

History – In para. 1, the words "local authority" substituted for the words "local education authority" by SI 2010/1172, art. 4 and Sch. 3, para. 26(2), with effect from 5 May 2010.
In para. 3, the words "local authority" substituted for the words "local education authority" by SI 2010/1172, art. 4 and Sch. 3, para. 26(2), with effect from 5 May 2010.

PART II – SCHOOLS: SCOTLAND

1 Any public school.

2 Any self-governing school.

3 Any grant-aided school.

4 Any independent school managed by an educational charity.

PART III – ESTABLISHMENTS OF FURTHER AND HIGHER EDUCATION: ENGLAND AND WALES

1   Any university.

2   Any institution within the higher education sector (within the meaning of section 91(5) of the Further and Higher Education Act 1992) other than a university.

3   [Omitted by SI 1993/561.]

4   Any institution of further or higher education (or both) maintained or assisted by a local authority or in receipt of grant under regulations made under section 100(1)(b) of the Education Act 1944.

5   Any institution within the further education sector (within the meaning of section 91(3) of the Further and Higher Education Act 1992).

6-22   [Omitted by SI 1993/561.]

23   Any other establishment providing further or higher education (or both) which is conducted by an educational charity.

History – Para. 2 substituted, para. 3 omitted, para. 4 and 5 substituted, and para. 6–22 omitted, by SI 1993/561, reg. 2, operative from 1 April 1993.
In para. 4, the words "local authority" substituted for the words "local education authority" by SI 2010/1172, art. 4 and Sch. 3, para. 26(3), with effect from 5 May 2010.

PART IV – ESTABLISHMENTS OF FURTHER AND HIGHER EDUCATION: SCOTLAND

1   Any university.

2   Any central institution, college of education or any institution established under section 77 of the 1980 Act.

3   Any establishment for the provision of further education under the management of

(a)   an education authority, or

(b)   a company by virtue of section 65 of the 1989 Act.

4   Any other establishment for the provision of further or higher education (or both) managed by an educational charity.

PORTS ACT 1991 (LEVY ON DISPOSALS OF LAND, ETC.) ORDER 1992

(SI 1992/58)

Notes – This statutory instrument made on 15 January 1992 modifies tax legislation in connection with levy charged on certain asset disposals of successor companies involved in the reorganisation of port authorities. The modifications are contained in Sch. 2 of the Order, which is reproduced below together with the interpretation paragraph.

INTERPRETATION

2(1) In this Order, unless the context otherwise requires–

"**the 1970 Act**" means the Income and Corporation Taxes Act 1970;

"**the 1988 Act**" means the Income and Corporation Taxes Act 1988;

"**the 1991 Act**" means the Ports Act 1991;

"**annual reporting date**", in relation to a disposal period, means–

(a) the day falling 180 days after the last day of that period; or

(b) if the last disposal period ends with a date other than the last day of a financial year, then, in relation to that disposal period, the day falling 180 days after the last day of the financial year in which that disposal period ends;

or, if that day is not a business day, the next succeeding business day;

"**base rate**" shall be construed in accordance with paragraph (3) of article 15;

"**business day**" means any day other than a non-business day within the meaning of section 92 of the Bills of Exchange Act 1882;

"**chargeable disposal**" has the meaning given to it by article 6;

"**company**" means any body corporate or unincorporated association but does not include a partnership, a local authority or a local authority association;

"**disposal date**", in relation to a disposal, means, subject to the provisions of this Order, the date on which the disposal is made for the purposes of the 1979 Act;

"**disposal period**", in relation to a chargeable company, means a financial year, provided that–

(a) the first disposal period shall begin with the first day of the levy period and end with the final day of the financial year in which that day falls; and

(b) the last disposal period shall end with the last day of the levy period, whether or not that day is the end of a financial year;

"**disposal statement**" means a statement required to be furnished under article 36;

"**disregarded disposal**" means a disposal on which, by virtue of paragraph (6) of article 8, no gain is regarded as having accrued;

"**financial year**", in relation to a chargeable company, means the financial year of that company within the meaning given by section 223 of the Companies Act 1985;

"**group**", in relation to a chargeable company, means (except in the expression "**wholly-owned group**") the group formed by–

(a) that chargeable company;

(b) any company or other person of which that chargeable company is an effective subsidiary;

(c) any company which is an effective subsidiary of that chargeable company; and

(d) any company which is an effective subsidiary of any company or other person of which the chargeable company is an effective subsidiary;

and for this purpose a company ("A") is an effective subsidiary of another company or other person ("B") if–

(i) A would be an effective 51 per cent subsidiary of B for the purposes referred to in subsection (1) of section 272 of the 1970 Act by virtue of subsections (1E) and (1F) of that section if paragraph (a) of subsection (1) of that section and the words in parenthesis in subsection (2) of that section were omitted and the word "and" between paragraphs (a) and (b) of subsection (1E) were replaced by the word "or"; or

(ii) B, or B together with any person connected with B, has control of A (and for this purpose any question whether a person is connected with another shall be determined in accordance with the provisions of section 839 of the 1988 Act, but as if the exception in subsection (4) were omitted; and **"control"** has the meaning given by section 840 of that Act);

"lease" has the same meaning as it has for the purposes of paragraph 10(1)(a) of Schedule 3 to the 1979 Act (and accordingly includes, amongst other things, a sub-lease);

"market value", subject to article 18, has the meaning given by section 150 of the 1979 Act;

"quarter date" shall be construed in accordance with paragraphs (2) to (5) of article 13;

"referee" means a person appointed under article 38;

"retail prices index" means the general index of retail prices (for all items) published by the Central Statistical Office of the Chancellor of the Exchequer, and, if that index is not published for any month, any substituted index or index figures published by that Office for that month;

"section 278 disposal" means a disposal which is treated as taking place by virtue of section 278(3) or (3C) of the 1970 Act or section 17(6) of the 1991 Act;

"small disposal" means a disposal on which, by virtue of article 8(2), no gain is regarded as having accrued;

"wholly-owned group", in relation to a chargeable company, means the group formed by–

(a) the chargeable company; and

(b) every company which would be a member of the same group as the chargeable company for the purposes of section 272 of the 1970 Act [TCGA 1992, s. 170] if–

     (i) subsections (1B) to (1D) of that section were omitted (and subsections (1)(b), (1A) and (1F) were construed accordingly); and

     (ii) the references to *75 per cent*, *51 per cent* and *more than 50 per cent* in that section and in subsection (1)(b) of section 838 and Schedule 18 to the 1988 Act were each references to 100 per cent.

2(2) In this Order a reference to the **1979 Act** or to any provision of that Act or to any other statutory provision relating to corporation tax on chargeable gains is, except in so far as it applies in determining whether there is a disposal of land or an interest in land for the purposes of section 17 of the 1991 Act, a reference to that Act or that provision as it applies immediately before the coming into force of this Order; and references to the purposes of the 1979 Act or of the statutory provisions relating to corporation tax on chargeable gains include references to the purposes of the 1979 Act as it applies by virtue of subsection (6) of section 17 of the 1991 Act.

SCHEDULE 2 – MODIFICATION OF TAX PROVISIONS APPLYING TO LEVY

Article 9

1 Sections 267 and 268A of the 1970 Act [TCGA 1992, s. 139, 140] shall not apply for the purposes of section 17 of the 1991 Act and this Order.

2 Subsection (4) of section 21 of the 1979 Act [TCGA 1992, s. 23(4)] shall apply for the purposes of section 17 of the 1991 Act and this Order as if the reference in it to the inspector were a reference to the appropriate Minister; and subsection (7) of that section shall not apply for those purposes.

3 Section 31(1) of the 1979 Act [TCGA 1992, s. 37(1)] shall not apply for the purposes of section 17 of the 1991 Act and this Order.

4(1) Subject to sub-paragraph (2) below, paragraph (a) of section 32(1) of the 1979 Act [TCGA 1992, s. 38(1)(a)] shall, in relation to the computation of any gain accruing on the disposal of relevant land or a relevant interest in land (other than land or an interest in land acquired within the levy period), apply for the purposes of section 17 of the 1991 Act and this Order as if that paragraph referred, and referred only, to the market value of the land or interest disposed of for its existing use at the beginning of the levy period, that value being determined in accordance with valuation principles and methods provided for in paragraphs (7) and (8) of article 36 (and in this paragraph **"existing use"** means the purpose for which the land or interest is used at that time).

4(2) This paragraph shall not apply in relation to any relevant land or relevant interest in land where there has, or there is to be regarded as having, been within the levy period a previous disposal of that land or interest from one member of the chargeable company's group to another member of that group.

5(1) In the application, for the purposes of section 17 of the 1991 Act and this Order, of section 32(1)(b) of the 1979 Act [TCGA 1992, s. 38(1)(b)] there shall, in relation to relevant land and a relevant interest in land, be excluded from the sums allowable thereunder any expenditure incurred before the beginning of the levy period.

5(2) Paragraphs (b) and (c) of section 32(1) of the 1979 Act [TCGA 1992, s. 38(1)(b), (c)] shall apply for the purposes of section 17 of the 1991 Act and this Order as if—

(a)   in paragraph (b) the words "or in the market value" appeared after the words "in the state or nature"; and

(b)   paragraph (c) included a reference to the costs of obtaining a valuation for the purposes of—

     (i)   article 36(5); or

     (ii)   paragraph 6 or 7 of Schedule 3 to this Order.

6   Subsections (1) and (2) of section 33 of the 1979 Act [TCGA 1992, s. 39(1), (2)] shall not apply for the purposes of section 17 of the 1991 Act and this Order to a sum applied in the manner specified in paragraph (a) or (b) of subsection (1) of section 21 of the 1979 Act or in subsection (3), (4) or (5) of that section.

7   Sections 40(2) and 41(2) of the 1979 Act [TCGA 1992, s. 48, 49(2)] shall apply for the purposes of section 17 of the 1991 Act and this Order as if the references in those provisions to the inspector were references to the appropriate Minister.

8(1)   In the application for the purposes of section 17 of the 1991 Act and this Order of subsection (4) of section 43 of the 1979 Act [TCGA 1992, 52(4)], the words from "and the method of apportionment" to the end of that subsection shall not apply; and, instead, the method of apportionment adopted for the purposes of any computation under Chapter II of Part II of the 1979 Act as applied for the purposes of section 17 of the 1991 Act and this Order shall, subject to the express provisions of that Chapter as so applied, be such method as appears to the appropriate Minister or, in the event of a dispute, to a referee to be just and reasonable.

8(2)   The said subsection (4) shall apply as if the words "necessary apportionments" referred to any apportionments which appear to the appropriate Minister or, in the event of a dispute (in which case article 38 shall apply for the purpose of resolving it), to a referee to be necessary for the purposes of this Order.

9   Section 108(4) of the 1979 Act [TCGA 1992, s. 243(4)] shall apply for the purposes of section 17 of the 1991 Act and this Order as if the words "not being an estate or interest which is a wasting asset" were omitted.

10   Sections 111A and 115 to 121 of the 1979 Act [TCGA 1992, s. 152–158, 247] shall not apply for the purposes of section 17 of the 1991 Act and this Order.

11   Section 113 of the 1979 Act [TCGA 1992, s. 250] shall not apply for the purposes of section 17 of the 1991 Act and this Order.

12(1)   Section 87(2) of the Finance Act 1982 [TCGA 1992, s. 54(2)] shall apply for the purposes of section 17 of the 1991 Act and this Order as if in the definition of "RI" there were substituted for the reference to the retail prices index for March 1982 a reference to the retail prices index for the month in which the chargeable company's levy period begins.

12(2)   For the avoidance of doubt section 68(4) of the Finance Act 1985 [TCGA 1992, s. 55(1)] shall not apply for the purposes of section 17 of the 1991 Act and this Order.

13   Sections 96 and 97 of, and Schedules 8 and 9 to, the Finance Act 1988 [TCGA 1992, s. 35, 36 and Sch. 3, 4] shall not apply for the purposes of section 17 of the 1991 Act and this Order.

INSURANCE COMPANIES (PENSION BUSINESS) (TRANSITIONAL PROVISIONS) REGULATIONS 1992

(SI 1992/2326, as amended by SI 1995/3134, SI 1993/3109, SI 1994/3036, SI 1995/3134, SI 1996/1 and SI 1997/2865)

Made on 29 September 1992 by the Commissioners of Inland Revenue, in exercise of the powers conferred on them by para. 4 and 5(4) of Sch. 19AB of the Income and Corporation Taxes Act 1988.

CITATION AND COMMENCEMENT

1 These Regulations may be cited as the Insurance Companies (Pension Business) (Transitional Provisions) Regulations 1992 and shall come into force on 2nd October 1992.

History – In reg. 1, the word "Pension" substituted by SI 1996/1, reg. 3, operative from 24 January 1996.

INTERPRETATION

2 In these Regulations unless the context otherwise requires–

"**accounting period**" means any accounting period in relation to which Schedule 19AB has effect;

"**the Board**" means the Commissioners of Inland Revenue;

"**the closing transitional date**" shall be construed in accordance with regulation 3(2);

"**the corresponding accounting period**", in relation to a provisional repayment period, is the accounting period in which that provisional repayment period falls;

"**insurance company**" means a company to which Part II of the Insurance Companies Act 1982 applies;

"**the Management Act**" means the Taxes Management Act 1970;

"**maximum reduced entitlement**" has the meaning given by paragraph 4(6) of Schedule 19AB;

"**notional repayment**" shall be construed in accordance with paragraph 1A of Schedule 19AB (treated as inserted by regulation 6 of the Insurance Companies (Gilt-edged Securities) (Periodic Accounting for Tax on Interest) Regulations 1995) [SI 1995/3224] and, in relation to a notional repayment,

"**provisional repayment period**" shall be construed in accordance with that paragraph of that Schedule; and

"**the opening transitional date**" shall be construed in accordance with regulation 3(1);

"**paragraph 4**" and "**paragraph 5**" mean, respectively, paragraph 4 and paragraph 5 of Schedule 19AB;

"**provisional repayment**" has the meaning given by paragraph 6(1) of Schedule 19AB, in relation to a provisional repayment, and "**provisional repayment period**" shall be construed in accordance with paragraph 1 of that Schedule;

"**Schedule 19AB**" means Schedule 19AB to the Taxes Act;

"**the Taxes Act**" means the Income and Corporation Taxes Act 1988.

History – In reg. 2, the definition of "notional repayment" and in the definition of "provisional repayment", the words ", in relation to a provisional repayment," inserted by SI 1996/1, reg. 4, operative from 24 January 1996.

SPECIFICATION OF "THE OPENING TRANSITIONAL DATE" AND "THE CLOSING TRANSITIONAL DATE"

3(1) The date specified by these Regulations as "**the opening transitional date**" for the purpose of paragraph 4 is 2nd October 1992.

3(2) The date specified by these Regulations as "**the closing transitional date**" for the purpose of paragraph 4 is 1st January 1999.

REDUCTION OF PROVISIONAL REPAYMENT BY PRESCRIBED PERCENTAGE

4(1) This regulation prescribes the percentage by which the amount of any provisional repayment or any notional repayment to which an insurance company would otherwise be entitled under Schedule 19AB for any of the accounting periods specified in paragraphs (2) to (5) (being accounting periods ending after the opening transitional date and before the closing transitional date) shall be reduced.

4(2) The prescribed percentage is 7.5 per cent for an accounting period ending after 2nd October 1992 and before 1st January 1994.

4(3) The prescribed percentage is 12.5 per cent for an accounting period ending after 31st December 1993 and before 1st January 1995.

4(4) The prescribed percentage is 10 per cent for an accounting period ending after 31st December 1994 and before 1st January 1996.

4(5) The prescribed percentage is 7.5 per cent for an accounting period ending after 31st December 1995 and before 1st January 1998.

History – In reg. 4(1), words from "of the accounting periods" to the end substituted by SI 1997/2865, reg. 3(a), operative from 31 December 1997.
In reg. 4(1), the words "or any notional repayment" inserted by SI 1996/1, reg. 5, operative from 24 January 1996.
Reg. 4(2) substituted and former para. (3) inserted by SI 1993/3109, reg. 3, operative from 31 December 1993.
Reg. 4(3) and former reg. 4(4) substituted for former reg. 4(3) by SI 1994/3036, operative from 21 December 1994.
Reg. 4(4) and former reg. (5) substituted for former reg. 4(4) by SI 1995/3134, operative from 31 December 1995.
Reg. 4(5) substituted by SI 1997/2865, reg. 3(b), operative from 31 December 1997.

REQUIREMENTS TO BE SPECIFIED IN CLAIM FOR PROVISIONAL REPAYMENT

5 An insurance company claiming a provisional repayment or a notional repayment for a provisional repayment period falling within any accounting period specified in regulation 4 shall specify in the claim–

(a)   the maximum amount to which it could have been entitled by way of provisional repayment for that provisional repayment or notional repayment period apart from these Regulations;

(b)   the maximum reduced entitlement for that provisional repayment period; and

(c)   the amount of the provisional repayment or the notional repayment claimed for that provisional repayment period.

History – Words in reg. 5 "specified in regulation (4)" substituted by SI 1997/2865, reg. 4, operative from 31 December 1997.
In reg. 5, the words "or a notional repayment" were inserted by SI 1996/1, reg. 6 operative from 24 January 1996.
In reg. 5(a), the words "or notional repayment" were inserted by SI 1996/1, operative from 24 January 1996.
In reg. 5(c), the words "or the notional repayment" were inserted by SI 1996/1, operative from 24 January 1996.

INTEREST WHERE A PROVISIONAL REPAYMENT EXCEEDS THE MAXIMUM REDUCED ENTITLEMENT FOR A PROVISIONAL REPAYMENT PERIOD

6(1) Where in relation to a provisional repayment period falling within an accounting period specified in regulation 4 an insurance company claims, and is paid, by way of provisional repayment an amount in excess of the maximum reduced entitlement for that period, interest shall be charged for the period specified in paragraph (2) at the rate specified in paragraph (3).

6(2) The period specified in this paragraph is a period beginning on the date on which the amount of the excess is paid to the company and ending on the first occurrence of any of the following–

(a)   the date on which that amount is repaid to the Board;

(b)   the date on which the company becomes entitled to that amount when effect is given to a claim such as is mentioned in section 7(6) of the Taxes Act, in section 42(5A) of the Management Act or in sub-paragraph (2) of paragraph 5, made in respect of the corresponding accounting period; and

(c)   the date on which the company becomes entitled to that amount when the assessment to corporation tax for the corresponding accounting period becomes final and conclusive.

6(3) The rate specified in this paragraph is the rate applicable under section 178 of the Finance Act 1989 for the purposes of section 87A of the Management Act.

6(4) Interest charged by virtue of paragraph (1) shall be treated for the purposes of section 30 of the Management Act as if it were an amount of corporation tax which had been repaid and which ought not to have been repaid.

6(5) In relation to an amount assessed to corporation tax under section 30 of the Management Act by virtue of these Regulations, section 87A of that Act shall apply with the modifications specified in paragraph (6).

6(6) The modifications specified in this paragraph are that–

(a)   the amount assessed to corporation tax under section 30 of the Management Act by virtue of these Regulations shall be taken to have become due and payable on the date on which that assessment was made; and

(b)   the words "(in accordance with section 10 of the principal Act)" in subsection (1) shall accordingly be disregarded.

History – In reg. 6(1), words from beginning to "for that period" substituted by SI 1997/2865, reg. 5, operative from 31 December 1997.

In reg. 6(2), the word "and" immediately preceding subpara. (c) substituted by SI 1993/3109, reg. 4, operative from 31 December 1993.

CLAIMS DURING TRANSITIONAL APPLICATION OF PAY AND FILE PROVISIONS

7 A claim under sub-paragraph (2) of paragraph 5 shall be made at the time of the delivery of the return under section 11 of the Management Act for the accounting period to which the claim relates.

INCOME TAX (INSURANCE COMPANIES) (EXPENSES OF MANAGEMENT) REGULATIONS 1992

(SI 1992/2744)

Made on 2 November 1992 by the Treasury, in exercise of the powers conferred on them by s. 76(7A) and (8) of the Income and Corporation Taxes Act 1988.

CITATION, COMMENCEMENT AND EFFECT

1 These Regulations may be cited as the Income Tax (Insurance Companies) (Expenses of Management) Regulations 1992 and shall come into force on 24th November 1992, but shall have effect with respect to sums paid before, as well as after, their coming into force.

INTERPRETATION

2 In these Regulations unless the context otherwise requires–

"**LAUTRO**" means the Life Assurance and Unit Trust Regulatory Organisation Limited;

"**the Lautro (Compensation Schemes) Rules 1991**" means the rules so entitled which were made by the Board of directors of LAUTRO on 26th November 1991;

"**the Lautro Indemnity Scheme**" means the scheme established by rules 8.2 and 8.3 in Part VIII of the Lautro Rules 1988 as amended by the Lautro (Compensation Schemes) Rules 1991;

"**the Lautro Rules 1988**" means the rules so entitled which were made by the Board of directors of LAUTRO on 26th April 1988.

SUMS TREATED AS EXPENSES OF MANAGEMENT

3 Any sums paid by a company to which section 76 of the Income and Corporation Taxes Act 1988 applies under a levy imposed under the Lautro Indemnity Scheme established under the rules of LAUTRO shall be treated for the purposes of that section as part of the company's expenses of management.

Statutory Instruments

INCOME TAX (MANUFACTURED OVERSEAS DIVIDENDS) REGULATIONS 1993

(SI 1993/2004 as amended by SI 1995/1324, SI 1996/1229, SI 1996/2643, SI 1997/987, SI 1997/988, SI 1997/2706, SI 2001/403, SI 2003/2582, SI 2003/3143, SI 2004/2310, SI 2007/2487, SI 2009/2811, SI 2010/925, SI 2011/1787, SI 2011/2503 and SI 2013/504)

Made on 9 August 1993 by the Treasury, in exercise of the powers conferred on them by para. 1(1), 4(6)–(8) and 8 of Sch. 23A to the Income and Corporation Taxes Act 1988. Operative from 1 October 1993.

CITATION AND COMMENCEMENT

1(1) These Regulations may be cited as the Income Tax (Manufactured Overseas Dividends) Regulations 1993 and shall come into force on 1st October 1993.

INTERPRETATION

2(1) In these Regulations unless the context otherwise requires–

"**approved United Kingdom collecting agent**" means a person who is a collecting agent and who is resident in the United Kingdom or, if not so resident, is carrying on a trade in the United Kingdom through a permanent establishment and who is approved by the Board for the purposes of these Regulations;

"**approved United Kingdom intermediary**" means an overseas dividend manufacturer who is resident in the United Kingdom or, if not so resident, is carrying on a trade in the United Kingdom through a permanent establishment and who is approved as an intermediary by the Board for the purposes of these Regulations;

"**the Board**" means the Commissioners of Inland Revenue;

"**chargeable period**" has the meaning given by regulation 2A;

"**collecting agent**" means a person who, in the course of carrying on a trade in the United Kingdom, collects or secures payment of overseas dividends for another person or acts as custodian of any overseas securities;

"**foreign permanent establishment payment**" means a payment made by a company in the course of a trade carried on through a permanent establishment in a territory outside the United Kingdom where section 18A of the Corporation Tax Act 2009 has effect in relation to the company for the accounting period in which the payment is made;

"**foreign permanent establishment receipt**" means a receipt by a company for the purposes of a trade carried on by the company through a permanent establishment in a territory outside the United Kingdom where section 18A of the Corporation Tax Act 2009 has effect in relation to the company for the accounting period in which the payment is received;

"**gross amount of the manufactured overseas dividend**" has the meaning given by paragraph 4(5)(b) of Schedule 23A;

"**gross amount of the overseas dividend**" has the meaning given by–

(a)   section 589(4) of the Income Tax Act 2007 for income tax purposes, and

(b)   section 813(3) of the Corporation Tax Act 2010 for corporation tax purposes;

"**the Income Tax Acts**" has the meaning given by section 831(1)(b) of the Taxes Act;

"**the Management Act**" means the Taxes Management Act 1970;

"**manufactured overseas dividend**" shall be construed in accordance with paragraph 4(1) of Schedule 23A;

"**overseas dividend**", "**overseas dividend manufacturer**", "**overseas securities**", "**overseas tax**" and "**overseas tax credit**" have the meanings given by paragraph 1(1) of Schedule 23A;

"**relevant withholding tax**" has the meaning given by paragraph 4(5)(a) of Schedule 23A;

"**Schedule 23A**" means Schedule 23A to the Taxes Act;

"**the Taxes Act**" means the Income and Corporation Taxes Act 1988;

"**the Tax Acts**" has the meaning given by section 831(2) of the Taxes Act;

"United Kingdom recipient" has the meaning given in section 918(5) and (5A) of the Income Tax Act 2007.

2(2)   References in regulations 3 to 11, 14 and 15 to manufactured overseas dividends do not include references to manufactured overseas dividends to which regulation 2B applies, and references in those regulations to overseas dividends do not include references to any overseas dividend of which a manufactured overseas dividend to which regulation 2B applies would be representative.

2(3)   In these Regulations references to a permanent establishment shall be read, in relation to accounting periods beginning before 1st January 2003, as references to a branch or agency.

History – In reg. 2(1), the definitions of "foreign permanent establishment payment" and "foreign permanent establishment receipt" inserted by SI 2011/1787, reg. 3(2), with effect in relation to manufactured overseas dividends paid or treated as paid on or after 11 August 2011.

In reg. 2(1), the definition of "United Kingdom recipient" substituted by SI 2011/1787, reg. 3(3), with effect in relation to manufactured overseas dividends paid or treated as paid on or after 11 August 2011. The former definition read as follows:

    "**"United Kingdom recipient"** shall be construed in accordance with paragraph 4(3A) of Schedule 23A.".

In reg. 2(1), definition of "gross amount of the overseas dividend" inserted by SI 2010/925, reg. 3, with effect in relation to manufactured overseas dividends made or treated as made on or after 14 April 2010.

In reg. 2(1) words "permanent establishment " substituted for "branch or agency " in two places, definition of "the Double Taxation Relief Regulations" omitted, and the definition of "United Kingdom recipient " substituted by SI 2003/2582, reg. 3(2), with effect from 1 November 2003.

In reg. 2(1), the definition of "collecting agent" substituted by SI 2001/403, reg. 2, operative from 9 March 2001 in relation to manufactured overseas dividends paid or received on or after 1 April 2001. The former wording was as follows:

    "has the meaning given by section 118C(1) of the Taxes Act for the purposes of Chapter VIIA of Part IV of that Act;"

In reg. 2(1), in the definition of "approved United Kingdom collecting agent", former words "for the purposes of Chapter VIIA of Part IV of the Taxes Act" omitted, and definition of "collecting agent" inserted, by SI 1996/2643, reg. 3(2), operative from 6 November 1996.

In reg. 2(1), definition of "chargeable period" substituted by SI 1995/1324, reg. 3, operative from 7 June 1995.

In reg. 2(1), former definitions of "unapproved manufactured overseas dividend" and "unapproved manufactured payment" omitted, in definition of "approved United Kingdom collecting agent" words "a collecting agent … and who is" and "is approved by" to the end substituted, and in definition of "approved United Kingdom intermediary" words "approved as an intermediary" to the end substituted, by SI 1996/1229, reg. 3, operative from 28 May 1996.

Reg. 2(2) inserted by SI 1996/2643, reg. 3(3), operative from 6 November 1996.

Reg. 2(3) inserted by SI 2003/2582, reg. 3(3), with effect from 1 November 2003.

Cross references – SI 1993/1957: Double Taxation Relief (Taxes on Income) (General) (Manufactured Overseas Dividends) Regulations 2003.

CHARGEABLE PERIOD

2A(1)   In these Regulations **"chargeable period"**–

(a)   as respects a company, means its accounting period for the purposes of corporation tax;

(b)   as respects a person other than a company who draws up accounts for any period ("the accounts period"), means one of the periods specified in paragraph (2) below;

(c)   as respects a person other than a company who does not draw up accounts, means a year of assessment.

2A(2)   The periods specified in this paragraph are–

(a)   the period which begins at the beginning of the accounts period and ends at the expiration of 12 months from that date or, if earlier, at the end of the accounts period;

(b)   any subsequent period which–

    (i)   begins at the end of the immediately preceding period, being a period specified in this paragraph, and

    (ii)   ends at the expiration of 12 months from that date or, if earlier, at the end of the accounts period.

2A(3)   [Omitted by SI 1997/988, reg. 3(b).]

History – Reg. 2A inserted by SI 1995/1324, reg. 4, with effect from 7 June 1995.

In reg. 2A(1)(b) words "draws up accounts for any period ("the accounts period"), means" substituted for "pays a manufactured overseas dividend in a period for which he draws up accounts ("the accounts period"), means the period in which the payment is made, being"by SI 1997/988, reg. 3(a)(i), with effect from 1 July 1997.

In reg. 2A(1)(c) words "does not draw up accounts, means a year of assessment" substituted for "pays a manufactured overseas dividend on a date falling within a time for which he does not draw up accounts ("the non-accounts period"), means the period in which the payment is made, being one of the periods specified in paragraph (3) below" by SI 1997/988, reg. 3(a)(ii), with effect from 1 July 1997.

Reg. 2A(3) omitted by SI 1997/988, reg. 3(b), with effect from 1 July 1997.

TAX TREATMENT OF MANUFACTURED OVERSEAS DIVIDENDS PAID IN CONNECTION WITH LOAN RELATIONSHIPS

2B(1)   For the purposes of the provisions of the Tax Acts relating to the charge to tax under Schedule D, paragraph 4(2) and (3), of Schedule 23A shall not apply to a manufactured overseas dividend paid in the circumstances prescribed in paragraph (2).

Statutory Instruments

2B(2) The circumstances prescribed are where the manufactured overseas dividend is representative of an overseas dividend on an overseas security that represents a loan relationship.

2B(3) Where the payer of a manufactured overseas dividend to which paragraph (2) applies is neither a company nor carrying on a trade in circumstances where the manufactured overseas dividend is taken into account in computing the profits of that trade, the manufactured overseas dividend shall be treated, for the purposes of the provisions of the Tax Acts relating to the charge to tax under Schedule D and so far as the payer is concerned, as if the amount paid was an annual payment, within section 349(1) of the Taxes Act, but so that no amount is required to be deducted on account of income tax from the amount of the payment, or accounted for under section 350 of that Act.

2B(4) Where the recipient of a manufactured overseas dividend to which paragraph (2) applies is neither a company nor carrying on a trade in circumstances where the manufactured overseas dividend is taken into account in computing the profits of that trade, the manufactured overseas dividend shall be treated, for the purposes of the provisions of the Tax Acts relating to the charge to tax under Schedule D and so far as the recipient is concerned, as an overseas dividend of an amount equal to the amount of the manufactured overseas dividend received by him, but not so as to entitle the recipient to claim relief under Part XVIII of the Taxes Act in respect of any tax attributable to the manufactured overseas dividend received.

2B(5) For the purposes of paragraph (2), an overseas security shall be taken to represent a loan relationship if a company holding that security would have a loan relationship within the meaning of section 81 of the Finance Act 1996.

2B(6) References in paragraph (4) to the recipient of a manufactured overseas dividend include references to any person claiming title to the manufactured overseas dividend through or under the recipient.

History – In reg. 2B(1), the words ", and paragraph 5" which followed the words "paragraph 4(2) and (3)" were omitted by SI 1997/987, reg. 8(2) with effect from 1 July 1997.
Reg. 2B inserted by SI 1996/2643, reg. 4, operative from 6 November 1996.

PRESCRIBED RATES OF RELEVANT WITHHOLDING TAX

3(1) Subject to paragraph (5) and (6), the rate of relevant withholding tax which is prescribed in relation to any manufactured overseas dividend is the rate which is equal to the rate (or, if more than one, the highest rate) at which tax would have been payable (and not repayable) under the law of the overseas territory specified in paragraph (3) in respect of–

(a) an overseas dividend paid on the same date that the manufactured overseas dividend is paid to a person who is–

    (i) resident in the United Kingdom and not carrying on a trade outside the United Kingdom through a permanent establishment,

    (ii) subject to tax under the law of the United Kingdom, and

    (iii) not subject to a special relationship with any other person as respects any commercial or financial dealings,

    in respect of the same kind of overseas securities as those in respect of which the manufactured overseas dividend was paid, and

(b) the overseas tax credit, if any, relating to that overseas dividend.

3(2) The reference in paragraph (1) above to tax which would have been payable is a reference to tax which would have been eligible for relief either–

(a) pursuant to arrangements made with the government of the overseas territory specified in paragraph (3) which have effect by virtue of section 788 of the Taxes Act and relate to the overseas dividend concerned, or

(b) by virtue of other provisions of Part XVIII of the Taxes Act other than section 790(5)(c)(ii) of that Act.

3(3) The overseas territory specified in this paragraph is the territory of the government or public or local authority which issued the securities in question or, where the securities were issued by any other body of persons not resident in the United Kingdom, the territory under whose law that tax would have been payable.

3(4) [Omitted by SI 2003/2582, reg. 4(3).]

3(5) Where the recipient of the manufactured overseas dividend is a company, the reference in paragraph (1) to the highest rate is a reference to the highest rate that would have applied in relation to the overseas dividend specified in paragraph (1)(a) paid to a company which is within paragraphs (i) to (iii) of that paragraph.

3(6)   Where the manufactured overseas dividend—

(a)   is paid to, or for the benefit of, a registered pension scheme (within the meaning given in Part 4 of the Finance Act 2004), or

(b)   is linked solely to pension business for the purposes of section 438 of the Taxes Act at the time that the payment is made,

the reference in paragraph (1) to the highest rate is a reference to the rate that would have been suffered by the recipient in relation to the overseas dividend of which that manufactured overseas dividend is representative.

History – In reg. 3(1) the words "paragraphs (5) and (6)" substituted for "paragraph (4)" by SI 2007/2487, reg. 3(2), with effect from 1 October 2007, in relation to manufactured overseas dividends made or treated as made on or after that day.
In reg. 3(1)(a)(i) words "permanent establishment" substituted for "branch or agency" by SI 2003/2582, reg. 4(2), with effect from 1 November 2003.
Reg. 3(4) omitted by SI 2003/2582, reg. 4(3), with effect from 1 November 2003. Reg. 3(4) previously read as follows:

> "**3(4)**   Where a manufactured overseas dividend is paid–
> (a)   to or for the benefit of–
>   (i)   an individual beneficially entitled to the payment who is resident in a territory outside the United Kingdom, or
>   (ii)   a company beneficially entitled to the payment whose central management and control is situated in a territory outside the United Kingdom and which is not resident in the United Kingdom, or
>   (iii)   any other body of persons resident in a territory outside the United Kingdom, and
> (b)   in respect of securities issued by the government, or a public or local authority, of that territory or any other body of persons resident in that territory, and
> (c)   in circumstances where arrangements, if any, made between the United Kingdom and the government of that territory which have effect under section 788 of the Taxes Act do not contain an article providing for exemption from United Kingdom tax in respect of the payment as constituting income not expressly mentioned in other articles of the arrangements, the rate prescribed in relation to that manufactured overseas dividend is the rate which is equal to the rate at which tax would have fallen to be deducted under the law of that territory in respect of–
>   (i)   an overseas dividend paid to that recipient in respect of those securities, and
>   (ii)   the overseas tax credit, if any, relating to that overseas dividend.".

Reg. 3(5) and (6) inserted by SI 2007/2487, reg. 3(3), with effect from 1 October 2007, in relation to manufactured overseas dividends made or treated as made on or after that day.

TAX TREATMENT OF APPROVED MANUFACTURED OVERSEAS DIVIDENDS PAID TO APPROVED UNITED KINGDOM INTERMEDIARIES OR APPROVED UNITED KINGDOM COLLECTING AGENTS

4(1)   For the purposes of the provisions of the Tax Acts relating to the charge to tax under Schedule D other than paragraph 4(3) of Schedule 23A, a manufactured overseas dividend paid in the circumstances prescribed in paragraph (2)–

(a)   shall not be treated as an annual payment pursuant to paragraph 4(2) of Schedule 23A;

(b)   shall be paid without deduction of an amount on account of income tax;

(c)   [revoked by SI 2004/2310, Schedule, para. 3(2);]

4(2)   The circumstances prescribed by this paragraph are where–

(a)   a manufactured overseas dividend is paid to an approved United Kingdom intermediary or an approved United Kingdom collecting agent by an overseas dividend manufacturer who–

     (i)   is resident in the United Kingdom or, if not so resident, makes the payment in the course of a trade which he carries on through a permanent establishment in the United Kingdom, and

     (ii)   is not an approved United Kingdom intermediary;

(b)   the manufactured overseas dividend is not representative of the overseas dividend received by the overseas dividend manufacturer, and

(c)   the receipt of the manufactured overseas dividend by the approved United Kingdom intermediary or approved United Kingdom collecting agent is not a foreign permanent establishment receipt.

4(3)   Subject to paragraph (4), the approved United Kingdom intermediary or approved United Kingdom collecting agent referred to in paragraph (2) shall account for and pay an amount of tax in respect of the manufactured overseas dividend which he receives equal to that which the maker of the payment would have been required to account for and pay had paragraph 4(2) of Schedule 23A applied to the payment.

4(4)   Paragraph (3) shall not apply where either paragraph (5) or (6) applies.

4(5) This paragraph applies where the approved United Kingdom intermediary or approved United Kingdom collecting agent pays, in accordance with regulation 5, and without deduction of tax, a manufactured overseas dividend representative of the same overseas dividend as is represented by the manufactured overseas dividend received by him.

4(6) This paragraph applies where the approved United Kingdom collecting agent is required to pay to an approved United Kingdom intermediary a manufactured overseas dividend representative of the same overseas dividend as is represented by the manufactured overseas dividend received by him and the approved United Kingdom intermediary–

(a)   pays as mentioned in paragraph (5) the manufactured overseas dividend, and

(b)   issues a notice to the approved United Kingdom collecting agent authorising him to make the payment without deduction of tax.

History – In reg. 4, words "a manufactured overseas dividend" and " the manufactured overseas dividend" substituted, wherever occurring, for former references to an approved manufactured overseas dividend or the approved manufactured overseas dividend, by SI 1996/1229, reg. 4, operative from 28 May 1996.

Reg. 4(1)(c) revoked by SI 2004/2310, Schedule, para. 73(2), with effect in relation to accounting periods beginning on or after 1 April 2004 subject to the transitional provisions at FA 2004, s. 43 and 44. Former reg. 4(1)(c) read as follows:

"(c)   where the maker of the payment is an investment company within the meaning of section 130 of the Taxes Act, shall be treated as if it was an expense of management in relation to that company."

Reg. 4(2)(c) inserted (and the "and" at the end of reg. 4(2)(a) omitted, and the ", and" at the end of reg. 4(2)(b) inserted) by SI 2011/1787, reg. 4, with effect in relation to manufactured overseas dividends paid or treated as paid on or after 11 August 2011.

In reg. 4(2)(a)(i) words "permanent establishment" substituted for "branch or agency" by SI 2003/2582, reg. 5(2), with effect from 1 November 2003.

Reg. 4(2) substituted by SI 1997/988, reg. 4 with effect from 1 July 1997.

Reg. 4(4)–(6) substituted for reg. 4(4) by SI 2003/2582, reg. 5(3), with effect from 1 November 2003. Reg. 4(4) previously read as follows:

"4(4)   Paragraph (3) shall not apply where–

(a)   the approved United Kingdom intermediary is entitled under regulation 5 to pay without deduction of tax a manufactured overseas dividend representative of the same overseas dividend as is represented by the manufactured overseas dividend received by him, or

(aa)   the approved United Kingdom intermediary is required to pay a manufactured overseas dividend representative of the same overseas dividend as is represented by the manufactured overseas dividend received by him, in circumstances where regulation 3(4) applies to the payment, or

(b)   the approved United Kingdom collecting agent has entered into arrangements with the Board under the Double Taxation Relief Regulations enabling him to pay without deduction of tax a manufactured overseas dividend representative of the same overseas dividend as is represented by the manufactured overseas dividend received by him, or

(c)   the approved United Kingdom collecting agent is required to pay to an approved United Kingdom intermediary a manufactured overseas dividend representative of the same overseas dividend as is represented by the manufactured overseas dividend received by him, the approved United Kingdom intermediary is entitled as mentioned in sub-paragraph (a) above and issues a notice to the approved United Kingdom collecting agent authorising him to make the payment without deduction of tax.".

Reg. 4(4)(aa) inserted by SI 1996/2643, reg. 5, operative from 6 November 1996.

TAX TREATMENT OF APPROVED MANUFACTURED OVERSEAS DIVIDENDS PAID TO PERSONS RESIDENT OUTSIDE THE UNITED KINGDOM

5(1) Subject to paragraph (1A), for the purposes of the provisions of the Tax Acts relating to the charge to tax under Schedule D, a manufactured overseas dividend paid in either of the circumstances prescribed by paragraphs (1B) and (2) shall not be treated as an annual payment pursuant to paragraph 4(2) of Schedule 23A, and accordingly shall be paid without deduction of an amount on account of income tax.

5(1A) Where a manufactured overseas dividend is paid in the circumstances prescribed by paragraph (1B) by a person who is not within the charge to corporation tax and who is not an approved United Kingdom intermediary, the dividend shall be treated, for the purposes of the provisions of the Tax Acts relating to the charge to tax under Schedule D and so far as the payer is concerned, as if the amount paid was an annual payment, within section 349(1) of the Taxes Act, but so that no amount is required to be deducted on account of income tax from the amount of the payment, or accounted for under section 350 of that Act.

5(1B) The circumstances prescribed by this paragraph are where–

(a)   a manufactured overseas dividend is paid by a person who is resident in the United Kingdom, or, if not so resident, makes the payment in the course of a trade which he carries on through a permanent establishment in the United Kingdom;

(b)   the payment is to or for the benefit of a person beneficially entitled to it who is not a United Kingdom recipient; and

(c)   regulation 4(1) does not apply.

5(2) The circumstances prescribed by this paragraph are where–

(a) a manufactured overseas dividend is paid by an approved United Kingdom intermediary who, if not resident in the United Kingdom, makes the payment in the course of a trade which he carries on through a permanent establishment in the United Kingdom; and

(b) the payment is made to another approved United Kingdom intermediary or to an approved United Kingdom collecting agent as part of a chain of payments where–

    (i) each payment in the chain is a payment by an approved United Kingdom intermediary or an approved United Kingdom collecting agent of a manufactured overseas dividend representative of the same overseas dividend,

    (ii) the maker of the last payment in the chain, if not resident in the United Kingdom, makes the payment in the course of a trade which he carries on through a permanent establishment in the United Kingdom and makes the payment to or for the benefit of a person beneficially entitled to it who is not a United Kingdom recipient,

    (iii) each recipient of a payment in the chain, apart from the last, has issued a notice to the maker of the payment authorising him to make the payment without deduction of tax, and

    (iv) none of the payments are foreign permanent establishment payments.

History – In reg. 5, words "a manufactured overseas dividend" substituted, wherever occurring, for former references to an approved manufactured overseas dividend by SI 1996/1229, reg. 4, operative from 28 May 1996.

In reg. 5(1A) the words "who is not within the charge to corporation tax and" inserted by SI 2004/2310, Schedule, para. 73(3), with effect in relation to accounting periods beginning on or after 1 April 2004 subject to the transitional provisions at FA 2004, s. 43 and 44.

In reg. 5(1) words "Subject to paragraph (1A)," inserted by SI 2003/2582, reg. 6(2), and words"either of the circumstances prescribed by paragraphs (1B) and (2)" substituted for "the circumstances prescribed by paragraph (2)" with effect from 1 November 2003.

In reg. 5(2)(b)(iii), the words ", apart from the last," inserted by SI 2011/2503, reg. 3, with effect in relation to manufactured overseas dividends paid or treated as paid on or after 10 November 2011.

Reg. 5(2)(b)(iv) inserted (and the "and" at the end of reg. 5(2)(b)(ii) omitted, and the ", and" at the end of reg. 5(2)(b)(iii) inserted) by SI 2011/1787, reg. 5, with effect in relation to manufactured overseas dividends paid or treated as paid on or after 11 August 2011.

In reg. 5(2) the word "where–" and reg. 5(2)(a) immediately following it substituted for words from "where a manufactured overseas dividend " to the word "or" immediately preceding reg. 5(2)(b), by SI 2003/2582, reg. 6(3) with effect from 1 November 2003.

Reg. 5(1A) and (1B) inserted by SI 2003/2582, reg. 6(3) with effect from 1 November 2003.

In reg. 5(2)(b)(ii) words "permanent establishment in the United Kingdom and makes the payment to or for the benefit of a person beneficially entitled to it who is not a United Kingdom recipient" substituted for "in the United Kingdom and has either entered into arrangements under the Double Taxation Relief Regulations enabling him to make the payment without deduction of tax or makes the payment in circumstances where regulation 3(4) applies" by SI 2003/2582, reg. 6(4) with effect from 1 November 2003.

In reg. 5(2)(b)(ii), words "either" and " or makes the payment" to the end inserted by SI 1996/2643, reg. 6, operative from 6 November 1996.

CHAINS OF PAYMENTS WHERE LAST PAYMENT MADE TO, OR FOR BENEFIT OF, REGISTERED PENSION SCHEME OR IS LINKED SOLELY TO PENSION BUSINESS

5A(1) This regulation applies where–

(a) a person (the "original payer") pays a manufactured overseas dividend, and

(b) the payment is made to an approved United Kingdom intermediary or to an approved United Kingdom collecting agent as part of a chain of payments where conditions A to E are met.

5A(2) Condition A is that each payment in the chain, apart from the first, is a payment by an approved United Kingdom intermediary or an approved United Kingdom collecting agent of a manufactured overseas dividend representative of the same overseas dividend.

5A(3) Condition B is that the last payment in the chain–

(a) is made to, or for the benefit of, a registered pension scheme (within the meaning given in Part 4 of the Finance Act 2004), or

(b) is linked solely to pension business for the purposes of section 438 of the Taxes Act at the time that the payment is made.

5A(4) Condition C is that the last payment in the chain is made by a person who–

(a) is resident in the United Kingdom, or

(b) is not resident in the United Kingdom, but makes the payment in the course of a trade carried on through a permanent establishment.

5A(5) Condition D is that each recipient of payment in the chain, apart from the last, has issued a notice to the original payer to make the payment at the applicable rate of relevant withholding tax.

5A(5A)   Condition E is that none of the payments are foreign permanent establishment payments.

5A(6)   The applicable rate of relevant withholding tax for each payment in the chain to an approved United Kingdom intermediary or to an approved United Kingdom collecting agent shall be determined in accordance with paragraphs (7) and (8).

5A(7)   If the last payment in the chain is made to, or for the benefit of, a registered pension scheme, the applicable rate shall be determined as if the person to whom the payment is made were the registered pension scheme to which the last payment in the chain is made.

5A(8)   If the last payment in the chain is linked solely to pension business at the time that the payment is made, the applicable rate shall be determined as if the person to whom the payment is made were the person to whom the last payment in the chain is made.

5A(9)   For the purposes of condition A (see paragraph (2)) it does not matter whether or not the first payment in the chain was made by an approved United Kingdom intermediary or an approved United Kingdom collecting agent.

History – In reg. 5A(1)(b), "E" substituted for "D" by SI 2011/1787, reg. 6(2), with effect in relation to manufactured overseas dividends paid or treated as paid on or after 11 August 2011.
In reg. 5A(5), the words ", apart from the last," inserted by SI 2011/2503, reg. 4(2), with effect in relation to manufactured overseas dividends paid or treated as paid on or after 10 November 2011.
Reg. 5A(5A) inserted by SI 2011/1787, reg. 6(3), with effect in relation to manufactured overseas dividends paid or treated as paid on or after 11 August 2011.
Reg. 5A inserted by SI 2007/2487, reg. 3(4), with effect from 1 October 2007, in relation to manufactured overseas dividends made or treated as made on or after that day.
In reg. 5A(6), the words "to an approved United Kingdom intermediary or to an approved United Kingdom collecting agent" inserted by SI 2011/2503, reg. 4(3), with effect in relation to manufactured overseas dividends paid or treated as paid on or after 10 November 2011.

CHAINS OF PAYMENTS INVOLVING CENTRAL COUNTERPARTIES

5B(1)   This regulation applies where–

(a)   a person pays a manufactured overseas dividend, and

(b)   the payment is made as part of a chain of payments ("a CCP chain"), which may form part of a chain of payments to which regulation 5(2) or 5A applies, where conditions A to C are met.

5B(2)   Condition A is that each payment in the CCP chain is a payment of a manufactured overseas dividend representative of the same overseas dividend.

5B(3)   Condition B is that each payment in the CCP chain is made–

(a)   by or to a central counterparty,

(b)   to a clearing member acting in the capacity as clearing member for another person where a corresponding payment is made by the clearing member to a central counterparty, or

(c)   by a clearing member acting in the capacity as clearing member for another person where a corresponding payment is made to the clearing member by a central counterparty.

5B(4)   Condition C is that a notice has been issued by or on behalf of the central counterparty to the first CCP payer and the final CCP recipient–

(a)   confirming that conditions A and B are met, and

(b)   either–

(i)   stating names and registered addresses of the first CCP payer and the final CCP recipient, or

(ii)   containing sufficient information to enable the parties to the CCP chain to meet their tax obligations in the United Kingdom with respect to the manufactured overseas dividend.

5B(5)   For the purposes of Chapter 9 of Part 15 of the Income Tax Act 2007 and these Regulations–

(a)   the first CCP payer is treated as required to pay to the final CCP recipient a manufactured overseas dividend representative of an overseas dividend on overseas securities paid under an arrangement for the transfer of securities,

(b)   the payments in the CCP chain are disregarded, and

(c)   a manufactured overseas dividend representative of the same overseas dividend is treated as paid by the first CCP payer to the final CCP recipient.

5B(6)   In this regulation–

"central counterparty" means a recognised clearing house, EEA central counterparty, third country central counterparty or recognised investment exchange which carries on a business of providing a central counterparty clearing service in relation to arrangements for the transfer of overseas securities;

"**central counterparty clearing service**" means the service provided to parties to an arrangement for the transfer of overseas securities, or to a clearing member acting on behalf of either of those parties, where there are contracts between each of those parties, or a clearing member, and the central counterparty in place of, or as an alternative to, a contract directly between those parties;

"**clearing member**" means a party who provides clearing arrangements between a party to an arrangement for the transfer of overseas securities and a central counterparty;

"**EEA central counterparty**" has the meaning given by section 285(1)(c) of the Financial Services and Markets Act 2000;

"**final CCP recipient**" means the party to whom the last payment in the CCP chain is made;

"**first CCP payer**" means the maker of the first payment in the CCP chain;

"**recognised clearing house**" has the meaning given by section 285(1)(b) of the Financial Services and Markets Act 2000;

"**recognised investment exchange**" means–

(a)   a recognised investment exchange within the meaning of the Financial Services and Markets Act 2000 (see section 285),

(b)   a regulated market within the meaning of Directive 2004/39/EC of the European Parliament and of the Council of 21 April 2004 on markets in financial instruments, or

(c)   a multilateral trading facility within the meaning of that Directive.

"**third country central counterparty**" has the meaning given by section 285(1)(d) of the Financial Services and Markets Act 2000.

History – In reg. 5B(6), in the definition of "central counterparty", the words ", EEA central counterparty, third country central counterparty " inserted by SI 2013/504, reg. 31(2)(a), with effect from 1 April 2013, immediately after Finance Services Act 2012, s. 6 comes fully into force.
In reg. 5B(6), in the definition of "recognised clearing house", the words "section 285(1)(b)" substituted for the words "section 285" by SI 2013/504, reg. 31(2)(b), with effect from 1 April 2013, immediately after Finance Services Act 2012, s. 6 comes fully into force.
In reg. 5B(6), definitions of "EEA central counterparty" and "third country central counterparty" inserted by SI 2013/504, reg. 31(2)(c), with effect from 1 April 2013, immediately after Finance Services Act 2012, s. 6 comes fully into force.
Reg. 5B inserted by SI 2011/2503, reg. 5, with effect in relation to manufactured overseas dividends paid or treated as paid on or after 10 November 2011.

RETENTION AND RECORD OF NOTICES GIVEN UNDER REGULATION 4 TO 5B

6(1)   A notice given under regulation 4(6)(b), 5(2)(b)(iii), 5A(5) or 5B(4) shall be in the form provided, or in a form authorised, by the Board.

6(2)   A recipient of such a notice–

(a)   shall retain the notice for a period of six years and, whenever required to do so within that period, shall make it available for inspection by an officer of the Board, and

(b)   if he receives more than one such notice during any chargeable period, shall in addition maintain a record showing–

(i)   the date of each such notice received in that period, and

(ii)   a description and the amount of the manufactured overseas dividend referred to in each such notice received in that period.

6(3)   A person who issues such a notice–

(a)   shall retain a copy of it for a period of six years and, whenever required to do so within that period, shall make that copy available for inspection by an officer of the Board, and

(b)   if he issues more than one such notice during any chargeable period, shall in addition maintain a record showing–

(i)   the date of each such notice issued in that period, and

(ii)   a description and the amount of the manufactured overseas dividend referred to in each such notice issued in that period.

6(4)   Any record required to be maintained by the recipient of a notice under paragraph (2)(b) or by the issuer of a notice under paragraph (3)(b), shall be retained by that person for a period of six years from the end of the chargeable period to which the record relates.

6(4A)   In the case of a record retained under paragraph (2)(b) or (3)(b) which is in electronic form the person retaining it shall afford an officer of the Board such assistance and facilities as the officer may reasonably require in order to read the record.

6(5)   Where the issuer of a notice fails to retain a copy of it for the period specified in paragraph (3)(a), or fails to maintain any such record as is specified in paragraph (3)(b) or to retain any such record for the period specified in paragraph (4), the Board may require that person to carry out, at his own expense, an audit of manufactured overseas dividends received by that person in order to ascertain the amount of tax, if any, liable to be deducted under paragraph 4(2) of Schedule 23A which was not deducted.

6(6)   The scope and method of the audit referred to in paragraph (5) shall be agreed between the Board and the issuer of the notice or, in the absence of agreement, determined by the Board, and the issuer of the notice shall account for and pay any tax which on the basis of the findings of the audit was liable to be deducted but which was not deducted from manufactured overseas dividends received by him.

History – In the heading to reg. 6, "4 to 5B" substituted for "4 and 5" by SI 2011/2503, reg. 6(2), with effect in relation to manufactured overseas dividends paid or treated as paid on or after 10 November 2011.
In reg. 6(1), the words ", 5(2)(b)(iii), 5A(5) or 5B(4)" substituted for the words "or regulation 5(2)(b)(iii)" by SI 2011/2503, reg. 6(2), with effect in relation to manufactured overseas dividends paid or treated as paid on or after 10 November 2011.
In reg. 6(1) words "(6)(b)" substituted for "(4)(c)" by SI 2003/2582, reg. 7 with effect from 1 November 2003.
Reg. 6(4A) inserted by SI 2003/3143, reg. 5(2) with effect from 1 January 2004.

REDUCTION OF TAX PAYABLE UNDER PARAGRAPH 4(3) OF SCHEDULE 23A

6A(1)   Where, in a case to which paragraph 4(3) of Schedule 23A applies, overseas tax was charged on, or in respect of, the making of the manufactured overseas dividend received by the United Kingdom recipient, the amount of tax to be accounted for and paid under that provision shall, for the purposes of the provisions of the Tax Acts relating to the charge to tax under Schedule D, be taken as reduced in accordance with paragraph (2) or, as the case may be, paragraph (3).

6A(2)   Where the amount specified in paragraph (4) exceeds the amount specified in paragraph (5), the amount of tax shall be reduced so as to equal the amount of the excess.

6A(3)   Where the amount specified in paragraph (4) is equal to or less than the amount specified in paragraph (5), the amount of tax shall be reduced to nil.

6A(4)   The amount specified in this paragraph is the amount of the manufactured overseas dividend received by the United Kingdom recipient.

6A(5)   The amount specified in this paragraph is the amount which the United Kingdom recipient would have received by way of the overseas dividend of which the manufactured overseas dividend is representative, had the overseas dividend been paid to him.

6A(6)   Relief claimed by the United Kingdom recipient under Part XVIII of the Taxes Act in a case to which paragraph (2) applies shall not exceed the aggregate of the amount of tax accounted for and paid by the United Kingdom recipient under paragraph 4(3) of Schedule 23A and the amount of overseas tax charged on, or in respect of, the making of the manufactured overseas dividend received by him.

History – In reg. 6A(6), the words ", other than relief given by virtue of section 811 of that Act,", which appeared after "paragraph (2) applies", omitted by SI 2010/925, reg. 4, with effect in relation to manufactured overseas dividends made or treated as made on or after 14 April 2010.
Reg. 6A inserted by SI 1996/2643, reg. 7, operative from 6 November 1996.

DISAPPLICATION OF PARAGRAPH 4(3) OF SCHEDULE 23A

7(1)   For the purposes of the provisions of the Tax Acts relating to the charge to tax under Schedule D, tax shall not be required to be accounted for and paid pursuant to paragraph 4(3) of Schedule 23A by a United Kingdom recipient of a manufactured overseas dividend which is received by him in any of the circumstances prescribed by paragraph (2).

7(2)   The circumstances prescribed by this paragraph are where the United Kingdom recipient–

(a)   pays, in accordance with regulation 5, and without deduction of tax, a manufactured overseas dividend representative of the same overseas dividend as is represented by the manufactured overseas dividend received by him, or;

(b)   [omitted by SI 2003/2582, reg. 8];

(c)   is an approved United Kingdom collecting agent and the person beneficially entitled to the manufactured overseas dividend received by the approved United Kingdom collecting agent is not resident in the United Kingdom and receipt of the manufactured overseas dividend by the person beneficially entitled to it would be otherwise than in the course of a trade carried on through a branch or agency in the United Kingdom, or

(ca)   is an approved United Kingdom collecting agent and receipt of the manufactured overseas dividend by the person beneficially entitled to it would be a foreign permanent establishment receipt, or

(d) is an approved United Kingdom collecting agent who is required to pay to an approved United Kingdom intermediary a manufactured overseas dividend representative of the same overseas dividend as is represented by the manufactured overseas dividend received by him, the approved United Kingdom intermediary is enabled or authorised as mentioned in sub-paragraph (a) above and issues a notice to the approved United Kingdom collecting agent authorising him to pay the manufactured overseas dividend without deduction of tax, or

(e) is an approved United Kingdom collecting agent or an approved United Kingdom intermediary in receipt of a manufactured overseas dividend who shows that the overseas dividend manufacturer concerned was entitled to payment of the overseas dividend of which the manufactured overseas dividend is representative either–

　(i) as the holder of the overseas securities concerned, or

　(ii) directly or indirectly from a person from whom he acquired those securities, or to whom he transferred them, and who was so entitled as the holder of those securities.

7(3)　A notice given under paragraph (2)(d) shall be in the form provided, or in a form authorised, by the Board.

7(3A)–(3E)　[Omitted by SI 2009/2811, reg. 2(2).]

7(4)　The United Kingdom recipient–

(a) shall maintain a record of all manufactured overseas dividends received by him in any chargeable period in the circumstances prescribed by paragraph (2), showing–

　(i) a description and the amount of each such manufactured overseas dividend, and the date on which it was received, and

　(ii) the total amount of all such manufactured overseas dividends received in that period;

(b) where he is an approved United Kingdom intermediary within sub-paragraph (b) or an approved United Kingdom collecting agent within sub-paragraph (c), of paragraph (2), shall in addition maintain a record of all manufactured overseas dividends paid by him as mentioned in sub-paragraph (b) or, as the case may be, sub-paragraph (c), of that paragraph in any chargeable period, showing–

　(i) the name and address of the person beneficially entitled to each such payment,

　(ii) a description and the amount of each such payment, and the date of the payment, and

　(iii) the total amount of all such payments made in that period;

(c) shall retain any such record as is specified in sub-paragraph (a) or (b) of this paragraph for a period of six years from the end of the chargeable period to which the record relates, and shall make any such record available for inspection by an officer of the Board whenever required to do so during the period of retention;

(d) where he is an approved United Kingdom collecting agent within sub-paragraph (d) of paragraph (2), shall in addition–

　(i) retain for a period of six years any notice received by him as mentioned in that sub-paragraph and, whenever required to do so, make it available for inspection by an officer of the Board, and

　(ii) if he receives more than one such notice during any chargeable period, maintain a record showing the date of each such notice received in that period and a description and the amount of the manufactured overseas dividend referred to in each such notice, and retain the record for a period of six years from the end of the chargeable period to which the record relates.

7(4A)　In the case of a record retained under paragraph (4) which is in electronic form the person retaining it shall afford an officer of the Board such assistance and facilities as the officer may reasonably require in order to read the record.

7(5)　Where the United Kingdom recipient fails to maintain, or to retain for the requisite period, any such record as is referred to in paragraph (4), or fails to retain for the requisite period any such notice as is referred to in that paragraph, the Board may require that person to carry out, at his own expense, an audit of manufactured overseas dividends received by him in order to ascertain the amount of tax, if any, for which he was liable to account under paragraph 4(3) of Schedule 23A.

7(6)　The scope and method of the audit referred to in paragraph (5) shall be agreed between the Board and the United Kingdom recipient or, in the absence of agreement, shall be determined by the Board, and the United Kingdom recipient shall account for and pay any tax which on the basis of the findings of the audit he was liable under paragraph 4(3) of Schedule 23A to account for and pay.

History – In reg. 7(2)(c), the words "and receipt of the manufactured overseas dividend by the person beneficially entitled to it would be otherwise than in the course of a trade carried on through a branch or agency in the United Kingdom" inserted by SI 2011/1787, reg. 7(a), with effect in relation to manufactured overseas dividends paid or treated as paid on or after 11 August 2011.

Reg. 7(2)(ca) inserted by SI 2011/1787, reg. 7(b), with effect in relation to manufactured overseas dividends paid or treated as paid on or after 11 August 2011.

In reg. 7(2), words "a manufactured overseas dividend" and "the manufactured overseas dividend" substituted for former references to an approved manufactured overseas dividend or the approved manufactured dividend, by SI 1996/1229, reg. 4, operative from 28 May 1996.

Reg. 7(2)(a) substituted and reg. 7(2)(b) omitted by SI 2003/2582, reg. 8 with effect from 1 November 2003. Reg. 7(2)(a) and (b) previously read as follows:

> "(a)   is an approved United Kingdom intermediary who has entered into arrangements with the Board under the Double Taxation Relief Regulations enabling him to pay without deduction of tax a manufactured overseas dividend representative of the same overseas dividend as is represented by the manufactured overseas dividend received by him, or who is authorised by a notice under regulation 5(2)(b)(iii) to make such a payment without deduction of tax, or
>
> (b)   is an approved United Kingdom intermediary who is required to pay a manufactured overseas dividend representative of the same overseas dividend as is represented by the manufactured overseas dividend received by him, in circumstances where regulation 3(4) applies in relation to the payment, or".

Reg. 7(2)(e) inserted by SI 1996/2643, reg. 8, operative from 6 November 1996.

Reg. 7(3A)–(3E) omitted by SI 2009/2811, reg. 2(2), with effect in relation to manufactured overseas dividends made or treated as made on or after 1.15 pm on 21 October 2009. Former reg. 7(3A)–(3E) read as follows:

> **7(3A)**   Paragraphs (3B) to (3D) apply where, by virtue of paragraph (1), tax is not required to be accounted for and paid in the circumstances prescribed by paragraph (2)(e).
>
> **7(3B)**   For the purposes of the Corporation Tax Acts, paragraph 4(4) of Schedule 23A shall apply as if the amount of tax required under section 923 of the Income Tax Act 2007 to be accounted for and paid were amount A or amount B (whichever should be the lower) and as if that amount of tax had been accounted for and paid.
>
> **7(3C)**   For the purposes of the Income Tax Acts, section 923 of the Income Tax Act 2007 shall apply as if the amount of tax which the recipient must account for and pay were amount A or amount B (whichever should be the lower).
>
> **7(3D)**   For the purposes of paragraphs (3B) and (3C)–
> (a)   amount A is an amount equal to the excess of the gross amount of the overseas dividend over the amount of that overseas dividend received by the overseas dividend manufacturer, and
> (b)   amount B is an amount equal to the excess of the gross amount of the overseas dividend over the amount of the manufactured overseas dividend paid by the overseas dividend manufacturer which represents that dividend.
>
> **7(3E)**   In paragraph (3D)(b) the reference to the manufactured overseas dividend paid by the overseas dividend manufacturer does not include any payment treated as made treated as made under–
> (a)   section 736B of the Income and Corporation Taxes Act 1988 (deemed manufactured payments in the case of stock lending arrangements), or
> (b)   section 737A of the Income and Corporation Taxes Act 1988 (sale and repurchase of securities: deemed manufactured payments).".

Former reg. 7(3A)–(3E) substituted for previous reg. 7(3A) by SI 2007/2487, reg. 4, with effect from 1 October 2007, in relation to manufactured overseas dividends made or treated as made on or after that day.

In former reg. 7(3A), the words "were an amount equal to the excess…received by the overseas dividend manufacturer and" were inserted by SI 1997/988, reg. 5 with effect from 1 July 1997.

Reg. 7(3A) inserted by SI 1996/2643, reg. 8, operative from 6 November 1996.

Reg. 7(4A) inserted by SI 2003/3143, reg. 5(3) with effect from 1 January 2004.

DISAPPLICATION OF PARAGRAPH 5 OF SCHEDULE 23A

7A   [Omitted by SI 1997/987, reg. 8(3), with effect from 1 July 1997.]

TAX TREATMENT OF MANUFACTURED OVERSEAS DIVIDENDS TO WHICH REGULATIONS 4, 5 AND 7 APPLY – FURTHER PROVISION

8   For all purposes of the Tax Acts as they apply in relation to persons resident in the United Kingdom or to persons not so resident but carrying on a business through a permanent establishment in the United Kingdom, any manufactured overseas dividend to which regulation 4,5 or 7 applies shall be treated in relation to the recipient, and all persons claiming title through or under him–

(a)   as if it were an overseas dividend of an amount equal to the amount of the manufactured overseas dividend, or

(b)   where paragraph (3) of regulation 4 applies and the amount of tax required under that paragraph in respect of the manufactured overseas dividend has been accounted for and paid, as if it were an overseas dividend of an amount equal to the gross amount of the manufactured overseas dividend, but paid after the withholding therefrom, on account of overseas tax, of the amount accounted for and paid; and the amount accounted for and paid shall accordingly be treated in relation to the recipient, and all persons claiming title through or under him, as an amount so withheld instead of an amount on account of income tax.

History – In reg. 8 words "permanent establishment" substituted for "branch or agency" by SI 2003/2582, reg. 9 with effect from 1 November 2003.

OFFSETTING OF TAX BY OVERSEAS DIVIDEND MANUFACTURERS

9(1) In the circumstances prescribed by paragraph (2) and subject to paragraph (4), a person who is an overseas dividend manufacturer in any chargeable period shall be entitled to set off the amounts specified in paragraph (1A) against the sums specified in paragraph (1B). This is subject to regulation 9ZA.

9(1A) The amounts specified in this paragraph are–

(a) amounts of overseas tax in respect of overseas dividends received by the overseas dividend manufacturer in the chargeable period otherwise than as foreign permanent establishment receipts;

(b) amounts of overseas tax charged on, or in respect of, the making of manufactured overseas dividends so received by him otherwise than as foreign permanent establishment receipts;

(c) amounts deducted under paragraph 4(2) of Schedule 23A from manufactured overseas dividends so received by him;

(d) amounts accounted for and paid under paragraph 4(3) of Schedule 23A in respect of manufactured overseas dividends so received by him;

(e) amounts accounted for and paid under regulation 4(3) in respect of manufactured overseas dividends so received by him.

9(1B) The sums specified in this paragraph are sums due from the overseas dividend manufacturer on account of the amounts deducted by him under paragraph 4(2) of Schedule 23A from the manufactured overseas dividends paid by him in the chargeable period.

9(2) The circumstances prescribed by this paragraph are where–

(a) the overseas dividend manufacturer is an approved United Kingdom intermediary,

(aa) [omitted by SI 1996/2643, reg. 10(b)(i),]

(b) the overseas dividends and manufactured overseas dividends referred to in paragraph (1A), if received by an overseas dividend manufacturer within sub-paragraph (a) of this paragraph who carries on a business in the ordinary course of which he receives overseas dividends and manufactured overseas dividends and pays manufactured overseas dividends, are such that a profit on the sale of the overseas securities to which those overseas dividends and manufactured overseas dividends relate would form part of the trading profits of that business,

(c) [omitted by SI 1996/1229, reg. 5,]

(d) except in a case to which paragraph (3) applies, the overseas dividends or, as the case may be, the manufactured overseas dividends received by him, do not fall to be matched, in accordance with regulation 10(1), against manufactured overseas dividends paid by him in that period.

9(3) This paragraph applies to a case where, under regulation 10(1), overseas dividends in respect of which overseas tax is payable received by the overseas dividend manufacturer in any chargeable period, and manufactured overseas dividends so received on or in respect of the making of which overseas tax has been charged or from which tax has been deducted or in respect of which tax falls to be accounted for and paid as mentioned in paragraph (1A) above, are matched against manufactured overseas dividends paid by him under deduction of tax in that period.

9(4) Where paragraph (3) applies in respect of any chargeable period, the overseas dividend manufacturer shall be entitled to set off against each other–

(a) the tax referred to in that paragraphs that is attributable to the matched overseas dividends and manufactured overseas dividends received, and

(b) the tax referred to in that paragraphs that is attributable to the matched manufactured overseas dividends paid.

9(4A) Subject to paragraphs (4B) and (5), where overseas dividends or manufactured overseas dividends received by the overseas dividend manufacturer in any chargeable period fall to be matched, in accordance with regulation 10(1), against manufactured overseas dividends paid by him in that period, relief under Part XVIII of the Taxes Act may not be claimed by the overseas dividend manufacturer in respect of any tax referred to in paragraph (1A) that is attributable to those overseas dividends or manufactured overseas dividends received.

9(4B) Where–

(a) overseas dividends or manufactured overseas dividends received by the overseas dividend manufacturer in any chargeable period fall to be matched, in accordance with regulation 10(1), against manufactured overseas dividends to which regulation 3(6), 5 or 5A applies that are paid by him in that period, and

(b)   the gross amount of the overseas dividends or the manufactured overseas dividends is brought into account by the overseas dividend manufacturer as income for the purposes of income tax or corporation tax for that period,

relief under section 112 of the Taxation (International and Other Provisions) Act 2010 (deduction from income for foreign tax (instead of credit against UK tax)) shall be given to the overseas dividend manufacturer in respect of any tax referred to in paragraph (1A) that is attributable to those overseas dividends or manufactured overseas dividends received.

9(4C)   Subject to paragraph (5), where tax referred to in paragraph (1A) that is attributable to overseas dividends or manufactured overseas dividends received by the overseas dividend manufacturer in any chargeable period is set off, in accordance with this regulation, against tax referred to in paragraph (1B) that is attributable to manufactured overseas dividends paid by him in that period, relief under Part XVIII of the Taxes Act may not be claimed by the overseas dividend manufacturer in respect of any tax referred to in paragraph (1A) that is attributable to those overseas dividends or manufactured overseas dividends received.

9(5)   Except in a case to which paragraph (3) applies, where in accordance with this regulation tax is set off by an overseas dividend manufacturer in any chargeable period and in relation to that period the sum of the overseas tax and amounts referred to in paragraph (1A) exceeds the total amount of the sums due as mentioned in paragraph (1B), relief under Part XVIII of the Taxes Act may be claimed by the overseas dividend manufacturer in respect of the amount of the excess.

9(6)   Where in accordance with this regulation tax is set off by an overseas dividend manufacturer in any chargeable period and in relation to that period the total amount of the sums due from the overseas dividend manufacturer as mentioned in paragraph (1B) exceeds the sum of the overseas tax and amounts referred to in paragraph (1A), the amount of the excess shall be payable to the Board.

9(7)   References to overseas tax in this regulation are references to the amount of such tax which is eligible for relief under Part XVIII of the Taxes Act either–

(a)   pursuant to arrangements made with the government of the overseas territory specified in paragraph (8) which have effect by virtue of section 788 of the Taxes Act and relate to the overseas dividend or manufactured overseas dividend concerned, or

(b)   by virtue of other provisions of Part XVIII of the Taxes Act other than section 790(5)(c)(ii) of that Act.

9(8)   The overseas territory specified in this paragraph–

(i)   so far as overseas dividends are concerned, is the territory of the government or public or local authority which issued the securities in question or, where the securities were issued by any other body of persons not resident in the United Kingdom, the territory under whose law that tax would have been payable;

(ii)   so far as manufactured overseas dividends are concerned, is the territory of the government by which tax is charged on, or in respect of, the making of the manufactured overseas dividend concerned.

History – In reg. 9(1), the words "This is subject to regulation 9ZA." inserted by SI 2010/925, reg. 5(2), with effect in relation to manufactured overseas dividends made or treated as made on or after 14 April 2010.
In reg. 9 words "regulation 3(6), 5 or 5A" substituted for "regulation 5" by SI 2007/2487, reg. 6, with effect from 1 October 2007, in relation to manufactured overseas dividends made or treated as made on or after that day.
In reg. 9(1A)(a), the words "otherwise than as foreign permanent establishment receipts" inserted by SI 2011/1787, reg. 8(a), with effect in relation to manufactured overseas dividends paid or treated as paid on or after 11 August 2011.
In reg. 9(1A)(b), the words "otherwise than as foreign permanent establishment receipts" inserted by SI 2011/1787, reg. 8(b), with effect in relation to manufactured overseas dividends paid or treated as paid on or after 11 August 2011.
Reg. 9(1), (1A), (1B) substituted for former reg. 9(1) by SI 1996/2643, reg. 10(a), operative from 6 November 1996.
Former reg. 9(2)(aa), which was inserted by SI 1995/1324, reg. 5 operative from 7 June 1995, omitted by SI 1996/2643, reg. 10(b)(i), operative from 6 November 1996.
In reg. 9(2)(b), reference to paragraph (1A) substituted for former reference to paragraph (1)(a) by SI 1996/2643, reg. 10(b)(ii), operative from 6 November 1996.
Reg. 9(2)(c) omitted by SI 1996/1229, reg. 5, operative from 28 May 1996.
In reg. 9(3), words from "on or in respect of" to "charged or" inserted, and reference to paragraph (1A) substituted for former reference to paragraph (1)(a), by SI 1996/2643, reg. 10(c), operative from 6 November 1996.
In reg. 9(4)(a), (b), words "referred to in that paragraph that is" inserted by SI 1996/2643, reg. 10(d), operative from 6 November 1996.
In reg. 9(4A), in para. (b), words "referred to in paragraph (3) that is" and "referred to in that paragraph that is", and, in the endpiece, words "referred to in paragraph (3) that is", inserted by SI 1996/2643, reg. 10(e), operative from 6 November 1996.
Reg. 9(4A)–(4C) substituted for former reg. 9(4A) by SI 1997/988, reg. 6 with effect from 1 July 1997.
Former reg. 9(4A) inserted by SI 1995/1324, reg. 5, operative from 7 June 1995.
Reg. 9(4B) substituted by SI 2010/925, reg. 5(3), with effect in relation to manufactured overseas dividends made or treated as made on or after 14 April 2010. Former reg. 9(4B) read as follows:

    "**9(4B)**   Where overseas dividends or manufactured overseas dividends received by the overseas dividend manufacturer in any chargeable period fall to be matched, in accordance with regulation 10(1), against manufactured overseas dividends to which regulation 3(6), 5 or 5A applies that are paid by him in that period, relief under section 811 of the

Taxes Act shall be given to the overseas dividend manufacturer in respect of any tax referred to in paragraph (1A) that is attributable to those overseas dividends or manufactured overseas dividends received.".

In reg. 9(5), (6), references to paragraph (1A) and paragraph (1B) substituted respectively for former references to paragraph (1)(a) and paragraph (1)(b) by SI 1996/2643, reg. 10(f), operative from 6 November 1996.

In reg. 9(7)(a), words "or manufactured overseas dividend" inserted by SI 1996/2643, reg. 10(g), operative from 6 November 1996.

In reg. 9(8), words from "in this paragraph" to the end substituted by SI 1996/2643, reg. 10(h), operative from 6 November 1996.

ENTITLEMENT TO OFFSETTING

9ZA(1)   There shall be no entitlement to set off under regulation 9(1) in relation to overseas dividends or manufactured overseas dividends received by an overseas dividend manufacturer in any chargeable period if–

(a)   the overseas dividends or the manufactured overseas dividends do not fall to be matched, in accordance with regulation 10(1), against manufactured overseas dividends paid by the overseas dividend manufacturer in that period, and

(b)   the gross amount of the overseas dividends or manufactured overseas dividends is not brought into account in accordance with generally accepted accounting practice by the overseas dividend manufacturer as income for the purposes of income tax or corporation tax for that period.

This is subject to paragraph (2).

9ZA(2)   Paragraph (1) does not apply if the overseas dividend manufacturer elects to bring into account the gross amount of the overseas dividends or manufactured overseas dividends received in any chargeable period as income for the purpose of calculating his liability to income tax or corporation tax for that period.

9ZA(3)   An election under paragraph (2)–

(a)   must be made in writing to Her Majesty's Revenue and Customs,

(b)   applies in relation to overseas dividends and manufactured overseas dividends received in the chargeable period in which the election is made and in subsequent periods, and

(c)   may be revoked by notice in writing to Her Majesty's Revenue and Customs with effect from the chargeable period in which the notice is given.

History – Reg. 9ZA inserted by SI 2010/925, reg. 6, with effect in relation to manufactured overseas dividends made or treated as made on or after 14 April 2010.

OFFSETTING OF TAX BY OVERSEAS DIVIDEND MANUFACTURERS WHO ARE NOT UNITED KINGDOM INTERMEDIARIES

9A(1)   An overseas dividend manufacturer who is not an approved United Kingdom intermediary shall be entitled to set off in any chargeable period amounts of overseas tax in respect of overseas dividends received by him in that chargeable period otherwise than as a foreign permanent establishment receipt against sums due from him on account of the amounts deducted by him under paragraph 4(2) of Schedule 23A from manufactured overseas dividends paid by him in that chargeable period that are representative of those overseas dividends.

9A(2)   Where overseas tax referred to in paragraph (1) is set off against sums referred to in that paragraph, relief under Part XVIII of the Taxes Act may not be claimed by the overseas dividend manufacturer in respect of that overseas tax.

9A(2A)   This paragraph applies where an overseas dividend manufacturer who is not an approved United Kingdom intermediary receives in any chargeable period overseas dividends or manufactured overseas dividends and pays in that period manufactured overseas dividends to which regulation 3(6), 5 or 5A applies that are representative of those overseas dividends or manufactured overseas dividends received.

9A(2B)   Where paragraph (2A) applies–

(a)   relief under section 811 of the Taxes Act shall be given to the overseas dividend manufacturer in respect of any tax referred to in regulation 9(1A) that is attributable to the overseas dividends or manufactured overseas dividends received by him; and

(b)   no other relief under Part 18 of the Taxes Act may be claimed by him in respect of any such tax.

9A(2C)   But paragraph (2B) only applies to a case where the gross amount of the overseas dividends or, as the case may be, the manufactured overseas dividends received by the overseas dividend manufacturer in any chargeable period is brought into account as income for the purposes of income tax or corporation tax for that period.

9A(3) References in this regulation to overseas tax shall be construed in accordance with regulation 9(7).

History – In reg. 9A(1), the words "otherwise than as a foreign permanent establishment receipt" inserted by SI 2011/1787, reg. 9, with effect in relation to manufactured overseas dividends paid or treated as paid on or after 11 August 2011.
In reg. 9A(2A) words "regulation 3(6), 5 or 5A" substituted for "regulation 5" by SI 2007/2487, reg. 7, with effect from 1 October 2007, in relation to manufactured overseas dividends made or treated as made on or after that day.
Reg. 9A(2A) and (2B) inserted by SI 2003/2582, reg. 10(2) with effect from 1 November 2003.
Reg. 9A(2C) inserted by SI 2010/925, reg. 7, with effect in relation to manufactured overseas dividends made or treated as made on or after 14 April 2010.
Reg. 9A inserted by SI 1997/988, reg. 7 with effect from 1 July 1997.

MATCHING OF DIVIDENDS AND MANUFACTURED OVERSEAS DIVIDENDS

10(1) For the purpose of paragraph (2)(d) and (3) of regulation 9, overseas dividends paid on overseas securities of a particular kind in respect of a particular dividend date which are received in any chargeable period by an overseas dividend manufacturer, and manufactured overseas dividends representative of those overseas dividends which are received by him in that period–

(a)   shall be matched against manufactured overseas dividends representative of those overseas dividends which are paid by him in that period in accordance with the following order of priority–

(i)   manufactured overseas dividends received without deduction of tax other than manufactured overseas dividends in respect of which tax falls to be accounted for and paid under paragraph 4(3) of Schedule 23A or regulation 4(3);

(ii)   overseas dividends received; and

(iii)   manufactured overseas dividends received to which tax referred to in regulation 9(1A) is attributable; and

(b)   shall first be matched against manufactured overseas dividends paid without deduction of tax under paragraph 4(2) of Schedule 23A by virtue of regulation 3(6), 5 or 5A

and the balance, if any, shall be matched against manufactured overseas dividends paid by him from which tax has been deducted under paragraph 4(2) of Schedule 23A.

10(1A) But the following cannot be matched under paragraph (1)–

(a)   overseas dividends received as foreign permanent establishment receipts,

(b)   manufactured overseas dividends received as foreign permanent establishment receipts, and

(c)   manufactured overseas dividends paid as foreign permanent establishment payments.

10(2)-(4) [Omitted by SI 2011/2503, reg. 7.]

History – In reg. 10(1)(a)(i), the words "other than" to the end substituted for the words "pursuant to notices issued by him under regulation 4(4)(c), 5(2)(b)(iii), or 7(2)(d)" by SI 1995/1324, reg. 6, operative from 7 June 1995.
In reg. 10(1)(a)(iii), the reference to "9(1A)" substituted for the reference to "9(3)" by SI 1997/988, reg. 8 with effect from 1 July 1997.
In reg. 10(1)(a)(iii), the words "to which tax referred to in regulation 9(3) is attributable" substituted by SI 1996/2643, reg. 11(a)6, operative from 6 November 1996.
In reg. 10(1)(b) words "regulation 3(6), 5 or 5A" substituted for "regulation 5" by SI 2007/2487, reg. 8, with effect from 1 October 2007, in relation to manufactured overseas dividends made or treated as made on or after that day.
In reg. 10(1)(b) words "by virtue of regulation 5" substituted for:
"by reason of–
   (i)   notices issued to him under regulation 5(2)(b)(iii), or
   (ii)   arrangements entered into with the Board under the Double Taxation Relief Regulations, or
   (iii)   in cases to which paragraph (4) of regulation 3 applies, the application of that paragraph resulting in a rate of relevant withholding tax of nil per cent,"
by SI 2003/2582, reg. 11(2) with effect from 1 November 2003.
Reg. 10(1A) inserted by SI 2011/1787, reg. 10, with effect in relation to manufactured overseas dividends paid or treated as paid on or after 11 August 2011.
Reg. 10(2)–(4) omitted by SI 2011/2503, reg. 7, with effect in relation to manufactured overseas dividends paid or treated as paid on or after 10 November 2011. Former reg. 10(2)–(4) read as follows:

"**10(2)**   Where under paragraph (1) an overseas dividend or manufactured overseas dividend received is matched with a manufactured overseas dividend paid to a United Kingdom recipient, any voucher relating to the deduction of overseas tax from the overseas dividend or manufactured overseas dividend received shall, subject to paragraph (3), be forwarded to the United Kingdom recipient.

10(3)   Where under paragraph (1) an overseas dividend received, or a manufactured overseas dividend received on or in respect of the making of which overseas tax has been charged, is matched with more than one manufactured overseas dividend paid to a United Kingdom recipient, the overseas dividend manufacturer–
   (a)   shall endeavour to obtain from the payer of the overseas dividend or manufactured overseas dividend received a voucher corresponding to each manufactured overseas dividend so paid, or
   (b)   if, despite reasonable attempts to do so, he is unable to obtain such a voucher, shall prepare a voucher corresponding to each manufactured overseas dividend so paid and showing the following amounts–
      (i)   so much of the gross amount of the overseas dividend or manufactured overseas dividend received as corresponds to the gross amount of the manufactured overseas dividend so paid,
      (ii)   so much of the overseas tax in respect of the overseas dividend or manufactured overseas dividend received as would be eligible for relief as mentioned in regulation 9(7) and relates to the amount of the overseas dividend or manufactured overseas dividend calculated in paragraph (i) above, and

       (iii)   so much of the actual amount of the overseas dividend or manufactured overseas dividend received as corresponds to the amount of the manufactured overseas dividend so paid, and

(c)   shall forward the voucher obtained or, as the case may be, prepared by him to the United Kingdom recipient of the manufactured overseas dividend paid by him to which the voucher relates, instead of the voucher referred to in paragraph (2).

10(4)   Where a voucher has been forwarded as mentioned in paragraph (3)(c) and subsequently a manufactured overseas dividend received by an overseas dividend manufacturer to which that voucher relates is matched under paragraph (1) with more than one manufactured overseas dividend paid to a United Kingdom recipient, the overseas dividend manufacturer—

(a)   shall endeavour to obtain from the payer of the overseas dividend of which the manufactured overseas dividend received is representative or (as the case may be) from the payer of the manufactured overseas dividend received a voucher corresponding to each such manufactured overseas dividend so paid, or

(b)   if, despite reasonable attempts to do so, he is unable to obtain such a voucher, shall prepare a voucher corresponding to each such manufactured overseas dividend so paid and showing the details specified in paragraphs (i) to (iii) of paragraph (3)(b), and

(c)   shall forward the voucher obtained or, as the case may be, prepared by him to the United Kingdom recipient of the manufactured overseas dividend to which the voucher relates.".

In former reg. 10(2) words "to a United Kingdom recipient" inserted after "paid", and "United Kingdom recipient" substituted for "recipient of the manufactured overseas dividend paid" by SI 2003/2582, reg. 11(3), with effect from 1 November 2003.

In former reg. 10(3) words "to a United Kingdom recipient" inserted after "paid", in the first instance and in reg. 10(3)(a) and (b) "so paid" substituted for "paid" by SI 2003/2582, reg. 11(4), with effect from 1 November 2003.

In former reg. 10(3)(c) words "United Kingdom recipient" substituted for "recipient" by SI 2003/2582, reg. 11(4), with effect from 1 November 2003.

Former reg. 10(2), (3) substituted by SI 1996/2643, reg. 11(b), operative from 6 November 1996.

In former reg. 10(4) words "to a United Kingdom recipient" inserted after "paid", in the first instance and in reg. 10(4)(a) and (b) "so paid" substituted for "paid" by SI 2003/2582, reg. 11(5), with effect from 1 November 2003.

In former reg. 10(4)(a), words from "or (as the case" to "dividend received" inserted by SI 1996/2643, reg. 11(c), operative from 6 November 1996.

In former reg. 10(4)(c) words "United Kingdom recipient" substituted for "recipient" by SI 2003/2582, reg. 11(5), with effect from 1 November 2003.

ACCOUNTING FOR TAX PAYABLE UNDER PARAGRAPH 4(2) AND (3) OF SCHEDULE 23A AND THESE REGULATIONS

11(1)   Within 30 days of the end of a chargeable period—

(a)   an overseas dividend manufacturer shall pay to the Board all amounts which he was liable to deduct under paragraph 4(2) of Schedule 23A on account of income tax from manufactured overseas dividends paid by him in that period;

(b)   an overseas dividend manufacturer who is an approved United Kingdom intermediary shall pay to the Board the amount of any excess payable under regulation 9(6) attributable to that period;

(c)   a United Kingdom recipient shall pay to the Board all amounts of tax for which he was liable to account under paragraph 4(3) of Schedule 23A in respect of manufactured overseas dividends received by him in that period;

(d)   an approved United Kingdom intermediary or an approved United Kingdom collecting agent shall pay to the Board all amounts of tax for which he was liable to account under regulation 4(3) in respect of manufactured overseas dividends received by him in that period.

11(2)   Within 30 days of the end of a chargeable period—

(a)   an overseas dividend manufacturer shall make a return to the Board or an inspector, in such form as the Board may prescribe, showing—

    (i)   the amounts which he was liable to deduct under paragraph 4(2) of Schedule 23A on account of income tax from manufactured overseas dividends paid by him in that period,

    (ii)   [Omitted by SI 1996/1299, reg. 6(b), and]

    (iii)   the amount of any excess payable under regulation 9(6) attributable to that period;

(b)   a United Kingdom recipient shall make a return to the Board or an inspector, in such form as the Board may prescribe, showing the amounts of tax for which he was liable to account under paragraph 4(3) of Schedule 23A in respect of manufactured overseas dividends received by him in that period;

(c)   an approved United Kingdom intermediary or an approved United Kingdom collecting agent shall make a return to the Board or an inspector, in such form as the Board may prescribe, showing the amounts of tax for which he was liable to account under regulation 4(3) in respect of manufactured overseas dividends received by him in that period.

11(3)   Any amount referred to in paragraph (1) shall be due at the end of the period of 30 days specified in that paragraph and shall be payable without the making of any assessment but may be assessed on the overseas dividend manufacturer or, as the case may be, the United Kingdom recipient, approved United Kingdom intermediary or approved United Kingdom collecting agent (whether or not it has been paid when the assessment is made) if it is not paid in full on or before that date.

Statutory Instruments

11(4) In any case where—

(a) it appears to the inspector that there is—

(i) a manufactured overseas dividend paid, or an overseas dividend or a manufactured overseas dividend received, by an overseas dividend manufacturer in a chargeable period, or

(ii) an overseas dividend or a manufactured overseas dividend received by a United Kingdom recipient, an approved United Kingdom intermediary or an approved United Kingdom collecting agent in a chargeable period,

which ought to have been but which has not been included in a return under paragraph (2) relating to that period, or

(b) the inspector is dissatisfied with any return under paragraph (2),

the inspector may make an assessment to the best of his judgment on the overseas dividend manufacturer or, as the case may be, the United Kingdom recipient, approved United Kingdom intermediary or approved United Kingdom collecting agent.

11(5) Any income tax due under an assessment made by virtue of paragraph (4) shall be treated for the purposes of interest on unpaid tax as having been payable at the end of the period of 30 days specified in paragraph (1).

11(6) Any amount for which an approved United Kingdom intermediary is liable to account under regulation 6(6), and any amount for which a United Kingdom recipient is liable to account under regulation 7(6), in respect of manufactured overseas dividends received by them in a chargeable period, shall be due at the end of the period of 30 days from the end of that period, and shall be payable without the making of any assessment but may be assessed on the approved United Kingdom intermediary or, as the case may be, the United Kingdom recipient (whether or not it has been paid when the assessment is made) if it is not paid in full on or before that date.

11(7) The like provisions as are contained in the Income Tax Acts with respect to the time within which an assessment may be made, so far as they refer or relate to the year of assessment for which an assessment is made, or the year to which an assessment relates, shall have effect in relation to an assessment under this regulation notwithstanding that, under this regulation, the assessment may be said to relate to a period which is not a year of assessment; and the like provisions as are contained in section 36 of the Management Act as to the circumstances in which an assessment may be made out of time shall have effect accordingly on the footing that any such assessment relates to the year of assessment in which the period in question ends.

11(8) Income tax assessed on a person under this regulation shall be due at the end of the period of 30 days after the issue of the notice of assessment (unless due earlier under paragraph (3) or (6)).

11(9) Any tax assessable under any one or more of the provisions of this regulation may be included in one assessment if the tax so included is all due on the same date.

11(10) Section 31 and Part V of the Management Act shall apply to an appeal against any assessment to tax under this regulation.

11(11) Subsections (1), (7) and (8) of section 87 of the Management Act shall apply to tax assessable under this regulation as they apply to tax assessable in accordance with Schedule 13 and 16 to the Taxes Act, and accordingly those subsections shall have effect as if references to those Schedules included references to this regulation.

11(12) Section 98 of the Management Act shall apply in relation to a return under paragraph (2) with the modification specified in paragraph (13).

11(13) At the end of the second column of the Table in section 98 of the Management Act there shall be inserted–

"Regulation 11(2) of the Income Tax (Manufactured Overseas Dividends) Regulations 1993".

History – In reg. 11(1)(d), (2)(a)(i) and (c), word "approved" which appeared before "manufactured overseas dividends", and reg. 9(2)(a)(ii), omitted by SI 1996/1299, reg. 6, operative from 28 May 1996.
In reg. 11(2), "30" substituted for "90" by SI 1997/988, reg. 9 with effect in relation to chargeable periods ending on or after 1 July 1997.

TAX TREATMENT OF MANUFACTURED OVERSEAS DIVIDENDS REPRESENTATIVE OF FOREIGN DIVIDENDS

12(1) This regulation applies to a case where a manufactured overseas dividend is paid to a collecting agent in circumstances where, had it been the overseas dividend of which it is representative, it would have been–

(a)   a foreign dividend (as defined in section 18(3D) of the Taxes Act, or

(b)   interest on a quoted Eurobond (as defined by section 124 of that Act) held in a recognised clearing system.

12(2)   Where this regulation applies–

(a)   deduction of an amount determined by reference to the gross amount of the manufactured overseas dividend shall be made by the collecting agent from the manufactured overseas dividend on account of income tax similar to the deduction that would, in the case of the overseas dividend of which the manufactured overseas dividend is representative, have been made under Chapter VIIA of Part IV of the Taxes Act; and

(b)   the provisions of that Chapter relating to collecting agents shall apply in relation to amounts falling to be deducted under sub-paragraph (a) as if references in that Chapter to relevant dividends, or the proceeds of sale or other realisation of coupons for relevant dividends, included references to manufactured overseas dividends to which this regulation applies or, as the case may be, the proceeds of sale or other realisation of manufactured overseas dividends to which this regulation applies.

12(3)   [Omitted by SI 1997/2706, reg. 2(b), operative from 9 December 1997].

History – Reg. 12(1) substituted by SI 1996/2643, reg. 12(a), operative from 6 November 1996.
In reg. 12(2)(a), words "subject to paragraph (3)" inserted, and former words "approved United Kingdom" which appeared before "collecting agent" omitted, by SI 1996/2643, reg. 12(b), operative from 6 November 1996.
Reg. 12(2) amended by SI 1996/1229, reg. 7(b), operative from 28 May 1996, by substituting, in reg. 12(2)(a), reference to ICTA 1988, Pt. IV, Ch. VIIA, and by substituting reg. 12(2)(b).
In reg. 12(2)(a), words at beginning "Subject to paragraph (3)" omitted by SI 1997/2706, reg. 2(a), operative from 9 December 1997.
Reg. 12(3) omitted by SI 1997/2706, reg. 2(b), operative from 9 December 1997.

FURTHER PROVISION RELATING TO MANUFACTURED OVERSEAS DIVIDENDS REPRESENTATIVE OF FOREIGN DIVIDENDS

13   [Omitted by SI 1996/2643, reg. 13, operative from 6 November 1996.]

RECORDS TO BE KEPT IN RESPECT OF CERTAIN MANUFACTURED OVERSEAS DIVIDENDS PAID WITHOUT DEDUCTION OF TAX

14(1)   An overseas dividend manufacturer or an approved United Kingdom collecting agent shall maintain a record in respect of any manufactured overseas dividend paid by him to which this regulation applies showing–

(a)   the date of payment and the amount of the manufactured overseas dividend,

(b)   the name of the person to whom payment was made,

(ba)   his grounds for believing that the payment should be made without deduction of tax, and

(c)   particulars of the overseas securities and the overseas dividend on those securities to which the manufactured overseas dividend relates.

14(2)   This regulation applies to any manufactured overseas dividend which an overseas dividend manufacturer or an approved United Kingdom collecting agent, by virtue of regulation 5(1B), pays without deduction of tax.

14(3)   An overseas dividend manufacturer or an approved United Kingdom collecting agent–

(a)   shall retain for a period of six years–

　　(i)   any record required to be maintained by him under paragraph (1), and

　　(ii)   any evidence relevant to his grounds for believing that the payment should be made without deduction of tax; and

(b)   whenever required to do so within that period, shall make any such record or evidence available for inspection by an officer of the Board.

14(3A)   In the case of evidence or a record retained under paragraph (3) which is in electronic form the person retaining it shall afford an officer of the Board such assistance and facilities as the officer may reasonably require in order to read the record or certificate.

14(4)   Where an overseas dividend manufacturer or an approved United Kingdom collecting agent fails to maintain, or to retain for the requisite period, any such record, or fails to retain any such evidence for the requisite period, the Board may require that person to carry out, at his own expense, an audit of manufactured overseas dividends paid by him in order to ascertain the amount of tax, if any, liable to be deducted under paragraph 4(2) of Schedule 23A which was not deducted.

14(5)   The scope and method of the audit referred to in paragraph (4) shall be agreed between the Board and the person concerned or, in the absence of agreement, shall be determined by the Board.

History – Reg. 14(1)(b) and (ba) substituted for reg. 14(1)(b) by SI 2003/2582, reg. 12(2) with effect from 1 November 2003. Reg. 14(1)(b) previously read as follows:

> "(b)   the name of the person beneficially entitled to the payment, and the territory in which he was resident at the date of payment, and".

Reg. 14(2) and (3) substituted for reg. 14(1)(b) by SI 2003/2582, reg. 12(3) with effect from 1 November 2003. Reg. 14(2) and (3) previously read as follows:

> "**14(2)**   This regulation applies to any manufactured overseas dividend in respect of which arrangements have been entered into with the Board by an overseas dividend manufacturer or an approved United Kingdom collecting agent under the Double Taxation Relief Regulations enabling him to make the payment without deduction of tax.
>
> **14(3)**   An overseas dividend manufacturer or an approved United Kingdom collecting agent shall retain for a period of six years–
> (a)   any record required to be maintained by him under paragraph (1), and
> (b)   any certificate under the Double Taxation Relief Regulations received by him,
>
> and, whenever required to do so within that period, shall make any such record or certificate available for inspection by an officer of the Board.".

Reg. 14(3A) inserted by SI 2003/3143, reg. 5(4) with effect from 1 January 2004.

In reg. 14(4) word "evidence " substituted for "certificate" by SI 2003/2582, reg. 12(4) with effect from 1 November 2003.

ISSUE OF VOUCHERS IN RESPECT OF MANUFACTURED OVERSEAS DIVIDENDS PAID UNDER DEDUCTION OF TAX

15(1)   Subject to paragraph (3), where an overseas dividend manufacturer makes a payment of a manufactured overseas dividend from which an amount is deducted by him under paragraph 4(2) of Schedule 23A, he shall furnish the recipient of the payment with a voucher showing the details specified in paragraph (4).

15(2)   [Omitted by SI 2011/2503, reg. 8(3).]

15(3)   Where the overseas dividend manufacturer is an approved United Kingdom intermediary, he shall not be required to furnish the recipient of a payment with the voucher referred to in paragraph (1) unless the recipient requests such a voucher.

15(4)   The details specified in this paragraph are that the voucher shall show–

(a)   the gross amount of the payment,

(b)   the amount deducted or, where more than one amount has been deducted, each such amount separately, and

(c)   the actual amount paid.

15(5)   An approved United Kingdom collecting agent, where requested to do so by the person beneficially entitled to a manufactured overseas dividend in respect of which tax has been paid or is due to be paid by the approved United Kingdom collecting agent under paragraph 4(3) of Schedule 23A or regulation 4(3), shall furnish that person with a voucher showing–

(a)   the gross amount of the manufactured overseas dividend received by him,

(b)   the amount of tax paid or due to be paid by him in respect of the manufactured overseas dividend, and

(c)   the actual amount paid.

History – In reg. 15(1), the words "paragraph (3)" substituted for the words "paragraphs (2) and (3)" by SI 2011/2503, reg. 8(2), with effect in relation to manufactured overseas dividends paid or treated as paid on or after 10 November 2011.

In reg. 15(1), references to amounts deducted under reg. 13(2)(a) omitted by SI 1996/2643, reg. 14, operative from 6 November 1996.

Reg. 15(2) omitted by SI 2011/2503, reg. 8(3), with effect in relation to manufactured overseas dividends paid or treated as paid on or after 10 November 2011. Former reg. 15(2) read as follows:

> "**15(2)**   Paragraph (1) shall not apply in any case where, pursuant to paragraph (2), (3)(c) or (4)(c) of regulation 10, a voucher is forwarded to the recipient of a manufactured overseas dividend.".

In former reg. 15(2), references to amounts deducted under reg. 13(2)(a) omitted by SI 1996/2643, reg. 14, operative from 6 November 1996.

MODIFICATIONS OF SECTION 21 OF THE MANAGEMENT ACT IN RELATION TO OVERSEAS DIVIDEND MANUFACTURERS

16   [Omitted by SI 1997/987, reg. 8(4), (5).]

History – Reg. 16 omitted by SI 1997/987, reg. 8(4), (5) with effect in relation to transactions entered into on or after 1 July 1997 in respect of which information may be obtained under TMA 1970, s. 21 and with effect to payments made on or after that date (whether under transactions entered into before or on or after that date) in respect of which information may be obtained under that section.

EXCHANGE GAINS AND LOSSES (TRANSITIONAL PROVISIONS) REGULATIONS 1994

(SI 1994/3226 as amended by SI 1995/408, SI 1996/1349, SI 2000/3315 and SI 2002/1969)

Made on 15 December 1994 by the Treasury, in exercise of the powers conferred on them by s. 164(14), 165(4) and (5) and 167(1) and (4) to (6) of, and Sch. 16 to, the Finance Act 1993. Operative from 23 March 1995.

ARRANGEMENT OF REGULATIONS

PART I – INTRODUCTORY PROVISIONS

CITATION, COMMENCEMENT AND INTERPRETATION

1(1) These Regulations may be cited as the Exchange Gains and Losses (Transitional Provisions) Regulations 1994.

1(2) These Regulations shall come into force on 23rd March 1995.

1(3) In these Regulations, subject to any contrary intention–

(a)   **"the 1992 Act"** means the Taxation of Chargeable Gains Act 1992;

Statutory Instruments

(b)   **"the 1993 Act"** means the Finance Act 1993;

(ba)   **"discounted debt"** has the same meaning as **"relevant discounted security"** as that term is defined for the purposes of Schedule 13 to the Finance Act 1996 by paragraphs 3 and 14(1) of that Schedule;

(c)   any reference to **Chapter II** is a reference to Chapter II of Part II of the 1993 Act;

(d)   any reference to a particular **section** is a reference to that section of that Act;

(e)   any reference to **an exchange gain or loss** is a reference to an exchange gain or loss of a trade or part of a trade or a non-trading exchange gain or loss;

(f)   any reference to **an exchange difference** is a reference to any gain or loss which is attributable to fluctuations in currency exchange rates;

(g)   **"a regulation 6(3) asset"** means an existing asset the basic valuation of which was determined for the purposes of Chapter II in accordance with regulation 6(3) of these Regulations;

(h)   **"the regulation 2(2) provisions"** means the provisions specified in regulation 2(2); and

(i)   **"the relevant accounting period"**, in relation to a company, means the company's first accounting period to begin on or after 1st October 2002.

1(4)   In determining for the purposes of these Regulations whether any gain or loss or other amount has or has not been taken into account for the purposes of corporation tax in computing a company's profits and gains (or the profits and gains of a trade) for an accounting period, or would have been or would not have been so taken into account if the company had been within the charge to corporation tax at the time the gain or loss accrued, there shall be disregarded, subject to any contrary intention, any insufficiency of profits or gains for that period.

1(5)   In computing the chargeable profits for an accounting period of a controlled foreign company as respects which–

(a)   a direction under section 747 of the Income and Corporation Taxes Act 1988 has been given for the company's accounting period which includes the day preceding the day on which these Regulations come into force, or

(b)   it can reasonably be assumed that such a direction would have been given for that accounting period but for the fact that the company pursues, within the meaning of Part I of Schedule 25 to that Act, an acceptable distribution policy,

it shall be assumed for the purposes of these Regulations (if it would not otherwise be so assumed) that the company is resident in the United Kingdom for the period as respects which the computation is being made for any other period (whether earlier or later than the period referred to in paragraph (a) or (b) above), and any gain or loss or other amount which is, or has been, taken into account in computing the company's chargeable profits for any period (or which would have been so taken into account if such a computation had been made) shall be treated for those purposes as being, or having been, taken into account for the purposes of corporation tax in computing the company's profits and gains for that period.

History – Reg. 1(3)(ba) inserted by SI 1996/1349, reg. 3, operative from 30 June 1996.
Reg. 1(3)(g) substituted by SI 2002/1969, reg. 3(a), with effect in relation to accounting periods beginning on or after 1 October 2002.
Reg. 1(3)(i) and the word "and" preceding it inserted by SI 2002/1969, reg. 3(b), with effect in relation to accounting periods beginning on or after 1 October 2002.

Cross references – SI 2002/1969, reg. 3: saving, subject to modifications, of reg. 1 in respect of the change of tax treatment of exchange gains and losses by FA 2002.

INTERACTION WITH OTHER EXCHANGE GAINS AND LOSSES PROVISIONS

2(1)   Subject to any provision to the contrary, in any case where a calculation falls to be made in relation to an existing asset, liability or contract in accordance with any of these Regulations and at the same time or in relation to the same event a calculation also falls to be made in relation to that asset, liability or contract in accordance with any of the provisions specified in paragraph (2) below, then the calculation to be made in accordance with these Regulations shall be made first and shall have effect for the purposes of the calculation falling to be made in accordance with any of those provisions.

2(2)   The provisions referred to above are the following–

The Exchange Gains and Losses (Alternative Method of Calculation of Gain or Loss) Regulations 1994;

History – In reg. 2(2) words "Sections 136, 137 and 139 to 141 of the 1993 Act;", and "The Exchange Gains and Losses (Deferral of Gains and Losses) Regulations 1994.", omitted by SI 2002/1969, reg. 4, with effect in relation to accounting periods beginning on or after 1 October 2002.

Cross references – SI 2002/1969, reg. 4: saving, subject to modifications, of reg. 2 in respect of the change of tax treatment of exchange gains and losses by FA 2002.

PART II – MISCELLANEOUS TRANSITIONAL PROVISIONS

DELAYED APPLICATION OF CHAPTER II IN RELATION TO CERTAIN FLUCTUATING DEBTS

3 [Omitted by SI 2002/1969, reg. 5.]

History – Reg. 3 omitted by SI 2002/1969, reg. 5, with effect in relation to accounting periods beginning on or after 1 October 2002.

Cross references – SI 2002/1969, reg. 5: omission of reg. 3 in respect of the change of tax treatment of exchange gains and losses by FA 2002.

BAD DEBTS

4 [Omitted by SI 2002/1969, reg. 5.]

History – Reg. 4 omitted by SI 2002/1969, reg. 5, with effect in relation to accounting periods beginning on or after 1 October 2002.

Cross references – SI 2002/1969, reg. 5: omission of reg. 4 in respect of the change of tax treatment of exchange gains and losses by FA 2002.

EXCHANGE RATE AT TRANSLATION TIMES

5 [Omitted by SI 2002/1969, reg. 5.]

History – Reg. 5 omitted by SI 2002/1969, reg. 5, with effect in relation to accounting periods beginning on or after 1 October 2002.

Cross references – SI 2002/1969, reg. 5: omission of reg. 5 in respect of the change of tax treatment of exchange gains and losses by FA 2002.

BASIC VALUATION

6 [Omitted by SI 2002/1969, reg. 5.]

History – Reg. 6 omitted by SI 2002/1969, reg. 5, with effect in relation to accounting periods beginning on or after 1 October 2002.

Previously in reg. 6(2)(a), words "30th September 1995" substituted, and in reg. 6(2)(b) words ", subject to paragraph (2A) below," inserted, and reg. 6(2A) inserted by SI 1996/1349, reg. 4, operative from 30 June 1996.

Cross references – SI 2002/1969, reg. 5: omission of reg. 6 in respect of the change of tax treatment of exchange gains and losses by FA 2002.

HMRC interpretations – IRInt. 109: "grandfathering" and other elections may be made on behalf of a CFC by a UK resident company which alone or jointly with other UK resident companies has a majority interest in the CFC, on the specific authority of the secretary or director of the CFC.

IRInt. 131: basic valuation of a deep discount or qualifying indexed security held by a company at its commencement day.

PART III – PRE-COMMENCEMENT GAINS AND LOSSES: CASE I ASSETS AND LIABILITIES AND CAPITAL ASSETS

INTERPRETATION

7(1) For the purposes of any computation required to be made for the purposes of regulation 10 or 11 below, an amount which is a gain shall be taken to be a positive figure and an amount which is a loss shall be taken to be a negative figure, but for the purposes of regulations 12 and 13 all amounts shall be taken to be positive.

7(2) In this Part–

"**attributed gain**", in relation to any asset or liability, means a gain which is attributed to the asset or liability under regulation 8(3) or 9(2) below;

"**attributed loss**", in relation to any asset or liability, means a loss which is attributed to the asset or liability under regulation 8(3) or 9(2) below;

"**current period**" has the meaning given by regulation 10 below;

"**the cumulative gain**" has the meaning given by regulation 10 below;

"**the cumulative loss**" has the meaning given by regulation 10 below;

"**the cumulative taxed gain**" has the meaning given by regulation 11 below;

"**the cumulative taxed loss**" has the meaning given by regulation 11 below;

"the final accounting period", in relation to a company, means the company's accounting period preceding the relevant accounting period;

History – In reg. 7(2) definition of "the final accounting period" inserted, and the words "and any reference to **exempt circumstances** shall be construed as if it were contained in paragraph 2 of Schedule 15 to the 1993 Act." omitted by SI 2002/1969, reg. 6, in relation to accounting periods beginning on or after 1 October 2002.

Cross references – SI 2002/1969, reg. 6: saving, subject to modifications, of reg. 7 in respect of the change of tax treatment of exchange gains and losses by FA 2002.

ATTRIBUTED GAINS AND LOSSES: TRADE ASSETS AND LIABILITIES

8(1) Paragraph (3) below applies in relation to an existing asset held by a qualifying company–

(a) if a profit or loss would have accrued to the company if it had disposed of the asset immediately before the company's commencement day for a consideration equal to the asset's basic valuation; and

(b) that profit or loss would have been taken into account in computing for the purposes of corporation tax the profits and gains of a trade carried on by the company for the accounting period which includes the day immediately before the company's commencement day.

8(2) Paragraph (3) below applies in relation to an existing liability owed by a qualifying company–

(a) if a profit or loss would have accrued to the company–

(i) in a case falling within section 153(2)(a), if the liability had been satisfied in full by the company immediately before the company's commencement day, or

(ii) in a case falling within section 153(2)(c) or (d), if the right to settlement or the share or shares in question (as the case may be) had been acquired by the company immediately before the company's commencement day for a consideration equal to the consideration for the company becoming subject to the liability, and

(b) that profit or loss (if it had accrued) would have been taken into account in computing for the purposes of corporation tax the profits and gains of a trade carried on by the company for the accounting period ending immediately before the company's commencement day.

8(3) The amount of any such profit or loss as is mentioned in paragraph (1) or (2) above reduced in accordance with paragraph (4) below if applicable, shall be attributed to the asset or liability (as the case may be) and–

(a) in the case of a profit shall be attributed as a gain, and

(b) in the case of a loss shall be attributed as a loss.

8(4) In any case where unrealised exchange differences which have accrued in respect of the asset or liability are taken into account for the purposes of corporation tax for the accounting period ending immediately before the company's commencement day or any earlier accounting period, the amount of the profit or loss referred to in paragraph (3) above shall be reduced by an amount equal to the amount of those differences.

8(5) Section 159 applies for the purposes of this regulation as modified by regulation 6 of these regulations.

History – In reg. 8(5) words "of these regulations", substituted for "above" by SI 2002/1969, reg. 7 with effect in relation to accounting periods beginning on or after 1 October 2002.

Cross references – SI 2002/1969, reg. 7: saving, subject to modifications, of reg. 8 in respect of the change of tax treatment of exchange gains and losses by FA 2002.

ATTRIBUTED GAINS AND LOSSES: REGULATION 6(3) ASSETS

9(1) This regulation applies in relation to any regulation 6(3) asset held by a qualifying company a disposal of which by that company immediately before its commencement day at the asset's market value at that time would have given rise to a chargeable gain or allowable loss, but does not apply in any case where any such disposal of the asset by the company would fall within section 116(10)(b) of the 1992 Act.

9(2) Subject to paragraph (3) below, an amount equal to any chargeable gain or allowable loss (as the case may be) which would have accrued to the company had it disposed of the asset as mentioned in paragraph (1) above shall be attributed to the asset and–

(a) if a chargeable gain would have accrued, it shall be attributed as a gain, and

(b) if an allowable loss would have accrued, it shall be attributed as a loss.

9(3) In any case where–

(a) the asset was held by a company which at any time before its commencement day was not resident in the United Kingdom, and

(b)   if the asset had been disposed of at that time and a gain had accrued to the company on that disposal, it would not have been included in the company's chargeable profits by virtue of section 10(3) of the 1992 Act,

then for the purposes of paragraph (1) above the company shall be deemed to have acquired the asset, at market value, on the first day on which any gain which would have accrued to the company if the asset had been disposed of on that day (assuming that the disposal gave rise to a gain and disregarding any allowable losses which might be available for deduction under section 8(1) of, or Schedule 7A to, the 1992 Act) would have been included in the company's chargeable profits for the purposes of corporation tax (whether because the company became resident or the asset became situated in the United Kingdom on that day or for any other reason).

9(4)   In any case where the company referred to in paragraph (1) above acquired the asset on a no gain/no loss disposal, then the reference in paragraph (3) above to a company includes the company from which it acquired the asset, and if that company also acquired the asset on such a disposal, to the company from which it acquired the asset, and so on for a series of such disposals.

9(5)   The disposal referred to in paragraph (1) above shall be taken not to be a no gain/no loss disposal, and for the purposes of this regulation a disposal is a no gain/no loss disposal if, by virtue of any enactment specified in section 35(3)(d) of the 1992 Act, neither a gain nor a loss accrues to the person making the disposal.

9(6)   In any case where section 176 of the 1992 Act would have applied in relation to the disposal referred to in paragraph (1) above if that disposal had actually taken place, that section shall apply for the calculation of any allowable loss for the purposes of that paragraph.

9(7)   Any expression used in this regulation which is not defined in Chapter II shall have the same meaning as in the 1992 Act.

THE CUMULATIVE GAIN AND THE CUMULATIVE LOSS

10(1)   Subject to regulation 15, in the case of any existing asset or liability held or owed by a company as respects which an initial exchange gain or loss accrues to the company for an accrual period (**"the current period"**), there shall be calculated the aggregate amount of initial exchange gains and losses which have accrued as respects the asset or liability in question for all earlier accrual periods and for the current period, and that aggregate amount–

(a)   if positive, shall be the cumulative gain for that asset or liability for the current period, and

(b)   if negative, shall be the cumulative loss for that asset or liability for the current period,

but in cases where that aggregate amount is zero there shall be either a cumulative gain or a cumulative loss equal to zero for the period, according to whether there was a cumulative gain or a cumulative loss of any amount (including zero) for the accrual period immediately preceding the current period.

10(2)   For the purposes of paragraph (1) above, the amount of any initial exchange gain or loss shall be determined disregarding the following provisions of this Part and the regulation 2(2) provisions.

10(3)   Where–

(a)   the asset held or the liability owed by the company consists of a discounted debt, and

(b)   the company did not cease on 31st March 1996 to be entitled to the asset or (as the case may be) subject to the liability,

it shall be regarded, for the purposes of paragraph (1) above and section 158 (translation times and accrual periods), as ceasing on that date to be so entitled or subject, and references in this regulation and in regulations 11 and 12 to accrual periods (including references to an accrual period as the current period) shall, as respects that asset or liability, be construed accordingly.

History – Reg. 10(3) added by SI 1996/1349, reg. 5, operative from 30 June 1996.

THE CUMULATIVE TAXED GAIN AND THE CUMULATIVE TAXED LOSS

11(1)   In the case of any asset or liability to which regulation 10 applies, there shall be calculated the aggregate amount of the initial exchange gains and losses which have accrued to the company as respects the asset or liability for accrual periods earlier than the current period, and–

(a)   if that aggregate amount is positive it shall be the cumulative taxed gain for that asset or liability for the current period,

(b)   if it is negative it shall be the cumulative taxed loss for that asset or liability for the current period, and

(c)   if that aggregate amount is zero or, by virtue of regulation 12, there is no aggregate amount, there shall be taken to be a cumulative taxed loss equal to zero for the period.

11(2) For the purposes of paragraph (1) above–

(a)   the question whether any initial exchange gain or loss has accrued for any period other than the current period shall be determined in accordance with this Part but as if the regulation 2(2) provisions had never come into force; and

(b)   there shall be disregarded any gain or loss which accrued for an accrual period other than the current period unless–

    (i)   it has been taken into account in computing the profits or gains of the company holding or owing the asset or liability for the purposes of corporation tax for accounting periods ending before the beginning of the current period, or

    (ii)   it would have been so taken into account if the regulation 2(2) provisions had never come into force; or

    (iii)   it is equal to zero.

ASSETS AND LIABILITIES AS RESPECTS WHICH THERE IS AN ATTRIBUTED GAIN OR LOSS

12(1) Subject to regulation 15, in relation to an asset or liability held or owed by a company as respects which–

(a)   there is an attributed gain, E, or an attributed loss, F, and

(b)   an initial exchange gain or loss (**"the actual gain or loss"**) accrues to the company for the current period,

Table A or Table B below (as appropriate) shall apply and in any case falling within the first column of that Table, the actual gain or loss shall be deemed not to accrue but, subject to any conditions specified in the second column, the gain or loss specified in relation thereto in the third column shall be deemed to accrue and shall be an initial exchange gain or loss (as the case may be) accruing in the place of the actual gain or loss.

12(2) For the purposes of paragraph (1)(b) above, the question whether any initial exchange gain or loss has accrued shall be determined disregarding this Part and the regulation 2(2) provisions.

TABLE A

If there is an attributed gain E

Case for the current period	Condition		Deemed gain or loss	
1. Cumulative loss B and no cumulative taxed gain or loss	B is greater than E		Loss equal to B−E	
2. Cumulative loss B and a cumulative taxed loss C	(i)	B is not greater than E and C is greater than zero	(i)	Gain equal to C
	(ii)	B is greater than E and C is less than (B−E)	(ii)	Loss equal to (B−E)−C
	(iii)	B is greater than E and C is greater than (B−E)	(iii)	Gain equal to C−(B−E)
3. Cumulative loss B and a cumulative taxed gain D	(i)	B is greater than E	(i)	Loss equal to (B−E)+D
	(ii)	B is not greater than E	(ii)	Loss equal to D
4. Cumulative gain A and a cumulative taxed gain D	(i)	A is greater than D	(i)	Gain equal to A−D
	(ii)	D is greater than A	(ii)	Loss equal to D−A
5. Cumulative gain A and a cumulative taxed loss C			Gain equal to C+A	

TABLE B

If there is an attributed loss F

Case for the current period	Condition		Deemed gain or loss	
1. Cumulative gain A and no cumulative taxed gain or loss	A is greater than F		Gain equal to A−F	
2. Cumulative gain A and a cumulative taxed gain D	(i)	A is not greater than F	(i)	Loss equal to D
	(ii)	A is greater than F and D is less than (A−F)	(ii)	Gain equal to (A−F)−D
	(iii)	A is greater than F and D is greater than (A−F)	(iii)	Loss equal to D−(A−F)
3. Cumulative loss A and a cumulative taxed loss C	(i)	A is greater than F	(i)	Gain equal to (A−F)+C
	(ii)	A is not greater than F and C is greater than zero	(ii)	Gain equal to C
4. Cumulative loss B and a cumulative taxed loss C	(i)	B is greater than C	(i)	Loss equal to B−C
	(ii)	C is greater than B	(ii)	Gain equal to C−B
5. Cumulative loss B and a cumulative taxed gain D	Loss equal to B+D			

GAINS AND LOSSES ON DISPOSAL OF ASSETS AND LIABILITIES

13(1)   Subject to regulations 14 and 14A, paragraph (2) or (3) below applies where–

(a)   an accrual period ends as respects an existing asset or liability held or owed by a company which is the last accrual period as respects that asset or liability, and

(b)   there is as respects the asset or liability an attributed gain or loss.

13(1A)   For the purposes of paragraph (1)(a) above, the final accounting period shall be treated as the last accrual period as respects any asset or liability held or owed by the company immediately after the end of the final accounting period.

13(2)   If there is an attributed gain, E, as respects the asset or liability, then–

(a)   if there is a cumulative gain, A, as respects the asset or liability for the last period, an amount equal to E shall be deemed to be a relevant gain, accruing to the company as respects that asset or liability immediately after the end of the final accounting period;

(b)   if there is a cumulative loss, B, as respects the asset or liability for the last period, and E exceeds B, an amount equal to the excess shall be deemed to be a relevant gain, accruing to the company as respects that asset or liability immediately after the end of the final accounting period; and

(c)   if there is neither a cumulative loss nor a cumulative gain as respects the asset or liability for the last period, an amount equal to E shall be deemed to be a relevant gain, accruing to the company as respects that asset or liability immediately after the end of the final accounting period.

13(3)   If there is an attributed loss, F, as respects the asset or liability, then–

(a)   if there is a cumulative loss, B, as respects the asset or liability for the last period, an amount equal to F shall be deemed to be a relevant loss, accruing to the company as respects that asset or liability immediately after the end of the final accounting period;

(b)   if there is a cumulative gain, A, as respects the asset or liability for the last period, and F exceeds A, an amount equal to the excess shall be deemed to be a relevant loss, accruing to the company as respects that asset or liability immediately after the end of the final accounting period; and

(c)   if there is neither a cumulative loss nor a cumulative gain as respects the asset or liability for the last period, an amount equal to F shall be deemed to be a relevant loss, accruing to the company as respects that asset or liability immediately after the end of the final accounting period.

13(4) In paragraphs (2) and (3) above, a relevant gain or loss in relation to a regulation 6(3) asset is a chargeable gain or an allowable loss.

13(4A) In relation to any asset other than a regulation 6(3) asset or any liability, an amount equal to the amount of any relevant gain or loss that is deemed to accrue to the company under paragraph (2) or (3) above shall be treated for the purposes of Chapter 2 of Part 4 of the Finance Act 1996 (according to whether it is a relevant gain or loss)–

(a)   as a credit in respect of a loan relationship of the company, or

(b)   as a debit in respect of a loan relationship of the company,

which falls to be brought into account under section 82(2) of that Act.

13(5) [Omitted by SI 2002/1969, reg. 8(6).]

13(6) [Omitted by SI 2002/1969, reg. 8(6).]

13(7) [Omitted by SI 2002/1969, reg. 8(6).]

13(8) [Omitted by SI 2002/1969, reg. 8(6).]

History – In reg. 13(1) "14 and 14A" substituted for "14(1) and 15(1)", by SI 2002/1969, reg. 8(2), with effect in relation to accounting periods beginning on or after 1 October 2002.

Reg. 13(1A) inserted by SI 2002/1969, reg. 8(3), with effect in relation to accounting periods beginning on or after 1 October 2002.

In reg. 13(2)(a), (b), (c) and reg. 13(3)(a), (b), (c) words "after the end of the final accounting period" substituted for "before the end of the last accrual period" by SI 2002/1969, reg. 8(4), with effect in relation to accounting periods beginning on or after 1 October 2002.

Reg. 13(4) substituted and reg. 13(4A) inserted by SI 2002/1969, reg. 8(5), with effect in relation to accounting periods beginning on or after 1 October 2002.

Cross references – SI 2002/1969, reg. 8: saving, subject to modifications, of reg. 13 in respect of the change of tax treatment of exchange gains and losses by FA 2002.

ELECTIONS TO DEFER BRINGING INTO ACCOUNT RELEVANT GAINS AND LOSSES DEEMED TO ACCRUE IMMEDIATELY AFTER THE END OF THE FINAL ACCOUNTING PERIOD

14(1) In any case where, apart from this regulation, relevant gains or losses would accrue to a company immediately after the end of the final accounting period by virtue of regulation 13, the company may elect, by notice to the inspector within two years of the end of the final accounting period, that this regulation shall apply as respects–

(a)   subject to paragraph (3) below, all relevant gains or losses to which paragraph (4) of regulation 13 would apply;

(b)   all relevant gains or losses to which paragraph (4A) of that regulation would apply; or

(c)   both.

An election under this paragraph shall be irrevocable.

14(2) Where an election is made under paragraph (1) above, every gain or loss to which this regulation applies shall be treated as accruing only when the asset or liability to which the gain or loss relates ceases to be held or owed by the company.

14(3) No election may be made under paragraph (1) above as respects relevant gains or losses to which regulation 13(4) would apply if an election under regulation 14A is made as regards such losses.

History – Reg. 14 substituted by SI 2002/1969, reg. 9, with effect in relation to accounting periods beginning on or after 1 October 2002.

Cross references – SI 2002/1969, reg. 9: saving, subject to modifications, of reg. 14 in respect of the change of tax treatment of exchange gains and losses by FA 2002.

ELECTIONS TO TREAT LOSSES DEEMED TO ACCRUE IMMEDIATELY AFTER THE END OF THE FINAL ACCOUNTING PERIOD AS DEBITS IN RESPECT OF LOAN RELATIONSHIPS

14A(1) In any case where–

(a)   apart from this regulation, relevant losses would accrue to a company as respects regulation 6(3) assets immediately after the end of the final accounting period by virtue of regulation 13; and

(b)   if relevant gains would accrue as respects such assets at that time by virtue of that regulation, such losses would exceed them,

the company may elect, by notice to the inspector within two years of the end of the final accounting period, that this regulation shall apply as respects such losses or, in a case where sub-paragraph (b) applies, such losses to the extent that they exceed the relevant gains.

An election under this paragraph shall be irrevocable.

14A(2) Where an election is made under paragraph (1) above, an amount equal to the amount of the losses to which this regulation applies shall be treated for the purposes of Chapter 2 of Part 4 of the Finance Act 1996 as a debit in respect of a loan relationship of the company for the new accounting period and not falling to be brought into account under section 82(2) of that Act.

History – Reg. 14A inserted by SI 2002/1969, reg. 9, with effect in relation to accounting periods beginning on or after 1 October 2002.

TREATMENT OF LOSSES AVAILABLE TO BE CARRIED FORWARD AT THE END OF THE FINAL ACCOUNTING PERIOD AS A RESULT OF AN ELECTION MADE UNDER REGULATION 14(5) OR 16(1)

14B(1) This regulation applies where, as a result of an election made under regulation 14(5) or 16(1) of these Regulations, an amount of available losses ("the relevant amount") was available at the end of the final accounting period to be carried forward and, apart from this regulation, to be set against a company's exchange gains.

14B(2) Where this regulation applies an amount equal to the relevant amount shall be treated for the purposes of Chapter 2 of Part 4 of the Finance Act 1996 as a debit in respect of a loan relationship of the company for the new accounting period and not falling to be brought into account under section 82(2) of that Act.

History – Reg. 14B inserted by SI 2002/1969, reg. 9, with effect in relation to accounting periods beginning on or after 1 October 2002.

ELECTIONS TO TREAT PRE-COMMENCEMENT DAY GAINS AND LOSSES AS ACCRUING AFTER COMMENCEMENT DAY OVER 6 YEAR PERIOD

15 [Omitted by SI 2002/1969, reg. 10.]

History – Reg. 15 omitted by SI 2002/1969, reg. 10, with effect in relation to accounting periods beginning on or after 1 October 2002.
In reg. 15(1), words "30th September 1996" and "paragraphs (6) and (7)" substituted, in reg. 15(1)(a) words "day, and subject to paragraph (1A) below," substituted, and reg. 15(1A) and (7) added, by SI 1996/1349, reg. 8, operative from 30 June 1996.
Cross references – SI 2002/1969, reg. 10: omission of reg. 15 in respect of the change of tax treatment of exchange gains and losses by FA 2002.
HMRC interpretations – IRInt. 109: "grandfathering" and other elections may be made on behalf of a CFC by a UK resident company which alone or jointly with other UK resident companies has a majority interest in the CFC, on the specific authority of the secretary or director of the CFC.

SET OFF OF CERTAIN PRE-COMMENCEMENT LOSSES AGAINST EXCHANGE GAINS

16 [Omitted by SI 2002/1969, reg. 10.]

History – Reg. 16 omitted by SI 2002/1969, reg. 10, with effect in relation to accounting periods beginning on or after 1 October 2002.
Cross references – SI 2002/1969, reg. 10: omission of reg. 16 in respect of the change of tax treatment of exchange gains and losses by FA 2002.

PART IV – PRE-COMMENCEMENT GAINS AND LOSSES: DEBTS OF FIXED AMOUNTS

[Part 4 omitted by SI 2002/1969, reg. 11, with effect in relation to accounting periods beginning on or after 1 October 2002.]

EXCHANGE GAINS AND LOSSES (ALTERNATIVE METHOD OF CALCULATION OF GAIN OR LOSS) REGULATIONS 1994

(SI 1994/3227 as amended by SI 1996/1347, SI 2000/3315, SI 2001/3629 and SI 2002/1969)

Made on 15 December 1994 by the Treasury, in exercise of the powers conferred on them by s. 164(14), 167(1) and (4) to (6) of, and Sch. 15 to, the Finance Act 1993. Operative from 23 March 1995.

ARRANGEMENT OF REGULATIONS

GENERAL

CITATION, COMMENCEMENT AND INTERPRETATION

1(1) These Regulations may be cited as the Exchange Gains and Losses (Alternative Method of Calculation of Gain or Loss) Regulations 1994.

1(2) These Regulations shall come into force on 23rd March 1995.

1(3) In these Regulations **"the 1993 Act"** means the Finance Act 1993.

ASSETS ETC. HELD IN EXEMPT CIRCUMSTANCES

REDUCTION IN EXCHANGE GAINS AND LOSSES

2 [Omitted by SI 2002/1969, reg. 13.]

History – Reg. 2 omitted by SI 2002/1969, reg. 13, with effect in relation to accounting periods beginning on or after 1 October 2002.

Previously in reg. 2(4) "long-term" substituted (twice) for "long term" by SI 2001/3629, art. 137 which came into force on 1 December 2001.

Cross references – SI 2002/1969, reg. 13: omission of reg. 2 in respect of the change of tax treatment of exchange gains and losses by FA 2002.

UNREMITTABLE INCOME

REDUCTION IN EXCHANGE GAINS AND LOSSES

3   [Omitted by SI 2002/1969, reg. 13.]

History – Reg. 3 omitted by SI 2002/1969, reg. 13, with effect in relation to accounting periods beginning on or after 1 October 2002.

Cross references – SI 2002/1969, reg. 13: omission of reg. 3 in respect of the change of tax treatment of exchange gains and losses by FA 2002.

MATCHING

INTERPRETATION

4(1)   This regulation has effect for the interpretation of regulations 5 to 11.

4(2)   In those regulations–

"**the Taxes Act**" means the Income and Corporation Taxes Act 1988;

"**the 1992 Act**" means the Taxation of Chargeable Gains Act 1992;

"**accounts**", in relation to a company, means the accounts of the company prepared in accordance with normal accountancy practice being either–

(i)   the annual accounts of the company prepared in accordance with Part VII of the Companies Act 1985, or

(ii)   if the company is not required to prepare such accounts, the accounts which it is required to keep under the law of its home State or, if it is not so required to keep accounts, such of its accounts as most closely correspond to accounts which it would have been required to prepare if the provisions of that Part applied to the company;

"**branch**" shall be construed in accordance with section 93(7) of the 1993 Act;

"**chargeable gain**" has the same meaning as it has for the purposes of the 1992 Act;

"**a liability**" means–

(a)   a liability falling within section 153(2)(a) of the 1993 Act, or

(b)   in relation to a currency contract held by a company, the duty of the company under that contract to pay in exchange for one currency an amount of a second currency;

and in relation to a currency contract references to initial exchange gains or losses shall be construed as references to initial exchange gains or losses accruing as regards the second currency.

"**qualifying asset**" shall be construed in accordance with subsection (1) of section 153 of the 1993 Act, read with subsections (3) and (4) of that section.

"**the relevant foreign currency**" has the meaning given by section 93(7) of the 1993 Act.

4(3)   For the purposes of this regulation and regulations 5 to 11, any reference to an asset being matched in part only shall include a reference to any asset matched in accordance with an election under regulation 10(2)(c).

4(4)   A liability is matched by an asset at any time only to the extent that the value of the liability at that time is matched by the value of the asset at that time and, subject to that, if the election concerned is made under regulation 10(2)(c) so that the asset is matched in part only, the liability shall be taken to be matched only to a corresponding extent.

4(5)   The value of a company's asset or liability at any time shall be taken to be the value attributed to the asset or liability as at that time by the company for the purposes of its accounts for the accounting period which includes that time (expressed in the currency in which those accounts are prepared).

4(6)   Any reference to the disposal of an asset and to the time of the disposal of an asset shall be construed as a reference to any event which is a disposal for the purposes of the 1992 Act and the time at which the disposal occurs for the purposes of that Act, and for the purposes of the foregoing, any reference to a disposal includes a part disposal.

History – In reg. 4(2), definition of "qualifying assets" added by SI 1996/1347, reg. 3, operative from 30 June 1996.
In reg. 4(2), definitions of "branch" and "the relevant foreign currency" added and the definition of "a local currency election" omitted by SI 2000/3315, reg. 7; with effect for company accounting periods beginning on or after 1 January 2000, where FA 2000, s. 105 and s. 106 apply.

GAINS AND LOSSES ACCRUING AS REGARDS MATCHED LIABILITIES TO BE
FOUND BY THE ALTERNATIVE METHOD OF CALCULATION

5(1) This regulation applies in any case where–

(a) a liability is owed by a company, and

(b) the liability is eligible to be matched with an asset on a day which falls within an accrual period for that liability, and

(c) an election made under regulation 10 is in effect for that day matching the liability (wholly or in part) with an eligible asset held by the company;

and in this regulation **"the current period"** means that accrual period.

5(2) In any case where this regulation applies, then, subject to paragraphs (3) and (3A) below–

(a) the amount of the initial exchange gain or initial exchange loss which, apart from this regulation, would accrue to the company for the current period as respects the liability shall be found in accordance with the alternative method of calculation, and

(b) the accrued amount for each day in that period during which the liability and asset are matched shall–

   (i) if the whole of the liability is matched, be reduced to nil, or

   (ii) if only a proportion of the liability is matched, be reduced by a corresponding proportion.

5(3) If in any case where this regulation applies–

(a) at any time during the current period there is a major change in the extent to which the liability is matched, and

(b) there is a significant change in the rate of exchange relevant to the computation of the accrued amounts during the current period, and

(c) that time is not (disregarding this regulation) a translation time as respects the liability,

then, subject to paragraph (3A) below, the initial exchange gain or loss as respects the liability for the current period shall be calculated, in accordance with paragraph (2) above, as if that time were a translation time (but not so as to create more than one accrual period) so that separate calculations are made for different parts of the period.

5(3A) If in a case where this regulation applies–

(a) only a proportion of a liability owed by the company is matched with an asset, not being an asset that is a ship or an aircraft, or

(b) another liability owed by the company is eligible to be matched with that asset at the time the election is made, but is not matched, and

(c) an exchange loss in relation to–

   (i) the whole of the liability referred to in sub-paragraph (a) or (b), or

   (ii) a proportion of that liability, being in the case of the liability referred to in sub-paragraph (a), a greater proportion than the proportion matched,

is shown in the company's accounts for the period which is or includes the current period, in the reserves,

the amount of the initial exchange loss as respects that liability for the current period, calculated in accordance with this regulation, shall be reduced by the amount by which the exchange loss shown in the reserves and relating to that liability exceeds the exchange loss relating to the proportion (if any) of the liability that was matched.

5(4) A liability (not being a duty under a currency contract) is eligible to be matched with an asset if–

(a) the liability does not represent either–

   (i) a duty to settle under a debt in respect of goods or services supplied to the company in the ordinary course of its trade, or

   (ii) accrued interest, and

(b) the nominal currency of the liability is such that borrowing in that currency could reasonably be expected to eliminate or substantially reduce the economic risk of holding the asset which is attributable to fluctuations in exchange rates.

Where the asset is matched in part only, references in this paragraph to the asset are to the part matched.

5(5) In the case of a liability which is a duty under a currency contract, the liability is eligible to be matched with an asset if the second currency to which it relates is such that the company could by entering into that contract reasonably expect to eliminate or substantially reduce the economic risk of holding the asset which is attributable to fluctuations in exchange rates.

Where the asset is matched in part only, references in this paragraph to the asset are to the part matched.

5(6) An asset held by a company which prepares its accounts as a whole in sterling is an eligible asset at any time if at that time–

(a)   it is shares in a company which is not resident in the United Kingdom, but this sub-paragraph only applies if at the time the election is made the company is an associated company of the company making the election; or

(b)   it is shares in a company which–

    (i)   is resident in the United Kingdom, and

    (ii)   is a company to which section 93 of the 1993 Act applies by virtue of its accounts as a whole being prepared in a currency other than sterling in accordance with normal accounting practice, and

    (iii)   is a **90 per cent subsidiary** (within the meaning of paragraph (7) below) of the company making the election; or

(c)   it is a debt on a security which under the terms of issue can be converted into or exchanged for shares falling within sub-paragraph (a) or (b) above and which is not a qualifying asset; or

(d)   it is the company's net investment in a branch through which the company carries on a business or part of a business and, by virtue of section 93 of the 1993 Act, the profits and losses of that business or that part are to be computed and expressed in a currency other than sterling; or

(e)   it is a ship or an aircraft.

5(6A) An asset held by a company which prepares its accounts as a whole in a currency other than sterling is an eligible asset at any time if at that time–

(a)   it is shares which–

    (i)   are denominated in a currency other than the relevant foreign currency for the company making the election, and

    (ii)   are in a company that is not resident in the United Kingdom and is, at the time the election is made, an associated company of the company making the election; or

(b)   it is shares in a company which–

    (i)   is resident in the United Kingdom, and

    (ii)   prepares its accounts as a whole either in sterling or in a currency other than sterling which is not the relevant foreign currency for the company making the election, and

    (iii)   is a 90 per cent subsidiary (within the meaning of paragraph (7) below) of the company making the election; or

(c)   it is a debt on a security which under the terms of issue can be converted into or exchanged for shares falling within sub-paragraph (a) or (b) above and which is not a qualifying asset; or

(d)   it is the company's net investment in a branch through which the company carries on a business or part of a business and, by virtue of section 93 of the 1993 Act, the profits and losses of that business or that part are to be computed and expressed in a currency other than the relevant foreign currency for the company; or

(e)   it is a ship or an aircraft.

5(7) For the purposes of paragraph (6) above–

(a)   **"shares"** includes stock but does not include any asset which is a qualifying asset,

(aa)   all shares in the same company shall constitute a single asset,

(ab)   all debts on a security issued by the same company shall constitute a single asset, and

(b)   a company is a 90 per cent subsidiary of another company if it is a 90 per cent subsidiary of that other within the meaning of section 838 of the Taxes Act or would be if "directly or indirectly" were substituted for "directly" in subsection (1)(c) of that section.

5(8) An asset held by a company is also an eligible asset at any time (whether or not it also falls within any provision of paragraph (6)) if at that time–

(a)   a gain accruing on the disposal of the asset by a person resident in the United Kingdom would be a chargeable gain, and

(b)   the asset is not a qualifying asset, and

(c)   the asset is held by a branch of the company outside the United Kingdom through which the company carries on a business or part of a business, and

    (i)   where the company prepares its accounts as a whole in sterling, the profits and losses of that business or that part are not to be computed and expressed in a currency other than sterling by virtue of section 93 of the 1993 Act, or

    (ii)   where the company prepares its accounts as a whole in a currency other than sterling, the profits and losses of that business or that part are not to be computed and expressed in a currency other than the relevant foreign currency for the company by virtue of that section.

5(9)   For the purposes of paragraphs (6), (6A) and (8) above–

(a)   a company is an associated company of another if that other directly controls 20 per cent or more of the voting power in the company;

(b)   the net investment of a company in a branch is the value of the assets of that branch less the liabilities of the branch and any other liabilities owed by the company for the purposes of the business or part business carried on through the branch.

History – Reg. 5(3A) and references to it in reg. 5(2), (3) inserted, in reg. 5(6)(c) the words "and which is not a qualifying asset" added, and reg. 5(7)(aa), (ab) inserted, by SI 1996/1347, reg. 4, with effect as respects accrual periods ending on or after 30 June 1996.

In reg. 5(6), the words "which prepares its accounts as a whole in sterling" inserted by SI 2000/3315, reg. 8(1)(a); with effect for company accounting periods beginning on or after 1 January 2000, where FA 2000, s. 105 and s. 106 apply.

Reg. 5(6)(b)(ii), substituted by SI 2000/3315, reg. 8(1)(b); with effect for company accounting periods beginning on or after 1 January 2000, where FA 2000, s. 105 and s. 106 apply.

Reg. 5(6)(d)(ii), substituted from "in a branch" to the end, by SI 2000/3315, reg. 8(1)(c); with effect for company accounting periods beginning on or after 1 January 2000, where FA 2000, s. 105 and s. 106 apply.

Reg. 5(6A), inserted by SI 2000/3315, reg. 8(2); with effect for company accounting periods beginning on or after 1 January 2000, where FA 2000, s. 105 and s. 106 apply.

Reg. 5(8)(b) substituted; and 5(8)(c) inserted by SI 2000/3315, reg. 8(3); with effect for company accounting periods beginning on or after 1 January 2000, where FA 2000, s. 105 and s. 106 apply.

In reg. 5(9), the reference to para. (6A) inserted; and the word "business" substituted (twice) in place of the word "trade"; by SI 2000/3315, reg. 8(4); with effect for company accounting periods beginning on or after 1 January 2000, where FA 2000, s. 105 and s. 106 apply.

Cross references – SI 2000/3315, reg. 11: where reg. 5(2)(b), above, applies so as to reduce the amount of an initial exchange gain/loss which, apart from that regulation, would accrue to a company as respects a liability, and FA 1993, s. 146 applies; then s. 146 shall have effect as if the reduction provided by reg. 5(2)(b) had not been made.

FA 1993, s. 146: early termination of currency contract.

Statements of practice – SP 4/98, para. 33: Revenue accept that partnerships which have eligible liabilities as described in reg. 5(4) or (5) can make a matching election for the full range of eligible assets described in reg. 5(6), so long as the election is signed by all partners subject to UK corporation tax.

HMRC interpretations – IRInt. 146: sets out how Revenue will apply reg. 5(3A) (broadly, not intended to deny relief for losses arising on liabilities on which exchange differences are taken to reserves in accordance with SSAP20 where no matching election has been made in respect of an asset).

CONTROLLED FOREIGN COMPANIES

6(1)   Where an accounting period of a controlled foreign company is or includes an accrual period, then, for the purposes of computing in accordance with Schedule 24 to the Taxes Act the company's chargeable profits for that accounting period, an election for matching may be made by a company resident in the United Kingdom which has, or jointly by companies resident in the United Kingdom which together have, a majority interest in the foreign company, notwithstanding that in such a case the company owing any liability or acquiring or holding any asset will not be the company making the election.

6(2)   Paragraph 4(3) and (4) of that Schedule shall apply for the purposes of determining whether one or more companies has a majority interest in another company and, for that purpose, the relevant accounting period is the accounting period referred to in paragraph (1) above.

DEEMED GAINS AND LOSSES ON DISPOSAL OF MATCHED ASSETS

7(1)   Paragraphs (3) to (5) below apply in any case where a disposal of an asset is deemed by virtue of paragraph (1A) below to have been made by a company immediately before the first day of its first accounting period to begin on or after 1st October 2002 (**"the disposal time"**) and at any time before the disposal time it was (to any extent) a matched asset for the purposes of an election for matching made by the company (**"the relevant election"**).

7(1A)   For the purposes of paragraph (1) above, any asset held by the company at the beginning of the first day of its first accounting period to begin on or after 1st October 2002 shall be deemed to have been disposed of by the company immediately before that first day.

7(2)   [Omitted by SI 2002/1969, reg. 14.]

7(3) There shall be found as respects the liability or liabilities matched with the asset for each accrual period for which the relevant election has had effect–

(a) the amount of the initial exchange gain (if any) calculated in accordance with the preceding regulations, and

(b) the amount of the initial exchange gain which would have accrued if the relevant election had not had effect;

and the excess of the amount found under sub-paragraph (b) over that found under sub-paragraph (a), or if no amount is found under sub-paragraph (a) the amount found under sub-paragraph (b), for each period is referred to below as the amount by which the initial exchange gain for the period has been reduced.

7(4) There shall be found as respects the liability or liabilities matched with the asset for each accrual period for which the relevant election has had effect–

(a) the amount of the initial exchange loss (if any) calculated in accordance with the preceding regulations, and

(b) the amount of the initial exchange loss which would have accrued if the relevant election had not had effect;

and the excess of the amount found under sub-paragraph (b) over that found under sub-paragraph (a), or if no amount is found under sub-paragraph (a) the amount found under sub-paragraph (b), for each period is referred to below as the amount by which the initial exchange loss for the period has been reduced.

7(5) There shall be found–

(a) the aggregate of the amounts by which the initial exchange gains accruing as respects the liability for accrual periods for which the relevant election has effect have been reduced, and

(b) the aggregate of the amounts by which the initial exchange losses accruing as respects the liability for accrual periods for which the relevant election has effect have been reduced.

7(6) [Omitted by SI 2002/1969, reg. 14.]

7(7) [Omitted by SI 2002/1969, reg. 14.]

7(8) [Omitted by SI 2002/1969, reg. 14.]

History – In reg. 7(1) words "Paragraphs (3) to (5) below apply in any case where a disposal of an asset is deemed by virtue of paragraph (1A) below to have been made by a company immediately before the first day of its first accounting period to begin on or after 1st October 2002" substituted for "Subject to paragraph (2) below, paragraphs (3) to (8) below apply in any case where there is a disposal of an asset by a company at any time" and reg. 7(1A) inserted, by SI 2002/1969, reg. 14 with effect in relation to accounting periods beginning on or after 1 October 2002.
Reg. 7(2), (6), (7) and (8) omitted by SI 2002/1969, reg. 14, with effect in relation to accounting periods beginning on or after 1 October 2002.

Cross references – SI 2002/1969, reg. 14: saving, subject to modifications, of reg. 7 in respect of the change of tax treatment of exchange gains and losses by FA 2002.

Statements of practice – SP 4/98, para. 35ff.: treatment of chargeable gain or allowable loss produced by reg. 7 in case of corporate partners.

DEFERRAL ETC. OF DEEMED GAINS AND LOSSES IN CERTAIN CASES

8 [Omitted by SI 2002/1969, reg. 15.]

History – Reg. 8 omitted by SI 2002/1969, reg. 15, with effect in relation to accounting periods beginning on or after 1 October 2002.

Cross references – SI 2002/1969, reg. 15: omission of reg. 8 in respect of the change of tax treatment of exchange gains and losses by FA 2002.

TRANSACTIONS TO WHICH SECTION 116 OR 127 OF THE 1992 ACT APPLIES

9 [Omitted by SI 2002/1969, reg. 15.]

History – Reg. 9 omitted by SI 2002/1969, reg. 15, with effect in relation to accounting periods beginning on or after 1 October 2002.

Cross references – SI 2002/1969, reg. 15: omission of reg. 9 in respect of the change of tax treatment of exchange gains and losses by FA 2002.

ELECTIONS FOR MATCHING

10(1) Subject to the provisions of these Regulations, an election under this regulation–

(a) may be made by notice given to the inspector by the company which owes the liability to be matched by the election,

(b) shall have effect as from the day on which it is made, and

(c)   shall be irrevocable.

10(2)   An election for matching must identify–

(a)   [omitted by SI 1996/1347, reg. 5(a)(i);]

(b)   the asset to be matched;

(c)   if the liability to be matched by the election is not being matched with the whole of the asset either–

    (i)   a fixed percentage of the asset which is to be available for matching; or

    (ii)   the value of the whole asset as at the time the election is made and a specific amount which is to be available for matching; or

    (iii)   a proportion or part of the asset which is to be available for matching where the value of the proportion or part is to be determined by reference to a formula or other method of calculation specified in the election and may vary from time to time in accordance with that formula or other method of calculation;

(d)   [omitted by SI 1996/1347, reg. 5(a)(i);]

(e)   the provision of these Regulations by virtue of which the asset is an eligible asset.

10(3)   An election under paragraph (2)(c)(i) or (ii) above may be varied by a subsequent election under this regulation so as to increase the percentage or amount which is specified in the election.

10(4)   An election to match a liability with an asset falling within regulation 5(6)(a), (b), (c) or (d) or 5(6A)(a), (b), (c) or (d) or 5(8), shall not have effect for any accrual period for which an initial exchange gain accrues as respects the liability unless–

(a)   any exchange difference arising in relation to the asset, and

(b)   at least part of any exchange difference arising in relation to the liability,

are shown, in the company's accounts for the period which is or includes the accrual period in which those differences arise, in the reserves, and if only part of the exchange differences relating to the liability are shown in the reserves, the elections shall have effect for that period only to that part.

Where the liability or asset (or both) are matched in part only, references in this paragraph to the liability or asset are to the part matched.

10(5)   An election shall not cease to have effect at any time by reason only that the liability matched by the election ceased at that time to match the asset to which the election refers either at all or to the same extent to which it matched it at the time the election was made (either by reason of its ceasing to be owed by the company or because it is reduced or its value changes), but where in any such case at any time after the election is made or, in the case of an election to which regulation 11(2) applies, has effect, the company is subject to another eligible liability which might have been matched by the election if the election had been made at that time, the election shall continue to have effect in relation to that other liability.

This paragraph shall apply with the necessary modifications in relation to any such other liability as it applies in relation to the liability originally matched by the election.

10(6)   In any case where the asset to which the election refers was original shares as defined by section 126 of the 1992 Act and by reason of a reorganisation (as so defined) the asset ceased at any time to match the liability matched by the election, then if the whole or any part of the new holding (as so defined) might have been specified in the election if the election had been made at the time of the reorganisation, the election shall not cease to have effect but shall continue to have effect in relation to the new holding or part as the case may be.

10(7)   Any question as to which liability is matched with which asset shall be determined on a just and reasonable basis.

History – Reg. 10(2)(a), (d) omitted, and in reg. 10(2)(c) words "to be matched by the election" inserted, by SI 1996/1347, reg. 5(a), operative from 6 June 1996.
In reg. 10(4), the reference to reg. 5(6A) inserted; by SI 2000/3315, reg. 9; with effect for company accounting periods beginning on or after 1 January 2000, where FA 2000, s. 105 and s. 106 apply.
In reg. 10(5), words "matched by" substituted for "specified in" in each place, and words "in any such case ... eligible liability" substituted, by SI 1996/1347, reg. 5(b), operative from 6 June 1996.
In reg. 10(6), words "matched by" substituted for "specified in" by SI 1996/1347, reg. 5(c), operative from 6 June 1996.

EFFECTIVENESS OF ELECTIONS

11(1)   An election which does not comply with regulation 10(2) shall be of no effect.

11(1A)   Notwithstanding the following provisions of this regulation, an election made under regulation 10 or this regulation–

(a)   shall have effect only in relation to accounting periods beginning before 1st October 2002, and

(b)   an election which specifies a day as the day from which the election is to have effect must specify a day that falls within an accounting period beginning before 1st October 2002.

11(2)   Notwithstanding regulation 10(1) above, if an election–

(a)   specifies as an eligible asset an asset which the company acquired not more than 92 days before the day on which the election is made, and

(b)   specifies the date of acquisition as the date as from which the election is to have effect,

the election shall have effect, so far as it relates to that asset and any liability to be matched with that asset, as from that date.

11(3)   Notwithstanding regulation 10(1) above, an election under regulation 10(3) may specify a day not more than 92 days earlier than the day on which the election is made as the date as from which the election is to have effect, and in such a case the election shall have effect as from that date.

11(4)   Notwithstanding regulation 10(1) above, if an election specifies an asset as an eligible asset which the company held on its commencement day and the election is made before the expiry–

(a)   of the period of 183 days beginning with 23rd March 1995, or

(b)   of the period of 92 days beginning with the company's commencement day,

whichever is the later, and the election specifies the company's commencement day as the date as from which the election is to have effect, the election shall have effect, so far as it relates to that asset and any liability to be matched with that asset, as from that specified day.

11(5)   Notwithstanding regulation 10(1) above, an election expressed to be made under this paragraph and made–

(a)   in pursuance of regulation 6 above in relation to a controlled foreign company as respects which a direction under section 747 of the Taxes Act is given on or after 23rd March 1995 for an accounting period of the company, whenever beginning, (and a direction under that section has not been given with respect to an earlier accounting period of that company or, where the direction is given on or after 1st April 1996, no earlier accounting period of that company is an ADP exempt period), and

(b)   before the expiry of the period of 92 days beginning with the date of that direction,

shall have effect from the latest of the following days, that is to say, the first day of the first accounting period as respects which the direction has effect, the first day of the first accounting period beginning on or after 23rd March 1995, and the day on which the asset in question is acquired by the company.

11(6)   In paragraph (5) above **"ADP exempt period"** means an accounting period of the company–

(a)   which begins on or after 28th November 1995, and

(b)   in respect of which the company has pursued, within the meaning of Part I of Schedule 25 to the Taxes Act, an acceptable distribution policy .

History – Reg. 11(1A) inserted by SI 2002/1969, reg. 16 with effect in relation to accounting periods beginning on or after 1 October 2002.

In reg. 11(5)(a), words "or, where the direction … ADP exempt period", and reg. 11(6), inserted by SI 1996/1347, reg. 6, operative from 30 June 1996.

Cross references – SI 2002/1969, reg. 16: saving, subject to modifications, of reg. 11 in respect of the change of tax treatment of exchange gains and losses by FA 2002.

TRANSACTIONS NOT AT ARM'S LENGTH

DISREGARD OF REGULATIONS 2 AND 4 TO 11

12   [Omitted by SI 2002/1969, reg. 17.]

History – Reg. 12 omitted by SI 2002/1969, reg. 17 with effect in relation to accounting periods beginning on or after 1 October 2002.

Cross references – SI 2002/1969, reg. 17: omission of reg. 12 in respect of the change of tax treatment of exchange gains and losses by FA 2002.

LOCAL CURRENCY ELECTIONS REGULATIONS 1994
(SI 1994/3230)

Made on 16 March 1993 by the Treasury, in exercise of the powers conferred on them by s. 158(3)–(6) of the Finance Act 1989.

CITATION AND COMMENCEMENT

1(1) These Regulations may be cited as the Local Currency Elections Regulations 1994.

1(2) These Regulations shall come into force on 23rd March 1995.

DEFINITIONS

2 In these Regulations, except where the context otherwise requires–

"**the 1993 Act**" means the Finance Act 1993;

"**accounts**" in relation to a company, means–

(i) the annual accounts of the company prepared in accordance with Part VII of the Companies Act 1985, or

(ii) if the company is not required to prepare such accounts, the accounts which it is required to keep under the law of its home State or, if it is not so required to keep accounts, such of its accounts as most closely correspond to accounts which it would have been required to prepare if the provisions of that Part applied to the company;

"**commencement day**", in relation to any company, means the first day of the company's first accounting period beginning on or after 23rd March 1995;

"**local currency**" means a currency other than sterling;

"**overseas branch**" means a branch outside the United Kingdom;

"**specified**", in relation to an election, means specified in the election;

and references to **an election are references** to an election under regulation 3 or 4.

ELECTIONS FOR TRADES

3(1) Subject to the following provisions of these Regulations, a company carrying on a trade may by notice given to the inspector elect to have the basic profits and losses of the trade computed and expressed for the purposes of corporation tax in a specified local currency.

3(2) A company may not make an election under this regulation for a trade for an accounting period if there is in force an election under regulation 4 for that accounting period and any part of that trade.

ELECTIONS FOR PART TRADES

4(1) Subject to the following provisions of these Regulations, a company carrying on a trade may by notice given to the inspector elect to have the basic profits and losses of a specified part of the trade computed and expressed for the purposes of corporation tax in a specified local currency.

4(2) A company may make an election under this regulation–

(a) for a trade which it carries on, wholly or in part, through one or more overseas branches, or

(b) for a ring fence trade as respects which the condition mentioned in section 94A(2) of the 1993 Act is fulfilled,

but not in relation to any other trade (and accordingly an election under paragraph (1) of this regulation may, subject to these Regulations, be made for a part of the trade which is carried on in the United Kingdom).

4(3) An election under this regulation may specify different currencies for different parts of the trade but if the company makes an election for each part of the trade, at least two currencies must be specified.

4(4) Where a company makes more than one election for different parts of one trade, paragraph (3) above shall apply cumulatively to the elections.

4(5) Where a company carries on part of a trade through two or more branches situated in the same country, an election under paragraph (2)(a) above for that part of the trade must specify the same currency to be used for all those branches, and for the purposes of this paragraph the United Kingdom shall be taken to be one country.

4(6) In any case where a company makes an election under this regulation for one or more parts of a trade but not for all the parts of the trade, the basic profits and losses of any part of the trade for which there is no election shall be computed and expressed for the purposes of corporation tax in sterling.

4(7) A company may not make an election under this regulation for part of a trade for an accounting period if there is in force an election under regulation 3 for that trade and that accounting period.

FACTORS AFFECTING DETERMINATION OF LOCAL CURRENCY

5(1) This regulation applies in relation to any election made by a company for the purpose of determining what currency (if any) may be specified in the election.

5(2) A currency may be specified in an election as a local currency if, but only if–

(a)   it is the currency of the primary economic environment in which the trade or part of the trade is carried on, and

(b)   one of the conditions set out in paragraphs (3), (4), (5) and (6) below is satisfied.

5(3) A currency may be specified in any election as a local currency if the accounts are prepared in that currency in accordance with normal accountancy practice.

5(4) A currency may be specified in an election made by a company resident in the United Kingdom as a local currency if the accounts, so far as they relate to the trade or part in question, are prepared from the financial statements relating to the trade or part using the closing rate/net investment method, and those statements are prepared in that currency.

The reference above to the closing rate/net investment method is a reference to that method as described under the title "Foreign currency translation" in the Statement of Standard Accounting Practice issued in April 1983 by the Institute of Chartered Accountants in England and Wales.

5(5) A currency may be specified in an election made by a company not resident in the United Kingdom as a local currency if it is the currency in which the financial statements relating to that trade or part are prepared in accordance with normal accountancy practice.

5(6) Subject to paragraph (7) below, a currency may be specified as a local currency in any election which is not for a trade or part of a trade carried on in the United Kingdom if–

(a)   the company making the election was within the charge to corporation tax as respects the trade or part in question immediately before its commencement day, and

(b)   for accounting periods ending within the two years before that day, the basic profits and losses of the trade or part were computed and expressed for corporation tax purposes in that currency.

5(7) An election made by virtue of paragraph (6) above shall be of no effect unless it is made before the expiry of the period of 92 days beginning with the company's commencement day.

FACTORS RELEVANT TO THE DETERMINATION OF THE PRIMARY ECONOMIC ENVIRONMENT

6 In determining whether a currency is the currency of the primary economic environment in which a trade or any part of a trade is carried on, regard shall be had to all relevant circumstances including in particular (in so far as they may be relevant) the following factors, that is to say–

(a)   the currency in which the net cash flows of the trade or part are generated or expressed in the relevant accounting records;

(b)   the currency in which the company manages the profitability of the trade or part so far as it is affected by currency exposure;

(c)   in the case of a company which is resident in the United Kingdom, the currency in which the company's share capital and its reserves are denominated;

(d)   the currency to which the company, or, where the trade or part is carried on through a branch, that branch, is exposed in its long term capital borrowing (of any kind whatsoever);

(e)   the currency which is the generally recognised currency in which trading in the principal market of the trade or part is carried on.

PROVISIONS SUPPLEMENTARY TO REGULATIONS 4, 5 AND 6

7(1) Where the election specifies more than one currency for parts of a trade, regulations 4, 5 and 6 shall apply separately in relation to each currency and each part of the trade.

7(2)   In regulations 4, 5 and 6, except where the context otherwise requires—

(a)   any reference to accounts, in relation to an election, is a reference to the accounts of the company making the election for the accounting period for which the election is to have effect; and

(b)   any reference to relevant accounting records, in relation to an election, is a reference to the accounting records, relating to the trade or that part of a trade to which the election refers, for the accounting period for which the election is to have effect.

DETERMINATION OF RATE OF EXCHANGE

8(1)   A company may in an election for a trade or part of a trade state that for accounting periods for which the election has effect an average arm's length exchange rate will be used in translating the basic profits or losses of the trade or part into sterling for the purposes of section 93(4) or 94(8) of the 1993 Act (as the case may be).

8(2)   In paragraph (1) above–

"arm's length exchange rate" means such exchange rate as might reasonably be expected to be agreed between persons dealing at arm's length; and

"average arm's length exchange rate" means the rate which represents the average of the arm's length exchange rates for all the days in the accounting period in question.

8(3)   Subject to paragraph (4) below, where an election contains a statement in accordance with paragraph (1) above, the average arm's length exchange rate shall be used in translating the basic profits or losses of the trade or part into sterling for the purposes of section 93(4) or 94(8) of the 1993 Act (as the case may be) for all accounting periods for which the election has effect.

8(4)   The company may by notice given to the inspector terminate the statement referred to above with effect from the first day of the first accounting period beginning on or after the date of the notice.

PERIODS FOR WHICH ELECTIONS HAVE EFFECT

9(1)   Subject to the following provisions of these Regulations, an election for a trade or part of a trade shall have effect as respects that trade or part for all accounting periods beginning on or after the date on which the election is made.

9(2)   Subject to the following provisions of these Regulations, an election for a trade or part of a trade made by a company which, as respects that trade or part, is within the charge to corporation tax immediately before its commencement day shall have effect as respects that trade or part of all accounting periods beginning on or after that day if the election is made before the end of the period of 92 days beginning with that day.

9(3)   Subject to the following provisions of these Regulations, an election for a trade or part of a trade made by a company which, as respects that trade or part, is not within the charge to corporation tax immediately before its commencement day shall have effect as respects that trade or part for all accounting periods beginning on or after the first day on which it comes within that charge as respects that trade or part if the election is made before the end of the period of 92 days beginning with that first day.

INFORMATION TO BE SUBMITTED WITH ELECTIONS
AND EFFECTIVENESS OF ELECTIONS

10(1)   An election by a company for a trade or part of a trade shall include–

(a)   a statement of the reasons why the company believes that such of the requirements of these Regulations as are applicable to the election will be met as respects that trade or part for the first accounting period of the company for which the election is to have effect; and

(b)   particulars of the nature of the trade or part and the place where it is carried on.

10(2)   An election which does not comply with paragraph (1) above and regulation 5(7) (if applicable) shall be of no effect.

10(3)   Without prejudice to paragraphs (1) and (2) above, an election made by a company for a trade or part of a trade shall be of no effect if the requirements of regulation 5 (so far as they are applicable to the election) are not complied with as respects that trade or part for the first accounting period of the company for which the election is intended to have effect.

10(4) If at any time in an accounting period of the company, the currency specified in an election made by the company ceases to be eligible to be specified in an election as the local currency of the trade or part, the election shall cease to have effect at the end of that accounting period.

10(5) In any case where an election has ceased to have effect by virtue of paragraph (4) above, the company shall notify the inspector in writing of that fact as soon as is reasonably practicable after becoming aware of it.

10(6) In a case where paragraph (4) above applies the inspector may notify the company in writing that by virtue of that paragraph the election is no longer effective.

EXCHANGE GAINS AND LOSSES (INSURANCE COMPANIES) REGULATIONS 1994

(SI 1994/3231 as amended by SI 1996/673, SI 1996/1485, SI 1997/1155, SI 2001/3629 and SI 2002/1969)

Made on 15 December 1994 by the Treasury, in exercise of the powers conferred on them by s. 167(1) and 168(2) to (5) of the Finance Act 1993. Operative from 23 March 1995.

Notes – SI 1994/3231 saved by SI 2002/1969 with modifications as incorporated below.

1(1) These Regulations may be cited as the Exchange Gains and Losses (Insurance Companies) Regulations 1994.

1(2) These Regulations shall come into force on 23rd March 1995.

1(3) In these Regulations unless the context otherwise requires–

"**basic valuation**" shall be construed in accordance with section 159(1) of the 1993 Act;

"**the final accounting period**", in relation to a company, means the company's accounting period preceding the first accounting period to begin on or after 1st October 2002;

"**loan relationship**" shall be construed in accordance with the Corporation Tax Acts, except that a relationship shall not be a loan relationship where the profits or gains chargeable to tax under Case III of Schedule D which arise from the relationship are confined to interest;

"**new holding**" and "**original shares**" have the meanings given by section 126(1) of the 1992 Act;

"**regulation 7 asset**" shall be construed in accordance with regulation 7(1);

"**the Taxes Act**" means the Income and Corporation Taxes Act 1988;

"**the 1992 Act**" means the Taxation of Chargeable Gains Act 1992;

"**the 1993 Act**" means the Finance Act 1993.

History – In reg. 1(3) definition of "the final accounting period" inserted by SI 2002/1969, reg. 19 with effect in relation to accounting periods beginning on or after 1 October 2002.
Reg. 1(3) substituted by SI 1996/673, reg. 2, with effect from 31 March 1996.

Cross references – SI 2002/1969, reg. 19: saving, subject to modifications, of reg. 1 in respect of the change of tax treatment of exchange gains and losses by FA 2002.

2 [Omitted by SI 2002/1969, reg. 20.]

History – Reg. 2 omitted by SI 2002/1969, reg. 20 with effect in relation to accounting periods beginning on or after 1 October 2002.

Cross references – SI 2002/1969, reg. 20: omission of reg. 2 in respect of the change of tax treatment of exchange gains and losses by FA 2002.

3 [Omitted by SI 2002/1969, reg. 20.]

History – Reg. 3 omitted by SI 2002/1969, reg. 20 with effect in relation to accounting periods beginning on or after 1 October 2002.

Cross references – SI 2002/1969, reg. 20: omission of reg. 3 in respect of the change of tax treatment of exchange gains and losses by FA 2002.

4 [Omitted by SI 2002/1969, reg. 20.]

History – Reg. 4 omitted by SI 2002/1969, reg. 20 with effect in relation to accounting periods beginning on or after 1 October 2002.

Cross references – SI 2002/1969, reg. 20: omission of reg. 4 in respect of the change of tax treatment of exchange gains and losses by FA 2002.

5 [Omitted by SI 2002/1969, reg. 20.]

History – Reg. 5 omitted by SI 2002/1969, reg. 20 with effect in relation to accounting periods beginning on or after 1 October 2002.

Cross references – SI 2002/1969, reg. 20: omission of reg. 5 in respect of the change of tax treatment of exchange gains and losses by FA 2002.

5A [Omitted by SI 2002/1969, reg. 20.]

History – Reg. 5A omitted by SI 2002/1969, reg. 20 with effect in relation to accounting periods beginning on or after 1 October 2002.
Former reg. 5A inserted by SI 1996/1485, with effect in relation to accounting periods ending on or after 30 June 1996.

Cross references – SI 2002/1969, reg. 20: omission of reg. 5A in respect of the change of tax treatment of exchange gains and losses by FA 2002.

6 [Revoked by SI 1996/673, reg. 6 with effect in relation to accounting periods ending after 31 March 1996.]

7(1) An asset specified by this regulation is referred to in regulations 7A and 8 to 12 as a **"regulation 7 asset"**.

7(2) An asset is specified by this regulation if it is an asset which, at the time of its disposal–

(a) represents a loan relationship of a company;

(b) is an asset to which paragraph (3), (4), (5) or (6) below applies; and

(c) is held in exempt circumstances.

7(3) This paragraph applies to an asset if–

(a) the settlement currency of the debt to which it relates is a currency other than sterling; and

(b) that debt is not a debt on a security.

7(4) This paragraph applies to an asset if the debt to which it relates is a debt on a security and is in a foreign currency.

7(5) This paragraph applies to an asset if it is comprised in a relevant holding and is denominated in a currency other than sterling.

7(6) This paragraph applies to an asset if–

(a) it is a qualifying corporate bond,

(b) it would not, apart from this paragraph, be a regulation 7 asset,

(c) it constitutes a new holding, and

(d) the original shares, in relation to the new holding, consisted of a regulation 7 asset by virtue of paragraph (3), (4) or (5) above.

7(7) For the purposes of paragraph (4) above a debt is a debt in a foreign currency if it is–

(a) a debt expressed in a currency other than sterling;

(b) a debt the amount of which in sterling falls at any time to be determined by reference to the value at that time of a currency other than sterling; or

(c) subject to paragraph (8) below, a debt as respects which provision is made for its conversion into, or redemption in, a currency other than sterling.

7(8) A debt is not a debt in a foreign currency for the purposes of paragraph (4) above by reason only that provision is made for its redemption on payment of an amount in a currency other than sterling equal, at the rate prevailing at the date of redemption, to a specified amount in sterling.

7(9) For the purposes of paragraph (5) above an asset is comprised in a relevant holding if it consists of–

(a) a unit in a unit trust scheme, or

(b) a relevant interest in an offshore fund to which section 212 of the 1992 Act does not apply or would not apply if the asset were an asset of the company's long-term insurance fund.

7(10) For the purposes of paragraph (5) above–

(a) a unit in a unit trust scheme, or

(b) a right (other than a share in a company) which constitutes a relevant interest in an offshore fund, or

(c) a share in an open-ended investment company,

shall be taken to be denominated in a currency other than sterling if the price at which it may be acquired from, or disposed of to, persons concerned in the management of the trust or fund is fixed by those persons in a currency other than sterling.

7(11) For the purposes of paragraph (5) above shares constituting a relevant interest in an offshore fund shall be taken to be denominated in a currency other than sterling if their nominal value is expressed in such a currency; and shares of a given class in an open-ended investment company shall be taken to be denominated in a currency other than sterling if the price at which they may be acquired from, or disposed of to, the company or its authorised corporate director is fixed by the company or director in a currency other than sterling, or (as the case may be) the price or prices at which they are quoted in The Stock Exchange Daily Official List is in a currency other than sterling.

7(12) The reference in paragraph (2)(c) above to exempt circumstances shall be construed in accordance with paragraph 3 of Schedule 17 to the 1993 Act, but as if references in that paragraph to a currency were references to the debt to which the relationship relates.

7(13) In this regulation–

  "debt on a security" shall be construed in accordance with section 132 of the 1992 Act;

  "long-term insurance fund" has the meaning given by section 431(2) of the Taxes Act;

"open-ended investment company" and **"authorised corporate director"** in relation to such a company have the meanings given by subsection (10) of section 468 of the Taxes Act, read with subsections (11) to (18) of that section, as those subsections are added in relation to open-ended investment companies by regulation 10(4) of the Open-ended Investment Companies (Tax) Regulations 1997; and accordingly references in subsections (11) to (16) of that section to "the Tax Acts" shall be construed as if they included references to these Regulations;

"qualifying corporate bond" has the same meaning as in the 1992 Act;

"relevant interest in an offshore fund" has the meaning given by section 212(5) of the 1992 Act;

"security" includes a debenture that is deemed to be a security for the purposes of section 251 of the 1992 Act by virtue of subsection (6) of that section;

"unit trust scheme" shall be construed in accordance with section 99 of the 1992 Act.

History – Reg. 7(1) substituted by SI 2002/1969, reg. 21 with effect in relation to accounting periods begining on or after 1 October 2002.

Reg. 7 inserted by SI 1996/673 with effect in relation to disposals taking place after 1 April 1996.

In reg. 7(9) and (13), "long-term insurance" substituted for "long term business" by SI 2001/3629, art. 138 which came into force on 1 December 2001.

Cross references – SI 2002/1969, reg. 21: saving, subject to modifications, of reg. 7 in respect of the change of tax treatment of exchange gains and losses by FA 2002.

7A(1) An asset shall be deemed to have been disposed of by an insurance company immediately before its first accounting period to begin on or after 1st October 2002 where–

(a) the asset was a regulation 7 asset at the time of its deemed disposal, and

(b) at that time, the insurance company had made no election under regulation 8A of these Regulations.

7A(2) Subject to regulation 7B, any chargeable gain or allowable loss accruing on the deemed disposal under paragraph (1) above of an asset shall be brought into account as if it had accrued immediately after the end of the final accounting period.

History – Reg. 7A inserted by SI 2002/1969, reg. 22 with effect in relation to accounting periods beginning on or after 1 October 2002, in respect of the change of tax treatment of exchange gains and losses by FA 2002.

7B In any case where, apart from this regulation, chargeable gains or allowable losses would accrue to an insurance company immediately after the end of the final accounting period by virtue of regulation 7A–

(a) the insurance company may elect, by notice to the inspector within two years of the end of the final accounting period, that this regulation shall apply as respects all such gains or losses, and

(b) where such an election is made, every such gain or loss to which this regulation applies shall be treated as accruing only when the asset or liability to which the gain or loss relates ceases to be held or owed by the insurance company.

History – Reg. 7B inserted by SI 2002/1969, reg. 22 with effect in relation to accounting periods beginning on or after 1 October 2002, in respect of the change of tax treatment of exchange gains and losses by FA 2002.

8(1) The amount of the chargeable gain accruing on the deemed disposal under regulation 7A(1) of an asset shall, subject to paragraphs (5) and (6) below and to regulations 9 to 12, be computed by ascertaining the amount specified in paragraph (3) below ("the first amount") and the amount specified in paragraph (4) below ("the second amount").

8(2) Where the second amount exceeds the first amount the excess shall be a chargeable gain; where the first amount exceeds the second amount the excess shall be an allowable loss; and where the first amount and the second amount are equal there shall be neither a chargeable gain nor an allowable loss.

8(3) The first amount is the basic valuation of the asset translated into sterling at the time immediately after the company becomes entitled to the asset.

8(4) The second amount is the basic valuation of the asset translated into sterling at the time immediately before the company ceases to be entitled to the asset.

8(5) Where any profit on the sale of a regulation 7 asset would be treated wholly as a receipt falling to be brought into account in computing profits or gains charged under Case I of Schedule D, neither a chargeable gain nor an allowable loss shall be treated as arising.

8(6) Where any profit on the sale of a regulation 7 asset would be treated partly as a receipt falling to be brought into account in computing profits or gains charged under Case I of Schedule D, any chargeable gain or allowable loss accruing by virtue of this regulation shall be reduced on a just and reasonable basis.

8(7)   Any translation into sterling required by this regulation shall be made by reference to the London closing rate.

8(8)   The provisions of Chapters III and IV of Part II of the 1992 Act shall not apply to any computation required by this regulation.

8(9)   All regulation 7 assets which are the subject of the computation required by this regulation shall be treated as relevant securities within the meaning given by subsection (1) of section 108 of the 1992 Act; and that section shall apply accordingly.

8(10)   Nothing in this regulation shall be taken as preventing any gain or loss which is deemed to accrue by virtue of section 116(10)(b) of the 1992 Act from being brought into charge to tax.

History – In reg. 8(1) words "the deemed disposal under regulation 7A(1) of an asset" substituted for "disposal of a regulation 7 asset", and "9" substituted for "8A", by SI 2002/1969, reg. 23 with effect in relation to accounting periods beginning on or after 1 October 2002.

In reg. 8(1), reference to reg. 8A to 12 substituted for former reference to reg. 9 to 12 by SI 1996/1485, reg. 4, operative from 30 June 1996. Reg. 8 inserted by SI 1996/673, reg. 4 with effect in relation to disposals taking place on or after 1 April 1996.

Cross references – SI 2002/1969, reg. 23: saving, subject to modifications, of reg. 8 in respect of the change of tax treatment of exchange gains and losses by FA 2002.

8A   [Omitted by SI 2002/1969, reg. 24.]

History – Reg. 8A omitted by SI 2002/1969, reg. 24 with effect in relation to accounting periods beginning on or after 1 October 2002.

Former reg. 8A inserted by SI 1996/1485, reg. 5, operative from 30 June 1996.

Cross references – SI 2002/1969, reg. 24: omission of reg. 8A in respect of the change of tax treatment of exchange gains and losses by FA 2002.

9(1)   This regulation applies in any case where—

(a)   an insurance company has acquired a regulation 7 asset, and

(b)   the asset was held by the company immediately before 1st April 1996.

9(2)   Regulation 8 shall apply on the deemed disposal under regulation 7A(1)of the asset with the modification that the first amount shall be the basic valuation of the asset translated into sterling by reference to the London closing rate on 1st April 1996.

History – In reg. 9(2) words "deemed disposal under regulation 7A(1) of the asset" substituted for "disposal of the asset" by SI 2002/1969, reg. 25, with effect in relation to accounting periods beginning on or after 1 October 2002.

Reg. 9 inserted by SI 1996/673, reg. 4 with effect in relation to disposals on or after 1 April 1996.

Cross references – SI 2002/1969, reg. 25: saving, subject to modifications, of reg. 9 in respect of the change of tax treatment of exchange gains and losses by FA 2002.

10(1)   This regulation applies in any case where, for the purposes of sections 126 to 131 of the 1992 Act–

(a)   a regulation 7 asset constitutes the original shares, and

(b)   another regulation 7 asset constitutes the new holding.

10(2)   Regulation 8 shall apply on the disposal of the new holding with the modifications specified in paragraphs (3) and (4) below.

10(3)   The modification specified in this paragraph is that the first amount shall be the aggregate of–

(a)   the basic valuation of the original shares translated into sterling at the time immediately after the company became entitled to the original shares, and

(b)   the basic valuation of the new holding translated into sterling at the time immediately after the company became entitled to the new holding.

10(4)   The modification specified in this paragraph is that the second amount shall be the aggregate of–

(a)   the basic valuation of the original shares translated into sterling at the time immediately before the company became entitled to the new holding, and

(b)   the basic valuation of the new holding translated into sterling at the time immediately before the company ceased to be entitled to the new holding.

History – Reg. 10 inserted by SI 1996/673, reg. 4 with effect in relation to disposals on or after 1 April 1996.

11(1)   This regulation applies in any case where–

(a)   an asset is a regulation 7 asset by virtue of paragraph (5) of that regulation, and

(b)   the asset has at any time after 31st March 1996 and during the company's period of ownership been an asset which did not represent a loan relationship.

11(2)   Regulation 8 shall apply on the deemed disposal under regulation 7A(1) of the asset with the modification that the first amount shall be the basic valuation of the asset translated into sterling at the beginning of the accounting period in which the asset first became a regulation 7 asset by virtue of paragraph (5) of that regulation.

History – In reg. 11(2) words "deemed disposal under regulation 7A(1) of the asset" substituted for "disposal of the asset" by SI 2002/1969, reg. 26, with effect in relation to accounting periods beginning on or after 1 October 2002.
Reg. 11 inserted by SI 1996/673, reg. 4 with effect in relation to disposals on or after 1 April 1996.

Cross references – SI 2002/1969, reg. 26: saving, subject to modifications, of reg. 11 in respect of the change of tax treatment of exchange gains and losses by FA 2002.

12(1) This regulation applies in any case where an asset is a regulation 7 asset by virtue of paragraph (6) of that regulation.

12(2) Regulation 8 shall apply on the deemed disposal under regulation 7A(1) of the asset with the modifications that–

(a)   the first amount shall be the basic valuation of the original shares in relation to the asset translated into sterling at the time immediately after the company became entitled to the original shares, and

(b)   the second amount shall be the basic valuation of the original shares in relation to the asset translated into sterling at the time immediately before the company ceased to be entitled to the original shares.

History – In reg. 12(2) words "deemed disposal under regulation 7A(1) of the asset" substituted for "disposal of the asset" by SI 2002/1969, reg. 27, with effect in relation to accounting periods beginning on or after 1 October 2002.
Reg. 12 inserted by SI 1996/673, reg. 4, with effect in relation to disposals on or after 1 April 1996.

Cross references – SI 2002/1969, reg. 27: saving, subject to modifications, of reg. 12 in respect of the change of tax treatment of exchange gains and losses by FA 2002.

LLOYD'S UNDERWRITERS (TAX) REGULATIONS 1995

(SI 1995/351, as amended by SI 1996/781, SI 2001/3629 and SI 2005/3338)

Made on 15 February 1995 by the Commissioners of Inland Revenue, in exercise of the powers conferred on them by s. 179(2), 179A(3)(b), 182(1), (4) and (5), and 184(1) and (3) of the Finance Act 1993, and s. 227(2), 229(a) and 230(1) and (3) of the Finance Act 1994. Operative from 9 March 1995.

Cross references – SI 1997/2681, reg. 3(1)(b): application of SI 1995/351 to Lloyd's Scottish limited partnership, where ICTA 1988, s. 111(2) applies, as though partnership were an individual member, and where ICTA 1988, s. 114(1) applies, as though partnership were a corporate member, and in each case with the omission of regs. 9–17.

ARRANGEMENT OF REGULATIONS

REGULATION

PRELIMINARY

CITATION, COMMENCEMENT AND EFFECT

1 These Regulations may be cited as the Lloyd's Underwriters (Tax) Regulations 1995 and shall come into force on 9th March 1995, but except as otherwise provided shall have effect–

(a)   in their application to members who are individuals, with respect to the year 1992–93 and subsequent years of assessment;

(b)   in their application to corporate members, with respect to the underwriting year 1994 and subsequent underwriting years.

INTERPRETATION

2(1)   In these Regulations unless the context otherwise requires–

"ancillary trust fund" in relation to a member who is an individual has the meaning given by section 184(1) of the Finance Act 1993, and in relation to a corporate member has the meaning given by section 230(1) of the Finance Act 1994;

"the Board" means the Commissioners of Inland Revenue;

"Chapter III" means Chapter III of Part II of the Finance Act 1993, and

"Chapter V" means Chapter V of Part IV of the Finance Act 1994;

"inspector" includes any officer of the Board;

"Management Act" means the Taxes Management Act 1970;

"managing agent" in relation to a member who is an individual has the meaning given by section 184(1) of the Finance Act 1993 as extended by regulation 3, and in relation to a corporate member has the meaning given by section 230(1) of the Finance Act 1994 as extended by that regulation;

"member" means a member of Lloyd's who is an individual or, as the case may be, a corporate member and who is or has been an underwriting member;

"quota share contract" in relation to a member who is an individual has the meaning given by section 178(4) of the Finance Act 1993, and in relation to a corporate member has the meaning given by section 225(4) of the Finance Act 1994;

"Schedule 19" and **"Schedule 20"** mean respectively Schedule 19 and Schedule 20 to the Finance Act 1993;

"the Taxes Act" means the Income and Corporation Taxes Act 1988;

"section 179" and **"section 179A"** mean respectively, section 179 and section 179A of the Finance Act 1993;

"tax credit" means a tax credit under section 231 of the Taxes Act;

"underwriting business" in relation to a member who is an individual has the meaning given by section 184(1) of the Finance Act 1993, and in relation to a corporate member has the meaning given by section 230(1) of the Finance Act 1994.

2(2)   For the purposes of these Regulations an underwriting year and a year of assessment shall be deemed to correspond to each other if the underwriting year ends in the year of assessment.

2(3)   References in these Regulations to the profits or losses of the underwriting business of a member who is an individual are references to profits or losses of that business within Chapter III, and references to the profits or losses of a corporate member's underwriting business are references to the profits or losses of that business within Chapter V.

History – Definition of "tax credit" inserted by SI 1996/781, reg. 3, operative from 5 April 1996.

MANAGING AGENTS

3 [Revoked by SI 2005/3338, reg. 18.]

History – Reg. 3 revoked by SI 2005/3338, reg. 18, which has effect for members who are individuals for 2006–07 and subsequent years of assessment and for corporate members, for accounting periods ending after 31 December 2005 (but not in relation to profits and losses arising to corporate members mentioned in FA 1994, s. 220(2) and which are declared in 2005).

ASSESSMENT AND COLLECTION OF TAX

ASSESSMENT AND COLLECTION – GENERAL

4 Subject to regulations 5 to 8 below and regulations 6 to 12, 14 and 15 of the Lloyd's Underwriters (Tax) (1992–93 to 1996–97) Regulations 1995, the like provisions as are contained in the Management Act and the Tax Acts relating to the assessment and collection of tax shall have effect in relation to tax charged in accordance with section 171 of the Finance Act 1993 or, as the case may be, section 219 of the Finance Act 1994.

AMOUNT PAYABLE UNDER STOP-LOSS INSURANCE – INDIVIDUAL MEMBER

5(1) This regulation applies where–

(a) any insurance money payable to a member under a stop-loss insurance in respect of a loss in his underwriting business, or any amount payable to a member out of the High Level Stop Loss Fund in respect of such a loss, falls to be treated by virtue of section 178(2) of the Finance Act 1993 as a trading receipt in computing the profits arising from the business for the year of assessment which corresponds to the underwriting year in which the loss arose or, as respects an amount payable in respect of a loss declared in the underwriting year 1997 or a subsequent underwriting year, the underwriting year in which the loss was declared;

(b) the amount so treated operates to reduce or extinguish the amount of the loss sustained by the member in his underwriting business for that year of assessment;

(c) section 178(3) of the Finance Act 1993 does not apply as respects the payment of that amount; and

(d) the inspector is precluded–

    (i) by section 34 of the Management Act from making an assessment under section 29(3)(c) of that Act or, as respects the year 1996–97 and subsequent years of assessment, section 29(1)(c) of that Act, in respect of the whole or any part of that amount, or

    (ii) by section 30(5) of the Management Act from making an assessment under that section in respect of the whole or any part of that amount.

5(2) An assessment under section 29(3)(c) or, as the case may be, section 29(1)(c) or 30 of the Management Act in respect of the whole or any part of that amount shall not be out of time if made before the end of the underwriting year following the underwriting year in which the amount was received.

AMOUNT PAYABLE UNDER STOP-LOSS INSURANCE – CORPORATE MEMBER

6(1) This regulation applies where–

(a) any insurance money is payable to a corporate member under a stop-loss insurance in respect of a loss in its underwriting business, and the insurance money or, as the case may be, the apportioned part of the insurance money falls to be treated by virtue of section 225(2) of the Finance Act 1994 as a trading receipt in computing the profits arising from the business for an accounting period;

(b) the amount so treated operates to reduce or extinguish the amount of the loss sustained by the corporate member in its underwriting business for that accounting period;

(c) section 225(3) of the Finance Act 1994 does not apply as respects the payment of the insurance money; and

(d) the inspector is precluded–

    (i) by section 34 of the Management Act from making an assessment under section 29(3)(c) of that Act or, as respects an accounting period ending on or after such day as is appointed under section 199(3) of the Finance Act 1994, section 29(1)(c) of the Management Act, in respect of the whole or any part of the amount so treated, or

    (ii) by section 30(5) of the Management Act from making an assessment under that section in respect of the whole or any part of that amount.

6(2) An assessment under section 29(3)(c) or, as the case may be, section 29(1)(c) or 30 of the Management Act in respect of the whole or any part of that amount shall not be out of time if made before the end of the underwriting year following the underwriting year in which the amount was received.

NON-DELIVERY OF RETURN – REASONABLE EXCUSE

7 [Revoked by SI 2005/3338, reg. 18.]

History – Reg. 7 revoked by SI 2005/3338, reg. 18, which has effect for members who are individuals for 2006–07 and subsequent years of assessment and for corporate members, for accounting periods ending after 31 December 2005 (but not in relation to profits and losses arising to corporate members mentioned in FA 1994, s. 220(2) and which are declared in 2005).

PAYMENT OF INCOME TAX – TAXED INCOME AND TAX CREDITS

7A The like provisions as are contained in sections 59A and 59B of the Management Act shall have effect for the year 1996–97 and subsequent years of assessment in relation to tax which–

(a)   is charged on income in accordance with section 171 of the Finance Act 1993, being income falling within section 172(1)(c) of that Act, and

(b)   either–

     (i)   was paid by way of deduction at source, or

     (ii)   is represented by a tax credit,

as if references to income tax deducted or treated as deducted from any income or treated as paid on any income in respect of a year of assessment were references to income tax deducted or treated as deducted or paid in respect of the underwriting year corresponding to that year of assessment.

History – Reg. 7A inserted by SI 1996/781, reg. 4, operative from 5 April 1996.

7B   The like provisions as are contained in section 824 of the Taxes Act shall have effect for the year 1996–97 and subsequent years of assessment in relation to–

(a)   any repayment of tax which was paid by way of deduction at source in respect of income charged to tax in accordance with section 171, and falling within section 172(1)(c), of the Finance Act 1993, and

(b)   any payment of the whole or part of a tax credit (to which section 824 of the Taxes Act applies by virtue of subsection (2) of that section) in respect of such income,

as if the reference in subsection (3)(b) of that section to the year of assessment for which the tax was charged was a reference to the year of assessment for which the tax was assessed on the member concerned.

History – Reg. 7B inserted by SI 1996/781, reg. 4, operative from 5 April 1996.

YEAR OF ASSESSMENT TO WHICH TAXED INCOME AND TAX CREDITS ATTRIBUTABLE

7C   The like provision as is contained in paragraph (a) of section 835(6) of the Taxes Act (total income) shall have effect for the year 1994–95 and subsequent years of assessment as if it provided that income falling within that paragraph and within section 172(1)(c) of the Finance Act 1993 should be deemed to be income of the year of assessment corresponding to the underwriting year in which it was received by the member concerned, and not income of the year of assessment referred to in that paragraph.

History – Reg. 7C inserted by SI 1996/781, reg. 4, operative from 5 April 1996.

DETERMINATIONS AND NOTICES OF DETERMINATIONS

8   [Revoked by SI 2005/3338, reg. 18.]

History – Reg. 8 revoked by SI 2005/3338, reg. 18, which has effect for members who are individuals for 2006–07 and subsequent years of assessment and for corporate members, for accounting periods ending after 31 December 2005 (but not in relation to profits and losses arising to corporate members mentioned in FA 1994, s. 220(2) and which are declared in 2005).

CESSATION OF MEMBER'S UNDERWRITING BUSINESS

CESSATION OF INDIVIDUAL MEMBER'S UNDERWRITING BUSINESS – FINAL YEAR OF ASSESSMENT

9(1)   Where a member who is an individual ceases to carry on his underwriting business, whether by reason of death or otherwise, the member's final year of assessment shall, in the cases specified in paragraphs (2) to (5) below and subject to subsection (3) of section 179, be ascertained in accordance with the provisions of those paragraphs.

9(2)   In any case where a letter is issued by the Membership Department of Lloyd's to the member or his agent inviting an application for the repayment of the member's deposit, the member's final year of assessment shall be not later than the year of assessment in which falls the date which is 180 days after the date of issue of the letter.

9(3)   In any case where the member's deposit at Lloyd's is paid over to a person other than the member or his personal representatives or assigns, the member's final year of assessment shall be that which corresponds to the underwriting year in which his deposit is so paid over or, where paragraph (2) above applies and the year of assessment specified in that paragraph is earlier, that earlier year of assessment.

9(4) In any case where the member or another person is released from any arrangement entered into by the member or that person in order to satisfy the requirement on the part of the member to provide a deposit at Lloyd's, the member's final year of assessment shall, except in a case to which paragraph (5) below applies, be that which corresponds to the underwriting year in which the release occurs.

9(5) In any case where the member's deposit at Lloyd's is extinguished or released before the last open year of account of any syndicate of which he is a member is closed, the member's final year of assessment shall be either–

(a)   the year of assessment next following the year of assessment which corresponds to the underwriting year in which the last open year of account of any syndicate of which he is a member is closed or, if later,

(b)   the year of assessment which corresponds to the underwriting year in which he ceases to be a member of Lloyd's under the rules or practice of Lloyd's.

9(6) This regulation has effect in relation to any member–

(a)   whose deposit at Lloyd's is paid over to him or another person or, as the case may be, released or extinguished, on or after 1st January 1993, and

(b)   in whose case the last open year of account of any syndicate of which he was a member is closed on or after that date.

9(7) For the purposes of this regulation, the last open year of account of a syndicate of which a person is a member shall be regarded as having closed either–

(a)   when the member is treated under the rules or practice of Lloyd's as having been discharged of all his liabilities in relation to that syndicate, whether by the syndicate closing its accounts or by the member or his personal representatives or assigns entering into a quota share contract, or

(b)   in a case where the member enters, or his personal representatives or assigns enter, into a quota share contract before the end of the closing year of the syndicate, at the end of the underwriting year in which the contract is made.

Cross references – SI 1997/2681, reg. 3(1)(b)(ii): where ICTA 1988, s. 111(2) or s. 114(1) apply in relation to a Lloyd's Scottish limited partnership, SI 1995/351 has effect in relation to that partnership as if reg. 9 were omitted.

CESSATION OF INDIVIDUAL MEMBER'S UNDERWRITING BUSINESS BY REASON OF DEATH ON OR AFTER 6TH APRIL 1994 – DATE OF CESSATION OF BUSINESS

10(1) For the purposes of the Income Tax Acts, where a member ceases to carry on his underwriting business by reason of his death, the business shall, in the cases specified in paragraphs (2) to (5) below, be treated as continuing until the date specified in those paragraphs in relation to the appropriate case.

10(2) In any case where a letter is issued by the Membership Department of Lloyd's to the member's agent, or his personal representatives or assigns, inviting an application for the repayment of the member's deposit, the member's business shall be treated as continuing until the date which is 180 days after the date of issue of the letter.

10(3) In any case where the member's deposit at Lloyd's is paid over to a person other than the member's personal representatives or assigns, the member's business shall be treated as continuing until his deposit is so paid over or, where paragraph (2) above applies and the date specified in that paragraph occurs earlier, that earlier date.

10(4) In any case where the member's personal representatives are, or another person is, released from any arrangement entered into by the member or that person in order to satisfy the requirement on the part of the member to provide a deposit at Lloyd's, the member's business shall, except in a case to which paragraph (5) below applies, be treated as continuing until the date on which the release occurs.

10(5) In any case where the member's deposit at Lloyd's is extinguished or released before the last open year of account of any syndicate of which he was a member is closed, the member's business shall be treated as continuing until either–

(a)   the end of the year of assessment next following the year of assessment which corresponds to the underwriting year in which the last open year of account of any syndicate of which he was a member is closed or, if later,

(b)   the end of the year of assessment which corresponds to the underwriting year in which he ceased to be a member of Lloyd's under the rules or practice of Lloyd's.

10(6) For the purposes of paragraph (5) above, the last open year of account of a syndicate of which a person was a member shall be regarded as having closed either–

(a)   when the member is treated under the rules or practice of Lloyd's as having been discharged of all his liabilities in relation to that syndicate, whether by the syndicate closing its accounts or by the member or his personal representatives entering into a quota share contract, or

(b)   in a case where the member enters, or his personal representatives enter, into a quota share contract before the end of the closing year of the syndicate, at the end of the underwriting year in which the contract is made.

10(7) This regulation has effect in relation to any member whose death occurs on or after 6th April 1994.

Cross references – SI 1997/2681, reg. 3(1)(b)(ii): where ICTA 1988, s. 111(2) or s. 114(1) apply in relation to a Lloyd's Scottish limited partnership, SI 1995/351 has effect in relation to that partnership as if reg. 10 were omitted.

CESSATION OF INDIVIDUAL MEMBER'S UNDERWRITING BUSINESS BY REASON OF DEATH PRIOR TO 6TH APRIL 1994 – PROFITS OR LOSSES ARISING AFTER DEATH

11 For the purposes of the provisions of Chapter III other than Schedule 20, where–

(a)   the death of a member occurred before 6th April 1994;

(b)   the member's deposit at Lloyd's, if paid over to him or his personal representatives or assigns, was not paid over prior to 1st January 1993; and

(c)   income arises to, or expenses are incurred or paid by, his personal representatives after his death from the carrying on by them of the member's underwriting business in circumstances where the income or expenses would have been taken into account, by virtue of those provisions, in computing the profits or losses arising to the member from his underwriting business had they arisen or been incurred or paid prior to his death,

the income and expenses shall be regarded as arising to, or incurred or paid by, the member and are accordingly to be taken into account in computing profits or losses arising to the member from his underwriting business for the purposes of those provisions.

Cross references – SI 1997/2681, reg. 3(1)(b)(ii): where ICTA 1988, s. 111(2) or s. 114(1) apply in relation to a Lloyd's Scottish limited partnership, SI 1995/351 has effect in relation to that partnership as if reg. 11 were omitted.

CESSATION OF INDIVIDUAL MEMBER'S UNDERWRITING BUSINESS BY REASON OF DEATH ON OR AFTER 6TH APRIL 1994 – PROFITS OR LOSSES ARISING AFTER DEATH

12 For the purposes of the provisions of Chapter III other than Schedule 20, where–

(a)   the death of a member occurs on or after 6th April 1994; and

(b)   income arises to, or expenses are incurred or paid by, his personal representatives after his death from the carrying on by them of the member's underwriting business in circumstances where the income or expenses would have been taken into account, by virtue of those provisions, in computing the profits or losses arising to the member from his underwriting business had they arisen or been incurred or paid prior to his death,

the profits or losses arising to the personal representatives from the income and expenses shall be computed as if references in those provisions to profits and losses arising to the member from his underwriting business included references to the profits and losses arising to the personal representatives.

Cross references – SI 1997/2681, reg. 3(1)(b)(ii): where ICTA 1988, s. 111(2) or s. 114(1) apply in relation to a Lloyd's Scottish limited partnership, SI 1995/351 has effect in relation to that partnership as if reg. 12 were omitted.

CESSATION OF INDIVIDUAL MEMBER'S UNDERWRITING BUSINESS – CLAIM FOR RELIEF WHERE BUSINESS COMMENCED BEFORE 1ST JANUARY 1972

13(1) This regulation applies where–

(a)   a member who is an individual has ceased to be a member of Lloyd's under the rules or practice of Lloyd's or, if earlier, has given notice of resignation of membership under the rules or practice of Lloyd's which has not been withdrawn; and

(b)   the member's underwriting business as an underwriting member of Lloyd's commenced before 1st January 1972.

13(2) The member may claim that–

(a) for the last year of assessment in which profits or losses of his underwriting business arising directly from his membership of one or more syndicates, or from assets forming part of a premiums trust fund of one or more syndicates, being profits or losses declared in the underwriting year following the closing year, fall to be included by virtue of the provisions of Chapter III, he shall be charged to tax in respect of those profits on the amount of the actual profits of the period beginning on 6th April and ending on 31st December in that underwriting year (but subject to any deduction or set-off to which he may be entitled under section 385 of the Taxes Act); and

(b) for the year of assessment immediately preceding that referred to in sub-paragraph (a) above, there shall be deducted in computing profits arising as mentioned in that sub-paragraph an amount equal to the lesser of–

  (i)   the amount of those profits, and

  (ii) the amount of the profits of his underwriting business for the underwriting year 1972.

13(3)   For the purposes only of determining the last year of assessment under paragraph (2) above in any case where the member enters into a quota share contract in relation to a syndicate before the end of the closing year of the syndicate, any loss declared by that syndicate following the making of the contract shall be treated as if it were a declared profit.

13(4)   A member may not make more than one claim under paragraph (2) above.

Cross references – SI 1997/2681, reg. 3(1)(b)(ii): where ICTA 1988, s. 111(2) or s. 114(1) apply in relation to a Lloyd's Scottish limited partnership, SI 1995/351 has effect in relation to that partnership as if reg. 13 were omitted.

CESSATION OF INDIVIDUAL MEMBER'S UNDERWRITING BUSINESS – TERMINAL LOSS RELIEF

14(1)   This regulation applies where a member ceases to carry on his underwriting business, whether by reason of death or otherwise, and either–

(a) his deposit at Lloyd's is paid over to him or his personal representatives or assigns on or after 1st January 1993, or

(b) the last open year of account of any syndicate of which he is a member is closed after 31st December 1992.

14(2)   Notwithstanding section 179 or section 179A, or regulation 9 or 10 of these Regulations, the date on which the member's underwriting business is permanently discontinued for the purposes of section 388 of the Taxes Act (carry-back of terminal losses) shall be deemed to be the 5th April in the last year of assessment in which profits or losses of that business which arise directly from his membership of one or more syndicates, or from assets forming part of a premium trust fund, fall to be included by virtue of the provisions of Chapter III.

14(3)   No claim may be made by a member under section 388 of the Taxes Act until–

(a) he has ceased to be a member under the rules or practice of Lloyd's or, if earlier,

(b) he has given (and not withdrawn) notice of resignation of membership under the rules or practice of Lloyd's.

14(4)   A member may not make more than one claim under section 388 of the Taxes Act in respect of the same underwriting business.

14(5)   For the purposes of paragraph (1)(b) above, the last open year of account of a syndicate of which a person is a member shall be regarded as having closed either–

(a) when the member is treated under the rules or practice of Lloyd's as having been discharged of all his liabilities in relation to that syndicate, whether by the syndicate closing its accounts or by the member or his personal representatives or assigns entering into a quota share contract; or

(b) in a case where the member enters, or his personal representatives or assigns enter, into a quota share contract before the end of the closing year of the syndicate, at the end of the underwriting year in which the contract is made.

14(6)   For the purposes only of determining the last year of assessment under paragraph (2) above in any case where the member enters into a quota share contract in relation to a syndicate before the end of the closing year of the syndicate, any loss declared by that syndicate following the making of the contract shall be treated as if it were a declared profit.

History – In reg. 14(2), "premium" substituted for "premiums" by SI 2001/3629, art. 139 which came into force on 1 December 2001.

Cross references – SI 1997/2681, reg. 3(1)(b)(ii): where ICTA 1988, s. 111(2) or s. 114(1) applies in relation to a Lloyd's Scottish limited partnership, SI 1995/351 has effect in relation to that partnership as if reg. 14 were omitted.

CESSATION OF INDIVIDUAL MEMBER'S UNDERWRITING BUSINESS BY REASON OF DEATH – WINDING UP OF OLD-STYLE SPECIAL RESERVE FUND

15(1)   In any case where–

(a)   a member ceases to carry on his underwriting business by reason of his death;

(b)   the member's final year of assessment, ascertained in accordance with the provisions of Chapter III and these Regulations, is the year 1992–93 or any subsequent year of assessment; and

(c)   prior to his death no new-style fund had been set up in relation to the member;

subsection (4) of section 175 of the Finance Act 1993 (winding-up of old-style fund) shall apply as if paragraph (b) of that subsection was omitted.

15(2)   In paragraph (1) above, **"new-style fund"** and **"old-style fund"** have the meanings given by paragraph 12(1) of Schedule 20.

Cross references – SI 1997/2681, reg. 3(1)(b)(ii): where ICTA 1988, s. 111(2) or s. 114(1) apply in relation to a Lloyd's Scottish limited partnership, SI 1995/351 has effect in relation to that partnership as if reg. 15 were omitted.

CESSATION OF CORPORATE MEMBER'S UNDERWRITING BUSINESS – FINAL UNDERWRITING YEAR

16(1)   Where a corporate member ceases to carry on its underwriting business, whether by reason of being wound up or otherwise, its final underwriting year shall, in the cases specified in paragraphs (2) to (5) below, be ascertained in accordance with the provisions of those paragraphs.

16(2)   In any case where a letter is issued by the Membership Department of Lloyd's to the corporate member or its agent inviting an application for the repayment of the corporate member's deposit, the corporate member's final underwriting year shall be not later than the underwriting year in which falls the date which is 180 days after the date of issue of the letter.

16(3)   In any case where the corporate member's deposit at Lloyd's is paid over to a person other than the corporate member, its final underwriting year shall be the underwriting year in which its deposit is so paid over or, where paragraph (2) above applies and the underwriting year specified in that paragraph is earlier, that earlier underwriting year.

16(4)   In any case where the corporate member or another person is released from any arrangement entered into by the corporate member or that person in order to satisfy the requirement on the part of the corporate member to provide a deposit at Lloyd's, the corporate member's final underwriting year shall, except in a case to which paragraph (5) below applies, be the underwriting year in which the release occurs.

16(5)   In any case where the corporate member's deposit at Lloyd's is extinguished or released before the last open year of account of any syndicate of which it is a member is closed, the corporate member's final underwriting year shall be either–

(a)   the underwriting year next following the underwriting year in which the last open year of account of any syndicate of which it was a member is closed or, if later,

(b)   the underwriting year in which the corporate member ceases to be a member of Lloyd's under the rules or practice of Lloyd's.

16(6)   For the purposes of this regulation, the last open year of account of a syndicate of which a person is a corporate member shall be regarded as having closed when the member is treated under the rules or practice of Lloyd' s as having been discharged of all its liabilities in relation to that syndicate, whether by the syndicate closing its accounts or by the member entering into a quota share contract.

Cross references – SI 1997/2681, reg. 3(1)(b)(ii): where ICTA 1988, s. 111(2) or s. 114(1) applies in relation to a Lloyd's Scottish limited partnership, SI 1995/351 has effect in relation to that partnership as if reg. 16 were omitted.

SUPPLEMENTAL

REVOCATIONS

17(1)   The Lloyd's Underwriters (Tax) Regulations 1974, the Lloyd's Under-writers (Tax) (No. 2) Regulations 1974 and the Lloyd's Underwriters (Schedule 19A to the Income and Corporation Taxes Act 1988) Regulations 1990 are hereby revoked.

17(2)   A claim made under regulation 21 of the Lloyd's Underwriters (Tax) Regulations 1974 which was valid for the purposes of that regulation immediately before the coming into force of these Regulations but which had not been finally determined at that time (**"a pending claim"**) shall have effect as if made under regulation 13 of these Regulations, and accordingly references in that regulation to a claim shall be construed as including references to a pending claim.

Cross references – SI 1997/2681, reg. 3(1)(b)(ii): where ICTA 1988, s. 111(2) or s. 114(1) apply in relation to a Lloyd's Scottish limited partnership, SI 1995/351 has effect in relation to that partnership as if reg. 17 were omitted.

Notes – The Lloyd's Underwriters (Tax) Regulations 1974 (SI 1974/896), reg. 21 formerly read as follows:

"CESSATION OF BUSINESS

21(1) When a member ceases to be a member of Lloyd's, or when his underwriting business ceases (if earlier), he may claim–

(a)   in the computation of his underwriting profits for the year of assessment preceding the year of assessment in which the cessation occurs, a deduction equal to the lesser of–

       (i)   an amount equal to those profits; and

       (ii)   an amount equal to his underwriting profits for the underwriting year 1972; and

(b)   that, for the year of assessment in which the cessation occurs, he shall be charged to tax in respect of his underwriting profits on the amount of the actual profits of the period beginning on 6th April in that year and ending on the relevant date (but subject to any deduction or set-off to which he may be entitled under Section 171 of the Income and Corporation Taxes Act 1970 [ICTA 1988, s. 385] in respect of any loss).

21(2) For the purposes of sub-paragraph (b) of paragraph (1) above the relevant date is the actual date of cessation or, where the cessation occurs by reason of the member's death or resignation, such other date as, under the rules and practice of the syndicates in which the member participates, is the latest of the dates on which he is deemed to cease to participate in any of those syndicates.

21(3) The provisions of this Regulation shall not apply more than once to any individual."

LLOYD'S UNDERWRITERS (TAX)
(1992–93 TO 1996–97) REGULATIONS 1995

(SI 1995/352, as amended by SI 1996/782 and SI 2005/3338)

Made on 15 February 1995 by the Commissioners of Inland Revenue, in exercise of the powers conferred on them by s. 182(1), (3) and (4) and 184(1) and (3) of the Finance Act 1993 and s. 209(2) and (6) of the Taxation of Chargeable Gains Act 1992. Operative from 9 March 1995.

CITATION, COMMENCEMENT AND EFFECT

1(1) These Regulations may be cited as the Lloyd's Underwriters (Tax) (1992–93 to 1996–97) Regulations 1995 and shall come into force on 9th March 1995.

1(2) Except as otherwise provided these Regulations shall have effect for the years of assessment 1992–93 to 1996–97.

INTERPRETATION

2(1) In these Regulations unless the context otherwise requires–

    "the Board" means the Commissioners of Inland Revenue;

    "Management Act" means the Taxes Management Act 1970;

    "Schedule 19" means Schedule 19 to the Finance Act 1993;

    "syndicate gains" means the chargeable gains accruing to a member on the disposal of assets forming part of a premiums trust fund;

    "the Taxes Act" means the Income and Corporation Taxes Act 1988;

    "the Taxes Acts" means the Management Act and

    (a)   the Tax Acts, and

    (b)   the Taxation of Chargeable Gains Act 1992 and all other enactments relating to capital gains tax; **"tax credit"** means a tax credit under section 231 of the Taxes Act.

2(2) For the purposes of these Regulations an underwriting year and a year of assessment shall be deemed to correspond to each other if the underwriting year ends in the year of assessment.

History – Definitions of "the Taxes Act" and "tax credit" inserted by SI 1996/782, reg. 3, operative from 5 April 1996.

MEMBERS' AGENTS

3   [Revoked by SI 2005/3338, reg. 18.]

History – Reg. 3 revoked by SI 2005/3338, reg. 18, with effect for 2006–07 and subsequent years of assessment (individuals) and for accounting periods ending on or after 31 December 2005 (corporate members). Former Reg. 3 read as follows:

    "**3(1)**   For the purposes of Part II of Schedule 19 and of these Regulations, if the person who is acting as a members' agent in respect of an underwriting year corresponding to a year of assessment (in this regulation referred to as "**the original year of assessment**") is different from the person who was so acting at the end of that underwriting year (in this regulation referred to as "**the original agent**"), then "**members' agent**" has the meaning given by sub-paragraph (a) or, as the case may be, sub-paragraph (b) of paragraph (2) below.

    3(2)   If the original agent ceases to act–
    (a)   before the beginning of the year of assessment next but two following the original year of assessment, then "**members' agent**" means–
       (i)   the person who is so acting at the beginning of that year of assessment, or
       (ii)   if that person ceases so to act, such person as the Board may determine having regard to all the circumstances;
    (b)   after the end of the year of assessment next but one following the original year of assessment, then "**member's agent**" means such person as the board may determine having regard to all the circumstances.

    3(3)   This regulation shall have effect for the years of assessment 1992–93 and 1993–94 only.".

ASSESSMENT AND COLLECTION: GENERAL

4   The like provisions as are contained in the Taxes Acts relating to the assessment and collection of tax shall have effect in relation to income tax charged in accordance with section 171 of the Finance Act 1993, but subject to regulations 6 to 12, 14 and 15 below and regulations 5 to 8 of the Lloyd's Underwriters (Tax) Regulations 1995.

5(1) The like provisions as are contained in the Taxes Acts relating to the assessment and collection of tax shall have effect in relation to capital gains tax charged in accordance with section 207 of the Taxation of Chargeable Gains Act 1992 but subject to regulations 6 to 12 and 14 below and regulations 5 to 8 of the Lloyd's Underwriters (Tax) Regulations 1995.

5(2) This regulation shall have effect for the years of assessment 1992–93 and 1993–94 only.

EXTENSION OF TIME LIMITS FOR MAKING CERTAIN ASSESSMENTS

6(1) The like provisions as are specified in paragraph (2) below shall have effect in relation to the assessment of tax as if the modifications specified in that paragraph had been made.

6(2) In the Management Act–

(a)   in subsection (1) of sections 34 and 36, for the words "the chargeable period to which the assessment relates" there shall be substituted the words "the year of assessment 1994–95";

(b)   in subsections (1) and (2) of section 40, for the words from "the third year next following" to the end of each subsection there shall be substituted the words "the year of assessment 1997–98".

6(3) This regulation shall have effect for the year of assessment 1992–93 only.

7 [Revoked by SI 2005/3338, reg. 18.]

History – Reg. 7 revoked by SI 2005/3338, reg. 18, with effect for 2006–07 and subsequent years of assessment (individuals) and for accounting periods ending on or after 31 December 2005 (corporate members). Former reg. 7 read as follows:

> "**7(1)**   The like provisions as are specified in paragraph (2) shall have effect in relation to the assessment of tax as if the modifications specified in that paragraph had been made.
>
> **7(2)**   In the Management Act–
> (a)   in subsection (1) of sections 34 and 36, for the words "the chargeable period to which the assessment relates" there shall be substituted the words "the year of assessment 1995–96";
> (b)   in subsections (1) and (2) of section 40, for the words from "the third year next following" to the end of each subsection there shall be substituted the words "the year of assessment 1998–99".
>
> **7(3)**   This regulation shall have effect for the years of assessment 1993–94 and 1994–95 only.".

DATE FOR PAYMENT

8 [Revoked by SI 2005/3338, reg. 18.]

History – Reg. 8 revoked by SI 2005/3338, reg. 18, with effect for 2006–07 and subsequent years of assessment (individuals) and for accounting periods ending on or after 31 December 2005 (corporate members). Former reg. 8 read as follows:

> "**8(1)**   Subject to paragraph (2) below–
> (a)   tax charged by an assessment on the profits arising to a member from his underwriting business shall be payable on or before 31st January 1997, and
> (b)   tax charged by an assessment on syndicate gains shall be payable on or before 1st January 1996.
>
> **8(2)**   Tax charged by an assessment made less than 30 days before, or made after, the date specified in sub-paragraph (a) or (b) of paragraph (1) above shall be payable at the expiration of a period of 30 days beginning with the date of the issue of the notice of assessment.
>
> **8(3)**   This regulation shall have effect for the year of assessment 1992–93 only.".

9(1) Subject to paragraph (2) below–

(a)   tax charged by an assessment on the profits arising to a member from his underwriting business shall be payable on or before 31st January 1998, and

(b)   tax charged by an assessment on syndicate gains shall be payable on or before 1st January 1997.

9(2) Tax charged by an assessment made less than 30 days before, or made after, the date specified in sub-paragraph (a) or (b) of paragraph (1) above shall be payable at the expiration of a period of 30 days beginning with the date of the issue of the notice of assessment.

9(3) This regulation shall have effect for the year of assessment 1993–94 only.

10(1) Subject to paragraph (2) below, tax charged by an assessment on the profits of a member's underwriting business shall be payable on or before 31st January 1998.

10(2) Tax charged by an assessment made less than 30 days before, or made after, 31st January 1998 shall be payable at the expiration of a period of 30 days beginning with the date of the issue of the notice of assessment.

10(3) This regulation shall have effect for the years of assessment 1994–95 to 1996–97 only.

REPAYMENT OF TAX – TAXED INCOME AND TAX CREDITS

10A(1) The like provisions as are contained in section 824 of the Taxes Act (as that section has effect for the year of assessment 1995–96) shall have effect in relation to–

(a)   any repayment of tax which was paid by way of deduction at source in respect of income charged to tax in accordance with section 171, and falling within section 172(1)(c), of the Finance Act 1993, and

(b)   any payment of the whole or part of a tax credit (to which section 824 of the Taxes Act applies by virtue of subsection (2) of that section) in respect of such income,

as if **"the relevant time"** for the purposes of subsection (1) of that section was the end of the period of 12 months following the year of assessment for which the tax was assessed on the member concerned.

10A(2)   This regulation shall have effect for the year of assessment 1995–96 only.

History – Reg 10A inserted by SI 1996/782, operative from 5 April 1996.

REASONABLE EXCUSE

11(1)   For the purposes of paragraph 10 of Schedule 19, a members' agent shall be deemed not to have failed to deliver a return of the member's profit within the time specified in sub-paragraph (5) of that paragraph if he delivered it within such further time, if any, as the inspector may have allowed.

11(2)   Where a members' agent had a reasonable excuse for not delivering the return of the member's profit, he shall be deemed not to have failed to deliver it unless the excuse had ceased and, after the excuse ceased, not to have failed to deliver it if he did so without unreasonable delay after the excuse had ceased.

11(3)   This regulation shall have effect for the years of assessment 1992–93 and 1993–94 only.

ERROR OR MISTAKE

12(1)   If a members' agent alleges that a statement of the amount of tax payable in the case of a member's profit under paragraph 10(1)(c) of Schedule 19 was excessive because of some error or mistake in a return made by him under paragraph 10(1) of that Schedule, he may by notice in writing at any time not later than six years after the end of the closing year relating to the year of assessment make a claim to the Board for relief.

12(2)   On receiving the claim the Board shall inquire into the matter and having regard to all the relevant circumstances of the case, but subject to paragraph (3) below, give by way of repayment or otherwise such relief in respect of the error or mistake as is reasonable and just.

12(3)   No relief shall be given under this regulation in respect of an error or mistake as to the basis on which a syndicate profit or loss, or as the case may be a member's profit, ought to have been computed where the return was in fact made on the basis or in accordance with the practice generally prevailing at the time when the return was made.

12(4)   An appeal may be brought against the decision of the Board on the claim by giving written notice to the Board within 30 days of receipt of written notice of that decision, and the Special Commissioners shall hear and determine the appeal in accordance with the principles to be followed by the Board in determining claims under this regulation; and either the appellant or the Board shall be entitled to appeal against the determination of the Special Commissioners under the like provisions as are contained in section 56A of the Management Act but only on a point of law arising in connection with the computation of the amount of tax payable in the case of the member's profit.

12(5)   In this regulation **"return"** includes the documents referred to in paragraphs (a) and (b) of paragraph 10(1) of Schedule 19.

12(6)   This regulation shall have effect for the years of assessment 1992–93 and 1993–94 only.

RUNNING-OFF SYNDICATES

13(1)   Where for an underwriting year corresponding to a year of assessment (in this regulation called **"the basis year"**) the accounts of a syndicate remain open beyond the end of the closing year, any profits or losses of a member's underwriting business which arise–

(a)   directly from his membership of that syndicate, or from assets forming part of a premiums trust fund of that syndicate, and

(b)   in an underwriting year corresponding to a year of assessment after the closing year,

shall be deemed, for the purposes of section 171 of the Finance Act 1993 and all other purposes of the Income Tax Acts and subject to paragraph (2) below, to be referable or, as the case may be, to be allocated to the last underwriting year but one preceding the year in which they arise, and not to the basis year.

13(2)   Where in a case to which paragraph (1) above applies the member dies and the underwriting year corresponding to the year of assessment in which he died is earlier than the underwriting year to which the profits or losses of his underwriting business referred to in that paragraph are deemed to be referable or allocated by virtue of that paragraph, the profits or losses in question shall be deemed, for the purposes of section 171 of the Finance Act 1993 and all other purposes of the Income Tax Acts, to be referable or allocated to the underwriting year corresponding to the year of assessment in which he died.

13(3)   This regulation shall have effect in relation to profits or losses of a member's underwriting business arising in the underwriting year 1994 or 1995.

EXTENSION OF TIME LIMITS – MEMBER AND SPOUSE

14(1) Where a claim or application or election falls to be made by a member or his spouse (or both) under a provision specified in the first column of the Schedule to these Regulations, that provision shall have effect as if it imposed the extended time limit specified in the second column of that Schedule.

14(2) This regulation shall have effect for the years of assessment 1992–93 and 1993–94 only.

15(1) Where a claim or application or election falls to be made by a member or his spouse (or both) under a provision specified in the first column of the Schedule to these Regulations, that provision shall have effect as if it imposed an extended time limit which is one year less than the extended time limit specified in the second column of that Schedule.

15(2) This regulation shall have effect for the year of assessment 1994–95 only.

SCHEDULE

Provision	*Extended time limit*
Taxes Management Act 1970 (c. 9)	
section 33(1)	Eight years after the end of the year of assessment or accounting period.
section 43(1)	Eight years from the end of the chargeable period.
Income and Corporation Taxes Act 1988 (c. 1)	
section 96(8)	Four years after the end of the second of the years of assessment to which the claim relates.
section 257B(3)	Eight years after the end of the year of assessment.
section 257BB(5)	Eight years after the end of the year of assessment.
section 257D(9)	Eight years after the end of the year of assessment.
section 265(5)	Eight years after the end of the year of assessment.
section 306(1)(b)	Four years in each case.
section 356B(2)	Three years.
section 356B(4)	Three years.
section 380(1)	Four years after the year of assessment.
section 381(1)	Four years after the year of assessment.
section 574(1)	Four years after the year of assessment in which the disposal took place.
Finance Act 1988 (c. 39)	
paragraph 4(4) of Schedule 6	Four years after the end of the chargeable period.
Capital Allowances Act 1990 (c. 1)	
section 11(3)	Four years after the date on which the lease takes effect.
section 25(3)	Four years after the end of the chargeable period.
section 31(3)	Four years after the end of the chargeable period.
section 33(1)	Four years after the end of the chargeable period.
section 37(2)	Four years after the end of the chargeable period or its basis period.
section 53(2)	The expiry of the period of four years beginning with the end of the chargeable period.
section 55(3)	Four years after the date on which the lease takes effect.
section 77(3)	Four years after the date of succession to the trade.
section 129(2)	Four years after the end of the chargeable period.
section 141(3)	Four years after the end of the year of assessment.
Finance Act 1991 (c. 31)	
section 72(1)	Four years after the year of assessment.

LLOYD'S UNDERWRITERS (SPECIAL RESERVE FUNDS) REGULATIONS 1995

(SI 1995/353, as amended by SI 1995/1185)

Made on 15 February 1995 by the Commissioners of Inland Revenue, in exercise of the powers conferred on them by s. 182(1)(c) and (4) and 184(1) and (3) of the Finance Act 1993 and para. 3(2), 4(8), 5(10), 6(1) and (3) and 11(5) of Sch. 20 to that Act. Operative from 9 March 1995.

CITATION, COMMENCEMENT AND EFFECT

1 These Regulations may be cited as the Lloyd's Underwriters (Special Reserve Funds) Regulations 1995, shall come into force on 9th March 1995 and, except as otherwise provided by these Regulations, shall have effect for the year 1992–93 and subsequent years of assessment.

INTERPRETATION

2 In these Regulations **"Schedule 20"** means Schedule 20 to the Finance Act 1993.

SYNDICATE PROFIT OR LOSS – MODIFICATION OF DEFINITION – RUNNING-OFF SYNDICATES

3(1) Paragraph 1(2) of Schedule 20 shall apply with the following modifications.

3(2) Immediately following paragraph (a) the word "and" shall be omitted.

3(3) After paragraph (b) there shall be added the following paragraph–

"(c) where the accounts of a syndicate remain open beyond the end of the underwriting year which is the closing year for that syndicate, profits or losses shown in the accounts of the syndicate as arising to a member in any subsequent underwriting year shall be profits or losses of the member for the last underwriting year but one preceding that subsequent underwriting year.".

CASH CALLS – RUNNING-OFF SYNDICATES – MODIFICATION OF PARAGRAPH 4 OF SCHEDULE 20

4(1) Paragraph 4 of Schedule 20 shall apply with the following modification.

4(2) After sub-paragraph (1) there shall be inserted the following sub-paragraph–

"**4(1A)** References in sub-paragraph (1) above to a cash call include references to a cash call made in respect of an underwriting year determined by paragraph 1(2)(c) above (**"the relevant cash call"**) if and to the extent that the aggregate amount of the relevant cash call and any previous cash calls made on the member in respect of the syndicate concerned exceeds the net amount of losses arising to the member from that syndicate which have been declared before the date of the relevant cash call after deducting the amount of profits arising to him from that syndicate which have been so declared.".

PAYMENTS INTO OR OUT OF SPECIAL RESERVE FUND – PRESCRIBED PERIODS

5(1) The period prescribed for the purposes of paragraph 3(1) of Schedule 20 is the period which begins on 1st January in the calendar year in which the profits and losses comprising the syndicate profit made by the member for the underwriting year concerned are declared and ends on 31st October in that calendar year or, if earlier, on the date on which payment is made to or on behalf of the member of an amount representing any part of the syndicate profit made by the member for that underwriting year.

5(2) The period prescribed for the purposes of any payments required by paragraph 4(1) of Schedule 20–

(a) where the accounts of the syndicate have remained open beyond the end of the closing year and the cash call concerned is made–

(i) in respect of an underwriting year determined by reference to paragraph 1(2)(c) of Schedule 20, and

(ii) in a calendar year (**"the relevant calendar year"**) after the end of the closing year, is the period which begins on 1st January in the relevant calendar year and ends on the date which is 90 days after the date on which the cash call is made on the member;

(b)   in any other case, is the period which begins on 1st January in the calendar year next but one preceding the underwriting year which is the closing year for the syndicate concerned and ends on the earlier of the following dates, namely—

(i)   the date which is 90 days after the date on which the cash call concerned is made on the member, and

(ii)   the date which is 90 days after the end of the closing year.

5(3) The period prescribed for the purposes of any payments required by paragraph 4(2) of Schedule 20 is the period which begins on 1st January in the calendar year in which the profits and losses comprising the syndicate profit or loss of the member for the underwriting year concerned are declared and ends on the earlier of the following dates, namely—

(a)   31st October in that calendar year;

(b)   where there is a syndicate profit made by the member for the underwriting year concerned, the date on which payment is made to or on behalf of the member of an amount representing any part of that profit.

5(4) The period prescribed for the purposes of any payment required by paragraph 4(3) of Schedule 20 is the period of 90 days following the date on which the stop-loss payment is made to the member in respect of his syndicate loss.

5(5) The period prescribed for the purposes of any payments required by paragraph 4(6) of Schedule 20 is the period of 90 days following the date on which the whole or part of the stop-loss payment made to the member is repaid by him.

5(6) The period prescribed for the purposes of any payments required by paragraph 5(1) of Schedule 20 is the period which begins on 1st January in the calendar year in which the profits and losses comprising the syndicate loss sustained by the member for the underwriting year concerned are declared and ends on 31st October in that calendar year.

5(7) The period prescribed for the purposes of any payment required by paragraph 5(4) of Schedule 20 is the period of 90 days following the date on which the stop-loss payment is made to the member in respect of his syndicate loss.

5(8) The period prescribed for the purposes of any payments required by paragraph 5(7) of Schedule 20 is the period of 90 days following the date on which the whole or part of the stop-loss payment made to the member is repaid by him.

5(9) The period prescribed for the purposes of any payments required by paragraph 6(2) of Schedule 20 is the period of 90 days following the last day of the underwriting year in respect of which the valuation giving rise to the payments is made.

History – In reg. 5(2)(a)(i) words "of Schedule 20" substituted for the word "above" by SI 1995/1185, reg. 3, operative from 23 May 1995.

VALUATION OF SPECIAL RESERVE FUND

6(1) Paragraph (2) below prescribes the manner in which the value of a member's special reserve fund as at the end of an underwriting year shall be determined, and paragraph (3) below prescribes the matters which, in addition to the value of the fund, are to be stated by the fund manager in his report to the member of the value of the fund.

6(2) The value of the fund shall be determined so as to be in accordance with—

(a)   the market value of the assets of the fund, and

(b)   the rules of Lloyd's relating to the method of valuation of the fund.

6(3) The matters prescribed are—

(a)   the amount of any payment made in the underwriting year to which the valuation relates under any of the paragraphs of Schedule 20 specified in paragraph (4) below, and

(b)   the date on which each such payment was made.

6(4) The paragraphs specified are paragraphs 3(1), 4(1), (2), (3) and (6), 5(1), (4) and (7), 6(2) and 7(1).

6(5) This regulation shall have effect for the underwriting year 1994 and subsequent underwriting years.

CESSATION OF UNDERWRITING BUSINESS – MODIFICATIONS OF PART I OF SCHEDULE 20

7(1) For the purposes of the Income Tax Acts and these Regulations–

(a)　references in paragraphs 1, 3 to 6, 8 and 10 of Schedule 20 to a member, other than references relating to a member's special reserve fund, shall be construed, in the circumstances specified in paragraph (2) below and unless the context otherwise requires, as including references to the member's personal representatives;

(b)　references in those paragraphs to a member's special reserve fund shall be construed, in the circumstances specified in paragraph (2) below and unless the context otherwise requires, as including references to income arising after the death of the member from assets of the fund and retained by the trustees, and profits arising from the investment of that income.

7(2) The circumstances specified in this paragraph are where–

(a)　the member dies on or after 6th April 1994, and

(b)　the member's personal representatives carry on his underwriting business after his death.

7(3) This regulation shall have effect–

(a)　in its application to paragraphs 1, 3 to 6 and 8 of Schedule 20, for the year 1994–95 and subsequent years of assessment;

(b)　in its application to paragraph 10 of Schedule 20, for the year 1997–98 and subsequent years of assessment.

History – See history note to reg. 7A below.

7A(1) Paragraph 9 of Schedule 20 (tax exemption for profits arising from assets of fund) shall apply with the modifications specified in paragraphs (2) and (3) below.

7A(2) In sub-paragraph (1) after the words "special reserve fund" there shall be inserted the words "or arising after the death of the member from the investment of income retained by the trustees".

7A(3) In sub-paragraphs (2) and (3) after the words "special reserve fund" in both places where they occur there shall be inserted the words "or arising after the death of the member as mentioned in sub-paragraph (1) above".

7A(4) This regulation shall have effect for the year 1994–95 and subsequent years of assessment.

History – Reg. 7, 7A substituted for former reg. 7 by SI 1995/1185, reg. 4, operative from 23 May 1995. Reg. 7 formerly read as follows:

> "**7(1)** For the purposes of the Income Tax Acts and these Regulations, references in paragraphs 1, 3 to 6, 8 and 10 of Schedule 20 to a member, other than references relating to a member's special reserve fund, shall be construed, in the circumstances specified in paragraph (2) below and unless the context otherwise requires, as including references to the member's personal representatives.
>
> **7(2)** The circumstances specified in this paragraph are where–
> (a)　the member dies on or after 6th April 1994, and
> (b)　the member's personal representatives carry on his underwriting business after his death.
>
> **7(3)** This regulation shall have effect–
> (a)　in its application to paragraphs 1, 3 to 6 and 8 of Schedule 20, for the year 1994–95 and subsequent years of assessment;
> (b)　in its application to paragraph 10 of Schedule 20, for the year 1997–98 and subsequent years of assessment."

8(1) Paragraph 11 of Schedule 20 (tax consequences of cessation) shall apply with the modifications specified in paragraphs (1A) to (5) below.

8(1A) In sub-paragraph (2) for the words from "under paragraph 7(1) above" to "assigns" there shall be substituted the words "which is made by the trustees to him or his personal representatives or assigns out of his special reserve fund under paragraph 7(1) above, or otherwise than".

8(2) In sub-paragraph (5) in the definition of **"the penultimate underwriting year"** for the words from "immediately preceding" to the end there shall be substituted the words "corresponding to the year of assessment immediately preceding the member's final year of assessment;".

8(3) In sub-paragraph (5) for the definition of **"the relevant underwriting year"** there shall be substituted the following definition–

> **"the relevant underwriting year"** means–
> (a)　where a member dies before the occurrence of any of the events specified in sub-paragraph (6) below, the underwriting year immediately preceding that corresponding to the relevant year of assessment; and
> (b)　in any other case, the underwriting year corresponding to the year of assessment immediately preceding the member's final year of assessment.".

8(4) In sub-paragraph (5) for paragraph (a) of the definition of **"the relevant year of assessment"** there shall be substituted the following paragraph–

"(a)   where a member dies before the occurrence of any of the events specified in sub-paragraph (6) below, the year of assessment at the end of which he is treated, by virtue of section 179A(2) of this Act, as having died;".

8(5)   After sub-paragraph (5) there shall be added the following sub-paragraphs–

"**11(6)**   For the purposes of the definitions of "**the relevant underwriting year**" and "**the relevant year of assessment**" in sub-paragraph (5) above the events specified before the occurrence of which a member dies are the following–

(a)   the member's deposit at Lloyd's is paid over to him or his assigns, or to a person other than the member or his assigns;

(b)   the member or another person is released from any arrangement entered into by the member or that person in order to satisfy the requirement on the part of the member to provide a deposit at Lloyd's;

(d)   the last open year of account of any syndicate of which he was a member is closed.

11(7)   For the purposes of sub-paragraph (6)(c) above, the last open year of account of any syndicate of which a person was a member shall be regarded as having closed either–

(a)   when the member is treated under the rules or practice of Lloyd's as having been discharged of all his liabilities in relation to that syndicate, whether by the syndicate closing its accounts or by the member or his personal representatives or assigns entering into a quota share contract, or

(b)   in a case where the member entered, or his personal representatives or assigns have entered, into a quota share contract before the end of the closing year of the syndicate, at the end of the underwriting year in which the contract was made.".

8(6)   This regulation shall have effect for the year 1994–95 and subsequent years of assessment.

History – Reg. 8(1A) inserted, and the reference to it in reg. 8(1) substituted for former reference to reg. 8(2), by SI 1995/1185, reg. 5(1), with effect for the year 1994–95 and subsequent years of assessment.

PROFIT-RELATED PAY (SHORTFALL RECOVERY) REGULATIONS 1995

(SI 1995/917)

Made on 29 March 1995 by the Commissioners of Inland Revenue, in exercise of the powers conferred on them by s. 179(2) and 203 of the Income and Corporation Taxes Act 1988 [ITEPA 2003, s. 684(1) and (2)]. Operative from 19 April 1995.

CITATION AND COMMENCEMENT

1 These Regulations may be cited as the Profit-Related Pay (Shortfall Recovery) Regulations 1995 and shall come into force on 19th April 1995.

INTERPRETATION

2 In these Regulations—

> **"the Board"** means the Commissioners of Inland Revenue;
> **"collector"** means a collector of taxes;
> **"the Management Act"** means the Taxes Management Act 1970;
> **"the principal Regulations"** means the Income Tax (Employments) Regulations 1993;
> **"the Taxes Act"** means the Income and Corporation Taxes Act 1988;
> **"year"** means year of assessment.

INFORMATION

3(1) Where the registration of a profit-related pay scheme registered under Chapter III of Part V of the Taxes Act is cancelled by the Board, the scheme employer shall, within 60 days of being required by the Board to do so, make a return to the Board, in such form as the Board may prescribe, containing the particulars specified in paragraph (2) below.

3(2) The particulars specified in this paragraph are particulars of—

(a)   the aggregate amount of the shortfall in the deductions made in accordance with the principal Regulations (an amount equal to which is payable by the scheme employer to the Board pursuant to section 179(2) of the Taxes Act);

(b)   the amount of the shortfall attributable to each year where the shortfall relates to more than one year.

RECOVERY

4(1) Within 60 days of his being required to make a return in accordance with regulation 3, the scheme employer shall pay to the Board an amount equal to the aggregate amount of the shortfall shown in the return.

4(2) Subject to these Regulations, the amount payable to the Board pursuant to paragraph (1) above shall be recoverable from the scheme employer as if it were an amount of tax which the scheme employer was liable under regulation 40 or 41 of the principal Regulations to pay to the collector.

EVIDENCE

5(1) Where an amount equal to the aggregate amount of the shortfall shown in a return has not been paid or fully paid within the period specified in regulation 4(1), an officer of the Board may certify the amount due to the collector.

5(2) The production of a certificate under paragraph (1) above shall be sufficient evidence that the scheme employer is liable to pay to the collector the amount shown in the certificate.

5(3) A certificate of a collector that an amount payable pursuant to regulation 4(1) has not been paid to him or, to the best of his knowledge and belief, to any other collector shall be sufficient evidence that the amount specified in the certificate is unpaid and due to the Crown.

5(4) Any document purporting to be a certificate under paragraph (1) or (3) above shall be deemed to be such a certificate until the contrary is proved.

DETERMINATIONS

6(1) Where it appears to the Board that there is an amount payable pursuant to regulation 4(1) which has not been paid or fully paid, the Board may determine to the best of their judgment the amount so unpaid, and shall serve notice of the determination on the scheme employer.

6(2) A determination under paragraph (1) above shall be subject to the like provisions as are contained in Parts IV, V and VI of the Management Act as if it were an assessment and as if the amount determined were income tax charged on the scheme employer, and those Parts of that Act shall, subject to these Regulations, apply accordingly with any necessary modifications.

6(3) An appeal against a determination under paragraph (1) above may be brought before either–

(a) the General Commissioners for the division where the trade, profession or vocation of the scheme employer is carried on or in which the head office or principal place of business of the scheme employer is situated, or

(b) the Special Commissioners.

INTEREST ON UNPAID AMOUNTS OF SHORTFALL

7(1) Where–

(a) there is an amount payable pursuant to regulation 4(1), or

(b) the Board make a determination of an amount under regulation 6, and

(c) in either case the amount in question is not paid or fully paid on or before the 14th day after the end of the year to which it is attributable,

the amount unpaid shall carry interest at the prescribed rate from the reckonable date until payment.

7(2) In paragraph (1) above **"the prescribed rate"** means the rate applicable under section 178 of the Finance Act 1989 for the purposes of section 86 of the Management Act; and where that rate changes on an operative date within the meaning given by regulation 2 of the Taxes (Interest Rate) Regulations 1989 by virtue of those Regulations, the change shall have effect for periods beginning on or after the operative date in relation to interest running from before that date as well as from or from after that date.

7(3) In this regulation **"the reckonable date"** means–

(a) where the amount referred to in sub-paragraph (a) or (b) of paragraph (1) above arises from a cancellation by the Board of the registration of a scheme under section 178(3) of the Taxes Act, the day immediately following the last day of the period specified in subsection (2) or, as the case may be, subsection (3) of section 180 of that Act;

(b) in any other case, the 14th day after the end of the year to which the amount is attributable.

7(4) The amount unpaid referred to in paragraph (1) above shall carry interest from the reckonable date even if that date is a non-business day within the meaning of section 92 of the Bills of Exchange Act 1882.

7(5) Interest payable under this regulation shall be recoverable as if it were an amount of tax which an employer is liable under regulation 40 or 41 of the principal Regulations to pay to the collector.

DEATH OF A SCHEME EMPLOYER

8 If a scheme employer dies, anything which he would have been liable to do under these Regulations shall be done by his personal representatives.

REVOCATIONS

9(1) The Profit-Related Pay (Shortfall Recovery) Regulations 1988 ("the 1988 Regulations"), so far as not previously revoked, are hereby revoked.

9(2) Regulation 14 of the Income Tax (Employments) (Amendment) Regulations 1993 is hereby revoked.

9(3) Anything done pursuant to the 1988 Regulations which, if done on or after the coming into force of these Regulations, could have been done pursuant to these Regulations, shall have effect as if done pursuant to these Regulations.

INSURANCE COMPANIES (TAXATION OF REINSURANCE BUSINESS) REGULATIONS 1995

(SI 1995/1730, as amended by SI 1996/1621, SI 2001/3629, SI 2002/1409, SI 2003/1828, SI 2003/2573, SI 2003/2642, SI 2004/2189 (though this was revoked before coming into effect), SI 2004/2257, SI 2004/2310, SI 2007/2087, SI 2008/1944 and SI 2008/2670)

Made on 7 July 1995 by the Commissioners of Inland Revenue, in exercise of the powers conferred on them by s. 431C(1), 439 and 442A(2)–(6) of the Income and Corporation Taxes Act 1988, and para. 58 of Sch. 8 to the Finance Act 1995. Operative from 28 July 1995.

CITATION, COMMENCEMENT AND EFFECT

1 These Regulations may be cited as the Insurance Companies (Taxation of Reinsurance Business) Regulations 1995, shall come into force on 28th July 1995, and shall have effect with respect to accounting periods beginning on or after 1st January 1995.

INTERPRETATION

2 In these Regulations unless the context otherwise requires—

"**accounting period**" means an accounting period of a cedant company during which a reinsurance arrangement is in force;

"**basic life assurance and general annuity business**" has the meaning given by section 431F of the Taxes Act;

"**deposit-back arrangement**" has the meaning given to "deposit back arrangements" by section 431(2)(d) of the Taxes Act;

"**EEA Agreement**" and "**EEA State**" have the meanings given in Schedule 1 to the Interpretation Act 1978;

"**expense risk**" means the risk that the amount of expenses attributable to a policy or contract over its duration is greater than the amount expected by the cedant company when it entered into the policy or contract;

"**insurance business transfer scheme**" has the meaning given by section 431(2) of the Taxes Act;

"**internal linked fund**" has the meaning given by section 431(2) of the Taxes Act;

"**investment return**" means the investment return to be treated as accruing to a cedant company in respect of a policy pursuant to subsection (1) of section 442A in an accounting period;

"**linked assets**" has the meaning given by section 432ZA(1) of the Taxes Act, and "**non-linked assets**" means assets other than linked assets;

"**linked business**" means business which comprises the effecting and carrying out by an insurance company of policies where benefits provided for under each policy are to be determined by reference to the value of linked assets;

"**morbidity risk**" in relation to a policy means the risk that the person whose life is insured by the policy will suffer any sickness, accident or infirmity;

"**mortality risk**" in relation to a policy means the risk that the person whose life is insured by the policy will die;

"**periodical return**" has the meaning given by section 431(2) of the Taxes Act;

"**policy**" includes an annuity contract;

"**the Prudential Sourcebook (Insurers)**" has the meaning given by section 431(2) of the Taxes Act;

"**reinsurance arrangement**" means a reinsurance arrangement to which section 442A applies;

"**relevant profits**" has the meaning given by section 88(3) of the Finance Act 1989;

"**section 431C**", "**section 431G**" and "**section 442A**" mean respectively section 431C, section 431G and section 442A of the Taxes Act;

"**90% subsidiary**" means a body corporate 90 per cent or more of whose ordinary share capital is owned directly or indirectly by another body corporate;

"the Taxes Act" means the Income and Corporation Taxes Act 1988.

History – In reg. 2, the definition of "the Board" omitted by SI 2008/1944, reg. 3(a), with effect in relation to accounting periods beginning on or after 1 January 2008. Former definition read as follows:
    "**"the Board"** means the Commissioners of Inland Revenue;"
In reg. 2, the definition of "deposit-back arrangement" substituted by SI 2008/1944, reg. 3(b), with effect in relation to accounting periods beginning on or after 1 January 2008. Former definition read as follows:
    "**"deposit-back arrangement"** means an arrangement whereby an amount is deposited with the cedant company by the reinsurer;"
In reg. 2, the definition of "inspector" omitted by SI 2008/2670, reg. 3, with effect from 29 October 2008. The former definition read:
    "**"inspector"** means any officer of Revenue and Customs;"
In reg. 2, the definition of "inspector" substituted by SI 2008/1944, reg. 3(b), with effect in relation to accounting periods beginning on or after 1 January 2008. Former definition read as follows:
    "**"inspector"** includes any officer of the Board;"
In reg. 2, the definitions of "EEA Agreement" and "EEA State" and "internal linked fund" substituted by SI 2007/2087, reg. 3, with effect in relation to periods of account beginning on or after 1 January 2007 and ending on or after 13 August 2007.
In reg. 2, in the definition of "section 439A", the words "431G" substituted for the words "439A", with effect in relation to periods of account beginning on or after 1 January 2007 and ending on or after 13 August 2007.
In reg. 2 the definition of "expense risk" and "insurance business transfer scheme" inserted by SI 2003/2573, reg. 3(a) and (b), operative from 28 October 2003, in relation to periods of account beginning on or after 1 November 2003.
In reg. 2 the definition of "the Prudential Sourcebook (Insurers)" inserted by SI 2003/2573, reg. 3(c), operative from 28 October 2003, in relation to periods of account beginning on or after 1 January 2001.
Notes – In Schedule 1 to the Interpretation Act 1978, the terms "EEA Agreement" and "EEA State" are given the following meanings:
    "EEA agreement" means the agreement on the European Economic Area signed at Oporto on 2nd May 1992, together with the Protocol adjusting that Agreement signed at Brussels on 17th March 1993, as modified or supplemented from time to time. [The date of the coming into force of this paragraph.]
    "EEA state", in relation to any time, means–
    (a)   a state which at that time is a member State; or
    (b)   any other state which at that time is a party to the EEA agreement. [The date of the coming into force of this paragraph.]

CALCULATION OF INVESTMENT RETURN IN SOLE ACCOUNTING PERIOD

3(1)   Where the period during which a reinsurance arrangement is in force falls wholly within a single accounting period, the amount of the investment return in that accounting period ("I") shall be calculated in accordance with the formula–

$$I = (C - P) \times R$$

where–

C   is the aggregate of–

    (a)   so much of any amount payable by the reinsurer to the cedant company during that accounting period as a result of the death, illness, or infirmity of, or accident to, any person as does not exceed the amount which would have been paid by the reinsurer if the policy had been surrendered immediately before the death, illness, or infirmity of, or accident to, that person, and

    (b)   other amounts paid by the reinsurer to the cedant company during that accounting period, being sums paid by way of commission or as a result of the surrender in whole or in part of the rights under the policy or otherwise, but excluding any sum which forms part of the relevant profits of the cedant company or is paid by way of commission that has been charged to tax;

P   is the aggregate of the sums paid by the cedant company to the reinsurer during that accounting period by way of premium or otherwise, or treated as paid where that company makes a payment to another person, and in pursuance of any arrangements that other person or a person connected with it (within the meaning of section 839 of the Taxes Act 1988) puts the reinsurer in funds; and

R   is the percentage rate of return prescribed by paragraph (2) below.

3(2)   The percentage rate of return prescribed is 100 per cent.

History – In reg. 3(1)(b) of the definition of "C", the words "under section 85 of the Finance Act 1989" omitted by SI 2008/1944, reg. 4, with effect in relation to accounting periods beginning on or after 1 January 2008.
In reg. 3(1) in para. (b) of the definition of "C", the words "charged to tax under section 85 of the Finance Act 1989" substituted for the words "deducted from expenses of management pursuant to section 76(1)(ca) of the Taxes Act" by SI 2004/2310, Schedule, para. 74(2), with effect in relation to accounting periods beginning on or after 1 April 2004, subject to the transitional provisions at FA 2004, s. 43 and 44.
In reg. 3(1), words from "C is" to "Taxes Act" substituted by SI 1996/1621, reg. 3, with effect with respect to accounting periods beginning on or after 1 January 1995.
In reg. 3(1) in the definition of "P", the words from "or otherwise" to the word "funds" inserted by SI 2004/2257, reg. 3, with effect from 15 September 2004.

CALCULATION OF INVESTMENT RETURN IN FIRST ACCOUNTING PERIOD

4 Where the period during which a reinsurance arrangement is in force falls within more than one accounting period, the amount of the investment return in the first accounting period ("I_1") shall be calculated in accordance with the formula–

$$I_1 = (P - C) \times R$$

where–

P   is the aggregate of the sums paid by the cedant company to the reinsurer during that accounting period by way of premium or otherwise, or treated as paid where that company makes a payment to another person, and in pursuance of any arrangements that other person or a person connected with it (within the meaning of section 839 of the Taxes Act 1988) puts the reinsurer in funds;

C   is the aggregate of the sums paid by the reinsurer to the cedant company during that accounting period by way of commission or as a result of the surrender in part of the rights under the policy or otherwise (but excluding any such sums paid by way of a loan or otherwise creating a debt such as is mentioned in paragraph 9(3)(a)(i) of Appendix 9.4 of the Prudential Sourcebook (Insurers)); and

R   is the percentage rate of return prescribed by regulation 7(2);
but where C is greater than P, taking the amount to be zero.

History – In reg. 4 in the definition of "C", the figure "9(3)" substituted for "12(4)" by SI 2007/2087, reg. 4, operative from 13 August 2007, with effect for accounting periods ending on or after 31 January 2005.
In reg. 4 in the definition of "P", the words from "or treated" to the word "funds" inserted by SI 2004/2257, reg. 4(3)(a), with effect for accounting periods beginning on or after 1 January 2003 though, under SI 2004/2257, reg. 1(3), no amount shall be treated as an amount of investment return given by SI 1995/1730, reg. 4 for an accounting period ending before 1 January 2004 if that amount arises solely by virtue of this amendment.
In reg. 4 the words from "(but excluding" to "Prudential Sourcebook (Insurers))" which appeared at the end of item P omitted by SI 2004/2257, reg. 4(2), with effect for accounting periods beginning on or after 1 January 2003.
In reg. 4 the words from "(but excluding" to "Prudential Sourcebook (Insurers))" inserted in item C and P, and the words "C is greater than P" substituted for the words "the result is less than zero" by SI 2003/2573, reg. 4, operative from 28 October 2003, in relation to periods of account beginning on or after 1 January 2001.

CALCULATION OF INVESTMENT RETURN IN SECOND AND SUBSEQUENT ACCOUNTING PERIODS OTHER THAN FINAL ACCOUNTING PERIOD

5(1) Where the period during which a reinsurance arrangement is in force falls within more than one accounting period, the amount of the investment return in the second or any subsequent accounting period other than the final accounting period ("I_n") shall be calculated in accordance with the formula–

$$I_n = ((P_n - C_n) + I_{n-1}) \times R$$

where–

Pn   is the aggregate of the sums paid by the cedant company to the reinsurer during that accounting period and earlier accounting periods by way of premium or otherwise, or treated as paid where that company makes a payment to another person, and in pursuance of any arrangements that other person or a person connected with it (within the meaning of section 839 of the Taxes Act 1988) puts the reinsurer in funds;

Cn   is the aggregate of the sums paid by the reinsurer to the cedant company during that accounting period and earlier accounting periods by way of commission or as a result of the surrender in part of the rights under the policy or otherwise (but excluding any such sums paid by way of a loan or otherwise creating a debt such as is mentioned in paragraph 9(3)(a)(i) of Appendix 9.4 of the Prudential Sourcebook (Insurers));

In – 1 is the aggregate amount of the net investment return in previous accounting periods, that is to say, net of tax at the appropriate rate or rates prescribed by paragraph (2) below; and

R   is the percentage rate of return prescribed by regulation 7(4) or (6), as the case may be;
but where (($P_n - C_n$) + I_{n-1}) is less than zero, taking the amount to be zero.

5(2) The rates prescribed by this paragraph are–

(a)   as respects an accounting period ending before the financial year 1996, the rate applicable in accordance with section 88(1) of the Finance Act 1989;

(b)   as respects an accounting period commencing in or after the financial year 1996 and ending before the financial year 2003, the rate applicable in accordance with section 88A(1) of the Finance Act 1989;

(c)   as respects an accounting period part of which falls in the financial year 1995 ("the 1995 part") and part in the financial year 1996 ("the 1996 part"), the rate applicable in accordance with section 88(1) of the Finance Act 1989 in relation to the proportion of the amount of the investment return attributable to the 1995 part, and the rate applicable in accordance with section 88A(1) of that Act in relation to the proportion of the amount of the investment return attributable to the 1996 part;

(d)   as respects an accounting period commencing in or after the financial year 2003, the rate applicable in accordance with section 88(1) of the Finance Act 1989;

(e)   as respects an accounting period part of which falls in the financial year 2002 ("the 2002 part") and part in the financial year 2003 ("the 2003 part"), the rate applicable in accordance with section 88A(1) of the Finance Act 1989 in relation to the proportion of the amount of the investment return attributable to the 2002 part, and the rate applicable in accordance with section 88(1) of that Act in relation to the proportion of the amount of the investment return attributable to the 2003 part.

History – In reg. 5(1) in the definition of "Cn", the figure "9(3)" substituted for "12(4)" by SI 2007/2087, reg. 4, operative from 13 August 2007, with effect for accounting periods ending on or after 31 January 2005.
In reg. 5(1) in the definition of "Pn", the words from "or treated" to the word "funds" inserted by SI 2004/2257, reg. 4(3), with effect for accounting periods beginning on or after 1 January 2003.
In reg. 5(1) the words from "(but excluding" to "Prudential Sourcebook (Insurers))" which appeared at the end of item Pn omitted by SI 2004/2257, reg. 4(2), operative from 15 September 2004, with effect for accounting periods beginning on or after 1 January 2003.
In reg. 5(1) the words from "(but excluding" to "Prudential Sourcebook (Insurers))" inserted in item Pn and Cn, and the words "((Pn – Cn) + In – 1)" substituted for the words "the result" by SI 2003/2573, reg. 5, operative from 28 October 2003, in relation to periods of account beginning on or after 1 January 2001.
In reg. 5(2)(b) words "and ending before the financial year 2003" inserted by SI 2003/1828, reg. 3(a), with effect in relation to accounting periods ending in the financial year 2003 and subsequent financial years.
Reg. 5(2)(d) and (e) inserted by SI 2003/1828, reg. 3(b), with effect in relation to accounting periods ending in the financial year 2003 and subsequent financial years.
Reg. 5(2), and in reg. 5(1) the words "at the appropriate rate or rates prescribed", substituted by SI 1996/1621, reg. 4, with effect with respect to accounting periods beginning on or after 1 January 1995.

Cross references – SI 2004/2257, reg. 1(4): the rate prescribed under reg. 5(2) where an amount in an accounting period ending before 1 January 2004 is not regarded as an amount of investment return because it arises solely by virtue of the amendment made to that regulation by SI 2004/2257, reg. 4(3) shall be treated as nil.

CALCULATION OF INVESTMENT RETURN IN FINAL ACCOUNTING PERIOD

6(1)   Where the period during which a reinsurance arrangement is in force falls within more than one accounting period, the amount of the investment return in the final accounting period is the amount by which the profit over the whole period during which the policy and the reinsurance arrangement was in force (**"the whole period"**) exceeds the aggregate of the amounts of the investment returns treated as accruing in earlier accounting periods.

6(2)   For the purposes of paragraph (1) above, the profit over the whole period is the amount by which the aggregate of the amounts specified in paragraph (3) below exceeds the aggregate of all amounts paid to the reinsurer by way of premiums in respect of the policy.

6(3)   The amounts specified in this paragraph are–

(a)   any amount payable by the reinsurer to the cedant company as a result of the maturity of the policy concerned;

(b)   so much of any amount payable by the reinsurer as a result of the death, illness, or infirmity of, or accident to, any person as does not exceed the amount which would have been paid by the reinsurer if the policy had been surrendered immediately before the death, illness, infirmity or accident;

(c)   any amount payable by the reinsurer as a result of the surrender in whole of the rights conferred by the policy;

(d)   any amount payable by the reinsurer as a result of the surrender in part of the rights conferred by the policy;

(e)   any amount not falling within any of sub-paragraphs (a) to (d) above which is payable by the reinsurer to the cedant company in respect of the policy, other than an amount which–

(i)   forms part of the relevant profits of the cedant company, or

(ii)   is paid by way of commission that has been charged to tax.

6(4)   For the purposes of paragraph (1) above, the aggregate of the amounts of the investment returns treated as accruing in earlier accounting periods are the amounts treated as accruing in those accounting periods but–

(a)   prior to any setting off permitted by regulation 7A(2)(c), calculated in accordance with regulations 4 and 5 as if in regulation 7(7) the formula were–

$$\frac{(X \times 100)}{Y}; \text{ and}$$

(b)   in any case falling within paragraph (10)(b)(iii) of regulation 7, adjusted by such an amount as is just and reasonable in the circumstances after taking into account the factor specified in paragraph (12)(d) of that regulation.

History – In reg. 6(3)(e)(ii), the words "under section 85 of the Finance Act 1989" omitted by SI 2008/1944, reg. 5, with effect in relation to accounting periods beginning on or after 1 January 2008.
In reg. 6(3)(e)(ii) the words "charged to tax under section 85 of the Finance Act 1989" substituted for the word "deducted from expenses of management pursuant to section 76(1)(ca) of the Taxes Act" by SI 2004/2310, Schedule, para. 74(3), with effect in relation to accounting periods beginning on or after 1 April 2004, subject to the transitional provisions at FA 2004, s. 43 and 44.
In reg. 6(4)(b), the words "is" substituted for the words "the inspector determines to be" by SI 2008/2670, reg. 4, with effect from 29 October 2008.
In reg. 6 the words "treated as accruing" and reg. 6(4) inserted by SI 2003/2573, reg. 6, operative from 28 October 2003, in relation to periods of account beginning on or after 1 January 2001.

PRESCRIBED PERCENTAGE RATES OF RETURN FOR THE PURPOSES OF REGULATIONS 4 AND 5

7(1)   Where the period during which a reinsurance arrangement is in force falls within more than one accounting period, the percentage rate of return–

(a)   in relation to the first accounting period, is the rate prescribed by paragraph (2) below;

(b)   in relation to any subsequent accounting period other than the final accounting period or an accounting period falling within paragraph (6) below, is the rate prescribed by paragraph (4) below.

7(2)   The rate prescribed by this paragraph is the rate ("R") found by the formula–

$$\frac{R = (D - E)}{G} \times F$$

where–

D   is such percentage rate as is specified in any of paragraphs (7) to (10) below and is applicable to the reinsurance arrangement concerned and, if more than such rate is so applicable, is the first applicable rate specified in the order of those paragraphs;

E   is the percentage rate which results from applying the formula specified in paragraph (3) below;

F   is the number of days in the first accounting period falling after the date prescribed by regulation 8(2); and

G   is the number of days in that accounting period.

7(3)   The formula specified in this paragraph is–

$$\frac{A}{P - C}$$

where–

A   is the amount of any payment made by the reinsurer to the cedant company which forms part of the relevant profits of that company for the first accounting period, other than a payment which falls to be taken into account under these Regulations in calculating the investment return to be treated as accruing to that company in that accounting period; and

P and C   have the meanings given by regulation 4.

7(4)   The rate prescribed by this paragraph is the rate ("R") found by the formula–

$$R = (D - H)$$

where–

D   has the meaning given by paragraph (2) above; and

H   is the percentage rate which results from applying the formula specified in paragraph (5) below.

7(5)   The formula specified in this paragraph is–

Statutory Instruments

$$\frac{B}{((P_n - C_n) + I_{n-1})}$$

where—

B   is the amount of any payment made by the reinsurer to the cedant company which forms part of the relevant profits of that company for the subsequent accounting period concerned, other than a payment which falls to be taken into account under these Regulations in calculating the investment return to be treated as accruing to that company in that accounting period; and

P_n, C_n and I_{n-1} have the meanings given by regulation 5(1).

7(6) In any case where a subsequent accounting period other than the final accounting period is less than 12 months in duration, the percentage rate of return prescribed in relation to that accounting period is the rate ("R") found by the formula—

$$R = \frac{J \times K}{365}$$

where—

J   is the rate prescribed by paragraph (4) above, and

K   is the number of days in that accounting period.

7(7) In any case where—

(a)   assets by reference to the value of which benefits payable under the reinsurance arrangement concerned are to be determined are held by the reinsurer in an internal linked fund, or by another company in an internal linked fund, or

(b)   such assets are held directly by the reinsurer, that is to say, without being appropriated to an internal linked fund,

the percentage rate of return specified is the rate, expressed as a rate per annum, which is found by the formula—

$$\frac{(X \times 100)}{Y} \times the\ Relevant\ Fraction, \text{ and}$$

where—

X   is the amount of investment income arising from those assets for the accounting period concerned, increased by the amount of any increase in the value of those assets which is identified in the records of the reinsurer or (as the case may be) the other company, or reduced by the amount of any reduction in the value of those assets which is so identified; and

Y   is the mean of the value of those assets at the beginning and end of the accounting period concerned, as identified in those records.

7(7A) For the purposes of paragraph (7) above, the Relevant Fraction is—

(a)   in a case where, in finding X, the amount of investment income is increased by the amount of an increase in the value of the assets mentioned in sub-paragraphs (a) and (b) of that paragraph—

$$\frac{(X - X1)}{X};$$

(b)   in a case where, in finding X, the amount of investment income is decreased by the amount of a reduction in the value of those assets and, after being so decreased, is not less than zero—

$$\frac{(X2 - X1)}{X2}; \text{ or}$$

(c)   in a case where X is an amount that is less than zero—

$$1 + \left(0.5 \times \frac{X1}{X2}\right).$$

where—

X is the same as for the purposes of that paragraph;

X1 is the amount included in the amount of investment income used in finding X which represents dividends and other distributions that are not chargeable to corporation tax by virtue of section 208 of the Taxes Act (which provides that dividends and other distributions of a company resident in the United Kingdom are not generally so chargeable); and

X2 is the amount of investment income before it is decreased by the amount of any reduction in the value of the assets mentioned in sub-paragraphs (a) and (b) of that paragraph.

7(8) In any case where—

(a)   there is in force a deposit-back arrangement as part of the reinsurance arrangement, and

(b)   the calculation of the rate of return on the deposit is capable of being expressed as a percentage rate per annum,

the percentage rate of return specified is such of the calculated rates of return on the deposit as is applicable to a period which includes any part of the accounting period concerned and is capable of being expressed not later than six months after the end of that accounting period and, if there is more than one such rate of return, is the average of those rates for periods beginning with the period which includes the date of commencement of the accounting period and ending with the period which includes the date of the end of the accounting period.

7(9) In any case where the policy being reinsured provides for a percentage rate of return which is fixed or is capable of being determined for the accounting period concerned not later than six months after the end of that period, the percentage rate of return specified is that percentage rate plus 1 per cent.

7(10) In any case not falling within paragraph (7), (8) or (9) above, the percentage rate of return specified is either—

(a)   the rate found by expressing the amount of the expected income from non-linked assets for the accounting period concerned as a percentage of the value of the total non-linked assets (other than assets not providing income) as identified in the relevant part of the periodical return of the cedant company specified in paragraph (11) below; or

(b)   where—

(i)   that periodical return contains no relevant part, or

(ii)   the cedant company is not required to make a periodical return, or

(iii)   the cedant company shows that in the circumstances the calculation specified in sub-paragraph (a) above would not produce a reasonable result,

such rate as is just and reasonable in the circumstances after taking into account the factors specified in paragraph (12) below.

7(11) The periodical return specified in this paragraph is the periodical return for the period of account immediately preceding the period of account in which the accounting period concerned falls, and **"the relevant part"** of that return means—

(a)   in the case of a cedant company which is resident in the United Kingdom, the part which shows the expected income from non-linked assets in respect of the whole of the company's long-term business;

(b)   in the case of a cedant company which is an overseas life insurance company—

(i)   the part which shows the expected income from non-linked assets of the company's long-term insurance fund relating exclusively to business carried on through a permanent establishment in the United Kingdom or, if there is no such part,

(ii)   the part which shows the expected income from non-linked assets of the company's long-term insurance fund relating exclusively to business carried on through permanent establishments in the United Kingdom and EEA States taken together.

7(12) The factors specified in this paragraph are—

(a)   the nature of the policy concerned;

(b)   the rate of interest assumed by the cedant company in determining the valuation of its liabilities in respect of the policy for the purposes of its periodical return;

(c)   any undertaking by the cedant company with respect to—

(i)   the nature of the assets in which the premiums it receives will be invested, or

(ii)   the rate of return which it is offering or has offered on that or any similar policy.

(d)   the extent to which the reinsurer is in receipt of dividends and other distributions which–

(i)   arise from assets held by the reinsurer which may reasonably be regarded as related to the reinsurance arrangement in question; and

(ii)   are not chargeable to corporation tax by virtue of section 208 of the Taxes Act.

7(13)   [Omitted by SI 2008/2670, reg. 5(3).]

7(14)   [Omitted by SI 2008/2670, reg. 5(3).]

History – In reg. 7(2), (4) and (7) the words "but where the result is less than zero, taking the rate to be zero" omitted by SI 2003/2573, reg. 7, operative from 28 October 2003, in relation to periods of account beginning on or after 1 January 2001.
In reg. 7(7) formula substituted by SI 2003/2573, reg. 7(3), operative from 28 October 2003, in relation to periods of account beginning on or after 1 January 2001.
In reg. 7(7A)(c), formula substituted by SI 2003/2642, reg. 2(2), operative from 28 October 2003, immediately after SI 2003/2573, in relation to periods of account beginning on or after 1 January 2001, in order to correct an error in SI 2003/2573.
Reg. 7(7A) inserted by SI 2003/2573, reg. 7(4), operative from 28 October 2003, in relation to periods of account beginning on or after 1 January 2001.
Reg. 7(10)(a) substituted, by SI 2003/2573, reg.7(5), operative from 28 October 2003, in relation to periods of account beginning on or after 1 January 2001.
In reg. 7(10), in the closing words, the words "is" substituted for the words "the inspector determines to be" by SI 2008/2670, reg. 5(2), with effect from 29 October 2008.
In reg. 7(11)(a), the words "which is resident" substituted for the words "whose head office is", in reg. 7(11)(b)(i) the words "permanent establishment" substituted for the words "branch or agency" and in reg. 7(11)(b)(ii) the words "permanent establishments" substituted for the words "branches and agencies" by SI 2008/1944, reg. 6, with effect in relation to accounting periods beginning on or after 1 January 2008.
In reg. 7(11), in sub-para. (a) "long-term" substituted for "long term" and in sub-para. (b)(i) and (ii) "long-term insurance" substituted for "long term business", by SI 2001/3629, art. 140 which came into force on 1 December 2001.
Reg. 7(12)(d) inserted by SI 2003/2573, reg. 7(6), operative from 28 October 2003, in relation to periods of account beginning on or after 1 January 2001.
Reg. 7(13) omitted by SI 2008/2670, reg. 5(3), with effect from 29 October 2008. Former reg. 7(13) read:

"**7(13)**   An appeal may be brought against a determination of the inspector under regulation 6(4)(d) or paragraph (10)(b) above by giving written notice to the inspector within 30 days of receipt of written notice of the decision.".
In former reg. 7(13) words "regulation 6(4)(d) or" inserted by SI 2003/2573, reg. 7(7), operative from 28 October 2003, in relation to periods of account beginning on or after 1 January 2001.
Reg. 7(14) omitted by SI 2008/2670, reg. 5(3), with effect from 29 October 2008. Former reg. 7(14) read:

"**7(14)**   An appeal under paragraph (13) above shall lie to the Special Commissioners who may confirm or vary the determination appealed against (whether or not the variation is to the advantage of the appellant).".

TREATMENT OF AMOUNTS OF INVESTMENT RETURN WHICH ARE LESS THAN ZERO

7A(1)   This regulation applies where the amount of investment return on a policy or contract, as calculated in accordance with regulation 3, 4 or 5, is less than zero ("the negative amount").

7A(2)   The negative amount may be set off in the following order against the following amounts–

(a)   first, the amount of any income (other than any investment return which is treated under these Regulations as accruing) which–

(i)   accrues in the same accounting period as that in which the negative amount is treated as accruing; and

(ii)   is referable to basic life assurance and general annuity business and is charged to tax under Case VI of Schedule D;

(b)   secondly, the amount of any investment return which–

(i)   is treated under these Regulations as accruing in the same accounting period as that in which the negative amount is treated as accruing; and

(ii)   is more than zero; and

(c)   thirdly, the amount of any investment return which is treated under these Regulations as accruing–

(i)   in an accounting period subsequent to that in which the negative amount is treated as accruing; and

(ii)   in respect of the same policy or contract as that in respect of which the negative amount is treated as accruing;

and is more than zero.

7A(3)   Any setting off under paragraph (2)(c) above shall, so far as possible, reduce amounts accruing in an earlier accounting period before reducing amounts accruing in a later one.

7A(4)   Except as is provided for by paragraph (2) above, the negative amount shall be treated for the purposes of section 396 of the Taxes Act as if it were zero.

7A(5)   Where section 442A of the Taxes Act applies to the life or endowment business carried on by friendly societies subject to the modification prescribed by regulation 19 of the Friendly Societies

(Modification of the Corporation Tax Acts) Regulations 2005, this regulation shall have effect as if the reference in paragraph (2)(a)(ii) above to basic life assurance and general annuity business were a reference to taxable basic life assurance and general annuity business (within the meaning given by section 431(2) of the Taxes Act as modified by regulation 6 of those regulations).

History – Reg. 7A(5) inserted by SI 2007/2087, reg. 5, with effect in relation to periods of account beginning on or after 1 January 2007 and ending on or after 13 August 2007.

Reg. 7A inserted by SI 2003/2573, reg. 8(6), operative from 28 October 2003, in relation to periods of account beginning on or after 1 January 2001.

ASCERTAINMENT OF INVESTMENT RETURN – PRESCRIBED DATES OF PAYMENTS MADE UNDER REINSURANCE ARRANGEMENTS

8(1) For the purposes of ascertaining the investment return in each accounting period, the payments specified in paragraphs (2) to (6) below shall be treated as paid on the dates prescribed by those paragraphs in relation to the payment concerned.

8(2) In any case where under the reinsurance arrangement a premium or any other amount is payable to the reinsurer within 30 days of the date on which the first premium is paid to the reinsurer, the date prescribed as the date on which that premium or other amount is to be treated as paid is the date on which the first premium is paid.

8(3) In any case where under the reinsurance arrangement commission or any other amount is payable by the reinsurer in respect of the policy concerned at the same time as the first premium is paid to the reinsurer or within 30 days of the date on which the first premium is paid to the reinsurer, the date prescribed as the date on which that commission or other amount is to be treated as paid is the date on which the first premium is paid.

8(4) In any case where under the reinsurance arrangement–

(a)   a premium other than the first premium or a premium falling within paragraph (2) above, or any other amount not being an amount falling within paragraph (2) above, is paid to the reinsurer before the end of the accounting period in which the first premium is paid, or

(b)   commission or any other amount, not being commission or an amount falling within paragraph (3) above, is paid by the reinsurer to the cedant company before the end of that accounting period,

the date prescribed as the date on which that premium or other amount is to be treated as paid to the reinsurer, or that commission or other amount is to be treated as paid by the reinsurer, is the first day of the next accounting period.

8(5) The dates prescribed as the dates on which any premium or any other amount paid to the reinsurer under the reinsurance arrangement, other than a premium or amount falling within paragraph (2) or (4)(a) above, is to be treated as paid are the following–

(a)   as to one half of the amount of the premium or other amount, the date on which the premium or other amount is paid;

(b)   as to the other half, the first day of the accounting period next following that in which the premium or other amount is paid.

8(6) The dates prescribed as the dates on which any commission or any other amount paid by the reinsurer under the reinsurance arrangement, not being commission or an amount falling within paragraph (3) or (4)(b) above, is to be treated as paid are the following–

(a)   as to one half of the commission or other amount, the date on which the commission or other amount is paid;

(b)   as to the other half, the first day of the accounting period next following that in which the commission or other amount is paid.

EXCLUSION OF CERTAIN REINSURANCE ARRANGEMENTS FROM SECTION 442A

9(1) There shall be excluded from the operation of section 442A any reinsurance arrangement in respect of a policy which falls within any of the descriptions prescribed by paragraphs (2) to (4) below.

9(2) The description prescribed by this paragraph is of any reinsurance arrangement where–

(a)   both the cedant company and the reinsurer are insurance companies which are either resident in the United Kingdom or, as respects the reinsurance arrangement or, as the case may be, the business to which the reinsurance is attributable, are within the charge to corporation tax by virtue of section 11 of the Taxes Act;

(b)   the cedant company is a 90% subsidiary of the reinsurer, or the reinsurer is a 90% subsidiary of the cedant company, or each is a 90% subsidiary of another body corporate; and

(c)   the reinsurer is not a company which is charged to tax under Case I of Schedule D by virtue of section 431G(3)(a) of the Taxes Act.

9(3)   The description prescribed by this paragraph is of any reinsurance arrangement where–

(a)   the reinsurer is a company which in the relevant period is chargeable to tax under the laws of the territory in which it is domiciled or resident in respect of amounts to which the reinsurance arrangement gives rise;

(b)   the head office of the reinsurer is in an EEA State;

(c)   the charge to tax in the relevant period is such a charge made otherwise than by reference to profits as (by disallowing their deduction in computing the amount chargeable) to require sums payable and other liabilities arising under reinsurance arrangements to be treated as sums or liabilities falling to be met out of amounts subject to tax in the hands of the reinsurer;

(d)   the rate of tax fixed for the purposes of that charge in relation to the amounts subject to tax in the hands of the reinsurer (not being amounts arising or accruing in respect of investments that are of a particular description for which a special relief or exemption is generally available) has in the relevant period been at least 20 per cent;

(e)   none of the obligations of the reinsurer under the reinsurance arrangement to pay any sum or meet any other liability, other than obligations in respect of mortality risk or morbidity risk, has itself been the subject of a reinsurance arrangement;

(f)   no deposit-back arrangements are in force in respect of the reinsurance arrangement; and

(g)   the reinsurer is not subject in the relevant period to a restriction in the amount of the expenses which may be deducted in computing its liability to tax, where the restriction is calculated by reference to the amount of its profits.

9(4)   The description prescribed by this paragraph is of any reinsurance arrangement under which–

(a)

    (i)   the mortality risk or the morbidity risk (but no other risk other than the expense risk) is being reinsured, or both the mortality risk and the morbidity risk (but no other risk other than the expense risk) are being reinsured, and

    (ii)   no payment by way of surrender value is capable of being made by the reinsurer to the cedant company; or

(b)   either–

    (i)   no profit such as is referred to in regulation 6(2) is capable of arising; or

    (ii)   such profit is capable of arising only as a result of the death, illness or infirmity of, or accident to, a person or the lapsing of the policy.

9(4A)   [Revoked by SI 2004/2257, reg. 5(1)(b).]

9(5)   In paragraph (3) above, **"the relevant period"** means a period for which the reinsurer draws up accounts and which ends in or at the end of an accounting period of the cedant company or, if there is more than one such period ending in or at the end of the same accounting period, the period which is the first to end.

9(6)   For the purposes of paragraph (4) above, the fact that a premium payable by the cedant company under the reinsurance arrangement is calculated so as to reflect a guarantee by that company under the terms of the policy that it will issue a different policy at a future date shall not be taken to mean that risks other than mortality risk or morbidity risk are being reinsured under the reinsurance arrangement.

History – In reg. 9(1), "(4)" subsituted for "(4A)" by SI 2004/2257, reg. 5(1)(a), with effect for accounting periods beginning on or after 1 November 2003.

In reg. 9(2)(c), the words "by virtue of section 431G(3)(a) of the Taxes Act" inserted by SI 2008/1944, reg. 7, with effect in relation to accounting periods beginning on or after 1 January 2008.

In reg. 9, "4A" substituted for "4", and para. (4)(a)(i) substituted by SI 2003/2573, reg. 9, operative from 28 October 2003, in relation to periods of account beginning on or after 1 November 2003. Reg. 9(4)(a)(i) previously read as follows:
    "(i)   only the mortality risk or the morbidity risk is being reinsured, or both the mortality risk and the morbidity risk (but no other risk) are being reinsured, and".

Reg. 9(4A) revoked by SI 2004/2189, reg. 5(1)(b), with effect for accounting periods beginning on or after 1 November 2003.

Reg. 9(4A) inserted by SI 2003/2573, reg. 9(4), operative from 28 October 2003, in relation to periods of account beginning on or after 1 November 2003.

EXCLUSION OF POLICY AND CONTRACT FROM SECTION 442A

10(1)   There shall be excluded from the operation of section 442A–

(a)   any policy which evidences a contract of long-term insurance which is neither–

Statutory Instruments

   (i) a qualifying contract of insurance, nor

   (ii) a reinsurance contract; and

 (b) any annuity contract under which–

   (i) payment of the annuity is to commence not later than 12 months after the date of the contract, and

   (ii) no surrender value is capable of being produced.

10(2) In paragraph (1)(a) above, **"contract of long-term insurance"** means any contract which falls within Part 2 of Schedule 1 to the Financial Services and Markets Act 2000 (Regulated Activities) Order 2001 and ;**"qualifying contract of insurance"** has the meaning by article 3(1) of that Order.

History – Reg. 10(1)(a) substituted and reg. 10(2) inserted by SI 2002/1409, reg. 4(2), (3) with effect from 2 July 2002.

EXCLUSION OF CERTAIN BUSINESS FROM SECTION 431C

11 There shall be excluded from section 431C any reinsurance business where–

 (a) in relation to the reinsurance arrangement–

   (i) the cedant company is a 90% subsidiary of the reinsurer, or the reinsurer is a 90% subsidiary of the cedant company, or each is a 90% subsidiary of another body corporate,

   (ii) the cedant company is either resident in the United Kingdom or is an overseas life insurance company which, as respects the reinsurance arrangement or, as the case may be, the business being reinsured, is within the charge to corporation tax by virtue of section 11 of the Taxes Act, and

   (iii) the business being reinsured is basic life assurance and general annuity business in the hands of the cedant company; or

 (b) [omitted by SI 2003/2573, reg. 10;]

 (c) the business–

   (i) is the reinsurance of the business of a company which is not resident in the United Kingdom,

   (ii) is not business which is overseas life assurance business within the meaning given by section 431D(1) of the Taxes Act being business for which the policy or contract concerned was made on or after 1st November 1994 and before the first accounting period of the company to begin on or after 1st January 2007, and

   (iii) is linked business where the linked assets concerned consist wholly or substantially of land in the United Kingdom. or

 (d) the business is business in relation to which an election under regulation 11A has been made.

History – In reg. 11(c)(ii), the words "and before the first accounting period of the company to begin on or after 1st January 2007" inserted by SI 2007/2087, reg. 6, with effect in relation to periods of account beginning on or after 1 January 2007 and ending on or after 13 August 2007.

Reg. 11(b) omitted by SI 2003/2573, reg. 10, operative from 28 October 2003, in relation to periods of account beginning on or after 1 November 2003. Reg. 11(b) previously read as follows:

 "(b) the business is overseas life assurance business within the meaning given by section 431D(1) of the Taxes Act being business for which the policy or contract concerned was made on or after 1st November 1994; or".

Previously, in reg. 11(b) words "overseas life assurance business within the meaning given by section 431D(1)", and in reg. 11(c)(ii) words "which is overseas life assurance business within the meaning given by section 431D(1)" substituted for "of any of the descriptions specified in section 431D(1)(b)", by SI 2003/1828, reg. 3(4), with effect in relation to any policy or contract for any life assurance business made on or after 22 August 2000.

In reg. 11(b), (c)(ii), words "being business for which … 1st November 1994" added by SI 1996/1621, reg. 4(a), with effect with respect to accounting periods ending on or after 15 July 1996.

Reg. 11(d) substituted by SI 2003/2573, reg. 10, operative from 28 October 2003, in relation to periods of account beginning on or after 1 November 2003. Reg. 11(d) previously read as follows:

 "(d) the business is business the contract for which–

   (i) was effected by a company resident in the United Kingdom at or through a branch or agency outside the United Kingdom where none, or no significant part, of the reinsurance business carried on relates to life assurance business with policy holders or annuitants residing in the United Kingdom, and

   (ii) was made before 1st November 1994.".

Reg. 11(d) originally added by SI 1996/1621, reg. 5(b), with effect with respect to accounting periods beginning on or after 1 January 1995.

ELECTION FOR CERTAIN BUSINESS TO BE EXCLUDED FROM SECTION 431C

11A(1) A company may make an election under this regulation in relation to–

 (a) any period of account beginning on or after 1st November 2003; and

 (b) any of its reinsurance business which is business of the kind specified in paragraph (2), (3) or (4) below.

11A(2)   The business specified in this paragraph is business–

(a)   which is of any of the descriptions specified in section 431D(1)(b) of the Taxes Act (as it has effect before the substitution made by paragraph 9(2) of Schedule 7 to the Finance Act 2007), being business for which the policy or contract concerned was made on or after 1st November 1994; and

(b)   the contract for which was made before the beginning of the company's first period of account to begin on or after 1st November 2003.

11A(3)   The business specified by this paragraph is business the contract for which–

(a)   was effected by a company resident in the United Kingdom at or through a branch or agency outside the United Kingdom where none, or no significant part, of the reinsurance business carried on relates to life assurance business with policy holders or annuitants residing in the United Kingdom; and

(b)   was made before 1st November 1994.

11A(4)   The business specified by this paragraph is business the contract for which was made after the beginning of the company's first period of account to begin on or after 1st November 2003 and replaces–

(a)   a contract made before the beginning of the company's first period of account to begin on or after 1st November 2003 such as is mentioned in paragraph (2) above;

(b)   a contract made before 1st November 1994 such as is mentioned in paragraph (3) above; or

(c)   a contract that replaced a contract such as is mentioned in sub-paragraph (a) or (b).

11A(5)   For the purposes of paragraph (4) above, a contract replaces a contract if it results in–

(a)   no significant difference in the type of business being reinsured; and

(b)   no significant variation in the terms on which that business is reinsured.

11A(6)   For the purposes of paragraph (5) above, where more than one contract replaces a contract–

(a)   there is no significant difference in the type of business being reinsured if the replacement contracts, when taken together, do not result in such a difference; and

(b)   there is no significant variation in the terms on which business is reinsured if the replacement contracts, when taken together, do not result in such a variation.

11A(7)   Where there is a relevant transfer from one person ("the transferor") to another ("the transferee") and the transferor makes an election under this regulation in relation to that business, the transferee is to be treated for the purposes of these Regulations as making the election.

11A(8)   In paragraph (7) above, "a relevant transfer" means a transfer of reinsurance business that is effected by–

(a)   novation; or

(b)   an insurance business transfer scheme.

11A(9)   A company may revoke an election under this regulation with effect for any period of account in relation to which it would have effect.

11A(10)   A revocation under paragraph (9) above must be in respect of all elections under this regulation which a company has made or is treated as having made.

11A(11)   An election made by a company under this regulation ceases to have effect at the end of the accounting period immediately preceding the first accounting period of the company which begins on or after 1st January 2007.

History – In reg. 11A(2)(a), the words "(as it has effect before the substitution made by paragraph 9(2) of Schedule 7 to the Finance Act 2007)" inserted by SI 2007/2087, reg. 7(2), with effect in relation to periods of account beginning on or after 1 January 2007 and ending on or after 13 August 2007.
Reg. 11A(11) inserted by SI 2007/2087, reg. 7(3), with effect in relation to periods of account beginning on or after 1 January 2007 and ending on or after 13 August 2007.
Reg. 11A inserted by SI 2003/2573, reg. 11, operative from 28 October 2003, in relation to periods of account beginning on or after 1 November 2003.

EXCLUSION OF CERTAIN REINSURANCE BUSINESS FROM SUBSECTION (3) OF SECTION 431G

12   There shall be excluded from subsection (3) of section 431G any reinsurance business carried on by a company **("the reinsurer")** whose reinsurance business is limited to arrangements where–

(a)   the cedant company is a 90% subsidiary of the reinsurer, or the reinsurer is a 90% subsidiary of the cedant company, or each is a 90% subsidiary of another body corporate, and

(b)   the cedant company either–

(i)   is resident in the United Kingdom, or

(ii)   is not so resident but, as respects all the business reinsured with the reinsurer, is within the charge to corporation tax by virtue of section 11 of the Taxes Act.

History – In reg. 12, the heading changed to "Exclusion of certain reinsurance business from subsection (3) of section 431G" from "Exclusion of certain reinsurance business from section 439A" by SI 2007/2087, reg. 8(2), with effect in relation to periods of account beginning on or after 1 January 2007 and ending on or after 13 August 2007.

In reg. 12, the words "subsection (3) of section 431G" substituted for the words "section 439A" by SI 2007/2087, reg. 8(1), with effect in relation to periods of account beginning on or after 1 January 2007 and ending on or after 13 August 2007.

TRANSFERS OF REINSURANCE ARRANGEMENTS EFFECTED BY NOVATION OR INSURANCE BUSINESS TRANSFER SCHEMES

13(1)   Where a transfer of a reinsurance arrangement from one insurance company ("the transferor") to another ("the transferee") is effected by novation or an insurance business transfer scheme, these Regulations shall apply in relation to the reinsurance arrangement concerned as follows.

13(2)   Regulation 3 shall not apply.

13(3)   For the purposes of regulations 4 to 7–

(a)   if there is no accounting period of the transferor ending on the day of the transfer, an accounting period of the transferor shall be treated as ending on that day;

(b)   an accounting period of the transferor which ends (or is treated as ending) on the day of the transfer shall not be treated as the final accounting period during which the reinsurance arrangement concerned is in force;

(c)   if there is no accounting period of the transferee beginning on, or immediately after, the day of the transfer an accounting period of the transferee shall be treated as beginning immediately after that day; and

(d)   an accounting period of the transferee which begins on, or immediately after, (or is treated as beginning immediately after) the day of the transfer shall not be treated as the first accounting period during which the reinsurance arrangement concerned is in force.

13(4)   For the purposes of regulation 5, 6 and 9, the references in regulations 5(1), 6(3) and 9(6) respectively to the cedant company shall be treated as including (as well as the transferee)–

(a)   the transferor; and

(b)   any insurance company from which the reinsurance arrangement concerned was transferred on an earlier transfer effected by novation or an insurance business transfer scheme.

13(5)   For the purposes of regulation 5, the reference in paragraph (1) of that regulation to previous accounting periods shall be treated as including (as well as the previous accounting periods of the transferee)–

(a)   previous accounting periods of the transferor; and

(b)   previous accounting periods of any insurance company from which the reinsurance arrangement concerned was transferred on an earlier transfer effected by novation or an insurance business transfer scheme.

13(6)   For the purposes of regulation 6, the reference in paragraph (1) of that regulation to the amounts of the investment returns in earlier accounting periods shall be treated as including (as well as the amounts of the investment returns in earlier accounting periods of the transferee)–

(a)   the amounts of the investment returns in earlier accounting periods of the transferor; and

(b)   the amounts of the investment returns in earlier accounting periods of any insurance company from which the reinsurance arrangement concerned was transferred on an earlier transfer effected by novation or an insurance business transfer scheme.

13(6A)   For the purposes of regulation 7A, any negative amount that is available before the transfer to be set off by the transferor in accordance with paragraph (2)(c) of that regulation shall be treated as if it had accrued in an earlier accounting period of the transferee.

13(7)   The following questions shall be determined in respect of the transferor as the cedant company before the transfer and then, as a separate matter, in respect of the transferee as the cedant company after the transfer–

(a)   whether the reinsurance arrangement concerned falls within the description prescribed by regulation 9(2);

(b)   whether, in relation to the reinsurance arrangement concerned, any of the circumstances set out in regulations 11(a) and 12 exist.

13(8)   [Omitted by SI 2003/2573, reg. 12(2).]

History – Reg. 13(3) substituted by SI 2008/1944, reg. 8, with effect in relation to accounting periods beginning on or after 1 January 2008. Former reg. 13(3) read as follows:

"**13(3)**   For the purposes of regulations 4 to 7, an accounting period of the transferor shall be treated as ending with the day of the transfer and a new accounting period of the transferee shall be treated as beginning with that day but–

(a)   the new accounting period of the transferee so treated as beginning shall not be treated as the first accounting period during which the reinsurance arrangement concerned is in force; and

(b)   the accounting period of the transferor which is so treated as ending shall not treated as the final accounting period during which the reinsurance arrangement concerned is in force."

Reg. 13(6A) inserted by SI 2003/2573, reg. 12(2), operative from 28 October 2003, in relation to transfers of reinsurance arrangements taking place on or after 1 January 2003.

Reg. 13(8) omitted by SI 2003/2573, reg. 12(3), operative from 28 October 2003, in relation to periods of account beginning on or after 1 November 2003. Reg. 13(8) previously read as follows:

"**13(8)**   In this regulation, **"insurance business transfer scheme"** has the meaning given by section 431(2) of the Taxes Act.".

Reg. 13 originally inserted by SI 2003/1828, reg. 5, with effect in relation to transfers of reinsurance arrangements taking place on or after 1 January 2003.

VENTURE CAPITAL TRUST REGULATIONS 1995

(SI 1995/1979 as amended by SI 1999/819, SI 2008/1893 and SI 2009/56)

Made on 26 July 1995 by the Treasury, in exercise of the powers conferred on them by s. 73(1)–(4) of the Finance Act 1995. Operative from 6 April 1995.

Statutory Instruments

ARRANGEMENT OF REGULATIONS

REGULATION

PART I – INTRODUCTORY

PART II – APPROVAL OF A COMPANY FOR PURPOSES OF PART 6

PART III – RELIEF FROM INCOME TAX

PART IV – RETURN OF PARTICULARS OF INVESTMENTS, KEEPING OF RECORDS AND PROVISION OF INFORMATION

PART I – INTRODUCTORY

CITATION AND COMMENCEMENT

1 These Regulations may be cited as the Venture Capital Trust Regulations 1995 and shall come into force on 16th August 1995.

INTERPRETATION

2(1) In these Regulations unless the context otherwise requires–

"accounting date" has the meaning given by section 834(1) of the Income and Corporation Taxes Act 1988;

"accounting period" shall be construed in accordance with section 12 of the Income and Corporation Taxes Act 1988;

"the Board" means the Commissioners for Her Majesty's Revenue and Customs;

"director" means a person appointed as a director of the trust company;

"eligible shares" has the meaning given by section 273(1);

"full approval" means approval in pursuance of section 274;

"investor" means a person who holds shares in a company which is, or has been, a trust company;

"period of account" has the meaning given by section 989;

"provisional approval" means approval in pursuance of section 275(2);

"qualifying holding" shall be construed in accordance with Chapter 4 of Part 6;

"trust company" means a venture capital trust within the meaning given by section 259(1);

"VCT approval" has the meaning it has in section 259(2);

"year" means a year beginning with 6th April in any year and ending with 5th April in the following year.

2(2) In these Regulations, a reference to a "section" or "Part" without more is a reference to a section or Part of the Income Tax Act 2007.

History – In reg. 2(1), in the definition of "accounting date" the words "of the Income and Corporation Taxes Act 1988" added by SI 2008/1893, reg. 3(2)(a), with effect from 1 September 2008.
In reg. 2(1), the definition of "accounting period" inserted by SI 2008/1893, reg. 3(2)(j), with effect from 1 September 2008.
In reg. 2(1), in the definition of "the Board" the words "for Her Majesty's Revenue and Customs" substituted for the words "of Inland Revenue" by SI 2008/1893, reg. 3(2)(b), with effect from 1 September 2008.
In reg. 2(1), the definition of "director" inserted by SI 2008/1893, reg. 3(2)(j), with effect from 1 September 2008.
In reg. 2(1), in the definition of "eligible shares" the words "section 273(1)" substituted for the words "paragraph 6(1) of Schedule 15B" by SI 2008/1893, reg. 3(2)(c), with effect from 1 September 2008.
In reg. 2(1), in the definition of "full approval" the words "section 274" substituted for the words "subsection (2) of section 842AA" by SI 2008/1893, reg. 3(2)(d), with effect from 1 September 2008.
In reg. 2(1), the definition of "the Management Act" omitted by SI 2008/1893, reg. 3(2)(e), with effect from 1 September 2008.
In reg. 2(1), in the definition of "period of account" the words "989" substituted for the words "834(1)" by SI 2008/1893, reg. 3(2)(f), with effect from 1 September 2008.
In reg. 2(1), in the definition of "provisional approval" the words "section 275(2)" substituted for the words "subsection (4) of section 842AA" by SI 2008/1893, reg. 3(2)(g), with effect from 1 September 2008.
In reg. 2(1), in the definition of "qualifying holding" the words "Chapter 4 of Part 6" substituted for the words "Schedule 28B" by SI 2008/1893, reg. 3(2)(h), with effect from 1 September 2008.
In reg. 2(1), in the definition of "trust company" the words "259(1)" substituted for the words "842AA" by SI 2008/1893, reg. 3(i), with effect from 1 September 2008.
In reg. 2(1), in the definition of "VCT approval" inserted by SI 2008/1893, reg. 3(2)(j), with effect from 1 September 2008.
In reg. 2(1), the definitions of "enduring declaration" and "permitted maximum" were removed by SI 1999/819, with effect from 6 April 1999.
Reg. 2(2) substituted by SI 2008/1893, reg. 3(3), with effect from 1 September 2008.

PART II – APPROVAL OF A COMPANY FOR PURPOSES OF PART 6

History – In the heading the words "Part 6" substituted for the words "section 842AA" by SI 2008/1893, reg. 4, with effect from 1 September 2008.

APPLICATIONS FOR APPROVAL

3(1) A company making an application for approval as a venture capital trust for the purposes of Part 6 shall apply to the Board in writing.

3(2) The application shall be either for full approval or for provisional approval.

3(3) An application for full approval shall contain a declaration–

(a) that the conditions for full approval were fulfilled in relation to the most recent complete accounting period of the company;

(b) that to the best of the company's knowledge and belief, the conditions for full approval will also be fulfilled in relation to the accounting period of the company which is current when the application for full approval is made; and

(c) that to the best of the company's knowledge and belief, the particulars given in the application are true and correct.

3(4) An application for provisional approval shall contain a declaration that to the best of the company's knowledge and belief–

(a) the conditions for full approval will be fulfilled within the periods specified in section 275(3); and

(b) the particulars given in the application are true and correct.

3(5) An application for approval for the purposes of Part 6 shall be signed by the secretary or by a director of the company.

History – In reg. 3(1) the words "Part 6" substituted for the words "section 842AA" by SI 2008/1893, reg. 5(a), with effect from 1 September 2008.
In reg. 3(4)(a) the words "section 275(3)" substituted for the words "subsection (4) of section 842AA" by SI 2008/1893, reg. 5(b), with effect from 1 September 2008.
In reg. 3(5) the words "Part 6" substituted for the words "section 842AA" by SI 2008/1893, reg. 5(a), with effect from 1 September 2008.

APPROVAL OF A COMPANY

4(1) The Board's approval of a company as a trust company for the purposes of Part 6 shall be given to the company by notice in writing.

4(2) The notice shall specify–

(a) the date on which the Board's approval is given, and

(b) the date from which the approval shall have effect.

4(3) A notice giving provisional approval may include conditions designed to ensure that the company will fulfil the conditions specified in section 274.

4(4) The company may appeal against the inclusion of any of the conditions mentioned in paragraph (3) above.

History – In reg. 4(1) the words "Part 6" substituted for the words "section 842AA" by SI 2008/1893, reg. 6(a), with effect from 1 September 2008.
In reg. 3(4)(a) the words "section 274" substituted for the words "subsection (4) of section 842AA" by SI 2008/1893, reg. 6(b), with effect from 1 September 2008.
In reg. 4(4), the words "to the Special Commissioners", which appeared after "appeal", omitted by SI 2009/56, art. 3(2) and Sch. 2, para. 24, operative from 1 April 2009 subject to transitional and saving provisions in SI 2009/56, Sch. 3.

REFUSAL OF APPROVAL OF A COMPANY

5(1) The Board's refusal of approval of a company as a trust company for the purposes of Part 6 shall be given to the company by notice in writing.

5(2) The notice shall specify–

(a) the date on which the Board's refusal of approval is given, and

(b) the reasons for the Board's refusal of approval.

5(3) The company may appeal against the refusal of approval.

History – In reg. 5(1) the words "Part 6" substituted for the words "section 842AA" by SI 2008/1893, reg. 7, with effect from 1 September 2008.
In reg. 5(3), the words "to the Special Commissioners", which appeared after "appeal", omitted by SI 2009/56, art. 3(2) and Sch. 2, para. 25, operative from 1 April 2009 subject to transitional and saving provisions in SI 2009/56, Sch. 3.

WITHDRAWAL OF APPROVAL OF A COMPANY

6(1) The Board's withdrawal of approval of a company as a trust company for the purposes of Part 6 shall be given to the company by notice in writing.

6(2)   The notice shall specify–

(a)   the date from which the Board's withdrawal of approval shall have effect, and

(b)   the reasons for the Board's withdrawal of approval.

6(3)   The company may appeal against the withdrawal of approval.

History – In reg. 6(1) the words "Part 6" substituted for the words "section 842AA" by SI 2008/1893, reg. 8, with effect from 1 September 2008.

In reg. 6(3), the words "to the Special Commissioners", which appeared after "appeal", omitted by SI 2009/56, art. 3(2) and Sch. 2, para. 26, operative from 1 April 2009 subject to transitional and saving provisions in SI 2009/56, Sch. 3.

APPEALS TO THE TRIBUNAL

7(1)   This regulation applies where a company appeals pursuant to regulation 4(4), 5(3) or 6(3).

7(2)   The appeal shall be made by notice in writing given to the Board before the end of the period of 30 days beginning with the day on which the notice of provisional approval, refusal of approval or withdrawal of approval, as the case may be, was given to the company.

7(3)   Subject to paragraph (4) below, the tribunal shall, on an appeal notified to it, confirm the notice unless satisfied that the notice ought to be quashed.

7(4)   Where the appeal is against the inclusion of any of the conditions mentioned in regulation 4(3), the tribunal may vary any of those conditions.

7(5)   If the tribunal allows an appeal against a refusal of approval, the tribunal shall specify the date from which the approval is to have effect.

History – In the heading to reg. 7, "tribunal" substituted for "Special Commissioners" by SI 2009/56, art. 3(2) and Sch. 2, para. 27(2), operative from 1 April 2009 subject to transitional and saving provisions in SI 2009/56, Sch. 3.

In reg. 7(1), the words "to the Special Commissioners", which appeared after "appeals", omitted by SI 2009/56, art. 3(2) and Sch. 2, para. 27(3), operative from 1 April 2009 subject to transitional and saving provisions in SI 2009/56, Sch. 3.

In reg. 7(3), the words "tribunal shall, on an appeal notified to it," substituted for the words "Special Commissioners shall on appeal" by SI 2009/56, art. 3(2) and Sch. 2, para. 27(4)(a), operative from 1 April 2009 subject to transitional and saving provisions in SI 2009/56, Sch. 3.

In reg. 7(3), the words "they are", which appeared before "satisfied", omitted by SI 2009/56, art. 3(2) and Sch. 2, para. 27(4)(b), operative from 1 April 2009 subject to transitional and saving provisions in SI 2009/56, Sch. 3.

In reg. 7(4), "tribunal" substituted for "Special Commissioners" by SI 2009/56, art. 3(2) and Sch. 2, para. 27(5), operative from 1 April 2009 subject to transitional and saving provisions in SI 2009/56, Sch. 3.

In reg. 7(5), the words "tribunal allows" substituted for the words "Special Commissioners allow" by SI 2009/56, art. 3(2) and Sch. 2, para. 27(6)(a), operative from 1 April 2009 subject to transitional and saving provisions in SI 2009/56, Sch. 3.

In reg. 7(5), the words "the tribunal" substituted for the word "they" by SI 2009/56, art. 3(2) and Sch. 2, para. 27(6)(b), operative from 1 April 2009 subject to transitional and saving provisions in SI 2009/56, Sch. 3.

NOTIFICATION OF BREACH OF CONDITIONS FOR APPROVAL

8(1)   Where a trust company has been given full approval and–

(a)   any condition specified in section 274 has ceased to be met or is broken, or

(b)   the company considers that it is likely that any such condition will cease to be met or will be broken,

the company shall as soon as reasonably possible give notice in writing to the Board of that fact.

8(2)   Where a trust company has been given provisional approval and–

(a)   either–

    (i)   any condition specified in section 274 has not been met in relation to the period specified in section 275(3) in respect of that condition, or

    (ii)   the company considers that it is likely that any such condition will not be met in relation to the period so specified;

(b)   any condition included in a notice giving provisional approval and given under regulation 4(3) has not been met or has been broken, or the company considers that it is likely that any such condition will not be met or will be broken; or

(c)   after meeting the conditions specified in section 274 within the periods specified in section 275(3) any condition has ceased to be met, or the company considers that it is likely that any such condition will cease to be met or will be broken;

the company shall as soon as reasonably possible give notice in writing to the Board of that fact.

8(3)   A notice required under this regulation to be given by a company must–

(a)   specify the circumstances that caused or are likely to cause any condition to cease to be met or to be broken or not met,

(b)   so far as possible, state the extent to which any condition–

    (i)   has ceased or will cease to be met, or

    (ii)   has been or will be broken or not met, and

(c) where the company considers that any condition is likely to cease to be met or to be broken or not met by or on a date occurring after the date of the notice, specify (if possible) that future date.

History – Reg. 8–8J substituted for former reg. 8 by SI 2008/1893, reg. 9, with effect from 1 September 2008.

8(4) A notice required under this regulation must be signed by the secretary or a director of the company.

8(5) Paragraph (6) below applies if a company has given notice under this regulation in respect of circumstances that are likely to cause any condition to cease to be met or to be broken or not met ("the notified circumstances").

8(6) If this paragraph applies, no further notice under this regulation is required in relation to the notified circumstances where any condition ceases to be met or is broken or not met in, or as a result of, the notified circumstances.

8(7) Paragraph (6) above does not prevent a company giving a further notice under this regulation in respect of the notified circumstances for the purpose of enabling an application under regulation 8A(1) to be made.

History – Reg. 8–8J substituted for former reg. 8 by SI 2008/1893, reg. 9, with effect from 1 September 2008.

BREACH OF CONDITIONS FOR VCT APPROVAL: APPLICATIONS FOR APPROVAL TO CONTINUE

8A(1) If a trust company has not met or is likely not to meet the conditions for its VCT approval to continue in force in, or as a result of, the circumstances notified under regulation 8 it may apply in writing to the Board for a determination that the Board will not exercise their power conferred by section 281(1) to withdraw the company's VCT approval.

This is subject to paragraph (3) below.

8A(2) An application under paragraph (1) above–

(a) may only be made by being included in or with a notice under regulation 8;

(b) must specify the measures, if any, the company has taken or intends to take to rectify or avoid the failure or likely failure to meet the conditions for its VCT approval to continue in force; and

(c) must specify–

　(i) the date on which the failure to meet the conditions for its VCT approval to continue in force was rectified, or

　(ii) the date by which it expects to meet the conditions for its VCT approval to continue in force where the conditions are not met at the time of the application or will cease to be met after the time of the application.

8A(3) In a case where a company considers that it is likely not to meet the conditions for its VCT approval to continue in force, an application under paragraph (1) above may only be made if the likely failure to meet the conditions is expected to arise or occur within the period of 90 days commencing on the date on which notice under regulation 8 is given by the company.

History – Reg. 8–8J substituted for former reg. 8 by SI 2008/1893, reg. 9, with effect from 1 September 2008.

RECTIFYING A BREACH OF A CONDITION REQUIRED TO BE MET THROUGHOUT A PERIOD

8B(1) This regulation applies where–

(a) a condition for a trust company's VCT approval to continue in force must be met throughout, or satisfied at all times during, a relevant period,

(b) the condition has not been so met or satisfied, and

(c) after the failure to so meet or satisfy the condition, the circumstances of the company become such that were they to exist, or had they existed, throughout the relevant period, the condition would be or would have been, so met or satisfied.

8B(2) The failure to meet or satisfy the condition is to be treated for the purposes of this Part of these Regulations as having been rectified on the date when the circumstances of the company became such as are mentioned in paragraph (1)(c) above.

8B(3) In this regulation a reference to **"a relevant period"**, in relation to a condition, means–

(a) where the company has been given full approval, the relevant period as defined by section 274(2) in relation to the condition,

(b) where the company has been given provisional approval, the relevant period as defined by section 275(3) in relation to the condition, or

(c) where the condition is included in a notice giving provisional approval and given under regulation 4(3), the period specified in the notice in relation to the condition.

History – Reg. 8–8J substituted for former reg. 8 by SI 2008/1893, reg. 9, with effect from 1 September 2008.

DETERMINATION OF APPLICATIONS: BREACH OF CONDITIONS RECTIFIED AT TIME OF APPLICATION

8C(1) This regulation applies where–

(a) an application under regulation 8A(1) is in respect of the trust company's failure to meet the conditions for its VCT approval to continue in force, and

(b) the failure has been rectified at the date of the application.

8C(2) Where this regulation applies, the Board shall determine that they will not exercise their power under section 281(1) (power to withdraw VCT approval of a company) if the Board are satisfied that–

(a) the failure was as a result of circumstances outside the control of the company,

(b) those circumstances prevented the company from meeting the conditions for its VCT approval to continue in force,

(c) the company took all reasonable measures to continue to meet the conditions for its VCT approval to continue in force, and

(d) the failure was–
   (i) rectified by the company as soon as reasonably possible after the circumstances causing the failure arose, or
   (ii) rectified notwithstanding that no measures could be taken by the company to rectify it.

This is subject to regulation 8E (circumstances within the control of the company: investment managers).

History – Reg. 8–8J substituted for former reg. 8 by SI 2008/1893, reg. 9, with effect from 1 September 2008.

DETERMINATION OF APPLICATIONS: BREACH OF CONDITIONS NOT RECTIFIED AT TIME OF APPLICATION

8D(1) This regulation applies where–

(a) an application under regulation 8A(1) is in respect of the trust company's failure to meet the conditions for its VCT approval to continue in force, and

(b) the failure has not been rectified at the date of the application or the failure is likely to occur after the date of the application.

8D(2) Where this regulation applies, the Board shall determine that they will not exercise their power under section 281(1) (power to withdraw VCT approval of a company) if the they are satisfied that–

(a) the failure is or will be as a result of circumstances outside the control of the company,

(b) those circumstances prevent or will prevent the company from meeting the conditions for its VCT approval to continue,

(c) the company took and will take all reasonable measures to rectify or avoid the failure to meet the conditions for its VCT approval to continue, and

(d) either–
   (i) measures were taken or will be taken to rectify or avoid the failure as soon as possible and in any event within a reasonable period from the date of the application, or
   (ii) where no measures to rectify or avoid the failure can be taken, the failure will nevertheless become rectified or be avoided within a reasonable period from the date of the application.

This is subject to regulation 8E.

History – Reg. 8–8J substituted for former reg. 8 by SI 2008/1893, reg. 9, with effect from 1 September 2008.

CIRCUMSTANCES WITHIN THE CONTROL OF THE COMPANY: INVESTMENT MANAGERS

8E(1) For the purposes of regulations 8C and 8D, circumstances within the control of any investment manager of a company are to be treated as being within the control of the company.

8E(2) In paragraph (1) above **"investment manager"**, in relation to a company, means a person appointed by, or acting for or on behalf of, the company who–

(a) manages investments in an account or portfolio on a discretionary basis under the terms of an agreement with the company which confers discretionary management of those investments on that person, or

(b) manages investments in an account or portfolio without exercising any discretion in relation to those investments under the terms of an agreement with the company.

History – Reg. 8–8J substituted for former reg. 8 by SI 2008/1893, reg. 9, with effect from 1 September 2008.

DETERMINATIONS: SUPPLEMENTAL PROVISIONS

8F(1) A determination under regulation 8C(2) or 8D(2) shall be given by notice in writing to the company which applied for it.

8F(2) Where the Board make a determination under regulation 8D(2), the determination shall have effect for the period of 90 days commencing on the date on which they give notice to the company of it.

8F(3) A company given notice of a determination under regulation 8D(2) must give written notice to the Board when the failure or likely failure has been rectified or avoided.

8F(4) A notice under paragraph (3) above must–

(a) confirm that the failure or likely failure has been rectified or avoided,

(b) specify the date on which the failure or likely failure was rectified or avoided, and

(c) be given within 14 days of the date on which the failure or likely failure is rectified or avoided.

History – Reg. 8–8J substituted for former reg. 8 by SI 2008/1893, reg. 9, with effect from 1 September 2008.

DETERMINATION IN FORCE: FURTHER CIRCUMSTANCES CAUSING BREACH OF CONDITIONS

8G(1) This regulation applies where–

(a) the Board have made a determination under regulation 8D(2), and

(b) during the period in which that determination has effect further circumstances arise or occur which–

(i) have caused, cause or are likely to cause the company to fail to meet or to cease to meet any condition (including a condition imposed under regulation 4(3)) for its VCT approval to continue in force, or

(ii) in relation to a condition to which the determination relates, have caused, cause or are likely to cause that condition to be broken further or to increase the extent of the failure to meet the condition by the company.

8G(2) In relation to the further circumstances referred to in paragraph (1)(b) above, the company–

(a) must give notice in accordance with regulation 8, and

(b) may make an application in accordance with regulation 8A(1).

History – Reg. 8–8J substituted for former reg. 8 by SI 2008/1893, reg. 9, with effect from 1 September 2008.

FURTHER DETERMINATIONS IN RESPECT OF SAME APPLICATION

8H After the expiry of a determination made under regulation 8D(2), the Board may make a further determination under that regulation in respect of the same application if–

(a) the company requests in writing that a further determination be made in respect of that application,

(b) a return made in accordance with regulation 8I accompanies the request for the further determination, and

(c) the Board continue to be satisfied in relation to the matters specified in regulation 8D(2).

History – Reg. 8–8J substituted for former reg. 8 by SI 2008/1893, reg. 9, with effect from 1 September 2008.

MONITORING OF BREACH OF CONDITIONS: RETURNS

8I(1) If a company requests under regulation 8H that a further determination be made in respect of an application under regulation 8A(1) a return must be made by the company in accordance with this regulation and must be included in or with that request.

8I(2) A return under this regulation must be made–

(a) in relation to a first request under regulation 8H, in respect of the period from the date of the application under regulation 8A(1) to the date on which the first determination under regulation 8D(2) ceases to have effect, and

(b) in relation to a subsequent request under regulation 8H, in respect of the period commencing on the day after the end of the period to which the last return under this regulation relates and ending on the date on which the most recent determination under regulation 8D(2) ceases to have effect.

This is subject to paragraph (5) below.

8I(3) The return must–

(a) so far as is possible, state the extent to which the conditions for the company's VCT approval to continue in force–

    (i) have ceased or will cease to be met, or

    (ii) have been or will be broken or not met,

(b) specify what measures, if any, have been taken during that period to rectify or avoid the failure, or the likely failure, to meet the conditions for the company's VCT approval to continue in force,

(c) specify any alterations to the measures specified in the application made under regulation 8A(1), or in the last return under this regulation if later, that the company intends to take to rectify or avoid the failure, or likely failure, to meet the conditions for its VCT approval to continue,

(d) specify the date by which the company expects to meet the conditions for its VCT approval to continue, and

(e) be signed by the secretary or a director of the company.

8I(4) A return under this regulation must be made within 7 days after the date on which the period to which it relates ends.

8I(5) If more than one determination of the Board is in effect at the same time in relation to the same company, the Board may direct that one return applicable to those determinations is made in relation to a specified period.

8I(6) A return under this regulation shall be in such form as the Board may specify or authorise.

History – Reg. 8–8J substituted for former reg. 8 by SI 2008/1893, reg. 9, with effect from 1 September 2008.

WITHDRAWAL OF VCT APPROVAL WHERE DETERMINATION HAS BEEN MADE

8J(1) A determination under regulation 8C(2) or 8D(2) shall not prevent the Board from exercising their power under section 281(1) to withdraw the company's VCT approval where they have grounds for doing so in relation to other circumstances not the subject of an application under regulation 8A(1) to which the determination relates.

8J(2) A determination under 8D(2) shall not prevent the Board from exercising their power under section 281(1) to withdraw the company's VCT approval where the failure or likely failure to which the determination relates has not been rectified or avoided within a reasonable period from the date of the application to which the determination relates.

History – Reg. 8–8J substituted for former reg. 8 by SI 2008/1893, reg. 9, with effect from 1 September 2008.

PART III – RELIEF FROM INCOME TAX

Chapter I – Relief in Respect of Investments in Trust Companies

CERTIFICATE TO BE GIVEN TO INVESTOR

9(1) If an individual to whom eligible shares have been issued so requires, a trust company shall, within 30 days, give him a certificate containing the particulars specified in paragraph (2) below and certifying as specified in paragraph (3) below.

9(2) The particulars specified are–

(a) the name of the investor,

(b) his permanent address including postcode,

(c) the date on which the eligible shares were issued to him,

(d) the amount payable in respect of those shares and the date on which that amount will be payable, and

(e) the amount paid in respect of those shares and the date on which that amount was paid.

9(3) The certificate shall certify–

(a) that eligible shares have been issued to the investor,

(b) that to the best of the trust company's knowledge and belief the shares were both subscribed for and issued as mentioned in section 261(3), and

(c) that to the best of the trust company's knowledge and belief the shares were not issued in a case where the investor is not entitled to relief under Chapter 2 of Part 6 because the case is one to which section 264 applies.

9(4) The trust company shall keep a record of the information contained in any certificate given under this regulation.

History – In reg. 9(3)(b), the words "section 261(3)" substituted for the words "paragraph 1(9) of Schedule 15B" by SI 2008/1893, reg. 10(a), with effect from 1 September 2008.

In reg. 9(3)(c), the words "Chapter 2 of Part 6" substituted for the words "Part I of Schedule 15B" and the words "section 264" substituted for the words "paragraph 2 of that Schedule" by SI 2008/1893, reg. 10(b), with effect from 1 September 2008.

Chapter II – Relief in Respect of Distributions by Trust Companies

GENERAL

SCHEME OF RELIEF IN RESPECT OF DISTRIBUTIONS

10(1) Relief from income tax in respect of a distribution by a trust company shall not be given except where the trust company–

(a) has complied with the requirements imposed by regulations 11 and 14, and

(b) has made a claim in accordance with this Chapter.

10(2) Where a trust company has complied with the requirements imposed by regulations 11 and 14 and has made a claim in accordance with this Chapter, a tax credit to which an investor is entitled in respect of a distribution by the trust company shall not be set against income tax but shall be claimed by and paid to the trust company.

10(3) Where a tax credit has been claimed by and paid to a trust company pursuant to paragraph (2) above, an amount equal to the tax credit shall be paid by the trust company to the person who is entitled to receive the distribution.

Enduring Declaration

REQUIREMENT AS TO OBTAINING OF ENDURING DECLARATION

11 Relief from income tax in respect of a distribution by a trust company shall not be given except where the trust company has obtained an enduring declaration in respect of the shares to which the distribution relates.

ENDURING DECLARATION

12(1) An enduring declaration shall be in writing and shall be given to the trust company by an individual beneficially entitled to shares in that trust company.

12(2) The enduring declaration shall contain the particulars relating to the individual specified in paragraph (3) below, the particulars relating to the shares in the trust company specified in paragraph (4) below and the declaration by the individual specified in paragraph (5) below.

12(3) The particulars relating to the beneficial owner are–

(a) his full name,

(b) his permanent address including postcode,

(c) his date of birth, and

(d) if he has one, his national insurance number.

12(4) The particulars relating to the shares in the trust company are–

(a) the identity of the shares acquired,

(b) the date on which those shares were acquired,

(c) the market value of those shares at the time of their acquisition, and

(d) the extent to which those shares were acquired in excess of the permitted maximum for the year in which the acquisition was made.

12(5)   The declaration by the individual is–

(a)   that he is beneficially entitled to the shares in the trust company, and

(b)   that to the best of his knowledge and belief the particulars given in the declaration are correct.

RETURN CONTAINING PARTICULARS OF ENDURING DECLARATIONS

13(1)   A company which is, or has been, a trust company shall deliver to the Board, in respect of the period specified in paragraph (2) below ("the specified period"), and within the time limit specified in paragraph (3) below, a return containing, in respect of each enduring declaration received by the trust company during the specified period, the particulars specified in paragraph (4) below.

13(2)   The specified period is–

(a)   a year, or

(b)   a period beginning on 6th April and ending on the day on which that company ceased to be approved as a trust company, whichever is the shorter.

13(3)   The time limit specified is–

(a)   six months after the end of the year, or

(b)   six months after the day on which the company ceased to be approved as a trust company, whichever is the shorter.

13(4)   The particulars specified in respect of each enduring declaration are–

(a)   the full name of the investor,

(b)   his permanent address, including postcode,

(c)   his date of birth,

(d)   if he has one, his national insurance number,

(e)   the acquisition value of the shares to which the enduring declaration relates, and

(f)   the date on which those shares were acquired.

13(5)   A return under this regulation shall be in such form as the Board may specify or authorise.

REQUIREMENT FOR TRUST COMPANY TO BE SATISFIED THAT ENDURING DECLARATION CORRECT

14   Relief from income tax in respect of a distribution by a trust company shall not be given except where the trust company has no reason to believe, by reference to the information in its possession, that the enduring declaration relating to the shares in the trust company in respect of which the distribution is made is or has become incorrect.

POSITION WHERE TRUST COMPANY CEASES TO BE SATISFIED THAT ENDURING DECLARATION CORRECT

15(1)   This regulation applies where a trust company has reason to believe, by reference to the information in its possession, that an enduring declaration is or has become incorrect.

15(2)   The company shall deliver to the Board, within three months of having reason so to believe, a statement containing the particulars specified in paragraph (3) below.

15(3)   The particulars are–

(a)   a copy of the enduring declaration,

(b)   the reason why the trust company believes that the enduring declaration is or has become incorrect,

(c)   the tax credits claimed by the trust company in respect of distributions made in respect of the shares to which the enduring declaration relates, and

(d)   the amounts equal to the tax credits referred to in sub-paragraph (c) above which have been paid to the person who is entitled to the distribution.

15(4)   Section 252 shall have effect with the modification specified in paragraph (5) below in relation to any tax credit claimed as mentioned in paragraph (3)(c) above as it has effect in relation to any set-off or payment of tax credit mentioned in subsection (1)(b) of that section which ought not to have been made.

15(5)   Subsection (1) of section 252 shall be modified so as to apply only where a trust company has been fraudulent, reckless or negligent in claiming tax credits in respect of distributions made in respect of the shares to which the enduring declaration relates.

Claims

INTRODUCTORY

16(1) A claim made by a trust company in accordance with this Chapter shall be made to the Board in writing, and shall be in such form and contain such particulars as the Board may require or authorise.

16(2) A claim shall be either an interim claim or an annual claim.

16(3) A claim shall contain a declaration by the trust company that it has continued to satisfy the conditions for approval for the purposes of section 842AA since the date on which approval for the purposes of section 842AA was given or, if later, since the date it last delivered a return under regulation 22.

16(4) The Board shall not be under an obligation to make a payment to a trust company earlier than the end of the month following that in which the claim was received.

INTERIM CLAIMS

17(1) An interim claim may be made for a period which–

(a) consists of one month or a number of months (not exceeding six) beginning on the 6th day of a month and ending on the 5th day of the relevant following month, and

(b) does not fall within more than one year.

17(2) No interim claim may be made for the month ending 5th July or any subsequent month until the return under regulation 13 due in respect of the preceding year has been duly made and received by the Board.

17(3) No interim claim may be made for the month ending 5th October or any subsequent month until the annual claim due in respect of the preceding year has been duly made and received by the Board.

17(4) A claim under this regulation may not be based on an estimate but may only be made to claim tax credits in respect of distributions made during the period covered by the claim.

17(5) If the Board are satisfied that the trust company may claim the amount specified in a claim under paragraph (4) above in relation to the period for which the claim is made, they shall pay that amount to the trust company and, if they are not so satisfied, they shall pay any lesser amount which they are satisfied may be claimed.

ANNUAL CLAIMS

18(1) An annual claim in respect of a year shall be made within six months after the end of that year.

18(2) No payment shall be made by the Board under an annual claim which is made more than six years after the end of the year for which it is made.

18(3) A claim under this regulation–

(a) may not be based on an estimate but may only be made to claim tax credits in respect of distributions made during the year, and

(b) shall bring into account aggregate interim payments made for the year, and for the purposes of this regulation **"aggregate interim payments"** means the aggregate of payments made (and not repaid) on interim claims.

18(4) If the Board are satisfied that the trust company may claim the amount specified in a claim under paragraph (3) above in relation to the year for which the claim is made, they shall pay the amount to the trust company and, if they are not so satisfied, they shall pay any lesser amount which they are satisfied may be claimed.

18(5) If the aggregate interim payments shown by an annual claim exceeds the aggregate tax credits which the trust company may claim by virtue of regulation 10(2) in respect of distributions made during the year, the trust company shall repay the amount of the excess to the Board with the claim.

18(6) If a trust company fails to make an annual claim within six months following the end of the year, the Board may issue a notice to the trust company showing the aggregate interim payments made to the trust company for the year, and stating that the Board are not satisfied that the amount due to the trust company for that year exceeds the lower amount stated in the notice.

18(7) If an annual claim for the year is not delivered to the Board within 14 days after the issue of a notice under paragraph (6) above, the amount of the difference between the aggregate interim payments and the lower amount stated in the notice shall immediately be recoverable by the Board in the same manner as tax charged by an assessment on the trust company which has become final and conclusive; and section 88 of the Management Act shall apply from the 6th October following the end of the year.

18(8) Where an annual claim has been made and the trust company which made it subsequently discovers that an error or mistake has been made in the claim, the trust company may make a supplementary annual claim within six years after the end of the year for which the annual claim was made.

18(9) If the Board so wish, forms required or authorised for annual claims may require a report to be given by a person qualified for appointment as auditor of a company.

SUPPLEMENTARY PROVISIONS

19(1) Section 42 of the Management Act shall not apply to a claim under this Chapter of these Regulations.

19(2) No appeal shall lie from the Board's decision on an interim claim.

19(3) An appeal from the Board's decision on an annual claim may be made to the Special Commissioners; and the appeal shall be made by notice in writing given to the Board before the end of the period of 30 days beginning with the day of receipt of the Board's decision.

19(4) No payment or repayment made or other thing done on or in relation to an interim claim or a notice under regulation 18(6) shall prejudice the Board's decision on an annual claim.

19(5) On appeal the Special Commissioners may vary the decision appealed against whether or not the variation is to the advantage of the appellant.

19(6) All such assessments, payments and repayments shall be made as are necessary to give effect to the Board's decision on an annual claim or to any variation of that decision on appeal.

Supplementary Provisions

LIABILITY FOR TAX WHERE PROVISIONAL APPROVAL WITHDRAWN

20 Where the provisional approval of a company as a trust company is withdrawn, section 252 shall have effect in relation to any tax credit paid under this Chapter as it has effect in relation to any set-off or payment of tax credit mentioned in subsection (1)(b) of that section which ought not to have been made.

ISSUE OF TAX CREDIT VOUCHERS IN CERTAIN CIRCUMSTANCES

21(1) This regulation applies where–

(a)   a trust company makes a distribution which is not included in a claim, or

(b)   a trust company makes a distribution which is the subject of a claim which is refused, or

(c)   a tax credit in respect of a distribution made by a trust company is recovered pursuant to regulation 15(3) or 20.

21(2) Section 234 shall have effect in relation to the distribution.

PART IV – RETURN OF PARTICULARS OF INVESTMENTS, KEEPING OF RECORDS AND PROVISION OF INFORMATION

RETURN CONTAINING PARTICULARS OF AMOUNTS SUBSCRIBED FOR ELIGIBLE SHARES

21A(1) A company which at any time in the period specified in paragraph (2) below ("the specified period") is a trust company, shall deliver to the Board, in respect of the specified period and within the time limit specified in paragraph (3) below, a return containing, in respect of each amount subscribed by any investor for eligible shares in the specified period, the particulars specified in paragraph (4) below.

21A(2) The specified period is–

(a)   a year, or

(b)   a period beginning on the 6th April and ending on the day on which that company ceased to be approved as a trust company,

whichever is the shorter.

21A(3) The time limit specified is—

(a) six months after the end of the year, or

(b) six months after the day on which the company ceased to be approved as a trust company, whichever is the earlier.

21A(4) The particulars specified are–

(a) the full name of the investor,

(b) his permanent residential address, including postcode,

(c) his date of birth,

(d) if he has one, his national insurance number,

(e) the amount paid in respect of eligible shares subscribed for in that period, and

(f) the date on which that amount was paid.

21A(5) A return under this regulation shall be in such form as the Board may prescribe or authorise.

History – Reg. 21A inserted by SI 1999/819, reg. 5, with effect from 6 April 1999.

RETURN CONTAINING PARTICULARS OF INVESTMENTS

22(1) A company which is, or has been, a trust company shall deliver to the Board, in respect of the period specified in paragraph (2) below ("the specified period"), and within the time limit specified in paragraph (3) below, a return containing the particulars specified in paragraph (4) below, the certificate specified in paragraph (5) below and the declaration specified in paragraph (6) below.

22(2) The specified period is–

(a) an accounting period of a trust company,

(b) a period beginning on the date from which the Board's approval of a company for the purposes of Part 6 has effect and ending on an accounting date of the company, or

(c) a period beginning at the commencement of an accounting period of a company and ending on the day on which that company ceased to be approved for the purposes of Part 6, whichever is the shortest.

22(3) The time limit specified is–

(a) twelve months after the end of the accounting period of the trust company, or

(b) twelve months after the day on which the company ceased to be approved for the purposes of Part 6, whichever is the shorter.

22(4) The particulars specified are–

(a) in respect of each investment held by the company at the beginning of the specified period, the value of that investment computed in accordance with section 278;

(b) in respect of any new investment made by the company during the specified period–

(i) the date on which that investment was made, and

(ii) the value of that investment together with any revaluation of investments, computed in accordance with section 278, which is required as a result of the making of that investment;

(c) in relation to each investment, whether or not it is a qualifying holding;

(d) in relation to each qualifying holding–

(i) the name of the company in which the investment has been made, and

(ii) the address of that company's registered or principal office; and

(e) in respect of each disposal of an investment by the company during the specified period–

(i) the name of the company in which the investment was held,

(ii) the address of that company's registered or principal office,

(iii) the date of the disposal, and

(iv) the value, immediately after the disposal, computed in accordance with section 278, of the remainder of any holding of investments from which the disposal was made.

22(5) The certificate specified is–

(a) where the trust company has been given full approval or has been given provisional approval three years or more before the beginning of the specified period, that the trust company satisfied all the conditions in section 274 throughout the specified period; or

(b)   where the trust company has been given provisional approval less than three years before the beginning of the specified period, that the trust company satisfied all the conditions of section 274 and any other conditions attached to the provisional approval throughout the specified period; or

(c)   that the company has ceased to be approved for the purposes of Part 6.

22(6)   The declaration specified is a declaration that the particulars contained in the return are, to the best of the company's knowledge and belief, true and correct.

22(7)   The declaration specified in paragraph (6) above shall be signed by the secretary or by a director of the company.

22(8)   A return under this regulation shall be in such form as the Board may specify or authorise.

History – In reg. 22(2)(b) and (c), the words "Part 6" substituted for the words "section 842AA" by SI 2008/1893, reg. 11(a), with effect from 1 September 2008.
In reg. 22(3)(b), the words "Part 6" substituted for the words "section 842AA" by SI 2008/1893, reg. 11(a), with effect from 1 September 2008.
In reg. 22(4)(a), (b)(ii) and (e)(iv), the words "section 278" substituted for the words "subsections (5) and (11) of section 842AA" by SI 2008/1893, reg. 11(b), with effect from 1 September 2008.
In reg. 22(4), the word "and" immediately following sub-para. (c) was removed by SI 1999/819, reg. 6(a) with effect from 6 April 1999.
In reg. 22(4), the word "and" immediately following sub-para. (d) was inserted by SI 1999/819, reg. 6(b) with effect from 6 April 1999.
In reg. 22(4), sub-para. (e) was inserted by SI 1999/819, reg. 6(b) with effect from 6 April 1999.
In reg. 22(5)(a), the words "section 274" substituted for the words "subsection (2) of section 842AA" and in reg. 22(5)(b)the words "section 274" substituted for the words "subsection (4) of section 842AA" by SI 2008/1893, reg. 11(c), with effect from 1 September 2008.
In reg. 22(5)(c), the words "Part 6" substituted for the words "section 842AA" by SI 2008/1893, reg. 11(a), with effect from 1 September 2008.

RECORDS TO BE KEPT BY TRUST COMPANY

23(1)   A company which is or has been a trust company shall at all times during the relevant period keep sufficient accounts, records and other information to enable the requirements of Part 6 and these Regulations to be satisfied.

23(2)   In paragraph (1) above, the **"relevant period"** means–

(a)   in the case of a company which has ceased to be approved for the purposes of Part 6, the period of six years from the date on which the company ceased to be so approved, and

(b)   in any other case, the period of six years from the end of the period of account or the year to which the accounts, records and information relate, whichever is the longer.

History – In reg. 23(1), the words "Part 6" substituted for the words "section 842AA, Schedule 15B" by SI 2008/1893, reg. 12(a), with effect from 1 September 2008.
In reg. 23(2)(a), the words "Part 6" substituted for the words "section 842AA" by SI 2008/1893, reg. 12(b), with effect from 1 September 2008.

INFORMATION TO BE PROVIDED TO THE BOARD

24(1)   The Board may by notice require any company which is or has been a trust company or any person who holds or has held shares in such a company, within such period as may be specified in the notice, to furnish them with such information as they may reasonably require for the purposes of Part 6 or these Regulations.

24(2)   The period specified in a notice given under paragraph (1) above shall be not less than 14 days.

History – In reg. 24(1), the words "Part 6" substituted for the words "section 842AA, Schedule 15B" by SI 2008/1893, reg. 13, with effect from 1 September 2008.

INSPECTION OF RECORDS BY OFFICER OF THE BOARD

25(1)   The Board may by notice require any company which is or has been a trust company or any person who holds or has held shares in such a company, within such period as may be specified in the notice, to make available for inspection by an officer of the Board authorised for that purpose such accounts, records and other information as are in that person's possession or under that person's control as the Board may reasonably require for the purposes of Part 6 or these Regulations.

25(2)   The period specified in a notice given under paragraph (1) above shall be not less than 14 days.

25(3)   Where records are maintained by computer the person required to make them available for inspection shall provide the officer making the inspection with all the facilities necessary for obtaining information from them.

History – In reg. 25(1), the words "Part 6" substituted for the words "section 842AA, Schedule 15B" by SI 2008/1893, reg. 14, with effect from 1 September 2008.

Statutory Instruments

INCOME TAX (DEALERS IN SECURITIES) (TRADEPOINT) REGULATIONS 1995

(SI 1995/2050)

Made on 1 August 1995 by the Treasury, in exercise of the powers conferred on them by s. 732(2A) and (7) of the Income and Corporation Taxes Act 1988. Operative from 25 August 1995.

CITATION AND COMMENCEMENT

1   These Regulations may be cited as the Income Tax (Dealers in Securities) (Tradepoint) Regulations 1995 and shall come into force on 25th August 1995.

INTERPRETATION

2   In these Regulations unless the context otherwise requires–

"**Board of directors**" means the Board of directors of Tradepoint;

"**clearing participant**" means a member (as defined by this regulation) who is also a member of The London Clearing House Limited and who as such is permitted by the Board of directors and that clearing house to clear transactions made on the Exchange for a traded security;

"**equity securities**" means securities within the meaning given by section 731(9) of the Taxes Act which are issued by a company;

"**the Exchange**" means Tradepoint Investment Exchange;

"**first buyer**" shall be construed in accordance with section 731(2) of the Taxes Act;

"**member**" in relation to Tradepoint means a person approved by the Board of Directors as a participant in the Exchange;

"**subsection (1)**" and "**subsection (2A)**" mean subsection (1) and subsection (2A) respectively of section 732 of the Taxes Act;

"**Taxes Act**" means the Income and Corporation Taxes Act 1988;

"**Tradepoint**" means Tradepoint Financial Networks plc.

PRESCRIBED PERSONS AND DATE FOR THE PURPOSES OF SUBSECTION (2A)

3   For the purposes of subsection (2A)–

(a)   The London Clearing House Limited is a recognised clearing house which is prescribed;

(b)   Tradepoint is a recognised investment exchange which is prescribed;

(c)   a member in relation to Tradepoint who is a clearing participant is prescribed as a class or description of member of Tradepoint;

(d)   the date which is referred to in paragraph (b) of subsection (2A) and which is prescribed is 25th August 1995.

PRESCRIBED CIRCUMSTANCES FOR THE PURPOSES OF SUBSECTION (2A)

4(1)   Paragraphs (2) and (3) below prescribe for the purposes of subsection (2A) the circumstances in which subsection (1) shall not apply.

4(2)   If the first buyer is The London Clearing House Limited, the circumstances prescribed are where–

(a)   the securities referred to in subsection (1) as purchased by the first buyer are equity securities, and

(b)   those securities were purchased by The London Clearing House Limited as the first buyer acting in its capacity as a person providing clearing services in connection with a transaction made on the Exchange.

4(3)   If the first buyer is a member in relation to Tradepoint and is a clearing participant, the prescribed circumstances are where–

(a)   the securities referred to in subsection (1) as purchased by the first buyer are equity securities, and

(b)   those securities were purchased by the member as the first buyer and in his capacity as a clearing participant–

(i) from a person in circumstances where the member is required to sell equity securities under a matching transaction to The London Clearing House Limited, or

(ii) from The London Clearing House Limited in circumstances where he is required to sell equity securities under a matching transaction to another person.

4(4) In paragraph (3) above **"matching transaction"** means a transaction under which–

(a) the equity securities to be sold by the member are of the same kind as the equity securities purchased by him, and

(b) the number and price of the equity securities to be sold by the member are identical to the number and price of the equity securities purchased by him.

Statutory Instruments

TAXATION OF INCOME FROM LAND (NON-RESIDENTS) REGULATIONS 1995

(SI 1995/2902, as amended by SI 2009/56)

Made on 10 November 1995 by the Commissioners of Inland Revenue, in exercise of the powers conferred on them by s. 42A of the Income and Corporation Taxes Act 1988. Operative from 1 December 1995.

ARRANGEMENT OF REGULATIONS

PRELIMINARY

CITATION, COMMENCEMENT AND EFFECT

1(1) These Regulations may be cited as the Taxation of Income from Land (Non-residents) Regulations 1995 and shall come into force on 1st December 1995.

1(2) These Regulations shall have effect with respect to any payment made on or after 6th April 1996 which–

(a)   constitutes income of a Schedule A business carried on by a non-resident, and

(b)   either–

(i)   is made by a person falling within subsection (2)(a) of section 42A who is a prescribed person in respect of the non-resident, or

(ii)   is received by an agent who is a prescribed person in respect of the non-resident or by another person at the direction of that agent.

INTERPRETATION

2 In these Regulations unless the context otherwise requires–

"agent" means a person falling within subsection (2)(b) of section 42A;

"annual period" means the period commencing on 1st April and ending on the following 31st March;

"the Board" means the Commissioners of Inland Revenue;

"deductible expense" means an expense which is deductible under the Tax Acts in computing the profits or gains of a non-resident's Schedule A business;

"Management Act" means the Taxes Management Act 1970;

"non-resident" means a person who has his usual place of abode outside the United Kingdom;

"notice" means notice in writing;

"prescribed person" means a person prescribed by regulation 3;

"professional trustee" means a person who carries on, or is employed by, a business which consists of or includes the management of trusts, and who acts as trustee in the course of that business or employment;

"quarter" means–

(a)   the period from 6th April 1996 to 30th June 1996;

(b)   any subsequent period of 3 months ending with the last day of September, December, March or June;

"section 42A" means section 42A of the Taxes Act;

"Schedule A business" shall be construed in accordance with subsection (8)(a) of section 42A;

"Taxes Act" means the Income and Corporation Taxes Act 1988;

"year" means year of assessment.

PRESCRIBED PERSONS

PRESCRIBED PERSONS FOR THE PURPOSES OF SECTION 42A

3(1) In any case where a person falling within subsection 2(a) or (b) of section 42A is issued with a notice by the Board stating that he is a prescribed person for the purposes of subsection (1) of that section in respect of the Schedule A business of a non-resident, or a part of that business, that person is prescribed for the purposes of subsection (1) of that section in respect of that business or, as the case may be, the part referred to in the notice.

3(2) Except where it relates to a part of a non-resident's Schedule A business, a notice under paragraph (1) above need not specify the name of the non-resident concerned or describe his Schedule A business.

3(3) In any case where–

(a)   no notice has been issued by the Board under paragraph (1) above in respect of a non-resident's Schedule A business, or there is a part of his business in respect of which no notice has been issued under that paragraph; and

(b)   a person whose usual place of abode is in the United Kingdom–

    (i)   is an agent in respect of that business or that part,

    (ii)   has power to receive income in respect of that business or that part or has control over the direction of that income, and

    (iii)   is not an excluded person,

that person is, subject to paragraph (4) below, prescribed for the purposes of subsection (1) of section 42A in respect of that business or, as the case may be, that part.

3(4) Where in a case falling within paragraph (3) above there is more than one person to whom sub-paragraph (b) of that paragraph applies as respects the same business or the same part of a business, the person who is the elected agent or, if there is no elected agent, the last agent is the person prescribed for the purposes of subsection (1) of section 42A in respect of that business or, as the case may be, that part.

3(5) In any case where–

(a)   no notice has been issued by the Board under paragraph (1) above in respect of a non-resident's Schedule A business, or there is a part of his business in respect of which no notice has been issued under that paragraph;

(b)   there is no person to whom paragraph (3)(b) above applies in respect of that business or that part; and

(c)   a person whose usual place of abode is in the United Kingdom–

      (i)   is a tenant of premises owned by the non-resident in connection with that business or that part, and

     (ii)   is liable to pay to the non-resident in respect of his occupation of those premises sums exceeding in the aggregate £5,200 per annum or, where he occupies the premises for less than one year, the proportionate amount of that sum which is determined by the duration of his occupation,

that person is prescribed for the purposes of subsection (1) of section 42A in respect of that business or, as the case may be, that part.

INTERPRETATION OF REGULATION 3

4(1) In regulation 3–

(a)   **"excluded person"** means an agent whose activity on behalf of the non-resident in connection with the management or administration of his Schedule A business or part thereof (as the case may be) is confined to the provision of legal advice or legal services;

(b)   **"elected agent"** means the agent who is elected jointly by the last agent and himself to assume the responsibilities of a prescribed person for the purposes of subsection (1) of section 42A in relation to the Schedule A business or part thereof (as the case may be);

(c)   **"last agent"** means the agent by whom sums constituting income from the non-resident's Schedule A business or part thereof (as the case may be) are paid directly to the non-resident or to an agent whose usual place of abode is outside the United Kingdom or to a person who is not an agent.

4(2) An election shall be made by notice to the Board signed by the last agent and the person to be elected, and any such notice shall state–

(a)   the name and address of the agent elected, and

(b)   the date from which the election has effect, not being a date earlier than the first day of the quarter in which the election is made.

4(3) An election may be revoked by notice to the Board given by either of the agents who made the election, and any such revocation shall have effect–

(a)   from the first day of the quarter next following the date on which the notice is received by the Board, or

(b)   after the expiry of 30 days following the date on which the notice is received by the Board,

whichever is the later to occur.

PARTNERSHIPS

5 In any case where a liability to make any payment to the Board under these Regulations arises from amounts payable or things done in the course of a business carried on by any persons in partnership, that partnership as such shall be treated for the purposes of these Regulations as a person falling within subsection (2)(a) or (b) (as the case may be) of section 42A.

MULTIPLE BRANCHES

6(1) In any case where an agent–

(a)   is a prescribed person by virtue of regulation 3 in respect of the Schedule A business, or part thereof, of more than one non-resident,

(b)   acts on behalf of those non-residents through branches of his business in circumstances where the average number of non-residents in each branch at the relevant time is not less than five, and

(c)   is a person approved by the Board for the purposes of this regulation, that person shall be treated for the purposes of these Regulations as if in respect of each branch he were a separate and distinct person.

6(2) An application for approval under paragraph (1) above shall be made to the Board in a form provided or authorised by the Board which shall contain–

(a)   such information as is necessary to identify the branches concerned,

(b)   the number of non-residents in each branch, and

(c)   a declaration by the prescribed person that he does not act on behalf of any non-residents other than those whose business is managed by the branches so identified.

6(3) An approval under paragraph (1) above shall, unless revoked or withdrawn, have effect for the quarter following that in which it is given and for any subsequent quarter.

6(4) An approval may be revoked by the prescribed person by notice to the Board and, subject to paragraph (5) below, such revocation shall have effect for the quarter following that in which it is given and for any subsequent quarter.

6(5) Notwithstanding the revocation of approval under paragraph (4) above, a further application for approval may be made by the prescribed person in accordance with paragraph (2) above at any time following the revocation; and paragraph (3) above shall apply accordingly in relation to an approval given in response to that application.

6(6) The Board may, by notice to the prescribed person, refuse approval where they have reason to believe that–

(a)   the average number of non-residents in each branch is less than five at the relevant time, or

(b)   there is likely to be a failure on the part of the prescribed person to comply with the obligations imposed on him under these Regulations in relation to any branch, or

(c)   the declaration given by the prescribed person pursuant to paragraph (2)(c) above is incorrect.

6(7) The Board may, by notice to the prescribed person, withdraw approval where they have reason to believe that–

(a)   the average number of non-residents in each branch was at the relevant time, or has since become, less than five, or

(b)   there has been a failure on the part of the prescribed person to comply with the obligations imposed on him under these Regulations in relation to any branch, or

(c)   the declaration given by the prescribed person pursuant to paragraph (2)(c) above was, or has become, incorrect.

6(8) The prescribed person may appeal against a notice under paragraph (6) above refusing approval, or a notice under paragraph (7) above withdrawing approval, by notice to the Board within 30 days of the date of issue of the notice of refusal or, as the case may be, the notice of withdrawal.

6(9) [Omitted by SI 2009/56, art. 3(2) and Sch. 2, para. 29(2).]

6(10) The tribunal shall, on an appeal notified to it, confirm the notice of refusal or withdrawal unless satisfied that it ought to be quashed.

6(11) In this regulation–

(a)   references to branches of an agent's business are references to the units (of whatever kind) into which the agent has divided his business;

(b)   references to **"the relevant time"** are references to the time at which an application for approval is made by the prescribed person.

History – Reg. 6(9) omitted by SI 2009/56, art. 3(2) and Sch. 2, para. 29(2), operative from 1 April 2009 subject to transitional and saving provisions in SI 2009/56, Sch. 3. Former reg. 6(9) read as follows:

    "**6(9)**   The appeal shall be to the General Commissioners except that the prescribed person may elect (in accordance with section 46(1) of the Management Act) to appeal to the Special Commissioners.".

In reg. 6(10), the words "The tribunal shall, on an appeal notified to it," substituted for the words "The General Commissioners or, as the case may be, the Special Commissioners shall on appeal to them" by SI 2009/56, art. 3(2) and Sch. 2, para. 29(3)(a), operative from 1 April 2009 subject to transitional and saving provisions in SI 2009/56, Sch. 3.

In reg. 6(10), the words "they are", which appeared before "satisfied", omitted by SI 2009/56, art. 3(2) and Sch. 2, para. 29(3)(b), operative from 1 April 2009 subject to transitional and saving provisions in SI 2009/56, Sch. 3.

REGISTRATION BY PRESCRIBED PERSONS

7(1) The person prescribed by paragraph (2) below shall, within the period of 30 days following the date specified in paragraph (3) below, register with the Board the following details–

(a)   his name and address, and

(b)   his tax office reference, if he has one.

Statutory Instruments

7(2) The person prescribed by this paragraph is any person who is–

(a)   an agent in respect of the Schedule A business, or part thereof, of a non-resident, and

(b)   a person prescribed by regulation 3 in respect of that business or that part.

7(3) The date specified in this paragraph is the date on which the agent became a person prescribed by regulation 3 in respect of that business or that part.

PAYMENT AND RECOVERY OF TAX

CALCULATION OF PAYMENT OF TAX BY PERSON FALLING WITH SUBSECTION (2)(A) OF SECTION 42A

8(1) A person falling within subsection (2)(a) of section 42A who is a prescribed person in respect of the Schedule A business, or part thereof, of a non-resident shall calculate for each quarter the amount of any payment to be made to the Board in respect of tax which is or may become chargeable on the income from that business or that part.

8(2) The amount of the payment to be calculated by that person is the amount of tax at the basic rate on the aggregate of all income which falls to be treated as a receipt of that business or that part, other than income specified in paragraph (3) below, and which either–

(a)   was paid by him in the quarter to the non-resident, or

(b)   was paid by him in the quarter to a person other than the non-resident, not being a payment which he can reasonably be satisfied is a deductible expense.

8(3) The income specified in this paragraph is any income which–

(a)   is attributable to a branch of the non-resident in the United Kingdom, and

(b)   is chargeable to corporation tax.

CALCULATION OF PAYMENT OF TAX BY AGENT

9(1) An agent who is a prescribed person in respect of the Schedule A business, or part thereof, of a non-resident shall calculate for each quarter the amount of any payment to be made to the Board in respect of tax which is or may become chargeable on the income from that business or that part.

9(2) The amount of the payment to be calculated is the amount of tax at the basic rate on the amount which results after deducting from the income specified in paragraph (3) below–

(a)   the expenses specified in paragraph (4) below, and

(b)   any excess amount of expenses falling to be deducted from that income in accordance with paragraph (5) below.

9(3) The income specified is all income which falls to be treated as a receipt of that business or that part, other than income specified in regulation 8(3), and which either–

(a)   was received by the prescribed person in the quarter concerned, or

(b)   was income which it was in his power to receive or over whose direction he had control but which was paid at his direction to another person in that quarter without being received by him.

9(4) The expenses specified are all amounts paid in the quarter by the prescribed person or by another person at his direction that he can reasonably be satisfied are deductible under the Tax Acts in computing the profits or gains of that business or that part.

9(5) Where in any quarter in an annual period the expenses specified in paragraph (4) above exceed the income specified in paragraph (3) above–

(a)   the amount of the excess shall first be deducted from the income specified in paragraph (3) above for previous quarters in that annual period, taking later quarters before earlier quarters, and

(b)   any balance remaining of that amount shall be carried forward and deducted from the income specified in paragraph (3) above for subsequent quarters, including quarters after the end of that annual period, taking earlier quarters before later quarters.

9(6) Where an amount paid by a prescribed person in a previous quarter becomes repayable as a result of an excess amount being deducted from income pursuant to paragraph (5)(a) above, the amount repayable–

(a)   shall first be set off by the prescribed person against payments due under this regulation in respect of other non-residents in respect of whose Schedule A business or part thereof he is a prescribed person for the quarter in which the excess amount arises, and

(b)   any balance remaining shall, on a claim being made to the Board by the prescribed person, be repaid to him.

9(7)   A claim under paragraph (6)(b) above ("a repayment claim") shall be made in a quarterly return under regulation 10.

9(8)   An appeal from the Board's decision on a repayment claim shall be brought by giving notice to the Board within 30 days of receipt of notice of the decision.

9(9)   All such assessments, payments and repayments shall be made as are necessary to give effect to the Board's decision on a repayment claim or to any variation of that decision on appeal.

History – In reg. 9(8), the words "shall lie to the Special Commissioners", which appeared after "appeal", omitted by SI 2009/56, art. 3(2) and Sch. 2, para. 30(2), operative from 1 April 2009 subject to transitional and saving provisions in SI 2009/56, Sch. 3. In reg. 9(8), the words ", and the appeal", which appeared before "shall be brought", omitted by SI 2009/56, art. 3(2) and Sch. 2, para. 30(3), operative from 1 April 2009 subject to transitional and saving provisions in SI 2009/56, Sch. 3.

ACCOUNTING FOR TAX – QUARTERLY RETURNS

10(1)   In the circumstances specified in paragraph (2) below and within 30 days after the end of a quarter, a prescribed person shall make a return to the Board, in such form as the Board may prescribe, containing the information specified in paragraph (3) below and the declaration specified in paragraph (4) below.

10(2)   The circumstances specified are where–

(a)   an amount is payable by the prescribed person in respect of the quarter, calculated in accordance with regulation 8 or 9 as the case may be, or

(b)   a repayment of tax is due under regulation 9(6)(b), or

(c)   the Board have issued a notice to the prescribed person requiring a return to be made in respect of that quarter.

10(3)   The information specified is–

(a)   the name and address of the prescribed person;

(b)   where the prescribed person is a person falling within subsection (2)(a) of section 42A, the aggregate of the amounts payable by him for that quarter, calculated in accordance with regulation 8, in respect of all non-residents in respect of whose Schedule A businesses (or parts thereof) he is a prescribed person;

(c)   where the prescribed person is an agent, the aggregate of the amounts payable by him for that quarter, calculated in accordance with regulation 9, in respect of all non-residents in respect of whose Schedule A businesses (or part thereof) he is a prescribed person, after set off of any amounts repayable pursuant to paragraph (6)(a) of that regulation; and

(d)   a claim for repayment of an amount pursuant to regulation 9(6)(b), where appropriate.

10(4)   The declaration specified is a declaration by the prescribed person that the particulars given in the return are to the best of his knowledge correct and complete.

10(5)   The aggregate amount referred to in paragraph (3)(b) or (c) above shall be due at the time by which the return under paragraph (1) above is to be made, and that amount so due–

(a)   shall be payable by the prescribed person without the making of an assessment, and

(b)   may be assessed on the prescribed person (whether or not it has been paid when the assessment is made) if it, or any part of it, is not paid on or before the due date.

10(6)   The amount so due shall carry interest at the rate applicable under section 178 of the Finance Act 1989 to section 87 of the Management Act from the date when the amount becomes due until payment.

10(7)   Where an amount paid by a prescribed person in a previous quarter is repaid pursuant to a claim under regulation 9(6)(b), the repayment shall not affect interest under paragraph (6) above on the amount repaid for such time as is specified in paragraph (8) below but, subject to that, paragraph (6) above shall apply as if any such amount which is repaid had never become payable.

10(8)   The time for which interest is not affected is–

(a)   any time before the expiration of the period of 30 days from the end of the quarter in which the excess of expenses giving rise to the repayment arose, unless the return for that quarter is made earlier in that period; and

(b)   if that return is made earlier in that period, any time ending before the date on which the return is made.

10(9)   If it appears to the Board that there is an amount which ought to have been but has not been included in a quarterly return as payable to the Board, or if the Board are dissatisfied with any quarterly return, they may make an assessment on the prescribed person to the best of their judgment in respect of that amount.

10(10)   The like provisions as are contained in paragraph 10 of Schedule 16 to the Taxes Act (assessments and due date of tax) shall have effect in relation to an assessment under paragraph (9) above as if–

(a)   for references to an assessment under that Schedule there were substituted references to an assessment under paragraph (9) above;

(b)   the references to paragraphs 4(1) and 9 of that Schedule were omitted;

(c)   sub-paragraph (5) were omitted.

10(11)   Any income tax due under an assessment made by virtue of paragraph (9) above shall carry interest at the rate applicable under section 178 of the Finance Act 1989 to section 87 of the Management Act from the date when the tax becomes due until payment; and for that purpose the tax shall be treated as having become due at the time when it would have become due if a correct return had been made.

ANNUAL RETURNS

11(1)   Not later than the 5th July following the end of an annual period, a prescribed person, other than a person specified in paragraph (3) below, shall make a return to the Board for that period–

(a)   in respect of the non-resident or, if more than one, each non-resident separately, in respect of whose Schedule A business (or part thereof) he was a prescribed person at any time falling within that period, and

(b)   containing the information specified in paragraph (4) below and the declaration specified in paragraph (5) below.

11(2)   A return under paragraph (1) above shall be in such form as the Board may prescribe.

11(3)   The person specified is any tenant who, as a result of a notice given by the Board under regulation 17(5)(b), was not obligated to make payments to the Board in respect of any payments made to a non-resident in that period.

11(4)   The information specified is–

(a)   the name of the non-resident;

(b)   where the non-resident is–

(i)   an individual, or

(ii)   a trustee other than a corporate or a professional trustee, the principal residential address of the non-resident;

(c)   where the non-resident is a company, the address of its registered office or its principal place of business;

(d)   where the non-resident is a professional trustee, the address of his employment or principal place of business;

(e)   where the prescribed person is an agent, the amount of income which, before deduction of any expenses, fell to be taken into account in the annual period in calculating under regulation 9 amounts of tax payable by him in respect of the Schedule A business (or part thereof) of the non-resident, or which would have fallen so to be taken into account if the non-resident had not been an approved person for the purposes of regulation 17 in that period;

(f)   where the prescribed person is a person falling within subsection (2)(a) of section 42A, the aggregate of the following amounts of income–

(i)   the amount of income which fell to be taken into account in the annual period in calculating under regulation 8 amounts of tax payable by him in respect of the Schedule A business (or part thereof) of the non-resident, or which would have fallen so to be taken into account if the non-resident had not been an approved person for the purposes of regulation 17 in that period, and

(ii)   the amount of income which did not fall so to be taken into account because it was paid to a person other than the non-resident in circumstances where the prescribed person could reasonably be satisfied that the amount of the payment was a deductible expense;

(g)   except where the non-resident is an approved person for the purposes of regulation 17, the aggregate of—

(i)   all amounts paid during the annual period on behalf of the non-resident by or at the direction of the prescribed person which the prescribed person could reasonably be satisfied constituted deductible expenses, and

(ii)   amounts carried forward to that period from a previous period pursuant to regulation 9(5)(b);

(h)   the aggregate of the amounts specified as payable to the Board in quarterly returns made by the prescribed person for the annual period;

(j)   the reference number relating to an approval by the Board of the non-resident under regulation 17.

11(5)   The declaration specified is a declaration by the prescribed person that the particulars given in the return are to the best of his knowledge correct and complete.

CERTIFICATE OF TAX LIABILITY

12(1)   Not later than the 5th July following the end of an annual period, a prescribed person who is liable under these Regulations to make any payments to the Board for any quarter falling within that period in respect of tax chargeable on the income of a non-resident, shall provide the non-resident with a certificate which shall include the particulars specified in paragraph (2) below and the declaration specified in paragraph (3) below.

12(2)   The particulars specified are—

(a)   the name of the non-resident;

(b)   where the non-resident is—

(i)   an individual, or

(ii)   a trustee other than a corporate or a professional trustee, the principal residential address of the non-resident:

(c)   where the non-resident is a company, the address of its registered office or its principal place of business;

(d)   where the non-resident is a professional trustee, the address of his employment or principal place of business;

(e)   the name and address of the prescribed person;

(f)   the annual period to which the certificate relates;

(g)   the aggregate amount of the liability referred to in paragraph (1) above for all quarters falling within the annual period.

12(3)   The declaration specified is a declaration by the prescribed person that the certificate is to the best of his knowledge correct and complete.

PROVISION OF INFORMATION AND INSPECTION AND KEEPING OF RECORDS

INFORMATION TO BE PROVIDED TO THE BOARD BY PRESCRIBED PERSONS

13   The Board may by notice require a prescribed person to furnish them, within such time (not being less than 14 days) as may be provided by the notice, such information as they may reasonably require to satisfy themselves that the prescribed person has complied with the requirements of these Regulations.

INSPECTION OF RECORDS BY OFFICER OF THE BOARD

14(1)   The Board may by notice require a prescribed person, within such time (not being less than 14 days) as may be provided by the notice, to make available for inspection by an officer of the Board authorised for that purpose all such books, documents and other records in his possession or under his control as they may reasonably require to satisfy themselves that the prescribed person has complied with the requirements of these Regulations.

14(2)   Where a document or other record is maintained by computer, the prescribed person shall provide the officer making the inspection with all the facilities necessary for obtaining information from that document or other record.

KEEPING OF RECORDS

15 A prescribed person shall at all times maintain and retain sufficient records to enable an officer of the Board to satisfy himself on inspection of those records that the prescribed person has complied with the requirements of these Regulations.

USE OF INFORMATION

16(1) Subject to paragraph (2) below, information obtained by the Board under regulation 13 or 14–

(a) shall not be used for the purpose of ascertaining the tax liability (if any) of any person other than–

   (i) a person whose usual place of abode is outside the United Kingdom, or

   (ii) a person falling within subsection (2)(a) of section 42A, or

   (iii) an agent.

16(2) Paragraph (1) above shall not be construed as preventing any disclosure of information within section 182(5) of the Finance Act 1989.

GROSS PAYMENT OF PROPERTY INCOME

APPLICATION FOR GROSS PAYMENT OF PROPERTY INCOME

17(1) A non-resident may apply to the Board for the obligation imposed under these Regulations to make payments to the Board not to apply in relation to payments falling to be treated as receipts of a Schedule A business carried on by him.

17(2) An application under paragraph (1) above shall be made on a form provided by the Board and shall contain the information specified in paragraph (3) below and the undertakings specified in paragraph (4) below.

17(3) The information specified is–

(a) the name of the applicant;

(b) the date of the application;

(c) where the applicant is–

   (i) an individual, or

   (ii) a trustee other than a corporate or a professional trustee,
        the principal residential address of the applicant;

(d) where the applicant is a company, the address of its registered office or its principal place of business, and the names and principal residential addresses of its directors;

(e) where the applicant is a professional trustee, the address of his employment or principal place of business;

(f) the applicant's national insurance number, if he has one;

(g) the applicant's United Kingdom tax office reference, if he has one;

(h) the name and address of the prescribed person or, if more than one, each of the prescribed persons by or through whom payments falling to be treated as receipts of the applicant's Schedule A business are made;

(j) a statement that–

   (i) the applicant has complied with all obligations imposed on him by or under the Tax Acts or the Management Act prior to the date of the application; or

   (ii) the applicant has not had any obligations imposed on him by or under the Tax Acts or the Management Act prior to the date of the application; or

   (iii) he does not expect to be liable to pay any amount by way of United Kingdom income tax for the year in which the application is made.

17(4) The undertakings specified are that–

(a) where the applicant makes a statement falling within paragraph (3)(j)(iii) above, he will notify the Board in writing if he becomes liable to pay any such amount;

(b) the applicant will fully comply with all obligations imposed on him by or under the Tax Acts or the Management Act;

(c)   the applicant will inform the Board if his usual place of abode ceases to be outside the United Kingdom.

17(5)   Where the Board approve an application under paragraph (1) above, they shall give–

(a)   notice of the approval to the non-resident, and

(b)   notice to the prescribed person or, if more than one, each prescribed person, specifying the date from which the obligations referred to in paragraph (1) above shall cease to apply in relation to payments falling to be treated as receipts of the applicant's Schedule A business and made on or after that date.

17(6)   The Board may, by notice to the applicant, refuse an application under paragraph (i) above where–

(a)   they are not satisfied that the statement contained in the application and falling within paragraph (3)(j)(i), (ii) or (iii) above, as the case may be, is correct; or

(b)   they are not satisfied that the applicant will comply with the undertakings contained in the application.

17(7)   The applicant may appeal against the Board's refusal of his application under paragraph (6) above by giving notice to the Board within 90 days of receipt of the notice of refusal.

17(8)   [Omitted by SI 2009/56, art. 3(2) and Sch. 2, para. 31(2).]

17(9)   The tribunal shall, on an appeal notified to it, confirm the notice refusing approval unless satisfied that the notice ought to be quashed.

History – Reg. 17(8) omitted by SI 2009/56, art. 3(2) and Sch. 2, para. 31(2), operative from 1 April 2009 subject to transitional and saving provisions in SI 2009/56, Sch. 3. Former reg. 17(8) read as follows:

> "**17(8)**   The appeal shall be to the General Commissioners, except that the appellant may elect (in accordance with section 46(1) of the Management Act) to bring the appeal before the Special Commissioners instead of the General Commissioners.".

In reg. 17(9), the words "The tribunal shall, on an appeal notified to it," substituted for the words "The General Commissioners or the Special Commissioners, as the case may be, shall on appeal to them" by SI 2009/56, art. 3(2) and Sch. 2, para. 31(3)(a), operative from 1 April 2009 subject to transitional and saving provisions in SI 2009/56, Sch. 3.
In reg. 17(9), the words "they are", which appeared before "satisfied", omitted by SI 2009/56, art. 3(2) and Sch. 2, para. 31(3)(b), operative from 1 April 2009 subject to transitional and saving provisions in SI 2009/56, Sch. 3.

REVIEW OF APPROVAL UNDER REGULATION 17 – FURNISHING OF INFORMATION

18   Where the Board have approved an application under regulation 17, they may by notice require the non-resident by whom the application was made to furnish them, within such time (not being less than 42 days) as may be provided by the notice, such information as they may reasonably require to enable them to review the approval.

WITHDRAWAL OF APPROVAL UNDER REGULATION 17

19(1)   An approval of an application under regulation 17 may be withdrawn by the Board by notice to the non-resident by whom the application was made specifying–

(a)   the reasons for the withdrawal, and

(b)   the date from which the withdrawal of approval shall take effect.

19(2)   The Board may withdraw their approval of an application where–

(a)   they cease to be satisfied that the statement contained in the application and falling within regulation 17(3)(j)(i), (ii) or (iii), as the case may be, is correct; or

(b)   they cease to be satisfied that the non-resident will comply with the undertakings contained in the application; or

(c)   the non-resident fails to furnish information to the Board in accordance with regulation 18.

19(3)   Where the Board withdraw their approval of an application under paragraph (1) above, they shall give notice to the prescribed person or, if more than one, each prescribed person, specifying the date from which the obligations imposed under these Regulations to make payments to the Board shall apply in relation to payments falling to be treated as receipts of the applicant's Schedule A business and made on or after that date.

19(4)   A non-resident may appeal against the Board's withdrawal of approval under paragraph (1) above by giving notice to the Board within 90 days of the date of issue of the notice withdrawing approval.

19(5) [Omitted by SI 2009/56, art. 3(2) and Sch. 2, para. 32(2).]

19(6) The tribunal shall, on an appeal notified to it, confirm the notice withdrawing approval unless satisfied that the notice ought to be quashed.

History – Reg. 19(5) omitted by SI 2009/56, art. 3(2) and Sch. 2, para. 32(2), operative from 1 April 2009 subject to transitional and saving provisions in SI 2009/56, Sch. 3. Former reg. 19(5) read as follows:

"**19(5)**   The appeal shall be to the General Commissioners, except that the non-resident may elect (in accordance with section 46(1) of the Management Act) to bring the appeal before the Special Commissioners instead of the General Commissioners.".

In reg. 19(6), the words "The tribunal shall, on an appeal notified to it," substituted for the words "The General Commissioners or the Special Commissioners, as the case may be, shall on appeal to them" by SI 2009/56, art. 3(2) and Sch. 2, para. 32(3)(a), operative from 1 April 2009 subject to transitional and saving provisions in SI 2009/56, Sch. 3.

In reg. 19(6), the words "they are", which appeared before "satisfied", omitted by SI 2009/56, art. 3(2) and Sch. 2, para. 31(3)(b), operative from 1 April 2009 subject to transitional and saving provisions in SI 2009/56, Sch. 3.

PROVISIONS RELATING TO SELF-ASSESSMENT

SELF-ASSESSMENT – PAYMENTS ON ACCOUNT

20 Section 59A of the Management Act (payments on account of income tax) ("section 59A") shall have effect in relation to payments to be made to the Board by virtue of section 42A in respect of any tax as if any reference in section 59A to income tax deducted at source included a reference to such payments.

SELF-ASSESSMENT – CONSEQUENTIAL PROVISIONS

21(1) A non-resident may set off against either of the amounts specified in paragraph (2) below the aggregate amount of the payments which–

(a)   were liable to be made to the Board under these Regulations for each quarter ending in a year by any person who is a prescribed person in respect of the Schedule A business (or part thereof) carried on by the non-resident in that year, and

(b)   were retained by the prescribed person out of sums due from him to the non-resident in order to meet that liability.

21(2) The amounts specified are–

(a)   the amount in which the non-resident is chargeable to income tax for the year in question, and

(b)   the amount of the first payment on account of his liability to income tax for that year.

21(3) Where pursuant to paragraph (1) above an amount is set off against the amount specified in paragraph (2)(a) above, section 59A (as modified by regulation 20) shall have effect as if the reference in subsection (1) of that section to the amount which is the assessed amount were a reference to that assessed amount reduced by the amount set off.

21(4) Where pursuant to paragraph (1) above an amount is set off against the amount specified in paragraph (2)(b) above, section 59A (as so modified) shall have effect as if the reference in subsection (2) of that section to the first payment on account were a reference to the amount of that payment reduced by the amount set off.

21(5) In any case where–

(a)   by virtue of regulation 17 the obligations imposed under these Regulations to make payments to the Board do not apply in any year in relation to payments falling to be treated as receipts of a Schedule A business carried on by a non-resident in that year, and

(b)   those obligations applied to such payments in the immediately preceding year,

subsection (1) of section 59A (as so modified) shall have effect as if those obligations did not apply in the immediately preceding year.

MANUFACTURED PAYMENTS AND TRANSFER OF SECURITIES (TAX RELIEF) REGULATIONS 1995

(SI 1995/3036, as amended by SI 1998/1871 and SI 2006/745)

Made on 28 November 1995 by the Treasury, in exercise of the powers conferred on them by s. 730A(7) and 737D(1) of the Income and Corporation Taxes Act 1988. Operative from 2 January 1996.

CITATION, COMMENCEMENT AND EFFECT

1(1) These Regulations may be cited as the Manufactured Payments and Transfer of Securities (Tax Relief) Regulations 1995 and shall come into force on 2nd January 1996.

1(2) These Regulations have effect in relation to–

(a)   any manufactured payment made on or after 2nd January 1996, and

(b)   any payment of interest deemed to be made on or after that date under an agreement to sell securities entered into on or after 1st May 1995.

INTERPRETATION

2   In these Regulations–

"manufactured payment" has the meaning given by section 737D(2) of the Taxes Act;

"the Taxes Act" means the Income and Corporation Taxes Act 1988.

TAX RELIEF FOR MANUFACTURED PAYMENTS

3(1) Any manufactured payment made to a person for the benefit of–

(a)   a pension scheme referred to in section 186(1) of the Finance Act 2004, or

(b)   any fund referred to in section 613(4)(a) or 614(2), (3) or (4) of the Taxes Act,

shall be treated as comprised in income of that person that is eligible for relief from tax by virtue of that section.

3(2) Any manufactured payment made to an insurance company shall be treated, to the extent of so much of the payment as is referable to the company's pension business, or individual savings account business within the meaning of regulation 3 of the Individual Savings Account (Insurance Companies) Regulations 1998, as comprised in income of that company that is eligible for relief from tax by virtue of section 438 of the Taxes Act.

History – In reg. 3(1)(a) the words "a pension scheme" substituted for the words "a scheme", and the words "186(1) of the Finance Act 2004" substituted for the words "592(2) or 643(2) of the Taxes Act" and in reg. 3(1)(b) the words "613(4)(a) or 614(2), (3) or (4) of the Taxes Act" substituted for the words "608(2)(a), 613(4), 614(2), (3) or (4) or 620(6) of that Act" by SI 2006/745, art. 22(2), with effect from 6 April 2006.

In reg. 3(2), words "or individual savings account" to "Regulations 1998" inserted by SI 1998/1871, reg. 24, operative from 6 April 1999.

TAX RELIEF FOR DEEMED PAYMENTS OF INTEREST

4(1) Where, pursuant to section 730A(2) of the Taxes Act (treatment of price differential on sale and repurchase of securities), a payment of interest is deemed to be made to a person in circumstances where, if it were actually made, it would be received by that person for the benefit of–

(a)   a pension scheme specified in section 186(1) of the Finance Act 2004, or

(b)   any fund referred to in section 613(4)(a) or 614(2), (3) or (4) of the Taxes Act,

the amount of the payment shall be treated as comprised in income that is eligible for relief from tax by virtue of that section.

4(2) Where, pursuant to section 730A(2) of the Taxes Act, a payment of interest is deemed to be made to an insurance company, it shall be treated, to the extent of so much of the deemed payment as is referable to the company's pension business, or individual savings account business within the meaning of regulation 3 of the Individual Savings Account (Insurance Companies) Regulations 1998, as comprised in income that is eligible for relief from tax by virtue of section 438 of the Taxes Act.

History – In reg. 4(1)(a) the words "a pension scheme" substituted for the words "a scheme", and the words "186(1) of the Finance Act 2004" substituted for the words "592(2) or 643(2) of the Taxes Act" and in reg. 4(1)(b) the words "613(4)(a) or 614(2), (3) or (4) of the Taxes Act" substituted for the words "608(2)(a), 613(4), 614(2), (3) or (4) or 620(6) of that Act" by SI 2006/745, art. 22(2), with effect from 6 April 2006.

In reg. 4(2), words "or individual savings account" to "Regulations 1998" inserted by SI 1998/1871, reg. 24, operative from 6 April 1999.

INSURANCE COMPANIES (OVERSEAS LIFE ASSURANCE BUSINESS) (COMPLIANCE) REGULATIONS 1995

(SI 1995/3237 as amended by SI 1997/481, SI 1998/1872, SI 1999/2839, SI 2000/2104, SI 2001/3629, SI 2004/3273, SI 2006/3271, SI 2007/2088 and SI 2008/2627)

Made by the Commissioners of Inland Revenue, in exercise of the powers conferred on them by s. 431E of the Income and Corporation Taxes Act 1988 and para. 58 of Sch. 8 to the Finance Act 1995. Operative from 2 January 1996.

History – In SI 1995/3237, "long-term" substituted for "long term" wherever it appeared by SI 2001/3629, art. 142 which came into force on 1 December 2001.

ARRANGEMENT OF REGULATIONS

REGULATION

PRELIMINARY

13.   BUSINESS OTHER THAN REINSURANCE BUSINESS EFFECTED BY A COMPANY RESIDENT IN THE UNITED KINGDOM OUTSIDE THE UNITED KINGDOM

14.   BUSINESS OTHER THAN REINSURANCE BUSINESS EFFECTED EITHER BY A COMPANY RESIDENT IN THE UNITED KINGDOM OTHERWISE THAN OUTSIDE THE UNITED KINGDOM OR BY AN OVERSEAS LIFE INSURANCE COMPANY

14A. BUSINESS OTHER THAN REINSURANCE BUSINESS EFFECTED EITHER BY A COMPANY RESIDENT IN THE UNITED KINGDOM OTHERWISE THAN OUTSIDE THE UNITED KINGDOM OR BY AN OVERSEAS LIFE INSURANCE COMPANY – POLICY HOLDER NOT WITHIN REGULATION 7

15.   REINSURANCE BUSINESS EFFECTED BY A COMPANY RESIDENT IN THE UNITED KINGDOM OUTSIDE THE UNITED KINGDOM

16.   REINSURANCE BUSINESS EFFECTED EITHER BY A COMPANY RESIDENT IN THE UNITED KINGDOM OTHERWISE THAN OUTSIDE THE UNITED KINGDOM OR BY AN OVERSEAS LIFE INSURANCE COMPANY

16A. REINSURANCE BUSINESS EFFECTED EITHER BY A COMPANY RESIDENT IN THE UNITED KINGDOM OTHERWISE THAN OUTSIDE THE UNITED KINGDOM OR BY AN OVERSEAS LIFE INSURANCE COMPANY – POLICY HOLDER NOT WITHIN REGULATION 7

CERTIFICATES TO BE OBTAINED ON THE HAPPENING OF SPECIFIED EVENTS

17.   BUSINESS OTHER THAN REINSURANCE BUSINESS EFFECTED EITHER BY A COMPANY RESIDENT IN THE UNITED KINGDOM OTHERWISE THAN OUTSIDE THE UNITED KINGDOM OR BY AN OVERSEAS LIFE INSURANCE COMPANY

SANCTIONS

18.   RECLASSIFICATION OF POLICY OR CONTRACT FROM DATE WHEN IT WAS EFFECTED

18A. RECLASSIFICATION OF POLICY OR CONTRACT AS RELATING TO OVERSEAS LIFE ASSURANCE BUSINESS FROM DATE WHEN IT WAS MADE OR TRANSFERRED

19.   RECLASSIFICATION OF POLICY OR CONTRACT FROM DATE AFTER IT WAS EFFECTED

20.   CHARGE TO TAX WHERE NO CERTIFICATE UNDER REGULATION 17

KEEPING AND INSPECTION OF RECORDS AND PROVISION OF INFORMATION

21.   RECORDS TO BE KEPT AND TRANSFERS OF RECORDS
22.   INFORMATION TO BE PROVIDED TO THE BOARD
23.   INSPECTION OF RECORDS

PRELIMINARY

CITATION, COMMENCEMENT AND EFFECT

1 These Regulations may be cited as the Insurance Companies (Overseas Life Assurance Business) (Compliance) Regulations 1995, shall come into force on 2nd January 1996, and shall have effect in relation to accounting periods beginning on or after 1st November 1994.

INTERPRETATION

2(1) In these Regulations unless the context otherwise requires–

"basic life assurance and general annuity business" has the meaning given by section 431F;

"beneficiary" has the meaning given by regulation 2 of the Excluded Business Regulations;

"the Board" means the Commissioners for Her Majesty's Revenue and Customs;

"branch" includes agency;

"child trust fund business" has the meaning given by section 431BA;

"company tax return" has the meaning given by paragraph 3 of Schedule 18 to the Finance Act 1998;

"the Consolidated Life Assurance Directive" means the Directive of the European Parliament and of the Council of 5th November 2002 concerning life assurance (2002/83/EC);

"excepted business" means pension business, individual savings account business, child trust fund business, life reinsurance business and long-term business which is not life assurance business;

"excluded business" means business which is excluded from section 431D (as amended by section 108 of the Finance Act 2000 and from time to time) by the Excluded Business Regulations;

"the Excluded Business Regulations" means the Insurance Companies (Overseas Life Assurance Business) (Excluded Business) Regulations 2000;

"the first long-term insurance Directive" means Council Directive 79/267 of 5th March 1979;

"individual savings account business" has the meaning given by section 431BB;

"life reinsurance business" has the meaning given by section 431C;

"pension business" has the meaning given by section 431B;

"policy holder" includes annuitant;

"relevant business" means–

(a) in the case of an overseas life insurance company, life assurance business carried on through a permanent establishment in the United Kingdom which is not excepted business, and

(b) in any other case, life assurance business which is not excepted business;

"relevant policy" means any policy or contract which has at any time been treated as relating to overseas life assurance business, or any policy or contract for business to which regulation 5(3) applies;

"relevant record" means–

(a) any certificate, declaration, undertaking or other document which in these Regulations is either prescribed or specified, or

(b) any other document relating to a relevant policy;

"term assurance business" means life assurance business in relation to which the policy or contract, or the underlying policy, is one which–

(a) is for a specified term; and

(b) is not capable of acquiring a surrender value that exceeds the amount of premiums paid;

"the third long-term insurance Directive" means Council Directive 92/96 of 10th November 1992.

2(2)   Subject to paragraph (3) below, in any case where the obligations under any policy or contract of the body that issued, entered into or effected it (**"the original insurer"**) are at any time the obligations of another body (**"the transferee"**) to whom there has been a transfer of the whole or any part of a business previously carried on by the original insurer, any reference to an insurance company (however expressed) shall, unless the context otherwise requires, include the transferee.

2(3)   Paragraph (2) above does not apply to regulations 5 to 7A, or 21 to 23.

2(4)   In these Regulations any reference to a particular provision, without more, is a reference to that provision of the Income and Corporation Taxes Act 1988.

2(5)   Save where otherwise indicated, any reference in these Regulations to any of the provisions of section 431D is a reference to that provision as it had effect prior to the amendment of that section by section 108 of the Finance Act 2000.

History – In reg. 2(1), in the definition of "the Board", the words "for Her Majesty's Revenue and Customs" substituted for the words "of Inland Revenue" by SI 2008/2627, reg. 2(2), with effect from 27 October 2008.
In reg. 2(1), the definitions of "child trust fund business" and "excepted business" inserted by SI 2007/2088, reg. 3(2), with effect in relation to accounting periods beginning on or after 1 January 2007 and ending on or after 13 August 2007.
In reg. 2(1), the definitions of "individual savings account business" and "relevant business" substituted, in the definition of "relevant policy" the words ", or any underlying policy," omitted, and the definition of "underlying policy" omitted by SI 2007/2088, reg. 3(2), with effect in relation to accounting periods beginning on or after 1 January 2007 and ending on or after 13 August 2007.
The former wording of the definitions "individual savings account business", "relevant business" and "underlying policy" were as follows:

"individual savings account business" has the meaning given by regulation 3 of the Individual Savings Account (Insurance Companies) Regulations 1998;
"relevant business" means–
(a) in the case of an overseas life insurance company, life assurance business carried on through a branch or agency in the United Kingdom other than pension business, individual savings account business or life reinsurance business, or
(b) in any other case, life assurance business other than pension business, individual savings account business or life reinsurance business;
"underlying policy" means a policy or contract any risk arising from which is reinsured by a reinsurer in a reinsurance arrangement, and **"underlying policy holder"** shall be construed accordingly.

In reg. 2(1), definition of the Consolidated Life Assurance Directive inserted by SI 2004/3273, reg. 3(2), with effect from 31 December 2004.
See History note at start of SI 1995/3237 re substitution of "long-term" for "long term".
In reg. 2(1), definitions of "company tax return", "the first long term insurance Directive", "term assurance business", and "the third long term insurance Directive" inserted, and in the definition of "relevant policy" the words ", or any policy or contract for business to which regulation 5(3) applies;" added by SI 1999/2839, reg. 3, operative from 8 November 1999.
In reg. 2(1), definition of "individual savings account business" inserted, and in definition of "relevant pension business" words "other than pension business, individual savings account business or" substituted in both places for "which is neither pension business nor" by SI 1998/1872, reg. 2, operative from 6 April 1999.
In reg. 2(1), definitions of "beneficiary" and "term assurance business" substituted, definition of "settlor" omitted and definitions of "excluded business" and "the Excluded Business Regulations" inserted by SI 2000/2104, reg. 3(2) with effect from 23 August 2000 in relation to policies or contracts made by, or, as the case may be, transferred to, an insurance company on or after 22 August 2000. The former wording of the definitions of "beneficiary", "term assurance business" and "settlor" were as follows:

> **"beneficiary"** shall be construed in accordance with section 431D(6);
> **"term assurance business"** means life assurance business in relation to which the policy or contract, or the underlying policy, has no surrender value, or a surrender value the amount of which does not exceed the amount of the premiums paid, throughout its term;
> **"settlor"** shall be construed in accordance with section 431D(6)(a);

In reg. 2(3) "9, 10" which followed the words "regulations 5 to 7A," omitted by SI 2007/2088, reg. 3(3), with effect in relation to accounting periods beginning on or after 1 January 2007 and ending on or after 13 August 2007.
In reg. 2(3), "7" substituted for "7A" by SI 2000/2104, reg. 3(3), with effect from 23 August 2000 in relation to policies or contracts made by, or, as the case may be, transferred to, an insurance company on or after 8 November 1999.
Reg. 2(5) inserted by SI 2000/2104, reg. 3(4), operative from 23 August 2000.

Cross references – SI 2004/2200, reg. 12: modification of the definition of "relevant business" in reg. 2(1) for the purposes of the taxation of overseas life insurance companies.
SI 2006/3271, reg. 42: modification of para. 2(1) with effect from 31 December 2006 in relation to accounting periods ending on or after that date.

MEANING OF SPECIFIED EVENT

3   [Omitted by SI 1999/2839.]

History – Reg. 3 omitted by SI 1999/2839, reg. 4, with effect from 8 November 1999.

EXCLUSION OF BUSINESS OF FRIENDLY SOCIETY WHICH IS EXEMPT FROM TAX

3A   These Regulations do not apply to any business of a friendly society the profits arising from which are exempt from income tax and corporation tax under section. 460(1).

History – Reg. 3A inserted by SI 1997/481, reg. 2, operative from 19 March 1997.

EXCLUSION OF TAX EXEMPT LIFE ASSURANCE BUSINESS

3B   These Regulations do not apply to any business of an insurance company the profits arising from which are exempt from corporation tax by virtue of section 460(11) or (12) of the Income and Corporation Taxes Act 1988.

History – Reg. 3B inserted by SI 2007/2088, reg. 4, with effect in relation to accounting periods beginning on or after 1 January 2007 and ending on or after 13 August 2007.

BUSINESS WHICH IS OVERSEAS LIFE ASSURANCE BUSINESS

GENERAL

4   In the circumstances prescribed in regulations 5 to 8, any issue as to whether business is overseas life assurance business shall be determined by reference to the matters prescribed in those regulations.

History – In reg. 4, the figure "8" substituted for the figure "11" by SI 2007/2088, reg. 5, with effect in relation to accounting periods beginning on or after 1 January 2007 and ending on or after 13 August 2007.

BUSINESS OTHER THAN REINSURANCE BUSINESS EFFECTED BY A COMPANY RESIDENT IN THE UNITED KINGDOM OUTSIDE THE UNITED KINGDOM

5(1)   This regulation applies in circumstances where–

(a)   an insurance company has entered into relevant business which is not reinsurance business,

(b)   that business is with a policy holder not residing in the United Kingdom,

(c)   the policy or contract for that business was effected by an insurance company resident in the United Kingdom at or through a permanent establishment outside the United Kingdom,

(d)   the policy or contract was made on or after 1st January 1996, and

(e)   to the best of the company's knowledge and belief the policy or contract is not for excluded business.

5(1A) This regulation also applies in circumstances where–

(a) on or after 8th November 1999 business is transferred to an insurance company in accordance with an authorisation granted outside the United Kingdom for the purposes of–

(i) Article 31a.2 of the first long-term insurance Directive, or

(ii) Article 11 of the third long-term insurance Directive,

(b) that business is with a policy holder not residing in the United Kingdom,

(c) that business is, immediately after the transfer, carried on by an insurance company resident in the United Kingdom at or through a permanent establishment outside the United Kingdom, and

(d) to the best of the company's knowledge and belief the policy or contract is not for excluded business.

5(1B) This regulation also applies in circumstances where–

(a) on or after 19th December 2002 business is transferred to an insurance company in accordance with an authorisation granted outside the United Kingdom for the purposes of Article 14 or 53(2) of the Consolidated Life Assurance Directive,

(b) that business is with a policy holder not residing in the United Kingdom,

(c) that business is, immediately after the transfer, carried on by an insurance company resident in the United Kingdom at or through a permanent establishment outside the United Kingdom, and

(d) to the best of the company's knowledge and belief the policy or contract is not for excluded business.

5(2) Except in relation to business to which paragraph (3) below applies, the business referred to in paragraphs (1) to (1B) above shall be overseas life assurance business.

5(3) This paragraph applies to business–

(a) which is not term assurance business, and

(b) for which the policy or contract is one–

(i) in respect of which the insurance company completes the certificate prescribed in paragraph (4) below, or

(ii) which falls within a class of policies or contracts in respect of which the company completes the certificate prescribed in paragraph (4A) below.

5(4) The certificate prescribed is a certificate–

(a) showing the date on which it is given,

(b) stating the territory in which the permanent establishment is situated, and

(c) identifying the policy or contract by stating the name of the policy holder and any unique identifying designation given to the policy or contract.

5(4A) The certificate prescribed is a certificate–

(a) stating the territory in which the permanent establishment is situated,

(b) setting out the unique characteristics of a class of policies or contracts which is not being treated by the insurance company as relating to overseas life assurance business, and

(c) confirming that any policy or contract within the class is capable of being identified readily in the books and records of the company by virtue of a unique identifying designation given to policies or contracts within that class.

5(5) A certificate under this regulation shall be given by an employee of the insurance company, and shall show the name of that employee and his position within the company.

5(6) Paragraph (7) below applies in any case where–

(a) policies or contracts for business to which paragraph (2) above applies were effected at or through a particular permanent establishment outside the United Kingdom, or, where paragraph (1A) or (1B) above applies, transferred to an insurance company so as to be carried on at or through a particular permanent establishment outside the United Kingdom, and

(b) those policies or contracts were effected by, or transferred to, an insurance company within the same accounting period.

5(7) The insurance company may combine a certificate under paragraph (3)(b)(i) above with another certificate under paragraph (3)(b)(i) above in a single document.

5(8) The insurance company shall complete the certificate prescribed in this regulation before the date on which it makes its company tax return for the accounting period in which the policy or contract was made or, where paragraph (1A) or (1B) above applies, transferred.

History – In reg. 5, the words "permanent establishment" substituted for the word "branch" wherever occurring by SI 2007/2088, reg. 6(a), with effect in relation to accounting periods beginning on or after 1 January 2007 and ending on or after 13 August 2007. See History note at start of SI 1995/3237 re substitution of "long-term" for "long term".

Reg. 5(1), the word "and" immediately following sub-para. (c) omitted and the word "and", and sub-para. (e) inserted after sub-para. (d), reg. 5(1A) inserted, reg. 5(2)–(4) substituted by SI 1999/2839, with effect from 8 November 1999. These amendments have effect in relation to–

(a)   accounting periods ending on or after 31 December 1999, or

(b)   where an insurance company so elects by written notice given to an officer of the Board on or before 31 December 1999, the first accounting period beginning on or after 1 October 1999 and ending after 31 December 1999 and subsequent accounting periods.

In reg. 5(1)(e) the words "for excluded business" substituted for "one to which section 431D(2) or (4) applies" by SI 2000/2104, reg. 4(2), with effect from 23 August 2000 in relation to policies or contracts made by, or, as the case may be, transferred to, an insurance company on or after 22 August 2000.

In reg. 5(1A)(d) the words "is not for excluded business" substituted for "for that business is not one to which section 431D(2) or (4) applies", by SI 2000/2104, reg. 4(3), with effect from 23 August 2000 in relation to policies or contracts made by, or, as the case may be, transferred to, an insurance company on or after 22 August 2000.

Reg. 5(1A) inserted by SI 1999/2839, reg. 5(3), with effect from 31 December 2004. This amendment has effect in relation to–

(a)   accounting periods ending on or after 31 December 1999, or

(b)   where an insurance company so elects by written notice given to an officer of the Board on or before 31 December 1999, the first accounting period beginning on or after 1 October 1999 and ending after 31 December 1999 and subsequent accounting periods.

Reg. 5(1B) inserted by SI 2004/3273, reg. 4(2), with effect from 31 December 2004.

In reg. 5(2) the words "to (1B)" substituted for the words "and (1A)" by SI 2004/3273, reg. 4(3), with effect from 31 December 2004.

Reg. 5(4A) inserted by SI 1999/2839, reg. 5, with effect from 8 November 1999 in relation to–

(a)   accounting periods ending on or after 31 December 1999, or

(b)   where an insurance company so elects by written notice given to an officer of the Board on or before 31 December 1999, the first accounting period beginning on or after 1st October 1999 and ending after 31 December 1999 and subsequent accounting periods.

In reg. 5(6)(a) the words "or (1B)" inserted after "(1A)" by SI 2004/3273, reg. 4(4), with effect from 31 December 2004.

In reg. 5(6)(a), words "paragraph (2) above" substituted for "this regulation" and after the words "United Kingdom" the words " or, where paragraph (1A) above applies, transferred to an insurance company so as to be carried on at or through a particular branch outside the United Kingdom," inserted by SI 1999/2839, reg. 5, with effect from 8 November 1999, in relation to–

(a)   accounting periods ending on or after 31 December 1999, or

(b)   where an insurance company so elects by written notice given to an officer of the Board on or before 31 December 1999, the first accounting period beginning on or after 1 October 1999 and ending after 31 December 1999 and subsequent accounting periods.

In reg. 5(6)(b), after the words "effected by" the words ", or transferred to," inserted by SI 1999/2839, reg. 5, with effect from 8 November 1999, in relation to–

(a)   accounting periods ending on or after 31 December 1999, or

(b)   where an insurance company so elects by written notice given to an officer of the Board on or before 31 December 1999, the first accounting period beginning on or after 1 October 1999 and ending after 31st December 1999 and subsequent accounting periods.

Reg. 5(7) substituted by SI 1999/2839, reg. 5, with effect from 8 November 1999, in relation to–

(a)   accounting periods ending on or after 31 December 1999, or

(b)   where an insurance company so elects by written notice given to an officer of the Board on or before 31 December 1999, the first accounting period beginning on or after 1 October 1999 and ending after 31 December 1999 and subsequent accounting periods.

In reg. 5(8) the words "or (1B)" inserted after "(1A)" by SI 2004/3273, reg. 4(5), with effect from 31 December 2004.

In reg. 5(8) the words "before the date on which it makes its company tax return for the accounting period in which the policy or contract was made or, where paragraph (1A) above applies, transferred" substituted for the words from "within" to the end by SI 1999/2839, reg. 5, with effect from 8 November 1999, in relation to–

(a)   accounting periods ending on or after 31 December 1999, or

(b)   where an insurance company so elects by written notice given to an officer of the Board on or before 31 December 1999, the first accounting period beginning on or after 1 October 1999 and ending after 31 December 1999 and subsequent accounting periods.

BUSINESS OTHER THAN REINSURANCE BUSINESS EFFECTED EITHER BY A COMPANY RESIDENT IN THE UNITED KINGDOM OTHERWISE THAN OUTSIDE THE UNITED KINGDOM OR BY AN OVERSEAS LIFE INSURANCE COMPANY – POLICIES OR CONTRACTS MADE BEFORE 1ST JANUARY 1996

6(1)   This regulation applies in circumstances where–

(a)   an insurance company has entered into relevant business which is not reinsurance business,

(b)   that business is with a policy holder not residing in the United Kingdom,

(c)   the policy or contract for that business was effected either by an insurance company resident in the United Kingdom otherwise than at or through a branch outside the United Kingdom, or by an overseas life insurance company, and

(d)   the policy or contract was made before 1st January 1996.

6(2)   The business shall be overseas life assurance business where the insurance company completes–

(a)   the certificate prescribed in paragraph (3) below, and

(b)   the declaration prescribed–

(i)   in a case where the policy holder is an individual, in paragraph (4) below, or

(ii)   in a case where the policy holder is not an individual, in paragraph (5) below.

Statutory Instruments

6(3)   The certificate prescribed is a certificate–

(a)   stating that to the best of the company's knowledge and belief the policy holder was not residing in the United Kingdom on the date the policy or contract was made, and

(b)   specifying the territory in which to the best of the company's knowledge and belief the policy holder was residing on that date.

6(4)   The declaration prescribed is a declaration that to the best of the company's knowledge and belief–

(a)   the policy or contract is not one to which section 431D(2) applies, and

(b)   where the policy or contract is one to which section 431D(2) does not apply solely by virtue of section 431D(5), that the conditions specified in section 431D(5) are fulfilled.

6(5)   The declaration prescribed is a declaration that to the best of the company's knowledge and belief–

(a)   the policy or contract is one to which subsection (5) of section 431D applies and that the conditions specified in that subsection are fulfilled, or

(b)   the policy or contract is one to which subsection (7) of section 431D applies and that the conditions specified in that subsection are fulfilled.

6(6)   A certificate or declaration under this regulation shall be given by an employee of the insurance company, and shall show the name of that employee and his position within the company.

6(7)   The insurance company shall complete any certificate or declaration prescribed in this regulation either within six months following the end of the insurance company's accounting period in which the policy or contract was made, or by 1st March 1996, whichever is the later.

BUSINESS OTHER THAN REINSURANCE BUSINESS EFFECTED EITHER BY A COMPANY RESIDENT IN THE UNITED KINGDOM OTHERWISE THAN OUTSIDE THE UNITED KINGDOM OR BY AN OVERSEAS LIFE INSURANCE COMPANY – POLICIES OR CONTRACTS MADE ON OR AFTER 1ST JANUARY 1996

7(1)   This regulation applies in circumstances where–

(a)   an insurance company has entered into relevant business which is neither reinsurance business nor term assurance business,

(b)   that business is with a policy holder who is an individual not residing in the United Kingdom and either–

   (i)   is a British citizen, or

   (ii)   is a person in respect of whose business the company has treated this regulation as applying,

(c)   the policy or contract for that business was effected either by an insurance company resident in the United Kingdom otherwise than at or through a permanent establishment outside the United Kingdom, or by an overseas life insurance company, and

(d)   the policy or contract was made on or after 1st January 1996.

7(1A)   This regulation also applies where–

(a)   on or after 8th November 1999 relevant business which is neither reinsurance business nor term assurance business is transferred to an insurance company in accordance with an authorisation granted outside the United Kingdom for the purposes of–

   (i)   Article 31a.2 of the first long-term insurance Directive, or

   (ii)   Article 11 of the third long-term insurance Directive,

(b)   that business has not been treated by the transferor as relating to overseas life assurance business,

(c)   that business is with a policy holder who is an individual not residing in the United Kingdom and either–

   (i)   is a British citizen, or

   (ii)   is a person in respect of whose business with the company has treated this regulation as applying, and

(d)   that business is, immediately after the transfer, carried on by an insurance company resident in the United Kingdom otherwise than at or through a branch outside the United Kingdom, or by an overseas life insurance company.

7(1B)   This regulation also applies in circumstances where–

(a) on or after 19th December 2002 business is transferred to an insurance company in accordance with an authorisation granted outside the United Kingdom for the purposes of Article 14 or 53(2) of the Consolidated Life Assurance Directive,

(b) that business has not been treated by the transferor as relating to overseas life assurance business;

(c) that business is with a policy holder who is an individual not residing in the United Kingdom and either–

  (i) is a British citizen, or

  (ii) is a person in respect of whose business the company has treated this regulation as applying, and

(d) that business is, immediately after the transfer, carried on by an insurance company resident in the United Kingdom otherwise than at or through a permanent establishment outside the United Kingdom, or by an overseas life insurance company.

7(2) The business shall be overseas life assurance business where the insurance company obtains–

(a) the document prescribed in paragraph (3) below from the policy holder, and

(b) in any case where the business is of a description falling within the circumstances set out in regulation 5 of the Excluded Business Regulations and the policy or contract is held otherwise than by the trustees of the trust, the certificate prescribed in paragraph (8) below from the trustees of the trust.

7(3) The document prescribed is a document containing–

(a) the certificate prescribed in paragraph (4) below,

(b) the declaration prescribed in paragraph (5) below, and

(c) the undertaking prescribed in paragraph (7) below.

7(4) The certificate prescribed is a certificate–

(a) stating that the policy holder was not residing in the United Kingdom on the date the policy or contract was made or, where paragraph (1A) or (1B) above applies, transferred, and

(b) specifying the territory in which the policy holder was residing on that date.

7(5) The declaration prescribed is a declaration that the policy or contract is not for excluded business.

7(6) [Omitted by SI 1999/2839.]

7(7) The undertaking prescribed is an undertaking that the policy holder will notify the company if–

(a) the policy holder begins residing in the United Kingdom, or

(b) the rights conferred by the policy or contract come to be held subject to a trust, or

(c) the declaration prescribed in paragraph (5) above ceases to be true.

7(8) The certificate prescribed is a certificate stating that the circumstances are as set out in paragraph (1)(b) or (c), as the case may be, of regulation 5 of the Excluded Business Regulations.

7(9) The insurance company shall obtain the document prescribed in paragraph (3) above and, in any case where the business is of a description falling within the circumstances set out in regulation 5 of the Excluded Business Regulations and the policy or contract is held otherwise than by the trustees of the trust, the certificate prescribed in paragraph (8) above, before the date on which it makes its company tax return for the accounting period in which the policy or contract was made or, where paragraph (1A) above applies, transferred.

History – In reg. 7, the words "permanent establishment" substituted for the word "branch" wherever occurring (except in paragraph (1A)) by SI 2007/2088, reg. 6(b), with effect in relation to accounting periods beginning on or after 1 January 2007 and ending on or after 13 August 2007.

See History note at start of SI 1995/3237 re substitution of "long-term" for "long term".

In reg. 7(1)(a) the words "neither reinsurance business nor term assurance business" substituted for the words "not reinsurance business" by SI 1999/2839, reg. 6, with effect from 8 November 1999, in relation to policies or contracts made by or, as the case may be, transferred to, an insurance company on or after 8 November 1999.

In reg. 7(1)(b) the words
"who is an individual not residing in the United Kingdom and either–
  (i) is a British citizen, or
  (ii) is a person in respect of whose business the company has treated this regulation as applying,"
substituted for the words "not residing in the United Kingdom" by SI 1999/2839, reg. 6, with effect from 8 November 1999, in relation to policies or contracts made by or, as the case may be, transferred to, an insurance company on or after 8 November 1999. Reg. 7(1A) inserted by SI 1999/2839, reg. 6, with effect from 8 November 1999, in relation to policies or contracts made by or, as the case may be, transferred to, an insurance company on or after 8 November 1999.

Reg. 7(1B) inserted by SI 2004/3273, reg. 5(2), with effect from 31 December 2004.

In reg. 7(2)(b) the words "the business is of a description falling within the circumstances set out in regulation 5 of the Excluded Business Regulations" substituted for "section 431D(5) applies" by SI 2000/2104, reg. 5(2), with effect from 23 August 2000, in relation to policies or contracts made by, or, as the case may be, transferred to, an insurance company on or after 22 August 2000.
In reg. 7(3)(b) the words "the declaration prescribed in paragraph (5) below, and" substituted for sub-para. (b) and the word "and" immediately following it by SI 1999/2839, reg. 6, with effect from 8 November 1999, in relation to policies or contracts made by or, as the case may be, transferred to, an insurance company on or after 8 November 1999.
In reg. 7(4) the words "or (1B)" inserted after the words "paragraph (1A)" by SI 2004/3273, reg. 5(3), with effect from 31 December 2004.
In reg. 7(4)(a) the words "or, where paragraph (1A) above applies, transferred " inserted after the word "made" by SI 1999/2839, reg. 6, with effect from 8 November 1999, in relation to policies or contracts made by or, as the case may be, transferred to, an insurance company on or after 8 November 1999.
Reg. 7(5) substituted by SI 2000/2104, reg. 5(3), with effect from 23 August 2000, in relation to policies or contracts made by, or, as the case may be, transferred to, an insurance company on or after 22 August 2000.
Reg. 7(6) omitted by SI 1999/2839, reg. 6, with effect from 8 November 1999, in relation to policies or contracts made by or, as the case may be, transferred to, an insurance company on or after 8 November 1999.
In reg. 7(7)(c) the word "above" substituted for the words "or (6) above, as the case may be," by SI 1999/2839, reg. 6, with effect from 8 November 1999, in relation to policies or contracts made by or, as the case may be, transferred to, an insurance company on or after 8 November 1999.
Reg. 7(8) substituted by SI 2000/2104, reg. 5(4), with effect from 23 August 2000, in relation to policies or contracts made by, or, as the case may be, transferred to, an insurance company on or after 22 August 2000.
In reg. 7(9) the words "the business is of a description falling within the circumstances set out in regulation 5 of the Excluded Business Regulations" substituted for "section 431D(5) applies" by SI 2000/2104, reg. 5(5), with effect from 23 August 2000, in relation to policies or contracts made by, or, as the case may be, transferred to, an insurance company on or after 22 August 2000.
In reg. 7(9) the words "before the date on which it makes its company tax return for the accounting period in which the policy or contract was made or, where paragraph (1A) above applies, transferred." substituted for the words "within six months following the end of the insurance company's accounting period in which the policy or contract was made." by SI 1999/2839, reg. 6, with effect from 8 November 1999, in relation to policies or contracts made by or, as the case may be, transferred to, an insurance company on or after 8 November 1999.

BUSINESS OTHER THAN REINSURANCE BUSINESS EFFECTED EITHER BY A COMPANY RESIDENT IN THE UNITED KINGDOM OTHERWISE THAN OUTSIDE THE UNITED KINGDOM OR BY AN OVERSEAS LIFE INSURANCE COMPANY – POLICY HOLDER NOT WITHIN REGULATION 7

7A(1)   This regulation applies in circumstances where–

(a)   an insurance company has entered into relevant business which is neither reinsurance business nor term assurance business,

(b)   that business is with a policy holder not residing in the United Kingdom who either–

(i)   is not an individual, or

(ii)   if an individual, is not one falling within regulation 7(1)(b)(i) or (ii),

(c)   the policy or contract for that business was effected either by an insurance company resident in the United Kingdom otherwise than at or through a permanent establishment outside the United Kingdom, or by an overseas life insurance company, and

(d)   the policy or contract was made on or after 8th November 1999.

7A(2)   This regulation also applies where–

(a)   on or after 8th November 1999 relevant business which is neither reinsurance business nor term assurance business is transferred to an insurance company in accordance with an authorisation granted outside the United Kingdom for the purposes of–

(i)   Article 31a.2 of the first long-term insurance Directive, or

(ii)   Article 11 of the third long-term insurance Directive,

(b)   that business has not been treated by the transferor as relating to overseas life assurance business,

(c)   that business is with a policy holder not residing in the United Kingdom who either–

(i)   is not an individual, or

(ii)   if an individual, is not one falling within regulation 7(1)(b)(i) or (ii), and

(d)   that business is, immediately after the transfer, carried on by an insurance company resident in the United Kingdom otherwise than at or through a branch outside the United Kingdom, or by an overseas life insurance company.

7A(2A)   This regulation also applies in circumstances where–

(a)   on or after 19th December 2002 relevant business which is neither reinsurance business nor term assurance business is transferred to an insurance company in accordance with an authorisation granted outside the United Kingdom for the purposes of Article 14 or 53(2) of the Consolidated Life Assurance Directive,

(b)   that business has not been treated by the transferor as relating to overseas life assurance business;

(c)   that business is with a policy holder not residing in the United Kingdom who–

(i)   is not an individual, or

(ii)   if an individual is not one falling within regulation 7(1)(b)(i) or (ii), and

(d)   that business is, immediately after the transfer, carried on by an insurance company resident in the United Kingdom otherwise than at or through a permanent establishment outside the United Kingdom, or by an overseas life insurance company.

7A(3)   The business shall be overseas life assurance business where the insurance company completes the certificate prescribed in paragraph (4) or (5) below.

7A(4)   The certificate prescribed is a certificate–

(a)   showing the date on which it is given,

(b)   stating the name of the policy holder,

(c)   stating any unique identifying designation given to the policy or contract,

(d)   stating the territory which, to the best of the company's knowledge and belief, is the territory in which the policy holder resides,

(e)   stating that the company has no knowledge of any information making it reasonable for the company to assume that the policy holder was residing in the United Kingdom at the time the policy or contract was made or, where paragraph (2) or (2A) above applies, transferred,

(f)   stating that to the best of the company's knowledge and belief the policy or contract is not for excluded business,

(g)   [omitted by SI 2000/2104]

(h)   where the company makes the statement mentioned in sub-paragraph (f) above, stating that the company is in possession of information enabling it to make that statement, and stating the nature of that information.

7A(5)   The certificate prescribed is a certificate–

(a)   showing the date on which it is given,

(b)   stating the name of the policy holder,

(c)   stating any unique identifying designation given to the policy or contract, and

(d)   stating that to the best of the company's knowledge and belief the policy or contract is for business of a description falling within regulation 7(b) of the Excluded Business Regulations.

7A(6)   A certificate under this regulation shall be given by an employee of the insurance company, and shall show the name of that employee and his position within the company.

7A(7)   Paragraph (8) below applies in any case where policies or contracts for business to which this regulation applies were effected by, or where paragraph (2) or (2A) above applies, transferred to, an insurance company within the same accounting period.

7A(8)   The insurance company may–

(a)   combine a certificate under paragraph (4) above with another certificate under paragraph (4) above in a single document, or

(b)   combine a certificate under paragraph (5) above with another certificate under paragraph (5) above in a single document,

but a certificate under paragraph (4) above shall not be combined with a certificate under paragraph (5) above in a single document.

7A(9)   The insurance company shall complete the certificate prescribed in this regulation before the date on which it makes its company tax return for the accounting period in which the policy or contract was made or, where paragraph (2) or (2A) above applies, transferred.

History – In reg. 7A, the words "permanent establishment" substituted for the word "branch" wherever occurring (except in paragraph (2)) by SI 2007/2088, reg. 6(c), with effect in relation to accounting periods beginning on or after 1 January 2007 and ending on or after 13 August 2007.
See History note at start of SI 1995/3237 re substitution of "long-term" for "long term".
Reg. 7A(1) inserted by SI 1999/2839, reg. 7, with effect from 8 November 1999, in relation to policies or contracts made by or, as the case may be, transferred to, an insurance company on or after 8 November 1999.
Reg. 7A(2A) inserted by SI 2004/3273, reg. 6(2), with effect from 31 December 2004.
Reg. 7A(3) substituted by SI 2000/2104, reg. 6(2), with effect from 23 August 2000 in relation to policies or contracts made by, or, as the case may be, transferred to, an insurance company on or after 22 August 2000.
In reg. 7A(4) the words "or (2A)" inserted after the words "paragraph (2)" by SI 2004/3273, reg. 6(3), with effect from 31 December 2004.
In reg. 7A(4)–
(a)   in sub-para. (f) the words "for excluded business" substituted for "one to which section 431D(2) applies";
(b)   sub-para. (g) omitted; and
(c)   in sub-para. (h) "(f)" substituted for "(g)"

Statutory Instruments

by SI 2000/2104, reg. 6(3), with effect from 23 August 2000 in relation to policies or contracts made by, or, as the case may be, transferred to, an insurance company on or after 22 August 2000.

Reg. 7A(5) substituted by SI 2000/2104, reg. 6(4), with effect from 23 August 2000 in relation to policies or contracts made by, or, as the case may be, transferred to, an insurance company on or after 22 August 2000.

In reg. 7A(7) the words "or (2A)" inserted after the words "paragraph (2)" by SI 2004/3273, reg. 6(4), with effect from 31 December 2004.

In reg. 7A(8)(b) the words "a single document," substituted for "a single document." by SI 2000/2104, reg. 6(5), operative from 23 August 2000.

In reg. 7A(9) the words "or (2A)" inserted after the words "paragraph (2)" by SI 2004/3273, reg. 6(5), with effect from 31 December 2004.

CERTAIN BUSINESS OTHER THAN REINSURANCE BUSINESS WHERE THE COMPANY COMES INTO POSSESSION OF ADDITIONAL INFORMATION

8(1) This regulation applies in circumstances where–

(a) an insurance company has entered into relevant business which is neither reinsurance business nor term assurance business,

(b) that business was entered into by the insurance company with a policy holder referred to in regulation 7(1)(b);

(c) the policy or contract for that business was effected either by an insurance company resident in the United Kingdom otherwise than at or through a permanent establishment outside the United Kingdom, or by an overseas life insurance company, and

(d) the insurance company comes to be in possession of information making it reasonable for the company to assume either–

(i) that there has been a change in the identity of the policy holder and the new policy holder is a person referred to in regulation 7(1)(b), or

(ii) that the policy holder (being a person referred to in regulation 7(1)(b)) has ceased to be beneficially entitled to the rights conferred by the policy or contract.

8(1A) This regulation also applies in circumstances where–

(a) on or after 8th November 1999 relevant business which is neither reinsurance business nor term assurance business is transferred to an insurance company in accordance with an authorisation granted outside the United Kingdom for the purposes of–

(i) Article 31a.2 of the first long-term insurance Directive, or

(ii) Article 11 of the third long-term insurance Directive,

(b) that business was entered into with a policy holder referred to in regulation 7(1)(b),

(c) that business is, immediately after the transfer, carried on by an insurance company resident in the United Kingdom otherwise than at or through a branch outside the United Kingdom, or by an overseas life insurance company, and

(d) the insurance company to whom the business is transferred comes to be in possession of information making it reasonable for the company to assume either–

(i) that there has been a change in the identity of the policy holder and the new policy holder is a person referred to in regulation 7(1)(b), or

(ii) that the policy holder (being a person referred to in regulation 7(1)(b)) has ceased to be beneficially entitled to the rights conferred by the policy or contract.

8(1B) This regulation also applies in circumstances where–

(a) on or after 19th December 2002 relevant business which is neither reinsurance business nor term assurance business is transferred to an insurance company in accordance with an authorisation granted outside the United Kingdom for the purposes of Article 14 or 53(2) of the Consolidated Life Assurance Directive,

(b) that business was entered into with a policy holder referred to in regulation 7(1)(b);

(c) that business is, immediately after the transfer, carried on by an insurance company resident in the United Kingdom otherwise than at or through a permanent establishment outside the United Kingdom, or by an overseas life insurance company, and

(d) the insurance company to whom the business is transferred comes to be in possession of information making it reasonable for the company to assume either–

(i) that there has been a change in the identity of the policy holder and the new policy holder is a person referred to in regulation 7(1)(b), or

(ii) that the policy holder (being a person referred to in regulation 7(1)(b)) has ceased to be entitled to the rights conferred by the policy or contract.

8(2) The business shall continue to be overseas life assurance business where the insurance company obtains–

(a)   the document prescribed in paragraph (3) below from the policy holder, and

(b)   in any case where the business is of a description falling within the circumstances set out in regulation 5 of the Excluded Business Regulations, the certificate prescribed in paragraph (8) below from the trustees of the trust.

8(3) The document prescribed is a document containing–

(a)   the certificate prescribed in paragraph (4) below,

(b)   the declaration prescribed in paragraph (5) below, and

(c)   the undertaking prescribed in paragraph (7) below.

8(4) The certificate prescribed is a certificate–

(a)   stating that the policy holder was not residing in the United Kingdom–

    (i)   in a case where it is reasonable for the company to assume that there has been a change in the identity of the policy holder, on the date he became the policy holder, or

    (ii)   in a case where it is reasonable for the company to assume that the policy holder has ceased to be beneficially entitled to the rights conferred by the policy or contract, on the date on which he ceased to be beneficially entitled to those rights, and

(b)   specifying the territory in which the policy holder was residing on that date.

8(5) The declaration prescribed is a declaration that the policy or contract is not for excluded business.

8(6) [Omitted by SI 1999/2839.]

8(7) The undertaking prescribed is an undertaking that the policy holder will notify the company if–

(a)   the policy holder begins residing in the United Kingdom, or

(b)   the rights conferred by the policy or contract come to be held subject to a trust, or

(c)   the declaration prescribed in paragraph (5) above ceases to be true.

8(8) The certificate prescribed is a certificate stating that the circumstances are as set out in regulation 5(1)(b) or (c) of the Excluded Business Regulations.

8(9) The insurance company shall obtain the document prescribed in paragraph (3) above and, in any case where the business is of a description falling within the circumstances set out in regulation 5 of the Excluded Business Regulations, the certificate prescribed in paragraph (8) above, before the date on which the insurance company makes its company tax return for the accounting period in which the insurance company comes to be in possession of information making it reasonable for the company to assume that there has been a change in the identity of the policy holder or that the policy holder has ceased to be beneficially entitled to the rights conferred by the policy or contract, as the case may be.

History – In reg. 8, the words "permanent establishment" substituted for the word "branch" wherever occurring (except in paragraph (1A)) by SI 2007/2088, reg. 6(d), with effect in relation to accounting periods beginning on or after 1 January 2007 and ending on or after 13 August 2007.

See History note at start of SI 1995/3237 re substitution of "long-term" for "long term".

In reg. 8(1)(a) the words "neither reinsurance business nor term assurance business" substituted for the words "not reinsurance business" by SI 1999/2839, reg. 8, with effect from 8 November 1999, where the date on which–

(a)   the insurance company comes to be in possession of information making it reasonable for the company to assume that there has been a change in the identity of the policy holder, or

(b)   the policy holder ceased to be beneficially entitled to the rights conferred by the policy or contract, falls after 8 November 1999.

Reg. 8(1)(b) substituted by SI 1999/2839, reg. 8, with effect from 8 November 1999, where the date on which–

(a)   the insurance company comes to be in possession of information making it reasonable for the company to assume that there has been a change in the identity of the policy holder, or

(b)   the policy holder ceased to be beneficially entitled to the rights conferred by the policy or contract, falls after 8 November 1999.

In reg. 8(1)(d) the words

    "either–

    (i)   that there has been a change in the identity of the policy holder and the new policy holder is a person referred to in regulation 7(1)(b), or

    (ii)   that the policy holder (being a person referred to in regulation 7(1)(b)) has ceased to be beneficially entitled to the rights conferred by the policy or contract"

substituted for the words from "either" to the end by SI 1999/2839, reg. 8, with effect from 8 November 1999, where the date on which–

(a)   the insurance company comes to be in possession of information making it reasonable for the company to assume that there has been a change in the identity of the policy holder, or

(b)   the policy holder ceased to be beneficially entitled to the rights conferred by the policy or contract, falls after 8 November 1999.

Reg. 8(1A) inserted by SI 1999/2839, reg. 8, with effect from 8 November 1999, where the date on which–

(a)   the insurance company comes to be in possession of information making it reasonable for the company to assume that there has been a change in the identity of the policy holder, or

    (b)   the policy holder ceased to be beneficially entitled to the rights conferred by the policy or contract, falls after 8 November 1999.

Reg. 8(1B) inserted by SI 2004/3273, reg. 7(2), with effect from 31 December 2004.

In reg. 8(2)(b) the words "the business is of a description falling within the circumstances set out in regulation 5 of the Excluded Business Regulations" substituted for "section 431D(5) applies" by SI 2000/2104, reg. 7(2), with effect from 23 August 2000, in relation to policies or contracts made by, or, as the case may be, transferred to, an insurance company on or after 22 August 2000.

Reg. 8(3)(b) substituted by SI 1999/2839, reg. 8, with effect from 8 November 1999, where the date on which–

    (a)   the insurance company comes to be in possession of information making it reasonable for the company to assume that there has been a change in the identity of the policy holder, or

    (b)   the policy holder ceased to be beneficially entitled to the rights conferred by the policy or contract, falls after 8 November 1999.

Reg. 8(5) substituted by SI 2000/2104, reg. 7(3), with effect from 23 August 2000, in relation to policies or contracts made by, or, as the case may be, transferred to, an insurance company on or after 22 August 2000.

Reg. 8(6) omitted by SI 1999/2839, reg. 8, with effect from 8 November 1999, where the date on which–

    (a)   the insurance company comes to be in possession of information making it reasonable for the company to assume that there has been a change in the identity of the policy holder, or

    (b)   the policy holder ceased to be beneficially entitled to the rights conferred by the policy or contract, falls after 8 November 1999.

In reg. 8(7)(c) the word "above" substituted for the words "or (6) above, as the case may be," by SI 1999/2839, reg. 8, with effect from 8 November 1999, where the date on which–

    (a)   the insurance company comes to be in possession of information making it reasonable for the company to assume that there has been a change in the identity of the policy holder, or

    (b)   the policy holder ceased to be beneficially entitled to the rights conferred by the policy or contract, falls after 8 November 1999.

Reg. 8(8) substituted by SI 2000/2104, reg. 7(4), with effect from 23 August 2000, in relation to policies or contracts made by, or, as the case may be, transferred to, an insurance company on or after 22 August 2000.

In reg. 8(9) the words "the business is of a description falling within the circumstances set out in regulation 5 of the Excluded Business Regulations" substituted for "section 431D(5) applies", by SI 2000/2104, reg. 7(5), with effect from 23 August 2000, in relation to policies or contracts made by, or, as the case may be, transferred to, an insurance company on or after 22 August 2000.

In reg. 8(9) the words "before the date on which the insurance company makes its company tax return for the accounting period in which" substituted for the words "within six months after" by SI 1999/2839, reg. 8, with effect from 8 November 1999, where the date on which–

    (a)   the insurance company comes to be in possession of information making it reasonable for the company to assume that there has been a change in the identity of the policy holder, or

    (b)   the policy holder ceased to be beneficially entitled to the rights conferred by the policy or contract, falls after 8 November 1999.

REINSURANCE OF BUSINESS EFFECTED BY A COMPANY RESIDENT IN THE UNITED KINGDOM OUTSIDE THE UNITED KINGDOM

9   [Omitted by SI 2007/2088.]

History – Reg. 9 omitted by SI 2007/2088, reg. 7(a), with effect in relation to accounting periods beginning on or after 1 January 2007 and ending on or after 13 August 2007. Former reg. 9 read as follows:

    "**9(1)**   This regulation applies in circumstances where–

        (a)   an insurance company has entered into relevant business which is not term assurance business,

        (b)   that business is reinsurance of life assurance business with a policy holder not residing in the United Kingdom,

        (c)   the underlying policy in relation to that business was effected by an insurance company resident in the United Kingdom at or through a branch outside the United Kingdom, and

        (d)   the underlying policy in relation to that business was made on or after 1st January 1996.

    9(2)   The business shall be overseas life assurance business where the insurance company obtains from the cedant company–

        (a)   the certificate prescribed in paragraph (3) below, and

        (b)   the undertaking prescribed in paragraph (4) below.

    9(3)   The certificate prescribed is a certificate that–

        (a)   the underlying policy in relation to the business is not one in respect of which the cedant company has completed the certificate prescribed in regulation 5(4) or (4A), or

        (b)   in relation to an underlying policy which was made in an accounting period for which regulation 5(2) to (4) did not have effect, the cedant company had complied with the requirements of regulation 5(2) as it applied for that accounting period.

    9(4)   The undertaking prescribed is an undertaking that the cedant company will notify the insurance company if the cedant company comes to be in possession of information making it reasonable for the cedant company to assume that–

    (a)   [Omitted by SI 1999/2839.]

        (b)   the underlying policy in relation to the business has ceased to be life assurance business with a policy holder who was not residing in the United Kingdom at the time the policy or contract was made or at any time within twelve months thereafter, or

        (c)   the underlying policy holder, not being the person with whom the policy or contract was originally effected, was residing in the United Kingdom at the time the underlying policy was made or at any time thereafter.

    9(5)   The insurance company shall obtain the certificate prescribed in paragraph (3) above and the undertaking prescribed in paragraph (4) above before the date on which it makes its company tax return for the accounting period in which the reinsurance arrangement was made.

History – In reg. 9(1)(a) the words "which is not term assurance business" inserted after the words "relevant business" by SI 1999/2839, reg. 9, with effect from 8 November 1999, in relation to–

    (a)   accounting periods ending on or after 31 December 1999, or

    (b)   where an insurance company so elects by written notice given to an officer of the Board on or before 31 December 1999, the first accounting period beginning on or after 1st October 1999 and ending after 31 December 1999 and subsequent accounting periods.

In reg. 9(3)(a), the words "or (4A)" inserted by SI 2000/2104, reg. 8, with effect from 23 August 2000, shall have effect in relation to–

    (a)   accounting periods ending on or after 31 December 1999; or

(b)   where an insurance company has so elected by written notice given to an officer of the Board on or before 31 December 1999, the first accounting period beginning on or after 1 October 1999 and ending after 31 December 1999 and subsequent accounting periods.

In reg. 9(3) the words "that" to the end substituted by SI 1999/2839, reg. 9, with effect from 8 November 1999, in relation to–

(a)   accounting periods ending on or after 31 December 1999, or

(b)   where an insurance company so elects by written notice given to an officer of the Board on or before 31 December 1999, the first accounting period beginning on or after 1 October 1999 and ending after 31 December 1999 and subsequent accounting periods.

Reg. 9(4)(a) and the word "or" immediately following it omitted by SI 1999/2839, reg. 9, with effect from 8 November 1999, in relation to–

(a)   accounting periods ending on or after 31 December 1999, or

(b)   where an insurance company so elects by written notice given to an officer of the Board on or before 31 December 1999, the first accounting period beginning on or after 1st October 1999 and ending after 31 December 1999 and subsequent accounting periods.

In reg. 9(4)(b) the word "twelve" substituted for the word "six" by SI 1999/2839, reg. 9, with effect from 8 November 1999, in relation to–

(a)   accounting periods ending on or after 31 December 1999, or

(b)   where an insurance company so elects by written notice given to an officer of the Board on or before 31 December 1999, the first accounting period beginning on or after 1 October 1999 and ending after 31 December 1999 and subsequent accounting periods.

In reg. 9(5) the words from "before" to the end substituted by SI 1999/2839, reg. 9, with effect from 8 November 1999, in relation to–

(a)   accounting periods ending on or after 31 December 1999, or

(b)   where an insurance company so elects by written notice given to an officer of the Board on or before 31 December 1999, the first accounting period beginning on or after 1 October 1999 and ending after 31 December 1999 and subsequent accounting periods."

REINSURANCE OF BUSINESS EFFECTED EITHER BY A COMPANY RESIDENT IN THE UNITED KINGDOM OTHERWISE THAN OUTSIDE THE UNITED KINGDOM OR BY AN OVERSEAS LIFE INSURANCE COMPANY

10   [Omitted by by SI 2007/2088.]

History – Reg. 10 omitted by SI 2007/2088, reg. 7(b), with effect in relation to accounting periods beginning on or after 1 January 2007 and ending on or after 13 August 2007. Former reg. 10 read as follows:

"**10(1)**   This regulation applies in circumstances where–

(a)   an insurance company has entered into relevant business which is not term assurance business,

(b)   that business is reinsurance of life assurance business with a policy holder referred to in regulation 7(1)(b),

(c)   the underlying policy in relation to that business was effected either by an insurance company resident in the United Kingdom otherwise than at or through a branch outside the United Kingdom, or by an overseas life insurance company, and

(d)   the underlying policy in relation to that business was made on or after 1st January 1996.

10(2)   The business shall be overseas life assurance business where the insurance company obtains from the cedant company–

(a)   the certificate prescribed in paragraph (3) below, and

(b)   the undertaking prescribed in paragraph (4) below.

10(3)   The certificate prescribed is a certificate that the cedant company either–

(a)   has completed the certificate prescribed in regulation 6(3) and, in any case where section 431D(5) applies, the declaration prescribed in regulation 6(4) or (5), or

(b)   has obtained the document prescribed in regulation 7(3) from the underlying policy holder and, in any case where the business is of a description falling within the circumstances set out in regulation 5 of the Excluded Business Regulations and the policy or contract is held otherwise than by the trustees of the trust, the certificate prescribed in regulation 7(8) from the trustees of the trust.

10(4)   The undertaking prescribed is an undertaking that the cedant company will notify the insurance company if the cedant company comes to be in possession of information making it reasonable for the cedant company to assume that–

(a)   any part of the certificate prescribed in regulation 6(3) or any part of the declarations prescribed in paragraphs (4) and (5) of regulation 6 or, as the case may be, any part of the document prescribed in regulation 7(3) has ceased to be true, or

(b)   in any case where the business is of a description falling within the circumstances set out in regulation 5 of the Excluded Business Regulations and the policy or contract is held otherwise than by the trustees of the trust, any part of the certificate prescribed in regulation 7(8) has ceased to be true, or

(c)   the underlying policy in relation to the business has ceased to be life assurance business with a policy holder who was not residing in the United Kingdom at the time the policy or contract was made or at any time within six months thereafter, or

(d)   the underlying policy holder, not being the person with whom the policy or contract was originally effected, was residing in the United Kingdom at the time the underlying policy was made or at any time thereafter.

10(5)   The insurance company shall obtain the certificate prescribed in paragraph (3) above and the undertaking prescribed in paragraph (4) above before the date on which it makes its company tax return for the accounting period in which the reinsurance arrangement was made.

History – In reg. 10(1)(a) the words "which is not term assurance business" added by SI 1999/2839, reg. 10, with effect from 8 November 1999, in relation to policies or contracts made by or, as the case may be, transferred to, an insurance company on or after 8 November 1999.

In reg. 10(1)(b) the words "referred to in regulation 7(1)(b)" substituted for the words "not residing in the United Kingdom" by SI 1999/2839, reg. 10, with effect from 8 November 1999, in relation to policies or contracts made by or, as the case may be, transferred to, an insurance company on or after 8 November 1999.

In reg. 10(3)(a) the words "declaration prescribed in regulation 6(4) or (5)" substituted for the words "certificate prescribed in regulation 6(4)" by SI 1999/2839, reg. 10, with effect from 8 November 1999, in relation to policies or contracts made by or, as the case may be, transferred to, an insurance company on or after 8 November 1999.

In reg. 10(3)(b) the words "the business is of a description falling within the circumstances set out in regulation 5 of the Excluded Business Regulations" substituted for "section 431D(5) applies", by SI 2000/2104, reg. 9, with effect from 23 August 2000, in relation to policies or contracts made by, or, as the case may be, transferred to, an insurance company on or after 22 August 2000.

In reg. 10(3)(b) the words from "within six months" to the end omitted by SI 1999/2839, reg. 10, with effect from 8 November 1999, in relation to policies or contracts made by or, as the case may be, transferred to, an insurance company on or after 8 November 1999.

In reg. 10(4)(b) the words "the business is of a description falling within the circumstances set out in regulation 5 of the Excluded Business Regulations" substituted for "section 431D(5) applies", by SI 2000/2104, reg. 9, with effect from 23 August 2000, in relation to policies or contracts made by, or, as the case may be, transferred to, an insurance company on or after 22 August 2000.

In reg. 10(5) the words "before the date on which it makes its company tax return for the accounting period in which the reinsurance arrangement was made." substituted for the words

"within–
(a) nine months following the end of the cedant company's accounting period in which the underlying policy was made, or
(b) three months following the making of the reinsurance arrangement,
whichever is the later."

by SI 1999/2839, reg. 10, with effect from 8 November 1999, in relation to policies or contracts made by or, as the case may be, transferred to, an insurance company on or after 8th November 1999."

REINSURANCE OF BUSINESS EFFECTED EITHER BY A COMPANY RESIDENT IN THE UNITED KINGDOM OTHERWISE THAN OUTSIDE THE UNITED KINGDOM OR BY AN OVERSEAS LIFE INSURANCE COMPANY – POLICY HOLDER NOT WITHIN REGULATION 7

10A   [Omitted by SI 2007/2088.]

History – Reg. 10A omitted by SI 2007/2088, reg. 7(c), with effect in relation to accounting periods beginning on or after 1 January 2007 and ending on or after 13 August 2007. Former reg. 10A read as follows:

"**10A(1)**   This regulation applies in circumstances where–
(a) an insurance company has entered into relevant business which is not term assurance business,
(b) that business is reinsurance of life assurance business with a policy holder not residing in the United Kingdom who either–
    (i)   is not an individual, or
    (ii)   if an individual, is not one falling within regulation 7(1)(b)(i) or (ii),
(c) the underlying policy in relation to that business was effected either by an insurance company resident in the United Kingdom otherwise than at or through a branch outside the United Kingdom, or by an overseas life insurance company, and
(d) the underlying policy in relation to that business was made on or after 8th November 1999.
10A(2)   The business shall be overseas life assurance business where the insurance company obtains from the cedant company–
(a) the certificate prescribed in paragraph (3) below, and
(b) where the cedant company has completed the certificate prescribed in regulation 7A(4), the undertaking prescribed in paragraph (4) below.
10A(3)   The certificate prescribed is a certificate that the cedant company has complied with the requirements of regulation 7A(3).
10A(4)   The undertaking prescribed is an undertaking that the cedant company will notify the insurance company if the cedant company comes to be in possession of information making it reasonable for the cedant company to assume that–
(a) any part of the certificate prescribed in regulation 7A(4) has ceased to be true, or
(b) the underlying policy in relation to the business has ceased to be life assurance business with a policy holder who was not residing in the United Kingdom at the time the policy or contract was made or at any time within six months thereafter, or
(c) the underlying policy holder, not being the person with whom the policy or contract was originally effected, was residing in the United Kingdom at the time the underlying policy was made or at any time thereafter.
10A(5)   The insurance company shall obtain the certificate prescribed in paragraph (3) above and the undertaking prescribed in paragraph (4) above before the date on which it makes its company tax return for the accounting period in which the reinsurance arrangement was made.

History – Reg. 10A inserted by SI 1999/2839, reg. 11, with effect from 8 November 1999, in relation to policies or contracts made by or, as the case may be, transferred to, an insurance company on or after 8 November 1999.

In reg. 10A(2) the words "where the cedant company has completed the certificate prescribed in regulation 7A(4)," inserted by SI 2000/2104, reg. 10(2), with effect from 23 August 2000, in relation to policies or contracts made by, or, as the case may be, transferred to, an insurance company on or after 22 August 2000.

In reg. 10A(4) the words "regulation 7A(4)" substituted for "paragraph (4) or (5) of regulation 7A, as the case may be," by SI 2000/2104, reg. 10(3), with effect from 23 August 2000, in relation to policies or contracts made by, or, as the case may be, transferred to, an insurance company on or after 22 August 2000. "

CERTAIN REINSURANCE BUSINESS WHERE THE COMPANY COMES INTO POSSESSION OF ADDITIONAL INFORMATION

11   [Omitted by SI 2007/2088.]

History – Reg. 11 omitted by SI 2007/2088, reg. 7(d), with effect in relation to accounting periods beginning on or after 1 January 2007 and ending on or after 13 August 2007. Former reg. 11 read as follows:

"**11(1)**   This regulation applies in circumstances where–
(a) an insurance company has entered into relevant business which is not term assurance business,
(b) that business is reinsurance of life assurance business and was entered into by the insurance company with a policy holder referred to in regulation 7(1)(b),
(c) the underlying policy in relation to that business was effected by an insurance company resident in the United Kingdom otherwise than at or through a branch outside the United Kingdom, or by an overseas life insurance company, and
(d) the insurance company comes to be in possession of information making it reasonable for the company to assume either–
    (i)   that there has been a change in the identity of the underlying policy holder and the new underlying policy holder is a person referred to in regulation 7(1)(b), or

(ii)   that the underlying policy holder (being a person referred to in regulation 7(1)(b)) has ceased to be beneficially entitled to the rights conferred by the policy or contract.

11(2)   The business shall continue to be overseas life assurance business where the insurance company obtains from the cedant company–

(a)   the certificate prescribed in paragraph (3) below, and

(b)   the undertaking prescribed in paragraph (4) below.

11(3)   The certificate prescribed is a certificate that the cedant company has obtained the document prescribed in regulation 8(3) from the policy holder and, in any case where the business is of a description falling within the circumstances set out in regulation 5 of the Excluded Business Regulations, the certificate prescribed in regulation 8(8) from the trustees of the trust, within six months after the cedant company came to be in possession of information making it reasonable for the cedant company to assume that there had been a change in the identity of the policy holder or that the policy holder had ceased to be beneficially entitled to the rights conferred by the policy or contract, as the case may be.

11(4)   The undertaking prescribed is an undertaking that the cedant company will notify the insurance company if the cedant company comes to be in possession of information making it reasonable for the cedant company to assume that–

(a)   any part of the document prescribed in regulation 8(3) has ceased to be true, or

(b)   in any case where the business is of a description falling within the circumstances set out in regulation 5 of the Excluded Business Regulations, any part of the certificate prescribed in regulation 8(8) has ceased to be true, or

(c)   the underlying policy in relation to the business has ceased to be life assurance business with a policy holder not residing in the United Kingdom.

11(5)   The insurance company shall obtain the certificate prescribed in paragraph (3) above and the undertaking prescribed in paragraph (4) above before the date on which it makes its company tax return for the accounting period in which the reinsurance arrangement was made.

History – In reg. 11(1)(a) words "which is not term assurance business" inserted by SI 1999/2839, reg. 12, with effect from 8 November 1999, where the date on which–

(a)   the insurance company comes to be in possession of information making it reasonable for the company to assume that there has been a change in the identity of the policy holder, or

(b)   the policy holder ceased to be beneficially entitled to the rights conferred by the policy or contract, falls after 8 November 1999.

In reg. 11(1)(b) words "and was entered into by the insurance company with a policy holder referred to in regulation 7(1)(b)" substituted for "with a policy holder not residing in the United Kingdom," by SI 1999/2839, reg. 12, with effect from 8 November 1999, where the date on which–

(a)   the insurance company comes to be in possession of information making it reasonable for the company to assume that there has been a change in the identity of the policy holder, or

(b)   the policy holder ceased to be beneficially entitled to the rights conferred by the policy or contract, falls after 8 November 1999.

In reg. 11(1)(d) the words

"either–

(i)   that there has been a change in the identity of the underlying policy holder and the new underlying policy holder is a person referred to in regulation 7(1)(b), or

(ii)   that the underlying policy holder (being a person referred to in regulation 7(1)(b)) has ceased to be beneficially entitled to the rights conferred by the policy or contract."

substituted by SI 1999/2839, reg. 12, with effect from 8 November 1999, where the date on which–

(a)   the insurance company comes to be in possession of information making it reasonable for the company to assume that there has been a change in the identity of the policy holder, or

(b)   the policy holder ceased to be beneficially entitled to the rights conferred by the policy or contract, falls after 8 November 1999.

In reg. 11(3) and (4)(b) the words "the business is of a description falling within the circumstances set out in regulation 5 of the Excluded Business Regulations" substituted for "section 431D(5) applies" by SI 2000/2104, reg. 11, with effect from 23 August 2000, in relation to policies or contracts made by, or, as the case may be, transferred to, an insurance company on or after 22 August 2000.

In reg. 11(5) the words "before the date on which it makes its company tax return for the accounting period in which the reinsurance arrangement was made." substituted by SI 1999/2839, reg. 12, with effect from 8 November 1999, where the date on which–

(a)   the insurance company comes to be in possession of information making it reasonable for the company to assume that there has been a change in the identity of the policy holder, or

(b)   the policy holder ceased to be beneficially entitled to the rights conferred by the policy or contract, falls after 8 November 1999."

TERRITORIES IN WHICH POLICY HOLDERS RESIDING

GENERAL

12   In the circumstances prescribed in regulations 13 to 14A, any issue as to whether a policy holder is residing in the United Kingdom or in some other territory shall be determined by reference to the matters prescribed in those regulations.

History – In reg. 12, the words "14A" substituted for "16A" by SI 2007/2088, reg. 8, with effect in relation to accounting periods beginning on or after 1 January 2007 and ending on or after 13 August 2007.

In reg. 12 the words "16A" substituted for "16" by SI 2000/2104, reg. 12, with effect from 23 August 2000, in relation to policies or contracts made by, or, as the case may be, transferred to, an insurance company on or after 8 November 1999.

BUSINESS OTHER THAN REINSURANCE BUSINESS EFFECTED BY A COMPANY RESIDENT IN THE UNITED KINGDOM OUTSIDE THE UNITED KINGDOM

13(1)   This regulation applies in circumstances where–

(a)   an insurance company has entered into relevant business which is not reinsurance business, and

(b)   the policy or contract for that business was effected by an insurance company resident in the United Kingdom at or through a permanent establishment outside the United Kingdom.

13(1A)   This regulation also applies where–

(a)   on or after 8th November 1999 relevant business which is not reinsurance business is transferred to an insurance company in accordance with an authorisation granted outside the United Kingdom for the purposes of–

(i)   Article 31a.2 of the first long-term insurance Directive, or

(ii)   Article 11 of the third long-term insurance Directive, and

(b)   that business is, immediately after the transfer, carried on by an insurance company resident in the United Kingdom at or through a branch outside the United Kingdom.

13(1B)   This regulation also applies in circumstances where–

(a)   on or after 19th December 2002 relevant business which is neither reinsurance business nor term assurance business is transferred to an insurance company in accordance with an authorisation granted outside the United Kingdom for the purposes of Article 14 or 53(2) of the Consolidated Life Assurance Directive, and

(c)   that business is, immediately after the transfer, carried on by an insurance company resident in the United Kingdom at or through a permanent establishment or agency outside the United Kingdom.

13(2)   Subject to paragraph (3) below, the territory in which the policy holder was residing at the time the policy or contract was made or, where paragraph (1A) [or (1B) apply], transferred shall be the territory in which the permanent establishment was situated.

13(3)   Where, at the time the policy or contract was made or transferred or at any time within eighteen months thereafter, the company was in possession of information making it reasonable for the company to assume that the policy holder was residing in the United Kingdom at the time the policy or contract was made or transferred or at any time within twelve months thereafter, the territory in which the policy holder was residing at the time the policy or contract was made or transferred shall be the United Kingdom.

13(4)   Where, pursuant to paragraph (2) or (3) above, a policy holder has been treated as residing in a particular territory at the time the policy or contract was made or transferred, the territory in which the policy holder is residing at any time thereafter shall, subject to paragraph (5) below, be that same territory.

13(5)   Subject to paragraph (3) above, where at any time after the policy or contract was made or transferred the company comes to be in possession of information making it reasonable for the company to assume that the policy holder, being neither–

(a)   the person with whom the policy or contract was originally effected, nor

(b)   a person to whom the rights conferred by the policy or contract have been assigned in circumstances where the assignment did not constitute a chargeable event within the meaning of section 484 of the Income Tax (Trading and Other Income) Act 2005, nor

(c)   a personal representative in whom those rights have been vested by operation of law,

was residing in the United Kingdom at the time he became the policy holder or at any time thereafter, the territory in which the policy holder is residing shall, from the date on which it is reasonable for the company so to assume, be the United Kingdom.

History – In reg. 13, the words "permanent establishment" substituted for the word "branch" wherever occurring (except in paragraph (1A)) by SI 2007/2088, reg. 9(a), with effect in relation to accounting periods beginning on or after 1 January 2007 and ending on or after 13 August 2007.

See History note at start of SI 1995/3237 re substitution of "long-term" for "long term".

In reg. 13(2), the words "paragraph (1A) or (1B) apply" substituted for the words "paragraphs (1A) applies" by SI 2004/3273, reg. 8(2). SI 2004/3273 actually reads as follows:

"**8(2)**   In paragraph (1)(a) for "paragraph (1) or (1A)" substitute "paragraph (1), (1A) or (1B)""

However, CCH is of the opinion that the former wording and new wording should read "paragraph (1A)" and "paragraph (1A) or (1B)" respectively and not as stated in reg. 8(2).

Reg. 13(1A) inserted by SI 1999/2839, reg. 13, with effect from 8 November 1999.

Reg. 13(1B) inserted by SI 2004/3273, reg. 8(3), with effect from 31 December 2004.

Reg. 13(2) the words "or, where paragraph (1A) applies, transferred" inserted by SI 1999/2839, reg. 13, with effect from 8 November 1999.

In reg. 13(3) the word "eighteen" substituted for the word "twelve", the word "twelve" substituted for the word "six", and after the word "made", in each place where it occurs, the words "or transferred" inserted by SI 1999/2839, reg. 13, with effect from 8 November 1999, in relation to policies or contracts made by or, as the case may be, transferred to, an insurance company on or after 8 November 1999.

In reg. 13(4) after the word "made" the words "or transferred" inserted by SI 1999/2839, reg. 13, with effect from 8 November 1999.

In reg. 13(5)(b), the words "section 484 of the Income Tax (Trading and Other Income) Act 2005" substituted for the words "section 540, 542 or 545" by SI 2008/2627, reg. 2(3)(a), with effect from 27 October 2008.

In reg. 13(5) after the word "made" the words "or transferred" inserted by SI 1999/2839, reg. 13, with effect from 8 November 1999.

In reg. 13(5) the words
"being neither–
  (a)   the person with whom the policy or contract was originally effected, nor
  (b)   a person to whom the rights conferred by the policy or contract have been assigned in circumstances where the assignment did not constitute a chargeable event within the meaning of section 540, 542 or 545, nor
  (c)   a personal representative in whom those rights have been vested by operation of law"substituted for the words
"not being the person with whom the policy or contract was originally effected"
by SI 1999/2839, reg. 13, with effect from 8 November 1999.

BUSINESS OTHER THAN REINSURANCE BUSINESS EFFECTED EITHER BY A COMPANY RESIDENT IN THE UNITED KINGDOM OTHERWISE THAN OUTSIDE THE UNITED KINGDOM OR BY AN OVERSEAS LIFE INSURANCE COMPANY

14(1)   This regulation applies in circumstances where–

(a)   an insurance company has entered into relevant business which is not reinsurance business, and

(b)   the policy or contract for that business was effected either by an insurance company resident in the United Kingdom otherwise than at or through a permanent establishment outside the United Kingdom, or by an overseas life insurance company and

(c)   that business is with a policy holder referred to in regulation 7(1)(b).

14(1A)   This regulation also applies in circumstances where–

(a)   on or after 8th November 1999 relevant business which is not reinsurance business is transferred to an insurance company in accordance with an authorisation granted outside the United Kingdom for the purposes of–

  (i)   Article 31a.2 of the first long-term insurance Directive, or

  (ii)   Article 11 of the third long-term insurance Directive,

(b)   that business has not been treated by the transferor as relating to overseas life assurance business,

(c)   that business is, immediately after the transfer, carried on either by an insurance company resident in the United Kingdom otherwise than at or through a branch outside the United Kingdom, or by an overseas life insurance company, and

(d)   that business is with a policy holder referred to in regulation 7(1)(b).

"**14(1B)**   This regulation also applies in circumstances where–

(a)   on or after 19th December 2002 business is transferred to an insurance company in accordance with an authorisation granted outside the United Kingdom for the purposes of Article 14 or 53(2) of the Consolidated Life Assurance Directive,

(b)   that business has not been treated by the transferor as relating to overseas life assurance business,

(c)   that business is, immediately after the transfer, carried on by an insurance company resident in the United Kingdom at or through a permanent establishment outside the United Kingdom, or by an overseas life insurance company; and

(d)   that business is with a policy holder referred to in regulation 7(1)(b)."

14(2)   Subject to paragraph (3) and (3A) below, the territory in which the policy holder was residing at the time the policy or contract was made or, where paragraph (1A) or (1B) applies, transferred shall be the territory specified in the certificate prescribed in regulation 6(3) or, as the case may be, 7(4).

14(3)   Where, at the time the policy or contract was made or transferred or at any time within eighteen months thereafter, the company was in possession of information making it reasonable for the company to assume that the policy holder was residing in the United Kingdom at the time the policy or contract was made or transferred or at any time within twelve months thereafter, the territory in which the policy holder was residing at the time the policy or contract was made or transferred shall be the United Kingdom.

14(3A)   Subject to paragraph (3) above, where the policy is for term assurance business, the territory in which the policy holder was residing at the time the policy was made or transferred shall be the territory in which, to the best of the company's knowledge or belief, the policy holder was residing at the time the policy was made or transferred.

14(4)   Where, pursuant to paragraph (2) , (3) or (3A) above, a policy holder has been treated as residing in a particular territory at the time the policy or contract was made or transferred, the territory in which the policy holder is residing at any time thereafter shall, subject to paragraph (5) below, be that same territory.

14(5) Subject to paragraph (3) above, where at any time after the policy or contract was made or transferred the company comes to be in possession of information making it reasonable for the company to assume that the policy holder, being neither–

(a)   the person with whom the policy or contract was originally effected, nor

(b)   any person to whom the rights conferred by the policy or contract have been assigned in circumstances where the assignment did not constitute a chargeable event within the meaning of section 484 of the Income Tax (Trading and Other Income) Act 2005, nor

(c)   a personal representative in whom those rights have been vested by operation of law,

was residing in the United Kingdom at the time he became the policy holder or at any time thereafter, the territory in which the policy holder is residing shall, from the date on which it is reasonable for the company so to assume, be the United Kingdom.

History – In reg. 14, the words "permanent establishment" substituted for the word "branch" wherever occurring (except in paragraph (1A)) by SI 2007/2088, reg. 9(b), with effect in relation to accounting periods beginning on or after 1 January 2007 and ending on or after 13 August 2007.
See History note at start of SI 1995/3237 re substitution of "long-term" for "long term".
Reg. 14(1)(c) and the word "and" immediately preceding it inserted by SI 1999/2839, reg. 14, with effect from 8 November 1999.
Reg. 14(1A) inserted by SI 1999/2839, reg. 14, with effect from 8 November 1999.
Reg. 14(1B) inserted by SI 2004/3273, reg. 9(2), with effect from 31 December 2004.
In reg. 14(2) the words "or (1B)" inserted after the words "paragraph (1A)" by SI 2004/3273, reg. 9(2), with effect from 31 December 2004.
In reg. 14(2) the words "paragraphs (3) and (3A)" substituted for "paragraph (3)" by SI 2000/2104, reg. 13(2), with effect from 23 August 2000, in relation to policies or contracts made by, or, as the case may be, transferred to, an insurance company on or after 22 August 2000.
In reg. 14(2) the words "or, where paragraph (1A) applies, transferred" inserted by SI 1999/2839, reg. 14, with effect from 8 November 1999.
In reg. 14(3) the word "eighteen" substituted for the word "twelve", the word "twelve" substituted for the word "six", and after the word "made", in each place where it occurs, the words "or transferred" inserted by SI 1999/2839, reg. 13, with effect from 8 November 1999, in relation to policies or contracts made by or, as the case may be, transferred to, an insurance company on or after 8 November 1999.
Reg. 14(3A) inserted by SI 2000/2104, reg. 13(3), with effect from 23 August 2000, in relation to policies or contracts made by, or, as the case may be, transferred to, an insurance company on or after 22 August 2000.
In reg. 14(4) the words ", (3) or (3A)" substituted for "or (3)" by SI 2000/2104, reg. 13(4), with effect from 23 August 2000, in relation to policies or contracts made by, or, as the case may be, transferred to, an insurance company on or after 22 August 2000.
In reg. 14(4) after the word "made" the words "or transferred" inserted by SI 1999/2839, reg. 14, with effect from 8 November 1999.
In reg. 14(5)(b), the words "section 484 of the Income Tax (Trading and Other Income) Act 2005" substituted for the words "section 540, 542 or 545" by SI 2008/2627, reg. 2(3)(b), with effect from 27 October 2008.
In reg. 14(5) after the word "made" the words "or transferred" inserted and the words from "being neither" to the end of sub-para. (c) (i.e. including sub-para. (a), (b) and (c)) substituted for the words "not being the person with whom the policy or contract was originally effected" by SI 1999/2839, reg. 14, with effect from 8 November 1999.

BUSINESS OTHER THAN REINSURANCE BUSINESS EFFECTED EITHER BY A COMPANY RESIDENT IN THE UNITED KINGDOM OTHERWISE THAN OUTSIDE THE UNITED KINGDOM OR BY AN OVERSEAS LIFE INSURANCE COMPANY – POLICY HOLDER NOT WITHIN REGULATION 7

14A(1) This regulation applies in circumstances where–

(a)   an insurance company has entered into relevant business which is not reinsurance business,

(b)   that business is with a policy holder not residing in the United Kingdom who either–

    (i)   is not an individual, or

    (ii)   if an individual, is not one falling within regulation 7(1)(b)(i) or (ii),

(c)   the policy or contract for that business was effected either by an insurance company resident in the United Kingdom otherwise than at or through a permanent establishment outside the United Kingdom, or by an overseas life insurance company, and

(d)   the policy or contract was made on or after 8th November 1999.

14A(2) This regulation also applies where–

(a)   on or after 8th November 1999 relevant business which is not reinsurance business is transferred to an insurance company in accordance with an authorisation granted outside the United Kingdom for the purposes of–

    (i)   Article 31a.2 of the first long-term insurance Directive, or

    (ii)   Article 11 of the third long-term insurance Directive,

(b)   that business has not been treated by the transferor as relating to overseas life assurance business,

(c)   that business is with a policy holder not residing in the United Kingdom who either–

(i)   is not an individual, or

(ii)   if an individual, is not one falling within regulation 7(1)(b)(i) or (ii), and

(d)   that business is, immediately after the transfer, carried on by an insurance company resident in the United Kingdom otherwise than at or through a branch outside the United Kingdom, or by an overseas life insurance company.

14A(2A)   This regulation also applies in circumstances where–

(a)   on or after 19th December 2002 relevant business which is neither reinsurance business nor term assurance business is transferred to an insurance company in accordance with an authorisation granted outside the United Kingdom for the purposes of Article 14 or 53(2) of the Consolidated Life Assurance Directive,

(b)   that business has not been treated by the transferor as relating to overseas life assurance business;

(c)   that business is with a policy holder not residing in the United Kingdom who–

(i)   is not an individual, or

(ii)   if an individual is not one falling within regulation 7(1)(b)(i) or (ii), and

(d)   that business is, immediately after the transfer carried on by an insurance company resident in the United Kingdom otherwise than at or through a permanent establishment outside the United Kingdom, or by an overseas life insurance company.

14A(3)   Subject to paragraphs (4), (4A) and (4B) below, the territory in which the policy holder was residing at the time the policy or contract was made or, where paragraph (2) or paragraph (2A) above applies, transferred shall be the territory specified in the certificate prescribed in regulation 7A(4) above.

14A(4)   Where, at the time the policy or contract was made or transferred or at any time within eighteen months thereafter, the company was in possession of information making it reasonable for the company to assume that the policy holder was residing in the United Kingdom at the time the policy or contract was made or transferred or at any time within twelve months thereafter, the territory in which the policy holder was residing at the time the policy or contract was made or transferred shall be the United Kingdom.

14A(4A)   Subject to paragraph (4) above, where the policy is for term assurance business, the territory in which the policy holder was residing at the time the policy was made or transferred shall be the territory in which, to the best of the company's knowledge or belief, the policy holder was residing at the time the policy was made or transferred.

14A(4B)   Where the policy or contract is for business of a description falling within regulation 7(b) of the Excluded Business Regulations, the territory in which the policy holder was residing at the time the policy or contract was made or transferred shall be the territory under the law of which the scheme mentioned in that regulation is established.

14A(5)   Where, pursuant to paragraph (3), (4), (4A) or (4B) above, a policy holder has been treated as residing in a particular territory at the time the policy or contract was made or transferred, the territory in which the policy holder is residing at any time thereafter shall, subject to paragraph (6) below, be that same territory.

14A(6)   Subject to paragraph (4) above, where at any time after the policy or contract was made or transferred the company comes to be in possession of information making it reasonable for the company to assume that the policy holder, being neither–

(a)   the person with whom the policy or contract was originally effected, nor

(b)   a person to whom the rights conferred by the policy or contract have been assigned in circumstances where the assignment did not constitute a chargeable event within the meaning of section 484 of the Income Tax (Trading and Other Income) Act 2005, nor

(c)   a personal representative in whom those rights have been vested by operation of law,

was residing in the United Kingdom at the time he became the policy holder or at any time thereafter, the territory in which the policy holder is residing shall, from the date on which it is reasonable for the company so to assume, be the United Kingdom.

History – In reg. 14A, the words "permanent establishment" substituted for the word "branch" wherever occurring (except in paragraph (2)) by SI 2007/2088, reg. 9(c), with effect in relation to accounting periods beginning on or after 1 January 2007 and ending on or after 13 August 2007.
See History note at start of SI 1995/3237 re substitution of "long-term" for "long term".
Reg. 14A inserted by SI 1999/2839, reg. 15, with effect from 8 November 1999, in relation to policies or contracts made by or, as the case may be, transferred to, an insurance company on or after 8 November 1999.
Reg. 14A(2A) inserted by SI 2004/3273, reg. 10(2), with effect from 31 December 2004.

In reg. 14A(3) the words "or paragraph (2A)" inserted after the words "paragraph (2)" by SI 2004/3273, reg. 10(3), with effect from 31 December 2004.

In reg. 14A(3) the words "paragraphs (4), (4A) and (4B) below" substituted for "paragraph (4) below" and the words "regulation 7A(4) above" substituted for "paragraph (4) of regulation 7A or, as the case may be, paragraph (5) of that regulation" by SI 2000/2104, reg. 14(2), with effect from 23 August 2000 in relation to policies or contracts made by, or, as the case may be, transferred to, an insurance company on or after 22 August 2000.

Reg. 14A(4A) and (4B) inserted by SI 2000/2104, reg. 14(3), with effect from 23 August 2000 in relation to policies or contracts made by, or, as the case may be, transferred to, an insurance company on or after 22 August 2000.

In reg. 14A(5) the words ", (4), (4A) or (4B)" substituted for "or (4)" by SI 2000/2104, reg. 14(4), with effect from 23 August 2000 in relation to policies or contracts made by, or, as the case may be, transferred to, an insurance company on or after 22 August 2000.

In reg. 14A(6)(b), the words "section 484 of the Income Tax (Trading and Other Income) Act 2005" substituted for the words "section 540, 542 or 545" by SI 2008/2627, reg. 2(3)(c), with effect from 27 October 2008.

REINSURANCE BUSINESS EFFECTED BY A COMPANY RESIDENT IN THE UNITED KINGDOM OUTSIDE THE UNITED KINGDOM

15   [Omitted by SI 2007/2088.]

History – Reg. 15 omitted by SI 2007/2088, reg. 10(a), with effect in relation to accounting periods beginning on or after 1 January 2007 and ending on or after 13 August 2007. Former reg. 15 read as follows:

"**15(1)**   This regulation applies in circumstances where–
(a)   an insurance company has entered into relevant business which is reinsurance business, and
(b)   the underlying policy in relation to that business was effected by an insurance company resident in the United Kingdom at or through a branch outside the United Kingdom.

15(2)   Subject to paragraph (3) below, the territory in which the underlying policy holder was residing at the time the underlying policy was made shall be the territory in which the branch was situated.

15(3)   Where, at the time the underlying policy was made or at any time within eighteen months thereafter, the company was in possession of information making it reasonable for the company to assume that the underlying policy holder was residing in the United Kingdom at the time the underlying policy was made or at any time within twelve months thereafter, the territory in which the underlying policy holder was residing at the time the underlying policy was made shall be the United Kingdom.

15(4)   Where, pursuant to paragraph (2) or (3) above, an underlying policy holder has been treated as residing in a particular territory at the time the underlying policy was made, the territory in which the underlying policy holder is residing at any time thereafter shall, subject to paragraph (5) below, be that same territory.

15(5)   Subject to paragraph (3) above, where at any time after the underlying policy was made the company comes to be in possession of information making it reasonable for the company to assume that the underlying policy holder, being neither–
(a)   the person with whom the policy or contract was originally effected, nor
(b)   a person to whom the rights conferred by the policy or contract have been assigned in circumstances where the assignment did not constitute a chargeable event within the meaning of section 540, 542 or 545, nor
(c)   a personal representative in whom those rights have been vested by operation of law,
was residing in the United Kingdom at the time he became the underlying policy holder or at any time thereafter, the territory in which the underlying policy holder is residing shall, from the date on which it is reasonable for the company so to assume, be the United Kingdom.

History – In reg. 15(3) the word "eighteen" substituted for the word "twelve", and the word "twelve" substituted for the word "six" by SI 1999/2839, reg. 16, with effect from 8 November 1999, in relation to policies or contracts made by or, as the case may be, transferred to, an insurance company on or after 8 November 1999.

In reg. 15(5) the words from "being neither" to the end of sub-para. (c) (i.e. including sub-para. (a), (b) and (c)) substituted for the words "not being the person with whom the policy or contract was originally effected" by SI 1999/2839, reg. 16, with effect from 8 November 1999."

REINSURANCE BUSINESS EFFECTED EITHER BY A COMPANY RESIDENT IN THE UNITED KINGDOM OTHERWISE THAN OUTSIDE THE UNITED KINGDOM OR BY AN OVERSEAS LIFE INSURANCE COMPANY

16   [Omitted by SI 2007/2088.]

History – Reg. 16 omitted by SI 2007/2088, reg. 10(b), with effect in relation to accounting periods beginning on or after 1 January 2007 and ending on or after 13 August 2007. Former reg. 16 read as follows:

"**16(1)**   This regulation applies in circumstances where–
(a)   an insurance company has entered into relevant business which is reinsurance business, and
(b)   the underlying policy in relation to that business was effected either by an insurance company resident in the United Kingdom otherwise than at or through a branch outside the United Kingdom, or by an overseas life insurance company and
(c)   the underlying policy holder in relation to that business is a person referred to in regulation 7(1)(b).

16(2)   Subject to paragraphs (3) and (3A) below, the territory in which the underlying policy holder was residing at the time the underlying policy was made shall be the territory specified in the certificate prescribed in regulation 6(3) or, as the case may be, 7(4).

16(3)   Where, at the time the underlying policy was made or at any time within eighteen months thereafter, the company was in possession of information making it reasonable for the company to assume that the underlying policy holder was residing in the United Kingdom at the time the underlying policy was made or at any time within twelve months thereafter, the territory in which the underlying policy holder was residing at the time the underlying policy was made shall be the United Kingdom.

16(3A)   Subject to paragraph (3) above, where the underlying policy is for term assurance business, the territory in which the policy holder was residing at the time the underlying policy was made or transferred shall be the territory in which, to the best of the company's knowledge or belief, the policy holder was residing at the time the underlying policy was made or transferred.

16(4)   Where, pursuant to paragraph (2) , (3) or (3A) above, an underlying policy holder has been treated as residing in a particular territory at the time the underlying policy was made, the territory in which the underlying policy holder is residing at any time thereafter shall, subject to paragraph (5) below, be that same territory.

16(5) Subject to paragraph (3) above, where at any time after the underlying policy was made the company comes to be in possession of information making it reasonable for the company to assume that the underlying policy holder, being neither–

(a) the person with whom the policy or contract was originally effected, nor

(b) a person to whom the rights conferred by the policy or contract have been assigned in circumstances where the assignment did not constitute a chargeable event within the meaning of section 540, 542 or 545, nor

(c) a personal representative in whom those rights have been vested by operation of law, was residing in the United Kingdom at the time he became the underlying policy holder or at any time thereafter, the territory in which the underlying policy holder is residing shall, from the date on which it is reasonable for the company so to assume, be the United Kingdom.

History – Reg. 16(1)(c) and the word "and" immediately preceding it inserted by SI 1999/2839, reg. 17, with effect from 8 November 1999.

In reg. 16(2) the words "paragraphs (3) and (3A)" substituted for "paragraph (3)" by SI 2000/2104, reg. 15(2), with effect from 23 August 2000 in relation to policies or contracts made by, or, as the case may be, transferred to, an insurance company on or after 22 August 2000.

In reg. 16(3) the word "eighteen" substituted for the word "twelve", and the word "twelve" substituted for the word "six" by SI 1999/2839, reg. 17, with effect from 8 November 1999.

Reg. 16(3A) inserted by SI 2000/2104, reg. 15(3), with effect from 23 August 2000 in relation to policies or contracts made by, or, as the case may be, transferred to, an insurance company on or after 22 August 2000.

In reg. 16(4) the words ", (3) or (3A)" substituted for "or (3)" by SI 2000/2104, reg. 15(4), with effect from 23 August 2000 in relation to policies or contracts made by, or, as the case may be, transferred to, an insurance company on or after 22 August 2000.

In reg. 16(5) the words from "being neither" to the end of sub-para. (c) (i.e. including sub-paras (a), (b) and (c)) substituted for the words " not being the person with whom the policy or contract was originally effected" by SI 1999/2839, reg. 17, with effect from 8 November 1999."

REINSURANCE BUSINESS EFFECTED EITHER BY A COMPANY RESIDENT IN THE UNITED KINGDOM OTHERWISE THAN OUTSIDE THE UNITED KINGDOM OR BY AN OVERSEAS LIFE INSURANCE COMPANY – POLICY HOLDER NOT WITHIN REGULATION 7

16A [Omitted by SI 2007/2088.]

History – Reg. 16A omitted by SI 2007/2088, reg. 10(c), with effect in relation to accounting periods beginning on or after 1 January 2007 and ending on or after 13 August 2007. Former reg. 16A read as follows:

"**16A(1)** This regulation applies in circumstances where–

(a) an insurance company has entered into relevant business,

(b) that business is reinsurance of life assurance business with a policy holder not residing in the United Kingdom who either–

(i) is not an individual, or

(ii) if an individual, is not one falling within regulation 7(1)(b)(i) or (ii),

(c) the underlying policy in relation to that business was effected either by an insurance company resident in the United Kingdom otherwise than at or through a branch outside the United Kingdom, or by an overseas life insurance company, and

(d) the underlying policy in relation to that business was made on or after 8th November 1999.

16A(2) Subject to paragraphs (3), (3A) and (3B) below, the territory in which the underlying policy holder was residing at the time the underlying policy was made shall be the territory specified in the certificate prescribed in regulation 7A(4) above.

16A(3) Where, at the time the underlying policy was made or at any time within eighteen months thereafter, the company was in possession of information making it reasonable for the company to assume that the underlying policy holder was residing in the United Kingdom at the time the underlying policy was made or at any time within twelve months thereafter, the territory in which the underlying policy holder was residing at the time the underlying policy was made shall be the United Kingdom.

16A(3A) Subject to paragraph (3) above, where the underlying policy is for term assurance business, the territory in which the policy holder was residing at the time the underlying policy was made or transferred shall be the territory in which, to the best of the company's knowledge or belief, the policy holder was residing at the time the underlying policy was made or transferred.

16A(3B) Where the underlying policy is for business of a description falling within regulation 7(b) of the Excluded Business Regulations, the territory in which the policy holder was residing at the time the underlying policy was made or transferred shall be the territory under the law of which the scheme mentioned in that regulation is established.

16A(4) Where, pursuant to paragraph (2), (3), (3A) or (3B) above, an underlying policy holder has been treated as residing in a particular territory at the time the underlying policy was made, the territory in which the underlying policy holder is residing at any time thereafter shall, subject to paragraph (5) below, be that same territory.

16A(5) Subject to paragraph (3) above, where at any time after the underlying policy was made the company comes to be in possession of information making it reasonable for the company to assume that the underlying policy holder, being neither–

(a) the person with whom the policy or contract was originally effected, nor

(b) a person to whom the rights conferred by the policy or contract have been assigned in circumstances where the assignment did not constitute a chargeable event within the meaning of section 540, 542 or 545, nor

(c) a personal representative in whom those rights have been vested by operation of law, was residing in the United Kingdom at the time he became the underlying policy holder or at any time thereafter, the territory in which the underlying policy holder is residing shall, from the date on which it is reasonable for the company so to assume, be the United Kingdom.

History – Reg. 16A inserted by SI 1999/2839, reg. 18, with effect from 8 November 1999.

In reg. 16A(2) the words "paragraphs (3), (3A) and (3B)" substituted for "paragraph (3)" and the words "regulation 7A(4) above" substituted for "paragraph (4) of regulation 7A or, as the case may be, paragraph (5) of that regulation" by SI 2000/2104, reg. 16(2) with effect from 23 August 2000 in relation to policies or contracts made by, or, as the case may be, transferred to, an insurance company on or after 22 August 2000.

Reg. 16A(3A) and (3B) inserted by SI 2000/2104, reg. 16(3) with effect from 23 August 2000 in relation to policies or contracts made by, or, as the case may be, transferred to, an insurance company on or after 22 August 2000.

In reg. 16A(4) the words ", (3), (3A) or (3B)" substituted for "or (3)" by SI 2000/2104, reg. 16(4) with effect from 23 August 2000 in relation to policies or contracts made by, or, as the case may be, transferred to, an insurance company on or after 22 August 2000."

CERTIFICATES TO BE OBTAINED ON THE HAPPENING OF SPECIFIED EVENTS

BUSINESS OTHER THAN REINSURANCE BUSINESS EFFECTED EITHER BY A COMPANY RESIDENT IN THE UNITED KINGDOM OTHERWISE THAN OUTSIDE THE UNITED KINGDOM OR BY AN OVERSEAS LIFE INSURANCE COMPANY

17   [Omitted by SI 1999/2839.]

History – Reg. 17 omitted by SI 1999/2839, reg. 4, with effect from 8 November 1999, except in relation to specified events occurring before 8 November 1999.

SANCTIONS

RECLASSIFICATION OF POLICY OR CONTRACT FROM DATE WHEN IT WAS EFFECTED

18(1)   Subject to paragraph (2) below, this regulation applies in any case where an insurance company—

(a)   treats a policy or contract as relating to overseas life assurance business–

    (i)   in the circumstances prescribed in regulation 6(1) where the insurance company has not completed the certificate prescribed in regulation 6(3) or one of the declarations prescribed in paragraphs (4) and (5) of regulation 6 within the period limited in regulation 6(7), or

    (ii)   in the circumstances prescribed in regulation 7(1) where the insurance company has not obtained the document prescribed in regulation 7(3) or, in any case where section 431D(5) applies, or where the business is of a description falling within the circumstances set out in regulation 5 of the Excluded Business Regulations, and the policy or contract is held otherwise than by the trustees of the trust, the certificate prescribed in regulation 7(8) within the period limited in regulation 7(9), or

    (iii)   in the circumstances prescribed in regulation 7A(1) where the insurance company has not completed the certificate prescribed in regulation 7A(4) or (5) within the period limited in regulation 7A(9), or

(aa)   [omitted by SI 2007/2088]

(b)   [omitted by SI 2007/2088]

(ba)   [omitted by SI 2007/2088]

(c)   treats a policy or contract as relating to overseas life assurance business in the circumstances prescribed in regulation 13(3), 14(3) or 14A(4), or

(d)   [omitted by SI 2007/2088]

(e)   treats a policy or contract as relating to overseas life assurance business in circumstances where the insurance company, at the time the policy or contract was made or transferred, was in possession of information making it reasonable for the insurance company to assume that–

    (i)   any of the requirements of section 431D (other than those relating to where the policy holder is residing) was not fulfilled (notwithstanding its possession of any certificate, declaration or other document), or

    (ii)   the business was excluded business.

18(2)   [Omitted by SI 2007/2088.]

18(3)   The company shall treat the policy or contract as relating to basic life assurance and general annuity business from the date the policy or contract was made or transferred.

18(4)   All necessary adjustments, whether by way of assessment self-assessment, or otherwise, shall be made to give effect to paragraph (3) above; and any such assessment may be made without limits on time.

History – In reg. 18(1)(a)(ii) the words ", or where the business is of a description falling within the circumstances set out in regulation 5 of the Excluded Business Regulations," inserted by SI 2000/2104, reg. 17(2)(a) with effect from 23 August 2000 in relation to policies or contracts made by, or, as the case may be, transferred to, an insurance company on or after 22 August 2000. In reg. 18(1)(a), para. (iii) the words "7A(1)" substituted for "7(A)(1)" by SI 2000/2104, reg. 17(2)(b) operative from 23 August 2000.

Reg. 18(1)(a)(iii) inserted by SI 1999/2839, reg. 19, with effect from 8 November 1999.

Reg. 18(1)(aa) omitted by SI 2007/2088, reg. 11(2)(a), with effect in relation to accounting periods beginning on or after 1 January 2007 and ending on or after 13 August 2007. Former reg. 18(1)(aa) read as follows:

> "(aa)   treats an underlying policy as relating to overseas life assurance business in the circumstances prescribed in regulation 9 where the insurance company has not obtained the certificate prescribed in regulation 9(3) or the undertaking prescribed in regulation 9(4) within the period limited in regulation 9(5), or"

Reg. 18(1)(aa) inserted by SI 1999/2839, reg. 19, with effect from 8 November 1999.

Reg. 18(1)(b) omitted by SI 2007/2088, reg. 11(2)(a), with effect in relation to accounting periods beginning on or after 1 January 2007 and ending on or after 13 August 2007. Former reg. 18(1)(b) read as follows:

> "(b)   treats an underlying policy as relating to overseas life assurance business in the circumstances prescribed in regulation 10(1) where the insurance company has not obtained the certificate prescribed in regulation 10(3) or the undertaking prescribed in regulation 10(4) within the period limited in regulation 10(5), or"

Reg. 18(1)(ba) omitted by SI 2007/2088, reg. 11(2)(a), with effect in relation to accounting periods beginning on or after 1 January 2007 and ending on or after 13 August 2007. Former reg. 18(1)(b) read as follows:

> "(ba)   treats an underlying policy as relating to overseas life assurance business in the circumstances prescribed in regulation 10A(1) where the insurance company has not obtained the certificate prescribed in regulation 10A(3) or the undertaking prescribed in regulation 10A(4) within the period limited in regulation 10A(5), or"

Reg. 18(1)(ba) inserted by SI 1999/2839, reg. 19, with effect from 8 November 1999.

In reg. 18(1)(c) the words ", 14(3) or 14A(4)" substituted for the words "or 14(3)" by SI 1999/2839, reg. 19, with effect from 8 November 1999.

Reg. 18(1)(d) omitted by SI 2007/2088, reg. 11(2)(a), with effect in relation to accounting periods beginning on or after 1 January 2007 and ending on or after 13 August 2007. Former reg. 18(1)(d) read as follows:

> "(d)   treats an underlying policy as relating to overseas life assurance business in the circumstances prescribed in regulation 15(3), 16(3) or 16A(3), or"

In reg. 18(1)(d) the words ", 16(3) or 16A(3)" substituted for the words "or 16(3)" by SI 1999/2839, reg. 19, with effect from 8 November 1999.

In reg. 18(1)(e), the words "policy or contract" substituted for the words "policy, contract or underlying policy", the words "or the relevant business in relation to that underlying policy was entered into" (which followed the words "was made or transferred") omitted, and the numbers "(i)" and "(ii)" substituted respectively for the letters "(a)" and "(b)" by SI 2007/2088, reg. 11(2)(b), with effect in relation to accounting periods beginning on or after 1 January 2007 and ending on or after 13 August 2007.

In reg. 18(1)(e), the word "that–" and sub-paras (a) and (b) which followed it substituted for the words "that any of the requirements of section 431D (other than those relating to where the policy holder is residing) was not fulfilled (notwithstanding its possession of any certificate, declaration or other document)." by SI 2000/2104, reg. 17(3) with effect from 23 August 2000 in relation to policies or contracts made by, or, as the case may be, transferred to, an insurance company on or after 22 August 2000. In reg. 18(1)(e) the words "or transferred" inserted by SI 1999/2839, reg. 19, with effect from 8 November 1999.

Reg. 18(2) omitted by SI 2007/2088, reg. 11(3), with effect in relation to accounting periods beginning on or after 1 January 2007 and ending on or after 13 August 2007. Former reg. 18(2) read as follows:

> "**18(2)**   This regulation shall not apply in any case specified in sub-paragraph (aa), (b), (ba), (d) or (e) of paragraph (1) above where the insurance company is a company to which section 439A applies."

In reg. 18(2) the words "(aa), (b), (ba), (d) or (e)" substituted for the words "(b), (d) or (e)" by SI 1999/2839, reg. 19, with effect from 8 November 1999.

Reg. 18(3) substituted by SI 2007/2088, reg. 11(4), with effect in relation to accounting periods beginning on or after 1 January 2007 and ending on or after 13 August 2007. Former reg. 18(3) read as follows:

> "**18(3)**   The company shall–
> (a)   in the case of business other than reinsurance business, treat the policy or contract as relating to basic life assurance and general annuity business from the date the policy or contract was made or transferred, or
> (b)   in the case of reinsurance business, treat the business relating to the underlying policy as basic life assurance and general annuity business from the date the underlying policy was made."

In reg. 18(3)(a) the words "or transferred" inserted by SI 1999/2839, reg. 19, with effect from 8 November 1999.

In reg. 18(4) the word "self-assessment" inserted by SI 1999/2839, reg. 19, with effect from 8 November 1999.

RECLASSIFICATION OF POLICY OR CONTRACT AS RELATING TO OVERSEAS LIFE ASSURANCE BUSINESS FROM DATE WHEN IT WAS MADE OR TRANSFERRED

18A(1)   This regulation applies in any case where an insurance company–

(a)   does not treat a policy or contract as relating to overseas life assurance business in the circumstances prescribed in regulation 5(1) (1A) or (1B), and

(b)   has not completed the certificate prescribed in regulation 5(4) or (4A) within the period limited in regulation 5(8).

18A(2)   The company shall treat the policy or contract as relating to overseas life assurance business from the date the policy or contract was made or transferred.

18A(3)   All necessary adjustments, whether by way of assessment or otherwise, shall be made to give effect to paragraph (2).

History – In reg. 18A(1)(a) the words "(1A) or (1B)" substituted for the words "or (1A)" by SI 2004/3273, reg. 11(2), with effect from 31 December 2004.

In reg. 18A(1)(b) the words "or (4A)" inserted by SI 2000/2104, reg. 18, with effect from 23 August 2000 in relation to cases occurring on or after 8 November 1999.

Reg. 18A inserted by SI 1999/2839, reg. 20, with effect from 8 November 1999.

RECLASSIFICATION OF POLICY OR CONTRACT FROM DATE AFTER IT WAS EFFECTED

19(1) Subject to paragraph (2) below, this regulation applies in any case where an insurance company—

(a) treats a policy or contract as relating to overseas life assurance business in the circumstances prescribed in regulation 8(1) where the insurance company has not obtained the document prescribed in regulation 8(3) or, in any case where section 431D(5) applies, or the business is of a description falling within the circumstances set out in regulation 5 of the Excluded Business Regulations, the certificate prescribed in regulation 8(8) within the period limited in regulation 8(9), or

(b) [omitted by SI 2007/2088]

(c) treats a policy or contract as relating to overseas life assurance business in the circumstances prescribed in regulation 13(5), 14(5) or 14A(6), or

(d) [omitted by SI 2007/2088]

(e) treats a policy or contract as relating to overseas life assurance business in circumstances where the insurance company, at any time after the policy or contract was made or transferred, was in possession of information making it reasonable for the insurance company to assume that—

  (i) any of the requirements of section 431D (other than those relating to where the policy holder is residing) was not fulfilled (notwithstanding its possession of any certificate, declaration or other document), or

  (ii) the business was excluded business.

19(2) [Omitted by SI 2007/2088.]

19(3) Subject to paragraphs (3A) and (3B) below, the company shall treat the policy or contract as relating to basic life assurance and general annuity business from the end of the accounting period in which the relevant date falls.

19(3A) Paragraph (3) above shall not apply where—

(a) the case concerned falls within paragraph (1)(e) above,

(b) section 431D(7) applied to the policy or contract when it was made or transferred, or the underlying policy when it was made,

(c) the case falls within paragraph (1)(e) above by reason of the fact that, at some time that is—

  (i) more than three years after the date on which the policy or contract was made or transferred, or the underlying policy was made, but

  (ii) is not earlier than 8th November 1999,

  the number of persons for or in respect of whom benefits were to be provided under the policy or contract, or the underlying policy, and who were not relevant overseas employees within the meaning of section 431D(8), became a not insignificant number ("the relevant number") for the purposes of section 431D(7), and

(d) the relevant number has at no time exceeded the number which is equal to twenty per cent of the total number of persons for or in respect of whom benefits are to be provided under the policy or contract or the underlying policy.

19(3B) Paragraph (3) above shall not apply where—

(a) the case concerned falls within paragraph (1)(e) above,

(b) the policy or contract fell within the description set out in regulation 7(c) of the Excluded Business Regulations when it was made or transferred, or the underlying policy fell within that description when it was made,

(c) the case falls within paragraph (1)(e) above by reason of the fact that, at some time that is more than three years after the date on which the policy or contract was made or transferred, or the underlying policy was made, the number of persons for or in respect of whom benefits were to be provided under the policy or contract, or the underlying policy, and who were not relevant overseas employees within the meaning of regulation 2 of the Excluded Business Regulations, became a not insignificant number ("the relevant number") for the purposes of regulation 7(c) of those Regulations, and

(d)   the relevant number has at no time exceeded the number which is equal to twenty per cent. of the total number of persons for or in respect of whom benefits are to be provided under the policy or contract or the underlying policy.

19(4)   All necessary adjustments, whether by way of assessment or otherwise, shall be made to give effect to paragraph (3) above; and any such assessment may be made without limits on time.

19(5)   In paragraph (3) above **"the relevant date"** means–

(a)   in any case specified in sub-paragraph (a) or (b) of paragraph (1) above, the last day by which the insurance company should have obtained any certificate, document or undertaking mentioned in either of those sub-paragraphs, or

(b)   in any case specified in sub-paragraph (c) or (d) of paragraph (1) above, the date when it became reasonable for the company to assume as mentioned in regulation 13(5), 14(5), 14A(5), 15(5) 16(5) or 16A(5) as the case may be, or

(c)   in any case specified in sub-paragraph (e) of paragraph (1) above, the date when it became reasonable for the insurance company to assume as mentioned in that sub-paragraph.

History – In reg. 19(1)(a) the words ", or the business is of a description falling within the circumstances set out in regulation 5 of the Excluded Business Regulations," inserted by SI 2000/2104, reg. 19(2) with effect from 23 August 2000 in relation to policies or contracts made by, or, as the case may be, transferred to, an insurance company on or after 22 August 2000.
Reg. 19(1)(b) omitted by SI 2007/2088, reg. 12(2)(a), with effect in relation to accounting periods beginning on or after 1 January 2007 and ending on or after 13 August 2007. Former reg. 19(1)(b) read as follows:
> "(b)   treats an underlying policy as relating to overseas life assurance business in the circumstances prescribed in regulation 11(l) where the insurance company has not obtained the certificate prescribed in regulation 11(3) or the undertaking prescribed in regulation 11(4) within the period limited in regulation 11(5), or"
In reg. 19(1)(c) the words ", 14(5) or 14A(6)" substituted for the words "or 14(5)" by SI 1999/2839, reg. 21, with effect from 8 November 1999, in relation to–
(a)   accounting periods ending on or after 31 December 1999, or
(b)   where an insurance company so elects by written notice given to an officer of the Board on or before 31 December 1999, the first accounting period beginning on or after 1 October 1999 and ending after 31 December 1999 and subsequent accounting periods.
Reg. 19(1)(d) omitted by SI 2007/2088, reg. 12(2)(a), with effect in relation to accounting periods beginning on or after 1 January 2007 and ending on or after 13 August 2007. Former reg. 19(1)(d) read as follows:
> "(d)   treats an underlying policy as relating to overseas life assurance business in the circumstances prescribed in regulation 15(5), 16(5) or 16A(5), or"
In reg. 19(1)(d) the words ", 16(5) or 16A(5)" substituted for the words "or 16(5)" by SI 1999/2839, reg. 21, with effect from 8 November 1999, in relation to–
(a)   accounting periods ending on or after 31 December 1999, or
(b)   where an insurance company so elects by written notice given to an officer of the Board on or before 31 December 1999, the first accounting period beginning on or after 1 October 1999 and ending after 31 December 1999 and subsequent accounting periods.
In reg. 19(1)(e) the word "that–" and sub-para. (a) and (b) which followed it substituted for the words "that any of the requirements of s. 431D (other than those relating to where the policy holder is residing) was not fulfilled (notwithstanding its possession of any certificate, declaration or other document)." by SI 2000/2104, reg. 19(3) with effect from 23 August 2000 in relation to policies or contracts made by, or, as the case may be, transferred to, an insurance company on or after 22 August 2000.
In reg. 19(1)(e), the words "policy or contract" substituted for the words "policy, contract or underlying policy", the words "or the relevant business in relation to that underlying policy was entered into" (which followed the words "was made or transferred") omitted, and the numbers "(i)" and "(ii)" substituted respectively for the letters "(a)" and "(b)" by SI 2007/2088, reg. 12(2)(b), with effect in relation to accounting periods beginning on or after 1 January 2007 and ending on or after 13 August 2007.
In reg. 19(1)(e) the words "or transferred" inserted by SI 1999/2839, reg. 21, with effect from 8 November 1999, in relation to–
(a)   accounting periods ending on or after 31 December 1999, or
(b)   where an insurance company so elects by written notice given to an officer of the Board on or before 31 December 1999, the first accounting period beginning on or after 1 October 1999 and ending after 31 December 1999 and subsequent accounting periods.
Reg. 19(2) omitted by SI 2007/2088, reg. 12(3), with effect in relation to accounting periods beginning on or after 1 January 2007 and ending on or after 13 August 2007. Former reg. 19(2) read as follows:
> "**19(2)**   This regulation shall not apply in any case specified in sub-paragraph (b), (d) or (e) of paragraph (1) above where the insurance company is a company to which section 439A applies."
Reg. 19(3) substituted by SI 2007/2088, reg. 12(4), with effect in relation to accounting periods beginning on or after 1 January 2007 and ending on or after 13 August 2007. Former reg. 19(3) read as follows:
> "**19(3)**   Subject to paragraphs (3A) and (3B) below, the company shall–
> (a)   in the case of business other than reinsurance business, treat the policy or contract as relating to basic life assurance and general annuity business from the end of the accounting period in which the relevant date falls, or
> (b)   in the case of reinsurance business, treat the business relating to the underlying policy as basic life assurance and general annuity business from the end of the accounting period in which the relevant date falls."
In reg. 19(3) the words "paragraphs (3A) and (3B)" substituted for "paragraph (3A)" by SI 2000/2104, reg. 19(4) with effect from 23 August 2000 in relation to policies or contracts made by, or, as the case may be, transferred to, an insurance company on or after 22 August 2000, the words "Subject to paragraph (3A) below" having been inserted previously by SI 1999/2839, reg. 21, with effect from 8 November 1999, in relation to–
(a)   accounting periods ending on or after 31 December 1999, or
(b)   where an insurance company so elects by written notice given to an officer of the Board on or before 31 December 1999, the first accounting period beginning on or after 1 October 1999 and ending after 31 December 1999 and subsequent accounting periods.
Reg. 19(3A) inserted by SI 1999/2839, reg. 21, with effect from 8 November 1999, in relation to–
(a)   accounting periods ending on or after 31 December 1999, or
(b)   where an insurance company so elects by written notice given to an officer of the Board on or before 31 December 1999, the first accounting period beginning on or after 1 October 1999 and ending after 31 December 1999 and subsequent accounting periods.

Statutory Instruments

Reg. 19(3B) inserted by SI 2000/2104, reg. 19(5) with effect from 23 August 2000 in relation to policies or contracts made by, or, as the case may be, transferred to, an insurance company on or after 22 August 2000.
In reg. 19(5)(b) the words "14(5), 14A(5), 15(5), 16(5) or 16A(5)," substituted for "14(5), 15(5) or 16(5)" by SI 2000/2104, reg. 19(6) with effect from 23 August 2000 in relation to—

(a)   accounting periods ending on or after 31 December 1999; or

(b)   where an insurance company has so elected by written notice given to an officer of the Board on or before 31 December 1999, the first accounting period beginning on or after 1 October 1999 and ending after 31 December 1999 and subsequent accounting periods.

CHARGE TO TAX WHERE NO CERTIFICATE UNDER REGULATION 17

20 [Omitted by SI 1999/2839.]

History – Reg. 20 omitted by SI 1999/2839, reg. 4, with effect from 8 November 1999, except in relation to specified events occurring before 8 November 1999.

KEEPING AND INSPECTION OF RECORDS AND PROVISION OF INFORMATION

RECORDS TO BE KEPT AND TRANSFERS OF RECORDS

21(1) A company (including any transferee) shall at all times keep sufficient records in respect of each relevant policy to enable the requirements of these Regulations to be satisfied.

21(2) Without prejudice to the generality of paragraph (1) above, any relevant record shall be preserved by the company, in such manner as may be approved by the Board, so as to be available for inspection under regulation 23 for a period of six years after the termination of the policy or contract.

21(3) In any case where the obligations under any policy or contract of the body that issued, entered into or effected it ("the original insurer") are at any time the obligations of another body (in this regulation and in regulations 22 and 23 referred to as the "transferee") to whom there has been a transfer of the whole or any part of a business previously carried on by the original insurer, the original insurer shall deliver any relevant record to the transferee within the period of three months after the transfer.

21(4) Paragraph (3) above has effect in relation to transfers on or after 1st January 1996.

INFORMATION TO BE PROVIDED TO THE BOARD

22 An officer of the Board authorised for the purposes of this regulation may by notice require any company which has at any time effected a relevant policy or any transferee, within such time as may be provided by the notice (not being less than 30 days), to furnish him with such information relating to any relevant policy as he may reasonably require for the purposes of these Regulations.

INSPECTION OF RECORDS

23(1) An officer of the Board authorised for the purposes of this regulation may by notice require any company which has at any time effected a relevant policy or any transferee, within such time as may be provided in the notice (not being less than 30 days), to make available for inspection by him such books, documents and other records as are in the company's possession or under the company's control containing such information relating to any relevant policy as he may reasonably require for the purposes of these Regulations.

23(2) The officer to whom the books, documents and other records are made available shall be entitled to take copies, or make extracts from, any book, document or record made available to him by virtue of paragraph (1) above.

INSURANCE COMPANIES (OVERSEAS LIFE ASSURANCE BUSINESS) (TAX CREDIT) REGULATIONS 1995

(SI 1995/3238)

Made by the Commissioners of Inland Revenue, in exercise of the powers conferred on them by s. 431E(2) and (3) and 441A(3) to (5) of the Income and Corporation Taxes Act 1988 and para. 58 of Sch. 8 to the Finance Act 1995. Operative from 2 January 1996.

PRELIMINARY

CITATION, COMMENCEMENT AND EFFECT

1 These Regulations may be cited as the Insurance Companies (Overseas Life Assurance Business) (Tax Credit) Regulations 1995, shall come into force on 2nd January 1996, and shall have effect in relation to accounting periods beginning on or after 1st November 1994.

INTERPRETATION

2(1) In these Regulations unless the context otherwise requires—

"**the Board**" means the Commissioners of Inland Revenue;

"**branch**" includes agency;

"**the Compliance Regulations**" means the Insurance Companies (Overseas Life Assurance Business) (Compliance) Regulations 1995;

"**linked liabilities**" means liabilities in respect of benefits to be determined by reference to the value of linked assets;

"**policy holder**" includes annuitant;

"**relevant overseas policy holders**" shall be construed in accordance with regulation 3;

"**relevant tax credit**" has the meaning given by regulation 8;

"**tax credit territory**" shall be construed in accordance with regulation 4.

2(2) In regulations 9 to 12, in any case where the obligations under any policy or contract of the body that issued, entered into or effected it ("the original insurer") are at any tune the obligations of another body ("the transferee") to whom there has been a transfer of the whole or any part of a business previously carried on by the original insurer, any reference to an insurance company (however expressed) shall, unless the context otherwise requires, include the transferee.

2(3) In these Regulations, any reference to a particular provision, without more, is a reference to that provision of the Income and Corporation Taxes Act 1988.

MEANING OF RELEVANT OVERSEAS POLICY HOLDERS

3(1) For the purposes of these Regulations, and subject to paragraph (2) below, policy holders are relevant overseas policy holders of a company if—

(a) in relation to business other than reinsurance business, the company's life assurance business with them is overseas life assurance business, or

(b) in relation to reinsurance business—

    (i) the cedant company's life assurance business with them is overseas life assurance business, or

    (ii) the reinsurance of the cedant company's business with them is overseas life assurance business.

3(2) Policy holders shall not be relevant overseas policy holders where the business is reinsurance of business within sub-paragraph (i) or (ii) of section 431D(1)(b).

MEANING OF TAX CREDIT TERRITORY

4 For the purposes of these Regulations a territory is a tax credit territory if an individual resident in the territory and receiving a distribution would be entitled, under arrangements having effect by virtue of section 788, to a tax credit in respect of a qualifying distribution made to him by a company resident in the United Kingdom.

ENTITLEMENT TO TAX CREDIT

5(1)   Subject to paragraph (2) below, an insurance company shall be entitled, under section 441A(3), to an amount of tax credit in the case of a distribution in respect of an asset of the company's overseas life assurance fund if any of the company's relevant overseas policy holders is residing in a tax credit territory.

5(2)   An insurance company shall not be entitled, under section 441A(3), to an amount of tax credit as mentioned in paragraph (1) above to the extent that the company is entitled to that amount under any other provision of the Corporation Tax Acts.

AMOUNT OF TAX CREDIT

6   The amount of tax credit to which an insurance company is entitled by virtue of regulation 5 in respect of an asset shall be calculated by–

(a)   taking, for each tax credit territory in which any of its relevant overseas policy holders is residing, the appropriate fraction of the relevant tax credit, and

(b)   aggregating the amounts arrived at under paragraph (a) above.

APPROPRIATE FRACTION

7(1)   In regulation 6 **"the appropriate fraction"** means–

(a)   in any case where the asset is linked to overseas life assurance business, the fraction specified in paragraph (2) below, and

(b)   in any case where the asset is not linked to overseas life assurance business, the fraction specified in paragraph (3) below.

7(2)   The fraction referred to in paragraph (1)(a) above is the fraction of which–

(a)   the numerator is the aggregate amount of the company's linked liabilities which are liabilities in respect of–

    (i)   its relevant overseas policy holders within regulation 3(1)(a) residing in the tax credit territory, or

    (ii)   its cedant companies in respect of the company's relevant overseas policy holders within regulation 3(1)(b) residing in the tax credit territory, and

(b)   the denominator is the aggregate amount of the company's linked liabilities which are liabilities in respect of–

    (i)   all its relevant overseas policy holders within regulation 3(1)(a), or

    (ii)   its cedant companies in respect of all the company's relevant overseas policy holders within regulation 3(1)(b).

7(3)   The fraction referred to in paragraph (1)(b) above is the fraction of which–

(a)   the numerator is the aggregate amount of the company's liabilities, other than its linked liabilities, in respect of–

    (i)   its relevant overseas policy holders within regulation 3(1)(a) residing in the tax credit territory, or

    (ii)   its cedant companies in respect of the company's relevant overseas policy holders within regulation 3(1)(b) residing in the tax credit territory, and

(b)   the denominator is the aggregate amount of the company's liabilities, other than its linked liabilities, in respect of–

    (i)   all its relevant overseas policy holders within regulation 3(1)(a), or

    (ii)   its cedant companies in respect of all the company's relevant overseas policy holders within regulation 3(1)(b).

7(4)   In its application to an overseas life insurance company this regulation shall be modified so that the word "liabilities" wherever it occurs is construed in accordance with the definition given in paragraph 6(2) of Schedule 19AC.

RELEVANT TAX CREDIT

8   In regulation 6 the **"relevant tax credit"** means the amount of tax credit which would be paid under arrangements having effect by virtue of section 788, after taking into account any tax to be charged or deducted and any reduction in the amount received to be made by reference to the aggregate of the distribution and tax credit under those arrangements, if the distribution were received by an individual resident in the tax credit territory.

TERRITORIES IN WHICH POLICY HOLDERS RESIDING

GENERAL

9   Any issue as to the territory in which a relevant overseas policy holder is residing for the purposes of these Regulations shall be determined in accordance with regulations 10 to 12.

POLICIES OR CONTRACTS EFFECTED BY A COMPANY RESIDENT IN THE UNITED KINGDOM OUTSIDE THE UNITED KINGDOM

10(1)   This regulation applies in circumstances where a policy or contract is effected by a company resident in the United Kingdom at or through a branch outside the United Kingdom.

10(2)   Subject to paragraph (3) below, the territory in which the policy holder was residing at the time the policy or contract was made shall be the territory in which the branch was situated.

10(3)   Where–

(a)   the policy or contract was made at or through a branch situated in a tax credit territory, and

(b)   at the time the policy or contract was made the company was in possession of information making it reasonable for the company to assume that the policy holder was residing in a non-qualifying territory at that time,

the territory in which the policy holder was residing at the time the policy was made shall be that non-qualifying territory.

10(4)   Where, pursuant to paragraph (2) or (3) above, a policy holder has been treated as residing in a territory at the time the policy or contract was made, the territory in which the policy holder is residing at any time thereafter shall, subject to paragraphs (5) and (6) below, be that same territory.

10(5)   Where–

(a)   the policy or contract was made at or through a branch situated in a tax credit territory, and

(b)   at any time after the policy or contract was made the company comes to be in possession of information making it reasonable for the company to assume that the policy holder was residing in a non-qualifying territory at the time the policy or contract was made or at any time thereafter,

the territory in which the policy holder is residing shall, from the relevant date, be that non-qualifying territory.

10(6)   If at any time after paragraph (5) above has applied, the company comes to be in possession of information making it reasonable for the company to assume that the policy holder, after residing in a non-qualifying territory, has begun residing in a tax credit territory, the territory in which the policy holder is residing shall, from the relevant date, be that tax credit territory.

POLICIES OR CONTRACTS EFFECTED EITHER BY A COMPANY RESIDENT IN THE UNITED KINGDOM OTHERWISE THAN OUTSIDE THE UNITED KINGDOM OR BY AN OVERSEAS LIFE INSURANCE COMPANY

11(1)   This regulation applies in circumstances where a policy or contract is effected either by a company resident in the United Kingdom otherwise than at or through a branch outside the United Kingdom, or by an overseas life insurance company.

11(2)   Subject to paragraph (6) below, in a case where the business is not reinsurance business, the territory in which the policy holder was residing at the time the policy or contract was made shall be the territory specified in the certificate prescribed in regulation 6(3) or, as the case may be, 7(4) of the Compliance Regulations.

11(3)   Subject to paragraphs (4) to (6) below, in a case where the business is reinsurance business, the territory in which the policy holder was residing at the time the policy or contract was made shall be a non-qualifying territory.

11(4)   Subject to paragraph (6) below, in a case where–

(a)   the business is reinsurance business, and

(b)   the relevant overseas policy holder is a policy holder with a cedant company whose business with him is overseas life assurance business,

the territory in which the policy holder was residing at the time the policy or contract was made shall be the territory which the cedant company notifies the company is the territory specified in the certificate prescribed in regulation 6(3) or, as the case may be, 7(4) of the Compliance Regulations.

11(5)   Subject to paragraph (6) below, in a case where–

(a)   the business is reinsurance business other than reinsurance business in a case falling within paragraph (4) above, and

(b)   the reinsurer notifies the company of the territory in which it reasonably believes the relevant overseas policy holder to reside,

the territory in which the policy holder was residing at the time the policy or contract was made shall be the territory notified.

11(6)   Where, at the time the policy or contract was made, the company was in possession of information making it reasonable for the company to assume that the policy holder was residing in a non-qualifying territory at that time, the territory in which the policy holder was residing at the time the policy or contract was made shall be that non-qualifying territory.

11(7)   Where, pursuant to any of paragraphs (2) to (6) above, a policy holder has been treated as residing in a territory at the time the policy or contract was made, the territory in which the policy holder is residing at any time thereafter shall, subject to paragraphs (8) and (9) below, be that same territory.

11(8)   Where, at any time after the policy or contract was made, the company comes to be in possession of information making it reasonable for the company to assume that the policy holder was residing in a non-qualifying territory at the time the policy was made or at any time thereafter, the territory in which the policy holder is residing shall, from the relevant date, be that non-qualifying territory.

11(9)   If at any time after paragraph (8) has applied, the company comes to be in possession of information making it reasonable for the company to assume that the policy holder, after residing in a non-qualifying territory, has begun residing in a tax credit territory, the territory in which the policy holder is residing shall, from the relevant date, be that tax credit territory.

11(10)   The company shall obtain the notification mentioned in paragraph (4) above within–

(a)   nine months following the end of the cedant company's accounting period in which the cedant company entered into the business with the relevant overseas policy holder, or

(b)   three months following the making of the reinsurance arrangement, or

(c)   three months following the end of the company's accounting period in which the company first receives a distribution from an asset of its overseas life assurance fund to which a tax credit is attached,

whichever is the last to occur.

INTERPRETATION OF REGULATIONS 10 AND 11

12(1)   In regulations 10 and 11 a **"non-qualifying territory"** means–

(a)   the United Kingdom, or

(b)   a territory which is not a tax credit territory, or

(c)   a territory which is a tax credit territory, but where the amount of the relevant tax credit is nil.

12(2)   In each of the provisions to which this paragraph applies, **"the relevant date"** means the date from which it is reasonable for the company to assume that the policy holder is residing as mentioned in that provision; and this paragraph applies to regulations 10(5), 10(6), 11(8) and 11(9).

KEEPING AND INSPECTION OF RECORDS AND PROVISION OF INFORMATION

RECORDS TO BE KEPT AND TRANSFERS OF RECORDS

13(1) An insurance company (including any transferee) shall at all times keep sufficient records to enable the requirements of these Regulations to be satisfied.

13(2) In any case where the obligations under any policy or contract of the body that issued, entered into or effected it (**"the original insurer"**) are at any time the obligations of another body (in this regulation referred to as the **"transferee"**) to whom there has been a transfer of the whole or any part of a business previously carried on by the original insurer, the original insurer shall deliver any relevant record (within the meaning given by the Compliance Regulations) to the transferee within the period of three months after the transfer.

13(3) Paragraph (2) above has effect in relation to transfers on or after 1st January 1996.

INFORMATION TO BE PROVIDED TO THE BOARD

14 An officer of the Board authorised for the purposes of this regulation may by notice in writing require any insurance company to which these Regulations apply or any cedant company with which the insurance company has entered into a reinsurance arrangement, within such time as may be provided by the notice (not being less than 30 days), to furnish him with such information as he may reasonably require for the purposes of these Regulations.

INSPECTION OF RECORDS

15(1) An officer of the Board authorised for the purposes of this regulation may by notice in writing require any insurance company to which these Regulations apply or any cedant company with which the insurance company has entered into a reinsurance arrangement, within such time as may be provided in the notice (not being less than 30 days), to make available for inspection by that officer in the United Kingdom, such books, documents and other records as are in the company's possession or under the company's control containing information relating to the territory in which any policy holder is, or has been, treated under these Regulations as residing.

15(2) The officer to whom the books, documents and other records are made available shall be entitled to take copies, or make extracts from, any books, documents or records made available to him by virtue of paragraph (1) above.

Statutory Instruments

TAX-EXEMPT SPECIAL SAVINGS ACCOUNT (RELEVANT EUROPEAN INSTITUTIONS) REGULATIONS 1995

(SI 1995/3239)

Made on 12 December 1995 by the Commissioners of Inland Revenue, in exercise of the powers conferred on them by s. 326C(1) and (1A) and 326D of the Income and Corporation Taxes Act 1988. Operative from 12 December 1995.

PART I – GENERAL

CITATION AND COMMENCEMENT

1   These Regulations may be cited as the Tax-exempt Special Savings Account (Relevant European Institutions) Regulations 1995 and shall come into force on 2nd January 1996.

INTERPRETATION

2   In these Regulations–

"**the Board**" means the Commissioners of Inland Revenue;

"**notice**" means notice in writing and "**notify**" shall be construed accordingly;

"**the principal Regulations**" means the Tax-exempt Special Savings Account Regulations 1990;

"**a relevant European institution**" has the meaning given by section 326A(10) of the Taxes Act;

"**the Taxes Act**" means the Income and Corporation Taxes Act 1988;

and in Part III of these Regulations "**regulation**" means a regulation of the principal Regulations.

PART II – TAX REPRESENTATIVES

ACCOUNTS HELD WITH RELEVANT EUROPEAN INSTITUTIONS

3(1)   An account held with a relevant European institution shall not be a tax-exempt special savings account at the time it is opened, or shall cease to be a tax-exempt special savings account at a given time, unless at the time concerned one of the following three requirements is fulfilled.

3(2)   The first requirement is that–

(a)   a person who falls within subsection (5) of section 326D of the Taxes Act is appointed by the institution to be responsible for securing the discharge of the duties prescribed by regulation 4 which fall to be discharged by the institution, and

(b)   his identity and the fact of his appointment have been notified to the Board by the institution.

3(3)   The second requirement is that there are other arrangements with the Board for a person other than the institution to secure the discharge of such duties.

3(4)   The third requirement is that there are other arrangements with the Board designed to secure the discharge of such duties.

PRESCRIBED DUTIES OF TAX REPRESENTATIVES

4   The duties prescribed by this regulation are those that fall to be discharged by a society or institution under the principal Regulations.

TERMINATION OF APPOINTMENT

5   The appointment of a person in pursuance of the first requirement mentioned in regulation 3(2) shall be treated as terminated in circumstances where–

(a)   the Board have reason to believe that the person concerned–

> (i)   has failed to secure the discharge of any of the duties prescribed by regulation 4, or
>
> (ii)   does not have adequate resources to discharge those duties; and

(b)   the Board have notified the institution and that person that they propose to treat his appointment as having terminated with effect from the date specified in the notice.

POWERS AND LIABILITIES OF TAX REPRESENTATIVE

6   Where, in accordance with the first requirement mentioned in regulation 3(2), a person is at any time appointed to be responsible for securing the discharge of duties, the person concerned–

(a)   shall be entitled to act on the institution's behalf for any of the purposes of the provisions relating to the duties;

(b)   shall secure (where appropriate by acting on the institution's behalf) the institution's compliance with and discharge of the duties;

(c)   shall be personally liable in respect of any failure of the institution to comply with or discharge any such duty as if the duties imposed on the institution were imposed jointly and severally on the institution and the person concerned.

EFFECT OF SECTION 326B(3) OF THE TAXES ACT

7   Section 326B(3) of the Taxes Act shall have effect as if the reference to subsection (1) included a reference to this Part of these Regulations.

PART III – AMENDMENTS TO THE PRINCIPAL REGULATIONS

8-11   Not reproduced here: amendments consolidated in text of SI 1990/2361

CAPITAL GAINS TAX (PENSION FUNDS POOLING SCHEMES) REGULATIONS 1996

(SI 1996/1583, as amended by SI 2001/3629)

Made on 19 June 1996 by the Treasury, in exercise of the powers conferred on them by s. 99(3) of the Taxation of Chargeable Gains Act 1992. Operative from 11 July 1996.

1   These regulations may be cited as the Capital Gains Tax (Pension Funds Pooling Schemes) Regulations 1996 and shall come into force on 11th July 1996.

2   In these Regulations–

> **"pension funds pooling scheme"** means a unit trust scheme of the description specified in regulation 4 of the Income Tax (Pension Funds Pooling Schemes) Regulations 1996;

> **"unit trust scheme"** has the meaning given by section 237(1) of the Financial Services and Markets Act 2000.

History – In reg. 2, in the definition of "unit trust scheme", the words "237(1) of the Financial Services and Markets Act 2000" substituted for "75(8) of the Financial Services Act 1986" by SI 2001/3629, art. 143 which came into force on 1 December 2001.

3   A unit trust scheme which is a pension funds pooling scheme shall be treated as not being a unit trust scheme for the purposes of the Taxation of Chargeable Gains Act 1992.

INCOME TAX (PENSION FUNDS POOLING SCHEMES) REGULATIONS 1996

(SI 1996/1585 as amended by SI 2001/3629, SI 2006/745 and SI 2006/1162)

Made on 19 June by the Treasury, in exercise of the powers conferred on them by s. 469(7) and (8) of the Income and Corporation Taxes Act 1988. Operative from 11 July 1996.

CITATION AND COMMENCEMENT

1 These Regulations may be cited as the Income Tax (Pension Funds Pooling Schemes) Regulations 1996 and shall come into force on 11th July 1996.

INTERPRETATION

2(1) In these Regulations unless the context otherwise requires—

"address" in relation to any person means—

(a) where that person is an individual, the address of his principal place of business or, if he has none, his principal residential address;

(b) where that person is a company, the address of its registered or principal office;

"the Board" means the Commissioners of Inland Revenue;

"cancellation event" means an occasion when the rights and interests of a participant in the scheme property of a unit trust scheme are wholly redeemed, or otherwise wholly purchased or wholly cancelled, by the trustee of that scheme, other than an occasion when the rights and interests of the participant in the scheme property become the rights and interests of its successor in the scheme property;

"descendant" in relation to a former participant in a unit trust scheme ("the relevant participant") means the participant for the time being in the scheme which is either the successor of the relevant participant or the successor of another former participant in the scheme which, at the time it so participated, was part of the line of succession of participants that commenced with the relevant participant;

"employee" and **"employer"** have the meaning given in section 279(1) of the Finance Act 2004);

"notice" means notice in writing;

"recognised overseas pension scheme" has the meaning given in section 150(8) of the 2004 Act;

"pension funds pooling scheme" means a unit trust scheme of the description specified in regulation 4;

"pension scheme" has the meaning given by section 150(1) of the 2004 Act;

"registered pension scheme" in section 150(2) of the 2004 Act, (for the purpose of these Regulations), must also be an "occupational pension scheme" within the meaning of section 150(5) of that Act;

"relevant period" in relation to a unit trust scheme means a period which—

(a) commences when the trustee of the scheme first incurs expenditure in respect of which an allowance under the 1990 Act is to be, or may be, made, or next incurs such expenditure after the end of a relevant period, and

(b) ends when it is first the case that the trustee of the scheme has disposed of all interests in respect of which such expenditure is incurred, unless immediately after that time the scheme incurs further expenditure in respect of which an allowance under the 1990 Act is to be, or may be, made;

"scheme property" in relation to a unit trust scheme means property of any description, including money, which is held on trust for the participants in the scheme;

"section 469" means section 469 of the Taxes Act;

"sponsor" in relation to a pension funds scheme means any person who established the scheme or who for the time being has authority to vary the terms of, or to terminate, the scheme, or to appoint or replace a manager of the scheme;

"successor" in relation to a former participant in a unit trust scheme means the participant which–

(a) was not a participant in the scheme immediately before the time when that former participant ceased to participate in the scheme, and

(b) immediately after that time became entitled to all the rights and interests in the scheme property to which that former participant was entitled immediately before ceasing so to participate;

"tax year" means a year beginning on 6th April and ending on 5th April in the following calendar year;

"Taxes Act" means the Income and Corporation Taxes Act 1988;

"trustee" in relation to a unit trust scheme means the person or persons for the time being holding the scheme property on trust for the participants in that scheme;

"units" and

"unit trust scheme" have the meanings given by section 237 of the Financial Services and Markets Act 2000;

"1990 Act" means the Capital Allowances Act 1990;

"1992 Act" means the Taxation of Chargeable Gains Act 1992.

"2004 Act" means the Finance Act 2004.

2(2)   [Omitted by SI 2006/745, art. 23(2)(b).]

2(3)   References in these Regulations to a superannuation fund are references to a superannuation fund which either–

(a)   falls within subsection (6) of section 615 of the Taxes Act, or

(b)   is before the Board in order for them to decide whether the superannuation fund falls within that subsection.

2(4)   References in these Regulations to a registered pension scheme, a superannuation fund or a recognised overseas pension scheme as a participant in a unit trust scheme, are references to the appropriate person or persons specified in paragraph (5) who is or are for the time being a participant or participants in the unit trust scheme and, for the purposes of this paragraph, "participant" shall be construed in accordance with section 235 of the Financial Services and Markets Act 2000.

2(5)   The persons specified are–

(a)   in the case of a registered pension scheme set up under trust or a superannuation fund, the trustees of that scheme or fund;

(b)   in the case of a registered pension scheme not set up under trust, the sponsor of that scheme;

(c)   in the case of a recognised overseas pension scheme, the persons who are for the time being parties to the arrangements constituting that scheme, other than an employee in his capacity as a beneficiary of the scheme.

2(6)   The like provisions as are contained in section 159(2) to (8) of the 1990 Act shall have effect to determine when capital expenditure is to be taken to be incurred for the purposes of these Regulations.

History – In reg. 2(1), the definitions of "employee" and "employer" substituted, the definition of "recognised overseas pension scheme" substituted for the definition of "overseas scheme", the definitions of "retirement benefits scheme" and "scheme" omitted, the definitions of "registered pension scheme", "pension scheme" and "2004 Act" inserted by SI 2006/745, art. 23(2)(a), with effect from 6 April 2006.

In reg. 2(1), in the definition of "units" and "unit trust scheme", the words "237 of the Financial Services and Markets Act 2000" substituted for "75(8) of the Financial Services Act 1986" and, in reg. 2(4), the words "and, for the purposes of this paragraph, "participant" shall be construed in accordance with section 235 of the Financial Services and Markets Act 2000" substituted for the words "within the meaning given by section 75(1) and (2) of the Financial Services Act 1986", by SI 2001/3629, art. 145 which came into force on 1 December 2001.

Reg. 2(2) omitted by SI 2006/745, art. 23(2)(b), with effect from 6 April 2006.

In reg. 2(4), the words "a recognised overseas pension scheme" substituted for the words "an overseas scheme" by SI 2006/745, art. 23(3), with effect from 6 April 2006.

In reg. 2(4) and (5) (twice), the words "a registered pension scheme" substituted for the words "an exempt approved scheme" by SI 2006/745, art. 23(2)(c), with effect from 6 April 2006.

In reg. 2(5)(c), the words "a recognised overseas pension scheme" substituted for the words "an overseas scheme" by SI 2006/745, art. 23(3), with effect from 6 April 2006.

EXCEPTION OF PENSION FUNDS POOLING SCHEME FROM SECTION 469

3   A unit trust scheme which is a pension funds pooling scheme shall be treated as not being a unit trust scheme for the purposes of section 469.

DESCRIPTION OF A PENSION FUNDS POOLING SCHEME

4(1) Subject to paragraph (2), a unit trust scheme is a pension funds pooling scheme at any time if at that time it has the characteristics specified in paragraph (3).

4(2) Subject to paragraph (2A), a unit trust scheme which at any time in a tax year, or at the end of a tax year, ceases to have the characteristics specified in paragraph (3) is not a pension funds pooling scheme as regards that year.

4(2A) Paragraph (2) does not apply if the unit trust scheme ceases to have the characteristics specified in paragraph (3) solely because it is wound up.

4(3) The characteristics specified in this paragraph are that–

(a)   subject to regulation 9(10) and (11), each participant in the scheme is–

    (i)   a registered pension scheme, or

    (ii)   a superannuation fund, or

    (iii)   a recognised overseas pension scheme;

(b)   each participant in the scheme has been approved by the Board in accordance with regulation 7 as eligible to participate in the scheme and, subject to regulation 9(10) and (11), that approval has not subsequently been revoked or withdrawn under regulation 7(8) or (9);

(c)   all the participants in the scheme are jointly absolutely entitled as against the trustee of that scheme, within the meaning of section 60 of the 1992 Act, to the scheme property;

(d)   subject to paragraph (4), the scheme property consists of any or all of the following–

    (i)   land;

    (ii)   buildings or structures on land;

    (iii)   shares, stock or other investments which are the subject of transactions falling within subsection (12) of section 127 of the Finance Act 1995 (read with subsection (13) of that section);

    (iv)   investments comprising futures contracts or options contracts relating to land (including contracts falling within subsection (13) of that section);

(e)   except as provided in paragraph (5), the contributions of the participants are expended on any or all of the following–

    (i)   the acquisition of, or of rights in or over, land, or the management or development of that land;

    (ii)   the acquisition or construction of, or the purchase of interests in, buildings or structures on land, or the management or development of those buildings or structures;

    (iii)   the provision of machinery or plant which is an integral part of those buildings or structures, or the management, alteration or improvement of that machinery or plant;

    (iv)   the making of any investments falling within sub-paragraph (d)(iii) or (iv) above, or the management of those investments;

(f)   where expenditure falling within sub-paragraph (e) is expenditure in respect of which an allowance under the 1990 Act is to be, or may be, made, the terms of the scheme secure that the conditions specified in regulation 5 (read with regulation 6) are satisfied;

(g)   the terms of the scheme secure that no participant has rights or interests in any part of the scheme property that are different in nature from the rights or interests which any other participant has in that part of the scheme property;

(h)   the terms of the scheme secure that, in relation to any arrangements which are entered into on or after the date of coming into force of these Regulations–

    (i)   a participant is obliged to give to the trustee of the scheme, in the situation described, and within the period of time specified, in paragraph (1) of regulation 8, the notification specified in that regulation;

    (ii)   the trustee of the scheme is irrevocably authorised and obliged to undertake on behalf of the participants the responsibilities specified in regulation 10 and the duties specified in regulations 9 and 11;

(j)   the trustee of the scheme has given notice to the Board electing for the scheme to be treated, pursuant to these Regulations, the Capital Gains Tax (Pension Funds Pooling Schemes) Regulations 1996, and the Stamp Duty and Stamp Duty Reserve Tax (Pension Funds Pooling Schemes) Regulations 1996, as not being a unit trust scheme for the purposes specified in each of the Regulations.

4(4) A unit trust scheme is a pension funds pooling scheme notwithstanding that the scheme property at any time consists wholly or partly of–

(a)   cash held temporarily by the trustee that is subsequently expended as mentioned in sub-paragraph (e) of paragraph (3), or for purposes incidental to, or arising out of, any of the expenditure referred to in that sub-paragraph,

(b)   cash held temporarily by the trustee that is subsequently expended in making payment to a participant or former participant in the scheme following the redemption, purchase or cancellation of any of the rights or interests of that participant or former participant in the scheme property,

(c)   cash held temporarily by the trustee that is subsequently expended by way of distribution to the participants generally,

(d)   cash held temporarily by the trustee that is subsequently expended on the management of the scheme, or the management or development of the scheme property,

(e)   cash held temporarily by the trustee that is subsequently expended on the acquisition or maintenance of assets falling within sub-paragraph (f) below, or

(f)   other assets held by the trustee in connection with the management of the scheme, or the management or development of the scheme property.

4(5) A unit trust scheme is a pension funds pooling scheme notwithstanding that the contributions of the participants are expended–

(a)   for purposes incidental to, or arising out of, the expenditure referred to in paragraph (3)(e),

(b)   for any of the purposes mentioned in sub-paragraphs (a) to (e) of paragraph (4), or

(c)   on the acquisition or maintenance of assets falling within sub-paragraph (f) of that paragraph.

4(6) In this regulation–

   "management" includes insurance, repair and maintenance;

   "development" includes alteration or improvement.

History – In reg. 4(2) the words "Subject to paragraph (2A)" inserted by SI 2006/1162, reg. 2(2), with effect from 16 May 2006. Reg. 4(2A) inserted by SI 2006/1162, reg. 2(3), with effect from 16 May 2006.
In reg. 4(3)(a)(i), the words "a registered pension scheme" substituted for the words "an exempt approved scheme" by SI 2006/745, art. 23(4), with effect from 6 April 2006.
In reg. 4(3)(a)(iii), the words "a recognised overseas pension scheme" substituted for the words "an overseas scheme" by SI 2006/745, art. 23(3), with effect from 6 April 2006.

EXPENDITURE QUALIFYING FOR CAPITAL ALLOWANCES – SPECIFICATION OF CONDITIONS

5(1) The conditions specified for the purposes of regulation 4(3)(f) are those set out in paragraphs (2) to (6).

5(2) The first condition is that each participant in the scheme in a relevant period is either–

(a)   an enduring participant, or

(b)   a participant that is a descendant of a former participant in the scheme which was a participant at the commencement of that period.

5(3) The second condition is that, during a relevant period, no participant in the scheme is the successor of more than one former participant which ceased to participate in the scheme–

(a)   immediately before the commencement of that period, or

(b)   at the time of the commencement of that period, or

(c)   at any subsequent time before the end of that period.

5(4) The third condition is that during a relevant period–

(a)   an enduring participant's share of the scheme property remains the same as it was at the commencement of that period, and

(b)   the share of a participant which is a descendant of a former participant which was a participant at the commencement of the relevant period remains the same as the share of that former participant was at the commencement of that period,

until such time as a cancellation event occurs, or, if earlier, the rights and interests in the scheme property of the participant concerned become the rights and interests in the scheme property of its successor.

5(5) The fourth condition is that, immediately after the occurrence of a cancellation event during a relevant period, the ratio that the shares of the scheme property belonging to the participants at that time bear to each other is the same as the ratio that the shares of the scheme property belonging to those participants bore to each other immediately before the occurrence of that event.

5(6) The fifth condition is that, following the occurrence of a cancellation event during a relevant period, every participant's share of the scheme property remains the same as it was immediately after the occurrence of that event or, where a participant is a descendant of a former participant which was a participant immediately after the occurrence of that event, the same as the share of that former participant was at that time, until that period ends or, if earlier, a further cancellation event occurs or the rights and interests in the scheme property of the participant concerned become the rights and interests in the scheme property of its successor.

5(7) In this regulation **"enduring participant"** in relation to a relevant period means a participant which has been a participant since the commencement of that period.

EXPENDITURE QUALIFYING FOR CAPITAL ALLOWANCES – PROVISIONS SUPPLEMENTARY TO REGULATION 5

6(1) Where the rights and interests of a participant in the scheme property become the rights and interests of its successor in the scheme property at the time when a relevant period commences or a cancellation event occurs during a relevant period, those rights and interests shall be treated, for the purposes of regulation 5, as having become the rights and interests of the successor before the commencement of the relevant period or (as the case may be) the occurrence of the cancellation event.

6(2) Where the rights and interests of a participant in the scheme property become the rights and interests of its successor in the scheme property at the time when a relevant period ends, those rights and interests shall be treated, for the purposes of regulation 5, as having become the rights and interests of the successor after the end of that period.

6(3) Where contributions by participants in the scheme are made at the time when–

(a)   a relevant period commences, or

(b)   a cancellation event occurs during a relevant period, or

(c)   a relevant period ends,

those contributions shall be treated, for the purposes of regulation 5, as having been made before the commencement of the relevant period or the occurrence of the cancellation event, or after the end of the relevant period (as the case may be).

6(4) Where during a relevant period the rights and interests of a participant in the scheme property become the rights and interests of its successor in the scheme property at the same time as the trustee of the scheme makes a disposal of any interest or rights in or over an asset which, immediately before that disposal was made, formed part of the scheme property, the disposal shall be treated, for the purposes of regulation 5, as having been made after the participant's rights and interests in the scheme property have become the successor's rights and interests in the scheme property.

6(5) Where, as a result of a business reorganisation, amalgamation or other form of reconstruction, a merger of participants occurs, that is, the whole of the rights and interests of two or more participants in the scheme property become the whole of the rights and interests of a single participant in the scheme property, then for the purposes of regulation 5–

(a)   where the merger occurs at the time when a relevant period commences, it shall be treated as having occurred before that time;

(b)   where the merger occurs at the time when a relevant period ends, it shall be treated as having occurred after that time;

(c)   where the merger occurs during a relevant period, it shall be treated as never having occurred.

6(6) Where, as a result of a business reorganisation, fragmentation or other form of reconstruction, a demerger relating to participants occurs, that is, the whole of the rights and interests of a single participant in the scheme property ("the demerging participant") become the whole of the rights and interests of two or more participants in the scheme property ("the replacement participants"), then for the purposes of regulation 5–

(a)   where the demerger occurs at the time when a relevant period commences or a cancellation event occurs during a relevant period, it shall be treated as having occurred before that time;

(b)   where the demerger occurs at the time when a relevant period ends, it shall be treated as having occurred after that time;

(c)   where the demerger occurs during a relevant period, the demerging participant shall be treated as having been comprised of participants whose successors are the replacement participants.

6(7) For the purposes of paragraph (6)(c), where one of the replacement participants is the demerging participant, that participant shall be treated as if, in its capacity as a replacement participant, it were a separate and distinct participant from the demerging participant.

6(8) In paragraph (4) "disposal" shall be construed in accordance with the provisions of Chapter II of Part II of the 1992 Act relating to disposals of assets.

6(9) Where during a relevant period of a unit trust scheme it first occurs that the scheme has the characteristics specified in regulation 4(3), that period shall be treated, for the purposes of regulation 5 and this regulation, as having commenced at the time of that first occurrence.

APPROVAL OF PARTICIPANTS

7(1) An application for approval of a scheme or fund as eligible to participate in a pension funds pooling scheme shall be made in writing by the trustee of that pension funds pooling scheme to the Board and shall contain the information specified in paragraph (2) or, as the case may be, in paragraph (3).

7(2) As regards a registered pension scheme or a superannuation fund, the information is–

(a)   the full title of the scheme or fund;

(b)   the Board's reference number relating to the scheme or fund.

7(3) As regards a recognised overseas pension scheme, the information is–

(a)   the full title of the scheme;

(b)   where the scheme is established under trust, the names and addresses of the sponsors and trustees of the scheme;

(c)   where the scheme is not established under trust, the names and addresses of the sponsors and managers of the scheme;

(d)   the names and addresses of any employers who contribute to, but are not sponsors of, the scheme;

(e)   where the arrangements constituting the scheme are made between two or more persons, details of any undertakings or promises made between any of those persons that are, or are likely to be, relevant to the custodianship of any rights or interests of that scheme in the pension funds pooling scheme, and the name and address of each of those persons;

(f)   either–

      (i)   evidence demonstrating that the scheme fulfils the requirements set out in regulations 2 and 3 of the Pension Schemes (Categories of Country and Requirements for Overseas Pension Schemes and Recognised Overseas Pension Schemes) Regulations 2006; or

      (ii)   in respect of information which has already been provided in accordance with section 169 of the Finance Act 2004 (recognised transfers) to an officer of Her Majesty's Revenue and Customs, notification of any reference used by an officer of Her Majesty's Revenue and Customs in respect of that information;

(g)   [effectively omitted by SI 2006/745, art. 23(5)(c)(ii);]

(h)–(o)[omitted by SI 2006/745, art. 23(5)(c)(iii).]

7(4) [Omitted by SI 2006/745, art. 23(5)(c)(iv).]

7(5) Where the Board determine to approve a scheme or fund pursuant to an application under paragraph (1), they shall give notice of the approval to the trustee of the pension funds pooling scheme.

7(6) Approval may be given by the Board in full where they are satisfied that the scheme or fund is eligible to participate in the pension funds pooling scheme, or may be given on a provisional basis–

(a)   in the case of a scheme falling within paragraph (3), pending the Board's consideration of information received by them pursuant to that paragraph, or

(b)   in the case of a superannuation fund which is before the Board for the purposes referred to in regulation 2(3)(b).

7(7) On receipt of a notice of approval, the trustee of the pension funds pooling scheme may admit the scheme or fund which is the subject of the notice to be a participant in the pension funds pooling scheme.

7(8) The Board shall, by notice to the trustee, either convert to full approval or revoke an approval given on a provisional basis and, where the approval is revoked, the notice shall state the reason why it is considered by the Board that the participant is not eligible to participate in the pension funds pooling scheme.

7(9) The Board may, by notice to the trustee, withdraw approval of a participant where they are satisfied that a participant is not eligible to participate in the pension funds pooling scheme, and the notice shall state the reason why it is considered by the Board that the participant is not so eligible.

7(10) In this regulation references to a pension funds pooling scheme include references to any arrangements which, although not constituting such a scheme at the time an application for approval is made under paragraph (1), have been entered into with the intention that they will constitute such a scheme, and references to the trustee of a pension funds pooling scheme shall be construed accordingly.

History – In reg. 7(1) the words "or (4)" omitted by SI 2006/745, art. 23(5)(a), with effect from 6 April 2006.
In reg. 7(2) the words "a registered pension scheme" substituted for the words "an exempted approved scheme" by SI 2006/745, art. 23(5)(b), with effect from 6 April 2006.
In reg. 7(3) the words "a recognised overseas pension scheme" substituted for the words "an overseas scheme other than a scheme falling within paragraph (4) below", reg. 7(3)(f) substituted for former reg. 7(3)(f) and (g) and reg. 7(3)(h) to (o) omitted by SI 2006/745, art. 23(5)(c), with effect from 6 April 2006.
Reg. 7(4) omitted by SI 2006/745, art. 23(5)(d), with effect from 6 April 2006.
Reg. 7(6)(b) substituted by SI 2006/745, art. 23(5)(e), with effect from 6 April 2006.

NOTIFICATION BY PARTICIPANT OF NON-ELIGIBILITY

8(1) On becoming aware that, by reason of a change in its circumstances or otherwise, it is not, or may not be, eligible to participate in a pension funds pooling scheme, a participant shall notify the trustee of the scheme in writing of that fact within seven days after its becoming so aware.

8(2) A notification under paragraph (1)–

(a) shall state the reason why the participant considers that it is not, or may not be, so eligible, and

(b) shall be accompanied by a copy of any document in the participant's possession that confirms or suggests that it is not, or may not be, so eligible.

DUTIES OF TRUSTEE OF A PENSION FUNDS POOLING SCHEME – PARTICIPANTS CEASING TO BE ELIGIBLE TO PARTICIPATE

9(1) On receiving a notification by a participant in accordance with regulation 8(1), the trustee of a pension funds pooling scheme shall, within 14 days after the date of receipt of the notification, give notice to the Board that a notification has been received by him.

9(2) A notice under paragraph (1) shall state the full title of the participant concerned and, in the case of a notification received from a participant which is a registered pension scheme or a superannuation fund, the Board's reference number relating to that participant.

9(3) A notice under paragraph (1) shall be accompanied by–

(a) a copy of the notification received from the participant, and

(b) a copy of the information provided by the participant to the trustee in accordance with regulation 8(2)(b), together with a translation of that information into English where the document in which the information is comprised is in a language other than English.

9(4) Where, as a result of receiving any information, other than information provided in accordance with regulation 8(1), the trustee of a pension funds pooling scheme has reason to believe that–

(a) in the case of a participant which is a registered pension scheme or a superannuation fund, the participant is not eligible to participate in the scheme, or

(b) in the case of a participant which is a recognised overseas pension scheme, the Board would be likely, were they to be in possession of the information received by the trustee, to have reason to revoke or withdraw their approval of the participant under regulation 7(8) or (9),

the trustee shall, within 14 days after the date of receipt of that information, give notice to the Board containing the information specified in paragraph (5).

9(5) The information specified in this paragraph is–

(a) the full title of the participant,

(b) in the case of a participant which is a registered pension scheme or a superannuation fund, the Board's reference number relating to the scheme or fund concerned,

(c) details of the information received by the trustee;

(d) a statement setting out the reasons for the trustee's belief that–

    (i) in the case of a participant which is a registered pension scheme or a superannuation fund, the participant is not eligible to participate in the scheme, or

    (ii) in the case of a participant which is a recognised overseas pension scheme, the Board would be likely to have reason to revoke or withdraw their approval of the participant.

9(6)   A notice under paragraph (4) above shall be accompanied by a copy of any document in the trustee's possession that contains information in support of his belief as mentioned in paragraph (5)(d), together with a translation of that information into English where the document is in a language other than English.

9(7)   Where a notice is given by the trustee under paragraph (1) or (4) in relation to a participant which is a recognised overseas pension scheme, an officer of the Board may, for the purpose of ascertaining whether or not the participant is eligible to participate in the scheme, by notice require the trustee to furnish him, within such time (not being less than 21 days) as may be provided by the notice, such information relating to the participant as is specified in regulation 7(3).

9(8)   On receiving a notice given by the Board revoking or withdrawing approval under regulation 7(8) or (9), the trustee of the scheme shall forthwith give notice to the participant concerned that every unit in the scheme held by the participant, or by a nominee on its behalf, will be sold or cancelled by the trustee within 28 days after the date on which the notice given by the Board was received by the trustee.

9(9)   A notice given by the trustee under paragraph (8) shall state the reason why the participant is not eligible to participate in the scheme.

9(10)   Where all the units referred to in paragraph (8) are sold or cancelled by the trustee within the period of 28 days referred to in that paragraph, the unit trust scheme shall not cease to have the characteristics specified in regulation 4(3)(a) and (b).

9(11)   Where any of the units referred to in paragraph (8) are not sold or cancelled by the trustee within the period of 28 days referred to in that paragraph, the unit trust scheme shall be regarded as ceasing to satisfy the characteristics specified in regulation 4(3)(a) and (b) with effect from the date on which the notice given by the Board under regulation 7(8) or (9) was received by the trustee.

9(12)   References in this regulation to a participant which is a registered pension scheme or a superannuation fund include references to a participant which is no longer a registered pension scheme or a superannuation fund but which was such a scheme or fund at the time when notice of approval was given by the Board to the trustee in accordance with regulation 7(5).

History – In reg. 9(2), the words "a registered pension scheme" substituted for the words "an exempt approved scheme" by SI 2006/745, art. 23(6)(a), with effect from 6 April 2006.
In reg. 9(4)(a), the words "a registered pension scheme" substituted for the words "an exempt approved scheme" by SI 2006/745, art. 23(6)(a), with effect from 6 April 2006.
In reg. 9(4)(b), the words "a recognised overseas pension scheme" substituted for the words "an overseas scheme" by SI 2006/745, art. 23(3), with effect from 6 April 2006.
In reg. 9(5)(b), the words "a registered pension scheme" substituted for the words "an exempt approved scheme" by SI 2006/745, art. 23(6)(a), with effect from 6 April 2006.
In reg. 9(5)(d)(i), the words "a registered pension scheme" substituted for the words "an exempt approved scheme" by SI 2006/745, art. 23(6)(a), with effect from 6 April 2006.
In reg. 9(5)(d)(ii), the words "a recognised overseas pension scheme" substituted for the words "an overseas scheme" by SI 2006/745, art. 23(3), with effect from 6 April 2006.
In reg. 9(7) the words "(whether or not the participant is an overseas scheme to which regulation 7(4) applies)" omitted by SI 2006/745, art. 23(6)(b), with effect from 6 April 2006.
In reg. 9(7) (twice), the words "a recognised overseas pension scheme" substituted for the words "an overseas scheme" by SI 2006/745, art. 23(3), with effect from 6 April 2006.
In reg. 9(12) (twice), the words "a registered pension scheme" substituted for the words "an exempt approved scheme" by SI 2006/745, art. 23(6)(a), with effect from 6 April 2006.

RESPONSIBILITIES OF TRUSTEE OF A PENSION FUNDS POOLING SCHEME

10(1)   The trustee of a pension funds pooling scheme shall be responsible for negotiating and agreeing with an officer of the Board on behalf of the participants the matters specified in paragraph (2).

10(2)   The matters specified in this paragraph are–

(a)
    (i)   a method of calculating the amount of any income arising from the scheme property in each accounting period of the scheme, and of attributing to each participant the appropriate allocation of that amount;

    (ii)   the amount of any income arising from the scheme property in each accounting period of the scheme, and the amount of that income that is attributable to each participant;

(b)   the amount of any profits or gains arising in each accounting period of the scheme in respect of rents or receipts from the scheme property in that period that are attributable to each of those participants in the scheme which are chargeable on such profits or gains under Schedule A;

(c)   the amount of any interest of money or other annual profits or gains from the scheme property arising in each accounting period of the scheme that are attributable to each of those participants in the scheme which are chargeable on such interest or other annual profits or gains under Schedule D;

(d)   the amount of any dividends or other distributions from the scheme property arising in each accounting period of the scheme that are attributable to each of those participants in the scheme which are chargeable on such dividends or other distributions under Schedule F;

(e)

> (i)   where in an accounting period an event occurs that gives rise, or may give rise, to a balancing allowance or a balancing charge under the 1990 Act to or on those participants which were participants immediately before or immediately after that event, a method of computing the amount of the balancing allowance or charge attributable to each of those participants;
>
> (ii)   the amount of the balancing allowance or charge referred to in paragraph (i) of this sub-paragraph that is attributable to each of the participants concerned;

(f)   in relation to expenditure to which regulation 4(3)(f) applies, the amount of any such expenditure incurred in each accounting period of the scheme which is–

> (i)   capital expenditure for a chargeable period in relation to which Part I of the 1990 Act applies, or
>
> (ii)   capital expenditure on the provision of machinery or plant in respect of which a writing-down allowance is to be, or may be, made in accordance with sections 24 to 26 of the 1990 Act;

(g)   the amount of the expenditure calculated in accordance with sub-paragraph (f) for an accounting period that is attributable to each participant;

(h)   where, in relation to a building or structure which forms part of the scheme property, an event occurs in an accounting period which gives rise, or may give rise, to a balancing allowance or a balancing charge under the 1990 Act to or on each of the participants which were participants immediately before or immediately after that event, the amount of any sale, insurance, salvage or compensation moneys within the meaning of section 156 of the 1990 Act which are relevant to that event;

(j)   the disposal value, calculated in accordance with section 26 of the 1990 Act, of any plant and machinery forming part of the scheme property which is or may be required to be brought into account for a chargeable period;

(k)   the form of the certificate referred to in paragraph (3).

10(3)   The trustee of a pension funds pooling scheme shall also be responsible for providing within three months after the end of each accounting period of the scheme to each participant in the scheme in that period, a certificate in relation to that participant showing the information specified in paragraph (4).

10(4)   The information specified in this paragraph is–

(a)   the amount of the income agreed with the officer of the Board under paragraph (2)(a)(ii) which is attributable to that participant for the accounting period concerned;

(b)   the amount (if any) agreed with the officer of the Board under paragraph (2)(b) to be chargeable under Schedule A which is attributable to that participant for the accounting period concerned;

(c)   the amount (if any) agreed with the officer of the Board under paragraph (2)(c) to be chargeable under Schedule D which is attributable to that participant for the accounting period concerned;

(d)   the amount (if any) agreed with the officer of the Board under paragraph (2)(d) to be chargeable under Schedule F which is attributable to that participant for the accounting period concerned;

(e)   where in the accounting period concerned an event occurs that gives rise to a balancing allowance or a balancing charge under the 1990 Act, the amount (if any) of that allowance or charge agreed with the officer of the Board under paragraph (2)(e)(ii) which is attributable to that participant for that period;

(f)   the amount (if any) of the expenditure agreed with the officer of the Board under paragraph (2)(g) which is attributable to that participant for the accounting period concerned;

(g)   where applicable, the parts of amounts of sale, insurance, salvage or compensation moneys in relation to events occurring in the accounting period concerned, and of the disposal values of plant and machinery agreed with the officer of the Board under paragraph (2)(h) and (j), which are attributable to that participant for that period.

10(5)   In this regulation any reference to a participant in the scheme in relation to an accounting period includes a reference to a participant which, although not a participant throughout that period, was a participant at some time during that period.

DUTIES OF TRUSTEE OF A PENSION FUNDS POOLING SCHEME – ANNUAL PROVISION OF INFORMATION

11(1)   Where, at the end of a tax year, a unit trust scheme has the characteristics specified in regulation 4(3), the trustee of that scheme shall, within three months after the end of that year ("the relevant year"), provide to an officer of the Board, in a form authorised, or in the form provided, by the Board–

(a)   the information concerning each participant in the scheme specified in paragraph (2) or, as the case may be, paragraph (3), and

(b)   a declaration made by the trustee and signed by him or, if the trustee is a company, signed by the company secretary or other person authorised by the company for that purpose, that the information so provided is correct to the best of the declarant's knowledge and belief.

11(2)   As regards a participant in the relevant year which is a registered pension scheme or a superannuation fund, the information is–

(a)   the full title of the scheme or fund;

(b)   the Board's reference number relating to the scheme or fund;

(c)   a copy of any certificate referred to in regulation 10(3) which was supplied by the trustee to the participant in respect of any accounting period of the scheme ending in or at the end of the relevant year;

(d)   where the trustee has in the relevant year received a notice given by the Board under regulation 7(8) or (9) revoking or withdrawing approval in relation to that participant–

(i)   a copy of the notice given to the participant by the trustee under regulation 9(8);

(ii)   the date or dates (if any), whether during the relevant year or subsequently but prior to the making of the declaration under paragraph (1)(b), on which units held by the participant, or by a nominee on its behalf, at the time the notice given by the Board was received by the trustee, were sold or cancelled;

(iii)   if applicable, the date on which the participant ceased to participate in the scheme;

(e)   where the trustee has not, whether in the relevant year or subsequently but prior to the making of the declaration under paragraph (1)(b), received a notice given by the Board under regulation 7(8) or (9) revoking or withdrawing approval in relation to that participant, confirmation that the participant had not at any time in that year received notification from the Board that it was not a registered pension scheme or, as the case may be, a superannuation fund.

11(3)   As regards a participant in the relevant year which is a recognised overseas pension scheme, the information is–

(a)   the full title of the scheme;

(b)   details of any matters falling within sub-paragraphs (b) to (f) of regulation 7(3) which, by reason of changes to those matters having occurred in the relevant year, differ from–

(i)   the details of those matters which were included in the trustee's application under regulation 7(1) in respect of the participant, or

(ii)   (if applicable) the details of those matters which were most recently provided in accordance with this sub-paragraph in respect of the participant in relation to tax years ending before the relevant year;

(c)   the like information as is specified in paragraph (2)(c);

(d)   if applicable, the like information as is specified in paragraph (2)(d).

11(4)   As regards a participant in the relevant year which is a recognised overseas pension scheme, an officer of the Board may, at any time after the form referred to in paragraph (1) has been provided to him by the trustee of the scheme, by notice require the trustee to furnish him, within such time (not being less than 21 days) as may be provided by the notice, with a statement in writing setting out details of matters–

(a)   falling within sub-paragraphs (b) to (f)of regulation 7(3) with respect to that scheme, and

(b)   subsisting at any time during the relevant year.

11(5)   In this regulation any reference to a participant in the relevant year which is a registered pension scheme or a superannuation fund or a recognised overseas pension scheme (as the case may be)–

(a)   includes a reference to a participant which, although not a participant throughout that year, was a participant at some time during that year, and

(b)   includes a reference to a participant which is no longer a registered pension scheme or a superannuation fund or a recognised overseas pension scheme but which was such a scheme or fund at the time when notice of approval was given by the Board to the trustee of the scheme in accordance with regulation 7(5).

History – In reg. 11(2) (twice), the words "a registered pension scheme" substituted for the words "an exempt approved scheme" by SI 2006/745, art. 23(6)(a), with effect from 6 April 2006.

In reg. 11(3), the words "a recognised overseas pension scheme" substituted for the words "an overseas scheme" by SI 2006/745, art. 23(3), with effect from 6 April 2006.

In reg. 11(3)(b) the word "(f)" substituted for the words "(g) and, where the scheme is not one to which regulation 7(4) applies, sub-paragraphs (h) to (o)" by SI 2006/745, art. 23(7), with effect from 6 April 2006.

In reg. 11(4), the words "a recognised overseas pension scheme" substituted for the words "an overseas scheme" by SI 2006/745, art. 23(3), with effect from 6 April 2006.

In reg. 11(4)(a) the word "(f)" substituted for the words "(g) and, where the scheme is not one to which regulation 7(4) applies, sub-paragraphs (h) to (o)" by SI 2006/745, art. 23(7), with effect from 6 April 2006.

In reg. 11(5) (twice), the words "a recognised overseas pension scheme" substituted for the words "an overseas scheme" by SI 2006/745, art. 23(3), with effect from 6 April 2006.

In reg. 11(5), the words "a registered pension scheme" substituted for the words "an exempt approved scheme" by SI 2006/745, art. 23(6)(a), with effect from 6 April 2006.

Statutory Instruments

INCOME TAX (PAYMENTS ON ACCOUNT) REGULATIONS 1996

(SI 1996/1654, as amended by SI 1997/2491 and SI 2008/838)

Made on 26 June 1996 by the Commissioners of Inland Revenue, in exercise of the powers conferred on them by s. 59A(1) of the Taxes Management Act 1970. Operative from 17 July 1996.

1(1) These Regulations may be cited as the Income Tax (Payments on Account) Regulations 1996 and shall come into force on 17th July 1996.

1(2) Regulation 3 shall have effect as respects the year 1996–97 and subsequent years of assessment.

1(3) Regulation 4 shall have effect as respects the year 1997–98 and subsequent years of assessment.

2 In these Regulations "subsection (1)" means subsection (1) of section 59A of the Taxes Management Act 1970.

3 The prescribed amount for the purposes of paragraph (c) of subsection (1) is the amount of £1,000.

History – In reg. 3 the sum of "£1,000" substituted for "£500" by SI 2008/838, reg. 2, with effect from 6 April 2009 in relation to 2009–10 and subsequent years of assessment.

4 The prescribed proportion for the purposes of paragraph (d) of subsection (1), that is to say, the proportion which the relevant amount as mentioned in paragraph (c) of subsection (1) bears to the assessed amount as mentioned in paragraph (b) of subsection (1), is the proportion of one to five.

History – In reg. 4, word "five" substituted for "four" by SI 1997/2491, reg. 2, operative from 7 November 1997.

MANUFACTURED OVERSEAS DIVIDENDS (FRENCH INDEMNITY PAYMENTS) REGULATIONS 1996

(SI 1996/1826, as amended by SI 1996/2642 and SI 2007/2484)

Made on 12 July 1996 by the Treasury, in exercise of the powers conferred on them by para. 1(1) and 8 of Sch. 23A to the Income and Corporation Taxes Act 1988. Operative from 1 August 1996.

CITATION AND COMMENCEMENT

1 These Regulations may be cited as the Manufactured Overseas Dividends (French Indemnity Payments) Regulations 1996 and shall come into force on 1st August 1996.

INTERPRETATION

2(1) In these Regulations–

"French equities" means shares of any company resident in France;

"French indemnity payment" means a payment, representative of a dividend on French equities, that a party to a transaction for the sale of those equities is required, under the rules of the Society of French Stock Exchanges, to make to the other party to that transaction;

"manufactured overseas dividend" shall be construed in accordance with paragraph 4(1) of Schedule 23A;

"Schedule 23A" means Schedule 23A to the Taxes Act;

"the Tax Acts" has the meaning given by section 831(2) of the Taxes Act;

"the Taxes Act" means the Income and Corporation Taxes Act 1988.

2(2) References in these Regulations to "the dividend concerned" are references to the dividend of which a French indemnity payment is representative.

2(3) For the purposes of the Income Tax Acts references in these Regulations to "the sale and repurchase of French equities" include an arrangement which–

(a)   involves the sale of French equities and the subsequent purchase of French equities, and

(b)   is a repo.

2(4) In paragraph (3) "repo" shall be construed in accordance with section 569 of the Income Tax Act 2007 (read, if appropriate, with the modifications made by the Sale and Repurchase of Securities (Modification of Enactments) Regulations 2007).

2(5) For the purposes of the Corporation Tax Acts references in these Regulations to "the sale and repurchase of French equities" include an arrangement which–

(a)   involves the sale of French equities and the subsequent purchase of French equities, and

(b)   is a debtor repo, a debtor quasi-repo, a creditor repo or a creditor quasi-repo.

2(6) In paragraph (5) "debtor repo", "debtor quasi-repo", "creditor repo" and "creditor quasi-repo" shall be construed in accordance with Schedule 13 to the Finance Act 2007 (read, if appropriate, with the modifications made by the Sale and Repurchase of Securities (Modification of Schedule 13 to the Finance Act 2007) Regulations 2007).

History – Reg. 2(3)–(6) substituted for reg. 2(3) by SI 2007/2484, reg. 2(2), with effect from 1 October 2007, in relation to arrangements that come into force on or after that day.

TAX TREATMENT OF FRENCH INDEMNITY PAYMENTS

3(1) This regulation applies where a person makes or receives a payment of a manufactured overseas dividend that is a French indemnity payment, other than a payment which arises from an arrangement for the sale and repurchase of French equities.

3(2) For the purposes of the Tax Acts–

(a)   paragraph 4 of Schedule 23A shall not apply in relation to the indemnity payment, but where the maker of the payment receives the dividend concerned, he (and no other person) shall be chargeable to tax in respect of that dividend;

(b)   subject to paragraph (3)–

(i)   relief by way of deduction in computing profits or gains, or deduction or set off against income or total profits, shall not be given under any provision of the Tax Acts in respect of the indemnity payment to the maker of the payment, and

(ii)   the indemnity payment shall not be chargeable to tax.

Statutory Instruments

3(3)   For the purposes of the Tax Acts and the Taxation of Chargeable Gains Act 1992 the amount paid or payable in respect of the sale of the French equities to which the dividend concerned relates shall, as respects both the seller and the purchaser of those equities, be taken as reduced by the amount of the indemnity payment.

3(4)   Any entitlement to relief under Part XVIII of the Taxes Act (double taxation relief) in respect of the indemnity payment shall be extinguished.

History – In reg. 3(2)(a), former reference to ICTA 1988, Sch. 23A, para. 5 omitted by SI 1996/2642, operative from 6 November 1996.

4(1)   This regulation applies where a person makes or receives a payment of a manufactured overseas dividend that is a French indemnity payment arising from an arrangement for the sale and repurchase of French equities.

4(2)   For the purposes of the Tax Acts–

(a)   paragraph 4 of Schedule 23A shall not apply in relation to the indemnity payment, but where the maker of the payment receives the dividend concerned, he (and no other person) shall be chargeable to tax in respect of that dividend;

(b)   the indemnity payment shall be treated as an annual payment, within section 349(1) of the Taxes Act, but so that no amount is required to be deducted on account of income tax from the amount of the payment, or accounted for under section 350 of that Act;

(c)   in relation to a recipient of the indemnity payment, or a person claiming title to it through or under him, who is resident in the United Kingdom or, if not so resident, is carrying on business through a branch or agency in the United Kingdom, the payment shall be treated as if it were an overseas dividend of an amount equal to the amount of the payment, but without prejudice to paragraph (3).

4(3)   Any entitlement to relief under Part XVIII of the Taxes Act in respect of the indemnity payment shall be extinguished.

History – In reg. 4(2)(a), former reference to ICTA 1988, Sch. 23A, para. 5 omitted by SI 1996/2642, operative from 6 November 1996.

TAXATION OF BENEFITS UNDER PILOT SCHEMES (EARNINGS TOP-UP) ORDER 1996

(SI 1996/2396)

Made on 13 September 1996 by the Treasury, in exercise of the powers conferred on them by s. 151(1)(a), (2), (5) and (7) of the Finance Act 1996. Operative from 8 October 1996.

CITATION, COMMENCEMENT AND EFFECT

1(1) This Order may be cited as the Taxation of Benefits under Pilot Schemes (Earnings Top-up) Order 1996 and shall come into force on 8th October 1996.

1(2) This Order shall have effect in relation to amounts of Earnings Top-up payable on or after 8th October 1996.

INTERPRETATION

2 In this Order–

"**benefit**" shall be construed in accordance with section 151(6) of the Finance Act 1996;

"**Earnings Top-up**" means the benefit payable under that name by virtue of a Government pilot scheme;

"**Government pilot scheme**" has the meaning given by subsections (3) and (4) of section 151 of the Finance Act 1996.

EXEMPTION OF EARNINGS TOP-UP FROM INCOME TAX

3 The Income Tax Acts shall have effect in relation to any amount of Earnings Top-up as if it were wholly exempt from income tax and, accordingly, to be disregarded in computing the amount of any receipts brought into account for income tax purposes.

Statutory Instruments

INSURANCE COMPANIES (RESERVES) (TAX) REGULATIONS 1996

(SI 1996/2991 as amended by SI 1999/1408, SI 2001/3629, SI 2002/1409, SI 2004/3260, SI 2006/3218, SI 2006/3389, SI 2008/954, SI 2008/2679 and FA 2012)

Made on 27 November 1996 by the Treasury, in exercise of the powers conferred on them by s. 444BA(10), 444BB(1), (3), (4) and (5), 444BC and 444BD(1), (4) and (5) of the Income and Corporation Taxes Act 1988. Operative from 23 December 1996.

PART I – GENERAL

CITATION, COMMENCEMENT AND EFFECT

1   These Regulations may be cited as the Insurance Companies (Reserves) (Tax) Regulations 1996, shall come into force on 23rd December 1996, and shall have effect for accounting periods of insurance companies ending on or after that day.

INTERPRETATION

2(1)   In these Regulations unless the context otherwise requires–

"the Board" means the Commissioners for Her Majesty's Revenue and Customs;

"company tax return" has the meaning given by paragraph 3(1) of Schedule 18 to the Finance Act 1998;

"credit insurance business" has the meaning given by subsection (7) of section 444BD;

"credit insurance equalisation reserve" means a reserve which is an equivalent reserve for the purposes of section 444BD by virtue of subsection (3) of that section;

"double taxation relief" has the meaning given by subsection (6) of section 444BB;

"EEA firm" means an EEA firm of the kind mentioned in paragraph 5(d) or (da) of Schedule 3 to the Financial Services and Markets Act 2000;

"equivalent reserve" shall be construed in accordance with section 444BD;

"equalisation reserve rules" means the rules in Chapter 1.4 of INSPRU made by the Financial Services Authority under the Financial Services and Markets Act 2000;

"INSPRU" means the Prudential Sourcebook for Insurers made by the Financial Services Authority under the Financial Services and Markets Act 2000;

"paragraph 58 method of accounting on a non-annual basis" means the method of accounting on a non-annual basis described in paragraph 58 of Schedule 3 to the Large and Medium-sized Companies and Groups (Accounts and Reports) Regulations 2008;

"return period" means the period covered in a document prepared by an insurance company for the purposes of section 9.3 of the Prudential Sourcebook (Insurers);

"section 444BA",

"section 444BB",

"section 444BC" and

"section 444BD" mean sections 444BA, 444BB, 444BC and 444BD respectively of the Taxes Act;

"the Taxes Act" means the Income and Corporation Taxes Act 1988;

"Treaty firm" means a firm which has permission under paragraph 4 of Schedule 4 to the Financial Services and Markets Act 2000 (as a result of qualifying for authorisation under paragraph 2 of that Schedule) to effect or carry out contracts of insurance in the United Kingdom and, in this definition, **"contract of insurance"** has the meaning given by Article 3(1) of the Financial Services and Markets Act 2000 (Regulated Activities) Order 2001;

2(2)   In these Regulations **"statutory accounts"**, in relation to a company, means–

(a)   the annual accounts of the company prepared in accordance with Part 15 of the Companies Act 2006, or

(b)   if the company is not required to prepare such accounts, the accounts which it is required to keep under the law of its home state or, if it is not so required to keep accounts, such of its accounts as most closely correspond to accounts which it would have been required to prepare if the provisions of that Part applied to the company.

2(3)   For the purposes of these Regulations a return period and an accounting period are related if any day falls within both the return period and the accounting period.

History – In reg. 2(1), in the definition of "the Board", the words "Commissioners for Her Majesty's Revenue and Customs" substituted for the words "Commissioners of Inland Revenue" by SI 2008/2679, reg. 3(2), with effect in relation to accounting periods beginning on or after 6 April 2008 and ending on or after 30 October 2008.
In reg. 2(1), the definition of "branch" omitted by SI 2008/2679, reg. 3(3), with effect in relation to accounting periods beginning on or after 6 April 2008 and ending on or after 30 October 2008.
In reg. 2(1), in the definition of "EEA firm", the words "or (da)" inserted by SI 2008/2679, reg. 3(4), with effect in relation to accounting periods beginning on or after 6 April 2008 and ending on or after 30 October 2008.
In reg. 2(1), in the definition of "equalisation reserve rules", the words "Chapter 1.4 of INSPRU" substituted for the words "Chapter 7.5 of the Integrated Prudential Sourcebook" by SI 2008/2679, reg. 3(5), with effect in relation to accounting periods beginning on or after 6 April 2008 and ending on or after 30 October 2008.
In reg. 2(1), the definition of "paragraph 52 method of accounting on a non-annual basis" omitted by SI 2008/2679, reg. 3(6), with effect in relation to accounting periods beginning on or after 6 April 2008 and ending on or after 30 October 2008.
In reg. 2(1), the definition of "the Prudential Sourcebook (Insurers)" omitted by SI 2008/2679, reg. 3(7), with effect in relation to accounting periods beginning on or after 6 April 2008 and ending on or after 30 October 2008.
In reg. 2(1), the definition of "INSPRU" inserted by SI 2008/2679, reg. 3(8), with effect in relation to accounting periods beginning on or after 6 April 2008 and ending on or after 30 October 2008.
In reg. 2(1), the definition of "paragraph 58 method of accounting on a non-annual basis" inserted by SI 2008/2679, reg. 3(8), with effect in relation to accounting periods beginning on or after 6 April 2008 and ending on or after 30 October 2008.
In reg. 2(1) the definition of "equalisation reserve rules" substituted by SI 2004/3260, reg. 2(2), with effect for accounting periods of insurance companies ending on or after 31 December 2004.
In reg. 2(1):
(1)   the definition of "company tax return" inserted;
(2)   the definition of "EEA firm" substituted for that of "EC company" (which formerly read "has the same meaning as in the 1982 Act;")
(3)   the definition of "equalisation reserves rules" inserted;
(4)   the definition of "the Management Act" (which formerly read "means the Taxes Management Act 1970") omitted;
(5)   the definition of "the Prudential Sourcebook (Insurers)" inserted;
(6)   in the definition of "return period", the words "9.3 of the Prudential Sourcebook (Insurers)" substituted for "17 of the 1982 Act";
(7)   the definition of "section 34A regulations" (which formerly read "means regulations made under section 34A of the 1982 Act") omitted;
(8)   the definition of "Treaty firm" inserted; and
(9)   the definition of "the 1982 Act" (which formerly read "means the Insurance Companies Act 1982") omitted,
all by SI 2001/3629, art. 146 and 147 which came into force on 1 December 2001, except that the amendments made by (1), (3) to (7) and (9) above have effect in relation to periods of account ending on or after 1 December 2001.
In reg. 2(2)(a) the words "Part 15 of the Companies Act 2006" substituted for "Part VII of the Companies Act 1985" by SI 2008/954, art. 46, with effect from 6 April 2008.

DIFFERING TREATMENTS OF RESERVES

3(1)   This regulation applies in any case where for any accounting period–

(a)   an insurance company maintains any reserve to which these Regulations apply, and

(b)   the amount of that reserve for the purposes of the Tax Acts is different from the amount of that reserve as maintained for regulatory purposes.

3(2)   A separate computation of the amount of the reserve for the purposes of the Tax Acts and of the amount of the reserve as maintained for regulatory purposes shall be made for each accounting period until, in any later accounting period, the two computations produce the same opening balance for the reserve.

3(3)   For the purposes of this regulation a reserve is maintained by a company for regulatory purposes if it is maintained–

(a)   by virtue of equalisation reserves rules, or

(b)   for the purposes of the company's statutory accounts, or

(c)   for the purposes of any credit insurance business in accordance with requirements specified in subsection (3) of section 444BD.

History – In reg. 3(3)(a), the words "equalisation reserves rules" substituted for "section 34A regulations" by SI 2001/3629, art. 146 and 151 in relation to periods of account ending on or after 1 December 2001.

PART II – EQUALISATION RESERVES, ETC.

SCOPE OF THIS PART

4(1)   Subject to paragraph (2), this Part of these Regulations applies to–

(a)   any equalisation reserve which an insurance company is required to maintain by virtue of equalisation reserves rules, and

(b)   any reserve which is an equivalent reserve by virtue of subsection (2) of section 444BD.

4(2)   This part of these Regulations does not apply to any credit insurance equalisation reserve.

History – In reg. 4(1)(a), the words "equalisation reserves rules" substituted for "section 34A regulations" by SI 2001/3629, art. 146 and 151 in relation to periods of account ending on or after 1 December 2001

ACCOUNTING ON A NON-ANNUAL BASIS

Non-annual Accounts: Tax Returns Prepared on an Annual Basis

5   [Omitted by SI 2008/2679, reg. 4.]

History – Reg. 5 omitted by SI 2008/2679, reg. 4, with effect in relation to accounting periods beginning on or after 6 April 2008 and ending on or after 30 October 2008.
In former reg. 5(2), the words "equalisation reserves rules" substituted for "section 34A regulations" (twice) by SI 2001/3629, art. 146 and 151 and, in former reg. 5(2):
(a)   the words "9.3 of the Prudential Sourcebook (Insurers)" substituted for "17 of the 1982 Act"; and
(b)   the words "company tax return" substituted for "return under section 11 of the Management Act" and,
in former reg. 5(4), the words "Financial Services Authority pursuant to Chapter 9 of the Prudential Sourcebook (Insurers)" substituted for "Secretary of State pursuant to section 22 of the 1982 Act"; and the words "prescribed by the Accounts and Statements Rules contained in that Chapter" substituted for "prescribed by the Insurance Companies (Accounts and Statements) Regulations 1996", by SI 2001/3629, art. 146 and 148, all the above amendments being with effect in relation to periods of account ending on or after 1 December 2001, the date on which SI 2001/3629 came into force.

GENERAL PROVISIONS

Companies Carrying on Mutual Business and Business other than Mutual Business

6(1)   This regulation applies in any case where an insurance company which, in accordance with equalisation reserves rules, is required to make transfers into or out of an equalisation reserve in respect of any business carried on by that company for any accounting period, is carrying on both mutual business and business other than mutual business for the whole or any part of that period.

6(2)   Paragraphs (a) and (b) of subsection (2) of section 444BA shall be modified so as to provide that, for the purposes of corporation tax, the amounts of the net premiums earned, the net premiums written and the net claims incurred which, in accordance with equalisation reserves rules, are used for the purpose of computing the amounts transferred into or out of the equalisation reserve or the amount of the maximum reserve in relation to the equalisation reserve for the accounting period in question, shall be restricted to the amounts attributed to business other than mutual business.

6(3)   For the purposes of corporation tax, the modification specified in paragraph (2) shall be made before subsections (4) to (6) of section 444BA are applied.

6(4)   In paragraph (2) **"net premiums earned"**, **"net premiums written"**, **"net claims incurred"** and **"maximum reserve"** have the meanings given by equalisation reserves rules.

History – In reg. 6(1), (2) and (4), the words "equalisation reserves rules" substituted for "section 34A regulations" by SI 2001/3629, art. 146 and 151 in relation to periods of account ending on or after 1 December 2001

EEA FIRMS AND TREATY FIRMS

History – Heading to reg. 7 substituted by SI 2001/3629, art. 146 and 149 which came into force on 1 December 2001. Formerly, it read "EC COMPANIES".

7(1)   This regulation applies in any case where for any accounting period–

(a)   an equivalent reserve is maintained, otherwise than by virtue of equalisation reserves rules, by an EEA firm or a Treaty firm carrying on business in the United Kingdom through a permanent establishment, and

(b)   the three conditions specified in paragraphs (2) to (4) are satisfied.

7(2)   The first condition is that the permanent establishment in the United Kingdom has submitted, together with its company tax return, a balance sheet **("the permanent establishment balance sheet")** in respect of the trade of the permanent establishment.

7(3)   The second condition is that the permanent establishment balance sheet includes as a liability an amount in respect of an equalisation reserve which is equal to the amount which it would have been required to include as a liability in respect of an equalisation reserve maintained by virtue of equalisation reserves rules if the permanent establishment had been subject to such rules.

7(4) The third condition is that a balance sheet drawn up on the same day as the permanent establishment balance sheet for the purposes of the company's statutory accounts (**"the company balance sheet"**), either–

(a)   includes as a liability an amount in respect of an equalisation reserve equal to or greater than the amount in respect of the equalisation reserve included in the permanent establishment balance sheet, or

(b)   in a case where the amount in respect of the equalisation reserve included in the permanent establishment balance sheet exceeds the amount in respect of the equalisation reserve included in the company balance sheet, shows the amount of the excess in the company balance sheet otherwise than as funds belonging to, or available for distribution either immediately or prospectively to, the proprietors of the company.

7(5) For the purpose of calculating the amount of the excess referred to in paragraph (4), any amount in the company balance sheet denominated in a currency other than sterling is to be translated into sterling at the London closing exchange rate on the last day of the accounting period in question.

7(6) Section 444BA shall have effect, subject to the modification specified in paragraph (7), in relation to the equalisation reserve included in the permanent establishment balance sheet as it has effect in relation to equalisation reserves maintained by virtue of equalisation reserves rules.

7(7) Section 444BA shall be modified so as to provide in addition that in any case where, after the conditions specified in paragraphs (2) to (4) have been satisfied in an earlier accounting period, any of those conditions ceases to be satisfied in a later accounting period, then, for the purposes of the Tax Acts–

(a)   any balance which exists in the reserve at the end of the later accounting period shall be deemed to have been transferred out of the reserve immediately before the end of that accounting period;

(b)   that transfer shall be deemed to be a transfer in respect of that company's business for that accounting period; and

(c)   the amount of the reserve shall thereupon be deemed to be nil.

History – In reg. 7, in each place, the words "permanent establishment" substituted for the word "branch" in each place by SI 2008/2679, reg. 5, with effect in relation to accounting periods beginning on or after 6 April 2008 and ending on or after 30 October 2008.

In reg. 7(1)(a), the words "EEA firm or a Treaty firm" substituted for "EC company" by SI 2001/3629, art. 146 and 149 which came into force on 1 December 2001 and, the words "equalisation reserves rules" substituted for "section 34A regulations" by SI 2001/3629, art. 146 and 151 in relation to periods of account ending on or after 1 December 2001.

In reg. 7(2) the words "company tax return" substituted for "return under section 11 of the Management Act" by SI 2001/3629, art. 146 and 149, in relation to periods of account ending on or after 1 December 2001.

In reg. 7(3) and (6), the words "equalisation reserves rules" substituted for "section 34A regulations" by SI 2001/3629, art. 146 and 151 in relation to periods of account ending on or after 1 December 2001.

In reg. 7(3) the word "rules" substituted for the word "regulations" by SI 2002/1409, reg. 5 with effect from 2 July 2001.

CERTAIN INSURANCE BUSINESS CARRIED ON OUTSIDE THE UNITED KINGDOM

8(1) Subject to regulation 8B, this regulation applies in any case where for any accounting period–

(a)   an equivalent reserve is maintained, otherwise than by virtue of equalisation reserves rules, in respect of any insurance business which is carried on outside the United Kingdom by a company resident in the United Kingdom, and

(b)   the condition specified in paragraph (2) is satisfied.

8(2) The condition is that the company prepares statutory accounts in which the balance sheet includes as a liability an amount in respect of an equalisation reserve which is equal to the amount which it would have been required to include as a liability in respect of an equalisation reserve maintained by virtue of equalisation reserves rules if the company had been subject to such rules.

8(3) For the purpose of calculating the amount of the liability referred to in paragraph (2), any amount in the company balance sheet denominated in a currency other than sterling is to be translated into sterling at the London closing exchange rate on the last day of the accounting period in question.

8(4) Section 444BA shall have effect, subject to the modification specified in paragraph (5), in relation to the equalisation reserve included in the statutory accounts as it has effect in relation to equalisation reserves maintained by virtue of equalisation reserves rules.

8(5) Section 444BA shall be modified so as to provide in addition that in any case where, after the condition specified in paragraph (2) has been satisfied in an earlier accounting period, that condition ceases to be satisfied in a later accounting period, then, for the purposes of the Tax Acts–

(a)   any balance which exists in the reserve at the end of the later accounting period shall be deemed to have been transferred out of the reserve immediately before the end of that accounting period;

(b)   that transfer shall be deemed to be a transfer in respect of that company's business for that accounting period; and

(c)   the amount of the reserve shall thereupon be deemed to be nil.

8(6)   In paragraph (1)(a) **"insurance business"** means business which consists of the effecting or carrying out of contracts of insurance and, for the purposes of this definition, "contract of insurance" has the meaning given by Article 3(1) of the Financial Services and Markets Act 2000 (Regulated Activities) Order 2001.

History – In reg. 8(1), the words "Subject to regulation 8B," were inserted by SI 1999/1408, reg. 7(2) which is operative from 10 June 1999.

In reg. 8(1)(a), the words "(within the meaning of the 1982 Act)", which appeared after the words "in respect of any insurance business", omitted by SI 2001/3629, art. 146 and 150 which came into force on 1 December 2001.

In reg. 8(1)(a), (2) and (4), the words "equalisation reserves rules" substituted for "section 34A regulations" by SI 2001/3629, art. 146 and 151 in relation to periods of account ending on or after 1 December 2001.

In reg. 8(2) the word "rules" substituted for the word "regulations" by SI 2002/1409, reg. 5 with effect from 2 July 2001.

Reg. 8(6) inserted by SI 2001/3629, art. 146 and 150 which came into force on 1 December 2001.

Cross references – SI 2006/3389, reg. 12: modification of reg. 8 with effect from 8 January 2007 with effect for periods of account beginning on or after 1 April 2006.

SI 2008/2646, reg. 4: modification of reg. 8 in relation to EEA general insurers with effect for accounting periods beginning on or after 28 October 2008.

CERTAIN INSURANCE BUSINESS CARRIED ON OUTSIDE THE UNITED KINGDOM BY A CONTROLLED FOREIGN COMPANY – NON-ANNUAL ACCOUNTS BUT RETURNS PREPARED ON AN ANNUAL BASIS

8A(1)   Subject to regulation 8B, this regulation applies in any case where–

(a)   paragraphs (1) and (2) of regulation 8 apply in respect of an accounting period of a CFC (within the meaning of Part 9A of the Taxation (International and Other Provisions) Act 2010), and

(b)   the statutory accounts drawn up by the CFC for that period use a paragraph 58 method of accounting on a non-annual basis.

(c)   [Omitted by SI 2008/2679, reg. 6(2).]

8A(2)   Paragraph (3) of regulation 8 shall apply in relation to this regulation as it applies in relation to that regulation.

8A(3)   Section 444BA shall have effect, subject to the modifications specified in paragraph (5) of regulation 8 and in paragraph (4) of this regulation, in relation to the equalisation reserve included in the statutory accounts as it has effect in relation to equalisation reserves maintained by virtue of equalisation reserves rules.

8A(4)   The operation of paragraphs (a) and (b) of subsection (2) of section 444BA shall be modified so as to provide that, for the purposes of the Tax Acts, the amounts which are transferred into or out of the equalisation reserve in respect of the CFC's business for the accounting period in question shall be the amounts which would have been transferred into or out of the equalisation reserve if the CFC had been required to maintain an equalisation reserve by reference to accounts prepared on an accident year basis.

8A(5)   [Omitted by SI 2008/2679, reg. 6(3).]

8A(6)   For the purposes of paragraph (4), accounts are prepared on an accident year basis where the accounts and statements required to be deposited with the Financial Services Authority pursuant to Chapter 9 of IPRU(INS) are prepared using Forms 21, 22 and 23 prescribed by the Accounts and Statements Rules contained in that Chapter.

8A(7)   For the purposes of paragraph (6), **"IPRU(INS)"** means the Interim Prudential Sourcebook for Insurers made by the Financial Services Authority under the Financial Services and Markets Act 2000.

History – In reg. 8A(1)(a), the words "CFC (within the meaning of Part 9A of the Taxation (International and Other Provisions) Act 2010)" substituted for the words "controlled foreign company" by FA 2012, s. 180 and Sch. 20, para. 47(2)(a), with effect in relation to accounting periods of controlled foreign companies beginning on or after 1 January 2013.

In reg. 8A(1)(a), the word "and" inserted at the end by SI 2008/2679, reg. 6(2), with effect in relation to accounting periods beginning on or after 6 April 2008 and ending on or after 30 October 2008.

In reg. 8A(1)(b), "CFC" substituted for the words "controlled foreign company" by FA 2012, s. 180 and Sch. 20, para. 47(2)(b), with effect in relation to accounting periods of controlled foreign companies beginning on or after 1 January 2013.

In reg. 8A(1)(b), "paragraph 58" substituted for "paragraph 52" and the word "but" at the end omitted, by SI 2008/2679, reg. 6(2), with effect in relation to accounting periods beginning on or after 6 April 2008 and ending on or after 30 October 2008.

Reg. 8A(1)(c) omitted by SI 2008/2679, reg. 6(2), with effect in relation to accounting periods beginning on or after 6 April 2008 and ending on or after 30 October 2008.

In reg. 8A(3), the words "equalisation reserves rules" substituted for "section 34A regulations" by SI 2001/3629, art. 146 and 151 in relation to periods of account ending on or after 1 December 2001.

In reg. 8A(4), "CFC's" substituted for the words "controlled foreign company's" by FA 2012, s. 180 and Sch. 20, para. 47(3)(a), with effect in relation to accounting periods of controlled foreign companies beginning on or after 1 January 2013.

In reg. 8A(4), "the CFC" substituted for the words "the company" by FA 2012, s. 180 and Sch. 20, para. 47(3)(b), with effect in relation to accounting periods of controlled foreign companies beginning on or after 1 January 2013.

Reg. 8A(5) omitted by SI 2008/2679, reg. 6(3), with effect in relation to accounting periods beginning on or after 6 April 2008 and ending on or after 30 October 2008.

Reg. 8A(6) substituted by SI 2008/2679, reg. 6(4), with effect in relation to accounting periods beginning on or after 6 April 2008 and ending on or after 30 October 2008.

Reg. 8A(7) inserted by SI 2008/2679, reg. 6(5), with effect in relation to accounting periods beginning on or after 6 April 2008 and ending on or after 30 October 2008.

Reg. 8A introduced by SI 1999/1408, reg. 7, with respect to accounting periods ending after 30 June 1999.

DISAPPLICATION OF REGULATIONS 8 AND 8A WHERE CONTROLLED FOREIGN COMPANY PREPARES NON-ANNUAL ACCOUNTS AND FINAL REPLACEMENT OF THE TECHNICAL PROVISION DOES NOT TAKE PLACE IN CONFORMITY WITH THE COMPANIES ACT

8B Regulations 8 and 8A shall not apply in any case where for an accounting period a CFC (within the meaning of Part 9A of the Taxation (International and Other Provisions) Act 2010)–

(a) draws up its statutory accounts for that period using a paragraph 58 method of accounting on a non-annual basis, and

(b) the final replacement of the technical provision, as described in sub-paragraph (4) of that paragraph does not take place on or before the end of the year referred to in that sub-paragraph as the third year following the underwriting year.

History – In reg. 8B, the words "CFC (within the meaning of Part 9A of the Taxation (International and Other Provisions) Act 2010)" substituted for the words "controlled foreign company" by FA 2012, s. 180 and Sch. 20, para. 48, with effect in relation to accounting periods of controlled foreign companies beginning on or after 1 January 2013.

In reg. 8B(a), "paragraph 58" substituted for "paragraph 52" by SI 2008/2679, reg. 7, with effect in relation to accounting periods beginning on or after 6 April 2008 and ending on or after 30 October 2008.

Reg. 8B introduced by SI 1999/1408, reg. 7, with respect to accounting periods ending after 30 June 1999.

UNITED KINGDOM BRANCHES OF COMPANIES NOT RESIDENT IN THE UNITED KINGDOM WHICH MAINTAIN EQUALISATION RESERVES BY VIRTUE OF EQUALISATION RESERVES RULES

History – See history note after this regulation for details of the change in wording of the above heading made by SI 2001/3629.

9(1) If the three conditions prescribed in paragraphs (2) to (4) below are satisfied, section 444BA shall have effect in the case of an equalisation reserve maintained by an insurance company which–

(a) is not resident in the United Kingdom, and

(b) carries on business in the United Kingdom through a permanent establishment.

9(2) The first condition is that the permanent establishment in the United Kingdom has submitted, together with its "company tax return", a balance sheet (**"the permanent establishment balance sheet"**) in respect of the trade of the permanent establishment.

9(3) The second condition is that the permanent establishment balance sheet includes as a liability an amount in respect of an equalisation reserve maintained by virtue of equalisation reserves rules.

9(4) The third condition is that a balance sheet drawn up on the same day as the permanent establishment balance sheet for the purposes of the company's statutory accounts (**"the company balance sheet"**), either–

(a) includes as a liability an amount in respect of an equalisation reserve equal to or greater than the amount in respect of the equalisation reserve included in the permanent establishment balance sheet, or

(b) in a case where the amount in respect of the equalisation reserve included in the permanent establishment balance sheet exceeds the amount in respect of the equalisation reserve included in the company balance sheet, shows the amount of the excess in the company balance sheet otherwise than as funds belonging to, or available for distribution either immediately or prospectively to, the proprietors of the company.

9(5) For the purpose of calculating the amount of the excess referred to in paragraph (4), any amount in the company balance sheet denominated in a currency other than sterling is to be translated into sterling at the London closing exchange rate on the last day of the accounting period in question.

9(6) Where, after the conditions prescribed in paragraphs (2) to (4) have been satisfied in an earlier accounting period, any of those conditions ceases to be satisfied in a later accounting period, then, for the purposes of the Tax Acts–

(a) any balance which exists in the reserve at the end of the later accounting period shall be deemed to have been transferred out of the reserve immediately before the end of that accounting period;

(b)   that transfer shall be deemed to be a transfer in respect of that company's business for that accounting period; and

(c)   the amount of the reserve shall thereupon be deemed to be nil.

History – In reg. 9, "permanent establishment" substituted for "branch" in each place by SI 2008/2679, reg. 8(2), with effect in relation to accounting periods beginning on or after 6 April 2008 and ending on or after 30 October 2008.

In reg. 9(2), "company tax return" substituted for "return under section 11 of the Management Act" by SI 2008/2679, reg. 8(3), with effect in relation to accounting periods beginning on or after 6 April 2008 and ending on or after 30 October 2008.

In the heading to reg. 9 and in reg. 9(3), the words "equalisation reserves rules" substituted for "section 34A regulations" by SI 2001/3629, art. 146 and 151 in relation to periods of account ending on or after 1 December 2001.

DOUBLE TAXATION RELIEF

10(1)   This regulation applies in any case where an insurance company which, in accordance with equalisation reserves rules, is required to make transfers into or out of an equalisation reserve in respect of any business carried on by that company for any accounting period, is carrying on any business by reference to which double taxation relief is afforded in respect of any income or gains.

10(2)   Paragraphs (a) and (b) of subsection (2) of section 444BA shall be modified so as–

(a)   to require that the amounts which, in accordance with equalisation reserves rules, are transferred into or out of the equalisation reserve in respect of the company's business for the accounting period in question shall be apportioned amongst each permanent establishment outside the United Kingdom through which the company carries on business and business which is not carried on through permanent establishments outside the United Kingdom; and

(b)   to provide that only those amounts which, pursuant to sub-paragraph (a), are apportioned to each permanent establishment outside the United Kingdom through which the company carries on business shall be brought into account for the purposes of computing the profits or losses by reference to which double taxation relief is afforded.

10(3)   The apportionment of each transfer into the equalisation reserve which is required by this regulation shall be made in accordance with the formula–

$$\frac{A \times B}{C}$$

where–

A   is the amount which, in accordance with equalisation reserves rules, is transferred into the equalisation reserve in respect of the company's business for the accounting period in question;

B   is the amount of net premiums written by reference to which A is calculated that is attributable to business carried on through the permanent establishment outside the United Kingdom for the accounting period in question; and

C   is the amount of net premiums written by reference to which A is calculated for the accounting period in question.

10(4)   In paragraph (3) **"net premiums written"** means gross premiums written net of reinsurance premiums payable under reinsurance ceded.

10(5)   The apportionment of each transfer out of the equalisation reserve which is required by this regulation shall be made in accordance with the formula–

$$\frac{D \times E}{F}$$

where–

D   is the amount which, in accordance with equalisation reserves rules, is transferred out of the equalisation reserve in respect of the company's business for the accounting period in question;

E   is the amount of claims attributable to business carried on through the permanent establishment outside the United Kingdom that is to be taken into account in determining whether, by comparison with premiums, any transfer out of the equalisation reserve needs to be made for the period in question; and

F   is the amount of claims to be taken into account in determining whether, by comparison with premiums, any transfer out of the equalisation reserve needs to be made for the period in question.

10(6)   Paragraph (7) applies where–

(a)   an insurance company carries on business through one or more branches outside the United Kingdom,

(b)   an amount is transferred into an equalisation reserve in respect of the business of that company for any accounting period, and

(c)   the company has made an election for the purposes of subsection (4) of section 444BA so that there is an unrelieved transfer in relation to that accounting period.

10(7) The company—

(a)   shall apportion the amount transferred into the equalisation reserve in accordance with paragraph (3) without having regard to the existence of the unrelieved transfer, and

(b)   may then set the amount of the unrelieved transfer, or any part of that amount, against the amount transferred into the equalisation reserve for that accounting period (and the action of the company under this sub-paragraph is called **"the allocation"** in paragraph (8)).

10(8) The allocation may be made—

(a)   in such amounts, and

(b)   in relation to such of the apportioned amounts transferred into the equalisation reserve pursuant to paragraph (7)(a) (and whether in relation to business carried on in the United Kingdom or in relation to business which the company carries on through a permanent establishment outside the United Kingdom),

as the company thinks fit.

10(9) Paragraph (10) applies where—

(a)   an insurance company carries on business through one or more branches outside the United Kingdom,

(b)   an amount is transferred out of an equalisation reserve in respect of the business of that company for any accounting period, and

(c)   the accounting period is one to which any amount representing one or more unrelieved transfers has been carried forward under subsection (4) of section 444BA.

10(10) The company—

(a)   shall ascertain the amount to which the rule mentioned in subsection (2)(b) of section 444BA applies by virtue of the operation of subsection (5) of that section (in this paragraph and in paragraph (11) referred to as **"the ascertained amount"**), and

(b)   shall then apportion the ascertained amount.

10(11) Paragraph (5) shall apply for the purposes of the apportionment of the ascertained amount as it applies for the purposes of the apportionment of each transfer out of the equalisation reserve which is required by this regulation, with the modification that in the formula set out in that paragraph D shall be the ascertained amount.

10(12) In paragraphs (6), (7) and (9) **"unrelieved transfer"** shall be construed in accordance with subsection (4) of section 444BA.

History – In reg. 10, "permanent establishment" substituted for "branch" in each place by SI 2008/2679, reg. 9(2), with effect in relation to accounting periods beginning on or after 6 April 2008 and ending on or after 30 October 2008.
In reg. 10(1), (2)(a), (3) and (5), the words "equalisation reserves rules" substituted for "section 34A regulations" by SI 2001/3629, art. 146 and 151 in relation to periods of account ending on or after 1 December 2001.
In reg. 10(2)(a), "permanent establishments" substituted for "branches" by SI 2008/2679, reg. 9(3), with effect in relation to accounting periods beginning on or after 6 April 2008 and ending on or after 30 October 2008 (note that similar substitutions are not made by SI 2008/2679 in reg. 10(6)(a) and (9)(a); this may be an oversight).

PART III – RESERVES MAINTAINED FOR THE PURPOSES OF CREDIT INSURANCE BUSINESS

SCOPE OF THIS PART

11 This Part of these Regulations applies to any credit insurance equalisation reserve.

APPLICATION OF SECTION 444BA

12 Where for any accounting period an insurance company maintains a credit insurance equalisation reserve, section 444BA shall have effect in relation to that reserve as it has effect in relation to equalisation reserves maintained by virtue of equalisation reserves rules.

History – In reg. 12, the words "equalisation reserves rules" substituted for "section 34A regulations" by SI 2001/3629, art. 146 and 151 in relation to periods of account ending on or after 1 December 2001.

TRANSITIONAL PROVISION

13(1) This regulation applies in any case where an insurance company was required, pursuant to regulations 76 to 78 of, and Schedule 14 to, the Insurance Companies Regulations 1994, to maintain a credit insurance equalisation reserve.

13(2) Paragraph 2(2) of Schedule 2 to the Insurance Companies (Reserves) Regulations 1996 shall be disregarded for the purposes of the Tax Acts in determining how much is required, on any occasion, to be transferred into the credit insurance equalisation reserve.

APPLICATION OF PROVISIONS CONTAINED IN PART II OF THESE REGULATIONS

14 Subject to regulation 13, regulations 6, 9 and 10 shall have effect in relation to any credit insurance equalisation reserve as they have effect in relation to any reserve to which Part II of these Regulations applies.

History – In reg. 15, "5", which appeared after "regulations", omitted by SI 2008/2679, reg. 10, with effect in relation to accounting periods beginning on or after 6 April 2008 and ending on or after 30 October 2008.

INTERNATIONAL ORGANISATIONS (MISCELLANEOUS EXEMPTIONS) ORDER 1997

(SI 1997/168)

Made on 27 January 1997 by the Treasury, in exercise of the powers conferred on them by s. 582A(1) of the Income and Corporation Taxes Act 1988.

1 This Order may be cited as the International Organisations (Miscellaneous Exemptions) Order 1997.

2 The following international organisations are designated for the purposes of subsections (2) and (4) to (6) of section 582A and subsection (4) of section 118B of the Income and Corporation Taxes Act 1988–

Asian Development Bank

European Bank for Reconstruction and Development

International Bank for Reconstruction and Development

International Development Association

Multilateral Investment Guarantee Agency.

3 The following international organisations are designated for the purposes of subsection (5) of section 582A and subsection (4) of section 118B of the Income and Corporation Taxes Act 1988–

African Development Bank

European Investment Bank

Inter-American Development Bank.

4 The International Organisations (Miscellaneous Exemptions) Order 1991 and the International Organisations (Miscellaneous Exemptions) Order 1992 are hereby revoked.

13,411   **Life Assurance and Other Policies etc. Regulations 1997**   **SI 1997/265**

Statutory Instruments

LIFE ASSURANCE AND OTHER POLICIES (KEEPING OF INFORMATION AND DUTIES OF INSURERS) REGULATIONS 1997

(SI 1997/265, as amended by SI 2002/444, SI 2008/2628 and SI 2013/1820)

Made on 10 February 1997 by the Commissioners of Inland Revenue, in exercise of the powers conferred on them by s. 552(4A)(b), (4B) and (4C) of the Income and Corporation Taxes Act 1988. Operative from 1 April 1997.

CITATION AND COMMENCEMENT

1 These Regulations may be cited as the Life Assurance and Other Policies (Keeping of Information and Duties of Insurers) Regulations 1997 and shall come into force on 1st April 1997

INTERPRETATION

2(1) In these Regulations unless the context otherwise requires–

"**the Board**" means the Commissioners for Her Majesty's Revenue and Customs;

"**relevant records**", in respect of a policy or contract, means the books, documents and records specified in regulation 3;

"**Schedule 15**" means Schedule 15 to the Taxes Act;

"**section 552**" means section 552 of the Taxes Act and a reference to that section without more includes, where necessary, a reference to section 552ZA of the Taxes Act;

"**the Taxes Act**" means the Income and Corporation Taxes Act 1988.

2(2) For the purposes of these Regulations, an "**insurer**"–

(a) in a case where the obligations under any policy or contract of the body that issued, entered into or effected it ("the original insurer") are at any time the obligations of another body ("the transferee") to whom there has been a transfer of the whole or any part of a business previously carried on by the original insurer, means the transferee, and

(b) in any other case, means the body by or with whom the policy or contract was issued, entered into or effected.

2(3) For the purposes of these Regulations and in relation to an insurer, a policy or contract is a relevant policy or contract if–

(a) on the happening of a chargeable event within the meaning of Chapter 9 of Part 4 of the Income Tax (Trading and Other Income) Act 2005 in relation to the policy or contract, the insurer is under the duty to deliver a certificate pursuant to section 552; and, for the purposes of this paragraph, the words "unless satisfied that no gain is to be treated as arising by reason of the event" in subsection (1)(a) shall be disregarded, or

(b) it is a qualifying policy.

2(4) For the purposes of these Regulations and in respect of any policy or contract, any reference to books, documents and records includes books, documents and records (including material prepared for the purposes of advertising or publicity) which contain information–

(a) relating to the terms of the policy or contract, or

(b) required for the purposes of a certificate to be delivered under section 552.

History – In reg. 2(1), in the definition of "the Board", the words "for Her Majesty's Revenue and Customs" substituted for the words "of Inland Revenue" by SI 2008/2628, reg. 2(2)(a), with effect from 27 October 2008.

In reg. 2(1) the definition of ICTA 1988, s. 552 amended and extended to include s. 552ZA by SI 2002/444, reg. 3(2), with effect from 6 April 2002.

In reg. 2(3), the words "if– (a) on" substituted for the words "if, on" and the words ", or (b) it is a qualifying policy" inserted by SI 2013/1820, reg. 6(2), with effect from 12 August 2013.

In reg. 2(3), the words "Chapter 9 of Part 4 of the Income Tax (Trading and Other Income) Act 2005" substituted for the words "Chapter II of Part XIII of the Taxes Act" by SI 2008/2628, reg. 2(2)(b), with effect from 27 October 2008.

In reg. 2(3) the words: "the words "unless satisfied that no gain is to be treated as arising by reason of the event" in subsection (1)(a) shall be disregarded" substituted by SI 2002/444, reg. 3(3), with effect from 6 April 2002.

KEEPING OF RECORDS – GENERAL

3 An insurer shall, in respect of each relevant policy or contract, keep sufficient books, documents and records to enable the Board–

(a)   to ascertain the terms of the policy or contract,

(b)   to ascertain whether there has been or is likely to be any contravention of the requirements of section 552,

(c)   to verify any certificate delivered under that section,

(d)   to ascertain whether there has been or is likely to be any contravention of the requirements of the regulations made under section 552ZB(1), and

(e)   to verify any information provided to an officer of Revenue and Customs as required by the regulations made under section 552ZB(1).

History – Reg. 3(d) and (e) inserted (and the "and" after (b) omitted) by SI 2013/1820, reg. 6(3), with effect from 12 August 2013.

PERIOD FOR WHICH RECORDS TO BE KEPT

4(1)   Subject to paragraph (2), an insurer shall, in respect of each relevant policy or contract, keep the relevant records for a period of three years after the termination of the policy or contract.

4(2)   In any case where–

(a)   a relevant policy is connected with another policy for the purposes of paragraph 13 or 14 of Schedule 15, or

(b)   in relation to a relevant policy under which a single premium only is payable, liability for that payment is discharged in accordance with paragraph 15(2) of Schedule 15, or

(c)   a relevant policy is issued in substitution for, or on the maturity of and in consequence of an option conferred by, another policy,

an insurer shall, in respect of each policy, keep the relevant records for a period of three years after the termination of the final policy which is in force.

TRANSFERS OF RECORDS

5(1)   This regulation applies in any case where the obligations under any policy or contract of the body that issued, entered into or effected it (**"the original insurer"**) are at any time the obligations of another body (**"the transferee"**) to whom there has been a transfer of the whole or any part of a business previously carried on by the original insurer.

5(2)   The original insurer shall, in respect of that policy or contract, deliver the relevant records to the transferee within the period of three months after the transfer.

5(3)   This regulation has effect in relation to transfers on or after 1st April 1997.

6(1)   This regulation applies in any case where each of the three conditions specified in paragraphs (2) to (4) is fulfilled.

6(2)   The first condition is that one policy (the **"new policy"**) is issued in substitution for another policy (the **"old policy"**).

6(3)   The second condition is that the new policy is issued in substitution for an old policy issued by an insurance company (the **"old insurer"**) which was resident outside the United Kingdom at the time the old policy was issued.

6(4)   The third condition is that the new policy is issued by an insurance company (the **"new insurer"**) pursuant to arrangements made between the old insurer and the new insurer for the issue of policies in substitution for ones held by persons becoming resident in the United Kingdom.

6(5)   The new insurer shall, in respect of the old policy, obtain the relevant records from the old insurer within the period of three months after the issue of the new policy.

6(6)   This regulation has effect in relation to any new policy where the insurance for that new policy is made, and that new policy is issued, on or after 1st April 1997.

7(1)   This regulation applies in any case where each of the conditions specified in paragraphs (2) and (3) is fulfilled.

7(2)   The first condition is that one policy (**"the new policy"**) is issued in substitution for, or on the maturity of and in consequence of an option conferred by, another policy (**"the old policy"**).

7(3)   The second condition is that, at the time the new policy is issued, the insurance company issuing the new policy (**"the new insurer"**) and the insurance company which issued the old policy (**"the old insurer"**) are both members of a group of companies.

7(4)   For the purposes of paragraph (3) two companies are members of a group of companies if one is the 51 per cent subsidiary of the other or both are 51 per cent subsidiaries of a third company.

7(5) The original insurer shall, in respect of the old policy, deliver the relevant records to the new insurer within the period of three months beginning with the date on which the new policy was substituted for the old policy or, as the case may be, the date of the exercise of the option on the maturity of the old policy.

7(6) This regulation has effect in relation to any new policy where the insurance for that new policy is made, and that new policy is issued, on or after 1st April 1997.

INFORMATION TO BE PROVIDED TO THE BOARD

8(1) The Board may by notice require any person to whom premiums under any policy are or have at any time been payable, within such period as may be specified in the notice, to furnish them with such information as they may reasonably require to enable them—

(a)   to ascertain whether there has been or is likely to be any contravention of the requirements of section 552, and

(b)   to verify any certificate delivered under that section.

8(2) The period specified in a notice given under paragraph (1) shall be a period of not less than 14 days beginning with the date on which the notice is given.

INSPECTION OF RECORDS BY OFFICER OF THE BOARD

9(1) The Board may by notice require any person to whom premiums under any policy are or have at any time been payable, to make available for inspection by an officer of the Board authorised for that purpose, at such time as that officer may reasonably require, all such books, documents and records as are in that person's possession or under that person's control and are such as may be required by the Board under regulation 8 or required by regulation 3(d) and (e).

9(2) The time specified in a notice given under paragraph (1) shall not fall within the period of 14 days beginning with the date on which the notice is given.

History – In reg. 9(1), the words "or required by regulation 3(d) and (e)." inserted by SI 2013/1820, reg. 6(4), with effect from 12 August 2013.

LLOYD'S UNDERWRITERS (DOUBLE TAXATION RELIEF) REGULATIONS 1997

(SI 1997/405)

Made on 21 February 1997 by the Commissioners of Inland Revenue, in exercise of the powers conferred on them by section 182(1) of the Finance Act 1993. Operative from 14 March 1997.

CITATION, COMMENCEMENT AND EFFECT

1(1) These Regulations may be cited as the Lloyd's Underwriters (Double Taxation Relief) Regulations 1997 and shall come into force on 14th March 1997.

1(2) These Regulations shall have effect for the year 1996–97 and subsequent years of assessment.

INTERPRETATION

2(1) In these Regulations–

> **"Canadian tax"** means the appropriate income tax or income taxes imposed by the Government of Canada;
>
> **"final year of assessment"** shall be construed in accordance with section 179(2);
>
> **"foreign tax"** means tax chargeable under the law of a territory outside the United Kingdom;
>
> **"member"** means a member of Lloyd's who is an individual and who is or has been an underwriting member;
>
> **"Part XVIII"** means Part XVIII of the Taxes Act;
>
> **"the Taxes Act"** means the Income and Corporation Taxes Act 1988;
>
> **"United States tax"** means the appropriate Federal income tax or Federal income taxes of the United States of America imposed by the Internal Revenue Code.

2(2) For the purposes of these Regulations an underwriting year and a year of assessment shall be deemed to correspond to each other if the underwriting year ends in the year of assessment.

2(3) References to a section, without more, are references to that section of the Finance Act 1993.

POOLED FOREIGN TAX

3(1) For the purposes of Part XVIII foreign tax paid in respect of profits or losses arising from a member's underwriting business in a year of assessment shall be taken into account in accordance with paragraph (2).

3(2) Foreign tax paid as mentioned in paragraph (1) shall be taken into account by reference to the aggregate amount of such amounts of foreign tax as are paid (whether or not under the law of more than one territory outside the United Kingdom) in respect of income that is taken into account in computing the profits or losses of the member's underwriting business; and accordingly the provisions of Part XVIII shall apply as if–

(a)   references, however expressed, to tax paid under the law of a territory outside the United Kingdom were references to that aggregate amount paid as a single payment in respect of a single source of income, and

(b)   references to United Kingdom tax chargeable in respect of any income were references to United Kingdom tax chargeable in respect of the total profits of the member's underwriting business.

ALLOCATION OF FOREIGN TAX TO UNITED KINGDOM YEARS OF ASSESSMENT – SYNDICATE PROFITS

4(1) For the purposes of regulation 3, foreign tax referred to in that regulation that is paid in respect of income specified in paragraph (2), other than foreign tax to which regulation 6 or 7 applies, shall be allocated to the year of assessment specified in paragraph (3).

4(2) The income specified is the income that is taken into account in computing the profits or losses of the member's underwriting business falling within section 172(1)(a) or (b).

4(3) The year of assessment specified is the same year of assessment as the year of assessment to which, by virtue of section 172, the profits or losses referred to in paragraph (2) relate.

ALLOCATION OF FOREIGN TAX TO UNITED KINGDOM YEARS OF ASSESSMENT – NON-SYNDICATE PROFITS

5(1) For the purposes of regulation 3, foreign tax referred to in that regulation that is paid in respect of income specified in paragraph (2), other than foreign tax to which regulation 6 or 7 applies, shall be allocated to the year of assessment specified in paragraph (3).

5(2) The income specified is the income that is taken into account in computing the profits or losses of the member's underwriting business falling within section 172(1)(c).

5(3) The year of assessment specified is the same year of assessment as the year of assessment to which, by virtue of section 172, the profits or losses referred to in paragraph (2) relate.

ALLOCATION OF FOREIGN TAX TO UNITED KINGDOM YEARS OF ASSESSMENT – UNITED STATES TAX

6(1) This regulation applies to foreign tax that is United States tax paid by Lloyd's in accordance with a United States tax return rendered by them for a calendar year in respect of income that is taken into account in computing the profits or losses of the member's underwriting business.

6(2) For the purposes of regulation 3 and subject to paragraph (3), United States tax paid as mentioned in paragraph (1) shall be allocated to the year of assessment next but one following the year of assessment to which the underwriting year for which the return is made corresponds.

6(3) Where the member's final year of assessment is the year 1996/97, United States tax paid as mentioned in paragraph (1) which under paragraph (2) would have been eligible for relief in a later year of assessment had not the member's final year of assessment been the year 1996/97 and which has not been used for relief in an earlier year of assessment, shall be allocated to the year 1996/97.

ALLOCATION OF FOREIGN TAX TO UNITED KINGDOM YEARS OF ASSESSMENT – CANADIAN TAX

7(1) This regulation applies to foreign tax that is Canadian tax paid by Lloyd's in accordance with a Canadian tax return rendered by them for a calendar year in respect of income that is taken into account in computing the profits or losses of the member's underwriting business.

7(2) For the purposes of regulation 3 and subject to paragraph (3), Canadian tax paid as mentioned in paragraph (1) shall be allocated to the year of assessment next following the year of assessment to which the underwriting year for which the return is made corresponds.

7(3) Where the member's final year of assessment is the year 1996/97, Canadian tax paid as mentioned in paragraph (1) which under paragraph (2) would have been eligible for relief in a later year of assessment had not the member's final year of assessment been the year 1996/97 and which has not been used for relief in an earlier year of assessment, shall be allocated to the year 1996/97.

ALLOCATION OF FOREIGN TAX TO UNITED KINGDOM YEARS OF ASSESSMENT – ADDITIONAL PAYMENTS OF FOREIGN TAX

8(1) Where–

(a) payment of foreign tax (**"the primary payment"**) is made for an underwriting year in respect of income that falls to be taken into account in computing the profits or losses of a member's underwriting business, and

(b) payment of an additional amount of foreign tax in respect of that income is subsequently required,

then, notwithstanding anything in regulations 4 to 7 but subject to paragraph (2), the additional amount paid shall, for the purposes of regulation 3, be treated as foreign tax paid for the underwriting year in which it was paid and not as foreign tax paid for the underwriting year for which the primary payment was made.

8(2) Where the underwriting year in which the additional amount of foreign tax is paid is an underwriting year that is subsequent to the underwriting year corresponding to the member's final year of assessment, the additional amount paid shall, for the purposes of regulation 3, be treated as foreign tax paid for the underwriting year corresponding to the member's final year of assessment.

REFUNDS OF FOREIGN TAX

9(1)   Where–

(a)   income that is taken into account in computing the profits or losses of a member's underwriting business is treated as reduced by foreign tax under section 811 of the Taxes Act, and

(b)   an amount of that foreign tax is subsequently repaid to the member,

the amount repaid shall be treated as a payment received as mentioned in section 172(1)(c).

9(2)   Subject to paragraph (3), where–

(a)   relief for foreign tax is given by way of credit against United Kingdom tax on profits arising from a member's underwriting business, and

(b)   an amount of that foreign tax is subsequently repaid to the member,

the amount of United Kingdom tax charged on the profits arising from the member's underwriting business for the relevant year of assessment shall be treated as increased by the amount repaid.

9(3)   Where–

(a)   relief by way of credit against United Kingdom tax on profits arising from a member's underwriting business is claimed for an amount of foreign tax,

(b)   relief is given in respect of part only of the amount of the foreign tax claimed, and

(c)   an amount of the foreign tax claimed is subsequently repaid to the member,

the amount of United Kingdom tax charged on the profits arising from the member's underwriting business for the relevant year of assessment shall be treated as increased by the amount (if any) which is equal to so much of the amount received as exceeds the amount of the foreign tax in respect of which relief was not given.

9(4)   In paragraphs (2) and (3) **"the relevant year of assessment"**–

(a)   where the underwriting year in which the repayment of foreign tax was received is an underwriting year subsequent to the underwriting year corresponding to the member's final year of assessment, means the member's final year of assessment;

(b)   in any other case, means the year of assessment corresponding to the underwriting year in which the repayment of foreign tax was received.

MANUFACTURED DIVIDENDS (TAX) REGULATIONS 1997

(SI 1997/993, as amended by SI 1999/621 and SI 2006/3271)

Made on 20 March 1997 by the Treasury, in exercise of the powers conferred on them by para. 1(1), 2(3) to (5) and 8(1) and (2) to (4) of Sch. 23A to the Income and Corporation Taxes Act 1988. Operative from 1 July 1997.

CITATION AND COMMENCEMENT

1 These Regulations may be cited as the Manufactured Dividends (Tax) Regulations 1997 and shall come into force on 1st July 1997.

INTERPRETATION

2(1) In these Regulations unless the context otherwise requires–

"**the Board**" means the Commissioners of Inland Revenue;

"**chargeable period**" has the meaning given by regulation 3;

"**dividend**" means a dividend on United Kingdom equities, not being a foreign income dividend within Chapter VA of Part VI of the Taxes Act;

"**the Management Act**" means the Taxes Management Act 1970;

"**manufactured dividend**" shall be construed in accordance with paragraph 2(1) of Schedule 23A;

"**relevant period**" means–

    (a)   each complete quarter falling within a chargeable period, that is to say, each of the periods of three months ending with 31st March, 30th June, 30th September or 31st December which falls within that period;

    (b)   each part of the chargeable period which is not a complete quarter and ends on the first (or only), or begins immediately after the last (or only), of those dates which falls within the chargeable period;

    (c)   if none of those dates falls within a chargeable period which is an accounting period, the whole chargeable period;

"**the Taxes Act**" means the Income and Corporation Taxes Act 1988.

2(2) References in these Regulations to a "creditable amount" in respect of a dividend or manufactured dividend received in any period–

(za)   are references to such an amount in respect of a dividend or manufactured dividend other than a dividend or manufactured dividend that is paid on or after 6th April 1999, and either

(a)   are references to the tax credit in respect of that dividend or manufactured dividend, not being an amount of tax credit to which paragraph (3) applies, or

(b)   where the recipient of the dividend or manufactured dividend is a company that is not resident in the United Kingdom and the dividend or manufactured dividend is attributable to a branch or agency through which the company trades in the United Kingdom, are references to an amount of tax equal to the amount of advance corporation tax payable in respect of that dividend or manufactured dividend, or (as the case may be) the amount of advance corporation tax that would have been payable in respect of that dividend or manufactured dividend if–

    (i)   the person by whom the dividend or manufactured dividend was paid were a company resident in the United Kingdom, and

    (ii)   the manufactured dividend were a distribution by that company.

2(3) This paragraph applies to the amount of tax credit in respect of a distribution which–

(a)   [Revoked by SI 2006/3271, reg. 43 and Sch., Pt. 2.]

(b)   is a distribution in respect of which that company has claimed or may claim the payment of a tax credit under section 438(4) or 441A(7).

2(4) References in these Regulations to a section or Schedule, without more, are references to that section of, or that Schedule to, the Taxes Act.

History – Reg. 2(2)(za) inserted by SI 1999/621, reg. 2 which came into force on 30th March 1999.

Reg. 2(3)(a) revoked by SI 2006/3271, reg. 43 and Sch., Pt. 2 with effect from 31 December 2006 in relation to accounting periods ending on or after that date. Subpara. (a) read as follows:

"(a)   is comprised in the UK distribution income (within the meaning given by paragraph 5B(4) of Schedule 19AC of an overseas life insurance company falling within that Schedule, and".

CHARGEABLE PERIOD

3(1) In these Regulations **"chargeable period"** means—

(a)   as respects a company, its accounting period;

(b)   as respects a person other than a company who draws up accounts for any period (**"the accounts period"**), one of the periods specified in paragraph (2);

(c)   as respects a person other than a company who does not draw up accounts, a year of assessment.

3(2) The periods specified in this paragraph are—

(a)   the period which begins at the beginning of the accounts period and ends at the expiration of 12 months from that date or, if earlier, at the end of the accounts period;

(b)   any subsequent period which—

    (i)   begins at the end of the immediately preceding period, being a period specified in this paragraph, and

    (ii)   ends at the expiration of 12 months from that date or, if earlier, at the end of the accounts period.

ACCOUNTABILITY FOR TAX

4(1) Where—

(a)   a manufactured dividend is paid by any person other than a company resident in the United Kingdom, and

(b)   the payment is one in relation to which either the dividend manufacturer or the recipient of the payment is a person to whom paragraph (2) below applies (**"the appropriate person"**),

the appropriate person shall be liable to account to the Board, to the extent and in the manner specified in these Regulations, for tax as mentioned in paragraph 2(3) of Schedule 23A.

4(2) Subject to regulation 5, the appropriate person is—

(a)   where paragraph 2(5) of Schedule 23A applies in relation to the manufactured dividend, the dividend manufacturer;

(b)   where sub-paragraph (a) above does not apply in relation to the manufactured dividend and either of the conditions specified in paragraph (3) below applies, the recipient of the payment.

4(3) The conditions specified in this paragraph are—

(a)   that the recipient is a person resident in the United Kingdom;

(b)   that the recipient is a company that is not so resident but carries on a trade in the United Kingdom through a branch or agency, and the manufactured dividend is attributable to the carrying on of that trade through that branch or agency.

LIABILITY FOR TAX WHERE THE MANUFACTURER RECEIVES THE DIVIDEND OF WHICH THE MANUFACTURED DIVIDEND IS REPRESENTATIVE

5(1) Regulation 4(2)(b) shall not apply in any case where the recipient of the manufactured dividend shows that—

(a)   the dividend manufacturer was entitled to payment of the dividend of which the manufactured dividend is representative either—

    (i)   as the holder of the securities concerned, or

    (ii)   directly or indirectly from a person from whom he acquired those securities, or to whom he transferred them, and who was so entitled as the holder of those securities, and

(b)   the aggregate of the amount of the dividend received by the dividend manufacturer and any amount paid to him in respect of a tax credit in relation to that dividend (**"the aggregate amount"**) does not exceed the amount of the dividend.

5(2) Where paragraph (1) applies, the dividend manufacturer concerned shall be liable for tax, in respect of the manufactured dividend paid by him, in an amount equal to the amount (if any) of a tax credit in respect of the dividend received by him which, assuming him to have made a claim under arrangements having effect by virtue of section 788, the dividend manufacturer is entitled to have paid to him in respect of the dividend received by him.

5(3) The amount of tax for which the dividend manufacturer is liable shall be set against the amount of the tax credit to which, on the assumption made in paragraph (2), he is entitled as mentioned in that paragraph.

5(4) Where paragraph (1) does not apply by reason only of the fact that sub-paragraph (b) of that paragraph does not apply, the amount of tax for which the recipient of the manufactured dividend shall be liable to account under paragraph 2(3) of Schedule 23A shall be reduced to an amount equal to the amount by which the aggregate amount exceeds the amount of the dividend.

ACCOUNTING FOR TAX BY RECIPIENTS THAT ARE UNITED KINGDOM RESIDENT COMPANIES

6(1) This regulation applies in any case where a recipient of a manufactured dividend–

(a)   is liable under regulation 4 to account to the Board for any tax in respect of that manufactured dividend, and

(b)   is a company resident in the United Kingdom.

6(2) Paragraphs 1 to 3, 8 and 10 of Schedule 13 (collection of advance corporation tax) and, on or after the appointed day referred to in section 137(2) of the Finance Act 1996, paragraph 7A of that Schedule, shall apply in relation to the amount of tax for which the company is liable to account in respect of that manufactured dividend as if–

(a)   manufactured dividends received by the company in each of its accounting periods and the tax for which it is liable to account in respect of those manufactured dividends;

(b)   paragraph 2(1) of that Schedule required a return for any return period to include in addition the amount of any manufactured dividends received by the company in that period, and the amount of tax for which it is liable to account in respect of those manufactured dividends;

(c)   references in paragraph 3 of that Schedule to franked payments and advance corporation tax in respect of such payments included references to manufactured dividends required to be included in a return under that Schedule by virtue of this regulation and tax for which the company is liable to account in respect of those manufactured dividends;

(d)   paragraph 8 of that Schedule included a reference to a manufactured dividend included in a return under that Schedule by virtue of this regulation;

(e)   paragraph 10 of that Schedule included a reference to tax for which the company is liable to account in respect of manufactured dividends received in any accounting period.

ACCOUNTING FOR TAX BY PERSONS OTHER THAN UNITED KINGDOM RESIDENT COMPANIES

7(1) This regulation applies in any case where the payer or recipient of a manufactured dividend (**"the relevant person"**)–

(a)   is liable under regulation 4 to account to the Board for any tax in respect of that manufactured dividend, and

(b)   is not a company resident in the United Kingdom.

7(2) The relevant person shall be liable to account in respect of any relevant period for an amount of tax equal to the sum of the following–

(a)   the amount (if any) by which for that period the aggregate amount of tax for which he is accountable in respect of manufactured dividends paid by him exceeds the aggregate amount of creditable amounts in respect of dividends and manufactured dividends received by him, and

(b)   the amount (if any) for that period of the aggregate amount of tax for which he is accountable in respect of manufactured dividends received by him.

7(3) Tax for which the relevant person is accountable under paragraph (2)–

(a)   shall be due not later than 14 days after the end of the relevant period concerned, and

(b)   shall be payable without the making of an assessment.

7(4) Tax due under paragraph (3) shall, whether or not an assessment is made under paragraph (10) of this regulation or under regulation 8(4), carry interest at the rate applicable under section 178 of the Finance Act 1989 to section 87 of the Management Act from the end of the period of 14 days referred to in that paragraph until payment.

7(5) Where the aggregate amount of creditable amounts in respect of dividends and manufactured dividends received by the relevant person in a relevant period exceeds the aggregate amount of tax for which he is accountable in respect of manufactured dividends paid by him in that period, the amount of the excess may be carried forward to any subsequent relevant period falling within the same chargeable period for the purposes of offsetting, pursuant to paragraph (2)(a), that excess amount against the aggregate amount of tax for which he is accountable in respect of manufactured dividends paid by him in respect of that subsequent relevant period.

7(6) Where—

(a) the aggregate amount of tax for which the relevant person is accountable in respect of manufactured dividends paid by him in a relevant period **("the first period")** exceeds the aggregate amount of creditable amounts in respect of dividends and manufactured dividends received by him in that period, and

(b) in any subsequent relevant period falling within the same chargeable period there is an excess of the aggregate amount of creditable amounts in respect of dividends and manufactured dividends received by him over the aggregate amount of tax for which he is accountable in respect of manufactured dividends paid by him,

that excess amount may be set off, for the purposes of paragraph (2)(a), against the aggregate amount of tax for which the relevant person is accountable in respect of manufactured dividends paid by him in the first period, and a repayment of tax shall be made accordingly.

7(7) Where—

(a) the relevant person is a company that is not resident in the United Kingdom, and

(b) the aggregate amount of creditable amounts in respect of dividends and manufactured dividends received by him in a chargeable period exceeds the aggregate amount of tax for which the company is accountable in respect of manufactured dividends paid by him in that period,

the amount of that excess may be carried forward so as to be regarded, for the purposes of paragraph (2), as a creditable amount in respect of dividends or manufactured dividends received by him in the first relevant period of the next chargeable period.

7(8) Where—

(a) the relevant person was under an obligation to make a return under regulation 20 of the Income Tax (Dividend Manufacturing) Regulations 1992 in respect of the return period ending 30th June 1997, and

(b) surplus tax credits received by the relevant person fell to be carried forward on that date to its next accounting period under paragraph (10)(a) of that regulation or would have fallen so to be carried forward if its accounting period had ended on that date,

references in these Regulations to creditable amounts shall, as respects the relevant period commencing 1st July 1997, be taken as including references to those surplus tax credits.

7(9) The same creditable amount shall not be taken into account both under this regulation and under any other provision of the Tax Acts.

7(10) Tax which has become due from a person under paragraph (3) may be assessed on that person (whether or not it has been paid when the assessment is made) if that tax, or any part of it, is not paid on or before the due date.

RETURNS BY PERSONS OTHER THAN UNITED KINGDOM RESIDENT COMPANIES

8(1) This regulation applies in any case where under regulation 7 the relevant person is liable to account for an amount of tax in respect of any relevant period falling within a chargeable period.

8(2) The relevant person shall, within 30 days from the end of the chargeable period, make a return for that period to the Board.

8(3) A return under paragraph (2) shall show—

(a) the aggregate amount of the manufactured dividends received by the relevant person in the chargeable period in respect of which he is liable to account for tax under regulation 7,

(b) the aggregate amount of the manufactured dividends paid by the relevant person in the chargeable period in respect of which he is liable to account for tax under regulation 7,

(c) the aggregate amount of creditable amounts in respect of dividends and manufactured dividends received by the relevant person in the chargeable period,

(d) the amount of creditable amounts brought forward from the previous chargeable period under regulation 7(7);

(e) the amount of creditable amounts carried forward to the next chargeable period under regulation 7(7);

Statutory Instruments

(f)   the aggregate amount of tax for which he is liable to account under regulation 7 for the chargeable period which is the subject of the return.

8(4)   If it appears to an officer of the Board that there is a manufactured dividend which ought to have been and has not been included in a return under paragraph (2), or if he is otherwise dissatisfied with any such return, he may make an assessment on the relevant person to the best of his judgment.

8(5)   Section 98 of the Management Act (**"section 98"**) shall apply in relation to a return under paragraph (2) with the modification specified in paragraph (6).

8(6)   At the end of the second column of the Table in section 98 there shall be added–

"Regulation 8(2) of the Manufactured Dividends (Tax) Regulations 1997."

SET OFF OF TAX BY COMPANIES NOT RESIDENT IN THE UNITED KINGDOM

9(1)   Subject to the modification specified in paragraph (2), the provisions of section 239 other than subsection (7) of that section, section 246(5) and section 797(4) shall apply in relation to the aggregate amount of tax for which a company that is not resident in the United Kingdom is liable in accordance with regulation 7(2)(a) to account for all relevant periods falling within any chargeable period in respect of manufactured dividends paid by it, as if that tax were advance corporation tax paid by the company in respect of distributions made by it in that chargeable period.

9(2)   Subsection (3) of section 239 shall apply as if the reference in that subsection to any of the company's accounting periods beginning in the six years preceding the accounting period concerned were a reference to any of the company's accounting periods ending on or after 1st July 1997 and beginning in the six years preceding that accounting period.

INCOME TAX (SCHEDULE 22 TO THE FINANCE ACT 1995) (PRESCRIBED AMOUNTS) REGULATIONS 1997

(SI 1997/1158)

Made on 3 April 1997 by the Commissioners of Inland Revenue, in exercise of the powers conferred on them by para. 1(3), 2(4)(b), 3(3), 5(4)(b), 6(3), 7(3), 9(3)(a) and 10(3) of Sch. 22 to the Finance Act 1995. Operative from 25 April 1997.

CITATION AND COMMENCEMENT

1 These Regulations may be cited as the Income Tax (Schedule 22 to the Finance Act 1995) (Prescribed Amounts) Regulations 1997 and shall come into force on 25th April 1997.

INTERPRETATION

2(1) In these Regulations **"appropriate period"** means–

(a)   where paragraph 1(3) applies, "the transitional period" within the meaning given by paragraph 1(4);

(b)   where paragraph 3(3) applies so as to modify paragraph 1(3), "the transitional overlap period" within the meaning given by paragraph 3(4);

(c)   where paragraph 6(3) applies so as to modify paragraph 1(3), the years of assessment 1995–96 and 1996–97;

(d)   where paragraph 7(3) applies so as to modify paragraph 1(3), "the transitional overlap period" within the meaning given by paragraph 7(4).

2(2) References in these Regulations to a paragraph are to that paragraph of Schedule 22 to the Finance Act 1995.

AMOUNTS PRESCRIBED UNDER PARAGRAPH 1(3) – PERSONS OTHER THAN PARTNERS

3 As respects a trade, profession or vocation carried on by any person (other than in partnership)–

(a)   the amount prescribed for the purposes of paragraph 1(3)(a) and of that provision as applied by paragraphs 3(3), 6(3) and 7(3) is £10,000;

(b)   the amount prescribed for the purposes of paragraphs 1(3)(c) and of that provision as applied by paragraphs 3(3), 6(3) and 7(3) is £50,000.

AMOUNT PRESCRIBED UNDER PARAGRAPH 1(3)(A) – PERSONS IN PARTNERSHIP

4 As respects a trade, profession or vocation carried on by persons in partnership, the amount prescribed for the purposes of paragraph 1(3)(a) and of that provision as applied by paragraphs 3(3), 6(3) and 7(3)–

(a)   where the maximum number of partners comprising the partnership in the appropriate period does not exceed 20, is the amount determined by the formula–

$$£7,500 \times A$$

where A is the maximum number of partners comprising the partnership in the appropriate period–

(b)   where the maximum number of partners comprising the partnership in the appropriate period exceeds 20, is the amount determined by the formula

$$£150,000 + (£1,000 \times B)$$

where B is the number by which the maximum number of partners comprising the partnership in the appropriate period exceeds 20.

Statutory Instruments

AMOUNT PRESCRIBED UNDER PARAGRAPH 1(3)(C) – PERSONS IN PARTNERSHIP

5 As respects a trade, profession or vocation carried on by persons in partnership, the amount prescribed for the purposes of paragraph 1(3)(c) and of that provision as applied by paragraphs 3(3), 6(3) and 7(3) is the amount determined by the formula–

$$£50,000 \times C$$

where C is the maximum number of partners comprising the partnership in the appropriate period.

AMOUNT PRESCRIBED UNDER PARAGRAPH 2(4)(B)

6 The amount prescribed for the purposes of paragraph 2(4)(b) is £15,000.

AMOUNT PRESCRIBED UNDER PARAGRAPH 5(4)(B)

7 The amount prescribed for the purposes of paragraph 5(4)(b) is £7,500.

AMOUNT PRESCRIBED UNDER PARAGRAPH 9(3)(A)

8 The amount prescribed for the purposes of paragraph 9(3)(a) and of that provision as applied by paragraph 10(3) is £7,500.

LLOYD'S UNDERWRITERS (PARTNERSHIPS) (TAX) REGULATIONS 1997

(SI 1997/2681, as amended by SI 2006/111)

Made on 7 November 1997 by the Commissioners of Inland Revenue, in exercise of the powers conferred on them by s. 182(1) of the Finance Act 1993 and s. 229 of the Finance Act 1994. Operative from 1 December 1997.

History – The words "Scottish Limited", which previously preceded the word "Partnerships", omitted from the title by SI 2006/111, reg. 3 with effect from 14 February 2006 in relation to accounting periods of Lloyd's partnerships ending on or after that date.

PRELIMINARY

CITATION, COMMENCEMENT AND EFFECT

1   These Regulations may be cited as the Lloyd's Underwriters (Partnerships) (Tax) Regulations 1997, shall come into force on 1st December 1997 and shall have effect with respect to accounting periods of Lloyd's partnerships ending on or after that date.

History – The words "Scottish limited", which previously preceded the word "Partnerships", omitted from the citation in both places by SI 2006/111, reg. 3 with effect from 14 February 2006 in relation to accounting periods of Lloyd's partnerships ending on or after that date.

INTERPRETATION

2(1)   In these Regulations unless the context otherwise requires–

"accounting period" in relation to a Lloyd's partnership has the meaning given by regulation 6(2);

"corporate member" has the meaning given by section 230(1) of the Finance Act 1994;

"Lloyd's partnership" means–

(a)   a Lloyd's Scottish limited partnership, or

(b)   a limited liability partnership formed under the law of any part of the United Kingdom which is a member of Lloyd's.

"Lloyd's Scottish limited partnership" means a limited partnership formed under the laws of Scotland which is a member of Lloyd's;

"member" means a member of Lloyd's who is or has been an underwriting member;

"the Taxes Act" means the Income and Corporation Taxes Act 1988.

2(2)   For the purposes of these Regulations an underwriting year and a year of assessment shall be deemed to correspond to each other if the underwriting year ends in the year of assessment.

History – In reg. 2(1) words "Scottish limited" which previously followed the word "Lloyd's", omitted from the definition of "accounting period" by SI 2006/111, reg. 4 with effect from 14 February 2006 in relation to accounting periods of Lloyd's partnerships ending on or after that date.
In reg. 2(1) definition of "Lloyd's partnership" inserted by SI 2006/111, reg. 5 with effect from 14 February 2006 in relation to accounting periods of Lloyd's partnerships ending on or after that date.

PROVISIONS RELATING TO BOTH INDIVIDUAL AND CORPORATE PARTNERS IN A LLOYD'S PARTNERSHIP

OPERATION OF PARTNERSHIP ASSESSMENT RULES

3(1)   Where section 849 of the Income Tax (Trading and Other Income) Act 2005 applies in relation to a Lloyd's partnership–

(a)   the provisions of Chapter III of Part II of the Finance Act 1993 shall apply, subject to the amendments made by these Regulations, as if the partnership were a member who is an individual;

(b)   the Lloyd's Underwriters (Tax) Regulations 1995 shall have effect in relation to that partnership–

(i)   as if it were a member who is an individual, and

(ii)   with the omission of regulations 9 to 17;

(ba)   the Lloyd's Underwriters (Tax) Regulations 2005 shall have effect in relation to the partnership as if it were a member who is an individual.

Statutory Instruments

(c)   the Lloyd's Underwriters (Double Taxation Relief) Regulations 1997 shall have effect in relation to that partnership as if it were a member who is an individual.

3(2)   Where section 114(1) of the Taxes Act applies in relation to a Lloyd's partnership–

(a)   the provisions of Chapter V of Part IV of the Finance Act 1994 shall apply, subject to the amendments made by these Regulations, as if the partnership were a member which is a corporate member;

(b)   the Lloyd's Underwriters (Tax) Regulations 1995 shall have effect in relation to that partnership–

   (i)   as if it were a member which is a corporate member, and

   (ii)   with the omission of regulations 9 to 17; and

(c)   the Lloyd's Underwriters (Tax) Regulations 2005 shall have effect in relation to the partnership as if it were a member which is a corporate member.

History – The words "Scottish limited", which previously followed the word "Lloyd's", omitted from the heading and from the opening words of reg. 3(1) and (2) by SI 2006/111, reg. 4 with effect from 14 February 2006 in relation to accounting periods of Lloyd's partnerships ending on or after that date.
In reg. 3(1) the words "section 849 of the Income Tax (Trading and Other Income) Act 2005" substituted for the words "section 111(2) of the Taxes Act" and reg. 3(1)(ba) inserted by SI 2006/111, reg. 6 with effect from 14 February 2006 in relation to accounting periods of Lloyd's partnerships ending on or after that date.
Reg. 3(2)(c) inserted by SI 2006/111, reg. 7 with effect from 14 February 2006 in relation to accounting periods of Lloyd's partnerships ending on or after that date.

DISAPPLICATION OF CESSATION PROVISIONS

4(1)   Sections 179 and 179A of the Finance Act 1993 shall not apply in relation to a Lloyd's partnership which, by virtue of regulation 3(1), is treated as a member who is an individual.

4(2)   Section 227 of the Finance Act 1994 shall not apply in relation to a Lloyd's partnership which, by virtue of regulation 3(2), is treated as a member which is a corporate member.

History – The words "Scottish limited", which previously followed the word "Lloyd's", omitted from reg. 4(1) and 4(2) by SI 2006/111, reg. 4 with effect from 14 February 2006 in relation to accounting periods of Lloyd's partnerships ending on or after that date.

ANCILLARY TRUST FUNDS RELATING TO A LLOYD'S PARTNERSHIP

5(1)   An ancillary trust fund set up in relation to a Lloyd's partnership shall be regarded as an ancillary trust fund of that partnership, irrespective of whether the fund is established by the partnership itself or by one or more of the partners in the partnership; and, subject to the modification specified in paragraph (2), section 176 of the Finance Act 1993 and section 223 of the Finance Act 1994 shall apply accordingly.

5(2)   Subsections (3) and (4) of section 176 of the Finance Act 1993 shall be omitted.

5(3)   In paragraph (1)

   "ancillary trust fund"–

   (a)   where regulation 3(1) applies, has the meaning given by section 184(1) of the Finance Act 1993;

   (b)   where regulation 3(2) applies, has the meaning given by section 230(1) of the Finance Act 1994.

History – The words "Scottish limited", which previously preceded the word "partnership", omitted from the opening words of reg. 5(1) by SI 2006/111, reg. 4 with effect from 14 February 2006 in relation to accounting periods of Lloyd's partnerships ending on or after that date.

PROVISIONS RELATING TO INDIVIDUAL PARTNERS IN A LLOYD'S PARTNERSHIP

BASIS OF ASSESSMENT

6(1)   Where regulation 3(1) applies in relation to a Lloyd's partnership–

(a)   Chapter 15 of Part 2 of the Income Tax (Trading and Other Income) Act 2005 shall not apply in relation to that partnership;

(b)   section 172 of the Finance Act 1993 shall apply in relation to that partnership as if–

   (i)   in each of paragraphs (a) and (b) of subsection (1) of that section for the reference to the corresponding underwriting year there were substituted a reference to the accounting period ending in the corresponding underwriting year;

   (ii)   in paragraph (c) of that subsection for the reference to profits or losses derived from payments made or received in the corresponding underwriting year there were substituted a reference to profits or losses attributable to the accounting period ending in the corresponding underwriting year.

6(2) In paragraph (1)(b)(i) and (ii) **"accounting period"** in relation to a Lloyd's partnership means the period

(a) beginning on the 1st January in each year, or the date on which the partnership was formed (if later in that year), and

(b) ending on—

    (i) the 31st December in that year, or the date when the partnership is terminated (if earlier), or

    (ii) where the partnership was formed later than 1st January in that year, the 31st December in the following year, or the date when the partnership is terminated (if earlier).

History – The words "Scottish limited", which previously followed the word "Lloyd's", omitted from the heading and from opening words of reg. 6(1) and (2) by SI 2006/111, reg. 4 with effect from 14 February 2006 in relation to accounting periods of Lloyd's partnerships ending on or after that date.
In reg. 6(1)(a) the words "Chapter 15 of Part 2 of the Income Tax (Trading and Other Income) Act 2005" substituted for the words "section 60(2) to (5), and sections 61 to 63A, of the Taxes Act" by SI 2006/111, reg. 8 with effect from 14 February 2006 in relation to accounting periods of Lloyd's partnerships ending on or after that date.

DISAPPLICATION OF SECTION 175 OF THE FINANCE ACT 1993 (SPECIAL RESERVE FUNDS)

7(1) Section 175 of, and Schedule 20 to, the Finance Act 1993 shall not apply in relation to a Lloyd's partnership which, by virtue of regulation 3(1), is treated as a member who is an individual.

7(2) Paragraph (1) shall not prevent the setting up of a special reserve fund in relation to an individual who is both a member of Lloyd's and a partner in a Lloyd's partnership, but in such a case the special reserve fund shall take account only of the underwriting business carried on by that person as a member.

History – The words "Scottish limited", which previously followed the word "Lloyd's", omitted from reg. 7(1) and (2) by SI 2006/111, reg. 4 with effect from 14 February 2006 in relation to accounting periods of Lloyd's partnerships ending on or after that date.

DISAPPLICATION OF SECTION 180 OF THE FINANCE ACT 1993 (UNDERWRITING PROFITS TO BE EARNED INCOME)

8 Section 180 of the Finance Act 1993 shall not apply in relation to the profits arising to an individual as a partner in a Lloyd's Scottish limited partnership.

DEATH OF PARTNER

9(1) This regulation applies where—

(a) regulation 3(1) applies in relation to a Lloyd's partnership, and

(b) an individual who is a partner in the partnership dies.

9(2) The carrying on of the deceased partner's partnership business by his personal representatives shall not be treated for the purposes of the Income Tax Acts as a change in the persons engaged in the carrying on of that business.

9(3) The deceased partner's partnership business shall be treated for the purposes of the Income Tax Acts as continuing until either—

(a) any security provided by him in relation to that business is released or repaid by Lloyd's to his personal representatives, or

(b) his interest in the partnership is assigned by his personal representatives.

History – The words "Scottish limited", which previously followed the word "Lloyd's", omitted from the heading and from opening words of reg. 9(1)(a) by SI 2006/111, reg. 4 with effect from 14 February 2006 in relation to accounting periods of Lloyd's partnerships ending on or after that date.

TERMINAL LOSS RELIEF

10(1) This regulation applies where—

(a) regulation 3(1) applies in relation to a Lloyd's partnership, and

(b) an individual who is a partner in the partnership ceases to carry on his partnership business, whether by reason of death or otherwise.

10(2) The date on which the individual's partnership business is permanently discontinued for the purposes of section 388 of the Taxes Act (carry-back of terminal losses) ("section 388") shall be deemed to be the 5th April in the last year of assessment in which his share of the profits or losses of that business arising from the partnership's membership of one or more syndicates, or from assets forming part of a premiums trust fund, fall to be included in a calculation under Part 9 of the Income Tax (Trading and Other Income) Act 2005.

10(3) A partner may not make more than one claim under section 388 in respect of the same partnership business.

History – The words "Scottish limited", which previously followed the word "Lloyd's", omitted from the heading and from opening words of reg. 10(1)(a) by SI 2006/111, reg. 4 with effect from 14 February 2006 in relation to accounting periods of Lloyd's partnerships ending on or after that date.

In reg. 10 the words "calculation under Part 9 of the Income Tax (Trading and Other Income) Act 2005" substituted for the words "computation under section 111 of the Taxes Act" by SI 2006/111, reg. 9 with effect from 14 February 2006 in relation to accounting periods of Lloyd's partnerships ending on or after that date.

GIFTS FOR RELIEF IN POOR COUNTRIES (DESIGNATION) ORDER 1998

(SI 1998/1868)

Made on 31 July 1998 by the Treasury, in exercise of the powers conferred on them by s. 47(8) and 48(9) of the Finance Act 1998. Operative from 21 August 1998.

1 This Order may be cited as the Gifts for Relief in Poor Countries (Designation) Order 1998 and shall come into force on 21st August 1998.

2 The descriptions of countries specified for the purposes of sections 47 and 48 of the Finance Act 1998 are–

(a)   the countries included in the lists of countries which are eligible for lending by the International Development Association ("the Association"), and by the Association and the International Bank for Reconstruction and Development ("the Bank"), published by the Association and the Bank (under the name of The World Bank) in Appendix 5 to The World Bank Annual Report 1997, under the headings "Countries eligible for IDA funds only" and "Countries eligible for a blend of IBRD and IDA funds", and

(b)   any further countries included in those lists as published in The World Bank Annual Reports issued between the date on which this Order is made and 31st December 2000.

INDIVIDUAL SAVINGS ACCOUNT REGULATIONS 1998

(SI 1998/1870, as amended by SI 1998/3174, SI 2000/809, SI 2000/2079, SI 2000/3112, SI 2001/908, SI 2001/3629, SI 2001/3778, SI 2002/453, SI 2002/1409, SI 2002/1974, SI 2002/3158, SI 2003/2066, SI 2003/2096, SI 2003/2155, SI 2003/2747, SI 2004/1677, SI 2004/2996, SI 2004/3379, SI 2005/609, SI 2005/2078, SI 2005/2561, SI 2005/3230, SI 2005/3350, SI 2006/1722, SI 2006/3194, SI 2007/2119, SI 2008/704, SI 2008/1934, SI 2008/3025, SI 2009/56, SI 2009/1550, SI 2009/1994, SI 2010/835, SI 2010/2957, SI 2011/22, SI 2011/782, SI 2011/1780, SI 2012/705, SI 2012/1871, SI 2013/267, SI 2013/605, SI 2013/623, SI 2013/1743, SI 2013/1765, SI 2013/1773, SI 2014/654, SI 2014/1450 and FA 2014)

Made on 31 July 1998 by the Treasury, in exercise of the powers conferred on them by s. 333, 333A and 333B of the Income and Corporation Taxes Act 1988, s. 151 of the Taxation of Chargeable Gains Act 1992 and s. 75 and 76(3) of the Finance Act 1998. Operative in accordance with reg. 1.

Cross references – SI 2009/317, reg. 3: modification of SI 1998/1870 as it applies in relation to liquidation and administration.

Other material – HMRC guidance on individual savings accounts is available at http://www.hmrc.gov.uk/isa/index.htm.

ARRANGEMENT OF REGULATIONS

34.   CAPITAL GAINS TAX – ADAPTATION OF ENACTMENTS
35.   ADMINISTRATION OF TAX IN RELATION TO ACCOUNTS – SUPPLEMENTARY
36.   APPLICATION OF THE PROVISIONS OF CHAPTER II OF PART XIII OF THE TAXES
       ACT AND OF CHAPTER 9 OF PART 4 OF ITTOIA 2005 TO POLICIES WHERE AN
       INVESTOR CEASES TO BE OR WAS NOT ENTITLED TO RELIEF FROM TAX

CITATION AND COMMENCEMENT

1   These Regulations may be cited as the Individual Savings Account Regulations 1998 and shall
come into force for the purposes of–

(a)   applications under regulations 12 and 13 relating to the year 1999–00, to subscribe to an
       account in that year,

(b)   applications under regulation 14 to be approved as an account manager to manage accounts in
       the year 1999–00 and subsequent years, and

(c)   regulations 16 to 18 and 20, so far as they relate to applications referred to in paragraph (b),

on 1st October 1998, and for all other purposes on 6th April 1999.

Notes – Amendments made by SI 1998/3174 to reg. 2, 6(4)(ii), 7, 8(2), 9, 14(2)(b)(iii), 25(5), 26(2), 35(6), and reg. 36 inserted,
operative from 6 April 1999.

INTERPRETATION

2(1)   In these Regulations unless the context otherwise requires–

(a)

    "account", except in the case of–

      (i)   an account with a deposit-taker,

      (ii)   [Omitted by SI 2007/2119, reg. 3(a)]

      (iii)   a share or deposit account with a building society, or

      (iv)   a deposit account with a person falling within section 991(2) of the Income Tax Act 2007,

    shall be construed in accordance with regulation 4(1) and, where appropriate, regulation 2B(b)
and shall include a personal equity plan treated on and from the 6th April 2008 as a stocks and
shares account;

    an **"account investment"** is an investment under the account which is a qualifying investment
for a stocks and shares component, or a cash component, as the case may be, within the
meaning of regulation 7 or 8;

    an **"account investor"** has the meaning given in regulation 2A;

    an **"account manager"** is a person who fulfils the conditions of these Regulations and is
approved by the Board for the purposes of these Regulations as an account manager;

    "approved profit sharing scheme" has the same meaning as in Chapter IV of Part V of the
Taxes Act;

    an **"assurance undertaking"** means an assurance undertaking within the meaning of Article 6
of Directive 2002/83/EC of the European Parliament and of the Council of 5th November 2002
concerning life assurance;

    "bank" has the meaning given by section 991(2) to (5) of the Income Tax Act 2007;

    "the Board" means the Commissioners for Her Majesty's Revenue and Customs;

    "building society" means a building society within the meaning of the Building Societies Act
1986, or the Irish Building Societies Act 1989;

    "building society bonus" except in regulation 22(1)(a)(i), excludes any bonus, distribution of
funds or the conferring of rights in relation to shares–

    (a)   in connection with an amalgamation, transfer of engagements or transfer of business of a
       building society, and

    (b)   mentioned in section 96 or 100 of the Building Societies Act 1986,

    and "payment under a building society bonus scheme" shall be construed accordingly;

    "business day" means any day except–

    (a)   a Saturday, Sunday, Good Friday or Christmas Day;

    (b)   a bank holiday under the Banking and Financial Dealings Act 1971;

"**ceasing to be subject to the plan**", in relation to plan shares under a Schedule 2 SIP, shall be construed in accordance with the SIP code (see section 488(3) of ITEPA 2003);

"**child**" means an individual under 18;

"**child trust fund**" has the meaning given by section 1 of the Child Trust Funds Act 2004;

"**company**", except in regulation 7(4), means any body corporate having a share capital other than–

(i) an open-ended investment company, within the meaning given by section 236 of the Financial Services and Markets Act 2000,

(ii) a UK UCITS, recognised UCITS or non-UCITS retail scheme,

(iii) an industrial and provident society, or

(iv) a body corporate which is a 51% subsidiary of any industrial and provident society;

"**credit union**" means a society registered as a credit union under the Industrial and Provident Societies Act 1965 or the Credit Unions (Northern Ireland) Order 1985;

"**CTA 2010**" means the Corporation Tax Act 2010;

"**deposit-taker**" has the meaning given by section 853 of ITA 2007;

"**the Director of Savings**" has the same meaning as in the National Debt Act 1972;

"**dormant account**" means a cash account which is a "relevant dormant account" within the meaning given in section 39(2) of the Finance Act 2008, omitting the words–

(a) "is to be, or"; and

(b) "will apply, or" (in both places they appear);

"**EEA Agreement**" means the agreement on the European Economic Area signed at Oporto on 2nd May 1992, together with the Protocol adjusting that Agreement signed at Brussels on 17th March 1993, as modified or supplemented from time to time;

"**EEA State**", in relation to any time, means a state which at that time is a member State, or any other state which at that time is a party to the EEA Agreement;

"**eligible child**" means a child–

(a) born–

(i) on or after 3rd January 2011; or

(ii) before the time mentioned in paragraph (i) but who is not an "**eligible child**" within the meaning given in the Child Trust Funds Act 2004; and

(b) who, at the time when the application to open an account pursuant to a junior ISA application described in regulation 12A is made, is–

(i) resident in the United Kingdom;

(ii) a person who has general earnings from overseas Crown employment subject to United Kingdom tax within the meaning given by section 28 of ITEPA 2003;

(iii) married to, or in a civil partnership with, a person mentioned in paragraph (ii); or

(iv) a dependant of a person mentioned in paragraph (ii);

"**European institution**" means an EEA firm of the kind mentioned in paragraph 5(a) to (d), (f) and (h) of Schedule 3 to the Financial Services and Markets Act 2000 which is an authorised person for the purposes of that Act as a result of qualifying for authorisation under paragraph 12(1) to (4) and (7) of that Schedule;

"**51% subsidiary**" and "**75% subsidiary**" have the same meanings as they do in section 1154 of CTA 2010;

"**gains**", except in regulations 22(1)(a)(ii) to (v) and 35(6), means "chargeable gains" within the meaning of the Taxation of Chargeable Gains Act 1992;

"**gilt-edged securities**" has the meaning given by paragraphs 1 and 1A of Schedule 9 to the Taxation of Chargeable Gains Act 1992;

an "**incorporated friendly society**" means a society incorporated under the Friendly Societies Act 1992;

an "**industrial and provident society**" means a society registered or deemed to be registered under the Industrial and Provident Societies Act 1965 or under the Industrial and Provident Societies (Northern Ireland) Act 1969;

"**investment trust**" is a company that is such a trust for the purposes of the Corporation Tax Acts, or would be such a trust but for section 1158(3) of the Corporation Tax Act 2010;

"**ITA 2007**" means the Income Tax Act 2007;

"**ITEPA 2003**" means the Income Tax (Earnings and Pensions) Act 2003;

"**ITTOIA 2005**" means the Income Tax (Trading and Other Income) Act 2005;

"**junior ISA account**" has the meaning given in regulation 2B;

"**Looked After Child**" has the meaning given in regulation 2F (special provision in respect of Looked After Children);

"**the Management Act**" means the Taxes Management Act 1970;

"**market value**" shall be construed in accordance with section 272 of The Taxation of Chargeable Gains Act 1992;

"**named child**" means a child who holds an account opened pursuant to a junior ISA application described in regulation 12A;

"**notice**", except in regulations 9 and 36, means notice in writing and "**notify**" shall be construed accordingly;

"**parental responsibility**" means–

(a) parental responsibility within the meaning of the Children Act 1989 or the Children (Northern Ireland) Order 1995, or

(b) parental responsibilities within the meaning of the Children (Scotland) Act 1995;

"**qualifying distribution**" has the same meaning as in section 1136 of the Corporation Tax Act 2010;

"**recognised stock exchange**" has the same meaning as in section 1005 of ITA 2007;

a "**registered friendly society**" has the meaning given by the Friendly Societies Act 1992, and includes any society that by virtue of section 96(2) of that Act is to be treated as a registered friendly society;

"**release date**" has the meaning given by section 187(2) of the Taxes Act;

"**relevant authorised person**" has the same meaning as in section 697(2)(b) of ITTOIA 2005;

"**responsible person**" means a person who is the responsible person in respect of the management of a junior ISA account in accordance with regulation 2C(4);

"**security**", except in regulations 7(2)(c) to (cc) and (8)(b), 8(2)(f) and 34(3), means any loan stock or similar security of a company whether secured or unsecured, and in regulation 7(2)(cc) has the same meaning but with the omission of the words "of a company";

"**the Stakeholder Products Regulations**" means the Financial Services and Markets Act 2000 (Stakeholder Products) Regulations 2004;

"**tax**" where neither income tax nor capital gains tax is specified means either of those taxes;

"**tax credit**" means a tax credit under section 231 of the Taxes Act;

"**the Taxes Act**" means the Income and Corporation Taxes Act 1988;

"**year**" means a year of assessment, and "**the year 1999–00**" means the year of assessment beginning on 6th April 1999;

(b)

"**authorised fund**" means–

(i) an authorised unit trust, or

(ii) an open-ended investment company;

"**authorised unit trust**" means a unit trust scheme in the case of which an authorisation order made by the Financial Services Authority under section 243 of the Financial Services and Markets Act 2000 is in force;

"**collective investment scheme**" has the meaning in section 235 of FISMA 2000;

"**the Collective Investment Schemes Sourcebook**" means the sourcebook of that name made by the Financial Services Authority under the Financial Services and Markets Act 2000;

"**depositary interest**" means the rights of the person mentioned in paragraph (b), under a certificate or other record (whether or not in the form of a document) acknowledging–

(a) that a person holds relevant investments or evidence of the right to them, and

(b) that another person is entitled to rights in or in relation to those or identical relevant investments, including the right to receive such investments, or evidence of the right to them or the proceeds from such investments, from the person mentioned in paragraph (a), where **"relevant investments"** means investments which are exclusively qualifying investments for a stocks and shares component falling within any of regulation 7(2)(a) to (h), and the rights mentioned in paragraph (b) are exclusively rights in or in relation to relevant investments;

"insolvency event" means the procedures listed in the definition of "insolvency event" in regulation 19(15) of the Payment Services Regulations 2009;

"FISMA 2000" means the Financial Services and Markets Act 2000;

"non-UCITS retail scheme"–

(a) has the meaning in the Collective Investment Schemes Sourcebook (that is, a scheme to which, or to whose authorised fund manager and depositary, COLL 5.1, 5.4 and 5.6 apply),

(b) includes a "recognised scheme" by virtue of section 272 of the Financial Services and Markets Act 2000, which would fall within paragraph (a) of this definition if it were an authorised fund, and

(c) includes a sub-fund of an umbrella which the terms of the scheme identify as a sub-fund which would fall within paragraph (a) or (b) of this definition if it were itself an authorised fund or a recognised scheme.

In this definition, expressions defined in the Glossary forming part of the Financial Services Authority Handbook have those defined meanings;

"open-ended investment company" means a company incorporated in the United Kingdom to which section 236 of the Financial Services and Markets Act 2000 applies;

"participant", in relation to a Schedule 2 SIP, shall be construed in accordance with the SIP code (see section 488(3) of ITEPA 2003);[See History note.]

"plan shares", in relation to a Schedule 2 SIP, shall be construed in accordance with the SIP code (see section 488(3) of ITEPA 2003) except that–[See History note.]

(a) paragraph 87(6) of Schedule 2 to ITEPA 2003 (meaning of the word "shares" in the context of company reconstructions) shall not apply, and

(b) in paragraph 88(2) of that Schedule (treatment of shares acquired under rights issue) the words "or securities or rights" shall be treated as omitted;

"qualifying units in or shares of a non-UCITS retail scheme" means that–

(a) the instrument constituting the scheme secures that redemption of the units or shares in question shall take place no less frequently than bi-monthly (see Rule 6.2.16(6) of the Collective Investment Schemes Sourcebook omitting the words "Except where (7) applies, and", read with Rule 6.3.4(1), whether or not those Rules apply to the scheme), and

(b) a provision for suspension of dealings in exceptional conditions in accordance with Rule 7.2 of that Sourcebook (or any foreign procedure which is a direct foreign equivalent of that Rule) shall not be treated as a provision contrary to paragraph (a) of this definition;

a **"recognised UCITS"** means–

(a) a collective investment scheme constituted in an EEA State, which is a "recognised scheme" under section 264 of FISMA 2000, and complies with the requirements to be a "UCITS scheme" for the purposes of the Collective Investment Schemes Sourcebook (see in particular COLL 1.2.2); or

(b) a part of a recognised UCITS mentioned in paragraph (a) of this definition, which would be a sub-fund of an umbrella scheme which is a recognised UCITS;

"Schedule 2 SIP" shall be construed in accordance with the SIP code (see section 488(3) of ITEPA 2003);

"Schedule 3 SAYE option scheme" shall be construed in accordance with the SAYE code (see section 516(3) of ITEPA 2003);

"UK UCITS" means —

(a) a collective investment scheme authorised under section 31(1)(a) of FISMA 2000, which complies with the requirements to be a "UCITS scheme" for the purposes of the Collective Investment Schemes Sourcebook (see in particular COLL 1.2.2); or

(b) a part of a UK UCITS mentioned in paragraph (a) of this definition which would be a sub-fund of an umbrella scheme which is a UK UCITS;

"umbrella scheme" means an authorised fund which according to the terms of the scheme is an umbrella scheme belonging to the category under that name established by the Financial Services Authority, and

(i)   in the case of an authorised fund which is an authorised unit trust, references to a part of an umbrella scheme shall be construed in accordance with subsection (8) of section 468 of the Taxes Act, and sub-paragraphs (6) and (7) of regulation 7 of the Authorised Investment Funds (Tax) Regulations 2006 shall apply for the purposes of these Regulations as they apply for the purposes of those Regulations, and

(ii)   in the case of an authorised fund which is an open-ended investment company, references to a part of an umbrella scheme shall be construed in accordance with subsection (4) of section 468A of the Taxes Act, and sub-paragraphs (2) and (3) of regulation 7 of the Authorised Investment Funds (Tax) Regulations 2006 shall apply for the purposes of these Regulations as they apply for the purposes of those Regulations;

"unit holder", means a person entitled to a share of the investments subject to the trusts of a unit trust scheme;

"unit trust scheme" has the meaning given by section 237 of the Financial Services and Markets Act 2000;

"units", in relation to an authorised unit trust, means the rights or interests (however described) of the unit holders in that authorised unit trust and, in relation to a part of an umbrella scheme, means the rights or interests for the time being of the unit holders in that part;

"units in, or shares of, a UK UCITS or recognised UCITS" means the rights or interests (however described) of the holders of the units or shares in that UK UCITS or recognised UCITS;

2(1A)   In these Regulations–

(a)   a **"bulk transfer of accounts"** occurs where two or more accounts are transferred by an account manager ("the transferor") to another account manager ("the transferee")–

(i)   pursuant to an agreement made between the transferor and the transferee where the transfers are not made pursuant to requests made by a person who is the account investor or registered contact in relation to the accounts transferred; or

(ii)   pursuant to an insurance business transfer scheme or a banking business transfer scheme under Part 7 (Control of Business Transfers) of the Financial Services and Markets Act 2000;

(b)   a **"group transfer of accounts"** occurs where a bulk transfer of accounts is made between account managers that are members of the same group of companies when the transfer occurs;

(c)   two companies are members of the same group of companies if–

(i)   one is a 75% subsidiary of the other, or

(ii)   both are 75% subsidiaries of a third company.

2(2)   The Table below indexes other definitions in these Regulations:

Term defined	Regulation
Account	4(1)
Cash account	4(1A)(a) and (c)
Component	4(1A)(b) and (c)
The disqualifying circumstances	17(1)
Interim claim	25
Qualifying circumstances	14(1)
Qualifying individual	10
Qualifying investments for a stocks and shares component	7
Qualifying investments for a cash component	8
Qualifying securities	7(2)(b)

Term defined	Regulation
Registered contact	2C
Stocks and shares account	4(1A)(a) and (b)
Subscription limit – junior ISA account	4ZB
Subscription limit – other accounts	4ZA

History – In reg. 2(1)(a), in the definition of "account", the words "section 991(2) of the Income Tax Act 2007" substituted for the words "section 840A(1)(b) of the Taxes Act, or a relevant European institution" by SI 2014/654, reg. 3(a), with effect from 6 April 2014.

In reg. 2(1)(a), in the definition of "account", the words "regulation 4(1) and, where appropriate, regulation 2B(b)" substituted for the words "regulation 4(1)" by SI 2011/1780, reg. 3(a), with effect from 1 November 2011.

In reg. 2(1)(a), in the former definition of "account", para. (ii) and the word "and" which preceded it omitted and the words "and shall include a personal equity plan treated on and from the 6th April 2008 as a stocks and shares account" inserted at the end by SI 2007/2119, reg. 3(a), with effect from 6 April 2008.

In reg. 2(1)(a), the former definition of "account" amended by SI 2001/3629, reg. 169 which came into force on 1 December 2001.

In reg. 2(1)(a), the definition of "account investment" amended by SI 2004/2996, reg. 3(a), with effect from 6 April 2005.

In reg. 2(1)(a), the definition of "account investor" substituted by SI 2011/1780, reg. 3(b), with effect from 1 November 2011. The former definition read: "an "account investor" is an individual who subscribes to an account and who is a qualifying individual within the meaning of regulation 10;".

In reg. 2(1)(a), the former definition of "approved employee share ownership plan" inserted by SI 2000/2079, reg. 3, with effect from 21 August 2000.

In reg. 2(1)(a) the definition of "approved SAYE option scheme" omitted by FA 2014, s. 51 and Sch. 8, para. 144(a), with effect from 6 April 2014 (subject to the provisions of Sch. 8, para. 147–157). The former definition read as follows:

""approved SAYE option scheme" shall be construed in accordance with the SAYE code (see section 516 of ITEPA 2003);"

In reg. 2(1)(a) the definition of "approved SIP" omitted by FA 2014, s. 51 and Sch. 8, para. 85(a), with effect from 6 April 2014 (subject to the provisions of Sch. 4, para. 89–96). The former definition read as follows:

""approved SIP" shall be construed in accordance with the SIP code (see section 488(3) of ITEPA 2003);"

In reg. 2(1)(a), the former definitions of "approved SAYE option scheme" and "approved SIP" substituted for "approved employee share ownership plan" (and the other expressions defined with that expression), by SI 2008/704, reg. 3(2), with effect from 6 April 2008.

In reg. 2(1)(a), in the definition of "assurance undertaking", the words "Article 6 of Directive 2002/83/EC of the European Parliament and of the Council of 5th November 2002 concerning life assurance" substituted for the words "Article 8 of the First Council Directive 79/267 as extended by the EEA Agreement" by SI 2004/3379, reg. 12, with effect from 11 January 2005.

In reg. 2(1)(a), in the definition of "assurance undertaking", the words "2 of the Council Directive of 5th November 2002 concerning life assurance (No. 2002/83)" substituted for "8 of the First Council Directive 79/267 as extended by the EEA Agreement" by SI 2004/2996, reg. 3(b), with effect from 7 December 2004.

In reg. 2(1)(a), the definition of "bank" inserted by SI 2014/654, reg. 3(b), with effect from 6 April 2014.

In reg. 2(1)(a), the definition of "the Board" substituted by SI 2005/2561, reg. 3, with effect from 6 October 2005.

In reg. 2(1)(a), the definition of "building society bonus" inserted by SI 2006/3194, reg. 3 with effect from 1 January 2007.

In reg. 2(1)(a), the definition of "business day" inserted by SI 2011/1780, reg. 3(c), with effect from 1 November 2011.

In reg. 2(1)(a) in the definition of "ceasing to be subject to the plan", words "a Schedule 2" substituted for the words "an approved" by FA 2014, s. 51 and Sch. 8, para. 85(b), with effect from 6 April 2014 (subject to the provisions of Sch. 8, para. 90–96).

In reg. 2(1)(a), the definition of "ceasing to be subject to the plan" inserted by SI 2008/704, reg. 3(2), with effect from 6 April 2008.

In reg. 2(1)(a), the definition of "child" inserted by SI 2011/1780, reg. 3(d), with effect from 1 November 2011.

In reg. 2(1)(a), the definition of "child trust fund" inserted by SI 2012/1871, reg. (5)(a), with effect from 1 November 2011.

In reg. 2(1)(a), in (iv) of the definition of "company", "51%" substituted for the words "51 per cent." by SI 2012/1871, reg. 5(b), with effect from 9 November 2011.

In reg. 2(1)(a), in the definition of "company", para. (ii) substituted by SI 2009/1994, reg. 3(a)(i), with effect from 11 August 2009.

In reg. 2(1)(a), the definition of "company" amended by SI 2001/3629, reg. 169 which came into force on 1 December 2001.

In reg. 2(1)(a), the definition of "credit union" inserted by SI 2005/3350, reg. 3, with effect from 27 December 2005.

In reg. 2(1)(a), the definition of "CTA 2010" inserted by SI 2012/1871, reg. 5(c), with effect from 9 November 2011.

In reg. 2(1)(a), in the definition of "deposit-taker", the words "section 853 of ITA 2007" substituted for "section 481(2) of the Taxes Act" by SI 2008/704, reg. 3(2), with effect from 6 April 2008.

In reg. 2(1)(a), the definition of "the Director of Savings" inserted by SI 1998/3174, reg. 3, with effect from 6 April 1999.

In reg. 2(1)(a), the definition of "dormant account" inserted by SI 2011/22, reg. 9(2), with effect from 1 February 2011.

In reg. 2(1)(a), definition of "EEA Agreement" substituted by SI 2013/1743, reg. 3(a), with effect from 5 August 2013.

In reg. 2(1)(a), in the former definition of "EEA Agreement", the words ", as modified or supplemented from time to time" inserted by SI 2009/1994, reg. 3(a)(ii), with effect from 11 August 2009.

In reg. 2(1)(a), definition of "EEA State" substituted by SI 2013/1743, reg. 3(a), with effect from 5 August 2013.

In reg. 2(1)(a), in para. (b)(i) in the definition of "eligible child", the words "and ordinarily resident" omitted by SI 2013/605, reg. 4(2), with effect for the purposes of a person's liability to income tax for the tax year 2013–14 or any subsequent tax years.

In reg. 2(1)(a), the definition of "eligible child" inserted by SI 2011/1780, reg. 3(e), with effect from 1 November 2011.

In reg. 2(1)(a), in the definition of "European institution", the words "paragraph 5(a) to (d), (f) and (h)" substituted for the words "paragraph 5(a), (b) or (c)" and the words "(1) to (4) and (7)" inserted by SI 2014/654, reg. 3(c), with effect from 15 August 2013.

In reg. 2(1)(a), the definition of "European Institution" substituted by SI 2001/3629, reg. 169 which came into force on 1 December 2001.

In reg. 2(1)(a), the definitions of "51% subsidiary" and "75% subsidiary" substituted by SI 2012/1871, reg. 5(d), with effect from 9 November 2011.

In reg. 2(1)(a), the definition of "gilt-edged securities" amended by SI 1998/3174, reg. 3, with effect from 6 April 1999.

In reg. 2(1)(a), the definition of "income tax quarter" omitted by SI 2008/704, reg. 3(2), with effect from 6 April 2008.

In reg. 2(1)(a), for the meaning of "investment trust" substituted by SI 2014/654, reg. 3(d), with effect from 6 April 2014.

In reg. 2(1)(a), in the definition of "investment trust", the words from ", and references" to the end of that definition omitted, by SI 2008/704, reg. 3(2), with effect from 6 April 2008.

In reg. 2(1)(a), the definitions of "ITA 2007", "ITEPA 2003" and "ITTOIA 2005" inserted by SI 2008/704, reg. 3(2), with effect from 6 April 2008.

In reg. 2(1)(a), the definition of "junior ISA account" inserted by SI 2011/1780, reg. 3(f), with effect from 1 November 2011.

In reg. 2(1)(a), the definition of "Looked After Child" inserted by SI 2012/1871, reg. 5(e), with effect from 8 August 2012.

In reg. 2(1)(a), the definition of "long term business" omitted by SI 2001/3629, reg. 169 which came into force on 1 December 2001.

In reg. 2(1)(a), the definition of "named child" inserted by SI 2011/1780, reg. 3(g), with effect from 1 November 2011.

In reg. 2(1)(a), the definition of "notice" amended by SI 1998/3174, reg. 3, with effect from 6 April 1999.

In reg. 2(1)(a), the definition of "parental responsibility" inserted by SI 2011/1780, reg. 3(h), with effect from 1 November 2011.

In reg. 2(1)(a), in the definition of "qualifying distribution", the words "section 1136 of the Corporation Tax Act 2010" substituted for the words "section 832(1) of the Taxes Act" by SI 2011/1780, reg. 3(i), with effect from 1 November 2011.

In reg. 2(1)(a), in the definition of "recognised stock exchange", the words "section 1005 of ITA 2007" substituted for the words "section 841 of the Taxes Act" by SI 2011/1780, reg. 3(j), with effect from 1 November 2011.

In reg. 2(1)(a), in the definition of "relevant authorised person", the words "section 697(2)(b) of ITTOIA 2005" substituted for "section 333A(12) of the Taxes Act", by SI 2008/704, reg. 3(2), with effect from 6 April 2008.

In reg. 2(1)(a), the definition of "relevant European institution" omitted by SI 2014/654, reg. 3(e), with effect from 6 April 2014.

In reg. 2(1)(a), in the definition of "relevant European institution", the words "section 697(2)(a) of ITTOIA 2005" substituted for "section 326A(10) of the Taxes Act", by SI 2008/704, reg. 3(2), with effect from 6 April 2008.

In reg. 2(1)(a), the definition of "responsible person" inserted by SI 2011/1780, reg. 3(k), with effect from 1 November 2011.

In reg. 2(1)(a), the definition of "savings-related share option scheme" omitted by SI 2008/704, reg. 3(2), with effect from 6 April 2008.

In reg. 2(1)(a), in the definition of "security", "(cc) and (8)(b), 8(2)(f)" substituted for "(cb) and (8)(b), 8(2)(e) and (f), 31(4)(b)" by SI 2008/3025, reg. 3(a), with effect from 16 December 2008.

In reg. 2(1)(a), in the definition of "security", the words ", and in regulation 7(2)(cc) has the same meaning but with the omission of the words "of a company"" inserted by SI 2008/3025, reg. 3(b), with effect from 16 December 2008.

In reg. 2(1)(a), the definition of "security" amended by SI 1998/3174, reg. 3, with effect from 6 April 1999.

In reg. 2(1)(a), the definition of "the Stakeholder Products Regulations" inserted by SI 2004/2996, reg. 3(c), with effect from 6 April 2005.

In reg. 2(1)(a), the definition of "tax-exempt special savings account" omitted by SI 2007/2119, reg. 3(b), with effect from 6 April 2008.

In reg. 2(1), the definitions of "participant" and "plan shares" inserted by SI 2008/704, reg. 3(2), however there appears to be an error in the amending instrument as the insertions are stated as being in reg. 2(1)(a) after the definition of "open-ended investment company" but that definition appears to be in reg. 2(1)(b), with effect from 6 April 2008.

In reg. 2(1)(b), in the definition of "authorised fund", the words following "investment company" omitted by SI 2008/704, reg. 3(3), with effect from 6 April 2008.

In reg. 2(1)(b), the definition of "authorised unit trust" amended by SI 2001/3629, reg. 169 with effect from 1 December 2001.

In reg. 2(1)(b), the definition of "Chapter 5 UCITS" omitted by SI 2009/1994, reg. 3(b)(i), with effect from 11 August 2009.

In reg. 2(1)(b), the definition of "Chapter 5 UCITS", substituted by SI 2008/704, reg. 3(3), with effect from 6 April 2008.

In reg. 2(1)(b), the definition of "Chapter 5 UCITS" substituted by SI 2004/1677, reg. 3(b), with effect from 22 July 2004.

In reg. 2(1)(b), the definition of "Chapter 5 UCITS" inserted by SI 2003/2747, reg. 3(a), with effect from 17 November 2003.

In reg. 2(1)(b), the definition of "collective investment scheme" inserted by SI 2009/1994, reg. 3(b)(v), with effect from 11 August 2009.

In reg. 2(1)(b), the definition of "the Collective Investment Schemes Sourcebook" inserted by SI 2003/2747, reg. 3(a), with effect from 17 November 2003.

In reg. 2(1)(b), the definition of "depositary interest" inserted by SI 2000/3112, reg. 3, operative from 13 December 2000.

In reg. 2(1)(b), the definition of "the first condition" omitted by SI 2008/704, reg. 3(3), with effect from 6 April 2008.

In reg. 2(1)(b), in the former definition of "the first condition", the words "warrant schemes or Chapter 5 UCITS;" substituted for the words "or warrant schemes" by SI 2004/1677, reg. 3(c), with effect from 22 July 2004.

In reg. 2(1)(b), the former definition of "the first condition" amended by SI 2001/3629, reg. 169, with effect from 1 December 2001.

In reg. 2(1)(b), the former definition of "the first condition" inserted by SI 1998/3174, reg. 3, with effect from 6 April 1999.

In reg. 2(1)(b), the definition of "FISMA 2000" inserted by SI 2009/1994, reg. 3(b)(v), with effect from 11 August 2009.

In reg. 2(1)(b), the definition of "fund of funds scheme" omitted by SI 2008/704, reg. 3(3), with effect from 6 April 2008.

In reg. 2(1)(b), in the former definition of "fund of funds scheme" the word "or" substituted for the word "and" by SI 2005/3350, reg. 4(b), with effect from 27 December 2005.

In reg. 2(1)(b), the former definition of "fund of funds" amended and re-termed "fund of funds" by SI 2001/3629, reg. 169, with effect from 1 December 2001.

In reg. 2(1)(b), the former definition of "fund of funds" amended by SI 1998/3174, reg. 3, with effect from 6 April 1999.

In reg. 2(1)(b), the definition of "insolvency event" inserted by SI 2011/1780, reg. 4, with effect from 1 November 2011.

In reg. 2(1)(b), the definition of "money market scheme" omitted by SI 2008/704, reg. 3(3), with effect from 6 April 2008.

In reg. 2(1)(b), the former definition of "money market fund" amended and re-termed "money market scheme" by SI 2001/3629, reg. 169, with effect from 1 December 2001.

In reg. 2(1)(b), the definition of "the New Collective Investment Schemes Sourcebook" omitted by SI 2008/704, reg. 3(3), with effect from 6 April 2008.

In reg. 2(1)(b), the former definition of "the New Collective Investment Schemes Sourcebook" inserted by SI 2004/1677, reg. 3(a), with effect from 22 July 2004.

In reg. 2(1)(b), in the definition of "non-UCITS retail scheme", in para. (b), the words "270 or" omitted by SI 2013/1773, reg. 81 and Sch. 2, para. 4, with effect from 22 July 2013.

In reg. 2(1)(b), in the definition of "non-UCITS retail scheme", the words "COLL 5.1, 5.4 and 5.6" substituted for the words "Sections 5.1, 5.4 and 5.6 of that Sourcebook" by SI 2009/1994, reg. 3(b)(ii), with effect from 11 August 2009.

In reg. 2(1)(b), in the definition of "non-UCITS retail scheme", the word "New" omitted by SI 2008/704, reg. 3(3), with effect from 6 April 2008.

In reg. 2(1)(b), the definition of "non–UCITS retail scheme" inserted by SI 2005/3350, reg. 4(c), with effect from 27 December 2005.

In reg. 2(1)(b), the definition of "open-ended investment company", substituted by SI 2008/704, reg. 3(3), with effect from 6 April 2008.

In reg. 2(1)(b) (though the amending provision says 2(1)(a)), in the definitions of "participant" and "plan shares" the words "a Schedule 2" substituted for the words "an approved" by FA 2014, s. 51 and Sch. 8, para. 85(b), with effect from 6 April 2014 (subject to Sch. 8, para. 90–96).

In reg. 2(1)(b), the definition of "qualifying units in or shares of a non-UCITS retail scheme", the word "New" omitted by SI 2008/704, reg. 3(3), with effect from 6 April 2008.

In reg. 2(1)(b), the definition of "qualifying units in or shares of a non-UCITS retail scheme" inserted by SI 2005/3350, reg. 4(c), with effect from 27 December 2005.

In reg. 2(1)(b), the definition of "recognised UCITS" substituted for the definition of "relevant UCITS" by SI 2009/1994, reg. 3(b)(iii), with effect from 11 August 2009.

In reg. 2(1)(b), in the definition of a "relevant UCITS" the words following paragraph (ii) omitted by SI 2003/2747, reg. 3(b), with effect from 17 November 2003

In reg. 2(1)(b), the definition of "relevant UCITS" amended by SI 2001/3629, reg. 169, with effect from 1 December 2001.

In reg. 2(1)(b), the definition of "relevant UCITS" substituted by SI 1998/3174, reg. 3, with effect from 6 April 1999.

In reg. 2(1)(b), the definition of "the second condition" omitted by SI 2008/704, reg. 3(3), with effect from 6 April 2008.

In reg. 2(1)(b), in para. (i) of the former definition of "the second condition", "264," inserted by SI 2005/3350, reg. 4(a), with effect from 27 December 2005.

In reg. 2(1)(b), in the former definition of "the second condition", the words "warrant scheme or Chapter 5 UCITS," substituted for the words "or warrant scheme" by SI 2004/1677, reg. 3(d), with effect from 22 July 2004.

In reg. 2(1)(b), the former definition of "the second condition" amended by SI 2001/3629, reg. 169, with effect from 1 December 2001.

In reg. 2(1)(b), the former definition of "the second condition" inserted by SI 1998/3174, reg. 3, with effect from 6 April 1999.

In reg. 2(1)(b), the definition of "securities scheme" omitted by SI 2008/704, reg. 3(3), with effect from 6 April 2008.

In reg. 2(1)(b), the definition of "securities scheme" substituted for the definitions of "securities company" and "securities fund" by SI 2001/3629, reg. 169, with effect from 1 December 2001.

In reg. 2(1)(b), the definition of "the 1997 Regulations", omitted by SI 2008/704, reg. 3(3), with effect from 6 April 2008.

In reg. 2(1)(b), the definition of "UCITS" omitted by SI 2009/1994, reg. 3(b)(i), with effect from 11 August 2009.

In reg. 2(1)(b), in the former definition of "UCITS" the words "Council Directive 85/611/EEC, as last amended by European Parliament and Council Directive 2001/108/EC" substituted for the words "Council Directive 85/611" by SI 2003/2066, reg. 13(4), with effect from 13 February 2004.

In reg. 2(1)(b) the definition of "Schedule 2 SIP" inserted by FA 2014, s. 51 and Sch. 8, para. 85(c), with effect from 6 April 2014 (subject to the provisions of Sch. 8, para. 90–96).

In reg. 2(1)(b), the definition of "Schedule 3 SAYE option scheme" inserted by FA 2014, s. 51 and Sch. 8, para. 144(b), with effect from 6 April 2014 (subject to the provisions of Sch. 8, para. 147–157).

In reg. 2(1)(b), the definition of "UK UCITS" inserted by SI 2009/1994, reg. 3(b)(v), with effect from 11 August 2009.

In reg. 2(1)(b), in the definition of "umbrella scheme" the words "and sub-paragraphs (6) and (7) of regulation 7 of the Authorised Investment Funds (Tax) Regulations 2006 shall apply for the purposes of these Regulations as they apply for the purposes of those Regulations, and" substituted for the words following "Taxes Act,", and the words "subsection (4) of section 468A of the Taxes Act, and sub-paragraphs (2) and (3) of regulation 7 of the Authorised Investment Funds (Tax) Regulations 2006 shall apply for the purposes of these Regulations as they apply for the purposes of those Regulations;" substituted for the words following "in accordance with", by SI 2008/704, reg. 3(3), with effect from 6 April 2008.

In reg. 2(1)(b), the definition of "umbrella scheme" substituted for the former definitions of "umbrella company" and "umbrella scheme" by SI 2001/3629, reg. 169, with effect from 1 December 2001.

In reg. 2(1)(b), the definition of "unit holder" substituted by SI 2008/704, reg. 3(3), with effect from 6 April 2008.

In reg. 2(1)(b), in the definition of "units in, or shares of, a UCITS", the words "UK UCITS or recognised" inserted in both places by SI 2009/1994, reg. 3(b)(iv), with effect from 11 August 2009.

In reg. 2(1)(b), in the definition of "units in, or shares of, a relevant UCITS", the word "relevant" omitted immediately before the word "UCITS" in both places by SI 2003/2747, reg. 3(c), with effect from 17 November 2003.

In reg. 2(1)(b), the definition of "unit trust scheme" substituted by SI 2008/704, reg. 3(3), with effect from 6 April 2008.

In reg. 2(1)(b), the definition of "warrant scheme" omitted by SI 2008/704, reg. 3(3), with effect from 6 April 2008.

In reg. 2(1)(b), the former definition of "warrant scheme" substituted for the former definitions of "warrant company" and "warrant fund" by SI 2001/3629, reg. 169, with effect from 1 December 2001.

Reg. 2(1A)(a)(i) and (ii) substituted by SI 2013/1743, reg. 3(b), with effect from 5 March 2013.

Reg. 2(1A) inserted by SI 2012/1871, reg. 6, with effect from 9 November 2011.

In reg. 2(2), in the Table, in the entry relating to "Cash account", "4(1A)(a) and (c)" substituted for "4(1)(a) and (c)" by SI 2011/1780, reg. 5(a), with effect from 1 November 2011.

In reg. 2(2), in the Table, the entry for "Cash account" inserted by SI 2007/2119, reg. 4(c), with effect from 6 April 2008.

In reg. 2(2), in the Table, in the entry relating to "Component", "4(1A)(b) and (c)" substituted for "4(1)(b) and (c)" by SI 2011/1780, reg. 5(b), with effect from 1 November 2011.

In reg. 2(2), in the Table, in the entry relating to "Component", the words "4(1)(b) and (c)" substituted for "4(1)(a)" by SI 2007/2119, reg. 4(a), with effect from 6 April 2008.

In reg. 2(2), in the Table, the entry relating to "Maxi-account" omitted by SI 2007/2119, reg. 4(b), with effect from 6 April 2008.

In reg. 2(2), in the Table, the entry relating to "Mini-account" omitted by SI 2007/2119, reg. 4(b), with effect from 6 April 2008.

In reg. 2(2), in the Table, the entry relating to "Overall subscription limit" omitted by SI 2011/1780, reg. 5(d), with effect from 1 November 2011. The former entry referred to reg. 4(2).

In reg. 2(2), in the Table, the former entry for "Overall subscription limit" inserted by SI 2007/2119, reg. 4(c), with effect from 6 April 2008.

In reg. 2(2), in the Table, the definition of "qualifying investments for an insurance component" omitted by SI 2004/2996, reg. 4, with effect from 6 April 2005.

In reg. 2(2), in the Table, the entry relating to "Registered contact" inserted by SI 2011/1780, reg. 5(e), with effect from 1 November 2011.

In reg. 2(2), in the Table, in the entry relating to "Stocks and shares account", "4(1A)(a) and (b)" substituted for "4(1)(a) and (b)" by SI 2011/1780, reg. 5(c), with effect from 1 November 2011.

In reg. 2(2), in the Table, the entry for "Stocks and shares account" inserted by SI 2007/2119, reg. 4(c), with effect from 6 April 2008.

In reg. 2(2), in the Table, the entry relating to "Subscription limits" omitted by SI 2011/1780, reg. 5(d), with effect from 1 November 2011. The former entry referred to reg. 4(2)–(4).

In reg. 2(2), in the Table, "Subscription limit – junior ISA account" substituted for "Subscription limits – junior ISA accounts" by SI 2014/1450, reg. 3, with effect from 1 July 2014.

In reg. 2(2), in the Table, the entry relating to "Subscription limits – junior ISA accounts" inserted by SI 2011/1780, reg. 5(e), with effect from 1 November 2011.

In reg. 2(2), in the Table, "Subscription limit – other accounts" substituted for "Subscription limits – other accounts" by SI 2014/1450, reg. 3, with effect from 1 July 2014.

In reg. 2(2), in the Table, the entry relating to "Subscription limits – other accounts" inserted by SI 2011/1780, reg. 5(e), with effect from 1 November 2011.

In reg. 2(2), in the Table, the entry relating to "TESSA only account" omitted by SI 2007/2119, reg. 4(b), with effect from 6 April 2008.

MEANING OF ACCOUNT INVESTOR

2A(1)   This regulation makes provision for the meaning of **"account investor"** in these Regulations.

2A(2)   In relation to an account that is not a junior ISA account, **"account investor"** means an individual who subscribes to an account and who is a qualifying individual within the meaning of regulation 10.

2A(3)   In relation to a junior ISA account, **"account investor"** has different meanings in relation to the application of the regulations specified in paragraphs (4) and (5) as provided for in those paragraphs.

2A(4) For the purposes of the application of regulations 5C, 5D to 5DC, 5DF, 6(3), 7, 8, 9 (other than regulation 9(3)(b)(iii) and (6)), 21A(1) (other than its first occurrence therein), 21A(2) and (3), 22, 24, 28, 31, 34, 35 (other than regulation 35(10)) and 36, **"account investor"** means the named child in relation to the account in question.

2A(5) For the purposes of the application of regulations 4, 9(6), 15, 17, 19, 20, 21A(7), 35(10) and its first occurrence in regulation 21A(1), **"account investor"** means the registered contact in relation to the account in question.

History – In reg. 2A(4), the words "5D to 5DC, 5DF," inserted by SI 2012/1871, reg. 7, with effect from 8 August 2012. Reg. 2A inserted by SI 2011/1780, reg. 6, with effect from 1 November 2011.

MEANING OF JUNIOR ISA ACCOUNT

2B In these Regulations–

(a) an account opened pursuant to a junior ISA application described in regulation 12A is a junior ISA account at any time when it is held by a child;

(b) references to **"account"** shall be construed as including a reference to an account that is a junior ISA account except where the context otherwise requires; and

(c) references to an account held by a child are references to an account in respect of which the child is the beneficial owner of the account investments under that account.

History – Reg. 2B inserted by SI 2011/1780, reg. 6, with effect from 1 November 2011.

MEANING OF "REGISTERED CONTACT" ETC.

2C(1) In these Regulations **"registered contact"** means the person who may give instructions in respect of the management of a junior ISA account to the person who is the account manager in relation to that account.

2C(2) The person who may give instructions in respect of the management of a junior ISA account to the account manager of that account is–

(a) the named child who holds the account if the application to open the account in accordance with regulation 12A was made by that child,

(b) the named child who holds the account if–

    (i) the child has attained the age of 16 years,

    (ii) paragraph (3) does not apply in relation to the child, and

    (iii) the child has assumed responsibility for the management of the account in accordance with paragraph (6), or

(c) in any other case, the responsible person in relation to the account.

2C(3) For the purposes of paragraph (2)(b)(ii) this paragraph applies in relation to the child–

(a) if the child is resident in England and Wales and lacks capacity in relation to the management of the junior ISA account under section 2(1) of the Mental Capacity Act 2005;

(b) if the child is resident in Scotland, the child is suffering mental disorder within the meaning given by section 328 of the Mental Health (Care and Treatment) (Scotland) Act 2003;

(c) if the child is resident in Northern Ireland, the child is suffering mental disorder within the meaning given by Article 3 of the Mental Health (Northern Ireland) Order 1986.

2C(4) A person is the responsible person in relation to a junior ISA account if–

(a) that person–

    (i) makes the application to open the account in question in accordance with regulation 12A; or

    (ii) assumes responsibility for the management of the account in accordance with paragraph (6); and

(b) that person has parental responsibility in relation to the named child who holds the account at the time when that person–

    (i) makes the application described in sub-paragraph (a)(i); or

    (ii) assumes responsibility for the management of the account as described in sub-paragraph (a)(ii).

2C(5) A person ceases to be the person who may give instructions in respect of the management of a junior ISA account to the person who is the account manager in relation to that account when another person assumes responsibility for the management of the account in accordance with paragraph (6).

2C(6) A person assumes responsibility for the management of a junior ISA account if–

(a)   the person makes an application to assume responsibility for the management of the account in accordance with paragraph (7), and

(b)   the account manager of the account in question accepts the application.

2C(7)   An application by a person ("the applicant") to assume responsibility for the management of a junior ISA account must–

(a)   be made to the account manager of the account in question;

(b)   contain–

    (i)   the applicant's full name,

    (ii)   the applicant's address (including postcode),

    (iii)   the named child's full name and date of birth,

    (iv)   the named child's address (including postcode),

    (v)   the named child's national insurance number if the child is over 16 and has been issued with a national insurance number, and

    (vi)   the authorisation specified in paragraph (8);

(c)   contain a declaration by the applicant that the applicant–

    (i)   is 16 years of age or over,

    (ii)   is the named child who holds the account in question or has parental responsibility in relation to the named child who holds the account in question, and

    (iii)   is to be the registered contact for the account.

2C(8)   The authorisation specified by this paragraph is authority given by the applicant to the account manager (on behalf of the named child who holds the account where appropriate)–

(a)   to hold the subscriptions, account investments, interest, dividends and any other rights or proceeds in respect of those investments and cash;

(b)   to make on behalf of the named child any claims to relief from tax in respect of account investments; and

(c)   to make a record in writing in accordance with paragraph (11) where that paragraph requires the account manager to do so.

2C(9)   An account manager must not accept an application to assume responsibility for the management of a junior ISA account if–

(a)   except in the circumstances specified in paragraph (10), the person who is the registered contact in relation to the account at the time when the application is made does not consent to the applicant assuming responsibility for the management of the account; or

(b)   the account manager has reason to believe that the applicant has given untrue information in the application.

2C(10)   The circumstances specified in this paragraph are–

(a)   the death of the most recent registered contact,

(b)   the incapacity of the registered contact,

(c)   where the registered contact cannot be contacted,

(d)   the bringing to an end of a Court order under which the registered contact is a responsible person,

(e)   where the applicant is the named child who holds the account and is aged 16 or over,

(f)   where, under an adoption order, the applicant is the adopter of the named child who holds the account,

(g)   where a Court so orders,

(h)   where the applicant has been appointed to be a guardian or special guardian of the named child who holds the account,

2C(11)   Where the application to assume responsibility for the management of a junior ISA account is not in writing or the account manager operates a record system under which all original written applications are not retained–

(a)   the account manager must, immediately after receiving the application, record, in writing, on behalf of the applicant the declaration required by paragraph (7)(c) and the authorisation required by paragraphs (7)(b)(vi) and (8);

(b)   the account manager must notify the applicant of the contents of the written record within 5 business days of making it; and

(c)   the written record (as amended by any corrections notified to the account manager by the applicant within 30 days of the notification mentioned in sub-paragraph (b)) shall be treated as the applicant's declaration required by paragraph (7)(c) and authorisation required by paragraphs (7)(b)(vi) and (8).

History – Reg. 2C(3) and para. (a) substituted by SI 2014/654, reg. 4(a), with effect from 6 April 2014.
In reg. 2C(3)(b), the words "if the child is resident in Scotland, the child is suffering mental disorder within the meaning given by" substituted for the words "in relation to a child resident in Scotland," by SI 2014/654, reg. 4(b), with effect from 6 April 2014.
In reg. 2C(3)(b), the words "if the child is resident in Northern Ireland, the child is suffering mental disorder within the meaning given by" substituted for the words "in relation to a child resident in Northern Ireland," by SI 2014/654, reg. 4(c), with effect from 6 April 2014.
Reg. 2C inserted by SI 2011/1780, reg. 6, with effect from 1 November 2011.

REGULATIONS THAT DO NOT APPLY TO JUNIOR ISA ACCOUNTS

2D   Regulations 4(6)(fa), 4ZA, 4A, 4B, 5B, 5DI to 5DM, 7(2)(h), 10, 11, 12, 21 and 30, do not apply to a junior ISA account.

History – In reg. 2D, "4C, 4D," and ", 23" omitted by SI 2014/1450, reg. 4, with effect from 1 July 2014.
In reg. 2D, the words "5DI to 5DM," inserted by SI 2012/1871, reg. 8, with effect from 8 August 2012.
Reg. 2D inserted by SI 2011/1780, reg. 6, with effect from 1 November 2011.

CONTRACTS ENTERED INTO BY OR ON BEHALF OF A CHILD WHO IS 16 OR OVER

2E   Where, by virtue of the opening of an account pursuant to a junior ISA application described in regulation 12A, a contract is entered into by a child who is–

(a)   aged 16 or over; and

(b)   the child who–

    (i)   holds the account, or

    (ii)   has parental responsibility in relation to the child who holds the account,

the contract has effect as if the child who opened the account had been 18 or over when the contract was entered into.

History – Reg. 2E inserted by SI 2011/1780, reg. 6, with effect from 1 November 2011.

SPECIAL PROVISION IN RESPECT OF LOOKED AFTER CHILDREN

2F(1)   A child is a Looked After Child where, after 2nd January 2011, there is a continuous period of at least 12 months during which paragraph (2) applies in relation to the child.

2F(2)   This paragraph applies in relation to a child where the child is–

(a)   looked after by a local authority within the meaning of section 22(1) of the Children Act 1989 (general duty of local authority in relation to children looked after by them);

(b)   provided with accommodation by an authority by virtue of article 21 of the Children (Northern Ireland) Order 1995 (provision of accommodation for children: general);

(c)   the subject of an order made under article 50(1)(a) of the Children (Northern Ireland) Order 1995 (care orders and supervision orders);

(d)   provided with accommodation by a local authority by virtue of section 25 of the Children (Scotland) Act 1995 (provision of accommodation for children, etc.);

(e)   the subject of a supervision requirement made under section 70(1) of the Children (Scotland) Act 1995 (disposal of referral by children's hearing: supervision requirements, including residence in secure accommodation);

(ea)   the subject of a compulsory supervision order within section 83 of the Children's Hearings (Scotland) Act 2011 ("the 2011 Act") (meaning of compulsory supervision order);

(eb)   the subject of an interim compulsory supervision order within section 86 of the 2011 Act (meaning of interim compulsory supervision order);

(f)   the subject of a permanence order made under section 80 of the Adoption and Children (Scotland) Act 2007 (permanence orders); or

(g)   treated as if the child were subject to an order described in sub-paragraph (f) by virtue of article 13(1) of the Adoption and Children (Scotland) Act 2007 (Commencement No. 4, Transitional and Savings) Order 2009.

2F(3)   In relation to a Looked After Child, regulations 2C(4)(b) (meaning of "registered contact" etc.) and 12A(4)(b)(i) (conditions for application to open an account that is a junior ISA account) must be construed as if the Share Foundation has parental responsibility in respect of that child.

2F(4) In relation to an application to assume responsibility for the management of a junior ISA account by the Share Foundation, regulation 2C(7)(c) must be construed as requiring a declaration that–

(a) the applicant is the Share Foundation;

(b) the application is in relation to a Looked After Child; and

(c) the Share Foundation is to be the registered contact for the account.

2F(5) Where an application to assume responsibility for the management of a junior ISA account is made in relation to which the registered contact is the Share Foundation, regulation 2C(9)(a) must be construed as referring only to sub-paragraphs (e) and (g) of paragraph (10).

2F(6) Where the registered contact in relation to a junior ISA account is the Share Foundation, any reference in these Regulations to the residence of the registered contact must be construed as meaning a reference to the registered offices of the Share Foundation.

2F(7) In this regulation **"the Share Foundation"** means the company limited by guarantee (number 4500923) and charity registered with the Charity Commission of England and Wales (number 1108068) as "The Share Foundation".

History – Reg. 2F inserted by SI 2012/1871, reg. 9, with effect from 8 August 2012.
Reg. 2F(ea) and (eb) inserted by SI 2013/1743, reg. 4, with effect from 24 June 2013.

INTRODUCTORY

3 These Regulations provide for the setting up of plans in the form of an account, by account managers approved by the Board, under which individuals may make certain investments, for the conditions under which they may invest and under which those accounts are to operate, for relief from tax in respect of account investments and generally for the administration of tax in relation to such accounts.

GENERAL CONDITIONS FOR ACCOUNTS AND SUBSCRIPTIONS TO ACCOUNTS

4(1) An account is a scheme of investment, to which a subscription may be made, and in respect of which–

(a) the conditions and requirements contained in paragraphs (1A) and (5) to (8) are fulfilled; and

(b) either–

(i) the conditions contained in paragraph (1B) are fulfilled, or

(ii) at the time when the subscription to the account is made, the account is a junior ISA account.

4(1A) The conditions in this paragraph are–

(a) the account is set up as a stocks and shares account or a cash account;

(b) a stocks and shares account is made up of a single stocks and shares component only;

(c) a cash account is made up of a single cash component only;

(d) the application to open the account is made in accordance with regulation 12 or 12A.

4(1B) The conditions in this paragraph are–

(a) a qualifying individual who is 16 or over may only subscribe to a single cash account that is not a junior ISA account in a particular year;

(b) a qualifying individual who is 18 or over may only subscribe to a single stocks and shares account that is not a junior ISA account in a particular year;

(c) it is an account to which only one qualifying individual subscribes;

(d) subject to regulation 7(2)(h), it is an account to which the qualifying individual subscribes only by payment to the account manager of a sum or sums of the individual's cash; and

(e) the subscriptions made by the qualifying individual to accounts (ignoring transfers and payments from account managers to the individual) do not in the aggregate in any year exceed the subscription limit in regulation 4ZA(1).

4(2) [Omitted by SI 2011/1780, reg. 7(c).]

4(3) [Omitted by SI 2011/1780, reg. 7(c).]

4(4) [Omitted by SI 2011/782, reg. 5.]

4(5) An account must at all times be managed in accordance with these Regulations by an account manager and under terms agreed in a recorded form between the account manager and the account investor.

4(6) Apart from other requirements of these Regulations the terms agreed to which paragraph (5) refers shall secure–

(a)   that the account investments shall be in the beneficial ownership of–

    (i)   in the case of an account that is not a junior ISA account, the account investor; or

    (ii)   in the case of a junior ISA account, the named child;

(b)   that, except in relation to qualifying investments for a cash component within regulation 8(2)(a), (b) or (e), and subject to regulation 15–

    (i)   in relation to an account that is not a junior ISA account, the title to all account investments shall be vested in the account manager or his nominee or jointly in one of them and the account investor, and

    (ia)   in relation to an account that is a junior ISA account, title to all investments shall be vested in the account manager or his nominee or jointly in one of them and either one of the registered contact or named child to the account in question as the account manager considers appropriate,

    (ii)   where a share certificate or other document evidencing title to an account investment is issued, it shall be held by the account manager or as he may direct;

(c)   that, in relation to a stocks and shares component, and qualifying investments falling within sub-paragraph (h) of regulation 8(2)), the account manager shall, if the account investor so elects, arrange for the account investor to receive a copy of the annual report and accounts issued to investors by every company, unit trust, open-ended investment company or other entity in which he has account investments;

(d)   that, in relation to a stocks and shares component, and qualifying investments falling within sub-paragraph (h) of regulation 8(2), the account manager shall be under an obligation (subject to any provisions made under any enactment and if the account investor so elects) to arrange for the account investor to be able–

    (i)   to attend any meetings of investors in companies, unit trusts, open-ended investment companies and other entities in which he has account investments,

    (ii)   to vote, and

    (iii) to receive, in addition to the documents referred to in sub-paragraph (c), any other information issued to investors in such companies, unit trusts, open-ended investment companies and other entities;

(e)   that the account manager shall satisfy himself that any person to whom he delegates any of his functions or responsibilities under the terms agreed with the account investor is competent to carry out those functions or responsibilities;

(f)   that on the instructions of the account investor ("the transfer instructions") and within such time as is stipulated by the account investor in the transfer instructions –

    (i)   an account, with all rights and obligations of the parties to it, or

    (ii)   such parts thereof as may be agreed between the account investor and the account manager,

shall be transferred to another account manager subject to and in accordance with regulation 21 or 21B and, where it applies, regulation 21A;

(fa)   that on the instructions, subject to regulation 9(3)(b), of the account investor ("the withdrawal instructions") and within such time as is stipulated by the account investor in the withdrawal instructions, account investments, interest, dividends, rights or other proceeds in respect of such investments or any cash shall be transferred or paid to him;

(g)   that the account manager shall notify the account investor if by reason of any failure to satisfy the provisions of these Regulations an account is or will become no longer exempt from tax by virtue of regulation 22(1).

4(7)   The time stipulated in the transfer instructions or withdrawal instructions shall be subject to any reasonable business period of the account manager required for the practical implementation of the instructions, but such period–

(a)   must not exceed 30 days; and

(b)   must be consistent with regulation 21A where it applies.

4(8)   Where an account holds units in or shares of a UK UCITS, recognised UCITS or non-UCITS retail scheme, and dealings in the units or shares are suspended in accordance with Rule 7.2 of the Collective Investment Schemes Sourcebook (COLL 7.2), or any direct foreign equivalent of that Rule, the business period in paragraph (7) may be extended to 7 days after the end of such suspension.

History – Reg. 4(1) substituted by SI 2011/1780, reg. 7(a), with effect from 1 November 2011.

Former reg. 4(1)(a)–(h) substituted by SI 2007/2119, reg. 5, with effect from 6 April 2008.
In former reg. 4(1)(a), the words "and an insurance component" omitted by SI 2004/2996, reg. 5(a), with effect from 6 April 2005.
In former reg. 4(1)(c)(i), the words ", save that a maxi-account ... include a cash component" inserted by SI 2001/908, reg. 3, operative from 6 April 2001.
In former reg. 4(1)(f)(i), the words "paragraph (ia) and" inserted by SI 2001/908, reg. 3, operative from 6 April 2001.
Former reg. 4(1)(f)(ia) inserted by SI 2001/908, reg. 3, operative from 6 April 2001.
In reg. 4(1B)(e), "limit" substituted for "limits" and "and (2)" omitted by SI 2014/1450, reg. 5(a), with effect from 1 July 2014.
Reg. 4(1A) and (1B) inserted by SI 2011/1780, reg. 7(b), with effect from 1 November 2011.
Reg. 4(2) and (3) omitted by SI 2011/1780, reg. 7(c), with effect from 1 November 2011.
Former reg. 4(2) and (3) substituted by SI 2011/782, reg. 4, with effect for the tax year 2011–12 and all subsequent tax years.
In former reg. 4(2), "£10,200" substituted for "£7,200" and in para. (b) "£5,100" substituted for "£3,600" by SI 2009/1550, reg. 7, with effect for the tax year 2010–11 and succeeding tax years.
In former reg. 4(2), the words "£7, 200 unless" inserted by SI 2009/1550, reg. 3(a), with effect for the tax year 2009–10 and succeeding tax years.
Former reg. 4(2)(a) substituted by SI 2009/1550, reg. 3(b), with effect for the tax year 2009–10 only. The substituted reg. 4(2)(a) read: "the qualifying investor is 50 years of age or over, or is due to be aged 50 not later than 5th April 2010, where it is £10,200, or", and the former reg. 4(2)(a) read: "£7,200, unless".
Former reg. 4(2)–(4) substituted by SI 2007/2119, reg. 6, with effect from 6 April 2008.
In former reg. 4(2), the words "2009–10" substituted for the words "2005–06 and £5,000 for subsequent years" and the words "each year" substituted for the words "the years 1999–00 to 2005–06, and £1,000 in subsequent years," by SI 2005/2561, reg. 4(a), with effect from 6 October 2005.
In former reg. 4(2), the words "and no more than £1,000 may be allocated in any year to an insurance component" omitted by SI 2004/2996, reg. 5(b), with effect from 6 April 2005.
In former reg. 4(2), the words "Subject to paragraphs (2A) and (2B), the" substituted for "The" and "to 2005–06" substituted for "and 2000–01" in both places where it appeared by SI 2001/908, reg. 3, operative from 6 April 2001.
In former reg. 4(2), the words "the years 1999–00 and 2000–01" substituted by SI 2000/809, reg. 2, operative from 6 April 2000.
In reg. 4(2A), the words "2009–10" substituted for the words "2005–06, and £1,000 in subsequent years" by SI 2005/2561, reg. 4(b), with effect from 6 October 2005.
In reg. 4(2B), the words "2009–10" substituted for the words "2005–06, and £1,000 in subsequent years" by SI 2005/2561, reg. 4(b), with effect from 6 October 2005.
Reg. 4(2A) and (2B) inserted by SI 2001/908, reg. 3, operative from 6 April 2001.
In former reg. 4(3), "£5,100" substituted for "£3,600" by SI 2009/1550, reg. 8, with effect for the tax year 2010–11 and succeeding tax years.
In former reg. 4(3), the words ", unless the qualifying investor is 50 years of age or over, or is due to be aged 50 not later than 5th April 2010, when he or she may invest £5,100 in the year 2009–10." inserted at the end by SI 2009/1550, reg. 4 with effect for the tax year 2009–10 only.
In former reg. 4(3), the words "2009–10" substituted for the words "2005–06, and £1,000 in subsequent years" by SI 2005/2561, reg. 4(c), with effect from 6 October 2005.
In former reg. 4(3), the words "in the case of an account made up of an insurance component, £1,000" omitted by SI 2004/2996, reg. 5(c), with effect from 6 April 2005.
In former reg. 4(3)(a), the words "to 2005–06" substituted for "and 2000–01" by SI 2001/908, reg. 3, operative from 6 April 2001.
In former reg. 4(3)(c), "£4,000" substituted for "£3,000" by SI 2004/2996, reg. 5(d), with effect from 6 April 2005.
In former reg. 4(3)(a), the words "the years 1999–00 and 2000–01" substituted by SI 2000/809, reg. 2, operative from 6 April 2000.
Reg. 4(4) omitted by SI 2011/782, reg. 5, with effect for the tax year 2011–12 and all subsequent tax years.
In former reg. 4(4)(a), "£5,100" substituted for "£3,600" (twice), in para. (b) "£8,200" substituted for "£5,200", in para. (c) "£10,200" substituted for "£7,200" and in words following para. (c) "£5,100" substituted for "£3,600" by SI 2009/1550, reg. 9, with effect for the tax year 2010–11 and succeeding tax years.
In former reg. 4(4), the words "(who is not aged 50 or over, or due to be aged 50 not later than 5th April 2010)" inserted after "qualifying investor" by SI 2009/1550, reg. 5 with effect for the tax year 2009–10 only.
In reg. 4(6)(c) and (d), the words "and qualifying investments falling within sub-paragraph (h) of regulation 8(2)" substituted for "and qualifying investments falling within paragraphs (g), (h), (k), (l) and (m) of regulation 8(2)" by SI 2014/1450, reg. 5(b), with effect only in respect of investments purchased or made on or after 1 July 2014.
In reg. 4(6), in the opening words, the word "secure" substituted for the words "include the following conditions" by SI 2011/1780, reg. 7(d), with effect from 1 November 2011.
Reg. 4(6)(a) substituted by SI 2011/1780, reg. 7(e), with effect from 1 November 2011.
In reg. 4(6)(b)(i), the words "in relation to an account that is not a junior ISA account," inserted by SI 2011/1780, reg. 7(f), with effect from 1 November 2011.
Reg. 4(6)(b)(ia) inserted by SI 2011/1780, reg. 7(g), with effect from 1 November 2011.
In reg. 4(6)(f), the words "regulation 21 or 21B" substituted for the words "regulation 21" by SI 2011/1780, reg. 7(h), with effect from 1 November 2011.
In reg. 4(6)(c), the words "paragraphs (g), (h), (k), (l) and (m) of regulation 8(2)" substituted for "regulation 8(2)(c) and (d)" by SI 2008/704, reg. 4, with effect from 6 April 2008.
In reg. 4(6)(d), the words "paragraphs (g), (h), (k), (l) and (m) of regulation 8(2)" substituted for "regulation 8(2)(c) and (d)" by SI 2008/704, reg. 4, with effect from 6 April 2008.
In reg. 4(6)(f), the words "and, where it applies, regulation 21A" inserted by SI 2010/2957, reg. 3(1), with effect from 6 April 2011.
In reg. 4(6)(f) words "on the instructions of the account investor ("the transfer instructions") and within such time as is stipulated by the account investor in the transfer instructions " substituted for "at the request of the account investor and within such time as shall be agreed", and the word "shall" substituted for the word "may", by SI 2002/1974, reg. 3(2), with effect from 1 October 2002 in relation to all accounts set up before or after that date.
Reg. 4(6)(fa) and reg. 4(7) inserted by SI 2002/1974, reg. 3, with effect from 1 October 2002 in relation to all accounts set up before or after that date.
Reg. 4(7) substituted by SI 2010/2957, reg. 3(2), with effect from 6 April 2011.
Reg. 4(8) inserted by SI 2009/1994, reg. 4, with effect from 11 August 2009.

SUBSCRIPTIONS TO AN ACCOUNT OTHER THAN A JUNIOR ISA ACCOUNT

4ZA(1)   The overall subscription limit for any qualifying individual for any year (that is the aggregate of the qualifying individual's subscriptions to all accounts that are not junior ISA accounts in that year) is £15,000.

(a)   [omitted by SI 2014/1450, reg. 6(a)]

Statutory Instruments

(b) [omitted by SI 2014/1450, reg. 6(a)]

4ZA(2) [omitted by SI 2014/1450, reg. 6(b)]

4ZA(3) A qualifying individual may not subscribe to an account that was a junior ISA account while it was held by the qualifying individual as the named child for the account unless the account manager of that account has been provided with–

(a) the qualifying individual's national insurance information specified by paragraph (4);

(b) a declaration specified by paragraph (5);

(c) the authorisation specified by paragraph (6); and

(d) if the account manager of the account requires, an authorisation specified by paragraph (7).

4ZA(4) The national insurance information specified by this paragraph is–

(a) the qualifying individual's national insurance number; or

(b) a declaration by the qualifying individual that the qualifying individual does not have a national insurance number.

4ZA(5) The declaration specified by this paragraph is a declaration by the qualifying individual that, if the qualifying individual were making an application to open an account pursuant to regulation 12, would be in accordance with paragraph (3)(c) to (f) of that regulation.

4ZA(6) The authorisation specified by this paragraph is an authorisation by the qualifying individual that, if the qualifying individual were making an application to open an account pursuant to regulation 12, would be in accordance with paragraphs (4)(e) and (4A)(c) of that regulation.

4ZA(7) The authorisation specified by this paragraph is an authorisation by the qualifying individual that, if the qualifying individual were making an application to open an account pursuant to regulation 12, would be in accordance with paragraphs (4)(e) and (4A)(a) and (b) of that regulation.

4ZA(8) Regulation 12(7), (9) and (10) apply in relation to the declaration specified by paragraph (5) and authorisations specified by paragraphs (6) and (7) as if they were made in relation to an application made by the qualifying individual to open an account pursuant to regulation 12.

4ZA(9) For the purposes of paragraphs (5) to (8)–

(a) references in regulation 12 to **"the applicant"** are references to the qualifying individual making the declaration specified by paragraph (5) or giving an authorisation specified in paragraphs (6) and (7);

(b) references in regulation 12(3)(c) to (f) to **"the year in which paragraph (2) refers"** (the first year to which the application to open the account relates) are references to the year in which the declaration specified by paragraph (5) is made by the qualifying individual.

History – In reg. 4ZA(1), "£15,000." substituted for "—" and sub-para. (a) and (b) omitted by SI 2014/1450, reg. 6(a), with effect from 1 July 2014. Former sub-para. (a) and (b) read as follows:
"(a) where the qualifying individual is 16 or over but less than 18 at the end of the year, £5,940; and
(b) in all other cases, £11,880, but subject to paragraph (2)."
In reg. 4ZA(1)(a), the figure "£5,940" substituted for "£5,760" by SI 2014/654, reg. 5(a), with effect from 6 April 2014.
In reg. 4ZA(1)(a), the figure "£5,760" substituted for "£5,640" by SI 2013/267, reg. 2(a), with effect from 6 April 2013.
In reg. 4ZA(1)(a), the figure "£5,640" substituted for "£5,340" by SI 2012/705, reg. 2(a), with effect from 6 April 2012.
In reg. 4ZA(1)(b), the figure "£11,880" substituted for "£11,520" by SI 2014/654, reg. 5(b), with effect from 6 April 2014.
In reg. 4ZA(1)(b), the figure "£11,520" substituted for "£11,280" by SI 2013/267, reg. 2(b), with effect from 6 April 2013.
In reg. 4ZA(1)(b), the figure "£11,280" substituted for "£10,680" by SI 2012/705, reg. 2(b), with effect from 6 April 2012.
In reg. 4ZA(2) omitted by SI 2014/1450, reg. 6(a), with effect from 1 July 2014. Former reg. 4ZA(2) read as follows:
"**4ZA(2)** Where the qualifying individual is 18 or over at the end of the year, the qualifying individual may only invest up to 50 per cent of the overall subscription limit specified in paragraph (1)(b) in any year to a cash account."
Reg. 4ZA inserted by SI 2011/1780, reg. 8, with effect from 1 November 2011.

SUBSCRIPTIONS TO A JUNIOR ISA ACCOUNT

4ZB(1) Any person may subscribe to a junior ISA account provided the overall amount subscribed by that person and any other person for any year in respect of the same named child does not exceed £4,000.

4ZB(2) An amount paid to a junior ISA account in excess of the amount mentioned in paragraph (1) is not an amount subscribed to a junior ISA account and must not be held in that account.

4ZB(3) A single subscription for an amount equal to the amount mentioned in paragraph (1) or any number of smaller amounts that, when aggregated, do not exceed the amount mentioned in paragraph (1), may be made in respect of the same named child–

(a) to a cash account held by that child,

(b) to a stocks and shares account held by that child, or

(c) in any proportion between such accounts.

4ZB(4) No subscription may be made to a cash account that is a junior ISA account held by a named child where–

(a) the balance in the account is less than one penny; and

(b) that child holds another cash account opened pursuant to a junior ISA application described in regulation 12A after the time when the account mentioned in sub-paragraph (a) was opened.

4ZB(5) No subscription may be made to a stocks and shares account that is a junior ISA account held by a named child where–

(a) the balance in the account is less than one penny; and

(b) that child holds another stocks and shares account opened pursuant to a junior ISA application described in regulation 12A after the time when the account mentioned in sub-paragraph (a) was opened.

History – In reg. 4ZB(1), the figure "£4,000" substituted for "£3,840" by SI 2014/1450, reg. 7, with effect from 1 July 2014.
In reg. 4ZB(1), the figure "£3,840" substituted for "£3,720" by SI 2014/654, reg. 6, with effect from 6 April 2014.
In reg. 4ZB(1), the figure "£3,720" substituted for "£3,600" by SI 2013/267, reg. 3, with effect from 6 April 2013.
Reg. 4ZB inserted by SI 2011/1780, reg. 8, with effect from 1 November 2011.

INALIENABILITY OF A JUNIOR ISA ACCOUNT

4ZC(1) Any assignment of, or agreement to assign, investments under a junior ISA account, and any charge on or agreement to charge any such investments, is void.

4ZC(2) On the bankruptcy of the named child holding a junior ISA account, the entitlement to investments under it does not pass to any trustee or other person acting on behalf of the child's creditors.

4ZC(3) "Assignment" includes assignation; and "assign" is to be construed accordingly.

4ZC(4) "Charge on or agreement to charge" includes a right in security over or an agreement to create a right in security over.

4ZC(5) "Bankruptcy", in relation to a named child, includes the sequestration of the child's estate.

4ZC(6) Paragraph (1) shall not render void anything done to vest title to an account investment as required by regulation 4(6)(b)(ia) or 15(a) by virtue of–

(a) a transfer of an account in accordance with regulation 21B; or

(b) a change of registered contact in relation to a junior ISA account.

History – Reg. 4ZC inserted by SI 2011/1780, reg. 8, with effect from 1 November 2011.

PERMITTED WITHDRAWALS FROM A JUNIOR ISA ACCOUNT

4ZD Withdrawals from a junior ISA account may only be made–

(a) by the account manager, to settle any management charges and other incidental expenses, which are due by or under the management agreement,

(b) in accordance with regulation 4ZE, or

(c) where the account manager is satisfied that the named child who held the account has died.

History – Reg. 4ZD inserted by SI 2011/1780, reg. 8, with effect from 1 November 2011.

PERMITTED WITHDRAWALS FROM A JUNIOR ISA ACCOUNT WHERE THE NAMED CHILD IS TERMINALLY ILL

4ZE(1) A registered contact may make a claim to the Board for withdrawals from a junior ISA account to be permitted in accordance with this regulation.

4ZE(2) The claim shall be–

(a) made in a manner prescribed by the Board, which shall include the giving of any consent necessary for the verification or consideration of the claim, and

(b) accepted in either of the following cases:

Case 1

The named child holding the account:

(i) in England and Wales or Scotland, falls within either section 72(5) of the Social Security Contributions and Benefits Act 1992 (special rules for terminally ill person's entitlement to care component of disability living allowance) or section 82(4) of the Welfare Reform Act 2012 (terminal illness); or

(ii) in Northern Ireland, falls within section 72(5) of the Social Security Contributions and Benefits (Northern Ireland) Act 1992 (the care component).

Case 2

Evidence that the named child holding the account is terminally ill has been supplied to the satisfaction of the Board.

4ZE(3) The Board shall issue a letter to the registered contact authorising withdrawals from the account under this regulation.

4ZE(4) Once a claim has been accepted, withdrawals of any amount (including the proceeds from a policy of life insurance and an amount sufficient to close the account) may be made by the registered contact at any time (but this does not include the transfer of a policy of life insurance otherwise than in accordance with regulation 21B).

4ZE(5) Where account investments are withdrawn in a form other than sterling currency, the named child shall be treated as having sold the account investments in question, and as having reacquired them in his personal capacity, for a consideration equal to their market value at the time of their withdrawal.

4ZE(6) In this regulation, **"terminally ill"** has the meaning

(a)   for England and Wales and Scotland in section 66(2)(a) of the Social Security Contributions and Benefits Act 1992 or section 82(4) of the Welfare Reform Act 2012 (terminal illness); or

(b)   for Northern Ireland, section 72(5) of the Social Security Contributions and Benefits (Northern Ireland) Act 1992 (the care component).

History – In reg. 4ZE(2)(b), the entry "Case 1" substituted by SI 2014/654, reg. 7(1), with effect from 6 April 2014.
In reg. 4ZE(3), the words ", and shall also notify the account manager" omitted by SI 2014/654, reg. 7(2), with effect from 6 April 2014.
In reg. 4ZE(6), the words "(a) for England and Wales and Scotland" inserted by SI 2014/654, reg. 7(3)(a), with effect from 6 April 2014.
In reg. 4ZE(6), the words "or section 82(4) of the Welfare Reform Act 2012 (terminal illness); or (b) for Northern Ireland, section 72(5) of the Social Security Contributions and Benefits (Northern Ireland) Act 1992 (the care component)" inserted by SI 2014/654, reg. 7(3)(b), with effect from 6 April 2014.
Reg. 4ZE inserted by SI 2011/1780, reg. 8, with effect from 1 November 2011.

REPAIR OF CERTAIN INCOMPATIBLE ACCOUNTS AND EXCESS SUBSCRIPTIONS – ACCOUNTS OTHER THAN JUNIOR ISA ACCOUNTS

4A(1) An invalid account is "eligible for repair" if, in relation to the year in which the subscriptions to the account were made (**"the relevant year"**), it satisfies–

(a)   both the First and Second Conditions below, or

(b)   the Third Condition.

First Condition

The account is invalid because a subscription to the account causes the account investor to breach the conditions in regulation 4(1B)(a) or (b) (which, taken together, allow an individual to subscribe to a single cash account and a single stocks and shares account, in a particular year) and for no other reason.

Second Condition

The account is (disregarding any account exempt from tax under regulation 4B) the earliest account in the relevant year, the subscriptions to which caused the account investor to breach the conditions in regulation 4(1B)(a) or (b), as the case may be (that is, it was first subscribed to earlier in that year than any other such account).

Third Condition

The account is invalid because a subscription to the account breaches the overall subscription limit in regulation 4ZA(1), and for no other reason.

4A(2) In this regulation–

(a)   where an account investor subscribes to a particular account in more than one year, each year's subscriptions shall be treated as a separate account for the purposes of this regulation, and regulation 4B (except for determining when an account is closed) only;

(b)   **"date of discovery"** means the date on which an officer of the Board gives a notice ("notice of discovery") to the account manager or account investor that the account is invalid, and (if appropriate) directions under paragraph (5) below;

(c)   [Omitted by SI 2007/2119, reg. 7]

(d)   **"valid account"** means an account which (apart from under this regulation) is exempt from tax under regulation 22;

(e)   **"invalid account"** means a scheme of investment which is not exempt from tax under these Regulations but which (if so exempt) would be an account, within the meaning in regulation

4(1A)(a) and, in relation to an invalid account, references to an account and component have corresponding meanings; and

(f)   (for the avoidance of doubt) "repair" of an account is without prejudice to loss of, and accounting to the Board for, any relief from tax given for the period up to the date of discovery.

4A(3)   An invalid account which is eligible for repair shall be treated as–

(a)   exempt from tax under this regulation (as if under regulation 22), and

(b)   complying with the conditions of regulation 4(1B)(a) or (b), or 4ZA(1), as the case may be,

as from the date of discovery, to the extent of the relevant proportion mentioned in paragraph (4)(b).

4A(4)

(a)   Calculate the extent to which the subscriptions made (and counting towards the subscription limit) during the relevant year–

        (i)   to that account, any other account which is eligible for repair, and any valid account (but ignoring subscriptions to any closed account within the meaning in regulation 4B) do not exceed,

        (ii)   the subscriptions limit in regulation 4ZA(1), and

(b)   an officer of the Board shall apportion that result between the accounts mentioned in sub-paragraph (a)(i), and the amount apportioned to the account mentioned in paragraph (3) is the relevant proportion.

4A(5)   The account manager must comply within 30 days with any directions in the notice of discovery which–

(a)   make the apportionment under paragraph (4)(b) and identify the account and component from which excess subscriptions or allocations (if any) are to be removed;

(b)   direct the removal of subscriptions and proceeds representing them from an account; or

(c)   direct the removal of subscriptions and proceeds representing them from a component.

4A(6)   For the purposes of this regulation, a subscription to an account that is a junior ISA account shall be disregarded.

History – Heading to reg. 4A substituted by SI 2011/1780, reg. 9(a), with effect from 1 November 2011.
In the former heading to reg. 4A the words "and excess subscriptions" inserted at the end by SI 2007/2119, reg. 7(a), with effect from 6 April 2008.
In reg. 4A(1), under the Third Condition, "4ZA(1)" substituted for "4ZA(1)(b)" by SI 2014/1450, reg. 8(a), with effect from 1 July 2014.
In reg. 4A(1), in the parts headed "First Condition" and "Second Condition", the words "regulation 4(1B)(a) or (b)" substituted for the words "regulation 4(1)(d) or (e)" by SI 2011/1780, reg. 9(b)(i), with effect from 1 November 2011.
In reg. 4A(1), in the part headed "Third Condition", the words "regulation 4ZA(1)(b)" substituted for the words "regulation 4(2)(a)" by SI 2011/1780, reg. 9(b)(ii), with effect from 1 November 2011.
Reg. 4A(1)(a) and (b) and Three Conditions substituted for reg. 4A(1)(a) and (b) and the Four Conditions, by SI 2007/2119, reg. 7(b), with effect from 6 April 2008.
In reg. 4A(2)(e), the words "regulation 4(1A)(a)" substituted for the words "regulation 4(1)(a)" by SI 2011/1780, reg. 9(c), with effect from 1 November 2011.
Reg. 4A(2)(c) omitted and in sub-para. (e) the words "and component" substituted for the words ", a component and subscriptions pursuant to regulation 5(1)" by SI 2007/2119, reg. 7(c), with effect from 6 April 2008.
In reg. 4A(3)(b), "or (2)" omitted by SI 2014/1450, reg. 8(b), with effect from 1 July 2014.
In reg. 4A(3)(b), the words "regulation 4(1B)(a) or (b), or 4ZA(1) or (2)" substituted for the words "regulation 4(1)(d) or (e), or 4(2)(a)" by SI 2011/1780, reg. 9(d), with effect from 1 November 2011.
In reg. 4A(3)(b), the words "4(1)(d) or (e), or 4(2)(a)" substituted for the words "4(1)(c)(ii) or (d)(ii)" by SI 2007/2119, reg. 7(d), with effect from 6 April 2008.
In reg. 4A(4)(a),"limit" substituted for "limits" and in reg. 4A(4)(a)(ii) "limit" substituted for "limits" and "and (2), as the case may be" omitted by SI 2014/1450, reg. 8(c), with effect from 1 July 2014.
In reg. 4A(4)(a)(ii), the words "regulation 4ZA(1) and (2)" substituted for the words "regulation 4(2) and (3)" by SI 2011/1780, reg. 9(e), with effect from 1 November 2011.
Reg. 4A(4)(a) substituted by SI 2007/2119, reg. 7(e), with effect from 6 April 2008.
Reg. 4A(6) inserted by SI 2011/1780, reg. 9(f), with effect from 1 November 2011.
Reg. 4A inserted by SI 2002/3158, reg. 3 with effect from 8 January 2003, where a notice of discovery is given on or after that date in relation to subscriptions to accounts made on or after 6 April 2001.

CLOSURE OF CASH ACCOUNT THAT IS NOT A JUNIOR ISA ACCOUNT PRIOR TO THE OPENING OF THE SAME TYPE OF ACCOUNT TO BE DISREGARDED ONCE

4B(1)   Where–

(a)   an account investor, within the same year–

        (i)   subscribes to a cash account,

        (ii)   then closes it ("the closed account"), and

        (iii)   subsequently first subscribes to another cash account and (b)　the closed account was (apart from under this regulation) exempt from tax under regulation 22(1),

the earliest account in that year to fall within the terms of sub-paragraph (a)(iii) (the **"first later account"**) shall be eligible for the relief in paragraph (2).

4B(2)　The first later account shall be treated, as from the date of the first subscription to it mentioned in paragraph (1)(a)(iii) as complying with the conditions of regulation 4(1B)(a) in the same manner as the closed account.

4B(3)　In this regulation, an account is closed where—

(a)　the account investor withdraws from the account all account investments, other proceeds in respect of such investments and cash, representing subscriptions to the account (and closure shall be treated as occurring at the date of such withdrawal), and

(b)　no further subscriptions to the account are made during the remainder of the year, after such withdrawal.

History – In the heading to reg. 4B the words "that is not a junior ISA account" inserted by SI 2011/1780, reg. 10(a), with effect from 1 November 2011.
In the heading to reg. 4B the words "cash" substituted for the words "mini-account or TESSA only" by SI 2007/2119, reg. 8(a), with effect from 6 April 2008.
Reg. 4B inserted by SI 2002/3158 reg. 4, with effect from 8 January 2003, in relation to subscriptions to accounts made on or after 6 April 2003.
In reg. 4B(1)(a)(i) the words "cash" substituted for the words "mini-account or TESSA only" by SI 2007/2119, reg. 8(b), with effect from 6 April 2008.
In reg. 4B(1)(a)(iii) the words "cash account" substituted for the words "account which has the same designation and type of component as the closed account," by SI 2007/2119, reg. 8(c), with effect from 6 April 2008.
In reg. 4B(2) the words "regulation 4(1B)(a)" substituted for the words "regulation 4(1)(d)" by SI 2011/1780, reg. 10(b), with effect from 1 November 2011.
In reg. 4B(2) the words "as complying with the conditions of regulation 4(1)(d)" substituted for sub-para. (a) and (b) and the hyphen which precedes them by SI 2007/2119, reg. 8(d), with effect from 6 April 2008.

REMOVAL OF INSURANCE COMPONENTS AT 6TH APRIL 2005

4C　[Omitted by SI 2014/1450, reg. 9.]

History – Reg. 4C omitted by SI 2014/1450, reg. 9, with effect from 1 July 2014. Former reg. 4C read as follows:
　　"**4C(1)**　This regulation applies to accounts which include (or are made up of) an insurance component immediately before 6th April 2005 ("the transitional time").
　　4C(2)　Where all the policies of life insurance falling within regulation 9, held under the component at the transitional time, were issued in respect of an insurance made before 6th April 2004, the component–
　　(a)　if the account is, or had been, designated as a maxi-account, shall be treated on and from 6th April 2005 as merged into the stocks and shares component for that account; and
　　(b)　if the account is, or had been, designated as a mini-account, shall be treated on and from 6th April 2005 as a stocks and shares component of the same account.
　　4C(3)　Where any of the policies of life insurance falling within regulation 9, held under the component at the transitional time, were issued in respect of an insurance made on or after 6th April 2004–
　　(a)　the condition in regulation 7(15) shall be applied to those policies on 6th April 2005, modified as if for "the date" to "five years" there were substituted "6th April 2005";
　　(b)　if all those policies satisfy that condition, paragraph (2)(a) or (b), as the case may be, shall apply to the component;
　　(c)　if any of those policies does not satisfy that condition, the component–
　　　(i)　if the account is, or had been, designated as a maxi-account including a cash component, shall be treated on and from 6th April 2005 as merged into the cash component for that account; and
　　　(ii)　in any other case, shall be treated on and from 6th April 2005 as a cash component for the same account.
　　History – Reg. 4C(3)(a) substituted by SI 2005/609, reg. 3, with effect from 6 April 2005.
　　Reg. 4C inserted by SI 2004/2996, reg. 6, with effect from 6 April 2005."

REMOVAL OF MAXI-ACCOUNTS, MINI-ACCOUNTS AND TESSA ONLY ACCOUNTS AT 6TH APRIL 2008

4D　[Omitted by SI 2014/1450, reg. 10.]

History – Reg. 4D omitted by SI 2014/1450, reg. 10, with effect from 1 July 2014. Former reg. 4D read as follows:
　　"**4D(1)**　This regulation applies to accounts in existence immediately before 6th April 2008 ("the transitional time").
　　4D(2)　An account that, at the transitional time, is or has been designated as a TESSA only account shall be treated as a cash account on and from 6th April 2008.
　　4D(3)　An account that, at the transitional time, is or has been designated as a mini-account made up of a cash component shall be treated as a cash account on and from 6th April 2008.
　　4D(4)　An account that, at the transitional time, is or has been designated as a mini-account made up of a stocks and shares component shall be treated as a stocks and shares account on and from 6th April 2008.
　　4D(5)　An account that, at the transitional time, is or has been designated as a maxi-account and is made up of a stocks and shares component only, shall be treated as a stocks and shares account on and from 6th April 2008.
　　4D(6)　Where an account, at the transitional time, is or has been designated as a maxi-account and is made up of two components–
　　(a)　the stocks and shares component, if it holds investments or cash at the transitional time, shall be treated as a stocks and shares account on and from 6th April 2008; and
　　(b)　the cash component, if it holds investments or cash at the transitional time, shall be treated as a separate cash account on and from 6th April 2008.
　　History – Reg. 4D inserted by SI 2007/2119, reg. 9, with effect from 6 April 2008."

TRANSFERS FROM MATURED TAX-EXEMPT SPECIAL SAVINGS ACCOUNTS

5 [Omitted by SI 2007/2119, reg. 10, with effect from 6 April 2008.]

TREATMENT OF SUMS HELD IN ACCOUNTS MANAGED BY ICESAVE BANK

5A [Omitted by SI 2011/1780, reg. 11, with effect from 1 November 2011.]

TREATMENT OF CERTAIN SUMS HELD IN ACCOUNTS MANAGED BY KEYDATA INVESTMENT SERVICES LIMITED

5B [Omitted by SI 2012/1871, reg. 10.]

History – Reg. 5B omitted by SI 2012/1871, reg. 10, with effect from 8 August 2012. Former reg. 5B read as follows:
> "**5B(1)** This regulation applies if–
>> (a)   at 8th June 2009, an account investor had an account holding SLS Capital S.A. Secure Income Bonds, issue 1, 2 or 3 ("the Bonds"), for which the account manager was Keydata Investment Services Limited ("Keydata") which went into administration on that date;
>> (b)   the investor has received from the Administrators of Keydata a certificate containing the following information–
>>> (i)   the investor's full name and permanent residential address, including postcode;
>>> (ii)   the investor's Keydata client reference number;
>>> (iii)   the date of investment in the Bonds;
>>> (iv)   the amount (if any) subscribed in cash;
>>> (v)   the amount (if any) subscribed by an ISA transfer;
>>> (vi)   the total amount subscribed (for investment in the Bonds); and
>>> (vii)   the maximum amount that can be reinvested using the certificate.
> **5B(2)** Where this regulation applies, the account investor may make a single subscription to a stocks and shares account held by him or her with another account manager–
>> (a)   not exceeding the maximum stated in the certificate under paragraph (1)(b)(vii);
>> (b)   not later than 5th April 2011; and
>> (c)   giving the certificate to the new account manager.
> **5B(3)** The subscription made under this regulation shall not count towards the subscription limits in regulation 4ZA(1).
> **5B(4)** The new account manager must–
>> (a)   treat the subscription made under this regulation in the same way as an account transferred from another account manager to him; and
>> (b)   retain either the certificate mentioned in paragraph (1)(b), or a copy of it.".

In former reg. 5B(3), the words "regulation 4ZA(1)" substituted for the words "regulation 4(2)" by SI 2011/1780, reg. 12, with effect from 1 November 2011.
Former reg. 5B inserted by SI 2010/835, reg. 3, with effect from 30 December 2009.

TREATMENT OF CERTAIN SUMS HELD IN DORMANT ACCOUNTS

5C(1) Regulations 30 and 31 (information by account managers) shall not apply to a dormant account, while section 1 or 2 of the Dormant Bank and Building Society Accounts Act 2008 ("the 2008 Act") applies in relation to that account.

5C(2) Where, following a repayment claim, the balance of a dormant account is paid–

(a)   back into the account (in a case where the original cash account can be reinstated with the same account manager, the same account investor and number), or

(b)   into another cash account in the same account investor's name, with the same account manager (in any other case),

the payment into the account shall not count towards the subscription limit in regulation 4ZA(1).

5C(3) In this regulation, **"repayment claim"** means a repayment claim mentioned in section 5(6) of the 2008 Act, and other terms used in this regulation and that Act have the same meaning in this regulation as in that Act.

History – In reg. 5C(2)"limit" substituted for "limits" and "regulation 4ZA(1)" substituted for "regulation 4ZA(2)" by SI 2014/1450, reg. 11, with effect from 1 July 2014.
In reg. 5C(2), the words "regulation 4ZA(2)" substituted for the words "regulation 4(2) and (3)" by SI 2011/1780, reg. 13, with effect from 1 November 2011.
Reg. 5C inserted by SI 2011/22, reg. 9(3), with effect from 1 February 2011.

SUBSCRIPTIONS DISREGARDED FOR THE PURPOSES OF THE SUBSCRIPTION LIMITS IN REGULATIONS 4ZA AND 4ZB

5D(1) A subscription to an account made in accordance with this regulation must be disregarded for the purposes of the subscription limits in regulations 4ZA (subscriptions to an account other than a junior ISA account) and 4ZB (subscriptions to a junior ISA account).

5D(2) A subscription to an account held by an account investor is made in accordance with this regulation if–

(a)   the subscription is–

(i)   a defaulted cash account subscription;

Statutory Instruments

   (ii) a defaulted investment subscription; or

   (iii) permitted in accordance with regulation 5DE; and

(b) the account manager of the account to which the subscription is made is provided with the information specified in regulation 5DF as relevant to the subscription.

History – Reg. 5D inserted by SI 2012/1871, reg. 11, with effect from 8 August 2012.

DEFAULTED CASH ACCOUNT SUBSCRIPTION

5DA A subscription is a defaulted cash account subscription if–

(a)   it is made to an account (which may be a stocks and shares account or a cash account) held by an account investor who held a cash account ("defaulted cash account") in respect of which a default event occurred no more than 180 days before the subscription is made; and

(b)   it does not exceed the amount held in the defaulted cash account immediately before the default event occurred (including interest accrued but not paid at that time).

History – Reg. 5DA inserted by SI 2012/1871, reg. 11, with effect from 8 August 2012.

DEFAULTED INVESTMENT SUBSCRIPTION

5DB A subscription is a defaulted investment subscription if–

(a)   it is made to an account held by the account investor who held the account in respect of which a defaulted investment payment has been made no more than 180 days before the subscription is made; and

(b)   it does not exceed the amount of the defaulted investment payment.

History – In reg. 5DB(a) "an account" substituted for "a stocks and shares account" by SI 2014/1450, reg. 12, with effect from 1 July 2014.
Reg. 5DB inserted by SI 2012/1871, reg. 11, with effect from 8 August 2012.

DEFAULT EVENT IN RESPECT OF CASH ACCOUNT

5DC A default event in respect of a cash account held by an account investor occurs where the account manager of that account is determined to be unable or likely to be unable to satisfy claims against the account manager in accordance with the rules of the scheme for compensation established pursuant to section 213 of the Financial Services and Markets Act 2000.

History – Reg. 5DC inserted by SI 2012/1871, reg. 11, with effect from 8 August 2012.

DEFAULTED INVESTMENT PAYMENT

5DD A defaulted investment payment occurs where a payment is made (otherwise than by accretion to a stocks and shares account) by way of compensation in respect of the poor performance, loss, depreciation or risk of depreciation of an investment described in regulation 7 ("defaulted investment") held in a stocks and shares account (whether or not the defaulted investment continues to be held in the account at the time of the payment).

History – Reg. 5DD inserted by SI 2012/1871, reg. 11, with effect from 8 August 2012.

ADDITIONAL PERMITTED SUBSCRIPTION TO A JUNIOR ISA ACCOUNT

5DE A subscription is permitted by this regulation if it is made to a junior ISA account that is a cash account but would have been a defaulted investment subscription if it had been made to a stocks and shares account.

History – Reg. 5DE inserted by SI 2012/1871, reg. 11, with effect from 8 August 2012.

INFORMATION REQUIRED BY REGULATION 5D

5DF(1) The information specified by this regulation is–

(a)   in relation to a defaulted cash account subscription–

   (i) the amount held in the defaulted cash account to which the subscription relates immediately before the default event occurred (including interest accrued but not paid at that time);

   (ii) the current year's subscription made to that account; and

   (iii) the date on which the first subscription (if any) was made to that account, in the year in which the defaulted cash subscription is made;

(b)   in relation to a defaulted investment subscription or a subscription permitted by regulation 5DE–

     (i)   evidence of the amount of the defaulted investment payment to which the subscription relates and the date it was paid;

     (ii)   details of the defaulted investment in respect of which the defaulted investment payment was made;

     (iii)   the full name and address (including postcode) of the account manager of the stocks and shares account in which the defaulted investment was held;

     (iv)   the full name and address (including postcode) of the maker of the defaulted investment payment.

5DF(2)   In this regulation–

"current year's subscription" in relation to a defaulted cash account means–

   (a)   subscriptions made to the account in the year in which the defaulted cash account subscription is made, but before the default event; and

   (b)   subscriptions made to any other account held by the account investor in the year in which the defaulted cash account subscription is made and transferred to the account before the subscription is made.

History – Reg. 5DF inserted by SI 2012/1871, reg. 11, with effect from 8 August 2012.

SINGLE REGULATION 5D SUBSCRIPTION

5DG   Only one defaulted cash account subscription, defaulted investment subscription or subscription permitted by regulation 5DE may be made in respect of a defaulted cash account or a defaulted investment payment as the case may be even if the subscription made is an amount less than that which could have been made by way of such subscription in accordance with regulation 5D.

History – Reg. 5DG inserted by SI 2012/1871, reg. 11, with effect from 8 August 2012.

DEFAULT EVENT OR DEFAULT INVESTMENT PAYMENT OCCURRING IN THE PERIOD BEGINNING ON 6TH APRIL 2011 AND ENDING ON 7TH AUGUST 2012

5DH   Anything occurring in the period commencing on 6th April 2011 and ending on 7th August 2012 that, if it had occurred after that period, would have been–

(i)   a default event in respect of a cash account within regulation 5DC, or

(ii)   a defaulted investment payment within regulation 5DD,

shall be treated as occurring on 8th August 2012 for the purposes of regulations 5D to 5DG.

History – Reg. 5DH inserted by SI 2012/1871, reg. 11, with effect from 8 August 2012.

SPECIAL PROVISION IN RESPECT OF LEHMAN BROTHERS INVESTMENTS AND KEYDATA INVESTMENTS

5DI(1)   Regulations 5DJ to 5DM make special provision in respect of an investment that is a Lehman Brothers investment or a Keydata investment.

5DI(2)   An investment is a Lehman Brothers investment if–

(a)   the investment was a qualifying investment held by an account investor in a stocks and shares account on 15th September 2008;

(b)   Lehman Brothers Holdings Inc. acted as the sole counterparty underwriting the investment on that day; and

(c)   the investment was not sold or otherwise disposed of on that day so as to cause it to cease to be a qualifying investment of the account on that day or any other day.

5DI(3)   An investment is a Keydata investment if–

(a)   the investment was a qualifying investment held by an account investor in a stocks and shares account on 8th June 2009;

(b)   Keydata Investment Services Limited (Keydata) on that day–

     (i)   was the account manager of the account, or

     (ii)   administered the account for another account manager; and

(c)   the investment was not sold or otherwise disposed of on that day so as to cause it to cease to be a qualifying investment of the account on that day or any other day.

History – Reg. 5DI inserted by SI 2012/1871, reg. 11, with effect from 8 August 2012.

SPECIAL APPLICATION OF REGULATIONS 5DB, 5DD, 5DF AND 5DH IN RESPECT OF A LEHMAN BROTHERS INVESTMENT

5DJ In respect of a Lehman Brothers investment–

(a) regulation 5D shall apply as if after paragraph (2) there is added–

"**5D(3)** No defaulted investment subscription may be made in respect of a defaulted investment payment made or treated as made on 8th August 2012 other than a single defaulted investment payment treated as made by virtue of regulation 5DL(2).";

(b) regulation 5DB shall apply as if paragraph (b) provided that a defaulted investment subscription must not exceed the amount of the defaulted investment payment determined in accordance with regulation 5DL;

(c) regulation 5DD is subject to regulation 5DL(2);

(d) regulation 5DF(1)(b) shall apply as if the information specified by it is–

  (i) the information specified in paragraphs (i)–(iv) of that regulation;

  (ii) the value of the defaulted investment at the opening of trading on the London Stock Exchange on 15th September 2008;

  (iii) the date and amount of any earlier defaulted investment subscriptions in respect of the Lehman Brothers investment in question made before the making of the defaulted investment subscription;

  (iv) the name and address (including postcode) of the account manager to whom any subscription referred to in sub-paragraph (iii) of this paragraph was made;

(e) regulation 5DH–

  (i) shall apply as if the period mentioned in that regulation were the period commencing on 16th September 2008 and ending on 7th August 2012;

  (ii) is subject to regulation 5DL(2).

History – Reg. 5DJ inserted by SI 2012/1871, reg. 11, with effect from 8 August 2012.

DEEMED DEFAULTED INVESTMENT PAYMENT IN RESPECT OF A LEHMAN BROTHERS INVESTMENT

5DK A defaulted investment payment shall be treated as made on 8th August 2012 in respect of a Lehman Brothers investment to the account investor who held it.

History – Reg. 5DK inserted by SI 2012/1871, reg. 11, with effect from 8 August 2012.

SPECIFIED AMOUNT FOR THE PURPOSES OF A DEFAULTED INVESTMENT SUBSCRIPTION IN RESPECT OF A LEHMAN BROTHERS INVESTMENT

5DL(1) This regulation determines the amount which a defaulted investment subscription must not exceed for the purposes of regulation 5DB(b) in relation to a defaulted investment payment made or treated as made in respect of a Lehman Brothers investment.

5DL(2) Where one or more defaulted investment payments in respect of a Lehman Brothers investment are made on 8th August 2012 or are treated as made on that day by virtue of regulations 5DH or 5DK, they shall be treated as if they comprised a single defaulted investment payment made on that day of an amount which is the greater of–

(a) the value of the investment at the opening of trading on the London Stock Exchange on 15th September 2008; or

(b) the total of the payments made or treated as made by virtue of regulation 5DH on 8th August 2012.

5DL(3) Where a defaulted investment payment in respect of a Lehman Brothers investment is made after 8th August 2012, its amount for the purposes of regulation 5DB(b) is the greater of–

(a) the amount determined by the formula $A - B$ where–

  (i) "A" is the total of the single defaulted investment payment treated as made on 8th August 2012 in respect of the investment by virtue of paragraph (2) and all defaulted investment payments made in respect of it in the period commencing immediately after that day and ending immediately after the defaulted investment payment in question;

  (ii) "B" is the total of all defaulted investment subscriptions made in respect of the Lehman Brothers investment before the subscription in question; or

(b) the amount determined by the formula $C - D$ where–

(i) "C" is the value of the investment at the opening of trading on the London Stock Exchange on 15th September 2008;

(ii) "D" is the total of all defaulted investment subscriptions made in respect of the Lehman Brothers investment before the subscription in question.

History – Reg. 5DL inserted by SI 2012/1871, reg. 11, with effect from 8 August 2012.

SPECIAL APPLICATION OF REGULATIONS 5DJ TO 5DL IN RESPECT OF A KEYDATA INVESTMENT

5DM In respect of a Keydata investment–

(a) regulations 5DJ to 5DL shall apply as if–

(i) a reference to a Lehman Brothers investment were a reference to a Keydata investment;

(ii) the reference in regulation 5DJ(e)(i) to 16th September 2008 were a reference to 9th June 2009;

(b) regulation 5DJ(d)(ii) shall apply as if the information it requires is the amount for which the Keydata investment in question was acquired;

(c) regulation 5DL(2)(a) shall apply as if it referred to the amount of subscriptions made to the account (or any other account or personal equity plan) and other proceeds (including income) representing those subscriptions used to purchase the investment;

(d) regulation 5DL(3)(a)(i) shall apply as if element "A" is the amount described in regulation 5DL(2)(a) as construed in accordance with paragraph (c) of this regulation;

(e) regulation 5DL(3)(b)(i) shall apply as if element "C" is the total of the single defaulted investment payment treated as made on 8th August 2012 in respect of the investment by virtue of regulation 5DL(2) and all defaulted investment payments made in respect of it in the period commencing immediately after that day and ending immediately after the defaulted investment payment in question.

History – Reg. 5DM inserted by SI 2012/1871, reg. 11, with effect from 8 August 2012.

SUBSCRIPTIONS MADE BY ACCOUNT INVESTORS ISSUED WITH CERTIFICATES BY ROYAL BANK OF SCOTLAND GROUP DISREGARDED FOR THE PURPOSES OF REGULATIONS 4ZA AND 31(3)(C)(II)

5E(1) A subscription to an account made in accordance with this regulation on or before 5th April 2013 must be disregarded for the purposes of–

(a) the subscription limit in regulation 4ZA (subscriptions to an account other than a junior ISA account); and

(b) regulation 31(3)(c)(ii) (returns of information by account manager).

5E(2) A subscription to an account is made in accordance with this regulation if–

(a) it is made to a cash account held by an account investor;

(b) a withdrawal was made during the relevant period from a cash account held by the account investor with the account manager holding the cash account to which the subscription is made;

(c) the account manager of the account to which the subscription is made holds the certificate issued to the account investor in accordance with paragraph (3) (or a copy of it);

(d) the subscription does not exceed the amount determined in accordance with paragraph (4); and

(e) no earlier subscription in accordance with this regulation has been made to an account held by the account investor with the account manager holding the cash account to which the subscription in question is made.

5E(3) A certificate is issued to an account investor in accordance with this paragraph if–

(a) it is issued to the account investor by a RBSG bank;

(b) it contains the name and address (including postcode) of the account investor;

(c) it identifies the period in respect of which the delay certified in accordance with sub–paragraph (d) occurred; and

(d) it certifies–

(i) that the account investor held with a RBSG bank a banking facility (other than an account opened in accordance with regulation 12), in respect of which the updating of the records of deposits made to and payments from the facility was delayed during the relevant period; or

(ii) that a deposit, payment or other transfer of money to the account investor was delayed in the relevant period by reason of the delay described in paragraph (i).

5E(4) The amount referred to in paragraph (2)(d) is the total of all withdrawals made in the relevant period from any cash account held with the account manager holding the cash account to which the subscription in question is made.

5E(5) In this regulation–

(a) a bank is a **"RBSG bank"** if it is–

(i) The Royal Bank of Scotland plc, a company incorporated in Scotland (Company Number 090312);

(ii) National Westminster Bank plc, a company incorporated in England and Wales (Company Number 00929027);

(iii) Ulster Bank, Limited, a company incorporated in Northern Ireland (Company Number R0000733);

(b) the **"relevant period"** is 19th June to 6th July 2012 (but to 22nd July 2012 where the bank in paragraph (3)(d) is Ulster Bank, Limited).

History – In reg. 5E(1)(a) "limit" substituted for "limits" by SI 2014/1450, reg. 13, with effect from 1 July 2014. Reg. 5E inserted by SI 2013/623, reg. 2(2), with effect from 5 April 2013.

GENERAL INVESTMENT RULES

6(1) All transactions by way of purchase by an account manager of investments under an account shall be made–

(a) in the case of an authorised fund which is a dual priced unit trust, at the manager's price for the sale of the relevant class of units within the meaning of, and complying with the requirements of, rules 6.3.5 and 6.3.5B of the Collective Investment schemes sourcebook;

(b) in the case of an authorised fund which is a single priced unit trust or an open-ended investment company, at the price of a unit or share within the meaning of, and complying with the requirements of, rules 6.3.5 and 6.3.5A of the Collective Investment schemes sourcebook; and

(c) in the case of all other account investments, at the price for which those investments might reasonably be expected to be purchased in the open market.

6(1ZA) In paragraph (1)(a) and (b)–

"a dual priced unit trust" means an authorised unit trust in respect of which the manager gives different prices for buying and selling units at the same time;

"a single priced unit trust" means an authorised unit trust in respect of which the manager gives the same price for buying and selling units at the same time.

6(2) All other transactions by way of sale or otherwise by an account manager in investments under an account shall be made at the price for which those investments might reasonably be expected to be sold or otherwise transacted, as the case may be, in the open market.

6(3) Investments, or rights in respect of investments, may not at any time–

(a) be purchased or made otherwise than out of cash which an account manager holds under an account and component, for which those investments or rights are qualifying investments; or

(b) be purchased from–

(i) an account investor, or

(ii) the spouse or civil partner of an account investor,

so as to become account investments under an account to which the account investor subscribes or has subscribed.

6(4) Subject to paragraphs (5) and (6), cash subscriptions and other cash held by an account manager under an account shall be held only in sterling and be deposited in–

(i) an account with a deposit-taker (including for this purpose a credit union), or a deposit account or a share account with a building society, or

(ii) in the case where the account manager is the Director of Savings, an account with the Director of Savings,

which is designated as an ISA account for the purposes of these Regulations only.

6(5) An account manager who is a European institution, a relevant authorised person or an assurance undertaking may hold cash subscriptions and other cash held under an account in the currency of the EEA State in which he has his principal place of business and may deposit such cash in an account, which is designated as mentioned in paragraph (4), with any person authorised under the law of that State to accept deposits.

6(6) Cash by way of dividends, interest, distributions, and other rights or proceeds in respect of qualifying investments for any account shall at all times be recorded and accounted for separately from that for any other account, and may be invested only–

(a)   in qualifying investments for the appropriate component; or

(b)   by way of cash deposit in accordance with paragraphs (4) and (5).

History – In reg. 6(1)(a), the words "rules 6.3.5 and 6.3.5B of the Collective Investment schemes sourcebook" substituted for "rule 15.4.4 of the Collective Investment Schemes Sourcebook" by SI 2008/704, reg. 5(2), with effect from 6 April 2008.
In reg. 6(1)(b), the words "rules 6.3.5 and 6.3.5A of the Collective Investment schemes sourcebook" substituted for "rule 4.3.11 of the Collective Investment Schemes Sourcebook" by SI 2008/704, reg. 5(3), with effect from 6 April 2008.
Reg. 6(1)(a), (b) substituted, and subreg. (1ZA) inserted by SI 2001/3629, reg. 171 which came into force on 1 December 2001.
In reg. 6(1ZA) the definition of "the Collective Investment Schemes Sourcebook" omitted by SI 2003/2747, reg. 4, with effect from 17 November 2003.
In reg. 6(3)(a), the words "and component" substituted for the words "at that time, and which has been allocated to the particular component of that account" by SI 2007/2119, reg. 11(a), with effect from 6 April 2008.
In reg. 6(3)(b)(ii) the words "or civil partner" inserted by SI 2005/3230, reg. 10(2), with effect from 5 December 2005.
In reg. 6(4), the words "cash subscriptions and other cash" substituted for the words "an account investor's cash subscription and any other cash" by SI 2011/1780, reg. 14, with effect from 1 November 2011.
In reg. 6(4)(i), the words "(including for this purpose a credit union)" inserted by SI 2005/3350, reg. 5, with effect from 27 December 2005.
Reg. 6(4)(ii) amended by SI 1998/3174, reg. 4, operative from 6 April 1999.
In reg. 6(5), the words "cash subscriptions and other cash" substituted for the words "an account investor's cash subscription and any other cash" by SI 2011/1780, reg. 14, with effect from 1 November 2011.
In reg. 6(6), in the words preceding sub-para. (a), the word "account" substituted for the word "component" twice and in sub-para. (a) the word "appropriate" substituted for the word "same" by SI 2007/2119, reg. 11(b), with effect from 6 April 2008.

QUALIFYING INVESTMENTS FOR A STOCKS AND SHARES COMPONENT

7(1) This regulation specifies the kind of investments ("qualifying investments for a stocks and shares component") which may be purchased, made or held under a stocks and shares component, and in this regulation and regulations 31 and 34, "shares" without more includes stock.

7(2) Qualifying investments for a stocks and shares component to which paragraph (1) refers are–

(a)   shares, not being shares in an investment trust–

    (i)   issued by a company wherever incorporated, and

    (ii)   subject to paragraph (3), either officially listed on a recognised stock exchange or, in the European Economic Area, admitted to trading on a recognised stock exchange.

    (iii)   [omitted by SI 2014/1450, reg. 14]

(b)   securities ("qualifying securities")–

    (i)   issued by a company wherever incorporated,

    (ii)   where the securities in question satisfy at least one of the conditions specified in paragraph (5); and

    (iii)   in the case of securities of an investment trust, purchased or acquired by the account manager in circumstances where the trust satisfies the conditions specified in paragraph (8);

(c)   gilt-edged securities;

(ca)   any securities issued by or on behalf of a government of any EEA State;

(cb)   any securities which, in relation to a security mentioned in sub-paragraph (ca), would be a strip of that security if "strip" had the same meaning as in section 47 of the Finance Act 1942, with the omission of the words "issued under the National Loans Act 1968"

(cc)   securities issued by a multilateral institution, contributions to which may be reported as official development assistance, listed in Part I of Annex 2 to the DAC Statistical Reporting Directive (approved by the Development Assistance Committee of the Organisation for Economic Co-operation and Development), where the securities satisfy the condition in paragraph (5)(b;

(d)   shares in an investment trust, in circumstances where the trust satisfies the conditions specified in paragraph (8);

(e)   [Omitted by SI 2008/704, reg. 6(3);]

(f)   units in, or shares of, a UK UCITS or recognised UCITS;

(g)   qualifying units in or shares of a non-UCITS retail scheme;

(h)   subject to the conditions specified in paragraph (10)–

    (i)   shares which the qualifying individual has exercised the right to acquire in accordance with the provisions of a Schedule 3 SAYE option scheme,

    (ii)   shares which have been appropriated to the qualifying individual in accordance with the provisions of an approved profit sharing scheme, or

    (iii)   plan shares of a Schedule 2 SIP which cease to be subject to the plan but have remained in the beneficial ownership of the participant,

and such shares shall be treated as fulfilling the condition as to payment of cash in regulation 4(1B)(d);

(ha)   a depositary interest;

(j)   cash deposited in accordance with regulation 6(4) to (6);

(k)   investments which–

    (i)   were held under a stocks and shares component or a personal equity plan on 28th November 2001,

    (ii)   on that date were admitted to trading on a recognised stock exchange in an EEA State and were not listed by a competent authority in an EEA State for the purposes of Council Directive 2001/34,

    (iii)   since that date have not ceased to be so admitted and have not become so listed,

    (iv)   do not fall within any of the other sub-paragraphs of this paragraph, and

    (v)   are not investments which, having fallen within any of those sub-paragraphs, have ceased so to fall on or after that date.

(l)   investments which–

    (i)   were held under the stocks and shares component or a personal equity plan on 6th April 2004; and

    (ii)   immediately before that date, fell within sub-paragraphs (e), (f) or (g), or sub-paragraph (ha) so far as the relevant investments (within the meaning in the definition of "depositary interest") fell within any of those sub-paragraphs.

(m)   units in a relevant collective investment scheme specified as a stakeholder product by regulation 5 of the Stakeholder Products Regulations;

(n)   policies of life insurance falling within regulation 9, issued in respect of an insurance made on or after 6th April 2005;

(o)   [omitted by SI 2014/1450, reg. 14]

(p)   in the case of a personal equity plan which is treated on and from 6th April 2008 as a stocks and shares account, investments which, immediately before that date, were qualifying investments for the plan under regulation 6(2)(m) of the Personal Equity Plan Regulations 1989;

(q)   core capital deferred shares within the meaning of regulation 2 of the Building Societies (Core Capital Deferred Shares) Regulations 2013, provided that such shares are listed on the official list of a recognised stock exchange.

7(3)   An investment in shares fulfils the conditions as to official listing and admission to trading in paragraph (2)(a), if–

(a)   in pursuance of a public offer, the account manager applies for the allotment or allocation to him of shares in a company which are due to be admitted to such listing or admitted to such trading within 30 days of the allocation or allotment, and which, when admitted to such listing, or trading would be qualifying investments for a stocks and shares component, and

(b)   the shares are not allotted or allocated to the account manager in the circumstances specified in paragraph (4).

7(4)   The circumstances specified in this paragraph are where–

(a)   the allotment or allocation of the shares was connected with the allotment or allocation of–

    (i)   shares in the company or trust of a different class, or

    (ii)   rights to shares in the company or trust of a different class, or

    (iii)   shares or rights to shares in another company or trust, or

    (iv)   units in or shares in, or rights to units in or shares in, an authorised fund or a part of an umbrella scheme, or

    (v)   [omitted by SI 2001/3629, reg. 172]

    (vi)   securities or rights to securities of the company or trust, or of another company or trust, to the account manager, the account investor or any other person; and

(b) the terms on which the first-mentioned shares in this paragraph were offered were significantly more favourable to the account manager or account investor than they would have been if their allotment or allocation had not been connected as described in sub-paragraph (a).

7(5) The conditions specified in this paragraph are—

(a) that the shares in the company issuing the securities are listed on the official list of a recognised stock exchange;

(b) that the securities are so listed;

(c) that the company issuing the securities is a 75% subsidiary of a company whose shares are so listed.

7(6) [Omitted by SI 2014/1450, reg. 14.]

7(7) [Omitted by SI 2008/704, reg. 6(5).]

7(8) The condition specified in this paragraph is that not more than 50% in value of the investments of the investment trust are either—

(a) securities which would not be qualifying securities, or

(b) securities which would not fall within any of sub-paragraphs (c) to (cb) of paragraph (2).

7(9) [Omitted by SI 2008/704, reg. 6(7).]

7(10) The conditions specified in this paragraph are—

(a) in relation to shares which the individual has exercised his right to acquire in accordance with the provisions of a Schedule 3 SAYE option scheme, that the shares are transferred to the account manager or his nominee before the expiry of the period of 90 days following the exercise of that right;

(b) in relation to shares appropriated to the individual in accordance with the provisions of an approved profit-sharing scheme, that the shares are transferred to the account manager or his nominee before the expiry of the period of 90 days following the date when the individual directed the trustees to transfer the ownership of the shares to him or, if earlier, the release date in relation to the shares;

(ba) in relation to plan shares mentioned in paragraph (2)(h)(iii), that the shares are transferred to the account manager or his nominee before the expiry of the period of 90 days following the date when the plan shares ceased to be subject to the plan;

(c) that the aggregate market value at the date of transfer of any shares transferred to the account manager or his nominee in accordance with sub-paragraphs (a), (b) or (ba) in any year, and the individual's cash subscriptions in that year to that account, do not together exceed the overall subscription limit in regulation 4ZA(1) in that year, reduced by the subscriptions by the individual in that year to a cash account.

7(11) In paragraph (4)(a), **"company"** means any body corporate having a share capital.

7(12) [Omitted by SI 2014/1450, reg. 14.]

7(13) The references to "shares" in paragraphs (2)(h) and (10) shall include references to a depositary interest where the relevant investments in question (referred to in paragraphs (a) and (b) of the definition of "depositary interest") are shares falling within both paragraphs (2)(h) and (10).

7(14) [Omitted by SI 2014/1450, reg. 14.]

7(15) [Omitted by SI 2014/1450, reg. 14.]

7(16) In this regulation, references, in relation to qualifying investments, to the value, are to be construed in accordance with regulation 6(2), but deducting the incidental costs that would be incurred by a disposal and, in the case of a policy of life insurance, omitting any benefits payable in the event of the death of the account investor.

7(17) [Omitted by SI 2014/1450, reg. 14.]

History – In reg. 7(2)(a)(i) "and " inserted at end, in reg. 7(2)(a)(ii) "." substituted for "," and "and" at end and reg. 7(2)(a)(iii) omitted by SI 2014/1450, reg. 14, with effect from 1 July 2014. Former reg. 7(2)(a)(iii) read as follows:
"(iii)   in circumstances where the shares in question satisfy the condition specified in paragraph (15), or were held under the component on 6th October 2005;"
Reg. 7(2)(a)(i)–(iii) substituted for the words ", issued by a company wherever incorporated and, subject to paragraph (3), officially listed on a recognised stock exchange;" by SI 2005/2561, reg. 5(a), with effect from 6 October 2005.
In reg. 7(2)(a)(ii), the words "either officially listed on a recognised stock exchange or, in the European Economic Area, admitted to trading on a recognised stock exchange, and" substituted for the words "officially listed on a recognised stock exchange, and" by SI 2013/1743, reg. 5(a), with effect from 5 August 2013.
Reg. 7(2)(b)(ii) substituted by SI 2014/1450, reg. 14, with effect from 1 July 2014. Former reg. 7(2)(b)(ii) read as follows:
"(ii)   where the securities in question satisfy—

    (a)   at least one of the conditions specified in paragraph (5), and

    (b)   the condition specified in paragraph (6), "

Reg. 7(2)(b)(ii) substituted by SI 2005/2561, reg. 5(b), with effect from 6 October 2005.

In reg. 7(2)(b)(ii)(a) the word "and" inserted, reg. 7(2)(b)(ii)(c) (and the word and which preceded it) omitted, in reg. 7(2)(e) the words ", fund of funds scheme or" substituted for the words "or a", in reg. 7(2)(f) the words "or Chapter 5 UCITS" inserted and reg. 7(2)(g) substituted for former reg 7(2)(g) and (ga) by SI 2005/3350, reg. 6, with effect from 27 December 2005.

In reg. 7(2)(b)(iii), the word "paragraph" substituted for "paragraphs (7) and" by SI 2008/704, reg. 6(2), with effect from 6 April 2008.

In reg. 7(2)(c) "which satisfy the condition specified in paragraph (12)" omitted by SI 2014/1450, reg. 14, with effect from 1 July 2014.

In reg. 7(2)(ca) ", which satisfy the condition specified in paragraph (12)" omitted by SI 2014/1450, reg. 14, with effect from 1 July 2014.

Reg. 7(2)(cb) substituted by SI 2014/1450, reg. 14, with effect from 1 July 2014. Former reg. 7(2)(cb) read as follows:

    "(cb)   any securities which–

          (i)   in relation to a security mentioned in sub-paragraph (ca), would be a strip of that security if "strip" had the same meaning as in section 47 of the Finance Act 1942, with the omission of the words "issued under the National Loans Act 1968", and

          (ii)   satisfy the condition specified in paragraph (12);"

Reg. 7(2)(c)–(cb) substituted, reg. 7(8) amended, and reg. 7(12) inserted, by SI 1998/3174, reg. 5, operative from 6 April 1999. In reg. 7(2)(cc) "condition " substituted for "conditions" and "paragraph" substituted for "paragraphs" and "and (6)" omitted by SI 2014/1450, reg. 14, with effect from 1 July 2014.

Reg. 7(2)(cc) inserted by SI 2008/3025, reg. 4, with effect from 16 December 2008.

In reg. 7(2)(d), the words "listed in the Official List of the Stock Exchange," omitted by SI 2014/654, reg. 8(a), with effect from 6 April 2014.

In reg. 7(2)(d), the word "paragraph" substituted for "paragraphs (7) and" by SI 2008/704, reg. 6(2), with effect from 6 April 2008.

Reg. 7(2)(e) omitted by SI 2008/704, reg. 6(3), with effect from 6 April 2008.

In reg. 7(2)(e) and (g) the words "units or shares satisfy the condition specified in paragraph (15)" substituted for the words "scheme satisfies the condition specified in paragraph (8)", and "scheme satisfies the condition specified in paragraph (9)" respectively, by SI 2003/2747, reg. 5(a), with effect from 6 April 2004.

In reg. 7(2)(f) ", in circumstances where the units or shares satisfy the condition specified in paragraph (15)" omitted by SI 2014/1450, reg. 14, with effect from 1 July 2014.

In reg. 7(2)(f), the words "UK UCITS or recognised UCITS" substituted for the words "relevant UCITS or Chapter 5 UCITS" by SI 2009/1994, reg. 6, with effect from 11 August 2009.

In reg. 7(2)(f) the words "units or shares satisfy the condition specified in paragraph (15)" substituted for the words "UCITS satisfies the condition specified in paragraph (8)", by SI 2003/2747, reg. 5(b), with effect from 6 April 2004.

In reg. 7(2)(g) ", in circumstances where the units or shares satisfy the condition specified in paragraph (15)" omitted by SI 2014/1450, reg. 14, with effect from 1 July 2014.

Reg. 7(2)(ga) inserted by SI 2003/2747, reg. 5(c), with effect from 17 November 2003.

In reg. 7(2)(h)(iii), the words "a Schedule 2" substituted for the words "an approved" by FA 2014, s. 51 and Sch. 8, para. 86, with effect from 6 April 2014 (subject to Sch. 8, para. 90–96).

In reg. 7(2)(h), the words "regulation 4(1B)(d)" substituted for the words "regulation 4(1)(h)" by SI 2011/1780, reg. 15(a), with effect from 1 November 2011.

In reg. 7(2)(h) the words: ", shares which the qualifying individual has exercised the right to acquire, or which have been appropriated to the qualifying individual, in accordance with the provisions of a savings-related share option scheme or an approved profit-sharing scheme," substituted by SI 2000/2079, reg. 4, operative from 21 August 2000.

In reg. 7(2)(h)(i), the words "a Schedule 3" substituted for the words "an approved" by FA 2014, s. 51 and Sch. 8, para. 145, with effect from 6 April 2014 (subject to the provisions of Sch. 8, para. 147–157).

In reg. 7(2)(h)(i), the words "an approved SAYE option scheme" substituted for "a savings-related share option scheme" by SI 2008/704, reg. 6(4), with effect from 6 April 2008.

In reg. 7(2)(h)(iii), the word "SIP" substituted for "employee share ownership plan" by SI 2008/704, reg. 6(4), with effect from 6 April 2008.

Reg. 7(2)(ha) inserted by SI 2000/3112, reg. 4, operative from 13 December 2000.

In reg. 7(2)(j) "which an account manager holds for the purpose of investment in investments which are qualifying investments for a stocks and shares component" omitted by SI 2014/1450, reg. 14, with effect from 1 July 2014.

In reg. 7(2)(k) inserted by SI 2001/3778, reg. 3(2), with effect from 19 December 2001.

In reg. 7(2)(k)(i) and (l)(i), the words "or a personal equity plan" inserted after the word "component" by SI 2007/2119, reg. 12(a), with effect from 6 April 2008.

In reg. 7(2)(l) inserted by SI 2003/2747, reg. 5(d), with effect from 6 April 2004.

In reg. 7(2)(m) ", in circumstances where the units satisfy the condition in paragraph (15)" omitted by SI 2014/1450, reg. 14, with effect from 1 July 2014.

In reg. 7(2)(n) ", in circumstances where the policy satisfies the condition in paragraph (15)" omitted by SI 2014/1450, reg. 14, with effect from 1 July 2014.

Reg. 7(2)(o) omitted by SI 2014/1450, reg. 14, with effect only in respect of investments purchased or made on or after 1 July 2014. Former reg. 7(2)(o) read as follows:

    "(o)   policies of life insurance falling within regulation 9, issued in respect of an insurance made before–

          (i)   6th April 2004, in a case where regulation 4C(2)(a) or (b) applies, or

          (ii)   6th April 2005, in a case where regulation 4C(3)(b) applies."

Reg. 7(2) (m), (n) and (o) inserted by SI 2004/2996, reg.7, with effect from 6 April 2005.

Reg. 7(2)(p) inserted by SI 2007/2119, reg. 12(b), with effect from 6 April 2008.

Reg. 7(2)(q) inserted and ";" substituted for "." at end of sub-para (p) by SI 2014/1450, reg. 14, with effect from1 July 2014.

In reg. 7(3), the words "An investment in shares fulfils the conditions as to official listing and admission to trading in paragraph (2)(a)" substituted for the words "An investment in shares fulfils the condition as to official listing in paragraph (2)(a) or (d), or the condition as to admission to trading in paragraph (2)(a)" by SI 2014/654, reg. 8(b), with effect from 6 April 2014.

In reg. 7(3), the words ", or the condition as to admission to trading in paragraph (2)(a)," inserted by SI 2013/1743, reg. 5(b), with effect from 5 August 2013.

In reg. 7(3)(a), the words "or trust" omitted by SI 2014/654, reg. 8(c), with effect from 6 April 2014.

In reg. 7(3)(a), the words "or admitted to such trading" and the words "or trading" inserted by SI 2013/1743, reg. 5(c), with effect from 5 August 2013.

In reg. 7(4)(a), ", or" substituted for ";" by SI 2002/1409, art. 7, with effect from 2 July 2002.

In reg. 7(5)(c), "75%" substituted for the words "75 per cent." by SI 2012/1871, reg. 12(a), with effect from 8 August 2012.

Reg. 7(6) omitted by SI 2014/1450, reg. 14, with effect from 1 July 2014. Former reg. 7(6) read as follows:

"**7(6)**   The condition specified in this paragraph is that, judged at the date when each of the securities is first held under the account, the terms on which it was issued do not–

(a)   require the loan to be repaid or the security to be re-purchased or redeemed, or

(b)   allow the holder to require the loan to be repaid or the security to be re-purchased or redeemed except in circumstances which are neither certain nor likely to occur,

within the period of five years from that date."

Reg. 7(7), omitted by SI 2008/704, reg. 6(5), with effect from 6 April 2008.

In reg. 7(8)(b) "." substituted for "," and "if paragraph (6), or paragraph (6) as it applies with the modifications in paragraph (12), as the case may be, required the terms on which they were issued to be judged at the date when they first became investments of the investment trust." which followed sub-para. (b) omitted by SI 2014/1450, reg. 14, with effect from 1 July 2014.

In reg. 7(8),"50%" substituted for the words "50 per cent." by SI 2012/1871, reg. 12(b), with effect from 8 August 2012.

In reg. 7(8), the words "investment trust" substituted for "trust, scheme or UCITS, or investments subject to the trusts of the scheme, as the case may be," by SI 2008/704, reg. 6(6), with effect from 6 April 2008.

In reg. 7(8), the words "investment trust" substituted for the words from "trust," to the end by SI 2008/704, reg. 6(6), with effect from 6 April 2008.

Reg. 7(8) amended and reg. 7(2)(e), (g); (4)(a)(iv), (v); and (9) substituted by SI 2001/3629, reg. 172 which came into force on 1 December 2001. The word "or" at the end of (4)(a)(iv) did not appear in the original substitution of reg. 7(4)(a)(iv), (v) with new (4)(a)(iv) but this was corrected by SI 2002/1409, reg. 7, with effect from 2 July 2002. Prior to this date the drafting error omission is presumed to apply.

Reg. 7(9) omitted by SI 2008/704, reg. 6(7), with effect from 6 April 2008.

In reg. 7(1)(a) the words "a Schedule 3" substituted for the words "an approved" by FA 2014, s. 51 and Sch. 8, para. 145, with effect from 6 April 2014 (subject to the provisions of Sch. 8, para. 147–157).

In reg. 7(10)(a), the words "an approved SAYE option scheme" substituted for the words "a savings-related share option scheme" by SI 2008/704, reg. 6(8), with effect from 6 April 2008.

Reg. 7(10)(ba) inserted by SI 2000/2079, reg. 4(2), operative from 21 August 2000.

In reg. 7(10)(c) "regulation 4ZA(1)" substituted for "regulation 4ZA(1)(b)" by SI 2014/1450, reg. 14, with effect from 1 July 2014.

In reg. 7(10)(c), the words "regulation 4ZA(1)(b)" substituted for the words "regulation 4(2)(a)" by SI 2011/1780, reg. 15(b), with effect from 1 November 2011.

In reg. 7(10)(c) the words "to that account, do not together exceed the overall subscription limit in regulation 4(2)(a) in that year, reduced by the subscriptions by the individual in that year to a cash account" substituted for the words below by SI 2007/2119, reg. 13, with effect from 6 April 2008.

"(c)   which are allocated to the stocks and shares component of that account–

(i)   in the case of a maxi-account do not together exceed the subscription limit in regulation 4(2) in that year, reduced by the cash subscriptions in that year which are allocated to a cash component of the account; and

(ii)   in the case of a mini-account, do not together exceed the subscription limit in regulation 4(3)(c) in that year.".

In former reg. 7(10)(c)(i) the words "or an insurance component" omitted by SI 2004/2996, reg. 8, with effect from 6 April 2005.

In reg. 7(10)(c) the words "(a), (b) or (ba)" substituted for "(a) or (b)" by SI 2000/2079, reg. 4(3), operative from 21 August 2000.

Reg. 7(12) omitted by SI 2014/1450, reg. 14, with effect from 1 July 2014. Former reg. 7(12) read as follows:

"**7(12)**   The condition specified in this paragraph is the condition specified in paragraph (6), omitting sub-paragraph (b) of that paragraph and the word "or" after sub-paragraph (a)."

Reg. 7(13) inserted by SI 2000/3112, reg. 4, operative from 13 December 2000.

Reg. 7(14) omitted by SI 2014/1450, reg. 14, with effect from 1 July 2014. Former reg. 7(14) read as follows:

"**7(14)**   Qualifying investments for a stocks and shares component falling within sub-paragraph (ha) of paragraph (2), so far as the relevant investments (within the meaning given in the definition of "depositary interest") fall within any of sub-paragraphs (a), (f), or (g) of that paragraph, must satisfy the condition specified in paragraph (15)."

In former reg. 7(14), the reference to "(e)," omitted and "or (g)" substituted for ", (g) or (ga)" by SI 2008/704, reg. 6(9), with effect from 6 April 2008.

In former reg. 7(14) "(b)," omitted by SI 2005/3350, reg. 7, with effect from 27 December 2005.

In former reg. 7(14) the words "(a), (b)," inserted by SI 2005/2561, reg. 5(c), with effect from 6 October 2005.

Reg. 7(15) omitted by SI 2014/1450, reg. 14, with effect from 1 July 2014. Former reg. 7(15) read as follows:

"**7(15)**   The condition specified in this paragraph is that, judged at the date on which the qualifying investments in question become held in the account (and having regard to the contractual terms and conditions then in existence) the account investor will not be entitled to a secured minimum return at any time falling within the following 5 years.

The account investor is entitled to a secured minimum return if–

(a)   the contract under which the investments were acquired, or any other transaction entered into by the account investor or any other person, or

(b)   the nature of the underlying subject matter of the investments,

have the effect that the account investor is not exposed, or not exposed to any significant extent, to the risk of loss from fluctuations in the value of the investments exceeding 5% of the capital consideration paid or payable for the acquisition of those investments."

Former reg. 7(15) substituted by SI 2005/3350, reg. 8, with effect from 27 December 2005.

In former reg. 7(15) the words "at the date on which the qualifying investments in question become held in the account, and at any later time (if any) which has elapsed during the succeeding five years" substituted for the words "during the period of five years from the date on which the qualifying investments in question became held in the account, there was no time when", the words "do not have" substituted for the word "had" and the words "is not" substituted for the words "was not" by SI 2005/609, reg. 4, with effect from 6 April 2005.

In former reg. 7(15) the word "became" substituted for the words "were first" by SI 2004/2996, reg. 9, with effect from 6 April 2005.

Reg. 7(16) substituted by SI 2014/1450, reg. 14, with effect from 1 July 2014. Former reg. 7(16) read as follows:

"**7(16)**   In this regulation references, in relation to qualifying investments, to–

(a)   the underlying subject matter are references to or to the value of the investments, currencies or other matters to which, or to the value of which, those qualifying investments or their value is referable, and in the case of a policy of life insurance, under whose terms some or all of the benefits are determined by reference to fluctuations in, or in an index of, the value of any property of any description (whether or not specified in the policy or contract), that property or that index;

(b)   the capital consideration paid or payable include premiums paid or payable under a policy of life insurance, and include the incidental costs of acquisition; and (c)　　the value are to be construed applying regulation 6(2), but deducting the incidental costs that would be incurred by a disposal and, in the case of a policy of life insurance, omitting any benefits payable in the event of the death of the account investor."

In former reg. 7(16)(a) the words ", and in the case of a policy of life insurance, under whose terms some or all of the benefits are determined by reference to fluctuations in, or in an index of, the value of any property of any description (whether or not specified in the policy or contract), that property or that index" inserted by SI 2004/2996, reg. 10(a), with effect from 6 April 2005.

In former reg. 7(16)(b) the words "or payable include premiums paid or payable under a policy of life insurance, and" inserted by SI 2004/2996, reg. 10(b), with effect from 6 April 2005.

In former reg. 7(16)(c) the words "and, in the case of a policy of life insurance, omitting any benefits payable in the event of the death of the account investor" inserted by SI 2004/2996, reg. 10(c), with effect from 6 April 2005.

Reg. 7(14), (15) and (16) inserted by SI 2003/2747, reg. 6, with effect from 17 November 2003 (as far as those provisions relate to reg. 7(2)(ga)).

Reg. 7(17) omitted by SI 2014/1450, reg. 14, with effect from 1 July 2014. Former reg. 7(17) read as follows:

"**7(17)** Where a policy of life insurance confers on the person to whom it is issued an option to have another policy issued for it or to have any of its terms changed, the condition in paragraph (15) shall only be satisfied if it would also be satisfied if each or any of the changes capable of being made in pursuance of such an option had been made."

Former reg. 7(17) inserted by SI 2004/2996, reg. 11, with effect from 6 April 2005.

QUALIFYING INVESTMENTS FOR A CASH COMPONENT

8(1) This regulation specifies the kind of investments ("qualifying investments for a cash component") which may be purchased, made or held under a cash component.

8(2) Qualifying investments for a cash component to which paragraph (1) refers are, subject to paragraph (3)–

(a)　　cash deposited in a deposit account with–

　　(i)　　a building society,

　　(ii)　　a credit union,

　　(iii)　　a bank, other than of a type at paragraph (a), (d) or (e) of section 991(2) of the ITA 2007,

　　(iv)　　[Omitted by SI 2014/654, reg. 9(b).]

(b)　　cash deposited in a share account with a building society;

(c)　　[omitted by SI 2008/704, reg. 7(2);]

(d)　　[omitted by SI 2008/704, reg. 7(2);]

(e)　　such investment deposits with the National Savings Bank which, according to the terms and conditions subject to which they are made, are expressly permitted to be held under a cash component of an account;

(f)　　any securities issued under the National Loans Act 1968–

　　(i)　　for the purpose of or in connection with raising money under the auspices of the Director of Savings within the meaning of section 11(1)(a) of the National Debt Act 1972, and

　　(ii)　　other than national savings certificates, premium savings bonds, national savings stamps and national savings gift tokens,

　　which, according to the terms and conditions subject to which they are issued and purchased, are expressly permitted to be held under a cash component of an account.

(g)　　[omitted by SI 2014/1450, reg. 15(a)]

(h)　　a depositary interest (with the references in that definition to a stocks and shares component and to regulation 7(2)(a) to (h) being replaced with references to a cash component and to regulation 8(2)(a) to (f)).

(j)　　a deposit account specified as a stakeholder product by regulation 4 of the Stakeholder Products Regulations;

(k)　　[omitted by SI 2014/1450, reg. 15(a);]

(l)　　[omitted by SI 2014/1450, reg. 15(a);]

(m)　　[omitted by SI 2014/1450, reg. 15(a);]

(n)　　arrangements falling within section 47 of the Finance Act 2005 (alternative finance arrangements) under which the person referred to in that section as Y is a financial institution;

(o)　　arrangements falling within section 49 of that Act;

(p)　　a short-term money market fund which meets the conditions in COLL section 5.9.3.R;

(q)　　a money market fund which meets the conditions in COLL section 5.9.5R.

8(3) A deposit account or share account which is a qualifying investment for a cash component falling within sub-paragraphs (a) or (b) of paragraph (2) respectively ("Account A") must not be connected with any other account falling within the descriptions in those sub-paragraphs ("Account B"), held by the account investor or any other person.

8(4) For the purposes of paragraph (3), Account A is connected with Account B if all of the following circumstances apply–

(a)   either of the accounts was opened with reference to the other, or with a view to enabling the other to be opened on particular terms, or with a view to facilitating the opening of the other on particular terms,

(b)   the terms on which Account A was opened would have been significantly less favourable to the holder if Account B had not been opened, and

(c)   Account B is not a tax exempt account.

8(5) The following are tax exempt accounts for the purposes of paragraph (4)–

(a)   an account opened (or treated as opened) in accordance with regulation 12 or 12A;

(b)   a child trust fund.

History – Reg. 8(2)(a) substituted by SI 2008/1934, reg. 4, with effect from 12 August 2008.
In reg. 8(2)(a) the words "(including for this purpose a credit union)" inserted, in reg. 8(2)(g) the words "(b)," and ", securities" omitted and reg. 8(2)(n) and (o) inserted by SI 2005/3350, reg. 9, with effect from 27 December 2005.
Reg. 8(2)(a)(iii) substituted by SI 2014/654, reg. 9(a), with effect from 6 April 2014.
Reg. 8(2)(a)(iv) omitted by SI 2014/654, reg. 9(b), with effect from 6 April 2014.
Reg. 8(2)(a) amended and 8(2)(c) and (d) substituted by SI 2001/3629, reg. 173 which came into force on 1 December 2001.
Reg. 8(2)(c) and (d) omitted by SI 2008/704, reg. 7(2), with effect from 6 April 2008.
Reg. 8(2)(d)–(f) substituted by SI 1998/3174, reg. 6, operative from 6 April 1999.
Reg. 8(2)(g) omitted by SI 2014/1450, reg. 15(a), with effect only in respect of investments purchased or made on or after 1 July 2014. Former reg. 8(2)(g) read as follows:
    "(g)   investments falling within sub-paragraphs (a), (f) or (g) of regulation 7(2), in circumstances where the units or shares do not satisfy the condition specified in regulation 7(15);"
In former reg. 8(2)(g) the reference to "(e)," omitted and "or (g)" substituted for ", (g) or (ga)" by SI 2008/704, reg. 7(3), with effect from 6 April 2008.
In former reg. 8(2)(g) the words "(a), (b)," and ", securities" inserted by SI 2005/2561, reg. 6, with effect from 6 October 2005.
In reg. 8(2)(h) "8(2)(a) to (f)" substituted for "8(2)(a) to (g)" by SI 2014/1450, reg. 15(b), with effect only in respect of investments purchased or made on or after 1 July 2014.
Former reg. 8(2)(g) and (h) inserted by SI 2003/2747, reg. 7, with effect from 17 November 2003.
Reg. 8(2)(k) omitted by SI 2014/1450, reg. 15(a), with effect only in respect of investments purchased or made on or after 1 July 2014. Former reg. 8(2)(k) read as follows:
    "(k)   units in a relevant collective investment scheme specified as a stakeholder product by regulation 5 of the Stakeholder Products Regulations, in circumstances where the units do not satisfy the condition in regulation 7(15);"
Reg. 8(2)(l) omitted by SI 2014/1450, reg. 15(a),with effect only in respect of investments purchased or made on or after 1 July 2014. Former reg. 8(2)(l) read as follows:
    "(l)   policies of life insurance, falling within regulation 9, issued in respect of an insurance made on or after 6th April 2005, in circumstances where the policy does not satisfy the condition in regulation 7(15);"
Reg. 8(2)(m) omitted by SI 2014/1450, reg. 15(a), with effect only in respect of investments purchased or made on or after 1 July 2014. Former reg. 8(2)(m) read as follows:
    "(m)   policies of life insurance, falling within regulation 9, issued in respect of an insurance made before 6th April 2005, in a case where regulation 4C(3)(c)(i) or (ii) applies."
Reg. 8(2)(j) and former (k), (l) and (m) inserted by SI 2004/2996, reg. 12, with effect from 6 April 2005.
Reg. 8(2)(p) inserted (and ";" substituted for "." at end of sub-para. (o)) by SI 2014/1450, reg. 15(c), with effect from 1 July 2014.
Reg. 8(2)(q) inserted by SI 2014/1450, reg. 15(c), with effect from 1 July 2014.
Reg. 8(3) substituted, and (4) and (5) inserted, by SI 2012/1871, reg. 13, with effect from 1 November 2011.

INSURANCE POLICIES

9(1) Policies referred to in regulation 7(2)(n) or (o) must, subject to compliance with paragraphs (4) to (9) as appropriate, satisfy the conditions specified in paragraph (3).

9(2) In paragraph (1) "policies" includes rights under a linked long-term contract specified as a stakeholder product by regulation 6 of the Stakeholder Products Regulations.

9(3) The conditions specified in this paragraph are that–

(a)   the insurance is on the life of the account investor only;

(b)   the terms and conditions of the policy provide–

    (i)   that the policy may only be owned or held as a qualifying investment for an account which satisfies the provisions of these Regulations;

    (ii)   in the case of a policy that is held under an account that is not a junior ISA account, that the policy shall automatically terminate if it comes to the notice of the account manager, in any manner, that either of the events specified in paragraph (8) has occurred in relation to the policy;

    (iia)   in the case of a policy that is held under an account that is a junior ISA account, that the policy shall automatically terminate if it comes to the notice of the account manager, in any manner, that the event specified in paragraph (8A) has occurred in relation to the policy;

    (iii)   subject to paragraph (3B), for an express prohibition of any transfer, assignment or (in Scotland) assignation of the policy to the account investor who holds the account under which the policy is held or, in the case of a policy held under an account that is a junior ISA account, the registered contact or named child in relation to that account;

    (iv)   [omitted by SI 2011/1780, reg. 16(e),]

(c)   the policy evidences or secures a contract of insurance which–

    (i)   falls within paragraph I or III of Part II of Schedule 1 to the Financial Services and Markets Act 2000 (Regulated Activities) Order 2001, or

    (ii)   would fall within either of those paragraphs if the insurer was a company with permission under Part 4 of the Financial Services and Markets Act 2000 to effect or carry out contracts of insurance;

(d)   the policy is not–

    (i)   a contract to pay an annuity on human life, or

    (ii)   a personal portfolio bond within the meaning given by section 516 of ITTOIA 2005, or

    (iii)   a contract, the effecting and carrying out of which constitutes "pension business" within the meaning given by section 431B(1) of the Taxes Act; and

(e)   after the first payment in respect of a premium in relation to the policy has been made, there is no contractual obligation on any person to make any other such payment.

9(3A)   In paragraphs (3)(b)(iii) and (3B), **"policy"** includes–

(a)   the rights conferred by a policy; and

(b)   any share or interest in the rights conferred by a policy.

9(3B)   The prohibition required by paragraph (3)(b)(iii) must not prohibit–

(a)   the cash proceeds from the termination of the policy or a partial surrender of the policy ownership–

    (i)   being paid to the account investor where the policy is held under an account that is not a junior ISA account;

    (ii)   being withdrawn in accordance with regulation 4ZD (permitted withdrawals from a junior ISA account) and (4ZE) (permitted withdrawals from a junior ISA account where the named child is terminally ill);

(b)   the transfer of title to the policy so that it is vested as required from time to time by regulations 4(6)(b)(i) and (ia) (general conditions for accounts) and 15(a) (special provisions relating to insurer-managers) by virtue of–

    (i)   a transfer of an account in accordance with regulations 21 or 21B;

    (ii)   a change of registered contact in relation to a junior ISA account; or

    (iii)   an account ceasing to be a junior ISA account upon the named child in relation to the account attaining 18 years;

(c)   the vesting of the policy in the personal representatives of the account investor.

9(4)   A policy must not be connected with any other policy ("the linked policy"), held by the account investor or any other person, and for this purpose a policy is connected with another if–

(a)   either policy was issued in respect of an insurance made with reference to the other, or with a view to enabling the other to be made on particular terms, or with a view to facilitating the making of the other on particular terms, and

(b)   the terms on which the first-mentioned policy in this paragraph was issued would have been significantly less favourable to the holder if the linked policy had not been issued.

9(5)   References to "the linked policy" in paragraph (4) shall include a contract of insurance, and references to the issuing of the linked policy shall include the making of such a contract.

9(6)   No sum may at any time, at or after the making of the insurance, be lent to or at the direction of the account investor by or by arrangement with the insurer for the time being responsible for the obligations under the policy.

9(7)   Where any of the events specified in paragraphs (8) or (8A) occurs in relation to a policy, the policy shall nevertheless be treated, for the purposes of these Regulations, excepting paragraphs (3)(b)(ii) and (iia), (8) and (8A) and regulation 36, as if it had satisfied the conditions in paragraph (3)(b)(i) during the period–

(a)   commencing at the time at which the specified event occurred, and

(b)   ending immediately before–

    (i)   the end of the final insurance year in relation to the policy, within the meaning given by section 499 of ITTOIA 2005, or

(ii) the time at which the specified event came to the notice of the account manager,

whichever first occurs (the "termination event").

9(8) The events specified in this paragraph are–

(a) that the policy has ceased to be one in respect of which the conditions in paragraph (3)(b)(i) are satisfied; and

(b) that those conditions were not satisfied in relation to the policy at the date on which the insurance was made.

9(8A) The event specified in this paragraph is that–

(a) the policy has ceased to be one in respect of which the conditions in paragraph (3)(b)(i) are satisfied or those conditions were not satisfied in relation to the policy at the date on which the insurance was made; and

(b) the breach or non-compliance cannot be remedied in accordance with regulation 21C or has not been remedied within a reasonable time.

9(9) Where–

(a) it comes to the notice of the account manager, in any manner, that an event specified in paragraph (8) or (8A) has occurred in relation to a policy, and

(b) the account manager is not the insurer for the time being responsible for the obligations under the policy or, where the policy is not still in existence, the person who was the last such insurer,

the account manager shall, within 30 days of the event coming to his notice, give notice to that insurer, specifying the event mentioned in sub-paragraph (a), and the termination event.

History – The heading to reg. 9 substituted for former heading "QUALIFYING INVESTMENTS FOR AN INSURANCE COMPONENT" by SI 2004/2996, reg. 13(a), with effect from 6 April 2005.
In reg. 9(1)"or 8(2)(l) or (m)" omitted by SI 2014/1450, reg. 16, with effect from 1 July 2014.
In reg. 9(1), the words "paragraphs (4) to (9) as appropriate" substituted for the words "paragraphs (4) to (7)" by SI 2011/1780, reg. 16(a), with effect from 1 November 2011.
Reg. 9(1) and (2) substituted for former reg. 9(1) and (2) by SI 2004/2996, reg. 13(b), with effect from 6 April 2005.
In reg. 9(3)(b)(i) the words "an insurance component of" which appeared after the words "a qualifying investment for" omitted by SI 2004/2996, reg. 13(c), with effect from 6 April 2005.
In reg. 9(3)(b)(ii), the words "in the case of a policy that is held under an account that is not a junior ISA account," inserted by SI 2011/1780, reg. 16(b), with effect from 1 November 2011.
Reg. 9(3)(b)(iia) inserted by SI 2011/1780, reg. 16(c), with effect from 1 November 2011.
Reg. 9(3)(b)(iii) substituted by SI 2011/1780, reg. 16(d), with effect from 1 November 2011.
Reg. 9(3)(b)(iv) omitted by SI 2011/1780, reg. 16(e), with effect from 1 November 2011.
In reg. 9(3)(d)(ii) the words "section 516 of ITTOIA 2005" substituted for "regulation 2(1) of the Personal Portfolio Bonds (Tax) Regulations 1999" by SI 2008/704, reg. 8(2), with effect from 6 April 2008.
Reg. 9(3A) and (3B) inserted by SI 2011/1780, reg. 16(f), with effect from 1 November 2011.
In reg. 9(4) the words "which is a qualifying investment for an insurance component falling within paragraph (2)(a)" omitted by SI 2004/2996, reg. 13(d), with effect from 6 April 2005.
Reg. 9(3)(c) substituted by SI 2001/3629, reg. 174 which came into force on 1 December 2001.
In reg. 9(3)(d)(ii) the words "regulation 2(1) of the Personal Portfolio Bonds (Tax) Regulations 1999, or" substituted for "sub-section (7) of section 89 of the Finance Act 1998, as varied by Regulations made under that section, or" by SI 2001/908, reg. 4, operative from 6 April 2001.
Reg. 9(3)(b)(ii) amended, and reg. 9(7) substituted and reg. 9(8), (9) inserted, by SI 1998/3174, reg. 7, operative from 6 April 1999.
In reg. 9(7), the words "any of the events specified in paragraphs (8) or (8A)" substituted for the words "either of the events specified in paragraph (8)" by SI 2011/1780, reg. 16(g)(i), with effect from 1 November 2011.
In reg. 9(7), the words "excepting paragraphs (3)(b)(ii) and (iia), (8) and (8A)" substituted for the words "excepting paragraphs (3)(b)(ii) and (8)" by SI 2011/1780, reg. 16(g)(ii), with effect from 1 November 2011.
In reg. 9(7)(b)(i) the words "final insurance year in relation to the policy, within the meaning given by section 499 of ITTOIA 2005" substituted for "final year in relation to the policy, within the meaning of section 546(4) of the Taxes Act" by SI 2008/704, reg. 8(3), with effect from 6 April 2008.
Reg. 9(8A) inserted by SI 2011/1780, reg. 16(h), with effect from 1 November 2011.
In reg. 9(9)(a), the words "paragraph (8) or (8A)" substituted for the words "paragraph (8)" by SI 2011/1780, reg. 16(i), with effect from 1 November 2011.

QUALIFYING INDIVIDUALS WHO MAY INVEST UNDER AN ACCOUNT THAT IS NOT A JUNIOR ISA ACCOUNT

10(1) This regulation specifies the description of individual ("qualifying individual") who may invest under an account that is not a junior ISA account.

10(2) A qualifying individual to whom paragraph (1) refers is an individual–

(a) who, in the case of a cash account, is 16 years of age or over and, in the case of a stocks and shares account, is 18 years of age or over;

(b) who, in the case of a stocks and shares account, has not subscribed, and will not subscribe, to any other stocks and shares account, in the year in which the subscription is made;

(c) who, in the case of a cash account, has not subscribed, and will not subscribe, to any other cash account, in the year in which the subscription is made;

Statutory Instruments

(ca)   who has not exceeded the overall subscription limit in regulation 4ZA(1) in that year;

(d)

    (i)   who is resident in the United Kingdom, or

    (ii)   who, though not resident in the United Kingdom, has general earnings from overseas Crown employment subject to United Kingdom tax within the meaning given by section 28 of ITEPA 2003,

    (iii)   who, though not resident in the United Kingdom, is married to or in a civil partnership with a person mentioned in paragraph (ii).

10(3)   For the purposes of paragraph (2)(b) and (c), a subscription to a junior ISA account shall be disregarded.

History – In the heading to reg. 10, the words "that is not a junior ISA account" inserted by SI 2011/1780, reg. 17(a), with effect from 1 November 2011.
Reg. 10(1) substituted by SI 2011/1780, reg. 17(b), with effect from 1 November 2011.
In reg. 10(2)(a) the words ", in the cases of a maxi-account or of a mini-account made up of a cash component, is 16 years of age or over and, in any other case," inserted by SI 2001/908, reg. 5, operative from 6 April 2001.
In reg. 10(2)(ca) the word "appropriate" and the words ", or the applicable subscription limit in regulation 4ZA(2)," omitted by SI 2014/1450, reg. 17, with effect from 1 July 2014.
In reg. 10(2)(ca), the words "regulation 4ZA(1)" substituted for the words "regulation 4(2)" by SI 2011/1780, reg. 17(c)(i), with effect from 1 November 2011.
In reg. 10(2)(ca), the words "regulation 4ZA(2)" substituted for the words "regulation 4(3)" by SI 2011/1780, reg. 17(c)(ii), with effect from 1 November 2011.
In reg. 10(2)(ca) the word "applicable" substituted for the word "other" by SI 2009/1550, reg. 6, with effect for the tax year 2009–10.
Reg. 10(2)(a)–(c) substituted for reg. 10(2)(a)–(c) by SI 2007/2119, reg. 14, with effect from 6 April 2008.
In reg. 10(2)(d)(i), the words "and ordinarily resident" omitted by SI 2013/605, reg. 4(3), with effect for the purposes of a person's liability to income tax for the tax year 2013–14 or any subsequent tax years.
Reg. 10(2)(d)(ii) substituted by SI 2008/704, reg. 9, with effect from 6 April 2008.
In reg. 10(2)(d)(iii) the words "or in a civil partnership with" inserted by SI 2005/3230, reg. 10(3), with effect from 5 December 2005.
In reg. 10(2)(d) the words
", or
    (iii)   who, though not resident in the United Kingdom, is married to a person mentioned in paragraph (ii)."
added by SI 2001/908, reg. 5, operative from 6 April 2001.
Reg. 10(3) inserted by SI 2011/1780, reg. 17(d), with effect from 1 November 2011.

ACCOUNT INVESTOR CEASING TO QUALIFY

11   Notwithstanding any other provision of these Regulations an account investor who, after subscribing to an account, at any time ceases to fulfil the conditions of regulation 10(2)(d) may retain the benefits of the account (including the right to any relief or exemption due under the account) subsisting at that time but, so long as he fails to fulfil those conditions, shall not be entitled to subscribe further to such an account.

CONDITIONS FOR APPLICATION TO OPEN AN ACCOUNT THAT IS NOT A JUNIOR ISA ACCOUNT

12(1)   An application by an individual to open an account in the year in which he first subscribes to that account, and in the year following a year in which that individual has not subscribed to the account, must be made to an account manager in a statement and must fulfil the conditions specified in paragraphs (2), (3) and (4).

12(2)   An application must specify the first year to which the application relates.

12(3)   An application must contain a declaration by the applicant that–

(a)   his application is to open a stocks and shares account or cash account, as the case may be;

(b)   the declaration shall have effect for the year to which paragraph (2) refers, and each successive year following that year, in which the applicant subscribes to the account;

(c)   all cash subscriptions made, and to be made, to the account are the applicant's cash;

(d)   in the case of a stocks and shares account, the applicant–

    (i)   has not subscribed, and will not subscribe, to any other stocks and shares account, in the year to which paragraph (2) refers, and

    (ii)   will not subscribe to any other stocks and shares account, in each successive year following that year, in which the declaration has effect;

(e)   in the case of a cash account, the applicant–

    (i)   has not subscribed, and will not subscribe, to any other cash account, in the year to which paragraph (2) refers, and

    (ii)   will not subscribe to any other cash account, in each successive year following that year, in which the declaration has effect;

(ea)   that the applicant has not subscribed, and will not subscribe, more than the overall subscription limit in regulation 4ZA(1) (aggregating subscriptions to all accounts)–

        (i)   in the year to which paragraph (2) refers, and

        (ii) in each successive year following that year, in which the declaration has effect;

(eb)   [omitted by SI 2014/1450, reg. 18(b);]

(f)   the applicant is 16 years of age or over, and–

        (i)   is resident in the United Kingdom, or

        (ii) is a person who has general earnings from overseas Crown employment subject to United Kingdom tax within the meaning given by section 28 of ITEPA 2003,

        (iii) is married to or in a civil partnership with a person mentioned in paragraph (ii),

    and will inform the account manager if he ceases to be so resident, or to perform such duties, or to be married to or in a civil partnership with a person who performs such duties, as the case may be;

(g)   [omitted by SI 2011/1780, reg. 18(c)(v).]

12(4) An application must contain–

(a)   the applicant's full name,

(b)   the address of his permanent residence, including postcode,

(c)   his national insurance number, or confirmation that he does not have one,

(d)   his date of birth,

(e)   the authorisation specified in paragraph (4A).

12(4A) The authorisation specified by this paragraph is authority given by the applicant to the account manager–

(a)   to hold the subscriptions, account investments, interest, dividends and any other rights or proceeds in respect of those investments and cash;

(b)   to make on behalf of the applicant any claims to relief in respect of account investments; and

(c)   to make a record in writing in accordance with paragraph (7) where that paragraph requires the account manager to do so.

12(5) [Omitted by SI 2007/2119, reg. 16.]

12(6) An account manager may not accept as an account investor any individual if he has reason to believe that–

(a)   he is not or might not be a qualifying individual, or

(b)   he has given untrue information in his application.

12(7) Where an application is not in writing or the manager operates a record system under which all original written applications are not retained–

(a)   the account manager must, immediately after receiving the application, record in writing on behalf of the applicant, the declaration required by paragraph (3) and authorisation required by paragraphs (4)(e) and (4A);

(b)   the account manager must notify the applicant of the contents of the written record within 5 business days of making it; and

(c)   the written record (as amended by any corrections notified to the account manager by the applicant within 30 days of the notification mentioned in sub-paragraph (b)) shall be treated as the applicant's declaration required by paragraph (3) and authorisation required by paragraphs (4)(e) and (4A).

12(7A) [Omitted by SI 2011/1780, reg. 18(g).]

12(8) Section 95 of the Management Act shall have effect as if–

(a)   the statement and declarations to which paragraphs (1), (3) and (7) refer were a statement or declarations, as the case may be, within the meaning of subsection (1)(b), and

(b)   there were substituted for subsection (3) the following words–

"(3) The relevant years of assessment for the purposes of this section are the year of assessment in respect of which any claim to relief or exemption from tax in connection with which the statement or declarations are relevant, is made, the next following, and any preceding year of assessment."

12(9) An application furnished by an individual under this regulation shall be regarded as in writing if it is furnished–

(a)   by telephonic facsimile transmission containing the signature of the individual, or

(b)   by electronic communication containing an electronic signature of the individual.

12(10) Where an account manager is required by paragraph (7) to make a record in writing–

(a)   a record shall be regarded as being a written record if it is produced by electronic means;

(b)   the notification of the contents of the record by the account manager to the applicant required by paragraph (7)(b) may be sent to the applicant by telephonic facsimile transmission or by electronic communication.

12(11) In this regulation–

"**electronic communication**" includes any communication conveyed by means of an electronic communications network.

"**electronic signature**" has the meaning given by section 7(2) of the Electronic Communications Act 2000.

12(11A) In paragraph (3), references to subscriptions to an account do not include subscriptions to an account that is a junior ISA account.

12(12) An application may be made on an individual's behalf–

(a)   if the individual is resident in England and Wales–

    (i)   pursuant to an order under section 16(2)(a) of the Mental Capacity Act 2005; or

    (ii)   by a deputy appointed under section 16(2)(b) of that Act; or

(b)   if the individual is resident in Scotland or Northern Ireland and is suffering from mental disorder, by a parent, guardian, spouse, civil partner, son or daughter of the individual.

12(13) In paragraph (12) "**mental disorder**" has the meaning given by in Scotland, section 328 of the Mental Health (Care and Treatment) (Scotland) Act 2003 or, in Northern Ireland, Article 3 of the Mental Health (Northern Ireland) Order 1986.

History – Heading to reg. 12 substituted by SI 2011/1780, reg. 18(a), with effect from 1 November 2011.
In reg. 12(1), the words ", subject to paragraph (5)," omitted by SI 2012/1871, reg. 14, with effect from 8 August 2012.
In reg. 12(1), the word "open" substituted for the words "subscribe to" by SI 2011/1780, reg. 18(b), with effect from 1 November 2011.
In reg. 12(3), in the opening words, the words "must contain" substituted for the words "shall provide for" by SI 2011/1780, reg. 18(c)(i), with effect from 1 November 2011.
In reg. 12(3)(a), the word "open" substituted for the words "subscribe to" by SI 2011/1780, reg. 18(c)(ii), with effect from 1 November 2011.
Reg. 12(3)(a) substituted by SI 2007/2119, reg. 15(a), with effect from 6 April 2008.
In reg. 12(3)(ea) the word "appropriate" omitted by SI 2014/1450, reg. 18(a), with effect from 1 July 2014.
In reg. 12(3)(ea), the words "regulation 4ZA(1)" substituted for the words "regulation 4(2)" by SI 2011/1780, reg. 18(c)(iii), with effect from 1 November 2011.
Reg. 12(3)(eb) omitted by SI 2014/1450, reg. 18(b), with effect from 1 July 2014. Former reg. 12(3)(eb) read as follows:
    "(eb)   that in the case of a cash account, the applicant has not subscribed, and will not subscribe, more than the subscription limit in regulation 4ZA(1)(a) or (2)–
      (i)   in the year to which paragraph (2) refers, and
      (ii)   in each successive year following that year, in which the declaration has effect;"
In former reg. 12(3)(eb), the words "regulation 4ZA(1)(a) or (2)" substituted for the words "regulation 4(3)" by SI 2011/1780, reg. 18(c)(iv), with effect from 1 November 2011.
Reg. 12(3)(d)–(eb) substituted for (d) and (e) by SI 2007/2119, reg. 15(b), with effect from 6 April 2008.
In reg. 12(3)(f) and (i), the words "and ordinarily resident" omitted by SI 2013/605, reg. 4(4), with effect for the purposes of a person's liability to income tax for the tax year 2013–14 or any subsequent tax years.
Reg. 12(3)(f)(ii) substituted by SI 2008/704, reg. 10(2), with effect from 6 April 2008.
In reg. 12(3)(f) the words "or in a civil partnership with" inserted twice by SI 2005/3230, reg. 10(4), with effect from 5 December 2005.
Reg. 12(3)(f) substituted by SI 2001/908, reg. 6, operative from 6 April 2001.
Reg. 12(3)(g) omitted by SI 2011/1780, reg. 18(c)(v), with effect from 1 November 2011.
Reg. 12(3)(g)(iii) omitted by SI 2002/1974, reg. 4, with effect from 1 October 2002 in relation to all accounts set up before or after that date.
In former reg. 12(3)(g)(iv) the words "a written declaration is required by paragraph (7)" substituted for "the application is not in writing" by SI 2008/704, reg. 10(3), with effect from 6 April 2008.
Reg. 12(4)(e) inserted (and the "and" immediately preceding reg. 12(4)(d) omitted) by SI 2011/1780, reg. 18(d), with effect from 1 November 2011.
Reg. 12(4A) inserted by SI 2011/1780, reg. 18(e), with effect from 1 November 2011.
Reg. 12(5) omitted by SI 2007/2119, reg. 16, with effect from 6 April 2008.
Reg. 12(7) substituted by SI 2011/1780, reg. 18(f), with effect from 1 November 2011.
Reg. 12(7) and (7A) substituted by SI 2009/1994, reg. 7, with effect from 11 August 2009.
In former reg. 12(7) the words "Where the application is not in writing or the manager operates a record system under which all original written applications are not retained" substituted for "Where paragraph (3)(g)(iv) applies" and "referred to in paragraph (3)(g)(iv)" substituted for "therein referred to" by SI 2008/704, reg. 10(4), with effect from 6 April 2008.
Reg. 12(7A) omitted by SI 2011/1780, reg. 18(g), with effect from 1 November 2011.
In reg. 12(9) words "or regulation 13" repealed by SI 2002/3158 reg. 5(a), with effect from 8 January 2003.
Reg. 12(10) substituted by SI 2011/1780, reg. 18(h), with effect from 1 November 2011.
In former reg. 12(10) the reference to "(7)" substituted for "(3)(g)(iv) of this regulation" and "of this regulation" omitted preceding the words "may be sent", by SI 2008/704, reg. 10(5), with effect from 6 April 2008.
In former reg. 12(10) words "or regulation 13(4)(h)(iv)" repealed, and words "this regulation" substituted for "either this regulation or regulation 13" by SI 2002/3158 reg. 5, with effect from 8 January 2003.

Reg. 12(9)–(11) added by SI 2001/908, reg. 6, operative from 6 April 2001.
In reg. 12(11), the definition of "electronic communication" substituted by SI 2003/2155, art. 3(2) and Sch. 1, para. 24, with effect from 17 September 2003.
Reg. 12(11A) inserted by SI 2011/1780, reg. 18(i), with effect from 1 November 2011.
Reg. 12(12) substituted by SI 2014/654, reg. 10(a), with effect from 6 April 2014.
In reg. 12(12) the words "civil partner," inserted by SI 2005/3230, reg. 10(4), with effect from 5 December 2005.
Reg. 12(12) inserted by SI 2002/3158 reg. 5(c), with effect from 8 January 2003.
In reg. 12(13), the words "section 1(2) of the Mental Health Act 1983 or," omitted by SI 2014/654, reg. 10(b), with effect from 6 April 2014.
In reg. 12(13), the words "section 328 of the Mental Health (Care and Treatment) (Scotland) Act 2003" substituted by SI 2005/2078, art. 15 and Sch. 2, para. 19 and by SI 2005/445, art. 2 and Sch, para. 28 – both with effect from 5 October 2005.
Reg. 12(13) inserted by SI 2002/3158, reg. 5(c), with effect from 8 January 2003.

CONDITIONS FOR APPLICATION TO OPEN AN ACCOUNT THAT IS A JUNIOR ISA ACCOUNT

12A(1)   An application ("junior ISA application") to open a junior ISA account with an account manager may only be made if the account will be held by an eligible child immediately following the opening of the account.

12A(2)   An eligible child may hold–

(a)   only one account set up as a cash account; and

(b)   only one account set up as a stocks and shares account.

12A(3)   For the purposes of paragraphs (2) and (7), an account holding an amount of less than one penny shall be disregarded.

12A(4)   A junior ISA application may be made by a person who–

(a)   is over 16, and

(b)   in relation to the junior ISA account to be opened pursuant to the application is–

    (i)   a person who has parental responsibility in relation to the eligible child who will hold the account; or

    (ii)   the eligible child who will hold the account.

12A(5)   A junior ISA application must be made to an account manager in a statement and must fulfil the conditions specified in paragraphs (6), (7) and (8).

12A(6)   A junior ISA application must specify the eligible child as being the beneficial owner of the account investments under that account.

12A(7)   A junior ISA application must contain a declaration by the applicant that–

(a)   the application is made to open a junior ISA account;

(b)   the information provided in accordance with paragraph (8) is true;

(c)   the child who will hold the account opened pursuant to the application is an **"eligible child"** within the meaning given in the Child Trust Funds Act 2004;

(d)   the child who will hold the account opened pursuant to the application is–

    (i)   resident in the United Kingdom,

    (ii)   a person who has general earnings from overseas Crown employment subject to United Kingdom tax within the meaning given by section 28 of ITEPA 2003,

    (iii)   married to or in a civil partnership with a person mentioned in paragraph (ii), or

    (iv)   a dependant of a person mentioned in paragraph (ii);

(e)   the applicant is the person who, upon the opening of the account, will be the registered contact in relation to the account;

(f)   the application is to open a stocks and shares account or cash account, as the case may be;

(g)   in the case of a stocks and shares account, the applicant–

    (i)   has not subscribed, and will not subscribe, to any other stocks and shares account that is a junior ISA account held by the same eligible child, and

    (ii)   is not aware of any other stocks and shares account held by the eligible child that is a junior ISA account;

(h)   in the case of a cash account, the applicant–

    (i)   has not subscribed, and will not subscribe, to any other cash account that is a junior ISA account held by the same eligible child, and

    (ii)   is not aware of any other cash account held by the eligible child that is a junior ISA account;

(i) as far as the applicant is aware, the applicant has not subscribed amounts to the account (or any other account) that, when aggregated with other subscriptions, exceed the overall subscription limit in regulation 4ZB(1) (subscriptions to accounts opened in accordance with this regulation) in relation to the eligible child who will hold the account in the year in which the junior ISA application is made; and

(j) the applicant will not knowingly subscribe amounts to the account that, when aggregated with other subscriptions, exceed the overall subscription limit in regulation 4ZB(1) applicable from time to time (subscriptions to accounts opened in accordance with this regulation) in each successive year following the year in which the junior ISA application is made.

12A(8) A junior ISA application must contain–

(a) the applicant's full name,

(b) the address of the applicant's permanent residence, including postcode,

(c) the full name of the eligible child,

(d) the date of birth of the eligible child,

(e) where the applicant is not the eligible child, the address of the eligible child's permanent residence, including postcode,

(f) the eligible child's national insurance number if the child–

 (i) is 16 or over, and

 (ii) has been issued with a national insurance number,

(g) the authorisation specified in paragraph (9).

12A(9) The authorisation specified by this paragraph is authority given by the applicant to the account manager (on behalf of the child who holds the account where appropriate)–

(a) to hold the subscriptions, account investments, interest, dividends and any other rights or proceeds in respect of those investments and cash;

(b) to make on behalf of the child any claim to relief from tax in respect of account investments; and

(c) to make a record in writing in accordance with paragraph (11) where that paragraph requires the account manager to do so.

12A(10) An account manager must not accept a junior ISA application if the account manager has reason to believe that the applicant has given untrue information in the application.

12A(11) Where the junior ISA application is not in writing, or the account manager operates a record system under which all original written applications are not retained–

(a) the account manager must, immediately after receiving the application, record in writing on behalf of the applicant, the declaration required by paragraph (7) and authorisation required by paragraphs (8)(g) and (9);

(b) the account manager must notify the applicant of the contents of the written record within 5 business days of making it; and

(c) the written record (as amended by any corrections notified to the account manager by the applicant within 30 days of the notification mentioned in sub-paragraph (b)) shall be treated as the applicant's declaration required by paragraph (7) and authorisation required by paragraphs (8)(g) and (9).

12A(12) An application furnished by an applicant under this regulation shall be regarded as in writing if it is furnished–

(a) by telephonic facsimile transmission containing the signature of the applicant, or

(b) by electronic communication containing an electronic signature of the applicant.

12A(13) Where an account manager is required by paragraph (11) to make a record in writing–

(a) a record shall be regarded as being a written record if it is produced by electronic means;

(b) the notification of the contents of the record by the account manager to the applicant required by paragraph (11)(b) may be sent to the applicant by telephonic facsimile transmission or by electronic communication.

12A(14) In this regulation–

 "electronic communication" includes any communication conveyed by means of an electronic communications network;

"electronic signature" has the meaning given by section 7(2) of the Electronic Communications Act 2000.

History – In reg. 12A(7)(d)(i), the words "and ordinarily resident" omitted by SI 2013/605, reg. 4(5), with effect for the purposes of a person's liability to income tax for the tax year 2013–14 or any subsequent tax years.
Reg. 12A inserted by SI 2011/1780, reg. 19, with effect from 1 November 2011.

APPLICATION BY CURATOR BONIS

13 [Repealed by SI 2002/3158, reg. 6.]

History – Reg. 13 repealed by SI 2002/3158, reg. 6, with effect from 8 January 2003.
Previously in reg. 13(4)(g) the words ", or to perform such duties, … as the case may be" added at the end by SI 2001/908, reg. 7, operative from 6 April 2001.
Reg. 13(4)(h)(iii) previously omitted by SI 2002/1974, reg. 5, with effect from 1 October 2002 in relation to all accounts set up before or after that date.

ACCOUNT MANAGER – QUALIFICATIONS AND BOARD'S APPROVAL

14(1) This regulation specifies the circumstances ("qualifying circumstances") in which a person may be approved by the Board as an account manager.

14(2) The qualifying circumstances to which paragraph (1) refers are the following–

(a) the person must make an application to the Board for approval in a form prescribed by the Board;

(aa) if the person intends to be an account manager in relation to a junior ISA account, the person must undertake to the Board to–

    (i) publicise (and update where appropriate) statements of the minimum amount which may be subscribed to a junior ISA account on a single occasion, and the permitted means of payment of subscriptions; and

    (ii) inform persons proposing to make a subscription to a junior ISA account (other than the named child) that the subscription is a gift to the child;

(b) an account manager must be–

    (i) an authorised person within the meaning of section 31(1)(a) or (c) of, or Schedule 5 to, the Financial Services and Markets Act 2000 who has permission to carry on one or more of the activities specified in Articles 14, 21, 25, 37,40, 45, 51 and 53 and, in so far as it applies to any of those activities, Article 64 of the Financial Services and Markets Act 2000 (Regulated Activities) Order 2001 but excluding any person falling within paragraph (iv) below; or

    (ii) European institution which carries on one or more of those activities; or

    (iia) in the case of a credit union, an authorised person within the meaning of FISMA 2000, who has permission to carry on one or more of the activities specified in Article 5 of the Financial Services And Markets Act 2000 (Regulated Activities) Order 2001;

    (iii) the Director of Savings, a building society or a person falling within section 991(2)(b) or (c) or (3)(c) of ITA 2007 (bank or credit union); or

    (iv) an insurance company, within the meaning given by section 431 of the Taxes Act, an incorporated friendly society, or a registered friendly society; or

    (v) any assurance undertaking which does not fall within paragraph (iv) above;

(c) an account manager must not be prevented from acting as such by any requirement imposed under sections 42 and 43 of the Financial Services and Markets Act 2000, or by any prohibition imposed by or under any rules made by the Financial Services Authority under that Act, by or under the rules of any recognised self-regulating organisation of which the account manager is a member, or by or under the rules of any recognised professional body by which the account manager is certified, or by a prohibition imposed under section 65 of the 1986 Act; and

(d) an account manager who–

    (i) is a European institution or a relevant authorised person and who does not have a branch or business establishment in the United Kingdom, or has such a branch or business establishment but does not intend to carry out all his functions as an account manager at that branch or business establishment, or

    (ii) falls within sub-paragraph (b)(v),

    must fulfil one of the three requirements specified in regulation 16.

14(3) The terms of the Board's approval may–

(a)   approve a person to set up and administer cash accounts only, or stocks and shares accounts only, or both

    (i)   [Omitted by SI 2007/2119, reg. 17.]

    (ii)   [Omitted by SI 2007/2119, reg. 17.]

    (iii)   [Omitted by SI 2004/2996, reg. 15(b).]

(b)   include conditions designed to ensure that the provisions of these Regulations are satisfied.

History – Reg. 14(2)(aa) inserted by SI 2011/1780, reg. 20(a), with effect from 1 November 2011.
In reg. 14(2)(b)(iia), the words "FISMA 2000" substituted for the words "section 31(1)(a) of the Financial Services and Markets Act 2000" by SI 2013/1765, art. 3, with effect from 1 September 2013.
Reg. 14(2)(b)(iia) inserted by SI 2005/3350, reg. 10, with effect from 27 December 2005.
In reg. 14(2)(b)(iii), the words "or a person falling within section 991(2)(b) or (c) or (3)(c) of ITA 2007 (bank or credit union)" substituted for ", a person falling within section 840A(1)(b) of the Taxes Act or a relevant European institution" by SI 2014/654, reg. 11, with effect from 6 April 2014.
In reg. 14(2)(b)(iii) the words "in the case of an account manager approved to set up and administer accounts made up of a cash component only," which appeared before the words "the Director of Savings" omitted by SI 2004/2996, reg. 14(a)(i), with effect from 6 April 2005.
In reg. 14(2)(b)(iv) the words "in the case of an account manager approved to set up and administer accounts made up of an insurance component only," which appeared before the words "an insurance company" omitted by SI 2004/2996, reg. 14(a)(ii), with effect from 6 April 2005.
In reg. 14(2)(b)(v) the word "any" substituted for the words "in the case of an account manager approved to set up and administer accounts made up of an insurance component only, an" by SI 2004/2996, reg. 14(a)(iii), with effect from 6 April 2005.
In reg. 14(2)(c), the words "sections 42 and 43" substituted for the words "section 43" by SI 2011/1780, reg. 20(b), with effect from 1 November 2011.
In reg. 14(3)(a), the words "cash accounts only, or stocks and shares accounts only, or both" substituted for the word "accounts–" and para. (i) and (ii) by SI 2007/2119, reg. 17, with effect from 6 April 2008.
In reg. 14(3)(a)(ii) the word "any" which appeared before the words "two specified components" omitted by SI 2004/2996, reg. 14(b)(i), with effect from 6 April 2005.
Reg. 14(3)(a)(iii) omitted and the word "and" preceding reg. 14(3)(a)(iii) substituted for the word "or" by SI 2004/2996, reg. 14(b)(ii), with effect from 6 April 2005.
Reg. 14(2)(b)(i), (ii), (iii) and (c) amended by SI 2001/3629, reg. 175 which came into force on 1 December 2001.
Reg. 14(2)(b)(iii) amended by SI 1998/3174, reg. 8, operative from 6 April 1999.

SPECIAL REQUIREMENTS RELATING TO INSURER-MANAGERS

15   If and so long as a person falling within regulation 14(2)(b)(iv) or (v) acts as account manager of an account, and the account investments include a policy of life insurance–

(a)   the title to all such policies shall be vested in the account investor; and

(b)   where a policy document or other document evidencing title to such policies of life insurance is issued, it shall be held by the account investor.

ACCOUNT MANAGER – APPOINTMENT OF TAX REPRESENTATIVE

16(1)   This regulation specifies the requirements mentioned in regulation 14(2)(d).

16(2)   The first requirement specified in this regulation is that–

(a)   a person who falls within section 698(2)(b) of ITTOIA 2005 is for the time being appointed by the account manager to be responsible for securing the discharge of the duties prescribed by paragraph (5) which fall to be discharged by the account manager, and

(b)   his identity and the fact of his appointment have been notified to the Board by the account manager.

16(3)   The second requirement specified in this regulation is that there are for the time being other arrangements with the Board for a person other than the account manager to secure the discharge of such duties.

16(4)   The third requirement specified in this regulation is that there are for the time being other arrangements with the Board designed to secure the discharge of such duties.

16(5)   The duties prescribed by this paragraph are those that fall to be discharged by an account manager under these Regulations.

16(6)   The appointment of a person in pursuance of the first requirement shall be treated as terminated in circumstances where–

(a)   the Board have reason to believe that the person concerned–

    (i)   has failed to secure the discharge of any of the duties prescribed by paragraph (5), or

    (ii)   does not have adequate resources to discharge those duties, and

(b)   the Board have notified the account manager and that person that they propose to treat his appointment as having terminated with effect from the date specified in the notice.

16(7) Where, in accordance with the first requirement, a person is at any time responsible for securing the discharge of duties, the person concerned–

(a) shall be entitled to act on the account manager's behalf for any of the purposes of the provisions relating to the duties;

(b) shall secure (where appropriate by acting on the account manager's behalf) the account manager's compliance with and discharge of the duties; and

(c) shall be personally liable in respect of any failure of the account manager to comply with or discharge any such duty as if the duties imposed on the account manager were imposed jointly and severally on the account manager and the person concerned.

History – In reg. 16(2)(a) the words "section 698(2)(b) of ITTOIA 2005" substituted for "subsection (5) of section 333A of the Taxes Act", by SI 2008/704, reg. 11, with effect from 6 April 2008.

ACCOUNT MANAGER – WITHDRAWAL BY BOARD OF APPROVAL

17(1) This regulation specifies the circumstances ("the disqualifying circumstances") in which the Board may by notice withdraw their approval of a person as an account manager in relation to an account.

17(2) The disqualifying circumstances to which paragraph (1) refers are that the Board have reason to believe–

(a) that any provision of these Regulations is not or at any time has not been satisfied in respect of an account managed by the account manager; or

(b) that a person to whom they have given approval to act as an account manager is not qualified so to act.

17(3) The notice to which paragraph (1) refers–

(a) may withdraw an approval in part, that is, in respect of particular types of accounts specified in the notice;

(b) shall specify the date from which the Board's approval is withdrawn; and

(c) shall specify the disqualifying circumstances.

17(4) On receiving the notice referred to in paragraph (1), subject to any appeal in accordance with regulation 18, the account manager shall notify the person who is the account investor in relation to the account held with the account manager of the right to transfer the account under regulations 21 or 21B (as appropriate), and the provision made by regulation 20(3).

History – Reg. 17(4) inserted by SI 2011/1780, reg. 21, with effect from 1 November 2011.

ACCOUNT MANAGER – APPEAL AGAINST WITHDRAWAL OF BOARD'S APPROVAL

18(1) An account manager to whom notice of withdrawal of approval has been given under regulation 17 may appeal against the withdrawal by notice given to the Board within 30 days after the date of the notice of withdrawal.

18(2) [Omitted by SI 2009/56, art. 3(2) and Sch. 2, para. 46(2).]

18(3) The like provisions are contained in Part V of the Management Act (appeals and other proceedings) shall apply to an appeal and the tribunal, on an appeal notified to it, shall confirm the notice unless satisfied that the notice ought to be quashed.

History – Reg. 18(2) omitted by SI 2009/56, art. 3(2) and Sch. 2, para. 46(2), operative from 1 April 2009 subject to transitional and saving provisions in SI 2009/56, Sch. 3. Former reg. 18(2) read as follows:
"**18(2)** The appeal shall be to the Special Commissioners.".
In reg. 18(3), the words "tribunal, on an appeal notified to it, shall" substituted for the words "Special Commissioners shall on appeal to them" by SI 2009/56, art. 3(2) and Sch. 2, para. 46(3)(a), operative from 1 April 2009 subject to transitional and saving provisions in SI 2009/56, Sch. 3.
In reg. 18(3), the words "they are", which appeared before "satisfied", omitted by SI 2009/56, art. 3(2) and Sch. 2, para. 46(3)(b), operative from 1 April 2009 subject to transitional and saving provisions in SI 2009/56, Sch. 3.

ACCOUNT MANAGER'S INTENTION TO MAKE A BULK TRANSFER OF ACCOUNTS OR TO CEASE TO ACT AS AN ACCOUNT MANAGER

19(1) An account manager must give notice to the Board if the account manager–

(a) intends to cease to act as an account manager; or

(b) intends to make a bulk transfer of accounts.

19(2) An account manager must give notice to a person who is the account investor in relation to an account held with the account manager if the account manager–

(a)   intends to cease to act as an account manager; or

(b)   intends that the account will be one of the accounts transferred in a bulk transfer of accounts.

19(3)   The notices described in paragraphs (1) and (2) must–

(a)   specify whether the account manager–

    (i)   intends to cease to act as an account manager; or

    (ii)   intends to make a bulk transfer of accounts;

(b)   where the notice specifies an intention to cease to act as an account manager,–

    (i)   specify the day on or after which the account manager intends to cease to act as an account manager; and

    (ii)   be given no less than 30 days before that day;

(c)   where the notice specifies an intention to make a bulk transfer of accounts,–

    (i)   specify the day on or after which the account manager intends to make the first transfer in the bulk transfer of accounts;

    (ii)   be given no less than 30 days before that day; and

    (iii)   advise the name and address of the person to whom the account manager intends to transfer accounts.

19(4)   The notice described in paragraph (2) must also–

(a)   identify the account to which it relates;

(b)   advise the account investor that the account may be transferred in accordance with regulation 21 or 21B otherwise than in a bulk transfer of accounts if sufficient instructions are provided to enable the account manager to do so;

(c)   advise the day by which the account manager must receive sufficient instructions for the account to be transferred otherwise than in a bulk transfer of accounts.

19(5)   Where an account manager intends to make a bulk transfer of accounts in consequence of an intention to cease to act as an account manager, such intention may be specified in the same notice to the Board or an account investor (as appropriate) provided the requirements of paragraphs (3) and (4) are met.

History – Reg. 19 (and the heading immediately preceding it) substituted by SI 2012/1871, reg. 15, with effect from 8 August 2012. Former reg. 19 read as follows:

"ACCOUNTING MANAGER CEASING TO ACT

19   A person shall give notice to the Board and to the account investor in the account which he manages of his intention to cease to act as the account manager not less than 30 days before he so ceases so that his obligations to the Board under the account can be conveniently discharged at or about the time he ceases so to act, and the notice to the account investor shall inform him of his right to transfer the account under regulation 21 or 21B.".

In former reg. 19, the words "or 21B" inserted by SI 2011/1780, reg. 22, with effect from 1 November 2011.

ACCOUNT MANAGER CEASING TO QUALIFY

20(1)   A person shall cease to qualify as an account manager and shall notify the Board within 30 days of the relevant event in sub-paragraphs (a) to (e), of that relevant event, where–

(a)   the person no longer fulfils the conditions of regulation 14;

(b)   there is an insolvency event in relation to the account manager;

(c)   an application has been made for a bank insolvency order or a bank administration order;

(d)   in the case of a building society, a person falling within section 991 of ITA 2007 or a credit union–

    (i)   it ceases to be a building society or to fall within section 991 of ITA 2007 or to be a credit union, as the case may be;

    (ii)   its directors have made a proposal under Part 1 of the Insolvency Act 1986 for a composition in satisfaction of its debts or a scheme of arrangement of its affairs; or

    (iii)   a receiver or manager of its property has been appointed; or

(e)   in the case of a European institution, a relevant authorised person or an assurance undertaking which falls within regulation 14(2)(b)(iv) and (v), action corresponding to any described in sub-paragraphs (b) to (d) has been taken by or in relation to the institution, person or undertaking under the law of an EEA State.

20(2)   On giving the notice referred to in paragraph (1), the person shall also notify the account investor of his right to transfer the account under regulation 21 or 21B (as appropriate), and the notice shall inform the account investor of his rights under paragraph (3).

20(3)   Where the account investor–

(a)   receives a notice under paragraph (2), or regulation 17(4) or 19, and

(b)   within 30 days of the sending of the notice to him, transfers the account to another account manager pursuant to regulation 21 or 21B (as appropriate),

the period between the transferor ceasing to act or to qualify as an account manager, and the transfer to the transferee, shall be ignored in determining whether the account has at all times been managed by an account manager.

History – Reg. 20(1) substituted by SI 2011/1780, reg. 23(a), with effect from 1 November 2011.
In former reg. 20(1)(b), the words "or is the subject of a bankruptcy restrictions order or an interim order" inserted by SI 2006/1722, art. 2(2) and Sch. 2, para. 12, with effect from 29 June 2006.
In former reg. 20(1)(d)(iii) the words "it enters administration" substituted for "an administration order is made in relation to it" by SI 2003/2096, art. 5 and Schedule, para. 73 with effect from 15 September 2003. Transitional provisions are contained in art. 6. Former reg. 20(1)(d) amended by SI 2001/3629, reg. 176 which came into force on 1 December 2001.
In reg. 20(2), the words "or 21B (as appropriate)" inserted by SI 2011/1780, reg. 23(b), with effect from 1 November 2011.
In reg. 20(3)(a), the words "regulation 17(4) or 19" substituted for the words "regulation 19" by SI 2011/1780, reg. 23(c), with effect from 1 November 2011.
In reg. 20(3)(b), the words "or 21B (as appropriate)" inserted by SI 2011/1780, reg. 23(d), with effect from 1 November 2011.
Transitional – SI 2003/2096, art. 6 contains transitional provisions so that the former rules remain in effect where a petition for an administration order was presented prior to 15 September 2003.

TRANSFERS RELATING TO ACCOUNTS OTHER THAN JUNIOR ISA ACCOUNTS

21(1)   In this regulation, in relation to a transfer of an account that is not a junior ISA account–

"**the current year's subscriptions**" means–

(a)   subscriptions made to the account by the account investor in the year in which the transfer takes place, but before the transfer,

(b)   subscriptions made to any other account by the account investor in the year in which the transfer takes place and transferred to the account before the transfer, and

(c)   the qualifying investments and other proceeds (including income) representing the subscriptions in sub-paragraphs (a) and (b) of this definition;

"**the previous years' subscriptions**" means–

(a)   subscriptions made to the account (or any other account or former personal equity plan) in any earlier year or years, and

(b)   the qualifying investments and other proceeds (including income) representing those subscriptions.

21(2)   Any transfer relating to an account or part of an account shall be made–

(a)   directly between one account manager ("the transferor") and another account manager ("the transferee"), or

(b)   where the same person is account manager before and after the transfer, solely by that manager (who shall maintain the records of both transferor and transferee required by this regulation).

21(3)   The current year's subscriptions may only be transferred as a whole (with or without the whole or part of any previous years' subscriptions).

21(4)   The current year's subscriptions and the previous years' subscriptions may only be transferred to–

(a)   a stocks and shares account (if the account investor is 18 years of age or over), or

(b)   a cash account,

belonging to the same account investor.

21(4A)   [Omitted by SI 2014/1450, reg. 19(1)(b).]

21(4B)   Where the current year's subscriptions (with or without other subscriptions) are transferred under paragraph (4), the subscriptions in sub-paragraphs (a) and (b) in the definition of "the current year's subscriptions" in paragraph (1) shall be treated, for all purposes including regulation 31(1)(c), as if they had been made to the account held with the transferee.

21(4C)   Where the current year's subscriptions (with or without other subscriptions) are transferred from–

(a)   a cash account to a cash account, or

(b)   a stocks and shares account to a stocks and shares account,

the subscriptions transferred, and no other subscriptions, shall be treated as the same account, for the purpose of making any remaining permitted subscriptions in that year.

Statutory Instruments

21(4CA) Regulation 12(1) does not prevent the current year's subscriptions and the previous years' subscriptions being transferred to an account that was held immediately before the transfer but to which no subscription has been made in the year in which the transfer occurs or the year immediately before that year.

21(4D) The account investor shall, subject to paragraph (4DA), make a fresh application under regulation 12 (with any necessary modifications to reflect that it is made on a transfer) to the transferee.

21(4DA) Paragraph (4D) does not apply where–

(a)   an account is transferred in a bulk transfer of accounts;

(b)   a cash account (whether or not in a bulk transfer of accounts) is transferred to a cash account held with the transferee immediately before the time when the transfer is made;

(c)   a stocks and shares account (whether or not in a bulk transfer of accounts) is transferred to a stocks and shares account held with the transferee immediately before the time when the transfer is made;

(d)   a cash account is transferred (otherwise than in a bulk transfer of accounts) to a stocks and shares account held with the transferee immediately before the time when the transfer is made, or

(e)   a stocks and shares account is transferred (otherwise than in a bulk transfer of accounts) to a cash account held with the transferee immediately before the time when the transfer is made.

21(4DB) Where an account is transferred in a bulk transfer of accounts that is not also a transfer described in paragraph (4DA)(b) or (c), a subscription to the account after the transfer may only be made if–

(a)   the subscription is made after the account investor has, during the period of time determined in accordance with paragraph (4DC), made an application to the transferee in relation to the account in accordance with regulation 12 (with any necessary modifications where appropriate to reflect that the account has been transferred in a bulk transfer of accounts);

(b)   the subscription is made in the year immediately following a year in which a subscription has been made to the account other than a subscription permitted by virtue of paragraph (4DE); or

(c)   the subscription is permitted by virtue of paragraph (4DE).

21(4DC) The period of time referred to in paragraph (4DB)(a) is the period–

(a)   starting at the beginning of the year immediately preceding the year in which the subscription is made, and

(b)   ending immediately before the subscription is made.

21(4DD) For the purposes of paragraphs (4DB) and (4DE), the current year's subscriptions and the previous years' subscriptions transferred are not subscriptions to the account.

21(4DE) A subscription to an account is permitted by this paragraph if–

(a)   the account has been transferred to the transferee in a bulk transfer of accounts pursuant to a scheme described in regulation 2(1A)(a)(ii) or in a group transfer of accounts;

(b)   the most recent application in accordance with regulation 12 relating to the transferred account made before its transfer is available to the transferee; and

(c)   the subscription is made–

(i)   in the year in which the account is transferred (provided a subscription has been made to the account in that year before the account was transferred); or

(ii)   in a year immediately following a year in which a subscription has been made to the transferred account (including a subscription made before the transfer).

21(4DF) For the purposes of paragraph (4DE)(b), an application in accordance with regulation 12 as described in that paragraph is available to a transferee if–

(a)   paragraph (4DG) or (4DH) applies; and

(b)   the transferor has advised the transferee whether a subscription has been made to the transferred account in the year immediately preceding the year in which the transfer takes place.

21(4DG) This paragraph applies where the application described in paragraph (4DE)(b) (or a copy of it) is held by the transferee.

21(4DH) This paragraph applies where–

(a)   the application described in paragraph (4DE)(b) (or a copy of it) is held by the transferor; and

(b)   the transferee can require the transferor to make it available to the transferee for any purpose necessary to ensure the transferee's compliance with these regulations.

21(4DI) An account transferred in accordance with this regulation in a bulk transfer of accounts is an account opened in accordance with regulation 12 for the purposes of these Regulations whether or not an application in accordance with regulation 12 as described in paragraph (4DB)(a) is made.

21(4E) This regulation shall also apply where an account is transferred in consequence of an account manager ("the transferor") ceasing to act or to qualify as an account manager.

21(5) Where an account is transferred, the transferor must, subject to paragraph (5B), give to the transferee a notice containing the information specified in paragraph (6) before the relevant time specified in paragraph (5A).

21(5A) The relevant time specified in this paragraph is–

(a)   in the case of an account transferred in a bulk transfer of accounts, the time of the transfer;

(b)   in any other case, the expiry of 30 days after the day of the transfer.

21(5B) Paragraph (5) does not apply where a transferor provides information to a transferee in accordance with regulation 21A(2)(b)(ii).

21(6) The information specified in this paragraph is–

(a)   as regards the account investor–

       (i)   his full name,

       (ii)   the address of his permanent residence, including postcode,

       (iii)   his date of birth, and

       (iv)   if he has one, his national insurance number, and

(b)   as regards an account or any part of an account transferred pursuant to paragraph (2)–

       (i)   whether the account is a cash account or stocks and shares account,

       (ii)   the date of the transfer,

       (iii)   the total amount of cash subscribed to the account during the period from the beginning of the year in which the transfer takes place to the date of the transfer,

       (iv)   the date on which the first subscription (if any) was made to the account, in the year in which the transfer takes place, and

       (v)   the amount of any dividends on account investments which are payable to, but have not been received by, the transferor at the date of the transfer.

       (vi)   [omitted by SI 2014/1450, reg. 19(3)]

(c)   [Omitted by SI 2007/2119, reg. 18(d).]

21(7) [Omitted by SI 2009/1994, reg. 8(b).]

History – The heading to reg. 21 substituted by SI 2011/1780, reg. 24(a), with effect from 1 November 2011. The heading formerly read: "TRANSFERS RELATING TO ACCOUNTS".
The former heading to reg. 21 substituted for "Transfer of accounts to other account managers" by SI 2007/2119, reg. 18(a), with effect from 6 April 2008.
In reg. 21(1), the words "In this regulation, in relation to a transfer of an account that is not a junior ISA account" substituted for the words "In this regulation, in relation to a transfer" by SI 2011/1780, reg. 24(b), with effect from 1 November 2011.
In reg. 21(4) the words "In the case of a cash account," omitted and the word "The" substituted for "the" by SI 2014/1450, reg. 19(1)(a), with effect from 1 July 2014.
Reg. 21(4A) omitted by SI 2014/1450, reg. 19(1)(b), with effect from 1 July 2014. Former reg. 21(4A) read as follows:
     "**21(4A)** In the case of a stocks and shares account, the current year's subscriptions and the previous years' subscriptions may only be transferred to a stocks and shares account belonging to the same account investor."
Reg. 21(4B) substituted by SI 2014/1450, reg. 19(1)cb), with effect from 1 July 2014. Former reg. 21(4B) read as follows:
     "**21(4B)** Where the current year's subscriptions (with or without other subscriptions) are transferred from a cash account to a stocks and shares account (under paragraph (4)(a))–
     (a)   the subscriptions in sub-paragraphs (a) and (b) of the definition of "the current year's subscriptions" in paragraph (1) shall be treated, for all purposes including regulation 31(3)(c), as if they had been made to the stocks and shares account, and
     (b)   accordingly, shall not count towards the cash subscription limit in regulation 4ZA. "
Reg. 21(1)–(4E) substituted for former reg. 21(1)–(4) by SI 2007/2119, reg. 18(b), with effect from 6 April 2008.
In reg. 21(4B)(b), the words "regulation 4ZA" substituted for the words "regulation 4(3)" by SI 2012/1871, reg. 16(a), with effect from 8 August 2012.
Reg. 21(4CA) inserted by SI 2012/1871, reg. 16(b), with effect from 9 November 2011.
In reg. 21(4D), the words ", subject to paragraph (4DA)," inserted by SI 2012/1871, reg. 16(c), with effect from 9 November 2011.
Reg. 21(4DA)(e) inserted and the word "or" at end of sub-para. (c) omitted and ", or" at end of sub-para. (d) substituted for "." by SI 2014/1450, reg. 19(2), with effect from 1 July 2014.
In reg. 21(4DE)(a), the words "in a bulk transfer of accounts pursuant to a scheme described in regulation 2(1A)(a)(ii) or" inserted by SI 2013/1743, reg. 6, with effect from 5 March 2013.
Reg. 21(4DA)–(4DI) inserted by SI 2012/1871, reg. 16(d), with effect from 9 November 2011.
Reg. 21(5) substituted, and (5A) and (5B) inserted, by SI 2012/1870, reg. 16(e), with effect from 8 August 2012.
In former reg. 21(5), the words "Except where the transferor has provided information to the transferee in accordance with regulation 21A(2)(b)(ii), the" substituted for the word "The" by SI 2010/2957, reg. 4, with effect in relation to instructions given on or after 4 January 2011 for a cash account or part of a cash account held by an account investor with an account manager to be transferred, subject to and in accordance with reg. 21, to a cash account belonging to the account investor which is held with

another account manager. For this purpose, "account investor" and "account manager" have the meanings given in reg. 2(1)(a), and "cash account" has the same meaning as in reg. 4(1).

In former reg. 21(5), the words "and the declaration specified in paragraph (7)", which appeared at the end, omitted by SI 2009/1994, reg. 8(a), with effect from 11 August 2009.

Reg. 21(6)(b)(vi) omitted and the word "and" inserted at end of sub-para. (b)(iv) and "." at end of sub-para. (b)(v) substituted for ", and" by SI 2014/1450, reg. 19(3), with effect from 1 July 2014. Former reg. 21(6)(b)(vi) read as follows:

> "(vi)   any amount which is, or will become, due under regulation 23 which has not been paid to the Board at the date of the transfer."

In reg. 21(6)(b), in the words preceding para. (i), the words "or any part of an account" inserted after the word "account"; in para. (i) the words "cash account or stocks and shares account," substituted for the words "maxi-account, a mini-account made up of a specified component or a TESSA only account," and in para. (iii) the words ", and the amounts respectively allocated to each component of the account" omitted by SI 2007/2119, reg. 18(c), with effect from 6 April 2008.

Reg. 21(6)(b)(iv) inserted by SI 2007/2119, reg. 18(c), with effect from 6 April 2008.

Reg. 21(6)(c) and the word "and" which preceded it omitted by SI 2007/2119, reg. 18(d), with effect from 6 April 2008.

Reg. 21(7) omitted by SI 2009/1994, reg. 8(b), with effect from 11 August 2009.

FURTHER REQUIREMENTS RELATING TO TRANSFERS BETWEEN CASH ACCOUNTS

21A(1)   This regulation applies where an account investor, through the agency of an account manager ("the transferee"), gives instructions ("transfer instructions") to an account manager with whom the account investor holds a cash account ("the transferor") for that account or part of that account to be transferred, subject to and in accordance with regulations 21 or 21B, to a cash account held by the account investor with the transferee.

21A(2)   Where this regulation applies–

(a)   the transferee shall, within 5 business days beginning on the instruction day, send to the transferor–

    (i)   the transfer instructions; and

    (ii)   a notice specifying that the transferee consents to the transfer ("the consent notice");

(b)   the transferor shall, within 5 business days beginning on the day that the transferor receives the transfer instructions and the consent notice,–

    (i)   transfer to the transferee the subscriptions specified in the transfer instructions; and

    (ii)   send to the transferee a notice containing the information specified in paragraph (3); and

(c)   the transferee shall ensure that the subscriptions specified in the transfer instructions are transferred to a cash account held by the account investor with the transferee within 3 business days beginning on the day that the transferee receives the subscriptions and the notice referred to in subparagraph (b)(ii).

21A(3)   The information specified in this paragraph is–

(a)   as regards the account investor–

    (i)   the full name of the account investor,

    (ii)   the address of the account investor's permanent residence, including postcode,

    (iii)   the date of birth of the account investor, and

    (iv)   the national insurance number of the account investor (if any),

(b)   as regards the cash account or any part of the cash account–

    (i)   the date of the transfer,

    (ii)   the total amount of cash subscribed to the account during the period from the beginning of the year in which the transfer takes place to the date of the transfer,

    (iii)   in relation to the transfer of an account that is not a junior ISA account, the date on which the first subscription (if any) was made to the account in the year in which the transfer takes place,

    (iiia)   in relation to the transfer of an account that is a junior ISA account, the date on which the subscription described in paragraph (3A) was made (if appropriate), and

    (iv)   the reference number or other means used by the transferor to identify the account belonging to the account investor in respect of which the transfer is made, and

    in relation to an account that is a junior ISA account–

    (i)   the full name of the registered contact,

    (ii)   the address of the registered contact's permanent residence, including postcode.

21A(3A)   The subscription referred to in paragraph (3)(b)(iiia) is the first subscription to the account provided the subscription is made in the same year as the transfer.

21A(4) For the purposes of paragraph (2)(a) and (b), the transfer instructions and the notices (as appropriate) shall be treated as sent if they are–

(a)   posted to, or left at, the proper address of the transferor or the transferee (as appropriate); or

(b)   transmitted by electronic communication.

21A(5) For the purposes of paragraph (2)(b), where the transferor receives the transfer instructions and consent notice on different days, they must both be treated as received on the latest of those days.

21A(6) For the purposes of paragraph (2)(c), where the transferee receives subscriptions specified in the transfer instructions and the notice described in paragraph (2)(b) on different days, they must all be treated as received on the latest of those days.

21A(7) In this regulation–

> **"electronic communication"** includes any communication conveyed by means of an electronic communications network;

> **"instruction day"** means–

> > (a)   the day stipulated by the account investor for the transferee to begin the transfer process, or

> > (b)   if no day is stipulated, the day that the transfer instructions are received by the transferee;

> **"subscriptions"** means the current year's subscriptions and the previous years' subscriptions as described in regulation 21(1).

21A(8) For the purposes of this regulation–

(a)   a document is **"posted"** if it is sent pre-paid by a postal service which seeks to deliver documents by post within the United Kingdom no later than the next business day in all or the majority of cases, and to deliver by post outside the United Kingdom within such a period as is reasonable in all the circumstances; and

(b)   the **"proper address"** to which a document is to be sent is any current address provided by the transferor or transferee as an address for service of such documents, but if no current address is provided then it shall be the address of its registered or principal office in the United Kingdom.

History – In reg. 21A(1), the words "regulations 21 or 21B, to a cash account held by the account investor with the transferee." substituted for the words "regulation 21, to a cash account belonging to the account investor which is held with the transferee." by SI 2011/1780, reg. 25(a), with effect from 1 November 2011.
In reg. 21A(2)(c), the words "held by the account investor" substituted for the words "belonging to the account investor which is held" by SI 2011/1780, reg. 25(b), with effect from 1 November 2011.
Reg. 21A(3)(b)(iii) substituted and (iiia) inserted by SI 2012/1871, reg. 17(a), with effect from 8 August 2012. Former reg. 21A(3)(b)(iii) read as follows:
> "(iii)   the date on which the first subscription (if any) was made to the account, in the year in which the transfer takes place, and".
Reg. 21A(3)(c) inserted (and the "and" at the end of reg. 21A(3)(a) omitted, and the ", and" at the end of reg. 21A(3)(b) inserted) by SI 2011/1780, reg. 25(c) and (d), with effect from 1 November 2011.
Reg. 21A(3A) inserted by SI 2012/1871, reg. 17(b), with effect from 8 August 2012.
In reg. 21A(7), the definition of "business day" omitted by SI 2011/1780, reg. 25(e), with effect from 1 November 2011.
Reg. 21A inserted by SI 2010/2957, reg. 5, with effect in relation to instructions given on or after 4 January 2011 for a cash account or part of a cash account held by an account investor with an account manager to be transferred, subject to and in accordance with reg. 21, to a cash account belonging to the account investor which is held with another account manager. For this purpose, "account investor" and "account manager" have the meanings given in reg. 2(1)(a), and "cash account" has the same meaning as in reg. 4(1).

TRANSFERS RELATING TO JUNIOR ISA ACCOUNTS

21B(1) This regulation only applies to an account that is a junior ISA account.

21B(2) In this regulation, in relation to a transfer–

> **"the current year's subscriptions"** means–

> > (a)   subscriptions made to the account in the year in which the transfer takes place, but before the transfer;

> > (b)   subscriptions made in the year in which the transfer takes place to any other account held by the named child and transferred to the account before the transfer, and

> > (c)   the qualifying investments and other proceeds (including income) representing the subscriptions in sub-paragraphs (a) and (b) of this definition;

> **"the previous years' subscriptions"** means–

> > (a)   subscriptions made to the account (or any other account) in any earlier year or years, and

> > (b)   the qualifying investments and other proceeds (including income) representing those subscriptions.

21B(3) Any transfer relating to an account or part of an account shall be made–

(a)   directly between one account manager ("the transferor") and another account manager ("the transferee"), or

(b)   where the same person is account manager before and after the transfer, solely by that manager (who shall maintain the records of both transferor and transferee required by this regulation).

21B(4)   The current year's subscriptions may only be transferred as a whole (with or without the whole or part of any previous years' subscriptions).

21B(5)   In the case of a cash account—

(a)   all or part of the previous years' subscriptions and, if current year's subscriptions are to be transferred, all of the current year's subscriptions made to the cash account, may be transferred to a junior ISA account that is a stocks and shares account belonging to the same named child, or

(b)   all of the subscriptions made to the cash account ("old cash account") that are held in the account immediately before the transfer may be transferred to a junior ISA account that is a cash account ("new cash account") belonging to the same named child (and, for the avoidance of doubt, no transfer may be made to a new cash account if the transfer does not comprise all of the subscriptions held in the old cash account immediately before the transfer).

21B(6)   In the case of a stocks and shares account—

(a)   all or part of the previous years' subscriptions and, if current year's subscriptions are to be transferred, all of the current year's subscriptions made to the stocks and shares account, may be transferred to a junior ISA account that is a cash account belonging to the same named child, or

(b)   all of the subscriptions made to the stocks and shares account ("old stocks and shares account") that are held in the account immediately before the transfer may be transferred to a junior ISA account that is a stocks and shares account ("new stocks and shares account") belonging to the same named child (and, for the avoidance of doubt, no transfer may be made to a new stocks and shares account if the transfer does not comprise all of the subscriptions held in the old stocks and shares account immediately before the transfer).

21B(7)   Where current year's subscriptions are transferred from a junior ISA account to another junior ISA account, the current year's subscriptions transferred shall count towards the overall subscription limit for the child holding the account for that year.

21B(8)   The registered contact shall, subject to paragraph (8A), make a fresh application under regulation 12A (with any necessary modifications to reflect that it is made on a transfer) to the transferee.

21B(8A)   Paragraph (8) does not apply where an account is transferred in a bulk transfer of accounts.

21B(8B)   Where an account is transferred in a bulk transfer of accounts, a subscription to the account after the transfer may only be made if—

(a)   an application to the transferee in relation to the account in accordance with regulation 12A (with any necessary modifications where appropriate to reflect that the account has been transferred in a bulk transfer of accounts) has been made; or

(b)   the subscription is permitted by virtue of paragraph (8D).

21B(8C)   For the purposes of paragraphs (8B) and (8E), the current year's subscriptions and the previous years' subscriptions transferred are not subscriptions to the account.

21B(8D)   A subscription to an account is permitted by this paragraph where—

(a)   the account has been transferred to the transferee in a bulk transfer of accounts pursuant to a scheme described in regulation 2(1A)(a)(ii) or in a group transfer of accounts; and

(b)   the most recent application in accordance with regulation 12A relating to the transferred account made before its transfer is available to the transferee.

21B(8E)   For the purposes of paragraph (8D)(b), an application in accordance with regulation 12A as described in that paragraph is available to a transferee if—

(a)   paragraph (8F) or (8G) applies; and

(b)   the transferor has advised the transferee whether a subscription has been made to the transferred account in the year immediately preceding the year in which the transfer takes place.

21B(8F)   This paragraph applies where the application described in paragraph (8D)(b) (or a copy of it) is held by the transferee.

21B(8G)   This paragraph applies where—

(a)   the application described in paragraph (8D)(b) (or a copy of it) is held by the transferor; and

(b)   the transferee can require the transferor to make it available to the transferee for any purpose necessary to ensure the transferee's compliance with these regulations.

21B(8H)   An account transferred in accordance with this regulation in a bulk transfer of accounts is a junior ISA account opened pursuant to an application in accordance with regulation 12A for the purposes of these Regulations whether or not an application in accordance with regulation 12A as described in paragraph (8B)(a) is made.

21B(9)   This regulation shall also apply where an account is transferred in consequence of an account manager ("the transferor") ceasing to act or qualify as an account manager.

21B(10)   Where an account is transferred, the transferor must, subject to paragraph (10B), give to the transferee a notice containing the information specified in paragraph (11) before the relevant time specified in paragraph (10A).

21B(10A)   The relevant time specified in this paragraph is–

(a)   in the case of an account transferred in a bulk transfer of accounts, the time of the transfer;

(b)   in any other case, the expiry of 30 days after the day of the transfer.

21B(10B)   Paragraph (10) does not apply where a transferor provides information to a transferee in accordance with regulation 21A(2)(b)(ii).

21B(11)   The information specified in this paragraph is–

(a)   as regards the named child who holds the account transferred–

    (i)   the full name of the child,

    (ii)   the address (including postcode) of the permanent residence of the child,

    (iii)   the date of birth of the child,

    (iv)   the national insurance number of the child (if any); and

(b)   as regards an account from which the transfer is made–

    (i)   whether the account is a cash account or stocks and shares account,

    (ii)   the date of the transfer,

    (iii)   the total amount of cash subscribed to the account during the period from the beginning of the year in which the transfer takes place to the date of the transfer,

    (iv)   the date on which the subscription described in paragraph (12) was made (if appropriate), and

    (v)   the amount of any dividends on account investments which are payable to, but have not been received by, the transferor at the date of the transfer,

    (vi)   the full name of the person who is the registered contact in relation to the account, and

    (vii)   the address of the registered contact's permanent residence, including postcode.

21B(12)   The subscription referred to in paragraph (11)(b)(iv) is the first subscription to the account provided the subscription is made in the same year as the transfer.

History – In reg. 21B(8), the words ", subject to paragraph (8A)," inserted by SI 2012/1871, reg. 18(a), with effect from 9 November 2011.
In reg. 21B(8D)(a), the words "in a bulk transfer of accounts pursuant to a scheme described in regulation 2(1A)(a)(ii) or" inserted by SI 2013/1743, reg. 7, with effect from 5 March 2013.
Reg. 21B(8A)–(8H) inserted by SI 2012/1871, reg. 18(b), with effect from 9 November 2011.
Reg. 21B(10) substituted, and (10A) and (10B) inserted, by SI 2012/1871, reg. 18(c), with effect from 8 August 2012. Former reg. 21B(10) read as follows:

"**21B(10)**   Except where the transferor has provided information to the transferee in accordance with regulation 21A(2)(b)(ii), the transferor shall within 30 days after the date of the transfer give the transferee a notice containing the information specified in paragraph (11).".

Reg. 21B(11)(b)(iv) substituted by SI 2012/1871, reg. 18(d), with effect from 8 August 2012. Former reg. 21B(11)(b)(iv) read as follows:

"(iv)   the date on which the first subscription (if any) was made to the account, in the year in which the transfer takes place,".

Reg. 21B(12) inserted by SI 2012/1871, reg. 18(e), with effect from 8 August 2012.
Reg. 21B inserted by SI 2011/1780, reg. 26, with effect from 1 November 2011.

REPAIR OF INVALID JUNIOR ISA ACCOUNTS

21C(1)   It is an overriding requirement to be satisfied in relation to a junior ISA account that the account manager and registered contact, as the case may be, take any steps necessary to remedy any breach of these Regulations.

21C(2)   Where a breach is remedied as mentioned in paragraph (1), the account shall, to the extent of that breach, be treated as having been a valid account at all times.

History – Reg. 21C inserted by SI 2011/1780, reg. 26, with effect from 1 November 2011.

EXEMPTION FROM TAX OF ACCOUNT INCOME AND GAINS

22(1)   Subject to these Regulations–

(a)   no tax shall be chargeable on the account manager or his nominee or on the account investor–

     (i)   in respect of interest, dividends, distributions or gains in respect of account investments (excluding any building society bonus), or

     (ia)   in respect of alternative finance return paid by a financial institution in accordance with Part 10A of ITA 2007, or

     (ib)   in respect of a payment under a building society bonus scheme, so far as the payment is calculated by reference to account investments (and if paid directly by the society into the account, the payment shall not count towards the subscription limit in regulations 4ZA(1) and 4ZB(1)); or

     (ii)   on any annual profits or gains treated under Part 12 of ITA 2007 (accrued income profits) as having been received by any of them in respect of account investments, or

     (iii)   on an offshore income gain to which a disposal by any of them of an account investment would otherwise give rise to a charge to tax under regulation 17 of the Offshore Funds (Tax) Regulations 2009, or

     (iv)   on a profit on the disposal of a deeply discounted security within the meaning given by section 430 of ITTOIA 2005,

     (v)   in respect of gains treated by under Chapter 9 of Part 4 of ITTOIA 2005 as arising in connection with a policy of life insurance which is an account investment;

(b)   losses in respect of account investments shall be disregarded for the purposes of capital gains tax;

(ba)   any gain or loss accruing on and attributable to a payment within paragraph (ib) of sub-paragraph (a) shall not be a chargeable gain or allowable loss for capital gains tax purposes;

(c)   a deficiency arising in a tax year and falling within section 539(1) of ITTOIA 2005, so far as it relates to an account investment, shall not be allowable as a deduction from the total income of the account investor;

(d)   relief in respect of tax shall be given in the manner and to the extent provided by these Regulations;

(e)   in relation to an account that is not a junior ISA account, interest on a cash deposit which is an account investment held under a cash component shall not, except for the purposes of section 629 of ITTOIA 2005, be regarded as income for any income tax purposes,

(f)   in relation to a junior ISA account, income arising from account investments shall not be regarded as income for any income tax purposes (including section 629 of ITTOIA 2005).

22(2)   An account investor who, after the opening of an account, at any time ceases to be resident in the United Kingdom, shall be treated as if he were resident in the United Kingdom for the purposes of determining his entitlement to, or to payment of, tax credits in respect of qualifying distributions, so far as they relate to account investments under an account held by him.

22(3)   A reference to **"interest"** in this regulation includes a reference to any bonus and to a dividend paid or credited in respect of a share account with a building society.

History – In reg. 22(1)(a)(i) the words "(excluding any building society bonus)" inserted by SI 2006/3194, reg. 4(a) with effect from 1 January 2007.

Reg. 22(1)(a)(ia) substituted by SI 2011/1780, reg. 27(a), with effect from 1 November 2011.

After former reg. 22(1)(a)(ia) the word "or" inserted by SI 2006/3194, reg. 4(b) with effect from 1 January 2007.

Former reg. 22(1)(a)(ia) inserted by SI 2005/3350, reg. 11, with effect from 27 December 2005.

In reg. 22(1)(a)(ib) "limit" substituted for "limits" and "4ZA(1) and 4ZB(1)" substituted for "4ZA(1) and (2) and 4ZB(1)" by SI 2014/1450, reg. 20, with effect from 1 July 2014.

In reg. 22(1)(a)(ib), the words "regulations 4ZA(1) and (2) and 4ZB(1)" substituted for the words "regulation 4(2) to (3)" by SI 2011/1780, reg. 27(b), with effect from 1 November 2011.

Reg. 22(1)(a)(ib) inserted by SI 2006/3194, reg. 4(b) with effect from 1 January 2007.

In reg. 22(1)(a)(ii) the words "under Part 12 of ITA 2007 (accrued income profits)" substituted for "by section 714(2) of the Taxes Act", by SI 2008/704, reg. 12(2), with effect from 6 April 2008.

Reg. 22(1)(a)(iii) substituted by SI 2011/1780, reg. 27(c), with effect from 1 November 2011.

In reg. 22(1)(a)(v) the words "under Chapter 9 of Part 4 of ITTOIA 2005" substituted for "by section 541 of the Taxes Act" by SI 2008/704, reg. 12(4), with effect from 6 April 2008.

In reg. 22(1)(a)(ii) the words "under Part 12 of ITA 2007 (accrued income profits)" substituted for "by section 714(2) of the Taxes Act", by SI 2008/704, reg. 12(2), with effect from 6 April 2008.

In reg. 22(1)(a)(v) the words "held under an insurance component" which appeared after the words "an account investment" omitted by SI 2004/2996, reg. 15(a), with effect from 6 April 2005.

Reg. 22(1)(ba) inserted by SI 2006/3194, reg. 5 with effect from 1 January 2007.

Reg. 22(1)(c) substituted by SI 2008/704, reg. 12(5), with effect from 6 April 2008.

In former reg. 22(1)(c), the words "held under an insurance component" which appeared after the words "an account investment" omitted by SI 2004/2996, reg. 15(b), with effect from 6 April 2005.

In reg. 22(1)(d), the "and" at the end omitted by SI 2011/1780, reg. 27(d), with effect from 1 November 2011.

In reg. 22(1)(e), the words "in relation to an account that is not a junior ISA account," inserted by SI 2011/1780, reg. 27(e), with effect from 1 November 2011.

In reg. 22(1)(e) the words "section 629 of ITTOIA 2005" substituted for "section 660B of the Taxes Act" by SI 2008/704, reg. 12(6), with effect from 6 April 2008.

In reg. 22(1)(e) the words ", except for the purposes of section 660B of the Taxes Act," inserted by SI 2001/908, reg. 8, operative from 6 April 2001.

Reg. 22(1)(f) inserted by SI 2011/1780, reg. 27(f), with effect from 1 November 2011.

In reg. 22(2), the words "the opening of" substituted for the words "subscribing to" by SI 2011/1780, reg. 27(g), with effect from 1 November 2011.

Reg. 22(3) inserted by SI 2011/1780, reg. 27(h), with effect from 1 November 2011.

INTEREST ON CASH DEPOSITS HELD UNDER A STOCKS AND SHARES COMPONENT OF AN ACCOUNT THAT IS NOT A JUNIOR ISA ACCOUNT

23 [Omitted by SI 2014/1450, reg. 2.]

History – Reg. 23 omitted by SI 2014/1450, reg. 21, with effect from 1 July 2014. Former reg. 23 read as follows:

"**23(1)** When in any year, a sum of interest is paid or credited in respect of a cash deposit which is held under a stocks and shares component of an account that is not a junior ISA account in accordance with regulation 6(4) to (6)–
(a)   no relief from tax shall apply to such interest, but
(b)   paragraph (2) shall apply, and the amount determined in accordance with that paragraph shall be taken to represent the tax on such interest, in the place of the liabilities to tax which would otherwise arise.

23(2) Where this paragraph applies–
(a)   the account manager shall pay to the Board an amount representing income tax at the basic rate in force for the year on all sums of interest referred to in paragraph (1) paid or credited in that year; and
(b)   any amount so payable–
        (i)   may be set-off against any repayment in respect of tax due under regulation 25, and subject thereto
        (ii)   shall be treated as an amount of tax due under an assessment which is final and conclusive and payable not later than 6 months after the end of the year in which the interest was paid or credited.

23(3) The interest referred to in paragraph (1) shall in all other respects be regarded as if it were not income for any income tax purposes, and no repayment of tax or amounts representing tax shall be made to the account investor receiving or entitled to such interest.

23(4) The reference to interest in paragraph (1), and in regulation 22, includes a reference to any bonus and to a dividend paid or credited in respect of a share account with a building society.

History – Heading to reg. 23 substituted by SI 2011/1780, reg. 28(a), with effect from 1 November 2011.

In the former heading to reg. 23, the wording "or insurance component" which appeared after the words "shares component" omitted by SI 2004/2996, reg. 16, with effect from 6 April 2005.

In reg. 23(1), the words "of an account that is not a junior ISA account" inserted by SI 2011/1780, reg. 28(b), with effect from 1 November 2011.

In reg. 23(1) the words "or insurance component" which appeared after the words "share component" omitted by SI 2004/2996, reg. 16, with effect from 6 April 2005.

In reg. 23(2), the words "basic rate" substituted for the words "lower rate" by SI 2008/1934, reg. 5, with effect from 12 August 2008. "

TAX LIABILITIES AND RELIEFS – ACCOUNT MANAGER TO ACT ON BEHALF OF ACCOUNT INVESTOR

24(1) An account manager may under these Regulations make claims, conduct appeals and agree on behalf of the account investor liabilities for and reliefs from tax in respect of an account.

24(2) Claims shall be made to the Board in accordance with the provisions of regulations 25 and 26.

24(3) Where any relief or exemption from tax previously given in respect of an account has by virtue of these Regulations become excessive, in computing the relief due on any claim there shall be deducted (so that amounts equal to that excess are set off or repaid to the Board, as the case may be) notwithstanding that those amounts have been invested–

(a)   any amount repaid in respect of income tax or paid in respect of a tax credit; and

(b)   [omitted by SI 2014/1450, reg. 22;]

(c)   any other amount due to the Board by an account manager in respect of any tax liability in respect of account investments under an account including (but without prejudice to the making of an assessment under the provisions of that Schedule) any amount falling due in respect of a liability under Chapter 9 of Part 15 of ITA 2007.

24(4) Any amount deducted under paragraph (3) shall be treated as an amount of income tax deducted at source and not repayable within the meaning and for the purposes of section 95(2)(a) of the Management Act.

History – Reg. 24(3)(b) omitted and the word "and" inserted at end of sub-para (a) by SI 2014/1450, reg. 22, with effect from 1 July 2014. Former reg. 24(3)(b) read as follows:

"(b)   any sum representing income tax which is payable under regulation 23 on amounts of interest paid or credited as mentioned in that regulation; and"

In reg. 24(3)(c) the words "Chapter 9 of Part 15 of ITA 2007" substituted for "paragraph 3 or 4 of Schedule 23A to the Taxes Act", by SI 2008/704, reg. 13, with effect from 6 April 2008.

REPAYMENTS IN RESPECT OF TAX TO ACCOUNT MANAGER – INTERIM CLAIMS

25(1) Notwithstanding the provisions of any other enactment, the Board shall not be under an obligation to make any repayment in respect of tax under these Regulations earlier than the end of the month following the month in which the claim for the repayment is received.

25(2) A claim for repayment in respect of tax which is not an annual claim ("interim claim") may be made only for a period of a month (or a number of months not exceeding six) beginning on the 6th day of the month and ending on the 5th day of the relevant following month.

25(3) No claim for repayment may be made for the month ending 5th October or any subsequent month until the annual return under regulation 26(2) due in respect of an account for the preceding year has been duly made by the account manager and received by the Board.

25(4) Where, on the occasion of a claim, there is due to the Board an amount in respect of tax, that amount shall be recoverable by the Board in the same manner as tax charged by an assessment on the account manager which has become final and conclusive.

25(5) This regulation and regulation 26 shall not apply to any repayment in respect of tax on policies of life insurance falling within regulation 9, or on distributions and other rights or proceeds in respect of such policies except in so far as a return is required in respect of any gain treated as arising in accordance with regulation 36(3)(a) or (b).

History – In reg. 25(5) the words "a return is required in respect of" substituted for the words "regulation 26(2) requires a return of all sums of interest referred to in regulation 23(2)(a) and" by SI 2014/1450, reg. 23, with effect from 1 July 2014.
In reg. 25(5) the words "policies of life insurance falling within regulation 9" substituted for the words "qualifying investments for an insurance component of any account" by SI 2004/2996, reg. 17(a), with effect from 6 April 2005.
In reg. 25(5) the words "such policies" substituted for "the qualifying investments held under any such component" by SI 2004/2996, reg. 17(b), with effect from 6 April 2005.
Reg. 25(5) amended by SI 1998/3174, reg. 9, operative from 6 April 1999.

REPAYMENTS IN RESPECT OF TAX TO ACCOUNT MANAGER – ANNUAL RETURNS AND ANNUAL CLAIMS

26(1) An annual claim is a claim for repayment in respect of tax for a year and may not be made at any time more than six years after the end of the year.

26(2) An account manager shall within six months after the end of the year make a return of all income and any gain treated as arising in accordance with regulation 36(3)(a) or (b), and in addition an annual claim to establish the total of repayments due under an account for that year.

26(3) Where the aggregate of the repayments in respect of interim claims for the year shown by an annual claim exceeds the amount repayable for the year shown on the claim, the account manager shall repay the amount of the excess to the Board with the claim.

26(4) If an account manager fails to make the return and the annual claim required under this regulation within the time limited, the Board may issue a notice to the account manager showing the aggregate of payments in respect of the interim claims for the year, and stating that the Board are not satisfied that the amount due to the account manager for that year exceeds the lower amount stated in the notice.

26(5) If a return and an annual claim are not delivered to the Board within 14 days after the issue of such a notice under paragraph (4) the amount of the difference between the aggregate and the lower amount stated in the notice shall immediately be recoverable by the Board in the same manner as tax charged by an assessment on the account manager which has become final and conclusive.

26(6) Where a return and an annual claim have been made and the account manager subsequently discovers that an error or mistake has been made in the return or claim the account manager may make a supplementary return or annual claim within the time allowed in paragraph (1).

History – In reg. 26(2) the words ", and of all sums of interest referred to in regulation 23(2)(a)" and ", and the total amount payable under regulation 23(2)(a)" omitted by SI 2014/1450, reg. 24, with effect from 1 July 2014.
Reg. 26(2) amended by SI 1998/3174, reg. 10, operative from 6 April 1999.

ACCOUNT MANAGER'S RETURNS AND CLAIMS – SUPPLEMENTARY PROVISIONS

27(1) Section 42 of the Management Act shall not apply to claims under these Regulations.

27(2) No appeal shall lie from the Board's decision on an interim claim.

27(3) An appeal from the Board's decision on an annual claim shall be brought by giving notice to the Board within 30 days of receipt of notice of the decision.

27(4) No payment or repayment made or other thing done on or in relation to an interim claim or a notice under regulation 26(4) shall prejudice the decision on an annual claim.

27(5) The like provisions as are contained in Part V of the Management Act (appeals and other proceedings) shall apply to an appeal under paragraph (3) above, and on an appeal that is notified to the tribunal, the tribunal may vary the decision appealed against whether or not the variation is to the advantage of the appellant.

27(6) All such assessments, payments and repayments shall be made as are necessary to give effect to the Board's decision on an annual claim or to any variation of that decision on appeal.

27(7) Returns and claims under these Regulations shall be in such form and contain such particulars as the Board prescribe and, subject to regulation 31(1) and (2), shall be signed by the account manager, and forms prescribed for annual claims may require a report to be given by a person qualified for appointment as auditor of a company.

History – In reg. 27(3), the words "shall be to the Special Commissioners", which appeared after "appeal", omitted by SI 2009/56, art. 3(2) and Sch. 2, para. 47(2)(a), operative from 1 April 2009 subject to transitional and saving provisions in SI 2009/56, Sch. 3. In reg. 27(3), the words ", and the appeal", which appeared before "shall be brought", omitted by SI 2009/56, art. 3(2) and Sch. 2, para. 47(2)(b), operative from 1 April 2009 subject to transitional and saving provisions in SI 2009/56, Sch. 3.
In reg. 27(5), the words "on an appeal that is notified to the tribunal, the tribunal" substituted for the words "on appeal the Special Commissioners" by SI 2009/56, art. 3(2) and Sch. 2, para. 47(3), operative from 1 April 2009 subject to transitional and saving provisions in SI 2009/56, Sch. 3.

ASSESSMENTS FOR WITHDRAWING RELIEF AND RECOVERING TAX

28(1) Where–

(a) any relief or exemption from tax given in respect of income or gains under an account is found not to be due or to be excessive, or

(b) the full amount of tax in respect of the income or gains under an account has not otherwise been fully accounted for and paid to the Board by or on behalf of the account investor,

an assessment to tax may be made by the Board in the amount or further amount which in their opinion ought to be charged.

28(2) An assessment to which paragraph (1) refers may be made on the account manager or on the account investor.

28(3) If the assessment is made to recover tax in respect of income (including any amount in respect of a tax credit) under an account it shall be made under Chapter 8 of Part 5 of ITTOIA 2005.

History – In reg. 28(3), the words "Chapter 8 of Part 5 of ITTOIA 2005" substituted for the words "Case VI of Schedule D" by SI 2011/1780, reg. 29, with effect from 1 November 2011.

RECORDS TO BE KEPT BY ACCOUNT MANAGER

29(1) An account manager shall at all times keep sufficient records in respect of an account to enable the requirements of these Regulations to be satisfied.

29(2) Where an account is transferred by an account manager ("the transferor") to another account manager ("the transferee") in a group transfer of accounts, any records (or copies of records) kept by the transferor in respect of the account at the time when it is transferred shall be treated for the purposes of this regulation as kept by the transferee for so long as sub-paragraphs (a), (b) and (c) of paragraph (3) apply.

29(3) For the purposes of paragraph (2)–

(a) this sub-paragraph applies if the records described in paragraph (2) are kept by the transferor;

(b) this sub-paragraph applies if the transferor and transferee are members of the same group of companies; and

(c) this sub-paragraph applies if the transferee can require the transferor to make the records available to the transferee for any purpose necessary to ensure the transferee's compliance with these regulations.

History – Reg. 29(2) and (3) inserted (and the existing provision renumbered as "(1)") by SI 2012/1871, reg. 19, with effect from 9 November 2011.

INFORMATION TO BE GIVEN TO ACCOUNT INVESTOR BY ACCOUNT MANAGER IN RELATION TO AN ACCOUNT THAT IS NOT A JUNIOR ISA ACCOUNT

30(1) [Omitted by SI 2013/623, reg. 2(3).]

30(2) An account manager who makes a payment to an account investor out of or in respect of which tax, or a sum representing tax, has been deducted shall, if the account investor so requests in writing, furnish the account investor with a statement in writing showing the gross amount of the payment, the amount deducted and the amount actually paid.

30(3) On the transfer to an account investor of an account investment, subject to regulation 9(3)(b), the account manager shall provide for the account investor details in writing of the market value on the date of transfer.

History – In the heading to reg. 30, the words "in relation to an account that is not a junior ISA account" inserted by SI 2011/1780, reg. 30(a), with effect from 1 November 2011.

Reg. 30(1) omitted by SI 2013/623, reg. 2(3), with effect from 5 April 2013. Former reg. 30(1) read as follows:

> "**30(1)** An account manager shall give notice to the account investor, at the commencement of, and in respect of, each successive year following the year in which the investor first subscribed to the account, during which the declaration referred to in regulation 12(3) has or may have effect, that—
>
> (a)   in the case of a stocks and shares account, if the account investor subscribes to that account in the year to which the notice relates, the account investor may not subscribe to any other stocks and shares account, in that year;
>
> (b)   in the case of a cash account, if the account investor subscribes to that account in the year to which the notice relates, the account investor may not subscribe to any other cash account, in that year;
>
> (c)   the account investor must not subscribe more than the appropriate overall subscription limit in regulation 4ZA(1) in that year (aggregating subscriptions to all accounts); and
>
> (d)   in the case of a cash account, the account investor must not subscribe more than the subscription limit in regulation 4ZA(2), in that year.".

In former reg. 30(1)(c), the words "regulation 4ZA(1)" substituted for the words "regulation 4(2)" by SI 2011/1780, reg. 30(b), with effect from 1 November 2011.

In former reg. 30(1)(d), the words "regulation 4ZA(2)" substituted for the words "regulation 4(3)" by SI 2011/1780, reg. 30(c), with effect from 1 November 2011.

Former reg. 30(1)(a)–(d) substituted for reg. 30(1)(a) and (b) by SI 2007/2119, reg. 19, with effect from 6 April 2008.

RETURNS OF INFORMATION BY ACCOUNT MANAGER

31(1) An account manager shall within 60 days after the end of each year (beginning with the year 1999–00) in which he acts as an account manager, and after ceasing to act or to qualify as an account manager, deliver to the Board a return for that year, or for the part of that year in which he so acted or qualified, which contains the information specified in paragraphs (3), (4), (5), (7) and (7A), and is accompanied by a certificate as to the contents of the return, in the form prescribed by the Board, signed by the account manager or on his behalf.

31(2) [Omitted by SI 2008/704, reg. 14(3).]

31(3) The information specified in this paragraph is information relating to each account, in respect of which he acted as account manager, in the year or the part of the year for which the return is made, other than accounts transferred to another account manager under Regulation 21(2) in that year or part of a year, as to–

(a)   as regards the account investor–

     (i)   his full name,

     (ii)   the address of his permanent residence, including postcode,

     (iii)   his date of birth, and

     (iv)   if he has one, his national insurance number;

(b)   as regards each such account–

     (i)   the number allocated to the account by the account manager, and

     (ii)   the market value of the account investments held under the component of the account, the value of each account investment being determined either as at 5th April in that year, or any other valuation date in that year, not falling earlier than 5th October, and

(c)   as regards each such account, to which subscriptions or a transfer under regulation 21, were made in that year or part of a year–

     (i)   whether the account is a cash account or stocks and shares account,

     (ia)   whether the account was a junior ISA account at any time in the year or part of the year for which the return is made,

     (ii)   subject to paragraphs (3A) and (3AB)(a), the total amount of cash subscribed to the account, in the year or the part of the year for which the return is made;

     (iii)   subject to paragraphs (3AB)(b) and (3B), the date on which the first subscription (being either cash or shares pursuant to regulation 7(2)(h)) was made to the account, in the year or the part of the year for which the return is made,

(iv)   the aggregate market value at the date of transfer of any shares transferred to the account manager or his nominee in accordance with regulation 7(2)(h) in the year or the part of the year for which the return is made, and–

(v)   subject to paragraph (3C), the date when any such cash account was closed, where that occurred during the year or the part of the year for which the return was made.

31(3A) Where a subscription is made to an account that ceases to be a junior ISA account in the year or part of the year for which the return is made, the return must show, as separate amounts, the total amount of cash subscribed to the account at times–

(a)   when the account is a junior ISA account; and

(b)   when the account is not a junior ISA account.

31(3AB) Where a defaulted cash account subscription in accordance with regulation 5D (subscriptions disregarded for the purposes of the subscription limits in regulations 4ZA and 4ZB) is made to an account in the year or part of the year for which a return required by this regulation is made–

(a)   the amount of subscriptions reported to an account manager in accordance with regulation 5DF(1)(a)(ii) (current year's subscriptions made to the defaulted cash account) must be included as part of the total amount of cash subscribed to the account required by paragraph (3)(c)(ii);

(b)   paragraph (3)(c)(iii) must be construed as requiring (in addition to the information specified in that paragraph) the date reported to the account manager in accordance with regulation 5DF(1)(a)(iii).

31(3B) In relation to an account that is a junior ISA account, the information described in paragraph (3)(c)(iii) shall only be provided in the return for the year or part of the year in which the application to open the account in accordance with regulation 12A is made.

31(3C) The information provided in accordance with paragraph (3)(c)(v) must not include information relating to an account that was a junior ISA account immediately before it was closed.

31(4) Subject to paragraph (5), the information specified in this paragraph is–

(a)   the respective market values at the end of the year or the part of the year for which the return is made of account investments held under stocks and shares components, by him or a nominee for him on behalf of account investors, under all the accounts in respect of which he acted as account manager in that year or part, with separate values for–

   (i)   shares, not being shares in an investment trust or in a UK UCITS, recognised UCITS or non-UCITS retail scheme, officially listed on a recognised stock exchange;

  (ia)   such shares admitted to trading on a recognised stock exchange in an EEA State,

  (ii)   qualifying securities,

  (iia)   government securities falling within regulation 7(2)(c), (ca) or (cb);

  (iii)   shares in investment trusts,

  (iv)   units in an authorised unit trust,

  (via)   the surrender value of life insurance policies,

  (v)   units in, or shares of, a recognised UCITS, or non-UCITS retail scheme (constituted outside the United Kingdom),

  (vi)   shares in an open-ended investment company,

  (vii)   cash, including cash represented in share accounts with building societies,

with depositary interests being included in the paragraph to which their relevant investments (referred to in paragraphs (a) and (b) of the definition of "depositary interest") relate.

(b)   the respective market values at the end of the year or the part of the year for which the return is made of account investments held under cash components, by him or a nominee for him on behalf of account investors, under all the accounts in respect of which he acted as account manager in that year or part, with separate values for–

  (i)   cash, including cash represented in share accounts with building societies, and

  (ii)   investments other than those specified in paragraph (i); and

  (iii)   [effectively omitted by SI 2014/1450, reg. 25(c)]

(c)   the aggregate market value at that date of all such account investments held by him or his nominee.

31(5) Paragraph (4) shall apply to policies of life insurance falling within regulation 9 with the omission of the words "by him or a nominee for him on behalf of account investors," with references to the market value of account investments, in the case of policies of life insurance, being replaced with references to the surrender value of such policies, and as if separate valuations were required of such policies.

31(6) [Omitted by SI 2008/704, reg. 14(8).]

31(7) The information specified in this paragraph is information relating to all accounts to which subscriptions were made in the year or part of the year, in respect of which he was acting as account manager immediately before the end of the year or part of the year for which the return is made, or in the case of an account that was closed during the year, in respect of which he was acting as manager at the date the account was closed, as to–

(a)   the total number of accounts to which subscriptions were made, with separate figures for–

    (i)   cash accounts holding policies of life insurance falling within regulation 9,

    (ii)   all cash accounts,

    (iii)   stocks and shares accounts holding policies of life insurance falling within regulation 9, and

    (iv)   all stocks and shares accounts,

(b)   the total amount of cash subscriptions made in the year or part of the year–

    (i)   to stocks and shares components of accounts;

    (ii)   to cash components of accounts;

    (iii)   invested in policies (within the meaning in regulation 9(1)) under stocks and shares components; and

    (iv)   invested in policies (within that meaning) under cash components.

31(7A) The information specified in this paragraph is information relating to all accounts in respect of which the account manager was acting as account manager immediately before the end of the year or part of the year for which the return is made that were junior ISA accounts at the end of the period covered by the return (whether or not a subscription was made to the account during that period) with separate figures for cash accounts and stocks and shares accounts.

31(8) No claim for repayment, or repayment, may be made under regulations 25 and 26 until the returns which have become due under this regulation have been duly made by the account manager and received by the Board.

History – In reg. 31(1), the words "paragraphs (3), (4), (5), (7) and (7A)" substituted for the words "paragraphs (3), (4), (5) and (7)" by SI 2011/1780, reg. 31(a), with effect from 1 November 2011.
In reg. 31(1) the words ", (5) and (7)" substituted for "and (5)", by SI 2008/704, reg. 14(2), with effect from 6 April 2008.
Reg. 31(2) omitted by SI 2008/704, reg. 14(3), with effect from 6 April 2008.
In reg. 31(3)(b)(ii), the words "subject to paragraph (6)," omitted by SI 2014/654, reg. 12(a), with effect from 6 April 2014.
In reg. 31(3)(b)(ii) the word "the" substituted for the word "each" (where it appears first) by SI 2007/2119, reg. 20(a), with effect from 6 April 2008.
In reg. 31(3)(c), in the words preceding para. (i), the words "account, to which subscriptions or a transfer under regulation 21" substituted for the words "maxi-account or mini-account, to which subscriptions,", in para. (i) the words "cash account or stocks and shares account" substituted for the words "maxi-account or a mini-account made up of a specified component or a TESSA only account", para. (ii) substituted and in para. (v) the word "cash" substituted for the words "mini-account or TESSA only" by SI 2007/2119, reg. 20(b), with effect from 6 April 2008.
In reg. 31(3)(c) words "other than those made pursuant to regulation 5(1)" repealed by SI 2002/3158, reg. 7, with effect on or after 6 April 2003.
In reg. 31(3)(c)(i) words "or a TESSA only account" inserted by SI 2002/3158, reg. 7, with effect on or after 6 April 2003.
Reg. 31(3)(c)(ia) inserted by SI 2011/1780, reg. 31(b), with effect from 1 November 2011.
In reg. 31(3)(c)(ii), the words "paragraphs (3A) and (3AB)(a)" substituted for the words "paragraph (3A)" by SI 2012/1871, reg. 20(a), with effect from 8 August 2012.
In reg. 31(3)(c)(ii) the words "subject to paragraph (3A)," inserted by SI 2011/1780, reg. 31(c), with effect from 1 November 2011.
In reg. 31(3)(c)(iii), the words "paragraphs (3AB)(b) and (3B)" substituted for the words "paragraph (3B)" by SI 2012/1871, reg. 20(b), with effect from 8 August 2012.
In reg. 31(3)(c)(iii) the words "subject to paragraph (3B)," inserted by SI 2011/1780, reg. 31(d), with effect from 1 November 2011.
In reg. 31(3)(c)(iii) the word "and" at the end omitted by SI 2011/1780, reg. 31(e), with effect from 1 November 2011.
In reg 31(3)(c)(iii) words ", other than pursuant to regulation 5(1)," repealed by SI 2002/3158, reg. 7, with effect on or after 6 April 2003.
In reg. 31(3)(c)(v) the words "subject to paragraph (3C)," inserted by SI 2011/1780, reg. 31(f), with effect from 1 November 2011.
Reg. 31(3)(c)(v) inserted by SI 2002/3158, reg. 7, with effect on or after 6 April 2003.
Reg. 31(3A), (3B) and (3C) inserted by SI 2011/1780, reg. 31(g), with effect from 1 November 2011.
Reg. 31(3AB) inserted by SI 2012/1871, reg. 20(c), with effect from 8 August 2012.
Reg. 31(4)(a)(via) the words "which satisfy the condition of regulation 7(15)" omitted by SI 2014/1450, reg. 25(a), with effect from 1 July 2014. ;
Reg. 31(4)(b)(ii) substituted for former reg. 31(4)(b)(ii) and (iii) (and the word "and" inserted at end of sub-para. (b)(i)) by SI 2014/1450, reg. 25(c), with effect from 1 July 2014. Former reg. 31(4)(b)(ii) and (iii) read as follows:
    "(ii)   the surrender value of life insurance policies which do not satisfy the condition in regulation 7(15), and
    (iii)   investments (other than those specified in paragraphs (i) and (ii)) which do not satisfy the condition in regulation 7(15); and"
In reg. 31(4)(a)(i), the words "officially listed on a recognised stock exchange;" inserted by SI 2014/654, reg. 12(b), with effect from 6 April 2014.

In reg. 31(4)(a)(i). the words "UK UCITS, recognised UCITS or non-UCITS retail scheme" substituted for the "UCITS" by SI 2009/1994, reg. 9(a), with effect from 11 August 2009.

Reg. 31(4)(a)(ia) inserted by SI 2014/654, reg. 12(c), with effect from 6 April 2014.

Reg. 31(4)(a)(iia) inserted by SI 2005/2561, reg. 7(a), with effect from 6 October 2005.

Reg. 31(4)(b)(ii) omitted by SI 2005/2561, reg. 7(b), with effect from 6 October 2005.

In reg. 31(4) the words "Subject to paragraph (5), the" substituted for "The" by SI 2004/2996, reg. 18(a), with effect from 6 April 2005.

Reg. 31(4)(a)(iv) substituted by SI 2008/704, reg. 14(4), with effect from 6 April 2008.

Reg. 31(4)(a)(vi) substituted by SI 2008/704, reg. 14(5), with effect from 6 April 2008.

Reg. 31(4)(a)(iv), (vi) and (b)(i) substituted by SI 2001/3629, reg. 177 which came into force on 1 December 2001.

In reg. 31(4)(a)(v), the words "recognised UCITS, or non-UCITS retail scheme (constituted outside the United Kingdom)" substituted for "relevant UCITS" by SI 2009/1994, reg. 9(b), with effect from 11 August 2009.

In reg. 31(4)(a) the words "with depositary interests being included ... definition of "depositary interest") relate", added by SI 2000/3112, reg. 5, operative from 13 December 2000.

Reg. 31(4)(a)(via) substituted by SI 2008/704, reg. 14(6), with effect from 6 April 2008.

Former reg. 31(4)(a)(via), and also reg. 31(4)(b)(ia) inserted by SI 2003/2747, reg. 8, with effect from 6 April 2004.

Reg. 31(4)(b) substituted by SI 2008/704, reg. 14(7), with effect from 6 April 2008.

In reg. 31(5) the words "Paragraph (4) shall apply to policies of life insurance falling within regulation 9" substituted for "The information specified in this paragraph is such information in relation to insurance components, as if paragraph (4) applied" by SI 2004/2996, reg. 18(b)(i), with effect from 6 April 2005.

In reg. 31(5) the words ", and of cash" omitted by SI 2004/2996, reg. 18(b)(ii), with effect from 6 April 2005.

Reg. 31(6) omitted by SI 2008/704, reg. 14(8), with effect from 6 April 2008.

In reg. 31(7) the words "The information specified in this paragraph is information relating to all accounts to which subscriptions were made in the year or part of the year, in respect of which he was acting as account manager immediately before the end of the year or part of the year for which the return is made, or in the case of an account that was closed during the year, in respect of which he was acting as manager at the date the account was closed, as to" substituted for the words from the beginning to "for which the return is made, as to" by SI 2008/704, reg. 14(9), with effect from 6 April 2008.

Reg. 31(7)(a)(i)–(iv) substituted for reg. 31(7)(a)(i)–(iii) by SI 2007/2119, reg. 21, with effect from 6 April 2008.

Reg. 31(7)(b) the words "year or part of the year" substituted for "quarter or other period" by SI 2008/704, reg. 14(9), with effect from 6 April 2008.

Reg. 31(7)(b)(iii) and (iv) inserted by SI 2005/2561, reg. 7(c), with effect from 6 October 2005.

Former reg. 31(7)(b)(iii) and the word "and" which preceded it omitted by SI 2004/2996, reg. 19, with effect from 6 April 2005.

Reg. 31(7A) inserted by SI 2011/1780, reg. 31(h), with effect from 1 November 2011.

INFORMATION TO BE PROVIDED TO THE BOARD

32 [Omitted by SI 2011/1780, reg. 32, with effect from 1 November 2011.]

INSPECTION OF RECORDS BY OFFICER OF THE BOARD

33 [Omitted by SI 2011/1780, reg. 32, with effect from 1 November 2011.]

CAPITAL GAINS TAX – ADAPTATION OF ENACTMENTS

34(1) For the purposes of capital gains tax on the occasion when the title to account investments is transferred from an account manager to an account investor there shall be deemed to be a disposal and reacquisition by the account investor of those investments for a consideration equal to their market value at the date of the transfer.

34(2) Sections 104 to 114 of the Taxation of Chargeable Gains Act 1992 shall apply for the purposes of pooling and identifying account investments as if–

(a)   in section 106A(b) after subsection (11) there were added–

"**106A(12)** This section and sections 104, 110, 110A and 114–

(a)   shall apply separately in relation to any securities which are held by a person as account investments so long as they are so held, and

(b)   shall apply in relation to any such securities which became account investments by being transferred or renounced to an account manager or to a nominee for an account manager in the circumstances specified in regulation 7(2)(h) and (10)(a), (b) or (ba) as if they had been account investments–

(i)   in the case of securities acquired by that person in accordance with the provisions of a savings-related share option scheme, which were transferred in the circumstances specified in regulation 7(2)(h)(i) and (10)(a), from the date of their acquisition by him, or

(ii)   in the case of securities appropriated to that person in accordance with the provisions of an approved profit sharing scheme, which were transferred in the circumstances specified in regulation 7(2)(h)(ii) and (10)(b), from the date when he directed the trustees to transfer the ownership of the securities to him or, if earlier, the release date in relation to those securities, or

    (iii)   in the case of securities which were plan shares of a Schedule 2 SIP before being transferred in the circumstances specified in regulation 7(2)(h)(iii) and (10)(ba), from the date when the securities ceased to be subject to the plan, and

  (c)   while applying separately to any such securities, shall have effect as if that person held them in a capacity other than that in which he holds any other securities of the same class whether under another such account or otherwise.

106A(13)   In this section–

  (a)   **"account"**, **"account investment"** and **"account manager"** have the same meanings as in the Individual Savings Account Regulations 1998 and **"regulation"** means a regulation of those Regulations;

  (b)   **"approved profit sharing scheme"** has the same meaning as in Chapter IV of Part V of the Taxes Act and **"savings-related share option scheme"** has the meaning given by paragraph 1 of Schedule 9 to that Act;

  (c)   **"Schedule 2 SIP"** and **"ceased to be subject to the plan"** shall be construed in accordance with the SIP code (see section 488(3) of ITEPA 2003); and

  (d)   **"plan shares"**, in relation to a Schedule 2 SIP, shall be construed in accordance with the SIP code (see section 488(3) of ITEPA 2003) except that–

    (i)   paragraph 87(6) of Schedule 2 to ITEPA 2003 (meaning of the word "shares" in the context of company reconstructions) shall not apply, and

    (ii)   in paragraph 88(2) of that Schedule (treatment of shares acquired under rights issue) the words "or securities or rights" shall be treated as omitted."; and

(b)   in section 110A after subsection (5) there were added–

"**110A(6)**   Where part of a section 104 holding is treated by section 106A(12)(b)(ii) as having been account investments since a particular date–

  (a)   an operative event shall be regarded as having occurred for the purposes of this section immediately before that date, consisting of the disposal of the part of that section 104 holding which is so treated, and

  (b)   this section shall apply in relation to the occurrence of that operative event as it would have applied if it had always applied separately in relation to the part of that section 104 holding which is so treated."

34(3)   Section 106A of the Taxation of Chargeable Gains Act 1992 shall apply for the purposes of identifying securities within the meaning of that section which are eligible to become account investments as if–

(a)   in subsection (4), there were added at the beginning the words "Subject to subsection (14) below";

(b)   in subsection (6), the words "subsections (4) and (5) above" were replaced with the words "subsections (4), (5) and (14)"; and

(c)   after subsections (12) and (13), as added by paragraph (2), there were added–

"**106A(14)**   Where a person disposes of securities and securities of the same class which were eligible for transfer to an account under regulation 7(2)(h) were–

  (a)   held by him immediately before that disposal, or

  (b)   acquired by him on the same day as that disposal, or

  (c)   acquired by him within the period of thirty days after that disposal,

and those securities were acquired in the circumstances specified in that regulation, he shall be treated as having first disposed of any securities of that class held or acquired by him which were not so eligible."

34(4)   Sections 127 to 131 of the Taxation of Chargeable Gains Act 1992 shall not apply in relation to qualifying investments falling within any of sub-paragraphs (a), (b), (d), (e), (f), (g) and (h) of regulation 7(2) which are held under an account if there is by virtue of any allotment for payment as is mentioned in section 126(2) of that Act a reorganisation affecting those shares or securities.

History – In reg. 34(2)(a), in the notionally added TCGA 1992, s. 106A(12)(b)(iii) and (13)(d) the words "a Schedule 2" substituted for the words "an approved" and in (13)(c) the words "Schedule 2" substituted for the word "approved" by FA 2014, s. 51 and Sch. 8, para. 87, with effect from 6 April 2014 (subject to the provisions of Sch. 8, para. 90–96).
In reg. 34(2)(a), in the notionally added TCGA 1992, s. 106A(12)(b)(iii), the word "SIP" substituted for "employee share ownership plan" by SI 2008/704, reg. 15(2), with effect from 6 April 2008.
In reg. 34(2)(a), in the notionally added TCGA 1992, s. 106A(13), para. (c) and (d) substituted for para. (c) by SI 2008/704, reg. 15(3), with effect from 6 April 2008.
Reg. 34(4) amended by SI 2001/3629, reg. 178 which came into force on 1 December 2001.

In reg. 34(2)(a) under the subsection (12)(b) treated as added to section 106A of the Taxation of Chargeable Gains Act 1992–
- (a)   "(10)(a), (b) or (ba)" is substituted for "(10)(a) or (b)";
- (b)   in paragraph (b)(i) "7(2)(h)(i)" is substituted for "7(2)(h)";
- (c)   in paragraph (b)(ii) "7(2)(h)(ii)" is substituted for "7(2)(h)"; and
- (d)   the word "and" following paragraph (b)(ii) is substituted by–
  - "(iii)   in the case of securities which were plan shares of an approved employee share ownership plan before being transferred in the circumstances specified in regulation 7(2)(h)(iii) and (10)(ba), from the date when the securities ceased to be subject to the plan, and".

These amendments are made by SI 2000/2079, reg. 5(2), operative from 21 August 2000.

In reg. 34(2)(a) under the subsection (13) treated as added to section 106A of the Taxation of Chargeable Gains Act 1992– paragraph (c) is added by SI 2000/2079, reg. 5(3), operative from 21 August 2000.

ADMINISTRATION OF TAX IN RELATION TO ACCOUNTS – SUPPLEMENTARY

35(1)   Nothing in these Regulations shall be taken to prejudice any powers conferred or duties imposed by or under any enactment in relation to the making of returns of income or gains, or for the recovery of tax, penalties or interest by means of an assessment or otherwise.

35(2)   Notwithstanding the provisions of these Regulations an account manager shall not be released from obligations under these Regulations in relation to an account except under conditions agreed in writing with and notified to that person by the Board.

35(3)   The like provisions as are contained in the Management Act shall apply to any assessment under these Regulations as if it were an assessment to tax for the year in which, apart from these Regulations, the account investor would have been liable (by reason of his ownership of the investments).

35(4)   In the application of the like provisions as are contained in section 86 of the Management Act by virtue of paragraph (3) in relation to any sums due and payable by virtue of an assessment made on an account manager under these Regulations, the relevant date–

- (a)   is the 1st January in the year for which the account investor would have been liable where the account manager has made an interim claim for a period falling within that year; and

- (b)   in any other case, is the later of the following dates, that is to say–
  - (i)   the 1st January in that year; or
  - (ii)   the date of the making of the repayment by the Board following receipt of the annual claim for that year.

35(5)   The like provisions as are contained in section 97(1) of the Management Act shall apply as if–

- (a)   there were inserted after the words "section 95 above" the words "or the Individual Savings Account Regulations 1998", and

- (b)   there were inserted after the words "that they were" the words "or have become".

35(6)   If–

- (a)   a chargeable event, within the meaning given by Chapter 9 of Part 4 of ITTOIA 2005, has happened in relation to a policy of life insurance which is an account investment; and

- (b)   the body by whom the policy was issued is satisfied that no gain is to be treated as chargeable to tax on the happening of the event by virtue of regulation 22(1)(a)(v),

the body shall not be obliged to deliver the certificates mentioned in section 552(1) of that Act.

This paragraph does not prevent the operation of section 552(1) in a case to which regulation 36(1) applies.

35(7)   A termination of a policy of insurance pursuant to regulation 9(3)(b)(ii) shall be treated as the surrender of all rights under the policy for the purposes of section 484(1)(a)(i) of ITTOIA 2005.

35(8)   Where there are in force relevant insurances within the meaning given by section 552A of the Taxes Act then, so far as they consist of policies of life insurance which are account investments, they shall be disregarded in calculating the amount or value of gross premiums, for the purposes of subsection (4)(b) of that section.

35(9)   Any form prescribed by the Board for the purposes of these Regulations shall provide for a declaration that all the particulars given in the form are correctly stated to the best of the knowledge and belief of the person concerned.

35(10)   No obligation as to secrecy imposed by statute or otherwise shall preclude the Board from disclosing to an account manager or account investor that any provision of these Regulations has not been satisfied or that relief has been given or claimed in respect of investments under an account.

History – In reg. 35(5)(a), the words "section 95" substituted for "sections 95 and 96" by SI 2008/704, reg. 16(2), with effect from 6 April 2008.

In reg. 35(6)(a), the words "Chapter 9 of Part 4 of ITTOIA 2005" substituted for "Chapter 2 of Part 13 of the Taxes Act" by SI 2008/704, reg. 16(3), with effect from 6 April 2008.

In reg. 35(6)(a), the words "held under an insurance component" which appeared after the words "an account investment" omitted by SI 2004/2996, reg. 20, with effect from 6 April 2005.
Reg. 35(6) substituted by SI 2002/453, reg. 4, with effect for the tax year 2002–03 and subsequent years.
Prior to being substituted, reg. 35(6) was amended by SI 1998/3174, reg. 11, operative from 6 April 1999.
Reg. 35(7) substituted by SI 2008/704, reg. 16(4), with effect from 6 April 2008.
In reg. 35(8), the words "held under an insurance component" which appeared after the words "account investments" omitted by SI 2004/2996, reg. 21, with effect from 6 April 2005.

APPLICATION OF THE PROVISIONS OF CHAPTER II OF PART XIII OF THE TAXES ACT AND OF CHAPTER 9 OF PART 4 OF ITTOIA 2005 TO POLICIES WHERE AN INVESTOR CEASES TO BE OR WAS NOT ENTITLED TO RELIEF FROM TAX

36(1) This paragraph applies to a case where–

(a) an event specified in regulation 9(8) has occurred in relation to a policy of life insurance, and

(b) a termination event within the meaning given by regulation 9(7) occurs in relation to that policy.

36(2) Where–

(a) there is a case to which paragraph (1) applies, and

(b) a chargeable event in relation to the policy, falling within section 484(1) of ITTOIA 2005, has occurred prior to the time at which the termination event mentioned in paragraph (1)(b) occurs,

the account investor shall cease to be, and shall be treated as not having been, entitled to relief from tax under regulation 22(1)(a)(v), in respect of gains treated as arising on the occurrence of any chargeable event mentioned in sub-paragraph (b).

36(3) The provisions of Chapter II of Part XIII of the Taxes Act and of Chapter 9 of Part 4 of ITTOIA 2005 shall apply, in a case to which paragraph (1) applies, to–

(a) the termination event mentioned in paragraph (1)(b), and

(b) any chargeable event mentioned in paragraph (2)(b),

with the modifications provided for in regulation 35(7) and paragraphs (4) to (7) of this regulation, and the account investor and the account manager shall account to the Board in accordance with this regulation for tax from which relief under regulation 22(1)(a)(v) has been given on the basis that the account investor was so entitled, or in circumstances such that the account investor was not so entitled.

36(4) Section 530 of ITTOIA 2005 does not apply to a gain in a case in which paragraph (1) applies.

36(5) Relief under section 535 of ITTOIA 2005 shall be computed as if paragraph (4) had not been enacted.

36(6) In section 552 of the Taxes Act–

(a) in subsection (1)(b) for the words "policy holder" there shall be substituted "account investor";

(b) in subsection (3)–

(i) [omitted by SI 2008/1934, reg. 6(2);]

(ii) [omitted by SI 2008/1934, reg. 6(2);]

(iii) the words "and the corresponding financial year," shall be omitted;

(c) in subsection (5)–

(i) for the words "the appropriate policy holder" there shall be substituted "the account investor";

(ii) sub-paragraph (b)(ii) shall be omitted;

(iii) paragraph (c) shall be omitted;

(iv) in paragraph (d) the words "except where paragraph (c) above applies," shall be omitted; and

(v) paragraph (f) shall be omitted;

(d) in subsection (6)–

(i) paragraph (b) shall be omitted;

(ii) for paragraph (c) there shall be substituted–

"(c) if the event is a death, the period of three months beginning with the receipt of written notification of the death;";

(iii) after paragraph (c) there shall be inserted–

"(d) if the event is–

(i) a termination event, or

        (ii) a chargeable event preceding such a termination event (as mentioned in regulation 36(2) of the Individual Savings Account Regulations 1998),

the period of three months beginning with the date on which the insurer received notice under regulation 9(9)(b) of those Regulations or, if earlier, actual notice of the termination event.";

(e)   in subsection (7)–

    (i)   [omitted by SI 2008/1934, reg. 6(2);]

    (ii) paragraph (b) shall be omitted;

    (iii) for paragraph (c) there shall be substituted–

      "(c) if the event is a death, the period of three months beginning with the receipt of written notification of the death;";

    (iv) after paragraph (c) there shall be inserted–

      "(ca) if the event is–

        (i) a termination event, or

        (ii) a chargeable event preceding such a termination event (as mentioned in regulation 36(2) of the Individual Savings Account Regulations 1998),

the period of three months beginning with the date on which the insurer received notice under regulation 9(9)(b) of those Regulations or, if earlier, actual notice of the termination event;";
and

    (v) in paragraph (d) for the words "paragraph (c)" there shall be substituted "paragraph (c) or (ca)";

(f)   in subsection (8)–

    (i)   in paragraph (b) for "policy holder" there shall be substituted "account investor in respect";

    (ii) [omitted by SI 2008/1934, reg. 6(2);]

(g)   [omitted by SI 2008/1934, reg. 6(2);]

(h)   in subsection 10–

    (i)   before the definition of "amount" there shall be inserted–
""account investor" has the same meaning as in the Individual Savings Account Regulations 1998;";

    (ii) the definition of "appropriate policy holder" shall be omitted; and

    (iii) [omitted by SI 2008/1934, reg. 6(2);]

    (iv) [omitted by SI 2008/1934, reg. 6(2);]

    (v) after the definition of "section 546 excess" there shall be inserted–
""termination event" has the same meaning as in the Individual Savings Account Regulations 1998;";
and

(i)   [omitted by SI 2008/1934, reg. 6(2);]

36(6A) In Section 552ZA of the Taxes Act–

(a)   in subsection (2)(b) the words "or an assignment" shall be omitted; and

(b)   subsections (3) and (4) shall be omitted.

36(7) [Omitted by SI 2002/453, reg. 5(4).]

36(8) The account manager shall account for and pay income tax at the basic rate in force for the year of assessment in which the termination event, or the chargeable event mentioned in paragraph (2)(b), occurred, as the case may be, and any amount so payable–

(a)   may be set off against any repayment in respect of tax due under regulation 25 or regulation 26 and, subject thereto,

(b)   shall be treated as an amount of tax due not later than 6 months after the end of the year in which the event specified in regulation 9(8) came to the notice of the account manager, and

(c)   shall be payable without the making of an assessment.

36(9) Where tax is charged in accordance with paragraph (3)(a) or (b)–

(a)   an assessment to income tax at the basic rate determined in pursuance of section 6(2) of ITA 2007 in force for the relevant year of assessment may be made on the account manager or on the account investor, and

(b)   an assessment to income tax may be made on the account investor at the higher rate and additional rate (determined in pursuance of section 6(2) of ITA 2007) for that year of assessment as appropriate to the account investor's income tax liability calculated in accordance with section 23 of ITA 2007,

not more than 4 years after the end of that year of assessment, and regulation 28 shall not apply.

History – In the heading to reg. 36, the words "and of Chapter 9 of Part 4 of ITTOIA 2005" inserted by SI 2008/704, reg. 17(2), with effect from 6 April 2008.
In reg. 36(2)(b), the words "falling within section 484(1) of ITTOIA 2005" substituted for "within the meaning given by section 540 of the Taxes Act" by SI 2008/704, reg. 17(3), with effect from 6 April 2008.
In reg. 36(3), the words "and of Chapter 9 of Part 4 of ITTOIA 2005" inserted by SI 2008/704, reg. 17(4), with effect from 6 April 2008.
Reg. 36(4) substituted by SI 2008/704, reg. 17(5), with effect from 6 April 2008.
In reg. 36(5) the words "section 535 of ITTOIA 2005" substituted for "section 550 of the Taxes Act" by SI 2008/704, reg. 17(6), with effect from 6 April 2008.
Reg. 36(6)(b)(i) and (ii) omitted by SI 2008/1934, reg. 6(2), with effect from 12 August 2008.
Reg. 36(6)(e)(i) omitted by SI 2008/1934, reg. 6(2), with effect from 12 August 2008.
Reg. 36(6)(f)(ii) omitted by SI 2008/1934, reg. 6(2), with effect from 12 August 2008.
Reg. 36(6)(g) omitted by SI 2008/1934, reg. 6(2), with effect from 12 August 2008.
Reg. 36(6)(h)(iii) and (iv) omitted and the word "and" at end of reg. 36(6)(ii) inserted by SI 2008/1934, reg. 6(2), with effect from 12 August 2008.
Reg. 36(6)(i), and the word "and" which preceded it, omitted by SI 2008/1934, reg. 6(2), with effect from 12 August 2008.
In reg. 36(6) the para. (d) and (ca) which are treated as inserted in ICTA 1988, s. 552(6) and s. 552(7) respectively, substituted by SI 2002/3158, reg. 8, with effect from 8 January 2003.
Reg. 36(6) previously substituted by SI 2002/453, reg. 5(2), with effect for the tax year 2002–03 and subsequent years.
Reg. 36 inserted by SI 1998/3174, reg. 12, operative from 6 April 1999.
Reg. 36(6A) inserted by SI 2002/453, reg. 5(3), with effect for the tax year 2002–03 and subsequent years.
Reg. 36(7) omitted by SI 2002/453, reg. 5(4), with effect for the tax year 2002–03 and subsequent years.
In reg. 36(8), the word "lower" substituted for the word "basic" by SI 2004/2996, reg. 22, with effect from 6 April 2005.
In reg. 36(8), the words "basic rate" substituted for the words "lower rate" by SI 2008/1934, reg. 6(3), with effect from 12 August 2008.
In reg. 36(9)(a), the words "determined in pursuance of section 6(2) of ITA 2007" inserted by SI 2011/1780, reg. 33(a), with effect from 1 November 2011.
In reg. 36(9)(a), the word "lower" substituted for the word "basic" by SI 2004/2996, reg. 22, with effect from 6 April 2005.
Reg. 36(9)(b) substituted by SI 2011/1780, reg. 33(b), with effect from 1 November 2011.
In reg. 36(9), the words "not more than 4 years after the end of" substituted for the words "within five years after the 31st January next following" by SI 2011/1780, reg. 33(c), with effect from 1 November 2011.
In reg. 36(9), the words "basic rate" substituted for the words "lower rate" by SI 2008/1934, reg. 6(4), with effect from 12 August 2008.

CONTROLLED FOREIGN COMPANIES (EXCLUDED COUNTRIES) REGULATIONS 1998

(SI 1998/3081, as amended by SI 2001/3629, SI 2002/1963, SI 2002/2406, SI 2005/185 and SI 2005/186)

Made on 9 December 1998 by the Commissioners of Inland Revenue, in exercise of the powers conferred on them by s. 748(1)(e) and (1A) of the Income and Corporation Taxes Act 1988. Operative from 31 December 1998.

ARRANGEMENT OF REGULATIONS

CITATION, COMMENCEMENT AND EFFECT

1(1) These Regulations may be cited as the Controlled Foreign Companies (Excluded Countries) Regulations 1998, shall come into force on 31st December 1998, and shall have effect with respect to any appropriate accounting period of a relevant company.

1(2) In this regulation–

"**appropriate accounting period**" means an accounting period ending on or after the day to be appointed under section 199 of the Finance Act 1994 (corporation tax self-assessment);

"**relevant company**" means a company resident in the United Kingdom that had a relevant interest in a controlled foreign company at any time during an accounting period of the controlled foreign company ending in an appropriate accounting period of the relevant company;

"**relevant interest**" shall be construed in accordance with section 752A of the Taxes Act.

INTERPRETATION

2(1) In these Regulations unless the context otherwise requires–

"**controlled foreign company**" shall be construed in accordance with section 747(2) of the Taxes Act;

"**gains**" in relation to a controlled foreign company means any gains of that company other than a gain accruing to the company on a disposal of an asset which, on the assumption that the company was within the charge to corporation tax, would have fallen to be treated as a chargeable gain and would not have been taken into account as a receipt in computing the company's income or profits or gains or losses for the purposes of the Income Tax Acts;

"**insurance company**" means a company carrying on the business of effecting or carrying out contracts which fall within Part I or II of Schedule 1 to the Financial Services and Markets Act 2000 (Regulated Activities) Order 2001;

"**Schedule 1**" and "**Schedule 2**" mean Schedule 1 and Schedule 2 respectively to these Regulations;

"**section 748(1)(e)**" means section 748(1)(e) of the Taxes Act;

"the Taxes Act" means the Income and Corporation Taxes Act 1988.

2(2) For the purposes of these Regulations a company is resident in a territory if–

(a) by reason of the law of that territory relating to domicile, residence or place of management, the company is liable to tax in that territory, or

(b) if there is either no such law or such law does not apply to the company, the company is incorporated in that territory and liable to tax in that territory on its profits;

and references in these Regulations to the territory of residence of a company shall be construed accordingly.

2(3) For the purposes of these Regulations a controlled foreign company is resident in a territory, within the meaning of paragraph (2), in an accounting period only if it is so resident throughout that accounting period.

2(4) References in these Regulations to a branch or agency of a controlled foreign company are references to a branch or agency situated in a territory other than the territory of residence of the controlled foreign company.

History – In reg. 2(1) the words "the business of effecting or carrying out contracts which fall within Part I or II of Schedule 1 to the Financial Services and Markets Act 2000 (Regulated Activities) Order 2001" substituted for ""long-term business" or "general business" within the meaning of section 1 of the Insurance Companies Act 1982" by SI 2001/3629, reg. 180 which came into force on 1 December 2001.

In reg. 2(2)(b) the words "incorporated in that territory and liable to tax in that territory on its profits;" substituted for the words "incorporated in that territory;" by SI 2005/185, reg. 3, with effect in relation to accounting periods of companies resident outside the UK beginning on or after 3 December 2004 (subject to the transitional provision at SI 2005/185, reg. 6 – reproduced below).

"TRANSITIONAL PROVISION

6   Where an accounting period of a company resident outside the United Kingdom–
(a)   would, without amendment, have ended on or after 2nd December 2004; but
(b)   is amended on or after that date so as end before that date
an accounting period of the company shall, for the purposes of Controlled Foreign Companies (Excluded Countries) Regulations 1998, be treated as having ended on that date."

LIMITATION ON APPORTIONMENT OF CHARGEABLE PROFITS OF A CONTROLLED FOREIGN COMPANY — SPECIFIED TERRITORIES

3 The territory in which a controlled foreign company is required to be resident as respects an accounting period for the purposes of section 748(1)(e) is–

(a) as respects an accounting period beginning before 9th July 1998, any territory specified in Part I or in Part II of Schedule 1;

(b) as respects an accounting period beginning on or after that date, any territory specified in Part I or in Part II of Schedule 2.

LIMITATION ON APPORTIONMENT OF CHARGEABLE PROFITS OF A CONTROLLED FOREIGN COMPANY — CONDITIONS TO BE SATISFIED

4(A1) Paragraph (A2) specifies the condition which is required to be satisfied as respects an accounting period by a controlled foreign company, wherever it is resident in that accounting period.

4(A2) The condition specified in this paragraph is that, during the accounting period, the company has not been involved in a scheme or arrangement the purpose, or one of the main purposes, of which is to achieve a reduction in United Kingdom tax.

In this paragraph–

"arrangement" means an arrangement of any kind, whether in writing or not; and

"United Kingdom tax" means corporation tax or any tax chargeable as if it were corporation tax.

4(1) Paragraph (2) specifies the condition which is required to be satisfied as respects an accounting period, for the purposes of section 748(1)(e), by a controlled foreign company which is resident in a territory specified in Part I of Schedule 1 or, as the case may be, in Part I of Schedule 2, in that accounting period.

4(2) The condition specified is that the requirement with respect to the controlled foreign company's income and gains specified in regulation 5 is satisfied by the controlled foreign company in relation to that accounting period.

4(3) Paragraph (4) specifies the conditions which are required to be satisfied as respects an accounting period, for the purposes of section 748(1)(e), by a controlled foreign company which is resident in a territory specified in column 1 of Part II of Schedule 1 or, as the case may be, in column 1 of Part II of Schedule 2, in that accounting period.

4(4)   The conditions specified in this paragraph are that the controlled foreign company–

(a)   satisfies the requirement with respect to its income and gains specified in regulation 5 in relation to that accounting period, and

(b)   at no time during that accounting period–

   (i)   is entitled to any tax exemption, tax reduction or other benefit, or

   (ii)   falls within any condition,

specified in column 2 of Part II of Schedule 1 or, as the case may be, in column 2 of Part II of Schedule 2, opposite the specification of the territory in which the controlled foreign company is resident.

History – Reg. 4(A1) and (A2) inserted by SI 2005/186 reg. 2(2), with effect in relation to accounting periods of companies resident outside the UK beginning on or after 31 March 2005 (subject to the transitional provision at SI 2005/186, reg. 3 – reproduced below).

"TRANSITIONAL PROVISION

3   Where an accounting period of a company resident outside the United Kingdom–
(a)   would, without amendment, have ended on or after 31st March 2005, but
(b)   is amended on or after that date so as end before that date,
an accounting period of the company shall, for the purposes of Controlled Foreign Companies (Excluded Countries) Regulations 1998, be treated as having ended on that date."

INCOME AND GAINS REQUIREMENT

5(1)   The requirement with respect to the income and gains of a controlled foreign company as respects an accounting period is that the amount of its non-local source income arising in that accounting period does not exceed whichever is the greater of–

(a)   £50,000 or, where that accounting period is less than twelve months in duration, that amount proportionately reduced, and

(b)   an amount equal to ten per cent of its commercially quantified income arising in that accounting period.

5(2)   In paragraphs (1) and (3) **"commercially quantified income"** means the amount of profits of the controlled foreign company before tax, determined in accordance with generally accepted accounting standards other than an equity basis of accounting, subject to the qualifications in paragraphs (2A) and (2C).

5(2A)   In computing a controlled foreign company's commercially quantified income capital profits and losses shall be disregarded.

5(2B)   Paragraph (2C) applies if a controlled foreign company–

(a)   has invested, whether directly or indirectly, in an entity which is not a company, but is engaged in economic activity;

(b)   is capable of exercising control over the entity; and

(c)   the entity receives, whether directly or indirectly, at least 50 per cent. of its commercially quantified income, computed in accordance with paragraphs (2) and (2A) above from bodies which are associated or connected with the company, the reference to paragraph (2C) in paragraph (2) being disregarded for this purpose.

5(2C)   Where this paragraph applies, that part of the income and gains of the entity mentioned in paragraph (2B)(a), which bears to the whole the same proportion as the extent of control, determined in accordance with regulation 7(1A) below, bears to the whole (the controller's share), shall be treated, for the purposes of these Regulations, as the income and gains of the controlled foreign company by which the entity is controlled (if not already included in that income or those gains).

5(3)   Subject to paragraphs (3A) to (4) (special rules about connected persons and about banks and insurance companies), for the purposes of paragraph (1) the amount of a controlled foreign company's non-local source income arising in an accounting period is the aggregate of the following amounts, namely–

(a)   the gross amount of income consisting of distributions recognised as income in computing the commercially quantified income of that company for that period from the profits of companies not resident in the territory of residence of that company, other than branch or agency income;

(b)   the gross amount of income and gains recognised as income in computing the commercially quantified income of that company for that period and deriving from loans to, or deposits with, persons not resident in the territory of residence of that company, or branches or agencies situated outside that territory of companies resident in that territory, other than branch or agency income and gains;

(c)   the gross amount of income and gains recognised as income in computing the commercially quantified income of that company for that period in relation to royalties payable by persons not resident in the territory of residence of that company, or by branches or agencies situated outside that territory of companies resident in that territory, other than branch or agency income and gains;

(d)   the gross amount of income and gains recognised as income in computing the commercially quantified income of that company for that period in relation to premiums and rents payable in respect of property situated outside the territory of residence of that company by persons not resident in that territory, or by branches situated outside that territory of companies resident in that territory, other than branch or agency income and gains;

(e)   the amount of any branch or agency income and gains recognised as income in computing the commercially quantified income of that company for that period, calculated in accordance with regulation 6;

(f)   the gross amount of any income not falling within any of sub-paragraphs (a) to (e) above that is recognised as income in computing the commercially quantified income of that company for that period and does not constitute income which either–

     (i)   is treated under the laws of the territory of residence of that company as accruing or arising in, or derived from, that territory, or

     (ii)   where there are no laws of that territory treating that income as accruing or arising in, or derived from, that territory or another territory, would be treated as accruing or arising in, or derived from, that territory if there were such laws in force in that territory and those laws were identical to the laws of the United Kingdom treating income as accruing or arising in, or derived from, a territory for the purposes of the Corporation Tax Acts, and which

     (iii)   in either case is within that territory's charge to tax.

5(3A)   Where a controlled foreign company–

(a)   has entered into one or more transactions with one or more connected or associated persons;

(b)   the value to the company of that transaction, or the aggregate value to the company of all of those transactions, exceeds fifty per cent. of the commercially quantified income of the company; and

(c)   the income and gains arising to, or the expenditure incurred by, the connected or associated person as a result of that transaction is taken into account–

     (i)   in computing the company's profits for tax purposes in the territory in which resides but not in computing its chargeable profits, or

     (ii)   in computing the company's chargeable profits, but not in computing its profits for tax purposes in the territory in which it resides;

paragraph (3B) applies.

5(3B)   If this paragraph applies–

(a)   the income and gains to which paragraph (3A)(c) applies shall be treated as nonlocal source income of the controlled foreign company; and

(b)   an amount equal to which paragraph (3A)(c) applies shall be treated as non-local source income (and accordingly added to the amounts produced by sub-paragraphs (a) to (f) of paragraph (3) for the purpose of computing the amount of non-local source income).

5(4)   Where–

(a)   the controlled foreign company concerned is an institution carrying on the business of banking, or an insurance company, and

(b)   income of that company falling within any of sub-paragraphs (a) to (d) of paragraph (3)–

     (i)   is an integral part of income arising or accruing to the company from the trade of banking or insurance carried on by the company, being income which, if the company were resident in the United Kingdom, would be income arising to the company from a trade for the purposes of the Corporation Tax Acts, and

     (ii)   is within the charge to tax of the territory of residence of that company,

the aggregate amount of that income shall be disregarded in computing the aggregate amount of the company's non-local source income.

History – In reg. 5(2) the words "subject to the qualifications in paragraphs (2A) and (2C)" substituted for the words "but disregarding capital profits or losses" by SI 2005/185 reg. 4(2), with effect in relation to accounting periods of companies resident outside the UK beginning on or after 3 December 2004 (subject to the transitional provision at SI 2005/185, reg. 6 – reproduced at reg. 2 above).

Reg. 5(2A)–(2C) inserted by SI 2005/185 reg. 4(3), with effect in relation to accounting periods of companies resident outside the UK beginning on or after 3 December 2004 (subject to the transitional provision at SI 2005/185, reg. 6 – reproduced at reg. 2 above).

In reg. 5(3) the words "paragraphs (3A) to (4) (special rules about connected persons and about banks and insurance companies)" substituted for the words "paragraph (4) (special rules for banks and insurance companies)" by SI 2005/185 reg. 4(4), with effect in relation to accounting periods of companies resident outside the UK beginning on or after 3 December 2004 (subject to the transitional provision at SI 2005/185, reg. 6 – reproduced at reg. 2 above).

Reg. 5(3A) and (3B) inserted by SI 2005/185 reg. 4(5), with effect in relation to accounting periods of companies resident outside the UK beginning on or after 3 December 2004 (subject to the transitional provision at SI 2005/185, reg. 6 – reproduced at reg. 2 above).

BRANCH OR AGENCY INCOME AND GAINS

6(1) The amount of any branch or agency income and gains as mentioned in regulation 5(3)(e) is–

(a) where the conditions specified in paragraph (2) are satisfied with respect to the branch or agency for the accounting period concerned, the amount (being not more than 10 per cent of the net amount of the profits of that branch or agency for that period) by reference to which the condition specified in sub-paragraph (d) of that paragraph is satisfied by that branch or agency;

(b) where the conditions specified in paragraph (2) are not satisfied with respect to the branch or agency for the accounting period concerned, the net amount or, where paragraph (3) applies, the gross amount of the branch or agency income and gains for that accounting period.

6(2) The conditions specified in this paragraph are that–

(a) the branch or agency is situated in a territory specified in Part I or in Part II of Schedule 1 or, as the case may be, in Part I or in Part II of Schedule 2, and where the territory is one specified in Part II of Schedule 1 or in Part II of Schedule 2, at no time during the accounting period–

   (i)   is entitled to any tax exemption, tax reduction or other benefit, or

   (ii) falls within any condition,

specified in column 2 of that Part opposite the specification of that territory;

(b) the profits of the branch or agency are within the charge to tax of that territory;

(c) the profits attributed to the branch or agency for tax purposes in that territory are those which it might be expected to make if it were a distinct and separate enterprise from the company of which it is a branch or agency, engaged in the same or similar activities under the same or similar conditions and dealing wholly independently with the company of which it is a branch or agency;

(d) not more than 10 per cent of the net amount of the profits of the branch or agency for the accounting period would, on the assumption that the branch or agency was not a branch or agency of the controlled foreign company but a separate controlled foreign company, be attributable to the aggregate of the gross amounts of any income and gains falling within any of sub-paragraphs (a) to (d) of regulation 5(3) and arising outside the territory in which the branch or agency is situated;

(e) amounts falling to be deducted in computing the taxable profits of the branch or agency, being amounts which are paid to, or are in respect of costs incurred by, the head office of the company of which it is a branch or agency, either–

   (i)   are liable to tax, or are disallowed as an expense, in the territory of residence of that company, or

   (ii) where that company is liable to tax in its territory of residence in respect of the whole of its profits wherever arising, are not allowed as a deduction in computing the taxable profits of that company except where the amount in question is paid by that company to another person.

6(3) This paragraph applies to a case where the net amount of the income and gains referred to in paragraph (1) in the accounting period concerned does not exceed an amount which would be equal to the aggregate of the gross amounts of any income and gains falling within any of sub-paragraphs (a) to (d) of regulation 5(3) in that period if branch or agency income and gains fell within those sub-paragraphs.

INTERPRETATION OF REGULATIONS 5 AND 6

7(1) In regulation 5(2) **"capital profits or losses"** means profits or losses arising in relation to chargeable assets.

7(1A) For the purposes of regulation 5(2B) a company ("C") is capable of exercising control over another entity–

(a) where C is entitled to a share of more than one half of the assets, or more than one half of the income of the entity; or

(b) where, if the entity were a company and C were resident in the United Kingdom, C would be treated as having control of it for the purposes of Chapter 4 of Part 17 of the Taxes Act (tax avoidance: controlled foreign companies).

7(2) In regulations 5(3) and 6 references to **"branch or agency income"** or to **"branch or agency income and gains"** are references to income and gains that–

(a) arise in or are derived from any branch or agency of a controlled foreign company, and

(b) fall within sub-paragraph (e) of regulation 5(3) in the accounting period concerned.

7(3) In regulation 5(3)–

(a) the references to **"the gross amount"** of any income in sub-paragraphs (a) and (f) are references to the amount of that income before deduction of expenses or reserves;

(b) the reference to **"the gross amount"** of any income and gains in sub-paragraph (b) is a reference to the amount of that income and those gains found–

    (i) after excluding any gain or loss arising on any loan or deposit referred to in that sub-paragraph which is offset by a loss or gain on a contract ancillary to that loan or deposit which is a derivative contract, and

    (ii) after deducting any exchange losses attributable to the loans or deposits referred to in that sub-paragraph to the extent that those losses have not already been excluded by virtue of paragraph (i) above, but

    (iii) before deducting other expenses or reserves;

(c) the references to **"the gross amount"** of any income and gains in sub-paragraphs (c) and (d) are references to the amount of that income and those gains found after deducting any exchange losses attributable to the royalties, premiums or rents referred to in those sub-paragraphs but before deducting other expenses or reserves;

and the references to **"the gross amounts"** in regulation 6(2)(d) and (3) shall be construed accordingly.

7(4) In regulation 5(3) references to persons not resident in the territory of residence of a controlled foreign company do not include references to a company not so resident in circumstances where–

(a) the branch or agency of the company is situated in that territory, and

(b) the transaction giving rise to the income and gains in question of the controlled foreign company is made with that branch or agency.

7(5) In regulation 6(l)(b) the reference to the gross amount of income and gains is a reference to the amount of that income or of those gains before deduction of expenses or reserves.

7(6) In regulation 6(1)(b) the reference to "the net amount" of the branch or agency income and gains, and in regulation 6(2)(d) the reference to "the net amount" of the profits of the branch or agency concerned, are references to the amount of that income, or of those profits, after deduction of expenses but before tax, as determined in accordance with a generally accepted method of accounting for profits of branches or profits of agencies of companies.

7(7) In paragraph (l) of this regulation a **"chargeable asset"** is any asset in the case of which one of the following conditions is satisfied, that is to say–

(a) a gain accruing to the company on a disposal of that asset on or after the date of coming into force of these Regulations would, on the assumption that the company was within the charge to corporation tax, have fallen to be treated in relation to the company as a chargeable gain and would not have been taken into account as a receipt in computing the company's income or profits or gains or losses for the purposes of the Income Tax Acts;

(b) a chargeable gain or allowable loss would, on the assumption mentioned in sub-paragraph (a), be deemed to have accrued to the company on any disposal of that asset on or after the date mentioned in that sub-paragraph.

7(8)   [Omitted by SI 2002/1963.]

History – Reg. 7(1A) inserted by SI 2005/185 reg. 5(2), with effect in relation to accounting periods of companies resident outside the UK beginning on or after 3 December 2004 (subject to the transitional provision at SI 2005/185, reg. 6 – reproduced at reg. 2 above).

In reg. 7(3)(b)(i) words "is a derivative contract" substituted for "would be a qualifying contract if the company were a qualifying company", by SI 2002/1963, reg. 2(2) with effect from 1 October 2002 in relation to accounting periods beginning on or after that date.

Reg. 7(8) omitted by SI 2002/1963, reg. 2(3) with effect from 1 October 2002 in relation to accounting periods beginning on or after that date. Reg. 7(8) formerly read as follows:

"**7(8)**   In paragraph (3)(b)(i) of this regulation–

"**qualifying company**"–

(a)   as respects a contract falling within section 126(1) of the Finance Act 1993, has the meaning given by section 152 of that Act;

(b)   as respects a contract falling within section 147(1) of the Finance Act 1994, has the meaning given by section 154 of that Act;

"**qualifying contract**" means a contract falling within section 126(1) of the Finance Act 1993 or section 147(1) of the Finance Act 1994, as the case may be, other than a contract which, in the case of branch or agency income or gains which would be income or gains falling within sub-paragraph (b) of regulation 5(3) if branch or agency income and gains fell within that sub-paragraph, is not entered into by the branch or agency concerned.".

SCHEDULES

SCHEDULE 1 – ACCOUNTING PERIODS BEGINNING BEFORE 9TH JULY 1998

Regulations 3, 4 and 6(2)(a)

Part I

SPECIFIED TERRITORIES

Australia	Japan
Austria	Korea, Republic of
Bangladesh	Lesotho
Bolivia	Malawi
Botswana	Mexico
Brazil	New Zealand
Canada	Nigeria
Colombia	Norway
Czech Republic	Papua New Guinea
Denmark	Poland
Dominican Republic	Romania
Falkland Islands	Senegal
Fiji	Sierra Leone
Finland	Slovak Republic
France	Solomon Islands
Gambia	South Africa
Germany	Spain
Ghana	Swaziland
Honduras	Sweden
Hungary	Trinidad and Tobago
Iceland	Turkey
India	Zambia
Indonesia	Zimbabwe
Ivory Coast	

Part II

SPECIFIED TERRITORIES WITH QUALIFICATIONS

Argentina	Companies obtaining exemption from tax on income from transactions, activities or operations carried on in, or from goods located in, tax free areas in accordance with Law 19640 of 16th May 1972.
Belgium	1. Companies which are regarded as Foreign Sales Corporations in section 922(a) of the United States Internal Revenue Code 1954 and which accordingly qualify for reduced Belgian taxation.
	2. Companies approved under Royal Decree No. 187 of 30th December 1982 as Co-ordination Centres.
Brunei	Companies qualifying as "pioneer companies" under the Investment Incentives Enactment 1975.
Bulgaria	Any company obtaining a tax benefit under Article 111 of Decree 56 of 9th January 1989 (Free Zone legislation).
Chile	Companies obtaining exemption from tax under Law 16,441 of 1st March 1966 on income from property located in the Department of Isla da Pascua or from activities developed in that Department.
China	Companies deriving income in or from the Hong Kong Special Administrative Region and submitting tax returns to the authorities of that Region.
Egypt	Companies which do not fall within the scope of Article 111, Book 2 of Law 157 of 1981 because they do not operate in Egypt.
Faroe Islands	Companies deriving interest from Faroese financial institutions from which tax is deducted at source under Law 4 of 26th March 1953.
Greece	1. Companies whose profits are exempt from tax under Article 6(2)(c) of Law 3843/1958 (profits from the operation of ships under the Greek flag).
	2. Companies having profits exempt from company income tax by virtue of Article 25 of Law 25/1975 or by virtue of Law 89/1967 (profits from shipping and associated activities).
Ireland	1. Companies obtaining relief or exemption from tax under Chapters 1 and 2 of Part 14 of the Taxes Consolidation Act 1997.
	2. Holding companies having income exempted from tax under section 44 in Chapter 3 of Part 3 of the Taxes Consolidation Act 1997.
Italy	Companies benefiting from paragraphs 12 to 14 of Article 11 of Law 413 of 30th December 1991 (Trieste Free Zone Financial and Insurance Centre).
Kenya	Companies having income exempted from tax under paragraph 11 of Schedule 1 to the Income Tax Act 1973.
Luxembourg	1. Companies obtaining any special tax benefit under the Law of 31st July 1929, the decree of 17th December 1938 or the Grand Ducal Regulation of 29th July 1977 (holding companies).
	2. Any reinsurance company established in Luxembourg requiring authorisation under Article 92 of the Law of 6th December 1991.
Malaysia	1. Companies exempt from tax in accordance with section 54A of the Income Tax Act 1967 (shipping).
	2. Companies subject to tax at 5 per cent in accordance with sections 60A and 60B of the Income Tax Act 1967 (inward reinsurance and offshore insurance).
	3. Companies deriving dividends from a company or companies deriving income from one or more of the activities referred to in paragraphs 1 and 2 above.
	4. Companies obtaining a tax benefit under the Offshore Companies Act (Island of Labuan) 1990.
Malta	1. Companies entitled to exemption or relief from tax under section 11(2) of the Income Tax Act 1948.

2. Companies obtaining exemption from tax under section 86 of the Merchant Shipping Act 1973.

3. Companies obtaining exemption or relief from tax under section 30 of the Malta International Business Activities Act 1988.

4. Companies obtaining exemption or relief from tax under section 18 of the Malta Freeports Act 1989.

Morocco	Companies receiving a tax benefit under Law 58–90 of 1992 (offshore financial centres).
Netherlands	Companies which are regarded as Foreign Sales Corporations under section 922(a) of the United States Internal Revenue Code 1954.
Pakistan	Companies deriving royalties, commissions or fees which are exempt from tax under paragraph 139 in Part I of the second Schedule to the Income Tax Ordinance 1979.
Philippines	1. Companies authorised under Presidential Decree 1034 of 30th September 1976, or under Presidential Decree 1035 of 30th September 1976, to operate an offshore Banking Unit or a Foreign Currency Deposit Unit as defined in those Decrees.
	2. Companies receiving interest on deposits with a Foreign Currency Deposit Unit, or other interest subject to the reduced rates of tax under section 27(D) of the National Internal Revenue Code 1997.
Portugal	Companies obtaining tax benefits under Decree Law 502/85 of 30th December 1985, Articles 41 and 51(g) of the Tax Benefits statute (EBF) approved by Decree Law 215/90 of 31st August 1989 (free zone in Madeira), or Decree Law 501/85 of 28th December 1985 as implemented by Decree Law 63/87 of 5th February 1987 (free zone in the Azores).
Puerto Rico	1. Companies obtaining a tax benefit under section 2(o) of the Industrial Incentive Act 1978 (designated service industries).
	2. Companies obtaining a tax benefit under section 25 of the International Banking Centre Regulatory Act 1989 (International Banking Entities).
Singapore	1. Any company obtaining tax concessions under Ministry of Finance Regulations pursuant to section 43A, and sections 43C to 43J, of the Income Tax Act.
	2. Companies obtaining exemption from tax on the income of a shipping enterprise in accordance with section 13A of the Income Tax Act.
	3. Companies obtaining relief from tax in accordance with sections 45 to 55 (international trade incentives), and sections 75 to 84 (warehouse and service incentives), of the Economic Expansion Incentives (Relief from Income Tax) Act.
	4. Companies deriving dividends from a company or companies deriving income from one or more of the activities falling within paragraphs 1 to 3 above.
Sri Lanka	Companies obtaining relief or exemption from income tax under any of the following provisions of the Inland Revenue Act 1979—
	(a) section 8(c)(iv) (foreign currency banking units);
	(b) sections 10(d) and 15(b) (income derived from approved bank accounts);
	(c) section 10(e) (interest of newly resident companies);
	(d) section 15(cc) (services rendered outside Sri Lanka);
	(e) section 15(p) (re-export of approved products).
Tanzania	Companies relieved or exempted from income tax under section 15(1) or (1A) of the Income Tax Act 1973.
Thailand	Companies obtaining a tax benefit under Royal Decree 280 of 22nd September 1992 (offshore banking units).
Tunisia	Companies obtaining exemption from, or reduction of, tax under Law 76/63 of 12th July 1976 (financial and banking institutions dealing with non-residents).
United States	Domestic International Sales Corporations as defined in section 992(a) of the Internal Revenue Code 1954.

SCHEDULE 2 – ACCOUNTING PERIODS BEGINNING ON OR AFTER 9TH JULY 1998

Regulations 3, 4 and 6(2)(a)

Part I

SPECIFIED TERRITORIES

Australia	Ivory Coast
Austria	Japan
Bangladesh	Korea, Republic of
Bolivia	Lesotho
Botswana	Malawi
Brazil	Mexico
Bulgaria	New Zealand
Canada	Nigeria
Colombia	Norway
Czech Republic	Papua New Guinea
Denmark	Poland
Dominican Republic	Romania
Falkland Islands	Senegal
Fiji	Sierra Leone
Finland	Slovak Republic
France	Solomon Islands
Gambia	South Africa
Germany	Swaziland
Ghana	Sweden
Honduras	Trinidad and Tobago
Iceland	Turkey
India	Zambia
Indonesia	Zimbabwe

Part II

SPECIFIED TERRITORIES WITH QUALIFICATIONS

Argentina — Companies obtaining exemption from tax on income from transactions, activities or operations carried on in, or from goods located in, tax free areas in accordance with Law 19640 of 16th May 1972.

Belgium — 1. Companies which are regarded as Foreign Sales Corporations in section 922(a) of the United States Internal Revenue Code 1954 and which accordingly qualify for reduced Belgian taxation.

2. Companies approved under Royal Decree No. 187 of 30th December 1982 as Co-ordination Centres.

Brunei — Companies qualifying as "pioneer companies" under the Investment Incentives Enactment 1975.

Chile — Companies obtaining exemption from tax under Law 16,441 of 1st March 1966 on income from property located in the Department of Isla da Pascua or from activities developed in that Department.

China — 1. Companies deriving income in or from the Hong Kong Special Administrative Region and submitting tax returns to the authorities of that Region.

	2. From 20th December 1999, companies deriving income in or from the Macao Special Administrative Region and submitting tax returns to the authorities of that Region.
Egypt	Companies which do not fall within the scope of Article 111, Book 2 of Law 157 of 1981 because they do not operate in Egypt.
Faroe Islands	Companies deriving interest from Faroese financial institutions from which tax is deducted at source under Law 4 of 26th March 1953.
Greece	1. Companies whose profits are exempt from tax under Article 6(2)(c) of Law 3843/1958 (profits from the operation of ships under the Greek flag).
	2. Companies having profits exempt from company income tax by virtue of Article 25 of Law 25/1975 or by virtue of Law 89/1967 (profits from shipping and associated activities).
Hungary	Companies benefiting from the reduced rate of tax for extra-territorial companies under section 19(2) of Act LXXXI of 1996 on Corporate Tax and Dividend Tax.
Italy	Companies benefiting from paragraphs 12 to 14 of Article 11 of Law 413 of 30th December 1991 (Trieste Free Zone Financial and Insurance Centre).
Kenya	Companies having income exempted from tax under paragraph 11 of Schedule 1 to the Income Tax Act 1973.
Luxembourg	1. Companies obtaining any special tax benefit under the Law of 31st July 1929, the decree of 17th December 1938 or the Grand Ducal Regulation of 29th July 1977 (holding companies).
	2. Any reinsurance company established in Luxembourg requiring authorisation under Article 92 of the Law of 6th December 1991.
Malaysia	1. Companies exempt from tax in accordance with section 54A of the Income Tax Act 1967 (shipping).
	2. Companies subject to tax at 5 per cent in accordance with sections 60A and 60B of the Income Tax Act 1967 (inward reinsurance and offshore insurance).
	3. Companies deriving dividends from a company or companies deriving income from one or more of the activities referred to in paragraphs 1 and 2 above.
	4. Companies obtaining a tax benefit under the Offshore Companies Act (Island of Labuan) 1990.
Malta	1. Companies entitled to exemption or relief from tax at the discretion of the Minister responsible for finance under section 12(2) of the Income Tax Act 1948.
	2. Companies obtaining exemption from tax under section 86 of the Merchant Shipping Act 1973.
	3. Companies obtaining exemption or relief from tax under section 30 of the Malta International Business Activities Act 1988 or section 30 of the Malta Financial Services Centre Act 1988.
	4. Companies obtaining exemption or relief from tax under section 18 of the Malta Freeports Act 1989.
Morocco	Companies receiving a tax benefit under Law 58–90 of 1992 (offshore financial centres).
Netherlands	1. Companies which are regarded as Foreign Sales Corporations under section 922(a) of the United States Internal Revenue Code 1954.
	2. A company ("The first company") receiving interest, rents or royalties in an accounting period directly or indirectly from a Dutch company ("the second company") which is connected with the first company within the meaning of section 839 of the Taxes Act, in circumstances where—
	(a) the second company does not satisfy the income and gains requirement in regulation 5 as respects its accounting period in which the interest, rents or royalties were paid, and

(b)   the aggregate of the non-local source income of the first company in its accounting period in question and the interest, rents and royalties received by it from the second company in that period exceeds whichever is the greater of–

    (i)   £50,000 or, where that period is less than twelve months in duration, that amount proportionately reduced, and

    (ii)   an amount equal to ten per cent of its commercially quantified income arising in that period.

Pakistan	Companies deriving royalties, commissions or fees which are exempt from tax under paragraph 139 in Part I of the second Schedule to the Income Tax Ordinance 1979.
Philippines	1. Companies authorised under Presidential Decree 1034 of 30th September 1976, or under Presidential Decree 1035 of 30th September 1976, to operate an offshore Banking Unit or a Foreign Currency Deposit Unit as defined in those Decrees.
	2. Companies receiving interest on deposits with a Foreign Currency Deposit Unit, or other interest subject to the reduced rates of tax under section 27(D) of the National Internal Revenue Code 1997.
Portugal	Companies obtaining tax benefits under Decree Law 502/85 of 30th December 1985, Articles 41 and 51(g) of the Tax Benefits statute (EBF) approved by Decree Law 215/90 of 31st August 1989 (free zone in Madeira), or Decree Law 501/85 of 28th December 1985 as implemented by Decree Law 63/87 of 5th February 1987 (free zone in the Azores).
Puerto Rico	1. Companies obtaining a tax benefit under section 2(o) of the Industrial Incentive Act 1978 (designated service industries).
	2. Companies obtaining a tax benefit under section 25 of the International Banking Centre Regulatory Act 1989 (International Banking Entities).
Singapore	1. Any company obtaining tax concessions under Ministry of Finance Regulations pursuant to section 43A, and sections 43C to 43K, of the Income Tax Act.
	2. Companies obtaining exemption from tax on the income of a shipping enterprise in accordance with section 13A of the Income Tax Act.
	3. Companies obtaining relief from tax in accordance with sections 45 to 55 (international trade incentives), and sections 75 to 84 (warehouse and service incentives), of the Economic Expansion Incentives (Relief from Income Tax) Act.
	4. Companies deriving dividends from a company or companies deriving income from one or more of the activities falling within paragraphs 1 to 3 above.
Spain	1. Companies which are registered in the official register of the Canary Islands Special Zone (Zona Especial Canaria) established under Law 19/1994 and which benefit from the special low tax rate applied to such companies.
	2. Companies benefiting from the alternative taxation regime for co-ordination centres established by the provincial governments of the Basque Country under laws pursuant to Norma Foral 3/1996 of 26th June 1996, Norma Foral 7/1996 of 4th July 1996, and Norma Foral 24/1996 of 5th July 1996.
Sri Lanka	Companies obtaining relief or exemption from income tax under any of the following provisions of the Inland Revenue Act 1979–
	(a) section 8(c)(iv) (foreign currency banking units);
	(b) sections 10(d) and 15(b) (income derived from approved bank accounts);
	(c) section 10(e) (interest of newly resident companies);
	(d) section 15(cc) (services rendered outside Sri Lanka);
	(e) section 15(p) (re-export of approved products).
Tanzania	Companies relieved or exempted from income tax under section 15(1) or (1A) of the Income Tax Act 1973.

Thailand	Companies obtaining a tax benefit under Royal Decree 280 of 22nd September 1992 (offshore banking units).
Tunisia	Companies obtaining exemption from, or reduction of, tax under Law 76/63 of 12th July 1976 (financial and banking institutions dealing with non-residents).
United States	Domestic International Sales Corporations as defined in section 992(a) of the Internal Revenue Code 1954.

History – Entry in respect of Ireland omitted by SI 2002/2406, reg. 2 with effect from 11 October 2002 in relation to accounting periods beginning on or after that date.

CIVIL PROCEDURE RULES 1998

(SI 1998/3132 as amended by SI 1999/1008, SI 2000/2092, SI 2002/2058, SI 2003/364 and SI 2007/3543)

Made on 10 December 1998 by the Civil Procedure Rule Committee under section 2 of the Civil Procedure Act 1997. Operative from 26 April 1999.

Statutory Instruments

ARRANGEMENT OF RULES

PART 50 – APPLICATION OF THE SCHEDULES

50(1) The Schedules to these Rules set out, with modifications, certain provisions previously contained in the Rules of the Supreme Court 1965 and the County Court Rules 1981.

50(2) These Rules apply in relation to the proceedings to which the Schedules apply subject to the provisions in the Schedules and the relevant practice directions.

50(3) A provision previously contained in the Rules of the Supreme Court 1965–

(a) is headed "RSC";

(b) is numbered with the Order and rule numbers it bore as part of the RSC; and

(c) unless otherwise stated in the Schedules or the relevant practice direction, applies only to proceedings in the High Court.

50(4) A provision previously contained in the County Court Rules 1981

(a) is headed "CCR";

(b) is numbered with the Order and rule numbers it bore as part of the CCR; and

(c) unless otherwise stated in the Schedules or the relevant practice direction, applies only to proceedings in the county court.

50(5) A reference in a Schedule to a rule by number alone is a reference to the rule so numbered in the Order in which the reference occurs.

50(6) A reference in a Schedule to a rule by number prefixed by "CPR" is a reference to the rule with that number in these Rules.

50(7) In the Schedules, unless otherwise stated, **"the Act"** means–

(a) in a provision headed "RSC", the Supreme Court Act 1981; and

(b) in a provision headed "CCR", the County Courts Act 1984.

PART 54 – JUDICIAL REVIEW AND STATUTORY REVIEW

History – The words "and statutory review" inserted in the heading to Pt. 54 by SI 2003/364, r. 3, with effect from 1 April 2003 (SI 2003/754).

Pt. 54 inserted by SI 2000/2092, r. 22, with effect from 2 October 2000 subject to the transitional provisions at SI 2000/2092, r. 29 and 30, which read as follows:

"**29** Where a person has, before 2nd October 2000, filed a notice of appeal in a claim allocated to the small claims track–

(a)   Part 52 shall not apply to the appeal to which that notice relates; and

(b)   rules 27.12 and 27.13 shall apply to that appeal as if they had not been revoked.

30 Where a person has, before 2nd October 2000, filed an application for permission to make an application for judicial review in accordance with RSC Order 53–

(a)   Part 54 shall not apply to that application for permission or the application for judicial review to which it relates; and

(b)   RSC Order 53 shall apply to those applications as if it had not been revoked."

SECTION I – JUDICIAL REVIEW

SCOPE AND INTERPRETATION

54.1(1) This Section of this Part contains rules about judicial review.

54.1(2) In this Section–

(a) a **"claim for judicial review"** means a claim to review the lawfulness of–

(i) an enactment; or

(ii) a decision, action or failure to act in relation to the exercise of a public function.

(b) an order of mandamus is called a **"mandatory order"**;

(c) an order of prohibition is called a **"prohibiting order"**;

(d) an order of certiorari is called a **"quashing order"**;

(e) **"the judicial review procedure"** means the Part 8 procedure as modified by this Section;

(f) **"interested party"** means any person (other than the claimant and defendant) who is directly affected by the claim; and

(g) **"court"** means the High Court, unless otherwise stated.

(Rule 8.1(6)(b) provides that a rule or practice direction may, in relation to a specified type of proceedings, disapply or modify any of the rules set out in Part 8 as they apply to those proceedings)

History – In r. 54.1(1) the words "This section of this Part" substituted for the words "This Part" by SI 2003/364, r. 5(a), with effect from 1 April 2003 (SI 2003/754).

In r. 54.1(2) the words "In this Section" substituted for the words "In this Part" by SI 2003/364, r. 5(b), with effect from 1 April 2003 (SI 2003/754).

In r. 54.1(2)(e) the words "this Section" substituted for the words "this Part" by SI 2003/364, r. 5(b), with effect from 1 April 2003 (SI 2003/754).

WHEN THIS SECTION MUST BE USED

54.2 The judicial review procedure must be used in a claim for judicial review where the claimant is seeking–

(a) a mandatory order;

(b) a prohibiting order;

(c) a quashing order; or

(d) an injunction under section 30 of the Supreme Court Act 1981 (restraining a person from acting in any office in which he is not entitled to act).

History – In the heading to r. 54.2 the word "Section" substituted for the word "Part" by SI 2003/364, r. 5(c), with effect from 1 April 2003 (SI 2003/754).

WHEN THIS SECTION MAY BE USED

54.3(1) The judicial review procedure may be used in a claim for judicial review where the claimant is seeking–

(a) a declaration; or

(b) an injunction.

(Section 31(2) of the Supreme Court Act 1981 sets out the circumstances in which the court may grant a declaration or injunction in a claim for judicial review)

(Where the claimant is seeking a declaration or injunction in addition to one of the remedies listed in rule 54.2, the judicial review procedure must be used)

54.3(2) A claim for judicial review may include a claim for damages but may not seek damages alone.

(Section 31(4) of the Supreme Court Act 1981 sets out the circumstances in which the court may award damages on a claim for judicial review)

History – In the heading to r. 54.3 the word "Section" substituted for the word "Part" by SI 2003/364, r. 5(c), with effect from 1 April 2003 (SI 2003/754).

PERMISSION REQUIRED

54.4 The court's permission to proceed is required in a claim for judicial review whether started under this Section or transferred to the Administrative Court.

History – In r. 54.4 the word "Section" substituted for the word "Part" by SI 2003/364, r. 5(d), with effect from 1 April 2003 (SI 2003/754).

TIME LIMIT FOR FILING CLAIM FORM

54.5(1) The claim form must be filed–

(a) promptly; and

(b) in any event not later than 3 months after the grounds to make the claim first arose.

54.5(2) The time limit in this rule may not be extended by agreement between the parties.

54.5(3) This rule does not apply when any other enactment specifies a shorter time limit for making the claim for judicial review.

CLAIM FORM

54.6(1) In addition to the matters set out in rule 8.2 (contents of the claim form) the claimant must also state–

(a) the name and address of any person he considers to be an interested party;

(b) that he is requesting permission to proceed with a claim for judicial review; and

(c) any remedy (including any interim remedy) he is claiming.

(Part 25 sets out how to apply for an interim remedy)

54.6(2) The claim form must be accompanied by the documents required by the relevant practice direction.

SERVICE OF CLAIM FORM

54.7 The claim form must be served on–

(a) the defendant; and

(b) unless the court otherwise directs, any person the claimant considers to be an interested party,

within 7 days after the date of issue.

ACKNOWLEDGMENT OF SERVICE

54.8(1) Any person served with the claim form who wishes to take part in the judicial review must file an acknowledgment of service in the relevant practice form in accordance with the following provisions of this rule.

54.8(2) Any acknowledgment of service must be–

(a) filed not more than 21 days after service of the claim form; and

(b) served on–

(i) the claimant; and

(ii)   subject to any direction under rule 54.7(b), any other person named in the claim form, as soon as practicable and, in any event, not later than 7 days after it is filed.

54.8(3)   The time limits under this rule may not be extended by agreement between the parties.

54.8(4)   The acknowledgment of service–

(a)   must–

   (i)   where the person filing it intends to contest the claim, set out a summary of his grounds for doing so; and

   (ii)   state the name and address of any person the person filing it considers to be an interested party; and

(b)   may include or be accompanied by an application for directions.

54.8(5)   Rule 10.3(2) does not apply.

FAILURE TO FILE ACKNOWLEDGMENT OF SERVICE

54.9(1)   Where a person served with the claim form has failed to file an acknowledgment of service in accordance with rule 54.8, he–

(a)   may not take part in a hearing to decide whether permission should be given unless the court allows him to do so; but

(b)   provided he complies with rule 54.14 or any other direction of the court regarding the filing and service of–

   (i)   detailed grounds for contesting the claim or supporting it on additional grounds; and

   (ii)   any written evidence,

may take part in the hearing of the judicial review.

54.9(2)   Where that person takes part in the hearing of the judicial review, the court may take his failure to file an acknowledgment of service into account when deciding what order to make about costs.

54.9(3)   Rule 8.4 does not apply.

PERMISSION GIVEN

54.10(1)   Where permission to proceed is given the court may also give directions.

54.10(2)   Directions under paragraph (1) may include a stay of proceedings to which the claim relates.

(Rule 3.7 provides a sanction for the non-payment of the fee payable when permission to proceed has been given)

SERVICE OF ORDER GIVING OR REFUSING PERMISSION

54.11   The court will serve–

(a)   the order giving or refusing permission; and

(b)   any directions,

on–

   (i)   the claimant;

   (ii)   the defendant; and

   (iii)   any other person who filed an acknowledgment of service.

PERMISSION DECISION WITHOUT A HEARING

54.12(1)   This rule applies where the court, without a hearing–

(a)   refuses permission to proceed; or

(b)   gives permission to proceed–

   (i)   subject to conditions; or

   (ii)   on certain grounds only.

54.12(2)   The court will serve its reasons for making the decision when it serves the order giving or refusing permission in accordance with rule 54.11.

54.12(3)   The claimant may not appeal but may request the decision to be reconsidered at a hearing.

54.12(4)   A request under paragraph (3) must be filed within 7 days after service of the reasons under paragraph (2).

54.12(5)   The claimant, defendant and any other person who has filed an acknowledgment of service will be given at least 2 days' notice of the hearing date.

DEFENDANT ETC. MAY NOT APPLY TO SET ASIDE

54.13   Neither the defendant nor any other person served with the claim form may apply to set aside an order giving permission to proceed.

RESPONSE

54.14(1)   A defendant and any other person served with the claim form who wishes to contest the claim or support it on additional grounds must file and serve—

(a)   detailed grounds for contesting the claim or supporting it on additional grounds; and

(b)   any written evidence,

within 35 days after service of the order giving permission.

54.14(2)   The following rules do not apply—

(a)   rule 8.5(3) and 8.5(4) (defendant to file and serve written evidence at the same time as acknowledgment of service); and

(b)   rule 8.5(5) and 8.5(6) (claimant to file and serve any reply within 14 days).

WHERE CLAIMANT SEEKS TO RELY ON ADDITIONAL GROUNDS

54.15   The court's permission is required if a claimant seeks to rely on grounds other than those for which he has been given permission to proceed.

EVIDENCE

54.16(1)   Rule 8.6(1) does not apply.

54.16(2)   No written evidence may be relied on unless—

(a)   it has been served in accordance with any—

     (i)   rule under this Section; or

     (ii)   direction of the court; or

(b)   the court gives permission.

History – In r. 54.16 the word "Section" substituted for the word "Part" by SI 2003/364, r. 5(d), with effect from 1 April 2003 (SI 2003/754).
In r. 54.16, "(1)" inserted by SI 2002/2058, r. 21, with effect from 2 December 2002.

COURT'S POWERS TO HEAR ANY PERSON

54.17(1)   Any person may apply for permission—

(a)   to file evidence; or

(b)   make representations at the hearing of the judicial review.

54.17(2)   An application under paragraph (1) should be made promptly.

JUDICIAL REVIEW MAY BE DECIDED WITHOUT A HEARING

54.18   The court may decide the claim for judicial review without a hearing where all the parties agree.

COURT'S POWERS IN RESPECT OF QUASHING ORDERS

54.19(1)   This rule applies where the court makes a quashing order in respect of the decision to which the claim relates.

54.19(2)   The court may—

(a)

     (i)   remit the matter to the decision-maker; and

     (ii)   direct it to reconsider the matter and reach a decision in accordance with the judgment of the court; or

(b)   in so far as any enactment permits, substitute its own decision for the decision to which the claim relates.

(Section 31 of the Supreme Court Act 1981 enables the High Court, subject to certain conditions, to substitute its own decision for the decision in question.)

54.19(3) [Revoked by SI 2007/3543, r. 7.]

History – R. 54.19(2) substituted by SI 2007/3543, r. 7, with effect from 6 April 2008.
R. 54.19(3) revoked by SI 2007/3543, r. 7, with effect from 6 April 2008.

TRANSFER

54.20 The court may–

(a)   order a claim to continue as if it had not been started under this Section; and

(b)   where it does so, give directions about the future management of the claim.

(Part 30 (transfer) applies to transfers to and from the Administrative Court)

History – In r. 54.20(a) the word "Section" substituted for the word "Part" by SI 2003/364, r. 5(e), with effect from 1 April 2003 (SI 2003/754).

SECTION II – STATUTORY REVIEW UNDER THE NATIONALITY, IMMIGRATION AND ASYLUM ACT 2002

[Section II of Pt. 54 is not relevant to tax and is therefore not reproduced here.]

SCHEDULE 1

RSC ORDER 53 – APPLICATIONS FOR JUDICIAL REVIEW

History – RSC Order 53 revoked by SI 2000/2092, r. 23, with effect from 2 October 2000 subject to the transitional provisions at SI 2000/2092, r. 29 and 30 which read as follows:

"**29**   Where a person has, before 2nd October 2000, filed a notice of appeal in a claim allocated to the small claims track–
(a)   Part 52 shall not apply to the appeal to which that notice relates; and
(b)   rules 27.12 and 27.13 shall apply to that appeal as if they had not been revoked.
30   Where a person has, before 2nd October 2000, filed an application for permission to make an application for judicial review in accordance with RSC Order 53–
(a)   Part 54 shall not apply to that application for permission or the application for judicial review to which it relates; and
(b)   RSC Order 53 shall apply to those applications as if it had not been revoked."

RSC ORDER 55 – APPEALS TO HIGH COURT FROM COURT, TRIBUNAL OR PERSON: GENERAL

BRINGING AN APPEAL

3(1)   An appeal to which this Order applies shall be by way of rehearing and must be brought by notice of appeal.

3(2)   Every notice by which such an appeal is brought must state the grounds of the appeal and, if the appeal is against a judgment, order or other decision of a court, must state whether the appeal is against the whole or a part of that decision and, if against a part only, must specify the part.

3(3)   The bringing of such an appeal shall not operate as a stay of proceedings on the judgment, determination or other decisions against which the appeal is brought unless the Court by which the appeal is to be heard or the court, tribunal or person by which or by whom the decision was given so orders.

SERVICE OF NOTICE OF APPEAL AND ENTRY OF APPEAL

4(1)   The persons to be served with the notice of appeal are the following:–

(a)   if the appeal is against a judgment, order or other decision of a court, the registrar or clerk of the court and any party to the proceedings in which the decision was given who is directly affected by the appeal;

(b)   if the appeal is against an order, determination, award or other decision of a tribunal, Minister of the Crown, government department or other person, the chairman of the tribunal, Minister, government department or person, as the case may be, and every party to the proceedings (other than the appellant) in which the decision appealed against was given.

4(2)   The notice must be served, and the appeal entered, within 28 days after the date of the judgment, order, determination or other decision against which the appeal is brought.

4(3) In the case of an appeal against a judgment, order or decision of a court, the period specified in paragraph (2) shall be calculated from the date of the judgment or order or the date on which the decision was given.

4(4) In the case of an appeal against an order, determination, award or other decision of a tribunal, Minister, government department or other person, the period specified in paragraph (2) shall be calculated from the date on which notice of the decision, or, in a case where a statement of the reasons for a decision was given later than such notice, on which such a statement was given to the appellant by the person who made the decision or by a person authorised in that behalf to do so.

History – In r. 4(1) the words "the notice of appeal" substituted for the previous words "notice of the motion by which an appeal to which this Order applies is brought" by SI 1999/1008, r. 1, 34 as from 26 April 1999.

DATE OF HEARING OF APPEAL

5 Unless the Court having jurisdiction to determine the appeal otherwise directs, an appeal to which this Order applies shall not be heard sooner than 21 days after service of notice of the motion by which the appeal is brought.

RSC ORDER 91 – REVENUE PROCEEDINGS

ASSIGNMENT TO CHANCERY DIVISION, ETC.

1 The following proceedings, namely–

(a)   any case stated for the opinion of the High Court under–

(i)   section 13 of the Stamp Act 1891, or

(ii)   section 705A of the Income and Corporation Taxes Act 1988, or

(iii)   regulation 22 of the General Commissioners (Jurisdiction and Procedure) Regulations 1994;

(b)   any appeal to the High Court under–

(i)   section 53, 56A or 100C(4) of the Taxes Management Act 1970, or

(ii)   section 222(3), 225, 249(3) or 251 of the Inheritance Tax Act 1984, or

(iii)   regulation 8(3) or 10 of the Stamp Duty Reserve Tax Regulations 1986;

(c)   any application for permission to appeal under the said section 222(3) or the said regulation 8(3); and

(d)   proceedings to which the provisions of section 56A of the Taxes Management Act 1970 apply under any enactment or regulation,

shall be assigned to the Chancery Division and heard and determined by a single judge.

APPEAL UNDER SECTION 222 OF THE INHERITANCE ACT 1984

2(1) Order 55 shall not apply in relation to an appeal to the High Court under section 222(3) of the Inheritance Tax Act 1984 or Regulation 8(3) of the Stamp Duty Reserve Tax Regulations 1986.

2(2) Such an appeal must be brought by a notice of appeal which must–

(a)   state the date on which the Commissioners of Inland Revenue (in this rule referred to as the "Board") gave notice to the appellant under section 221 of the said Act or Regulation 6 of the said Regulations of the determination which is the subject of the appeal;

(b)   state the date on which the appellant gave to the Board notice of appeal under section 222(1) of the said Act, or Regulation 8(1) of the said Regulations and, if the notice was not given within the time limited, whether the Board or the Special Commissioners have given consent to the appeal being brought out of time and if they have, the date on which it was given; and

(c)   either state that the appellant and the Board have agreed that the appeal may be to the High Court or contain an application for permission to appeal to the High Court.

2(3) At the time of issuing the notice of appeal the appellant shall file in Chancery Chambers–

(a)   two copies of the notice referred to in paragraph (2)(a);

(b)   two copies of the notice of appeal (under section 222(1) of the said Act, or Regulation 8(1) of the said Regulations) referred to in paragraph (2)(b); and

(c)   where the notice of appeal contains an application for permission to appeal, a witness statement or affidavit setting out the grounds on which it is alleged that the matters to be decided on the appeal are likely to be substantially confined to questions of law.

2(4) The notice of appeal must be issued and served on the Board within 30 days of the date on which the appellant gave to the Board notice of appeal under section 222(1) of the said Act or Regulation

(8)(1) of the said Regulations or, if the Board or the Special Commissioners have given consent to the appeal being brought out of time, within 30 days of the date on which such consent was given.

2(5) The notice of appeal, must specify a date of hearing being not less than 40 days from the issue of the notice of appeal.

2(6) Where the notice of appeal contains an application for permission to appeal to the High Court, a copy of the witness statement or affidavit lodged pursuant to paragraph (3)(c) shall be served on the Board with the notice of appeal and the Board may, within 30 days after service, file in the judge's chambers a witness statement or affidavit in answer and a copy of any such witness statement or affidavit shall be served by the Board on the appellant.

2(7) Except with the permission of the Court, the appellant shall not be entitled on the hearing of an appeal to rely on any grounds of appeal not specified in the notice referred to in paragraph (2)(b).

SETTING DOWN CASE STATED UNDER TAXES MANAGEMENT ACT 1970

3(1) At any time after a case stated under section 705A of the Income and Corporation Taxes Act 1988 or Regulation 22 of the General Commissioners (Jurisdiction and Procedure) Regulations 1994 has been filed in Chancery Chambers either party may set down the case for hearing.

3(2) On setting down the case the party who sets it down must give notice to the other party that he has done so.

CASE STATED: NOTICE TO BE GIVEN OF CERTAIN MATTERS

4 Not less than 10 days before the hearing of such a case as is mentioned in rule 1(a) either party must give notice to the other of any point which he intends to take at the hearing and which might take the other party by surprise and leave at Chancery Chambers two copies of the notice for the use of the Court.

APPEALS UNDER SECTION 53 AND 100C(4) OF THE TAXES MANAGEMENT ACT 1970

5(1) The notice of appeal by which an appeal under section 53 or 100C(4) of the Taxes Management Act 1970 or section 249(3) or 251 of the Inheritance Tax Act 1984 is brought must be issued out of Chancery Chambers.

5(2) Order 55, rule 3(2), shall apply in relation to the notice of appeal as if the decision, award or determination appealed against were the decision of a court.

5(3) The persons to be served with the notice are the General or Special Commissioners against whose decision, award or determination the appeal is brought and–

(a)   in the case of an appeal brought under section 100C(4) of the Taxes Management Act 1970 or section 249(3) of the Inheritance Tax Act 1984 by any party other than the defendant in the proceedings before the Commissioners, that defendant;

(b)   in any other case, the Commissioners of Inland Revenue.

5(4) Order 55, rules 4(2) and 5, shall apply in relation to any such appeal as if for the period of 28 days and 21 days therein specified there were substituted a period of 30 days and 35 days respectively.

5(5) Within 30 days after the service on them of the notice by which any such appeal is brought, the General or Special Commissioners, as the case may be, must file in Chancery Chambers two copies of a note of their findings and of the reasons for their decision, award or determination and must serve a copy of the note on every other party to the appeal.

5(6) Any document required or authorised to be served on the General or Special Commissioners in proceedings to which this rule relates may be served by delivering or sending it to their clerk.

5(7) Order 57 shall not apply to proceedings to which this rule applies.

APPEALS UNDER SECTION 56A OF THE TAXES MANAGEMENT ACT 1970, SECTION 225 OF THE INHERITANCE ACT 1984 AND REGULATION 10 OF THE STAMP DUTY RESERVE TAX REGULATIONS 1986

5A(1) This rule applies to appeals under section 56A of the Taxes Management Act 1970, section 225 of the Inheritance Tax Act 1984 and regulation 10 of the Stamp Duty Reserve Tax Regulations 1986.

5A(2) The notice of appeal by which such an appeal is brought must be issued out of Chancery Chambers.

5A(3) Order 55, rule 3(2) shall apply in relation to the notice of appeal as if the decision or determination appealed against were the decision of a court.

5A(4) Order 55, rule 4(2) shall apply in relation to such an appeal as if for the period of 28 days specified in that rule there were substituted a period of 56 days, except where the appeal is made following the refusal of the Special Commissioners to issue a certificate under section 56A(2)(b) of the Taxes Management Act 1970 or the refusal of permission to appeal to the Court of Appeal under section 56A(2)(c) of that Act.

5A(5) Where the appeal is made following the refusal of the Special Commissioners to issue a certificate under section 56A(2)(b) of the Taxes Management Act 1970, the period of 28 days specified in Order 55, rule 4(2) shall be calculated from the date of the release of the decision of the Special Commissioners containing the refusal.

5A(6) Where the appeal is made following the refusal of permission to appeal to the Court of Appeal under section 56A(2)(c) of the Taxes Management Act 1970, the period of 28 days specified in Order 55, r.4(2) shall be calculated from the date when permission is refused.

5A(7) Order 57 shall not apply to proceedings to which this rule applies.

CORPORATION TAX (INSTALMENT PAYMENTS) REGULATIONS 1998

(SI 1998/3175, as amended by SI 1999/1929, SI 2000/892, SI 2001/3629, SI 2005/889, SI 2008/2649, SI 2009/56, SI 2011/1785 and FA 2002)

Made on 17 December 1998 by the Treasury, in exercise of the powers conferred on them by s. 59DA(8) and 59E of the Taxes Management Act 1970, s. 826A of the Income and Corporation Taxes Act 1988 and s. 30 of the Finance Act 1998. Operative from 7 January 1999.

ARRANGEMENT OF REGULATIONS

REGULATION

CITATION, COMMENCEMENT AND EFFECT

1(1) These Regulations may be cited as the Corporation Tax (Instalment Payments) Regulations 1998 and shall come into force on 7th January 1999.

1(2) These Regulations have effect in relation to accounting periods of companies ending on or after 1st July 1999.

INTERPRETATION

2(1) In these Regulations–

"**accounting period**" shall be construed in accordance with Chapter 2 of Part 2 of CTA 2009;

"**applicable accounting period**" means any accounting period for which bank levy is chargeable in respect of the chargeable period determined in accordance with–

(a) paragraph 50 of Schedule 19 where bank levy is charged in relation to a relevant group; or

(b) paragraph 51 of that Schedule where bank levy is charged in relation to a relevant entity;

"**large company**" has the meaning given by regulation 3;

"**Schedule 18**" means Schedule 18 to the Finance Act 1998;

"**Schedule 19**" means Schedule 19 to the Finance Act 2011;

"**the bank levy**" means the tax charged in accordance with Schedule 19;

"**the chargeable period**" has the meaning given by paragraph 4 or paragraph 5 of Schedule 19 (as the case may be);

"**the relevant entity**" has the meaning given by paragraph 5 of Schedule 19;

"**the relevant group**" has the meaning given by paragraph 4 of Schedule 19;

"**the responsible member**" has the meaning given by paragraph 54 of Schedule 19;

"**the Management Act**" means the Taxes Management Act 1970; and

"**the Taxes Act**" means the Income and Corporation Taxes Act 1988.

2(2) References in these Regulations to profits of a company in any accounting period are references to the company's augmented profits within the meaning given by section 32 of CTA 2010.

2(3) References in these Regulations to the total liability of a company for an accounting period are references to the amount of tax payable for that period by the company as calculated in accordance with paragraph 8(1) of Schedule 18.

History – Reg. 2 substituted by SI 2011/1785, reg. 3, with effect from 11 August 2011 in relation to accounting periods ending on or after 1 January 2011.

LARGE COMPANIES

3(1) Subject to paragraphs (1A) to (3A), a large company is a company whose profits in any accounting period exceed the upper limit in force at the end of that period.

3(1A) In relation to any applicable accounting period an entity which is the relevant entity or the responsible member for the purposes of Schedule 19 is a large company for that period for the purposes of these Regulations.

3(2) A company is not a large company as respects an accounting period if the amount of its total liability for that period does not exceed £10,000 or, where the accounting period is less than twelve months, that amount proportionately reduced. This paragraph does not apply if a company is the relevant entity or the responsible member.

3(3) A company is not a large company as respects an accounting period if–

(a) its profits for that accounting period do not exceed £10,000,000 and

(b) apart from this paragraph, it was not a large company in the twelve months preceding that accounting period.

This paragraph does not apply if a company is the relevant entity or the responsible member.

3(3A) Any question whether a company is, or is not, a large company as respects an accounting period beginning on or after 17th April 2002 shall, so far as not falling to be determined by reference to the company's total liability, be determined as it would have been determined apart from sections 330 (supplementary charge in respect of ring fence trades) and 331 (meaning of "financing costs" etc) of CTA 2010.

3(4) [Omitted by SI 2011/1785, reg. 4(7).]

3(5) Sections 24 to 30 of CTA 2010 (the lower limit and the upper limit) shall apply so as to reduce the amount specified in paragraph (3)(a) in accordance with those sections as they apply to reduce the upper and lower limits, except that—

(a)   the number of associated companies referred to in section 24(3) of CTA 2010 shall be determined by reference to the number existing at the end of the immediately preceding accounting period of the company or, if there is no immediately preceding accounting period or the immediately preceding accounting period did not end on the day before the accounting period concerned commenced, by reference to the number existing at the commencement of the accounting period concerned; and

(b)   section 434(3A) of the Taxes Act (franked investment income) and section 88(4) of the Finance Act 1989 (corporation tax policy holders' share of profits) shall be disregarded.

3(6) For the purposes of paragraph (3)(b) a company shall be treated as not being a large company in the period of twelve months preceding the accounting period in question in either of the following circumstances—

(a)   during any part of the period of twelve months it either did not exist or did not have an accounting period;

(b)   a relevant accounting period of the company either falls within or ends in that period of twelve months.

3(7) In paragraph (6) **"relevant accounting period"** means an accounting period as respects which, by virtue of the provisions of this regulation other than paragraph (3), the company was not a large company.

In this regulation **"upper limit"** and **"lower limit"** shall be construed in accordance with section 24 of CTA 2010 (the lower limit and the upper limit).

History – In reg. 3(1), "(1A)" substituted for "2" by SI 2011/1785, reg. 4(2)(a), with effect from 11 August 2011 in relation to accounting periods ending on or after 1 January 2011.
In reg. 3(1), the word "limit" substituted for the words "relevant maximum amount" by SI 2011/1785, reg. 4(2)(b), with effect from 11 August 2011 in relation to accounting periods ending on or after 1 January 2011.
In reg. 3(1), the words "paragraphs (2) to (3A)," substituted by FA 2002, s. 92(6).
Reg. 3(1A) inserted by SI 2011/1785, reg. 4(3), with effect from 11 August 2011 in relation to accounting periods ending on or after 1 January 2011.
In reg. 3(2), the words "This paragraph does not apply if a company is the relevant entity or the responsible member." inserted by SI 2011/1785, reg. 4(4), with effect from 11 August 2011 in relation to accounting periods ending on or after 1 January 2011.
In reg. 3(2) the figure of "£10,000" substituted by SI 2000/892, reg. 2, operative from 19 April 2000.
In reg. 3(3), the words "This paragraph does not apply if a company is the relevant entity or the responsible member." inserted by SI 2011/1785, reg. 4(5), with effect from 11 August 2011 in relation to accounting periods ending on or after 1 January 2011.
In reg 3(3A), the words "sections 330 (supplementary charge in respect of ring fence trades) and 331 (meaning of "financing costs" etc) of CTA 2010" substituted for the words "section 501A of the Taxes Act (supplementary charge in respect of ring fence trades)" by SI 2011/1785, reg. 4(6), with effect from 11 August 2011 in relation to accounting periods ending on or after 1 January 2011.
Reg. 3(3A) inserted by FA 2001, s. 92(7).
Reg. 3(4) omitted by SI 2011/1785, reg. 4(7), with effect from 11 August 2011 in relation to accounting periods ending on or after 1 January 2011.
In former reg. 3(4), "and (3B)", which appeared after "section 434(3A)", omitted by SI 2008/2649, reg. 2(a), with effect from 28 October 2008.
Reg. 3(5) substituted by SI 2011/1785, reg. 4(8), with effect from 11 August 2011 in relation to accounting periods ending on or after 1 January 2011.
In former reg. 3(5)(b), "and (3B)", which appeared after "section 434(3A)", omitted by SI 2008/2649, reg. 2(b), with effect from 28 October 2008.
Reg. 3(8) inserted by SI 2011/1785, reg. 4(9), with effect from 11 August 2011 in relation to accounting periods ending on or after 1 January 2011.

INSTALMENT PAYMENTS – TRANSITIONAL PROVISION

4(1) In relation to an accounting period of a large company ending on or after 1st July 1999 but before 1st July 2000—

(a)   an amount equal to 60 per cent of the company's total liability for that period shall be treated as becoming due and payable in accordance with regulation 5;

(b)   the balance of the company's total liability for that period shall be payable in accordance with section 59D(1) of the Management Act, that is, on the day following the expiry of nine months from the end of the accounting period ("the due and payable date").

4(2) In relation to an accounting period of a large company ending on or after 1st July 2000 but before 1st July 2001—

(a)   an amount equal to 72 per cent of the company's total liability for that period shall be treated as becoming due and payable in accordance with regulation 5;

(b)   the balance of the company's total liability for that period shall be payable on the due and payable date.

4(3) In relation to an accounting period of a large company ending on or after 1st July 2001 but before 1st July 2002–

(a) an amount equal to 88 per cent of the company's total liability for that period shall be treated as becoming due and payable in accordance with regulation 5;

(b) the balance of the company's total liability for that period shall be payable on the due and payable date.

INSTALMENT PAYMENTS – TRANSITIONAL PROVISIONS: THE BANK LEVY (APPLICABLE ACCOUNTING PERIODS ENDING ON OR BEFORE 19TH JULY 2011 WHERE COMPANY BECOMES A LARGE COMPANY BY VIRTUE OF REGULATION 3(1A))

4A(1) This regulation applies if–

(a) an entity ("E") is the relevant entity or the responsible member in relation to an applicable accounting period ("the period") which ended on or before 19th July 2011;

(b) E is a large company for the purposes of these Regulations only by virtue of regulation 3(1A); and

(c) accordingly, E would not otherwise be liable to make instalment payments in relation to the period.

4A(2) The total liability of E for the period shall be treated as becoming due and payable in accordance with regulation 5, but this is subject to paragraphs (3) to (5).

4A(3) An instalment payment which apart from this regulation would be treated as becoming due and payable on a date falling before 11th August 2011 shall be treated as not being due and payable.

4A(4) If there is no instalment payment which is treated as becoming due and payable on a date falling on or after 11th August 2011, the total liability of E shall be treated as becoming due and payable on 18th August 2011.

4A(5) If in relation to the period there is an instalment payment which is treated as becoming due and payable on a date falling on or after 11th August 2011, the amount of that instalment payment, or the amount of the first of those instalment payments, shall be increased by the adjustment amount.

4A(6) In paragraph (5) the adjustment amount is the aggregate of the amounts of the instalment payments which would have been treated as being due and payable, on a date falling before 11th August 2011, determined on the basis that–

(a) the provisions of Schedule 19 had effect on the date on which each instalment payment would have been treated as becoming due and payable; and

(b) paragraph (3) does not apply in relation to each instalment payment.

History – Reg. 4A inserted by SI 2011/1785, reg. 5, with effect from 11 August 2011 in relation to accounting periods ending on or after 1 January 2011.

INSTALMENT PAYMENTS – TRANSITIONAL PROVISIONS: THE BANK LEVY (APPLICABLE ACCOUNTING PERIODS ENDING ON OR BEFORE 19TH JULY 2011 WHERE COMPANY IS A LARGE COMPANY OTHERWISE THAN BY VIRTUE OF REGULATION 3(1A))

4B(1) This regulation applies if–

(a) an entity ("E") is the relevant entity or the responsible member in relation to an applicable accounting period ("the period") which ended on or before 19th July 2011; and

(b) E is a large company for the purposes of these Regulations otherwise than by virtue of regulation 3(1A).

4B(2) The total liability of E for the period shall be treated as becoming due and payable in accordance with regulation 5, but this is subject to paragraphs (3) to (5).

4B(3) An instalment payment which apart from this regulation would be treated as becoming due and payable on a date falling before 11 August 2011 shall be treated as not being due and payable to the extent that it includes an amount in respect of the bank levy.

4B(4) If, apart from paragraph (5), in relation to the period there is an instalment payment, or more than one instalment payment, which is treated as becoming due and payable on a date falling or after 11th August 2011, the amount of that instalment payment, or the amount of the first of those instalment payments, shall be increased by the adjustment amount.

4B(5) If, apart from this paragraph, in relation to the period there is no instalment payment which is treated as becoming due and payable on a date falling on or after 11th August 2011, a further instalment payment of an amount equal to the adjustment amount shall be treated as becoming due and payable on 18th August 2011.

4B(6) For the purposes of paragraphs (4) and (5) the adjustment amount is the difference between–

(a) the aggregate amount of the instalment payments which were treated as becoming due and payable before 11th August 2011, determined on the basis that the total liability of E did not include any liability to the bank levy; and

(b) the aggregate amount of those instalment payments including E's liability to the bank levy determined on the basis that paragraph (3) does not apply in relation to those instalment payments.

History – Reg. 4B inserted by SI 2011/1785, reg. 5, with effect from 11 August 2011 in relation to accounting periods ending on or after 1 January 2011.

INSTALMENT PAYMENTS – TRANSITIONAL PROVISIONS: THE BANK LEVY (APPLICABLE ACCOUNTING PERIODS BEGINNING ON OR BEFORE 19TH JULY 2011 AND ENDING AFTER THAT DATE WHERE COMPANY IS A LARGE COMPANY BY VIRTUE OF REGULATION 3(1A))

4C(1) This regulation applies if–

(a) an entity ("E") is the relevant entity or the responsible member in relation to an applicable accounting period ("the period") which began on or before 19th July 2011 and ends after that date;

(b) E is a large company for the purposes of these Regulations only by virtue of regulation 3(1A); and

(c) accordingly, E would not otherwise be liable to make instalment payments in relation to the period.

4C(2) The total liability of E for the period shall be treated as becoming due and payable in accordance with regulation 5, but this is subject to paragraphs (3) and (4).

4C(3) An instalment payment which apart from this regulation would be treated as becoming due and payable on a date falling before 11th August 2011 shall be treated as not being due and payable.

4C(4) The amount of the first instalment payment which is treated as becoming due and payable on a date falling on or after 11th August 2011 shall be increased by the adjustment amount.

4C(5) In paragraph (4) the adjustment amount is the aggregate of the amounts of instalment payments which would have been treated as becoming due and payable before 11th August 2011, determined on the basis that–

(a) the provisions of Schedule 19 had effect at the date on which each instalment payment would have been treated as becoming due and payable; and

(b) paragraph (3) does not apply in relation to each instalment.

History – Reg. 4C inserted by SI 2011/1785, reg. 5, with effect from 11 August 2011 in relation to accounting periods ending on or after 1 January 2011.

INSTALMENT PAYMENTS – TRANSITIONAL PROVISIONS: THE BANK LEVY (APPLICABLE ACCOUNTING PERIODS BEGINNING ON OR BEFORE 19TH JULY 2011 BUT ENDING AFTER THAT DATE WHERE COMPANY IS A LARGE COMPANY OTHERWISE THAN BY VIRTUE OF REGULATION 3(1A))

4D(1) This regulation applies if–

(a) an entity ("E") is the relevant entity or the responsible member in relation to an applicable accounting period ("the period") which began on or before 19th July 2011 and ends after that date; and

(b) E is a large company for the purposes of these Regulations otherwise than by virtue of regulation 3(1A).

4D(2) The total liability of E for the period shall be treated as becoming due and payable in accordance with regulation 5, but this is subject to paragraphs (3) and (4).

4D(3) An instalment payment which apart from this regulation would be treated as becoming due and payable on a date falling before 11 August 2011 shall be treated as not being due and payable to the extent that it includes an amount in respect of the bank levy.

4D(4) In relation to the period, the amount of the first instalment payment which is treated as becoming due and payable on a date falling on or after 11th August 2011 shall be increased by the adjustment amount.

4D(5) For the purposes of paragraph (4) the adjustment amount is the difference between–

(a) the aggregate amount of the instalment payments which were treated as becoming due and payable on a date falling before 11th August 2011, determined on the basis that the total liability of E did not include any liability to the bank levy; and

(b) the aggregate amount of those instalment payments including E's liability to the bank levy determined on the basis that paragraph (3) does not apply in relation to those instalment payments.

History – Reg. 4D inserted by SI 2011/1785, reg. 5, with effect from 11 August 2011 in relation to accounting periods ending on or after 1 January 2011.

INSTALMENT PAYMENTS – PRINCIPAL PROVISION

5(1) Save as regards any amount falling within regulation 4(1)(b), (2)(b), (3)(b) or regulation 5A, amounts in respect of the total liability of a large company for an accounting period shall be treated as becoming due and payable as follows.

5(2) Subject to paragraph (4), the amount of the company's total liability for that period or, as the case may be, the specified percentage amount shall be treated as becoming due and payable in instalments (not exceeding four) on the dates specified in paragraph (3).

5(3) The first instalment payment shall be treated as becoming due and payable on the date which is six months and thirteen days from the start of the accounting period.

The final instalment payment shall be treated as becoming due and payable on the date which is three months and fourteen days from the end of the accounting period.

An additional instalment payment or additional instalment payments shall, where the length of the accounting period so allows, each be treated as becoming due and payable on the date which is three months after the date of the immediately preceding instalment payment.

5(4) Where the length of the accounting period is such that the date which is three months and fourteen days from the end of the accounting period falls earlier than the date which is six months and thirteen days from the start of the accounting period, the amount of the company's total liability for that period or, as the case may be, the specified percentage amount shall be treated as becoming due and payable on the date which is three months and fourteen days from the end of the accounting period.

5(5) Where in accordance with paragraph (2) amounts in respect of the amount of the company's total liability for an accounting period or in respect of the specified percentage amount are treated as becoming due and payable in instalments, the amount treated as becoming due and payable on any instalment payment date shall be calculated in accordance with paragraphs (6) to (8) and by reference to the formula–

$$\frac{3 \times CTI}{n}$$

where–

CTI is the amount of the company's total liability for that accounting period or the specified percentage amount less any amounts falling within regulation 5A(1), and

n is the number of whole months falling within that accounting period plus the appropriate decimal.

5(6) The amount treated as becoming due and payable on the first instalment payment date is the smaller of CTI and the amount resulting from the formula specified in paragraph (5).

5(7) The amount treated as becoming due and payable on each subsequent instalment payment date other than the final instalment payment date is the smaller of–

(a) the balance of the company's total liability for that accounting period or of the specified percentage amount carried forward from the immediately preceding instalment payment date, and

(b) the amount resulting from the formula specified in paragraph (5).

5(8) The amount treated as becoming due and payable on the final instalment payment date is the balance of the company's total liability for that accounting period or of the specified percentage amount carried forward from the immediately preceding instalment payment date.

5(9) In this regulation–

"**the appropriate decimal**" is a decimal, calculated to two places rounded arithmetically where necessary, representing the number of days in the accounting period falling outside the whole months falling within that period and corresponding to the fraction of which the numerator is the number of those days and the denominator is 30;

"**the specified percentage amount**" means an amount equal to the percentage specified in regulation 4(1)(a), (2)(a) or (3)(a), as the case may be.

History – In reg. 5(1) the words ", (3)(b) or regulation 5A" substituted for the words "or (3)(b)" by SI 2005/889, reg. 3(2), with effect in relation to accounting periods of companies ending on or after 1 July 2005, but do not affect any amount which is treated as becoming due and payable, by virtue of SI 1998/3175 as it had effect before 13 April 2005, before the commencement date. In reg. 5(5) the words "less any amounts falling within regulation 5A(1)" inserted by SI 2005/889, reg. 3(3), with effect in relation to accounting periods of companies ending on or after 1 July 2005, but do not affect any amount which is treated as becoming due and payable, by virtue of SI 1998/3175 as it had effect before 13 April 2005, before the commencement date.

Other material – Tax Bulletin TB02/00-2: article on aspects of quarterly instalment payments (QIPs): over and under-payments of early QIPs.

INSTALMENT PAYMENTS – RING FENCE PROFITS AND ADJUSTED RING FENCE PROFITS

5A(1) This regulation applies to amounts in respect of the liability to corporation tax and supplementary charge in relation to the ring fence profits and adjusted ring fence profits of a large company for an accounting period ("the ring fence amount").

5A(2) The ring fence amount shall be treated as becoming due and payable in instalments (not exceeding three) on the dates specified in paragraph (3).

5A(3) The first instalment payment shall be treated, subject to paragraph (4), as being due and payable on the date which is six months and 13 days from the start of the accounting period.

The final instalment payment shall be treated as being due and payable on the date which is 14 days from the end of the accounting period.

An additional instalment payment shall, where the length of the accounting period so allows, be treated as becoming due and payable on the date which is three months after the date of the first instalment payment.

5A(4) Where the length of the accounting period is such that the date which is 14 days from the end of the accounting period falls earlier than the date which is six months and 13 days from the start of the accounting period, the ring fence amount shall be treated as becoming due and payable on the date which is 14 days from the end of the accounting period.

5A(5) Where in accordance with paragraph (2) ring fence amounts are treated as becoming due and payable in instalments, the amount treated as becoming due and payable on any instalment payment date shall be calculated in accordance with paragraphs (6) to (8) and by reference to the formula–

(a)   in relation to an accounting period of a large company ending on or after 1st July 2005 but before 1st July 2006, $3 \times RFA/n$, and

(b)   thereafter, $4 \times RFA/n$

where–

RFA is the ring fence amount, and

n is the number of whole months falling within that accounting period plus the appropriate decimal.

5A(6) The amount treated as becoming due and payable on the first instalment payment date is the smaller of RFA and the amount resulting from the formula in paragraph (5).

5A(7) The amount treated as becoming due and payable on any subsequent instalment payment date other than the final instalment payment date is the smaller of–

(a)   the balance of the company's ring fence amount for that accounting period carried forward from the immediately preceding instalment payment date, and

(b)   the amount resulting from the formula specified in paragraph (5).

5A(8) The amount treated as becoming due and payable on the final instalment payment date is the balance of the company's ring fence amount for that accounting period carried forward from the immediately preceding instalment payment date.

5A(9) In this regulation–

"**adjusted ring fence profits**" has the meaning given in section 330(2) of CTA 2010;

"**the appropriate decimal**" is a decimal, calculated to two places rounded arithmetically where necessary, representing the number of days in the accounting period falling outside the whole months falling within that period and corresponding to the fraction of which the numerator is the number of those days and the denominator is 30;

"**ring fence profits**" has the meaning given in section 276 of CTA 2010;

"**supplementary charge**" means the charge imposed by section 330(1) of CTA 2010.

History – In reg. 5A(9), in the definition of "adjusted ring fence profits" the words "330(2) of CTA 2010" substituted for the words "501A(2) of the Taxes Act" by SI 2011/1785, reg. 6(2)(a), with effect from 11 August 2011 in relation to accounting periods ending on or after 1 January 2011.
In reg. 5A(9), in the definition of "ring fence profits" the words "276 of CTA 2010" substituted for the words "502(1) of the Taxes Act" by SI 2011/1785, reg. 6(2)(b), with effect from 11 August 2011 in relation to accounting periods ending on or after 1 January 2011.
In reg. 5A(9), in the definition of "supplementary charge" the words "330(1) of CTA 2010" substituted for the words "501A(1) of the Taxes Act" by SI 2011/1785, reg. 6(2)(c), with effect from 11 August 2011 in relation to accounting periods ending on or after 1 January 2011.
Reg. 5A inserted by SI 2005/889, reg. 4, with effect in relation to accounting periods of companies ending on or after 1 July 2005, but do not affect any amount which is treated as becoming due and payable, by virtue of SI 1998/3175 as it had effect before 13 April 2005, before the commencement date.

INSTALMENT PAYMENTS – THE BANK LEVY – ANTI-AVOIDANCE

5B(1) Paragraphs (3) and (4) apply if on or after 31st March 2011 there is a relevant amendment–

(a) in relation to the accounting period of an entity (E) which is the chargeable member; or

(b) in relation to the accounting periods of E and any other chargeable member; and

as a consequence of the relevant amendment there is no chargeable member which meets, or would meet, the requirements of paragraph 54(3) or (5) of Schedule 19 (meaning of the responsible member) at the end of the chargeable period.

5B(2) In relation to E and, where relevant, any other chargeable member a relevant amendment is an alteration to–

(a) the ending of an accounting period, as a result of an event referred to in section 10 (end of accounting period) or section 12 (companies being wound up) of CTA 2009; or

(b) the commencement of an accounting period, as a result of an event referred to in section 9 (beginning of an accounting period) or section 12(5) of CTA 2009;

the main purpose, or one of the main purposes, of which is to obtain a tax advantage.

5B(3) Where this paragraph applies for the purposes of ascertaining the dates on which instalment payments are treated as becoming due and payable in accordance with regulation 5(3), the applicable accounting period of the entity that is the responsible member in relation to the chargeable period is to be treated as beginning and ending on the dates on which the chargeable period begins and ends ("the assumption").

5B(4) Where paragraph (3) applies, the assumption will apply in relation to any applicable accounting periods that relate to a subsequent chargeable period where there is no chargeable member which meets the requirements of paragraph 54(3) or (5) of Schedule 19.

5B(5) In this regulation–

"**tax advantage**" has the same meaning as in section 1139 of CTA 2010; and

"**the chargeable member**" has the meaning given by paragraph 54(2) of Schedule 19.

History – Reg. 5B inserted by SI 2011/1785, reg. 7, with effect from 11 August 2011 in relation to accounting periods ending on or after 1 January 2011.

REPAYMENT OF AMOUNTS IN RESPECT OF A LARGE COMPANY'S TOTAL LIABILITY FOR AN ACCOUNTING PERIOD

6(1) This regulation applies where a large company–

(a) has paid an amount or amounts by way of instalments in respect of its total liability for an accounting period in accordance with regulation 4A, 4B, 4C, 4D, 5, 5A or 5B (as the case may be), and

(b) subsequently has grounds for believing that, by reason of a change in the circumstances of the company since the payment or payments were made–

(i) the amount of its total liability for that period is likely to be less than previously calculated, and

(ii) the aggregate amount so paid exceeds the aggregate amount ("the revised aggregate amount") that would have been treated as becoming due and payable by the relevant date having regard to the revised calculation of that liability.

6(2) The company may, by notice given to an officer of Revenue and Customs, make a claim to an officer of Revenue and Customs for the repayment of so much of the aggregate amount so paid as in the company's view exceeds the revised aggregate amount.

6(3) The notice under paragraph (2) must state–

(a)   the amount which the company considers should be repaid, and

(b)   the grounds referred to in paragraph (1)(b).

6(4) If the company has appealed against an amendment of an assessment, or an assessment, in respect of the amount of its total liability for the accounting period concerned, and the appeal has not been finally determined, it may apply to the tribunal to whom the appeal stands referred for a determination of the amount which should be repaid to the company pending determination of the amount of its total liability for that accounting period.

6(5) Any claim under paragraph (2) or application under paragraph (4) is to be subject to the relevant provisions of Part 5 of the Taxes Management Act 1970 (see, in particular, section 48(2)(b) of that Act).

6(6) If the company makes an application under section 55(3) or (4) of the Management Act (application to postpone payment pending determination of appeal), that application may be combined with an application under paragraph (4).

6(7) In paragraph (1)(b) **"the relevant date"** means the date on which a claim under paragraph (2) is made.

6(8) Section 59DA of the Management Act (claim for repayment in advance of liability being established) shall not apply in any case where this regulation applies.

History – In reg. 6(1)(a), the words "4A, 4B, 4C, 4D, 5, 5A or 5B (as the case may be)" substituted for "5 or 5A" by SI 2011/1785, reg. 8(2), with effect from 11 August 2011 in relation to accounting periods ending on or after 1 January 2011.
In reg. 6(1)(a) the words "or 5A" inserted by SI 2005/889, reg. 5, with effect in relation to accounting periods of companies ending on or after 1 July 2005, but do not affect any amount which is treated as becoming due and payable, by virtue of SI 1998/3175 as it had effect before 13 April 2005, before the commencement date.
In reg. 6(2), the words "Revenue and Customs" substituted for the words "the Board" in both places by SI 2011/1785, reg. 8(3), with effect from 11 August 2011 in relation to accounting periods ending on or after 1 January 2011.
In reg. 6(4), "tribunal" substituted for "Commissioners" by SI 2009/56, art. 3(2) and Sch. 2, para. 49(2), operative from 1 April 2009 subject to transitional and saving provisions in SI 2009/56, Sch. 3.
Reg. 6(5) substituted by SI 2009/56, art. 3(2) and Sch. 2, para. 49(3), operative from 1 April 2009 subject to transitional and saving provisions in SI 2009/56, Sch. 3. Former reg. 6(5) read as follows:

> "**6(5)** Any claim under paragraph (2) or application under paragraph (4) shall be heard and determined in the same way as an appeal.".

Cross references – FA 2013, s. 202(11): references to regulation 4A, 4B, 4C, 4D, 5, 5A or 5B in reg. 6(1)(a) to be read as including a reference to FA 2013, s. 202(6)–(10) (bank levy).

Other material – Tax Bulletin TB02/00-2: article on aspects of quarterly instalment payments (QIPs): over and under-payments of early QIPs.

ALLOCATION OF PAYMENTS

6A(1) This regulation applies where–

(a)   an entity (E) is either–

       (i)   the relevant entity; or

       (ii)   the responsible member; and

(b)   there has been an underpayment of E's total liability for an applicable accounting period.

6A(2) Any payment made by E in respect of that applicable accounting period shall be treated–

(a)   as a payment in respect of any amount of the bank levy which is unpaid for the applicable accounting period; and

(b)   to the extent that the payment exceeds the unpaid amount of the bank levy, as a payment in respect of corporation tax other than the bank levy for the applicable accounting period.

6A(3) Whether there has been an underpayment of E's total liability shall be ascertained in accordance with the provisions of Schedule 18.

History – Reg. 6A inserted by SI 2011/1785, reg. 9, with effect from 11 August 2011 in relation to accounting periods ending on or after 1 January 2011.

INTEREST ON UNPAID AMOUNTS OF A LARGE COMPANY'S TOTAL LIABILITY FOR AN ACCOUNTING PERIOD

7(1) Section 87A of the Management Act shall apply in relation to any unpaid amount in respect of the total liability of a large company for an accounting period, with the modifications specified in paragraphs (2) to (5).

7(2) After subsection (1) there shall be inserted the following subsection–

       "**87A(1A)** An amount or amounts treated as becoming due and payable in respect of the total liability of a large company for an accounting period in accordance with regulation 4A, 4B, 4C, 4D, 5, 5A or 5B (as the case may be) of the Corporation Tax (Instalment Payments) Regulations

1998 shall carry interest at the rate applicable under section 178 of the Finance Act 1989 from the date or dates specified in the regulation in question as the date or dates when that amount or those amounts are treated as becoming due and payable until payment."

7(3) In subsection (2)–

(a) for the words "Subsection (1) above applies" there shall be substituted "Subsections (1) and (1A) above apply";

(b) for the words "that subsection" there shall be substituted "those subsections".

7(4) In subsection (3) there shall be added at the end the words ", and the reference in subsection (1A) above to the date or dates when an amount or amounts are treated as becoming due and payable in respect of the total liability of a large company for an accounting period is a reference to the date or dates when that amount or those amounts are treated as having become due and payable by the company".

7(5) After subsection (9) there shall be added–

"**87A(10)** In subsections (1A) and (3) above **"large company"** has the meaning given by regulation 3 of the Corporation Tax (Instalment Payments) Regulations 1998."

History – In reg. 7(2), in the inserted text, the words "4A, 4B, 4C, 4D, 5, 5A or 5B (as the case may be)" substituted for "5 or 5A" by SI 2011/1785, reg. 10(a), with effect from 11 August 2011 in relation to accounting periods ending on or after 1 January 2011. In reg. 7(2), in the inserted text, the words "the regulation in question" substituted for the words "that regulation" by SI 2011/1785, reg. 10(b), with effect from 11 August 2011 in relation to accounting periods ending on or after 1 January 2011. In reg. 7(2), in para. (1A) notionally inserted into TMA 1970, s. 87A, the words "or 5A" inserted by SI 2005/889, reg. 6, with effect in relation to accounting periods of companies ending on or after 1 July 2005, but do not affect any amount which is treated as becoming due and payable, by virtue of SI 1998/3175 as it had effect before 13 April 2005, before the commencement date.

Cross references – FA 2013, s. 202(11): references to regulation 4A, 4B, 4C, 4D, 5, 5A or 5B in reg. 7(2) to be read as including a reference to FA 2013, s. 202(6)–(10) and reference to "the regulation in question" to be read accordingly (bank levy).

Other material – Tax Bulletin TB02/00-2: article on aspects of quarterly instalment payments (QIPs): over and under-payments of early QIPs.

INTEREST ON OVERPAID AMOUNTS OF A COMPANY'S TOTAL LIABILITY FOR AN ACCOUNTING PERIOD

8(1) Section 826 of the Taxes Act shall apply in relation to–

(a) an amount or amounts paid by a large company in accordance with regulation 4A, 4B, 4C, 4D, 5, 5A or 5B, in respect of its total liability for an accounting period, and

(b) an amount or amounts paid by a company that is not a large company in an accounting period in respect of its total liability for that accounting period, where the payment is made prior to the day following the expiry of nine months from the end of that accounting period,

with the modifications specified in paragraphs (2) and (3).

8(2) In subsection (1)–

(a) after paragraph (c) there shall be inserted "or

    (ca) the total amount paid by a large company (as defined in regulation 3 of the Corporation Tax (Instalment Payment) Regulations 1998) up to a point in time in respect of its total liability for an accounting period in accordance with regulation 4A, 4B, 4C, 4D, 5, 5A or 5B of those Regulations exceeds the amount that is treated as having become due and payable by the company for that period at that time in accordance with that regulation, or

    (cb) an amount paid by a company that is not a large company in an accounting period in respect of the amount of its total liability for that period is paid prior to the day following the expiry of nine months from the end of that period ("the normal due date",)";

(b) for the words "the repayment or payment shall" there shall be substituted the words "or, in a case to which paragraph (ca) above applies, until the date on which the excess amount arising as mentioned in that paragraph is extinguished or, in a case to which paragraph (cb) above applies, until the normal due date, the repayment or payment or excess amount shall".

8(3) After subsection (3) there shall be inserted–

"**826(3ZA)** In relation to an excess amount in respect of a company's total liability arising as mentioned in subsection (1)(ca) above, the material date is the date on which the first instalment payment for the accounting period concerned is treated as becoming due as mentioned in regulation regulation 4A, 4B, 4C, 4D, 5(3), 5A(3) or 5B(3) of the Corporation Tax (Instalment Payments) Regulations 1998 or, if later, the date on which the excess amount arises.

826(3ZB) In relation to a case falling within subsection (1)(cb) above–

    (a) if the payment for the accounting period concerned was made on or before the date which, if the company had been a large company, would have been the date on which the first instalment payment for that accounting period would have been treated as becoming due as mentioned in regulation 5(3) or 5A(3) of the Regulations referred to in subsection (3ZA) above, the material date is that date, or

(b)   if the payment for the accounting period concerned was made later than the date referred to in paragraph (a) above, the material date is the date on which that payment was made."

History – In reg. 8(1), the words "4A, 4B, 4C, 4D, 5, 5A or 5B," substituted for "5 or 5A" by SI 2011/1785, reg. 11(2), with effect from 11 August 2011 in relation to accounting periods ending on or after 1 January 2011.
In reg. 8(1)(a) the words "or 5A" inserted by SI 2005/889, reg. 7(2), with effect in relation to accounting periods of companies ending on or after 1 July 2005, but do not affect any amount which is treated as becoming due and payable, by virtue of SI 1998/3175 as it had effect before 13 April 2005, before the commencement date.
In reg. 8(2)(a), the inserted para. (ca) renamed (previously named (d)) and the words "4A, 4B, 4C, 4D, 5, 5A or 5B" substituted for "5 or 5A" by SI 2011/1785, reg. 11(3)(a)(i), with effect from 11 August 2011 in relation to accounting periods ending on or after 1 January 2011.
In reg. 8(2)(a), in former para. (d) notionally inserted into ICTA 1988, s. 826, the words "or 5A" inserted by SI 2005/889, reg. 7(3), with effect in relation to accounting periods of companies ending on or after 1 July 2005, but do not affect any amount which is treated as becoming due and payable, by virtue of SI 1998/3175 as it had effect before 13 April 2005, before the commencement date.
In reg. 8(2)(a), the inserted para. (cb) renamed (previously named (e)) by SI 2011/1785, reg. 11(3)(a)(ii), with effect from 11 August 2011 in relation to accounting periods ending on or after 1 January 2011.
In reg. 8(2)(b), "(ca)" substituted for "(d)" by SI 2011/1785, reg. 11(3)(b)(i), with effect from 11 August 2011 in relation to accounting periods ending on or after 1 January 2011.
In reg. 8(2)(b), "(cb)" substituted for "(e)" by SI 2011/1785, reg. 11(3)(b)(ii), with effect from 11 August 2011 in relation to accounting periods ending on or after 1 January 2011.
In reg. 8(3), the inserted subsection (3ZA) renamed (previously named (3A)), and "(1)(ca)" substituted for "(1)(d)", and "4A, 4B, 4C, 4D, 5(3), 5A(3) or 5B(3)" substituted for "5(3) or 5A(3)" by SI 2011/1785, reg. 11(4)(a), with effect from 11 August 2011 in relation to accounting periods ending on or after 1 January 2011.
In reg. 8(3), the inserted subsection (3ZB) renamed (previously named (3B)), and "(1)(cb)" substituted for "(1)(e)", and "(3ZA)" substituted for "(3A)" by SI 2011/1785, reg. 11(4)(b), with effect from 11 August 2011 in relation to accounting periods ending on or after 1 January 2011.
In reg. 8(3), in former subsections (3A) and (3B) notionally inserted into ICTA 1988, s. 826, the words "or 5A(3)" inserted by SI 2005/889, reg. 7(4), with effect in relation to accounting periods of companies ending on or after 1 July 2005, but do not affect any amount which is treated as becoming due and payable, by virtue of SI 1998/3175 as it had effect before 13 April 2005, before the commencement date.

Cross references – FA 2013, s. 202(11): references to regulation 4A, 4B, 4C, 4D, 5, 5A or 5B in reg. 8(1)(a) and (2)(a) to be read as including a reference to FA 2013, s. 202(6)–(10) and the reference in reg. 8(2) to "that regulation" to be read accordingly (bank levy).

Other material – Tax Bulletin TB02/00-2: article on aspects of quarterly instalment payments (QIPs): over and under-payments of early QIPs.

CONSEQUENTIAL AMENDMENT OF CHAPTER 4 OF PART 22 OF CTA 2010

9(1)   Chapter 4 of Part 22 of CTA 2010 (surrender of tax refund within a group) applies with the modifications specified in paragraphs (2) to (5) in any case where a tax refund is due to be made to the surrendering company in respect of an amount paid in respect of its total liability for an accounting period and–

(a)   either the surrendering company or the recipient company referred to in that Chapter is a large company as respects that accounting period; or

(b)   both the surrendering company and the recipient company referred to in that Chapter are large companies as respects that accounting period.

9(2)   In section 963 (power to surrender tax refund), after subsection (2) insert–

"**963(2A)**   If, and to the extent that, the tax refund surrendered is within subsection (4)(c) and is of an amount paid in respect of the surrendering company's bank levy liability for the accounting period, the requirement in subsection (2)(b) is to be read as a requirement that the surrendering company and the recipient company are both entities which are jointly and severally liable for the surrendering company's bank levy liability for that period in accordance with paragraph 53 of Schedule 19 to the Finance Act 2011.

963(2B)   In subsection (2A) the reference to the surrendering company's bank levy liability for the accounting period is to any liability within paragraph 53(8) of that Schedule which the company has for that accounting period."

9(3)   In subsection (4) of that section–

(a)   omit the "or" at the end of paragraph (a); and

(b)   after paragraph (b) insert–

", or

(c)   the repayment in whole or in part of any amount paid by way of an instalment under the Corporation Tax (Instalment Payments) Regulations 1998 in respect of the company's total liability for the period (within the meaning of regulation 2(3))."

9(4)   In section 964 (effects of surrender of tax refund), in subsection (6), after "refund" insert "other than a refund of instalment corporation tax".

9(5)   After that subsection insert–

"**964(6A)**   For the purpose of this Chapter **"the relevant date"**, in relation to a refund of instalment corporation tax, means–

(a)   in so far as the refund falls to be treated in accordance with subsections (6C) to (6E) as consisting of a repayment of the whole or any part of a payment made on or before the earliest due date, that date, and

(b)   in so far as the refund falls to be treated in accordance with those subsections as consisting of the repayment of the whole or any part of a payment made after the earliest due date, the date on which the payment was made.

964(6B)   For the purposes of subsection (6A), the earliest due date, in relation to a refund of instalment corporation tax, is–

(a)   where the surrendering company is a large company for the relevant accounting period, the earliest date on which any amount is treated as having become due and payable by that company under regulation 4A, 4B, 4C, 4D, 5, 5A or 5B of the Corporation Tax (Instalment Payments) Regulations 1998 in respect of that company's total liability for that period, and

(b)   where the surrendering company is not a large company for that accounting period, the date that would have been the earliest due date under paragraph (a) had it been a large company for that period.

964(6C)   For the purposes of subsection (6A), at the same time as giving notice under section 963(2) in the case of any refund of instalment corporation tax relating to any accounting period, the surrendering company must also give notice to an officer of Revenue and Customs identifying the extent to which it requires the refund to be treated as consisting of amounts comprised in any payment or payments made for that period.

964(6D)   Where, in a case to which subsection (6C) applies, an officer of Revenue and Customs notifies the surrendering company that the amount of the refund of instalment corporation tax relating to the accounting period is less than the aggregate of the amounts identified under that subsection, the company must, no later than 30 days after the notification, give a revised notice under that subsection to the officer of Revenue and Customs.

964(6E)   Where in a case to which subsection (6D) applies–

(a)   a notification has been given to the surrendering company under that subsection, and

(b)   the surrendering company does not give a revised notice in accordance with the requirements of that subsection,

the same consequences follow as if a notice had not been given in accordance with section 963(2) in relation to the refund.

964(6F)   In this section–

(a)   references to a refund of instalment corporation tax are references to any refund of tax for any accounting period which falls in relation to that accounting period within paragraph (c) of the definition of "tax refund" in section 963(4),

(b)   **"large company"** has the same meaning as in regulation 3 of the Corporation Tax (Instalment Payments) Regulations 1998, and

(c)   references to the total liability of a company for an accounting period are to be construed in accordance with regulation 2(3) of those Regulations.""

History – Reg. 9 substituted by SI 2011/1785, reg. 12, with effect from 11 August 2011 in relation to accounting periods ending on or after 1 January 2011.

Cross references – FA 2013, s. 202(11): references to regulation 4A, 4B, 4C, 4D, 5, 5A or 5B in reg. 9(5) to be read as including a reference to FA 2013, s. 202(6)–(10) and reference in reg. 9(3) the reference to SI 1998/3175 is to be read as including a reference to FA 2013, s. 202(6)–(10) (bank levy).

ENTITY NOT LIABLE TO THE BANK LEVY

9A(1)   This regulation applies where–

(a)   a relevant entity (E) has made a payment for an accounting period which includes an amount in respect of the bank levy for the chargeable period; but

(b)   another member of the relevant group (OM) is the responsible member for that chargeable period.

9A(2) Where this regulation applies–

(a) no repayment of the amount paid by E in respect of the bank levy shall be made to or be due to E;

(b) E shall not be entitled, as a result of the payment of the amount in respect of the bank levy, to set off or otherwise treat as discharged any liability to corporation tax or to any other tax or duty for any period;

(c) the amount of the payment made by E in respect of the bank levy for the chargeable period shall be treated as if it were a payment made by OM, on the date on which the payment was made by E; and

(d) if OM does not have an applicable accounting period which is the same as the chargeable period,

  (i) the payment made by E shall be treated as a payment of an amount of the bank levy due and payable in respect of the earliest instalment payment in relation to the earliest applicable accounting period of OM for the chargeable period; and

  (ii) the balance, if any, shall be treated as a payment of the bank levy due and payable in respect of OM's next instalment payment in relation to the earliest applicable accounting period and so on in relation to that applicable accounting period and any subsequent applicable accounting period.

9A(3) In paragraph (2)(d) the reference to an applicable accounting period being the same as the chargeable period shall be construed in accordance with paragraph 54 of Schedule 19.

History – Reg. 9A inserted by SI 2011/1785, reg. 13, with effect from 11 August 2011 in relation to accounting periods ending on or after 1 January 2011.

INFORMATION TO BE PROVIDED TO HMRC

History – In the heading to reg. 10, "HMRC" substituted for "The Board" by SI 2011/1785, reg. 14(2), with effect from 11 August 2011 in relation to accounting periods ending on or after 1 January 2011.

10(1) HMRC may, at any time following the relevant date, by notice require any company to furnish them, within such time (not being less than thirty days) as may be provided by the notice–

(a) such information relating to the computation of any amount paid in respect of the company's total liability for an accounting period in accordance with regulation 4A, 4B, 4C, 4D, 5, 5A or 5B, as the case may be, as they may reasonably require for ascertaining whether the amount of the payment was consistent with the quality and quantity of the information available to the company, at the time the payment was due, regarding its total liability for that period;

(b) such information as they may reasonably require for ascertaining the reasons for non-payment by the company at any time in accordance with regulation 4A, 4B, 4C, 4D, 5, 5A or 5B, as the case may be, of any amount in respect of the company's total liability for an accounting period;

(c) such information as they may reasonably require for ascertaining whether a claim for repayment of an amount under regulation 6(2) was properly made.

10(2) In paragraph (1) **"the relevant date"** means the date specified in paragraph 14(1) of Schedule 18 as the filing date for the company tax return for the accounting period concerned.

History – In reg. 10(1), "HMRC" substituted for "The Board" by SI 2011/1785, reg. 14(3)(a), with effect from 11 August 2011 in relation to accounting periods ending on or after 1 January 2011.
In reg. 10(1), in both places, the words "4A, 4B, 4C, 4D, 5, 5A or 5B, as the case may be," substituted for "5 or 5A" by SI 2011/1785, reg. 14(3)(b), with effect from 11 August 2011 in relation to accounting periods ending on or after 1 January 2011.
In reg. 10(1)(a) and (b) the words "or 5A" inserted by SI 2005/889, reg. 9, with effect in relation to accounting periods of companies ending on or after 1 July 2005, but do not affect any amount which is treated as becoming due and payable, by virtue of SI 1998/3175 as it had effect before 13 April 2005, before the commencement date.

Cross references – FA 2013, s. 202(11): references to regulation 4A, 4B, 4C, 4D, 5, 5A or 5B in reg. 10(1) to be read as including a reference to FA 2013, s. 202(6)–(10) (bank levy).

ADDITIONAL INFORMATION TO BE PROVIDED TO HMRC WHERE THE LARGE COMPANY IS AN ENTITY WHICH IS RESPONSIBLE FOR THE PAYMENT OF THE BANK LEVY

10A(1) This regulation applies if the relevant entity or the responsible member ("E") makes an instalment payment which includes an amount in respect of the bank levy.

10A(2) Subject to paragraph (4), E must provide written notice (a "quantification notice") identifying the amount of the instalment payment which is in respect of the bank levy.

10A(3) A quantification notice must be given to an officer of Revenue and Customs on or before the date on which payment is made.

10A(4)   Where E is a member of a group payment arrangement under section 59F of the Management Act (arrangements for paying tax on behalf of group members), but E is not the member which is responsible for discharging the liability of the group under that arrangement–

(a)   E shall provide the quantification notice to the member (M) which, in accordance with the group payment arrangement, is responsible for discharging the liability of all the members of the group; and

(b)   accordingly M shall be responsible for providing the quantification notice to the officer of Revenue and Customs as required by paragraphs (2) and (3) and for the purposes of paragraph (5).

10A(5)   The requirement to provide a quantification notice under this regulation shall be treated as a requirement to comply with an information notice for the purposes of Part 7 of Schedule 36 to the Finance Act 2008 (information and inspection powers).

History – Reg. 10A inserted by SI 2011/1785, reg. 15, with effect from 11 August 2011 in relation to accounting periods ending on or after 1 January 2011.

PRODUCTION OF RECORDS

11(1)   HMRC may, at any time following the relevant date, by notice require a company to produce, within such time (not being less than thirty days) as may be provided by the notice–

(a)   all such books, documents and other records in its possession or power relating to the computation of any amount paid in respect of the company's total liability for an accounting period in accordance with regulation 4A, 4B, 4C, 4D, 5, 5A or 5B (as the case may be) as they may reasonably require for ascertaining whether the amount of the payment was consistent with the quality and quantity of the information available to the company, at the time the payment was due, regarding its total liability for that period;

(b)   all such books, documents and other records in its possession or power as they may reasonably require for ascertaining the reasons for non-payment by the company at any time in accordance with regulation 4A, 4B, 4C, 4D, 5, 5A or 5B (as the case may be) of any amount in respect of the company's total liability for an accounting period;

(c)   all such books, documents and other records in its possession or power as they may reasonably require for ascertaining whether a claim for repayment of an amount under regulation 6(2) was properly made.

11(2)   In complying with a notice under paragraph (1) copies of books, documents and other records may be produced instead of originals, but–

(a)   the copies must be photographic or other facsimiles, and

(b)   an officer of Revenue and Customs may require the original to be made available for inspection in accordance with regulation 12.

11(3)   In paragraph (1) **"the relevant date"** has the same meaning as in regulation 10.

History – In reg. 11(1), "HMRC" substituted for "the Board" by SI 2011/1785, reg. 16(2)(a), with effect from 11 August 2011 in relation to accounting periods ending on or after 1 January 2011.
In reg. 11(1), in both places, "4A, 4B, 4C, 4D, 5, 5A or 5B (as the case may be)" substituted for "5 or 5A" by SI 2011/1785, reg. 16(2)(b), with effect from 11 August 2011 in relation to accounting periods ending on or after 1 January 2011.
In reg. 11(1)(a) and (b) the words "or 5A" inserted by SI 2005/889, reg. 10, with effect in relation to accounting periods of companies ending on or after 1 July 2005, but do not affect any amount which is treated as becoming due and payable, by virtue of SI 1998/3175 as it had effect before 13 April 2005, before the commencement date.
In reg. 11(2)(b), the words "Revenue and Customs" substituted for "the Board" by SI 2011/1785, reg. 16(3), with effect from 11 August 2011 in relation to accounting periods ending on or after 1 January 2011.

Cross references – FA 2013, s. 202(11): references to regulation 4A, 4B, 4C, 4D, 5, 5A or 5B in reg. 11(1) to be read as including a reference to FA 2013, s. 202(6)–(10) (bank levy).

INSPECTION OF RECORDS

12(1)   An officer of Revenue and Customs authorised to do so may, at any time following the relevant date, by notice require a company to make available for inspection, at such time as that officer may reasonably require, all such books, documents and other records in its possession or power as could be required to be produced by notice under regulation 11.

12(2)   Where records are maintained by computer the officer making the inspection shall be provided by the company with all the facilities necessary for obtaining information from them.

12(3)   In paragraph (1) **"the relevant date"** has the same meaning as in regulation 10.

History – In reg. 12(1), the words "of Revenue and Customs" substituted for the words "of the Board" by SI 2011/1785, reg. 17(a), with effect from 11 August 2011 in relation to accounting periods ending on or after 1 January 2011.
In reg. 12(1), the words "by the Board", which appeared after the words "by notice", omitted by SI 2011/1785, reg. 17(b), with effect from 11 August 2011 in relation to accounting periods ending on or after 1 January 2011.
Para. 12(1) amended by SI 1999/1929, reg. 3, with effect in relation to accounting periods of companies ending on or after 1 July 1999.

PENALTY FOR UNPAID TAX

13   The circumstances prescribed for the purposes of section 59E(4) of the Management Act (penalty not exceeding twice the amount of interest charged by virtue of regulation 7 on any unpaid amount in respect of the total liability of a company for an accounting period) are where–

(a)   the company, or a person acting on its behalf, deliberately or recklessly fails to pay the amount in question in accordance with regulation 4A, 4B, 4C, 4D, 5, 5A or 5B (as the case may be);

(b)   the company, or a person acting on its behalf fraudulently or negligently makes a claim for repayment of an amount under regulation 6(2).

History – In reg. 13(a), the words "4A, 4B, 4C, 4D, 5, 5A or 5B (as the case may be)" substituted for "5 or 5A" by SI 2011/1785, reg. 18, with effect from 11 August 2011 in relation to accounting periods ending on or after 1 January 2011.

In reg. 13(a) the words "or 5A" inserted by SI 2005/889, reg. 11, with effect in relation to accounting periods of companies ending on or after 1 July 2005, but do not affect any amount which is treated as becoming due and payable, by virtue of SI 1998/3175 as it had effect before 13 April 2005, before the commencement date.

Cross references – FA 2013, s. 202(11): references to regulation 4A, 4B, 4C, 4D, 5, 5A or 5B in reg. 13 to be read as including a reference to FA 2013, s. 202(6)–(10) (bank levy).

ANTI-AVOIDANCE PROVISION

14   [Omitted by SI 2011/1785, reg. 19(a).]

History – Reg. 14 omitted by SI 2011/1785, reg. 19(a), with effect from 11 August 2011 in relation to accounting periods ending on or after 1 January 2011.

INSURANCE COMPANIES AND FRIENDLY SOCIETIES – SUPPLEMENTARY PROVISION

15   [Omitted by SI 2011/1785, reg. 19(b).]

History – Reg. 15 omitted by SI 2011/1785, reg. 19(b), with effect from 11 August 2011 in relation to accounting periods ending on or after 1 January 2011.

EUROPEAN SINGLE CURRENCY (TAXES) REGULATIONS 1998

(SI 1998/3177 as amended by SI 2000/3315, SI 2002/1971, SI 2004/2310, SI 2007/2484 and SI 2008/2647)

Made on 17 February 1998 and laid before the House of Commons on 17 February 1998. Operative from 1 January 1999.

ARRANGEMENT OF REGULATIONS

REGULATION

PART I – INTRODUCTORY

CITATION AND COMMENCEMENT

1 These Regulations may be cited as the European Single Currency (Taxes) Regulations 1998 and shall come into force on 1st January 1999.

INTERPRETATION

2(1) In these Regulations unless the context otherwise requires–

"**commodity or financial futures**" has the meaning given by subsection (2)(a) of section 143 of the 1992 Act, and references in these Regulations to commodity or financial futures include references to a commodity or financial futures contract referred to in subsection (7)(a) or (b);

"**debt**" other than a debt on a security, includes a debt owed by a bank which is not in sterling and which is represented by a sum standing to the credit of a person in an account in the bank;

"**derivative**" means any commodity or financial futures or an option;

"**ecu**" shall be construed in accordance with section 95(5) of the Finance Act 1993;

"euro" means the single currency adopted or proposed to be adopted as its currency by a member State in accordance with the Treaty establishing the European Community;

"euroconversion" has the meaning given by regulation 3;

"member State" means a member State other than the United Kingdom;

"participating member State" means a member State that adopts the euro as its currency;

"reconventioning" in relation to a relevant asset means a change, consequent on simple redenomination, in the terms of the asset as a result of which the new terms become aligned to the prevailing terms of equivalent marketable relevant assets denominated in euro;

"relevant asset" means a debt (whether or not a debt on a security), an option, or any commodity or financial futures;

"renominalisation" in relation to a relevant asset means a change, consequent on simple redenomination, in the minimum nominal amount in which the asset can be held or traded to a new round amount;

"security" has the meaning given by section 132(3)(b) of the 1992 Act;

"simple redenomination" means the conversion of the currency in which an asset, liability, contract or instrument is expressed from the currency of a participating member State into euro, and any rounding of the resulting amount to the nearest euro cent;

"the Taxes Act" means the Income and Corporation Taxes Act 1988;

"the 1992 Act" means the Taxation of Chargeable Gains Act 1992.

2(2)   In these Regulations references to an option, without more, are references to an option to which section 144 or 144A of the 1992 Act applies.

History – In reg. 2(1) the following definitions omitted by SI 2002/1971, reg. 3 with effect from 1 October 2002 in relation to accounting periods beginning on or after that date:

"**"long-term capital asset and long-term capital liability"** have the meaning given in relation to both those expressions by section 143(4) of the Finance Act 1993;

"qualifying contract" shall be construed in accordance with sections 147, 147A and 148 of the Finance Act 1994;".

In reg. 2(1) in the definition of "relevant asset" the words "an option" substituted for "a long-term capital asset, a long-term capital liability, an option, a qualifying contract" by SI 2002/1971, reg. 3 with effect from 1 October 2002 in relation to accounting periods beginning on or after that date.

DEFINITION OF EUROCONVERSION

3(1)   **"Euroconversion"** means–

(a)   in relation to any currency, or an amount expressed in any currency, of a participating member State, the conversion or restating of that currency or that amount into euro and any rounding of the resulting amount within a euro;

(b)   in relation to any asset, liability, contract or instrument–

(i)   the simple redenomination of that asset, liability, contract or instrument, or

(ii)   in the case of a relevant asset, the simple redenomination of that asset accompanied by either or both of renominalisation and reconventioning, or

(iii)   the substitution (whether by way of exchange, conversion, replacement or otherwise) for the asset, liability, contract or instrument of an equivalent replacement asset, liability, contract or instrument.

3(2)   An equivalent replacement asset, liability, contract or instrument means an asset, liability, contract or instrument whose amount, terms and conditions are identical to what it is reasonable to assume would be the amount, terms and conditions of the original asset, liability, contract or instrument were it to undergo a simple redenomination, or (in the case of a relevant asset) a simple redenomination accompanied by either or both of renominalisation and reconventioning.

3(3)   For the purposes of paragraphs (1) and (2) a simple redenomination is accompanied (in the case of a relevant asset) by renominalisation or reconventioning if either–

(a)   the renominalisation or reconventioning is effected simultaneously, or

(b)   it is effected within a period of time following the simple redenomination which is such as to enable it reasonably to be inferred that the renominalisation or reconventioning is associated with the simple redenomination.

PART II – DEDUCTIBILITY OF COSTS OF EUROCONVERSION OF SHARES AND OTHER SECURITIES

INTERPRETATION

4 References in this Part of these Regulations to a euroconversion in relation to shares and other securities of a company ("the original shares and other securities") are references to a euroconversion that is effected solely by the issue of shares and other securities in replacement of the original shares and other securities.

TRADING COMPANIES

5 Costs incurred in respect of a euroconversion of its shares or other securities by a company carrying on a trade shall be deductible in computing the amount of its profits chargeable to corporation tax under Case I of Schedule D as if those costs constituted money wholly and exclusively laid out or expended for the purposes of the trade within section 74(1)(a) of the Taxes Act.

INVESTMENT COMPANIES AND INSURANCE COMPANIES – DEEMED EXPENSES OF MANAGEMENT

6(1) Costs which—

(a) are incurred by an investment company or a company carrying on life assurance business in respect of a euroconversion of its shares or other securities, and

(b) except where the costs are referable to life assurance business of a company whose profits in relation to that business are charged to tax under the I minus E basis, are not deductible under regulation 5,

shall be treated in accordance with paragraph (1A).

6(1A) If the company–

(a) is a company with investment business, the costs shall be treated as expenses of management deductible under section 75 to the extent they otherwise would not be, or

(b) is one in relation to which section 76 applies, the costs shall be treated for the purposes of that section as expenses payable which fall to be brought into account at Step 1 in subsection (7) of that section to the extent that they otherwise would not be.

6(2) [Revoked by SI 2004/2310, Schedule, para. 77(c).]

6(3) [Revoked by SI 2004/2310, Schedule, para. 77(c).]

6(4) In this regulation–

"**investment company**" and "**company with investment business**" have the meanings given by section 130 of the Taxes Act;

"**life assurance business**" shall be construed in accordance with section 431(2) of the Taxes Act.

History – In reg. 6(1)(b), "under the I minus E basis" substituted for "otherwise than under Case I of Schedule D" by SI 2008/2647, reg. 2, with effect from 28 October 2008.

In reg. 6(1) the words "shall be treated in accordance with paragraph (1A)" substituted for the words "shall be treated as sums disbursed as expenses of management to which section 75(1) of the Taxes Act (deduction in computing total profits of an investment company for an accounting period) applies" by SI 2004/2310, Schedule, para. 77(2)(a), with effect in relation to accounting periods beginning on or after 1 April 2004 subject to the transitional provisions at FA 2004, s. 43 and 44.

Reg. 6(1A) inserted by SI 2004/2310, Schedule, para. 77(2)(b), with effect in relation to accounting periods beginning on or after 1 April 2004 subject to the transitional provisions at FA 2004, s. 43 and 44.

Reg. 6(2) revoked by SI 2004/2310, Schedule, para. 77(2)(c), with effect in relation to accounting periods beginning on or after 1 April 2004 subject to the transitional provisions at FA 2004, s. 43 and 44. Former reg. 6(2) read as follows:

"**6(2)** Costs incurred by a company carrying on life assurance business in respect of a euroconversion of its shares or other securities shall be deductible in computing the profits of that company chargeable to corporation tax under Case VI of Schedule D as if those costs were allowances falling to be made under Part II of the Capital Allowance Act 1990 and referred to in subsection (4) of section 434D of the Taxes Act; and accordingly those costs shall be apportioned in accordance with that subsection between the different classes of life assurance business carried on by that company."

Reg. 6(3) revoked by SI 2004/2310, Schedule, para. 77(2)(c), with effect in relation to accounting periods beginning on or after 1 April 2004 subject to the transitional provisions at FA 2004, s. 43 and 44. Former reg. 6(3) read as follows:

"**6(3)** Section 76 of the Taxes Act (expenses of management: insurance companies) shall have effect as if the reference in subsection (1)(d) of that section (disallowance of certain expenses as expenses of management) to expenses referable to different classes of life assurance business included a reference to costs apportioned to those classes of business under paragraph (2)."

In reg. 6(4) the words "and "company with investment business" have the meanings" substituted for the words "has the meaning" by SI 2004/2310, Schedule, para. 77(2)(d), with effect in relation to accounting periods beginning on or after 1 April 2004 subject to the transitional provisions at FA 2004, s. 43 and 44.

PART III – EXCHANGE GAINS AND LOSSES, INTEREST RATE AND CURRENCY CONTRACTS AND OPTIONS, DEBT CONTRACTS AND OPTIONS, AND RELEVANT DISCOUNTED SECURITIES

DEFERRAL OF UNREALISED GAINS

7   [Omitted by SI 2002/1971.]

History – Reg. 7 omitted by SI 2002/1971, reg. 4 with effect from 1 October 2002 in relation to accounting periods beginning on or after that date. Reg. 7 formerly read as follows:

> "**7(1)**   Where, as a result of a euroconversion of a long-term capital asset or of a long-term capital liability, that asset ("**the original long-term capital asset**") or that liability ("**the original long-term capital liability**") is replaced by a new long-term capital asset or a new long-term capital liability–
>
> (a)   the new long-term capital asset or the new long-term capital liability shall be treated as if it were the same asset or liability as the original long-term capital asset or the original long-term capital liability, acquired when the original long-term capital asset or the original long-term capital liability was acquired; and
>
> (b)   any gain which accrued as respects the original long-term capital asset or the original long-term capital liability for the accrual period in which the euroconversion of that asset or liability took place shall, without prejudice to regulation 2 of the Exchange Gains and Losses (Deferral of Gains and Losses) Regulations 1994 (settlement and replacement of debts), be deemed to be unrealised, and sections 139 to 143 (apart from section 143(7)) of the Finance Act 1993 shall have effect accordingly.
>
> **7(2)**   In paragraph (1) "**accrual period**" shall be construed in accordance with section 158(4) of the Finance Act 1993.".

INTEREST RATE CONTRACTS (INCLUDING OPTIONS) – CHANGE IN RATE OF INTEREST

8   [Omitted by SI 2002/1971.]

History – Reg. 8 omitted by SI 2002/1971, reg. 4 with effect from 1 October 2002 in relation to accounting periods beginning on or after that date. Reg. 8 formerly read as follows:

> "**8**   Where, as a result of the adoption of the euro by a member State–
>
> (a)   there is a change in the variable rate of interest resulting in a change in the variable rate payment specified in a contract ("**the original contract**") in accordance with subsection (2) of section 149 of the Finance Act 1994, and
>
> (b)   the change in the variable rate payment is such as to result in the rescission of the original contract and the making of a new contract,
>
> the new contract shall be treated for the purposes of that section as if it were the same contract as the original contract, made when the original contract was made.".

CURRENCY CONTRACTS (INCLUDING OPTIONS) – CHANGE IN RATE OF INTEREST

9   [Omitted by SI 2002/1971.]

History – Reg. 9 omitted by SI 2002/1971, reg. 4 with effect from 1 October 2002 in relation to accounting periods beginning on or after that date. Reg. 9 formerly read as follows:

> "**9**   Where, as a result of the adoption of the euro by a member State–
>
> (a)   there is a change in the rate of interest specified in a currency contract ("**the original contract**") in accordance with subsection (3) of section 150 of the Finance Act 1994, and
>
> (b)   the change is such as to result in the rescission of the original contract and the making of a new contract,
>
> the new contract shall be treated for the purposes of that section as if it were the same contract as the original contract, made when the original contract was made.".

CURRENCY CONTRACTS (INCLUDING OPTIONS) – CONVERSION INTO EURO

10   [Omitted by SI 2002/1971.]

History – Reg. 10 omitted by SI 2002/1971, reg. 4 with effect from 1 October 2002 in relation to accounting periods beginning on or after that date. Reg. 10 formerly read as follows:

> "**10(1)**   This regulation applies in a case where, as a result of the adoption of the euro by member States–
>
> (a)   the amounts of both the currencies specified in a currency contract referred to in section 126 of the Finance Act 1993 ("**section 126**"), or in a currency contract referred to in section 150 of the Finance Act 1994 ("**section 150**"), are converted into euro, and
>
> (b)   the effect is that the currency contract ("**the original currency contract**") is rescinded and replaced by a new contract which, but for the adoption of the euro, would have been a currency contract.
>
> **10(2)**   This regulation also applies in a case where–
>
> (a)   one of the currencies ("**the former currency**") specified in a currency contract referred to in section 126 or section 150 is in a currency other than euro and the other currency is either in euro or expressed to be in the single currency;
>
> (b)   as a result of the adoption of the euro by a member State, the former currency is converted into euro, and

(c)   the effect is that the currency contract (**"the original currency contract"**) is rescinded and replaced by a new contract which, but for the adoption of the euro, would have been a currency contract.

10(3)   In each of the cases referred to in paragraphs (1) and (2) the new contract shall be treated for the purposes of section 126 or, as the case may be, section 150 as if it were a currency contract and were the same contract as the original currency contract, made when the original currency contract was made.".

DEBT CONTRACTS (INCLUDING OPTIONS) – CONVERSION INTO EURO

11   [Omitted by SI 2002/1971.]

History – Reg. 11 omitted by SI 2002/1971, reg. 4 with effect from 1 October 2002 in relation to accounting periods beginning on or after that date. Reg. 11 formerly read as follows:

"**11(1)**   Where as a result of the adoption of the euro by a member State–
(a)   there is a euroconversion of the loan relationship to which, under a debt contract, a qualifying company has any entitlement, or is subject to any duty, to become a party, or
(b)   a qualifying company has any entitlement, or is subject to any duty, to become treated as a person with rights and liabilities corresponding to those of a party to a loan relationship and there is a euroconversion of any of those rights and liabilities, and
(c)   in either of the cases referred to in sub-paragraphs (a) and (b) the effect is that the original debt contract is rescinded and replaced by a new debt contract,

the new debt contract shall be treated for the purposes of section 150A of the Finance Act 1994 (debt contracts and options) as if it were the same contract as the original debt contract, made when the original debt contract was made.

"**11(2)**   In paragraph (1)–
"**debt contract**" has the meaning given by section 150A(1) and (2) of the Finance Act 1994;
"**loan relationship**" has the meaning given by section 81 of the Finance Act 1996, read with section 150A(10) of the Finance Act 1994;
"**qualifying company**" shall be construed in accordance with section 154 of the Finance Act 1994.".

EXCHANGE OR CONVERSION OF RELEVANT DISCOUNTED SECURITIES

12(1)   A euroconversion of relevant discounted securities that is effected solely by means of an exchange or conversion of those securities shall be treated as not constituting either–

(a)   a transfer of those securities within the meaning of paragraph 4 of Schedule 13 to the Finance Act 1996 ("Schedule 13"), or

(b)   a conversion of those securities for the purposes of paragraph 5 of Schedule 13.

12(2)   The relevant discounted securities ("the new securities") resulting from the exchange or conversion referred to in paragraph (1) shall be deemed for the purposes of Schedule 13 to have been acquired for the amount resulting from the formula–

$$A - B$$

where–

A   is the amount equal to the acquisition cost of the relevant discounted securities replaced by the new securities, and

B   is the amount of any cash payment received by a person in respect of the euroconversion, to the extent that that amount does not exceed A.

12(3)   Where a cash payment is received by a person in respect of relevant discounted securities as a result of a euroconversion of those securities which–

(a)   involves a simple redenomination of those securities, accompanied by either or both of renominalisation and reconventioning as a consequence of that simple redenomination, and

(b)   is effected otherwise than by means of–
(i)   a transfer of those securities, or
(ii)   an exchange or conversion of those securities,

those securities shall be deemed for the purposes of Schedule 13 to have been acquired for the amount resulting from the formula–

$$C - D$$

where–

C   is the amount equal to the acquisition cost of the relevant discounted securities, and

D   is the amount of the cash payment received, to the extent that that amount does not exceed C.

12(4)   Where–

(a)   the amount of the cash payment referred to in the description of B in paragraph (2) exceeds the amount referred to in the description of A in that paragraph, or

(b)   the amount of the cash payment referred to in the description of D in paragraph (3) exceeds the amount referred to in the description of C in that paragraph, an amount equal to the excess in either case shall constitute a profit realised by a person from the discount on a relevant discounted security for the purposes of paragraph 1 of Schedule 13 (charge to tax on realised profit comprised in discount).

12(5) In this regulation **"relevant discounted security"** has the meaning given by paragraph 3 of Schedule 13.

PART IV – AGREEMENTS FOR SALE AND REPURCHASE OF SECURITIES

INTERPRETATION

13 In this Part of these Regulations–

"**capital payment**" means any payment on the euroconversion of securities other than any interest, dividend or other annual payment payable in respect of the securities;

"**original owner**" and "**interim holder**" shall be construed in accordance with section 730A(1) of the Taxes Act;

"**transferor**" shall be construed in accordance with sections 727A(1) and 737A(1) of the Taxes Act.

REPLACEMENT OF SECURITIES IN A EUROCONVERSION

14(1) This regulation applies in a case where–

(a) there is an agreement for the sale of securities, and

(b) there is a euroconversion of the securities to which the agreement relates ("the old securities"), effected wholly or in part by the issue of new securities to replace them.

14(2) The new securities which replace the old securities shall be regarded for the purposes of sections 727A(1), 730A(1) and 737A(1) of the Taxes Act, and section 263A(1) of the 1992 Act, as similar securities in relation to the old securities.

14(3) In paragraph (2) the reference to similar securities shall be construed in accordance with section 727A(4), 730B(4) or 737B(6), as the case may be.

14(4) The new securities which replace the old securities shall be regarded as similar securities for the purposes of paragraphs 2 and 7 of Schedule 13 to the Finance Act 2007.

14(5) In paragraph (4) the reference to similar securities shall be construed in accordance with paragraph 14(4) of Schedule 13 to the Finance Act 2007.

History – Reg. 14(4) and (5) inserted by SI 2007/2484, reg. 3(2), with effect from 1 October 2007, in relation to arrangements that come into force on or after that day.

PAYMENT OR BENEFIT RECEIVED BY INTERIM HOLDER ON EUROCONVERSION

15(1) This regulation applies in a case where–

(a) there is an arrangement for the sale and repurchase of securities to which section 263A(1) of the 1992 Act applies,

(b) a capital payment, but for the arrangement, would be received by the original owner on the euroconversion of those securities,

(c) the interim holder is not required under the arrangement to pay to the original owner an amount representative of that capital payment, and an amount representative of that capital payment is not required under the arrangement to be taken into account in computing the repurchase price of the securities, and

(d) the amount of the capital payment would not exceed 500 euros.

15(2) The interim holder shall not be regarded, for the purposes of section 263A of the 1992 Act, as receiving a benefit under subsection (3)(b) of that section equal to the amount of the capital payment.

PAYMENT DEEMED TO BE MADE BY INTERIM HOLDER ON EUROCONVERSION

16(1)   This regulation applies in a case where–

(a)   there is an arrangement for the sale and repurchase of securities to which section 730A(1) of the Taxes Act, or section 263A(1) of the 1992 Act, applies, or to which section 730A(1) of the Taxes Act would apply if the sale price and the repurchase price were different,

(b)   there is a euroconversion of those securities prior to their being repurchased, and

(c)   it is reasonable to assume that an amount that is representative of a capital payment in respect of the euroconversion is taken into account in computing the repurchase price of those securities.

16(2)   The amount referred to in paragraph (1)(c) shall be treated as if it were a separate representative payment in respect of the euroconversion made by the interim holder to the person required or entitled under the arrangement to repurchase the securities.

16(3)   The repurchase price of the securities shall be treated, for the purposes of section 730A of the Taxes Act and the 1992 Act, as increased by an amount equal to the amount of the separate payment treated as made by paragraph (2).

RENOMINALISATION RESULTING IN NEW MINIMUM DENOMINATION IN WHICH SECURITIES CAN BE HELD OR TRADED

17(1)   This regulation applies in a case where–

(a)   there is an arrangement for the sale and repurchase of securities to which section 730A(1) or 737A(1) of the Taxes Act, or section 263A(1) of the 1992 Act, applies, or to which section 730A(1) of the Taxes Act would apply if the sale price and the repurchase price were different,

(b)   there is a euroconversion of those securities prior to their being repurchased,

(c)   the aggregate nominal value (expressed in euros) of the securities sold, or of securities issued to replace them in a euroconversion is, as a result of renominalisation, not a whole multiple of the new minimum denomination in which those securities can be traded at the time of repurchase under the arrangement,

(d)   securities the aggregate nominal value of which is equal to the largest whole multiple of the new minimum denomination which does not exceed the aggregate nominal value referred to in sub-paragraph (c) are required under the arrangement to be sold back to the original owner or the transferor or a person connected with him, and

(e)   the interim holder is required under the arrangement to pay to the original owner or transferor, or person connected with him, an amount which either–

   (i)   is equal to the amount of what would, but for the arrangement, have been the proceeds of disposal of the remainder of the securities on the renominalisation received by the original owner, or

   (ii)   is equal to the value, at the time of the repurchase of securities pursuant to the arrangement, of the remainder if the remainder could still be held at that time though not traded.

17(2)   Where this regulation applies, the requirement for payment of the amount specified in paragraph (1)(e) is to to be regarded for the purposes of sections 727A, 730A and 737A of the Taxes Act, and section 263A of the 1992 Act, as equivalent to a requirement on the original owner, transferor or person connected with him to repurchase the remainder of the securities.

17(3)   The value referred to in paragraph (1)(e)(ii) is the appropriate proportion (based on nominal value) of the market value of the minimum amount of the original securities that, at the time of the repurchase of the securities pursuant to the arrangement, could be traded.

17(4)   Where the amount calculated in accordance with sub-paragraph (e) of paragraph (1) does not exceed 500 euros, and the arrangement does not require payment of a sum equal to this amount, this regulation shall have effect as if the amount calculated in accordance with that sub-paragraph were nil and the requirement specified in that sub-paragraph were satisfied.

17(5)   Where, in a case to which paragraph (1)(a) to (d) applies–

(a)   no amount is paid as mentioned in paragraph (1)(e) by the interim holder to the original owner, transferor or person connected with him in respect of securities that, as a result of the renominalisation, could not be traded, but

(b)   it is reasonable to assume that an amount that is representative of an amount that could have been paid as mentioned in sub-paragraph (a) was taken into account in computing the repurchase price of the securities,

that amount shall be treated as if it were a separate payment made by the interim holder to the original owner, transferor or person connected with him that is representative of a capital payment on the euroconversion of the securities, and the repurchase price of the securities shall be treated as increased by an amount equal to the amount of that separate payment so treated as made.

PAYMENT MADE OR DEEMED TO BE MADE BY INTERIM HOLDER IN RESPECT OF EUROCONVERSION – CHARGEABLE GAINS CONSEQUENCES

18(1)   This regulation applies in a case where–

(a)   there is an arrangement for the sale and repurchase of securities to which section 263A(1) of the 1992 Act applies, and

(b)   as a result of a euroconversion of those securities, a payment representative of a capital payment is made, or treated under regulation 16(2) or 17(5) as made ("deemed payment"), by the interim holder to the original owner or the transferor or a person connected with him.

18(2)   The payment or deemed payment shall be treated, for the purposes of the 1992 Act–

(a)   where the original owner and the repurchaser are the same person, as a capital payment received by the original owner in respect of the euroconversion of the securities concerned on such date as, on a just and reasonable view, may be inferred from the terms of the arrangement to be the date when the original owner would, but for the arrangement, have received a capital payment in respect of which the payment or deemed payment is made;

(b)   where the original owner and the repurchaser are not the same person and so far as concerns persons other than the interim holder, as reducing the repurchase price; and

(c)   as deductible by the interim holder in computing any capital gain arising–

    (i)   on a disposal of the securities received by the interim holder under the arrangement, or

    (ii)   where there has been an exchange of those securities as a result of the euroconversion, on a disposal of the securities received by the interim holder in exchange for the original securities received by him under the arrangement.

EUROCONVERSION – LOAN RELATIONSHIPS CONSEQUENCES

19   [Revoked by SI 2007/2484, reg. 3(3).]

History – Reg. 19 revoked by SI 2007/2484, reg. 3(3), with effect from 1 October 2007, in relation to arrangements that come into force on or after that day. Reg. 19 read as follows:

    "**19(1)**   Paragraph 15 of Schedule 9 to the Finance Act 1996 (loan relationships – repo transactions and stock-lending) shall have effect as if the definition of "repo or stock-lending arrangements" in sub-paragraph (3) of that paragraph also included provision under an agreement or series of agreements for the original owner, or a person connected with him, subsequently to be or become entitled, or required, to have transferred to him either–

    (a)   the rights accruing on a euroconversion of the loan relationship, or

    (b)   where the rights include a payment on the euroconversion, other than interest, of an amount which, when aggregated with all other payments on the euroconversion of loan relationships with equivalent rights which are the subject of the same repo or stock-lending arrangement, results in an aggregate amount that does not exceed 500 euros, either the whole of those rights or the whole of those rights apart from that payment.

    19(2)   In paragraph (1)(b) "equivalent rights" shall be construed in accordance with paragraph 15(4) of Schedule 9 to the Finance Act 1996.".

PART V – STOCK LENDING ARRANGEMENTS

INTERPRETATION

20   In this Part of these Regulations–

    "**capital payment**" means any payment on the euroconversion of securities other than any interest, dividend or other annual payment payable in respect of the securities;

    "**stock lending arrangement, borrower and lender**" have the meanings given by section 263B(1) of the 1992 Act.

DEEMED CAPITAL PAYMENT

21(1)   This regulation applies in a case where–

(a)   there is a stock lending arrangement in relation to securities,

(b)   a capital payment resulting from the euroconversion of those securities would, but for the arrangement, be received by the lender, and

(c)   the stock lending arrangement does not include a requirement for the borrower to make a payment to the lender that is representative of the capital payment referred to in sub-paragraph (b).

21(2)   Subject to paragraph (3), the lender shall be treated, for all purposes of the Taxes Acts, as having received a capital payment in respect of the euroconversion of the securities concerned–

(a)   on such date as it is reasonable to assume would have been, but for the arrangement, the first date on which the lender could have received the payment mentioned in paragraph (1)(b), and

(b)   in an amount equal to the amount of the payment he could have received.

21(3)   Paragraph (2) shall not apply where the amount of the capital payment that the lender could have received is less than 500 euros.

RENOMINALISATION RESULTING IN NEW MINIMUM AMOUNT IN WHICH SECURITIES CAN BE HELD OR TRADED

22(1)   This regulation applies in a case where–

(a)   there is a stock lending arrangement in relation to securities,

(b)   there is a euroconversion of those securities prior to their being transferred back to the lender under the arrangement,

(c)   the aggregate nominal value (expressed in euros) of the securities transferred to the borrower under the arrangement, or of the securities issued to replace them in the euroconversion, is, as a result of renominalisation, not a whole multiple of the new minimum denomination in which those securities can be traded at the time of the transfer of securities back to the lender under the arrangement,

(d)   securities the aggregate nominal value of which is equal to the largest whole multiple of the new minimum denomination which does not exceed the aggregate nominal value referred to in sub-paragraph (c) are transferred back to the lender pursuant to the arrangement, and

(e)   the borrower is required under the arrangement to pay to the lender an amount which either–

     (i)   is equal to the amount of what would, but for the arrangement, have been the proceeds of disposal of the remainder of the securities on the renominalisation received by the lender, or

     (ii)   is equal to the value, at the time of the transfer of securities back to the lender under the arrangement, of the remainder of the securities if the remainder could still be held at that time though not traded.

22(2)   Where this regulation applies, the requirement for payment of the amount specified in paragraph (1)(e) is to be regarded for the purposes of section 263B of the 1992 Act as a requirement on the part of the borrower to transfer the remainder of the securities back to the lender.

22(3)   The value referred to in paragraph (1)(e)(ii) is the appropriate proportion (based on nominal value) of the market value of the minimum amount of the original securities that, at the time of the transfer back of securities to the lender under the arrangement, could be traded.

22(4)   Where the value, or proceeds of disposal, of the remainder of the securities referred to in sub-paragraph (e) of paragraph (1) does not exceed 500 euros, and the arrangement does not require payment of a sum equal to this amount, this regulation shall have effect as if the amount calculated in accordance with that sub-paragraph were nil and the requirement specified in that sub-paragraph were satisfied.

PAYMENT MADE BY BORROWER TO LENDER IN RESPECT OF EUROCONVERSION – CHARGEABLE GAINS CONSEQUENCES

23(1)   This regulation applies in a case where–

(a)   there is a stock lending arrangement in relation to securities, and

(b)   a payment representative of a capital payment resulting from a euroconversion of those securities is made by the borrower to the lender.

23(2)   The representative payment shall be treated, for all purposes of the Taxes Acts–

(a)   as a capital payment received by the lender in respect of the euroconversion of the securities concerned on such date as it is reasonable to assume would have been, but for the arrangement, the first date on which the lender could have received the capital payment, and

(b)   as deductible by the borrower in computing any capital gain arising–

     (i)   on a disposal of the securities received by the borrower under the arrangement, or

     (ii)   where the euroconversion is effected by means of an exchange of securities, on a disposal of the securities received by the borrower in exchange for the original securities received by him under the arrangement.

PART VI – REPURCHASES AND STOCK LENDING – STAMP DUTY AND STAMP DUTY RESERVE TAX

INTERPRETATION

24   In this Part of these Regulations **"capital payment"** means any payment on the euroconversion of securities other than any interest, dividend or other annual payment payable in respect of the securities.

REPLACEMENT OF STOCK IN A EUROCONVERSION

25(1)   This regulation applies in a case where–

(a)   there is an arrangement involving the transfer of stock to which subsection (1)(a) of section 80C of the Finance Act 1986 (repurchases and stock lending – exemption from stamp duty) applies, and

(b)   there is a euroconversion of that stock ("the old stock"), effected wholly or in part by the issue of new stock to replace the old stock.

25(2)   The new stock shall be regarded, for the purposes of section 80C of the Finance Act 1986, as stock of the same kind and amount as the old stock.

REPLACEMENT OF CHARGEABLE SECURITIES IN A EUROCONVERSION

26(1)   This regulation applies in a case where–

(a)   there is an arrangement involving the transfer of chargeable securities to which subsection (1)(a) of section 89AA of the Finance Act 1986 (repurchases and stock lending – exemption from stamp duty reserve tax) applies, and

(b)   there is a euroconversion of those chargeable securities ("the old chargeable securities"), effected wholly or partly by the issue of new chargeable securities to replace the old chargeable securities.

26(2)   The new chargeable securities shall be regarded, for the purposes of section 89AA of the Finance Act 1986, as chargeable securities of the same kind and amount as the old chargeable securities.

PAYMENT OR BENEFIT RECEIVED BY TRANSFEREE OF STOCK ON EUROCONVERSION

27(1)   This regulation applies in a case where–

(a)   there is an arrangement involving the transfer of stock to which subsection (1) of section 80C of the Finance Act 1986 applies,

(b)   a capital payment would, but for the arrangement, be received by the person referred to as B in that section or by his nominee on the euroconversion of that stock,

(c)   neither the person referred to as A in that section nor his nominee is required under the arrangement to pay to B or to B's nominee an amount equivalent to the amount of that capital payment, and an amount equivalent to the amount of that capital payment is not required under the arrangement to be taken into account in computing the price of stock to be transferred to B or his nominee under the arrangement, and

(d)   the amount of the capital payment would not exceed 500 euros.

27(2)   A shall not be regarded, for the purposes of section 80C of the Finance Act 1986, as a person to whom a benefit consisting of an amount equal to the capital payment referred to in paragraph (1) accrues as mentioned in subsection (4)(b) of that section.

PAYMENT OR BENEFIT RECEIVED BY TRANSFEREE OF CHARGEABLE SECURITIES ON EUROCONVERSION

28(1) This regulation applies in a case where—

(a) there is an arrangement involving the transfer of chargeable securities to which subsection (1) of section 89AA of the Finance Act 1986 applies,

(b) a capital payment would, but for the arrangement, be received by the person referred to as Q in that section or by his nominee on the euroconversion of those chargeable securities,

(c) neither the person referred to as P in that section nor his nominee is required under the arrangement to pay to Q or to Q's nominee an amount equivalent to the amount of that capital payment, and an amount equivalent to the amount of that capital payment is not required under the arrangement to be taken into account in computing the price of the chargeable securities to be transferred to Q or his nominee under the arrangement, and

(d) the amount of the capital payment would not exceed 500 euros.

28(2) P shall not be regarded, for the purposes of section 89AA of the Finance Act 1986, as a person to whom a benefit consisting of an amount equal to the capital payment referred to in paragraph (1) accrues as mentioned in subsection (4)(b) of that section.

RENOMINALISATION RESULTING IN NEW MINIMUM DENOMINATION IN WHICH STOCK CAN BE HELD OR TRADED

29(1) This regulation applies in a case where—

(a) there is an arrangement involving the transfer of stock to which subsection (1) of section 80C of the Finance Act 1986 applies,

(b) there is a euroconversion of that stock prior to the transfer of stock under the arrangement by A or his nominee to B or his nominee as mentioned in subsection (1)(b) of that section,

(c) the aggregate nominal value (expressed in euros) of the stock transferred by B to A or his nominee as mentioned in subsection (1)(a) of that section, or of stock issued to replace that stock in a euroconversion is, as a result of renominalisation, not a whole multiple of the new minimum denomination in which that stock can be traded at the time of the transfer of stock referred to in sub-paragraph (b),

(d) stock the aggregate nominal value of which is equal to the largest whole multiple of the new minimum denomination which does not exceed the aggregate nominal value referred to in sub-paragraph (c) is required under the arrangement to be transferred by A or his nominee to B or his nominee, and

(e) A or his nominee is required under the arrangement to pay to B or his nominee an amount which either—

   (i) is equal to the amount of what would, but for the arrangement, have been the proceeds of disposal of the remainder of the stock on the renominalisation received by B, or

   (ii) is equal to the value, at the time of the transfer of stock referred to in sub-paragraph (b), of the remainder of the stock if the remainder could still be held at that time though not traded.

29(2) Where this regulation applies, the requirement for payment of the amount specified in paragraph (1)(e) is to be regarded, for the purposes of section 80C of the Finance Act 1986, as equivalent to a requirement for the remainder of the stock to be transferred by A or his nominee to B or his nominee.

29(3) The value referred to in paragraph (1)(e)(i) is the appropriate proportion (based on nominal value) of the market value of the minimum amount of the original stock that, at the time of the transfer of stock referred to in sub-paragraph (b), could be traded.

29(4) Where the amount calculated in accordance with sub-paragraph (e) of paragraph (1) does not exceed 500 euros, and the arrangement does not require payment of a sum equal to this amount, this regulation shall have effect as if the amount calculated in accordance with that sub-paragraph were nil and the requirement specified in that sub-paragraph were satisfied.

RENOMINALISATION RESULTING IN NEW MINIMUM DENOMINATION IN WHICH CHARGEABLE SECURITIES CAN BE HELD OR TRADED

30(1)   This regulation applies in a case where–

(a)   there is an arrangement involving the transfer of chargeable securities to which subsection (1) of section 89AA of the Finance Act 1986 applies,

(b)   there is a euroconversion of those chargeable securities prior to the transfer of chargeable securities under the arrangement by P or his nominee to Q or his nominee as mentioned in subsection (1)(b) of that section,

(c)   the aggregate nominal value (expressed in euros) of the chargeable securities transferred by Q to P or his nominee as mentioned in subsection (1)(a) of that section, or of chargeable securities issued to replace those chargeable securities in a euroconversion is, as a result of renominalisation, not a whole multiple of the new minimum denomination in which those chargeable securities can be traded at the time of the transfer of chargeable securities referred to sub-paragraph (b),

(d)   chargeable securities the aggregate nominal value of which is equal to the largest whole multiple of the new minimum denomination which does not exceed the aggregate nominal value referred to in sub-paragraph (c) are required under the arrangement to be transferred by P or his nominee to Q or his nominee, and

(e)   P or his nominee is required under the arrangement to pay to Q or his nominee an amount which either–

     (i)   is equal to the amount of what would, but for the arrangement, have been the proceeds of disposal of the remainder of the chargeable securities on the renominalisation received by Q, or

     (ii)   is equal to the value, at the time of the transfer of chargeable securities referred to in sub-paragraph (b), of the remainder of the chargeable securities if the remainder could still be held at that time though not traded.

30(2)   Where this regulation applies, the requirement for payment of the amount specified in paragraph (1)(e) is to be regarded, for the purposes of section 89AA of the Finance Act 1986, as equivalent to a requirement for the remainder of the chargeable securities to be transferred by P or his nominee to Q or his nominee.

30(3)   The value referred to in paragraph (1)(e) is the appropriate proportion (based on nominal value) of the market value of the minimum amount of the original chargeable securities that, at the time of the transfer of chargeable securities referred to in paragraph (1)(b), could be traded.

30(4)   Where the amount calculated in accordance with sub-paragraph (e) of paragraph (1) does not exceed 500 euros, and the arrangement does not require payment of a sum equal to this amount, this regulation shall have effect as if the amount calculated in accordance with that sub-paragraph were nil and the requirement specified in that sub-paragraph were satisfied.

PART VII – ACCRUED INCOME SCHEME

INTERPRETATION

31   In this Part of these Regulations–

"**the accrued amount**" has the meaning given by section 713(4) of the Taxes Act;

"**the accrued income provisions**" means sections 710 to 728 of the Taxes Act;

"**interest period**" shall be construed in accordance with section 711(3) and (4) of the Taxes Act except that, where securities are issued on an exchange of securities to which regulation 32 (exchange of securities resulting from euroconversion) applies, paragraph (a) of section 711(3) of that Act (commencement of interest period) shall have effect for the purposes of regulation 33 as if the reference in that paragraph to the day following that on which securities are issued were a reference to the day on which they are issued;

"**the rebate amount**" has the meaning given by section 713(5) of the Taxes Act;

"**securities**" has the meaning given by section 710(2) to (4) of the Taxes Act;

"**transfer**" in relation to a transfer of securities has the meaning given by subsection (5), read with subsection (13), of section 710 of the Taxes Act.

DISAPPLICATION OF ACCRUED INCOME PROVISIONS IN RESPECT OF AN EXCHANGE OR CONVERSION OF SECURITIES RESULTING FROM A EUROCONVERSION

32 An exchange or conversion of securities that arises solely as a result of actions to effect a euroconversion of those securities shall not constitute, or be treated as, a transfer of those securities for the purposes of the accrued income provisions.

DISAPPLICATION OF VARIABLE INTEREST RATE PROVISION IN CERTAIN CIRCUMSTANCES

33(1) This regulation applies in a case where, solely to provide for actions reasonably required to effect a euroconversion of a security—

(a) there may be a change in the rate of interest carried by the security in relation to the interest period in which the euroconversion occurs, or

(b) there may be a change in the rate of interest carried by the security in relation to subsequent periods but, throughout the subsequent periods, the new rate of interest falls within one, and one only, of the categories specified in paragraphs (a) to (c) of section 717(2) of the Taxes Act, or

(c) there may be a change in the rate of interest as mentioned in sub-paragraph (a) and a change in the rate of interest as mentioned in sub-paragraph (b).

33(2) The provision for change in the rate of interest referred to in paragraph (1)(a) or (b) shall not cause the security concerned to be one to which section 717 of the Taxes Act applies.

CALCULATION OF ACCRUED AMOUNT OR REBATE AMOUNT IN THE EVENT OF A EUROCONVERSION OF SECURITIES

34(1) This regulation applies in a case where—
(a) there is a transfer of securities at any time in an interest period, and

(b) at any time in that interest period there is a euroconversion of the securities transferred in that period.

34(2) The accrued amount or, as the case may be, the rebate amount arising in respect of the transferred securities on the transfer shall be such amount as is just and reasonable.

TREATMENT OF CAPITAL SUM RECEIVABLE ON EUROCONVERSION OF SECURITIES

35(1) This regulation applies in a case where—

(a) otherwise than as a result of a transfer of securities that is not an exchange or conversion of securities to which regulation 32 applies, a person becomes entitled in an interest period to a capital sum in connection with a euroconversion of securities, and

(b) any part of that sum is, on a just and reasonable view—

(i) attributable to a reduction in the interest payable on those securities, or

(ii) by way of compensation for a deferral of the interest payable on those securities.

35(2) The person entitled to a capital sum in an interest period as mentioned in paragraph (1)(a) shall be regarded as entitled in that interest period to a sum on the securities, for the purposes of section 713(2)(a) or (3)(a), in an amount equal to the part of the sum referred to in paragraph (1)(b).

PART VIII – CHARGEABLE GAINS

EQUATION OF HOLDING OF NON-STERLING CURRENCY WITH NEW EURO HOLDING ON EUROCONVERSION

36 A euroconversion of currency ("the original currency") shall not be treated for the purposes of the 1992 Act as involving any disposal of the original currency or any acquisition of the new euro holding or any part of it, but the original currency (taken as a single asset) and the new euro holding (taken as a single asset) shall be treated for those purposes as the same asset acquired as the original currency was acquired.

EQUATION OF DEBT (OTHER THAN A DEBT ON A SECURITY) ON EUROCONVERSION

37   A euroconversion of a debt other than a debt on a security ("the original debt") shall not be treated for the purposes of the 1992 Act as involving any disposal of that debt by the creditor or any acquisition by him of a new debt or any part of it, but the original debt and the new debt shall be treated for those purposes (to the extent that they are not already so treated) as the same asset acquired as the original asset was acquired.

DERIVATIVES OVER ASSETS THE SUBJECT OF EUROCONVERSION

38(1)   This regulation applies where–

(a)   a derivative represents rights or obligations in respect of any asset or liability or other amount ("the underlying asset"),

(b)   there is a euroconversion of the underlying asset,

(c)   a transaction is entered into in relation to that derivative that would, but for this regulation, result in a disposal for the purposes of the 1992 Act of the derivative ("the original derivative") and the acquisition of a new derivative,

(d)   the terms of the new derivative differ from the terms of the original derivative only to the extent necessary to reflect the euroconversion of the underlying asset, and

(e)   no party to the transaction receives any consideration in respect of the original derivative other than the new derivative.

38(2)   The transaction described at paragraph (1)(c) shall not be treated for the purposes of the 1992 Act as involving any disposal of the original derivative or any acquisition of the new derivative, but the original derivative and the new derivative shall be treated for those purposes as the same asset acquired as the original derivative was acquired.

CASH PAYMENTS RECEIVED ON EUROCONVERSION OF SECURITIES

39   Chapter II of Part IV of the 1992 Act shall have effect as if after section 133 of that Act (premiums on conversion of securities) there were inserted the following section–

    "133A   Cash payments received on euroconversion of securities

    133A(1)   This section applies where, under a euroconversion of a security that does not involve a disposal of the security and accordingly is not a conversion of securities within section 132(3)(a), a person receives, or becomes entitled to receive, any sum of money ("the cash payment").

    133A(2)   If the cash payment is small, as compared with the value of the security concerned–

    (a)   receipt of the cash payment shall not be treated for the purposes of this Act as a disposal of part of the security, and

    (b)   the cash payment shall be deducted from any expenditure allowable under this Act as a deduction in computing a gain or a loss on a disposal of the security by the person receiving or becoming entitled to receive the cash payment.

    133A(3)   Where the allowable expenditure is less than the cash payment (or is nil)–

    (a)   subsection (2) above shall not apply, and

    (b)   if the recipient so elects (and there is any allowable expenditure)–

       (i)   the amount of the cash payment shall be reduced by the amount of the allowable expenditure, and

       (ii)   none of that expenditure shall be allowable as a deduction in computing a gain accruing on the occasion of the euroconversion or on any subsequent occasion.

    133A(4)   In this section–

    "allowable expenditure" means expenditure which immediately before the euroconversion was attributable to the security under paragraphs (a) and (b) of section 38(1);

    "euroconversion" has the meaning given by regulation 3 of the European Single Currency (Taxes) Regulations 1998."

PART IX – CONTROLLED FOREIGN COMPANIES

REPLACEMENT OF CURRENCY USED IN ACCOUNTS OF CONTROLLED FOREIGN COMPANY BY EURO

40(1)　This regulation applies in a case where, as a result of the adoption of the euro by a participating member State, the currency used in the accounts of a controlled foreign company for the first relevant accounting period of the company is to be replaced by the euro.

40(2)　Section 747A(2) of the Taxes Act shall have effect as if it provided that–

(a)　where the currency used in the accounts of the controlled foreign company for the first relevant accounting period was the ecu, the chargeable profits for any subsequent accounting period ending on or after 1st January 1999 should be computed and expressed in the euro;

(b)　where the currency used in the accounts of the controlled foreign company for the first relevant accounting period was a currency other than the ecu–

　　(i)　the chargeable profits for any subsequent accounting period in which, or in any part of which, the currency continues to exist as a legal sub-unit of the euro should be computed and expressed in either the currency so used or the euro;

　　(ii)　the chargeable profits for any accounting period beginning after the end of the latest accounting period referred to in paragraph (i) should be computed and expressed in the euro.

PART X – AMENDMENTS TO THE LOCAL CURRENCY ELECTIONS REGULATIONS

History – Pt. X (Reg. 41–47) revoked by SI 2000/3315, reg. 10, with effect for company accounting periods beginning on or after 1 January 2000, where FA 2000, s. 105 and s. 106 apply.

41-47　[Reg. 41–47 revoked by SI 2000/3315, reg. 10.]

CORPORATION TAX (TREATMENT OF UNRELIEVED SURPLUS ADVANCE CORPORATION TAX) REGULATIONS 1999

(SI 1999/358, as amended by SI 2003/1861, SI 2010/669 and SI 2013/157)

Made on 15 February 1999 by the Treasury, in exercise of the powers conferred on them by s. 32 of the Finance Act 1998. Operative from 6 April 1999

Statutory Instruments

ARRANGEMENT OF REGULATIONS

CITATION AND COMMENCEMENT

1 These Regulations may be cited as the Corporation Tax (Treatment of Unrelieved Surplus Advance Corporation Tax) Regulations 1999 and shall come into force on 1999.

INTRODUCTORY

2(1) These Regulations make provision for and in connection with enabling unrelieved surplus ACT that a company has as at 6th April 1999 to be set against its liability to corporation tax on profits charged to corporation tax for an accounting period beginning on or after that date, other than an accounting period that is subsequent to the company's final accounting period.

2(2)   In paragraph (1) the reference to unrelieved surplus ACT of a company includes, where the company is a member of a group at any time in an accounting period to which that paragraph applies, a reference to unrelieved surplus ACT that another company, which is a member of the same group at any time in that accounting period, has as at 6th April 1999.

INTERPRETATION

3(1)   In these Regulations unless the context otherwise requires–

"**abnormal dividend**" has the meaning given by regulation 6A;

"**accounting period**" shall be construed in accordance with regulation 2(1);

"**ACT**" means advance corporation tax;

"**company**" in regulation 6A means a company referred to in section 733 (company liable to counteraction of corporation tax advantage) of the Corporation Tax Act 2010;

"**the CTA**" means the Corporation Tax Act 2010;

"**distribution**" has the meaning given by section 832(1);

"**final accounting period**" shall be construed in accordance with regulations 4 and 5;

"**franked distribution**" means the sum of the amount or value of a relevant distribution and such proportion of that amount or value as corresponds to the rate of shadow ACT specified in regulation 11(9), and references in these Regulations to any accounting period in which a franked distribution is made are references to the accounting period in which the relevant distribution in question is made;

"**franked investment income**" means income of a company resident in the United Kingdom which consists of a distribution in respect of which the company is entitled to a tax credit (and which accordingly represents income equal to the aggregate of the amount or value of the distribution and the amount of that credit), except that it does not include income to which regulations 7, 8(4), 9 or 10A refer, nor income falling within regulation 10 where paragraph (4) of that regulation does not apply;

"**group**" has the meaning given by regulation 6;

"**notification**" means notification in writing;

"**parent company**" in relation to a group shall be construed in accordance with regulation 6(1) to (7); and

"**immediate parent company**" shall be construed in accordance with regulation 6(8);

"**relevant distribution**" means a distribution made on or after 6th April 1999;

"**shadow ACT**" means a notional amount of ACT treated as paid by a company in respect of a relevant distribution and computed in accordance with regulation 11;

"**straddling accounting period**" means an accounting period beginning before, and ending on or after, 6th April 1999, and includes a separate accounting period mentioned in sections 245(2), 245A(2) and 245B(2);

"**surplus franked investment income**"–

(a)   as respects an accounting period beginning on or after 6th April 1999, has the meaning given by regulation 11(13);

(b)   as respects an accounting period beginning before that date, has the meaning given by section 238(1A);

"**surplus shadow ACT**" means the excess amount of shadow ACT over the total amount of shadow ACT set against a company's liability to corporation tax for an accounting period in accordance with regulation 12(1);

"**the Taxes Act**" means the Income and Corporation Taxes Act 1988;

"**unrelieved surplus ACT**" means the ACT (if any) which, apart from sub-paragraph (3) of paragraph 12 of Schedule 3 to the Finance Act 1998 but otherwise in accordance with that paragraph, would be treated by virtue of section 239(4) as paid in respect of distributions made by a company in the first accounting period of the company to begin on or after 6th April 1999.

3(2)   References in these Regulations to the profits of a company charged to corporation tax for any accounting period are references to the amount of the company's profits for that period on which corporation tax falls finally to be borne.

3(3) References in these Regulations, however expressed, to a company's liability to corporation tax for an accounting period include references to a company's liability in respect of any sums chargeable on the company for that period under section 747(4)(a) (controlled foreign companies).

3(4) For the purposes only of these Regulations, a straddling accounting period shall be treated as if–

(a) it were composed of two accounting periods, the one ending on 5th April 1999 and the other beginning on 6th April 1999;

(b) there were apportioned to each of those accounting periods the proportionate part of the profits of the company charged to corporation tax for the straddling accounting period.

3(5) References in these Regulations to an accounting period beginning on or after 6th April 1999 include references to–

(a) an accounting period deemed by virtue of paragraph (4) of this regulation to begin on 6th April 1999, and

(b) a separate accounting period referred to in regulations 16(2) and 17(2) that begins on or after that date.

3(6) References in these Regulations, other than the reference in paragraph (4)(b) above, to a requirement for profits charged to corporation tax for an accounting period to be apportioned between two separate parts of that accounting period are references to a requirement for those profits to be apportioned either–

(a) on a time basis, or

(b) where that basis would be unjust and unreasonable, on such basis as would be just and reasonable.

3(7) In these Regulations any reference to a particular provision, without more, is a reference to that provision of the Taxes Act.

History – In reg. 3(1), the definitions of "abnormal dividend", "company" and "the CTA" inserted by SI 2010/669, reg. 3(a) and (c), with effect from 1 April 2010.

In reg. 3(1), the definition of "the Board" omitted by SI 2010/669, reg. 3(b), with effect from 1 April 2010. The former definition read as follows:

"**"the Board"** means the Commissioners of Inland Revenue;"

In reg. 3(1) the definition of "franked investment income" substituted by SI 2010/669, reg. 3(d), with effect from 1 April 2010. The former definition read as follows:

"**"franked investment income"** means income of a company resident in the United Kingdom which consists of a distribution in respect of which the company is entitled to a tax credit (and which accordingly represents income equal to the aggregate of the amount or value of the distribution and the amount of that credit), except that it does not include income to which regulation 7, 8(4) or 9 refers, or income falling within regulation 10 to which paragraph (4) of that regulation does not apply;"

DEFINITION OF FINAL ACCOUNTING PERIOD – COMPANY NOT A MEMBER OF A GROUP

4(1) For the purpose of regulation 2(1) and subject to paragraphs (3) to (5) of this regulation and to regulation 5(10), where a company is not a member of a group at any time in the relevant accounting period, the final accounting period of that company is the accounting period beginning in the period of twelve months immediately following the end of the relevant accounting period or, if there is more than one accounting period beginning in that period of twelve months, the latest accounting period beginning in that period.

4(2) In paragraph (1) **"the relevant accounting period"** is the first accounting period of the company after which no amount of unrelieved surplus ACT is available to be set against the company's liability to corporation tax in accordance with these Regulations.

4(3) Paragraph (1) shall not apply where, at any time in the first of its accounting periods to begin on or after 6th April 1999, the company notifies an officer of Revenue and Customs that it will not seek or, as the case may be, will cease to seek recovery of unrelieved surplus ACT in respect of that accounting period or any subsequent accounting period.

4(4) Where, otherwise than in a case to which paragraph (3) applies, the company notifies an officer of Revenue and Customs at any time in an accounting period that it wishes that accounting period to be its final accounting period and that it will not seek recovery of unrelieved surplus ACT in respect of any subsequent accounting period, the final accounting period of that company is, subject to paragraph (5), the accounting period in which the notification is made.

4(5) Where–

(a) there is an amount of surplus shadow ACT in respect of an accounting period of the company beginning in the period of twelve months (**"the relevant period"**) immediately following the end of the accounting period in which the company notifies an officer of Revenue and Customs as mentioned in paragraph (4) or, if there is more than one such accounting period, the latest accounting period beginning in the relevant period, and

(b)   that amount or any part of it falls to be carried back in accordance with regulation 12(7) to the accounting period in which that notification is made,

the final accounting period shall be the accounting period or, as the case may be, the latest accounting period beginning in the relevant period from which an amount of surplus shadow ACT falls to be carried back as mentioned in sub-paragraph (b) of this paragraph, and not the accounting period in which the notification is made.

History – In reg. 4 the words "an officer of Revenue and Customs" substituted for the words "an officer of the Board" three times by SI 2010/669, reg. 6, with effect from 1 April 2010.

DEFINITION OF FINAL ACCOUNTING PERIOD – COMPANY A MEMBER OF A GROUP

5(1) For the purpose of regulation 2 and subject to paragraphs (3) to (10), where a company is a member of a group at any time in the relevant accounting period, the final accounting period of that company in its capacity as a member of that group is the accounting period beginning in the period of twelve months immediately following the end of the relevant accounting period or, if there is more than one accounting period beginning in that period of twelve months, the latest accounting period beginning in that period.

5(2) In paragraph (1) **"the relevant accounting period"** is the first accounting period of the company after which no amount of unrelieved surplus ACT belonging to the company or any other company which is a member of the group at any time in that accounting period is available to be set against any liability to corporation tax in accordance with these Regulations; and for this purpose unrelieved surplus ACT belonging to another company that is a member of the group at any time in that accounting period shall be regarded as so available until the end of that other company's accounting period.

5(3) Paragraph (1) shall not apply where–

(a)   the company is a member of the group as at 6th April 1999, and

(b)   at any time in the first accounting period of the parent company of the group to begin on or after that date, the parent company notifies an officer of Revenue and Customs on behalf of the group that the group will not seek or, as the case may be, will cease to seek recovery of unrelieved surplus ACT in respect of any accounting period of any member of the group that begins on or after that date.

5(4) A notification made in accordance with paragraph (3) shall, subject to paragraph (9), be binding on each company that was a member of the group as at 6th April 1999.

5(5) Where, otherwise than in a case to which paragraph (3) applies, at any time in an accounting period of the parent company of the group the parent company notifies an officer of Revenue and Customs on behalf of the group that the group wishes the accounting period of any member of the group in which the notification is made to be the final accounting period of that member and that it will not seek recovery of amounts of unrelieved surplus ACT available to that member in respect of any subsequent accounting period, the final accounting period of that member and the final accounting period of the parent company is, subject to paragraphs (7) to (10), the accounting period of the parent company in which the notification by the parent company is made.

5(6) A notification made in accordance with paragraph (5) shall, subject to paragraph (10), be binding on each company that was a member of the group when the notification was made or that subsequently becomes a member of the group prior to the end of the parent company's final accounting period.

5(7) Where paragraph (5) applies and the accounting period of a company in the group other than the parent company that would otherwise be its final accounting period in accordance with that paragraph begins before the end of, but ends after, the accounting period of the parent company in which the notification by the parent company is made, the accounting period of the company concerned shall be treated as if the part ending with the last day of the parent company's accounting period, and the part after, were two separate accounting periods; and the part ending with the last day of the parent company's accounting period shall, subject to paragraph (10), be treated as the company's final accounting period for the purposes of this regulation.

5(8) Where–

(a)   there is an amount of surplus shadow ACT in respect of an accounting period of any company that is a member of the group beginning in the period of twelve months ("the relevant period") immediately following the end of the accounting period of the company in which the parent company notifies an officer of Revenue and Customs as mentioned in paragraph (5), and

(b)   all or any part of that surplus amount falls to be carried back under regulation 12 or 13 to an accounting period of a company that is a member of the group ending before the relevant period of the company referred to in sub-paragraph (a),

the final accounting period of any company that is a member of the group at any time in the relevant period shall, subject to paragraph (10), be the accounting period or, if more than one, the latest accounting period beginning in the relevant period from which an amount of surplus shadow ACT falls to be carried back as mentioned in sub-paragraph (b) of this paragraph, and not the accounting period referred to in paragraph (5).

5(9)   Where in an accounting period ("the material period") subsequent to the accounting period in which the parent company notifies an officer of Revenue and Customs as mentioned in paragraph (3), a company which has an amount of unrelieved surplus ACT becomes a member of the group, these Regulations shall apply in relation to the material period (but not earlier accounting periods) as if no notification had been made in accordance with that paragraph, but not so as to entitle any company to whom that notification, when made, applied to seek recovery of any amount of unrelieved surplus ACT.

5(10)   Where in an accounting period ("the material period") subsequent to the final accounting period as determined in accordance with paragraph (1), (5), (7) or (8), a company which has an amount of unrelieved surplus ACT becomes a member of the group, these Regulations shall apply in relation to the material period (but not earlier accounting periods) as if the final accounting period had not yet been determined in accordance with any of those paragraphs, but not so as to entitle a company whose final accounting period had previously been determined in accordance with those provisions to seek recovery of any amount of unrelieved surplus ACT.

5(11)   Where–

(a)   a company is a member of two or more groups,

(b)   its final accounting period as a member of one or more, but not all, of the groups concerned has been determined in accordance with the previous provisions of this regulation, and

(b)   at least one of those determinations is as a result of a notification made by a parent company in accordance with paragraph (5) of this regulation,

these Regulations shall have effect in relation to the group or groups in respect of which the final accounting period of the company has not been determined as if the total amount of its unrelieved surplus ACT had been set against its liability to corporation tax in accordance with regulation 14.

History – In reg. 5 the words "an officer of Revenue and Customs" substituted for the words "an officer of the Board" four times by SI 2010/669, reg. 6, with effect from 1 April 2010.

DEFINITION OF GROUP

6(1)   In these Regulations **"group"** means a company resident in an EEA state ("the parent company") which has one or more 51 per cent subsidiaries together with that or those subsidiaries.

6(2)   For the purposes of paragraph (1)–

(a)   **"51 per cent subsidiary"** means a 51 per cent subsidiary that is a company resident in the United Kingdom;

(b)   a company is not the parent company within a group if–

     (i)   it has no 51 per cent subsidiary but is itself a 51 per cent subsidiary of another company, or

     (ii)   it and its 51 per cent subsidiaries are all members of another group;

(c)   the question whether a company is a 51 per cent subsidiary of the parent company shall be determined, subject to paragraph (3), in accordance with section 838, except that the parent company shall be treated as not being the owner–

     (i)   of any share capital which it owns directly in a company if a profit on the sale of the shares would be treated as a trading receipt of its trade; or

     (ii)   of any share capital which it owns indirectly, and which is owned directly by a body corporate for which a profit on the sale of the shares would be treated as a trading receipt of its trade; or

     (iii)   of any share capital which it owns directly or indirectly in a body corporate not resident in the United Kingdom.

6(3) Where a company would otherwise not be a 51 per cent subsidiary, but–

(a)   persons, whether company members or not, enjoy extraordinary rights or powers under the articles of association or under any other document regulating the company, and

(b)   because of that fact, ownership of the ordinary share capital (for the purposes of the definition of "51 per cent subsidiary" in section 838(1)(a)) may not be an appropriate test of whether a company is a 51 per cent subsidiary of the parent company,

then in considering whether a company is a 51 per cent subsidiary of the parent company for the purposes of paragraph (1), holdings of all kinds of share capital, including preference shares, or of any particular category of share capital, or voting power or any other kind of special power may be taken into account instead of ordinary share capital.

6(4) Notwithstanding that, apart from this paragraph, a company ("the subsidiary company") would at any time be a 51 per cent subsidiary of the parent company for the purposes of this regulation, the subsidiary company shall not be treated at that time as a 51 per cent subsidiary for those purposes–

(a)   if arrangements are in existence by virtue of which any person has or could obtain, or any persons together have or could obtain, control of the subsidiary company but not of the parent company; and

(b)   unless the following conditions are also fulfilled, namely–

   (i)   that the parent company is beneficially entitled to more than 50 per cent of any profits available for distribution to equity holders of the subsidiary company; and

   (ii)   that the parent company would be beneficially entitled to more than 50 per cent of any assets of the subsidiary company available for distribution to its equity holders on a winding up.

6(5) In paragraph (4)–

   "arrangements" means arrangements of any kind, whether in writing or not, other than arrangements whose sole or main purpose is to reduce the amount of surplus shadow ACT available to be utilised by a company other than the subsidiary company in accordance with regulation 13;

   "control" has the meaning given by section 840.

6(6) Where by virtue of any enactment a Minister of the Crown or Northern Ireland department has power to give directions to a statutory body as to the disposal of assets belonging to, or to a subsidiary of, that body, the existence of that power shall not be regarded as constituting (or as having at any time constituted) an arrangement within the meaning of paragraph (4)(a).

6(7) The provisions of Schedule 18 shall apply for the purposes of paragraph (4)(b) as if–

(a)   for any reference to section 413(7) to (9) there were substituted a reference to paragraph (4)(b);

(b)   paragraph 7(1) of that Schedule were omitted and for any reference to "the relevant accounting period" there were substituted a reference to the accounting period current at the time in question.

6(8) For the purposes of these Regulations, a company ("A") is the "immediate parent company" of another company ("B") if, disregarding any other company of which B is a 51 per cent subsidiary by virtue of section 838 and this regulation, A would be the parent company of B by virtue of section 838 and this regulation.

History – In reg. 6(1), the words "an EEA state" substituted for the words "the United Kingdom" by SI 2013/157, reg. 2(1), with effect in relation to distributions made on or after 11 March 2013.

ABNORMAL DIVIDENDS: GENERAL

6A(1) In regulation 10A an abnormal dividend has been received by a company where section 740 (abnormal dividends: general) of the CTA as modified by paragraph (2) has been applied to it.

6A(2) For the purposes of regulation 10A, an amount received by way of dividend in subsection (1) of section 740 of the CTA shall, for the avoidance of doubt, be interpreted as being in connection with–

(a)   the purchase of securities where the purchase is followed by the sale of the same or other securities,

(b)   the sale of securities where the sale is followed by the purchase of the same or other securities,

(c)   the distribution, transfer or realisation of assets of a company, or

(d)   the application of such assets in discharge of liabilities.

History – Reg. 6A inserted by SI 2010/669, reg. 4, with effect from 1 April 2010.

RESTRICTION ON FRANKED INVESTMENT INCOME – REPLACEMENT OF INCOME

7 Where a company takes any action the effect of which is that income consisting of interest to which a company is or will be entitled becomes or is replaced by income consisting of a distribution, and the main purpose of that action is to reduce the amount of shadow ACT which it would be treated as having paid under regulation 11 for an accounting period, the income consisting of the distribution shall not be regarded for the purposes of these Regulations as franked investment income.

RESTRICTION ON FRANKED INVESTMENT INCOME – ARRANGEMENTS TO PASS ON VALUE OF FRANKED INVESTMENT INCOME

8(1) This regulation applies in any case where–

(a)   a person ("A") who is a company is entitled to franked investment income;

(b)   arrangements subsist such that another person ("B") obtains, whether directly or indirectly, a payment representing any of the value of that franked investment income, in excess of the payment that would have been made in the circumstances specified in paragraph (2);

(c)   the arrangements (whether or not made directly between A and B) were entered into for an unallowable purpose, and

(d)   neither A nor B is a company whose final accounting period has been determined in accordance with regulation 4 or 5.

8(2) The circumstances specified in this paragraph are where–

(a)   the payment representing any of the value of that franked investment income was made under a transaction between persons at arm's length both of whom were companies;

(b)   neither company was or had been at any time a member of a group, and

(c)   neither company was entitled to an amount of unrelieved surplus ACT as at 6th April 1999.

8(3) This regulation does not apply if and to the extent that any provision of the Tax Acts has the effect of cancelling or reducing the tax advantage which would otherwise be obtained by virtue of the arrangements.

8(4) Where this regulation applies, the franked investment income referred to in paragraph (1) shall not be regarded for the purposes of these Regulations as franked investment income.

8(5) For the purposes of this regulation, the question whether any arrangements were entered into for an "unallowable purpose" shall be determined in accordance with paragraphs (6) and (7).

8(6) Arrangements are entered into for an unallowable purpose if the purposes for which A is a party to the arrangements include the purpose of reducing the amount of shadow ACT treated as paid, in accordance with regulation 11, on relevant distributions made–

(a)   by A, or

(b)   where A is a member of a group, by any other company which is a member of that group,

at any time in, or after the end of, the accounting period in which the arrangements are entered into.

8(7) In determining for the purposes of paragraph (6) whether a company could have used franked investment income for the purpose of reducing shadow ACT, the company shall be taken to use its actual franked investment income for that purpose before using the franked investment income in question.

8(8) In this regulation–

"arrangements" means arrangements of any kind, whether in writing or not (and includes a series of arrangements, whether or not between the same parties);

"tax advantage" has the same meaning as in Chapter I of Part XVII of the Taxes Act.

RESTRICTION ON FRANKED INVESTMENT INCOME – DEALERS

9(1) Where a dealer receives–

(a)   a distribution which is made by a company resident in the United Kingdom ("a UK distribution"), or any payment which is representative of a UK distribution, and

(b)   the distribution or, as the case may be, the payment is taken into account in computing the profits of the dealer which are chargeable to tax in accordance with the provisions of the Taxes Act applicable to Case I or II of Schedule D, the distribution or payment shall not be regarded for the purposes of these Regulations as franked investment income.

9(2) In paragraph (1) **"dealer"** means a person who is a dealer in relation to a distribution within the meaning of section 95(2).

RESTRICTION ON FRANKED INVESTMENT INCOME – INTRA-GROUP DISTRIBUTIONS

10(1) A distribution received by a company which is a member of a group from another company within the group, or from another company in the circumstances specified in paragraph (2) or (3) shall, subject to paragraph (4), not be regarded for the purposes of these Regulations as franked investment income.

10(2) The circumstances specified in this paragraph are where the company making the distribution in question is not a member of the group at the time the distribution is received but arrangements in place at that time are such as to give rise to a reasonable expectation that the company will join or, as the case may be, rejoin the group.

10(3) The circumstances specified in this paragraph are where the distribution in question was made by reference to the shareholdings existing at a time when both the company making the distribution and the company owning the shares at that time were members of the same group.

10(4) Where the distribution is a relevant distribution and the company making the relevant distribution has elected as mentioned in regulation 11(3)(b), paragraph (1) of this regulation shall not apply to so much of the franked distribution in respect of which that election is made.

RESTRICTION ON FRANKED INVESTMENT INCOME – ABNORMAL DIVIDENDS

10A(1) For the purposes of these Regulations an abnormal dividend shall not be regarded as franked investment income where it has been received by–

(a)   company (R1) from company (P1) where P1 and R1 are not members of a group, or

(b)   company (R2) from company (P2) where P2 and R2 are members of the same group.

10A(2) Sub-paragraph (b) of paragraph (1) shall apply notwithstanding that company P2 has made an election under regulation 11(3)(b).

History – Reg. 10A inserted by SI 2010/669, reg. 5, with effect from 1 April 2010.

COMPUTATION OF SHADOW ACT

11(1) Where a company resident in the United Kingdom makes a relevant distribution, other than a relevant distribution to which paragraph (2) applies, shadow ACT shall, for the purposes of determining the amount of unrelieved surplus ACT that may be set against a company's liability to corporation tax for an accounting period in accordance with regulation 14, be treated as having been paid by the company in accordance with the provisions of this regulation.

11(2) This paragraph applies to a relevant distribution–

(a)   which is a manufactured dividend to which paragraph 2(2) of Schedule 23A applies, or

(b)   which is made, otherwise than in the circumstances specified in paragraph (3), by a company that is a member of a group to another company within the group.

11(3) The circumstances specified in this paragraph are where the company making the distribution–

(a)   has received, in the accounting period in which the distribution is made, franked investment income of an amount sufficient to ensure that the amount of shadow ACT that, apart from paragraph (2)(b), would be treated as having been paid in respect of that distribution would have been less than it would have been had the company not received that amount of franked investment income;

(b)   has elected in its tax return for the accounting period in which the distribution is made, or in an amendment to that tax return, that an amount of the franked distribution equal to the whole or a stated amount of that franked investment income (multiplied by nine-eighths) should not be excluded in computing its shadow ACT for that period; and

(c)   has informed the company receiving the distribution that sub-paragraphs (a) and (b) of this paragraph apply in relation to the distribution, and of the amount of the distribution to which the election under sub-paragraph (b) applies.

Statutory Instruments

11(4)   An election to which paragraph (3)(b) refers–

(a)   shall be made not later than two years after the end of the accounting period in which the distribution is made, and

(b)   shall be irrevocable.

11(5)   Where a relevant distribution to which paragraph (1) applies does not fall within an accounting period of the company making the distribution, it shall be treated, for all purposes of these Regulations, as falling within an accounting period that–

(a)   begins–

   (i)   on the same date as the date on which the accounting period of the company's immediate parent company in which the distribution falls begins or, if later

   (ii)   on the date immediately following the end of the last accounting period of the company making the distribution that precedes the date on which the distribution is made, and

(b)   ends–

   (i)   on the same date as the date on which the accounting period of the company's immediate parent company in which the distribution falls ends or, if earlier

   (ii)   on the date immediately before the beginning of an accounting period of the company making the distribution.

11(6)   For the purposes of paragraph (5), where the distribution referred to in that paragraph is made at a time when there is no accounting period of the company's immediate parent company, that paragraph shall have effect as if for the references to the accounting period of the company's immediate parent company there were substituted references to the accounting period of the immediate parent company of the company's immediate parent company (and so on until the accounting period of an immediate parent company in which the distribution falls is found).

11(7)   Where a company ceases to be a member of a group, shadow ACT shall be computed in accordance with paragraph (1) in relation to the accounting period of the company in which it ceases to be a member of the group as if the part ending on the date on which the company ceases to be member of the group, and the part after, were two separate accounting periods.

11(8)   Where there is a change of ownership of a company and the change–

(a)   is not such as to cause the company to cease to be a member of a group, but

(b)   occurs in circumstances where either regulation 16 or regulation 17 applies,

shadow ACT shall be computed in accordance with paragraph (1) in relation to the accounting period of the company in which the change occurs as if the part ending with the change, and the part after, were two separate accounting periods.

11(9)   Subject to paragraphs (10) to (12), for the financial year 1999 and any subsequent financial year, shadow ACT shall be treated as having been paid at the rate of 25 per cent on an amount equal to the amount or value of the relevant distribution.

11(10)   Where in any accounting period a company receives franked investment income, subject to regulation 22(1), shadow ACT shall not be treated as having been paid by the company in respect of relevant distributions made by it in that period unless the amount of franked distributions made by it in that period exceeds the aggregate of–

(a)   nine-eighths of the amount of franked investment income consisting of distributions made to the company in that period, and

(b)   the amount of any surplus of franked investment income carried forward from the previous accounting period in accordance with paragraph (12).

11(11)   If in an accounting period there is such an excess, shadow ACT shall be treated as having been paid on an amount which, when the shadow ACT treated as having been paid thereon is added to it, is equal to the excess.

11(12)   Where a company has a surplus of franked investment income in any accounting period, the surplus shall be carried forward to the next accounting period for the purposes of paragraphs (3), (10) and (13).

11(13)   A company has a surplus of franked investment income in an accounting period for the purposes of paragraph (12) if an amount equal to the aggregate of nine-eighths of the franked investment income consisting of distributions made to the company in that period and the surplus of franked investment income carried forward from the previous accounting period in accordance with paragraph (12) exceeds the amount of the franked distributions made by it in that period; and the amount of that excess shall be regarded as the amount of the surplus of franked investment income for the purposes of paragraph (12).

11(14)   In the application of paragraphs (12) and (13) to a straddling accounting period of a company, or to the case where an accounting period of a company ends on 5th April 1999 and its next accounting period begins on 6th April 1999—

(a)   there shall be ascertained the amount of surplus franked investment income in the accounting period ending or, in the case of a straddling accounting period, deemed by virtue of regulation 3(4) to end, on 5th April 1999;

(b)   that amount shall be treated as carried forward to the accounting period beginning or, in the case of a straddling accounting period, deemed by virtue of regulation 3(4) to begin, on 6th April 1999 and shall be treated as mentioned in paragraph (10).

UTILISATION OF SHADOW ACT

12(1)   Shadow ACT which a company is treated as having paid in accordance with regulation 11 in respect of any relevant distribution made by it in an accounting period shall, for the purposes mentioned in regulation 11(1) and in accordance with the provisions of this regulation, be set against the company's liability to corporation tax on any profits charged to corporation tax for that accounting period, but not so as to reduce the amount of that liability.

12(2)   Subject to paragraph (7)(b), shadow ACT shall be utilised as mentioned in paragraph (1) before any amount of unrelieved surplus ACT is set against a company's liability to corporation tax in accordance with regulation 14.

12(3)   The amount of shadow ACT to be set against a company's liability for any accounting period under paragraph (1)—

(a)   shall not exceed the amount of shadow ACT that would have been treated as paid (apart from regulation 11(10) to (12)) in respect of a relevant distribution made at the end of that period of an amount which, together with the shadow ACT treated as paid in respect of it, is equal to the company's profits charged to corporation tax for that period;

(b)   shall be computed, where applicable, by reference to the like provisions with respect to separate accounting periods on a change of ownership of a company that are contained in regulations 16 and 17 for the purposes of computing the amount of unrelieved surplus ACT to be set against the company's liability for an accounting period.

12(4)   Where an amount of credit for foreign tax falls to be allowed in accordance with section 797 against corporation tax attributable to any income or chargeable gain ("the relevant income or gain"), then—

(a)   paragraph (3) shall have effect only in relation to so much of the company's profits chargeable to corporation tax for the relevant accounting period as does not include the relevant income or gain;

(b)   in so far as the company's liability to corporation tax for the relevant accounting period relates to the relevant income or gain, it shall be taken to be reduced by the amount of the credit for foreign tax attributable to that income or gain, as determined in accordance with subsections (2) and (3) of section 797; and

(c)   the amount of shadow ACT which may be set against that liability, so far as it relates to the relevant income or gain, shall not exceed whichever is the lower of the limits specified in paragraph (5).

12(5)   The limits specified in this paragraph are—

(a)   the limit which would apply under paragraph (3) if the amount of the relevant income or gain, determined in accordance with subsection (3) of section 797, were the company's only income or gain for the relevant accounting period; and

(b)   the amount of corporation tax for which, after taking account of the reduction mentioned in paragraph (4) (b), the company is liable in respect of that income or gain.

12(6)   In paragraph (4) **"the relevant accounting period"** shall be construed in accordance with subsection (2) of section 797.

12(7)   Where in respect of any accounting period of a company ("the principal period") there is an amount of surplus shadow ACT, that amount shall be treated as if it were shadow ACT which the company is treated as having paid in respect of relevant distributions made by it in any of its accounting periods beginning on or after 6th April 1999 and in the six years preceding the principal period, but so that that amount—

(a)   is set, so far as possible, against the company's liability for a more recent accounting period before a more remote one,

(b)   does not cause the amount of shadow ACT specified in paragraph (3)(a) as respects an accounting period of the company to be exceeded,

(c)   where the company is a member of a group, is not set against the liability of another company in the group for an accounting period, and

(d)   except in relation to the period beginning twenty four months before the end of the principal period and ending the day before the commencement of the principal period, does not displace any amount of unrelieved surplus ACT that, by virtue of regulation 14, is set against the company's liability for an accounting period.

12(8)   For the purposes of paragraph (7)–

(a)   the reference to any of the company's accounting periods beginning on or after 6th April 1999 includes a reference to a separate accounting period mentioned in regulations 16 and 17 beginning on or after that date;

(b)   where an accounting period begins before, but ends during, the period of twenty four months referred to in sub-paragraph (d) of that paragraph, the amount of unrelieved surplus ACT falling to be displaced as mentioned in that sub-paragraph shall be proportionately reduced by reference to the part of that accounting period that falls outside the period of twenty four months.

12(9)   Subject to regulation 13 (intra-group allocation of shadow ACT), where in respect of any accounting period of a company there is an amount of surplus shadow ACT which has not been dealt with under paragraph (7), that amount shall be treated for the purposes of this regulation (including any further application of this paragraph) as if it were shadow ACT which the company is treated as having paid in the next accounting period.

INTRA-GROUP ALLOCATION OF SURPLUS SHADOW ACT

13(1)   Where in respect of any accounting period of a company that is a member of a group at any time in that accounting period, there is an amount of surplus shadow ACT that has not been utilised as mentioned in regulation 12(7), the whole or part of that amount shall, for the purposes mentioned in regulation 11(1) and in accordance with the provisions of this regulation, be allocated by the parent company to another company, or other companies, that are members of the group ("the potential recipients").

13(2)   Where an amount of surplus shadow ACT is allocated to another company in the group under paragraph (1), that amount shall be set against the balance (if any) of that company's liability to corporation tax on any profits charged to corporation tax for an accounting period to which that amount is attributed in accordance with paragraph (8), that remains after the amount of that company's shadow ACT in respect of its own distributions for that period (together with the amount of any surplus shadow ACT treated as belonging to that company under paragraph (6)) has been set against that liability in accordance with regulation 12(1), but not so as to reduce the amount of that liability or so as to exceed the capacity of that company to utilise that amount.

13(3)   No company that is a member of a group at any time in an accounting period shall be entitled to set an amount of unrelieved surplus ACT against its liability to corporation tax for that accounting period in accordance with regulation 14 until all surplus shadow ACT of that company for that period has been allocated under paragraph (1).

13(4)   Where the amount of surplus shadow ACT referred to in paragraph (1) is insufficient in relation to the capacity of all the potential recipients fully to utilise surplus shadow ACT, the parent company in the group shall determine the recipients to whom that amount shall be allocated under that paragraph, and the proportion of that amount to be allocated to each of those recipients in accordance with the capacity of each of those recipients to utilise that amount.

13(5)   Where the amount referred to in paragraph (1) exceeds the amount which could be utilised by all the potential recipients–

(a)   so much of that amount as is able to be utilised by the potential recipients shall be allocated to them by the parent company under that paragraph in accordance with the capacity of each of the potential recipients to utilise that amount, and

(b)   the balance shall, subject to paragraph (6), be retained by the company in which the amount arose and shall be treated by that company (in accordance with regulation 12(9)) as if it were shadow ACT which the company is treated as having paid in the next accounting period.

13(6) Where, in a case to which paragraph (1) applies, the company concerned ceases to be a member of the group, otherwise than by reason of a transaction or arrangements between that company or that company's immediate parent company (or the latter company's immediate parent company and so on) and another person who is not connected with that company within the meaning of section 839, the amount of surplus shadow ACT shall be treated for the purposes of this regulation as belonging to the immediate parent company of that company at the time it ceases to be a member of the group or, where the immediate parent company ceases to be a member of the group at the same time as that company, as belonging to the next immediate parent company (and so on as necessary until an immediate parent company is found who has not ceased to be a member of the group at the same time as that company).

13(7) An amount of surplus shadow ACT allocated to a company under paragraph (1) may subsequently be reallocated at any time under that paragraph, but not so as to reduce the amount allocated to a company to an amount below its capacity to utilise surplus shadow ACT after the time limit for amending that company's tax return has expired.

13(8) Where the whole or part of an amount of surplus shadow ACT is allocated to a company under paragraph (1), it shall be attributed to a relevant accounting period, or relevant accounting periods, of that company in the following order—

(a)   an accounting period beginning and ending on the same dates as, or otherwise contained within, the accounting period of the company whose surplus shadow ACT is allocated ("the transferring company's accounting period");

(b)   an accounting period beginning before, but ending in, the transferring company's accounting period;

(c)   an accounting period beginning in, but ending after, the end of the transferring company's accounting period;

(d)   any further period (whether the whole or part of an accounting period) beginning twenty four months or less prior to the end of the transferring company's accounting period.

13(9) In paragraph (8) **"relevant accounting period"** means an accounting period in which both the transferring company and the company receiving the amount were at some time members of the group.

13(10) Where the further period referred to in paragraph (8)(d) is a part of an accounting period, the capacity of the company to utilise the amount attributed to that further period shall be proportionately reduced by reference to the part of its accounting period which falls outside that further period.

13(11) Where in accordance with paragraph (8) amounts of surplus shadow ACT in respect of accounting periods of two or more companies are attributed to a relevant accounting period, or relevant accounting periods, of a company, the parent company in the group shall determine the order of priority in which those amounts are attributed, and the order of priority so determined shall apply on any subsequent reallocation of those amounts.

13(12) Where a company is a member of more than one group and there is an allocation to that company under paragraph (1) of an amount of surplus shadow ACT by the parent company of more than one group, the order of priority in which allocations are attributed to an accounting period, or accounting periods, of that company in accordance with paragraph (8) shall be determined by reference to the date on which an allocation is made (an earlier allocation having priority over a later allocation).

13(13) Where in accordance with paragraph (8) an amount falls to be attributed to an accounting period which is either the first or the last accounting period in which both the transferring company and the company receiving the amount were members of the group, then for the purpose of determining the amount to be attributed to that accounting period—

(a)   the capacity of the company receiving the amount to utilise the amount to be attributed to that accounting period—

    (i)   shall be proportionately reduced by reference to the part of that period during which the transferring company and the company receiving the amount were not both members of the group, and

    (ii)   shall be further reduced by any prior attribution to that period by reason of the allocation to the company receiving the amount of the surplus shadow ACT of another company, and

(b)   the amount shall be treated as attributed to a separate accounting period comprising the part of that accounting period during which both the transferring company and the company receiving the amount were members of the group.

13(14) Where in accordance with paragraph (8) an amount is attributed to a relevant accounting period referred to in sub-paragraph (b) or (d) of that paragraph, that amount—

(a)   shall displace any amount of unrelieved surplus ACT that, by virtue of regulation 14, was set against the company's liability to corporation tax on any profits charged to corporation tax for that accounting period, but

(b)   shall not displace any amount of surplus shadow ACT that, in accordance with regulation 12, has previously been set against that company's liability for corporation tax for that accounting period or (as the case may be) has been treated as shadow ACT which that company is treated as having paid in respect of any relevant distributions made by the company in that accounting period.

13(15)   Where the parent company fails to allocate an amount of surplus shadow ACT in accordance with this regulation–

(a)   that amount may be allocated in accordance with this regulation by an officer of Revenue and Customs;

(b)   if that amount is subsequently allocated by the parent company in accordance with this regulation, any allocation by an officer of Revenue and Customs under sub-paragraph (a) shall be treated as if it had not been made.

History – In reg. 13 the words "an officer of Revenue and Customs" substituted for the words "an officer of the Board" twice by SI 2010/669, reg. 6, with effect from 1 April 2010.

SET-OFF OF UNRELIEVED SURPLUS ACT AGAINST LIABILITY TO CORPORATION TAX

14(1)   Subject to paragraphs (2) to (4), a company's unrelieved surplus ACT shall be set against its liability to corporation tax on any profits charged to corporation tax for an accounting period beginning on or after 6th April 1999, and shall accordingly discharge a corresponding amount of that liability.

14(2)   Unrelieved surplus ACT shall not be set against a company's liability to corporation tax for an accounting period under paragraph (1) to the extent that it can be set against the company's liability to corporation tax for an earlier accounting period.

14(3)   Where section 116(2) applies in relation to a company which is a member of a partnership, no unrelieved surplus advance corporation tax may be set against its liability to corporation tax on its share in the profits of the relevant accounting period of the partnership.

14(4)   The amount of unrelieved surplus ACT to be set against a company's liability for an accounting period under paragraph (1) shall not exceed the amount calculated in accordance with the formula–

$$A - B$$

where–

A   is the amount of the company's capacity to utilise unrelieved surplus ACT calculated in accordance with regulation 12, and

B   is the amount of any shadow ACT attributed to that period in accordance with regulations 12 and 13.

14(5)   References to **"the relevant accounting period"** in paragraph (3) shall be construed in accordance with section 116(3).

RESTRICTION ON SET-OFF OF COMPANY'S UNRELIEVED SURPLUS ACT AGAINST SUBSIDIARY COMPANY'S LIABILITY TO CORPORATION TAX

15(1)   Subject to paragraph (2) and regulation 17, unrelieved surplus ACT consisting of ACT which a subsidiary is treated as having paid by virtue of section 240(2) shall be set off against the subsidiary's liability to corporation tax for an accounting period in accordance with regulation 14 before unrelieved surplus ACT consisting of ACT paid in respect of any distribution made by the subsidiary.

15(2)   No unrelieved surplus ACT consisting of ACT which a subsidiary is treated as having paid by virtue of section 240(2) shall be set against the subsidiary's liability to corporation tax in accordance with regulation 14 for any accounting period in which, or in any part of which, it was not a subsidiary of the surrendering company, unless throughout that period or part both companies were subsidiaries of a third company.

15(3)   In this regulation **"surrendering company"** and **"subsidiary"** have the same meanings as in section 240.

CALCULATION OF UNRELIEVED SURPLUS ACT ON CHANGE OF OWNERSHIP OF COMPANY

16(1)   This regulation applies where–

(a)   within any period of three years there is both a change in the ownership of a company and, either earlier or later in that period, or at the same time, a major change in the nature or conduct of a trade or business carried on by the company; or

(b)   at any time after the scale of the activities in a trade or business carried on by a company has become small or negligible, and before any considerable revival of the trade or business, there is a change in the ownership of the company.

16(2)   Regulation 14 shall apply in relation to an accounting period in which the change of ownership occurs as if the part ending with the change of ownership, and the part after, were two separate accounting periods; and for that purpose the profits of the company charged to corporation tax for the accounting period shall be apportioned between those parts.

16(3)   No unrelieved surplus ACT of the company shall be set off against the company's liability to corporation tax on any profits charged to corporation tax for an accounting period ending after the change of ownership; and for this purpose an accounting period in which the change of ownership occurs shall be treated as if the part ending with the change of ownership, and the part after, were two separate accounting periods.

16(4)   Paragraph (3) applies to unrelieved surplus ACT consisting of ACT which a subsidiary is treated as having paid by virtue of section 240(2) as it applies to unrelieved surplus ACT consisting of ACT paid in respect of any distribution made by the subsidiary.

16(5)   Sections 768(8) and (9) and 769 shall apply for the purposes of this regulation as if in subsection (3) of section 769 the reference to the benefit of the losses were a reference to the benefit of unrelieved surplus ACT.

16(6)   In paragraph (1) **"a major change in the nature or conduct of a trade or business"** includes–

(a)   a major change in the type of property dealt in, or services or facilities provided, in the trade or business;

(b)   a major change in customers, outlets or markets of the trade or business;

(c)   a change whereby the company ceases to be a trading company and becomes an investment company or vice versa; or

(d)   where the company is an investment company, a major change in the nature of the investments held by the company;

and this paragraph applies even if the change is the result of a gradual process which began outside the period of three years mentioned in paragraph (1).

16(7)   In this regulation–

"trading company" means a company whose business consists wholly or mainly in the carrying on of a trade or trades;

"investment company" means a company (other than a holding company) whose business consists wholly or mainly in the making of investments and the principal part of whose income is derived therefrom;

"holding company" means a company whose business consists wholly or mainly in the holding of shares or securities of companies which are its 90 per cent subsidiaries and which are trading companies;

"90 per cent subsidiary" has the meaning given by section 838.

RESTRICTION ON APPLICATION OF REGULATION 15 ON CHANGE OF OWNERSHIP OF COMPANY

17(1)   This regulation applies where–

(a)   there is a change in the ownership of a company ("the relevant company"),

(b)   there is an amount of unrelieved surplus ACT which the relevant company, as a subsidiary company, is treated as having paid by virtue of section 240(2), and

(c)   within the period of six years beginning three years before the change, there is a major change in the nature or conduct of a trade or business of the company which is for the purposes of regulation 15 the surrendering company in relation to that amount.

17(2) The amount of unrelieved surplus ACT referred to in paragraph (1)(b) shall not be set off in accordance with regulation 14 against the relevant company's liability to corporation tax on profits charged to corporation tax for an accounting period ending after the change of ownership; and for this purpose an accounting period in which the change of ownership occurs shall be treated as if the part ending with the change of ownership, and the part after, were two separate accounting periods.

17(3) Paragraphs (5) to (7) of regulation 16 shall apply for the purposes of this regulation as they apply for the purposes of that regulation and as if the reference in paragraph (6) of regulation 16 to the period of three years mentioned in paragraph (1) of that regulation were a reference to the period mentioned in paragraph (1)(c) of this regulation.

RESTRICTION ON SET-OFF UNDER REGULATION 14 WHERE ASSET TRANSFERRED AFTER CHANGE OF OWNERSHIP OF COMPANY

18(1) This regulation applies where–

(a) there is a change in the ownership of a company ("the relevant company"),

(b) after the change the relevant company acquires an asset from another company in circumstances such that section 171(1) of the Taxation of Chargeable Gains Act 1992 applies to the acquisition, and

(c) a chargeable gain accrues to the relevant company on the disposal of the asset within the period of three years beginning with the change of ownership.

18(2) For the purposes of paragraph (1)(c) an asset acquired by the relevant company as mentioned in paragraph (1)(b) shall be treated as the same as an asset owned at a later time by that company if the value of the second asset is derived in whole or in part from the first asset, and in particular where the second asset is a freehold, and the first asset was a leasehold and the lessee has acquired the reversion.

18(3) In relation to the accounting period in which the chargeable gain accrues to the relevant company ("the relevant period"), regulation 14 shall have effect as if the limit imposed by paragraph (4) of that regulation on the amount of unrelieved surplus ACT to be set against the relevant company's liability to corporation tax were reduced by an amount equal to 20 per cent of the amount of the chargeable gain.

18(4) Paragraph (5) of regulation 16 shall apply for the purposes of this regulation as it applies for the purposes of that regulation.

RECOVERY OF UNRELIEVED SURPLUS ACT WRONGLY SET OFF

19 If an officer of Revenue and Customs discovers that any set off of unrelieved surplus ACT of a company by virtue of regulation 14 ought not to have been made, or has become excessive, the officer may make any such assessments as may in his judgment be required for recovering any tax that ought to have been paid and generally for securing that the resulting liability to tax (including interest on unpaid tax) of the company is what it would have been if only such set off had been made as ought to have been made.

History – In reg. 19 the words "an officer of Revenue and Customs" substituted for the words "an officer of the Board" by SI 2010/669, reg. 6, with effect from 1 April 2010.

SET OFF OF UNRELIEVED SURPLUS ACT AGAINST LIABILITY TO CORPORATION TAX ON PROFITS OF A CONTROLLED FOREIGN COMPANY APPORTIONED TO A COMPANY

20(1) In any case where–

(a) an amount of chargeable profits ("Chapter IV profits") of a controlled foreign company is apportioned to a company resident in the United Kingdom under the provisions of Chapter IV of Part XVII of the Taxes Act, and

(b) the company to whom the amount is apportioned has an amount of surplus shadow ACT, calculated in accordance with regulation 12 and (where applicable) regulation 13, available to be set against the company's liability to corporation tax for the appropriate accounting period (including, by virtue of regulation 3(3), its liability to tax under section 747(4) for that period),

then so much of that amount as does not exceed the relevant maximum shall be set against the company's liability to tax under that section in respect of the Chapter IV profits.

20(2) So much of any unrelieved surplus ACT of the company as does not exceed the relevant amount may be set against the company's liability to tax in respect of the Chapter IV profits.

20(3) Where—

(a) the whole of the amount of the company's surplus shadow ACT has not been set off against the company's liability to tax as mentioned in paragraph (1), and

(b) the company is a member of a group,

the part of that amount that has not been so utilised may be allocated by the parent company to any other company in the group to whom an amount of Chapter IV profits has been apportioned, and the provisions of this regulation shall apply accordingly to that other company.

20(4) In this regulation—

(a) **"the appropriate accounting period"** has the same meaning as in paragraph 1 of Schedule 26;

(b) **"the relevant amount"** is the amount (if any) which is the difference between the amount of the relevant maximum and the amount of surplus shadow ACT set against the company's liability in respect of the Chapter IV profits in accordance with paragraph (1);

(c) **"the relevant maximum"** is the amount calculated in accordance with the formula—

$$C - D$$

where—

C   is the amount of shadow ACT that would have been treated as paid (apart from regulation 11(10) to (12)) in respect of a relevant distribution made at the end of the company's appropriate accounting period of an amount which, together with the shadow ACT treated as paid in respect of it, is equal to the amount calculated in accordance with the formula specified in paragraph (5), and

D   is the portion of the controlled foreign company's creditable tax (if any) which is apportioned to the company for that accounting period as mentioned in section 747(4)(a).

20(5) The formula specified in this paragraph is—

$$E - F$$

where—

E   is the amount of the Chapter IV profits on which the company is chargeable to corporation tax for the appropriate accounting period, and

F   is the total of any relevant allowances which are to be regarded, by virtue of paragraph 1(5) of Schedule 26, as having been allowed as a deduction against the company's profits together with any such additional amount as would fall to be so regarded if a claim under paragraph 1(1) of Schedule 26 were made in respect of all relevant allowances that are available under that paragraph.

DISPLACEMENT OF UNRELIEVED SURPLUS ACT – CONSEQUENTIAL PROVISION

21(1) Where, with respect to an accounting period of a company ("the affected company") that is a member of a group at any time in that accounting period—

(a) an amount of unrelieved surplus ACT is displaced under regulation 12(7)(d) or 13(8)(b) or (d), and

(b) as a consequence the affected company is assessed to, or an amendment of its self-assessment is made in respect of, an amount of corporation tax for that accounting period,

then, if the whole of that amount of corporation tax is not paid by the affected company within six months from the date determined under paragraph (2), any other company that is a member of the group at any time in that accounting period may, at any time within two years from that date, be assessed and charged (in the name of the affected company) to the whole or, as the case may be, the unpaid part of that amount; and a company paying any amount of corporation tax under this paragraph shall be entitled to recover from the affected company a sum equal to the aggregate of the amount paid and any interest paid by the company under section 87A of the Taxes Management Act 1970 on that amount.

21(2) The date referred to in paragraph (1) is whichever is the later of—

(a) the date when the amount of corporation tax became due and payable by the affected company or, as the case may be, the date when that amount is treated as having become due and payable under the Corporation Tax (Instalment Payments) Regulations 1998; and

(b) the date when an amendment of the affected company's self-assessment was made.

LIFE ASSURANCE COMPANIES

22(1) So much of the policy holders' share of the franked investment income from investments of a company's long-term insurance fund as is referable to its life assurance business–

(a) shall not be used (for the purposes of computing the amount of shadow ACT which the company is treated as having paid for an accounting period under regulation 11(10)) to frank relevant distributions made by the company in that period;

(b) shall be disregarded in determining whether the company has a surplus of franked investment income as mentioned in regulation 11(13), or the amount of the surplus.

22(2) For the purposes of regulations 12 to 14, the profits charged to corporation tax for any accounting period of a company carrying on life assurance business shall be reduced by deducting the policy holders' share of the relevant profits.

22(3) In this regulation–

"life assurance business" and **"long-term insurance fund"** shall be construed in accordance with section 431(2);

"policy holders' share of the franked investment income" shall be construed in accordance with section 434(6A)(a);

"policy holders' share of the relevant profits" shall be construed in accordance with section 89 of the Finance Act 1989.

History – In reg. 22(1) words "So much of the policy holders' share of the franked investment income from investments of a company's long-term insurance fund as is referable to its" substituted for "The policy holders' share of the franked investment income from investments held in connection with a company's", by SI 2003/1861, reg. 2(2), with effect from 7 August 2003, in relation to distributions made on or after 9 April 2003 in accounting periods beginning before (as well as accounting periods ending on or after) 7 August 2003.

In reg. 22(3) words "and "long-term insurance fund"" inserted by SI 2003/1861, reg. 2(3), with effect from 7 August 2003, in relation to distributions made on or after 9 April 2003 in accounting periods beginning before (as well as accounting periods ending on or after) 7 August 2003.

CANCELLATION OF TAX ADVANTAGE

23 [Omitted by SI 2010/669, reg. 7.]

History – Reg. 23 omitted by SI 2010/669, reg. 7, with effect from 1 April 2010.

> "**23(1)** Section 704 shall have effect in relation to any relevant distribution with the modification specified in paragraph (2).
>
> **23(2)** In paragraph A after sub-paragraph (d) there shall be inserted–
>
> "**(da)** the application of franked investment income for the purpose of regulations made under section 32 of the Finance Act 1998, or"."

INSURANCE COMPANIES (CAPITAL REDEMPTION BUSINESS) (MODIFICATION OF THE CORPORATION TAX ACTS) REGULATIONS 1999

(SI 1999/498, as amended by SI 2004/2310 and SI 2006/3271)

Made on 1 March 1999 by the Treasury, in exercise of the powers conferred on them by section 458A of the Income and Corporation Taxes Act 1988. Operative from 23 March 1999.

ARRANGEMENT OF REGULATIONS

CITATION, COMMENCEMENT AND EFFECT

1 These Regulations may be cited as the Insurance Companies (Capital Redemption Business) (Modification of the Corporation Tax Acts) Regulations 1999, shall come into force on 23rd March 1999 and shall have effect with respect to accounting periods of insurance companies ending on or after 1st July 1999.

INTERPRETATION

2 In these Regulations–

> **"capital redemption business"** means any capital redemption business within the meaning of section 458 of the Taxes Act other than business referred to in subsection (4) of that section;
>
> **"the life assurance provisions of the Corporation Tax Acts"** shall be construed in accordance with section 458A(4) of the Taxes Act;
>
> **"the Taxes Act"** means the Income and Corporation Taxes Act 1988.

APPLICATION OF LIFE ASSURANCE PROVISIONS OF THE CORPORATION TAX ACTS TO CAPITAL REDEMPTION BUSINESS

3 The life assurance provisions of the Corporation Tax Acts specified in regulations 4 to 16 shall have effect in relation to any insurance company carrying on capital redemption business–

(a)   as if the company's capital redemption business were life assurance business; and

(b)   as respects its capital redemption business, with the modifications provided for in those regulations.

MODIFICATIONS OF SECTION 76 OF THE TAXES ACTS

4 [Reg. 4 revoked by SI 2004/2310, Schedule, para. 78.]

History – Reg. 4 revoked by SI 2004/2310, Schedule, para. 78, with effect in relation to accounting periods beginning on or after 1 April 2004 subject to the transitional provisions at FA 2004, s. 43 and 44. Former reg. 4 read as follows:

> "**4(1)** Section 76 of the Taxes Act shall be modified as follows.
>
> **4(2)** Subsection (5A) shall be omitted.
>
> **4(3)** In subsection (6) the words from "or to any" to the end shall be omitted.
>
> **4(4)** In subsection (8) the definition of "capital redemption business" shall be omitted."

MODIFICATIONS OF SECTION 431 OF THE TAXES ACT

5(1) Section 431 of the Taxes Act shall be modified as follows.

5(2) In subsection (2)–

(a) after the definition of "basic life assurance and general annuity business" there shall be inserted the following definition–

"**"capital redemption business"** has the same meaning as in section 458;";

(b) in the definition of "life assurance business" there shall be added at the end the words "and capital redemption business".

MODIFICATION OF SECTION 431B OF THE TAXES ACT

6(1) Section 431B of the Taxes Act shall be modified as follows.

6(2) In subsection (1) after the words "life assurance business" there shall be inserted the words ", other than its capital redemption business,".

MODIFICATION OF SECTION 458 OF THE TAXES ACT

7(1) Section 458 of the Taxes Act shall be modified as follows.

7(2) Subsections (1) and (2) shall be omitted.

MODIFICATION OF SCHEDULE 19AC TO THE TAXES ACT

8 [Reg. 8 revoked by SI 2006/3271, reg. 43 and Sch., Pt. 2.]

History – Reg. 8 revoked by SI 2006/3271, reg. 43 and Sch., Pt. 2 with effect from 31 December 2006 in relation to accounting periods ending on or after that date. Reg. 8 read as follows:

> "**8(1)** Schedule 19AC to the Taxes Act shall be modified as follows.
>
> **8(2)** In paragraph 5(1), in paragraph (a) of the subsection (6A) notionally inserted in section 76 of the Taxes Act, the words "or capital redemption business" shall be omitted.".

MODIFICATION OF SECTION 44 OF THE FINANCE ACT 1989

9(1) Section 44 of the Finance Act 1989 shall be modified as follows.

9(2) After subsection (12) there shall be inserted the following subsection–

"**44(12A)** In subsection (12) above "life assurance business" has the same meaning as in Chapter I of Part XII of the Taxes Act 1988."

MODIFICATION OF SECTION 82 OF THE FINANCE ACT 1989

10(1) Section 82 of the Finance Act 1989 shall be modified as follows.

10(2) After subsection (8) there shall be added the following subsection–

"**82(9)** In this section and in sections 83, 83AA, 85, 86, 88, 88A and 89, and in paragraph 1A(1) of Schedule 8A, "life assurance business" has the same meaning as in Chapter I of Part XII of the Taxes Act 1988."

MODIFICATION OF SECTION 213 OF THE TAXATION OF CHARGEABLE GAINS ACT 1992

11(1) Section 213 of the Taxation of Chargeable Gains Act 1992 shall be modified as follows.

11(2) In subsection (1A) for the words from "which" to the end there shall be substituted the words "which are referable to basic life assurance and general annuity business".

MODIFICATION OF SECTION 214 OF THE TAXATION OF CHARGEABLE GAINS ACT 1992

12(1) Section 214 of the Taxation of Chargeable Gains Act 1992 shall be modified as follows.

12(2) In subsection (1)(c) (definition of "relevant linked liabilities") after the words "general annuity business" there shall be inserted the words ", other than capital redemption business,".

MODIFICATION OF SECTION 65 OF THE FINANCE (NO. 2)ACT 1992

13(1) Section 65 of the Finance (No. 2) Act 1992 shall be modified as follows.

13(2) In subsection (3)(b) there shall be added at the end the words "and capital redemption business".

MODIFICATION OF SCHEDULE 18 TO THE FINANCE ACT 1994

14(1) Schedule 18 to the Finance Act 1994 shall be modified as follows.

14(2) In paragraph 1A(1) the words "or capital redemption business" shall be omitted.

MODIFICATIONS OF SCHEDULE 11 TO THE FINANCE ACT 1996

15(1) Schedule 11 to the Finance Act 1996 shall be modified as follows.

15(2) In paragraph 1(1)(a) and (2) the words "or capital redemption business", in both places where they occur, shall be omitted.

15(3) In paragraph 2–

(a)   for sub-paragraph (1) there shall be substituted the following paragraph–

"**2(1)** Where an insurance company carries on basic life assurance and general annuity business, a separate computation, using only the non-trading credits and non-trading debits referable to that business, shall be made for the purposes of this Chapter in relation to that business.";

(b)   in sub-paragraph (3) for the words from "Where" to "capital redemption business," there shall be substituted the words "Where an insurance company carries on life assurance business or any category of life assurance business,".

15(4) In paragraph 4–

(a)   in sub-paragraph (1) for the words from "paragraph 2 above" to "capital redemption business," there shall be substituted the words "paragraph 2 above for basic life assurance and general annuity business,";

(b)   in sub-paragraph (2)(a) for the words "the relevant category of business" there shall be substituted the words "basic life assurance and general annuity business";

(c)   in sub-paragraph (7) for the words "the relevant category of business" there shall be substituted the words "its basic life assurance and general annuity business";

(d)   in sub-paragraph (10) for the words "the relevant category of business" there shall be substituted the words "basic life assurance and general annuity business";

(e)   in sub-paragraph (16) the definition of "the relevant category of business" and the word "and" immediately preceding it shall be omitted.

15(5) In paragraph 6–

(a)   the definition of "capital redemption business" shall be omitted;

(b)   in the definition of "life assurance business" after the words "annuity business" there shall be inserted the words "or capital redemption business".

MODIFICATION OF PARAGRAPH 19 OF SCHEDULE 12 TO THE FINANCE ACT 1997

16(1) Paragraph 19 of Schedule 12 to the Finance Act 1997 shall be modified as follows.

16(2) After sub-paragraph (4) there shall be added the following sub-paragraph–

"**19(5)** In this paragraph **"life assurance business"** has the same meaning as in Chapter I of Part XII of the Taxes Act 1988."

Statutory Instruments

FRIENDLY SOCIETIES (PROVISIONAL REPAYMENTS FOR EXEMPT BUSINESS) REGULATIONS 1999

(SI 1999/622, as amended by SI 2001/3269 and SI 2001/3973)

Made on 9 March 1999 by the Treasury, in exercise of the powers conferred on them by s. 121 of the Finance Act 1993. Operative from 30 March 1999.

CITATION, COMMENCEMENT AND EFFECT

1(1) These Regulations may be cited as the Friendly Societies (Provisional Repayments for Exempt Business) Regulations 1999 and shall come into force on 30th March 1999.

1(2) These Regulations shall have effect in relation to accounting periods of friendly societies ending on or after 1st July 1999.

INTERPRETATION

2 In these Regulations unless the context otherwise requires–

"**exempt business**" means any business of a friendly society the profits arising from which are exempt from income tax and corporation tax under section 460(1) of the Taxes Act, not being a business carried on by a friendly society all of whose profits are so exempt;

"**Schedule 3**" means Schedule 3 to the Finance (No. 2) Act 1997;

"**Schedule 19AB**" means Schedule 19AB to the Taxes Act;

"**the Taxes Act**" means the Income and Corporation Taxes Act 1988.

History – In reg. 2, the words ", 461(1) or 461B(1)" omitted by SI 2001/3973, reg. 3, with effect for accounting periods of friendly societies beginning after 31 December 2001.

APPLICATION OF SCHEDULE 19AB – GENERAL

3(1) Schedule 19AB shall have effect, in accordance with paragraphs (2) and (3) below, in relation to exempt business of a friendly society.

3(2) Schedule 19AB, as it is deemed to have effect, by virtue of paragraph 12(1) of Schedule 3 for the purposes of section 121 of the Finance Act 1993, without the amendments made by Schedule 3, shall have effect as mentioned in paragraph (1) above with the modifications and exceptions specified in regulations 4, 5 and 8 to 12.

3(3) [Omitted by SI 2001/3973, reg. 5.]

History – In reg. 3(1), the words "as it has effect in relation to the pension business of an insurance company" omitted by SI 2001/3973, reg. 4, with effect for accounting periods of friendly societies beginning after 31 December 2001.

Reg. 3(3) omitted by SI 2001/3973, reg. 5, with effect for accounting periods of friendly societies beginning after 31 December 2001.

SUBSTITUTION OF PARAGRAPH 1(1) OF SCHEDULE 19AB (AS UNAMENDED BY SCHEDULE 3)

4(1) Paragraph (2) substitutes the following sub-paragraph for sub-paragraph (1) of paragraph 1 of Schedule 19AB (as unamended by Schedule 3) in relation to exempt business of a friendly society.

4(2) For that sub-paragraph (1) there shall be substituted–

"**1(1)** A friendly society carrying on both tax exempt business and business other than tax exempt business shall for each provisional repayment period in an accounting period be entitled on a claim made in that behalf to a payment (in this Schedule referred to as a "**provisional repayment**") of an amount equal to–

(a)   [omitted by SI 2001/3973, reg. 6(b)]

(b)   [omitted by SI 2001/3973, reg. 6(b)]

(c)   respects any distribution made on or after 6th April 1999 and before 6th April 2004 that–

    (i)   is received by the society in that provisional repayment period, and

    (ii)   is referable to its tax exempt business,

    (iii) [omitted by SI 2001/3973, reg. 6(d)]

the appropriate portion of any tax credit in respect of that distribution.".

History – In reg. 4(2), in substituted sub-para. (1), the words "the aggregate of the following amounts" and sub-para. (a) and (b) and (c)(iii) omitted and the word "and" at the end of sub-para. (c)(i) inserted by SI 2001/3973, reg. 6, with effect for accounting periods of friendly societies beginning after 31 December 2001.

SUBSTITUTION OF PARAGRAPH 1(5) OF SCHEDULE 19AB WHERE REGULATION 4 APPLIES

5(1) Paragraph (2) substitutes the following sub-paragraphs for sub-paragraph (5) of paragraph 1 of Schedule 19AB in circumstances where regulation 4(2) applies.

5(2) For sub-paragraph (5) there shall be substituted–

"**1(5)** [omitted by SI 2001/3973, reg. 7(a)]

1(5A) In sub-paragraph (1)(c) above **"the appropriate portion"** means–

(a) where the distribution in question is income arising from assets linked to tax exempt basic life assurance and general annuity business or to tax exempt class IV business the profits of which are exempt from tax by virtue of section 460(1) (**"section 460(1) exempt business"**), the whole;

(b) where the distribution in question is income arising from assets of the society's overseas life assurance fund, the fraction whose numerator is the mean of the opening and closing liabilities to policyholders in respect of the society's tax exempt overseas life assurance business and whose denominator is the opening and closing liabilities to policyholders in respect of the whole of the society's overseas life assurance business;

(c) if and to the extent that the distribution in question is income arising from assets of the society's long-term insurance fund but, on the assumption that section 460(1) exempt business were a separate category of business within section 432A, is not referable to a category of business by virtue of subsection (3) or (4) of that section, the provisional fraction;

(d) except as provided by paragraph (a), (b) or (c) above, none.

1(5B) [Omitted by SI 2001/3973, reg. 7(a).]

1(5C) In determining the provisional fraction for the purposes of sub-paragraph (5)(c) above, tax exempt basic life assurance and general annuity business and tax exempt class IV business shall be taken to be a single category of business for the purposes of section 432A(5).

1(5D) In sub-paragraph (5A) above references to assets of the society's long-term insurance fund–

(a) as respects societies to which regulation 13(1) of the Friendly Societies (Modification of the Corporation Tax Acts) Regulations 1997 applies, shall be construed in accordance with the definition in subsection (11) of section 432A, read with subsections (12) to (14) of that section, as those subsections are added by regulation 13(5) of those Regulations;

(b) as respects other societies, shall be construed in accordance with the definitions of "long-term business" (as substituted by regulation 6(4) of those Regulations) and "long-term insurance fund" in section 431(2).

1(5E) In sub-paragraphs (5A) and (5C) above–

"tax exempt basic life assurance and general annuity business" shall be construed in accordance with the definition inserted in section 431(2) by regulation 6(2) of the Friendly Societies (Modification of the Corporation Tax Acts) Regulations 1997;

"tax exempt class IV business" shall be construed in accordance with the definition inserted in section 431(2) by regulation 7(2) of those Regulations;

"tax exempt overseas life assurance business" shall be construed in accordance with section 441(4D)."

History – In reg. 5(2), in sub-para. (5)–(5E) of Sch. 19AB, para. 1, sub-para. (5) and (5B) omitted, in (5D) the words "sub-paragraph" substituted and in sub-para. (5E) the words "(5A) and" substituted by SI 2001/3973, reg. 7, with effect for accounting periods of friendly societies beginning after 31 December 2001.

In reg. 5(2), in sub-para (5)–(5E) of Sch. 19AB, para. 1, in former (5)(a)(ii) and (c) and (5A)(c) and (5D) (twice) the words "long-term insurance fund" substituted for the words "long term business fund", and in sub-para (5D)(b) the words "long-term" substituted for the words "long term" by SI 2001/3629, art. 182, with effect from 1 December 2001.

SUBSTITUTION OF PARAGRAPH 1(1) OF SCHEDULE 19AB (AS AMENDED BY SCHEDULE 3)

6 [Omitted by SI 2001/3973, reg. 8.]

History – Reg. 6 omitted by SI 2001/3973, reg. 8, with effect for accounting periods of friendly societies beginning after 31 December 2001.

Statutory Instruments

SUBSTITUTION OF PARAGRAPH 1(5) OF SCHEDULE 19AB WHERE REGULATION 6 APPLIES

7 [Omitted by SI 2001/3973, reg. 8.]

History – Reg. 7 omitted by SI 2001/3973, reg. 8, with effect for accounting periods of friendly societies beginning after 31 December 2001.

MODIFICATIONS OF PARAGRAPH 1(2) TO (4), (7), (10) AND (11) OF SCHEDULE 19AB

8(1) Paragraphs (2) to (7) specify modifications of sub-paragraphs (2) to (4), (7), (10) and (11) of paragraph 1 of Schedule 19AB in relation to exempt business of a friendly society.

8(2) In sub-paragraph (2)–

(a) for the words "a company" there shall be substituted the words "a society";

(b) for paragraph (a) there shall be substituted–

"(a) shall begin whenever–

(i) the society begins, at a time when it is carrying on only tax exempt business, to carry on business other than tax exempt business;

(ii) the society begins, at a time when it is carrying on only business other than tax exempt business, to carry on tax exempt business;

(iii) an accounting period of the society begins at a time when the society is carrying on both tax exempt business and business other than tax exempt business; or

(iv) a provisional repayment period of the society ends, at a time when the society is carrying on both tax exempt business and business other than tax exempt business; and";

(c) in paragraph (b)(ii) for the word "company" there shall be substituted the word "society".

8(3) Sub-paragraph (3) shall be omitted.

8(4) For sub-paragraph (4) there shall be substituted the following sub-paragraph–

"**1(4)** The provisional fraction for the purposes of this paragraph for an accounting period which begins before 6th April 2004 shall be such fraction as the society may reasonably estimate, being a fraction which is not likely to be greater than the relevant fraction for its tax exempt business which would be determined in accordance with subsections (5) to (9B) of section 432A for that accounting period."

8(5) In sub-paragraph (7)–

(a) for the words "pension business" (wherever occurring) there shall be substituted the words "tax exempt business";

(b) for the word "company" (wherever occurring) there shall be substituted the word "society".

(c) the words "or repaid" shall be omitted;

(d) paragraph (a) shall be omitted;

(e) for "9(2)" there shall be substituted "9(3)";

(f) for words "or section 42(4) of the Management Act" shall be omitted.

8(6) Paragraphs (10) and (11) shall be omitted.

8(7) [Effectively omitted by SI 2001/3973, reg. 9(5).]

History – Reg. 8(3) substituted by SI 2001/3973, reg. 9(2), with effect for accounting periods of friendly societies beginning after 31 December 2001.
Reg. 8(4) substituted by SI 2001/3973, reg. 9(3), with effect for accounting periods of friendly societies beginning after 31 December 2001.
Reg. 8(5)(c)–(e) inserted by SI 2001/3973, reg. 9(4), with effect for accounting periods of friendly societies beginning after 31 December 2001.
Reg. 8(6) substituted for former reg. 8(6) and (7) by SI 2001/3973, reg. 9(5), with effect for accounting periods of friendly societies beginning after 31 December 2001.

DISAPPLICATION OF PARAGRAPH 2 OF SCHEDULE 19AB

9 Paragraph 2 of Schedule 19AB shall not apply to exempt business of a friendly society.

History – Reg. 9 substituted by SI 2001/3973, reg. 10, with effect for accounting periods of friendly societies beginning after 31 December 2001.

MODIFICATIONS OF PARAGRAPH 3 OF SCHEDULE 19AB

10(1) Paragraphs (2) to (7) specify modifications of paragraph 3 of Schedule 19AB in relation to exempt business of a friendly society.

10(2) In sub-paragraph (1)–

(a) for the words "an insurance company's" there shall be substituted the words "a friendly society's";

(b) for the words "the company" there shall be substituted the words "the society";

(c) for the words "the insurance company" there shall be substituted the words "the friendly society".

10(3) In sub-paragraph (1A)–

(a) for the word "company" (wherever occurring) there shall be substituted the word "society";

(b) for the words "pension business" (wherever occurring) there shall be substituted the words "tax exempt business".

(c) for the words "assumptions in sub-paragraphs (1B) and (1C)" there shall be substituted the words "assumption in sub-paragraph (1B)";

(d) the words "or repaid" shall be omitted;

(e) for "9(2)" there shall be substituted "9(3)";

(f) the words "or section 42(4) of the Management Act" shall be omitted;

(g) paragraph (a) shall be omitted.

10(4) In sub-paragraph (1B)–

(a) for the words "the company" there shall be substituted the words "the society";

(b) for the words "the company's" there shall be substituted the words "the society's".

(c) the word "first" shall be omitted;

(d) the words "or repayments" shall be omitted;

(e) paragraph (a) shall be omitted;

(f) in paragraph (b) for the words "that sub-paragraph" there shall be substituted the words "sub-paragraph (1A) above".

10(5) Sub-paragraph (1C) shall be omitted.

10(6) In sub-paragraph (5) for the word "company" there shall be substituted the word "society".

10(7) In sub-paragraph (8)–

(a) for the word "company" (wherever occurring) there shall be substituted the word "society";

(b) the words "or repaid" shall be omitted;

(c) paragraph (a) shall be omitted;

(d) in paragraph (b) for the words "that sub-paragraph" there shall be substituted the words "sub-paragraph (1A) above".

History – Reg. 10(3)(c)–(g) inserted by SI 2001/3973, reg. 11(2), with effect for accounting periods of friendly societies beginning after 31 December 2001.
Reg. 10(4)(c)–(f) inserted by SI 2001/3973, reg. 11(3), with effect for accounting periods of friendly societies beginning after 31 December 2001.
Reg. 10(5) substituted by SI 2001/3973, reg. 11(4), with effect for accounting periods of friendly societies beginning after 31 December 2001.
Reg. 10(7) substituted by SI 2001/3973, reg. 11(5), with effect for accounting periods of friendly societies beginning after 31 December 2001.

DISAPPLICATION OF PARAGRAPHS 4 AND 5 OF SCHEDULE 19AB

11 Paragraphs 4 and 5 of Schedule 19AB shall not apply to exempt business of a friendly society.

MODIFICATIONS OF PARAGRAPH 6 OF SCHEDULE 19AB

12(1) Paragraphs (2) and (3) specify modifications of paragraph 6 of Schedule 19AB in relation to exempt business of a friendly society.

12(2) In sub-paragraph (1)–

(a) after the definition of "provisional repayment period" there shall be added the following definition–

""**tax exempt business**" means any business of a friendly society the profits arising from which are exempt from income tax and corporation tax under section 460(1)."

(b)　　in the definition of "provisional fraction" for the words "paragraphs 1(4) and 2" there shall be substituted "paragraph 1(4)".

12(3)　　Sub-paragraphs (4) to (6) shall be omitted.

History – Reg. 12(2) split into para. (a) and (b) and in new para. (a), in the definition of "tax exempt business" the words ", 461(1) or 461B(1)" omitted by SI 2001/3973, reg. 12(3), with effect for accounting periods of friendly societies beginning after 31 December 2001.

Reg. 12(3) substituted by SI 2001/3973, reg. 12(3), with effect for accounting periods of friendly societies beginning after 31 December 2001.

REVOCATIONS

13　　The Friendly Societies (Provisional Repayments for Exempt Business) Regulations 1993 and the Friendly Societies (Provisional Repayments for Exempt Business) (Amendment) Regulations 1997 are hereby revoked as respects accounting periods in relation to which, by virtue of regulation 1(2), these Regulations have effect.

INSURANCE COMPANIES (GILT-EDGED SECURITIES) (PERIODIC ACCOUNTING FOR TAX ON INTEREST) REGULATIONS 1999

(SI 1999/623)

Made on 9 March 1999 by the Treasury, in exercise of the powers conferred on them by s. 51B(1) to (4) of the Income and Corporation Taxes Act 1988. Operative from 30 March 1999.

ARRANGEMENT OF REGULATIONS

CITATION, COMMENCEMENT AND EFFECT

1(1) These Regulations may be cited as the Insurance Companies (Gilt-edged Securities) (Periodic Accounting for Tax on Interest) Regulations 1999 and shall come into force on 30th March 1999.

1(2) These Regulations have effect as respects payments of interest on relevant gilt-edged securities made without deduction of tax to an insurance company carrying on pension business that fall within an accounting period of that company beginning before 1st April 1999 and ending on or after 1st July 1999, not being payments to which section 51B(5A) of the Taxes Act refers.

INTERPRETATION

2 In these Regulations unless the context otherwise requires–

   "amount of excess gilt interest received" has the same meaning as in the Gilts Regulations;

   "the Gilts Regulations" means the Gilt-edged Securities (Periodic Accounting for Tax on Interest) Regulations 1995;

   "pension business" has the meaning given by section 431B of the Taxes Act;

   "relevant gilt-edged securities" has the meaning given by section 51B(5) of the Taxes Act;

   "return period" has the same meaning as in the Gilts Regulations;

   "Schedule 19AB" means Schedule 19AB to the Taxes Act;

   "the Taxes Act" means the Income and Corporation Taxes Act 1988.

BASIC RULE

3(1) Notwithstanding the provisions of the Gilts Regulations, an insurance company carrying on pension business shall not be required to include in its return for a return period–

(a)   the amount of tax on the amount of excess gilt interest received in relation to which the condition specified in paragraph (2) below is satisfied, or

(b)   the appropriate portion of the amount of excess gilt interest received.

3(2) The condition specified is that the amount of tax referred to in paragraph (1)(a) above is identified in a claim, made by the specified date, for a notional repayment made pursuant to paragraph 1A(1) of Schedule 19AB (as inserted by regulation 6 of these Regulations).

3(3) In paragraph (1)(b) above **"the appropriate portion"** has the meaning given by paragraph 1A(7) of Schedule 19AB (as so inserted).

3(4) In paragraph (2) above

"the specified date" means–

    (a)   the date which is 14 days after the end of the return period, or

    (b)   where the return for the return period is made on a date less than 14 days after the end of the return period, that date.

MODIFICATIONS OF SCHEDULE 19AB

4 Regulations 5 to 9 make provision modifying the operation of Schedule 19AB in relation to cases where payments of interest on relevant gilt-edged securities are made without deduction of tax to an insurance company carrying on pension business.

5(1) Paragraphs (2) and (3) below specify modifications of paragraph 1 of Schedule 19AB.

5(2) In sub-paragraph (2), before the words "For the purposes of this paragraph" there shall be inserted the words "Subject to sub-paragraphs (2A) and (2B) below,".

5(3) After sub-paragraph (2) there shall be inserted the following sub-paragraphs–

    "**1(2A)** Sub-paragraph (2B) below has effect where payments of interest on relevant gilt-edged securities are made without deduction of tax to insurance companies carrying on pension business.

    1(2B) For the purposes of this paragraph, a **"provisional repayment period"** of a company–

        (a)   shall begin–

            (i)   on the date on which the company begins to carry on pension business; or

            (ii)   on the date on which the accounting period of the company beginning before 1st April 1999 and ending on or after 1st July 1999 begins, where the company is carrying on pension business at that time; or

            (iii)   if different from either of the dates referred to in sub-paragraphs (i) and (ii) above, on 1st October 1998 or 1st January 1999, where that date falls within the accounting period referred to in sub-paragraph (ii) above; and

        (b)   shall end on the expiration of a period ending on 30th September 1998, 31st December 1998 or 31st March 1999, where that date falls within the accounting period referred to in paragraph (a)(ii) above."

5(4) Where by virtue of paragraph 1(2B)(b) of Schedule 19AB (inserted by paragraph (3) above) a provisional repayment period of a company ends on 31st March 1999, being a time when the company is carrying on pension business, a provisional repayment period of the company shall be taken also to have ended on that date for the purposes of paragraph 1(2)(a)(iii) of that Schedule.

6 After paragraph 1 of Schedule 19AB there shall be inserted the following paragraph–

"ENTITLEMENT TO CERTAIN NOTIONAL PAYMENTS ON ACCOUNT

    1A(1) An insurance company carrying on pension business shall for each provisional repayment period in its accounting period beginning before 1st April 1999 and ending on or after 1st July 1999 be entitled on a claim made in that behalf by the specified date to a notional payment (in this Schedule referred to as a "notional repayment") of an amount equal, subject to paragraph 2 below, to the tax on the appropriate portion of the amount of excess gilt interest received in that provisional repayment period and referable to its pension business, or to a notional repayment of such lesser amount as may be specified in the claim.

    1A(2) No repayment shall be made to a company in respect of any claim to a notional repayment; but the notional repayment shall be taken to be the amount of tax referred to in regulation 3(1) of the Insurance Companies (Gilt-edged Securities) (Periodic Accounting for Tax on Interest) Regulations 1999.

    1A(3) For the purposes of this paragraph a **"provisional repayment period"** of a company–

        (a)   shall begin–

            (i)   on the date on which the company begins to carry on pension business; or

            (ii)   on the date on which the accounting period of the company beginning before 1st April 1999 and ending on or after 1st July 1999 begins, where the company is carrying on pension business at that time; or

(iii) if different from either of the dates referred to in sub-paragraphs (i) and (ii) above, on 1st October 1998 or 1st January 1999, where that date falls within the accounting period referred to in sub-paragraph (ii) above; and

(b)   shall end on the expiration of a period ending on 30th September 1998, 31st December 1998 or 31st March 1999, where that date falls within the accounting period referred to in paragraph (a)(ii).

1A(4) In sub-paragraph (1) above **"the specified date"** means the earlier of the following dates—

(a)   the date which is 14 days after the end of a provisional repayment period, or

(b)   where a provisional repayment period coincides with a return period within the meaning of the Gilts Regulations and the return for the return period is made on a date less than 14 days after the end of the return period, that date.

1A(5) In the application of subsections (5) to (9) of section 432A for the purpose of determining the amounts to which a company is entitled by way of notional repayments, the reference in subsection (5) to "the relevant fraction" shall be taken as a reference to the fraction determined in accordance with subsections (6) to (9)—

(a)   for the latest preceding accounting period of the company for which an inspector is satisfied that the company has supplied him with such information as would enable the relevant fraction for that accounting period to be estimated with reasonable accuracy, and

(b)   by reference to that information,

and, subject to sub-paragraph (6)(b) below, any reference in this paragraph to "the provisional fraction" is a reference to the fraction so determined.

1A(6) For the purposes of sub-paragraph (5) above—

(a)   **"information"** means any information, accounts, statements or reports delivered under section 11 of the Management Act; and

(b)   unless and until an inspector is satisfied as mentioned in paragraph (a) of that sub-paragraph, the provisional fraction shall be taken to be nil;

but this sub-pararaph is subject to paragraph 2 below.

1A(7) In sub-paragraph (1) above **"the appropriate portion"** means—

(a)   in the case of an insurance company carrying on pension business and no other category of long term business, the whole; and

(b)   in the case of an insurance company carrying on more than one category of long term business—

(i) where the payment in question is of interest on relevant gilt-edged securities arising from an asset linked to pension business, the whole;

(ii) where the payment in question is an amount of manufactured gilt interest received derived from an asset which at the time of its transfer (being the transfer referred to in paragraph 3 of Schedule 23A) was linked to pension business, the whole;

(iii) where the payment in question is an amount of manufactured gilt interest paid in respect of an asset linked to pension business, the whole;

(iv) if and to the extent that the payment in question is income which is not referable to a category of business by virtue of subsection (3) or (4) of section 432A, the provisional fraction, and

(v) except as provided by sub-paragraphs (i) to (iv) above, none.

1A(8) For the purposes of sub-paragraph (7)(b)(iv) above and in relation to a manufactured payment, the provisional fraction shall be found by applying subsections (5) to (9) of section 432A to the payment as if it were an amount of income arising from the assets of the company's long term fund.

1A(9) In sub-paragraph (1) above **"the amount of excess gilt interest received"**, in relation to a provisional repayment period, means the amount ascertained in accordance with the formula—

$$(A + B) - C$$

where—

A   is the amount of manufactured gilt interest received in that provisional repayment period;

B   is the amount of real gilt interest received in that provisional repayment period; and

Statutory Instruments

C   is the amount of manufactured gilt interest paid in that provisional repayment period;
and where the aggregate of A and B exceeds C.

1A(10) Where a claim made pursuant to sub-paragraph (1) above is for a lesser amount as mentioned in that sub-paragraph, the appropriate portion of each of the amounts A, B and C specified in sub-paragraph (9) above shall be ascertained in accordance with the formula–

$$\frac{D}{E}$$

where–

    D   is the lesser amount of the notional repayment claimed, and

    E   is the maximum amount of the notional repayment which it is possible for the company to claim.

1A(11) Paragraphs 57 to 60 of Schedule 18 to the Finance Act 1998 (general provisions as to procedure on claims and elections) shall not apply to a claim for a notional repayment.

1A(12) A claim for a notional repayment shall be in such form as the Board may determine and the form of claim shall provide for a declaration to the effect that all the particulars given in the form are correctly stated to the best of the knowledge and belief of the person making the claim.

1A(13) In this paragraph **"manufactured payment"** means any payment which for the purposes of Schedule 23A is a payment of manufactured interest, and to which paragraph 3A(2)(a) of that Schedule applies."

7(1) Paragraphs (2) to (6) below specify modifications of paragraph 2 of Schedule 19AB.

7(2) In sub-paragraph (1)(a) and (c), after the words "a provisional repayment", in both places where they occur, there shall be inserted the words "or a notional repayment".

7(3) In sub-paragraph (2)(a)–

(a)   after the words "any provisional repayment" there shall be inserted the words "or notional repayment";

(b)   after the words "sub-paragraph (3)" there shall be inserted the words "or (3A)".

7(4) In sub-paragraph (3), at the beginning, there shall be inserted the words "In the case of provisional repayments,".

7(5) After sub-paragraph (3) there shall be inserted the following sub-paragraphs–

    "**2(3A)** In the case of notional repayments, the amount referred to in sub-paragraph (2)(a) above is the amount (if any) by which total notional entitlement exceeds total notional past payments, and for this purpose–

"total notional entitlement" means the aggregate of the notional repayments to which the company would have been entitled (apart from this paragraph) for–

    (a)   the provisional repayment period to which the claim relates, and

    (b)   any earlier provisional repayment period in the same accounting period,

had the substituted provisional fraction been the provisional fraction for the accounting period as from the beginning of that period; and

"total notional past payments" means the aggregate of any amounts already taken into account by way of notional repayments for provisional repayment periods falling within that accounting period.

2(3B) In a case where, following the application of sub-paragraph (3A) above, the notional repayment for a provisional repayment period is less than the amount to which the company would be entitled for that provisional repayment period (apart from that sub-paragraph), the appropriate portion of each of the amounts A, B and C specified in paragraph 1A(9) above shall be ascertained in accordance with the formula–

$$\frac{F}{G}$$

where–

    F   is the amount of any notional repayment ascertained in accordance with sub-paragraph (3A) above, and

G   is the maximum amount of the notional repayment which it is possible for the company to claim (apart from that sub-paragraph).".

7(6) In sub-paragraph (4), at the end there shall be added "; and expressions used in this paragraph and in paragraph 1A above have the same meaning in this paragraph as they have in that paragraph".

8(1) Paragraphs (2) to (5) below specify modifications of paragraph 3 of Schedule 19AB.

8(2) In sub-paragraph (1), for paragraph (b) there shall be substituted the following paragraph–

> "(b)   the aggregate amount of the provisional repayments made to the company for that accounting period and of the notional repayments to which the company is entitled in respect of that accounting period exceeds the aggregate of the appropriate amount and the relevant final amount,".

8(3) After sub-paragraph (1C) there shall be inserted the following sub-paragraph–

> "**3(1CA)** For the purposes of sub-paragraph (1)(b) above, the relevant final amount for the accounting period of a company is the amount (if any) which, on the assumptions in sub-paragraphs (1B) and (1C) above, the company would have been entitled to be repaid, when its self-assessment for the period became final, in respect of income tax borne by deduction on the amount of manufactured gilt interest received and real gilt interest received if those amounts had been paid under deduction of tax, in respect of its pension business for that accounting period on a claim such as is mentioned in section 7.".

8(4) In sub-paragraph (5), at the end there shall be added–

> "; and so much of the principal as does not exceed the amount of the last notional repayment made to the company for the accounting period in question shall be taken to have become outstanding on the date on which the company made the claim referred to in paragraph 1A(1) above".

8(5) In sub-paragraph (6)–

(a)   in paragraph (a), after the words "provisional repayment" there shall be inserted the words "or, as the case may be, notional repayment,";

(b)   in paragraph (b), after the words "preceding provisional repayment" there shall be inserted the words "or, as the case may be, preceding notional repayment,";

(c)   after the words "that preceding provisional repayment" there shall be inserted the words "or, as the case may be, that preceding notional repayment,";

(d)   after the words "any preceding provisional repayments" there shall be inserted the words "or, as the case may be, any preceding notional repayments".

9(1) Paragraphs (2) and (3) below specify modifications of paragraph 6 of Schedule 19AB.

9(2) In sub-paragraph (1)–

(a)   before the definition of "provisional fraction" there shall be inserted the following definitions–

> **"the Gilts Regulations"** means the Gilt-edged Securities (Periodic Accounting for Tax on Interest) Regulations 1995;
>
> **"notional repayment"** means a notional repayment under paragraph 1A above;";

(b)   in the definition of "provisional fraction" after "1(4)" there shall be inserted ", 1A(7) and (9)";

(c)   in the definition of "provisional repayment period" after "1" there shall be inserted "or 1A";

(d)   at the end there shall be added the following definitions–

> **"relevant gilt-edged securities"** has the meaning given by section 51B(5);
>
> **"amount of manufactured gilt interest paid"**, **"amount of manufactured gilt interest received"** and **"amount of real gilt interest received"** have the same meanings in this Schedule in relation to a provisional repayment period as they have in the Gilts Regulations in relation to a return period.".

9(3) After sub-paragraph (2) there shall be inserted the following sub-paragraph–

> "**6(2A)** Any reference in this Schedule to a notional repayment for an accounting period is a reference to a notional repayment for a provisional repayment period falling within that accounting period."

REVOCATIONS

10(1) The Regulations referred to in paragraph (2) below are, to the extent specified in that paragraph, hereby revoked as respects any payments of interest on relevant gilt-edged securities to which, by virtue of regulation 1(2) of these Regulations, these Regulations apply.

10(2)   The Regulations referred to are–

(a)   the Insurance Companies (Gilt-edged Securities) (Periodic Accounting for Tax on Interest) Regulations 1995 – the whole;

(b)   the Insurance Companies (Gilt-edged Securities) (Periodic Accounting for Tax on Interest) (Amendment) Regulations 1996 – the whole;

(c)   the Stock Lending and Manufactured Payments (Revocations and Amendments) Regulations 1997 – regulation 7(2)(c).

FRIENDLY SOCIETIES (GILT-EDGED SECURITIES) (PERIODIC ACCOUNTING FOR TAX ON INTEREST) REGULATIONS 1999

(SI 1999/624)

Made on 9 March 1999 by the Treasury, in exercise of the powers conferred on them by s. 51B(1)–(4) of the Income and Corporation Taxes Act 1988 and s. 121 of the Finance Act 1993. Operative from 30 March 1999.

CITATION, COMMENCEMENT AND EFFECT

1(1) These Regulations may be cited as the Friendly Societies (Gilt-edged Securities) (Periodic Accounting for Tax on Interest) Regulations 1999 and shall come into force on 30th March 1999 immediately after the coming into force of the Insurance Companies (Gilt-edged Securities) (Periodic Accounting for Tax on Interest) Regulations 1999 and the Friendly Societies (Provisional Repayments for Exempt Business) Regulations 1999.

1(2) These Regulations have effect as respects payments of interest on relevant gilt-edged securities made without deduction of tax to a friendly society that fall within an accounting period of that society beginning before 1st April 1999 and ending on or after 1st July 1999, not being payments to which section 51B(5A) of the Taxes Act refers.

INTERPRETATION

2 In these Regulations unless the context otherwise requires–

"amount of excess gilt interest received" has the same meaning as in the Gilts Regulations;

"exempt business" means any business of a friendly society the profits arising from which are exempt from income tax and corporation tax under section 460(1), 461(1) or 461B(1) of the Taxes Act, not being a business carried on by a friendly society all of whose profits are so exempt;

"the Friendly Societies Regulations" means the Friendly Societies (Provisional Repayments for Exempt Business) Regulations 1999;

"the Gilts Regulations" means the Gilt-edged Securities (Periodic Accounting for Tax on Interest) Regulations 1995;

"relevant gilt-edged securities" has the meaning given by section 51B(5) of the Taxes Act;

"return period" has the same meaning as in the Gilts Regulations;

"Schedule 19AB" means Schedule 19AB to the Taxes Act;

"the Taxes Act" means the Income and Corporation Taxes Act 1988.

BASIC RULE

3(1) Notwithstanding the provisions of the Gilts Regulations, a friendly society carrying on both exempt business and business other than exempt business shall not be required to include in its return for a return period–

(a)   the amount of tax on the amount of excess gilt interest received in relation to which the condition specified in paragraph (2) below is satisfied, or

(b)   the appropriate portion of the amount of excess gilt interest received.

3(2) The condition specified is that the amount of tax referred to in paragraph (1)(a) above is identified in a claim, made by the specified date, for a notional repayment made pursuant to paragraph 1A(1) of Schedule 19AB (as inserted by regulation 6 of the Insurance Companies (Gilt-edged Securities) (Periodic Accounting for Tax on Interest) Regulations 1999).

3(3) In paragraph (1)(b) above **"the appropriate portion"** has the meaning given by paragraph 1A(7) of Schedule 19AB (as so inserted).

3(4) In paragraph (2) above **"the specified date"** means–

(a)   the date which is 14 days after the end of the return period, or

(b)   where the return for the return period is made on a date less than 14 days after the end of the return period, that date.

Statutory Instruments

MODIFICATIONS OF THE FRIENDLY SOCIETIES REGULATIONS

4   In relation to cases where payments of interest on relevant gilt-edged securities are made without deduction of tax to friendly societies carrying on exempt business, the Friendly Societies Regulations shall have effect with the modifications specified in regulations 5 to 8.

5(1)   Paragraph (2) below specifies a modification of regulation 8.

5(2)   After paragraph (2) of that regulation there shall be inserted the following paragraphs–

"**8(2A)**   In sub-paragraph (2A) for the words "insurance companies carrying on pension business" there shall be substituted the words "friendly societies carrying on tax exempt business".

8(2B)   In sub-paragraph (2B)–

(a)   for the words "a company" there shall be substituted the words "a society";

(b)   for paragraphs (a) and (b) there shall be substituted the following paragraphs–

"(a)   shall begin whenever–

(i)   the society begins, at a time when it is carrying on only tax exempt business, to carry on business other than tax exempt business;

(ii)   the society begins, at a time when it is carrying on only business other than tax exempt business, to carry on tax exempt business; or

(iii)   the accounting period of the society beginning before 1st April 1999 and ending on or after 1st July 1999 begins, at a time when the society is carrying on both tax exempt business and business other than tax exempt business; and

(b)   shall end on 31st March 1999.""

6   After regulation 8 there shall be inserted the following regulation–

"MODIFICATIONS OF PARAGRAPH 1A OF SCHEDULE 19AB

8A(1)   Paragraphs (2) to (10) specify modifications of paragraph 1A of Schedule 19AB in relation to exempt business of a friendly society.

8A(2)   In sub-paragraph (1)–

(a)   for the words "An insurance company carrying on pension business" there shall be substituted the words "A friendly society carrying on both tax exempt business and business other than tax exempt business";

(b)   for the words "its pension business" there shall be substituted the words "its tax exempt business".

8A(3)   For sub-paragraph (2) there shall be substituted the following sub-paragraph–

"1A(2)   No repayment shall be made to a society in respect of any claim to a notional repayment; but the notional repayment shall be taken to be the amount of tax referred to in regulation 3(1) of the Friendly Societies (Gilt-edged Securities) (Periodic Accounting for Tax on Interest) Regulations 1999."

8A(4)   In sub-paragraph (3)–

(a)   for the words "a company" there shall be substituted the words "a society";

(b)   for paragraphs (a) and (b) there shall be substituted the following paragraphs–

"(a)   shall begin whenever–

(i)   the society begins, at a time when it is carrying on only tax exempt business, to carry on business other than tax exempt business;

(ii)   the society begins, at a time when it is carrying on only business other than tax exempt business, to carry on tax exempt business; or

(iii)   the accounting period of the society beginning before 1st April 1999 and ending on or after 1st July 1999 begins, at a time when the society is carrying on both tax exempt business and business other than tax exempt business; and

(b)   shall end on 31st March 1999."

8A(5)   In sub-paragraph (5) for the word "company" (wherever occurring) there shall be substituted the word "society".

8A(6)   For sub-paragraph (7) there shall be substituted the following paragraphs–

"1A(7)   In sub-paragraph (1) above **"the appropriate portion"** means–

(a)   where the payment in question is either an amount of manufactured gilt interest received or an amount of real gilt interest received and is income arising from–

       (i)   assets linked to tax exempt basic life assurance and general annuity business or to tax exempt class IV business, or

      (ii)   assets other than those of the society's long term business fund,

the whole;

(b)   where the payment in question is as mentioned in paragraph (a) above but is income arising from the society's overseas life assurance fund, the fraction whose numerator is the mean of the opening and closing liabilities to policyholders in respect of the society's tax exempt overseas life assurance business and whose denominator is the mean of the opening and closing liabilities to policyholders in respect of the whole of the society's overseas life assurance business;

(c)   where the payment in question is as mentioned in paragraph (a) above but is not referable to a category of business by virtue of subsection (3) or (4) of section 432A, the provisional fraction;

(d)   where the payment in question is an amount of manufactured gilt interest paid in respect of–

       (i)   assets linked to tax exempt basic life assurance and general annuity business or to tax exempt class IV business, or

      (ii)   assets other than those of the society's long term business fund,

the whole;

(e)   where the payment in question is as mentioned in paragraph (d) above but is paid in respect of income arising from assets of the society's overseas life assurance fund, the fraction whose numerator is the mean of the opening and closing liabilities to policyholders in respect of the society's tax exempt overseas life assurance business and whose denominator is the mean of the opening and closing liabilities to policyholders in respect of the whole of the society's overseas life assurance business;

(f)   where the payment in question is as mentioned in paragraph (d) above but is not referable to a category of business by virtue of subsection (3) or (4) of section 432A, the provisional fraction;

(g)   except as provided by paragraphs (a) to (f) above, none.

1A(7A) In determining the provisional fraction for the purposes of sub-paragraph (7)(c) and (f) above, tax exempt basic life assurance and general annuity business and tax exempt class IV business shall be taken to be a single category for the purposes of section 432A(5).

1A(7B) In sub-paragraph (7) above references to assets of the society's long term business fund–

(a)   as respects societies referred to in paragraph (1) of regulation 13 of the Friendly Societies (Modification of the Corporation Tax Acts) Regulations 1997, shall be construed in accordance with the definition in subsection (11) of section 432A, read with subsections (12) to (14) of that section, as those subsections are added by paragraph (5) of regulation 13 of those Regulations;

(b)   as respects other societies, shall be construed in accordance with the definitions of "long term business" (as substituted by regulation 6(4) of those Regulations) and "long term business fund" in section 431(2).

1A(7C) In sub-paragraphs (7) and (7A) above–

"tax exempt basic life assurance and general annuity business" shall be construed in accordance with the definition inserted in section 431(2) by regulation 6(2) of the Friendly Societies (Modification of the Corporation Tax Acts) Regulations 1997;

"tax exempt class IV business" shall be construed in accordance with the definition inserted in section 431(2) by regulation 7(2) of those Regulations;

"tax exempt overseas life assurance business" shall be construed in accordance with section 441(4D)."

8A(7) In sub-paragraph (8)–

(a)   for the words "sub-paragraph (7)(b)(iv)" there shall be substituted the words "sub-paragraph (7)(c) and (f)";

(b)   for the word "company's" there shall be substituted the word "society's"."

7(1)   Paragraph (2) below specifies a modification of regulation 9.

7(2)   In paragraph (2) of that regulation after "(3)" there shall be inserted ", (3A) and (3B)".

8(1)   Paragraphs (2) to (4) below specify modifications of regulation 10.

8(2)   In paragraph (2)(b) of that regulation after the words ""the company"" there shall be inserted the words "(wherever occurring)".

8(3)   After paragraph (5) of that regulation there shall be inserted the following paragraph–

> "**10(5A)**   In sub-paragraph (1CA)–
>
> (a)   for the word "company" (wherever occurring) there shall be inserted the word "society";
>
> (b)   for the words "pension business" there shall be substituted the words "tax exempt business"."

8(4)   In paragraph (6) of that regulation after the word ""company"" there shall be inserted the words "(wherever occurring)".

REVOCATIONS

9   The Friendly Societies (Gilt-edged Securities) (Periodic Accounting for Tax on Interest) Regulations 1996 and the Friendly Societies (Gilt-edged Securities) (Periodic Accounting for Tax on Interest) (Amendment) Regulations 1997 are hereby revoked as respects any payments of interest on relevant gilt-edged securities in relation to which, by virtue of regulation 1(2) of these Regulations, these Regulations have effect.

OVERSEAS INSURERS (TAX REPRESENTATIVES) REGULATIONS 1999

(SI 1999/881, as amended by SI 2001/2726, SI 2002/443, SI 2004/3272, SI 2008/2626 and SI 2009/56)

Made on 18 March 1999 by the Commissioners of Inland Revenue, in exercise of the powers conferred on them by s. 552A of the Income and Corporation Taxes Act 1988. Operative from 6 April 1999.

CITATION AND COMMENCEMENT

1 These Regulations may be cited as the Overseas Insurers (Tax Representatives) Regulations 1999 and shall come into force on 6th April 1999.

INTERPRETATION

2 In these Regulations–

"**the Board**" means the Commissioners for Her Majesty's Revenue and Customs;

"**EEA Agreement**" means the Agreement on the European Economic Area signed at Oporto on 2nd May 1992 as adjusted by the Protocol signed at Brussels on 17th March 1993;

"**EEA State**" means a State which is a Contracting Party to the EEA Agreement other than the United Kingdom;

"**the Management Act**" means the Taxes Management Act 1970;

"**notice**" means notice given either in writing or in such form and by such means of electronic communications as may be approved by directions given by the Board, and

"**notify**" and "**notification**" shall be construed accordingly;

"**the relevant duties**" has the meaning given for the purposes of section 552B by subsection (2) of that section;

"**the Taxes Act**" means the Income and Corporation Taxes Act 1988, and a reference to a numbered section, without more, is a reference to the section of the Taxes Act bearing that number.

History – In reg. 2, in the definition of "the Board", the words "for Her Majesty's Revenue and Customs" substituted by SI 2008/2626, reg. 2 and 3, with effect from 27 October 2008.
In reg. 2 the definition of "notice" substituted by SI 2002/443, reg 4(a); the definitions of "section 552A" and "section 552B" omitted by SI 2002/443, reg 4(b); and the definition of "the Taxes Act" amended (with the addition of the wording that follows "1988") by SI 2002/443, reg 4(c): all with effect from 6 April 2002.

DESIGNATED DAY

3 The day specified for the purpose of the definition of "the designated day" in subsection (12) of section 552A is 6th April 1999.

NOMINATION OF TAX REPRESENTATIVE BY OVERSEAS INSURER

4(1) A nomination to the Board of a tax representative by an overseas insurer must be in writing and must contain the following information–

(a) the full name or title under which the overseas insurer is registered in the country in which his principal place of business is situated and the address in that country of that principal place of business;

(b) the business address of any branch or agency which the overseas insurer has in the United Kingdom;

(c) the name of the person nominated and–

(i) if he is an individual, the address of that person's fixed place of residence in the United Kingdom, or

(ii) if he is not an individual, the address of his business establishment in the United Kingdom;

(d) the consent of the person nominated that he is willing to secure that the relevant duties are discharged by or on behalf of the overseas insurer signed–

(i) if he is an individual, by that individual, or

(ii)   if he is not an individual, by the proper officer of the company as defined for the purposes of section 108 of the Management Act by subsection (3) of that section in the case of a company and by any partner who is an individual in the case of a partnership;

(e)   the office of Her Majesty's Revenue and Customs to which, and the tax reference under which, the person nominated submits tax returns.

4(2)   A nomination which does not contain the information required by paragraph (1) is invalid.

History – In reg. 4(1)(e), the words "office of Her Majesty's Revenue and Customs" substituted by SI 2008/2626, reg. 2 and 3, with effect from 27 October 2008.

BOARD'S DECISION ON NOMINATION

5(1)   Within the period of thirty days after receipt of a nomination the Board must give notice to the overseas insurer and the person nominated that they–

(a)   approve the person nominated by the overseas insurer as his tax representative; or

(b)   refuse to approve the person nominated by the overseas insurer as his tax representative on one or more of the grounds specified in sub-paragraphs (a), (b) and (c) of paragraph (4); or

(c)   require the overseas insurer or the person nominated or both of them to supply within the period of thirty days after the date of the notice such further information as may be reasonably required before the Board can be satisfied that the person nominated is a fit and proper person to be a tax representative.

5(2)   A notice under sub-paragraph (c) of paragraph (1) must specify the information that the Board require.

5(3)   Where the overseas insurer or the person nominated, or both of them, supplies information pursuant to a notice under sub-paragraph (c) of paragraph (1), the Board must within the period of thirty days after receiving the information–

(a)   give notice to the overseas insurer and the person nominated–

(i)   that they approve the person nominated, or

(ii)   that they refuse to approve the person nominated, stating on which of the grounds specified in sub-paragraphs (a), (b) and (c) of paragraph (4) they rely, or

(b)   give a further notice under sub-paragraph (c) of paragraph (1).

5(4)   The grounds on which the Board may refuse to approve the person nominated by the overseas insurer as his tax representative are that–

(a)   he does not satisfy the requirements of subsection (7) of section 552A;

(b)   they have reason to believe that he cannot or will not secure that the relevant duties are properly discharged by or on behalf of the overseas insurer;

(c)   information which was specified by a notice given under sub-paragraph (c) of paragraph (1) has not been supplied.

5(5)   If at any time there is a change in the information required by regulation 4, or in the further information required by paragraph (1)(c) of this regulation, the overseas insurer must notify the Board of that change.

5(6)   Where the Board have refused to approve the person nominated, and subject to paragraph (5) of regulation 13, the overseas insurer must nominate another person to be his tax representative within the period of three months after the date of the notice of that refusal.

5(7)   Where the overseas insurer nominates another person in accordance with paragraph (6) that nomination must contain the information required by regulation 4 and paragraphs (1) to (4) of this regulation apply to that nomination in the same way that they applied to the original nomination.

5(8)   Where the Board approve the person nominated the date of his appointment is the date on which notice was given under paragraph (1) or (3).

TERMINATION BY THE BOARD OF APPOINTMENT OF PERSON NOMINATED

6(1)   The Board may at any time give notice to both the overseas insurer and the person nominated that they have decided to withdraw the approval which they have given to the person nominated on the grounds that–

(a)   he no longer satisfies the requirements of subsection (7) of section 552A; or

(b)   they have reason to believe that he cannot or will not secure that the relevant duties are properly discharged by or on behalf of the overseas insurer; or

(c)   they have reason to believe that he has failed to secure that relevant duties have been properly discharged by or on behalf of the overseas insurer.

6(2) Where the Board have given notice of their decision to withdraw their approval under paragraph (1) of a person nominated–

(a)   that person continues to be the tax representative of the overseas insurer until they give notice of their approval of the nomination of another person or themselves appoint another person in his place;

(b)   subject to paragraph (5) of regulation 13, the overseas insurer must nominate another person to be his tax representative within the period of three months after the date on which the Board gave notice of their decision; and

(c)   any such information must contain the information required by regulation 4 and the Board must give their decision on that nomination in accordance with regulation 5.

TERMINATION BY OVERSEAS INSURER OF APPOINTMENT OF PERSON NOMINATED

7(1) The overseas insurer may at any time after the Board have approved the person nominated by him as his tax representative give notice to the Board that he no longer wishes that person to be his tax representative.

7(2) Where notice is given by the overseas insurer under paragraph (1), the appointment of the person nominated continues until such time as the Board approve the nomination of another person in his place.

7(3) At the same time as the Board give notice of their decision approving the nomination of another person they must give notice to the person originally nominated that this appointment ceased on the date of that notice.

TERMINATION BY PERSON NOMINATED OF HIS APPOINTMENT

8(1) The person nominated may at any time after the Board have approved him as the tax representative of the overseas insurer give notice to the Board and to the overseas insurer that he no longer wishes to be the overseas insurer's tax representative and in that event the overseas insurer must nominate another person to be his tax representative within the period of three months after the date of that notice.

8(2) Where the overseas insurer nominates another person in accordance with paragraph (1), that nomination must contain the information required by regulation 4 and the Board must give their decision on that nomination in accordance with regulation 5.

8(3) At the same time as the Board give notice of their decision approving the nomination of another person they must give notice to the person originally nominated that his appointment ceased on the date of that notice.

TERMINATION OF APPOINTMENT ON BANKRUPTCY OR DEATH OR ON DISSOLUTION OR WINDING-UP OF A COMPANY OR PARTNERSHIP

9(1) Where the person nominated by an overseas insurer is an individual who becomes bankrupt, or in Scotland his estate is sequestrated, or makes any arrangement or composition with his creditors generally or dies, or is a company or a partnership which is dissolved or wound up, the appointment of that person ceases and the overseas insurer must nominate another person to be his tax representative within the period of three months after the event in question.

9(2) Any such nomination must contain the information required by regulation 4 and the Board must give their decision on that nomination in accordance with regulation 5.

APPOINTMENT BY THE BOARD OF AN OVERSEAS INSURER'S TAX REPRESENTATIVE

10(1) In circumstances where the overseas insurer has failed–

(a)   to nominate a person to be his tax representative in accordance with subsection (6) of section 552A; or

(b)   following the refusal of the Board to approve a person nominated by him, to nominate another person to be his tax representative in accordance with paragraph (6) of regulation 5; or

(c) following the withdrawal by the Board of their approval of a person nominated, to nominate another person to be his tax representative in accordance with paragraph (2)(b) of regulation 6; or

(d) following the notification by a person nominated under paragraph (1) of regulation 8 that he no longer wishes to be the overseas insurer's tax representative or on the occurrence of one of the events described in paragraph (1) of regulation 9, to nominate another person in accordance with the paragraph in question; or

(e) following the giving of a notice by the Board in accordance with paragraph (3) of regulation 11, to nominate a person to be his tax representative in accordance with paragraph (4) of that regulation; or

(f) following–

    (i) the refusal of the Board to agree to release him from the requirement that there be a tax representative, or

    (ii) the disclosure to the Board of information with respect to relevant insurances ceasing to be a criminal offence under the law of the EEA state in which he is resident, or

    (iii) notification by him to the Board that the total amount or value of gross premiums paid under relevant insurances is £1 million or more, or

    (iv) the giving of a notice by the Board of their intention to withdraw from their agreement to release him from the requirement that there be a tax representative,

to nominate a person to be his tax representative in accordance with paragraph (9) of regulation 12; or

(g) to notify the Board that the total amount or value of gross premiums paid under relevant insurances is £1 million or more; or

(h) following the termination of the appointment of a person appointed under this paragraph, to nominate another person in accordance with paragraph (4) of this regulation; the Board may appoint a person who satisfies the description in paragraph (2) to be the overseas insurer's tax representative.

10(2) A person appointed by the Board to be the tax representative of an overseas insurer must be a person who has a significant business or economic connection with the overseas insurer and may in particular (but without prejudice to the generality of the preceding words) be–

(a) a company which is connected with the overseas insurer within the meaning of section 839 (connected persons); or

(b) the branch or agency in the United Kingdom of any such company.

10(3) The Board must give notice of their decision to the person appointed under this regulation and to the overseas insurer and, subject to paragraph (6) of regulation 13, the date of the appointment is the date of the notice.

10(4) The Board may at any time terminate the appointment of the person appointed by them as the tax representative of an overseas insurer by giving notice to the person appointed and to the overseas insurer and in that event the overseas insurer must nominate another person to be his tax representative within the period of three months after the date of that notice.

10(5) The overseas insurer may at any time nominate a person to be his tax representative in place of the person appointed by the Board and, if the Board approve the nomination of that person, at the same time as the Board give notice of their decision approving the nomination they must give notice to the person appointed by them that his appointment ceased on the date of the notice.

10(6) Where the overseas insurer nominates another person in accordance with paragraph (4) or (5), that nomination must contain the information required by regulation 4 and the Board must give their decision on that nomination in accordance with regulation 5.

History – In reg. 10(1)(f)(ii), the word "state" substituted by SI 2008/2626, reg. 5, with effect from 27 October 2008.
In reg. 10(2)(a) the words "of the Taxes Act" (which followed "section 839") omitted by SI 2002/443, reg. 5, with effect from 6 April 2002.

OTHER ARRANGEMENTS

11(1) An overseas insurer may make other arrangements with the Board for the purpose of securing the discharge by him or on his behalf of the relevant duties.

11(2) Where such arrangements have been made with the Board by the overseas insurer, section 552A is to be regarded as never having applied to the overseas insurer so long as those arrangements remain in force.

11(3) If the Board have reason to believe that any arrangements which have been made do not secure the discharge by the overseas insurer or on his behalf of the relevant duties, they may give notice to the overseas insurer that those arrangements are no longer in force with effect from the date of the notice.

11(4) Where notice is given by the Board in accordance with paragraph (3)—

(a)   subject to paragraph (5) of regulation 13, the overseas insurer must nominate a person to be his tax representative within the period of three months after the date of the notice;

(b)   that nomination must contain the information required by regulation 4; and

(c)   the Board must give their decision on that nomination in accordance with regulation 5.

RELEASE OF OVERSEAS INSURER FROM REQUIREMENT TO NOMINATE A TAX REPRESENTATIVE

12(1) The Board may agree to release an overseas insurer to whom section 552A applies from the requirement that there must be a tax representative where—

(a)   the overseas insurer is resident in an EEA State and the disclosure by him to the Board of information with respect to holders of relevant insurances is a criminal offence under the law of that state and was such an offence on 17th March 1998; or

(b)   subject to the condition specified in paragraph (2), at any time after section 552A first applies to the overseas insurer the total amount or value of the gross premiums paid under the relevant insurances referred to in paragraph (b) of subsection (4) of that section is nil or a negligible amount; or

(c)   subject to paragraph (5), the overseas insurer enters into an undertaking—

    (i)   in relation to relevant insurances referred to in paragraph (3), in the terms set out in Part II of the Schedule;

    (ii)   in relation to relevant insurances referred to in paragraph (4), in the terms set out in Part III of the Schedule.

12(2) The condition specified in this paragraph is that the overseas insurer gives notice of the fact to the Board forthwith if, at any time following the agreement to release the overseas insurer from the requirement that there must be a tax representative, the total amount or value of the gross premiums paid under the relevant insurances referred to in paragraph (b) of subsection (4) of section 552A is £1 million or more.

12(3) The relevant insurances referred to in this paragraph are—

(a)   policies of life insurance issued in respect of insurances made before 6th April 2000;

(b)   contracts for life annuities made before 6th April 2000;

(c)   capital redemption policies where the contract was effected before 6th April 2000.

12(4) The relevant insurances referred to in this paragraph are—

(a)   policies of life insurance issued in respect of insurances made on or after 6th April 2000;

(b)   contracts for life annuities made on or after 6th April 2000;

(c)   capital redemption policies where the contract was effected on or after 6th April 2000.

12(5) The Board may at any time give notice to the overseas insurer of their decision to withdraw from their agreement to release him from the requirement that there be a tax representative where that agreement has been given in the circumstances described in sub-paragraph (c) of paragraph (1).

12(6) An application by an overseas insurer to be released from the requirement that there must be a tax representative must be by notice to the Board specifying which of the circumstances described in sub-paragraphs (a), (b) and (c) of paragraph (1) apply to his case and the Board must, within the period of thirty days after the receipt of the notice of any such application, give notice to the overseas insurer that they—

(a)   agree to release him from the requirement that there be a tax representative, or

(b)   refuse to agree to release him from that requirement, or

(c)   require him to supply within the period of thirty days after the date of that notice such information as may be reasonably required before they can be satisfied that he comes within the relevant circumstances.

12(7) A notice under sub-paragraph (c) of paragraph (6) must specify the information which the Board require.

12(8) Where the overseas insurer supplies information pursuant to a notice under sub-paragraph (c) of paragraph (6), the Board must within the period of thirty days after receiving the information—

(a)   give notice to the insurer that they agree or refuse to agree to release him from the requirement that there be a tax representative, or

(b)   give a further notice under sub-paragraph (c) of paragraph (6).

12(9)   Where–

(a)   the Board give notice that they refuse to agree to release the overseas insurer from the requirement that there be a tax representative, or

(b)   it ceases to be a criminal offence under the law of the EEA state in which the overseas insurer is resident for him to disclose to the Board information with respect to the holders of relevant insurances, or

(c)   the overseas insurer gives notice to the Board in accordance with the condition in paragraph (2) that the total amount or value of the gross premiums paid under relevant insurances is £1 million or more, or

(d)   the Board give notice to the overseas insurer of their decision to withdraw from their agreement to release him from the requirement that there be a tax representative,

and subject to paragraph (5) of regulation 13, the overseas insurer must nominate a person to be his tax representative within the period of three months after the date of the notice or the date when disclosure to the Board ceased to be a criminal offence, as the case may be.

12(10)   Where the overseas insurer nominates a person to be his tax representative in accordance with paragraph (9), that nomination must contain the information required by regulation 4 and the Board must give their decision in accordance with regulation 5.

History – In reg. 12(1)(a), the words "state" substituted by SI 2008/2626, reg. 6, with effect from 27 October 2008. In reg. 12(9)(b), the word "state" substituted by SI 2008/2626, reg. 6, with effect from 27 October 2008.

Statutory instruments – SI 2002/443, reg. 10: transitional provision which states that: "For the purposes of regulation 12(1)(c) of the Principal Regulations [i.e. SI 1998/881] (release of overseas insurer from requirement to nominate a tax representative), an undertaking given by an overseas insurer before the coming into force of these Regulations [i.e. SI 2002/443, which came into force on 6 April 2002], which complied with the terms of Parts II and III of the Schedule to the Principal Regulations as then in force, shall have effect as if it were an undertking in the terms required by the Schedule as amended by these Regulations. Accordingly any agreement by the Board to release the insurer under regulation 12(1)(c) given before the coming into force of these Regulations shall continue to have effect until the Board give notice of their decision to withdraw from it."

APPEALS AGAINST DECISIONS OF THE BOARD

13(1)   An overseas insurer to whom notice has been given of a decision of the Board–

(a)   refusing to approve a person nominated by him as his tax representative,

(b)   withdrawing their approval of a person nominated by him as his tax representative,

(c)   appointing a person to be his tax representative,

(d)   that arrangements made under regulation 11 are no longer in force,

(e)   refusing to agree to release him from the requirement that there be a tax representative, or

(f)   to withdraw from their agreement to release him from the requirement that there be a tax representative,

may appeal against the decision contained in that notice by notice given to the Board within the period of thirty days after the date of the notice of the decision in question.

13(2)   A person to whom notice has been given of a decision of the Board appointing him to be the tax representative of an overseas insurer under regulation 10 may appeal against the decision contained in that notice within the period of thirty days after the date of the notice of that decision.

13(3)   [Omitted by SI 2009/56, art. 3(2) and Sch. 2, para. 58(2).]

13(4)   The like provisions as are contained in Part V of the Management Act (appeals and other proceedings) apply to an appeal under this regulation and the tribunal, on an appeal notified to it, shall confirm the decision contained in the notice unless satisfied that it ought to be quashed.

13(5)   Where an overseas insurer appeals against a decision of the Board referred to in sub-paragraph (a), (b), (d), (e) or (f) of paragraph (1), and the decision of the Board is confirmed on appeal, the period of three months within which he must nominate another person, or a person, as his tax representative does not begin until such time as there is no possibility of a further appeal against that decision.

13(6)   Where an overseas insurer appeals against a decision of the Board appointing a person to be his tax representative, or the person appointed by the Board to be the tax representative of an overseas insurer appeals against the decision of the Board appointing him, and the decision of the Board is confirmed on appeal, the date of the appointment of that person is the first date on which there is no possibility of a further appeal against that decision.

13(7)   Where an overseas insurer appeals against a decision of the Board referred to in sub-paragraph (a) of paragraph (1) and the decision of the Board is quashed on appeal, the date of the appointment of the person nominated as the tax representative of the overseas insurer is the first date on which there is no possibility of a further appeal against the decision quashing the decision of the Board.

History – Reg. 13(3) omitted by SI 2009/56, art. 3(2) and Sch. 2, para. 58(2), operative from 1 April 2009 subject to transitional and saving provisions in SI 2009/56, Sch. 3. Former reg. 13(3) read as follows:

"**13(3)**   An appeal under paragraph (1) or (2) is to the Special Commissioners.".
In reg. 13(4), the words "and in regulations made under sections 56B to 56D of that Act", which appeared after "proceedings)", omitted by SI 2009/56, art. 3(2) and Sch. 2, para. 58(3)(a), operative from 1 April 2009 subject to transitional and saving provisions in SI 2009/56, Sch. 3.
In reg. 13(4), the words "tribunal, on an appeal notified to it, shall" substituted for the words "Special Commissioners must on appeal to them" by SI 2009/56, art. 3(2) and Sch. 2, para. 58(3)(b), operative from 1 April 2009 subject to transitional and saving provisions in SI 2009/56, Sch. 3.
In reg. 13(4), the words "they are", which appeared before "satisfied", omitted by SI 2009/56, art. 3(2) and Sch. 2, para. 58(3)(c), operative from 1 April 2009 subject to transitional and saving provisions in SI 2009/56, Sch. 3.

SCHEDULE

Regulation 12(1)(c)

Part I

INTERPRETATION

1   In this Schedule–

"**basic rate limit**" has the meaning given by section 20(2) of the Income Tax Act 2007;

"**gain**" means a gain which is treated as arising in connection with a policy or contract under Chapter 9 of Part 4 of ITTOIA 2005;

"**tax year**" has the meaning given by section 4(2) of the Income Tax Act 2007;

History – In para. 1, in the definition of "basic rate limit", the words "section 20(2) of the Income Tax Act 2007" substituted by SI 2008/2626, reg. 7, with effect from 27 October 2008.
In para. 1, the definition of "financial year" revoked by SI 2008/2626, reg. 7, with effect from 27 October 2008.
In para. 1, in the definition of "gain", the words "Chapter 9 of Part 4 of ITTOIA 2005" substituted by SI 2008/2626, reg. 7, with effect from 27 October 2008.
In para. 1, in the definition of "gain", the words "of the Taxes Act" (which followed "545 or 546C") omitted by SI 2002/443, reg. 6, with effect from 6 April 2002.
In para. 1, in the definition of "gain", the reference to "546C" inserted by SI 2001/2726, reg. 2, operative from 17 August 2001.
In para. 1, the definition of "inspector" revoked by SI 2008/2626, reg. 7, with effect from 27 October 2008.
In para. 1, the definition of "tax year" inserted by SI 2008/2626, reg. 7, with effect from 27 October 2008.
In para. 1, the definition of "year of assessment" revoked by SI 2008/2626, reg. 7, with effect from 27 October 2008.

2   [Revoked by SI 2008/2626, reg. 7.]

History – Para. 2 revoked by SI 2008/2626, reg. 7, with effect from 27 October 2008.

Part II

UNDERTAKING BY OVERSEAS INSURER – PRE 6 APRIL 2000 INSURANCES

3   The terms of the undertaking referred to in regulation 12(1)(c)(i) are that the overseas insurer undertakes, within three months after the end of each tax year, to supply to the Board the information referred to in paragraph 6 about relevant events occurring in that tax year in connection with a policy or contract held by a policy holder where to the best of the overseas insurer's information and belief the policy holder was resident in the United Kingdom immediately before the relevant event occurred.

History – In para. 3, the words "tax year" (twice) and "Board" substituted and the words "or where the policy holder is a company each financial year," revoked by SI 2008/2626, reg. 7, with effect from 27 October 2008.

4   For the purposes of this undertaking a relevant event is a chargeable event within the meaning of Chapter 9 of Part 4 of ITTOIA 2005–

(a)   in respect of which an insurer is under an obligation to deliver a certificate under section 552 (as read with section 552ZA);

(b)   which occurs three months or more after section 552A first applies to the overseas insurer;

(c)   which is the last such event to occur in relation to the policy or contract;

(d)   by reason of which the aggregate sum payable, or other benefits to be conferred, by the overseas insurer exceeds twice the basic rate limit for the tax year in which it occurs.

History – In para. 4, the words "Chapter 9 of Part 4 of ITTOIA 2005" and para. (d) substituted by SI 2008/2626, reg. 7, with effect from 27 October 2008.
Para. 4(a) amended, with insertion of a reference to section 552ZA, by SI 2002/443, reg.7, with effect from 6 April 2002.

5   In determining whether the aggregate sum payable, or other benefits to be conferred, by reason of a relevant event exceeds twice the basic rate limit for the tax year in which it occurs, all sums payable and benefits to be conferred are to be taken into account which are payable or to be conferred by reason of relevant events occurring in that tax year in connection with policies or contracts–

(a)   under which immediately before the relevant event in question the same insurer has obligations, and

(b)   which are held by the same policy holder.

History – In para. 5, the words "the tax year in which it occurs," and "tax year" substituted and the words "or for the year of assessment corresponding to the financial year in which it occurs, as the case may be," and "or that financial year" revoked by SI 2008/2626, reg. 7, with effect from 27 October 2008.

6   The information referred to in this paragraph is–

(a)   the name and address of the policy holder;

(b)   any unique identifying designation given to the policy or contract in connection with which a relevant event has occurred;

(c)   the date and nature of each such relevant event;

(d)   the aggregate of the sums payable, or other benefits to be conferred, as a result of all such relevant events.

Part III

UNDERTAKING BY OVERSEAS INSURER – POST 5 APRIL 2000 INSURANCES

7   The terms of the undertaking referred to in regulation 12(1)(c)(ii) are that the overseas insurer undertakes–

(a)   within three months after a relevant event occurs in connection with a policy or contract, to deliver to the policy holder a certificate containing the information referred to in paragraph 10; and

(b)   within three months after the end of each tax year in which such a certificate is delivered, and in the circumstances described in paragraph 9, to supply to the Board a copy of that certificate;

where to the best of the overseas insurer's information and belief the policy holder was resident in the United Kingdom immediately before the relevant event occurred.

History – In para. 7(b), the words "tax year" and "Board" substituted and the words ", or where the policy holder is a company each financial year," revoked by SI 2008/2626, reg. 7, with effect from 27 October 2008.

8   For the purpose of this undertaking a relevant event is a chargeable event within the meaning of Chapter 9 of Part 4 of ITTOIA 2005 in respect of which an insurer is under an obligation to deliver a certificate under section 552.

History – Para. 8 and 8A substituted for former para. 8 by SI 2008/2626, reg. 7, with effect from 27 October 2008.
Former para. 8 substituted by SI 2002/443, reg.8, with effect from 6 April 2002.

8A   For the purposes of this Part of this Schedule, in the determination of the amount of a gain in connection with a policy or contract, no account is to be taken of the effect of section 541A of ITTOIA 2005.

History – Para. 8 and 8A substituted for former para. 8 by SI 2008/2626, reg. 7, with effect from 27 October 2008.

9   The circumstances described in this paragraph are where the aggregate amount of connected gains in the tax year exceeds one half of the basic rate limit for that tax year and, for the purposes of this paragraph, a gain is connected with another gain where–

(a)   both gains arise in connection with policies or contracts containing obligations which, immediately before the relevant event in question, were obligations of the same overseas insurer;

(b)   the policy holder of those policies and contracts is the same; and

(c)   both gains arise in the same tax year.

History – In para. 9, the words "in the tax year" and "that tax year" and para. (c) substituted by SI 2008/2626, reg. 7, with effect from 27 October 2008.

10   The information referred to in this paragraph is–

(a)   the name and address of the policy holder;

(b)   any unique identifying designation given to the policy or contract in connection with which the relevant event has occurred;

(c)   the date and nature of the relevant event;

(d)   the amount of the gain;

(e)   the number of years relevant for computing the appropriate fraction of the gain for the purposes of section 536, apart from section 536(7), of ITTOIA 2005;

(f)   whether the policy holder is to be treated as having paid income tax at the basic or lower rate on the amount of the gain in accordance with section 530, apart from section 528, of ITTOIA 2005.

History – In para. 10(e), the words "section 536, apart from section 536(7), of ITTOIA 2005" substituted by SI 2008/2626, reg. 7, with effect from 27 October 2008.
In para. 10(f), the words "section 530, apart from section 528, of ITTOIA 2005" substituted by SI 2008/2626, reg. 7, with effect from 27 October 2008.
In para. 10(f) the words "or lower" inserted after the word "basic" by SI 2004/3272, with effect from 31 December 2004.
Para. 10(e) and 10(f) amended with references to section 553(3) and section 553(8) inserted by SI 2002/443, reg. 9, with effect from 6 April 2002.

PERSONAL PORTFOLIO BONDS (TAX) REGULATIONS 1999

(SI 1999/1029, as amended by SI 2001/2724, SI 2001/3629 and SI 2002/455)

Made on 30 March 1999 by the Treasury, in exercise of the powers conferred on them by s. 553C of the Income and Corporation Taxes Act 1988, hereby make the following Regulations. Operative from 6 April 1999.

ARRANGEMENT OF REGULATIONS

CITATION, COMMENCEMENT AND EFFECT

1(1) These Regulations may be cited as the Personal Portfolio Bonds (Tax) Regulations 1999 and shall come into force on 6th April 1999.

1(2) These Regulations shall have effect, in relation to personal portfolio bonds, with respect to any year ending on or after 6th April 2000.

INTERPRETATION

2(1) In these Regulations unless the context otherwise requires–

"**building society**" means a building society within the meaning of the Building Societies Act 1986, or the Irish Building Societies Act 1989;

"**collective investment scheme**" has the meaning given by section 235 of the Financial Services and Markets Act 2000, and "**interest**" in relation to a collective investment scheme means the beneficial entitlement (however described) of a participant (within the meaning of that section);

"**company**" has the meaning given by section 832(1) and (2) of the Taxes Act;

"**insurance company**" means an undertaking carrying on the business of effecting or carrying out contracts of insurance and, for the purposes of this definition, "**contract of insurance**" has the meaning given by Article 3(1) of the Financial Services and Markets Act 2000 (Regulated Activities) Order 2001;

"**internal linked fund**" has the meaning given by section 11.1 of the Prudential Sourcebook (Insurers) and in this definition "**the Prudential Sourcebook (Insurers)**" means the Interim Prudential Sourcebook for Insurers made by the Financial Services Authority under the Financial Services and Markets Act 2000;

"**market value**" shall be construed in accordance with section 272 of the Taxation of Chargeable Gains Act 1992;

"**personal portfolio bond**" has the meaning given by regulation 4, subject to regulation 3;

"**policy holder**", except in regulation 4(1), includes a holder of a life annuity contract;

"**recognised stock exchange**" has the meaning given by section 841 of the Taxes Act;

"**security**" has the same meaning as in section 132(3)(b) of the Taxation of Chargeable Gains Act 1992;

"**share**" includes stock;

"**the Taxes Act**" means the Income and Corporation Taxes Act 1988;

"**unit trust scheme**" has the meaning given by subsection (6) of section 468 of the Taxes Act;

"**warrant**" has the same meaning as in paragraph 14 of Schedule 2 to the Financial Services and Markets Act 2000;

"**year**" in relation to a personal portfolio bond means a year as defined in section 546(4) of the Taxes Act, and "**the final year**" has the meaning given by that section.

2(2) In these Regulations references to the premium paid, or the amount of the premium paid, include–

(a)   references to lump sum, or any other, consideration,

(b)   where more than one amount is payable by way of premium in respect of the policy or contract, references to the aggregate of the premiums paid, and

(c)   references to the market value at the date of transfer of any property other than cash transferred to the insurance company in satisfaction of any premium.

2(3) In these Regulations references to a section, without more, are to that section of the Taxes Act.

History – In reg. 2(1) the definitions of "collective investment scheme", "insurance company", "internal linked fund" and "warrant" amended by SI 2001/3629, reg. 184 which came into force on 1 December 2001. The amendment to the definition of "internal linked fund" is effective in relation to periods of account ending on or after 1 December 2001

POLICIES OR CONTRACTS ISSUED OR MADE BEFORE 17 MARCH 1998 WHICH ARE THE SUBJECT OF SPECIAL EXCLUSIONS FROM BEING PERSONAL PORTFOLIO BONDS

3(1) A policy or contract is not a personal portfolio bond if it is a policy or contract–

(a)   which, in the case of a policy, was issued in respect of an insurance made before 17th March 1998 and, in the case of a contract, was made before 17th March 1998,

(b)   whose terms are not varied on or after 16th July 1998 so as to increase the benefits secured or to extend the term of the policy or contract (any exercise of rights conferred by the policy or contract being regarded for this purpose as a variation), and

(c)   which is a policy or contract to which either paragraph (2) or paragraph (3) applies.

3(2) This paragraph applies to a policy or contract under whose terms the benefits have at no time during its existence been capable of being determined either in whole or in part by reference to any index other than those referred to in regulation 4(7), or to any property other than–

(a)   shares or securities listed on a recognised stock exchange,

(b)   shares or securities of a company which are dealt in on the Unlisted Securities Market or the Alternative Investment Market, and which satisfy the conditions specified in paragraph (4), and

(c)   property described in regulation 4(3) and (4).

3(3) This paragraph applies to a policy or contract–

(a)   under whose terms the benefits were at some time during its existence capable of being determined either in whole or in part by reference to property other than that referred to in paragraph (2)(a), (b) and (c), or by reference to an index other than those referred to in regulation 4(7), but at no time during its existence have been so determined, and

(b)   whose terms are varied before the end of the first year, in relation to that policy or contract, which commences on or after 6th April 1999, subject to paragraph (5), so that the only property that may be selected as mentioned in regulation 4(1) consists of property referred to in paragraph (2)(a), (b) and (c), and the only index that may be so selected consists of an index referred to in regulation 4(7).

3(4) The conditions specified in this paragraph are that–

(a)   any holding of shares or securities of a company, by reference to which any benefits under the policy or contract are or have been capable of being determined during any period, does not at any time during that period exceed 10 per cent. of the issued share capital of the company concerned; and

(b)   the amount invested in any shares or securities of a single company to which this condition applies does not at any time exceed 10 per cent. of the premium paid in respect of the policy or contract (and "**amount invested**" includes the market value at the date of transfer of any property other than cash transferred to the insurance company in satisfaction of any premium).

3(5) In a case where–

(a)   the policy holder was not resident in the United Kingdom on 17th March 1998, and

(b)   after that date, the policy holder is at any time resident in the United Kingdom, paragraph (3)(b) shall apply with the modification that, for the year mentioned in that sub-paragraph, there is substituted a reference to whichever is the later of that year, and the first year, in relation to that policy or contract, which commences after the time mentioned in sub-paragraph (b) of this paragraph or, where there is more than one such time, the earliest such time.

3(6) Any reference in paragraphs (2) and (3) to the period of existence of a policy or contract, or to a period in paragraph (4), or to a time during either such period, shall be construed ignoring any such period of time before 6th April 1994, but shall include any other such period or time (whether before or after the coming into force of these Regulations).

3(7) Any reference in paragraphs (2)(a) and (b) and (4) to shares or securities, or to a holding of shares or securities, includes a reference to any option, warrant or other right to acquire shares or securities.

DEFINITION OF PERSONAL PORTFOLIO BOND (APPLYING TO ALL POLICIES OR CONTRACTS WHENEVER ISSUED OR MADE)

4(1) Subject to paragraph (2) and regulation 3, **"personal portfolio bond"** means a policy of life insurance, contract for a life annuity or capital redemption policy under whose terms–

(a) some or all of the benefits are determined by reference to the value of, or the income from, property of any description (whether or not specified in the policy or contract) or fluctuations in, or in an index of, the value of property of any description (whether or not so specified); and

(b) some or all of the property, or such an index, may be selected by, or by a person acting on behalf of, the holder of the policy or contract or a person connected with him (or the holder of the policy or contract and a person connected with him).

4(2) A policy or contract is not a personal portfolio bond if–

(a) the only property which may be selected as mentioned in paragraph (1)(b) is of the description prescribed by either or both of paragraphs (3) and (4), and

(b) the only index which may be selected as mentioned in paragraph (1)(b) is of the description prescribed by paragraph (7).

4(3) The description prescribed by this paragraph is of property which the insurance company has appropriated to an internal linked fund, where the property satisfies the condition specified in paragraph (5).

4(4) The description prescribed by this paragraph is of property consisting of any of the following–

(a) units in an authorised unit trust within the meaning of subsection (6) of section 468, read with subsections (7) to (9) of that section,

(b) shares in an investment trust within the meaning of section 842,

(c) shares in an open-ended investment company within the meaning of section 236 of the Financial Services and Markets Act 2000,

(d) cash, including cash deposited in a deposit account or share account with a building society, or in a bank account or similar account, except where the acquisition of the cash was made wholly or partly for the purpose of realising a gain from the disposal of it,

(e) policies or contracts to which Chapter II of Part XIII of the Taxes Act applies, which satisfy the conditions specified in paragraph (6), and

(f) an interest in a collective investment scheme which is constituted by–

   (i) a company, not being an open-ended investment company, which is resident outside the United Kingdom,

   (ii) a unit trust scheme the trustees of which are not resident in the United Kingdom, or

   (iii) any arrangements which do not fall within paragraph (i) or (ii), which take effect by virtue of the law of a territory outside the United Kingdom and which, under that law, create rights in the nature of co-ownership (without restricting that expression to its meaning in the law of any part of the United Kingdom),

where the property concerned satisfies, or further satisfies, as the case may be, the condition specified in paragraph (5).

4(5) The condition specified in this paragraph is that, at the time when the property is available to be selected, the opportunity to select property of the same description as the first-mentioned property is available to, or to persons acting on behalf of, all the policy holders of the insurance company concerned or one, or more than one, class of policy holders of that insurance company, as mentioned in paragraph (8)(a) to (c).

4(6)   The conditions specified in this paragraph are that neither–

(a)   the policy or contract, nor

(b)   any property by reference to which the value of any benefits under the policy or contract is or has been directly or indirectly capable of being determined, nor

(c)   any property which, in relation to the policy or contract, or the premium paid in respect thereof, is **"derived property"** within the meaning of section 660A(10) of the Taxes Act,

is a personal portfolio bond.

4(7)   The description prescribed by this paragraph is of indices consisting of any of the following–

(a)   the retail prices index,

(b)   any similar general index of prices which is published by the government of any foreign state, or by an agent of such a government, or

(c)   any published index of prices of shares listed on a recognised stock exchange,

in circumstances where, at the time when the index is available to be selected, the opportunity to select the same index is available to, or to persons acting on behalf of, all the policy holders of the insurance company concerned or one, or more than one, class of policy holders of that insurance company, as mentioned in paragraph (8)(a) to (c).

4(8)   In paragraphs (5) and (7) a **"class"** of policy holders means a number of policy holders to whom the opportunity is given to select property or an index as mentioned in paragraphs (5) and (7) in circumstances where–

(a)   that opportunity is clearly identified in marketing or other promotional literature published by the insurance company concerned to members of the public, or members of the public who are intending investors, as available generally to any person falling within its terms,

(b)   the class and the opportunity are not limited to connected persons, and

(c)   the composition of the class (which means the inclusion in or exclusion from the class of any person, or the ability of that person to take the opportunity, if he so chooses) is determined by the insurance company alone.

History – In reg. 4(4)(c) the words "236 of the Financial Services and Markets Act 2000" substituted for "75(8) of the Financial Services Act 1986" by SI 2001/3629, reg. 185 which came into force on 1 December 2001.

PERSONAL PORTFOLIO BONDS – COMPUTATION OF GAIN

5(1)   This regulation makes provision for amounts to be treated as gains arising in connection with a personal portfolio bond in any year ending on or after 6th April 2000 other than the final year (a "relevant year") for the purposes of charging those gains to tax in accordance with the provisions of Chapter II of Part XIII of the Taxes Act applied (with modifications) by regulation 6.

5(2)   There shall be treated as a gain arising in a relevant year the amount calculated in accordance with the formula–

$$0.15 \times (A + - C)$$

Here–

A   is the amount of the premium paid in respect of the personal portfolio bond;

B   is the sum of the amounts found by applying the formula at the end of each of the previous years during which the personal portfolio bond was in existence in succession starting with the first such year; and

C   is the amount calculated in accordance with the formula in paragraph (2A).

5(2A)   C is the amount calculated in accordance with the formula

$$R - G$$

(a)   at the end of the year immediately preceding the relevant year if the calculation produces an excess; and

(b)   at the end of any earlier year during the existence of the bond when the calculation produces an excess; and

(c)   adding together all the amounts produced by sub-paragraphs (a) and (b).

Here–

R   is the reckonable aggregate value mentioned in section 546(2); and

G   is the allowable aggregate amount referred to in section 546(3).

5(2B)   For the purposes of the computation of C–

(a)   section 546(1)(a) shall be read as if the words "or assignment" and "assigned for money or money's worth, or" and sub-paragraph (ii) and the word "; or" preceding it were omitted;

(b)   section 546(6) shall be disregarded; and

(c)   sections 546B to 546D shall be disregarded.

5(3)   The gain calculated in accordance with paragraph (2) shall be treated as arising at the end of the relevant year concerned.

This is subject to paragraph (4) and (4A).

5(4)   The references–

(a)   in paragraph (3) to the end of a relevant year, and

(b)   in paragraph (2), in the definition of "B", to the end of any previous year,

shall each be construed as a reference to the time immediately before any gain treated as arising in connection with the same policy or contract at the end of that year under section 541, 543 or 545, on the occurrence of such an excess as is mentioned in section 540(1)(a)(v), 542(1)(c) or 545(1)(d).

5(4A)   For the purposes of paragraphs (2) to (3), any gain treated as arising under section 546C shall be treated as arising immediately after the gain calculated in accordance with paragraph (2).

5(5)   Where the terms of a policy or contract, to which regulation 3(3) applies as modified by regulation 3(5), are varied, within the alternative period permitted by regulation 3(5), (that is, the first year which commences after the time mentioned in regulation 3(5)(b) falls later than the year mentioned in regulation 3(3)(b)), no gain shall be treated as arising under paragraph (2) at the end of the first year, in relation to the policy or contract, which ends after the time mentioned in regulation 3(5)(b).

History – Reg. 5(2) inserted by SI 2001/2724, reg. 3, operative from 17 August 2001, with effect as respects gains treated as arising on or after that day.
In reg. 5(3) reference to "(4A)" inserted by SI 2001/2724, reg. 3, operative from 17 August 2001, with effect as respects gains treated as arising on or after that day.
Reg. 5(4A) inserted by SI 2001/2724, reg. 3, operative from 17 August 2001, with effect as respects gains treated as arising on or after that day.

APPLICATION OF CHAPTER II OF PART XIII OF THE TAXES ACT

6(1)   The gain treated as arising in accordance with regulation 5(2) shall be treated, for the purposes of section 547 and paragraph (2) (other than sub-paragraph (b) of that paragraph), as arising on the happening of a chargeable event, which takes place at the time given by regulation 5(3) and (4).

6(2)   The provisions of Chapter II of Part XIII of the Taxes Act (other than section 553C) shall, so far as concerns policies or contracts that are also personal portfolio bonds, apply, subject to the omissions and modifications specified in paragraphs (3) to (8), both in relation to–

(a)   the gain treated as arising on the happening of a chargeable event in accordance with regulation 5(2) and paragraph (1), and

(b)   other gains treated as arising in accordance with that Chapter.

6(3)   In section 547 (method of charging gain to tax)–

(a)   in subsection (1) after "545 or 546C" there shall be inserted the words "or regulations 5(2) and 6(1) of the Personal Portfolio Bonds (Tax) Regulations 1999";

(b)   in each of subsections (5A) and (7) after "543 or 546C(7)(b)" there shall be inserted the words "or regulations 5(2) and 6(1) of the Personal Portfolio Bonds (Tax) Regulations 1999".

6(4)   In each of paragraphs (a), (b) and (c) of section 541(1), after sub-paragraph (ii) there shall be added–

"and

(iii)   the total amount treated under regulation 5 of the Personal Portfolio Bonds (Tax) Regulations 1999 as a gain arising in a relevant year in relation to the policy, prior to the happening of the chargeable event;"

6(5)   In each of paragraphs (a) and (b) of section 543(1), after sub-paragraph (ii) there shall be added–

"and

(iii)   the total amount treated under regulation 5 of the Personal Portfolio Bonds (Tax) Regulations 1999 as a gain arising in a relevant year in relation to the contract, prior to the happening of the chargeable event;"

6(6)   Section 550 (relief where gain charged at a higher rate) shall be omitted.

6(7)   In section 552–

(a)   in subsection (1)–

   (i)   in paragraph (a) the words "unless satisfied that no gain is to be treated as arising by reason of the event," shall be omitted;

   (ii)   in paragraph (b), for "paragraph (a) or (b) of subsection (2)" there shall be substituted "subsection (2)";

(b)   for subsection (2) there shall be substituted–

   "**552(2)**   For the purposes of this section the condition is that the amount of the gain, or the aggregate amount of the gain and any other gains connected with it, exceeds one half of the basic rate limit for the relevant year of assessment.";

(c)   in subsection (5)

   (i)   for paragraph (b) there shall be substituted–

      "(b)   the nature of the chargeable event and the date on which it is treated as having happened;";

   (ii)   paragraph (c) shall be omitted;

   (iii)   for paragraph (d) there shall be substituted–

      "(d)   the amount of the gain treated as arising in accordance with regulations 5(2) and 6(1) of the Personal Portfolio Bonds (Tax) Regulations 1999;";

   (iv)   in paragraph (f)(ii) the words ", except in a case where paragraph (c) above applies," shall be omitted;

(d)   for subsection (6) there shall be substituted–

   "**552(6)**   For the purposes of subsection (1)(a) above, the relevant three month period is the period of three months beginning with the time given by regulation 5(3), (4) and (4A) of the Personal Portfolio Bonds (Tax) Regulations 1999."

(e)   for subsection (7) there shall be substituted–

   "**552(7)**   For the purposes of subsection (1)(b) above, the relevant three month period is whichever of the following periods ends later–

   (a)   the period of three months following the end of the year of assessment or, where the policy holder is a company, the financial year, in which the event happened; or

   (b)   if a certificate under subsection (1)(b) would not be required in respect of the event apart from the happening of another event, and that other event is a death or an assignment, the period of three months beginning with receipt of written notification of the death or the assignment.";

(f)   for subsection (9) there shall be substituted–

   "**552(9)**   For the purposes of this section, the year of assessment or financial year to which a gain is attributable is the year in which the gain, treated as arising under regulations 5(2) and 6(1) of the Personal Portfolio Bonds (Tax) Regulations 1999, is treated as arising in accordance with regulation 5(3), (4) and (4A) of those Regulations.";

(g)   in subsection (10)–

   (i)   for the definition of "appropriate policy holder" there shall be substituted– "**"appropriate policy holder"** means the person who is the policy holder immediately before the happening of the event;"; and

   (ii)   the definition of "section 546 excess" shall be omitted; and

(h)   each of the references to a chargeable event shall be taken to include a reference to the chargeable event treated as occurring by reason of paragraph (1)

6(7A)   In section 552ZA subsection (3) shall be omitted.

6(8)   In section 553–

(a)   in each of subsections (3) and (6) after "section 541 or 546C(7)(b)" there shall be inserted the words "or regulations 5(2) and 6(1) of the Personal Portfolio Bonds (Tax) Regulations 1999"; and

(b)   in subsection (10) after "545 or 546C(7)(a)" there shall be inserted the words "or, in relation to a gain treated as arising in relation to a policy under regulations 5(2) and 6(1) of the Personal Portfolio Bonds (Tax) Regulations 1999, the same meaning as in section 553C(4)(b)".

History – In reg. 6(3) references to "546C" and "546C(7)(b)" inserted by SI 2001/2724, reg. 4, operative from 17 August 2001, with effect as respects gains treated as arising on or after that day.

Statutory Instruments

Reg. 6(7) substituted with effect from 6 April 2002, as respects gains treated as arising on or after that date, by SI 2002/455, reg. 2.
Reg. 6(7A) inserted with effect from 6 April 2002, as respects gains treated as arising on or after that date, by SI 2002/455, reg. 2.
In reg. 6(8) references to "546C(7)(b)" and "546C(7)(a)" inserted by SI 2001/2724, reg. 4, operative from 17 August 2001, with effect as respects gains treated as arising on or after that day.

Cross references – SI 1999/881, reg. 8: use of reg. 6(1) in defining a "relevant event".

NON-RESIDENT COMPANIES (GENERAL INSURANCE BUSINESS) REGULATIONS 1999

(SI 1999/1408, as amended by SI 2008/954 and SI 2008/2643)

Made on 20 May 1999 by the Treasury, in exercise of the powers conferred on them by s. 444BB(5), 444BD(1), (4) and (5), 755B(5) and 755C of the Income and Corporation Taxes Act 1988. Operative from 10 June 1999

ARRANGEMENT OF REGULATIONS

CITATION, COMMENCEMENT AND EFFECT

1(1) These Regulations may be cited as the Non-resident Companies (General Insurance Business) Regulations 1999 and shall come into force on 10 June 1999.

1(2) These Regulations have effect with respect to any appropriate accounting period of a relevant company.

INTERPRETATION

2(1) In these Regulations unless the context otherwise requires–

"appropriate accounting period" means an accounting period ending on or after 1 July 1999;

"controlled foreign company" shall be construed in accordance with section 747(2);

"general insurance business" has the meaning given by section 755B(6);

"non-resident company" means a company resident outside the United Kingdom;

"relevant company" means a company resident in the United Kingdom that had a relevant interest in a non-resident company at any time during an accounting period of the non-resident company ending in an appropriate accounting period of the relevant company;

"relevant interest" shall be construed in accordance with section 752A on the assumption that the non-resident company is a controlled foreign company;

"the Taxes Act" means the Income and Corporation Taxes Act 1988.

2(2) In these Regulations references to a particular provision, without more, are references to that provision of the Taxes Act.

MODIFICATIONS OF CHAPTER IV OF PART XVII OF THE TAXES ACT

3 Chapter IV of Part XVII of the Taxes Act shall have effect with the modifications prescribed in regulations 4 to 6 in any case where a non-resident company–

(a)   carries on general insurance business, and

(b)   draws up accounts relating to that business using a method falling within subsection (2) of section 755B.

4 After section 754A there shall be inserted–

"754AA   Returns where it is not established whether a non-resident company carrying on general insurance business is a controlled foreign company

754AA(1)   This section applies where–

(a)   if an apportionment were made in accordance with section 747 of the chargeable profits for an accounting period of a company resident outside the United Kingdom ("the non-resident company"), a company resident in the United Kingdom ("the UK company") would be chargeable to tax by virtue of subsection (5) of that section with reference to the whole or a part of the non-resident company's chargeable profits for that accounting period ("the relevant accounting period");

(b)   the non-resident company carries on general insurance business within the meaning given by section 755B(6) and draws up accounts relating to that business using a method falling within section 755B(2);

(c)   the UK company delivers a company tax return for the accounting period in which the relevant accounting period of the non-resident company ends; and

(d)   at the time when the UK company delivers the company tax return for that accounting period, it is not established whether in the relevant accounting period the non-resident company is subject to a lower level of taxation in the territory in which it is resident so as to constitute a controlled foreign company.

754AA(2)   Prior to delivering its company tax return for the accounting period mentioned in paragraph (1)(c), the UK company shall consider whether or not the non-resident company is likely, in the relevant accounting period, to be subject to a lower level of taxation in the territory in which it is resident so as to constitute a controlled foreign company.

754AA(3)   If the UK company is of the opinion that in the relevant accounting period the non-resident company is likely to be subject to a lower level of taxation in the territory in which it is resident so as to constitute a controlled foreign company, the UK company shall make the company tax return on the basis that the relevant accounting period is an accounting period of a company which is a controlled foreign company.

754AA(4)   If the UK company is of the opinion that in the relevant accounting period the non-resident company is not likely to be subject to a lower level of taxation in the territory in which it is resident so as to constitute a controlled foreign company, the UK company shall make the company tax return on the basis that the relevant accounting period is an accounting period of a company which is not a controlled foreign company.

754AA(5)   In any case where–

(a)   the UK company makes the company tax return on the basis mentioned in subsection (3) above, but

(b)   it becomes established that in the relevant accounting period the non-resident company is not subject to a lower level of taxation in the territory in which it is resident,

the UK company shall amend the company tax return on the basis that the relevant accounting period is an accounting period of a company which is not a controlled foreign company.

754AA(6)   In any case where–

(a)   the UK company makes the company tax return on the basis mentioned in subsection (4) above, but

(b)   it becomes established that in the relevant accounting period the non-resident company is subject to a lower level of taxation in the territory in which it is resident, the UK company shall amend the company tax return on the basis that the relevant accounting period is an accounting period of a company which is a controlled foreign company.

754AA(7)   Any amendment required to be made to the company tax return by virtue of subsection (5) or (6) above shall be made by the UK company before the expiration of the period commencing immediately following the close of the underwriting year and ending on the date which is eighteen months plus thirty days thereafter.

754AA(8)   Subject to subsection (9) below, an amendment of a company tax return in accordance with subsection (7) above is subject to, and must be in accordance with, the other provisions of the Corporation Tax Acts as they apply for the purposes of this Chapter.

754AA(9)   The time limits otherwise applicable to amendment of a company tax return do not apply to an amendment of a company tax return in accordance with subsection (7) above.

754AA(10) A company which fails to make an amendment required by subsection (6) above in accordance with subsection (7) above shall be liable to a tax-related penalty under paragraph 20 of Schedule 18 to the Finance Act 1998 (penalty, not exceeding amount of tax understated, for incorrect or uncorrected return).

754AA(11) In subsection (7) above
"the close of the underwriting year" means–

(a) the date on which final replacement of the technical provision, as described in sub-paragraph (4) of paragraph 58 of Schedule 3 to the Large and Medium-sized Companies and Groups (Accounts and Reports) Regulations 2008, takes place, or

(b) where there is no final replacement of the technical provision in the three years following the underwriting year, the date referred to in section 755B(4), that is, the end of the third year following the underwriting year."

History – In reg. 4, in modified ICTA 1988, s. 754AA(11)(a), the words "sub-paragraph (4) of paragraph 58 of Schedule 3 to the Large and Medium-sized Companies and Groups (Accounts and Reports) Regulations 2008" substituted for "sub-paragraph (4) of paragraph 52 of Schedule 9A to the Companies Act 1985" by SI 2008/954, art. 47, with effect from 6 April 2008.

5(1) Section 755B shall be modified as follows.

5(2) After subsection (4) there shall be inserted–

"755B(4A) Where in accordance with subsection (4) above the technical provision is treated as finally replaced by a provision for estimated claims outstanding ("the deemed provision"), the amount of the deemed provision which may be deducted from the chargeable profits of the controlled foreign company for the accounting period concerned shall not exceed the amount that, on the assumptions in Schedule 24, would have been deductible from those profits if the deemed provision had been an actual provision as mentioned in subsection (2)(a) above."

6 [Revoked by SI 2008/2643, reg. 2.]

History – Reg. 6 revoked by SI 2008/2643, reg. 2, with effect in relation to accounting periods of relevant companies ending on or after 28 October 2008. Former reg. 6 read:

"**6(1)**   Paragraph 2 of Schedule 25 shall be modified as follows.
6(2)   In sub-paragraph (1), in each of paragraphs (b) and (d) there shall be inserted at the beginning "subject to sub-paragraphs (1AA) to (1AC) below,".
6(3)   After sub-paragraph (1) there shall be inserted–
"**2(1AA)**   sub-paragraph (1AB) below applies where, in a case to which section 754AA(1) applies–
(a)   a company resident in the United Kingdom ("the UK company") either–
  (i)   has made a company tax return for an accounting period on the basis mentioned in section 754AA(3), that is, that an accounting period of a non-resident company ("the relevant accounting period") ending in the accounting period of the UK company for which the company tax return is made is an accounting period of a controlled foreign company, and has not subsequently been required to amend the company tax return in accordance with section 754AA(5) on the basis that the relevant accounting period of the non-resident company is an accounting period of a company which is not a controlled foreign company, or
  (ii)   has made a company tax return for an accounting period on the basis mentioned in section 754AA(4), that is, that the relevant accounting period of a non-resident company is an accounting period of a company which is not a controlled foreign company, but has subsequently amended the company tax return in accordance with section 754AA(6) to (8) on the basis that the relevant accounting period of the non-resident company is an accounting period of a controlled foreign company; and
(b)   the final replacement of the technical provision in the accounts of the non-resident company for the relevant accounting period–
  (i)   takes place on a date falling within the period of three years ("the three year period") following the relevant accounting period, or
  (ii)   where no final replacement of the technical provision takes place in the three year period, is treated by virtue of section 755B(4) as having taken place on the date that is the end of that period,
and each of those dates is referred to in sub-paragraphs (1AB), (1AD) and (1AE) below as, "the close of the underwriting year".
2(1AB)   Where this sub-paragraph applies–
(a)   the dividend referred to in sub-paragraph (1) above shall be due on or before the date which is eighteen months after the close of the underwriting year, or on or before such later date as the Board may, in any particular case, allow;
(b)   the amount of the dividend or, if there is more than one, of the aggregate of those dividends which is paid to persons resident in the United Kingdom is the aggregate of the following amounts–
  (i)   an amount equal to 90 per cent of the company's net chargeable profits for the relevant accounting period or, where sub-paragraph (4) or (5) below applies, of the appropriate portion of those profits, and
  (ii)   in respect of each dividend that is paid to persons resident in the United Kingdom later than the date which is eighteen months after the end of the relevant accounting period, an amount calculated at the date of the dividend concerned in accordance with the formula–

$$\frac{D \times i}{(1 + i)}$$

2(1AC)   In sub-paragraph (1AB) above–
(a)   D is the amount of the dividend concerned, and
(b)   "i" is the interest factor calculated in accordance with the rates applicable under section 178 of the Finance Act 1989 to section 87A of the Management Act from the date that is eighteen months after the end of the relevant accounting period until the date of payment of that dividend.
2(1AD)   Where–
(a)   sub-paragraphs (1AA) to (1AC) above apply in relation to an accounting period of the UK company,

Statutory Instruments

(b)   the UK company has made a company tax return for that accounting period on the basis that the dividend referred to in sub-paragraph (1) above will be paid to persons resident in the United Kingdom not later than the date which is eighteen months after the close of the underwriting year or not later than the date allowed by the Board as mentioned in sub-paragraph (1AB)(a) above, and

(c)   that dividend is not paid on or before that date,

the UK company shall amend the company tax return so as to record that the controlled foreign company has not pursued an acceptable distribution policy in respect of the relevant accounting period.

2(1AE)   An amendment required to be made to the company tax return by virtue of sub-paragraph (1AD) above shall be made by the UK company before the expiration of the period of thirty days next following the date which is eighteen months after the close of the underwriting year or next following the date allowed by the Board as mentioned in sub-paragraph (1AB)(a) above.

2(1AF)   A company which fails to make an amendment required by sub-paragraph (1AD) above before the expiry of the period specified in sub-paragraph (1AE) above shall be liable to a tax-related penalty under paragraph 20 of Schedule 18 to the Finance Act 1998.""

AMENDMENTS TO THE INSURANCE COMPANIES (RESERVES)(TAX) REGULATIONS 1996

7(1)   The Insurance Companies (Reserves) (Tax) Regulations 1996 shall be amended as follows.

7(2)   In regulation 8(1) there shall be inserted at the beginning "Subject to regulation 8B,".

7(3)   After regulation 8 there shall be inserted–

"CERTAIN INSURANCE BUSINESS CARRIED ON OUTSIDE THE UNITED KINGDOM BY A CONRTOLLED FOREIGN COMPANY – NON-ANNUAL ACCOUNTS BUT RETURNS PREPARED ON AN ANNUAL BASIS

8A(1)   Subject to regulation 8B, this regulation applies in any case where–

(a)   paragraphs (1) and (2) of regulation 8 apply in respect of an accounting period of a controlled foreign company,

(b)   the statutory accounts drawn up by the controlled foreign company for that period use a paragraph 52 method of accounting on a non-annual basis, but

(c)   returns of chargeable profits of that company for that period are based on accounts prepared on an annual basis.

8A(2)   Paragraph (3) of regulation 8 shall apply in relation to this regulation as it applies in relation to that regulation.

8A(3)   Section 444BA shall have effect, subject to the modifications specified in paragraph (5) of regulation 8 and in paragraph (4) of this regulation, in relation to the equalisation reserve included in the statutory accounts as it has effect in relation to equalisation reserves maintained by virtue of section 34A regulations.

8A(4)   The operation of paragraphs (a) and (b) of subsection (2) of section 444BA shall be modified so as to provide that, for the purposes of the Tax Acts, the amounts which are transferred into or out of the equalisation reserve in respect of the controlled foreign company's business for the accounting period in question shall be the amounts which would have been transferred into or out of the equalisation reserve if the company had been required to maintain an equalisation reserve by reference to accounts prepared on an accident year basis.

8A(5)   The reference in paragraph (1)(c) to accounts prepared on an annual basis shall be construed in accordance with regulation 5(3).

8A(6)   The reference in paragraph (4) to accounts prepared on an accident year basis shall be construed in accordance with regulation 5(4).

DISAPPLICATION OF REGULATIONS 8 AND 8A WHERE CONTROLLED FOREIGN COMPANY PREPARES NON-ANNUAL ACCOUNTS AND FINAL REPLACEMENT OF THE TECHNICAL PROVISION DOES NOT TAKE PLACE IN CONFORMITY WITH THE COMPANIES ACT

8B   Regulations 8 and 8A shall not apply in any case where for an accounting period a controlled foreign company–

(a)   draws up its statutory accounts for that period using a paragraph 52 method of accounting on a non-annual basis, and

(b)   the final replacement of the technical provision, as described in sub-paragraph (4) of that paragraph does not take place on or before the end of the year referred to in that sub-paragraph as the third year following the underwriting year."

CORPORATION TAX (SIMPLIFIED ARRANGEMENTS FOR GROUP RELIEF) REGULATIONS 1999

(SI 1999/2975)

Made on 1 November 1999 by the Treasury, in exercise of the powers conferred on them by para. 77 of Sch. 18 to the Finance Act 1998. Operative from 23 November 1999.

Cross references – SI 2009/317, reg. 3: modification of SI 1999/2975 as it applies in relation to liquidation and administration.

ARRANGEMENT OF REGULATIONS

CITATION AND COMMENCEMENT

1 These Regulations may be cited as the Corporation Tax (Simplified Arrangements for Group Relief) Regulations 1999 and shall come into force on 23rd November 1999.

INTRODUCTORY

2 These Regulations make provision for arrangements for the surrendering and claiming of group relief in relation to any accounting period of a claimant company ending on or after 1st July 1999.

INTERPRETATION

3(1) In these Regulations unless the context otherwise requires—

"the arrangements" means the arrangements made by these Regulations as mentioned in regulation 2;

"authorised company" has the meaning given by regulation 4;

"authorising companies" has the meaning given by regulation 5;

"the Board" means the Commissioners of Inland Revenue;

"claimant company" has the meaning given by section 402(1);

"consortium company" has the meaning given by section 406(1)(b);

"group of companies" means a collection of companies such that every pair of companies within that collection comprises companies that are members of the same group of companies within the meaning of section 413(3)(a);

"group relief" has the meaning given by subsection (1) of section 402, read with subsection (2) of that section (group claim) and subsection (3) of that section and section 406 (consortium claim);

"insolvency practitioner" in relation to a company means a liquidator, provisional liquidator, administrator, administrative receiver, or a supervisor of a voluntary arrangement under Part I of the Insolvency Act 1986;

"the Management Act" means the Taxes Management Act 1970;

"member of the consortium" shall be construed in accordance with section 413(6);

"Schedule 18" means Schedule 18 to the Finance Act 1998;

"three month date" shall be construed in accordance with regulation 7(1).

3(2) In these Regulations references to a section, without more, are to that section of the Income and Corporation Taxes Act 1988.

AUTHORISED COMPANY

4 A company is an "authorised company" for the purposes of these Regulations if–

(a)   it is authorised by companies within regulation 5 to act on their behalf in relation to the arrangements, and

(b)   it is a member of the same group of companies as that referred to in regulation 5(1)(a).

AUTHORISING COMPANY

5(1) In these Regulations an **"authorising company"** means a company which for the time being–

(a)   is a member of a group of companies, or

(b)   is a consortium company in circumstances where a company falling within sub-paragraph (a) is a member of the consortium concerned, and

(c)   in either case satisfies one of the conditions specified in paragraph (2).

5(2) Those conditions are that the company–

(a)   is one of the companies named in the application made by the authorised company in accordance with regulation 6;

(b)   following the making of that application, is treated for the purposes of these Regulations, by agreement between the company, the authorised company and the Board, as if it had been one of the companies named in that application.

APPLICATION BY AUTHORISED COMPANY

6(1) An application by the authorised company on behalf of itself and the authorising companies to enter into the arrangements must be made in writing to an officer of the Board.

6(2) The application must specify–

(a)   the name and the tax office reference of the authorised company,

(b)   the names and the tax office references of the authorising companies, and

(c)   details relating to the authorised company and each of the authorising companies that are sufficient to demonstrate that the company concerned is a member of the group of companies or, as the case may be, a consortium company.

6(3) The application must contain a statement by the authorised company and the authorising companies that they agree to be covered by the arrangements and to be bound by claims, surrenders and withdrawals made under the arrangements.

6(4) The application must be accompanied–

(a)   by a specimen copy of the statement referred to in regulation 10(2) that the authorised company proposes to use for the purpose of making and withdrawing surrenders and claims on behalf of itself and the authorising companies;

(b)   in the case of a company which is a consortium company, by an agreement, signed by each member of the consortium and the consortium company, consenting to the authorised company acting on their behalf in relation to the arrangements.

6(5) The application must be signed on behalf of each of the companies concerned by a person referred to in section 108(1) of the Management Act as a person through whom that company may act.

6(6) The application must be sent to the tax office dealing with the tax affairs of the authorised company.

MATTERS CONSEQUENTIAL TO THE MAKING OF AN APPLICATION

7(1) Except where paragraph (2), (3) or (4) applies and subject to regulation 9, the authorised company may enter into the arrangements on behalf of itself and the authorising companies at any time on or after the date ("the three month date") that is three months after the date on which the application is delivered to the tax office in accordance with regulation 6(6).

7(2) An officer of the Board may, prior to the three month date, accept the application and permit the authorised company to enter into the arrangements on behalf of itself and the authorising companies with effect from the date notified to the authorised company by the officer of the Board.

7(3) An officer of the Board may, prior to the three month date, accept the application and permit the authorised company to enter into the arrangements with effect from the date notified to the company by the officer of the Board, but exclude from the arrangements any of the authorising companies on the grounds that he has reason to believe that that company–

(a) has failed to comply with its obligations under the Corporation Tax Acts in relation to any accounting period (whether an accounting period ending before, or on or after, 1st July 1999), or

(b) is a company in relation to which a person is acting as an insolvency practitioner.

7(4) An officer of the Board may, prior to the three month date, refuse the application on the grounds that–

(a) he has reason to believe that one or more of the companies named in the application is not a member of a group of companies, or is not a consortium company in circumstances where a company which is a member of that group is a member of the consortium concerned,

(b) he has reason to believe that one or more of the companies named in the application has failed to comply with its obligations under the Corporation Tax Acts in relation to any accounting period (whether an accounting period ending before, or on or after, 1st July 1999),

(c) the case is not one in which all, or substantially all, of the companies named in the application deliver their company tax returns to the same tax office, or

(d) the specimen copy of the statement referred to in regulation 6(4)(a) is not adequate for the purpose of enabling an officer of the Board to deal with claims for group relief.

7(5) Where following the making of an application by an authorised company under regulation 6 a company is treated by agreement in accordance with regulation 5(2)(b) as if it had been one of the companies named in the application, the authorised company may enter into the arrangements on behalf of that company from the date of the agreement.

CHANGE IN MEMBERS OF CONSORTIUM

8(1) Where following the making of an application under regulation 6 there is a change in the members of the consortium referred to in paragraph (4)(b) of that regulation, as from the date of the change the authorised company may not act in accordance with the provisions of regulation 10 in relation to the consortium company concerned unless it takes the action specified in paragraph (2).

8(2) The action specified in this paragraph is that the company must ensure that a new agreement, signed by the consortium company concerned and each company that is a member of the consortium immediately after the change, consenting to the authorised company acting on their behalf in relation to the arrangements, is sent to the tax office referred to in regulation 6(6).

8(3) Where in accordance with paragraph (2) a new agreement is entered into and sent to the tax office, that agreement is effective for the purposes of the arrangements as from the date on which acceptance of the agreement is notified by an officer of the Board to the authorised company.

EXCLUSION OF COMPANY FROM THE ARRANGEMENTS

9 An officer of the Board may, at any time on or after the three month date or, if earlier, the date on which an application under regulation 6 was accepted, exclude from the arrangements a company named, or treated under regulation 5(2)(b) as named, in that application, on the grounds that he has reason to believe that that company–

(a) is not an authorising company at that time by reason of the company not falling within regulation 5(1)(a) or (b);

(b) has failed to comply with its obligations under the Corporation Tax Acts in relation to any accounting period (whether an accounting period ending before, or on or after, 1st July 1999); or

(c) is a company in relation to which a person is acting as an insolvency practitioner.

GROUP RELIEF CLAIMS UNDER THE ARRANGEMENTS NOT ACCOMPANIED BY COPY OF NOTICE OF CONSENT TO SURRENDER

9A(1) Where an application by an authorised company is accepted by an officer of the Board under regulation 7, any of the authorising companies may make a claim for group relief in accordance with the following provisions of this regulation.

9A(2) A claim may be made without being accompanied by the copy of the notice of consent required under paragraph 70(4) of Schedule 18 if the authorised company gives authority for the claim being so made.

Statutory Instruments

9A(3) The authority given by the authorised company must–

(a) be included in the company tax return of the authorising company for the accounting period for which the claim is made,

(b) be included in that return as originally made, and

(c) be signed on behalf of the authorised company by a person referred to in section 108(1) of the Management Act as a person through whom that company may act.

History – Reg. 9A inserted by SI 2000/3228, reg. 2, operative from 29 December 2000.

GROUP RELIEF CLAIMS AND SURRENDERS UNDER THE ARRANGEMENTS

10(1) Where an application by an authorised company is accepted by an officer of the Board under regulation 7, the authorised company may act in accordance with the following provisions of this regulation in relation to itself and to any of the authorising companies, other than a company excluded from the arrangements in accordance with regulation 7(3) or 9.

10(2) The authorised company may from time to time furnish to an officer of the Board on behalf of itself and the authorising companies a statement in writing, in the form provided, or in a form authorised, by the Board, containing information necessary for the amendment in accordance with the provisions of Part VIII of Schedule 18 of the company tax returns of itself and the authorising companies for the purpose of making and withdrawing claims and surrenders of group relief.

10(3) Where a statement is furnished to an officer of the Board as mentioned in paragraph (2)–

(a) the provisions of Part VIII of Schedule 18, other than paragraph 70(4) (claim for group relief ineffective unless accompanied by copy of notice of consent to surrender) and paragraph 71(4) (notice of withdrawal of consent to surrender ineffective unless accompanied by notice of consent of claimant company to withdrawal), shall apply in relation to the authorised company as if references to the claimant company and the surrendering company included references to the authorised company;

(b) amendments made in accordance with the provisions of Part VIII of Schedule 18 to the company tax returns of the authorising companies in reliance on the information contained in the statement shall have effect for the purposes of the Corporation Tax Acts as if the amendments had been made by those companies.

10(4) Without prejudice to the generality of paragraph (2), the information to be contained in the statement must include in particular–

(a) as regards the amount claimed, the same information as is specified in paragraph 68 of Schedule 18,

(b) as regards the amount surrendered, the same information as is specified in paragraph 71(1) of Schedule 18,

(c) where applicable, details showing the effect of the claim on each company's self-assessment included in its company tax return, and

(d) where applicable, details showing which of the company tax returns of the companies concerned are returns into which an enquiry is in progress under Part IV of Schedule 18.

10(5) A statement provided under paragraph (2) that does not contain information that is sufficient for the amendment of the company tax returns of the authorised company and the authorising companies in accordance with the provisions of Part VIII of Schedule 18 is ineffective.

10(6) An authorising company remains liable, in accordance with the provisions of Schedule 18, for any incorrect claim or incorrect company tax return arising from a statement provided by the authorised company under paragraph (2).

TERMINATION OF ARRANGEMENTS AND EXCLUSION OF APPLICANT COMPANY FROM ARRANGEMENTS

11(1) Either the Board or the authorised company may at any time give notice in writing to the other terminating the arrangements with effect from the date of issue of the notice.

11(2) The authorised company may at any time give notice in writing to the Board excluding an authorising company from the arrangements with effect from the date of issue of the notice.

LLOYD'S UNDERWRITERS (SPECIAL RESERVE FUNDS) REGULATIONS 1999

(SI 1999/3308)

Made on 9 December 1999 by the Commissioners of Inland Revenue, in exercise of the powers conferred on them by s. 182(1)(b) and (c) of the Finance Act 1993. Operative from 31 December 1999.

Whereas the Commissioners of the Inland Revenue, in consequence of a variation to the arrangements referred to in section 175(1) of the Finance Act 1993, think it expedient to make the provision made by regulation 3 of these Regulations:

Now, therefore, the Commissioners of Inland Revenue, in exercise of the powers conferred on them by section 182(1)(b) and (c) of the finance act 1993, hereby make the following regulations:

CITATION, COMMENCEMENT AND EFFECT

1(1) These Regulations may be cited as the Lloyd's Underwriters (Special Reserve Funds) Regulations 1999.

1(2) These Regulations shall come into force on 31st December 1999, but except for regulation 3 shall have effect–

(a)   for the year 2000–01 and subsequent years of assessment, and

(b)   in relation to payments and transfers of assets made on or after 1st January 2000.

INTERPRETATION

2 In these Regulations **"Schedule 20"** means Schedule 20 to the Finance Act 1993.

AMENDMENTS TO AND MODIFICATIONS OF SCHEDULE 20

3 In paragraph 6(2) of Schedule 20–

(a)   for the words "of the fund as so determined in respect" there shall be substituted the words "(determined under sub-paragraph (1) above) of the fund as at the end";

(b)   for paragraph (a) the following paragraph shall be substituted–

"(a)   the higher of–

    (i)   the member's overall premium limit for that year, and

    (ii)   his overall premium limit for the immediately preceding year; or";

(c)   in paragraph (b) for the words "that year" there shall be substituted the words "either of those years".

4 In paragraph 8(1) of Schedule 20 after "(2)" there shall be inserted the words "and paragraph 11(2) to (4)".

5 In paragraph 10(4) of Schedule 20 after the word "above" there shall be inserted the words "(including where they are also made under paragraph 7(1) above)".

6(1) Paragraph 11 of Schedule 20 is modified as follows.

6(2) In sub-paragraph (2)–

(a)   for the words "any payment which is" there shall be substituted the words "the aggregate of any payments which are";

(b)   after the word "above" there shall be inserted the words "(except where they are also made under paragraph 6(2) above)";

(c)   in paragraph (a) at the beginning there shall be inserted the words "subject to sub-paragraph (2A) below,";

(d)   in paragraph (b) after the words "being a" there shall be inserted the word "single".

6(3) After sub-paragraph (2) the following sub-paragraph shall be inserted–

"**11(2A)** Where the member ceases to carry on his underwriting business by reason of his death, any payment falling within sub-paragraph (2) above shall be treated, for the purposes of sections 59C and 86 of the Management Act, as if made immediately after the commencement of his final year of assessment."

6(4) In sub-paragraph (3)–

(a)   in paragraph (b) after the word "paragraph" there shall be inserted "3(1),";

(b)   the word "and" which immediately follows paragraph (b) shall be omitted;

(c)   at the end the following paragraphs shall be added–

   "(d)   as increased by an amount equal to any profits, and reduced by an amount equal to any losses, arising to the trustees from assets after the end of that year (excluding any gains or losses on assets whose transfer is treated as an acquisition by sub-paragraph (4)(a) or (b) below); and

   (e)   as increased by the aggregate amount of any payments made–

      (i)   by the trustees to the member or his personal representatives or assigns,

      (ii)   out of his special reserve fund under paragraph 7(1) above (except where they are also made under paragraph 6(2) above), or otherwise than out of his special reserve fund, and

      (iii)   before the end of that year,

   and for this purpose the amount of any payment which is made by way of the transfer of an asset shall be taken to be the market value of the asset at the date of the transfer and **"market value"** shall be construed in accordance with section 272 of the Taxation of Chargeable Gains Act 1992."

6(5) In sub-paragraph (4)–

(a)   after the word "above" there shall be inserted the words "or otherwise than out of his special reserve fund";

(b)   for the words from ", to be" to the end there shall be substituted–

   "(a)   in a case where the asset was held by the trustees at the end of the penultimate underwriting year, as an acquisition of the asset by the member or his personal representatives or assigns at the end of that year for a consideration equal to its market value at that time;

   (b)   in a case where the asset was acquired by the trustees after the end of the penultimate underwriting year, as an acquisition of the asset by the member or his personal representatives or assigns, at the date on which, and for the consideration for which, the asset was acquired by the trustees; and

   (c)   in a case where the asset was both acquired by the trustees and transferred by them to the member or his personal representatives or assigns before the end of the penultimate underwriting year, as an acquisition of the asset by the member or his personal representatives or assigns at the date of the transfer and for a consideration equal to its market value at that time."

DOUBLE TAXATION RELIEF (TAXES ON INCOME) (FOREIGN INTEREST AND DIVIDENDS) REGULATIONS 1999

(SI 1999/3330)

Made on 13 December 1999 by the Commissioners of Inland Revenue, in exercise of the powers conferred on them by s. 798B(4) of the Income and Corporation Taxes Act 1988. Operative from 3 January 2000

ARRANGEMENT OF REGULATIONS

REGULATION

1. CITATION AND COMMENCEMENT
2. INTERPRETATION
3. DETERMINATION OF THE SUM WHICH IT IS JUST AND REASONABLE TO ATTRIBUTE TO THE EARNING OF FOREIGN INTEREST OR FOREIGN DIVIDENDS – MATTERS TO BE TAKEN INTO ACCOUNT
4. DETERMINATION OF INTERBANK BID RATES OF INTEREST
5. REVOCATION

CITATION AND COMMENCEMENT

1 These Regulations may be cited as the Double Taxation Relief (Taxes on Income) (Foreign Interest and Dividends) Regulations 1999 and shall come into force on 3rd January 2000.

INTERPRETATION

2(1) In these Regulations unless the context otherwise requires–

"the cost of acquiring the asset", in relation to a foreign dividend, means–

(a)   the cost of acquiring the right to the dividend (if any), and

(b)   the cost of acquiring the stocks, funds, shares or securities (if any) out of which, or in respect of which, the dividend is paid;

"interbank market" means the market that exists between banks in a particular place for the purpose of borrowing and lending funds and dealing in currencies, and **"the relevant interbank market"** means the interbank market which is most appropriate in relation to a loan having regard to all the terms on which it was made;

"interest period", in relation to a loan, means–

(a)   any period specified in the loan agreement as a period for which interest is to be calculated, or, as the case may be, selected in accordance with that agreement by one of the parties thereto, beginning either on the date on which the loan was first made or on the expiry of the preceding interest period; or

(b)   where no such period is specified in the loan agreement, but interest is to be calculated under that agreement by reference to a period of at least 360 days, and is payable on two or more specified dates within that period, any period beginning immediately after one and ending on the next of those dates; or

(c)   in any other case, any period not exceeding one year which is appropriate in the circumstances of the loan;

"loan agreement" means, in relation to a loan, any agreement in pursuance of which the loan is made;

"qualifying taxpayer" has the meaning given by section 798(4) and (5);

"the specified circumstances" means circumstances in which–

(a)   section 798 applies, and

(b)   the amount of the qualifying taxpayer's financial expenditure in relation to the earning of the foreign interest or foreign dividends in question is not readily ascertainable;

"subsection (3)" means subsection (3) of section 798B.

2(2) References in these Regulations to a particular section, without more, are to that section of the Income and Corporation Taxes Act 1988.

DETERMINATION OF THE SUM WHICH IT IS JUST AND REASONABLE TO ATTRIBUTE TO THE EARNING OF FOREIGN INTEREST OR FOREIGN DIVIDENDS – MATTERS TO BE TAKEN INTO ACCOUNT

3(1) This regulation specifies, for the purpose of supplementing subsection (3), matters to be taken into account in determining such sum as it is just and reasonable to attribute to the earning of foreign interest or foreign dividends, in the specified circumstances.

3(2) Subject to paragraph (6), in relation to a loan there shall be taken into account (whether or not the interest rate payable is determined by reference to rates at which deposits are offered in an interbank market) the interbank bid rates, determined in accordance with regulation 4, which at any time are most appropriate in the circumstances of the loan, having regard to–

(a)   the amount of principal outstanding on the loan during each interest period,

(b)   the currency in which the loan is denominated, and

(a)   the length of each interest period.

3(3) In relation to foreign interest other than loan interest, paragraph (2), regulation 4 and the definitions of "interbank market", "the relevant interbank market" and "interest period" shall apply, with the modifications that–

(a)   references to the loan, or to the loan agreement, are replaced with references to the obligations, under which the right to interest arises;

(b)   the reference to the date on which the loan was first made is replaced with a reference to the date on which any of those obligations first came into existence; and

(c)   the reference to principal outstanding is replaced with a reference to any amount other than interest which is owing (whether or not yet due and payable) by the payer of the foreign interest to the qualifying taxpayer.

3(4) In relation to foreign dividends, paragraph (2), regulation 4 and the definitions of "interbank market" and "the relevant interbank market" shall apply as if–

(a)   so much of the cost of acquiring the asset as has not been repaid to the qualifying taxpayer represented a loan from the payee of the dividend to the payer thereof and the dividend represented interest on that loan;

(b)   the date on which any of the cost of acquiring the asset was first expended by the qualifying taxpayer were the date on which that loan was made; and

(c)   the interest periods were periods of one year, beginning either–

(i)   on the date on which the loan is treated as made by sub-paragraph (b), or

(ii)   on the expiry of the preceding interest period,

(d)   except in a case where the loan so treated as made subsists for less than a year, where the interest period shall be equal to the period for which the loan so treated as made subsists.

3(5) Where, in relation to a loan it would be impracticable to establish the interbank bid rates, there shall be taken into account such amount as would, when deducted from the foreign interest payable on the loan in the interest period, provide the lender with a margin no greater than would be usual in the case of loans of that description.

3(6) Where a qualifying taxpayer establishes to the satisfaction of the inspector that, in relation to all loans, obligations and assets referred to in this regulation ("arrangements") made or held by him, on which foreign interest or foreign dividends arose in any chargeable period, the sums attributable under paragraphs (2) to (5) would be greater than the total amount of the expenditure incurred in financing those arrangements, there shall be taken into account the best estimate of such total expenditure, and in determining that figure, regard is to be had to the cost to the qualifying taxpayer of obtaining funds for such financing, to the terms on which the arrangements were made and to any other relevant matters.

DETERMINATION OF INTERBANK BID RATES OF INTEREST

4 The interbank bid rates referred to in regulation 3(2) shall be taken to be the average of the bids that would be made in relation to each interest period applicable to the loan in the relevant interbank market on terms corresponding to the terms of the loan.

REVOCATION

5(1)   The Double Taxation Relief (Taxes on Income) (Foreign Loan Interest) Regulations 1988 are hereby revoked.

5(2)   Anything whatsoever begun under any regulation revoked by these Regulations may be continued under these Regulations as if begun under these Regulations.

EDUCATION (STUDENT LOANS) (REPAYMENT) REGULATIONS 2000

(SI 2000/944, as amended by SI 2001/971, SI 2002/2087, SI 2002/2859, SI 2004/1175, SI 2004/2752, SI 2005/2690, SI 2006/745, SI 2006/2009, SI 2007/1683, SI 2008/546 and SI 2009/56)

Made on 31 March 2000 by the Secretary of State for Education and Employment, in exercise of the powers conferred on the Secretary of State by s. 22 and 42(6) of the Teaching and Higher Education Act 1998 and s. 73(f) and 73B of the Education (Scotland) Act 1980. Operative from 1 April 2000.

ARRANGEMENT OF REGULATIONS

REGULATION

PART V – REPAYMENTS BY OVERSEAS RESIDENTS

PART 6 – REPAYMENT BY OVERSEAS BORROWERS

PART I – GENERAL

CITATION, COMMENCEMENT AND EXTENT

1(1)   These Regulations may be cited as the Education (Student Loans) (Repayment) Regulations 2000, and shall come into force on 1st April 2000.

1(2)   Subject to paragraph (3) these Regulations extend to England and Wales only.

1(3)   These Regulations extend to all of the United Kingdom in so far as they impose any obligation or confer any power on the Board, an employer or a borrower in relation to repayments under Part III or IV.

INTERPRETATION

2 In these Regulations–

"**the Act**" means the Teaching and Higher Education Act 1998;

"**the 1970 Act**" means the Taxes Management Act 1970 as amended from time to time both before and after the date of these Regulations;

"**the 1988 Act**" means the Income and Corporation Taxes Act 1988 as amended from time to time both before and after the date of these Regulations;

"**the Assembly**" means the National Assembly for Wales;

"**the Board**" means the Commissioners of Inland Revenue;

"**borrower**" means a person to whom the Secretary of State has lent money pursuant to regulations made under section 22 of the Act and who has not received a notice from him that it has been repaid in full or cancelled, and also has the meaning given it in regulation 3(3);

"**collector**" means a Collector of Taxes;

"**eligible employment**" has the same meaning as in the Teachers' Regulations;

"**eligible teacher**" means a teacher with a student loan made when he was resident in England or Wales who is eligible for a reduction in respect of that loan under the Teachers' Regulations;

"**full-time**" employment is full-time if the contract of employment so provides;

"**inspector**" means an Inspector of Taxes;

"**part-time**" employment is part-time if the contract of employment requires the employee to work for less than the whole of the working week;

"**repayment**" means a repayment of a student loan;

"**Secretary of State**" includes any person exercising functions on behalf of a Secretary of State pursuant to section 23(4) of the Act, and also has the meanings given it in regulation 3(3);

"**student loan**" means the total outstanding principal, interest, penalties and charges owed by a borrower to the Secretary of State pursuant to these or any other regulations made under section 22 of the Act, excluding any interest, penalties or charges payable under Part III or IV, and also has the meaning given to it in regulation 3(3);

"**the Teachers' Regulations**" means the Education (Teacher Student Loans) (Repayment etc.) Regulations 2002;

"**year of assessment**" means the period 6th April to the following 5th April.

History – In reg. 2, the definition of "the Assembly" inserted by SI 2006/2009, reg. 3, with effect from 1 September 2006.
In reg. 2, the definition of "eligible employment" inserted by SI 2002/2087, reg. 2(2) with effect from 1 September 2002.
In reg. 2, the definition of "eligible teacher" inserted by SI 2002/2087, reg. 2(2) with effect from 1 September 2002.
In reg. 2, the definition of "full-time" inserted by SI 2002/2087, reg. 2(2) with effect from 1 September 2002.
In reg. 2, the definition of "part-time" inserted by SI 2002/2087, reg. 2(2) with effect from 1 September 2002.
In reg. 2, in the definition of "Secretary of State", the words "and (5)" deleted by SI 2001/971, reg. 9 and Schedule, para. 1, with effect from 6 April 2001.
In reg. 2, the definition of "the Teachers' Regulations" inserted by SI 2002/2087, reg. 2(2) with effect from 1 September 2002.

Notes – SI 2001/971, reg. 9 and Schedule, para. 1 requires the words "as amended from time to time both before and after the date of these Regulations" to be inserted into the definition of "the 1998 Act" with effect from 6 April 2001. As no such definition exists and those words are already in the definition of "the 1988 Act" no amendment has been made.

APPLICATION

3(1) These Regulations apply to repayments of student loans made under the Act.

3(2) Where the Scottish Ministers have determined that repayments of student loans made under the Education (Scotland) Act 1980 shall be collected by the Board under Parts III and IV they shall give notices to the borrower and to the Board in accordance with regulation 11.

3(3) Where the Scottish Ministers have given notices in accordance with regulation 11(5)(a) or (b) Parts III and IV, and the provisions of Parts I and II so far as they relate to the application of Parts III and IV, shall apply to repayments of students loans made under the Education (Scotland) Act 1980 as they apply to student loans made under the Act, and for those purposes in these Regulations–

"**borrower**" means a person to whom the Secretary of State or the Scottish Ministers have lent money pursuant to regulations made under section 73(f) of the Education (Scotland) Act 1980 and who has not received a notice from them that it has been repaid in full or cancelled;

"**Secretary of State**" means, other than in this regulation and regulation 4, the Scottish Ministers, and includes any person exercising functions on behalf of the Secretary of State or the Scottish Ministers pursuant to section 73A(4) of the Education (Scotland) Act 1980; and "**student loan**" means the total outstanding principal, interest and charges owed by a borrower to the Scottish Ministers pursuant to regulations made under section 73(f) of the Education (Scotland) Act 1980, excluding any interest, penalties or charges payable under Part III or IV.

3(4)   No provision of Part 3 or 4 nor any provision of Part 1 or 2 so far as it relates to the application of Parts 3 and 4 applies in relation to student loans made by the Assembly under section 22 of the Act unless the Assembly–

(a)   has determined, in relation to any student loan or description of student loan, that repayments are to be collected by the Board, and

(b)   has given notice to the Secretary of State and to the borrower.

3(5)   Where Parts 3 and 4 of these Regulations and any provision of Part 1 or 2 of these Regulations so far as it relates to the application of Parts 3 and 4 apply to student loans made by the Assembly pursuant to paragraph (4), they apply with the following modifications–

"**borrower**" means a person to whom the Assembly has lent money pursuant to Regulations made by it under section 22 of the Act and who has not received a notice from the Assembly that it has been repaid in full or cancelled;

"**Secretary of State**" means, other than in this regulation and regulation 4, the Assembly, and includes any person exercising functions on behalf of the Assembly pursuant to section 23(4) of the Act; and

"**student loan**" means the total outstanding principal, interest and charges owed by a borrower to the Assembly pursuant to Regulations made under section 22 of the Act, excluding any interest, penalties or charges payable under Part 3 or 4.

History – Reg. 3(4) inserted by SI 2006/2009, reg. 4, with effect from 1 September 2006.
Reg. 3(5) inserted by SI 2006/2009, reg. 4, with effect from 1 September 2006.

FUNCTIONS OF THE INLAND REVENUE

4(1)   The Board shall collect repayments from borrowers in accordance with Parts III and IV, and the provisions of section 1 of the 1970 Act shall apply for those purposes as they apply for the purposes of income tax.

4(2)   The Board shall, at such times and in such manner as the Treasury may direct, account to the Secretary of State for, and pay to him the sums estimated by the Board (in the manner so directed) to have been collected by them as repayments in accordance with Parts III and IV.

4(3)   Repayments shall not include any interest, penalties or charges payable under Part III or IV, and the Board shall cause any such sums which they recover to be paid, at such times and under such regulations as the Treasury may from time to time prescribe, to accounts, to be intituled "The Account of Her Majesty's Exchequer", at the Bank of England, and the sums so paid shall form part of the Consolidated Fund.

INSPECTORS AND COLLECTORS

5   Any legal proceedings or administrative act authorised by or done for the purposes of these Regulations and begun by one inspector or collector may be continued by another inspector or, as the case may be, collector; and any inspector or collector may act for any division or other area.

SERVICE BY POST

6   Any notice or other document which is authorised or required to be given, served or issued under these Regulations may be sent by post.

PENALTIES ETC IN RELATION TO PARTS III AND IV

7(1)   Section 98 of the 1970 Act (special returns etc.) shall apply for the purposes of repayments under Part III or IV as if any reference to a provision in the Table in that section were a reference to a provision in those Parts other than regulation 16.

7(2)   Section 99 of the 1970 Act (assisting in the preparation of incorrect returns etc.) shall apply in the case of returns, statements, declarations, accounts, information or documents for the purposes of repayments under Part III or IV as they apply for the purposes of income tax.

7(2A)   For years of assessment–

(a)   ending on or before 5 April 2008 sections 100 (determination of penalties by officer of Board), 100A (provisions supplementary to section 100) and 100B (appeals against policy determinations) of the 1970 Act shall apply to the penalties outlined in regulation 26(3) in connection with repayments under Part III as they apply in connection with income tax;

(b) commencing on or after 6 April 2008, where the date on which the return is due to be filed is on or after 6 April 2009, Schedule 24 of the Finance Act 2007 (penalties for errors) shall apply in relation to the assessment of penalties and appeals against the assessment of penalties in connection with Part III as it applies to penalties in connection with income tax.

7(2B) Sections 100 (determination of penalties by officer of Board), 100A (provisions supplementary to section 100) and 100B (appeals against penalty determinations) of the 1970 Act shall apply to penalties other than those outlined in regulations 26(3) and 26(4) in connection with repayment under Part III and all penalties under Part IV as they apply to penalties in connection with income tax.

7(3) Sections 100C (penalty proceedings before the tribunal), 100D (penalty proceedings before court), 102 (mitigation of penalties), 103(3) and (4) (time limits for penalties), 103A (interest on penalties), 104 (savings for criminal proceedings) and 105 (evidence in case of fraudulent conduct) of the 1970 Act shall apply to penalties in connection with repayments under Part III or IV as they apply to penalties in connection with income tax.

7(4) Sections 112 to 115A of and Schedule 3A to the 1970 Act (documents) shall apply to assessments, returns or any other documents made, required, issued, served, sent or lodged for the purposes of or in connection with repayments under Part III or IV as they apply to documents for the purposes of or in connection with income tax.

7(5) Section 118(2) of the 1970 Act (failure to act within limited time) shall apply in relation to anything required to be done under Part III or IV as it applies in relation to anything required to be done under that Act.

7(6) For the purposes of these Regulations the amount of a repayment covered by any assessment under Part III shall not be deemed to be finally determined until that assessment can no longer be varied, whether by the tribunal on appeal or by the order of any court.

History – Reg. 7(2A) inserted by SI 2008/546, reg. 3, with effect from 1 April 2008.
Reg. 7(2B) inserted by SI 2008/546, reg, 3, with effect from 1 April 2008.
In reg. 7(3), the words "the tribunal" substituted for the word "Commissioners" by SI 2009/56, art. 2 and Sch. 2, para. 73(2), with effect from 1 April 2009 (subject to the transitional provisions at SI 2009/56, Sch. 3).
In reg. 7(3), the words "100 and 100A (determination of penalties by officer of Board), 100B (appeals against penalty determinations)," omitted by SI 2008/546, reg. 3, with effect from 1 April 2008.
In reg. 7(6), the words "by the tribunal" substituted for the words "by any Commissioners" by SI 2009/56, art. 2 and Sch. 2, para. 73(2), with effect from 1 April 2009 (subject to the transitional provisions at SI 2009/56, Sch. 3).

REVOCATION

8 Regulation 27 of the Education (Student Support) Regulations 1999 is hereby revoked.

PART II – PROVISIONS APPLICABLE TO ALL REPAYMENTS

INTERPRETATION

9(1) In this Part—

"the 1998 to 2005 Regulations" means the Education (Student Support) Regulations 1998, the Education (Student Support) Regulations 1999, the Education (Student Support) Regulations 2000, the Education (Student Support) Regulations 2001, the Education (Student Support) Regulations 2002, the Education (Student Support) (No.2) Regulations 2002 and the Education (Student Support) Regulations 2005;

"the 2006 Regulations" means the Education (Student Support) Regulations 2006;

"date of receipt" in relation to a repayment shall be construed in accordance with paragraph (2);

"disability-related benefit" means long term incapacity benefit or short term incapacity benefit at the higher rate, severe disablement allowance, disability living allowance, industrial injuries benefit and disability working allowance, all payable under the Social Security Contributions and Benefits Act 1992, or the amount of any disability premium and severe disability premium included in the applicable amount in calculating the income support payable under the Income Support (General) Regulations 1987.

"end-on course" means—

(a)   a full-time first degree course (other than a first degree course for the initial training of teachers) which, disregarding any intervening vacation, a student begins immediately after ceasing to attend a full-time course mentioned in paragraph (5) for which the student received or was entitled to receive an award made under the Education (Mandatory Awards) Regulations 1998 (other than an award within the meaning of the Education (Mandatory Awards) Regulations 2003), or financial support under the 1998 to 2005 Regulations; and

(b)   a full-time honours degree course beginning on or after 1st September 2006 which, disregarding any intervening vacation, a student begins immediately after ceasing to attend a full-time foundation degree course and for which the student received or was entitled to receive any of the financial support mentioned in paragraph (a);

9(2)   For the purposes of this Part a repayment shall be considered to have been paid by the borrower and received by the Secretary of State as follows:

(a)   where an amount is paid by the borrower directly to the Secretary of State, a repayment of that amount shall be considered to have been received by him on the date on which the amount is in fact received;

(b)   where the Board has notified the Secretary of State that an amount has become payable to the Board in respect of a year of assessment under Part III, a repayment of that amount shall be considered to have been received by him on 31st January following the year of assessment, whether or not the borrower has in fact paid any or all of that amount to the Board; and

(c)   where an amount is deducted by an employer under Part IV that amount shall be aggregated with all other such amounts deducted in the same year of assessment and repayments of the aggregate amount shall be considered to have been received by the Secretary of State in equal instalments received on the days during the year of assessment which are—

(i)   the last days of a month,

(ii)   days after the date on which the Secretary of State has given notice under regulation 11(5)(b) that payment should be deducted, and

(iii)   days before the date on which he has given notice under regulation 11(5)(e) that payment should cease to be deducted.

9(3)   In this Part a document is to be treated as served on a person when it is delivered to him or sent to him by post.

9(4)   The definitions of "the 1998 to 2005 Regulations", "the 2006 Regulations" and "end-on course" do not apply to Part 2 in its application to Wales.

9(5)   The courses mentioned in this paragraph are a course for the Diploma of Higher Education; and a course for the Higher National Diploma or Higher National Certificate of–

(a)   the Business & Technician Education Council; or

(b)   the Scottish Qualifications Authority.

History – In reg. 9(1), the definition of "the 1998 to 2005 Regulations" inserted by SI 2006/2009, reg. 5(a), with effect from 1 September 2006.
In reg. 9(1), the definition of "the 2006 Regulations" inserted by SI 2006/2009, reg. 5(a), with effect from 1 September 2006.
In reg. 9(1), the definition of "end-on course" inserted by SI 2006/2009, reg. 5(a), with effect from 1 September 2006.
In reg. 9(1), the words "paragraph (2)" substituted for the words "paragraphs (2) and (3)" by SI 2001/971, reg. 9 and Schedule, para. 2, with effect from 6 April 2001.
Reg. 9(3) inserted by SI 2004/2752, reg. 4, with effect from 22 November 2004.
Reg. 9(4) inserted by SI 2006/2009, reg. 5(b), with effect from 1 September 2006.
Reg. 9(5) inserted by SI 2006/2009, reg. 5(b), with effect from 1 September 2006.

INTEREST AND PENALTIES

10(1)   Interest or penalties charged under Parts III or IV shall not be added to the principal outstanding, and payment of such interest or penalties shall not be credited against the principal outstanding.

10(2)   Any repayment received by the Secretary of State shall be applied by him in reduction or in satisfaction of:

(a)   first, any outstanding penalties, costs or expenses under regulation 13C or regulation 13D,

(b)   second, any outstanding penalties or charges under Part 5 in relation to Wales and Part 6 in relation to England,

(c)   third, any outstanding interest, and

(d)   fourth, any outstanding principal, which shall be reduced or satisfied from the date of receipt.

History – In reg. 10(2)(b) the words "Part 5 in relation to Wales and Part 6 in relation to England" substituted for the words "Part V" by SI 2006/2009, reg. 6, with effect from 1 September 2006.
Reg. 10(2) substituted by SI 2004/2752, reg. 5, with effect from 22 November 2004.

TIME FOR REPAYMENTS

11(1)   A borrower may repay all or any part of his student loan to the Secretary of State at any time.

11(2)   A borrower shall not be required to repay any of his student loan before 6th April 2000.

11(3)   A borrower shall not be required to repay such part of his student loan as relates to a particular notification of eligibility under the Education (Student Support) Regulations 2000 until the year of assessment beginning after the date on which that eligibility terminates under regulation 8 or 35 of those Regulations.

11(4)   A borrower—

(a)   whose student loan was made in connection with his attendance at a course for the initial training of teachers, other than a course leading to a first degree; and

(b)   who has notified the Secretary of State in writing that he does not wish to repay that loan during any period in which he is required to repay a loan made under the Education (Student Loans) Act 1990 or the Education (Student Loans) (Northern Ireland) Order 1990;

shall not be required to repay any of his student loan during any such period.

11(4A)   A borrower who is an eligible teacher in full-time eligible employment shall not be required to repay any of his student loan during the period he remains eligible under regulation 3(1) of the Teachers' Regulations.

11(4B)   A borrower who is an eligible teacher in part-time eligible employment shall not be required to repay the proportion of any of his student loan for which he is eligible for a reduction under the Teachers' Regulations during the period he remains eligible under regulation 3(1) of the Teachers' Regulations.

11(5)   Subject to paragraph (7) the Secretary of State shall notify the borrower and the Board of–

(a)   the first, or as the case may be next, year of assessment in respect of which the borrower may be required to make repayments under Part III;

(b)   the date on and after which a borrower may be required to make repayments by way of deduction from his emoluments under Part IV;

(c)   where the borrower has given the Secretary of State notification in accordance with paragraph (4), the year of assessment in respect of which the borrower shall cease to be required to make repayments under Part III;

(d)   the year of assessment in respect of which the borrower shall cease to be required to make repayments under Part III because–

     (i)   the loan has been repaid to the Secretary of State in full, or

     (ii)   an amount sufficient to repay the balance owing to the Secretary of State in full is likely to be received by the Board under Part IV and by the Secretary of State under Part 5 in relation to Wales and Part 6 in relation to England by the 30th April in the year of assessment immediately following the year of assessment in which the notice is issued, or

     (iii)   the loan has been cancelled; or

     (iv)   the borrower is an eligible teacher in full-time eligible employment; and

(e)   the date after which a borrower shall not be required to make repayments by way of deduction from his emoluments under Part IV because–

     (i)   the loan has been repaid to the Secretary of State in full, or

     (ii)   an amount sufficient to repay the balance owing to the Secretary of State in full is likely to be received by the Board under Parts III and IV and by the Secretary of State under Part 5 in relation to Wales and Part 6 in relation to England by that date, or

     (iii)   the loan has been cancelled; or

     (iv)   the borrower has given the Secretary of State notification in accordance with paragraph (4) or

     (v)   the borrower is an eligible teacher in full-time eligible employment or

     (vi)   the borrower has undertaken to repay the loan in full after that date by fixed instalments or a lump sum.

11(6) The Secretary of State shall not issue a notice under paragraph (5)(d) after the end of the calendar year during which the year of assessment specified in the notice ends.

11(7) Where the Secretary of State has notified a borrower and the Board that repayments under Parts III and IV shall no longer be made but at a later date it appears to him that the student loan has not been fully repaid he may give further notices in accordance with paragraph (5).

11(8) The Secretary of State shall not be required to give notices under paragraph (5)(a) or (b) where the borrower's student loan does not exceed £120.

11(8A) Where a borrower is an eligible teacher in full-time eligible employment the Secretary of State shall not issue a notice under paragraphs (5)(a) to (d).

11(8B) Paragraph (5) shall apply where–

(i) a person ceases to be eligible for a reduction under the Teachers' Regulations; or

(ii) an eligible teacher in full-time eligible employment changes to part-time eligible employment.

11(9) Where under paragraph (8) the Secretary of State is not requested to give notices under paragraph (5)(a) or (b) he may require the borrower to repay his student loan in such manner and over such period of time as in all the circumstances seems appropriate.

11(10) Without prejudice to regulation 6 a notice may be given to the Board by the Secretary of State under this regulation by transmitting it electronically to the Board.

11(11) A notice is transmitted electronically for the purposes of paragraph (10) where the particulars contained in the notice are transmitted by electronic means from a computer system operated by or on behalf of the Secretary of State to the Board's computer system and accepted by the Board's computer system.

11(12) If notices under paragraph (5) or (7) fall to be given to the Board in respect of two or more borrowers, one notice may be given by the Secretary of State in respect of all of those borrowers containing, in respect of each of them, the particulars specified in paragraph (5).

History – In reg. 11(3), the words "Education (Student Support) Regulations 2000" substituted for the words "Education (Student Support) Regulations 1999" and "or 35" inserted by SI 2001/971, reg. 9 and Schedule, para. 3, with effect from 6 April 2001.
Reg. 11(4A) inserted by SI 2002/2087, reg. 3(2), with effect from 1 September 2002.
Reg. 11(4B) inserted by SI 2002/2087, reg. 3(2), with effect from 1 September 2002.
In reg. 11(5) the words "Part 5 in relation to Wales and Part 6 in relation to England" substituted for the words "Part V" by SI 2006/2009, reg. 7, with effect from 1 September 2006.
Reg. 11(5)(d)(iv) and word "or" which precedes it inserted by SI 2002/2087, reg. 3(3), with effect from 1 September 2002.
Reg. 11(5)(e)(v) and word "or" which precedes it inserted by SI 2002/2087, reg. 3(4), with effect from 1 September 2002.
Reg. 11(5)(e)(vi) and word "or" which precedes it inserted by SI 2007/1683, reg. 3, with effect from 20 July 2007.
In reg. 11(5)(d) the words "the year of assessment in respect of which the borrower shall cease to be required to make repayments under Part III because" substituted for the words "the final year of assessment in respect of which the borrower shall be required to make repayments under Part III because" by SI 2001/971, reg. 3(1), with effect from 6 April 2001.
In reg. 11(5)(d)(ii) the words "in the year of assessment immediately following the year of assessment in which the notice is issued" substituted for the words "following the date of issue of the notice" by SI 2001/971, reg. 3(2), with effect from 6 April 2001.
In reg. 11(6) the words "final" deleted by SI 2001/971, reg. 3(3), with effect from 6 April 2001.
Reg. 11(8A) inserted by SI 2002/2087, reg. 3(5), with effect from 1 September 2002.
Reg. 11(8B) inserted by SI 2002/2087, reg. 3(5), with effect from 1 September 2002.
Reg. 11(10) inserted by SI 2001/971, reg. 3(4), with effect from 6 April 2001.
Reg. 11(11) inserted by SI 2001/971, reg. 3(4), with effect from 6 April 2001.
Reg. 11(12) inserted by SI 2001/971, reg. 3(4), with effect from 6 April 2001.

CANCELLATION

12(A1) This regulation applies in relation to Wales only.

12(1) Subject to paragraph (4) where a borrower is not in breach of any obligation to repay his loan in accordance with Part V or in breach of any obligation to repay any other loan mentioned in paragraph (2) and the Secretary of State is satisfied that he–

(a) has died;

(b) has attained the age of 65; or

(c) receives a disability related benefit and because of his disability he is permanently unfit for work the Secretary of State shall cancel his liability to repay his student loan

the Secretary of State shall cancel his liability to repay his student loan.

12(2) The loans mentioned in this paragraph are loans made under the Education (Student Loans) Act 1990, the Education (Student Loans) (Northern Ireland) Order 1990, the Education (Scotland) Act 1980 and regulations made thereunder and the Education (Student Support) (Northern Ireland) Order 1998 and regulations made thereunder.

12(3) For the purposes of this Part the cancellation of a student loan shall have effect on the date on which it is cancelled, not on the date the event giving rise to the right to cancellation takes place.

12(4) The cancellation of a borrower's liability to repay his student loan under paragraph (1) shall not affect his liability to make repayments under Part III subject to and in accordance with that Part in respect of any year of assessment–

(a) in the case of cancellation under paragraph (1)(a) during which the borrower was alive; and

(b) in any other case preceding the year of assessment during which the loan is cancelled.

12(5) The cancellation of a borrower's liability to repay his student loan under paragraph (1) shall not affect his liability to make repayments by way of deductions made under Part IV subject to and in accordance with that Part in respect of any earnings period ending before the date of cancellation.

History – Reg. 12(A1) inserted by SI 2006/2009, reg. 8, with effect from 1 September 2006.

12A(1) This regulation applies in relation to England only.

12A(2) This regulation shall apply where a borrower is not in breach of any obligation to repay his student loan under Part 6 or any obligation to repay any loan mentioned in paragraph (5).

12A(3) In this regulation **"post-2006 student loan"** means any student loan paid under the 2006 Regulations or any subsequent Regulations made under section 22 of the Act and taken out by the following–

(a) a borrower who takes out a student loan for the first time in respect of an academic year beginning on or after 1st September 2006; or

(b) a borrower who takes out a student loan in respect of a course which satisfies the following conditions–

   (i) it begins on or after 1st September 2006;

   (ii) it is not an end-on course following on from a course which he began before 1st September 2006; and

   (iii) it is not one to which he had his status as a student eligible for support under Regulations made under section 22 of the Act transferred from another course which he began before 1st September 2006.

12A(4) The Secretary of State shall cancel the borrower's liability to repay his student loan when one of the following occurs–

(a) the borrower dies;

(b) the borrower receives a disability related benefit and because of his disability is permanently unfit for work;

(c) in the case of post-2006 student loans, the 25th anniversary of the date on which the borrower became liable to repay the student loan; or

(d) in the case of student loans which are not post-2006 student loans, the borrower reaches the age of 65.

12A(5) The loans mentioned in this paragraph are loans made under the Education (Student Loans) Act 1990, the Education (Student Loans) (Northern Ireland) Order 1990, the Education (Scotland) Act 1980 and Regulations made under it and the Education (Student Support) (Northern Ireland) Order 1998 and Regulations made under it.

12A(6) The cancellation of the borrower's liability to repay his student loan under paragraph (4) shall not affect his liability to make repayments under Part 3 subject to and in accordance with that Part in respect to any year of assessment–

(a) in the case of cancellation under paragraph (4)(a) during which the borrower was alive; and

(b) in any other case preceding the year of assessment during which the student loan was cancelled.

12A(7) The cancellation of a borrower's liability to repay his student loan under paragraph (4) shall not affect his liability to make repayments by way of deductions made under Part 4 subject to and in accordance with that Part in respect of any earnings period ending before the date of cancellation.

History – Reg. 12A inserted by SI 2006/2009, reg. 9, with effect from 1 September 2006.

REFUNDS

13(1) Where the Secretary of State has received a repayment either directly from the borrower or from the Board under Part IV–

(a) which results in the student loan being paid in full, or

(b) when the student loan has already been paid in full

he shall refund to the borrower any amount not required to repay the loan in full together with interest calculated as if it were the principal of a student loan outstanding from the date of receipt of the repayment to the date of the refund.

13(2) Where the Secretary of State is considered to have received a payment from the Board under Part III in respect of a year of assessment–

(a) which results in the student loan being paid in full, or

(b) when the student loan has already been paid in full

the repayment shall be considered to have been received by the Secretary of State on the 31st January next following the year of assessment in accordance with regulation 9(2)(b), and the Secretary of State shall refund to the Board for the account of the borrower any overpayment which results from the receipt.

13(3) A refund under paragraph (2) shall not carry interest, and the Board shall be considered to have received the refund on the date on which the amount refunded was considered to have been received by the Secretary of State in accordance with regulation 9.

13(4) Where in accordance with Part IV the Secretary of State has received a repayment by way of deduction from a borrower's emoluments for a year of assessment and those emoluments do not exceed £15,000 the Secretary of State shall on application by the borrower refund the amount deducted.

13(5) Where the Secretary of State has received a voluntary payment not required under these Regulations in relation to loans of a borrower who is an eligible teacher after he has commenced eligible employment or 1st September 2002 whichever is the later he may refund to the borrower–

(a) who is a full-time eligible teacher, an amount equal to that payment, or

(b) who is a part-time eligible teacher, an amount equal to the part of that payment which is not required to pay the loan in full not including the proportion of the loan for which he is eligible for a reduction under the Teachers' Regulations.

History – In reg. 13(4), "£15,000" substituted for "£10,000" by SI 2004/2752, reg. 7, with effect from 6 April 2005.
Reg. 13(5) inserted by SI 2002/2087, reg. 4, with effect from 1 September 2002.

INFORMATION REQUESTS

13A Every borrower must, within six weeks, inform the Secretary of State and provide him with particulars if either of the following occurs–

(a) his home address changes; or

(b) his name changes.

History – Reg. 13A inserted by SI 2004/2752, reg. 6, with effect from 22 November 2004.

13B(1) The Secretary of State may serve a notice ("an Information Notice") on a borrower at his home address.

13B(2) An Information Notice under paragraph (1) requires the borrower to provide some or all of the following, together with documentary evidence in support where relevant–

(a) his full name;

(b) his telephone number;

(c) his national insurance number or a valid reason for not having one;

(d) his date of birth;

(e) a statement of whether he is employed, self-employed or not employed;

(f) the following particulars of his employment and income during the period specified in the notice–

    (i) for each part of that period during which he was employed, the dates on which the employment began and (unless it is still continuing) ended, the name and address of his employer, his employee number and his gross earnings,

    (ii) for each part of that period during which he was self-employed, the dates on which it began and (unless it is still continuing) ended and his gross earnings, and

    (iii) the amount, source and date of receipt of any other income.

13B(3) An Information Notice under paragraph (1) must set out the provisions contained in regulation 13C.

13B(4) Where the Secretary of State has served an Information Notice on a borrower under paragraph (1), the borrower must comply with it within a period of 28 days beginning with the day on which the Information Notice was served.

History – Reg. 13B inserted by SI 2004/2752, reg. 6, with effect from 22 November 2004.

13C(1) Where a borrower has failed to comply with regulation 13A, the Secretary of State may require the borrower to pay a penalty of £50.

13C(2) Where a borrower has failed to comply with regulation 13B(4), the Secretary of State may require the borrower to pay a penalty of £50.

13C(3) Where a borrower has been liable to a penalty under paragraph (2) in respect of an Information Notice and has not paid it, upon expiry of the time limit for payment the Secretary of State may require the borrower to pay one additional penalty of £100 in respect of that Information Notice.

13C(3A) Where a borrower has been liable to a penalty under paragraph (2) in respect of an Information Notice and has paid it, but does not comply with the Information Notice within a period of 28 days from the date of payment, the Secretary of State may require the borrower to pay one additional penalty of £100 in respect of that Information Notice;

13C(4) The Secretary of State must notify the borrower of a penalty imposed under paragraph (1), (2), (3) or (3A) by serving a notice ("a Penalty Notice") on the borrower at his home address.

13C(4) Notwithstanding the provisions of regulation 11(3), (4), (4A) and (4B), a penalty imposed under paragraph (1), (2), (3) or (3A) is payable within a period of 28 days beginning with the day on which the Penalty Notice was served and may be added to the borrower's loan account.

History – Reg. 13C(3A) inserted by SI 2006/2009, reg. 10(a), with effect from 1 September 2006.
In reg. 13C(4) the words "(3) or (3A)" substituted for "or (3)" by SI 2006/2009, reg. 10(b), with effect from 1 September 2006.
In reg. 13C(5) the words "(3) or (3A)" substituted for "or (3)" by SI 2006/2009, reg. 10(b), with effect from 1 September 2006.
Reg. 13C inserted by SI 2004/2752, reg. 6, with effect from 22 November 2004.

13D Where the Secretary of State incurs reasonable costs or expenses in taking steps to–

(a)   serve an Information Notice on a borrower under regulation 13B(1),

(b)   serve a Penalty Notice on a borrower under regulation 13C(4), or

(c)   obtain the information requested in an Information Notice served under regulation 13B(1),

he may require the reimbursement of those costs or expenses by the borrower and may add them to the borrower's loan account.

History – Reg. 13D inserted by SI 2004/2752, reg. 6, with effect from 22 November 2004.

13E Where the Secretary of State considers that having regard to all the circumstances of a particular case a time limit in regulation 13B(4), 13C(3A) or regulation 13C(5) should be relaxed, he may specify another time limit.

History – In reg. 13E, the words ", 13C(3A)" inserted by SI 2006/2009, reg. 11, with effect from 1 September 2006.
Reg. 13E inserted by SI 2004/2752, reg. 6, with effect from 22 November 2004.

13F Where a borrower has failed to comply with a Penalty Notice or an Information Notice or both the Secretary of State may require him to repay his loan in full immediately.

History – Reg. 13F inserted by SI 2006/2009, reg. 11, with effect from 1 September 2006.

PART III – REPAYMENTS BY ASSESSMENT TO INCOME TAX

REPAYMENTS OF STUDENT LOANS BY ASSESSMENT TO INCOME TAX

14 Repayments by a borrower who in respect of any year of assessment is required to make and deliver to the Board a return under section 8 of the 1970 Act shall be made, accounted for and recovered in like manner as income tax payable under the Taxes Acts; and in such case the provisions of this Part (which with extensions and modifications include provisions of the Taxes Acts) shall apply to and for the purposes of such repayments.

TIME FOR AND AMOUNT OF REPAYMENTS

15(1) Every borrower who has received notice from the Secretary of State under regulation 11(5)(a) that he may be required to make repayments of his student loan shall make a repayment in respect of any year of assessment–

(a)   which is specified in a notice under regulation 11(5)(a) or which, subject to paragraph (2), is any subsequent year up to and including any year specified in a notice under regulation 11(5)(d); and

(b)   in respect of which he has been required to make and deliver a return under section 8 of the 1970 Act.

15(2) A borrower shall not be required to make repayments in respect of any year of assessment specified in a notice under regulation 11(5)(c) or any subsequent year falling before a year specified in a subsequent notice under regulation 11(5)(a).

15(3) The repayment shall be an amount equal to 9% of the borrower's total income for that year calculated in accordance with the Taxes Acts.

15(4) In calculating a borrower's total income for the purposes of paragraph (3) any deduction which falls to be made by way of personal reliefs provided for in Chapter I of Part VII of the 1988 Act shall not be made

15(5) In calculating a borrower's total income for the purposes of paragraph (3) there shall be excluded:

(a) the first £15,000 of that income;

(aa) where a borrower is an eligible teacher in part-time eligible employment, any amount of his income from that employment in excess of £15,000;

(b) income on which the borrower could not become liable to tax under a self-assessment made under section 9 of the 1970 Act for that year;

(c) unearned income unless the amount of such income for that year exceeds £2,000;

(d) incapacity benefit payable under the Social Security Contributions and Benefits Act 1992;

(e) amounts chargeable to tax under sections 145, 146, 154, 157, 158, 159AA, 159A, 160 or 162 of the 1988 Act (benefits in kind);

(f) amounts in respect of which relief is given under Part XIV of the 1988 Act (pension schemes, social security benefits, life annuities etc.) or Part 4 of the Finance Act 2004 (pension schemes etc.);

(g) the amount of any loss in respect of which relief is given under section 380 of the 1988 Act (trade etc. losses set-off against general income);

(h) the amount of any payment in respect of which relief is given under section 109A of the 1988 Act (relief for post-cessation expenditure); and

(i) amounts of any reduction or repayment made under the Teachers' Regulations.

15(6) For the purposes of this regulation unearned income is income other than—

(a) earned income within the meaning of section 833(4) and (5) of the 1988 Act;

(b) income referred to in section 127(1) of that Act (enterprise allowance);

(c) the profits arising from a business chargeable to tax under Case I of Schedule D pursuant to section 503(1) of that Act (furnished holiday accommodation);

(d) payments and other benefits chargeable to tax under section 148(1) of that Act (payments and benefits in connection with termination of employment);

(e) income treated as earned income under section 107 of that Act (receipts after cessation of trade);

(f) sums treated as earned income under section 491(5) of that Act (certain receipts from bodies corporate carrying on mutual business); and

(g) an amount treated as earned income under section 531(6) of that Act (consideration in respect of the disposal of know-how);

(h) [omitted by SI 2006/745, art. 25(2)(b)]

(i) [omitted by SI 2006/745, art. 25(2)(b)]

History – In reg. 15(3), the word "the" deleted by SI 2001/971, reg. 9 and Schedule, para. 4, with effect from 6 April 2001.
In reg. 15(4), the words "paragraph (3)" substituted for "paragraph (1)" by SI 2004/2752, reg. 8, with effect from 22 November 2004.
In reg. 15(5), the words "paragraph (3)" substituted for "paragraph (1)" by SI 2004/2752, reg. 8, with effect from 22 November 2004.
In reg. 15(5)(a), and (aa), "£15,000" substituted for "£10,000" by SI 2004/2752, reg. 7, with effect from 6 April 2005.
Reg. 15(5)(aa) inserted, and the word "and" which appeared at end of para. (g) deleted by SI 2002/2087, reg. 5, with effect from 1 September 2002.
In reg. 15(5)(f) the words "or Part 4 of the Finance Act 2004 (pension schemes etc.)" inserted by SI 2006/745, art. 25(2)(a), with effect from 6 April 2006.
Reg. 15(6)(h) and (i) omitted and the word "and" at the end of para. (f) inserted by SI 2006/745, art. 25(2)(b), with effect from 6 April 2006.
Former reg. 15(5)(i) inserted by SI 2002/2087, reg. 5, with effect from 1 September 2002.

PERSONAL RETURN

16 For the purposes of establishing the amount of the repayment which a borrower is required to make for a year of assessment under regulation 14 an inspector or an officer of the Board may require him–

Statutory Instruments

(a)   to include in a return required to be made and delivered under section 8 of the 1970 Act such information as may reasonably be required, and

(b)   to deliver with the return such accounts, statements and documents, relating to information contained in the return by virtue of sub-paragraph (a), as may reasonably be required.

RETURNS TO INCLUDE SELF-ASSESSMENT

17(1)   Subject to subsection (2), every return made and delivered by a borrower under section 8 of the 1970 Act shall include a self-assessment, that is to say—

(a)   an assessment of the amount of the repayment which, on the basis of the information contained in the return and taking into account any relief or allowance mentioned in regulation 15 he is required to make for the year of assessment under regulation 15; and

(b)   an assessment of the amount payable by him by way of repayment, that is to say, the difference between the amount of the repayment which he is assessed to make for the year of assessment under sub-paragraph (a) and the aggregate amount of any repayments deducted from emoluments under Part IV during that year.

17(2)   Section 9(2) to (6) (self-assessment) and section 9A (power to enquire into returns) of the 1970 Act shall apply to a self-assessment under this regulation as they apply to a self-assessment under section 9(1) of that Act, and any reference in the Taxes Acts to those sections shall be construed as a reference to them as extended by this regulation.

RECORDS

18   Section 12B of the 1970 Act (records to be kept for the purposes of returns) shall apply in the case of a borrower as if any reference to a return includes reference to a return including the information required by regulation 16(a).

OTHER RETURNS AND INFORMATION

19(1)   Part III of the 1970 Act (other returns and information) shall apply for the purposes of establishing the amount of the repayment a borrower may be required to make under this Part as it applies for the purposes of establishing the amounts in which a person is chargeable to income tax.

19(2)   Section 19A of the 1970 Act (power to call for documents for purposes of certain enquiries) shall apply where an officer of the Board gives notice under section 9A(1) of that Act in relation to a self-assessment under regulation 16 of these Regulations as it applies to a self-assessment under section 9 of that Act.

ASSESSMENTS, CLAIMS AND APPEALS

20(1)   Subject to paragraph (2) Parts IV (assessment and claims) and V (appeals and other proceedings) of the 1970 Act shall apply with any necessary modifications for the purposes of—

(a)   assessing the amount of the repayment a borrower is required to make under this Part,

(b)   claims or other matters concerning any such assessment, and

(c)   appeals against any such assessment

as if any reference to an assessment or a self-assessment included a reference to an assessment or self-assessment for the purposes of this Part.

20(2)   An officer of the Board shall not make a determination of the amount of a repayment a borrower may be required to make under this Part under section 28C of the 1970 Act (determination of tax where no return delivered).

PAYMENT

21(1)   Any repayment by a borrower under this Part shall be paid as if the repayment were an amount of income tax payable by him under section 59B of the 1970 Act (payment of income tax and capital gains tax) in accordance with the following paragraphs.

21(2)   In a case where the borrower—

(a)   gave the notice required by section 7 of that Act within six months from the end of the year of assessment, but

(b)   was not given notice under section 8 of that Act until after the 31st October next following that year any repayment by a borrower shall be made at the end of the period of three months beginning with the day on which the notice under section 8 was given.

21(3) In any other case the repayment shall be made on or before the 31st January next following the year of assessment.

21(4) Section 59B(4A), (5) or (6) of that Act shall apply where an enquiry, an amendment of a self-assessment or an assessment is made in respect of a repayment under this Part respectively, and any reference to tax payable in those subsections shall be treated as a reference to a repayment by a borrower.

21(5) Section 59B(5A), (7) and (8) of that Act shall not apply for the purposes of this regulation.

SURCHARGES

22 Section 59C of the 1970 Act (surcharges on unpaid income tax and capital gains tax) shall apply to repayments which have become payable by a borrower under this Part as it applies to income tax payable in accordance with section 55 or 59B of that Act.

COLLECTION AND RECOVERY

23 Part VI of the 1970 Act (collection and recovery) shall apply to repayments, interest and penalties which have become due and payable by a borrower under this Part as it applies to income tax and interest charged and penalties imposed under that Act.

PERSONS CHARGEABLE IN REPRESENTATIVE CAPACITY

24 Sections 72 (trustees, guardians, etc. of incapacitated persons), 74 (personal representatives), 75 (receivers appointed by a court) and 76 (protection for certain trustees, agents and receivers) of the 1970 Act shall apply in the case of repayments due and payable by a borrower under this Part as they apply in the case of income tax chargeable to any person.

INTEREST

25(1) Any repayment due and payable under this Part shall carry interest at the rate applicable under section 178 of the Finance Act 1989 for the purposes of section 86 of the 1970 Act from whichever of the following days is applicable–

(a) the last day of the period referred to in regulation 21(2), or

(b) the date mentioned in regulation 21(3),

until payment, whether or not the applicable day is a non-business day within the meaning of section 92 of the Bills of Exchange Act 1882.

25(2) Sections 90 and 91 of the 1970 Act shall apply to interest under this regulation as they apply to interest on income tax.

25(3) A refund by the Board to a borrower of an overpayment of amounts payable under this Part shall carry interest at the rate applicable under section 178 of the Finance Act 1989 from the date on which the overpayment arose to the date on which the order for the refund is issued.

PENALTIES

26(1) Section 93 of the 1970 Act (failure to make return for income tax and capital gains tax) shall apply to returns under section 8 of that Act which are required to include information under regulation 16 as it applies to any other such returns.

26(2) In the case of such returns the references in section 93 to liability to tax which would have been shown in the return shall be references to the aggregate of the amounts which, if a proper return had been delivered on the filing date, would have been payable–

(a) by the taxpayer under section 59B of the Act (payment of income tax and capital gains tax), and

(b) where the taxpayer is a borrower by way of a repayment under regulation 15.

26(3) For years of assessment ending on or before 5 April 2008–

(a) section 95 of the 1970 Act (incorrect return or accounts for income tax or capital gains tax) shall apply in relation to anything done for the purposes of or in connection with the ascertainment of liability of a borrower to make a repayment under this Part as it applies for the purposes of or in connection with the ascertainment of liability to income tax, and for that purpose the difference referred to in section 95(2) shall be the difference between–

    (i) the amount calculated under regulation 15(1) and

Statutory Instruments

(ii) the amount which would have been the amount so calculated if the return, statement, declaration or accounts as made or submitted by the borrower had been correct.

(b) section 97 (incorrect return or accounts: supplemental) of the 1970 Act shall apply in the case of returns, statements, declarations, accounts, information or documents for the purposes of repayments under this Part as it applies for the purposes of income tax.

26(4) For years of assessment commencing on or after 6 April 2008, where the date on which the return is due to be filed is on or after 6 April 2009, Schedule 24 of the Finance Act 2007 (penalties for errors) shall apply–

(a) in relation to anything done for the purposes of or in connection with the ascertainment of liability of a borrower to make a repayment under this Part as it applies for the purposes of or in connection with the ascertainment of liability to income tax;

(b) in the case of returns, statements, declarations, accounts, information or documents for the purposes of repayments under this Part as it applies for the purposes of income tax.

History – Reg. 26(3) substituted by SI 2008/546, reg. 4, with effect from 1 April 2008.
Reg. 26(4) substituted by SI 2008/546, reg. 4, with effect from 1 April 2008.

PART IV – DEDUCTION OF REPAYMENTS BY EMPLOYERS

INTERPRETATION

27 In this Part–

"**the 2003 Act**" means the Income Tax (Earnings and Pensions) Act 2003;

"**the Contributions Regulations**" means the Social Security (Contributions) Regulations 1979;

"**deductions working sheet**" means any form of record on or in which are to be kept the matters required by the Contributions Regulations in connection with an employee's emoluments and deductions;

"**emoluments**" means, subject to regulation 30 of these Regulations, such sums as–

(a) constitute earnings for the purposes of section 3 of the Social Security Contributions and Benefits Act 1992 as calculated for the purposes of the Contributions Regulations as amended from time to time, and

(b) are to be taken into account for the purposes of the computation of secondary Class 1 contributions under section 9 of the Social Security Contributions and Benefits Act 1992;

"**employee**" means any person in receipt of emoluments;

"**employer**" means any person paying emoluments to an employee, including the Crown;

"**Form P45**" has the same meaning as in the PAYE Regulations;

"**Form P46**" has the same meaning as in the PAYE Regulations;

"**income tax month**" means the period beginning on the 6th day of any calendar month and ending on the 5th day of the following calendar month;

"**income tax period**" means income tax quarter where regulation 39(2) has effect, but otherwise means income tax month;

"**income tax quarter**" means the period beginning on 6th April and ending on 5th July, or beginning on 6th July and ending on 5th October, or beginning on 6th October and ending on 5th January, or beginning on 6th January and ending on 5th April;

"**national insurance number**" means the national insurance number allocated within the meaning of the Contributions Regulations.

"**the PAYE Regulations**" means the Income Tax (Pay As You Earn) Regulations 2003.

History – In reg. 27, the definition of "the 2003 Act" inserted by SI 2004/1175, reg. 3(a), with effect from 17 May 2004.
In reg. 27, the definition of "Form P45" inserted by SI 2005/2690, reg. 3, with effect from 6 April 2006.
In reg. 27, the definition of "Form P46" inserted by SI 2005/2690, reg. 3, with effect from 6 April 2006.
In reg. 27, the definition of "the Income Tax Regulations" omitted by SI 2004/1175, reg. 3(b), with effect from 17 May 2004.
In reg. 27, the definition of "the PAYE Regulations" inserted by SI 2004/1175, reg. 3(c), with effect from 17 May 2004.

REPAYMENT OF STUDENT LOANS BY EMPLOYEES

28 Subject to the provisions contained in this Part, repayments by a borrower who is an employee shall be made, accounted for and recovered in like manner as income tax deducted from the emoluments of an office or employment by virtue of regulations under section 684 of the 2003 Act.
History – Reg. 28 substituted by SI 2004/1175, reg. 4, with effect from 17 May 2004.

FORM P46

28A Where at the commencement of employment a borrower is required to complete a Form P46, he must state in the Form P46 whether he has a student loan which he is required to repay.
History – Reg. 28A inserted by SI 2005/2690, reg. 4, with effect from 6 April 2006.

AMOUNT OF REPAYMENTS

29(1) The repayment deducted shall be 9% of any emoluments paid to, or provided to or for the benefit of, the borrower in respect of the employment which exceed the threshold specified in paragraph (2).

29(2) The threshold shall be–

(a) where the earnings period specified in respect of those emoluments is a year, £15,000; or

(b) in any other case, the amount which bears the same relation to £15,000 as the number of days, weeks or months of the earnings period specified in respect of those emoluments bears to the number of days, weeks or months in the year respectively.

29(3) Where a repayment calculated under paragraph (1) includes pence as well as pounds the pence shall be ignored.

29(4) In the alternative the repayment specified in the last preceding paragraph may be calculated in accordance with the appropriate scale prepared by the Secretary of State.

29(5) Where the amount of emoluments to which the appropriate scale is to be applied does not appear in the scale, the amount of the repayment shall be calculated by reference to the next smaller amount of emoluments in the appropriate column in the scale.

29(6) Where a scale would, but for the period to which it relates, be appropriate and the earnings period in question is a multiple of the period in the scale, the scale shall be applied by dividing the emoluments in question so as to obtain the equivalent emoluments for the period to which the scale relates and by multiplying the amount of repayments shown in the scale as appropriate to those equivalent emoluments by the same factor as the earnings were divided.
History – In reg. 29(2)(a) and (b), "£15,000" substituted for "£10,000" by SI 2004/2752, reg. 7, with effect from 6 April 2005.

CALCULATION OF EMOLUMENTS

30(1) In calculating emoluments for the purposes of these Regulations emoluments paid to or for the benefit of an employee shall be aggregated or not aggregated as they are for the purposes of the Contributions Regulations.

30(2) The Board may, where they are satisfied as to the existence of any practice in respect of the payment of emoluments whereby the incidence of repayments is avoided or reduced by means of the payment of emoluments to or for the benefit of an employee by different persons in respect of different employments, give directions for securing that such repayments are made as if that practice were not followed.

30(3) The Board may, where they are satisfied as to the existence of any practice in respect of the payment of emoluments whereby the incidence of repayments is avoided or reduced by means of irregular or unequal payments, give directions for securing that such repayments are made as if that practice were not followed.

EARNINGS PERIODS

31(1) The amount of repayments, if any, which shall be deducted by the employer shall, subject to the provisions of paragraphs (2) and (3), be calculated by reference to the amount of emoluments paid to, or provided to or for the benefit of, the borrower in respect of the employment, in the earnings period specified or determined in respect of those emoluments for the purposes of the Contributions Regulations.

31(2) Where emoluments in respect of two or more employments–

(a) fall to be aggregated for the purposes of the Contributions Regulations; and

Statutory Instruments

(b)   the earnings periods in respect of those emoluments are, by virtue of the Contributions Regulations, of different lengths

the earnings period specified in respect of the aggregated emoluments shall be the shorter or shortest of those earnings periods.

31(3) Regulation 6B of the Contributions Regulations shall not apply in determining the earnings period specified in respect of a payment of statutory maternity pay or statutory sick pay.

MULTIPLE EMPLOYERS

32(1) Where–

(a)   an employer has made an election under regulation 98(1) of the PAYE Regulations (Multiple PAYE schemes), and

(b)   no improper purpose notice has been issued under regulation 99(1) of those Regulations (Multiple PAYE schemes: election made for improper purpose ineffective), or if one has been issued it has been withdrawn under regulation 99(5),

he shall be treated as having made an election for the purposes of these Regulations.

32(2) Where emoluments in respect of two or more employments fall to be aggregated under regulation 12(1)(a) of the Contributions Regulations, the amount to be deducted shall be apportioned between the employers in the same proportions as secondary Class 1 contributions are apportioned between them under that regulation.

History – Reg. 32(1) substituted by SI 2004/1175, reg. 5, with effect from 17 May 2004.

INTERMEDIATE EMPLOYERS

33(1) Where an employee works for a person who is not his immediate employer, that person ("the principal employer") shall be deemed to be the employer for the purposes of these Regulations, and the immediate employer shall furnish the principal employer with such particulars of the employee's emoluments as may be necessary to enable the principal employer to comply with these Regulations.

33(2) If the employee's emoluments are actually paid to him by the immediate employer–

(a)   the immediate employer shall be notified by the principal employer of the amount of repayments which shall be deducted when the emoluments are paid to the employee, and shall deduct the amount so notified to him accordingly; and

(b)   the principal employer may make a corresponding deduction on making to the immediate employer the payment out of which the said emoluments will be paid.

33(3) Paragraphs (1) and (2) apply only in the circumstances that a direction has been given by the Board under section 691 of the 2003 Act (PAYE: mobile UK workforce).

33(4) In paragraphs (1) and (2)–

(a)   **"the principal employer"** means the person specified as the relevant person in the direction referred to in paragraph (3), and

(b)   **"the immediate employer"** means the person specified as the contractor in that direction.

History – In reg. 33(3) the words "section 691 of the 2003 Act" substituted for the words "section 203E of the 1988 Act" by SI 2004/1175, reg. 6, with effect from 17 May 2004.

NOTICE TO EMPLOYERS

34(1) Where the Board have been given notice by the Secretary of State under regulation 11(5)(b) that a borrower may be required to make repayments under this Part on and after a specified date the Board shall give notice to any person who to their knowledge is an employer of the borrower requiring the employer to make deductions of repayments from emoluments paid to the borrower in accordance with these Regulations.

34(2) A notice under paragraph (1) shall contain–

(a)   the employee's name;

(b)   his national insurance number;

(c)   the date on and after which the employer is required to make deductions.

34(3) Where the Board have been given notice by the Secretary of State under regulation 11(5)(e) that repayments shall no longer be required to be made by a borrower under this Part after a particular date the Board shall give notice to any person who to their knowledge is an employer of that borrower requiring him not to make deductions, or to cease making such deductions accordingly.

34(4) A notice under paragraph (3) shall contain—

(a)   the employee's name;

(b)   his national insurance number;

(c)   the date on and after which no deduction is required to be made.

34(5) If notices under paragraph (1) or (3) fall to be given by the Board to the employer of two or more borrowers, one notice may be given by the Board in respect of all of those borrowers containing, in respect of each of them, the particulars specified in paragraph (2) or (4) as the case requires.

History – Reg. 34(5) inserted by SI 2001/971, reg. 4, with effect from 6 April 2001.

DEDUCTION OF REPAYMENTS

35(1) Every employer who has received—

(a)   a notice under regulation 34(1), or

(b)   a Form P45 containing a statement under regulation 50 of these Regulations, or

(c)   a Form P46 stating that the employee has a student loan which he is required to repay,

shall, on making to that employee any payment of emoluments on the first available pay day after the date referred to in paragraph (2) and at any time after that pay day but before the date referred to in paragraph (3), deduct the appropriate repayment in accordance with these Regulations.

35(2) The date referred to in this paragraph is–

(a)   where the employer has received notice from the Board under regulation 34(1) the date specified in the notice as the date on or after which he is required to make deductions; or

(b)   where the employer has received a Form P45 the date on which he first receives the Form P45. or

(c)   where the employer has received a Form P46 stating that the employee has a student loan which he is required to repay, the date on which he first receives the Form P46.

35(3) The date referred to in this paragraph is the date specified in the notice given by the Board under regulation 34(3) as the date on or after which he is required not to make or to cease to make deductions.

35(3A) The employer shall not make or shall cease to make deductions on the first available pay day after the date referred to in paragraph (3).

35(4) [Omitted by SI 2007/1683, reg. 4(c).]

35(5) Where two or more payments of emoluments fall to be aggregated for the purposes of calculating the amount of a repayment required to be deducted the employer may deduct that amount either wholly from one such payment or partly from one and partly from the other or any one or more of the others.

35(6) If the employer on making any payment of emoluments to an employee does not deduct from it the full amount of a repayment he was required to deduct he may deduct the amount so underdeducted from any subsequent payment or payments of emoluments to that employee during the same year of assessment but–

(a)   a subsequent deduction shall not be made after the date referred to in paragraph (3); and

(b)   the amount of any subsequent deduction shall be an amount in addition to but not in excess of the amount deductible from the payment under the other provisions of this Part.

35(7) If the employer deducts any repayment from the emoluments of an employee who is a borrower in accordance with these Regulations he shall not be required to repay any amount to the employee only because that amount was not owed by the employee to the Secretary of State as all or part of a student loan.

35(8) Paragraph (1) shall not apply to an employer of an eligible teacher in respect of eligible employment where the employer has received a written notification from the Secretary of State to that effect.

History – In reg. 35(1) the words "shall, on making to that employee any payment of emoluments on the first available pay day after the date referred to in paragraph (2) and at any time after that pay day but before the date referred to in paragraph (3), deduct the appropriate repayment in accordance with these Regulations." substituted for the words "shall on making to that employee any payment of emoluments on or after the date referred to in paragraph (2) and before the date referred to in paragraph (3) deduct the appropriate repayment in accordance with these Regulations." by SI 2007/1683, reg. 4(a), with effect from 6 April 2008.
Reg. 35(1) substituted by SI 2005/2690, reg. 5(2), with effect from 6 April 2006.
In former reg. 35(1) the words "regulation 40 of the PAYE Regulations, which contains a statement under regulation 50 of these Regulations" substituted for the words "regulation 25 of the Income Tax Regulations (form P45), which contains a statement under regulation 50 of those Regulations" by SI 2004/1175, reg. 7(a), with effect from 17 May 2004.
Reg. 35(2)(b) substituted by SI 2005/2690, reg. 5(3), with effect from 6 April 2006.

In former reg. 35(2)(b) the words "regulation 40 of the PAYE Regulations" substituted for the words "regulation 25 of the Income Tax Regulations" by SI 2004/1175, reg. 7(b), with effect from 17 May 2004.
Reg. 35(2)(c) and the word "or" preceding it inserted by SI 2005/2690, reg. 5(4), with effect from 6 April 2006.
Reg. 35(4) omitted by SI 2007/1683, reg. 4(c), with effect from 6 April 2008.
Reg. 35(3A) inserted by SI 2007/1683, reg. 4(b), with effect from 6 April 2008.
Reg. 35(8) inserted by SI 2002/2087, reg. 6, with effect from 1 September 2002.

PRIORITY WHERE OTHER DEDUCTIONS REQUIRED

36(1)   Where an employer is required to deduct repayments from a payment under regulation 35 but the aggregate of the deduction and any deductions on account of income tax and national insurance contributions exceeds the amount of the payment he shall make the deductions on account of income tax and national insurance first, and the amount of the repayment required to be deducted shall be the remaining balance.

36(2)   Where an employer is required to deduct repayments from a payment under regulation 35 and is also required to comply with one or more–

(a)   attachment of earnings orders made under the Attachment of Earnings Act 1971 ("the 1971 Act"), the Community Charge (Administration and Enforcement) Regulations 1989 ("the Community Charge Regulations"), the Council Tax (Administration and Enforcement) Regulations 1992 ("the Council Tax Regulations"), the Judgements Enforcement (Northern Ireland) Order 1981, the Magistrates' Courts (Northern Ireland) Order 1981; or

(b)   deduction of earnings orders made under the Child Support (Collection and Enforcement) Regulations 1992, or with one or more of these types of order or notice paragraph (3) shall apply; or

(c)   income support deduction notices made under regulation 20 of the Social Security (Payments on Account, Overpayments and Recovery) Regulations 1988 ("the Social Security Regulations"),

36(3)   An employer shall deduct repayments as if they were amounts required to be deducted pursuant to an order under the 1971 Act which–

(a)   was not made to secure the repayment of a judgment debt or payments under an administration order,

(b)   was the most recent order under that Act not so made, and

(c)   specifies a protected earnings rate equal to the protected earnings rate specified in the most recent attachment of earnings order, deduction of earnings order or income support deduction notice not so made which specifies such a rate, unless there is no such order or notice.

36(4)   Where under paragraph (3) an employer is required to comply with an attachment of earnings order made under the Community Charge Regulations or the Council Tax Regulations or an income support deduction notice made under regulation 20 of the Social Security Regulations before deducting a repayment under regulation 35, he shall not deduct any repayment.

36(5)   Where an employer is required to deduct repayments from a payment under regulation 35 and is also required to comply with one or more earnings arrestments, current maintenance arrestments or conjoined arrestment orders within the meaning of the Debtors (Scotland) Act 1987 (whether or not he is also required to comply with an attachment of earnings order, deduction of earnings order or income support deduction notice), he shall not deduct repayments under that regulation.

36(6)   Where repayments to be deducted in accordance with paragraph (3) are reduced as a result of sub-paragraph (c) of that paragraph and the total of the reduced repayments includes pence as well as pounds the pence shall be ignored.

History – Reg. 36(2)(c) inserted and the words "these types of order or notice" substituted for the words "both types of order" by SI 2002/2859, reg. 3(1), with effect from 16 December 2002.
In reg. 36(3)(c), the words ", deduction of earnings order or income support deduction notice" substituted for the words "or deductions of earnings order" and the words "or notice" inserted by SI 2002/2859, reg. 3(2), with effect from 16 December 2002.
In reg. 36(4), the words "or an income support deduction notice made under regulation 20 of the Social Security Regulations." inserted by SI 2002/2859, reg. 3(3), with effect from 16 December 2002.
In reg. 36(5), the words ", deduction of earnings order or income support deduction notice" substituted for the words "or a deduction of earnings order" by SI 2002/2859, reg. 3(4), with effect from 16 December 2002.
Reg. 36(6) inserted by SI 2002/2859, reg. 3(5), with effect from 16 December 2002.

DEDUCTIONS WORKING SHEET

37(1)   The employer shall record on the deductions working sheet for an employee the amount of any deduction from any payment of emoluments under these Regulations.

37(2)   Where two or more payments of emoluments fall to be aggregated for the purposes of calculating the amount of repayments required to be deducted the employer, instead of recording separate amounts in respect of each such payment shall record a single amount, being the total of the amount required to be deducted in respect of the aggregated payments.

CERTIFICATE OF REPAYMENTS

38(1)   Where the employer is required to give an employee a certificate in accordance with regulation 67 of the PAYE Regulations or paragraph 25 of Schedule 1 to the Contributions Regulations (form P60) he shall enter thereon in respect of the year to which the certificate relates the amount of repayments deducted by him.

38(2)   Where the employer is not required to give an employee who is in his employment on the last day of the year a certificate as described in paragraph (1) but has deducted repayments in respect of a year the employer shall nevertheless give the employee such a certificate showing thereon the amount of repayments deducted.

History – In reg. 38(1) the words "regulation 67 of the PAYE Regulations" substituted for the words "regulation 39 of the Income Tax Regulations" by SI 2004/1175, reg. 8, with effect from 17 May 2004.

PAYMENT OF REPAYMENTS DEDUCTED TO THE INLAND REVENUE

39(1)   Subject to paragraphs (1A), (2), (2A) and (3) the employer shall pay an amount equal to the repayments–

(a)   which he has deducted under these Regulations during an income tax month, or

(b)   which he is required to deduct under these Regulations during that income tax month,

whichever is the smaller amount, to the collector within 14 days of the end of that month.

39(1A)   Where the employer makes a payment in accordance with paragraph (1) by an approved method of electronic communications, he shall make the payment within 17 days of the end of the income tax month.

39(2)   Subject to paragraphs (2A) and (3) the employer shall pay an amount equal to the repayments–

(a)   which he has deducted during an income tax quarter, or

(b)   which he is required to deduct during that quarter,

whichever is the smaller amount, to the collector within 14 days of the end of that quarter where under paragraph 26A of Schedule 1 to the Contributions Regulations he is required to pay national insurance contributions due in respect of emoluments paid in that quarter within 14 days of its end.

39(2A)   Where an employer makes a payment in accordance with paragraph (2) by an approved method of electronic communications, he shall make the payment within 17 days of the end of the income tax quarter.

39(3)   Where the employer has, under regulation 7(2) of the Tax Credit (Payment by Employers) Regulations 1999, funded the payment of tax credit out of repayments deducted under these Regulations, the amount required to be paid to the collector under paragraph (1) or (2) shall be reduced by the amount of tax credit which the employer has so funded in the income tax period.

39(4)   If the employer has paid to the collector on account of repayments under this regulation an amount which he was not liable to pay, the amounts which he is liable to pay subsequently in respect of other payments of emoluments made by him during the same year shall be reduced by the amount overpaid, so however that if there was a corresponding overdeduction from any payment of emoluments to an employee the provisions of this paragraph shall apply only in so far as the employer has reimbursed the employee for that overdeduction.

History – In reg. 39(1) the words "paragraphs (1A), (2), (2A) and (3)" substituted for the words "paragraphs (2) and (3)" by SI 2004/1175, reg. 9(a), with effect from 17 May 2004.
Reg. 39(1A) inserted by SI 2004/1175, reg. 9(b), with effect from 17 May 2004.
In reg. 39(2) the words "paragraphs (2A) and (3)" substituted for the words "paragraph (3)" by SI 2004/1175, reg. 9(c), with effect from 17 May 2004.
Reg. 39(2A) inserted by SI 2004/1175, reg. 9(d), with effect from 17 May 2004.

NOTICE AND CERTIFICATE WHEN REPAYMENTS DEDUCTED NOT PAID

39A(1)   This regulation applies where, within 17 days of the end of any income tax period, the employer has paid no amount in respect of student loan repayments to the collector under regulation 39 for that income tax period, and the collector is unaware of the amount, if any, which the employer is liable so to pay.

39A(2)   Where this regulation applies, the collector may give notice to the employer, requiring him to render, within 14 days, a return in such form as the Board may prescribe showing the amount in respect of student loan repayments which the employer is liable to pay to the collector under regulation 39 in respect of the income tax period in question.

39A(3) Where a notice given by the collector under paragraph (2) extends to two or more consecutive income tax periods, these Regulations shall have effect as if the consecutive income tax periods were one income tax period.

39A(4) The collector may give a notice under paragraph (2) notwithstanding that an amount in respect of student loan repayments has been paid to him by the employer under regulation 39 for an income tax period, if he is not satisfied that the amount so paid is the full amount which the employer is liable to pay to him for the income tax period in question.

39A(5) Upon receipt of a return made by the employer under paragraph (2), the collector may prepare a certificate showing the amount in respect of student loan repayments which the employer is liable to pay to the collector in respect of the income tax period in question.

39A(6) The production of the return made by the employer under paragraph (2) and of the certificate of the collector under paragraph (5) shall be sufficient evidence that the amount shown in the certificate is the amount of student loan repayment which the employer is liable to pay to the collector in respect of the income tax period in question.

39A(7) Any document purporting to be a certificate under paragraph (5) shall be deemed to be such a certificate until the contrary is proved.

History – In reg. 39A(1) the words "17 days" substituted for the words "14 days" by SI 2004/1175, reg. 10, with effect from 17 May 2004.
Reg. 39A inserted by SI 2001/971, reg. 5, with effect from 6 April 2001.

NOTICE OF SPECIFIED AMOUNT AND CERTIFICATE WHEN REPAYMENTS DEDUCTED NOT PAID

39B(1) This regulation applies where, after 17 days following the end of any income tax period, the employer has paid no amount in respect of student loan repayments to the collector under regulation 39 for that income tax period and there is reason to believe that the employer is liable so to pay.

39B(2) Where this regulation applies, the collector, upon consideration of the employer's record of past payments, may to the best of his judgment specify the amount in respect of student loan repayments which he considers the employer is liable to pay, and serve notice on the employer of that amount.

39B(3) Where the employer has paid no amount under regulation 39 for the relevant income tax periods, the collector may give a notice under paragraph (2) which extends to two or more consecutive income tax periods, and these Regulations shall have effect as if those income tax periods were the latest income tax period specified in the notice.

39B(4) The collector may give a notice under paragraph (2) notwithstanding that an amount in respect of student loan repayments has been paid to him by the employer under regulation 39 for any income tax period, if he is not satisfied, after seeking the employer's explanation, that the amount so paid is the full amount which the employer is liable to pay to him for that income tax period, and this regulation shall have effect accordingly.

39B(5) If, during the period allowed in a notice given by the collector under paragraph (2), the employer claims, but does not satisfy the collector, that the payment made in respect of the income tax period specified in the notice is the full amount he is liable to pay to the collector for that income tax period, then–

(a)   the employer may require the collector to inspect the employer's documents and records as if the collector had called upon the employer to produce those documents and records in accordance with regulation 43, and

(b)   regulation 43 shall apply to that inspection, and the notice given by the collector under paragraph (2) shall be disregarded.

39B(6) Subject to paragraph (7), if the specified amount in respect of student loan repayments, or any part of it, is unpaid on the expiration of the period of seven days allowed in the notice, the amount so unpaid–

(a)   shall be deemed to be an amount in respect of student loan repayments which the employer was liable to pay for that income tax period in accordance with regulation 39, and

(b)   may be certified by the collector.

39B(7) Paragraph (6) shall not apply if, during the period allowed in the notice–

(a)   the employer pays the full amount in respect of student loan repayments which he is liable to pay to the collector under regulation 39 for that income tax period, or

(b)   the employer satisfies the collector that no amount, or no further amount, is due for that income tax period.

39B(8)   The production of a certificate under paragraph (6) shall be sufficient evidence that the employer is liable to pay the amount shown in the certificate to the collector.

39B(9)   Any document purporting to be a certificate under paragraph (6) shall be deemed to be such a certificate until the contrary is proved.

39B(10)   Notwithstanding anything in this regulation, if the employer pays any amount certified by the collector under this regulation and that amount exceeds the amount which he would have been liable to pay in respect of that income tax period apart from this regulation, he shall be entitled to set off such excess against any amount which he is liable to pay to the collector under regulation 39 for any subsequent income tax period.

39B(11)   If the employer renders the return required by regulation 42(1) after the end of the year, and pays the total net amount in respect of student loan repayments which he is liable to pay, any excess amount paid, and not otherwise recovered by set-off in accordance with this regulation shall be repaid.

History – In reg. 39B(1) the words "17 days" substituted for the words "14 days" by SI 2004/1175, reg. 11, with effect from 17 May 2004.
Reg. 39B inserted by SI 2001/971, reg. 5, with effect from 6 April 2001.

RECOVERY OF REPAYMENTS DEDUCTED

40(1)   The provisions of the Taxes Acts and of any regulations under section 684 of the 2003 Act relating to the recovery of tax shall apply to the recovery of any amount which the employer is liable to pay to the collector under regulation 39, 39A, 39B, 42 or 43 as if that amount had been tax charged by way of an assessment on the employer under Schedule E.

40(1A)   Without prejudice to paragraph (1), regulation 84 of the PAYE Regulations shall apply to the amount shown in a certificate under regulation 39A(5), 39B(6), 42(4) or 43(7) with the modification that summary proceedings for the recovery of the amount in respect of student loan repayments, or such part of it as remains unpaid, may be brought at any item before the expiry of twelve months after the date of the certificate.

40(2)   In the application to any proceedings taken by virtue of this regulation of any provisions referred to in paragraph (1) limiting the amount which is recoverable in those proceedings, there shall be disregarded any amount of tax which may by virtue of the following paragraph be included as part of the cause of action or matter of complaint in those proceedings.

40(3)   Proceedings may be brought for the recovery of—

(a)   the total amount which the employer is liable to pay to the collector under regulation 39, or

(b)   the total amount which the employer is liable to pay to the collector under regulation 39 in addition to any tax which the employer is liable to pay to the collector for any income tax period, or

(c)   the total amount which the employer is liable to pay to the collector under regulation 39 in addition to any national insurance contributions which the employer is liable to pay to the collector, or

(d)   the total amount which the employer is liable to pay to the collector under regulation 39 in addition to any national insurance contributions and tax which the employer is liable to pay to the collector

without specifying the respective amounts or distinguishing the amounts which the employer is liable to pay in respect of each employee and without specifying the employees in question, and for the purposes of proceedings under section 66 or 67 of the 1970 Act (including proceedings under that section as applied by the provisions of this regulation) and for the purposes of summary proceedings (including in Scotland proceedings in the sheriff court), the said total amount shall, subject to the provisions of paragraph (2), be one cause of action or one matter of complaint; but nothing in this paragraph shall prevent the bringing of separate proceedings for the recovery of each of the several amounts referred to in this paragraph which the employer is liable to pay to the collector for any income tax period in respect of his several employees.

History – In reg. 40(1) the words "section 684 of the 2003 Act" substituted for the words "section 203 of the 1988 Act" by SI 2004/1175, reg. 12(a), with effect from 17 May 2004.
In reg. 40(1), the words ", 39A, 39B, 42 or 43" inserted by SI 2001/971, reg. 6, with effect from 6 April 2001.
In reg. 40(1A) the words "regulation 84 of the PAYE Regulations" substituted for the words "paragraphs (1) to (5) of regulation 54 of the Income Tax (Employments) Regulations 1993 (being regulations made under section 203 of the 1988 Act)" by SI 2004/1175, reg. 12(b), with effect from 17 May 2004.
Reg. 40(1A) inserted by SI 2001/971, reg. 6, with effect from 6 April 2001.
In reg. 40(3), the words "the employer" inserted by SI 2001/971, reg. 9 and Schedule, para. 5, with effect from 6 April 2001.

INTEREST ON UNPAID REPAYMENTS

41(1) Subject to paragraph (1A) where an employer has not on or before the 14th day after the end of a year of assessment paid an amount which he is liable to pay to the collector under regulation 39 in that year that amount shall carry interest at the rate applicable under section 178 of the Finance Act 1989 for the purposes of section 86 of the 1970 Act from that date until payment.

41(1A) Where payment is made by an approved method of electronic communications, the interest payable under paragraph (1) shall be calculated as if the date in paragraph (1) was the 17th day after the year of assessment.

41(2) Interest payable under this regulation shall be recoverable as if it were an amount which the employer is liable to pay under regulation 39.

41(3) An amount to which paragraph (1) applies shall carry interest from the day mentioned in that paragraph even if that date is a non-business day within the meaning of section 92 of the Bills of Exchange Act 1882.

41(4) A certificate of the collector that any amount of interest payable under this regulation has not been paid to him, or to the best of his knowledge and belief, to any other collector or to any person acting on his behalf or on behalf of another collector, shall be sufficient evidence that the employer is liable to pay to the collector the amount of interest shown on the certificate and that the sum is unpaid and due to be paid, and any document purporting to be such a certificate shall be deemed to be a certificate until the contrary is proved.

41(5) Where an employer has paid interest on an amount under this regulation and it is found not to have been due to be paid, although the amount in respect of which it was paid was due to be paid, that interest shall be repaid to him.

History – In reg. 41(1) the words "Subject to paragraph (1A)" inserted by SI 2004/1175, reg. 13(a), with effect from 17 May 2004. Reg. 41(1A) inserted by SI 2004/1175, reg. 13(b), with effect from 17 May 2004.

RETURNS BY EMPLOYERS

42(1) Not later than 44 days after the end of the year of assessment the employer shall render to the inspector or, if so required to the collector in such form as the Board may approve or prescribe, a return showing in respect of each employee, in respect of whom he was required at any time during the year of assessment to prepare or maintain a deductions working sheet in accordance with regulation 37–

(a) such particulars as the Board may require for the identification of the employee,

(b) the year of assessment to which the return relates, and

(c) the total amount of repayments deducted for the year of assessment from the emoluments paid to the employee.

42(2) The return required by paragraph (1) shall include a statement and declaration in the form approved or prescribed by the Board containing a list of all deductions working sheets on which the employer was obliged to keep records in accordance with these Regulations in respect of the year of assessment, and shall also include a certificate showing the total amount of repayments deducted for the year of assessment in respect of each employee.

42(3) Where the employer is a body corporate, the declaration and the certificate referred to in paragraph (2) shall be signed by the secretary or by a director of the body corporate.

42(4) If within 17 days of the end of any year of assessment an employer has failed to pay to the collector the total amount of repayments he is liable to pay under regulation 39 the collector may prepare a certificate showing the amount of repayments remaining unpaid for the year of assessment in question.

42(5) Where an employer fails to make a return in accordance with paragraph (1) he shall be liable–

(a) to a penalty or penalties of the relevant monthly amount for each month (or part of a month) during which the failure continues, but excluding any month after the twelfth or for which a penalty under this paragraph has already been imposed, and

(b) if the failure continues beyond twelve months, without prejudice to any penalty under paragraph (a) above, to a penalty not exceeding so much of the amount payable by him in accordance with the regulations for the year of assessment to which the return relates as remained unpaid at the end of the 22nd April after the end of that year.

42(6) For the purposes of subsection (5) the relevant monthly amount in the case of a failure to make a return–

(a) where the number of persons in respect of whom particulars should be included in the return is fifty or less, £100, and

(b)   where that number is greater than fifty, is £100 for each fifty such persons and an additional £100 where that number is not a multiple of fifty.

42(7)   Where a return under this regulation is required to be made–

(a)   at the same time as–

(i)   any specified return required to be made in accordance with regulations made by the Inland Revenue under section 684 of the 2003 Act or section 566(1) (sub-contractors) of the 1988 Act to which section 98A of the 1970 Act (penalties) applies; or

(ii)   any specified return required to be made in accordance with regulations made by the Board under paragraph 6 of Schedule 1 to the Social Security Contributions and Benefits Act 1992 in respect of which section 98A of the 1970 Act has been applied by such regulations, or

(b)   if the circumstances are such that a return mentioned in paragraph (a) does not fall to be made, at a time defined by reference to the time for making that return, had it fallen to be made

and a person has been required to pay a penalty under section 98A(2)(a) of the 1970 Act (first twelve months' default in consequence of a failure in respect of a tax return) in respect of the tax return or in respect of the national insurance contributions return or in respect of both he shall not also be required to pay a penalty in respect of any failure to submit the return under this regulation.

42(8)   Where an employer fraudulently or negligently makes an incorrect return under paragraph (1) he shall be liable to a penalty not exceeding £3,000 for each employee in respect of whom incorrect particulars are included in the return.

42(9)   A certificate of the collector under paragraph (4) that the net amount in respect of student loan repayments remaining unpaid for that year has not been paid to him or, to the best of his knowledge and belief, to any other collector or to any person acting on his behalf or on behalf of another collector, shall be sufficient evidence that the sum mentioned in the certificate is unpaid and is due to the Crown.

42(10)   Any document purporting to be a certificate under paragraph (4) shall be deemed to be such a certificate until the contrary is proved.

History – In reg. 42(4) the words "17 days" substituted for the words "14 days" by SI 2004/1175, reg. 14(a), with effect from 17 May 2004.
In reg. 42(4), the words ", and the provisions of regulation 40 shall apply with any necessary modifications to the amount shown in the said certificate" deleted by SI 2001/971, reg. 7, with effect from 6 April 2001.
In reg. 42(5)(b) the words "22nd April" substituted for the words "19th April" by SI 2004/1175, reg. 14(b), with effect from 17 May 2004.
In reg. 42(7) the words "section 684 of the 2003 Act or section" substituted for the words "section 203(2) (PAYE) or" by SI 2004/1175, reg. 14(c), with effect from 17 May 2004.
In reg. 42(7)(a)(ii), the words "the Board" substituted for the words "the Secretary of State" by SI 2001/971, reg. 9 and Schedule, para. 6, with effect from 6 April 2001.
Reg. 42(9) inserted by SI 2001/971, reg. 7, with effect from 6 April 2001.
Reg. 42(10) inserted by SI 2001/971, reg. 7, with effect from 6 April 2001.

INSPECTION OF EMPLOYER'S RECORDS

43(1)   Every employer, whenever called upon to do so by an officer authorised by the Board, shall produce to that officer for inspection, at such time as that officer may reasonably require, at the prescribed place–

(a)   all wages sheets, deductions working sheets, and other documents and records whatsoever relating to the calculation of payment of the emoluments of his employees in respect of the years of assessment specified by such officer or to the amount of the repayments required to be deducted in respect of those emoluments under these Regulations;

(b)   all wages sheets, deductions working sheets, and other documents and records whatsoever relating to the amount of repayments in fact deducted during the years of assessment specified by such officer; or

(c)   such of those wages sheets, deductions working sheets or other documents and records as may be specified by such officer.

43(2)   In paragraph (1) **"the prescribed place"** means–

(a)   such place in the United Kingdom as the employer and the authorised officer may agree upon; or

(b)   in default of such agreement, the place in the United Kingdom at which the documents and records referred to in paragraph (1) are normally kept;

(c)   in default of such agreement and if there is no such place as is referred to in sub-paragraph (b), the employer's principal place of business in the United Kingdom; or

(d)   any notification received under regulation 35(8).

43(3)　The authorised officer may–

(a)　take copies of, or make extracts from, any documents produced to him for inspection in accordance with paragraph (1);

(b)　if it appears to him to be necessary to do so, at a reasonable time and for a reasonable period, remove any document so produced, and, if he does so, shall provide a receipt for any documents so removed; and where a lien is claimed on a document produced in accordance with paragraph (1), the removal of the document under this sub-paragraph shall not be regarded as breaking the lien;

and where a document removed in accordance with sub-paragraph (1) is reasonably required for the proper conduct of a business the authorised officer shall within 7 days provide a copy of the document, free of charge, to the person by whom it was produced or caused to be produced.

43(4)　Where records are maintained by computer, the person required to make them available for inspection shall provide the authorised officer with all facilities necessary for obtaining information from them.

43(5)　For the purposes of paragraph (1) the wages sheets, deductions working sheets (not being deductions working sheets issued under regulation 26 of the PAYE Regulations) and other documents and records therein mentioned shall be retained by the employer for not less than three years after the end of the year of assessment to which they relate.

43(6)　Section 98 of the 1970 Act (penalties for failure to furnish information) shall apply in relation to an employer's duties under this regulation as they apply to a person's duties under provisions specified in the Table below section 98.

43(7)　By reference to the information obtained from an inspection of the documents and records produced under paragraph (1) the collector may, on the occasion of each inspection, prepare a certificate showing–

(a)　the amount in respect of student loan repayments which it appears from the documents and records so produced that the employer is liable to pay to the collector for the years or income tax periods covered by the inspection; and

(b)　any amount in respect of such student loan repayments which has not been paid to him or, to the best of his knowledge and belief, to any other collector or to any person acting on his behalf or on behalf of another collector.

43(8)　The production of a certificate under paragraph (7) shall be sufficient evidence that the employer is liable to pay the amount shown in the certificate pursuant to paragraph (7)(b) to the collector in respect of the years or income tax periods mentioned in the certificate.

43(9)　Any document purporting to be a certificate under paragraph (7) shall be deemed to be such a certificate until the contrary is proved.

History – Reg. 43(1)(d), and the word "or" preceding it, inserted and the word "or" at end of para. (1)(b) deleted by SI 2002/2087, reg. 7, with effect from 1 September 2002.
In reg. 43(5) the words "regulation 26 of the PAYE Regulations" substituted for the words "regulation 21 of the Income Tax Regulations" by SI 2004/1175, reg. 15, with effect from 17 May 2004.
Reg. 43(7) inserted by SI 2001/971, reg. 8, with effect from 6 April 2001.
Reg. 43(8) inserted by SI 2001/971, reg. 8, with effect from 6 April 2001.
Reg. 43(9) inserted by SI 2001/971, reg. 8, with effect from 6 April 2001.

POWERS TO OBTAIN INFORMATION

44(1)　Section 20 of the 1970 Act (power to call for documents etc.), and section 20B of that Act (restrictions on powers) so far as relating to section 20, shall apply in relation to an employer's compliance with this Part as they apply in relation to a person's tax liability or its amount.

44(2)　Those sections as they so apply shall have effect as if–

(a)　any reference to the taxpayer, a taxpayer or a class of taxpayer were a reference to the employer, an employer or a class of employers;

(b)　any reference to any provision of the Taxes Acts were a reference to this Part;

(c)　any reference to the proper assessment or collection of tax were a reference to the proper repayment of student loans;

(d)　the reference in section 20(8) to the taxpayer with whose liability the inspector or the Board is concerned were a reference to the employer with whose compliance with this Part the inspector or the Board is concerned;

(e)　the reference in section 20B(2) to an appeal relating to tax were a reference to an appeal relating to compliance with this Part; and

(f)   the reference in section 20B(6) to reasonable ground for believing that tax has, or may have been, lost to the Crown owing to the fraud of the taxpayer were a reference to reasonable ground for believing that student loan repayments have, or may have been, incorrectly deducted owing to the fraud of the employer.

44(3)   Section 20BB of the 1970 Act (falsification etc. of documents) shall apply in relation to documents to be delivered, or to be delivered or made available for inspection, under section 20 or 20B(1) as applied by this regulation.

FORMAL DETERMINATION OF REPAYMENTS PAYABLE BY EMPLOYER

45(1)   This regulation applies where it appears to the inspector that there may be repayments payable by an employer under regulation 39 which–

(a)   have not been paid to the collector, and

(b)   have not been certified by the collector under regulation 42.

45(2)   Where this regulation applies, the inspector may determine the amount of those repayments to the best of his judgment, and shall serve notice of his determination on the employer.

45(3)   A determination under this regulation may–

(a)   cover the repayments payable by the employer under regulation 39 for any one or more tax periods in a year, and

(b)   extend to the whole of the repayments or to such part of them as is payable in respect of a class or classes of employees specified in the notice of determination (without naming the individual employees) or of one or more named employees so specified.

45(4)   A determination under this regulation shall be subject to the like provisions as are contained in Parts IV (Assessments and Claims), V (Appeals and Other Proceedings), except section 55, and VI (Collection and Recovery) of the 1970 Act as if it were an assessment, and as if the amount of repayments determined was income tax charged on the employer, and those Parts of that Act shall apply with any necessary modifications.

45(5)   [Omitted by SI 2009/56, art. 2 and Sch. 2, para. 73.]

History – Reg. 45(5) omitted by SI 2009/56, art. 2 and Sch. 2, para. 73(3), with effect from 1 April 2009 (subject to the transitional provisions at SI 2009/56, Sch. 3). Former reg. 45(5) read as follows:

"**45(5)**   An appeal against a determination under this regulation that is to be brought before the General Commissioners shall be brought before the General Commissioners for the division in which the determination was made."

INTEREST ON UNPAID REPAYMENTS WHICH HAVE BEEN FORMALLY DETERMINED

46(1)   Where–

(a)   an employer has not paid an amount of repayments to the collector under regulation 39, and

(b)   the inspector makes a determination of the amount of such repayments under regulation 45, and

(c)   repayments are payable pursuant to that determination,

the repayments so payable shall carry interest at the applicable rate under section 178 of the Finance Act 1989 for the purposes of section 86 of the 1970 Act from the 14th day after the end of the year of assessment in which they are payable until payment.

46(2)   Interest payable under this regulation shall be recoverable as if it were an amount which the employer is liable to pay under regulation 39.

DEATH OF EMPLOYER

47   If an employer dies, anything which he would have been liable to do under these Regulations shall be done by his personal representative, or in the case of an employer who paid emoluments on behalf of another person, by the person succeeding him, or if no person succeeds him, the person on whose behalf he paid emoluments.

SUCCESSION TO A BUSINESS

48(1)   This regulation applies where there has been a change in the employer from whom an employee receives emoluments in respect of his employment in any trade, business, concern or undertaking, or in connection with any property, or from whom an employee receives any annuity other than a pension.

48(2) Subject to paragraph (3), where this regulation applies in relation to any matter arising after the change the employer after the change shall be liable to do anything which the employer before the change would have been liable to do under these Regulations if the change had not taken place.

48(3) An employer after the change shall not be liable for the payment of any repayment which was deductible from emoluments paid to the employee before, unless they are also deductible from emoluments paid to the employee after, the change took place.

PAYMENT BY CHEQUE

49 For the purposes of regulations 39 to 41 where–

(a) any payment to the collector is made by cheque, and

(b) the cheque is paid on its first presentation to the banker on whom it is drawn,

the payment shall be treated as paid on the day on which the cheque was received by the collector, and **"pay"**, **"paid"**, **"unpaid"** and **"overpaid"** shall be construed accordingly.

CESSATION OF EMPLOYMENT

50 Where an employer sends a Form P45, if on the date of the Form P45 he–

(a) has received notice that the employee is a borrower as described in regulation 34(1); or

(b) has received a Form P46 stating that the employee has a student loan which he is required to repay; and

(c) (in either case) he has not received notice from the Board under regulation 34(3) requiring him to cease making deductions on and after a date which is before the date on which he ceased to employ the employee

he shall state in the Form P45 that the employee is a borrower.

History – Reg. 50 substituted by SI 2005/2690, reg. 6, with effect from 6 April 2006.
In former reg. 50, the words "regulation 36(2)(a) of the PAYE Regulations" substituted for the words "regulation 23(1) of the Income Tax Regulations" by SI 2004/1175, reg. 16, with effect from 17 May 2004.

PENALTIES

51(1) Subject to paragraph (3) where in the case of any employee an employer fraudulently or negligently–

(a) makes incorrect deductions, or

(b) makes or receives incorrect payments in a year of assessment

in pursuance of this Part he shall be liable to a penalty not exceeding £3,000 for each employee in respect of whom incorrect deductions or payments are made.

51(2) A penalty under paragraph (1) shall not be imposed before the end of the year of assessment in question; and no more than one such penalty may be imposed by reference to any one employee in relation to any year of assessment.

51(2) This regulation shall not apply where an employer has paid an electronic payment default surcharge to the Board in respect of an incorrect payment.

History – In reg. 51(1), the words "Subject to paragraph (3)" inserted by SI 2004/1175, reg. 17(a), with effect from 17 May 2004. Reg. 51(3) inserted by SI 2004/1175, reg. 17(b), with effect from 17 May 2004.

COLLECTION AND RECOVERY OF PENALTIES

52 Section 69 of the 1970 Act (recovery of penalties etc.) shall apply to penalties imposed under this Part as it applies to penalties imposed under that Act.

52A In the application of regulation 202 of the PAYE Regulations (default notice and appeal) for the purposes of these Regulations the only ground for appeal shall be that the employer is not in default.

History – Reg. 52A inserted by SI 2004/1175, reg. 18, with effect from 17 May 2004.

52B In the application of regulation 203 of the PAYE Regulations (default surcharge) for the purposes of these Regulations–

    "A" is the total amount of repayments payable for the year of assessment in which were made the relevant deductions to which the specified payment relates; and

    "B" is the total of the amounts deducted from A under regulations 39(3) and 39(4) of these Regulations.

History – Reg. 52B inserted by SI 2004/1175, reg. 18, with effect from 17 May 2004.

52C In the application of regulation 210 of the PAYE Regulations (penalties and appeals) for the purposes of these Regulations an employer shall not be liable to a penalty as a result of this regulation if the employer has been liable to a penalty for failing to comply with regulation 205 of the PAYE Regulations or regulation 90N of the Social Security (Contributions) Regulations 2001 in relation to the same year of assessment.

History – Reg. 52C inserted by SI 2004/1175, reg. 18, with effect from 17 May 2004.

PART V – REPAYMENTS BY OVERSEAS RESIDENTS

INTERPRETATION

52D This Part applies in relation to Wales only.

History – Reg. 52D inserted by SI 2006/2009, reg. 13, with effect from 1 September 2006.

53 In this Part–

"**gross income**" means income from all sources before deductions for or relief from tax or other statutory charge;

"**residence**" in or outside the United Kingdom shall have the same meaning as it has in the Taxes Acts.

NOTICE OF OVERSEAS RESIDENCE

54(1) A borrower shall notify the Secretary of State of any period of residence outside the United Kingdom which exceeds three months.

54(2) A borrower shall provide such information about any period of residence outside the United Kingdom which exceeds three months as the Secretary of State may require, including–

(a)   the purpose of the residence outside the United Kingdom,

(b)   whether the borrower is employed, or self-employed, during that residence,

(c)   the likely duration of the residence outside the United Kingdom, and

(d)   the amount of any repayments likely to be payable under Part III and deducted or likely to be deducted under Part IV in respect of any year or years of assessment during which the residence occurs.

NOTICE OF LIABILITY TO MAKE REPAYMENTS

55(1) Where the Secretary of State is satisfied that–

(a)   a borrower is resident outside the United Kingdom,

(b)   he is not likely to be resident in the United Kingdom for any year or years of assessment during which the period of residence falls

he may serve a notice on the borrower requiring the borrower to repay his loan in monthly instalments in accordance with regulation 56.

55(2) In a notice served under paragraph (1) the Secretary of State may require a borrower who has failed to–

(a)   give the notice required by regulation 54(1), or

(b)   provide any information required by the Secretary of State under regulation 54(2),

to repay forthwith such part of his student loan as will reduce the amount outstanding to the amount which the Secretary of State considers would have been outstanding if the borrower had given the notice or provided the information required of him.

55(3) When he serves a notice under paragraph (1) the Secretary of State may determine that a student loan shall bear interest at three times the rate or rates which would otherwise be applicable during any period–

(a)   beginning when the borrower fails to give notice or provide information as described in paragraph (2), and

(b)   ending when the borrower has given the notice and provided the information required and made any repayment required under paragraph (2).

History – In reg. 55(3), the word "and" inserted between para. (a) and (b) by SI 2001/971, reg. 9 and Schedule, para. 7, with effect from 6 April 2001.

REPAYMENT BY INSTALMENTS

56(1) Subject to paragraph (2) a borrower shall not later than the day specified in a notice served under regulation 55 and on the same day of each subsequent month pay the Secretary of State an instalment of £246.

56(2) Instead of paying the monthly instalment referred to in paragraph (1) a borrower shall be entitled to pay monthly instalments determined by the Secretary of State under paragraph (3) in respect of the twelve months referred to in the determination.

56(3) On application by a borrower the Secretary of State may determine that the amount of each of the twelve monthly instalments beginning with such date as may be determined by the Secretary of State, being a date not more than three months earlier or two months later than the date of the determination, shall be one twelfth of the relevant amount.

56(4) The relevant amount shall be 9% of the gross income which the Secretary of State considers that the borrower is likely to receive during the twelve month period in respect of which the instalments will be paid, disregarding–

(a)   the first £15,000 of such income; and

(b)   income in respect of which the Secretary of State is satisfied that repayments are likely to be made under Part III or IV.

56(5) After the expiry of the twelve months referred to in a determination under paragraph (3) the borrower shall pay instalments in accordance with paragraph (1), subject to any further determination under paragraph (3).

56(6) If a borrower does not pay an instalment or other amount when it is due the Secretary of State may require him to repay his student loan in full immediately.

56(7) The Secretary of State may allow a borrower to pay an instalment late or to fail to pay all or part of an instalment, but such indulgence shall not affect any rights or duties in relation to any other instalment.

History – In reg. 56(4)(a), "£15,000" substituted for "£10,000" by SI 2004/2752, reg. 7, with effect from 6 April 2005.

APPLICATION TO CEASE REPAYMENT BY INSTALMENTS

57(1) A borrower who–

(a)   is required to make repayments in accordance with regulation 56, and

(b)   who has not been required to repay his student loan in full immediately under regulation 56(6),

may apply to the Secretary of State for a determination that he shall no longer be required to make such payments.

57(2) The Secretary of State may determine that a borrower who has applied under paragraph (1) shall not be required to make repayments under this Part from a date specified in his determination, being a date not more than three months earlier and two months later than the date of the determination, if he is satisfied that–

(a)   the borrower is resident in the United Kingdom, and

(b)   he is likely to be resident in the United Kingdom for the year of assessment during which the date specified in his determination will fall.

57(3) A determination under paragraph (2) shall have effect until any further notice under regulation 55 is served on the borrower.

PART 6 – REPAYMENT BY OVERSEAS BORROWERS

58 This Part applies in relation to England only.

History – Reg. 58 inserted by SI 2006/2009, reg. 14, with effect from 1 September 2006.

INTERPRETATION

59 In this Part–

     "gross income" means income from all sources before deductions for or relief from tax or other statutory charge;

     "residence" in or outside the United Kingdom has the same meaning as it has in the Taxes Acts;

     "Eurostat" means the Statistical Office for the European Communities.

History – Reg. 59 inserted by SI 2006/2009, reg. 14, with effect from 1 September 2006.

NOTICE OF OVERSEAS RESIDENCE

60(1) A borrower shall notify the Secretary of State of any period of residence outside the United Kingdom which exceeds three months.

60(2) A borrower shall provide such information about his income during any such period of residence as the Secretary of State may require.

History – Reg. 60 inserted by SI 2006/2009, reg. 14, with effect from 1 September 2006.

NOTICE OF LIABILITY TO MAKE REPAYMENTS

61(1) Subject to regulation 63, where the Secretary of State is satisfied that a borrower is resident outside the United Kingdom he may serve a notice on the borrower requiring the borrower to repay his student loan in accordance with regulation 62.

61(2) In a notice served under paragraph (1) the Secretary of State may require a borrower who has failed to—

(a)   give the notice required by regulation 60(1), or

(b)   provide any information required by the Secretary of State under regulation 60(2)

to repay immediately such part of his student loan as well reduce the amount outstanding to the amount which the Secretary of State considers would have been outstanding if the borrower had given the notice or provided the information required of him.

History – Reg. 61 inserted by SI 2006/2009, reg. 14, with effect from 1 September 2006.

REPAYMENT BY FIXED INSTALMENTS

62 A borrower shall not later than the day specified in a notice served under regulation 61 and not later than the same day of each subsequent month pay the Secretary of State a fixed instalment, calculated in accordance with regulation 64.

History – Reg. 62 inserted by SI 2006/2009, reg. 14, with effect from 1 September 2006.

REPAYMENT BY INCOME-RELATED INSTALMENTS

63(1) Where the Secretary of State is satisfied that a borrower to whom regulation 61 applies has complied with a requirement to provide information under regulation 60, he may determine that the borrower may repay his loan by income-related instalments, in accordance with this regulation.

63(2) The first such instalment must be paid on a date determined by the Secretary of State, being a date not more than two months later than the date of the determination, and subsequent instalments shall be paid not later than the same date in each subsequent month for up to twelve months.

63(3) Each instalment shall be one twelfth of the relevant amount.

63(4) The relevant amount shall be 9% of the gross income which the Secretary of State considers the borrower is likely to receive during the twelve month period following the date of the determination referred to in paragraph (2), disregarding—

(a)   income up to the applicable threshold, calculated in accordance with regulation 64; and

(b)   income in respect of which the Secretary of State is satisfied that repayments are likely to be made under Part 3 or 4.

63(5) The amount of the instalment shall be stated in the determination.

63(6) At the end of the period for payment of instalments referred to in paragraph (2), the borrower shall pay fixed instalments under regulation 62, subject to a further determination under paragraph (1).

63(7) At any time during the period for payment of instalments referred to in paragraph (2) the Secretary of State may make a re-determination under paragraph (1).

History – Reg. 63 inserted by SI 2006/2009, reg. 14, with effect from 1 September 2006.

CALCULATION OF FIXED INSTALMENT AND APPLICABLE THRESHOLD

64(1) The fixed instalment in regulation 62 and the applicable threshold in regulation 63 shall be determined by reference to the most recent price level index for the borrower's country of residence and in accordance with the following tables–

Band	Price Level Index	Fixed Instalment
A	0<30	£49.20
B	30<50	£98.40
C	50<70	£147.60
D	70<90	£196.80
E	90<110	£246
F	110<130	£295.20
G	130+	£344.40

Band	Price Level Index	Applicable Threshold
A	0<30	£3,000
B	30<50	£6,000
C	50<70	£9,000
D	70<90	£12,000
E	90<110	£15,000
F	110<130	£18,000
G	130+	£21,000

64(2)　The price level index for the United Kingdom is 100.

64(3)　Price level indices shall be calculated using the most recent provisional comparative price level indices measured in gross domestic product produced by Eurostat.

64(4)　Where a price level index cannot be calculated because Eurostat does not hold the necessary data, it shall be calculated using the most recent provisional comparative price level indices measured in gross domestic product produced by the World Bank's World Development Indicators.

64(5)　Where a price level index cannot be calculated under paragraph (3) or (4), the applicable threshold and fixed instalment shall be those for band A.

64(6)　The Secretary of State may determine that the applicable threshold or fixed instalment for a borrower shall be that for a country other than his country of residence.

History – Reg. 64 inserted by SI 2006/2009, reg. 14, with effect from 1 September 2006.

APPLICATION TO CEASE REPAYMENT BY INSTALMENTS

65(1)　A borrower who–

(a)　is required to make repayments under this Part, and

(b)　who has not been required to repay his student loan in full immediately under regulation 66

may apply to the Secretary of State for a determination that he shall no longer be required to make such repayments.

65(2)　Where the Secretary of State is satisfied that–

(a)　the borrower is resident in the United Kingdom, and

(b)　he is likely to be resident in the United Kingdom for the year of assessment during which the date specified in his determination will fall

he may determine that a borrower who has applied under paragraph (1) shall not be required to make repayments under this Part from a date specified in his determination, being a date not more than two months later than the date of the determination.

65(3)　A determination under paragraph (2) shall have effect until the borrower again becomes liable to repay his loan under regulation 62 or 63.

History – Reg. 65 inserted by SI 2006/2009, reg. 14, with effect from 1 September 2006.

PENALTIES

66　If borrower does not pay an instalment or other amount when it is due the Secretary of State may require him to repay his loan in full immediately.

History – Reg. 66 inserted by SI 2006/2009, reg. 14, with effect from 1 September 2006.

DONATIONS TO CHARITY BY INDIVIDUALS (APPROPRIATE DECLARATIONS) REGULATIONS 2000

(SI 2000/2074 as amended by SI 2003/2155 and SI 2005/2790)

Made on 28 July 2000 by the Commissioners of Inland Revenue, in exercise of the powers conferred on them by s. 25(3) and (3A) of the Finance Act 1990, s. 132(1)(a), (2)(a), (8), (9) and (10) and 133(1) and (2) of the Finance Act 1999 and s. 39(10) of the Finance Act 2000. Operative from 21 August 2000.

ARRANGEMENT OF REGULATIONS

CITATION, COMMENCEMENT AND EFFECT

1(1) These Regulations may be cited as the Donations to Charity by Individuals (Appropriate Declarations) Regulations 2000 and shall come into force on 21st August 2000.

1(2) These Regulations shall have effect in relation to—

(a)   gifts made on or after 6th April 2000 which are not covenanted payments; and

(b)   covenanted payments falling to be made on or after that date.

INTERPRETATION

2 in these Regulations–

> **"appropriate declaration"** has the same meaning as in section 25(1)(c) of the Finance Act 1990;

> **"the Commissioners"** means the Commissioners for Her Majesty's Revenue and Customs;

> **"donor"** has the same meaning as in section 25(1) of the Finance Act 1990;

> **"electronic communications"** includes any communications conveyed by means of an electronic communications network.

History – In reg. 2, the definition of "the Commissioners" substituted for the definition of "the Board" by SI 2005/2790, reg. 3, with effect from 1 November 2005.

In reg. 2, the definition of "electronic communications" substituted by SI 2003/2155, art. 3(1) and Schedule, para. 23(1)(c) and (2), with effect from 17 September 2003.

MANNER IN WHICH AN APPROPRIATE DECLARATION MAY BE GIVEN

3 An appropriate declaration may be given by a donor to a charity–

(a)   in writing; or

(b)   orally;

including the use of written or oral methods of electronic communications, as the case may be.

History – Reg. 3(b) and words following substituted for reg. 3(b) and (c) by SI 2005/2790, reg. 4, with effect from 1 November 2005.

GIVING APPROPRIATE DECLARATIONS

4(1) An appropriate declaration must–

(a)   contain the name and home address of the donor,

(b)   name the charity (or be made in circumstances where the charity is identified),

(c)   identify the gift or gifts to which the declaration relates, and

Statutory Instruments

(d) confirm that the identified gift or gifts are to be qualifying donations for the purposes of section 25 of the Finance Act 1990 (Donations to charity by individuals).

4(2) The explanation of section 25(8) of the Finance Act 1990 referred to in regulation 5(2)(b) or (4)(b), as the case may be, must be given to the donor in order for an appropriate declaration to have effect (subject to regulation 6).

History – Reg. 4 substituted by SI 2005/2790, reg. 5, with effect from 1 November 2005.

RECORDING AND AUDIT OF APPROPRIATE DECLARATIONS

5(1) A charity must either–

(a) maintain an auditable record of appropriate declarations given to it, or

(b) comply with paragraphs (4) to (6) in relation to each declaration.

This is subject to paragraph (3).

5(2) An auditable record is a record of evidence–

(a) of appropriate declarations and the making of them, and

(b) that (whether or not separate from the declaration) statements explaining the effect of section 25(8) of the Finance Act 1990 were given to donors at the time the declarations were made,

in a form, and to a standard, which can be inspected and audited by the Commissioners.

5(3) If the Commissioners notify the charity that the record, or the records relating to particular declarations or classes of declarations, do not meet with their satisfaction, the charity must comply with paragraphs (4) to (6) in relation to the declarations in question.

5(4) Where paragraph (1)(b) or (3) applies, the charity shall in each case send the donor a statement in writing ("written statement") containing–

(a) the information required by regulation 4(1)(a) to (d),

(b) an explanation of the effect of section 25(8) of the Finance Act 1990,

(c) the date on which the charity sends the statement to the donor, and

(d) a statement that the donor is entitled to cancel his declaration by giving notice in writing to the charity not later than 30 days following the date in sub-paragraph (c).

5(5) Where paragraph (4) applies, the donor is entitled to cancel the declaration by giving notice of cancellation to the charity in accordance with paragraph (4)(d).

5(6) The charity shall maintain an auditable record of–

(a) written statements, and

(b) any cancellation notices,

in a form, and to a standard, which can be inspected and audited by the Commissioners.

5(7) Where a donor who has given an appropriate declaration to a charity notifies the charity of any change to his name or home address, the charity must keep a record of those changes with the declaration.

History – Reg. 5 substituted by SI 2005/2790, reg. 5, with effect from 1 November 2005.

PRESCRIBED CIRCUMSTANCES IN WHICH APPROPRIATE DECLARATIONS ARE DEEMED NEVER TO HAVE HAD EFFECT

6 An appropriate declaration shall be treated for the purposes of the Taxes Acts as never having had effect where–

(a) the charity has not sent the written statement to the donor in a case where it is required to do so by regulation 5(4);

(b) the donor cancels the declaration by giving notice in accordance with regulation 5(5); or

(c) the Commissioners notify the charity that the records relating to that declaration under regulation 5(6) do not meet with their satisfaction.

History – Reg. 6 substituted by SI 2005/2790, reg. 5, with effect from 1 November 2005.

PRESCRIBED CIRCUMSTANCES IN WHICH APPROPRIATE DECLARATIONS CEASE TO HAVE EFFECT

7 An appropriate declaration shall cease to have effect for the purposes of the Taxes Acts where—

(a)   the donor notifies the charity of the cancellation of his declaration (other than in accordance with regulation 5(5)), and

(b)   the cancellation takes effect from (or after) the date of its receipt by the charity.

History – Reg. 7 substituted by SI 2005/2790, reg. 5, with effect from 1 November 2005.

INDIVIDUAL LEARNING ACCOUNTS (SEPARATE EMPLOYERS UNDER THE CROWN) REGULATIONS 2000

(SI 2000/2076)

Made on 28 July 2000 by the Treasury, in exercise of the powers conferred on them by s. 200G(3) of the Income and Corporation Taxes Act 1988 [ITEPA 2003, s. 260(3)–(5)]. Operative from 21 August 2000.

1 These Regulations may be cited as the Individual Learning Accounts (Separate Employers under the Crown) Regulations 2000 and shall come into force on 21st August 2000.

2(1) For the purposes of section 200G of the Income and Corporation Taxes Act 1988, Crown servants mentioned in paragraphs (2) and (3) shall be treated as holding office or employment in accordance with those paragraphs.

2(2) Any Crown servant who is in–

(a)   employment under or for the purposes of a Government department,

(b)   service as a member of staff of the Scottish Administration, or holds an office in that Administration which is not a ministerial office,

(c)   service as a member of the staff of the National Assembly for Wales,

(d)   employment under or for the purposes of a Northern Ireland department, or

(e)   service as a member of staff of the Northern Ireland Assembly,

shall be treated as holding office or employment under the organisation concerned.

2(3) Service as a member of–

(a)   the Royal Navy and Royal Marines,

(b)   the Military Forces of the Crown, or

(c)   the Regular Air Force,

shall be treated as employment of the organisation concerned (and each of those organisations shall be treated as an entity for the purposes of these Regulations).

INCOME TAX (BENEFITS IN KIND) (EXEMPTION FOR WELFARE COUNSELLING) REGULATIONS 2000

(SI 2000/2080)

Made on 28 July 2000 by the Treasury, in exercise of the powers conferred on them by s. 155ZB of the Income and Corporation Taxes Act 1988 [ITEPA 2003, s. 210]. Operative from 21 August 2000.

1 These Regulations may be cited as the Income Tax (Benefits in Kind) (Exemption for Welfare Counselling) Regulations 2000 and shall come into force on 21st August 2000.

2(1) There shall be exempted from section 154 of the Income and Corporation Taxes Act 1988 a benefit consisting of welfare counselling that is made available to an employer's employees generally on similar terms.

2(2) In paragraph (1) **"welfare counselling"** means counselling of any kind other than–

(a)   medical treatment of any kind, or

(b)   advice specified in paragraph (3).

2(3) The advice specified in this paragraph is advice on finance (other than on debt problems), advice on tax, or on leisure or recreation, and legal advice.

INSURANCE COMPANIES (OVERSEAS LIFE ASSURANCE BUSINESS) (EXCLUDED BUSINESS) REGULATIONS 2000

(SI 2000/2089, as amended by SI 2001/3629, SI 2004/3274, SI 2005/3230, SI 2007/2086, SI 2007/3445 and SI 2008/2625)

Made on 1 August 2000 by the Commissioners of Inland Revenue, in exercise of the powers conferred on them by s. 431D of the Income and Corporation Taxes Act 1988. Operative from 22 August 2000.

ARRANGEMENT OF REGULATIONS

CITATION, COMMENCEMENT AND EFFECT

1(1) These Regulations may be cited as the Insurance Companies (Overseas Life Assurance Business) (Excluded Business) Regulations 2000 and shall come into force on 22nd August 2000.

1(2) These Regulations shall have effect in relation to policies or contracts made by an insurance company on or after 22nd August 2000.

INTERPRETATION

2(1) In these Regulations–

"**beneficiary**" means any person who is, or will or may become, entitled to any benefit under a trust, including–

(a) any person who may become so entitled on the exercise of a discretion; and

(b) a settlor who has an interest in the trust property for the purpose of section 660A;

"**the Board**" means the Commissioners of Inland Revenue;

"**charity**" means a person or body of persons established for charitable purposes only;

"**collective investment scheme**" has the meaning given by section 235 of the Financial Services and Markets Act 2000;

"**discretionary trust**" means any trust under which–

(a) the income arising to the trustees is to be accumulated and no person other than the trustees is entitled to that income before it is distributed; or

(b) the beneficiaries may become entitled to a benefit on the exercise of a discretion (whether or not the trustees have power to accumulate income) and no person is entitled to any benefit before the exercise of that discretion;

"**holding company**" means a company whose assets all, or all but an insignificant part, consist of shares in companies which, for the purposes of the Tax Acts, are deemed to be its 51 per cent subsidiaries by virtue of section 838;

"**investment company**" means any company whose business consists wholly or mainly in the making of investments and the principal part of whose income is derived therefrom, but excludes any holding company or collective investment scheme;

"**relevant overseas employees**" means persons who are not residing in the United Kingdom and are–

(a) employees of a policy holder or annuitant; or

(b) employees of a person connected with a policy holder or annuitant; or

(c) employees in respect of whose employment there is established a superannuation fund to which section 615(3) applies;

and, for the purpose of paragraph (b), whether a person is connected with a policy holder or annuitant shall be determined in accordance with section 839;

"**relevant former employees**" means–

(a) former employees of a policy holder or annuitant; or

(b) former employees of a person connected with a policy holder or annuitant; or

(c) former employees in respect of whose employment there is established a superannuation fund to which section 615(3) applies;

and, for the purpose of paragraph (b), whether a person is connected with a policy holder or annuitant shall be determined in accordance with section 839;

"**settlor**" means the person, or each of the persons, by whom the trust was directly or indirectly created, and for this purpose a person shall, in particular, be regarded as having created a trust if he provided or undertook to provide funds directly or indirectly for the purposes of the trust, or made with any other person a reciprocal arrangement for that other person to create the trust;

"**term assurance business**" means life assurance business in relation to which the policy or contract, or the underlying policy, is one which–

(a) is for a specified term; and

(b) is not capable of acquiring a surrender value that exceeds the amount of premiums paid.

2(2) In these Regulations any reference to a particular provision, without more, is a reference to that provision of the Income and Corporation Taxes Act 1988.

History – In reg. 2(1) definition of "collective investment scheme" the words "235 of the Financial Services and Markets Act 2000" substituted for "75 of the Financial Services Act 1986" by SI 2001/3629, reg. 187 which came into force on 1 December 2001.

LIFE ASSURANCE BUSINESS PRESCRIBED FOR THE PURPOSES OF SECTION 431D(1A)(D)

3(1) Subject to paragraph (2), life assurance business is prescribed for the purposes of section 431D(1A)(d) (meaning of "overseas life assurance business") if it is of a description–

(a) that does not fall within any of the circumstances set out in regulations 4 to 7; or

(b) that falls within the circumstances set out in regulation 9.

3(2) Where a policy or contract for business is owned by two or more policy holders or annuitants who do not hold the policy or contract as trustees of the same trust, the business is prescribed for the purposes of section 431D(1A)(d) where, if any of the policy holders or annuitants were the only policy holder or annuitant, paragraph (1) would so prescribe it.

History – Reg. 3 substituted by SI 2007/2086, reg. 3(1), with effect for accounting periods beginning on or after 13 August 2007.

CIRCUMSTANCES WHERE BUSINESS NOT PRESCRIBED FOR THE PURPOSES OF SECTION 431D(1A)(D)

History – Heading to reg. 4–7 substituted by SI 2007/2086, reg. 3(1), with effect for accounting periods beginning on or after 13 August 2007.

4 The circumstances set out in this regulation are where–

(a) the business is with a policy holder or annuitant who–

    (i) is not a company, or

    (ii) is a company which holds the policy or contract for the business in a fiduciary or representative capacity;

(b) the rights conferred by the policy or contract for the business are not held subject to a trust; and

(c) not less than 65 per cent of any benefit under the policy or contract for the business is payable to–

(i)   persons residing outside the United Kingdom; and

(ii)   charities.

5(1)   The circumstances set out in this paragraph are where–

(a)   the rights conferred by the policy or contract for the business are held subject to a trust;

(b)   in the case of a discretionary trust, each beneficiary is either an individual not residing in the United Kingdom or a charity; and

(c)   in the case of a non-discretionary trust, beneficiaries who are–

     (i)   not residing in the United Kingdom, or

     (ii)   charities,

have an interest in not less than 65 per cent of the capital of the trust;

5(2)   For the purposes of paragraph (1)(b), an individual who, as a trustee of any trust, is a beneficiary under the trust referred to in paragraph (1)(a) shall not be regarded as an individual.

6(1)   The circumstances set out in this paragraph are where–

(a)   the business is with a policy holder or annuitant which–

     (i)   is a company, and

     (ii)   does not hold the policy or contract for the business in a fiduciary or representative capacity;

(b)   in a case where the company is an investment company which is not controlled, or is not treated as controlled, by the trustees of any trust, the company is not controlled, or is not treated as controlled, by persons residing in the United Kingdom; and

(c)   in a case where the company is an investment company which is controlled, or is treated as controlled, by the trustees of any trust, the business would, if the trustees were the policy holders or the annuitants, be of a description falling within the circumstances set out in regulation 5.

6(2)   For the purposes of paragraph (1)(b), whether a company is not controlled, or is not treated as controlled, by persons residing in the United Kingdom shall be determined in accordance with section 416 but as if in subsection (6) of that section the words "five or fewer participators" read "persons residing in the United Kingdom".

6(3)   For the purposes of paragraph (1)(c), whether a company is controlled, or is treated as controlled, by the trustees of any trust shall be determined in accordance with section 416 but as if in subsection (6) of that section the words "five or fewer participators" read "the trustees of any trust".

7   The circumstances set out in this regulation are where–

(a)   the business is term assurance business; or

(b)   the policy or the contract for the business is held for the purposes of, or in connection with, a scheme which is for the time being a recognised overseas pension scheme within the meaning given by section 150(8) of the Finance Act 2004;

(c)   the policy or contract for the business is held solely to provide benefits for or in respect of–

     (i)   persons all, or all but an insignificant number, of whom are relevant overseas employees or relevant former employees, or

     (ii)   spouses, widows, widowers, civil partners, surviving civil partners, children or dependants of such persons.

History – In reg. 7(b) the words "recognised overseas pension scheme within the meaning given by section 150(8) of the Finance Act 2004" substituted for "qualifying overseas pension scheme within the meaning of paragraph 5 of Schedule 33 to the Finance Act 2004" by SI 2007/3445, reg. 2(2), with effect from 28 December 2007 in relation to policies or contracts made by an insurance company on or after that date.
Reg. 7(b) substituted by SI 2007/2086, reg. 4, with effect in relation to policies or contracts made by an insurance company on or after 13 August 2007.
In reg. 7(b), the words "where the Board" omitted from the words preceding reg. 7(b)(i) and inserted at the start of reg. 7(b)(i) and (ii) and the word "or" at the end of reg. 7(b)(i) omitted by SI 2004/3274, reg. 3(2)–(5), with effect from 31 December 2004.
In reg. 7(b)(ii), the words following the words "section 596(2)(b)" by SI 2004/3274, reg. 3(6), with effect from 31 December 2004.
Reg. 7(b)(iii), inserted by SI 2004/3274, reg. 3(7), with effect from 31 December 2004.
In reg. 7(c)(ii) the words "civil partners, surviving civil partners," inserted by SI 2005/3230, reg. 12(2), with effect from 5 December 2005.

TRUSTEES RESIDING IN THE UNITED KINGDOM

8(1)   A trustee who is a policy holder or annuitant residing in the United Kingdom shall be treated for the purposes of section 431D as not so residing where the policy or contract for the business is held for the purposes set out in regulation 7(b) or (c).

8(2)   Nothing in Chapter 9 of Part 4 of the Income Tax (Trading and Other Income) Act 2005 shall apply to a policy or contract which–

(a)   constitutes overseas life assurance business by virtue of paragraph (1), and

(b)   is held for the purposes set out in regulation 7(b).

History – In reg. 8(2) the words "Chapter 9 of Part 4 of the Income Tax (Trading and Other Income) Act 2005" substituted for the words "Chapter II of Part XIII of the Income and Corporation Taxes Act 1988" by SI 2008/2625, reg. 4, with effect from 27 October 2008.

CIRCUMSTANCES WHERE BUSINESS PRESCRIBED FOR THE PURPOSES OF SECTION 431D(1A)(D)

9(1)   The circumstances set out in this regulation are where the benefits provided for under the policy or contract for the business are determined by reference to the value of assets consisting of or including land in the United Kingdom.

9(2)   In paragraph (1), "land" includes buildings and other structures, land covered with water and any estate, interest, easement, servitude, right or licence in or over land.

History – Reg. 9 inserted by SI 2007/2086, reg. 5, with effect for accounting periods beginning on or after 13 August 2007.

Statutory Instruments

EMPLOYEE SHARE OWNERSHIP PLANS (PARTNERSHIP SHARES – NOTICE OF EFFECTS ON BENEFITS, STATUTORY SICK PAY AND STATUTORY MATERNITY PAY) REGULATIONS 2000

(SI 2000/2090, as amended by SI 2007/109)

Made on 1 August 2000 by the Commissioners of Inland Revenue in exercise of the powers conferred upon them by s. 47 of, and para. 38 of Sch. 8 to the Finance Act 2000, and of all other powers enabling them in that behalf. Operative from 22 August 2000.

ARRANGEMENT OF REGULATIONS

REGULATION
1. CITATION AND COMMENCEMENT
2. PRESCRIBED FORM OF NOTICE OF EFFECT OF DEDUCTIONS FROM SALARY ON ENTITLEMENT TO SOCIAL SECURITY BENEFIT

CITATION AND COMMENCEMENT

1 These Regulations may be cited as the Employee Share Ownership Plans (Partnership Shares – Notice of Effects on Benefits, Statutory Sick Pay and Statutory Maternity Pay) Regulations 2000 and shall come into force on 4th August 2000.

PRESCRIBED FORM OF NOTICE OF EFFECT OF DEDUCTIONS FROM SALARY ON ENTITLEMENT TO SOCIAL SECURITY BENEFIT

2 The form of notice prescribed under paragraph 38 of Schedule 8 to the Finance Act 2000 (employee share ownership plans – notice of possible effect of deductions on benefit entitlement) to be included in a partnership share agreement under the rules of the employee share plan is set out below.

Notice Deductions from your pay to buy partnership shares under this agreement may affect your entitlement to or the level of, some contributory social security benefits, statutory maternity pay and statutory sick pay.

They may also have a similar effect in respect of some contributory social security benefits paid to your spouse or civil partner.

With this agreement you should have been given information on the effect of deductions from your pay to buy partnership shares on entitlement to social security benefits, statutory sick pay and statutory maternity pay. The effect is particularly significant if your earnings are brought below the lower earnings limit for National Insurance purposes, and is explained in the information: it is therefore important that you read it. If you have not been given a copy, ask your employer for it. Otherwise a copy may be obtained from any office of the Inland Revenue, the Department of Social Security, or, in Northern Ireland, the Department for Social Development. You should take the information you have been given into account in deciding whether to buy partnership shares.

History – In reg. 2 words "spouse or civil partner" substituted for "wife or husband" by SI 2007/109, art. 2(2) with effect from 13 February 2007.

TONNAGE TAX (TRAINING REQUIREMENT) REGULATIONS 2000

(SI 2000/2129, as amended by SI 2003/2320, SI 2010/2158, SI 2011/2185, SI 2013/5 and SI 2013/2245)

Made on 3 August 2000 by the Secretary of State for the Environment, Transport and the Regions, in exercise of the powers conferred by para. 24, 27 to 33, 34(2) and 36 of Sch. 22 to the Finance Act 2000 and of all other powers enabling him in that behalf. Operative from 31 August 2000.

CITATION AND COMMENCEMENT

1   These Regulations may be cited as the Tonnage Tax (Training Requirement) Regulations 2000 and shall come into force on 31st August 2000.

INTERPRETATION

2(1)   In these Regulations–

"**the Act**" means the Finance Act 2000;

"**back-up officer**" means a master or a deck or engineer officer required for the purpose of enabling a ship to be operated on an indefinite basis, allowing for leave, in addition to the officers required by the safe manning document;

"**base rate**" means the interest rate set by the Bank of England which is used as the basis for other banks' rates;

"**British citizen**" means a person who is a British citizen within the meaning of the British Nationality Act 1981;

"**British citizen from the Channel Islands or Isle of Man**" means a person who holds British citizenship by virtue of the fact that he, a parent or grandparent was born, adopted, naturalised or registered in one of those islands, and neither he nor any parent or grandparent was born, adopted, naturalised or registered in the United Kingdom, and he has never been ordinarily resident in the United Kingdom for five years;

"**Chamber of Shipping**" means the trade association for the United Kingdom shipping industry, incorporated under that name as a company limited by guarantee;

"**conversion training**" means training of at least ten months' duration for a merchant navy rating, a person formerly employed in Her Majesty's Navy or a skipper or crew member of a fishing vessel, which leads to a first certificate of competency;

"**EEA Agreement**" and "**EEA State**" have the meaning given in Schedule 1 to the Interpretation Act 1978.

"**effective officer complement**" means the class comprising the relevant officers and back-up officers for a ship, and is calculated in accordance with regulation 4;

"**eligible officer trainee**" has the meaning given by regulation 7;

"**first certificate of competency**" means any of the following certificates referred to in the STCW Convention–

(a)   the appropriate certificate for an officer in charge of a navigational watch referred to in Regulation II/1.1, II/3.1 or II/3.3,

(b)   the appropriate certificate for an officer in charge of an engineering watch referred to in Regulation III/1.1;

"**IMO number**" means the number assigned to the ship in accordance with Resolution A.600(15) of 19th November 1987 of the International Maritime Organization;

"**Maritime Training Trust**" means the body of that name which has been set up by the Chamber of Shipping, the National Union of Marine, Aviation and Shipping Transport Officers (NUMAST) and the National Union of Rail, Maritime and Transport Workers (RMT) to hold and allocate monies contributed by organisations for the purpose of promoting the training of seafarers;

"**Merchant Navy Training Board**" means the body of that name which is recognised by the Secretary of State under section 2 of the Employment and Training Act 1973 as a national training organisation for maintaining and enhancing skills in the shipping industry;

"**nationality groups**" means the following groups:

(a)   British citizens,

(b)   nationals of EEA States other than the United Kingdom, and

(c)   people who do not fall within paragraph (a) or (b);

"**Ratings Task Force**" means the ad hoc group of that name comprising representatives from industry, trade unions and government and chaired by the Chamber of Shipping;

"**relevant course**" means a course which leads to a first certificate of competency;

"**relevant four month period**" means a period of four months commencing 1st October, 1st February or 1st June;

"**relevant officer**" means a master or a deck or engineer officer;

"**safe manning document**" means a document described as such or as a safe manning certificate and issued, in the case of a United Kingdom ship, by the Secretary of State, and in the case of any other ship, by or on behalf of the government of the State whose flag the ship is entitled to fly;

"**the STCW Convention**" means the International Convention on Standards of Training, Certification and Watchkeeping for Seafarers, 1978, as amended on 7th July 1995;

"**United Kingdom ship**" means a ship registered in the United Kingdom under Part II of the Merchant Shipping Act 1995; and

"**year**" means a twelve month period beginning on 1 October.

History – In reg. 2, definition of ""EEA Agreement" and "EEA State"" substituted for definitions of "EEA Agreement" and "EEA State" by SI 2013/2245, reg. 3(2), with effect for the purposes of calculating the payments in lieu of training in respect of a relevant four month period (a period of four months commencing on 1 February, 1 June or 1 October in any year) falling after 30 September 2013.

THE MINIMUM TRAINING OBLIGATION

3   The minimum obligations of a tonnage tax company as regards the training of seafarers shall be calculated as set out in regulations 4 and 5.

4(1)   Subject to the provisions of this regulation–

(a)   for every 15 posts in the effective officer complement for the qualifying ships operated by the company during a year, and

(b)   in any case where there are less than 15 posts in that effective officer complement,

a tonnage tax company shall during that year provide the first year of training on a relevant course for not less than one eligible officer trainee.

4(2)   Where a safe manning document is required to be carried on board a qualifying ship, the number of posts in the effective officer complement shall be calculated by adding the number of relevant officers required by the safe manning document for the ship and the number of back-up officers required for that ship.

4(3)   Where a safe manning document is not required to be carried on board a qualifying ship, the number of posts in the effective officer complement shall be deemed to be three.

4(4)   Where the number of posts in the effective officer complement is more than 15 but is not a multiple of 15, the calculation of the number of eligible officer trainees for whom training is to be provided under paragraph (1) is as follows–

(a)   divide the number of posts in the effective officer complement by 15,

(b)   if the resulting number involves a fraction of less than a half, round it down to the nearest whole number, and

(c)   if the resulting number involves a fraction of a half or more, round it up to the nearest whole number.

4(5)   For the purposes of paragraph (2) and regulation 8(4)(b)(iv)(bb), the number of back-up officers required for a ship shall be calculated by reference to the ratio of leave to work for officers on that ship, but shall not in any event be less than 50% of the number of relevant officers required by the safe manning document for that ship.

4(6)   In addition to the training provided under paragraph (1) during a year, the company shall during that year provide training on a relevant course for not less than the same number of eligible officer trainees as the number referred to in paragraph (7).

4(7)   The number referred to in paragraph (6) is the total number of eligible officer trainees who, in a previous year when the company was a tonnage tax company–

(a)   started a relevant course which continues in the year in question; but this number shall not include any eligible officer trainee who started a relevant course more than two years before the year in question, or

(b)   would have started a relevant course which would have continued in the year in question, if the company had provided the first year of training for the minimum number of eligible officer trainees for whom such training was required under paragraph (1); and for these purposes such a course shall be deemed to continue for three years.

4(8)   Where the training provided for an eligible officer trainee consists of conversion training, the trainee shall count as half a trainee for the purposes of paragraphs (1) and (6).

History – Reg. 4(7) substituted by SI 2003/2320, reg. 3, with effect from 1 October 2003, for the purpose of calculating the payments in lieu of training in respect of a relevant four month period falling on or after that date.

5   The Board of directors of a tonnage tax company shall each year review the feasibility of adopting the options agreed by the Ratings Task Force for the training of ratings.

6   Where a company is a member of a tonnage tax group, references in regulations 3, 4 and 5 to "tonnage tax company" and "company" shall be treated as references to "tonnage tax group" and "group" respectively.

MEANING OF "ELIGIBLE OFFICER TRAINEE"

7   For the purposes of these Regulations, an **"eligible officer trainee"** means a person on a relevant course who is–

(a)   a national of an EEA State, or a British citizen from the Channel Islands or Isle of Man, and

(b)   ordinarily resident in the United Kingdom.

THE TRAINING COMMITMENT

8(1)   Except where paragraph (2) applies, a tonnage tax company shall annually produce a training commitment in respect of the coming year.

8(2)   Where a company is a member of a tonnage tax group, the tonnage tax group shall annually produce a training commitment in respect of the coming year.

8(3)   The tonnage tax company in paragraph (1), or the tonnage tax group in paragraph (2), shall submit the training commitment to the Secretary of State for approval.

8(4)   The training commitment submitted to the Secretary of State shall contain the following information–

(a)   either–

    (i)   the total numbers of relevant officers and of ratings, and the breakdowns of these numbers in terms of nationality groups, employed in each ship which the company or group expects to operate as a qualifying ship during the coming year, or

    (ii)   the total numbers of relevant officers and of ratings, and the breakdowns of these numbers in terms of nationality groups, employed in all ships which the company or group expects to operate as qualifying ships during the coming year;

(b)   in respect of each ship which the company or group expects to operate as a qualifying ship during the coming year–

    (i)   the name of the ship,

    (ii)   the IMO number, if assigned,

    (iii)   the State or territory in which the ship is registered, or if it is not registered in any State or territory, the State whose flag the ship is entitled to fly,

    (iv)   where a safe manning document is required to be carried on board the ship–

        (aa)   the number of relevant officers required by that document, and

        (bb)   the figure, calculated by reference to the number of back-up officers required for a ship, by which the number referred to in sub-paragraph (aa) is to be multiplied to obtain the number of posts in the effective officer complement, and

    (v)   the number of posts in the effective officer complement;

(c)   the total number of eligible officer trainees for whom the company or group expects to provide the first year of training on approved courses during the coming year;

(d)   details of the company's or group's proposals to meet the minimum training obligation by making payments in lieu of training, and the reasons for meeting the obligation in this way;

(e)   details of the company's or group's proposals for adopting the options agreed by the Ratings Task Force for the training of ratings or, where applicable, reasons for not adopting those options; and

(f)   the number of ratings who the company or group expects to be involved in the adoption of any options referred to in paragraph (e).

8(5) In addition to the information required under paragraph (4), the training commitment submitted to the Secretary of State shall contain an undertaking by the company or group–

(a)   to comply with the minimum training obligation;

(b)   to exercise best endeavours to provide the training referred to in regulation 4(1) and (6), and to make payments in lieu of training where such training is not provided;

(c)   to make payments in lieu of training, in any case where–

    (i)   a qualifying ship is operated by the company or group in addition to those which were expected to be operated, but

    (ii)   it is not practicable to train the additional trainees required to meet the minimum training obligation; and

(d)   to comply with the requirements of regulation 12 and with any direction to the company or group under regulation 19.

9 When considering whether to approve a training commitment, the Secretary of State may consult the Merchant Navy Training Board or the Maritime Training Trust or both.

10(1) Where the Secretary of State is minded not to approve a training commitment, he shall notify the company or group and shall invite representations.

10(2) If the Secretary of State and the company or group are unable to reach agreement on the contents of the training commitment by the end of the period of 30 days beginning with the date of the Secretary of State's notification, the Secretary of State may set the training commitment for the year.

10(3) On the application of the company or group concerned, made after consultation with the Maritime Training Trust, the Secretary of State may vary the training commitment set by him under paragraph (2).

11(1) On the application of the company or group concerned, the Secretary of State may adjust a training commitment (to any extent) to take account of changed circumstances.

11(2) Such an application shall contain the following information–

(a)   details of the changed circumstances, and

(b)   reasons why the training commitment should be adjusted.

11(3) When considering an application for adjustment, the Secretary of State may consult the Merchant Navy Training Board or the Maritime Training Trust or both.

"END OF PERIOD ADJUSTMENTS"

12(1) A tonnage tax company or tonnage tax group shall make a return (known as an **"end of period adjustment"**) within 30 days after the end of each relevant four month period.

12(2) The return shall be made to the Secretary of State and to the Maritime Training Trust.

12(3) The return shall contain the following information–

(a)   the number of eligible officer trainees for whom training on a relevant course has been provided, determined as at the first day of each month in the relevant four month period;

(b)   where there is an increase in the total number of qualifying ships operated by the company or group, compared with the training commitment, which occurs during the relevant four month period and relates to a period of not less than one month, details of–

    (i)   the additional ships, and

    (ii)   any consequent increase in the number of eligible officer trainees for whom training should have been provided in order to meet the minimum training obligation of the company or group referred to in regulation 3; and

(c)   details of the payments made or proposed to be made in lieu of training in respect of the relevant four month period.

PAYMENTS IN LIEU OF TRAINING

13 Where a company or group is unable to provide the training required by regulation 4(1) or (6), it may propose in its training commitment to meet the minimum training obligation by making payments in lieu of training.

14 A company or group shall make payments in lieu of training–

(a)   where its training commitment provides for such payments, or

(b)   where training is not provided in accordance with its training commitment.

15(1) The payments in lieu of training shall be calculated in respect of each relevant four month period as follows–

(a)   in respect of each eligible officer trainee for whom training is required to be provided under regulation 4(1) or (6), calculate the number of months in that period during which–

   (i)   the training commitment of the company or group provided for payment in lieu of training, or

   (ii)   the company or group did not provide training in accordance with its training commitment, or both sub-paragraphs (i) and (ii) applied; and

(b)   multiply that number of months by £1,176, and the total is the amount of the payments in lieu of training which is due for that period.

15(2) For the purposes of the calculation in paragraph (1)(a), any surplus (as compared with the requirements in regulation 4(1) and (6)) in the number of months when training is provided during the relevant four month period shall be offset against any shortfall (as compared with those requirements) in that period.

History – In reg. 15(1)(b), "£1,176" substituted for "£1,092" by SI 2013/2245, reg. 3(3), operative from 1 October 2013, for the purposes of calculating the payments in lieu of training in respect of a relevant four month period falling after 30 September 2013. A relevant four month period is a period of four months commencing on 1 February, 1 June or 1 October in any year.
In reg. 15(1)(b) "£1,092" substituted for "£798" by SI 2013/5, reg. 3(2), operative from 1 February 2013, for the purposes of calculating the payments in lieu of training in respect of a relevant four month period falling after 31 January 2013. A relevant four month period is a period of four months commencing on 1 February, 1 June or 1 October in any year.
In reg. 15(1)(b) "£798" substituted for "£743" by SI 2011/2185, reg. 3(2), operative from 1 October 2011, for the purpose of calculating the payments in lieu of training in respect of a relevant four month period falling after 30 September 2011. A relevant four month period is a period of four months commencing on 1 October, 1 February or 1 June.
In reg. 15(1)(b) "£743" substituted for "£685" by SI 2010/2158, reg. 3(2), operative from 1 October 2010, for the purpose of calculating the payments in lieu of training in respect of a relevant four month period falling after 30 September 2010. A relevant four month period is a period of four months commencing on 1 October, 1 February or 1 June.
In reg. 15(1)(b) "£685" substituted for "£671" by SI 2009/2304, reg. 3(2), operative from 1 October 2009, for the purpose of calculating the payments in lieu of training in respect of a relevant four month period falling after 30 September 2009. A relevant four month period is a period of four months commencing on 1 October, 1 February or 1 June. SI 2009/2304 was revoked by SI 2010/2158, reg. 4, with effect from 1 October 2010.

16 The payments in lieu of training shall be made to the Maritime Training Trust, and shall become due 30 days after the end of each relevant four month period.

17 If in any case there is a failure in relation to a company or group to comply with the requirements of Part IV of Schedule 22 to the Act with respect to–

(a)   the submission of training commitments, or

(b)   the making of returns or provision of information, the Secretary of State may determine to the best of his information and belief the amount of the payments in lieu of training to be made by the company or group.

18(1) A payment in lieu of training that has become due but is unpaid–

(a)   is a debt to the Maritime Training Trust, and

(b)   carries interest at an annual rate equivalent to base rate plus two per cent per annum.

18(2) The costs or expenses of any legal or other proceedings for recovering the debt or interest shall be recoverable, and carry interest, in the same way as the debt.

DIRECTIONS TO PROVIDE INFORMATION

19 The Secretary of State may direct any person to provide such information as the Secretary of State may reasonably require for the purposes of ascertaining–

(a)   what the minimum training obligation of a company or group should be,

(b)   whether the proposals in a training commitment are adequate to meet the minimum training obligation of a company or group, or

(c)   whether a company or group has complied with its training commitment.

AUDITS

20 The Secretary of State may appoint one or more persons to carry out on his behalf an audit of the accounts or other records–

(a)   of a qualifying single company, or

(b)   of the qualifying companies in a group, for the purpose of checking that any return or information provided to the Secretary of State is correct.

HIGHER RATE OF PAYMENT IN CASE OF FAILURE TO MEET TRAINING REQUIREMENT

21(1) Subject to paragraph (3), a company or group is to be treated as failing to meet its training commitment in any year where it fails to provide training on a relevant course for at least 50% of the total number of eligible officer trainees for whom the company or group proposed to provide such training in its training commitment.

21(2) Subject to paragraph (3)–

(a)   if a company fails to meet its training commitment in a particular year, the basic rate of any payments in lieu of training that fall to be made by the company in the following year shall be increased by 50%;

(b)   if a group fails to meet its training commitment in a particular year, the basic rate of any payments in lieu of training that fall to be made by any member of the group in the following year shall be increased by 50%; and

(c)   if a company or group fails to meet its training commitment in two or more successive years, the basic rate of any payments in lieu of training shall be increased by 100% in the third and subsequent years.

21(3) The higher rate shall not be payable where the Secretary of State is satisfied that there are mitigating circumstances for the company's or group's failure to meet the training commitment.

21(4) For the purposes of paragraph (2), "the basic rate" is £1,094 per eligible officer trainee per month.

History – In reg. 21(4) "£1,094" substituted for "£1,020" by SI 2013/2245, reg. 3(4), operative from 1 October 2013, for the purposes of calculating the payments in lieu of training in respect of a relevant four month period falling after 30 September 2013. A relevant four month period is a period of four months commencing on 1 February, 1 June or 1 October in any year.
In reg. 21(4) "£1,020" substituted for "£726" by SI 2013/5, reg. 3(3), operative from 1 February 2013, for the purposes of calculating the payments in lieu of training in respect of a relevant four month period falling after 31 January 2013. A relevant four month period is a period of four months commencing on 1 February, 1 June or 1 October in any year.
In reg. 21(4) "£726" substituted for "£676" by SI 2011/2185, reg. 3(3), operative from 1 October 2011, for the purpose of calculating the payments in lieu of training in respect of a relevant four month period falling after 30 September 2011. A relevant four month period is a period of four months commencing on 1 October, 1 February or 1 June.
In reg. 21(4) "£676" substituted for "£623" by SI 2010/2158, reg. 3(2), operative from 1 October 2010, for the purpose of calculating the payments in lieu of training in respect of a relevant four month period falling after 30 September 2010. A relevant four month period a period of four months commencing on 1 October, 1 February or 1 June.
In reg. 21(4) "£623" substituted for "£610" by SI 2009/2304, reg. 3(3), operative from 1 October 2009, for the purpose of calculating the payments in lieu of training in respect of a relevant four month period falling after 30 September 2009. A relevant four month period is a period of four months commencing on 1 October, 1 February or 1 June. SI 2009/2304 was revoked by SI 2010/2158, reg. 4, with effect from 1 October 2010.

CERTIFICATE OF NON-COMPLIANCE

22(1) The Secretary of State may issue a certificate of non-compliance in respect of a single company if–

(a)   the company fails to meet its training commitment for successive periods amounting to not less than two years, or

(b)   the company, or any of its officers, commits an offence under Schedule 22 to the Act.

22(2) The Secretary of State may issue a certificate of non-compliance in respect of a group if–

(a)   the group fails to meet its training commitment for successive periods amounting to not less than two years, or

(b)   a member of the group, or an officer of a member, commits an offence under Schedule 22 to the Act.

22(3) The Secretary of State shall issue a certificate of non-compliance if any circumstances referred to in paragraph (1) or (2) arise, unless the Secretary of State is satisfied that there are good reasons why a certificate should not be issued.

23(1) A company or group in respect of which a certificate of non-compliance has been issued may apply to the Secretary of State to cancel the certificate.

23(2)   Any such application shall contain information showing that–

(a)   the training commitment has been complied with for at least one year since the period in relation to which the certificate was issued, and

(b)   the company or group has made arrangements to ensure that its training commitment for the current and future years will be complied with.

24   When considering an application to cancel a certificate of non-compliance, the Secretary of State may consult the Merchant Navy Training Board or the Maritime Training Trust or both.

DISCLOSURE OF INFORMATION

25   For the purposes of paragraph 34(2) of Schedule 22 to the Act, the following persons are prescribed persons involved in the training of seafarers–

(a)   the Merchant Navy Training Board, and

(b)   the Maritime Training Trust.

TONNAGE TAX REGULATIONS 2000

(SI 2000/2303)

Made on 24 August 2000 by the Commissioners of Inland Revenue, in exercise of the powers conferred on them by para. 47, 85(3), 112(7), 113(4), and 130 to 136 of Sch. 22 to the Finance Act 2000. Operative from 31 August 2000.

CITATION AND COMMENCEMENT

1 These Regulations may be cited as the Tonnage Tax Regulations 2000 and shall come into force on 31st August 2000.

INTERPRETATION

2(1) In these Regulations–

"corporate partner" means a company which carries on activities in partnership;

"the 1990 Act" means the Capital Allowances Act 1990;

"the paragraph 85(2)(a) amount", in relation to an asset, means the amount determined under paragraph 85(2)(a) of Schedule 22 for that asset, subject to regulation 8(2)(a), and **"the paragraph 112(2) amount"** and **"the paragraph 113(2) amount"** shall have corresponding meanings;

"qualifying expenditure" has the meaning in paragraph 135 of Schedule 22;

"Schedule 22" means Schedule 22 to the Finance Act 2000;

"Schedule 28AA" means Schedule 28AA to the Taxes Act;

"the 75% limit" has the meaning given in paragraph 37(4) of Schedule 22;

"the Taxes Act" means the Income and Corporation Taxes Act 1988.

2(2) In these Regulations, the following expressions have the same meaning as in Schedule 22–

"bareboat charter terms"

"company"

"core qualifying activities"

"group" (and "member" of a group)

"leaving tonnage tax"

"operating (a ship)"

"qualifying company"

"qualifying ship"

"relevant shipping profits"

"ship"

"ship-related activities"

"subject to tonnage tax"

"tonnage tax company"

"tonnage tax group" (and "member" of such a group)

"tonnage tax profits"

"tonnage tax trade".

2(3) References in regulation 3(3)(a) to (j) and (4) to a qualifying ship operated by a company, where the company is a member of a tonnage tax group, include references to a qualifying ship operated by another qualifying company in the same tonnage tax group.

2(4) For the purposes of the definition of "arm's length provision" (regulation 3(3)(a)(ii)), where any provision is made or imposed as between a company's tonnage tax trade and other activities carried on by it, the assumptions in paragraph 59(1)(a) to (c) of Schedule 22 and paragraph 1(3) of Schedule 28AA shall apply.

QUALIFYING SECONDARY ACTIVITIES

3(1) The descriptions of activity to be regarded as qualifying secondary activities shall be determined in accordance with the following paragraphs.

Statutory Instruments

3(2) **A tonnage tax company's qualifying secondary activities** means its ship-related activities, other than commercial activities which form part of the operation of a port carried on for profit, that–

(a)   have a substantial connection with the company's core qualifying activities or, where the company is a member of a tonnage tax group, the core qualifying activities of another qualifying company in that group,

(b)   fall within the descriptions in paragraph (3) or (4), and

(c)   in the case of paragraph (3) are carried on at any level and in the case of paragraph (4) are carried on at the permitted level.

3(3)   The descriptions in this paragraph are–

(a)   the carriage of passengers or cargo otherwise than on board a qualifying ship operated by the company, where–

      (i)   there is a single contract with the customer for a journey which includes a voyage on the qualifying ship, and

      (ii)   the transport for the remainder of the journey is purchased or obtained by the company by provision ("arm's length provision") which would have been made as between independent enterprises;

(b)   administrative and insurance services which are directly related to the carriage of passengers or cargo, including under a contract described in sub-paragraph (a)(i);

(c)   the embarkation and disembarkation of passengers on a qualifying ship operated by the company, and the provision of relevant facilities by the company;

(d)   the provision of excursions for passengers of a qualifying ship operated by the company, where any cabin for the passenger remains available for his exclusive use;

(e)   the provision of holidays, sold to the customer under a single contract, where–

      (i)   part of the holiday is a voyage on a qualifying ship operated by the company, and the remaining part is land-based ("the land-based part"),

      (ii)   the land-based part is purchased or obtained by the company by arm's length provision, and

      (iii)   the cost to the company of the land-based part in accordance with paragraph (ii) is less than one half of the price paid by the customer under the single contract;

(f)   sales and facilities which are normally provided to customers by seagoing passenger ships, including–

      (i)   the provision of food or drink,

      (ii)   entertainment, but not betting or gambling (see paragraph (4)(b)(i)),

      (iii)   the sale of alcoholic beverages, perfume and tobacco, but not luxury goods (see paragraph (4)(b)(ii)),

      (iv)   the exchange of amounts of different currencies for personal expenditure;

(g)   the loading and unloading of cargo carried on a qualifying ship operated by the company, and the provision by the company of facilities used exclusively for those purposes;

(h)   the consolidation or breaking of cargo carried on a qualifying ship operated by the company, immediately before or after the voyage, where the activity is not haulage-related;

(i)   the temporary placement of cargo carried on a qualifying ship operated by the company, on or at the dockside, where the activity is not part of a long-term storage operation;

(j)   the rental or provision to customers of containers for goods to be carried on a qualifying ship operated by the company;

(k)   activities carried on by the company in relation to a qualifying ship operated by another qualifying company in the same tonnage tax group, which would be core qualifying activities of the first-mentioned company if carried on in relation to a qualifying ship operated by that company.

3(4)   The descriptions and permitted levels in this paragraph are–

(a)   services which, if carried out in relation to qualifying ships operated by the company, would be core qualifying activities of the company or activities of the company which would fall within the descriptions in paragraph (3), but only to the level where–

      (i)   the relevant staff and assets are needed by the company to carry out the company's main function, and the services are undertaken to make full use of those staff and assets, and

      (ii)   the services are minimal compared to the main function;

(b)

    (i)   betting or gambling facilities normally offered to customers by seagoing passenger ships for entertainment, and

    (ii)   the sale to passengers on seagoing ships of luxury goods of a kind normally offered to such passengers,

but only to the level where the turnover from those activities is negligible compared to the turnover from the company's core qualifying activities.

3(5) In paragraph (4)(a) **"the company's main function"** means the company's core qualifying activities and those of its activities which fall within the descriptions in paragraph (3).

PLANT AND MACHINERY OTHER THAN EXPENSIVE MOTOR CARS AND LONG-LIFE ASSETS – WRITING-DOWN BASIS

4(1) This regulation applies to any asset mentioned in paragraph 85(2) of Schedule 22, where the provisions of Part II of the 1990 Act would have applied to the asset on the footing that the company had not been subject to tonnage tax ("the tax condition"), other than–

(a)   a motor car, to which the provisions of section 34 of the 1990 Act (expensive motor cars) would have effect on that condition, or

(b)   a long-life asset, where Chapter IVA of Part II of the 1990 Act would have applied to the capital expenditure incurred on the provision of the asset, on that condition.

4(2) The written down value of the paragraph 85(2)(a) amount for the asset shall be determined by multiplying that amount by the percentage given by the table in paragraph (3).

4(3) That table is as follows–

Length of qualifying holding period for the asset	Percentage of the paragraph 85(2)(a) amount which is qualifying expenditure under Part II of the 1990 Act
Less than or equal to 1 year	75
1 year and one day to 2 years	55
2 years and one day to 3 years	40
3 years and one day to 4 years	30
4 years and one day to 5 years	25
5 years and one day to 6 years	15
6 years and one day to 7 years	12
7 years and one day to 8 years	10
8 years and one day to 9 years	5
More than 9 years	Nil

4(4) References in this regulation and regulations 5 and 6 to the qualifying holding period for an asset are references to the period between–

(a)   the date on which the expenditure represented by the paragraph 85(2)(a) amount, or the part thereof, was incurred, and

(b)   the date on which the company leaves tonnage tax.

EXPENSIVE MOTOR CARS – WRITING-DOWN BASIS

5(1) This regulation applies to motor cars described in regulation 4(1)(a).

5(2) The written down value of the paragraph 85(2)(a) amount for the motor car shall be determined in accordance with the following provisions:

Rule 1

The paragraph 85(2)(a) amount for the motor car shall be reduced by £3,000 for each complete year in the qualifying holding period, subject to Rule 2.

Rule 2

Rule 1 shall cease to apply at the end of the complete year where the paragraph 85(2)(a) amount is first reduced below £12,000, and Rule 3 shall thereafter apply to that amount as reduced at the end of that year ("the reduced amount").

Rule 3

The table in regulation 4(3) shall apply to the reduced amount, in relation to any subsequent period in the qualifying holding period, as if for the date mentioned in regulation 4(4)(a) there were substituted a reference to the end of the year mentioned in Rule 2.

LONG-LIFE ASSETS – WRITING-DOWN BASIS

6(1) This regulation applies to long-life assets described in regulation 4(1)(b).

6(2) The written down value of the paragraph 85(2)(a) amount for the asset shall be determined by multiplying that amount by the percentage given by the table in paragraph (3).

6(3) That table is as follows–

Length of qualifying holding period for the asset	Percentage of the paragraph 85(2)(a) amount which is qualifying expenditure under Part II of the 1990 Act
Less than or equal to 1 year	94
From 1 year and one day to 2 years	88
From 2 years and one day to 3 years	83
From 3 years and one day to 4 years	78
From 4 years and one day to 5 years	73
From 5 years and one day to 6 years	69
From 6 years and one day to 7 years	65
From 7 years and one day to 8 years	61
From 8 years and one day to 9 years	57
From 9 years and one day to 10 years	54
From 10 years and one day to 11 years	51
From 11 years and one day to 13 years	47
From 13 years and one day to 16 years	40
From 16 years and one day to 19 years	33
From 19 years and one day to 22 years	27
From 22 years and one day to 25 years	23
From 25 years and one day to 30 years	18
From 30 years and one day to 35 years	13

From 35 years and one day to 40 years	10
From 40 years and one day to 45 years	7
From 45 years and one day to 50 years	5
From 50 years and one day to 60 years	3
From 60 years and one day to 70 years	2
More than 70 years	Nil

PLANT AND MACHINERY USED FOR THE PURPOSES OF THE COMPANY'S OFFSHORE ACTIVITIES – WRITING-DOWN BASIS

7(1) This regulation applies to any asset mentioned in paragraph 110(2)(a) of Schedule 22, where–

(a) the provisions of Part II of the 1990 Act apply to the asset by virtue of paragraph 110(2) of Schedule 22, and

(b) the paragraph 112(2) amount or the paragraph 113(2) amount for the asset, as the case may be ("the relevant amount"), falls to be written down under paragraph 112(6) or 113(3) of Schedule 22.

7(2) The written down value of the relevant amount shall be determined by applying regulation 4, 5 or 6, as the case may be, as if–

(a) the tax condition were omitted,

(b) for references to the paragraph 85(2)(a) amount there were substituted references to the relevant amount, and

(c) for regulation 4(4)(a) and (b) there were substituted a reference to the period mentioned in paragraph 112(6) or 113(3) of Schedule 22, as the case may be.

ADJUSTMENTS TO BE MADE FOR CAPITAL ALLOWANCE PURPOSES TO THE AMOUNT OF QUALIFYING EXPENDITURE FOR ASSETS WHERE A CORPORATE PARTNER LEAVES TONNAGE TAX

8(1) This regulation applies where–

(a) a corporate partner leaves tonnage tax,

(b) an asset has been used by the corporate partner for the purposes of tonnage tax activities which it carries on as a member of a partnership, and

(c) as at the beginning of the partnership chargeable period in which the corporate partner leaves tonnage tax (the beginning of which period is referred to in this regulation as "the relevant time") the asset–

    (i) was partnership property of the partnership concerned, or

    (ii) would have been so treated by regulation 9(2), or by section 65 of the 1990 Act if the corporate partner had not been subject to tonnage tax,

and applies to the corporate partner and all the other members of the partnership.

In this paragraph **"the partnership chargeable period"** means the accounting period or period of account used by the partnership in its partnership computation under section 114(1) of the Taxes Act or section 111(2) of that Act, as the case may be.

8(2) In relation to any asset mentioned in paragraph (1)(b) and (c)–

(a) there shall be determined the amount for that asset which is referred to in paragraph 85(2)(a) of Schedule 22 (which amount is referred to in this regulation as "the paragraph 85(2)(a) amount" for the asset), on the assumptions–

    (i) that the corporate partner left tonnage tax at the relevant time, and

    (ii) (where it is not otherwise the case) that the asset was held by the corporate partner at that time; and

(b)   where the asset is counted in a calculation under paragraphs (3) to (7) of this regulation, it shall not be counted again in any determination under paragraph 85(1) of Schedule 22 on the same occasion of the corporate partner leaving tonnage tax.

8(3)   In the following paragraphs of this regulation–

"unrelieved qualifying expenditure", in relation to an asset, means the balance of qualifying expenditure attributable to that asset that would otherwise have been carried forward under Part II of the 1990 Act, including postponed allowances attributable to that asset; and

"postponed allowances" means qualifying expenditure which is unrelieved by virtue of notice having been given under–

(a)   section 30(1) of the 1990 Act (postponement or reduction of first allowances), or

(b)   section 31(3) of that Act (postponement of writing-down allowance in respect of expenditure in single ship pool).

8(4)   The unrelieved qualifying expenditure for any asset mentioned in paragraph (1)(b) and (c), so far as it is not represented by postponed allowances, that would otherwise have been carried forward as at the relevant time, shall be adjusted to the amount resulting from the calculation in paragraph (5) or (6), as the case may be.

8(5)   Except in the case described in paragraph (6), the calculation is–

$$(A\% \times B) + ((100\% - A\%) \times C)$$

where–

A   equals the corporate partner's share (expressed as a percentage) in the partnership property of the partnership concerned at the relevant time, subject to paragraph (8);

B   equals the written down value of the paragraph 85(2)(a) amount for the asset calculated by applying regulation 4, 5 or 6, as the case may be–

        (a)   as if for regulation 4(4)(b), there were substituted a reference to the relevant time; and

        (b)   on the assumptions contained in paragraph (2)(a) where applicable;

C   equals the unrelieved qualifying expenditure for the asset, so far as it is not represented by postponed allowances, as at the relevant time.

8(6)   In a case where all the members of the partnership other than the corporate partner are–

(a)   persons who (within the meaning in section 161 of the 1990 Act) are not within the charge to tax in the United Kingdom on the profits of the trade carried on in the partnership in question, or

(b)   companies which are subject to tonnage tax,

the calculation is of B, which has the same meaning as in paragraph (5).

8(7)   The unrelieved qualifying expenditure for any asset mentioned in paragraph (1)(b) and (c), so far as it is represented by postponed allowances, that would otherwise have been carried forward as at the relevant time (the amount of which is referred to as "D" in this paragraph), shall be reduced to the percentage of D which is represented by the following calculation–

$$(100\% - A\%) \times D$$

where A has the same meaning as in paragraph (5).

8(8)   Where the share of the corporate partner in the partnership property (expressed as a proportion of the whole) varied during the period–

(a)   beginning on the last to occur of–

        (i)   the date on which the corporate partner became a member of the partnership concerned,

        (ii)   the date on which the corporate partner entered tonnage tax, or

        (iii)   the date six years before the relevant time, and

(b)   ending at the relevant time,

the calculation of A in paragraphs (5) and (7) shall be made according to the average of the corporate partner's interest in the property of the relevant partnership during that period, and any necessary apportionment on a daily basis shall be made.

8(9)   A payment made by a corporate partner to another corporate partner in the same partnership which is compensation for any adjustment carried out under paragraphs (4) to (7)–

(a)   shall not be taken into account in computing profits or losses of either company for corporation tax purposes, and

(b)   shall not for any of the purposes of the Corporation Tax Acts, (within the meaning in section 831(1)(a) of the Taxes Act) be regarded as a distribution or a charge on income.

CORPORATE PARTNERS – MODIFICATIONS OF THE REQUIREMENTS FOR BEING A QUALIFYING COMPANY (WITH SUPPLEMENTARY PROVISION RELATING TO FINANCE LEASES)

9(1)   Paragraphs (1) to (3), (5) and (6) of this regulation prescribe modifications to the requirements for determining whether–

(a)   a corporate partner operates qualifying ships within the meaning in paragraphs 16(1)(b) and 18(1) to (4) of Schedule 22, and

(b)   those ships are strategically and commercially managed in the United Kingdom within the meaning in paragraph 16(1)(c) of Schedule 22.

9(2)   Where–

(a)   a qualifying ship is owned by, or (other than by a charter described in paragraph (3)) chartered to, one or more of the members of a partnership but is not partnership property, and

(b)   activities of the partnership business which, if carried on by a tonnage tax company, would be tonnage tax activities, are carried on in relation to the ship, the ship shall be treated as if it were owned by, or chartered to, all the partners, as the case may be, and as if everything done by or to any of the partners in relation to it had been done by or to all the partners.

9(3)   Any charter of a ship from one or more members of the partnership to the other partners, or to the partnership, for use in the tonnage tax activities carried on in that partnership, shall be treated for the purposes of paragraph 18(4) of Schedule 22 as a charter to a person who is not a third party.

9(4)   A finance lease (within the meaning in section 82A of the 1990 Act) of a qualifying ship where the lessee is one or more members of a partnership which includes a tonnage tax company as a member, or is such a partnership, and the ship is used in the tonnage tax activities which the tonnage tax company carries on as a member of the partnership, shall be treated for the purposes of Part X of Schedule 22 as if–

(a)   the qualifying ship were provided (within the meaning in paragraph 89(1) of Schedule 22) to the tonnage tax company;

(b)   the tonnage tax company were the "lessee" for the purposes of paragraphs 98 and 99 of Schedule 22; and

(c)   the references in paragraph 92 of Schedule 22 to the ship being owned by a tonnage tax company included references to the ship being owned by one or more of the partners, or by the partnership.

9(5)   Paragraph 16(1)(c) of Schedule 22 shall be modified as if, in relation to activities carried on by a corporate partner in a partnership, the reference to those ships were replaced with a reference to the requisite proportion of those ships.

9(6)   In paragraph (5) **"the requisite proportion of those ships"** means a proportion of those ships such that–

$$\frac{E}{F} \text{ is not less than } G$$

where–

E   equals the aggregate net tonnage of all the qualifying ships which are–

     (a)   operated by the partners of the partnership concerned, in their capacity as such partners, and

     (b)   strategically and commercially managed in the United Kingdom;

F   equals the aggregate net tonnage of all the qualifying ships which are operated by the partners of the partnership concerned, in their capacity as such partners; and

G   equals the share of the corporate partner, expressed as a fraction, in the partnership property of the partnership concerned.

RULES FOR CALCULATING THE TONNAGE TAX PROFITS AND RELEVANT SHIPPING PROFITS OF A CORPORATE PARTNER

10(1) Paragraph (2) applies to any corporate partner which is a tonnage tax company (but only in relation to the share of profits or losses which such a partner derives from the activities carried on in the partnership concerned).

10(2) Section 114 of the Taxes Act shall apply to the profits and losses of the partnership as if the partnership were a tonnage tax company, for the purpose of calculating–

(a)   the tonnage tax profits, and

(b)   the relevant shipping profits (or such of the corresponding losses as fall within paragraph 3(2) of Schedule 22),

of any corporate partner to whom this paragraph applies (but not the share of profits or losses of any other partner).

10(3) Where a ship falls to be counted as operated by a partnership in a calculation under paragraph (2)(a) carried out in relation to a corporate partner, it shall not be counted again in any computation of the tonnage tax profits of that corporate partner, and the same provision shall apply as between a calculation under paragraph (2)(b) and the relevant shipping profits (or relevant corresponding losses) of a corporate partner.

SHIPS CHARTERED TO PARTNERS – FURTHER PROVISION RELATING TO CHARTERING IN

11(1) Where a corporate partner carries on activities in partnership which include the operation of a qualifying ship, the calculation whether the 75% limit is exceeded by–

(a)   that corporate partner (if it is a single company), or

(b)   a group of which that corporate partner is a member, so far as the calculation relates to the corporate partner, shall be made in accordance with this regulation.

11(2) The calculation is as follows:

Step One

Find out the aggregate net tonnage of the qualifying ships that are operated by the members of the partnership concerned, in their capacity as such partners.

Step Two

Find out the proportion, in percentage terms, of the result of Step One which represents tonnage of ships which are chartered to the partners, or to the partnership, otherwise than on bareboat charter terms ("chartered in"), ignoring any such charters which are from another qualifying member of any group of which the corporate partner is also a member.

Step Three

Determine the corporate partner's share of the results of Steps One and Two according to the interests of the partners in the partnership property in the accounting period in question, expressed as a figure of net tonnage and the percentage of it which is chartered in.

Step Four

Follow Steps One to Three for each partnership of which the corporate partner is a member and aggregate the results, to arrive at a total figure of net tonnage and the percentage of it which is chartered in.

Step Five

Aggregate the results of Step Four with the results of the calculation for the purposes of paragraph 37(1)(a) or (b) of Schedule 22, as the case may be, in relation to any ships other than those which the corporate partner operates as a member of a partnership.

Step Six

Apply paragraph 37(1)(a) or (b) of Schedule 22, as the case may be, to the results of Step Five.

11(3) Where the interests of the partners in the partnership property, expressed as a proportion of the whole, vary in the course of an accounting period, the interest of a corporate partner for that period shall be calculated according to the average interest of that partner during that period.

CHARGEABLE GAINS: USE OF ASSETS BY PARTNERSHIPS WHICH INCLUDE CORPORATE PARTNERS

12 Where–

(a) an asset has been used wholly and exclusively for the purposes of activities of a partnership which are (or would be, if the partnership were a tonnage tax company) tonnage tax activities;

(b) throughout the period of use of the asset as mentioned in sub-paragraph (a), there was a corporate partner member of the partnership which was also a tonnage tax company; and

(c) the asset is disposed of by that corporate partner, or by another member of a group of which that corporate partner is a member,

references in paragraph 65(1) and (3) of Schedule 22 to a tonnage tax asset, or to any time at which or period during which an asset was a tonnage tax asset, shall respectively include references to the asset and period mentioned in this regulation, and references to a period during which an asset was not a tonnage tax asset shall be construed accordingly.

TRANSACTIONS NOT AT ARM'S LENGTH BETWEEN A PARTNERSHIP (WHERE A CORPORATE PARTNER IS A TONNAGE TAX COMPANY) AND ANOTHER PARTNER

13(1) Where a corporate partner which is a tonnage tax company ("the relevant company") carries on tonnage tax activities in partnership, paragraph 58 of Schedule 22 shall apply to provision made or imposed as between–

(a) the partnership, and

(b) another partner,

if the condition in paragraph (2) is satisfied, and in that event on the assumptions in paragraph (3).

13(2) The condition is that the relevant company (in addition to the partner referred to in paragraph (1)(b)) is a major participant in the partnership's enterprise, within the meaning of that expression in paragraph 4(7) of Schedule 28AA.

13(3) The assumptions are that the partnership–

(a) is a tonnage tax company, and

(b) is regarded for the purposes of paragraph 58(1)(a) of Schedule 22 as carrying on the tonnage tax trade of the relevant company, so far as that trade consists of activities carried on by the relevant company in the partnership in question.

ORDERS FOR THE DELIVERY OF DOCUMENTS (PROCEDURE) REGULATIONS 2000

(SI 2000/2875, as amended by SI 2005/1131 and SI 2007/881)

Made on 23 October 2000 by the Commissioners of Inland Revenue, in exercise of the powers conferred on them by para. 2(2), 3(2), 6, 7(1) and (2), 10 and 11(a) of Sch. 1AA to the Taxes Management Act 1970. Operative from 13 November 2000.

CITATION AND COMMENCEMENT

1 These Regulations may be cited as the Orders for the Delivery of Documents (Procedure) Regulations 2000 and shall come into force on 13th November 2000.

INTERPRETATION

2 In these Regulations–

"the appropriate judicial authority" has the meaning given by section 20D(1) of the Management Act;

"the Commissioners" means the Commissioners for Her Majesty's Revenue and Customs;

"the court" has the meaning given by paragraph 9(2) of Schedule 1AA to the Management Act;

"items subject to legal privilege" has the meaning given by paragraph 5(2) of Schedule 1AA to the Management Act;

"the Management Act" means the Taxes Management Act 1970;

"notice of application" means the notice of intention to apply for an order to which a person is entitled under paragraph 3(1) of Schedule 1AA to the Management Act;

"order" means an order under section 20BA of the Management Act;

"working day" means any day other than a Saturday, Sunday or public holiday.

History – In reg. 2 the definition of "the Commissioners" inserted by SI 2005/1131, reg. 3(b), with effect from 18 April 2005, In reg. 2 the definition of "the Board" omitted by SI 2005/1131, reg. 3(a), with effect from 18 April 2005.

APPROVAL OF DECISION TO APPLY FOR AN ORDER

3 Before the hearing of an application for an order, an officer of Her Majesty's Revenue and Customs who is a member of the Senior Civil Service in the Criminal Investigation Directorate must approve in writing the decision to apply for that order.

History – Reg. 3 substituted by SI 2007/881, reg. 2, with effect from 9 April 2007.
In former reg. 3 the words "Her Majesty's Revenue and Customs" substituted for the words "the Board", in para. (a) the words "the Cross-Cutting Policy branch of Her Majesty's Revenue and Customs" substituted for the words "the Cross-Cutting Policy branch of the Inland Revenue" and in para. (b) the words "the Special Compliance Office of Her Majesty's Revenue and Customs" substituted for the words "the Special Compliance Office of the Inland Revenue" by SI 2005/1131, reg. 4, with effect from 18 April 2005.

NOTICE OF APPLICATION

4(1) Notice of application must be given in writing and must contain the following details–

(a)　　the date, time and place of the hearing of the application;

(b)　　the specifications or descriptions of documents which are the subject of the application;

(c)　　a description of the suspected offence to which the application relates; and

(d)　　the name of the person suspected of committing, having committed or being about to commit the suspected offence.

4(2) Notice of application must be given to the person entitled to it not less than five working days before the hearing of the application.

NOTICE OF AN ORDER, OR NOTICE OF APPLICATION, TREATED AS HAVING BEEN GIVEN

5(1) Where notice of an order, or notice of application, is delivered to a person, or left at his proper address, notice shall be treated as having been given to that person on the day on which it is delivered or left or, where that day is not a working day, on the next working day.

5(2) Where notice of application, or notice of an order, is sent to a person's proper address by facsimile transmission or other similar means which produce a document containing a text of the communication, notice shall be treated as given when the text is received in a legible form.

5(3) For the purposes of this regulation, a person's proper address is–

(a) the usual or last known place of residence, or the place of business or employment, of that person; or

(b) in the case of a company, the address of the company's registered office; or

(c) in the case of a liquidator of a company, the liquidator's address for the purposes of the liquidation.

COMPLYING WITH AN ORDER

6(1) A person complies with an order by producing the documents specified or described in the order to the officer of the Board specified in the order within–

(a) the period mentioned in section 20BA(2) of the Management Act; or

(b) such further period, if any, as is agreed with that officer.

6(2) For the purposes of paragraph (1), documents are produced to an officer of Revenue and Customs if they are either–

(a) delivered to the officer; or

(b) left for the officer at an address specified in the relevant order.

6(3) Where documents are sent to an officer of Revenue and Customs at the address specified in the relevant order by post, they shall be treated, unless the contrary is proved, as having been produced to the officer–

(a) if first class post is used, on the second working day after posting;

(b) if second class post is used, on the fourth working day after posting.

History – In reg. 6 the words "an officer of Revenue and Customs" substituted for the words "an officer of the Board" twice by SI 2005/1131, reg. 5, with effect from 18 April 2005.

RESOLUTION OF DISPUTES AS TO LEGAL PRIVILEGE

7(1) This regulation applies where there is a dispute between the Commissioners and a person against whom an order has been made as to whether a document, or part of a document, is an item subject to legal privilege.

7(2) The person against whom an order has been made may apply to the appropriate judicial authority to resolve the dispute.

7(3) All the documents to which an application under paragraph (2) relates must be lodged in the court at the same time as the application is made and shall be held by the court until the appropriate judicial authority resolves the dispute.

7(4) The court shall give the Commissioners notice of an application made under paragraph (2) not less than five working days before the hearing of the application, and the Commissioners shall be entitled to appear and be heard at that hearing in addition to the person making the application.

7(5) On the hearing of an application made under paragraph (2), the appropriate judicial authority shall–

(a) resolve the dispute by confirming whether the document, or part of the document, is or is not an item subject to legal privilege; and

(b) order the costs of the application to be met by the Commissioners except where it holds that no document, or no part of any document, to which the application relates is an item subject to legal privilege.

7(6) Where a person makes an application under paragraph (2) within the period mentioned in regulation 6(1), he shall be treated as having complied with the order in relation to the documents to which the application relates until the appropriate judicial authority resolves the dispute.

7(7) A dispute may be resolved at any time by the Commissioners and the person against whom an order has been made reaching an agreement, whether in writing or otherwise, and, for all purposes, the consequences of such an agreement shall be the same as those which would have ensued if, at the time when the agreement was reached, the appropriate judicial authority had resolved the dispute.

History – In reg. 7 the words "the Commissioners" substituted for the words "the Board" five times by SI 2005/1131, reg. 6, with effect from 18 April 2005.

CONTROLLED FOREIGN COMPANIES (DESIGNER RATE TAX PROVISIONS) REGULATIONS 2000

(SI 2000/3158)

Made on 29 November 2000 by the Commissioners of Inland Revenue, in exercise of the powers conferred upon them by s. 750A(2) to (4) of the Income and Corporation Taxes Act 1988. Operative from 20 December 2000.

Cross references – FA 2012, Sch. 20, para. 59: application of SI 2000/3158 for the purposes of TIOPA 2010, s. 371ND.

CITATION, COMMENCEMENT AND EFFECT

1(1) These Regulations may be cited as the Controlled Foreign Companies (Designer Rate Tax Provisions) Regulations 2000 and shall come into force on 20th December 2000.

1(2) These Regulations have effect in relation to any accounting period of a company resident outside the United Kingdom which begins on or after 6th October 1999.

INTERPRETATION

2 In these Regulations **"the Board"** means the Commissioners of Inland Revenue.

SPECIFIED DESIGNER RATE TAX PROVISIONS

3 For the purposes of section 750A(1) of the Income and Corporation Taxes Act 1988 (deemed lower level of taxation: designer rate tax provisions) the following provisions are specified, being provisions which appear to the Board to be designed to enable companies to exercise significant control over the amount of tax which they pay–

(a)　the provisions contained in Part XVIIA (international bodies) of the Income Tax (Guernsey) Law, 1975;

(b)　Article 123B (international business companies) of the Income Tax (Jersey) Law 1961;

(c)　the provisions contained in Part 1 (International Companies) of the Isle of Man International Business Act 1994, and the provisions contained in Part 3 (Miscellaneous and Supplemental) of that Act so far as relating to Part 1 of that Act;

(d)　section 41 (rates for qualifying companies) of the Gibraltar Income Tax Ordinance.

EXCHANGE GAINS AND LOSSES (MISCELLANEOUS MODIFICATIONS) REGULATIONS 2000

(SI 2000/3315, as amended by SI 2002/1969)

Made on 18 December 2000 by the Treasury, in exercise of the powers conferred upon them by s. 164(14) and 167(1) and (4) to (6) of, and Sch. 15 and 16 to, the Finance Act 1993 and s. 163 of the Finance Act 1998. Operative from 9 January 2001.

CITATION COMMENCEMENT AND EFFECT

1(1) These Regulations may be cited as the Exchange Gains and Losses (Miscellaneous Modifications) Regulations 2000 and shall come into force on 9th January 2001.

1(2) Regulations 2 to 10 shall have effect in relation to any accounting period of a company beginning on or after 1st January 2000 for which sections 105 and 106 of the Finance Act 2000 have effect.

MODIFICATION OF THE EXCHANGE GAINS AND LOSSES (TRANSITIONAL PROVISIONS) REGULATIONS 1994

2 [Omitted by SI 2002/1969, reg. 29.]

History – Reg. 2 omitted by SI 2002/1969, reg. 29 with effect in relation to accounting periods beginning on or after 1 October 2002.

3 [Omitted by SI 2002/1969, reg. 29.]

History – Reg. 3 omitted by SI 2002/1969, reg. 29 with effect in relation to accounting periods beginning on or after 1 October 2002.

4 [Omitted by SI 2002/1969, reg. 29.]

History – Reg. 4 omitted by SI 2002/1969, reg. 29 with effect in relation to accounting periods beginning on or after 1 October 2002.

5 [Omitted by SI 2002/1969, reg. 29.]

History – Reg. 5 omitted by SI 2002/1969, reg. 29 with effect in relation to accounting periods beginning on or after 1 October 2002.

MODIFICATION OF THE EXCHANGE GAINS AND LOSSES (ALTERNATIVE METHOD OF CALCULATION OF GAIN OR LOSS) REGULATIONS 1994

6 Apply the Exchange Gains and Losses (Alternative Method of Calculation of Gain or Loss) Regulations 1994 with the modifications set out in regulations 7 to 9.

7 In regulation 4(2)–

(a)   after the definition of "accounts" insert–
"**"branch"** shall be construed in accordance with section 93(7) of the 1993 Act;";

(b)   omit the definition of "a local currency election";

(c)   after the definition of "qualifying asset" add–
"**"the relevant foreign currency"** has the meaning given by section 93(7) of the 1993 Act."

8(1) In regulation 5(6)–

(a)   after "An asset held by a company" insert "which prepares its accounts as a whole in sterling";

(b)   for sub-paragraph (b)(ii) substitute–
"**(ii)** is a company to which section 93 of the 1993 Act applies by virtue of its accounts as a whole being prepared in a currency other than sterling in accordance with normal accounting practice, and";

(c)   in sub-paragraph (d) for "in a branch" to "other than sterling" substitute "in a branch through which the company carries on a business or part of a business and, by virtue of section 93 of the 1993 Act, the profits and losses of that business or that part are to be computed and expressed in a currency other than sterling".

8(2) After regulation 5(6) insert–

"**5(6A)** An asset held by a company which prepares its accounts as a whole in a currency other than sterling is an eligible asset at any time if at that time–

(a)   it is shares which–

(i)   are denominated in a currency other than the relevant foreign currency for the company making the election, and

(ii)   are in a company that is not resident in the United Kingdom and is, at the time the election is made, an associated company of the company making the election; or

(b)   it is shares in a company which–

(i)   is resident in the United Kingdom, and

(ii)   prepares its accounts as a whole either in sterling or in a currency other than sterling which is not the relevant foreign currency for the company making the election, and

(iii)   is a 90 per cent. subsidiary (within the meaning of paragraph (7) below) of the company making the election; or

(c)   it is a debt on a security which under the terms of issue can be converted into or exchanged for shares falling within sub-paragraph (a) or (b) above and which is not a qualifying asset; or

(d)   it is the company's net investment in a branch through which the company carries on a business or part of a business and, by virtue of section 93 of the 1993 Act, the profits and losses of that business or that part are to be computed and expressed in a currency other than the relevant foreign currency for the company; or

(e)   it is a ship or an aircraft.".

8(3) For regulation 5(8)(b) substitute–

"(b)   the asset is not a qualifying asset, and

(c)   the asset is held by a branch of the company outside the United Kingdom through which the company carries on a business or part of a business, and

(i)   where the company prepares its accounts as a whole in sterling, the profits and losses of that business or that part are not to be computed and expressed in a currency other than sterling by virtue of section 93 of the 1993 Act, or

(ii)   where the company prepares its accounts as a whole in a currency other than sterling, the profits and losses of that business or that part are not to be computed and expressed in a currency other than the relevant foreign currency for the company by virtue of that section.".

8(4) In regulation 5(9)–

(a)   for "(6) and (8)" substitute "(6), (6A) and (8)";

(b)   for "trade" in both places where it occurs substitute "business".

9 In regulation 10(4) after "regulation 5(6)(a), (b), (c) or (d)" insert "or 5(6A)(a), (b), (c) or (d)".

REVOCATION OF THE EUROPEAN SINGLE CURRENCY (TAXES) REGULATIONS 1998

10 Part X of the European Single Currency (Taxes) Regulations 1998 is revoked to the extent that it is not previously revoked.

MODIFICATION OF THE EFFECT OF SECTION 146 OF THE FINANCE ACT 1993

11 [Omitted by SI 2002/1969, reg. 29.]

History – Reg. 11 omitted by SI 2002/1969, reg. 29 with effect in relation to accounting periods beginning on or after 1 October 2002.

INCOME TAX (ELECTRONIC COMMUNICATIONS) (INCENTIVE PAYMENTS) REGULATIONS 2001

(SI 2001/56, as amended by SI 2001/1081)

Made on 11 January 2001 by the Commissioners of Inland Revenue, in exercise of the powers conferred upon them by s. 143(1) of, and Sch. 38 to, the Finance Act 2000. Operative from 1 February 2001.

CITATION, COMMENCEMENT AND EFFECT

1(1) These Regulations may be cited as the Income Tax (Electronic Communications) (Incentive Payments) Regulations 2001 and shall come into force on 1st February 2001.

1(2) Nothing in these Regulations affects the operation of the Electronic Lodgement of Tax Returns Order 1997 or the Income Tax (Electronic Communications) Regulations 2000.

INTERPRETATION

2   In these Regulations–

"**the Board**" means the Commissioners of Inland Revenue;

"**employer**" means any person paying emoluments;

"**Employments Regulations**" means the Income Tax (Employments) Regulations 1993;

"**incentive payment**" means a payment by way of an incentive to use electronic communications for the delivery of information under regulation 3, 4 or 5;

"**the Management Act**" means the Taxes Management Act 1970;

"**tax credit**" means working families' tax credit or, as the case may be, disabled person's tax credit.

INCENTIVE PAYMENT – RETURN UNDER SECTIONS 8 AND 9 OF THE MANAGEMENT ACT

3(1) The Board shall make an incentive payment in the amount of £10 to any individual who–

(a)   makes and delivers a return under sections 8 and 9 of the Management Act for a year of assessment using electronic communications, and

(b)   satisfies the conditions specified in any direction given by the Board under paragraph (2).

3(2) The Board may give a direction specifying any or all of the following conditions–

(a)   a condition that the year of assessment for which the return is to be made and delivered is one specified in the direction,

(b)   a condition specifying the form of electronic communication by which the return is to be delivered,

(c)   a condition that the individual by whom the return is to be made and delivered is one who is authorised to use the form of electronic communication specified in the direction,

(d)   a condition that where the individual by whom the return is made and delivered becomes liable to pay an amount by way of income tax for the year of assessment concerned, the payment or, if more than one, at least one of the payments, made by him in meeting that liability is made using one of the forms of electronic payment specified in the direction,

(e)   a condition that the return is made and delivered using the form of electronic communication specified in the direction,

(f)   a condition that the return is made and delivered by the individual on or before the day mentioned in section 8(1A) of the Management Act,

(g)   a condition that any amount payable by way of income tax by the individual for the year of assessment concerned is paid in accordance with the provisions for payment of income tax contained in sections 59A and 59B of the Management Act.

3(3) Where an officer of the Board considers that the individual has failed to satisfy one or more of the conditions specified in the direction, he may give notice to the individual that the conditions are not met or, where the incentive payment has already been authorised or made, notice withdrawing the incentive payment.

3(4) Where prior to the giving of a notice under paragraph (3) an incentive payment has already been made to the individual, an officer of the Board may recover the amount of the incentive payment in accordance with paragraph (5).

3(5) For the purposes of paragraph (4), subsections (1), (4), (5) and (6) of section 30 of the Management Act (recovery of overpayment of tax, etc) and section 30A of that Act (assessing procedure) shall apply as if the amount of the incentive payment to be recovered were an amount of income tax repaid to that individual which ought not to have been repaid to him.

3(6) The Board may give a direction relating to appeals against notices under paragraph (3) and appeals against assessments made in pursuance of paragraph (5).

Cross references – Direction of the Board, 19 February 2001: direction setting the conditions to be satisfied by an individual in order to qualify for an incentive payment, when delivering a 1999–2000 tax return under TMA 1970, s. 8 or 9, to the Revenue over the Internet.
Direction of the Board, 10 April 2001: direction providing for appeals by a taxpayer in respect of a failure to obtain or the withdrawal of an incentive payment.

INCENTIVE PAYMENT – RETURN UNDER REGULATION 43 OF THE EMPLOYMENTS REGULATIONS

4(1) The Board shall make an incentive payment in the amount of £50 to any employer who–

(a)   renders a return under regulation 43 of the Employments Regulations for a year of assessment using electronic communications, and

(b)   satisfies the conditions specified in any direction given by the Board under paragraph (2).

4(2) The Board may give a direction specifying any or all of the following conditions–

(a)   a condition that the year of assessment for which the return is to be rendered is one specified in the direction;

(b)   a condition specifying the form of electronic communication by which the return is to be rendered,

(c)   a condition that the employer by whom the return is to be rendered is one who is authorised to use the form of electronic communication specified in the direction,

(d)   a condition that at least one of the payments made by the employer under regulation 40 or 41 of the Employments Regulations in the year of assessment concerned is made using one of the forms of electronic payment specified in the direction,

(e)   a condition that the return is rendered by the employer, or by an agent of the employer authorised to render the return, using the form of electronic communication specified in the direction,

(f)   a condition that, where the return is rendered by the employer's agent on the employer's behalf–

    (i)   the employer has registered on line to use the form of electronic communication specified in the direction,

    (ii)   the employer has used that form of electronic communication to notify the Board of his agent's name and address, and

    (iii) his agent is authorised by him to render the return on his behalf and to use that form of electronic communication,

(g)   a condition that the return is rendered not later than the end of the period mentioned in regulation 43(1) of the Employments Regulations,

(h)   a condition that each of the payments required to be made by the employer under regulation 40 or 41 for the year of assessment concerned is made not later than the end of the period mentioned in regulation 40(1) or, as the case may be, regulation 41(1).

4(3) Where an officer of the Board considers that the employer has failed to satisfy one or more of the conditions specified in the direction, he may give notice to the employer that the conditions are not met or, where the incentive payment has already been authorised or made, notice withdrawing the incentive payment.

4(4) Where prior to the giving of a notice under paragraph (3) an incentive payment has already been made to the employer, an officer of the Board may recover the amount of the incentive payment in accordance with paragraph (5).

4(5) For the purposes of paragraph (4), subsections (1), (4), (5) and (6) of section 30 of the Management Act and section 30A of that Act shall apply as if the amount of the incentive payment to be recovered were an amount of income tax repaid to a person which ought not to have been repaid to him.

Statutory Instruments

4(6)   The Board may give a direction relating to appeals against notices under paragraph (3) and appeals against assessments made in pursuance of paragraph (5).

History – In reg. 4(1) the word "shall" substituted in place of the word "may" by SI 2001/1081, reg. 22, with effect from 9 April 2001.

Cross references – Direction of the Board, 10 April 2001: direction setting the conditions to be satisfied by an employer in order to qualify for an incentive payment, when making a 2000–01 employer's return to the Revenue over the Internet.
Direction of the Board, 10 April 2001: direction providing for appeals by an employer in respect of a failure to obtain or the withdrawal of an incentive payment.

INCENTIVE PAYMENT – RETURN OF PAYMENTS OF TAX CREDIT

5(1)   The Board shall make an incentive payment in the amount of £50 to any employer who–

(a)   pays tax credit to one or more of his employees during a year of assessment,

(b)   in accordance with regulation 6(7) of the Tax Credits (Payment by Employers) Regulations 1999 records on the certificate contained in a return under regulation 43 of the Employments Regulations the total tax credit paid to his employees for that year,

(c)   renders that return using electronic communications, and

(d)   satisfies the conditions specified in any direction given by the Board under paragraph (2).

5(2)   The Board may give a direction specifying any or all of the following conditions–

(a)   a condition that the year of assessment for which the return is to be rendered is one specified in the direction,

(b)   a condition specifying the form of electronic communication by which the return is to be rendered,

(c)   a condition that the employer by whom the return is to be rendered is one who is authorised to use the form of electronic communication specified in the direction,

(d)   a condition that the employer satisfies each of the conditions specified in a direction made under regulation 4(2) of these Regulations,

(e)   a condition that the employer has paid tax credit in the year of assessment concerned in accordance with regulation 6 of the Tax Credits (Payment by Employers) Regulations 1999 (obligation to pay tax credit on paying emoluments to employees entitled to tax credit).

5(3)   Where an officer of the Board considers that the employer has failed to satisfy one or more of the conditions specified in the direction, he may give notice to the employer that the conditions are not met or, where the incentive payment has already been authorised or made, notice withdrawing the incentive payment.

5(4)   Where prior to the giving of a notice under paragraph (3) an incentive payment has already been made to the employer, an officer of the Board may recover the amount of the incentive payment in accordance with paragraph (5).

5(5)   For the purposes of paragraph (4), subsections (1), (4), (5) and (6) of section 30 of the Management Act and section 30A of that Act shall apply as if the amount of the incentive payment to be recovered were an amount of income tax repaid to a person which ought not to have been repaid to him.

5(6)   The Board may give a direction relating to appeals against notices under paragraph (3) and appeals against assessments made in pursuance of paragraph (5).

Cross references – Direction of the Board, 10 April 2001: direction setting the conditions to be satisfied by an employer in order to qualify for an incentive payment, when including a certificate of tax credit payments in the making of an employer's return, under SI 1993/744, reg. 43, over the Internet.
Direction of the Board, 10 April 2001: direction providing for appeals by an employer in respect of a failure to obtain or the withdrawal of an incentive payment.

INVESTMENT TRUSTS (APPROVAL OF ACCOUNTING METHODS FOR CREDITOR RELATIONSHIPS) ORDER 2001

(SI 2001/391)

Made on 14 February 2001. Operative from 7 March 2001.

Whereas it appears to the Treasury that the accounting methods referred to in Art. 3 of this Order as "the main method" and "the simple method" are recognised by normal accounting practice for use in the case of investment trusts:

Now, therefore the Treasury, in exercise of the powers conferred on them by para. 1 and 9(1) of Sch. 10 to the Finance Act 1996, hereby make the following Order:

CITATION, COMMENCEMENT AND EFFECT

1   This Order may be cited as the Investment Trusts (Approval of Accounting Methods for Creditor Relationships) Order 2001 and shall come into force on 7th March 2001, but shall have effect in relation to accounting periods of investment trusts ending after 31st March 1996.

INTERPRETATION

2(1)   In this Order—

"**Chapter II**" means Chapter II of Part IV of the Finance Act 1996;

"**creditor relationship**" has the same meaning as in section 103(1);

"**investment trust**" has the meaning given by section 842 of the Taxes Act;

"**statutory accounts**" shall be construed in accordance with section 86(8);

"**the Taxes Act**" means the Income and Corporation Taxes Act 1988.

2(2)   References in this Order to a section, or a Schedule, without more, are references to that section of, or that Schedule to, the Finance Act 1996.

APPROVAL OF THE USE OF ACCOUNTING METHODS

3   The accounting methods that are approved for use for the creditor relationships of investment trusts for the purposes of paragraph 1 of Schedule 10 are—

(a)   the method ("**the main method**") contained in a Statement of Recommended Practice issued by the Association of Investment Trust Companies bearing the date December 1995 ("**the Statement**"), as modified by article 4 of this Order;

(b)   the method contained in the Statement as varied by a Guidance Note issued by that Association on 8th January 1997 ("**the simple method**"), and as modified by article 4.

MODIFICATIONS OF THE MAIN METHOD AND THE SIMPLE METHOD

4(1)   The main method and the simple method shall be modified as follows.

4(2)   For paragraph R604 in the Statement there shall be substituted the following paragraph—

"R604 An ITC shall be under an obligation—

(a)   to make proper provision for allocating payments under a creditor relationship to accounting periods (and that expression has the same meaning as in sub-section (3) of section 85 of the Finance Act 1996, on the assumption that the words "loan relationship" in that sub-section were replaced with the words "creditor relationship"), and

(b)   not to make any provision (other than provision comprised in authorised arrangements for bad debt, within the meaning in section 85(5)(a) of the Finance Act 1996) that gives debits by reference to the valuation at different times of any asset representing a creditor relationship (within the meaning in section 103(1) of the Finance Act 1996)."

4(3)   Paragraph R606 in the Statement shall be omitted.

4(4)   In this Order, "**the modified main method**" and "**the modified simple method**" mean the main method, and the simple method, as so modified, respectively.

PURPOSES FOR WHICH ACCOUNTING METHODS ARE APPROVED

5(1)   This article has effect for the purpose of determining which of the accounting methods approved under article 3 is to be used as respects the creditor relationships of an investment trust.

5(2)   The same method shall be used as respects all creditor relationships of an investment trust for any single accounting period.

5(3)   The modified main method shall be used for any accounting period where–

(a)   the investment trust uses the main method or the modified main method for the purposes of its statutory accounts for that accounting period;

(b)   the investment trust has in an earlier accounting period (not being an accounting period described in paragraph (4)) used the modified main method as an authorised accounting period for the purposes of Chapter II; or

(c)   the investment trust has, at any time during the accounting period referred to in the words preceding sub-paragraph (a), held–

    (i)   a relevant discounted security within the meaning of Schedule 13; or

    (ii)   a security to which section 717 of the Taxes Act applies.

5(4)   The accounting period described in this paragraph is one–

(a)   which ended before the coming into force of this Order; and

(b)   during which the investment trust did not at any time hold any of the securities referred to in paragraph (3)(c)(i) or (ii).

DOUBLE TAXATION RELIEF (TAXES ON INCOME) (UNDERLYING TAX ON DIVIDENDS AND DUAL RESIDENT COMPANIES) REGULATIONS 2001

(SI 2001/1156)

Made on 26 March 2001 by the Treasury in exercise of the powers conferred by s. 801(2A)(b) of the Income and Corporation Taxes Act 1988. Operative from 31 March 2001.

CITATION, COMMENCEMENT AND APPLICATION

1(1) These Regulations may be cited as the Double Taxation Relief (Taxes on Income) (Underlying Tax on Dividends and Dual Resident Companies) Regulations 2001.

1(2) These Regulations shall come into force on 31st March 2001 and shall apply in relation to any claim for an allowance by way of credit made on or after that date in respect of a dividend paid by an overseas company to a company resident in the United Kingdom, unless the dividend was paid before that date.

INTERPRETATION

2 In these Regulations–

"**the Act**" means the Income and Corporation Taxes Act 1988, and a reference to a numbered section is a reference to the section of the Act which is so numbered;

"**dual resident company**" means a company which is liable, by reason of its domicile, residence or place of management or of incorporation, or other similar criterion, to tax in two or more territories;

"**overseas company**" has the meaning given in section 801(1) (dividends paid between related companies: relief for UK and third country taxes); and

"**third company**" means the company referred to as such in section 801(2).

ADDITIONAL CASES PRESCRIBED FOR THE PURPOSES OF SECTION 801(2) OF THE ACT

3(1) The cases specified in paragraphs (2) and (3) are prescribed for the purposes of section 801(2) (cases where the overseas company receives a dividend from a related third company and in respect of which relief allowable for underlying tax is subject to a restriction under section 799(1)(b)).

3(2) The case specified in this paragraph is that the overseas company is a dual resident company as respects an accounting period and, although resident in the same territory as the third company–

(a)   it is treated for the purposes of Chapter IV of Part XVII of the Act (tax avoidance: controlled foreign companies) as resident in a different territory; or

(b)   it would be so treated in accordance with paragraphs (a) to (c) of subsection (3) of section 749 (residence of controlled foreign companies) if that subsection applied to it.

3(3) The case specified in this paragraph is that the third company is a dual resident company as respects an accounting period and although resident in the same territory as the overseas company–

(a)   it is treated for the purposes of Chapter IV of Part XVII of the Act as resident in a different territory; or

(b)   it would be so treated in accordance with paragraphs (a) to (c) of subsection (3) of section 749 if that subsection applied to it.

DOUBLE TAXATION RELIEF (SURRENDER OF RELIEVABLE TAX WITHIN A GROUP) REGULATIONS 2001

(SI 2001/1163, as amended by SI 2001/3873, SI 2003/1829 and SI 2008/2681)

Made on 23 March 2001 by the Commissioners of Inland Revenue, in exercise of the powers conferred upon them by s. 806H of the Income and Corporation Taxes Act 1988. Operative from 31 March 2001.

CITATION, COMMENCEMENT AND EFFECT

1(1) These Regulations may be cited as the Double Taxation Relief (Surrender of Relievable Tax Within a Group) Regulations 2001 and shall come into force on 31st March 2001.

1(2) These Regulations shall have effect in relation to any claim made on or after 31st March 2001 for the surrender of an amount of EUFT arising in respect of a dividend falling within section 806A(2) that is paid by a company resident outside the United Kingdom to a company resident in the United Kingdom, unless the dividend was paid before that date.

INTERPRETATION

2(1) In these Regulations–

"**EUFT**" means eligible unrelieved foreign tax;

"**group**" shall be construed in accordance with subsection (3)(a) of section 413, read with subsections (4), (5) and (7) of that section;

"**the Taxes Act**" means the Income and Corporation Taxes Act 1988.

2(2) In these Regulations the following expressions have the meanings given by section 413(2)–

"**claimant company**"

"**company**"

"**group relief**"

"**surrendering company**".

2(3) In these Regulations references to a section, without more, are to that section of the Taxes Act.

INTRODUCTORY

3 These Regulations make provision for, and in connection with, allowing a company which is a member of a group to surrender an amount of EUFT arising to it in an accounting period to another company which is a member of the same group.

AMOUNT OF EUFT AVAILABLE FOR SURRENDER

4(1) Subject to paragraph (2), the amount of EUFT arising in an accounting period in the cases set out in sections 806A and 806B that may be surrendered by the surrendering company to a claimant company must not exceed the amount (if any) that remains (**"the remaining amount"**) after the surrendering company has fully utilised in accordance with the relevant provisions of sections 806D to 806G the EUFT arising in that accounting period.

4(2) For the purposes of paragraph (1), where the surrendering company chooses not to utilise section 806D(4)(c) or (5)(c) (carry back provision), the remaining amount shall be computed in accordance with that paragraph as if the surrendering company had in fact fully utilised that provision.

4(3) Where the surrendering company carries on life assurance business, the policy holders' share of the amount of EUFT attributable to BLAGAB may not be surrendered to another company in the group.

4(4) Where–

(a)   an amount of EUFT is surrendered to a claimant company, and

(b)   the claimant company carries on life assurance business,

the amount surrendered may not be set against the policy holders' share of the corporation tax attributable by virtue of section 797(1) to any single dividend referable by virtue of section 432A to the claimant company's BLAGAB.

4(5) In this regulation–

"**BLAGAB**" means basic life assurance and general annuity business within the meaning given by section 431F;

"**the policy holders' share of the amount of EUFT attributable to BLAGAB**" means the relevant fraction of–

(a) where all of the company's long-term business within the meaning given by section 431(2) is BLAGAB, the whole of the amount of EUFT;

(b) in any other case, so much of the amount of EUFT as is attributable to BLAGAB by virtue of section 804B(3) or (4);

"**the policy holders' share of the corporation tax attributable to any single dividend referable to the claimant company's BLAGAB**" means the relevant fraction of that tax;

"**the relevant fraction**" means the fraction arrived at by dividing–

(a) the policy holders' share of the company's relevant profits for the relevant accounting period, by

(b) the company's BLAGAB profits for that period,

and, for the purposes of this definition, "the policy holders' share of the company's relevant profits" shall be construed in accordance with sections 88(3) and 89 of the Finance Act 1989 and "the company's BLAGAB profits" shall be construed in accordance with section 431(2YB) of the Income and Corporation Taxes Act 1988;

"**the relevant provisions of sections 806D to 806G**" means all provisions of those sections other than section 806D(4)(b) and (5)(b) (carry forward provision);

"**single dividend**" has the meaning given by section 806E(6).

History – In reg. 4(4) words "by virtue of section 797(1)" and "by virtue of section 432A" inserted by SI 2003/1829, reg. 2(2), with effect from 7 August 2003, in relation to distributions made on or after 9 April 2003 in accounting periods ending on or after 7 August 2003.
In reg. 4(5), in the definition of "the relevant fraction", the words "section 431(2YB) of the Income and Corporation Taxes Act 1988" substituted for the words "section 89(1B) of that Act" by SI 2008/2681, with effect in relation to accounting periods beginning on or after 1 January 2008 and ending after 30 October 2008.
In reg. 4(5) definition of "attributable" omitted by SI 2003/1829, reg. 2(3), with effect from 7 August 2003, in relation to distributions made on or after 9 April 2003 in accounting periods ending on or after 7 August 2003.
In reg. 4(5), in the definition of "BLAGAB" words "within the meaning given by section 431F" inserted by SI 2003/1829, reg. 2(3), with effect from 7 August 2003, in relation to distributions made on or after 9 April 2003 in accounting periods ending on or afer 7 August 2003.
In reg. 4(5), definitions of "the policy holders' share of the amount of EUFT attributable to BLAGAB", "the policy holders' share of the corporation tax attributable to any single dividend referable to the claimant company's BLAGAB" and "the relevant fraction" substituted for definitions of "the policy holder's share of the amount of EUFT attributable to BLAGAB" and "the policy holders' share of the corporation tax attributable to any single dividend referable to the claimant company's BLAGAB" by SI 2003/1829, reg. 2(3), with effect from 7 August 2003, in relation to distributions made on or after 9 April 2003 in accounting periods ending on or afer 7 August 2003.

CLAIMING OF EUFT

5(1) The claimant company may claim the whole or part of the amount of EUFT available for surrender in accordance with regulation 4.

5(2) The amount of EUFT claimed by the claimant company may be utilised by the claimant company in accordance with the provisions of sections 806D to 806G.

ACCOUNTING PERIODS OF SURRENDERING COMPANY AND CLAIMANT COMPANY

6(1) The surrendering company and the claimant company must be members of the same group throughout the accounting period of the surrendering company in which the amount of EUFT available for surrender arises.

6(2) Where the accounting period of the surrendering company in which the amount of EUFT available for surrender arises and the accounting period of the claimant company are not coterminous–

(a) the amount of EUFT arising in that accounting period of the surrendering company which is surrendered to the claimant company in accordance with regulations 4 and 5 shall be treated as if it arose on a dividend received by the claimant company, and

(b) that dividend shall be treated as arising in that one of the claimant company's accounting periods in which falls the last day of the accounting period of the surrendering company in which the amount of EUFT surrendered arises.

Statutory Instruments

CALCULATION OF SCHEDULE D CASE V INCOME WHEN EUFT CLAIMED

7   An amount of EUFT that is utilised by the claimant company in accordance with the provisions of sections 806D to 806G shall not be taken into account as underlying tax under section 795(2)(b) in computing the amount of income of the claimant company.

FORM OF CLAIM AND WITHDRAWAL OF CLAIM

8(1)   The like provisions as those contained in Part VIII of Schedule 18 to the Finance Act 1998 ("Schedule 18") and listed below shall have effect, with necessary modifications, in relation to claims for amounts of EUFT available for surrender as they have effect in relation to claims for group relief.

8(2)   Those provisions of Schedule 18 are paragraphs 67, 68, 70(1), (3) and (4), 71, 72(1) and (4), 73, 75, 75A and 76.

TIME LIMIT FOR CLAIMS

9(1)   A claim for the whole or part of the amount of EUFT available for surrender in an accounting period of the surrendering company may only be made or withdrawn before the expiration of–

(a)   six years after the expiration of that accounting period or, if later,

(b)   one year after the end of the accounting period in which the foreign tax in question is paid.

9(2)   The time limits otherwise applicable to amendment of a company tax return under the Corporation Tax Acts do not apply to an amendment to the extent that it makes or withdraws a claim for the surrender of an amount of EUFT in accordance with these Regulations within the time allowed under paragraph (1).

MISCELLANEOUS PROVISIONS

10(1)   The like provisions as those contained in Chapter IV of Part X of the Taxes Act ("Chapter IV") and listed below shall have effect, with necessary modifications, in relation to claims for amounts of EUFT available for surrender as they have effect in relation to claims for group relief.

10(2)   Those provisions of Chapter IV are sections 402(1), (2), (5) and (6), 410(1), (4) and (5) to (7) and 411(1).

History – In reg. 10(2) reference to "404" omitted by SI 2001/3873, reg. 2, with effect from 5 December 2001.

GENERAL INSURANCE RESERVES (TAX) REGULATIONS 2001

(SI 2001/1757, as amended by SI 2001/3629, SI 2003/2862, SI 2003/2096, SI 2005/3289, SI 2006/3218 and SI 2006/3389)

Made on 8 May 2001 by the Commissioners of Inland Revenue, in exercise of the powers conferred on them by s. 107 of the Finance Act 2000. Operative from 29 May 2001.

CITATION, COMMENCEMENT AND EFFECT

1   These Regulations may be cited as the General Insurance Reserves (Tax) Regulations 2001 and shall come into force on 29th May 2001, and shall have effect for periods of account of general insurers–

(a)   beginning on or after 1st January 2001, and

(b)   ending on or after 29th May 2001.

INTERPRETATION

2(1)   In these Regulations unless the context otherwise requires–

"controlled foreign company" has the meaning in Chapter IV of Part XVII of the Income and Corporation Taxes Act 1988 ("the Taxes Act");

"corporate general insurer" means a general insurer which is a company;

"Schedule 9A" means Schedule 9A to the Companies Act 1985;

"section 107" means section 107 of the Finance Act 2000;

other references to a section, without more, are to that section of the Taxes Act; and **"statutory accounts"**, in relation to a company other than an underwriting member, has the meaning given by section 86(8)(a) and (c) to (e) of the Finance Act 1996.

2(2)   References to a company being connected with another company shall be construed in accordance with section 839(5) to (7).

2(3)   In these Regulations a reference to a numbered Rule is a reference to the Rule in regulation 3 bearing that number.

History – In reg. 2(1) definition of "corporate general insurer" inserted by SI 2003/2862, reg. 4(2), with effect from 5 December 2003, in relation to periods of account ending on or after that date.

Reg. 2(3) inserted by SI 2003/2862, reg. 4(3), with effect from 5 December 2003, in relation to periods of account ending on or after that date.

Cross references – Reg. 10: modification of the concept of "the first earlier period of account".

RECALCULATION OF TECHNICAL PROVISIONS FOR THE PURPOSES OF SECTION 107

3(1)   This regulation and regulation 4 apply for determining for the purposes of section 107 whether an amount representing the whole or part of the technical provisions made and taken into account in computing for tax purposes the profits of a general insurer other than an underwriting member (see regulation 7(2)) for a period of account was excessive or insufficient, and the amount of the excess or deficiency.

3(2)   In the following provisions of this regulation and regulation 4–

"the balance sheet date" means the end of the earlier period of account (as the latter expression is defined in paragraph (3));

"the recalculation date" means the end of the later period of account (as the latter expression is defined in paragraph (3)); and

"relevant transaction" means any disposal or acquisition (in whole or in part) of the rights or liabilities of–

(a)   a corporate general insurer under a contract of insurance; or

(b)   a reinsurer under a contract of reinsurance;

"taken into account" means taken into account in computing for tax purposes the profits of the general insurer's trade for the relevant period of account;

and expressions which are used in Schedule 9A have the same meanings as in that Schedule.

3(3) As at the end of each period of account which begins on or after 1st January 2001 (and the period which is relevant to the calculation in question is referred to as **"the later period of account"**), recalculate the provisions for claims outstanding made and taken into account for each earlier period of account which–

(a)   began on or after 1st January 2000,

(b)   [Omitted by SI 2003/2862, reg. 5(3).]

History – In reg. 3(2) definition of "relevant transaction" inserted by SI 2003/2862, reg. 5(2), with effect from 5 December 2003, in relation to periods of account ending on or after that date.
Reg. 3(3)(b), and the word "and"preceding it, omitted by SI 2003/2862, reg. 5(3), with effect from 5 December 2003, in relation to periods of account ending on or after that date.

Cross references – Reg. 10: modification of the concept of "the first earlier period of account".

Rule 1

1.1. Subject to regulation 5, the calculation under Rules 2 to 9 shall be carried out in sterling, and the sterling discount rate in paragraph (a) of Rule 5.4. shall apply.

Rule 2

2.1. Find out the amount of the provisions for claims outstanding made and taken into account for the earlier period of account which–

(a)   where the earlier period of account is the general insurer's first period of account which began on or after 1st January 2000, were provisions made and taken into account for that period, and

(b)   in any other case, were provisions made and taken into account for that period for liabilities which (according to their treatment in the statutory accounts of the general insurer) arose in respect of that period.

History – In Rule 2.1 para. (a) substituted and in (b) the words "were provisions" substituted for "was provision" by SI 2003/2862, reg. 5(3)(b), with effect from 5 December 2003, in relation to periods of account ending on or after that date.

2.2. The result of this Rule is referred to as **"the original provisions for the earlier period of account"**.

Rule 3

3.1. In relation to the original provisions for the earlier period of account, find out (subject to Rule 4) the cost of settling the liabilities to which the provisions relate, including the amount of–

(a)   claims paid (gross amount, less reinsurer's share), between the balance sheet date and the recalculation date, (calculated in accordance with Note 4 on the profit and loss account format in section B of Chapter I of Part I of Schedule 9A, but as if the references to the addition and deduction of provisions for claims were omitted),

(b)   bonuses and rebates (if any), net of reinsurance (calculated in accordance with Note 5 on that profit and loss account format),

(c)   premiums (if any) paid, or treated as paid, between the balance sheet date and the recalculation date, under a reinsurance to close contract, qualifying contract or relevant transaction, and

(d)   provisions (if any) for claims outstanding, net of reinsurance, which are carried forward as at the recalculation date (calculated in accordance with paragraphs 43 and 47 of Schedule 9A), and which are taken into account for the later period of account.

History – In Rule 3.1 the words ", qualifying contract or relevant transaction" substituted for "or qualifying contract" by SI 2003/2862, reg. 5(3)(c), with effect from 5 December 2003, in relation to periods of account ending on or after that date.

3.2. Any such payment, bonus, rebate, deemed payment or provision is referred to in Rule 5 (except in paragraph (a) of Rule 5.2.) as a **"liability"**.

Rule 4

4.1 This Rule applies where either Rule 4.1A or 4.1B is satisfied.

History – Rule 4.1–4.1C substituted for 4.1 by SI 2003/2862, reg. 5(3)(d), with effect from 5 December 2003, in relation to periods of account ending on or after that date.
In Rule 4.2 the words "or the relevant transaction" inserted after "qualifying contract" by SI 2003/2862, reg. 5(3)(e), with effect from 5 December 2003, in relation to periods of account ending on or after that date.
In Rule 4.2(a) the words "or that transaction" inserted after "under that contract" by SI 2003/2862, reg. 5(3)(e), with effect from 5 December 2003, in relation to periods of account ending on or after that date.

4.1A This Rule is satisfied if–

(a)   on or after 1st January 2004 a corporate general insurer enters into a qualifying contract, other than a reinsurance to close contract, with another person ("the reinsurer") and–

　　(i)   the corporate general insurer and the reinsurer are connected companies; or

　　(ii)   the qualifying contract is, or forms part of, a transaction, as a result of which a company connected with the corporate general insurer ("the connected company") directly or indirectly agrees to meet a liability of the corporate general insurer or any further liability representing that liability, through any number of such agreements ("the replacement agreements"); and

(b)   Rule 4.1C applies.

History – Rule 4.1–4.1C substituted for 4.1 by SI 2003/2862, reg. 5(3)(d), with effect from 5 December 2003, in relation to periods of account ending on or after that date.

4.1B   This Rule is satisfied if–

(a)   on or after 1st January 2004, as a result of–

    (i)   a relevant transaction between a corporate general insurer and a company with which it is connected ("a connected company"), or

    (ii)   a series of transactions having the same effect as a relevant transaction between a corporate general insurer and a connected company,

the connected company directly or indirectly replaces the corporate general insurer as a party to a contract of insurance including by way of novation; and

(b)   Rule 4.1C applies.

History – Rule 4.1–4.1C substituted for 4.1 by SI 2003/2862, reg. 5(3)(d), with effect from 5 December 2003, in relation to periods of account ending on or after that date.

4.1C   This Rule applies if the person assuming the liabilities–

(a)   is not within the charge to corporation tax in respect of income arising from the qualifying contract or the relevant replacement agreement, assuming there were such income; and

(b)   is not a controlled foreign company in relation to which–

    (i)   an apportionment under section 747(3) falls to be made regarding, or

    (ii)   section 748(1)(a) applies to,

the accounting period in which the qualifying contract is made.

This is subject to the following qualification.

This Rule applies only to the extent that the qualifying contract reinsures liabilities represented in technical provisions which the corporate general insurer has previously taken into account.

In this Rule **"the person assuming the liabilities"** means, as the case requires, the reinsurer referred to in Rule 4.1A(a) or the connected company referred to in Rule 4.1A(a)(ii).

History – Rule 4.1–4.1C substituted for 4.1 by SI 2003/2862, reg. 5(3)(d), with effect from 5 December 2003, in relation to periods of account ending on or after that date.

4.2.   Where, or to the extent that, this Rule applies, the qualifying contract or the relevant transaction shall be ignored for the purposes of Rule 3, and accordingly–

(a)   premiums paid under that contract or that transaction shall be ignored for the purposes of paragraph (c) of Rule 3.1., and

(b)   the claims paid, bonuses and rebates and provisions for claims for the purposes of paragraphs (a), (b) and (d) of Rule 3.1. shall be calculated without deduction for reinsurance, so that each such liability shall be calculated gross.

History – In Rule 4.2 the words "or the relevant transaction" inserted after "qualifying contract" by SI 2003/2862, reg. 5(3)(e), with effect from 5 December 2003, in relation to periods of account ending on or after that date.
In Rule 4.2(a) the words "or that transaction" inserted after "under that contract" by SI 2003/2862, reg. 5(3)(e), with effect from 5 December 2003, in relation to periods of account ending on or after that date.

Rule 5

5.1.   Discount the amount of each liability as defined in Rule 3 to the present value of the liability as at the balance sheet date, by the application of a discount factor, reflecting the time value of money between the balance sheet date and the date of payment of the liability (the period between those dates being referred to as **"the discount period"**), subject to Rule 5.2.

5.2.   The discount period for any liability shall not extend later than 10 years after–

(a)   the date on which the corresponding liability to which the provisions relate (as referred to in Rule 3.1. in the words preceding paragraph (a)) arose (within the meaning in paragraph (b) of Rule 2.1.), or

(b)   the end of the general insurer's first period of account which began on or after 1st January 2000, whichever is the later.

5.3.   It shall be assumed for the purposes of this calculation that the provisions mentioned in paragraph (d) of Rule 3.1. were a single payment made by the general insurer on the recalculation date.

5.4.   The discount rate for the whole of the discount period to be used in calculating the discount factor shall be determined as follows–

(a) in a case where the sterling discount rate is to apply (see Rule 1), the discount rate shall be found from the formula–

$(A - 2.3$ per cent), or nil per cent, whichever is the greater;

(b) in a case where the calculations under these Regulations are carried out in Australian dollars, Canadian dollars, euro, Japanese yen, Swiss francs or United States dollars ("the relevant foreign currency"), the discount rate shall be found from the formula–

$(A - 2.3$ per cent) $+ (B - C)$, or nil per cent, whichever is the greater.

History – In Rule 5.4 the words "where the calculations under these Regulations are carried out in Australian dollars, Canadian dollars, euro, Japanese yen, Swiss francs or United States dollars ("the relevant foreign currency")" substituted for "where a foreign currency discount rate is to apply (see regulation 5)" by SI 2003/2862, reg. 5(3)(f), with effect from 5 December 2003, in relation to periods of account ending on or after that date.

5.5. In this Rule–

A is the average of the gross redemption yields, expressed as a percentage, applicable to 5-year British Government Stocks as compiled by the Financial Times, the Institute of Actuaries and the Faculty of Actuaries, which were compiled for each of the first five business days beginning with the day on which the balance sheet date fell or, if that day was not a business day, the first business day thereafter;

B is the London Interbank Offered Rate, in the market which exists between banks in London for the purpose of borrowing and lending funds and dealing in currencies, at which deposits for a term of 12 months were offered in the relevant foreign currency on the day on which the balance sheet date fell (or if that day was not a business day, the first business day thereafter) as determined by the British Banking Association; and

C has the same meaning as B, but with the word **"sterling"** substituted for the words **"the relevant foreign currency"**.

5.6. The discount shall in principle be computed separately for each liability, save that statistical methods may be used where they may be expected to give approximately the same result as individual calculations.

5.7. Aggregate the discounted liabilities and the result is referred to as **"the recalculated provisions"** for the earlier period of account.

Rule 6

6.1. Compare the difference between–

(a) the original provisions for the earlier period of account, and

(b) the recalculated provisions for the earlier period of account,

with a margin for error of 5 per cent of the recalculated provisions for the earlier period of account.

Rule 7

7.1. If the amount of the difference does not exceed the margin for error, the difference is assumed to be nil, for the purposes of that period's recalculation.

7.2. If the amount of the difference exceeds the margin for error, deduct the margin for error from the difference, for the purposes of that period's recalculation.

7.3. The result of Rule 7 represents the cumulative excess or deficiency found from the recalculation under this regulation–

(a) in the later period of account, and

(b) in any periods of account which fell between the earlier period of account and the later period of account **("intervening periods")**,

in relation to the same earlier period of account.

Rule 8

8.1. Compare–

(a) the result of Rule 7, with

(b) the aggregate excess or deficiency found by combining the results of the recalculation under this regulation in any intervening periods in relation to the same earlier period of account

and find out the adjustment (if any) to the amount mentioned in paragraph (b) above which is necessary to make it equal the amount mentioned in paragraph (a) above. If the adjustment is an excess, that is the amount of the excess referred to in section 107(2). If the adjustment is a deficiency, that is subject to Rule 8A the amount of the deficiency referred to in section 107(3).

History – In Rule 8.1 the words "the same earlier period of account" inserted in para. (b), the words "subject to Rule 8A" inserted following para. (b), and (b)(i) and (ii) omitted by SI 2003/2862, reg. 5(3)(g), with effect from 5 December 2003, in relation to periods of account ending on or after that date.

8.2. Where there has been no intervening period (as mentioned in paragraph (b) of Rule 7.3.), or the result of paragraph (b) of Rule 8.1. is neither an excess nor a deficiency, the result of Rule 7 shall be the amount of the excess referred to in section 107(2), or the amount of the deficiency referred to in section 107(3), as the case may be.

8A.1 This Rule applies if, in respect of the provisions made for the earlier period of account–

(a)   an election has been made under section 107(4) for the earlier period of account in question, and

(b)   the result of applying Rule 8 is a deficiency.

History – Rule 8A.1 inserted by SI 2003/2862, reg. 5(3)(h), with effect from 5 December 2003, in relation to periods of account ending on or after that date.

8A.2 Where Rule 8A.1 applies, apply Rules 6 to 8 but, in carrying out the calculation made at the end of the later period of account, add to the amount of the original provisions–

(a)   the amount of any losses set off, under section 393 of the Taxes Act (losses other than terminal losses of a trade) against the trading income of the company's general insurance business for the period of account for which an election under section 107(4) was made in respect of the provisions for the earlier period of account; and

(b)   any amount which remains to be set off against the profits of the company's general insurance business for the period of account for which an election under section 107(4) was made in respect of the provisions for the earlier period of account under–

    (i)   section 393A of the Taxes Act (trading losses: set off against the profits of the same or an earlier accounting period);

    (ii)   Chapter 4 of Part 10 of the Taxes Act (group relief);

    (iii)   section 83 of, and Schedule 8 to the Finance Act 1996 (non-trading deficit on loan relationships);

    (iv)   paragraph 35 of Schedule 29 to the Finance Act 2002 (non-trading losses on intangible fixed assets); and

    (v)   other charges on the income of the company;

    after treating any other profits of the general insurer for the earlier period as being reduced in priority to the profits of its general insurance business.

    This is subject to the following qualifications.

History – Rule 8A.2 inserted by SI 2003/2862, reg. 5(3)(h), with effect from 5 December 2003, in relation to periods of account ending on or after that date.

8A.3 The qualifications referred to in Rule 8A.2 are that–

(a)   the total amount added in accordance with it to the provisions for all earlier periods of account taken together shall not exceed the sum of the amounts found under paragraphs (a) and (b) of that Rule; and

(b)   the adjustment made under that Rule shall not exceed the amount of the technical provisions for the earlier period of account for which an election under section 107(4) was made in respect of the provision for the earlier period.

History – In Rule 8A.3 the words "for which an election under section 107(4) was made in respect of the provision for the earlier period" inserted by SI 2005/3289, reg. 3(2), with effect from 21 December 2005.
Rule 8A.3 inserted by SI 2003/2862, reg. 5(3)(h), with effect from 5 December 2003, in relation to periods of account ending on or after that date.

8A.4 Compare the result of applying Rule 8A.2 with that found before applying it.

If both the amounts are deficiencies, for the purposes only of Rule 9 the smaller deficiency is the amount referred to in section 107(3).

If the result of applying Rule 8A.2 is an excess–

(a)   it is disregarded for the purposes of section 107(2); and

(b)   the deficiency produced by Rule 8 is disregarded for the purposes of section 107(3).

History – Rule 8A.4 inserted by SI 2003/2862, reg. 5(3)(h), with effect from 5 December 2003, in relation to periods of account ending on or after that date.

8A.5 If any amount mentioned in Rule 8A.2 is amended in accordance with any provision of the Taxes Act, the adjustment made under that Rule shall be amended accordingly.

History – Rule 8A.5 inserted by SI 2003/2862, reg. 5(3)(h), with effect from 5 December 2003, in relation to periods of account ending on or after that date.

Rule 9

9.1. Interest shall be calculated on the amount of the result of Rule 8, at the rate or rates specified in respect of the period mentioned below in Regulation 3ZA(1) of the Taxes (Interest Rate) Regulations 1989–

(a)   but as if there were deducted from the amount of such interest corporation tax at the rate fixed for companies generally (within the meaning in section 13(1) of the Taxes Act) for the later period of account, and

(b)   save that the rate of interest is a compound rate, with annual rests,

from the date when corporation tax for the earlier period of account became due and payable until the stop date.

History – In Rule 9.1 the words "at the rate or rates specified in respect of the period mentioned below" substituted for "at the rate specified ", "from the amount of such interest" substituted for "therefrom", and "until the stop date" substituted for "until the date when corporation tax for the later period of account becomes due and payable (in both cases, determined in accordance with section 59D of the Taxes Management Act 1970, treating those periods as if they were accounting periods)" by SI 2003/2862, reg. 5(3)(i), with effect from 5 December 2003, in relation to periods of account ending on or after that date.

9.1A Interest shall be calculated on the amount of the result of Rule 8 or 8A (as the case requires) in respect of the period–

(a)   beginning with the stop date, and

(b)   ending with the date when corporation tax for the later period of account becomes due and payable at the rate specified in regulation 3ZA(1) of the Taxes (Interest Rate) Regulations 1989,

but as if there were deducted from the amount of such interest corporation tax at the rate fixed for companies generally (within the meaning of section 13(1) of the Taxes Act) for the later period of account.

History – Rule 9.1A inserted by SI 2003/2862, reg. 5(3)(j), with effect from 5 December 2003, in relation to periods of account ending on or after that date.

9.1B In Rules 9.1 and 9.1A the "stop date" is the earlier of–

(a)   the date when corporation tax for the later period of account becomes due and payable; and

(b)   the tenth anniversary of the date on which corporation tax for the earlier period of account became due and payable.

Subsection (1) of section 59D of the Taxes Management Act 1970 (day when corporation tax due and payable) applies for the purposes of this Rule and Rules 9.1 and 9.1A as it applies for the purposes of that section but as if the references in that subsection to an accounting period were to a period of account.

History – Rule 9.1B inserted by SI 2003/2862, reg. 5(3)(j), with effect from 5 December 2003, in relation to periods of account ending on or after that date.

9.2. Where the later period of account falls in more than one financial year, the rates of corporation tax for those financial years shall be apportioned to the later period of account on a daily basis.

9.3. The amount of interest so calculated is the amount to be treated as a receipt or an expense, as the case may be, in accordance with section 107, and is the amount of a receipt or expense, as the case may be, referred to, or to be taken into account in a computation of profits and losses under, [sections] 92 to 92C of the Finance Act 1993, in a case where those sections apply.

History – In Rule 9.3 the words"sections 92 to 92C" substituted for the words "sections 92 to 93A" by SI 2005/3289, reg. 3(3), with effect from 21 December 2005.
In Rule 9.3 the words "92 to 93A" substituted for "sections 92 to 94" by SI 2003/2862, reg. 5(3)(k), with effect from 5 December 2003, in relation to periods of account ending on or after that date.
Notes – SI 2001/1757 and FA 2000, s. 107 require use of interest rate as set out in Rule 9. For periods of account ending on 31 December 2002 the rate is 5 per cent and for periods of account ending on 31 December 2001 the rate is 5.25 per cent.

Rule 10

10.1. No amount representing provisions for unearned premiums or provisions for unexpired risks shall be determined as excessive or insufficient for the purposes of section 107.

PROVISIONS SUPPLEMENTING REGULATION 3

4(1) Paragraph (2) applies where a general insurer (**"the transferor"**) transfers the whole or part of its general business to another body (**"the transferee"**) by–

(a)   a transfer effected under a scheme falling within section 105 of the Financial Services and Markets Act 2000, including an excluded scheme falling within Case 2, 3 or 4 of subsection (3) of that section, or

(ab)   a scheme which would be an insurance business transfer scheme but for section 105(1)(b) of the Financial Services and Markets Act 2000;

(b)   a transfer in accordance with an authorisation granted outside the United Kingdom for the purposes of Article 12 of Council Directive 92/49/EC on the co-ordination of the laws, regulations and administrative provisions relating to direct insurance other than life assurance and amending Directives 73/329/EEC and 88/357/EEC,

on or after the date on which these Regulations come into force.

4(1A)   Paragraph (2) also applies where, as a result of–

(a)   a relevant transaction effected after 5th December 2003 between a corporate general insurer and another company–

     (i)   with which it is connected, and

     (ii)   which is within the charge to corporation tax in respect of that transaction, or

(b)   a series of transactions having the same effect as a relevant transaction effected after 5th December 2003 between two companies which–

     (i)   have been connected with each other at any time in the course of that series of transactions, and

     (ii)   are within the charge to corporation tax in respect of the relevant transaction,

     one of those companies directly or indirectly replaces the other as the insurer under a contract of insurance, or as the reinsurer under a contract of reinsurance, including (in either case) by way of novation.

4(2)   Where this paragraph applies, the transferor and the transferee shall be treated for the purposes of section 107 and regulation 3 as if–

(a)   technical provisions made and taken into account by the transferor, so far as they relate to the general business transferred, had been made and taken into account by the transferee,

(ab)   an election made under section 107(4) by the transferor had been made by the transferee; and

(b)   any other act or thing mentioned in Rules 1 to 9 in regulation 3(3) and regulation 5 which was done to or by the transferor, so far as it relates to the general business transferred, had been done to or by the transferee.

4(2A)   In paragraph (2)(a) **"technical provisions made and taken into account by the transferor"** means, in relation to a period of account in which a transfer of business occurs, the technical provisions which would have been made and taken into account had the transferor's period of account ended immediately before the transfer.

The time at which the technical provisions are treated as made and taken into account by this paragraph shall be treated as the end of a period of account for the purposes of regulation 3(3) (and an election under section 107(4) may accordingly be made in respect of that period).

4(3)   Where Rule 4 in regulation 3(3) would apply but for the condition in Rule 4.1C. not being satisfied, in a case falling within Rule 4.1A(a)(i). the reinsurer, and in a case falling withinRule 4.1A(a)(ii) the connected company (and the relevant person is referred to as **"the transferee"**), and the corporate general insurer, shall be treated for the purposes of section 107 and regulation 3 as if–

(a)   technical provisions made and taken into account by the corporate general insurer, so far as they relate to the liabilities reinsured, had been made and taken into account by the transferee,

(b)   premiums paid under the contract were ignored, and

(c)   any other act or thing mentioned in Rules 1 to 10 in regulation 3(3) and regulation 5 which was done to or by the corporate general insurer, so far as it relates to the liabilities reinsured, had been done to or by the transferee.

History – Reg. 4(1)(a) substituted by SI 2001/3629, art. 193 with effect in relation to any transfer under a scheme falling within s. 105 of the Financial Services and Markets Act 2000, including an excluded scheme falling within Case 2, 3 or 4 of subs. (3) of that section.

Reg. 4(1)(ab) and (b) substituted for reg. 4(1)(b) by SI 2003/2862, reg. 6(2), with effect from 5 December 2003, in relation to periods of account ending on or after that date.

Reg. 4(1)(b) previously amended by SI 2001/3629, art. 193 with effect in relation to any transfer in relation to which section 116 of the Financial Services and Markets Act 2000 applies.

Reg. 4(1A) inserted by SI 2003/2862, reg, 6(3), with effect from 5 December 2003, in relation to periods of account ending on or after that date.

In reg. 4(2) the word "and" omitted at the end of para. (a), and para. (ab) inserted by SI 2003/2862, reg. 6(4), with effect from 5 December 2003, in relation to periods of account ending on or after that date.

Reg. 4(2A) inserted by SI 2003/2862, reg, 6(5), with effect from 5 December 2003, in relation to periods of account ending on or after that date.

In reg. 4(3) the following amendments made by SI 2003/2862, reg. 6(6), with effect from 5 December 2003, in relation to periods of account ending on or after that date:

- words "Rule 4.1C" substituted for "paragraph (c) of Rule 4.1";
- words "Rule 4.1A(a)(i)" substituted for "paragraph (b)(i) of Rule 4.1";
- words "Rule 4.1A(a)(ii)" substituted for "paragraph (b)(ii) thereof";

Statutory Instruments

- words "the corporate general insurer" substituted for "the general insurer (as defined in that Rule)";
- words "corporate" inserted before " general insurer" in paras. (a) and (c);
- words "Rules 1 to 10" substituted for "Rules 1 to 9" in para. (c).

Cross references – Reg. 10: modification of the concept of "the first earlier period of account".

CURRENCY ACCOUNTING AND RELEVANT DISCOUNT RATE

5(1) Subject to paragraph (3), in respect of a general insurer's business to which section 92B of the Finance Act 1993 applies, any calculation required under these Regulations shall be made in the functional currency.

5(2) Subject to paragraph (3), in respect of a general insurer's business to which section 92C of the Finance Act 1993 applies, any calculation required under these Regulations shall be made in the accounts currency.

5(3) In respect of any foreign operation, so much of any calculation required under these Regulations as relates to that operation shall be made in the currency in which the activities of the foreign operation are conducted.

5(4) Where paragraph (3) applies any amount of interest calculated in accordance with these Regulations to be treated as a receipt or expense under Rule 9.3 shall be translated into the currency in which profits or losses are required to be computed under sections 92 to 92C of the Finance Act 1993 by reference to the appropriate exchange rate.

5(5) If the currency determined by paragraphs (1) to (3) to be used in calculations under these Regulations is one of the currencies mentioned in paragraph (b) of Rule 5.4, the discount rate to be applied to those calculations shall be found in accordance with the formula in that paragraph, and in any other case shall be found in accordance with the formula in paragraph (a) of Rule 5.4.

5(6) In this regulation–

"**accounts currency**" has the meaning given in section 92C(1) and (2) of the Finance Act 1993;

"**appropriate exchange rate**" has the meaning given in section 92D(2) of the Finance Act 1993;

"**foreign operation**" means–

(a) in the case of a general insurer not resident in the United Kingdom, its permanent establishment in the United Kingdom, and

(b) in any other case, an entity that is a subsidiary, associate, joint venture or branch of a general insurer the activities of which are conducted in a currency other than the functional currency;

"**functional currency**" has the meaning given in section 92E(3) of the Finance Act 1993.

History – Reg. 5 substituted by SI 2005/3289, reg. 4(1), with effect from 21 December 2005, subject to the following transitional provisions at SI 2005/3289, reg. 4(2) and (3) – which read as follows:

"**4(2)** If an election was made before 31 December 2003 under regulation 5(1) as it stood immediately before the substitution of regulation 5 made by the General Insurance Reserves (Tax) (Amendment) Regulations 2003, the currency chosen under regulation 5(5) as it stood before that substitution may continue to be used as it might have been had the substitution made by paragraph (1) not occurred.

4(3) The currency determined by regulation 5 as it stood immediately before the substitution made by paragraph (1) to be used in calculations in respect of part of a general insurer's business may continue to be used in relation to that part of the general insurer's business as it might have been had the substitution not occurred."

Former reg. 5 read as follows:

"ACCOUNTING IN FOREIGN CURRENCIES AND RELEVANT DISCOUNT RATES

5(1) In respect of that part of a general insurer's business to which subsection (1) of section 747A of the Taxes Act applies, any calculation required under these Regulations shall be made in the same currency as that required to be used, for the purposes of Chapter 4 of Part 17 of the Taxes Act, by subsection (2) of that section.

5(2) In respect of that part of a general insurer's business to which section 93A of the Finance Act 1993 applies, so much of any calculation required under these Regulations as relates to business in respect of which financial statements and records are prepared in the relevant foreign currency (within the meaning of that section) shall be made in that currency.

5(3) In respect of that part of a general insurer's business to which section 93 of the Finance Act 1993 applies–

(a) any calculation required under these Regulations shall be made in the relevant foreign currency (within the meaning of that section); and

(b) the exchange rate to be used for determining the sterling equivalent of the amount of the receipt or expense found under Rule 9.3 is the London closing exchange rate.

5(4) In respect of so much of general insurer's business as does not fall within the previous provisions of this regulation section 94AA of the Finance Act 1993 shall apply to the calculation of an excess or deficiency under regulation 3 as it applies to a computation under section 92(1) of that Act.

5(5) If the foreign currency used in the calculations under paragraphs (1) to (3) is one of the currencies mentioned in paragraph (b) of Rule 5.4, the discount rate to be applied to those calculations shall be found in accordance with the formula in that paragraph, and in any other case shall be found in accordance with the formula in paragraph (a) of Rule 5.4."

EXCLUDED DESCRIPTIONS OF GENERAL INSURER

6(1)   The descriptions of general insurer which are excluded from the operation of section 107(1) to (4) are–

(a)   a company which is in insolvent liquidation (within the meaning in section 214(6) of the Insolvency Act 1986 (**"the Act"**) or Article 178(6) of the Insolvency (Northern Ireland) Order 1989 (**"the Order"**)), where the exclusion takes effect from the date on which it goes into liquidation (within the meaning in section 247(2) of the Act or Article 6(2) of the Order);

(b)   a company in relation to which an administration order has been made under Article 21 of the Order or a company which is in administration within the meaning of Schedule B1 to the Act;

(c)   a company in respect of which a provisional liquidator is appointed under section 135 of the Act or Article 115 of the Order; and

(d)   a company in respect of which a relevant arrangement or compromise (within the meaning in section 74(2) of the Taxes Act) is in force.

This is subject to the following qualification.

6(2)   A general insurer is not excluded from the operation of section 107 by virtue of paragraph (1)(c) or (d) unless–

(a)   it is insolvent at the time the provisional liquidator is appointed or the relevant arrangement or compromise comes into force; or

(b)   in a case falling within paragraph (1)(d), it would be insolvent but for the relevant arrangement or compromise coming into force.

History – In reg. 6(1)(b) (reference to para. (1) omitted from SI 2003/2096 in error) the words "section 8 of the Act or" omitted, and the words "or a company which is in administration within the meaning of Schedule B1 to the Act" substituted by SI 2003/2096, art. 5 and Sch., para. 78, with effect from 15 September 2003. Transitional provisions are contained in art. 6.
In reg. 6 the following amendments made by SI 2003/2862, reg. 8(3), with effect from 5 December 2003, in relation to periods of account ending on or after that date:
- Reg. 6 renumbered as reg. 6(1);
- words "is in" substituted for "has gone into" in para. 1(a);
- words "is" substituted for "has been" in para. 1(c);
- words "is in force" substituted for "has taken effect" in para. 1(d);
- words "This is subject to the following qualification." inserted at the end of reg. 6(1).
Reg. 6(2) inserted by SI 2003/2862, reg. 8(4), with effect from 5 December 2003, in relation to periods of account ending on or after that date:

Cross references – Reg. 10: modification of the concept of "the first earlier period of account".

Transitional – SI 2003/2096, art. 6, contains transitional provisions so that the former rules remain in effect where a petition for an administration order was presented prior to 15 September 2003.

"TECHNICAL PROVISIONS" IN RELATION TO AN UNDERWRITING MEMBER

7(1)   **"Technical provisions"** in relation to an underwriting member and the premium paid or treated as paid by him under a reinsurance to close contract means–

(a)   where the member is a continuing member, that is, a member not only of the syndicate as a member of which he pays, or is treated as paying, the premium (**"the reinsured syndicate"**) but also of the syndicate as a member of which he receives or is treated as receiving it or part of it (**"the reinsurer syndicate"**), so much of the premium as equals–

    (i)   the amount of the premium which he pays or is treated as paying, or

    (ii)   the amount of the premium which he receives or is treated as receiving,

whichever is the lesser (subject to sub-paragraph (b)); and

(b)   where the member is not entitled to participate in the underwriting business of the reinsurer syndicate, or his entitlement to participate in either of the reinsured syndicate or the reinsurer syndicate is less than 4 per cent of the whole, none of the premium.

7(2)   Regulations 3 to 5 shall apply to–

(a)   any premium or part of a premium treated as **"technical provisions"** by paragraph (1)(a), with the modifications to regulation 3(3) contained in paragraphs (3) to (5), and

(b)   any provisions or part of provisions treated as **"technical provisions"** by paragraph (8), with the modifications contained in paragraphs (3), (4), (5)(c) and (7).

7(3)   In regulation 3(3) in the words preceding sub-paragraph (a), for the reference to provisions for claims outstanding there shall be substituted a reference to technical provisions.

7(4)   In Rule 2–

(a)   for the reference to provisions for claims outstanding, there shall be substituted a reference to technical provisions, and

(b)   for paragraph (b) of Rule 2.1. there shall be substituted–

"(b)   in any other case, were provisions for liabilities arising directly from the underwriting member's membership of one or more syndicates, whose closing year was the year immediately preceding the earlier period of account, but excluding liabilities which the member acquired by means of a reinsurance to close contract, the premium for which was treated as a technical provision for the same member for that preceding year."

7(5)   In Rule 3–

(a)   in paragraph (a) **"claims paid"** shall be construed as a reference to claims paid by the member in consequence of his membership of the reinsurer syndicate or of any further syndicate which, directly or indirectly, reinsures the liabilities to which the provisions relate under any further reinsurance to close contracts;

(b)   where any claim, bonus, rebate or premium was paid by the member as a member of the reinsurer syndicate, the payment shall be treated for the purposes of Rules 3 and 5 as made one year later than the date of the actual payment; and

(c)   in Rule 3.1.(d) for the reference to provisions for claims outstanding, there shall be substituted a reference to provisions made for the unpaid liabilities of the reinsurer syndicate where it is an open syndicate.

7(6)   [Reg. 7(6) omitted by SI 2003/2862, reg. 9(4).]

7(7)   The modification contained in this paragraph is the modification to Rule 3 in paragraph (5)(b) omitting the words "as a member of the reinsurer syndicate".

7(8)   **"Technical provisions"** in relation to an underwriting member and the provisions made for the unpaid liabilities of an open syndicate of which he is a member means–

(a)   where the member's entitlement to participate in the underwriting business of the open syndicate is equal to or more than 4 per cent of the whole, the share of those provisions which corresponds to his proportionate entitlement; and

(b)   in any other case, none of the provisions.

7(9)   In determining a member's entitlement to participate in the business of a syndicate, or share of a premium, for the purposes of paragraphs (1) and (8), there shall be attributed to a member which is a company any entitlement to participate in the relevant syndicate of any company which is connected with the member.

7(10)   In a case falling within the provisions of both paragraphs (1) and (9), where–

(a)   there is a change in the entitlement of a company to participate, as between the reinsured syndicate and the reinsurer syndicate, such that,

(b)   the reinsurance to close contract has the same financial effect as if a liability were transferred from that company to a company connected with it,

the provisions of sub-paragraphs (a), (ab) and (b) of regulation 4(2) shall to that extent apply as if there were a transfer of business between those companies.

7(11)   A syndicate's managing agent (within the meaning in Chapter III of Part II of the Finance Act 1993) shall, on request from a member or former member of the syndicate, provide the member with the information which he needs, and which is within the agent's possession or power, to make a recalculation under regulation 3 (as applied by paragraph (2)) in relation to his proportionate entitlement in the syndicate.

History – In reg. 7 the following amendments made by SI 2003/2862, reg. 9, with effect from 5 December 2003, in relation to periods of account ending on or after that date:
- words "(5)" substituted for "(6)" in para. 2(a);
- words ", (6)" omitted from para. 2(b);
- words "were provisions" substituted for "was provision" in para. 4(b);
- words "sub-paragraphs (a), (ab) and (b) of regulation 4(2)" substituted for "regulation 4(2)(a) and (b)" in reg. 7(10).
Reg. 7(6) omitted by SI 2003/2862, reg. 9(4), with effect from 5 December 2003, in relation to periods of account ending on or after that date.

Cross references – Reg. 10: modification of the concept of "the first earlier period of account".

ELECTIONS UNDER SECTION 107(4), OR PARAGRAPH 4(2) OF SCHEDULE 24 TO THE TAXES ACT

8(1)   An election by a general insurer for the purposes of section 107(4) or for the purposes of paragraph 4(2) of Schedule 24 to the Taxes Act may be made or withdrawn at any time up to whichever is the last of the following dates–

(a)   the first anniversary of the filing date for the company tax return of the company making the election for the period of account in respect of which the election is made;

(b)   if notice of enquiry is given into that return, 30 days after the enquiry is completed;

(c)   if, after such an enquiry, the Board amend the return under paragraph 34(2) of Schedule 18 to the Finance Act 1998, 30 days after the notice of the amendment is issued; and

(d)   if an appeal is brought against such an amendment, 30 days after the date on which the appeal is finally determined.

8(1A)   Paragraph (1) applies to an underwriting member other than a body corporate with the substitution for paragraphs (a) to (c) of—

> "(a)   the first anniversary of 31st January next following the end of the year of assessment in which falls the end of the period of account in respect of which the election is made;
>
> (b)   if notice of enquiry is given into the underwriting member's tax return for that year of assessment, 30 days after the enquiry is completed;
>
> (c)   if after such an enquiry the Board amend the return under section 28A of the Taxes Management Act 1970, 30 days after the amendment of the return;".

8(2)   Where a general insurer delivers a tax return based wholly or partly on accounts drawn up using the method described in paragraph 52 of Schedule 9A (which provides for a technical provision to be made in the accounts which is later replaced by a provision for estimated claims outstanding) the period in paragraph (1)(a) is extended until two years from the date on which the provision was replaced.

8(3)   Where a general insurer which is a controlled foreign company draws up accounts using a method falling within section 755B(2), the period of twenty months mentioned in paragraph 4(2) of Schedule 24 to the Taxes Act (elections by a United Kingdom resident company or companies) shall be extended until two years immediately following the close of the underwriting year (within the meaning in section 754AA(11)).

8(4)   An election under section 107(4) by a controlled foreign company may be communicated, on its behalf, by the person or persons resident in the United Kingdom by whom it is controlled to the Board.

8(5)   An election under section 107(4) shall be made in writing and shall specify—

(a)   the period of account in respect of which the election is made;

(b)   the earlier period or periods of account to which the technical provisions in question relate;

(c)   the amount of technical provisions being disclaimed in respect of each such period; and

(d)   the currency in which the technical provisions being disclaimed are expressed.

History – Reg. 8(1) and (1A) substituted for reg. 8(1) by SI 2003/2862, reg. 10(2), with effect from 5 December 2003, in relation to periods of account ending on or after that date.
In reg. 8(2) the words "paragraph (1)(a)" substituted for "paragraph (1)" by SI 2003/2862, reg. 10(3), with effect from 5 December 2003, in relation to periods of account ending on or after that date. Reg. 8(1).
Reg. 8(4) inserted by SI 2003/2862, reg. 10(4), with effect from 5 December 2003, in relation to periods of account ending on or after that date.
Reg. 8(5) inserted by SI 2003/2862, reg. 10(4), with effect from 5 December 2003, in relation to periods of account ending on or after that date.

Cross references – Reg. 10: modification of the concept of "the first earlier period of account".

GENERALLY

9   For the purposes of any computation under these Regulations any necessary apportionments shall be made and the method of apportionment adopted shall, subject to the express provisions of these Regulations, be just and reasonable.

Cross references – Reg. 10: modification of the concept of "the first earlier period of account".

MODIFICATION: COMPANIES SUBJECT TO THESE REGULATIONS ON OR AFTER 5TH DECEMBER 2003

10(1)   Paragraph (2) applies to a company if any of the following Cases applies.

Case 1

The company is one to which these Regulations first apply on or after 5th December 2003 by reason of its becoming—

(a)   a controlled foreign company on or after that date; or

(b)   subject to corporation tax for the first time on or after that date.

Case 2

The company, already being subject to corporation tax in respect of its general insurance business, is charged to tax under Case I of Schedule D in respect of that business for the first time for a period of account beginning on or after 5th December 2003.

Case 3

The company is a controlled foreign company and the first period of account in respect of which–

(a)   an apportionment falls to be made under section 747(3), or

(b)   section 748(1)(a) applies,

is a period of account ending on or after 5th December 2003.

Case 4

The company is one to which these Regulations apply on 5th December 2003 by reason only of the amendments made by regulation 8 of the General Insurance Reserves (Tax) (Amendment) Regulations 2003 to regulation 6 of these Regulations.

10(2)   In the case of a company to which this paragraph applies, regulations 2 to 9 of these Regulations shall apply as if references to the first earlier period of account were to the period of account preceding that during which the company first becomes subject to these Regulations and references to original technical provisions shall be construed accordingly.

10(3)   If paragraph (2) applies, an election may be made under section 107(4) in respect of the original technical provisions of the period of account preceding that during which the company in question first becomes subject to these Regulations.

History – Reg. 10 inserted by SI 2003/2862, reg. 11, with effect from 5 December 2003, in relation to periods of account ending on or after that date.

Cross references – SI 2006/3218, reg. 11 (revoked as contained technical error): formerly modified reg. 10(1) with effect from 26 December 2006 in relation to periods of account beginning on or after 1 April 2006.
SI 2006/3389, reg. 11: modification of reg. 10(1) with effect from 8 January 2007 with effect for periods of account beginning on or after 1 April 2006.

CAPITAL ALLOWANCES (ENERGY-SAVING PLANT AND MACHINERY) ORDER 2001

(SI 2001/2541, as amended by SI 2002/1818, SI 2003/1744, SI 2004/2093, SI 2005/2424, SI 2006/2233, SI 2007/2165, SI 2008/1916, SI 2009/1863, SI 2010/2286, SI 2011/2221, SI 2012/1832 and SI 2013/1763)

Made on 16 July 2001 by the Treasury, in exercise of the powers conferred upon them by s. 45A(3) and (4), 45B(1), 45C(2)(b) and (3)(b) and 180A(2) of the Capital Allowances Act 2001. Operative from 7 August 2001.

CITATION AND COMMENCEMENT

1   This Order may be cited as the Capital Allowances (Energy-saving Plant and Machinery) Order 2001 and shall come into force on 7th August 2001.

INTERPRETATION

2   In this Order–

"Capital Allowances Act" means the Capital Allowances Act 2001;

"the Energy Technology Criteria List" means the list dated 8 July 2013 and issued by the Secretary of State for Energy and Climate Change on 10 July 2013;

"the Energy Technology Product List" means the list dated 8 July 2013 and issued by the Secretary of State for Energy and Climate Change on 10 July 2013.

History – In art. 2, in the definitions of "Energy Technology Criteria List" and "Energy Technology Product List", "8 July 2013" substituted for "4 July 2012" and "10 July 2013" substituted for "5 July 2012" by SI 2013/1763, art. 3, with effect from 7 August 2013.

In art. 2, in the definition of "Energy Technology Criteria List "4 July 2012" substituted for "25th August 2011" and "5 July 2012" substituted for "1st September 2011" by SI 2012/1832, art. 3, with effect from 2 August 2012.

In art. 2, definition of "Energy Technology Criteria List" substituted by SI 2011/2221, art. 3(a), with effect from 1 October 2011.

In art. 2, definition of "Energy Technology Product List" substituted by SI 2011/2221, art. 3(b), with effect from 1 October 2011.

In art. 2, in the definition of "Energy Technology Criteria List", the words "3rd August 2010" substituted for the words "6th July 2009" in both places by SI 2010/2286, art. 3, with effect from 8 October 2010.

In art. 2, definition of "Energy Technology Criteria List" substituted by SI 2009/1863, art. 2 with effect from 4 August 2009.

Former definition of "Energy Technology Criteria List" substituted by SI 2008/1916, art. 2 with effect from 11 August 2008.

Former definition of "Energy Technology Criteria List" substituted by SI 2007/2165, art. 2(2), with effect from 16 August 2007.

Former definition of "Energy Technology Criteria List" substituted by SI 2006/2233, art. 2(2), with effect from 7 September 2006.

Former definition of "Energy Technology Criteria List" substituted by SI 2005/2424, art. 3, with effect from 22 September 2005.

Former definition of "Energy Technology Criteria List" substituted by SI 2004/2093 reg. 2(2), with effect from 26 August 2004.

Former definition of "Energy Technology Criteria List" substituted by SI 2003/1744 reg. 3(2), with effect from 5 August 2003.

Former definitions of "Energy Technology Criteria List" and "Energy Technology Product List" substituted by SI 2002/1818, art. 3 with effect from 5 August 2002.

In art. 2, in the definition of "Energy Technology Product List "4 July 2012" substituted for "25th August 2011" and "5 July 2012" substituted for "1st September 2011" by SI 2012/1832, art. 3, with effect from 2 August 2012.

In art. 2, in the definition of "Energy Technology Product List", the words "3rd August 2010" substituted for the words "6th July 2009" in both places by SI 2010/2286, art. 3, with effect from 8 October 2010.

In art. 2, definition of "Energy Technology Product List" substituted by SI 2009/1863, art. 2, with effect from 4 August 2009.

Former 2 definition of "Energy Technology Product List" substituted by SI 2008/1916, art. 2, with effect from 11 August 2008.

Former definition of "Energy Technology Criteria List" substituted by SI 2007/2165, art. 2(2), with effect from 16 August 2007.

Former definition of "Energy Technology Product List" substituted by SI 2006/2233 art. 2(2), with effect from 7 September 2006.

Former definition of "Energy Technology Product List" substituted by SI 2005/2424 art. 3, with effect from 22 September 2005.

Former definition of "Energy Technology Product List" substituted by SI 2004/2093 reg. 2(3), with effect from 26 August 2004.

Former definition of "Energy Technology Product List" substituted by SI 2003/1744 reg. 3(3), with effect from 5 August 2003.

DESCRIPTION OF ENERGY-SAVING PLANT AND MACHINERY

3(1)   Plant or machinery is energy-saving plant or machinery for the purposes of section 45A of the Capital Allowances Act (expenditure on energy-saving plant or machinery) if–

(a)   it falls within a technology class specified in the Energy Technology Criteria List,

(b)   it meets the energy-saving criteria set out in that List, and

(c)   subject to paragraphs (3) and (4) in the case of plant or machinery falling within any of the technology classes specified in paragraph (2), it is of a type that–

   (i)   is specified in, and has not been removed from, the Energy Technology Product List, or

   (ii)   has been accepted for inclusion in the Energy Technology Product List.

3(2)   The technology classes specified for the purposes of paragraph (1)(c) are–

(a)   boilers,

(b)   motors and drives,

(c)   refrigeration,

(d)   [omitted by SI 2006/2233, art. 2(3),]

(e)   heat pumps,

(f)   radiant and warm air heaters,

(g)   compressed air equipment,

(h)   solar thermal systems,

(i)   automatic monitoring and targeting equipment;

(j)   air-to-air energy recovery equipment;

(k)   [omitted by SI 2010/2286, art. 4;]

(l)   heating, ventilation and air conditioning equipment;

(m)   uninterruptible power supplies;

(n)   high speed hand air dryers.

3(3)   In the case of solar thermal systems either the solar thermal system or the solar collector included in the system must be of a type within paragraph (i) or (ii) of article 3(1)(c).

3(4)   In the case of automatic monitoring and targeting equipment–

(a)   portable equipment must be of a type within paragraph (i) or (ii) of article 3(1)(c),

(b)   component based fixed systems are within article 4.

History – In art. 3(1)(c) words "paragraphs (3) and (4)" substituted for the words "paragraph (3)" by SI 2003/1744, art. 4(1) with effect from 5 August 2003.
In art. 3(1)(c) words "subject to paragraph (3)" inserted by SI 2002/1818, art. 4(2) with effect from 5 August 2002.
In art. 3(2) class (d) "thermal screens," omitted by SI 2006/2233, art. 2(3) with effect from 7 September 2006.
Art. 3(2)(e)–(h) inserted by SI 2002/1818, art. 4(3) with effect from 5 August 2002.
Art. 3(2)(i) inserted by SI 2003/1744, art. 4(3) with effect from 5 August 2003.
Art. 3(2)(k) omitted by SI 2010/2286, art. 4, with effect from 8 October 2010. Former art. 3(2)(k) read as follows:
     "(k)   compact heat exchangers;".
In art. 3(2)(l), the word "equipment;" substituted for the words "zone controls." by SI 2009/1863, art. 4(a), with effect from 4 August 2009.
Art. 3(2)(j)–(l) inserted by SI 2004/2093, art. 2(3) with effect from 26 August 2004.
Art. 3(2)(m) inserted by SI 2009/1863, art. 4(a), with effect from 4 August 2009.
Art. 3(2)(n) inserted by SI 2011/2221, art. 4, with effect from 1 October 2011.
Art. 3(3) inserted by SI 2002/1818, art. 4(4) with effect from 5 August 2002.
Art. 3(4) inserted by SI 2003/1744, art. 4(4) with effect from 5 August 2003.

CERTIFICATION OF ENERGY-SAVING PLANT AND MACHINERY

4(1)   In the case of plant or machinery falling within the technology class "Combined Heat and Power" specified in the Energy Technology Criteria List no section 45A allowance may be made unless a relevant certificate of energy efficiency is in force with respect to that plant or machinery.

4(2)   In paragraph (1) "section 45A allowance" and "relevant certificate of energy efficiency" have the meanings given by section 45B of the Capital Allowances Act.

History – Art. 4(1) substituted by SI 2011/2221, art. 5, with effect from 1 October 2011.

ENERGY-SAVING COMPONENTS OF PLANT OR MACHINERY

5   Where one or more components of certain plant or machinery (but not all of that plant or machinery)–

(a)   meets the conditions set out in sub-paragraphs (a) to (c) of article 3(1), and

(b)   falls within any of the technology classes specified in sub-paragraphs (a) to (c), (f), (g), (j), (l) and (m) of article 3(2),

the amount specified in respect of each such component for the purposes of section 45C of the Capital Allowances Act is the amount specified in the Energy Technology Product List in relation to that component.

History – Art. 5(a) substituted by SI 2005/2424, art. 4, with effect from 22 September 2005.
In art. 5(b), "," substituted for "and", and the words "and (m)" inserted, by SI 2009/1863, art. 5, with effect from 4 August 2009.
Art. 5(b) substituted by SI 2005/2424, art. 4, with effect from 22 September 2005.
In former art. 5(b) words "and (g)" inserted by SI 2002/1818, art. 5 with effect from 5 August 2002.

ENERGY SERVICES PROVIDERS

6   The class of plant or machinery specified for the purposes of section 180A(2) of the Capital Allowances Act is the technology class "Combined Heat and Power" specified in the Energy Technology Criteria List.

INCOME TAX (EXEMPTION OF MINOR BENEFITS) REGULATIONS 2002

(SI 2002/205, as amended by SI 2003/1434, SI 2004/3087, SI 2007/2090 and SI 2012/1808)

Made on 4 February 2002 by the Treasury, in exercise of the powers conferred upon them by s. 155ZB of the Income and Corporation Taxes Act 1988 [ITEPA 2003, s. 210]. Operative from 6 April 2002.

CITATION, COMMENCEMENT AND EFFECT

1(1) These Regulations may be cited as the Income Tax (Exemption of Minor Benefits) Regulations 2002 and shall come into force on 6th April 2002.

1(2) These Regulations have effect for the year 2002–03 and subsequent years of assessment.

INTERPRETATION

2 In these Regulations–

"bus" and **"minibus"** mean a bus, or a minibus, by means of which is provided a works bus service to which section 242 of ITEPA applies;

"employment" includes an office and related expressions have a corresponding meaning;

"health screening" means an assessment to identify employees who might be at a particular risk of ill health;

"ITEPA" means the Income Tax (Earnings and Pensions) Act 2003;

"medical check-up" means a physical examination of an employee by a health professional which is limited to determining that employee's state of health;

"working day" in relation to an employee, means a day on which his attendance at a workplace is necessary in the performance of the duties of the employment;

"workplace", in relation to an employee, means a place at which his attendance is necessary in the performance of the duties of the employment.

History – In reg. 2 the definition of "cycle" omitted by SI 2012/1808, reg. 2(a), with effect for the tax year 2013–14 and subsequent tax years.
In reg. 2 the definitions of "health screening" and "medical check-up" inserted by SI 2007/2090, reg. 2(2), with effect for the tax year 2007–08 and subsequent tax years.
In reg. 2 in the definition of "bus and minibus" the words "section 242 of ITEPA" substituted for the words "section 197AA of the Taxes Act" by SI 2003/1434, reg. 2(2), with effect from 25 June 2003.
In reg. 2 the definition of "ITEPA" inserted and the definition of "the Taxes Act" repealed by SI 2003/1434, reg. 2, with effect from 25 June 2003.

EXEMPTION IN RESPECT OF THE PROVISION OF QUALIFYING MEALS

3 [Omitted by SI 2012/1808, reg. 2(b).]

History – Reg. 3 omitted by SI 2012/1808, reg. 2(b), with effect for the tax year 2013–14 and subsequent tax years. Former reg. 3(1) substituted and former reg. 3(2) repealed by SI 2003/1434, reg. 3(2) and (3) respectively, with effect from 25 June 2003.

EXEMPTION IN RESPECT OF THE PROVISION OF BUS OR MINIBUS

4(1) There is no charge to tax under Chapter 10 of Part 3 of ITEPA in respect of the provision for employees of a bus, or a minibus, for conveying employees of one or more employers on relevant journeys.

4(2) For the purposes of this regulation, a **"relevant journey"**, in relation to an employee, is a journey which–

(a)   is a single journey of a distance of not more than 10 miles;

(b)   is between his workplace and shops or other amenities; and

(c)   is made on a working day.

History – In reg. 4(1) the words "Chapter 10 of Part 3 of ITEPA" substituted for the words "section 154 of the Taxes Act (taxable benefits: general charging provision)" by SI 2003/1434, reg. 4, with effect from 25 June 2003.

EXEMPTION IN RESPECT OF THE PROVISION OF PENSIONS ADVICE

5(1) There is no charge to tax under Chapter 10 of Part 3 of ITEPA in respect of the provision to an employee, on behalf of an employer, of pension information and advice.

5(2) The exemption conferred by paragraph (1) applies only if the cash equivalent of the benefit of provision of pension information and advice to an employee does not exceed £150 in total in a year of assessment.

History – Reg. 5 inserted by SI 2004/3087, reg. 2, with effect for 2005–06 and subsequent tax years of assessment.

EXEMPTION IN RESPECT OF THE PROVISION OF RECREATIONAL FACILITIES AND SUBSIDISED MEALS TO THIRD PARTIES

6(1) Where there is no charge to tax under–

(a)   section 261 of ITEPA (exemption of recreational benefits), or

(b)   section 317 of ITEPA (subsidised meals)

in respect of the provision of recreational facilities or subsidised meals to employees, paragraph (2) applies.

6(2) If this paragraph applies, the provision of the facilities or meals referred to in paragraph (1) to other persons who work on the premises of the employer in question shall be exempt notwithstanding that the conditions set out in section 261 or section 317 respectively of ITEPA may not be satisfied in respect of those persons.

History – Reg. 6 inserted by SI 2004/3087, reg. 2, with effect for 2005–06 and subsequent tax years of assessment.

EXEMPTION IN RESPECT OF THE PROVISION OF HEALTH SCREENING AND MEDICAL CHECK-UPS

7(1) There is no charge to tax under Chapter 10 of Part 3 (taxable benefits: residual liability to charge) of ITEPA in respect of the provision to an employee, on behalf of an employer, of one health screening and one medical check-up each year.

7(2) In order for this regulation to apply–

(a)   health screenings must be available to all employees, and

(b)   medical check-ups must be available to either–

    (i)   all employees, or

    (ii)   those employees who have been identified in a health screening as requiring a medical check-up.

History – Reg. 7 inserted by SI 2007/2090, reg. 2(3), with effect for the tax year 2007–08 and subsequent tax years.

INCOME TAX (EMPLOYMENT AND ELECTRONIC COMMUNICATIONS) (MISCELLANEOUS PROVISIONS) REGULATIONS 2002

(SI 2002/680)

Made on 13 March 2002 by the Commissioners of Inland Revenue, in exercise of the powers conferred upon them by s. 203(10) of the Income and Corporation Taxes Act 1988 [ITEPA 2003, s. 684(1) and (2)] and s. 132 of the Finance Act 1999. Operative from 8 April 2002.

CITATION, COMMENCEMENT AND INTERPRETATION

1(1) These Regulations may be cited as the Income Tax (Employment and Electronic Communications) (Miscellaneous Provisions) Regulations 2002 and shall come into force on 8th April 2002.

1(2) In these Regulations **"the Board"** means the Commissioners of Inland Revenue.

NOTICES GIVEN BY THE BOARD UNDER REGULATION 34 OF THE EDUCATION (STUDENT LOANS) (REPAYMENT) REGULATIONS 2000

2(1) Any notice to be given by the Board under regulation 34 of the Education (Student Loans) (Repayment) Regulations 2000 (notices to employers by the Board to deduct repayments from emoluments) ("regulation 34") may be given, either to the employer or a person acting on his behalf, in such form and by such means of electronic communications as are for the time being approved by directions issued by the Board if the employer–

(a)   has given his consent to the delivery of documents by the Board by that means; and

(b)   has not notified the Board that that consent has been withdrawn.

2(2) If it is recorded on an official computer system that a notice under regulation 34 has been given to any person by an approved means of electronic communications, it shall be presumed, unless the contrary is proved, that a notice–

(a)   was given by that means;

(b)   was given to the person recorded on that system as the recipient;

(c)   was given at the time recorded on that system as the time of delivery; and

(d)   contained the information recorded on that system in respect of that notice.

2(3) A document certified by an officer of the Board to be a printed-out version of a notice, given by means of electronic communications in accordance with paragraph (1), which is recorded on an official computer system as at a particular date shall be presumed unless the contrary is proved–

(a)   to have been recorded on an official computer system at that date;

(b)   to constitute the entirety of the electronic communication so recorded.

2(4) A document purporting to be such a certificate as is mentioned in paragraph (3) shall be presumed to be such a certificate unless the contrary is proved.

2(5) For the purposes of this regulation "employers" and "official computer system" have the same meanings as they have in the Income Tax (Employments) Regulations 1993.

INCOME TAX (BENEFITS IN KIND) (EXEMPTION FOR EMPLOYMENT COSTS RESULTING FROM DISABILITY) REGULATIONS 2002

(SI 2002/1596)

Made on 18 June 2002 by the Treasury in exercise of the powers conferred on them by s. 155ZB of the Income and Corporation Taxes Act 1988 [ITEPA 2003, s. 210(1)]. Operative from 9 July 2002.

1   These Regulations may be cited as the Income Tax (Benefits in Kind) (Exemption for Employment Costs resulting from Disability) Regulations 2002 and shall come into force on 9th July 2002.

2   In these Regulations–

(a)   **"the Access to Work programme"** means the programme known by that name and provided in pursuance of arrangements made by or on behalf of the Secretary of State under section 2 of the Employment and Training Act 1973, in Scotland, made under section 2(3) of the Enterprise and New Towns (Scotland) Act 1990 or, in Northern Ireland, made by or on behalf of the Department of Employment and Learning under section 1 of the Employment and Training (Northern Ireland) Act 1950; and

(b)   any reference to a section, without more, is to that section of the Income and Corporation Taxes Act 1988.

3   There shall be exempted from section 154 any benefit which satisfies each of the following conditions.

Condition 1

The benefit is provided to a disabled employee.

Condition 2

The main purpose of providing the benefit is to enable the employee to perform the duties of his employment.

Condition 3

The benefit consists in the provision of a hearing aid or other equipment, services or facilities, excepting any excluded benefit within the meaning in section 155ZA and Regulations made under that section.

Condition 4

The benefit is provided under, or within the terms of the provisions of, the Disability Discrimination Act 1995, the Access to Work programme, or any other statutory provision or arrangements, whether or not the employer has any legal duty to provide the benefit.

Condition 5

The benefit is made available to the employer's employees generally on similar terms (which include terms identical to Conditions 1 to 4).

RELIEF FOR COMMUNITY AMATEUR SPORTS CLUBS (DESIGNATION) ORDER 2002

(SI 2002/1966)

Made on 25 July 2002 by the Treasury, in exercise of the powers conferred upon them by para. 14(1) of Sch. 18 to the Finance Act 2002. Operative from 15 August 2002.

1 This Order may be cited as the Relief for Community Amateur Sports Clubs (Designation) Order 2002 and shall come into force on 15th August 2002.

2 A sport is designated as an eligible sport for the purposes of Schedule 18 to the Finance Act 2002 where that sport appears on the list maintained by the National Sports Councils of activities recognised by them.

Other material – Activities recognised by the National Sports Council are: Aikido, Archery, Arm Wrestling, Association Football, Athletics, Australian Rules Football, Badminton, Ballooning, Baseball, Basketball, Baton Twirling, Biathlon, Bicycle Polo, Billiards and Snooker, Bobsleigh, Boccia, Bowls, Boxing, Camogie, Canoeing, Caving, Chinese Martial Arts, Cricket, Croquet, Crossbow, Curling, Cycling, Disability Sport, Dragon Boat Racing, Equestrian, Fencing, Fives, Flying, Gaelic Football, Gliding, Golf, Gymnastics, Handball, Hang/Para Gliding, Highland Games, Hockey, Horse Racing, Hovering, Hurling, Ice Hockey, Ice Skating, Jet Skiing, Ju Jitsu, Judo, Kabaddi, Karate, Kendo, Korfball, Lacrosse, Lawn Tennis, Life Saving, Luge, Modern Pentathlon , Motor Cycling, Motor Sports, Mountaineering, Movement Dance Exercise & Fitness, Netball, Orienteering, Parachuting, Petanque, Polo, Pony Trekking, Pool, Quoits, Racketball, Rackets, Raquetball, Rambling, Real Tennis, Roller Hockey, Roller Skating, Rounders, Rowing, Rugby League, Rugby Union, Sailing Sand/Land Yachting, Shinty, Shooting, Skateboarding, Skiing, Skipping, Snowboarding, Softball, Sombo Wrestling, Squash, Skater/Street Hockey, Sub-Aqua, Surf Life Saving, Surfing, Swimming & Diving, Table Tennis, Taekwondo, Tang Soo Do, Tenpin Bowling, Trampolining, Triathlon, Tug of War, Unihoc, Volleyball, Water Skiing , Weightlifting, Wrestling, Yoga.

Registered Community Amateur Sports Clubs are: 3D Dynamos Football Club, Abercorn Sports Club, Abernethy Golf Club, Abernethy Highland Games Association, Acton Reynald Cricket Club, Aldershot Cricket Club, Annbank Angling Club, Antrim Rugby Football & Ladies Hockey Club, Ards Rugby Football Club, Assheton Bowmen Archery Club, Astwood Bank Cricket Club, Aylesbury Vale Seido Karate, Badenoch Riding Club, Bainsford Bowling Club, Balfron Golf Society, Ballinamallard United Football Club, Ballyhegan Davitts GAA Club, Banstead Neville Bowling Club Limited, Belfast United, Belfast Wado Karate Club, Belgrave Harriers, Bere Alston Bowling Club, Beverley and East Riding Lawn Tennis Club, Bewdley Rowing Club, Biggar Rugby Football Club, Billingham Synthonia Cricket Club, Birmingham Rowing Club, Bishop Sutton Tennis Club, Blaydon Rugby Football Club, Boat of Garten Golf & Tennis Club, Bon Accord Thistle Amateur Swimming Club, Bough Beech Sailing Club, Brackley Golf Club, Bradford Ice Skating Club, Bradford Sub-Aqua Club, Brecon Sub Aqua Club, Brighton Swimming Club, Brigstock Cricket Club, Bristol Croquet Club, Bristol Orienteering Klub, Broadstairs & St Peters Lawn Tennis Club, Broughty Ferry Lawn Tennis Club, Budleigh Salterton Cricket Club, Budleigh Salterton Croquet Club, Bullmershe Gymnastics Club, Burnopfield Cricket Club, Burntisland Sailing Club, Bury Croquet Club, Calday Grange Amateur Swimming Club, Canterbury & District Indoor Bowling Association Ltd, Car Colston Cricket Club, Carrickfergus Rugby Football Club, Carshalton Beeches Badminton Club, Castle Cove Sailing Club, Castleford Rugby Union Football Club, Charlestown Bowling Club, Chester Le Street Town FC, Chipping Campden Tennis Club, Chorley Buccaneers American Football, Christ Church Lawn Tennis Club, Cirencester Town Juniors FC, Clacton Swimming Club (1931), Cleator Moor Celtic Football Club, Cliftonville Cricket Club, Clwb Chwaraeon Pwllheli, Clydesdale Cricket Club, Coleraine Rugby Football & Cricket Club, Collegeland O'Rahillys Gaelic Football Club, Coolhurst Lawn Tennis and Squash Rackets Club, Craignish Boat Club, Criccieth Golf Club, Cromer Marrams Bowls Club, Croquet in Pendle, Crowstone & St Saviours Lawn Tennis Club, Culter Boys Club, Cwmcarn United RFC, Dabchicks Sailing Club, Dalgety Bay Sailing Club, Dalmally Golf Club, Dedham Cricket Club, Derby Congregational Cricket Club, Dinnington Rugby Union Football Club, Donaghadee Sailing Club, Dorchester Rifle & Pistol Club, Doune Cricket Club, Duddingston Golf Club, Dulwich Runners AC, Dunbar Golf Club, Dundee Sailing Club, Dunfermline Tennis & Bridge Club Limited, Durham Amateur Rowing Club, Dysart Sailing Club, Ealing Southall & Middlesex AC, Eastbourne Sovereign Sailing Club, Eastcote Hockey & Badminton Club Ltd, Edmonton Bowls Club, Ely Rugby Union Football Club, Epping Archers, Evercreech Cricket Club, Eversley Cricket Club, Failsworth Dynamos Junior Football Club, Fairlie Yacht Club, Falcon Bowling & Social Club (Chelmsford) Ltd, Falkirk Indoor Bowling Club, Falkirk Lawn Tennis Club, Felixstowe Lawn Tennis Club, Fife Athletic Club, Forth Corinthian Yacht Club, Friary Bowling Club, Fromeside Gymnastics Club (1987) Limited, Garleton Football Club, Girton Golf Club (Cambridge) Ltd, Glan Aber Tennis Club, Glenrothes Rugby Football Club, Golcar Cricket & Athletic Club, Gordonians Hockey Club, Gracemount Ibex Gymnastics Club, Grampian Speleological Group, Grantown-on-Spey Golf Club, Gravesend Sailing Club, Grovelands Bowling Club, Guildford City Boys Football Club, Haddington Rugby Football Club, Hallam Cricket Club, Halstead Cricket Club, Hampton Junior Football Club, Harborough Flyers Basketball Club, Hawkwell Athletic Football Club, Haywards Heath Swimming Club, Helensburgh Sailing Club, Herne Bay Lawn Tennis Club, Herne Bay Lifeguard & Swimming Club, Hertford Cricket Club, Heywood Sports AFC, Higham Town Colts Junior Football Club, Highworth Tennis Club, Hindsford Junior Football Club, Hollowell Sailing Club, Hook Norton Sports & Social Club, Hutton Cranswick SRA Cricket Club, Ice Rink Club (Curling), Ickleford Sports & Recreation Club, Ilmington Tennis Club, Island Cruising Club Limited, Isle of Wight Athletics Club, Ivybridge Cricket Club, Jesmond Lawn Tennis Club, Kendal Cricket Club, Kingussie Golf Club, Kirkintilloch Golf Club, Knaresborough Tennis Club, Knockin & Kinnerley Cricket Club, Lakeland Cross Country Ski Club, Langleybury Cricket Club, Langtons Cricket Club, Largs Golf Club, Lighcliffe and District Cricket and Lawn Tennis Club, Linlithgow Sports Club, Lisburn Rugby Football Club, Liverpool Yacht Club, Llandudno Golf Club (Maesdu) Ltd, Llandudno Rugby Club Ltd, Llandudno Sailing Club, Lochaber Camanachd Club, Lochaber Yacht Club, Lochcarron Camanachd, Lochcarron Golf Club, Locks Sailing Club, Lundin Sports Club, Macclesfield Tennis Club, Madras College Former Pupils RFC, Malpas & District Sports Club Ltd, Mansfield Rugby Union Football Club, Margate Lawn Tennis Club, Merioneth Yacht Club Ltd, Morriston Town AFC, Nairn Golf Club, Naunton County Cricket Club, Newark Rowing Club, Newbury & Thatcham Hockey Club, Newick Bowling Club, North Down Cricket Club, Northampton Rowing Club, Nottingham Kayak Club, Octavian Droobers Orienteering Club, Oldmeldrum Golf Club, Oxford City & County Bowls Club Ltd, Parkside Raiders Junior Football Club, Pendle Ski Club, Perthshire Table Tennis Club, Peterborough City Rowing Club, Peterculter Golf Club, Peterlee Amateur Rugby League Football Club, Pevensy Bay Sailing Club Ltd, Philadelphia Cricket Club, Pirbright Tennis Club, Plockton Small Boat Sailing Club, Port Edgar Yacht Club, Portadown Rugby Football Club, Porthmadog Golf Club, Portishead Yacht & Sailing Club, Prestatyn Cricket Club, Prestwick Symington & Ayr Fort Community Tennis Club, Purley Sports Club, Pwllheli Sailing Club Ltd, Rame Gig Club, Reading Branch British Sub-aqua Club, Rogate Bowling Club, Ross County Cricket Club, Rothley Ivanhoe Tennis Club, Royal Solent Yacht Club, Royal Tunbridge Wells Croquet Club, Rustlings Lawn Tennis Club, Rye Harbour Sailing Club, Salcombe Rugby Football Club, Scarborough & District

Statutory Instruments

Indoor Bowls Club, Scholes Cricket Club, Scottish Carriage Driving Association, Sevenoaks Athletics Club, Shadwell Cricket Club, Shipley Juniors AFC, Silverdale Cricket Club, Snettisham Beach Sailing Club, Sons Of The Thames Rowing Club, South Antrim Hockey Club, South Cerney Sailing Club Ltd, South Cliff Bowling Club, South Gower Sports Club, South Hampstead Club Limited, South Northumberland Cricket Club, Southampton Amateur Rowing Club, Sowerby Tennis & Bowling Club, Spey Valley Sailing Club, Spofforth Cricket Club, Springfield Cricket Club, St Andrews Fencing Club, St Andrews Lawn Tennis Club, St Just Cricket Club, St Mary's Cricket Club, St Mary's Loch Sailing Club, St Michael's Cricket Club, Staddiscombe Colts Football Club, Stanley Sports & Social (Cricket & Rugby League), Stirling County Cricket Club, Stone-In-Oxney Sports Club, Stranraer Golf Club, Strathpeffer Spa Golf Club, Street Sub Aqua Club, Surbiton Postal Rifle Club, Sutton Coldfield Cricket & Hockey Club Ltd, Swaffham Cricket Club, Sydenham Lawn Tennis Croquet Club Ltd, Taunton Deane Bowling Club, Taynuilt Golf Club, Teddington Hockey Club, Tempest United Association Football Club, Thames Ditton Cricket Club, Thames Ditton Lawn Tennis Club Ltd, Thames Valley Harriers, The Rough-Stuff Fellowship, The Trojans Club, Toward Sailing Club, Troon Lawn Tennis Club, Twinstead Cricket Club, Victoria Hall Badminton Club, Walshaw Sports Club, Walton-Le-Dale Cricket Club, Warborough & Shillingford Cricket Club, Warrington and District Rifle and Pistol Club, Wealden Bowls Centre Ltd, Weirs Cricket Club, Wembley Sports Association, Wessex Mountaineering Club, West Bridgford Hockey Club, West Cheshire Athletic Club, West Kirby Sailing Club, West of Scotland Cricket Club, Western Baths Club, Weybridge Rowing Club, Weyfarers Rowing Club, White Roding Social & Sports Club, Widmer End Lawn Tennis Club, Wigton Moor Junior AFC, Wigtownshire County Golf Club, Wollaston Lawn Tennis Club, Woodford Green Athletic Club with Essex Ladies Woodford Rugby Football Club, Wootton Bassett Rugby Football Club, Worthing Chippingdale Cricket Club, Wyre Villa Football Club, York Railway Institute, Yoxford Cricket Club.

3 **"The National Sports Councils"** means UK Sport, Sport England, Sport Scotland, the Sports Council of Wales and the Sports Council of Northern Ireland.

CORPORATION TAX (FINANCE LEASING OF INTANGIBLE ASSETS) REGULATIONS 2002

(SI 2002/1967)

Made on 25 July 2002 by the Treasury, in exercise of the powers conferred upon them by para. 104 of Sch. 29 to the Finance Act 2002. Operative from 15 August 2002.

CITATION, COMMENCEMENT AND EFFECT

1 These Regulations may be cited as the Corporation Tax (Finance Leasing of Intangible Assets) Regulations 2002, shall come into force on 15th August 2002, and shall have effect from 1st April 2002.

INTERPRETATION

2 In these regulations–

"financial asset" shall be construed in accordance with paragraph 75 of Schedule 29;

"finance lease", **"finance lessor"** and **"finance lessee"** shall be construed in accordance with paragraph 104(4) and (5) of Schedule 29;

"Schedule 29" means Schedule 29 to the Finance Act 2002 (gains and losses of a company from intangible fixed assets).

APPLICATION OF SCHEDULE 29

3 Schedule 29 shall apply in relation to a company that is the finance lessor of an intangible asset that is the subject of a finance lease as if, notwithstanding that the asset is accounted for by the finance lessor as a financial asset, it were an intangible fixed asset of the lessor and not a financial asset.

4 References in Schedule 29 to capitalised expenditure on an intangible fixed asset shall accordingly be taken as including references to any amount accounted for by the finance lessor as a financial asset as a consequence of the finance lease of the asset, except that–

(a) no election may be made under paragraph 10 of Schedule 29 (election for writing down on fixed rate basis) in respect of that amount,

(b) that amount is not to be treated as capitalised expenditure for the purposes of paragraph 39(1)(b) of Schedule 29 (roll-over relief in case of realisation and reinvestment: conditions to be met in relation to expenditure on other assets), and

(c) accordingly any amount treated by paragraph 57(2) of Schedule 29 (roll-over relief on reinvestment: acquisition of group company treated as equivalent to acquisition of underlying assets) as expenditure on acquiring the financial asset is not to be treated as capitalised expenditure for the purposes of paragraph 39(1)(b) of that Schedule.

INTANGIBLE FIXED ASSET BECOMING FINANCIAL ASSET – CONSEQUENTIALS

5 Where an asset formerly recognised by the lessor for accounting purposes as an intangible fixed asset becomes subject to a finance lease (and accordingly comes to be accounted for as a financial asset)–

(a) a realisation of the intangible fixed asset shall be treated, for the purposes of Part 4 of Schedule 29 (realisation of intangible fixed assets), as having occurred on the commencement of the finance lease,

(b) the accounting value of the financial asset so created shall be recognised as realisation proceeds of the intangible fixed asset for the purposes of that Part, and

(c) that amount shall not be taken into account in determining the accounting value of the financial asset immediately after the realisation for the purposes of paragraph 22(2) of that Schedule (apportionment in case of part realisation).

FINANCIAL ASSETS EXCLUDED FROM SCHEDULE 29

6(1) Assets partially excluded from Schedule 29 by virtue of paragraphs 78 to 81 (assets excluded except as regards royalties) shall be entirely excluded from that Schedule as regards the finance lessor if they are subject to a finance lease and are accounted for by the lessor as financial assets.

Accordingly in relation to such assets–

(a)   Schedule 29 applies only to royalties recognised for accounting purposes prior to the asset becoming subject to the finance lease, or after it ceases to be subject to the finance lease,

(b)   to the extent that such royalties are brought into account for tax purposes under Schedule 29, they shall not be brought into account for tax purposes again, and

(c)   to the extent that such royalties are brought into account for tax purposes otherwise than under Schedule 29, they shall not be brought into account for tax purposes under that Schedule.

6(2)   Except for the purposes of regulation 5, an asset shall be excluded from Schedule 29 if it is used by the finance lessee for the purposes of a trade or business in respect of which he is within the charge to income tax.

6(3)   Nothing in these Regulations shall be read as enabling Schedule 29 to apply to existing assets excluded from the application of that Schedule by paragraph 118 of that Schedule.

6(4)   An asset shall count as an existing asset in the hands of the finance lessor for the purposes of paragraph 118 of Schedule 29 if the finance lessee–

(a)   is a company for whom the asset was the whole or part of an existing asset, or

(b)   is a person who is a related party in relation to such a company.

6(5)   References in paragraph (1) to royalties being brought into account for tax purposes include references to royalties which would have been so brought into account if the person concerned had been within the charge to corporation tax.

6(6)   In paragraph (4)(b) **"related party"** shall be construed in accordance with paragraph 95, read with paragraphs 96 to 101, of Schedule 29.

EXCHANGE GAINS AND LOSSES (TRANSITIONAL PROVISIONS AND SAVINGS) REGULATIONS 2002

(SI 2002/1969)

Made on 25 July 2002 by the Treasury, in exercise of the powers conferred upon them by s. 81 of the Finance Act 2002. Operative from 1 October 2002.

PART 1 – INTRODUCTION

CITATION, COMMENCEMENT AND EFFECT

1(1) These Regulations may be cited as the Exchange Gains and Losses (Transitional Provisions and Savings) Regulations 2002 and shall come into force on 1st October 2002.

1(2) These Regulations have effect in relation to accounting periods beginning on or after 1st October 2002.

PART 2 – SAVING OF THE EXCHANGE GAINS AND LOSSES (TRANSITIONAL PROVISIONS) REGULATIONS 1994 WITH MODIFICATIONS

INTRODUCTION

2 The Exchange Gains and Losses (Transitional Provisions) Regulations 1994 are modified in accordance with regulations 3 to 11 below and, as modified, continue to have effect (notwithstanding the repeal of sections 164(14), 165(4) to (6) and 167(1) and (4) to (6) of, and Schedule 16 to, the Finance Act 1993 by sections 79(1)(b) and 141 of, and Part 3(10) of Schedule 40 to, the Finance Act 2002).

MODIFICATION OF REGULATION 1

3 In regulation 1(3)–

(a)   for sub-paragraph (g) substitute–

"(g)   **"a regulation 6(3) asset"** means an existing asset the basic valuation of which was determined for the purposes of Chapter II in accordance with regulation 6(3) of these Regulations;";

(b)   at the end of sub-paragraph (h) add
"; and

(i)   **"the relevant accounting period"**, in relation to a company, means the company's first accounting period to begin on or after 1st October 2002.".

MODIFICATION OF REGULATION 2

4 In regulation 2(2)–

(a)   omit "Sections 136, 137 and 139 to 141 of the 1993 Act;";

(b)   omit "The Exchange Gains and Losses (Deferral of Gains and Losses) Regulations 1994.".

OMISSION OF REGULATIONS 3 TO 6

5 Omit regulations 3 to 6.

MODIFICATION OF REGULATION 7

6 [I]n regulation 7(2)–

(a)   after the definition of "the cumulative taxed loss" insert–
""the final accounting period"**, in relation to a company, means the company's accounting period preceding the relevant accounting period;";

(b)   omit the words from "and any reference" to the end.

Statutory Instruments

MODIFICATION OF REGULATION 8

7 In regulation 8(5) for "above" substitute "of these Regulations".

MODIFICATION OF REGULATION 13

8(1) Modify regulation 13 as follows.

8(2) In paragraph (1) for "14(1) and 15(1)" substitute "14 and 14A".

8(3) After paragraph (1) insert–

"**13(1A)** For the purposes of paragraph (1)(a) above, the final accounting period shall be treated as the last accrual period as respects any asset or liability held or owed by the company immediately after the end of the final accounting period.".

8(4) In paragraphs (2)(a), (b) and (c) and (3)(a), (b) and (c) for "before the end of the last accrual period" substitute "after the end of the final accounting period".

8(5) For paragraph (4) substitute–

"**13(4)** In paragraphs (2) and (3) above, a relevant gain or loss in relation to a regulation 6(3) asset is a chargeable gain or an allowable loss.

13(4A) In relation to any asset other than a regulation 6(3) asset or any liability, an amount equal to the amount of any relevant gain or loss that is deemed to accrue to the company under paragraph (2) or (3) above shall be treated for the purposes of Chapter 2 of Part 4 of the Finance Act 1996 (according to whether it is a relevant gain or loss)–

(a)   as a credit in respect of a loan relationship of the company, or

(b)   as a debit in respect of a loan relationship of the company,

which falls to be brought into account under section 82(2) of that Act.".

8(6) Omit paragraphs (5) to (8).

SUBSTITUTION OF REGULATION 14

9 For regulation 14 substitute–

"ELECTIONS TO DEFER BRINGING INTO ACCOUNT RELEVANT GAINS AND LOSSES DEEMED TO ACCRUE IMMEDIATELY AFTER THE END OF THE FINAL ACCOUNTING PERIOD

14(1) In any case where, apart from this regulation, relevant gains or losses would accrue to a company immediately after the end of the final accounting period by virtue of regulation 13, the company may elect, by notice to the inspector within two years of the end of the final accounting period, that this regulation shall apply as respects–

(a)   subject to paragraph (3) below, all relevant gains or losses to which paragraph (4) of regulation 13 would apply;

(b)   all relevant gains or losses to which paragraph (4A) of that regulation would apply; or

(c)   both.

An election under this paragraph shall be irrevocable.

14(2) Where an election is made under paragraph (1) above, every gain or loss to which this regulation applies shall be treated as accruing only when the asset or liability to which the gain or loss relates ceases to be held or owed by the company.

14(3) No election may be made under paragraph (1) above as respects relevant gains or losses to which regulation 13(4) would apply if an election under regulation 14A is made as regards such losses.

ELECTIONS TO TREAT LOSSES DEEMED TO ACCRUE IMMEDIATELY AFTER THE END OF THE FINAL ACCOUNTING PERIOD AS DEBITS IN RESPECT OF LOAN RELATIONSHIPS

14A(1) In any case where–

(a)   apart from this regulation, relevant losses would accrue to a company as respects regulation 6(3) assets immediately after the end of the final accounting period by virtue of regulation 13; and

(b) if relevant gains would accrue as respects such assets at that time by virtue of that regulation, such losses would exceed them,

the company may elect, by notice to the inspector within two years of the end of the final accounting period, that this regulation shall apply as respects such losses or, in a case where sub-paragraph (b) applies, such losses to the extent that they exceed the relevant gains.

An election under this paragraph shall be irrevocable.

14A(2) Where an election is made under paragraph (1) above, an amount equal to the amount of the losses to which this regulation applies shall be treated for the purposes of Chapter 2 of Part 4 of the Finance Act 1996 as a debit in respect of a loan relationship of the company for the new accounting period and not falling to be brought into account under section 82(2) of that Act.

TREATMENT OF LOSSES AVAILABLE TO BE CARRIED FORWARD AT THE END OF THE FINAL ACCOUNTING PERIOD AS A RESULT OF AN ELECTION MADE UNDER REGULATION 14(5) OR 16(1)

14B(1) This regulation apples where, as a result of an election made under regulation 14(5) or 16(1) of these Regulations, an amount of available losses ("the relevant amount") was available at the end of the final accounting period to be carried forward and, apart from this regulation, to be set against a company's exchange gains.

14B(2) Where this regulation applies an amount equal to the relevant amount shall be treated for the purposes of Chapter 2 of Part 4 of the Finance Act 1996 as a debit in respect of a loan relationship of the company for the new accounting period and not falling to be brought into account under section 82(2) of that Act.".

OMISSION OF REGULATIONS 15 AND 16

10 Omit regulations 15 and 16.

OMISSION OF PART 4

11 Omit the whole of Part 4.

PART 3 – SAVING OF THE EXCHANGE GAINS AND LOSSES (ALTERNATIVE METHOD OF CALCULATION) REGULATIONS 1994 WITH MODIFICATIONS

INTRODUCTION

12 The Exchange Gains and Losses (Alternative Method of Calculation) Regulations 1994 are modified in accordance with regulations 13 to 17 below and, as modified, continue to have effect (notwithstanding the repeal of sections 164(14) and 167(1) and (4) to (6) of, and Schedule 15 to, the Finance Act 1993 by sections 79(1)(b) and 141 of, and Part 3(10) of Schedule 40 to, the Finance Act 2002).

OMISSION OF REGULATIONS 2 AND 3

13 Omit regulations 2 and 3.

MODIFICATION OF REGULATION 7

14(1) Modify regulation 7 as follows.

14(2) In paragraph (1) for the words from "Subject to" to "by a company at any time" substitute "Paragraphs (3) to (5) below apply in any case where a disposal of an asset is deemed by virtue of paragraph (1A) below to have been made by a company immediately before the first day of its first accounting period to begin on or after 1st October 2002".

14(3) After paragraph (1) insert–

"**7(1A)** For the purposes of paragraph (1) above, any asset held by the company at the beginning of the first day of its first accounting period to begin on or after 1st October 2002 shall be deemed to have been disposed of by the company immediately before that first day.".

14(4) Omit paragraph (2).

14(5) Omit paragraphs (6) to (8).

OMISSION OF REGULATIONS 8 AND 9

15 Omit regulations 8 and 9.

MODIFICATION OF REGULATION 11

16 In regulation 11 after paragraph (1) insert–

"**11(1A)** Notwithstanding the following provisions of this regulation, an election made under regulation 10 or this regulation–

(a) shall have effect only in relation to accounting periods beginning before 1st October 2002, and

(b) an election which specifies a day as the day from which the election is to have effect must specify a day that falls within an accounting period beginning before 1st October 2002.".

OMISSION OF REGULATION 12

17 Omit regulation 12.

PART 4 – SAVING OF THE EXCHANGE GAINS AND LOSSES (INSURANCE COMPANIES) REGULATIONS 1994 WITH MODIFICATIONS

INTRODUCTION

18 The Exchange Gains and Losses (Insurance Companies) Regulations 1994 are modified in accordance with regulations 19 to 27 below and, as modified, continue to have effect (notwithstanding the repeal of 167(1) and 168(2) to (5) of the Finance Act 1993 by sections 79(1)(b) and 141 of, and Part 3(10) of Schedule 40 to, the Finance Act 2002).

MODIFICATION OF REGULATION 1

19 In regulation 1 after the definition of "basic valuation" insert–

""**the final accounting period**", in relation to a company, means the company's accounting period preceding the first accounting period to begin on or after 1st October 2002;".

OMISSION OF REGULATIONS 2 TO 5A

20 Omit regulations 2 to 5A.

MODIFICATION OF REGULATION 7

21 In regulation 7 for paragraph (1) substitute–

"**7(1)** An asset specified by this regulation is referred to in regulations 7A and 8 to 12 as a "regulation 7 asset"."

INSERTION OF REGULATIONS 7A AND 7B

22 After regulation 7 insert–

"**7A(1)** An asset shall be deemed to have been disposed of by an insurance company immediately before its first accounting period to begin on or after 1st October 2002 where–

(a) the asset was a regulation 7 asset at the time of its deemed disposal, and

(b) at that time, the insurance company had made no election under regulation 8A of these Regulations.

7A(2) Subject to regulation 7B, any chargeable gain or allowable loss accruing on the deemed disposal under paragraph (1) above of an asset shall be brought into account as if it had accrued immediately after the end of the final accounting period.

7B In any case where, apart from this regulation, chargeable gains or allowable losses would accrue to an insurance company immediately after the end of the final accounting period by virtue of regulation 7A–

(a) the insurance company may elect, by notice to the inspector within two years of the end of the final accounting period, that this regulation shall apply as respects all such gains or losses, and

(b) where such an election is made, every such gain or loss to which this regulation applies shall be treated as accruing only when the asset or liability to which the gain or loss relates ceases to be held or owed by the insurance company.".

MODIFICATION OF REGULATION 8

23 In regulation 8(1)–

(a) for "disposal of a regulation 7 asset" substitute "the deemed disposal under regulation 7A(1) of an asset";

(b) for "8A" substitute "9".

OMISSION OF REGULATION 8A

24 Omit regulation 8A.

MODIFICATION OF REGULATION 9

25 In regulation 9(2) for "disposal of the asset" substitute "deemed disposal under regulation 7A(1) of the asset".

MODIFICATION OF REGULATION 11

26 In regulation 11(2) for "disposal of the asset" substitute "deemed disposal under regulation 7A(1) of the asset".

MODIFICATION OF REGULATION 12

27 In regulation 12(2) for "disposal of the asset" substitute "deemed disposal under regulation 7A(1) of the asset".

PART 5 – SAVING OF THE EXCHANGE GAINS AND LOSSES (MISCELLANEOUS MODIFICATIONS) REGULATIONS 2000 WITH MODIFICATIONS

INTRODUCTION

28 The Exchange Gains and Losses (Miscellaneous Modifications) Regulations 2000 are modified in accordance with regulations 29 and 30 below and, as modified, continue to have effect (notwithstanding the repeal of sections 164(14), and 167(1) and (4) to (6) of, and Schedules 15 and 16 to, the Finance Act 1993 by sections 79(1)(b) and 141 of, and Part 3(10) of Schedule 40 to, the Finance Act 2002).

OMISSION OF REGULATIONS 2 TO 5

29 Omit regulations 2 to 5.

OMISSION OF REGULATION 11

30 Omit regulation 11.

EXCHANGE GAINS AND LOSSES (BRINGING INTO ACCOUNT GAINS OR LOSSES) REGULATIONS 2002

(SI 2002/1970, as amended by SI 2004/3259, SI 2005/2013, SI 2010/809 and SI 2013/1843)

Made on 25 July 2002 by the Treasury, in exercise of the powers conferred upon them by s. 84A(8)–(10) of the Finance Act 1996 and para. 26(5) of Sch. 23, and para. 16(8)–(10) of Schedule 26, to the Finance Act 2002. Operative from 1 October 2002.

CITATION, COMMENCEMENT AND EFFECT

1(1) These Regulations may be cited as the Exchange Gains and Losses (Bringing into Account Gains or Losses) Regulations 2002 and shall come into force on 1st October 2002 immediately after the Exchange Gains and Losses (Transitional Provisions and Savings) Regulations 2002.

1(2) These Regulations have effect in relation to accounting periods beginning on or after 1st October 2002.

INTERPRETATION

2(1) In these Regulations–

"Chapter 2" means Chapter 2 of Part 4 of the Finance Act 1996;

"chargeable gain" and **"allowable loss"** have the same meaning as they have for the purposes of the 1992 Act;

"foreign business asset" means, in relation to a company, an asset of an operation of the company which for accounting purposes is a foreign operation consisting of a branch;

"a no gain/no loss disposal" means a disposal on which, by virtue of any of the no gain/no loss provisions (within the meaning of section 288(3A) of the 1992 Act), neither a gain nor a loss accrues;

"original shares" and **"new holding"** have the same meaning as in section 127 of the 1992 Act or (as the case may be) that section as applied by virtue of any enactment relating to chargeable gains;

"paragraph 16" means paragraph 16 of Schedule 26 to the Finance Act 2002;

"section 84A" means section 84A of the Finance Act 1996;

"statement of recognised gains and losses and statement of changes in equity" mean the statements mentioned in subsection (3) of section 84A or sub-paragraph (3) of paragraph 16;

"the 1992 Act" means the Taxation of Chargeable Gains Act 1992;

"the 1994 Regulations" means the Exchange Gains and Losses (Alternative Method of Calculation of Gain or Loss) Regulations 1994.

"the Disregard Regulations" means the Loan Relationships and Derivative Contracts (Disregard and Bringing into Account of Profits and Losses) Regulations 2004.

2(1A) For the purposes of these Regulations a relevant transaction to which section 116(10) of the 1992 Act applies shall be treated as a disposal.

2(2) In these Regulations–

(a) any reference to a disposal of an asset shall be construed as a reference to any event which is or is treated as a disposal for the purposes of the 1992 Act; and

(b) any reference to the time of the disposal of an asset shall be construed as a reference to the time at which the disposal occurs for the purposes of that Act,

and, for the purposes of this paragraph, any reference to a disposal includes a part disposal.

2(2A) In these Regulations any reference to the amount or value of the consideration for the disposal of the asset is a reference to any amount treated as disposal consideration by any provision of the 1992 Act.

2(3) In these Regulations–

(a) any reference to an asset which is a ship or aircraft includes a reference to a contract–

   (i) to which section 67 of the Capital Allowances Act 2001 applies; and

   (ii) which relates to plant or machinery which is a ship or aircraft; and

(b)   any reference to a disposal of an asset which is a ship or aircraft by a person includes a reference to the case where a person ceases to be entitled to the benefit of such a contract and does not then in fact become the owner of the plant or the machinery to which the contract relates.

History – In reg. 2(1) the definition of "a no gain/no loss disposal" substituted by SI 2010/809, reg. 3(2), with effect in relation to a disposal of an asset made on or after 6 April 2010, subject to SI 2010/809, reg. 13 and 14(4). The former definition read as follows:

"**"a no gain/no loss disposal"** means a disposal on which neither a gain nor a loss accrues by virtue of any of the following provisions of the 1992 Act–

    (a)   section 139;
    (b)   section 140A;
    (c)   section 171;
    (d)   section 215; and
    (e)   section 216;".

In reg. 2(1) the definition of "foreign business asset" substituted by SI 2004/3259, reg. 3, with effect from 1 January 2005.
In reg. 2(1) the definitions of "statement of recognised gains and losses and statement of changes in equity" and "the Disregard Regulations" inserted by SI 2004/3259, reg. 3, with effect from 1 January 2005.
Reg. 2(1A) inserted by SI 2010/809, reg. 3(3), with effect in relation to a disposal of an asset made on or after 6 April 2010, subject to SI 2010/809, reg. 13 and 14(4).
Reg. 2(2A) inserted by SI 2010/809, reg. 3(4), with effect in relation to a disposal of an asset made on or after 6 April 2010, subject to SI 2010/809, reg. 13 and 14(4).

PRESCRIBED CIRCUMSTANCES IN WHICH REGULATION 4 APPLIES

3(1)   Regulation 4 applies in any of the circumstances prescribed by paragraphs (1A), (2) and (3) below.

3(1A)   The circumstances prescribed by this paragraph are that–

(a)   there is a disposal of an asset by a company in an accounting period beginning on or after 1st January 2005; and

(b)   in relation to a liability representing a loan relationship of the company or an obligation under a derivative contract of the company, an exchange gain or loss arose to the company which–

    (i)   was recognised in the company's statement of recognised gains and losses or statement of changes in equity and was set off by or against an amount which represents the whole or part of an exchange gain or loss arising in relation to the asset, or

    (ii)   was prescribed by regulation 3 or 4 of the Disregard Regulations.

3(2)   The circumstances prescribed by this paragraph are where there is a disposal of an asset by a company and–

(a)   any exchange gain or loss arose to the company in relation to the asset in an accounting period beginning on or after 1st October 2002 but before 1st January 2005; and

(b)   in accordance with generally accepted accounting practice an amount representing the whole or part of an exchange loss or gain which arises to the company in relation to a liability representing a loan relationship of the company or an obligation under a derivative contract–

    (i)   was carried to or sustained by the reserve mentioned in subsection (5) of section 84A or sub-paragraph (4) of paragraph 16; and

    (ii)   was set off by or against an amount which represents the whole or part of an exchange gain or loss arising in relation to the asset and falls within subsection (6) of section 84A or sub-paragraph (5) of paragraph 16.

3(3)   The circumstances prescribed by this paragraph are where there is a disposal of an asset by a company and there is in relation to the asset any of the following–

(a)   a deemed disposal under regulation 7(1A) of the 1994 Regulations (as modified by the Exchange Gains and Losses (Transitional Provisions and Savings) Regulations 2002);

(b)   a deferred gain or loss under regulation 8 of the 1994 Regulations in relation to which paragraph (3) or (4) of that regulation did not apply immediately before the relevant day;

(c)   a deferred gain or loss under regulation 9 of the 1994 Regulations in relation to which paragraph (3)(a) or (b) or paragraph (4)(a) or (b) of that regulation, as the case may be, did not apply immediately before the relevant day.

3(4)   In paragraph (3)(b) and (c) above "the relevant day" means the first day of the company's first accounting period to begin on or after 1st October 2002.

3(5)   In this regulation an obligation under a derivative contract is the obligation of the company to pay in exchange for one currency an amount in a second currency.

History – In reg. 3(1) the word "any" substituted for the word "either" and "(1A)," inserted after the word "paragraphs" by SI 2004/3259, reg. 4(2), with effect from 1 January 2005.
In reg. 3(1A)(b), the words "of the company" (appearing after "loan relationship") and "an obligation under" inserted by SI 2005/2013, reg. 3(2) which came into force on 11 August 2005.

Reg. 3(1A) originally inserted by SI 2004/3259, reg. 4(3), with effect from 1 January 2005.
Reg. 3(5) inserted by SI 2005/2013, reg. 3(3) which came into force on 11 August 2005.

GENERAL RULE FOR BRINGING AMOUNTS INTO ACCOUNT

4(1) For the purposes of the 1992 Act, the amount or value of the consideration for the disposal of the asset shall be—

(a) increased by the amount of any net gain, and

(b) subject to paragraph (2) below, reduced by the amount of any net loss.

This is subject to paragraph (4) below and regulations 6 and 8.

4(2) If the amount of any net loss exceeds the amount or value of the consideration that would be brought into account but for the application of this regulation, the amount of the excess of the net loss shall be treated as consideration for the acquisition of the asset for the purposes of section 38(1)(a) of the 1992 Act.

4(3) If section 42 of the 1992 Act applies, this regulation shall not apply to determine the amount or value of the consideration for the disposal referred to as "A" in that section in apportioning the sums attributable to the asset.

4(4) Paragraph (1) above does not apply if, immediately before the disposal, the asset is a foreign business asset other than shares not held on trading account.

History – Reg. 4 substituted by SI 2010/809, reg. 4, with effect in relation to a disposal of an asset made on or after 6 April 2010, subject to SI 2010/809, reg. 13 and 14(4). Former reg. 4 read as follows:

> "**4(1)** For the purposes of the 1992 Act, there shall be brought into account for the accounting period in which the disposal of the asset occurs–
> (a) as a chargeable gain accruing to the company at the time of the disposal, the amount of any net gain; or
> (b) as an allowable loss accruing to the company at the time of the disposal, the amount of any net loss.
> **4(2)** Paragraph (1) above does not have effect if the asset disposed of–
> (a) is a foreign business asset immediately before its disposal; or
> (b) consists of shares or an asset related to shares on the disposal of which no chargeable gain is treated as accruing by virtue of Part 1 of Schedule 7AC to the 1992 Act.
> **4(3)** Paragraph (1) above is subject to regulations 6 and 8.".

CALCULATION OF THE AMOUNT OF ANY NET GAIN OR NET LOSS FOR THE PURPOSES OF REGULATION 4

5(1) The amount of any net gain or net loss referred to in regulation 4(1) shall be calculated in accordance with this regulation.

5(1A) The net gain or net loss must be calculated in the company's relevant currency at the time of the disposal of the asset.

5(2) The amount of any net gain or loss shall be calculated by finding the aggregate of the amounts representing exchange gains or losses which accrued in relation to liabilities matched with the asset disposed of during the period in which the asset was held by the company disposing of it.

5(2A) Where section 9C of the Corporation Tax Act 2010 (chargeable gains and losses of companies) applies in relation to the asset disposed of, in determining the amounts representing accrued exchange gains or losses–

(a) exchange gains and losses must be calculated in the relevant currency of the company for the period in which the gains or losses arose,

(b) if there is a change in the company's relevant currency before the asset is disposed of, the amount of any accrued exchange gains or losses must be translated (or if it has previously been translated under this paragraph, further translated) into the relevant currency of the company immediately following the change by reference to the spot rate of exchange for the day of the change, and

(c) if sub-paragraph (b) applies as a result of more than one change in the company's relevant currency, it is to be applied in relation to each change in the order the changes were made (with the earliest first).

5(3) The aggregate referred to in paragraph (2) above shall be found in any manner that is just and reasonable having regard to–

(a) the effect of regulation 6 in the accounting period in which the disposal occurs or in any earlier accounting period; and

(b) the way in which such an aggregate was found for any earlier accounting period in accordance with this regulation.

5(4) [Omitted by SI 2010/809, reg. 5(3).]

5(5) Subject to paragraph (6), for the purposes of this regulation and regulation 8, a company's relevant currency at any time is its functional currency at that time.

5(6) If at any time–

(a) a company is a UK resident investment company, and

(b) the company has a designated currency which is different from its functional currency,

the company's relevant currency at that time is that designated currency.

5(7) In this regulation–

"**designated currency**" means the currency a company elects as its designated currency under section 9A of the Corporation Tax Act 2010;

"**functional currency**" has the same meaning as in section 17(4) of that Act;

"**investment company**" has the meaning given by section 17(3A) of that Act.

History – Reg. 5(1A) inserted by SI 2013/1843, reg. 2(2)(a), with effect in relation to a disposal of an asset made on or after 1 September 2013.

In reg. 5(2) the words "Subject to paragraph (4) below,", which appeared at the beginning, omitted by SI 2010/809, reg. 5(2), with effect in relation to a disposal of an asset made on or after 6 April 2010, subject to SI 2010/809, reg. 13 and 14(4).

Reg. 5(2A) inserted by SI 2013/1843, reg. 2(2)(b), with effect in relation to a disposal of an asset made on or after 1 September 2013.

Reg. 5(4) omitted by SI 2010/809, reg. 5(3), with effect in relation to a disposal of an asset made on or after 6 April 2010, subject to SI 2010/809, reg. 13 and 14(4). Former reg. 5(4) read as follows:

"**5(4)** Notwithstanding that a loss accruing to a company on the disposal of the asset is not deductible except from a chargeable gain of the kind mentioned in section 18(3) of the 1992 Act, where the aggregate referred to in paragraph (2) would be an amount of net gain for the purposes of regulation 4(1) in relation to that disposal, the amount of such a loss may be deducted from the aggregate.".

Reg. 5(5)–(7) inserted by SI 2013/1843, reg. 2(2)(c), with effect in relation to a disposal of an asset made on or after 1 September 2013.

ASSETS REPRESENTING CERTAIN LOAN RELATIONSHIPS AND SHIPS OR AIRCRAFT

6(1) This paragraph applies to an accounting period beginning on or after 1st January 2005 where the asset disposed of–

(a) represents a loan relationship of the company, or

(b) is a ship or aircraft.

6(2) Where paragraph (1) above applies, the amount of any net gain or net loss referred to in regulation 4 shall not be brought into account under that regulation but instead, for the purposes of Part 5 of the Corporation Tax Act 2009, shall be brought into account for the accounting period in which the disposal of the asset occurs as a credit or a debit (according to whether it is an amount of net gain or net loss) in respect of the loan relationships of the company.

6(3) [Omitted by SI 2004/3259, reg. 5(4).]

6(4) [Omitted by SI 2004/3259, reg. 5(4).]

History – In reg. 6(1) the words "to an accounting period beginning on or after 1st January 2005" inserted by SI 2004/3259, reg. 5(2), with effect from 1 January 2005.

In reg. 6(1)(a) the words "other than one which falls within section 92 or 93 of the Finance Act 1996 at the time of the disposal" which followed the word "company" omitted by SI 2004/3259, reg. 5(3), with effect from 1 January 2005.

Reg. 6(2) substituted by SI 2010/809, reg. 6, with effect in relation to a disposal of an asset made on or after 6 April 2010, subject to SI 2010/809, reg. 13 and 14(4). Former reg. 6(2) read as follows:

"**6(2)** Where paragraph (1) applies, the amount to be brought into account under regulation 4(1) shall not be brought into account, for the purposes of the 1992 Act, as a chargeable gain or allowable loss but instead, for the purposes of Chapter 2, as a credit or a debit (according to whether it is an amount of net gain or net loss) in respect of the loan relationships of the company.".

Reg. 6(3) and (4) omitted by SI 2004/3259, reg. 5(4), with effect from 1 January 2005.

REGULATIONS 5 AND 6: SUPPLEMENTARY

7(1) This regulation has effect for the purposes of regulations 5 and 6.

7(2) References to the asset disposed of include references to any predecessor asset which was–

(a) original shares; or

(b) "the old asset" construed in accordance with section 116 of the 1992 Act.

7(3) References to the company disposing of the asset include references to any predecessor company which was "the disposing company" for the purposes of regulation 8 of the 1994 Regulations and these Regulations.

7(4) In respect of any time falling within an accounting period beginning before 1st October 2002 a liability or obligation is matched with an asset to the extent that it is matched in accordance with an election under regulation 10 of the 1994 Regulations.

7(5) In respect of any time falling within an accounting period beginning on or after 1st October 2002 but before 1st January 2005–

(a)　a liability or obligation is fully matched with an asset where an amount representing the whole of an exchange gain or loss arising in relation to the liability or obligation is treated as mentioned in subsection (5) of section 84A or sub-paragraph (4) of paragraph 16; and

(b)　where the amount treated as mentioned in that subsection or that sub-paragraph represents only part of an exchange gain or loss, the liability shall be treated as being matched only to the corresponding extent.

7(5A) In respect of any time falling within an accounting period beginning on or after 1st January 2005–

(a)　a liability or obligation is fully matched with an asset if–

　(i)　an amount representing the whole of an exchange gain or loss arising in relation to the liability or obligation is recognised in the company's statement of recognised gains and losses or statement of changes in equity, and

　(ii)　the whole of an exchange gain or loss arising in relation to the asset is also so recognised, or

　(iii)　it is matched with that asset in accordance with regulation 3 or 4 of the Disregard Regulations; and

(b)　a liability or obligation is partly matched with an asset if–

　(i)　an amount representing part of an exchange gain or loss arising in relation to the liability or obligation is recognised in the company's statement of recognised gains and losses or statement of changes in equity, and

　(ii)　part of an exchange gain or loss arising in relation to the asset is also so recognised, or

　(iii)　an amount representing part of an exchange gain or loss arising in relation to the liability or obligation is matched with that asset in accordance with regulation 3 or 4 of the Disregard Regulations.

7(6) Where in any accounting period beginning on or after 1st October 2002 but before 1st January 2005–

(a)　a company holds more than one asset in relation to which there are amounts falling within subsection (6) of section 84A or sub-paragraph (5) of paragraph 16; and

(b)　the assets are denominated and the liabilities are expressed in the same currency,

the extent to which an asset is matched shall be determined in accordance with the rules set out in paragraph (7) below.

7(7) The following rules shall apply in relation to–

(a)　any disposal of an asset occurring before the relevant disposal;

(b)　any asset held at the time of the relevant disposal.

Rule 1

Liabilities or obligations are to be regarded as having been matched to the greatest possible extent with assets which–

(a)　represent loan relationships of the company; or

(b)　are ships or aircraft.

Rule 2

Subject to Rule 1, liabilities or obligations are to be regarded as having been matched to the greatest possible extent with assets (other than foreign business assets) on the disposal of which a chargeable gain accrues or would accrue.

Rule 3

Subject to Rules 1 and 2, liabilities or obligations are to be regarded as having been matched with assets–

(a)　on the disposal of which no chargeable gain is treated as accruing by virtue of Part 1 of Schedule 7AC to the 1992 Act;

(b)   on a disposal of which no chargeable gain would be treated as accruing by virtue of that Part if the disposal were made on a date falling more than twelve months after the date of the relevant disposal but excluding assets which–

(i)   are actually disposed of on a date falling less than twelve months after the date of the relevant disposal, and

(ii)   have been held for less than twelve months at the date of the actual disposal; or

(c)   which are foreign business assets held at the time of the relevant disposal.

7(8)   For the purposes of paragraph (6), the currency in which a liability or obligation is expressed is to be treated as the currency in which an asset is denominated if–

(a)   borrowing in that currency, or

(b)   the entering into a derivative contract whose underlying subject matter is that currency,

could reasonably be expected to eliminate or substantially reduce the economic risk of holding the asset which is attributable to fluctuations in exchange rates.

7(9)   In paragraph (7) above, **"the relevant disposal"** means the disposal referred to in regulation 4.

History – In reg. 7(3), the words "and these Regulations" inserted by SI 2010/809, reg. 7, with effect in relation to a disposal of an asset made on or after 6 April 2010, subject to SI 2010/809, reg. 13 and 14(4).
In reg. 7(4) and (5)(a) the words "or obligation" inserted after "liability" in each place it occurred by SI 2005/2013, reg. 4(2) which came into force on 11 August 2005.
In reg. 7(5) the words "but before 1st January 2005" inserted by SI 2004/3259, reg. 6(2) and the words "(other than ones which fall within section 93 of the Finance Act 1996)" omitted by reg. 6(4), with effect from 1 January 2005.
In reg. 7(5A)(a), (a)(i), (b), (b)(i) and (b)(iii) the words "or obligation" inserted after "liability" in each place it occurred by SI 2005/2013, reg. 4(2) which came into force on 11 August 2005.
Reg. 7(5A) originally inserted by SI 2004/3259, reg. 6(3), with effect from 1 January 2005.
In reg. 7(6) the words "but before 1st January 2005" inserted by SI 2004/3259, reg. 6(2) and the words "(other than ones which fall within section 93 of the Finance Act 1996)" omitted by reg. 6(4), with effect from 1 January 2005.
In reg. 7(7), r. 1, 2 and 3, the words "or obligations" inserted after the word "liabilities" in each place it occurs by SI 2005/2013, reg. 4(3) which came into force on 11 August 2005.
In reg. 7(8) the words "or obligation" inserted after "liability" by SI 2005/2013, reg. 4(2) which came into force on 11 August 2005.
Reg. 7(8) originally substituted by SI 2004/3259, reg. 6(5), with effect from 1 January 2005.

NO GAIN/NO LOSS DISPOSALS

8(1)   This regulation applies where the disposal of the asset is a no gain/no loss disposal.

8(2)   Where this regulation applies, regulation 4 shall not apply to bring into account the net gain or net loss on the occasion of the no gain/no loss disposal but shall instead apply to bring that net gain or net loss into account on the first relevant disposal of the asset.

8(2A)   Where section 9C of the Corporation Tax Act 2010 applies in relation to the asset on or before the first relevant disposal, for the purposes of determining the net gain or net loss to be brought into account on the first relevant disposal of the asset–

(a)   where the relevant currency of the company disposing of the asset is different from the relevant currency of the company acquiring the asset, the net gain or net loss must be translated into the relevant currency of the company acquiring the asset at the time of the no gain/no loss disposal by reference to the spot rate of exchange at that time,

(b)   if there is a change in the acquiring company's relevant currency before the asset is disposed of, the amount of the net gain or net loss must be translated (or if it has previously been translated under this paragraph, further translated) into the relevant currency of the company immediately following the change by reference to the spot rate of exchange for the day of the change,

(c)   if sub-paragraph (b) applies as a result of more than one change in the company's relevant currency, it is to be applied in relation to each change in the order the changes were made (with the earliest first), and

(d)   sub-paragraphs (a) and (b) apply in relation to each no gain/no loss disposal of the asset before the first relevant disposal of the asset.

8(3)   In this regulation, in relation to the disposal of an asset which is a no gain/no loss disposal, "the first relevant disposal" means the first subsequent disposal of that asset which is not a no gain/no loss disposal.

History – Reg. 8(2) substituted by SI 2010/809, reg. 8(2), with effect in relation to a disposal of an asset made on or after 6 April 2010, subject to SI 2010/809, reg. 13 and 14(4). Former reg. 8(2) read as follows:

"**8(2)**   Where this regulation applies, the amount to be brought into account under regulation 4(1) as a chargeable gain or allowable loss–
(a)   shall not be brought into account for the accounting period in which the disposal of the asset occurs, but instead
(b)   for the purposes of the 1992 Act, shall be brought into account as a chargeable gain or allowable loss, as the case may be, by the company making the first relevant disposal of the asset for the accounting period in which the first relevant disposal occurs.".

In reg. 8(3), "(b)", which appeared after "paragraph (2)", omitted by SI 2010/809, reg. 8(3), with effect in relation to a disposal of an asset made on or after 6 April 2010, subject to SI 2010/809, reg. 13 and 14(4).

Reg. 8(2A) inserted by SI 2013/1843, reg. 2(3)(a), with effect in relation to a disposal of an asset made on or after 1 September 2013.

In reg. 8(3), the words "this regulation" substituted for the words "paragraph (2) above" by SI 2013/1843, reg. 2(3)(b), with effect in relation to a disposal of an asset made on or after 1 September 2013.

CASES WHERE THERE IS NO DISPOSAL OF THE ASSET BY VIRTUE OF SECTION 116(10) OF THE 1992 ACT

9   [Omitted by SI 2010/809, reg. 9.]

History – Reg. 9 omitted by SI 2010/809, reg. 9, with effect in relation to a disposal of an asset made on or after 6 April 2010, subject to SI 2010/809, reg. 13 and 14(4). Former reg. 9 read as follows:

"**9(1)** This regulation applies in the circumstances prescribed by paragraph (2) below.

9(2) The circumstances prescribed by this paragraph are where the circumstances prescribed by regulation 3(1A) and (2) would exist but for there being no disposal of the asset for the purposes of the 1992 Act by virtue of section 116(10) of that Act ("section 116(10)").

9(3) Where this regulation applies, the amount which, but for section 116(10), would be brought into account under regulation 4(1) as a chargeable gain or allowable loss shall be found and paragraph (4) below shall apply.

9(4) Where this paragraph applies–

(a)   if the amount found under paragraph (3) above would be brought into account as a chargeable gain, the market value of the asset shall, for the purposes of paragraph (a) of section 116(10), be increased by an amount equal to that amount;

(b)   if the amount found under paragraph (3) above would be brought into account as an allowable loss

    (i)   the market value of the asset shall, for the purposes of paragraph (a) of section 116(10), be reduced by an amount equal to that amount; and

    (ii)   if that amount exceeds the amount of the market value, an allowable loss equal in amount to the excess shall be treated as accruing on the subsequent disposal of the new asset (within the meaning of section 116(4) of the 1992 Act).".

CASES WHERE, BUT FOR SECTION 116, SECTION 127 OF THE 1992 ACT WOULD APPLY IN RELATION TO ASSETS AS REGARDS WHICH PARAGRAPH (2)(A), BUT NOT PARAGRAPH (2)(B), OF REGULATION 8 HAS HAD EFFECT

10   [Omitted by SI 2010/809, reg. 10.]

History – Reg. 10 omitted by SI 2010/809, reg. 10, with effect in relation to a disposal of an asset made on or after 6 April 2010, subject to SI 2010/809, reg. 13 and 14(4). Former reg. 10 read as follows:

"**10(1)** This regulation applies in the circumstances prescribed by paragraph (2) below.

10(2) The circumstances prescribed by this paragraph are where, but for section 116 of the 1992 Act, section 127 of that Act would apply in relation to a transaction involving original shares which are or include an asset as regards which paragraph (2)(a), but not paragraph (2)(b), of regulation 8 has had effect.

10(3) Where this regulation applies, regulation 9(4) shall apply to the amount which, by virtue of regulation 8(2)(a), is not brought into account as a chargeable gain or an allowable loss for the accounting period in which the disposal of the asset occurs in the same way as it applies to an amount found under regulation 9(3).".

CASES WHERE THERE IS NO DISPOSAL OF THE ASSET BY VIRTUE OF SECTION 127 OF THE 1992 ACT

11   [Omitted by SI 2010/809, reg. 11.]

History – Reg. 11 omitted by SI 2010/809, reg. 11, with effect in relation to a disposal of an asset made on or after 6 April 2010, subject to SI 2010/809, reg. 13 and 14(4). Former reg. 11 read as follows:

"**11(1)** This regulation applies in the circumstances prescribed by paragraph (2) below.

11(2) The circumstances prescribed by this paragraph are where the circumstances prescribed by regulation 3(1A) and (2) would exist but for there being no disposal of the asset for the purposes of the 1992 Act by virtue of section 127 of that Act ("section 127").

11(3) Where this regulation applies, the amount which, but for section 127, would be brought into account under regulation 4(1) as a chargeable gain or allowable loss shall be found and paragraph (4) below shall apply.

11(4) Where this paragraph applies–

(a)   if the amount found under paragraph (3) above would be brought into account as a chargeable gain, in computing the amount of any chargeable gain or allowable loss accruing on the subsequent disposal of the new holding, the consideration received on that disposal shall be increased by an amount equal to that amount;

(b)   if the amount found under paragraph (3) above would be brought into account as an allowable loss–

    (i)   in computing the amount of any chargeable gain or allowable loss accruing on the subsequent disposal of the new holding, the consideration received on that disposal shall be reduced by an amount equal to that amount; and

    (ii)   if that amount exceeds the amount of the consideration, an allowable loss equal in amount to the excess shall be treated as accruing on that disposal.".

CASES WHERE SECTION 127 OF THE 1992 ACT APPLIES IN RELATION TO ASSETS AS REGARDS WHICH PARAGRAPH (2)(A), BUT NOT PARAGRAPH (2)(B), OF REGULATION 8 HAS HAD EFFECT

12   [Omitted by SI 2010/809, reg. 12.]

History – Reg. 12 omitted by SI 2010/809, reg. 12, with effect in relation to a disposal of an asset made on or after 6 April 2010, subject to SI 2010/809, reg. 13 and 14(4). Former reg. 12 read as follows:

"**12(1)** This regulation applies in the circumstances prescribed by paragraph (2) below.

12(2) The circumstances prescribed by this paragraph are where section 127 of the 1992 Act applies in relation to a transaction involving original shares which are or include an asset as regards which paragraph (2)(a), but not paragraph (2)(b), of regulation 8 has had effect.

12(3) Where this regulation applies, regulation 11(4) shall apply to the amount which, by virtue of regulation 8(2)(a), has not been brought into account as a chargeable gain or an allowable loss for the accounting period in which the disposal of the asset occurs in the same way as it applies to an amount found under regulation 11(3).".

CASES WHERE MATCHED ASSETS REPRESENT LOAN RELATIONSHIPS

History – The heading to reg. 13 substituted by SI 2004/3259, reg. 9(2), with effect from 1 January 2005. The former heading read as follows: "CASES WHERE EXCHANGE GAINS OR LOSSES FALL WITHIN SUBSECTION (4) OF SECTION 84A".

13(1) This regulation applies in the circumstances prescribed by paragraph (2) and (2A) below.

13(2) The circumstances prescribed by this paragraph are where there is a disposal of an asset by a company and the asset disposed of represents a loan relationship of the company in relation to which exchange gains or losses have fallen within subsection (4) of section 84A.

13(2A) The circumstances prescribed by this paragraph are where there is a disposal of an asset in an accounting period beginning on or after 1st January 2005 representing a loan relationship in relation to which exchange gains or losses were recognised in the company's statement of recognised gains and losses or statement of changes in equity.

13(3) Where this regulation applies, an amount equal to the amount of any net gain or net loss shall be brought into account, for the purposes of Chapter 2, as a credit or a debit (according to whether it is an amount of net gain or net loss) in respect of the loan relationship for the accounting period in which the disposal occurs.

13(4) For the purposes of this regulation, the amount of any net gain or net loss shall be calculated by finding the aggregate of the amounts representing the exchange gains and losses which fell within paragraphs (2) and (2A).

History – In reg. 13(1) the words "paragraphs (2) and (2A)" substituted for the words "paragraph (2)" by SI 2004/3259, reg. 9(3), with effect from 1 January 2005.
Reg. 13(2A) inserted by SI 2004/3259, reg. 9(4), with effect from 1 January 2005.
In reg. 13(4) the words "paragraphs (2) and (2A)" substituted for the words "subsection (4) of section 84A" by SI 2004/3259, reg. 9(3), with effect from 1 January 2005.

CASES WHERE THERE ARE NO MATCHING ASSETS

14 [Omitted by SI 2005/2013, reg. 5.]

History – Reg. 14 omitted by SI 2005/2013, reg. 5 which came into force on 11 August 2005.
Reg. 14 previously inserted by SI 2004/3259, reg. 10, with effect from 1 January 2005.

Statutory Instruments

VENTURE CAPITAL TRUST (EXCHANGE OF SHARES AND SECURITIES) REGULATIONS 2002

(SI 2002/2661)

Made on 22 October 2002 by the Treasury, in exercise of the powers conferred on them by s. 842AA(5AD) of the Income and Corporation Taxes Act 1988 and para. 11B of Sch. 28B to that Act. Operative from 13 November 2002.

CITATION, COMMENCEMENT AND EFFECT

1(1)   These Regulations may be cited as the Venture Capital Trust (Exchange of Shares and Securities) Regulations 2002 and shall come into force on 13th November 2002.

1(2)   These Regulations have effect in relation to exchanges of shares or securities occurring on or after 21st March 2000.

INTERPRETATION

2(1)   In these Regulations unless the context otherwise requires—

"earn-out right" has the meaning in section 138A(1) of the 1992 Act (references to "debentures" being read as references to "securities" as defined below);

the **"issue"** of any shares or securities has the meaning in section 135 of the 1992 Act, except for a security consisting in a liability in respect of an unsecured loan where it has effect as a reference to the making of the loan;

"market value" shall be construed in accordance with sections 272 and 273 of the 1992 Act;

"a monetary right" means a right under an agreement to receive a monetary amount at a future time in respect of shares or securities, whether or not the amount is ascertainable at the date of the agreement;

"original shares or securities" has the meaning in paragraph 11B(2) of Schedule 28B;

"recognised stock exchange" has the meaning given by section 841;

"Schedule 28B" means Schedule 28B to the Taxes Act;

"securities" has the meaning given by section 842AA(12);

"the 1992 Act" means the Taxation of Chargeable Gains Act 1992;

"the Taxes Act" means the Income and Corporation Taxes Act 1988;

"venture capital trust" has the meaning given by section 842AA(1).

2(2)   References in these Regulations (except regulation 5(1)(a), (b) and (d)) to an exchange of shares or securities shall be construed in accordance with paragraph 11B(2) of Schedule 28B, and **"exchanged"** has a corresponding meaning.

2(3)   For the purposes of these Regulations, old shares and new shares are matching shares in relation to each other if the old shares are the shares for which the new shares are exchanged under the arrangements, and the same provision shall apply, with any necessary modifications, as between old securities and new securities, and old securities and new shares.

2(4)   References in these Regulations to a section, without more, are to that section of the Taxes Act.

SCOPE OF REGULATIONS

3   These Regulations apply to any exchange of shares or securities held by a venture capital trust—

(a)   which falls within the terms of paragraph 11B(1)(a) to (c) of Schedule 28B,

(b)   which falls within one of the cases described in regulations 4 to 6, and

(c)   where the trust company receives, in respect of the old shares or old securities, new shares or new securities, with or without other consideration.

EXCHANGE OF SHARES OR SECURITIES FOR THOSE IN THE SAME COMPANY

4(1)   The case described in this regulation is an exchange of shares or securities where—

(a)   persons are, whether for payment or not, issued shares in or securities of a company in respect of and in proportion to (or as nearly as may be in proportion to) their holdings of shares in or securities of the company or of any class of shares in or securities of the company,

(b)   the person in question is a venture capital trust,

(c)   the new shares are issued in respect of old shares or old securities, and the new securities are issued solely in respect of old securities,

(d)   immediately after the exchange, the old shares and old securities are cancelled or otherwise extinguished, and

(e)   the exchange is not an exchange of convertibles for shares to which paragraph 10D of Schedule 28B applies.

4(2)   In paragraph (1) and regulation 7—

(a)   expressions have the same meanings as in section 126(2) of the 1992 Act;

(b)   the shares or securities issued to the trust company are referred to as the "new shares" and the "new securities" respectively, and the trust company's former holding mentioned in paragraph (1)(a) is referred to, separately and as the case may be, as the "old shares" and the "old securities" respectively.

EXCHANGE OF SHARES OR SECURITIES FOR THOSE IN ANOTHER COMPANY

5(1)   The case described in this regulation is where—

(a)   a company ("company B") issues shares or securities to a person in exchange for the shares in or securities of another company ("company A"),

(b)   either—

    (i)   in consequence of the exchange, company B will hold more than 50% of the ordinary share capital of company A, or

    (ii)   company B issues the shares or securities in exchange for shares in or securities of company A as the result of a general offer made to members of company A or any class of them (with or without exceptions for persons connected with company B), and made in the first instance on a condition such that if it were satisfied company B would have control of company A,

(c)   the person in question is a venture capital trust,

(d)   the new shares are issued in exchange for old shares or old securities, and the new securities are issued solely in exchange for old securities, and

(e)   the arrangements under which the exchange takes place are not arrangements to which paragraph 10C of Schedule 28B (acquisitions for restructuring purpose) applies.

5(2)   In paragraph (1)(a), (b) and (d) and regulation 8—

(a)   expressions (other than "securities") have the same meanings as in section 135 of the 1992 Act;

(b)   the shares in or securities of company B issued to the trust company are referred to as the "new shares" and the "new securities" respectively, and the shares in or securities of company A held by the trust company and mentioned in paragraph (1)(a) are referred to as the "old shares" and the "old securities" respectively.

SCHEME OF RECONSTRUCTION INVOLVING ISSUE OF SHARES OR SECURITIES

6(1)   The case described in this regulation is where—

(a)   an arrangement between a company ("company A") and—

    (i)   the persons holding shares in or securities of the company, or

    (ii)   where there are different classes of shares in or securities of the company, the persons holding any class of those shares or securities,

is entered into for the purposes of, or in connection with, a scheme of reconstruction,

(b)   under the arrangement—

    (i)   another company ("company B") issues shares or securities to those persons in respect of and in proportion to (or as nearly as may be in proportion to) their original holding, but

    (ii)   the shares in or securities of company A comprised in their original holding are either retained by those persons or cancelled, redeemed or otherwise extinguished,

(c)   the person in question is a venture capital trust, and

(d)   the new shares are issued in respect of old shares or old securities, and the new securities are issued solely in respect of old securities.

6(2)   In paragraph (1) and regulation 9–

(a)   expressions (other than "securities") have the same meanings as in section 136(1) and (3) to (5) of the 1992 Act (references to "debentures" in those provisions being read as references to "securities" as defined above);

(b)   the shares in or securities of company B issued to the trust company are referred to as the "new shares" and the "new securities" respectively, and the trust company's original holding in company A is referred to, separately and as the case may be, as the "old shares" and the "old securities" respectively.

PROVISION WHERE THERE IS AN EXCHANGE OF SHARES OR SECURITIES IN THE SAME COMPANY

7(1)   In relation to any case described in regulation 4 the following paragraphs have effect.

7(2)   For the purposes of subsection (2)(b) to (d) of section 842AA, the aggregate value of the new shares and new securities shall be determined, immediately after the exchange and until such time as those shares or securities fall to be revalued in accordance with subsection (5) of that section, in accordance with the following formula:

$$Nv = Ov \times \frac{Nmv}{Nmv + C}$$

Where–

Nv is the aggregate value of the new shares and new securities to be determined in accordance with this paragraph,

Ov is the aggregate value of the old shares and old securities when last valued in accordance with subsection (5) of section 842AA ("historic values"),

Nmv is the aggregate market value, immediately after the exchange, of the new shares and new securities,

C is the aggregate market value, immediately after the exchange, of–

(i)   any monetary amount,

(ii)   any monetary right (without any discount for postponement of the right to receive the payment or any part of it), and

(iii)   any other consideration or receipt (except the new shares and new securities),

received by the venture capital trust as consideration for, or in respect of, the old shares or old securities, and

"immediately after the exchange" in this regulation means immediately after the events mentioned in regulation 4(1)(d).

7(3)   For the purposes of subsection (2)(b) to (d) of section 842AA, where the venture capital trust retains original shares or securities in the company which are not included in the exchange of old shares or old securities for new shares or new securities, such original shares or securities shall, immediately after the exchange, continue to be valued at their value, or apportioned value, as the case may be, when last valued before the exchange in accordance with subsection (5) of section 842AA, until such time as they fall to be revalued in accordance with that subsection.

7(4)   For the purposes of paragraph 10B of Schedule 28B the like provisions as are contained in paragraphs (2) and (3) shall apply (substituting references to valuations in accordance with paragraph 10B for references to valuations in accordance with subsection (5) of section 842AA).

7(5)   Where the company in which the venture capital trust holds the old shares or old securities is deemed to satisfy the requirements of paragraph 2 of Schedule 28B (unquoted company) by virtue of sub-paragraph (6) of that paragraph for a period of five years after ceasing to be an unquoted company, the company shall be deemed to satisfy those requirements in relation to the new shares or new securities for the same five year period.

7(6)   Subject to paragraph (7), where the old shares or old securities are shares or securities in relation to which the requirements of paragraphs 6 and 8 of Schedule 28B were (or were deemed to be[)] satisfied to any extent immediately before the exchange, those requirements shall be deemed, at all times after that time, to be satisfied to the same extent in relation to the matching new shares or new securities.

7(7)   Where there is a time following the exchange when (apart from the exchange) the requirements of paragraph 6 of Schedule 28B would have ceased under–

(a)   sub-paragraph (2) of that paragraph, or

(b)   this paragraph,

to be satisfied in relation to the old shares or old securities, those requirements shall cease at that time to be satisfied in relation to the matching new shares or new securities.

7(8) For the purposes of paragraph 7 of Schedule 28B any new shares or new securities shall be deemed—

(a)   to have been issued at the time when the matching old shares or old securities were issued (or, as the case may be, were deemed to have been issued), and

(b)   by virtue of that issue, to have raised the same amount of money as was raised (or, as the case may be, was deemed to be raised) by virtue of the issue of the matching old shares or old securities.

7(9) In determining whether the requirements of paragraph 9 of Schedule 28B are satisfied in relation to the company at any time in the period for giving effect to the exchange, the exchange shall be disregarded.

7(10) The reference in paragraph (9) to the period for giving effect to the exchange is to the period which—

(a)   begins on the day when a shareholder disposes of, redeems or otherwise ceases to possess shares or securities in consequence of the exchange or, where there is more than one exchange of shares or securities involved in a company reorganisation, the exchanges, and is the first shareholder to do so, and

(b)   ends on the earlier of—

   (i)   the date when the last of the shares or securities to be issued in consequence of the exchange or exchanges is issued, and

   (ii)   the day six months after the date in sub-paragraph (a) (or such later date as the Board may by notice in writing allow).

PROVISION WHERE EXCHANGE OF SHARES OR SECURITIES FOR THOSE IN ANOTHER COMPANY

8(1) In relation to a case described in regulation 5, the following paragraphs have effect.

8(2) For the purposes of subsection (2)(b) to (d) of section 842AA, the aggregate value of the new shares and new securities issued to the venture capital trust shall be determined, immediately after the exchange and until such time as those shares or securities fall to be revalued in accordance with subsection (5) of that section, in accordance with the formula in regulation 7(2) (substituting references to the period for giving effect to the exchange for references to the events mentioned in regulation 4(1)(d)).

8(3) For the purposes of paragraph 10B of Schedule 28B, the like provisions as are contained in paragraph (2) shall apply (substituting references to valuations in accordance with paragraph 10B for references to valuations in accordance with subsection (5) of section 842AA).

8(4) The new shares and new securities held by the venture capital trust shall be treated, during the period for giving effect to the exchange, as meeting the requirements of Schedule 28B.

8(5) The requirements of and arrangements referred to in paragraph 9 of Schedule 28B, to the extent that they are incidental to the exchange, shall be disregarded before and during that period.

8(6) The new shares and new securities shall be treated at all times following the end of the period for giving effect to the exchange as having met the requirements of paragraphs 6 and 7 of Schedule 28B.

8(7) Where, immediately after the end of the period for giving effect to the exchange, any of the new shares or new securities are found not to meet the requirements of paragraph 2 of Schedule 28B, or of that paragraph and any other paragraphs of that Schedule (other than paragraph 6 or 7), those shares or securities shall be treated as meeting those requirements until the end of the period specified in paragraph (8) or the disposal by the venture capital trust of those shares or securities, whichever is the earlier to occur.

8(8) The period specified is the period that—

(a)   begins on the date when new shares or new securities are first issued to the venture capital trust or, if later, on the date on which all the new shares or new securities issued to the venture capital trust become fully tradeable, and

(b)   ends immediately before the second anniversary of that date.

8(9) Where, immediately after the end of the period for giving effect to the exchange, any of the new shares or new securities are found not to meet the requirements of any paragraph of Schedule 28B other than paragraph 2, 6 or 7, those shares or securities shall be treated as meeting those requirements until the end of the period–

(a)   beginning on the date when new shares or new securities are first issued to the venture capital trust ("the first issue date"), and

(b)   ending on the earlier of–

    (i)   the disposal by the venture capital trust of those shares or securities, or

    (ii)   subject to paragraph (10), in the case of shares, the day 3 years after the first issue date and, in the case of securities, the day 5 years after the first issue date.

8(10)   Where, in a case falling within the terms of paragraph (9)(b)(ii), before the relevant date there mentioned, the new shares or new securities become marketed to the general public (within the meaning of paragraph 2(3) of Schedule 28B), there shall be substituted for that date the second anniversary of the date on which the new shares or new securities became so marketed or, if later, the second anniversary of the date on which those shares or securities became fully tradeable.

8(11)   References in this regulation to the period for giving effect to the exchange are references to the period which–

(a)   begins when a shareholder or holder of securities ceases to possess shares in or securities of company A in consequence of the exchange, and is the first shareholder or holder of securities to do so, and

(b)   ends when the last of the shares in or securities of company B to be issued in consequence of the exchange (excluding shares or securities issued in pursuance of an earn-out right) is issued.

8(12)   Shares or securities become fully tradeable for the purposes of this regulation and regulation 9 when, in circumstances where they are offered for issue to the shareholders or holders of securities of company A, they cease to be subject to–

(a)   rules of the recognised stock exchange (or other exchange) governing the offer that prohibit or restrict the disposal of the shares or securities to any other person, and

(b)   conditions prohibiting or restricting the disposal of the shares or securities to any other person that are contained in any contract entered into by any of the following persons–

    (i)   company B, or a company disposing of the shares or securities,

    (ii)   the person or persons sponsoring, underwriting or organising the offer, and

    (iii)   the venture capital trust in question.

PROVISION WHERE SCHEME OF RECONSTRUCTION INVOLVING ISSUE OF SHARES OR SECURITIES

9(1)   In relation to a case described in regulation 6 the following paragraphs have effect as regards–

(a)   any shares in or securities of company A that are retained by the venture capital trust after the scheme of reconstruction, whether old shares or old securities or original shares or securities, not included in the scheme of reconstruction (the "company A shares or securities"), and

(b)   the shares in or securities of company B issued to the venture capital trust as mentioned in regulation 6(2)(b) (the "new shares" and the "new securities" respectively).

9(2)   For the purposes of subsection (2)(b) to (d) of section 842AA, the aggregate value of the new shares and new securities and any company A shares or securities shall be determined, immediately after the reorganisation period and until such time as those shares or securities fall to be revalued in accordance with subsection (5) of that section, in accordance with the formula in regulation 7(2) but where–

    Nv is the aggregate value of the new shares and new securities, and of the company A shares or securities, to be determined in accordance with that paragraph,

    Nmv is the aggregate market value, immediately after the reorganisation period, of the new shares and new securities and the company A shares or securities, and

any reference to events mentioned in regulation 4(1)(d) is replaced with a reference to the reorganisation period.

9(3)   For the purposes of paragraph 10B of Schedule 28B, the like provisions as are contained in paragraph (2) shall apply (substituting references to valuations in accordance with paragraph 10B for references to valuations in accordance with subsection (5) of section 842AA).

9(4)   The new shares and new securities held by the venture capital trust shall be treated, during the reorganisation period, as meeting the requirements of Schedule 28B.

9(5)   The requirements of and arrangements referred to in paragraph 9 of Schedule 28B, to the extent that they are incidental to the scheme of reconstruction, shall be disregarded before and during the reorganisation period.

9(6)   The new shares or new securities held by the venture capital trust shall be treated at all times following the date on which they were issued to the trust company as having met the requirements of paragraphs 6 and 7 of Schedule 28B.

9(7)   Where, immediately after the date on which the new shares or new securities were issued to the venture capital trust, those shares or securities are found not to meet the requirements of paragraph 2 of that Schedule, or of that paragraph and any other paragraph of that Schedule excepting paragraph 6 or 7, those shares or securities shall be treated as meeting those requirements until the end of the period specified in paragraph (8) or the disposal by the venture capital trust of those shares or securities, whichever is the earlier to occur.

9(8)   The period specified is the period that–

(a)   begins on the date on which the new shares or new securities were issued to the venture capital trust or, if later, on the date on which all those shares or securities become fully tradeable, and

(b)   ends immediately before the second anniversary of that date.

9(9)   Where, immediately after the date on which the new shares or new securities were issued to the venture capital trust, those shares or securities are found not to meet the requirements of any paragraph of Schedule 28B other than paragraph 2, 6 or 7, those shares or securities shall be treated as meeting the requirements of that Schedule until the end of the period–

(a)   beginning on the date when new shares or new securities are first issued to the venture capital trust **("the first issue date")**, and

(b)   ending on the earlier of–

(i)   the disposal by the venture capital trust of those shares or securities, or

(ii)   subject to paragraph (10), in the case of shares, the day 3 years after the first issue date and, in the case of securities, the day 5 years after the first issue date.

9(10)   Where, in a case falling within the terms of paragraph (9)(b)(ii), before the relevant date there mentioned, the new shares or new securities become marketed to the general public (within the meaning of paragraph 2(3) of Schedule 28B), there shall be substituted for that date the second anniversary of the date on which the new shares or new securities became so marketed or, if later, the second anniversary of the date on which those shares or securities became fully tradeable.

9(11)   In this regulation references to the reorganisation period are to the period which–

(a)   begins when a shareholder or holder of securities receives shares in or securities of company B in consequence of the scheme of reconstruction, and is the first person to do so, and

(b)   ends when the last of the shares in or securities of company B to be issued in consequence of the scheme of reconstruction (excluding shares or securities issued in pursuance of an earn-out right) is issued.

EARN-OUTS

10(1)   Where, in a case described in either regulation 5 or 6–

(a)   shares in or securities of company B **("earn-out shares or securities")** are issued to a venture capital trust in pursuance of an earn-out right, which was conferred on the trust company in exchange for old shares or old securities, and

(b)   the requirements of regulation 5(1)(d) or 6(1)(d), as the case may be, would be satisfied if the earn-out right were treated as replaced by the earn-out shares or securities that are issued in pursuance of it–

(i)   regulation 8(4) to (12) or regulation 9(4) to (11), as the case may be, shall apply to the earn-out shares and securities as they apply to new shares and new securities; and

(ii)   the trust company may elect to recalculate the formula in regulation 7(2) (as applied by regulation 8(2) or (3) or 9(2) or (3)).

10(2)   The recalculation shall be made–

(a)   including the earn-out shares and securities in the calculation of Nv and Nmv (but at their market value immediately after they were issued), and

(b)   omitting the earn-out right from the calculation of C.

10(3)   An election under this regulation in respect of any right–

Statutory Instruments

(a)   must be made, by a notice given to an officer of the Board, within the period of one year from the end of the accounting period in which the relevant earn-out shares and securities are issued, and

(b)   shall be irrevocable.

APPORTIONMENT

11(1)   For the purposes of these Regulations (and of subsection (2)(b) to (d) of section 842AA and paragraph 10B of Schedule 28B), where it is necessary to apportion any value between the new shares or new securities issued to the venture capital trust (or one or more classes thereof), such apportionment shall be carried out–

(a)   in the first instance, having regard to the historic values of any old shares or old securities in relation to which the new shares or new securities are matching shares or securities,

(b)   otherwise according to such method as is just and reasonable, and

(c)   in any event, with a view to securing that the requirements of section 842AA(2)(b) to (d), or paragraph 10B of Schedule 28B, as the case may be, do not cease to be met.

11(2)   In the application of paragraph (1) to regulation 9, references to new shares and new securities shall be construed as extending to company A shares or securities (as defined in that regulation) with any necessary modifications.

COMMUNITY INVESTMENT TAX RELIEF (ACCREDITATION OF COMMUNITY DEVELOPMENT FINANCE INSTITUTIONS) REGULATIONS 2003

(SI 2003/96 amended by SI 2008/383, SI 2009/56 and SI 2013/417)

Made on 23 January 2003 by the Treasury, in exercise of the powers conferred upon them by para. 4(2)(b), (4), (5), (6) and 5 of Sch. 16 to the Finance Act 2002. Operative from 13 February 2003.

PART 1 – INTRODUCTORY

CITATION AND COMMENCEMENT

1 These Regulations may be cited as the Community Investment Tax Relief (Accreditation of Community Development Finance Institutions) Regulations 2003 and shall come into force on 13th February 2003.

INTERPRETATION

2 In these Regulations–

"**accreditation**" means accreditation as a community development finance institution;

"**CDFI**" means a body accredited as a community development finance institution under Chapter 2 of Part 7 of the Income Tax Act 2007;

"**the five year period**" means the period of five years beginning with the day the investment is made;

"**the first investment**" in relation to an investment made in a CDFI means the first investment made in the CDFI in its current period of accreditation;

"**investment**"

(a) in relation to an individual, shall be construed in accordance with section 336 of the Income Tax Act 2007

(b) in relation to a company, has the meaning given in section 221 of the Corporation Tax Act 2010;

"**investment fund**" has the meaning given in regulation 9;

"**notice**" means notice in writing;

"**qualifying enterprise**" has the meaning given in regulation 10;

"**qualifying investment**"

(a) in relation to an investment made by an individual, means an investment in respect of which the individual is eligible under section 334 of the Income Tax Act 2007 for community investment tax relief; and

(b) in relation to an investment made by a company, has the meaning given in section 225 of the Corporation Tax Act 2010;

"**relevant investment**" has the meaning given in regulation 11;

"**residential property**" has the meaning given in Annex D of the Material Concerning the Accreditation of Community Development Finance Institutions published by the Secretary of State;

"**retail community development finance institution**" shall be construed in accordance with section 340(6)(b), (7) and (8) of the Income Tax Act 2007;

"**tax relief certificate**" means a certificate issued by the CDFI in respect of the investment which is in the form specified by the Commissioners for Her Majesty's Revenue and Customs;

History – In reg. 2, in the definition of "CDFI" the words "Chapter 2 of Part 7 of the Income Tax Act 2007" substituted for "Schedule 16 to the Finance Act 2002" by SI 2008/383, reg. 3(2), with effect from 11 March 2008.
In reg. 2, the definition of "the Board" omitted by SI 2008/383, reg. 3(3), with effect from 11 March 2008.
In reg. 2, the definition of "the Director of Enterprise Environment" omitted by SI 2013/417, reg. 5(a), with effect from 1 April 2013.
In reg. 2, the former definition of "the Director of Enterprise Environment" inserted by SI 2008/383, reg. 3(4), with effect from 11 March 2008.
In reg. 2, the definition of "five year period" substituted by SI 2008/383, reg. 3(5), with effect from 11 March 2008.
In reg. 2, the definition of "the first investment" inserted by SI 2013/417, reg. 5(b), with effect from 1 April 2013.
In reg. 2, the definition of "the Investment Director" omitted by SI 2008/383, reg. 3(6), with effect from 11 March 2008.

In reg. 2, in the definition of "investment" the words "section 221 of the Corporation Tax Act 2010" substituted for the words "paragraph 2 of Schedule 16 to the Finance Act 2002" by SI 2013/417, reg. 5(c), with effect from 1 April 2013.

In reg. 2, the definition of "investment" substituted by SI 2008/383, reg. 3(7), with effect from 11 March 2008.

In reg. 2, in the definition of "qualifying investment" the words "section 225 of the Corporation Tax Act 2010" substituted for the words "paragraph 2 of Schedule 16 to the Finance Act 2002" by SI 2013/417, reg. 5(d), with effect from 1 April 2013.

In reg. 2, the definition of "qualifying investment" substituted by SI 2008/383, reg. 3(8), with effect from 11 March 2008.

In reg. 2, in the definition of "retail community development finance institution", the words "section 340(6)(b), (7) and (8) of the Income Tax Act 2007" substituted for "paragraph 4(6) and (7) of Schedule 16 to the Finance Act 2002" by SI 2008/383, reg. 3(9), with effect from 11 March 2008.

In reg. 2, the definition of "the Small Business Service" omitted by SI 2008/383, reg. 3(10), with effect from 11 March 2008.

In reg. 2, the definition of "tax relief certificate" substituted by SI 2008/383, reg. 3(11), with effect from 11 March 2008.

PART 2 – APPLICATION AND CRITERIA FOR ACCREDITATION

CRITERIA FOR ACCREDITATION

3   For the purposes of section 340(2)(b) of the Income Tax Act 2007 the criteria to be satisfied for accreditation are specified in Part 2 (Application and Criteria for Accreditation) of the Material Concerning the Accreditation of Community Development Finance Institutions published by the Secretary of State.

History – In reg. 3, the words "section 340(2)(b) of the Income Tax Act 2007" substituted for "paragraph 4(2)(b) of Part 2 of Schedule 16 to the Finance Act 2002" by SI 2008/383, reg. 4, with effect from 11 March 2008.

NOTIFICATION OF ACCREDITATION OR REFUSAL

4   The Secretary of State must give notice to a body of the grant of an accreditation specifying the date of the grant of accreditation and the date on which the period of accreditation begins.

5   The Secretary of State must give notice to a body of a refusal to grant accreditation specifying the date of the refusal and the reasons for the refusal.

PART 3 – TERMS AND CONDITIONS OF ACCREDITATION

6   An accreditation is subject to the terms set out in this Part.

PUBLICATION OF DETAILS

7(1)   It is a term of accreditation that the CDFI agrees to the publication of the information specified in paragraph (2) in a list which the Secretary of State may publish from time to time.

7(2)   The information specified for the purpose of paragraph (1) is–

(a)   the name of the CDFI;

(b)   the business address of the CDFI;

(c)   the name of an individual who may be contacted at the CDFI;

(d)   the date the CDFI was granted accreditation; and

(e)   an outline of the aims and business operations of the CDFI.

7(3)   The CDFI must give notice to the Secretary of State of–

(a)   any change to the information specified in subparagraphs (a) to (d) of paragraph (2), and

(b)   any material change to the information specified in subparagraph (e) of paragraph (2),

within 30 days of the relevant change.

7(4)   The CDFI is liable to a penalty of £100 payable to the Department for Business, Enterprise and Regulatory Reform for each failure to notify a change to the specified information in accordance with paragraph (3) unless the Secretary of State is satisfied that the CDFI had a reasonable excuse for failing to notify the change.

History – In reg. 7(4), the words "Secretary of State" substituted for the words "Director of Enterprise Environment" by SI 2013/417, reg. 12(a), with effect from 1 April 2013.

In reg. 7(4), the words "Department for Business, Enterprise and Regulatory Reform" substituted for "Small Business Service" by SI 2008/383, reg. 5, with effect from 11 March 2008.

In reg. 7(4), the words "Director of Enterprise Environment" substituted for "Investment Director" by SI 2008/383, reg. 5, with effect from 11 March 2008.

GENERAL CDFI INVESTMENT TERMS

8(1)   It is a term of accreditation that–

(a)   on or before the first anniversary of the date the first investment was made in the CDFI, at least 25% of the amount of the investment fund is invested in relevant investments in qualifying enterprises;

(b)   on or before the second anniversary of the date the first investment was made in the CDFI, at least 50% of the amount of the investment fund is invested in relevant investments in qualifying enterprises;

(c)   on or before the third anniversary of the date the first investment was made in the CDFI at least 75% of the amount of the investment fund is invested in relevant investments in qualifying enterprises; and

(d)   at the end of each year ending on a subsequent anniversary of the date the first investment was made in the CDFI, an average of at least 75% of the amount of the investment fund has been invested in relevant investments in qualifying enterprises.

8(2)   For the purpose of paragraph (1)(d), the average percentage of the investment fund invested in relevant investments in qualifying enterprises is to be found on the last day of the year in question by calculating–

(a)   the average of the percentages so invested as at close of business on each day of that year, or

(b)   the average of the percentages so invested as at close of business on the relevant dates.

8(3)   **"The relevant dates"**, in relation to a year, means–

(a)   a date falling within the first three months of the year,

(b)   a date falling within the second three months of the year,

(c)   a date falling within the third three months of the year, and

(d)   a date falling within the final three months of the year,

8(4)   A date falling within any of the time periods specified in paragraph (3)(b), (c) and (d) must be at least 87 days but not more than 95 days after the preceding date.

8(5)   If the percentage of the investment fund invested in relevant investments in qualifying enterprises at close of business on any day exceeds 100% of the investment fund, the excess shall be disregarded.

History – In reg. 8(1)(a) the words "the date the first investment was made in the CDFI" substituted for the words "the date the CDFI was first granted accreditation ("the accreditation date")" by SI 2013/417, reg. 6(a), with effect from 1 April 2013 (but only in relation to a CDFI whose current accreditation period starts on or after 1 April 2013).
In reg. 8(1)(b), (c) and (d) the words "the date the first investment was made in the CDFI" substituted for the words "the accreditation date" by SI 2013/417, reg. 6(b), with effect from 1 April 2013 (but only in relation to a CDFI whose current accreditation period starts on or after 1 April 2013).
Reg. 8 substituted by SI 2008/383, reg. 6, with effect from 11 March 2008.

MEANING OF THE "INVESTMENT FUND"

9(1)   The amount of the investment fund at a given date (**"the relevant date"**) is the sum of–

$$A - (B + C)$$

Here–

A is the amount of qualifying investments and investments by other CDFIs in the CDFI made on or before the relevant date and held continuously since the investment was made until the relevant date, but does not include any qualifying investments or investments by other CDFIs in the CDFI made at any time during the three months prior to the relevant date;

B is any amount payable by the CDFI at the relevant date or at any time during the three months following the relevant date to repay, redeem or buy-back the capital element of any qualifying investment;

C is the amount of any investment made by the CDFI from the investment fund which has been written-off in accordance with generally accepted accounting practice.

9(2)   For the purpose of paragraph (1) where a qualifying investment is a loan which authorises the CDFI to draw down amounts of the loan over a period of time, the amount of the qualifying investment is the amount drawn down at the relevant date.

MEANING OF "QUALIFYING ENTERPRISE"

10(1)   For the purposes of these Regulations an enterprise is a qualifying enterprise if–

(a)   the enterprise is a small or medium-sized enterprise;

(b)   the CDFI can demonstrate that at the time the investment in the enterprise was made the enterprise was unable to obtain finance from other sources; and

(c)   the enterprise falls within one of the following Cases.

Case 1

The enterprise is located in a geographic area identified in Annex A of the Material Concerning the Accreditation of Community Development Finance Institutions published by the Secretary of State.

Case 2

The enterprise is located in an area which the CDFI, by reference to Government-recognised measures of disadvantage relating to–

(i)   income;

(ii)   employment;

(iii)   health, deprivation and disability;

(iv)   education, skills and training;

(v)   geographical access to services, and

(vi)   housing,

can demonstrate has a level of disadvantage comparable to those identified in Annex A of the Material Concerning the Accreditation of Community Development Finance Institutions published by the Secretary of State.

Case 3

The enterprise is owned and operated by, or intended to serve, individuals recognised as being disadvantaged on account of their ethnicity, gender, age, disability or other similar defining characteristic.

10(2) For the purpose of paragraph (1)(a), a **"small or medium-sized enterprise"** means a micro, small or medium-sized enterprise as defined in Commission Recommendation 2003/361/EC of 6th May 2003 ("the Recommendation", references to the Annex being references to the Annex to the Recommendation), subject to the qualification set out in paragraph (3).

10(3) If a company ("C") is a micro, small or medium-sized enterprise, disregarding any partner enterprise or linked enterprise, and, taken alone, it would satisfy the employee limit and a least one of the financial limits, but–

(a)   the number of employees, annual turnover or annual balance sheet total (as the case may be) of a partner enterprise or linked enterprise to which it is related has been taken into account in determining whether the employee limit or the financial limits have been exceeded, and

(b)   a partner enterprise or linked enterprise to which C is related would, disregarding the number of employees, and the annual turnover and balance sheet totals of C, exceed the employee limit or both of the financial limits,

Article 4(2) of the Annex shall be disregarded in determining whether C is a small or medium-sized enterprise for an accounting period in which it exceeds the employee or financial limits.

10(4) For the purpose of paragraph (3), references to the employee limit and the financial limits are to the limits respectively on the number of employees, and the annual turnover and balance sheet totals, contained in Article 2(1) of the Annex.

History – Reg. 10(2)–(4) substituted for reg. 10(2) by SI 2008/383, reg. 9, with effect from 11 March 2008.

MEANING OF "RELEVANT INVESTMENT"

11(1) Subject to paragraph (4), for the purposes of these Regulations a relevant investment is an investment made by the CDFI in an enterprise where–

(a)   it makes a loan (whether secured or unsecured) to the enterprise, or

(b)   an issue of securities of or shares in the enterprise, for which the CDFI has subscribed, is made to the CDFI.

11(2) For the purposes of paragraph (1)(a)–

(a)   the CDFI does not make a loan to an enterprise where–

(i)   the enterprise uses overdraft facilities provided by the CDFI, or

(ii)   the CDFI subscribes for or otherwise acquires securities of the enterprise;

(b)   where the loan agreement authorises the enterprise to draw down amounts of the loan over a period of time the loan is treated as made at the time when the first amount is drawn down.

11(3) For the purpose of these Regulations where a relevant investment is a loan within paragraph (2)(b) the amount of the relevant investment is the amount drawn down at a given date.

11(4) The investments specified in Schedule 1 are not relevant investments.

LIMITS ON QUALIFYING INVESTMENTS

12(1) The CDFI must give notice to the Secretary of State at least one month before entering into any arrangements or commitments with the aim of increasing qualifying investments in the CDFI to more than 125% of the amount stated in its application for accreditation ("the 125% limit").

12(2) The Secretary of State may approve the increase by notice to the CDFI.

12(3) Where–

(a)   the CDFI fails to give notice in accordance with paragraph (1), or

(b)   the Secretary of State does not approve the increase in accordance with paragraph (2),

the Secretary of State may treat all or some of the investments made by the CDFI after the date on which the qualifying investments exceed the 125% limit as not being relevant investments for the purposes of regulation 8 up to an amount equal to the amount by which the qualifying investments exceed the 125% limit.

History – In reg. 12(1), the words "Secretary of State" substituted for the words "Director of Enterprise Environment" by SI 2013/417, reg. 12(b), with effect from 1 April 2013.
In reg. 12(1), the words "Director of Enterprise Environment" substituted for "Investment Director" by SI 2008/383, reg. 5, with effect from 11 March 2008.
In reg. 12(2), the words "Secretary of State" substituted for the words "Director of Enterprise Environment" by SI 2013/417, reg. 12(b), with effect from 1 April 2013.
In reg. 12(2), the words "Director of Enterprise Environment" substituted for "Investment Director" by SI 2008/383, reg. 5, with effect from 11 March 2008.
In reg. 12(3), the words "Secretary of State" substituted (twice) for the words "Director of Enterprise Environment" by SI 2013/417, reg. 12(b), with effect from 1 April 2013.
In reg. 12(3), the words "Director of Enterprise Environment" substituted for "Investment Director" in both places by SI 2008/383, reg. 5, with effect from 11 March 2008.

NOTICE OF FIRST INVESTMENT IN A CDFI

12A(1) A CDFI must notify the Secretary of State in writing of the date the first investment is made in the CDFI, no later than three months after that date.

12A(2) A CDFI that does not comply with paragraph (1) is liable to a penalty of £500 payable to the Department for Business, Innovation and Skills.

12A(3) But paragraph (2) does not apply if in the opinion of the Secretary of State the CDFI had a reasonable excuse for failing to comply with paragraph (1).

History – Reg. 12A inserted by SI 2013/417, reg. 7, with effect from 1 April 2013 (but only in relation to a CDFI whose current accreditation period starts on or after 1 April 2013).

REPORTING REQUIREMENTS

13(1) The CDFI must make an annual report to the Department for Business, Enterprise and Regulatory Reform–

(a)   within three months of each anniversary of the date the first investment was made in the CDFI, or

(b)   subject to paragraph (2), on such other date coincident with the CDFI's reporting cycle and agreed with the Department for Business, Enterprise and Regulatory Reform.

13(2) The first annual report made by the CDFI must be made no later than 18 months after the date the first investment was made in the CDFI.

13(3) The annual report shall be in the form provided by the Secretary of State for this purpose.

13(4) Subject to paragraph (5), the CDFI is liable to a penalty of £500 payable to the Department for Business, Enterprise and Regulatory Reform where the annual report is not made within three months of date on which it was due under paragraph (1).

13(5) Paragraph (4) does not apply if in the opinion of the Secretary of State the CDFI had reasonable excuse for failing to make an annual return.

History – In reg. 13(1)(a) the words "the date the first investment was made in the CDFI" substituted for the words "the date on which the CDFI was last granted accreditation" by SI 2013/417, reg. 8(a), with effect from 1 April 2013 (but only in relation to a CDFI whose current accreditation period starts on or after 1 April 2013).
In reg. 13(1), the words "Department for Business, Enterprise and Regulatory Reform" substituted for "Small Business Service" in both places by SI 2008/383, reg. 5, with effect from 11 March 2008.
In reg. 13(2) the words "the date the first investment was made in the CDFI" substituted for the words "the date accreditation was granted" by SI 2013/417, reg. 8(b), with effect from 1 April 2013 (but only in relation to a CDFI whose current accreditation period starts on or after 1 April 2013).
In reg. 13(4), the words "Department for Business, Enterprise and Regulatory Reform" substituted for "Small Business Service" by SI 2008/383, reg. 5, with effect from 11 March 2008.
In reg. 13(5), the words "Secretary of State" substituted for the words "Director of Enterprise Environment" by SI 2013/417, reg. 12(c), with effect from 1 April 2013.
In reg. 13(5), the words "Director of Enterprise Environment" substituted for "Investment Director" by SI 2008/383, reg. 5, with effect from 11 March 2008.

Statutory Instruments

TAX RELIEF CERTIFICATE

14(1)　Subject to paragraph (2), the CDFI must issue a tax relief certificate to the investor or its nominee within 30 days of receiving an investment from an individual or a company.

14(2)　Where the investment is received before the grant of accreditation but an application for accreditation is made before 6th April 2003, the CDFI must issue a tax relief certificate within 30 days of the grant of accreditation.

PART 4 – GENERAL PROVISIONS

WITHDRAWAL OF ACCREDITATION

15(1)　The Secretary of State must withdraw the CDFI's accreditation–

(a)　subject to regulations 15A to 15E, with effect from the time of the failure, where the CDFI fails to satisfy the terms of regulation 8;

(b)　subject to paragraph (2), where the CDFI makes a direct or indirect investment in residential property from the investment fund; and

(c)　subject to paragraph (3), where the CDFI fails to make an annual report within 12 months of the date on which it was due under paragraph (1) of regulation 13.

15(2)　Paragraph (1)(b) does not apply where–

(a)　the CDFI can demonstrate that to the best of its knowledge and belief it had not invested in residential property, and

(b)　the CDFI divested itself of the investment within three months of–

　　(i)　the date it discovered that the investment was in residential property, or

　　(ii)　the date of receipt of a notice from the Department for Business, Enterprise and Regulatory Reform that the investment is in residential property,

　　whichever is the earlier.

15(3)　Paragraph (1)(c) does not apply if in the opinion of the Secretary of State the CDFI had reasonable excuse for failing to make an annual return.

15(4)　A withdrawal of an accreditation must be given by notice by the Secretary of State specifying the date from which accreditation is withdrawn and the reasons for the withdrawal.

15(5)　The CDFI must within 30 days of receiving notice under paragraph (4) of withdrawal of accreditation give notice to each of the investors to which it has issued a tax relief certificate in respect of investments made within the specified period stating that accreditation has been withdrawn and specifying the date from which accreditation is withdrawn.

15(6)　For the purpose of paragraph (5) **"specified period"** means the five years immediately preceding the date from which accreditation is withdrawn.

History – In reg. 15(1)(a) the words "subject to regulations 15A to 15E," inserted by SI 2008/383, reg. 7, with effect from 11 March 2008.
In reg. 15(2)(b)(ii), the words "Department for Business, Enterprise and Regulatory Reform" substituted for "Small Business Service" by SI 2008/383, reg. 5, with effect from 11 March 2008.
In reg. 15(3), the words "Secretary of State" substituted for the words "Director of Enterprise Environment" by SI 2013/417, reg. 12(d), with effect from 1 April 2013.
In reg. 15(3), the words "Director of Enterprise Environment" substituted for "Investment Director" by SI 2008/383, reg. 5, with effect from 11 March 2008.

APPLICATIONS RELATING TO FAILURES TO SATISFY THE CONDITIONS OF REGULATION 8

15A(1)　This regulation applies where after the end of a year ending upon the anniversary of the date the first investment was made in the CDFI a CDFI becomes aware of a failure to satisfy the conditions of regulation 8 in respect of that year.

15A(2)　Where this regulation applies, the CDFI may apply in writing to the Secretary of State within 3 months after the end of that year for a determination that the accreditation shall not be withdrawn notwithstanding the failure to satisfy the conditions of regulation 8.

15A(3)　An application under this regulation must specify–

(a)　the circumstances that have led to the failure to satisfy the conditions of regulation 8, and

(b)　the measures taken by the CDFI to avoid the failure.

15A(4) Where the failure relates to a condition specified in regulation 8(1)(a), (b) or (c), the application must state–

(a)   the maximum percentage of the investment fund that was suitably invested during that year, and

(b)   the maximum percentage that would have been so invested had it not been for the circumstances that led to the failure.

15A(5) Where the failure relates to the condition specified in regulation 8(1)(d), the application must state–

(a)   the average percentage of the investment fund suitably invested as calculated in accordance with regulation 8(2), and

(b)   the average percentage of the investment fund that would have been suitably invested as calculated in accordance with regulation 8(2) had it not been for the circumstances that led to the failure.

History – In reg. 15A(1) the words "the date the first investment was made in the CDFI" substituted for the words "the date that the CDFI was first granted accreditation" by SI 2013/417, reg. 9, with effect from 1 April 2013 (but only in relation to a CDFI whose current accreditation period starts on or after 1 April 2013).
Reg. 15A inserted by SI 2008/383, reg. 8, with effect from 11 March 2008.

APPLICATIONS RELATING TO ANTICIPATED FAILURES TO SATISFY CONDITIONS OF REGULATION 8

15B(1) This regulation applies where during a year ending upon the anniversary of the date the first investment was made in a CDFI the CDFI anticipates likely failure to satisfy the conditions of regulation 8 in respect of that year.

15B(2) Where this regulation applies the CDFI may apply in writing to the Secretary of State for a decision that, should the anticipated likely failure occur at the end of the year as a result of the circumstances specified in the application, the Secretary of State will determine after the end of the year in respect of which the application relates, that accreditation will not be withdrawn.

15B(3) An application under this regulation must specify–

(a)   the circumstances that are anticipated will lead to the failure to satisfy the conditions of regulation 8, and

(b)   any measures that have been taken or that will be taken by the CDFI in that year–
    (i)   to avoid that failure, and
    (ii) to ensure that the maximum amount of the investment fund that is possible in all the circumstances will be suitably invested.

15B(4) Where the failure relates to a condition specified in regulation 8(1)(a), (b), or (c) the application must state–

(a)   the maximum percentage of the investment fund suitably invested at the time the application under this regulation is submitted to the Secretary of State,

(b)   the maximum percentage of the investment fund that would have been so invested had it not been for the circumstances that are anticipated to lead to the failure, and

(c)   as far as possible, the maximum possible percentage of the investment fund that the CDFI anticipates will be so invested as a result of the measures taken under paragraph (3)(b).

15B(5) Where the anticipated failure relates to a condition specified in regulation 8(1)(d), the application must state–

(a)   the average percentage of the investment fund suitably invested as calculated in accordance with regulation 8(2)(a) for each day of that year before the day on which the application is submitted to the Secretary of State, and

(b)   as far as possible the average percentage of the investment fund that will be suitably invested on the final day of that year as calculated in accordance with regulation 8(2) (a) or (b) further to the measures taken under paragraph (3)(b).

15B(6) Where a CDFI submits an application under this regulation further to which the Secretary of State decides under regulation 15D that after the end of the year to which the application relates accreditation will not be withdrawn and the CDFI thereafter anticipates that it will fail–

(a)   to take the measures as specified in the application, or

(b)   to ensure that the maximum or average amount of the investment fund as specified in the application will be suitably invested, it may make a further application under this paragraph (2) in respect of that anticipated failure and this regulation will apply to that failure as it would apply to an application in respect of an anticipated failure to satisfy the conditions of regulation 8.

History – In reg. 15B(1) the words "the date the first investment was made in a CDFI" substituted for the words "the date a CDFI was first granted accreditation" by SI 2013/417, reg. 10, with effect from 1 April 2013 (but only in relation to a CDFI whose current accreditation period starts on or after 1 April 2013).
Reg. 15B inserted by SI 2008/383, reg. 8, with effect from 11 March 2008.

APPLICATIONS UNDER REGULATION 15A: FAILURES THAT HAVE OCCURRED

15C(1)   This regulation applies where an application under regulation 15A has been made in respect of a failure to meet the conditions of regulation 8.

15C(2)   Where the Secretary of State is satisfied that–

(a)   the failure to satisfy the conditions of regulation 8 was as a result of the circumstances specified in the application,

(b)   those circumstances were outside the control of the CDFI and, where applicable, any person connected with it, and

(c)   the CDFI acted reasonably in its attempts to avoid failing to satisfy the conditions of regulation 8 and to minimise the extent of failure,

the Secretary of State must determine that accreditation shall not be withdrawn and shall notify the CDFI of the determination.

15C(3)   Where the Secretary of State does not have sufficient information to make a determination under this regulation he may ask the CDFI to supply further information prior to making a determination.

History – Reg. 15C inserted by SI 2008/383, reg. 8, with effect from 11 March 2008.

APPLICATIONS UNDER REGULATION 15B: ANTICIPATED FAILURES

15D(1)   This regulation applies where an application under regulation 15B has been made in respect of an anticipated failure to meet the conditions of regulation 8.

15D(2)   Where the Secretary of State is satisfied that–

(a)   the anticipated failure to satisfy the conditions of regulation 8 arises from the circumstances specified in the application,

(b)   those circumstances are outside the control of the CDFI and, where applicable, any person connected with it, and

(c)   the measures specified in the application that have been taken or that will be taken to prevent failure or to minimise the extent of failure are reasonable in all the circumstances,

he must, subject to paragraphs (4) and (5), decide that where such measures as are specified in the application are taken by the CDFI but the CDFI thereafter fails to meet the conditions of regulation 8 as a result of the circumstances specified in the application the accreditation shall not be withdrawn after the end of that year if failure occurs as a result of those circumstances.

15D(3)   The Secretary of State must notify the CDFI of his decision made under paragraph (2).

15D(4)   Where the Secretary of State does not have sufficient information to make a decision under this regulation he may request the CDFI to provide more information prior to making a decision.

15D(5)   Where the Secretary of State decides under paragraph (2) that accreditation will not be withdrawn after the end of the year to which the application relates and the CDFI–

(a)   becomes aware that the measures specified in the application will not prevent the failure or minimise the extent of failure, or

(b)   becomes unable to implement such measures,

the CDFI may submit a further application under regulation 15B in respect of the same circumstances specifying further measures that will be taken to avoid or minimise the extent of failure.

15D(6)   Where the Secretary of State notifies the CDFI under paragraph (3) that accreditation may be withdrawn the CDFI may submit a further application under regulation 15B.

History – Reg. 15D inserted by SI 2008/383, reg. 8, with effect from 11 March 2008.

REGULATIONS 15A TO 15D: SUPPLEMENTARY

15E(1)   Where a CDFI has submitted an application under regulation 15B but the Secretary of State does not make a decision under regulation 15D before the end of the year in question and the CDFI thereafter fails to satisfy the conditions of regulation 8 for that year it must submit an application under regulation 15A.

15E(2) Where the Secretary of State has received one or more applications under regulation 15B upon which no decision has yet been made, the Secretary of State must not make a decision that accreditation will not be withdrawn until he is satisfied that it should not be withdrawn in respect of each and every application.

15E(3) A determination under regulation 15C not to withdraw accreditation and a decision under regulation 15D that accreditation may not be withdrawn shall not prevent the Secretary of State from withdrawing accreditation where he has grounds for doing so as a result of other circumstances which are not the subject of an application under regulation 15A or 15B.

15E(4) For the purposes of regulations 15A and 15B "suitably invested" means invested in relevant investments in qualifying enterprises.

15E(5) For the purposes of regulations 15C and 15D–

(a)   a person who acts on behalf of a CDFI to manage its investment is treated as a CDFI, and

(b)   section 993 of the Income Tax Act 2007 shall apply for determining whether a person is connected with a CDFI.

History – Reg. 15E inserted by SI 2008/383, reg. 8, with effect from 11 March 2008.

APPEALS AGAINST REFUSAL TO GRANT ACCREDITATION OR WITHDRAWAL OF ACCREDITATION

16(1) An appeal may be brought against a refusal to grant accreditation or a withdrawal of accreditation.

16(2) Notice of an appeal under this regulation must be given–

(a)   in writing,

(b)   within 30 days of the date of the notification of the refusal under regulation 5 or the withdrawal under regulation 15(4), and

(c)   to the Secretary of State.

16(3) The notice of appeal must require the Secretary of State to transmit to the tribunal–

(a)   in an appeal against a refusal to grant accreditation, the application for accreditation, together with any information or particulars provided by the body to the Secretary of State in support of the application, or

(b)   in an appeal against a withdrawal of accreditation, the notice under regulation 15(4) together with any information or particulars prepared by the Department for Business, Enterprise and Regulatory Reform leading to the issue of that notice.

16(4) The tribunal may allow the appeal and–

(a)   in an appeal against a refusal to grant accreditation, direct that the Secretary of State accredit the body within 14 days of its decision, or

(b)   in an appeal against a withdrawal of accreditation, direct that the withdrawal was ineffective.

16(5) Notwithstanding the provisions of sections 11 and 13 of the Tribunals, Courts and Enforcement Act 2007, the decision of the tribunal shall be final.

History – In reg. 16(1), the words "to the Special Commissioners", which appeared after "An appeal", omitted by SI 2009/56, art. 3(2) and Sch. 2, para. 83(2), operative from 1 April 2009 subject to transitional and saving provisions in SI 2009/56, Sch. 3. In reg. 16(2)(c), the words "Secretary of State" substituted for the words "Director of Enterprise Environment" by SI 2013/417, reg. 12(e), with effect from 1 April 2013.
In reg. 16(2)(c), the words "Director of Enterprise Environment" substituted for "Investment Director" by SI 2008/383, reg. 5, with effect from 11 March 2008.
In reg. 16(3), the words "Secretary of State" substituted for the words "Director of Enterprise Environment" by SI 2013/417, reg. 12(e), with effect from 1 April 2013.
In reg. 16(3), "tribunal" substituted for "Special Commissioners" by SI 2009/56, art. 3(2) and Sch. 2, para. 83(3), operative from 1 April 2009 subject to transitional and saving provisions in SI 2009/56, Sch. 3.
In reg. 16(3)(b), the words "Department for Business, Enterprise and Regulatory Reform" substituted for "Small Business Service" by SI 2008/383, reg. 5, with effect from 11 March 2008.
In reg. 16(3), the words "Director of Enterprise Environment" substituted for "Investment Director" by SI 2008/383, reg. 5, with effect from 11 March 2008.
In reg. 16(4), "tribunal" substituted for "Special Commissioners" by SI 2009/56, art. 3(2) and Sch. 2, para. 83(3), operative from 1 April 2009 subject to transitional and saving provisions in SI 2009/56, Sch. 3.
Reg. 16(5) substituted by SI 2009/56, art. 3(2) and Sch. 2, para. 83(4), operative from 1 April 2009 subject to transitional and saving provisions in SI 2009/56, Sch. 3. Former reg. 16(5) read as follows:

"**16(5)** The decision of the Special Commissioners shall be final.".

SCHEDULE 1 – INVESTMENTS WHICH ARE NOT RELEVANT INVESTMENTS

Regulation 11(4)

GENERAL INVESTMENTS

1   Any investment which benefits directly or indirectly from the security offered by a Phoenix Fund guarantee or by any similar publicly-funded underwriting or guarantee arrangement.

2(1)   Any loan to a profit-distributing enterprise–

(a)   which is not made on terms that are equivalent to those offered by conventional sources of finance, or

(b)   as a consequence of which, and for so long as, the total amount of loans to that enterprise exceeds £100,000 ("the £100,000 limit").

2(2)   Where the £100,000 limit is exceeded–

(a)   by two or more loans made on the same day, or

(b)   in any other circumstances where it is not possible to establish which loan caused the limit to be exceeded,

the Secretary of State shall determine which of those loans shall not constitute relevant investments so that the amount of relevant investments in the enterprise approximates to but does not exceed the £100,000 limit.

History – In para. 2(2), the words "Secretary of State" substituted for the words "Director of Enterprise Environment" by SI 2013/417, reg. 12(f), with effect from 1 April 2013.
In para. 2(2), the words "Director of Enterprise Environment" substituted for "Investment Director" by SI 2008/383, reg. 5, with effect from 11 March 2008.

3(1)   Any loan to a profit-distributing enterprise which is not made at market rates or above, or, where interest is not charged on loans the fee structure is not at an equivalent level.

3(2)   In paragraph (1) **"market rate"** means the European Commission's Hurdle Rate, which is the Reference Rate (as published at http://europa.eu.int/comm/competition/state_aid/others/reference_rates. html) plus four percentage points, or more.

3A   Any equity investment in a profit-distributing enterprise.

History – Para. 3A inserted by SI 2008/383, reg. 10, with effect from 11 March 2008.

4(1)   Any loan to a non-profit-distributing enterprise for the purposes of undertaking community projects as a consequence of which, and for so long as, the total amount invested in that enterprise exceeds £250,000 ("the £250,000 limit").

4(2)   For the purpose of paragraph (1) **"community projects"** means–

(a)   public sector projects,

(b)   projects which benefit charities and other non-profit distributing bodies which are engaged entirely in public functions, non-competitive and non-commercial activity, or

(c)   projects which are commercial in the sense that there is remuneration for the service provider and competition for their supply, but which are small-scale and purely local in nature.

4(3)   Where the £250,000 limit is exceeded–

(a)   by two or more loans made on the same day, or

(b)   in any other circumstances where it is not possible to establish which loan caused the limit to be exceeded,

the Secretary of State shall determine which of those loans shall not constitute relevant investments so that the amount of relevant investments in the enterprise approximates to but does not exceed the £250,000 limit.

History – In para. 4(1) the words "or equity investment in" omitted by SI 2013/417, reg. 11(2)(a), with effect from 1 April 2013 (but only in relation to investments made in a CDFI on or after 1 April 2013).
In para. 4(3), the words "Secretary of State" substituted for the words "Director of Enterprise Environment" by SI 2013/417, reg. 12(f), with effect from 1 April 2013.
In para. 4(3)(a) the words "or equity investments" omitted, in para. 4(b) the words "or investment" omitted and the words "shall determine which of those loans shall not" substituted for the words "shall determine which of those loans or investments shall not" by SI 2013/417, reg. 11(2)(b), with effect from 1 April 2013 (but only in relation to investments made in a CDFI on or after 1 April 2013).
In para. 4(3), the words "Director of Enterprise Environment" substituted for "Investment Director" by SI 2008/383, reg. 5, with effect from 11 March 2008.

5   Any investment in an enterprise as a consequence of which, and for so long as, the total amount invested by the CDFI in that enterprise exceeds 20% of the amount of the investment fund at–

(a)   for the first year following accreditation, the date the investment is made by the CDFI, and

(b)   thereafter, the immediately preceding anniversary of the accreditation date.

6(1)   Any investment in an enterprise within Case 2 of regulation 10 as a consequence of which, and for so long as–

(a)   the total amount invested out of the investment fund by the CDFI in enterprises in Case 2 exceeds the amount invested in enterprises within Cases 1 and 3; or

(b)   the number of investments out of the investment fund by the CDFI in enterprises in Case 2 exceeds the number of investments in enterprises within Cases 1 and 3.

6(2)   For the purposes of paragraph (1) an investment in an enterprise which is within both Case 2 and Case 3 shall be treated as being only within Case 3.

PROPERTY INVESTMENTS, WHICH ARE NOT RELEVANT INVESTMENTS

7   Any investment which funds directly or indirectly the acquisition, construction or development of residential property.

8(1)   Any investment which funds directly or indirectly the acquisition, construction or development of non-residential property where, on the next anniversary of the date on which the CDFI was granted accreditation, in consequence of that investment–

(a)   the total amount of investment within Case 1 below exceeds the amount of relevant investments other than those in Case 1, or

(b)   the total amount of investment within Case 2 below exceeds one half of the relevant investments within Case 1.

Case 1

1.1   Investment in a non profit-distributing enterprise, the main activity of which is to hold and invest in or to develop non-residential property.

1.2   Investment in a development trust or other social enterprise for the purpose of investment in or development of non-residential property, whether owned by the trust or by others.

Case 2

2.1   Investment in a profit-distributing enterprise, the main activity of which is holding land with the aim of benefiting from capital appreciation of that land, or with the aim of receiving income through the exploitation of an interest in it.

2.2   Investment in a profit-distributing enterprise, the main activity of which is non-residential property development.

8(2)   For the purposes of paragraph (1) where a investment is a loan which authorises the CDFI to draw down amounts of the loan over a period of time, the amount of the investment is the amount drawn down at the relevant date.

INVESTMENTS BY RETAIL COMMUNITY INVESTMENT FINANCE INSTITUTIONS

9   Where the CDFI has been accredited as a retail community investment finance institution, any investment in another CDFI or in any other body whose objective is to provide finance for enterprises in or for disadvantaged communities where, as a consequence of that investment, and for so long as, for more than three months the total amount invested in such bodies exceeds 10% of the amount of the investment fund at–

(a)   for the first year following the date the first investment is made in the CDFI, the date the investment is made by that CDFI, and

(b)   thereafter, the immediately preceding anniversary of the date the first investment is made in the CDFI.

History – Para. 9(a) substituted by SI 2013/417, reg. 11(3)(a), with effect from 1 April 2013 (but only in relation to a CDFI whose current accreditation period starts on or after 1 April 2013). Former para. 9(a) read as follows:
"(a)   for the first year following accreditation, the date the investment is made by the CDFI, and"
In para. 9(b), the words "date the first investment is made in the CDFI" substituted for the words "accreditation date" by SI 2013/417, reg. 11(3)(b), with effect from 1 April 2013 (but only in relation to a CDFI whose current accreditation period starts on or after 1 April 2013).

10   Any investment by a retail community investment finance institution in a body other than a CDFI whose objective is to provide finance for enterprises in or for disadvantaged communities as a consequence of which, and for so long as, the total amount of investment in such enterprises exceeds £250,000.

INVESTMENTS BY WHOLESALE CDFIS

11(1) Any investment made by a wholesale CDFI in an enterprise where as a consequence of which, and for so long as, the total amount of investment in that enterprise exceeds–

(a)   20% of the amount of the investment fund at–

    (i)   for the first year following the date the first investment is made in the CDFI, the date the investment is made by that CDFI, and

    (ii)   thereafter, the immediately preceding anniversary of the date the first investment is made in the CDFI, or

(b)   £2,500,000

whichever is the lesser amount.

11(2) Any investment made by a wholesale CDFI in a body other than a CDFI whose objective is to provide finance for enterprises in or for disadvantaged communities as a consequence of which, and for so long as, the total amount invested in that body exceeds £250,000.

11(3) A **"wholesale CDFI"** means a CDFI which is not accredited as a retail community investment finance institution.

History – Para. 11(a)(i) substituted by SI 2013/417, reg. 11(4)(a), with effect from 1 April 2013 (but only in relation to a CDFI whose current accreditation period starts on or after 1 April 2013). Former para. 11(a)(i) read as follows:

    "(i)   for the first year following accreditation, the date the investment is made by the CDFI, and"

Para. 11(a)(ii), the words "date the first investment is made in the CDFI" substituted for the words "accreditation date" by SI 2013/417, reg. 11(3)(b), with effect from 1 April 2013 (but only in relation to a CDFI whose current accreditation period starts on or after 1 April 2013).

INCOME AND CORPORATION TAXES (ELECTRONIC COMMUNICATIONS) REGULATIONS 2003

(SI 2003/282, as amended by SI 2005/3338, SI 2009/3218, SI 2010/2942 and SI 2014/489)

Made on 12 February 2003 by the Commissioners of Inland Revenue, in exercise of the powers conferred upon them by s. 132 and 133(2) of the Finance Act 1999. Operative from 5 March 2003.

PART 1 – INTRODUCTION

CITATION, COMMENCEMENT AND INTERPRETATION

1(1) These Regulations may be cited as the Income and Corporation Taxes (Electronic Communications) Regulations 2003 and shall come into force on 5th March 2003.

1(2) In these Regulations–

"the Board" means the Commissioners of Inland Revenue;

"the Management Act" means the Taxes Management Act 1970;

"official computer system" means a computer system maintained by or on behalf of the Board–

(a) to send or receive information or payments, or

(b) to process or store information;

"secure mailbox" means a facility or feature which–

(a) forms part of an official computer system, and

(b) can be accessed by an individual permitted to use electronic communications by an authorisation given by means of a direction by the Board; and

"the Taxes Act" means the Income and Corporation Taxes Act 1988.

1(2A) The provision these Regulations make for company tax returns relates to Schedule 18 to the Finance Act 1998 (corporation tax – company tax returns, etc), consequently where they refer to–

(a) **"company tax return"**, it has the meaning in paragraph 3 of that Schedule,

(b) **"return period"**, it means the period for which a company tax return is required under paragraph 5 of that Schedule,

(c) **"amendment"**, it has the meaning in paragraph 15 of that Schedule, and

(d) **"filing date"**, it has the meaning in paragraph 14 of that Schedule (but it has the meaning in paragraph 35(2) when in connection with a company tax return for an "outstanding period" in paragraph 35(1)).

1(2B) The **"extra time"** in connection with the filing date mentioned in regulation 3(8)(c) refers to a stage–

(a) for which there is an excuse for late delivery of the company tax return under paragraph 19 of Schedule 18 to the Finance Act 1998 (delivery of accounts to registrar of companies in time); or,

(b) arising under section 117(2) of that Act in conjunction with section 118(2) of the Management Act (further time allowed by the Board, reasonable excuse for being late, etc).

1(3) References in these Regulations to information and to the delivery of information shall be construed in accordance with section 132(8) of the Finance Act 1999.

Such references shall be construed in accordance with section 135(8) of the Finance Act 2002 (mandatory e-filing) when in connection with a company tax return.

History – In reg. 1(2), in the definition of "official computer system" the word "and" omitted by SI 2014/489, reg. 3(a), with effect from 27 March 2014.
In reg. 1(2), the definition of "secure mailbox" inserted by SI 2014/489, reg. 3(b), with effect from 27 March 2014.
Reg. 1(2A) inserted by SI 2009/3218, reg. 2 and Schedule, para. 1, with effect from 1 January 2010.
Reg. 1(2B) inserted by SI 2009/3218, reg. 2 and Schedule, para. 1, with effect from 1 January 2010.
In reg. 1(3) the words "Such references shall be construed in accordance with section 135(8) of the Finance Act 2002 (mandatory e-filing) when in connection with a company tax return." inserted by SI 2009/3218, reg. 2 and Schedule, para. 2, with effect from 1 January 2010.

SCOPE OF THESE REGULATIONS

2(1) These Regulations apply to–

(a)   the delivery of information, to or by the Board, the delivery of which is authorised or required by or under–

    (i)   any provision of section 8, 8A, 8B, 9, 9ZA, 9ZB, 9A, 9B, 9C, 9D, 12AA, 12AAA, 12AB, 12ABA, 12ABB, 12AC, 12AD, 12AE, 28A, 28B, 28C, 30B, 59C, 59DA, 59E or 100 of the Management Act,

    (ii)   Schedule 1A to the Management Act,

    (iia)   the Lloyd's Underwriters (Tax) Regulations 2005,

    (iii)   section 36 of the Finance Act 1998,

    (iv)   Schedule 18 to the Finance Act 1998 (and in connection with which they also make specific provision for mandatory e-filing of company tax returns as mentioned in regulation 1(3)),

    (v)   paragraph 13 of Schedule 24 to the Finance Act 2007,

    (vi)   paragraph 1 or 46 of Schedule 36 to the Finance Act 2008, or

    (vii)   paragraph 17A, 17B or 18 of Schedule 55, or paragraph 11 of Schedule 56, to the Finance Act 2009; and

(b)   the making of any payment or repayment of tax or other sums in connection with the operation of those provisions, or the making of any payment in connection with the operation of section 87A of the Management Act (interest on overdue corporation tax etc), and they apply in such a way that the corporation tax-related payments in regulation 3(2C) are subject to the mandatory electronic payment envisaged by section 204 of the Finance Act 2003.

2(2)   Nothing in these Regulations affects the operation of the Electronic Lodgement of Tax Returns Order 1997.

History – In reg. 2(1)(a)(i), the word "8B," inserted by SI 2014/489, reg. 4(a)(i), with effect from 27 March 2014.
In reg. 2(1)(a)(i), the words "9ZA, 9ZB," inserted by SI 2014/489, reg. 4(a)(ii), with effect from 27 March 2014.
In reg. 2(1)(a)(i), the word "12AAA," inserted by SI 2014/489, reg. 4(a)(iii), with effect from 27 March 2014.
In reg. 2(1)(a)(i), the word "12ABA, 12ABB," inserted by SI 2014/489, reg. 4(a)(iv), with effect from 27 March 2014.
In reg. 2(1)(a)(i), the words "28A, 28B, 28C, 30B, 59C," inserted by SI 2014/489, reg. 4(a)(v), with effect from 27 March 2014.
In reg. 2(1)(a)(i), the words "59DA, 59E or 100" substituted for "59DA or 59E" by SI 2014/489, reg. 4(a)(vi), with effect from 27 March 2014.
Reg. 2(1)(a)(iia) inserted by SI 2005/3338, reg. 15, with effect for 2006–07 and subsequent years of assessments (individuals) and for accounting periods ending after 31 December 2005 (corporate members).
In reg. 2(1)(a)(iii), the word "or" omitted by SI 2014/489, reg. 4(b), with effect from 27 March 2014.
In reg. 2(1)(a)(iii), the words "30 or" repealed by Statute Law (Repeals) Act 2013, s. 1 and Sch. 1, Pt. 10, with effect from 31 January 2013.
In reg. 2(1)(a)(iv), for "; and" substituted for "," by SI 2014/489, reg. 4(c), with effect from 27 March 2014.
In reg. 2(1)(a)(iv) the words "and in connection with which they also make specific provision for mandatory e-filing of company tax returns as mentioned in regulation 1(3))" inserted by SI 2009/3218, reg. 2 and Schedule, para. 3, with effect from 1 January 2010.
Reg. 2(1)(a)(v)–(vii) inserted by SI 2014/489, reg. 4(d), with effect from 27 March 2014.
In reg. 2(1)(b) the words ", or the making of any payment in connection with the operation of section 87A of the Management Act (interest on overdue corporation tax etc), and they apply in such a way that the corporation tax-related payments in regulation 3(2C) are subject to the mandatory electronic payment envisaged by section 204 of the Finance Act 2003" inserted by SI 2009/3218, reg. 2 and Schedule, para. 4, with effect from 1 January 2010.

PART 2 – ELECTRONIC COMMUNICATIONS – GENERAL PROVISIONS

USE OF ELECTRONIC COMMUNICATIONS

History – The heading to reg. 3 substituted by SI 2009/3218, reg. 2 and Schedule, para. 5, with effect from 1 January 2010. Former heading read "RESTRICTION ON THE USE OF ELECTRONIC COMMUNICATIONS".

3(1)   The Board may only use electronic communications in connection with the matters referred to in regulation 2(1) if–

(a)   the recipient has indicated that he consents to the Board using electronic communications in connection with those matters; and

(b)   the Board have not been informed that that consent has been withdrawn.

3(1ZA)   The Board may specify by specific or general direction the manner in which consent may be provided and withdrawn, including the time from which consent and withdrawal of consent is to take effect.

3(1A)   Paragraphs (1) and (1ZA) do not apply to a company tax return delivered by, or a corporation tax-related payment made by, electronic communications under paragraphs (2A) to (2C).

3(2) A person other than the Board may only use electronic communications in connection with the matters referred to in regulation 2(1) if the conditions specified in paragraphs (3) to (6) are satisfied.

3(2A) Such a person must use electronic communications to deliver a company tax return, and in doing so need only satisfy the second to fourth of those conditions.

This paragraph only applies to a company tax return delivered on 1 April 2011 or later, relating to a return period ending on 1 April 2010 or later.

It does not apply to an amendment to such a company tax return.

3(2B) The payer must use electronic communications to make the corporation tax-related payments in paragraph (2C), and in doing so need only satisfy the second and third of those conditions (excluding those in paragraphs (4)(a) (authenticating identity) and (4)(c) (authenticating information)).

This paragraph only applies to payments made on 1 April 2011 or later.

The Board need not accept such payments tendered in breach of this paragraph.

3(2C) Paragraph (2B) applies to payment of each of the following–

(a)   any amount of corporation tax that must be calculated as payable under paragraph 8 of Schedule 18 to the Finance Act 1998 (calculation of corporation tax payable);

(b)   any amount treated as such under regulation 5 or 5A of the Corporation Tax (Instalment Payments) Regulations 1998;

(c)   any interest payable on overdue corporation tax etc under section 87A of the Management Act and regulation 7 of those Regulations;

(d)   a flat-rate penalty for failing to deliver a company tax return by the filing date under paragraph 17 of that Schedule;

(e)   a tax-related penalty for failing to deliver a company tax return for an accounting period under paragraph 18 of that Schedule.

3(3) The first condition is that the person is for the time being permitted to use electronic communications for the purpose in question by an authorisation given by means of a direction of the Board.

3(4) The second condition is that the person uses–

(a)   an approved method for authenticating the identity of the sender of the communication;

(b)   an approved method of electronic communications; and

(c)   an approved method for authenticating any information delivered by means of electronic communications.

3(5) The third condition is that any information or payment sent by means of electronic communications is in a form approved for the purpose of these Regulations, and Extensible Business Reporting Language (XBRL), Inline XBRL and other electronic data handling techniques are among the forms that may be so approved.

Here **"form"** includes the manner in which the information is presented.

3(6) The fourth condition is that the person maintains such records in written or electronic form as may be specified in a general or specific direction of the Board.

3(7) In this regulation **"approved"** means approved, for the purposes of these Regulations and for the time being, by means of a general or specific direction of the Board.

3(8) The conditions mentioned in paragraph (2A) (company tax returns) are to be taken to be satisfied in connection with that paragraph only where the Board is satisfied about one or more of the following–

(a)   there are no contraventions or failures to comply;

(b)   the accumulated contraventions or failures to comply do not undermine the purpose of that paragraph (delivery of company tax returns by approved electronic means);

(c)   at least one of the contraventions or failures to comply was necessary in order to deliver the company tax return by the filing date or within any extra time arising, despite genuine efforts not to undermine that purpose.

3(9) The consequences of contravening or failing to comply with paragraph (2A) (company tax returns) are–

(a)   that the Board must accept delivery of the return, but only if satisfied about paragraph (8)(b) or (8)(c), or about both; otherwise,

(b)   the Board must disregard the return and treat it as not having been delivered.

3(10) Electronic communications need not be used to deliver a company tax return while the company required to deliver it by the notice under paragraph 3(1) of Schedule 18 to the Finance Act 1998 is–

(a) the subject of a winding-up order,

(b) having its affairs, business and property managed by an administrator, or

(c) in administrative receivership.

The expressions **"winding-up order"**, **"administrator"** and **"in administrative receivership"** each has the same meaning here as it does in section 81 of the Value Added Tax Act 1994 (insolvency procedures, etc).

3(10A) Electronic communications need not be used to deliver a company tax return while the company required to deliver it by the notice mentioned in paragraph (10)–

(a) has a liquidator appointed for the purposes of a creditors' voluntary winding up (within sections 90 and 100 of the Insolvency Act 1986 or Articles 76 and 86 of the Insolvency (Northern Ireland) Order 1989);

(b) has a liquidator provisionally appointed by a court (within section 135 of that Act or Article 115 of that Order);

(c) has a supervisor carrying out functions in relation to a company voluntary arrangement (within section 7(2) of or Schedule A1, paragraph 39(2) to that Act or Article 20(2) of or Schedule A1, paragraph 49(2) to that Order);

(d) has a compromise or arrangement in effect (within Part 26 of the Companies Act 2006); or

(e) is a limited liability partnership, and

   (i) has a liquidator appointed, or

   (ii) is the subject of a winding up order by the court,

   (within section 1273(4)(a) of the Corporation Tax Act 2009).

3(11) Paragraph (2A) (company tax returns) does not apply to the use of electronic communications in a way incompatible with the beliefs of a religious society or order of which–

(a) all the company's directors (and, if there is one, the company's secretary) are practising members, or

(b) all the individuals in the unincorporated association are such members.

3(12) The exceptions created by paragraphs (10) to (11) also apply in circumstances corresponding to those listed or described there but governed by the law of a place outside the United Kingdom.

History – Reg. 3(1ZA) inserted by SI 2014/489, reg. 5, with effect from 27 March 2014.
In reg. 3(1A), the words "Paragraphs (1) and (1ZA) do" substituted for "Paragraph (1) does" by SI 2014/489, reg. 6, with effect from 27 March 2014.
Reg. 3(1A) inserted by SI 2009/3218, reg. 2 and Schedule, para. 6, with effect from 1 January 2010.
Reg. 3(2A) inserted by SI 2009/3218, reg. 2 and Schedule, para. 7, with effect from 1 January 2010.
Reg. 3(2B) inserted by SI 2009/3218, reg. 2 and Schedule, para. 7, with effect from 1 January 2010.
Reg. 3(2C) inserted by SI 2009/3218, reg. 2 and Schedule, para. 7, with effect from 1 January 2010.
In reg. 3(5) the words ", and Extensible Business Reporting Language (XBRL), Inline XBRL and other electronic data handling techniques are among the forms that may be so approved" inserted by SI 2009/3218, reg. 2 and Schedule, para. 8, with effect from 1 January 2010.
Reg. 3(8) inserted by SI 2009/3218, reg. 2 and Schedule, para. 9, with effect from 1 January 2010.
Reg. 3(9) inserted by SI 2009/3218, reg. 2 and Schedule, para. 9, with effect from 1 January 2010.
Reg. 3(10) inserted by SI 2009/3218, reg. 2 and Schedule, para. 9, with effect from 1 January 2010.
Reg. 3(10A) inserted by SI 2010/2942, reg. 2(2), with effect from 4 January 2011.
Reg. 3(11) inserted by SI 2009/3218, reg. 2 and Schedule, para. 9, with effect from 1 January 2010.
Reg. 3(12) inserted by SI 2010/2942, reg. 2(3), with effect from 4 January 2011.

Other material – HMRC Direction 8/12/10: electronic communications in relation to company tax returns made under FA 1998, Sch. 18.

CORPORATION TAX-RELATED PAYMENTS BY CHEQUE

3A(1) Paragraph (2) applies instead of section 70A of the Management Act to each of the corporation tax-related payments in regulation 3(2C) tendered by cheque, but only if the Board receives that cheque on 1 April 2011 or later and that cheque is paid on its first presentation by the Board to the banker on whom it is drawn.

3A(2) The payment is to be treated as made on the second business day after the day on which the Board received that cheque.

3A(3) For these purposes, a **"business day"** is any day except–

(a) Saturday, Sunday, Good Friday or Christmas Day;

(b) a bank holiday under the Banking and Financial Dealings Act 1971;

(c)   a day appointed by Royal proclamation as a public fast or thanksgiving day;

(d)   a day declared by an order under section 2 of the Banking and Financial Dealings Act 1971 to be a non-business day.

History – Reg. 3A inserted by SI 2009/3218, reg. 2 and Schedule, para. 10, with effect from 1 January 2010.

USE OF INTERMEDIARIES

4   The Board may use intermediaries in connection with–

(a)   the delivery of information or the making of payments or repayments by means of electronic communications in connection with the matters referred to in regulation 2(1), and

(b)   the authentication or security of anything transmitted by such means,

and may require other persons to use intermediaries in connection with those matters.

PART 3 – ELECTRONIC COMMUNICATIONS – EVIDENTIAL PROVISIONS

EFFECT OF DELIVERING INFORMATION BY MEANS OF ELECTRONIC COMMUNICATIONS

5(1)   Information to which these Regulations apply, and which is delivered by means of electronic communications, shall be treated as having been delivered, in the manner or form required by any provision of the Taxes Act, the relevant Finance Acts or the Management Act if, but only if, all the conditions imposed by–

(a)   these Regulations,

(b)   any other applicable enactment (except to the extent that the condition thereby imposed is incompatible with these Regulations), and

(c)   any specific or general direction given by the Board,

are satisfied or, but only in the case of the conditions mentioned in regulation 3(2A) (electronic delivery of company tax returns), are taken to be satisfied under regulation 3(8).

5(2)   Information delivered by means of electronic communications shall be treated as having been delivered on the day on which the last of the conditions imposed as mentioned in paragraph (1) is satisfied.

This is subject to paragraphs (3) and (4).

5(3)   The Board may by a general or specific direction provide for information to be treated as delivered upon a different date (whether earlier or later) than that given by paragraph (2).

5(4)   Information shall not be taken to have been delivered to an official computer system by means of electronic communications unless it is accepted by the system to which it is delivered.

5(5)   For the purposes of this Part, information which is delivered by means of electronic communications includes information delivered to a secure mailbox.

5(6)   For the purposes of paragraph (1) **"the relevant Finance Acts"** means the Finance Act 2007, the Finance Act 2008 or the Finance Act 2009.

History – In reg. 5(1), the words ", the relevant Finance Acts" inserted by SI 2014/489, reg. 7(a), with effect from 27 March 2014.
In reg. 5(1) the words "or, but only in the case of the conditions mentioned in regulation 3(2A) (electronic delivery of company tax returns), are taken to be satisfied under regulation 3(8)" inserted by SI 2009/3218, reg. 2 and Schedule, para. 11, with effect from 1 January 2010.
Reg. 5(5) and (6) inserted by SI 2014/489, reg. 7(b), with effect from 27 March 2014.

PROOF OF CONTENT

6(1)   A document certified by an officer of the Board to be a printed-out version of any information delivered by means of electronic communications under these Regulations on any occasion shall be evidence, unless the contrary is proved, that that information–

(a)   was delivered by means of electronic communications on that occasion; and

(b)   constitutes the entirety of what was delivered on that occasion.

6(2)   A document purporting to be a certificate given in accordance with paragraph (1) shall be presumed to be such a certificate unless the contrary is proved.

PROOF OF SENDER OR RECIPIENT

7   The identity of–

(a)   the sender of any information delivered to an official computer system by means of electronic communications under these Regulations, or

(b)   the recipient of any information delivered by means of electronic communications from an official computer system,

shall be presumed, unless the contrary is proved, to be the person recorded as such on an official computer system.

INFORMATION DELIVERED ELECTRONICALLY ON ANOTHER'S BEHALF

8   Any information delivered by an approved method of electronic communications on behalf of any person shall be deemed to have been delivered by him unless he proves that it was delivered without his knowledge or connivance.

PROOF OF DELIVERY OF INFORMATION AND PAYMENTS

9(1)   The use of an authorised method of electronic communications shall be presumed, unless the contrary is proved, to have resulted in the making of a payment or the delivery of information–

(a)   in the case of information falling to be delivered, or a payment falling to be made, to the Board, if the making of the payment or the delivery of the information has been recorded on an official computer system; and

(b)   in the case of information falling to be delivered, or a payment falling to be made, by the Board, if the despatch of that payment or information has been recorded on an official computer system.

9(2)   The use of an authorised method of electronic communications shall be presumed, unless the contrary is proved, not to have resulted in the making of a payment, or the delivery of information–

(a)   in the case of information falling to be delivered, or a payment falling to be made, to the Board, if the making of the payment or the delivery of the information has not been recorded on an official computer system; and

(b)   in the case of information falling to be delivered, or a payment falling to be made, by the Board, if the despatch of that payment or information has not been recorded on an official computer system.

9(3)   The time of receipt of any information or payment sent by an authorised means of electronic communications shall be presumed, unless the contrary is proved, to be that recorded on an official computer system.

USE OF UNAUTHORISED MEANS OF ELECTRONIC COMMUNICATIONS

10(1)   Paragraph (2) applies to information which is required to be delivered to the Board in connection with the matters mentioned in regulation 2(1).

10(2)   The use of a means of electronic communications, for the purpose of delivering any information to which this paragraph applies, shall be conclusively presumed not to have resulted in the delivery of that information, unless–

(a)   that means of electronic communications is for the time being approved for delivery of information of that kind; and

(b)   the sender is approved, if necessary, for the use of that means of electronic communications in relation to information of that kind.

10(3)   A company tax return delivered under regulation 3(2A) by means of electronic communications must meet standards of accuracy and completeness set by a specific or general direction given by the Board.

The Board may treat failure to meet those standards as failure to deliver that return.

History – In reg. 10(2) the words ", if necessary," inserted by SI 2009/3218, reg. 2 and Schedule, para. 12, with effect from 1 January 2010.

Reg. 10(3) inserted by SI 2009/3218, reg. 2 and Schedule, para. 13, with effect from 1 January 2010.

Other material – HMRC Direction 8/12/10: electronic communications in relation to company tax returns made under FA 1998, Sch. 18.

PART 4 – REVOCATIONS

REVOCATION AND SAVING

11(1) There are revoked–

(a) the Income Tax (Electronic Communications) Regulations 2000; and

(b) Part 2 of the Income Tax (Electronic Communications) (Miscellaneous Amendments) Regulations 2001 and, in regulation 1(2) of those Regulations, the definition of "the Electronic Communications Regulations".

11(2) Notwithstanding the revocations in paragraph (1), any direction given by the Board under the provisions revoked, to the extent that it could be given under these Regulations, shall continue to have effect as if given under these Regulations.

INCOME TAX (AUTHORISED UNIT TRUSTS) (INTEREST DISTRIBUTIONS) REGULATIONS 2003
(SI 2003/1830)

Made on 16 July 2003 by the Commissioners of Inland Revenue, in exercise of the powers conferred upon them by s. 468PB of the Income and Corporation Taxes Act 1988. Operative from 7 August 2003.

CITATION, COMMENCEMENT AND EFFECT

1(1) These Regulations may be cited as the Income Tax (Authorised Unit Trusts) (Interest Distributions) Regulations 2003 and shall come into force on 7th August 2003.

1(2) These Regulations have effect in relation to interest distributions made on or after 16th October 2002.

INTERPRETATION

2 In these Regulations–

"**authorised unit trust**" and "**unit holder**" have the meanings given by section 468(6) of the Taxes Act;

"**the Board**" means the Commissioners of Inland Revenue;

"**interest distribution**" has the meaning given by section 468L(3) of the Taxes Act;

"**the Taxes Act**" means the Income and Corporation Taxes Act 1988 and references to a section number without more are references to a section of that Act;

"**the Tax Acts**" has the meaning given by section 831(2) of the Taxes Act;

"**unit trust scheme**" has the meaning given by section 469(7) of the Taxes Act.

Cross references – SI 1997/1154, reg. 28(3): modifications of reg. 2 in relation to open-ended investment companies.

MODIFICATION OF SECTIONS 468M(1)(A), 468O AND 468P IN RELATION TO INTEREST DISTRIBUTIONS MADE TO OR RECEIVED UNDER A TRUST

3 Except in a case to which regulation 7 applies, section 468M(1)(a), section 468O and section 468P shall apply in relation to an interest distribution made to or received under a trust (other than a unit trust scheme) with the modifications specified in regulations 4, 5 and 6.

4 In section 468M(1)(a) after the word "company" insert the words "except where the company is the trustee of the trust to which or under which the interest distribution is made or received,".

5 In section 468O for subsection (1) substitute the following subsection–

"**468O(1)** For the purposes of section 468M, the residence condition is fulfilled with respect to a unit holder in the case of an interest distribution made to or received under a trust if there is a valid declaration made by the trustees of that trust that–

(a)   the trustees are not resident in the United Kingdom, and

(b)   each beneficiary of the trust is either not ordinarily resident or, in the case of a beneficiary which is a company, not resident in the United Kingdom.

468O(1ZA) In subsection (1) and in section 468P, references to a beneficiary are references to any person who is known to the trustees of the trust to be either–

(a)   a person who is, or will or may become, entitled to any income of the trust, whether in the form of income or not, or

(b)   a person to whom any such income may be paid, or for whose benefit any such income may be applied, whether in the form of income or not, in the exercise of a discretion by them.".

Cross references – SI 1997/1154, reg. 28(4): modifications of reg. 5 in relation to open-ended investment companies.

6 In section 468P–

(a)   in subsection (1)(c) for the words "subsections (2) or (3)" substitute the words "subsection (2)";

(b)   for subsection (2) substitute the following subsection–

"**468P(2)** A declaration made as mentioned in section 468O(1) must contain–

(a)   the names and principal residential addresses of the trustees of the trust or, in the case of a trustee which is a company, the name of the company and the address of its registered or principal office;

(b) the names and principal residential addresses of the beneficiaries of the trust or, in the case of a beneficiary which is a company, the name of the company and the address of its registered or principal office; and

(c) an undertaking that the trustees of the trust will notify the trustees of the authorised unit trust in question if–

   (i) they become resident in the United Kingdom,

   (ii) any beneficiary of the trust named in the declaration becomes ordinarily resident or, in the case of a company, resident in the United Kingdom, or

   (iii) any person who becomes a beneficiary of the trust after the making of the declaration either is at the time of becoming a beneficiary, or subsequently becomes, ordinarily resident or, in the case of a company, resident in the United Kingdom.";

(c) omit subsection (3);

(d) in subsection (5)(a) for the words "the person in question" substitute the words "the trustees of the trust have become resident in the United Kingdom, or any beneficiary of the trust";

(e) in subsection (5)(b) for the words "the person in question" substitute the words "the trustees of the trust are or may be resident in the United Kingdom, or any beneficiary of the trust".

Cross references – SI 1997/1154, reg. 28(5): modifications of reg. 6(b) in relation to open-ended investment companies.

MODIFICATION OF SECTION 468O IN CASES WHERE AN INTEREST DISTRIBUTION MADE TO OR RECEIVED UNDER A TRUST IS INCOME OF A PERSON OTHER THAN THE TRUSTEES

7(1) This regulation applies in any case where the whole of an interest distribution made to or received under a trust (other than a unit trust scheme) is, or falls to be treated as, or under any provision of the Tax Acts is deemed to be, the income of a person other than the trustees of that trust.

7(2) Where this regulation applies, sections 468M, 468O and 468PA shall apply as if references to a unit holder in those sections were references to the person referred to in paragraph (1).

Cross references – SI 1997/1154, reg. 28(6): modifications of reg. 7(2) in relation to open-ended investment companies.

INFORMATION TO BE PROVIDED TO THE BOARD – INTEREST DISTRIBUTIONS MADE WITHOUT DEDUCTION OF TAX

8 The Board may by notice require the trustees of an authorised unit trust, within such time (not being less than 14 days) as may be provided by the notice, to supply them with such information (including copies of any relevant books, documents or other records) as they may reasonably require for the purpose of determining whether, having regard to section 468M, section 468O and section 468P, interest distributions were properly made by that authorised unit trust without deduction of tax.

Cross references – SI 1997/1154, reg. 28(7): modifications of reg. 8 in relation to open-ended investment companies.

INSPECTION OF RECORDS

9 The trustees of an authorised unit trust shall, whenever required to do so, make available for inspection by an officer of the Board authorised for that purpose, at such time as that officer may reasonably require, all such copies of books, documents or other records in their possession or under their control as may be required by the Board under regulation 8.

Cross references – SI 1997/1154, reg. 28(8): modifications of reg. 9 in relation to open-ended investment companies.

USE OF INFORMATION

10(1) Subject to paragraph (3), information obtained by the Board under regulation 8 or 9 shall not be used for the purpose of ascertaining the tax liability (if any) of any person other than the persons specified in paragraph (2) and shall otherwise be used only for the purposes of these Regulations.

10(2) The persons specified in this paragraph are–

(a) the trustees of the authorised unit trust in question;

(b) a unit holder beneficially entitled to an interest distribution made without deduction of tax to whom the information obtained relates;

(c) where an interest distribution is made to or received under a trust without deduction of tax and sub-paragraph (d) does not apply, the trustees of that trust and any beneficiary of the trust to whom the information obtained relates; and

(d)   where the whole of an interest distribution made to or received under a trust without deduction of tax is, or falls to be treated as, or under any provision of the Tax Acts is deemed to be, the income of a person other than the trustees of that trust, that person in so far as the information obtained relates to him.

10(3)   Paragraph (1) shall not be construed as preventing any disclosure of information within section 182(5) of the Finance Act 1989.

10(4)   In paragraph (2)(c), **"any beneficiary of the trust"** means–

(a)   any person who is, or will or may become, entitled to any income of the trust, whether in the form of income or not, and

(b)   any person to whom any such income may be paid, or for whose benefit any such income may be applied, whether in the form of income or not, in the exercise of a discretion by the trustees of the trust.

Cross references – SI 1997/1154, reg. 28(9): modifications of reg. 10(2) in relation to open-ended investment companies.

REVOCATION

11   The Income Tax (Authorised Unit Trusts) (Interest Distributions) Regulations 1994 are revoked.

LIFE ASSURANCE (APPORTIONMENT OF RECEIPTS OF PARTICIPATING FUNDS) (APPLICABLE PERCENTAGE) ORDER 2003

(SI 2003/1860)

Made on 17 July 2003 by the Treasury, in exercise of the power conferred upon them by s. 432E(4) of the Income and Corporation Taxes Act 1988. Operative from 7 August 2003.

CITATION, COMMENCEMENT AND EFFECT

1(1) This Order may be cited as the Life Assurance (Apportionment of Receipts of Participating Funds) (Applicable Percentage) Order 2003 and shall come into force on 7th August 2003.

1(2) This Order has effect for periods of account ending on or after 7th August 2003.

DETERMINATION OF APPLICABLE PERCENTAGE

2   The applicable percentage for the purposes of subsection (3) of section 432E of the Income and Corporation Taxes Act 1988 is–

$$\frac{A \times 100}{B} \text{ per cent}$$

Here–

A   is the net amount referred to in subsection (1) of that section as brought into account for the period in question for the purposes of section 83(2) of the Finance Act 1989 in respect of the relevant business less the part of that net amount which is attributable to linked assets, and

B   is the mean of the opening and closing liabilities of the relevant business reduced by the opening and closing values of any assets of the relevant business which are linked assets.

REVOCATIONS

3   The following orders are revoked–

(a)   the Life Assurance (Apportionment of Receipts of Participating Funds) (Applicable Percentage) Order 1990;

(b)   the Life Assurance (Apportionment of Receipts of Participating Funds) (Applicable Percentage) (Amendment) Order 1990;

(c)   the Life Assurance (Apportionment of Receipts of Participating Funds) (Applicable Percentage) (Amendment) Order 1995;

(d)   the Life Assurance (Apportionment of Receipts of Participating Funds) (Applicable Percentage) (Amendment) Order 1998.

CAPITAL ALLOWANCES (ENVIRONMENTALLY BENEFICIAL PLANT AND MACHINERY) ORDER 2003

(SI 2003/2076, as amended by SI 2004/2094, SI 2005/2423, SI 2006/2235, SI 2007/2166, SI 2008/1917, SI 2009/1864, SI 2010/2483, SI 2011/2220, SI 2012/1838, SI 2012/2602 and SI 2013/1762)

Made on 11 August 2003 by the Treasury, in exercise of the powers conferred upon them by s. 45H(3) and (4) and 45J(3)(b) of the Capital Allowances Act 2001. Operative from 1 September 2003.

CITATION AND COMMENCEMENT

1 This Order may be cited as the Capital Allowances (Environmentally Beneficial Plant and Machinery) Order 2003 and shall come into force on 1st September 2003.

INTERPRETATION

2 In this Order–

"the Capital Allowances Act" means the Capital Allowances Act 2001;

"the Water Technology Criteria List" means the list dated 23 June 2013 and issued by the Secretary of State for the Environment, Food and Rural Affairs on 1 July 2013;

"the Water Technology Product List" means the list dated 23 June 2013 and issued by the Secretary of State for the Environment, Food and Rural Affairs on 1 July 2013.

History – In art. 2, in the definitions of "the Water Technology Criteria List" and "the Water Technology Product List", "23 June 2013" substituted for "17 September 2012" and "1 July 2013" substituted for "10 October 2012" by SI 2013/1762, art. 3, with effect from 7 August 2013.

In art. 2, in the definitions of the Water Technology Criteria List and the Water Technology Product List, "17 September 2012" substituted for "22 June 2012" and "10 October 2012" substituted for "5 July 2012" by SI 2012/2602, art. 3, with effect from 7 November 2012.

In art. 2, in the definitions of Water Technology Criteria List and Water Technology Product List, "22 June 2012" substituted for "26th June 2011" and "5 July 2012" substituted for "2nd September 2011" by SI 2012/1838, art. 3, with effect from 2 August 2012.

In art. 2, in the definitions of Water Technology Criteria List and Water Technology Product List, "26th June 2011" substituted for "13 September 2010" and "2nd September 2011" substituted for "28 September 2010" by SI 2011/2220, art. 2(2), with effect from 1 October 2011.

In art. 2, in the definitions of Water Technology Criteria List and Water Technology Product List, "13 September 2010" substituted for "27th June 2009" and "28 September 2010" substituted for "7th July 2009" by SI 2010/2483, art. 2(2), with effect from 8 November 2010.

In art. 2, the definition of the Water Technology Criteria List substituted by SI 2009/1864, art. 2(2), with effect from 4 August 2009.

Former definition of the Water Technology Criteria List substituted by SI 2008/1917, art. 2(2), with effect from 11 August 2008.

Former definition of the Water Technology Criteria List substituted by SI 2007/2166, art. 2(2), with effect from 16 August 2007.

Former definition of the Water Technology Criteria List substituted by SI 2006/2235, art. 2(2), with effect from 7 September 2006.

Former definition of the Water Technology Criteria List substituted by SI 2005/2423, art. 3, with effect from 22 September 2005.

Former definition of the Water Technology Criteria List substituted by SI 2004/2094, reg. 2(2)(a), with effect from 26 August 2004.

In art. 2, the definition of the Water Technology Product List substituted by SI 2009/1864, art. 2(2), with effect from 4 August 2009.

Former definition of the Water Technology Product List substituted by SI 2008/1917, art. 2(2), with effect from 11 August 2008.

Former definition of the Water Technology Product List substituted by SI 2007/2166, art. 2(2), with effect from 16 August 2007.

Former definition of the Water Technology Product List substituted by SI 2006/2235, art. 2(2), with effect from 7 September 2006.

Former definition of the Water Technology Product List substituted by SI 2005/2423, art. 3, with effect from 22 September 2005.

Former definition of the Water Technology Product List substituted by SI 2004/2094, reg. 2(2)(b), with effect from 26 August 2004.

DESCRIPTION OF ENVIRONMENTALLY BENEFICIAL PLANT AND MACHINERY

3(1) Plant or machinery is environmentally beneficial plant or machinery for the purposes of section 45H of the Capital Allowances Act (expenditure on environmentally beneficial plant or machinery) if–

(a)   it falls within a technology class specified in the Water Technology Criteria List,

(b)   it meets the environmental criteria set out in that List, and

(c)   in the case of plant or machinery falling within any of the technology classes specified in paragraph (2), it is of a type that–

      (i)   is specified in, and has not been removed from, the Water Technology Product List, or

      (ii)   has been accepted for inclusion in the Water Technology Product List.

3(2)   The technology classes specified for the purposes of paragraph (1)(c) are–

(a)   flow controllers;

(b)   leakage detection equipment;

(c)   meters and monitoring equipment;

(d)   efficient taps;

(e)   efficient toilets;

(f)   rainwater harvesting equipment;

(g)   water reuse systems;

(h)   cleaning in place equipment;

(i)   efficient showers;

(j)   efficient washing machines;

(k)   small scale slurry and sludge dewatering equipment.

(l)   vehicle wash waste reclaim units;

(m)   water efficient industrial cleaning equipment;

(n)   water management equipment for mechanical seals.

(o)   greywater recovery and reuse equipment.

History – Art. 3(2)(o) inserted by SI 2013/1762, art. 3, with effect from 7 August 2013.
In art. 3(2), para. (c)–(e) substituted by SI 2008/1917, art. 2(3)(a), with effect from 11 August 2008.
In art. 3(2), para. (g) substituted by SI 2008/1917, art. 2(3)(b), with effect from 11 August 2008.
In art. 3(2), para. (m) and (n) substituted by SI 2008/1917, art. 2(3)(c), with effect from 11 August 2008.
In art. 3(2), para. (l), (m) and (n) inserted by SI 2007/2166, art. 3, with effect from 16 August 2007.
In art. 3(2) para. (j) and (k) inserted by SI 2006/2235, art. 2(3) with effect from 7 September 2006.
Art. 3(2) substituted by SI 2005/2423, art. 4, with effect from 22 September 2005.
Former art. 3(2)(ca) inserted by SI 2004/2094, reg. 2(3), with effect from 26 August 2004.

Other material – Water Technology Criteria and Water Technology Product Lists (not reproduced) are accessible from www.eca-water.gov.uk.

ENVIRONMENTALLY BENEFICIAL COMPONENTS OF PLANT OR MACHINERY

4   Where one or more components of certain plant or machinery (but not all of that plant or machinery)–

(a)   meets the conditions set out in article 3(1)(a) to (c), and

(b)   falls within any of the technology classes specified in article 3(2)(a) to (c),

the amount specified in respect of each such component for the purposes of section 45J of the Capital Allowances Act is the amount specified in the Water Technology Product List in relation to that component.

Other material – Water Technology Criteria and Water Technology Product Lists (not reproduced) specify amount of components for purposes of CAA 2001, s. 45J. Lists are accessible from www.eca-water.gov.uk.

CERTIFICATION OF ENVIRONMENTALLY BENEFICIAL PLANT AND MACHINERY

5(1)   In a case in which paragraph (2) applies, no section 45H allowance may be made unless a relevant certificate of environmental benefit is in force.

5(2)   This paragraph applies in the case of expenditure on–

(a)   efficient membrane filtration systems for the treatment of wastewater for recovery and reuse; and

(b)   efficient wastewater recovery and reuse systems,

falling within the technology class "water reuse systems" specified in the Water Technology Criteria List.

5(3)   In paragraph (1), "section 45H allowance" has the meaning given by section 45I(1) of the Capital Allowances Act, and "relevant certificate of environmental benefit" means a certificate of environmental benefit, as defined in subsection (2) of section 45I of the Capital Allowances Act, and which has been issued in accordance with subsection (3) of that section.

History – Art. 5(2) substituted by SI 2008/1917, art. 2(4), with effect from 11 August 2008.
Art. 5 inserted by SI 2005/2423, art. 5, with effect from 22 September 2005.

INSURANCE COMPANIES (CALCULATION OF PROFITS: POLICY HOLDERS' TAX) REGULATIONS 2003

(SI 2003/2082, as amended by SI 2008/1906 and SI 2010/2932)

Made on 11 August 2003 by the Treasury, in exercise of the powers conferred upon them by s. 82A of the Finance Act 1989. Operative from 1 September 2003.

CITATION, COMMENCEMENT AND EFFECT

1(1) These Regulations may be cited as the Insurance Companies (Calculation of Profits: Policy Holders' Tax) Regulations 2003 and shall come into force on 1st September 2003.

1(2) These Regulations have effect in relation to periods of account beginning on or after 1st January 2003 and ending on or after these Regulations come into force.

CALCULATION OF PROFITS: POLICY HOLDERS' TAX

2 Tax expended on behalf of policy holders or annuitants is allowed as a deduction in calculating the profits for a period of account to the extent permitted by–

(a)   subject to regulation 5, the basis of deduction specified in regulation 3 or 3A; and

(b)   regulation 5.

History – In reg. 2(a), "or 3A" inserted by SI 2010/2932, reg. 3, with effect in relation to periods of account ending on or after 31 December 2010.

3 For the purpose of regulation 2 the basis of deduction is–

(a)   the basis used in the company's latest company tax return to determine the amount of tax expended on behalf of policy holders or annuitants allowed as a deduction in calculating the profits for that accounting period; or

(b)   where the company has no latest company tax return–

      (i)   where the company was the transferee of life assurance business under an insurance business transfer scheme, the basis used in the latest company tax return of the transferor company to determine the amount of tax expended on behalf of policy holders or annuitants allowed as a deduction in calculating the profits for that accounting period; or

      (ii)   in any other case, the basis the company would have used to determine the amount of tax expended on behalf of policy holders or annuitants allowed as a deduction in calculating the profits for an accounting period had it been required to deliver a company tax return for an accounting period beginning before 1st January 2003.

This regulation does not apply for a period of account in which there has been a substantial change in the business of the company, except to the extent permitted by regulation 3A(2)(a), or for any subsequent period of account

History – In reg. 3, the final paragraph inserted by SI 2010/2932, reg. 4, with effect in relation to periods of account ending on or after 31 December 2010.

BASIS OF DEDUCTION FOLLOWING A SUBSTANTIAL CHANGE IN THE BUSINESS OF A COMPANY

3A(1) This regulation applies for the purposes of regulation 2 where there has been a substantial change in the long-term business of a company.

3A(2) Where the change occurred or occurs on or before 31st December 2010–

(a)   in the first period of account ending on or after 31st December 2010 the basis of deduction is either–

      (i)   the basis specified in regulation 3; or

      (ii)   such other basis to determine the amount of tax expended on behalf of policy holders or annuitants as is just and reasonable; and

(b)   for any subsequent period of account, the basis of deduction is such basis to determine the amount of tax expended on behalf of policy holders or annuitants as is just and reasonable.

3A(3) Where the change occurs in a period of account beginning on or after 1st January 2011, the basis of deduction to be used in relation to the period of account in which the change occurs and in relation to each subsequent period of account shall be such basis to determine the amount of tax expended on behalf of policy holders or annuitants as is just and reasonable.

3A(4) For the purpose of determining whether a substantial change in the long-term business of a company has occurred in relation to–

(a) the first period of account ending on or after 31st December 2010, the long-term business of the company as at the end of the last day of that period of account is to be compared with the long-term business of the company as at the end of the last day of the first period of account to which these regulations applied; and

(b) a period of account beginning on or after 1st January 2011, the long-term business of the company as at the end of the last day of the period of account in which the substantial change occurs is to be compared with the long-term business of the company as at the end of the last day of the immediately preceding period of account.

3A(5) For the purposes of this regulation, a basis to determine the amount of tax expended on behalf of policy holders and annuitants is just and reasonable if it takes account of and is consistent with–

(a) the long-term business activities of the company; and

(b) the structure of the long-term insurance fund.

3A(6) In this regulation **"a substantial change in the long-term business of a company"** includes but is not limited to–

(a) an insurance business transfer scheme;

(b) the commencement of a new category of long-term business;

(c) ceasing to write a category of long-term business; or

(d) a change in the structure of the long-term insurance fund.

History – Reg. 3A and the heading before it inserted by SI 2010/2932, reg. 5, with effect in relation to periods of account ending on or after 31 December 2010.

INTERPRETATION OF REGULATIONS 3 AND 3A

4(1) In regulation 3 **"the latest company tax return"** means the company tax return for the latest preceding accounting period of the company or the transferor company for which such a return has been delivered before the day on which these Regulations come into force.

4(2) In regulation 3 and 3A **"an insurance business transfer scheme"** means a scheme falling within section 105 of the Financial Services and Markets Act 2000, including an excluded scheme falling within Case 2, 3, 4 or 5 of subsection (3) of that section.

4(3) In regulation 3A–

"long-term business"; and

"long-term insurance fund"

have the meanings given by section 431(2) of the Income and Corporation Taxes Act 1988.

History – Reg. 4 and the heading before it substituted for former reg. 4 by SI 2010/2932, reg. 6, with effect in relation to periods of account ending on or after 31 December 2010. Former reg. 4 read as follows:
"4 In regulation 3–
(a) **"the latest company tax return"** means the company tax return for the latest preceding accounting period of the company or the transferor company for which such a return has been delivered before the day on which these Regulations come into force;
(b) **"an insurance business transfer scheme"** means a scheme falling within section 105 of the Financial Services and Markets Act 2000, including an excluded scheme falling within Case 2, 3, 4 or 5 of subsection (3) of that section.".
In former reg. 4(b), the words ", 4 or 5" substituted for "or 4" by SI 2008/1906, reg. 2, with effect for periods of account beginning on or after 1 January 2008 and ending on or after 8 August 2008.

5 A deduction for tax expended on behalf of policy holders or annuitants but not brought into account shall be allowed but only where such an amount has been included in any value deemed to be brought into account by virtue of section 83(2B) of the Finance Act 1989.

FINANCE ACT 1995, SECTION 127(12) (DESIGNATED TRANSACTIONS) REGULATIONS 2003

(SI 2003/2172)

Made on 21 August 2003 by the Treasury, in exercise of the powers conferred upon them by s. 127(12)(c) of the Finance Act 1995. Operative from 12 September 2003.

CITATION AND COMMENCEMENT

1 These Regulations may be cited as the Finance Act 1995, Section 127(12) (Designated Transactions) Regulations 2003 and shall come into force on 12th September 2003.

DESIGNATED TRANSACTION

2(1) In this regulation **"section 127(12)"** means section 127(12) of the Finance Act 1995 (meaning of "investment transaction" for the purposes of determining whether person capable of being the UK representative of a non-resident taxpayer).

2(2) For the purposes of section 127(12) a transaction falling within paragraph (3) is designated.

2(3) A transaction falls within this paragraph if it is a contract, not otherwise falling within section 127(12), whose terms–

(a)   provide that–

    (i)   after setting off their obligations to each other under the contract, a cash payment is to be made by one party to the other in respect of the excess, if any, or

    (ii)   each party is liable to make to the other party one or more cash payments in respect of that party's obligations to the other under the contract, and

(b)   do not provide for the delivery of any property other than currency.

This is subject to the following qualification.

2(4) A transaction does not fall within paragraph (3) if it is–

(a)   a contract which relates to land;

(b)   a contract of insurance; or

(c)   a contract effected in the course of capital redemption business within the meaning of section 458 of the Income and Corporation Taxes Act 1988.

FINANCE ACT 2003, SCHEDULE 26, PARAGRAPH 3(3) (DESIGNATED TRANSACTIONS) REGULATIONS 2003

(SI 2003/2173)

Made on 21 August 2003 by the Treasury, in exercise of the powers conferred upon them by para. 3(3)(c) of Sch. 26 to the Finance Act 2003. Operative from 12 September 2003.

CITATION AND COMMENCEMENT

1 These Regulations may be cited as the Finance Act 2003, Schedule 26 Paragraph 3(3) (Designated Transactions) Regulations 2003 and shall come into force on 12th September 2003.

DESIGNATED TRANSACTION

2(1) In these Regulations **"paragraph 3(3)"** means paragraph 3(3) of Schedule 26 to the Finance Act 2003 (meaning of "investment transaction" for the purposes of determining whether a person is an agent of independent status in respect of investment transactions).

2(2) For the purposes of paragraph 3(3) a transaction falling within paragraph (3) is designated.

2(3) A transaction falls within this paragraph if it is a contract, not otherwise falling within paragraph 3(3), whose terms–

(a)   provide that–

    (i)   after setting off their obligations to each other under the contract, a cash payment is to be made by one party to the other in respect of the excess, if any, or

    (ii)   each party is liable to make to the other party one or more cash payments in respect of that party's obligations to the other under the contract, and

(b)   do not provide for the delivery of any property other than currency.

This is subject to the following qualification.

2(4) A transaction does not fall within paragraph (3) if it is–

(a)   a contract which relates to land;

(b)   a contract of insurance; or

(c)   a contract effected in the course of capital redemption business within the meaning of section 458 of the Income and Corporation Taxes Act 1988.

TAXATION OF BENEFITS UNDER GOVERNMENT PILOT SCHEMES (RETURN TO WORK CREDIT AND EMPLOYMENT RETENTION AND ADVANCEMENT SCHEMES) ORDER 2003

(SI 2003/2339)

Made on 10 September 2003 by the Treasury, in exercise of the powers conferred upon them by s. 151(1)(a), (2), (5) and (7) of the Finance Act 1996. Operative from 1 October 2003.

CITATION AND COMMENCEMENT

1 This Order may be cited as the Taxation of Benefits under Government Pilot Schemes (Return to Work Credit and Employment Retention and Advancement Schemes) Order 2003 and shall come into force on 1st October 2003.

INTERPRETATION

2 In this Order–

"benefit" has the meaning given by subsection (6) of section 151 of the Finance Act 1996;

"Employment Retention and Advancement Scheme payment" means a payment of benefit under the Government pilot scheme known as the Employment Retention and Advancement Scheme;

"Government pilot scheme" has the meaning given by subsections (3) and (4) of section 151 of the Finance Act 1996; and

"Return to Work Credit payment" means a payment of benefit under the Government pilot scheme known as the Return to Work Credit Scheme.

EXEMPTIONS FROM INCOME TAX

3 The Income Tax Acts shall not have effect in relation to any amount of an Employment Retention and Advancement Scheme payment, and any amount of a Return to Work Credit Scheme payment, as if that amount were wholly exempt from income tax and accordingly to be disregarded in computing the amount of any receipts brought into account for income tax purposes.

INCOME TAX (INCENTIVE PAYMENTS FOR VOLUNTARY ELECTRONIC COMMUNICATION OF PAYE RETURNS) REGULATIONS 2003

(SI 2003/2495 as amended by SI 2005/826, SI 2006/777, SI 2009/56 and SI 2009/1890)

Made on 29 September 2003 by the Commissioners of Inland Revenue, in exercise of the powers conferred upon them by s. 143(1) of, and Sch. 38 to, the Finance Act 2000. Operative from 20 October 2003.

CITATION, COMMENCEMENT AND INTERPRETATION

1(1) These Regulations may be cited as the Income Tax (Incentive Payments for Voluntary Electronic Communication of PAYE Returns) Regulations 2003 and shall come into force on 20th October 2003.

1(2) In these Regulations–

"**approved**" means approved by means of a general or specific direction of the Board;

"**the Board**" means the Commissioners of Inland Revenue;

"**direction**" means a direction given by the Board;

"**employee**" has the meaning given in section 4 of ITEPA 2003, and cognate expressions shall be construed accordingly;

"**incentive payment**" has the meaning given in Schedule 38;

"**ITEPA 2003**" means the Income Tax (Earnings and Pensions) Act 2003;

"**the Management Act**" means the Taxes Management Act 1970;

"**the PAYE Regulations**" means the Income Tax (Pay As You Earn) Regulations 2003;

"**Schedule 38**" means Schedule 38 to the Finance Act 2000;

"**the specified date**" means, in relation to a year of assessment, such date in the immediately preceding year of assessment as is announced annually by means of a direction given by the Board not later than 30th November of that preceding year; and

references to the delivery of information have the same meaning as they have in section 132 of the Finance Act 1999.

1(3) In these Regulations "a small employer" is a person treated as paying PAYE income to 49 or fewer recipients at the specified date.

A person is treated as paying PAYE income to a recipient at the specified date if at that date–

(a)   he is required by the PAYE Regulations or by paragraph 6 of Schedule 4 to the Social Security (Contributions) Regulations 2001 to prepare or maintain a deductions working sheet in respect of the recipient; and

(b)   he has not delivered, sent or transmitted to the inspector a statement required by regulation 23 of the PAYE Regulations for the recipient.

History – In reg. 1(2) the definitions of "employee" and "ITEPA 2003" inserted and the definition of "the PAYE regulations" substituted by SI 2005/826, reg. 3(2), with effect from 8 April 2005.
In reg. 1(3)(a) the words "PAYE Regulations or by" substituted for the words "PAYE Regulations," and the words ", or by regulation 6(6) of the Working Tax Credit (Payment by Employers) Regulations 2002" omitted by SI 2006/777, reg. 6, with effect from the tax year 2007–08.
In reg. 1(3) the words ", paragraph 6 of Schedule 4 to the Social Security (Contributions) Regulations 2001, or by regulation 6(6)" substituted for the words "or by regulation 6(6)" by SI 2005/826, reg. 3(3), with effect from 8 April 2005.

CONSTRUCTION OF REFERENCES TO NUMBERS OF EMPLOYEES

2(1) If an election has been made under regulation 98 of the PAYE Regulations (multiple employers) and–

(a)   no notice under regulation 99 of those Regulations (elections for improper purposes) has been given, or

(b)   any notice under that regulation has been withdrawn,

paragraph (2) applies.

2(2) Where this paragraph applies, a reference in these Regulations to a number of recipients shall be construed as a reference to the number of such employees treated as employed in a separate undertaking by virtue of regulation 98 of the PAYE Regulations.

History – In reg. 2(2) the words "regulation 98" substituted for the words "regulation 3", in reg. 2(1)(a) the words "regulation 99 of those Regulations" substituted for the words "paragraph (6) of that regulation" and in reg. 2(1)(b) the words "that regulation" substituted for the words "that paragraph" by SI 2005/826, reg. 4(2), with effect from 8 April 2005.
In reg. 2(2) the words "regulation 98" substituted for the words "regulation 3(1)" by SI 2005/826, reg. 4(3), with effect from 8 April 2005.

SCOPE

3(1) These Regulations apply to the persons specified in paragraph (2) who deliver, or cause to be delivered, the return and supporting information required under regulation 73 of the PAYE Regulations by an approved method of electronic communications if–

(a)   the return and that information are delivered in respect of a year of assessment specified in paragraph (3); and

(b)   the return satisfies the conditions mentioned in regulation 4(1)(b).

3(2) The persons specified in this paragraph are those who–

(a)   are small employers on the specified date; or

(b)   not being small employers on that date, are treated as making payments of PAYE income for the first time after that date.

3(3) The years of assessment specified in this paragraph are 2004–05 to 2008–09.

History – In reg. 3(1) the words "regulation 73" substituted for the words "regulation 43" by SI 2005/826, reg. 5(2), with effect from 8 April 2005.

INCENTIVE PAYMENT – RETURN UNDER REGULATION 73 OF THE PAYE REGULATIONS

History – In the heading the words "REGULATION 73" substituted for the words "REGULATION 43" by SI 2005/826, reg. 6(2), with effect from 8 April 2005.

4(1) The Board shall make an incentive payment in the amount prescribed in paragraph (3) to a person specified in regulation 3(2) for the year of assessment in question, if–

(a)   he delivers, or causes to be delivered, a return under regulation 73 of the PAYE Regulations for that year of assessment by an approved method of electronic communications; and

(b)   the return satisfies the conditions as to accuracy and completeness specified in any direction given by the Board.

This is subject to paragraphs (2) and (2A).

4(2) An incentive payment shall not be made in respect of a return which contains only information supplied in accordance with any of the provisions and arrangements mentioned in regulation 141 of the PAYE Regulations.

4(2A) An incentive payment shall not be made where a small employer–

(a)   has been established,

(b)   employs employees, or

(c)   makes payments of PAYE income (within the meaning of section 683 of ITEPA 2003),

wholly or mainly for an impermissible purpose.

4(2B) For the purpose of paragraph (2A)–

(a)   a small employer is "established" where–

     (i)   persons enter into partnership, within the meaning of section 4 of the Partnership Act 1894, in accordance with the principles set out in section 2 of that Act,

     (ii)   a limited partnership is registered in accordance with the Limited Partnerships Act 1907,

     (iii)   a limited liability partnership is incorporated in accordance with section 2 of the Limited Liability Partnerships Act 2000,

     (iv)   a company is incorporated under the Companies Act 2006, or

     (v)   an unincorporated association, or a body corporate, not falling within the previous paragraphs, is created,

   and it is intended at the time of incorporation, formation or creation that it should be a small employer;

(b)   a small employer is established for an impermissible purpose if it is established for the purpose of–

     (i)   obtaining an advantage in relation to income tax, corporation tax or national insurance contributions;

     (ii)   obtaining an incentive under these Regulations; or

   (iii)   avoiding an obligation to file a return by means of electronic communications under any enactment relating to income tax, corporation tax or national insurance.

4(2C) For the purposes of paragraph (2B)(b)(i) **"advantage"**—

(a)   in relation to income tax and corporation tax, has the meaning given by section 318 of the Finance Act 2004 (interpretation for the purposes of Part 7: tax avoidance schemes); and

(b)   in relation to national insurance, has the meaning which would be given by that section were national insurance a tax to which it applied.

4(3) The amounts prescribed are those shown in the Table 1 for the relevant year of assessment.

Year of assessment	Amount of incentive payment
2004–05	£250
2005–06	£250
2006–07	£150
2007–08	£100
2008–09	£75

4(3A) If an officer of the Board considers that, by virtue of paragraph (2A), a person will not be entitled to an incentive payment for a year of assessment, he may give notice to that effect to that person.

4(4) Where an officer of the Board considers that a person, who has claimed to be entitled to an incentive under these Regulations—

(a)   does not satisfy one or more of the requirements of these Regulations or the directions made under them, or

(b)   is not entitled to an incentive payment by virtue of paragraph (2) or (2A).

the officer shall give notice to that person that the conditions are not met or, where the incentive payment has already been authorised or made, notice withdrawing the incentive payment.

4(5) Where, prior to the giving of a notice under paragraph (4), an incentive payment has already been made to the person referred to in that paragraph, an office of the Board may recover the amount of the incentive payment in accordance with paragraph (6).

4(6) For the purpose of paragraph (5), subsections (1), (4), (5) and (6) of section 30 and section 30A of the Management Act (recovery of overpayment of tax, etc and assessing procedure) shall apply as if the amount to be recovered were an amount of income tax repaid to a person which ought not to have been repaid to him.

History – In reg. 4(1)(a) the words "regulation 73" substituted for the words "regulation 43" by SI 2005/826, reg. 6(3)(a), with effect from 8 April 2005.

In reg. 4(1) the words "paragraphs (2) and (2A)" substituted for the words "the following qualification" by SI 2005/826, reg. 6(3)(b), with effect from 19 March 2005 subject to the commencement rules at SI 2005/826, reg. 1 which read as follows:

    "**1(1)** These Regulations may be cited as the Income Tax (Incentive Payments for Voluntary Electronic Communication of PAYE Returns) (Amendment) Regulations 2005 and shall come into force—

    (a)   for the purposes of the amendments made—

        (i)   by regulations 6(3)(b) and 6(5) to (7), and regulation 6(1) so far as it relates to those provisions, and

        (ii)   by regulation 8,

    on 19th March 2005; and

    (b)   for all other purposes on 8th April 2005.

    1(2)   The amendments made by regulations the provisions listed in paragraph (1)(a) above shall have effect—

    (a)   if the obligation to maintain a deductions working sheet under any of the provisions listed in paragraph (3) arises for the first time in relation to the year of assessment 2004–05 after the coming into force of these Regulations, in relation to any return delivered in respect of that year; and

    (b)   except as provided by sub-paragraph (a), in relation to any return delivered in respect of the years of assessment 2005–06 to 2008–09.

    1(3)   The provisions referred to in paragraph (2)(a) are—

    (a)   paragraph 6 of Schedule 4 to the Social Security (Contributions) Regulations 2001;

    (b)   regulation 6(6) of the Working Tax Credit (Payment by Employers) Regulations 2002; and

    (c)   regulation 66 of the Income Tax (Pay As You Earn) Regulations 2003."

In reg. 4(2) the words "regulation 141" substituted for the words "regulation 102(2)" by SI 2005/826, reg. 6(4), with effect from 8 April 2005.

In reg. 4(2B)(a)(iii), the words " or section 2 of the Limited Liability Partnerships Act (Northern Ireland) 2002" omitted by SI 2009/1890, art. 3(7), with effect from 1 October 2009.

In reg. 4(2B)(a)(iv), the words "section 1 of" (which preceded the words "the Companies Act") omitted, "2006" substituted for "1985", and the words "or article 12 of the Companies (Northern Ireland) Order 1986" (which followed "1985") omitted by SI 2009/1890, art. 3(8), with effect from 1 October 2009.

Reg. 4(2A)–(2C) inserted by SI 2005/826, reg. 6(5), with effect from 19 March 2005 subject to the commencement rules at SI 2005/826, reg. 1 which are reproduced as part of the history note for reg. 4(1) above.

Reg. 4(3A) inserted by SI 2005/826, reg. 6(6), with effect from 19 March 2005 subject to the commencement rules at SI 2005/826, reg. 1 which are reproduced as part of the history note for reg. 4(1) above.

In reg. 4(4)(b) "(2) or (2A)" substituted for "(2)" by SI 2005/826, reg. 6(7), with effect from 19 March 2005 subject to the commencement rules at SI 2005/826, reg. 1 which are reproduced as part of the history note for reg. 4(1) above.

Cross references – Direction of the Board, 21 October 2003: direction providing that the methods of electronic communication approved for the purposes of reg. 4(1)(a) are the EDI services (Electronic Data Interchange) and the Internet services provided through PAYE Online for Employers and PAYE Online for Agents.

DESCRIPTIONS OF INCENTIVES

4A(1) Any incentive under these Regulations shall take the form of–

(a) in the case of a person, from whom a sum of any of the descriptions mentioned in paragraph (3) has become due to the Board, a reduction in the person's liability for that sum;

(b) in the case of a person in respect of whom an account is maintained by the Board, not falling within sub-paragraph (a), a credit to that account; or

(c) in any other case, or at the request of a person who would be entitled to a credit to his account as mentioned in sub-paragraph (b), a payment by the Board.

4A(2) Where the amount of an incentive due to a person falling within paragraph (1)(a) exceeds the amount of his liability, the excess shall be credited to any account maintained in respect of that person by the Board, or, if that person so requests, paid to him by the Board

4A(3) The sums referred to in paragraph (1) are those which a person is liable to pay to a collector of inland revenue in pursuance of an obligation as an employer, contractor or a sub-contractor.

4A(4) If an incentive is given as mentioned in paragraph (1)(a) or (b) an officer of the Board shall notify the person entitled to the incentive of the form it has taken.

History – Reg. 4A inserted by SI 2005/826, reg. 7, with effect from 8 April 2005.

NOTICE OF NON-ENTITLEMENT TO INCENTIVE PAYMENT

5 If, during the year of assessment 2003–04, an officer of the Board considers that a person–

(a) is not a small employer in respect of the year of assessment 2004–05; but

(b) is treated as paying PAYE income to less than 250 employees at the specified date in respect of that year;

the officer shall give notice to that person that he is not entitled to an incentive payment under these Regulations for the year of assessment 2004–05.

APPEALS

6(1) An appeal lies, subject to paragraph (1A) against a decision made by an officer of the Board under regulation 4(3A) or (4) or 5 and may be brought–

(a) by notice in writing to an officer of the Board; and

(b) within 30 days of the issue of the officer's notice under that regulation.

6(1A) A person may not appeal against a decision under regulation 4(4)(b) where he has already appealed unsuccessfully against a notice given under regulation 4(3A) in respect of the same year of assessment.

6(2) An appeal may be brought against an officer's notice under regulation 4(3A) or (4) on the grounds that the recipient of the notice–

(a) has satisfied all the requirements of these Regulations and the directions made under them so far as they apply to him; and

(b) is not precluded from receiving an incentive payment by virtue of regulation 4(2) or (2A).

6(3) The recipient of an officer's notice under regulation 5 may appeal against it on the grounds that he is entitled to an incentive payment for the year of assessment 2004–05.

6(4) Section 31A(5) of the Management Act applies to an appeal under these Regulations as it applies to an appeal under section 31 of that Act.

History – In reg. 6(1) the words ", subject to paragraph (1A)" and "in writing" inserted and the words "regulation 4(3A) or (4)" substituted for the words "regulation 4(4)" by SI 2005/826, reg. 8(2), with effect from 19 March 2005 subject to the commencement rules at SI 2005/826, reg. 1 which read as follows:

> "**1(1)** These Regulations may be cited as the Income Tax (Incentive Payments for Voluntary Electronic Communication of PAYE Returns) (Amendment) Regulations 2005 and shall come into force–
> (a) for the purposes of the amendments made–
>   (i) by regulations 6(3)(b) and 6(5) to (7), and regulation 6(1) so far as it relates to those provisions, and
>   (ii) by regulation 8,
> on 19th March 2005; and
> (b) for all other purposes on 8th April 2005.
> **1(2)** The amendments made by regulations the provisions listed in paragraph (1)(a) above shall have effect–
> (a) if the obligation to maintain a deductions working sheet under any of the provisions listed in paragraph (3) arises for the first time in relation to the year of assessment 2004–05 after the coming into force of these Regulations, in relation to any return delivered in respect of that year; and

(b)   except as provided by sub-paragraph (a), in relation to any return delivered in respect of the years of assessment 2005–06 to 2008–09.

1(3)   The provisions referred to in paragraph (2)(a) are—

(a)   paragraph 6 of Schedule 4 to the Social Security (Contributions) Regulations 2001;

(b)   regulation 6(6) of the Working Tax Credit (Payment by Employers) Regulations 2002; and

(c)   regulation 66 of the Income Tax (Pay As You Earn) Regulations 2003."

Reg. 6(1A) inserted by SI 2005/826, reg. 8(3), with effect from 19 March 2005 subject to the commencement rules at SI 2005/826, reg. 1 which are reproduced at the history note for reg. 6(1) above.

In reg. 6(2) the words "regulation 4(3A) and (4)" substituted for the words "regulation 4(4)" and in reg. 6(2)(b) the words "regulation 4(2) or (2A)" substituted for the words "regulation 4(2)" by SI 2005/826, reg. 8(4), with effect from 19 March 2005 subject to the commencement rules at SI 2005/826, reg. 1 which are reproduced at the history note for reg. 6(1) above.

Reg. 6(4) substituted for former reg. 6(4)–(7) by SI 2009/56, art. 3(2) and Sch. 2, para. 91, operative from 1 April 2009 subject to transitional and saving provisions in SI 2009/56, Sch. 3. Former reg. 6(4)–(7) read as follows:

"**6(4)**   The following provisions of the Management Act apply to an appeal under these Regulations as they apply to an appeal under section 31 of that Act–

(a)   section 31A(5) and (6) (notice of appeal);

(b)   section 31B (appeals to General Commissioners); and

(c)   section 31D (election to bring appeal before Special Commissioners).

6(5)   Paragraphs 3 and 8 of Schedule 3 to the Management Act (rules for assigning proceedings to General Commissioners) shall apply for the purposes of an appeal under these Regulations as they apply to an appeal under the PAYE Regulations.

6(6)   In relation to an appeal under these Regulations the "relevant place" for the purposes of paragraph 3 of Schedule 3 to the Management Act (as applied by paragraph (5) of this regulation) is–

(a)   the appellant's place of business in the United Kingdom; or

(b)   where the appellant has no place of business in the United Kingdom, the appellant's place of residence in the United Kingdom.

6(7)   For the purposes of paragraph (6) **"place of business"** and **"place of residence"** have the same meanings as they have for the purposes of paragraph 2(2) of Schedule 3 to the Management Act.".

INCOME TAX (PAY AS YOU EARN) REGULATIONS 2003

(SI 2003/2682, as amended by SI 2004/851, SI 2005/2691, SI 2006/243, SI 2006/745, SI 2006/777, SI 2007/1077, SI 2007/2069, SI 2007/2296, SI 2007/2969, SI 2008/782, SI 2008/2601, SI 2009/56, SI 2009/588, SI 2009/2029, SI 2010/466, SI 2010/668, SI 2010/2496, SI 2011/729, SI 2011/1054, SI 2011/1584, SI 2012/822, SI 2012/1895, SI 2013/521, SI 2013/630, SI 2013/2300, SI 2014/472, SI 2014/474, SI 2014/992, SI 2014/1017 and FA 2014)

Made on 21 October 2003 by the Commissioners of Inland Revenue in exercise of the powers conferred on them by s. 684, 685(4), 692, 704, 705, 706, 707, 708 and 710 of the Income Tax (Earnings and Pensions) Act 2003, s. 59A(10), 59B(8), 98A and 113(1) of the Taxes Management Act 1970, s. 132 and 133(2) of the Finance Act 1999, s. 136 of the Finance Act 2002, and s. 145(4) and 205 of the Finance Act 2003. Operative from 6 April 2004.

ARRANGEMENT OF REGULATIONS
PART 1 – INTRODUCTION

PART 1 – INTRODUCTION

CITATION AND COMMENCEMENT

Citation and commencement

1 These Regulations may be cited as The Income Tax (Pay As You Earn) Regulations 2003 and shall come into force on 6th April 2004.

Origin – Drafting.

INTERPRETATION

Interpretation

2(1) In these Regulations, unless the context otherwise requires–

"**additional pay**" means the appropriate amount, established from an employee's code (where it is a K code not used on the cumulative basis) and the tax tables, to be added to the relevant payments made to an employee in order to determine the taxable payments;

"**additional rate**" in relation to the charging of income tax for any tax year, means the rate of income tax determined under section 6(2) of ITA;

"**agency**" has the meaning given in section 44 of ITEPA;

"**agency worker**" means a worker whose services are treated by section 44 of ITEPA as the duties of an employment held with the agency;

"**approved method of electronic communications**" has the meaning given in regulation 189;

"**basic rate**", in relation to the charging of income tax for any tax year, means the rate of income tax determined under section 1(2)(a) of ICTA;

"**Board of Inland Revenue**" means the Commissioners of Inland Revenue (as to which see in particular the Inland Revenue Regulation Act 1890);

"**closed tax year**" means any tax year preceding the current year, and cognate expressions shall be construed accordingly;

"**code**" and related expressions have the meanings given in regulation 7;

"**cumulative basis**" means the basis of deduction or repayment of tax provided for in regulation 23;

"**combined amount**" means an amount which includes tax due under these regulations and one or more of the following–

(a) earnings-related contributions due under the SSC Regulations;

(b) amounts due under the Income Tax (Construction Industry Scheme) Regulations 2005;

(c) payments of repayments of student loans due under the Student Loan Regulations;

"**deductions working sheet**" means–

(a) any form of record in which are to be kept the matters required by these Regulations in connection with an employee's relevant payments and tax;

(b) [Omitted by SI 2014/472, reg. 3;]

"**earnings**" has the meaning given in sections 62 and 721(7) of ITEPA;

"**electronic communications**" has the meaning given in regulation 189;

"**employee's code**" has the meaning given in regulation 8(1);

"**employer reference**" means the combination of letters, numbers or both used by the Inland Revenue to identify an employer for the purposes of these Regulations;

"**employer's PAYE reference**", in relation to an employer, means the combination of the employer's employer reference and the Inland Revenue office number;

"**employment**", subject to regulations 10 to 12, has the meaning given in sections 4 and 5 of ITEPA; and "**employer**" and "**employee**" have corresponding meanings;

"**excluded business expenses**" has the meaning given in regulation 5;

"**family**" and "**family or household**", in relation to a person, have the meanings given in section 721(4) and (5) of ITEPA;

"**free pay**" means the appropriate amount, established from an employee's code (where not used on the cumulative basis) and the tax tables, to be subtracted from relevant payments to arrive at taxable payments (and accordingly represents an appropriate part of reliefs allowable against those payments);

"**general earnings**" has the meaning given in section 7(3) of ITEPA;

"**higher rate**", in relation to the charging of income tax for any tax year, means the rate of income tax determined under section 1(2)(b) of ICTA;

"**HMRC**" means Her Majesty's Revenue and Customs;

"**ICTA**" means the Income and Corporation Taxes Act 1988;

"**Inland Revenue**" means any officer of the Board of Inland Revenue;

"**Inland Revenue office**", in relation to an employer, means the office of the Inland Revenue from which codes are normally issued to the employer;

"**Inland Revenue office number**" means the number which identifies an employer's Inland Revenue office;

"**ITA**" means the Income Tax Act 2007;

"**ITEPA**" means the Income Tax (Earnings and Pensions) Act 2003;

"**large employer**" has the meaning given in regulation 198A;

"**lower earnings limit**" means the lower earnings limit for Class 1 contributions for the purposes of section 5(1) of the Social Security Contributions and Benefits Act 1992;

"**national insurance number**" means the national insurance number allocated within the meaning of regulation 9 of the Social Security (Crediting and Treatment of Contributions, and National Insurance Numbers) Regulations 2001;

"**net PAYE income**" has the meaning given in regulation 3;

"**non-cumulative basis**" means the basis of deduction of tax provided for in regulation 27;

"**non-Real Time Information employer**" means an employer other than one within regulation 2A;

"**non-Real Time Information pension payer**" means a pension payer other than one within regulation 2B;

"**notice**" means as follows and "**notify**" must be read accordingly–

    (a)   notice in writing, or in a form authorised (in relation to the case in question) by directions under section 118 of the Finance Act 1998 (which allows certain claims etc to be made by telephone)

    (b)   for the purpose of regulation 19 (Amendment of code), notice in writing or by telephone;

"**notional payment**" has the meaning given in section 710(2)(a) of ITEPA;

"**objects**" means gives a notice of objection to the Inland Revenue;

"**official computer system**" has the meaning given in regulation 189;

"**other payee**" means a person receiving relevant payments in a capacity other than employee, agency worker or pensioner;

"**other payer**" means a person making relevant payments in a capacity other than employer, agency or pension payer;

"**overriding limit**" means the limit on the amount of tax to be deducted from a relevant payment, where the tax due in accordance with the appropriate tax tables in respect of any taxable payments or total taxable payments to date at the relevant date has been calculated by reference to additional pay or total additional pay to date, and that limit is an amount equal to 50% of the amount of the relevant payment;

"**PAYE income**" has the meaning given in section 683 of ITEPA;

"**PAYE pension income**" has the meaning given in section 683(3) of ITEPA;

"**PAYE threshold**" must be determined in accordance with regulation 9;

"**payee**" means an employee, agency worker, pensioner or other payee;

"**payer**" means an employer, agency, pension payer or other payer;

"**pension**" means a pension, annuity or other payments of PAYE pension income;

"**pensioner**" means a person receiving PAYE pension income;

"**pension payer**" means a person making payments of PAYE pension income;

"**PSA**" means a PAYE settlement agreement made in accordance with regulation 105;

"**qualifying general earnings**", in relation to a PSA, has the meaning given in regulation 106;

"qualifying payment" means a payment which becomes retrospective employment income as a relevant payment (including a notional payment);

"Real Time Information employer" has the meaning given in regulation 2A;

"Real Time Information pension payer" has the meaning given in regulation 2B;

"relevant payments" has the meaning given in regulation 4;

"relevant pension payments" has the meaning given in regulation 6;

"the relevant time", in relation to retrospective employment income, has the meaning given by section 710(7) of ITEPA, as modified by subsection (7A) of that section, but subject to section 94(5) of the Finance Act 2006;

"reliefs from income tax" includes allowances and deductions;

"retrospective contributions regulations" has the meaning given by regulation 1(2) of the SSC Regulations;

"retrospective employment income" means payments which are retrospectively treated as payments of employment income by virtue of a retrospective tax provision;

"retrospective tax provision" means a provision of the Income Tax Acts charging to income tax amounts of employment income paid before the enactment containing the provision was passed;

"seconded expatriate" means an employee meeting one of the following descriptions–

(a) an employee in section 689 of ITEPA (employee of non-UK employer); or

(b) an employee in a branch of an employer where–

　(i) these Regulations would not apply to that employer but for that branch,

　(ii) the employer seconded the employee to that branch, and

　(iii) the employee was not employed in the United Kingdom immediately before the secondment;

"specified date" for the purposes of Chapter 3 of Part 10, has the meaning given in regulation 198A;

"SSC Regulations" means the Social Security (Contributions) Regulations 2001;

"Student Loan Regulations" means the Education (Student Loans) (Repayment) Regulations 2009 or, in Northern Ireland, the Education (Student Loans) (Repayment) Regulations (Northern Ireland) 2009;

"taxable payments" means relevant payments reduced by free pay or, as the case may be, increased by additional pay (where the employee's code is not used on the cumulative basis);

"tax month" means the period beginning on the 6th day of a calendar month and ending on the 5th day of the following calendar month;

"tax not deducted because of the overriding limit" means any tax–

(a) which is due at the relevant date in accordance with the appropriate tax tables in respect of any taxable payments or total taxable payments to date, but

(b) which has not been deducted because of the overriding limit;

"tax period" means–

(a) tax quarter, if regulation 70 (quarterly tax periods) applies, or

(b) tax month, in every other case;

"tax quarter" means any of the following (inclusive) periods–

　6th April to 5th July,

　6th July to 5th October,

　6th October to 5th January, and

　6th January to 5th April;

"tax tables" means the tax tables prepared by the Board of Inland Revenue under section 685 of ITEPA;

"tax week" means 6th April to 12th April (inclusive) and each successive period of 7 days, except that the final tax week in a tax year ("Week 53") is just the last day of the tax year (or last 2 days in a leap year);

"tax year" means a year for which any Act provides for income tax to be charged;

"TMA" means the Taxes Management Act 1970;

"**total additional pay to date**" means the appropriate amount, established from an employee's code (where it is a K code to be used on the cumulative basis) and the tax tables, to be added to the total payments to date in order to determine the total taxable payments to date;

"**total free pay to date**", in relation to any date, means the appropriate amount, established from an employee's code (where used on the cumulative basis) and the tax tables, to be subtracted from total payments to date to arrive at total taxable payments to date (and accordingly represents an appropriate part of reliefs allowable against those payments);

"**total net tax deducted**", in relation to the relevant payments made to an employee during any period, means the total tax deducted from those payments plus any tax accounted for in accordance with regulation 62(5) (notional payments), less any tax repaid to the employee;

"**total payments to date**", in relation to any date, means the sum of all relevant payments made by the employer to the employee from the beginning of the tax year up to and including that date;

"**total tax to date**" means the tax due at any date in accordance with the appropriate tax tables in respect of any total taxable payments to date;

"**total taxable payments to date**" means total payments to date reduced by total free pay to date or, as the case may be, increased by total additional pay to date (where the employee's code is used on the cumulative basis);

"**trade dispute**" has the meaning given in section 35(1) of the Jobseekers Act 1995 or, in Northern Ireland, in article 2(2) of the Jobseekers (Northern Ireland) Order 1995.

"**tribunal**" means the First-tier Tribunal or, where determined by or under Tribunal Procedure Rules, the Upper Tribunal.

2(2)   References in these Regulations to income tax in respect of PAYE income (however expressed) are references to income tax in respect of that income if reasonable assumptions are, when necessary, made about other income.

History – In reg. 2(1), definition of "reckonable date" omitted by SI 2014/992, art. 9(2), with effect from 6 May 2014 in relation to payments which are due and payable in respect of the tax year 2014–15 and subsequent tax years.
In reg. 2(1), in the definition of "deductions working sheet", para. (b) omitted by SI 2014/472, reg. 3, with effect from 6 April 2014.
In reg. 2(1), in para. (b) of the definition of "deductions working sheet", the words "regulations 34 and 35 (simplified deduction scheme), and" omitted by SI 2013/521, reg. 6(a), with effect from 6 April 2014.
In reg. 2(1), in para. (a) of the definition of "tax period", the words "regulation 34 (simplified deduction scheme for personal employees) or" omitted by SI 2013/521, reg. 6(b), with effect from 6 April 2014.
In reg. 2(1), the definitions of "lower earnings limit", "seconded expatriate" inserted and the definition of "Student Loan Regulations" substituted by SI 2012/822, reg. 60, with effect from 6 April 2012.
In reg. 2(1), the definitions of "non-Real Time Information employer", "non-Real Time Information pension payer", "Real Time Information employer" and "Real Time Information pension payer" inserted by SI 2012/822, reg. 3, with effect from 6 April 2012.
In reg. 2(1), the definition of "additional rate" inserted by SI 2011/729, reg. 3(a), with effect from 6 April 2011.
In reg. 2(1), the definition of "large employer" substituted for the definition of "large employer" and "large or medium employer" by SI 2010/668, reg. 15(a), with effect in relation to the tax year 2011–12 and subsequent tax years.
In reg. 2(1), the definition of "notice" substituted by SI 2011/729, reg. 3(b), with effect from 6 April 2011.
In reg. 2(1), the definition of "specified date" substituted by SI 2010/668, reg. 15(b), with effect in relation to the tax year 2011–12 and subsequent tax years.
In reg. 2, definition of "tribunal" inserted by SI 2009/56, art. 3(2) and Sch. 2, para. 93, operative from 1 April 2009 subject to transitional and saving provisions in SI 2009/56, Sch. 3.
In reg. 2, definitions of "combined amount", "ITA" and "Student Loan Regulations" inserted by SI 2008/782, reg. 3, with effect from 6 April 2008.
In reg. 2, definition of "starting rate" omitted by SI 2008/782, reg. 3, with effect from 6 April 2008.
In reg. 2, definitions of "closed tax year", "HMRC", "qualifying payment", "the relevant time", "retrospective contributions regulations", "retrospective employment income", "retrospective tax provision", and "SSC Regulations" inserted by SI 2007/1077, reg. 3, with effect from 6 April 2007.

Origin – "additional pay", "approved method of electronic communications", "basic rate", "code", "electronic communications", "employee's code", "free pay", "higher rate", "ICTA", "net PAYE income", "official computer system", "overriding limit", "starting rate", "taxable payments", "tax month", "tax not deducted because of the overriding limit", "tax period", "tax quarter", "tax tables", "tax year", "TMA", "total additional pay to date", "total free pay to date", "total payments to date", "total tax to date", "total taxable payments to date", "trade dispute": SI 1993/744, reg. 2(1).
"agency", "agency worker", "excluded business expenses", "pension": see *Rewrite: Changes in Law* notes below.
"Board of Inland Revenue": ITEPA 2003, s. 720(2), SI 1993/744, reg. 2(1).
"cumulative basis", "employer reference", "employer's PAYE reference", "Inland Revenue office", "Inland Revenue office number", "ITEPA", "national insurance number", "non-cumulative basis", "objects", "PSA", "qualifying general earnings", "relevant payments", "relevant pension payments", "specified date", "tax week": drafting.
"deductions working sheet", "Inland Revenue", "other payee", "other payer", "payee", "payer", "pensioner", "pension payer", "reliefs from income tax": SI 1993/744, reg. 2(1) and see *Rewrite: Changes in Law* notes below.
"employment": ITEPA 2003, s. 4, 5 and see *Rewrite: Changes in Law* notes below.
"notice": SI 1993/744, reg. 2(1) and drafting.
"PAYE pension income": ITEPA 2003, s. 683(3) and SI 1993/744, reg. 2(1).
"PAYE threshold": SI 1993/744, reg. 2(2)(part), 28(2) and see *Rewrite: Changes in Law* notes below.
"reckonable date": SI 1993/744, reg. 51(3).
"total net tax deducted": SI 1993/744, reg. 2(1) and SI 1994/1212, reg. 13(3).

Reg. 2(2): ITEPA 2003, s. 684(7B).

Rewrite: Changes in Law – Commentary, App. 1, Change 1: reg. 2 refers to "the Inland Revenue" (meaning any officer of the Board) rather than "the Board" or "the inspector".

Commentary, App. 1, Change 6: reg. 9 (PAYE threshold) sets out rules for deciding whether a payment exceeds the PAYE threshold by looking at the total payments to an employee in the interval in which they are normally paid, and sets additional rules for employees with no normal interval.

Commentary, App. 1, Change 7: reg. 10–12 make clear which regulations apply (and which do not apply) and with what modifications to pension payers and pensioners, agencies and agency workers, and other payers and other payees.

Real Time Information Employers

2A(1)   The following are Real Time Information employers–

(a)   an employer who has entered into an agreement with HMRC to comply with the provisions of these Regulations which are expressed as relating to Real Time Information employers,

(b)   an employer within paragraph (2),

(c)   [omitted by SI 2013/521, reg. 14(a),] and

(d)   on and after 6th October 2013, all employers except employers within paragraph (3).

2A(2)   An employer is within this paragraph if the employer has been given a general or specific direction by the Commissioners for Her Majesty's Revenue and Customs before 6th October 2013 to deliver to HMRC returns under regulation 67B (real time returns of information about relevant payments).

2A(3)   An employer is within this paragraph if the employer–

(a)   has an existing special arrangement under regulation 141 (direct collection and special arrangements), and

(b)   has not been given a direction under paragraph (2) by the Commissioners for Her Majesty's Revenue and Customs.

History – Reg. 2A(1)(c) (but not the "and" after it) omitted by SI 2013/521, reg. 14(a)(i), with effect for the tax year 2013–14 and subsequent tax years. Former reg. 2A(1)(c) read as follows:

     "(c)   on and after 6th April 2013, employers to whom regulation 67D (exceptions to regulation 67B) applies, and".

In reg. 2A(1)(d), the words ", except employers within paragraph (3)" inserted by SI 2013/521, reg. 14(a)(ii), with effect for the tax year 2013–14 and subsequent tax years.

Reg. 2A inserted by SI 2012/822, reg. 4, with effect from 6 April 2012.

Reg. 2A(3) inserted by SI 2013/521, reg. 14(b), with effect for the tax year 2013–14 and subsequent tax years.

Cross references – SI 2012/822, reg. 53: transitional provisions.

Real Time Information Pension Payers

2B(1)   The following are Real Time Information pension payers–

(a)   a pension payer who has entered into an agreement with HMRC to comply with the provisions of these Regulations which are expressed as relating to Real Time Information pension payers or Real Time Information employers,

(b)   a pension payer within paragraph (2),

(c)   [omitted by SI 2012/521, reg. 15,]

(c)   on and after 6th October 2013, all pension payers.

2B(2)   A pension payer is within this paragraph if the pension payer has been given a general or specific direction by the Commissioners for Her Majesty's Revenue and Customs before 6th October 2013 to deliver to HMRC returns under regulation 67B (real time returns of information about relevant payments).

History – Reg. 2B(1)(c) (the first) omitted by SI 2013/521, reg. 15, with effect for the tax year 2013–14 and subsequent tax years. Former reg. 2B(1)(c) read as follows:

     "(c)   on and after 6th April 2013, pension payers to whom regulation 67D (exceptions to regulation 67B) applies, and".

Reg. 2B inserted by SI 2012/822, reg. 4, with effect from 6 April 2012.

Other material – HMRC Direction under reg. 2A(1)(b) and (2) of 19 and 20 August 2013.

Net PAYE income

3(1)   "Net PAYE income" means PAYE income less any–

(a)   allowable pension contributions, and

(b)   allowable donations to charity.

3(2)   In paragraph (1)–

     "allowable pension contributions" means any contribution under a registered pension scheme which is withheld from the payment of PAYE income which is allowed to be deducted from employment income by the sponsoring employer under section 193(2) of the Finance Act 2004 (relief under net pay arrangements);

"**registered pension scheme**" and "**sponsoring employer**" have the meanings given by section 150(2) and (6) respectively, of the Finance Act 2004.

"**allowable donations to charity**" means any donation which is withheld from the payment of PAYE income and for which a deduction must be allowed under section 713 of ITEPA (donations to charity: payroll deduction scheme).

History – In reg. 3(2) the definition of "allowable pension contributions" substituted and the definitions of "registered pension scheme" and "sponsoring employer" inserted by SI 2006/745, art. 27(2), with effect from 6 April 2006.

Origin – Reg. 3(1): SI 1993/744, reg. 2(1) ("emoluments") (part) and drafting.

Reg. 3(2): SI 1993/744, reg. 2(1) ("allowable superannuation contributions", "emoluments" and see *Rewrite: Changes in Law* note below.

Cross references – SI 2003/2682, reg. 2(1): "PAYE income" defined by ITEPA 2003, s. 683.

Rewrite: Changes in Law – Commentary, App. 1, Change 2: "Net pay arrangement" applies only to contributions to pension schemes made through payroll and not to FSAVCS contributions made direct by employees. Reg. 3(2) extends (to FSAVCS contributions) and restricts (to avoid giving double relief) what can be taken into account in PAYE.

Relevant payments

4(1) In these Regulations, any reference (however expressed) to relevant payments means payments of, or on account of, net PAYE income, except payments of, or on account of,–

(a) PAYE social security income, except in so far as it is provided for in Part 8,

(b) United Kingdom social security pensions,

(c) excluded relocation expenses,

(d) excluded business expenses,

(e) excluded pecuniary liabilities, and

(f) excluded notional payments.

4(2) In paragraph (1)–

"**excluded business expenses**" has the meaning given in regulation 5;

"**excluded notional payments**" means notional payments which an employer is treated as making by section 694 or 695 of ITEPA (non-cash vouchers and credit tokens) as a result of an employee using a non-cash voucher or credit token on behalf of the employer, except where the voucher or token is used as, or as part of, any scheme or arrangement the purpose, or one of the main purposes, of which is–

   (a) to provide the employee with money or an asset, or

   (b) to avoid the making of a relevant payment;

"**excluded pecuniary liabilities**" means payments made to a person other than an employee to meet the employee's liability to that other person, but which are not made–

   (a) in fulfilment (in whole or in part) of the employee's right to a sum of money, nor

   (b) as, or as part of, any scheme or arrangement the purpose, or one of the main purposes, of which is to avoid the making of a relevant payment;

"**excluded relocation expenses**" means payments in respect of removal expenses, as defined by section 272 of ITEPA (removal benefits and expenses to which section 271 applies), if, and to the extent that, they are payments of net PAYE income;

"**PAYE social security income**" has the meaning given in section 683(5) of ITEPA;

"**United Kingdom social security pensions**" means income which is taxable income in accordance with section 578 of ITEPA (UK social security pensions).

Origin – Reg. 4: SI 1993/744, reg. 2(3)(part) and see *Rewrite: Changes in Law* note below.

Rewrite: Changes in Law – Commentary, para. 88–95 and App. 1, Change 3: "relevant payments" exclude most social security pensions and benefits and certain business expenses, pecuniary liabilities and notional payments.

Excluded business expenses

5(1) "**Excluded business expenses**" means expenses within Chapter 3 of Part 3 of ITEPA (earnings and benefits treated as earnings) which the Inland Revenue have authorised the employer to exclude from relevant payments in accordance with this regulation.

5(2) The Inland Revenue may authorise an employer to exclude any payment of expenses from relevant payments if the Inland Revenue are of the opinion that a deduction or relief will, or is likely to, result in no tax being payable as a result of the payment.

5(3) The Inland Revenue may authorise the exclusion of–

(a) specific expenses or a class of expenses,

(b) expenses paid by a specific employer or a class of employers, and

(c) expenses paid to a specific employee or a class of employees.

Statutory Instruments

5(4) The Inland Revenue must notify an employer of any excluded business expenses and the date from which the exclusion is to apply.

5(5) The Inland Revenue may revoke the authorisation to exclude business expenses by giving notice to the employer specifying the date of the notice or a subsequent date as the date from which the revocation has effect.

Origin – Reg. 5: see *Rewrite: Changes in Law* note below.

Rewrite: Changes in Law – Commentary, para. 88–95, 98 and App. 1, Change 3: "relevant payments" exclude certain business expenses.

Relevant pension payments

6 In these Regulations, any reference (however expressed) to relevant pension payments means relevant payments in respect of PAYE pension income.

Origin – Reg. 6: SI 1993/744, reg. 2(1) ("pension emoluments").

Cross references – ITEPA 2003, s. 683(3): "PAYE pension income" defined.

Meaning of "code" etc

7(1) In these Regulations,

"**code**" means–

(a) a combination of letters, numbers or both for use in accordance with the tax tables to establish free pay, additional pay, total free pay to date or total additional pay to date;

(b) any of the special codes (whether expressed in words or represented by a combination of letters, numbers or both) for use in accordance with the tax tables or otherwise.

7(2) "**K code**" means a code which gives rise to additional pay or total additional pay to date.

7(3) The special codes are–

(a) the basic rate code, which effects deductions of tax wholly at the basic rate;

(b) the higher rate code, which effects deductions of tax wholly at the higher rate;

(ba) the additional rate code, which effects deductions of tax wholly at the additional rate;

(c) the nil tax code, which requires no deductions of tax;

(ca) the 0T code, which without allowing for personal allowances, effects deductions of tax at the basic rate, higher rate and additional rate so that during the tax year the amounts subject to deductions at the rate or rates concerned are in accordance with section 10 of ITA (income charged at the basic, higher and additional rates: individuals);

(d) the emergency code, which, after allowing for the personal allowance, effects deductions of tax at

  (i) the basic rate, or

  (ii) the basic and higher rates, or

  (iii) the basic, higher and additional rates

so that during the tax year the amounts subject to deductions at the rate or rates concerned are in accordance with section 10 of ITA (income charged at the basic, higher and additional rates: individuals);

(e) the emergency IB codes which, after allowing for the personal allowance and the blind person's allowance, effect deductions at the basic rate, so that during the tax year the amounts subject to deductions at that rate are in accordance with section 10 of ITA.

7(4) In paragraph (3)–

"**blind person's allowance**" means an allowance claimed under either section 265 of ICTA (blind person's allowance) or section 38 of ITA (blind person's allowance);

"**personal allowance**" means an allowance claimed under either section 257(1) of ICTA (personal allowance) or section 35 of ITA (personal allowances for those aged under 65).

History – Reg. 7(3)(ba) inserted by SI 2011/729, reg. 4(a), with effect from 6 April 2011.
Reg. 7(3)(ca) inserted by SI 2011/729, reg. 4(b), with effect from 6 April 2011.
Reg. 7(3)(d)(i), (ii) and (iii) and the closing words of reg. 7(3)(d) substituted for the words "either or both of the basic rate and the higher rate, so that during the tax year the amounts subject to deductions at the rate or rates concerned are in accordance with section 10 of ITA (income charged at basic and higher rates: individuals);" by SI 2011/729, reg. 4(c), with effect from 6 April 2011.
Reg. 7(3)(d) and (e) substituted by SI 2008/782, reg. 4, with effect from 6 April 2008.
Reg. 7(4) inserted by SI 2008/782, reg. 4, with effect from 6 April 2008.

Origin – Reg. 7(1): SI 1993/744, reg. 2(1) ("code")(part), drafting.
Reg. 7(2): SI 1993/744, reg. 2(1) ("code")(part), drafting.
Reg. 7(3): drafting.
"basic rate code": see *Rewrite: Changes in Law* note below.
"higher rate code": SI 1993/744, reg. 9(1)(part), (3)(part) and see *Rewrite: Changes in Law* note below.

"nil tax code": SI 1993/744, reg. 9(1)(part), (3)(part) and see *Rewrite: Changes in Law* note below.
"emergency code": SI 1993/744, reg. 29(2)(part), (3)(part), 30(2)(part), (3)(part), 32(part), 84(7)(part).
"emergency IB codes": SI 1993/744, reg. 98C(1)(part), (3), (4).

Rewrite: Changes in Law – Commentary, App. 1, Change 4: reg. 7 expressly defines "basic rate code", "higher rate code" and "nil tax code".

Employee's code

8(1) An employee's code is the code–

(a)　issued to an employer for use in respect of the employee for a tax year,

(b)　applied by these Regulations for use by an employer in respect of the employee, or

(c)　issued to an employee in accordance with regulation 142 (direct collection).

8(2) A code is issued to an employer if it is contained in a document that is sent–

(a)　to the employer, or

(b)　to a person acting on behalf of the employer,

by the Inland Revenue, and any code so issued is received by the employer for the purposes of these Regulations.

Origin – Reg. 8(1): SI 1993/744, reg. 2(1)("code authorisation"), 13(6)(part), 104(1)(part) and see *Rewrite: Changes in Law* notes below.
Reg. 8(2): SI 1993/744, reg. 6(4)(part) and see *Rewrite: Changes in Law* notes below.

Cross references – SI 2003/2682, reg. 7: meaning of "code".

Rewrite: Changes in Law – Commentary, App. 1, Change 1: reg. 8 refers to "Inland Revenue" (meaning any officer of the Board) rather than "inspector".
Commentary, App. 1, Change 4: "code" includes certain special codes.
Commentary, App. 1, Change 5: reg. 8(2)(b): notices of codes may be sent to an employer's agent.

Notes – In reg. 8(1)(b), "applied by these Regulations" covers codes determined by General Commissioners under SI 2003/2682, reg. 18.

PAYE threshold

9(1) The rules set out in Table 1 apply in order to determine whether a relevant payment made by an employer to an employee is a relevant payment which exceeds the PAYE threshold.

9(2) Rules 1 to 5 apply if the employer normally pays the employee at regular intervals.

9(3) If the employer does not normally pay the employee at regular intervals–

(a)　rule 6 applies to determine whether a relevant payment made less than a week since the previous relevant payment exceeds the PAYE threshold, and

(b)　rule 7 applies to determine whether any other relevant payment exceeds the PAYE threshold.

Table 1
Determination of PAYE threshold

Employee's payment interval	Rule to determine whether relevant payment exceeds PAYE threshold
1. Weekly	1. If the sum of the relevant payment and any other relevant payments made earlier in the same tax week is more than the weekly PAYE threshold.
2. Monthly	2. If the sum of the relevant payment and any other relevant payments made earlier in the same tax month is more than the monthly PAYE threshold.
3. Regular intervals which are multiples of a week	3. If the sum of the relevant payment and any other relevant payments made earlier in the same interval is more than the corresponding multiple of the weekly PAYE threshold.
4. Regular intervals, longer than a week, which are fractions or multiples of a month	4. If the sum of the relevant payment and any other relevant payments made earlier in the same interval is more than the corresponding fraction or multiple of the monthly PAYE threshold.
5. Regular intervals, longer than a week, which are not within rules 1 to 4	5. If the sum of the relevant payment and any other relevant payments made earlier in the same interval is more than the corresponding proportion of the weekly PAYE threshold.

Employee's payment interval	*Rule to determine whether relevant payment exceeds PAYE threshold*
6. Intervals shorter than a week, whether regular or irregular	6. If the sum of the relevant payment and any other relevant payments made earlier in the same tax week is more than the weekly PAYE threshold.
7. Irregular intervals longer than a week	7. If the relevant payment is more than the corresponding proportion of the weekly PAYE threshold since– (a) any previous relevant payment in the tax year, or (b) if none, the start of the employment or the start of the tax year (whichever is later).

9(4)   Regulations 24 and 30 (employee not paid weekly or monthly)–

(a)   apply for the purpose of establishing an employee's normal payment interval, but

(b)   must otherwise be ignored for the purpose of determining whether a relevant payment exceeds the PAYE threshold.

9(5)   If an employee has more than one normal payment interval in respect of payments made by the same employer, the rules must be applied on the basis of the shorter or shortest of those intervals.

9(6)   If an employee's normal payment interval is longer than a year, the rules must be applied as if the normal payment interval were a year.

9(7)   **"Weekly PAYE threshold"** means 1/52 of the personal allowance specified in section 257(1) of ICTA, rounded to the nearest pound.

9(8)   **"Monthly PAYE threshold"** means 1/12 of the personal allowance specified in section 257(1) of ICTA, rounded to the nearest pound.

9(9)   The **"corresponding proportion of the weekly PAYE threshold"** is established by dividing the number of days in the payment interval by 7, and multiplying the result by the weekly PAYE threshold.

Origin – Reg. 9(1): SI 1993/744, reg. 28(1) and see *Rewrite: Changes in Law* note below.
Reg. 9(2): see *Rewrite: Changes in Law* note below.
Reg. 9(3): SI 1993/744, reg. 28(1) and see *Rewrite: Changes in Law* note below.
Table 1: SI 1993/744, reg. 18(part) and see *Rewrite: Changes in Law* note below.
Reg. 9(4): SI 1993/744, reg. 18(part), 28(1)(part) and see *Rewrite: Changes in Law* note below.
Reg. 9(5), (6): SI 1993/744, reg. 28(1)(part) and see *Rewrite: Changes in Law* note below.
Reg. 9(7), (8): SI 1993/744, reg. 28(2)(part).
Reg. 9(9): SI 1993/744, reg. 28(1)(part) and see *Rewrite: Changes in Law* note below.

Rewrite: Changes in Law – Commentary, App. 1, Change 6: reg. 9 sets out rules for deciding whether a payment exceeds the PAYE threshold by looking at the total payments to an employee in the interval in which they are normally paid, and sets additional rules for employees with no normal interval.

APPLICATION TO PAYERS AND PAYEES

Rewrite: Technical Points – Commentary, para. 129: examples of payers who could be within PAYE besides employers paying their employees include:

(a)   pension payers paying their pensioners,
(b)   agencies paying their agency workers,
(c)   employers making payments to someone else's employee,
(d)   clients making payments of earnings directly to agency workers,
(e)   receivers making payments of earnings to former employees,
(f)   relevant persons within ITEPA 2003, s. 689 treated as making payments to employees of non-UK employers,
(g)   someone who is neither employer, pension payer nor agency making payments (which may be payments of employment income or pension income) on behalf of another person (who may or may not be an employer, agency or pension payer).

Application to agencies and agency workers

10(1)   For the purposes of these Regulations–

(a)   agencies are treated as employers; and

(b)   agency workers are treated as employees.

10(2)   For the purposes of the regulations listed in paragraph (3), an agency ceases to employ an agency worker at the earlier of–

(a)   the end of the relationship between the agency and agency worker, or

(b)   the end of a period of 3 months during which the agency makes no relevant payments to the agency worker,

and not each time the agency worker stops providing services to a client of the agency.

10(3)   The regulations are—

regulation 36	cessation of employment: Form P45
regulation 37	PAYE income paid after employment ceased
regulation 46(6)	employer to ignore code relating to employment which has ceased
regulation 51(5) to (7)	effects of employment ceasing on Form P45 procedure
regulation 94(3) to (7)	information to former employees of other earnings.

10(4)   The following regulations do not apply to agencies or agency workers in their capacity as such—

regulation 91	termination awards: information to be provided
regulation 92	termination awards: return if award changes
regulation 93	termination awards: return if more than one employer
regulation 96	termination awards: information to employees
Part 6	PAYE settlement agreements
regulation 167	jobseeker's allowance paid by employer
regulation 168	regulation 167 cases: application of other regulations.

History – In reg. 10(4), in the list, references to reg. 34 and 35 omitted by SI 2013/521, reg. 7, with effect from 6 April 2014.
Origin – Reg. 10(1): SI 1993/744, reg. 2(1)("employee")(part), ("employer")(part) and see *Rewrite: Changes in Law* notes below.
Reg. 10(2), (3): see *Rewrite: Changes in Law* notes below.
Reg. 10(4): SI 1993/744, reg. 2(1)("employee")(part), ("employer")(part) and see *Rewrite: Changes in Law* notes below.
Cross references – Reg. 2(1): meaning of "agency" and "agency worker".
Rewrite: Changes in Law – Commentary, App. 1, Change 7: reg. 10 specifies which PAYE regulations apply to agencies and agency workers and which do not.
Commentary, App. 1, Change 8: reg. 10 provides for an agency to issue a P45 to an agency worker only when the worker stops doing work for the agency or when the agency has not paid them for 3 months (and not after every job the worker undertakes for a different client).

Application to pension payers and pensioners

11(1)   For the purposes of these Regulations—

(a)   pension payers are treated as employers;

(b)   pensioners are treated as employees; and

(c)   a pensioner's "employment" with a pension payer starts when the pension starts and ends when the pension ends.

11(2)   The following regulations do not apply to pension payers or pensioners in their capacity as such—

regulation 25	cumulative basis: subsidiary PAYE income of employee paid weekly or at greater intervals
regulation 38	death of employee (other than pensioner)
Chapter 2 of Part 3	new employees (other than pensioners): Forms P45 and P46
regulation 63	repayment during unpaid leave
regulation 64	trade disputes
regulation 65	repayment if no longer employed
regulation 71	modification of regulations 67G and 68 in case of trade dispute
regulation 75	additional return in case of trade dispute
regulations 85 to 89	employers: annual return of other earnings
regulation 90	quarterly return if car becomes available or unavailable
regulation 91	termination awards: information to be provided
regulation 92	termination awards: return if award changes
regulation 93	termination awards: return if more than one employer
regulation 94	employers: information to employees of other earnings
regulation 95	third parties: information to employees of other earnings
regulation 96	termination awards: information to employees
regulation 100	tips: special arrangements
regulation 102(1)	succession to a business etc: employees (other than pensioners)
regulation 104	succession to a business: trade disputes
Part 6	PAYE settlement agreements
Chapter 3 of Part 7	holiday pay funds
regulation 151	obtaining the claimant's Form P45

regulation 167	jobseeker's allowance paid by employer
regulation 168	regulation 167 cases: application of other regulations.

History – In reg. 11(2), in the list, references to reg. 34 and 35 omitted by SI 2013/521, reg. 7, with effect from 6 April 2014. In reg. 11(2), in the list, in the entry relating to reg. 71, the words "regulations 67G and 68" substituted for the words "regulation 68" by SI 2012/822, reg. 5, with effect from 6 April 2012.

Origin – SI 1993/744, reg. 2(1)("employee")(part), ("employer")(part) and see *Rewrite: Changes in Law* note below.

Cross references – SI 2003/2682, reg. 2(1): meaning of "pension payer" and "pensioner".

Rewrite: Changes in Law – Commentary, App. 1, Change 7: reg. 11 specifies which PAYE regulations apply to pension payers and pensioners and which do not.

Application to other payers and payees

12(1) For the purposes of these Regulations–

(a) other payers are treated as employers;

(b) other payees are treated as employees; and

(c) an other payee's "employment" with an other payer starts when relevant payments start and ends when relevant payments end.

12(2) The following regulations do not apply to other payers or other payees in their capacity as such–

regulation 85 to 88	employers: annual return of other earnings
regulation 90	quarterly return if car becomes available or unavailable
regulation 91	termination awards: information to be provided
regulation 92	termination awards: return if award changes
regulation 93	termination awards: return if more than one employer
regulation 94	employers: information to employees of other earnings
regulation 95	third parties: information to employees of other earnings
regulation 96	termination awards: information to employees
Part 6	PAYE settlement agreements
regulation 134	interpretation of Chapter 3 (holiday pay funds)
regulation 167	jobseeker's allowance paid by employer
regulation 168	regulation 167 cases: application of other regulations.

12(3) Paragraph (2) is subject to regulation 91(9) (termination awards: former employers and employees).

12(4) The following regulation does not apply to other payees in their capacity as such–

regulation 64	trade disputes.

History – In reg. 12(2), in the list, references to reg. 34 and 35 omitted by SI 2013/521, reg. 7, with effect from 6 April 2014.

Origin – Reg. 12(1), (2): SI 1993/744, reg. 2(1)("employee")(part), ("employer")(part) and see *Rewrite: Changes in Law* note below.

Reg. 12(3): drafting and see *Rewrite: Changes in Law* note below.

Reg. 12(4): SI 1993/744, reg. 2(1)("employee")(part) and see *Rewrite: Changes in Law* note below.

Cross references – SI 2003/2682, reg. 2(1): meaning of "other payer" and "other payee".

Rewrite: Changes in Law – Commentary, App. 1, Change 7: reg. 12 specifies which PAYE regulations apply to other payers and payees and which do not.

Other material – ICAEW Technical Release TR 799 (not reproduced): an administrator acting under the Insolvency Act 1986 is liable to account for PAYE/NIC deductions as an employer paying emoluments to the company's employees.

PART 2 – CODES

DETERMINATION OF CODE

Determination of code by Inland Revenue

13 The Inland Revenue must determine the code for use by an employer in respect of an employee for a tax year.

Origin – SI 1993/744, reg. 7(1) and see *Rewrite: Changes in Law* note below.

Rewrite: Changes in Law – Commentary, App. 1, Change 1: reg. 13 refers to "Inland Revenue" (meaning any officer of the Board) rather than "inspector".

Matters relevant to determination of code

14(1) If the Inland Revenue determine a code under this regulation, they must have regard to the following matters so far as known to them–

(a)   the reliefs from income tax to which the employee is entitled for the tax year in which the code is determined, so far as the employee's title to those reliefs has been established at the time of the determination;

(b)   any PAYE income of the employee (other than the relevant payments in relation to which the code is being determined);

(c)   any tax overpaid for any previous tax year which has not been repaid;

(d)   any tax remaining unpaid for any previous tax year which is not otherwise recovered;

(e)   any tax repaid to the employee in excess of the amount properly due to the employee which may be recovered as if it were unpaid tax under section 30(1) of TMA (recovery of overpayment of tax etc) and which is not otherwise recovered;

(f)   unless the employee objects, any other income of the employee which is not PAYE income; and

(g)   such other adjustments as may be necessary to secure that, so far as possible, the tax in respect of the employee's income in relation to which the code is determined will be deducted from the relevant payments made during that tax year.

14(2)   If the Inland Revenue determine the code before the beginning of the tax year for which it is determined, the Inland Revenue–

(a)   must have regard to any expected change in the amount of any relief referred to in paragraph (1)(a), but

(b)   may disregard any such relief if they are not satisfied that the employee will be entitled to it for the tax year for which the code is determined.

14(3)   Paragraphs (1)(c) and (d) are subject to regulations 186 and 187 (recovery and repayment: adjustment of employee's code).

Origin – Reg. 14(1): SI 1993/744, reg. 7(1)(part), (2)(part) and see *Rewrite: Changes in Law* notes below.
Reg. 14(2): SI 1993/744, reg. 7(2)(part), (3) and see *Rewrite: Changes in Law* notes below.
Reg. 14(3): see *Rewrite: Changes in Law* notes below.

Rewrite: Changes in Law – Commentary, App. 1, Change 1: reg. 14 refers to "Inland Revenue" (meaning any officer of the Board) rather than "inspector".
Commentary, App. 1, Change 9: in reg. 14(1), "must have regard" removes the scope for anyone to argue that, although some matter which is to be taken into account in setting a code is known, it should be ignored.
Commentary, App. 1, Change 10: reg. 14(1)(f) Revenue may take account of non-PAYE income in setting code unless taxpayer objects.
Commentary, App. 1, Change 120: reg. 186 and 187 provide for PAYE codes to be adjusted for underpayments and overpayments of tax in a self-assessment unless taxpayer objects.

Determination of code in respect of recovery of relevant debts

14A(1)   HMRC may determine a code so as to effect recovery of all or part of a relevant debt within the meaning of section 684 of ITEPA (sums owed to HMRC).

14A(2)   A determination in reliance on paragraph (1) does not prevent recovery by other means (whether or not under a provision of TMA) of all or any part of a relevant debt that is not recovered by deduction in accordance with the code (whether or not it was at any stage expected to be recovered by deduction).

14A(3)   Sums deducted or to be deducted as a result of a determination made in reliance on paragraph (1) are to be treated, for the purposes of employers' obligations and enforcement, in the same way as amounts of tax which the employer is liable to pay under provisions of these Regulations (so, for example, regulation 84 applies for the purposes of recovery).

14A(4)   Sums deducted as a result of a determination made in reliance on paragraph (1) are to be treated for the purposes of interest on the relevant debt as having been paid on the first day of the tax year in respect of which the determination is made.

History – Reg. 14A inserted by SI 2011/1584, reg. 2(2), with effect from 6 April 2012.

Determination of code in respect of high income child benefit charge

14B   HMRC may determine a code, if and to the extent that the payee does not object, to secure that–

(a)   income tax payable for a tax year by the payee by virtue of section 681B of ITEPA (high income child benefit charge) is deducted from PAYE income of the payee paid during that year, and

(b)   repayments are made in a tax year in respect of any amounts overpaid on account of income tax under that section for that tax year.

History – Reg. 14B inserted by SI 2013/521, reg. 3, with effect for the tax year 2013–14 and subsequent tax years.

Flat rate codes

15(A1) HMRC may determine that the code for use by an employer in respect of an employee for a tax year is the additional rate code, if they have reason to believe that the employee will be chargeable at the additional rate on all or a substantial part of the employee's relevant payments.

15(1) The Inland Revenue may determine that the code for use by an employer in respect of an employee for a tax year is the higher rate code, if they have reason to believe that the employee will be chargeable at the higher rate on all or a substantial part of the employee's relevant payments.

15(2) The Inland Revenue may determine that the code for use by an employer in respect of an employee for a tax year is the basic rate code, if they have reason to believe that the employee will be chargeable at the basic rate on all or a substantial part of the employee's relevant payments.

15(3) The Inland Revenue may determine that the code for use by an employer in respect of an employee for a tax year is the nil tax code, if–

(a) the employee's PAYE income will be taken into account as taxable income other than PAYE income in any assessment,

(b) the Inland Revenue are not satisfied that the employee's income will be chargeable, or

(c) the Inland Revenue have reason to believe that the employee will be entitled to a deduction under Chapter 6 of Part 5 of ITEPA (deductions from seafarers' earnings) in respect of the employee's PAYE income or so much of it as remains after any deductions under sections 188 to 195 of the Finance Act 2004 (members' contributions).

15(4) References in this regulation to an employee's relevant payments, PAYE income and income are references to the payments or income in respect of which the employee's code is being determined for the purposes of the employment in question.

History – Reg. 15(A1) inserted by SI 2011/729, reg. 5, with effect from 6 April 2011.
In reg. 15(3)(c) the words "sections 188 to 195 of the Finance Act 2004 (members' contributions)" substituted for the words "section 592(7) or 594(1) of ICTA (exempt approved schemes and exempt statutory schemes)" by SI 2006/745, art. 27(3), with effect from 6 April 2006.
Origin – Reg. 15(1): SI 1993/744, reg. 9(1) and see *Rewrite: Changes in Law* notes below.
Reg. 15(2): see *Rewrite: Changes in Law* notes below.
Reg. 15(3): SI 1993/744, reg. 9(2) and see *Rewrite: Changes in Law* notes below.
Reg. 15(4): drafting.
Cross references – SI 2003/2682, reg. 7: meaning of "code".
Rewrite: Changes in Law – Commentary, App. 1, Change 1: reg. 15 refers to "Inland Revenue" (meaning any officer of the Board) rather than "inspector".
Commentary, App. 1, Change 4: "code" includes certain special codes.
Commentary, para. 151–154 and App. 1, Change 11: reg. 15(1) higher rate code may only be determined if Revenue have reason to believe that a substantial part of income in question will be liable to higher rate tax.
Commentary, App. 1, Change 12: reg. 15(2) specifies the circumstances in which the basic rate code may be set.
Commentary, App. 1, Change 13: reg. 15(3): nil tax code may be used to cover not only Sch. D income but all income that may be assessed in another way.

Continued application of employee's code

16(1) If the Inland Revenue determine that the code for use by an employer in respect of an employee for a tax year remains the same as at the previous 5th April, the Inland Revenue need not issue a code to the employer.

16(2) If for any tax year the employer does not receive a code for an employee who was in that employer's employment on the previous 5th April, the code which applied on that date is treated as having been issued by the Inland Revenue for the tax year in question.

Origin – Reg. 16(1): SI 1993/744, reg. 8(1) and see *Rewrite: Changes in Law* note below.
Reg. 16(2): SI 1993/744, reg. 8(2) and see *Rewrite: Changes in Law* note below.
Rewrite: Changes in Law – Commentary, App. 1, Change 1: reg. 16 refers to "Inland Revenue" (meaning any officer of the Board) rather than "inspector".

Notice to employee of code

17(1) The Inland Revenue must give notice to an employee of the code which they have determined for use in respect of that employee for any tax year.

17(2) But notice need not be given if–

(a) the code for use in respect of the employee remains the same as at the previous 5th April; or

(b) the change in the code is solely because of an alteration or proposed alteration in the rates of any of the personal reliefs allowable under sections 257 and 257A of ICTA (personal allowance and married couple's allowance) or in the tax tables.

Origin – Reg. 17(1): SI 1993/744, reg. 10(1) and see *Rewrite: Changes in Law* note below.
Reg. 17(2): SI 1993/744, reg. 10(1), (2).
Rewrite: Changes in Law – Commentary, App. 1, Change 1: reg. 17 refers to "Inland Revenue" (meaning any officer of the Board) rather than "inspector".

APPEALS AND AMENDMENT

Objections and appeals against employee's code

18(1) An employee who objects to the determination of a code must state the grounds of objection.

18(2) On receiving the notice of objection the Inland Revenue may amend the determination of the code by agreement with the employee.

18(3) If the Inland Revenue and employee do not reach agreement, the employee may appeal against the determination of the code by giving notice to the Inland Revenue.

18(4) On an appeal that is notified to the tribunal, the tribunal must determine the code in accordance with these Regulations.

18(5) [Omitted by SI 2009/56, art. 3(2) and Sch. 2, para. 94(4).]

History – In reg. 18(3), the words "to the General Commissioners", which appeared after "appeal", omitted by SI 2009/56, art. 3(2) and Sch. 2, para. 94(2), operative from 1 April 2009 subject to transitional and saving provisions in SI 2009/56, Sch. 3. In reg. 18(4), the words "On an appeal that is notified to the tribunal, the tribunal" substituted for the words "On appeal, the General Commissioners" by SI 2009/56, art. 3(2) and Sch. 2, para. 94(3), operative from 1 April 2009 subject to transitional and saving provisions in SI 2009/56, Sch. 3.
Reg. 18(5) omitted by SI 2009/56, art. 3(2) and Sch. 2, para. 94(4), operative from 1 April 2009 subject to transitional and saving provisions in SI 2009/56, Sch. 3. Former reg. 18(5) read as follows:

> "**18(5)** For the purposes of paragraph 3(1)(a) of Schedule 3 to TMA (rules for assigning proceedings to General Commissioners), the relevant place for an appeal under this regulation is–
> (a)   the place where the employment is situated, or
> (b)   if there is no such place, the place where the employee lives.".

Origin – Reg. 18(1): SI 1993/744, reg. 11(1) and see *Rewrite: Changes in Law* notes below.
Reg. 18(2), (3): SI 1993/744, reg. 11(2)(part) and see *Rewrite: Changes in Law* notes below.
Reg. 18(4): SI 1993/744, reg. 11(5) and see *Rewrite: Changes in Law* notes below.
Reg. 18(5): SI 1993/744, reg. 11(3) and see *Rewrite: Changes in Law* notes below.

Rewrite: Changes in Law – Commentary, App. 1, Change 1: reg. 18 refers to "Inland Revenue" (meaning any officer of the Board) rather than "inspector".
Commentary, App. 1, Change 14: reg. 18 applies if employee "objects", whether or not employee is "aggrieved".
Commentary, App. 1, Change 15: employees may object to and appeal against determinations by General Commissioners, as well as determinations by Inland Revenue.
Commentary, App. 1, Change 16: reg. 18(4) enables General Commissioners to determine a flat rate code.
Commentary, App. 1, Change 17: reg. 18(5): if taxpayer has no place of employment, appeal to be heard by Commissioners for place where employee lives.

Amendment of code

19(1) Paragraph (2) applies if the code for use by an employer in respect of an employee is found to be inappropriate because the actual circumstances are different from the circumstances by reference to which it was determined, whether by the Inland Revenue or the tribunal.

19(2) The Inland Revenue may, and if required by the employee must, amend the code by reference to the actual circumstances.

19(3) The Inland Revenue must give notice of the amended code to the employee by the date on which the notice under regulation 20(1) is issued to the employer.

19(4) But notice need not be given where the change in the code is solely because of an alteration or proposed alteration in the rates of any of the personal reliefs allowable under sections 257 and 257A of ICTA (personal allowance and married couple's allowance) or in the tax tables.

19(5) Regulation 18 (objections and appeals) applies in relation to the amended code as it applies in relation to the original code.

19(6) Regulation 18 also applies if the Inland Revenue do not agree that the circumstances have changed and so refuse to amend the code in accordance with paragraph (2).

History – In reg. 19(1), "tribunal" substituted for "General Commissioners" by SI 2009/56, art. 3(2) and Sch. 2, para. 95, operative from 1 April 2009 subject to transitional and saving provisions in SI 2009/56, Sch. 3.

Origin – Reg. 19(1), (2): SI 1993/744, reg. 12(1)(part) and see *Rewrite: Changes in Law* notes below.
Reg. 19(3): SI 1993/744, reg. 12(2) and see *Rewrite: Changes in Law* notes below.
Reg. 19(4): SI 1993/744, reg. 12(3).
Reg. 19(5): SI 1993/744, reg. 12(4).
Reg. 19(6): see *Rewrite: Changes in Law* notes below.

Rewrite: Changes in Law – Commentary, App. 1, Change 1: reg. 19 refers to "Inland Revenue" (meaning any officer of the Board) rather than "inspector".
Commentary, App. 1, Change 18: employee's right of appeal against Revenue's refusal to amend code when they do not agree circumstances have changed.

Notice to employer of amended code

20(1) If the code for use by an employer in respect of an employee is amended after notice of it has been issued to the employer, the Inland Revenue must issue the amended code to the employer.

Statutory Instruments

20(2) An amended code is issued to an employer if it is contained in a document that is sent to the employer or a person acting on behalf of the employer by the Inland Revenue, and any code so issued is received by the employer for the purposes of these Regulations.

20(3) On making any subsequent relevant payment to the employee, the employer must deduct or repay tax by reference to the amended code.

20(4) Paragraphs (5) and (6) apply if there is a change or proposed change in the rates of any of the personal reliefs allowable under sections 257 and 257A of ICTA (personal allowance and married couple's allowance).

20(5) If the change or proposed change relates to the current tax year, the Inland Revenue may give notice requiring the employer, with effect from the date specified in the notice, to amend specified codes as directed.

20(6) If the change relates to the following tax year, the Inland Revenue may give notice requiring the employer to carry forward to the following tax year specified codes of the current tax year and adjust them as directed in the notice.

20(7) A code which has–

(a) been amended by virtue of paragraph (5) in respect of the current tax year, or

(b) been carried forward to the following tax year and adjusted by virtue of paragraph (6),

is treated as having been determined and issued by the Inland Revenue as the employee's code for that tax year.

20(8) A notice under paragraphs (5) and (6) may be issued to the employer or to a person acting on behalf of the employer.

Origin – Reg. 20(1): SI 1993/744, reg. 13(1)(part) and see *Rewrite: Changes in Law* note below.
Reg. 20(2): SI 1993/744, reg. 6(4)(part), 13(1)(part), (6)(part).
Reg. 20(3): SI 1993/744, reg. 13(2).
Reg. 20(4): SI 1993/744, reg. 13(4)(part).
Reg. 20(5), (6): SI 1993/744, reg. 13(4)(part) and see *Rewrite: Changes in Law* note below.
Reg. 20(7): SI 1993/744, reg. 8(5), 13(5) and see *Rewrite: Changes in Law* note below.
Reg. 20(8): SI 1993/744, reg. 13(6)(part).

Rewrite: Changes in Law – Commentary, App. 1, Change 1: reg. 20 refers to "Inland Revenue" (meaning any officer of the Board) rather than "inspector".

PART 3 – DEDUCTION AND REPAYMENT OF TAX
Chapter 1 – Deduction and Repayment

DEDUCTION AND REPAYMENT BY REFERENCE TO EMPLOYEE'S CODE

Deduction and repayment of tax by reference to employee's code

21(1) On making a relevant payment to an employee during a tax year, an employer must deduct or repay tax in accordance with these Regulations by reference to the employee's code, if the employer has one for the employee.

21(2) The employer must deduct or repay tax by reference to the employee's code, even if the code is the subject of an objection or appeal.

Origin – Reg. 21(1): SI 1993/744, reg. 6(1), (2).
Reg. 21(2): SI 1993/744, reg. 6(3).

THE CUMULATIVE BASIS

The cumulative basis

22 An employer must deduct or repay tax on the cumulative basis, unless these Regulations provide otherwise.

Origin – SI 1993/744, reg. 14(1)(part) and drafting.

Cumulative basis: deduction and repayment

23(1) This regulation provides for deductions and repayments on the basis of total payments to date (the cumulative basis).

23(2) In this regulation–

(a) TT is the total tax to date relating to an employee;

(b)   UT is any tax not deducted because of the overriding limit when the last relevant payment was made to the employee, and is nil if the payment in question is the first relevant payment to the employee in any tax year;

(c)   PT is the previous total tax to date relating to the employee, and is nil if the payment in question is the first relevant payment to the employee in any tax year.

23(3) The employer must, before making any relevant payment to the employee, calculate TT.

23(4) If TT + UT exceeds PT, the employer must deduct the excess from the relevant payment on making the payment.

23(5) But if the employee's code is a K code, the deduction is not to exceed the overriding limit, subject to 62(6) (notional payments).

23(6) If TT + UT is less than PT, the employer must repay the difference to the employee on making the payment, subject to regulations 25(4) (extra payment made before main payment) and 64 (trade disputes).

23(7) If TT + UT equals PT, the employer must neither deduct nor repay tax when making the payment.

23(8) **"Previous total tax to date"** means the total tax to date corresponding to the employee's total payments to date and the employee's code—

(a)   at the date of the last preceding relevant payment, or

(b)   if later, at the date on which the employer complied with this regulation as if a relevant payment had been made.

23(9) But—

(a)   if the employee's code is an amended code, and

(b)   the employee's previous code was not used on the cumulative basis,

"previous total tax to date" means the total net tax deducted by the employer.

23(10) Paragraphs (2)(c), (8) and (9) are subject to regulations 43(9) and (10), 52(11) and (12), 53(4) and 61(4) (which modify the meaning of previous total tax to date in certain circumstances).

Origin – Reg. 23(1): drafting.
Reg. 23(2): SI 1993/744, reg. 14(1)(part), (2)(part), 15(part) and drafting.
Reg. 23(3): SI 1993/744, reg. 14(1)(part) and see *Rewrite: Changes in Law* notes below.
Reg. 23(4): SI 1993/744, reg. 14(2) and 15(part).
Reg. 23(5): SI 1993/744, reg. 14(2)(part) and 15.
Reg. 23(6): SI 1993/744, reg. 14(3) and drafting.
Reg. 23(7): SI 1993/744, reg. 14(4).
Reg. 23(8): SI 1993/744, reg. 2(1) ("previous cumulative tax").
Reg. 23(9): see *Rewrite: Changes in Law* notes below.
Reg. 23(10): drafting, and see *Rewrite: Changes in Law* notes below.

Rewrite: Changes in Law – Commentary, App. 1, Change 20: reg. 23 omits unnecessary requirement for employers to ascertain intermediate figures each time they undertake calculation.
Commentary, App. 1, Change 21: reg. 23(9): on change from non-cumulative basis to cumulative basis, in computing first deduction or repayment, employer compares total tax to date with total net tax deducted previously.
Commentary, para. 213–221 and App. 2, Change 22: reg. 23(10) repairs missed consequential effects of introduction of K codes, so that deductions on cumulative basis are maintained or restored when employees change jobs.

Notes – In reg. 23(5), "subject to 62(6)" is evidently typo for "subject to regulation 62(6)"; *cf*. reg. 28(5).

Cumulative basis: employee not paid weekly or monthly

24(1) This regulation applies if—

(a)   an employer normally makes main relevant payments to an employee at regular intervals which are longer than a week, other than monthly, and

(b)   the employee's code is used on the cumulative basis.

24(2) The first main relevant payment in a tax year is treated for the purposes of calculating the deduction or repayment of tax as having been made at the end the period which—

(a)   starts on the first day of the tax year, and

(b)   finishes at the end of the employee's normal regular payment interval.

24(3) Subsequent main relevant payments in the tax year are treated for the purposes of calculating the deduction or repayment of tax as having been made at the end of the period which—

(a)   starts the day after the date on which the previous main relevant payment is treated as having been made (by paragraph (2) or this paragraph), and

(b)   finishes at the end of the employee's normal regular payment interval or the last day of the tax year (if earlier).

24(4)   If the employee's main relevant payments are normally made at regular intervals which are longer than a year, any such payment in a tax year is treated, for the purposes of calculating the deduction or repayment of tax, as made on the last day of that tax year.

24(5)   But, in every case, the employer must record the actual date of every payment in the deductions working sheet.

24(6)   This regulation does not apply if the payment falls within regulation 31(1) (payments in short payment periods).

Origin – Reg. 24(1)–(4): SI 1993/744, reg. 18(part) and see *Rewrite: Changes in Law* note below.
Reg. 24(5): SI 1993/744, reg. 18(part).
Reg. 24(6): drafting.

Rewrite: Changes in Law – Commentary, para. 226–232 and App. 1, Change 23: only an employee's *main* relevant payments, paid at regular intervals of *more* than a week, treated as paid later for the purposes of calculating deductions and repayments; date of payment cannot be deemed to be in next tax year.

Cumulative basis: subsidiary PAYE income of employee paid weekly or at greater intervals

25(1)   This regulation applies if–

(a)   an employee's main relevant payments are normally made at regular intervals of a week or more,

(b)   the employee's code is used on the cumulative basis, and

(c)   the employer makes a payment in respect of overtime or other extra earnings (the "extra payment").

25(2)   For the purposes of calculating the deduction or repayment of tax, the extra payment is treated as made on the same date as that on which the main relevant payment in the payment period is due to be paid or is due to be treated as paid by regulation 24 (employee not paid weekly or monthly).

25(3)   But paragraph (4) applies if the extra payment is actually made before the date on which the main relevant payment in the payment period is due to be paid (disregarding the effects of regulation 24).

25(4)   A repayment which would (but for this paragraph) be due under regulation 23(6) on making the extra payment must not be paid to the employee, but must instead be added to the previous total tax (as defined by regulation 23(8)) on making the next relevant payment.

25(5)   This regulation does not apply if the extra payment is made in a short payment period (but regulation 31 applies instead if that period contains an extra pay day).

25(6)   "Payment period–"

(a)   in the case of an employee normally paid weekly, means a tax week,

(b)   in the case of an employee normally paid monthly, means a tax month,

(c)   in the case of an employee normally paid at other regular intervals, has the meaning given in paragraph (7).

25(7)   In the case mentioned in paragraph (6)(c)–

(a)   the first payment period in a tax year starts on 6th April and finishes at the end of the employee's normal regular payment interval, and

(b)   subsequent payment periods in the tax year start the day after the end of the previous payment period and finish–

  (i)   at the end of the employee's normal regular payment interval, or

  (ii)   on 5th April (if earlier).

25(8)   "Short payment period" means the last payment period in a tax year if, because of paragraph (7)(b)(ii), it is shorter than the previous payment periods.

25(9)   "Extra pay day" has the meaning given in regulation 31(4).

Origin – Reg. 25(1): SI 1993/744, reg. 19(1)(part) and see *Rewrite: Changes in Law* notes below.
Reg. 25(2): SI 1993/744, reg. 19(2)(part) and see *Rewrite: Changes in Law* notes below.
Reg. 25(3): SI 1993/744, reg. 19(1)(part), (2)(part) and see *Rewrite: Changes in Law* notes below.
Reg. 25(4): SI 1993/744, reg. 19(2)(part) and see *Rewrite: Changes in Law* notes below.
Reg. 25(5): SI 1993/744, reg. 17(1) and see *Rewrite: Changes in Law* notes below.
Reg. 25(6)–(9): see *Rewrite: Changes in Law* notes below.

Cross references – SI 2003/2682, reg. 31: "week 53" basis.

Rewrite: Changes in Law – Commentary, App. 1, Change 24: reg. 25 only applies if main relevant payments are made at regular intervals.
Commentary, App. 1, Change 25: reg. 25 applies to employees normally paid at weekly or at greater intervals.
Commentary, App. 1, Change 26: reg. 25(2)–(4) require employers to treat any extra payment as made when the next relevant payment is due, refer explicitly to the actual date a normal payment is due to be made, and provide for the previous total tax to date to be adjusted for any repayment not made because of reg. 25. This requires employers to calculate tax on extra payments

when they make them (but as if they were made at the date of the normal payment) and then use that calculation as the starting point for the next relevant payment, instead of making the calculation using the actual date and then erasing their calculation. Commentary, App. 1, Change 30: "week 53" basis extended to employees paid at greater intervals than a week.

THE NON-CUMULATIVE BASIS

The non-cumulative basis

26(1) An employer must deduct tax in accordance with regulation 27 (the non-cumulative basis) from any relevant payment made to an employee if–

(a)   the Inland Revenue direct, or

(b)   these Regulations provide,

that the non-cumulative basis is to apply.

26(2) If this regulation applies then regulation 22 (cumulative basis) does not apply.

Origin – Reg. 26(1): SI 1993/744, reg. 17(1)(part) and drafting.
Reg. 26(2): SI 1993/744, reg. 17(2)(part).

Non-cumulative basis: general rule for deductions

27(1) On making a relevant payment, the employer must deduct the amount of tax which would have been deductible in accordance with the appropriate tax tables, by reference to the employee's code, if the payment had been made on the first day of the tax year.

27(2) This is subject to–

regulation 28   modification of general rule

regulation 29   aggregation of payments.

Origin – Reg. 27(1): SI 1993/744, reg. 17(2)(part) and see *Rewrite: Changes in Law* note below.
Reg. 27(2): drafting.

Rewrite: Changes in Law – Commentary, App. 1, Change 27: reg. 27 refers not to "the preceding 6 April" but to "the first day of the tax year", to avoid any question of treating payments made on 6 April as made a year earlier.

Non-cumulative basis: modification of general rule

28(1) Paragraphs (2) to (5) modify the general rule in regulation 27(1) (the non-cumulative basis) in certain circumstances.

28(2) If regulation 30 (employee not paid weekly or monthly) applies to the employee's main relevant payments, the employer must deduct from a relevant payment the amount of tax which would have been deductible, by reference to the employee's code, if the payment (whether or not it is a main relevant payment) had been made on the date given by that regulation.

28(3) If the employer does not normally make relevant payments to the employee at regular intervals, the employer must deduct from a relevant payment the amount of tax which would have been deductible, by reference to the employee's code–

(a)   if the payment is the first payment in the tax year, on the date it is made, or

(b)   in any other case, on the date found by counting forward x days starting on 5th April, where x is the number of days found by starting with the date of the previous relevant payment and counting forward to the date of the payment in question.

28(4) But if two or more relevant payments are made in the same tax week, the employer must deduct from the second or subsequent relevant payment the amount of tax which (subject to regulation 29(5)) would have been deductible, by reference to the employee's code, if that payment were made at the date given by paragraph (3) for the first payment.

28(5) If the employee's code is a K code, the deduction is not to exceed the overriding limit, subject to regulation 62(6) (notional payments).

Origin – Reg. 28(1): drafting.
Reg. 28(2): SI 1993/744, reg. 17(2)(part), 18(part) and see *Rewrite: Changes in Law* notes below.
Reg. 28(3), (4): see *Rewrite: Changes in Law* notes below.
Reg. 28(5): SI 1993/744, reg. 14(2)(part).

Rewrite: Changes in Law – Commentary, para. 261–263 and App. 1, Change 28: reg. 28(2) treats all relevant payments to employee with regular payments (other than weekly or monthly payments) as paid at the same date.
Commentary, para. 264–267 and App. 1, Change 29: reg. 28(3) gives employees paid at irregular intervals whatever slice of their annual allowances is unused since their previous relevant payment (or since the start of the tax year, if it is the first relevant payment); reg. 28(4) modifies this rule for payments actually made in the same tax week.

Non-cumulative basis: aggregation of payments

29(1) Paragraph (2) applies if–

(a)   relevant payments are normally made to an employee at regular intervals of a week or more, and

(b)   the employee's code is used on the non-cumulative basis.

Statutory Instruments

29(2)   If the relevant payment is the second or subsequent relevant payment made to the employee during the payment period (as defined by regulation 25(6)), the amount of tax to be deducted must be–

(a)   calculated by reference to the aggregate of the relevant payments made to the employee during the payment period (as defined by regulation 25(6)),

(b)   increased by any tax not deducted because of the overriding limit when the previous relevant payment in that payment period was made to the employee, and

(c)   reduced by the amount of tax calculated when the employer made the previous relevant payment in that payment period.

29(3)   But, for the purposes of the aggregate, any effects of regulation 30(2) (regular payments treated as made at later date) must be disregarded.

29(4)   Paragraph (5) applies if relevant payments to an employee–

(a)   are normally made at regular intervals of less than a week, or

(b)   are made at irregular intervals of less than a week.

29(5)   If the relevant payment is the second or subsequent relevant payment made to the employee during a tax week, the amount of tax to be deducted must be–

(a)   calculated by reference to the aggregate of the relevant payments made to the employee in the tax week,

(b)   increased by any tax not deducted because of the overriding limit when the previous relevant payment in that tax week was made to the employee, and

(c)   reduced by the amount of tax calculated when the employer made the previous relevant payment in that tax week.

Origin – Reg. 29(1): SI 1993/744, reg. 21(part) and see *Rewrite: Changes in Law* note below.
Reg. 29(2): SI 1993/744, reg. 14(2)(part), reg. 21(part); and see *Rewrite: Changes in Law* note below.
Reg. 29(3): drafting.
Reg. 29(4): SI 1993/744, reg. 21(part).
Reg. 29(5): SI 1993/744, reg. 14(2)(part), 21(part).

Rewrite: Changes in Law – Commentary, App. 1, Change 28: reg. 29 extends aggregation of payments where PAYE operated on non-cumulative basis to all payment intervals, rather than just periods of week or month, and provides for all payments in payment period to be treated as paid at same time for the purposes of calculating deductions of tax.

Non-cumulative basis: employee not paid weekly or monthly

30(1)   This regulation applies if–

(a)   an employer normally makes main relevant payments to an employee at regular intervals which are longer than a week, other than monthly, and

(b)   the employee's code is used on the non-cumulative basis.

30(2)   Each main relevant payment in a tax year is treated for the purposes of calculating the deduction of tax as having been made at the end the period which–

(a)   starts on 6th April, and

(b)   finishes at the end of the employee's regular payment interval.

30(3)   If the employee's main relevant payments are normally made at regular intervals which are longer than a year, any such payment in a tax year is treated, for the purposes of calculating the deduction of tax, as made on 5th April in that tax year.

30(4)   But, in every case, the employer must record the actual date of every payment in the deductions working sheet.

Origin – Reg. 30(1)–(3): SI 1993/744, reg. 18(part) and see *Rewrite: Changes in Law* note below.
Reg. 30(4): SI 1993/744, reg. 18(part).

Rewrite: Changes in Law – Commentary, App. 1, Change 23: only an employee's *main* relevant payments, paid at regular intervals of *more* than a week, treated as paid later for the purposes of calculating deductions and repayments; date of payment cannot be deemed to be in next tax year.

Notes – In reg. 30(2), "… at the end the period …" is evidently typo for "… at the end of the period …"

Payments in short payment periods

31(1)   An employer must deduct tax on the non-cumulative basis from any relevant payment made to an employee in a short payment period which includes an extra pay day, even if the employee's code is normally used on the cumulative basis.

31(2)   Paragraph (1) does not apply if the employee's code is the basic rate code.

31(3)   If–

(a)   the employee's total payments to date do not exceed the employee's total free pay to date, and

(b)   the employee's code is normally used on the cumulative basis, the employer must not deduct any tax from relevant payments made in a short payment period which includes an extra pay day.

31(4) "**Extra pay day**" means the last day in a tax year on which a main relevant payment is due to be made to an employee if–

(a) the employee's main relevant payments are normally made weekly or at greater intervals which results in the number of pay days varying from tax year to tax year (solely because of the number of days in a calendar year), and

(b) the day falls in a short payment period.

31(5) "**Short payment period**" has the meaning given in regulation 25(8).

Origin – Reg. 31(1): SI 1993/744, reg. 17(1)(part) and see *Rewrite: Changes in Law* notes below.
Reg. 31(2), (3): see *Rewrite: Changes in Law* notes below.
Reg. 31(4): SI 1993/744, reg. 17(1)(part) and see *Rewrite: Changes in Law* notes below.
Reg. 31(5): see *Rewrite: Changes in Law* notes below.

Rewrite: Changes in Law – Commentary, App. 1, Change 4: reg. 7 defines "basic rate code".
Commentary, App. 1, Change 30: reg. 31 extends "week 53 basis" (which prevents exceptionally large deductions from pay of weekly paid employees paid 53 times in a year) to employees paid at other regular intervals, and provides exception for employees with cumulative PAYE codes who would have no tax deducted from such payments if PAYE were operated on cumulative basis, so that they continue to have no tax deducted.

HIGHER RATE, ADDITIONAL RATE AND NIL TAX CODES

History – The heading above was substituted by SI 2011/729, reg. 6, with effect from 6 April 2011.

Higher rate code: deductions

32 If an employee's code is the higher rate code the employer must deduct tax at the higher rate, and regulations 22 and 26 (cumulative and non-cumulative basis) do not apply.

Origin – SI 1993/744: reg. 16(1)(part), (2)(part) and see *Rewrite: Changes in Law* notes below.

Cross references – SI 2003/2682, reg. 8: meaning of "employee's code" covers codes determined by either Inland Revenue or General Commissioners.

Rewrite: Changes in Law – Commentary, App. 1, Change 4: reg. 7 defines "higher rate code".
Commentary, App. 1, Change 31: reg. 32 provides for use of higher rate code determined by General Commissioners.

Additional rate code: deductions

32A If the employee's code is the additional rate code the employer must deduct tax at the additional rate and regulations 22 and 26 (cumulative and non-cumulative basis) do not apply.

History – Reg. 32A inserted by SI 2011/729, reg. 7, with effect from 6 April 2011.

Nil tax code: no deductions or repayments

33(1) If an employee's code is the nil tax code the employer must not deduct or repay any tax, and so regulation 22 (cumulative basis) does not apply.

33(2) But–

(a) if the nil tax code is an amended code, and

(b) the Inland Revenue so direct,

regulation 22 applies to the next relevant payment the employer makes in the same tax year, and the employer must make any repayment of tax due.

Origin – Reg. 33(1): SI 1993/744, reg. 16(1)(part), (2)(part) and see *Rewrite: Changes in Law* notes below.
Reg. 33(2): SI 1993/744, reg. 16(3) and see *Rewrite: Changes in Law* notes below.

Cross references – SI 2003/2682, reg. 8: meaning of "employee's code" covers codes determined by either Inland Revenue or General Commissioners.

Rewrite: Changes in Law – Commentary, App. 1, Change 4: reg. 7 defines "nil tax code".
Commentary, App. 1, Change 31: reg. 33 provides for use of nil tax code determined by General Commissioners.

SIMPLIFIED DEDUCTION SCHEME

Simplified deduction scheme for personal employees

34 [Omitted by SI 2013/521, reg. 5.]

History – Reg. 34 omitted by SI 2013/521, reg. 5, with effect from 6 April 2014.
Reg. 34(A1) inserted by SI 2013/521, reg. 4, with effect for the tax year 2013–14 only.
In reg. 34(1) the words ", subject to paragraph (1A)," inserted by SI 2012/822, reg. 64(a), with effect from 6 April 2012.
Reg. 34(1A) inserted by SI 2012/822, reg. 64(b), with effect from 6 April 2012.

Origin – Reg. 34(1): SI 1993/744, reg. 20(1)(part), (2)(part) and see *Rewrite: Changes in Law* notes below.
Reg. 34(2): SI 1993/744, reg. 21(part), 14(2)(part) and see *Rewrite: Changes in Law* notes below.
Reg. 34(3): SI 1993/744, reg. 2(1)("simplified tax tables")(part), 20(1)(part) and see *Rewrite: Changes in Law* notes below.
Reg. 34(4): SI 1993/744, reg. 20(4) and see *Rewrite: Changes in Law* notes below.

Rewrite: Changes in Law – Commentary, App. 1, Change 1: reg. 34 refers to "Inland Revenue" (meaning any officer of the Board) rather than "inspector".
Commentary, App. 1, Change 28: reg. 34(2)(a) requires relevant payments to be aggregated.

Commentary, App. 1, Change 32: simplified deduction scheme only applies to "personal employees", but extends to employees who are not paid fixed wages.
Commentary, App. 1, Change 33: reg. 34(2)(b) provides that only the net additional tax must be deducted.
Commentary, App. 1, Change 34: reg. 34(4) does not disapply SI 2003/2682, reg. 40 (duty of employee to give new employer P45).

Simplified deduction schemes: records

35   [Omitted by SI 2013/521, reg. 5.]

History – Reg. 35 omitted by SI 2013/521, reg. 5, with effect from 6 April 2014.
Origin – Reg. 35(1): SI 1993/744, reg. 20(2)(part) and see *Rewrite: Changes in Law* notes below.
Reg. 35(2): SI 1993/744, reg. 20(2)(part); SI 1994/1212, reg. 13(1)(2); and see *Rewrite: Changes in Law* notes below.
Reg. 35(3): SI 1993/744, reg. 20(2)(part) and see *Rewrite: Changes in Law* notes below.
Reg. 35(4): SI 1993/744, reg. 20(3)(part) and see *Rewrite: Changes in Law* notes below.
Reg. 35(5): SI 1993/744, reg. 43(1)(part), (1A)(part), (2)(part), (3)(part) and see *Rewrite: Changes in Law* notes below.
Reg. 35(6): SI 1993/744, reg. 43(4)(part) and see *Rewrite: Changes in Law* notes below.
Reg. 35(7), (8): drafting.
Rewrite: Changes in Law – Commentary, App. 1, Change 1: reg. 35 refers to "Inland Revenue" (meaning any officer of the Board) rather than "inspector".
Commentary, App. 1, Change 32: simplified deduction scheme only applies to "personal employees", but extends to employees who are not paid fixed wages.
Commentary, App. 1, Change 35: reg. 35(2)(e) requires employers to record any tax "*to be* deducted or accounted for" in respect of notional payments as well as tax *actually* deducted or accounted for.
Commentary, App. 1, Change 36: reg. 35(5)–(7) make special provision for employers' returns under simplified deduction scheme.

CESSATION OF EMPLOYMENT

Cessation of employment: Form P45

36(1)   On ceasing to employ an employee in respect of whom a code has been issued, the employer must complete Form P45.

36(1A)   If Part 3 of Form P45 is not available–

(a)   the employer is not required to complete that Part of the Form, and

(b)   where the employer does not complete that Part, any requirement, however expressed, in these Regulations which relates only to Part 3 does not apply.

36(2)   The employer must then–

(a)   send Part 1 of that form to the Inland Revenue if the employer is one to whom paragraph (2A) applies, and

(b)   provide Parts 1A,2 and 3 to the employee,

on the day on which the employment ceases or, if that is not practicable, without unreasonable delay.

36(2A)   This paragraph applies to–

(a)   non-Real Time Information employers, and

(b)   Real Time Information employers to whom HMRC has given a notice requiring the employer to send to HMRC Form P45 or Form P46 on the commencement of a new employee's employment.

36(3)   Retirement on pension is not a cessation of employment for the purposes of this regulation if the PAYE pension income is paid by the same employer after retirement.

36(4)   The information listed in column 1 of Table 2 must, subject to the conditions set out in column 2, be provided in the various Parts of Form P45 as indicated in columns 3 to 5.

Table 2
Information which must be provided in Form P45

1. Information to be provided	2. Conditions	3–5. Form P45 Part
	1A	1, 2, 3
1. the employer's PAYE reference		yes yes yes
2. the employee's national insurance number	if known	yes yes yes
3. the employee's name		yes yes yes
3A. the employee's date of birth	yes	no no
3B. the employee's sex	yes	no no

1. Information to be provided	2. Conditions 1A	3–5. Form P45 Part 1, 2, 3		
4. the date on which the employment ceased		yes	yes	yes
5. the employee's code or, if more than one, the latest code, issued by the Inland Revenue for the tax year during which the employment ceased		yes	yes	yes
6. whether the employee's code is used on the cumulative basis		yes	yes	yes
7. the tax week or month in which the last relevant payment was made to the employee or, in a case falling within regulation 24, was treated as having been made	if the employee's code is used on the cumulative basis	yes	yes	yes
8. the total payments to date and the corresponding total net tax deducted	if the employee's code is used on the cumulative basis	yes	yes	yes
9. the total payments to date relating to the employment in question and the corresponding total net tax deducted	if the employee's code is used on the cumulative basis, and if different from the information supplied under item 8	yes	yes	no
10. the total payments to date relating to the employment in question and the corresponding total net tax deducted	if the employee's code is not used on the cumulative basis	yes	yes	no
11. the number used by the employer to identify the employee	if any	yes	no	no
12. the department or branch in which the employee was employed	if any	yes	no	no
13. the employee's address	if known	yes	no	no
14. the employer's name		yes	yes	no
15. the employer's address		yes	yes	no
16. the date the Form is completed		yes	yes	no

36(5) This regulation is subject to regulations 38, 39 and 180 (death of employee etc).

History – Reg. 36(1A) inserted by SI 2013/521, reg. 16, with effect for the tax year 2013–14 and subsequent tax years. In reg. 36(2)(a), the words "if the employer is one to whom paragraph (2A) applies" inserted by SI 2012/822, reg. 6(a), with effect from 6 April 2012.
Reg. 36(2A) inserted SI 2012/822, reg. 6(b), with effect from 6 April 2012.
In reg. 36(4), in Table 2, items 3A and 3B inserted by SI 2007/2969, reg. 3, with effect from 6 April 2009.

Origin – Reg. 36(1): SI 1993/744, reg. 23(1)(part).
Reg. 36(2): SI 1993/744, reg. 23(1)(part), (3)(part) and see *Rewrite: Changes in Law* notes below.
Reg. 36(3): SI 1993/744, reg. 26(1)(part).
Reg. 36(4): SI 1993/744, reg. 23(1)(part), (3)(part) and see *Rewrite: Changes in Law* notes below.
Table 2: SI 1993/744, reg. 23(1)(part), (2), (3)(part) and see *Rewrite: Changes in Law* notes below.
Reg. 36(5): drafting.

Rewrite: Changes in Law – Commentary, App. 1, Change 1: reg. 36 refers to "Inland Revenue" (meaning any officer of the Board) rather than "inspector".
Commentary, App. 1, Change 37: reg. 36(2) indicates that P45 is multi-part form.
Commentary, App. 1, Change 38: Table 2 brings into line with practice the information which employers are required to provide in Form P45.

Income subject to retrospective tax provision — information to employee

36A(1) This regulation applies if–

(a) a payment is made to an employee;

(b) the employment in connection with which it was paid ceases;

(c) the payment becomes a qualifying payment after the cessation of the employment;

(d)   the tax year in which the payment was actually made is not closed, and

(e)   the amount of the qualifying payment was not included in Form P45.

36A(2)   If this regulation applies the person who made the payment must provide to the employee, without unreasonable delay after the relevant time, details of–

(a)   the date on which the qualifying payment was actually made;

(b)   the amount of the qualifying payment; and

(c)   the amount of tax deducted under regulation 62(4) or (5).

History – Reg. 36A inserted by SI 2007/1077, reg. 4, with effect from 6 April 2007.

PAYE income paid after employment ceased

37(1)   This regulation applies if a relevant payment is made to an employee after the employment has ceased–

(a)   by the former employer in respect of the former employment, or

(b)   by any other person in respect of an obligation of the former employer,

and the payment has not been included in Form P45.

37(1A)   But this regulation does not apply if regulation 37A applies.

37(2)   The person making the payment must deduct tax on the non-cumulative basis using the 0T Code.

37(2A)   [Omitted by SI 2012/822, reg. 65(b).]

37(2B)   [Omitted by SI 2012/822, reg. 65(c).]

37(3)   But–

(a)   the payment does not affect the cessation of employment, and

(b)   the provisions listed in paragraph (4) do not apply.

37(4)   The provisions are–

regulation 21	deduction and repayment of tax by reference to employee's code
regulations 22 and 23	cumulative basis
Chapters 2 and 3 of this Part	new employees and new pensioners: Forms P45 and P46.

37(5)   The person making the payment must record the following information in a deductions working sheet (which the person must prepare for the purpose if one has not already been prepared for that tax year).

37(6)   The information is–

(a)   the date of the payment,

(b)   the amount of the relevant payment, and

(c)   the amount of tax deducted on making the payment, or to be deducted or accounted for under regulation 62(4) or (5) (notional payments).

37(7)   The person making the payment must also notify the employee of the information mentioned in paragraph (6) without unreasonable delay.

History – Reg. 37(1A) inserted by SI 2007/1077, reg. 5, with effect from 6 April 2007.
In reg. 37(2) the word "The" substituted for the words "Subject to paragraph (2A), the" by SI 2012/822, reg. 65(a), with effect from 6 April 2012.
Reg. 37(2A) and (2B) omitted by SI 2012/822, reg. 65(b) and (c), with effect from 6 April 2012. Former reg. 37(2A) and (2B) read as follows:

> "**37(2A)**   If the payment is in the form of securities, an interest in securities or securities options which gives rise to earnings within Chapter 1 of Part 3 of ITEPA or which counts as employment income by virtue of Part 7 of ITEPA, the person making the payment must deduct tax at the basic rate in force for the tax year in which the payment is made.
>
> **37(2B)**   In paragraph (2A)—
> "**interest**",
> "**securities**", and
> "**securities options**"
> have the meaning indicated in section 420 of ITEPA."

Reg. 37(2), and former (2A) and (2B) substituted for former reg. 37(2) by SI 2011/1054, reg. 3, with effect from 6 April 2011, immediately after the coming into force of SI 2011/729 (which amended former reg. 37(2); see below).
In former reg. 37(2), the words "using the 0T code" substituted for the words "at the basic rate in force for the tax year in which the payment is made" by SI 2011/729, reg. 8(a), with effect from 6 April 2011.
In reg. 37(4), in the list, the entry for "regulations 26 and 27   non-cumulative basis" omitted SI 2011/729, reg. 8(a), with effect from 6 April 2011.

Origin – Reg. 37(1): SI 1993/744, reg. 24(1).
Reg. 37(2): SI 1993/744, reg. 24(2)(part).
Reg. 37(3): SI 1993/744, reg. 24(2)(part) and see *Rewrite: Changes in Law* notes below.

Reg. 37(4): SI 1993/744, reg. 24(2)(part) and drafting.
Reg. 37(5): SI 1993/744, reg. 24(2)(part).
Reg. 37(6): SI 1993/744, reg. 24(2)(part); SI 1994/1212, reg. 13(1), (2); and see *Rewrite: Changes in Law* notes below.
Reg. 37(7): see *Rewrite: Changes in Law* notes below.

Rewrite: Changes in Law – Commentary, App. 1, Change 7: SI 2003/2682, reg. 10 applies reg. 37 to agencies and agency workers.

Commentary, App. 1, Change 35: reg. 37(6)(c): requirement to record any tax "*to be* deducted or accounted for" in respect of notional payments as well as tax *actually* deducted or accounted for.

Commentary, App. 1, Change 40: reg. 37(7) requires former employer or person acting on behalf of former employer to notify former employee of payments made and tax deducted after end of employment.

Income paid after cessation of employment subsequently becoming subject to PAYE

37A(1)   This regulation applies if–

(a)   a payment has been made, after the cessation of the employment, to a former employee–

    (i)   by the former employer, or

    (ii)   by any other person in respect of an obligation of the former employer;

(b)   that payment becomes a qualifying payment after the employment ceased; and

(c)   the amount of the qualifying payment has not been included in Form P45.

37A(2)   Where a qualifying payment has been made in a closed year, the employer must deduct tax, from any other payment made to the former employee in the tax period at the relevant time–

(a)   in accordance with the last code used for the tax year in which the qualifying payment was made, or

(b)   if the employer has not been notified of a code for that tax year, at the additional rate of tax applicable for that year.

37A(3)   Where a qualifying payment has been made in an open year, the employer must deduct tax from any other payment made to the former employee–

(a)   in accordance with the code in force in the final tax period in which the employee was employed, or

(b)   if the employer has not been notified of a code, at the additional rate of tax applicable for that year.

37A(4)   Neither the making of the qualifying payment, nor its subsequently becoming taxable, affect the cessation of the employment, and the provisions listed in regulation 37(4) do not apply in relation that payment.

37A(5)   The employer must record the following information in a deductions working sheet for the tax year in which that payment was made.

If a deductions working sheet has not already been prepared for that tax year, the employer must prepare one.

37A(6)   The information is–

(a)   the date on which the qualifying payment was actually made;

(b)   the amount of that payment; and

(c)   the amount of tax to be deducted or accounted for under regulation 62(4) or(5) (notional payments).

37A(7)   The employer must also notify the employee of the information listed in paragraph (6) without unreasonable delay after the relevant time.

History – In reg. 37A(2)(b), the word "additional" substituted for the word "higher" by SI 2011/729, reg. 9(a), with effect from 6 April 2011.

In reg. 37A(3)(b), the word "additional" substituted for the word "higher" by SI 2011/729, reg. 9(b), with effect from 6 April 2011.

Reg. 37A inserted by SI 2007/1077, reg. 6, with effect from 6 April 2007.

Death of employee

38(A1)   This regulation applies to–

(a)   non-Real Time Information employers, and

(b)   Real Time Information employers to whom HMRC has given a notice requiring the employer to send to HMRC Form P45 or Form P46 on the commencement of a new employee's employment.

38(1)   On the death of an employee (other than a pensioner) in respect of whom a code has been issued by the Inland Revenue, the employer must–

(a)   complete Form P45 indicating in Part 1 that the employee has died, and

(b)   send it to the Inland Revenue.

38(2)   The employer must comply with paragraph (1)–

(a)   on the day on which the employer learns of the employee's death, or

(b)   if that is not practicable, without unreasonable delay.

38(3)   The employer must, on making a relevant payment after learning of the employee's death but before completing Form P45, deduct or repay tax as if the deceased employee were still alive and employed by the employer at the date of the payment.

38(4)   Regulation 37(2) to (6) applies to any relevant payment which–

(a)   is made in respect of the employee's employment after the date of the employee's death, and

(b)   is not included in Form P45.

History – Reg. 38(A1) inserted by SI 2012/822, reg. 7, with effect from 6 April 2012.

Origin – Reg. 38(1), (2): SI 1993/744, reg. 27(1) and see *Rewrite: Changes in Law* notes below.
Reg. 38(3): SI 1993/744, reg. 27(2)(part).
Reg. 38(4): see *Rewrite: Changes in Law* notes below.

Rewrite: Changes in Law – Commentary, App. 1, Change 1: reg. 38 refers to "Inland Revenue" (meaning any officer of the Board) rather than "inspector".
Commentary, App. 1, Change 37: reg. 38 indicates that P45 is multi-part form.
Commentary, App. 1, Change 39: reg. 38 provides for P45 to be completed on learning of death of employee or, if that is not practicable, without unreasonable delay (rather than "forthwith").
Commentary, App. 1, Change 41: reg. 38 omits requirement to provide information about personal representatives and about future payments.
Commentary, App. 1, Change 42: reg. 38(4) gives the same rule for payments following death or departure of employee.

Death of pensioner

39(A1)   This regulation applies to–

(a)   non-Real Time Information pension payers, and

(b)   Real Time Information pension payers to whom HMRC has given a notice requiring the pension payer to send to HMRC Form P45 or Form P46(Pen) on the commencement of a new pensioner's pension.

39(1)   On the death of a pensioner in respect of whom a code has been issued by the Inland Revenue, the pension payer must–

(a)   complete Form P45 indicating in Part 1 that the pensioner has died, and

(b)   send it to the Inland Revenue.

39(2)   The pension payer must comply with paragraph (1)–

(a)   on the day on which the pension payer learns of the pensioner's death, or

(b)   if that is not practicable, without unreasonable delay.

39(3)   Paragraph (4) applies if the pension payer makes any relevant pension payments after the date of the pensioner's death–

(a)   before completing Form P45, or

(b)   after completing Form P45 but during the tax year in which the pensioner died.

39(4)   The pension payer must, on making any such payment, deduct or repay tax as if the deceased pensioner were still alive and in receipt of a pension at the date of the payment.

39(5)   Regulation 37(2) to (6) applies to any relevant pension payment which–

(a)   is made in a tax year following the tax year in which the pensioner died, and

(b)   is not included in Form P45.

History – Reg. 39(A1) inserted by SI 2012/822, reg. 8, with effect from 6 April 2012.

Origin – Reg. 39(1), (2): SI 1993/744, reg. 27(1)(part) and see *Rewrite: Changes in Law* notes below.
Reg. 39(3): SI 1993/744, reg. 27(2)(part) and see *Rewrite: Changes in Law* notes below.
Reg. 39(4): SI 1993/744, reg. 27(2)(part).
Reg. 39(5): see *Rewrite: Changes in Law* notes below.

Rewrite: Changes in Law – Commentary, App. 1, Change 1: reg. 39 refers to "Inland Revenue" (meaning any officer of the Board) rather than "inspector".
Commentary, App. 1, Change 37: reg. 39 indicates that P45 is multi-part form.
Commentary, App. 1, Change 39: reg. 39 provides for P45 to be completed on learning of death of pensioner or, if that is not practicable, without unreasonable delay (rather than "forthwith").
Commentary, App. 1, Change 41: reg. 39 omits requirement to provide information about personal representatives and about future payments.
Commentary, App. 1, Change 42: reg. 39 requires pension payers to deduct basic rate tax from payments made in years after year of death.

EMPLOYEE'S DUTY TO PROVIDE FORM P45

Duty of employee to give new employer Form P45

40(1)   An employee who has Parts 2 and 3 of Form P45 must give them to the new employer on commencing a new employment.

40(2)   If an employee receives Parts 2 and 3 of Form P45 after commencing a new employment, the employee must immediately give them to the new employer.

40(3)   But paragraphs (4) and (6) apply if an employee objects to the disclosure of the total payments to date to the new employer.

40(4)   If the employer is a non-Real Time Information employer or a Real Time Information employer to whom HMRC has given a notice requiring the employer to send to HMRC Form P45 or Form P46 on the commencement of a new employee's employment, the employee may, instead of complying with paragraph (1) or (2), send Parts 2 and 3 of Form P45 to the Inland Revenue before commencing the new employment or as soon as the employee receives Form P45 (as the case may be).

40(5)   The Inland Revenue–

(a)   must then issue a code in respect of the employee to the new employer, and

(b)   may direct that the non-cumulative basis is to apply to all relevant payments which the new employer makes to the employee.

40(6)   If the employer is a Real Time Information employer, the employee need not comply with paragraphs (1) and (2).

History – In reg. 40(3), the words "But paragraphs (4) and (6) apply" substituted for the words "But paragraph (4) applies" by SI 2012/822, reg. 9(a), with effect from 6 April 2012.
In reg. 40(4), the words "If the employer is a non-Real Time Information employer or a Real Time Information employer to whom HMRC has given a notice requiring the employer to send to HMRC Form P45 or Form P46 on the commencement of a new employee's employment, the" substituted for the word "The" by SI 2012/822, reg. 9(b), with effect from 6 April 2012.
Reg. 40(6) inserted by SI 2012/822, reg. 9(c), with effect from 6 April 2012.

Origin – Reg. 40(1): SI 1993/744, reg. 25(1)(part) and see *Rewrite: Changes in Law* notes below.
Reg. 40(2): see *Rewrite: Changes in Law* notes below.
Reg. 40(3): SI 1993/744, reg. 25(11)(part).
Reg. 40(4), (5): SI 1993/744, reg. 25(11)(part) and see *Rewrite: Changes in Law* notes below.

Rewrite: Changes in Law – Commentary, App. 1, Change 1: reg. 40 refers to "Inland Revenue" (meaning any officer of the Board) rather than "inspector".
Commentary, App. 1, Change 37: reg. 40 indicates that P45 is multi-part form.
Commentary, App. 1, Change 43: reg. 40 requires employees receiving a P45 after starting new employment to give Parts 2 and 3 to new employer immediately.
Commentary, App. 1, Change 44: reg. 40 requires Revenue to issue code if employee sends P45 Parts 2 & 3 to Revenue instead of giving them to new employer.

Duty of employee to assist with completion of new employee fields in returns under regulations 67B and 67D

40A(1)   An employee who commences employment with a Real Time Information employer must provide the information required to allow the employer to complete the new employee fields in the first return required by regulation 67B (real time returns of information about relevant payments) or 67D (exceptions to regulation 67B) which includes information in respect of the employee.

40A(2)   The employer must verify the information given under paragraph (1) before making that return.

40A(3)   In this regulation, **"the new employee fields"** means the information required under paragraphs 36 to 44 of Schedule A1.

History – Reg. 40A inserted by SI 2012/822, reg. 10, with effect from 6 April 2012.

Chapter 2 – New Employees (Other Than Pensioners): Forms P45 and P46

Scope of Chapter 2

41   This Chapter sets out the procedure to be followed for deductions and repayments (Form P45 and P46 procedure) in cases to which Chapter 3 (new pensioners: Forms P45 and P46) does not apply (see regulation 54).

Origin – Drafting.

Procedure if employer receives Form P45

42(1) This regulation applies–

(a)   if an employee gives Parts 2 and 3 of Form P45 to the employer on commencing employment, and

(b)   in the circumstances mentioned in regulation 51(2) (late presentation of Form P45: before employer required to send Form P46).

42(2) The new employer must prepare a deductions working sheet and record on it the following information shown in Parts 2 and 3 of Form P45–

(a)   the employee's name,

(b)   the employee's national insurance number.

42(3) If Parts 2 and 3 of Form P45 show that the earlier employment ended in the current tax year, the new employer must comply with regulation 43.

42(4) If–

(a)   Parts 2 and 3 of Form P45 show that the earlier employment ended in the previous tax year, and

(b)   the new employment commences on or before 24th May,

the new employer must comply with regulation 44.

42(5) If–

(a)   Parts 2 and 3 of Form P45 show that the employment ended in the previous tax year, and

(b)   the employment commences after 24th May,

the new employer must comply with regulation 45.

42(6) If Parts 2 and 3 of Form P45 show that the employment ended in any earlier tax year, the new employer must comply with regulation 45.

42(6A) Paragraphs (7) and (8) apply if the employer is either–

(a)   a non-Real Time Information employer, or

(b)   a Real Time Information employer to whom HMRC has given a notice requiring the employer to send to HMRC Form P45 or Form P46 on the commencement of a new employee's employment.

42(7) In all cases the new employer must then insert in Part 3 of Form P45–

(a)   the employer's employer reference,

(b)   the date on which the new employment commenced,

(c)   any number used to identify the employee,

(d)   the employee's code in use by the employer if different from the code shown in Parts 2 and 3 of Form P45,

(e)   any figure recorded in accordance with paragraph (5)(c) or (6)(c) of regulation 43 (Form P45 for current tax year), if different from the total tax to date shown on Parts 2 and 3 of Form P45,

(f)   the employee's address,

(g)   the employee's date of birth,

(ga)   the employee's sex,

(h)   the employee's job title or description,

(i)   the employer's name, and

(j)   the employer's address.

42(8) The employer must then send Part 3 of Form P45 to the employer's Inland Revenue office.

History – Reg. 42(6A) inserted by SI 2012/822, reg. 11, with effect from 6 April 2012.
In reg. 42(7), in para. (g), the words "if known" omitted, and para. (ga) inserted by SI 2007/2969, reg. 4, with effect from 6 April 2009.
Origin – Reg. 42(1): SI 1993/744, reg. 25(1)(part), 24(2)(part); drafting; and see *Rewrite: Changes in Law* notes below.
Reg. 42(2): SI 1993/744, reg. 25(3)(part) and see *Rewrite: Changes in Law* notes below.
Reg. 42(3): SI 1993/744, reg. 25(1) and see *Rewrite: Changes in Law* notes below.
Reg. 42(4), (5): SI 1993/744, reg. 25(8)(part) and see *Rewrite: Changes in Law* notes below.
Reg. 42(6): see *Rewrite: Changes in Law* notes below.
Reg. 42(7), (8): SI 1993/744, reg. 25(2)(part) and see *Rewrite: Changes in Law* notes below.
Rewrite: Changes in Law – Commentary, App. 1, Change 37: reg. 42 indicates that P45 is multi-part form.
Commentary, App. 1, Change 38: reg. 42(7) brings into line with practice the information which employers are required to provide in Form P45.
Commentary, App. 1, Change 45: under reg. 42, P45 refers to date when old employment ended, rather than date when last payment was made.
Commentary, App. 1, Change 46: reg. 42 deals explicitly with cases in which P45 given to new employer relates to year before previous tax year.

Form P45 for current tax year

43(1) The new employer must record in the deductions working sheet the code shown in Parts 2 and 3 of Form P45 as the employee's code.

43(2) Paragraphs (3) to (10) apply if Parts 2 and 3 of Form P45 show that the cumulative basis was used.

43(3) The employer must record in the deductions working sheet the total payments to date (if any) shown in Parts 2 and 3 of Form P45.

43(4) The employer must record in the deductions working sheet the following additional information, or keep such records as enable its production.

43(5) If the code shown in Parts 2 and 3 of Form P45 is a K code, the additional information is–

(a)   the total additional pay to date,

(b)   the total taxable payments to date, and

(c)   the lower of the total tax to date as at the week or month shown in Parts 2 and 3 of Form P45 and the total net tax deducted shown in it.

43(6) In any other case, the additional information is–

(a)   the total free pay to date,

(b)   the total taxable payments to date, and

(c)   the corresponding total tax to date as at the week or month shown in Parts 2 and 3 of Form P45.

43(7) The amounts required by paragraphs (5)(a) and(b) and (6)(a) and (b) must be arrived at by the employer by reference to the information shown in Parts 2 and 3 of Form P45.

43(8) On making any relevant payment to the employee, the employer must deduct or repay tax by reference to the employee's code on the cumulative basis.

43(9) For the purposes of–

(a)   paragraph (8), and

(b)   item 8 of Table 2 in regulation 36(4) (Form P45), and

(c)   regulation 55(4)(f) (Form P46(Pen)),

the total payments to date recorded in the deductions working sheet in accordance with paragraph (3), and the figure recorded in accordance with paragraph (5)(c) or (6)(c) must be treated as if they were relevant payments made to the employee by, and tax deducted by, the new employer.

43(10) For the purposes of regulation 23(8) (cumulative basis: meaning of previous total tax to date) the figure recorded in accordance with paragraph (5)(c) or (6)(c) must be treated as the previous total tax to date when the employer next makes a relevant payment to the employee.

43(11) If Parts 2 and 3 of Form P45 show that the non-cumulative basis has been used, on making any relevant payment to the employee the employer must, subject to regulation 32 (higher rate code: deductions), deduct or repay tax by reference to the employee's code on the non-cumulative basis.

43(12) The receipt by the employer of Parts 2 and 3 of Form P45 is treated as the issue by the Inland Revenue of the code shown in Parts 2 and 3 of Form P45 as the code for use in respect of the employee.

History – In reg. 43(9)(c), the words "(Form P46(Pen))" substituted for "(retirement statement)" by SI 2007/2969, reg. 5, with effect from 6 April 2009.

Origin – Reg. 43(1): SI 1993/744, reg. 25(3)(part) and see *Rewrite: Changes in Law* notes below.
Reg. 43(2): SI 1993/744, reg. 27(1)(part) and see *Rewrite: Changes in Law* notes below.
Reg. 43(3): SI 1993/744, reg. 25(3)(part) and see *Rewrite: Changes in Law* notes below.
Reg. 43(4): SI 1993/744, reg. 25(4)(part).
Reg. 43(5), (6): SI 1993/744, reg. 25(4)(part) and see *Rewrite: Changes in Law* notes below.
Reg. 43(7): SI 1993/744, reg. 25(4)(part), 34(2)(part) and see *Rewrite: Changes in Law* notes below.
Reg. 43(8): SI 1993/744, reg. 25(5)(part).
Reg. 43(9), (10): SI 1993/744, reg. 25(5)(part) and see *Rewrite: Changes in Law* notes below.
Reg. 43(11): SI 1993/744, reg. 25(7); drafting; and see *Rewrite: Changes in Law* notes below.
Reg. 43(12): SI 1993/744, reg. 25(9) and see *Rewrite: Changes in Law* notes below.

Rewrite: Changes in Law – Commentary, para. 213–221 and App. 2, Change 22: reg. 23 repairs missed consequential effects of introduction of K codes, so that deductions on cumulative basis are maintained or restored when employees change jobs.
Commentary, App. 1, Change 37: reg. 43 indicates that P45 is multi-part form.
Commentary, App. 1, Change 47: reg. 43 treats code taken from P45 in accordance with the PAYE regulations as code issued for the PAYE regulations generally.
Commentary, App. 1, Change 48: reg. 43 provides that, for various purposes, new employer must take into account relevant payments made by old employer when receiving P45 with code used on cumulative basis.

Form P45 for previous tax year: employment starting on or before 24th May

44(1) The new employer must–

(a) record in the deductions working sheet the code shown in Parts 2 and 3 of Form P45 as the employee's code, and

(b) deduct or repay tax by reference to that code on the cumulative basis, subject to regulation 32 (higher rate code: deductions).

44(2) The receipt by the employer of Parts 2 and 3 of Form P45 is treated as the issue by the Inland Revenue of the code shown in Parts 2 and 3 of Form P45 as the code for use in respect of the employee.

Origin – Reg. 44(1): SI 1993/744, reg. 25(8) and see *Rewrite: Changes in Law* notes below.
Reg. 44(2): SI 1993/744, reg. 25(9) and see *Rewrite: Changes in Law* notes below.
Rewrite: Changes in Law – Commentary, App. 1, Change 37: reg. 44 indicates that P45 is multi-part form.
Commentary, App. 1, Change 47: reg. 44 treats code taken from P45 in accordance with the PAYE regulations as code issued for the PAYE regulations generally.

Other Forms P45

45(1) The new employer must–

(a) record in the deductions working sheet the emergency code as the employee's code, and

(b) deduct tax from each relevant payment using the emergency code on the non-cumulative basis.

45(2) The emergency code is treated as having been issued to the employer by the Inland Revenue as the code for use in respect of the employee.

Origin – Reg. 45(1): SI 1993/744, reg. 25(8)(part), 32.
Reg. 45(2): SI 1993/744, reg. 25(8)(part), 32 and see *Rewrite: Changes in Law* notes below.
Rewrite: Changes in Law – Commentary, App. 1, Change 47: reg. 45 treats code taken from P45 in accordance with the PAYE regulations as code issued for the PAYE regulations generally.

APPLICATION OF REGULATIONS 46 TO 49E: REAL TIME INFORMATION EMPLOYERS AND NON-REAL TIME INFORMATION EMPLOYERS

45A(1) Regulations 46 to 49 (procedure where no Form P45) apply in relation to–

(a) non-Real Time Information employers, and

(b) Real Time Information employers to whom HMRC has given a notice requiring the employer to send to HMRC Form P45 or Form P46 on the commencement of a new employee's employment.

45A(2) Regulations 49A to 49E (procedure where employee fails to assist with completion of new employee fields or no Form P45) apply in relation to Real Time Information employers other than those within paragraph (1)(b).

History – Reg. 45A inserted by SI 2012/822, reg. 12, with effect from 6 April 2012.

Form P46 where employer does not receive Form P45 and code not known

46(1) This regulation applies if–

(a) an employee commences employment without giving the employer Parts 2 and 3 of Form P45, and

(b) a code in respect of the employee has not otherwise been issued to the employer.

46(1A) The employee must provide the following information in Form P46.

46(1B) The information is–

(a) the employee's national insurance number (if known),

(b) the employee's full name,

(c) the employee's sex,

(d) the employee's date of birth, and

(e) the employee's full address including postcode.

A seconded expatriate who is a national of an EEA state (see section 56(3)(za) of ITA) must provide confirmation of this as additional information.

46(1C) [Omitted by SI 2012/822, reg. 61.]

46(2) The employee must indicate in Form P46 which of the following statements applies–

Statement A: that the employment referred to in paragraph (1)(a) is the employee's first employment since the preceding 6th April, and the employee has not since that date received–

(a) jobseeker's allowance, incapacity benefit or employment and support allowance which is subject to income tax, or

(b) a retirement pension or an occupational pension;

Statement B: that the employee is not receiving a retirement pension or an occupational pension and since the preceding 6th April–

(a)　has had another employment, but is not now in receipt of employment income from it, or

(b)　has received jobseeker's allowance, incapacity benefit or employment and support allowance which is subject to income tax, but payment of that allowance or benefit has ceased;

Statement C: that the employee either has another employment (which is continuing) or is in receipt of a retirement pension or an occupational pension.

A seconded expatriate must indicate instead which of the following statements applies–

Statement A: the employee intends to live in the United Kingdom for 183 days or more;

Statement B: the employee intends to live in the United Kingdom for less than 183 days;

Statement C: the employee will work both inside and outside the United Kingdom, but will live outside.

46(2A)　A Form P46 must be–

(a)　signed by the employee; or

(b)　delivered by the employer by an approved method of electronic communications after he has complied with paragraph (2B).

46(2B)　To the extent that the information contained in it relates to the employee, the employer must verify the content of a Form P46 before it is delivered.

46(2C)　If, despite the requirements of paragraphs (2) to (2B), a Form P46 is sent or delivered to an officer of Revenue and Customs without the requirements of those paragraphs being satisfied, the employer must deduct tax on the non-cumulative basis using code 0T from the employee's earnings.

46(3)　The employer must provide the following information in the Form P46–

(a)　the date on which the employment started;

(b)　the employee's works payroll number and the department or branch (if any) in which the employee is employed;

(c)　the title of the job;

(d)　the employer's PAYE reference;

(e)　the employer's name;

(f)　the employer's full address, including the postcode; and

(g)　the tax code used in relation to the employee's earnings.

46(4)　The employer must keep the Form P46 until required to send it to the Inland Revenue in accordance with regulations 47 to 49.

46(5)　Before sending the Form P46, the employer must indicate in the Form which code is being used in respect of the employee and whether it is being used on the non-cumulative basis.

46(6)　For the purposes of paragraph (1)(b), the employer must ignore any code issued to the employer in respect of an employee's earlier employment which has ceased.

46(7)　This regulation ceases to apply in the circumstances mentioned in regulation 51(2)(a) (late presentation of Form P45: before employer required to send Form P46).

History – In reg. 46(1B), the words ", or is a Commonwealth citizen (see section 278(2)(a) of ICTA),", which appeared after "ITA)", omitted by SI 2012/822, reg. 66, with effect from 6 April 2012.

In reg. 46(1B), the sentence "A seconded expatriate who is a national of an EEA state (see section 56(3)(za) of ITA), or is a Commonwealth citizen (see section 278(2)(a) of ICTA), must provide confirmation of this as additional information." added by SI 2009/588, reg. 3(1), with effect from 6 April 2009.

Reg. 46(1A) and (1B) inserted by SI 2005/2691, reg. 3(2), with effect from 6 April 2006.

Reg. 46(1C) omitted by SI 2012/822, reg. 61, with effect from 6 April 2012. Former reg. 46(1C) read as follows:

"**46(1C)**　In this regulation and in regulations 47 to 49, a **"seconded expatriate"** is an employee meeting one of the following descriptions.

Description 1: An employee in section 689 ITEPA (employee of non-UK employer) whose "work" in section 689(6) starts on 6 April 2009 or later.

Description 2: An employee in a branch of an employer. These Regulations would not apply to that employer but for that branch. The employer seconded the employee to that branch. The employee was not employed in the United Kingdom immediately before the secondment. The secondment starts on 6 April 2009 or later."

Former reg. 46(1C) inserted by SI 2009/588, reg. 3(2), with effect from 6 April 2009.

In reg. 46(2), in para. (a) of the first Statement A, the words ", incapacity benefit or employment and support allowance" substituted for the words "or incapacity benefit" by SI 2013/521, reg. 17(a), with effect for the tax year 2013–14 and subsequent tax years.

In reg. 46(2), in para. (b) of the first Statement B, the words ", incapacity benefit or employment and support allowance" substituted for the words "or incapacity benefit" by SI 2013/521, reg. 17(a), with effect for the tax year 2013–14 and subsequent tax years.

In reg. 46(2), in the second Statement A, the words "183 days or more" substituted for the words "more than 6 months" by SI 2013/521, reg. 17(b), with effect for the tax year 2013–14 and subsequent tax years.

In reg. 46(2), in the second Statement B, the words "183 days" substituted for the words "6 months" by SI 2013/521, reg. 17(c), with effect for the tax year 2013–14 and subsequent tax years.

In reg. 46(2), the words "A seconded expatriate must indicate instead which of the following statements applies–" and Statements A, B and C that follow those words added by SI 2009/588, reg. 3(3), with effect from 6 April 2009.

In reg. 46(2) the words "(if any)" which were after the words "Form P46 which" omitted and the word "supplies" substituted for the word "supply" and Statements A to C substituted and the words "and must sign and date the form" which followed Statement C omitted by SI 2005/2691, reg. 3(3), with effect from 6 April 2006.

In reg. 46(2C), the words "on the non-cumulative basis using code 0T" substituted for the words "at the basic rate" by SI 2011/729, reg. 10, with effect from 6 April 2011.

Reg. 46(2A)–(2C) inserted by SI 2005/2691, reg. 3(4), with effect from 6 April 2006.

Reg. 46(3) substituted by SI 2005/2691, reg. 3(5), with effect from 6 April 2006.

In reg. 46(7), "51(2)(a)" substituted for "51(2)" by SI 2012/822, reg. 13, with effect from 6 April 2012.

Origin – Reg. 46(1): SI 1993/744, reg. 28(1)(part), (4)(part) and see *Rewrite: Changes in Law* notes below.

Reg. 46(2): SI 1993/744, reg. 29(1)(part), 30(1)(part); drafting; and see *Rewrite: Changes in Law* notes below.

Reg. 46(3): SI 1993/744, reg. 28(1A)(part), (1B)(part) and see *Rewrite: Changes in Law* notes below.

Reg. 46(4): SI 1993/744, reg. 28(1A)(part) and see *Rewrite: Changes in Law* notes below.

Reg. 46(5): SI 1993/744, reg. 28(1B)(part) and see *Rewrite: Changes in Law* notes below.

Reg. 46(6): see *Rewrite: Changes in Law* notes below.

Reg. 46(7): SI 1993/744, reg. 28(4)(part).

Rewrite: Changes in Law – Commentary, App. 1, Change 1: reg. 46 refers to "Inland Revenue" (meaning any officer of the Board) rather than "inspector".

Commentary, App. 1, Change 37: reg. 46 indicates that P45 is multi-part form.

Commentary, App. 1, Change 38: reg. 46 brings into line with practice the information which employers are required to provide in Form P46.

Commentary, App. 1, Change 49: reg. 46 allows employees and employers to complete P46 before they are required to send it to the Revenue.

Commentary, App. 1, Change 50: reg. 46, 57 and 58 simplify conditions for P46 procedures and avoid them leading to basic rate deductions for employees with no other employment.

Commentary, para. 345 and App. 1, Change 51: reg. 46 explicitly applies P46 procedures when employee returns to employment of former employer (i.e. "old" codes and deductions working sheets cannot be resurrected).

Procedure in Form P46 cases: (a) seconded expatriate is national of EEA state or Commonwealth citizen, or (b) employee is not seconded expatriate and Statement A applies

History – Heading of reg. 47 changed to "Procedure in Form P46 cases: (a) seconded expatriate is national of EEA state or Commonwealth citizen, or (b) employee is not seconded expatriate and Statement A applies" from "Procedure in Form P46 cases: Statement A applies" by SI 2009/588, reg. 3(4), with effect from 6 April 2009.

In the heading to reg. 47 the words "Statement A applies" substituted for the words "former full time students" by SI 2005/2691, reg. 4(2), with effect from 6 April 2006.

47(1) This regulation applies in the case of an employee (not a seconded expatriate) who indicates that Statement A applies.

It also applies to a seconded expatriate who confirms being a national of an EEA state (see regulation 46(1B)).

47(2) On making the first relevant payment which equals or exceeds the lower earnings limit to the employee, the employer must–

(a)   send the Form P46 to Her Majesty's Revenue and Customs,

(b)   prepare a deductions working sheet and enter the total payments to date, and

(c)   deduct tax on the cumulative basis using the emergency code.

47(2A) To comply with paragraph (2)(a)–

(a)   the employer must send the Form P46 to Her Majesty's Revenue and Customs even if the employee has not provided all of the information required by regulation 46, and

(b)   the employer must provide any of the information required by regulation 46(1B) that the employee has not provided.

47(3) On making any subsequent relevant payment before the Inland Revenue issue a code for use in respect of the employee, the employer must continue to deduct or repay tax on the cumulative basis using the emergency code.

47(4) [Omitted by SI 2012/822, reg. 62.]

History – In reg. 47(1), the words "or being a Commonwealth citizen", which appeared after "state", omitted by SI 2012/822, reg. 67, with effect from 6 April 2012.

In reg. 47(1), the words "(not a seconded expatriate)" inserted and the sentence "It also applies to a seconded expatriate who confirms being a national of an EEA state or being a Commonwealth citizen (see regulation 46(1B))." added by SI 2009/588, reg. 3(5), with effect from 6 April 2009.

Reg. 47(1) substituted by SI 2005/2691, reg. 4(3), with effect from 6 April 2006.

In reg. 47(2), the words "equals or exceeds the lower earnings limit" substituted for "exceeds the PAYE threshold" by SI 2007/2969, reg. 6(a), with effect from 6 April 2008.

Reg. 47(2)(a) substituted by SI 2007/2969, reg. 6(b), with effect from 6 April 2008.

Reg. 47(2A) inserted by SI 2007/2969, reg. 6(c), with effect from 6 April 2008.

Reg. 47(4) omitted by SI 2012/822, reg. 62, with effect from 6 April 2012. Former reg. 47(4) read as follows:

"**47(4)**   In this regulation, **"lower earnings limit"** means the lower earnings limit for Class 1 contributions for the
            purposes of section 5(1) of the Social Security Contributions and Benefits Act 1992."
Former reg. 47(4) inserted by SI 2007/2969, reg. 6(d), with effect from 6 April 2008.
Origin – Reg. 47(1): SI 1993/744, reg. 29(1)(part).
Reg. 47(2): SI 1993/744, reg. 28(1)(part), (1A)(part), 29(2) and see *Rewrite: Changes in Law* notes below.
Reg. 47(3): SI 1993/744, reg. 29(3)(part).
Rewrite: Changes in Law – Commentary, App. 1, Change 1: reg. 47 refers to "Inland Revenue" (meaning any officer of the
Board) rather than "inspector".
Commentary, App. 1, Change 52: reg. 47 requires employers to record the total payments to date made to new employee in
deductions working sheet once PAYE threshold is exceeded.

Procedure in Form P46 cases: (a) Statement B applies (not seconded expatriate), or (b) Statement B or C applies (seconded expatriate)

History – Heading of reg. 48 changed to "Procedure in Form P46 cases: (a) Statement B applies (not seconded expatriate), or (b)
Statement B or C applies (seconded expatriate)" from "Procedure in Form P46 cases: Statement B applies" by SI 2009/588,
reg. 3(6), with effect from 6 April 2009.
In the heading to reg. 48 the words "Statement B applies" substituted for the words "employee taking up only or main
employment" by SI 2005/2691, reg. 5(2), with effect from 6 April 2006.

48(1)   This regulation applies in the case of an employee (not a seconded expatriate) who indicates in
the Form P46 that Statement B applies.

It also applies in the case of a seconded expatriate who indicates in the Form P46 that Statement B or C
applies.

48(2)   On making the first relevant payment which equals or exceeds the lower earnings limit to the
employee, the employer must–

(a)   send the P46 to Her Majesty's Revenue and Customs,

(b)   prepare a deductions working sheet and enter the total payments to date, and

(c)   deduct tax on the non-cumulative basis using the emergency code.

48(2A)   To comply with paragraph (2)(a)–

(a)   the employer must send the Form P46 to Her Majesty's Revenue and Customs even if the
        employee has not provided all of the information required by regulation 46, and

(b)   the employer must provide any of the information required by regulation 46(1B) that the
        employee has not provided.

48(3)   On making any subsequent relevant payment before the employee's code is issued, the
employer must continue to deduct or repay tax on the non-cumulative basis using the emergency code.

48(4)   [Omitted by SI 2012/822, reg. 62.]

History – In reg. 48(1), the words "(not a seconded expatriate)" inserted and the sentence "It also applies in the case of a
seconded expatriate who indicates in the Form P46 that Statement B or C applies." added by SI 2009/588, reg. 3(7), with effect
from 6 April 2009.
In reg. 48(1) the word "only" which was after the words "Form P46 that" omitted by SI 2005/2691, reg. 5(3), with effect from
6 April 2006.
In reg. 48(2), the words "equals or exceeds the lower earnings limit" substituted for "exceeds the PAYE threshold" by
SI 2007/2969, reg. 7(a), with effect from 6 April 2008.
Reg. 48(2)(a) substituted by SI 2007/2969, reg. 7(b), with effect from 6 April 2008.
Reg. 48(2A) inserted by SI 2007/2969, reg. 7(c), with effect from 6 April 2008.
Reg. 48(4) omitted by SI 2012/822, reg. 62, with effect from 6 April 2012. Former reg. 48(4) read as follows:

    "**48(4)**   In this regulation, **"lower earnings limit"** means the lower earnings limit for Class 1 contributions for the
            purposes of section 5(1) of the Social Security Contributions and Benefits Act 1992."
Former reg. 48(4) inserted by SI 2007/2969, reg. 7(d), with effect from 6 April 2008.
Origin – Reg. 48(1): SI 1993/744, reg. 30(1)(part).
Reg. 48(2): SI 1993/744, reg. 28(1)(part), (1A)(part), 30(2) and see *Rewrite: Changes in Law* notes below.
Reg. 48(3): SI 1993/744, reg. 30(3)(part).
Rewrite: Changes in Law – Commentary, App. 1, Change 1: reg. 48 refers to "Inland Revenue" (meaning any officer of the
Board) rather than "inspector".
Commentary, App. 1, Change 52: reg. 48 requires employers to record the total payments to date made to new employee in
deductions working sheet once PAYE threshold is exceeded.

Procedure in Form P46 cases: (a) Statement C applies (not seconded expatriate), or (b) Statement A applies (seconded expatriate)

History – In the heading to reg. 49, the words ", or (c) Form P46 not signed when required", which appeared at the end, omitted
by SI 2011/729, reg. 11, with effect from 6 April 2011.
Heading to reg. 49 substituted by SI 2009/588, reg. 3(8), with effect from 6 April 2009.
In the former heading to reg. 49 the words "Statement C applies or Form P46 not signed when required" substituted for the words
"other new employees" by SI 2005/2691, reg. 5(2), with effect from 6 April 2006.

49(1)   This regulation applies in any case which is not dealt with by regulation 47 or 48 which
concerns an employee to whom regulation 46(1) applies.

49(2)   On making the first relevant payment to the employee, the employer must–

(a)   send the Form P46 to Her Majesty's Revenue and Customs,

(b)   prepare a deductions working sheet and enter both the total payments to date and the total tax to date before the first payment as nil,

(c)   deduct tax on the cumulative basis using the basic rate code.

49(2A)   To comply with paragraph (2)(a)–

(a)   the employer must send the Form P46 to Her Majesty's Revenue and Customs even if the employee has not provided all of the information required by regulation 46, and

(b)   the employer must provide any of the information required by regulation 46(1B) that the employee has not provided.

49(3)   On making any subsequent relevant payment before the employee's code is issued, the employer must continue to deduct tax on the cumulative basis using the basic rate code.

49(4)   In the case of a seconded expatriate, the emergency code must be used instead of the basic rate code mentioned in paragraphs (2)(c) and (3) (see also regulation 7(3) about the codes).

History – Reg. 49(2)(a) substituted by SI 2007/2969, reg. 8(a), with effect from 6 April 2008.
Reg. 49(2A) inserted by SI 2007/2969, reg. 8(b), with effect from 6 April 2008.
Reg. 49(4) inserted by SI 2009/588, reg. 3(9), with effect from 6 April 2009.

Origin – Reg. 49(1): SI 1993/744, reg. 31(1).
Reg. 49(2): SI 1993/744, reg. 28(1)(part), (1A)(part), 31(2) and see *Rewrite: Changes in Law* notes below.
Reg. 49(3): SI 1993/744, reg. 31(4)(part).

Rewrite: Changes in Law – Commentary, App. 1, Change 1: reg. 49 refers to "Inland Revenue" (meaning any officer of the Board) rather than "inspector".
Commentary, App. 1, Change 52: reg. 49 requires employers to record the total payments to date made to new employee in deductions working sheet once PAYE threshold is exceeded.

Procedure where employee fails to assist with completion of new employee fields in returns under regulations 67B and 67D

49A(1)   If, despite the requirements of regulation 40A(1) and (2) (duty of employee to assist with completion of new employee fields in returns under regulations 67B and 67D) and regulations 67B (real time returns of information about relevant payments) and 67D (exceptions to regulation 67B), a return is sent to HMRC under those regulations without the new employee fields being completed in respect of the employee, the employer must deduct tax on the non-cumulative basis using code 0T.

49A(2)   In paragraph (1), **"the new employee fields"** has the same meaning as in regulation 40A.

History – Reg. 49A inserted by SI 2012/822, reg. 14, with effect from 6 April 2012.

Procedure where no Form P45 and code not known: application of regulations 49C to 49E

49B(1)   Regulations 49C to 49E (procedure where no Form P45) apply if–

(a)   regulation 49A does not apply,

(b)   an employee commences employment without giving the employer Parts 2 and 3 of Form P45 and the circumstances mentioned in regulation 51(2)(b) (late presentation of Form P45) do not apply, and

(c)   a code in respect of the employee has not otherwise been issued to the employer.

49B(2)   For the purposes of paragraph (1)(c), the employer must ignore any code issued to the employer in respect of an employee's earlier employment which has ceased.

History – Reg. 49B inserted by SI 2012/822, reg. 14, with effect from 6 April 2012.

Procedure where no Form P45 and: (a) employee is not a seconded expatriate and paragraph 41(a) of Schedule A1 applies; or (b) seconded expatriate is national of EEA state

49C(1)   This regulation applies where–

(a)   the employee is not a seconded expatriate and has indicated in accordance with regulation 40A(1) (duty of employee to assist with completion of new employee fields in returns under regulations 67B and 67D) that the statement in paragraph 41(a) of Schedule A1 (real time returns) is correct, or

(b)   the employee is a seconded expatriate and has confirmed in accordance with regulation 40A(1) being a national of an EEA state.

49C(2)   On making the first relevant payment which equals or exceeds the lower earnings limit to the employee, the employer must–

(a)   prepare a deductions working sheet and enter the total payments to date, and

(b) deduct tax on the cumulative basis using the emergency code.

49C(3) On making any subsequent relevant payment before HMRC issue a code for use in respect of the employee, the employer must continue to deduct or repay tax on the cumulative basis using the emergency code.

History – Reg. 49C inserted by SI 2012/822, reg. 14, with effect from 6 April 2012.

Procedure where no Form P45 and: (a) employee is not a seconded expatriate and paragraph 41(b) of Schedule A1 applies; or (b) employee is a seconded expatriate and paragraph 43(b) or 43(c) of Schedule A1 applies

49D(1) This regulation applies where–

(a) the employee is not a seconded expatriate and has indicated in accordance with regulation 40A(1) that the statement in paragraph 41(b) of Schedule A1 is correct, or

(b) the employee is a seconded expatriate to whom regulation 49C does not apply and has indicated in accordance with regulation 40A(1) that the statement in paragraph 43(b) or 43(c) of Schedule A1 is correct.

49D(2) On making the first relevant payment which equals or exceeds the lower earnings limit to the employee, the employer must–

(a) prepare a deductions working sheet and enter the total payments to date, and

(b) deduct tax on the non-cumulative basis using the emergency code.

49D(3) On making any subsequent relevant payment before the employee's code is issued, the employer must continue to deduct or repay tax on the non-cumulative basis using the emergency code.

History – Reg. 49D inserted by SI 2012/822, reg. 14, with effect from 6 April 2012.

Procedure where no Form P45 and: (a) employee is not a seconded expatriate and paragraph 41(c) of Schedule A1 applies; or (b) employee is a seconded expatriate and paragraph 43(a) of Schedule A1 applies

49E(1) This regulation applies in any case which is not dealt with by regulation 49C or 49D.

49E(2) On making the first relevant payment to the employee, the employer must–

(a) prepare a deductions working sheet and enter both the total payments to date and the total tax to date before the first payment as nil,

(b) deduct tax on the cumulative basis using the basic rate code.

49E(3) On making any subsequent relevant payment before the employee's code is issued, the employer must continue to deduct tax on the cumulative basis using the basic rate code.

49E(4) In the case of a seconded expatriate, the emergency code must be used instead of the basic rate code mentioned in paragraphs (2)(b) and (3).

History – Reg. 49E inserted by SI 2012/822, reg. 14, with effect from 6 April 2012.

No Form P45: code treated as issued by HMRC

History – Heading to reg. 50 substituted by SI 2012/822, reg. 15, with effect from 6 April 2012.

50(1) Code 0T, the emergency code or the basic rate code used by the employer in accordance with regulations 46 to 49E is treated, for the purposes of Parts 2 to 4 (codes; deduction and repayment of tax; payments, returns and information) as having been issued by the Inland Revenue as the code for use in respect of the employee.

50(2) This does not apply for the purposes of regulation 18 (objections and appeals) and regulations 46 to 49E and 51 to 53 (late presentation of Form P45).

History – In reg. 50(1), the words "Code 0T, the" substituted for the word "The" by SI 2012/822, reg. 16(a), with effect from 6 April 2012.

In reg. 50(1), "46" substituted for "47" by SI 2012/822, reg. 16(b), with effect from 6 April 2012.

In reg. 50(1) and (2), "49E" substituted for "49" by SI 2012/822, reg. 16(c), with effect from 6 April 2012.

In reg. 50(2), the words "Form P46 procedure and", which appeared before the words "late presentation of Form P45", omitted by SI 2012/822, reg. 16(d), with effect from 6 April 2012.

Origin – Reg. 50(1): SI 1993/744, reg. 32(part) and see *Rewrite: Changes in Law* notes below.

Reg. 50(2): SI 1993/744, reg. 32(part) and see *Rewrite: Changes in Law* notes below.

Rewrite: Changes in Law – Commentary, App. 1, Change 1: reg. 50 refers to "Inland Revenue" (meaning any officer of the Board) rather than "inspector".

Commentary, App. 1, Change 47: reg. 50 treats code applied as part of P46 procedure as code issued for PAYE regulations generally.

PROCEDURE IN CASES OF RETROSPECTIVE EARNINGS: CODE TREATED AS ISSUED BY HMRC

50A(1) If–

(a)   as a result of a retrospective tax provision, a qualifying payment was made in a year (whether open or closed) to a person, and

(b)   a code has never been issued to the employer in respect of employment with whom that qualifying payment was made,

paragraph (2) applies.

50A(2) Where this paragraph applies the higher rate code applicable to the year in which the qualifying payment was made is treated, for the purposes of Parts 2 to 4 (codes, deduction and repayment of tax, payments, information and returns) as having been issued by HMRC as the code for use in respect of the employee in relation to that year.

50A(3) Paragraph (2) does not apply for the purposes of regulation 18 (objections and appeals) and regulations 46 to 49E and 51 to 53 (Form P46 procedure and late presentation of Form P45).

History – In reg. 50A(3), "49E" substituted for "49" by SI 2012/822, reg. 17, with effect from 6 April 2012.
Reg. 50A inserted by SI 2007/1077, reg. 7, with effect from 6 April 2007.

Late presentation of Form P45

51(1) This regulation applies if an employee gives Parts 2 and 3 of Form P45 to the employer after commencing employment.

51(2) If the employee gives Parts 2 and 3 of Form P45 to the employer before, as the case may be–

(a)   the employer is required to send Form P46 to HMRC under regulations 47 to 49, or

(b)   the employer is required to send the first return in relation to the employee under regulation 67B (real time returns of information about relevant payments) or 67D (exceptions to regulation 67B) to HMRC,

regulation 42 (procedure if employer receives Form P45) applies.

51(3) If the employee gives Parts 2 and 3 of Form P45 to the employer–

(a)   after, as the case may be–

     (i)   Form P46 is required to have been sent to HMRC, or

     (ii)   the employer is required to send the first return in relation to the employee under regulation 67B or 67D to HMRC,

     but

(b)   before the employee's code has been issued to the employer,

this regulation and regulation 52 (late presentation of Form P45: employer's duties) apply.

51(4) If the employee gives Parts 2 and 3 of Form P45 to the employer after the employee's code has been issued to the employer, they must be destroyed.

51(5) If Parts 2 and 3 of Form P45 show that the employment ended in the current tax year then, unless the employer has already ceased to employ the employee–

(a)   the code shown in Parts 2 and 3 of Form P45 is treated as having been issued by the Inland Revenue to the employer on the day the employee gives them to the employer, and

(b)   the employer must comply with regulation 52.

51(6) If Parts 2 and 3 of Form P45 show that the employment ended in the previous tax year and the employee gives them to the employer on or before 24th May then, unless the employer has already ceased to employ the employee–

(a)   the code shown in Parts 2 and 3 of Form P45 is treated as having been issued by the Inland Revenue to the employer on the day the employee gives them to the employer,

(b)   the employer must deduct or repay tax by reference to that code using the cumulative basis, subject to regulation 32 (higher rate code: deductions), and

(c)   the employer must comply with paragraphs (2) and (3) of regulation 52.

51(7) Parts 2 and 3 of Form P45 must be destroyed–

(a)   if they show that the employment ended in the previous tax year and the employee gives them to the employer after 24th May, or

(b)   if they show that the employment ended in an earlier tax year.

History – Reg. 51(2) substituted by SI 2012/822, reg. 18(a), with effect from 6 April 2012.

Reg. 51(3)(a) substituted by SI 2012/822, reg. 18(b), with effect from 6 April 2012.

Origin – Reg. 51(1): SI 1993/744, reg. 34(1)(part) and see *Rewrite: Changes in Law* notes below.
Reg. 51(2): SI 1993/744, reg. 34(1)(part), (2)(part) and see *Rewrite: Changes in Law* notes below.
Reg. 51(3): SI 1993/744, reg. 34(1)(part) and see *Rewrite: Changes in Law* notes below.
Reg. 51(4): see *Rewrite: Changes in Law* notes below.
Reg. 51(5): SI 1993/744, reg. 34(2)(part) and see *Rewrite: Changes in Law* notes below.
Reg. 51(6), (7): SI 1993/744, reg. 34(3)(part) and see *Rewrite: Changes in Law* notes below.

Rewrite: Changes in Law – Commentary, App. 1, Change 1: reg. 51 refers to "Inland Revenue" (meaning any officer of the Board) rather than "inspector".
Commentary, App. 1, Change 37: reg. 51 indicates that P45 is multi-part form.
Commentary, App. 1, Change 45: under reg. 51, P45 refers to date when old employment ended, rather than date when last payment was made.
Commentary, App. 1, Change 46: reg. 51 deals explicitly with cases in which P45 given to new employer relates to year before previous tax year.
Commentary, App. 1, Change 47: reg. 51 treats code taken from P45 as code issued for PAYE regulations generally.
Commentary, App. 1, Change 53: reg. 51 allows employers to use in normal way P45 received before P46 has been sent to the Revenue.
Commentary, App. 1, Change 54: reg. 51 tells employers to destroy Forms P45 handed in by new employees after Revenue have issued codes for them.
Commentary, App. 1, Change 55: reg. 51 omits SI 1993/744, reg. 34(4) (which relates to Forms P45 from 1992–93) as effectively spent.

Late presentation of Form P45: employer's duties

52(1) This regulation applies in the circumstances mentioned in regulation 51(5); and paragraphs (2) and (3) of this regulation also apply in the circumstances mentioned in regulation 51(6).

52(1A) Paragraphs (2) and (3) apply if the employer is either

(a)   a non-Real Time Information employer, or

(b)   a Real Time Information employer to whom HMRC has given a notice requiring the employer to send to HMRC Form P45 or Form P46 on the commencement of a new employee's employment.

52(2) The employer must insert in Part 3 of Form P45–

(a)   the employer's employer reference,

(b)   the date on which the new employment commenced,

(c)   any number used to identify the employee,

(d)   the employee's code in use by the employer if different from the code shown in Parts 2 and 3 of Form P45,

(e)   if Parts 2 and 3 of the Form P45 show that the cumulative basis has been used, the figure (if any) recorded in accordance with paragraph (7)(c) or (8)(c) if different from the total tax to date shown on Parts 2 and 3 of Form P45,

(f)   the employee's address,

(g)   the employee's date of birth,

(ga)   the employee's sex,

(h)   the employee's job title or description,

(i)   the employer's name, and

(j)   the employer's address.

52(3) The employer must then send Part 3 of Form P45 to the employer's Inland Revenue office.

52(4) The employer must prepare a deductions working sheet (unless the employer has already prepared one) in accordance with the following information shown in Parts 2 and 3 of Form P45–

(a)   the employee's name,

(b)   the employee's national insurance number, and

(c)   the employee's code.

52(5) The employer must record in the deductions working sheet the sum of–

(a)   the total payments to date (if any) shown in Parts 2 and 3 of Form P45, and

(b)   the relevant payments which have been made by the employer since the employment commenced which have not already been recorded in the deductions working sheet.

52(6) If Parts 2 and 3 of Form P45 show that the cumulative basis has been used, the employer must also record the following additional information in the deductions working sheet, or keep such records as enable its production.

52(7) If the code shown in Parts 2 and 3 of Form P45 is a K code, the additional information is–

(a)   the total additional pay to date,

(b)   the total taxable payments to date, and

(c)   the lower of the total tax to date as at the week or month shown in Parts 2 and 3 of Form P45 or the total net tax deducted shown in it.

52(8)   In any other case, the additional information is–

(a)   the total free pay to date,

(b)   the total taxable payments to date, and

(c)   the corresponding total tax to date as at the week or month shown in Parts 2 and 3 of Form P45.

52(9)   The employer must ascertain the amounts required by paragraphs (7)(a) and (b) and (8)(a) and (b) by reference solely to the information shown in Parts 2 and 3 of Form P45.

52(10)   If Parts 2 and 3 of Form P45 show that the cumulative basis has been used, the employer, on making any subsequent relevant payment to the employee, must deduct or repay tax by reference to the code shown in Parts 2 and 3 of Form P45 on the cumulative basis.

52(11)   For the purposes of–

(a)   paragraph (10), and

(b)   item 8 of Table 2 in regulation 36(4) (Form P45), and

(c)   regulation 55(4)(f) (Form P46(Pen)),

the total payments to date recorded in the deductions working sheet in accordance with paragraph (5) and the figure recorded in accordance with paragraph (7)(c) or (8)(c) must be treated as if they were relevant payments made to the employee by, and tax deducted by, the new employer.

52(12)   For the purposes of regulation 23(8) (cumulative basis: meaning of previous total tax to date), the figure recorded in accordance with paragraph (7)(c) or (8)(c) must be added to any actual previous total tax to date, and the total treated as the previous total tax to date when the employer next makes a relevant payment to the employee.

52(13)   If Parts 2 and 3 of Form P45 show that the non-cumulative basis has been used, on making any relevant payment to the employee, the employer must, subject to regulation 32 (higher rate code: deductions), deduct tax by reference to the code shown in Parts 2 and 3 of Form P45 on the non-cumulative basis.

History – Reg. 52(1A) inserted by SI 2012/822, reg. 19, with effect from 6 April 2012.
In reg. 52(2)(g) the words "if known," omitted by SI 2007/2969, reg. 9(a)(i), and para. (ga) inserted by reg. 9(a)(ii) with effect from 6 April 2009.
In reg. 52(11) the words "(Form P46(Pen))" substituted for "(retirement statement)" by SI 2007/2969, reg. 9(b) with effect from 6 April 2009.

Origin – Reg. 52(1): drafting.
Reg. 52(2): SI 1993/744, reg. 25(2)(part), 34(2)(part), (3)(part) and see *Rewrite: Changes in Law* notes below.
Reg. 52(3): SI 1993/744, reg. 25(2)(part), 34(2)(part), and see *Rewrite: Changes in Law* notes below.
Reg. 52(4): SI 1993/744, reg. 25(3)(part) and see *Rewrite: Changes in Law* notes below.
Reg. 52(5): SI 1993/744, reg. 25(3)(part), 34(2)(part) and see *Rewrite: Changes in Law* notes below.
Reg. 52(6): SI 1993/744, reg. 25(4)(part), (7)(part), 34(2)(part) and see *Rewrite: Changes in Law* notes below.
Reg. 52(7), (8): SI 1993/744, reg. 25(4)(part), 34(2)(part) and see *Rewrite: Changes in Law* notes below.
Reg. 52(9): SI 1993/744, reg. 25(4)(part) and see *Rewrite: Changes in Law* notes below.
Reg. 52(10), (11): SI 1993/744, reg. 25(5)(part), 34(2)(part); drafting; and see *Rewrite: Changes in Law* notes below.
Reg. 52(11), (12): SI 1993/744, reg. 25(5)(part), 34(2)(part) and see *Rewrite: Changes in Law* notes below.
Reg. 52(13): SI 1993/744, reg. 25(7)(part), 34(2)(part) and see *Rewrite: Changes in Law* notes below.

Rewrite: Changes in Law – Commentary, App. 1, Change 1: reg. 52 refers to "Inland Revenue" (meaning any officer of the Board) rather than "inspector".
Commentary, App. 1, Change 22: reg. 23 repairs missed consequential effects of introduction of K codes, so that deductions on cumulative basis are maintained or restored when employees change jobs.
Commentary, App. 1, Change 37: reg. 52 indicates that P45 is multi-part form.
Commentary, App. 1, Change 38: reg. 52 brings into line with practice the information which employers are required to provide in Form P46.
Commentary, App. 1, Change 48: reg. 52 provides that, for various purposes, new employer must take into account relevant payments made by the old employer when receiving a P45 with a code used on cumulative basis.

No Form P45: subsequent procedure on issue of employee's code

History – Heading to reg. 53 substituted by SI 2012/822, reg. 20, with effect from 6 April 2012.

53(1)   On making any relevant payment to an employee falling within regulation 47 to 49E (procedure where no Form P45) after the Inland Revenue have issued a code to the employer for use in respect of the employee, the employer must deduct or repay tax by reference to that code.

53(2)   For the purposes of paragraph (1) and regulation 66 (deductions working sheets)–

(a)   any total payments to date notified to the employer by the Inland Revenue are treated as if they represented relevant payments made by the employer; and

(b)   the total net tax deducted before the first payment made in accordance with this regulation is taken to be the sum of–

> (i)   the total net tax deducted, if any, notified to the employer by the Inland Revenue, and
>
> (ii)   any tax which the employer was liable to deduct from the employee's relevant payments under regulation 47, 48, 49, 49C, 49D or 49E.

53(3)   For the purposes of–

(a)   item 8 of Table 2 in regulation 36(4) (Form P45), and

(b)   regulation 55(4)(f) (Form P46(Pen)),

any total payments to date and total net tax deducted which are notified to the employer by the Inland Revenue must be treated as if they were relevant payments made to the employee by, and tax deducted by, the employer.

53(4)   If the employee's previous code was used on the cumulative basis, any amount notified to the employer under paragraph (2)(b)(i) must be added to the previous total tax to date for the purposes of regulation 23(8) (cumulative basis: meaning of previous total tax to date).

History – In reg. 53(1), the words "49E (procedure where no Form P45)" substituted for the words "49 (procedure in Form P46 cases)" by SI 2012/822, reg. 21(a), with effect from 6 April 2012.
In reg. 53(2)(b)(ii), ", 49, 49C, 49D or 49E" substituted for "or 49" by SI 2012/822, reg. 21(b), with effect from 6 April 2012.
In reg. 53(3) the words "(Form P46(Pen))" substituted for "(retirement statement)" by SI 2007/2969, reg. 10 with effect from 6 April 2009.

Origin – SI 1993/744, reg. 33 and see *Rewrite: Changes in Law* notes below.

Rewrite: Changes in Law – Commentary, App. 1, Change 1: reg. 53 refers to "Inland Revenue" (meaning any officer of the Board) rather than "inspector".
Commentary, App. 1, Change 22: reg. 23 repairs missed consequential effects of introduction of K codes, so that deductions on cumulative basis are maintained or restored when employees change jobs.
Commentary, App. 1, Change 48: reg. 53 provides that, for various purposes, new employer must take into account relevant payments made by the old employer when receiving a P45 with a code used on cumulative basis
Commentary, App. 1, Change 56: reg. 53 removes any doubt about Revenue issuing code to be used on non-cumulative basis after submission of P46.

Chapter 3 – New Pensioners: Forms P45 And P46(Pen)

History – Heading to Ch. 3 substituted by SI 2007/2969, reg. 11 with effect from 6 April 2009.

Scope of Chapter 3

54   This Chapter applies (instead of Chapter 2) when a pension starts and either–

(a)   the pensioner will be continuing in employment and will be receiving relevant pension payments in addition to relevant payments from their employer, or

(b)   the pensioner will not be receiving relevant payments other than relevant pension payments.

History – Reg. 54 substituted by SI 2011/729, reg. 12, with effect from 6 April 2011.

APPLICATION OF THIS CHAPTER TO REAL TIME INFORMATION PENSION PAYERS

54ZA(1)   Any requirement in this Chapter to complete (howsoever expressed) and send to HMRC Part 3 of Form P45 or Form P46(Pen) applies only to–

(a)   non-Real Time Information pension payers, and

(b)   Real Time Information pension payers to whom HMRC has given a notice requiring the pension payer to send to HMRC Form P45 or Form P46(Pen) on the commencement of a new pensioner's pension.

54ZA(2)   Paragraph (1) is without prejudice to the requirement in regulation 55(3)(b) (PAYE pension income paid by former employer) to complete and give Form P46(Pen) to the pensioner.

History – Reg. 54ZA inserted by SI 2012/822, reg. 22, with effect from 6 April 2012.

Relevant pension payments and relevant payments being received by a pensioner

54A(1)   This regulation applies if the pensioner begins to receive relevant pension payments whilst continuing to receive relevant payments from their employer.

54A(2)   On making relevant pension payments to the pensioner, the pension payer must deduct tax on the non-cumulative basis using the 0T tax code.

54A(3)   The pension payer must send to HMRC the following information in the Form P46(Pen)–

(a)   the pensioner's national insurance number, if known,

(b)   the pensioner's full name,

(c)   the pensioner's sex,

(d)   the pensioner's date of birth,

(e)   the pensioner's full address including postcode,

(f)   the date upon which the pension payments started,

(g)   the pensioner's work payroll number and the department or branch (if any) in which the pensioner is employed,

(h)   confirmation that the recipient of the relevant payments is a pensioner,

(i)   the pension payer's PAYE reference,

(j)   the pension payer's name,

(k)   the pension payer's full address including postcode, and

(l)   the tax code used in relation to the pension.

54A(4)   Before sending the Form P46(Pen), the pension payer must indicate in the form that code 0T is being used on a non-cumulative basis in respect of the pension.

History – Reg. 54A inserted by SI 2011/729, reg. 13, with effect from 6 April 2011.

Procedure in regulation 54A cases: code treated as issued by HMRC

History – Heading to reg. 54B substituted by SI 2012/822, reg. 23, with effect from 6 April 2012.

54B(1)   The 0T code used by the pension payer in accordance with regulation 54A is treated, for the purposes of Parts 2 to 4 (codes; deduction and repayment of tax; payments, returns and information), as having been issued by HMRC as the code for use in respect of the pensioner.

54B(2)   This does not apply for the purposes of regulation 18 (objections and appeals) and regulations 58, 60 and 61 late presentation of Form P45 etc).

History – In reg. 54B(2), the words "Form P46(Pen)) procedure,", which appeared before the words "late presentation of Form P45 etc", omitted by SI 2012/822, reg. 24, with effect from 6 April 2012.
Reg. 54B inserted by SI 2011/729, reg. 13, with effect from 6 April 2011.

PAYE pension income paid by former employer

55(1)   This regulation applies if the pension payer was, immediately before the pensioner's retirement, the pensioner's employer and so, in accordance with regulation 36(3), no Form P45 was completed.

55(2)   On making relevant pension payments to the pensioner, the pension payer must deduct tax on the non-cumulative basis, subject to regulation 32 (higher rate code: deductions), for the remainder of the tax year in which the pension starts or until directed otherwise by the Inland Revenue.

55(3)   Within 14 days after the pensioner's retirement, the pension payer must prepare a Form P46(Pen) and–

(a)   send it to the Inland Revenue, and

(b)   give a copy of the information to the pensioner.

55(4)   The Form P46(Pen) must contain the following information–

(a)   the pensioner's name,

(b)   the pensioner's address,

(ba)   the pensioner's date of birth,

(bb)   the pensioner's sex,

(c)   the pensioner's national insurance number, if known,

(d)   the pension payer's PAYE reference,

(e)   the date of retirement,

(f)   the total payments to date at the date of retirement,

(g)   the total payments to date relating to the employment in question at the date of retirement,

(h)   the total net tax deducted corresponding to the total payments to date relating to the employment in question,

(i)   the amount of pension payable annually,

(j)   any number used to identify the pensioner,

(k)   whether the pensioner's code is use on the cumulative basis,

(l)   the pension payer's name, and

(m)   the pension payer's address.

55(5) Paragraph (4) is subject to regulation 212 (modifications for electronic version of Form P46(Pen)).

History – In reg. 55(3), (4) and (5) the words "Form P46(Pen)" substituted for "retirement statement" by SI 2007/2969, reg. 12(a) with effect from 6 April 2009.
In reg. 55(3)(b) the words "a copy of the information" substituted for "a copy" by SI 2007/2969, reg. 12(b) with effect from 6 April 2009.
In reg. 55(4)(b) the words "if known," omitted by SI 2007/2969, reg. 12(c)(i) with effect from 6 April 2009.
Reg. 55(4)(ba) and (bb) inserted by SI 2007/2969, reg. 12(c)(ii) with effect from 6 April 2009.
In reg. 55(4)(i) the word "annually" substituted for "and the frequency of the payments" by SI 2007/2969, reg. 12(c)(iii) with effect from 6 April 2009.
In reg. 55(5) the words "delivered to Inland Revenue" omitted by SI 2007/2969, reg. 12(d) with effect from 6 April 2009.
Origin – Reg. 55(1): SI 1993/744, reg. 26(1)(part).
Reg. 55(2): SI 1993/744, reg. 17(1)(part), 26(1)(part) and drafting.
Reg. 55(3): SI 1993/744, reg. 26(1)(part), (1A)(part) and see *Rewrite: Changes in Law* notes below.
Reg. 55(4): SI 1993/744, reg. 26(2) and see *Rewrite: Changes in Law* notes below.
Reg. 55(5): drafting.
Rewrite: Changes in Law – Commentary, App. 1, Change 38: reg. 55 brings into line with practice the information which certain employers are required to provide on pensioner's retirement.
Commentary, App. 1, Change 57: reg. 55 allows retirement statements made on paper to be made other than "on the form provided".

PAYE pension income paid by other pension payer

56(1) This regulation applies if the pensioner gives Parts 2 and 3 of Form P45 to the pension payer when a pension starts.

56(2) The pension payer must insert in Part 3 of Form P45—

(a) the pensioner's address,

(b) any number used to identify the pensioner,

(c) the date on which the pension started.

(d) the pensioner's date of birth, and

(e) the pensioner's sex.

56(3) The pension payer must then send Part 3 of Form P45 to the pension payer's Inland Revenue office.

56(4) The receipt by the pension payer of Parts 2 and 3 of Form P45 under paragraph (1) is treated as the issue by the Inland Revenue of the code shown in Parts 2 and 3 of Form P45 as the code for use in respect of the pensioner.

56(5) On making relevant pension payments to the pensioner, the pension payer must, subject to regulation 32 (higher rate code: deductions), deduct or repay tax—

(a) on the non-cumulative basis, for the remainder of the tax year to which Parts 2 and 3 of Form P45 relate;

(b) on the cumulative basis, for subsequent tax years.

56(6) Paragraph (5) applies until the pension payer is directed otherwise by the Inland Revenue.

History – In reg. 56(2) the word "and" following sub-para. (b) omitted by SI 2007/2969, reg. 13(a) with effect from 6 April 2009.
Reg. 56(2)(d) and (e) inserted by SI 2007/2969, reg. 13(b) with effect from 6 April 2009.
Origin – Reg. 56(1): SI 1993/744, reg. 26(3)(part) and see *Rewrite: Changes in Law* notes below.
Reg. 56(2): SI 1993/744, reg. 25(2)(part), 26(3)(part) and see *Rewrite: Changes in Law* notes below.
Reg. 56(3): SI 1993/744, reg. 26(3)(part), (4)(part) and see *Rewrite: Changes in Law* notes below.
Reg. 56(4): see *Rewrite: Changes in Law* notes below.
Reg. 56(5): SI 1993/744, reg. 17(1)(part), 26(3)(part) and drafting.
Reg. 56(6): drafting.
Rewrite: Changes in Law – Commentary, App. 1, Change 1: reg. 56 refers to "Inland Revenue" (meaning any officer of the Board) rather than "inspector".
Commentary, App. 1, Change 37: reg. 56 indicates that P45 is multi-part form.
Commentary, App. 1, Change 47: reg. 56 treats code taken from P45 in accordance with PAYE Regulations as code issue for PAYE Regulations generally.
Commentary, App. 1, Change 58: reg. 56 omits requirement for pension payer to give pensioner who provides Form P45 copy of Part 3 of the Form.

Information to be provided in Form P46(Pen) if code not known: non UK residents
History – Heading to reg. 57 substituted by SI 2007/2969, reg. 14(a) with effect from 6 April 2009.

57(1) This regulation applies if a pension payer pays a pension, which does not arise wholly from an employment carried on abroad, to a pensioner—

(a) who is not resident in the United Kingdom,

(b) who has not given Parts 2 and 3 of Form P45 to the pension payer, and

(c) in respect of whom a code has not otherwise been issued by the Inland Revenue.

57(2) On making the first payment which exceeds the PAYE threshold, the pension payer must send to the Inland Revenue the following information in Form P46(Pen).

57(3) The information is–

(a)   the pensioner's national insurance number (if known),

(b)   the pensioner's full name,

(c)   the pensioner's sex,

(d)   the pensioner's date of birth,

(e)   the pensioner's full address including postcode,

(f)   date upon which payment of the pension started,

(g)   the pensioner's works payroll number and the department or branch (if any),

(h)   the fact that the recipient is a pensioner,

(i)   the pension payer's PAYE reference,

(j)   the pension payer's name,

(k)   the pension payer's full address, including the postcode.

57(4) For the purposes of paragraph (1)(c), the pension payer must ignore any code issued to the pension payer in respect of a previous pension of the pensioner which has ended.

History – In reg. 57(2) the words "Form P46(Pen)" substituted for "Form P46" by SI 2007/2969, reg. 14(b) with effect from 6 April 2009.
Reg. 57(3) substituted by SI 2005/2691, reg. 7(2), with effect from 6 April 2006.
Origin – Reg. 57(1): SI 1993/744, reg. 28(4)(part), (5)(part) and see *Rewrite: Changes in Law* notes below.
Reg. 57(2): SI 1993/744, reg. 28(5)(part), (5A)(part) and see *Rewrite: Changes in Law* notes below.
Reg. 57(3): SI 1993/744, reg. 28(5B) and see *Rewrite: Changes in Law* notes below.
Rewrite: Changes in Law – Commentary, App. 1, Change 1: reg. 57 refers to "Inland Revenue" (meaning any officer of the Board) rather than "inspector" or "Board".
Commentary, App. 1, Change 37: reg. 57 indicates that P45 is multi-part form.
Commentary, App. 1, Change 38: reg. 57 brings into line with practice the information which pension payer must provide on P46.
Commentary, App. 1, Change 51: reg. 57 explicitly applies P46 procedures in case in which pensioner returns to pension payer after end of previous pension.

Procedure if no Form P45 and code not known: UK pensioners
History – Heading to reg. 58 substituted by SI 2012/822, reg. 25, with effect from 6 April 2012.
Heading to reg. 58 substituted by SI 2007/2969, reg. 15(a) with effect from 6 April 2009.

58(1) This regulation applies if–

(a)   a pension payer starts to make relevant pension payments to a pensioner,

(b)   the pensioner is resident in the United Kingdom,

(c)   the pensioner does not give to the pension payer Parts 2 and 3 of Form P45, and

(d)   a code in respect of the pensioner has not otherwise been issued to the pension payer.

58(1A) This regulation does not apply where the relevant pension payment is a relevant lump sum payment.

58(2) On making any relevant pension payments to the pensioner before the Inland Revenue issue a code for use in respect of the pensioner, the pension payer must deduct tax on the non-cumulative basis applying the emergency code.

58(3) The pension payer must send the Inland Revenue the following information in Form P46(Pen).

58(4) The information is–

(a)   the pensioner's national insurance number (if known),

(b)   the pensioner's full name,

(c)   the pensioner's sex,

(d)   the pensioner's date of birth,

(e)   the pensioner's full address including postcode,

(f)   date upon which payment of the pension started,

(g)   the pensioner's works payroll number and the department or branch (if any),

(h)   the fact that the recipient is a pensioner,

(i)   the pension payer's PAYE reference,

(j)   the pension payer's name,

(k)   the pension payer's full address, including the postcode, and

(l)   the tax code used in relation to the pension.

58(5)   The pension payer must also indicate in the Form that the emergency code is being used on the non-cumulative basis.

58(6)   For the purposes of paragraph (1)(d), the pension payer must ignore any code issued to the pension payer in respect of a previous pension of the pensioner which has ended.

58(7)   In this regulation, and in regulation 58A (procedure if no Form P45 and code not known where payment is a relevant lump sum payment)(g), a "relevant lump sum payment" is–

(a)   a payment of taxable pension income under section 636B or 636C of ITEPA, or treated as such a payment, and

(b)   which is made at a time when the pension payer is not making any other payments of PAYE pension income to the pensioner under the same registered pension scheme.

History – Reg. 58(1A) inserted by SI 2013/521, reg. 12(a), with effect for the tax year 2013–14 and subsequent tax years.
In reg. 58(3) the words "Form P46(Pen)" substituted for "Form P46" by SI 2007/2969, reg. 15(b) with effect from 6 April 2009.
Reg. 58(4) substituted by SI 2005/2691, reg. 8(2), with effect from 6 April 2006.
Reg. 58(7) inserted by SI 2013/521, reg. 12(b), with effect for the tax year 2013–14 and subsequent tax years.

Origin – Reg. 58(1): SI 1993/744, reg. 28(1)(part), (4)(part) and see *Rewrite: Changes in Law* notes below.
Reg. 58(2): SI 1993/744, reg. 31(1), (3)(part), (4).
Reg. 58(3): SI 1993/744, reg. 28(1A)(part) and see *Rewrite: Changes in Law* notes below.
Reg. 58(4), (5): SI 1993/744, reg. 28(1B)(part) and see *Rewrite: Changes in Law* notes below.
Reg. 58(6): see *Rewrite: Changes in Law* notes below.

Rewrite: Changes in Law – Commentary, App.1, Change 1: reg. 58 refers to "Inland Revenue" (meaning any officer of the Board) rather than "inspector" or "Board".
Commentary, App. 1, Change 37: reg. 58 indicates that P45 is multi-part form.
Commentary, App. 1, Change 38: reg. 58 brings into line with practice the information which pension payer must provide in P46.
Commentary, para. 342, 343, App. 1, Change 50: reg. 58 simplifies conditions for P46 procedures and avoids them leading to basic rate deductions for employees with no other employment.
Commentary, App. 1, Change 51: reg. 58 explicitly applies P46 procedures in case in which pensioner returns to pension payer after end of previous pension.

Procedure if no Form P45 and code not known where payment is a relevant lump sum payment

58A(1)   This regulation applies if–

(a)   a pension payer makes a payment of a relevant lump sum payment,

(b)   the pensioner is resident in the United Kingdom,

(c)   the pensioner does not give to the pension payer Parts 2 and 3 of Form P45, and

(d)   a code in respect of the pensioner has not otherwise been issued to the pension payer.

58A(2)   On making a relevant lump sum payment to the pensioner before HMRC issue a code for use in respect of the pensioner, the pension payer must deduct tax using the basic rate code on the non-cumulative basis.

58A(3)   Where the pension payer is one to whom paragraph (6) applies on the day on which the relevant lump sum payment is made, or if that is not practicable, without unreasonable delay, the pension payer must complete Form P45 and provide–

(a)   Part 1 of Form P45 to HMRC, and

(b)   Parts 1A, 2 and 3 to the pensioner.

58A(4)   Where paragraph (6) does not apply, on the day on which the relevant lump sum payment is made, or if that is not practicable, without unreasonable delay, the pension payer must complete and provide Parts 1A, 2 and 3 of Form P45 to the pensioner.

58A(5)   The information listed in rows 1 to 6, and 10 to 16 of column 1 of Table 2 to regulation 36 must, subject to the conditions set out in column 2, be provided in the various Parts of Form P45 as indicated in columns 3 to 5, as if–

(a)   references to "employer" were to "pension payer", and

(b)   references to "employee" were to "pensioner"

58A(6)   This paragraph applies to–

(a)   a pension payer who is a non-Real Time Information pension payer, and

(b)   a Real Time Information pension payer to whom HMRC has given a notice requiring the pension payer to send to HMRC Form P45.

History – Reg. 58A inserted by SI 2013/521, reg. 13, with effect for the tax year 2013–14 and subsequent tax years.

UK resident pensioner's code treated as issued by Inland Revenue

59(1) The emergency code used by the pension payer in accordance with regulation 58 is treated, for the purposes of Parts 2 to 4 (codes; deduction and repayment of tax; payments, returns and information) as having been issued by the Inland Revenue as the code for use in respect of the pensioner.

59(2) This does not apply for the purposes of regulation 18 (objections and appeals) and regulations 58, 60 and 61 (late presentation of Form P45 etc).

History – In reg. 59(2) the words "Form P46(Pen) procedure,", which appeared before the words "late presentation of Form P45 etc", omitted by SI 2012/822, reg. 26, with effect from 6 April 2012.
In reg. 59(2) the words "Form P46(Pen)" substituted for "Form P46" by SI 2007/2969, reg. 16 with effect from 6 April 2009.
Origin – Reg. 59(1), (2): SI 1993/744, reg. 32(part) and see *Rewrite: Changes in Law* notes below.
Rewrite: Changes in Law – Commentary, App. 1, Change 1: reg. 59 refers to "Inland Revenue" (meaning any officer of the Board) rather than "inspector".
Commentary, App. 1, Change 47: reg. 59 treats code applied as part of the P46 procedure as code issued for the PAYE regulations generally.

Late presentation of Form P45

60(1) Paragraphs (2) to (6) apply if the pensioner gives Parts 2 and 3 of Form P45 to the pension payer after the pension has started but before a code has been issued.

60(2) The pension payer must insert in Part 3 of Form P45–

(a) the pensioner's address,

(b) any number used to identify the pensioner, and

(c) the date on which the pension started.

60(3) The pension payer must then send Part 3 of Form P45 to the pension payer's Inland Revenue office.

60(4) The receipt by the pension payer of Parts 2 and 3 of Form P45 under paragraph (1) is treated, except for the purposes of paragraph (1), as the issue by the Inland Revenue of the code shown in that Form as the pensioner's code.

60(5) On making relevant pension payments to the pensioner, the pension payer must, subject to regulation 32 (higher rate code: deductions), deduct or repay tax–

(a) on the non-cumulative basis, for the remainder of the tax year to which Parts 2 and 3 of Form P45 relate;

(b) on the cumulative basis, for subsequent tax years.

60(6) Paragraph (5) applies until the pension payer is directed otherwise by the Inland Revenue.

60(7) If Parts 2 and 3 of Form P45 are given to the pension payer after the pension has started and after a code has been issued by the Inland Revenue, they must be destroyed.

Origin – Reg. 60(1): SI 1993/744, reg. 34(1)(part) and see *Rewrite: Changes in Law* notes below.
Reg. 60(2), (3): SI 1993/744, reg. 25(2)(part), 34(2)(part), (3)(part) and see *Rewrite: Changes in Law* notes below.
Reg. 60(4): SI 1993/744, reg. 34(2)(part), (3)(part) and see *Rewrite: Changes in Law* notes below.
Reg. 60(5): SI 1993/744, reg. 25(5)(part), (7)(part), 34(2)(part), (3)(part); drafting; and see *Rewrite: Changes in Law* notes below.
Reg. 60(6): drafting.
Reg. 60(7): see *Rewrite: Changes in Law* notes below.
Rewrite: Changes in Law – Commentary, App. 1, Change 1: reg. 60 refers to "Inland Revenue" (meaning any officer of the Board) rather than "inspector".
Commentary, App. 1, Change 37: reg. 60 indicates that P45 is multi-part form.
Commentary, App. 1, Change 47: reg. 60 treats code taken from P45 in accordance with PAYE regulations as code issued for PAYE regulations generally.
Commentary, App. 1, Change 54: reg. 60 tells pension payer to destroy P45 handed in by new pensioner after Revenue have issued code.
Commentary, App. 1, Change 59: if pension payer receives P45 after P46 has to be submitted, reg. 60 requires pension payer to operate code in P45 on non-cumulative basis.

Subsequent procedure on issue of UK resident pensioner's code

61(1) On making any relevant pension payment to a pensioner falling within regulation 58 after the Inland Revenue have issued a code to the pension payer for use in respect of the pensioner, the pension payer must deduct or repay tax by reference to that code.

61(2) For the purposes of paragraph (1) and regulation 66 (deductions working sheets).

(a) any total payments to date notified to the pension payer by the Inland Revenue are treated as if they represented relevant pension payments made by pension payer; and

(b) the total net tax deducted before the first payment made in accordance with this regulation is taken to be the sum of–

    (i)   the total net tax deducted, if any, notified to the pension payer by the Inland Revenue, and

    (ii)   any tax which the pension payer was liable to deduct from the pensioner's relevant pension payments under regulation 58.

61(3)   For the purposes of–

(a)   item 8 of Table 2 in regulation 36(4) (Form P45), and

(b)   regulation 55(4)(f) (P46(Pen)),

any total payments to date and total net tax deducted which are which are notified to the employer by the Inland Revenue must be treated as if they were relevant pension payments made to the pensioner by, and tax deducted by, the pension payer.

61(4)   If the pensioner's previous code was used on the cumulative basis, any amount notified to the pension payer under paragraph (2)(b)(i) must be added to the previous total tax to date for the purposes of regulation 23(8) (meaning of previous total tax to date).

History – In reg. 61(3)(b) the words "(P46(Pen))" substituted for "(retirement statement)" by SI 2007/2969, reg. 17 with effect from 6 April 2009.

Origin – SI 1993/744, reg. 33(part) and see *Rewrite: Changes in Law* notes below.

Rewrite: Changes in Law – Commentary, App. 1, Change 1: reg. 61 refers to "Inland Revenue" (meaning any officer of the Board) rather than "inspector".

Commentary, para. 213–221 and App. 1, Change 22: reg. 23 repairs some missed consequential effects of the introduction of K codes so that deductions on cumulative basis are maintained or restored when employees change jobs.

Commentary, App. 1, Change 48: reg. 61 provides that new employer must take into account relevant payments made by old employer when receiving P45 with code used on cumulative basis.

Commentary, App. 1, Change 56: reg. 61 removes any doubt about Inland Revenue issuing a code to be used on non-cumulative basis after submission of P46.

Chapter 4 – Miscellaneous

Deductions in respect of notional payments

62(1)   This regulation applies if an employer makes a relevant payment which is a notional payment (including a notional payment arising by virtue of a retrospective tax provision) to an employee.

62(2)   The employer must, so far as possible, deduct tax required to be deducted in respect of a notional payment in accordance with any of the provisions listed in paragraph (3) from any relevant payment or payments which the employer actually makes to the employee at the same time as the notional payment.

62(3)   The provisions are–

regulations 22 to 25	cumulative basis
regulations 26 to 31	non-cumulative basis
regulation 32	higher rate code: deductions
regulation 37	PAYE income paid after employment ceased.
paragraphs (2) and (3) of regulation 37A	Income paid after cessation of employment becoming subject to PAYE.

62(4)   If the employer cannot deduct the full amount of tax as required by paragraph (2) from another relevant payment made at the same time as the notional payment, the employer must, so far as possible, deduct the tax from any payment or payments which the employer makes later in the same tax period.

62(5)   If the relevant payments actually made are insufficient to enable the employer to deduct the full amount of tax due in respect of notional payments, the employer must account to the Board of Inland Revenue for any amount which the employer is unable to deduct.

62(6)   Regulations 23(5) and 28(5) (deductions on cumulative or non-cumulative basis not to exceed the overriding limit) do not apply to the extent that the tax to be deducted is in respect of a notional payment.

History – In reg. 62(1) the words "(including a notional payment arising by virtue of a retrospective tax provision)" inserted by SI 2007/1077, reg. 8(2), with effect from 6 April 2007.

In reg. 62(2) the words "the provisions listed in paragraph (3)" substituted for "the following regulations" by SI 2007/1077, reg. 8(3), with effect from 6 April 2007.

In reg. 62(3), in the list, the reference to reg. 34 omitted by SI 2013/521, reg. 8, with effect from 6 April 2014.

In reg. 62(3) the words "The provisions are–" substituted for the opening words by SI 2007/1077, reg. 8(4)(a), with effect from 6 April 2007.

In the table in reg. 62(3) the entry relating to reg. 37A inserted by SI 2007/1077, reg. 8(4)(b), with effect from 6 April 2007.

Origin – Reg. 62(1): drafting.

Reg. 62(2): SI 1993/744, reg. 6(1)(part), 24(2)(part).

Reg. 62(3)–(5): new.
Reg. 62(6): SI 1993/744, reg. 14(2).

Repayment during unpaid leave

63(1) This regulation applies if–

(a) an employee is not entitled to receive any relevant payments on a normal pay day because of absence from work,

(b) the cumulative basis would have been used in relation to a payment made on that day,

(c) the employee does not fall within regulation 64(1) (absence from work due to participation in trade dispute), and

(d) the employee, or the employee's authorised representative, makes an application in person to the employer.

63(2) The employer must–

(a) comply with regulation 23 (cumulative basis: deduction and repayment) and accordingly repay any tax due to the employee, and

(b) comply with regulation 66(4) to (6) (completion of deductions working sheet),

as if the pay day were one on which relevant payments of nil had been made.

Origin – Reg. 63(1): SI 1993/744, reg. 35(1)(part), (2), (3).
Reg. 63(2): SI 1993/744, reg. 35(1)(part).

Trade disputes

64(1) This regulation applies if an employee–

(a) is absent from work because of a trade dispute at the employee's place of work, and

(b) is participating or directly interested in the trade dispute.

64(2) The employer must–

(a) on making any relevant payment, calculate the amount of tax to be deducted or repaid, and

(b) comply with paragraphs (5) to (8).

64(3) If no relevant payments are to be made on the normal pay day but the employee's code would be used on the cumulative basis if a relevant payment were made on that day, the employer must–

(a) calculate, in accordance with regulation 23 (cumulative basis: deduction and repayment) whether any tax is due to be repaid on that day as if it were a day on which relevant payments of nil had been paid, and

(b) comply with paragraphs (5) to (8).

64(4) Paragraphs (2) and (3) are subject to paragraphs (9) and (10).

64(5) The employer–

(a) must not repay any tax due to be repaid until the end of the employee's strike action, but

(b) must deduct any tax due to be deducted, less any repayment for the tax year which has not been made.

64(6) The amount of any repayment–

(a) made at the end of the employee's strike action under paragraph (5)(a), or

(b) set against tax due to be deducted under paragraph (5)(b),

must be reduced by any amount previously set off in accordance with paragraph (5)(b).

64(7) If the absence of an employee extends beyond the end of the tax year, the employer must–

(a) before 1st June following the end of the tax year, give notice to the employee of the amount of any repayment of tax for the tax year in question calculated in accordance with paragraph (2) which has not been set off against any tax due to be deducted under paragraph (5)(b); and

(b) complete the certificate which must be given under regulation 67 (Form P60) and the return which must be sent under regulation 73 (Form P35 and P14) as if that tax had been repaid to the employee.

64(8) If the employer has not made any repayment of tax withheld under paragraph (5) within 42 days after the end of the employee's strike action, the employer must instead immediately pay the tax not repaid to the Inland Revenue, and regulation 69(2) (receipt where requested) applies to that payment.

64(9) An employee from whom a repayment of tax has been withheld in accordance with paragraph (5) may request a benefit officer to certify that–

(a)   section 14 of the Jobseekers Act 1995, or

(b)   in Northern Ireland, article 16 of the Jobseekers (Northern Ireland) Order 1995,

(no allowance to those involved in trade dispute) does not disqualify the employee from receiving jobseeker's allowance, whether or not the employee is in fact entitled to receive jobseeker's allowance.

64(10)   If a benefit officer certifies in accordance with paragraph (9), the employer must make such repayment to the employee as may be due.

64(11)   In this regulation–

"**benefit officer**" means the appropriate officer.

(a)   of the Department for Work and Pensions or,

(b)   in Northern Ireland, of the Department for Social Development;

"**end of the employee's strike action**" means any of the following.

(a)   the employee is no longer absent from work because of the trade dispute,

(b)   the employer ceases to employ the employee,

(c)   the employee has become genuinely employed elsewhere in the occupation which the employee usually follows,

(d)   the employee has become regularly engaged in some other occupation, or

(e)   the employee dies;

"**jobseeker's allowance**" has the same meaning as in regulation 148;

"**place of work**" has the meaning given in section 14(4) of the Jobseekers Act 1995 or, in Northern Ireland, in article 16(4) of the Jobseekers (Northern Ireland) Order 1995.

Origin – Reg. 64(1): SI 1993/744, reg. 36(1), (2)(part).
Reg. 64(2), (3): SI 1993/744, reg. 36(2)(part).
Reg. 64(4): drafting.
Reg. 64(5), (6): SI 1993/744, reg. 36(3)(part).
Reg. 64(7): SI 1993/744, reg. 36(4) and see *Rewrite: Changes in Law* notes below.
Reg. 64(8): SI 1993/744, reg. 36(5), 42(7) and see *Rewrite: Changes in Law* notes below.
Reg. 64(9), (10): SI 1993/744, reg. 36(6)(part).
Reg. 64(11): SI 1993/744, reg. 36(3)(part), (7).

Rewrite: Changes in Law – Commentary, App. 1, Change 1: reg. 64 refers to "Inland Revenue" (meaning any officer of the Board) rather than "inspector".
Commentary, App. 1, Change 60: reg. 64 introduces time limit on issue of notices to employees concerning tax repayments not made by employers because of trade dispute, bringing legislation into line with timetable for Forms P60.

Repayment if no longer employed

65(1)   This regulation applies if, in a tax year, a person ("P")–

(a)   was employed,

(b)   is no longer employed, and

(c)   applies for a repayment of tax.

65(2)   P must give the Inland Revenue–

(a)   Parts 2 and 3 of Form P45,

(b)   either certificate A or B, depending on P's circumstances, and

(c)   such evidence of P's unemployment as the Inland Revenue may require.

65(3)   Certificate A is one which certifies that P is unemployed and, to the best of P's knowledge and belief, P–

(a)   will not be a claimant during the period starting with the date on which the application is made and ending at the end of the tax year, and

(b)   will not be employed during that period.

65(4)   Certificate B is one which certifies that P is unemployed and is not a claimant when the application is made.

65(5)   On receiving P's application, the Inland Revenue must make any repayment of tax which is appropriate, having regard to P's employee's code and the following information.

65(6)   If P gives certificate A the information is–

(a)   the total payments to date and the corresponding total tax to date as at the week or month shown in Parts 2 and 3 of Form P45 (or, if lower, the total net tax deducted shown in it),

(b)   any other relevant payments received by P in the tax year to date, and

(c)   any other payments P will receive in the tax year.

65(7)   If P does not give certificate A the information is—

(a)   the total payments to date and the corresponding total tax to date as at the week or month shown in Parts 2 and 3 of Form P45 (or, if lower, the total net tax deducted shown in it), and

(b)   any other relevant payments received by P in the tax year to date.

65(8)   For the purposes of this regulation, **"claimant"** means a person who is—

(a)   a claimant as defined by regulation 148 (jobseeker's allowance), or

(b)   a claimant in receipt of taxable benefit as defined by regulation 173 (incapacity benefit).

Origin – Reg. 65(1): SI 1993/744, reg. 37(1), (2)(part) and see *Rewrite: Changes in Law* notes below.
Reg. 65(2)–(4): SI 1993/744, reg. 37(2)(part) and see *Rewrite: Changes in Law* notes below.
Reg. 65(5)–(7): SI 1993/744, reg. 37(3)(part) and see *Rewrite: Changes in Law* notes below.
Reg. 65(8): SI 1993/744, reg. 37(2)(part), (3)(part).

Rewrite: Changes in Law – Commentary, App. 1, Change 1: reg. 65 refers to "Inland Revenue" (meaning any officer of the Board) rather than "inspector" or "Board".
Commentary, App. 1, Change 37: reg. 65 indicates that P45 is multi-part form.
Commentary, para. 406 and App. 1, Change 61: under reg. 65, Revenue need an application before making a repayment.
Commentary, App. 1, Change 62: reg. 65 clarifies period for which applicants must certify they were unemployed and not benefit claimants.
Commentary, para. 408–414 and App. 1, Change 63: reg. 65 sets out more of the information which Revenue may take into account when deciding what unemployment repayment is appropriate.

Deductions working sheets

66(1)   Paragraph (2) applies if a code has been issued to an employer in respect of an employee.

66(2)   The employer must, on making a relevant payment to the employee, prepare a deductions working sheet (unless the employer has already done so).

66(3)   The employer must record in the deductions working sheet—

(a)   the employee's name,

(b)   the employee's national insurance number, if known,

(c)   the employee's code, and

(d)   the tax year to which the deductions working sheet relates.

66(4)   The employer must record in the deductions working sheet in respect of every relevant payment which the employer makes to the employee—

(a)   the date of the payment,

(b)   the amount of the payment, and

(c)   the amount of tax, if any, deducted or repaid on making the payment, or to be deducted or accounted for under regulation 62(4) or (5) (notional payments).

66(4A)   For the purposes of paragraphs (4)(a) and (6)(a), (b), (c), and (e)(i), a relevant payment—

(a)   which comprises an amount of retrospective employment income, and

(b)   which was actually paid during a tax year which is not closed,

shall be treated, for the purpose of computing the amount of tax to be deducted, as paid at the earlier of the relevant time and the end of the last tax period in which the former employee was employed.

66(5)   If the employee's code is used on the cumulative basis, the employer must, in respect of every relevant payment which the employer makes to the employee, either—

(a)   record the following information in the deductions working sheet, or

(b)   keep such records as enable its production.

66(6)   The information is—

(a)   the total payments to date in relation to the date of payment,

(b)   the total free pay to date or, as the case may be, the total additional pay to date, in relation to that date,

(c)   the total taxable payments to date in relation to that date,

(d)   the corresponding total tax to date,

(e)   if the employee's code is a K code—

   (i)   the tax due to be deducted at that date (subject to the overriding limit),

   (ii)   the overriding limit, if any, in relation to the payment,

   (iii)   the amount of any tax not deducted at that date because of the overriding limit, and

(f)   any amount of tax which is not to be repaid because of regulation 64 (trade disputes).

66(7)   If the employee's code is not used on the cumulative basis, the employer must, in respect of every relevant payment which the employer makes to the employee, either–

(a)   record the following information in the deductions working sheet, or

(b)   keep such records as enable its production.

66(8)   The information is–

(a)   the free pay, or, as the case may be, the additional pay for the employee's code,

(b)   the taxable payments, and

(c)   if the employee's code is a K code, the tax due to be deducted and the overriding limit.

66(9)   Nothing in this regulation applies to a closed tax year (see regulation 66A).

History – Reg. 66(4A) inserted by SI 2007/1077, reg. 9(2), with effect from 6 April 2007.
Reg. 66(9) inserted by SI 2007/1077, reg. 9(3), with effect from 6 April 2007.
Origin – Reg. 66(1), (2): SI 1993/744, reg. 38(1)(part).
Reg. 66(3): SI 1993/744, reg. 38(1)(part), (2) and see *Rewrite: Changes in Law* notes below.
Reg. 66(4): SI 1993/744, reg. 17(3)(part), 38(3); SI 1994/1212, reg. 13(1), (2) and see *Rewrite: Changes in Law* notes below.
Reg. 66(5), (6): SI 1993/744, reg. 38(4)(part).
Reg. 66(7): SI 1993/744, reg. 17(3).
Reg. 66(8): SI 1993/744, reg. 17(4).
Rewrite: Changes in Law – Commentary, App. 1, Change 35: reg. 66(4)(c) provides for employer to record tax "*to be* deducted or accounted for" in respect of notional payments in the same way as tax *actually* accounted for.
Commentary, App. 1, Change 38: reg. 66 brings into line with practice the information to be provided on deductions working sheets.

DEDUCTION WORKING SHEETS: RETROSPECTIVE EMPLOYMENT INCOME IN CLOSED TAX YEAR

66A(1)   Paragraph (2) applies if–

(a)   a code has been issued to an employer in respect of an employee for a tax year which has subsequently become a closed tax year ("the relevant tax year"); and

(b)   after the end of that tax year a payment made during it to that employee becomes a qualifying payment.

66A(2)   The employer must at the relevant time–

(a)   in a case where there was a deductions working sheet for the employee for the relevant tax year, revise it to reflect the effect of the retrospective tax provision on the total PAYE income including the retrospective employment income for that year; and

(b)   in a case where there was no deductions working sheet for the employee for the relevant year, produce one showing that effect on that income for that year.

66A(3)   In a case falling within paragraph (2)(b) the employer must record in the deductions working sheet–

(a)   the employee's name,

(b)   the employee's national insurance number, if known,

(c)   the employee's final code for the relevant tax year, and

(d)   details of the relevant tax year.

66A(4)   The employer must record in the deductions working sheet in respect of every qualifying payment–

(a)   the date on which the payment is made,

(b)   the amount of the payment, and

(c)   the amount of tax, if any, to be deducted or accounted for under regulation 62(4) or (5) (notional payments).

66A(5)   Despite paragraph (4)(a), in completing the deductions working sheet, the amount of any retrospective employment income shall be treated, for the purpose of computing the amount of tax to be deducted, as if it were paid in the final tax period, in which the employee was employed, in the relevant tax year.

History – Reg. 66A inserted by SI 2007/1077, reg. 10, with effect from 6 April 2007.

Information to employees about payments and tax deducted (Form P60)

67(1)   Before 1st June following the end of the tax year, an employer must give a certificate (Form P60) to every employee–

(a)   who was in the employer's employment on the last day of the tax year, and

(b)   from whose relevant payments the employer was required to deduct tax at any time during that tax year.

67(2)   The certificate must show–

(a)   the tax year to which it relates,

(b)   the employer's PAYE reference,

(c)   the employee's name,

(d)   the employee's national insurance number, if known,

(e)   any number used by the employer to identify the employee,

(f)   the total amount of the relevant payments made by the employer to the employee during the tax year in respect of the employment in question,

(g)   the total net tax deducted in relation to those payments, subject to regulation 64(7)(b) (trade disputes),

(h)   the employee's code,

(i)   the employer's name, and

(j)   the employer's address.

67(3)   In the case of an employee taken into employment after the beginning of the tax year, the certificate must also show–

(a)   any amounts required by regulation 43(9), 52(11), 53(3) or 61(3) to be treated as relevant payments made by the employer to the employee during the tax year,

(b)   any amounts treated as tax deducted by the employer at the end of the tax year by any of those regulations,

(c)   the sum of the figures given under sub-paragraph (a) of this paragraph and paragraph (2)(f),

(d)   the sum of the figures given under sub-paragraph (b) of this paragraph and paragraph (2)(g).

Origin – Reg. 67(1): SI 1993/744, reg. 39(1).
Reg. 67(2): SI 1993/744, reg. 39(2) and see *Rewrite: Changes in Law* notes below.
Reg. 67(3): SI 1993/744, reg. 39(3) and see *Rewrite: Changes in Law* notes below.
Rewrite: Changes in Law – Commentary, App. 1, Change 38: reg. 67 brings into line with practice the information to be provided on P60.
Commentary, App. 1, Change 64: reg. 67 omits requirement for substitute P60s to show that Revenue has approved them.

REVISED INFORMATION TO EMPLOYEES ABOUT PAYMENTS AND TAX DEDUCTED (FORM P60)

67A(1)   This regulation applies where–

(a)   an enactment containing a retrospective tax provision applicable to a closed tax year is passed; and

(b)   in consequence of the passing of that enactment an employee's employment income in that closed tax year is increased.

67A(2)   Before 1st January next following the passing of the enactment–

(a)   if the employer has previously given the employee a certificate (Form P60), the employer must give the employee a revised certificate (Form P60); and

(b)   if the employer has not previously given the employee such a certificate, the employer must give the employee a copy of the revised form P14 completed in accordance with regulation 73A (amended return of relevant payments (Forms P14 and P35(RL)).

67A(3)   Paragraphs (2) and (3) of regulation 67 apply, in a case falling within paragraph (2)(a), for the purposes of this regulation as they apply for the purposes of that regulation, save that–

(a)   sub-paragraph (f) of paragraph (2) shall have effect as if for "the total amount" there were substituted "the revised total amount"; and

(b)   sub-paragraph (g) of that paragraph shall have effect as if for "total net tax" there were substituted "the revised total amount of net tax";

with references to revised amounts being construed as references to the amounts of relevant payments and net tax deducted computed after the application of the retrospective tax provision.

67A(4)   Where a revised certificate is given under this regulation–

(a)   the employer must endorse it to show that it supersedes an earlier certificate; and

(b)   the employee must not use the certificate which it supersedes.

History – Reg. 67A inserted by SI 2007/1077, reg. 11, with effect from 6 April 2007.

PART 4 – PAYMENTS, RETURNS AND INFORMATION

Chapter 1 – Payment of Tax and Associated Returns

History – Cross-heading before reg. 68 omitted, and reg. 67B to 67H and related cross-headings inserted, by SI 2012/822, reg. 27, with effect from 6 April 2012.

Cross references – FA 2009, Sch. 56: penalties for failure to make PAYE payments on time.

Other material – HMRC guidance on operating PAYE in real time is available at http://www.hmrc.gov.uk/rti/index.htm. HMRC guidance on PAYE real time information penalties, returns and payments for 2012–13 and 2013–14 is available at http://www.hmrc.gov.uk/news/payerti-payments.htm.

REAL TIME RETURNS

Real time returns of information about relevant payments

67B(1) Subject to paragraph (1A), on or before making a relevant payment to an employee, a Real Time Information employer must deliver to HMRC the information specified in Schedule A1 in accordance with this regulation unless the employer is not required by regulation 66 (deductions working sheets) to maintain a deductions working sheet for any employees.

67B(1A) But a Real Time Information employer–

(a) which for the tax year 2014–15 meets Conditions A and B, or

(b) which for the tax year 2015–16 meets Conditions A and C,

may instead for that tax year deliver to HMRC the information specified in Schedule A1 (real time returns) in respect of all relevant payments made to an employee in a tax month on or before making the last relevant payment in that month.

67B(1B) Condition A is that, at 5th April 2014, the Real Time Information employer is one to whom HMRC has issued an employer's PAYE reference.

67B(1C) Condition B is that, at 6th April 2014, the Real Time Information employer employs no more than 9 employees.

67B(1D) Condition C is that, at 6th April 2015, the Real Time Information employer employs no more than 9 employees.

67B(2) The information must be included in a return.

67B(3) Subject to paragraph (4), if relevant payments are made to more than one employee at the same time, the return under paragraph (2) must include the information required by Schedule A1 in respect of each employee to whom a relevant payment is made at that time.

67B(4) If relevant payments are made to more than one employee at the same time but the employer operates more than one payroll, the employer must make a return in respect of each payroll.

67B(5) The return is to be made using an approved method of electronic communications.

67B(6) [Omitted by SI 2013/521, reg. 18.]

67B(7) [Omitted by SI 2013/521, reg. 18.]

History – In reg. 67B(1), the words "paragraph (1A)" substituted for "paragraphs (1A) and (1B)" by SI 2014/472, reg. 4(a), with effect from 6 April 2014.

In reg. 67B(1), the words "Subject to paragraphs (1A) and (1B)," inserted by SI 2013/2300, reg. 2(a), with effect in relation to relevant payments made in the period beginning on 6 October 2013 and ending on 5 April 2014.

Reg. 67B(1A)–(1D) substituted for reg. 67B(1A) and (1B) by SI 2014/472, reg. 4(a), with effect from 6 April 2014.

Reg. 67B(1A) and (1B) inserted by SI 2013/2300, reg. 2(b), with effect in relation to relevant payments made in the period beginning on 6 October 2013 and ending on 5 April 2014.

Reg. 67B(6) and (7) omitted by SI 2013/521, reg. 18, with effect for the 2013–14 tax year and subsequent tax years. Former reg. 67B(6) and (7) read as follows:

"**67B(6)** Section 98A of TMA (special penalties in case of certain returns) applies to returns within paragraph (7).

67B(7) A return is within this paragraph if it is one of the following–

(a) a return under this regulation which relates to the relevant payments made on the final normal pay day in the tax year 2012–13 for any of the employees in respect of whom information is included in the return, or

(b) a return under this regulation which contains information about the final relevant payment made to any employee in the tax year 2012–13 where–

(i) the relevant payment is made after the employee's final normal pay day in the tax year, or

(ii) the employee is paid at irregular intervals.".

Reg. 67B inserted by SI 2012/822, reg. 27(b), with effect from 6 April 2012.

Cross references – SI 2012/822, reg. 54, 55 and 56: transitional provisions.

Employees in respect of whom employer is not required to maintain deductions working sheets

67BA(1) This regulation applies if an employer makes a relevant payment to an employee in respect of whom the employer is not required by regulation 66 (deductions working sheets) to maintain a deductions working sheet.

67BA(2)   The employer need not deliver the information required by regulation 67B(1) on or before making the payment.

67BA(3)   The employer must deliver that information no later than the end of the period of 7 days starting with the day following the day on which the payment is made.

History – Reg. 67BA inserted by SI 2013/521, reg. 19, with effect for the tax year 2013–14 and subsequent tax years.

Employees paid in specified circumstances

67BB(1)   This regulation applies if an employer makes a payment to an employee and all of the circumstances in paragraph (2) apply.

67BB(2)   The circumstances are that–

(a)   the payment includes an amount which is a relevant payment for work undertaken by the employee on–

     (i)   the day the payment is made, or

     (ii)   provided that the payment is made before the employee leaves the place of work at the end of the employee's period of work, the day before the payment is made,

(b)   in respect of the work mentioned in sub-paragraph (a), it was not reasonably practicable for the employer to calculate the payment due before the completion of the work, and

(c)   it is not reasonably practicable for the employer to deliver the information required by regulation 67B(1) on making the payment.

67BB(3)   The employer need not deliver the information required by regulation 67B(1) on or before making the payment.

67BB(4)   The employer must deliver that information no later than the end of the period of 7 days starting with the day following the day on which the payment is made.

History – Reg. 67BB inserted by SI 2013/521, reg. 19, with effect for the tax year 2013–14 and subsequent tax years.

Regulations 67BA and 67BB: supplementary

67BC   Where regulation 67BA or 67BB applies, the information required by regulation 67B(1) in respect of the relevant payment may be included in a return with the information for any other relevant payment.

History – Reg. 67BC inserted by SI 2013/521, reg. 19, with effect for the tax year 2013–14 and subsequent tax years.

Modification of the requirements of regulation 67B: notional payments

67C(1)   This regulation applies if an employer makes a relevant payment which is a notional payment (including a notional payment arising by virtue of a retrospective tax provision) to an employee.

67C(2)   If the employer is unable to comply with the requirements in regulation 67B(1) to deliver the information required by that regulation on or before making the relevant payment, the employer must instead deliver the information as soon as reasonably practicable after the payment is made and in any event no later than 14 days after the end of the tax month in which the payment is made.

History – Reg. 67C(2) substituted by SI 2013/521, reg. 20, with effect for the 2013–14 tax year and subsequent tax years. Former reg. 67C(2) read as follows:

> "**67C(2)**   If the employer is unable to comply with the requirement in regulation 67B(1) to deliver the information required by that regulation on or before making the relevant payment, the employer must instead deliver the information as soon as reasonably practicable after the payment is made and in any event no later than–
> (a)   the time at which the employer deducts tax in respect of the relevant payment in accordance with regulation 62 (deductions in respect of notional payments), or
> (b)   14 days after the end of the tax month the payment is made in, whichever is the earliest.",

Reg. 67C inserted by SI 2012/822, reg. 27(b), with effect from 6 April 2012.

Notifications of relevant payments to and by providers of certain electronic payment methods

67CA(1)   A Real Time Information employer who makes a relevant payment using an approved method of electronic communications which falls to be included in a return under regulation 67B must–

(a)   generate a reference under paragraph (3) and include it in that return,

(b)   notify the service provider that the payment is a relevant payment, and

(c)   generate a sub-reference under paragraph (3) in respect of the relevant payment and notify the service provider of that sub-reference.

67CA(2)   A service provider who receives a notification under paragraph (1)(b) must notify HMRC of the information it holds that is required for generating a reference under paragraph (3) in relation to the relevant payment.

67CA(3)   A reference and sub-reference under this paragraph is to be generated using the method specified by the Commissioners for Her Majesty's Revenue and Customs in a direction.

67CA(4)   In paragraphs (1) and (2), **"service provider"** means the provider of the approved method of electronic communications using which the payment is made.

67CA(5)   For the purposes of paragraphs (1) and (4), an **"approved method of electronic communications"** is any method of electronic communications which has been approved for the purposes of regulation 199 (large employers required to make specified payments electronically).

67CA(6)   A direction under paragraph (3) may also–

(a)   specify circumstances in which paragraphs (1) and (2) are not to apply, and

(b)   specify the form and manner of the notifications required by paragraphs (1)(b) and (c) and (2).

History – Reg. 67CA inserted by SI 2012/1895, reg. 2, with effect in relation to relevant payments (within the meaning given in reg. 4) made on and after 1 September 2012.

Cross references – HMRC Direction of 28 August 2012 made under reg. 67CA.

Exceptions to regulation 67B

67D(1)   This regulation applies to–

(a)   an individual who is a practising member of a religious society or order whose beliefs are incompatible with the use of electronic communications,

(b)   a partnership, if all the partners fall within sub-paragraph (a),

(c)   a company, if all the directors and the company secretary fall within sub-paragraph (a)

(d)   a care and support employer, and

(e)   an employer to whom a direction has been given under paragraph (11),

but this is subject to paragraph (2B).

67D(2)   A Real Time Information employer to whom this regulation applies may proceed in accordance this regulation instead of regulation 67B.

67D(2A)   Before 6th April 2014, a Real Time Information employer to whom this regulation applies may proceed as if the employer were a non-Real Time Information employer and the provisions of these Regulations apply accordingly to such an employer.

67D(2B)   This regulation does not apply if a Real Time Information employer within paragraph (1) makes a return using an approved method of electronic communications.

67D(3)   On and after 6th April 2014, a Real Time Information employer must deliver to HMRC the information specified in Schedule A1 in respect of each employee to whom relevant payments are made in a tax quarter unless the employer is not required by regulation 66 (deductions working sheets) to maintain a deductions working sheet for any employees and, for the purposes of this regulation, references in Schedule A1 to a relevant payment shall be read as if they were references to all the relevant payments made to the employee in the tax quarter.

67D(4)   The information must be included in a return.

67D(5)   The return required under paragraph (4) must be delivered within 14 days after the end of the tax quarter the return relates to.

67D(6)   If relevant payments have been made to more than one employee in the tax quarter, the return under paragraph (4) must include the information required by Schedule A1 in respect of each employee to whom a relevant payment has been made.

67D(7)   [Omitted by SI 2013/521, reg. 21(d).]

67D(8)   [Omitted by SI 2013/521, reg. 21(d).]

67D(9)   In paragraph (1)(c), **"company"** means a body corporate or unincorporated association but does not include a partnership.

67D(10)   In paragraph (1)(d), **"a care and support employer"** means an individual ("the employer") who employs a person to provide domestic or personal services at or from the employer's home where–

(a)   the services are provided to the employer or a member of the employer's family,

(b)   the recipient of the services has a physical or mental disability, or is elderly or infirm, and

(c)   it is the employer who delivers the return (and not some other person on the employer's behalf).

67D(11)   Where the Commissioners for Her Majesty's Revenue and Customs are satisfied that–

(a)   it is not reasonably practicable for an employer to make a return using an approved method of electronic communication, and

(b)   it is the employer who delivers the return (and not some other person on the employer's behalf)

they may make a direction specifying that the employer is not required to make a return using an approved method of electronic communication.

History – In reg. 67D(1)(e), the words ", but this is subject to paragraph (2B).", inserted by SI 2014/472, reg. 5(a), with effect from 6 April 2014.

Reg. 67D(1)(e) (and the ", and" before it) inserted (and the "and" after (c) omitted) by SI 2013/521, reg. 21(a), with effect for the tax year 2013–14 and subsequent tax years.

Reg. 67D(2A) inserted by SI 2013/521, reg. 21(b), with effect for the tax year 2013–14 and subsequent tax years.

Reg. 67D(2B) inserted by SI 2014/472, reg. 5(b), with effect from 6 April 2014.

In reg. 67D(3), the word "quarter" substituted for the word "month" by SI 2014/472, reg. 5(c), with effect from 6 April 2014.

In reg. 67D(3), the words "On and after 6th April 2014, a" substituted for the word "A" by SI 2013/521, reg. 21(c), with effect for the tax year 2013–14 and subsequent tax years.

In reg. 67D(5), the word "quarter" substituted for the word "month" by SI 2014/472, reg. 5(c), with effect from 6 April 2014.

In reg. 67D(6), the word "quarter" substituted for the word "month" by SI 2014/472, reg. 5(c), with effect from 6 April 2014.

Reg. 67D(7) and (8) omitted by SI 2013/521, reg. 21(d), with effect for the tax year 2013–14 and subsequent tax years. Former reg. 67D(7) and (8) read as follows:

"**67D(7)** Section 98A of TMA (special penalties in case of certain returns) applies to returns within paragraph (8).

67D(8) A return is within this paragraph if it is one of the following–

(a)   a return under this regulation which contains information about the relevant payments made on the final normal pay day in the tax year 2012–13 for any of the employees in respect of whom information is included in the return, or

(b)   a return under this regulation which contains information about the final relevant payment made to any employee in the tax year 2012–13 where–

     (i)   the relevant payment is made after the employee's final normal pay day in the tax year, or

     (ii)   the employee is paid at irregular intervals.".

Reg. 67D(11) inserted by SI 2013/521, reg. 21(e), with effect for the tax year 2013–14 and subsequent tax years.

Reg. 67D inserted by SI 2012/822, reg. 27(b), with effect from 6 April 2012.

Cross references – SI 2012/822, reg. 53, 54 and 56: transitional provisions.

Returns under regulations 67B and 67D: amendments

67E(1) This regulation applies where there is an inaccuracy in a return made under regulation 67B (real time returns of information about relevant payments) or 67D (exceptions to regulation 67B), whether careless or deliberate, and paragraph (2), (3) or (4) applies.

67E(2) This paragraph applies where the inaccuracy relates to the information given in the return in respect of an employee under paragraph 16 or 17 of Schedule A1 (real time returns).

67E(3) This paragraph applies where the inaccuracy was the omission of details of a relevant payment to an employee.

67E(4) This paragraph applies where the inaccuracy arises because, as a result of a retrospective tax provision, the total amount of the relevant payments made by an employer to an employee increases for any tax year in which the employer was a Real Time Information employer.

67E(5) Where an employer becomes aware of an inaccuracy in a return submitted under regulation 67B or 67D, the employer must provide the correct information in the next return for the tax year in question.

67E(6) But if the information has not been corrected before 20th April following the end of the tax year in question, the employer must make a return under this paragraph.

67E(7) A return under paragraph (6)–

(a)   must include the following–

     (i)   the information specified in paragraphs 2 to 4, 8 to 13, 15 and 22A of Schedule A1,

     (ii)   [omitted by SI 2013/521, reg. 22(b),]

     (iii)   the value of the adjustment to the information given under paragraphs 16 or 17 of Schedule A1 in the final return under regulation 67B or 67D containing information in respect of the employee in the tax year in question,

     (iv)   the tax code used by the employer in respect of the employee in the tax year in question and,

     (iv)   in any case where information given under paragraph 17 of Schedule A1 is corrected, the tax code operated in arriving at the value of the correction, and

     (v)   if paragraph (8) applies, the information specified in paragraphs 36 to 43 of Schedule A1,

(b)   must be made as soon as reasonably practicable after the employer becomes aware of the inaccuracy, and

(c)   must be made by an approved method of electronic communications.

67E(8) This paragraph applies if–

(a)   the inaccuracy is within paragraph (3),

(b)   the relevant payment was the first relevant payment to the employee in the employment, and

(c)   the information specified in paragraphs 36 to 43 of Schedule A1 has not otherwise been provided.

67E(9) In the application of paragraphs (6) and (7) to cases within paragraph (3), if no information was given in any returns under regulation 67B or 67D in respect of the employee in the tax year, the value of the adjustments required must be calculated as if there was a final return containing information for the employee in the year and the figure requiring adjustment was zero.

67E(10) Paragraph (7)(c) does not apply if the employer is one to whom regulation 67D applies.

History – In reg. 67E(1), the words "there is an inaccuracy in a return" substituted for the words "an employer discovers an error in a return" by SI 2014/472, reg. 6(a), with effect from 6 April 2014.
In reg. 67E(2)–(4) and (8)(a), the word "inaccuracy" substituted for the word "error" by SI 2014/472, reg. 6(b), with effect from 6 April 2014.
Reg. 67E(5) substituted by SI 2014/472, reg. 6(c), with effect from 6 April 2014.
In reg. 67E(7)(a)(i), the words "13, 15 and 22A" substituted for the words "13 and 15" by SI 2013/521, reg. 22(a), with effect for the tax year 2013–14 and subsequent tax years.
Reg. 67E(7)(a)(ii) omitted by SI 2013/521, reg. 22(b), with effect for the tax year 2013–14 and subsequent tax years.
Reg. 67E(7)(a)(iv) substituted by SI 2013/521, reg. 22(c), with effect for the tax year 2013–14 and subsequent tax years. Former reg. 67E(7)(a)(iv) read as follows:
    "(iv)   in any case where information given under paragraph 17 of Schedule A1 is corrected, the tax code operated in arriving at the value of the correction, and".
In reg. 67E(7)(a)(v) and (8)(c), "43" substituted for "44" by SI 2013/521, reg. 22(d), with effect for the tax year 2013–14 and subsequent tax years.
In reg. 67E(7)(b), the words "employer becomes aware of the inaccuracy" substituted for the words "discovery of the error" by SI 2014/472, reg. 6(d), with effect from 6 April 2014.
Reg. 67E inserted by SI 2012/822, reg. 27(b), with effect from 6 April 2012.

Failure to make a return under regulation 67B or 67D

67EA(1) This regulation applies where an employer does not make a return as required by regulation 67B (real time returns of information about relevant payments) or 67D (exceptions to regulation 67B).

67EA(2) The employer must provide the information in the next return made under regulation 67B or 67D for the tax year in question.

67EA(3) If the information has not been provided before 20th April following the end of the tax year in question, the employer must make a return under this paragraph.

67EA(4) A return under paragraph (3) must—

(a)   include the information specified in Schedule A1,

(b)   be made as soon as reasonably practicable after the discovery of the failure to make the return, and

(c)   be made using an approved method of electronic communications.

67EA(5) If a return under paragraph (3) is not made before 20th May following the end of the tax year in question section 98A of TMA 1970 (special penalties in case of certain returns) will apply to the return.

History – Reg. 67EA inserted by SI 2013/521, reg. 23, with effect for the tax year 2013–14 and subsequent tax years.

Additional information about payments

67F(1) A Real Time Information employer may send to HMRC a notification if—

(a)   for a tax period, the employer was not required to make any returns in accordance with regulation 67B or 67D because no relevant payments were made during the tax period, or

(b)   the employer has sent the final return under regulation 67B or 67D that the employer expects to make—

    (i)   in the circumstances described in paragraph 5 of Schedule A1 (real time returns), or

    (ii)   for the tax year.

67F(2) A notification under paragraph (1)(b) must—

(a)   include the information specified in paragraph 7 of Schedule A1,

(b)   be sent within 14 days of the end of final tax period of the tax year.

(c)   the notification is under paragraph (1)(b)(i), include the date on which the PAYE scheme ceased

67F(3) A notification under this regulation must—

(a)   state—

    (i)   the tax year to which it relates,

    (ii)   the employer's HMRC office number,

    (iii)   the employer's PAYE reference, and

    (iv)   the employer's accounts office reference, and

(b)   be sent using an approved method of electronic communications unless the employer is one to whom regulation 67D applies.

History – Reg. 67F(2)(c) inserted by SI 2013/521, reg. 24, with effect for the tax year 2013–14 and subsequent tax years.
Reg. 67F inserted by SI 2012/822, reg. 27(b), with effect from 6 April 2012.

PAYMENT AND RECOVERY OF TAX BY EMPLOYER

Payments to and recoveries from HMRC for each tax period by real time information employers

67G(1) For each tax period, a Real Time Information employer must pay to, or may recover from, HMRC the amount arrived at under the formula in paragraph (4).

67G(2) If the amount arrived at under the formula in paragraph (4) is a positive amount, the employer must pay the excess to HMRC.

67G(3) If the amount arrived at under the formula in paragraph (4) is a negative amount, the employer may recover that amount either–

(a)   by deducting it from the amount which the employer is liable to pay under paragraph (2) for a later period in the tax year, or

(b)   from the Commissioners for Her Majesty's Revenue and Customs.

67G(3A) Where a return for a tax period contains a correction under regulation 67E(5) (returns under regulations 67B and 67D: amendments)) and paragraph (3) of this regulation applies, the negative amount is treated as having been paid to HMRC–

(a)   17 days after the end of the tax period in respect of which that return is delivered, where payment is made using an approved method of electronic communications, or

(b)   14 days after the end of the tax period in respect of which that return is delivered, in any other case.

67G(4) The formula in this paragraph is $A - B$, where–

     A is the sum total of the relevant amounts for each of the employer's employees, and

     B is amount A for the previous tax period in the tax year, if any.

67G(5) For the purposes of paragraph (4), a **"relevant amount"** is the amount shown under paragraph 17 of Schedule A1 (real time returns) for an employee in the most recent return made in the tax year by the employer under regulation 67B (real time returns of information about relevant payments) or 67D (exceptions to regulation 67B) which contains information about that employee.

67G(5A) If the employer makes a return under regulation 67EA(3) (failure to make a return under regulation 67B or 67D) a **"relevant amount"** for the purposes of paragraph (4) is the amount shown under paragraph 17 of Schedule A1 (real time returns) for an employee in that return for the tax year to which that return relates.

67G(6) In paragraph (5) **"the most recent return"** means the return which, as at the end of the tax period, contains the most up to date information under paragraph 17 of Schedule A1 about the employee.

67G(7) This regulation is subject to regulations 67H (payments to and recoveries from HMRC for each tax period by Real Time Information employers: returns under regulation 67E(6)), 71 (modification of regulations 67G and 68 in case of trade dispute) and 75B (certificates under regulation 75A: excess payments).

History – Reg. 67G(3A) inserted by SI 2014/1017, reg. 2(a), with effect in relation to amounts which are due and payable for the tax year 2014–15 and subsequent tax years.
Reg. 67G(5A) inserted by SI 2013/521, reg. 25, with effect for the tax year 2013–14 and subsequent tax years.
Reg. 67G inserted by SI 2012/822, reg. 27(b), with effect from 6 April 2012.

Payments to and recoveries from HMRC for each tax period by Real Time Information employers: returns under regulation 67E(6)

67H(1) This regulation applies if, during any tax period, an employer makes a return under regulation 67E(6) (returns under regulations 67B and 67D: amendments) other than by virtue of regulation 67E(4).

67H(2) If the return shows an adjustment under regulation 67E(7)(a)(iii) and the value of the adjustment is a positive amount, that amount is an amount due to be paid to HMRC for the final tax period of the tax year the return relates to.

67H(3) If the return shows such an adjustment and the value of the adjustment is a negative amount, that amount is an amount due to be repaid to the employer for the final tax period of the tax year the return relates to and, the employer may recover that amount–

(a)   by setting it off against the amount the employer is liable to pay under regulation 67G for the tax period the return was made in, or

(b)   from the Commissioners for Her Majesty's Revenue and Customs.

67H(4)   Where the value of the adjustment is a negative amount, that amount is treated as having been paid to HMRC–

(a)   17 days after the end of the final tax period of the tax year the return relates to, if payment is made using an approved method of electronic communications, or

(b)   14 days after the end of the final tax period of the tax year the return relates to, in any other case.

History – Reg. 67H(2) substituted by SI 2013/521, reg. 26(a), with effect for the tax year 2013–14 and subsequent tax years. In reg. 67H(3), the words "if the return shows such an adjustment and the value of the adjustment is a negative amount, that amount is an amount due to be repaid to the employer for the final tax period of the tax year the return relates to and" substituted for the words "if the value of the adjustment required by paragraph (2) is a negative amount" by SI 2013/521, reg. 26(b), with effect for the tax year 2013–14 and subsequent tax years.
Reg. 67H(4) inserted by SI 2014/1017, reg. 2(b), with effect in relation to amounts which are due and payable for the tax year 2014–15 and subsequent tax years.
Reg. 67H inserted by SI 2012/822, reg. 27(b), with effect from 6 April 2012.

Periodic payments to and recoveries from HMRC: non-Real Time Information employers

History – Heading to reg. 68 substituted by SI 2012/822, reg. 28, with effect from 6 April 2012.

68(1)   This regulation applies to determine how much a non-Real Time Information employer must pay or can recover for a tax period.

68(2)   If A exceeds B, the employer must pay the excess to the Inland Revenue.

68(3)   But if B exceeds A, the employer may recover the excess either–

(a)   by deducting it from the amount which the employer is liable to pay under paragraph (2) for a later tax period in the tax year, or

(b)   from the Board of Inland Revenue.

68(4)   In this Regulation–

A is–

(a)   the total amount of tax which the employer was liable to deduct from relevant payments made by the employer in the tax period, plus

(b)   the total amount of tax for which the employer was liable to account in respect of notional payments made or treated by virtue of a retrospective tax provision as made, by the employer in that period under regulation 62(5) (notional payments);

B is the total amount which the employer was liable to repay in the tax period.

68(5)   Paragraphs (2) and (3) are subject to regulation 71 (modification in case of trade disputes).

68(6)   Paragraph (2) is also subject to regulation 78(11) (entitlement to set off excess payments).

68(7)   In the application of paragraph (4) to notional payments arising by reason of the coming into force of the Finance Act 2006, the reference to section 710(7A)(a) of ITEPA 2003 shall be modified as mentioned in section 94(5)(c) of the Finance Act 2006.

History – In reg. 68(1), the words "a non-Real Time Information employer" substituted for the words "an employer" by SI 2012/822, reg. 29, with effect from 6 April 2012.
In reg. 68(4)(b) the words "or treated by virtue of a retrospective tax provision as made," inserted by SI 2007/1077, reg. 12(2), with effect from 6 April 2007.
Reg. 68(7) inserted by SI 2007/1077, reg. 12(3), with effect from 6 April 2007.
Origin – Reg. 68(1): drafting.
Reg. 68(2): SI 1993/744, reg. 40(1)(part), (2)(part), 41(1)(part), (2)(part) and see *Rewrite: Changes in Law* notes below.
Reg. 68(3): SI 1993/744, reg. 42(6) and see *Rewrite: Changes in Law* notes below.
Reg. 68(4): SI 1993/744, reg. 40(2)(part), 41(2)(part), 42(6)(part); SI 1994/1212, reg. 13(5)(part), (6)(part).
Reg. 68(5): SI 1993/744, reg. 40(2)(part), 41(2)(part).
Reg. 68(6): SI 1993/744, reg. 40(1)(part), 41(1)(part).
Rewrite: Changes in Law – Commentary, App. 1, Change 1: reg. 68 refers to "Inland Revenue" (meaning any officer of the Board) rather than "inspector" or "Board".
Commentary, App. 1, Change 65: reg. 68 puts limit on employer recovering amounts due from Revenue by offset against later payments due to Revenue.
Hansard – HC Written Answer, 22 February 1984 (vol. 54, col. 543) (not reproduced): for payment which is less than an employer's full (PAYE) tax and NIC liability, collector is instructed to agree basis of apportionment.

Due date and receipts for payment of tax

69(1)   An employer must pay amounts due under regulation 67G(2), as adjusted by regulation 67H(2) where appropriate, or 68(2)–

(a)   within 17 days after the end of the tax period, where payment is made by an approved method of electronic communications, or

(b)   within 14 days after the end of the tax period, in any other case.

69(1A)   In paragraph (1), the reference to amounts due under regulation 67G(2) includes any amount the employer was liable to deduct from employees during the tax period whether or not that amount was included in any return under regulation 67B (real time returns of information about relevant payments) or 67D (exceptions to regulation 67B).

69(2)   The Inland Revenue must give a receipt to the employer for the total amount paid under regulation 67G(2), as adjusted by regulation 67H(2) where appropriate, or 68(2) if asked.

69(3)   But no separate receipt for tax only need be given if a receipt is given for the total amount of tax and any earnings-related contributions (as defined by regulation 1(2) of the SSC Regulations) paid at the same time.

69(4)   In paragraph (1) "the tax period", in relation to an amount of retrospective employment income, means the tax period immediately following the relevant time.

History – In reg. 69(1) and (2), the words ", as adjusted by regulation 67H(2) where appropriate," inserted by SI 2013/521, reg. 27, with effect for the tax year 2013–14 and subsequent tax years.
In reg. 69(1) and (2), "67G(2) or" inserted by SI 2012/822, reg. 30, with effect from 6 April 2012.
Reg. 69(1A) inserted by SI 2014/1017, reg. 2(c), with effect in relation to amounts which are due and payable for the tax year 2014–15 and subsequent tax years.
In reg. 69(3) "the SSC Regulations" substituted for "the Social Security (Contributions) Regulations 2001" by SI 2007/1077, reg. 13(2), with effect from 6 April 2007.
Reg. 69(4) inserted by SI 2007/1077, reg. 13(3), with effect from 6 April 2007.

Origin – Reg. 69(1): SI 1993/744, reg. 40(1)(part), 41(1)(part).
Reg. 69(2): SI 1993/744, reg. 42(1)(part) and see *Rewrite: Changes in Law* note below.
Reg. 69(3): SI 1993/744, reg. 2(1)("earnings related contributions"), 42(1)(part).

Cross references – Direction of the Board, 5 April 2004: direction consolidates and revokes various directions in respect of the electronic delivery of information and specifies the approved methods of electronic payments of sums due.

Rewrite: Changes in Law – Commentary, App. 1, Change 1: reg. 69 refers to "Inland Revenue" (meaning any officer of the Board) rather than "inspector" or "Board".

Circumstances in which payment of a lesser amount is to be treated as payment in full for the purposes of paragraph 6(2) of Schedule 56 to the Finance Act 2009

69A(1)   A payment that is less than the full amount due under regulation 67G(2) (payments to and recoveries from HMRC for each tax period), as adjusted by regulation 67H (payments due and recoveries from HMRC for each tax period: returns under regulation 67E(6)) where appropriate, will for the purposes of paragraph 6(2) of Schedule 56 to the Finance Act 2009 (amount of penalty: PAYE and CIS) be treated as payment of the full amount if the difference between the full amount and the amount paid is no more than £100 ("the tolerance"), but this is subject to paragraphs (2) and (3).

69A(2)   Paragraph (1) does not apply where–

(a)   the payment relates to a return which is correcting information given in a return filed in respect of a relevant payment made in an earlier tax month, and

(b)   the return is delivered after 19th April following the end of the tax year in question.

69A(3)   If the total sum paid by the employer to HMRC for the tax period includes not only the amount due under regulation 67G(2), as adjusted by regulation 67H where appropriate, but also one or more of–

(a)   any earnings-related contributions (as defined by regulation 1(2) of the SSC Regulations 2001),

(b)   any payment under regulation 7(1) of the Income Tax (Construction Industry Scheme) Regulations 2005, or

(c)   any repayment due under the Student Loans Regulations,

the tolerance is applied to the total sum paid to HMRC for the tax period to which the payments relate.

History – Reg. 69A and the heading immediately preceding it inserted by SI 2014/472, reg. 7, with effect in relation to a payment made in relation to the tax year 2014–15 and subsequent tax years.

Quarterly tax periods

70(1)   This regulation applies, so that the tax period is a tax quarter, if an employer–

(a)   has reasonable grounds for believing that the average monthly amount will be less than £1,500, and

(b)   chooses to pay tax quarterly.

70(1A)   But this regulation does not apply, so that the tax period remains a month, in respect of amounts of retrospective employment income.

70(2)   "The average monthly amount" is the average, for tax months falling within the current tax year, of the amounts found by the formula–

$$(P + N + L + S) - (SP + CD).$$

70(3)   In paragraph (2)–

P is the amount which would be payable to the Inland Revenue under regulation 67G, as adjusted by regulation 67H(2) where appropriate, or 68 but disregarding any amount payable in respect of retrospective employment income;

N is the amount which would be payable to the Inland Revenue under the SSCBA and the SSC Regulations disregarding–

(a) any amount of secondary Class 1 contributions in respect of which liability has been transferred to the employed earner by an election made jointly by the employed earner and the secondary contributor for the purposes of paragraph 3B(1) of Schedule 1 to the SSCBA (transfer of liability to be borne by earner);

(aa) any amount payable under retrospective contributions regulations (see paragraph 1(2) of Schedule 4 to the SSC Regulations) in respect of retrospective earnings (within the meaning of those Regulations);

L is the amount which would be payable to the Inland Revenue under 54(1) or, in Northern Ireland, 49(1) of the Student Loans Regulations (payment of repayments deducted to the Inland Revenue) disregarding–

(a) the reduction referred to in paragraph (3) of those regulations,

S is the amount which would be payable by the employer to the Inland Revenue under sections 559 and 559A of ICTA (deduction on account of tax etc from payments to certain sub-contractors) and regulation 8 of the Income Tax (Sub-contractors in the Construction Industry) Regulations 1993;

SP is the amount which would be payable by the employer to employees by way of statutory sick pay, statutory maternity pay, ordinary statutory paternity pay, additional statutory paternity pay and statutory adoption pay under the SSCBA; and

CD is–

(a) if the employer is a company, the amount which others would deduct from payments to it, in its position as a sub-contractor, under section 559 of ICTA (deduction on account of tax etc from payments to certain sub-contractors);

(b) in any other case, nil.

70(4) In this regulation–

"employed earner" has the same meaning as in the SSCBA;

"SSCBA" means the Social Security Contributions and Benefits Act 1992 or, in Northern Ireland, the Social Security Contribution and Benefits (Northern Ireland) Act 1992;

History – Reg. 70(1A) inserted by SI 2007/1077, reg. 14(2), with effect from 6 April 2007.
In reg. 70(2), the formula substituted by SI 2006/777, reg. 3(a), with effect from 6 April 2006.
In reg. 70(3), the words ", as adjusted by regulation 67H(2) where appropriate," inserted by SI 2013/521, reg. 28, with effect for the tax year 2013–14 and subsequent tax years.
In reg. 70(3), in the definition of "L", "54(1) or, in Northern Ireland, 49(1)" substituted for the words "39(1)" and the words "those regulations" substituted for the words "that regulation" by SI 2012/822, reg. 63, with effect from 6 April 2012.
In reg. 70(3), in the definition of "P", "67G or" inserted by SI 2012/822, reg. 31, with effect from 6 April 2012.
In reg. 70(3), in the definition of "SP", the words "ordinary statutory paternity pay, additional statutory paternity pay" substituted for the words "statutory paternity pay" by SI 2010/2496, reg. 3, with effect from 14 November 2010.
In reg. 70(3), in the definition of "P" the words "but disregarding any amount payable in respect of retrospective employment income" inserted by SI 2007/1077, reg. 14(3)(a), with effect from 6 April 2007.
In reg. 70(3), in the definition of "N" para. (aa) inserted by SI 2007/1077, reg. 14(3)(b), with effect from 6 April 2007.
In reg. 70(3), in definition of "P" the words "disregarding any WTC adjustment", in the description of "S" the words ", disregarding any WTC adjustment", in the description of "N" and "L" para. (b) and the word "and" preceding and the description of "C" omitted by SI 2006/777, reg. 3(b), with effect from 6 April 2006.
In reg. 70(4) the definitions of "SSC Regulations" and "Student Loan Regulations" omitted by SI 2008/782, reg. 5, with effect from 6 April 2008.
In reg. 70(4), the definitions of "WTC adjustment" and "WTC Regulations" omitted by SI 2006/777, reg. 3(c), with effect from 6 April 2006.
Origin – Reg. 70(1): SI 1993/744, reg. 41(1)(part), (3)(part).
Reg. 70(2): SI 1993/744, reg. 41(3)(part).
Reg. 70(3): SI 1993/744, reg. 41(3)(part) and see *Rewrite: Changes in Law* notes below.
Reg. 70(4): SI 1993/744, reg. 2(1)("employed earner"); drafting.
Rewrite: Changes in Law – Commentary, App. 1, Change 1: reg. 70 refers to "Inland Revenue" (meaning any officer of the Board) rather than "inspector" or "Board".
Commentary, para. 437 and App. 1, Change 66: definition of "S" disregards any WTC adjustment.

Modification of regulations 67G and 68 in case of trade dispute

History – In the heading to reg. 71, the words "regulations 67G and 68" substituted for the words "regulation 68" by SI 2012/822, reg. 32, with effect from 6 April 2012.

71(1) This regulation modifies the amount payable or recoverable by an employer under regulations 67G and 68 in cases where regulation 64 (trade disputes) applies–

(a)   by providing for the amount which would otherwise be payable by the employer for a tax period to be reduced by an amount of repayments ("R") that cannot be made to employees in the tax period, and

(b)   by providing–

     (i)   for amounts which would otherwise be payable in later tax periods to be increased, or

     (ii)   for amounts which would otherwise be recoverable in later tax periods to be reduced, by a total of R.

71(2)   This regulation applies for consecutive tax periods–

(a)   starting with the first tax period at the end of which there is an amount calculated as due to be repaid but which is required to be withheld by regulation 64(5) (tax to be withheld during strike action), and

(b)   ending with the next tax period at the end of which no amount is required to be withheld by that regulation.

71(3)   Column 3 of Table 3 shows the amount payable under regulation 67G(2), as adjusted by regulation 67H(2) where appropriate, or, as the case may be, 68(2) in the cases set out in column 2 for the first and subsequent tax periods.

Table 3

Modified amount payable under regulation 67G or 68

1. Tax period	2. Case	3. Amount payable
First tax period	if B equals or exceeds A	nil
First tax period	any other case	A − B, reduced by P (or by so much of P as reduces the amount payable to nil)
Subsequent tax periods	if B equals or exceeds (A + Q)	nil
Subsequent tax periods	any other case	(A + Q) − B, reduced by P (or by so much of P as reduces the amount payable to nil).

71(4)   The amount (if any) recoverable under regulation 67G, as adjusted by regulation 67H(2) where appropriate, or, as the case may be, 68(3) must be reduced to the extent that it includes amounts–

(a)   for which reduction was made under paragraph (3) in an earlier tax period, or

(b)   which are otherwise being recovered.

71(5)   In this regulation–

     A is–

     (a)   the total amount of tax which the employer was liable to deduct from relevant payments made by the employer in the tax period, plus

     (b)   the total amount of tax for which the employer was liable to account in respect of notional payments made by the employer in that period under regulation 62(5) (notional payments);

     B is the total amount which the employer is liable to repay in the tax period, not including any amounts–

     (a)   for which a reduction was made under paragraph (3) in an earlier tax period; or

     (b)   which are being recovered under paragraph (4);

     P is the total of amounts calculated as due to be repaid in the tax period but required to be withheld during that tax period by regulation 64(5);

     Q is the total of amounts–

     (a)   which, because of regulation 64(5)(b), are set off against tax due to be deducted in the tax period, and

     (b)   which also, under paragraph (3), have reduced the amount payable in an earlier tax period.

History – In reg. 71(1), the words "regulations 67G and 68" substituted for the words "regulation 68" by SI 2012/822, reg. 33(a), with effect from 6 April 2012.
In reg. 71(3), the words ", as adjusted by regulation 67H(2) where appropriate," inserted by SI 2013/521, reg. 29(a), with effect for the tax year 2013–14 and subsequent tax years.
In reg. 71(3), the words "67G(2) or, as the case may be," inserted by SI 2012/822, reg. 33(b)(i), with effect from 6 April 2012.
In reg. 71(3), in the heading to Table 3, "67G or" inserted by SI 2012/822, reg. 33(b)(ii), with effect from 6 April 2012.

In reg. 71(4), the words ", as adjusted by regulation 67H(2) where appropriate," inserted by SI 2013/521, reg. 29(b), with effect for the tax year 2013–14 and subsequent tax years.

In reg. 71(4), the words "67G or, as the case may be," inserted by SI 2012/822, reg. 33(c), with effect from 6 April 2012.

Origin – Reg. 71(1): drafting.
Reg. 71(2): SI 1993/744, reg. 40(2)(part), 41(2)(part); drafting.
Reg. 71(3): drafting.
Table 3: SI 1993/744, reg. 40(2)(part); 41(2)(part); drafting; and see *Rewrite: Changes in Law* notes below.
Reg. 71(4): SI 1993/744, reg. 42(6)(part).
Reg. 71(5): SI 1993/744, reg. 40(2)(part), 41(2)(part); SI 1994/1212, reg. 13(5)(part), (6)(part) and see *Rewrite: Changes in Law* notes below.

Rewrite: Changes in Law – Commentary: App 1, Change 67: reg. 71 provides explicitly that in "trade dispute cases" relief is given in tax period for tax actually repayable to employees before relief is available for amounts not yet repayable to employees. Commentary: App 1, Change 68: reg. 71 alters definition of "Q" (formerly "B" in SI 1993/744, reg. 40(2) and 41(2)) to prevent employer being required to repay relief in connection with trade dispute which was not actually given.

Recovery from employee of tax not deducted by employer

72(1)   This regulation applies if–

(a)   it appears to the Inland Revenue that the deductible amount exceeds the amount actually deducted, and

(b)   condition A or B is met.

72(2)   In this regulation and regulations 72A and 72B–

"the deductible amount" is the amount which an employer was liable to deduct from relevant payments made to an employee in a tax period;

"the amount actually deducted" is the amount actually deducted by the employer from relevant payments made to that employee during that tax period;

"the excess" means the amount by which the deductible amount exceeds the amount actually deducted.

72(3)   Condition A is that the employer satisfies the Inland Revenue–

(a)   that the employer took reasonable care to comply with these Regulations, and

(b)   that the failure to deduct the excess was due to an error made in good faith.

72(4)   Condition B is that the Inland Revenue are of the opinion that the employee has received relevant payments knowing that the employer wilfully failed to deduct the amount of tax which should have been deducted from those payments.

72(5)   The Inland Revenue may direct that the employer is not liable to pay the excess to the Inland Revenue.

72(5A)   Any direction under paragraph (5) must be made by notice ("the direction notice"), stating the date the notice was issued, to–

(a)   the employer and the employee if condition A is met;

(b)   the employee if condition B is met.

72(5B)   A notice need not be issued to the employee under paragraph (5A)(a) if neither the Inland Revenue nor the employer are aware of the employee's address or last known address.

72(6)   If a direction is made, the excess must not be added under regulation 185(5) or 188(3)(a) (adjustments to total net tax deducted for self-assessments and other assessments) in relation to the employee.

72(7)   If condition B is met, tax payable by an employee as a result of a direction carries interest, as if it were unpaid tax due from an employer, in accordance with section 101 of the Finance Act 2009.

72(8)   [Omitted by SI 2014/992, art. 9(3)(b).]

History – In reg. 72(2) words "regulations 72A and 72B" inserted by SI 2004/851, reg. 3(2), with effect from 12 April 2004.
Reg. 72(5A) and (5B) inserted by SI 2004/851, reg. 3(3), with effect from 12 April 2004.
In reg. 72(7), the words "section 101 of the Finance Act 2009" substituted for the words "regulation 82 (interest on tax overdue)" by SI 2014/992, art. 9(3)(a), with effect from 6 May 2014 in relation to payments which are due and payable in respect of the tax year 2014–15 and subsequent tax years.
Reg. 72(8) omitted by SI 2014/992, art. 9(3)(b), with effect from 6 May 2014 in relation to payments which are due and payable in respect of the tax year 2014–15 and subsequent tax years.

Origin – Reg. 72(1): SI 1993/744, reg. 42(2)(part), (3)(part) and see *Rewrite: Changes in Law* notes below.
Reg. 72(2): SI 1993/744, reg. 42(2)(part), (3)(part); SI 1994/1212, reg. 13(7)(part); drafting; and see *Rewrite: Changes in Law* notes below.
Reg. 72(3): SI 1993/744, reg. 42(2)(part) and see *Rewrite: Changes in Law* notes below.
Reg. 72(4): SI 1993/744, reg. 42(3)(part) and see *Rewrite: Changes in Law* notes below.
Reg. 72(5): SI 1993/744, reg. 42(2)(part), (3)(part) and see *Rewrite: Changes in Law* notes below.
Reg. 72(6): SI 1993/744, reg. 42(2)(part), (3)(part), 101(6)(part) and 101A(2)(part).
Reg. 72(7), (8): SI 1993/744, reg. 42(4)(part).

Rewrite: Changes in Law – Commentary, App. 1, Change 1: reg. 72 refers to "Inland Revenue" (meaning any officer of the Board) rather than "inspector" or "Board".

Commentary, App. 1, Change 69: reg. 72 makes it clearer that direction to recover tax from an employee must relate to tax that employer did not deduct from payments to the particular employee concerned.

Employer's request for a direction and appeal against refusal

72A(1) In relation to condition A in regulation 72(3), the employer may by notice to the Inland Revenue ("the notice of request") request that the Inland Revenue make a direction under regulation 72(5).

72A(2) The notice of request must–

(a) state–

    (i) how the employer took reasonable care to comply with these Regulations; and

    (ii) how the error resulting in the failure to deduct the excess occurred;

(b) specify the relevant payments to which the request relates;

(c) specify the employee or employees to whom those relevant payments were made; and

(d) state the excess in relation to each employee.

72A(3) The Inland Revenue may refuse the employer's request under paragraph (1) by notice to the employer ("the refusal notice") stating–

(a) the grounds for the refusal, and

(b) the date on which the refusal notice was issued.

72A(4) The employer may appeal against the refusal notice–

(a) by notice to the Inland Revenue,

(b) within 30 days of the issue of the refusal notice,

(c) specifying the grounds of the appeal.

72A(5) For the purpose of paragraph (4) the grounds of appeal are that–

(a) the employer did take reasonable care to comply with these Regulations, and

(b) the failure to deduct the excess was due to an error made in good faith.

72A(6) If on appeal under paragraph (4) that is notified to the tribunal it appears to the tribunal that the refusal notice should not have been issued the tribunal may direct that the Inland Revenue make a direction under regulation 72(5) in an amount the tribunal determines is the excess for one or more tax periods falling within the relevant tax year.

History – In reg. 72A(6), the words "that is notified to the tribunal" inserted by SI 2009/56, art. 3(2) and Sch. 2, para. 96(2), operative from 1 April 2009 subject to transitional and saving provisions in SI 2009/56, Sch. 3.
In reg. 72A(6), "tribunal" substituted for "Commissioners" by SI 2009/56, art. 3(2) and Sch. 2, para. 96(3), operative from 1 April 2009 subject to transitional and saving provisions in SI 2009/56, Sch. 3.
In reg. 72A(6), immediately before "may direct","the tribunal" substituted for "they" by SI 2009/56, art. 3(2) and Sch. 2, para. 96(4), operative from 1 April 2009 subject to transitional and saving provisions in SI 2009/56, Sch. 3.
In reg. 72A(6), the words "tribunal determines" substituted for the words "Commissioners determine" by SI 2009/56, art. 3(2) and Sch. 2, para. 96(5), operative from 1 April 2009 subject to transitional and saving provisions in SI 2009/56, Sch. 3.
Reg. 72A inserted by SI 2004/851, reg. 4, with effect from 12 April 2004.

Employee's appeal against a direction notice where Condition A is met

72B(1) An employee may appeal against a direction notice under regulation 72(5A)(a)–

(a) by notice to the Inland Revenue,

(b) within 30 days of the issue of the direction notice,

(c) specifying the grounds of the appeal

72B(2) For the purpose of paragraph (1) the grounds of appeal are that–

(a) the employer did not act in good faith,

(b) the employer did not take reasonable care, or

(c) the excess is incorrect.

72B(3) On an appeal under paragraph (1) that is notified to the tribunal, the tribunal may–

(a) if it appears that the direction notice should not have been made, set aside the direction notice; or

(b) if it appears that the excess specified in the direction notice is incorrect, increase or reduce the excess specified in the notice accordingly.

History – In reg. 72B(3), the words "that is notified to the tribunal, the tribunal" substituted for the words "the Commissioners" by SI 2009/56, art. 3(2) and Sch. 2, para. 97(2), operative from 1 April 2009 subject to transitional and saving provisions in SI 2009/56, Sch. 3.
In reg. 72B(3)(a) and (b), the words "to them", which appeared after "appears" in each place, omitted by SI 2009/56, art. 3(2) and Sch. 2, para. 97(3), operative from 1 April 2009 subject to transitional and saving provisions in SI 2009/56, Sch. 3.
Reg. 72B inserted by SI 2004/851, reg. 4, with effect from 12 April 2004.

Employee's appeal against a direction notice where Condition B is met

72C(1) An employee may appeal against a direction notice under regulation 72(5A)(b)–

(a)   by notice to the Inland Revenue,

(b)   within 30 days of the issue of the direction notice,

(c)   specifying the grounds of the appeal.

72C(2) For the purpose of paragraph (1) the grounds of appeal are that–

(a)   the employee did not receive the payments knowing that the employer wilfully failed to deduct the amount of tax which should have been deducted from those payments, or

(b)   the excess is incorrect.

72C(3) On an appeal under paragraph (1) that is notified to the tribunal, the tribunal may–

(a)   if it appears that the direction notice should not have been made, set aside the direction notice; or

(b)   if it appears that the excess specified in the direction notice is incorrect, increase or reduce the excess specified in the notice accordingly.

History – In reg. 72C(3), the words "that is notified to the tribunal, the tribunal" substituted for the words "the Commissioners" by SI 2009/56, art. 3(2) and Sch. 2, para. 98(2), operative from 1 April 2009 subject to transitional and saving provisions in SI 2009/56, Sch. 3.
In reg. 72C(3)(a) and (b), the words "to them", which appeared after "appears" in each place, omitted by SI 2009/56, art. 3(2) and Sch. 2, para. 98(3), operative from 1 April 2009 subject to transitional and saving provisions in SI 2009/56, Sch. 3.
Reg. 72C inserted by SI 2004/851, reg. 4, with effect from 12 April 2004.

Appeals: supplementary provisions

72D(1) This regulation applies to appeals under regulations 72A(4), 72B, 72C, 72G and 81A

72D(2) [Omitted by SI 2009/56, art. 3(2) and Sch. 2, para. 99(2).]

72D(3) [Omitted by SI 2009/56, art. 3(2) and Sch. 2, para. 99(2).]

72D(4) This paragraph applies if in respect of the same error by an employer in relation to condition A in regulation 72(3)–

(a)   more than one employee is appealing under regulation 72B; or

(b)   there is an appeal by an employer under regulation 72A(4) and by an employee under regulation 72B.

72D(5) [Omitted by SI 2009/56, art. 3(2) and Sch. 2, para. 99(2).]

72D(6) [Omitted by SI 2009/56, art. 3(2) and Sch. 2, para. 99(2).]

72D(7) [Omitted by SI 2009/56, art. 3(2) and Sch. 2, para. 99(2).]

72D(8) Where paragraph (4) applies or the appeal is material to the liability to tax of the employer and the employee, all the persons concerned are entitled to be parties to the appeal.

72D(9) [Omitted by SI 2009/56, art. 3(2) and Sch. 2, para. 99(2).]

History – In reg. 72D(1) the words "72C, 72G and 81A" substituted for "72C and 81A" by SI 2008/782, reg. 6, with effect from 6 April 2008.
Reg. 72D(2) omitted by SI 2009/56, art. 3(2) and Sch. 2, para. 99(2), operative from 1 April 2009 subject to transitional and saving provisions in SI 2009/56, Sch. 3. Former reg. 72D(2) read as follows:

     "**72D(2)** Subject to paragraph (4), an appeal is to the General Commissioners but the employer or employee as appropriate may elect (in accordance with section 46(1) of TMA) to bring the appeal before the Special Commissioners instead.".

Reg. 72D(3) omitted by SI 2009/56, art. 3(2) and Sch. 2, para. 99(2), operative from 1 April 2009 subject to transitional and saving provisions in SI 2009/56, Sch. 3. Former reg. 72D(3) read as follows:

     "**72D(3)** Section 31D(2) to (7) of TMA (election to bring appeal before Special Commissioners) has effect in relation to an election under paragraph (2) (as in relation to an election under subsection (1) of that section).".

In reg. 72D(4), the words "This paragraph applies if" substituted for the word "If" by SI 2009/56, art. 3(2) and Sch. 2, para. 99(3)(a), operative from 1 April 2009 subject to transitional and saving provisions in SI 2009/56, Sch. 3.
In reg. 72D(4), the words "the Commissioners who are to determine the appeals are given in paragraphs (5) to (7)", which appeared after para. (b), omitted by SI 2009/56, art. 3(2) and Sch. 2, para. 99(3)(b), operative from 1 April 2009 subject to transitional and saving provisions in SI 2009/56, Sch. 3.
Reg. 72D(5) omitted by SI 2009/56, art. 3(2) and Sch. 2, para. 99(2), operative from 1 April 2009 subject to transitional and saving provisions in SI 2009/56, Sch. 3. Former reg. 72D(5) read as follows:

     "**72D(5)** If–
     (a)   the same body of General Commissioners has jurisdiction with respect to all the persons concerned, and
     (b)   none of those persons has elected in accordance with section 46(1) of TMA to bring the appeal before the Special Commissioners

     the appeals are to be determined by that body of General Commissioners.".

Reg. 72D(6) omitted by SI 2009/56, art. 3(2) and Sch. 2, para. 99(2), operative from 1 April 2009 subject to transitional and saving provisions in SI 2009/56, Sch. 3. Former reg. 72D(6) read as follows:

     "**72D(6)** If–
     (a)   different bodies of General Commissioners have jurisdiction with respect to the persons concerned, and

(b)   none of those persons has elected in accordance with section 46(1) of TMA to bring the appeal before the Special Commissioners

the appeals are to be determined by such of those bodies as the Board of Inland Revenue determine.".

Reg. 72D(7) omitted by SI 2009/56, art. 3(2) and Sch. 2, para. 99(2), operative from 1 April 2009 subject to transitional and saving provisions in SI 2009/56, Sch. 3. Former reg. 72D(7) read as follows:

"**72D(7)**   In any other case, the appeals are to be determined by the Special Commissioners.".

Reg. 72D(8) substituted by SI 2009/56, art. 3(2) and Sch. 2, para. 99(4), operative from 1 April 2009 subject to transitional and saving provisions in SI 2009/56, Sch. 3. Former reg. 72D(8) read as follows:

"**72D(8)**   Where paragraph (4) applies or the appeal is material to the liability to tax of the employer and the employee, all the persons concerned are entitled–

(a)   to appear before and be heard by the Commissioners, or

(b)   to make representations in writing".

Reg. 72D(9) omitted by SI 2009/56, art. 3(2) and Sch. 2, para. 99(2), operative from 1 April 2009 subject to transitional and saving provisions in SI 2009/56, Sch. 3. Former reg. 72D(9) read as follows:

"**72D(9)**   On hearing an appeal the General Commissioners or the Special Commissioners may allow the employer or employee as appropriate to put forward grounds not specified in the notice, and take them into consideration, if satisfied that the omission was not wilful or unreasonable.".

Reg. 72D inserted by SI 2004/851, reg. 4, with effect from 12 April 2004.

Conditions where regulation 72F applies

72E(1)   Regulation 72F applies where–

(a)   one or more employees have received a relevant payment;

(b)   it appears to HMRC that an amount intended to represent tax on the payment–

    (i)   is likely to have been self-assessed by one or more of the employees, or

    (ii)   has not been self-assessed, but has been paid under section 59A TMA (payments on account of income tax), section 559A of ICTA (treatment of sums deducted under s. 559 (sub-contractors)) or section 62 of the Finance Act 2004 (treatment of sums deducted (sub-contractors));

(c)   any of conditions A, B and C is met;

(d)   a trigger event has occurred; and

(e)   a trigger event did not occur before 6th April 2008.

72E(2)   Condition A is that it appears to HMRC that the amount which the employer was liable to deduct–

(a)   from the relevant payment; or

(b)   in the case of a notional payment, from other relevant payments,

exceeds the amount actually deducted.

72E(3)   Condition B is that it appears to HMRC that the amount for which the employer was required to account under regulation 62(5) (notional payments) in respect of the relevant payment exceeds the amount actually accounted for.

72E(4)   Condition C is that–

(a)   tax on the relevant payment was included in a determination under regulation 80 (determination of unpaid tax and appeal against determination); and

(b)   the full amount of the determination is not paid within 30 days from the date on which the determination became final and conclusive.

72E(5)   The following are trigger events–

(a)   HMRC serve notice of a determination under regulation 80 that includes tax on the relevant payment;

(b)   HMRC receive a return under section 8 of TMA (personal return) which includes a self-assessment which includes tax on the relevant payment as tax treated as deducted;

(c)   HMRC receive–

    (i)   an amended return under section 9ZA of TMA (amendment of personal or trustee return by taxpayer), or

    (ii)   a claim under section 33 of TMA (error or mistake),

    which includes tax on the relevant payment as tax treated as deducted;

(d)   HMRC receive a letter of offer.

72E(6)   In paragraph (5)–

"**letter of offer**" means an offer in writing by the employer to agree an amount in settlement of the employer's liability to pay an amount that includes tax on the relevant payment;

"**tax treated as deducted**" has the meaning given by regulation 185(6).

72E(7) For the purposes of this regulation tax is self-assessed if–

(a)   it is included in a return under section 8 of TMA which includes a self-assessment; and

(b)   ignoring any relevant credit, the tax is or would be assessed as payable by way of income tax.

72E(8) In paragraph (7), **"relevant credit"** means–

(a)   a payment made under section 59A of TMA (payments on account of income tax) or 59B (payment of income tax and capital gains tax); or

(b)   tax deducted at source or tax treated as deducted (within the meaning given by regulation 185(6)).

History – In reg. 72E(1)(a), the words "one or more employees have" substituted for the words "an employee has" by SI 2014/472, reg. 8(a), with effect from 6 April 2014.
Reg. 72E(1)(b)(i) substituted by SI 2014/472, reg. 8(b), with effect from 6 April 2014.
Reg. 72E inserted by SI 2008/782, reg. 7, with effect from 6 April 2008.

Recovery from employee of tax that has been self-assessed etc.

72F(1) Where this regulation applies, HMRC may direct that the employer is not liable to pay an amount of tax to them.

72F(2) The direction may be in respect of one or more amounts that appear to HMRC to fall within regulation 72E(1)(b)(i) and (ii).

72F(3) A direction must be made by notice to both the employer and the employee, stating–

(a)   the date the notice was issued;

(b)   the–

    (i)   amount (or amounts) within regulation 72E(1)(b) to which it relates, or

    (ii)   employment in respect of which the relevant payment within regulation 72E(1)(a) was received and in respect of which the amount within regulation 72E(1)(b)(i) is likely to have been self-assessed, and

(c)   which of conditions A, B and C in regulation 72E have been met.

72F(4) A direction may be combined with one or more other directions relating to the same employer and may be made by issuing one notice to the employer, but each employee must be issued with a separate notice.

72F(5) A notice need not be issued to the employee if neither HMRC nor the employer are aware of the employee's address or last known address.

72F(6) The amount specified in a notice to the employee must not be added under regulation 185(5) or 188(3)(a) (adjustments to total net tax deducted for self-assessments and other assessments) in relation to the employee.

History – Reg. 72F(3)(b) substituted by SI 2014/472, reg. 9, with effect from 6 April 2014.
Reg. 72F inserted by SI 2008/782, reg. 7, with effect from 6 April 2008.

Employee's appeal against a direction notice

72G(1) An employee may appeal against a direction notice under regulation 72F–

(a)   by notice to HMRC,

(b)   within 30 days of the issue of the direction notice,

(c)   specifying the grounds of the appeal.

72G(2) For the purposes of paragraph (1) the grounds of appeal are that–

(a)   the employee did not receive a relevant payment;

(b)   the amount specified in the notice is incorrect, because all or part of it did not fall within regulation 72E(1)(b)(i) or (ii);

(c)   no trigger event within regulation 72E(5) occurred; or

(d)   a trigger event within regulation 72E(5) occurred before 6th April 2008.

72G(3) On an appeal under paragraph (1) that is notified to the tribunal, the tribunal may–

(a)   if it appears that the direction should not have been made, set aside the direction; or

(b)   if it appears that the amount specified in the notice is incorrect, increase or reduce the amount accordingly.

History – In reg. 72G(3), the words "that is notified to the tribunal, the tribunal" substituted for the words "the Commissioners" by SI 2009/56, art. 3(2) and Sch. 2, para. 100(2), operative from 1 April 2009 subject to transitional and saving provisions in SI 2009/56, Sch. 3.
In reg. 72G(3)(a) and (b), the words "to them", which appeared after "appears" in each place, omitted by SI 2009/56, art. 3(2) and Sch. 2, para. 100(3), operative from 1 April 2009 subject to transitional and saving provisions in SI 2009/56, Sch. 3.
Reg. 72G inserted by SI 2008/782, reg. 7, with effect from 6 April 2008.

ANNUAL RETURNS OF RELEVANT PAYMENTS AND TAX

Application of regulations 73 to 75

72H   Regulations 73 to 75 apply to–

(a)   non-Real Time Information employers,

(b)   Real Time Information employers in relation to tax years in which they were, for the whole of the tax year, non-Real Time Information employers, and

(c)   Real Time Information employers to whom HMRC has given a notice requiring a return under regulation 73 in respect of a tax year.

History – Reg. 72H inserted by SI 2012/822, reg. 34, with effect from 6 April 2012.

Annual return of relevant payments liable to deduction of tax (Forms P35 and P14)

73(1)   Before 20th May following the end of a tax year, an employer must deliver to the Inland Revenue a return containing the following information.

73(2)   The information is–

(a)   the tax year to which the return relates,

(b)   the total amount of the relevant payments made by the employer during the tax year to all employees in respect of whom the employer was required at any time during that year to prepare or maintain deductions working sheets, and

(c)   the total net tax deducted in relation to those payments.

73(3)   The return must be supported by the following information in respect of each of the employees mentioned in paragraph (2)(b).

73(4)   The supporting information is–

(a)   the employee's name,

(b)   the employee's address, if known,

(c)   either–

      (i)   the employee's national insurance number, or

      (ii)   if that number is not known, the employee's date of birth, if known, and sex,

(d)   the employee's code,

(e)   the tax year to which the return relates,

(f)   the total amount of the relevant payments made by the employer to the employee during that tax year, and

(g)   the total net tax deducted in relation to those payments.

73(5)   Paragraphs (2)(c) and (4)(g) are subject to regulation 64(7) (trade disputes).

73(6)   If an employee was taken into employment after the beginning of the tax year, the employer must also provide the total amounts of–

(a)   any amounts required by regulation 43(9), 52(11), 53(3) or 61(3) to be treated as relevant payments made by the employer to the employee during the tax year,

(b)   any amounts treated as tax deducted by the employer by any of those regulations,

(c)   the sum of the figures given under sub-paragraph (a) of this paragraph and paragraph (4)(f),

(d)   the sum of the figures given under sub-paragraph (b) of this paragraph and paragraph (4)(g).

73(7)   The return must include–

(a)   a statement and declaration containing a list of all deductions working sheets which the employer was required to prepare or maintain at any time during that tax year; and

(b)   a certificate showing–

      (i)   the total net tax deducted or the total net tax repaid in the case of each employee, and

      (ii)   the total net tax deducted or repaid in respect of all the employees, during that tax year.

73(8)   The statement and declaration and the certificate must be–

(a)   signed by the employer, or

(b)   if the employer is a body corporate, signed either by the secretary or by a director.

73(9)   Paragraph (8) is subject to regulation 211(5) (authentication in approved manner if return sent electronically).

73(10)   Section 98A of TMA (special penalties in case of certain returns) applies to paragraph (1).

Origin – Reg. 73(1): SI 1993/744, reg. 43(1)(part) and see *Rewrite: Changes in Law* notes below.

Reg. 73(2): SI 1993/744, reg. 43(1A)(part).
Reg. 73(3): SI 1993/744, reg. 43(1B)(part).
Reg. 73(4): SI 1993/744, reg. 43(2) and see *Rewrite: Changes in Law* notes below.
Reg. 73(5): SI 1993/744, reg. 43(1A)(part), (2)(part).
Reg. 73(6): SI 1993/744, reg. 43(1B)(part), (6).
Reg. 73(7): SI 1993/744, reg. 43(3), (3A)(part), (4)(part), (5)(part) and see *Rewrite: Changes in Law* notes below.
Reg. 73(8): SI 1993/744, reg. 43(4)(part), (5)(part), (7).
Reg. 73(9): SI 1993/744, reg. 43(3A)(part), (3B)(part).
Reg. 73(10): SI 1993/744, reg. 43(12).

Rewrite: Changes in Law – Commentary, App. 1, Change 1: reg. 73 refers to "Inland Revenue" (meaning any officer of the Board) rather than "inspector" or "Board".
Commentary, App. 1, Change 38: reg. 73 brings into line with practice the information to be provided on P35 and P14.

Amended returns of relevant payments and tax (Forms P14 and P35(RL))

73A(1) This regulation applies where, as a result of a retrospective tax provision, the total amount of the relevant payments made by an employer to employees increases for any closed tax year.

73A(2) Where this regulation applies, before 20th May following the end of the tax year in which the enactment containing the retrospective tax provision is passed, the employer must deliver to HMRC a return containing the following information.

73A(3) The information is–

(a)   the tax year to which the return relates,

(b)   the revised total amounts of the relevant payments made, or treated as made, during the tax year to all employees in respect of whom the employer was required, or has subsequently become required, to prepare or maintain deductions working sheets for any time during that year,

(c)   the total net tax deducted in respect of those payments.

73A(4) The return must be supported by the same information in respect of each of the employees mentioned in paragraph (3)(b) as is required by regulation 73(3) to support a return under that regulation.

73A(5) The return must include–

(a)   a statement and declaration containing a list of all deductions working sheets which the employer was required to prepare or maintain at any time during that year, and

(b)   a certificate showing–

> (i)   the total original net tax deducted or repaid in the case of each employee,
>
> (ii)   the revised total net tax deducted or repaid in the case of each employee;
>
> (iii)   the total original net tax deducted or repaid in respect of all the employees,
>
> (iv)   the revised total net tax deducted or repaid in respect of all the employees, and
>
> (v)   the difference between the figures given in paragraphs (iii) and (iv) above.

73A(6) The statement and declaration and the certificate must be–

(a)   signed by the employer, or

(b)   if the employer is a body corporate, signed either by the secretary or by a director.

73A(7) Section 98A of TMA (special penalties in case of certain returns) applies to a return under paragraph (2).

History – Reg. 73A inserted by SI 2007/1077, reg. 15, with effect from 6 April 2007.

Annual return of relevant payments not liable to deduction of tax (Form P38A)

74(1) Before 20th May following the end of a tax year, an employer must deliver a return to the Inland Revenue in respect of every relevant employee.

74(2) The return must contain the following information–

(a)   the employee's name,

(b)   the employee's address, if known,

(c)   the employee's national insurance number, if known,

(d)   the employee's job title or description,

(e)   the tax year to which the return relates,

(f)   the dates during which the employee was employed in the tax year, and

(g)   the total amount of the relevant payments made by the employer to the employee during the tax year.

74(3) A **"relevant employee"** is one–

(a)   to whom relevant payments exceeding the PAYE threshold were made at any time during the tax year,

(b)   who was employed for more than a week, or

(c)   who was paid more than £100 during the tax year.

74(4)   But the following are not relevant employees–

(a)   an employee included on a return under regulation 73 (Forms P35 and P14),

(b)   an employee who has indicated that statement A or statement B applies on Form P46 (see regulation 46), and to whom the employer has not made relevant payments exceeding the PAYE threshold at any time during that tax year.

History – In reg. 74(4)(b) the word "applies" substituted for the words "(or both) apply" by SI 2005/2691, reg. 9(2), with effect from 6 April 2006.

Origin – Reg. 74(1): SI 1993/744, reg. 44(1)(part), (2)(part) and see *Rewrite: Changes in Law* notes below.
Reg. 74(2): SI 1993/744, reg. 44(2).
Reg. 74(3), (4): SI 1993/744, reg. 44(1)(part) and see *Rewrite: Changes in Law* notes below.

Rewrite: Changes in Law – Commentary, App. 1, Change 1: reg. 74 refers to "Inland Revenue" (meaning any officer of the Board) rather than "inspector" or "Board".
Commentary, App. 1, Change 70: reg. 74 sets out the information required in the return of relevant payments not liable to deduction of tax, the form it must take and the time by which it is required.

Additional return in case of trade dispute

75(1)   An employer must immediately deliver an additional return to the Inland Revenue on each occasion that–

(a)   the employer has not made any repayment of tax withheld under regulation 64(5) (trade disputes) within 42 days after the end of the employee's strike action, and

(b)   a return has been made under regulation 73 which, in accordance with regulation 64(7)(b), treats that tax as if it were repaid.

75(2)   The return must contain the following information–

(a)   the tax year to which it relates,

(b)   such information as the Board of Inland Revenue may require for identifying each of the employees in question, and

(c)   the amount of tax not repaid to each of those employees.

75(3)   The return must be accompanied by a statement containing the following information–

(a)   a list of all employees in respect of whom the additional return is made,

(b)   the amount of tax not repaid to each of those employees,

(c)   the total tax not repaid by the employer to those employees for that tax year.

Origin – Reg. 75(1): SI 1993/744, reg. 45(1)(part), (2).
Reg. 75(2): SI 1993/744, reg. 45(1)(part), (3).
Reg. 75(3): SI 1993/744, reg. 45(1)(part), (4).

FAILURE TO ACCOUNT FOR DEDUCTIBLE TAX

Power of HMRC to issue a notice and certificate in cases where regulation 67B or 67D returns are not made, etc

75A(1)   This regulation applies if, 17 days or more after the end of a tax period, condition A or B or C is met.

75A(2)   Condition A is that a Real Time Information employer

(a)   has not paid to HMRC any tax for that tax period,

(b)   has not made any returns under regulation 67B (real time returns of information about relevant payments) or 67D (exceptions to regulation 67B) in respect of the tax period, and

(c)   has not sent HMRC a notification under regulation 67F(1)(a) (additional information about payments),

and HMRC are not satisfied that no relevant payments have been made in the tax period.

75A(3)   Condition B is that–

(a)   a Real Time Information employer has paid an amount of tax for that tax period, whether or not the amount is the amount due under regulation 67G (payments to and recoveries from HMRC for each tax period by Real Time Information employers), as adjusted by regulation 67H(2) where appropriate, but

(b)   HMRC are not satisfied, after seeking the employer's explanation, that the amount due under regulation 67G, as adjusted by regulation 67H(2) where appropriate is the amount which would have been due had any tax returned under regulation 67B or 67D as deducted from each of the employer's employees during the period been the amount that the employer was liable to deduct.

75A(4) Condition C is that a Real Time Information employer has not paid to HMRC the amount of tax due under regulation 67G, as adjusted by regulation 67H(2) where appropriate.

75A(5) HMRC, on consideration of the matters specified in paragraph (6), may–

(a) specify to the best of their judgment, the amount of tax, or a combined amount, they consider the employer is liable to pay, and

(b) serve notice on the employer requiring payment of that amount within 7 days of the issue of the notice ("the notice period").

75A(6) The matters specified in this paragraph are–

(a) the employer's record of past payments, whether of tax or combined amounts,

(b) any returns made by the employer under regulation 67B or 67D in respect of the tax period,

(c) any returns made by the employer under regulation 67B or 67D in respect of earlier tax periods,

(d) any returns made by the employer under regulation 67E(6),

(e) any returns made by the employer under regulation 73 (annual return of relevant payments liable to deduction of tax (Forms P35 and P14)) in relation to previous tax years.

75A(7) If the notice extends to two or more consecutive tax periods in a tax year, this regulation has effect as if they were the latest period specified in the notice.

75A(8) If, during the notice period, the employer–

(a) claims that the amount paid in respect of the tax period specified in the notice represents the full amount of tax the employer was liable to deduct from each of the employer's employees during the period, but

(b) does not satisfy HMRC that this is the case,

the employer may require HMRC to inspect the employer's PAYE records as if the employer had been required to produce those records under Schedule 36 to the Finance Act 2008 (information and inspection powers).

75A(9) If there is an inspection by virtue of paragraph (8), the notice given by HMRC under paragraph (5) must be disregarded.

75A(10) If the amount specified in the notice, or any part of it, is not paid during the notice period–

(a) the amount unpaid is treated as an amount of tax or as including an amount of tax which the employer was liable to pay for that tax period under regulation 67G, where appropriate, and

(b) HMRC may prepare a certificate showing how much of that amount remains unpaid.

75A(11) Regulation 218 deals with the use of certificates as evidence that sums are due and unpaid.

History – In reg. 75A(3)(a), the words "as adjusted for regulation 67H(2) where appropriate," inserted by SI 2013/521, reg. 30(a)(i), with effect for the tax year 2013–14 and subsequent tax years.
In reg. 75A(3)(b), the words ", as adjusted by regulation 67H(2) where appropriate" inserted by SI 2013/521, reg. 30(a)(ii), with effect for the tax year 2013–14 and subsequent tax years.
In reg. 75A(4), the words ", as adjusted by regulation 67H(2) where appropriate," inserted by SI 2013/521, reg. 30(b), with effect for the tax year 2013–14 and subsequent tax years.
In reg. 75A(10)(a), the words ", where appropriate" inserted by SI 2013/521, reg. 30(c), with effect for the tax year 2013–14 and subsequent tax years.
Reg. 75A inserted by SI 2012/822, reg. 35, with effect from 6 April 2012.

Certificates under regulation 75A: excess payments

75B(1) This regulation applies if, as a consequence of paying a certified amount of tax under regulation 75A in relation to the tax year, the total amount of tax paid to HMRC for the tax year under these Regulations by an employer exceeds the amount which would have been paid had it not been necessary for HMRC to prepare the certificate.

75B(2) The employer is entitled to set off the excess tax against any amount which the employer is liable to pay under regulation 67G, as adjusted by regulation 67H(2) where appropriate, for any subsequent tax period or, if the tax year in question has ended, the excess of tax paid may be repaid.

History – In heading to reg. 75B, the word "regulation" substituted for the word "regulations" by SI 2013/521, reg. 31(a), with effect for the tax year 2013–14 and subsequent tax years.
In reg. 75B, the words ", as adjusted by regulation 67H(2) where appropriate," inserted by SI 2013/521, reg. 31(b), with effect for the tax year 2013–14 and subsequent tax years.
Reg. 75B inserted by SI 2012/822, reg. 35, with effect from 6 April 2012.

Certificate if tax in regulation 73 return is unpaid

76(1) Paragraph (2) applies if an employer–

(a)   delivers a return under regulation 73 showing an amount of total net tax deducted by the employer for a tax year, and

(b)   does not pay that amount to the Inland Revenue before 20th April following the end of the tax year.

76(2)   The Inland Revenue may prepare a certificate showing how much of that amount remains unpaid.

76(3)   Regulation 218 deals with the use of certificates as evidence that sums are due and unpaid.

Origin – Reg. 76(1), (2): SI 1993/744, reg. 43(8)(part) and see *Rewrite: Changes in Law* note below.
Reg. 76(3): drafting.

Rewrite: Changes in Law – Commentary, App. 1, Change 1: reg. 76 refers to "Inland Revenue" (meaning any officer of the Board) rather than "inspector" or "Board".

Return and certificate if tax may be unpaid: amounts due under regulation 68

History – In the heading to reg. 77, the words "; amounts due under regulation 68" inserted by SI 2012/822, reg. 36, with effect from 6 April 2012.

77(1)   This regulation applies if, 17 days or more after the end of a tax period, condition A or B is met.

77(2)   Condition A is that–

(a)   an employer has not paid any tax under regulation 68 for that tax period, and

(b)   the Inland Revenue are unaware of the amount (if any) which the employer is liable to pay.

77(3)   Condition B is that–

(a)   an employer has paid an amount of tax under regulation 68 for that period, but

(b)   the Inland Revenue are not satisfied that it is the full amount which the employer is liable to pay for that period.

77(4)   The Inland Revenue may give notice to the employer requiring the employer within 14 days of the issue of the notice to deliver a return showing the amount of tax which the employer is liable to pay under regulation 68 in respect of the tax period.

77(5)   If the notice extends to two or more consecutive tax periods in a tax year, this regulation has effect as if they were one tax period.

77(6)   On receiving a return made by the employer under paragraph (4), the Inland Revenue may prepare a certificate showing the amount of tax which the employer is liable to pay for the tax period and how much (if any) of that amount remains unpaid.

77(7)   Regulation 218 deals with the use of certificates as evidence that sums are due and unpaid.

Origin – Reg. 77(1): SI 1993/744, reg. 47(1)(part).
Reg. 77(2): SI 1993/744, reg. 47(1)(part) and see *Rewrite: Changes in Law* notes below.
Reg. 77(3): SI 1993/744, reg. 47(4) and see *Rewrite: Changes in Law* notes below.
Reg. 77(4): SI 1993/744, reg. 47(2)(part) and see *Rewrite: Changes in Law* notes below.
Reg. 77(5): SI 1993/744, reg. 47(3) and see *Rewrite: Changes in Law* notes below.
Reg. 77(6): SI 1993/744, reg. 47(5), 54(6)(part) and see *Rewrite: Changes in Law* notes below.
Reg. 77(7): drafting.

Rewrite: Changes in Law – Commentary, App. 1, Change 1: reg. 77 refers to "Inland Revenue" (meaning any officer of the Board) rather than "inspector" or "Board".
Commentary, App. 1, Change 71: reg. 77 makes explicit the date on which the period begins for return to be delivered.
Commentary, App. 1, Change 72: reg. 77(5) limits the treatment of consecutive tax periods as a single tax period; such treatment applies only for the purpose of reg. 77 and consecutive tax periods must fall within the same tax year.

Notice and certificate if tax may be unpaid: amounts due under regulation 68

History – In the heading to reg. 78, the words "; amounts due under regulation 68" inserted by SI 2012/822, reg. 37, with effect from 6 April 2012.

78(1)   This regulation applies if, 17 days or more after the end of a tax period, condition A or B is met.

78(2)   Condition A is that–

(a)   an employer has not paid any tax under regulation 68 for that tax period, and

(b)   HMRC have reason to believe that the employer is liable to pay an amount of tax.

78(3)   Condition B is that–

(a)   an employer has paid an amount of tax under regulation 68 for that tax period, but

(b)   HMRC are not satisfied, after seeking the employer's explanation, that it is the full amount which the employer is liable to pay for that period.

78(4)   HMRC, on consideration of the employer's record of past payments whether of tax or of combined amounts, may–

(a)   specify, to the best of their judgment, the amount of tax or a combined amount which they consider the employer is liable to pay, and

(b) serve notice on the employer requiring payment of that amount within 7 days of the issue of the notice ("the notice period").

78(5) If the notice extends to two or more consecutive tax periods in a tax year, this regulation has effect as if they were the latest tax period specified in the notice.

78(6) If, during the notice period, the employer–

(a) claims that any payment made in respect of the tax period specified in the notice is or includes the full amount of tax the employer is liable to pay, but

(b) does not satisfy HMRC that this is the case,

the employer may require HMRC to inspect the employer's PAYE records as if the employer had been required to produce those records under Schedule 36 to the Finance Act 2008 (information and inspection powers).

78(7) If there is an inspection by virtue of paragraph (6) the notice given by HMRC under paragraph (4) must be disregarded.

78(8) If the amount specified in the notice, or any part of it, is not paid during the notice period–

(a) the amount unpaid is treated as an amount of tax or as including an amount of tax which the employer was liable to pay for that tax period under regulation 68, and

(b) HMRC may prepare a certificate showing how much of that amount remains unpaid.

78(9) But paragraph (8) does not apply if during the notice period–

(a) the employer pays the full amount of tax which the employer is liable to pay under regulation 68 for that tax period, or

(b) the employer satisfies HMRC that no amount, or no further amount, is due for that tax period.

78(10) Paragraph (11) applies if the employer pays an amount of tax, whether separately or as part of a combined amount, which is certified under this regulation and which exceeds the amount the employer would have been liable to pay in respect of that tax period apart from this regulation.

78(11) The employer is entitled to set off the excess tax against any amount which the employer is liable to pay under regulation 68 for any subsequent tax period in the tax year.

78(12) Paragraph (13) applies if the employer–

(a) delivers the return required by regulation 73(1) after the end of the tax year, and

(b) pays the total net tax which the employer is liable to pay.

78(13) Any excess of tax paid, and not otherwise recovered by set-off in accordance with this regulation, must be repaid.

78(14) Regulation 218 deals with the use of certificates as evidence that sums are due and unpaid.

History – In reg. 78(2)(b) "HMRC" substituted for "the Inland Revenue" by SI 2008/782, reg. 8, with effect from 6 April 2008.
In reg. 78(3)(b) "HMRC" substituted for "the Inland Revenue" by SI 2008/782, reg. 8, with effect from 6 April 2008.
In reg. 78(4) "HMRC" substituted for "The Inland Revenue" by SI 2008/782, reg. 8, with effect from 6 April 2008.
In reg. 78(4) "whether of tax or of combined amounts" inserted by SI 2008/782, reg. 8, with effect from 6 April 2008.
In reg. 78(4)(a) "or a combined amount" inserted by SI 2008/782, reg. 8, with effect from 6 April 2008.
In reg. 78(6)(a) "or includes" and "of tax" inserted by SI 2008/782, reg. 8, with effect from 6 April 2008.
In reg. 78(6), the words "under Schedule 36 to the Finance Act 2008 (information and inspection powers)" substituted for the words "in accordance with regulation 97 (inspection of employer's PAYE records)" by SI 2009/588, reg. 4(a), with effect from 1 April 2009.
In reg. 78(6) "HMRC" substituted for "the Inland Revenue" in each place by SI 2008/782, reg. 8, with effect from 6 April 2008.
In reg. 78(7), the words ", regulation 97 applies to that inspection and", which appeared after the words "by virtue of paragraph (6)", omitted by SI 2009/588, reg. 4(b), with effect from 1 April 2009.
In reg. 78(7) "HMRC" substituted for "the Inland Revenue" in each place by SI 2008/782, reg. 8, with effect from 6 April 2008.
In reg. 78(8) the words "of tax" omitted from the first line by SI 2008/782, reg. 8, with effect from 6 April 2008.
In reg. 78(8)(a) the words "or as including an amount of tax" omitted by SI 2008/782, reg. 8, with effect from 6 April 2008.
In reg. 78(8)(b) "HMRC" substituted for "the Inland Revenue" by SI 2008/782, reg. 8, with effect from 6 April 2008.
In reg. 78(8)(b) the word "amount" substituted for "tax" by SI 2008/782, reg. 8, with effect from 6 April 2008.
In reg. 78(9)(b) "HMRC" substituted for "the Inland Revenue" by SI 2008/782, reg. 8, with effect from 6 April 2008.
In reg. 78(10) the words "of tax, whether separately or as part of a combined amount, which is" inserted and "and" inserted after the words "certified under this regulation" by SI 2008/782, reg. 8, with effect from 6 April 2008.
In reg. 78(11) the word "and" inserted after the words "set off the excess" by SI 2008/782, reg. 8, with effect from 6 April 2008.

Origin – Reg. 78(1): SI 1993/744, reg. 48(1)(part).
Reg. 78(2): SI 1993/744, reg. 48(1)(part) and see *Rewrite: Changes in Law* notes below.
Reg. 78(3): SI 1993/744, reg. 48(4)(part) and see *Rewrite: Changes in Law* notes below.
Reg. 78(4): SI 1993/744, reg. 48(2), (6)(part) and see *Rewrite: Changes in Law* notes below.
Reg. 78(5): SI 1993/744, reg. 48(3) and see *Rewrite: Changes in Law* notes below.
Reg. 78(6), (7): SI 1993/744, reg. 48(5)(part) and see *Rewrite: Changes in Law* notes below.
Reg. 78(8): SI 1993/744, reg. 48(6)(part) and see *Rewrite: Changes in Law* notes below.
Reg. 78(9): SI 1993/744, reg. 48(7) and see *Rewrite: Changes in Law* notes below.
Reg. 78(10), (11): SI 1993/744, reg. 48(11)(part) and see *Rewrite: Changes in Law* notes below.
Reg. 78(12), (13): SI 1993/744, reg. 48(12)(part).
Reg. 78(14): drafting.

Rewrite: Changes in Law – Commentary, App. 1, Change 1: reg. 78 refers to "Inland Revenue" (meaning any officer of the Board) rather than "inspector" or "Board".
Commentary, App. 1, Change 71: reg. 78(4)(b) makes explicit the date on which the period begins for employer to pay tax.
Commentary, App. 1, Change 72: reg. 78(5) limits the treatment of consecutive periods as a single tax period; such treatment only applies for the sake of 78(5) and consecutive tax periods must fall within the same tax year.
Commentary, App. 1, Change 73: notice under reg. 78 may cover consecutive tax periods even if an amount has been paid for any of those periods.

Certificate after inspection of PAYE records

79(1) This regulation applies if there is an inspection of an employer's PAYE records under Schedule 36 to the Finance Act 2008 (information and inspection powers).

79(2) The Inland Revenue may, by reference to the information obtained from the inspection, prepare a certificate showing–

(a)   the amount of tax which it appears that the employer is liable to pay for the tax years or tax periods covered by the inspection; and

(b)   any amount of that tax which remains unpaid.

79(3) Regulation 218 deals with the use of certificates as evidence that sums are due and unpaid.

History – In reg. 79(1), the words "Schedule 36 to the Finance Act 2008 (information and inspection powers)" substituted for the words "regulation 97" by SI 2009/588, reg. 5, with effect from 1 April 2009.

Origin – Reg. 79(1): drafting.
Reg. 79(2): SI 1993/744, reg. 55(8)(part) and see *Rewrite: Changes in Law* notes below.
Reg. 79(3): drafting.

Rewrite: Changes in Law – Commentary, App. 1, Change 1: reg. 79 refers to "Inland Revenue" (meaning any officer of the Board) rather than "inspector" or "Board".

Determination of unpaid tax and appeal against determination

80(1) This regulation applies if it appears to HMRC that there may be tax payable for a tax year under regulation 67G, as adjusted by regulation 67H(2) where appropriate, or 68 by an employer which has neither been–

(a)   paid to HMRC, nor

(b)   certified by HMRC under regulation 75A, 76, 77, 78 or 79.

80(1A) In paragraph (1), the reference to tax payable for a tax year under regulation 67G includes a reference to any amount the employer was liable to deduct from employees during the tax year whether or not that amount was included in any return under regulation 67B (real time returns of information about relevant payments) or 67D (exceptions to regulation 67B).

80(2) HMRC may determine the amount of that tax to the best of their judgment, and serve notice of their determination on the employer.

80(3) A determination under this regulation must not include tax in respect of which a direction under regulation 72(5) has been made; and directions under that regulation do not apply to tax determined under this regulation.

80(3A) A determination under this regulation must not include tax in respect of which a direction under regulation 72F has been made.

80(4) A determination under this regulation may–

(a)   cover the tax payable by the employer under regulation 67G, as adjusted by regulation 67H(2) where appropriate, or 68 for any one or more tax periods in a tax year, and

(b)   extend to the whole of that tax, or to such part of it as is payable in respect of–

     (i)   a class or classes of employees specified in the notice of determination (without naming the individual employees), or

     (ii)   one or more named employees specified in the notice.

80(5) A determination under this regulation is subject to Parts 4, 5, 5A and 6 of TMA (assessment, appeals, collection and recovery) as if–

(a)   the determination were an assessment, and

(b)   the amount of tax determined were income tax charged on the employer,

and those Parts of that Act apply accordingly with any necessary modifications.

80(6) [Omitted by SI 2009/56, art. 3(2) and Sch. 2, para. 101(3).]

History – In reg. 80(1), the words ", as adjusted by regulation 67H(2) where appropriate," inserted by SI 2013/521, reg. 32, with effect for the tax year 2013–14 and subsequent tax years.
In reg. 80(1), the words "67G or" and "75A," inserted by SI 2012/822, reg. 38(a), with effect from 6 April 2012.
In reg. 80(1) "HMRC" substituted for each iteration of "the Inland Revenue" by SI 2008/782, reg. 9, with effect from 6 April 2008.
Reg. 80(1A) inserted by SI 2012/822, reg. 38(b), with effect from 6 April 2012.
In reg. 80(2) "HMRC" substituted for "The Inland Revenue" in each place by SI 2008/782, reg. 9, with effect from 6 April 2008.

Reg. 80(3A) inserted by SI 2008/782, reg. 9, with effect from 6 April 2008.

In reg. 80(4)(a), the words ", as adjusted by regulation 67H(2) where appropriate," inserted by SI 2013/521, reg. 32, with effect for the tax year 2013–14 and subsequent tax years.

In reg. 80(4), the words "67G or" inserted by SI 2012/822, reg. 38(c), with effect from 6 April 2012.

In reg. 80(5), ", 5A" inserted by SI 2010/668, reg. 3, with effect in relation to the tax year 2010–11 and subsequent tax years.

In reg. 80(5), the words "(other than section 55)", which appeared after "Parts 4, 5", omitted by SI 2009/56, art. 3(2) and Sch. 2, para. 101(2), operative from 1 April 2009 subject to transitional and saving provisions in SI 2009/56, Sch. 3.

Reg. 80(6) omitted by SI 2009/56, art. 3(2) and Sch. 2, para. 101(3), operative from 1 April 2009 subject to transitional and saving provisions in SI 2009/56, Sch. 3. Former reg. 80(6) read as follows:

"**80(6)** For the purposes of paragraph 3(1)(a) of Schedule 3 to TMA (rules for assigning proceedings to General Commissioners), the relevant place for an appeal against a determination under this regulation is the place where the determination was made.".

Origin – Reg. 80(1): SI 1993/744, reg. 49(1) and see *Rewrite: Changes in Law* note below.

Reg. 80(2): SI 1993/744, reg. 49(2) and see *Rewrite: Change in Law* note below.

Reg. 80(3): SI 1993/744, reg. 49(3).

Reg. 80(4): SI 1993/744, reg. 49(4).

Reg. 80(5): SI 1993/744, reg. 49(7).

Reg. 80(6): SI 1993/744, reg. 49(8).

Rewrite: Changes in Law – Commentary, App. 1, Change 1: reg. 80 refers to "Inland Revenue" (meaning any officer of the Board) rather than "inspector" or "Board".

HMRC Manuals – Employer Compliance Handbook ECH 20002: employer compliance officer may make formal determination if settlement cannot be negotiated.

Employee liability if tax unpaid after regulation 80 determination

81(1) This regulation applies if–

(a)   any part of the tax determined under regulation 80 is not paid within 30 days from the date on which the determination became final and conclusive, and

(b)   condition A or B is met in relation to an employee.

81(2) Condition A is that the Inland Revenue are of the opinion that the employee in respect of whose relevant payments the determination was made has received those payments knowing that the employer has wilfully failed to deduct the amount of tax which should have been deducted from those payments.

81(3) Condition B is that the unpaid tax represents an amount for which the employer was required to account under regulation 62(5) (notional payments) in relation to a notional payment to the employee.

81(4) The Inland Revenue may direct that the employer is not liable to pay the amount of tax which appears to them should have been but was not–

(a)   deducted on making those relevant payments, or

(b)   accounted for under regulation 62(5).

81(4A) If condition A or B is met, any direction under paragraph (4) must be made by notice ("the direction notice") to the employee stating the date the notice was issued.

81(5) If a direction is made, the amount of tax must not be added under regulation 185(5) or 188(3)(a) (adjustments for self-assessments and other assessments) in relation to the employee.

81(6) Tax payable by an employee as a result of a direction carries interest, as if it were unpaid tax due from an employer, in accordance with section 101 of the Finance Act 2009.

81(7) [Omitted by SI 2014/992, art. 9(4)(b).]

History – Reg. 81(4A) inserted by SI 2004/851, reg. 5, with effect from 12 April 2004.

In reg. 81(6), the words "section 101 of the Finance Act 2009" substituted for the words "regulation 82 (interest on tax overdue)" by SI 2014/992, art. 9(4)(a), with effect from 6 May 2014 in relation to payments which are due and payable in respect of the tax year 2014–15 and subsequent tax years.

Reg. 81(7) omitted by SI 2014/992, art. 9(4)(b), with effect from 6 May 2014 in relation to payments which are due and payable in respect of the tax year 2014–15 and subsequent tax years.

Origin – Reg. 81(1): SI 1993/744, reg. 49(5)(part).

Reg. 81(2): SI 1993/744, reg. 49(5) and see *Rewrite: Changes in Law* notes below.

Reg. 81(3): SI 1993/744, reg. 49(5)(part), SI 1994/1212, reg. 13(7)(part) and see *Rewrite: Changes in Law* notes below.

Reg. 81(4): SI 1993/744, reg. 49(5)(part), SI 1994/1212, reg. 13(7)(part) and see *Rewrite: Changes in Law* notes below.

Reg. 81(5): SI 1993/744, reg. 49(5)(part), 101(6)(part) and 101A(2)(part).

Reg. 81(6), (7): SI 1993/744, reg. 49(6)(part).

Rewrite: Changes in Law – Commentary, App. 1, Change 1: reg. 81 refers to "Inland Revenue" (meaning any officer of the Board) rather than "inspector" or "Board".

Commentary, App. 1, Change 35: reg. 81 refers to tax in respect of notional payments.

EMPLOYEE'S APPEAL AGAINST DIRECTION NOTICE

81A(1) An employee may appeal against a direction notice under regulation 81(4A)–

(a)   by notice to the Inland Revenue,

(b)   within 30 days of the issue of the direction notice,

(c)   specifying the grounds of the appeal.

81A(2) For the purpose of paragraph (1) the grounds of appeal are that–

(a)   in relation to condition A in regulation 81, the employee did not receive the payments knowing that the employer wilfully failed to deduct the amount of tax which should have been deducted from those payments,

(b)   in relation to condition B in regulation 81, the relevant payment was not a notional payment, or

(c)   the excess is incorrect.

81A(3)   On an appeal under paragraph (1) that is notified to the tribunal, the tribunal may–

(a)   if it appears that the direction notice should not have been made, set aside the notice; or

(b)   if it appears that the amount of tax specified in the direction notice is incorrect, increase or reduce the amount specified in the notice accordingly.

81A(4)   Regulation 72D applies to appeals under this regulation.

History – In reg. 81A(3), the words "that is notified to the tribunal, the tribunal" substituted for the words "the Commissioners" by SI 2009/56, art. 3(2) and Sch. 2, para. 102(2), operative from 1 April 2009 subject to transitional and saving provisions in SI 2009/56, Sch. 3.
In reg. 81A(3)(a) and (b), the words "to them", which appeared after "appears" in each place, omitted by SI 2009/56, art. 3(2) and Sch. 2, para. 102(3), operative from 1 April 2009 subject to transitional and saving provisions in SI 2009/56, Sch. 3.
Reg. 81A inserted by SI 2004/851, reg. 6, with effect from 12 April 2004.

INTEREST

Interest on tax overdue

82   [Omitted by SI 2014/992, art. 9(5).]

History – Reg. 82 omitted by SI 2014/992, art. 9(5), with effect from 6 May 2014 in relation to payments which are due and payable in respect of the tax year 2014–15 and subsequent tax years.
In former reg. 82(1) "HMRC" substituted for "the Inland Revenue" by SI 2008/782, reg. 10, with effect from 6 April 2008.
In former reg. 82(4) "regulation 72(5), 72F" substituted for "regulation 72(5)" by SI 2008/782, reg. 10, with effect from 6 April 2008.
In former reg. 82(6)(a), the words ", as adjusted by regulation 67H(2) where appropriate," inserted by SI 2013/521, reg. 33, with effect for the tax year 2013–14 and subsequent tax years.
In former reg. 82(6), the words "67G or" and "67G(3)(b) or" inserted by SI 2012/822, reg. 39, with effect from 6 April 2012.
In former reg. 82(8) the words "Except where tax is due in respect of a closed tax year by virtue of a retrospective tax provision," inserted by SI 2007/1077, reg. 16(2), with effect from 6 April 2007.
Former reg. 82(9) inserted by SI 2007/1077, reg. 16(3), with effect from 6 April 2007.
Origin – Former reg. 82(1): SI 1993/744, reg. 51(1)(part); SI 1994/1212, reg. 13(5)(part) and (6)(part) and see *Rewrite: Changes in Law* notes below.
Former reg. 82(2): SI 1993/744, reg. 51(1)(part).
Former reg. 82(3): SI 1993/744, reg. 52(2)(part).
Former reg. 82(4): SI 1993/744, reg. 52(2)(part) and see *Rewrite: Changes in Law* notes below.
Former reg. 82(5): SI 1993/744, reg. 51(1)(part).
Former reg. 82(6): SI 1993/744, reg. 51(1)(part); SI 1994/1212, reg. 13(5)(part) and (6)(part); and see *Rewrite: Changes in Law* notes below.
Former reg. 82(7): SI 1993/744, reg. 52(1).
Former reg. 82(8): SI 1993/744, reg. 51(3).
Cross references – SI 1989/1297: rate applicable under FA 1989, s. 178.
Direction of the Board, 5 April 2004: direction consolidates and revokes various directions in respect of the electronic delivery of information and specifies the approved methods of electronic payments of sums due.
Rewrite: Changes in Law – Commentary, App. 1, Change 1: former reg. 82 refers to "Inland Revenue" (meaning any officer of the Board) rather than "inspector" or "Board".
Commentary, para. 492 and App. 1, Change 35: former reg. 82 refers to tax "payable" in order to cover tax in respect of notional payments.
Commentary, App. 1, Change 74: former reg. 82 prevents interest being charged on amounts for which employer has been relieved of liability under reg. 81(4).
Commentary, App. 1, Change 75: former reg. 82 defines the "total net tax payable" for a year on which an employer may be liable to pay interest.

Interest on tax overpaid

83   [Omitted by SI 2014/992, art. 9(5).]

History – Reg. 83 omitted by SI 2014/992, art. 9(5), with effect from 6 May 2014 in relation to payments which are due and payable in respect of the tax year 2014–15 and subsequent tax years.
Origin – Former reg. 83(1): SI 1993/744, reg. 53A(1)(part).
Former reg. 83(2): SI 1993/744, reg. 53A(1)(part) and see *Rewrite: Changes in Law* note below.
Former reg. 83(3): SI 1993/744, reg. 53A(2)(part).
Cross references – SI 1989/1297: rate applicable under FA 1989, s. 178.
Rewrite: Changes in Law – Commentary, App. 1, Change 76: former reg. 83 provides explicit date from which employer may be liable to pay interest.

RECOVERY

Recovery of tax and interest

84(1)   In this regulation, **"the unpaid amount"** means any amount of tax or interest which–

(a)   an employer is liable to pay under regulation 75A(10), 76(2), 77(6), 78(8) or 79(2)(b);

(b)   an employee is liable to pay under regulation 72(7) or regulation 81(6).

84(2)   Part 6 of TMA (collection and recovery) applies to the recovery of the unpaid amount or combined amount and any interest on it as if it were income tax charged on the employer or employee (as the case may be) but with the modification indicated in paragraph (3).

84(3)   Summary proceedings for the recovery of the unpaid amount may be brought in England and Wales or Northern Ireland at any time before the end of the period which applies for the purposes of the regulation in question, as shown in Table 4.

Table 4

Period for summary proceedings for the recovery of unpaid amount

1. Regulation	2. Period
Regulation 76(2)	(a) 12 months after the date by which the statement specified in regulation 73(7) must be delivered, or
	(b) if that statement is delivered after that date, 12 months after its delivery.
Regulations 75A(10),77(6) and 78(8)	(a) 12 months after the date on which the unpaid amount or combined amount and any interest on it became payable, or
	(b) if a return has been required under regulation 77, 12 months after the date of the delivery of that return to the Inland Revenue.
Regulation 79(2)(b)	12 months after the date of the certificate.
Regulations 72(7) and 81(6)	12 months after the date on which the unpaid amount became payable.

84(4)   Proceedings against an employer may be brought for the recovery of the unpaid amount or combined amount and any interest on it without distinguishing the amounts which the employer is liable to pay in respect of each employee and without specifying the employees in question.

84(5)   The unpaid amount or combined amount and any interest on it is one cause of action or one matter of complaint for the purposes of proceedings under sections 65, 66 and 67 of TMA (magistrates' courts, county courts and inferior courts in Scotland).

84(6)   But paragraphs (4) and (5) do not prevent the bringing of separate proceedings for the recovery of each of the amounts which the employer is liable to pay for any tax period in respect of each of the employees.

History – In reg. 84(1), the words "75A(10)," and, in Table 4, para. (3), the words "75A(10)," inserted by SI 2012/822, reg. 40, with effect from 6 April 2012.
In reg. 84(1)(a), the words "or 79(2)(b)" substituted for the words ", 79(2)(b) or 82(2)" by SI 2014/992, art. 9(6), with effect from 6 May 2014 in relation to payments which are due and payable in respect of the tax year 2014–15 and subsequent tax years.
In reg. 84(2) the words "or combined amount and any interest on it" inserted by SI 2008/782, reg. 11, with effect from 6 April 2008.
In reg. 84(3), in the second entry in column 1 of Table 4, the words "and 82(2)" omitted (and the "and" after "77(6)" inserted) by SI 2014/992, art. 9(6), with effect from 6 May 2014 in relation to payments which are due and payable in respect of the tax year 2014–15 and subsequent tax years.
In reg. 84(3), in para. (a) in column 2 of the second item in Table 4, the words "or combined amount and any interest on it" inserted by SI 2008/782, reg. 11, with effect from 6 April 2008.
In reg. 84(4) the words "or combined amount and any interest on it" inserted by SI 2008/782, reg. 11, with effect from 6 April 2008.
In reg. 84(5) the words "or combined amount and any interest on it" inserted by SI 2008/782, reg. 11, with effect from 6 April 2008.

Origin – Reg. 84(1): SI 1993/744, reg. 54(1)(part), (2)(part).
Reg. 84(2): SI 1993/744, reg. 54(1)(part) and see *Rewrite: Change in Law* note below.
Reg. 84(3): drafting.
Table 4: SI 1993/744, reg. 43(9), 47(6), 48(6)(part), 52(3), 54(3), 55(9).
Reg. 84(4), (5): SI 1993/744, reg. 54(4)(part).
Reg. 84(6): SI 1993/744, reg. 54(5).

Rewrite: Changes in Law – Commentary, App. 1, Change 84: reg. 84 restricts recovery procedures to those available under TMA 1970, Pt. 6.

CONTINENTAL SHELF WORKERS: PROVISIONS RELATING TO CERTIFICATES

Application for certificate

84A(1)   An employer who meets the conditions in paragraph (2) may apply to HMRC for the issue of a UKCS continental shelf workers certificate.

84A(2)   The conditions are that—

(a)   the employer supplies or intends to supply a continental shelf worker for whom the oil field licensee is the relevant person;

(b)   the employer has or intends to have a contractual relationship under which the employer acts, directly or indirectly, as an agent of the oil field licensee in connection with these Regulations; and

(c)   the employer or an associated company has not had a certificate cancelled previously for a failure to comply with their obligations under regulation 84B.

84A(3)   An application under this regulation must be made in writing and must include–

(a)   the name and address of the employer and employer's PAYE reference;

(b)   the name and address of a person in the United Kingdom who is authorised to accept service on behalf of the employer;

(c)   confirmation that the employer understands and intends to comply with their obligations contained in regulation 84B; and

(d)   the name, address, and employer's PAYE reference of any associated company which is a current or former holder of a UKCS continental shelf workers certificate.

84A(4)   When the employer makes the first application under this regulation, the employer may also comply with the obligation under regulation 84B(e) by including those details (if known) in the application.

84A(5)   An application made under this regulation may be combined with an application made under regulation 114A of the SSC Regulations.

84A(6)   Upon receipt of an application under this regulation, an officer of Revenue and Customs may, if they are satisfied the conditions in paragraph (2) are met, issue a UKCS continental shelf workers certificate.

84A(7)   A UKCS continental shelf workers certificate must include–

(a)   the name of the UKCS continental shelf workers certificate holder;

(b)   the employer's PAYE reference of the UKCS continental shelf workers certificate holder; and

(c)   the date on which the certificate is issued.

84A(8)   A UKCS continental shelf workers certificate may be issued to–

(a)   the person authorised to accept service on behalf of the employer;

(b)   the employer; or

(c)   both the person authorised to accept service on behalf of the employer and the employer.

84A(9)   A certificate may be combined with a certificate issued under regulation 114A of the SSC Regulations.

84A(10)   Where an employer ceases to meet the conditions in paragraph (2) or to comply with its obligations under regulation 84B, or regulation 114B of the SSC Regulations, an officer of Revenue and Customs may, by notice in writing to the person authorised to accept service on behalf of the employer, cancel the UKCS continental shelf workers certificate from the date specified in the notice of cancellation.

84A(11)   The date specified in paragraph (10) may not be earlier than 10 working days after the date of the notice.

84A(12)   A notice under paragraph (10) may be combined with a notice under regulation 114A of the SSC Regulations.

84A(13)   In this regulation **"associated company"** means any company within the meaning of section 449 of the Corporation Tax Act 2010.

History – Reg. 84A inserted by SI 2014/474, reg. 2(2), with effect from 6 April 2014.

UKCS continental shelf workers certificate holder: obligations

84B(1)   A UKCS continental shelf workers certificate holder must–

(a)   make such deductions, returns and repayments as are required of a relevant person;

(b)   keep written records of–

     (i)   the name, date of birth, and national insurance number of the continental shelf workers supplied;

     (ii)   the name, registered office and oil field licence number of the oil field licensee to whom each of the workers were supplied;

     (iii)   the offshore installation to which each of the workers were supplied; and

(iv)   the dates between which the workers worked on the offshore installation;

(c)   keep the records required by sub-paragraph (b) for a period of 6 years from the end of the tax year to which they relate;

(d)   where an officer of Revenue and Customs requires them in writing to do so, provide copies of the records required by sub-paragraph (b) to HMRC within 30 days of the date of the request; and

(e)   before supplying the oil field licensee with continental shelf workers for the first time, inform HMRC in writing of the details of the oil field licensee including name, business address, and oil field licence number of the oil field licensee.

84B(2)   In this regulation **"offshore installation"** means a structure which is, is to be, or has been, put to a relevant use while in water but a structure is not an offshore installation if—

(a)   it has permanently ceased to be put to a relevant use,

(b)   it is not, and is not to be, put to any other relevant use, and

(c)   since permanently ceasing to be put to a relevant use, it has been put to a use which is not a relevant use.

84B(3)   In paragraph (2) a use is a relevant use if it is—

(a)   for the purposes of exploiting mineral resources,

(b)   for the purposes of exploration with a view to exploiting mineral resources,

(c)   for the storage of gas in or under the shore or the bed of any waters,

(d)   for the recovery of gas so stored,

(e)   for the conveyance of things by means of a pipe,

(f)   mainly for the provision of accommodation for individuals who work on or from a structure which is, is to be, or has been put to any of the above uses while in the water,

(g)   for the purposes of decommissioning any structure which has been used for or in connection with any of the relevant uses above.

84B(4)   For the purposes of paragraphs (3) and (4) a structure is put to use while in water if it is put to use while—

(i)   standing in any waters,

(ii)   stationed (by whatever means) in any waters, or

(iii)   standing on the foreshore or other land intermittently covered with water.

84B(5)   For the purposes of paragraphs (2), (3) and (4) a **"structure"** includes a ship or other vessel except where it is used wholly or mainly—

(a)   for the transport of supplies;

(b)   as a safety vessel;

(c)   for a combination of (a) and (b); or

(d)   for the laying of cables.

History – Reg. 84B inserted by SI 2014/474, reg. 2(2), with effect from 6 April 2014.

UKCS oil field licensee certificate

84C(1)   Where a UKCS continental shelf workers certificate holder has notified HMRC that the employer intends to supply continental shelf workers to an oil field licensee an officer of Revenue and Customs must issue a UKCS oil field licensee certificate to the oil field licensee.

84C(2)   The UKCS oil field licensee certificate must include—

(a)   the name of the oil field licensee;

(b)   the registered office of that oil field licensee;

(c)   the oil field licence number;

(d)   the name of the UKCS continental shelf workers certificate holder;

(e)   the date on which it is issued; and

(f)   a description of the continental shelf workers to whom it applies.

84C(3)   Where a UKCS oil field licensee certificate is in force the holder of that certificate is not liable to make deductions in respect of any continental shelf worker of a description set out in the certificate.

84C(4)   If a UKCS continental shelf workers certificate is cancelled by an officer of Revenue and Customs that officer must also, by notice in writing, cancel the UKCS oil field licensee certificate.

84C(5)   A notice under paragraph (4) must—

(a)   be sent on the same day as the notice cancelling the UKCS continental shelf workers certificate;

(b)   specify the date of cancellation of the UKCS oil field licensee certificate; and

(c)   notify the oil field licensee that it is liable to meet its obligations as a relevant person.

84C(6)   The date of cancellation of the UKCS oil field licensee certificate must be the same date as that specified in the UKCS continental shelf workers certificate cancellation notice.

84C(7)   In this regulation **"UKCS oil field licensee certificate"** means a certificate issued under paragraph (1).

History – Reg. 84C inserted by SI 2014/474, reg. 2(2), with effect from 6 April 2014.

Interpretation of regulations 84A to 114C

84D   In regulations 84A to 84C–

"oil field licensee" means the holder of a licence under Part 1 of the Petroleum Act 1998 in respect of the area in which the duties of the continental shelf worker's employment are performed;

"UKCS continental shelf workers certificate" means a certificate issued under regulation 84A.

History – Reg. 84D inserted by SI 2014/474, reg. 2(2), with effect from 6 April 2014.

Chapter 2 – Other Returns and Information

RETURNS INVOLVING PAYE INCOME OTHER THAN PAYMENTS

Employers: annual return of other earnings (Forms P11D and P9D)

85(1)   Before 7th July following the end of a tax year, the employer must provide the Inland Revenue–

(a)   with the information listed in regulation 86 for each employee, and

(b)   with the additional information listed in regulation 87 for each employee whose employment is subject to the benefits code.

85(2)   At the same time and in the same manner as the employer provides that information, the employer must also provide a declaration stating that–

(a)   all information required to be provided has been provided, and

(b)   the information is complete and accurate to the best of the employer's knowledge and belief.

85(3)   For the purposes of this regulation an employment is "subject to the benefits code" if, for the purposes of the benefits code in ITEPA, it is a taxable employment under Part 2 of ITEPA (as defined by section 66(3) of ITEPA) which is not an excluded employment under section 216(1) of ITEPA (lower-paid employment and certain types of company director).

Origin – Reg. 85(1): SI 1993/744, reg. 46(1)(part) and see *Rewrite: Changes in Law* note below.
Reg. 85(2): SI 1993/744, reg. 46(7A)(part), (7B)(part).
Reg. 85(3): drafting.
Rewrite: Changes in Law – Commentary, App. 1, Change 1: reg. 85 refers to "Inland Revenue" (meaning any officer of the Board) rather than "inspector" or "Board".

Information employer must provide for each employee

86(1)   Particulars of the following information must be provided in the case of each employee–

(a)   any earnings which the employee receives from the employer or related third party otherwise than in money, including the amount of those earnings;

(b)   any payments made on behalf of the employee by the employer or related third party and not repaid, including the amounts;

(c)   any non-cash voucher provided by the employer or related third party by reason of which the employee is treated by section 87(1) of ITEPA (benefit of non-cash voucher treated as earnings) as receiving earnings in that tax year, including the amount of those earnings;

(d)   any use of a credit-token provided by the employer or related third party by reason of which the employee is treated by section 94(1) of ITEPA (benefit of credit-token treated as earnings) as receiving earnings in that tax year, including the amount of those earnings;

(e)   the due amount in respect of any notional payment where that amount is treated by section 222 of ITEPA (payments on account of tax where deduction not possible) as earnings of the employee received in that tax year;

(f)　　any living accommodation which has been provided for the employee or a member of the employee's family or household by the employer or related third party, including the amount that is treated as earnings for that tax year by section 102 of ITEPA (benefit of living accommodation treated as earnings);

(g)　　any earnings consisting of the amount by which the value of the exemption under subsection (2) of section 287 of ITEPA (limit on exemption of removal expenses and removal benefits) exceeds the limit specified in subsection (1) of that section and having effect in relation to the employee.

86(2)　　Particulars of removal expenses and removal benefits to which section 271 of ITEPA (limited exemption of removal benefits and expenses) applies are required–

(a)　　only under paragraph (1)(g), and

(b)　　only to the extent that they exceed the limit in section 287(1) of ITEPA which applies to the change of residence of the employee in question.

86(3)　　In the case of any earnings relating to business entertainment, as defined by section 577 of ICTA, the employer must also inform the Inland Revenue whether the amount of the earnings has been or will be disallowed as a deduction or inclusion as mentioned in section 577(1)(a) of that Act in any tax computation relating to the trade, business, profession or vocation of the employer.

86(4)　　**"Related third party"** means a person making payments or providing benefits to an employee, if the making or provision of the payments or benefits by that person has been arranged, guaranteed or in any way facilitated by the employer.

Origin – Reg. 86(1): SI 1993/744, reg. 46(1)(part), (2), (5)(part) and see *Rewrite: Changes in Law* notes below.
Reg. 86(2): SI 1993/744, reg. 46(1)(part), (7)(part).
Reg. 86(3): SI 1993/744, reg. 46(1)(part), (4)(part) and see *Rewrite: Changes in Law* notes below.
Reg. 86(4): SI 1993/744, reg. 46(8)(part).

Cross references – ITTOIA 2005, s. 45(2), 46(1) and (3), 47(1) and (4) and 867(6): provisions which rewrite ICTA 1988, s. 577(1) for income tax purposes.
CTA 2009, s. 1298(1), (2): provisions which rewrite ICTA 1988, s. 577(1) for corporation tax purposes.

Rewrite: Changes in Law – Commentary, App. 1, Change 1: reg. 86 refers to "Inland Revenue" (meaning any officer of the Board) rather than "inspector" or "Board".
Commentary, para. 510 and App. 1, Change 37: reg. 86(1)(a), (b) bring into line with practice the information which employer must provide on P9D and P11D.
Commentary, App. 1, Change 78: reg. 86 limits the P11D/P9D return of payments made on behalf of employee to those made by employer or related third party.

Information employer must also provide for benefits code employees

87(1)　　Particulars of the following information must also be provided in the case of each employee whose employment is subject to the benefits code–

(a)　　any payments made by the employer or related third party to the employee by reason of the employment in respect of expenses;

(b)　　any sums put by the employer or related third party at the disposal of the employee by reason of the employment and paid away by the employee;

(c)　　any benefits provided by the employer or related third party for the employee such as give rise to any amount treated by Chapters 6 to 10 of Part 3, and section 223, of ITEPA (cars and vans, loans, shares, other benefits and payments on account of director's tax) as earnings of the employee received in that tax year, including the amount of those earnings.

87(2)　　Particulars are not required under paragraph (1) of removal expenses and removal benefits to which section 271 of ITEPA (limited exemption of removal benefits and expenses) applies (as to which see regulation 86(2)).

87(3)　　In the case of any earnings relating to business entertainment, as defined by section 577 of ICTA, the employer must also inform the Inland Revenue whether the amount of the earnings has been or will be disallowed as a deduction or inclusion as mentioned in section 577(1)(a) of that Act in any tax computation relating to the trade, business, profession or vocation of the employer.

87(4)　　**"Related third party"** has the meaning given in regulation 86(4).

87(5)　　Regulation 85(3) (meaning of employment "subject to benefits code") applies for the purposes of this regulation.

Origin – Reg. 87(1): SI 1993/744, reg. 46(1)(part), (3), (5)(part).
Reg. 87(2): SI 1993/744, reg. 46(1)(part), (7)(part).
Reg. 87(3): SI 1993/744, reg. 46(1)(part), (4)(part) and see *Rewrite: Changes in Law* note below.
Reg. 87(4): SI 1993/744, reg. 46(8)(part),
Reg. 87(5): drafting.

Cross references – ITTOIA 2005, s. 45(2), 46(1) and (3), 47(1) and (4) and 867(6): provisions which rewrite ICTA 1988, s. 577(1) for income tax purposes.
CTA 2009, s. 1298(1), (2): provisions which rewrite ICTA 1988, s. 577(1) for corporation tax purposes.

Rewrite: Changes in Law – Commentary, App. 1, Change 1: reg. 87 refers to "Inland Revenue" (meaning any officer of the Board) rather than "inspector" or "Board".

Annual return of other earnings: amounts

88(1) Paragraph (2) applies if an employer is required by regulations 85 to 87 to provide an amount which is or is treated as earnings.

88(2) The employer must make all deductions and other adjustments which the employer is able to show, by reference to information in the employer's possession or otherwise available to the employer, are authorised or required by Part 3 of ITEPA (earnings and benefits etc treated as earnings).

Origin – SI 1993/744, reg. 46(6).

Annual return of other earnings: exclusion for notional payments

89 The employer is not required to provide particulars in the return under regulation 85 of any notional payment which is a relevant payment made by the employer to the employee (as particulars of it may be required under regulation 73 or 74 (annual returns of relevant payments)).

Origin – SI 1993/744, reg. 744, reg. 46(7)(part).

Quarterly return if a car becomes available or unavailable (Form P46 (Car))

90(1) This regulation applies if–

(a) section 120 of ITEPA (benefit of car treated as earnings) treats the benefit of a car as giving rise to an amount as earnings of an employee received in a tax year, and

(b) one or more of the following occurs in a tax quarter–

    (i) the car becomes available;

    (ii) the car becomes unavailable;

    (iii) the car is available and the employee's employment becomes subject to the benefits code (as defined by regulation 85(3)).

90(1A) This regulation does not apply if the reason a car becomes available or unavailable is that one car is replaced with another.

90(2) The employer must provide the HMRC with the following information in respect of the employee not later than 28 days after the end of the tax quarter.

90(3) The information is–

(a) the employee's name,

(b) the employee's national insurance number, if known,

(c) details of the car in question,

(d) the interim sum determined at step 4 of section 121(1) of ITEPA (method of calculating cash equivalent of benefit of a car),

(e) any capital sum contributed by the employee to expenditure on the provision of the car or on any qualifying accessory which is taken into account in so determining the interim sum in respect of the car,

(f) any amount which, as a condition of the car being available for the employee's private use, the employee is required to pay in the tax year concerned for that use (whether by way of deduction from relevant payments or otherwise),

(g) whether any fuel is provided for private use.

90(4) In this regulation–

"**available**" and "**unavailable**" are to be read in accordance with sections 116(1) and 143(2) of ITEPA (meaning of when car is available and unavailable to employee);

"**qualifying accessory**" has the meaning given in section 125 of ITEPA (meaning of accessory etc).

History – Reg. 90(1A) inserted by SI 2009/588, reg. 9(a), with effect from 6 April 2009.
In reg. 90(2), the word "HMRC" substituted for the words "Inland Revenue" by SI 2009/588, reg. 9(b), with effect from 6 April 2009.

Origin – Reg. 90(1): SI 1993/744, reg. 46A(1)(part), (2).
Reg. 90(2): SI 1993/744, reg. 46A(1)(part) and see *Rewrite: Changes in Law* note below.
Reg. 90(3): SI 1993/744, reg. 46A(3), (4).
Reg. 90(4): SI 1993/744, reg. 46A(5).

Rewrite: Changes in Law – Commentary, App. 1, Change 1: reg. 90 refers to "Inland Revenue" (meaning any officer of the Board) rather than "inspector" or "Board".

Termination awards: information to be provided

91(1) Before 7th July following the end of the tax year, an employer must, in respect of each employee who received a termination award, provide the Inland Revenue with the information specified in paragraph (3) relating to that award.

91(2) "**Termination award**" means an award consisting of payments combined with other benefits, or consisting solely of other benefits–

(a)   which were awarded in that tax year in connection with the termination of the employee's employment with the employer, or any change in the duties of or earnings from that employment,

(b)   which when provided (whether in that or a subsequent tax year) would constitute payments and other benefits received to which Chapter 3 of Part 6 of ITEPA applies (payments and benefits on termination of employment etc), and

(c)   the total amount of which is estimated by the employer to exceed £30,000, when aggregated with other payments and other benefits provided or to be provided (whether in that or a subsequent tax year) in respect of the same person as mentioned in section 404(1) of ITEPA (aggregation of payments in respect of other related employments).

91(3) The information to be provided is–

(a)   the total amount of the payments and other benefits awarded;

(b)   the total amount of the payments made in that tax year in connection with the award;

(c)   details of the non-cash benefits provided in that tax year in connection with the award, other than benefits previously contained in a return for that tax year under regulation 85, and the total amount of their amounts calculated in accordance with section 415(2) of ITEPA (valuation of benefits);

(d)   the estimated total number of the tax years in which payments and non-cash benefits are to be provided in connection with the award and, if the duration of any of those payments and non-cash benefits is capable of being reduced in certain circumstances, details of those circumstances;

(e)   the estimated total amount of the payments to be made in subsequent tax years in connection with the award;

(f)   a description of each of the other benefits to be provided in subsequent tax years in connection with the award, and the terms of their provision.

91(4) In calculating the cash equivalents of non-cash benefits for the purposes of this regulation, the employer must make all deductions and other adjustments which the employer is able to show, by reference to information in the employer's possession or otherwise available to the employer, are authorised or required by any of the provisions of the benefits code as applied by section 415 of ITEPA.

91(5) In calculating the total amount of the payments and other benefits for the purposes of paragraphs (2)(c) and (3)(a), the employer–

(a)   must have regard to the provisions of Chapter 3 of Part 6 of ITEPA,

(b)   must take into account the matters referred to in paragraph (3)(d),(e) and (f), and

(c)   in valuing the amount of non-cash benefits for future tax years in connection with the award, must assume that the provisions of ITEPA relating to those benefits will remain unchanged with respect to those years.

91(6) Information required to be provided by an employer in accordance with paragraphs (1) and (3) may be provided after the termination award is made but before the end of the tax year in which it is made.

91(7) If information is provided in accordance with paragraph (6), paragraph (3)(b) and (c) have effect, so far as concerns the providing of information relating to the tax year, as if they required the amounts and benefits there specified to be estimated by the employer as accurately as possible.

91(8) This regulation is subject to regulation 93 (return if more than one employer).

91(9) In this regulation and regulations 92, 93 and 96 (further provisions about termination awards)–

"**employee**" includes a former employee; and

"**employer**" includes a former employer.

Origin – Reg. 91(1): SI 1993/744, reg. 46ZA(1)(part) and see *Rewrite: Changes in Law* note below.
Reg. 91(2): SI 1993/744, reg. 46ZA(1)(part); drafting.
Reg. 91(3): SI 1993/744, reg. 46ZA(2).
Reg. 91(4): SI 1993/744, reg. 46ZA(3).
Reg. 91(5): SI 1993/744, reg. 46ZA(4).

Reg. 91(6), (7): SI 1993/744, reg. 46ZA(11)(part).
Reg. 91(8): SI 1993/744, reg. 46ZA(10)(part).
Reg. 91(9): SI 1993/744, reg. 46ZA(12); drafting.
Rewrite: Changes in Law – Commentary, App. 1, Change 1: reg. 91 refers to "Inland Revenue" (meaning any officer of the Board) rather than "inspector" or "Board".

Termination awards: return if award changes

92(1)   Paragraph (3) applies if–

(a)   information has not been provided by the employer under regulation 91(1) solely because either–

    (i)   the total amount of payments and other benefits awarded in the tax year in respect of the employee is estimated in accordance with regulation 91(2)(c) not to exceed £30,000, or

    (ii)   the award made in the tax year consisted of payments only, and

(b)   there is a change in the award in a subsequent tax year.

92(2)   **"Change in the award"** means–

(a)   that there is a change in–

    (i)   the amount of the payments awarded, or

    (ii)   the nature and amounts of the other benefits awarded,

so that the total amount of those payments and other benefits is estimated in accordance with regulation 91(2)(c) to exceed £30,000; or

(b)   that the nature of the award is changed so that it consists–

    (i)   of payments combined with other benefits, or

    (ii)   solely of other benefits,

estimated in accordance with regulation 91(2)(c) to exceed £30,000.

92(3)   The employer must, before 7th July following the tax year in which the change in the award occurred, provide the Inland Revenue with the information specified in regulation 91(3) with respect to those payments and other benefits.

92(4)   Paragraph (5) applies if, after the employer has provided information in accordance with regulation 91(1) or paragraph (3) above, there is a material change–

(a)   in the amount of the payments awarded, or

(b)   in the nature and amounts of the other benefits awarded,

in relation to the employee.

92(5)   The employer must, before 7th July following the end of the tax year in which the material change occurred, give details of the material change to the Inland Revenue.

92(6)   For the avoidance of doubt, an employer is not required to provide details under this regulation of a change which arises solely because of amendments to the provisions of ITEPA which relate to non-cash benefits.

92(7)   This regulation is subject to regulation 93 (return if more than one employer).

Origin – Reg. 92(1): SI 1993/744, reg. 46ZA(5)(part) and see *Rewrite: Changes in Law* notes below.
Reg. 92(2): SI 1993/744, reg. 46ZA(5)(part) and see *Rewrite: Changes in Law* notes below.
Reg. 92(3): SI 1993/744, reg. 46ZA(6) and see *Rewrite: Changes in Law* notes below.
Reg. 92(4): SI 1993/744, reg. 46ZA(9)(part).
Reg. 92(5): SI 1993/744, reg. 46ZA(9)(part) and see *Rewrite: Changes in Law* notes below.
Reg. 92(6): new.
Reg. 92(7): SI 1993/744, reg. 46ZA(10)(part).
Rewrite: Changes in Law – Commentary, App. 1, Change 1: reg. 92 refers to "Inland Revenue" (meaning any officer of the Board) rather than "inspector" or "Board".
Commentary, App. 1, Change 79: clarifies that there is no exclusion from reg. 92 solely for changes made from 6 April to 6 July of tax year following that in which award is made.
Commentary, App. 1, Change 80: reg. 92 removes requirement to make return under reg. 92 where changed award does not exceed £30,000 threshold.

Termination awards: return if more than one employer

93(1)   This regulation applies if the payments and other benefits aggregated in accordance with regulation 91(2)(c) include amounts in respect of different employments with more than one employer.

93(2)   The person who must provide information to the Inland Revenue under regulation 91 or 92, or to the employee under regulation 96, is the employer providing the greatest amount of payments and other benefits so aggregated.

Origin – SI 1993/744, reg. 46ZA(10)(part).

INFORMATION TO BE GIVEN TO EMPLOYEES

Employers: information to employees of other earnings (Forms P11D and P9D)

94(1) Before 7th July following the end of a tax year, the employer must give a statement to every current employee in respect of whom particulars are to be provided under regulation 85(1) by the employer for that tax year.

94(2) The statement must contain the particulars provided under regulations 86 and 87 in so far as they relate to the employee.

94(3) If a person who was a current employee ceases to be an employee at any time before 7th July following the end of the tax year, the statement is given to the employee if it is sent or delivered to, or left at, that person's usual or last known address.

94(4) A former employee in respect of whom particulars are to be provided under regulation 85(1) by the employer for a tax year may by notice require the employer to give the statement specified in paragraph (2) to that former employee–

(a)   before 7th July following the end of the tax year, or

(b)   within 30 days of receiving the notice,

whichever is the later.

94(5) The notice may be given to the employer at any time up to 3 years after the end of the tax year.

94(6) A former employee who has received a statement from the employer under paragraph (4) in respect of a tax year may not require a further statement from the employer under that paragraph in respect of the same tax year.

94(7) In this regulation–

    "current employee" means a person who was an employee on 5th April in the tax year to which the particulars provided under regulation 85(1) relate;

    "former employee" means a person who was an employee during a part of the tax year to which the particulars provided under regulation 85(1) relate, but who was no longer an employee on 5th April in that tax year.

Origin – Reg. 94(1): SI 1993/744, reg. 46AA(1)(part).
Reg. 94(2): SI 1993/744, reg. 46AA(1)(part), (4)(part).
Reg. 94(3): SI 1993/744, reg. 46AA(2).
Reg. 94(4), (5): SI 1993/744, reg. 46AA(3)(part).
Reg. 94(6): SI 1993/744, reg. 46AA(5).
Reg. 94(7): SI 1993/744, reg. 46AA(6)(part).

Third parties: information to employees of other earnings

95(1) This regulation applies if a person ("the third party") has, in a tax year–

(a)   made any unrelated payments to, or on behalf of, another person's employee, or

(b)   provided any unrelated benefits to, or in respect of, another person's employee.

95(2) Before 7th July following the end of the tax year, the third party must give the employee a statement containing such of the particulars specified by regulations 86 and 87 as relate to the unrelated payments or unrelated benefits.

95(3) A benefit or payment is **"unrelated"** if–

(a)   the employee's employer is not required to provide particulars about it under regulation 85(1), and

(b)   the third party would have been required to provide particulars about it under regulation 85(1) had the third party been the employee's employer.

Origin – Reg. 95(1): SI 1993/744, reg. 46AB(1)(part).
Reg. 95(2): SI 1993/744, reg. 46AB(2), (3).
Reg. 95(3): SI 1993/744, reg. 46AB(1)(part), (4).

Termination awards: information to employees

96(1) This regulation applies if an employer is required to provide the information specified in regulation 91(3) to the Inland Revenue by–

(a)   regulation 91(1) (termination award), or

(b)   regulation 92(3) (change in termination award).

96(2) The employer must also give a copy of that information to the employee before 7th July following the end of the tax year.

96(3) A copy of the information is given to the employee if it is sent or delivered to, or left at, the employee's usual or last known address.

96(4) As to the person who is the employer in cases where there is more than one employer, see regulation 93.

Origin – Reg. 96(1): SI 1993/744, reg. 46ZA(7)(part) and see *Rewrite: Changes in Law* note below.
Reg. 96(2): SI 1993/744, reg. 46ZA(7)(part).
Reg. 96(3): SI 1993/744, reg. 46ZA(8).
Reg. 96(4): SI 1993/744, reg. 46ZA(10)(part).

Rewrite: Changes in Law – Commentary, App. 1, Change 1: reg. 96 refers to "Inland Revenue" (meaning any officer of the Board) rather than "inspector" or "Board".

Chapter 3 – PAYE Records

Retention by employer of PAYE records

97(1) An employer must keep and preserve for not less than three years after the end of the tax year to which they relate all PAYE records which are not required to be sent to HMRC by other provisions in these Regulations.

97(2) The duty under paragraph (1) to keep and preserve PAYE records may be discharged by preserving them in any form or by any means.

97(3) "PAYE records" means the following documents and records–

(a) all wages sheets, deductions working sheets, documents completed under regulation 46 (Form P46), information provided under regulation 40A(1) (duty of employee to assist with completion of new employee fields in returns under regulations 67B and 67D) and other documents and records relating to–

     (i) the calculation of the PAYE income of the employees,

     (ii) relevant payments to the employees, or

     (iii) the deduction of tax from, or accounting for tax in respect of, such payments, and

(b) all documents relating to any information which an employer is required to provide to HMRC under regulation 85 (Forms P11D and P9D).

History – In reg. 97(3)(a), the words ", information provided under regulation 40A(1) (duty of employee to assist with completion of new employee fields in returns under regulations 67B and 67D)" inserted by SI 2012/822, reg. 41, with effect from 6 April 2012. Reg. 97 substituted by SI 2009/588, reg. 6, with effect from 1 April 2009.

Chapter 3A – Certain Debts of Companies under Chapter 7 of Part 2 of ITEPA (Agencies)

History – Ch. 3A inserted by FA 2014, s. 17(1), with effect in relation to relevant PAYE debts that are to be deducted, accounted for or paid on or after 6 April 2014.

Interpretation of Chapter 3A

97ZA In this Chapter–

"**company**" includes a limited liability partnership;

"**HMRC**" means Her Majesty's Revenue and Customs;

"**director**" has the meaning given by section 67 of ITEPA;

"**personal liability notice**" has the meaning given by regulation 97ZB(2);

"**relevant PAYE debt**", in relation to a company, means–

(a) any amount that the company is to deduct, or account for, in accordance with these Regulations by virtue of–

     (i) section 44(4) to (6) of ITEPA (persons providing fraudulent documents), or

     (ii) section 46A of that Act (anti-avoidance), and

(b) any interest or penalty, in respect of an amount within paragraph (a), for which the company is liable;

"**the relevant date**", in relation to a relevant PAYE debt, means–

(a) in a case where the relevant PAYE debt is to be deducted or accounted for, or arises, by virtue of subsections (4) to (6) of section 44 of ITEPA, the date on which the fraudulent document was provided as mentioned in subsection (4) of that section, or

(b) in a case where the relevant PAYE debt is to be deducted or accounted for, or arises, by virtue of section 46A of ITEPA, the date the arrangements mentioned in subsection (1)(b) of that section were entered into;

"the specified amount" has the meaning given by regulation 97ZB(2)(a).

History – Reg. 97ZA inserted by FA 2014, s. 17(1), with effect in relation to relevant PAYE debts that are to be deducted, accounted for or paid on or after 6 April 2014.

Liability of directors for relevant PAYE debts

97ZB(1) This regulation applies in relation to an amount of relevant PAYE debt of a company if the company does not deduct, account for or (as the case may be) pay that amount by the time by which the company is required to do so.

97ZB(2) HMRC may serve a notice (a "personal liability notice") on any person who was, on the relevant date, a director of the company–

(a) specifying the amount of relevant PAYE debt in relation to which this regulation applies ("the specified amount"), and

(b) requiring the director to pay to HMRC–

(i) the specified amount, and

(ii) specified interest on that amount.

97ZB(3) The interest specified in the personal liability notice–

(a) is to be at the rate applicable under section 178 of the Finance Act 1989 for the purposes of section 86 of TMA, and

(b) is to run from the date the notice is served.

97ZB(4) A director who is served with a personal liability notice is liable to pay to HMRC the specified amount and the interest specified in the notice within 30 days beginning with the day the notice is served.

97ZB(5) If HMRC serve personal liability notices on more than one director of the company in respect of the same amount of relevant PAYE debt, the directors are jointly and severally liable to pay to HMRC the specified amount and the interest specified in the notices.

History – Reg. 97ZB inserted by FA 2014, s. 17(1), with effect in relation to relevant PAYE debts that are to be deducted, accounted for or paid on or after 6 April 2014.

Appeals in relation to personal liability notices

97ZC(1) A person who is served with a personal liability notice in relation to an amount of relevant PAYE debt of a company may appeal against the notice.

97ZC(2) A notice of appeal must–

(a) be given to HMRC within 30 days beginning with the day the personal liability notice is served, and

(b) specify the grounds of the appeal.

97ZC(3) The grounds of appeal are–

(a) that all or part of the specified amount does not represent an amount of relevant PAYE debt, of the company, to which regulation 97ZB applies, or

(b) that the person was not a director of the company on the relevant date.

97ZC(4) But a person may not appeal on the ground mentioned in paragraph (3)(a) if it has already been determined, on an appeal by the company, that–

(a) the specified amount is a relevant PAYE debt of the company, and

(b) the company did not deduct, account for, or (as the case may be) pay the debt by the time by which the company was required to do so.

97ZC(5) Subject to paragraph (6), on an appeal that is notified to the tribunal, the tribunal is to uphold or quash the personal liability notice.

97ZC(6) In a case in which the ground of appeal mentioned in paragraph (3)(a) is raised, the tribunal may also reduce or increase the specified amount so that it does represent an amount of relevant PAYE debt, of the company, to which regulation 97ZB applies.

History – Reg. 97ZC inserted by FA 2014, s. 17(1), with effect in relation to relevant PAYE debts that are to be deducted, accounted for or paid on or after 6 April 2014.

Withdrawal of personal liability notices

97ZD(1)   A personal liability notice is withdrawn if the tribunal quashes it.

97ZD(2)   An officer of Revenue and Customs may withdraw a personal liability notice if the officer considers it appropriate to do so.

97ZD(3)   If a personal liability notice is withdrawn, HMRC must give notice of that fact to the person upon whom the notice was served.

History – Reg. 97ZD inserted by FA 2014, s. 17(1), with effect in relation to relevant PAYE debts that are to be deducted, accounted for or paid on or after 6 April 2014.

Recovery of sums due under personal liability notice: application of Part 6 of TMA

97ZE(1)   For the purposes of this Chapter, Part 6 of TMA (collection and recovery) applies as if–

(a)   the personal liability notice were an assessment, and

(b)   the specified amount, and any interest on that amount under regulation 97ZB(2)(b)(ii), were income tax charged on the director upon whom the notice is served,

and that Part of that Act applies with the modification in paragraph (2) and any other necessary modifications.

97ZE(2)   Summary proceedings for the recovery of the specified amount, and any interest on that amount under regulation 97ZB(2)(b)(ii), may be brought in England and Wales or Northern Ireland at any time before the end of the period of 12 months beginning with the day after the day on which personal liability notice is served.

History – Reg. 97ZE inserted by FA 2014, s. 17(1), with effect in relation to relevant PAYE debts that are to be deducted, accounted for or paid on or after 6 April 2014.

Repayment of surplus amounts

97ZF(1)   This regulation applies if–

(a)   one or more personal liability notices are served in respect of an amount of relevant PAYE debt of a company, and

(b)   the amounts paid to HMRC (whether by directors upon whom notices are served or the company) exceed the aggregate of the specified amount and any interest on it under regulation 97ZB(2)(b)(ii).

97ZF(2)   HMRC is to repay the difference on a just and equitable basis and without unreasonable delay.

97ZF(3)   HMRC is to pay interest on any sum repaid.

97ZF(4)   The interest–

(a)   is to be at the rate applicable under section 178 of the Finance Act 1989 for the purposes of section 824 of ICTA, and

(b)   is to run from the date the amounts paid to HMRC come to exceed the aggregate mentioned in subsection (1)(b).

History – Reg. 97ZF inserted by FA 2014, s. 17(1), with effect in relation to relevant PAYE debts that are to be deducted, accounted for or paid on or after 6 April 2014.

Chapter 4 – Debts of Managed Service Companies

History – Ch. 4 inserted by SI 2007/2069, reg. 2, with effect from 6 August 2007.

Interpretation of Chapter 4

97A(1)   In this Chapter–

> **"HM Revenue and Customs"** means Her Majesty's Revenue and Customs;
>
> **"lower amount"** means the amount mentioned in regulation 97C(5);
>
> **"managed service company"** has the meaning given by section 61B of ITEPA;
>
> **"paragraph (b) associate"** means a person who–
>
> (a)   is within section 688A(2)(d), and
>
> (b)   is within that provision by virtue of a connection with a person who is within section 688A(2)(b);
>
> **"paragraph (c) associate"** means a person who–
>
> (a)   is within section 688A(2)(d), and

(b)   is within that provision by virtue of a connection with a person who is within section 688A(2)(c);

"qualifying period" means a tax period beginning on or after 6th August 2007;

"relevant PAYE debt " means a debt specified in regulation 97B;

"specified amount" means the amount mentioned in regulation 97C(1)(b);

"transfer notice" means the notice mentioned in regulation 97C(4);

"transferee" means the person mentioned in regulation 97C(4).

97A(2)   In this Chapter references to section 688A, however expressed, are references to section 688A of ITEPA.

History – Reg. 97A inserted by SI 2007/2069, reg. 2, with effect from 6 August 2007.

Relevant PAYE debts of managed service companies

97B(1)   A managed service company has a relevant PAYE debt if–

(a)   a managed service company must pay an amount of tax for a qualifying period, and

(b)   one of conditions A to E is met.

97B(2)   Condition A is met if–

(a)   an amount of tax for a qualifying period has been determined in accordance with regulation 80 (determination of unpaid tax and appeal against determination), and

(b)   any part of the tax determined has not been paid within 14 days from the date on which the determination became final and conclusive.

97B(2A)   Condition A2 is met if–

(a)   HMRC serve a notice on an employer under regulation 75A(5) (power of HMRC to issue a notice and certificate in cases where regulation 67B or 67D returns are not made, etc) requiring payment of the amount of tax they consider the employer is liable to pay, and

(b)   any part of that amount remains unpaid at the end of a period of 14 days beginning with the date on which the notice is prepared.

97B(3)   Condition B is met if–

(a)   an employer delivers a return under regulation 73 (annual return of relevant payments) for the tax year 2007–08, or any later tax year, showing an amount of total net tax deducted by the employer for that tax year,

(b)   HM Revenue and Customs prepare a certificate under regulation 76 (certificate if tax in regulation 73 return is unpaid) showing how much of that amount remains unpaid, and

(c)   any part of that amount remains unpaid at the end of a period of 14 days beginning with the date on which the certificate is prepared.

97B(4)   Condition C is met if–

(a)   HM Revenue and Customs prepare a certificate under regulation 77(6) (return and certificate if tax may be unpaid) showing an amount of tax which the employer is liable to pay for a qualifying period, and

(b)   any part of that amount remains unpaid at the end of a period of 14 days beginning with the date on which the certificate is prepared.

97B(5)   Condition D is met if–

(a)   HM Revenue and Customs serve notice on an employer under regulation 78(4) (notice and certificate if tax may be unpaid) requiring payment of the amount of tax which they consider the employer is liable to pay, and

(b)   any part of that amount remains unpaid at the end of a period of 14 days beginning with the date on which the notice is prepared.

97B(6)   Condition E is met if–

(a)   HM Revenue and Customs prepare a certificate under regulation 79(2) (certificate after inspection of PAYE records) showing an amount of tax which it appears that the employer is liable to pay for a qualifying period,

(b)   HM Revenue and Customs make a written demand for payment of that amount of tax, and

(c)   any part of that amount remains unpaid at the end of a period of 14 days beginning with the date on which the written demand for payment is made.

History – Reg. 97B(2A) inserted by SI 2012/822, reg. 42, with effect from 6 April 2012.
Reg. 97B inserted by SI 2007/2069, reg. 2, with effect from 6 August 2007.

Transfer of debt of managed service company

97C(1) This regulation applies if—

(a)   a managed service company has a relevant PAYE debt, and

(b)   an officer of Revenue and Customs is of the opinion that the relevant PAYE debt or a part of the relevant PAYE debt (the "specified amount") is irrecoverable from the managed service company within a reasonable period.

97C(2) HM Revenue and Customs may make a direction authorising the recovery of the specified amount from the persons specified in section 688A(2) (managed service companies: recovery from other persons).

97C(3) Upon the making of a direction under paragraph (2), the persons specified in section 688A(2) become jointly and severally liable for the relevant PAYE debt, but subject to what follows.

97C(4) HM Revenue and Customs may not recover the specified amount from any person in accordance with a direction made under paragraph (2) until they have served a notice (a "transfer notice") on the person in question (the "transferee").

97C(5) If an officer of Revenue and Customs is of the opinion that it is appropriate to do so, HM Revenue and Customs may accept an amount less than the specified amount (the "lower amount") from a transferee; but this acceptance shall not prejudice the recovery of the specified amount from any other transferee.

97C(6) HM Revenue and Customs may not serve a transfer notice on a person mentioned in section 688A(2)(c), or on a paragraph (c) associate, if the relevant PAYE debt is incurred before 6th January 2008.

97C(7) HM Revenue and Customs may not serve a transfer notice on a person mentioned in section 688A(2)(c), or on a paragraph (c) associate, unless an officer of Revenue and Customs certifies that, in his opinion, it is impracticable to recover the specified amount from persons mentioned in paragraphs (a) and (b) of section 688A(2) and from paragraph (b) associates.

97C(8) In determining, for the purposes of paragraph (7), whether it is impracticable to recover the specified amount from persons mentioned in paragraphs (a) and (b) of section 688A(2) and from paragraph (b) associates, the officer of Revenue and Customs may have regard to all managed service companies in relation to which a person is a person mentioned in paragraph (a) or (b) of section 688A(2) or a paragraph (b) associate.

97C(9) In determining which of the persons mentioned in section 688A(2)(c) and which of the paragraph (c) associates are to be served with transfer notices and the amount of those notices, HM Revenue and Customs must have regard to the degree and extent to which those persons are persons who (directly or indirectly) have encouraged or been actively involved in the provision by the managed service company of the services of the individual mentioned in that provision.

History – Reg. 97C inserted by SI 2007/2069, reg. 2, with effect from 6 August 2007.

Time limits for issue of transfer notices

97D(1) A transfer notice must be served before the end of the period determined in accordance with this regulation.

97D(2) Paragraphs (3) to (7) apply if the transfer notice is served on a person mentioned in paragraph (a) or (b) of section 688A(2) or on a paragraph (b) associate.

97D(3) In a case in which condition A in regulation 97B is met, the transfer notice must be served before the end of a period of 12 months beginning with the date on which the determination became final and conclusive.

97D(3A) In a case in which condition A2 in regulation 97B is met, the transfer notice must be served before the end of a period of 12 months beginning with the date on which HMRC serve notice to the employer under regulation 75A(5).

97D(4) In a case in which condition B in regulation 97B is met, the transfer notice must be served before the end of a period of 12 months beginning with the date on which HM Revenue and Customs received the return delivered under regulation 73.

97D(5) In a case in which condition C in regulation 97B is met, the transfer notice must be served before the end of a period of 12 months beginning with the date on which HM Revenue and Customs prepare the certificate under regulation 77(6).

97D(6) In a case in which condition D in regulation 97B is met, the transfer notice must be served before the end of a period of 12 months beginning with the date on which HM Revenue and Customs serve notice to the employer under regulation 78(4).

97D(7) In a case in which condition E in regulation 97B is met, the transfer notice must be served before the end of a period of 12 months beginning with the date on which HM Revenue and Customs carry out the inspection of the employer's PAYE records.

97D(8) If the transfer notice is served on a person mentioned in paragraph (c) of section 688A(2) or on a paragraph (c) associate, the transfer notice must be served before the end of a period of three months beginning with the date on which the officer of Revenue and Customs certifies the matters specified in regulation 97C(7).

History – Reg. 97D(3A) inserted by SI 2012/822, reg. 43, with effect from 6 April 2012.
In reg. 97D(8) the words "three months" substituted for "12 months" by SI 2007/2296, reg. 2, with effect from 6 August 2007 (immediately after the insertion of reg. 97D by SI 2007/2069).
Reg. 97D inserted by SI 2007/2069, reg. 2, with effect from 6 August 2007.

Contents of transfer notice

97E(1) A transfer notice must contain the following information–

(a)   the name of the managed service company to which the relevant PAYE debt relates;

(b)   the address of the managed service company to which the relevant PAYE debt relates;

(c)   the amount of the relevant PAYE debt;

(d)   the tax periods to which the relevant PAYE debt relates;

(e)   if the tax periods to which the relevant PAYE debt relates are comprised in more than one tax year, the apportionment of the relevant PAYE debt among those tax years;

(f)   which of the conditions A to E specified in regulation 97B is met;

(g)   the transferee's name;

(h)   the transferee's address;

(j)   whether the transferee is a person mentioned in paragraph (a), (b) or (c) of section 688A, a paragraph (b) associate or a paragraph (c) associate;

(k)   if the transferee is a person mentioned in paragraph (c) of section 688A or a paragraph (c) associate–

    (i)   the date on which the officer of Revenue and Customs certified the matters specified in regulation 97C(7), and

    (ii)   the names of the persons from whom it has been impracticable to recover the specified amount;

(l)   the specified amount;

(m)   the tax periods to which the specified amount relates;

(n)   if the tax periods to which the specified amount relates are comprised in more than one tax year, the apportionment of the specified amount among those tax years;

(o)   the address to which payment must be sent;

(p)   the address to which an appeal must be sent.

97E(2) The transfer notice may specify the lower amount if HM Revenue and Customs are prepared to accept the lower amount from the transferee.

97E(3) The transfer notice must also contain a statement, made by the officer of Revenue and Customs serving the notice, that in his opinion the specified amount is irrecoverable from the managed service company within a reasonable period.

History – Reg. 97E inserted by SI 2007/2069, reg. 2, with effect from 6 August 2007.

Payment of the specified amount

97F(1) If a transfer notice is served, the transferee must pay the specified amount to HM Revenue and Customs at the address specified in the transfer notice.

97F(2) The transferee must pay the specified amount within 30 days beginning with the date on which the transfer notice is served (the "specified period").

97F(3) If a transfer notice is served on a person mentioned in paragraph (a) or (b) of section 688A(2), or on a paragraph (b) associate, the specified amount carries interest from the reckonable date until the date on which payment is made.

97F(4) If a transfer notice is served on a person mentioned in paragraph (c) of section 688A(2), or on a paragraph (c) associate, the specified amount carries interest from the day following the expiry of the specified period until the date on which payment is made.

History – Reg. 97F inserted by SI 2007/2069, reg. 2, with effect from 6 August 2007.

Appeals

97G(1)   A transferee may appeal against the transfer notice.

97G(2)   A notice of appeal must–

(a)   be given to HM Revenue and Customs at the address specified in the transfer notice within 30 days beginning with the date on which the transfer notice was served, and

(b)   specify the grounds of appeal.

97G(3)   The grounds of appeal are any of the following–

(a)   that the relevant PAYE debt (or part of the relevant PAYE debt) is not due from the managed service company to HM Revenue and Customs;

(b)   that the specified amount does not relate to a company which is a managed service company;

(c)   that the specified amount is not irrecoverable from the managed service company within a reasonable period;

(d)   that the transferee is not a person mentioned in section 688A(2);

(e)   that the transferee was not a person mentioned in section 688A(2) during the tax periods to which the specified amount relates;

(f)   that the transferee was not a person mentioned in section 688A(2) during some part of the tax periods to which the specified amount relates;

(g)   that the transfer notice was not served before the end of the period specified in regulation 97D;

(h)   that the transfer notice does not satisfy the requirements specified in regulation 97E;

(j)   in the case of a transferee mentioned in section 688A(2)(c) or of a paragraph (c) associate, that it is not impracticable to recover the specified amount from persons mentioned in paragraphs (a) and (b) of section 688A(2) or from paragraph (b) associates;

(k)   in the case of a transferee mentioned in section 688A(2)(c) or of a paragraph (c) associate, that the amount specified in the transfer notice does not have regard to the degree and extent to which the transferee is a person who (directly or indirectly) has encouraged or been actively involved in the provision by the managed service company of the services of the individual mentioned in that provision.

97G(4)   Paragraph (3)(a) is subject to regulation 97H(4).

97G(5)   [Omitted by SI 2009/56, art. 3(2) and Sch. 2, para. 103.]

History – Reg. 97G(5) omitted by SI 2009/56, art. 3(2) and Sch. 2, para. 103, operative from 1 April 2009 subject to transitional and saving provisions in SI 2009/56, Sch. 3. Former reg. 97G(5) read as follows:

         "**97G(5)**   The appeal is to the Special Commissioners.".

Reg. 97G inserted by SI 2007/2069, reg. 2, with effect from 6 August 2007.

Procedures on appeals

97H(1)   On an appeal that is notified to the tribunal, the tribunal shall uphold or quash the transfer notice.

97H(2)   The general rule in paragraph (1) is subject to the following qualifications.

97H(3)   In the case of the ground of appeal specified in regulation 97G(3)(a), the tribunal shall investigate the matter and shall–

(a)   uphold the amount of the relevant PAYE debt specified in the transfer notice, or

(b)   reduce or increase the amount of the relevant PAYE debt specified in the transfer notice to such amount as in the tribunal's opinion is just and reasonable.

97H(4)   If the tribunal determines the amount of the relevant PAYE debt of a managed service company under paragraph (3), that amount is conclusive as to the amount of that relevant PAYE debt in any later appeal relating to that debt.

97H(5)   In the case of the ground of appeal specified in regulation 97G(3)(f), the tribunal may reduce the amount specified in the transfer notice to an amount determined in accordance with the equation–

$$RA = \frac{P}{TP} \times AS$$

97H(6)   In paragraph (5)–

RA means the reduced amount;

P means the number of days in the tax periods specified in the transfer notice during which the transferee was a person mentioned in section 688A(2);

TP means the number of days in the tax periods specified in the transfer notice;

AS means the amount specified in the transfer notice.

97H(7)　In the case of the ground of appeal specified in regulation 97G(3)(k), the tribunal may reduce the amount specified in the transfer notice to such amount as in the tribunal's opinion is just and reasonable.

History – In reg. 97H(1), the words "that is notified to the tribunal, the tribunal" substituted for the words "the Special Commissioners" by SI 2009/56, art. 3(2) and Sch. 2, para. 104(2), operative from 1 April 2009 subject to transitional and saving provisions in SI 2009/56, Sch. 3.
In reg. 97H(3), "tribunal" substituted for "Special Commissioners" by SI 2009/56, art. 3(2) and Sch. 2, para. 104(3)(a), operative from 1 April 2009 subject to transitional and saving provisions in SI 2009/56, Sch. 3.
In reg. 97H(3)(b), the words "the tribunal's opinion" substituted for the words "their opinion" by SI 2009/56, art. 3(2) and Sch. 2, para. 104(3)(b), operative from 1 April 2009 subject to transitional and saving provisions in SI 2009/56, Sch. 3.
In reg. 97H(4), the words "tribunal determines" substituted for the words "Special Commissioners determine" by SI 2009/56, art. 3(2) and Sch. 2, para. 104(4), operative from 1 April 2009 subject to transitional and saving provisions in SI 2009/56, Sch. 3.
In reg. 97H(5), "tribunal" substituted for "Special Commissioners" by SI 2009/56, art. 3(2) and Sch. 2, para. 104(5), operative from 1 April 2009 subject to transitional and saving provisions in SI 2009/56, Sch. 3.
In reg. 97H(7), "tribunal" substituted for "Special Commissioners" by SI 2009/56, art. 3(2) and Sch. 2, para. 104(6)(a), operative from 1 April 2009 subject to transitional and saving provisions in SI 2009/56, Sch. 3.
In reg. 97H(7), the words "the tribunal's opinion" substituted for the words "their opinion" by SI 2009/56, art. 3(2) and Sch. 2, para. 104(6)(b), operative from 1 April 2009 subject to transitional and saving provisions in SI 2009/56, Sch. 3.
Reg. 97H inserted by SI 2007/2069, reg. 2, with effect from 6 August 2007.

Withdrawal of transfer notices

97J(1)　A transfer notice shall be withdrawn if the tribunal quashes it.

97J(2)　A transfer notice may be withdrawn if, in the opinion of an officer of Revenue and Customs, it is appropriate to do so.

97J(3)　If a transfer notice is withdrawn, HM Revenue and Customs must give written notice of that fact to the transferee.

History – In reg. 97J(1), the words "tribunal quashes" substituted for the words "Special Commissioners quash" by SI 2009/56, art. 3(2) and Sch. 2, para. 105, operative from 1 April 2009 subject to transitional and saving provisions in SI 2009/56, Sch. 3.
Reg. 97J inserted by SI 2007/2069, reg. 2, with effect from 6 August 2007.

Application of Part 6 of TMA

97K(1)　For the purposes of this Chapter, Part 6 of TMA (collection and recovery) applies as if–

(a)　the transfer notice were an assessment, and

(b)　the amount specified in the transfer notice, and any interest payable on that amount under paragraph (3) or (4) of regulation 97F, were income tax charged on the transferee;

97K(2)　Summary proceedings for the recovery of the specified amount may be brought in England and Wales or Northern Ireland at any time before the end of a period of 12 months beginning immediately after the expiry of the period mentioned in regulation 97F(2).

97K(3)　The specified amount is one cause of action or one matter of complaint for the purposes of proceedings under sections 65, 66 and 67 of TMA (magistrates' courts, county courts and inferior courts in Scotland).

97K(4)　But paragraph (3) does not prevent the bringing of separate proceedings for the recovery of each of the amounts which the transferee is liable to pay for any tax period.

History – Reg. 97K inserted by SI 2007/2069, reg. 2, with effect from 6 August 2007.

Repayment of surplus amounts

97L(1)　This regulation applies if the amounts paid to HM Revenue and Customs in respect of a relevant PAYE debt exceed the specified amount.

97L(2)　HM Revenue and Customs shall repay the difference on a just and equitable basis and without unreasonable delay.

97L(3)　Interest on any sum repaid shall be paid in accordance with regulation 83 (interest on tax overpaid).
History – Reg. 97L inserted by SI 2007/2069, reg. 2, with effect from 6 August 2007.

PART 4A – SECURITY FOR PAYMENT OF PAYE

History – Pt. 4A inserted by SI 2012/822, reg. 58, with effect from 6 April 2012.

INTERPRETATION

97M　In this Part–

　　"a further notice" has the meaning given in regulation 97U(3); and

　　"PGS" has the meaning given in regulation 97S(1).

History – Reg. 97M inserted by SI 2012/822, reg. 58, with effect from 6 April 2012.

REQUIREMENT FOR SECURITY

97N(1) In circumstances where an officer of Revenue and Customs considers it necessary for the protection of the revenue, the officer may require a person described in regulation 97P(1) (persons from whom security can be required) to give security or further security for the payment of amounts in respect of which an employer described in regulation 97O (employers) is or may be accountable to HMRC under regulation 67G, as adjusted by regulation 67H(2) where appropriate, 68 or 80 (payments to HMRC and determination of unpaid amounts).

97N(2) Paragraph (1) does not apply to any amount which the employer is required to pay to HMRC that relates to income to which Part 8 (social security benefits) applies.

History – In reg. 97N(1), the words ", as adjusted by regulation 67H(2) where appropriate" inserted by SI 2013/521, reg. 34, with effect for the tax year 2013–14 and subsequent tax years.
Reg. 97N inserted by SI 2012/822, reg. 58, with effect from 6 April 2012.

EMPLOYERS

97O(1) The employer is any employer other than–

(a) the Crown,

(b) an employer to whom paragraph (2) applies,

(c) [omitted by SI 2013/521, reg. 9,]

(d) a care and support employer within the meaning given by regulation 206(4) (employers).

97O(2) This paragraph applies to employers who at the relevant time could not be liable to a penalty under Schedule 56 to the Finance Act 2009 by virtue of paragraph 10 of that Schedule (suspension of penalty for failure to make payments on time during currency of agreement for deferred payment).

97O(3) In paragraph (2), the relevant time is a time at which, but for paragraph (1)(b), the officer would require security.

History – Reg. 97O(1)(c) omitted by SI 2013/521, reg. 9, with effect from 6 April 2014.
Reg. 97O inserted by SI 2012/822, reg. 58, with effect from 6 April 2012.

PERSONS FROM WHOM SECURITY CAN BE REQUIRED

97P(1) The persons are–

(a) the employer,

(b) any of the following in relation to the employer–

    (i) a director,

    (ii) a company secretary,

    (iii) any other similar officer, or

    (iv) any person purporting to act in such a capacity, and

(c) in a case where the employer is a limited liability partnership, a member of the limited liability partnership.

97P(2) An officer of Revenue and Customs may require–

(a) a person to give security or further security of a specified value in respect of the employer, or

(b) more than one person to give security or further security of a specified value in respect of the employer, and where the officer does so those persons shall be jointly and severally liable to give that security or further security.

History – Reg. 97P inserted by SI 2012/822, reg. 58, with effect from 6 April 2012.

NOTICE OF REQUIREMENT

97Q(1) An officer of Revenue and Customs must give notice of a requirement for security to each person from whom security is required and the notice must specify–

(a) the value of security to be given,

(b) the manner in which security is to be given,

(c) the date on or before which security is to be given, and

(d) the period of time for which security is required.

97Q(2) The notice must include, or be accompanied by, an explanation of–

(a) the employer's right to make a request under paragraph 10(1) of Schedule 56 to the Finance Act 2009, and

(b) the effect of regulation 97R(2) and (3) (date on which security is due).

97Q(3) In a case which falls within regulation 97P(2)(b), the notice must include, or be accompanied by, the names of each other person from whom security is required.

97Q(4) The notice may contain such other information as the officer considers necessary.

97Q(5) A person shall not be treated as having been required to provide security unless HMRC comply with this regulation and regulation 97R(1).

History – Reg. 97Q inserted by SI 2012/822, reg. 58, with effect from 6 April 2012.

DATE ON WHICH SECURITY IS DUE

97R(1) The date specified under regulation 97Q(1)(c) (notice of requirement) may not be earlier than the 30th day after the day on which the notice is given.

97R(2) If, before the date specified under regulation 97Q(1)(c), the employer makes a request under paragraph 10(1) of Schedule 56 to the Finance Act 2009, the requirement to give security on or before that date does not apply.

97R(3) In a case which falls within paragraph (2), if HMRC does not agree to the employer's request, security is to be given on or before the 30th day after the day on which HMRC notifies the employer of that decision.

History – Reg. 97R inserted by SI 2012/822, reg. 58, with effect from 6 April 2012.

APPLICATION FOR REDUCTION IN THE VALUE OF SECURITY HELD

97S(1) A person who has given security ("PGS") may apply to an officer of Revenue and Customs for a reduction in the value of security held by HMRC if–

(a)   PGS' circumstances have changed since the day the security was given because–

     (i)   of hardship, or

     (ii)   PGS has ceased to be a person mentioned in regulation 97P(1) (person from whom security can be required), or

(b)   since the day the security was given there has been a significant reduction in the number of employees of the employer to whom the security relates or that employer has ceased to be an employer.

97S(2) Where regulation 97P(2)(b) applies, a person who has not contributed to the value of the security given may not make an application under paragraph (1).

History – Reg. 97S inserted by SI 2012/822, reg. 58, with effect from 6 April 2012.

OUTCOME OF APPLICATION FOR REDUCTION IN THE VALUE OF SECURITY HELD

97T(1) If an application under regulation 97S(1) (application for reduction in the value of security held) is successful, the officer must inform PGS of the reduced value of security that is still required or, where that value is nil, that the requirement for security has been cancelled.

97T(2) HMRC may make such arrangements as they think fit to ensure the necessary reduction in the value of security held.

History – Reg. 97T inserted by SI 2012/822, reg. 58, with effect from 6 April 2012.

OUTCOME OF APPLICATION FOR REDUCTION IN THE VALUE OF SECURITY HELD: FURTHER PROVISION

97U(1) This regulation applies–

(a)   in cases which fall within regulation 97P(2)(b), and

(b)   where PGS' application is made under regulation 97S(1)(a).

97U(2) As a consequence of arrangements made under regulation 97T(2) (outcome of application for reduction in the value of security held), an officer of Revenue and Customs may require any other person who was given notice under regulation 97Q (notice of requirement) in relation to the security ("the original security"), or any other person mentioned in regulation 97P(1), to provide security in substitution for the original security.

97U(3) Where an officer of Revenue and Customs acts in reliance on paragraph (2), the officer must give notice ("a further notice").

97U(4) Regulation 97Q and regulation 97R (date on which security is due) apply in relation to a further notice.

97U(5) Subject to paragraph (6), regulation 97V(1) (appeals) applies in relation to a further notice.

97U(6)   A person who is given a further notice and who was also given notice under regulation 97Q in relation to the original security may only appeal on the grounds the person is not a person mentioned in regulation 97P(1).

History – Reg. 97U inserted by SI 2012/822, reg. 58, with effect from 6 April 2012.

APPEALS

97V(1)   A person who is given notice under regulation 97Q may appeal against the notice or any requirement in it.

97V(2)   PGS may appeal against–

(a)   the rejection by an officer of Revenue and Customs of an application under regulation 97S(1), and

(b)   a smaller reduction in the value of security held than PGS applied for.

97V(3)   Notice of an appeal under this regulation must be given–

(a)   before the end of the period of 30 days beginning with–

    (i)   in the case of an appeal under paragraph (1), the day after the day on which the notice was given, and

    (ii)   in the case of an appeal under paragraph (2), the day after the day on which PGS was notified of the outcome of the application, and

(b)   to the officer of Revenue and Customs by whom the notice was given or the decision on the application was made, as the case may be.

97V(4)   Notice of an appeal under this regulation must state the grounds of appeal.

97V(5)   On an appeal under paragraph (1) that is notified to the tribunal, the tribunal may–

(a)   confirm the requirements in the notice,

(b)   vary the requirements in the notice, or

(c)   set aside the notice.

97V(6)   On an appeal under paragraph (2) that is notified to the tribunal, the tribunal may–

(a)   confirm the decision on the application, or

(b)   vary the decision on the application.

97V(7)   On the final determination of an appeal under this regulation–

(a)   subject to any alternative determination by a tribunal or court, any security to be given is due on the 30th day after the day on which the determination is made, or

(b)   HMRC may make such arrangements as it sees fit to ensure the necessary reduction in the value of security held.

97V(8)   An appeal under this regulation is subject to the provisions of Part 5 of TMA (appeals and other proceedings) apart from–

(a)   section 46D,

(b)   section 47B,

(c)   section 50(6) to (9), and

(d)   sections 54A to 57.

History – Reg. 97V inserted by SI 2012/822, reg. 58, with effect from 6 April 2012.

APPEALS: FURTHER PROVISION FOR CASES WHICH FALL WITHIN REGULATION 97R(2)

97W   In a case which falls within regulation 97R(2) (date on which security is due), if the request mentioned in that provision is made before an appeal under regulation 97V(1) (appeals), regulation 97V(3)(a)(i) applies as if the words "the day after the day on which the notice was given" were "the day after the day on which HMRC notifies the employer of its decision".

History – Reg. 97W inserted by SI 2012/822, reg. 58, with effect from 6 April 2012.

OFFENCE

97X(1)   For the purposes of section 684(4A) of ITEPA (PAYE regulations – security for payment of PAYE: offence)–

(a)   in relation to a requirement for security under a notice under regulation 97Q (notice of requirement) the period specified is the period which starts with the day the notice is given and ends with–

     (i)   the first day after the date specified under regulation 97Q(1)(c), or

     (ii) in a case which falls within regulation 97R(2), the first day after the date determined under regulation 97R(3),

(b)   in relation to a requirement for security under a further notice the period specified is the period which starts with the day the further notice is given and ends with–

     (i)   the first day after the date specified under regulation 97Q(1)(c) as it applies in relation to the further notice, or

     (ii) in a case which falls within regulation 97R(2), the first day after the date determined under regulation 97R(3) as it applies in relation to the further notice, and

(c)   in relation to a requirement for security to which regulation 97V(7)(a) applies the period specified is the period which starts with the day the determination is made and ends with the first day after–

     (i)   the day the tribunal or court determines to be the day that the security is to be given, or

     (ii) the day determined in accordance with that regulation,

    as the case may be.

History – Reg. 97X inserted by SI 2012/822, reg. 58, with effect from 6 April 2012.

PART 5 – EMPLOYERS

SPECIAL ARRANGEMENTS

Multiple PAYE schemes

98(1)   An employer may elect, for the purposes of these Regulations, to be treated as different employers in relation to different groups of employees.

98(2)   Where the employer makes an election, these Regulations apply as if–

(a)   in respect of each group the employer were a different employer;

(b)   each group constituted all of the employer's employees;

(c)   each group were employed in a separate undertaking from the others; and

(d)   an employee who has moved from one group to another has left one employment and started employment with a new employer.

98(3)   While an election is in force, an employer must allocate any new employees to one of the groups.

98(4)   An election must be made by notice to the Inland Revenue containing–

(a)   such information as may be necessary to identify the groups of employees, and

(b)   a certificate that each employee falls into one of the groups.

98(5)   An employer must, subject to paragraph (6), make an election before the beginning of the tax year for which it is to have effect.

98(6)   An employer who acquires the whole or a part of any business of another employer may, within 90 days of the acquisition, elect–

(a)   to be treated as a different employer in relation to the acquired employees, or two or more different employers in relation to groups of the acquired employees, whether or not an election is already in force in respect of the existing employees, or

(b)   to add some or all of the acquired employees to existing groups of employees in respect of whom an election is already in force,

and such an election has effect for the tax year in which the acquisition takes place.

98(7)   In paragraph (6)–

    "business" includes any trade, concern or undertaking;

    "acquired employee" means an employee who was employed in the acquired business.

98(8)   An election continues in effect until revoked by a notice given to the Inland Revenue.

98(9)   A notice of revocation must be given before the beginning of the tax year for which the election is to be revoked, but the revocation of an election does not prevent the making of a new election for that or a later tax year.

98(10) An election which has not yet come into effect may be revoked at any time before the beginning of the tax year for which it is to have effect.

98(11) This regulation is subject to regulation 99.

Origin – Reg. 98(1), (2): SI 1993/744, reg. 3(1)(part).
Reg. 98(3): drafting.
Reg. 98(4): SI 1993/744, reg. 3(2) and see *Rewrite: Changes in Law* notes below.
Reg. 98(5): SI 1993/744, reg. 3(3) and see *Rewrite: Changes in Law* notes below.
Reg. 98(6): SI 1993/744, reg. 3(4)(part) and see *Rewrite: Changes in Law* notes below.
Reg. 98(7): SI 1993/744, reg. 3(4)(part); drafting.
Reg. 98(8): SI 1993/744, reg. 3(3)(part) and see *Rewrite: Changes in Law* notes below.
Reg. 98(9), (10): SI 1993/744, reg. 3(5)(part) and see *Rewrite: Changes in Law* notes below.
Reg. 98(11): SI 1993/744, reg. 3(1)(part).

Rewrite: Changes in Law – Commentary, App. 1, Change 1: reg. 98 refers to "Inland Revenue" (meaning any officer of the Board) rather than "inspector" or "Board".
Commentary, para. 561, 562 and App. 1, Change 82: reg. 98 allows employers more flexibility as to when they may make or revoke election to operate separate PAYE schemes, and as to how they allocate employees to PAYE schemes after acquiring new employees.

Multiple PAYE schemes: election made for improper purpose ineffective

99(1) An election made under regulation 98 must be disregarded if the Inland Revenue–

(a) issue a notice to the employer stating that it appears to them that the election is made wholly or mainly for an improper purpose ("an improper purpose notice"), and

(b) issue the improper purpose notice within 60 days of the making of the election.

99(2) An election is made for an **"improper purpose"** if it is made for the purpose of–

(a) avoiding the requirement imposed by regulation 199 (large employers required to make specified payments electronically),

(b) [omitted by SI 2010/668, reg. 16(c),]

(c) [omitted by SI 2010/668, reg. 16(b).]

99(3) An employer may appeal against an improper purpose notice by giving notice to the Inland Revenue within 30 days of the issue of the improper purpose notice.

99(4) The grounds of appeal are–

(a) that the election was not made wholly or mainly for an improper purpose, or

(b) that the improper purpose notice was not issued within 60 days of the election.

99(5) If the appeal is successful the improper purpose notice must be withdrawn.

99(6) Regulation 217 (appeals: supplementary provisions) applies to appeals under this regulation.

History – Reg. 99(2)(b) omitted by SI 2010/668, reg. 16(c), with effect in relation to the tax year 2011–12 and subsequent tax years.
In former reg. 99(2)(b), "205A" substituted for "205" by SI 2010/668, reg. 16(a), with effect from 6 April 2010.
Reg. 99(2)(c) omitted by SI 2010/668, reg. 16(b), with effect from 6 April 2010.
Origin – Reg. 99(1): SI 1993/744, reg. 3(6).
Reg. 99(2): SI 1993/744, reg. 3(7)
Reg. 99(3)–(5): SI 1993/744, reg. 3(8)(part).
Reg. 99(6): SI 1993/744, reg. 3(9).

Tips: special arrangements

100(1) This regulation applies if an organised arrangement exists for tips to be shared among employees by a person ("T") who is not the principal employer.

100(2) On becoming aware of the existence of an arrangement, the principal employer must notify the Inland Revenue about the arrangement giving T's name, if known.

100(3) For the purposes of these Regulations–

(a) every payment made to an employee by way of the employee's share of tips by T (including the retention by T of T's own share if T is also an employee) is regarded as a relevant payment by T; and

(b) to the extent of any such payment, T is regarded as the employer.

100(4) But if in any case the Inland Revenue are satisfied that T has failed to comply with any of the requirements of these Regulations and they so direct, then–

(a) any tips paid to T through the principal employer for sharing among the employees are to be dealt with in accordance with paragraph (5), and

(b) any other tips may be taken into account by the Inland Revenue under regulation 14(1)(b) in determining the code for each employee.

100(5) If this paragraph applies–

(a) the principal employer is treated as the employer for the purposes of these Regulations in relation to the tips;

(b)   T must, before the principal employer pays any tips to T, give the principal employer such particulars of every payment by way of the sharing of tips to be made to an employee as may be necessary to enable the principal employer to comply with these Regulations;

(c)   the principal employer must, on making any payment of tips to T, deduct or repay tax in accordance with these Regulations in respect of the amount of such tips to be paid to each employee, and notify T of each amount so deducted or repaid.

100(6)   Paragraph (2) does not apply if the arrangement came into existence before 6th April 2004.

100(7)   In this regulation–

"**the principal employer**" means the person under whose general control and management the employees work;

"**tips**" means gratuities and service charges.

Origin – Reg. 100(1): SI 1993/744, reg. 5(1)(part).
Reg. 100(2): see *Rewrite: Changes in Law* notes below.
Reg. 100(3): SI 1993/744, reg. 5(2).
Reg. 100(4): SI 1993/744, reg. 5(3), (4A)(part) and see *Rewrite: Changes in Law* notes below.
Reg. 100(5): SI 1993/744, reg. 5(4).
Reg. 100(6): see *Rewrite: Changes in Law* notes below.
Reg. 100(7): SI 1993/744, reg. 5(1)(part), (5).

Rewrite: Changes in Law – Commentary, App. 1, Change 1: reg. 100 refers to "Inland Revenue" (meaning any officer of the Board) rather than "inspector" or "Board".
Commentary, App. 1, Change 83: reg. 100 requires employers to inform Revenue when they become aware that an organised arrangement for sharing tips is in existence, giving name of person who shares out tips if known.

DEATH OF EMPLOYER AND SUCCESSION

Death of employer

101(1)   This regulation applies if an employer dies.

101(2)   Anything which the employer would have been liable to do under these Regulations must be done by the employer's personal representatives.

101(3)   But if the employer made payments on behalf of another person ("the principal"), anything which the employer would have been liable to do under these Regulations in respect of or in connection with those payments must be done by the principal.

Origin – Reg. 101(1), (2): SI 1993/744, reg. 79(part).
Reg. 101(3): SI 1993/744, reg. 79(part) and see *Rewrite: Changes in Law* notes below.

Rewrite: Changes in Law – Commentary, App. 1, Change 84: reg. 101 makes clear that when agent paying net PAYE income on behalf of principal dies it is the principal who is responsible for implementing the PAYE regulations whether the agent is succeeded by another agent or not.
Commentary, App. 1, Change 87: reg. 101 makes clear who is to account for tax in respect of notional payments after death of employer or succession to business or both.

Succession to a business etc

102(1)   This regulation applies if there is a change in an employee's employer while the employee remains in employment in the same business.

102(2)   This regulation also applies if there is a change in the pension payer who pays a pension to a pensioner.

102(3)   The change is not to be treated as a cessation of employment for the purposes of regulation 36 (cessation of employment: Form P45).

102(4)   The new employer is, in relation to any matter arising after the change, liable to do anything which the former employer would have been liable to do under these Regulations if the change had not taken place.

102(5)   Paragraph (4) is subject to paragraphs (6) and (7) and regulation 104 (succession to a business: trade disputes).

102(6)   The new employer is not liable for the payment of any tax which was deductible from relevant payments made to the employee–

(a)   before the change took place, unless those payments were made by the new employer, or

(b)   by the former employer after the change took place.

102(7)   The new employer is not liable for the payment of any tax which was to be deducted or accounted for in accordance with regulation 62(4) or (5) (notional payments) in respect of notional payments made to the employee–

(a)   before the change took place, unless those payments were made by the new employer, or

(b)   by the former employer after the change took place.

102(8)   The former employer must give the new employer any particulars which the new employer needs in order to comply with this regulation.

PAYMENT OF TAX UNDER PSA

Calculation of tax payable under PSA

108(1) A PSA must provide for the sums in respect of income tax for which an employer is to be accountable to the Board of Inland Revenue under the PSA–

(a) to be computed in accordance with the factors specified in paragraph (2), and

(b) to be comprised of the amounts specified in paragraph (3).

108(2) The factors are–

(a) in the case of qualifying general earnings comprising sums paid in respect of expenses, the estimated aggregate amount of such payments on which income tax is chargeable, reduced by such amount (if any) as would have been deductible if the qualifying general earnings had not been included in the PSA;

(b) in the case of qualifying general earnings comprising benefits provided or made available, the estimated aggregate amount of the cash equivalents and other amounts on which income tax is chargeable, reduced by such amount (if any) as would have been deductible if the qualifying general earnings had not been included in the PSA;

(c) the total number of employees in receipt of qualifying general earnings comprised in the PSA;

(d) the number of those employees respectively chargeable to income tax–

   (i) at only the basic rate for the tax year to which the PSA relates, and

   (ii) at both the basic rate and the higher rate for that tax year; and

   (iii) at the basic, higher and additional rates for that tax year;

(e) such other matters as are agreed by HMRC and the employer to be relevant in relation to the qualifying general earnings comprised in the PSA.

108(3) The amounts specified for the purposes of paragraph (1)(b) are–

(a) an amount equal to income tax on the aggregate of the amounts computed in accordance with paragraph (2)(a) and (b), calculated so as to take account of the factor specified in paragraph (2)(d); and

(b) a further amount reflecting an estimate of the income tax on the benefit to the employees of having no tax liability on the qualifying general earnings included in the PSA.

History – Reg. 108(2)(d)(iii) (and the "and" at the end of reg. 108(2)(d)(ii)) inserted by SI 2011/729, reg. 14, with effect from 6 April 2011.

Reg. 108(2)(d) substituted by SI 2008/782, reg. 12, with effect from 6 April 2008.

In reg. 108(2)(e) "HMRC" substituted for "the Inland Revenue" by SI 2008/782, reg. 12, with effect from 6 April 2008.

Origin – Reg. 108(1): SI 1993/744, reg. 80F(1) and see *Rewrite: Changes in Law* notes below.

Reg. 108(2): SI 1993/744, reg. 80F(2) and see *Rewrite: Changes in Law* notes below.

Reg. 108(3): SI 1993/744, reg. 80F(3), (4) and see *Rewrite: Changes in Law* notes below.

Rewrite: Changes in Law – Commentary, App. 1, Change 1: reg. 108 refers to "Inland Revenue" (meaning any officer of the Board) rather than "inspector" or "Board".

Commentary, App. 1, Change 88: reg. 108(1)(b) and (3)(b) make it explicit that employers must gross up income tax on earnings covered by PSA.

Payment of tax and recovery proceedings

109(1) The employer must pay to the Inland Revenue by the due date the aggregate amount for which the employer is accountable to the Board of Inland Revenue under a PSA.

109(2) "**The due date**" means 19th October following the end of the tax year to which the PSA relates.

109(3) Part 6 of TMA (collection and recovery) applies to the recovery of the aggregate amount or any part of it ("the amount of tax") as if it were income tax charged on the employer.

109(4) But summary proceedings for the recovery of the amount of tax may be brought in England, Wales or Northern Ireland at any time before the expiry of 12 months beginning with the due date.

109(5) Proceedings may be brought for the recovery of the amount of tax without distinguishing the amounts which the employer is liable to pay in respect of each employee under the PSA and without specifying the employees in question.

109(6) The amount of tax is one cause of action or one matter of complaint for the purposes of proceedings under sections 65, 66 and 67 of TMA (magistrates' courts, county courts and inferior courts in Scotland).

Origin – Reg. 109(1): SI 1993/744, reg. 80G(1) and see *Rewrite: Changes in Law* notes below.

Reg. 109(2): SI 1993/744, reg. 80G(2).

Reg. 109(3): SI 1993/744, reg. 80G(3), (4) and see *Rewrite: Changes in Law* notes below.

Reg. 109(4): SI 1993/744, reg. 80G(5).

Reg. 109(5), (6): SI 1993/744, reg. 80G(6)(part).

Rewrite: Changes in Law – Commentary, App. 1, Change 1: reg. 109 refers to "Inland Revenue" (meaning any officer of the Board) rather than "inspector" or "Board".

Commentary, App. 1, Change 77: reg. 109 restricts recovery procedures to those available under TMA 1970, Pt. 6.

Formal determination of tax payable by the employer

110(1)   This regulation applies if it appears to the Inland Revenue that there may be an amount payable under regulation 109(1) for any tax year which has not been paid by the due date (as defined by regulation 109(2)).

110(2)   The Inland Revenue may determine the amount payable to the best of their judgment.

110(3)   If a determination is made, the Inland Revenue must serve notice of it on the employer.

110(4)   A determination under this regulation is subject to Parts 4, 5, 5A and 6 of TMA (assessment, appeals, collection and recovery) as if–

(a)   the determination were an assessment, and

(b)   the amount determined were income tax charged on the employer,

and those Parts of TMA apply accordingly with any necessary modifications.

110(5)   [Omitted by SI 2009/56, art. 3(2) and Sch. 2, para. 106.]

History – In reg. 110(4), ", 5A" inserted by SI 2010/668, reg. 3, with effect in relation to the tax year 2010–11 and subsequent tax years.

Reg. 110(5) omitted by SI 2009/56, art. 3(2) and Sch. 2, para. 106, operative from 1 April 2009 subject to transitional and saving provisions in SI 2009/56, Sch. 3. Former reg. 110(5) read as follows:

> "**110(5)**   For the purposes of paragraph 3(1)(a) of Schedule 3 to TMA (rules for assigning proceedings to General Commissioners), the relevant place for an appeal against a determination is the place where the determination was made.".

Origin – Reg. 110(1): SI 1993/744, reg. 80H(1).
Reg. 110(2), (3): SI 1993/744, reg. 80H(2)(part).
Reg. 110(4): SI 1993/744, reg. 80H(3).
Reg. 110(5): SI 1993/744, reg. 80H(4).

FORM AND COMMENCEMENT OF PSA

Form of PSA

111(1)   A PSA must be–

(a)   in writing, and

(b)   signed and dated by the employer and the Inland Revenue.

111(2)   A PSA must incorporate, whether by specification or indirect reference–

(a)   the qualifying general earnings included in the PSA,

(b)   the method of calculation, determined in accordance with regulation 108, of the amount of income tax for which the employer is to be accountable in respect of those qualifying general earnings, and

(c)   the due date by which, in accordance with regulation 109, income tax in respect of those qualifying general earnings is due and payable.

Origin – Reg. 111(1): SI 1993/744, reg. 80B(1)(part).
Reg. 111(2): SI 1993/744, reg. 80B(1)(part), (2).

Commencement of PSA

112(1)   A PSA may be entered into at any time before 6th July following the end of the tax year for which it is to have effect ("the year in question").

112(2)   A PSA entered into after the beginning of the year in question cannot apply to–

(a)   general earnings which, when the PSA is entered into, have been, or should have been, paid earlier in the year in question under deduction of tax in accordance with Part 3, or

(b)   general earnings consisting of benefits which, when the PSA is entered into, are or were reflected in the employee's code for the year in question in accordance with Part 2.

Origin – Reg. 112(1): SI 1993/744, reg. 80C(1).
Reg. 112(2): SI 1993/744, reg. 80C(2).

VARIATION AND CANCELLATION OF PSA

Variation of PSA

113(1)   The Inland Revenue and the employer may, by agreement and consistently with the provisions of this Part, vary the terms of a PSA entered into by them.

113(2)   The agreement must be–

Statutory Instruments

(a)   in writing, and

(b)   signed and dated by the employer and by the Inland Revenue.

113(3)   The last date for variation of a PSA is 6th July following the end of the tax year to which it relates.

Origin – Reg. 113(1): SI 1993/744, reg. 80D(1)(part) and see *Rewrite: Changes in Law* note below.
Reg. 113(2): SI 1993/744, reg. 80D(2).
Reg. 113(3): SI 1993/744, reg. 80D(1)(part), (3).

Rewrite: Changes in Law – Commentary, App. 1, Change 1: reg. 113 refers to "Inland Revenue" (meaning any officer of the Board) rather than "inspector" or "Board".

Cancellation of PSA

114(1)   The Inland Revenue may cancel a PSA if the employer has seriously or persistently failed–

(a)   to account to the Board of Inland Revenue for sums for which the employer is accountable under the PSA, or otherwise to comply with the terms of the PSA,

(b)   to produce records in accordance with regulation 117 (inspection of PSA records),

(c)   to deduct, or account for, tax in accordance with Parts 3 and 4 (deduction and repayment of tax; payments, returns and information), or

(d)   to deliver returns in accordance with Parts 3 and 4.

114(2)   Cancellation must be effected by notice to the employer.

114(3)   A cancellation comes into effect from the date of the notice.

114(4)   If a PSA is cancelled, this Part does not apply to general earnings–

(a)   to which the cancelled PSA related, and

(b)   which are paid, or (as the case may be) provided or made available, after the employer receives notice of the cancellation.

Origin – Reg. 114(1): SI 1993/744, reg. 80M(1)(part), (2) and see *Rewrite: Changes in Law* note below.
Reg. 114(2), (3): SI 1993/744, reg. 80M(1)(part).
Reg. 114(4): SI 1993/744, reg. 80M(3).

Rewrite: Changes in Law – Commentary, App. 1, Change 1: reg. 114 refers to "Inland Revenue" (meaning any officer of the Board) rather than "inspector" or "Board".

INTEREST

Interest on unpaid tax

115(1)   This regulation applies if an employer has not paid to the Inland Revenue by the due date (as defined by regulation 109(2)) the full amount for which the employer is liable under this Part.

115(2)   The unpaid amount carries interest at the prescribed rate from the due date until payment ("the interest period").

115(3)   Paragraph (2) applies even if the due date is a non-business day as defined by section 92 of the Bills of Exchange Act 1882.

115(4)   Any change made to the prescribed rate during the interest period applies to the unpaid amount from the date of the change.

115(5)   Interest is recoverable as if it were an amount payable under the PSA.

115(6)   **"The prescribed rate"** means the rate applicable under section 178 of the Finance Act 1989 for the purposes of section 86 of TMA.

Origin – Reg. 115(1): SI 1993/744, reg. 80J(1)(part), (2)(part) and see *Rewrite: Changes in Law* notes below..
Reg. 115(2): SI 1993/744, reg. 80J(1)(part), (2)(part).
Reg. 115(3): SI 1993/744, reg. 80J(7).
Reg. 115(4): SI 1993/744, reg. 80J(5)(part).
Reg. 115(5): SI 1993/744, reg. 80J(8).
Reg. 115(6): SI 1993/744, reg. 80J(5)(part).

Cross references – SI 1989/1297: rate applicable under FA 1989, s. 178.

Rewrite: Changes in Law – Commentary, App. 1, Change 1: reg. 115 refers to "Inland Revenue" (meaning any officer of the Board) rather than "inspector" or "Board".

Interest on overpaid tax

116(1)   This regulation applies if tax in respect of the tax year to which a PSA relates is repaid to the employer after the due date (as defined by regulation 109(2)).

116(2)   The tax repaid carries interest at the prescribed rate from the later of–

(a)   the due date, and

(b)   the date on which the tax was paid,

until the order for the repayment is issued ("the interest period").

116(3)   Any change made to the prescribed rate during the interest period applies to the tax repaid from the date of the change.

116(4)   **"The prescribed rate"** means the rate applicable under section 178 of the Finance Act 1989 for the purposes of section 824 of ICTA.

Origin – Reg. 116(1), (2): SI 1993/744, reg. 80K(1)(part).
Reg. 116(3), (4): SI 1993/744, reg. 80K(2)(part).

Cross references – SI 1989/1297: rate applicable under FA 1989, s. 178.

RECORDS

Inspection of PSA records

117(1)   An authorised officer may require an employer who has entered into a PSA to produce all PSA records, or such PSA records as may be specified by the authorised officer, for inspection–

(a)   at the prescribed place, and

(b)   at such time as that officer may reasonably require.

117(2)   **"PSA records"** means all books, documents and other records relating to–

(a)   the qualifying general earnings comprised in the PSA,

(b)   the calculation of amounts for which the employer is accountable to the Board of Inland Revenue in accordance with the PSA, and

(c)   the payment of those amounts to the Inland Revenue.

117(3)   **"The prescribed place"** means such place in the United Kingdom as the employer and the authorised officer may agree upon, or in the absence of agreement–

(a)   the place in the United Kingdom at which the PSA records are normally kept, or

(b)   if there is no such place, the employer's principal place of business in the United Kingdom.

117(4)   The authorised officer may–

(a)   take copies of, or make extracts from, any records produced for inspection in accordance with paragraph (1);

(b)   remove any records so produced if the officer considers it necessary to do so, at a reasonable time and for a reasonable period.

117(5)   If any record is removed in accordance with paragraph (4)(b), the authorised officer must provide–

(a)   a receipt for the record, and

(b)   a copy of the record, free of charge, to the person by whom it was produced or caused to be produced, within 7 days of that person requesting a copy, if the record is reasonably required for the proper conduct of a business.

117(6)   If a lien is claimed on a record produced in accordance with paragraph (1), the removal of the document under paragraph (4)(b) is not to be regarded as breaking the lien.

117(7)   If records are maintained by computer, the person required to make them available for inspection must provide the authorised officer with all facilities necessary for obtaining information from them.

117(8)   An employer must keep PSA records for not less than 3 years after the end of the most recent tax year to which they relate.

Origin – Reg. 117(1): SI 1993/744, reg. 80N(1), (2)(part) and see *Rewrite: Changes in Law* notes below.
Reg. 117(2): SI 1993/744, reg. 80N(2)(part) and see *Rewrite: Changes in Law* notes below.
Reg. 117(3): SI 1993/744, reg. 80N(3) and see *Rewrite: Changes in Law* notes below.
Reg. 117(4): SI 1993/744, reg. 80N(4) and see *Rewrite: Changes in Law* notes below.
Reg. 117(5): SI 1993/744, reg. 80N(5) and see *Rewrite: Changes in Law* notes below.
Reg. 117(6): SI 1993/744, reg. 80N(6).
Reg. 117(7): SI 1993/744, reg. 80N(7) and see *Rewrite: Changes in Law* notes below.
Reg. 117(8): SI 1993/744, reg. 80N(8).

Rewrite: Changes in Law – Commentary, App. 1, Change 1: reg. 117 refers to "Inland Revenue" (meaning any officer of the Board) rather than "inspector" or "Board".
Commentary, App. 1, Change 71: reg. 117 makes explicit date on which period begins for authorised officer to provide copy of removed document.
Commentary, App. 1, Change 89: reg. 117 limits to authorised officers the persons who can inspect PSA records.

PART 7 – SPECIAL CASES
Chapter 1 – Councillors' Allowances

Interpretation of Chapter 1

118(1) In this Chapter–

"allowances" means–

(a) payments by way of attendance allowance within section 173(1) or 175(1) of the Local Government Act 1972,

(b) payments within regulations made under section 18(1) of the Local Government and Housing Act 1989,

(c) payments within regulations made under section 100(1)(a) or (c) of the Local Government Act 2000,

(d) payments by way of attendance allowance within section 47(1) of the Local Government (Scotland) Act 1973, or

(e) payments within regulation 3(1), 4(1) or 5(1) of the Local Government (Payments to Councillors) Regulations (Northern Ireland) 1999;

"councillor" means a person entitled to receive any allowances;

"local council" means the local authority, council, joint authority or joint committee paying allowances.

118(2) For the purposes of paragraph (1)–

"council" and "joint committee" are to be read in accordance with section 148(1) of the Local Government Act (Northern Ireland) 1972; and

"local authority" in England and Wales has the meaning given in section 270(1) of the Local Government Act 1972, and in Scotland has the meaning given in section 235(1) of the Local Government (Scotland) Act 1973.

Origin – Reg. 118(1): SI 1993/744, reg. 56(part) and see *Rewrite: Changes in Law* note below.
Reg. 118(2): SI 1993/744, reg. 56(part).

Rewrite: Changes in Law – Commentary, App. 1, Change 90: reg. 118 extends option for basic rate deduction offered to councillors to other allowances which councillor may receive besides attendance allowance.

Councillor's option to have tax deducted at basic rate

119(1) A councillor may, by notice to the Inland Revenue, opt to have income tax deducted from allowances at the basic rate in force at the time of payment of the allowances (the "basic rate option").

119(2) On receiving any such notice the Inland Revenue must give notice to the local council of the councillor's exercise of the basic rate option.

119(3) On receiving a notice under paragraph (2), the local council must, when making any payment of allowances to the councillor, deduct income tax at the basic rate in force at the time of that payment on the non-cumulative basis.

119(4) Paragraph (5) applies if–

(a) a councillor has exercised the basic rate option, and

(b) the Inland Revenue consider that the councillor may incur deductible expenses.

119(5) The Inland Revenue may direct the local council to disregard an appropriate amount of the allowances in calculating the tax to be deducted.

119(6) In paragraph (4)(b), "deductible expenses" means expenses of a kind which would be deductible under sections 336 to 338 of ITEPA (expenses incurred wholly, exclusively and necessarily in performance of duties, and travel expenses).

Origin – Reg. 119(1): SI 1993/744, reg. 57(1), (2) and see *Rewrite: Changes in Law* notes below.
Reg. 119(2): SI 1993/744, reg. 57(3) and see *Rewrite: Changes in Law* notes below.
Reg. 119(3): SI 1993/744, reg. 57(4) and see *Rewrite: Changes in Law* notes below.
Reg. 119(4), (5): SI 1993/744, reg. 57(5)(part) and see *Rewrite: Changes in Law* notes below.
Reg. 119(6): SI 1993/744, reg. 57(5) and drafting.

Rewrite: Changes in Law – Commentary, App. 1, Change 1: reg. 119 refers to "Inland Revenue" (meaning any officer of the Board) rather than "inspector" or "Board".
Commentary, App. 1, Change 14: reg. 119 allows councillor to opt to have basic rate tax deducted from certain allowances, even if not "aggrieved" by code set by Inland Revenue.

Commentary, App. 1, Change 90: reg. 118 ("allowances") extends basic rate option to other allowances which councillor may receive besides attendance allowance

Particulars that local council must record

120(1)   This regulation applies if the Inland Revenue have given notice to the local council of the exercise by a councillor of the basic rate option.

120(2)   The local council must record, in a deductions working sheet (which it must prepare for the purpose unless it has already prepared one) the following particulars about every payment of allowances which it makes to the councillor.

120(3)   The particulars are–

(a)   the councillor's name,

(b)   the councillor's national insurance number, if known,

(c)   the date of the payment,

(d)   the amount of the allowances,

(e)   where regulation 119(5) applies, the net amount of the allowances from which tax has been deducted, and

(f)   the amount of tax deducted from the allowances.

Origin – Reg. 120(1): SI 1993/744, reg. 57(6)(part) and see *Rewrite: Changes in Law* notes below.
Reg. 120(2): SI 1993/744, reg. 57(6)(part); drafting.
Reg. 120(3): SI 1993/744, reg. 57(7) and see *Rewrite: Changes in Law* notes below.
Rewrite: Changes in Law – Commentary, App. 1, Change 1: reg. 120 refers to "Inland Revenue" (meaning any officer of the Board) rather than "inspector" or "Board".
Commentary, App. 1, Change 38: reg. 120 brings into line with practice the particulars that local council must record.
Commentary, App. 1, Change 90: reg. 118 ("allowances") extends option for basic rate deduction offered to councillors to other allowances which councillor may receive besides attendance allowance

Regulations apply as if basic rate option were issue of code

121   If a councillor exercises the basic rate option, these Regulations apply as if the Inland Revenue had issued the basic rate code in respect of the allowances.

Origin – See *Rewrite: Changes in Law* notes below.
Rewrite: Changes in Law – Commentary, App. 1, Change 4: SI 2003/2682, reg. 4 defines "basic rate code".
Commentary, App. 1, Change 91: reg. 121 deems basic rate code to be issued when councillor opts for deduction at basic rate from payments of certain allowances.

Chapter 2 – Reserve Forces' Pay

Interpretation of Chapter 2

122(1)   In this Chapter–

     "the Ministry" means the Ministry of Defence;

     "reserve forces" means the forces specified in paragraph (2);

     "reserve pay" means relevant payments made by the Ministry to members of the reserve forces, excluding such payments made on 6 April 2009 or later;

     "reservist" means any person in receipt of reserve pay, but does not include a person who is not resident in the United Kingdom and is serving outside the United Kingdom.

122(2)   The forces specified in this paragraph are–

(a)   the Royal Naval Reserve (including Queen Alexandra's Royal Naval Nursing Service Reserve),

(b)   the Royal Marines Reserve,

(c)   the Territorial Army,

(d)   the Royal Auxiliary Air Force,

(e)   the University Air Squadron, and

(f)   Officers, Adult Instructors and Adult Warrant Officers of the Sea Cadet Corps, Army Cadet Force, Air Training Corps or Combined Cadet Force.

History – In reg. 122(1), in the definition of "reserve pay", the words ", excluding such payments made on 6 April 2009 or later" inserted by SI 2009/588, reg. 10, with effect from 6 April 2009.
Origin – Reg. 122(1): SI 1993/744, reg. 59(1).
Reg. 122(2): SI 1993/744, reg. 59(2), (3)(part) and see *Rewrite: Changes in Law* notes below.
Rewrite: Changes in Law – Commentary, App. 1, Change 92: the Merchant Navy Reserve, the Royal Fleet Reserve, the Army Reserve and the Air Force Reserve (except the University Air Squadron) are removed from scope of reg. 122.

Application of other Parts

123(1) Parts 2 (codes) and 3 (deduction and repayment of tax) do not apply to reserve pay.

123(2) The rest of these Regulations apply as if the Inland Revenue had issued the basic rate code in respect of reserve pay.

Origin – Reg. 123(1): SI 1993/744, reg. 60.
Reg. 123(2): see *Rewrite: Changes in Law* notes below.

Rewrite: Changes in Law – Commentary, App. 1, Change 4: SI 2003/2682, reg. 4 defines "basic rate code".
Commentary, App. 1, Change 91: reg. 123 deems basic rate code to be issued when tax is deducted at basic rate from relevant payments to reservists.

Deduction of tax

124(1) On making any payment of reserve pay to a reservist during a tax year, the Ministry must deduct income tax at the basic rate in force when the payment is made.

124(2) But the Ministry must not deduct income tax if–

(a)   it has received notice from the Inland Revenue of a determination for that tax year under this Chapter that tax is not to be deducted from reserve pay, and

(b)   it has not received notice of any amendment of that determination.

124(3) This regulation applies even if an objection or appeal has been made under this Chapter.

Origin – Reg. 124(1): SI 1993/744, reg. 61(1).
Reg. 124(2): SI 1993/744, reg. 61(2) and see *Rewrite: Changes in Law* note below.
Reg. 124(3): SI 1993/744, reg. 61(4).

Rewrite: Changes in Law – Commentary, App. 1, Change 1: reg. 124 refers to "Inland Revenue" (meaning any officer of the Board) rather than "inspector" or "Board".

Determination by Inland Revenue

125(1) The Inland Revenue may make a determination that tax is not to be deducted from reserve pay if the Inland Revenue are satisfied that the reservist will not be liable to income tax on the full amount of the reserve pay in a tax year.

125(2) For the purpose of making a determination, it must be assumed–

(a)   that any reliefs from income tax to which the reservist is entitled are allowable primarily against the reservist's PAYE income from other sources, and

(b)   unless the reservist objects, that the balance (if any) of such reliefs is next allowable against the reservist's income other than PAYE income.

125(3) The Inland Revenue may make a determination before, or at any time during, the tax year.

125(4) On making a determination the Inland Revenue must notify the reservist and the Ministry.

Origin – Reg. 125(1), (2): SI 1993/744, reg. 62(1)(part) and see *Rewrite: Changes in Law* notes below.
Reg. 125(3): SI 1993/744, reg. 62(2) and see *Rewrite: Changes in Law* notes below.
Reg. 125(4): SI 1993/744, reg. 62(3) and see *Rewrite: Changes in Law* notes below.

Rewrite: Changes in Law – Commentary, App. 1, Change 1: reg. 125 refers to "Inland Revenue" (meaning any officer of the Board) rather than "inspector" or "Board".
Commentary, App. 1, Change 10: reg. 125 allows Revenue to take account of income of employee other than PAYE income when determining whether tax should be deducted from reservist's pay.

Objection against deduction of tax

126(1) A reservist who objects to tax being deducted in accordance with regulation 124 (deduction at basic rate) must state the grounds of objection.

126(2) On receiving the notice of objection, the Inland Revenue must make a determination whether income tax at the basic rate is to be deducted from the reserve pay.

126(3) Regulation 125(2) (assumptions) applies for the purpose of making the determination.

126(4) The Inland Revenue must notify the reservist of the determination.

126(5) The Inland Revenue may amend the determination by agreement with the reservist.

126(6) If the Inland Revenue and the reservist do not reach agreement, the reservist may appeal against the determination by giving notice to the Inland Revenue.

126(7) [Omitted by SI 2009/56, art. 3(2) and Sch. 2, para. 107.]

History – Reg. 126(7) omitted by SI 2009/56, art. 3(2) and Sch. 2, para. 107, operative from 1 April 2009 subject to transitional and saving provisions in SI 2009/56, Sch. 3. Former reg. 126(7) read as follows:

"**126(7)** An appeal under paragraph (6) may be made to the General or Special Commissioners.".

Origin – Reg. 126(1): SI 1993/744, reg. 63(1) and see *Rewrite: Changes in Law* notes below.
Reg. 126(2): SI 1993/744, reg. 63(2)(part) and see *Rewrite: Changes in Law* notes below.

Reg. 126(3): drafting.

Reg. 126(4): SI 1993/744, reg. 63(2)(part) and see *Rewrite: Changes in Law* notes below.

Reg. 126(5), (6): SI 1993/744, reg. 63(3) and see *Rewrite: Changes in Law* notes below.

Reg. 126(7): SI 1993/744, reg. 63(4).

Rewrite: Changes in Law – Commentary, App. 1, Change 1: reg. 126 refers to "Inland Revenue" (meaning any officer of the Board) rather than "inspector" or "Board".

Commentary, App. 1, Change 14: reg. 126 allows reservist to object to tax being deducted at basic rate without being "aggrieved".

Appeal to the tribunal

127(1) On an appeal that is notified to the tribunal, the tribunal must determine whether income tax at the basic rate is to be deducted from the reserve pay.

127(2) Regulation 125(2) (assumptions) applies for the purpose of making the determination.

127(3) If, on appeal, the tribunal determines that tax is not to be deducted from the reserve pay, the Inland Revenue must give notice of the determination to the Ministry.

127(4) [Omitted by SI 2009/56, art. 3(2) and Sch. 2, para. 108(5).]

History – In the heading to reg. 127, the words "the tribunal" substituted for the word "Commissioners" by SI 2009/56, art. 3(2) and Sch. 2, para. 108(2), operative from 1 April 2009 subject to transitional and saving provisions in SI 2009/56, Sch. 3.

In reg. 127(1), the words "an appeal that is notified to the tribunal, the tribunal" substituted for the words "appeal, the Commissioners" by SI 2009/56, art. 3(2) and Sch. 2, para. 108(3), operative from 1 April 2009 subject to transitional and saving provisions in SI 2009/56, Sch. 3.

In reg. 127(3), the words "tribunal determines" substituted for the words "Commissioners determine" by SI 2009/56, art. 3(2) and Sch. 2, para. 108(4), operative from 1 April 2009 subject to transitional and saving provisions in SI 2009/56, Sch. 3.

Reg. 127(4) omitted by SI 2009/56, art. 3(2) and Sch. 2, para. 108(5), operative from 1 April 2009 subject to transitional and saving provisions in SI 2009/56, Sch. 3. Former reg. 127(4) read as follows:

    "**127(4)** For the purposes of paragraph 3(1)(a) of Schedule 3 to TMA (rules for assigning proceedings to General Commissioners), the relevant place for the appeal is the place where the reservist lives.".

Origin – Reg. 127(1), (2): SI 1993/744, reg. 63(7).

Reg. 127(3): SI 1993/744, reg. 63(9) and see *Rewrite: Changes in Law* notes below.

Reg. 127(4): SI 1993/744, reg. 63(5), (6) and see *Rewrite: Changes in Law* notes below.

Rewrite: Changes in Law – Commentary, App. 1, Change 1: reg. 127 refers to "Inland Revenue" (meaning any officer of the Board) rather than "inspector" or "Board".

Commentary, App. 1, Change 17: reg. 127 makes it explicit that (in the absence of election by taxpayer or agreement between taxpayer and Revenue) appeal should be heard by Commissioners for area where taxpayer lives, if taxpayer has no place of employment, and allows reservists to elect for different place for hearing.

Amended determinations

128(1) This regulation applies if a determination by the Inland Revenue or the tribunal under regulation 125, 126 or 127 is found to be inappropriate because the actual circumstances are different from the circumstances by reference to which it was made.

128(2) The Inland Revenue must amend the determination.

128(3) The Inland Revenue must give notice of the amended determination to the reservist and the Ministry.

128(4) Regulations 126 and 127 apply in relation to an amended determination as they apply in relation to a determination under regulation 126(2).

History – In reg. 128(1), "tribunal" substituted for "Commissioners" by SI 2009/56, art. 3(2) and Sch. 2, para. 109, operative from 1 April 2009 subject to transitional and saving provisions in SI 2009/56, Sch. 3.

Origin – Reg. 128(1), (2): SI 1993/744, reg. 64(1) and see *Rewrite: Changes in Law* note below.

Reg. 128(3): SI 1993/744, reg. 64(2) and see *Rewrite: Changes in Law* note below.

Reg. 128(4): SI 1993/744, reg. 64(3).

Rewrite: Changes in Law – Commentary, App. 1, Change 1: reg. 128 refers to "Inland Revenue" (meaning any officer of the Board) rather than "inspector" or "Board".

Certificate of tax deducted

129(1) On making any payment of reserve pay from which tax is deducted, the Ministry may, and if the reservist so requires must, give the reservist a certificate showing the following particulars.

129(2) The particulars are—

(a)   the reservist's name,

(b)   the reservist's national insurance number, if known,

(c)   the date of the payment,

(d)   the amount of the payment, and

(e)   the amount of tax deducted.

Origin – Reg. 129(1): SI 1993/744, reg. 65(1).

Reg. 129(2): SI 1993/744, reg. 65(2) and see *Rewrite: Changes in Law* note below.

Statutory Instruments

Rewrite: Changes in Law – Commentary, App. 1, Change 38: reg. 129 brings into line with practice the information to be provided on certificate of tax deducted.

Repayment to reservist during tax year

130(1)   The Ministry must not repay tax in respect of reserve pay to a reservist.

130(2)   If a reservist applies for a repayment of tax deducted from reserve pay, the Inland Revenue may make such repayment at any time during the tax year as may be appropriate.

130(3)   In deciding what is appropriate the Inland Revenue must have regard to–

(a)   the reserve pay of the reservist for the period from the beginning of the tax year up to and including the date of the application,

(b)   the amount of tax deducted from the reserve pay as evidenced by certificates of pay and tax supplied under regulation 129,

(c)   any reliefs from income tax to which the reservist is entitled, and

(d)   the reservist's other PAYE income for the tax year and, unless the reservist objects, the reservist's income for the tax year from all other sources, and liability to tax on that income, as estimated by the Inland Revenue.

Origin – Reg. 130(1): SI 1993/744, reg. 66(1).
Reg. 130(2): SI 1993/744, reg. 66(2)(part) and see *Rewrite: Changes in Law* notes below.
Reg. 130(3): SI 1993/744, reg. 66(3)(part) and see *Rewrite: Changes in Law* notes below.
Rewrite: Changes in Law – Commentary, App. 1, Change 1: reg. 130 refers to "Inland Revenue" (meaning any officer of the Board) rather than "inspector" or "Board".
Commentary, App. 1, Change 10: reg. 130 allows Revenue to take account of income other than PAYE income into account when making repayment to reservist.

Particulars that Ministry must record

131(1)   The Ministry must record, in a deductions working sheet, the following particulars about every payment of reserve pay made to a reservist.

131(2)   The particulars are–

(a)   the reservist's name,

(b)   the reservist's national insurance number, if known,

(c)   the tax year to which the deductions working sheet relates,

(d)   the date of the payment,

(e)   the amount of the payment, and

(f)   the amount of tax (if any) deducted on making the payment.

Origin – Reg. 131(1): SI 1993/744, reg. 67(1).
Reg. 131(2): SI 1993/744, reg. 67(2) and see *Rewrite: Changes in Law* note below.
Rewrite: Changes in Law – Commentary, App. 1, Change 38: reg. 131 brings into line with practice the information to be provided on Ministry's deductions working sheet.

End of year certificate

132(1)   The Ministry must give an end of year certificate to a reservist in respect of whom the Ministry was required to prepare or maintain a deductions working sheet.

132(2)   The certificate must be given before 1st June following the end of the tax year to which it relates.

132(3)   The certificate must show–

(a)   the tax year to which it relates,

(b)   the reservist's name,

(c)   the reservist's national insurance number, if known,

(d)   the total amount of reserve pay paid by the Ministry to the reservist during the tax year,

(e)   the total tax deducted from the reserve pay,

(f)   the force in which the reservist was serving, and

(g)   the reservist's service number.

Origin – Reg. 132(1): SI 1993/744, reg. 68(1)(part), (3)(part) and see *Rewrite: Changes in Law* notes below.
Reg. 132(2): SI 1993/744, reg. 68(1)(part) and see *Rewrite: Changes in Law* notes below.
Reg. 132(3): SI 1993/744, reg. 68(2).
Rewrite: Changes in Law – Commentary, App. 1, Change 38: reg. 132 brings into line with practice the information to be provided on Ministry's end of year certificate.
Commentary, App. 1, Change 64: reg. 132 omits requirement for substitute Forms P60 to show that Inland Revenue have approved them.

Commentary, App. 1, Change 93: reg. 132 requires end of year certificate to be completed for and given to anyone who has served as a reservist in the tax year and for whom a deductions working sheet was prepared, even if no tax has been deducted from payments made to them in the year.

Other PAYE income of reservist

133   Nothing in this Chapter affects the application of these Regulations to any other PAYE income of a reservist.

Origin – SI 1993/744, reg. 70.

Chapter 2A – Social Security Lump Sums

INTERPRETATION OF CHAPTER 2A

133A(1)   In this Chapter–

"**the Act**" means the Finance (No.2) Act 2005 and a reference (without more) to a numbered provision is a reference to the provision of the Act bearing that number;

"**the Department**" means

(a)   in Great Britain, the Department for Work and Pensions; and

(b)   in Northern Ireland, the Department for Social Development;

"**lump sum**" means a social security pension lump sum as defined in section 9 of the Act;

"**the Recipient**" means a person who has become entitled to a lump sum.

History – Reg. 133A inserted by SI 2006/243, reg. 3 with effect from 6 April 2006.

APPLICATION OF OTHER PARTS

133B(1)   Parts 2 (codes) and 3 (deduction and repayment of tax) do not apply to lump sums.

133B(2)   The rest of these Regulations apply as if Her Majesty's Revenue and Customs had issued a code in respect of a social security pension lump sum at either–

(a)   the rate notified to the Department by the recipient pursuant to regulation 133D, or

(b)   the basic rate, if the recipient has not notified the Department of a rate.

History – Reg. 133B inserted by SI 2006/243, reg. 3 with effect from 6 April 2006.

DETERMINATION OF RATE OF DEDUCTION

133C(1)   On making any payment of a lump sum to a recipient during a tax year, the Department must deduct income tax at the marginal rate calculated in accordance with subparagraph (2).

133C(2)   For the purposes of this chapter the marginal rate is either–

(a)   the rate notified to the Department by the recipient in accordance with regulation 133D, or

(b)   in default of any such notification, the basic rate.

History – Reg. 133C inserted by SI 2006/243, reg. 3 with effect from 6 April 2006.

NOTIFICATION BY RECIPIENT OF NOTICE OF TAX RATE

133D(1)   The recipient shall notify the Department that he considers the nil tax code should be applied to the lump sum or that one of the following rates should be used–

(a)   [omitted by SI 2008/782, reg. 13]

(b)   the basic rate, or

(c)   the higher rate,

in accordance with section 7(5) of the Act.

133D(2)   Notification shall be in the form, and made within the period, specified by the Department.

History – Reg. 133D(1)(a) omitted by SI 2008/782, reg. 13, with effect from 6 April 2008.
Reg. 133D inserted by SI 2006/243, reg. 3 with effect from 6 April 2006.

CERTIFICATE OF TAX DEDUCTED

133E(1)   On making any payment of a lump sum from which tax is deducted, the Department may and if the recipient so requires, must, give the recipient an award notification showing the following particulars.

133E(2)   The particulars are–

(a)   the recipient's name,

(b)   the recipient's national insurance number, if known,

(c)   the date of the payment,

(d)   the amount of the payment, and

(e)   the amount of tax deducted.

History – Reg. 133E inserted by SI 2006/243, reg. 3 with effect from 6 April 2006.

REPAYMENT TO RECIPIENT DURING TAX YEAR

133F   The Department may repay tax deducted from a lump sum to a recipient at any time during the tax year in which it was paid, if it appears to the Department that the incorrect rate of income tax was applied to the payment due to an administrative error by the Department.

History – Reg. 133F inserted by SI 2006/243, reg. 3 with effect from 6 April 2006.

RECORDS AND NOTICES

133G(1)   The Department must record, in a deductions working sheet, the following particulars about any payment of a lump sum.

133G(2)   The particulars are–

(a)   the recipient's name,

(b)   the recipient's national insurance number, if known,

(c)   the amount of the payment,

(d)   the date of the payment,

(e)   the amount of tax (if any) deducted from the payment,

(f)   the tax rate (if any) notified by the recipient to the Department, and

(g)   the amount of any repayment made to the recipient in respect of the lump sum.

133G(3)   The Department shall notify an officer of Revenue and Customs when a lump sum payment is made.

133G(4)   The notification referred to in sub-paragraph (3) shall contain the following information–

(a)   the recipient's name and address,

(b)   the recipient's national insurance number, if known,

(c)   the date of the payment, and

(d)   the recipient's date of birth.

133G(5)   The Department shall administer a separate PAYE scheme for the lump sum payments.

History – Reg. 133G inserted by SI 2006/243, reg. 3 with effect from 6 April 2006.

OTHER PAYE INCOME OF RECIPIENT

133H   Nothing in this Chapter affects the application of these Regulations to any other PAYE income of a recipient.

History – Reg. 133H inserted by SI 2006/243, reg. 3 with effect from 6 April 2006.

Chapter 3 – Holiday Pay Funds

Interpretation of Chapter 3

Cross references – ITEPA 2003, s. 79 (voucher issued under approved scheme): Inland Revenue approval for holiday pay funds which operate PAYE: tax is deducted when stamps are exchanged, rather than when stamps are received.

134   In this Chapter–

    "fund" means a person who pays holiday pay–

    (a) to an individual who is not employed by the person, or

    (b) in respect of such an individual who has died;

    "holiday pay" means–

    (a) any payment received by an individual in exchange for a voucher, stamp or similar document purchased by a person who employs (or employed) that individual for any holiday period, or

(b)   if such an individual has died, any payment received by a person claiming in respect of that individual's right to such a payment;

"recipient" means a person who is paid holiday pay.

Origin – SI 1993/744, reg. 71.

Application of other Parts

135(1)   Parts 2 (codes) and 3 (deduction and repayment of tax) do not apply to holiday pay.

135(2)   The rest of these Regulations apply as if the Inland Revenue had issued the basic rate code in respect of holiday pay.

Origin – Reg. 135(1): SI 1993/744, reg. 72.
Reg. 135(2): see *Rewrite: Changes in Law* notes below.

Rewrite: Changes in Law – Commentary, App. 1, Change 4: SI 2003/2682, reg. 4 defines "basic rate code".
Commentary, App. 1, Change 91: reg. 135 deems basic rate code to be issued when payments are made by holiday pay funds.

Deduction of tax

136   On making any payment of holiday pay to a recipient, a fund must deduct income tax at the basic rate in force at the time the payment is made.

Origin – SI 1993/744, reg. 73.

Certificate of tax deducted

137(1)   On making any payment of holiday pay, a fund must give the recipient a certificate showing the following particulars.

137(2)   The particulars are–

(a)   the recipient's name,

(b)   the recipient's national insurance number, if known,

(c)   the tax year in which the payment is made,

(d)   the date of the payment,

(e)   the amount of the payment, and

(f)   the amount of tax deducted on making the payment.

Origin – Reg. 137(1): SI 1993/744, reg. 74(1).
Reg. 137(2): SI 1993/744, reg. 74(2) and see *Rewrite: Changes in Law* note below.

Rewrite: Changes in Law – Commentary, App. 1, Change 38: reg. 137 brings into line with practice the information to be provided on certificate of tax deducted.

Repayment to recipient during tax year

138(1)   A fund must not repay tax deducted from a payment of holiday pay to a recipient.

138(2)   If a recipient applies for a repayment of tax deducted from holiday pay, the Inland Revenue may make such repayment at any time during the tax year as may be appropriate.

138(3)   In deciding what is appropriate the Inland Revenue must have regard to–

(a)   the holiday pay of the recipient for the period from the beginning of the tax year up to and including the date of the application,

(b)   the amount of tax deducted from the holiday pay as evidenced by certificates supplied under regulation 137,

(c)   any entitlement of the recipient to relief from income tax, and

(d)   the recipient's other PAYE income for the tax year and, unless the recipient objects, the recipient's income for the tax year from all other sources, and liability to tax on that income, as estimated by the Inland Revenue.

Origin – Reg. 138(1): SI 1993/744, reg. 75(1).
Reg. 138(2): SI 1993/744, reg. 75(2)(part) and see *Rewrite: Changes in Law* notes below.
Reg. 138(3): SI 1993/744, reg. 75(3)(part) and see *Rewrite: Changes in Law* notes below.

Rewrite: Changes in Law – Commentary, App. 1, Change 1: reg. 138 refers to "Inland Revenue" (meaning any officer of the Board) rather than "inspector" or "Board".
Commentary, App. 1, Change 10: reg. 138 allows Revenue to take other income into account besides PAYE income when making repayment to recipient of payment from holiday pay fund.

Particulars that fund must record

139(1)   A fund must record, in a deductions working sheet, the following particulars about every payment of holiday pay made to a recipient.

139(2)   The particulars are–

(a)   the recipient's name,

(b)   the recipient's national insurance number, if known,

(c)   the tax year to which the deductions working sheet relates,

(d)   the date of the payment,

(e)   the amount of the payment, and

(f)   the amount of tax (if any) deducted on making the payment.

Origin – Reg. 139(1): SI 1993/744, reg. 76(1).
Reg. 139(2): SI 1993/744, reg. 76(2) and see *Rewrite: Changes in Law* note below.

Rewrite: Changes in Law – Commentary, App. 1, Change 38: reg. 138 brings into line with practice the particulars that fund must record.

Other PAYE income of recipient

140   Nothing in this Chapter affects the application of these Regulations to any other PAYE income of a recipient.

Origin – SI 1993/744, reg. 78.

Chapter 4 – Direct Collection and Special Arrangements

Direct collection and special arrangements

141(1)   In–

(a)   cases of casual employment, and

(b)   any other case in which HMRC are of the opinion that deduction of tax by reference to the tax tables is impracticable,

the direct collection procedure in regulation 142 applies to any PAYE income, unless HMRC makes special arrangements for the collection of tax in respect of that PAYE income.

141(2)   A special arrangement does not apply to PAYE income of an employer's employees if–

(a)   the arrangement has not been agreed with the employer, and

(b)   the employer does not proceed in accordance with the arrangement.

History – Reg. 141(1)(b) substituted by SI 2014/472, reg. 10, with effect from 6 April 2014.

Origin – Reg. 141(1): SI 1993/744, reg. 102(1)–(3) and see *Rewrite: Changes in Law* notes below.
Reg. 141(2): see *Rewrite: Changes in Law* notes below.

Rewrite: Changes in Law – Commentary, App. 1, Change 1: reg. 141 refers to "Inland Revenue" (meaning any officer of the Board) rather than "inspector" or "Board".
Commentary, App. 1, Change 95: reg. 141 makes explicit that employer cannot be compelled to operate special arrangements.

Direct collection: employee to report payments

142(1)   On receiving a relevant payment–

(a)   an employee (E) must proceed in accordance with paragraph (3) or paragraph (4), as the case may be, and

(b)   regulations 143 to 147A (direct collection) apply to E,

unless E objects to the application of the direct collection procedure.

142(2)   E may, within 30 days beginning with the date of receipt of written notification from HMRC that the direct collection procedure applies, object by written notice to HMRC to that procedure.

142(3)   E must deliver the information specified in Schedule A1 as if E were a Real Time Information employer for the purposes of regulations 67B (real time information returns of information about relevant payments), 67E (returns under regulations 67B and 67D: amendments), 67EA (failure to make a return under regulation 67B or 67D) and 67F (additional information about payments) and references to "an employer making a relevant payment" are to be read as if they were references to "the employee receiving a relevant payment".

142(4)   But if E–

(a)   is an individual who is a practising member of a religious society or order whose beliefs are incompatible with the use of electronic communications, or

(b)   has been given a direction under paragraph (5),

E may instead proceed as if E were a Real Time Information employer to whom regulations 67D (exceptions to regulation 67B), 67E (returns under regulations 67B and 67D: amendments), 67EA (failure to make a return under regulation 67B or 67D) and 67F (additional information about payments) apply with the modification referred to in paragraph (3).

142(5)   Where the Commissioners for Her Majesty's Revenue are satisfied that–

(a)   it is not reasonably practicable for E to make a return using an approved form of electronic communication, and

(b)   it is E who delivers the return (and not some other person on E's behalf),

they may make a direction specifying that E is not required to make a return using an approved method of electronic communication.

History – Reg. 142 and the heading immediately preceding it substituted by SI 2014/472, reg. 11, with effect from 6 April 2014.

Direct collection: employee to keep records

143(1)   Whenever the employee receives any relevant payment during the tax year, the employee must record in a deductions working sheet–

(a)   the amount of the payment,

(b)   the date on which it was received, and

(c)   the total payments to date.

143(2)   In addition, the employee must record in that deductions working sheet in relation to the last date in a tax quarter on which the employee receives a relevant payment–

(a)   the total free pay to date or, as the case may be, the total additional pay to date in relation to that date according to the employee's code, and

(b)   the corresponding total tax to date.

143(3)   If the employee does not receive any relevant payments in a tax quarter, the last day of the quarter must be used for the purposes of paragraph (2).

143(4)   If the employee receives relevant payments in more than one capacity, no account is to be taken for the purposes of this regulation and regulations 144 to 147 of the relevant payments received by the employee in any capacity other than that mentioned in that deductions working sheet.

143(5)   In this regulation and regulation 146, **"total payments to date"** means, in relation to any date, the sum of all relevant payments received by the employee from the beginning of the tax year up to and including that date, irrespective of the person or persons from whom it was received.

Prospective amendments – In reg. 143(5), the words "and regulation 146" omitted by SI 2014/472, reg. 13, with effect from 6 April 2015.

History – In reg. 143(1), the words "a deductions" substituted for the words "the deductions" by SI 2014/472, reg. 12(a), with effect from 6 April 2014.

In reg. 143(2) and (4), the words "that deductions" substituted for the words "the deductions" by SI 2014/472, reg. 12(b), with effect from 6 April 2014.

In reg. 143(5), the words "regulation 146" substituted for the words "regulations 145 and 146" by SI 2014/472, reg. 12(c), with effect from 6 April 2014.

Origin – Reg. 143(1), (2): SI 1993/744, reg. 104(2)(part).

Reg. 143(3): see *Rewrite: Changes in Law* note below.

Reg. 143(4): SI 1993/744, reg. 104(14).

Reg. 143(5): SI 1993/744, reg. 104(15).

Rewrite: Changes in Law – Commentary, para. 725 and App. 1, Change 97: reg. 143 brings law into line with practice on "direct collection".

Direct collection: payment

144(1)   In this regulation–

"the current total tax" means the amount required to be recorded at paragraph 17 of Schedule A1 (real time returns) in the most recent return which the employee is required to make in the tax year, or where the employee is required to make a return under regulation 67EA(3) (failure to make a return under regulation 67B), the amount required to be recorded at paragraph 17 of Schedule A1 for the tax year to which that return relates;

"the previous total tax" means the total tax to date (if any) required to be recorded for the previous tax quarter in the tax year.

144(2)   If, in relation to any tax quarter, the current total tax exceeds the previous total tax, the employee must pay the excess to the Inland Revenue, within 14 days after the end of the tax quarter.

144(3)   But if, in relation to any tax quarter, the previous total tax exceeds the current total tax, the employee may recover the excess–

Statutory Instruments

(a)　　by deducting it from the amount payable under paragraph (2) for a later quarter in the tax year, or

(b)　　from the Board of Inland Revenue.

144(4)　If the employee's code is a K code, the amount payable under paragraph (2) is not to exceed the overriding limit in relation to the relevant payments which the employee has received in that tax quarter.

144(5)　Any amount which is not payable because of the application of paragraph (4) must be added to the current total tax for the purpose of the calculation in paragraph (2) or (3) for the next tax quarter (if any) of that tax year.

History – In reg. 144(1), the definition of "the current total tax" substituted by SI 2014/472, reg. 14, with effect from 6 April 2014.

Origin – Reg. 144(1): drafting.
Reg. 144(2): SI 1993/744, reg. 104(3), (4) and see *Rewrite: Changes in Law* notes below.
Reg. 144(3): see *Rewrite: Changes in Law* notes below.
Reg. 144(4): SI 1993/744, reg. 104(2)(part) and see *Rewrite: Changes in Law* notes below.
Reg. 144(5): see *Rewrite: Changes in Law* notes below.

Rewrite: Changes in Law – Commentary, App. 1, Change 1: reg. 144 refers to "Inland Revenue" (meaning any officer of the Board) rather than "inspector" or "Board".
Commentary, para. 725 and App. 1, Change 97: reg. 144 brings law into line with practice on "direct collection".
Commentary, App. 1, Change 98: reg. 144 provides for employee to be entitled to repayment under direct collection arrangements.

Direct collection: return when relevant payments cease

145　[Omitted by SI 2014/472, reg. 15.]
History – Reg. 145 omitted by SI 2014/472, reg. 15, with effect from 6 April 2014.

Direct collection: end of year return

146(1)　Before 20th May following the end of the tax year, the employee must deliver a return to the Inland Revenue.

146(2)　The return must show–

(a)　　such particulars as the Board may require for identifying the employee,

(b)　　the tax year to which the return relates,

(c)　　the employee's total payments to date at the end of the tax year,

(d)　　the total tax to date calculated for the last tax quarter in the tax year, and

(e)　　if the employee's code is a K code, the amount, if any, of that total tax to date which is not payable because of regulation 144(4) (overriding limit).

146(3)　But paragraph (1) does not apply if the employee has already delivered a return under regulation 145 or section 8 of TMA (personal returns).

146(4)　If a return is required by paragraph (1), regulations 76, 84 and 218 (which relate to the certification and recovery of tax remaining unpaid by an employer for any tax year) apply with the necessary modifications in the case of any tax remaining unpaid by the employee.

146(5)　Section 98A of TMA (special penalties in case of certain returns) applies to paragraph (1).

Prospective amendments – Reg. 146 omitted by SI 2014/472, reg. 16, with effect from 6 April 2015.

Origin – Reg. 146(1): SI 1993/744, reg. 104(11)(part) and see *Rewrite: Changes in Law* notes below.
Reg. 146(2): SI 1993/744, reg. 104(12) and see *Rewrite: Changes in Law* notes below.
Reg. 146(3): SI 1993/744, reg. 104(11)(part).
Reg. 146(4): SI 1993/744, reg. 104(13).
Reg. 146(5): SI 1993/744, reg. 104(16).

Rewrite: Changes in Law – Commentary, App. 1, Change 1: reg. 146 refers to "Inland Revenue" (meaning any officer of the Board) rather than "inspector" or "Board".
Commentary, para. 725 and App. 1, Change 97: reg. 146 brings law into line with practice on "direct collection".

Direct collection: failure to pay

147(1)　This regulation applies if, within 14 days after the end of any tax quarter–

(a)　　the employee has not paid any tax for that quarter, and the Inland Revenue are unaware of the amount, if any, which the employee is liable to pay for that quarter, or

(b)　　the employee has paid an amount of tax for that quarter, but the Inland Revenue are not satisfied that it is the full amount which the employee is liable to pay for that quarter.

147(2)　The Inland Revenue may give notice to the employee requiring the employee, within 14 days of the issue of the notice, to deliver a return showing the amount of tax which the employee is liable to pay under regulation 144(2) in respect of the tax quarter in question.

147(3) If such a notice is given, regulations 77, 84 and 218(5) and (6) (which relate to the certification and recovery of tax unpaid by an employer) apply with the necessary modifications for the purposes of ascertaining, certifying and recovering the tax payable by the employee as if it were tax which the employee was liable to deduct from relevant payments paid by the employee.

Origin – Reg. 147(1): SI 1993/744, reg. 104(5) and see *Rewrite: Changes in Law* notes below.
Reg. 147(2): SI 1993/744, reg. 104(6)(part) and see *Rewrite: Changes in Law* notes below.
Reg. 147(3): SI 1993/744, reg. 104(6)(part).

Rewrite: Changes in Law – Commentary, App. 1: Change 1: reg. 147 refers to "Inland Revenue" (meaning any officer of the Board) rather than "inspector" or "Board".
Commentary, App. 1, 71: reg. 147 makes explicit the date on which period begins for employee to deliver return.

Circumstances in which payment of a lesser amount is to be treated as payment in full for the purposes of paragraph 6(2) of Schedule 56 to the Finance Act 2009

147A(1) A payment that is less than the full amount due under regulation 67G(2) (payments to and recoveries from HMRC for each tax period), as adjusted by regulation 67H (payments due and recoveries from HMRC for each tax period: returns under regulation 67E(6)) where appropriate, will for the purposes of paragraph 6(2) of Schedule 56 to the Finance Act 2009 (amount of penalty: PAYE and CIS) be treated as payment of the full amount if the difference between the full amount and the amount paid is no more than £100 ("the tolerance"), but this is subject to paragraphs (2) and (3).

147A(2) Paragraph (1) does not apply where–

(a)   the payment relates to a return which corrects information given in a return filed in respect of a relevant payment made in an earlier tax month, and

(b)   the return is delivered after 19th April following the end of the tax year in question.

147A(3) If the total sum paid by the employer to HMRC for the tax period includes not only the amount due under regulation 67G(2), as adjusted by regulation 67H where appropriate, but also one or more of–

(a)   any earnings-related contributions (as defined by regulation 1(2) of the SSC Regulations 2001),

(b)   any payment under regulation 7(1) of the Income Tax (Construction Industry Scheme) Regulations 2005, or

(c)   any repayment due under the Student Loans Regulations,

the tolerance is applied to the total sum paid to HMRC for the tax period to which the payments relate.

History – Reg. 147A and the heading immediately preceding it inserted by SI 2014/472, reg. 17, with effect in relation to a payment made in relation to the tax year 2014–15 and subsequent tax years.

PART 8 – SOCIAL SECURITY BENEFITS
Chapter 1 – Jobseeker's Allowance: Normal Cases

Interpretation of Chapters 1 and 2

148 In Chapters 1 and 2–

"**award**" means an award of a jobseeker's allowance;

"**claim**" means a claim for a jobseeker's allowance;

"**claimant**" means a person who has made a claim, or who is treated for the purposes of the JSA Regulations as having made a claim;

"**Chapter 2 claimant**" means–

(a)   a claimant who is entitled to a jobseeker's allowance by virtue of regulation 17 of the JSA Regulations (laid off and short time workers); or

(b)   a claimant who is a share fisherman–

     (i)   where the JSA Regulations apply, as defined in regulation 156 of those Regulations; and

     (ii)   where the Jobseeker's Allowance Regulations 2013 apply, as defined in regulation 67 of those Regulations;

"**Department**" means the Department for Work and Pensions or, in Northern Ireland, the Department for Social Development;

Statutory Instruments

"**JSA Regulations**" means the Jobseeker's Allowance Regulations 1996 or, in Northern Ireland, the Jobseeker's Allowance Regulations (Northern Ireland) 1996;

"**jobseeker's allowance**" means benefit payable under–

(a) the Jobseekers Act 1995, or

(b) in Northern Ireland, the Jobseekers (Northern Ireland) Order 1995;

"**taxable jobseeker's allowance**" means any amount of jobseeker's allowance which is chargeable to income tax under Chapter 2 of Part 10 of ITEPA (tax on social security income).

History – In reg. 148, in the entry for "Chapter 2 claimant", para. (b) substituted by SI 2013/630, reg. 83, with effect from 29 April 2013.

Origin – "award": drafting.
"claim", "claimant": SI 1993/744, reg. 81(part) and see *Rewrite: Changes in Law* notes below.
"Chapter 2 claimant": see *Rewrite: Changes in Law* notes below.
"Department": SI 1993/744, reg. 83(1), 94.
"JSA Regulations": drafting, and see *Rewrite: Changes in Law* notes below.
"jobseeker's allowance": SI 1993/744, reg. 81(part).
"taxable jobseeker's allowance": SI 1993/744, reg. 81(part) and see *Rewrite: Changes in Law* notes below.

Rewrite: Changes in Law – Commentary, App. 1, Change 99: reg. 148 expressly limits SI 2003/2682, Pt. 8 Ch. 1 and 2 to JSA. Commentary, para. 759 and App. 1, Change 100: reg. 148 distinguishes between JSA payments subject to the "normal" PAYE regulations for JSA and those subject to the special procedures for JSA for share fishermen et al.

Scope of Chapter 1

149 This Chapter applies to claimants who are not Chapter 2 claimants.

Origin – Drafting.

Application of other regulations

150(1) The following regulations apply to payments of taxable jobseeker's allowance made to a claimant with the modifications mentioned in paragraphs (2) and (3)–

regulation 2 interpretation
regulation 14 matters relevant to determination of code
regulation 15 flat rate codes
regulation 16 continued application of employee's code
regulation 17 notice to employee of code
regulation 18 objections and appeals against employee's code
regulation 19 amendment of code
regulation 20 notice to employer of amended code
regulation 21 deduction and repayment of tax by reference to employee's code
regulation 97 retention by employer of PAYE records
regulation 98 multiple PAYE schemes
regulation 1022 succession to a business etc
regulation 185 adjusting total net tax deducted for purposes of sections 59A(1) and 59B(1) TMA
regulation 188 assessments other than self-assessments
regulation 211 how information must or may be delivered by employers
regulation 214 how information must be provided by employees
regulation 216 service by post.

150(2) In the application of those regulations, the expressions listed in column 1 of Table 5 have the meanings shown in column 2 of the table.

Table 5
Meaning of expressions in application of other regulations

1. Expression	2. Meaning for purposes of this Chapter
employee	claimant
employer	Department
employment	award
relevant payments	taxable jobseeker's allowance.

150(3) In the application of regulations 20 and 21, any reference to the deduction or repayment of tax must be read as a reference to the tax calculation which the Department is required to make at the end of the tax year or on the cessation of an award (by virtue of regulations 157(2)(a) and 158(2) respectively).

History – In reg. 150(1), in column 2 of the list, the words "retention by employer of PAYE records" substituted for the words "inspection of employer's PAYE records" by SI 2009/588, reg. 7, with effect from 1 April 2009.

Origin – Reg. 150(1): SI 1993/744, reg. 82(1)(part), 85(1); drafting; and see *Rewrite: Changes in Law* note below.
Reg. 150(2): SI 1993/744, reg. 82(2)(part); drafting.
Table 5: SI 1993/744, reg. 82(2)(part); drafting.
Reg. 150(3): SI 1993/744, reg. 83(3).

Rewrite: Changes in Law – Commentary, App. 1, Change 101: reg. 150 makes explicit which regulations in other Parts apply and with what modifications to JSA payments within Pt. 8, Ch. 1.

Obtaining the claimant's Form P45

151(1) A claimant who has Parts 2 and 3 of Form P45 must deliver them to the Department on making a claim for a jobseeker's allowance which includes taxable jobseeker's allowance.

151(2) If, on making a claim, the claimant declares that the claimant's last employer did not provide Parts 2 and 3 of Form P45, the Department may require the employer to deliver them to a specified office of the Department.

Origin – Reg. 151(1): SI 1993/744, reg. 84(1)(part), (2)(part) and see *Rewrite: Changes in Law* note below.
Reg. 151(2): SI 1993/744, reg. 84(8) and see *Rewrite: Changes in Law* note below.

Rewrite: Changes in Law – Commentary, App. 1, Change 37: reg. 151 indicates that P45 is multi-part form.

Deductions working sheet for claimants awarded taxable jobseeker's allowance

152(1) The Department must prepare a deductions working sheet in respect of each claimant whose award includes taxable jobseeker's allowance.

152(2) If the Department obtains Parts 2 and 3 of Form P45 relating to the claimant, it must immediately prepare the deductions working sheet using the information shown in Parts 2 and 3 of Form P45 in accordance with regulation 153.

152(3) If the Department does not obtain Parts 2 and 3 of Form P45 relating to the claimant, it must prepare the deductions working sheet in accordance with regulation 154.

Origin – Reg. 152(1): SI 1993/744, reg. 84(3)(part).
Reg. 152(2): SI 1993/744, reg. 84(3)(part); drafting; and see *Rewrite: Changes in Law* note below.
Reg. 152(3): SI 1993/744, reg. 84(7)(part); drafting; and see *Rewrite: Changes in Law* note below.

Rewrite: Changes in Law – Commentary, App. 1, Change 37: reg. 152 indicates that P45 is multi-part form.

Form P45: deductions working sheet and return

153(1) If Parts 2 and 3 of Form P45 relate to the current tax year, the Department must record in the deductions working sheet the total payments to date shown in Parts 2 and 3 of Form P45.

153(2) If Parts 2 and 3 of Form P45 relate to the current tax year and show that the cumulative basis has been used, the Department must also–

(a) record the following information from Parts 2 and 3 of Form P45 in the deductions working sheet, or

(b) keep such records as enable production of the information.

153(3) If the code shown in Parts 2 and 3 of Form P45 is a K code, the information is–

(a) the total additional pay to date,

(b) the total taxable payments to date, and

(c) the lower of the total tax to date as at the week or month shown in Parts 2 and 3 of Form P45 or the total net tax deducted shown in them.

153(4) In any other case the information is–

(a) the total free pay to date,

(b) the total taxable payments to date, and

(c) the corresponding total tax to date as at the week or month shown in Parts 2 and 3 of Form P45.

153(5) Paragraph (6) applies if–

(a) the claim is made by 24th May in a tax year, and

(b) Parts 2 and 3 of Form P45 show that the last relevant payment was made in the preceding tax year.

153(6) The Department must complete the deductions working sheet but without recording the total payments to date or total net tax deducted (if any) shown in Parts 2 and 3 of Form P45.

153(7) In cases falling within paragraphs (1) and (5), the code shown in Parts 2 and 3 of Form P45 must be treated as the claimant's code for the purposes of these Regulations.

153(8) If, in a case not falling within paragraph (5), Parts 2 and 3 of Form P45 show that the last relevant payment was made in a tax year preceding that in which the claim was made, the Department–

(a)   must complete the deductions working sheet but without recording the total payments to date or total net tax deducted (if any) shown in Parts 2 and 3 of Form P45, and

(b)   must record the emergency code as the claimant's code.

153(9) The Department must supply the information recorded under this regulation to the Inland Revenue together with such further information as may be required for the purposes of these Regulations.

Origin – Reg. 153(1)–(4): SI 1993/744, reg. 84(3)(part) and see *Rewrite: Changes in Law* notes below.
Reg. 153(5), (6): SI 1993/744, reg. 84(5)(part) and see *Rewrite: Changes in Law* notes below.
Reg. 153(7): SI 1993/744, reg. 84(6)(part) and see *Rewrite: Changes in Law* notes below.
Reg. 153(8): SI 1993/744, reg. 84(7)(part) and see *Rewrite: Changes in Law* notes below.
Reg. 153(9): SI 1993/744, reg. 84(3)(part) and see *Rewrite: Changes in Law* notes below.

Rewrite: Changes in Law – Commentary, App. 1, Change 1: reg. 153 refers to "Inland Revenue" (meaning any officer of the Board) rather than "inspector" or "Board".
Commentary, App. 1, Change 37: reg. 153 indicates that P45 is multi-part form.

No Form P45: deductions working sheet and return

154(1) In a case falling within regulation 152(3) (no Form P45), the Department must–

(a)   prepare the deductions working sheet within 14 days of the award of a taxable jobseeker's allowance, and

(b)   record the emergency code as the claimant's code.

154(2) The Department must also deliver a return to the Inland Revenue, giving–

(a)   the claimant's name,

(b)   the claimant's national insurance number,

(c)   the claimant's date of birth, if known,

(d)   the date on which the claim was made, and

(e)   the reference number of the benefit office submitting the return.

154(3) But the return need not be delivered if the claimant certifies that the claimant–

(a)   is undergoing a course of full-time education and has not had regular employment since the previous 6th April, or

(b)   has not had regular employment since finishing full-time education.

Origin – Reg. 154(1): SI 1993/744, reg. 84(7)(part); drafting; and see *Rewrite: Changes in Law* notes below.
Reg. 154(2): SI 1993/744, reg. 84(9)(part); drafting; and see *Rewrite: Changes in Law* notes below.
Reg. 154(3): SI 1993/744, reg. 84(10)(part).

Rewrite: Changes in Law – Commentary, App. 1, Change 1: reg. 154 refers to "Inland Revenue" (meaning any officer of the Board) rather than "inspector" or "Board".
Commentary, App. 1, Change 38: reg. 154 brings into line with practice the information to be provided on the deductions working sheet and return.
Commentary, App. 1, Change 102: reg. 154 allows 14 days for Department to prepare deductions working sheet for JSA claimant if it gets no P45 from claimant.

Claimant's code etc to be used for calculations

155(1) This regulation applies if, in respect of a claimant, the Department receives notification from the Inland Revenue of–

(a)   a code or amended code,

(b)   total payments to date, or

(c)   total net tax deducted.

155(2) The Department must record that notification in substitution for any previous record and use it for the purpose of all calculations required under this Chapter.

Origin – Reg. 155(1): SI 1993/744, reg. 85(2)(part) and see *Rewrite: Changes in Law* note below.
Reg. 155(2): SI 1993/744, reg. 85(2)(part).

Rewrite: Changes in Law – Commentary, App. 1, Change 1: reg. 155 refers to "Inland Revenue" (meaning any officer of the Board) rather than "inspector" or "Board".

Recording the amount of taxable jobseeker's allowance

156 Whenever a payment of jobseeker's allowance is made, the Department must record the taxable jobseeker's allowance included in the payment.

Origin – SI 1993/744, reg. 87.

Obligations at end of tax year

157(1) This regulation applies in respect of each award which includes taxable jobseeker's allowance and which continues beyond the end of a tax year.

157(2) Before 1st June following the end of the tax year, the Department must–

(a) make a tax calculation in accordance with regulation 161 if the claimant's code is used on the cumulative basis;

(b) subject to paragraph (3), issue a certificate to the claimant; and

(c) deliver a return to the Inland Revenue.

157(3) The Department need not issue the certificate if–

(a) no taxable jobseeker's allowance has been paid, and

(b) a tax calculation in accordance with regulation 161 is not required.

157(4) The certificate must show–

(a) the tax year to which it relates,

(b) the total jobseeker's allowance for the tax year excluding any amounts previously notified under regulation 159(2) or 160(2),

(c) the taxable jobseeker's allowance included in the total jobseeker's allowance,

(d) the claimant's code,

(e) the claimant's national insurance number,

(f) the claimant's name,

(g) the claimant's address, if known,

(h) any previous relevant payments and any tax deducted from those relevant payments which the Department was required to take into account under regulation 161,

(i) any total payments to date recorded by the Department in accordance with regulation 153(1) plus the total taxable jobseeker's allowance for the tax year, and the corresponding total net tax deducted, and

(j) the amount of tax refunded by the Department.

157(5) The return must show–

(a) the particulars specified in paragraph (4), and

(b) if a calculation is required under regulation 161, any amount of tax outstanding.

Origin – Reg. 157(1): SI 1993/744, reg. 88(1)(part).
Reg. 157(2): SI 1993/744, reg. 88(1)(part); drafting; and see *Rewrite: Changes in Law* notes below.
Reg. 157(3): SI 1993/744, reg. 88(2).
Reg. 157(4): SI 1993/744, reg. 88(4)(part); drafting; and see *Rewrite: Changes in Law* notes below.
Reg. 157(5): SI 1993/744, reg. 88(5)(part).

Rewrite: Changes in Law – Commentary, App. 1, Change 1: reg. 157 refers to "Inland Revenue" (meaning any officer of the Board) rather than "inspector" or "Board".
Commentary, App. 1, Change 38: reg. 157 brings into line with practice the information to be provided on the certificate.

When an award ceases

158(1) For the purposes of these Regulations an award ceases when entitlement to a jobseeker's allowance ceases.

158(2) When an award of a taxable jobseeker's allowance ceases the Department must make a tax calculation in accordance with regulation 161 if the claimant's code is used on the cumulative basis.

158(3) The relevant date for the purposes of that calculation is the date on which the award ceases.

158(4) The date on which the award ceases is the last day for which benefit was paid and was not recoverable, except that if the last day is 4th or 5th April the date is the preceding 3rd April.

158(5) But the Department need not amend a tax calculation solely because the date used for the purposes of the calculation is subsequently shown to be incorrect.

Origin – Reg. 158(1): SI 1993/744, reg. 89(1) and see *Rewrite: Changes in Law* note below.
Reg. 158(2): SI 1993/744, reg. 89(2)(part), 91(4).
Reg. 158(3), (4): SI 1993/744, reg. 89(3)(part).
Reg. 158(5): SI 1993/744, reg. 89(4).

Rewrite: Changes in Law – Commentary, App. 1, Change 103: under reg. 158, JSA award ends for PAYE purposes when entitlement to JSA ends.

Cessation of award: Form P45U

159(1) When an award of a taxable jobseeker's allowance ceases the Department must immediately complete Form P45U.

159(2) The Department must then–

(a) send Part 1 of Form P45U to the Inland Revenue, and

(b) provide Part 1A of Form P45U and Parts 2 and 3 of Form P45 to the claimant.

159(3) The information listed in column 1 of Table 6 must, subject to the conditions set out in column 2, be provided in Parts 1 and 1A of Form P45U and Parts 2 and 3 of Form P45 as indicated in columns 3 to 5.

Table 6
Information which must be provided in Form P45U

1. Information to be provided	2. Conditions	3. Form P45U Part 1	4. Form P45U Part 1A	5. Form P45 Parts 2 & 3
1. the tax reference as shown in the deductions working sheet		yes	yes	yes
2. the claimant's national insurance number		yes	yes	yes
3. the claimant's name		yes	yes	yes
4. the date on which the award ceased		yes	yes	yes
5. the claimant's code or, if more than one, the latest code for the tax year during which the award ceased		yes	yes	yes
6. whether the claimant's code is used on the cumulative basis		yes	yes	yes
7. the tax week or month in which the award ceased	if the claimant's code is used on the cumulative basis	yes	yes	yes
8. the total payments to date (including taxable jobseeker's allowance) at the date the award ceased, and the corresponding total net tax deducted	if the claimant's code is used on the cumulative basis	yes	yes	yes
9. the taxable jobseeker's allowance paid during the tax year by virtue of the award in question	if the claimant's code is used on the cumulative basis, and if different from the information supplied under item 8	yes	yes	no
10. the taxable jobseeker's allowance paid during the tax year by virtue of the award in question	if the claimant's code is not used on the cumulative basis	yes	yes	no
11. any amount of tax outstanding	if the claimant's code is used on the cumulative basis	yes	no	no
12. whether the claimant was self-employed immediately before the claim was made		yes	no	no
13. whether the claimant is receiving a pension by reason of a former employment		yes	no	no
14. the claimant's address	if known	yes	no	no
15. the address of the benefit officer		yes	yes	no
16. the date the form is completed		yes	yes	no

159(4) The Department must also give notice to the claimant of–

(a)   the total jobseeker's allowance for the tax year excluding any sums previously notified under this regulation or regulation 160, 171 or 172, and

(b)   the taxable jobseeker's allowance included in that total.

159(5) Expressions used in Parts 2 and 3 of Form P45 have the following meanings–

(a)   **"employee"** means "claimant",

(b)   **"leaving date"** means "date the award ceased", and

(c)   **"pay"** means "jobseeker's allowance".

159(6) Regulation 163 (death of claimant) modifies the requirements of this regulation if an award of taxable jobseeker's allowance has ceased on the death of the claimant.

Origin – Reg. 159(1): SI 1993/744, reg. 89(2)(part).
Reg. 159(2), (3), Table 6: SI 1993/744, reg. 89(2)(part) and see *Rewrite: Changes in Law* notes below.
Reg. 159(4): SI 1993/744, reg. 89(2)(part).
Reg. 159(5): drafting; and see *Rewrite: Changes in Law* notes below.
Reg. 159(6): drafting.

Rewrite: Changes in Law – Commentary, App. 1, Change 1: reg. 65 refers to "Inland Revenue" (meaning any officer of the Board) rather than "inspector" or "Board".
Commentary, App. 1, Change 37: reg. 159 indicates that P45 is multi-part form.
Commentary, App. 1, Change 38: reg. brings into line with practice the information to be provided in P45U.
Commentary, App. 1, Change 104: reg. 159 requires Department to provide JSA claimants and Revenue with the information given in practice in Forms P45U Parts 1 and 1A and in Parts 2 and 3 of Form P45.

Notification of taxable jobseeker's allowance adjustment

160(1) Paragraph (2) applies if–

(a)   after a certificate under regulation 157(2)(b) has been issued (or would have been issued but for regulation 157(3)), or

(b)   after a notice has been issued under regulation 159(4) or this regulation,

further taxable jobseeker's allowance is paid to, or taxable jobseeker's allowance overpaid is recovered from, the claimant.

160(2) The Department must–

(a)   give notice to the claimant of the revised figure of total jobseeker's allowance and the taxable jobseeker's allowance included in that revised figure in accordance with the relevant regulation, and

(b)   notify the Inland Revenue of the sums paid or refunded.

Origin – Reg. 160(1): SI 1993/744, reg. 88(3), 90(part).
Reg. 160(2): SI 1993/744, reg. 90(part) and see *Rewrite: Changes in Law* note below.

Rewrite: Changes in Law – Commentary, App. 1, Change 1: reg. 160 refers to "Inland Revenue" (meaning any officer of the Board) rather than "inspector" or "Board".

Tax calculation

161(1) This regulation applies, subject to regulation 162, if the Department is required by regulation 157 or 158 to make a tax calculation.

161(2) The Department must calculate in respect of the claimant as at the relevant date–

(a)   the total payments to date, and

(b)   the claimant's total tax–

161(3) If the recorded tax exceeds the claimant's total tax, the Department must repay the excess to the claimant.

161(4) But if the recorded tax is less than the claimant's total tax–

(a)   the difference is tax outstanding for the purposes of regulation 157(5)(b) or item 11 of Table 6 in regulation 159(3), and

(b)   the Department must treat the claimant's code as issued by the Inland Revenue on the non-cumulative basis from the relevant date.

161(5) In this regulation–

    "claimant's total tax" means–

    (a) if the claimant's code is a K code, the lesser of–

      (i)   50% of the claimant's total payments to date, and

      (ii)   the tax due in accordance with the appropriate tax tables in respect of the claimant's total taxable payments to date at the relevant date;

(b)   in any other case, the tax due in accordance with the appropriate tax tables in respect of the claimant's total taxable payments to date at the relevant date;

"recorded tax" means the total tax to date or (as the case may be) the total net tax deducted which was recorded in accordance with regulation 153(3) or (4) when the claim was made;

"relevant date" means–

(a)   the end of the tax year, if the calculation is required by regulation 157;

(b)   the date used for the purposes of the calculation, if the calculation is required by regulation 158;

"total payments to date" means any payments to date recorded by the Department in accordance with regulation 153(1), plus the total taxable jobseeker's allowance.

Origin – Reg. 161(1): SI 1993/744, reg. 91(1)(part).
Reg. 161(2): SI 1993/744, reg. 91(1)(part) and see *Rewrite: Changes in Law* notes below.
Reg. 161(3): SI 1993/744, reg. 91(3).
Reg. 161(4): SI 1993/744, reg. 91(2); drafting.
Reg. 161(5): SI 1993/744, reg. 91(1)(part), (6) and see *Rewrite: Changes in Law* notes below.

Rewrite: Changes in Law – Commentary, App. 1, Change 20: reg. 161 omits unnecessary requirement for Department to ascertain intermediate figures each time they undertake a calculation.
Commentary, para. 807 and App. 1, Change 105: reg. 161 makes clearer the tax calculation which the Department makes at the end of a JSA award or tax year.

No tax calculation required in certain cases

162(1)   A tax calculation under regulation 161 is not required in any of the following cases–

(a)   if the claimant does not give the Department Parts 2 and 3 of Form P45, and does not certify in accordance with regulation 154(3) (students etc);

(b)   if the claimant gives the Department Parts 2 and 3 of Form P45, but they do not relate to the claimant's last employment or award before the present award, whichever is later;

(c)   if the claimant is in receipt of a pension in respect of a former employment;

(d)   if it appears to the Department on the occasion of a claim that a previous award should have been treated as having ceased in accordance with regulation 158 (when an award ceases); or

(e)   if the claimant's code is a nil tax code, basic rate code or higher rate code.

162(2)   Those cases are treated as if the Inland Revenue had made a direction that the claimant's code must be used on the non-cumulative basis.

162(3)   Those cases are subject to a notification from the Inland Revenue under regulation 155 that revised particulars are to be substituted and used.

Origin – Reg. 162(1): SI 1993/744, reg. 91(4)(part), (5)(part) and see *Rewrite: Changes in Law* notes below.
Reg. 162(2), (3): SI 1993/744, reg. 91(5)(part) and see *Rewrite: Changes in Law* notes below.

Rewrite: Changes in Law – Commentary, App. 1, Change 1: reg. 162 refers to "Inland Revenue" (meaning any officer of the Board) rather than "inspector" or "Board".
Commentary, App. 1, Change 37: reg. 162 indicates that P45 is multi-part form.

Death of claimant

163(1)   On being informed of the death of a claimant whose award included taxable jobseeker's allowance, the Department must send the Inland Revenue the completed Form P45U indicating in Part 1 that the claimant has died.

163(2)   If the Department knows the name and address of the claimant's personal representative, the Department must send the notice referred to in regulation 159(4) to the personal representative.

163(3)   But if the Department has not been notified of the name and address of the claimant's personal representative within 30 days of the claimant's death, the Department is not required–

(a)   to make a tax calculation under regulation 161, nor

(b)   to issue the notice under regulation 159(4).

Origin – Reg. 163(1): SI 1993/744, reg. 92(1)(part) and see *Rewrite: Changes in Law* notes below.
Reg. 163(2): SI 1993/744, reg. 92(1)(part).
Reg. 163(3): SI 1993/744, reg. 92(2).

Rewrite: Changes in Law – Commentary, App. 1, Change 1: reg. 163 refers to "Inland Revenue" (meaning any officer of the Board) rather than "inspector" or "Board".
Commentary, App. 1, Change 106: reg. 163 requires Department to indicate in Form P45U Part 1 that JSA claimant has died.

Finance

164(1)   The Board of Inland Revenue must advance monies to the National Insurance Funds of Great Britain and Northern Ireland at intervals to be agreed with the Department for use in making repayments of income tax under these Regulations.

164(2)   The Department must provide the Board with a quarterly statement of receipts and payments.

Origin – Reg. 164(1): SI 1993/744, reg. 93(1).
Reg. 164(2): SI 1993/744, reg. 93(2)(part).

Chapter 2 – Jobseeker's Allowance: Special Cases

Scope of Chapter 2

165(1)   This Chapter applies only to Chapter 2 claimants (as defined by regulation 148).

165(2)   Except for regulation 148 (interpretation), Chapter 1 does not apply to Chapter 2 claimants.

Origin – Drafting.

Jobseeker's allowance paid directly to claimant

166(1)   This regulation applies if the Department makes a payment of taxable jobseeker's allowance directly to a Chapter 2 claimant.

166(2)   The Department must–

(a)   record the amount, and

(b)   pay the full sum without any deduction or repayment of income tax.

Origin – SI 1993/744, reg. 95(part).

Jobseeker's allowance paid by employer

167(1)   If–

(a)   a jobseeker's allowance is paid to a Chapter 2 claimant by the claimant's employer on behalf of the Department, and

(b)   the employer calculates the jobseeker's allowance payable by reference to instructions supplied by the Department,

the employer must also calculate the taxable jobseeker's allowance in accordance with those instructions.

167(2)   If–

(a)   a jobseeker's allowance is paid to a Chapter 2 claimant by the claimant's employer on behalf of the Department, and

(b)   paragraph (1)(b) does not apply,

the Department must notify the employer of the amount of jobseeker's allowance and of taxable jobseeker's allowance.

167(3)   If the employer has undertaken to pay a jobseeker's allowance on behalf of the Department, the Department must pay the full amount to the employer without any deduction on account of income tax.

Origin – Reg. 167(1): SI 1993/744, reg. 96(1).
Reg. 167(2): SI 1993/744, reg. 96(2).
Reg. 167(3): SI 1993/744, reg. 96(3).

Regulation 167 cases: application of other regulations

168(1)   Parts 2 to 4 (codes; deduction and repayment of tax; payments, returns and information) apply to the taxable jobseeker's allowance paid to a Chapter 2 claimant by the employer on behalf of the Department under regulation 167, as if it were a relevant payment from the employment.

168(2)   But this is subject to paragraph (3), which applies in any case in which it appears to the Inland Revenue that deduction of tax from the taxable jobseeker's allowance paid by the employer on behalf of the Department by reference to the tax tables is impracticable.

168(3)   The Inland Revenue may make such other arrangements as are appropriate for the collection of tax in respect of taxable jobseeker's allowance.

168(4)   Regulations 170 to 172 (information to be supplied etc) do not apply if–

(a)   the Chapter 2 claimant's employer has been paying the jobseeker's allowance in accordance with regulation 167, and

(b)   the employer provides the information in question.

Origin – Reg. 168(1): SI 1993/744, reg. 96(4).
Reg. 168(2): SI 1993/744, reg. 96(5)(part) and see *Rewrite: Changes in Law* notes below.
Reg. 168(3): see *Rewrite: Changes in Law* notes below.

Rewrite: Changes in Law – Commentary, App. 1, Change 1: reg. 168 refers to "Inland Revenue" (meaning any officer of the Board) rather than "inspector" or "Board".
Commentary, App. 1, Change 107: reg. 168 prevents JSA claimants paid by employers having taxable JSA reported twice.

When a Chapter 2 award ceases

169   For the purposes of this Chapter, an award ceases when entitlement to a jobseeker's allowance which depends on regulation 17 or 156 of the JSA Regulations ceases.

Origin – SI 1993/744, reg. 97(1)(part) and see *Rewrite: Changes in Law* note below.

Rewrite: Changes in Law – Commentary, App. 1, Change 108: reg. 169 defines the end of a "Chapter 2 award" as end of entitlement to JSA which depends on reg. 17 or 156 of the JSA Regulations.

Information to be supplied at end of tax year

170(1)   This regulation applies in respect of an award of taxable jobseeker's allowance which continues beyond the end of a tax year.

170(2)   Before 1st June following the end of the tax year, the Department must give notice to the Inland Revenue and the Chapter 2 claimant of–

(a)   the total jobseeker's allowance, and

(b)   the taxable jobseeker's allowance,

paid in respect of the award during that tax year.

Origin – Reg. 170(1): drafting.
Reg. 170(2): SI 1993/744, reg. 97(2)(part) and see *Rewrite: Changes in Law* notes below.

Rewrite: Changes in Law – Commentary, App. 1, Change 1: reg. 170 refers to "Inland Revenue" (meaning any officer of the Board) rather than "inspector" or "Board".
Commentary, App. 1, Change 109: reg. 170 introduces same time limit for Department to provide "Chapter 2" claimants with details of JSA paid as for other claimants (and employees generally).

Information to be supplied when an award of taxable jobseeker's allowance ceases

171(1)   When an award of taxable jobseeker's allowance ceases, the Department must give notice to the Inland Revenue and, except where the Chapter 2 claimant has died, the claimant, of–

(a)   the total jobseeker's allowance, and

(b)   the taxable jobseeker's allowance,

paid in respect of the award, showing the amounts appropriate to the award for the tax year in which it ceased.

171(2)   If the Department has been notified of the name and address of a deceased claimant's personal representative within 30 days of the claimant's death, the Department must send the notice to the personal representative.

Origin – Reg. 171(1): SI 1993/744, reg. 97(2)(part) and see *Rewrite: Changes in Law* notes below.
Reg. 171(2): drafting, and see *Rewrite: Changes in Law* notes below.

Rewrite: Changes in Law – Commentary, App. 1, Change 1: reg. 171 refers to "Inland Revenue" (meaning any officer of the Board) rather than "inspector" or "Board".
Commentary, App. 1, Change 110: reg. 171 requires Department, on death of Chapter 2 claimant, to give Chapter 2 claimant's personal representative details of benefit paid, if they know the personal representative within 30 days of the death.

Adjustments of taxable jobseeker's allowance

172(1)   Paragraph (2) applies if, after the issue of a notice under regulation 170 or 171(1)–

(a)   further taxable jobseeker's allowance is paid to the Chapter 2 claimant, or

(b)   taxable jobseeker's allowance overpaid is recovered from the Chapter 2 claimant.

172(2)   The Department must–

(a)   notify the Chapter 2 claimant of the revised figure of total jobseeker's allowance and the taxable jobseeker's allowance included in that revised figure, and

(b)   notify the Inland Revenue of any adjustment to the figure of taxable jobseeker's allowance, showing the amounts appropriate to each tax year.

Origin – SI 1993/744, reg. 98 and see *Rewrite: Changes in Law* notes below.

Rewrite: Changes in Law – Commentary, App. 1, Change 1: reg. 172 refers to "Inland Revenue" (meaning any officer of the Board) rather than "inspector" or "Board".
Commentary, App. 1, Change 111: reg. 172 requires Department to provide details of both total and taxable JSA paid to Chapter 2 claimants if benefit is paid or recovered after return is made under reg. 170 or reg. 171.

Chapter 3 – Incapacity Benefit

Interpretation of Chapter 3

173 In this Chapter–

 "award" means an award of incapacity benefit;

 "claim" means a claim for incapacity benefit;

 "claimant" means a person who has made a claim;

 "Department" means the Department for Work and Pensions or, in Northern Ireland, the Department for Social Development;

 "incapacity benefit" means short-term incapacity benefit or long-term incapacity benefit payable under–

 (a) sections 30A(1), 30A(5), 40 or 41 of the Social Security Contributions and Benefits Act 1992, or

 (b) in Northern Ireland, section 30A(1), 30A(5), 40 or 41 of the Social Security Contributions and Benefits (Northern Ireland) Act 1992;

 "single-income claimant" means a claimant who, for a tax year–

 (a) is not entitled to receive any relevant payments in addition to the payments of taxable incapacity benefit, or

 (b) is so entitled but has failed to provide any details relating to those payments when making the claim,

 and who is not a self-employed earner as defined by section 2 of the Social Security Contributions and Benefits Act 1992 or, in Northern Ireland, section 2 of the Social Security Contributions and Benefits (Northern Ireland) Act 1992;

 "taxable incapacity benefit" means any amount of incapacity benefit which is chargeable to income tax under Chapter 2 of Part 10 of ITEPA (tax on social security income).

Origin – "award": drafting.
"claim", "claimant": SI 1993/744, reg. 81(part).
"Department": SI 1993/744, reg. 98A.
"incapacity benefit": SI 1993/744, reg. 81(part).
"single-income claimant": SI 1993/744, reg. 98C(2) and see *Rewrite: Changes in Law* note below.
"taxable incapacity benefit": SI 1993/744, reg. 81(part).

Rewrite: Changes in Law – Commentary, App. 1, Change 112: reg. 173 defines "single-income claimant" to exclude incapacity benefit claimant with other PAYE income or income from self-employment.

Application of other regulations

174(1) The following regulations apply, subject to this Chapter, to payments of taxable incapacity benefit with the modifications mentioned in paragraphs (2) to (4)–

regulation 2	interpretation
regulation 15	flat rate codes
regulation 16	continued application of employee's code
regulation 17	notice to employee of code
regulation 18	objections and appeals against employee's code
regulation 19	amendment of code
regulation 20	notice to employer of amended code
regulation 21	deduction and repayment of tax by reference to employee's code
regulations 22 to 25	cumulative basis
regulations 26 to 31	non-cumulative basis
regulation 33	nil tax code: no deductions or repayments
regulation 36	cessation of employment: Form P45
regulation 66	deductions working sheets
regulation 67	information to employees about payments and tax deducted

regulation 68	periodic payments to and recoveries from the Revenue
regulation 69	due date and receipts for payments of tax
regulation 70	quarterly tax periods
regulation 72	recovery from employee of tax not deducted by employer
regulation 73	annual return of relevant payments liable to deduction of tax
regulation 74	annual return of relevant payments not liable to deduction of tax
regulation 76	certificate if tax in regulation 73 return is unpaid
regulation 79	certificate after inspection of PAYE records
regulation 84	recovery of tax and interest
regulation 97	retention by employer of PAYE records
regulation 98	multiple PAYE schemes
regulation 102	succession to a business etc
regulation 141	direct collection and special arrangements
regulation 185	adjusting total net tax deducted for purposes of sections 59A(1) and 59B(1) TMA
regulation 188	assessments other than self-assessments
regulation 211	how information must or may be delivered by employers
regulation 216	service by post
regulation 218	certificate that sum due
regulation 219	payment by cheque.

174(2) In the application of those regulations, the expressions listed in column 1 of Table 7 have the meanings shown in column 2 of the table.

Table 7
Meaning of expressions in application of other regulations

1. Expression	2. Meaning for purposes of this Chapter
employee	claimant
employer	Department
employment	award
relevant payments	taxable incapacity benefit.

174(3) In regulation 15 (flat rate codes)–

(a)   omit paragraph (1);

(b)   omit paragraph (3)(a); and

(c)   for paragraph (3)(c) substitute–

     "(c)   the Inland Revenue consider that the code which would otherwise be the claimant's code would result in too much tax being deducted for the tax year in question."

174(4) In regulation 21(1) (deduction and repayment of tax by reference to employee's code), for "in accordance with these Regulations" substitute "in accordance with Chapter 3 of Part 8".

History – In reg. 174(1), in column 2 of the list, the words "retention by employer of PAYE records" substituted for the words "inspection of employer's PAYE records" by SI 2009/588, reg. 7, with effect from 1 April 2009.

Origin – Reg. 174(1): SI 1993/744, reg. 82(1)(part), 98B, 98F(5), 98G(1), (2), 98H; drafting; and see *Rewrite: Changes in Law* notes below.
Reg. 174(2): SI 1993/744, reg. 82(2)(part) and drafting.
Table 7: SI 1993/744, reg. 82(2)(part), 98B(part) and drafting.
Reg. 174(3): SI 1993/744, reg. 98G(1) and see *Rewrite: Changes in Law* notes below.
Reg. 174(4): SI 1993/744, reg. 98B and see *Rewrite: Changes in Law* notes below.

Rewrite: Changes in Law – Commentary, App. 1, Change 4: SI 2003/2682, reg. 7 defines certain flat rate codes. Commentary, App. 1, Change 113: reg. 174 makes explicit which regulations in other Parts apply to incapacity benefit and with what modifications.

Emergency IB code to be used before claimant's code issued

175(1) Paragraph (2) applies if the Department makes a payment of taxable incapacity benefit during a tax year to a single-income claimant before a code has been issued by the Inland Revenue for that year in respect of that award.

175(2) The Department must–

(a)   deduct tax using an emergency IB code on the non-cumulative basis, and

(b)   keep records in a deductions working sheet which it must prepare for the purpose.

175(3) The use of an emergency IB code under this regulation is treated as the issue of a code for the purposes of regulations 21, 36 and 180.

Origin – Reg. 175(1): SI 1993/744, reg. 98C(1)(part), (2) and see *Rewrite: Changes in Law* notes below.
Reg. 175(2): SI 1993/744, reg. 98C(1)(part).
Reg. 175(3): drafting.

Rewrite: Changes in Law – Commentary, App. 1, Change 1: reg. 175 refers to "Inland Revenue" (meaning any officer of the Board) rather than "inspector" or "Board".

Return in respect of all claimants to taxable incapacity benefit

176(1) When the Department first makes a payment of taxable incapacity benefit to a claimant it must immediately deliver a return to the Inland Revenue containing the following information.

176(2) The information is–

(a) the claimant's name,

(b) the claimant's address,

(c) the claimant's date of birth, if known,

(d) the claimant's national insurance number,

(e) the date on which the claimant's entitlement to taxable incapacity benefit began,

(f) the weekly rate of taxable incapacity benefit being paid to the claimant,

(g) if a code is being used for the payment, that code and whether it is used on the noncumulative basis,

(h) if the payment was preceded by payment of incapacity benefit which was not taxable, the date that benefit was first paid, and

(i) the claimant's tax reference, if known.

Origin – Reg. 176(1): SI 1993/744, reg. 98D(1) and see *Rewrite: Changes in Law* notes below.
Reg. 176(2): SI 1993/744, reg. 98D(2) and see *Rewrite: Changes in Law* notes below.

Rewrite: Changes in Law – Commentary, App. 1, Change 1: reg. 176 refers to "Inland Revenue" (meaning any officer of the Board) rather than "inspector" or "Board".
Commentary, App. 1, Change 114: reg. 176 requires returns that Department makes when claimants are first paid incapacity benefit to reflect all the information the Department provides in practice.

Further return required in certain cases

177(1) On making a subsequent payment of taxable incapacity benefit to the claimant, the Department must deliver a further return in accordance with regulation 176 as if that subsequent payment were the first payment, if conditions A and B are met.

177(2) Condition A is that the Inland Revenue have previously determined the claimant's code in relation to the payments of incapacity benefit to be a nil tax code.

177(3) Condition B is that the subsequent payment is the first payment to be made at a different rate from the rate subsisting at the time of that determination.

177(4) In addition to providing the information listed in regulation 176(2), the Department must indicate in the further return that the weekly rate of taxable incapacity benefit being paid to the claimant represents a revised amount.

Origin – Reg. 177(1): SI 1993/744, reg. 98D(3)(part).
Reg. 177(2): SI 1993/744, reg. 98D(3)(part) and see *Rewrite: Changes in Law* notes below.
Reg. 177(3): SI 1993/744, reg. 98D(3)(part).
Reg. 177(4): see *Rewrite: Changes in Law* notes below.

Rewrite: Changes in Law – Commentary, App. 1, Change 1: reg. 177 refers to "Inland Revenue" (meaning any officer of the Board) rather than "inspector" or "Board".
Commentary, App. 1, Change 115: reg. 177 requires Department to indicate on further return for claimants with nil tax code whose rate of benefit changes that it is a revised rate of taxable incapacity benefit.

Delivery of Form P45 to Department

178(1) This regulation applies if a single-income claimant–

(a) has Parts 2 and 3 of Form P45, and

(b) has not made, and does not intend to make, a claim for repayment of tax.

178(2) The claimant must deliver Parts 2 and 3 of Form P45 when making a claim, and the Department must immediately send them to the Inland Revenue office.

Origin – Reg. 178(1): SI 1993/744, reg. 98E(1)(part), (2) and see *Rewrite: Changes in Law* notes below.
Reg. 178(2): SI 1993/744, reg. 98E(1)(part) and see *Rewrite: Changes in Law* notes below.

Rewrite: Changes in Law – Commentary, App. 1, Change 1: reg. 178 refers to "Inland Revenue" (meaning any officer of the Board) rather than "inspector" or "Board".
Commentary, App. 1, Change 37: reg. 178 indicates that P45 is multi-part form.

Determination of claimant's code by Inland Revenue

179(1) On receiving a return under regulation 176 relating to a single-income claimant, the Inland Revenue must determine the code for the claimant.

179(2) The Inland Revenue may determine the code for a claimant who is not a single-income claimant if they consider that it would be impractical to collect tax arising on the claimant's taxable incapacity benefit by other means.

179(3) In determining the code for a claimant under this regulation, regulation 14(1) (matters to which Revenue must have regard in determining an employee's code) does not apply.

179(4) If the Inland Revenue are satisfied the claimant is entitled, for the tax year for which the code is determined, to any of the following reliefs from income tax, they must have regard to that relief in determining the code for the claimant under this regulation.

179(5) The reliefs are–

(a)   personal allowance (section 257(1) of ICTA),

(b)   married couple's allowance (section 257A of ICTA), and

(c)   blind person's allowance (section 265(1) of ICTA).

179(6) If the Inland Revenue determine the code for a claimant before the beginning of the tax year for which it is determined, the Inland Revenue–

(a)   must have regard to any expected change in the amounts of those reliefs, but

(b)   may disregard any of those reliefs if they are not satisfied that the claimant will be entitled to it for the tax year for which it is determined.

Origin – Reg. 179(1): SI 1993/744, reg. 98F(1) and see *Rewrite: Changes in Law* notes below.
Reg. 179(2): see *Rewrite: Changes in Law* notes below.
Reg. 179(3): SI 1993/744, reg. 98F(2)(part).
Reg. 179(4): SI 1993/744, reg. 98F(2)(part) and see *Rewrite: Changes in Law* notes below.
Reg. 179(5): SI 1993/744, reg. 98F(3).
Reg. 179(6): SI 1993/744, reg. 98F(4) and see *Rewrite: Changes in Law* notes below.
Rewrite: Changes in Law – Commentary, App. 1, Change 1: reg. 179 refers to "Inland Revenue" (meaning any officer of the Board) rather than "inspector" or "Board".
Commentary, App. 1, Change 116: reg. 179 limits requirement on Revenue to issue code on receipt of return under reg. 164 to "single-income claimants".
Commentary, App. 1, Change 117: reg. 179 provides for Revenue to issue PAYE codes to Department for claimants other than "single-income claimants" if they consider it impractical to collect tax on taxable incapacity benefit by other means.

Death of claimant

180(1) On the death of a claimant in respect of whom a code has been issued by the Inland Revenue, the Department must–

(a)   complete Form P45 indicating in Part 1 that the claimant has died, and

(b)   send it to the Inland Revenue.

180(2) The Department must comply with paragraph (1)–

(a)   on the day on which it learns of the claimant's death, or

(b)   if that is not practicable, without unreasonable delay.

180(3) Paragraph (4) applies if the Department makes any payment of taxable incapacity benefit after the date of the claimant's death–

(a)   before completing Form P45, or

(b)   after completing Form P45 but during the tax year in which the claimant died.

180(4) The Department must, on making the payment, deduct or repay tax as if the deceased claimant were still alive and the award had not ceased at the date of payment.

180(5) Regulation 37(2) to (6) (PAYE income paid after employment ceased) applies to any payment of taxable incapacity benefit which–

(a)   is made in a tax year following the tax year in which the claimant died, and

(b)   is not included in Form P45.

Origin – Reg. 180(1): SI 1993/744, reg. 27(1)(part), 98B(part) and see *Rewrite: Changes in Law* notes below.
Reg. 180(2): drafting, and see *Rewrite: Changes in Law* notes below.
Reg. 180(3), (4): SI 1993/744, reg. 27(2)(part), 98B(part).
Reg. 180(5): SI 1993/744, reg. 27(2)(part), 98B(part) and see *Rewrite: Changes in Law* notes below.
Rewrite: Changes in Law – Commentary, App. 1, Change 1: reg. 180 refers to "Inland Revenue" (meaning any officer of the Board) rather than "inspector" or "Board".
Commentary, App. 1, Change 37: reg. 180 indicates that P45 is multi-part form.
Commentary, App. 1, Change 39: reg. 180 provides for Department to complete P45 when it learns of claimant's death or, if that is not practicable, without unreasonable delay.
Commentary, para. 862–865 and App. 1, Change 42: reg. 39 applies same rule to pension payments in tax year following death.

Chapter 4 – Income Support

Interpretation of Chapter 4

181 In this Chapter–

"**award**" means an award of income support;

"**claim**" means a claim for income support;

"**claimant**" means a person who has made a claim;

"**Department**" means the Department for Work and Pensions or, in Northern Ireland, the Department for Social Development;

"**income support**" means benefit payable under–

(a) section 124 of the Social Security Contributions and Benefits Act 1992, or

(b) in Northern Ireland, section 123 of the Social Security Contributions and Benefits (Northern Ireland) Act 1992;

"**taxable income support**" means any amount of income support which is chargeable to income tax under Chapter 2 of Part 10 of ITEPA (tax on social security income).

Origin – See *Rewrite: Changes in Law* note below.

Rewrite: Changes in Law – Commentary, App. 1, Change 118: SI 2003/2682, Pt. 8, Ch. 4 makes specific provision for information about payments of taxable income support to be given to claimants and Revenue.

Recording the amount of taxable income support

182 Whenever the Department makes a payment of taxable income support it must–

(a) record the amount, and

(b) pay the full sum without any deduction or repayment of income tax.

Origin – See *Rewrite: Changes in Law* note below.

Rewrite: Changes in Law – Commentary, App. 1, Change 118: SI 2003/2682, Pt. 8, Ch. 4 makes specific provision for information about payments of taxable income support to be given to claimants and Revenue.

Information to be supplied when an award of taxable income support ceases

183(1) This regulation applies when an award of taxable income support ceases.

183(2) The Department must give notice to the Inland Revenue and, except where the claimant has died, the claimant of–

(a) the total income support, and

(b) the taxable income support,

paid in respect of the award showing the amounts appropriate to each tax year.

183(3) If the Department has been notified of the name and address of a deceased claimant's personal representative within 30 days of the claimant's death, the Department must send the notice to the personal representative.

Origin – See *Rewrite: Changes in Law* note below.

Rewrite: Changes in Law – Commentary, App. 1, Change 118: SI 2003/2682, Pt. 8, Ch. 4 makes specific provision for information about payments of taxable income support to be given to claimants and Revenue.

Adjustments of taxable income support

184(1) Paragraph (2) applies if, after the issue of a notice under regulation 183(2)–

(a) further taxable income support is paid to the claimant, or

(b) taxable income support overpaid is recovered from the claimant.

184(2) The Department must–

(a) notify the claimant of the revised figure of total income support and the taxable income support included in that revised figure, and

(b) notify the Inland Revenue of any adjustment to the figure of taxable income support,

showing the amounts appropriate to each tax year.

Origin – See *Rewrite: Changes in Law* note below.

Rewrite: Changes in Law – Commentary, App. 1, Change 118: SI 2003/2682, Pt. 8, Ch. 4 makes specific provision for information about payments of taxable income support to be given to claimants and Revenue.

Chapter 5 – Employment and Support Allowance

Interpretation of Chapter 5

184A   In this Chapter–

"**award**" means an award of employment and support allowance;

"**claim**" means a claim for employment and support allowance;

"**claimant**" means a person who has made a claim;

"**Department**" means the Department for Work and Pensions or, in Northern Ireland, the Department for Social Development;

"**employment and support allowance**" means benefit payable under–

(a)   the Welfare Reform Act 2007, or

(b)   in Northern Ireland, the Welfare Reform Act (Northern Ireland) 2007;

"**taxable employment and support allowance**" means any amount of employment and support allowance which is chargeable to income tax under Chapter 2 of Part 10 of ITEPA (tax on social security income).

History – Reg. 184A inserted by SI 2008/2601, reg. 3, with effect from 27 October 2008.

Application of other regulations

184B(1)   The following regulations apply to payments of employment and support allowance made to a claimant with the modifications mentioned in paragraphs (2) to (5)–

regulation 2	interpretation
regulation 14	matters relevant to determination of code
regulation 15	flat rate codes
regulation 16	continued application of employee's code
regulation 17	notice to employee of code
regulation 18	objections and appeals against employee's code
regulation 19	amendment of code
regulation 20	notice to employer of amended code
regulation 21	deduction and repayment of tax by reference to employee's code
regulation 97	retention by employer of PAYE records
regulation 98	multiple PAYE schemes
regulation 102	succession to a business etc
regulation 185	adjusting total net tax deducted for purposes of sections 59A(1) and 59B(1) TMA
regulation 205	mandatory use of electronic communications
regulation 206	employers
regulation 207	specified information
regulation 209	standards of accuracy and completeness
regulation 210	penalty for failing to deliver specified information
regulation 210C	appeals and interest
regulation 211	how information must or may be delivered by employers
regulation 214	how information must be provided by employees
regulation 216	service by post.

184B(2)   In the application of those regulations, the expressions listed in column 1 of Table 7A have the meanings shown in column 2 of the table.

Table 7A
Meaning of expressions in application of other regulations

1. Expression	*2. Meaning for purposes of this Chapter*
Employee	claimant
Employer	Department
Employment	award
Relevant payments	taxable employment and support allowance

184B(3) In the application of regulations 20 (notice to employer of amended code) and 21 (deduction and repayment of tax by reference to employee's code), any reference to the deduction or repayment of tax shall be read as a reference to the tax calculation which the Department is required to make at the end of the tax year or on the cessation of an award (by virtue of regulation 184I(2)(a) and 184K(2)).

184B(4) In the application of regulation 207 (specified information) the reference to specified information shall be read as including references to–

(a) the return and accompanying information required by regulations 184G (return in respect of all claimants to taxable employment and support allowance) and 184J (annual return),

(b) Part 1 of Form P45ESA, and

(c) the information required under regulation 184E(9).

184B(5) In the application of regulation 210 (penalty for failing to deliver specified information)–

(a) where the specified information is the return and accompanying information required by regulation 184J (annual return) the penalty will be determined in accordance with regulation 210AA, and

(b) where the specified information is 184G (return in respect of all claimants to taxable employment and support allowance), Part 1 of Form P45ESA or the information required under regulation 184E(9) the penalty will be determined in accordance with regulations 210B and 210BA.

History – In reg. 184B(1), "(5)" substituted for "(4)" by SI 2010/668, reg. 17(a), with effect from 6 April 2010.
In reg. 184B(1), in the list, the entry for reg. 205 substituted for the entries for reg. 205A and 205B, the words "and specified employers" omitted from the entry for reg. 206 and the words "relevant annual returns and" omitted from the entry for reg. 210 by SI 2010/668, reg. 17(b), with effect in relation to the tax year 2011–12 and subsequent tax years.
In reg. 184B(1), in the list, the entry for reg. 208 omitted by SI 2010/668, reg. 17(b)(iii), with effect in relation to the tax year 2010–11 and subsequent tax years.
In reg. 184B(1), in the list, the entry for reg. 210B omitted by SI 2010/668, reg. 17(b)(v), with effect from 6 April 2010.
In reg. 184B(1), in the list, entries for reg. 205A–210C substituted for entries for reg. 205–210 by SI 2009/2029, reg. 3(a), with effect in relation to the tax year 2009–10.
In reg. 184B(1), in column 2 of the list, the words "retention by employer of PAYE records" substituted for the words "inspection of employer's PAYE records" by SI 2009/588, reg. 7, with effect from 1 April 2009.
In reg. 184B(2), in the first column of Table 7A, the words ", specified employer" omitted by SI 2010/668, reg. 17(c), with effect in relation to the tax year 2011–12 and subsequent tax years.
In reg. 184B(2), in the first column of Table 7A, the words "Employer, specified employer" substituted for the word "Employer" by SI 2009/2029, reg. 3(b), with effect in relation to the tax year 2009–10.
In reg. 184B(5), "210AA" substituted for "210A" and "regulations 210B and 210BA" substituted for "regulation 210B" by SI 2010/668, reg. 17(e), with effect in relation to the tax year 2011–12 and subsequent tax years.
Reg. 184B(5) inserted by SI 2010/668, reg. 17(d), with effect from 6 April 2010.
Reg. 184B inserted by SI 2008/2601, reg. 3, with effect from 27 October 2008.

Obtaining the claimant's Form p45

184C(1) A claimant who has Parts 2 and 3 of Form P45 must deliver them to the Department on making a claim for employment and support allowance which includes taxable employment and support allowance.

184C(2) If on making a claim, the claimant declares that the claimant's last employer did not provide Parts 2 and 3 of Form P45, the Department may require the employer to deliver them to a specified officer of the Department.

History – Reg. 184C inserted by SI 2008/2601, reg. 3, with effect from 27 October 2008.

Deductions working sheet for claimants awarded taxable employment and support allowance

184D(1) The Department must prepare a deductions working sheet in respect of each claimant whose award includes taxable employment and support allowance.

184D(2) If the Department obtains Parts 2 and 3 of Form P45 relating to the claimant, it must immediately prepare the deductions working sheet using the information shown in Parts 2 and 3 of Form P45 in accordance with regulation 184E.

184D(3) If the Department does not obtain Parts 2 and 3 of Form P45 relating to the claimant, it must prepare the deductions working sheet in accordance with regulation 184F.

History – Reg. 184D inserted by SI 2008/2601, reg. 3, with effect from 27 October 2008.

FORM P45: DEDUCTIONS WORKING SHEET AND RETURN

184E(1) If Parts 2 and 3 of Form P45 relate to the current tax year, the Department must record in the deductions working sheet the total payments to date shown in Parts 2 and 3 of Form P45.

184E(2)   If Parts 2 and 3 of Form P45 relate to the current tax year and show that the cumulative basis has been used, the Department must also–

(a)   record the following information from Parts 2 and 3 of Form P45 in the deductions working sheet, or

(b)   keep such records as enable production of the information.

184E(3)   If the code shown in Parts 2 and 3 of Form P45 is a K code, the information is–

(a)   the code show,

(b)   the total additional pay to date,

(c)   the total taxable payments to date, and

(d)   the lower of the total tax to date as at the week or month shown in Parts 2 and 3 of Form P45 or the total net tax deducted shown in them.

184E(4)   In any other case, the information is–

(a)   the code shown,

(b)   the total free pay to date,

(c)   the total taxable payments to date, and

(d)   the corresponding total tax to date as at the week or month shown in Parts 2 and 3 of Form P45.

184E(5)   Paragraph (6) applies if–

(a)   the claim is made by 24th May in a tax year, and

(b)   Parts 2 and 3 of Form P45 show that the last relevant payment was made in the preceding tax year.

184E(6)   The Department must complete the deductions working sheet but without recording the total payments to date or total net tax deducted (if any) shown in Parts 2 and 3 of Form P45.

184E(7)   In cases falling within paragraphs (1) and (6), the code shown in Parts 2 and 3 of Form P45 must be treated as the claimant's code for the purposes of these Regulations.

184E(8)   If, in a case not falling within paragraph (6), Parts 2 and 3 of Form P45 show that the last relevant payment was made in a tax year preceding that in which the claim was made, the Department–

(a)   must complete the deductions working sheet but without recording the total payments to date or total net tax deducted (if any) shown in parts 2 and 3 of Form P45, and

(b)   must record the emergency code as the claimant's code.

184E(9)   The Department must supply the information recorded under this regulation to HMRC together with such further information as may be required for the purposes of these Regulations.

History – Reg. 184E inserted by SI 2008/2601, reg. 3, with effect from 27 October 2008.

No Form P45: Deductions working sheet and return

184F   In a case falling within regulations 184D(3) (no Form P45), the Department must–

(a)   prepare the deductions working sheet within 14 days of the award of a taxable employment and support allowance, and

(b)   record the emergency code as the claimant's code.

History – Reg. 184F inserted by SI 2008/2601, reg. 3, with effect from 27 October 2008.

Return in respect of all claimants to taxable employment and support allowance

184G(1)   When the Department first makes a payment of taxable employment and support allowance to a claimant it must deliver a return to HMRC containing the following information.

184G(2)   The information is–

(a)   the claimant's name,

(b)   the claimant's address,

(c)   the claimant's date of birth, if known,

(d)   the claimant's national insurance number,

(e)   the date on which the claimant's entitlement to taxable employment and support allowance began,

(f)   the weekly rate of taxable employment and support allowance being paid to the claimant,

(g)   if the payment was preceded by a payment of employment and support allowance which was not taxable, the date that benefit was first paid, and

(h)   the claimant's tax reference, if known.

184G(3)   But the return need not be delivered if the claimant certifies that the claimant–

(a)   is undergoing a course of full-time education and has not had regular employment since the previous 6th April, or

(b)   has not had regular employment since finishing full-time education.

History – Reg. 184G inserted by SI 2008/2601, reg. 3, with effect from 27 October 2008.

Further return required in certain cases

184H(1)   On making a subsequent payment of taxable employment and support allowance to the claimant, the Department must deliver a further return in accordance with regulation 184G as if that subsequent payment were the first payment, if the condition set out in paragraph (2) is met.

184H(2)   The condition is that the subsequent payment is the first payment to be made at a different rate from the rate subsisting at the time of that determination.

184H(3)   In addition to providing the information listed in regulation 184G(2), the Department must indicate in the further return that the weekly rate of taxable employment and support allowance being paid to the claimant represents a revised amount.

History – Reg. 184H inserted by SI 2008/2601, reg. 3, with effect from 27 October 2008.

Obligations at the end of the year

184I(1)   This regulation applies in respect of each award which includes taxable employment and support allowance and which continues beyond the end of a tax year.

184I(2)   Before 1st June following the end of the tax year the Department must–

(a)   make a tax calculation in accordance with regulation 184N if the claimant's code is used on the cumulative basis; and

(b)   subject to paragraph (3), issue a certificate to the claimant.

184I(3)   The Department need not issue a certificate if–

(a)   no taxable employment and support allowance has been paid, and

(b)   a tax calculation in accordance with regulation 184N is not required.

184I(4)   The certificate must show–

(a)   the tax year to which it relates,

(b)   the total employment and support allowance for the tax year excluding any amounts previously notified under regulations 184L(4) and 184Q(2)(a),

(c)   the taxable employment and support allowance included in the total employment and support allowance,

(d)   the claimant's code,

(e)   the claimant's national insurance number,

(f)   the claimant's address (if known),

(h)   any previous relevant payments and any tax deducted from those relevant payments which the Department was required to take into account under regulation 184N,

(i)   any total payments to date recorded by the Department in accordance with regulation 184E(1) plus the total taxable employment and support allowance for the tax year, and the corresponding total net tax deducted, and

(j)   the amount of tax refunded by the Department.

History – Reg. 184I inserted by SI 2008/2601, reg. 3, with effect from 27 October 2008.

Annual return

184J(1)   This regulation applies in respect of each award which includes taxable employment and support allowance.

184J(2)   Before 1st June following the end of the tax year, the Department must deliver a return to HMRC.

184J(3)   The return must show–

(a)   the particulars specified in regulation 184I(4), and

(b)   if a calculation is required under regulation 184N any amount of tax outstanding.

History – Reg. 184J inserted by SI 2008/2601, reg. 3, with effect from 27 October 2008.

When an award ceases

184K(1)   For the purposes of these Regulations an award ceases when entitlement to an employment and support allowance ceases.

184K(2)   When an award of a taxable employment and support allowance ceases, the Department must make a tax calculation in accordance with regulation 184N.

184K(3)   The relevant date for the purposes of that calculation is the date on which the award ceases.

184K(4)   The date on which the award ceases is the last day for which benefit was paid and was not recoverable, except that if the last day is 4th or 5th April the date is the preceding 3rd April.

184K(5)   But the Department need not amend a tax calculation solely because the date used for the purposes of the calculation is subsequently shown to be incorrect.

History – Reg. 184K inserted by SI 2008/2601, reg. 3, with effect from 27 October 2008.

Cessation of award: Form P45ESA

184L(1)   When an award of a taxable employment and support allowance ceases, the Department must immediately complete Form P45ESA.

184L(2)   The Department must then–

(a)   send Part 1 of Form P45ESA to HMRC; and

(b)   provide Part 1A of P45ESA and Parts 2 and 3 of Form P45 to the claimant.

184L(3)   The information listed in column 1 of Table 7B must, subject to the conditions set out in column 2, be provided in Parts 1 and 1A of Form P45ESA and Parts 2 and 3 of Form P45 as indicated in columns 3 to 5.

Table 7B
Information which must be provided in Form P45ESA

1	2	3	4	5
Information to be provided	*Conditions*	*Form P45ESA*	*Form P45ESA*	*Form P45*
		Part 1	*Part 1A*	*Parts 2 and 3*
1. the tax reference as shown in the deductions working sheet		yes	yes	yes
2. claimant's national insurance number		yes	yes	yes
3. claimant's name		yes	yes	yes
4. the date on which the award ceased		yes	yes	yes
5. the claimant's code or, if more than one, the latest code for the tax year during which the award ceased		yes	yes	yes
6. whether the claimant's code is used on the cumulative basis		yes	yes	yes
7. the tax week or month in which the award ceased	if the claimant's code is used on the cumulative basis	yes	yes	yes

1	2	3	4	5
Information to be provided	Conditions	Form P45ESA Part 1	Form P45ESA Part 1A	Form P45 Parts 2 and 3
8. the total payments to date (including taxable employment and support allowance) at the date the award ceased, and the corresponding total net tax deducted	if the claimant's code is used on the cumulative basis	yes	yes	yes
9. the taxable employment and support allowance paid during the tax year by virtue of the award in question	if the claimant's code is used on the cumulative basis, and if different from the information supplied under item 8	yes	yes	no
10. the taxable employment and support allowance paid during the tax year in question by virtue of the award in question	if the claimant's code is not used on the cumulative basis	yes	yes	no
11. any amount of tax outstanding	if the claimant's code is used on the cumulative basis	yes	no	no
12. whether the claimant was self-employed immediately before the claim was made.		yes	no	no
13. whether the claimant is receiving a pension by reason of a former employment.		yes	no	no
14. the claimant's address	if known	yes	no	no
15. the address of the benefit office		yes	yes	no
16. the date the form is completed		yes	yes	no

184L(4) The Department must also give notice to the claimant of–

(a) the total employment and support allowance for the tax year excluding any sums previously notified under this regulation and regulation 184Q(2)(a), and

(b) the taxable employment and support allowance included in that total.

184L(5) Expressions used in Parts 2 and 3 of Form P45 have the following meanings–

(a) **"employee"** means "claimant";

(b) **"leaving date"** means "date the award ceased"; and

(c) **"pay"** means "employment and support allowance".

184L(6) Regulation 184M (death of claimant) modifies the requirements of this regulation if an award of taxable employment and support allowance has ceased on the death of the claimant.

Statutory Instruments

184L(7)   If Form P45ESA has not come into use when the award of taxable employment and support allowance ceases, the Department must complete form P45U and any references to form P45ESA in these regulations shall be read as a reference to form P45U.

History – Reg. 184L inserted by SI 2008/2601, reg. 3, with effect from 27 October 2008.

DEATH OF CLAIMANT

184M(1)   On being informed of the death of a claimant whose award included taxable employment and support allowance, the Department must send HMRC the completed Form P45ESA indicating in Part 1 that the claimant has died.

History – Reg. 184M inserted by SI 2008/2601, reg. 3, with effect from 27 October 2008.

184M(2)   If the Department knows the name and address of the claimant's personal representative the Department must send the notice referred to in regulation 184L(4) to the personal representative.

184M(3)   But if the Department has not been notified of the name and address of the claimant's personal representative within 30 days of the claimant's death, the Department is not required–

(a)   to make a tax calculation under regulation 184N, nor

(b)   to issue the notice under regulation 184L(4).

History – Reg. 184M inserted by SI 2008/2601, reg. 3, with effect from 27 October 2008.

Tax calculation

184N(1)   This regulation applies, subject to regulation 184O, if the Department is required by regulation 184 or 184K to make a tax calculation.

184N(2)   The Department must calculate in respect of the claimant as at the relevant date–

(a)   the total payments to date, and

(b)   the claimant's total tax.

184N(3)   If the recorded tax exceeds the claimant's total tax, the Department must repay the excess to the claimant.

184N(4)   But if the recorded tax is less than the claimant's total tax–

(a)   the difference is tax outstanding for the purposes of regulation 184J(3)(b) or item 11 of table 7B in regulation 184L(3), and

(b)   the Department must treat the claimant's code as issued by HMRC on the non-cumulative basis from the relevant date.

184N(5)   In this regulation–

"claimant's total tax" means–

(a)   if the claimant's code is a K code, the lesser of–

(i)   50% of the claimant's total payments to date, and

(ii)   the tax due in accordance with the appropriate tax tables in respect of the claimant's total taxable payments to date at the relevant date,

(b)   in any other case, the tax due in accordance with the appropriate tax tables in respect of the claimant's total taxable payments to date at the relevant date;

"recorded tax" means the total tax to date or (as the case may be) the total net tax deducted which was recorded in accordance with regulation 184E(3) or (4) when the claim was made;

"relevant date" means–

(a)   the end of the tax year, if the calculation is required by regulation 184I,

(b)   the date used for the purposes of the calculation, if the calculation is required by regulation 184K;

"total payments to date" means any payments to date recorded by the Department in accordance with regulation 184E(1) plus the total taxable employment and support allowance.

History – Reg. 184N inserted by SI 2008/2601, reg. 3, with effect from 27 October 2008.

No tax calculation required in certain cases

184O(1)   A tax calculation made under regulation 184N is not required in any of the following cases–

(a)   if the claimant does not give the Department Parts 2 and 3 of form P45 and does not certifiy in accordance with regulation 184G(3) (students etc),

(b)   if the claimant gives the Department Parts 2 and 3 of Form P45 but they do not relate to the claimant's last employment or award before the present award, whichever is the later,

(c)   if the claimant is in receipt of a pension in respect of a former employment,

(d)   if it appears to the Department on the occasion of a claim that a previous award should have been treated as having ceased in accordance with regulation 184K (when an award ceases), or

(e)   if the claimant's code is a nil tax code, basic rate code or higher rate code.

184O(2)   Those cases are treated as if HMRC had made a direction that the claimant's code must be used on the non-cumulative basis.

184O(3)   Those cases are subject to a notification from HMRC under regulation 184P that revised particulars are to be substituted and used.

History – Reg. 184O inserted by SI 2008/2601, reg. 3, with effect from 27 October 2008.

Claimant's code etc to be used for calculations

184P(1)   This regulation applies if, in respect of a claimant, the Department receives notification from HMRC of–

(a)   a code or amended code,

(b)   total payments to date, or

(c)   total net tax deducted.

184P(2)   The Department must record that notification in substitution for any previous record and use it for the purpose of all calculations required under this Chapter.

History – Reg. 184P inserted by SI 2008/2601, reg. 3, with effect from 27 October 2008.

Notification of taxable employment and support allowance

184Q(1)   Paragraph (2) applies if–

(a)   after a certificate under regulation 184I(2)(b) has been issued (or would have been issued but for regulation 184I(3)), or

(b)   after a notice has been issued under regulation 184L(4) or this regulation,

further taxable employment and support allowance is paid to, or taxable employment and support allowance overpaid is recovered from, the claimant.

184Q(2)   The Department must–

(a)   give notice to the claimant of the revised figure of total employment and support allowance and the taxable employment and support allowance included in that revised figure in accordance with the relevant regulation, and

(b)   notify HMRC of the sums paid or refunded.

History – Reg. 184Q inserted by SI 2008/2601, reg. 3, with effect from 27 October 2008.

Recording the amount of taxable employment and support allowance

184R   Whenever a payment of employment and support allowance is made, the Department must record the taxable employment and support allowance included in the payment.

History – Reg. 184R inserted by SI 2008/2601, reg. 3, with effect from 27 October 2008.

Finance

184S(1)   HMRC must advance monies to the National Funds of Great Britain and Northern Ireland at intervals to be agreed with the Department for use in making repayments of income tax under these Regulations.

184S(2)   The Department must provide HMRC with a quarterly statement of receipts and payments made under this Chapter.

History – Reg. 184S inserted by SI 2008/2601, reg. 3, with effect from 27 October 2008.

PART 9 – ASSESSMENT AND SELF-ASSESSMENT

Adjusting total net tax deducted for purposes of sections 59A(1) and 59B(1) TMA

185(1)   This regulation applies for the purpose of determining–

(a)   the excess mentioned in section 59A(1) of TMA (payments on account of income tax: income tax assessed exceeds amount deducted at source), and

(b)   the difference mentioned in section 59B(1) of TMA (payments of income tax and capital gains tax: difference between tax contained in self-assessment and aggregate of payments on account or deducted at source).

185(2)   For those purposes, the amount of income tax deducted at source under these Regulations is the total net tax deducted during the relevant tax year ("A") after making any additions or subtractions required by paragraphs (3) to (5).

185(3)   Subtract from A any repayments of A which are made before the taxpayer's return and self-assessment is made under section 8 or 8A of TMA (personal return and trustee's return).

185(4)   Add to A any overpayment of tax from a previous tax year, to the extent that it was taken into account in determining the taxpayer's code for the relevant tax year.

185(5)   Add to A any tax treated as deducted, other than any direction tax, but–

(a)   only if there would be an amount payable by the taxpayer under section 59B(1) of TMA on the assumption that there are no payments on account and no addition to A under this paragraph, and then

(b)   only to a maximum of that amount.

185(6)   In this regulation–

"**direction tax**" means any amount of tax which is the subject of a direction made under regulation 72(5), regulation 72F or regulation 81(4) in relation to the taxpayer in respect of one or more tax periods falling within the relevant tax year;

"**relevant tax year**" means–

(a)   in relation to section 59A(1) of TMA, the immediately preceding year referred to in that subsection;

(b)   in relation to section 59B(1) of TMA, the tax year for which the self-assessment referred to in that subsection is made;

"**tax treated as deducted**" means any tax which in relation to relevant payments made by an employer to the taxpayer in the relevant tax year–

(a)   the employer was liable to deduct from payments but failed to do so, or

(b)   the employer was liable to account for in accordance with regulation 62(5) (notional payments) but failed to do so;

"**the taxpayer**" means the person referred to in section 59A(1) of TMA or the person whose self-assessment is referred to in section 59B(1) of TMA (as the case may be).

History – Reg. 185(6), in the definition of "direction tax" the words "regulation 72(5), regulation 72F" substituted for "regulation 72(5)" by SI 2008/782, reg. 14, with effect from 6 April 2008.

Origin – Reg. 185(1), (2): SI 1993/744, reg. 101A(1)(part).
Reg. 185(3): SI 1993/744, reg. 101A(2)(part), (4).
Reg. 185(4): SI 1993/744, reg. 101A(4)(part), 101A(2)(part).
Reg. 185(5): SI 1993/744, reg. 101A(4)(part), (5), (6)(part), 101A(2)(part); SI 1994/1212, reg. 13(1)(part) and see *Rewrite: Changes in Law* notes below.
Reg. 185(6): drafting.

Rewrite: Changes in Law – Commentary, App. 1, Change 35: reg. 185 refers to tax in respect of notional payments.
Commentary, App. 1, Change 119: reg. 185 provides explicit cap on extent to which credit can be given under self-assessment for tax not actually deducted from taxpayer or not actually accounted for on notional payments.

Recovery: adjustment of employee's code

186(1)   This regulation applies if, on the assumption mentioned in paragraph (2), the difference for a tax year mentioned in section 59B(1) of TMA (difference between tax contained in a self-assessment and aggregate of payments on account) would be payable by the taxpayer.

186(2)   The assumption is that, in respect of the tax year, nothing will be deducted at source under these Regulations in a subsequent tax year.

186(3)   The Inland Revenue must have regard to the difference in determining a taxpayer's code for a subsequent tax year under regulation 14 (matters relevant to determination of code) if–

(a)   it is less than £3,000, and

(b)   the return for the tax year is–

(i)   delivered by an approved method of electronic communications before 31st December following the end of the tax year, or

(ii)   delivered by any other method before 1st November following the end of the tax year.

186(4)   In a case not falling within paragraph (3)(b)(i), the Inland Revenue may have regard to the difference in determining a taxpayer's code for a subsequent tax year under regulation 14 if–

(a)   it is less than £3,000, and

(b)   the return for the tax year is delivered on or after 1st November following the end of the tax year and the code is determined before 31st December.

186(5)   But the Inland Revenue must not have regard to the difference if the taxpayer objects at the time the return is delivered or subsequently.

History – In reg. 186(3)(a), "£3,000" substituted for "£2,000" by SI 2011/1584, reg. 2(3), with effect from 6 April 2012.
In reg. 186(3)(b)(ii) and (4)(b) the words "1st November" substituted for "1st October" by SI 2007/2969, reg. 18 with effect from 6 April 2008.
In reg. 186(4)(a), "£3,000" substituted for "£2,000" by SI 2011/1584, reg. 2(3), with effect from 6 April 2012.
Origin – Reg. 186(1): SI 1993/744, reg. 101A(3).
Reg. 186(2): drafting.
Reg. 186(3)–(5): see *Rewrite: Change in Law* note below.
Rewrite: Changes in Law – Commentary, App. 1, Change 120: reg. 186 provides for PAYE codes to be adjusted for underpayment of tax in self-assessment unless taxpayer objects.

Repayment: adjustment of employee's code

187(1)   This regulation applies if the difference for a tax year mentioned in section 59B(1) of TMA (difference between tax contained in a self-assessment and aggregate of payments on account) is payable to the taxpayer.

187(2)   The Inland Revenue may have regard to the difference in determining the employee's code for a subsequent tax year under regulation 14 (matters relevant to determination of code).

187(3)   But the Inland Revenue must not have regard to the difference if the taxpayer objects at the time the return is delivered or subsequently.

Origin – See *Rewrite: Change in Law* note below.
Rewrite: Changes in Law – Commentary, App. 1, Change 120: reg. 187 provides for PAYE codes to be adjusted for overpayments of tax in self-assessment unless taxpayer objects.

Assessments other than self-assessments

188(1)   In this regulation, **"assessment"** means an assessment other than one under section 9 of TMA (self-assessment).

188(2)   The tax payable by the employee is–

$$A - (B - C)$$

where

A is the tax payable under the assessment;

B is the total net tax deducted in relation to the employee's relevant payments during the tax year for which the assessment is made, adjusted as required by paragraph (3); and

C is so much, if any, of B as is subsequently repaid.

188(3)   For the purpose of determining the tax payable by the employee, and subject to paragraphs (4) and (5)–

(a)   add to B any tax which–

     (i)   the employer was liable to deduct from relevant payments but failed to do so, or

     (ii)   the employer was liable to account for in accordance with regulation 62(5) (notional payments) but failed to do so;

(b)   make any necessary adjustment to B in respect of any tax overpaid or remaining unpaid for any tax year; and

(c)   make any necessary adjustment to B in respect of any amount to be recovered as if it were unpaid tax under section 30(1) of TMA (recovery of overpayment of tax etc) to the extent that–

     (i)   HMRC took that amount into account in determining the employee's code, and

     (ii)   the total net tax deducted was in consequence greater than it would otherwise have been.

188(4)   No direction tax is to be included in calculating the amount of tax referred to in paragraph (3)(a).

188(5)   If a direction is made after the making of the assessment, the amount (if any) shown in the notice of assessment as a deduction from, or a credit against, the tax payable under the assessment is to be taken as reduced by so much of the direction tax as was included in calculating the amount of tax referred to in paragraph (3)(a).

188(6)   Instead of requiring payment by the employee, HMRC may take the tax payable by the employee into account in determining the employee's code for a subsequent tax year.

188(7) In this regulation–

"**direction**" means a direction made under regulation 72(5), regulation 72F or 81(4) in relation to the employee in respect of one or more tax periods falling within the tax year in question;

"**direction tax**" means any amount of tax which is the subject of a direction;

"**tax payable under the assessment**" means the amount of tax shown in the assessment as payable without regard to any amount shown in the notice of assessment as a deduction from, or a credit against, the amount of tax payable.

History – In reg. 188(3)(c)(i), "HMRC" substituted for "the Inland Revenue" by SI 2008/782, reg. 15, with effect from 6 April 2008.

In reg. 188(6), "HMRC" substituted for "the Inland Revenue" by SI 2008/782, reg. 15, with effect from 6 April 2008.

In reg. 188(7), in the definition of "direction" the words "regulation 72(5), regulation 72F" substituted for "regulation 72(5)" by SI 2008/782, reg. 15, with effect from 6 April 2008.

Origin – Reg. 188(1): SI 1993/744, reg. 101(7)(part).

Reg. 188(2): SI 1993/744, reg. 101(2)(part).

Reg. 188(3): SI 1993/744, reg. 101(3)(part), (4)(part); SI 1994/1212, reg. 13(1)(part); and see *Rewrite: Changes in Law* note below.

Reg. 188(4), (5): SI 1993/744, reg. 101(6)(part).

Reg. 188(6): SI 1993/744, reg. 101(2)(part).

Reg. 188(7): SI 1993/744, reg. 101(7)(part) and drafting.

Rewrite: Changes in Law – Commentary, App. 1, Change 35: reg. 188(3) provides explicitly that employee can get credit for tax that should have been accounted for but was not.

PART 10 – COMMUNICATIONS

Chapter 1 – Electronic Communications: Interpretation

Meaning of electronic communications etc

189 In these Regulations–

"**approved method of electronic communications**", in relation to the delivery of information or the making of a payment in accordance with a provision of these Regulations, means a method of electronic communications which has been approved, by specific or general directions issued by the Board of Inland Revenue, for the delivery of information of that kind or the making of a payment of that kind under that provision;

"**electronic communications**" has the meaning given in section 132(10) of the Finance Act 1999;

"**official computer system**" means a computer system maintained by or on behalf of the Board of Inland Revenue or an officer of the Board.

Origin – "approved method of electronic communications": SI 1993/744, reg. 2(1)("electronic communications"'"approved") (part) and see *Rewrite: Change in Law* notes below.

"electronic communications": SI 1993/744, reg. 2(1)("electronic communications")(part).

"official computer system": SI 1993/744, reg. 2(1)("official computer system")(part), (4)(part) and see *Rewrite: Changes in Law* notes below.

Cross references – HMRC Direction of 4 April 2011 made under reg. 189.

Rewrite: Changes in Law – Commentary, App. 1, Change 121: reg. 189 omits specific provisions for EDI and internet service for PAYE, leaving them (and any other) methods of electronic communications to be approved by the Board.

Commentary, App. 1, Change 122: reg. 189 provides for official computer systems to be maintained by or on behalf of the Board, in addition to its officers.

Specified date

190 [Omitted by SI 2010/668, reg. 4.]

History – Reg. 190 omitted by SI 2010/668, reg. 4, with effect in relation to the tax year 2011–12 and subsequent years.

Large and medium sized employers

191 [Omitted by SI 2010/668, reg. 4.]

History – Reg. 191 omitted by SI 2010/668, reg. 4, with effect in relation to the tax year 2011–12 and subsequent years.

Chapter 2 – Electronic Communications: General

Whether information has been delivered electronically

192   For the purpose of these Regulations, information is taken to have been delivered to an official computer system by an approved method of electronic communications only if it is accepted by that official computer system.

Origin – SI 1993/744, reg. 2A and see *Rewrite: Changes in Law* note below.

Rewrite: Changes in Law – Commentary, App. 1, Change 121: reg. 192 omits specific provisions for EDI and internet service for PAYE, leaving them (and any other) methods of electronic communications to be approved by the Board.

Proof of content of electronic delivery

193(1)   A document certified by the Inland Revenue to be a printed-out version of any information delivered by an approved method of electronic communications is evidence, unless the contrary is proved, that the information–

(a)   was delivered by an approved method of electronic communications on that occasion, and

(b)   constitutes everything which was delivered on that occasion.

193(2)   A document which purports to be a certificate given in accordance with paragraph (1) is presumed to be such a certificate unless the contrary is proved.

Origin – Reg. 193(1): SI 1993/744, reg. 2B(1), (2) and see *Rewrite: Changes in Law* notes below.
Reg. 193(2): SI 1993/744, reg. 2B(3).

Rewrite: Changes in Law – Commentary, App. 1, Change 121: reg. 193 omits specific provisions for EDI and internet service for PAYE, leaving them (and any other) methods of electronic communications to be approved by the Board.
Commentary, App. 1, Change 123: reg. 193 allows Revenue to produce as proof of delivery of information only information delivered by approved methods.

Proof of identity of person sending or receiving electronic delivery

194   The identity of–

(a)   the person sending any information delivered by an approved method of electronic communications to the Inland Revenue, or

(b)   the person receiving any information delivered by an approved method of electronic communications by the Inland Revenue,

is presumed, unless the contrary is proved, to be the person recorded as such on an official computer system.

Origin – SI 1993/744, reg. 2C and see *Rewrite: Changes in Law* note below.

Rewrite: Changes in Law – Commentary, App. 1, Change 121: reg. 194 omits specific provisions for EDI and internet service for PAYE, leaving them (and any other) methods of electronic communications to be approved by the Board.

Information sent electronically on behalf of a person

195(1)   Any information delivered by an approved method of electronic communications–

(a)   to the Inland Revenue, or

(b)   to an official computer system,

on behalf of a person is taken to have been delivered by that person.

195(2)   But this does not apply if the person proves that the information was delivered without the person's knowledge or connivance.

Origin – SI 1993/744, reg. 46ZB(part) and see *Rewrite: Changes in Law* notes below.

Rewrite: Changes in Law – Commentary, App. 1, Change 1: reg. 195 refers to "Inland Revenue" (meaning any officer of the Board) rather than "inspector" or "Board".
Commentary, App. 1, Change 121: reg. 195 omits specific provisions for EDI and internet service for PAYE, leaving them (and any other) methods of electronic communications to be approved by the Board.

Proof of delivery of information sent electronically

196(1)   The use of an approved method of electronic communications is presumed, unless the contrary is proved, to have resulted in the delivery of information–

(a)   to the Inland Revenue, if the delivery of the information has been recorded on an official computer system;

(b)   by the Inland Revenue, if the despatch of the information has been recorded on an official computer system.

196(2) The use of an approved method of electronic communications is presumed, unless the contrary is proved, not to have resulted in the delivery of information–

(a) to the Inland Revenue, if the delivery of the information has not been recorded on an official computer system;

(b) by the Inland Revenue, if the despatch of the information has not been recorded on an official computer system.

196(3) The time of receipt or despatch of any information delivered by an approved method of electronic communications is presumed, unless the contrary is proved, to be the time recorded on an official computer system.

Origin – Reg. 196(1): SI 1993/744, reg. 2D(1)(part), (4)(part) and see *Rewrite: Changes in Law* notes below.
Reg. 196(2): SI 1993/744, reg. 2D(2)(part), (4)(part) and see *Rewrite: Changes in Law* notes below.
Reg. 196(3): SI 1993/744, reg. 2D(3)(part), (4)(part) and see *Rewrite: Changes in Law* notes below.

Rewrite: Changes in Law – Commentary, App. 1, Change 1: reg. 196 refers to "Inland Revenue" (meaning any officer of the Board) rather than "inspector" or "Board".
Commentary, App. 1, Change 124: to remove doubt, reg. 196 provides for proof of time of despatch of information by electronic communications *from* Revenue as well as *to* Revenue.

Proof of payment sent electronically

197(1) The use of a method of electronic communications is presumed, unless the contrary is proved, to have resulted in the making of a payment–

(a) to the Inland Revenue, if the making of the payment has been recorded on an official computer system;

(b) by the Inland Revenue, if the despatch of the payment has been recorded on an official computer system.

197(2) The use of a method of electronic communications is presumed, unless the contrary is proved, not to have resulted in the making of a payment–

(a) to the Inland Revenue, if the making of the payment has not been recorded on an official computer system;

(b) by the Inland Revenue, if the despatch of the payment has not been recorded on an official computer system.

197(3) The time of receipt or despatch of any payment sent by a method of electronic communications is presumed, unless the contrary is proved, to be the time recorded on an official computer system.

197(4) In this regulation, **"the Inland Revenue"** means the Board of Inland Revenue or any officer of the Board.

Origin – Reg. 197(1): SI 1993/744, reg. 2D(1)(part).
Reg. 197(2): SI 1993/744, reg. 2D(2)(part).
Reg. 197(3): SI 1993/744, reg. 2D(3)(part) and see *Rewrite: Changes in Law* notes below.
Reg. 197(4): see *Rewrite: Changes in Law* notes below.

Rewrite: Changes in Law – Commentary, App. 1, Change 1: reg. 197 refers to "Inland Revenue" (meaning any officer of the Board) rather than "inspector" or "Board".
Commentary, App. 1, Change 124: to remove doubt, reg. 197 provides for proof of time of despatch of payments by electronic communications *from* Revenue as well as *to* Revenue.

Use of unauthorised method of electronic communications

198(1) This regulation applies to information which is required to be delivered to the Board of Inland Revenue or to the Inland Revenue under a provision of these Regulations.

198(2) The use of a method of electronic communications for the purpose of delivering such information is conclusively presumed not to have resulted in the delivery of that information, unless that method of electronic communications is for the time being approved for delivery of information of that kind under that provision.

Origin – Reg. 198(1): SI 1993/744, reg. 2E(1).
Reg. 198(2): SI 1993/744, reg. 2E(2).

Chapter 3 – Electronic Payment By Large Employers

Large employers

198A(1) **"Large employer"** means an employer treated as paying PAYE income to 250 or more employees at the specified date.

198A(2) An employer is treated as paying PAYE income to an employee at the specified date if the employer–

(a) is required at that date by these Regulations to prepare or maintain a deductions working sheet in respect of that employee, and

(b) has not sent to HMRC Part 1 of Form P45 in respect of that employee or, as the case may be, has not indicated in a return under regulation 67B or 67D that the employee's employment has ceased.

198A(3) The specified date for a particular tax year is 31st October in the preceding tax year.

History – In reg. 198A(2)(b) the words "or, as the case may be, has not indicated in a return under regulation 67B or 67D that the employee's employment has ceased" inserted by SI 2012/822, reg. 46, with effect from 6 April 2012.
Reg. 198A(3) substituted by SI 2011/729, reg. 15, with effect from 6 April 2011.
Reg. 198A inserted by SI 2010/668, reg. 5, with effect in relation to the tax year 2011–12 and subsequent tax years.

Large employers required to make specified payments electronically

199(1) A large employer must use an approved method of electronic communications to make specified payments.

199(2) **"Specified payments"**, in this regulation, means payments of tax under regulation 67G (payments to and recoveries from HMRC: Real Time Information employers, as adjusted by regulation 67H(2) where appropriate) or 68 (periodic payments to and recoveries from HMRC: non-Real Time Information employers).

199(3) The Board of Inland Revenue may give specific or general directions–

(a) suspending, for any period during which the use of an approved method of electronic communications for the making of specified payments is impossible or impractical, any requirement imposed by these Regulations relating to the use of such methods,

(b) substituting alternative requirements for the suspended ones, and

(c) making any provision that is necessary in consequence of the imposition of the substituted requirements.

199(4) This regulation does not apply to a payment of tax in respect of retrospective employment income for a closed year.

199(5) A specified payment is not treated as received in full by HMRC on or before the date by which that specified payment is required in accordance with regulation 69 unless it is made in a manner which secures (in a case where the specified payment is made otherwise than in cash) that, on or before that date, all transactions can be completed which need to be completed before the whole amount of the specified payment becomes available to the Commissioners for Her Majesty's Revenue and Customs.

History – In reg. 199(1), the words "to whom an e-payment notice in respect of a tax year has been issued" omitted by SI 2010/668, reg. 6(1)(a), with effect in relation to the tax year 2010–11 and subsequent tax years.
In reg. 199(2), the words", as adjusted by regulation 67H(2) where appropriate," inserted by SI 2013/521, reg. 36, with effect for the 2013–14 tax year and subsequent tax years.
In reg. 199(2) the words "67G (payments to and recoveries from HMRC: Real Time Information employers) or 68 (periodic payments to and recoveries from HMRC: non-Real Time Information employers)" substituted for the words "68 (periodic payments to and recoveries from HMRC)" by SI 2012/822, reg. 47, with effect from 6 April 2012.
Reg. 199(2) substituted by SI 2010/668, reg. 6(1)(b), with effect in relation to the tax year 2010–11 and subsequent tax years.
Reg. 199(4) inserted by SI 2007/1077, reg. 17(2), with effect from 6 April 2007.
Reg. 199(5) inserted by SI 2010/668, reg. 6(1)(c), with effect in relation to the tax year 2010–11 and subsequent tax years.
Origin – Reg. 199(1): SI 1993/744, reg. 42A(1)(part).
Reg. 199(2): SI 1993/744, reg. 42A(2)(part).
Reg. 199(3): SI 1993/744, reg. 42A(3).
Cross references – SI 2003/2682, reg. 200: meaning of "e-payment notice".
Direction of the Board, 5 April 2004: direction consolidates and revokes various directions in respect of the electronic delivery of information and specifies the approved methods of electronic payments of sums due.

E-payment notices and appeal

200 [Omitted by SI 2010/668, reg. 7.]

History – Reg. 200 omitted by SI 2010/668, reg. 7, with effect in relation to the tax year 2010–11 and subsequent tax years.

Employer in default if specified payment not received by applicable due date

201 [Omitted by SI 2010/668, reg. 7.]

History – Reg. 201 omitted by SI 2010/668, reg. 7, with effect in relation to the tax year 2010–11 and subsequent tax years.

Default notice and appeal

202 [Omitted by SI 2010/668, reg. 7.]

History – Reg. 202 omitted by SI 2010/668, reg. 7, with effect in relation to the tax year 2010–11 and subsequent tax years.

Default surcharge

203   [Omitted by SI 2010/466, art. 4(1) and (3).]

History – Reg. 203 omitted by SI 2010/466, art. 4(1) and (3), with effect from 6 April 2010 but not in relation to surcharges arising in respect of late payments of tax where the tax was chargeable in respect of a tax period ending on or before 5 April 2010. Relevant definitions in SI 2010/466, art. 2 are as follows:

"**tax quarter**" means any of the following (inclusive) periods–
6th April to 5th July, 6th July to 5th October, 6th October to 5th January and 6th January to 5th April;
"**tax month**" means the period beginning on the 6th day of a calendar month and ending on the 5th day of the following calendar month;
"**tax period**" means a tax quarter or tax month;"

Former reg. 203 read as follows:

"**203(1)**   An employer in default in respect of any specified payment to whom–
(a)   a default notice under regulation 202, and
(b)   a surcharge notice under regulation 204,
have been issued, is liable to a surcharge.
203(2)   The surcharge is the sum of the surcharges, calculated in accordance with paragraph (3), in respect of each default relating to the tax year in which were made the relevant payments to which the specified payment referred to in paragraph (1) relates.
203(3)   The surcharge in respect of each default is the specified percentage of (A − B).
203(4)   In paragraph (3)–
(a)   A is the total amount of tax due for the tax year in which the relevant payments to which the specified payment relates were made;
(b)   B is the total of the amounts deducted from A under–
     (i)   omitted by SI 2006/777, reg. 5.]
     (ii)   regulations 4, 5 and 6 of the Statutory Maternity Pay (Compensation of Employers) and Miscellaneous Amendment Regulations 1994,
     (iii)   regulations 3 and 5 of the Statutory Paternity Pay and Statutory Adoption Pay (Administration) Regulations 2002, and
     (iv)   regulation 44B of the Income Tax (Sub-contractors in the Construction Industry) Regulations 1993;
(c)   the specified percentage is determined by reference to the number of the default during a surcharge period in accordance with Table 8.

Table 8
Specified percentage for each default in a surcharge period

1. Default number (within a surcharge period)	2. Specified percentage
1st	0%
2nd	0%
3rd	0.17%
4th	0.17%
5th	0.17%
6th	0.33%
7th	0.33%
8th	0.33%
9th	0.58%
10th	0.58%
11th	0.58%
12th and subsequent defaults	0.83%

203(5)   A surcharge period is a period which–
(a)   begins on the day following the date by which payment is required in accordance with regulation 69 for the first specified payment in respect of which the employer is in default, and
(b)   ends at the end of a tax year in relation to which the employer has not been in default in respect of any specified payment.
203(6)   A surcharge payable under this regulation is payable 30 days after the issue of the surcharge notice.
203(7)   Section 102 of TMA (mitigation of penalties) applies to a surcharge payable under this regulation as if it were a penalty.
203(8)   Section 108 of the Finance Act 2009 (suspension of penalties during currency of agreement for deferred payment) applies to a surcharge payable under this regulation with the following modifications–
(a)   in the Table in subsection (5), insert at the end–

Amount	Penalty
Specified payments within the meaning of regulations 90M of the Social Security (Contributions) Regulations 2001	Surcharge under regulation 90K of the Social Security (Contributions) Regulations 2001", and

(b)   omit subsections (7), (8), (9) and (11).

History – Reg. 203(8) inserted by SI 2009/2029. reg. 4, with effect in relation to deferred payment agreements made on or after 13 August 2009.
Reg. 203(4)(b)(i) omitted by SI 2006/777, reg. 5, with effect from 6 April 2006.

Origin – Reg. 203(1), (2): SI 1993/744, reg. 42B(9)(part).
Reg. 203(3), (4): SI 1993/744, reg. 42B(10)(part).
Table 8: SI 1993/744, reg. 42B(10)(part).
Reg. 203(5): SI 1993/744, reg. 42B(10)(part).
Reg. 203(6): SI 1993/744, reg. 42B(16)(part).
Reg. 203(7): SI 1993/744, reg. 42B(17)(part)."

Surcharge notice and appeal

204 [Omitted by SI 2010/466, art. 4(1) and (3).]

History – Reg. 204 omitted by SI 2010/466, art. 4(1) and (3), with effect from 6 April 2010, but not in relation to surcharges arising in respect of late payments of tax where the tax was chargeable in respect of a tax period ending on or before 5 April 2010. Relevant definitions in SI 2010/466, art. 2 are as follows:

"**'tax quarter'** means any of the following (inclusive) periods–
     6th April to 5th July, 6th July to 5th October, 6th October to 5th January and 6th January to 5th April;
     'tax month' means the period beginning on the 6th day of a calendar month and ending on the 5th day of the following calendar month;
     'tax period' means a tax quarter or tax month;".

Former reg. 204 read as follows:
     "**204(1)**   The Inland Revenue must issue a surcharge notice to an employer who has been in default on three or more occasions during a surcharge period and consequently will be liable to a surcharge under regulation 203.
     204(2)   The surcharge notice must show the total surcharge liability for the tax year.
     204(3)   The surcharge notice must be issued within 6 years of–
     (a)   the end of the tax year, or
     (b)   if earlier, the date on which the employer delivered a return in accordance with regulation 73 (annual return of relevant payments liable to deduction of tax (Forms P35 and P14)).
     204(4)   An employer may appeal against a surcharge notice by giving notice to the Inland Revenue within 30 days of the issue of the surcharge notice.
     204(5)   The grounds of appeal are–
     (a)   that the number of defaults stated in the notice is incorrect, or
     (b)   that the amount of the surcharge is incorrect.
     204(6)   But paragraph (5)(a) does not apply in respect of a disputed default which has already been the subject of an appeal under regulation 202, following which the default notice was not withdrawn.
     204(7)   Parts 4, 5 and 6 of TMA (assessment, appeals, collection and recovery) apply to the surcharge notice as if it were an assessment and the amount of the surcharge was tax charged by the assessment, subject to paragraphs (4), (5) and (8).
     204(8)   On an appeal section 50(6) to (8) of TMA (procedure) do not apply, but the tribunal may–
     (a)   if it appears that no surcharge has been incurred, set the surcharge notice aside,
     (b)   if the amount of the total surcharge liability appears to be correct, confirm the surcharge notice, or
     (c)   if the amount of the total surcharge liability appears to be incorrect, increase or reduce it to the correct amount.
     204(9)   Regulation 217(3) (appeals: supplementary provisions) applies to appeals under this regulation.

History – In reg. 204(8), "tribunal" substituted for "Commissioners" by SI 2009/56, art. 3(2) and Sch. 2, para. 110(2), operative from 1 April 2009 subject to transitional and saving provisions in SI 2009/56, Sch. 3.

In reg. 204(8)(a), (b) and (c), the words "to them", which appeared after "appears" in each place, omitted by SI 2009/56, art. 3(2) and Sch. 2, para. 110(3), operative from 1 April 2009 subject to transitional and saving provisions in SI 2009/56, Sch. 3.

Origin – Reg. 204(1)–(3): SI 1993/744, reg. 42B(11)(part).
Reg. 204(4), (5): SI 1993/744, reg. 42B(12)(part).
Reg. 204(6): SI 1993/744, reg. 42B(13).
Reg. 204(7): SI 1993/744, reg. 42B(14).
Reg. 204(8): SI 1993/744, reg. 42B(15).
Reg. 204(9): drafting."

Chapter 4 – Mandatory Use Of Electronic Communications: Specified Information

History – In the heading to Ch. 4, the words ": Specified Information" inserted by SI 2012/822, reg. 48, with effect from 6 April 2012.

MANDATORY USE OF ELECTRONIC COMMUNICATIONS

205(1)   An employer (as to which see regulation 206) must deliver specified information by an approved method of electronic communications to HMRC.

205(2)   The Commissioners for Her Majesty's Revenue and Customs may make a general or specific direction requiring an employer to deliver specified information by a particular approved method of electronic communications.

205(3)   Specified information may be delivered by a person on behalf of an employer.

205(4)   This regulation does not apply to specified information which relates to payments of tax due under a retrospective tax provision for a closed year.

205(5)   References in this Chapter to information and to the delivery of information must be construed in accordance with section 135(8) of the Finance Act 2002 (mandatory e-filing).

History – Reg. 205 substituted for former reg. 205, 205A and 205B by SI 2010/668, reg. 8, with effect in relation to the tax year 2011–12 and subsequent tax years.

Cross references – HMRC Direction of 4 April 2011 made under reg. 205(2).

MANDATORY USE OF ELECTRONIC COMMUNICATION FOR DELIVERING SPECIFIED INFORMATION

205A   [Effectively omitted by SI 2010/668, reg. 8.]

History – Reg. 205 substituted for former reg. 205, 205A and 205B by SI 2010/668, reg. 8, with effect in relation to the tax year 2011–12 and subsequent tax years.

GENERAL PROVISIONS RELATING TO THIS CHAPTER

205B   [Effectively omitted by SI 2010/668, reg. 8.]

History – Reg. 205 substituted for former reg. 205, 205A and 205B by SI 2010/668, reg. 8, with effect in relation to the tax year 2011–12 and subsequent tax years.

Employers

History – Heading to reg. 206 substituted by SI 2010/668, reg. 9(1), with effect in relation to the tax year 2011–12 and subsequent tax years.
Heading to reg. 206 substituted by SI 2009/2029, reg. 6, with effect in relation to the tax year 2009–10 and subsequent tax years, except in the case of an employer who is not a specified employer (see reg. 206), who ceases paying PAYE income during the tax year 2009–10, and who submits the return and accompanying information required by reg. 73 before 6 April 2010. The former heading was "Specified employers"

206(1)   [Omitted by SI 2010/668, reg. 9.]

206(2)   For the purposes of this Chapter, the following shall not be regarded as employers–

(a)   an individual who is a practising member of a religious society or order whose beliefs are incompatible with the use of electronic communications;

(b)   a partnership, if all the partners fall within sub-paragraph (a);

(c)   a company, if all the directors and company secretary fall within sub-paragraph (a);

(d)   [omitted by SI 2013/521, reg. 10;]

(e)   a care and support employer and,

(f)   an employer to whom a direction has been given under regulation 67D (exceptions to regulation 67B) or regulation 142 (direct collection: employee to report payments)

206(3)   In paragraph (2)(c), **"company"** means a body corporate or unincorporated association but does not include a partnership.

206(4)   In paragraph (2)(e), **"a care and support employer"** means an individual ("the employer") who employs a person to provide domestic or personal services at or from the employer's home where–

(a)   the services are provided to the employer or a member of the employer's family;

(b)   the recipient of the services has a physical or mental disability, or is elderly or infirm;

(c)   the employer has not received an incentive payment in respect of any of the last 3 tax years; and

(d)   it is the employer who delivers the specified information (and not some other person on the employer's behalf).

206(5)   In this regulation an **"incentive payment"** means an incentive payment received under the Income Tax (Incentive Payments for Voluntary Electronic Communication of PAYE Returns) Regulations 2003.

History – Reg. 206(1) omitted by SI 2010/668, reg. 9(2)(a), with effect in relation to the tax year 2011–12 and subsequent tax years.
Reg. 206(2)(d) omitted by SI 2013/521, reg. 10, with effect from 6 April 2014.
Reg. 206(2)(f) and the word "and" (preceding it) inserted by SI 2014/472, reg. 18, with effect from 6 April 2014.
In reg. 206(2), the words "For the purposes of this Chapter, the following shall not be regarded as employers–" substituted for the words "The following are not specified employers, but, for the purposes of this Chapter, shall not be regarded as employers–" by SI 2010/668, reg. 9(2)(b), with effect in relation to the tax year 2011–12 and subsequent tax years.
Reg. 206(2) substituted by SI 2009/2029, reg. 7(a), with effect in relation to the tax year 2009–10 and subsequent tax years, except in the case of an employer who is not a specified employer (see reg. 206), who ceases paying PAYE income during the tax year 2009–10, and who submits the return and accompanying information required by reg. 73 before 6 April 2010. Former reg. 206(2) read as follows:

> "**206(2)**   But the following are not specified employers–
> (a)   an individual who is a practising member of a religious society or order whose beliefs are incompatible with the use of electronic communications,
> (b)   a partnership, if all the partners fall within sub-paragraph (a), and
> (c)   a company, if all the directors and the company secretary fall within sub-paragraph (a).".

In reg. 206(4)(d), the words "specified information" substituted for the words "relevant annual return" by SI 2010/668, reg. 9(2)(c), with effect in relation to the tax year 2011–12 and subsequent tax years.
Reg. 206(4) and (5) inserted by SI 2009/2029, reg. 7(b), with effect in relation to the tax year 2009–10 and subsequent tax years, except in the case of an employer who is not a specified employer (see reg. 206), who ceases paying PAYE income during the tax year 2009–10, and who submits the return and accompanying information required by reg. 73 before 6 April 2010.

Origin – Reg. 206(1): SI 1993/744, reg. 46ZD(1), (2)(part), (3)(part).
Reg. 206(2): SI 1993/744, reg. 46ZD(2)(part), (3)(part).
Reg. 206(3): SI 1993/744, reg. 46ZD(4)(part).

RELEVANT ANNUAL RETURN

206A   [Omitted by SI 2010/668, reg. 12(1)(a).]

History – Reg. 206A omitted by SI 2010/668, reg. 12(1)(a), with effect in relation to the tax year 2011–12 and subsequent tax years.

Specified information

207(1) In this Chapter, **"specified information"** means–

(a) Part 1 of Form P45;

(b) Part 3 of Form P45;

(c) Form P46;

(d) Form P46(Pen);

(e) the return and accompanying information required by regulation 73 (annual return of relevant payments liable to deduction of tax (Forms P35 and P14)).

207(2) [Omitted by SI 2014/472, reg. 19.]

History – Reg. 207(1)(e) inserted by SI 2010/668, reg. 10, with effect in relation to the tax year 2011–12 and subsequent tax years.
Former reg. 207(1)(e) omitted by SI 2009/2029, reg. 9, with effect in relation to the tax year 2009–10 and subsequent tax years, except in the case of an employer who is not a specified employer (see reg. 206), who ceases paying PAYE income during the tax year 2009–10, and who submits the return and accompanying information required by reg. 73 before 6 April 2010.
Reg. 207(1) substituted by SI 2007/2969, reg. 19 with effect from 6 April 2009.
Reg. 207(2) omitted by SI 2014/472, reg. 19, with effect from 6 April 2014.
Origin – Reg. 207(1): SI 1993/744, reg. 46ZE(1)(part).
Reg. 207(2): SI 1993/744, reg. 46ZE(2).

E-filing notice and appeals

208 [Omitted by SI 2010/668, reg. 12(1)(b).]

History – Reg. 208 omitted by SI 2010/668, reg. 12(1)(b), with effect in relation to the tax year 2010–11 and subsequent tax years.

Standards of accuracy and completeness

209(1) Any specified information delivered by a method of electronic communications must meet the standards of accuracy and completeness set by specific or general directions given by the Commissioners for Her Majesty's Revenue and Customs.

209(2) Any specified information which fails to meet those standards must be treated as not having been delivered.

History – In reg. 209(1) and (2), the words "relevant annual return or" preceding the words "specified information" omitted by SI 2010/668, reg. 12(2), with effect in relation to the tax year 2011–12 and subsequent tax years.
Reg. 209 substituted by SI 2009/2029, reg. 11, with effect in relation to the tax year 2009–10 and subsequent tax years, except in the case of an employer who is not a specified employer (see reg. 206), who ceases paying PAYE income during the tax year 2009–10, and who submits the return and accompanying information required by reg. 73 before 6 April 2010. Former reg. 209 read as follows:
    "**209(1)** Specified information delivered by a method of electronic communications must meet the standards of accuracy or completeness set by specific or general directions given by the Board of Inland Revenue.
    209(2) Specified information which fails to meet those standards must be treated as not having been delivered.".
Cross references – HMRC Direction of 30 September 2005 made under former reg. 209(1).
HMRC Direction of 22 September 2006 made under former reg. 209(1).
HMRC Direction of 23 July 2007 made under former reg. 209(1).
HMRC Direction of 16 July 2008 made under former reg. 209(1).
HMRC Direction of 14 August 2009 made under reg. 209.
HMRC Direction of 20 December 2010 (first of two Directions) made under reg. 209.
HMRC Direction of 20 December 2010 (second of two Directions) made under reg. 209.
HMRC Direction of 16 March 2012 made under reg. 209.
Other material – Tax Bulletin TB08/04-3: quality standards and online filing.

Penalty for failing to deliver specified information

History – In the heading to reg. 210, the words "relevant annual returns and" omitted by SI 2010/668, reg. 11(1), with effect in relation to the tax year 2011–12 and subsequent tax years.
Heading to reg. 210 substituted by SI 2009/2029, reg. 12, with effect in relation to the tax year 2009–10 and subsequent tax years, except in the case of an employer who is not a specified employer (see reg. 206), who ceases paying PAYE income during the tax year 2009–10, and who submits the return and accompanying information required by reg. 73 before 6 April 2010.

210(1) An employer who fails to deliver specified information or any part of it in accordance with regulation 205 is liable to a penalty.

210(2) Where the specified information is the return and accompanying information required by regulation 73 (annual return of relevant payments liable to deduction of tax (Forms P35 and P14) the penalty will be determined in accordance with regulation 210AA.

210(3) The penalty must be determined in accordance with regulations 210B and 210BA in all other cases.

210(4)   Regulation 210C applies irrespective of how the penalty falls to be determined.

History – Reg. 210(1) and (2) substituted for reg. 210(A1)–(2) by SI 2010/668, reg. 11(2)(a), with effect in relation to the tax year 2011–12 and subsequent tax years.

Former reg. 210(A1) inserted by SI 2009/2029, reg. 13(a), with effect in relation to the tax year 2009–10 and subsequent tax years, except in the case of an employer who is not a specified employer (see reg. 206), who ceases paying PAYE income during the tax year 2009–10, and who submits the return and accompanying information required by reg. 73 before 6 April 2010.

In former reg. 210(1), "205A" substituted for "205" by SI 2009/2029, reg. 13(b), with effect in relation to the tax year 2009–10 and subsequent tax years, except in the case of an employer who is not a specified employer (see reg. 206), who ceases paying PAYE income during the tax year 2009–10, and who submits the return and accompanying information required by reg. 73 before 6 April 2010.

Former reg. 210(2) substituted by SI 2009/2029, reg. 13(c), with effect in relation to the tax year 2009–10 and subsequent tax years, except in the case of an employer who is not a specified employer (see reg. 206), who ceases paying PAYE income during the tax year 2009–10, and who submits the return and accompanying information required by reg. 73 before 6 April 2010.

In reg. 210(3), the words "regulations 210B and 210BA" substituted for the words "regulation 210B" by SI 2010/668, reg. 11(2)(b), with effect in relation to the tax year 2011–12 and subsequent tax years.

Reg. 210–210C substituted for former reg. 210 by SI 2007/2969, reg. 20 with effect from 6 April 2009.

PENALTY: RELEVANT ANNUAL RETURN FOR THE TAX YEAR ENDING 5TH APRIL 2010

210A   [Omitted by SI 2010/668, reg. 12(1)(c).]

History – Reg. 210A omitted by SI 2010/668, reg. 12(1)(c), with effect in relation to the tax year 2011–12 and subsequent tax years.

PENALTY: FORMS P35 AND P14

History – Heading to reg. 210AA substituted by SI 2010/668, reg. 11(3), with effect in relation to the tax year 2011–12 and subsequent tax years.

210AA   Table 9ZA sets out the penalty for the tax year ending 5th April 2011 and subsequent years, depending on the number of employees for whom particulars should have been included with the specified information.

Table 9ZA

Penalties: tax years ending 5th April 2011 and subsequent years

1 Number of employees for whom particulars should have been included with the specified information	2 Penalty
1–5	£100
6–49	£300
50–249	£600
250–399	£900
400–499	£1200
500–599	£1500
600–699	£1800
700–799	£2100
800–899	£2400
900–999	£2700
1000 or more	£3000

History – In reg. 210AA (in the sentence preceding Table 9ZA) and in Table 9ZA itself, the words "specified information" substituted for the words "relevant annual return" by SI 2010/668, reg. 11(4), with effect in relation to the tax year 2011–12 and subsequent tax years.

Reg. 210A and 210AA substituted for former reg. 210A by SI 2009/2029, reg. 14, with effect in relation to the tax year 2009–10 and subsequent tax years, except in the case of an employer who is not a specified employer (see reg. 206), who ceases paying PAYE income during the tax year 2009–10, and who submits the return and accompanying information required by reg. 73 before 6 April 2010.

Penalty: form P45 (Part 1 or Part 3), P46 or P46 (Pen); tax years ending 5th April 2012 and 5th April 2013

History – Heading to reg. 210B substituted by SI 2010/668, reg. 11(5), with effect in relation to the tax year 2011–12 and subsequent tax years.

210B(1)   This regulation applies for the tax years ending 5th April 2012 and 5th April 2013 (the "relevant period").

210B(2)   Table 9A sets out the penalties for the relevant period depending on the number of items of specified information the employer has failed to deliver in each tax quarter falling within that period.

Table 9A

Penalties: tax years ending 5th April 2012 and 5th April 2013

1. Number of items of specified information the employer has failed to deliver in the tax quarter	2. Penalty
1–2	nil
3–49	£100
50–149	£300
150–299	£600
300–399	£900
400–499	£1,200
500–599	£1,500
600–699	£1,800
700–799	£2,100
800–899	£2,400
900–999	£2,700
1000 or more	£3,000

210B(3) Each of the types of specified information mentioned in sub-paragraphs (a) to (d) of regulation 207(1) counts as a separate item of specified information for this purpose.

210B(4) An item of specified information counts even if it relates to the same employee as one or more other items.

History – Reg. 210B(1) substituted by SI 2010/668, reg. 11(6)(a), with effect in relation to the tax year 2011–12 and subsequent tax years.
In reg. 210B(2), the heading to Table 9A substituted by SI 2010/668, reg. 11(6)(b), with effect in relation to the tax year 2011–12 and subsequent tax years.
In reg. 210B(2), in the first column of Table 9A, "1–2" substituted for "1–5" as the first entry and "3–49" substituted for "6–49" as the second entry by SI 2010/668, reg. 11(6)(c), with effect in relation to the tax year 2011–12 and subsequent tax years.
Reg. 210–210C substituted for former reg. 210 by SI 2007/2969, reg. 20 with effect from 6 April 2009.

Penalty: form P45 (Part 1 or Part 3), P46 or P46(Pen); tax years ending 5th April 2014 and subsequent years

210BA(1) Table 9AA sets out penalties depending on the number of items of specified information the employer has failed to deliver in each tax quarter falling within the tax year ending 5th April 2014 and subsequent years.

Table 9AA

Penalties: tax year ending 5th April 2014 and subsequent years

1 Number of items of specified information the employer has failed to deliver in the tax quarter	2 Penalty
1–49	£100
50–149	£300
150–299	£600
300–399	£900
400–499	£1,200
500–599	£1,500
600–699	£1,800
700–799	£2,100
800–899	£2,400
900–999	£2,700
1000+	£3,000

210BA(2) Each of the types of specified information mentioned in sub-paragraphs (a) to (d) of regulation 207(1) counts as a separate item of specified information for this purpose.

210BA(3) An item of specified information counts even if it relates to the same employee as one or more other items.

History – Reg. 210BA inserted by SI 2010/668, reg. 11(7), with effect in relation to the tax year 2011–12 and subsequent tax years.

Appeals and interest

210C(1) An employer is not liable to a penalty if the employer had a reasonable excuse for failing to comply with regulation 205 which had not ceased at the time the specified information was delivered.

210C(2)   A notice of appeal against a determination under section 100 of TMA of a penalty can only be on the grounds that–

(a)   [omitted by SI 2010/668, reg. 12(3)(c),]

(aa)   the employer is not regarded as an employer the purposes of this Chapter

(b)   the employer did comply with regulation 205,

(c)   the amount of the penalty is incorrect, or

(d)   paragraph (1) applies.

210C(3)   [Omitted by SI 2010/668, reg. 12(3)(d).]

210C(4)   Section 103A of TMA (interest on penalties) applies to this penalty.

History – In reg. 210C(1), the words "or regulation 205A" following the words "regulation 205 " omitted by SI 2010/668, reg. 12(3)(a) and the words "relevant annual return or" preceding the words "specified information" omitted by SI 2010/668, reg. 12(3)(b), in both cases with effect in relation to the tax year 2011–12 and subsequent tax years.
In reg. 210C(1), the words "or regulation 205A" and the words "relevant annual return or" inserted by SI 2009/2029, reg. 15(a), with effect in relation to the tax year 2009–10 and subsequent tax years, except in the case of an employer who is not a specified employer (see reg. 206), who ceases paying PAYE income during the tax year 2009–10, and who submits the return and accompanying information required by reg. 73 before 6 April 2010.
Reg. 210C(2)(a) omitted by SI 2010/668, reg. 12(3)(c), with effect in relation to the tax year 2011–12 and subsequent tax years.
Reg. 210C(2)(aa) inserted by SI 2009/2029, reg. 15(b)(i), with effect in relation to the tax year 2009–10 and subsequent tax years, except in the case of an employer who is not a specified employer (see reg. 206), who ceases paying PAYE income during the tax year 2009–10, and who submits the return and accompanying information required by reg. 73 before 6 April 2010.
In reg. 210C(2)(b), the words "or regulation 205A" omitted by SI 2010/668, reg. 12(3)(a), with effect in relation to the tax year 2011–12 and subsequent tax years.
In reg. 210C(2)(b), the words "or regulation 205A" inserted by SI 2009/2029, reg. 15(b)(ii), with effect in relation to the tax year 2009–10 and subsequent tax years, except in the case of an employer who is not a specified employer (see reg. 206), who ceases paying PAYE income during the tax year 2009–10, and who submits the return and accompanying information required by reg. 73 before 6 April 2010.
Reg. 210C(3) omitted by SI 2010/668, reg. 12(3)(d), with effect in relation to the tax year 2011–12 and subsequent tax years.
Reg. 210–210C substituted for former reg. 210 by SI 2007/2969, reg. 20 with effect from 6 April 2009.

Chapter 4A – Mandatory Use of Electronic Communications: Real Time Returns of Information about Relevant Payments of Tax and Associated Matters

History – Ch. 4A inserted by SI 2012/822, reg. 49, with effect from 6 April 2012.

Application of Chapter 4 to real time returns of information about relevant payments of tax and associated matters

210D   Regulation 205(3) applies to the delivery of the following as if they were specified information within the meaning given by regulation 207–

(a)   returns under regulation 67B (real time returns of information about relevant payments),

(b)   returns under regulation 67E(6) (returns under regulation 67B and 67D: amendments), unless the employer is one to whom regulation 67D (exceptions to regulation 67B) applies, and

(c)   notifications under regulation 67F (additional information about payments) unless the employer is one to whom regulation 67D applies.

Chapter 5 – Methods Of Providing Information Etc

How information must or may be delivered by employers

211(1)   Table 10 applies to determine how employers must or may comply with the requirements of the regulations listed in column 1.

211(2)   The requirements of the regulation must be complied with in a document or format provided or approved by the Board of Inland Revenue if so indicated in column 4.

211(3)   Where appropriate, the relevant form number is listed in column 3.

211(4)   Instead of sending a document to the Inland Revenue, the requirements of the regulation may be complied with by an employer arranging for the information it would contain to be delivered to the Inland Revenue by an approved method of electronic communications if so indicated in column 5.

Table 10

Regulations which require approved document or format, and which permit electronic delivery

1. Regulation	2. Description of information	3. Form number	4. Approved document or format	5. Electronic communications
36(1), (2)(a)	cessation of employment	Form P45, Part 1	yes	yes
36(1), (2)(b)	cessation of employment	Form P45, Parts 1A, 2, 3	yes	no
38(1)	death of employee	Form P45, Part 1	yes	yes
39(1)	death of pensioner	Form P45, Part 1	yes	yes
42(8)	procedure if new employer receives Form P45	Form P45, Part 3	yes	yes
46(4), 47(2)(a) 48(2)(a) 49(2)(a)	information to be provided if code not known	Form P46	yes	yes
52(3)	late presentation of Form P45	Form P45, Part 3	yes	yes
55(3)(a)	information on retirement	P46(Pen)	yes	yes
56(3)	procedure if new pension payer receives Form P45	Form P45, Part 3	yes	yes
57(2)	information to be provided if code not known (non-UK resident pensioners)	Form P46(Pen)	yes	yes
58(3)	information to be provided if code not known (UK resident pensioners)	Form P46(Pen)	yes	yes
60(3)	late presentation of Form P45	Form P45, Part 3	yes	yes
67(1)	information to employees about payments and tax deducted	Form P60	yes	not applicable
73	annual return of relevant payments liable to deduction of tax	Forms P35 and P14	yes	yes
73A	annual return of relevant payments by virtue of a retrospective tax provision	Form P35 (RL)	yes	no
74	annual return of relevant payments not liable to deduction of tax	Form P38A	yes	yes
77(4)	return of tax for which employer is liable under regulation 68	Form P100	yes	no
85(1)	employers: annual return of other PAYE income	Form P9D	yes	no
85(1)(a) and (b)	employers: annual return of other PAYE income: benefits code employee	Form P11D	yes	yes
85(2)	employers: annual return of other PAYE income: declaration	Form P11D(b)	yes	yes
90(2)	quarterly return of cars becoming available or unavailable	Form P46 (car)	yes	yes
129(1)	reserve forces' pay: certificate of tax deducted	Form P59	yes	no
132(1)	reserve forces' pay: end of year certificate	Form P60	yes	not applicable

1. Regulation	2. Description of information	3. Form number	4. Approved document or format	5. Electronic
137(1)	holiday pay funds: certificate of tax deducted	Form P403	yes	no
152(2)	deductions working sheet for claimants awarded taxable JSA	Form PB8	yes	no
153(9)	Department's return for claimant who delivers Form P45	Forms PB3 and P45 Part 3	yes	no
154(2)	Department's return for claimant who does not deliver Form P45	Form PB3	yes	no
157(2)(b)	claimant's end of year certificate	Form P60U	yes	not applicable
157(2)(c)	Department's end of year return	Form P14U	yes	no
159(2)	cessation of award of JSA	Form P45U	yes	no
160(2)(b)	Department's notification of taxable JSA adjustment	Form P180	yes	no
164(2)	Department's quarterly statement to Board of receipts and payments in respect of taxable JSA	–	yes	no
184D	deductions working sheet for claimants awarded taxable ESA	Form PB8	yes	no
184E(9)	Department's return for claimant who delivers form P45	Forms PB8 and P45 Part 3	yes	yes
184G(1)	Department's return for claimant who does not deliver form P45	Form PB3	yes	yes
184I(2)(b)	claimant's end of year certificate	Form P60ESA	yes	not applicable
184J(2)	Department's end of year return	Form P14U	yes	yes
184L(1)	cessation of award of ESA	Form P45ESA	yes	yes
184Q(2)(b)	Department's notification of taxable ESA adjustment	Form P180	yes	no
184S(2)	Department's quarterly statement to HMRC of receipts and payments in respect of taxable ESA		yes	no

211(5) If an employer delivers electronically the return required by regulation 73 (annual return of relevant payments liable to deduction of tax (Forms P35 and P14)), the statement and declaration and the certificate must, instead of being signed as required by regulation 73(8), be authenticated by or on behalf of the employer in such manner as may be approved by the Board of Inland Revenue.

211(6) For the purposes of this regulation **"ESA"** means employment and support allowance.

History – In reg. 211(4), in Table 10, references to reg. 35 omitted by SI 2013/521, reg. 11, with effect from 6 April 2014.
In reg. 211(4), in Table 10, in entries relating to regulation 184G(1), in column 1 the words "184G(1)" substituted for "184(G)(1)" by SI 2012/822, reg. 68(b), with effect from 6 April 2012.
In reg. 211(4), in Table 10, in entries relating to regulations 67(1), 132(1), 157(2)(b) and 184I(2)(b), in column 5 the words "not applicable" substituted for the word "yes" by SI 2012/822, reg. 68(a), with effect from 6 April 2012.
In reg. 211(4), in Table 10, in column 5, of the entries relating to reg. 67(1), 132(1), 157(2)(b) and 184I(2)(b), the word "yes" substituted for the word "no" by SI 2010/668, reg. 13, with effect in relation to the tax year 2010–11 and subsequent tax years.
In reg. 211(4), in Table 10, in column 3, of the entries relating to reg. 57(2) and 58(3), the words "Form P46(Pen)" substituted for "Form P46" by SI 2007/2969, reg. 21(b) with effect from 6 April 2009.
In reg. 211(4), in Table 10, the entry relating to reg. 55(3)(a) substituted by SI 2007/2969, reg. 21(a) with effect from 6 April 2009.
In reg. 211(4), in Table 10, the entry relating to reg. 73A inserted by SI 2007/1077, reg. 19, with effect from 6 April 2007.
In reg. 211(4), in Table 10, the entry relating to reg. 184D inserted by SI 2008/2601, reg. 4(2), with effect from 27 October 2008.
In reg. 211(4), in Table 10, the entry relating to reg. 184E(9) inserted by SI 2008/2601, reg. 4(2), with effect from 27 October 2008.
In reg. 211(4), in Table 10, the entry relating to reg. 184(G)(1) (sic) inserted by SI 2008/2601, reg. 4(2), with effect from 27 October 2008.
In reg. 211(4), in Table 10, the entry relating to reg. 184I(2)(b) inserted by SI 2008/2601, reg. 4(2), with effect from 27 October 2008.
In reg. 211(4), in Table 10, the entry relating to reg. 184J(2) inserted by SI 2008/2601, reg. 4(2), with effect from 27 October 2008.
In reg. 211(4), in Table 10, the entry relating to reg. 184L(1) inserted by SI 2008/2601, reg. 4(2), with effect from 27 October 2008.

In reg. 211(4), in Table 10, the entry relating to reg. 184Q(2)(b) inserted by SI 2008/2601, reg. 4(2), with effect from 27 October 2008.

In reg. 211(4), in Table 10, the entry relating to reg. 184S(2) inserted by SI 2008/2601, reg. 4(2), with effect from 27 October 2008.

Reg. 211(6) inserted by SI 2008/2601, reg. 4(3), with effect from 27 October 2008.

Origin – Reg. 211(1): drafting.

Reg. 211(2): SI 1993/744, reg. 20(3)(part), 23(1)(part), (3)(part), 25(2)(part), 26(1A)(part), (4)(part), 27(1)(part), 28(1A)(part), (5A)(part), 29(1)(part), 30(1)(part), 39(2)(part), 43(1)(part), (1C)(part), (4)(part), 46(1A)(part), (7A)(part), 46A(1)(part), 47(2)(part), 65(1)(part), 68(2), 74(1)(part), 84(3)(part), 88(4)(part), (5)(part), 89(2)(part), 90(part), 93(2)(part); drafting; and see *Rewrite: Changes in Law* notes below.

Reg. 211(3): drafting.

Reg. 211(4): SI 1993/744, reg. 20(3)(part), 23(1)(part), 25(2)(part), 26(1A)(part), (4)(part), 27(1)(part), 28(1A)(part), (5A)(part), 43(1)(part), (1C)(part), 44(2)(part), 46(1)(part), (1A)(part), (7A)(part), (7B)(part), 46A(1)(part); drafting; and see *Rewrite: Changes in Law* notes below.

Table 10: SI 1993/744, reg. 20(2)(part), (3)(part), 23(1)(part), (3)(part), 25(2)(part), 26(1A)(part), (4)(part), 27(1)(part), 28(1A)(part), (5A)(part), 29(1)(part), 30(1)(part), 39(2)(part), 43(1)(part), (1C)(part), (4)(part), 44(2)(part), 46(1)(part), (1A)(part), (7A)(part), (7B)(part), 46A(1), 47(2)(part), 65(1)(part), 68(2)(part), 74(1)(part), 84(3)(part), 88(4)(part), (5)(part), 89(2)(part), 90(part), 93(2)(part); drafting; and see *Rewrite: Changes in Law* notes below.

Reg. 211(5): SI 1993/744, reg. 43(3B) and see *Rewrite: Changes in Law* notes below.

Cross references – HMRC Direction of 4 April 2011 made under reg. 211(5).

Rewrite: Changes in Law – Commentary, App. 1, Change 1: reg. 211 refers to "Inland Revenue" (meaning any officer of the Board) rather than "inspector" or "Board".

Commentary, App. 1, Change 36: reg. 35 makes special provision for year-end return by employers operating simplified PAYE scheme.

Commentary, App. 1, Change 37: reg. 211 indicates that P45 is multi-part form.

Commentary, App. 1, Change 57: reg. 55 allows retirement statements made on paper to be made other than "on the form provided".

Commentary, App. 1, Change 70: reg. 74 and 211 set out information required in return of relevant payments not liable to deduction of tax, the form it must take and the time by which it is required.

Other material – Direction of the Board, 30 May 2001: directions authorising information required under SI 1993/744, reg. 28 and 46 to be transmitted over the Internet and specifying certain approved methods for authenticating and delivering information.

Direction of the Board, 16 October 2001: directions authorising, that from 16 October 2001, information required under SI 1993/744, reg. 23, 25 and 26 may be transmitted over the Internet and specifying certain approved methods for authenticating and delivering information.

Direction of the Board, 5 April 2002: directions approving, from 8 April 2002, the Internet service for PAYE for the delivery of authenticated deduction working sheet details and employers' end of year returns and specifying certain approved methods of authenticating and delivering information.

Modifications for electronic version of Form P46(Pen)

History – Heading to reg. 212 substituted by SI 2007/2969, reg. 22(a) with effect from 6 April 2009.

212(1) This regulation applies if instead of sending to the Inland Revenue Form P46(Pen) a pension payer delivers the information it would contain to the Inland Revenue by an approved method of electronic communications (as permitted by regulation 211).

212(2) For sub-paragraphs (a) to (m) of regulation 55(4) (information to be provided in Form P46(Pen)) substitute–

    "(a)   the pension payer's PAYE reference,

    (b)   the pensioner's name,

    (c)   the date of retirement,

    (d)   the date on which the pension started,

    (e)   the pensioner's code immediately before retirement and whether it was being used on the cumulative basis,

    (f)   if the pensioner's code immediately before retirement was used on the cumulative basis–

         (i)   the tax week or tax month in which the last relevant payment before retirement was made to the pensioner or, in a case falling within regulation 24, was treated as having been made,

         (ii)   the total payments to date at the date of retirement,

         (iii)   the total net tax deducted,

    (g)   any number used to identify the pensioner,

    (h)   the tax code in use for the pensioner, and whether it is being used on the cumulative basis,

    (i)   the pensioner's address,

    (j)   the pensioner's sex,

    (k)   the pensioner's national insurance number, if known,

    (l)   the pensioner's date of birth,

    (m)   the amount of pension payable annually."

History – In reg. 212(1) the words "Form P46(Pen)" substituted for "the statement required by regulation 55(3)(a) (pensioner's retirement statement: Form P160)" by SI 2007/2969, reg. 22(b) with effect from 6 April 2009.
In reg. 212(2) the words "Form P46(Pen)" substituted for "retirement statement" by SI 2007/2969, reg. 22(c)(i) with effect from 6 April 2009.
In reg. 212(2)(i) and (l) the words "if known," omitted by SI 2007/2969, reg. 22(c)(ii) with effect from 6 April 2009.
Origin – SI 1993/744, reg. 26(2)(part) and see *Rewrite: Changes in Law* note below.
Rewrite: Changes in Law – Commentary, App. 1, Change 38: reg. 212 brings into line with practice the information to be provided in electronic version of P160.

How information may be delivered by Inland Revenue

213(1) Table 11 applies to determine how the Inland Revenue may comply with requirements of the regulations listed in column 1.

213(2) Instead of sending a document to the employer or (where relevant) the employer's agent, the requirements of the regulation may be complied with by the Inland Revenue arranging for the information it would contain to be delivered to the employer or (where relevant) the employer's agent by an approved method of electronic communications if so indicated in column 4.

213(3) The relevant form number is listed in column 3.

Table 11
Regulations which permit electronic delivery by Inland Revenue

1. Regulation	2. Description of information	3. Form number	4. Electronic communications
8(2), 20(2)	issue of code to employer or agent	Form P6 or P9	yes
20(5), (6)	notice to employer to amend codes	Form P7X or P9X	yes
53(2)	notice to employer of payments and total net tax deducted	Form P6	yes
97Q(1), 97U(3)	notice of requirement for security	notice of requirement	yes
61(2)	notice to pension payer of payments and total net tax deducted	Form P6	yes

213(4) But the Inland Revenue may only deliver information by an approved method of electronic communications if the employer or employer's agent (as the case may be) has consented to delivery of information in that way, and the Inland Revenue have not been notified that the consent has been withdrawn.

213(5) References in paragraphs (2) and (4) to–

(a) an employer include, in relation to regulations 97Q(1) (notice of requirement) and 97U(3) (outcome of application for reduction in the value of security held: further provision), any person to whom a notice under those regulations is given, and

(b) an employer's agent are to a person acting on behalf of the employer.

History – In reg. 213(3), in Table 11, the entry relating to reg. 97Q(1) and 97U(3) inserted by SI 2012/822, reg. 9(a), with effect from 6 April 2012.
In reg. 213(3), in Table 11, the entry relating to reg. 206(1) omitted by SI 2010/668, reg. 14(b), with effect in relation to the tax year 2011–12 and subsequent tax years.
In reg. 213(3), in Table 11, the entry relating to reg. 199(1) omitted by SI 2010/668, reg. 14(a), with effect in relation to the tax year 2010–11 and subsequent tax years.
In reg. 213(3), in Table 11, the entries relating to reg. 199(1) and reg. 206(1) inserted by SI 2007/2969, reg. 23 with effect from 6 April 2008.
Reg. 213(5) substituted by SI 2012/822, reg. 9(b), with effect from 6 April 2012. Former reg. 213(5) read as follows:
     "**213(5)** References in paragraphs (2) and (4) to an employer's agent are to a person acting on behalf of the employer."
Origin – Reg 213(1): drafting.
Reg 213(2): SI 1993/744, reg. 6(4)(part), 13(6)(part), 33(part) and see *Rewrite: Changes in Law* note below.
Reg 213(3): drafting.
Table 11: SI 1993/744, reg. 6(4)(part), 13(6)(part), 33(part) and see *Rewrite: Changes in Law* note below.
Reg 213(4), (5): SI 1993/744, reg. 13(6) and see *Rewrite: Changes in Law* note below.

Cross references – Direction of the Board, 5 April 2004: direction consolidates and revokes various directions in respect of the electronic delivery of information and specifies the approved methods of electronic payments of sums due.

Rewrite: Changes in Law – Commentary, App. 1, Change 5: reg. 213 permits Revenue to send electronically figures of payments and total net tax deducted if new employer consents.

Other material – Direction of the Board, 11 January 2002: directions approving, from 14 January 2002, the Internet service for PAYE for the delivery of notices to employers.
Direction of the Board, 5 April 2002: directions approving, from 8 April 2002, the Internet service for PAYE for the delivery of amended notices of coding and, additionally, the use of EDI for student loan details to employers.

How information must be provided by employees

214(1) An employee must comply with the requirements of the regulations listed in column 1 of Table 12 in a document or format provided or approved by the Board of Inland Revenue.

214(2) Where appropriate, the relevant form number is listed in column 3 of the Table.

Table 12
Regulations which require employee to use approved document or format

1. Regulation	2. Subject	3. Form number
46(2)	Form P46 where employer does not receive Form P45 and code not known	Form P46
145(1)	direct collection: return when relevant payments cease	—
146(1)	direct collection: end of year return	Form P14
147(2)	direct collection: return of unpaid tax	—
154(3)	claimant's certificate of full-time education	Form P187
184G(3)	claimant's certificate of full-time education	Form P187

History – In reg. 214(2), in Table 12, the entry relating to reg. 184G(3) inserted by SI 2008/2601, reg. 5(2), with effect from 27 October 2008.

Origin – Reg. 214(1): SI 1993/744, reg. 29(1)(part), 30(1)(part), 84(10)(part), 104(6)(part), (9)(part), (11)(part).
Reg. 214(2): drafting.
Reg. 214(3): SI 1993/744, reg. 29(1)(part), 30(1)(part), 84(10)(part), 104(6)(part), (9)(part), (11)(part).

Meaning of Form P45, P46 and P46(Pen)

History – Heading to reg. 215 substituted by SI 2007/2969, reg. 24(a) with effect from 6 April 2009.

215 In these Regulations–

"**Form P45**" means the form provided or approved for use in accordance with regulations 36 (cessation of employment: Form P45), 38 (death of employee) or 39 (death of pensioner);

"**Parts 2 and 3 of Form P45**" means–

(a) the Parts 2 and 3 of the Form P45 provided to the employee or claimant (as the case may be) in accordance with regulation 36,

(b) the Parts 2 and 3 of the Form P45 provided to the claimant in accordance with regulation 159 (cessation of award: Form P45U) or,

(c) the Parts 2 and 3 of the Form P45 provided to the claimant in accordance with regulation 184L (cessation of award: Form P45ESA);

"**Form P45ESA**" means the form required to be completed in accordance with regulation 184L;

"**Form P45U**" means the form required to be completed in accordance with regulation 159 or 184L;

"**Form P46**" means the form provided or approved for use in accordance with regulation 46 (form P46 where employer does not receive P45 and code not known);

"**Form P46(Pen)**" means the form provided or approved for use in accordance with regulation 55(3)a), 57(2) or 58(3).

History – In reg. 215, in the definition of "Parts 2 and 3 of Form P45", para. (c) inserted (and the word "or" removed from the end of para. (a) and inserted at the end of para. (b) by SI 2008/2601, reg. 6(2), with effect from 27 October 2008.
In reg. 215, definition of "Form P45ESA" inserted by SI 2008/2601, reg. 6(3), with effect from 27 October 2008.
In reg. 215, in the definition of "Form P45U", the words "regulation 159 or 184L" substituted for the words "regulation 159" by SI 2008/2601, reg. 6(4), with effect from 27 October 2008.
In reg. 215, the definition of "Form P46" substituted by SI 2007/2969, reg. 24(b) with effect from 6 April 2009.
In reg. 215, the definition of "Form P46(Pen)" inserted by SI 2007/2969, reg. 24(c) with effect from 6 April 2009.

Origin – "Form P45": SI 1993/744, reg. 23(1), (2), (3); drafting; and see *Rewrite: Changes in Law* note below.
"Parts 2 and 3 of Form P45": SI 1993/744, reg. 23(1), (2), (3), 89(2); drafting; and see *Rewrite: Changes in Law* note below.
"Form P45U": SI 1993/744, reg. 89(2); drafting; and see *Rewrite: Changes in Law* note below.
"Form P46": drafting.

Rewrite: Changes in Law – Commentary, App. 1, Change 37: reg. 215 indicates that P45 is multi-part form.

Service by post

216 Any notice or deductions working sheet which is authorised or required to be given, served or issued under these Regulations may be sent by post.

Origin – SI 1993/744, reg. 109.

PART 11 – SUPPLEMENTARY PROVISIONS

MISCELLANEOUS APPEALS

Appeals: supplementary provisions

217(1) The following provisions of TMA apply to appeals under the regulations listed in paragraph (2) as they apply to an appeal under section 31 of TMA–

section 31A(5)   notice of appeal

217(2) The regulations are–

regulation 99(3)   appeal against improper purpose notice
regulation 200(3)   appeal against e-payment notice
regulation 202(2)   appeal against default notice
regulation 208(2)   appeal against e-filing notice.

217(3) [Omitted by SI 2009/56, art. 3(2) and Sch. 2, para. 111(3).]

217(4) [Omitted by SI 2009/56, art. 3(2) and Sch. 2, para. 111(3).]

History – In reg. 217(1), "and (6)", which appeared after "section 31A(5)", omitted by SI 2009/56, art. 3(2) and Sch. 2, para. 111(2), operative from 1 April 2009 subject to transitional and saving provisions in SI 2009/56, Sch. 3.
In reg. 217(1), the entries for s. 31B and 31D omitted by SI 2009/56, art. 3(2) and Sch. 2, para. 111(2), operative from 1 April 2009 subject to transitional and saving provisions in SI 2009/56, Sch. 3.
Reg. 217(3) omitted by SI 2009/56, art. 3(2) and Sch. 2, para. 111(3), operative from 1 April 2009 subject to transitional and saving provisions in SI 2009/56, Sch. 3. Former reg. 217(3) read as follows:

> "**217(3)**   In an appeal under the regulations listed in paragraph (2) and regulation 204(4) (appeal against surcharge notice), the relevant place for the purposes of paragraph 3(1)(a) of Schedule 3 to TMA (rules for assigning proceedings to General Commissioners) is the place which at the time of the notice of appeal is–
> (a)   the employer's place of business in the United Kingdom, or
> (b)   if there is no such place, the employer's place of residence in the United Kingdom."

Reg. 217(4) omitted by SI 2009/56, art. 3(2) and Sch. 2, para. 111(3), operative from 1 April 2009 subject to transitional and saving provisions in SI 2009/56, Sch. 3. Former reg. 217(4) read as follows:

> "**217(4)**   In paragraph (3)–
> "**place of business**" means–
> (a)   the place where the trade, profession, vocation or business with which the proceedings are concerned is carried out, or
> (b)   if more than one such place, the head office or place where it is mainly carried out; and
> "**place of residence**" means the employer's usual place of residence or, if that is unknown, the employer's last known place of residence."

Origin – Reg. 217(1), (2): SI 1993/744, reg. 46ZH(1)(part).
Reg. 217(3): SI 1993/744, reg. 46ZH(3).
Reg. 217(4): SI 1993/744, reg. 46ZH(4).

CERTIFICATE THAT SUM DUE AND PAYMENT BY CHEQUE

Certificate that sum due

218(1) A certificate of HMRC that, to the best of their knowledge and belief, any amount shown in a certificate under the regulations listed in paragraph (2) has not been paid by an employer, is sufficient evidence that the amount mentioned in the certificate is unpaid and due to the Crown.

218(2) The regulations are–

regulation 75A(10)   unpaid amounts from regulation 75A specification
regulation 76   unpaid amounts in regulation 73 return (Form P35)
regulation 77(6)   unpaid amounts in regulation 77 return
regulation 78(8)   unpaid amounts from regulation 78 specification
regulation 79   unpaid amounts following inspection under Schedule 36 to the Finance Act 2008.

218(2A) HMRC may prepare a certificate showing the whole or any part of a combined amount which includes tax without specifying the components of the combined amount.

Paragraph (1) shall apply with any necessary modifications to the certificate.

218(3) A certificate of HMRC that, to the best of their knowledge and belief, any amount of interest payable under the regulations listed in paragraph (4) has not been paid by an employer or employee is sufficient evidence that the amount mentioned in the certificate is unpaid and due to the Crown.

218(4) The regulations are–

regulation 72(7)	interest consequential on regulation 72 direction
regulation 81(6)	interest consequential on regulation 81 direction
regulation 115	interest on tax overdue under PSA.

218(4A)　HMRC may prepare a certificate showing the total amount of interest payable in respect of the whole or any part of the combined amount without specifying which components of the combined amount the interest relates to.

Paragraph (3) shall apply with any necessary modifications to the certificate.

218(5)　The production of–

(a)　the return made by the employer under paragraph (4) of regulation 77 (return and certificate if tax unpaid), and

(b)　the certificate of HMRC under paragraph (6) of that regulation,

is sufficient evidence that the amount shown in the certificate is the amount of tax which the employer is liable to pay to HMRC in respect of the tax period in question under that regulation.

218(6)　A document which purports to be a certificate under this regulation, or regulation 77(6), is treated as such a certificate until the contrary is proved.

History – In reg. 218(1), "HMRC" substituted for "the Inland Revenue" by SI 2008/782, reg. 16, with effect from 6 April 2008.
In reg. 218(2), the entry for reg. 75A(10) inserted by SI 2012/822, reg. 50, with effect from 6 April 2012.
In reg. 218(2), in column 2 of the list, the words "Schedule 36 to the Finance Act 2008" substituted for the words "regulation 97" by SI 2009/588, reg. 8, with effect from 1 April 2009.
Reg. 218(2A) inserted by SI 2008/782, reg. 16, with effect from 6 April 2008.
In reg. 218(3), "HMRC" substituted for "the Inland Revenue" by SI 2008/782, reg. 16, with effect from 6 April 2008.
In reg. 218(4), entry for reg. 82 omitted by SI 2014/992, art. 9(7), with effect from 6 May 2014 in relation to payments which are due and payable in respect of the tax year 2014–15 and subsequent tax years.
Reg. 218(4A) inserted by SI 2008/782, reg. 16, with effect from 6 April 2008.
In reg. 218(5), "HMRC" substituted for "the Inland Revenue" in each place by SI 2008/782, reg. 16, with effect from 6 April 2008.
In reg. 218(6), the words "this regulation" substituted for "paragraph (1) or (3)" in each place by SI 2008/782, reg. 16, with effect from 6 April 2008.
Origin – Reg. 218(1): SI 1993/744, reg. 43(10), 48(6)(part), (9), 54(6)(part), 55(8)(part), (10) and see *Rewrite: Changes in Law* notes below.
Reg. 218(2): drafting.
Reg. 218(3): SI 1993/744, reg. 42(8), 49(9), 51(4), 80J(3) and see *Rewrite: Changes in Law* notes below.
Reg. 218(4): drafting.
Reg. 218(5): SI 1993/744, reg. 47(7) and see *Rewrite: Changes in Law* notes below.
Reg. 218(6): SI 1993/744, reg. 42(9), 43(11), 47(8), 48(10), 49(10), 51(5), 54(7)(part), 55(11), 80J(4).
Rewrite: Changes in Law – Commentary, App. 1, Change 1: reg. 218 refers to "Inland Revenue" (meaning any officer of the Board) rather than "inspector" or "Board".
Commentary, App. 1, Change 125: reg. 218 increases the number of persons that Revenue must have regard to in connection with their "knowledge and belief" that payment has not been made.

Payment by cheque

219(1)　For the purposes of the following provisions, if–

(a)　any payment to the Inland Revenue is made by cheque, and

(b)　the cheque is paid on its first presentation to the banker on whom it is drawn,

the payment is treated as made on the day on which the cheque was received by the Inland Revenue.

219(2)　The provisions are–

regulation 69	due date and receipts for payments of tax
regulation 72	recovery from employee of tax not deducted by employer
regulation 75A	notice and certificate in cases where regulation 67B or 67D returns are not made
regulation 78	notice and certificate if tax may be unpaid
regulation 115	interest on tax due under PSA
regulation 116	interest due on tax overpaid under PSA.

History – In reg. 219(2), entry for reg. 82 and 83(2)(b) omitted by SI 2014/992, art. 9(7), with effect from 6 May 2014 in relation to payments which are due and payable in respect of the tax year 2014–15 and subsequent tax years.
In reg. 219(2), the entry for reg. 75A inserted by SI 2012/822, reg. 51, with effect from 6 April 2012.
Origin – Reg. 219(1): SI 1993/744, reg. 42(7A), 48(7A), 52(4)(part), 80J(6), 80K(3) and see *Rewrite: Changes in Law* notes below.
Reg. 219(2): drafting; see *Rewrite: Changes in Law* notes below.
Rewrite: Changes in Law – Commentary, App. 1, Change 1: reg. 219 refers to "Inland Revenue" (meaning any officer of the Board) rather than "inspector" or "Board".
Commentary, App. 1, Change 126: reg. 219 applies to reg. 83 the rules in other regulations in SI 1993/744 about cheques and dates of payment to the Revenue.

TRANSITIONAL PROVISIONS, SAVINGS AND REVOCATIONS

Transitional provisions, savings and revocations

220(1)   Schedule 1 (transitional provisions and savings) has effect.

220(2)   The regulations listed in column 1 of Schedule 2 are revoked to the extent specified in column 3 of that Schedule.

220(3)   Paragraph (2) is subject to Schedule 1.

SCHEDULES

SCHEDULE A1 – REAL TIME RETURNS

Regulations 67B and 67D

History – Sch. A1 inserted by SI 2012/822, reg. 52, with effect from 6 April 2012.

Cross references – SI 2012/822, reg. 53 and 54: transitional provisions.

1   The information specified in this Schedule is as follows.

INFORMATION ABOUT THE EMPLOYER

2   The employer's HMRC office number.

3   The employer's PAYE reference.

4   The employer's accounts office reference.

5   If applicable, an indication that this is the final return under regulation 67B (real time returns of information about relevant payments) or 67D (exceptions to regulation 67B) that the employer expects to make because this PAYE scheme has ceased (and, in that case, the date of cessation), unless that information will be included in a notification under regulation 67F (additional information about payments).

History – In para. 5, the words "(and, in that case, the date of cessation)" inserted by SI 2013/521, reg. 37(a), with effect for the 2013–14 tax year and subsequent tax years.

6   If applicable, an indication that this is the final return under regulation 67B or 67D that the employer expects to make for the tax year, unless that information will be included in a notification under regulation 67F.

History – Para. 21(b) and (bd) substituted for former para. (b) by SI 2014/472, reg. 20, with effect

7   Unless the information will be included in a notification under regulation 67F, if either paragraph 5 or 6 applies details of the following–

(a)   whether the employer made any taxable payments to an employee in respect of which the employer has borne the tax liability,

(b)   whether any person other than the employer paid expenses or provided benefits to any employees during their employment with the employer in the year,

(c)   whether anyone employed by a non-UK employer has undertaken work for the employer for 30 days or more in a row in the tax year,

(d)   whether any payments of employment income in respect of an employee have been made directly to a person other than the employee,

(e)   whether the employer is required to make a return under regulation 85 (employers: annual return of other earnings (Forms P11D and P9D)) for the tax year,

(f)   whether the return is being made by an intermediary within Chapter 8 of Part 2 of ITEPA.

History – In para. 7(f), the words "or a managed service company" omitted by SI 2013/521, reg. 37(b), with effect for the tax year 2013–14 and subsequent tax years.

INFORMATION ABOUT THE EMPLOYEE

8   The employee's name.

9   The employee's date of birth.

10   The employee's current gender.

11   If known, the employee's national insurance number.

12   If the employee's national insurance is not known, the employee's address.

13   The number used by the employer to identify the employee in this employment.

History – In para. 13, the words "in this employment" substituted for the words ", if any" by SI 2013/521, reg. 37(c), with effect for the tax year 2013–14 and subsequent tax years.

14 If the number used by the employer to identify the employee is different to that shown on the previous return for the employee (if any), an indication of that and the number shown on the previous return.

14A If applicable, an indication that the payment to which the return relates is a payment to any one of—

(a)   a body corporate,

(b)   a trustee of a trust of which the employee is a beneficiary,

(c)   if the employee has died, the employee's personal representative.

History – Para. 14A inserted by SI 2013/521, reg. 37(d), with effect for the tax year 2013–14 and subsequent tax years.

14B Where the return relates to a payment within paragraph 14A, the information required by paragraphs 8 to 12 need not be provided.

History – Para. 14B inserted by SI 2013/521, reg. 37(d), with effect for the tax year 2013–14 and subsequent tax years.

INFORMATION ABOUT PAYMENTS TO THE EMPLOYEE, ETC

15 The tax year to which the return relates.

16 The total payments to date in this employment.

17 The total net tax deducted in relation to those payments.

18 The employee's pay frequency or an indication that payments are made to the employee on an irregular basis.

19 The date of the payment the return relates to.

20 The tax week number or tax month number in which the payment is made.

21 An indication of which of the following bands the number of normal hours worked each week by the employee falls into—

(a)   up to 15.99,

(b)   16 to 23.99,

(ba)   24 to 29.99,

(c)   30 or more,

or an indication that none of the bands is applicable.

History – Para. 21(b) and (ba) substituted for former para. (b) by SI 2014/472, reg. 20, with effect from 6 April 2014.

22 The value of the payment the return relates to.

22A If applicable, an indication that comprised within the payment is—

(a)   a pension and if so—

    (i)   the amount of the pension.

    (ii)   an indication of whether it is an occupational pension, and

    (iii)   an indication of whether the pension is being paid because the pensioner is a bereaved spouse or civil partner,

(b)   a trivial commutation lump sum, within the meaning given by paragraph 7 or 7A of Schedule 29 to the Finance Act 2004 and, if so, the amount of that lump sum,

(c)   a lump sum that falls within regulation 11 (de minimis rule for pension schemes) or 12 (payments by larger pension schemes) of the Registered Pension Schemes (Authorised Payments) Regulations 2009 and, if so, the amount of that lump sum,

(d)   a lump sum that falls within regulation 11A (payments by schemes which are not public service pension schemes or occupational pension schemes) of those Regulations, and if so, the amount of that lump sum.

History – Para. 22A inserted by SI 2013/521, reg. 37(e), with effect for the tax year 2013–14 and subsequent tax years.

23 The tax code operated on the payment the return relates to.

24 If applicable, an indication that the employee's tax code is being operated on a non-cumulative basis.

25 The total net tax deducted from the payment the return relates to.

26 The value of any amount comprised within the payment made to the employee which falls to be reported under regulation 85 (employees: annual return of other earnings (Forms P11D and P9D)) and in respect of which tax has been deducted.

26A The value of the amounts referred to in paragraph 26 in the tax year to date.

History – Para. 26A inserted by SI 2013/521, reg. 37(f), with effect for the tax year 2013–14 and subsequent tax years.

Statutory Instruments

27 If the employer is required by regulation 67CA(1)(a) (notifications of relevant payments to and by providers of certain electronic payment methods) to include a reference in the return, the value of any amount which is not subject to tax or national insurance paid to the employee at the same time as the payment.

History – In para. 27, the words "If the employer is required by regulation 67CA(1)(a) (notifications of relevant payments to and by providers of certain electronic payment methods) to include a reference in the return, the" substituted for the word "The" by SI 2013/521, reg. 37(g), with effect for the tax year 2013–14 and subsequent tax years.

28 If the employer is required by regulation 67CA(1)(a) to include a reference in the return, the value of any deductions made from the payment which do not otherwise fall to be reported under this Schedule.

History – In para. 28, the words "If the employer is required by regulation 67CA(1)(a) to include a reference in the return, the" substituted for the word "The" by SI 2013/521, reg. 37(h), with effect for the tax year 2013–14 and subsequent tax years.

29 The value of the payment after allowable pension contributions within the meaning given by regulation 3(2) (net PAYE income) and the deduction of tax, national insurance and deductions due under the Student Loan Regulations.

30 The value, if any, of allowable pension contributions within the meaning given by regulation 3(2) deducted from the payment of PAYE income comprising the payment.

30A The value of the contributions referred to in paragraph 30 in the tax year to date.

History – Para. 30A inserted by SI 2013/521, reg. 37(i), with effect for the tax year 2013–14 and subsequent tax years.

31 The value, if any, of employee pension contributions other than allowable pension contributions within the meaning given by regulation 3(2) deducted from the payment.

31A The value of the contributions referred to in paragraph 31 in the tax year to date.

History – Para. 31A inserted by SI 2013/521, reg. 37(j), with effect for the tax year 2013–14 and subsequent tax years.

32 The value of any earnings for the purposes of the Social Security Contributions and Benefits Act 1992 comprised within the total payment which are included in the gross earnings from the employment for the purpose of calculating liability to Class 1 contributions under that Act but in respect of which tax is not deducted under these Regulations, excluding allowable pension contributions.

33 In paragraphs 15 to 31, **"payment"** means the relevant payment the information being given in accordance with this Schedule relates to.

34 In paragraph 32, **"total payment"** means the relevant payment the information being given in accordance with this Schedule relates to plus any other amount paid to the employee at the same time as the relevant payment.

34A If applicable, an indication that during the period since the employer last made a return under regulation 67B or 67D containing information about the employee–

(a)   regulation 64 (trade disputes) has at any time applied in relation to the employee, or

(b)   the employee has been absent from the employment without pay.

History – Para. 34A inserted by SI 2013/521, reg. 37(k), with effect for the tax year 2013–14 and subsequent tax years.

INFORMATION ON THE COMMENCEMENT OF EMPLOYMENT

35 If the return is the first return in respect of the employee in this employment the information required by paragraphs 36 to 44.

36 The date on which the employment commenced or will commence.

37 The employee's address.

38 If known, the employee's passport number.

39 An indication of which of the statements in paragraph 41 applies to the employee.

40 If the employee is a seconded expatriate, the information required by paragraph 42 and an indication of which of the statements in paragraph 43 applies to the employee.

41 The statements in this paragraph are–

(a)   the employment is the employee's first employment since the preceding 6th April, and the employee has not since that date received–

    (i)   jobseeker's allowance, incapacity benefit or employment and support allowance which is subject to income tax, or

    (ii)   a retirement pension or an occupational pension,

(b)   the employee is not receiving a retirement pension or an occupational pension and since the preceding 6th April–

(i)　　has had another employment, but is not now in receipt of employment income from it, or

(ii)　　has received jobseeker's allowance, incapacity benefit or employment and support allowance which is subject to income tax, but payment of that allowance or benefit has ceased,

(c)　　the employee either has another employment (which is continuing) or is in receipt of a retirement pension or an occupational pension.

History – In para. 41(a)(i) and (b)(ii), the words ", incapacity benefit or employment and support allowance" substituted for the words "or incapacity benefit" by SI 2013/521, reg. 37(l), with effect for the tax year 2013–14 and subsequent tax years.

42　　An indication of whether the employee is a seconded expatriate who is a national of an EEA state.

43　　The statements in this paragraph are–

(a)　　the employee intends to live in the United Kingdom for 183 days or more,

(b)　　the employee intends to live in the United Kingdom for less than 183 days, or

(c)　　the employee will work both inside and outside the United Kingdom, but will live outside.

History – In para. 43(a) and (b), the words "183 days" substituted for the words "six months" by SI 2013/521, reg. 37(m), with effect for the tax year 2013–14 and subsequent tax years.

44　　[Omitted by SI 2013/521, reg. 37(n).]

History – Para. 44 omitted by SI 2013/521, reg. 37(n), with effect for the tax year 2013–14 and subsequent tax years. Former para. 44 read as follows:

"**44**　　An indication of whether a pension is being paid and, if so–
(a)　　the amount of the pension, and
(b)　　an indication of whether the pension is being paid because the pensioner is a bereaved spouse or civil partner.".

INFORMATION ON THE CESSATION OF EMPLOYMENT

45　　If the employment has ceased, the date of cessation.

46　　If applicable, an indication that the payment to which the details under this Schedule relate was made after cessation of the employment.

SCHEDULE 1 – TRANSITIONAL PROVISIONS AND SAVINGS

Regulation 220

Part 1 – General Provisions

CONTINUITY OF THE LAW

1　　The revocation of provisions and their making in a rewritten form in these Regulations does not affect the continuity of the law.

2　　Paragraph 1 does not apply to any change in the law made by these Regulations.

3　　Anything which–

(a)　　has been done, or has effect as if done, under or for the purposes of a provision of the revoked Regulations, and

(b)　　is in force or effective immediately before the commencement of these Regulations,

has effect after that commencement as if done under or for the purposes of the corresponding provision of these Regulations.

4　　Any reference (express or implied) in these Regulations or any document made under these Regulations to–

(a)　　a provision of these Regulations, or

(b)　　things done or falling to be done under or for the purposes of a provision of these Regulations,

is to be read as including, in relation to times, circumstances or purposes in relation to which any corresponding provision of the revoked Regulations had effect, a reference to the provision of the revoked Regulations or to things done or falling to be done under or for the purposes of the provision of the revoked Regulations.

5　　Any reference (express or implied) in these Regulations to relevant payments, relevant payments exceeding the PAYE threshold or similar concepts created by these Regulations is to be read as including, in relation to times, circumstances or purposes in relation to which any corresponding concept of the revoked Regulations had effect, a reference to the concept of the revoked Regulations.

6   Any reference (express or implied) in these Regulations to—

(a)   a provision of ITEPA, or

(b)   things done or falling to be done under or for the purposes of a provision of ITEPA,

is to be read as including, in relation to times, circumstances or purposes in relation to which any corresponding provision repealed by ITEPA had effect, a reference to the repealed provision or to things done or falling to be done under or for the purposes of the repealed provision.

7   Any reference (express or implied) in these Regulations to general earnings, PAYE income or similar concepts created by ITEPA is to be read as including, in relation to times, circumstances or purposes in relation to which any corresponding concept which has been superseded by ITEPA had effect, a reference to the superseded concept.

8   Paragraphs 4, 5, 6 and 7 apply only in so far as the context permits.

9   Paragraph 5 is without prejudice to the generality of paragraph 4 and paragraph 7 is without prejudice to the generality of paragraph 6.

10   These Regulations have effect in relation to tax liable, under the Income Tax (Employments) Regulations 1993 or section 710 of ITEPA, to be deducted or accounted for in respect of payments made before 6th April 2004 as if the tax had been liable to be deducted or accounted for under these Regulations.

11   Paragraph 10 is without prejudice to the generality of paragraphs 1 to 9.

12   Paragraphs 1 to 11 have effect instead of paragraph (b) of section 17(2) of the Interpretation Act 1978.

Notes – INA 1978, s. 17(2)(a) (which is subject to INA 1978, s. 23(3)) ensures that references in regulations to (e.g.) NIC and student loans to the old PAYE regulations are read as references to the corresponding new PAYE regulations.

GENERAL SAVING FOR OLD SAVINGS

13(1)   The revocation by these Regulations of a provision previously revoked subject to savings does not affect the continued operation of those savings.

13(2)   The revocation by these Regulations of a saving on the previous revocation of a provision does not affect the operation of the saving in so far as it is not specifically reproduced in these Regulations but remains capable of having effect.

INTERPRETATION

14   In this Part of this Schedule, "**the revoked Regulations**" means the Regulations which are revoked by these Regulations.

Part 2 – Specific Provisions

MODIFICATION OF REFERENCE TO PAYMENT TO THE INLAND REVENUE IN REGULATION 68(2)

15   For the purposes of giving effect to any enactment or instrument which refers to an amount which is, or would in certain circumstances be, payable to the collector, paragraph (2) of regulation 68 has effect as if that paragraph required payment of the amount to which it refers to the collector.

Origin – Para. 15: SI 1993/744. reg. 40(1)(part), 41(1)(part).

FPCS INFORMATION FOR THE TAX YEAR ENDING 5TH APRIL 2002: EMPLOYEES NOT COVERED BY REGULATION 46(1) OF 1993 REGULATIONS

16(1)   This paragraph applies to a person (a "former FPCS employee")–

(a)   who was employed by an employer during a part of the tax year ending 5th April 2002, but who was no longer employed by that employer on 5th April 2002, and

(b)   in respect of whom the employer–

     (i)   has provided information to the Inland Revenue under the FPCS arrangement for the tax year ending 5th April 2002, or

     (ii)   has delivered information by an approved method of electronic communications to an official computer system under the FPCS arrangement for the tax year ending 5th April 2002, but

(c)   in respect of whom no particulars were required to be provided by the employer under regulation 46(1) of the 1993 Regulations for the tax year ending 5th April 2002.

16(2)   The former FPCS employee may by notice require the employer to give a statement to the former FPCS employee containing—

(a)   particulars of the amount of the taxable profit, if any, for the tax year ending 5th April 2002 in respect of car allowances and motor mileage allowances paid to the former FPCS employee in the tax year ending 5th April 2002 for business travel, calculated by reference to the FPCS arrangement, or

(b)   particulars of the total amount of the car allowances and motor mileage allowances paid to the former FPCS employee in the tax year ending 5th April 2002 for business travel, and the total amount of miles covered by the former FPCS employee in the tax year ending 5th April 2002 in the course of business travel for which the motor mileage allowances were paid.

16(3)   The former FPCS employee may give the notice to the employer at any time before 6th April 2005.

16(4)   The employer must give the statement to the former FPCS employee within 30 days of receiving the notice.

16(5)   A former FPCS employee who has received the statement from the employer may not require a further statement from the employer in respect of the tax year ending 5th April 2002.

16(6)   In this paragraph—

"business travel" has the meaning given by section 168(5)(c) of ICTA as that definition had effect for the tax year ending 5th April 2002 by virtue of regulation 46AA(6) of the 1993 Regulations;

"the FPCS arrangement" means the arrangement known as the Fixed Profit Car Scheme made between the employer and the Inland Revenue for providing information in respect of payments of car allowances and motor mileage allowances made to employees for business travel.

16(7)   The reference in sub-paragraph (1)(b)(ii) to the delivery of information by an approved method of electronic communications to an official computer system includes, in relation to information which was delivered before the commencement of these Regulations, a reference to the delivery of information to an official computer system within the meaning of regulation 2(1) of the 1993 Regulations by a means of electronic communications approved for the purposes of regulation 46AA(3) of those Regulations.

Origin – Para. 16(1): SI 1993/744, reg. 46AA(3)(part), (6)(part).
Para. 16(2): SI 1993/744, reg. 46AA(3)(part), (4)(part).
Para. 16(3), (4): SI 1993/744, reg. 46AA(3)(part).
Para. 16(5): SI 1993/744, reg. 46AA(5)(part).
Para. 16(6): SI 1993/744, reg. 46AA(6)(part).
Para. 16(7): SI 1993/744, reg. 46AA(3)(part).

FPCS INFORMATION FOR THE TAX YEAR ENDING 5TH APRIL 2002: EMPLOYEES COVERED BY REGULATION 46(1) OF 1993 REGULATIONS

17(1)   This paragraph applies to a former employee who would be a former FPCS employee were it not for the fact that the employer was required under regulation 46(1) of the 1993 Regulations to provide particulars in respect of the former employee for the tax year ending 5th April 2002.

17(2)   If the former employee gives notice to the employer under paragraph (4) of regulation 94 requiring a statement relating to the tax year ending 5th April 2002, the statement must contain (in addition to the particulars mentioned in paragraph (2) of that regulation)—

(a)   particulars of the amount of the taxable profit, if any, for the tax year ending 5th April 2002 in respect of car allowances and motor mileage allowances paid to the former employee in the tax year ending 5th April 2002 for business travel, calculated by reference to the FPCS arrangement, or

(b)   particulars of the total amount of the car allowances and motor mileage allowances paid to the former employee in the tax year ending 5th April 2002 for business travel, and the total amount of miles covered by the former employee in the tax year ending 5th April 2002 in the course of business travel for which the motor mileage allowances were paid.

17(3)   **"Former employee"** has the same meaning as in regulation 94(7).

17(4)   Expressions used in this paragraph which are defined in paragraph 16 have the same meaning in this paragraph as in that paragraph.

Origin – Para. 17(1): SI 1993/744, reg. 46AA(3)(part).
Para. 17(2): SI 1993/744, reg. 46AA(4)(part).
Para. 17(3), (4): SI 1993/744, reg. 46AA(6)(part).

Statutory Instruments

DUE DATE FOR PAYMENTS OF TAX IN RESPECT OF TAX PERIODS ENDING BEFORE 6TH APRIL 2004

18(1) The following provisions have effect with the following modifications in so far as the provisions apply in relation to tax periods ending before 6th April 2004.

18(2) For sub-paragraphs (a) and (b) of regulation 69(1) (due date for payments of tax) substitute "within 14 days after the end of the tax period".

18(3) In regulation 77(1) (return and certificate if tax may be unpaid) for "17 days" substitute "14 days".

18(4) In regulation 78(1) (notice and certificate if tax may be unpaid) for "17 days" substitute "14 days".

Origin – Para. 18(1): drafting.
Reg. 18(2): SI 1993/744, reg. 40(1)(part), 41(1)(part).
Reg. 18(3): SI 1993/744, reg. 47(1)(part).
Reg. 18(4): SI 1993/744, reg. 48(1)(part).

INTEREST ON UNPAID TAX: DISAPPLICATION OF REGULATION 82 FOR TAX YEARS BEFORE THE TAX YEAR ENDING 5TH APRIL 1993

19 Regulation 82 (interest on tax overdue) does not apply in relation to unpaid tax in respect of a tax year ending on or before 5th April 1992.

Origin – Para. 19: SI 1993/744, reg. 51(1).

INTEREST ON UNPAID TAX: PROVISIONS APPLYING TO TAX YEARS BEFORE THE TAX YEAR ENDING 5TH APRIL 1993

20(1) This paragraph applies if the Inland Revenue make a determination under regulation 80 (determination of unpaid tax) which relates to tax payable for a tax year ending on or before 5th April 1992.

20(2) This paragraph also applies if–

(a) the inspector, at any time after 19th April 1988, made a determination under regulation 49 of the 1993 Regulations (determination of tax payable by employer),

(b) the determination relates to tax payable for a tax year ending on or before 5th April 1992, and

(c) tax remains payable pursuant to the determination immediately before the commencement of these Regulations.

20(3) The tax payable pursuant to the determination carries interest at the prescribed rate from the relevant start date until payment ("the interest period").

20(4) Sub-paragraph (3) applies even if the relevant start date is a non-business day as defined by section 92 of the Bills of Exchange Act 1882.

20(5) Any change made to the prescribed rate during the interest period applies to the tax payable pursuant to the determination from the date of change.

20(6) Regulation 84 (recovery of tax and interest) applies to an amount of interest which an employer is liable to pay under this paragraph as if it were the unpaid amount for the purposes of that regulation.

20(7) Paragraphs (3) and (6) of regulation 218 (certificate of interest due) apply in relation to an amount which an employer is liable to pay under this paragraph as if this paragraph were a regulation included among those listed in paragraph (4) of that regulation.

20(8) Regulation 219 (payment by cheque) applies for determining when a payment is made for the purposes of this paragraph as if this paragraph were included among the provisions listed in paragraph (2) of that regulation.

20(9) In this paragraph–

    "inspector" means an inspector of taxes;

    "the prescribed rate" means the rate applicable under section 178 of the Finance Act 1989 for the purposes of section 86 of TMA;

    "the relevant start date" means–

    (a) in a case where the determination relates to tax payable for a tax year ending on or before 5th April 1988, 19th April 1988, and

    (b) in a case where the determination relates to tax payable for a tax year ending after 5th April 1988 but on or before 5th April 1992, the 14th day after the end of the tax year to which the determination relates.

Origin – Para. 20(1)–(3): SI 1993/744, reg. 50(1)(part).
Para. 20(4): SI 1993/744, reg. 52(2)(part).
Para. 20(5): SI 1993/744, reg. 52(1)(part).
Para. 20(6): SI 1993/744, reg. 52(3)(part), 54(1)(part), (2)(part).
Para. 20(7): SI 1993/744, reg. 52(3)(part), 54(6)(part), (7)(part).
Para. 20(8): SI 1993/744, reg. 52(4)(part).
Para. 20(9): SI 1993/744, reg. 2(1)("inspector"), 50(2), (3), 52(1)(part).
Para. 20(): SI 1993/744, reg. 52()(part).

Cross references – SI 1989/1297: prescribed rate under FA 1989, s. 178.

INTEREST ON TAX OVERDUE: APPLICATION OF REGULATION 82 TO TAX YEARS FROM 1992–93 TO 2003–04

21(1)   Regulation 82 (interest on tax overdue) has effect with the following modifications where the tax year in respect of which tax is unpaid is–

(a)   the tax year ending 5th April 1993, or

(b)   a tax year ending after 5th April 1993 but on or before 5th April 2004.

21(2)   In paragraph (1) for "the total net tax payable in respect of a tax year" substitute "the total net tax deductible by him in respect of all of his employees during a tax year".

21(3)   In paragraph (4) for "a direction made under regulation 72(5) or 81(4)" substitute "a direction made under regulation 42(2) or (3) or 49(5) of the 1993 Regulations or regulation 72(5), 72F or 81(4) of these Regulations".

21(4)   Omit paragraph (6).

21(5)   For paragraph (8) substitute–

     "**82(8)**   The **"reckonable date"** means 14 days after the end of the tax year."

21(6)   After that paragraph insert–

     "**82(9)**   **"The 1993 Regulations"** means the Income Tax (Employments) Regulations 1993."

History – In para. 21(3), the words "regulation 72(5), 72F" substituted for "regulation 72(5)" by SI 2008/782, reg. 17, with effect from 6 April 2008.

Origin – Para. 21(1): SI 1993/744, reg. 51(1)(part).
Para. 21(2): SI 1993/744, reg. 51(1)(part).
Para. 21(3): SI 1993/744, reg. 51(2)(part).
Para. 21(4): SI 1993/744, reg. 51(1)(part).
Para. 21(5): SI 1993/744, reg. 51(3)(part).
Para. 21(6): drafting.

INTEREST ON OVERPAID TAX: DISAPPLICATION OF REGULATION 83 FOR TAX YEARS BEFORE THE TAX YEAR ENDING 5TH APRIL 1997

22   Regulation 83 (interest on overpaid tax) does not apply to tax which was paid by an employer in respect of a tax year ending on or before 5th April 1996.

Origin – Para. 22: SI 1993/744, reg. 53A(1)(part).

INTEREST ON OVERPAID TAX: PROVISIONS APPLYING TO TAX YEARS FROM 1992–93 TO 1995–96

23(1)   This paragraph applies in relation to tax which–

(a)   was paid by an employer in respect of the tax year ending 5th April 1993 or in respect of a tax year ending after 5th April 1993 but on or before 5th April 1996, and

(b)   is repaid to the employer after the end of the tax year in respect of which the tax was paid.

23(2)   If the late repayment condition is met, the tax repaid carries interest at the prescribed rate from the relevant time until the order for the repayment is issued ("the interest period").

23(3)   The late repayment condition is that the tax is repaid–

(a)   after the end of the tax year following the tax year in respect of which the tax was paid, and

(b)   after the end of the tax year in which the tax was paid.

23(4)   Any change made to the prescribed rate during the interest period applies to the tax repaid from the date of change.

23(5)   Regulation 219 (payment by cheque) applies for determining when a payment is made for the purposes of this paragraph as if this paragraph were included among the provisions listed in paragraph (2) of that regulation.

23(6)   In this paragraph–

"the prescribed rate" means the rate applicable under section 178 of the Finance Act 1989 for the purposes of section 824 of ICTA;

"the relevant time" means–

    (a)   in a case where the tax was paid more than twelve months after the end of the tax year in respect of which the payment was made, the end of the tax year in which that tax was paid, and

    (b)   in any other case, the end of the tax year after the tax year in respect of which the payment was made.

Origin – Para. 23(1), (2); SI 1993/744, reg. 53(1).
Para. 23(3): SI 1993/744, reg. 53(2).
Para. 23(4): SI 1993/744, reg. 53(3)(part).
Para. 23(5): SI 1993/744, reg. 53(5).
Para. 23(6): SI 1993/744, reg. 53(3)(part), (4).
Cross references – SI 1989/1297: prescribed rate under FA 1989, s. 178.

OVERPAYMENTS AND UNDERPAYMENTS OF TAX: TAX YEARS BEFORE THE TAX YEAR ENDING 5TH APRIL 1997

24(1)   Despite the revocations made by these Regulations, regulation 101 of the 1993 Regulations (repayment of overpayments and recovery of underpayments) continues to apply in relation to an assessment for a tax year ending on or before 5th April 1996, but with the modifications mentioned in sub-paragraph (2).

24(2)   The modifications are–

(a)   the references in paragraphs (1) and (2) of regulation 101 to the appropriate code for a subsequent year are to be read as references to the employee's code for a subsequent tax year;

(b)   the references in paragraphs (1) and (2) of that regulation to the inspector and to the collector are to be read as references to the Inland Revenue;

(c)   the reference in paragraph (6) of that regulation to a direction made by the collector under regulation 42(2) of the 1993 Regulations in relation to the employee and in respect of one or more income tax periods falling within the year is to be read as including a reference to a direction under regulation 72(5) of these Regulations in relation to that employee in respect of one or more tax periods falling within the tax year;

(d)   the reference in that paragraph to a direction made by the Board under regulation 42(3) of the 1993 Regulations in relation to the employee and in respect of one or more income tax periods falling within the year is to be read as including a reference to a direction under regulation 72(5) of these Regulations in relation to that employee in respect of one or more tax periods falling within the tax year;

(e)   the reference in that paragraph to a direction made by the Board under regulation 49(5) of the 1993 Regulations in relation to the employee and in respect of one or more income tax periods falling within the year is to be read as including a reference to a direction under regulation 81(4) of these Regulations in relation to that employee in respect of one or more tax periods falling within the tax year.

24(3)   Any tax which is payable to the Inland Revenue under regulation 101(2) as it continues to have effect by virtue of this paragraph is payable within 14 days of the date on which the Inland Revenue first makes application for its payment.

Origin – Para. 24(3): SI 1993/744, reg. 105(2).

OVERPAYMENTS AND UNDERPAYMENTS OF TAX: TAX YEARS BEFORE THE TAX YEAR ENDING 5TH APRIL 2002

25(1)   Regulation 188 (assessments other than self-assessments)–

(a)   does not apply in relation to an assessment for a tax year ending on or before 5th April 1996, and

(b)   has effect in particular with the following modification in relation to an assessment, other than one under section 9 of TMA, for a tax year beginning on or after 6th April 1996 and ending on or before 5th April 2001.

25(2)   In paragraph (3), after sub-paragraph (a) insert–

    "(aa)   make any necessary adjustment to B in respect of any shortfall in deductions made in accordance with the Income Tax (Employments) Regulations 1993 from the employee, where–

(i)   payments of profit-related pay have been made to the employee in accordance with a profit-related pay scheme registered under Chapter 3 of Part 5 of ICTA,

(ii) in consequence of the relief given by that Chapter less tax has been deducted from those payments than would have been deducted if the scheme had not been registered, and

(iii) the registration of the scheme has subsequently been cancelled with effect from a time before that relevant for the purposes of the relief;".

Origin – Para. 25: SI 1993/744, reg. 101(3)(part), (4)(part).

ATTRIBUTION OF REPAYMENTS: TAX YEARS BEFORE THE TAX YEAR ENDING 5TH APRIL 1997

26(1)   Despite the revocations made by these Regulations, regulations 106 to 108 of the 1993 Regulations (attribution of repayments) continue to apply in relation to a repayment to which section 824(5) of ICTA applies for a tax year ending on or before 5th April 1996, but with the modification mentioned in sub-paragraph (2).

26(2)   The modification is that the reference to the collector in regulation 107(3) is to be read as including a reference to the Inland Revenue.

CERTIFICATE THAT SUM DUE: CERTIFICATE OF THE COLLECTOR

27(1)   A certificate of the collector that any amount shown in a certificate under the regulations listed in paragraph (2) of regulation 218 has not been paid by an employer to the collector or, to the best of the collector's knowledge and belief, to any other collector or to any person acting on the collector's behalf or on behalf of another collector is sufficient evidence that the amount mentioned in the collector's certificate is unpaid and due to the Crown.

27(2)   A certificate of the collector that any amount of interest payable under the regulations listed in paragraph (4) of regulation 218 has not been paid by an employer or employee to the collector or, to the best of the collector's knowledge and belief, to any other collector or to any person acting on the collector's behalf or on behalf of another collector is sufficient evidence that the amount mentioned in the certificate is unpaid and due to the Crown.

27(3)   A document which purports to be a certificate of the collector under sub-paragraph (1) or (2) is treated as such a certificate until the contrary is proved.

INTERPRETATION

28   In this Part of this Schedule–

"**the 1993 Regulations**" means the Income Tax (Employments) Regulations 1993;

"**collector**" means a collector of taxes.

Origin – Para. 28: SI 1993/744, reg. 2(1)("collector"); drafting.

SCHEDULE 2 – REVOCATIONS

REGULATION 220

[Revokes SI 1993/744, SI 1993/2276, SI 1994/775, SI 1994/1212, SI 1995/216, SI 1995/447, SI 1995/853, SI 1995/1223, SI 1995/1284, SI 1996/804, SI 1996/980, SI 1996/1312, SI 1996/3281, SI 1996/2554, SI 1996/2631, SI 1997/214, SI 1998/1891, SI 1998/2484, SI 1999/70, SI 1999/824, SI 1999/2155, SI 2000/1152, SI 2000/2742, reg. 3, SI 2002/680, reg. 3–8 and SI 2003/2494 and amends SI 2001/1081, reg. 1(2) and SI 2003/536, reg. 1(2)]

NON-RESIDENT INSURANCE COMPANIES REGULATIONS 2003

(SI 2003/2714 amended by SI 2008/954)

Made on 22 October 2003 by the Commissioners of Inland Revenue, in exercise of the powers conferred upon them by s. 11AA(5) of the Income and Corporation Taxes Act 1988 and s. 149(6) of the Finance Act 2003. Operative from 13 November 2003.

1 These Regulations may be cited as the Non-resident Insurance Companies Regulations 2003, shall come into force on 13th November 2003, and have effect in relation to accounting periods of non-resident insurance companies beginning on or after 1st January 2003.

2 In these Regulations–

"**non-resident insurance company**" means an insurance company that is not resident in the United Kingdom; and for this purpose "**insurance company**" has the meaning given by section 431(2) of the Income and Corporation Taxes Act 1988.

3(1) In applying subsection (2) of section 11AA of the Income and Corporation Taxes Act 1988 in relation to a non-resident insurance company, it shall be assumed that the permanent establishment has assets such that its free assets would be not less than they would be in the circumstances specified in that subsection.

3(2) "**Free assets**" means the amount by which–

(a) the value of the assets of the permanent establishment, exceeds

(b) the aggregate of the permanent establishment's loan capital and technical provisions;

and for this purpose, the reinsurers' share of technical provisions is not to be included in determining the assets of the permanent establishment.

3(3) "**Value**" means the amount that, at the time at which the value falls to be determined, the non-resident insurance company would obtain from an independent person for the transfer of all the company's rights in respect of the asset.

3(4) "**Technical provision**" means each of the following–

(a) provision for unearned premiums;

(b) long term business provision;

(c) claims outstanding;

(d) provision for bonuses and rebates;

(e) provision for unexpired risks;

(f) technical provisions for linked liabilities;

(g) deposits received from reinsurers;

and in the case of the items listed in sub-paragraphs (a) to (f), the amount to be brought into account is the amount by which the gross amount exceeds the reinsurance amount.

In this paragraph expressions also used in Schedule 3 to the Large and Medium-sized Companies and Groups (Accounts and Reports) Regulations 2008 have the same meaning as in that Schedule.

History – In reg. 3(4) the words "Schedule 3 to the Large and Medium-sized Companies and Groups (Accounts and Reports) Regulations 2008" substituted for "Schedule 9A to the Companies Act 1985" by SI 2008/954, art. 52, with effect from 6 April 2008.

4(1) In accordance with the separate enterprise principle, profits from assets attributable, by virtue of regulation 3, to the permanent establishment of a non-resident insurance company are attributed to that establishment.

4(2) "**The separate enterprise principle**" means the principle in subsection (2) of section 11AA of the Income and Corporation Taxes Act 1988 (read with subsection (3) of that section).

INCOME AND CORPORATION TAXES (ELECTRONIC CERTIFICATES OF DEDUCTION OF TAX AND TAX CREDIT) REGULATIONS 2003

(SI 2003/3143, as amended by SI 2009/2050)

Made on 4 December 2003 by the Commissioners of Inland Revenue, in exercise of the powers conferred upon them by s. 132 of the Finance Act 1999. Operative from 1 January 2004.

CITATION, COMMENCEMENT AND INTERPRETATION

1(1) These Regulations may be cited as the Income and Corporation Taxes (Electronic Certificates of Deduction of Tax and Tax Credit) Regulations 2003 and shall come into force on 1st January 2004.

1(2) In these Regulations references to the delivery of a document include that document being made available to a person in circumstances where–

(a)   the sender and that person have agreed to his having access to the document on a website,

(b)   the document is a document to which the agreement relates; and

(c)   the person is notified in a manner for the time being agreed for the purpose between him and the sender of–

     (i)   the placing of the document on the website;

     (ii)   the address of the website; and

     (iii)   the place on the website at which, and the manner in which, the document may be accessed.

Here **"document"** means anything authorised to be delivered by means of electronic communications under these Regulations.

1(3) In these Regulations–

"electronic communications" has the meaning given by section 132(10) of the Finance Act 1999;

"the sender" means–

(a)   in relation to a statement to which regulation 2 applies, the company making the qualifying distribution, or a person acting on its behalf;

(b)   in relation to a statement to which regulation 3 applies, the person under the duty to furnish the certificate, or another person acting on his behalf; and

(c)   in relation to statement, notice, certificate or voucher to which regulation 4 applies, the person required or authorised, under the relevant provision mentioned in paragraph (2) of that regulation, to deliver that statement, notice, certificate or voucher, or another person acting on his behalf; and

"the Taxes Act" means the Income and Corporation Taxes Act 1988.

DELIVERING INFORMATION ELECTRONICALLY ABOUT DISTRIBUTIONS, DIVIDENDS, INTEREST PAYMENTS AND ASSOCIATED TAX CREDITS

2(1) A statement under section 234(1) or 234A(2) or (3) of the Taxes Act (information relating to distributions, dividends, interest payments and associated tax credits) by a company making a qualifying distribution may be delivered by means of electronic communications if the following conditions are satisfied.

2(2) The first condition is that the sender has indicated to the proposed recipient that it intends to use electronic communications for the purposes of delivering statements under those sections.

2(3) The second condition is that the proposed recipient has consented to information being delivered by the sender by means of electronic communications, and that consent has not been withdrawn.

2(4) The third condition is that the statement is delivered in an electronic format–

(a)   in which the statement may be stored

(b)   which permits a paper copy of the information contained in the statement to be printed; and

(c)   which is designed to prevent alteration of the contents.

History – In reg. 2(1), "or (3)" inserted after "234A(2)" by SI 2009/2050, reg. 2(2), with effect from 1 September 2009.

DELIVERING INFORMATION ELECTRONICALLY ABOUT DEDUCTION OF TAX

3(1)   A statement under section 352 of the Taxes Act (certificates of deduction of tax) may be delivered by means of electronic communications if the following conditions are satisfied.

3(2)   The first condition is that the sender has indicated to the proposed recipient that he intends to use electronic communications to furnish statements under section 352.

3(3)   The second condition is that the proposed recipient has consented to information being delivered by the sender by means of electronic communications, and that consent has not been withdrawn

3(4)   The third condition is that the statement is delivered in an electronic format–

(a)   in which the statement may be stored;

(b)   which permits a paper copy of the information contained in the statement to be printed; and

(c)   which is designed to prevent alteration of the contents.

SENDING INFORMATION ELECTRONICALLY ABOUT MANUFACTURED DIVIDENDS

4(1)   A statement, notice, certificate or voucher required or authorised to be delivered under the provisions listed in paragraph (2) may be delivered by means of electronic communications if the conditions specified in paragraphs (3) to (5) are satisfied.

4(2)   The provisions referred to in paragraph (1) are–

(a)   paragraphs 2(6) and 3(8) of Schedule 23A to the Taxes Act (information about manufactured dividends); and

(b)   regulations 4(4)(c), 5(2)(b)(iii), 7(2)(d), 10(3)(b) and (4)(b) and 15(1) and (5) of the Income Tax (Manufactured Overseas Dividends) Regulations 1993.

4(3)   The first condition is that the sender has indicated to the proposed recipient that he intends to use electronic communications to deliver documents of that type.

4(4)   The second condition is that the proposed recipient has consented to information being delivered by the sender by means of electronic communications, and that consent has not subsequently been withdrawn.

4(5)   The third condition is that the document in question is delivered in an electronic format–

(a)   in which it may be stored;

(b)   which permits a paper copy of the information contained in it to be printed; and

(c)   which is designed to prevent alteration of its contents.

AMENDMENTS OF THE INCOME TAX (MANUFACTURED OVERSEAS DIVIDENDS) REGULATIONS 1993

5   [Not reproduced.]

REPORTING OF SAVINGS INCOME INFORMATION REGULATIONS 2003

(SI 2003/3297, as amended by SI 2005/1539, SI 2006/3286, SI 2008/2682 and SI 2012/756)

Made on 16 December 2003 by the Treasury, in exercise of the powers conferred upon them by s. 199 of the Finance Act 2003. Operative in accordance with reg. 1(2).

Other material – HMRC Brief 12/13: EU savings directive: accession of Croatia.
HMRC Brief 34/13: Reporting of interest payments.
HMRC Brief 16/14: Reporting of interest payments.

PART 1 – INTRODUCTORY PROVISIONS

CITATION AND COMMENCEMENT

1(1) These Regulations may be cited as the Reporting of Savings Income Information Regulations 2003.

1(2) These Regulations shall come into force on such date, being not earlier than 1st January 2005, as is determined by the Treasury and specified by notices in the London, Edinburgh and Belfast Gazettes.

Notes – These regulations came into effect on 1 July 2005 (London Gazette, 14 June 2005).

INTERPRETATION

2(1) In these Regulations–

"**the Savings Directive**" means Council Directive 2003/48/EC of 3rd June 2003 ("the Directive of 2003") on the taxation of savings income in the form of interest payments, as amended by Council Directive 2004/66/EC, and a reference, without more, to a numbered Article is a reference to the Article of the Directive of 2003, as so amended, which bears that number;

"**the Securities Directive**" means Directive 2001/34/EC of 28th May 2001 on the admission of securities to official stock exchange listing and on information to be published on those securities as amended;

"**the UCITS Directive**" means Council Directive 85/611/EEC of 20th December 1985 on the co-ordination of laws, regulations and administrative provisions relating to undertakings for collective investment in transferable securities as amended.

2(2) In these Regulations–

"**agent**" means paying agent or receiving agent as appropriate;

"**arrangements**" means agreements or arrangements made with a territory being a dependent or associated territory of a member State in relation to the automatic exchange of information or, during the transitional period defined in Article 10 of the Savings Directive, the application of a withholding tax referred to in paragraph 2(ii) of Article 17 of the Savings Directive;

"**country**" includes a territory;

"**economic operator**" is a paying agent established in another member State or in a territory (construed in accordance with the Savings Directive or the arrangements with the territory, as appropriate) with which arrangements have been made;

"**money debt**" is a debt arising from a transaction for the lending of money and which falls to be, or may be, settled–

(a) by the payment of money; or

(b) by the transfer of a right to settlement under a debt which is itself a money debt, subject to the qualification in regulation 17;

"**paying agent**", unless the context otherwise requires, has the meaning given in regulation 3;

"**a prescribed territory**" means another member State, Aruba, the British Virgin Islands, Gibraltar, Guernsey, the Isle of Man, Jersey, Montserrat or the Netherlands Antilles;

"**receiving agent**" has the meaning given in regulation 6;

"**relevant payee**" has the meaning given in regulation 7;

"**resident**" and "**residence**" shall be construed in accordance with regulation 9;

"**residual entity**" has the meaning given in regulation 4;

"Revenue and Customs", except in the expression "an officer of Revenue and Customs", means Her Majesty's Revenue and Customs (see section 4 of the Commissioners for Revenue and Customs Act 2005);

"savings income" has the meaning given in regulation 8;

"third country" means a territory other than a member State;

"UCITS" means an undertaking for collective investment in transferable securities within the UCITS Directive.

2(3) For the purposes of these Regulations a person makes savings income payments to another person if the person–

(a)   makes payments of savings income to another person, or

(b)   secures the payment of savings income for the other person.

History – In reg. 2(1) the definition of "the Savings Directive" substituted by SI 2005/1539, reg. 3(2), with effect from 1 July 2005 (London Gazette, 14 June 2005).
In reg. 2(2) the definition of "economic operator" substituted by SI 2005/1539, reg. 3(3)(b), with effect from 1 July 2005 (London Gazette, 14 June 2005).
In reg. 2(2) the definition of "paying agent" substituted by SI 2005/1539, reg. 3(3)(c), with effect from 1 July 2005 (London Gazette, 14 June 2005).
In reg. 2(2) the definition of "a prescribed territory" substituted by SI 2005/1539, reg. 3(3)(d), with effect from 1 July 2005 (London Gazette, 14 June 2005).
In reg. 2(2) the definitions of "arrangements" and "country" inserted by SI 2005/1539, reg. 3(3)(a), with effect from 1 July 2005 (London Gazette, 14 June 2005).
In reg. 2(2) the definition of "Revenue and Customs" inserted by SI 2005/1539, reg. 3(3)(e), with effect from 1 July 2005 (London Gazette, 14 June 2005).

MEANING OF PAYING AGENT

3 A paying agent is a person who–

(a)   is established in the United Kingdom;

(b)   makes savings income payments in the course of his business or profession; and

(c)   makes those payments–

    (i)   for the immediate benefit of a relevant payee; or

    (ii)   to a residual entity established in a prescribed territory.

Here a **"person"** includes any officer in any public office or in any government department and any savings income payments made by such a person will be treated as if the payment were made in the course of that person's business or profession.

MEANING OF RESIDUAL ENTITY

4(1) Subject to paragraph (2) a residual entity is an entity established in a member State or in a territory with respect to which arrangements have been made other than an entity–

(a)   which is a legal person;

(b)   the profits of which are taxed under the general arrangements for business taxation; or

(c)   which is a UCITS authorised in accordance with the UCITS Directive or an equivalent undertaking for collective investment established in a territory with which arrangements have been made.

4(2) In paragraph (1)(a) a legal person excludes–

(a)   in Finland, avoin yhtiö (Ay) and kommandiittiyhtiö (Ky)/ öppet bolag and kommanditbolag; and

(b)   in Sweden, handelsbolag (HB) and kommanditbolag (KB).

4(3) A paying agent shall regard an entity as a residual entity unless the paying agent has reason to believe, on the basis of official evidence produced by the entity to the paying agent, that sub-paragraph (a), (b) or (c) of paragraph (1) applies.

An entity which presents to the paying agent or economic operator a certificate–

(a)   issued by the member State in which that entity is established in accordance with Article 4(3), or

(b)   issued by the territory with which arrangements have been made in which that entity is established in accordance with provisions which are equivalent to Article 4(3),

shall, for the purposes of this regulation, be treated as if it were a UCITS authorised in accordance with the UCITS Directive or an equivalent undertaking for collective investment established in the territory with which arrangements have been made (as the case may be).

History – In reg. 4(1), the words "or in a territory with respect to which arrangements have been made" inserted after the words "member State" by SI 2005/1539, reg. 4(2)(i), with effect from 1 July 2005 (London Gazette, 14 June 2005).
At the end of reg. 4(1)(c), the words "or an equivalent undertaking for collective investment established in a territory with which arrangements have been made" inserted by SI 2005/1539, reg. 4(2)(ii), with effect from 1 July 2005 (London Gazette, 14 June 2005).
The second paragraph of reg. 4(3) substituted by SI 2005/1539, reg. 4(3), with effect from 1 July 2005 (London Gazette, 14 June 2005).

ELECTION BY AN ENTITY TO BE TREATED AS A UCITS

5(1)   An entity established in the United Kingdom may obtain a certificate to the effect that it is to be treated as a UCITS authorised in accordance with the UCITS Directive for the purposes of the Savings Directive in accordance with this regulation.

5(2)   A notice requesting the issue of a certificate shall be given to Revenue and Customs by or on behalf of the entity.

5(3)   The notice shall include the following information–

(a)   the name and address of the entity;

(b)   where the notice is given on behalf of the entity, the name, address and position of the person giving notice;

(c)   a statement that–

    (i)   the entity is established in the United Kingdom;

    (ii)   the entity is not a legal person;

    (iii)   the entity's profits are not taxed under the general arrangements for business taxation;

    (iv)   the entity is not a UCITS authorised in accordance with the UCITS Directive; and

    (v)   the entity elects to be treated as if it were a UCITS authorised in accordance with the UCITS Directive for the purposes of the Savings Directive; and

(d)   a signed and dated declaration by the person giving notice to the effect that it is to the best of his knowledge correct and complete.

5(4)   Revenue and Customs will issue a certificate to that entity confirming that it is to be treated as if it were a UCITS authorised in accordance with the UCITS Directive for the purposes of the Savings Directive and that certificate shall have effect from the date specified in that certificate.

History – In reg. 5(2), the words "Revenue and Customs" substituted for the words "the Inland Revenue" by SI 2005/1539, reg. 5(2), with effect from 1 July 2005 (London Gazette, 14 June 2005).
In reg. 5(4), the words "Revenue and Customs" substituted for the words "the Inland Revenue" by SI 2005/1539, reg. 5(3), with effect from 1 July 2005 (London Gazette, 14 June 2005).

MEANING OF RECEIVING AGENT

6   A receiving agent is an entity–

(a)   which is a residual entity;

(b)   which is established in the United Kingdom; and

(c)   to which a savings income payment is made for the benefit of a relevant payee by a person established in a member State or in a territory with which arrangements have been made in the course of his business or profession.

History – In reg. 6(c), the words "or in a territory with which arrangements have been made" inserted after the words "member State" by SI 2005/1539, reg. 6, with effect from 1 July 2005 (London Gazette, 14 June 2005).

MEANING OF RELEVANT PAYEE

7(1)   The agent shall regard a person as a relevant payee if he is an individual–

(a)   resident in a prescribed territory; and

(b)   who has received a savings income payment or for whom a savings income payment has been secured,

unless he provides evidence to the agent that the payment is not received or secured for his own benefit because of one of the reasons listed in paragraph (2).

7(2)   The reasons referred to in paragraph (1) are that the individual–

(a)   is acting as a paying agent or an economic operator;

(b)   acts on behalf of a residual entity;

(c)   acts on behalf of an entity–

    (i)   which is a legal person;

(ii)   the profits of which are taxed under the general arrangements for business taxation;

(iii)   which is a UCITS authorised in accordance with the UCITS Directive, or an equivalent undertaking for collective investment established in a territory with which arrangements have been made; or

(iv)   which is treated as being a UCITS authorised in accordance with the UCITS Directive for the purposes of the Savings Directive by virtue of Article 4(3);

(v)   which is treated as being an equivalent undertaking for collective investment established in a territory with which arrangements have been made for the purposes of those arrangements by virtue of provisions which are equivalent to Article 4(3); or

(d)   acts on behalf of another individual for whose benefit the payment is received or secured.

7(3)   An individual who provides evidence that he is acting on behalf of a residual entity must in addition provide the name and address of that residual entity to the agent.

7(4)   An individual who provides evidence that he acts on behalf of another individual must in addition provide the agent with the name and address, and where appropriate the tax identification number or date and place of birth, of that individual. The individual providing the evidence must obtain and verify this information in accordance with regulation 9.

7(5)   If the agent has information which suggests that the individual who receives a savings income payment or for whom a savings income payment is secured may not be the relevant payee for the reason referred to in paragraph (2)(d), then paragraph (6) applies.

7(6)   The agent must take reasonable steps to establish who is the relevant payee and if the agent payment or for whom a savings income payment is secured as the relevant payee. is unable to identify the relevant payee, he shall treat the individual who receives a savings income payment or for whom a savings income payment is secured as the relevant payee.

History – In reg. 7(2)(a), the words "a paying agent" substituted for the words "paying agent" by SI 2005/1539, reg. 7(2), with effect from 1 July 2005 (London Gazette, 14 June 2005).
In reg. 7(2)(c)(iii) the words "Directive, or an equivalent undertaking for collective investment established in a territory with which arrangements have been made;" substituted for the word "Directive" by SI 2005/1539, reg. 7(3)(a), with effect from 1 July 2005 (London Gazette, 14 June 2005).
In reg. 7(2)(c)(iv) the word "authorised" inserted after the words "a UCITS" and the word "or" at the end omitted by SI 2005/1539, reg. 7(3)(b), with effect from 1 July 2005 (London Gazette, 14 June 2005).
Reg. 7(2)(c)(v) inserted by SI 2005/1539, reg. 7(3)(b), with effect from 1 July 2005 (London Gazette, 14 June 2005).

MEANING OF SAVINGS INCOME

8(1)   Subject to paragraphs (3) to (6) and (8) savings income is–

(a)   interest;

(b)   interest accrued or capitalised at the sale, refund or redemption of a money debt;

(c)   income distributed by a collective investment fund which is derived directly or indirectly, via other collective investment funds or residual entities, from interest;

(d)   income realised upon the sale, refund or redemption of shares or units in a collective investment fund if that fund invests directly or indirectly, via other collective investment funds or residual entities, more than 40% of its assets in money debts.

8(2)   In paragraph (1) **"interest"**–

(a)   includes–

(i)   prizes attaching to money debts (including premium bonds);

(ii)   premiums and discounts derived from money debts;

(iii)   any dividend derived from shares (including permanent interest bearing shares) in a building society;

(iv)   any share interest paid by a registered industrial and provident society; and

(v)   any share interest paid by a credit union registered under the Credit Unions (Northern Ireland) Order 1985; and

(b)   excludes–

(i)   any interest which is not related to a money debt; and

(ii)   penalty charges for late payment.

8(3)   In respect of savings income described in paragraph (1)(b), where an agent has no information concerning the amount of interest which is accrued or capitalised at the sale, refund or redemption of a money debt the total amount of the proceeds of the sale, redemption or refund is savings income.

8(4)   In respect of savings income described in paragraphs (1)(c), where an agent has no information concerning the proportion of income which derives from interest the total amount of the income is savings income.

8(5)   In respect of savings income described in paragraphs (1)(c) and (d), subject to paragraph (9)–

(a)   where a collective investment fund established in the United Kingdom has invested 15% or less of its assets directly or indirectly, via other collective investment funds or residual entities, in money debts there is no savings income;

(b)   where a collective investment fund–

    (i)   is established in another member State which has derogated from paragraphs (1)(c) and (d) of Article 6 in accordance with Article 6(6); and

    (ii)   the collective investment fund has invested 15% or less of its assets in money debts in accordance with the law of that member State in the application of that derogation,

    there is no savings income.

(c)   where a collective investment fund–

    (i)   is established in a territory with which arrangements have been made which has made provisions equivalent to the derogation in the first sentence of Article 6(6); and

    (ii)   the collective investment fund has invested 15% or less of its assets in money debts in accordance with the law of that territory in the application of those provisions,

    there is no savings income

8(6)   In respect of savings income described in paragraph (1)(d)–

(a)   where an agent has no information concerning the percentage of assets invested in money debts or in shares or units in collective investment funds, that percentage shall be considered to be more than 40%;

(b)   where the agent cannot determine the amount of income realised by the relevant payee, the income shall be deemed to correspond to the proceeds of the sale, refund or redemption of the shares or units.

8(7)   From 1st January 2011 paragraphs (1)(d) and (6)(a) shall have the effect with the substitution of "25%" for "40%".

8(8)   Subject to paragraph (9)–

(a)   where a residual entity established in the United Kingdom invests 15% or less of its assets directly or indirectly, via collective investment funds or other residual entities, in money debts there is no savings income;

(b)   where a residual entity–

    (i)   is established in another member State which has derogated from paragraph 4 of Article 6 in accordance with Article 6(6); and

    (ii)   the residual entity has invested 15% or less of its assets in money debts in accordance with the law of that member State in the application of that derogation,

    there is no savings income.

8(9)   In the application of paragraphs (5) and (8), where the agent cannot ascertain whether or not the collective investment fund or residual entity, as appropriate, has invested 15% or less of its assets in money debts in accordance with those provisions, there is savings income.

8(10)   The percentages referred to in this regulation shall be determined by reference to the investment policy as laid down in the fund rules or instruments of incorporation of the collective investment fund or residual entity concerned and, failing which, by reference to the actual composition of the assets of the collective investment fund or residual entity.

8(11)   In this regulation a collective investment fund is–

(a)   a UCITS authorised in accordance with the UCITS Directive or an equivalent undertaking for collective investment established in a territory with which arrangements have been made;

(b)   an entity which is treated as being a UCITS authorised in accordance with the UCITS Directive for the purposes of the Savings Directive by virtue of Article 4(3); or

(ba)   an entity which is treated as being an equivalent undertaking for collective investment established in a territory with which arrangements have been made for the purposes of those arrangements by virtue of provisions which are equivalent to Article 4(3); or

(c)   an undertaking for collective investment which is not established in the Community or in a territory with which arrangements have been made.

This is subject to the following qualification.

If a collective investment fund provides arrangements for separate pooling of the contributions of the participants and the profits or income out of which payments are to be made to them and under which participants are entitled to exchange rights in one pool for rights in another, each separate pool shall be treated as a separate collective investment fund.

8(12)   In this regulation–

"building society" means a building society within the meaning of the Building Societies Act 1986;

"permanent interest bearing shares" has the meaning given in section 117(11) of the Taxation of Chargeable Gains Act 1992;

"registered industrial and provident society" has the meaning given in section 486(12) of the Income and Corporation Taxes Act 1988 as extended by section 486(9) of that Act; and

"share interest" has the meaning given in section 486(12) of the Income and Corporation Taxes Act 1988.

History – In reg. 8(2)(a)(iii), the word "and" omitted by SI 2005/1539, reg. 8(a), with effect from 1 July 2005 (London Gazette, 14 June 2005).
Reg. 8(2)(a)(v) inserted by SI 2005/1539, reg. 8(b), with effect from 1 July 2005 (London Gazette, 14 June 2005).
Reg. 8(5)(c) inserted by SI 2005/1539, reg. 8(e), with effect from 1 July 2005 (London Gazette, 14 June 2005).
In reg. 8(8)(b)(i) the words "paragraph 4 of Article 6" substituted for the words "paragraphs (1)(c) and (d) of Article 6" inserted by SI 2005/1539, reg. 8(d), with effect from 1 July 2005 (London Gazette, 14 June 2005).
At end of reg. 8(11)(a) the words "or an equivalent undertaking for collective investment established in a territory with which arrangements have been made" inserted by SI 2005/1539, reg. 8(f)(i), with effect from 1 July 2005 (London Gazette, 14 June 2005).
Reg. 8(11)(ba) inserted by SI 2005/1539, reg. 8(f)(ii), with effect from 1 July 2005 (London Gazette, 14 June 2005).
Reg. 8(11)(c) substituted by SI 2005/1539, reg. 8(f)(iii), with effect from 1 July 2005 (London Gazette, 14 June 2005).

PART 2 – INFORMATION TO BE OBTAINED, VERIFIED AND REPORTED

IDENTITY AND RESIDENCE OF RELEVANT PAYEES

9(1)   Where–

(a)   a paying agent makes a savings income payment to an individual whom he believes to be a relevant payee, or

(b)   a receiving agent receives or secures a savings income payment for an individual whom he believes to be a relevant payee,

the agent must establish the identity and country of residence of that individual in accordance with this regulation.

9(2)   Subject to the conditions set out in this regulation, for the purposes of this regulation the country of residence means the country where the individual has his permanent address.

9(3)   Where contractual relations between the agent and the individual are entered into before 1st January 2004 the agent must verify the name, address and country of residence of the individual by using the information at its disposal, including information obtained pursuant to the Money Laundering Regulations 1993 and the Money Laundering Regulations 2001.

9(4)   Where contractual relations between the agent and the individual are entered into, or transactions are carried out in the absence of contractual relations, on or after 1st January 2004, the agent shall obtain and verify–

(a)   the name and address of the individual, and

(i)   where the individual is resident for tax purposes in a member State, the tax identification number (if any) allocated by that member State but if it is not available the individual's date and place of birth,

(ii)   where the individual is resident for tax purposes other than in a member State, the individual's date and place of birth,

in accordance with paragraphs (5) and (7);

(b)   the country of residence of the individual in accordance with paragraphs (8) and (9).

9(5)   The information in paragraph (4)(a) shall be verified by the presentation by the individual of his passport or official identity card to the agent.

9(6)   If the address does not appear on that passport or official identity card, it shall be verified by the presentation by the individual of any other documentary proof of identity to the agent.

9(7)   If the tax identification number is not required or if it is and it is not mentioned on the passport, official identity card or any other documentary proof of identity presented by the individual, the agent shall instead verify the individual.s date and place of birth on the basis of his passport or official identity card.

9(8)   Subject to paragraph (9), the country of residence of the individual shall be determined on the basis of his address verified in accordance with paragraphs (5) and (6).

9(9)   Where an individual presents a passport or official identity card issued by a member State and declares himself to be resident in a third country–

(a)   the agent shall establish the country of residence by means of a certificate of residence for tax purposes issued by the competent authority of the third country which the individual claims to be his country of residence;

(b)   if the individual fails to present such a certificate, the member State that issued the passport or other official identity document shall be considered to be the country of residence.

9(10)   The individual may present a certified copy of any of the documents referred to in this regulation.

Here "certified copy" means a copy certified or otherwise authenticated in such manner as would make it admissible in evidence in proceedings before a court.

9(11)   In this regulation–

"**competent authority**" means the competent authority for the purposes of bilateral or multilateral tax conventions or, failing that, such other authority as is competent to issue certificates of residence for tax purposes;

"**other documentary proof of identity**" includes certificates of residence for tax purposes.

History – Reg. 9(4)(a) substituted by SI 2005/1539, reg. 9(a), with effect from 1 July 2005 (London Gazette, 14 June 2005). In reg. 9(7) the words "is not required or if it is and it" inserted after the words "tax identification number" by SI 2005/1539, reg. 9(b), with effect from 1 July 2005 (London Gazette, 14 June 2005).
In reg. 9(9) the words "Where an individual presents a passport or official identity card issued by a member State and declares himself to be resident in a third country–" substituted for the words preceding subpara. (a) by SI 2005/1539, reg. 9(c)(i), with effect from 1 July 2005 (London Gazette, 14 June 2005).
In reg. 9(9)(a) the words "if he presents a passport or official identity card issued by a member State, " which appeared at the start omitted by SI 2005/1539, reg. 9(c)(ii), with effect from 1 July 2005 (London Gazette, 14 June 2005).

INFORMATION TO BE REPORTED TO REVENUE AND CUSTOMS BY PAYING AGENTS MAKING PAYMENTS TO RELEVANT PAYEES

History – In the heading to reg. 10 the words "Revenue and Customs" substituted for the words "the Inland Revenue" by SI 2005/1539, reg. 10(2), with effect from 1 July 2005 (London Gazette, 14 June 2005).

10(1)   When a paying agent makes a savings income payment for the immediate benefit of a relevant payee the information prescribed by paragraph (2) must be reported by the paying agent to Revenue and Customs in accordance with regulations 14 and 15.

10(2)   The information prescribed is–

(a)   the name and address of the paying agent;

(b)   the name, address and country of residence of the relevant payee established in accordance with regulation 9;

(c)   where contractual relations between the relevant payee and the paying agent were entered into, or transactions are carried out in the absence of contractual relations, on or after 1st January 2004, the tax identification number, or if it is not available, the relevant payee's date and place of birth, established in accordance with regulation 9;

(d)   the account number of the relevant payee or, where there is none, identification of the money debt or other instrument giving rise to the savings income;

(e)   the amount and category of the savings income payments made to the relevant payee in accordance with regulation 13 and the currency in which they were paid.

History – In reg. 10(1) the words "Revenue and Customs" substituted for the words "the Inland Revenue" by SI 2005/1539, reg. 10(3), with effect from 1 July 2005 (London Gazette, 14 June 2005).
In reg. 10(2)(c), the words "is not required or if it is and it", which appeared after the words "tax identification number", omitted by SI 2012/756, reg. 2(2), with effect from 1 April 2012.
In reg. 10(2)(c) the words "is not required or if it is and it" inserted after the words "tax identification number" by SI 2005/1539, reg. 10(4), with effect from 1 July 2005 (London Gazette, 14 June 2005). This amendment does not appear to have made sense.

INFORMATION TO BE REPORTED TO REVENUE AND CUSTOMS BY PAYING AGENTS MAKING PAYMENTS TO RESIDUAL ENTITIES

History – In the heading to reg. 11 the words "Revenue and Customs" substituted for the words "the Inland Revenue" by SI 2005/1539, reg. 11(2), with effect from 1 July 2005 (London Gazette, 14 June 2005).

11(1) When a paying agent makes a savings income payment to a residual entity established in a prescribed territory the information prescribed by paragraph (2) must be reported by the paying agent to Revenue and Customs in accordance with regulations 14 and 15.

11(2) The information prescribed is–

(a)   the name and address of the paying agent;

(b)   the name and address of the residual entity (including the territory in which it is established); and

(c)   the total amount and category of the savings income payments made to the residual entity in accordance with regulation 13 and the currency in which they were paid.

History – In reg. 11(1) the words "Revenue and Customs" substituted for the words "the Inland Revenue" by SI 2005/1539, reg. 11(3), with effect from 1 July 2005 (London Gazette, 14 June 2005).

INFORMATION TO BE REPORTED TO REVENUE AND CUSTOMS BY RECEIVING AGENTS

History – In the heading to reg. 12 the words "Revenue and Customs" substituted for the words "the Inland Revenue" by SI 2005/1539, reg. 12(2), with effect from 1 July 2005 (London Gazette, 14 June 2005).

12(1) When a receiving agent receives or secures savings income the information prescribed by paragraph (2), in respect of each relevant payee the savings income is attributable to, must be reported by the receiving agent to Revenue and Customs in accordance with regulations 14 and 15.

12(2) The information prescribed is–

(a)   a statement that the savings income has been received or secured by the receiving agent in his capacity as such;

(b)   the name and address of the receiving agent;

(c)   the name, address and country of residence of the relevant payee established in accordance with regulation 9;

(d)   where contractual relations between the relevant payee and the receiving agent were entered into, or transactions are carried out in the absence of contractual relations, on or after 1st January 2004, the tax identification number, or if it is not available, the relevant payee's date and place of birth, established in accordance with regulation 9;

(e)   the account number of the relevant payee or, where there is none, identification of the money debt or other instrument giving rise to the savings income;

(f)   the amount and category of the savings income received or secured by the receiving agent in accordance with regulation 13 and the currency in which it was paid.

History – In reg. 12(1) the words "Revenue and Customs" substituted for the words "the Inland Revenue" by SI 2005/1539, reg. 12(3), with effect from 1 July 2005 (London Gazette, 14 June 2005).

In reg. 12(2)(d), the words "is not required or if it is and it", which appeared after the words "tax identification number", omitted by SI 2012/756, reg. 2(2), with effect from 1 April 2012.

In reg. 12(2)(d) the words "is not required or if it is and it" inserted after the words "tax identification number" by SI 2005/1539, reg. 12(4), with effect from 1 July 2005 (London Gazette, 14 June 2005). This amendment does not appear to have made sense.

THE AMOUNT OF SAVINGS INCOME TO BE REPORTED TO REVENUE AND CUSTOMS

History – In the heading to reg. 13 the words "Revenue and Customs" substituted for the words "the Inland Revenue" by SI 2005/1539, reg. 13(2), with effect from 1 July 2005 (London Gazette, 14 June 2005).

13(1) The information concerning the savings income prescribed by paragraph (2) must be reported by the agent to Revenue and Customs.

13(2) The agent shall identify under which of the following three categories he is reporting the savings income and where the savings income is of the type prescribed by–

(a)   regulation 8(1)(a), report the amount of savings income;

(b)   sub-paragraph (b) or (d) of regulation 8(1), report either the amount of savings income or the full amount of the proceeds from the sale, redemption or refund;

(c)   regulation 8(1)(c), report either the amount of savings income or the full amount of the distribution.

13(3) Where the agent has reported savings income under sub-paragraph (a) or (c) of paragraph (2) no further report of the same savings income is required under sub-paragraph (b) of that paragraph.

History – In reg. 13(1) the words "Revenue and Customs" substituted for the words "the Inland Revenue" by SI 2005/1539, reg. 13(3), with effect from 1 July 2005 (London Gazette, 14 June 2005).

PART 3 – REPORTING THE INFORMATION

PAYING AND RECEIVING AGENTS TO NOTIFY REVENUE AND CUSTOMS OF REPORTABLE PAYMENTS

History – In the heading to reg. 14 the words "Revenue and Customs" substituted for the words "the Inland Revenue" by SI 2005/1539, reg. 14(2), with effect from 1 July 2005 (London Gazette, 14 June 2005).

14(1) An agent who must report information to Revenue and Customs in accordance with these Regulations must notify Revenue and Customs in writing that he needs to make a report within 14 days of the end of the tax year in which–

(a)   in the case of a paying agent, the savings income payment was made, or

(b)   in the case of a receiving agent, the savings income was secured or received,

unless the agent has already received a notice under regulation 15 from Revenue and Customs in respect of that tax year.

14(2) An agent who fails to comply with paragraph (1) is liable to a penalty not exceeding £3000 determined in accordance with section 100 of the Taxes Management Act 1970.

14(3) Sections 100A, 100B, 102, 103(4) and 118(2) of the Taxes Management Act 1970 apply to a penalty determined in accordance with paragraph (2).

History – In reg. 14(1) the words "Revenue and Customs" substituted for the words "the Inland Revenue" (in each place it occurs) by SI 2005/1539, reg. 14(3), with effect from 1 July 2005 (London Gazette, 14 June 2005).

REPORTS BY PAYING AND RECEIVING AGENTS TO REVENUE AND CUSTOMS

History – In the heading to reg. 15 the words "Revenue and Customs" substituted for the words "the Inland Revenue" by SI 2005/1539, reg. 15(2), with effect from 1 July 2005 (London Gazette, 14 June 2005).

15(1) Revenue and Customs must send a notice to–

(a)   an agent who has notified Revenue and Customs in accordance with regulation 14(1);

(b)   any person Revenue and Customs considers should have notified it in accordance with regulation 14(1) but has not done so; and

(c)   any person who has notified Revenue and Customs in accordance with regulation 14(1) in respect of a previous tax year, unless–

(i)   the person has informed Revenue and Customs; or

(ii)   an officer of Revenue and Customs has reasonable grounds to believe,

that he is no longer an agent.

15(2) The notice must specify–

(a)   the information prescribed by these Regulations which must be reported;

(b)   the tax year in respect of which the report must be made and that the report must be in respect of all savings income payments for that tax year;

(c)   the form in which the report must be made;

(d)   the address to which the report must be delivered; and

(e)   the date by which the report must be delivered which shall be a date no earlier than 30 days after the date of the notice.

15(3) For the report for the tax year in which the commencement date falls, the reference to the tax year in paragraph (2)(b) means the period beginning on the commencement date and ending at the end of the tax year in which the commencement date falls.

Here "commencement date" is the date specified in the notices under regulation 1(2).

15(4) The notice may be combined with a notice issued under paragraph 1 of Schedule 23 to the Finance Act 2011 (data-gathering powers).

15(5) The agent or person, as appropriate, must make and deliver the report in accordance with the requirements specified in the notice.

15(6) Paragraph (5) applies regardless of whether any savings income is reportable in accordance with these Regulations.

History – In reg. 15(1) the words "Revenue and Customs" substituted for the words "The Inland Revenue" and the words "Revenue and Customs" substituted for the words "the Inland Revenue" (in each place it occurs) by SI 2005/1539, reg. 15(3), with effect from 1 July 2005 (London Gazette, 14 June 2005).

In reg. 15(4), the words "paragraph 1 of Schedule 23 to the Finance Act 2011 (data-gathering powers)" substituted for the words "section 17 or 18, or under both of those sections, of the Taxes Management Act 1970" by SI 2012/756, reg. 2(3), with effect from 1 April 2012.

PART 4 – AUDIT

AUDIT AND RELATED ISSUES

16(1)   An officer of Revenue and Customs may by notice require an agent, or a person who appears to that Officer to be an agent, to furnish them within such time, not being less than 14 days, as may be provided by the notice, such information (including copies of any relevant books, documents or other records) as they may reasonably require for the purposes of determining whether information contained in a report under these Regulations by that agent or person, as appropriate, was correct and complete.

16(2)   An agent or person, as appropriate, required to make and deliver a report under these Regulations shall, whenever required to do so within the period specified in paragraph (4)(c), make available for inspection by an officer of Revenue and Customs, at such time as that officer may reasonably require, all such copies of books, documents or other records in his possession or under his control as may be required by an officer of the Inland Revenue under paragraph (1).

16(3)   An agent or person, as appropriate, required to make and deliver a report under these Regulations shall retain, for the period specified in paragraph (4), all such books, documents and other records copies of which he may be required to make available for inspection under paragraph (2). These documents include copies of the documents presented by relevant payees in accordance with regulation 9.

16(4)   The period specified is–

(a)   in relation to information concerning the identity and country of residence of a relevant payee the period of two years beginning immediately after the end of the tax year in which transactions between the relevant payee and paying agent cease;

(b)   in relation to the official evidence referred to in regulation 4(3) the period of two years beginning immediately after the end of the tax year in which transactions between the entity and paying agent cease; and

(c)   in relation to information concerning savings income the period of two years beginning immediately after the end of the tax year to which the notice referred to in regulation 15(1) relates.

16(5)   Paragraphs (3) and (4) are without prejudice to the following provisions–

(i)   regulations 8(5) and 14(6) of the Income Tax (Deposit-takers and Building Societies) (Interest Payments) Regulations 2008;

(ii)   [Omitted by SI 2008/2682, Sch. 1, para. 2(b).]

(iii)   [Omitted by SI 2008/2682, Sch. 1, para. 2(b).]

(iv)   regulation 9 of the Income Tax (Authorised Unit Trusts) (Interest Distributions) Regulations 2003 including that regulation as modified by regulation 28(8) of the Open-ended Investment Companies (Tax) Regulations 1997.

16(6)   Subject to paragraph (7), information obtained by Revenue and Customs under this Regulation–

(a)   shall not be used for the purpose of ascertaining the tax liability (if any) of any person other than–

    (i)   a person beneficially entitled to a payment to whom the information obtained relates, and

    (ii)   the person by whom the payment was made or received; and

(b)   shall otherwise be used only for the purposes of–

    (i)   these Regulations, unless the notice issued under regulation 15(1) is combined with a notice under section 17 or 18, or both of those sections, of the Taxes Management Act 1970, in which case only for the purposes of these Regulations and with whichever of those sections the notice was combined,

    (ii)   the provisions of Chapter 2 of Part 15 of the Income Tax Act 2007 relating to the deduction of tax from payments by building societies and deposit-takers,

    (iii)   the Income Tax (Deposit-takers and Building Societies) (Interest Payments) Regulations 2008, and

    (iv)   [Omitted by SI 2008/2682, Sch. 1, para. 3(c).]

    (v)   the Income Tax (Authorised Unit Trusts) (Interest Distributions) Regulations 2003 including these Regulations as modified by the Open-ended Investment Companies (Tax) Regulations 1997.

16(7) Paragraph (6) shall not be construed as preventing any disclosure of information under section 182(5) of the Finance Act 1989.

History – In reg. 16(1) the words "Revenue and Customs" substituted for the words "The Inland Revenue" and the words "that officer" substituted for the words "the Revenue" by SI 2005/1539, reg. 16(2), with effect from 1 July 2005 (London Gazette, 14 June 2005).
In reg. 16(2) the words "an officer of Revenue and Customs" substituted for the words "an officer of the Inland Revenue" (in each place where that expression occurs) by SI 2005/1539, reg. 16(3), with effect from 1 July 2005 (London Gazette, 14 June 2005).
In reg. 16(4)(b) the word "entity" substituted for the words "residual entity" by SI 2005/1539, reg. 16(4), with effect from 1 July 2005 (London Gazette, 14 June 2005).
Reg. 16(5)(i) substituted by SI 2008/2682, Sch. 1, para. 2(a), with effect in relation to payments of interest made on or after 31 October 2008. Former reg. 16(5)(i) read:
　　　"(i)　　regulations 11(7) and 15(2) of the Income Tax (Building Societies) (Dividends and Interest) Regulations 1990;".
Reg. 16(5)(ii) omitted by SI 2008/2682, Sch. 1, para. 2(b), with effect in relation to payments of interest made on or after 31 October 2008. Former reg. 16(5)(ii) read:
　　　"(ii)　　regulation 12(2) of the Income Tax (Deposit-takers) (Interest Payments) Regulations 1990;".
Reg. 16(5)(iii) omitted by SI 2008/2682, Sch. 1, para. 2(b), with effect in relation to payments of interest made on or after 31 October 2008. Former reg. 16(5)(iii) read:
　　　"(iii)　　regulation 8 of the Income Tax (Deposit-takers) (Non-residents) Regulations 1992;".
In reg. 16(6)(b)(ii), "Chapter 2 of Part 15 of the Income Tax Act 2007" substituted for "Chapter 4 of Part 12 of the Income and Corporation Taxes Act 1988" by SI 2008/2682, Sch. 1, para. 3(a), with effect in relation to payments of interest made on or after 31 October 2008.
Reg. 16(6)(b)(iii) substituted by SI 2008/2682, Sch. 1, para. 3(b), with effect in relation to payments of interest made on or after 31 October 2008. Former reg. 16(6)(b)(iii) read:
　　　"(iii)　　the Income Tax (Building Societies) (Dividends and Interest) Regulations 1990, ".
Reg. 16(6)(b)(iv) omitted by SI 2008/2682, Sch. 1, para. 3(c), with effect in relation to payments of interest made on or after 31 October 2008. Former reg. 16(6)(b)(iv) read:
　　　"(iv)　　the Income Tax (Deposit-takers) (Interest Payments) Regulations 1990, and".
In reg. 16(6) the words "Revenue and Customs" substituted for the words "the Inland Revenue" by SI 2005/1539, reg. 16(5), with effect from 1 July 2005 (London Gazette, 14 June 2005).

PART 5 – TRANSITIONAL PROVISIONS

TRANSITIONAL PROVISIONS – NEGOTIABLE DEBT SECURITIES

17(1) Until 31st December 2010 negotiable debt securities to which paragraph (2) applies shall not be considered to be money debts.

17(2) This paragraph applies to negotiable debt securities–

(a)　which were first issued before 1st March 2001; or

(b)　for which the original prospectus was approved before that date by–

　　(i)　the competent authority within the meaning of the Securities Directive; or

　　(ii)　the responsible authorities in third countries,

provided that no further issues of such negotiable debt securities are made on or after 1st March 2002.

17(3) Where a further issue is made on or after 1st March 2002 of negotiable debt securities described in paragraphs (2)(a) and (b) issued by a Government or a related entity acting as a public authority or whose role is recognised by an international treaty, as defined in the Schedule, the entire issue of such security, consisting of the original issue and any further issue, shall be considered a money debt.

17(4) If a further issue is made on or after 1st March 2002 of a negotiable debt security described in paragraphs (2)(a) and (b) issued by a person not referred to in paragraph (3), such further issue shall be considered a money debt.

17(5) Where an agent cannot ascertain whether paragraphs (2) to (4) apply the entire issue of the negotiable debt security shall be considered a money debt.

17(6) A negotiable debt security is a security that can be transferred from one creditor to another without the approval of the debtor.

SCHEDULE

Regulation 17(3)

NEGOTIABLE DEBT SECURITIES: ENTITIES REFERRED TO IN REGULATION 17(3)

For the purposes of regulation 17(3), an entity is "a related entity acting as a public authority or whose role is recognised by an international treaty" if it is listed in Table 1 or Table 2 below or it is situate in a third country and meets the following criteria–

(a)　the entity is clearly considered to be a public entity according to the national criteria;

(b)   such public entity is a non-market producer which administers and finances a group of activities, principally providing non-market goods and services, intended for the benefit of the community and which are effectively controlled by general government;

(c)   such public entity is a large and regular issuer of debt; and

(d)   the State concerned is able to guarantee that such public entity will not exercise early redemption in the event of gross-up clauses.

Table 1   Entities within the European Union

Member State	Entity
Belgium	Vlaams Gewest (Flemish Region)
	Région wallonne (Walloon Region)
	Région bruxelloise/Brussels Gewest (Brussels Region)
	Communauté française (French Community)
	Vlaamse Gemeenschap (Flemish Community)
	Deutschsprachige Gemeinschaft (German-speaking Community)
Bulgaria	Общините (municipalities)
	Социалноосигурителни фондове (Social Security Funds)
France	La Caisse d'amortissement de la dette sociale (CADES) (Social Debt Redemption Fund)
	L'Agence française de développement (AFD) (French Development Agency)
	Réseau Ferré de France (RFF) (French Rail Network)
	Caisse Nationale des Autoroutes (CNA) (National Motorways Fund)
	Assistance publique Hôpitaux de Paris (APHP) (Paris Hospitals Public Assistance)
	Charbonnages de France (CDF) (French Coal Board)
	Entreprise minière et chimique (EMC) (Mining and Checmicals Company)
Greece	Organismsz Thlepikoinulnwv Elladoz (National Telecommunications Organisation)
	Organismsz Sidhrodrsmwn Elladoz (National Railways Organisation)
	Dhmssia Epíxeirhsh Hlektrismon (Public Electricity Company)
Italy	Regions
	Provinces
	Municipalities
	Cassa Depositi e Prestiti (Deposits and Loans Fund)
Latvia	Pašvaldības (Local governments)
Poland	Gminy (Communes)
	Powiaty (Provinces)
	Województwa (Districts)
	Związki gmin (Associations of Communes)
	Związki powiatów (Associations of Provinces)
	Związki województw (Associations of Districts)
	Miasto Stołeczne Warszawa (Capital City of Warsaw)
	Agencja Restrukturyzacji I Modernizacji Rolnictwa (Agency for Reconstruction and Modernisation of Agriculture)
	Agencja Nieruchomosci Rolnych (Agricultural Property Agency)
Portugal	Região Autónoma de Madeira (Autonomous Region of Madeira)
	Região Autónoma dos Açores (Autonomous Region of Azores)
	Municipalities
Romania	autoritățile administrației publice locale (local public administration authorities)
Slovakia	Mestá a Obce (Municipalities)
	Železnice Slovenskej republiky (Slovak Railway Company)
	Štátny Fond Cestného Hospodártsva (State Road Management Fund)
	Slovenské Elektrárne (Slovak Power Plants)
	Vodohospodárska výstavba (Water Economy Building Company)

Member State	Entity
Spain	Xunta de Galicia (Regional Executive of Galicia)
	Junta de Andalucía (Regional Executive of Andalusia)
	Junta de Extremadura (Regional Executive of Extremadura)
	Junta de Castilla-La Mancha (Regional Executive of Castilla-La Mancha)
	Junta de Castilla-León (Regional Executive of Castilla-León)
	Gobierno Foral de Navarra (Regional Government of Navarre)
	Govern de les Illes Balears (Government of the Balearic Islands)
	Generalitat de Catalunya (Autonomous Government of Catalonia)
	Generalitat de Valencia (Autonomous Government of Valencia)
	Diputación General de Aragón (Regional Council of Aragon)
	Gobierno de las Islas Canarias (Government of the Canary Islands)
	Gobierno de Murcia (Government of Murcia)
	Gobierno de Madrid (Government of Madrid)
	Gobierno de la Comunidad Autónoma del País Vasco/Euzkadi (Government of the Autonomous Community of the Basque Country)
	Diputación Foral de Guipúzcoa (Regional Council of Guipúzcoa)
	Diputación Foral de Vizcaya/Bizkaia (Regional Council of Vizcaya)
	Diputación Foral de Alava (Regional Council of Alava)
	Ayuntamiento de Madrid (City Council of Madrid)
	Ayuntamiento de Barcelona (City Council of Barcelona)
	Cabildo Insular de Gran Canaria (Island Council of Gran Canaria)
	Cabildo Insular de Tenerife (Island Council of Tenerife)
	Instituto de Crédito Oficial (Public Credit Institution)
	Instituto Catalán de Finanzas (Finance Institution of Catalonia)
	Instituto Valenciano de Finanzas (Finance Institution of Valencia)

History – In Table 1 the entries for Bulgaria and Romania inserted by SI 2006/3286, reg. 2, with effect from 1 January 2007. In Table 1 the entries for Latvia and Poland inserted after the entries for Italy by SI 2005/1539, reg. 17(a), with effect from 1 July 2005 (London Gazette, 14 June 2005).
In Table 1 the entries for Slovakia inserted after the entries for Portugal by SI 2005/1539, reg. 17(b), with effect from 1 July 2005 (London Gazette, 14 June 2005).
In Table 1, in the first entry for Spain, the word "Galicia" substituted for the word "Galacia" by SI 2005/1539, reg. 17(c), with effect from 1 July 2005 (London Gazette, 14 June 2005).

Table 2   International entities

European Bank for Reconstruction and Development
European Investment Bank
Asian Development Bank
African Development Bank
World Bank/IBRD/IMF
International Finance Corporation
Inter-American Development Bank
Council of Europe Social Development Fund
Euratom
European Community
Corporación Andina de Fomento (CAF) (Andean Development Corporation)
Eurofima
European Coal and Steel Community
Nordic Investment Bank
Caribbean Development Bank
Note: The provisions of regulation 17 are without prejudice to any international obligations that member States or territories with which arrangements have been made may have entered into with respect of the international entities listed in Table 2.

History – In the Note at the end of Table 2, the words "or territories with which arrangements have been made" inserted after the words "member States" by SI 2005/1539, reg. 17(d), with effect from 1 July 2005 (London Gazette, 14 June 2005).

Statutory Instruments

URBAN REGENERATION COMPANIES (TAX) (DESIGNATION) ORDER 2004

(SI 2004/439)

Made on 23 February 2004 by the Treasury, in exercise of the powers conferred upon them by s. 79B(5) of the Income and Corporation Taxes Act 1988, and being satisfied that each of the criteria listed in s. 79B(7) have been met. Operative from 24 February 2004.

CITATION, COMMENCEMENT AND EFFECT

1(1)   This Order may be cited as the Urban Regeneration Companies (Tax) (Designation) Order 2004 and shall come into force on 24th February 2004.

1(2)   Article 2 takes effect on 1st April 2003.

1(3)   Article 3 takes effect on 8th April 2003.

1(4)   Article 4 takes effect on 17th July 2003.

1(5)   Article 5 takes effect on 2nd December 2003.

DESIGNATION OF URBAN REGENERATION COMPANIES TAKING EFFECT ON 1ST APRIL 2003

2   For the purposes of section 79B of the Income and Corporation Taxes Act 1988 the following companies limited by guarantee are designated as urban regeneration companies–

(a)   Bradford City Centre Urban Regeneration Company Limited;

(b)   Camborne Pool Redruth Urban Regeneration Company Limited;

(c)   Corby Urban Regeneration Company Limited;

(d)   Hull Urban Regeneration Company Limited;

(e)   Leicester Regeneration Company Limited;

(f)   Liverpool Vision;

(g)   New East Manchester Limited;

(h)   Newport Urban Regeneration Company Limited;

(i)   Sheffield City Centre Urban Regeneration Company Limited;

(j)   Sunderland ARC Limited;

(k)   Swindon Urban Regeneration Company Limited; and

(l)   Tees Valley Urban Regeneration Company Limited.

DESIGNATION OF URBAN REGENERATION COMPANIES TAKING EFFECT ON 8TH APRIL 2003

3   For the purposes of section 79B of the Income and Corporation Taxes Act 1988 the following companies limited by guarantee are designated as urban regeneration companies–

(a)   Derby Cityscape Limited;

(b)   Sandwell Regeneration Company Limited; and

(c)   Furness West Cumbria New Vision Urban Regeneration Company Limited.

DESIGNATION OF URBAN REGENERATION COMPANY TAKING EFFECT ON 17TH JULY 2003

4   For the purposes of section 79B of the Income and Corporation Taxes Act 1988 Ilex Urban Regeneration Company Limited, a company limited by guarantee, is designated as an urban regeneration company.

DESIGNATION OF URBAN REGENERATION COMPANY TAKING EFFECT ON 2ND DECEMBER 2003

5   For the purposes of section 79B of the Income and Corporation Taxes Act 1988 Walsall Regeneration Company Limited, a company limited by guarantee, is designated as an urban regeneration company.

TAXATION OF BENEFITS UNDER GOVERNMENT PILOT SCHEMES (WORKING NEIGHBOURHOODS PILOT AND IN WORK CREDIT) ORDER 2004

(SI 2004/575)

Made on 4 March 2004 by the Treasury, in exercise of the powers conferred upon them by s. 151(1)(a) and (7)(a) of the Finance Act 1996. Operative from 6 April 2004.

CITATION AND COMMENCEMENT

1(1)   This Order may be cited as the Taxation of Benefits under Government Pilot Schemes (Working Neighbourhoods Pilot and In Work Credit) Order 2004.

1(2)   This Order shall come into force on 6th April 2004.

INTERPRETATION

2   In this Order–

"**benefit**" has the meaning given by subsection (6) of section 151 of the Finance Act 1996;

"**Government pilot scheme**" has the meaning given by subsections (3) and (4) of section 151 of the Finance Act 1996;

"**In-Work Credit**" and "**Working Neighbourhoods Pilot**" mean benefits under the Government pilot schemes known by those names.

EXEMPTIONS FROM INCOME TAX

3   The Income Tax Acts shall have effect in relation to any amount of payment by way of In-Work Credit or by way of the Working Neighbourhoods Pilot, as if that amount were wholly exempt from income tax and accordingly to be disregarded in computing the amount of any receipts brought into account for income tax purposes.

RESEARCH AND DEVELOPMENT (PRESCRIBED ACTIVITIES) REGULATIONS 2004

(SI 2004/712)

Made on 11 March 2004 by the Treasury, in exercise of the powers conferred upon them by s. 837A(3) of the Income and Corporation Taxes Act 1988. Operative from 1 April 2004.

CITATION, COMMENCEMENT AND EFFECT

1(1) These Regulations may be cited as the Research and Development (Prescribed Activities) Regulations 2004, come into force on 1st April 2004, and subject to paragraphs (2) to (9) have effect–

(a) for the purposes of corporation tax, for accounting periods ending on or after 1st April 2004, and

(b) for the purposes of income tax and capital gains tax, in relation to the year 2004–05 and subsequent years of assessment.

1(2) These Regulations have effect in relation to shares issued on or after 6th April 2004 in relation to Chapter 3 of Part 7 of the Income and Corporation Taxes Act 1988 (enterprise investment scheme).

1(3) Nothing in these Regulations affects the operation of the following provisions in relation to shares issued before 6th April 2004–

(a) Chapter 3 of Part 7 of the Income and Corporation Taxes Act 1988 (enterprise investment scheme);

(b) sections 573 and 574 of that Act (relief for losses on unlisted shares in trading companies); and

(c) Schedule 5B to the Taxation of Chargeable Gains Act 1992 (enterprise investment scheme: re-investment).

1(4) These Regulations have effect for the purpose of determining whether shares or securities issued on or after 6th April 2004 are, for the purposes of section 842AA of the Income and Corporation Taxes Act 1988 (venture capital trusts), to be regarded as comprised in a company's qualifying holdings.

1(5) Nothing in these Regulations affects the operation of Schedule 28B to the Income and Corporation Taxes Act 1988 as it has effect for the purpose of determining whether shares or securities issued before 6th April 2004 are, for the purposes of section 842AA of the Income and Corporation Taxes Act 1988, to be regarded as comprised in a company's qualifying holdings.

1(6) These Regulations have effect in relation to shares issued on or after 6th April 2004 in relation to Schedule 15 to the Finance Act 2000 (corporate venturing scheme).

1(7) Nothing in these Regulations affects the operation of the Schedule specified in paragraph (6) in relation to shares issued before 6th April 2004.

1(8) In relation to–

(a) Chapter 9 of Part 7 of the Income Tax (Earnings and Pensions) Act 2003 (enterprise management incentives), and

(b) Part 4 of Schedule 7D to the Taxation of Chargeable Gains Act 1992 (enterprise management incentives),

these Regulations have effect in relation to share options granted on or after 6th April 2004.

1(9) Nothing in these Regulations affects the operation of the provisions specified in paragraph (8) in relation to share options granted before 6th April 2004.

ACTIVITIES PRESCRIBED AS RESEARCH AND DEVELOPMENT

2 For the purposes of section 837A of the Income and Corporation Taxes Act 1988–

(a) activities that fall to be treated as research and development in accordance with the "Guidelines on the Meaning of Research and Development for Tax Purposes" issued by the Secretary of State for Trade and Industry on 5 March 2004, are research and development; and

(b) activities that do not fall to be treated as such in accordance with those guidelines are not research and development.

REVOCATION OF THE RESEARCH AND DEVELOPMENT (PRESCRIBED ACTIVITIES) REGULATIONS 2000

3 The Research and Development (Prescribed Activities) Regulations 2000 are revoked.

CHILD TRUST FUNDS REGULATIONS 2004

(SI 2004/1450, as amended by SI 2004/2676, SI 2004/3382, SI 2005/383, SI 2005/909, SI 2005/2919, SI 2005/3349, SI 2006/199, SI 2006/2684, SI 2006/3195, SI 2007/1898, SI 2009/56, SI 2009/475, SI 2009/694, SI 2010/582, SI 2010/836, SI 2010/1894, SI 2010/2599, SI 2011/781, SI 2011/992, SI 2011/2447, SI 2012/886, SI 2012/1870, SI 2013/263, SI 2013/1744, SI 2013/1765, SI 2013/1773, SI 2014/649 and SI 2014/1453)

Made on 27 May 2004 by the Treasury, in exercise of the powers conferred upon them by s. 3(1) to (5) and (7), 5(1), (4) and (5), 6, 7, 8(1), 9(2) and (10)(b), 11(1), 12(2), 13, 15, 16, 23(1) and 28(1) to (4) of the Child Trust Funds Act 2004. Operative from 27 May 2004.

ARRANGEMENT OF REGULATIONS

REGULATION

PART 1 – INTRODUCTORY

PART 2 – OTHER REQUIREMENTS TO BE SATISFIED IN RELATION TO ACCOUNTS

PART 3 – TAX AND ADMINISTRATION OF ACCOUNTS

PART 1 – INTRODUCTORY

CITATION AND COMMENCEMENT

1   These Regulations may be cited as the Child Trust Funds Regulations 2004 and shall come into force for the purposes of–

(a)   issuing vouchers (see regulation 3),

(b)   completing account-opening formalities (see regulation 5),

(c)   applications under regulation 13 to open an account with effect from the appointed day,

(d)   applications under regulation 14 to be approved as an account provider to manage accounts from the appointed day,

(e)   regulation 17, so far as it relates to applications referred to in paragraph (d),

(f)   [omitted by SI 2013/263, reg. 2(4)(a).]

on 1st January 2005, and for all other purposes on the appointed day.

History – Reg. 1(f) (and the "and" before it) omitted by SI 2013/263, reg. 2(4)(a), with effect from 16 March 2013, in respect of what would otherwise be fortnightly and initial return periods within reg. 30(1) beginning on or after that day. Former reg. 1(f) read as follows:

"(f)   making a fortnightly claim and financial return (see regulation 30),".

Notes – The appointed day is 6 April 2005 by virtue of SI 2004/3369, reg. 2.

INTERPRETATION

2(1)   In these Regulations–

(a)   the following expressions have the meanings given in the Child Trust Funds Act 2004 ("the Act")–

     "child"

     "child trust fund"

     "eligible child"

     "Inland Revenue"

     "Inland Revenue contributions" (see section 11(2) of the Act),

     "parental responsibility" (see section 3(9) of the Act);

     "relevant person" (see section 15(2) of the Act),

     "relevant social security benefit" (see section 9(6) of the Act) "**responsible person**", in relation to a child under 16 (see section 3(8) of the Act),

"**tax year**" (see section 9(6) of the Act)

"**the income threshold**" (see section 9(6) of the Act)

"**the person entitled to child benefit in respect of the child**" (see section 2(1)(a), (4) and (6) of the Act);

"**the relevant income**" (see section 9(6) of the Act)

(b)   except where the context otherwise requires–

"**account**" means a scheme of investment which (except in regulation 22(1)) qualifies as a child trust fund, other than in the cases of–

(i)   an account with a deposit-taker,

(ii)   a share or deposit account with a building society, or

(iii) a deposit account with a person falling within section 991(2) of the Income Tax Act 2007, or a credit union;

an "**account investment**" is an investment under the account which is a qualifying investment for an account within the meaning of regulation 12;

an "**account provider**" is a person who fulfils the conditions of these Regulations and is approved by the Board for the purpose of these Regulations as an account provider;

"**adoption order**" has the meaning in section 46(1) of the Adoption and Children Act 2002 or section 28 of the Adoption and Children (Scotland) Act 2007 or of "Adoption Order" in Article 2(2) of the Adoption (Northern Ireland) Order 1987, as the case may be, and includes any corresponding order under the Adoption (Scotland) Act 1978, and any order of a court in the Isle of Man or any of the Channel Islands which, under section 108 of the Adoption and Children Act 2002, is declared to correspond to an adoption order made under that Act;

"**appointed day**" means the day appointed under section 27 of the Act, for the purposes of sections 8 and 9 of the Act;

"**assurance undertaking**" has the meaning in Article 2 of the Council Directive of 5 November 2002 concerning life assurance (No. 2002/83);

"**Bank of England base rate**" means the rate announced from time to time by the Monetary Policy Committee of the Bank of England as the official dealing rate, being the rate at which the Bank is willing to enter into transactions for providing short-term liquidity in the money markets;

"**the Board**" means the Commissioners for Her Majesty's Revenue and Customs;

"**building society**" means a building society within the meaning of the Building Societies Act 1986, or the Irish Building Societies Act 1989;

"**building society bonus**", except in regulation 24(a)(i), excludes any bonus, distribution of funds or the conferring of rights in relation to shares–

(a)   in connection with an amalgamation, transfer of engagements or transfer of business of a building society, and

(b)   mentioned in section 96 or 100 of the Building Societies Act 1986, and "payment under a building society bonus scheme" shall be construed accordingly;

"**company**", except in regulation 12(4)(a), means any body corporate having a share capital other than–

(i)   an open-ended investment company, within the meaning given by section 236 of the Financial Services and Markets Act 2000,

(ii)   a UCITS,

(iii) an industrial and provident society, or

(iv)   a body corporate which is a 51 per cent. subsidiary of any industrial and provident society;

"**credit union**" means a society registered as a credit union under the Industrial and Provident Societies Act 1965 or the Credit Unions (Northern Ireland) Order 1985;

"**deposit-taker**" has the meaning given by section 853 (as extended under section 854) of ITA 2007);

"**the Director of Savings**" has the same meaning as in the National Debt Act 1972;

"**the Distance Marketing Directive**" means Directive 2002/65/EC of the European Parliament and of the Council of 23 September 2002, and includes any provisions by which an EEA State or the United Kingdom has transposed the Directive or has corresponding obligations in its domestic law, and "distance contract" has the meaning in that Directive;

"electronic communications" includes any communications by means of a telecommunication system (within the meaning in the Telecommunications Act 1984;

"EEA Agreement" means the agreement on the European Economic Area signed at Oporto on 2nd May 1992, together with the Protocol adjusting that Agreement signed at Brussels on 17th March 1993, as modified or supplemented from time to time;

"EEA State", in relation to any time, means a state which at that time is a member State, or any other state which at that time is a party to the EEA Agreement;

"European institution" means an EEA firm of the kind mentioned in paragraph 5(a) to (d), (f) and (h) of Schedule 3 to the Financial Services and Markets Act 2000 which is an authorised person for the purposes of that Act as a result of qualifying for authorisation under paragraph 12(1) to (4) and (7) of that Schedule;

"51 per cent. subsidiary" and **"75 per cent. subsidiary"** have the meanings given by section 838 of the Taxes Act;

"FISMA 2000" means the Financial Services and Markets Act 2000;

"gains", except in regulations 22(1) to (3), 24(a)(ii), (iii) and (v), 37(5) and 38, means "chargeable gains" within the meaning in the 1992 Act;

"gilt-edged securities" has the meaning given by paragraphs 1 and 1A of Schedule 9 to the 1992 Act;

"guardian" means a guardian of a child within the meaning in section 5 of the Children Act 1989, section 7 of the Children (Scotland) Act 1995 or Article 2(2) of the Children (Northern Ireland) Order 1995, as the case may be;

"incorporated friendly society" means a society incorporated under the Friendly Societies Act 1992;

"industrial and provident society" means a society registered or deemed to be registered under the Industrial and Provident Societies Act 1965 or under the Industrial and Provident Societies (Northern Ireland) Act 1969;

"investments under the account" has the same meaning as investments under a child trust fund in the Act;

"investment trust" refers to a company that is such a trust for the purposes of the Corporation Tax Acts, or would be such a trust but for section 1158(3) of the Corporation Tax Act 2010;

"ITA 2007" means the Income Tax Act 2007;

"ITTOIA 2005" means the Income Tax (Trading and Other Income) Act 2005;

"the Management Act" means the Taxes Management Act 1970;

"market value" shall be construed in accordance with section 272 of the 1992 Act;

"the 1992 Act" means the Taxation of Chargeable Gains Act 1992;

"non-UCITS retail scheme"–

(a)   has the meaning in the Collective Investment Schemes Sourcebook (that is, a scheme to which, or to whose authorised fund manager and depositary, Sections 5.1, 5.4 and 5.6 of that Sourcebook apply),

(b)   includes a "recognised scheme" by virtue of section 272 of the Financial Services and Markets Act 2000, which would fall within paragraph (a) of this definition if it were an authorised fund, and

(c)   includes a sub-fund of an umbrella which the terms of the scheme identify as a sub-fund which would fall within paragraph (a) or (b) of this definition if it were itself an authorised fund or a recognised scheme.

In this definition, expressions defined in the Glossary forming part of the Financial Services Authority Handbook have those defined meanings;

"notice", except in regulations 12(12) and 37(6)(a), means notice in writing;

"qualifying units in or shares of a non-UCITS retail scheme" means that–

(a)   the instrument constituting the scheme secures that redemption of the units or shares in question shall take place no less frequently than bi-monthly (see Rule 6.2.16(6) of the Collective Investment Schemes Sourcebook omitting the words "Except where (7) applies, and", read with Rule 6.3.4(1), whether or not those Rules apply to the scheme), and

(b) a provision for suspension of dealings in exceptional conditions in accordance with Rule 7.2 of that Sourcebook (or any foreign procedure which is a direct foreign equivalent of that Rule) shall not be treated as a provision contrary to paragraph (a) of this definition;

"recognised stock exchange" has the same meaning as in section 1005 of ITA 2007;

"registered friendly society" has the meaning given by the Friendly Societies Act 1992 and includes any society that by virtue of section 96(2) of that Act is to be treated as a registered friendly society;

"relevant authorised person" means a firm mentioned in section 697(2)(b) of ITTOIA 2005;

"security" means any loan stock or similar security of a company whether secured or unsecured;

"special guardian" has the meaning in section 14A of the Children Act 1989;

"subscriptions" has the meaning in section 12(1) of the Act (but excluding Inland Revenue contributions and income or gains arising from investments under the account);

"tax" where neither income tax nor capital gains tax is specified means either of those taxes;

"the Taxes Act" means the Income and Corporation Taxes Act 1988;

"year", except in the expression "subscription year" in regulations 9, 21(5)(b) and 32(2)(b)(iv), means a year of assessment (within the meaning in section 832(1) of the Taxes Act, or section 288(1) of the 1992 Act, as the case may be);

(c) **"authorised fund"** means–

(i) an authorised unit trust, or

(ii) an open-ended investment company in the case of which an authorisation order made by the Financial Services Authority under regulation 14 of the Open-Ended Investment Companies Regulations 2001 is in force;

"authorised unit trust" means a unit trust scheme in the case of which an authorisation order made by the Financial Services Authority under section 243 of the Financial Services and Markets Act 2000 is in force;

"the Collective Investment Schemes Sourcebook" means the sourcebook of that name made by the Financial Services Authority under the Financial Services and Markets Act 2000;

"depositary interest" means the rights of the person mentioned in paragraph (ii), under a certificate or other record (whether or not in the form of a document) acknowledging–

(i) that a person holds relevant investments or evidence of the right to them, and

(ii) that another person is entitled to rights in or in relation to those or identical relevant investments, including the right to receive such investments, or evidence of the right to them or the proceeds from such investments, from the person mentioned in paragraph (i),

where **"relevant investments"** means investments which are exclusively qualifying investments for an account falling within regulation 12(2)(a) to (i), and the rights mentioned in paragraph (ii) are exclusively rights in or in relation to relevant investments;

"insolvency event" means the procedures listed in the definition of "insolvency event" in regulation 19(15) of the Payment Services Regulations 2009;

"open-ended investment company" means a company to which section 236 of FISMA 2000 applies, and "shares" in relation to an open-ended investment company, includes shares of any class and of any denomination of a given class and, in relation to a part of an umbrella company, means shares in the company which confer for the time being rights in that part;

"recognised UCITS" means–

(a) a collective investment scheme constituted in an EEA State, which is a "recognised scheme" under section 264 of FISMA 2000, and complies with the requirements to be a "UCITS scheme" for the purposes of the Collective Investment Schemes Sourcebook (see in particular COLL 1.2.2), or

(b) a part of a recognised UCITS mentioned in paragraph (a) of this definition, which would be a sub-fund of an umbrella scheme which is a recognised UCITS;

"UK UCITS" means–

(a) a collective investment scheme authorised under section 31(1)(a) of FISMA 2000, which complies with the requirements to be a "UCITS scheme" for the purposes of the Collective Investment Schemes Sourcebook (see in particular COLL 1.2.2), or

Statutory instruments

(b)   a part of a UK UCITS mentioned in paragraph (a) of this definition which would be a sub-fund of an umbrella scheme which is a UK UCITS;

"umbrella scheme" means an authorised fund which according to the terms of the scheme is an umbrella scheme belonging to the category under that name established by the Financial Services Authority, and

    (i)   in the case of an authorised fund which is an authorised unit trust, references to a part of an umbrella scheme shall be construed in accordance with subsection (8) of section 468 of the Taxes Act and paragraphs (6) and (7) of regulation 7 of the Authorised Investment Funds (Tax) Regulations 2006 shall apply for the purposes of these Regulations as they apply for the purposes of those Regulations;

    (ii) in the case of an authorised fund which is an open-ended investment company, references to a part of an umbrella scheme shall be construed in accordance with subsection (4) of section 468A of the Taxes Act, and paragraphs (2) and (3) of regulation 7 of the Authorised Investment Funds (Tax) Regulations 2006 shall apply for the purposes of these Regulations as they apply for the purposes of those Regulations;

"units", in relation to an authorised unit trust, means the rights or interests (however described) of the unit holders in that unit trust and, in relation to a part of an umbrella scheme, means the rights or interests for the time being of the unit holders in that part;

"units in, or shares of, a UK UCITS or recognised UCITS" means the rights (however described) of the holders of the units or shares in that UK UCITS or recognised UCITS.

2(1A) In these Regulations–

(a)   a **"bulk transfer of accounts"** occurs where two or more accounts are transferred, without a break in the management of the accounts, by an account provider ("the transferor") direct to another account provider ("the transferee")–

    (i)   pursuant to an agreement made between the transferor and the transferee where the transfers are not made pursuant to requests made by the person who is the registered contact in relation to the accounts transferred; or

    (ii) pursuant to an insurance business transfer scheme or a banking business transfer scheme under Part 7 (Control of Business Transfers) of FISMA 2000;

(b)   a **"group transfer of accounts"** occurs where a bulk transfer of accounts is made between account providers that are members of the same group of companies when the transfer occurs;

(c)   two companies are members of the same group of companies if–

    (i)   one is a 75% subsidiary of the other, or

    (ii) both are 75% subsidiaries of a third company.

2(2)   The table below indexes other definitions in these Regulations:

Term defined	Regulation
"the applicant"	5
"the commencement date"	7(8)
"description" of an account	4
"the disqualifying circumstances"	16
"initial contribution"	7(1)
"interim tax claim"	26(2)
"local authority"	33(1)
"looked after child"	33(1)
"management agreement"	5
"the named child"	5 and 8(1)
"qualifying circumstances"	14
"qualifying investments for an account"	12
"registered contact"	8(1)(d)
"special contribution"	7(1)
"subscription year"	9(2)

Term defined	Regulation
"supplementary contribution"	7(5)
the "termination event"	12(12)
"the transfer instructions"	8(2)(h)
"the internal transfer instructions".	8(2)(i)

History – In reg. 2(1)(a), the definitions of "relevant social security benefit", "tax year", "the income threshold" and "the relevant income" inserted by SI 2009/475, reg. 3, with effect where the Child Benefit commencement date for the child (first day for which child benefit was paid in respect of the child) is on or after 6 April 2008.

In reg. 2(1)(b), in the definition of "account", the words "section 991(2) of the Income Tax Act 2007" substituted for the words "section 840A(1)(b) of the Taxes Act" by SI 2014/649, reg. 3(a), with effect from 6 April 2014.

In reg. 2(1)(b), in the definition of "account", the words "credit union" substituted for the words "relevant European institution" by SI 2010/582, reg. 3(1)(a), with effect from 6 April 2010.

In reg. 2(1)(b), in the definition of "deposit-taker", the words "section 853 (as extended under section 854) of ITA 2007)" substituted for the words "section 481(2) of the Taxes Act" by SI 2010/582, reg. 3(1)(b), with effect from 6 April 2010.

In reg. 2(1)(b), definition of "EEA Agreement" substituted by SI 2013/1744, reg. 3(a), with effect from 5 August 2013. Former definition read as follows:

""EEA Agreement" means the Agreement on the European Economic Area signed at Oporto on 2 May 1992, as adjusted by the Protocol signed at Brussels on 17 March 1993;".

In reg. 2(1)(b), definition of "EEA State" substituted by SI 2013/1744, reg. 3(a), with effect from 5 August 2013. Former definition read as follows:

""EEA State" means a State, other than the United Kingdom, which is a Contracting Party to the EEA Agreement;".

In reg. 2(1)(b), in the definition of "European institution", the words "paragraph 5(a) to (d), (f) and (h)" substituted for the words "paragraph 5(a), (b) or (c)" and the words "(1) to (4) and (7)" inserted by SI 2014/649, reg. 3(b), with effect from 6 April 2014.

In reg. 2(1)(b), the definition of "investment trust" substituted by SI 2014/649, reg. 3(c), with effect from 6 April 2014.

In reg. 2(1)(b), in the definition of "investment trust", the words ", and references to the "eligible rental income" of an investment trust have the same meaning as in that section" omitted by SI 2010/582, reg. 3(1)(c), with effect from 6 April 2010.

In reg. 2(1)(b), the definitions of "the New Collective Investment Schemes Sourcebook" and "relevant European institution" omitted by SI 2010/582, reg. 3(1)(d), with effect from 6 April 2010.

In reg. 2(1)(b), in paragraph (a) of the definitions of "non-UCITS retail scheme" and "qualifying units in or shares of a non-UCITS retail scheme", the word "New", which preceded the words "Collective Investment Schemes Sourcebook" in each case, omitted by SI 2010/582, reg. 3(1)(e), with effect from 6 April 2010.

In reg. 2(1)(b), in the definition of "non-UCITS retail scheme", in para. (b), the words "270 or" omitted by SI 2013/1773, reg. 81 and Sch. 2, para. 18, with effect from 22 July 2013.

In reg. 2(1)(b), in the definition of "recognised stock exchange", the words "section 1005 of ITA 2007" substituted for the words "section 841 of the Taxes Act" by SI 2013/1744, reg. 3(b), with effect from 5 August 2013.

In reg. 2(1)(b), the definition of "relevant authorised person" substituted by SI 2010/582, reg. 3(1)(f), with effect from 6 April 2010.

In reg. 2(1)(b), the definitions of "adoption order", "FISMA 2000", "guardian", "ITA 2007", "ITTOIA 2005" and "special guardian" inserted by SI 2010/582, reg. 3(1)(g), with effect from 6 April 2010.

In reg. 2(1)(b) the definition of "the Board" substituted by SI 2005/3349, reg. 3(a), with effect from 27 December 2005.

In reg. 2(1)(b) the definition of "building society bonus" inserted by SI 2006/3195, reg. 3 with effect from 1 January 2007.

In reg. 2(1)(b) the definitions of "the New Collective Investment Schemes Sourcebook", "non-UCITS retail scheme" and "qualifying units in or shares of a non-UCITS retail scheme" inserted by SI 2005/3349, reg. 3(b), with effect from 27 December 2005.

In reg. 2(1)(b) the definition of "credit union" inserted by SI 2005/909, reg. 3, with effect from 6 April 2005.

In reg. 2(1)(b) the definition of "Bank of England base rate" inserted by SI 2004/2676, reg. 3, with effect from the date SI 2004/1450 is brought into force (6 April 2005).

In reg. 2(1)(c), in the definition of "authorised fund" in paragraph (ii), the words "with variable capital incorporated in the United Kingdom", which followed the words "an open-ended investment company", omitted by SI 2010/582, reg. 3(2)(a), with effect from 6 April 2010.

In reg. 2(1)(c), the definitions of "fund of funds scheme", "money market scheme", "securities scheme", "the 1997 Regulations" and "warrant scheme" omitted by SI 2010/582, reg. 3(2)(b), with effect from 6 April 2010.

In reg. 2(1)(c), in the definition of "open-ended investment company", the words "means a company to which section 236 of FISMA 2000 applies" substituted for the words ", except in sub-paragraph (a), has the meaning given by subsection (10) of section 468 of the Taxes Act as that subsection is added in relation to openended investment companies by regulation 10(4) of the 1997 Regulations" by SI 2010/582, reg. 3(2)(c), with effect from 6 April 2010.

In reg. 2(1)(c), the definitions of "unit holder", "unit trust scheme" and "UCITS" omitted by SI 2010/582, reg. 3(2)(d), with effect from 6 April 2010.

In reg. 2(1)(c), in the definition of "umbrella scheme" in paragraph (i), the words "and paragraphs (6) and (7) of regulation 7 of the Authorised Investment Funds (Tax) Regulations 2006 shall apply for the purposes of these Regulations as they apply for the purposes of those Regulations" substituted for the words ", and, in relation to a part of an umbrella scheme, references to investments subject to the trusts of an authorised unit trust and to a unit holder shall be construed in accordance with subsection (9) of that section, and" by SI 2010/582, reg. 3(2)(e)(i), with effect from 6 April 2010.

In reg. 2(1)(c), in the definition of "umbrella scheme" in paragraph (ii), the words "subsection (4) of section 468A of the Taxes Act, and paragraphs (2) and (3) of regulation 7 of the Authorised Investment Funds (Tax) Regulations 2006 shall apply for the purposes of these Regulations as they apply for the purposes of those Regulations" substituted for the words "subsection (18) of section 468 of the Taxes Act as that subsection is added in relation to open-ended investment companies by regulation 10(4) of the 1997 Regulations, and, in relation to a part of an umbrella scheme, references to investments of the company shall be construed in accordance with subsection (12) of that section as so added" by SI 2010/582, reg. 3(2)(e)(ii), with effect from 6 April 2010.

In reg. 2(1)(c), the definitions of "insolvency event", "recognised UCITS", "UK UCITS" and "units in, or shares of, a UK UCITS or recognised UCITS" inserted by SI 2010/582, reg. 3(2)(f), with effect from 6 April 2010.

In the table in reg. 2(2), entries in relation to "first return period", "fortnightly period" and "second return period" omitted by SI 2013/263, reg. 2(4)(b), with effect from 16 March 2013, in respect of what would otherwise be fortnightly and initial return periods within reg. 30(1) beginning on or after that day.

Reg. 2(1A) inserted by SI 2013/1744, reg. 4, with effect from 5 August 2013.

VOUCHERS

3(1) The voucher to be issued under section 5(1) of the Act shall contain the following particulars–

(a)   the full name of the child,

(b)   his date of birth,

(c)   his unique reference number,

(d)   the short expiry date of the voucher, and

(e)   the amount of the initial contribution (see regulation 7(1)),

and a statement that the voucher cannot be exchanged for money.

3(2) The voucher shall be sent to the person who is entitled to child benefit in respect of the child (or, in the case of a child who is an eligible child because of section 2(3) of the Act, to a responsible person in relation to the child) by post.

3(3) The expiry date shall be whichever is the earlier of–

(a)   the date 12 months from the date of issue of the voucher, or

(b)   where the child is over 17 years of age, the date on which he will attain the age of 18 years.

3(4) But for references in these Regulations to the short expiry date of the voucher paragraph (3) applies with "60 days" instead of "12 months".

History – In reg. 3(1)(d), the words "short expiry date" substituted for the words "expiry date" by SI 2011/2447, reg. 3(a), with effect from 1 November 2011 but only in relation to vouchers issued on or after 1 January 2012.

In reg. 3(3), the words "(when the voucher shall cease to be valid)" omitted by SI 2006/199, reg. 3, with effect from 7 February 2006.

Reg. 3(4) inserted by SI 2011/2447, reg. 3(b), with effect from 1 November 2011 but only in relation to vouchers issued on or after 1 January 2012.

DESCRIPTIONS OF ACCOUNTS

4(1) An account may be of either of the following descriptions–

Stakeholder account

Where the account meets the characteristics and conditions in the Schedule to these Regulations.

Non-stakeholder account

Where any of those characteristics or conditions is not met.

4(2) Accounts opened by the Inland Revenue (see regulation 6) must be stakeholder accounts.

OPENING OF ACCOUNT BY RESPONSIBLE PERSON OR THE CHILD

5(1) For the purposes of these Regulations, subject to paragraphs (1A) and (2), an account is opened for a child ("the named child") with an account provider on the date the last of the following conditions is satisfied (in any order), where **"the applicant"** means–

(a)   if the named child is 16 or over, the child; and

(b)   in any other case, a responsible person in relation to the named child:

     Condition 1

     The applicant gives the voucher relating to the named child to the account provider not later than 7 days after its short expiry date or, where the account provider has chosen to open accounts without sight of the relevant voucher, the applicant gives the following information to the account provider:

     (a)   the short expiry date of the voucher,

     (b)   the amount of the initial contribution as specified on the voucher, and

     (c)   where the date of birth shown on the voucher differs from the actual date of birth of the child (see regulation 13(5)(c)), the date of birth shown on the voucher.

     Condition 2

     The applicant enters into an agreement with the account provider (the "management agreement") for the management of the account (see regulation 8(1) and (2)), which includes the application and declaration required by regulation 13.

     Condition 3

     Where that application is not in writing the applicant has agreed, or is treated as having agreed, the contents of the copy of the declaration required by regulation 13(3).

Condition 4

(a)   In any case where the management agreement is a distance contract, the agreement must be an initial service agreement for the purposes of the Distance Marketing Directive, and contain the instructions required by regulation 8(1)(f), and

(b)   in every case where there is any right to cancel (or automatic cancellation of) the management agreement, the period during which it may be exercised or occur has expired without that right being exercised or cancellation occurring.

5(1A)   The application to open the account must be made, and Condition 2 satisfied, not later than the short expiry date of the voucher.

5(2)   An account must satisfy the requirements that–

(a)   no subscription to the account is accepted by the account provider until the account has been opened in accordance with paragraph (1); and

(b)   where the account is so opened before the appointed day, it shall not be treated as open for the purpose of accepting subscriptions until the appointed day.

History – In reg. 5(1), in Condition 1, the words "short expiry date" substituted for the words "expiry date" in both places by SI 2011/2447, reg. 4, with effect from 1 November 2011 but only in relation to vouchers issued on or after 1 January 2012.
In reg. 5(1), in Condition 1, words after "expiry date" inserted by SI 2009/694, reg. 3, with effect in relation to applications to open an account made before 6th April 2009 where the account has not been opened before that date, and in relation to applications to open an account made on or after 6th April 2009.
In reg. 5(1), the words "paragraphs (1A) and (2)" substituted for the words "paragraph (2)" by SI 2006/199, reg. 4(a)(i), with effect from 7 February 2006.
In reg. 5(1), in Condition 1, the words "not later than 7 days after its expiry date" added by SI 2006/199, reg. 4(a)(ii), with effect from 7 February 2006.
In reg. 5(1A), the words "short expiry date" substituted for the words "expiry date" by SI 2011/2447, reg. 4, with effect from 1 November 2011 but only in relation to vouchers issued on or after 1 January 2012.
Reg. 5(1A) inserted by SI 2006/199, reg. 4(b), with effect from 7 February 2006.

OPENING OF ACCOUNT BY INLAND REVENUE – (REVENUE ALLOCATED ACCOUNTS)

6(1)   The Board shall apply to open an account for a child to whom section 6 of the Act applies, by forwarding to an account provider the particulars which would be required for a voucher (see regulation 3), but omitting paragraph (1)(d) of that regulation.

6(2)   The account provider shall immediately open a stakeholder account in the name of the child, which shall have the same effect as if a responsible person for the child (or the child if aged 16 or over) had entered into the account provider's standard management agreement for the stakeholder account in question, including the terms mentioned in Condition 2 of regulation 5(1) (but treating the reference to the application and declaration required by regulation 13 as a reference to the authorisation required by regulation 13(4)) and regulation 8(1)(f).

6(3)   The Inland Revenue shall maintain (and update from time to time) a list of account providers who have agreed to accept Revenue allocated accounts under this regulation, in the order of the date of their agreement, and the account provider shall be selected in rotation from the current list.

6(4)   Where the account provider offers two or more types of stakeholder account–

(a)   the account provider shall select the type or types to be used for the purposes of this regulation (subject to sub-paragraph (b)),

(b)   any type selected must be offered to the general public at the time of opening a Revenue allocated account of that type, and

(c)   if more than one type has been selected, the account to be opened shall be chosen by the account provider in rotation between the selected types of accounts.

6(5)   The Inland Revenue shall write to the person who is entitled to child benefit in respect of the child (or, in the case of a child who is an eligible child because of section 2(3) of the Act, to a responsible person in relation to the child) to inform them of the opening of the account and particulars of it.

History – Reg. 6(4)(a)–(c) substituted for the words ", the account to be opened shall be chosen by the account provider in rotation between those types" by SI 2005/3349, reg. 4, with effect from 27 December 2005.
Reg. 6(5) inserted by SI 2004/2676, reg. 4, with effect from the date SI 2004/1450 is brought into force (6 April 2005).

GOVERNMENT CONTRIBUTIONS

7(1)   The amounts of the contribution for the purposes of section 8(1) of the Act are set out in paragraphs (2) to (4B), (the amounts set out in paragraphs (2), (4)(a) and (4A) to be known as the "initial contribution", and the amounts set out in paragraphs (3), (4)(b) and (4B) as the "special contribution").

7(2) Where the child is an eligible child on the appointed day by virtue of section 2(1)(a) of the Act (by reason of a child benefit award), and–

(i)   was born after 31 August 2002 but before 6 April 2003, the amount is £277,

(ii)   was born between 6 April 2003 and 5 April 2004, the amount is £268, and

(iii)   was born between 6 April 2004 and the day preceding the appointed day, the amount is £256.

7(3) Where the child is an eligible child on the appointed day by virtue of section 2(1)(b) of the Act (by reason of being a child in the care of a local authority at that date) and–

(i)   was born after 31 August 2002 but before 6 April 2003, the amount is £554,

(ii)   was born between 6 April 2003 and 5 April 2004, the amount is £536, and

(iii)   was born between 6 April 2004 and the day preceding the appointed day, the amount is £512.

7(4) Subject to paragraphs (4A) and (4B), where the child becomes an eligible child on or after the appointed day and–

(a)   is first an eligible child by virtue of section 2(1)(a) of the Act, the amount is £250, and

(b)   is first an eligible child by virtue of section 2(1)(b) of the Act, the amount is £500.

7(4A) Where a child–

(a)   is first an eligible child by virtue of section 2(1)(a) of the Act, and

(b)   the commencement date for the child (see paragraph (8)) is after the relevant 2010 date (see paragraph (10E)),

the amount is £50.

7(4B) Where a child–

(a)   is first an eligible child by virtue of section 2(1)(b) of the Act, and

(b)   either–

     (i)   is born on or after the relevant 2010 date, or

     (ii)   is first in the United Kingdom (other than temporarily) on or after the relevant 2010 date, or

     (iii)   becomes an eligible child on or after 3 months (less one day) after the relevant 2010 date,

the amount is £100.

7(5) The amounts of the supplementary contribution for the purposes of section 9(2) of the Act (to be known as the "supplementary contribution") are set out in paragraphs (6) and (7).

7(6) Where the child is an eligible child on the appointed day (and is a child to whom section 9 of the Act applies), the amount–

(a)   if the commencement date was after 31 August 2002 but before 6 April 2003, is £266,

(b)   if the commencement date was between 6 April 2003 and 5 April 2004, is £258,

(c)   if the commencement date was between 6 April 2004 and the appointed day, is £250.

7(7) Subject to paragraph (7A), where the child becomes an eligible child after the appointed day (and is a child to whom section 9 of the Act applies), the amount is £250.

7(7A) Where the child is one to whom section 9 of the Act applies, and the commencement date for the child is after the relevant 2010 date, the amount is £50.

7(8) The **"commencement date"**, in relation to a child, means the first day for which child benefit was paid (under a decision mentioned in section 2(6) of the Act) in respect of the child, except that–

(a)   where entitlement to child benefit is wholly excluded by a directly applicable Community provision, it means the date on which that exclusion took effect,

(b)   [Omitted by SI 2010/1894, reg. 3(7).]

7(9) The Inland Revenue shall, following final determination of entitlement to child tax credit, write to the person who is entitled to child benefit in respect of the child (or, in the case of a child who is an eligible child because of section 2(3) of the Act, to a responsible person in relation to the child) to inform them that the supplementary contribution is being paid into the child's account.

7(10) A further contribution under section 10 of the Act of £50 is due for any child where–

(a)   the commencement date (for child benefit: see paragraph (8)) in relation to that child is after 5th April 2005, and

(b)   income support or income-based jobseeker's allowance was paid for that commencement date to a person whose applicable amount included an amount in respect of the child.

7(10A)   A further contribution under section 10 of the Act of £50 is due for any child if–

(a)   an account is held by the child,

(b)   the child was first an eligible child by virtue of section 2(1)(a) of the Act,

(c)   section 9 of the Act does not apply to the child,

(d)   a contribution is not, and has not been, due for the child under paragraph (10),

(e)   the child is an eligible child on the day identified under the provisions of paragraph (10B) or (10C) as the case may be, and

(f)   the condition in paragraph (10B) or (10C) is satisfied in relation to the child.

7(10B)   The condition in this paragraph is that it has been determined in accordance with the provision made by and by virtue of sections 18 to 21 of the Tax Credits Act 2002–

(a)   that a person was, or persons were, entitled to child tax credit in respect of the child for any day falling–

     (i)   after the commencement date, but

     (ii)   not later than three months immediately preceding the expiry date of the voucher for the child (see regulation 3), and

(b)   that either the relevant income of the person or persons for the tax year in which that day fell does not exceed the income threshold or the person, or either of those persons, was entitled to a relevant social security benefit for that day,

and that determination has not been overturned.

7(10C)   The condition in this paragraph is that income support, or income-based jobseeker's allowance, was paid for any day falling–

(a)   after the commencement date, but

(b)   not later than one month immediately preceding the expiry date of the voucher for the child (see regulation 3),

to a person whose applicable amount included an amount in respect of the child.

7(10D)   Her Majesty's Revenue and Customs must inform the account provider holding the child's account where an amount is payable to the account under paragraph (10) or (10A).

7(10E)   In this regulation, **"the relevant 2010 date"** means–

(a)   2nd August 2010; or

(b)   if later, the day on which regulation 3 of the Child Trust Funds (Amendment No. 3) Regulations 2010 came into force.

7(11)   On receipt of the further contribution mentioned in paragraph (10) or (10A) from the Inland Revenue the account provider must credit the account held by the child with the amount of the payment.

History – In reg. 7(1), "(4B)" substituted for "(4)" by SI 2010/1894, reg. 3(2)(a), with effect from 2 August 2010.
In reg. 7(1), "(2), (4)(a) and (4A)" substituted for "(2) and (4)(a)" by SI 2010/1894, reg. 3(2)(b), with effect from 2 August 2010.
In reg. 7(1), "(3), (4)(b) and (4B)" substituted for "(3) and (4)(b)" by SI 2010/1894, reg. 3(2)(c), with effect from 2 August 2010.
In reg. 7(4), the words "Subject to paragraphs (4A) and (4B), where" substituted for the word "Where" by SI 2010/1894, reg. 3(3), with effect from 2 August 2010.
In reg. 7(4) the words "becomes an eligible child" substituted for the words "is born" by SI 2004/2676, reg. 5(a), with effect from the date SI 2004/1450 is brought into force (6 April 2005).
Reg. 7(4A) inserted by SI 2010/1894, reg. 3(4), with effect from 2 August 2010.
Reg. 7(4B) inserted by SI 2010/1894, reg. 3(4), with effect from 2 August 2010.
In reg. 7(7), the words "Subject to paragraph (7A), where" substituted for the word "Where" by SI 2010/1894, reg. 3(5), with effect from 2 August 2010.
Reg. 7(7A) inserted by SI 2010/1894, reg. 3(6), with effect from 2 August 2010.
Reg. 7(8)(b) (and the "and" preceding it) omitted by SI 2010/1894, reg. 3(7), with effect from 2 August 2010. Former reg. 7(8)(b) read as follows:
    "where the child was prevented from being an eligible child by virtue of section 2(5) of the Act, it means the date on which the child became an eligible child.".
Reg. 7(9) inserted by SI 2004/2676, reg. 5(b), with effect from the date SI 2004/1450 is brought into force (6 April 2005).
In reg. 7(10), "£50" substituted for "£250" by SI 2010/1894, reg. 3(8), with effect where the commencement date for the child (within the meaning of reg. 7(8)) is after 2 August 2010.
Reg. 7(10) inserted by SI 2005/383, reg. 3, with effect from 6 April 2005.
In reg. 7(10A), "£50" substituted for "£250" by SI 2010/1894, reg. 3(8), with effect where the commencement date for the child (within the meaning of reg. 7(8)) is after 2 August 2010.
Reg. 7(10A) inserted by SI 2009/475, reg. 4(a), with effect where the Child Benefit commencement date for the child (first day for which child benefit was paid in respect of the child) is on or after 6 April 2008.
Reg. 7(10B) inserted by SI 2009/475, reg. 4(a), with effect where the Child Benefit commencement date for the child (first day for which child benefit was paid in respect of the child) is on or after 6 April 2008.

Reg. 7(10C) inserted by SI 2009/475, reg. 4(a), with effect where the Child Benefit commencement date for the child (first day for which child benefit was paid in respect of the child) is on or after 6 April 2008.

Reg. 7(10D) inserted by SI 2010/1894, reg. 3(9), with effect from 2 August 2010.

Reg. 7(10E) inserted by SI 2010/1894, reg. 3(9), with effect from 2 August 2010.

In reg. 7(11), the words "mentioned in paragraph (10) or (10A)" inserted by SI 2009/475, reg. 4(b), with effect where the Child Benefit commencement date for the child (first day for which child benefit was paid in respect of the child) is on or after 6 April 2008.

Reg. 7(11) inserted by SI 2005/383, reg. 3, with effect from 6 April 2005.

Notes – In reg. 7(10E), "the relevant 2010 date" means 2 August 2010, because reg. 3 of the *Child Trust Funds (Amendment No. 3) Regulations* 2010 (SI 2010/1894) came into force on 2 August 2010.

AGE 7 PAYMENTS

7A   [Omitted by SI 2010/1894, reg. 4, with effect from 1 August 2010.]

YEARLY DISABILITY PAYMENTS

7B(1)   A further contribution under section 10 of the Act is due for any eligible child who is entitled in the year 2009/10 or 2010/11 to a disability living allowance, in accordance with paragraphs (2) to (4).

7B(2)   Where it has been determined that the child is entitled to the care component of a disability living allowance at the highest weekly rate (see section 72(4)(a) of either the Social Security Contributions and Benefits Act 1992 or the Social Security Contributions and Benefits (Northern Ireland) Act 1992), at any time in the year (whether it is paid or not), the contribution payable for the year shall be £200.

7B(3)   In any other case where it has been determined that the child is entitled to a disability living allowance at any time in the year (whether it is paid or not), the contribution payable for the year shall be £100.

7B(4)   [Omitted by SI 2010/1894, reg. 5(3).]

7B(5)   Her Majesty's Revenue and Customs must inform the account provider holding the child's account where an amount is payable to that account under this regulation.

7B(6)   On receipt of each further contribution from Her Majesty's Revenue and Customs, the account provider must credit the child's account with the amount of the payment.

History – In reg. 7B(1), the words "the year 2009/10 or 2010/11" substituted for the words "any year" by SI 2010/1894, reg. 5(2), with effect from 1 August 2010.

Reg. 7B(4) omitted by SI 2010/1894, reg. 5(3), with effect from 1 August 2010.

Reg. 7B inserted by SI 2010/836, reg. 3, with effect where a child falls within the terms of reg. 7B for a year of assessment commencing on or after 6 April 2009.

PART 2 – OTHER REQUIREMENTS TO BE SATISFIED IN RELATION TO ACCOUNTS

GENERAL REQUIREMENTS FOR ACCOUNTS

8(1)   An account must satisfy the requirements that–

(a)   it is the account for a single child ("the named child");

(b)   the named child is or has been an eligible child;

(c)   no child may hold more than one account;

(d)   at any time–

     (i)   where the named child is under 16, only a single responsible person in relation to the named child, or

     (ii)   where the named child is 16 or over, only the child,

     ("the registered contact") may give instructions to the account provider with respect to its management;

(e)   the account must at all times be managed in accordance with these Regulations by an account provider and, subject to regulation 6(2), under terms agreed and recorded in a management agreement made between the account provider and the registered contact (on behalf of the named child where appropriate); and

(f)   the management agreement must include instructions to the provider as to the manner in which Inland Revenue contributions and any subscriptions made are to be invested under the account.

8(2)   Apart from other requirements of these Regulations the terms so agreed shall include the conditions that–

(a)   the account investments shall be in the beneficial ownership of the named child;

(b)   the title to all account investments, except those falling within regulation 12(2)(k), (l) or (m), shall be vested in the account provider or his nominee, subject to sub-paragraph (f);

(c)   where a share certificate or other document evidencing title to an account investment is issued, it shall be held by the account provider or as he may direct, subject to subparagraph (f);

(d)   in relation to qualifying investments falling within regulation 12(2)(a), (b) and (f) to (j), the account provider shall, if the registered contact so elects (and subject to any charge for the arrangement), arrange for the registered contact to receive a copy of the annual report and accounts issued to investors by every company, unit trust, open-ended investment company or other entity in which account investments are held;

(e)   in relation to qualifying investments falling within regulation 12(2)(a), (b) and (f) to (j), the account provider shall, if the registered contact so elects (subject to any charge for the arrangement, and to any provisions made under any enactment), be under an obligation to arrange for the registered contact to be able–

     (i)   to attend any meetings of investors in companies, unit trusts, open-ended investment companies and other entities in which account investments are held,

     (ii)   to vote, and

     (iii)   to receive, in addition to the documents referred to in sub-paragraph (d), any other information issued to investors in such companies, unit trusts, open-ended investment companies and other entities;

(f)   if and so long as a person falling within regulation 14(2)(d)(iv) acts as account provider of an account, and the account investments include a policy of life insurance–

     (i)   the title to all such policies shall be vested in the registered contact, and

     (ii)   where a policy document or other document evidencing title to such policies of life insurance is issued, it shall be held by the registered contact;

(g)   the account provider shall satisfy himself that any person to whom he delegates any of his functions or responsibilities under the management agreement is competent to carry out those functions or responsibilities;

(h)   on the instructions of the registered contact ("the transfer instructions") and within such time as is stipulated by the registered contact in the transfer instructions, the whole of an account, with all rights and obligations of the parties to it, shall be transferred free of expense (except any incidental expenses) to another account provider subject to and in accordance with regulation 21;

(ha)   where the account is or has been transferred to the account provider by a transfer under regulation 21, that no charges or expenses are due in respect of that transfer, except in accordance with sub-paragraph (h);

(i)   where the account provider offers accounts of another description or type, on the instructions of the registered contact ("the internal transfer instructions") and within such time as is stipulated by the registered contact in the internal transfer instructions, the account shall become (free of expense, except any incidental expenses) an account of that other description or type (any necessary change in the investments being made accordingly); and

(j)   the account provider shall notify the registered contact if by reason of any failure to satisfy the provisions of these Regulations an account is or will become no longer exempt from tax by virtue of regulation 24.

8(3)   Where the transfer instructions or internal transfer instructions, or any new management agreement entered into by the registered contact with the account provider (or a new account provider) under regulation 8(1)(e), is a distance contract, the transfer or internal transfer shall only take effect once those contracts satisfy Condition 4 in regulation 5(1).

8(4)   The time stipulated in transfer instructions or internal transfer instructions shall be subject to any reasonable business period (not exceeding 30 days) of the account provider required for the practical implementation of the instructions.

8(5)   In this regulation, **"incidental expenses"** means stamp duty and other dealing costs of disposing of or acquiring investments.

History – Reg. 8(2)(ha) inserted by SI 2004/2676, reg. 6, with effect from the date SI 2004/1450 is brought into force (6 April 2005).

Statutory Instruments

ANNUAL LIMIT ON SUBSCRIPTIONS

9(1) Any person (including the child) may make subscriptions to a child's account, subject to paragraphs (2) and (3).

9(2) Subscriptions to an account made during any subscription year, that is–

(a) the period beginning with the day on which the account is opened (or if opened before the appointed day, opened for the purpose of accepting subscriptions under regulation 5(2)(b)), and ending immediately before the child's next birthday, and

(b) any succeeding period of twelve months,

shall not in aggregate exceed the sum of £4,000.

9(3) Where the aggregate of subscriptions in any year falls short of £4,000 or is nil, there shall be no addition to the amount for any succeeding year.

History – In reg. 9(2)(b), the figure "£4,000" substituted for "£3,840" by SI 2014/1453, reg. 3, with effect from 1 July 2014.
In reg. 9(2)(b), the figure "£3,840" substituted for "£3,720" by SI 2014/649, reg. 4, with effect from 6 April 2014.
In reg. 9(2)(b), the figure "£3,720" substituted for "£3,600" by SI 2013/263, reg. 2(2), with effect from 6 April 2013.
In reg. 9(2)(b) "£3,600" previously substituted for "£1,200" by SI 2011/2447, reg. 5, with effect from 1 November 2011.
In reg. 9(3), the figure "£4,000" substituted for "£3,840" by SI 2014/1453, reg. 3, with effect from 1 July 2014.
In reg. 9(3), the figure "£3,840" substituted for "£3,720" by SI 2014/649, reg. 4, with effect from 6 April 2014.
In reg. 9(3), the figure "£3,720" substituted for "£3,600" by SI 2013/263, reg. 2(2), with effect from 6 April 2013.
In reg. 9(3) "£3,600" previously substituted for "£1,200" by SI 2011/2447, reg. 5, with effect from 1 November 2011.

STATEMENTS FOR AN ACCOUNT

10(1) The account provider must produce a statement for the account–

(a) subject to paragraphs (6) and (7), annually ("an annual statement"), and

(b) where an account is transferred to another account provider under regulation 21, as at the transfer date ("a transfer statement").

10(2) References in paragraphs (2A)(b), (3), (4), (5), (6) and (8) to a statement (without more) shall be construed as references to any statement required to be produced in accordance with this regulation.

10(2A) The account provider must produce an annual statement at a date (a "relevant date") not later than 12 months from the latest of–

(a) the date of the opening of the account;

(b) the date at which the most recent statement was produced; and

(c) the last date at which, but for paragraph (6), a previous annual statement would have had to have been produced.

10(3) A statement required to be produced in accordance with this regulation shall be sent–

(a) where the named child is the registered contact, to the child,

(b) where a responsible person is the registered contact, to the named child care of the registered contact,

(c) where the Official Solicitor or Accountant of Court has been appointed under section 3(10) of the Act, to the Official Solicitor or Accountant of Court, on behalf of the child, and

(d) in any other case, to the named child,

within 30 days of the date specified in paragraph (3A).

10(3A) The date specified in this paragraph is–

(a) in relation to an annual statement, the relevant date;

(b) in relation to a transfer statement, the transfer date; or

(c) where paragraph (7) applies, the later of the relevant date in relation to the annual statement requested and the date that the request is received by the account provider.

10(4) Statements shall include the following information–

(a) the full name of the child;

(b) his address;

(c) his date of birth;

(d) his unique reference number;

(e) the description of the account (see regulation 4);

(f) the name of the registered contact (if any);

(g) the relevant date;

(h)   the total market value of the investments under the account at the date at which the most recent statement was produced (if any);

(i)   the amount of any Government contributions (see regulation 7) received by the account provider, during the period between–

> (i)   the date at which the most recent statement was produced, or the opening of the account (whichever is the later), and

> (ii)   the relevant date;

(j)   the aggregate amount of subscriptions (if any) received during the period in subparagraph (i);

(k)   the total amount of deductions (including management charges) made during the period in sub-paragraph (i);

(l)   the total market value of the investments under the account at the relevant date;

(m)   the number or amount, description and market value of each of the investments under the account at the relevant date;

(n)   the basis used in calculating the market value of each investment under the account (together with a statement of any change from a basis used in the previous statement); and

(o)   the exchange rate used where any investment is, or is denominated in, a currency other than sterling.

10(5)   As an alternative to the information in paragraph (4)(k), the statement may include, in relation to any management charges or other incidental expenses deducted from the account during the period in paragraph (4)(i)–

(a)   the rate, expressed as an annual percentage rate, at which, and the period in relation to which, such deductions were made, or

(b)   where such deductions were made in relation to different periods at different rates–

> (i)   each rate, expressed as an annual percentage rate, at which those deductions were made; and

> (ii)   the period in relation to which they were made at that rate.

10(6)   Where, in relation to an annual statement, at a relevant date–

(a)   the aggregate market value of the account investments held under the account is less than £300, or

(b)   no subscriptions under regulation 9 have been made to the account during the relevant period,

then, subject to paragraph (7), the account provider need only produce the annual statement if it would be the first statement to be produced following the child's fourth, tenth or fifteenth birthday.

10(7)   Paragraph (6) shall not apply where any potential recipient of an annual statement (see paragraph (3)) requests such a statement.

10(8)   **"The relevant period"** means the period–

(a)   beginning on the latest of–

> (i)   the date of the opening of the account;

> (ii)   the date at which the most recent statement was produced; and

> (iii)   the last date as at which, but for paragraph (6), an annual statement would have had to have been produced; and

(b)   ending on the relevant date.

History – Reg. 10(1), (2) and (2A) substituted for former reg. 10(1), (2) by SI 2011/992, reg. 2(2), with effect from 20 April 2011.

In former reg. 10(2)(a) "61" substituted for "60" by SI 2004/2676, reg. 7(a), with effect from the date SI 2004/1450 is brought into force (6 April 2005).

In reg. 10(3), the words "A statement required to be produced in accordance with this regulation" substituted for the words "The statement" by SI 2011/992, reg. 2(3)(a), with effect from 20 April 2011.

In reg. 10(3), the words "date specified in paragraph (3A)" substituted for the words "statement date" by SI 2011/992, reg. 2(3)(b), with effect from 20 April 2011.

Reg. 10(3A) inserted by SI 2011/992, reg. 2(4), with effect from 20 April 2011.

In reg. 10(4)(g), (4)(i)(ii), (4)(l) and (4)(m), the words "relevant date" substituted for the words "statement date" by SI 2011/992, reg. 2(5), with effect from 20 April 2011.

Reg. 10(4)(h) substituted by SI 2011/992, reg. 2(6), with effect from 20 April 2011.

Reg. 10(4)(i)(i) substituted by SI 2011/992, reg. 2(7), with effect from 20 April 2011.

In reg. 10(4)(i) the words "(see regulation 7) received by the account provider" substituted for the words "claimed by the account provider under regulation 30" by SI 2004/2676, reg. 7(b), with effect from the date SI 2004/1450 is brought into force (6 April 2005).

Reg. 10(5) inserted by SI 2004/2676, reg. 7(c), with effect from the date SI 2004/1450 is brought into force (6 April 2005).

Reg. 10(6), (7) and (8) inserted by SI 2011/992, reg. 2(8), with effect from 20 April 2011.

GENERAL INVESTMENT RULES

11(1) All transactions by way of purchase by an account provider of investments under an account shall be made–

(a)   in the case of an authorised fund which is a dual priced unit trust, at the maximum sale price of a unit of the relevant class at the relevant valuation point within the meaning of, and complying with the requirements of, rules 6.3.5 and 6.3.5B of the Collective Investment Schemes Sourcebook;

(b)   in the case of an authorised fund which is a single priced unit trust or an open-ended investment company, at the price of a unit of the relevant class at the relevant valuation point within the meaning of, and complying with the requirements of, rules 6.3.5 and 6.3.5A of the Collective Investment Schemes Sourcebook; and

(c)   in the case of all other account investments, at the price for which those investments might reasonably be expected to be purchased in the open market.

11(2) In paragraph (1)–

"a dual priced unit trust" means an authorised unit trust in respect of which the manager gives different prices for buying and selling units at the same time;

"a single priced unit trust" means an authorised unit trust in respect of which the manager gives the same price for buying and selling units at the same time.

11(3) All other transactions by way of sale or otherwise by an account provider in investments under an account shall be made at the price for which those investments might reasonably be expected to be sold or otherwise transacted, as the case may be, in the open market.

11(4) Investments, or rights in respect of investments, may not at any time–

(a)   be purchased or made otherwise than out of cash which an account provider holds under an account at that time; or

(b)   be purchased from–

     (i)   the named child, or

     (ii)   the spouse or civil partner of the named child,

so as to become account investments under the account.

11(5) Subject to paragraph (6), contributions, subscriptions and any other cash held by an account provider under an account shall be held only in sterling and be deposited in an account with a deposit-taker (including for this purpose a credit union), or a deposit account or a share account with a building society, which is designated as a CTF account for the purposes of these Regulations only.

11(6) An account provider who is a European institution, a relevant authorised person or an assurance undertaking may hold an account investor's cash subscription and other cash held under an account in the currency of the EEA State in which he has his principal place of business and may deposit such cash in an account, which is designated as mentioned in paragraph (5), with any person authorised under the law of that State to accept deposits.

History – In reg. 11(1)(a), the words "maximum sale price of a unit of the relevant class at the relevant valuation point" substituted for the words "manager's price for the sale of the relevant class of units" and the words "rules 6.3.5 and 6.3.5B" substituted for the words "rule 15.4.4" by SI 2010/582, reg. 4(a), with effect from 6 April 2010.
In reg. 11(1)(b), the words "of the relevant class at the relevant valuation point" substituted for the words "or share" and the words "rules 6.3.5 and 6.3.5A" substituted for the words "rule 4.3.11" by SI 2010/582, reg. 4(b), with effect from 6 April 2010.
In reg. 11(4)(b)(ii), the words "or civil partner" inserted by SI 2005/2919, reg. 15(2), with effect from 5 December 2005.
In reg. 11(5) the words "(including for this purpose a credit union)" inserted by SI 2005/909, reg. 4, with effect from 6 April 2005.

QUALIFYING INVESTMENTS FOR AN ACCOUNT

12(1) This regulation specifies the kind of investments ("qualifying investments for an account") which may be purchased, made or held under an account.

12(2) Qualifying investments for an account to which paragraph (1) refers are–

(a)   shares, not being shares in an investment trust, issued by a company wherever incorporated and either officially listed on a recognised stock exchange or, in the European Economic Area, admitted to trading on a recognised stock exchange (see paragraph (3));

(b)   securities–

     (i)   issued by a company wherever incorporated, and

     (ii)   which satisfy at least one of the conditions specified in paragraph (5),

(c)   gilt-edged securities;

(d)   any securities issued by or on behalf of a government of any EEA State;

(e)   any securities which, in relation to a security mentioned in sub-paragraph (d), would be a strip of that security if "strip" had the same meaning as in section 47 of the Finance Act 1942, with the omission of the words "issued under the National Loans Act 1968";

(f)   shares in an investment trust;

(g–h)   [omitted by SI 2010/582, reg. 5(g);]

(i)   units in, or shares of, a UK UCITS or recognised UCITS;

(j)   a depositary interest;

(k)   cash deposited in a deposit account with a building society, or a person falling within section 991 of ITA 2007 (including for this purpose a credit union), subject to paragraph (8);

(l)   cash deposited in a share account with a building society, subject to paragraph (8);

(m)   policies of life insurance which satisfy the conditions specified in paragraphs (9) and (10);

(n)   any securities issued under the National Loans Act 1968–

    (i)   for the purpose of or in connection with raising money under the auspices of the Director of Savings within the meaning of section 11(1)(a) of the National Debt Act 1972, and

    (ii)   other than national savings certificates, premium savings bonds, national savings stamps and national savings gift tokens,

which, according to the terms and conditions subject to which they are issued and purchased, are expressly permitted to be held under an account.

(o)   arrangements falling within section 47 of the Finance Act 2005 (alternative finance arrangements) under which the person referred to in that section as Y is a financial institution;

(p)   arrangements falling within section 49 of that Act;

(q)   qualifying units in or shares of a non-UCITS retail scheme;

(r)   core capital deferred shares within the meaning of regulation 2 of the Building Societies (Core Capital Deferred Shares) Regulations 2013, provided that such shares are listed on the official list of a recognised stock exchange.

12(3)   An investment in shares fulfils the conditions as to official listing and admission to trading in paragraph (2)(a), if–

(a)   in pursuance of a public offer, the account provider applies for the allotment or allocation to him of shares in a company which are due to be admitted to such listing or admitted to such trading within 30 days of the allocation or allotment, and which, when admitted to such listing, or trading would be qualifying investments for an account, and

(b)   the shares are not allotted or allocated to the account provider in the circumstances specified in paragraph (4).

12(4)   The circumstances specified in this paragraph are where–

(a)   the allotment or allocation of the shares was connected with the allotment or allocation of–

    (i)   shares in the company or investment trust of a different class, or

    (ii)   rights to shares in the company or investment trust of a different class, or

    (iii)   shares or rights to shares in another company or investment trust, or

    (iv)   units in or shares in, or rights to units in or shares in, an authorised fund or a part of an umbrella scheme, or

    (v)   securities or rights to securities of the company or investment trust, or of another company or investment trust,

to the account provider, the registered contact or any other person; and

(b)   the terms on which the first-mentioned shares in this paragraph were offered were significantly more favourable to the account provider or the named child than they would have been if their allotment or allocation had not been connected as described in subparagraph (a).

12(5)   The conditions specified in this paragraph are–

(a)   that the shares in the company issuing the securities are listed on the official list of a recognised stock exchange;

(b)   that the securities are so listed;

(c)   that the company issuing the securities is a 75 per cent subsidiary of a company whose shares are so listed.

12(6)   [Omitted by SI 2010/582, reg. 5(f).]

12(7) In paragraph (4)(a), **"company"** means any body corporate having a share capital.

12(8) A deposit account or share account which is a qualifying investment for an account falling within paragraph (2)(k) or (l) must not be connected with any other investment, held by the named child or any other person.

12(8A) For the purposes of paragraph (8), a deposit account or share account described in that paragraph, is connected with another investment if–

(a)   either was opened or acquired with reference to the other, or with a view to enabling the other to be opened or acquired on particular terms, or with a view to facilitating the opening or acquisition of the other on particular terms,

(b)   the terms on which the deposit account or share account was opened would have been significantly less favourable to the holder if the other investment had not been held, and

(c)   the other investment is not a tax exempt investment.

12(8B) The following are tax exempt investments for the purposes of paragraph (8A)–

(a)   an account investment held under a child trust fund;

(b)   an account investment within the meaning given in the Individual Savings Account Regulations 1998 held under an account opened (or treated as opened) in accordance with regulation 12 or 12A of those regulations.

12(9) The conditions specified in this paragraph are that–

(a)   the insurance is on the life of the named child only;

(b)   the terms and conditions of the policy provide–

  (i)   that the policy may only be owned or held as a qualifying investment for an account which satisfies the provisions of these Regulations;

  (ii)   that the policy shall automatically terminate if it comes to the notice of the account provider, in any manner, that the event specified in paragraph (11) has occurred in relation to the policy;

  (iii)   for an express prohibition of any payment of the proceeds from the termination of the policy or a partial surrender of the rights conferred by the policy, to the named child (while he is still a child) except in accordance with regulation 18A (terminal illness); and

  (iv)   that the policy, the rights conferred by the policy and any share or interest in the policy or rights respectively, shall not be capable of assignment or (in Scotland) assignation, other than that they may be vested in the named child's personal representatives, and that the title to the policy may be transferred to a new account provider subject to and in accordance with regulations 8(2)(f) and 21;

(c)   the policy evidences or secures a contract of insurance which–

  (i)   falls within paragraph 1 or 3 of Part 2 of Schedule 1 to the Financial Services and Markets Act 2000 (Regulated Activities) Order 2001, or

  (ii)   would fall within either of those paragraphs if the insurer were a company with permission under Part 4 of the Financial Services and Markets Act 2000 to effect or carry out contracts of insurance;

(d)   the policy is not–

  (i)   a contract to pay an annuity on human life,

  (ii)   a personal portfolio bond within the meaning given by section 516 of ITTOIA 2005, or

  (iii)   a contract, the effecting and carrying out of which constitutes "pension business" within the meaning given by section 431B(1) of the Taxes Act; and

(e)   after the first payment in respect of a premium in relation to the policy has been made, there is no contractual obligation on any person to make any other such payment.

12(10) The condition specified in this paragraph is that no sum may at any time, at or after the making of the insurance, be lent to or at the direction of the named child or registered contact by or by arrangement with the insurer for the time being responsible for the obligations under the policy.

12(11) The event specified in this paragraph is that–

(a)   there has been a breach of any of the conditions in paragraph (9) or (10), or any of those conditions was not satisfied at the date on which the insurance was made; and

(b)   the breach or non-compliance cannot be remedied in accordance with regulation 23, or (in any other case), has not been remedied within a reasonable time.

12(12)   Where the event specified in paragraph (11) occurs in relation to a policy, the policy shall nevertheless be treated, for the purposes of these Regulations, excepting paragraphs (9)(b)(ii) and (11), and regulations 37(6) and 38, as if it had satisfied the conditions in paragraphs (9) and (10) during the period–

(a)   commencing at the time when that specified event occurred, and

(b)   ending immediately before–

    (i)   the end of the final insurance year in relation to the policy, within the meaning given by section 499 of ITTOIA 2005,

    (ii)   the time at which that specified event came to the notice of the account provider,

whichever first occurs (the "termination event").

History – In reg. 12(2)(a), the words "either officially listed on a recognised stock exchange or, in the European Economic Area, admitted to trading on a recognised stock exchange (see paragraph (3))" substituted for the words "officially listed on a recognised stock exchange (see paragraph (3))" by SI 2013/1744, reg. 5(a), with effect from 5 August 2013.
In reg. 12(2)(b), the word "and" at the end of paragraph (i) added and paragraph (iii) (together with the word "and" that preceded it) omitted by SI 2010/582, reg. 5(a), with effect from 6 April 2010.
In reg. 12(2)(f), the words ", listed in the Official List of the Stock Exchange (see paragraph 3)" omitted by SI 2014/649, reg. 5(a), with effect from 6 April 2014.
In reg. 12(2)(f), the words ", in circumstances where the trust satisfies the condition specified in paragraph (6)" omitted by SI 2010/582, reg. 5(b), with effect from 6 April 2010.
Reg. 12(2)(g) and (h) omitted by SI 2010/582, reg. 5(c), with effect from 6 April 2010.
Reg. 12(2)(i) substituted by SI 2010/582, reg. 5(d), with effect from 6 April 2010.
In reg. 12(2)(k), the words "section 991 of ITA 2007 (including for this purpose a credit union)" substituted for the words "section 840A(1)(b) of the Taxes Act (including for this purpose a credit union) or a relevant European institution" by SI 2010/582, reg. 5(e), with effect from 6 April 2010.
In reg. 12(2)(k) the words "(including for this purpose a credit union)" inserted by SI 2005/909, reg. 5, with effect from 6 April 2005.
In reg. 12(2)(q), ";" substituted for "." by SI 2014/1453, reg. 4(a), with effect from 1 July 2014.
Reg. 12(2)(o)–(q) inserted by SI 2005/3349, reg. 5, with effect from 27 December 2005.
Reg. 12(2)(r) inserted by SI 2014/1453, reg. 4(b), with effect from 1 July 2014.
In reg. 12(3), the words "An investment in shares fulfils the conditions as to official listing and admission to trading in paragraph (2)(a)" substituted for the words "An investment in shares fulfils the condition as to official listing in paragraph (2)(a) or (f), or the condition as to admission to trading in paragraph (2)(a)" by SI 2014/649, reg. 5(b), with effect from 6 April 2014.
In reg. 12(3), the words ", or the condition as to admission to trading in paragraph (2)(a)," inserted by SI 2013/1744, reg. 5(b), with effect from 5 August 2013.
In reg. 12(3)(a), the words "or investment trust" omitted by SI 2014/649, reg. 5(c), with effect from 6 April 2014.
In reg. 12(3)(a), the words "or admitted to such trading" and the words "or trading" inserted by SI 2013/1744, reg. 5(b), with effect from 5 August 2013.
Reg. 12(6) omitted by SI 2010/582, reg. 5(f), with effect from 6 April 2010.
Reg. 12(8) substituted, and (8A) and (8B) inserted, by SI 2012/1870, reg. 2, with effect from 8 August 2012. Former reg. 12(8) read as follows:
    "**12(8)**   A deposit account or share account which is a qualifying investment for an account falling within paragraph (2)(k) or (l) must not be connected with any other investment, held by the named child or any other person, and for this purpose such an account is connected with an investment if–
    (a)   either was opened or acquired with reference to the other, or with a view to enabling the other to be opened or acquired on particular terms, or with a view to facilitating the opening or acquisition of the other on particular terms, and
    (b)   the terms on which the account was opened would have been significantly less favourable to the holder if the investment had not been acquired.".
In reg. 12(9)(b)(iii) the words "except in accordance with regulation 18A (terminal illness)" inserted by SI 2004/2676, reg. 8, with effect from the date SI 2004/1450 is brought into force (6 April 2005).
In reg. 12(9)(d)(ii), the words "section 516 of ITTOIA 2005" substituted for the words "regulation 2(1) of the Personal Portfolio Bonds (Tax) Regulations 1999" by SI 2010/582, reg. 5(g), with effect from 6 April 2010.
Reg. 12(12)(b)(i) substituted by SI 2010/582, reg. 5(h), with effect from 6 April 2010.

CONDITIONS FOR APPLICATION BY RESPONSIBLE PERSON OR THE CHILD TO OPEN AN ACCOUNT (AND CHANGES TO AN ACCOUNT)

13(1)   An application by a responsible person in relation to a child or the child if 16 or over, as the case may be, ("the applicant") to open an account for the child with an account provider must be made to the account provider in a statement which must satisfy the conditions specified in paragraphs (2) to (6).

13(2)   An application must specify the description of account applied for.

13(3)   An application must incorporate a declaration by the applicant that he–

(a)   is aged 16 years of age or over,

(b)   is–

    (i)   (where the child is under 16) a responsible person in relation to the named child (that is, that he has parental responsibility or, in Scotland, parental responsibilities in relation to the child), or

    (ii)   the child if 16 or over, and

(c)   is to be the registered contact for the account;

and where the application is not in writing, must authorise the account provider to record the terms of the declaration in a written declaration made on behalf of the applicant.

13(4) The applicant must authorise the account provider (on behalf of the named child where appropriate)–

(a)   to hold the child's Inland Revenue contributions, subscriptions, account investments, interest, dividends and any other rights or proceeds in respect of those investments and cash, and

(b)   to make on his behalf any claims to relief from tax in respect of account investments,

and the authority must continue until a further application and declaration is made in accordance with paragraph (10).

13(5) An application must contain–

(a)   the applicant's full name,

(b)   his address, including postcode,

(c)   the named child's full name and date of birth,

(d)   his address, including postcode, and

(e)   the child's unique reference number on the voucher.

13(6) There may be only one declaration and authorisation under paragraphs (3) to (5) in force for an account at any time.

13(7) Except in the case–

(a)   of the death or incapacity of the registered contact,

(b)   where the registered contact cannot be contacted,

(c)   of the bringing to an end of a Court order, under which he is a responsible person for the named child,

(d)   of the named child attaining the age of 16 years,

(da)   where the new registered contact has been appointed to be a guardian or special guardian of the named child,

(db)   where the new registered contact is the adopter of the named child under an adoption order,

(e)   where the Official Solicitor or Accountant of Court is appointed under section 3(10) of the Act, or

(f)   where a Court so orders,

any change in the identity of the registered contact shall require confirmation by the current registered contact that his declaration and authorisation under paragraphs (3)(c) and (4) is cancelled, and in the cases in sub-paragraphs (a) to (f) it shall be treated as automatically cancelled.

13(8) An account provider must decline to accept an application if he has reason to believe that–

(a)   the voucher has expired, or is not or might not be genuine, or

(b)   the applicant has given untrue information in his application.

13(9) Where the application is not in writing, the account provider shall make the written declaration referred to in paragraph (3), and notify the applicant of its contents, and such declaration shall take effect from the date on which the applicant agrees the contents (subject to any corrections), and if he neither agrees or disagrees with the contents within 30 days, he shall be treated as having agreed them.

13(10) Where–

(a)   there is a change in the identity of the registered contact, the new registered contact, or

(b)   an account has been opened by the Inland Revenue under regulation 6 (Revenue allocated accounts) and a responsible person in relation to the child (or the child, if 16 or over) subsequently applies to the account provider to be the registered contact for the account, he,

shall make the application and declaration required by paragraphs (3) to (5).

13(11) Where the new registered contact is the Official Solicitor or the Accountant of Court, he shall make the declaration and authorisation required by paragraphs (3)(c) and (4) and shall be treated as a party to the existing management agreement for the account in question.

History – In reg. 13(3)(b)(i) the words "or, in Scotland, parental responsibilities" inserted by SI 2004/2676, reg. 9(a), with effect from the date SI 2004/1450 is brought into force 6 April 2005).
In reg. 13(5)(c) the words "and date of birth" inserted by SI 2004/2676, reg. 9(b), with effect from the date SI 2004/1450 is brought into force (6 April 2005).
Reg. 13(7)(da) and (db) inserted by SI 2010/582, reg. 6(a), with effect from 6 April 2010.
In reg. 13(7), the words "and in the cases in sub-paragraphs (a) to (f) it shall be treated as automatically cancelled" added by SI 2010/582, reg. 6(b), with effect from 6 April 2010.
In reg. 13(11) the words following "paragraphs (3)(c) and (4)" inserted by SI 2004/3382, reg. 3, with effect from 6 April 2005.
Reg. 13(11) inserted by SI 2004/2676, reg. 9(c), with effect from the date SI 2004/1450 is brought into force (6 April 2005).

ACCOUNT PROVIDER – QUALIFICATIONS AND BOARD'S APPROVAL

14(1) This regulation specifies the circumstances ("qualifying circumstances") in which a person may be approved by the Board as an account provider.

14(2) The qualifying circumstances are the following–

(a) the person must make an application to the Board for approval in a form specified by the Board;

(b) the person must undertake with the Board–

    (i) to either offer stakeholder accounts to the general public (whether or not accounts of another description are offered), or to fulfil the requirements in paragraph (3),

    (ii) to accept vouchers from any responsible person or the child if 16 or over (subject to paragraph (iia) and regulation 13(8)),

    (iia) in the case of a credit union, to accept vouchers from any responsible person or the child if 16 or over, if the child to which the voucher relates is a member, or fulfils or is treated as fulfilling a qualification for admission to membership, of the credit union (subject to regulation 13(8)),

    (iii) where the person accepts Revenue allocated accounts, to allow instructions for their management to be made or given by post (whether or not other methods are allowed),

    (iv) to publicise (and up-date where appropriate) statements of the minimum amount which may be subscribed to an account on a single occasion, and the permitted means of payment of subscriptions,

    (v) to inform persons proposing to make subscriptions to an account (other than the named child) that the subscription is a gift to the child,

    (vi) to publicise (and up-date where appropriate) statements of the extent to which social, environmental or ethical decisions are taken into account in selecting, retaining or realising investments,

    (vii) that a child's unique reference number shall only be used for the purposes of the child's account (and of fulfilling the requirements of these Regulations with regard to that account), and

    (viii) that whether there is an initial contribution or special contribution to an account, whether there is a supplementary contribution to the account, and whether the account is a Revenue allocated account is information held for the purposes mentioned in paragraph (vii) only, and shall not be used for other purposes (including marketing other products);

(c) [omitted by SI 2013/263, reg. 2(4)(c),]

(d) an account provider must be–

    (i) an authorised person within the meaning of section 31(1)(a) or (c) of, or Schedule 5 to, the Financial Services and Markets Act 2000, who has permission to carry on one or more of the activities specified in Articles 14, 21, 25, 37, 40, 45, 51, 53 and (in so far as it applies to any of those activities) 64 of the Financial Services and Markets Act 2000 (Regulated Activities) Order 2001, but excluding any person falling within paragraph (iv) below;

    (iia) in the case of a credit union, an authorised person within the meaning of FISMA 2000, who has permission to carry on one or more of the activities specified in Article 5 of the Financial Services and Markets Act 2000 (Regulated Activities) Order 2001;

    (ii) a European institution which carries on one or more of those activities;

    (iii) a building society or a person falling within section 991 of ITA 2007 (including for this purpose a credit union)

    (iv) an insurance company within the meaning given by section 431(2) of the Taxes Act, an incorporated friendly society or a registered friendly society, or any other assurance undertaking;

(e) an account provider must not be prevented from acting as such by any limitation or requirement imposed under section 42 or 43 of FISMA 2000, or by any prohibition or prohibition order in or made under that Act

(f) an account provider who–

    (i) is a European institution or a relevant authorised person and who does not have a branch or business establishment in the United Kingdom, or has such a branch or business establishment but does not intend to carry out all his functions as an account provider at that branch or business establishment, or

(ii) falls within the expression "any other assurance undertaking" in sub-paragraph (d)(iv),

must fulfil one of the three requirements specified in regulation 15.

14(3) The requirements in this paragraph are that the person provides to any potential applicant for a child trust fund (before commencement of completion of any application under regulation 13)–

(a) a statement that a stakeholder account is available from a named alternative account provider who offers it on the terms in paragraph (2)(b)(i) (omitting the words from ", or to" to the end);

(b) a detailed description of that stakeholder account; and

(c) sufficient information (according to the method of communication used, and including documentation where appropriate) to put the potential applicant in the position to make an application to that alternative account provider, complying with regulation 13.

14(4) The terms of the Board's approval may include conditions designed to ensure that the provisions of these Regulations are satisfied.

History – In reg. 14(2)(b)(ii), the words "paragraph (iia) and" inserted by SI 2005/909, reg. 6, with effect from 6 April 2005. Reg. 14(2)(b)(iia) and 14(2)(d)(ia) inserted by SI 2005/909, reg. 7 and 8, with effect from 6 April 2005.
Reg. 14(2)(c) omitted by SI 2013/263, reg. 2(4)(c), with effect from 16 March 2013, in respect of what would otherwise be fortnightly and initial return periods within reg. 30(1) beginning on or after that day. Former reg. 14(2)(c) read as follows:
  "(c) the person must demonstrate to the satisfaction of the Board that the person can correctly operate the procedures in regulation 30;".
In reg. 14(2)(d)(iia), the words "FISMA 2000" substituted for the words "section 31(1)(a) of the Financial Services and Markets Act 2000" by SI 2013/1765, art. 8, with effect from 1 September 2013.
Reg. 14(2)(d)(iia) renumbered (was formerly reg. 14(2)(d)(ia)) by SI 2005/3349, reg. 6, with effect from 27 December 2005.
In reg. 14(2)(d)(iii), the words "or a person falling within section 991 of ITA 2007 (including for this purpose a credit union)" substituted for the words ", a person falling within section 840A(1)(b) of the Taxes Act or a relevant European institution; or" by SI 2010/582, reg. 7(a), with effect from 6 April 2010.
In reg. 14(2)(e), the words "limitation or requirement imposed under section 42 or 43 of FISMA 2000, or by any prohibition or prohibition order in or made under that Act" substituted for the words "requirement imposed under section 43 of the Financial Services and Markets Act 2000, or by any prohibition imposed by or under any rules made by the Financial Services Authority under that Act; and" by SI 2010/582, reg. 7(b), with effect from 6 April 2010.
In reg. 14(3) the words "before commencement of completion of" substituted for the words "prior to discussing" by SI 2004/2676, reg. 10, with effect from the date SI 2004/1450 is brought into force (6 April 2005).

ACCOUNT PROVIDER – APPOINTMENT OF TAX REPRESENTATIVE

15(1) This regulation specifies the requirements mentioned in regulation 14(2)(f).

15(2) The first requirement specified in this regulation is that–

(a) a person who falls within section 698(2)(b) of ITTOIA 2005 is for the time being appointed by the account provider to be responsible for securing the discharge of the duties prescribed by paragraph (5) which fall to be discharged by the account provider, and

(b) his identity and the fact of his appointment have been notified to the Board by the account provider.

15(3) The second requirement specified in this regulation is that there are for the time being other arrangements with the Board for a person other than the account provider to secure the discharge of such duties.

15(4) The third requirement specified in this regulation is that there are for the time being other arrangements with the Board designed to secure the discharge of such duties.

15(5) The duties prescribed by this paragraph are those that fall to be discharged by an account provider under these Regulations.

15(6) The appointment of a person in pursuance of the first requirement shall be treated as terminated in circumstances where–

(a) the Board have reason to believe that the person concerned–

(i) has failed to secure the discharge of any of the duties prescribed by paragraph (5), or

(ii) does not have adequate resources to discharge those duties, and

(b) the Board have notified the account provider and that person that they propose to treat his appointment as having terminated with effect from the date specified in the notice.

15(7) Where, in accordance with the first requirement, a person is at any time responsible for securing the discharge of duties, the person concerned–

(a) shall be entitled to act on the account provider's behalf for any of the purposes of the provisions relating to the duties;

(b)   shall secure (where appropriate by acting on the account provider's behalf) the account provider's compliance with and discharge of the duties; and

(c)   shall be personally liable in respect of any failure of the account provider to comply with or discharge any such duty as if the duties imposed on the account provider were imposed jointly and severally on the account provider and the person concerned.

History – In reg. 15(2)(a), the words "section 698(2)(b) of ITTOIA 2005" substituted for the words "sub-section (5) of section 333A of the Taxes Act" by SI 2010/582, reg. 8, with effect from 6 April 2010.

ACCOUNT PROVIDER – WITHDRAWAL BY BOARD OF APPROVAL

16(1)   This regulation specifies the circumstances ("the disqualifying circumstances") in which the Board may by notice withdraw their approval of a person as an account provider in relation to an account.

16(2)   The disqualifying circumstances are that the Board have reason to believe–

(a)   that any provision of the Act or these Regulations, or any term of an undertaking given in accordance with regulation 14(2)(b) or condition under regulation 14(4), is not or at any time has not been satisfied, either in respect of an account managed by the account provider or otherwise; or

(b)   that a person to whom they have given approval to act as an account provider is not qualified so to act.

16(2A)   Where paragraph (2B) applies, a term of an undertaking given in accordance with regulation 14(2)(b) shall not be taken as not satisfied only by reason that the person to whom the Board's approval as an account provider has been given does not accept vouchers.

16(2B)   This paragraph applies where–

(a)   a person does not accept any voucher after a day specified by that person; and

(b)   no less than 30 days before the specified day, notice in writing is given to the Board of the person's intention not to accept vouchers after that day.

16(3)   The notice to which paragraph (1) refers shall specify–

(a)   the date from which the Board's approval is withdrawn; and

(b)   the disqualifying circumstances.

16(4)   On receiving the notice referred to in paragraph (1), subject to any appeal under section 22(1)(b) of the Act, the account provider shall notify the registered contact (or, if there is no registered contact, the named child) of the right to transfer the account under regulation 21, and of his or her rights under regulation 20(3).

History – Reg. 16(2A) inserted by SI 2010/2599, reg. 3(1), with effect from 16 November 2010.
Reg. 16(2B) inserted by SI 2010/2599, reg. 3(1), with effect from 16 November 2010.
Reg. 16(4) added by SI 2010/582, reg. 9, with effect from 6 April 2010.

ACCOUNT PROVIDER – APPEAL AGAINST NON-APPROVAL OR WITHDRAWAL OF BOARD'S APPROVAL

17   A person who has been notified of a decision by the Board not to approve that person as an account provider, or an account provider to whom notice of withdrawal of approval has been given under regulation 16, may appeal against the decision by notice given to the Board within 30 days after the date of the notification or notice.

PERMITTED WITHDRAWALS FROM AN ACCOUNT

18   Withdrawals from an account before the date on which the named child attains the age of 18 years may only be made–

(a)   by the account provider, to settle any management charges and other incidental expenses, which are due by or under the management agreement, or

(ab)   in accordance with regulation 18A, or

(b)   where the account provider is satisfied that the named child has died under that age.

History – Reg. 18(ab) inserted by SI 2004/2676, reg. 11, with effect from the date SI 2004/1450 is brought into force (6 April 2005).

PERMITTED WITHDRAWALS FROM AN ACCOUNT WHERE THE CHILD IS TERMINALLY ILL

18A(1) A person with parental responsibility (or, in Scotland, parental responsibilities) for the named child (including a local authority, but excluding a person under 16), or the named child if 16 or over, may make a claim to the Board, for withdrawals from an account to be permitted in accordance with this regulation.

18A(2) The claim shall be–

(a) made in a manner prescribed by the Board, which shall include the giving of any consent necessary for the verification or consideration of the claim, and

(b) accepted in either of the following cases:

Case 1

The child:

(i) in England and Wales or Scotland falls within either section 72(5) of the Social Security Contributions and Benefits Act 1992 (special rules for terminally ill person's entitlement to care component of disability living allowance) or section 82(4) of the Welfare Reform Act 2012 (terminal illness); or

(ii) in Northern Ireland, falls within section 72(5) of the Social Security Contributions and Benefits (Northern Ireland) Act 1992 (the care component).

Case 2

Evidence that the named child is terminally ill has been supplied to the satisfaction of the Board.

18A(3) The Board shall issue a letter to the claimant authorising withdrawals from the account under this regulation.

18A(4) Once a claim has been accepted, withdrawals may be made by the registered contact (on behalf of the named child, where he is not the child) at any time–

(a) provided that, immediately following any withdrawal, a balance sufficient to keep the account open is maintained in the account, and

(b) excepting any transfer of a policy of life insurance (as opposed to the proceeds from such a policy).

18A(5) Where account investments are withdrawn in a form other than sterling currency, regulation 36(1)(b) shall apply (with any necessary modifications) to any such investment immediately before it is withdrawn.

18A(6) In this regulation, **"terminally ill"** has the meaning

(a) for England, Wales and Scotland, in section 66(2)(a) of the Social Security Contributions and Benefits Act 1992 or in section 82(4) of the Welfare Reform Act 2012 (terminal illness); or

(b) for Northern Ireland, in section 72(5) of the Social Security Contributions and Benefits (Northern Ireland) Act 1992 (the care component).

History – In reg. 18A(2)(b), the entry "Case 1" substituted by SI 2014/649, reg. 6(1), with effect from 6 April 2014.
In reg. 18A(3), the words ", and shall also notify the account provider" omitted by SI 2014/649, reg. 6(2), with effect from 6 April 2014.
In reg. 18A(6), the words "(a) for England, Wales and Scotland," inserted by SI 2014/649, reg. 6(3)(a), with effect from 6 April 2014.
In reg. 18A(6), the words "or in section 82(4) of the Welfare Reform Act 2012 (terminal illness); or (b) for Northern Ireland, in section 72(5) of the Social Security Contributions and Benefits (Northern Ireland) Act 1992 (the care component)" inserted by SI 2014/649, reg. 6(3)(b), with effect from 6 April 2014.
Reg. 18A inserted by SI 2004/2676, reg. 12, with effect from the date SI 2004/1450 is brought into force (6 April 2005).

ACCOUNT PROVIDER'S INTENTION TO MAKE A BULK TRANSFER OF ACCOUNTS OR TO CEASE TO ACT AS AN ACCOUNT PROVIDER

19(1) An account provider must give notice to the Board if the account provider–

(a) intends to cease to act as an account provider; or

(b) intends to make a bulk transfer of accounts.

19(2) An account provider must give notice to the person who is the registered contact (or, if there is no registered contact, the named child) if the account provider–

(a) intends to cease to act as an account provider; or

(b) intends that the account will be one of the accounts transferred in a bulk transfer of accounts.

19(3) The notices described in paragraphs (1) and (2) must–

(a)   specify whether the account provider–

    (i)   intends to cease to act as an account provider; or

    (ii)   intends to make a bulk transfer of accounts;

(b)   where the notice specifies an intention to cease to act as an account provider–

    (i)   specify the day on or after which the account provider intends to cease to act as an account provider; and

    (ii)   be given no less than 30 days before that day;

(c)   where the notice specifies an intention to make a bulk transfer of accounts–

    (i)   specify the day on or after which the account provider intends to make the first transfer in the bulk transfer of accounts;

    (ii)   be given no less than 30 days before that day; and

    (iii)   advise the name and address of the person to whom the account provider intends to transfer accounts.

19(4)   The notice described in paragraph (2) must also–

(a)   identify the account to which it relates;

(b)   in the case of a notice under paragraph (2)(a), advise the registered contact of the right to transfer the account under regulation 21 and of his rights under regulation 20(3);

(c)   in the case of a notice under paragraph (2)(b)–

    (i)   advise the registered contact that the account may be transferred otherwise than in a bulk transfer of accounts, such that regulation 21 applies, if sufficient instructions are provided to enable the account provider to do so; and

    (ii)   advise the day by which the account provider must receive sufficient instructions for the account to be transferred otherwise than in a bulk transfer of accounts.

19(5)   Where an account provider intends to make a bulk transfer of accounts in consequence of an intention to cease to act as an account provider, such intention may be specified in a single notice to the Board or to a registered contact (or, if there is no registered contact, the named child) (as appropriate, respectively) provided the requirements of paragraphs (3), (4)(a) and (c) are met.

History – Reg. 19 (and the heading before it) substituted by SI 2013/1744, reg. 6, with effect from 5 August 2013. Former reg. 19 read as follows:

"ACCOUNT PROVIDER CEASING TO ACT (OR CEASING TO ACCEPT REVENUE ALLOCATED ACCOUNTS)

    19(1)   A person shall give notice to the Board and to the registered contact of the account which he manages (or, if there is no registered contact, the named child) of his intention to cease to act as the account provider not less than 30 days before he so ceases so that his obligations to the Board under the account can be conveniently discharged at or about the time he ceases so to act, and the notice to the registered contact or the named child shall inform him of the right to transfer the account under regulation 21, and of his rights under regulation 20(3).

    19(2)   A person shall also give notice to the Board of his intention to cease to accept further Revenue allocated accounts under regulation 6, not less than 30 days before he so ceases.".

ACCOUNT PROVIDER CEASING TO ACCEPT REVENUE ALLOCATED ACCOUNTS

19A   A person shall give notice to the Board of his intention to cease to accept further Revenue allocated accounts under regulation 6, not less than 30 days before he so ceases.

History – Reg. 19A inserted by SI 2013/1744, reg. 6, with effect from 5 August 2013.

ACCOUNT PROVIDER CEASING TO QUALIFY

20(1)   A person shall cease to qualify as an account provider and shall notify the Board within 30 days of the relevant event in sub-paragraphs (a) to (f), of that relevant event, where–

(a)   the person no longer fulfils the conditions of regulation 14;

(b)   there is an insolvency event in relation to the account provider;

(c)   an application has been made for a bank insolvency order or a bank administration order;

(d)   [effectively omitted by SI 2010/582, reg. 10(a);]

(e)   in the case of a building society, a person falling within section 991 of ITA 2007 or a credit union–

    (i)   it ceases to be a building society or to fall within section 991 of ITA 2007 or to be a credit union, as the case may be;

    (ii)   its directors have made a proposal under Part 1 of the Insolvency Act 1986 for a composition in satisfaction of its debts or a scheme of arrangement of its affairs; or

(iii)   a receiver or manager of its property has been appointed; or

(f)   in the case of a European institution, a relevant authorised person or an assurance undertaking which falls within regulation 14(2)(d)(iv), action corresponding to any described in sub-paragraph (b) to (e) has been taken by or in relation to the institution, person or undertaking under the law of an EEA State.

20(2)   On giving the notice referred to in paragraph (1), the person shall also notify the registered contact (or, if there is no registered contact, the named child) of the right to transfer the account under regulation 21, and the notice shall inform the recipient of the rights under paragraph (3).

20(3)   Where a registered contact–

(a)   receives a notice under paragraph (2), or regulation 16(4) or 19(2)(a), and

(b)   within 30 days of the sending of the notice, transfers the account to another account provider pursuant to regulation 21,

the period between the transferor ceasing to act or qualify as an account provider, and the transfer to the transferee, shall be ignored in determining whether the account has at all times been managed by an account provider.

History – Reg. 20(1)(b) and (c) substituted for former reg. 20(1)(b)–(d) by SI 2001/582, reg. 10(a), with effect from 6 April 2010.
In reg. 20(1)(e), the words "section 991 of ITA 2007 or a credit union" substituted for the words "section 840A(1)(b) of the Taxes Act or a relevant European institution" by SI 2010/582, reg. 10(b), with effect from 6 April 2010.
In reg. 20(1)(e)(i), the words "section 991 of ITA 2007 or to be a credit union" substituted for the words "section 840A(1)(b) of the Taxes Act or to be a relevant European institution" by SI 2010/582, reg. 10(c), with effect from 6 April 2010.
In reg. 20(3)(a), "19(2)(a)" substituted for "19(1)" by SI 2013/1744, reg. 7, with effect from 5 August 2013.
In reg. 20(3)(a), the words "16(4) or" inserted by SI 2010/582, reg. 10(d), with effect from 6 April 2010.

TRANSFER OF ACCOUNTS TO OTHER ACCOUNT PROVIDERS

21(1)   Where–

(a)   arrangements are made by a registered contact to transfer the whole of the investments under an account from one account provider ("the transferor") to another account provider ("the transferee"),

(b)   the whole of the investments under an account are so transferred in consequence of an account provider ("the transferor") ceasing to act or to qualify as an account provider, or

(c)   an account is transferred in a bulk transfer of accounts or in a group transfer of accounts,

the transfer shall be treated as a transfer of the account.

21(2)   The account and its description under regulation 4 shall not be affected for the purposes of these Regulations by reason of the transfer, save that, where the registered contact specifies in accordance with paragraph (3)(a) an account of a different description, the account shall, on the transfer, become an account of that other description.

21(3)   The registered contact shall make–

(a)   the application required by regulation 13(2) (modified as if the words "applied for" were replaced with "following the transfer"), and

(b)   the application and declaration required by regulation 13(3) to (5),

to the transferee.

21(3A)   Paragraph (3) does not apply where an account is transferred in a bulk transfer of accounts.

21(3B)   Where an account is transferred in a bulk transfer of accounts, a subscription to the account after the transfer may only be made if–

(a)   an application to the transferee in relation to the account in accordance with regulation 13 has been made; or

(b)   the subscription is permitted by virtue of paragraph (3C);

and regulation 13(2) is then modified for the purposes of this paragraph as if the words "applied for" were replaced with "following the transfer".

21(3C)   A subscription to an account is permitted by this paragraph where–

(a)   the account has been transferred to the transferee in a bulk transfer of accounts pursuant to a scheme described in regulation 2(1A)(a)(ii) or pursuant to a transfer of the type described in regulation 2(1A)(b); and

(b)   the most recent application in accordance with regulation 13 relating to the transferred account made before its transfer is available to the transferee.

21(3D)   For the purposes of paragraph (3C)(b), an application in accordance with regulation 13 as described in that paragraph is available to a transferee if paragraph (3E) or (3F) applies.

21(3E) This paragraph applies where the application described in paragraph (3C)(b) (or a copy of it) is held by the transferee.

21(3F) This paragraph applies where–

(a)   the application described in paragraph (3C)(b) (or a copy of it) is held by the transferor; and

(b)   the transferee can require the transferor to make it available to the transferee for any purpose necessary to ensure the transferee's compliance with these regulations.

21(3G) An account transferred in accordance with this regulation in a bulk transfer of accounts is an account opened pursuant to an application in accordance with regulation 13 for the purposes of these Regulations whether or not an application in accordance with regulation 13 as described in paragraph (3B)(a) is made.

21(3H) Where a registered contact applies in accordance with paragraph (3) to a potential transferee for a transfer under this regulation, specifying a stakeholder account offered by the transferee, the transferee shall not decline to accept that application (or the transfer in consequence of it) except where–

(a)   the transferee has reason to believe that the registered contact has given untrue information in his application;

(b)   the transferee demonstrates to the satisfaction of the Board that acceptance of transfers, or a class of transfers, during a particular period would jeopardise his ability to prevent any of the matters mentioned in regulation 16(2)(a); or

(c)   the transferor does not give the transferee the notice in accordance with paragraph (4).

21(4) The transferor shall on the date of the transfer give the transferee a notice containing the information specified in paragraph (5) and the declaration specified in paragraph (6).

21(5) The information specified in this paragraph is–

(a)   as regards the named child–
     (i)   his full name,
     (ii)   his date of birth,
     (iii)   his unique reference number;

(b)   as regards the account–
     (i)   the description of the account,
     (ii)   the date of the transfer,
     (iii)   the total amount subscribed to the account during the period from the beginning of the subscription year in which the transfer takes place to the date of the transfer,
     (iv)   any amount which has been claimed from the Board under regulations 26 or 27 and which has not been paid at the date of the transfer, and
     (v)   the total amount subscribed to the account during the previous subscription year, where that subscription year ended later than the 5th April preceding the date of the transfer.

(c)   the full name and address, including postcode, of the registered contact who has made the transfer arrangements.

21(6) The declaration specified in this paragraph is a declaration by the transferor that–

(a)   he has fulfilled all his obligations to the named child, the Board or otherwise, which are imposed by these Regulations;

(b)   he has transferred to the transferee or his nominee all the account investments and that, where registration of any such transfer is required, he has taken the necessary steps to ensure that those account investments can be registered in the name of the transferee or nominee;

(c)   he will forward any further payment received in respect of those account investments to the transferee, on receipt of the payment, and

(d)   the information contained in the notice is correct.

History – Reg. 21(1)(c) (and the "or" before it) inserted (and the "or" after (a) omitted) by SI 2013/1744, reg. 8, with effect from 5 August 2013.
In reg. 21(3)(a) the words "following the transfer" substituted for the word "transferred" by SI 2004/2676, reg. 13(a), with effect from the date SI 2004/1450 is brought into force (6 April 2005).
Reg. 21(3A)–(3G) inserted by SI 2013/1744, reg. 8(d), with effect from 5 August 2013.
Reg. 21(3A) renumbered as (3H) by SI 2013/1744, reg. 8(d), with effect from 5 August 2013.
Reg. 21(3A) inserted by SI 2004/2676, reg. 13(b), with effect from the date SI 2004/1450 is brought into force (6 April 2005).
In reg. 21(5)(b)(iv), "26 or 27" substituted for "26, 27 or 30" by SI 2013/263, reg. 2(4)(d), with effect from 16 March 2013, in respect of what would otherwise be fortnightly and initial return periods within reg. 30(1) beginning on or after that day.
Reg. 21(5)(b)(v) and the word ", and " which precedes it added by SI 2010/582, reg. 11, with effect from 6 April 2010.

RECOUPMENT OF INLAND REVENUE CONTRIBUTIONS TO VOID ACCOUNTS (AND OTHER ACCOUNTS)

22(1) Where—

(a) the named child has never been an eligible child (see regulation 8(1)(b)), or

(b) there is a breach of regulation 8(1)(c) in relation to an account,

the account is void, and the persons mentioned in paragraph (3) shall account to the Inland Revenue for Inland Revenue contributions paid in respect of the account, together with income and gains which have arisen in consequence of the crediting of any of those payments to the account.

22(2) Where—

(a) the condition in section 9(5) of the Act or regulation 7(10B) or 7A(4) was satisfied in relation to a child, but the determination under sections 18 to 21 of the Tax Credits Act 2002 has been overturned, or

(b) the condition in section 9(8) of the Act was satisfied in relation to a child, but it has subsequently been determined that payment of the relevant benefit or tax credit mentioned in that subsection should not have been made, or that the applicable amount or tax credit should not have included an amount or credit in respect of the child, or

(c) the requirements of regulation 7(10) were, or the condition in regulation 7(10C), 7A(5) or 7B(1) was, satisfied in relation to a child, but it has subsequently been determined that payment of the relevant benefit mentioned in the relevant provision should not have been made, or that the applicable amount should not have included an amount in respect of that child,

the persons mentioned in paragraph (3) shall account to the Inland Revenue for any supplementary contribution, or further contribution, as the case may be, paid in respect of the account, together with income and gains which have arisen in consequence of the crediting of any such payment to the account.

22(3) The persons mentioned in paragraphs (1) and (2) are—

(a) the account provider (to the extent that he has assets in his possession or control),

(b) the registered contact,

(c) the named child, and

(d) any person in whom the Inland Revenue contributions, income or gains, or any property directly or indirectly representing any of them, is vested (whether beneficially or otherwise)

and they shall be jointly and severally liable.

22(4) Where a person accountable under this regulation is notified by the Inland Revenue that an amount is due from him under it, that amount shall be treated for the purposes of Part 6 of the Management Act (collection and recovery) as if it were tax charged in an assessment on that person, and due and payable.

History – In reg. 22(2)(a), the words "or regulation 7(10B) or 7A(4)" inserted by SI 2009/475, reg. 6(a), with effect from 6 April 2009.

In reg. 22(2)(c), ", 7A(5) or 7B(1)" substituted for "or 7A(5)" by SI 2010/836, reg. 4, with effect where a child falls within the terms of reg. 7B for a year of assessment commencing on or after 6 April 2009.

In reg. 22(2)(c), or the condition in regulation 7(10C) or 7A(5) was," inserted and the words "the relevant provision" substituted for the words "that provision" by SI 2009/475, reg. 6(b), with effect from 6 April 2009.

Reg. 22(2)(c) and the word "or" which precedes it and the words ", or further contribution, as the case may be," inserted by SI 2005/383, reg. 4, with effect from 6 April 2005.

"REPAIR" OF INVALID ACCOUNTS

23(1) Except in the case of a breach of regulation 8(1)(b) or (c) (where no repair of an account is possible), it is an overriding requirement to be satisfied in relation to an account that the account provider and registered contact, as the case may be, take any steps necessary to remedy any breach of these Regulations.

23(2) Where a breach is remedied as mentioned in paragraph (1), the account shall, to the extent of that breach, be treated as having been a valid account at all times, except for determining whether there has been a breach of these Regulations for the purposes of section 20 of the Act (penalties).

PART 3 – TAX AND ADMINISTRATION OF ACCOUNTS

EXEMPTION FROM TAX OF ACCOUNT INCOME AND GAINS

24   Subject to compliance with these Regulations (and in particular regulation 9)–

(a)   no tax shall be chargeable on the account provider or his nominee, or on the named child or registered contact (on his behalf)–

     (i)   in respect of interest, dividends, distributions or gains in respect of account investments (excluding any building society bonus),

     (ia)   in respect of alternative finance return or profit share return paid by a financial institution (within the meanings in Chapter 5 of Part 2 of the Finance Act 2005);

     (ib)   in respect of a payment under a building society bonus scheme, so far as the payment is calculated by reference to account investments (and if paid directly by the society into the account, the payment shall not count towards the subscription limit in regulation 9);

     (ii)   on any annual profits or gains treated under Part 12 of ITA 2007 as having been received by any of them in respect of account investments,

     (iii)   on an offshore income gain to which a disposal made by any of them of an account investment gives rise, which is treated by section 761(1) of the Taxes Act as constituting profits or gains,

     (iv)   on a profit on the disposal of a deeply discounted security within the meaning given by section 430 of ITTOIA 2005;

     (v)   in respect of gains treated under Chapter 9 of Part 4 of ITTOIA 2005 as arising in connection with a policy of life insurance which is an account investment;

(b)   losses accruing on any disposal of account investments shall be disregarded for the purposes of capital gains tax;

(ba)   any gain or loss accruing on and attributable to a payment within paragraph (ib) of sub-paragraph (a) shall not be a chargeable gain or allowable loss for capital gains tax purposes;

(c)   section 935 of ITA 2007 shall apply with the following modifications–

     (i)   for references to a plan manager, substitute references to an account provider,

     (ii)   for references to a plan, substitute references to an account, and

     (iii)   for the reference to Chapter 3 of Part 6 of ITTOIA 2005, substitute a reference to the Act;

(d)   a deficiency arising in a tax year and falling within section 539(1) of ITTOIA 2005, so far as it relates to a policy of life insurance which is an account investment, shall not be allowable as a deduction from the total income of the named child;

(e)   relief in respect of tax shall be given in the manner and to the extent provided by these Regulations; and

(f)   income arising from account investments shall not be regarded as income for any income tax purposes (including section 629 of ITTOIA 2005).

History – In reg. 24(a)(ii), the words "under Part 12 of ITA 2007" substituted for the words "by section 714(2) of the Taxes Act" by SI 2010/582, reg. 12(a), with effect from 6 April 2010.

Reg. 24(a)(iv) substituted by SI 2010/582, reg. 12(b), with effect from 6 April 2010.

In reg. 24(a)(v), the words "under Chapter 9 of Part 4 of ITTOIA 2005" substituted for "by section 541 of the Taxes Act" by SI 2010/582, reg. 12(c), with effect from 6 April 2010.

In reg. 24(a)(i) words "(excluding any building society bonus)" inserted by SI 2006/3195, reg. 4(a) with effect from 1 January 2007.

Reg. 24(ia) inserted, in reg. 24(c)(iii) the words "Chapter 3 of Part 6 of ITTOIA 2005" substituted for the words "section 333 of the Taxes Act" and in reg. 24(f) the words "section 629 of ITTOIA 2005" substituted for the words "section 660B of the Taxes Act" by SI 2005/3349, reg. 7, with effect from 27 December 2005.

Reg. 24(a)(ib) inserted by SI 2006/3195, reg. 4(b) with effect from 1 January 2007.

Reg. 24(ba) inserted by SI 2006/3195, reg. 5 with effect from 1 January 2007.

In reg. 24(c), the words "section 935 of ITA 2007" substituted for the words "section 349B(4) of the Taxes Act" by SI 2010/582, reg. 12(d), with effect from 6 April 2010.

In reg. 24(d), the words "a deficiency arising in a tax year and falling within section 539(1) of ITTOIA 2005" substituted for the words "a corresponding deficiency occurring at the end of the final year, within the meaning of section 549(1) of the Taxes Act" by SI 2010/582, reg. 12(e), with effect from 6 April 2010.

TAX LIABILITIES AND RELIEFS – ACCOUNT PROVIDER TO ACT ON BEHALF OF THE NAMED CHILD

25(1) An account provider may under these Regulations make tax claims, conduct appeals and agree on behalf of the named child (or of the registered contact in respect of the child) liabilities for and reliefs from tax in respect of an account.

25(2) Tax claims shall be made to the Board in accordance with the provisions of regulations 26 and 27.

25(3) Where any relief or exemption from tax previously given in respect of an account has by virtue of these Regulations become excessive, in computing the relief due on any claim there shall be deducted (so that amounts equal to that excess are set-off or repaid to the Board, as the case may be) notwithstanding that those amounts have been invested, any other amount of tax due to the Board by the account provider in respect of any tax liability in respect of account investments under an account including (but without prejudice to the making of an assessment under that Schedule) any amount falling due in respect of a liability under Chapter 9 of Part 15 of ITA 2007.

History – In reg. 25(3), the words "Chapter 9 of Part 15 of ITA 2007" substituted for the words "paragraph 3 or 4 of Schedule 23A of the Taxes Act" by SI 2010/582, reg. 13, with effect from 6 April 2010.

REPAYMENTS IN RESPECT OF TAX TO ACCOUNT PROVIDER – INTERIM TAX CLAIMS

26(1) Notwithstanding the provisions of any other enactment, the Board shall not be under an obligation to make any repayment in respect of tax under these Regulations earlier than the end of the month following the month in which the claim for the repayment is received.

26(2) A claim for repayment in respect of tax which is not an annual claim ("interim tax claim") may be made only for a period of a month (or a number of months not exceeding six) beginning on the 6th day of the month and ending on the 5th day of the relevant following month.

26(3) No claim for repayment may be made for the month ending 5th October or any subsequent month in a year until the annual claim due under regulation 27(2) in respect of an account for the preceding year has been duly made by the account provider and received by the Board.

26(4) Where, on the occasion of a claim, there is due to the Board an amount in respect of tax, that amount shall be recoverable by the Board in the same manner as tax charged by an assessment on the account provider which has become final and conclusive.

26(5) This regulation and regulation 27 shall not apply to any repayment in respect of tax on account investments falling within regulation 12(2)(m) (life insurance), or on distributions and other rights or proceeds in respect of those investments.

REPAYMENTS IN RESPECT OF TAX TO ACCOUNT PROVIDER – ANNUAL TAX CLAIMS

27(1) An annual tax claim is a claim for repayment in respect of tax for a year and may not be made at any time more than six years after the end of the year.

27(2) Where the account provider–

(a) has made at least one interim tax claim during a year, or

(b) wishes to reclaim tax, or there is due to the Board an amount in respect of tax, following the end of the year,

the account provider shall within six months after the end of the year make an annual tax claim to establish the total of tax repayments due under an account for that year.

27(3) Where the aggregate of the repayments in respect of interim tax claims for the year shown by an annual tax claim exceeds the amount of tax repayable for the year shown on the claim, the account provider shall repay the amount of the excess to the Board with the claim.

27(4) If an account provider fails to make the annual tax claim required under paragraph (2)(a) within the time limited, the Board may issue a notice to the account provider showing the aggregate of payments in respect of the interim tax claims for the year, and stating that the Board are not satisfied that the amount due to the account provider for that year exceeds the lower amount stated in the notice.

27(5) If an annual tax claim is not delivered to the Board within 14 days after the issue of a notice under paragraph (4) the amount of the difference between the aggregate and the lower amount stated in the notice shall immediately become recoverable by the Board in the same manner as tax charged by an assessment on the account provider which has become final and conclusive.

27(6) Where an annual tax claim has been made and the account provider subsequently discovers that an error or mistake has been made in the claim the account provider may make a supplementary annual claim within the time allowed in paragraph (1).

ACCOUNT PROVIDER'S TAX CLAIMS – SUPPLEMENTARY PROVISIONS

28(1) Section 42 of the Management Act shall not apply to tax claims under these Regulations.

28(2) No appeal shall lie from the Board's decision on an interim tax claim.

28(3) An appeal from the Board's decision on an annual tax claim shall be brought by giving notice to the Board within 30 days of receipt of notice of the decision.

28(4) No payment or repayment made or other thing done on or in relation to an interim tax claim or a notice under regulation 27(4) shall prejudice the decision on an annual tax claim.

28(5) The provisions contained in Part 5 of the Management Act (appeals and other proceedings) shall apply to an appeal under paragraph (3) above and, on an appeal that is notified to the tribunal, the tribunal may vary the decision appealed against whether or not the variation is to the advantage of the appellant.

28(6) All such assessments, payments and repayments shall be made as necessary to give effect to the Board's decision on an annual tax claim or to any variation of that decision on appeal.

28(7) Claims under these Regulations shall be in such form and contain such particulars as the Board prescribe and, subject to regulation 32(1), shall be signed by the account provider, and forms prescribed for annual claims may require a report to be given by a person qualified for appointment as auditor of a company.

History – In reg. 28(3), the words "shall be to the Special Commissioners", which appeared after "An appeal", omitted by SI 2009/56, art. 3(2) and Sch. 2, para. 127(2)(a), operative from 1 April 2009 subject to transitional and saving provisions in SI 2009/56, Sch. 3.
In reg. 28(3), the words ", and the appeal", which appeared after "tax claim", omitted by SI 2009/56, art. 3(2) and Sch. 2, para. 127(2)(b), operative from 1 April 2009 subject to transitional and saving provisions in SI 2009/56, Sch. 3.
In reg. 28(5), the words "and, on an appeal that is notified to the tribunal, the tribunal" substituted for the words ", and on appeal the Special Commissioners" by SI 2009/56, art. 3(2) and Sch. 2, para. 127(3), operative from 1 April 2009 subject to transitional and saving provisions in SI 2009/56, Sch. 3.

ASSESSMENTS FOR WITHDRAWING RELIEF AND RECOVERING TAX

29(1) Where–

(a)   any relief or exemption from tax given in respect of income or gains under an account is found not to be due or to be excessive, or

(b)   the full amount of tax in respect of the income or gains under an account has not otherwise been fully accounted for and paid to the Board on behalf of the named child,

an assessment to tax may be made by the Board in the amount or further amount which in their opinion ought to be charged.

29(2) An assessment to which paragraph (1) refers may be made on the account provider or on the registered contact (in respect of the child where the child is under the age of 16).

29(3) If the assessment is made to recover tax in respect of income under an account it shall be made under Case VI of Schedule D.

29(4) [Omitted SI 2012/886, reg. 2(2).]

History – Reg. 29(4) omitted by SI 2012/886, reg. 2(2), with effect from 6 April 2012. Former reg. 29(4) read as follows:
> "**29(4)** Sections 72 and 73 of the Management Act shall be modified in relation to accounts, so that–
> (a)   references to a parent or guardian include a reference to the registered contact for an account held by the named child, and
> (b)   references to an incapacitated person, in relation to Scotland, are to a person under the age of 16 years.".

FORTNIGHTLY CLAIM AND FINANCIAL RETURNS

30 [Omitted by SI 2013/263, reg. 2(3).]

History – Reg. 30 omitted by SI 2013/263, reg. 2(3), with effect from 16 March 2013, in respect of what would otherwise be fortnightly and initial return periods within reg. 30(1) beginning on or after that day. Former reg. 30 read as follows:
> "**30(1)** In this regulation–
> "**fortnightly period**" means a period–
> (a)   beginning on the 1st, and ending on the 15th, day of a calendar month, or
> (b)   beginning on the 16th, and ending on the last, day of a calendar month;
> "**first return period**", in relation to account providers approved with effect from a date between 1st January 2005 and 28th February 2005, means the period beginning on the date on which the approval takes effect and ending on 28th February 2005;

"**second return period**", in relation to account providers approved with effect from a date between 1st January 2005 and 31st March 2005, means the period beginning on the later of 1st March 2005 and the date on which the approval takes effect, and ending on 31st March 2005;

"**initial return period**", in relation to account providers approved later, means the period–
(a)   beginning on the date on which the approval takes effect, or the appointed day (whichever is the later), and
(b)   ending simultaneously with the end of the current fortnightly period.

30(2)   The following provisions of this regulation apply to an account provider in relation to–
(a)   that provider's first, second or initial return period, and
(b)   each succeeding fortnightly period (other than succeeding a first return period),
during which, or during any part of which, he acted as an account provider.

30(3)   Within–
(a)   ten days of the end of a provider's first return period (if any), and
(b)   five days of the end of any other period mentioned in paragraph (2),
the account provider shall deliver by means of electronic communications to the Board, a return for that period, in a form specified by the Board.

30(4)   The return shall include a declaration of the information in paragraph (5), and a claim as mentioned in paragraph (6) (in each case, stated separately for each account, quoting the named child's unique reference number and date of birth).

30(5)   The information is that, during that period–
(a)   the account provider has opened an account in accordance with regulation 5;
(b)   the account provider has opened a Revenue allocated account in accordance with regulation 6;
(c)   an account has been transferred to the account provider in accordance with regulation 21, and is held with the account provider at the end of the period; or
(d)   an account has been closed, due to the named child dying under the age of 18 (and the date of death).

30(6)   The claim is–
(a)   where paragraph (5)(a) or (b) applies, a claim for the initial contribution or special contribution due to the account in accordance with regulation 7(1) to (4);
(b)   where the Inland Revenue have informed the account provider that section 9 of the Act applies to the named child, a claim for the supplementary contribution due to the account in accordance with regulation 7(5) to (7); and
(c)   where the Inland Revenue have informed the account provider that a further contribution is due for the named child in accordance with regulation 7(10) or (10A), regulation 7A, or regulation 7B(2) or (3), a claim for the further contribution due to the account in accordance with the relevant provision.

30(7)   Paragraphs (5)(a) and (b) and (6)(a) and (b) shall apply notwithstanding any transfer of the account to another account provider under regulation 21, before the end of the period in question.".

In former reg. 30(5)(a) the words "(by means of a voucher)" omitted by SI 2006/199, reg. 5, with effect from 7 February 2006.
In former reg. 30(6)(c), ", regulation 7A, or regulation 7B(2) or (3)" substituted for "or regulation 7A" by SI 2010/836, reg. 5, with effect where a child falls within the terms of reg. 7B for a year of assessment commencing on or after 6 April 2009.
In former reg. 30(6)(c), the words "a further contribution is due for" substituted for the words "paragraph (10) of regulation 7 applies to", the words "the relevant provision" substituted for the words "that paragraph", and the words "in accordance with regulation 7(10) or (10A) or regulation 7A" inserted by SI 2009/475, reg. 7, with effect from 6 April 2009.
Former reg. 30(6)(c) and the word "and" which precedes it inserted by SI 2005/383, reg. 5, with effect from 6 April 2005.

RECORDS TO BE KEPT BY ACCOUNT PROVIDER

31(1)   An account provider shall at all times keep sufficient records in respect of an account to enable the requirements of these Regulations to be satisfied.

31(2)   In particular, an account provider shall produce (when required to do so by an officer of the Board) any–
(a)   application made under regulation 13(1) or (10),
(b)   voucher given to him,
(c)   annual statement issued by him, and
(d)   transfer notice given to him under regulation 21(4),
or electronic copies, within the period of 3 years from when it was made, issued or given (notwithstanding any transfer of the account under regulation 21).

31(3)   Where an account is transferred by an account provider ("the transferor") to another account provider ("the transferee") in a group transfer of accounts, any records (or copies of records) kept by the transferor in respect of the account at the time when it is transferred shall be treated for the purposes of this regulation as kept by the transferee for so long as sub-paragraphs (a), (b) and (c) of paragraph (4) apply.

31(4)   For the purposes of paragraph (3)–
(a)   this sub-paragraph applies as if the records described in paragraph (3) are kept by the transferor;
(b)   this sub-paragraph applies if the transferor and transferee are members of the same group of companies; and
(c)   this sub-paragraph applies if the transferee can require the transferor to make the records available to the transferee for any purpose necessary to ensure the transferee's compliance with these regulations.

History – Reg. 31(3) and (4) inserted by SI 2013/1744, reg. 9, with effect from 5 August 2013.

RETURNS OF INFORMATION BY ACCOUNT PROVIDER

32(1) An account provider shall within 60 days after the end of each year in which he acts as an account provider, and after ceasing to act or to qualify as an account provider, deliver by means of electronic communications to the Board a return for that year, or for the part of that year in which he so acted or qualified, in a form specified by the Board, which contains the information specified in paragraph (2).

32(2) The information specified in this paragraph is information relating to each account in respect of which he acted as account provider, in the year or the part of the year for which the return is made, other than accounts transferred to another account provider under regulation 21 in that year or part of a year, as to–

(a)   as regards the named child–

     (i)   [omitted by SI 2005/909, reg. 9,]

     (ii)   [omitted by SI 2005/909, reg. 9,]

     (iii)   his unique reference number;

(b)   as regards each such account–

     (i)   whether or not the account is a stakeholder account,

     (ii)   whether or not there is a registered contact for the account,

     (iii)   the aggregate market value of the account investments held under the account, subject to paragraph (3), the value of each account investment being determined either as at 5th April in that year, or any other valuation date not falling earlier than 5th October in that year, and

     (iv)   the total amount of cash subscribed to the account, in the subscription year ending during the year or the part of the year for which the return is made.

32(2A) Where, during the year or part of the year, the named child reaches the age of 18 years or dies, there shall be substituted for paragraph (2)(b)(iii)–

     "(iii)   the aggregate market value of the account investments held under the account immediately before the relevant event mentioned in paragraph (2A),"

32(3) The reference in paragraph (2)(b)(iii) to market value shall be construed–

(a)   in the case of policies of life insurance, as a reference to their surrender value, and

(b)   as referring to separate values for–

     (i)   cash falling within regulation 12(2)(k) or (l), and

     (ii)   policies of life insurance and all other account investments.

32(4) No claim for repayment, or repayment, may be made under regulations 26 and 27 until the returns which have become due under this regulation have been duly made by the account provider and received by the Board.

History – Reg. 32(2)(a)(i) and (ii) omitted by SI 2005/909, reg. 9, with effect from 6 April 2005.
Reg. 32(2A) inserted by SI 2010/582, reg. 14, with effect from 6 April 2010.

INFORMATION ABOUT "LOOKED AFTER CHILDREN" FROM LOCAL AUTHORITIES

33 [Omitted by SI 2011/781, reg. 3.]

History – Reg. 33 omitted by SI 2011/781, reg. 3, with effect from 7 April 2011.

THE OFFICIAL SOLICITOR OR ACCOUNTANT OF COURT TO BE THE PERSON WHO HAS THE AUTHORITY TO MANAGE AN ACCOUNT

33A(1) Every local authority shall be under a duty to–

(a)   identify any child who–

     (i)   is born after 31st August 2002 and before 3rd January 2011,

     (ii)   is under 16 years of age at the end of the return period, and

     (iii)   during the return period falls within the circumstances specified in paragraph (2) for the first time since the child became looked after (in Scotland, looked after and accommodated) by the local authority; and

(b)   deliver to the Board, within 10 days of the end of each return period and by means of electronic communications, a return for that period in a form specified by the Board containing the information specified in paragraph (2A) for each child identified under sub-paragraph (a).

33A(2)   The circumstances specified are where–

(a)   the child is looked after (in Scotland, looked after and accommodated) by the local authority, and

(b)   at least one of the following conditions is satisfied.

Condition 1

There is no person, or no person other than the local authority, who has parental responsibility (in Scotland, parental responsibilities) for the child.

Condition 2

It is part of the care plan for the child that–

(a)   the child will live indefinitely away from home (or his former home), and

(b)   the child will not have face to face contact with any parent having parental responsibility (in Scotland, parental responsibilities) for the child.

Condition 3

An order has been made under section 34(4) of the Children Act 1989 or Article 53(4) of the Children (Northern Ireland) Order 1995, authorising the local authority to refuse to allow contact between the child and any person with parental responsibility (or, in Scotland, a supervision requirement made with a condition regulating contact under section 70(5)(b) of the Children (Scotland) Act 1995 that the child shall have no contact with a person with parental responsibilities), and there is no other individual with parental responsibility (in Scotland, parental responsibilities) for the child to act as registered contact.

Condition 4

The Court of Protection has–

(a)   appointed a deputy for a person with parental responsibility for the child, or

(b)   determined that such a person lacks capacity within the meaning of the Mental Capacity Act 2005 to manage the child's property and affairs,

and there is no other individual with parental responsibility for the child to act as registered contact. In Scotland, in this Condition for–

(a)   "Court of Protection" substitute "Sheriff",

(b)   "receiver" substitute "guardian appointed under section 58 of the Adults with Incapacity (Scotland) Act 2000",

(c)   the reference to a patient, substitute "incapable for the purposes of the Adults with Incapacity (Scotland) Act 2000," and

(d)   "parental responsibility" substitute "parental responsibilities".

Condition 5

The child has been lost or abandoned, and there is no prospect for the foreseeable future of reunification of the child with a parent having parental responsibility (in Scotland, parental responsibilities) for the child.

In this Condition, "lost or abandoned"–

(a)   in England and Wales, has the meaning in section 20(1)(b) of the Children Act 1989;

(b)   in Northern Ireland, has the meaning in Article 21(1)(b) of the Children (Northern Ireland) Order 1995; and

(c)   in Scotland, has the meaning in section 25(1)(b) of the Children (Scotland) Act 1995.

Condition 6

In England and Wales, an adoption agency or local authority has been authorised to place the child for adoption under section 19, or by a placement order under section 21, of the Adoption and Children Act 2002, or

in Northern Ireland, an Order has been made under Article 17 or 18 of the Adoption (Northern Ireland) Order 1987 to free the child for adoption.

33A(2A)   The information specified in this paragraph is–

(a)   the name, address and unique identifier of the local authority making the return;

(b)   the name of the local authority officer responsible for the return;

(c)   the full name, sex and date of birth of the child;

(d)   the full name and address of the child's mother, if known by the local authority (or failing that the full name and address of the child's father, if known), unless the local authority considers the child's situation to be particularly sensitive;

(e)   any information that the local authority has about whether the child is or may be a person subject to immigration control within the meaning of section 115(9) of the Immigration and Asylum Act 1999, and the nature of that information;

(f)   a correspondence address for the child; and

(g)   if known by the local authority, the child's unique reference number as stated on the voucher issued under section 5(1) of the Child Trust Funds Act 2004 (if any).

33A(2B)   The unique identifier of a local authority as referred to in paragraph (2A)(a) is the number allocated to the local authority by the Board for the purpose of these Regulations.

33A(3)   Where–

(a)   the local authority delivers to the Board a return under this regulation in respect of any child, and

(b)   the Board (subject to checking and if necessary correcting the contents of the form) delivers it to the Official Solicitor (where the child is in England and Wales or Northern Ireland) or the Accountant of Court (where the child is in Scotland),

the Official Solicitor or Accountant of Court, as the case may be, shall be the person who has the authority to manage the child's account for the purposes of section 3(6)(b) of the Act.

33A(4)   The Official Solicitor or Accountant of Court shall cease to be the person who has the authority to manage the child's account (and shall be discharged from the duties of registered contact) where–

(a)   the child attains the age of 16,

(b)   in any case where the child is under 16 and still looked after (in Scotland, looked after and accommodated) by a local authority–

     (i)   the local authority confirms to the Official Solicitor or Accountant of Court that there is a named responsible person in relation to the child, who is able to be the registered contact for the child's account, and that none of the Conditions in paragraph (2) applies, and

     (ii)   the Official Solicitor or Accountant of Court cancels his declaration and authorisation in accordance with regulation 13(7) and is replaced as registered contact by that responsible person, in accordance with regulation 13(10), or

(c)   in any case where the child is under 16 and is not looked after (in Scotland, looked after and accommodated) by a local authority–

     (i)   a responsible person for the child provides evidence to the satisfaction of the Official Solicitor or Accountant of Court, as the case may be, that he has parental responsibility for the child, and

     (ii)   the Official Solicitor or Accountant of Court cancels his declaration and authorisation in accordance with regulation 13(7) and is replaced as registered contact by that responsible person, in accordance with regulation 13(10).

33A(5)   A local authority shall, for the purposes of paragraph (4), confirm to the Official Solicitor or Accountant of Court, as the case may be–

(a)   whether the child is still looked after (in Scotland, looked after and accommodated) by the authority, and

(b)   the identity of the person or persons who had parental responsibility for the child at the date when he ceased to be looked after (in Scotland, looked after and accommodated) by the authority (or, at the option of the authority, any later date).

33A(6)   In this regulation–

     "local authority" includes an authority within the meaning of the Children (Northern Ireland) Order 1995;

     "looked after and accommodated child", in Scotland, means a child who is–

     (a)   both looked after, and provided with or placed in accommodation, by a local authority within the meaning of those expressions in Part 2 of the Children (Scotland) Act 1995, or

     (b)   accommodated by a local authority under section 22 of that Act,

     and related expressions shall be construed accordingly;

"looked after child"–

(a)   in England and Wales, has the meaning given in section 22(1) of the Children Act 1989, extended to include a child accommodated by a local authority under section 17 of that Act, and

(b)   in Northern Ireland, means a child accommodated under Part 4 of the Children (Northern Ireland) Order 1995,

and related expressions shall be construed accordingly;

"return period" means a period–

(a)   beginning on 7th April 2011 and ending on 6th May 2011, and

(b)   each succeeding period of one month.

History – Reg. 33A(1) substituted by SI 2011/781, reg. 4(a), with effect from 7 April 2011.
In reg. 33A(2), in condition 4, in para. (a) the word "deputy" and para. (b) substituted by SI 2007/1898, art. 6 and Sch. 1, para. 33, with effect from 1 October 2007.
In reg. 33A(2) Condition 6 inserted by SI 2006/2684, reg. 5 with effect from 31 October 2006.
Reg. 33A(2A) inserted by SI 2011/781, reg. 4(b), with effect from 7 April 2011.
Reg. 33A(2B) inserted by SI 2011/2447, reg. 6, with effect from 1 November 2011.
Reg. 33A(3)(a) substituted by SI 2011/781, reg. 4(c), with effect from 7 April 2011.
Reg. 33A(6) substituted by SI 2011/781, reg. 4(d), with effect from 7 April 2011.
Reg. 33A inserted by SI 2004/3382, reg. 5, with effect from 6 April 2005.

INFORMATION TO BE PROVIDED TO THE BOARD

34   [Omitted by SI 2010/582, reg. 16.]

History – Reg. 34 omitted by SI 2010/582, reg. 16, with effect from 6 April 2010.

INSPECTION OF RECORDS BY OFFICER OF THE BOARD

35   [Omitted by SI 2010/582, reg. 16.]

History – Reg. 35 omitted by SI 2010/582, reg. 16, with effect from 6 April 2010.

CAPITAL GAINS TAX – ADAPTATION OF ENACTMENTS

36(1)   For the purposes of capital gains tax–

(a)   any assets held by a named child as account investments shall be regarded as held by the child in a separate capacity from that in which he holds any other assets of the same description; and

(b)   the named child shall be treated as having sold all the account investments, and as having reacquired them in his personal capacity, for a consideration equal to their market value, immediately before he attains the age of 18 years (and ceases to be a child).

36(2)   Sections 127 to 131 of the 1992 Act shall not apply in relation to qualifying investments falling within any of sub-paragraphs (a), (b), and (f) to (i) of regulation 12(2) which are held under an account if there is by virtue of any allotment for payment as is mentioned in section 126(2) of that Act a reorganisation affecting those assets.

ADMINISTRATION OF TAX IN RELATION TO ACCOUNTS – SUPPLEMENTARY

37(1)   Nothing in these Regulations shall be taken to prejudice any powers conferred or duties imposed by or under any enactment in relation to the making of returns of income or gains, or for the recovery of tax, penalties or interest by means of an assessment or otherwise.

37(2)   Notwithstanding the provisions of these Regulations an account provider shall not be released from obligations under these Regulations in relation to an account except under conditions agreed in writing with and notified to that person by the Board.

37(3)   The provisions contained in the Management Act shall apply to any assessment under these Regulations as if it were an assessment to tax for the year in which, apart from these Regulations, the named child would have been liable (by reason of his ownership of the investments).

37(4)   No obligation as to secrecy imposed by statute or otherwise shall preclude the Board from disclosing to an account provider or registered contact that any provision of these Regulations has not been satisfied or that relief has been given or claimed in respect of investments under an account.

37(5)   If–

(a)   a chargeable event, within the meaning given by Chapter 9 of Part 4 of ITTOIA 2005, has happened in relation to a policy of life insurance which is an account investment, and

(b)   the body by whom the policy was issued is satisfied that no gain is to be treated as chargeable to tax on the happening of the event by virtue of regulation 24(a)(v), the body shall not be obliged to deliver the certificates mentioned in section 552(1) of the Taxes Act. This paragraph does not prevent the operation of section 552(1) in a case to which regulation 38(1) applies.

37(6) Where–

(a) it comes to the notice of the account provider, in any manner, that the event specified in regulation 12(11) has occurred in relation to a policy, and

(b) the account provider is not the insurer for the time being responsible for the obligations under the policy or, where the policy is not still in existence, the person who was the last such insurer,

the account provider shall, within 30 days of the event coming to his notice give notice to that insurer, specifying the event mentioned in sub-paragraph (a) and the termination event.

History – In reg 37(5)(a), the words "Chapter 9 of Part 4 of ITTOIA 2005" substituted for the words "Chapter 2 of Part 13 of the Taxes Act" by SI 2010/582, reg. 17(a), with effect from 6 April 2010.
In reg. 37(5)(b), the words "the Taxes Act" substituted for the words "that Act" by SI 2010/582, reg. 17(b), with effect from 6 April 2010.

APPLICATION OF THE PROVISIONS OF CHAPTER 2 OF PART 13 OF THE TAXES ACT AND OF CHAPTER 9 OF PART 4 OF ITTOIA 2005 TO POLICIES

38(1) This paragraph applies to a case where–

(a) the event specified in regulation 12(11) has occurred in relation to a policy of life insurance, and

(b) a termination event within the meaning in regulation 12(12) occurs in relation to that policy.

38(2) Where–

(a) there is a case to which paragraph (1) applies, and

(b) a chargeable event in relation to the policy, within the meaning given by section 540 of the Taxes Act, has occurred prior to the time at which the termination event mentioned in paragraph (1)(b) occurs,

the named child shall cease to be, and shall be treated as not having been, entitled to relief from tax under regulation 24(a)(v), in respect of gains treated as arising on the occurrence of any chargeable event mentioned in sub-paragraph (b).

38(3) The provisions of Chapter 2 of Part 13 of the Taxes Act shall apply, in a case to which paragraph (1) applies, to–

(a) the termination event mentioned in paragraph (1)(b), and

(b) any chargeable event mentioned in paragraph (2)(b),

with the modifications provided for in paragraphs (4) to (8) of this regulation, and the registered contact and the account provider shall account to the Board in accordance with this regulation for tax from which relief under regulation 24 has been given on the basis that the named child was so entitled, or in circumstances such that the named child was not so entitled.

38(4) A termination of a policy of insurance pursuant to regulation 12(9)(b)(ii) shall be treated as the surrender of all rights under the policy for the purposes of section 484(1)(a)(i) of ITTOIA 2005.

38(5) Section 530 of ITTOIA 2005 does not apply to a gain in a case to which paragraph (1) applies.

38(6) Relief under section 550 of the Taxes Act shall be computed as if paragraph (5) had not been enacted.

38(7) In section 552 of the Taxes Act–

(a) in subsection (1)(b) for "policy holder" substitute "named child";

(b) in subsection (3)–

    (i) omit "(or, where the appropriate policy holder is a company, the corresponding financial year)";

    (ii) for "the name and address of the appropriate policy holder" substitute "the name and address of the named child";

    (iii) omit "and the corresponding financial year,";

(c) in subsection (5)–

    (i) for "the appropriate policy holder" substitute "the named child";

    (ii) omit sub-paragraph (b)(ii);

    (iii) omit paragraph (c);

    (iv) in paragraph (d) omit "except where paragraph (c) above applies,";

    (v) omit paragraph (f);

(d)   in subsection (6)–

     (i)   omit paragraph (b);

     (ii)   for paragraph (c) substitute–

        "(c)   if the event is a death, the period of three months beginning with the receipt of written notification of the death;";

     (iii)   after paragraph (c) insert–

        "(d)   if the event is–

          (i)   a termination event, or

          (ii)   a chargeable event preceding a termination event (as mentioned in regulation 38(2) of the Child Trust Funds Regulations 2004),

        the period of three months beginning with the date on which the insurer received notice under regulation 37(6) of those Regulations or, if earlier, actual notice of the termination event.";

(e)   in subsection (7)–

     (i)   in paragraph (a) omit ", or, where the policy holder is a company, the financial year,";

     (ii)   omit paragraph (b);

     (iii)   for paragraph (c) substitute–

        "(c)   if the event is a death, the period of three months beginning with the receipt of written notification of the death;";

     (iv)   after paragraph (c) insert–

        "(ca)   if the event is–

          (i)   a termination event, or

          (ii)   a chargeable event preceding such a termination event (as mentioned in regulation 38(2) of the Child Trust Funds Regulations 2004,

        the period of three months beginning with the date on which the insurer received notice under regulation 37(6) of those Regulations or, if earlier, actual notice of the termination event."; and

     (v)   in paragraph (d) after "paragraph (c)" insert "or (ca)";

(f)   in subsection (8)–

     (i)   in paragraph (b) for "policy holder" substitute "named child in respect";

     (ii)   in paragraph (c) omit the words from "or" to the end;

(g)   in subsection (9) omit "or financial year" in each place where they occur;

(h)   in subsection (10)–

     (i)   before the definition of "amount" insert–

        ""**named child**" has the same meaning as in the Child Trust Funds Regulations 2004;";

     (ii)   omit the definitions of "appropriate policy holder" and "financial year";

     (iii)   for the definition of "the relevant year of assessment" substitute–

        ""**the relevant year of assessment**", in the case of any gain, means the year of assessment to which the gain is attributable;"; and

     (iii)   after the definition of "section 546 excess" insert–

        ""**termination event**" has the same meaning as in the Child Trust Funds Regulations 2004;"; and

     (iv)   omit subsection (11).

38(8)   In section 552ZA of the Taxes Act–

(a)   in subsection (2)(b) omit the words "or an assignment"; and

(b)   omit subsections (3) and (4).

38(9)   The account provider shall account for and pay income tax at the basic rate in force for the year in which the termination event, or the chargeable event mentioned in paragraph (2)(b) occurred, as the case may be, and any amount so payable–

(a)   may be set off against any repayment in respect of tax due under regulation 26 or 27 and subject thereto,

(b)   shall be treated as an amount of tax due not later than 6 months after the end of the year in which the event specified in regulation 12(11) came to the notice of the account provider, and

(c)   shall be payable without the making of an assessment.

38(10)   Where tax is charged in accordance with paragraph (3)(a) or (b)–

(a)   an assessment to income tax at the basic rate in force for the relevant year may be made on the account provider or on the registered contact (on behalf of the named child), and

(b)   an assessment to income tax at the higher rate within the meaning of section 10(3) of ITA 2007, for that year, may be made on the registered contact (on behalf of the named child) within five years after the 31 January next following that year, and regulation 29 shall not apply.

History – In the title to reg. 38, the words "and of Chapter 9 of Part 4 of ITTOIA 2005" inserted by SI 2010/582, reg. 18(a), with effect from 6 April 2010.
In reg. 38(4), the words "of all rights under the policy for the purposes of section 484(1)(a)(i) of ITTOIA 2005" substituted for the words "in whole of the rights conferred by the policy, for the purposes of section 540(1)(a)(iii) of the Taxes Act" by SI 2010/582, reg. 18(b), with effect from 6 April 2010.
Reg. 38(5) substituted by SI 2010/582, reg. 18(c), with effect from 6 April 2010.
In reg. 38(9), the word "basic" substituted for the word "lower" by SI 2010/582, reg. 18(d), with effect from 6 April 2010.
In reg. 38(10)(a), the word "basic" substituted for the word "lower" by SI 2010/582, reg. 18(d), with effect from 6 April 2010.
In reg. 38(10)(b), the words "section 10(3) of ITA 2007" substituted for the words "section 832(1) of the Taxes Act" by SI 2010/582, reg. 18(e), with effect from 6 April 2010.

SCHEDULE – STAKEHOLDER ACCOUNTS

DESCRIPTION OF STAKEHOLDER ACCOUNT

1   An account is a stakeholder account where it has the characteristics and complies with the conditions set out in paragraph 2.

CHARACTERISTICS OF STAKEHOLDER ACCOUNT ETC

2(1)   A stakeholder account must have the characteristics set out in sub-paragraph (2) and must comply with the conditions set out in sub-paragraphs (3) to (5).

2(2)   The characteristics of a stakeholder account are–

(a)   the account does not directly hold investments of any of the following kinds–

     (i)   those referred to in regulation 12(2)(f) (shares in an investment trust);

     (ii)   securities of an investment trust;

     (iii)   rights in with-profits endowment policies;

     (iv)   rights, under a contract of insurance, in a with-profits fund;

     (v)   units or shares in a relevant collective investment scheme unless it is a requirement of that scheme that the purchase and sale price of those units or shares shall, at any given time, not differ from each other and that the price must be made available to the public on a daily basis;

     (vi)   rights under a contract of insurance which are expressed as shares in funds held by the insurer unless it is a requirement of the contract of insurance that the purchase and sale price of those shares shall, at any given time, not differ from each other and that the price must be made available to the public on a daily basis;

     (via)   shares referred to in regulation 12(2)(a) (shares issued by a company wherever incorporated and officially listed on a recognised stock exchange or, in the European Economic Area, admitted to trading on a recognised stock exchange);

     (vii)   depositary interests, where the investments concerned are investments of any of the kinds listed above in this paragraph;

(b)   the requirement is fulfilled that the account provider, and any relevant person, ensure that, subject to the other provisions of this paragraph, the account has exposure to equities;

(ba)   interest accrues on investments referred to in regulation 12(2)(k) and (l) (cash deposited in a deposit account or in a share account) on a daily basis at a rate that is not less than the Bank of England base rate minus 1 per cent per annum, except where cash is held temporarily on deposit in the course of dealing in investments under the account;

(baa)   when the Bank of England base rate increases, the interest rate on investments referred to in regulation 12(2)(k) and (l) (cash deposited in a deposit account or in a share account) must be raised within one month of the date of that increase ;

(bb)   in relation to qualifying investments which are securities (other than in an investment trust) or a depositary interest where the relevant investments (within the meaning in that definition) are such securities, the requirement is fulfilled that–

(i)　　the securities fall within regulation 12(2)(c) (d) or (e), or

(ii)　　where the securities fall within regulation 12(2)(b) or (n), the contract under which the securities are or have been acquired, or any other transaction entered into by the registered contact or any other person, has the effect that the named child is not exposed, or not exposed to a significant extent, to the risk of loss from fluctuations in the value of the securities exceeding 20% of the capital consideration paid or payable for the acquisition of those securities, during the period when the securities in question are held in the account.

(c)　　the requirement is fulfilled that the account provider and any relevant person have regard to—

(i)　　the need for diversification of investments of the account, in so far as is appropriate to the circumstances of the account; and

(ii)　　the suitability for the purposes of the account of any investment, investment strategy or investment option proposed; and

(d)　　except where otherwise instructed by the registered contact, the account is subject to lifestyling.

2(3)　　The account provider must permit payment of subscriptions to the account by—

(a)　　cheque;

(b)　　direct debit;

(c)　　standing order;

(d)　　direct credit (other than standing order).

For the purposes of this sub-paragraph, those means of payment do not include payments by cash, credit card or debit card or any combination including a payment by cash, credit card or debit card.

2(4)　　The minimum amount which may be subscribed to the account on a single occasion is £10 except where the account provider permits a smaller amount.

2(5)　　Deductions from the account may only be made in the circumstances, and to the extent, set out in paragraph 3.

2(6)　　In this paragraph—

"**equities**" means shares issued by a company wherever incorporated and officially listed on a recognised stock exchange or, in the European Economic Area, admitted to trading on a recognised stock exchange;

"**insurer**" means—

(a)　　a person who has permission under Part 4 of the Financial Services and Markets Act 2000 to effect or carry out contracts of insurance, or

(b)　　an EEA firm of the kind mentioned in paragraph 5(d) of Schedule 3 to that Act, which has permission under paragraph 15 of that Schedule (as a result of qualifying for authorisation under paragraph 12 of that Schedule) to effect or carry out contracts of insurance;

"**lifestyling**" means the process beginning from a date on or before the child is 13 years of age, or from when the account is opened, whichever is later, and continuing until the child is 18 years of age, by which the account provider, and any relevant person, adopts an investment strategy which aims progressively to minimise the variation or potential variation in capital value of the account caused by market conditions from time to time;

"**relevant collective investment scheme**" means an authorised unit trust scheme, an authorised open-ended investment company or a recognised scheme, as the case may be, as defined in section 237(3) of the Financial Services and Markets Act 2000;

"**relevant person**" means any person to whom the account provider has delegated any of his functions or responsibilities under the management agreement; and

"**with-profits fund**" means a fund maintained by an insurer in respect of a particular part of its long-term business for which—

(a)　　separate accounting records are maintained by the insurer in respect of all income and expenditure relating to that part of its business; and

(b)　　the benefits payable in respect of policies allocated to that fund are determined partly by reference to a discretion exercisable by any person.

2(7)　　In this paragraph, the definitions of "contract of insurance" and "insurer" must be read with—

(a)　　section 22 of the Financial Services and Markets Act 2000,

(b)　　any relevant order made under that section, and

(c)　　Schedule 2 to that Act.

History – In para. 2(2)(a)(via), the words "or, in the European Economic Area, admitted to trading on a recognised stock exchange" inserted by SI 2013/1744, reg. 10(a), with effect from 5 August 2013.
Para. 2(2)(a)(via) inserted by SI 2004/2676, reg. 15(a), with effect from the date SI 2004/1450 is brought into force (6 April 2005).
In para. 2(2)(ba) words from ", except where" to the end added by SI 2006/2684, reg. 6 with effect from 31 October 2006.
Para. 2(2)(baa) inserted by SI 2004/3382, reg. 6(a), with effect from 6 April 2005.
In para. 2(2)(b) the words "the requirement is fulfilled that" inserted, the word "must" which appeared before the word "ensure" omitted and the words ", whether directly or indirectly" omitted by SI 2004/2676, reg. 15(b), with effect from the date SI 2004/1450 is brought into force (6 April 2005).
In para. 2(2)(bb)(i) the words "(d) or (e)" substituted for the words "or (d)" by SI 2004/3382, reg. 6(b), with effect from 6 April 2005.
In para. 2(2)(bb)(ii) the words ", (e)" omitted by SI 2004/3382, reg. 6(c), with effect from 6 April 2005.
Para. 2(2)(ba) and (bb) inserted by SI 2004/2676, reg. 15(c), with effect from the date SI 2004/1450 is brought into force (6 April 2005).
In para. 2(2)(c) the words "the requirement is fulfilled that" inserted and the word "must" which appeared before the word "ensure" omitted by SI 2004/2676, reg. 15(d), with effect from the date SI 2004/1450 is brought into force (6 April 2005).
In para. 2(3) the words "For the purposes of this sub-paragraph, those means of payment do not include payments by cash, credit card or debit card or any combination including a payment by cash, credit card or debit card." inserted by SI 2004/2676, reg. 15(e), with effect from the date SI 2004/1450 is brought into force 6 April 2005).
In para. 2(6), in the definition of "equities", the words "or, in the European Economic Area, admitted to trading on a recognised stock exchange" inserted by SI 2013/1744, reg. 10(b).

STAKEHOLDER ACCOUNTS – CHARGES ETC

3(1) Deductions from a stakeholder account may only be made to the extent set out in this paragraph.

3(2) Subject to sub-paragraph (5), charges for the management of, and other expenses in connection with, a stakeholder account may be recovered from the account to the extent that they do not exceed whichever is the greater of–

(a) 3/730 per cent of the value of the child's rights in the account for each day on which the account is held; or

(b) 3/730 per cent of the value of the investments under the account for each day on which the account is held.

3(3) For the purposes of sub-paragraph (2)–

(a) the frequency, which must be daily, weekly or monthly, with which rights or investments are to be valued; and

(b) where valuation is to take place weekly or monthly, the day of the week or, as the case may be, the date in the month on which it is to take place,

must be specified in advance in writing by the account provider to the registered contact, and the specification may not be amended during the period of 12 months after the date on which it is made.

3(4) When calculating the value of a child's rights or of investments for the purposes of subparagraph (2), where the account provider has specified under sub-paragraph (3) that they are to be valued weekly or monthly–

(a) where they are to be valued weekly, they are to be valued on such day of the week ("the specified day") as has been so specified by the account provider (except that, where that day is not a working day, the rights are to be valued on the next working day), and the value of the rights on each subsequent day prior to the next specified day is to be taken to be the value of the rights on the previous specified day; and

(b) where they are to be valued monthly, they are to be so valued on such date in each month ("the specified date") as has been so specified by the account provider (except that, where that date is not a working day, the rights are to be valued on the next working day), and the value of the rights on each subsequent day prior to the next specified date is to be taken to be the value of the rights on the previous specified date.

3(5) The following charges and expenses may be deducted in full from the account and are not subject to and do not count towards the limit provided for in sub-paragraph (2)–

(a) any stamp duty, stamp duty reserve tax, value added tax or other charges (including any dilution levy) incurred by the account provider directly or indirectly in the sale or purchase of investments held under the account;

(aa) where any amount of tax is paid or anticipated to be payable in respect of income received or capital gains realised by the account provider in respect of investments held for the purposes of the account, the amount so deducted or anticipated;

(b) any charges or expenses incurred by the account provider directly or indirectly in complying with an order of the court or any other requirements imposed by law; and

(c) expenses incurred by the account provider in complying with its obligations under regulation 8(2)(d) and (e).

3(6) Valuations for the purpose of sub-paragraph (2) shall be after the deduction of any charges or expenses properly deducted from the account under sub-paragraph (5).

History – In para. 3(5)(a) the words ", value added tax" and "(including any dilution levy)" inserted by SI 2004/2676, reg. 15(f), with effect from the date SI 2004/1450 is brought into force (6 April 2005).
Para. 3(5)(aa) inserted by SI 2004/2676, reg. 15(g), with effect from the date SI 2004/1450 is brought into force (6 April 2005).

THALIDOMIDE CHILDREN'S TRUST (APPLICATION OF SECTION 329AA OF THE INCOME AND CORPORATION TAXES ACT 1988) ORDER 2004

(SI 2004/1819)

Made on 14 July 2004 by the Treasury, in exercise of the powers conferred upon them by s. 329AB(3) of the Income and Corporation Taxes Act 1988 [ITTOIA 2005, s. 732(3)]. Operative from 5 August 2004.

CITATION, COMMENCEMENT AND INTERPRETATION

1(1) This Order may be cited as the Thalidomide Children's Trust (Application of Section 329AA of the Income and Corporation Taxes Act 1988) Order 2004 and shall come into force on 5th August 2004.

1(2) In this Order **"the Thalidomide Children's Trust"** means the Trust established by that name by a declaration of trust made on the 10th August 1973 by Sir Henry Gordon Willmer, Arthur Halsall Walton and Sir Donald Macleod Douglas.

MODIFIED APPLICATION OF SECTION 329AA OF THE INCOME AND CORPORATION TAXES ACT 1988

2(1) Section 329AA of the Income and Corporation Taxes Act 1988 (personal injury damages in the form of periodical payments) applies to periodical payments by the Thalidomide Children's Trust as it applies to payments to which subsection (1) of that section applies, but subject to the following modifications.

2(2) In subsection (1)–

(a)   after "Where" insert "the Thalidomide Children's Trust makes periodical payments to a beneficiary of that Trust"; and

(b)   omit paragraphs (a) and (b).

2(3) In subsection (2)–

(a)   for paragraph (a) substitute–

"(a)   the person ("A") entitled to the payments made by the Thalidomide Children's Trust;";

(b)   in paragraphs (b) and (c) for "whether in pursuance of the agreement or order or otherwise" substitute "whether under the terms of the Thalidomide Children's Trust or otherwise".

2(4) In subsection (3) omit ", if the agreement or order mentioned in that subsection or a subsequent agreement so provides,".

2(5) For subsection (5) substitute–

"**329AA(5)**   In this section **"the Thalidomide Children's Trust"** means the Trust established by that name by a declaration of trust made on the 10th August 1973 by Sir Henry Gordon Willmer, Arthur Halsall Walton and Sir Donald Macleod Douglas.".

2(6) Omit subsections (6) to (8).

TAX AVOIDANCE SCHEMES (PROMOTERS AND PRESCRIBED CIRCUMSTANCES) REGULATIONS 2004

(SI 2004/1865, as amended by SI 2004/2613 and SI 2012/1836 and modified by SI 2007/785)

Made on 22 July 2004 by the Commissioners of Inland Revenue, in exercise of the powers conferred upon them by s. 307(5) and 318(1) of the Finance Act 2004. Operative from 1 August 2004.

CITATION, COMMENCEMENT AND INTERPRETATION

Cross references – SI 2007/785, reg. 18(1): modification providing for all references to s. 306–313 to be construed as a reference to the corresponding provision within SI 2007/785.

1(1) These Regulations may be cited as the Tax Avoidance Schemes (Promoters and Prescribed Circumstances) Regulations 2004 and shall come into force on 1st August 2004.

1(2) In these Regulations–

    "notifiable arrangements" has the meaning given by section 306(1);

    "notifiable proposal" has the meaning given by section 306(2); and

    except where the context otherwise requires a reference without more to a numbered section is a reference to the section of the Finance Act 2004 which is so numbered.

1(3) For the purposes of these Regulations section 839 of the Income and Corporation Taxes Act 1988 applies to determine whether persons are connected.

Cross references – SI 2007/785, reg. 18(2): modification substituting reg. 1(2).

PERSONS NOT TO BE TREATED AS PROMOTERS – GROUPS

2(1) A person is not to be treated as a promoter where–

(a) the person carrying on the relevant business referred to in section 307(1) is a company ("company A"); and

(b) on the date specified in paragraph (2) the other person (or each of the other persons) to whom company A provides services in connection with a notifiable proposal or notifiable arrangements is a company which is a member of the same group as company A.

2(2) The date specified by this paragraph is–

(a) in relation to a notifiable proposal, the relevant date within the meaning given by section 308(2);

(b) in relation to notifiable arrangements, the date mentioned in section 308(3).

2(3) For the purposes of this regulation two companies are members of the same group if they would, by virtue of the provisions of section 170 of the Taxation of Chargeable Gains Act 1992, be members of the same group for the purposes of sections 171 to 181 of that Act if section 170 were modified as follows–

(a) for each of the references to a 75 per cent. subsidiary there were substituted a reference to a 51 per cent. subsidiary;

(b) subsection (3)(b) and subsections (6) to (8) were omitted.

PERSONS NOT TO BE TREATED AS PROMOTERS – EMPLOYEES

3(1) A person is not to be treated as a promoter in relation to a notifiable proposal or notifiable arrangements where he is an employee of an employer who is–

(a) a promoter in relation to the proposal or the arrangements; or

(b) a person who–

    (i) is to enter into any transaction forming part of the proposed arrangements; or

    (ii) enters into any transaction forming part of the arrangements.

3(2) In this regulation **"employee"** and **"employer"** have the same meanings as they have for the purposes of the employment income Parts of the Income Tax (Earnings and Pensions) Act 2003 (see section 4 of that Act) and–

(a) **"employee"** includes an office holder to whom the provisions of those Parts that are expressed to apply to employments apply equally (see section 5 of that Act); and

(b) **"employer"** includes a person under whom an office holder holds office and to whom those provisions similarly apply.

Statutory Instruments

3(3) For the purposes of this regulation an employee of a person who is connected with another person ("A") shall be treated as an employee of A.

PERSONS NOT TO BE TREATED AS PROMOTERS UNDER SECTION 307(1)(A)(I) OR (B)(I)

4(1) A person is not to be treated as a promoter under section 307(1)(a)(i) or (b)(i) where paragraph (2), (3) or (4) applies.

4(2) This paragraph applies where, in the course of providing tax advice, a person is not responsible for the design of any element of the proposed arrangements or arrangements (including the way in which they are structured) from which the tax advantage expected to be obtained arises.

4(3) This paragraph applies where—

(a) a person, in the course of a business that is a relevant business for the purposes of section 307 by virtue of subsection (2)(a) of that section, is to any extent responsible for the design of the proposed arrangements or arrangements; but

(b) does not provide tax advice in the course of carrying out his responsibilities in relation to the proposed arrangements or arrangements.

4(4) This paragraph applies where a person—

(a) is not responsible for the design of all the elements of the proposed arrangements or arrangements (including the way in which they are structured) from which the tax advantage expected to be obtained arises; and

(b) could not reasonably be expected to have—

    (i) sufficient information as would enable him to know whether or not the proposal is a notifiable proposal or the arrangements are notifiable arrangements; or

    (ii) sufficient information as would enable him to comply with section 308(1) or (3).

Cross references – SI 2007/785, reg. 18(2): modification of reg. 4.

PERSONS NOT TO BE TREATED AS PROMOTERS UNDER SECTION 307(1)(A)(II)

5 A person is not to be treated as a promoter under section 307(1)(b)(ii) where he is not connected with another person who is a promoter under section 307(1)(a) or (b)(i) in relation to—

(a) the arrangements; or

(b) arrangements which are substantially the same as those arrangements.

PERSONS NOT TO BE TREATED AS PROMOTERS: LEGAL PROFESSIONAL PRIVILEGE

6 A person is not to be treated as a promoter in relation to a notifiable proposal or notifiable arrangements where his involvement with the proposal or arrangements is such that he is not required to provide all of the information prescribed in regulation 4(1) of the Tax Avoidance Schemes (Information) Regulations 2012 by virtue of section 314 (legal professional privilege).

History – In reg. 6, the words "regulation 4(1) of the Tax Avoidance Schemes (Information) Regulations 2012" substituted for the words "paragraph (1) or (2) (as the case may be) of regulation 3 of the Tax Avoidance Schemes (Information) Regulations 2004" by SI 2012/1836, reg. 18, with effect from 1 September 2012.
Reg. 6 added by SI 2004/2613, reg. 2, with effect from 14 October 2004.

Cross references – SI 2007/785, reg. 18(2): modification of reg. 6.

VENTURE CAPITAL TRUST (WINDING UP AND MERGERS) (TAX) REGULATIONS 2004

(SI 2004/2199 amended by SI 2008/954, SI 2009/56 and SI 2011/660)

Made on 27 August 2004 by the Treasury, in exercise of the powers conferred upon them by para. 2 to 5, 7 to 9, 11 and 16 of Sch. 33 to the Finance Act 2002. Operative from 17 September 2004.

CITATION, COMMENCEMENT AND EFFECT

1(1) These Regulations may be cited as the Venture Capital Trust (Winding up and Mergers) (Tax) Regulations 2004 and shall come into force on 17th September 2004.

1(2) These Regulations have effect as follows–

(a) regulations 3 to 8 have effect in relation to any VCT-in-liquidation whose winding-up commences on or after 17th April 2002;

(b) regulations 9 to 13 have effect in relation to any merger where the transactions for effecting the merger take place on or after 17th April 2002; and

(c) regulation 14 has effect in relation to shares issued on or after 6th April 2004.

INTERPRETATION

2(1) In these Regulations, references to provisions of an Act or to Parts of an Act are to provisions or Parts of the Income Tax Act 2007 unless otherwise stated.

2(2) In these Regulations–

"the Commissioners" means the Commissioners for Her Majesty's Revenue and Customs;

"market value" shall be construed in accordance with sections 272 and 273 of the Taxation of Chargeable Gains Act 1992;

"the 1992 Act" means the Taxation of Chargeable Gains Act 1992;

"prescribed winding-up period", in relation to a VCT-in-liquidation, means the period–

(a) beginning on the commencement of the company's winding-up, and

(b) ending on the earliest of–

(i) the end of the company's winding-up;

(ii) the company's ceasing to be wound up;

(iii) the dissolution of the company;

(iv) the third anniversary of the commencement of the winding-up;

"qualifying holdings" shall be construed in accordance with Chapter 4 of Part 6;

"securities", except in regulation 12, has the same meaning as in section 285(2);

"statement of affairs" means a statement as to the affairs of a company, in the form prescribed under and complying with section 99 or 131 of the Insolvency Act 1986;

"the 15% test" means the 15% holding limit condition specified in the table in section 274(2) and as provided for in sections 275 to 279;

"the 70% tests" means the conditions specified in the last two entries in the table in section 274(2) and as provided for in sections 275, 278, 280 and 280A;

"the 30% test" means the condition which was specified in the table at section 274(2) and as provided for in sections 275, 278 and 280, ignoring the amendments made to section 274(2) by paragraph 2(2)(b) and (c) of Schedule 2 to the Finance (No. 3) Act 2010.

2(3) In regulations 9 to 14 and in this paragraph–

a **"section 323(1) merger"** means a merger described in section 323(1);

a **"section 323(2) merger"** means a merger described in section 323(2);

"share for business transfer" means an issue of shares as mentioned in section 323(1)(b)(ii) or 323(2)(b)(ii), as the case may be;

"share for share exchange;" means an exchange of shares as mentioned in section 323(1)(b)(i) or 323(2)(b)(i), as the case may be;

"shares issued to effect the merger" means–

(a)　in the case of a section 323(1) merger, shares in the successor company issued as mentioned in section 323(1); and

(b)　in the case of a section 323(2) merger, shares in the successor company issued as mentioned in section 323(2);

"**shares issued for new consideration**" means shares in the successor company issued in the period during which the merger takes place for a consideration other than as mentioned in section 323(1)(b) or 323(2)(b).

2(4)　Section 319(3) (references in sections 314 to 318 to things done by a VCT-in-liquidation to include things done by the liquidator of a VCT-in-liquidation) shall apply for the purposes of regulations 3 to 8 as it applies to Chapter 5 of Part 6.

2(5)　References to a resolution passed, or petition presented, to wind up a company (or other references to insolvency procedure) shall, where the winding up is wholly or partly other than under the law of England and Wales, include references to the corresponding local equivalents.

History – Reg. 2(1)–(4) substituted by SI 2011/660, reg. 3(2), with effect from 6 April 2011. Former reg. 2(1)–(4) read as follows:

"**2(1)**　In these Regulations unless the context otherwise requires–
"**the Board**" means the Commissioners of Inland Revenue;
"**eligible shares**" has the meaning in Part 1 of Schedule 15B;
"**the 15% test**" means the condition specified in s. 842AA(2)(d);
"**market value**" shall be construed in accordance with sections 272 and 273 of the 1992 Act;
"**merger**" of two or more companies (and the associated definitions of "**the merging companies**" and "**the successor company**") shall bear the appropriate meanings given by paragraph 10 of Schedule 33;
"**the 1992 Act**" means the Taxation of Chargeable Gains Act 1992;
"**prescribed winding-up period**", in relation to a VCT-in-liquidation, means the period–
(a)　beginning on the commencement of the company's winding up, and
(b)　ending on the earliest of–
　　(i)　the end of the company's winding up,
　　(ii)　the company ceasing to be wound up,
　　(iii)　the dissolution of the company, and
　　(iv)　the third anniversary of the commencement of the winding up;
"**qualifying holdings**" has the meaning in Schedule 28B;
"**Schedule 33**" means Schedule 33 to the Finance Act 2002;
"**securities**", except in regulation 12, has the same meaning as in section 842AA(12);
"**the 70% test**" means the condition specified in section 842AA(2)(b);
"**the 30% test**" means the condition specified in section 842AA(2)(c);
"**statement of affairs**" means a statement as to the affairs of a company, in the form prescribed under and complying with section 99 or 131 of the Insolvency Act 1986, as the case may be;
"**the Taxes Act**" means the Income and Corporation Taxes Act 1988;
"**VCT approval**" has the meaning given by paragraph 7(4) of Schedule 33, and any reference to such approval taking effect shall have the same meaning as in section 842AA;
"**VCT-in-liquidation**" has the meaning given by paragraph 1(1) of Schedule 33;
"**venture capital trust**" has the meaning given by section 842AA(1).

2(2)　In regulations 9 to 14 and this paragraph–
a "**paragraph 10(1) merger**" means a merger described in paragraph 10(1) of Schedule 33;
a "**paragraph 10(2) merger**" means a merger described in paragraph 10(2) of Schedule 33;
"**share for business transfer**" means an issue of shares as mentioned in paragraph 10(1)(b) or (2)(b) of Schedule 33 (in each case, omitting sub-paragraph (i) and the word "or" which follows it);
"**share for share exchange**" means an exchange of shares as mentioned in paragraph 10(1)(b) or (2)(b) of Schedule 33 (in each case, omitting sub-paragraph (ii) and the word "or" which follows sub-paragraph (i));
"**shares issued to effect the merger**"–
(a)　in the case of a paragraph 10(1) merger, means shares in the successor company issued as mentioned in paragraph 10(1)(b) of Schedule 33, and
(b)　in the case of a paragraph 10(2) merger, means shares in the successor company issued as mentioned in paragraph 10(2)(b) of Schedule 33;
"**shares issued for new consideration**" means shares in the successor company, issued in the period during which the merger takes place, for a consideration other than as mentioned in paragraph 10(1)(b) or (2)(b) of Schedule 33.

2(3)　References in these Regulations to a section or Schedule (excepting Schedule 33), without more, are to that section of or Schedule to the Taxes Act.

2(4)　Paragraph 7(5) of Schedule 33 (acts of a liquidator attributed to the company) shall apply for the purposes of regulations 3 to 8 as it applies to Part 1 of Schedule 33.".

WINDING UP OF VENTURE CAPITAL TRUSTS

3(1)　Regulations 4 to 8 apply, subject to paragraphs (2) and (3), in the case of a VCT-in-liquidation–

(a)　whose VCT approval has had effect for the continuous period of 3 years immediately preceding the commencement of its winding up, or

(b)　which is being wound up by the court under section 122(1) of the Insolvency Act 1986 (other than under paragraph (a) of that provision) or under any corresponding local equivalent, and which has given notice to the Commissioners that a resolution has been passed, or a petition presented, to wind up the company, pursuant to regulation 8(1) of the Venture Capital Trust Regulations 1995.

3(2)   Where a company–

(a)   on or after 6th April 2004 and before 6th April 2006, makes an issue of shares falling within the circumstances in section 280(1)(a) and (b) (that is, whether or not the company makes a further issue as mentioned in paragraph (c) of that provision), and

(b)   has not made an issue of shares falling within those circumstances, before 6th April 2004,

the period in paragraph (1)(a) shall be 5 years.

3(3)   Paragraph (1) shall not apply to any VCT-in-liquidation which is, or has at any time been, a merging company (other than a successor company).

History – In reg. 3(1), the word "Commissioners" substituted for the word "Board" by SI 2011/660, reg. 13, with effect from 6 April 2011.

In reg. 3(2)(a), "section 280(1)(a) and (b)" substituted for "section 842AA(5A)(a) and (b)" by SI 2011/660, reg. 4, with effect in relation to any VCT-in-liquidation whose winding-up commences on or after 6 April 2011.

4   For the purposes of section 268, the commencement of the winding up shall not affect the status of the VCT-in-liquidation as a venture capital trust.

History – In reg. 4, "section 268" substituted for "paragraph 3(9) of Schedule 15B" by SI 2011/660, reg. 5, with effect in relation to any VCT-in-liquidation whose winding-up commences on or after 6 April 2011.

5   Section 100(1) of the 1992 Act (read with section 16(2) of that Act as regards losses) shall have effect as if a VCT-in-liquidation that would not otherwise be a venture capital trust were treated as a venture capital trust, during its prescribed winding-up period, in relation to gains and losses accruing on the disposal of assets acquired by the trust company before the commencement of its winding up.

6(1)   Sections 151A (excepting subsection (3)) and 151B of the 1992 Act shall have effect as follows.

6(2)   During the VCT-in-liquidation's prescribed winding-up period those provisions shall have effect as if–

(a)   the conditions in section 274 were fulfilled, and

(b)   the VCT-in-liquidation, if not otherwise a venture capital trust, were so treated.

6(3)   At the end of the prescribed winding-up period, if–

(a)   the VCT-in-liquidation is still in existence, and

(b)   the conditions in section 274 are not fulfilled immediately following the end of that period,

VCT approval shall be treated, for the purposes of sections 151A(1) and 151B(6) and (7), as having been withdrawn from the VCT-in-liquidation immediately following the end of that period.

History – In reg. 6(2)(a) and (3)(b), "section 274" substituted for "section 842AA(2)" by SI 2011/660, reg. 6, with effect in relation to any VCT-in-liquidation whose winding-up commences on or after 6 April 2011.

7(1)   Paragraph 3(1) of Schedule 5C to the 1992 Act ("paragraph 3(1)") shall have effect as if–

(a)   the VCT-in-liquidation, if not otherwise a venture capital trust, were so treated during its prescribed winding-up period;

(b)   during its prescribed winding-up period, paragraph (f) of paragraph 3(1) were omitted;

(c)   in paragraph (g) of paragraph 3(1), for "(f)" there were substituted "(e)"; and

(d)   there were added at the end of paragraph 3(1)–

     "or

     (h)   a VCT-in-liquidation–

         (i)   to which regulation 7 of the Venture Capital Trust (Winding up and Mergers) (Tax) Regulations 2004 applies, and

         (ii)   in which those shares are shares,

     is still in existence immediately following the end of its prescribed winding-up period (within the meaning in those Regulations).".

7(2)   Paragraph 3(6) of that Schedule shall be modified as if for "(f)" there were substituted "(h)".

7(3)   Paragraph 5(1) of that Schedule shall be modified as if for paragraph (d) there were substituted–

     "(d)   to the person who holds the shares in question immediately following the end of the company's prescribed winding-up period (within the meaning in the Venture Capital Trust (Winding up and Mergers) (Tax) Regulations 2004),".

TRANSFER OF INVESTMENTS IN SPECIE FROM A VCT-IN-LIQUIDATION TO A VENTURE CAPITAL TRUST

8(1) This regulation applies where–

(a)   a VCT-in-liquidation has made all reasonable endeavours to sell shares or securities comprised in its qualifying holdings at, or as near as may be to, their market value, but has been unable to do so;

(b)   the VCT-in-liquidation, during its prescribed winding-up period, transfers the shares or securities to a venture capital trust by way of a bargain made at arm's length, or for a consideration not less than their market value; and

(c)   the value of all shares or securities transferred under this regulation by the VCT-in-liquidation to venture capital trusts during its prescribed winding-up period does not exceed 7.5% of the aggregate value of the investments of the VCT-in-liquidation at the commencement of its winding up.

8(2) For the purposes of paragraph (1)(c) the value of investments (including shares or securities) shall be taken to be–

(a)   those used in the VCT-in-liquidation's statement of affairs, or

(b)   where sub-paragraph (a) does not provide a value for the investment, its market value at the commencement of the winding up.

8(3) Where the requirements of any of sections 286(2)(b), 287, 293, 294, 297 and 331(2) and (3) were satisfied (or deemed to be satisfied) to any extent or for any period in relation to the investment when held by the VCT-in-liquidation (whether before or after the commencement of its winding up), they shall be treated as satisfied to the same extent or for the same period in relation to the investment when held by the venture capital trust.

History – In reg. 8(3), "sections 286(2)(b), 287, 293, 294, 297 and 331(2) and (3)" substituted for "paragraphs 1(2)(b) and 6 to 8 of Schedule 28B" by SI 2011/660, reg. 7, with effect in relation to any VCT-in-liquidation whose winding-up commences on or after 6 April 2011.

MERGERS OF VENTURE CAPITAL TRUSTS

9(1) Regulations 11 to 13 shall apply to a merger of two or more companies, each of which was a venture capital trust immediately before the merger begins to be effected, in any case where, before the transactions for effecting the merger take place, the Commissioners have notified their approval of the merger, subject to paragraph (2).

9(2) In the case of a section 323(2) merger, the approval of the merger (and the application of regulations 11 to 13) shall be conditional on the successor company having VCT approval, and on the VCT approval having taken effect, at any relevant time for the purposes of those regulations (excepting regulation 13(4)(a)).

9(3) The Commissioners shall not approve the merger unless, on the application of a merging company or a successor company, the Commissioners are satisfied that–

(a)   the merger is effected for bona fide commercial reasons and is not part of a scheme or arrangement the main purpose of which, or one of the main purposes of which, is the avoidance of tax;

(b)   in the case of a section 323(2) merger, that the shares issued to effect the merger will be issued only at times when there are no issued shares in the successor company, other than subscriber shares, such shares as may be required to obtain a trading certificate under section 761 of the Companies Act 2006 and shares previously issued to effect the merger;

(c)   where there is a share for share exchange, more than 50% of the issued share capital, immediately before the transactions for effecting the merger, of–

      (i)   each of the other merging companies (in a section 323(1) merger), or

      (ii)   each of the merging companies (in a section 323(2) merger),

    (or shares representing them) will be exchanged for shares issued to effect the merger;

(d)   where any consideration other than shares in the successor company is offered to–

      (i)   all or any members of another merging company (in a section 323(1) merger), or

      (ii)   all or any members of a merging company (in a section 323(2) merger),

    in exchange for their holdings in that company, the amount or value of such consideration does not exceed 10% of the aggregate amount or value of consideration offered to the members of that company;

(e)   where there is a share for business transfer, the shares are issued in respect of and in proportion to (or as nearly as may be in proportion to) the holdings of the persons to whom they are issued in the other merging company or companies (in a section 323(1) merger) or merging companies (in a section 323(2) merger);

(f)   where there is a transfer of part of the business of a merging company to the successor company as mentioned in section 323(1)(b)(ii) or section 323(2)(b)(ii), the market value of the part not so transferred is merely incidental in comparison with the market value of the part so transferred; and

(g)   the money raised by any shares issued for new consideration (or any assets directly or indirectly derived from that money) to be used for the purpose of the successor company purchasing its own shares, or those of any of the merging companies, shall not exceed the least of A, B and C, where:

A equals 20% of the amount of money raised by the shares issued for new consideration (or of the aggregate of those amounts if there has been more than one such share issue);

B equals 5% of the aggregate of all amounts subscribed for eligible shares issued before the merger in–

    (i)   the successor company, and

    (ii)   the merging companies, or other merging companies, as the case may be; and

C equals £3,000,000.

History – In reg. 9, in each place it occurs, "section 323(1) merger" substituted for "paragraph 10(1) merger" by SI 2011/660, reg. 8(1)(a), with effect in relation to any merger where the transactions bringing the merger into effect take place on or after 6 April 2011.

In reg. 9, in each place it occurs, "section 323(2) merger" substituted for "paragraph 10(2) merger" by SI 2011/660, reg. 8(1)(b), with effect in relation to any merger where the transactions bringing the merger into effect take place on or after 6 April 2011.

In reg. 9(1), the word "Commissioners" substituted for the word "Board" by SI 2011/660, reg. 13, with effect from 6 April 2011.

In reg. 9(3), in both places, the word "Commissioners" substituted for the word "Board" by SI 2011/660, reg. 13, with effect from 6 April 2011.

In reg. 9(3)(b) the words "section 761 of the Companies Act 2006" substituted for "section 117 of the Companies Act 1985" by SI 2008/954, art. 54, with effect from 6 April 2008.

In reg. 9(3)(f), "section 323(1)(b)(ii) or section 323(2)(b)(ii)" substituted for "paragraph 10(1)(b)(ii) or 10(2)(b)(ii) of Schedule 33" by SI 2011/660, reg. 8(2), with effect in relation to any merger where the transactions bringing the merger into effect take place on or after 6 April 2011.

PROCEDURE FOR COMMISSIONERS' APPROVAL

History – In the heading before reg. 10, the word "Commissioners'" substituted for the word "Board's" by SI 2011/660, reg. 13, with effect from 6 April 2011. (The wording of SI 2011/660 indicated that the word "Commissioner" should be substituted for the word "Board" here but, as this would have created the word "Commissioners's" in the heading, CCH have made an assumption regarding the intention in SI 2011/660, reg. 13.)

10(1)   Any application under regulation 9(3) shall be in writing and shall contain particulars of the transactions in connection with the merger that are to be effected and the Commissioners may, within 30 days of the receipt of the application or of any further particulars previously required under this paragraph, by notice require the applicant to furnish further particulars for the purposes of enabling the Commissioners to make their decision; and if any such notice is not complied with within 30 days or such longer period as the Commissioners may allow, the Commissioners need not proceed further on the application.

10(2)   The Commissioners shall notify their decision to the applicant within 30 days of receiving the application or, if they give a notice under paragraph (1), within 30 days of the notice being complied with.

10(3)   If the Commissioners notify the applicant that they are not satisfied as mentioned in regulation 9(3) or do not notify their decision to the applicant within the time required by paragraph (2), the applicant may within 30 days of the notification or of that time require the Commissioners to transmit the application, together with any notice given and further particulars furnished under paragraph (1), to the tribunal, and in that event any notification of approval by the tribunal shall have effect for the purposes of these Regulations as if it were a notification of approval by the Commissioners.

10(4)   If any particulars provided under this regulation do not fully and accurately disclose all facts and circumstances (including any change in circumstances) material for the decision of the Commissioners or the tribunal then, unless the applicant shows that the information in question was not in his possession or power, any resulting notification of approval by the Commissioners or tribunal shall be void.

10(5)   The Commissioners may supply to any joint applicant–

(a)   any information relating to the application, to a decision made on the application or to any change in circumstances relevant to the application or a decision; and

(b)   any communication made or received relating to the application, decision or any change in circumstances.

History – In reg. 10, in the following places, the word "Commissioners" substituted for the word "Board" by SI 2011/660, reg. 13, with effect from 6 April 2011: reg. 10(1) (four times); reg. 10(2); reg. 10(3) (three times); reg. 10(4) (twice); and reg. 10(5).
In reg. 10(3), "tribunal" substituted for "Special Commissioners" in both places by SI 2009/56, art. 3(2) and Sch. 2, para. 129(2), operative from 1 April 2009 subject to transitional and saving provisions in SI 2009/56, Sch. 3.
In reg. 10(4), "tribunal" substituted for "Special Commissioners" (which appeared before "then, unless"), and for "Commissioners" (which appeared before "shall be void"), by SI 2009/56, art. 3(2) and Sch. 2, para. 129(3), operative from 1 April 2009 subject to transitional and saving provisions in SI 2009/56, Sch. 3.

Cross references – SI 2009/275, art. 3(k): any decision under reg. 10(3) is an excluded decision for the purposes of TCEA 2007, s. 11(1) and 13(1).

11   An individual shall not be entitled to claim relief under Chapter 2 of Part 6 in respect of any shares issued to him to effect the merger by the successor company, and they shall be disregarded in determining whether the permitted maximum for the purposes of that Chapter has been exceeded (but this regulation does not extend to shares issued for new consideration).

History – In reg. 11, the words "Chapter 2 of Part 6" substituted for the words "Part 1 of Schedule 15B" and the words "that Chapter" substituted for the words "that Schedule" by SI 2011/660, reg. 9, with effect in relation to any merger where the transactions bringing the merger into effect take place on or after 6 April 2011.

12(1)   Where there has been a merger, the 70% tests, the 30% test and (subject to regulation 13(6)) the 15% test, and the requirements of section 274(2) and Chapter 4 of Part 6, shall apply to the successor company–

(a)   as if the property of the merging companies were vested in the successor company (transfers between a merging company and the successor company being disregarded accordingly),

(b)   disregarding, in the hands of the successor company, any assets that consist in rights against, or in shares or securities of, another company which is a merging company, and

(c)   disregarding, in the hands of the successor company, the use of any money which, in the hands of another company which is a merging company, would have been disregarded under section 280(2), for the same periods as are mentioned in that provision.

12(2)   Section 171(2)(cc) of the Taxation of Chargeable Gains Act 1992 shall not apply to a disposal following a merger, where the disposal is–

(a)   by a merging company to the successor company, and

(b)   of an asset held by the merging company immediately before, or in the period during which, the merger takes place.

History – In reg. 12(1), "70% tests" substituted for "70% test" by SI 2011/660, reg. 10(a), with effect in relation to any merger where the transactions bringing the merger into effect take place on or after 6 April 2011.
In reg. 12(1), "section 274(2)" substituted for "section 842AA(2)(a)" by SI 2011/660, reg. 10(b), with effect in relation to any merger where the transactions bringing the merger into effect take place on or after 6 April 2011.
In reg. 12(1), "Chapter 4 of Part 6" substituted for "Schedule 28B" by SI 2011/660, reg. 10(c), with effect in relation to any merger where the transactions bringing the merger into effect take place on or after 6 April 2011.
In reg. 12(1)(c), "section 280(2)" substituted for "section 842AA(5B)" by SI 2011/660, reg. 10(d), with effect in relation to any merger where the transactions bringing the merger into effect take place on or after 6 April 2011.

13(1)   Where there has been a merger, the following paragraphs apply.

13(2)   The relevant shares issued to effect the merger are referred to as the "new shares" and–

(a)   in the case of a share for share exchange, the corresponding shares for which they were exchanged, and

(b)   in the case of a share for business transfer, the corresponding shares in respect of which they were issued,

are referred to as the "old shares".

13(3)   For the purposes of Chapter 2 of Part 6, and of Schedule 5C to the 1992 Act–

(a)   any share for share exchange or share for business transfer shall not be treated as a disposal of the old shares, or as a chargeable event for the purposes of Schedule 5C to the 1992 Act,

(b)   any other act (including the giving of relief under Chapter 2 of Part 6, or under paragraph 2 of Schedule 5C to the 1992 Act) carried out, or failure to act, in relation to the old shares shall be treated as carried out, or omitted, in relation to the corresponding new shares, and

(c)   references to the company in which the old shares were held shall be read as references to the successor company.

13(4)   For the purposes of sections 151A and 151B of the 1992 Act, where the successor company–

(a)   was not a venture capital trust at the time when shares issued to effect the merger were acquired, but

(b)   is a venture capital trust at the time of a subsequent disposal of those shares,

it shall be treated as a venture capital trust at and from the former time.

13(5) Where the requirements of Chapter 4 of Part 6 (except section 296(1) and (2)) were satisfied (or deemed to be satisfied) to any extent or for any period, in relation to an investment when held by a merging company immediately before the merger, they shall be treated as satisfied to the same extent or for the same period, in relation to the investment when held by the successor company, as if the successor company and the other company were the same company.

13(6) For the purposes of section 296(1) and (2) and the 15% test—

(a)   the period during which the merger takes place shall be disregarded, and

(b)   if, as a result of the merger, the requirements of that section or that test, as the case may be, would not be met immediately after the merger, those requirements shall be treated as met for a further period of one year.

13(7) For the purposes of section 274(2) the value of investments in the hands of the successor company immediately after the merger shall be their value when last valued before the merger, in accordance with that section, unless there has been a transaction (other than the merger) whereby those investments would fall to be so revalued.

13(8) For the purposes of section 289 the like provisions as are contained in paragraph (7) shall apply (substituting references to valuations in accordance with section 289 for references to valuations in accordance with section 278(1) to (3)).

13(9) Where—

(a)   a merging company, other than a successor company, obtained VCT approval in exercise of the power conferred by section 275(1) to (3) (provisional approval), and

(b)   the approval is withdrawn following the merger,

section 281 shall apply to the withdrawal of approval with the modifications that, in subsection (2) the words "Subject to subsections (3) and (4)," and subsections (3) and (4), are omitted.

History – In reg. 13(3) in the opening words, "Chapter 2 of Part 6" substituted for "Schedule 15B" by SI 2011/660, reg. 11(2)(a), with effect in relation to any merger where the transactions bringing the merger into effect take place on or after 6 April 2011. In reg. 13(3)(b), "Chapter 2 of Part 6" substituted for "Part 1 of Schedule 15B" by SI 2011/660, reg. 11(2)(b), with effect in relation to any merger where the transactions bringing the merger into effect take place on or after 6 April 2011.
In reg. 13(5), the words "Chapter 4 of Part 6 (except section 296(1) and (2))" substituted for the words "any of the paragraphs of Schedule 28B (except paragraph 9)" by SI 2011/660, reg. 11(3), with effect in relation to any merger where the transactions bringing the merger into effect take place on or after 6 April 2011.
In reg. 13(6), "section 296(1) and (2)" substituted for "paragraph 9 of Schedule 28B" by SI 2011/660, reg. 11(4)(a), with effect in relation to any merger where the transactions bringing the merger into effect take place on or after 6 April 2011.
In reg. 13(6)(b), the words "that section" substituted for the words "that paragraph" by SI 2011/660, reg. 11(4)(b), with effect in relation to any merger where the transactions bringing the merger into effect take place on or after 6 April 2011.
In reg. 13(7), "section 274(2)" substituted for "section 842AA(2)(b) to (d)" and "in accordance with that section" substituted for "in accordance with subsection (5) of that section" by SI 2011/660, reg. 11(5), with effect in relation to any merger where transactions bringing the merger into effect take place on or after 6 April 2011.
In reg. 13(8), "section 289" substituted for "paragraph 10B of Schedule 28B" and "section 289" (in the parentheses) substituted for "paragraph 10B" by SI 2011/660, reg. 11(6)(a), with effect in relation to any merger where the transactions bringing the merger into effect take place on or after 6 April 2011.
In reg. 13(8), "section 278(1) to (3)" substituted for "section 842AA(5)" by SI 2011/660, reg. 11(6)(b), with effect in relation to any merger where the transactions bringing the merger into effect take place on or after 6 April 2011.
In reg. 13(9)(a), "section 275(1) to (3)" substituted for "section 842AA(4)" by SI 2011/660, reg. 11(7)(a), with effect in relation to any merger where the transactions bringing the merger into effect take place on or after 6 April 2011.
In reg. 13(9)(b), "section 281" substituted for "section 842AA" by SI 2011/660, reg. 11(7)(b), with effect in relation to any merger where the transactions bringing the merger into effect take place on or after 6 April 2011.
In reg. 13(9), "subsection (2)" substituted for "subsection (7)" by SI 2011/660, reg. 11(7)(c), with effect in relation to any merger where the transactions bringing the merger into effect take place on or after 6 April 2011.
In reg. 13(9), "subsections (3) and (4)", in both places where it occurs, substituted for "subsections (8) and (9)" by SI 2011/660, reg. 11(7)(d), with effect in relation to any merger where the transactions bringing the merger into effect take place on or after 6 April 2011.

LIMITING THE OPERATION OF SECTION 280

History – Heading before reg. 14 substituted by SI 2011/660, reg. 12(2), with effect in relation to shares issued on or after 6 April 2011. The former heading read: "LIMITING THE OPERATION OF SECTION 842AA(5B)".

14(1) Section 280(2) shall apply to a further issue of shares (in the circumstances mentioned in subsection (1) of that section) conditionally on the money being raised by that further issue for the purposes of investment (that is, for the purpose of the trust company acquiring additional investments which fulfil the 70% tests and the 30% test).

14(2) The condition mentioned in paragraph (1) shall be treated (in particular) as not fulfilled if—

(a)   any of the money raised by the further issue (or any assets directly or indirectly derived from that money) is used for the purpose of the trust company purchasing any of its own shares, and

(b)   either—

       (i)   the Commissioners are of the opinion that the shares being purchased are not insignificant in relation to the issued ordinary share capital of the company, or

(ii) the purchase is made as the result of a general offer to members (with or without exceptions for persons connected with the trust company).

14(3) Where the further issue of shares is of shares issued for new consideration, paragraph (1) shall be treated (in particular) as not fulfilled if—

(a) any of the money raised by the further issue (or any assets directly or indirectly derived from that money) is used for the purpose of the successor company purchasing shares in any of the merging companies, or the other merging companies, as the case may be, and

(b) the money so used exceeds the least of A, B and C in regulation 9(3)(g).

14(4) Where any of the money raised by the further issue (or any assets directly or indirectly derived from that money) is used for a purpose other than as mentioned in paragraph (1), section 280(2) shall be treated as not having applied to the further issue from the time immediately before that use of the money or other assets.

14(5) Where, in consequence of paragraph (4), the 70% tests and the 30% test fall to be applied immediately before the use of money mentioned in that paragraph, the trust company's investments for the purposes of s section 274 shall be treated as including any money raised by that further issue (or assets directly or indirectly derived from that money).

History – In reg. 14(1), "Section 280(2)" substituted for "Section 842AA(5B)" and "(1)" substituted for "(5A)" by SI 2011/660, reg. 12(3), with effect in relation to shares issued on or after 6 April 2011.
In reg. 14(1), "70% tests" substituted for "70% test" by SI 2011/660, reg. 12(6), with effect in relation to shares issued on or after 6 April 2011.
In reg. 14(2)(b)(i), the word "Commissioners" substituted for the word "Board" by SI 2011/660, reg. 13, with effect from 6 April 2011.
In reg. 14(4), "section 280(2)" substituted for "section 842AA(5B)" by SI 2011/660, reg. 12(4), with effect in relation to shares issued on or after 6 April 2011.
In reg. 14(5), "section 274" substituted for "section 842AA(2)(b) and (c)" by SI 2011/660, reg. 12(5), with effect in relation to shares issued on or after 6 April 2011.
In reg. 14(5), "70% tests" substituted for "70% test" by SI 2011/660, reg. 12(6), with effect in relation to shares issued on or after 6 April 2011.

Statutory Instruments

CORPORATION TAX (NOTICE OF COMING WITHIN CHARGE – INFORMATION) REGULATIONS 2004

(SI 2004/2502)

Made on 22 September 2004 by the Commissioners of Inland Revenue, in exercise of the powers conferred upon them by s. 55(2)(c), (3) and (5) of the Finance Act 2004. Operative from 13 October 2004.

CITATION, COMMENCEMENT AND INTERPRETATION

1(1)　These Regulations may be cited as the Corporation Tax (Notice of Coming within Charge – Information) Regulations 2004 and shall come into force on 13th October 2004.

1(2)　In these Regulations–

"**the section**" means section 55 of the Finance Act 2004; and

a reference, without more, to a numbered subsection is a reference to the subsection of the section which is so numbered.

INFORMATION PRESCRIBED FOR THE PURPOSES OF SECTION 55(2)(C) OF THE FINANCE ACT 2004

2(1)　For the purposes of subsection (2)(c) the information specified in the following paragraphs of this regulation is prescribed.

2(2)　In the case of the company's accounting period falling within either paragraph (a) or (b) of subsection (1), the prescribed information is the date on which that accounting period commenced (within the meaning of section 12(2) of the Income and Corporation Taxes Act 1988), together with the information in paragraph (3).

2(3)　The information to be given in respect of any company to which the section applies is–

(a)　the company's name and its registered number;

(b)　the address of the company's registered office;

(c)　the address of the company's principal place of business;

(d)　the nature of the business being carried on by the company;

(e)　the date to which the company intends to prepare accounts;

(f)　the full name and home address of each of the directors of the company;

(g)　if the company has taken over any business, including any trade, profession or vocation formerly carried on by another–

　(i)　the name and address of that former business; and

　(ii)　the name and address of the person from whom the business was acquired;

(h)　if the company is deemed, by virtue of section 413(3) of the Income and Corporation Taxes Act 1988, to be a member of a group of companies for the purposes of Chapter 4 of Part 10 of that Act, the name of the parent company and the address of its registered office; and

(i)　in the case of a company which, at the time it gives notice under the section, has been obliged to comply with the requirements of the Income Tax (Pay as You Earn) Regulations 2003, the date on which that obligation first arose.

OFFSHORE FUNDS REGULATIONS 2004

(SI 2004/2572)

Made on 30 September 2004 by the Treasury, in exercise of the powers conferred upon them by s. 758(7) and (8) of, and para. 21 of Sch. 27 and para. 9 of Sch. 28 to, the Income and Corporation Taxes Act 1988 and s. 145(2)(b) of the Finance Act 2004. Operative from 22 October 2004.

CITATION, COMMENCEMENT AND EFFECT

1(1) These Regulations may be cited as the Offshore Funds Regulations 2004 and shall come into force on 22nd October 2004.

1(2) These Regulations have effect in relation to account periods ending on or after 22nd July 2004.

INTERPRETATION

2 In these Regulations–

> **"class of interest"** has the meaning given by section 756C of ICTA 1988;
>
> **"ICTA 1988"** means the Income and Corporation Taxes Act 1988;
>
> **"main fund"** has the meaning given by section 756C(1) of ICTA 1988;
>
> **"umbrella fund"** has the meaning given by section 756B(1) of ICTA 1988; and
>
> references to a part of a fund are references to a part of an umbrella fund which is regarded as a separate offshore fund by virtue of section 756B(2) of ICTA 1988.

SECTION 758 OF ICTA 1988

3(1) Section 758 of ICTA 1988 applies to–

(a)   a part of an umbrella fund which is regarded as a separate offshore fund by virtue of section 756B(2) of that Act, and

(b)   a class of interest, within a main fund, which is regarded as separate offshore fund by virtue of section 756C(1) of that Act,

subject to the following modifications.

3(2) For subsection (1)(b) substitute–

> "(b)   the umbrella fund or main fund makes a distribution to–
>
> > (i)   a holder of units in a part of that fund which is regarded as a separate offshore fund by virtue of section 756B(2); or
> >
> > (ii) a holder of a class of interest in an offshore fund which is regarded as a separate offshore fund by virtue of section 756C(1);
>
> for a period which begins before the date of his acquisition of those units or that interest;".

3(3) After subsection (1) insert–

> "**758(1A)**   In this section in the case of–
>
> (a)   an umbrella fund, part of which is regarded as a separate offshore fund by virtue of section 756B(2), or
>
> (b)   a main fund, a class of interest in which is regarded as a separate offshore fund by virtue of section 756C(1),
>
> references to the equalisation arrangements or to the equalisation account of the offshore fund shall be construed respectively as references to the equalisation arrangements of, or to the equalisation account maintained by, the umbrella fund or the main fund in respect of the separate offshore fund in question.".

3(4) For subsection (2)(a) substitute–

> "(a)   his acquisition is by way of subscription for, or allotment of new shares, units or other classes of interest issued or created–
>
> > (i)   by an umbrella fund;
> >
> > (b)   in a fund which is regarded as a separate offshore fund by virtue of section 756B(2);
> >
> > (iii) by a main fund; or
> >
> > (iv) in a class of interest which is regarded as a separate offshore fund by virtue of section 756C(1);".

MODIFICATION OF SCHEDULE 27 TO ICTA 1988

4(1)   Schedule 27 to ICTA 1988 (distributing funds) applies to–

(a)   a part of a fund which is regarded as a separate offshore fund by virtue of section 756B(2) of that Act, and

(b)   a class of interest, within a main fund, which is regarded as a separate offshore fund by virtue of section 756C(1) of that Act,

subject to the following modifications.

4(2)   In paragraph 1 (requirements as to distributions)–

(a)   after sub-paragraph (2) add–

"**1(2A)**   In the case of a class of interest which is regarded as a separate offshore fund the reference in sub-paragraph (2)(b) to the amount of the gross income shall be a reference to the amount of the gross income of the main fund (as defined in section 756C(1)).";

(b)   after sub-paragraph (3) add–

"**1(3A)**   In the case of a part of a fund or a class of interest which is regarded as a separate offshore fund, the accounts referred to in sub-paragraph (3) shall be the accounts of the umbrella fund or the main fund, of which the part of the fund, or the class of interest forms part."; and

(c)   after sub-paragraph (6) add–

"**1(7)**   In sub-paragraph (6) references to–

(a)   the offshore fund do not include–

(i)   parts of an umbrella fund which are regarded as separate offshore funds by virtue of sections 756B(2); or

(ii)   classes of interest which are regarded as separate offshore funds by virtue of section 756C(1); or

(b)   the making of distributions, in relation to a part of an umbrella fund or to a class of interest in a main fund, are references to distributions made (as the case may be) by–

(i)   the umbrella fund to persons having an interest in part of that fund which is regarded as a separate offshore fund by virtue of section 756B(2); and

(ii)   the main fund to a person having an interest of that class which is regarded as a separate offshore fund by virtue of section 756C(1).".

4(3)   In paragraph 2 (funds operating equalisation arrangements) after sub-paragraph (2) add–

"**2(2A)**   In this paragraph in the case of–

(a)   an umbrella fund, part of which is regarded as a separate offshore fund by virtue of section 756B(2), or

(b)   a main fund, a class of interest in which is regarded as a separate offshore fund by virtue of section 756C(1),

references to the equalisation arrangements or to the equalisation account of the offshore fund shall be construed respectively as references to the equalisation arrangements of, or to the equalisation account maintained by, the umbrella fund or the main fund in respect of the separate offshore fund in question.

2(2B)   In this paragraph references to making a distribution, in relation to a part of an umbrella fund or to a class of interest in a main fund, is a reference to a distribution made (as the case may be) by–

(a)   the umbrella fund to persons having an interest in part of that fund which is regarded as a separate offshore fund by virtue of section 756B(2); and

(b)   the main fund to a person having an interest of that class which is regarded as a separate offshore fund by virtue of section 756C(1).".

4(4)   After paragraph 4(3) insert–

"**4(3A)**   For the purposes of sub-paragraph (3), in determining the relevant amount of expenditure attributable to–

(a)   each part of a fund which is regarded as a separate offshore fund by virtue of section 756B(2), or

(b)   each class of interest which is regarded as a separate offshore fund by virtue of section 756C(1),

any expenditure shall be apportioned in such manner as is just and reasonable.".

4(5) At the end of paragraph 5 (United Kingdom equivalent profits) add—

"**5(6)** In sub-paragraph (5) references to the offshore fund do not include—

(a) a part of a fund, within an umbrella fund, where that part is regarded as a separate offshore fund by virtue of section 756B(2); or

(b) a class of interest, within a main fund which is regarded as a separate offshore fund by virtue of section 756C(1).

5(7) For the purposes of sub-paragraph (5) if an offshore fund has within it—

(a) any part which is regarded as a separate offshore fund by virtue of section 756B(2); or

(b) any class of interest which is regarded as a separate offshore fund by virtue of section 756C(1),

the relevant amount of income attributable to each part, or each class of interest, within the fund, shall be apportioned between them in such manner as is just and reasonable.".

4(6) At the end of paragraph 11 (offshore funds with wholly-owned subsidiaries) add—

"**11(5)** In sub-paragraphs (1) to (2) references to the offshore fund do not include a class of interest which is regarded as a separate offshore fund by virtue of section 756C(1).

11(6) In the case of a class of interest, references to the offshore fund in sub-paragraphs (1), (2) and (4)(b) shall be to the main fund.

11(7) For the purposes of sub-paragraph (4) if—

(a) there are parts of an umbrella fund which are regarded as separate offshore funds by virtue of section 756B(2); or

(b) there are classes of interest in a main fund which are regarded as separate offshore funds by virtue of section 756C(1),

the receipts and expenditure shall be apportioned in such manner as is just and reasonable.".

4(7) In paragraph 15 (application for certification) for sub-paragraph (1)(b) substitute—

"(b) the application is accompanied by—

(i) the accounts of the fund for, or for a period which includes, the account period to which the application relates; or

(ii) in the case of—

(aa) part of an umbrella fund, or

(bb) a class of interest in a main fund,

which is regarded as a separate offshore fund, the accounts of the umbrella fund or the main fund (as the case may be) for, or for a period which includes, the account period to which the application relates; and".

MODIFICATION OF SCHEDULE 28 TO ICTA 1988

5(1) Schedule 28 to ICTA 1988 (computation of offshore income gains) applies to—

(a) a part of a fund which is regarded as a separate offshore fund by virtue of section 756B(2) of that Act, and

(b) a class of interest, within a main fund, which is regarded as a separate offshore fund by virtue of section 756C(1) of that Act,

subject to the following modifications.

5(2) At the end of paragraph 6 add—

"**6(7)** In this paragraph in the case of—

(a) an umbrella fund, part of which is regarded as a separate offshore fund by virtue of section 756B(2), or

(b) a main fund, a class of interest in which is regarded as a separate offshore fund by virtue of section 756C(1),

references to the equalisation account of the offshore fund shall be construed as references to the equalisation account maintained by the umbrella fund or the main fund in respect of the separate offshore fund in question.".

MODIFICATION OF SCHEDULE 26 TO THE FINANCE ACT 2004: NEW FUNDS WITHIN EXISTING UMBRELLA FUNDS

6(1)   This regulation applies to an umbrella fund established on or before 22nd July 2004 and which has not made an election under paragraph 1(3) or paragraph 2(3) of Schedule 26 to the Finance Act 2004 (elections in respect of computation of UK equivalent profits from creditor relationships and derivative contracts).

6(2)   Paragraph (3) applies to a part of a fund which–

(a)   is regarded as a separate offshore fund by virtue of section 756B(2) of ICTA 1988; and

(b)   is established after 22nd July 2004.

6(3)   In relation to a part of a fund to which this paragraph applies, the repeals contained in paragraph 1(2) or 2(2) of Schedule 26 to the Finance Act 2004 (as the case requires) shall be disregarded, and accordingly–

(a)   paragraph 3 of Schedule 10 to the Finance Act 1996, (assumptions to be made in relation to creditor relationships for the purposes of Schedule 27 to ICTA 1988), or

(b)   paragraph 35 of Schedule 26 to the Finance Act 2002 (assumptions to be made in relation to derivative contracts for those purposes),

(as the case requires) shall apply in relation to that part of the umbrella fund as they would have applied had those repeals not been enacted.

MODIFICATION OF SCHEDULE 26 TO THE FINANCE ACT 2004: NEW CLASSES OF INTEREST WITHIN EXISTING MAIN FUNDS

7(1)   This regulation applies in relation to a main fund established on or before 22nd July 2004 and which has not made an election under paragraph 1(3) or paragraph 2(3) of Schedule 26 to the Finance Act 2004.

7(2)   Paragraph (3) applies to a class of interest within a main fund which–

(a)   is regarded as a separate offshore fund by virtue of section 756C(1) of ICTA 1988; and

(b)   is established after 22nd July 2004.

7(3)   In relation to a class of interest to which this paragraph applies, the repeals contained in paragraph 1(2) or 2(2) of Schedule 26 to the Finance Act 2004 (as the case requires) shall be disregarded, and accordingly–

(a)   paragraph 3 of Schedule 10 to the Finance Act 1996, (assumptions to be made in relation to creditor relationships for the purposes of Schedule 27 to ICTA 1988), or

(b)   paragraph 35 of Schedule 26 to the Finance Act 2002 (assumptions to be made for the purposes of the Schedule in relation to derivative contracts for those purposes),

(as the case requires) shall apply in relation to that class of interest as they would have applied but for those repeals.

EXEMPTION FROM TAX FOR CERTAIN INTEREST PAYMENTS REGULATIONS 2004

(SI 2004/2622, as amended by SI 2009/56)

Made on 8 October 2004 by the Board, in exercise of the powers conferred upon them by s. 100 of the Finance Act 2004. Operative from 1 November 2004.

CITATION AND COMMENCEMENT

1   These Regulations may be cited as the Exemption From Tax For Certain Interest Payments Regulations 2004 and shall come into force on 1st November 2004.

INTERPRETATION

2   In these Regulations–

"the Act" means the Finance Act 2004;

"the Board" means the Commissioners of Inland Revenue;

"a company in Condition 1" means a company in Condition 1 in section 98(2) of the Act;

"a company in Condition 2" means a company in Condition 2 in section 98(3) of the Act;

"an exemption notice" is a notice issued by the Board under section 98(5) of the Act;

REQUEST FOR AND ISSUE OF AN EXEMPTION NOTICE AND NOTIFICATION OF REFUSAL

3(1)   An exemption notice may be issued only on the request of an officer of a company in Condition 2 or its appointed agent.

3(2)   On receipt of a request under paragraph (1) the Board must determine whether to issue an exemption notice within three months of receipt of the request and the certificate.

3(3)   An exemption notice must be given to the person requesting the issue of the notice and the company in Condition 1.

3(4)   The Board must notify in writing the person requesting the issue of the notice of a refusal to issue a notice specifying the date of the refusal and the reasons for the refusal.

INFORMATION TO BE PROVIDED IN THE CERTIFICATE

4(1)   A person requesting the issue of an exemption notice must provide a certificate certifying that Conditions 1 to 3 in section 98 of the Act are satisfied and that section 104 of the Act (anti-avoidance) does not apply.

4(2)   For the purposes of paragraph (1), the certificate must provide–

(a)   proof of the residence for tax purposes of the company in Condition 2 and, where necessary, the existence of a permanent establishment;

(b)   information as to the beneficial entitlement of the company in Condition 2 to the income in respect of which the payment is made;

(c)   details of the United Kingdom corporation tax or tax corresponding to that tax to which the company in Condition 2 is subject;

(d)   information establishing that the company in Condition 1 and the company in Condition 2 are 25% associates within section 99(4) of the Act; and

(e)   a copy of the loan agreement or other document providing the legal justification for the interest payment.

SPECIAL RELATIONSHIP

5   If section 103 of the Act (special relationship) applies or may apply to a payment of interest, an exemption notice may specify–

(a)   the amount of the payment, or

(b)   the method to be used for determining the amount of the payment

in relation to which the notice has effect.

REQUIREMENTS WHERE CONDITIONS FOR EXEMPTION CEASE TO BE SATISFIED

6(1) If the person who has requested the issue of an exemption notice becomes aware that any of Conditions 1 to 3 in section 98 of the Act has ceased to be satisfied he must as soon as possible notify the Board and the company in Condition 1.

6(2) If the company in Condition 1 becomes aware that any of Conditions 1 to 3 in section 98 of the Act has ceased to be satisfied it must as soon as possible notify the Board.

6(3) An exemption notice becomes ineffective if the company in Condition 1—

(a) receives notice under paragraph (1), or

(b) becomes aware that any of Conditions 1 to 3 in section 98 of the Act has ceased to be satisfied.

CANCELLATION OF EXEMPTION NOTICE

7 If—

(a) the Board receives notice under regulation 6,

(b) it appears to the Board that any of Conditions 1 to 3 in section 98 of the Act has ceased to be satisfied, or

(c) it appears to the Board that section 104 of the Act (anti-avoidance) applies,

the Board may cancel the exemption notice by notice in writing to the person who requested the issue of the exemption notice and the company in Condition 1.

RECOVERY OF TAX NOT DEDUCTED

8(1) If after an exemption notice has been issued, it is discovered that any of Conditions 1 to 3 in section 98 of the Act was not satisfied in the case of a payment of interest and tax deductible from the payment has not been deducted, that tax may be recovered—

(a) by assessment on the company in Condition 2 under Case VI of Schedule D, or

(b) if a direction to that effect is given by the Board, by deduction from subsequent payments by the company in Condition 1.

8(2) Any tax deducted in accordance with paragraph (1)(b) shall be treated as tax deductible under section 349 of the Income and Corporation Taxes Act 1988 in respect of the payment from which it is deducted.

APPEALS AGAINST REFUSAL TO ISSUE AN EXEMPTION NOTICE OR CANCELLATION OF AN EXEMPTION NOTICE

9(1) An officer of a company in Condition 2 or its appointed agent may appeal against a refusal to issue an exemption notice or the cancellation of an exemption notice.

9(2) An appeal under this regulation must be by notice in writing to the Board within 30 days of the date of notification of the refusal under regulation 3 or the cancellation under regulation 7.

9(3) The grounds of appeal are

(a) that Conditions 1 to 3 in section 98 of the Act are satisfied, and

(b) section 104 of the Act (anti-avoidance) does not apply.

9(4) If, on its being notified to the tribunal, the tribunal allows the appeal it may also—

(a) in an appeal against a refusal to issue an exemption notice, direct that the Board issue an exemption notice within 14 days of its decision, or

(b) in an appeal against the cancellation of an exemption notice, direct that the cancellation was ineffective.

9(5) Notwithstanding the provisions of sections 11 and 13 of the Tribunals, Courts and Enforcement Act 2007, the decision of the tribunal shall be final.

History – In reg. 9(1), the words "to the Special Commissioners", which appeared after "appeal", omitted by SI 2009/56, art. 3(2) and Sch. 2, para. 130(2), operative from 1 April 2009 subject to transitional and saving provisions in SI 2009/56, Sch. 3.

In reg. 9(4), the words "If, on its being notified to the tribunal, the tribunal allows the appeal it may also" substituted for the words "If the Special Commissioners allow the appeal, they may also" by SI 2009/56, art. 3(2) and Sch. 2, para. 130(3), operative from 1 April 2009 subject to transitional and saving provisions in SI 2009/56, Sch. 3.

Reg. 9(5) substituted by SI 2009/56, art. 3(2) and Sch. 2, para. 130(4), operative from 1 April 2009 subject to transitional and saving provisions in SI 2009/56, Sch. 3. Former reg. 9(5) read as follows:

    "**9(5)** The decision of the Special Commissioners shall be final.".

FREEDOM OF INFORMATION AND DATA PROTECTION (APPROPRIATE LIMIT AND FEES) REGULATIONS 2004

(SI 2004/3244)

Made on 7 December 2004 by the Secretary of State, in exercise of the powers conferred upon him by s. 9(3) and (4), 12(3), (4) and (5), and 13(1) and (2) of the Freedom of Information Act 2000, and by s. 9A(5) and 67(2) of the Data Protection Act 1998, and having consulted the Information Commissioner in accordance with s. 67(3) of the Data Protection Act 1998. Operative from 1 January 2005.

CITATION AND COMMENCEMENT

1   These Regulations may be cited as the Freedom of Information and Data Protection (Appropriate Limit and Fees) Regulations 2004 and come into force on 1st January 2005.

INTERPRETATION

2   In these Regulations–

"**the 2000 Act**" means the Freedom of Information Act 2000;

"**the 1998 Act**" means the Data Protection Act 1998; and

"**the appropriate limit**" is to be construed in accordance with the provision made in regulation 3.

THE APPROPRIATE LIMIT

3(1)   This regulation has effect to prescribe the appropriate limit referred to in section 9A(3) and (4) of the 1998 Act and the appropriate limit referred to in section 12(1) and (2) of the 2000 Act.

3(2)   In the case of a public authority which is listed in Part I of Schedule 1 to the 2000 Act, the appropriate limit is £600.

3(3)   In the case of any other public authority, the appropriate limit is £450.

ESTIMATING THE COST OF COMPLYING WITH A REQUEST – GENERAL

4(1)   This regulation has effect in any case in which a public authority proposes to estimate whether the cost of complying with a relevant request would exceed the appropriate limit.

4(2)   A relevant request is any request to the extent that it is a request–

(a)   for unstructured personal data within the meaning of section 9A(1) of the 1998 Act, and to which section 7(1) of that Act would, apart from the appropriate limit, to any extent apply, or

(b)   information to which section 1(1) of the 2000 Act would, apart from the appropriate limit, to any extent apply.

4(3)   In a case in which this regulation has effect, a public authority may, for the purpose of its estimate, take account only of the costs it reasonably expects to incur in relation to the request in–

(a)   determining whether it holds the information,

(b)   locating the information, or a document which may contain the information,

(c)   retrieving the information, or a document which may contain the information, and

(d)   extracting the information from a document containing it.

4(4)   To the extent to which any of the costs which a public authority takes into account are attributable to the time which persons undertaking any of the activities mentioned in paragraph (3) on behalf of the authority are expected to spend on those activities, those costs are to be estimated at a rate of £25 per person per hour.

ESTIMATING THE COST OF COMPLYING WITH A REQUEST – AGGREGATION OF RELATED REQUESTS

5(1)   In circumstances in which this regulation applies, where two or more requests for information to which section 1(1) of the 2000 Act would, apart from the appropriate limit, to any extent apply, are made to a public authority–

(a)   by one person, or

(b)   by different persons who appear to the public authority to be acting in concert or in pursuance of a campaign,

the estimated cost of complying with any of the requests is to be taken to be the total costs which may be taken into account by the authority, under regulation 4, of complying with all of them.

5(2)   This regulation applies in circumstances in which–

(a)   the two or more requests referred to in paragraph (1) relate, to any extent, to the same or similar information, and

(b)   those requests are received by the public authority within any period of sixty consecutive working days.

5(3)   In this regulation, **"working day"** means any day other than a Saturday, a Sunday, Christmas Day, Good Friday or a day which is a bank holiday under the Banking and Financial Dealings Act 1971 in any part of the United Kingdom.

MAXIMUM FEE FOR COMPLYING WITH SECTION 1(1) OF THE 2000 ACT

6(1)   Any fee to be charged under section 9 of the 2000 Act by a public authority to whom a request for information is made is not to exceed the maximum determined by the public authority in accordance with this regulation.

6(2)   Subject to paragraph (4), the maximum fee is a sum equivalent to the total costs the public authority reasonably expects to incur in relation to the request in–

(a)   informing the person making the request whether it holds the information, and

(b)   communicating the information to the person making the request.

6(3)   Costs which may be taken into account by a public authority for the purposes of this regulation include, but are not limited to, the costs of–

(a)   complying with any obligation under section 11(1) of the 2000 Act as to the means or form of communicating the information,

(b)   reproducing any document containing the information, and

(c)   postage and other forms of transmitting the information.

6(4)   But a public authority may not take into account for the purposes of this regulation any costs which are attributable to the time which persons undertaking activities mentioned in paragraph (2) on behalf of the authority are expected to spend on those activities.

MAXIMUM FEE FOR COMMUNICATION OF INFORMATION UNDER SECTION 13 OF THE 2000 ACT

7(1)   Any fee to be charged under section 13 of the 2000 Act by a public authority to whom a request for information is made is not to exceed the maximum determined by a public authority in accordance with this regulation.

7(2)   The maximum fee is a sum equivalent to the total of–

(a)   the costs which the public authority may take into account under regulation 4 in relation to that request, and

(b)   the costs it reasonably expects to incur in relation to the request in–

(i)   informing the person making the request whether it holds the information, and

(ii)   communicating the information to the person making the request.

7(3)   But a public authority is to disregard, for the purposes of paragraph(2)(a), any costs which it may take into account under regulation 4 solely by virtue of the provision made by regulation 5.

7(4)   Costs which may be taken into account by a public authority for the purposes of paragraph (2)(b) include, but are not limited to, the costs of–

(a)   giving effect to any preference expressed by the person making the request as to the means or form of communicating the information,

(b)   reproducing any document containing the information, and

(c)   postage and other forms of transmitting the information.

7(5)   For the purposes of this regulation, the provision for the estimation of costs made by regulation 4(4) is to be taken to apply to the costs mentioned in paragraph (2)(b) as it does to the costs mentioned in regulation 4(3).

LOAN RELATIONSHIPS AND DERIVATIVE CONTRACTS (DISREGARD AND BRINGING INTO ACCOUNT OF PROFITS AND LOSSES) REGULATIONS 2004

(SI 2004/3256 as amended by SI 2005/2012, SI 2005/3374, SI 2006/3236, SI 2007/948, SI 2007/3431, SI 2009/1886, SI 2011/698, SI 2011/2912, SI 2013/2781 and SI 2013/3209)

Made on 9 December 2004 by the Treasury, in exercise of the powers conferred upon them by s. 84A(3A), 85B(3)(a) and 85B(5)(b) of the Finance Act 1996 and para. 16(3A), 17C(1) and 17C(3)(b) of Sch. 26 to the Finance Act 2002. Operative from 1 January 2005.

CITATION, COMMENCEMENT AND EFFECT

1(1) These Regulations may be cited as the Loan Relationships and Derivative Contracts (Disregard and Bringing into Account of Profits and Losses) Regulations 2004 and shall come into force on 1st January 2005.

1(2) These Regulations have effect in relation to periods of account beginning on or after 1st January 2005.

INTERPRETATION

2(1) In these Regulations–

"deferred shares" has the same meaning as in the Building Societies Act 1986;

"derivative contract" has the same meaning as in Schedule 26 to the Finance Act 2002;

"exchange gain or loss" has the same meaning as in paragraph 54 of Schedule 26 to the Finance Act 2002;

"fair value accounting" has the meaning given in section 103 of the Finance Act 1996;

"fair value profit or loss" means the profit or loss brought into account in relation to a derivative contract or an asset or liability representing a loan relationship where for the period in question fair value accounting is used, and where fair value accounting is used in relation to only part of a contract it means the profit or loss brought into account in relation to that part;

"loan relationship" has the same meaning as in section 81 of the Finance Act 1996;

"a paragraph 50A credit or debit" means the credit or debit to be brought into account in accordance with paragraph 50A of Schedule 26 to the Finance Act 2002;

"a prior period adjustment credit or debit" means so much of any credit or debit as represents a prior period adjustment taken into account by virtue of paragraph 17B(1)(b) of Schedule 26 to the Finance Act 2002 as a result of a change of accounting basis;

"regulatory capital security" has the meaning given in regulation 2 of the Taxation of Regulatory Capital Securities Regulations 2013;

"underlying subject matter" has the same meaning as in Schedule 26 to the Finance Act 2002.

2(2) In these Regulations–

"for accounting purposes" means for the purposes of accounts drawn up in accordance with generally accepted accounting practice;

"generally accepted accounting practice" has the meaning given in section 50 of the Finance Act 2004; and

"amortised cost", **"consolidated accounts"**, **"designated"**, **"effective hedge"**, **"effective interest method"**, **"firm commitment"**, **"forecast transaction"**, **"foreign operation"** and **"net investment in a foreign operation"** have the same meaning as for accounting purposes.

2(3) In these Regulations any reference to an asset which is a ship or aircraft includes a reference to a contract–

(a) to which section 67 of the Capital Allowances Act 2001 applies; and

(b) which relates to plant or machinery which is a ship or aircraft.

2(3A) For the purposes of these Regulations, a liability representing a loan relationship or a derivative contract is treated as matched with shares, ships or aircraft from the date that, and to the extent that, either condition 1 or 2 of regulations 3(3) or 4(3) are satisfied.

2(4) In these Regulations–

(a) any reference to a hedging instrument includes a reference to part of an instrument; and

(b) any reference to a hedged item includes a reference to part of a hedged item.

2(5) For the purposes of these Regulations, a company has a hedging relationship between a derivative contract or a liability representing a loan relationship on the one hand ("the hedging instrument") and an asset, liability, receipt or expense on the other ("the hedged item") if and to the extent that–

(a) the hedging instrument and the hedged item are designated by the company as a hedge; or

(b) in any other case the hedging instrument is intended to act as a hedge of–

    (i) the exposure to changes in fair value of a hedged item which is a recognised asset or liability or an unrecognised firm commitment or an identified portion of such an asset, liability or commitment that is attributable to a particular risk and could affect profit or loss of the company;

    (ii) the exposure to variability in cash flows that is attributable to a particular risk associated with a hedged item that is a recognised asset or liability or a forecast transaction and could affect profit or loss of the company; or

    (iii) a net investment in a foreign operation of the company.

2(6) For the purposes of regulations 3 to 5, where an asset referred to is shares in a company, the asset comprises all the shares held in that company whenever acquired.

History – In reg. 2(1), the definition of "Additional Tier 1 instrument" omitted by SI 2013/3209, reg. 10(1)(a), with effect from 1 January 2014. Former definition read as follows:

    "**"Additional Tier 1 instrument"** means an instrument which qualifies as an Additional Tier 1 instrument under Article 52 of the Commission Regulation (EU) No 575/2013;"

In reg. 2(1), the definition of "regulatory capital security" inserted by SI 2013/3209, reg. 10(1)(b), with effect from 1 January 2014.

In reg. 2(1), definitions of "Additional Tier 1 instrument" and "deferred shares" inserted by SI 2013/2781, reg. 2(2), with effect in relation to loan relationships and derivative contracts entered into on or after 21 November 2013.

In reg. 2(1), the definition of "exchange gain or loss" substituted, and the definitions of "loan relationship", "a paragraph 50A credit or debit" and "a prior period adjustment credit or debit" inserted, by SI 2005/2012, reg. 3 in relation to periods of account beginning on or after 1 January 2005 and ending after 11 August 2005.

In reg. 2(2) the words ", consolidated accounts" inserted by SI 2007/3431, reg. 2(2)(a), with effect in relation to accounting periods beginning on or after 1 January 2008.

Reg. 2(3A) inserted by SI 2011/2912, reg. 3, with effect from 11.45 a.m. on 6 December 2011 in relation to shares, ships or aircraft which are matched on or after that date in accordance with reg. 3 or 4 of these Regulations.

Reg. 2(6) inserted by SI 2007/3431, reg. 2(2)(b), with effect in relation to accounting periods beginning on or after 1 January 2008.

EXCHANGE GAINS OR LOSSES ARISING FROM LIABILITIES OR ASSETS HEDGING SHARES ETC.

3(1) For the purposes of section 84A(3A) of the Finance Act 1996 there is prescribed an exchange gain or loss arising to a company in an accounting period in relation to a liability representing a loan relationship of the company which is matched with the whole or part of any shares, ships or aircraft.

3(1ZA) But where the matched shares, ships or aircraft are matched after the company became party to the loan relationship, paragraph (1) only applies to a just and reasonable proportion of any exchange gain or loss having regard to–

(a) the fraction of the accounting period for which the shares, ships or aircraft are matched with the loan relationship,

(b) the fraction of the accounting period for which the company was party to the loan relationship, and

(c) fluctuations in exchange rates during the accounting period.

3(1A) For the purposes of paragraph (1) a liability representing a loan relationship does not include any liability representing a relationship within section 100(1) of the Finance Act 1996.

3(2) This regulation does not apply if movements in the fair value, or profits or losses arising on the disposal, of any shares, ships or aircraft which are an asset falling within regulation 3(1) are brought into account by the company in computing, for the purposes of corporation tax, the profits of a trade carried on by it which consists of or includes dealing in shares, ships or aircraft.

3(3) Shares, ships or aircraft are matched to the greatest possible extent with–

(a) the liability representing the loan relationship designated as a hedge if condition 1 is satisfied;

(b) subject to paragraph (a), the liability representing the loan relationship referred to in condition 2 if that condition is satisfied;

Condition 1

The condition is that the shares, ships or aircraft are a hedged item under a designated hedge of exchange rate risk in which the liability is the hedging instrument.

Condition 2

The condition is that the currency in which the liability is expressed is such that the company intends, by entering into or continuing to be subject to that liability, to eliminate or substantially reduce the economic risk of holding the asset, or part of the asset, which is attributable to fluctuations in exchange rates.

3(4) If condition 2 applies, a liability is matched with an asset only to the extent that the carrying value of the liability does not exceed the unmatched carrying value of the asset at the relevant time.

3(5) For the purposes of section 84A(3A) of the Finance Act 1996 there is prescribed an exchange gain or loss arising to a company in an accounting period in relation to an asset representing a loan relationship of the company which is matched with the whole or part of–

(a)   any share capital of the company,

(b)   in relation to a building society, any deferred shares issued by the building society to the extent that they are accounted for as equity instruments in accordance with generally accepted accounting practice, or

(c)   a regulatory capital security issued by the company to the extent that it is accounted for as an equity instrument in accordance with generally accepted accounting practice.

3(6) An asset is matched with share capital in particular where for the accounting period of the company immediately preceding the first accounting period to which these Regulations apply–

(a)   exchange gains and losses on the asset were taken to a reserve; and

(b)   set off there against exchange gains and losses on the share capital.

3(7) In this regulation–

      "carrying value" means, in relation to a liability, the value as shown in the company's accounts of that liability; and

      "unmatched carrying value" means, in relation to an asset, an amount equal to the relevant value to the extent that that amount has not previously been matched in accordance with this regulation or regulation 4.

History – Reg. 3(1ZA) inserted by SI 2011/2912, reg. 4(1), with effect from 11.45 a.m. on 6 December 2011 in relation to shares, ships or aircraft which are matched on or after that date in accordance with reg. 3 or 4 of these Regulations.
Reg. 3(1A) inserted by SI 2005/2012, reg. 4 in relation to periods of account beginning on or after 1 January 2005 and ending after 11 August 2005.
In reg. 3(2), the words ", or profits or losses arising on the disposal," inserted by SI 2005/2012, reg. 4 in relation to periods of account beginning on or after 1 January 2005 and ending after 11 August 2005.
In reg. 3(3), in Condition 1, the words "for the accounting period,", which appeared after the words "The condition is that", omitted by SI 2011/2912, reg. 4(2), with effect from 11.45 a.m. on 6 December 2011 in relation to shares, ships or aircraft which are matched on or after that date in accordance with reg. 3 or 4 of these Regulations.
In reg. 3(3), in Condition 2, the word "or" substituted for the word "and" (which appeared after the words "by entering into") by SI 2011/698, reg. 3, with effect in relation to accounting periods beginning on or after 1 April 2011.
In reg. 3(3), the opening words (including subpara. (a) and (b)) substituted for the words "Shares, ships or aircraft are matched with a liability if any of the following conditions are satisfied." by SI 2005/2012, reg. 4 in relation to periods of account beginning on or after 1 January 2005 and ending after 11 August 2005.
In reg. 3(3), former Condition 1 omitted and former Condition 2 and 3 renumbered as Condition 1 and 2 by SI 2005/2012, reg. 4 in relation to periods of account beginning on or after 1 January 2005 and ending after 11 August 2005.
In reg. 3(3), in Condition 2 (formerly Condition 3), the word "intends" substituted for "could", the words "and continuing to be subject to" inserted and the words "reasonably expect" (which appeared before the words "to eliminate or substantially reduce") omitted by SI 2005/2012, reg. 4 in relation to periods of account beginning on or after 1 January 2005 and ending after 11 August 2005.
In reg. 3(4) the words "at the time when the liability is entered into or, if later, when the asset is acquired" omitted by SI 2007/3431, reg. 2(3)(a), with effect in relation to accounting periods beginning on or after 1 January 2008.
In reg. 3(4) the words "the relevant time" substituted for "that time" by SI 2007/3431, reg. 2(3)(b), with effect in relation to accounting periods beginning on or after 1 January 2008.
In reg. 3(4), "condition 2" substituted for "condition 3" and the words "or, if later, when the asset is acquired" inserted by SI 2005/2012, reg. 4 in relation to periods of account beginning on or after 1 January 2005 and ending after 11 August 2005.
Reg. 3(5)(a)–(c) (and the "of–" before them) substituted for the words "of any share capital of the company" by SI 2013/2781, reg. 2(3), with effect in relation to loan relationships and derivative contracts entered into on or after 21 November 2013.
In reg. 3(5)(c), the words "any Additional Tier 1 instrument" substituted by SI 2013/3209, reg. 10(3), with effect from 1 January 2014.
In reg. 3(6) the words "in particular where" substituted for the word "if" by SI 2005/3374, reg. 4, with effect from 29 December 2005 in relation to periods of account beginning on or after 1 January 2005.
In reg. 3(7) the words "relevant value" substituted for the words "value as shown in the company's accounts" by SI 2005/3374, reg. 3, with effect from 29 December 2005 in relation to periods of account beginning on or after 1 January 2005.

EXCHANGE GAINS OR LOSSES ARISING FROM DERIVATIVE CONTRACTS HEDGING SHARES ETC.

4(1) For the purposes of paragraph 16(3A) and 17C(1)(a) of Schedule 26 to the Finance Act 2002 there is prescribed an exchange gain or loss arising to a company in an accounting period in relation to a derivative contract of the company which is matched with the whole or part of any shares, ships or aircraft.

4(1A) But where the matched shares, ships or aircraft are matched after the company became party to the derivative contract, paragraph (1) only applies to a just and reasonable proportion of any exchange gain or loss having regard to—

(a)   the fraction of the accounting period for which the shares, ships or aircraft are matched with the derivative contract,

(b)   the fraction of the accounting period for which the company was party to the derivative contract, and

(c)   fluctuations in exchange rates during the period.

4(2) This regulation does not apply if movements in the fair value, or profits or losses arising on the disposal, of any shares, ships or aircraft which are an asset falling within regulation 4(1) are brought into account by the company in computing, for the purposes of corporation tax, the profits of a trade carried on by it which consists of or includes dealing in shares, ships or aircraft.

4(3) Shares, ships or aircraft are matched to the greatest possible extent with—

(a)   the derivative contract designated as a hedge if condition 1 is satisfied;

(b)   subject to paragraph (a), the derivative contract referred to in condition 2 if that condition is satisfied.

Condition 1

The condition is that the shares, ships or aircraft are a hedged item under a designated hedge of exchange rate risk in which the derivative contract is the hedging instrument.

Condition 2

The condition is that the underlying subject matter of the derivative contract is such that the company intends, by entering into or continuing to be party to that contract, to eliminate or substantially reduce the economic risk of holding the asset, or part of the asset, which is attributable to fluctuations in exchange rates.

4(4) If condition 2 applies, a derivative contract is matched with an asset only to the extent that the value of the obligation under the derivative contract does not exceed the unmatched carrying value of the asset at the relevant time.

4(4A) For the purposes of paragraph 16(3A) of Schedule 26 to the Finance Act 2002 there is prescribed an exchange gain or loss arising to a company in an accounting period in relation to a derivative contract of the company which is matched with the whole or part of—

(a)   any share capital of the company,

(b)   in relation to a building society, any deferred shares issued by the building society to the extent that they are accounted for as equity instruments in accordance with generally accepted accounting practice, or

(c)   a regulatory capital security issued by the company to the extent that it is accounted for as an equity instrument in accordance with generally accepted accounting practice.

4(4B) A derivative contract is matched with share capital in particular where for the accounting period of the company immediately preceding the first accounting period beginning on or after 1st January 2005—

(a)   exchange gains and losses on the derivative contract were taken to a reserve; and

(b)   set off there against exchange gains and losses on the share capital.

4(5) In this regulation—

"**unmatched carrying value**" means, in relation to an asset, an amount equal to the relevant value to the extent that that amount has not previously been matched in accordance with this regulation or regulation 3.

"**the value of the obligation under the derivative contract**" means the value of the obligation of the company to pay in exchange for one currency an amount of a second currency and includes any notional obligation to pay an amount of currency in respect of a contract for differences.

History – Reg. 4(1A) inserted by SI 2011/2912, reg. 5(1), with effect from 11.45 a.m. on 6 December 2011 in relation to shares, ships or aircraft which are matched on or after that date in accordance with reg. 3 or 4 of these Regulations.
In reg. 4(2), the words ", or profits or losses arising on the disposal," inserted by SI 2005/2012, reg. 5 in relation to periods of account beginning on or after 1 January 2005 and ending after 11 August 2005.
In reg. 4(3), in Condition 1, the words "for the accounting period,", which appeared after the words "The condition is that", omitted by SI 2011/2912, reg. 5(2), with effect from 11.45 a.m. on 6 December 2011 in relation to shares, ships or aircraft which are matched on or after that date in accordance with reg. 3 or 4 of these Regulations.
In reg. 4(3), in Condition 2, the word "or" substituted for the word "and" (which appeared after the words "by entering into") by SI 2011/698, reg. 4, with effect in relation to accounting periods beginning on or after 1 April 2011.
In reg. 4(3), the opening words (including subpara. (a) and (b)) substituted for the words "Shares, ships or aircraft are matched with a derivative contract if any of the following conditions are satisfied." by SI 2005/2012, reg. 5 in relation to periods of account beginning on or after 1 January 2005 and ending after 11 August 2005.
In reg. 4(3), former Condition 1 omitted and former Condition 2 and 3 renumbered as Condition 1 and 2 by SI 2005/2012, reg. 5 in relation to periods of account beginning on or after 1 January 2005 and ending after 11 August 2005.
In reg. 4(3), in Condition 2 (formerly Condition 3), the word "intends" substituted for "could", the words "and continuing to be a party to" inserted and the words "reasonably expect" (which appeared before the words "to eliminate or substantially reduce") omitted by SI 2005/2012, reg. 5 in relation to periods of account beginning on or after 1 January 2005 and ending after 11 August 2005.
In reg. 4(4), "condition 2" substituted for "condition 3", the words "value of the obligation under" substituted for "carrying value of" and the words "or, if later, when the asset is acquired" inserted by SI 2005/2012, reg. 5 in relation to periods of account beginning on or after 1 January 2005 and ending after 11 August 2005.
Reg. 4(4A)(a)–(c) (and the "of–" before them) substituted for the words "of any share capital of the company" by SI 2013/2781, reg. 2(3), with effect in relation to loan relationships and derivative contracts entered into on or after 21 November 2013.
In reg. 4(4A)(c), the words "an Additional Tier 1 instrument" substituted by 2013/3209, reg. 10(3), with effect from 1 January 2014.
Reg. 4(4A) and (4B) inserted by SI 2005/3374, reg. 5, with effect from 29 December 2005 in relation to periods of account beginning on or after 1 January 2005.
In reg. 4(5), the definition of "carrying value" omitted and the definition of "the value of the obligation under the derivative contract" inserted by SI 2005/2012, reg. 5 in relation to periods of account beginning on or after 1 January 2005 and ending after 11 August 2005.
In reg. 4(5) the words "relevant value" substituted for the words "value as shown in the company's accounts" by SI 2005/3374, reg. 3, with effect from 29 December 2005 in relation to periods of account beginning on or after 1 January 2005.
In reg. 4(4) the words "at the time when the contract is entered into or, if later, when the asset is acquired" omitted by SI 2007/3431, reg. 2(4)(a), with effect in relation to accounting periods beginning on or after 1 January 2008.
In reg. 4(4) the words "the relevant time" substituted for "that time" by SI 2007/3431, reg. 2(4)(b), with effect in relation to accounting periods beginning on or after 1 January 2008.

RELEVANT VALUE

4A(1) For the purposes of regulations 3(7) and 4(5), "relevant value" means–

(a)   in relation to shares held by the company in another company ("Company A"), where the company elects, the higher of–

     (i)   the net asset value underlying the shares in Company A, and

     (ii)   the value shown in the accounts of the company; and

(b)   in any other case, the value shown in the accounts of the company.

4A(2) In paragraph (1)(a)(i) the net asset value underlying the shares in Company A is an amount equal to–

(a)   the value of the assets, less

(b)   the value of the liabilities

of Company A and any direct or indirect subsidiary of Company A denominated in the relevant currency.

This is subject to paragraph (6).

4A(3) The value of assets and liabilities referred to in paragraph (2) is the value at the relevant time shown in–

(a)   a balance sheet of Company A, or

(b)   where Company A has a direct or indirect subsidiary, a notional consolidated balance sheet of Company A prepared in the relevant currency.

4A(4) For the purposes of paragraph (3) in determining whether an asset or liability would be recognised in the balance sheet or notional consolidated balance sheet and, if so recognised the value that would be accorded to it, regard shall be had to the accounting treatment of the asset or liability–

(a)   in any consolidated accounts prepared by the company, or

(b)   where the company does not prepare consolidated accounts, in any consolidated accounts prepared by a company that directly or indirectly controls the company.

4A(5) Nothing in paragraph (3) or (4) shall prevent an asset or liability, which might be eliminated in the preparation of any consolidated accounts, from being taken into account in paragraph (2).

4A(6) If the company does not directly hold the entire issued share capital in Company A, the net asset value underlying the shares in Company A shall be reduced by such amount as is just and reasonable having regard to–

(a)   the proportion of the issued shares held by the company, and

(b)   where there is more than one class of share, the rights attached to the shares held by the company.

4A(7) An election under paragraph (1)–

(a)   is irrevocable,

(b)   applies to all the shareholdings held by the company which are matched in accordance with regulation 3(3)(b) or 4(3)(b),

(c)   has effect from the beginning of the accounting period in which the election is made,

(d)   must be made in writing to Her Majesty's Revenue and Customs within the time limit specified in paragraph (8), and

(e)   must specify the review period.

This is subject to paragraph (8A).

4A(8) The time limit for making an election is–

(a)   in relation to shares held on and before the start of the first accounting period beginning on or after 1st January 2008, the later of–

    (i)   31st March 2008, and

    (ii)   30 days from the start of that accounting period; and

(b)   in any other case, within 30 days of shares being matched in accordance with regulation 3(3)(b) or 4(3)(b).

4A(8A) Where a company has made an election before 1st April 2011 and has specified a review period of 92 days or less, it may amend that election to increase the length of the review period specified.

4A(8B) An amendment to an election must be made by 1st June 2011 by notice in writing to Her Majesty's Revenue and Customs.

4A(6) In this regulation–

"relevant currency" means the currency which, as a result of exchange rate fluctuations, gives rise to the economic risk referred to in regulations 3(3) and 4(3);

"control" has the meaning given in section 840 of the Income and Corporation Taxes Act 1988.

History – In reg. 4A(7), the words "This is subject to paragraph (8A)." inserted by SI 2011/698, reg. 5(2), with effect in relation to accounting periods beginning on or after 1 April 2011.

Reg. 4A(8A) and (8B) inserted by SI 2011/698, reg. 5(3), with effect in relation to accounting periods beginning on or after 1 April 2011.

Reg. 4A(9) renumbered as such (it had originally been incorrectly numbered as a second para. (6) in reg. 4A) by SI 2011/698, reg. 5(4), with effect in relation to accounting periods beginning on or after 1 April 2011.

Reg. 4A, 4B and 4C substituted for former reg. 4A by SI 2007/3431, reg. 2(5), with effect in relation to accounting periods beginning on or after 1 January 2008.

In former reg. 4A(2)(c)(i) the word "an" substituted for "the first", and the words "('the new period')" inserted by SI 2007/948, reg. 3(2)(a) and (b) respectively, with effect from 11 April 2007, in relation to periods of account ending on or after 11 April 2007.

In former reg. 4A(3) the words "the new period" substituted for the words from "its" to the end by SI 2007/948, reg. 3(3), with effect from 11 April 2007, in relation to periods of account ending on or after 11 April 2007.

Former reg. 4A inserted by SI 2005/3374, reg. 6, with effect from 29 December 2005 in relation to periods of account beginning on or after 1 January 2005.

RELEVANT TIME

4B(1) For the purposes of regulations 3(4), 4(4) and 4A(3) **"relevant time"** is determined as follows.

4B(2) In a case within regulation 4A(1)(a) (relevant value determined by net asset value) the relevant time is the start of each review period in an accounting period.

4B(3) In a case within regulation 4A(1)(b) (relevant value determined by accounts value), the relevant time is the time when the liability or contract is entered into or, if later, when the asset is acquired.

History – Reg. 4A, 4B and 4C substituted for reg. 4A by SI 2007/3431, reg. 2(5), with effect in relation to accounting periods beginning on or after 1 January 2008.

REVIEW PERIOD

4C(1) For the purposes of regulations 4A(7)(e) and 4B(2), a review period is a period, or one of a series of successive periods, of a length specified by a company making an election in accordance with regulation 4A(1)(a).

This is subject to the provisions of this regulation.

4C(2)   A review period, or where more than one in an accounting period the first review period in that accounting period, begins on the first day of the accounting period or, if later, the date that a liability or derivative contract first becomes matched with shares in accordance with regulation 3(3)(b) or 4(3)(b).

4C(3)   A review period, or where more than one in an accounting period the last review period in that accounting period, must end on the last day of the accounting period.

4C(4)   If a company has matched shares in accordance with regulation 3(3)(b) or 4(3)(b) ("the first asset"), the first review period in relation to shares which are subsequently matched–

(a)   begins when the subsequent matching occurs, and

(b)   ends at the same time as the review period which is current in relation to the first asset when the subsequent matching occurs.

4C(5)   If during a review period ("the current period") there is a significant variation in the net asset value underlying shares which have been matched in accordance with regulation 3(3)(b) or 4(3)(b), there shall be a new review period in relation to those shares which–

(a)   begins on the day that any variation in the net asset value becomes a significant variation, and

(b)   ends at the same time as the current period.

4C(6)   In paragraph (5) **"significant variation"** means an increase or decrease of 10% or more in the net asset value underlying the matched shares.

4C(7)   In this regulation the net asset value underlying shares shall be determined in accordance with regulation 4A(2).

History – Reg. 4C substituted by SI 2011/698, reg. 6, with effect in relation to accounting periods beginning on or after 1 April 2011. The former reg. 4C read as follows:

"**4C(1)**   For the purposes of regulations 4A(7)(f) and 4B(2) a review period is one of a series of successive periods of a length specified by a company making an election in accordance with regulation 4A(1)(a), but not exceeding 92 days. This is subject to the provisions of this regulation.

4C(2)   The first review period in an accounting period begins on the first day of the accounting period or, if later, when any liability or derivative contract first becomes matched with an asset consisting of shares in accordance with regulation 3(3)(b) or 4(3)(b).

4C(3)   Where a company has matched an asset consisting of shares in accordance with regulation 3(3)(b) or 4(3)(b) ("the first asset"), the first review period in relation to shares which are subsequently matched–

(a)   begins when the matching occurs, and

(b)   ends at the same time as the review period which is current in relation to the first asset when the subsequent matching occurs.

4C(4)   The last review period in an accounting period must end on or before the last day of the accounting period.".
Reg. 4A, reg. 4B and the former reg. 4C substituted for reg. 4A by SI 2007/3431, reg. 2(5), with effect in relation to accounting periods beginning on or after 1 January 2008.

REGULATIONS 3 AND 4: SUPPLEMENTARY

5(1)   Where in any accounting period–

(a)   a company holds more than one asset in relation to which there are amounts of exchange gains and losses falling within regulations 3 or 4; and

(b)   the currency–

    (i)   in which the assets are denominated and the liability mentioned in regulation 3(1) expressed; or

    (ii)   which is the underlying subject matter of the derivative contract mentioned in regulation 4(1),

is the same currency, the extent to which an asset is matched is determined in accordance with the following rules.

Rule 1

Liabilities and contracts are regarded as matched to the greatest possible extent with assets which are ships or aircraft.

Rule 2

Subject to Rule 1, liabilities and contracts are regarded as matched to the greatest possible extent with assets on the disposal of which a chargeable gain would accrue if the disposal were made on a date falling more than 12 months after the date of acquisition of the asset.

Rule 3

Subject to Rules 1 and 2, liabilities and contracts are regarded as matched with assets on a disposal of which no chargeable gain would be treated as accruing by virtue of Part 1 of Schedule 7AC to the Taxation of Chargeable Gains Act 1992.

5(2)   If–

(a)   part only of a liability falling within the condition 2 in regulation 3, or

(b)   part only of a contract falling within the condition 2 in regulation 4,

could reasonably be expected to eliminate or substantially reduce the economic risk of holding the asset which is attributable to fluctuations in exchange rates, the liability or contract is to be treated as being matched with a corresponding amount of value of an asset.

5(3)   For the purposes of paragraph (1), a currency in which a liability is expressed or which is the underlying subject matter of a derivative contract, is to be treated, if it is not the case, as the same currency in which an asset is denominated if–

(a)   borrowing in that currency, or

(b)   the obligation to deliver that currency,

could reasonably be expected to eliminate or substantially reduce the economic risk of holding the asset, or part of the asset, which is attributable to fluctuations in exchange rates.

5(4)   Where regulation 3 or section 84A(3) of the Finance Act 1996 applies to a company in an accounting period in relation to a liability representing a loan relationship there is prescribed, for the purposes of regulation 3 or section 84A(3A) of that Act, an exchange gain or loss treated by virtue of paragraph 6D(2) of Schedule 28AA to the Taxes Act 1988 as arising in that accounting period to another company in relation to the same loan relationship.

History – In reg. 5:
- in reg. 5(1)(b)(i), the words "mentioned in regulation 3(1)" and in (1)(b)(ii), the words "mentioned in regulation 4(1)" inserted;
- at the end of reg. 5(1)(b), the words "the extent to which an asset is matched is determined in accordance with the following rules" omitted (apparently erroneously) and then reinserted;
- in reg. 5(1), Rule 1 substituted; and
- in reg. 5(1), the words "if the disposal were made on a date falling more than 12 months after the date of acquisition of the asset" inserted in Rule 2, whilst a similar form of words was deleted from the end of Rule 3 and the words "and contracts" inserted in Rule 3,

all by SI 2005/2012, reg. 6 in relation to periods of account beginning on or after 1 January 2005 and ending after 11 August 2005.

In reg. 5(2)(a) and (b) the words "condition 2" substituted for "third condition" by SI 2007/948, reg. 4, with effect from 11 April 2007, in relation to periods of account ending on or after 11 April 2007.

RULES ABOUT FAIR VALUE PROFITS AND LOSSES

6(1)   Regulations 7, 7A, 8 and 9 contain specific rules about excluding fair value profits and losses for the purposes of Schedule 26 to the Finance Act 2002.

6(2)   For the purposes of regulations 7, 7A, 8 and 9 it is immaterial that the hedging relationship is not an effective hedge for accounting purposes.

6(3)   Except where an election has been made under paragraph (3A) a company may elect that–

(a)   regulation 7 shall not apply to its currency contracts which satisfy the conditions contained in regulation 7(1); and

(b)   regulation 8 shall not apply to its commodity contracts or debt contracts which satisfy the conditions contained in that regulation.

6(3A)   A company may elect that regulation 9A shall apply and–

(a)   regulation 7 shall not apply, to its currency contracts which satisfy the conditions contained in regulation 7(1), and

(b)   regulation 8 shall not apply, to its commodity or debt contracts which satisfy the conditions contained in regulation 8(1).

6(4)   Any election made under paragraph (3) or (3A) shall apply to–

(a)   all of the currency contracts entered into by the company which satisfy the conditions contained in regulation 7(1); and

(b)   all of the commodity contracts or debt contracts entered into by the company which satisfy the conditions contained in regulation 8(1).

6(5)   Subject to paragraph (5A) and except where an election has been made under paragraph (5B) a company may elect that regulation 9 shall not apply to its interest rate contracts which satisfy the conditions contained in that regulation but that regulation 9A shall apply and any election under this regulation shall apply to all of the interest rate contracts entered into by the company which satisfy the conditions contained in regulation 9(1).

6(5A)   An election under paragraph (5) has no effect in relation to interest rate contracts–

(a)   where–

(i)   the contract or a portion of the contract ("the hedging instrument") is designated as a hedge in respect of any risks arising in respect of an asset, liability, receipt or expense ("the hedged item");

(ii)   fair value profits or losses arising on the hedged item or in relation to any of the risks, in relation to which the contract was intended to act as a hedge, arising in respect of the hedged item, or any portion of the hedged item, are not brought into account for the purposes of corporation tax for that period; and

(iii)   fair value profits or losses arising on the hedging instrument are not recognised in the company's statement of recognised gains and losses or statement of changes in equity;

(b)   where the hedged item is a loan relationship to which section 87(1) of the Finance Act 1996 applies, or

(c)   where the hedged item is a regulatory capital security in relation to which the company uses fair value accounting.

6(5B)   Subject to paragraph (5C), a company may elect that regulation 9 shall not apply to its interest rate contracts which satisfy the conditions contained in that regulation but that regulation 9A shall apply, and any election under this regulation shall apply to all of the interest rate contracts entered into by the company which satisfy the conditions contained in regulation 9(1).

6(5C)   An election under paragraph (5B) has no effect in relation to interest rate contracts—

(a)   where the conditions in paragraph (5A)(a) are met;

(b)   where the hedged item is an asset representing a loan relationship—

     (i)   to which section 87(1) of the Finance Act 1996 applies, and

     (ii)   in relation to which the company uses fair value accounting, or

(c)   where the hedged item is a regulatory capital security in relation to which the company uses fair value accounting.

6(6)   Subject to paragraph (6A) and (7), an election under paragraph (3) or (5) shall be made before the start of a company's first accounting period to which regulations 7 and 8, or regulation 9 applies to that company or, if later, before—

(a)   1st October 2005 in the case of an election under paragraph (3), or

(b)   31st March 2006 in the case of an election under paragraph (5),

and has effect for that accounting period and all subsequent accounting periods unless, in the case of an election under paragraph (3), revoked.

6(6A)   In any case where a company—

(a)   does not use fair value accounting in relation to its derivative contracts for an accounting period beginning on or after 1st January 2005, and

(b)   begins to use fair value accounting in a subsequent accounting period ("the subsequent period") in relation to contracts to which regulations 7 or 8, or regulation 9 apply and to which it is a party at the start of that period,

an election under paragraph (3), (3A), (5) or (5B) shall be made before the start of the subsequent period.

This paragraph does not apply to cases within paragraph (7).

6(7)   In any case where a company is not a party to any contracts to which regulations 7 or 8, or regulation 9 apply immediately before the start of the company's first accounting period to which the Regulations apply, an election under paragraph (3), (3A), (5) or (5A) shall be made within 90 days of the company entering into its first contract to which regulation 7 or 8, or regulation 9 applies, as the case may be or, if later, 31st March 2006.

6(7A)   An election under paragraph (3A) or (5B)—

(a)   must be made before the later of—

     (i)   1st April 2007, and

     (ii)   the date determined by paragraph (6A) or (7) as the date before which an election must be made;

(b)   must be made in writing to Her Majesty's Revenue and Customs;

(c)   is irrevocable; and

(d)   applies in relation to accounting periods beginning on or after 1st January 2006.

6(7B) An election–

(a)   under paragraph (3A) revokes any previous election under paragraph (3);

(b)   under paragraph (5B) revokes any previous election under paragraph (5).

6(8) A company may revoke an election under paragraph (3) with effect from the date on which notice is given of it, but contracts entered into before that date shall not be affected.

6(9) An election under paragraph (3) shall be made, and may be revoked by the company which made it, by notice in writing to Her Majesty's Revenue and Customs.

6(9A) An election under paragraph (5) shall be made in writing to Her Majesty's Revenue and Customs and is irrevocable except where revoked by an election made under paragraph (5B).

6(10) If–

(a)   a company ("the electing company") makes an election under paragraph (3), (3A), (5) or (5B) in relation to its contracts;

(b)   any other company which is a party to a derivative contract to which the election applies is a member of the same group of companies as the electing company; and

(c)   that other company has not made an election under paragraph (3), (3A), (5) or (5B) in relation to the contract, as the case may be,

then the other company is to be treated as if it had made the election but only in relation to that contract.

6(11) Paragraph (10) does not apply if the electing company, or the other company, entered into the contract in the ordinary course of a banking business or a business as a securities house.

6(12) If a contract to which regulation 7, 8 or 9 applies is transferred by a company in circumstances to which paragraph 28 of Schedule 26 to the Finance Act 2002 would apply but for paragraph 30 of that Schedule–

(a)   paragraph 30 shall not apply (and accordingly paragraph 28 shall apply) and paragraph 50A(3B) of that Schedule shall be modified in accordance with paragraph (12A); and

(b)   the transferee company is to be treated as not having made the election under paragraph (3), (3A), (5) or (5B) as the case may be ("the relevant election") in relation to that contract, if it has made a relevant election in relation to all of its contracts.

6(12A) The modification to paragraph 50A(3B) of Schedule 26 to the Finance Act is as follows–

(a)   in paragraph (a) delete "and";

(b)   after paragraph (b) insert–

       ", and

(c)   regulations 7, 8 and 9 of the Loan Relationships and Derivative Contracts (Disregard and Bringing into Account of Profits and Losses) Regulations 2004.".

6(13) If a company ("the electing company") makes an election under paragraph (3), (3A), (5) or (5B) in relation to its contracts–

(a)   a contract to which the election applies is transferred to another company ("the transferee company") in circumstances to which paragraph 28 of Schedule 26 to the Finance Act 2002 applies, or

(b)   would apply but for paragraph 30 of that Schedule,

and the transferee company has not made an election under paragraph (3), (3A), (5) or (5B) in relation to the contract as the case may be, then the transferee company is to be treated as if it had made the election but only in relation to that contract.

6(14) In this Regulation–

"**group of companies**" shall be construed in accordance with section 170 of the Taxation of Chargeable Gains Act 1992; and

"**securities house**" means a person–

(a)   who is authorised for the purposes of the Financial Services and Markets Act 2000; and

(b)   whose business consists wholly or mainly of dealing as a principal in financial instruments within the meaning of section 349(5) and (6) of the Taxes Act 1988.

History – In reg. 6(1), "7A," inserted by SI 2009/1886, reg. 4, with effect in relation to periods of account beginning on or after 1 January 2009 and have effect in relation to derivative contracts (a) entered into on or after 1 January 2009 and which formed part of a relevant hedging relationship up to and including 10 March 2009, or (b) entered into on or after 10 March 2009.
In reg. 6(2), "7A," inserted by SI 2009/1886, reg. 4, with effect in relation to periods of account beginning on or after 1 January 2009 and have effect in relation to derivative contracts (a) entered into on or after 1 January 2009 and which formed part of a relevant hedging relationship up to and including 10 March 2009, or (b) entered into on or after 10 March 2009.
In reg. 6(3) the words "Except where an election has been made under paragraph (3A)" inserted by SI 2007/948, reg. 5(2), with effect from 11 April 2007, in relation to periods of account ending on or after 11 April 2007.

In reg. 6(3A) the word "and" substituted for "to" by SI 2007/948, reg. 5(3)(a), with effect from 11 April 2007, in relation to periods of account ending on or after 11 April 2007.

In reg. 6(3A)(a) the words "regulation 7 shall not apply, to" inserted by SI 2007/948, reg. 5(3)(b), with effect from 11 April 2007, in relation to periods of account ending on or after 11 April 2007.

In reg. 6(3A)(b) the words "regulation 8 shall not apply, to" inserted by SI 2007/948, reg. 5(3)(c), with effect from 11 April 2007, in relation to periods of account ending on or after 11 April 2007.

In reg. 6(5) the words "and except where an election has been made under paragraph (5B)" inserted by SI 2007/948, reg. 5(4), with effect from 11 April 2007, in relation to periods of account ending on or after 11 April 2007.

In reg. 6(5A) and (5C), the word "or" at the end of para. (a) omitted and reg. 6(5A)(c) and 6(5C)(c) inserted by SI 2013/3209, reg. 10(4)(a), with effect from 1 January 2014.

In reg. 6(6A) the reference to "(5B)" substituted for the reference to "5A" by SI 2007/948, reg. 5(5), with effect from 11 April 2007, in relation to periods of account ending on or after 11 April 2007.

In reg. 6:
- reg. 6(3A) inserted;
- in reg. 6(4) the words "or (3A)" inserted;
- in reg. 6(5A)(ii) the words ", in relation to which the contract was intended to act as a hedge," inserted;
- reg. 6(5B) and (5C) inserted;
- in reg. 6(6A) and (7) the words "(3), (3A), (5) or (5A)" substituted for the words "(3) or (5)";
- reg. 6(7A) and (7B) inserted;
- in reg. 6(9) the word "the" omitted;
- in reg. 6(9A) the words "except where revoked by an election made under paragraph (5B)" inserted;
- in reg. 6(10)(a) and (c), 6(12)(b) and twice in 6(13) the words "(3), (3A), (5) or (5B)" substituted for the words "(3) or (5)"; and
- in reg. 6(12)(a) "(3B)" substituted for "(3A)",

all by SI 2006/3236, reg. 3, with effect from 27 December 2006 in relation to periods of account beginning on or after 1 January 2006 and ending on or after 27 December 2006.

In reg. 6:
- in reg. 6(3)(a) and (4)(a) "7(1)" substituted for "7(2)";
- in reg. 6(5) the words "Subject to paragraph (5A)" and the words "but that regulation 9A shall apply," inserted;
- reg. 6(5A) inserted;
- in reg. 6(6) the words from "before" to "revoked" substituted for "before 1st October 2005 and has effect for that accounting period and all subsequent accounting periods unless revoked.";
- in reg. 6(6A) the words "This paragraph does not apply to cases within paragraph (7)." inserted;
- in reg. 6(7) the words "or, if later, 31st March 2006" inserted;
- in reg. 6(8) and (9) the words "or (5)" deleted;
- in reg. 6(9) the words "Her Majesty's Revenue and Customs" substituted for "Inland Revenue";
- reg. 6(9A) inserted;
- in reg. 6(12)(a) the words from "and paragraph 50A(3A)" to "(12A)" inserted;
- reg. 6(12A) inserted;

all by SI 2005/3374, reg. 7, with effect from 29 December 2005 in relation to periods of account beginning on or after 1 January 2005.

In reg. 6:
- in reg. 6(6), the words "(6A) and" inserted, the words "regulations 7 and 8, or regulation 9 applies to that company" substituted for "these Regulations apply" and "1st October 2005" substituted for "31st March 2005";
- reg. 6(6A) inserted; and
- in reg. 6(7) "under" substituted for "within",

all by SI 2005/2012, reg. 7 in relation to periods of account beginning on or after 1 January 2005 and ending after 11 August 2005.

Cross references – HMRC Brief 22/07: election under reg. 6A: guidance for companies.

Notes – Revenue statement of 15 June 2005 stated that the deadline in the statement of 3 March 2005 would be extended further to 1 October 2005. This has since been achieved by the amendments referred to in the History note above. Previously, the Revenue statement of 3 March 2005 had stated that elections made before 1 July 2005 would be accepted as valid (rather than the date of 31 March 2005 in accordance with the regulations as originally drafted).

FAIR VALUE PROFITS OR LOSSES ARISING FROM DERIVATIVE CONTRACTS WHICH ARE CURRENCY CONTRACTS

7(1) For the purposes of paragraph 17C(1)(a) of Schedule 26 to the Finance Act 2002 there is prescribed in relation to a derivative contract whose underlying subject matter consists wholly of currency–

(a)   all credits and debits representing the whole or part of a company's fair value profit or loss in an accounting period if–

    (i)   there is a hedging relationship between the contract or part of the contract and a forecast transaction or a firm commitment ("the hedged item") of the company; and

    (ii)   the hedged item is not one for which fair value profits or losses are brought into account for the purposes of corporation tax;

(b)   a company's paragraph 50A credit or debit in relation to such a contract, if for the accounting period in which the paragraph 50A credit or debit falls to be brought into account sub-paragraph (a) applies to the contract; and

(c)   a company's prior period adjustment credit or debit in relation to such a contract, if for the accounting period in which the prior period adjustment credit or debit falls to be brought into account sub-paragraph (a) applies to the contract,

and the credits and debits mentioned in sub-paragraphs (a) to (c) together make up the regulation 7 fair value profits or losses.

7(2)   [Omitted by SI 2005/2012, reg. 8.]

7(3)   Where there is a hedging relationship between part of a currency contract and a hedged item, the part of the regulation 7 fair value profit or loss that is prescribed is the part which bears to the whole the proportion which the value of that part of the contract which is in the hedging relationship bears to the value of the whole of the contract.

7(4)   Paragraph 16(3) of Schedule 26 to the Finance Act 2002 does not apply to any regulation 7 fair value profit or loss.

History – In reg. 7(1)(a)(ii) the words "for which fair value profits or losses are brought into account for the purposes of corporation tax" substituted for the words "to which fair value accounting applies for that accounting period" by SI 2005/3374, reg. 8, with effect from 29 December 2005 in relation to periods of account beginning on or after 1 January 2005.
In reg. 7:
- reg. 7(1) substituted;
- reg. 7(2) omitted;
- in reg. 7(3), the reference to "regulation 7" inserted; and
- reg. 7(4) inserted,
all by SI 2005/2012, reg. 8 in relation to periods of account beginning on or after 1 January 2005 and ending after 11 August 2005.

EXCHANGE GAINS OR LOSSES ARISING FROM DERIVATIVE CONTRACTS HEDGING ANTICIPATED OR FUTURE PROCEEDS FROM CERTAIN ISSUES OF SHARES

7A(1)   For the purposes of section 598(1)(a) of the Corporation Tax Act 2009, an exchange gain or loss arising to a company is an excluded amount in an accounting period in relation to a derivative contract if–

(a)   the underlying subject matter of the contract consists wholly of currency; and

(b)   there is a relevant hedging relationship within the meaning of paragraph (2).

7A(2)   There is a relevant hedging relationship between a derivative contract (or part of a derivative contract) and the anticipated or future proceeds of an announced or proposed rights issue or open offer of shares ("relevant share issue") if, and to the extent that–

(a)   the contract (or part of the contract) is intended to hedge the economic risk to future capital raised under the relevant share issue ("the hedged item"); and

(b)   the economic risk is attributable to fluctuations in exchange rates between the currency in which the relevant share issue is denominated and the company's functional currency.

7A(3)   If there is a hedging relationship between part of a currency contract and a hedged item, the part of the fair value profit or loss that is an excluded amount is the part which bears to the whole the proportion which the value of that part of the contract which is in the hedging relationship bears to the value of the whole of the contract.

7A(4)   Paragraph (1) shall not apply to a derivative contract which is entered into with a person ("person A") to whom the company is connected unless–

(a)   a person who is connected to the company enters into a derivative contract with a person who is not connected with the company; and

(b)   that contract confers rights or imposes liabilities which are equivalent to those of A under the contract which A entered with the company.

7A(5)   Section 466 of the Corporation Tax Act 2009 (companies connected for an accounting period) applies for the purposes of paragraph (4).

7A(6)   A derivative contract to which this regulation applies may act as a hedge of the anticipated or future proceeds from a relevant share issue only to the extent that the value of the obligation under the derivative contract (within the meaning of regulation 4(5)) does not exceed the anticipated or future proceeds from the relevant share issue which, but for the derivative contract, would not be hedged.

7A(7)   Subsections (3) and (4) of section 606 of the Corporation Tax Act 2009 do not apply to any exchange gain or loss which is an excluded amount by virtue of paragraph (1).

7A(8)   In this regulation–

(a)   **"functional currency"**, in relation to a company, means the currency of the primary economic environment in which the company operates; and

(b)   **"rights issue or open offer of shares"** means an offer or invitation to existing shareholders to subscribe for or purchase further shares in proportion to (or as nearly as may be in proportion to) their current holdings.

History – Reg. 7A inserted by SI 2009/1886, reg. 5, with effect in relation to periods of account beginning on or after 1 January 2009 and have effect in relation to derivative contracts (a) entered into on or after 1 January 2009 and which formed part of a relevant hedging relationship up to and including 10 March 2009, or (b) entered into on or after 10 March 2009.

PROFITS OR LOSSES ARISING FROM DERIVATIVE CONTRACTS WHICH ARE COMMODITY CONTRACTS OR DEBT CONTRACTS

8(1) For the purposes of paragraph 17C(1)(a) of Schedule 26 to the Finance Act 2002 there is prescribed in relation to a commodity contract or debt contract–

(a) all credits and debits representing the whole or part of a company's fair value profit or loss arising in an accounting period if–

    (i) there is a hedging relationship between the contract or part of the contract and a forecast transaction or a firm commitment ("the hedged item") of the company; and

    (ii) the hedged item is not one for which fair value profits or losses are brought into account for the purposes of corporation tax;

(b) a company's paragraph 50A credit or debit, if for the accounting period in which the paragraph 50A credit or debit falls to be brought into account, sub-paragraph (a) applies to the contract; and

(c) a company's prior period adjustment credit or debit, if for the accounting period in which the prior period adjustment credit or debit falls to be brought into account, sub-paragraph (a) applies to the contract,

and the credits and debits mentioned in sub-paragraphs (a) to (c) together make up the regulation 8 fair value profits or losses.

8(2) In this regulation–

"**a commodity contract**" means a derivative contract whose underlying subject matter is commodities unless the contract is an interest rate contract within the meaning of regulation 9(4); and

"**a debt contract**" means a derivative contract whose underlying subject matter is an asset or liability representing a loan relationship unless the contract is an interest rate contract within the meaning of regulation 9(4).

8(3) Where there is a hedging relationship between part of a commodity contract or part of a debt contract as the case may be and a hedged item, the part of the regulation 8 fair value profit or loss that is prescribed is the part which bears to the whole the proportion which the value of that part of the contract which is in the hedging relationship bears to the value of the whole of the contract.

History – In reg. 8(1)(a)(ii) the words "for which fair value profits or losses are brought into account for the purposes of corporation tax" substituted for the words "to which fair value accounting applies for that accounting period" by SI 2005/3374, reg. 8, with effect from 29 December 2005 in relation to periods of account beginning on or after 1 January 2005.
Reg. 8(1) substituted and, in reg. 8(3), the reference to "regulation 8" inserted, by SI 2005/2012, reg. 9 in relation to periods of account beginning on or after 1 January 2005 and ending after 11 August 2005.

PROFITS OR LOSSES ARISING FROM DERIVATIVE CONTRACTS WHICH ARE INTEREST RATE CONTRACTS

9(1) For the purposes of paragraph 17C(1)(a) of Schedule 26 to the Finance Act 2002 there is prescribed all credits and debits representing the whole or part of the fair value profit or loss arising to a company in relation to its interest rate contracts in an accounting period if–

(a) there is a hedging relationship between the contract or a portion of the contract and any of the risks arising in respect of an asset, liability, receipt or expense ("the hedged item"); and

(b) fair value profits or losses arising on the hedged item or in relation to any of the risks, in relation to which the contract was intended to act as a hedge, arising in respect of the hedged item, or any portion of the hedged item, are not brought into account for the purposes of corporation tax for that period.

9(2) Where paragraph (1) applies, credits and debits shall be brought into account for the purposes of paragraph 17C(1)(b) of Schedule 26 to the Finance Act 2002 on the assumption that an appropriate accruals basis had been used in relation to the contract for that accounting period.

9(2A) Where an interest rate contract–

(a) becomes a contract to which paragraph (1) applies, or

(b) ceases to be a contract to which paragraph (1) applies,

the amount to be brought into account for the purposes of paragraph 17C(1)(b) of Schedule 26 to the Finance Act 2002 is such amount as is just and reasonable in the circumstances and with regard to whether as a result of the change any amounts cease to be brought into account or are brought into account more than once.

9(3) Where paragraph 16(3) of Schedule 26 to the Finance Act 2002 or regulation 4 apply to a contract to which this regulation applies nothing in this regulation is to require any exchange gains or losses in relation to that contract to be brought into account.

9(4) In this regulation–

"**an appropriate accruals basis**" in relation to a derivative contract is one where–

(a) the contract is shown in the company's accounts at cost (which may be nil), and the cost is adjusted for any cumulative amortisation of any premium or other amount falling to be recognised in arriving at the cost of the contract;

(b) the aggregate of–

(i) the amount of periodical payments under the contract, or in the case of a swap contract under which only a single payment is to be made, the value of the payment and

(ii) the credits or debits representing interest arising, on the assumption that an effective interest method is used, in respect of the asset or liability representing a loan relationship which is the hedged item,

represent the credits or debits that would be given by generally accepted accounting practice in relation to an asset or liability representing a loan relationship whose terms include those of both the hedged item and the interest rate contract;

(c) exchange gains and losses are recognised as a result of the translation of the contract at the balance-sheet date; and

(d) profits and losses which arise as a result of the contract coming to an end before its stated date of maturity are amortised and brought into account over the unexpired term of the hedged item.

"**an interest rate contract**" means–

(i) a derivative contract whose underlying subject matter is, or includes, interest rates, or

(ii) if not falling within paragraph (i), a swap contract in which payments fall to be made by reference to a rate of interest or to an index determined by reference to income or retail prices.

9(5) For the purposes of paragraph 17C(1)(a) of Schedule 26 to the Finance Act 2002, there is also prescribed for any period any credits and debits which–

(a) have for that or any previous period been brought into account in the statement of recognised gains and losses or statement of changes in equity ("equity statements"); and

(b) represent fair value profits or losses which are transferred in that period from an equity statement–

(i) to the profit and loss account or income statement, or

(ii) directly to the carrying value of an asset or liability.

9(6) Where credits and debits are prescribed by sub-paragraph (5) there is also prescribed, for the purposes of paragraph 17C(1)(a) of Schedule 26 to the Finance Act 2002, any debits and credits corresponding to the sub-paragraph (5) credits and debits which are brought into account in the profit and loss account or income statement when–

(a) the hedged item is recognised; or

(b) a forecast transaction is no longer expected to occur.

9(7) This regulation does not apply to any contract to which paragraphs 6, 7 or 8 of Schedule 26 to the Finance Act 2002 applies.

History – In reg. 9(1)(b) the words ", in relation to which the contract was intended to act as a hedge," inserted by SI 2006/3236, reg. 4, with effect from 27 December 2006 in relation to periods of account beginning on or after 1 January 2006 and ending on or after 27 December 2006.
Reg. 9(2A) inserted by SI 2005/3374, reg. 9, with effect from 29 December 2005 in relation to periods of account beginning on or after 1 January 2005.

9A(1) For the purposes of paragraph 17C(1)(a) of Schedule 26 to the Finance Act 2002 there is prescribed all credits and debits representing the whole or part of the fair value profit or loss arising to a company in relation to a currency contract, a commodity contract, a debt contract or an interest rate contract (as the case may be) in an accounting period if–

(a) the contract or a portion of the contract ("the hedging instrument") is designated as a hedge in respect of any risks arising in respect of an asset, liability, receipt or expense ("the hedged item");

(b)   fair value profits or losses arising on the hedging instrument are recognised in accordance with generally accepted accounting practice in the company's statement of recognised gains and losses or statement of changes in equity ("equity statements"); and

(c)   the company has made an election under regulation 6(3A), 6(5) or 6(5B) (as the case may be).

This is subject to paragraph (2).

9A(2)   Credits and debits which–

(a)   are brought into account in the profit and loss account or income statement (including debits and credits previously brought into account in an equity statement and transferred to the profit and loss account or income statement), or

(b)   are taken to the carrying value of an asset or liability, where the profit or loss for corporation tax purposes in relation to that asset or liability will not fall to be computed in accordance with generally accepted accounting practice

are not prescribed for the purposes of paragraph 17C(1)(a) of Schedule 26 to the Finance Act 2002. This is subject to paragraph (3).

9A(3)   In relation to credits or debits within paragraph (2)(a) or (b), there is prescribed for the purposes of paragraph 17C(1)(a) of Schedule 26 to the Finance Act 2002 any debits or credits corresponding to the paragraph (2)(a) or (b) debits or credits which are reflected in an equity statement.

9A(3A)   Where–

(a)   amounts in respect of a currency contract, a commodity contract or a debt contract are brought into account differently as a result of an election under regulation 6(3A), or

(b)   an interest rate contract ceases to be a contract to which regulation 9 applies as a result of an election under regulation 6(5B),

the amount to be brought into account for the purposes of paragraph 17C(1)(b) of Schedule 26 to the Finance Act 2002 is such amount as is just and reasonable in the circumstances and with regard to whether as a result of the change any amounts cease to be brought into account or are brought into account more than once, and that amount shall be brought into account on the first day of the first accounting period beginning on or after 1st January 2006.

9A(4)   In this regulation "an interest rate contract" has the same meaning as in regulation 9.

History – In reg. 9A:

- in reg. 9A(1) the words "a currency contract, a commodity contract, a debt contract or an interest rate contract (as the case may be)" substituted for the words "an interest rate contract";
- in reg. 9A(1)(c) the words "6(3A), 6(5) or 6(5B) (as the case may be)" substituted for the words "6(5)";
- in reg. 9A(2)(b) the words "where the profit or loss for corporation tax purposes in relation to that asset or liability will not fall to be computed in accordance with generally accepted accounting practice" inserted;
- reg. 9A(3) the words "or (b)" inserted (although not specifically stated in the amending provision this insertion has been made in both places where it could apply); and
- reg. 9A(3A) inserted,

all by SI 2006/3236, reg. 5, with effect from 27 December 2006 in relation to periods of account beginning on or after 1 January 2006 and ending on or after 27 December 2006.

Reg. 9A inserted by SI 2005/3374, reg. 10, with effect from 29 December 2005 in relation to periods of account beginning on or after 1 January 2005.

BRINGING FAIR VALUE PROFITS OR LOSSES INTO ACCOUNT ON CURRENCY AND COMMODITY CONTRACTS

10(1)   For the purposes of paragraph 17C(1)(c) of Schedule 26 to the Finance Act 2002–

(a)   there is prescribed the aggregate of the credits and debits representing any regulation 7 or 8 fair value profits or losses excluded in relation to a derivative contract of a company; and

(b)   the amount of that aggregate is brought into account for the period in which a termination event occurs.

This is subject to paragraphs (3), (5), (7) and (8).

10(2)   In paragraph (1) a "termination event" occurs–

(a)   on the company ceasing to be a party to the contract; or

(b)   if earlier, when the hedged item begins to affect the company's profit or loss.

10(3)   If the forecast transaction or firm commitment which is the hedged item mentioned in regulation 7 or regulation 8 is a forecast transaction of, or a firm commitment to a purchase of, anything the expenditure in relation to which–

(a)   falls to be taken into account in computing the profits of a trade or property business carried on by the company, or

(b)   would fall to be deducted but for any provision of the Corporation Tax Acts prohibiting the deduction of capital expenditure in respect of depreciation of an asset,

then the aggregate mentioned in paragraph (1)(a) in relation to the contract is, subject to paragraph (3A), to be brought into account in the accounting period in which the expenditure falls or would fall to be deducted.

10(3A)   Subject to paragraph (3B), if paragraph (3)(b) applies–

(a)   the amount to be brought into account in an accounting period is the product of

$$DA/E \times FVP,$$

where–

DA is the amount of depreciation recognised in the profit and loss account or income statement in relation to the hedged item in the accounting period,

E is the total expenditure on the hedged item, and

FVP is the aggregate amount of regulation 7 or 8 fair value profit;

(b)   where the hedged item is disposed of, the balance of the aggregate amount mentioned in paragraph (1)(a) which has not been brought into account under sub-paragraph (a) of this paragraph shall be brought into account in the accounting period in which the disposal takes place.

10(3B)   Where the disposal mentioned in paragraph (3A)(b) is to a company ("the transferee") which is a member of the same group of companies, in applying paragraph (3A)(a) to the transferee FVP shall be treated as meaning the fair value profits and losses of the transferor.

10(3C)   In paragraph (3B), **"group of companies"** has the meaning given in paragraph 28(6) of Schedule 26 to the Finance Act 2002.

10(4)   In paragraph (3) "property business" has the meaning given in paragraph 32(2) of Schedule 29 to the Finance Act 2002 (gains and losses of a company from intangible fixed assets).

10(5)   Where–

(a)   part of a contract to which this regulation applies terminates without the company ceasing to be a party to the contract, or

(b)   part only of the hedged item begins to be recognised in determining the company's profit and loss,

paragraph (1)(b) or paragraph (3) is to apply to a proportionate amount of the aggregate.

10(6)   In paragraph (5) **"proportionate amount"** means that proportion of the relevant aggregate amount which is–

(a)   in a case where it is part of the contract which matures, the proportion which the fair value of the part of the contract maturing bears to the fair value of the whole of the contract at that time, and

(b)   in any other case the proportion which the fair value of the hedged item which begins to be recognised bears to the fair value of the whole of the hedged item at that time.

10(7)   Where immediately on ceasing to be a party to the contract ("the old contract"), the company enters into another contract ("the new contract") which meets the conditions in regulation 7 or regulation 8 in relation to the same hedged item as was the hedged item in relation to the old contract–

(a)   paragraph (1)(b) shall not apply in relation to the old contract, and

(b)   the aggregate prescribed in paragraph (1)(a) in relation to the old contract shall be treated for the purposes of the application of this regulation to the new contract as included in the aggregate prescribed in relation to the new contract.

10(8)   Where as a result of the company ("the transferor company") ceasing to be a party to the contract ("the old contract")–

(a)   paragraph 28 of Schedule 26 to the Finance Act 2002 would apply but for paragraph 30 of that Schedule, and

(b)   the transferee company (within the meaning of paragraph 28 of that Schedule) meets the conditions in regulation 7 or regulation 8 in relation to the contract ("the new contract") and the same hedged item as was the hedged item in relation to the old contract,

paragraph (9) applies.

10(9)   Where this paragraph applies—

(a)   paragraph (1)(b) shall not apply in relation to the old contract; and

(b)   the aggregate prescribed in paragraph (1)(a) in relation to the old contract shall be treated for the purposes of the application of this regulation to the new contract as included in the aggregate prescribed in relation to the new contract.

10(10)   For the purposes of paragraph 17C(1)(a) of Schedule 26 to the Finance Act 2002, there is also prescribed for any period any credits and debits which–

(a)   have for that or any previous period been brought into account in the statement of recognised gains and losses and statement of changes in equity ("equity statements"); or

(b)   represent regulation 7 or 8 fair value profits or losses which are transferred in that period from an equity statement–

    (i)   to the profit and loss account or income statement, or

    (ii)   directly to the carrying value of an asset or liability.

10(11)   Where credits and debits are prescribed by sub-paragraph (10) there is also prescribed, for the purposes of paragraph 17C(1)(a) of Schedule 26 to the Finance Act 2002, any debits and credits corresponding to the sub-paragraph (10) credits and debits which are brought into account in the profit and loss account or income statement when–

(a)   the hedged item is recognised; or

(b)   a forecast transaction is no longer expected to occur.

History – In reg. 10:
- in reg. 10(3A) the words "Subject to paragraph (3B)," inserted;
- reg. 10(3B) and (3C) inserted;
- in reg. 10(10)(a) the word "and" substituted for the word "or",

all by SI 2005/3374, reg. 11, with effect from 29 December 2005 in relation to periods of account beginning on or after 1 January 2005.

In reg. 10:
- in reg. 10(1)(a), the reference to "regulation 7 or 8" inserted and the words "by virtue of regulation 7(1) or regulation 8(1)" (which previously appeared at the end of (1)(a)) omitted;
- in reg. 10(3), the words ", subject to paragraph (3A)," inserted;
- reg. 10(3A) inserted;
- in reg. 10(5), the words "or paragraph (3)" inserted;
- in reg. 10(6)(a), the word "proportion" substituted for the words "amount to" and, in (6)(b), the words "which begins" substituted for the words "on which exchange gains and losses begin";
- in reg. 10(8)(a), the words "would apply but for paragraph 30 of that Schedule" substituted for "applies"; and
- in reg. 10(10)(b), the references to "regulation 7 or 8" inserted,

all by SI 2005/2012, reg. 10 in relation to periods of account beginning on or after 1 January 2005 and ending after 11 August 2005.

BRINGING EXCHANGE GAINS INTO ACCOUNT ON CONTRACTS TO WHICH REGULATION 7A APPLIES

10A(1)   For the purposes of section 598(1)(c) of the Corporation Tax Act 2009 there is an amount to be brought into account which is equivalent to the amount of any exchange gain specified in paragraph (2).

10A(2)   The exchange gain specified is any exchange gain–

(a)   arising to a company in relation to a derivative contract to which regulation 7A applies or applied, and

(b)   which has been distributed to the shareholders of the company.

10A(3)   The amount to be brought into account by paragraph (1) is to be brought into account for the accounting period in which the distribution is made.

History – Reg. 10A inserted by SI 2009/1886, reg. 6, with effect in relation to periods of account beginning on or after 1 January 2009 and have effect in relation to derivative contracts (a) entered into on or after 1 January 2009 and which formed part of a relevant hedging relationship up to and including 10 March 2009, or (b) entered into on or after 10 March 2009.

PROFITS AND LOSSES ARISING FROM LOAN RELATIONSHIPS WITH EMBEDDED DERIVATIVES

11(1)   For the purposes of section 85B(3) of the Finance Act 1996 (amounts recognised in determining company's profits and loss) the amounts described in paragraph (2) are prescribed in relation to a company which is party to a creditor relationship to which–

(a)   either–

    (i)   section 92 (convertible securities etc: creditor relationships), or

    (ii)   section 93 (relationships linked to the value of chargeable assets),

    of the Finance Act 1996 applied immediately before the start of the first accounting period of the company to begin on or after 1st January 2005, and

(b)   section 94A of the Finance Act 1996 (loan relationships with embedded derivatives) applies in the first accounting period of the company to begin on or after 1st January 2005.

11(1A)   Where paragraph (1) does not apply, for the purposes of section 85B(3) of the Finance Act 1996 the amounts described in paragraph (3) are prescribed in relation to a company which is party to a creditor relationship to which—

(a)   section 92, or

(b)   section 93,

of the Finance Act 1996 applies immediately before the start of the first accounting period of the company to begin on or after 1st January 2005.

11(2)   The prescribed amounts are all credits and debits in respect of the host contract save for—

(a)   credits in relation to interest accruing in respect of the creditor relationship without regard to the amounts given by the effective interest method; and

(b)   where paragraph (1)(a)(i) applies, credits and debits in respect of exchange gains and losses.

11(3)   The prescribed amounts are all credits and debits save for—

(a)   credits in relation to interest, and

(b)   where paragraph (1A)(a) applies, credits and debits in respect of exchange gains and losses.

11(4)   Where there is a change of accounting policy in drawing up a company's accounts from one period of account to the next affecting the amounts to be brought into account for accounting purposes in respect of the company's loan relationships, the amounts prescribed in paragraphs (1) to (3) that would otherwise be brought into account for the purposes of Chapter 2 of the Finance Act 1996 shall not be brought into account.

History – Reg. 11(1) and (1A) substituted for former reg. 11(1) by SI 2006/3236, reg. 6(2), with effect from 27 December 2006 in relation to periods of account beginning on or after 1 January 2006 and ending on or after 27 December 2006.
In reg. 11(2)(b) the words "where paragraph (1)(a)(i) applies," inserted by SI 2006/3236, reg. 6(3), with effect from 27 December 2006 in relation to periods of account beginning on or after 1 January 2006 and ending on or after 27 December 2006.
In reg. 11(3)(b) the words "where paragraph (1A)(a) applies," inserted by SI 2006/3236, reg. 6(4), with effect from 27 December 2006 in relation to periods of account beginning on or after 1 January 2006 and ending on or after 27 December 2006.
Reg. 11(4) inserted by SI 2005/3374, reg. 12, with effect from 29 December 2005 in relation to periods of account beginning on or after 1 January 2005.
Reg. 11 inserted by SI 2005/2012, reg. 11 in relation to periods of account beginning on or after 1 January 2005 and ending after 11 August 2005.

12(1)   For the purposes of section 85B(3) of the Finance Act 1996 the amounts described in paragraph (2) are prescribed in relation to a company which is party to a debtor relationship to which—

(a)   either—

    (i)   section 92A (convertible securities etc: debtor relationships), or

    (ii)   section 93,

of the Finance Act 1996 applies immediately before the start of the first accounting period of the company to begin on or after 1st January 2005, and

(b)   section 94A of the Finance Act 1996 applies in the first accounting period of the company to begin on or after 1st January 2005.

This is subject to paragraph (4).

12(1A)   Where paragraph (1) does not apply, for the purposes of section 85B(3) of the Finance Act 1996 the amounts described in paragraph (2A) are prescribed in relation to a company which is party to a debtor relationship to which—

(a)   section 92A, or

(b)   section 93,

of the Finance Act 1996 applies immediately before the start of the first accounting period of the company to begin on or after 1st January 2005.

This is subject to paragraph (4).

12(2)   The prescribed amounts are—

(a)   where paragraph (1)(a)(i) applies, all debits and credits in respect of the host contract save for—

    (i)   debits in relation to interest accruing in respect of the debtor relationship,

    (ii)   credits and debits in respect of discounts, premiums, fees and other incidental costs to the extent that these amounts are not within section 92A(3) of the Finance Act 1996(c), and

    (iii)   debits and credits in respect of exchange gains and losses;

    without regard to the amounts given by the effective interest method, and

(b)   where paragraph (1)(a)(ii) applies, all debits and credits in respect of the host contract save for debits in relation to interest accruing in respect of the debtor relationship without regard to the amounts given by the effective interest method.

12(2A)   The prescribed amounts are—

(a)   where paragraph (1A)(a) applies, debits to the extent that they are within section 92A(3) of the Finance Act 1996;

(b)   where paragraph (1A)(b) applies, all debits and credits in respect of the host contract save for debits in relation to interest.

12(3)   Where there is a change of accounting policy in drawing up a company's accounts from one period of account to the next affecting the amounts to be brought into account for accounting purposes in respect of the company's loan relationships, the amounts prescribed in paragraphs (1) and (2) that would otherwise be brought into account for the purposes of Chapter 2 of the Finance Act 1996 shall not be brought into account.

12(4)   This regulation does not apply to a company which is a party to a debtor relationship in a case where—

(a)   the company is carrying on a banking business or a business consisting wholly or partly in dealing in securities, and

(b)   it entered into the debtor relationship in the ordinary course of that business.

History – In reg. 12(2)(a) the words from "all debits and credits" to the end of para. (a) substituted by SI 2007/948, reg. 6, with effect from 11 April 2007, in relation to periods of account ending on or after 11 April 2007, except where a company ceased to be party to a debtor relationship to which reg. 12(1)(a)(i) below applies before 11 April 2007 in which case regulation 6 shall not apply in respect of that relationship.
Reg. 12(1), (1A), (2) and (2A) substituted for former reg. 12(1) and (2) by SI 2006/3236, reg. 7, with effect from 27 December 2006 in relation to periods of account beginning on or after 1 January 2006 and ending on or after 27 December 2006.
In reg. 12:
- in reg. 12(1) the words "This is subject to paragraph (4)." inserted;
- reg. 12(2)(a) the words from "and credits" to "Finance Act 1996" inserted;
- reg. 12(3) and (4) inserted,
all by SI 2005/3374, reg. 13, with effect from 29 December 2005 in relation to periods of account beginning on or after 1 January 2005.
Reg. 12 inserted by SI 2005/2012, reg. 11 in relation to periods of account beginning on or after 1 January 2005 and ending after 11 August 2005.

TRANSITIONAL PROVISION: EXCHANGE LOSSES ARISING FROM CONTRACTS TO WHICH REGULATION 7A APPLIES

13(1)   This regulation applies to a derivative contract to which regulation 7A applies—

(a)   which was entered into on or after 1st January 2009;

(b)   which formed part of a relevant hedging relationship (within the meaning of regulation 7A) up to and including 10th March 2009; and

(c)   in respect of which an exchange loss would have arisen to the company had an accounting period ended on 9th March 2009.

13(2)   For the purposes of section 598(1)(c) of the Corporation Tax Act 2009 the amount to be brought into account is the lower of—

(a)   the exchange loss arising to the company which is incurred on the termination of the derivative contract; or

(b)   the exchange loss which would have arisen to the company in relation to the derivative contract had an accounting period ended on 9th March 2009.

13(3)   Paragraph (4) applies if there is more than one derivative contract to which regulation 7A applies in relation to the same hedged item.

13(4)   The total amount of the exchange loss in relation to those contracts which is to be brought into account under this regulation shall not exceed the aggregate net exchange losses (if any) which—

(a)   arose to the company on the termination of those contracts, or

(b)   would have arisen to the company in relation to those contracts had an accounting period ended on 9 March 2009.

13(5)   Where paragraph (4) applies, the amount of loss to be brought into account is to be apportioned between each of the contracts on a just and reasonable basis.

13(6)   For the purposes of this regulation, the termination of a derivative contract shall be regarded as having occurred on the earlier of—

(a)   the day on which the contract is terminated, or

(b)   the last day of the first accounting period which ends on or after 10th March 2009.

13(7)   The amount to be brought into account for the purposes of section 598(1)(c) of the Corporation Tax Act 2009 is nil in a case where–

(a)   no exchange loss arises to the company on the termination of the derivative contract;

(b)   there is more than one derivative contract to which regulation 7A applies in relation to the same hedged item and no aggregate net exchange loss arises to the companion the termination of those contracts; or

(c)   there is more than one derivative contract to which regulation 7A applies in relation to the same hedged item and no aggregate net exchange loss would have arisen to the company in relation to those contracts had an accounting period ended on 9th March 2009.

History – Reg. 13 inserted by SI 2009/1886, reg. 7, with effect in relation to periods of account beginning on or after 1 January 2009 and have effect in relation to derivative contracts (a) entered into on or after 1 January 2009 and which formed part of a relevant hedging relationship up to and including 10 March 2009, or (b) entered into on or after 10 March 2009.

LOAN RELATIONSHIPS AND DERIVATIVE CONTRACTS (CHANGE OF ACCOUNTING PRACTICE) REGULATIONS 2004

(SI 2004/3271, as amended by SI 2004/3347, SI 2005/3383, SI 2006/3238, SI 2007/950, SI 2007/3432 and SI 2008/3237)

Made on 9 December 2004 by the Treasury, in exercise of the powers conferred upon them by s. 85B(3) and (5) and 90A of, and para. 19B of Sch. 9 to, the Finance Act 1996 and para. 17C of Sch. 26 to, the Finance Act 2002. Operative from 1 January 2005.

CITATION, COMMENCEMENT AND EFFECT

1(1) These Regulations may be cited as the Loan Relationships and Derivative Contracts (Change of Accounting Practice) Regulations 2004 and shall come into force on 1st January 2005.

1(2) These Regulations have effect in relation to periods of account beginning on or after 1st January 2005.

INTERPRETATION

2　In these Regulations–

"**amortised cost basis of accounting**" has the meaning given by section 103(1) of the Finance Act 1996;

"**earlier period**" and "**later period**" have the meanings given in paragraph 19A of Schedule 9 to the Finance Act 1996;

"**exchange gains and losses**"–

(a)　in relation to a loan relationship shall be construed in accordance with sections 103(1A) and 103(1B) of the Finance Act 1996; and

(b)　in relation to a derivative contract shall be construed in accordance with paragraphs 54(2) and (3) of Schedule 26 to the Finance Act 2002;

"**fair value accounting**" has the meaning given by section 103(1) of the Finance Act 1996;

"**impairment**" and "**impairment loss**" have the meanings given by section 103(1) of the Finance Act 1996.

"**qualifying transfer**" means–

(a)　a transaction to which section 343(1) of the Income and Corporation Taxes Act 1988 (company reconstruction without a change of ownership) applies,

(b)　a transaction to which that section would apply if for "trade" there were substituted "investment business or property business", or

(c)　a transfer of a business which consists of the effecting or carrying out of contracts of long-term insurance from one person to another person ("the transferee");

"**successor**" has the meaning given by section 343(1) of the Income and Corporation Taxes Act 1988;

"**transferee**" shall be construed in accordance with paragraph (c) of "qualifying transfer"

History – In reg. 2 the definition of "earlier period" and "later period" inserted by SI 2005/3383, reg. 3 with effect from 29 December 2005, in relation to periods of account beginning on or after 1 January 2005.
In reg. 2, the definition of "exchange gains and losses" inserted by SI 2008/3237, reg. 3, with effect from 7 January 2009.
In reg. 2 the definitions of "qualifying transfer", "successor" and "transferee" inserted by SI 2007/3432, reg. 3, with effect from 27 December 2007, in relation to accounting periods beginning on or after 1 January 2008.

PRESCRIBED DEBITS AND CREDITS TO BE BROUGHT INTO ACCOUNT: GENERAL

History – The heading to reg. 3 substituted by SI 2006/3238, reg. 3, with effect from 27 December 2006.

3　Subject to regulation 3C, the debits and credits prescribed in regulation 4 shall be brought into account in accordance with regulations 3A and 3B in an accounting period of the company beginning on or after 1st January 2006.

History – Reg. 3 substituted by SI 2006/3238, reg. 3, with effect from 27 December 2006.

PRESCRIBED DEBITS AND CREDITS BROUGHT INTO ACCOUNT OVER PRESCRIBED PERIOD

3A(1) Subject to regulation 3B, debits and credits prescribed in regulation 4 ("the applicable amounts") shall be brought into account in accordance with this regulation.

3A(2) Subject to paragraphs (7A) and (7B), one tenth of the applicable amounts shall be brought into account for each year in the period of ten years ("the prescribed period") beginning with the later of–

(a)   the first accounting period of the company beginning on or after 1st January 2006, and

(b)   the later period.

3A(3) If amounts representing fractions of the applicable amounts fall to be brought into account under paragraph (2), those amounts shall be–

(a)   apportioned between the accounting periods beginning or ending in that year, and

(b)   brought into account in the periods to which they are allocated in accordance with that apportionment.

3A(4) An apportionment between accounting periods of amounts to be brought into account under paragraph (2) for any year shall be made according to how much of the year is included in each period, and, if that year and the accounting period are the same, the apportionment shall be effected by the allocation of the whole of the amounts to that accounting period.

3A(5) Subject to paragraphs (7A) and (7B), if a company ceases to be within the charge to corporation tax before the end of the prescribed period, the whole of the applicable amounts, so far as they have not fallen to be brought into account for an earlier accounting period, shall be brought into account as a credit or debit for the accounting period ending when the company ceases to be within that charge.

This paragraph does not apply if paragraph (6) applies.

3A(6) In a case where there is a qualifying transfer–

(a)   these Regulations apply to the successor or transferee for the remainder of the prescribed period for the purpose of bringing into account the applicable amounts, so far as they have not fallen to be brought into account for an earlier accounting period, and

(b)   if–

      (i)   there are two or more successors or transferees, or

      (ii)   the transfer is of part only of the business,

    those applicable amounts shall be apportioned between the parties in a manner that is just and reasonable in the circumstances.

3A(7) Paragraph (6) does not apply where the successor or transferee is resident outside the United Kingdom unless the business to which the qualifying transfer relates is carried on by the successor or transferee through a permanent establishment in the United Kingdom.

3A(7A) To the extent that the applicable amounts (or fractions of applicable amounts) represent debits or credits to which sub-paragraph (ca) or (da) of regulation 3C(2) would apply if those sub-paragraphs had been in force at the time that the debits or credits arose–

(a)   those amounts shall not be brought into account under paragraph (2) or (5) in relation to any accounting period beginning on or after 1st January 2009;

(b)   the relevant fraction of those amounts shall not be brought into account under paragraph (2) or (5) in relation to any accounting period beginning on or after 1st January 2008 and ending after 31st December 2008.

3A(7B) In paragraph (7A)(b) the relevant fraction is–

$$1 - \frac{A}{B}$$

where–

    A is the number of days in the accounting period up to, and including, 31st December 2008, and

    B is the total number of days in the accounting period.

3A(8) [Omitted by SI 2007/3432, reg. 4]

History – In reg. 3A(2), the words "Subject to paragraphs (7A) and (7B)," inserted by SI 2008/3237, reg. 4(2), with effect in relation to periods of account beginning on or after 1 January 2008 and ending after 31 December 2008.
In reg. 3A(5), the words "Subject to paragraphs (7A) and (7B)," inserted by SI 2008/3237, reg. 4(3), with effect in relation to periods of account beginning on or after 1 January 2008 and ending after 31 December 2008.

Reg. 3A(7A) inserted by SI 2008/3237, reg. 4(4), with effect in relation to periods of account beginning on or after 1 January 2008 and ending after 31 December 2008.

Reg. 3A(7B) inserted by SI 2008/3237, reg. 4(4), with effect in relation to periods of account beginning on or after 1 January 2008 and ending after 31 December 2008.

Reg. 3A(8) omitted by SI 2007/3432, reg. 4, with effect from 27 December 2007, in relation to accounting periods beginning on or after 1 January 2008.

Reg. 3A inserted by SI 2005/3383, reg. 5 with effect from 29 December 2005, in relation to periods of account beginning on or after 1 January 2005.

Cross references – SI 2007/3338: Securitisation Companies (Application of Section 83(1) of the Finance Act 2005: Accounting Standards) Regulations 2007, containing application and modifications.

SI 2009/2971, reg. 8: building societies: transfer of loan relationship or derivative contract: treatment of "relevant transfer" as a qualifying transfer for the purposes of reg. 3A(6).

PRESCRIBED DEBITS AND CREDITS IN RELATION TO DORMANT ACCOUNTS

3B(1) The debits and credits prescribed in regulation 4(1)(or (b) which are specified in paragraph (2) ("the specified amounts") shall be brought into account in accounting periods of the company beginning on or after 1st January 2008 in accordance with this regulation, but only to the extent that they represent the reversal of amounts that have been brought into account for corporation tax in accounting periods before the later period.

3B(2) The specified debits and credits are those which represent an adjustment in the value for accounting purposes of a liability owed by a bank or building society to a depositor which at the end of the earlier period had no carrying value.

3B(3) One tenth of the specified amounts shall be allocated to each year in the prescribed period.

3B(4) If amounts representing fractions of the specified amounts fall under paragraph (3) to be allocated to a year these amounts shall be–

(a) apportioned between the accounting periods beginning or ending in that year, and

(b) brought into account in the periods to which they are so apportioned, subject to paragraph (6).

3B(5) An apportionment between accounting periods of amounts allocated under paragraph (3) to any year shall be made according to how much of the year is included in each period, and, if that year and the accounting period are the same, the apportionment shall be effected by the allocation of the whole of the amounts to that accounting period.

3B(6) Where the prescribed period began before 1st January 2008, the debits and credits specified in paragraph (2) that would have been brought into account in accounting periods beginning before that date if regulation 3A had applied to those debits and credits from the beginning of the prescribed period shall be brought into account in the first accounting period beginning on or after that date.

3B(7) If a company ceases to be within the charge to corporation tax before the end of the prescribed period, the whole of the specified amounts, so far as they have not fallen to be brought into account for an earlier accounting period, shall be brought into account as a credit or debit for the accounting period ending when the company ceases to be within that charge.

This paragraph does not apply if paragraph (8) applies.

3B(8) In a case where there is a qualifying transfer–

(a) these Regulations apply to the successor or transferee for the remainder of the prescribed period for the purpose of bringing into account the specified amounts, so far as they have not fallen to be brought into account for an earlier accounting period, and

(b) if–

(i) there are two or more successors or transferees, or

(ii) the transfer is of part only of the business,

those specified amounts shall be apportioned between the parties in a manner that is just and reasonable in the circumstances.

3B(9) Paragraph 8 does not apply where the successor or transferee is resident outside the United Kingdom unless the business to which the qualifying transfer relates is carried on by the successor or transferee through a permanent establishment in the United Kingdom.

3B(10) In this regulation–

"**bank**" has the meaning given by section 840A of the Income and Corporation Taxes Act 1988(6);

"**building society**" has the meaning given by section 832(1) of that Act;

"**carrying value**" has the meaning given by paragraph 19A(4A) of Schedule 9 to the Finance Act 1996;

"**prescribed period**" has the meaning given by regulation 3A(2).

History – Reg. 3B substituted by SI 2007/3432, reg. 5, with effect from 27 December 2007, in relation to accounting periods beginning on or after 1 January 2008.
Previously in reg. 3B(1) the word "2008" substituted for the word "2007" by SI 2006/3238, reg. 4, with effect from 27 December 2006.
Reg. 3B inserted by SI 2005/3383, reg. 5 with effect from 29 December 2005, in relation to periods of account beginning on or after 1 January 2005.

PRESCRIBED DEBITS AND CREDITS NOT BROUGHT INTO ACCOUNT

3C(1)   The debits and credits prescribed in regulation 4(1) which are specified in paragraph (2) shall not be brought into account in determining a company's profit or loss for any period.

3C(2)   The specified debits and credits are–

(a)   debits and credits in relation to a derivative contract to which a company is treated as a party by section 94A(2)(b) of the Finance Act 1996 where section 92A of that Act (convertible securities etc: debtor relationships) applied to the debtor relationship in relation to that contract at the end of the company's period of account immediately preceding the first period of account to begin on or after 1st January 2005;

(aa)   debits and credits in relation to a derivative contract to which a company is treated as party by section 94A(2)(b) of the Finance Act 1996 where section 93 of that Act (relationships linked to the value of chargeable assets) applied to the debtor relationship in relation to that contract at the end of the company's period of account immediately preceding the first period of account to begin on or after 1st January 2005;

(b)   debits and credits in relation to a derivative contract to which paragraph 45L of Schedule 26 to the Finance Act 2002 (derivatives not embedded in a loan relationship) applies;

(c)   debits and credits in relation to a derivative contract which is an interest rate contract to which regulation 9 of the Disregard Regulations applies;

(ca)   debits and credits in relation to a derivative contract the underlying subject matter of which consists wholly or partly of a currency, to the extent that–

   (i)   those debits and credits represent the reversal of exchange gains and losses arising to the company in an accounting period before the later period, and

   (ii)   those exchange gains and losses have not been brought into account for the purposes of corporation tax by virtue of paragraph 16(3) of Schedule 26 to Finance Act 2002, regulations 4 to 11 of the Exchange Gains and Losses (Alternative Method of Calculation of Gain or Loss) Regulations 1994 or regulation 4 of the Disregard Regulations;

(d)   debits and credits in relation to a loan relationship specified in paragraph (3) representing the difference between the value of the loan relationship recognised for accounting purposes at the end of the earlier period and the value recognised at the beginning of the later period, where in accordance with generally accepted accounting practice–

   (i)   in the earlier period the loan relationship was brought into account at a contract rate, and

   (ii)   in the later period the loan relationship is brought into account at a spot rate of exchange, to the extent that the debit or credit is attributable to the different rates of exchange;

(da)   debits and credits in relation to a loan relationship which is denominated in a currency which is not, or was not, the company's functional currency, to the extent that–

   (i)   those debits and credits represent the reversal of exchange gains and losses arising to the company in an accounting period before the later period, and

   (ii)   those exchange gains and losses have not been brought into account for the purposes of corporation tax by virtue of section 84A(3) of the Finance Act 1996, regulations 4 to 11 of the Exchange Gains and Losses (Alternative Method of Calculation of Gain or Loss) Regulations 1994 or regulation 3 of the Disregard Regulations;

(e)   debits and credits in relation to an interest rate currency, commodity or debt contract which is designated as a cash flow hedge of a particular risk in respect of which an election has been made under regulation 6(3A), (5) or (5B) of the Disregard Regulations, to the extent that–

   (i)   they offset, or are expected to offset, variability in cash flows attributable to the risk being hedged, and

   (ii)   regulation 9A(2)(a) of the Disregard Regulations applies or will apply to them; and

(f)   debits and credits in relation to a loan relationship to which a company is treated as party by section 94A(2)(a) of the Finance Act 1996 where section 92A(4) of that Act (convertible securities etc: debtor relationships) applied to the debtor relationship in relation to that relationship at the end of the company's period of account immediately preceding the first period of account to begin on or after 1st January 2005.

3C(3)   A loan relationship is specified if–

(a)   it is denominated in a currency which is not the company's functional currency;

(b)   a hedging relationship exists between the loan relationship and a derivative contract, and

(c)   as a result of that hedging relationship, the derivative contract is within regulation 9 of the Disregard Regulations.

3C(4)   In this regulation–

"contract rate" means the rate of exchange implied by the derivative contract in paragraph 3(b);

"designated", **"cash flow hedge"** and **"income statement"** have the same meaning as for accounting purposes;

"the Disregard Regulations" means the Loan Relationships and Derivative Contracts (Disregard and Bringing into Account of Profits and Losses) Regulations 2004;

"functional currency" has the meaning given in section 92E(3) of the Finance Act 1993;

"hedging relationship" has the meaning given in regulation 2(5) of the Disregard Regulations.

"underlying subject matter" has the meaning given in paragraph 11 of Schedule 26 to the Finance Act 2002.

History – Reg. 3C(2)(ca) inserted by SI 2008/3237, reg. 5(2)(a), with effect in relation to periods of account beginning on or after 1 January 2009.
Reg. 3C(2)(da) inserted by SI 2008/3237, reg. 5(2)(b), with effect in relation to periods of account beginning on or after 1 January 2009.
In reg. 3C(2)(e) the words "currency, commodity or debt" inserted, "a particular risk" substituted for "an interest rate risk", and "6(3A), (5) or (5B)" substituted for "6(5)" by SI 2007/950, reg. 3(2)(a), with effect from 11 April 2007.
Reg. 3C(2)(e)(i) substituted by SI 2007/950, reg. 3(2)(a)(iv), with effect from 11 April 2007.
Reg. 3C(2)(f) the words "convertible securities etc: debtor relationships" substituted for "loan relationships with embedded derivatives" by SI 2007/950, reg. 3(2)(b), with effect from 11 April 2007.
Reg. 3C(2)(aa) inserted, in reg. 3C(2)(D) the word "and" at end omitted, in reg. 3C(2)(e) the word "and" at the end inserted and reg. 3C(2)(f) inserted by SI 2006/3238, reg. 5, with effect from 27 December 2006.
In reg. 3C(4), the definition of "underlying subject matter" inserted by SI 2008/3237, reg. 5(4), with effect in relation to periods of account beginning on or after 1 January 2009.
Reg. 3C inserted by SI 2005/3383, reg. 5 with effect from 29 December 2005, in relation to periods of account beginning on or after 1 January 2005.

PRESCRIBED DEBITS AND CREDITS

4(1)   Subject to paragraphs (1A) and (2), the debits and credits prescribed for the purpose of regulation 3 are any debits or credits in any accounting period of a company beginning on or after 1st January 2005 which must be brought into account in accordance with–

(a)   section 85B(1)(b) of the Finance Act 1996 (amounts recognised in determining company's profit or loss)where the debit or credit represents a prior period adjustment;

(b)   paragraph 19A(3) of Schedule 9 to the Finance Act 1996 (adjustment on change of accounting policy);

(c)   paragraph 17B(1)(b) of Schedule 26 to the Finance Act 2002 (amounts recognised in determining company's profit or loss) where the debit or credit represents a prior period adjustment;

(d)   paragraph 50A(2) of Schedule 26 to the Finance Act 2002 (adjustment on change of accounting policy).

4(1A)   In relation to a liability representing a loan relationship to which a company is treated as a party by section 94A(2)(a) of the Finance Act 1996 to which, immediately before the start of the first accounting period of the company beginning on or after 1st January 2005–

(a)   section 92A of that Act applied, but

(b)   section 92A(4) of that Act did not apply,

in determining whether credits must be brought into account in accordance with section 85B(1)(b) of, or paragraph 19A(3) of Schedule 9 to, that Act regulation 12(3) of the Disregard Regulations shall be treated as not applying to the extent that the amount otherwise falling to be brought into account does not exceed the relevant amount specified in paragraph (1B).

4(1B)   The relevant amount is an amount equal to A less B, where–

A is the amount of all debits and credits in an accounting period ending on or after 27th December 2006 and before 11th April 2007 ("the relevant period") in respect of the loan relationship save for–

(a)   debits in relation to interest accruing in respect of the debtor relationship,

(b)   credits and debits in respect of discounts, premiums, fees and other incidental costs to the extent that these amounts are not within [section] 92A(3) of the Finance Act 1996, and

(c)   debits and credits in respect of exchange gains and losses,

without regard to the amounts given by the effective interest method; and

B is the amount of debits in the relevant period in respect of the loan relationship to the extent that they are within section 92A(3) of the Finance Act 1996.

4(2)   The debits and credits falling within paragraph (3) and (4) are not prescribed.

4(3)   The debits or credits falling within this paragraph are debits or credits in relation to an asset or liability representing a loan relationship of a company (referred to in this regulation respectively as "a relevant asset" and "a relevant liability") where the latest date on which the asset or liability falls to be fully discharged is within the same accounting period as that in which the debits or credits falling within this paragraph arise.

4(4)   The debits and credits falling within this paragraph are debits and credits in relation to a derivative contract to which a company is a party where—

(a)   the company is treated as party to the contract by section 94A(2)(b) of the Finance Act 1996 and the corresponding loan relationship to which the company is treated as a party by paragraph (b) of that section is one to which paragraph (3) applies; or

(b)   the Disregard Regulations do not apply to that contract and there is a hedging relationship between the derivative contract and a hedged item which is a relevant asset or relevant liability.

4(5)   In this regulation "the Disregard Regulations" means the Loan Relationships and Derivative Contracts (Disregard and Bringing into Account of Profits and Losses) Regulations 2004 and expressions which are defined for the purposes of those Regulations have the same meanings in that paragraph (4) as they have in those Regulations.

4(6)   [Omitted by SI 2005/3383, reg. 6.]

4(7)   [Omitted by SI 2005/3383, reg. 6.]

History – In reg. 4(1) the words "paragraphs (1A) and" substituted for "paragraph", by SI 2007/950, reg. 4(2), with effect from 11 April 2007.

Reg. 4(1A) and (1B) inserted by SI 2007/950, reg. 4(3), with effect from 11 April 2007.

In reg. 4(3) the words "the asset or liability falls to be fully discharged is within the same accounting period as that in which the debits or credits falling within this paragraph arise." substituted for the words "it falls to be fully discharged is within an accounting period of the company which begins on or after 1st January 2005 and before 1st January 2006." by SI 2006/3238, reg. 6, with effect from 27 December 2006.

In reg. 4:

- in reg. 4(1) the word "any" substituted for the words "the first";
- in reg. 4(2) the words "paragraph (3) and (4)" substituted for the words "any of paragraphs (3), (4), (6) and (7)";
- in reg. 4(3) the word "ends" preceding "before 1st January 2006" omitted and the last sentence which read "This paragraph is subject to paragraphs (6) and (7)" omitted;
- reg. 4(4) substituted;
- reg. 4(6) and (7) omitted;

by SI 2005/3383, reg. 6 with effect from 29 December 2005, in relation to periods of account beginning on or after 1 January 2005.

In reg. 4(5) the words "this regulation" substituted for "paragraph (4)" by SI 2007/950, reg. 4(4), with effect from 11 April 2007.

In reg. 4(7) the words "a liability representing" substituted for the words "an asset representing", the words "the credit falling" substituted for the words "the debit falling" and the words "interest payable" substituted for the words "interest receivable" by SI 2004/3347, reg. 2(2), with effect from 1 January 2005.

Cross references – SI 2007/3338: Securitisation Companies (Application of Section 83(1) of the Finance Act 2005: Accounting Standards) Regulations 2007, containing application and modifications.

AMOUNTS RECOGNISED IN DETERMINING A COMPANY'S PROFIT OR LOSS IN RELATION TO HELD-TOMATURITY ASSETS

5(1)   Subject to paragraph (6), if the assets representing a loan relationship of a company satisfy the conditions prescribed in paragraph (5) and in accordance with generally accepted accounting practice those assets—

(a)   were previously dealt with for accounting purposes on an amortised cost basis of accounting and

(b)   are subsequently required to be dealt with for accounting purposes on the basis of fair value accounting,

the debits and credits to be brought into account for the purposes of Chapter 2 of Part 4 of the Finance Act 1996 shall continue to be determined on an amortised cost basis of accounting.

5(2)   Subject to paragraph (6), the amounts described in paragraphs (3) and (4) are excluded from section 85B(1) of the Finance Act 1996 in the circumstances specified in those paragraphs.

5(3) If the assets representing a loan relationship of a company satisfy the conditions prescribed in paragraph (5), the amount is any debit or credit representing the difference between the carrying value of the asset recognised for accounting purposes at the time the company ceased to treat the asset as held-to-maturity and the fair value of the asset immediately after that time.

5(4) If the assets representing a loan relationship of a company cease to satisfy the conditions prescribed in paragraph (5), the amount is any debit or credit representing profits or losses–

(a)   brought into account in the statement of realised gains or losses or statement of changes in equity for the periods in which the asset was treated as available-for-sale,

(b)   which are transferred from the statement of realised gains or losses or statement of changes in equity for the period in which the company ceased to satisfy the conditions in paragraph (5), and

(c)   which are brought into account in the company's profit and loss account or income statement for the period in which the company ceased to satisfy the conditions in paragraph (5) and any subsequent accounting period.

5(5) The conditions prescribed in relation to an asset are that–

(a)   in accordance with generally accepted accounting practice, it is treated at any time as available-for-sale,

(b)   in accordance with generally accepted accounting practice, it has at any previous time been treated as held-to-maturity,

(c)   it becomes treated as available-for-sale as a result of the disposal by the company of one or more assets previously treated as held-to-maturity, and

(d)   the amortised cost of the asset or assets disposed of (referred to in paragraph (c)) in the accounting period in which the disposal was made is less than 10% of the amortised cost of all the assets then treated by the company as held-to-maturity in that period.

5(6) A company may elect that this regulation does not apply.

5(7) An election under paragraph (6) applies to all of the company's assets which satisfy the conditions in paragraph (5).

5(8) An election under paragraph (6)–

(a)   shall be made by notice in writing to the Inland Revenue,

(b)   within 90 days of the end of the company's accounting period in which the disposal mentioned in paragraph (5)(c) took place.

has effect for the succeeding accounting period and all subsequent accounting periods until the assets representing a loan relationship of the company cease to satisfy the conditions prescribed in paragraph (5).

History – In reg. 5(5)(d) the word "less" substituted for the word "greater" by SI 2005/3383, reg. 7 with effect from 29 December 2005, in relation to periods of account beginning on or after 1 January 2005.

CHILD TRUST FUNDS (NON-TAX APPEALS) REGULATIONS 2005

(SI 2005/191, as amended by SI 2008/2683 and SI 2009/56)

Made on 3 February 2005 by the Treasury, in exercise of the powers conferred upon them by s. 23(1), 24(5) and 28(1) to (4) of the Child Trust Funds Act 2004. Operative from 25 February 2005.

CITATION, COMMENCEMENT AND DURATION

1(1)   These Regulations may be cited as the Child Trust Funds (Non-tax Appeals) Regulations 2005 and shall come into force on 25 February 2005.

1(2)   [Omitted by SI 2009/56, art. 3(2) and Sch. 2, para. 132.]

History – Reg. 1(2) omitted by SI 2009/56, art. 3(2) and Sch. 2, para. 132, operative from 1 April 2009 subject to transitional and saving provisions in SI 2009/56, Sch. 3. Former reg. 1(2) read as follows:

"**1(2)**   These Regulations shall cease to have effect on the day appointed by Order made under section 24(1) of the Child Trust Funds Act 2004 (temporary modifications).".

INTERPRETATION

2   In these Regulations–

"**the Act**" means the Child Trust Funds Act 2004;

"**appeal tribunal**" means an appeal tribunal constituted in Northern Ireland, under Chapter 1 of Part 2 of the 1998 Order (social security appeals: Northern Ireland);

"**child trust fund appeal**" means an appeal under section 22 of the Act which, by virtue of section 24 of the Act, is to an appeal tribunal or lies to a Social Security Commissioner or to the First-tier Tribunal or lies to the Upper Tribunal;

"**Social Security Commissioner**" means in Northern Ireland, the Chief Social Security Commissioner or any other Social Security Commissioner appointed under the Social Security Administration (Northern Ireland) Act 1992 or a tribunal of two or more Commissioners constituted under Article 16(7) of the 1998 Order;

"**the 1998 Act**" means the Social Security Act 1998;

"**the 1998 Order**" means the Social Security (Northern Ireland) Order 1998.

History – In reg. 2, in the definition of "appeal tribunal", para. (a) and the following "(b)" omitted by SI 2008/2683, art. 6 and Sch. 1, para. 261(a), with effect from 3 November 2008. The wording of former para. (a) was "in Great Britain, under Chapter 1 of Part 1 of the 1998 Act (social security appeals: Great Britain), or".
In reg. 2, in the definition of "child trust fund appeal", the words "or to the First-tier Tribunal or lies to the Upper Tribunal" inserted by SI 2008/2683, art. 6 and Sch. 1, para. 261(b), with effect from 3 November 2008.
In reg. 2, in the definition of "Social Security Commissioner",sub-para. (a) and the following "(b)" omitted by SI 2008/2683, art. 6 and Sch. 1, para. 261(a), with effect from 3 November 2008. The wording of former sub-para. (a) was "in Great Britain, the Chief Social Security Commissioner or any other Social Security Commissioner appointed under the 1998 Act or a tribunal of three or more Commissioners constituted under section 16(7) of that Act, and".

PRESCRIBED MANNER OF NOTICE OF APPEAL

3(1)   The prescribed manner of giving notice of appeal, in respect of an appeal to an appeal tribunal, to the Inland Revenue under section 23(1) of the Child Trust Funds Act 2004 is as follows.

3(2)   The notice must–

(a)   be given in writing,

(b)   contain sufficient information to identify the appellant and the decision against which the appeal is being made, and

(c)   be signed by or on behalf of the appellant.

3(3)   In paragraph (2)(a) "**writing**" includes writing produced by electronic communications if those electronic communications are approved by the Commissioners of Inland Revenue.

3(4)   In paragraph (2)(c) "**signed**", where the notice is in writing produced by electronic communications, means authenticated in any manner approved by those Commissioners.

History – In reg. 3(1), the words ", in respect of an appeal to an appeal tribunal," inserted by SI 2008/2683, art. 6 and Sch. 1, para. 262, with effect from 3 November 2008.

APPLICATION OF SECTION 54 OF THE TAXES MANAGEMENT ACT 1970

4(1)   Section 54 of the Taxes Management Act 1970 (settling of appeals by agreement) shall apply to a child trust fund appeal to an appeal tribunal or the First-tier Tribunal, with the following modifications.

4(2) In subsection (1) for "tribunal", in both places where that word occurs, substitute "appeal tribunal or the First-tier Tribunal".

4(3) In subsections (1) and (4) omit "assessment or", in each place where those words occur.

4(4) In subsections (1) to (3) and (4)(a) for "inspector or other proper officer of the Crown" substitute "officer of the Board".

4(5) In subsection (3)(a), (4)(b) and in the words following paragraph (b) in subsection (4), for "inspector or other proper officer" substitute "officer of the Board".

4(6) After subsection (5) add the following subsection–

> "**54(6)** In subsection (1) **"appeal tribunal"** means an appeal tribunal constituted in Northern Ireland, under Chapter 1 of Part 2 of the Social Security (Northern Ireland) Order 1998 (social security appeals: Northern Ireland).".

History – In reg. 4(1), the words "or the First-tier Tribunal" inserted by SI 2008/2683, art. 6 and Sch. 1, para. 263(a), with effect from 3 November 2008.
In reg. 4(2), ""tribunal"" substituted for ""Commissioners"" by SI 2009/56, art. 3(2) and Sch. 2, para. 133, operative from 1 April 2009 subject to transitional and saving provisions in SI 2009/56, Sch. 3.
In reg. 4(2), the words "or the First-tier Tribunal" inserted by SI 2008/2683, art. 6 and Sch. 1, para. 263(a), with effect from 3 November 2008.
In reg. 4(6), in the inserted TMA 1970, s. 53(6), sub-para. (a) and the following "(b)" omitted by SI 2008/2683, art. 6 and Sch. 1, para. 263(b), with effect from 3 November 2008. The wording of former sub-para. (a) was "in Great Britain, under Chapter 1 of Part 1 of the Social Security Act 1998 (social security appeals: Great Britain), and".

APPLICATION OF ARTICLES 6 TO 8 OF AND SCHEDULE 1 TO THE 1998 ORDER

5(1) Articles 6 to 8 of and paragraphs 7, 11 and 12 of Schedule 1 to the 1998 Order, shall apply to a child trust fund appeal to an appeal tribunal with the following modifications.

5(2) [Omitted by SI 2008/2683, art. 6 and Sch. 1, para. 264(c).]

5(3) In paragraph 12 in Schedule 1 to the 1998 Order, for references to officers authorised by the Department substitute references to the clerk to the appeal tribunal.

History – In the heading to reg. 5, the words "sections 5 to 7 and Schedule 1 to the 1998 Act or", which appeared before "articles", omitted by SI 2008/2683, art. 6 and Sch. 1, para. 264(a), with effect from 3 November 2008.
In reg. 5(1), the words "Sections 5 to 7 and paragraphs 7, 11 and 12 of Schedule 1 to the 1998 Act or, in Northern Ireland,", which appeared before "Articles", omitted by SI 2008/2683, art. 6 and Sch. 1, para. 264(b), with effect from 3 November 2008.
Reg. 5(2) omitted by SI 2008/2683, art. 6 and Sch. 1, para. 264(c), with effect from 3 November 2008. Former reg. 5(2) read–

> "**5(2)** In paragraph 12 in Schedule 1 to the 1998 Act, for references to officers authorised by the Secretary of State substitute references to the clerk to the appeal tribunal.".

APPLICATION OF SECTION 12 OF THE 1998 ACT OR ARTICLE 13 OF THE 1998 ORDER

6(1) Section 12 of the 1998 Act ("section 12") or, in Northern Ireland, Article 13 of the 1998 Order ("Article 13") (appeals to an appeal tribunal or the First-tier Tribunal), shall apply to a child trust fund appeal to an appeal tribunal or the First-tier Tribunal, with the following modifications.

6(2) Omit subsections (1) to (6) of section 12 and paragraphs (1) to (6) of Article 13.

6(3) In subsection (8) of section 12 for "an appeal under this section" substitute a child trust "fund appeal".

6(4) In paragraph (8) of Article 13 for "an appeal under this Article" substitute "a child trust fund appeal".

6(5) Omit subsections (8)(a) and (9) of section 12 and paragraphs (8)(a) and (9) of Article 13.

History – In reg. 6(1), the words "or the First-tier Tribunal" inserted in both places by SI 2008/2683, art. 6 and Sch. 1, para. 265, with effect from 3 November 2008.

APPLICATION OF SECTION 13 OF THE 1998 ACT OR ARTICLE 14 OF THE 1998 ORDER

7 Section 13 of the 1998 Act ("section 13") or, in Northern Ireland, Article 14 of the 1998 Order ("Article 14") (redetermination etc. of appeals by tribunal), shall apply to a decision of an appeal tribunal or the First-tier Tribunal on a child trust fund appeal (other than a decision on a penalty appeal under section 21(9) of the Act as modified by section 24(2) of the Act), with the modifications that subsections (3) and (4) of section 13, and paragraphs (3) and (4) of Article 14, are omitted.

History – In reg. 7, the words "or the First-tier Tribunal" inserted by SI 2008/2683, art. 6 and Sch. 1, para. 266, with effect from 3 November 2008.

APPLICATION OF SECTION 14 OF THE 1998 ACT OR ARTICLE 15 OF THE 1998 ORDER

8(1) Section 14(2) and (3) of the 1998 Act or, in Northern Ireland, Article 15(1) to (10) of the 1998 Order (Appeal from tribunal to Commissioner or the Upper Tribunal), shall apply to a decision of an appeal tribunal or the First-tier Tribunal on a child trust fund appeal (other than a decision on a penalty appeal under section 21(9) of the Act as modified by section 24(2) of the Act)), with the following modifications.

8(2) In section 14–

(a)   in subsection (3) for "under section 12 or 13 above" substitute "on a child trust fund appeal";

(b)   in subsection (3)(a) for "Secretary of State" substitute "Board";

(c)   for subsection (3)(b) substitute–

    "(b)   the appellant in the child trust fund appeal;"; and

(d)   omit subsections 3(c) and (d).

(e)   [omitted by SI 2008/2683, art. 6 and Sch. 1, para. 267(b)(iv).].

8(3) In Article 15–

(a)   in paragraph (1) for "under Article 13 or 14" substitute "on a child trust fund appeal";

(b)   in paragraph (3)(a) for "Department" substitute "Board";

(c)   for paragraph (3)(b) substitute–

    "(b)   the appellant in the child trust fund appeal;";

(d)   omit paragraphs (3)(c) and (d), and (4) to (6); and

(e)   in paragraph (7) for "principal parties" substitute "Board and the appellant".

History – In reg. 8(1), "14(2) and (3)" substituted for "14(1) to (10)" by SI 2008/2683, art. 6 and Sch. 1, para. 267(a)(i), with effect from 3 November 2008.
In reg. 8(1), the words "or the Upper Tribunal" inserted by SI 2008/2683, art. 6 and Sch. 1, para. 267(a)(ii), with effect from 3 November 2008.
In reg. 8(1), the words "or the First-tier Tribunal" inserted by SI 2008/2683, art. 6 and Sch. 1, para. 267(a)(iii), with effect from 3 November 2008.
In reg. 8(2)(a), "(3)" substituted for "(1)" by SI 2008/2683, art. 6 and Sch. 1, para. 267(b)(i), with effect from 3 November 2008.
In reg. 8(2)(c), the words "and" inserted at the end by SI 2008/2683, art. 6 and Sch. 1, para. 267(b)(ii), with effect from 3 November 2008
Reg. 8(2)(d) substituted by SI 2008/2683, art. 6 and Sch. 1, para. 267(b)(iii), with effect from 3 November 2008. The wording of former reg. 8(2)(d) was "omit paragraphs (3)(c) and (d), and (4) to (6); and".
Reg. 8(2)(e) omitted by SI 2008/2683, art. 6 and Sch. 1, para. 267(b)(iv), with effect from 3 November 2008. The wording of former reg. 8(2)(e) was "in subsection (7) for "principal parties" substitute "Board and the appellant"".

APPLICATION OF ARTICLE 15(11) TO (13) OF THE 1998 ORDER

9(1) Article 15(11) to (13) of the 1998 Order, (appeals and procedure before Commissioner), shall apply to a decision of an appeal tribunal on a child trust fund appeal, with the following modifications.

9(2) So far as concerns decisions of an appeal tribunal on a penalty appeal under paragraph (11) of Article 15, omit the words "and applications made for leave to appeal".

History – In the heading to reg. 9, the words "section 14(11) and (12) of and Schedule 4 to the 1998 Act or", which appeared before "Article", omitted by SI 2008/2683, art. 6 and Sch. 1, para. 268(a), with effect from 3 November 2008.
In reg. 9(1), the words "Section 14(11) and (12) of, and Schedule 4 to, the 1998 Act, or, in Northern Ireland,", which appeared before "Article", omitted by SI 2008/2683, art. 6 and Sch. 1, para. 268(b), with effect from 3 November 2008.
In reg. 9(2), the words "section 21(9) of the Act as modified by section 24(2) of the Act in subsection 11 of section 14 and", which appeared before "paragraph", omitted by SI 2008/2683, art. 6 and Sch. 1, para. 268(c), with effect from 3 November 2008.

APPLICATION OF SECTION 15 OF THE 1998 ACT

10 Section 15 of the 1998 Act (Applications for permission to appeal against a decision of the Upper Tribunal) shall apply to a decision of the Upper Tribunal on a child trust fund appeal.

History – In reg. 10, the words "Applications for permission to appeal against a decision of the Upper Tribunal" substituted for the words "appeal from Commissioner on point of law", and the words "the Upper Tribunal" substituted for the words "a Social Security Commissioner", by SI 2008/2683, art. 6 and Sch. 1, para. 269, with effect from 3 November 2008.

APPLICATION OF SECTION 16 OF THE 1998 ACT OR ARTICLE 16 OF THE 1998 ORDER

11(1) Section 16 ("section 16") of and Schedule 5 to the 1998 Act or, in Northern Ireland, Article 16 ("Article 16") of and Schedule 4 to the 1998 Order (procedure), shall apply for the purposes of a child trust fund appeal with the following modifications.

11(2) Omit subsection (3) of section 16.

11(3)   Omit paragraph (3)(b) of Article 16 and the word "and" immediately preceding it.

11(4)   Omit subsections (4) and (5) of section 16 and paragraphs (4) and (5) of Article 16.

11(5)   In Schedule 5 to the 1998 Act, in paragraph 1, omit "the Secretary of State," in both places where those words occur.

11(6)   In Schedule 4 to the 1998 Order, in paragraph 1, omit "the Department", in both places where those words occur.

History – Reg. 11(2) substituted by SI 2008/2683, art. 6 and Sch. 1, para. 270, with effect from 3 November 2008. The wording of former reg. 11(2) was "Omit subsection (3)(b) of section 16 and the word "and" immediately preceding it.".

APPLICATION OF SECTION 17 OF THE 1998 ACT OR ARTICLE 17 OF THE 1998 ORDER

12(1)   Section 17 of the 1998 Act ("section 17") or, in Northern Ireland, Article 17 of the 1998 Order ("Article 17") (finality of decisions), shall apply to a decision of an appeal tribunal, the First-tier Tribunal, the Upper Tribunal or a Social Security Commissioner on a child trust fund appeal, with the following modifications.

12(2)   For subsection (1) of section 17 substitute the following subsection–

> "**17(1)**   Subject to the provisions of–
>
> (a)   sections 12 to 16, and 28 of this Act (as modified by the Child Trust Funds (Nontax Appeals) Regulations 2004), and
>
> (b)   sections 21(9) and (10) and 22 to 24 of the Child Trust Funds Act 2004,
>
> any decisions made in accordance with those provisions in respect of a child trust fund appeal which, in accordance with section 24 of the Child Trust Funds Act 2004, is to the First-tier Tribunal or lies to the Upper Tribunal, shall be final.".

12(3)   For paragraph (1) of Article 17 substitute the following paragraph–

> "**17(1)**   Subject to the provisions of–
>
> (a)   Articles 13 to 16, and 28 of this Order (as modified by the Child Trust Funds (Non-tax Appeals) Regulations 2004),
>
> (b)   sections 21(9) and (10) and 22 to 24 of the Child Trust Funds Act 2004], and
>
> (c)   any provisions made by or under Chapter 2 of Part 1 of the Tribunals, Courts and Enforcement Act 2007 (c.15),
>
> any decisions made in accordance with those provisions in respect of a child trust fund appeal which, in accordance with section 24 of the Child Trust Funds Act 2004, is to an appeal tribunal or lies to a Commissioner, shall be final.".

12(4)   Omit subsection (2)(b) and (c) of section 17 and paragraph (2)(b) and (c) of Article 17.

History – In reg. 12(1), the words ", the First-tier Tribunal, the Upper Tribunal" inserted by SI 2008/2683, art. 6 and Sch. 1, para. 271(a), with effect from 3 November 2008.
In reg. 12(2), in the substituted SSA 1998, s. 17(1), sub-para. (c) inserted, and the "and" at the end of sub-para. (a) omitted, and the "and" at the end of sub-para. (c) inserted, by SI 2008/2683, art. 6 and Sch. 1, para. 271(b)(i)–(iii), with effect from 3 November 2008.
In reg. 12(2), the words "the First-tier Tribunal or lies to the Upper Tribunal" substituted for the words "an appeal tribunal or lies to a Commissioner" by SI 2008/2683, art. 6 and Sch. 1, para. 271(b)(iv), with effect from 3 November 2008.

APPLICATION OF ARTICLE 28 OF THE 1998 ORDER

13(1)   Article 28 of the 1998 Order ("Article 28") (correction of errors and setting aside of decisions), shall apply to a decision by an appeal tribunal or a Social Security Commissioner on a child trust fund appeal, with the following modifications.

13(2)   Omit paragraph (1A) of Article 28.

13(3)   For subsection (3) of section 28 substitute the following subsection–

> "**28(3)**   In this section **"relevant enactment"** means–

(a)   any of sections 12 to 17 above (as modified by the Child Trust Funds (Non-tax Appeals) Regulations 2004), and

(b)   sections 21(9) and (10) and 22 to 24 of the Child Trust Funds Act 2004.".

13(4)   [Omitted by SI 2008/2683, art. 6 and Sch. 1, para. 272(d).]

History – In the heading to reg. 13, the words "section 28 of the 1998 Act or", which appeared before "Article", omitted by SI 2008/2683, art. 6 and Sch. 1, para. 272(a), with effect from 3 November 2008.
In reg. 13(1), the words "Section 28 of the 1998 Act ("section 28") or, in Northern Ireland,", which appeared before "Article", omitted by SI 2008/2683, art. 6 and Sch. 1, para. 272(b), with effect from 3 November 2008.

In reg. 13(2), the words "subsection (1A) of section 28 and", which appeared before "paragraph", omitted by SI 2008/2683, art. 6 and Sch. 1, para. 272(c), with effect from 3 November 2008.

Reg. 13(3) omitted by SI 2008/2683, art. 6 and Sch. 1, para. 272(d), with effect from 3 November 2008. Former reg. 13(3) read as follows–

> "**13(3)**   For subsection (3) of section 28 substitute the following subsection–
> "**28(3)**   In this section **"relevant enactment"** means–
> (a)   any of sections 12 to 17 above (as modified by the Child Trust Funds (Non-tax Appeals) Regulations 2004), and
> (b)   sections 21(9) and (10) and 22 to 24 of the Child Trust Funds Act 2004.".".

APPLICATION OF SECTION 39 OF THE 1998 ACT OR ARTICLE 39 OF THE 1998 ORDER

14(1)   Section 39 of the 1998 Act or, in Northern Ireland, Article 39 of the 1998 Order (interpretation etc. of Chapter 2), shall apply for the purposes of a child trust fund appeal with the following modifications.

14(2)   In subsection (1) of section 39–

(a)   insert at the appropriate places–

> ""**the Board**" means the Commissioners of the Inland Revenue;
>
> "**child trust fund appeal**" means an appeal under section 22 of the Child Trust Funds Act 2004 which, by virtue of section 24 of that Act, is to the First-tier Tribunal or lies to the Upper Tribunal;";

(b)   omit the definitions of **"claimant"** and **"relevant benefit."**

14(3)   In paragraph (1) of Article 39–

(a)   for the definition of "Inland Revenue" substitute–

> ""**the Board**" means the Commissioners of Inland Revenue;
>
> "**child trust fund appeal**" means an appeal under section 22 of the Child Trust Funds Act 2004 which, by virtue of section 24 of that Act, is to an appeal tribunal or lies to a Social Security Commissioner;";

(b)   omit the definitions of **"claimant"** and **"relevant benefit."**

14(4)   Omit subsections (2) and (3) of section 39 and paragraphs (2) and (3) of Article 39.

History – In reg. 14(2), in the inserted definition of "child trust fund appeal", the words "the First-tier Tribunal or lies to the Upper Tribunal" substituted for the words "an appeal tribunal or lies to a Social Security Commissioner" by SI 2008/2683, art. 6 and Sch. 1, para. 273, with effect from 3 November 2008.

Reg. 14(2)(b) substituted by SI 2009/56, art. 3(2) and Sch. 2, para. 134(2), operative from 1 April 2009 subject to transitional and saving provisions in SI 2009/56, Sch. 3. Former reg. 14(2)(b) read as follows:

> "(b)   omit the definitions of "claimant", "relevant benefit" and "tax appeal Commissioners".".

Reg. 14(3)(b) substituted by SI 2009/56, art. 3(2) and Sch. 2, para. 134(2), operative from 1 April 2009 subject to transitional and saving provisions in SI 2009/56, Sch. 3. Former reg. 14(3)(b) read as follows:

> "(b)   omit the definitions of "claimant", "relevant benefit" and "tax appeal Commissioners".".

APPLICATION OF SECTIONS 79, 80 AND 84 OF THE 1998 ACT OR ARTICLES 74 AND 75 OF THE 1998 ORDER

15   [Omitted by SI 2008/2683, art. 6 and Sch. 1, para. 273.]

History – Reg. 15 omitted by SI 2008/2683, art. 6 and Sch. 1, para. 273, with effect from 3 November 2008. Former reg. 15 read as follows–

> "**15(1)**   Sections 79, 80 and 84 of the 1998 Act or, in Northern Ireland, Articles 74 and 75 of the 1998 Order shall apply to regulations for child trust fund appeals, made under provisions of the 1998 Act or the 1998 Order applied by these Regulations, with the following modifications.
>
> **15(2)**   In section 79–
> (a)   in subsection (1) for "subsections (2) and (2A) below" substitute "subsection (2)";
> (b)   omit subsections (2A) and (8).
>
> **15(3)**   In Article 74–
> (a)   in paragraph (1)–
>   (i)   for "paragraphs (2) and (2A)" substitute "paragraph (2)";
>   (ii)   for "Department" substitute "Treasury";
> (b)   omit paragraphs (2A) and (7).
>
> **15(4)**   In Article 75 omit paragraphs (1) and (3).".

ENERGY ACT 2004 (NUCLEAR DECOMMISSIONING) (EXEMPT ACTIVITIES AND FURTHER CONDITIONS) REGULATIONS 2005

(SI 2005/644)

Made on 10 March 2005 by the Treasury, with the concurrence of the Secretary of State, in exercise of the powers conferred upon them by s. 27(3)(b) and (5)(d) of the Energy Act 2004. Operative from 1 April 2005.

CITATION, COMMENCEMENT AND INTERPRETATION

1(1) These Regulations may be cited as the Energy Act 2004 (Nuclear Decommissioning) (Exempt Activities and Further Conditions) Regulations 2005 and shall come into force on 1st April 2005.

1(2) In these Regulations–

a reference, without more, to a **numbered section or Schedule** is a reference to the corresponding provision of the Energy Act 2004;

"**the NDA**" means the Nuclear Decommissioning Authority (see section 1); and

"**designated**" means designated by means of a direction given by the Secretary of State to the NDA under section 3(3); and

any other expression defined in section 37(1) bears the same meaning in these Regulations.

EXEMPT ACTIVITIES FOR THE PURPOSES OF SECTION 27 OF, AND SCHEDULE 4 TO, THE ENERGY ACT 2004

2(1) For the purposes of section 27 and Schedule 4 (tax exemptions for NDA activities) the activities mentioned in paragraph (2) are specified.

2(2) The activities are the operation of designated facilities for the treatment, storage, transportation or disposal of hazardous material, carried on for the purpose of thermal oxide reprocessing or mixed oxide manufacture where that reprocessing or manufacture is undertaken at Sellafield in Cumbria.

FURTHER CONDITIONS IN RESPECT OF NDA COMPANY WHICH IS A RELEVANT SITE LICENSEE

3(1) The further conditions referred to in section 27(5)(d) (conditions in respect of NDA company which is a relevant site licensee) are those in paragraphs (2) and (3).

3(2) The condition is that all the ordinary share capital of the company must have been transferred from the NDA or a wholly owned subsidiary of the NDA ("the original transfer").

3(3) The condition is that where–

(a)   a management contract is in force–

    (i)   which relates to the whole or part of the site, or to an installation or facility in or on that site, for which a nuclear site licence is in force; and

    (ii)   which is made between the NDA and the company, or between the NDA and a company which owns, directly or indirectly, at least 90 per cent of the ordinary share capital of the company; or

(b)   the company has control of a designated installation, site or facility and directions have been given to the company under section 18(3) in respect of that installation, site or facility;

the company's memorandum and articles must be such as to secure that the restrictions imposed by paragraphs (4) and (5) will always be met.

3(4) The company may not declare dividends on its shares.

3(5) A transfer of the company's shares–

(a)   may only be made to the NDA; or a wholly owned subsidiary of the NDA,

(b)   must comprise the whole of the company's share capital, and

(c)   must be for a consideration which is no greater than that given for the original transfer.

3(6) For the purposes of paragraph (5)(c) where consideration is given for share capital and for something else besides, a just and reasonable apportionment shall be made between the amount given for the share capital and the amount given for the other thing.

14,047   Charge to Income Tax etc. Regs 2005   SI 2005/724

Statutory Instruments

CHARGE TO INCOME TAX BY REFERENCE TO ENJOYMENT OF PROPERTY PREVIOUSLY OWNED REGULATIONS 2005

(SI 2005/724)

Made on 16 March 2005 by the Treasury, in exercise of the powers conferred upon them by para. 1, 4(5) and (6), 7(2), (4) and (5), 9(1) and (3), 14 and 20 of Sch. 15 to the Finance Act 2004, and the Commissioners of Inland Revenue, in exercise of powers conferred upon them by s. 104 of the Finance Act 1986. Operative from 6 April 2005.

CITATION AND COMMENCEMENT

1 These Regulations may be cited as the Charge to Income Tax by Reference to Enjoyment of Property Previously Owned Regulations 2005 and shall come into force on 6th April 2005.

PRESCRIBED VALUATION DATE

2 In paragraph 4 (chargeable amount in relation to land), paragraph 7 (chargeable amount in relation to chattels) and paragraph 9 (chargeable amount in relation to intangible property) of Schedule 15 to the Finance Act 2004 the valuation date in relation to a taxable period is 6th April in the relevant year of assessment or, if later, the first day of the taxable period.

PRESCRIBED RATE OF INTEREST

3(1) In paragraphs 7(2) and 9(1) of Schedule 15 to the Finance Act 2004 the prescribed rate is the official rate of interest at the valuation date.

3(2) In this regulation, "the official rate of interest" has the meaning given in section 181 of the Income Tax (Earnings and Pensions) Act 2003.

VALUATION AND RENTAL VALUE

4(1) The valuation of land or any interest in land for the purposes of paragraph 4 of Schedule 15 to the Finance Act 2004 and a chattel or any interest in a chattel for the purposes of paragraph 7 of Schedule 15 to the Finance Act 2004 is—

(a) before the first five-year anniversary, by reference to the first valuation date, and

(b) thereafter, by reference to the valuation date at the last five-year anniversary.

4(2) The rental value of land for the purposes of paragraph 4 of Schedule 15 to the Finance Act 2004 is determined in relation to a year of assessment—

(a) between the end of the first taxable period and the first five-year anniversary, by reference to the annual value in relation to the first year of assessment in which paragraph 3 of Schedule 15 to the Finance Act 2004 (land) applied, and

(b) thereafter, by reference to the rental value for the year of assessment commencing at the last five-year anniversary.

4(3) Subject to paragraph (4), in this regulation—

"**five-year anniversary**" means the fifth anniversary of 6th April in the year of assessment in which paragraph 3 (land) or paragraph 6 (chattels) of Schedule 15 to the Finance Act 2004 first applied to a chargeable person in relation to the relevant land or chattel or any interest in the relevant land or chattel, and subsequent anniversaries at five-year intervals;

"**first valuation date**" means the date on which paragraph 3 or paragraph 6 of Schedule 15 to the Finance Act 2004 first applied to a chargeable person in relation to the relevant land or chattel or any interest in the relevant land or chattel.

4(4) If there is no valuation date at a five-year anniversary, the date on which paragraph 3 or paragraph 6 of Schedule 15 to the Finance Act 2004 next apply to the chargeable person in relation to the relevant land or chattel, or any interest in the relevant land or chattel, shall be treated as the date on which, and being in the year of assessment in which, paragraph 3 or paragraph 6 of that Schedule first applied to that person in relation to that land, chattel or interest.

EXEMPTIONS FROM CHARGE

5(1)   Paragraph 3 (land) and paragraph 6 (chattels) do not apply to a person in relation to a disposal of part of an interest in any property if–

(a)   the disposal was by a transaction made at arm's length with a person not connected with him;

(b)   the disposal was by a transaction such as might be expected to be made at arm's length between persons not connected with each other, and

    (i)   the disposal was for a consideration not in money or in the form of readily convertible assets, or

    (ii)   the disposal was made before 7th March 2005.

5(2)   In this regulation "readily convertible asset" has the meaning given in section 702 of the Income Tax (Earnings and Pensions) Act 2003.

AVOIDING DOUBLE CHARGE

6(1)   This regulation provides for the avoidance, to the extent specified, of double charges to tax arising in the circumstances specified (in paragraph (2)) for the purposes of paragraph (d) of section 104(1) of the Finance Act 1986 (being circumstances which appear to the Board to be similar to those referred to in paragraphs (a) to (c) of that subsection).

6(2)   The specified circumstances are–

(a)   a person makes a transfer by way of gift–

    (i)   of property representing the proceeds of the disposal of relevant property,

    (ii)   by virtue of which property becomes comprised in a settlement,

(b)   the transfer is or proves to be a chargeable transfer,

(c)   the person dies on or after 6th April 2005 and within seven years of the transfer,

(d)   the person made an election under paragraph 21 of Schedule 15 to the Finance Act 2004 (election for application of inheritance tax provisions) in relation to the relevant property,

(e)   the relevant property–

    (i)   is by virtue of section 102(3) of the Finance Act 1986 treated for the purposes of the Inheritance Tax Act 1984 as property to which the person was beneficially entitled immediately before his death, or

    (ii)   ceased to be property subject to a reservation and became the subject of a potentially exempt transfer by virtue of section 102(4) of the Finance Act 1986, and

(f)   the chargeable proportion of the relevant property–

    (i)   is comprised in the estate of the person immediately before his death within the meaning of section 5(1) of the Inheritance Tax Act 1984 and the value attributable to it is transferred by a chargeable transfer under section 4 of that Act, or

    (ii)   is property transferred by the potentially chargeable transfer to which sub-paragraph (e)(ii) applies, value attributable to which is transferred by a chargeable transfer.

6(3)   Where this regulation applies, there shall be calculated, separately in accordance with subparagraphs (a) and (b), the total tax chargeable as a consequence of the death of the person–

(a)   disregarding so much of the value transferred by the transfer of value to which paragraph (2)(a) refers as represents the proceeds of the disposal of the relevant property to which paragraph (2)(f) refers, and

(b)   disregarding so much of the value transferred by the transfer of value to which paragraph (2)(f) refers as is represented by property to which paragraph (2)(a) refers.

6(4)   Where the amount calculated under paragraph (3)(a) is higher than the amount calculated under (3)(b)–

(a)   only so much of that higher amount shall be payable as remains after deducting, as a credit, from the amount comprised in the higher amount which is attributable to the value of the property to which paragraph (2)(f) refers, a sum (not exceeding the amount so attributable) equal to so much of the tax paid–

    (i)   as became payable before the person's death, and

    (ii)   as is attributable to the value disregarded under paragraph (3)(a), and

(b)   so much of the value transferred by the transfer of value to which paragraph (2)(a) refers as is attributable to the property to which paragraph (2)(f) refers shall (except in relation to chargeable transfers which were chargeable to tax, when made by the person, for the purposes of an occasion which occurred before the person's death on which tax was chargeable under section 64 or 65 of the Inheritance Tax Act 1984 (charge at ten year anniversary and charge at other times in relation to settlements without interests in possession)) be treated as reduced to a nil amount for all the purposes of the Inheritance Tax Act 1984.

6(5)   Where the amount calculated under paragraph (3)(a) is less than the amount calculated under paragraph (3)(b) the value of the property to which paragraph (2)(f) refers shall be reduced to a nil amount for all the purposes of the Inheritance Tax Act 1984.

6(6)   In this regulation, "relevant property" and "the chargeable proportion" have the meanings given in paragraph 21 of Schedule 15 to the Finance Act 2004.

CHILD TRUST FUNDS (APPEALS) REGULATIONS 2005

(SI 2005/990, as amended by SI 2008/2683 and SI 2009/56)

Made on 24 March 2005 by the Secretary of State for Work and Pensions, in exercise of the powers conferred upon him by s. 7(6) and (7), 12(7), 14(10)(a) and (11), 16(1) and (3)(a), 28(1), 79(1) and (4) to (7) and 84 of, and para. 7, 11 and 12 of Sch. 1 to, and para. 1 to 6 of Sch. 5 to, the Social Security Act 1998.

CITATION, COMMENCEMENT, DURATION AND INTERPRETATION

1(1) These Regulations may be cited as the Child Trust Funds (Appeals) Regulations 2005 and shall come into force on the day after they are made.

1(2) [Omitted by SI 2009/56, art. 3(2) and Sch. 2, para. 136.]

1(3) In these Regulations, unless the context otherwise requires–

"**the Act**" means the Social Security Act 1998;

"**the 2004 Act**" means the Child Trust Funds Act 2004;

"**appeal**" means an appeal under section 22 of the 2004 Act to the First-tier Tribunal;

"**the Board**" means the Commissioners of Inland Revenue;

"**notification period**" has the meaning given in regulation 3;

"**party to the proceedings**" means the Board and any person who brings an appeal;

1(4) [Omitted by SI 2008/2683, art. 6 and Sch. 1, para. 291(3).]

History – Reg. 1(2) omitted by SI 2009/56, art. 3(2) and Sch. 2, para. 136, operative from 1 April 2009 subject to transitional and saving provisions in SI 2009/56, Sch. 3. Former reg. 1(2) read as follows:

"**1(2)** These Regulations shall cease to have effect on such day as is appointed by order made under section 24(1) of the Child Trust Funds Act 2004.".

In reg. 1(3), in the definition of "appeal", "the First-tier Tribunal" substituted for "an appeal tribunal" by SI 2008/2683, art. 6 and Sch. 1, para. 291(2)(a), with effect from 3 November 2008.

In reg. 1(3) the definitions of the following terms omitted by SI 2008/2683, art. 6 and Sch. 1, para. 291(2)(b), with effect from 3 November 2008: "clerk to the appeal tribunal"; "decision notice"; "financially qualified panel member"; "legally qualified panel member"; and "the President".

Reg. 1(4) omitted by SI 2008/2683, art. 6 and Sch. 1, para. 291(3), with effect from 3 November 2008. Former reg. 1(4) read as follows–

"**1(4)** In these Regulations any reference to the chairman of the appeal tribunal shall, in the case of an appeal tribunal which has only one member, include reference to that member.".

SERVICE OF NOTICES OR DOCUMENTS

2 Where by any provision of these Regulations–

(a) any notice or other document is required to be given or sent to the Board, that notice or document shall be treated as having been so given or sent on the day that it is received by the Board, and

(b) any notice or other document is required to be given or sent to any person other than the Board, that notice or document shall, if sent to that person's last known address, be treated as having been given or sent on the day that it was posted.

History – In reg. 2(a), the words "the clerk to the appeal tribunal or to", which appeared before "the Board", omitted by SI 2008/2683, art. 6 and Sch. 1, para. 292(a)(i), with effect from 3 November 2008.

In reg. 2(a), the words "the clerk to the appeal tribunal or by", which appeared before "the Board", omitted by SI 2008/2683, art. 6 and Sch. 1, para. 292(a)(ii), with effect from 3 November 2008.

In reg. 2(b), the words "the clerk to the appeal tribunal or", which appeared before "the Board", omitted by SI 2008/2683, art. 6 and Sch. 1, para. 292(b), with effect from 3 November 2008.

DISPUTES ABOUT NOTICES OF APPEAL

3 Where a dispute arises as to whether notice of an appeal was given to the Board within the period of thirty days specified in section 23(1) of the 2004 Act ("the notification period") the dispute shall be referred to, and be determined by, the First-tier Tribunal.

History – In reg. 3, the words "the First-tier Tribunal" substituted for the words "a legally qualified panel member" by SI 2008/2683, art. 6 and Sch. 1, para. 293, with effect from 3 November 2008.

LATE APPEALS

4(1) Where the conditions specified in paragraphs (4) to (8) are satisfied, the Board may treat an appeal as made in time where an appeal is brought within a period of one year after the expiration of the notification period.

Statutory Instruments

4(2) [Omitted by SI 2008/2683, art. 6 and Sch. 1, para. 294(b).]

4(3) [Omitted by SI 2008/2683, art. 6 and Sch. 1, para. 294(b).]

4(4) The Board must not treat the appeal as made in time unless the Board is satisfied that it is in the interests of justice.

4(5) For the purposes of paragraph (4) it is not in the interests of justice to treat the appeal as made in time unless the Board are satisfied that–

(a)   the special circumstances specified in paragraph (6) are relevant; or

(b)   some other special circumstances exist which are wholly exceptional and relevant,

and as a result of those special circumstances, it was not practicable for the appeal to be brought within the notification period.

4(6) For the purposes of paragraph (5)(a), the special circumstances are that–

(a)   the appellant or a partner or dependant of the appellant has died or suffered serious illness;

(b)   the appellant is not resident in the United Kingdom; or

(c)   normal postal services were disrupted.

4(7) In determining whether it is in the interests of justice to treat the appeal as made in time, regard shall be had to the principle that the greater the amount of time that has elapsed between the expiration of the notification period and the submission of the notice of appeal, the more compelling should be the special circumstances.

4(8) In determining whether it is in the interests of justice to treat the appeal as made in time, no account shall be taken of the following–

(a)   that the appellant or any person acting for him was unaware of or misunderstood the law applicable to his case (including ignorance or misunderstanding of the notification period); or

(b)   that the Upper Tribunal or a court has taken a different view of the law from that previously understood and applied.

4(9) [Omitted by SI 2008/2683, art. 6 and Sch. 1, para. 294(h).]

4(10) [Omitted by SI 2008/2683, art. 6 and Sch. 1, para. 294(h).]

4(11) As soon as practicable after the decision is made a copy of the decision shall be sent or given to every party to the proceedings.

History – In reg. 4(1), the words "(4) to (8) are satisfied, the Board may treat an appeal as made in time where an appeal is" substituted for the words "(2) to (8) are satisfied, an appeal may be" by SI 2008/2683, art. 6 and Sch. 1, para. 294(a), with effect from 3 November 2008.

Reg. 4(2) omitted by SI 2008/2683, art. 6 and Sch. 1, para. 294(b), with effect from 3 November 2008. Former reg. 4(2) read as follows–

"**4(2)**   An application to bring a late appeal under this regulation shall be made in writing, signed by or on behalf of the appellant and sent to the Board and it shall include sufficient information to determine–
(a)   the identity of the appellant;
(b)   whether the appellant is a relevant person within the meaning of section 22(3) of the 2004 Act or a personal representative of a child in accordance with section 22(5), if the appellant is appealing in either capacity;
(c)   the subject of the appeal to which the application relates;
(d)   the decision against which the appeal is being made; and
(e)   the grounds on which the applicant seeks time to appeal, including details of any relevant special circumstances for the purposes of paragraph (4).".

Reg. 4(3) omitted by SI 2008/2683, art. 6 and Sch. 1, para. 294(b), with effect from 3 November 2008. Former reg. 4(3) read as follows–

"**4(3)**   An application to bring a late appeal under this regulation shall be determined by a legally qualified panel member, except that where the Board consider that the conditions in paragraphs (4)(b) to (8) are satisfied, the Board may grant the application.".

Reg. 4(4) substituted by SI 2008/2683, art. 6 and Sch. 1, para. 294(c), with effect from 3 November 2008. Former reg. 4(4) read as follows–

"**4(4)**   An application to bring a late appeal shall not be granted unless–
(a)   the panel member is satisfied that, if the application is granted, there are reasonable prospects that the appeal will be successful; or
(b)   the panel member is, or the Board are, satisfied that it is in the interests of justice for the application to be granted.".

In reg. 4(5), the words "treat the appeal as made in time unless the Board are" substituted for the words "grant an application unless the panel member is, or the Board are, as the case may be," by SI 2008/2683, art. 6 and Sch. 1, para. 294(d)(i), with effect from 3 November 2008.

In reg. 4(5)(a) and (b), the words "to the application", which appeared at the end of each sub-para, omitted by SI 2008/2683, art. 6 and Sch. 1, para. 294(d)(ii), with effect from 3 November 2008.

In reg. 4(6), "appellant" substituted for "applicant" in each place by SI 2008/2683, art. 6 and Sch. 1, para. 294(e), with effect from 3 November 2008.

In reg. 4(7), the words "treat the appeal as made in time" substituted for the words "grant the application" by SI 2008/2683, art. 6 and Sch. 1, para. 294(f)(i), with effect from 3 November 2008.

In reg. 4(7), the words "submission of the notice of appeal, the more compelling should be the special circumstances." substituted for the words "making of the application to bring a late appeal, the more compelling should be the special circumstances on which the application is based." by SI 2008/2683, art. 6 and Sch. 1, para. 294(f)(ii), with effect from 3 November 2008.

In reg. 4(8), the words "treat the appeal as made in time" substituted for the words "grant an application" by SI 2008/2683, art. 6 and Sch. 1, para. 294(g)(i), with effect from 3 November 2008.

In reg. 4(8)(a), "appellant" substituted for "applicant" by SI 2008/2683, art. 6 and Sch. 1, para. 294(g)(ii), with effect from 3 November 2008.

In reg. 4(8)(b), the words "the Upper Tribunal" substituted for the words "a Social Security Commissioner" by SI 2008/2683, art. 6 and Sch. 1, para. 294(g)(iii), with effect from 3 November 2008.

Reg. 4(9) omitted by SI 2008/2683, art. 6 and Sch. 1, para. 294(h), with effect from 3 November 2008. Former reg. 4(9) read as follows–

> "**4(9)**   An application under this regulation for a late appeal which has been refused may not be renewed.".

Reg. 4(10) omitted by SI 2008/2683, art. 6 and Sch. 1, para. 294(h), with effect from 3 November 2008. Former reg. 4(10) read as follows–

> "**4(10)**   The panel member who determines an application under this regulation shall record a summary of his decision in such written form as has been approved by the President.".

DEATH OF A PARTY TO AN APPEAL

5   In any proceedings relating to an appeal under section 22(2), (4), (5) or (6) of the 2004 Act, on the death of a party to the proceedings (other than the Board) the personal representative of the person who has died may represent him at any hearing.

COMPOSITION OF APPEAL TRIBUNALS

6   [Omitted by SI 2008/2683, art. 6 and Sch. 1, para. 295.]

History – Reg. 6 omitted by SI 2008/2683, art. 6 and Sch. 1, para. 295, with effect from 3 November 2008.

CLERK TO AN APPEAL TRIBUNAL

7   [Omitted by SI 2008/2683, art. 6 and Sch. 1, para. 295.]

History – Reg. 7 omitted by SI 2008/2683, art. 6 and Sch. 1, para. 295, with effect from 3 November 2008.

CONSIDERATION AND DETERMINATION OF APPEALS

8   [Omitted by SI 2008/2683, art. 6 and Sch. 1, para. 295.]

History – Reg. 8 omitted by SI 2008/2683, art. 6 and Sch. 1, para. 295, with effect from 3 November 2008.

CHOICE OF HEARING

9   [Omitted by SI 2008/2683, art. 6 and Sch. 1, para. 295.]

History – Reg. 9 omitted by SI 2008/2683, art. 6 and Sch. 1, para. 295, with effect from 3 November 2008.

WITHDRAWAL OF APPEAL

10   [Omitted by SI 2008/2683, art. 6 and Sch. 1, para. 295.]

History – Reg. 10 omitted by SI 2008/2683, art. 6 and Sch. 1, para. 295, with effect from 3 November 2008.

SUMMONING OF WITNESSES AND ADMINISTRATION OF OATHS

11   [Omitted by SI 2008/2683, art. 6 and Sch. 1, para. 295.]

History – Reg. 11 omitted by SI 2008/2683, art. 6 and Sch. 1, para. 295, with effect from 3 November 2008.

CONFIDENTIALITY IN APPEALS

12   [Omitted by SI 2008/2683, art. 6 and Sch. 1, para. 295.]

History – Reg. 12 omitted by SI 2008/2683, art. 6 and Sch. 1, para. 295, with effect from 3 November 2008.

APPEALS WHICH MAY BE STRUCK OUT

13   [Omitted by SI 2008/2683, art. 6 and Sch. 1, para. 295.]

History – Reg. 13 omitted by SI 2008/2683, art. 6 and Sch. 1, para. 295, with effect from 3 November 2008.

REINSTATEMENT OF STRUCK OUT APPEALS

14   [Omitted by SI 2008/2683, art. 6 and Sch. 1, para. 295.]

History – Reg. 14 omitted by SI 2008/2683, art. 6 and Sch. 1, para. 295, with effect from 3 November 2008.

PROCEDURE AT ORAL HEARINGS

15   [Omitted by SI 2008/2683, art. 6 and Sch. 1, para. 295.]

History – Reg. 15 omitted by SI 2008/2683, art. 6 and Sch. 1, para. 295, with effect from 3 November 2008.

MANNER OF PROVIDING EXPERT ASSISTANCE

16   [Omitted by SI 2008/2683, art. 6 and Sch. 1, para. 295.]

History – Reg. 16 omitted by SI 2008/2683, art. 6 and Sch. 1, para. 295, with effect from 3 November 2008.

POSTPONEMENT AND ADJOURNMENT

17   [Omitted by SI 2008/2683, art. 6 and Sch. 1, para. 295.]

History – Reg. 17 omitted by SI 2008/2683, art. 6 and Sch. 1, para. 295, with effect from 3 November 2008.

DECISIONS OF APPEAL TRIBUNALS

18   [Omitted by SI 2008/2683, art. 6 and Sch. 1, para. 295.]

History – Reg. 18 omitted by SI 2008/2683, art. 6 and Sch. 1, para. 295, with effect from 3 November 2008.

LATE APPLICATIONS FOR STATEMENTS OF REASONS OF TRIBUNAL DECISIONS

19   [Omitted by SI 2008/2683, art. 6 and Sch. 1, para. 295.]

History – Reg. 19 omitted by SI 2008/2683, art. 6 and Sch. 1, para. 295, with effect from 3 November 2008.

RECORD OF TRIBUNAL PROCEEDINGS

20   [Omitted by SI 2008/2683, art. 6 and Sch. 1, para. 295.]

History – Reg. 20 omitted by SI 2008/2683, art. 6 and Sch. 1, para. 295, with effect from 3 November 2008.

CORRECTION OF ACCIDENTAL ERRORS

21   [Omitted by SI 2008/2683, art. 6 and Sch. 1, para. 295.]

History – Reg. 21 omitted by SI 2008/2683, art. 6 and Sch. 1, para. 295, with effect from 3 November 2008.

SETTING ASIDE DECISIONS ON CERTAIN GROUNDS

22   [Omitted by SI 2008/2683, art. 6 and Sch. 1, para. 295.]

History – Reg. 22 omitted by SI 2008/2683, art. 6 and Sch. 1, para. 295, with effect from 3 November 2008.

PROVISIONS COMMON TO REGULATIONS 21 AND 22

23   [Omitted by SI 2008/2683, art. 6 and Sch. 1, para. 295.]

History – Reg. 23 omitted by SI 2008/2683, art. 6 and Sch. 1, para. 295, with effect from 3 November 2008.

SERVICE OF DECISION NOTICE BY ELECTRONIC MAIL

24   [Omitted by SI 2008/2683, art. 6 and Sch. 1, para. 295.]

History – Reg. 24 omitted by SI 2008/2683, art. 6 and Sch. 1, para. 295, with effect from 3 November 2008.

APPLICATION FOR LEAVE TO APPEAL TO A COMMISSIONER FROM AN APPEAL TRIBUNAL

25   [Omitted by SI 2008/2683, art. 6 and Sch. 1, para. 295.]

History – Reg. 25 omitted by SI 2008/2683, art. 6 and Sch. 1, para. 295, with effect from 3 November 2008.

REVENUE AND CUSTOMS (INSPECTIONS) REGULATIONS 2005

(SI 2005/1133)

Made on 7 April 2005 by the Treasury, in exercise of the powers conferred on them by s. 27(1) and (2) of the Commissioners for Revenue and Customs Act 2005. Operative from 29 April 2005.

CITATION AND COMMENCEMENT

1　　These Regulations may be cited as the Revenue and Customs (Inspections) Regulations 2005 and shall come into force on 29th April 2005.

INTERPRETATION

2(1)　　In these Regulations–

"**the Act**" means the Commissioners for Revenue and Customs Act 2005;

"**appropriate inspectors**" means in relation to–

(a)　an inspection in England and Wales, the inspectors of constabulary,

(b)　an inspection in Scotland, the inspectors of constabulary and the Scottish inspectors acting jointly,

(c)　an inspection in Northern Ireland, the Northern Ireland inspectors;

"**Chairman**" means the Commissioner for the time being designated as chairman of Her Majesty's Revenue and Customs in Letters Patent under section 1(1) of the Act;

"**civil penalty**" means any penalty for which the Commissioners have power under any enactment to make an assessment or a demand;

"**Commissioners**" means the Commissioners for Revenue and Customs;

"**criminal investigation**" means any investigation for the purpose of considering whether an offence has been committed or discovering by whom an offence has been committed;

"**Director**" means the Director of Revenue and Customs Prosecutions;

"**inspectors of constabulary**" means Her Majesty's Inspectors of Constabulary;

"**officer**" means an officer of Revenue and Customs;

"**revenue**" has the meaning given by section 5(4) of the Act;

"**risk**" means the likelihood of an officer or the Commissioners doing or omitting to do something which affects–

(a)　the prevention, detection or investigation of an offence by an officer or the Commissioners,

(b)　any criminal proceedings in England and Wales conducted by the Director,

(c)　any criminal proceedings conducted in Scotland under the direction of the Lord Advocate or a procurator fiscal, or

(d)　any criminal proceedings conducted in Northern Ireland by the Commissioners or the Director of Public Prosecutions for Northern Ireland,

and the possible effect of such an act or omission on the prevention, detection or investigation of that offence or those proceedings.

2(2)　　A reference to the Scottish inspectors or to the Northern Ireland inspectors has the same meaning as in section 27(6) of the Act.

INSPECTION FUNCTIONS: ENGLAND AND WALES

3(1)　　The inspectors of constabulary may carry out inspections in England and Wales for the purpose of assessing the effectiveness of the following conduct–

(a)　any acts or omissions of an officer or the Commissioners in connection with the prevention, detection or investigation of an offence by him or them, or

(b)　any acts or omissions of an officer or the Commissioners in connection with criminal proceedings conducted by the Director.

3(2)　　The inspectors of constabulary may carry out inspections in England and Wales to assess the effectiveness of any matter described in regulation 6.

3(3)   The inspectors of constabulary may exercise the powers under this regulation on their own initiative or at the request of the Chancellor of the Exchequer or the Commissioners but the Chancellor of the Exchequer may not make a request to carry out an inspection in relation to a particular person.

3(4)   The chief inspector of constabulary may include in his report under section 54(4) of the Police Act 1996 (annual reports) a report on the Commissioners and officers.

INSPECTION FUNCTIONS: SCOTLAND

4(1)   The inspectors of constabulary and the Scottish inspectors may jointly carry out inspections in Scotland for the purpose of assessing the effectiveness of the following conduct–

(a)   any acts or omissions of an officer or the Commissioners in connection with the prevention, detection or investigation of an offence by him or them, or

(b)   any acts or omissions of an officer or the Commissioners in connection with criminal proceedings conducted under the direction of the Lord Advocate or a procurator fiscal.

4(2)   The inspectors of constabulary and the Scottish inspectors may jointly carry out inspections in Scotland to assess the effectiveness of any matter described in regulation 6.

4(3)   The inspectors of constabulary and the Scottish inspectors may jointly exercise the powers under this regulation on their own initiative or at the request of the Chancellor of the Exchequer or the Commissioners but the Chancellor of the Exchequer may not make a request to carry out an inspection in relation to a particular person.

INSPECTION FUNCTIONS: NORTHERN IRELAND

5(1)   The Northern Ireland inspectors may carry out inspections in Northern Ireland for the purpose of assessing the effectiveness of the following conduct–

(a)   any acts or omissions of an officer or the Commissioners in connection with the prevention, detection or investigation of an offence by him or them, or

(b)   any acts or omissions of an officer or the Commissioners in connection with criminal proceedings conducted in Northern Ireland by the Commissioners or the Director of Public Prosecutions for Northern Ireland.

5(2)   The Northern Ireland inspectors may carry out inspections in Northern Ireland to assess the effectiveness of any of the matters described in regulation 6.

5(3)   The Northern Ireland inspectors may exercise the powers under this regulation on their own initiative or at the request of the Chancellor of the Exchequer or the Commissioners but the Chancellor of the Exchequer may not make a request to carry out an inspection in relation to a particular person.

INSPECTION OF MEANS OF DEALING WITH RISKS

6   The matters to which regulations 3(2), 4(2) and 5(2) apply are–

(a)   any method devised by or for Her Majesty's Revenue and Customs for identifying and dealing with a risk;

(b)   any measures devised by or for Her Majesty's Revenue and Customs for assuring that an officer or the Commissioners are properly applying that method, and

(c)   the operation of any such method or measures by an officer or the Commissioners.

ACCESS

7(1)   This regulation applies to an inspection carried out under regulation 3, 4 or 5.

7(2)   For the purposes of an inspection the Commissioners shall provide to the appropriate inspectors such of the following as are reasonably required by the appropriate inspectors–

(a)   access to any premises belonging to the Commissioners;

(b)   access to any system operated by or on behalf of the Commissioners for storing and retrieving information electronically;

(c)   any information or documents held by the Commissioners.

7(3)   For the purposes of an inspection an officer shall provide to the appropriate inspectors such information or documents held by him as are reasonably required by the inspectors.

INSPECTIONS OF GUIDANCE

8   The appropriate inspectors may, if the Chancellor of the Exchequer or the Commissioners request them to do so, carry out an inspection of–

(a)   the operation of any guidance issued by the Commissioners to officers for assessing or demanding a civil penalty instead of carrying out a criminal investigation into any matter or vice versa, or

(b)   the operation of any guidance issued by the Commissioners for using other powers to secure any revenue, for the collection and management of which the Commissioners are responsible, instead of assessing or demanding a civil penalty or carrying out a criminal investigation.

REPORTS

9(1)   Where–

(a)   the inspectors of constabulary carry out an inspection under regulation 3 or 8,

(b)   the inspectors of constabulary and the Scottish inspectors jointly carry out an inspection under regulation 4 or 8, or

(c)   the Northern Ireland inspectors carry out an inspection under regulation 5 or 8,

they shall provide a report of the inspection to the Chancellor of the Exchequer.

9(2)   Subject to paragraph (3), the Chancellor of the Exchequer shall arrange for any report received by him to be published.

9(3)   The Chancellor of the Exchequer may exclude from publication under paragraph (2) any part of a report if, in his opinion, the publication of that part–

(a)   would be against the interests of national security;

(b)   might jeopardise the safety of any person;

(c)   would contravene section 29(2) of the Act, or

(d)   might prejudice the prevention or detection of crime or the apprehension or prosecution of offenders.

9(4)   The Chancellor of the Exchequer shall send a copy of the published report to the Chairman.

9(5)   The Commissioners shall–

(a)   prepare comments on the published report;

(b)   send a copy of the comments to the Chancellor of the Exchequer before such date as may be specified by him;

(c)   publish the comments in such manner as appears to the Commissioners to be appropriate.

9(6)   Where the inspectors of constabulary and the Scottish inspectors provide a report of an inspection to the Chancellor of the Exchequer he shall send a copy of the published report to the Scottish Ministers.

APPOINTMENT OF ASSISTANT INSPECTORS AND STAFF OFFICERS

10(1)   Section 56 of the Police Act 1996 (appointment of assistant inspectors and staff officers) shall have effect subject to the following modifications–

(a)   in section 56(1) after "constabulary" insert "for the purpose of carrying out functions under the Revenue and Customs (Inspections) Regulations 2005", and

(b)   in section 56(2) for "Members of a police force" substitute "Officers of Revenue and Customs".

10(2)   Section 34 of the Police (Scotland) Act 1967 (appointment of assistant inspectors and staff officers) shall have effect subject to the following modifications–

(a)   in section 34(1) after "constabulary" insert "for the purpose of carrying out functions under the Revenue and Customs (Inspections) Regulations 2005", and

(b)   in section 34(1A) for "Constables" substitute "Officers of Revenue and Customs".

PAYMENT

11(1)   The Commissioners shall pay to the inspectors of constabulary, for functions carried out by those inspectors under these Regulations, such amount as may be agreed between the Commissioners and those inspectors or, in the absence of an agreement, such amount as the Treasury, after consultation with the Secretary of State, may determine.

Statutory Instruments

11(2) The Commissioners shall pay to the inspectors of constabulary and the Scottish inspectors, for functions carried out jointly by those inspectors under these Regulations, such amount as may be agreed between the Commissioners and those inspectors or, in the absence of an agreement, such amount as the Treasury, after consultation with the Secretary of State and Scottish Ministers, may determine.

11(3) The Commissioners shall pay to the Northern Ireland inspectors for functions carried out by those inspectors under these Regulations such amount as may be agreed between the Commissioners and those inspectors or, in the absence of an agreement, such amount as the Treasury, after consultation with the Secretary of State, may determine.

TONNAGE TAX (FURTHER OPPORTUNITY FOR ELECTION) ORDER 2005

(SI 2005/1449)

Made on 6 June 2005 by the Treasury, in exercise of the powers conferred upon them by para. 11 of Sch. 22 to the Finance Act 2000. Operative from 1 July 2005.

CITATION AND COMMENCEMENT

1 This Order may be cited as the Tonnage Tax (Further Opportunity for Election) Order 2005 and shall come into force on 1st July 2005.

FURTHER OPPORTUNITY FOR ELECTION INTO TONNAGE TAX

2 A tonnage tax election may be made at any time during the period beginning on 1st July 2005 and ending on 31st December 2006 ("the further period").

3(1) In the case of a tonnage tax election made during the further period, paragraph 12 of Schedule 22 to the Finance Act 2000 (when a tonnage tax election takes effect) is adapted as follows.

3(2) In sub-paragraph (2)–

(a)   after "A tonnage tax election" insert "made during the further period"; and

(b)   for "1st January 2000" substitute "1st January 2005".

3(3) In sub-paragraph (3)–

(a)   for "before the end of the initial period" substitute "during the further period"; and

(b)   for "1st January 2000" substitute "1st January 2005".

3(4) In sub-paragraph (4) for "before the end of the initial period" substitute "during the further period".

3(5) At the end of the paragraph add–

"**12(7)** In this paragraph **"the further period"** means the period provided for by article 2 of the Tonnage Tax (Further Opportunity for Election) Order 2005 (S.I. 2005/1449).".

TONNAGE TAX (EXCEPTION OF FINANCIAL YEAR 2005) ORDER 2005

(SI 2005/1480)

Made on 6 June 2005 by the Treasury, in exercise of the powers conferred upon them by para. 22B(2) of Sch. 22 to the Finance Act 2000. Operative from 1 July 2005.

CITATION AND COMMENCEMENT

1 This Order may be cited as the Tonnage Tax (Exception of Financial Year 2005) Order 2005 and shall come into force on 1st July 2005.

EXCEPTION OF FINANCIAL YEAR 2005

2 The financial year 2005 is designated as one in relation to which paragraph 22A of Schedule 22 to the Finance Act 2000 is not to have effect.

SERIOUS ORGANISED CRIME AND POLICE ACT 2005 (COMMENCEMENT NO. 1, TRANSITIONAL AND TRANSITORY PROVISIONS) ORDER 2005

(SI 2005/1521)

Made on 7 June 2005 by the Secretary of State, in exercise of the powers conferred upon him by (a) s. 178(7) of the Serious Organised Crime and Police Act 2005 as respects the provisions brought into force by art. 2 of this Order, after consulting the Scottish Ministers, and (b) s. 178(8), (9) and (10) of that Act as respects the other provisions.

CITATION AND INTERPRETATION

1(1) This Order may be cited as the Serious Organised Crime and Police Act 2005 (Commencement No.1, Transitional and Transitory Provisions) Order 2005.

1(2) In this Order **"the Act"** means the Serious Organised Crime and Police Act 2005.

PROVISIONS COMING INTO FORCE ON 1ST JULY 2005

2(1) Subject to paragraph (2), the following provisions of the Act shall come into force on 1st July 2005–

(a)   [Not relevant.]

(b)   section 99(2) and (3) (civil recovery: interim receivers' expenses etc.);

(c)   section 100 (detention of seized cash: meaning of "48 hours");

(d)   section 101 (appeal in proceedings for forfeiture of cash); and

(e)   [Not relevant.]

2(2) Section 101 of the Act does not apply to a decision of a court in Scotland to order the forfeiture of cash under section 298 of the Proceeds of Crime Act 2002 taken before section 101 comes into force.

3(1) Subject to paragraphs (4) and (5), the following provisions of the Act shall come into force on 1st July 2005–

(a)   section 97 (confiscation orders by magistrates' courts);

(b)   section 99(1) and (4) (civil recovery: interim receivers' expenses etc.);

(c)   sections 103 to 106 (money laundering);

(d)–(ee)   [Not relevant.]

3(2) Except to the extent that it has effect for the purposes of conferring functions on the Scottish Ministers, section 96 (mutual assistance in freezing property or evidence) of the Act shall come into force on 1st July 2005.

3(3) Except to the extent that they extend to Scotland, the following provisions of the Act shall come into force on 1st July 2005–

(a)   section 164 (criminal record checks: verification of identity);

(b)   section 165(1)(a) (certain references to police forces); and

(c)   section 166(2) (further amendments to Police Act 1997 as it applies to Scotland).

3(4) During the period from 1st July 2005 to 31st March 2006 the amendments made by section 104(3), (4) and (6) of the Act are to have effect so that the reference in sections 330(4)(b), 331(4) and 332(4) of the Proceeds of Crime Act 2002, as substituted by section 104 of the Act, to the Director General of the Serious Organised Crime Agency is to have effect as a reference to the Director General of the National Criminal Intelligence Service.

3(5) The references in section 133(2) (notice of demonstrations in designated area) of the Act to a demonstration starting are to take effect as if they were references to demonstrations starting or continuing on or after 1st August 2005.

PROVISIONS COMING INTO FORCE ON 1ST AUGUST 2005

4(1) [Not relevant.]

4(2) [Not relevant.]

PROVISIONS COMING INTO FORCE ON 1ST APRIL 2006

5(1)   Except to the extent that they extend to Scotland, Chapter 1 (investigatory powers of the DPP, etc.) (sections 60 to 70) and Chapter 4 (protection of witnesses and other persons) (sections 82 to 94 and Schedule 5) of Part 2 of the Act shall come into force on 1st April 2006.

5(2)   [Not relevant.]

PENSION PROTECTION FUND (TAX) (2005–06) REGULATIONS 2005

(SI 2005/1907, as amended by SI 2005/3230)

Made on 12 July 2005 by the Treasury, in exercise of the powers conferred upon them by s. 102 of the Finance Act 2005. Operative from 3 August 2005.

CITATION, COMMENCEMENT AND EFFECT

1(1) These Regulations may be cited as the Pension Protection Fund (Tax) (2005–06) Regulations 2005 and shall come into force on 3rd August 2005.

1(2) These Regulations have effect for the period beginning on 6th April 2005 and ending on 5th April 2006 only.

INTERPRETATION

2(1) In this regulation–

(a) paragraph (2) gives the meaning of the abbreviated references to Acts and instruments used in these Regulations, and

(b) paragraph (3) deals with other expressions used in these Regulations.

2(2) In these Regulations–

"the Pensions Act" (without more) means the Pensions Act 2004;

"the 1988 Act" means the Income and Corporation Taxes Act 1988;

"the 1992 Act" means the Taxation of Chargeable Gains Act 1992;

"the 2003 Act" means the Income Tax (Earnings and Pensions) Act 2003;

"the 2005 Order" means the Pensions (Northern Ireland) Order 2005.

2(3) In these Regulations–

"the Board of the Pension Protection Fund" means the body corporate established under section 107 of the Pensions Act;

"exempt approved scheme" means an exempt approved scheme within the meaning of Chapter 1 of Part 14 of the 1988 Act (see section 592(1) of that Act);

"the Fraud Compensation Fund" has the meaning given by regulation 3(1);

"fraud compensation payment"–

(a) in England, Wales and Scotland means a fraud compensation payment within the meaning of Part 2 of the Pensions Act (see section 182(1) of that Act), and

(b) in Northern Ireland means a fraud compensation payment within the meaning of Part 3 of the 2005 Order (see Article 165(1) of that Order);

"the Pension Protection Fund" has the meaning given by regulation 3(1);

"the Pensions Act Funds" has the meaning given by regulation 3(1);

"the Pensions Act levies" means the levies specified in paragraph (2) or (3) of regulation 3, as the case may require.

MEANING OF "THE PENSION PROTECTION FUND" AND OTHER EXPRESSIONS

3(1) In these Regulations–

"the Pension Protection Fund" means the Fund required to be held, managed and applied by the Board of the Pension Protection Fund under section 110(1)(a) of the Pensions Act;

"the Fraud Compensation Fund" means the Fund required to be held, managed and applied by the Board of the Pension Protection Fund under section 110(1)(b) of the Pensions Act;

"the Pensions Act Funds" means the Pension Protection Fund and the Fraud Compensation Fund.

3(2) In England, Wales and Scotland, "the Pensions Act levies" means–

(a) the administration levy referred to in section 117(1) of the Pensions Act;

(b) the initial levy referred to in section 174(1) of that Act;

(c) the risk-based pension protection levy referred to in section 175(1)(a) of that Act;

(d)   the scheme-based pension protection levy referred to in section 175(1)(b) of that Act;

(e)   the fraud compensation levy referred to in section 189(1) of that Act;

(f)   a levy in respect of eligible schemes imposed by regulations made under section 209(7) of that Act (the Ombudsman for the Board of the Pension Protection Fund).

3(3) In Northern Ireland, **"the Pensions Act levies"** means–

(a)   the administration levy referred to in Article 103(1) of the 2005 Order;

(b)   the initial levy referred to in Article 157(1) of that Order;

(c)   the risk-based pension protection levy referred to in Article 158(1)(a) of that Order;

(d)   the scheme-based pension protection levy referred to in Article 158(1)(b) of that Order;

(e)   the fraud compensation levy referred to in Article 171(1) of that Order;

(f)   a levy in respect of eligible schemes imposed by regulations made under Article 191(3) of that Order (the PPF Ombudsman).

APPLICATION OF THE TAX ACTS: GENERAL

4(1) The Tax Acts apply in relation to each of the Pensions Act Funds in the same way as they apply in relation to an exempt approved scheme.

4(2) The general rule in paragraph (1) is subject to the further provisions contained in these Regulations.

APPLICATION OF THE 1988 ACT: FURTHER PROVISIONS

5 Section 592(2) of the 1988 Act (exemption from income tax in respect of investments) applies in respect of income derived from investments or deposits held for each of the Pensions Act Funds–

(a)   as if for "income tax" there were substituted "corporation tax", and

(b)   as if after "income derived from investments or deposits" there were inserted "(including any profit, gain or loss on a loan relationship within the meaning of Chapter 2 of Part 4 of the Finance Act 1996)".

6 Section 592(3) of the 1988 Act (exemption from income tax in respect of underwriting commissions) applies in respect of underwriting commissions applied for the purposes of each of the Pensions Act Funds–

(a)   as if for "income tax" there were substituted "corporation tax", and

(b)   as if for "under Chapter 8 of Part 5 of ITTOIA 2005 (income not otherwise charged)" there were substituted "under Case VI of Schedule D".

7 Section 592(6A) of the 1988 Act (sums paid towards discharge of liability of an employer) applies in relation to the payment, by an employer, of any sum in respect of any of the Pensions Act levies as it applies in relation to the payment of any sum in or towards the discharge of any liability of an employer under the enactments specified in that subsection.

8(1) If at any time section 606 of the 1988 Act (default of scheme administrator etc.) applies in relation to the Pension Protection Fund, the Board of the Pension Protection Fund shall be responsible for the discharge of all duties imposed on the administrator under Chapter 1 of Part 14 of the 1988 Act (whenever arising), and liable for any tax due from the administrator in the administrator's capacity as such (whenever falling due).

8(2) Section 606 of the 1988 Act does not apply in relation to the Fraud Compensation Fund.

9(1) For the purposes of section 611AA of the 1988 Act (definition of the administrator), references to the administrator, in relation to the Pension Protection Fund, are to the person who is, or the persons who are, for the time being, appointed by the Board of the Pension Protection Fund to be responsible for the discharge of all duties imposed on the administrator under Chapter 1 of Part 14 of the 1988 Act.

9(2) Section 611AA of the 1988 Act does not apply in relation to the Fraud Compensation Fund.

10 Schedule 22 to the 1988 Act (reduction of pension fund surpluses) does not apply in relation to either of the Pensions Act Funds.

APPLICATION OF THE 1992 ACT: FURTHER PROVISIONS

11(1) For the purposes of the 1992 Act, any gain accruing to the Board of the Pension Protection Fund from its disposal of investments shall not be a chargeable gain if, or to the extent that, at the time of the disposal, those investments were held by the Board, or on its behalf, for the purposes of one of the Pensions Act Funds.

11(2) In paragraph (1) **"investments"** includes futures contracts and options contracts.

11(3) This regulation is to be construed as one with the 1992 Act.

APPLICATION OF THE FINANCE ACT 1996: FURTHER PROVISIONS

12(1) No credit or debit shall be required or allowed to be brought into account for the purposes of Chapter 2 of Part 4 of the Finance Act 1996 (loan relationships) in respect of the Pensions Compensation Board transfer in the case of the transferor.

12(2) In paragraph (1) **"the Pensions Compensation Board transfer"** means the transfer, by the Pensions Compensation Board to the Board of the Pension Protection Fund, of all property, rights and liabilities to which the Pensions Compensation Board was entitled immediately before the transfer.

APPLICATION OF THE 2003 ACT: FURTHER PROVISIONS

13 Step 5 of section 54(1) of the 2003 Act (calculation of deemed employment payment under arrangements made by intermediaries) applies in relation to a payment, by the intermediary, of any sum in respect of any of the Pensions Act levies in the same way as it applies in relation to any contributions that may be deducted under that step.

14 Section 307 of the 2003 Act (exemption from employment income for death or retirement benefit provision made by employer) applies in relation to the payment of any sum in respect of any of the Pensions Act levies in the same way as it applies in respect of provision made by an employee's employer for a retirement or death benefit.

15(1) Section 583 of the 2003 Act (unauthorised payments of pension income from approved retirement benefits schemes) applies in relation to a payment made out of funds which are held for the purposes of the Pension Protection Fund if the following two conditions are met.

15(2) The first condition is that the payment is not expressly authorised under Part 2 of the Pensions Act.

15(3) The second condition is that the payment is made to or for the benefit of—

(a) an employee, or

(b) an ex-spouse or former civil partner of an employee,

who has entitlements under a scheme for which the Board of the Pension Protection Fund has assumed responsibility under Chapter 3 of Part 2 of the Pensions Act.

History – In reg. 15(3)(b) the words "or former civil partner" inserted by SI 2005/3230, reg. 16(2), with effect from 5 December 2005.

FRAUD COMPENSATION PAYMENTS AND OTHER RELATED PAYMENTS

16(1) Receipt of a payment to which this regulation applies shall not be regarded as a disposal of an asset for the purposes of capital gains tax or for the purposes of corporation tax on chargeable gains.

16(2) This regulation applies to—

(a) a fraud compensation payment under section 185 of the Pensions Act;

(b) an interim payment under section 186 of the Pensions Act;

(c) a fraud compensation payment under Article 168 of the 2005 Order;

(d) an interim payment under Article 169 of the 2005 Order;

(e) a payment made by the Board of the Pension Protection Fund under section 83 of the Pensions Act 1995;

(f) a payment in anticipation made by the Board of the Pension Protection Fund under section 84 of that Act;

(g) a payment made by the Board of the Pension Protection Fund under Article 81 of the Pensions (Northern Ireland) Order 1995;

(h) a payment in anticipation made by the Board of the Pension Protection Fund under Article 82 of that Order.

Statutory Instruments

FRIENDLY SOCIETIES (MODIFICATION OF THE CORPORATION TAX ACTS) REGULATIONS 2005

(SI 2005/2014, as amended by SI 2007/2134 and SI 2008/1937)

Made on 21 July 2005 by the Treasury, in exercise of the powers conferred on them by s. 463 of the Income and Corporation Taxes Act 1988. Operative from 12 August 2005.

History – SI 2005/2014 revoked by SI 2012/3008, reg. 16, with effect in relation to accounting periods beginning on or after 1 January 2013. The text of former SI 2005/2014 read as follows:

"CITATION, COMMENCEMENT AND EFFECT

1(1) These Regulations may be cited as the Friendly Societies (Modification of the Corporation Tax Acts) Regulations 2005 and shall come into force on 12 August 2005.

1(2) These Regulations have effect for accounting periods beginning on or after 1 January 2005.

INTERPRETATION

2 In these Regulations–

"annual return society" means a non-directive friendly society which is required to submit an annual actuarial investigation to the Financial Services Authority under rule 5.1 of the Prudential Sourcebook (Friendly Societies);

"directive friendly society" and **"non-directive friendly society"** have the meanings in the Prudential Sourcebook (Friendly Societies);

"non annual return society" means a non-directive friendly society which is not required to submit an annual actuarial investigation to the Financial Services Authority under rule 5.1 of the Prudential Sourcebook (Friendly Societies);

"partnership pension society" has the meaning in the Prudential Sourcebook (Friendly Societies);

"pension business"–

(a) in relation to any time before 6th April 2006, has the meaning given by section 431B of the Taxes Act, and

(b) in relation to any time on or after 6th April 2006, has the meaning given by section 466(2B) of the Taxes Act;

"prescribed transactions" means any of the following transactions–

(a) the transfer of business as between a friendly society which maintains a separate fund for long-term insurance business and a friendly society which does not do so,

(b) the amalgamation of a friendly society which maintains a separate fund for long-term insurance business and a friendly society which does not do so,

(c) the transfer of the whole or part of the business of a friendly society which does not maintain a separate fund for long-term insurance business to a company which is not a friendly society, and

(d) the conversion of a friendly society which does not maintain a separate fund for long-term insurance business into a company which is not a friendly society,

and for the purposes of this definition a friendly society maintains a separate fund for long-term insurance business if it complies with rule 4.20 of the Prudential Sourcebook (Friendly Societies), whether that rule applies to it or voluntarily;

"the Prudential Sourcebook (Insurers)" means the Interim Prudential Sourcebook for Insurers made by the Financial Services Authority under the Financial Services and Markets Act 2000;

"the Prudential Sourcebook (Friendly Societies)" means the Interim Prudential Sourcebook for Friendly Societies made by the Financial Services Authority under the Financial Services and Markets Act 2000;

"the Taxes Act" means the Income and Corporation Taxes Act 1988.

History – In reg. 2 the definition of "child trust fund business" omitted by SI 2007/2134, reg. 3, with effect for accounting periods beginning on or after 1 January 2007.

In reg. 2 the definition of "individual savings account business" omitted by SI 2007/2134, reg. 3, with effect for accounting periods beginning on or after 1 January 2007.

3 In the Corporation Tax Acts, in their application to a friendly society–

"insurance business transfer scheme" means a scheme which effects–

(a) the transfer of the whole or part of the business of a friendly society to another friendly society;

(b) the amalgamation of two or more friendly societies;

(c) the transfer of the whole or part of the business of a friendly society to a company which is not a friendly society;

(d) the conversion of a friendly society into a company which is not a friendly society; or

(e) the transfer of the whole or part of the long-term business of an insurance company to a friendly society.

MODIFICATION OF SECTION 43F OF THE TAXES ACT

4 [Omitted by SI 2007/2134, reg. 4.]

History – Reg. 4 omitted by SI 2007/2134, reg. 4, with effect in relation to transactions entered into on or after 6 June 2006.

MODIFICATIONS OF SECTION 76 OF THE TAXES ACT

5(1) Paragraphs (2) to (6) prescribe modifications to section 76 of the Taxes Act so far as it applies to the life or endowment business carried on by friendly societies, subject to paragraph (7).

5(2) In subsection (2), after "referable to" insert "taxable";

5(3) In subsection (3), for "line 12, 22 or 25 of Form 40 (the revenue account)" substitute "line 12 or 25 of Form 40 (the revenue account) or column 1 of line 49 of Form 41 (long-term insurance business: analysis of premiums and expenses)";

5(4) In paragraph (a) of Step 1 in subsection (7), after "attributable to" insert "taxable";

5(5) In subsection (8)–

(a) after "attributable to" insert "taxable";

(b) in paragraph (b), for "the Prudential Sourcebook (Insurers)" substitute "the Prudential Sourcebook (Friendly Societies)";

5(5A) In paragraph (a) of subsection (9E)(c) before "basic life" insert "taxable".

5(6) [Omitted by SI 2007/2134, reg. 5.]

5(7) The modifications in paragraphs (3) and (5)(b) only apply to a non-directive friendly society.

History – Reg. 5(5A) inserted by SI 2008/1937, reg. 3, with effect in relation to accounting periods beginning on or after 1 January 2008.

Reg. 5(6) omitted by SI 2007/2134, reg. 5, with effect for accounting periods beginning on or after 1 January 2007.

MODIFICATIONS OF SECTION 431 OF THE TAXES ACT

6(1)   In this regulation–

(a)   paragraphs (2), (2A), (5A) and (5B) prescribe modifications of section 431 of the Taxes Act so far as it applies to long-term business carried on by friendly societies, and

(b)   paragraphs (3) to (5) and (6) prescribe modifications of that section so far as it applies to the long-term business carried on by non-directive friendly societies.

6(2)   In subsection (2) insert the following definitions in the appropriate places–

"annual return society" means a non-directive friendly society which is required to submit an annual actuarial investigation to the Financial Services Authority under rule 5.1 of the Prudential Sourcebook (Friendly Societies);

"directive friendly society" and **"non-directive friendly society"** have the meanings in the Prudential Sourcebook (Friendly Societies);

"non annual return society" means a non-directive friendly society which is not required to submit an annual actuarial investigation to the Financial Services Authority under rule 5.1 of the Prudential Sourcebook (Friendly Societies);

"partnership pension society" has the meaning in the Prudential Sourcebook (Friendly Societies);

"the Prudential Sourcebook (Friendly Societies)" means the Interim Prudential Sourcebook for Friendly Societies made by the Financial Services Authority under the Financial Services and Markets Act 2000;

"tax exempt basic life assurance and general annuity business" means basic life assurance and general annuity business the profits arising from which are exempt from tax by virtue of section 460(1);

"taxable basic life assurance and general annuity business" means basic life assurance and general annuity business other than tax exempt basic life assurance and general annuity business;

"tax exempt PHI business" means–

(a)   business specified in section 466(1)(b) the profits arising from which are exempt from tax by virtue of section 460(1), and

(b)   business other than that specified in section 466(1)(b) which is long term business the profits arising from which are exempt from tax by virtue of section 461(1) or 461B(1);

"taxable PHI business" means–

(a)   business specified in section 466(1)(b) other than tax exempt PHI business, and

(b)   business other than that specified in section 466(1)(b) which is PHI business the profits arising from which are not exempt from tax by virtue of section 461(1) or 461B(1);

"valuation report"–

(a)   in the case of an annual return society, means the abstract of the actuary's report referred to in rule 5.1(2) of the Prudential Sourcebook (Friendly Societies);

(b)   in the case of a non annual return society, means the abstract of the actuary's report referred to in section rule 5.2(2) of the Prudential Sourcebook (Friendly Societies);

6(2A)   In subsection (2) in the definition of "foreign currency assets" before "gross roll-up business" in each place insert "taxable".

6(2B)   In the definition of "foreign business assets" before "overseas life assurance business" in both places insert "taxable".

6(3)   In subsection (2) for the definition of **"liabilities"** substitute–

"liabilities"–

(a)   in relation to an annual return society, means the liabilities of the society estimated as for the purposes of its valuation report (excluding any that have fallen due or been reinsured and any not arising under or in connection with policies or contracts effected as part of the society's insurance business); and

(b)   in relation to a non annual return society means–

(i)   in the case of a society which has sent a valuation report as at the end of a period of account to the Financial Services Authority, the liabilities of the society estimated as for the purposes of its valuation report (excluding any that have fallen due or been reinsured and any not arising under or in connection with policies or contracts effected as part of the society's insurance business), and

(ii)   in the case of a society which has not sent a valuation report as at the end of a period of account to the Financial Services Authority but has caused the actuary to the society to prepare a report on the same basis as the actuary's report referred to in rule 5.2(2) of the Prudential Sourcebook (Friendly Societies), the liabilities of the society estimated as for the purposes of that report (excluding any that have fallen due or been reinsured and any not arising under or in connection with policies or contracts effected as part of the society's insurance business), and

(iii)   in any other case, the liabilities of the society ascertained in accordance with subsections (7) to (9) and (13) below;".

6(4)   In subsection (2) for the definition of **"periodical return"** substitute–

"periodical return"–

(a)   in the case of an annual return society, means the FSC1 return within the meaning in Chapter 5 of the Prudential Sourcebook (Friendly Societies); and

(b)   in the case of a non annual return society, means the FSC2 return within the meaning in that Chapter;".

6(5)   In subsection (2) for the definition of **"value"** substitute–

"value"–

(a)   in relation to an annual return society, means the value of the assets as taken into account for the purposes of the society's periodical return; and

(b)   in relation to the assets of a non annual return society means–

(i)   in the case of a society which has sent a valuation report as at the end of a period of account to the Financial Services Authority, the value of the assets as taken into account for the purposes of its valuation report,

(ii)   in the case of a society which has not sent a valuation report as at the end of a period of account to the Financial Services Authority but has caused the actuary to the society to prepare a report on the same basis as the actuary's report referred to in rule 5.2(2) of the Prudential Sourcebook (Friendly Societies), the value of the assets as taken into account for the purposes of that report, and

(iii)   in any other case, the value of the assets ascertained in accordance with subsections (10) to (13) below;".

6(5A)   In subsection (2YB) before "BLAGAB income" and before "BLAGAB deductions" insert "taxable".

6(5B)   In subsection (2YC)(a)(h) before "basic life assurance" insert "taxable".

6(6)   At the end of the section add the following subsections–

"**431(7)**   For the purposes of paragraph (b)(iii) of the definition of **"liabilities"** in subsection (2) above the closing liabilities of a society for a period of account ("the relevant period of account") shall be ascertained in accordance with the formula–

Statutory Instruments

$$L1 + \ (L2 - L1) \times \frac{T1}{T2}$$

where—

L1 is the liabilities as at the end of the last period of account ("the preceding period of account") which precedes the relevant period of account and for which a relevant report is drawn up;

L2 is the liabilities as at the end of the first period of account ("the subsequent period of account") which follows the relevant period of account and for which a relevant report is drawn up;

T1 is the number of days from the end of the preceding period of account to the end of the relevant period of account;

T2 is the number of days from the end of the preceding period of account to the end of the subsequent period of account;

and where the formula is used to ascertain the closing liabilities for a period of account, the liabilities so ascertained shall be the opening liabilities for the next period of account.

431(8) Where, for those purposes, it is necessary to ascertain the liabilities in any case where a relevant report has not been drawn up at the end of the relevant period of account, the liabilities shall be estimated on a basis compatible with that used in the previous relevant report, having regard to any changes in the nature or extent of the society's business since that report.

431(9) In any case where subsection (8) above has applied, subsection (7) above shall apply as soon as the society is able to ascertain the closing liabilities in accordance with the formula set out in that subsection; and all such adjustments to the liability to tax of the society shall be made, whether by assessment or otherwise, as may be required to give effect to subsection (7) above.

431(10) For the purposes of paragraph (b)(iii) of the definition of "value" in subsection (2) above the value of the assets of a society as at the end of a period of account ("the relevant period of account") shall be ascertained in accordance with the formula—

$$V1 + \ (V2 - V1) \times \frac{T1}{T2}$$

V1 is the value of the assets at the end of the last period of account ("the preceding period of account") which precedes the relevant period of account and for which a relevant report is drawn up;

V2 is the value of the assets as at the end of the first period of account ("the subsequent period of account") which follows the relevant period of account and for which a relevant report is drawn up;

T1 is the number of days from the end of the preceding period of account to the end of the relevant period of account;

T2 is the number of days from the end of the preceding period of account to the end of the subsequent period of account;

and where the formula is used to ascertain the value of the assets as at the end of a period of account, the value so ascertained shall be the value of the assets at the beginning of the next period of account.

431(11) Where, for those purposes, it is necessary to ascertain the value of the assets in any case where a relevant report has not been drawn up at the end of the relevant period of account, the value of the assets shall be estimated on a basis compatible with that used in the previous relevant report, having regard to any changes in the nature or extent of the society's business since that report.

431(12) In any case where subsection (11) above has applied, subsection (10) above shall apply as soon as the society is able to ascertain the value of the assets in accordance with the formula set out in that subsection; and all such adjustments to the liability to tax of the society shall be made, whether by assessment or otherwise, as may be required to give effect to subsection (10) above.

431(13) In subsections (7), (8), (10) and (11) above a "relevant report" means a valuation report or the report specified in paragraph (b)(ii) of the definition of "value" in subsection (2) above.".

History – Reg. 6(1) substituted by SI 2008/1937, reg. 4(2), with effect in relation to accounting periods beginning on or after 1 January 2008.

In reg. 6(2), in the definition of "tax exempt PHI business", in para. (2)(a) the words "section 466(1)(b)(c)" substituted for the words "section 466(1)(d)" and in para. (2)(b) the words "section 466(1)(b) which is long term business" substituted for the words "section 466(1)(d)" by SI 2008/1937, reg. 4(3), with effect in relation to accounting periods beginning on or after 1 January 2008.

In reg. 6(2), the definition of "taxable PHI business" substituted by SI 2008/1937, reg. 4(4), with effect in relation to accounting periods beginning on or after 1 January 2008.

In reg. 6(2), in the inserted definition of "tax exempt PHI business", "PHI" substituted for "class IV" by SI 2007/2134, reg. 6(a), with effect for accounting periods beginning on or after 1 January 2007.

In reg. 6(2), in the inserted definition of "taxable PHI business", "PHI" substituted twice for "class IV" by SI 2007/2134, reg. 6(b), with effect for accounting periods beginning on or after 1 January 2007.

Reg. 6(2A) inserted by SI 2008/1937, reg. 4(5), with effect in relation to accounting periods beginning on or after 1 January 2007.

Reg. 6(2B) inserted by SI 2008/1937, reg. 4(6), with effect in relation to accounting periods beginning on or after 1 January 2008.

Reg. 6(5A) inserted by SI 2008/1937, reg. 4(7), with effect in relation to accounting periods beginning on or after 1 January 2008.

Reg. 6(5B) inserted by SI 2008/1937, reg. 4(7), with effect in relation to accounting periods beginning on or after 1 January 2008.

MEANING OF "LONG-TERM INSURANCE FUND" FOR A SOCIETY WHICH DOES NOT MAINTAIN SEPARATE ASSETS

7 In the case of a friendly society which does not maintain a separate fund for long-term business, the following section shall be treated as inserted after section 431AA of the Taxes Act–

"431AB Friendly societies: meaning of "long-term insurance fund"

431AB(1) Long-term insurance fund means the fund made up of–

(a) assets held primarily for the purposes of long-term business carried on by a friendly society, and

(b) the relevant fraction of each asset held neither primarily for the purposes of long-term business nor primarily for the purposes of some other specific business carried on by that society.

431AB(2)   For the purposes of subsection (1) "the relevant fraction" means–

$$\frac{(0.5 \times (OLB + CLB)) - (0.5 \times (OLA + CLA))}{(0.5 \times (OTB + CTB)) - (0.5 \times (OTA + CTA))}$$

where–

OLB and CLB are respectively the balances brought forward and carried forward in the fund accounts for those accounts within which the society conducts its long-term business;

OLA and CLA are respectively the opening and closing values of the assets already recognised at the beginning and end of the period of account as held for the purposes of long-term business carried on by the society;

OTB and CTB are respectively the total balances brought forward and carried forward on all the society's fund accounts; and

OTA and CTA are respectively the opening and closing values of the assets already recognised at the beginning and end of the period of account as held for the purposes of long-term business or for the purposes of other specific business carried on by the society.

431AB(3)   In calculating the values and balances for the purpose of determining the relevant fraction in subsection (2), a balance on a general management fund or a general reserve fund shall be excluded.

431AB(4)   In subsection (2), references to balances brought forward and carried forward are references to balances brought forward and carried forward as shown in the society's periodical return.".

MODIFICATIONS OF SECTION 431H OF THE TAXES ACT

7A(1)   Paragraphs (2) to (4) prescribe modifications of section 431H of the Taxes Act so far as it applies to the long-term business carried on by friendly societies.

7A(2)   For subsection (1) substitute–

"**431H(1)**   This section applies in relation to a friendly society which carries on two or more of the following–

(a)   life assurance business,

(b)   taxable PHI business and taxable insurance business of any other kind (other than life assurance business), and

(c)   tax exempt PHI business and tax exempt business of any other kind.

(d)   [effectively omitted by SI 2008/1937, reg. 5(3)]".

7A(3)   In subsection (2)–

(a)   omit the word "and" immediately following paragraph (a),

(b)   after paragraph (a) insert–

"(aa)   taxable PHI business,

(ab)   tax exempt PHI business, and", and

(c)   in paragraph (b) for "the" substitute "any".

7A(4)   Omit subsections (3) and (4).

History – In reg. 7A(1), the words "long-term" substituted for the words "life or endowment" by SI 2008/1937, reg. 5(2), with effect in relation to accounting periods beginning on or after 1 January 2008.

In reg. 7A(2), substituted para. (a)–(c) substituted for former (a)–(d) by SI 2008/1937, reg. 5(3), with effect in relation to accounting periods beginning on or after 1 January 2008.

Reg. 7A inserted by SI 2007/2134, reg. 7, with effect for accounting periods beginning on or after 1 January 2007.

MODIFICATION OF SECTION 432 OF THE TAXES ACT

8   [Omitted by SI 2007/2134, reg. 8.]

History – Reg. 8 omitted by SI 2007/2134, reg. 8, with effect for accounting periods beginning on or after 1 January 2007.

MODIFICATIONS OF SECTION 432A OF THE TAXES ACT

9(1)   In this regulation–

(a)   paragraphs (1A), (2), (4) and (4A) prescribe modifications of section 432A of the Taxes Act so far as it applies to long-term business carried on by friendly societies, and

(b)   paragraph (3) prescribes a further modification of that section so far as it applies to the long-term business carried on by partnership pensions societies.

9(1A)   In subsection (1ZC) before "PHI" insert "taxable".

9(2)   After subsection (1A) insert the following subsections–

"**432A(1B)**   Subsections (1C) to (1E) below apply where a friendly society with branches carries on more than one category of business.

432A(1C)   In a case where–

(a)   the society has caused the actuary to the society to prepare, as at the end of an accounting period and as at the end of the previous accounting period, reports prepared on the same basis as–

   (i)   the society's valuation report but which are limited to an investigation of the matters referred to in Rule 5.1(3) of the Prudential Sourcebook (Friendly Societies), or

   (ii)   the society's periodical return but which are limited to an investigation of the matters referred to in Rule 9.4(2) of the Prudential Sourcebook (Insurers),

   in relation to the central body of the society (and not to any of its branches), and

(b)   the society so chooses,

the apportionment of the income, gains or losses of the central body shall be determined by reference to the liabilities and the value of the assets estimated for the purposes of those reports.

432A(1D)   Subject to subsection (1C) above, the apportionment shall be of the income, gains or losses of the society, together with all its branches.

432A(1E)   Where, by virtue of this section, income, gains or losses are referable to any of the following categories, namely–

(a)   gross roll-up business;

(b)   [effectively omitted by SI 2007/2134, reg. 9(3)(a),]

(c)   [effectively omitted by SI 2007/2134, reg. 9(3)(a),]

(d)   taxable basic life assurance and general annuity business, or

(e)   taxable PHI business,

that income, or those gains or losses, shall be attributable to the central body of the society and not to any of its branches unless the society shows that any business within any of those categories was written by a branch, in which case the income, gains or losses referable to any of those categories shall be attributed to any such branch in such manner as is just and reasonable.".

9(3) After subsection (1E) (inserted by paragraph (2)) insert the following subsection–

"**432A(1F)** In the case of a partnership pension society, the definitions of "liabilities" and "value" in section 431(2) shall not apply, and any apportionment required by this section shall be made in such manner as is just and reasonable.".

9(4) In subsection (2), for paragraphs (a) to (c) substitute–

"(a) taxable basic life assurance and general annuity business,

(b) tax exempt basic life assurance and general annuity business,

(c) gross roll-up business,

(d) taxable PHI business, and

(e) tax exempt PHI business;".

9(4A) For subsection (3A) substitute–

"**432A(3A)** Amounts falling within–

(a) section 442A, or

(b) section 85(2C) of the Finance Act 1989,

are directly referable to taxable basic life assurance and general annuity business to the extent that the amounts are referable to that business.".

9(5) For subsections (6) to (6C) substitute–

"**432A(6)** For the purposes of subsection (5) above, "the relevant fraction", in relation to taxable basic life assurance and general annuity business is–

$$\frac{A}{A+B+C+D+E}$$

where:

A is the aggregate of–

(a) the mean of the opening and closing liabilities of the taxable basic life assurance business (but taking that mean to be nil if it would otherwise be below nil) reduced (but not below nil) by the mean of the opening and closing net values of any assets directly referable to that category, and

(b) the mean of the appropriate parts (that is, the parts relating to that category) of the opening and closing amounts of the free assets amounts;

B is the aggregate of–

(a) the mean of the opening and closing liabilities of the tax exempt basic life assurance business (but taking that mean to be nil if it would otherwise be below nil) reduced (but not below nil) by the mean of the opening and closing net values of any assets directly referable to that category, and

(b) the mean of the appropriate parts (that is, the parts relating to that category) of the opening and closing amounts of the free assets amounts;

C is the aggregate of–

(a) the mean of the opening and closing liabilities of the gross roll-up business (but taking that mean to be nil if it would otherwise be below nil) reduced (but not below nil) by the mean of the opening and closing net values of any assets directly referable to that category, and

(b) the mean of the appropriate parts (that is, the parts relating to that category) of the opening and closing amounts of the free assets amounts;

D is the aggregate of–

(a) the mean of the opening and closing liabilities of the taxable PHI business (but taking that mean to be nil if it would otherwise be below nil) reduced (but not below nil) by the mean of the opening and closing net values of any assets directly referable to that category, and

(b) the mean of the appropriate parts (that is, the parts relating to that category) of the opening and closing amounts of the free assets amounts; and

E is the aggregate of–

(a) the mean of the opening and closing liabilities of the tax exempt PHI business (but taking that mean to be nil if it would otherwise be below nil) reduced (but not below nil) by the mean of the opening and closing net values of any assets directly referable to that category, and

(b) the mean of the appropriate parts (that is, the parts relating to that category) of the opening and closing amounts of the free assets amounts.

432A(6A) For the purposes of subsection (5) above, "the relevant fraction", in relation to tax exempt basic life assurance and general annuity business, is–

$$\frac{B}{A+B+C+D+E}$$

where *A*, *B*, *C*, *D* and *E* have the same meaning as in subsection (6) above.

432A(6B) For the purposes of subsection (5) above, "the relevant fraction", in relation to gross roll-up business, is–

$$\frac{C}{A+B+C+D+E}$$

where *A*, *B*, *C*, *D* and *E* have the same meaning as in subsection (6) above.

432A(6C) For the purposes of subsection (5) above, "the relevant fraction", in relation to taxable PHI business, is–

$$\frac{D}{A+B+C+D+E}$$

where *A*, *B*, *C*, *D* and *E* have the same meaning as in subsection (6) above.

432A(6D) For the purposes of subsection (5) above, "the relevant fraction", in relation to tax exempt PHI business, is–

$$\frac{E}{A+B+C+D+E}$$

where *A*, *B*, *C*, *D* and *E* have the same meaning as in subsection (6) above.

432A(6E) But if the denominator found in accordance with subsection (6), (6A), (6B), (6C) or (6D) above is nil, the relevant fraction for the purposes of subsection (5) above in relation to the category of business in question is such fraction as is just and reasonable."

9(6)   [Effectively omitted by SI 2007/2134, reg. 9(4) – see history note.]
9(7)   In subsection (7) for "and (6B)" substitute ", (6B), (6C) and (6D)".
9(8)   Omit–
(a)   paragraph (b) of subsection (8) and the word "and" which precedes it;
(b)   subsections (8ZA), (8A) and (8B).

History – Reg. 9(1) substituted by SI 2008/1937, reg. 6(2), with effect in relation to accounting periods beginning on or after 1 January 2008.
In reg. 9(1) words ", (4) to (8)" substituted for "and (4)" by SI 2007/2134, reg. 9(3)(a), with effect for accounting periods beginning on or after 1 January 2007.
Reg. 9(1A) inserted by SI 2008/1937, reg. 6(3), with effect in relation to accounting periods beginning on or after 1 January 2008.
In reg. 9(2), in the inserted subsection (1E), para. (a) substituted for former para. (a)-(c) by SI 2007/2134, reg. 9(3)(a), with effect for accounting periods beginning on or after 1 January 2007.
In reg. 9(2), in the inserted subsection (1E), in para. (e) "PHI" substituted for the words "class IV" by SI 2007/2134, reg. 9(3)(b), with effect for accounting periods beginning on or after 1 January 2007.
Reg. 9(4A) inserted by SI 2008/1937, reg. 6(4), with effect in relation to accounting periods beginning on or after 1 January 2008.
Reg. 9(4), (5), (7) and (8) substituted for former reg. 9(4)–(8) by SI 2007/2134, reg. 9(4), with effect for accounting periods beginning on or after 1 January 2007. It would appear that reg. 9(6) has not been used in error.

MODIFICATION OF SECTION 432B OF THE TAXES ACT
9A   [Omitted by SI 2008/1937, reg. 7.]

History – Reg. 9A omitted by SI 2008/1937, reg. 7, with effect in relation to accounting periods beginning on or after 1 January 2008.

MODIFICATIONS OF SECTION 432AA OF THE TAXES ACT
10(1)   Paragraphs (2) to (4) prescribe modifications of subsection (4) of section 432AA of the Taxes Act so far as it applies to the long-term business carried on by friendly societies.
10(2)   In paragraph (c) at the beginning, insert "taxable".
10(3)   After paragraph (c) insert the following paragraph–
"(ca)   tax exempt basic life assurance and general annuity business;".
10(4)   For paragraph (d) substitute the following paragraphs–
"(d)   taxable PHI business;
(e)   tax exempt PHI business."

History – In reg. 10(1), the words "long-term" substituted for the words "life or endowment" by SI 2008/1937, reg. 8, with effect for accounting periods beginning on or after 1 January 2008.
In reg. 10(4), in substituted para. (d) and (e), "PHI" substituted for "class IV" by SI 2007/2134, reg. 11, with effect for accounting periods beginning on or after 1 January 2007.

MODIFICATIONS OF SECTION 432AB OF THE TAXES ACT
11(1)   Paragraphs (2) and (3) prescribe modifications of section 432AB of the Taxes Act so far as it applies to the life or endowment business carried on by friendly societies.
11(2)   In subsection (3) before "basic" insert "taxable".
11(3)   In subsection (4) before "basic" insert "taxable".

MODIFICATIONS OF SECTION 432E OF THE TAXES ACT
12(1)   Section 432E of the Taxes Act shall apply to the life or endowment business of a friendly society with the following modifications.
12(2)   In subsection (1)(a), after the words "subsections (2) and (2A)" insert "or, as the case may be, subsection (2B)".
12(3)   After subsection (2A), the following subsection shall be treated as inserted–
"**432E(2B)**   In a case where an amount is taken into account under subsection (2) of section 83 of the Finance Act 1989 by virtue of subsection (2F) of that section, the amount determined under subsection (2) above is increased by

$$\frac{CAS}{AS} \times RP$$

where–
CAS and AS have the same meanings as in subsection (2) above; and
RP is the amount taken into account under subsection (2) of section 83 of the Finance Act 1989 by virtue of subsection (2F) of that section.".

History – In reg. 12(2) "(1)(a)" substituted for "(1)" by SI 2007/2134, reg. 12, with effect for accounting periods beginning on or after 1 January 2007.
13   [Omitted by SI 2007/2134, reg. 13.]

History – Reg. 13 omitted by SI 2007/2134, reg. 13, with effect for accounting periods beginning on or after 1 January 2007.

MODIFICATIONS OF SECTION 436A OF THE TAXES ACT
13A(1)   Paragraph (2) prescribes a modification of section 436A of the Taxes Act so far as it applies to the life or endowment business carried on by non annual return societies other than partnership pension societies.
13A(2)   At the end of subsection (2) add–
", and
(c)   the opening liabilities and the closing liabilities of the society shall be ascertained in accordance with paragraph (b) of the definition of "liabilities" in subsection (2) of section 431, and the definition of "closing liabilities" in that subsection shall not apply.".
13A(3)   Paragraph (4) prescribes a modification of section 436A of the Taxes Act so far as it applies to the life or endowment business carried on by partnership pension societies.
13A(4)   At the end add the following subsections–
"**436A(8)**   Subject to subsection (11) below, subsection (9) below applies where the amount shown in respect of Item 3 of Part I of Schedule 7 to the Friendly Societies (Accounts and Related Provisions) Regulations 1994 ("the Item 3 amount") is a positive amount; and subsection (10) below applies where the Item 3 amount is a negative amount.

436A(9)   The amount of the increase in liabilities to policy holders (that is to say, the excess of the society's closing liabilities to policy holders over its opening liabilities to policy holders) that is taken into account for the purpose of computing the profits arising to the society from pension business shall be the Item 3 amount.

436A(10)   The amount of the decrease in liabilities to policy holders (that is to say, the excess of the society's opening liabilities to policy holders over its closing liabilities to policy holders) that is taken into account for the purpose of computing the profits arising to the society from pension business shall be the Item 3 amount.

436A(11)   Subject to subsection (13) below, in a case where, for any period of account, income or gains arising to a society—

(a)   derive directly or indirectly from a transaction or transactions with a member or members of the society, and

(b)   exceed the amount of the income or gains which would have arisen to the society if any transaction mentioned in paragraph (a) above had been a transaction at arm's length,

436A(12)   For the purposes of subsection (11) above a person associated with a member shall be treated as a member; and "associated" shall be construed in accordance with section 783(10).

436A(13)   In any case where—

(a)   there has been a transaction consisting of the disposal of an asset to a friendly society ("the earlier disposal"),

(b)   section 17(1)(a) of the 1992 Act has applied on the earlier disposal,

(c)   the friendly society subsequently makes a disposal of the asset ("the later disposal"), and

(d)   subsection (11) above applies (or would, apart from this subsection, apply) to the later disposal,

any gains accruing to the society on the later disposal shall, for the purposes of subsection (11) above, be reduced by the excess (if any) of the amount treated, by virtue of the application of section 17(1)(a) of the 1992 Act, as the consideration for the earlier disposal over the actual amount of the consideration for the earlier disposal.".

History – Reg. 13A inserted by SI 2007/2134, reg. 14, with effect for accounting periods beginning on or after 1 January 2007.

MODIFICATIONS OF SECTION 437 OF THE TAXES ACT

14(1)   Paragraphs (2) and (3) prescribe modifications of section 437 of the Taxes Act so far as it applies to the life or endowment business carried on by friendly societies.

14(2)   In subsection (1C)(a), before "basic" insert "taxable".

14(3)   In subsection (1F) at the end insert–

""**taxable basic life assurance and general annuity business**" means basic life assurance and general annuity business the profits arising from which do not fall to be exempted from tax by virtue of section 460(1), and for the purposes of this definition it shall be assumed that the friendly society has made a claim for exemption from tax under that provision.".

MODIFICATIONS OF SECTION 438B OF THE TAXES ACT

15   [Omitted by SI 2007/2134, reg. 15.]

History – Reg. 15 omitted by SI 2007/2134, reg. 15, with effect for accounting periods beginning on or after 1 January 2007.

MODIFICATIONS OF SECTION 440 OF THE TAXES ACT

16(1)   The modifications of section 440 of the Taxes Act given in paragraphs (2) and (3) apply–

(a)   where a friendly society begins or ceases to maintain a separate fund for long-term insurance business, or

(b)   in relation to a prescribed transaction.

16(2)   In subsection (1), for "If" substitute "Subject to subsection (4A) below, if".

16(2A)   In subsection (3) after "(d)" insert "(da)".

16(3)   After subsection (4) insert the following subsection–

"**440(4A)**   Subsection (1) above shall not have effect in relation to any assets which–

(a)   cease to be within the category set out in paragraph (e) of subsection (4) above and come within the category set out in paragraph (f) of that subsection, or

(b)   cease to be within the category set out in paragraph (f) of subsection (4) above and come within the category set out in paragraph (e) of that subsection.".

16(4)   Paragraph (5) prescribes a modification of section 440(4) of the Taxes Act so far as it applies to the life or endowment business carried on by friendly societies.

16(5)   For paragraph (d) substitute–

"(d)   assets linked solely to taxable basic life assurance and general annuity business;

(da)   assets linked solely to tax exempt basic life assurance and general annuity business;".

History – Reg. 16(2A) inserted by SI 2007/2134, reg. 16, with effect for accounting periods beginning on or after 1 January 2007.

MODIFICATIONS OF SECTION 440A OF THE TAXES ACT

17(1)   Paragraphs (2) and (3) prescribe modifications of section 440A of the Taxes Act so far as it applies to the life or endowment business carried on by friendly societies.

17(2)   In subsection (2)(a)–

(a)   in sub-paragraph (i) before "basic life assurance" insert "taxable";

(b)   after sub-paragraph (i) insert–

"(ia)   tax exempt basic life assurance and general annuity business, or".

17(3)   Omit subsection (3).

History – Reg. 17 substituted by SI 2007/2134, reg. 17, with effect for accounting periods beginning on or after 1 January 2007.

MODIFICATIONS OF SECTION 441 OF THE TAXES ACT

18   [Omitted by SI 2007/2134, reg. 18(a).]

History – Reg. 18 omitted by SI 2007/2134, reg. 18(a), with effect for accounting periods beginning on or after 1 January 2007.

MODIFICATION OF SECTION 442A(1) OF THE TAXES ACT

19(1)   Paragraph (2) prescribes a modification of section 442A(1) of the Taxes Act so far as it applies to the life or endowment business carried on by friendly societies.

19(2)   Before "basic" insert "taxable".

MODIFICATION OF SECTION 460(2) OF THE TAXES ACT

20   [Omitted by SI 2007/2134, reg. 18(b).]

History – Reg. 20 omitted by SI 2007/2134, reg. 18(b), with effect for accounting periods beginning on or after 1 January 2007.

MODIFICATIONS OF SECTION 502H OF THE TAXES ACT

20A [Omitted by SI 2008/1937, reg. 9.]

History – Reg. 20A omitted by SI 2008/1937, reg. 9, with effect for accounting periods beginning on or after 1 January 2008.

MODIFICATION OF SECTION 587B OF THE TAXES ACT

21 [Omitted by SI 2007/2134, reg. 20.]

History – Reg. 21 omitted by SI 2007/2134, reg. 20, with effect for accounting periods beginning on or after 1 January 2007.

MODIFICATIONS OF SECTION 755A OF THE TAXES ACT

22(1) Paragraphs (2) to (9) prescribe modifications of section 755A of the Taxes Act so far as it applies to the life or endowment business carried on by friendly societies.

22(2) In subsections (3) and (10) before "BLAGAB apportioned profit", in each place where those words occur, insert "taxable".

22(3) In subsection (4) after "gross roll-up business" insert ", or tax exempt basic life assurance and general annuity business,".

22(4) In subsection (4A) before "basic life assurance" insert "taxable".

22(5) In subsection (6)(c) after "gross roll-up business" insert "or tax exempt basic life assurance and general annuity business".

22(6) In subsection (11) before "BLAGAB" insert "taxable".

22(7) [Effectively omitted by SI 2007/2134, reg. 21(2).]

22(8) In subsection (12), in the definition of "BLAGAB apportioned profit"–
(a)   before "BLAGAB" insert "taxable";
(b)   before "basic life assurance" insert "taxable".

22(9) In subsection (13)(a) before "basic life assurance" insert "taxable".

History – Reg. 22(3)–(6) substituted for former reg. 22(3)–(7) by SI 2007/2134, reg. 21(2), with effect for accounting periods beginning on or after 1 January 2007.
Reg. 22(9) substituted by SI 2007/2134, reg. 21(3), with effect for accounting periods beginning on or after 1 January 2007.

MODIFICATIONS OF SECTION 804B OF THE TAXES ACT

23(1) Paragraphs (2) to (5) prescribe modifications of section 804B of the Taxes Act so far as it applies to the long-term business carried on by friendly societies.

23(2) The modification of section 804B(4)(a) prescribed by paragraph (3)(a) shall not apply where section 804B(4) is applied by virtue of regulation 4(3) and (5) of the Double Taxation Relief (Surrender of Relievable Tax within a Group) Regulations 2001.

23(3) In subsection (4)–
(a)   in paragraph (a) before "basic" insert "taxable";
(b)   for paragraph (b) substitute–
"(b)   taxable PHI business,".

23(4) [Omitted by SI 2007/2134, reg. 22(3).]

23(5) [Omitted by SI 2007/2134, reg. 22(3).]

History – In reg. 23(1), the words "long-term" substituted for the words "life or endowment" by SI 2008/1937, reg. 10, with effect for accounting periods beginning on or after 1 January 2008.
In reg. 23(3)(b) "PHI" substituted for "class IV" by SI 2007/2134, reg. 22(2), with effect for accounting periods beginning on or after 1 January 2007.
Reg. 23(4) and (5) omitted by SI 2007/2134, reg. 22(3), with effect for accounting periods beginning on or after 1 January 2007.

MODIFICATIONS OF SECTION 804D OF THE TAXES ACT

24(1) Paragraphs (2) to (4) prescribe modifications of section 804D of the Taxes Act so far as it applies to the life or endowment business carried on by non annual return societies.

24(2) In subsection (2) for the words from "by which" to the end substitute–
"by which–
(a)   so much of the total of the amounts shown, in the society's accounts for that period, in respect of Item 1 of Part I of Schedule 7 to the Friendly Societies (Accounts and Related Provisions) Regulations 1994 as is referable to that category of business,
exceeds
(b)   so much of any commissions payable and any expenses of management incurred in connection with the acquisition of the business, as shown in those accounts in respect of Item 2(f) and (g) of Part I of that Schedule, as is referable to that category of business.".

24(3) In subsection (4) for the words from "claims incurred" to the end substitute "total income of that category determined under subsection (2) above.".

24(4) Omit subsection (5).

MODIFICATION OF PARAGRAPH 5 OF SCHEDULE 19AA TO THE TAXES ACT

25 [Omitted by SI 2007/2134, reg. 23.]

History – Reg. 25 omitted by SI 2007/2134, reg. 23, with effect for accounting periods beginning on or after 1 January 2007.

MODIFICATIONS OF SECTION 82 OF THE FINANCE ACT 1989

26(1) Where section 82(1)(b) of the Finance Act 1989 applies, as originally enacted, by virtue of paragraph 1(6) of Schedule 33 to the Finance Act 2003–
(a)   in the case of a friendly society, subsection (1)(b) of that section shall be modified so that for "section 9.6 of the Prudential Sourcebook (Insurers)" there is substituted "rule 5.1 of the Prudential Sourcebook (Friendly Societies)";
(b)   in the case of a non annual return society, at the end of that section there is treated as inserted–
"82(9)   Where a period of account ends on a day to which a valuation report has not been prepared, or begins on a day immediately following such a day, the amount of any unappropriated surplus on valuation for the purposes of subsections (1)(b) and (4) shall be the amount which was taken into account at the end of the last period of account for which a valuation report was prepared.".

MODIFICATIONS OF SECTION 82B OF THE FINANCE ACT 1989

27(1) In the case of a non-directive friendly society, section 82B of the Finance Act 1989 shall apply with the following modifications.

27(2) In paragraph (a) of subsection (1), for "section 9.6 of the Prudential Sourcebook (Insurers)" substitute "Rule 5.1 of the Prudential Sourcebook (Friendly Societies)".

27(3) In paragraph (b) of subsection (1), for "Rule 9.10(c) of the Prudential Sourcebook (Insurers)" substitute "Paragraph 2(6) of Appendix 4 to the Prudential Sourcebook (Friendly Societies)".

27(4) Where that friendly society is not required to submit an annual actuarial investigation to the Financial Services Authority under Rule 5.1 of the Prudential Sourcebook (Friendly Societies)—

(a)   in subsection (2) for "the period of account immediately preceding the period of account in question" substitute "the period of account for which a report was submitted which most closely precedes the period of account in question ("the most closely preceding period of account")";

(b)   in subsection (3), for "that immediately preceding period of account", wherever those words occur, substitute "the most closely preceding period of account".

MODIFICATION OF SECTION 83 OF THE FINANCE ACT 1989

28(1) Paragraph (2) prescribes a modification of section 83 of the Finance Act 1989 so far as it applies to the life or endowment business carried on by annual return societies.

28(2) After subsection (2E) insert the following subsections—

"**83(2F)** Where, in a case where the expenses charged in the management fund exceed the amount transferred from all revenue account funds, the amount determined in accordance with subsection (2G) below shall be taken into account as an increase in value of the assets of the long-term insurance fund.

83(2G) Subject to subsection (2I) below, that amount is the amount found by—

(a)   taking the aggregate amount of the society's investment income recognised in the account of the management fund;

(b)   either adding any increase in value of the assets of the management fund, or subtracting any decrease in value of the assets of the management fund, as the case may be; and

(c)   multiplying the amount so found by the fraction specified in subsection (2H) below.

83(2H) That fraction is the fraction of which—

(a)   the numerator is the amount transferred from the revenue account recognised for the purposes of section 83A(2), and

(b)   the denominator is the amount transferred from all revenue account funds.

83(2I) Where, apart from this subsection, the amount determined in accordance with subsection (2G) above would be a negative amount, the amount determined in accordance with that subsection shall be taken to be nil.".

MODIFICATION OF SECTION 83A OF THE FINANCE ACT 1989 – ANNUAL RETURN

29(1) Paragraph (2) prescribes a modification of section 83A of the Finance Act 1989 so far as it applies to the life or endowment business carried on by annual return societies.

29(2) For subsection (2) substitute—

"**83A(2)** The accounts recognised for the purposes of those sections are—

(a)   a revenue account included in, or supplied to the Financial Services Authority with, the society's valuation report which contains items relating to the society's life or endowment business in respect of the whole of the society's long-term business;

(b)   any separate revenue account included in, or supplied to the Financial Services Authority with, the society's valuation report which contains items relating to the society's life or endowment business in respect of a with-profits fund (see subsection (6)).

83A(2A) In subsection (2) above "life or endowment business" has the meaning given by section 466(1) of the Taxes Act 1988.".

MODIFICATIONS OF SECTION 83A OF THE FINANCE ACT 1989 – NON-ANNUAL RETURN SOCIETIES

30(1) Paragraphs (2) and (3) prescribe modifications of Section 83A of the Finance Act 1989 so far as it applies to the life or endowment business carried on by non annual return societies.

30(2) For subsection (2) substitute—

"**83A(2)** The account recognised for the purposes of those sections is the income and expenditure account prepared in accordance with the requirements of the Friendly Societies (Accounts and Related Provisions) Regulations 1994."

30(3) Omit subsections (3) to (4).

History – In reg. 30(3) "(3) to (4)" substituted for "(3) and (4)" by SI 2007/2134, reg. 24, with effect for accounting periods beginning on or after 1 January 2007.

MODIFICATIONS OF SECTION 85 OF THE FINANCE ACT 1989

31(1) Paragraph (2) prescribes a modification of section 85(1) and (2C) of the Finance Act 1989 so far as they apply to the life or endowment business carried on by friendly societies.

31(2) Before "basic life assurance", wherever those words occur, insert "taxable".

MODIFICATION OF SECTION 88 OF THE FINANCE ACT 1989

32(1) Paragraph (2) prescribes a modification of section 88(3)(a) of the Finance Act 1989 so far as it applies to the life or endowment business carried on by friendly societies.

32(2) Before "basic life assurance", wherever those words occur, insert "taxable".

History – In reg. 32, the words "88(3)(a)" substituted for the words "88(3A)(a) and (3B)" and the words "it applies" substituted for the words "they apply" by SI 2008/1937, reg. 11, with effect for accounting periods beginning on or after 1 January 2008.

Reg. 32 substituted by SI 2007/2134, reg. 25, with effect for accounting periods beginning on or after 1 January 2007.

MODIFICATION OF PARAGRAPH 16 OF SCHEDULE 7 TO THE FINANCE ACT 1991

33(1) Paragraph (2) prescribes a modification of paragraph 16 of Schedule 7 to the Finance Act 1991 so far as it applies to the life or endowment business carried on by friendly societies.

33(2) In sub-paragraph (7), in the definition of "general annuity contract", for "referable to general annuity business" substitute ""referable to taxable general annuity business", and "taxable general annuity business" means general annuity business the profits arising from which do not fall to be exempted from tax by virtue of section 460(1) of the Taxes Act 1988, and for the purposes of this definition it shall be assumed that the friendly society has made a claim for exemption from tax under that provision".

MODIFICATION OF PARAGRAPH 17 OF SCHEDULE 7 TO THE FINANCE ACT 1991

34 [Omitted by SI 2007/2134, reg. 26.]

History – Reg. 34 omitted by SI 2007/2134, reg. 26, with effect for accounting periods beginning on or after 1 January 2007.

MODIFICATION OF SECTION 210A OF THE 1992 ACT

34A(1) In the case of a friendly society, section 210A of the Taxation of Chargeable Gains Act 1992 shall be modified as follows.

34A(2) In subsection (13), in the definitions of "BLAGAB allowable losses" and "BLAGAB chargeable gains", before "basic life assurance" insert "taxable".

History – Reg. 34A inserted by SI 2007/2134, reg. 27, with effect for accounting periods beginning on or after 1 January 2007.

MODIFICATIONS OF SECTION 210B OF THE 1992 ACT

35(1) In the case of a friendly society, section 210B of the Taxation of Chargeable Gains Act 1992(d) shall be modified as follows.

35(2) In subsection (7)(a), before "BLAGAB internal linked fund" insert "taxable".

35(3) In subsection (8), for the definition of "BLAGAB internal linked fund" substitute–

""**taxable BLAGAB internal linked fund**" means an internal linked fund all the assets appropriated to which are linked solely to taxable basic life assurance and general annuity business,".

MODIFICATIONS OF SECTION 211ZA OF THE 1992 ACT

36(1) In the case of a friendly society, section 211ZA of the Taxation of Chargeable Gains Act 1992 shall be modified as follows.

36(2) In subsection (7), before "basic life assurance and general annuity business" insert "taxable".

36(3) In subsection (10), before "basic life assurance and general annuity business" insert "taxable".

MODIFICATION OF SECTION 212 OF THE 1992 ACT

37(1) Paragraph (2) prescribes a modification of section 212 of the 1992 Act so far as it applies to the life or endowment business carried on by friendly societies.

37(2) In subsection (2) after "gross roll-up business" insert "or tax exempt basic life assurance and general annuity business".

History – Reg. 37(2) substituted by SI 2007/2134, reg. 28, with effect for accounting periods beginning on or after 1 January 2007.

MODIFICATION OF SECTION 213 OF THE 1992 ACT

38(1) Paragraph (2) prescribes a modification of section 213(1A) of the 1992 Act so far as it applies to the life or endowment business carried on by friendly societies.

38(2) In paragraph (a) before "basic life" insert "taxable".

MODIFICATION OF SECTION 214(1) OF THE 1992 ACT

39 [Omitted by SI 2007/2134, reg. 29.]

History – Reg. 39 omitted by SI 2007/2134, reg. 29, with effect for accounting periods beginning on or after 1 January 2007.

MODIFICATION OF PARAGRAPH 12 OF SCHEDULE 9 TO THE FINANCE ACT 1996

39A(1) Paragraph (2) prescribes a modification of paragraph 12 of Schedule 9 to the Finance Act 1996 so far as it applies to the life or endowment business carried on by friendly societies.

39A(2) In sub-paragraph (3) after "(d)" insert ", (da)".

History – Reg. 39A inserted by SI 2007/2134, reg. 30, with effect for accounting periods beginning on or after 1 January 2007.

MODIFICATIONS OF SCHEDULE 11 TO THE FINANCE ACT 1996

40(1) Paragraphs (2) and (3) prescribe modifications of Schedule 11 to the Finance Act 1996 so far as it applies to the long-term business carried on by friendly societies.

40(2) In paragraph 4(1)(a), (2)(a), (7) and (10) before "basic life assurance", wherever those words occur insert "taxable".

40(2A) In paragraph 3A(5) before "PHI" insert "taxable" after "(6B)" insert ", (6C), (6D)".

40(3) [Omitted by SI 2007/2134, reg. 31(4).]

History – In reg. 40(1), the words "long-term" substituted for the words "life or endowment" by SI 2008/1937, reg. 12(2), with effect for accounting periods beginning on or after 1 January 2008.

In reg. 40(2), the word "paragraph" substituted for the words "paragraphs 2(1) and" by SI 2008/1937, reg. 12(3), with effect for accounting periods beginning on or after 1 January 2008.

In reg. 40(2), the words ", (2)(a), (7) and (10) before "basic life assurance", wherever those words occur" substituted for the words "before "basic life assurance"" by SI 2007/2134, reg. 31(2), with effect for accounting periods beginning on or after 1 January 2007.

Reg. 40(2A) inserted by SI 2007/2134, reg. 31(3), with effect for accounting periods beginning on or after 1 January 2007.

Reg. 40(3) omitted by SI 2007/2134, reg. 31(4), with effect for accounting periods beginning on or after 1 January 2007.

MODIFICATIONS OF SCHEDULE 11 TO THE FINANCE ACT 1996 AS MODIFIED IN RELATION TO CAPITAL REDEMPTION BUSINESS

41 [Omitted by SI 2007/2134, reg. 32(a).]

History – Reg. 41 omitted by SI 2007/2134, reg. 32(a), with effect for accounting periods beginning on or after 1 January 2007.

MODIFICATION OF PARAGRAPH 18 OF SCHEDULE 12 TO THE FINANCE ACT 1997

42 [Omitted by SI 2007/2134, reg. 32(b).]

History – Reg. 42 omitted by SI 2007/2134, reg. 32(b), with effect for accounting periods beginning on or after 1 January 2007.

Statutory Instruments

MODIFICATIONS OF PARAGRAPH 4 OF SCHEDULE 6 TO THE FINANCE ACT 1999

43   [Omitted by SI 2007/2134, reg. 32(c).]

History – Reg. 43 omitted by SI 2007/2134, reg. 32(c), with effect for accounting periods beginning on or after 1 January 2007.

MODIFICATION OF SECTION 255 OF THE CAPITAL ALLOWANCES ACT 2001

43A(1)   Paragraph (2) prescribes a modification of section 255 of the Capital Allowances Act 2001 so far as it applies to the long-term business carried on by friendly societies.

43A(2)   In subsection (1)–

(a)   for "basic life assurance and general annuity business" substitute "taxable basic life assurance and general annuity business, tax exempt basic life assurance and general annuity business", and

(b)   for "and PHI business" substitute ", taxable PHI business and tax exempt PHI business".

History – In reg. 43A(1), the words "long-term" substituted for the words "life or endowment" by SI 2008/1937, reg. 13(2), with effect for accounting periods beginning on or after 1 January 2008.

Reg. 43A(2) substituted by SI 2008/1937, reg. 13(3), with effect for accounting periods beginning on or after 1 January 2008.

Reg. 43A inserted by SI 2007/2134, reg. 33, with effect for accounting periods beginning on or after 1 January 2007.

MODIFICATIONS OF SECTION 256 OF THE CAPITAL ALLOWANCES ACT 2001

44(1)   Paragraphs (2) and (3) prescribe modifications of section 256 of the Capital Allowances Act 2001 so far as it applies to the life or endowment business carried on by friendly societies.

44(2)   In subsection (1)(a) before "basic life assurance and general annuity business" insert "taxable".

44(3)   In subsection (2)(a) before "basic life assurance and general annuity business" insert "taxable".

MODIFICATION OF PARAGRAPH 29 OF SCHEDULE 26 TO THE FINANCE ACT 2002

44A(1)   Paragraph (2) prescribes a modification of paragraph 29 of Schedule 26 to the Finance Act 2002 so far as it applies to the life or endowment business carried on by friendly societies.

44A(2)   In sub-paragraph (1) after "(d)" insert ", (da)".

History – Reg. 44A inserted by SI 2007/2134, reg. 34, with effect for accounting periods beginning on or after 1 January 2007.

MODIFICATION OF PARAGRAPH 36 OF SCHEDULE 29 TO THE FINANCE ACT 2002

45(1)   Paragraph (2) prescribes a modification of paragraph 36 of Schedule 29 to the Finance Act 2002 so far as it applies to the life or endowment business carried on by friendly societies.

45(2)   In sub-paragraph (3) after "carries on" insert "taxable".

SUPERSESSION OF EARLIER REGULATIONS

46   In consequence of the provisions of these Regulations, the Regulations specified in column (1) of the Schedule shall (to the extent mentioned in column (3) of that Schedule) cease to have effect for accounting periods beginning on or after 1 January 2005.

REVOCATIONS

Regulation 46

[Revokes SI 1997/473, SI 1997/2877, SI 1998/1871, reg. 25, SI 1999/2636, SI 2000/2710, SI 2001/3629 art. 152–165, SI 2001/3975, SI 2003/23, SI 2004/822 and SI 2005/2005]".

PARTNERSHIPS (RESTRICTIONS ON CONTRIBUTIONS TO A TRADE) REGULATIONS 2005

(SI 2005/2017, as amended by ITA 2007)

The Commissioners for Her Majesty's Revenue and Customs, in exercise of the powers conferred by s. 118ZN(2)–(4) of the Income and Corporation Taxes Act 1988 and s. 122A(2)–(4) of the Finance Act 2004, make the following Regulations.

CITATION, COMMENCEMENT AND EFFECT

1(1) These Regulations may be cited as the Partnerships (Restrictions on Contributions to a Trade) Regulations 2005 and shall come into force on 22nd July 2005.

1(2) These Regulations shall have effect from 2nd December 2004.

INTERPRETATION

2 In these Regulations–

"any other person", in relation to an individual, includes a partnership of which the individual is a member;

"arrangement" means any scheme, arrangement or understanding of any kind (whether or not it is, or is intended to be, legally enforceable);

"bank" has the meaning given by section 991 of ITA 2007;

"capital contribution"–

(a) for the purposes of section 114 of ITA 2007, means the contribution to the firm for the purposes of section 104 or 110 of that Act or the contribution to the LLP for the purposes of section 107 of that Act, and

(b) for the purposes of section 802 of ITA 2007, has the meaning given by section 801(3) of that Act;

"events" includes an omission to exercise a right;

"FA 2004" means the Finance Act 2004;

"ITA 2007" means the Income Tax Act 2007;

"loan" includes–

(a) an advance of money, or any form of credit and "takes out a loan" shall be construed accordingly; and

(b) except in regulation 4(4)(a), any loan which, directly or indirectly, replaces the original loan (and so on, through any number of such loans);

"repaying", where the context requires, includes part repayment.

History – In reg. 2, in the definition of "bank", the words "section 991 of ITA 2007" substituted for the words "section 840A of ICTA" by ITA 2007, s. 1031 and Sch. 2, para. 35(3)(a), with effect, for income tax purposes, from 6 April 2007, and, for corporation tax purposes, for accounting periods ending after 5 April 2007.
In reg. 2, the definition of "capital contribution" substituted for the definition of "contribution to the relevant trade" by ITA 2007, s. 1031 and Sch. 2, para. 35(3)(b), with effect, for income tax purposes, from 6 April 2007, and, for corporation tax purposes, for accounting periods ending after 5 April 2007.
In reg. 2, the definition of "ITA 2007" substituted for the definition of "ICTA" by ITA 2007, s. 1031 and Sch. 2, para. 35(3)(c), with effect, for income tax purposes, from 6 April 2007, and, for corporation tax purposes, for accounting periods ending after 5 April 2007.

SCOPE OF THESE REGULATIONS

3 These Regulations apply for the purposes of–

(a) the relevant provisions mentioned in section 114(1)(a) and (b) of ITA 2007, and

(b) except in regulation 5, applying section 730 of ITA 2007 as mentioned in section 735(2) of that Act,

in computing the amount of an individual's capital contribution.

History – In reg. 3, the words "capital contribution" substituted for the words "contribution to the relevant trade" by ITA 2007, s. 1031 and Sch. 2, para. 35(4), with effect, for income tax purposes, from 6 April 2007, and, for corporation tax purposes, for accounting periods ending after 5 April 2007.
In reg. 3(a), the words "section 114(1)(a) and (b) of ITA 2007" substituted for the words "section 118ZN of ICTA" by ITA 2007, s. 1031 and Sch. 2, para. 35(5)(a), with effect, for income tax purposes, from 6 April 2007, and, for corporation tax purposes, for accounting periods ending after 5 April 2007.

Statutory Instruments

In reg. 3(b), the words "section 730 of ITA 2007 as mentioned in section 735(2) of that Act" substituted for the words "section 119 FA 2004 as mentioned in section 122A(2) of that Act" by ITA 2007, s. 1031 and Sch. 2, para. 35(5)(b), with effect, for income tax purposes, from 6 April 2007, and, for corporation tax purposes, for accounting periods ending after 5 April 2007.

RESTRICTIONS ON COMPUTING THE AMOUNT OF AN INDIVIDUAL'S CONTRIBUTION TO A TRADE – LOANS

4(1)   This Regulation applies where–

(a)   an individual takes out a loan in connection with his financing of the whole or part of a capital contribution, and

(b)   at least one of the following conditions is satisfied.

Condition 1

There is, at any time an agreement or arrangement, under which all or any of the financial cost of repaying the loan is, will or may be borne, or ultimately borne, by any other person.

Condition 2

All or any of the financial cost of repaying the loan is at any time borne, or ultimately borne, by any other person (except under the terms of an agreement or arrangement falling within Condition 1).

Condition 3

The liability to repay the loan is at any time assumed or released by any other person.

Condition 4

The actual financial cost which the individual incurs in repaying the loan during a period mentioned in paragraph (4) is substantially less than what the financial cost to him would be on arm's length repayment terms (those costs being determined in accordance with paragraphs (3) and (4)), or is nil.

4(2)   Where any of Conditions 1 to 3 are satisfied, there shall be excluded when computing the amount of the individual's capital contribution at the time in question the financial cost of repaying the loan, which is, will or may be borne or ultimately borne by the other person, or the liability to repay which is assumed or released by the other person, as the case may be.

4(3)   In determining the final cost on arm's length repayment terms–

(a)   the actual amount of the loan shall be taken into account;

(b)   it shall be assumed that the individual repays the loan personally (without recourse to any other person or fund), and

(c)   the rate of interest, period of the loan, repayment terms and other terms of the loan shall be assumed to be such that might be expected to be applicable if the loan were made–

(i)   by a bank in the ordinary course of its lending business, and

(ii)   by way of a bargain made at arm's length.

4(4)   The comparison required by Condition 4 shall be carried out over five year periods, and computations shall be made to determine the earliest such period–

(a)   beginning on or after 2nd December 2004 (or the date when the loan was taken out, if later) and

(b)   for which Condition 4 is satisfied.

The end of that period is referred to in paragraph (5) as "the relevant time".

4(5)   Where Condition 4 is satisfied, there shall be excluded when computing the amount of the individual's capital contribution at the relevant time the capital liability outstanding under the loan at the relevant time, whether due from the individual or any other person or fund.

History – In reg. 4, the words "capital contribution" substituted for the words "contribution to the relevant trade" by ITA 2007, s. 1031 and Sch. 2, para. 35(4), with effect, for income tax purposes, from 6 April 2007, and, for corporation tax purposes, for accounting periods ending after 5 April 2007.

RESTRICTIONS ON COMPUTING THE AMOUNT OF AN INDIVIDUAL'S CONTRIBUTION TO A TRADE – REIMBURSEMENTS

5(1)   Where there is, at any time, an agreement or arrangement, under which all or any of the financial cost of making a contribution to the relevant trade will or may be directly or indirectly reimbursed to the individual by any other person, paragraph (3) shall apply.

5(2)   Where, at any time, all or any of the financial cost of making a contribution to the relevant trade is directly or indirectly reimbursed to the individual by any other person (except under the terms of an agreement or arrangement falling within paragraph (1)), paragraph (3) shall apply.

5(3) There shall be excluded when computing the amount of the individual's capital contribution at the time in question the financial cost of making the contribution which is, will or may be directly or indirectly reimbursed by the other person, as the case may be.

History – In reg. 5, the words "capital contribution" substituted for the words "contribution to the relevant trade" by ITA 2007, s. 1031 and Sch. 2, para. 35(4), with effect, for income tax purposes, from 6 April 2007, and, for corporation tax purposes, for accounting periods ending after 5 April 2007.

6　　No amount shall be excluded from the computations more than once, and the following shall not be excluded when computing the amount of the individual's capital contribution–

(a)　　any financial cost which is borne or reimbursed by another individual in the normal course of that individual's domestic, family or personal relationships;

(b)　　any loan repayments not made by the individual due to his financial inability to pay, arising as a result of events outside his control which occur after the loan was taken out; and

(c)　　any amount on which the individual is chargeable to income tax as profits of a trade.

History – In reg. 6, the words "capital contribution" substituted for the words "contribution to the relevant trade" by ITA 2007, s. 1031 and Sch. 2, para. 35(4), with effect, for income tax purposes, from 6 April 2007, and, for corporation tax purposes, for accounting periods ending after 5 April 2007.
In reg. 6(c), the words "a trade" substituted for the words "the trade" by ITA 2007, s. 1031 and Sch. 2, para. 35(6), with effect, for income tax purposes, from 6 April 2007, and, for corporation tax purposes, for accounting periods ending after 5 April 2007.

INCOME TAX (CONSTRUCTION INDUSTRY SCHEME) REGULATIONS 2005

(SI 2005/2045 as amended by SI 2007/672, SI 2008/740, SI 2008/1282, SI 2009/56, SI 2009/2030, SI 2010/466, SI 2010/717, SI 2010/1172, SI 2010/2495, SI 2011/2391, SI 2012/820, SI 2013/620, SI 2014/472 and SI 2014/992)

Made on 25 July 2005 by the Commissioners for Her Majesty's Revenue and Customs, in exercise of the powers conferred upon them by s. 205 of the Finance Act 2003, s. 60(7), 62(3), (6) and (7), 63(1), 65(2), 66(2) and (9), 68, 69, 70, 71, 73 and 75 of, and para. 2, 3(1) and (3), 4(3) and (5), 6, 7(1) and (3), 8(2), 10, 11(1) and (4), 12(2), 15 and 16 of Sch. 11 to the Finance Act 2004 and s. 98A(1) and 113(1) of the Taxes Management Act 1970. Operative in accordance with reg. 1.

ARRANGEMENT OF REGULATIONS

PART 1 – INTRODUCTION

CITATION AND COMMENCEMENT

1   These Regulations may be cited as the Income Tax (Construction Industry Scheme) Regulations 2005 and shall come into force on such day as may be appointed by the Commissioners for Her Majesty's Revenue and Customs by notice in the London, Edinburgh and Belfast Gazettes ("the appointed day").

History – The appointed day under reg. 1 is 6 April 2007 (London Gazette, 9 March 2007).

INTERPRETATION

2   In these Regulations–

"**the Act**" means the Finance Act 2004;

"**approved method of electronic communications**", in relation to the delivery of information or the making of a payment in accordance with a provision of these Regulations, means a method of electronic communications which has been approved, by specific or general directions issued by the Commissioners for Her Majesty's Revenue and Customs, for the delivery of information of that kind or the making of a payment of that kind under that provision;

"**combined amount**" means an amount which includes an amount the contractor is liable to pay under these regulations and one or more of the following–

(a)   earnings-related contributions due under the SSC Regulations;

(b)   tax due under the PAYE Regulations;

(c)   payments of repayments of student loans due under the Student Loan Regulations;

"**contract payment**" has the meaning given in section 60 of the Act;

"**contractor**" has the meaning given in section 57 of the Act;

"**construction contract**" has the meaning given in section 57 of the Act;

"**construction operations**" has the meaning given in section 74 of the Act;

"**electronic communications**" has the meaning given in section 132(10) of the Finance Act 1999;

"**employer reference**" means the combination of letters, numbers or both used by Her Majesty's Revenue and Customs to identify an employer for the purpose of the Income Tax (Pay As You Earn) Regulations 2003;

"**ICTA**" means the Income and Corporation Taxes Act 1988;

"**ITEPA**" means the Income Tax (Earnings and Pensions) Act 2003;

"**notice**" means notice in writing;

"**PAYE Regulations**" means the Income Tax (Pay As You Earn) Regulations 2003;

"**SSC Regulations**" means the Social Security (Contributions) Regulations 2001;

"**sub-contractor**" has the meaning given in section 58 of the Act;

"**Student Loan Regulations**" means the Education (Student Loans) (Repayment) Regulations 2009 or, in Northern Ireland, the Education (Student Loans) (Repayment) Regulations (Northern Ireland) 2009;

"**tax month**" means the period beginning on the 6th day of a calendar month and ending on the 5th day of the following calendar month;

"**tax year**" means a year for which any Act provides for income tax to be charged;

"**tax period**" means–

(a)   tax quarter if regulation 8 (quarterly tax periods) applies, or

(b)   tax month, in every other case;

"**tax quarter**" means any of the following (inclusive) periods–

6th April to 5th July,

6th July to 5th October,

6th October to 5th January, and

6th January to 5th April;

"**TMA**" means the Taxes Management Act 1970;

"**tribunal**" means the First-tier Tribunal or, where determined by or under Tribunal Procedure Rules, the Upper Tribunal.

History – In reg. 2, definition of "Student Loan Regulations" substituted by SI 2012/820, reg. 3, with effect from 6 April 2012. The former definition read as follows:

"**"Student Loan Regulations"** means the Education (Student Loans) (Repayment) Regulations 2000 or, in Northern Ireland, the Education (Student Loans) (Repayment) Regulations (Northern Ireland) 2000;".

In reg. 2, definition of "tax appeal Commissioners" omitted by SI 2009/56, art. 3(2) and Sch. 2, para. 138(2), operative from 1 April 2009 subject to transitional and saving provisions in SI 2009/56, Sch. 3. Former definition read as follows:

"**"tax appeal Commissioners"** means the General Commissioners or Special Commissioners as the case may be;".

In reg. 2, definition of "tribunal" inserted by SI 2009/56, art. 3(2) and Sch. 2, para. 138(3), operative from 1 April 2009 subject to transitional and saving provisions in SI 2009/56, Sch. 3.

In reg. 2, definitions of "combined amount", "SSC Regulations" and "Student Loan Regulations" inserted by SI 2008/740, reg. 2, with effect from 6 April 2008.

PART 2 – CONTRACTORS

MULTIPLE CONTRACTORS

3(1) A contractor may elect, for the purposes of these Regulations, to be treated as different contractors in relation to different groups of sub-contractors.

3(2) Where the contractor makes an election these Regulations apply as if–

(a) in respect of each group the contractor were a different contractor; and

(b) each group constituted all the sub-contractors to whom the contractor makes payments under contracts relating to construction operations.

3(3) While an election is in force, a contractor must allocate any new sub-contractors to one of the groups.

3(4) An election must be made by notice to an officer of Revenue and Customs containing–

(a) such information as may be necessary to identify the groups of sub-contractors, and

(b) a certificate that the contractor makes no payments under contracts relating to construction operations other than to sub-contractors in the groups so identified.

3(5) A contractor must, subject to paragraph (6), make an election before the beginning of the tax year for which it is to have effect.

3(6) A contractor who acquires the whole or part of any business of another contractor may, within 90 days of the acquisition, elect–

(a) to be treated as a different contractor in relation to the acquired sub-contractors, or two or more different contractors in relation to groups of the acquired sub-contractors, whether or not an election is already in force in respect of the existing sub-contractors, or

(b) to add some or all of the acquired sub-contractors to existing groups of sub-contractors in respect of whom an election is already in force,

and such election has effect for the tax year in which the acquisition takes place.

3(7) In paragraph (6)–

"**business**" includes any trade, concern or undertaking;

"**acquired sub-contractor**" means a sub-contractor who contracted with the acquired business.

3(8) An election continues in effect until revoked by notice given to an officer of Revenue and Customs.

3(9) A notice of revocation must be given before the beginning of the tax year for which the election is to be revoked, but the revocation of an election does not prevent the making of a new election for that or a later tax year.

3(10) An election which has not yet come into effect may be revoked at any time before the beginning of the tax year for which it is to have effect.

MONTHLY RETURN

4(1) A return must be made to the Commissioners for Her Majesty's Revenue and Customs in a document or format provided or approved by the Commissioners–

(a) not later than 14 days after the end of every tax month, by a contractor making contract payments or payments which would be contract payments but for section 60(4) of the Act (contract payments: exceptions), and

(b) not later than 14 days after the end of the tax month following the appointed day, by a contractor who has made a payment in the 12 months preceding the appointed day which would be a contract payment or a payment which would be a contract payment but for section 60(4) of the Act if made after the appointed day.

4(2) The return under paragraph (1) must contain the following information–

(a) the contractor's name,

(b) the contractor's unique taxpayer reference (UTR) and Accounts' Office reference,

(c) the tax month to which the return relates, and

(d) in respect of each sub-contractor to whom, or to whose nominee, payments under construction contracts were made by the contractor during that month,–

(i) the sub-contractor's name;

    (ii)   the sub-contractor's national insurance number (NINO) or company registration number (CRN), if known; and

    (iii) the information specified in paragraph (3).

4(3)   The information specified is–

(a)   if the sub-contractor is registered for gross payment–

    (i)   the sub-contractor's unique taxpayer reference (UTR), and

    (ii)   the total amount of payments which would be contract payments but for section 60(4) of the Act (contract payments: exceptions) made by the contractor to the sub-contractor during the tax month;

(b)   if the sub-contractor is registered for payment under deduction–

    (i)   the sub-contractor's unique taxpayer reference (UTR),

    (ii)   the total amount of contract payments made by the contractor to the sub-contractor during the tax month,

    (iii) the total amount included in those payments which the contractor is satisfied represents the direct cost to any person other than the contractor of materials used or to be used in carrying out the construction contract to which the contract payment relates, and

    (iv) the total amount deducted from the payments mentioned in paragraph (3)(b)(ii) under section 61 of the Act (deduction on account of tax from contract payments);

(c)   if the sub-contractor is not registered for gross payment or payment under deduction–

    (i)   the sub-contractor's unique taxpayer reference (UTR), if known,

    (ii)   the total amount of contract payments made by the contractor to the sub-contractor during the tax month,

    (iii) the total amount included in those payments which the contractor is satisfied represents the direct cost to any person other than the contractor of materials used or to be used in carrying out the construction contract to which the contract payment relates,

    (iv) the total amount deducted from the payments mentioned in paragraph (3)(c)(ii) under section 61 of the Act, and

    (v)   the verification reference for higher rate deduction.

4(4)   The return may be transmitted electronically to the Commissioners for Her Majesty's Revenue and Customs.

4(5)   The return must include a declaration by the person making the return–

(a)   that none of the contracts to which the return relates is a contract of employment;

(b)   indicating whether he has complied with the requirements of regulation 6 (verification etc of registration status of sub-contractor) in the case of each person to whom a payment to which the return relates is made; and

(c)   that the return contains all the information, particulars and supporting information required by this regulation to be included in the return, and such information, particulars and supporting information are complete and accurate to the best of the contractor's knowledge and belief.

4(6)   If the return is not transmitted electronically, it must be signed by the contractor or a person duly authorised by the contractor to make the return.

4(7)   The contractor must make and keep such records as will enable him to comply with this regulation.

4(8)   The contractor must give the following information in writing to the sub-contractor to whom it relates not later than 14 days after the end of the tax month either in respect of the total payments made in that month or in respect of each payment made in that month–

(a)   if the sub-contractor is registered for payment under deduction–

    (i)   the contractor's name,

    (ii)   the contractor's employer's reference,

    (iii) the tax month to which the payments relate or the date of the payment,

    (iv) the sub-contractor's name,

    (v)   the sub-contractor's unique taxpayer reference (UTR),

    (vi) the total amount of contract payments made by the contractor to the sub-contractor during the tax month,

(vii)   the total amount included in those payments which the contractor is satisfied represents the direct cost to any person other than the contractor of materials used or to be used in carrying out the construction contract to which the contract payment relates, and

(viii)   the total amount deducted from the payments mentioned in paragraph (vi) under section 61 of the Act;

and

(b)   if the sub-contractor is not registered under Chapter 3 of the Act, the verification reference.

4(9)   The information required under paragraph (8) may be given by means of electronic communications if–

(a)   the contractor has indicated to the sub-contractor that he intends to use electronic communications for the purposes of giving this information;

(b)   the sub-contractor has consented to information being given by the contractor by means of electronic communications, and that consent has not been withdrawn;

(c)   the information is given in an electronic format–

(i)   in which the statement may be stored; and

(ii)   which permits a paper copy of the information contained in the statement to be printed.

4(10)   If a contractor who has made a return, or should have made a return, under this regulation makes no payments under construction contracts in the tax month following that return, the contractor must make a nil return not later than 14 days after the end of that tax month.

This is subject to paragraph (11).

4(11)   Paragraph (10) does not apply if the contractor has notified the Commissioners for Her Majesty's Revenue and Customs that the contractor will make no further payments under construction contracts within the following six months.

4(12)   Subject to paragraph (13), section 98A of TMA (special penalties in the case of certain returns) applies to the requirements in–

(a)   paragraph (1),

(b)   paragraph (3)(b),

(c)   paragraph (3)(c),

(d)   paragraph (10).

4(13)   A penalty under section 98A of TMA in relation to a failure to make a return in accordance with paragraphs (1) or (10) arises for each month (or part of a month) during which the failure continues after the 19th day of the sixth month following the appointed day, but only arises where that failure relates to a return that must be made not later than 19th October 2011.

History – In reg. 4(13), the words ", but only arises where that failure relates to a return that must be made not later than 19th October 2011" inserted by SI 2011/2391, art. 3(3), with effect from 6 October 2011.

Cross references – FA 2009, Sch. 55: penalties in relation to returns for which the filing date is after 19 October 2011.

SCHEME REPRESENTATIVE

5(1)   A company ("the appointing company") which makes payments under construction contracts may appoint another company in the same group ("a scheme representative") to act on its behalf in connection with any such requirements imposed on the company by these Regulations as the appointment specifies.

5(2)   An appointment under paragraph (1) shall not have effect until the appointing company has notified the Commissioners for Her Majesty's Revenue and Customs.

5(3)   A scheme representative must make returns and payments under these Regulations in the name of the appointing company.

5(4)   The appointing company remains liable in relation to all the requirements imposed on it by these Regulations notwithstanding any appointment under paragraph (1).

5(5)   For the purposes of paragraph (1) section 413(3)(a) of ICTA applies to determine whether two companies are in the same group.

VERIFICATION ETC OF REGISTRATION STATUS OF SUB-CONTRACTOR AND NOMINEE

6(1)   A contractor must verify with the Commissioners for Her Majesty's Revenue and Customs whether a person to whom he is proposing to make–

(a)   a contract payment, or

(b)   a payment which would be a contract payment but for section 60(4) of the Act (contract payments:exceptions),

and, where that person has appointed a nominee, his nominee, are registered for gross payment, for payment under deduction or is not registered under Chapter 3 of the Act.

This is subject to paragraph (3).

6(2)   For the purpose of verification the contractor must provide–

(a)   his name, unique taxpayer reference (UTR), accounts office reference and employer's reference, and

(b)   in relation to the person to whom he is proposing to make the payment and, where that person has appointed a nominee, his nominee–

 (i)   if that person or nominee is an individual, his name, unique taxpayer reference (UTR) and national insurance number;

 (ii)   if that person or nominee is a partner in a firm, the name of the firm and that partner, the unique taxpayer reference (UTR) of the firm, and if the partner is an individual his unique taxpayer reference (UTR) or national insurance number or if the partner is a company the unique taxpayer reference (UTR) or the company registration number;

 (iii)   if that person or nominee is a company, the name of the company, unique taxpayer reference (UTR) and the company registration number.

6(3)   A contractor may not verify under paragraph (1) unless the contractor has a contract with the sub-contractor or has formally accepted a tender for work under a contract.

6(4)   A contractor need not verify if–

(a)   the person to whom he is proposing to make the payment has been included in a return under regulation 4 in the current or previous two tax years;

(b)   the payment is made within two years of the appointed day, if the person to whom he is proposing to make the payment has been included in a return under regulation 4 or a return under regulation 40A of the Income Tax (Sub-contractors in the Construction Industry) Regulations 1993 for the current or previous two years;

(c)   the contractor is a company and the person to whom he is proposing to make the payment has been included in a return under regulation 4 or a return under regulation 40A of the Income Tax (Sub-contractors in the Construction Industry) Regulations 1993 for the current or previous two tax years made by another company in the same group;

(d)   the contractor has made an election under regulation 3 and the person to whom he is proposing to make the payment has been included in a return under regulation 4 in the current or previous two years in respect of a different group of sub-contractors in relation to which the contractor is treated as a different contractor;

(e)   the contractor acquired the contract under which the payment is to be made in a transfer of a business as a going concern where the transferor was within one of paragraphs (a) to (d) and the contractor has notified the Commissioners for Her Majesty's Revenue and Customs of the transfer.

6(5)   For the purposes of paragraph (4)(c) section 413(3)(a) of ICTA applies to determine whether two companies are in the same group.

6(6)   The Commissioners for Her Majesty's Revenue and Customs must notify a contractor that–

(a)   a person registered for gross payment has become registered for payment under deduction or has ceased to be registered under Chapter 3 of the Act, or

(b)   a person registered for payment under deduction has become registered for gross payment or has ceased to be registered under Chapter 3 of the Act,

if a payment to that person has been included in the contractor's return under regulation 4, or a return under regulation 40A of the Income Tax (Sub-contractors in the Construction Industry) Regulations 1993, in the current or previous two tax years or that person has been verified under paragraph (1) by the contractor in that period.

6(7)   A contractor is entitled to assume that–

(a)   a person verified or notified as being registered for gross payment, or

(b)   a person verified or notified as being registered for payment under deduction,

has not subsequently ceased to be so registered.

PART 3 – PAYMENT AND RECOVERY OF AMOUNTS DEDUCTED UNDER SECTION 61

PAYMENT, DUE DATE FOR PAYMENT OF AMOUNTS DEDUCTED AND RECEIPTS

7(1) A contractor must pay to the Commissioners for Her Majesty's Revenue and Customs all amounts he was liable under section 61 of the Act to deduct on account of tax from contract payments made by him during that tax period–

(a)   within 17 days after the end of the tax period, where payment is made by an approved method of electronic communications, or

(b)   within 14 days after the end of the tax period, in any other case.

7(2) The Commissioners for Her Majesty's Revenue and Customs must give a receipt to the contractor for the total amount paid under paragraph (1) if asked.

7(3) But no separate receipt for the total amount paid under paragraph (1) need be given if a receipt is given for the total of–

(a)   the amount paid under paragraph (1),

(b)   any tax deducted under the PAYE Regulations, and

(c)   any earnings-related contributions (as defined by regulation 1(2) of the Social Security (Contributions) Regulations 2001,

paid at the same time.

History – In reg. 7(3)(b), the words "PAYE Regulations" substituted for "Pay As You Earn Regulations" by SI 2008/740, reg. 4, with effect from 6 April 2008.

7A(1) Payment of an amount that is less than the amount which the contractor was liable to pay to the Commissioners for Her Majesty's Revenue and Customs under regulation 7(1), will, for the purposes of paragraph 6(2) of Schedule 56 to the Finance Act 2009 (amounts of penalty: PAYE and CIS), be treated as a payment of the full amount if the difference between the full amount and the amount paid is no more than £100 ("the tolerance"), but this is subject to paragraph (2).

7A(2) If a contractor makes a payment under regulation 7(1) and the total sum paid to Her Majesty's Revenue and Customs for the tax period includes not only that payment but also one or more of–

(a)   any tax deducted under the PAYE Regulations,

(b)   any earnings-related contributions (as defined by regulation 1(2) of the SSC Regulations, or

(c)   any repayment due under the Student Loans Regulations 2009,

the tolerance is applied to the total sum paid to the Commissioners for Her Majesty's Revenue and Customs for the tax period to which the payments relate.

History – Reg. 7A inserted by SI 2014/472, reg. 21, with effect in relation to a payment made in relation to the tax year 2014–15 and subsequent tax years.

QUARTERLY TAX PERIODS

8(1) This regulation applies so that the tax period is a tax quarter if a contractor–

(a)   has reasonable grounds for believing that the average monthly amount will be less than £1,500, and

(b)   chooses to pay tax quarterly.

8(2) **"The average monthly amount"** is the average, for tax months falling within the current tax year, of the amounts found by the formula–

$$(P + N + L + S) - (SP + CD).$$

8(3) In paragraph (2)–

P is the amount which would be payable to an officer of Revenue and Customs under regulation 67G or 68 of the PAYE Regulations (periodic payments to and recoveries from the Revenue);

N is the amount which would be payable to an officer of Revenue and Customs under the SSCBA and the SSC Regulations disregarding any amount of secondary Class 1 contributions in respect of which liability has been transferred to the employed earner by an election made jointly by the employed earner and the secondary contributor for the purposes of paragraph 3B(1) of Schedule 1 to the SSCBA (transfer of liability to be borne by earner);

L is the amount which would be payable to an officer of Revenue and Customs under regulation 54(1) or, in Northern Ireland, 49(1) of the Student Loans Regulations (payment of repayments deducted to the Commissioners for Her Majesty's Revenue and Customs) disregarding the reduction referred to in paragraph (3) of those regulations;

S is the amount which would be payable by the contractor to the Commissioners for Her Majesty's Revenue and Customs under regulation 7 during the tax month;

SP is the amount which would be payable by the contractor to employees by way of statutory sick pay, statutory maternity pay, ordinary statutory paternity pay, additional statutory paternity pay and statutory adoption pay under the SSCBA; and

CD is—

(a)   if the contractor is a company, the amount which others would deduct from payments to it, in its position as a sub-contractor, under section 61 of the Act;

(b)   in any other case, nil.

8(4)   In this regulation—

"employed earner" has the same meaning as in the SSCBA;

"SSCBA" means the Social Security Contributions and Benefit Act 1992 or, in Northern Ireland, the Social Security Contributions and Benefit (Northern Ireland) Act 1992;

History – In reg. 8(3), in the definition of "P", "67G or" inserted by SI 2012/820, reg. 4(a), with effect from 6 April 2012.
In reg. 8(3), in the definition of "L", the words "54(1) or, in Northern Ireland, 49(1)" substituted for "39(1)" by SI 2012/820, reg. 4(b)(i), with effect from 6 April 2012.
In reg. 8(3), in the definition of "L", the words "those regulations" substituted for the words "that regulation" by SI 2012/820, reg. 4(b)(ii), with effect from 6 April 2012.
In reg. 8(3), in the definition of "SP", the words "ordinary statutory paternity pay, additional statutory paternity pay" substituted for the words "statutory paternity pay" by SI 2010/2495, reg. 3, with effect from 14 November 2010.
In reg. 8(4), definitions of "SSC Regulations" and "Student Loan Regulations" omitted by SI 2008/740, reg. 5, with effect from 6 April 2008.

RECOVERY FROM SUB-CONTRACTOR OF AMOUNT NOT DEDUCTED BY CONTRACTOR

9(1)   This regulation applies if—

(a)   it appears to an officer of Revenue and Customs that the deductible amount exceeds the amount actually deducted, and

(b)   condition A or B is met.

9(2)   In this regulation—

"the deductible amount" is the amount which a contractor is liable to deduct on account of tax from a contract payment under section 61 of the Act in a tax period;

"the amount actually deducted" is the amount actually deducted by the contractor on account of tax from a contract payment under section 61 of the Act during that tax period;

"the excess" means the amount by which the deductible amount exceeds the amount actually deducted.

9(3)   Condition A is that the contractor satisfies an officer of Revenue and Customs—

(a)   that he took reasonable care to comply with section 61 of the Act and these Regulations, and

(b)   that—

(i)   the failure to deduct the excess was due to an error made in good faith, or

(ii)   he held a genuine belief that section 61 of the Act did not apply to the payment.

9(4)   Condition B is that—

(a)   an officer of Revenue and Customs is satisfied that the person to whom the contractor made the contract payments to which section 61 of the Act applies either—

(i)   was not chargeable to income tax or corporation tax in respect of those payments, or

(ii)   has made a return of his income or profits in accordance with section 8 of TMA (personal return) or paragraph 3 of Schedule 18 to the Finance Act 1998 (company tax return), in which those payments were taken into account, and paid the income tax and Class 4 contributions due or corporation tax due in respect of such income or profits;

and

(b)   the contractor requests that the Commissioners for Her Majesty's Revenue and Customs make a direction under paragraph (5).

9(5)   An officer of Revenue and Customs may direct that the contractor is not liable to pay the excess to the Commissioners for Her Majesty's Revenue and Customs.

9(6) If condition A is not met an officer of Revenue and Customs may refuse to make a direction under paragraph (5) by giving notice to the contractor ("the refusal notice") stating–

(a) the grounds for the refusal, and

(b) the date on which the refusal notice was issued.

9(7) A contractor may appeal against the refusal notice–

(a) by notice to an officer of Revenue and Customs,

(b) within 30 days of the refusal notice,

(c) specifying the grounds of the appeal.

9(8) For the purpose of paragraph (7) the grounds of appeal are that–

(a) that the contractor took reasonable care to comply with section 61 of the Act and these Regulations, and

(b) that–

    (i) the failure to deduct the excess was due to an error made in good faith, or

    (ii) the contractor held a genuine belief that section 61 of the Act did not apply to the payment.

9(9) If on an appeal under paragraph (7) that is notified to the tribunal it appears that the refusal notice should not have been issued the tribunal may direct that an officer of Revenue and Customs make a direction under paragraph (5) in an amount the tribunal determines is the excess for one or more tax periods falling within the relevant year.

9(10) If a contractor has deducted an amount under section 61 of the Act, but has not paid it to the Commissioners for Her Majesty's Revenue and Customs as required by regulation 7 (payment, due date etc. and receipts), that amount is treated, for the purposes of determining the liability of any sub-contractor in respect of whose liability the sum was deducted, as having been paid to the Commissioners for Her Majesty's Revenue and Customs at the time required by regulation 8 (quarterly tax periods).

History – In reg. 9(9), the words "that is notified to the tribunal it appears" substituted for the words "it appears to the tax appeal Commissioners" by SI 2009/56, art. 3(2) and Sch. 2, para. 139(2), operative from 1 April 2009 subject to transitional and saving provisions in SI 2009/56, Sch. 3.
In reg. 9(9), the words "the tribunal" substituted for the word "they" by SI 2009/56, art. 3(2) and Sch. 2, para. 139(3), operative from 1 April 2009 subject to transitional and saving provisions in SI 2009/56, Sch. 3.
In reg. 9(9), the words "tribunal determines" substituted for the words "tax appeal Commissioners determine" by SI 2009/56, art. 3(2) and Sch. 2, para. 139(4), operative from 1 April 2009 subject to transitional and saving provisions in SI 2009/56, Sch. 3.

RETURN AND CERTIFICATE IF AMOUNT MAY BE UNPAID

10(1) This regulation applies if, 17 days or more after the end of a tax period, condition A, B or C is met.

10(2) Condition A is that–

(a) a contractor has not paid any amount under regulation 7 for that tax period, and

(b) an officer of Revenue and Customs is unaware of the amount (if any) which the contractor is liable to pay for that tax period.

10(3) Condition B is that–

(a) a contractor has paid an amount under regulation 7 for that tax period, but

(b) an officer of Revenue and Customs is not satisfied, that it is the full amount which the contractor is liable to pay for that period.

10(3A) Condition C is that–

(a) the contractor has made a return under regulation 4 showing the amount which the contractor is liable to pay under regulation 7 for that tax period, but

(b) the contractor has not paid the full amount shown in the return.

10(4) If condition A or B is met an officer of Revenue and Customs may give notice to the contractor requiring the contractor within 14 days of the issue of the notice to deliver a return showing the amount which the contractor is liable to pay under regulation 7 in respect of the tax period.

10(5) If–

(a) the notice extends to, or

(b) condition C is met in,

two or more consecutive tax periods in a tax year, this regulation has effect as if they were one tax period.

10(6) On receiving a return made by the contractor under paragraph (4) or if condition C is met, an officer of Revenue and Customs may prepare a certificate showing the amount which the contractor is liable to pay for the tax period and how much (if any) of that amount remains unpaid.

10(7) Regulation 57 (certificate that sum due) deals with the use of certificates as evidence that sums are due and unpaid.

History – In reg. 10(1) the reference to "A, B or C" substituted for "A or B" by SI 2007/672, reg. 3(2), with effect from 26 March 2007.
Reg. 10(3A) inserted by SI 2007/672, reg. 3(3), with effect from 26 March 2007.
In reg. 10(4) the words "If condition A or B is met" inserted by SI 2007/672, reg. 3(4), with effect from 26 March 2007.
In reg. 10(5) the words from "If– (a)... two" substituted for "If the notice extends to two" by SI 2007/672, reg. 3(5), with effect from 26 March 2007.
In reg. 10(6) the words "or if condition C is met" inserted by SI 2007/672, reg. 3(6), with effect from 26 March 2007.

NOTICE AND CERTIFICATE IF AMOUNT MAY BE UNPAID

11(1) This regulation applies if, 17 days or more after the end of a tax period, condition A or B is met.

11(2) Condition A is that–

(a) a contractor has not paid any amount under regulation 7 for that tax period, and

(b) an officer of Revenue and Customs has reason to believe that the contractor is liable to pay an amount for that tax period.

11(3) Condition B is that–

(a) a contractor has paid an amount under regulation 7 for that tax period, but

(b) an officer of Revenue and Customs is not satisfied, after seeking the contractor's explanation, that it is the full amount which the contractor is liable to pay for that period.

11(4) An officer of Revenue and Customs, on consideration of the contractor's record of past payments whether of deductions under section 61 of the Act (deductions on account of tax from contract payments) or of combined amounts, may–

(a) specify, to the best of his judgment, the amount due under regulation 7 or a combined amount which he considers the contractor is liable to pay, and

(b) serve notice on the contractor requiring payment of the specified amount within 7 days of the issue of the notice ("the notice period").

11(5) If condition A is met an officer of Revenue and Customs may give notice under paragraph (4) which extends to two or more consecutive tax periods in a tax year and these Regulations have effect as if they were the latest tax period specified in the notice.

11(6) If, during the notice period, the contractor–

(a) claims that any payment made in respect of the tax period specified in the notice is or includes the full amount the contractor is liable to pay under regulation 7, but

(b) does not satisfy an officer of Revenue and Customs that this is the case,

the contractor may require an officer of Revenue and Customs to inspect the contractor's documents and records as if the contractor had been required to produce those documents in accordance with regulation 51 (inspection of records of contractors and sub-contractors).

11(7) If there is an inspection by virtue of paragraph (6), regulation 51 applies to that inspection and the notice given by an officer of Revenue and Customs under paragraph (4) must be disregarded.

11(8) If the amount specified in the notice, or any part of it, is not paid during the notice period–

(a) the amount unpaid is treated as, or including, an amount which the contractor was liable to pay for that tax period under regulation 7, and

(b) an officer of Revenue and Customs may prepare a certificate showing how much of that amount remains unpaid.

11(9) But paragraph (8) does not apply if during the notice period–

(a) the contractor pays the full amount which the contractor is liable to pay under regulation 7 for that tax period, or

(b) the contractor satisfies an officer of Revenue and Customs that no amount, or no further amount, is due for that tax period.

11(10) Paragraph (11) applies if the contractor pays an amount of deductions under section 61 of the Act, whether separately or as part of a combined amount, certified under this regulation which exceeds the amount the contractor would have been liable to pay in respect of that tax period apart from this regulation.

11(11) The contractor is entitled to set off the excess of deductions under section 61 of the Act against any amount which the contractor is liable to pay under regulation 7 for any subsequent tax periods in the tax year.

11(12) Regulation 57 deals with the use of certificates as evidence that sums are due and unpaid.

History – In reg. 11(4), the words "whether of deductions under section 61 of the Act (deductions on account of tax from contract payments) or of combined amounts" inserted by SI 2008/740, reg. 6(2), with effect from 6 April 2008.
In reg. 11(4)(a), the words "due under regulation 7 or a combined amount" inserted by SI 2008/740, reg. 6(2), with effect from 6 April 2008.
In reg. 11(4)(b), the words "the specified" substituted for "that" by SI 2008/740, reg. 6(2), with effect from 6 April 2008.
Reg. 11(6)(a) substituted by SI 2008/740, reg. 6(3), with effect from 6 April 2008.
In reg. 11(8)(a), the words ", or including," inserted by SI 2008/740, reg. 6(4), with effect from 6 April 2008.
In reg. 11(10), the words "of deductions under section 61 of the Act, whether separately or as part of a combined amount," inserted by SI 2008/740, reg. 6(5), with effect from 6 April 2008.
In reg. 11(11), the words "of deductions under section 61 of the Act" inserted by SI 2008/740, reg. 6(6), with effect from 6 April 2008.

CERTIFICATE AFTER INSPECTION OF RECORDS OF CONTRACTORS AND SUB-CONTRACTORS

12(1) This regulation applies if there is an inspection of a contractor's documents and records under regulation 51.

12(2) An officer of Revenue and Customs may, by reference to the information obtained from the inspection, prepare a certificate showing–

(a)   the amount which it appears that the contractor is liable to pay for the tax years or tax periods covered by the inspection; and

(b)   any amount which remains unpaid.

12(3) Regulation 57 deals with the use of certificates as evidence that sums are due and unpaid.

DETERMINATION OF AMOUNTS PAYABLE BY CONTRACTOR AND APPEAL AGAINST DETERMINATION

13(1) This regulation applies if–

(a)   there is a dispute between a contractor and a sub-contractor as to–

    (i)   whether a payment is made under a construction contract, or

    (ii)   the amount, if any, deductible by the contractor under section 61 of the Act from a contract payment to a sub-contractor or his nominee, or

(b)   an officer of Revenue and Customs has reason to believe, as a result of an inspection under regulation 51 or otherwise, that there may be an amount payable for a tax year under these Regulations by a contractor that has not been paid to them, or

(c)   an officer of Revenue and Customs considers it necessary in the circumstances.

13(2) An officer of Revenue and Customs may determine the amount which to the best of his judgment a contractor is liable to pay under these Regulations, and serve notice of his determination on the contractor.

13(3) A determination under this regulation must not include amounts in respect of which a direction under regulation 9(5) has been made and directions under that regulation do not apply to amounts determined under this regulation.

13(4) A determination under this regulation may–

(a)   cover the amount payable by the contractor under section 61 of the Act for any one or more tax periods in a tax year, and

(b)   extend to the whole of that amount, or to such part of it as is payable in respect of–

    (i)   a class or classes of sub-contractors specified in the notice of determination (without naming the individual sub-contractors), or

    (ii)   one or more named sub-contractors specified in the notice.

13(5) A determination under this regulation is subject to Parts 4, 5, 5A and 6 of TMA (assessment, appeals, collection and recovery) as if–

(a)   the determination were an assessment, and

(b)   the amount determined were income tax charged on the contractor,

and those Parts of that Act apply accordingly with any necessary modifications, except that the amount determined is due and payable 14 days after the determination is made.

13(6) If paragraph (1)(a) applies and an officer of Revenue and Customs does not make a determination under paragraph (2), either the contractor or the sub-contractor may on giving notice to an officer of Revenue and Customs, apply to the tribunal to determine the matter.

13(7) [Omitted by SI 2009/56, art. 3(2) and Sch. 2, para. 140(3).]

13(8) If paragraph (1)(a) applies–

(a)   the contractor must make the deduction required by section 61 of the Act from the contract payment or the part of the contract payment, to which the dispute relates, and the amount so deducted is treated as a sum which he is liable to pay to the Commissioners for Her Majesty's Revenue and Customs under these Regulations; and

(b)   any amount which, on a final determination of the dispute, is shown not to have been so payable is, except where regulation 56 (application by the Commissioners for Her Majesty's Revenue and Customs of sums deducted under section 61 of the Act) applies, treated as an overpayment of income tax or corporation tax by the sub-contractor.

History – In reg. 13(5), ", 5A" inserted by SI 2010/717, reg. 3, with effect in relation to 2010–11 and subsequent tax years. In reg. 13(6), "tribunal" substituted for "General Commissioners" by SI 2009/56, art. 3(2) and Sch. 2, para. 140(2), operative from 1 April 2009 subject to transitional and saving provisions in SI 2009/56, Sch. 3. Reg. 13(7) omitted by SI 2009/56, art. 3(2) and Sch. 2, para. 140(3), operative from 1 April 2009 subject to transitional and saving provisions in SI 2009/56, Sch. 3. Former reg. 13(7) read as follows:

"**13(7)**   For the purposes of paragraph 3(1)(a) of Schedule 3 to TMA (rules for assigning proceedings to General Commissioners), the relevant place for an appeal against a determination under this regulation is the place where the determination was made.".

INTEREST ON AMOUNTS OVERDUE

14   [Omitted by SI 2014/992, art. 11(a).]

History – Reg. 14 omitted by SI 2014/992, art. 11(a), with effect from 6 May 2014 in relation to payments which are due and payable in respect of the tax year 2014–15 and subsequent tax years. Former reg. 14 read as follows:

"**14(1)**   This regulation applies if a contractor has not paid to the Commissioners for Her Majesty's Revenue and Customs the total amount which he is liable under these Regulations to pay in respect of a tax year by the reckonable date.

14(2)   Any unpaid amount carries interest at the prescribed rate from the reckonable date until payment ("the interest period").

14(3)   Paragraph (2) applies even if the reckonable date is a non-business day as defined by section 92 of the Bills of Exchange Act 1882.

14(4)   But paragraph (2) does not apply to any amount which the contractor does not have to pay as a result of a direction under regulation 9(5).

14(5)   Any change made to the prescribed rate during the interest period applies to the unpaid amount from the date of the change.

14(6)   The "**prescribed rate**" means the rate applicable under section 178 of the Finance Act 1989 (setting of rates of interest) for the purposes of section 86 of TMA (interest on overdue tax).

14(7)   The "**reckonable date**" means–

(a)   17 days after the end of the tax year, if payment is made using an approved method of electronic communication, or

(b)   14 days after the end of the tax year, in any other case.".

INTEREST ON AMOUNT OVERPAID

15   [Omitted by SI 2014/992, art. 11(b).]

History – Reg. 15 omitted by SI 2014/992, art. 11(b), with effect from 6 May 2014 in relation to payments which are due and payable in respect of the tax year 2014–15 and subsequent tax years. Former reg. 15 read as follows:

"**15(1)**   This regulation applies if an amount is repaid to a contractor after the end of the tax year in respect of which the amount was paid.

15(2)   The amount repaid carries interest at the prescribed rate from the relevant time until the order for the repayment is issued ("the interest period").

15(3)   In paragraph (2) "**the relevant time**" means–

(a)   in the case of a repayment of an amount which was paid more than 12 months after the end of the tax year in respect of which the payment was made, the end of the tax year in which that amount was paid; and

(b)   in any other case, the end of the tax year after the tax year in respect of which the payment was made.

15(4)   Any change made to the prescribed rate during the interest period applies to the amount repaid from the date of the change.

15(5)   "**The prescribed rate**" means the rate applicable under section 178 of the Finance Act 1989 for the purposes of section 824 of ICTA (repayment supplements)."

RECOVERY OF AMOUNT UNPAID AND INTEREST

16(1)   In this regulation, "**the unpaid amount**" means any amount or interest which a contractor is liable to pay under regulation 10(6), 11(8), 12(2)(b) or 13(2).

16(2)   Part 6 of TMA (collection and recovery) applies to the recovery of the unpaid amount or combined amount and any interest on it as if it were income tax charged on the contractor but with the modification indicated in paragraph (3).

16(3)   Summary proceedings for the recovery of the unpaid amount may be brought in England and Wales or Northern Ireland at any time before the end of the period which applies for the purposes of the regulation, as shown in Table 1.

Table 1

Period for summary proceedings for the recovery of unpaid amount

1. Regulation	*2. Period*
Regulation 10(6), 11(8) and 13(2)	(a) 12 months after the date on which the unpaid amount or combined amount and any interest on it became payable, or (b) if a return has been required under regulation 10, 12 months after the date of the delivery of that return to the Commissioners for Her Majesty's Revenue and Customs.
Regulation 12(2)	12 months after the date of the certificate.

16(4)   Proceedings against a contractor may be brought for the recovery of the unpaid amount or unpaid combined amount and any interest on it without distinguishing the amounts which the employer is liable to pay in respect of each sub-contractor and without specifying the sub-contractor in question.

16(5)   The unpaid amount or unpaid combined amount and any interest on it is one cause of action or one matter of complaint for the purposes of proceedings under sections 65, 66 and 67 of TMA (magistrates' courts, county courts and inferior courts in Scotland).

16(6)   But paragraphs (4) and (5) do not prevent the bringing of separate proceedings for the recovery of each of the amounts which the contractor is liable to pay for any tax period in respect of each of the sub-contractors.

History – In reg. 16(2), the words "or combined amount and any interest on it" inserted by SI 2008/740, reg. 7(2), with effect from 6 April 2008.
In reg. 16(3), in Table 1 the words "or combined amount and any interest on it" inserted by SI 2008/740, reg. 7(3), with effect from 6 April 2008.
In reg. 16(4) the words "or unpaid combined amount and any interest on it" inserted by SI 2008/740, reg. 7(4), with effect from 6 April 2008.
In reg. 16(5) the words "or unpaid combined amount and any interest on it" inserted by SI 2008/740, reg. 7(5), with effect from 6 April 2008.

IN-YEAR REPAYMENTS OF PROVISIONAL EXCESS CREDIT

17(1)   This regulation applies if–

(a)   a sub-contractor is an individual or a firm,

(b)   an application is made by that individual or a partner in the firm ("the applicant") to the Commissioners for Her Majesty's Revenue and Customs in accordance with paragraph (4),

(c)   any income tax and Class 4 contributions due from the applicant, or the sub-contractor, on the applicant's share of the annual profits or gains arising or accruing from the trade, profession or vocation of the sub-contractor, for any earlier year, have been paid, and

(d)   all relevant tax payment vouchers issued to the sub-contractor under regulation 7 of the Income Tax (Sub-contractors in the Construction Industry) Regulations 1993 in relation to payments made before the appointed day are produced to the Commissioners for Her Majesty's Revenue and Customs.

17(2)   If the Commissioners for Her Majesty's Revenue and Customs are satisfied by evidence produced by the applicant that A exceeds B, the applicant shall, subject to paragraph (5), be entitled to repayment of the excess by the Commissioners for Her Majesty's Revenue and Customs.

17(3)   In paragraph (2)–

A is the amount of the applicant's share of the total of sums deducted under section 61 of the Act from contract payments made to the sub-contractor and paid to the Commissioners for Her Majesty's Revenue and Customs, in so much of the year as has elapsed at the date when the application is made; and

B is the aggregate of the following amounts–

(a)   the income tax and any Class 4 contributions payable (whether or not yet due and payable) by the applicant, on his share of the annual profits or gains arising from the trade, profession or vocation of the sub-contractor which are chargeable to tax for the whole of that year, after deducting any cumulative entitlement of the applicant at the date of the application to an allowance under section 257 or 257A of ICTA (personal allowance and married couple's allowance);

Statutory Instruments

(b)   the income tax and any Class 4 contributions payable (whether or not yet due and payable) by the applicant, on any income arising during so much of the year as has elapsed at the date of the application, from which income tax has not been deducted at source, within the meaning given by section 59B(7) of TMA (payment of income tax and capital gains tax); and

(c)   any sum due and payable by the sub-contractor under ICTA or TMA, and, without prejudice to the generality of the foregoing, this includes any sums deducted by the sub-contractor in the capacity of a contractor, under section 61 of the Act.

17(4)   An application under this regulation must be made to the Commissioners for Her Majesty's Revenue and Customs containing a declaration that all of the information given in relation to paragraph (3) is correctly stated to the best of the knowledge and belief of the applicant, and where the applicant is a partner in a firm, the form shall be signed by all the partners in the firm who are individuals and, where the partner is a company, by the secretary or a director of the company.

17(5)   No repayment under this regulation shall be made after the end of the year to which the application relates.

PART 4 – PAYMENTS EXCEPTED FROM SECTION 60

SMALL PAYMENTS

18(1)   A payment under a construction contract is not a contract payment if–

(a)   the conditions prescribed in paragraph (2) in relation to the person making the payment are satisfied, and

(b)   the condition prescribed in paragraph (3) in relation to the payment is satisfied.

18(2)   The conditions prescribed in relation to the person making the payment are that–

(a)   the person is one to whom any of paragraphs (b) to (l) of section 59(1) of the Act (contractors) applies, and

(b)   the person has been approved by the Commissioners for Her Majesty's Revenue and Customs for the purposes of this regulation.

18(3)   The condition prescribed in relation to the payment is that the payment is not one made under a construction contract in respect of which the total payments so made (excluding the direct cost of materials) exceed or are likely to exceed £1000.

WORK CARRIED OUT ON LAND OWNED BY PERSON TO WHOM PAYMENT IS MADE

19(1)   A payment under a construction contract is not a contract payment if–

(a)   the conditions prescribed in paragraph (2) in relation to the person making the payment are satisfied, and

(b)   the conditions prescribed in paragraph (3) in relation to the payment are satisfied.

19(2)   The conditions prescribed in relation to the person making the payment are that–

(a)   the person is one to whom section 59(1)(a) of the Act applies, and

(b)   the person has been approved by the Commissioners for Her Majesty's Revenue and Customs for the purposes of this regulation.

19(3)   The conditions prescribed in relation to the payment are that the payment–

(a)   is made to a body or person in respect of construction operations carried out by that body or person in relation to–

(i)   property owned by that body or person, or

(ii)   agricultural property of which that body or person is a tenant, and

(b)   is not one made under a construction contract in respect of which the total payments so made (excluding the direct cost of materials) exceed or are likely to exceed £1000.

19(4)   For the purposes of paragraph (3)(a)(ii) **"agricultural property"** means–

(a)   agricultural land or pasture,

(b)   woodland or any building used in connection with the intensive rearing of livestock or fish if the woodland or building is occupied with agricultural land or pasture and the occupation is ancillary to that of the agricultural land or pasture,

(c)   cottages, farm buildings and farm houses, together with the land occupied with them, as are of a character appropriate to the property, and

(d)   land and buildings used for breeding and rearing horses on a stud farm and grazing of horses in connection with those activities.

History – In reg. 19(2)(a) the word "applies" inserted after "Act" by SI 2007/672, reg. 4, with effect from 26 March 2007.

REVERSE PREMIUMS

20(1)   Subject to paragraph (2), a payment under a construction contract is not a contract payment if the payment is a reverse premium within the meaning of Schedule 6 to the Finance Act 1999 (tax treatment of receipts by way of reverse premium) (see paragraph 1 of that Schedule) or section 99 of the Income Tax (Trading and Other Income) Act 2005 (reverse premiums).

20(2)   Paragraph 5 of Schedule 6 to the Finance Act 1999 (exclusion of receipts taken into account for capital allowances) and section 100(1) of the Income Tax (Trading and Other Income) Act 2005 (excluded cases) do not apply for the purposes of paragraph (1).

History – In reg. 20(1) the words "or section 99... premiums)" inserted by SI 2007/672, reg. 5(2), with effect from 26 March 2007.
In reg. 20(2) the words "and section 100(1)... do" substituted for "does" by SI 2007/672, reg. 5(3), with effect from 26 March 2007.

PAYMENT AS AGENT OF LOCAL AUTHORITY

21   A payment under a construction contract is not a contract payment if the payment is made by the governing body or head teacher of a maintained school as the agent of a local authority under section 49(5)(b) of the School Standards and Framework Act 1998 (delegated budget).

History – Reg. 21 substituted by SI 2010/1172, art. 4 and Sch. 3, para. 59, with effect from 5 May 2010. Former reg. 21 read as follows:

"PAYMENTS AS AGENT OF A LOCAL EDUCATION AUTHORITY
21   A payment under a construction contract is not a contract payment if the payment is made by the governing body or head teacher of a maintained school as the agent of a local education authority under section 49(5)(b) of the School Standards and Framework Act 1998 (delegated budgets).".

PAYMENTS IN RESPECT OF PROPERTY USED FOR BUSINESS

22(1)   A payment under a construction contract is not a contract payment if the payment is made by a person to whom section 59(1)(l) of the Act applies in respect of construction operations relating to property used for the purposes of the business of–

(a)   that person, or

(b)   another company in the same group or of another company of which that company owns 50% or more of the shares.

22(2)   For the purpose of paragraph (1)–

(a)   property is not used for the purposes of the business of a person if it is for sale or to let (except where the sale or letting of that property is purely incidental to the business of that person) or is held as an investment by that person;

(b)   in determining whether property is used for the purposes of the business of a person incidental use of that property by any other person is disregarded;

(c)   section 413(3)(a) of ICTA applies to determine whether two companies are in the same group.

History – In reg. 22(2)(a) the words "(except where the sale... that person)" inserted by SI 2007/672, reg. 6, with effect from 26 March 2007.

ARRANGEMENTS INVOLVING PUBLIC BODIES

23(1)   A payment under a construction contract is not a contract payment if–

(a)   the person making the payment ("the public body") is within any of paragraphs (b) to (k) of section 59(1) of the Act, and

(b)   the payment is made under a private finance transaction.

23(2)   For the purposes of this regulation, a transaction is a private finance transaction if–

(a)   the resources are provided partly by one or more public bodies and partly by one or more private persons;

(b)   it is designed wholly or mainly for the purpose of assisting a public body to discharge a function or is ancillary to the function of a public body; and

(c)   the public body makes payments by instalments at annual or more frequent intervals of fees determined in accordance with factors which include–

    (i)   the standard attained in the performance of services by the private person or persons in relation to the discharge of the function referred to in paragraph (b), or

    (ii)   the extent, rate or intensity of use of the resources or the asset which is constructed, enhanced, replaced or installed under the transaction.

23(3)   For the purposes of paragraph (2), **"resources"** includes–

(a)   funds (including payment for the provision of services or facilities),

(b)   assets,

(c)   professional skill,

(d)   the grant of a concession or franchise, and

(e)   any other commercial resource.

CHARITIES

24   A payment under a construction contract is not a contract payment if the payment is made by any body of persons or trust established for charitable purposes only.

PART 5 – REGISTRATION OF SUB-CONTRACTORS

REGISTRATION FOR GROSS PAYMENT OR FOR PAYMENT UNDER DEDUCTION AND CANCELLATION OF REGISTRATION FOR PAYMENT UNDER DEDUCTION

25(1)   On the application for registration for gross payment or for payment under deduction under section 63 of the Act (registration for gross payment or payment under deduction), the applicant must provide such documents, records and information to establish his identity as an officer of Revenue and Customs may require, which may include–

(a)   the applicant's birth certificate,

(b)   the name, address, national insurance number and unique taxpayer reference of–

    (i)   if the applicant is an individual, the applicant,

    (ii)   if the applicant is a partner in a firm, any partner,

    (iii)   if the applicant is a company, the directors of the company or, if the company is a close company, the persons who are the beneficial owners of shares in the company,

(c)   utility bills,

(d)   council tax bills,

(e)   current passport,

(f)   driving licence,

(g)   company registration number,

(h)   company's memorandum and articles of association.

25(2)   An officer of Revenue and Customs may require that any of the documents, records or information required under paragraph (1) be produced by the applicant in person.

25(3)   If the Commissioners for Her Majesty's Revenue and Customs are not satisfied with the documents, records or information provided under paragraph (1), they may refuse to register the applicant for payment under deduction by notice stating the reasons for the refusal ("the refusal notice").

25(4)   An officer of Revenue and Customs may at any time make a determination cancelling a person's registration for payment under deduction with immediate effect by notice stating the reasons for the cancellation ("the cancellation notice") if they have reasonable grounds to suspect that the person–

(a)   provided false or incorrect information under paragraph (1),

(b)   has fraudulently made an incorrect return or provided incorrect information (whether as a contractor or a sub-contractor) under any provision of Chapter 3 of the Act or these Regulations, or

(c)   has knowingly failed to comply (whether as a contractor or a sub-contractor) with any such provision.

25(5) A person may appeal against a notice or refusal specified in column 1 of Table 2 by giving notice to an officer of Revenue and Customs within 30 days of the event specified in column 2 stating the person's reasons for appeal stated in column 3.

Column 1: appeal	Column 2: timing event	Column 3: reasons for appeal
Appeal against a refusal notice.	Issue of the refusal notice.	Reasons for believing the application should not have been refused.
Appeal against a cancellation notice.	Issue of the cancellation notice.	Reasons for believing the registration should not have been cancelled.
Refusal to register for payment under deduction under section 66(7) of the Act (registration following cancellation of registration for gross payment).	Cancellation of registration for gross payment.	Reasons for believing the person should have been registered for payment under deduction.

25(6) [Omitted by SI 2009/56, art. 3(2) and Sch. 2, para. 141.]

History – Reg. 25(6) omitted by SI 2009/56, art. 3(2) and Sch. 2, para. 141, operative from 1 April 2009 subject to transitional and saving provisions in SI 2009/56, Sch. 3. Former reg. 25(6) read as follows:

"**25(6)** An appeal under paragraph (5) is to the General Commissioners or, if the person so elects in the notice, to the Special Commissioners.".

CANCELLATION OF REGISTRATION FOR GROSS PAYMENT

26 For the purpose of section 66(2) of the Act (cancellation of registration for gross payment) the prescribed period is 90 days from the date of the notice given under sub-section (5) of that section.

PART 6 – CONDITIONS TO BE SATISFIED FOR GROSS PAYMENT

Business test

EVIDENCE PRESCRIBED TO SATISFY THE BUSINESS TEST

27(1) The evidence required to satisfy an officer of Revenue and Customs for the purposes of section 64 of the Act (requirements for registration for gross payment) that the applicant or company is carrying on a business in the United Kingdom which satisfies the conditions mentioned in paragraph 2(a) and (b) of Schedule 11 to the Act is prescribed in paragraph (2).

27(2) The evidence is–

(a) the business address;

(b) invoices, contracts or purchase orders for construction work carried out by the applicant;

(c) details of payments for construction work;

(d) the books and accounts of the business;

(e) details of the business bank account, including bank statements.

Turnover test

MINIMUM TURNOVER

28(1) The minimum turnover for the purposes of paragraph 3(1) of Schedule 11 to the Act is £30,000.

28(2) The amount specified for the purposes of paragraph 7 of Schedule 11 to the Act is £200,000.

28(3) The amount specified for the purposes of paragraph 11 of Schedule 11 to the Act is £200,000.

EVIDENCE PRESCRIBED TO SATISFY THE TURNOVER TEST

29(1) The evidence prescribed for the purposes of paragraphs 3(1), 7(1) and 11(1) of Schedule 11 to the Act is–

(a)   evidence of turnover of the business mentioned in paragraph 3(1), 7(1) or 11(1) of Schedule 11 to the Act, as appropriate, during the qualifying period;

(b)   evidence of relevant payments which may include bank statements and paid cheques;

(c)   evidence that—

    (i)   the aggregate amount of relevant payments received in the qualifying period equalled or exceeded the relevant turnover threshold; or

    (ii)   for the purposes of section 66 of the Act (cancellation of registration for gross payment – continuing compliance), the aggregate amount of relevant payments received in the qualifying period equalled or exceeded the relevant turnover threshold or the average amount of relevant payments received in the qualifying period and the previous two years equalled or exceeded the relevant turnover threshold;

(d)   documentary evidence of operations carried out by the business during the qualifying period which demonstrate that the operations amounted to construction operations.

29(2)   In the case of a new business carried on by a firm or company where there is no evidence as prescribed in sub-paragraphs (a), (c) or (d) of paragraph 1, the evidence prescribed for the purposes of paragraphs 7(1) and 11(1) of Schedule 11 to the Act is—

(a)   evidence of relevant payments which may include bank statements and paid cheques;

(b)   in the case of a firm, evidence of turnover of partners during the qualifying period;

(c)   in the case of a company, evidence of turnover of relevant persons during the qualifying period;

(d)   evidence of construction contracts entered into by the firm or company including payment schedules where the aggregate value of these contracts exceeds £200,000 and payments of at least £30,000 have been made;

(e)   if the business mentioned in paragraph 11(1) of Schedule 11 was acquired from another person, firm or company ("the transferor"), the evidence specified in paragraph (3).

This is subject to paragraph (4).

29(3)   The evidence specified is—

(a)   evidence of turnover of the transferor in relation to carrying on the business during the qualifying period;

(b)   evidence that—

    (i)   the aggregate amount of relevant payments received by the transferor in relation to carrying on the business in the qualifying period equalled or exceeded the relevant turnover threshold; or

    (ii)   for the purposes of section 66(1)(a) of the Act (cancellation of registration for gross payment – continuing compliance), the aggregate amount of relevant payments received by the transferor in the qualifying period in relation to carrying on the business equalled or exceeded the relevant turnover threshold or the average amount of relevant payments in relation to the business received in the qualifying period and the previous two years equalled or exceeded the relevant turnover threshold;

(c)   invoices for operations carried out by the transferor during the qualifying period which demonstrate that the business operations amounted to construction operations;

(d)   evidence that the transferor would have satisfied the compliance test in paragraphs 4, 8 or 12 of Schedule 11 to the Act at the date of the transfer.

29(4)   The evidence prescribed in paragraph (2) may only be given in relation to one application for registration for gross payment.

29(5)   For the purposes of this regulation and regulation 31—

    "relevant payment" has the meaning given in paragraph 3(2) of Schedule 11 to the Act;

    "relevant turnover threshold" means—

    (a)   for the purposes of paragraph 3(1) of Schedule 11 of the Act, in relation to individuals, the minimum turnover specified in regulation 28(1);

    (b)   for the purposes of paragraph 7(1) of Schedule 11 of the Act, in relation to firms, the smaller of—

        (i)   the sum specified in paragraph 7(2) of Schedule 11 of the Act, and

        (ii)   the amount specified in regulation 28(2);

    (c)   for the purposes of paragraph 11(1) of Schedule 11 of the Act, in relation to companies, the minimum turnover for the purposes of that sub-paragraph.

NUMBER OF PARTNERS OR RELEVANT PERSONS

30 For the purposes of paragraphs 7(2)(a) and 11(2)(a) of Schedule 11 to the Act if the number of partners or relevant persons as the case may be has fluctuated over the qualifying period, the number of partners or relevant persons is the maximum number of partners or relevant persons at any one time in the qualifying period.

TURNOVER TEST TREATED AS SATISFIED IN PRESCRIBED CIRCUMSTANCES

31 A person, firm or company which does not satisfy the condition in paragraphs 3(1), 7(1) or 11(1) of Schedule 11 to the Act, as appropriate, is treated as satisfying that condition if an officer of Revenue and Customs is satisfied that—

(a)   the business of the person, firm or company does not mainly consist of construction operations,

(b)   in the year prior to making the application the total turnover of the business exceeded the relevant turnover threshold, and

(c)   in the year following making the application the person, firm or company is likely to receive relevant payments in relation to construction operations which are incidental to the main business of the person, firm or company.

COMPLIANCE TEST

32(1) The obligations and requests prescribed for the purposes of paragraphs 4(3), 8(2) and 12(2) of Schedule 11 to the Act are given in column 1 of Table 3.

32(2) The circumstances prescribed in which the applicant or company is to be treated as satisfying the conditions in paragraphs 4(1), 8(1) or 12(1) of Schedule 11 to the Act as regards each of the prescribed obligations are given in column 2 of Table 3.

1. Prescribed obligations	2. Prescribed circumstances
Obligation to submit monthly contractor return within the required period.	(1) Return is submitted not later than 28 days after the due date, and
	(2) the applicant or company—
	(a) has not otherwise failed to comply with this obligation within the previous 12 months, or
	(b) has failed to comply with this obligation on not more than two occasions within the previous 12 months.
Obligation to pay—	(1) Payment is made not later than 14 days after the due date, and
(a) the amount liable to be deducted under section 61 of the Act from payments made during that tax period, or	(2) the applicant or company— (a) has not otherwise failed to comply with this obligation within the previous 12 months, or
(b) tax liable to be deducted under the PAYE Regulations.	(b) has failed to comply with this obligation on not more than two occasions within the previous 12 months.
Obligation to pay income tax.	(1) Payment is made not later than 28 days after the due date, and
	(2) the applicant has not otherwise failed to comply with this obligation within the previous 12 months.
Obligation to submit a return under regulation 85 of the PAYE Regulations (annual return of other earnings) within the required period.	Return is submitted after the due date.
Obligation to pay corporation tax for which the applicant or company is liable.	(1) Payment is made not later than 28 days after the due date, and
	(2) any shortfall in that payment has incurred an interest charge but no penalty.

1. Prescribed obligations	2. Prescribed circumstances
Obligation to submit a self-assessment return within the required period.	Return is submitted after the due date.
Obligations and requests referred to in paragraphs 4(1), 8(1) and 12(1) of Schedule 11 to the Act.	The failure to comply occurred before the appointed day and was within section 562(10), 564(4) or 565(4) of ICTA (conditions to be satisfied: minor and technical failures).
Obligation to make a payment under the Tax Acts or Taxes Management Act 1970.	Late, or non-payment of an amount under £100.

History – In reg. 32, in Table 3, in the entry in column 1 relating to the obligation to submit a return under SI 2003/2682, reg. 67B, 67D, 73, 74 and 85, the words "67B or 67D (real time returns) and 73, 74 and" omitted by SI 2013/620, reg. 3(a), with effect from 6 April 2013 in relation to the tax year 2013–14 and subsequent years.

In reg. 32, in Table 3, in the entry in column 1 relating to the obligation to submit a return under SI 2003/2682, reg. 67B, 67D, 73, 74 and 85, the words "(annual return of other earnings)" substituted for the words "annual returns" by SI 2013/620, reg. 3(b), with effect from 6 April 2013 in relation to the tax year 2013–14 and subsequent years.

In reg. 32, in Table 3, in the entry in column 1 relating to the obligation to submit a return under SI 2003/2682, reg. 73, 74 and 85, the words "67B or 67D (real time returns) and" inserted by SI 2012/820, reg. 5, with effect from 6 April 2012.

In reg. 32, in Table 3, the words "Obligation to make a payment under the Tax Acts or Taxes Management Act 1970" and "Late, or non-payment of an amount under £100" inserted in column 1 and column 2 respectively by SI 2008/1282, reg. 2, with effect from 3 June 2008.

ABSENCE ABROAD – EVIDENCE OF LIVING OUTSIDE THE UNITED KINGDOM

33(1)   The evidence required to satisfy the Commissioners for Her Majesty's Revenue and Customs for the purposes of paragraph 4(5)(a) of Schedule 11 to the Act that the applicant was not subject to any one or more of the obligations mentioned in paragraph 4(1) of that Schedule because he has been outside the United Kingdom for the whole or part of the qualifying period is prescribed in paragraphs (2) and (3).

33(2)   Subject to paragraph (3), if the applicant claims to have been employed or self-employed outside the United Kingdom during any part of the qualifying period, the evidence is any document from the Revenue Department or equivalent department of the country in which he claims to have been living which confirms his presence throughout that part of the qualifying period.

33(3)   If the applicant claims–

(a)   not to have been employed or self-employed while outside the United Kingdom during any part of the qualifying period, or

(b)   to have been employed or self-employed outside the United Kingdom during any part of the qualifying period but not to have been liable to tax in the country in which he claims to have been living during that part of the qualifying period,

the evidence is any document from the Social Security Department or equivalent department, or from the immigration authorities, or from any other Government department of the country in which he claims to have been living which confirms his presence throughout that part of the qualifying period.

ABSENCE ABROAD – EVIDENCE OF COMPLIANCE WITH TAX OBLIGATIONS

34(1)   The evidence required to satisfy the Commissioners for Her Majesty's Revenue and Customs for the purposes of paragraph 4(5)(b) of Schedule 11 to the Act that the applicant has complied with any obligations imposed under the tax laws of any country in which he was living during any part of the qualifying period which are comparable to the obligations mentioned in paragraph 4(1) of that Schedule is prescribed in paragraph (2).

34(2)   The evidence is such notice or documents issued by the Revenue Department or equivalent department of the country in which the applicant claims to have been living as confirms that the obligations have been complied with.

EVIDENCE OF UNEMPLOYMENT

35(1)   The evidence required to satisfy the Commissioners for Her Majesty's Revenue and Customs for the purposes of paragraph 4(5)(a) of Schedule 11 to the Act that the applicant was not subject to any one or more of the obligations mentioned in paragraph 4(1) of that Schedule because he was unemployed is prescribed in paragraphs (2) and (3).

35(2)   If the applicant claims to have been living within the United Kingdom during any period, the evidence is–

(a)   a statement from the benefit officer certifying the period during which the applicant was registered as unemployed, or

(b)   during any period during which the applicant was not registered as unemployed, such other evidence as satisfied the Commissioners for Her Majesty's Revenue and Customs that he was unemployed during that period.

35(3)   If the applicant claims to have been living outside the United Kingdom during any period, the evidence is any document from the Social Security Department or equivalent department, or from the immigration authorities, or from any other Government Department of the country in which he claims to have been living, which confirms his presence there throughout that period.

35(4)   In paragraph (2), **"benefit officer"** means appropriate officer of the Department for Work and Pensions or, in Northern Ireland, the appropriate officer of the Department of Health and Social Services for Northern Ireland.

EVIDENCE OF FULL-TIME EDUCATION

36(1)   The evidence required to satisfy the Commissioners for Her Majesty's Revenue and Customs for the purposes of paragraph 4(5)(a) of Schedule 11 to the Act that the applicant was not subject to any one or more of the obligations mentioned in paragraph 4(1) of that Schedule because he was undergoing full-time education is prescribed in paragraphs (2) and (3).

36(2)   If the applicant claims to have been living within the United Kingdom, the evidence is a statement from the educational institution which the applicant attended, certifying the periods during which the applicant was undergoing full-time education at that institution.

36(3)   If the applicant claims to have been living outside the United Kingdom during any period, the evidence is a statement from the educational institution which the applicant attended, in the country in which the applicant claims to have been living, certifying the periods during which the applicant was undergoing full-time education at that institution.

INTERPRETATION

37   In this Part—

    "applicant" shall be construed in accordance with section 63 of and Schedule 11 to the Act;

    "qualifying period" has the meaning given in paragraph 14 of Schedule 11 to the Act.

PART 7 – ELECTRONIC COMMUNICATIONS

INTERPRETATION

38   In this Part—

    "official computer system" means a computer system maintained by or on behalf of the Commissioners for Her Majesty's Revenue and Customs or an officer of Revenue and Customs;

    "specified payment" means the amount due under regulation 7 (payment, due date for payment of amounts deducted and receipts) in respect of contract payments.

History – In reg. 38, in the definition of "specified payment", the words "made in the tax year to which the e-payment notice issued under regulation 199 of the PAYE Regulations relates (large employers required to make specified payments electronically)", which appeared at the end, omitted by SI 2010/717, reg. 4, with effect in relation to the tax year 2010–11 and subsequent tax years.

WHETHER INFORMATION HAS BEEN DELIVERED ELECTRONICALLY

39   For the purpose of these Regulations, information is taken to have been delivered to an official computer system by an approved method of electronic communications only if it is accepted by that official computer system.

PROOF OF CONTENT OF ELECTRONIC DELIVERY

40(1)   A document certified by an officer of Revenue and Customs to be a printed-out version of any information delivered by an approved method of electronic communications is evidence, unless the contrary is proved, that the information—

(a)   was delivered by an approved method of electronic communications on that occasion, and

(b)   constitutes everything which was delivered on that occasion.

Statutory Instruments

40(2) A document which purports to be a certificate given in accordance with paragraph (1) is presumed to be such a certificate unless the contrary is proved.

PROOF OF IDENTITY OF PERSON SENDING OR RECEIVING ELECTRONIC DELIVERY

41 The identity of–

(a)   the person sending any information by an approved method of electronic communications to Her Majesty's Revenue and Customs, or

(b)   the person receiving any information delivered by an approved method of electronic communications by Her Majesty's Revenue and Customs,

is presumed, unless the contrary is proved, to be the person recorded as such on an official computer system.

INFORMATION SENT ELECTRONICALLY ON BEHALF OF A PERSON

42(1) Any information delivered by an approved method of electronic communications–

(a)   to Her Majesty's Revenue and Customs, or

(b)   to an official computer system,

on behalf of a person is taken to have been delivered by that person.

42(2) But this does not apply if the person proves that the information was delivered without the person's knowledge or connivance.

PROOF OF DELIVERY OF INFORMATION SENT ELECTRONICALLY

43(1) The use of an approved method of electronic communications is presumed, unless the contrary is proved, to have resulted in the delivery of information–

(a)   to Her Majesty's Revenue and Customs, if the delivery of the information has been recorded on an official computer system;

(b)   by Her Majesty's Revenue and Customs, if the despatch of the information has been recorded on an official computer system.

43(2) The use of a method of electronic communications is presumed, unless the contrary is proved, not to have resulted in the delivery of information–

(a)   to Her Majesty's Revenue and Customs, if the delivery of the information has not been recorded on an official computer system;

(b)   by Her Majesty's Revenue and Customs, if despatch of the information has not been recorded on an official computer system.

43(3) The time of receipt or despatch of any information delivered by a method of electronic communications is presumed, unless the contrary is proved, to be the time recorded on an official computer system.

PROOF OF PAYMENT SENT ELECTRONICALLY

44(1) The use of a method of electronic communications is presumed, unless the contrary is proved, to have resulted in the making of a payment–

(a)   to Her Majesty's Revenue and Customs, if the making of the payment has been recorded on an official computer system;

(b)   by Her Majesty's Revenue and Customs, if despatch of the payment has been recorded on an official computer system.

44(2) The use of a method of electronic communications is presumed, unless the contrary is proved, not to have resulted in the making of a payment–

(a)   to Her Majesty's Revenue and Customs, if the making of the payment has not been recorded on an official computer system;

(b)   by Her Majesty's Revenue and Customs, if despatch of the payment has not been recorded on an official computer system.

44(3) The time of receipt or despatch of any payment sent by a method of electronic communications is presumed, unless the contrary is proved, to be the time recorded on an official computer system.

MANDATORY ELECTRONIC PAYMENT

45(1)   A contractor who is a large employer within the meaning of regulation 198A (large employers) of the PAYE Regulations must pay the specified payment using an approved method of electronic communications.

45(2)   Paragraph (1) applies regardless of whether a payment of tax is due under regulation 67G or 68 of the PAYE Regulations (payment and recovery of tax by employer).

45(3)   If the Commissioners for Her Majesty's Revenue and Customs have given directions under regulation 199(3) of the PAYE Regulations in relation to a contractor, the specified payment must be made in accordance with those directions.

45(4)   A specified payment is not treated as received in full by Her Majesty's Revenue and Customs on or before the date by which that specified payment is required in accordance with regulation 7 unless it is made in a manner which secures (in a case where the specified payment is made otherwise than in cash) that, on or before that date, all transactions can be completed which need to be completed before the whole amount of the specified payment becomes available to the Commissioners for Her Majesty's Revenue and Customs.

History – In reg. 45(1), the words "198A (large employers)" substituted for the words "191 (large and medium sized employers)" by SI 2010/717, reg. 5(b), with effect in relation to the tax year 2011–12 and subsequent tax years.
Reg. 45(1) substituted by SI 2010/717, reg. 5(a), with effect in relation to the tax year 2010–11 and subsequent tax years.
In reg. 45(2), "67G or" inserted by SI 2012/820, reg. 6, with effect from 6 April 2012.
Reg. 45(4) inserted by SI 2010/717, reg. 5(c), with effect in relation to the tax year 2010–11 and subsequent tax years.

CONTRACTOR IN DEFAULT IF SPECIFIED PAYMENT NOT RECEIVED BY APPLICABLE DUE DATE

46   [Omitted by SI 2010/717, reg. 6.]

History – Reg. 46 omitted by SI 2010/717, reg. 6, with effect in relation to the tax year 2010–11 and subsequent tax years.

DEFAULT NOTICE AND APPEAL

47   [Omitted by SI 2010/717, reg. 6.]

History – Reg. 47 omitted by SI 2010/717, reg. 6, with effect in relation to the tax year 2010–11 and subsequent tax years.

DEFAULT SURCHARGE

48   [Omitted by SI 2010/466, art. 4(2) and (3).]

History – Reg. 48 omitted by SI 2010/466, art. 4(2) and (3), with effect from 6 April 2010 but not in relation to surcharges arising in respect of late payments of tax where the tax was chargeable in respect of a tax period ending on or before 5 April 2010. Relevant definitions in SI 2010/466, art. 2 are as follows:

"**"tax quarter"** means any of the following (inclusive) periods–
6th April to 5th July, 6th July to 5th October, 6th October to 5th January and 6th January to 5th April;
"tax month" means the period beginning on the 6th day of a calendar month and ending on the 5th day of the following calendar month;
"tax period" means a tax quarter or tax month;"
Former reg. 48 read as follows:

"**48(1)**   A contractor in default in respect of any specified payment to whom–
(a)   a default notice under regulation 47, and
(b)   a surcharge notice under regulation 49,
have been issued, is liable to a surcharge.
48(2)   The surcharge is the sum of the surcharges, calculated in accordance with paragraph (3), in respect of each default relating to the tax year in which were made the contract payments to which the specified payment referred to in paragraph (1) relates.
48(3)   The surcharge in respect of each default is the specified percentage of (A - B).
48(4)   In paragraph (3)–
(a)   A is the total amount the contractor was liable to deduct under section 61 of the Act on account of tax from contract payments made in the tax year in which the contract payments to which the specified payment relates were made;
(b)   B is the total of the amounts deducted from A under–
  (i)   regulations 4, 5 and 6 of the Statutory Maternity Pay (Compensation of Employers) and Miscellaneous Amendment Regulations 1994,
  (ii)   regulations 3 and 5 of the Statutory Paternity Pay and Statutory Adoption Pay (Administration) Regulations 2002, and
  (iii)   regulation 56 (application by the Commissioners for Her Majesty's Revenue and Customs of sums deducted under section 61);
(c)   the specified percentage is determined by reference to the number of the default during a surcharge period in accordance with Table 4.

1. Default number (within a surcharge period)	2. Specified percentage
1st	0%
2nd	0%

1. Default number (within a surcharge period)	2. Specified percentage
3rd	0.17%
4th	0.17%
5th	0.17%
6th	0.33%
7th	0.33%
8th	0.33%
9th	0.58%
10th	0.58%
11th	0.58%
12th	0.83%

48(5) A surcharge period is a period which–

(a) begins on the day following the date by which payment is required in accordance with paragraph 7 for the first specified payment in respect of which the contractor is in default, and

(b) ends at the end of a tax year in relation to which the contractor has not been in default in respect of any specified payment.

48(6) A surcharge payable under this paragraph is payable 30 days after the issue of the surcharge notice.

48(7) Section 102 of TMA (mitigation of penalties) applies to a surcharge payable under this paragraph as if it were a penalty.

48(8) Section 108 of the Finance Act 2009 (suspension of penalties during currency of agreement for deferred payment) applies to a surcharge payable under this regulation with the following modifications–

(a) in the Table in subsection (5), insert at the end–

"Specified payments within the meaning of regulation 38 of the Income Tax (Construction Industry Scheme) Regulations 2005	Surcharge under regulation 48 of the Income Tax (Construction Industry Scheme) Regulations 2005"

, and

(b) omit subsections (7), (8), (9) and (11).

History – Former reg. 48(8) inserted by SI 2009/2030, reg. 2(2), with effect in relation to deferred payment agreements made on or after 13 August 2009."

SURCHARGE NOTICE AND APPEAL

49 [Omitted by SI 2010/466, art. 4(2) and (3).]

History – Reg. 49 omitted by SI 2010/466, art. 4(2) and (3), with effect from 6 April 2010 but not in relation to surcharges arising in respect of late payments of tax where the tax was chargeable in respect of a tax period ending on or before 5 April 2010. Relevant definitions in SI 2010/466, art. 2 are as follows:

"**"tax quarter"** means any of the following (inclusive) periods–

6th April to 5th July, 6th July to 5th October, 6th October to 5th January and 6th January to 5th April;

"tax month" means the period beginning on the 6th day of a calendar month and ending on the 5th day of the following calendar month;

"tax period" means a tax quarter or tax month;"

Former reg. 49 read as follows:

"**49(1)** An officer of Revenue and Customs must issue a surcharge notice to a contractor who has been in default on three or more occasions during a surcharge period and consequently will be liable to a surcharge under regulation 48.

49(2) The surcharge notice must show the total surcharge liability for the tax year.

49(3) The surcharge notice must be issued within 6 years of–

(a) the end of the tax year, or

(b) if earlier, the date on which the contractor delivered a return in accordance with regulation 73 of the PAYE Regulations (annual return of relevant payments liable to deduction of tax (Forms P35 and P14)).

49(4) A contractor may appeal against a surcharge notice by giving notice to an officer of Revenue and Customs within 30 days of the issue of the surcharge notice.

49(5) The grounds of appeal are–

(a) that the numbers of defaults stated in the notice is incorrect, or

(b) that the amount of the surcharge is incorrect.

49(6) But paragraph (5)(a) does not apply in respect of a disputed default which has already been the subject of an appeal under regulation 49, following which the default notice was not withdrawn.""

PART 8 – SUPPLEMENTARY PROVISIONS

DELEGATION OF COMMISSIONERS FOR HER MAJESTY'S REVENUE AND CUSTOMS' FUNCTIONS

50(1) The following may be done by an officer of Revenue and Customs on behalf of the Commissioners for Her Majesty's Revenue and Customs–

(a) the registration of persons under section 63 of the Act (registration for gross payment or payment under deduction);

(b)   the giving of directions under section 64(5) of the Act (power to make directions as to application of conditions to be satisfied by individuals applying for registration for gross payment);

(c)   the cancellation under section 66 of the Act of a person's registration for gross payment.

50(2)   This regulation is without prejudice to any other power of the Commissioners for Her Majesty's Revenue and Customs to delegate their functions.

INSPECTION OF RECORDS OF CONTRACTORS AND SUB-CONTRACTORS

51(1)   Whenever required to do so by a person nominated by the Commissioners for Her Majesty's Revenue and Customs, a contractor must produce to that person all contractor records, or such contractor records as may be specified by that person, for inspection at the prescribed place and at such time as that person may reasonably require.

51(2)   **"Contractor records"** means all documents and records relating to–

(a)   the calculation and payment of sums paid by the contractor to sub-contractors (or their nominees) under contracts relating to construction operations, and

(b)   the deductions made from such sums required under section 61 of the Act,

        in the tax years or tax periods specified by the nominated person.

51(3)   Whenever required to do so by a person nominated by the Commissioners for Her Majesty's Revenue and Customs, a person who is or has within the preceding three tax years been a sub-contractor must produce to that person all sub-contractor records, or such sub-contractor records as may be specified by that person, for inspection at the prescribed place and at such time as that person may reasonably require.

51(4)   **"Sub-contractor records"** means all documents and records relating to–

(a)   the calculation or payment of sums paid to the sub-contractor pursuant to any contract relating to construction operations under which he is or was a sub-contractor within the previous three years, and

(b)   the direct cost of materials relating to any such contract.

51(5)   **"The prescribed place"** means such place in the United Kingdom as the contractor or sub-contractor and the nominated person may agree upon, or in the absence of agreement–

(a)   the place in the United Kingdom at which the contractor records or sub-contractor records are normally kept, or

(b)   if there is no such place, the contractor's or sub-contractor's principal place of business in the United Kingdom.

51(6)   The nominated person may–

(a)   take copies of, or make extracts from, any document produced for inspection in accordance with paragraph (1) or (3);

(b)   remove any document so produced if it appears to the nominated person to be necessary to do so, at a reasonable time and for a reasonable period.

51(7)   If any document is removed in accordance with paragraph (6)(b), the nominated person must provide–

(a)   a receipt for the document, and

(b)   a copy of the document, free of charge, to the person by whom it was produced or caused to be produced, within seven days of that person requesting a copy, if the document is reasonably required for the proper conduct of a business.

51(8)   If a lien is claimed on a document produced in accordance with paragraph (1) or (3), the removal of the document under paragraph (6)(b) is not to be regarded as breaking the lien.

51(9)   If records are maintained by computer, the person required to make them available for inspection must provide the nominated person with all facilities necessary for obtaining information from them.

51(10)   For the purposes of this regulation, a contractor and a sub-contractor must keep, for not less than three years after the end of the tax year to which they relate, all contractor records or sub-contractor records as the case may be which are not required to be sent to the Commissioners for Her Majesty's Revenue and Customs by other provisions of these Regulations.

Statutory Instruments

INSPECTION OF RECORDS OF SUB-CONTRACTORS – ADDITIONAL PROVISIONS

52(1) Where a sum deducted under section 61 of the Act is treated as paid on account of the liabilities mentioned in regulation 56(2) (application by Commissioners for Her Majesty's Revenue and Customs of sums deducted under section 61), the sub-contractor, whose liabilities they are, shall–

(a)   maintain the records specified in paragraph (2), and

(b)   produce to a person nominated by the Commissioners for Her Majesty's Revenue and Customs for inspection those records, or such of them as may be specified by him, at such time as he may reasonably require, at the prescribed place.

52(2) The records are all documents and records relating to the calculation of–

(a)   the amounts which the sub-contractor would have been liable to pay to the Commissioners for Her Majesty's Revenue and Customs in the preceding three tax years, under the provisions mentioned in regulation 56(2), but for the withholding by a contractor of sums due to him; and

(b)   the amounts deducted by a contractor under section 61 of the Act which the sub-contractor claims to be entitled to set off against those liabilities.

52(3) **"The prescribed place"** means such place in the United Kingdom as the sub-contractor and the nominated person may agree upon, or in the absence of agreement—

(a)   the place in the United Kingdom at which the documents and records mentioned in paragraph (2) are normally kept, or

(b)   if there is no such place, the sub-contractor's principal place of business in the United Kingdom.

52(4) The nominated person may–

(a)   take copies of, or make extracts from, any document produced for inspection in accordance with paragraph (1)(b);

(b)   remove any document so produced if it appears to the nominated person to be necessary to do so, at a reasonable time and for a reasonable period.

52(5) If a lien is claimed on a document produced in accordance with paragraph (1)(b), the removal of the document under paragraph (4)(b) is not to be regarded as breaking the lien.

52(6) If records are maintained by computer, the person required to make them available for inspection must provide the nominated person with all facilities necessary for obtaining information from them.

INFORMATION AS TO CHANGE OF CONTROL OF CLOSE COMPANY

53(1) This regulation applies to a company which–

(a)   is a close company,

(b)   is a private company limited by shares, and

(c)   is registered for gross payment or is applying to be so registered.

53(2) Where there is a change in the control of the company by reason of an issue or transfer of shares in the company to a person who was not a shareholder in the company immediately before the issue or transfer, the company shall, within 30 days of the issue or of receiving information as to the transfer, give notice to the Commissioners for Her Majesty's Revenue and Customs of the name and address of the person to whom the shares were issued or transferred.

53(3) In this regulation **"control"** has the same meaning as in section 840 of ICTA.

DEATH OF CONTRACTOR

54 If a contractor dies, anything which he would have been liable to do under these Regulations must be done by his personal representatives.

SERVICE BY POST

55 Any notice which is authorised or required to be given, served or issued under these Regulations may be sent by post.

APPLICATION BY THE COMMISSIONERS FOR HER MAJESTY'S REVENUE AND CUSTOMS OF SUMS DEDUCTED UNDER SECTION 61

56(1) This regulation applies to sums deducted from contract payments made to a sub-contractor which is a company ("the qualifying sub-contractor").

56(2) So much of any sum deducted under section 61 of the Act by a contractor in a tax year and paid to the Commissioners for Her Majesty's Revenue and Customs as is required shall be applied–

(a)   first, in discharge of any liability of the qualifying sub-contractor to account for primary Class 1 contributions in respect of earnings paid to its employees in that year;

(b)   second, in discharge of any liability of the qualifying sub-contractor for secondary Class 1 contributions in respect of earnings paid to its employees in that year;

(c)   third, in discharge of any liability of the qualifying sub-contractor to account for tax deducted from the emoluments of its employees in accordance with Regulations made under section 684 of ITEPA (pay as you earn) in respect of that year;

(d)   fourth, in discharge of any liability of the qualifying sub-contractor to account for deductions made by it in that year from the emoluments of its employees in accordance with regulations made under section 22(5) of the Teaching and Higher Education Act 1998, section 73B of the Education (Scotland) Act 1980, or Article 3(5) of the Education (Student Support) (Northern Ireland) Order 1998;

(e)   fifth, in discharge of any liability of the qualifying sub-contractor to refund to the Commissioners for Her Majesty's Revenue and Customs any funding payment made by them in respect of statutory sick pay, statutory maternity pay, ordinary statutory paternity pay, additional statutory paternity pay or statutory adoption pay under the relevant recovery provision; and

(f)   last, in discharge of any liability of the qualifying sub-contractor to account for sums deducted by it (in its capacity as a contractor) under section 61 of the Act from payments made to other sub-contractors.

56(2A) For any tax period where as a consequence of paragraph (2) the qualifying sub-contractor pays an amount to the Commissioners for Her Majesty's Revenue and Customs in respect of any liability referred to in that paragraph that is less than the amount the qualifying sub-contractor would have paid but for that paragraph, paragraph (2B) applies if the qualifying sub-contractor is a Real Time Information employer for the purposes of the PAYE Regulations.

56(2B) The qualifying sub-contractor must deliver to the Commissioners for Her Majesty's Revenue and Customs a return under this paragraph stating the value of the sums deducted from contract payments made to the qualifying sub-contractor under section 61 of the Act in the tax year to date.

56(2C) The return required by paragraph (2B) must be delivered within 14 days after the end of the tax period.

56(2D) If an employer makes an error in a return under paragraph (2B), the employer must provide the correct information in the first return made under that paragraph after the discovery of the error.

56(2E) But if the information given has not been corrected before 20th April following the end of the year in question, the employer must provide the correct information for the year in question in a return under this paragraph.

56(3) So much of any sum deducted under section 61 of the Act as is not required to discharge the sub-contractor's liabilities specified in paragraph (2) shall be repaid to the qualifying sub-contractor. This is subject to the qualifications in paragraphs (5) and (6).

56(4) [Omitted by SI 2014/992, art. 11(c).]

56(5) The Commissioners for Her Majesty's Revenue and Customs shall not repay any sum deducted under section 61 of the Act to the qualifying sub-contractor unless–

(a)   the tax year in which the deduction was made, has ended; and

(b)   the qualifying sub-contractor has paid to the Commissioners for Her Majesty's Revenue and Customs–

   (i)   any amounts the qualifying sub-contractor deducted from contract payments in their capacity as a contractor during that tax year, and

   (ii)   any amounts due under the PAYE Regulations in respect of that tax year.

56(6) If it appears to an officer of Revenue and Customs that there is an outstanding liability of the qualifying sub-contractor in respect of corporation tax due for an accounting period ending before the relevant payment is made under section 61 of the Act, the amount required to discharge that liability shall be retained by the Commissioners for Her Majesty's Revenue and Customs and applied in discharge of that liability.

56(7)   In paragraph (2)(e), **"the relevant recovery provision"** means–

(a)   in respect of ordinary statutory paternity pay and statutory adoption pay, regulations 4, 5, 6 and 8 of either the Statutory Paternity Pay and Statutory Adoption Pay (Administration) Regulations 2002 or the Statutory Paternity Pay and Statutory Adoption Pay (Administration) Regulations (Northern Ireland) 2002;

(aa)   in respect of additional statutory paternity pay, regulations 4, 5, 6 and 8 of either the Additional Statutory Paternity Pay (Birth, Adoption and Adoptions from Overseas) (Administration) Regulations 2010 or the Additional Statutory Paternity Pay (Birth, Adoption and Adoptions from Overseas) (Administration) Regulations (Northern Ireland) 2010;

(b)   in respect of statutory maternity pay, regulations 5, 6, 6A and 7A of the Statutory Maternity (Compensation of Employers) and Miscellaneous Amendment Regulations 1994 or the Statutory Maternity (Compensation of Employers) and Miscellaneous Amendment Regulations (Northern Ireland) 1994.

56(8)   A return under this regulation must–

(a)   state–

    (i)   the employer's HMRC office number,

    (ii)   the employer's PAYE reference for the purposes of the PAYE Regulations,

    (iii)   the employer's accounts office reference, and

    (iv)   the tax year to which the return relates, and

(b)   be delivered using an approved method of electronic communications unless the qualifying sub-contractor is one to whom regulation 67D of the PAYE Regulations applies, in which case the return must be made in a document or format provided or approved by the Commissioners for Her Majesty's Revenue and Customs.

History – In reg. 56(2)(e), the words "ordinary statutory paternity pay, additional statutory paternity pay" substituted for the words "statutory paternity pay" by SI 2010/2495, reg. 4(a), with effect from 14 November 2010.
Reg. 56(2A), (2B), (2C), (2D) and (2E) inserted by SI 2012/820, reg. 7(a), with effect from 6 April 2012.
Reg. 56(4) omitted by SI 2014/992, art. 11(c), with effect from 6 May 2014 in relation to payments which are due and payable in respect of the tax year 2014–15 and subsequent tax years. Former reg. 56(4) read as follows:

    "**56(4)**   Regulation 83 of the PAYE Regulations (interest on tax overpaid) shall apply to any sum repaid under paragraph (3) and any such sum shall be treated as tax repaid for the purposes of that regulation.".
In reg. 56(5), the word "unless" substituted for the word "until" by SI 2012/820, reg. 7(b), with effect from 6 April 2012.
Reg. 56(5)(b) substituted by SI 2013/620, reg. 4, with effect from 6 April 2013 in relation to the tax year 2013–14 and subsequent tax years. Former reg. 56(5)(b) read as follows:
    "(b)   either–
        (i)   the qualifying sub-contractor has delivered the return required by regulation 73 of the PAYE Regulations (annual return of relevant payments liable to deduction of tax), or
        (ii)   the qualifying sub-contractor has delivered to the Commissioners for Her Majesty's Revenue and Customs each return required under paragraph (2B) for the tax year.".
Former reg. 56(5)(b) substituted by SI 2012/820, reg. 7(c), with effect from 6 April 2012. Former reg. 56(5)(b) read as follows:
    "(b)   the qualifying sub-contractor has delivered the return required by regulation 73 of the PAYE Regulations (annual return of relevant payments liable to deduction of tax).".
In reg. 56(7)(a), the words "ordinary statutory paternity pay" substituted for the words "statutory paternity pay" by SI 2010/2495, reg. 4(b), with effect from 14 November 2010.
Reg. 56(7)(aa) inserted by SI 2010/2495, reg. 4(c), with effect from 14 November 2010.
Reg. 56(8) inserted by SI 2012/820, reg. 7(d), with effect from 6 April 2012.

CERTIFICATE THAT SUM DUE

57(1)   A certificate of an officer of Revenue and Customs that, to the best of his knowledge and belief, any amount shown in a certificate under the regulations listed in paragraph (2) has not been paid by a contractor, is sufficient evidence that the amount mentioned in the certificate is unpaid and due to the Crown.

57(2)   The regulations are–

    regulation 10(6) (return and certificate if amount may be unpaid)

    regulation 11(8) (notice and certificate if amount may be unpaid)

    regulation 12(2) (certificate after inspection of records).

57(2A)   An officer of Revenue and Customs may prepare a certificate showing the whole or part of a combined amount which includes deductions under section 61 of the Act without specifying the components of the combined amount.

Paragraph (1) shall apply with any necessary modifications to the certificate.

57(3) A certificate of an officer of Revenue and Customs that, to the best of his knowledge and belief, any amount of interest payable under regulation 14 (interest on amounts overdue) has not been paid by a contractor, is sufficient evidence that the amount mentioned in the certificate is unpaid and due to the Crown.

57(3A) An officer of Revenue and Customs may prepare a certificate showing the total amount of interest payable in respect of the whole or any component of the combined amount without specifying which component of the combined amount the interest relates to.

Paragraph (3) shall apply with any necessary modifications to the certificate.

57(4) The production of–

(a)   the return made by the contractor under regulation 10(4), and

(b)   the certificate of an officer of Revenue and Customs under regulation 10(6),

is sufficient evidence that the amount shown in the certificate is the amount of tax which the contractor is liable to pay to the Commissioners for Her Majesty's Revenue and Customs in respect of the tax period in question.

57(5) A document which purports to be a certificate under this regulation is treated as such a certificate until the contrary is proved.

History – Reg. 57(2A) inserted by SI 2008/740, reg. 8(2), with effect from 6 April 2008.
In reg. 57(3) the word "the" omitted following "interest payable under" by SI 2008/740, reg. 8(3), with effect from 6 April 2008.
Reg. 57(3A) inserted by SI 2008/740, reg. 8(4), with effect from 6 April 2008.
In reg. 57(5) the words "this regulation" substituted for "paragraph (1) or (3)" by SI 2008/740, reg. 8(5), with effect from 6 April 2008.

PAYMENT BY CHEQUE

58(1) For the purposes of the following provisions, if–

(a)   any payment to the Commissioners for Her Majesty's Revenue and Customs is made by cheque, and

(b)   the cheque is paid on its first presentation to the banker on whom it is drawn,

the payment shall be treated as made on the day which the cheque was received by the Commissioners for Her Majesty's Revenue and Customs.

58(2) [Omitted by SI 2014/992, art. 11(d).]

History – Reg. 58(2) omitted by SI 2014/992, art. 11(d), with effect from 6 May 2014 in relation to payments which are due and payable in respect of the tax year 2014–15 and subsequent tax years. Former reg. 58(2) read as follows:

"**58(2)**   The provisions are–
regulation 7 payment, due date for payment of amounts deducted and receipts for payment of tax
regulation 9 recovery from sub-contractor of tax not deducted by contractor
regulation 11 notice and certificate if tax may be unpaid
regulation 14 interest on amounts overdue".

APPEALS: SUPPLEMENTARY PROVISIONS

59(1) Section 31A(5) and (6) of TMA applies to appeals under regulation 47 (default notice and appeal) as it applies to an appeal under section 31 of that Act.

59(2) [Omitted by SI 2009/56, art. 3(2) and Sch. 2, para. 142(3).]

59(3) [Omitted by SI 2009/56, art. 3(2) and Sch. 2, para. 142(3).]

History – Reg. 59(1) substituted by SI 2009/56, art. 3(2) and Sch. 2, para. 142(2), operative from 1 April 2009 subject to transitional and saving provisions in SI 2009/56, Sch. 3. Former reg. 59(1) read as follows:

"**59(1)**   The following provisions of TMA apply to appeals under regulation 47 (default notice and appeal), as they apply to an appeal under section 31 of TMA–
(a)   section 31A(5) and (6) (notice of appeal);
(b)   section 31B (appeals to General Commissioners);
(c)   section 31D (election to bring appeal before Special Commissioners).".
Reg. 59(2) omitted by SI 2009/56, art. 3(2) and Sch. 2, para. 142(3), operative from 1 April 2009 subject to transitional and saving provisions in SI 2009/56, Sch. 3. Former reg. 59(2) read as follows:

"**59(2)**   In an appeal under regulation 47 or regulation 49(4) (surcharge notice and appeal), the relevant place for the purposes of paragraph 3(1)(a) of Schedule 3 to TMA[40] (rules for assigning proceedings to General Commissioners) is the place which at the time of the notice of appeal is–
(a)   the contractor's place of business in the United Kingdom, or
(b)   if there is no such place, the contractor's place of residence in the United Kingdom.".
Reg. 59(3) omitted by SI 2009/56, art. 3(2) and Sch. 2, para. 142(3), operative from 1 April 2009 subject to transitional and saving provisions in SI 2009/56, Sch. 3. Former reg. 59(3) read as follows:

"**59(3)**   In paragraph (2)–
"**place of business**" means–
(a)   the place where the trade, profession, vocation or business with which the proceedings are concerned is carried out, or
(b)   if more than one such place, the head office or place where it is mainly carried out; and
"**place of residence**" means the contractor's usual place of residence or, if that is unknown, the contractor's last known place of residence.".

TRANSITIONAL PROVISIONS, SAVINGS AND REVOCATION

60(1)   Schedule 1 (transitional provisions and savings) has effect.

60(2)   The Regulations listed in column 1 of Schedule 2 are revoked to the extent specified in column 3 of that Schedule.

60(3)   Paragraph (2) is subject to Schedule 1.

SCHEDULES

SCHEDULE 1 – TRANSITIONAL PROVISIONS AND SAVINGS

Regulation 60

Part 1 – General Provisions

CONTINUITY OF THE LAW

1   The revocation of provisions and their making in a rewritten form in these Regulations does not affect the continuity of the law.

2   Paragraph 1 does not apply to any change in the law made by these Regulations.

3   Anything which–

(a)   has been done, or has effect as if done, under or for the purposes of a provision of the revoked Regulations, and

(b)   is in force or effective immediately before the commencement of these Regulations,

has effect after that commencement as if done under or for the purposes of the corresponding provision of these Regulations.

4   Any reference (express or implied) in these Regulations or any document made under these Regulations to–

(a)   a provision of these Regulations, or

(b)   things done or falling to be done under or for the purposes of a provision of these Regulations,

is to be read as including, in relation to times, circumstances or purposes in relation to which any corresponding provision of the revoked Regulations had effect, a reference to the provision of the revoked Regulations or to things done or falling to be done under or for the purposes of the provision of the revoked Regulations.

5   Any reference (express or implied) in these Regulations to–

(a)   a provision of the Act, or

(b)   things done or falling to be done under or for the purposes of a provision of the Act,

is to be read as including, in relation to times, circumstances or purposes in relation to which any corresponding provision repealed by the Act had effect, a reference to the repealed provision or to things done or falling to be done under or for the purposes of the repealed provision.

6   Any reference (express or implied) in these Regulations to contractors, sub-contractors, construction operations or similar concepts created by the Act is to be read as including, in relation to times, circumstances or purposes in relation to which any corresponding concept which has been superseded by the Act had effect, a reference to the superseded concept.

7   Paragraphs 4, 5 and 6 apply only in so far as the context permits.

8   Paragraph 6 is without prejudice to the generality of paragraph 5.

9   These Regulations have effect in relation to sums liable, under the Income Tax (Sub-contractors in the Construction Industry) Regulations 1993, to be deducted or accounted for in respect of payments made before the appointed day as if the sum had been liable to be deducted or accounted for under these Regulations.

10   Paragraph 9 is without prejudice to the generality of paragraphs 1 to 8.

11   Paragraphs 1 to 10 have effect instead of paragraph (b) of section 17(2) of the Interpretation Act 1978.

GENERAL SAVING FOR OLD SAVINGS

12(1) The revocation by these Regulations of a provision previously revoked subject to savings does not affect the continued operation of those savings.

12(2) The revocation by these Regulations of a saving on the previous revocation of a provision does not affect the operation of the saving in so far as it is not specifically reproduced in these Regulations but remains capable of having effect.

INTERPRETATION

13 In this Part of this Schedule, "the revoked Regulations" means the Regulations which are revoked by these Regulations.

Part 2 – Specific Provisions

INTEREST ON UNPAID AMOUNTS: DISAPPLICATION OF REGULATION 14 FOR TAX YEARS BEFORE THE TAX YEAR ENDING 5TH APRIL 1993

1 Regulation 14 (interest on amounts overdue) does not apply in relation to unpaid amounts in respect of a tax year ending on or before 5th April 1992.

INTEREST ON OVERPAID TAX: DISAPPLICATION OF REGULATION 15 FOR TAX YEARS BEFORE THE TAX YEAR ENDING 5TH APRIL 1993

2 Regulation 15 (interest on overpaid amount) does not apply to tax which was paid by an employer in respect of a tax year ending on or before 5th April 1993.

SCHEDULE 2 – REVOCATIONS

Regulation 60

1. Regulations revoked	2. Reference	3. Extent of revocation
The Income Tax (Sub-contractors in the Construction Industry) Regulations 1993	1993/743	The whole instrument.
The Income Tax (Sub-contractors in the Construction Industry) (Amendment) Regulations 1995	1995/217	The whole instrument.
The Income Tax (Sub-contractors in the Construction Industry) (Amendment No. 2) Regulations 1995	1995/448	The whole instrument.
The Income Tax (Sub-contractors in the Construction Industry) (Amendment) Regulations 1996	1996/981	The whole instrument.
The Income Tax (Sub-contractors in the Construction Industry) (Amendment) Regulations 1998	1998/2622	The whole instrument.
The Income Tax (Sub-contractors in the Construction Industry) (Amendemnt) Regulations 1999	1999/825	The whole instrument.
The Income Tax (Sub-contractors in the Construction Industry) (Amendment No. 2) Regulations 1999	1999/2159	The whole instrument.
The Income Tax (Sub-contractors in the Construction Industry) (Amendment) Regulations 2000	2000/1151	The whole instrument.
The Income Tax (Sub-contractors in the Construction Industry) (Amendment No. 2) Regulations 2000	2000/1880	The whole instrument.

1. Regulations revoked	2. Reference	3. Extent of revocation
The Income Tax (Sub-contractors in the Construction Industry and Employments) (Amendment) Regulations 2000	2000/2742	The whole instrument to the extent not already revoked.
The Income Tax (Sub-contractors in the Construction Industry) (Amendment) Regulations 2001	2001/1531	The whole instrument.
The Income Tax (Sub-contractors in the Construction Industry) (Amendment) Regulations 2002	2002/2225	The whole instrument.
The Income Tax (Sub-contractors in the Construction Industry and Employments) (Amendment) Regulations 2003	2003/536	The whole instrument to the extent not already revoked.
The Income Tax (Sub-contractors in the Construction Industry) (Amendment) Regulations 2004	2004/1075	The whole instrument.

REVENUE AND CUSTOMS (COMPLAINTS AND MISCONDUCT) REGULATIONS 2005

(SI 2005/3311, as amended by SI 2006/1748 and as revoked by SI 2010/1813 (see note below))

Made by the Treasury on 1st December 2005, in exercise of the powers conferred on them by s. 28(1) and (2), and 29(3) of the Commissioners for Revenue and Customs Act 2005.

History – SI 2005/3311 revoked by SI 2010/1813, reg. 2(a), with effect from 5 August 2010, but continue to have effect where an allegation in respect of the conduct by an officer came to the attention of the appropriate authority before 5 August 2010, in which case they continue to apply (SI 2010/1813, reg. 2(b)). For reference purposes the text of former SI 2005/3311 is reproduced below.

"CITATION, COMMENCEMENT AND EXTENT

1(1) These Regulations may be cited as the Revenue and Customs (Complaints and Misconduct) Regulations 2005 and shall come into force on 28th December 2005.

1(2) These Regulations extend to England and Wales.

INTERPRETATION

2 In these regulations–

"2002 Act" means the Police Reform Act 2002;

"Commission" means the Independent Police Complaints Commission;

"Commissioners" means the Commissioners for Her Majesty's Revenue and Customs;

"Complaints Regulations" means the Police (Complaints and Misconduct) Regulations 2004;

"conduct matter" has the meaning given by section 12 of the 2002 Act;

"functions" has the meaning given by section 51(2)(a) of the Commissioners for Revenue and Customs Act 2005;

"Investigatory Powers Order" means the Independent Police Complaints Commission (Investigatory Powers) Order 2004;

"officers" means officers of Revenue and Customs;

"Staff Conduct Regulations" means the Independent Police Complaints Commission (Staff Conduct) Regulations 2004.

3(1) The provisions specified in paragraphs (2), (3) and (4) shall apply for the purpose of conferring functions on the Commission in relation to the Commissioners and officers.

3(2) Sections 9 to 29 of the 2002 Act shall have effect with the modifications made by Schedule 1 to these Regulations.

3(3) Schedule 2 to the 2002 Act shall have effect with the modifications made by Schedule 2 to these Regulations.

3(4) Paragraphs 10 to 24, 27 and 29 of Schedule 3 to the 2002 Act shall have effect with the modifications made by Schedule 3 to these Regulations.

3(5) Paragraphs 1 to 9, 25, 26 and 28 of Schedule 3 to the 2002 Act shall have effect with the modifications made by Schedule 3 to these Regulations.

3(6) The provisions specified in–

(a) paragraphs (2), (3) and (4) shall have effect from the date these Regulations come into force;

(b) paragraph (5) shall have effect from 1st April 2006.

3(7) The references in regulations 5, 8 and 9(1) to Part 2 of the 2002 Act are references to Part 2 of the 2002 Act as modified by Schedules 1, 2 and 3 to these Regulations.

Notes – The originally enacted Police Reform Act 2002 can be found at http://www.opsi.gov.uk/acts/acts2002/ukpga_20020030_en.pdf. The parts of that Act mentioned in reg. 3 have been significantly amended by SOCPA 2005, Sch. 2, 4, 11, 12 and 17 – see http://www.opsi.gov.uk/acts/acts2005/ukpga_20050015_en.pdf.

APPLICATION OF THE INVESTIGATORY POWERS ORDER, THE COMPLAINTS REGULATIONS AND THE STAFF CONDUCT REGULATIONS WITH MODIFICATIONS

4(1) The provisions specified in paragraph (2) shall apply for the purpose of conferring functions on the Commission in relation to the Commissioners and officers.

4(2) From the date these Regulations come into force–

(a) the Investigatory Powers Order shall have effect,

(b) the Complaints Regulations shall have effect with the modifications made by Part 1 of Schedule 4 to these Regulations, and

(c) the Staff Conduct Regulations shall have effect with the modifications made by Part 2 of Schedule 4 to these Regulations.

4(3) The references in regulations 5, 8 and 9(1) to–

(a) the Complaints Regulations,

(b) the Staff Conduct Regulations,

are references to those Regulations as modified by Parts 1 and 2 of Schedule 4 to these Regulations.

4A(1) For the purpose of the application of the Complaints Regulations under regulation 4, the amendments made to those Regulations by the provisions specified in paragraph (2) shall apply.

4A(2) The provisions specified are–

(a) regulation 26 of the Serious Organised Crime and Police Act 2005 (Powers of Arrest) (Consequential Amendments) Order 2005, and

(b) regulation 2 of the Police (Complaints and Misconduct) (Amendment) Regulations 2006.

4A(3) This regulation has effect from 27th July 2006.

History – Reg. 4A was inserted by SI 2006/1748, reg. 3, operative from 27 July 2006.

DISCLOSURE OF INFORMATION

5 Where the Commission, or any person acting on its behalf, obtains information in the course of performing a function under these Regulations it or he may not disclose it except as permitted by Part 2 of the 2002 Act or the Complaints Regulations.

USE OF INFORMATION

6 Where the Commission, or any person acting on its behalf, obtains information in the course of performing a function under these Regulations it or he may not use it for any purpose other than the performance of a function under these Regulations.

7(1) The Commissioners shall pay such amount to the Secretary of State in respect of functions performed by the Commission under these Regulations as may be agreed between the Commissioners and the Commission.

7(2) In the absence of an agreement, the Commissioners shall pay such amount in respect of those functions as the Treasury, after consultation with the Secretary of State, shall determine.

COMPLAINTS ABOUT CONDUCT OCCURRING BEFORE 1ST APRIL 2006

8 Nothing in Part 2 of the 2002 Act, the Investigatory Powers Order, the Complaints Regulations or the Staff Conduct Regulations shall have effect in relation to a complaint made about the conduct of a Commissioner or an officer occurring before 1st April 2006.

CONDUCT MATTER OCCURRING BEFORE 1ST APRIL 2006

9(1) Subject to paragraph (2), nothing in Part 2 of the 2002 Act, the Investigatory Powers Order, the Complaints Regulations or the Staff Conduct Regulations shall have effect in relation to a conduct matter relating to the conduct of a Commissioner or an officer occurring before 1st April 2006.

9(2) Paragraph (1) does not apply to any conduct matter which the appropriate authority may refer to the Commission under paragraph 13(2) of Schedule 3 to the 2002 Act.

SCHEDULES

SCHEDULE 1 – MODIFICATION OF SECTIONS 9 TO 29 OF THE 2002 ACT

Regulation 3(2)

1 At the end of section 9(3) insert–
"(g) any person who holds or has held office or employment as a Commissioner or officer.".

2(1) Section 10 shall be modified as follows.

2(2) In subsection (1) after "the Commission" insert ", in relation to the Commissioners and officers,".

2(3) In subsection (1)(a) for "police authorities and chief officers" substitute "the Commissioners".

2(4) In subsection (1)(e) omit "and also of police practice in relation to other matters,".

2(5) Omit subsection (1)(f).

2(6) In subsection (2)(a) for "persons serving with the police" substitute–
"Commissioners or officers which the appropriate authority–
(i) has a duty to refer to the Commission under paragraph 4(1) of Schedule 3 or,
(ii) may refer to the Commission under paragraph 4(2) or (3) of Schedule 3;".

2(7) In subsection (2)(b) for the words from "appears that" to the end substitute–
"appears that
(i) there may have been conduct by such persons which constitutes or involves the commission of a criminal offence or behaviour justifying disciplinary proceedings, and
(ii) that conduct or behaviour is conduct or behaviour which the appropriate authority has a duty to refer to the Commission under paragraph 13(1) of Schedule 3 or may refer to the Commission under paragraph 13(2) or (3) of that Schedule.".

2(8) In subsection (2)(ba) for "a person serving with the police" insert "an officer".

2(9) Omit subsection (3).

2(10) In subsection (4)(a) for "subsections (1) and (3)" insert "subsection (1)".

2(11) In subsection (5)(a) after "functions" insert "in relation to the Commissioners and officers".

2(12) Omit subsections (7)(b) and (c).

2(13) In subsection (8) for the words from "control of a police force" to the end substitute "control of Her Majesty's Revenue and Customs by the Commissioners".

3(1) Section 11 shall be modified as follows.

3(2) In subsections (1), (2), (3), and (5) for "Secretary of State" insert "Chancellor of the Exchequer".

3(3) Omit subsection (4)(b).

3(4) In subsection (6) for the words from "under subsection (1)" to the end substitute "under subsection (1) to the Commissioners".

3(5) In subsection (7) for the words from "under subsection (3)" to the end substitute "under subsection (3) to the Commissioners".

3(6) Omit subsections (8) and (9).

3(7) In subsection (10) for paragraphs (a) to (g) substitute–
"(a) the Chancellor of the Exchequer, and
(b) the Commissioners.".

3(8) In the heading for "Reports to the Secretary of State" substitute "Reports to the Chancellor of the Exchequer".

4(1) Section 12 shall be modified as follows.

4(2) In subsections (1) and (2) for "a person serving with the police" substitute "a Commissioner or an officer".

4(3) In subsections (2B)(a), (2C)(a) and (2D) for "a person serving with the police" (on each occasion the words occur) substitute "an officer".

5(1) Section 14 shall be modified as follows.

5(2) In subsection (1) for the words from "control of a police force" to the end substitute "control of Her Majesty's Revenue and Customs by the Commissioners".

5(3) Omit subsections (2) and (3).

6(1) Section 15 shall be modified as follows.

6(2) In subsection (1)–
(a) for the words in paragraph (a) substitute "the Commissioners and";
(b) omit paragraph (b);
(c) for "it or he is" substitute "they are or he is" and for "that force" substitute "Her Majesty's Revenue and Customs".

6(3) In subsection (3)–
(a) for paragraph (a) substitute–

"(a)   the Commission requires the chief officer of a police force to provide a member of his force for appointment under paragraph 17A or 18A of Schedule 3,";

(b)   omit paragraphs (b) and (c);

(c)   omit "or Director General".

6(4)   In subsection (4)–

(a)   omit paragraphs (c) and (d), and

(b)   after paragraph (d) insert–

"(e)   the Commissioners,".

6(5)   In subsection (5)–

(a)   omit paragraphs (c) and (d);

(b)   for "16, 17 or 18" substitute "17A or 18A".

6(6)   After subsection (5) insert–

"**15(5A)**   It shall be the duty of the Head of the Home Civil Service, the Chairman and Commissioners to ensure that a person appointed under paragraph 16,17, 17A, 18 or 18A of Schedule 3 to carry out an investigation is given all such assistance and co-operation in the carrying out of that investigation as that person may reasonably require."

6(7)   Omit subsections (6) and (7).

7(1)   Section 16 shall be modified as follows.

7(2)   In subsection (1)–

(a)   in paragraph (a)–

    (i)   for "one" substitute "a";

    (ii)   omit "to another";

    (iii)   delete "or";

(b)   at the end of paragraph (b) insert "; or";

(c)   after paragraph (b) insert–

"(c)   a police force provides assistance by agreement under paragraph 17A(2) or 18A(2) of Schedule 3.".

7(3)   In subsection (2)–

(a)   in paragraph (a) for–

    (i)   "one police force to another" substitute "a police force",

    (ii)   "the first force ("the assisting force")" substitute "that force";

    (iii)   in sub-paragraph (i) for "a member of the other force" substitute "a Commissioner or an officer";

    (iv)   in sub-paragraph (ii) for "a member of the other force" substitute "an officer";

(b)   in paragraph (b)–

    (i)   omit "(the assisting force)";

    (ii)   in sub-paragraph (i) for "not a member of that force" substitute "a Commissioner or an officer";

    (iii)   in sub-paragraph (ii) for "not a member of that force" substitute "an officer".

7(4)   In subsection (3)–

(a)   for "one police force to another" substitute "a police force";

(b)   for "police authority maintaining that other police force" substitute "appropriate authority";

(c)   for "the assisting force" substitute "that force";

(d)   omit "(if any)";

(e)   in paragraph (b)(i) after "generally" insert "and the Commissioners", and

(f)   in paragraph (b)(ii) omit "by one police force to another".

7(5)   After subsection (3) there shall be inserted–

"**16(3A)**   Subsection (3) shall have effect in relation to assistance which a police force provides by agreement under paragraph 17A (2) or 18A (2) of Schedule 3 as if the reference in that subsection to required to be provided were a reference to provided by agreement under paragraph 17A(2) or 18A(2) of Schedule 3.".

7(6)   Omit subsections (5), (6) and (7).

8(1)   Section 17 shall be modified as follows.

8(2)   From the beginning of subsection (1) to the end of paragraph (b) of that subsection substitute "It shall be the duty of the Commissioners".

8(3)   In subsection (2)–

(a)   for the words "every police authority and of every chief officer" substitute "the Commissioners", and

(b)   in paragraph (a) for the words "that authority and or chief officer" substitute "the Commissioners".

8(4)   In subsection (4)–

(a)   for the words "a police authority or chief officer" substitute "the Commissioners", and

(b)   in paragraph (a) for the words "that authority and or chief officer" substitute "the Commissioners".

9(1)   Section 18 shall be modified as follows.

9(2)   In subsection (1)(a)–

(a)   for paragraphs (i) and (ii) substitute "the Commissioners"; and

(b)   for "that force" substitute "Her Majesty's Revenue and Customs".

9(3)   In subsection (1) for the words "the authority or, as the case may be, of the chief officer" substitute "the Commissioners".

9(4)   In subsection (2)(a) for "the force in question" substitute "the Commissioners".

9(5)   In subsection (3) for "the authority or chief officer" substitute "the Commissioners".

9(6)   In subsection (5)(b) for "police authorities and chief officers" substitute "the Commissioners".

9(7)   In the heading to the section for "police premises" substitute "Her Majesty's Revenue and Customs premises".

10(1)   Section 22 shall be modified as follows.

10(2)   In subsection (1) for the words from "guidance" to the end of paragraph (c) substitute "guidance to the Commissioners and officers".

10(3)   In subsection (3)–

(a)   for paragraph (a) substitute–

"(a)   the Commissioners and;";

(b)   omit paragraph (b).

10(4)   In subsection (4) for "the Secretary of State" substitute "the Chancellor of the Exchequer".

10(5)   Omit subsection (5)(c).

11   Omit sections 25 and 26.

12(1)   Section 29 shall be modified as follows.

12(2)   In subsection (1)–

(a)   for the definition of "the appropriate authority" substitute the following definition–

"**the appropriate authority**"–

(a)   in relation to the Chairman, the Deputy Chairman, a Commissioner or an officer or in relation to any complaint, matter or investigation relating to the conduct of such a person, means–

    (i)   if that person is the Chairman or Deputy Chairman, the Head of the Home Civil Service,

(ii)   if that person is a Commissioner, the Chairman, or

(iii)   if that person is an officer, the Commissioners and

(b)   in relation to a death or serious injury matter and the relevant officer, means the Commissioners";

(b)   after the definition of "the appropriate authority" insert–

"**the Chairman**" means the chairman of the Commissioners";

(c)   after the definition of "the Commission" insert–

"**the Commissioners**" means the Commissioners for Her Majesty's Revenue and Customs;";

(d)   after the definition of "conduct matter" insert–

"**the Deputy Chairman**" means the Deputy Chairman of the Commissioners";

(e)   for the definition of "disciplinary proceedings" substitute–

"**disciplinary proceedings**" means any proceedings or management process during which the conduct of the Chairman, Deputy Chairman, a Commissioner or an officer is considered in order to determine whether a sanction or punitive measure should be imposed against him in relation to that conduct;";

(f)   after the definition of "local resolution" insert the following definition–

"**officers**" means officers of Revenue and Customs;", and

(g)   omit the definitions of "local resolution" "relevant force", and "senior officer".

12(3)   In subsection (1A) for "person serving with the police (within the meaning of section 12(7))" substitute "officer" and for "such person" substitute "such officer".

12(4)   In subsection (1B) for "persons serving with the police" substitute "officers".

12(5)   Omit subsection (2).

12(6)   In subsection (3) for the words from "falling within" to the end of that subsection substitute "who is a Commissioner or an officer (whether at the time of the conduct or any subsequent time)".

12(7)   In subsection (4)–

(a)   for paragraph (a) substitute–

"(a)   a person who, at the time when the conduct was supposed to have taken place in relation to him, was a Commissioner or an officer (whether or not he was on duty in his capacity as a Commissioner or officer at that time).";

(b)   omit paragraph (b)(i);

(c)   for "person falling within subsection (3)(a) to (d)" substitute "Commissioner or officer".

SCHEDULE 2 –MODIFICATION OF SCHEDULE 2 TO THE 2002 ACT

Regulation 3(3)

1   After paragraph 6(2) insert–

"**6(2A)**   The Commission may make arrangements with the Commissioners under which officers of Revenue and Customs are engaged on temporary service with the Commission.".

2   In paragraph 17(1)(c) after "Secretary of State" insert ", the Treasury".

SCHEDULE 3 – MODIFICATION OF SCHEDULE 3 TO THE 2002 ACT

Regulations 3(4) and (5)

1(1)   Paragraph 1 shall be modified as follows.

1(2)   For sub-paragraph (1) substitute–

"**1(1)**   Where–

(a)   complaint is made to the Head of the Home Civil Service about the conduct of the Chairman or Deputy Chairman, or

(b)   the Head of the Home Civil Service becomes aware that a complaint about the conduct of the Chairman or Deputy Chairman has been made to the Commission,

the Head of the Home Civil Service shall take all such steps as appear to him to be appropriate for the purposes of Part 2 of this Act for obtaining and preserving evidence relating to the conduct complained of.".

1(3)   After sub-paragraph (1) insert–

"**1(1A)**   Where–

(a)   a complaint is made to the Chairman about the conduct of a Commissioner, or

(b)   the Chairman becomes aware that a complaint about the conduct of a Commissioner has been made to the Commission,

the Chairman shall take all such steps as appear to him to be appropriate for the purposes of Part 2 of this Act for obtaining and preserving evidence relating to the conduct complained of.".

1(4)   For sub-paragraph (2) substitute–

"**1(2)**   Where–

(a)   a complaint is made to the Commissioners about the conduct of an officer, or

(b)   the Commissioners become aware that a complaint about the conduct of an officer has been made to the Commission,

the Commissioners shall take all such steps as appear to them to be appropriate for the purposes of Part 2 of this Act for obtaining and preserving evidence relating to the conduct complained of.".

1(5)   For sub-paragraph (3) substitute–

"**1(3)**   The duty of the–

(a)   Head of the Home Civil Service under sub-paragraph (1);

(b)   Chairman under sub-paragraph (1A);

(c)   Commissioners under sub-paragraph (2),

must be performed as soon as practicable after the complaint is made or, as the case may be, he or they become aware of it.".

1(6)   In sub-paragraph (4) for–

(a)   "he shall" substitute "he or they shall";

(b)   "he is satisfied" substitute "he is or they are satisfied"; and

(c)   "appearing to him" substitute "appearing to him or them".

1(7)   Omit sub-paragraph (5).

1(8)   In sub-paragraph (6)–

(a)   for "a chief officer" substitute–

"the–

(a)   Head of the Home Civil Service;

(b)   Chairman;

(c)   Commissioners,";

(b)   the words after "a chief officer" become full out words;

(c)   for "he may" substitute "he or they may"; and

(d)   omit "by the police authority maintaining his force or".

2(1)   Paragraph 2 shall be modified as follows.

2(2)   In sub-paragraph (1)(a) for "police authority or chief officer who is" substitute "Head of the Home Civil Service, Chairman or Commissioners who is or are".

2(3)   In sub-paragraph (2)–

(a)   for "a police authority, it" substitute "the Head of the Home Civil Service or Chairman, he";

(b)   in paragraph (a) for "it is itself" substitute "he is himself"; and

(c)   in paragraph (b) for "it determines that it" substitute "he determines that he".

2(4)   In sub-paragraph (3) for–

(a)   "a chief officer, he shall" substitute "the Commissioners, they shall";

(b)   "he is himself" substitute "they are themselves"; and

(c)   "he determines that he is not" substitute "they determine that they are not".

2(5)   In sub-paragraph (5) for "a police authority or a chief officer gives" substitute "Head of the Home Civil Service, Chairman or Commissioners gives or give".

2(6)   For sub-paragraph (6) substitute–

"**2(6)**   Where–

(a)   the Head of the Home Civil Service or Chairman determines, in the case of any complaint made to him, that he is himself the appropriate authority,

(b)   the Commissioners determine, in the case of any complaint made to them, that they are themselves the appropriate authority, or

(c)   a complaint is notified to the Head of the Home Civil Service, Chairman or Commissioners under this paragraph,

the Head of the Home Civil Service, Chairman or Commissioners shall record the complaint.".

3(1)   Paragraph 3 shall be modified as follows.

3(2)   In sub-paragraph (1) for "a police authority or chief officer" substitute "the Head of the Home Civil Service, Chairman or Commissioners".

3(3)   In sub-paragraph (2)–

(a)   for "police authority or chief officer" and "authority or chief officer" substitute (on each occasion) "Head of the Home Civil Service, Chairman or Commissioners"

(b)   for "decides" substitute "decides or decide" and

(c)   in paragraph (c) for "that complainant's right to appeal" substitute "whether the complainant has a right to appeal".

3(4)   In sub-paragraph (3)–

(a)   for "police authority or chief officer" substitute "Head of the Home Civil Service, Chairman or Commissioners"; and

(b)   after "paragraph" insert "if, but only if, the failure is in respect of conduct which the Head of the Home Civil Service, Chairman or Commissioners is or are required to refer to the Commission under paragraph 4(1)(a) or (b).".

3(5)   In sub-paragraph (4)–

(a)   in paragraph (b) for "police authority or chief officer" substitute "Head of the Home Civil Service, Chairman or Commissioners"; and

(b)   for "a police authority or chief officer" substitute "the Head of the Home Civil Service, Chairman or Commissioners".

3(6)   In sub-paragraph (6) for–

(a)   "police authority or, as the case may be, the chief officer" substitute "Head of the Home Civil Service, Chairman or, as the case may be, the Commissioners"; and

(b)   "police authority or chief officer" substitute "Head of the Home Civil Service, Chairman or Commissioners".

4(1)   Paragraph 4 shall be modified as follows.

4(2)   In sub-paragraph (3)–

(a)   for "a police authority" substitute "the Head of the Home Civil Service";

(b)   in paragraph (a) for "chief officer of police of the police force maintained by that authority" substitute "Chairman"; and

(c)   in paragraph (b) for "the police authority" substitute "the Head of the Home Civil Service".

4(3)   In sub-paragraph (5)(b) for "a police authority or chief officer" substitute "the Head of the Home Civil Service, Chairman or Commissioners".

4(4)   In sub-paragraph (6)–

(a)   for "A police authority or chief officer which refers" substitute "Where the Head of the Home Civil Service, Chairman or Commissioners refers or refer";

(b)   after "paragraph" insert "he or they"; and

(c)   in paragraph (b) for "that authority or chief officer" substitute "the Head of the Home Civil Service, Chairman or Commissioners".

5(1)   Paragraph 5 shall be modified as follows.

5(2)   In sub-paragraph (1) for "a police authority or chief officer" substitute "the Head of the Home Civil Service, Chairman or Commissioners".

5(3)   For sub-paragraph (2) for "paragraph 6" substitute "sub-paragraph (2A)".

5(4)   After sub-paragraph (2) insert–

"In a case to which sub-paragraph (2) applies the appropriate authority shall not be required by virtue of any of the provisions of this Schedule to take any action in relation to the complaint but may handle the complaint in whatever manner it thinks fit, or take no action in relation to the complaint.".

5(5)   For sub-paragraph 3(b) substitute–

"(b)   to the person complained against.".

6(1)   Paragraph 6 shall be modified as follows.

6(2)   For sub-paragraph (2) substitute–

"**5(2)**   The appropriate authority shall not be required by virtue of any provisions of this Schedule to take any action in relation to the complaint but may handle the complaint in whatever manner it thinks fit or take no action in relation to the complaint.".

6(3)   Omit sub-paragraphs (3) to (7).

7   Omit paragraphs 7, 8 and 9.

8(1)   Paragraph 10 shall be modified as follows.

8(2)   In sub-paragraph (1)–

(a)   in paragraph (a) for–

(i) "a police authority or chief officer" (on both occasions where it occurs) substitute "the Head of the Home Civil Service, Chairman or Commissioners";

(ii) for "has received" substitute "has or have received"; and

(iii) for "that authority or chief officer" substitute "the Head of the Home Civil Service, Chairman or Commissioners";

(b) in paragraph (b) for "that authority or chief officer" substitute "the Head of the Home Civil Service, Chairman or Commissioners".

8(3) In sub-paragraph (2)–

(a) for "The authority or chief officer" substitute "The Head of the Home Civil Service, Chairman or Commissioners";

(b) in paragraph (a) for "it or, as the case may be, he is" substitute "he is or, as the case may be, they are"; and

(c) in paragraph (b) for "if it or he is not" substitute "if he is or they are not".

8(4) In sub-paragraph (3)–

(a) at the beginning insert "Subject to sub-paragraphs (3A) and (3B),";

(b) for "a police authority or chief officer determines" substitute "the Head of the Home Civil Service, Chairman or Commissioners determines or determine";

(c) for "it or, as the case may be, he is" substitute "he is, or as the case may be, they are", and

(d) for "it or he" substitute "he or they".

8(5) After sub-paragraph (3) insert–

"**10(3A)** Nothing in sub-paragraph (3) shall require the Head of the Home Civil Service, as the appropriate authority, to record a conduct matter if he is satisfied that matter falls within subsection 12(1)(b) of this Act.

10(3B) Nothing in sub-paragraph (3) shall require the Chairman or the Commissioners, as the appropriate authority, to record a conduct matter if he is or they are satisfied that–

(a) the matter falls within subsection 12(1)(b) of this Act; and

(b) any disciplinary proceedings which were brought would be unlikely to result in the termination of an office or employment.".

9(1) Paragraph 11 shall be modified as follows.

9(2) In sub-paragraph (1)–

(a) at the beginning insert "Subject to paragraphs (2A) and (2B),";

(b) in paragraph (a) for "police authority or chief officer who is" substitute "Head of the Home Civil Service, Chairman or Commissioners who is or are".

9(3) After sub-paragraph (2) insert–

"**11(2A)** Nothing in sub-paragraph (1) shall require the Head of the Home Civil Service, as the appropriate authority, to record a conduct matter if he is satisfied that the matter falls within section 12(1)(b) of this Act.

11(2B) Nothing in sub-paragraph (1) shall require the Chairman or the Commissioners, as the appropriate authority, to record a conduct matter if he is or they are satisfied that–

(a) the matter falls within section 12(1)(b) of this Act; and

(b) any disciplinary proceedings which were brought would be unlikely to result in the termination of an office or employment.".

10(1) Paragraph 12 shall be modified as follows.

10(2) Omit sub-paragraph (1).

10(3) For sub-paragraph (2) substitute–

"**12(2)** Where–

(a) the Head of the Home Civil Service becomes aware of any recordable matter relating to the conduct of the Chairman or Deputy Chairman;

(b) the Chairman becomes aware of any recordable matter relating to the conduct of a Commissioner; or

(c) the Commissioners become aware of any recordable matter relating to the conduct of an officer,

it shall be his or their duty to take all such steps as appear to him or them to be appropriate for the purposes of Part 2 of this Act for obtaining and preserving the evidence relating to that matter.".

10(4) For sub-paragraph (3) substitute–

"**12(3)** The duty under sub-paragraph (2) of–

(a) the Head of the Home Civil Service;

(b) the Chairman;

(c) the Commissioners,

must be performed as soon as practicable after he becomes or they become aware of the matter in question.".

10(5) In sub-paragraph (4) for–

(a) "he shall be under a duty, until he is" substitute "he or they shall be under a duty until he is or they are"; and

(b) "appearing to him" substitute "appearing to him or them".

10(6) Omit sub-paragraph (5).

10(7) In sub-paragraph (6)–

(a) for "the chief officer" substitute "the Chairman or Commissioners";

(b) for "he may be directed" substitute "he or they may be directed"; and

(c) omit "by the police authority maintaining his force or".

11(1) Paragraph 13 shall be modified as follows.

11(2) In sub-paragraph (1) for–

(a) "a police authority or a chief officer" substitute "the Head of the Home Civil Service, Chairman or Commissioners", and

(b) "the authority or chief officer is" substitute "any of those persons is or are".

11(3) In sub-paragraph (3)–

(a) for "a police authority maintaining any police force" substitute "the Head of the Home Civil Service";

(b) in paragraph (a) for "chief officer of police of that force" substitute "Chairman"; and

(c) in paragraph (b) for "police authority" substitute "Head of the Home Civil Service".

11(4) In sub-paragraph (5)(b) for "a police authority or chief officer" substitute "the Head of the Home Civil Service, Chairman or Commissioners".

11(5) In sub-paragraph (6)–

(a) in paragraph (a) for "a police authority or chief officer refers" substitute "the Head of the Home Civil Service, Chairman or Commissioners refers or refer";

(b) in paragraph (b) for "that authority or chief officer does not" substitute "the Head of the Home Civil Service, Chairman or Commissioners does or do not"; and

(c) for "that authority or chief officer" substitute "the Head of the Home Civil Service, Chairman or Commissioners".

12(1)   Paragraph 14 shall be modified as follows.

12(2)   In sub-paragraph (1) for "a police authority or chief officer" substitute "the Head of the Home Civil Service, Chairman or Commissioners".

12(3)   In sub-paragraph (2)–

(a)   after "recordable conduct matter" insert "referred by the Head of the Home Civil Service, Chairman or Commissioners";

(b)   for "appropriate authority" substitute "Head of the Home Civil Service, Chairman or Commissioners";

(c)   for "that authority" (on the first occasion those words appear) substitute "by him or them"; and

(d)   for "that authority" (on the second occasion those words appear) substitute "he or they".

13(1)   Paragraph 14A shall be modified as follows.

13(2)   For sub-paragraph (1) substitute–

"**14A(1)**   Where a DSI matter comes to the attention of the Commissioners, being the appropriate authority, it shall be their duty to record that matter.".

14(1)   Paragraph 14B shall be modified as follows.

14(2)   Omit sub-paragraph (1).

14(3)   In sub-paragraph (2)–

(a)   for the words from "Where" to the end of paragraph (b) substitute "Where a DSI matter comes to the attention of the Commissioners";

(b)   for "his duty" substitute "their duty"; and

(c)   for "to him" substitute "to them".

14(4)   In sub-paragraph (3) for "chief officer's" substitute "Commissioners'" and for "he becomes" substitute "they become".

14(5)   In sub-paragraph (4) for "he shall" substitute "they shall", "he is" substitute "they are" and "to him" substitute "to them".

14(6)   Omit sub-paragraph (5).

14(7)   In sub-paragraph (6) for "chief officer" substitute "Commissioners", for "he" substitute "they" and omit "by the police authority maintaining his force or".

15(1)   Paragraph 14D shall be modified as follows.

15(2)   In sub-paragraph (1) for "a police authority or a chief officer" substitute "the Commissioners".

16(1)   Paragraph 15 shall be modified as follows.

16(2)   After sub-paragraph (4)(b) insert–

"(bb) an investigation by a police force under the supervision of the Commission;".

16(3)   In sub-paragraph (4)(c) substitute "the appropriate authority" for "that authority".

16(4)   After sub-paragraph (4)(c) insert–

"(cc) an investigation by a police force under the management of the Commission;".

16(5)   After sub-paragraph (4) insert–

"**15(4A)**   An investigation relating to any conduct of the Chairman, Deputy Chairman or other Commissioners under this paragraph may only be carried out in the form specified in sub-paragraph (4)(bb), (4)(cc) or (4)(d).".

17(1)   Paragraph 16 shall be modified as follows.

17(2)   In sub-paragraph (1) omit paragraph (a).

17(3)   Omit sub-paragraph (2).

17(4)   In sub-paragraph (3) for the words from "appoint" to the end of the sub-paragraph substitute "appoint an officer to investigate the complaint or matter.".

17(5)   Omit sub-paragraph (5).

18(1)   Paragraph 17 shall be modified as follows.

18(2)   In sub-paragraph (2) for the words from "appoint" to the end of the sub-paragraph substitute "appoint an officer to investigate the complaint or matter.".

18(3)   In sub-paragraph (4)(a) for "sub-paragraph 2(a) or (b)" substitute "sub-paragraph (2)".

18(4)   Omit sub-paragraphs (6) and (6A).

19   After paragraph 17 insert–

"**17A(1)**   This paragraph applies where the Commission determines that there should be an investigation by a police force under the supervision of the Commission.

17A(2)   The Commission shall–

(a)   identify the police force whose force area includes the geographical area to which the subject matter of the complaint, recordable conduct matter or DSI matter most closely relates, and

(b)   take steps to obtain the agreement of–

    (i)   the chief officer of police of that force, and

    (ii)   the appropriate authority,

(b)   to the appointment by the Commission of that force to carry out the investigation.

17A(3)   In the event that no agreement is reached under sub-paragraph (2) the Commission may require the chief officer of police of any police force it considers appropriate to carry out the investigation.

17A(4)   A chief officer of police of a police force who agrees to or is required to carry out an investigation shall, if he has not already done so, appoint a person serving with the police who is a member of that force to investigate that complaint.

17A(5)   Sub-paragraphs (3) to (5) and (7) of paragraph 17 shall apply as they apply to an investigation by the appropriate authority which the Commission has determined is one that it should supervise and the references to the appropriate authority in those sub-paragraphs shall be treated as references to the chief officer of police concerned.

17A(6)   An appointment of a person under sub-paragraph (4) or (5) shall be notified by the chief officer of police concerned to the appropriate authority.".

20   After paragraph 18 insert–

"**18A(1)**   This paragraph applies where the Commission determines that there should be an investigation by a police force under the management of the Commission.

18A(2)   The Commission shall–

(a)   identify the police force whose force area includes the geographical area to which the subject matter of the complaint, recordable conduct matter or DSI matter most closely relates, and

(b)   take steps to obtain the agreement of–

    (i)   the chief officer of police of that force, and

    (ii)   the appropriate authority,

(b)   to the appointment by the Commission of that force to carry out the investigation.

18A(3)   In the event that no agreement is reached under sub-paragraph (2) the Commission may require the chief officer of police of any police force it considers appropriate to carry out the investigation.

Statutory Instruments

18A(4)   A chief officer of police of a police force who agrees to or is required to carry out an investigation shall, if he has not already done so, appoint a person serving with the police who is a member of that force to investigate that complaint or matter.

18A(5)   Sub-paragraphs (3) to (5) of paragraph 17 shall apply as they apply to an investigation by the appropriate authority which the Commission has determined is one that it should supervise and the references to the appropriate authority in those sub-paragraphs shall be treated as references to the chief officer of police concerned.

18A(6)   An appointment of a person under sub-paragraph (4) or (5) shall be notified by the chief officer of police concerned to the appropriate authority.

18A(7)   The person appointed to investigate the complaint or matter shall, in relation to that investigation, be under the direction and control of the Commission.".

21   Omit paragraphs 19(3) and (3A).

22(1)   Paragraph 20 shall be modified as follows.

22(2)   Omit sub-paragraph (1)(a).

22(3)   In paragraph 20(3) after "Director of Public Prosecutions" insert "or, as the case may be, the Director of Revenue and Customs Prosecutions".

23   Omit paragraphs 20A to 20I.

24(1)   Paragraph 21A shall be modified as follows.

24(2)   In sub-paragraphs (1) and (3) for "a person serving with the police" substitute "an officer".

24(3)   In sub-paragraph (1) after "18" insert "or 18A".

24(4)   In sub-paragraph (3) for "16 or 17" substitute "16, 17 or 17A".

25   In paragraph 22(2) for "17 or 18" substitute "17, 17A, 18 or 18A".

26(1)   In paragraph 23(2)(c) after "Director of Public Prosecutions" insert "or the Director of Revenue and Customs Prosecutions".

26(2)   In paragraphs 23(3), (4) and (6)(b) after "Director of Public Prosecutions" insert "or, as the case may be, the Director of Revenue and Customs Prosecutions".

27   In paragraphs 24(2)(b), (3), (4) and (6)(b) after "Director of Public Prosecutions" insert "or, as the case may be, the Director of Revenue and Customs Prosecutions".

28   In paragraphs 24A(4), 24B(1) and 24C(1) for "a person serving with the police" substitute (on each occasion where the words occur) "an officer".

29   Omit paragraph 25(2A).

30   In paragraph 27(3) for "any person serving with the police" substitute "any officer".

SCHEDULE 4

Regulation 4(2)

PART 1 – MODIFICATION OF THE COMPLAINTS REGULATIONS

1   Omit regulation 4.

2(1)   In regulation 6(2) for the words from "consent" to the end of the paragraph substitute–

"consent–

(i)   in the case of an investigation carried out by an appointed person who is an officer, of the Director of Revenue and Customs Prosecutions, or

(ii)   in any other case, of the Director of Public Prosecutions,

to the imposition thereof.".

2(2)   In regulation 6(3) for–

(a)   "a chief officer" substitute "the Head of the Home Civil Service, Chairman or Commissioners";

(b)   "consulting him" substitute "consulting him or them";

(c)   "he may make" substitute "he or they may make".

3   Omit regulations 7(2)(b) and 7(7)(c).

4(1)   In regulation 8(1) for "a police authority or chief officer" substitute "the Head of the Home Civil Service, Chairman or Commissioners".

4(2)   In regulation 8(2)(c) for "the police force or police authority which" substitute "the Head of the Home Civil Service, Chairman or Commissioners who".

4(3)   In regulations 8(3)(a) and (7) for "police authority or chief officer" substitute "Head of the Home Civil Service, Chairman or Commissioners".

4(4)   In regulation 8(5) for "A police authority or chief officer" substitute "The Head of the Home Civil Service, Chairman or Commissioners".

5   Omit regulation 9.

6(1)   Regulation 12 shall be modified as follows.

6(2)   After paragraph (1)(b) insert–

"(c)   preventing the disclosure of any information held by the Revenue and Customs in connection with a function of the Revenue and Customs which–

(i)   is obtained from the Head of the Home Civil Service, Chairman, Commissioners or an officer, and

(ii)   relates to a person whose identity is specified in the disclosure or can be deduced from it.".

6(3)   After paragraph (1) insert–

"**12(1A)**   Paragraph (1)(c) does not apply to any information about internal administrative arrangements of Her Majesty's Revenue and Customs (whether relating to Commissioners, officers or others).".

6(4)   After paragraph (2) insert–

"**12(2A)**   The Commission shall consult the appropriate authority in any case under paragraph (1)(c) before deciding whether or not it is satisfied under paragraph (2).".

6(5)   After paragraph (3) insert–

"**12(4)**   In this regulation **"the Revenue and Customs"** means–

"(a)   the Commissioners;

(b)   an officer;

(c)   a person acting on behalf of the Commissioners or an officer;

(d)   a committee established by the Conmmissioners;

(e)   a member of the committee established by the Commissioners;

(f)   the Commissioners of Inland Revenue (or any committee or staff of theirs or anyone acting on their behalf);

(g)   the Commissioners of Customs and Excise (or any committee or staff of theirs or anyone acting on their behalf), and

(h)   a person specified in section 6(2) or 7(3) of the Commissioners for Revenue and Customs Act 2005.".

7(1)   In regulation 18(1) for "17 or 18" substitute "17, 17A, 18 or 18A".

7(2)   Omit regulations 18(1)(d), (2) and (3).

8   In regulation 21 for "person serving with the police" substitute "Commissioner or an officer".

9   In regulation 24—

(a)   for "Every police authority and chief officer" substitute "The Head of the Home Civil Service, Chairman and Commissioners", and

(b)   in paragraphs (a) and (b) for "it or him" substitute "him or them".

10(1)   In regulation 25(1) for "a police authority or chief officer" substitute "the Head of the Home Civil Service, Chairman or Commissioners".

10(2)   In regulation 25(3) for "(a) and (b)" substitute "(a), (b) and (c)".

11(1)   Regulation 26 shall be modified as follows.

11(2)   In paragraph (1) for–

(a)   "chief officer" substitute "the Head of the Home Civil Service, Chairman or Commissioners";

(b)   "on him" substitute "on him or them"; and

(c)   "an officer" substitute "a person".

11(3)   In paragraph (2) for sub-paragraphs (a) to (c) substitute–

"(a)   in the case of the Head of the Home Civil Service, to a member of the Senior Civil Service;

(b)   in the case of the Chairman, to a member of the Senior Civil Service employed in the service of the Commissioners;

(c)   in the case of the Commissioners, to an officer."

11(4)   Omit paragraph (3).

11(5)   For paragraph (4) substitute–

"**26(4)**   The Head of the Home Civil Service, Chairman or Commissioners shall not, in any particular case, delegate any power or duty under paragraph (1) to a person who has acted as investigating officer in that case."

11(6)   In paragraph (5) for "a chief constable" substitute "the Head of the Home Civil Service, Chairman or Commissioners".

12   Omit regulations 28, 29 and 30.

PART 2 – MODIFICATION OF THE STAFF CONDUCT REGULATIONS

1   In regulation 2(3)(a)(i) for "person serving with the police" substitute "Commissioner or officer".

LLOYD'S UNDERWRITERS (TAX) REGULATIONS 2005

(SI 2005/3338, as amended by SI 2009/2889)

Made on 6 December 2005 by the Commissioners for Her Majesty's Revenue and Customs, in exercise of the powers conferred by s. 182(1)(a) and (6) and 184(1) of the Finance Act 1993, s. 229(1)(a) and (2) and 230(1) of the Finance Act 1994, s. 132 and 133(2) of the Finance Act 1999 and s. 45(11) and (12) of the Finance (No. 2) Act 2005. Operative from 27 December 2005.

PART 1 – GENERAL

CITATION, COMMENCEMENT AND EFFECT

1(1) These Regulations may be cited as the Lloyd's Underwriters (Tax) Regulations 2005 and shall come into force on 27th December 2005.

1(2) These Regulations shall have effect–

(a) in their application to members who are individuals, for the year 2006–07 (including any actions taken before 6th April 2006, in relation to the year 2006–07) and subsequent years of assessment; and

(b) in their application to corporate members, for accounting periods ending after 31st December 2005 (but not in relation to profits and losses arising to corporate members which are mentioned in section 220(2) of the Finance Act 1994 and are declared in 2005).

INTERPRETATION

2(1) In these Regulations–

"the Commissioners" means the Commissioners for Her Majesty's Revenue and Customs;

"managing agent", in relation to a syndicate and an underwriting year, means–

(a) the person registered as a managing agent at Lloyd's who is currently acting as such managing agent, or

(b) such person who has previously acted as managing agent in relation to that syndicate and underwriting year, as the Commissioners may determine;

"the Management Act" means the Taxes Management Act 1970;

"notice" has the meaning in section 832(1) of the Taxes Act;

"Schedule 18" means Schedule 18 to the Finance Act 1998;

"the Taxes Act" means the Income and Corporation Taxes Act 1988.

2(2) In relation to members who are individuals, other expressions which are defined in Chapter 3 of Part 2 of the Finance Act 1993 have those defined meanings.

2(3) In relation to corporate members, other expressions which are defined in Chapter 5 of Part 4 of the Finance Act 1994 have those defined meanings.

PART 2 – DETERMINATION OF A SYNDICATE'S PROFIT OR LOSS

PRELIMINARY

3 In this Part of these Regulations **"profit or loss"**, in relation to a syndicate, means the aggregate amount of such of the profits or losses of all the members of the syndicate (taken together) as arise–

(a) directly from their membership of the syndicate, or

(b) from assets forming part of premium trust funds;

and "profits" and "losses" shall be construed accordingly.

RETURNS BY MANAGING AGENT

4(1)   An officer of Revenue and Customs may, by notice to a syndicate's managing agent, require him to deliver a return (a "syndicate return") of the syndicate's profit or loss for an underwriting year (the amount of that profit or loss being referred to as a "syndicate determination").

4(2)   A notice under paragraph (1) may be given–

(a)   at any time after the closing year for the underwriting year in question; and

(b)   more than once, (in particular where the syndicate continues after the end of its closing year).

4(3)   The return shall–

(a)   contain such information as may reasonably be required by the notice; and

(b)   be accompanied by such accounts, statements and reports as may reasonably be so required.

4(4)   The filing date for any syndicate return required by a notice under paragraph (1) is whichever is the later of–

(a)   1st July in the underwriting year next following that closing year; and

(b)   the end of the period of three months beginning on the day following that on which the notice was served.

4(5)   If a syndicate's managing agent, having been required by a notice under paragraph (1) to deliver a return, fails to deliver the return on or before the filing date, he shall be liable to a flat-rate penalty equal to the prescribed amount multiplied by the number of days on which the failure continues.

4(6)   In paragraph (5) **"the prescribed amount"** means £60 for each fifty members of the syndicate (counting any number of members less than fifty, and any number left over, as fifty).

4(7)   If a syndicate's managing agent fraudulently or negligently delivers an incorrect return under paragraph (1), he shall be liable to a penalty not exceeding £3,000 multiplied by the number of members of the syndicate.

4(8)   In relation to a return required by a notice under paragraph (1)–

(a)   any reference in paragraph (4) or (5) to the filing date for, or delivery of, a return is a reference to its delivery together with the accompanying documents referred to in paragraph (3)(b); and

(b)   the reference in paragraph (7) to the return being incorrect includes a reference to any of those documents being incorrect.

AMENDMENT OF SYNDICATE DETERMINATIONS AND HMRC ENQUIRIES

5(1)   In relation to both members who are individuals and corporate members, the like provisions as are contained in paragraphs 15, 16, 24, 25, 27 to 29 and 31 to 34 of Schedule 18(a) shall apply with the modifications in paragraphs (2) to (6).

5(2)   For references to–

(a)   the company substitute references to the syndicate's managing agent;

(b)   the company tax return substitute references to the syndicate return;

(c)   the company's self-assessment, tax payable or tax liability, substitute references to the syndicate determination;

(d)   an accounting period (or periods) substitute references to the underwriting year to which the syndicate return relates (or would relate); and

(e)   the Inland Revenue substitute references to Her Majesty's Revenue and Customs.

5(3)   In paragraph 15(4) for "twelve" substitute "six".

5(4)   In paragraph 16(3) for "nine" substitute "three".

5(5)   In paragraph 24(2) for "twelve" substitute "six".

5(6)   Omit paragraphs 32(2) and (3) and 34(1)(a)(ii), (2)(a)(ii) and (5).

5(7)   The giving of a notice of enquiry to a syndicate's managing agent under the like provisions as are contained in paragraph 24 of Schedule 18 shall be deemed to include the giving of notice of enquiry–

(a)   under section 9A(1) of the Management Act to each member of the syndicate who is an individual, and who at that time has made a return under section 8 or 8A of that Act or at any subsequent time makes such a return; and

(b)   under paragraph 24 of Schedule 18 to each member of the syndicate who at that time has made a company tax return or at any subsequent time makes such a return.

NOTICE TO PROVIDE REPORT ON TECHNICAL PROVISIONS

5A   In relation to both members who are individuals and corporate members, paragraph 2 of Schedule 11 to the Finance Act 2007 (technical provisions made by general insurers: enforcement) shall apply with the following modifications–

(a)   in sub-paragraphs (1), (2), (4), (5) and (6) for "general insurer" in each place it occurs substitute "syndicate's managing agent"; and

(b)   in sub-paragraph (2)–

   (i)   for "general insurer's" substitute "managing agent's", and

   (ii)   for "the company tax return" substitute "the syndicate return".

History – Reg. 5A inserted by SI 2009/2889, reg. 2(2), with effect in relation to a syndicate return made in respect of profits or losses declared after 31 December 2009 (where "syndicate return" means a return of a syndicate's profit or loss for an underwriting year under reg. 4).

HMRC DETERMINATIONS

6(1)   In relation to both members who are individuals and corporate members, the like provisions as are contained in paragraphs 36 and 40 of Schedule 18 shall apply with the modifications in paragraphs (2) and (3).

6(2)   For references to–

(a)   the company substitute references to the syndicate's managing agent;

(b)   the company tax return substitute references to the syndicate return;

(c)   the company's self-assessment or tax payable, substitute references to the syndicate determination;

(d)   an accounting period (or periods) substitute references to the underwriting year to which the syndicate return relates (or would relate); and

(e)   the Inland Revenue substitute references to Her Majesty's Revenue and Customs.

6(3)   Omit paragraphs 36(3) and (6)(a) and 40(1)(b) and (2).

DISCOVERY DETERMINATIONS

7(1)   In relation to both members who are individuals and corporate members, the like provisions as are contained in paragraphs 41(2) to 44 and 46 to 49 of Schedule 18 (as they apply to discovery determinations) shall apply with the modifications in paragraphs (2) and (3).

7(2)   Except in paragraph 49 of Schedule 18, for references to–

(a)   the company substitute references to the syndicate's managing agent;

(b)   the company tax return substitute references to the syndicate return;

(c)   the company's self-assessment or tax payable, substitute references to the syndicate determination;

(d)   an accounting period (or periods) substitute references to the underwriting year to which the syndicate return relates (or would relate); and

(e)   the Inland Revenue substitute references to Her Majesty's Revenue and Customs.

7(3)   In paragraph 41(2) of Schedule 18, omit–

(a)   "for another accounting period" in paragraph (a), and

(b)   paragraph (b).

RELIEF IN CASE OF MISTAKE IN SYNDICATE RETURN

8(1)   In relation to both members who are individuals and corporate members, the like provisions as are contained in paragraph 51 of Schedule 18 shall apply with the modifications in paragraph (2).

8(2)   For references to–

(a)   the company substitute references to the syndicate's managing agent;

(b)   the payment of tax, an assessment or the profits of the company for corporation tax purposes substitute references to the syndicate determination;

(c)   the liability of the claimant or claimant company, treat them as including references to the liability of the members of the syndicate;

(d)   an accounting period (or periods) substitute references to the underwriting year to which the syndicate return relates (or would relate); and

(e)   the Inland Revenue substitute references to Her Majesty's Revenue and Customs.

APPORTIONMENTS OF SYNDICATE'S PROFIT OR LOSS

9(1)   Where a determination of a syndicate's profit or loss for an underwriting year is made, amended or corrected (whether under the foregoing provisions of these Regulations or on appeal), the officer may, by notice in writing to the syndicate's managing agent, require him to make to the officer, within the specified period, a return apportioning, between the members of the syndicate, the syndicate's profit or loss as stated in the determination as so made, amended or corrected.

9(2)   If a syndicate's managing agent, having been required by a notice under paragraph (1) to deliver a return within the specified period, fails to deliver the return within that period, he shall be liable to a penalty equal to the prescribed amount multiplied by the number of days on which the failure continues.

9(3)   In paragraph (2) **"the prescribed amount"** means £5 for each fifty members of the syndicate (counting any number of members less than fifty, and any number left over, as fifty).

9(4)   In this regulation **"the specified period"** means such period, not being less than thirty days and beginning with the day following the date of the notice under paragraph (1), as may be specified in that notice.

EFFECT OF DETERMINATIONS ON MEMBERS

10(1)   A determination of a syndicate's profit or loss for an underwriting year (whether as originally made or as amended or corrected) and any apportionment under regulation 9 shall, for the purpose of determining the liability to tax of each member of the syndicate, be conclusive against that member that the syndicate's profit or loss for that year, or the member's share of it, as the case may be, is as there stated.

10(2)   Where a determination of a syndicate's profit or loss for an underwriting year is amended or corrected at any time after the issue of a notice of assessment assessing any member of the syndicate to tax–

(a)

    (i)   in relation to members who are individuals, section 31A of the Management Act (notice of appeal) and section 55 of that Act (recovery of tax not postponed), and

    (ii) in relation to corporate members, paragraph 48 of Schedule 18,

shall have effect, in relation to that member, as if any reference to the date of the notice of assessment, or the date of the issue of the notice of assessment, were a reference to the date of the amendment or correction; and

(b)   in the case of an amendment, an assessment which gives effect to the determination as amended shall not be out of time if it is made within one year of the date of the amendment.

10(3)   Paragraph (2)(b) shall not apply in the case of an HMRC amendment under regulation 6 which is made later than six years after the end of the last year during which, or during any part of which, the syndicate continues.

ASSESSMENT OF INDIVIDUAL MEMBERS: TIME LIMITS

11   For the purposes of sections 36 and 40 of the Management Act and paragraph 46(2) of Schedule 18 (extension of time in cases of fraudulent or negligent conduct) anything done or omitted to be done by a syndicate's managing agent shall be deemed to have been done or omitted to be done by each member of the syndicate.

NON-DELIVERY OF RETURN – REASONABLE EXCUSE

12(1)   For the purposes of these Regulations, a managing agent shall be deemed not to have failed to deliver–

(a)   a syndicate return by the filing date referred to in regulation 4(4), or

(b)   a return apportioning a syndicate profit or loss within the period referred to in regulation 9(4),

if he delivered it within such further time, if any, as the officer of Revenue and Customs may have allowed.

12(2)   Where a managing agent had a reasonable excuse for not delivering a return mentioned in paragraph (1), he shall be deemed not to have failed to deliver it–

(a)   unless the excuse had ceased, and

(b)   if, after the excuse ceased, he delivered it without unreasonable delay.

DETERMINATIONS AND NOTICES OF DETERMINATIONS

13   The like provisions as are contained in section 113(1B) of the Management Act shall apply to a determination or notice of a determination under regulations 6 or 7 as if the determination were an assessment and the notice of a determination were a notice of an assessment.

PART 3

REPAYMENT OF TAX DEDUCTED ETC. FROM INVESTMENT INCOME

14(1)   In relation to an underwriting year, a syndicate's managing agent may, by notice in writing at any time during the period of six years beginning with the 1st March next following the end of the closing year for that year, make a claim to an officer of Revenue and Customs for the repayment of tax suffered by way of deduction on such of the syndicate's investment income as is allocated to that year in accordance with the rules or practice of Lloyd's.

14(2)   The syndicate's managing agent shall provide such information in support of the claim as the officer may reasonably require.

14(3)   Where an amount is repaid to a syndicate's managing agent under this regulation, he shall–

(a)   apportion that amount between the members of the syndicate in proportion to their interests in that part of the syndicate's investment income which has suffered tax by way of deduction; and

(b)   except in so far as it is required to meet a share of a loss of the syndicate, pay the amount so apportioned to each member, within 90 days of the repayment, to the members' agent of that member.

14(4)   The provisions of section 824 of the Taxes Act (repayment supplements: individuals and others) shall not apply to any repayment of tax made under this regulation.

14(5)   In this regulation "investment income", in relation to a syndicate, means the aggregate amount of the profits arising to all the members of the syndicate (taken together) from assets forming part of premium trust funds.

14(6)   In its application to a corporate member, this regulation shall have effect as if–

(a)   in paragraph (3)(b), the reference to the members' agent of each member were a reference to each corporate member itself; and

(b)   in paragraph (4), the reference to section 824 of the Taxes Act were a reference to section 826 of that Act (interest on tax overpaid).

PART 4 – ELECTRONIC COMMUNICATIONS, CONSEQUENTIAL PROVISIONS AND REPEALS

AMENDMENT TO THE INCOME AND CORPORATION TAXES (ELECTRONIC COMMUNICATIONS) REGULATIONS 2003

15   In regulation 2(1)(a) of the Income and Corporation Taxes (Electronic Communications) Regulations 2003, after paragraph (ii) insert–

"(iia)   the Lloyd's Underwriters (Tax) Regulations 2005,".

CONSEQUENTIAL PROVISIONS AND REPEALS

16   In section 184(1) of the Finance Act 1993, in the definition of "members' agent", for "Part II of Schedule 19 to this Act" substitute "the Lloyd's Underwriters (Tax) Regulations 2005".

17   In Schedule 1 to the Income Tax (Trading and Other Income) Act 2005 omit paragraph 465.

18   Regulations 3, 7 and 8 of the Lloyd's Underwriters (Tax) Regulations 1995 are hereby revoked.

PROCEEDS OF CRIME ACT 2002 (LEGAL EXPENSES IN CIVIL RECOVERY PROCEEDINGS) REGULATIONS 2005

(SI 2005/3382, as amended by SI 2008/523)

Made on 3 December 2005 by the Lord Chancellor in exercise of the powers conferred by s. 286A, 286B and 459(2) of the Proceeds of Crime Act 2002 and art. 198, 199 and 5(2) of SI 2005/3181. Operative from 1 January 2006.

PART 1 – INTRODUCTION

CITATION AND COMMENCEMENT

1   These Regulations may be cited as the Proceeds of Crime Act 2002 (Legal Expenses in Civil Recovery Proceedings) Regulations 2005 and shall come into force on 1st January 2006.

INTERPRETATION

2(1)   In these Regulations–

"**the 1990 Act**" means the Courts and Legal Services Act 1990;

"**the 2002 Act**" means the Proceeds of Crime Act 2002;

"**CPR**" means the Civil Procedure Rules 1998;

"**the Order in Council**" means the Proceeds of Crime Act 2002 (External Requests and Orders) Order 2005;

"**RSC (NI)**" means the Rules of the Supreme Court (Northern Ireland) 1980;

"**civil recovery proceedings**" means proceedings under Part 5 of the 2002 Act or Part 5 of the Order in Council;

"**notice**" means notice in writing;

"**relevant enforcement authority**" means the enforcement authority which is conducting the civil recovery proceedings concerned;

"**solicitor**" means a solicitor of the Supreme Court and, in relation to England and Wales, includes any other person who is an authorised litigator within the meaning of section 119(1) of the 1990 Act.

2(2)   Any reference in these Regulations to the assessment of legal expenses by the court shall, in relation to Northern Ireland, be interpreted as referring to the taxation of those expenses by the Master (Taxing Office).

History – In reg. 2(1), the definition of "relevant enforcement authority" inserted by SI 2008/523, reg. 2(2), with effect from 1 April 2008.

PART 2 – REQUIRED CONDITIONS: GENERAL

EFFECT OF THIS PART

3   This Part specifies the required conditions for the purposes of sections 245C(5) and 252(4) of the 2002 Act and articles 149(5) and 157(4) of the Order in Council.

CONDITION RELATING TO WORK COVERED BY EXCLUSION

4   An exclusion from a property freezing order or interim receiving order must specify–

(a)   the stage or stages in civil recovery proceedings to which it relates; and

(b)   the maximum amount which may be released in respect of legal expenses for each stage to which it relates.

Statutory Instruments

CONDITION RELATING TO NOTIFICATION

5   If the solicitor acting for the person to whose legal expenses the exclusion relates becomes aware that–

(a)   that person's legal expenses in respect of any stage in civil recovery proceedings have exceeded or will exceed the maximum amount specified in the exclusion for that stage; or

(b)   that person's total legal expenses in respect of all the stages to which the exclusion relates have exceeded or will exceed the total amount that may be released pursuant to the exclusion,

the solicitor must give notice to the relevant enforcement authority and the court as soon as reasonably practicable.

History – In reg. 5, the words "relevant enforcement authority" substituted for the word "Director" by SI 2008/523, reg. 2(3), with effect from 1 April 2008.

CONDITION RELATING TO PAYMENT OF EXPENSES

6   Where a person has incurred legal expenses in relation to a stage in civil recovery proceedings specified in an exclusion–

(a)   during any period when the property freezing order or interim receiving order has effect, a sum may only be released in respect of those expenses in accordance with Part 3;

(b)   where the court makes a recovery order which provides for the payment of that person's reasonable legal expenses in respect of civil recovery proceedings, the sum payable in respect of his legal expenses shall be determined in accordance with Part 4, regardless of whether a sum has been released in respect of any of those expenses under Part 3.

PART 3 – REQUIRED CONDITIONS: RELEASE OF INTERIM PAYMENTS

EFFECT OF THIS PART

7   This Part applies where, during a period when a property freezing order or interim receiving order has effect, a person to whose property the order applies seeks the release of a sum in respect of his legal expenses pursuant to an exclusion from the order.

REQUEST FOR RELEVANT ENFORCEMENT AUTHORITY'S AGREEMENT TO RELEASE OF INTERIM PAYMENT

History – In the heading, the words "relevant enforcement authority's" substituted for the word "Director's" by SI 2008/523, reg. 2(4), with effect from 1 April 2008.

8(1)   A request for the relevant enforcement authority's agreement to the release of a sum in respect of legal expenses pursuant to an exclusion must be made in writing to that authority by the person to whose expenses the exclusion relates.

8(2)   The request must–

(a)   describe the stage or stages in the civil recovery proceedings in relation to which the legal expenses were incurred;

(b)   summarise the work done in connection with each stage;

(c)   be accompanied by any invoices, receipts or other documents which are necessary to show that the expenses have been incurred; and

(d)   identify any item or description of property from which the person making the request wishes the sum to be released.

8(3)   A person may not make a request under this regulation–

(a)   in respect of legal expenses which he has not yet incurred; or

(b)   more than once in any 2 month period.

History – In reg. (8)(1), the words "relevant enforcement authority's" substituted for the word "Director's" and the words "that authority" substituted for the word "the Director" by SI 2008/523, reg. 2(4), with effect from 1 April 2008.

RELEVANT ENFORCEMENT AUTHORITY'S RESPONSE TO REQUEST

History – In the heading, the words "relevant enforcement authority's" substituted for the word "Director's" by SI 2008/523, reg. 2(5), with effect from 1 April 2008.

9(1)   Not later than 21 days after it receives the request, the relevant enforcement authority must give notice to the person who made the request stating–

(a)   whether it agrees to the release of the requested sum; and

(b)   if it does not agree to the release of the requested sum–

    (i)   the amount (if any) which it agrees may be released; and

    (ii)   the reasons for its decision.

9(2)   Where an interim receiving order applies to the property from which it is proposed that the requested sum should be released, the relevant enforcement authority must at the same time send copies of the request and the notice referred to in paragraph (1) to the interim receiver.

9(3)   In determining the amount which may be released in respect of legal expenses with its agreement, the relevant enforcement authority must have regard to the provisions of Part 5 which would apply on the assessment of those expenses by the court.

History – In reg. 9(1), the word "it" substituted for the word "he", the words "relevant enforcement authority" substituted for the word "Director" and the word "its" substituted for the word "his" by SI 2008/523, reg. 2(5), with effect from 1 April 2008.
In reg. 9(2), the words "relevant enforcement authority" substituted for the word "Director" by SI 2008/523, reg. 2(5), with effect from 1 April 2008.
In reg. 9(3), the words "relevant enforcement authority" substituted for the word "Director" and the word "its" substituted for the word "his" by SI 2008/523, reg. 2(5), with effect from 1 April 2008.

RELEASE OF INTERIM PAYMENT

10(1)   The sum which may be released pursuant to the exclusion is the greater of–

(a)   the amount which the relevant enforcement authority agrees may be released; and

(b)   65% of the requested sum.

10(2)   The sum may only be released to–

(a)   the solicitor who is instructed to act in the civil recovery proceedings for the person to whose legal expenses the exclusion relates; or

(b)   where appropriate, to the solicitor who was so instructed when the legal expenses to which the sum relates were incurred.

History – In reg. 10(1), the words "relevant enforcement authority" substituted for the word "Director" by SI 2008/523, reg. 2(6), with effect from 1 April 2008.

PART 4 – AGREEMENT OR ASSESSMENT OF EXPENSES AT CONCLUSION OF CIVIL RECOVERY PROCEEDINGS

EFFECT OF THIS PART

11   This Part specifies the procedure for determining the amount payable in respect of a person's reasonable legal expenses in civil recovery proceedings, where the court has made a recovery order which provides for the payment of those expenses.

AGREEMENT OF EXPENSES BY THE RELEVANT ENFORCEMENT AUTHORITY

History – In the heading, the words "relevant enforcement authority" substituted for the word "Director" by SI 2008/523, reg. 2(7), with effect from 1 April 2008.

12(1)   This regulation applies where a person seeks the relevant enforcement authority's agreement to the payment of a sum in respect of his legal expenses pursuant to section 266(8B)(a) of the 2002 Act or article 177(11)(a) of the Order in Council.

12(2)   In determining the amount which may be paid in respect of legal expenses with its agreement, the relevant enforcement authority must have regard to the provisions of Part 5 which would apply on the assessment of those expenses by the court.

12(3)   Where the relevant enforcement authority agrees to the payment of the sum which a person seeks in respect of his legal expenses–

(a)   it shall give that person and the trustee for civil recovery notice of the agreed sum; and

(b)   the sum payable in respect of those expenses shall be the agreed sum.

History – In reg. 12(1), the words "relevant enforcement authority's" substituted for the word "Director's" by SI 2008/523, reg. 2(7), with effect from 1 April 2008.
In reg. 12(2) and (3), the words "relevant enforcement authority" substituted for the word "Director" by SI 2008/523, reg. 2(7), with effect from 1 April 2008.
In reg. 12(2), the word "its" substituted for the word "his" by SI 2008/523, reg. 2(7), with effect from 1 April 2008.
In reg. 12(3)(a), the word "it" substituted for the word "he" by SI 2008/523, reg. 2(7), with effect from 1 April 2008.

EXPENSES TO BE ASSESSED IF NOT AGREED

13(1) Unless the relevant enforcement authority agrees to the payment of the sum which a person seeks in respect of his legal expenses pursuant to provision made in a recovery order, that person must commence proceedings for the assessment of those expenses in accordance with paragraph (2).

13(2) Where paragraph (1) requires a person to commence proceedings for the assessment of his legal expenses–

(a)   in relation to civil recovery proceedings in England and Wales, he must commence proceedings for the detailed assessment of those expenses in accordance with CPR Part 47, subject to the modifications that–

    (i)   rule 47.7 shall have effect as if it provided that he must commence those proceedings not later than 2 months after the date of the recovery order; and

    (ii)   rule 47.14(2) shall have effect as if it provided that he must file a request for a detailed assessment hearing not later than 2 months after the expiry of the period for commencing the detailed assessment proceedings;

(b)   in relation to civil recovery proceedings in Northern Ireland, he must begin proceedings for the taxation of those expenses in accordance with RSC (NI) Order 62, subject to the modification that rule 29(1) shall have effect as if it provided that he must begin those proceedings not later than 4 months after the date of the recovery order.

13(3) The court will assess the person's legal expenses in accordance with the provisions of Part 5 and the relevant rules of court, and the sum payable in respect of those expenses shall be the assessed amount.

History – In reg. 13(1), the words "relevant enforcement authority" substituted for the word "Director" by SI 2008/523, reg. 2(8), with effect from 1 April 2008.

PAYMENT OF EXPENSES

14(1) Where the sum payable in respect of a person's legal expenses–

(a)   exceeds the total amount which has been released in respect of those expenses in accordance with Part 3, the trustee for civil recovery must pay the balance out of the sums referred to in section 280(1) of the 2002 Act or article 191(1) of the Order in Council;

(b)   is less than the total amount which has been released in respect of those expenses in accordance with Part 3, the person to whose expenses the sum relates must repay the balance to the trustee.

14(2) The trustee for civil recovery may only make a payment in respect of a person's legal expenses to–

(a)   the solicitor who is instructed to act for that person; or

(b)   where appropriate, the solicitor who was so instructed when the legal expenses to which the sum relates were incurred.

PART 5 – BASIS FOR ASSESSMENT OF LEGAL EXPENSES

EFFECT OF THIS PART

15 This Part sets out the basis on which the court must assess the amount payable in respect of a person's reasonable legal expenses of civil recovery proceedings pursuant to provision made in a recovery order.

GENERAL PRINCIPLES

16(1) Subject to regulation 17, the court will assess a person's legal expenses on the standard basis.

16(2) The court must give effect to–

(a)   any provision made in the recovery order for the purpose of enabling the person to meet his reasonable legal expenses of civil recovery proceedings; and

(b)   subject to sub-paragraph (a), the terms of any exclusion made for the purpose of enabling that person to meet those legal expenses (including the required conditions).

16(3) In paragraph (1), **"the standard basis"** has the meaning given in–

(a)   CPR rule 44.4 in relation to proceedings in England and Wales;

(b)   RSC (NI) Order 62 rule 12 in relation to proceedings in Northern Ireland.

RATES OF REMUNERATION

17(1) Subject to the following paragraphs of this regulation, remuneration for work done by a legal representative may only be allowed at the appropriate hourly rate shown in the Table below.

17(2) The higher hourly rates specified in the third column of the Table may only be allowed where the case involves substantial novel or complex issues of law or fact.

17(3) The rates specified in the Table will be increased by–

(a) 20% for legal representatives whose offices are situated in Central London; and

(b) 10% for legal representatives whose offices are situated in Outer London.

17(4) In paragraph (3)–

(a) **"Central London"** means postcode districts EC1–4, SW1, W1 and WC1–2;

(b) **"Outer London"** means all other postcode districts in postcode areas BR, CR, DA, E, N, NW, SE, SW, UB and W.

and **"postcode area"** and **"postcode district"** shall be construed in accordance with the Postcode Address File within the meaning given in section 116 of the Postal Services Act 2000.

Table: rates of remuneration for legal representatives

Category of fee earner[1]	Standard hourly rate (excluding VAT)	Higher hourly rate (excluding VAT)
Solicitors and their employees		
Senior solicitor (of at least 8 years' standing)	£187.50	£225.00
Solicitor (of at least 4 years' and less than 8 years' standing)	£150.00	£187.50
Junior solicitor (of less than 4 years' standing)	£107.50	£131.25
Trainee solicitor, paralegal or other fee earner	£75.00	£93.75
Council		
Queen's Counsel	–	£275.00
Senior junior counsel (of at least 10 years' standing)	£150.00	£225.00
Junior counsel (of less than 10 years' standing)	£100.00	£150.00

[1] In relation to England and Wales, a reference to a number of years' standing as a solicitor or counsel to be interpreted as referring to that number of years' general qualification (within the meaning of section 71 of the 1990 Act).

LOAN RELATIONSHIPS AND DERIVATIVE CONTRACTS (EXCHANGE GAINS AND LOSSES USING FAIR VALUE ACCOUNTING) REGULATIONS 2005

(SI 2005/3422)

Made on 12 December 2005 by the Treasury, in exercise of the powers conferred upon them by s. 103(1AA) of the Finance Act 1996 and para. 54(2A) of Sch. 26 to the Finance Act 2002. Operative from 2 January 2006.

CITATION, COMMENCEMENT AND EFFECT

1   These Regulations may be cited as the Loan Relationships and Derivative Contracts (Exchange Gains and Losses using Fair Value Accounting) Regulations 2005 and shall come into force on 2nd January 2006 and shall have effect in relation to periods of account beginning on or after 1st January 2005.

INTERPRETATION

2(1)   In these Regulations–

"**derivative contract**" has the same meaning as in Schedule 26 to the Finance Act 2002;

"**fair value accounting**" has the meaning given in section 103 of the Finance Act 1996;

"**generally accepted accounting practice**" has the meaning given in section 50 of the Finance Act 2004;

"**loan relationship**" has the same meaning as in Chapter 2 of Part 4 of the Finance Act 1996; and "**designated**", "**fair value**", "**available-for-sale**" and "**fair value hedge**" have the same meanings as they have for accounting purposes.

CURRENCY

3   For the purposes of these Regulations the currency with which a company computes its profits and losses as determined by sections 92 to 92E of the Finance Act 1993 shall be known as the "base currency".

EXCHANGE GAIN OR LOSS : GENERAL

4   In these Regulations exchange gain or loss shall not include any debits or credits referred to in regulation 4(1), (3) and (4) of the Loan Relationships and Derivative Contracts (Change of Accounting Practice) Regulations 2004.

EXCHANGE GAIN OR LOSS ARISING FROM LOAN RELATIONSHIP ASSETS OR LIABILITIES

5(1)   Paragraphs (2) and (3) set out the rules for calculating the exchange gain or loss arising from loan relationship assets or liabilities in the following circumstances–

(a)   the asset or liability is accounted for at fair value, or

(b)   that asset or liability or part of it is a hedged item in a designated fair value hedge and the risk being hedged is or includes exchange risk.

5(2)   Where paragraph (1) applies and–

(a)   an amount is recognised in the company's profit and loss account or income statement which arises from comparing at different times the fair value of the asset or liability (or in the case of regulation 5(1)(b) any part of it), and

(b)   the change in fair value is attributable to any extent to fluctuations in the spot rate of exchange between the currency in which the asset or liability is denominated and the base currency of the company,

the exchange gain or loss is calculated as set out in paragraph (3).

5(3)   The exchange gain or loss for any accounting period is the change in fair value between the earlier and the later time in that period that is attributable only to fluctuations in the spot rate of exchange between the currency in which the asset or liability is denominated and the base currency of the company.

6   If an asset is accounted for as available-for-sale, the exchange gain or loss is the amount shown in the profit and loss account or income statement which fairly represents that gain or loss in accordance with generally accepted accounting practice.

EXCHANGE GAIN OR LOSS ARISING FROM DERIVATIVE CONTRACTS

7(1)   Paragraphs (2) and (3) set out the rules for calculating the exchange gain or loss arising from derivative contracts where such a contract is accounted for at fair value.

7(2)   Where–

(a)   an amount is recognised in the company's profit and loss account or income statement which arises from comparing at different times the fair value of the derivative contract, and

(b)   that change in fair value is attributable to any extent to fluctuations in the spot rate of exchange between the base currency of the company and one or more currencies that form part of–

    (i)   the underlying subject matter of the derivative contract, or

    (ii)   in a case in which that currency or those currencies do not form part of the underlying subject matter of the contract, the currency or currencies in which payments under the contract fall to be made,

the exchange gain or loss is calculated as set out in paragraph (3).

7(3)   The exchange gain or loss for any accounting period is the change in fair value between the earlier and the later time in that period that is attributable only to fluctuations in the spot rate of exchange between the currency or currencies and the base currency.

CALCULATION OF RESIDUAL PROFIT AND LOSS

8   Regulation 9 applies where there is a fair value profit or loss in relation to a loan relationship or derivative contract which is not wholly an exchange gain or loss (as determined by regulations 5 to 7).

9(1)   Where there is a fair value profit, the residual profit is calculated by subtracting from the profit any exchange gain, and adding to it the amount of any exchange loss.

9(2)   Where the exchange gain exceeds the fair value profit, the difference between the two is the residual loss.

9(3)   Where there is a fair value loss, the residual loss is calculated by adding to the loss any exchange gain or subtracting from it any exchange loss.

9(4)   Where the exchange loss exceeds the fair value loss the difference between the two is the residual profit.

9(5)   Residual profits and losses are amounts recognised in determining a company's profit or loss for a period for the purposes of section 85B(1) of the Finance Act 1996 and paragraph 17B(1) of Schedule 26 to the Finance Act 2002.

REGISTERED PENSION SCHEMES (RELIEF AT SOURCE) REGULATIONS

(SI 2005/3448, as amended by SI 2009/56 and SI 2009/571)

Made on 14 December 2005 by the Commissioners for Her Majesty's Revenue and Customs, in exercise of the powers conferred by s. 192(6), (7) and (8) of the Finance Act 2004. Operative from 6 April 2006.

CITATION AND COMMENCEMENT

1 These Regulations may be cited as the Registered Pension Schemes (Relief at Source) Regulations 2005 and shall come into force on 6th April 2006.

INTERPRETATION

2(1) In these Regulations **"section"**, without more, means a section of the Finance Act 2004.

2(2) In these Regulations, unless the context otherwise requires–

"the basic amount" has the meaning given by section 190(4);

"electronic signature" has the meaning given by section 7(2) of the Electronic Communications Act 2000;

"ITEPA 2003" means the Income Tax (Earnings and Pensions) Act 2003;

"ITTOIA 2005" means the Income Tax (Trading and Other Income) Act 2005;

"net contribution" means a contribution from which income tax at the basic rate is deductible in accordance with section 192;

"person with parental responsibility" means a person–

(a) in England and Wales, who has such responsibility within section 3 of the Children Act 1989;

(b) in Scotland means a person who has parental responsibilities as defined by section 1(3) of the Children (Scotland) Act 1995; and

(c) in Northern Ireland, who has such responsibility within the meaning of Article 6 of the Children (Northern Ireland) Order 1995;

"pension scheme" and **"registered pension scheme"** have the meanings given by section 150;

"relevant individual" means the person in respect of whom contributions are payable to a pension scheme;

"scheme administrator" has the meaning given by section 270;

"tax month" means a period beginning on the 6th day of any month and ending with the 5th day of the following month;

"TMA 1970" means the Taxes Management Act 1970;

"tribunal" means the First-tier Tribunal or, where determined by or under Tribunal Procedure Rules, the Upper Tribunal.

"year of assessment" means a year beginning with 6th April in any year and ending with 5th April in the following year.

History – In reg. 2(2), entry for "tribunal" inserted by SI 2009/56, art. 3(2) and Sch. 2, para. 144, operative from 1 April 2009 subject to transitional and saving provisions in SI 2009/56, Sch. 3.

PRESCRIBED CONDITIONS

3(1) Regulations 4, 5 and 6 specify the conditions subject to which relief under section 191 (methods of giving relief for pension contributions) shall be given in accordance with section 192(1) and (2) (relief at source).

3(2) The particulars specified in regulation 4(2) and the declarations required by regulations 5(2) and 6(2) must be given to the scheme administrator by the relevant individual.

This paragraph is subject to the qualifications in paragraph (3) and regulation 7.

3(3) In a case where–

(a) membership of a registered pension scheme is connected with a particular employment, and

(b)   an individual in such employment automatically becomes a member of a registered pension scheme, subject to the right of the individual to opt out of membership of the scheme,

the employer (rather than the relevant individual) may give the scheme administrator the particulars specified in regulation 4(2), and make the declarations required by regulation 5(2) and 6.

INFORMATION TO BE GIVEN TO THE SCHEME ADMINISTRATOR

4(1)   The scheme administrator must be given–

(a)   the particulars specified in paragraph (2), and

(b)   the declarations required by regulations 5(2) and 6(2),

before the time specified in paragraph (5).

4(2)   The particulars are–

(a)   the relevant individual's full name and permanent residential address including, where the address is in the United Kingdom, the postcode.

(b)   the relevant individual's date of birth;

(c)   unless the relevant individual is–

     (i)   aged under 16, or

    (ii)   a citizen of a country outside the United Kingdom who is not resident in the United Kingdom,

         the relevant individual's National Insurance number, or a statement that he does not have one;

(d)   except where the scheme is an occupational pension scheme within the meaning of section 150(5), the category of status specified in paragraph (3) applicable in the relevant individual's case or, if more than one category is applicable, the category which is that individual's principal source of income.

4(3)   The categories of status specified for the purposes of paragraph (2)(d) are–

(a)   employed, if the relevant individual is chargeable to tax under Chapter 2 of Part 2 of ITEPA 2003 for the year of assessment concerned in respect of employment income as defined in section 7 of that Act;

(b)   pensioner, where the relevant individual is chargeable to tax under Part 9 of that Act for the year of assessment concerned in respect of a pension;

(c)   self-employed, in the case of an individual chargeable to tax under Chapter 2 of Part 2 of ITTOIA 2005 for the year of assessment concerned in respect of annual profits or gains arising or accruing from any trade, profession or vocation carried on by the individual;

(d)   child, where the individual is under the age of 16;

(e)   other, in the case of a relevant individual not falling within any of sub-paragraphs (a) to (d).

4(4)   In the case of a relevant individual whose status falls within paragraph (3)(e), the particulars given must specify which of the following descriptors is applicable or, if more than one, the most applicable, namely–

(a)   caring for one or more children aged under 16;

(b)   caring for a person aged 16 or over;

(c)   in full time education;

(d)   unemployed; or

(e)   other.

4(5)   The time specified in relation to the particulars in paragraph (2)(a) to (d) is when the individual first pays a net contribution.

DECLARATION THAT RELEVANT INDIVIDUAL ENTITLED TO RELIEF

5(1)   Before a relevant individual pays a net contribution for the first time, the scheme administrator must be given the declaration specified in paragraph (2).

5(2)   The declaration is one that the total contributions to any registered pension schemes in respect of which he is entitled to relief under section 188 will not exceed the higher of–

(a)   the basic amount, or

(b)   the relevant individual's relevant UK earnings, within the meaning of section 189 for that tax year.

DECLARATION ABOUT ACCURACY OF INFORMATION

6(1) Whenever particulars are given in accordance with regulation 4 they must be accompanied by the declaration specified in paragraph (2).

6(2) The declaration is one to the effect that–

(a)   in relation to–

     (i)   the particulars specified in regulation 4(2), they are, to the best of the maker's knowledge and belief, correct and complete;

     (ii)   the declaration specified in regulation 5(2), it is, to the best of the maker's knowledge and belief, correct;

(b)   no later than the date specified in paragraph (3), the maker will give notice to the scheme administrator if an event occurs, as a result of which the relevant individual will no longer be entitled to relief for his contributions pursuant to section 188.

6(3) The date is the later of–

(a)   5th April in the year of assessment in which the event referred to in sub-paragraph (2)(b) occurs; and

(b)   the date which is 30 days after the occurrence of that event.

6(4) If a declaration given under this regulation or regulation 5 is in writing, it shall be signed by, or on behalf of, the maker.

PERSONS UNDER INCAPACITY AND DISABLED PERSONS

7(1) Where the obligations imposed by regulations 4 to 6 would fall to be discharged by a person who is–

(a)   a child under the age of 16,

(b)   a person incapable, by reason of mental disorder, of managing and administering his property and affairs, or

(c)   a person suffering from a physical disability, by reason of which he has difficulty executing documents in respect of the management and administration of his property and affairs,

the following provisions of this regulation apply.

7(2) In a case falling within paragraph (1)(a) those obligations shall be discharged by the child's parent or guardian, or a person with parental responsibility for the child.

7(3) In a case falling within paragraph (1)(b) those obligations shall be discharged–

(a)   in England and Wales or Northern Ireland, by the person's attorney or receiver, or the person managing and administering his property and affairs;

(b)   in Scotland, by the person's guardian within the meaning of the Adults with Incapacity (Scotland) Act 2000.

7(4) In a case falling within paragraph (1)(c) those obligations may be discharged by a person having a power of attorney in relation to the affairs of the person referred to in that sub-paragraph.

ELECTRONIC COMMUNICATIONS AND DOCUMENTS

8(1) If particulars or declarations given under regulations 4 to 7–

(a)   are not in writing, or

(b)   are given to the scheme administrator by someone other than the relevant individual,

the following provisions of this regulation apply.

8(2) In a case falling within paragraph (1) the scheme administrator shall–

(a)   make a declaration in writing on behalf of the relevant individual under regulations 4 to 6 that the particulars given or the terms of the declarations given are those recorded in the scheme administrator's declaration, and

(b)   send a copy of the declaration to the relevant individual.

8(3) Unless the relevant individual notifies the scheme administrator, within 30 days after the date when the copy of the declaration referred to in paragraph (2) ("the original declaration") was sent to him–

(a)   that he does not wish to become a member of the pension scheme, or

(b)   that the original declaration was incorrect,

the original declaration shall take effect as from the date on which the copy of it was sent to the relevant individual in accordance with that paragraph.

8(4) If the relevant individual notifies the scheme administrator that the original declaration should be corrected, the original declaration shall cease to have effect, and the scheme administrator shall make a new declaration and paragraphs (2) and (3) shall apply to the new declaration as they applied to the original declaration.

8(5) Particulars or declarations furnished under regulation 4, 5, 6 or 7 or this regulation shall be regarded as furnished in writing for the purposes of this regulation if, although not in writing, they are furnished by means of electronic communication and contain the electronic signature of the maker.

8(6) Declarations made by the scheme administrator under this regulation shall be regarded as made in writing if they are produced by electronic means.

8(7) The copy of a declaration to be sent in accordance with paragraph (2)(b) may be sent to the relevant individual by electronic communications.

8(8) In the case of a person to whom regulation 7 applies, references in this regulation to the relevant individual include any person authorised by that regulation to act on his behalf.

CLAIMS: INTRODUCTORY

9(1) Amounts recoverable by a scheme administrator under section 192(3)(a) shall be recovered on a claim made to Her Majesty's Revenue and Customs for the purpose of these Regulations.

9(2) A claim shall be for a year of assessment (an "annual claim").

This is subject to the following qualification.

9(3) A claim may also be made in accordance with regulation 10 for a tax month (an "interim claim").

INTERIM CLAIMS

10(1) An interim claim may be made by a scheme administrator within 6 months after the end of the tax month for which it is made.

This is subject to the following qualifications.

10(2) An interim claim may not be made for the tax month ending 5th October or for any subsequent month until the annual claim for the preceding year of assessment and any information required by a notice under regulation 15(1) in respect of that year has been made by the scheme administrator and received by an officer of Revenue and Customs.

10(3) An interim claim may not be based on an estimate but may only be made to recover an amount deducted in respect of contributions paid in the tax month to which it relates.

10(4) If the amount claimed is established to the satisfaction of Her Majesty's Revenue and Customs, they shall pay that amount to the claimant: if they are not so satisfied they shall pay to the claimant any lesser amount which is so established.

10(5) If a scheme administrator discovers that an amount paid by Her Majesty's Revenue and Customs under paragraph (4) was excessive the scheme administrator shall bring into account in the interim claim next made after the discovery ("the subsequent claim") the amount of the excess.

If that excess exceeds the amount deducted in respect of the tax month for which the subsequent claim is made–

(a)   the scheme administrator shall repay the amount of the excess to Her Majesty's Revenue and Customs with the claim; and

(b)   if the scheme administrator fails so to do that amount shall immediately be recoverable by Her Majesty's Revenue and Customs in the same manner as tax charged by an assessment on the scheme administrator which has become final and conclusive.

ANNUAL CLAIMS

11(1) An annual claim may be made at any time within 6 years after the end of the year of assessment to which it relates.

This is subject to the following qualification.

11(2) In relation to any year of assessment in which a scheme administrator has received and not repaid in full any amount on an interim claim, the administrator shall within 6 months after the end of the year of assessment make an annual claim.

11(3) An annual claim–

(a)   may not be based on an estimate but may only be made to recover an amount deducted in respect of contributions paid in respect of the year of assessment to which it relates, and

(b)   must bring into account payments made in respect of that year.

For the purpose of this regulation **"aggregate of the interim payments"** means the aggregate of payments made (and not repaid) on interim claims.

11(4) Where the aggregate of the interim payments shown by an annual claim exceeds the amount deducted for the year of assessment–

(a)   the scheme administrator shall repay the amount of the excess to Her Majesty's Revenue and Customs with the claim; and

(b)   if the administrator fails to do so, that amount shall immediately be recoverable by Her Majesty's Revenue and Customs in the same manner as tax charged by an assessment on the scheme administrator which has become final and conclusive.

11(5) If a scheme administrator fails to make an annual claim under paragraph (2) within the time limited by that paragraph, an officer of Revenue and Customs may issue a notice to the scheme administrator showing the aggregate of the interim payments for the year, and stating that they are not satisfied that the amount due to the scheme administrator for the year of assessment exceeds the lower amount stated in the notice.

11(6) If an annual claim is not delivered to Her Majesty's Revenue and Customs within 14 days after the issue of a notice under paragraph (5), the amount of the difference between the aggregate of the interim payments and the amount stated in the notice shall immediately be recoverable by Her Majesty's Revenue and Customs in the same manner as tax charged by an assessment on the scheme administrator which has become final and conclusive.

11(7) If an annual claim has been made and the scheme administrator subsequently discovers that an error or mistake has been made in the claim the scheme administrator may make a supplementary claim within the time limited by paragraph (1).

CLAIMS: SUPPLEMENTARY PROVISIONS

12(1) Section 42 of TMA 1970 (procedure for making claims) shall not apply to a claim under these Regulations.

12(2) No appeal shall lie from the decision of an officer of Revenue and Customs on an interim claim.

12(3) An appeal from the decision of an officer of Revenue and Customs on an annual claim shall be brought by giving written notice to the officer within 30 days of receipt of written notice of the decision.

12(4) No payment made or other thing done on or in relation to an interim claim shall prejudice the decision on an annual claim.

12(5) Part 5 of TMA 1970 (appeals and other proceedings) shall apply to an appeal under paragraph (3) and, on an appeal that is notified to the tribunal, the tribunal may vary the decision appealed against whether or not the variation is to the advantage of the appellant.

12(6) All such assessments, payments and repayments shall be made as are necessary to give effect to the decision of an officer of Revenue and Customs on an annual claim, or to any variation of that decision on appeal.

12(7) Claims under these Regulations must–

(a)   contain such information and be in such form as the Commissioners for Her Majesty's Revenue and Customs may prescribe (and forms prescribed for annual claims may require a report to be given by the scheme administrator's auditor);

(b)   contain declarations to the effect that–

    (i)   sufficient records in respect of the scheme are maintained so as to enable the requirements of these Regulations to be satisfied, and

    (ii)   the information contained in the claim (including the declaration referred to in paragraph (i)) is correct; and

(c)   be signed by the scheme administrator or an individual in the service of the scheme administrator authorised by him.

History – In reg. 12(3), the words "shall lie to the Special Commissioners", which appeared after "An appeal", omitted by SI 2009/56, art. 3(2) and Sch. 2, para. 145(2)(a), operative from 1 April 2009 subject to transitional and saving provisions in SI 2009/56, Sch. 3.
In reg. 12(3), the words ", and the appeal", which appeared after "annual claim", omitted by SI 2009/56, art. 3(2) and Sch. 2, para. 145(2)(b), operative from 1 April 2009 subject to transitional and saving provisions in SI 2009/56, Sch. 3.

In reg. 12(5), the words "and, on an appeal that is notified to the tribunal, the tribunal" substituted for the words "and on an appeal to the Special Commissioners" by SI 2009/56, art. 3(2) and Sch. 2, para. 145(3), operative from 1 April 2009 subject to transitional and saving provisions in SI 2009/56, Sch. 3.

RECOVERY ON DE-REGISTRATION OF SCHEMES

13(1) When a scheme administrator gives information to an officer of Revenue and Customs in accordance with regulation 15(2) the amount (if any) referred to in regulation 15(2)(b) must be paid to Her Majesty's Revenue and Customs.

13(2) If an amount payable by virtue of paragraph (1) is not paid as required, that amount shall immediately be recoverable by Her Majesty's Revenue and Customs in the same manner as tax charged by an assessment on the scheme administrator which has become final and conclusive.

RECOVERY OF AMOUNTS BY ASSESSMENT ETC.

14(1) Section 30 of TMA 1970 (recovery of overpayment of tax, etc.) shall apply in relation to the payment by Her Majesty's Revenue and Customs of an amount—

(a)   paid under these Regulations to which a scheme administrator was not entitled, or

(b)   recoverable from a scheme administrator under regulations 10(5), 11(4) or (6) or 13,

as if it had been income tax repaid to the scheme administrator to which he was not entitled.

14(2) An assessment made by virtue of this regulation shall be made by an officer of Revenue and Customs and, subject to the provisions of these Regulations, TMA 1970 shall apply as if the assessment were an assessment to tax for the year of assessment in respect of which the amount was paid or is recoverable.

14(3) For the purposes of section 86 TMA 1970 (interest on overdue income tax and capital gains tax) the relevant date shall be the later of—

(a)   1st January in the year in which the amount was paid or is recoverable; or

(b)   the date of the making of the repayment by Her Majesty's Revenue and Customs following receipt of the annual claim for that year.

14(4)   [Omitted by SI 2009/571, art. 8 and Sch. 2, para. 41.]

History – Reg. 14(4) omitted by SI 2009/571, art. 8 and Sch. 2, para. 41, with effect from 1 April 2009.

INFORMATION

15(1) An officer of Revenue and Customs may by notice in writing require any person who is, or who at any time has been—

(a)   a scheme administrator to whom net contributions have been paid, or

(b)   an individual or other person who has paid such contributions,

to give the officer, within such time (not being less than 14 days) as may be provided in the notice, such information and in such form as may be prescribed in the notice.

15(2) If an officer of Revenue and Customs by notice under section 157 withdraws the registration of a scheme under which net contributions have been paid, within 30 days the scheme administrator in relation to that scheme must give to that officer the following information—

(a)   the full name, address and national insurance number of each individual who has paid net contributions after the date specified in the notice in relation to the scheme ("the relevant contributions"); and

(b)   the amount of relief obtained under section 189 by means of the relevant contributions.

15(3) If the requirements of regulations 4 to 6 or 7(2) or (3) have not been met in relation to an individual who has paid net contributions, the scheme administrator to whom such contributions have been made shall give to an officer of Revenue and Customs the information prescribed in paragraph (2) within 30 days.

INSPECTION OF RECORDS

16(1) Every scheme administrator to whom net contributions have been paid shall, whenever required so to do, make available for inspection by an officer of Revenue and Customs all books, documents and other records (including all particulars and declarations furnished under regulations 4 to 6 and 7(2) to 7(4)) in the scheme administrator's possession or control relating to—

(a)   contributions paid to the scheme administrator,

(b)   the scheme under which those contributions were paid, and

(c)   the individual who paid the contributions.

16(2) Where records are maintained by computer, the scheme administrator shall provide the person making the inspection with all facilities necessary to obtain information from them.

16(3) All books, documents and records referred to in paragraph (1), shall be preserved by the scheme administrator so as to be available for inspection under this regulation for a period of six years following the end of the tax year to which they relate, or, where there is more than one such year, the later or latest of them.

This is subject to the following qualification.

16(4) All particulars and declarations furnished under regulations 4 to 8 shall be preserved for a period of six years following the end of the tax year in which the individual to whom they relate ceased to make net contributions.

TRANSITIONAL PROVISION

17(1) If information has been furnished to, or a declaration made to, the scheme administrator of a personal pension scheme in relation to an individual in accordance with any provision of the Personal Pension Schemes (Relief at Source) Regulations 1988 ("the 1988 Regulations"), paragraph (2) applies.

17(2) If this paragraph applies, and the scheme administrator to whom information or a declaration under these Regulations would fall to be made—

(a) is the same person as the scheme administrator to whom that information was furnished (whether in the form of particulars or a certificate), or that declaration was made, under the 1988 Regulations, or

(b) is the successor, as the scheme administrator of the scheme to which the 1988 Regulations applied, of the person to whom that information was furnished or that declaration was made,

the information furnished under the 1988 Regulations, and the declaration under those Regulations, shall be treated as having been furnished or made under these Regulations.

REGISTERED PENSION SCHEMES (PRESCRIBED INTEREST RATES FOR AUTHORISED EMPLOYER LOANS) REGULATIONS 2005

(SI 2005/3449)

Made on 14 December 2005 by the Commissioners for Her Majesty's Revenue and Customs, in exercise of the powers conferred by s. 179(2)(a) of the Finance Act 2004. Operative from 6 April 2006.

CITATION AND COMMENCEMENT

1 These Regulations may be cited as the Registered Pension Schemes (Prescribed Interest Rates for Authorised Employer Loans) Regulations 2005 and shall come into force on 6th April 2006.

INTERPRETATION

2(1) In these Regulations–

"**the operative date**" means the sixth working day of each month;

"**the reference date**" is the twelfth working day preceding the operative date in the following month;

"**working day**" means a day which is not a non-business day within the meaning of section 92 of the Bills of Exchange Act 1882.

2(2) In these Regulations the relevant interest rate found on a reference date is the percentage rate per annum found by the following steps.

Step 1

Find the average of the base lending rates of–

(a)   the Bank of Scotland;

(b)   Barclays Bank plc;

(c)   HSBC Bank plc;

(d)   Lloyds TSB Bank plc;

(e)   National Westminster Bank plc; and

(f)   the Royal Bank of Scotland plc.

Step 2

If the amount found by step 1 is a multiple of ¼%, that is the relevant interest rate.

If the amount found by step 1 is not such a multiple, round the amount up to the nearest amount which is such a multiple.

PRESCRIBED RATE OF INTEREST FOR THE PURPOSES OF SECTION 179 OF THE FINANCE ACT 2004

3(1) For the purposes of section 179 of the Finance Act 2004 (authorised employer loans) the prescribed rate of interest is found in accordance with paragraph (2).

3(2) The prescribed rate applicable for the period beginning on one operative date and ending on the day preceding the next operative date is the percentage rate found by the formula–

RIR + 1.

Here RIR is the relevant interest rate found on the reference date immediately preceding the operative date at the start of the period.

Statutory Instruments

REGISTERED PENSION SCHEMES (MINIMUM CONTRIBUTIONS) REGULATIONS 2005

(SI 2005/3450)

Made on 14 December 2005 by the Commissioners for Her Majesty's Revenue and Customs, in exercise of the powers conferred upon them by s. 202(5)(b) of the Finance Act 2004. Operative from 6 April 2006.

CITATION AND COMMENCEMENT

1 These Regulations may be cited as the Registered Pension Schemes (Minimum Contributions) Regulations 2005 and shall come into force on 6th April 2006.

RECOVERY OF AMOUNTS REPRESENTING BASIC RATE TAX

2(1) Subsections (1), (1B), (4) and (5) of section 30 of the Taxes Management Act 1970 (recovery of overpayments of tax, etc.) shall apply in relation to the payment by the Commissioners for Her Majesty's Revenue and Customs of an amount, by way of minimum contributions under section 202 of the Finance Act 2004, which–

(a) they were not required to pay, or

(b) they were required to pay, but which they paid to persons other than the scheme administrator of the registered pension scheme to whom they should have made the payment,

as if a sum representing income tax at the basic rate on the amount paid ("the notional repayment sum") had been income tax repaid to the person to whom, or in respect of whom, the amount was paid, and to which that person was not entitled.

2(2) An assessment made by virtue of paragraph (1) shall be made by an officer of Revenue and Customs and the provisions of the Taxes Management Act 1970 shall apply to the assessment as if it were an assessment to tax for the year of assessment in respect of which the amount of the notional repayment sum was paid.

REGISTERED PENSION SCHEMES (PRESCRIBED SCHEMES AND OCCUPATIONS) REGULATIONS 2005

(SI 2005/3451)

Made on 14 December 2005 by the Commissioners for Her Majesty's Revenue and Customs, in exercise of the powers conferred by para. 19(3)(c) and 23(4)(b) of Sch. 36 to the Finance Act 2004. Operative from 6 April 2006.

CITATION, COMMENCEMENT AND INTERPRETATION

1(1) These Regulations shall be cited as the Registered Pension Schemes (Prescribed Schemes and Occupations) Regulations 2005 and shall come into force on 6th April 2006.

1(2) In these Regulations **"Schedule 36"** means Schedule 36 to the Finance Act 2004 (pension schemes etc: transitional provisions and savings) and any other reference to a numbered Schedule is a reference to the corresponding Schedule to these Regulations.

SCHEMES PRESCRIBED FOR THE PURPOSES OF PARAGRAPH 19(3) OF SCHEDULE 36

2 A pension scheme is prescribed for the purposes of paragraph 19(3) of Schedule 36 if—

(a)   it is listed in Schedule 1; or

(b)   it is a scheme established solely for the receipt of additional voluntary pension contributions from members of a scheme listed in Schedule 1.

OCCUPATIONS PRESCRIBED FOR THE PURPOSES OF PARAGRAPH 23 OF SCHEDULE 36

3 The occupations listed in Schedule 2 are prescribed for the purposes of paragraph 23 of Schedule 36.

SCHEDULE 1

Regulation 2

PRESCRIBED SCHEMES

The Armed Forces Pension Scheme.
The British Transport Police Force Superannuation Fund.
The Firefighters' Pension Scheme.
The Firemen's Pension Scheme (Northern Ireland).
The Gurkha Pension Scheme
The Police Pension Scheme.
The Police Service of Northern Ireland Pension Scheme.
The Police Service of Northern Ireland Full Time Reserve Pension Scheme.

SCHEDULE 2

Regulation 3

PRESCRIBED OCCUPATIONS

Athletes
Badminton Players
Boxers
Cricketers
Cyclists
Dancers
Divers (Saturation, Deep Sea and Free Swimming)
Footballers

Golfers
Ice Hockey Players
Jockeys – Flat Racing
Jockeys – National Hunt
Members of the Reserve Forces
Models
Motor Cycle Riders (Motocross or Road Racing)
Motor Racing Drivers
Rugby League Players
Rugby Union Players
Skiers (Downhill)
Snooker or Billiards Players
Speedway Riders
Squash Players
Table Tennis Players
Tennis Players (including Real Tennis)
Trapeze Artistes
Wrestlers

REGISTERED PENSION SCHEMES (DISCHARGE OF LIABILITIES UNDER SECTIONS 267 AND 268 OF THE FINANCE ACT 2004) REGULATIONS 2005

(SI 2005/3452, as amended by SI 2012/886)

Made on 14 December 2005 by the Commissioners for Her Majesty's Revenue and Customs, in exercise of the powers conferred by s. 267(10) and 268(10) of the Finance Act 2004. Operative from 6 April 2006.

CITATION AND COMMENCEMENT

1 These Regulations may be cited as the Registered Pension Schemes (Discharge of Liabilities under Sections 267 and 268 of the Finance Act 2004) Regulations 2005 and shall come into force on 6th April 2006.

INTERPRETATION

2 In these Regulations–

"**a section 267 application**" means an application under subsection (2) or (5) of section 267 of the Finance Act 2004 (which concern the scheme administrator's liability to lifetime allowance charges);

"**a section 268 application**" means an application under subsection (2) or (5) of section 268 of the Finance Act 2004 (which concern liability to unauthorised payments surcharges and scheme sanctions charges);

"**applicant**" means a person making a section 267 application or a section 268 application; and

"**company**" and "**year of assessment**" have the meanings given to them in section 832 of the Income and Corporation Taxes Act 1988.

TIME LIMITS FOR, AND CONTENT OF SECTION 267 AND 268 APPLICATIONS

3(1) Any section 267 application or section 268 application must be made in writing–

(a) in the case of a company, not later than six years after the end of the accounting period to which it relates; or

(b) in the case of any other applicant, no later than five years after the 31st January next following the year of assessment to which it relates.

This is subject to the following qualification.

3(2) If an assessment is made under section 36 of the Taxes Management Act 1970 (assessments for the purpose of making good any loss to the Crown from a loss of income tax, etc.), the section 267 application or section 268 application (as the case may be) must be made within two years of the date on which the assessment is issued as stated in the notice of that assessment.

3(3) A section 267 application or section 268 application shall set out particulars of the ground relied on under the relevant section.

APPLICATIONS ON BEHALF OF PERSONS WHO ARE INCAPACITATED

4 [Omitted by SI 2012/886, reg. 3.]

History – Reg. 4 omitted by SI 2012/886, reg. 3, with effect from 6 April 2012. Former reg. 4 read as follows:
"**4** A section 267 application or 268 application may be made on behalf of an incapacitated person by his trustee, guardian or receiver.
Here "**incapacitated person**" has the meaning given by section 118 of the Taxes Management Act 1970.".

SUPPLEMENTARY APPLICATIONS

5 Where a section 267 application or section 268 application has been made and the applicant subsequently discovers that an error or mistake has been made in it, the applicant may make a supplementary application in the same manner, and within the same time, as is allowed for making the original application.

EMPLOYER-FINANCED RETIREMENT BENEFITS SCHEMES (PROVISION OF INFORMATION) REGULATIONS 2005

(SI 2005/3453)

Made on 14 December 2005 by the Commissioners for Her Majesty's Revenue and Customs, in exercise of the powers conferred by s. 251(1) and (2)(e) and (f) of the Finance Act 2004. Operative from 6 April 2006.

CITATION AND COMMENCEMENT

1   These Regulations may be cited as the Employer-Financed Retirement Benefits Schemes (Provision of Information) Regulations 2005 and shall come into force on 6th April 2006.

INTERPRETATION

2(1)   In these Regulations–

"**the Act**" means the Finance Act 2004; and

"**ITEPA 2003**" means the Income Tax (Earnings and Pensions) Act 2003.

2(2)   In these Regulations–

"**employer-financed retirement benefits scheme**" has the same meaning as in section 393A of ITEPA 2003;

"**relevant benefits**" has the same meaning as in section 393B of ITEPA 2003;

"**responsible person**" has the same meaning as in section 399A of ITEPA 2003;

"**year of assessment**" means a year beginning with 6th April in any year and ending with 5th April in the following year.

PRESCRIBED PERSON

3   The responsible person in relation to an employer-financed retirement benefits scheme is the person prescribed for the purposes of these Regulations.

PROVISION OF INFORMATION IN RELATION TO THE COMING INTO OPERATION OF SCHEMES

4(1)   The responsible person shall supply to the Board the particulars prescribed in paragraph (3) on or before 31st January next following the end of the year of assessment during which the, scheme first came into operation.

4(2)   For the purposes of this regulation a scheme "comes into operation" on whichever is the first date, on or after that on which these Regulations come into force, on which–

(a)   an employer makes a contribution to that scheme ; or

(b)   relevant benefits are provided.

4(3)   The prescribed information for the purposes of this paragraph is–

(a)   the name of the scheme;

(b)   the address of the responsible person; and

(c)   the date the scheme came into operation.

PROVISION OF INFORMATION IN RELATION TO RELEVANT BENEFITS

5(1)   The responsible person shall supply to the Board the particulars prescribed in paragraph (3) in respect of all relevant benefits provided during the year of assessment at the time prescribed by paragraph (4).

This is subject to the following qualification.

5(2)   Information is not required to be supplied under this regulation in respect of pensions which are chargeable to tax under Chapter 2 of Part 9 of ITEPA 2003.

5(3)   The prescribed information is–

(a)   the name, address and national insurance number of the recipient of the relevant benefit;

(b)　the nature of the relevant benefit provided; and

(c)　the amount of the relevant benefit calculated in accordance with section 398(2) of ITEPA 2003.

5(4)　The prescribed time is not later than 7th July following the end of the year of assessment in which the relevant benefit was provided.

(SI 2005/3453)

"the Act" means the Finance Act 2004; and

"ITEPA 2003" means the Income Tax (Earnings and Pensions) Act 2003.

2(2)　In these Regulations—

"employer-financed retirement benefits scheme" has the same meaning as in section 393A of ITEPA 2003;

(b)　relevant benefits are provided.

4(3)　The prescribed information for the purposes of this paragraph is—

(a)　the name of the scheme;

(b)　the address of the responsible person; and

REGISTERED PENSION SCHEMES (ACCOUNTING AND ASSESSMENT) REGULATIONS 2005

(SI 2005/3454, as amended by SI 2011/302, SI 2011/1751 and SI 2013/1111)

Made on 14 December 2005 by the Commissioners for Her Majesty's Revenue and Customs, in exercise of the powers conferred upon them by s. 254(4)(b), (6) and (7) and 255 of the Finance Act 2004. Operative from 6 April 2006.

CITATION AND COMMENCEMENT

1 These Regulations may be cited as the Registered Pension Schemes (Accounting and Assessment) Regulations 2005 and shall come into force on 6th April 2006.

INTERPRETATION

2(1) In these Regulations–

"**the Act**" means the Finance Act 2004;

"**ITEPA**" means the Income Tax (Earnings and Pensions) Act 2003;

"**TMA**" means the Taxes Management Act 1970.

2(2) In these Regulations a reference to a numbered case is a reference to the case bearing that number in Table 2.

THE PARTICULARS REQUIRED TO BE INCLUDED IN RETURNS UNDER SECTION 254

3(1) If the scheme administrator is liable to income tax in respect of a charge listed in column 1 of Table 1, the return under section 254 of the Act must include the particulars in respect of that liability specified in column 2.

Table 1

Column 1: charge	Column 2: specified particulars
Charge under section 207 of the Act (authorised surplus payments charge).	1. The number of employers to whom an authorised surplus payment was made.
	2. The name, registered address and, if appropriate, company registration number of each employer to whom an authorised surplus payment was made.
	3. The date the authorised surplus payment was made.
	4. The amount of tax due and payable in respect of each authorised surplus payment.
Charge under section 214 of the Act (lifetime allowance charge).	1. The number of individuals liable to a lifetime allowance charge.
	2. The name and national insurance number of each individual liable to a lifetime allowance charge.
	3. The date of the benefit crystallisation event in relation to the lifetime allowance charge.
	4. The amount of tax due in respect of each chargeable amount as constitutes a lump-sum amount and each chargeable amount as constitutes a retained amount.
Charge under section 227 of the Act (annual allowance charge).	1. The title, name and national insurance number of each individual in relation to whom the scheme administrator becomes liable to an annual allowance charge under section 237B(7) of the Act.
	2. The date on which the scheme administrator becomes liable to the annual allowance charge.

Column 1: charge	Column 2: specified particulars
	3. The amount of tax to which the scheme administrator became jointly liable in respect of each individual under section 237B(7) of the Act.
	4. The tax year to which the annual allowance charge relates.
Charge under section 242 of the Act (de-registration charge).	The date the registration of the registered pension scheme was withdrawn.

3(2) Where an individual provides the scheme administrator with written confirmation that the individual does not qualify for a national insurance number, the scheme administrator must–

(a) provide the Commissioners with the individual's date of birth and address in order to obtain an alternative number from them; and

(b) provide this alternative number in place of the national insurance number (where the national insurance number is required by paragraph (1)).

3(3) Paragraph (4) applies to any amended return (made in accordance with regulation 6)–

(a) delivered on or after 6th April 2011 in respect of a return under section 254 of the Act delivered before 6th April 2011, and

(b) which relates to an individual whose details were included in the return under section 254 of the Act in relation to which an amended return is being made.

3(4) Where paragraph (1) requires the scheme administrator to provide the Commissioners with an individual's national insurance number and where the national insurance number is not known to the scheme administrator–

(a) paragraph (2) does not apply, and

(b) the scheme administrator may provide the date of birth in place of the national insurance number.

History – In reg. 3(1), in Table 1, in the entry relating to the charge under s. 227 point 4 under the specified particulars inserted by SI 2013/1111, reg. 2(2), with effect from 31 May 2013.
In reg. 3(1), in Table 1, the entry relating to the charge under s. 227 inserted by SI 2011/1751, reg. 9(2), which came into force on 11 August 2011, with effect for the tax year 2011–12 and subsequent tax years.
In reg. 3(1), in Table 1, in column 2, the words ", date of birth, address", which appeared after the words "The name", omitted by SI 2011/302, reg. 2(b), with effect from 6 April 2011.
Reg. 3(1) created from existing text of reg. 3 by SI 2011/302, reg. 2(a), with effect from 6 April 2011.
Reg. 3(2), (3) and (4) inserted by SI 2011/302, reg. 2(c), with effect from 6 April 2011.

THE MAKING OF ASSESSMENTS

4(1) In the cases listed in column 1 of Table 2 an officer of Revenue and Customs must issue an assessment to tax to the assessable person specified in column 2.

Table 2

Column 1	Column 2: assessable person
Case 1: a charge to tax arises under section 208 of the Act (unauthorised payments charge) and the person liable to the charge is a company.	The person liable to the charge under section 208(2) of the Act.
Case 2: a charge to tax arises under section 209 of the Act (unauthorised payments surcharge) and the person liable to the charge is a company.	The person liable to the charge under section 209(3) of the Act.
Case 3: a charge to tax arises under section 217(2) of the Act (lifetime allowance charge on receipt of a lump sum death benefit).	The person liable under section 217(2) of the Act.
Case 4: a charge to tax arises under section 239 of the Act (scheme sanction charge).	The scheme administrator, or the person or persons liable to the scheme sanction charge under section 239(3) of the Act.
Case 5: the correct tax due under section 254 of the Act has not been paid on or before the due date.	The scheme administrator.

Column 1	Column 2: assessable person
Case 6: section 272 of the Act (trustees etc. liable as scheme administrator) applies.	The person specified as assuming liability under section 272(4) of the Act.
Case 7: section 273 of the Act (members liable as scheme administrator) applies.	The person liable under section 273(2) of the Act.
Case 8: a charge to tax arises under section 394(2) of ITEPA (employer-financed retirement benefits scheme).	The person who is, or persons who are, the responsible person in relation to an employer-financed retirement benefits scheme under section 394(2) of ITEPA.

4(2) Subject to paragraph (3), tax assessed under this regulation is payable within 30 days after the issue of the notice of assessment.

4(3) Tax assessed under cases 1 and 2 is payable on the day following the expiry of nine months from the end of the accounting period in which the unauthorised payment was made or, if later, within 30 days after the issue of the notice of assessment.

4(4) An assessment under case 3 may be made at any time not later than six years after an officer of Revenue and Customs is notified of the relevant lump sum death benefit, but cannot be made later than 20 years after 31st January following the end of the tax year in which the relevant lump sum death benefit was paid.

4(5) Any tax assessable under one or more cases of Table 1 may be included in one assessment if the tax so included is all due on the same date.

INTEREST ON TAX DUE UNDER SECTION 254 OR ASSESSED UNDER REGULATION 4

5(1) Tax which–

(a)   becomes due and payable in accordance with section 254(5) of the Act, or

(b)   is assessed under regulation 4,

carries interest at the prescribed rate from the reckonable date until payment ("the interest period").

5(2) The **"prescribed rate"** means the rate applicable under section 178 of the Finance Act 1989 for the purposes of section 86 of TMA.

5(3) In relation to each of the cases listed in column 1 of Table 3, the "reckonable date" is specified in column 2.

Table 3

Column 1	Column 2: reckonable date
Tax due under section 254 of the Act.	The due date under section 254(5) of the Act.
Tax assessed under case 1 or 2.	The day following the expiry of nine months from the end of the accounting period in which the unauthorised payment was made.
Tax assessed under case 3.	31st January following the end of the tax year in which the relevant lump sum death benefit was paid.
Tax assessed under case 4.	31st January following the end of the tax year in which the scheme sanction charge arose.
Tax assessed under case 5.	The due date under section 254(5) of the Act.
Tax assessed under case 6 or 7.	The date the tax was due before sections 272 or 273 of the Act applied in relation to the pension scheme.
Tax assessed under case 8.	31st January following the end of the tax year in which the benefit within section 393 of ITEPA is received.

5(4) Paragraph (1) applies even if the reckonable date is a non-business day as defined by section 92 of the Bills of Exchange Act 1882.

5(5) Any change made to the prescribed rate during the interest period applies to the unpaid amount from the date of the change.

THE MAKING OF AMENDED RETURNS

6   If the scheme administrator becomes aware–

(a)   that anything which ought to have been included in a return made under section 254 of the Act for any period has not been so included,

(b)   that anything which ought not to have been included in a return made under section 254 of the Act for any period has been so included, or

(c)   that any other error has occurred in a return made under section 254 of the Act for any period, the scheme administrator must immediately make an amended return to an officer of Revenue and Customs for that period.

ADJUSTMENTS, REPAYMENTS AND INTEREST ON TAX OVERPAID

7(1)   If the correct tax due under section 254 of the Act has not been paid on or before the due ate or if an amended return is made under regulation 6, an officer of Revenue and Customs may ake such adjustments or repayments as may be required for securing that the resulting liabilities to tax (including interest on unpaid or overpaid tax) whether of the scheme administrator or of any other person are the same as they would have been if the correct tax had been paid or if a correct return had been made.

7(2)   Tax overpaid which is repaid to the scheme administrator or any other person carries interest at the prescribed rate from the later of the due date and the date on which the tax was paid until the date of repayment ("the interest period").

7(3)   The **"prescribed rate"** means the rate applicable under section 178 of the Finance Act 1989 for the purposes of section 824 of the Income and Corporation Taxes Act 1988.

7(4)   Any change made to the prescribed rate during the interest period applies to the overpaid amount from the date of the change.

MODIFICATIONS AND APPLICATION OF TMA

8(1)   Section 9(1A)(c) of TMA (tax not to be assessed by a self-assessment) applies with the following modifications in relation to an assessment to tax under case 3, 6 or 7.

8(2)   At the end of paragraph (a) delete "or".

8(3)   After paragraph (b) insert–

"(c)   is chargeable on a person under section 217(2) of the Finance Act 2004 (liability to lifetime allowance charge by reason of the payment of a relevant lump sum death benefit),

(d)   is chargeable on a person or persons under section 272 of the Finance Act 2004 (trustees etc. liable as scheme administrator), or

(e)   is chargeable on a person or persons under section 273 of the Finance Act 2004 (members liable as scheme administrator).".

9(1)   Section 29(1)(a) of TMA (assessment where loss of tax discovered) applies with the following modification in relation to an assessment to tax under case 1, 2 or 3.

9(2)   After "any income" insert–

", unauthorised payments under section 208 of the Finance Act 2004 or surchargeable unauthorised payments under section 209 of that Act or relevant lump sum death benefit under section 217(2) of that Act".

10(1)   Section 34(1) of TMA (ordinary time limit of six years) applies with the following modifications in relation to an assessment to tax under case 8.

10(2)   For "income tax or" substitute "income tax,".

10(3)   After "capital gains tax" insert–

"or to tax chargeable under section 394(2) of the Income Tax (Earnings and Pensions) Act 2003".

11(1)   Section 36(1) of TMA (fraudulent or negligent conduct) applies with the following modifications in relation to an assessment to tax under case 8.

11(2)   For "income tax or" substitute "income tax,".

11(3)   After "capital gains tax" insert " or to tax chargeable under section 394(2) of the Income Tax (Earnings and Pensions) Act 2003".

12   In relation to any assessment under case 5–

(a)   section 34 of TMA applies notwithstanding that the assessment may relate to a quarter or other period which is not a year of assessment, and

(b)   for the purposes of section 36 of TMA any such assessment relates to the year of assessment in which the quarter or other period ends.

MODIFICATION OF SCHEDULE 18 TO THE FINANCE ACT 1998

13(1)   Schedule 18 to the Finance Act 1998 (company tax returns, assessments and related matters) applies with the following modification in relation to an assessment to tax under case 8.

13(2)   In paragraph 1 after "as if it was corporation tax" insert–

"but does not include any tax which is chargeable on the person who is (or persons who are) the responsible person in relation to an employer-financed retirement benefits scheme under section 394(2) of the Income Tax (Earnings and Pensions) Act 2003".

REGISTERED PENSION SCHEMES AND EMPLOYER-FINANCED RETIREMENT BENEFITS SCHEMES (INFORMATION) (PRESCRIBED DESCRIPTIONS OF PERSONS) REGULATIONS 2005

(SI 2005/3455)

Made on 14 December 2005 by the Commissioners of Inland Revenue, in exercise of the powers conferred upon them by s. 252(1) of the Finance Act 2004. Operative from 6 April 2006.

CITATION, COMMENCEMENT AND INTERPRETATION

1(1) These Regulations may be cited as the Registered Pension Schemes and Employer-Financed Retirement Benefits Schemes (Information) (Prescribed Descriptions of Persons) Regulations 2005 and shall come into force on 6th April 2006.

1(2) In these Regulations any reference, without more, to a numbered section, is a reference to the section of the Finance Act 2004 which is so numbered.

PRESCRIBED DESCRIPTIONS OF PERSONS FOR THE PURPOSES OF SECTION 252 OF THE FINANCE ACT 2004

2(1) For the purposes of section 252 (notices requiring documents or particulars about registered pension schemes and employer-financed retirement benefit schemes) the prescribed descriptions of persons are those prescribed in the following paragraphs.

For the purposes of this regulation **"the relevant period"** means the period which–

(a) begins with the time at which occurred the event in relation to which information is required by the notice under section 252, and

(b) ends with the end of the sixth tax year following that in which that event occurred.

2(2) In relation to a pension scheme referred to in subsection (3)(a), (b) or (c) of section 252 the prescribed descriptions of person are–

(a) any person who is, or at any time during the relevant period has been, the scheme administrator,

(b) any person who is, or at any time during the relevant period has been, a trustee of the scheme,

(c) any person who is, or at any time during the relevant period has been, a sponsoring employer in relation to the scheme, and

(d) any person who is, or at any time within the relevant period has been, a member of the scheme,

in respect of which the notice is given.

2(3) In relation to an annuity purchased with sums or assets held for the purposes of a registered pension scheme, the prescribed description of person is the insurance company or other person from whom the annuity has been purchased.

2(4) In relation to an employer-financed retirement benefits scheme, the prescribed description of person–

(a) for the purposes of section 252(3)(e), is the responsible person at the time the scheme comes into operation; and

(b) for the purposes of section 252(3)(f) is the responsible person at the time that the notice under that section is issued.

2(5) For the purposes of paragraph (4)–

(a) a scheme "comes into operation" on whichever is the first date, on or after that on which these Regulations come into force on which–

   (i) an employer makes a contribution to that scheme; or

   (ii) relevant benefits are provided; and

(b) **"responsible person"** has the meaning given in section 399A of the Income Tax Earnings and Pensions Act 2003.

REGISTERED PENSION SCHEMES (AUDITED ACCOUNTS) (SPECIFIED PERSONS) REGULATIONS 2005

(SI 2005/3456, as amended by SI 2008/954)

Made on 14 December 2005 by the Commissioners for Her Majesty's Revenue and Customs, in exercise of the powers conferred by s. 250(6) of the Finance Act 2004. Operative from 6 April 2006.

CITATION AND COMMENCEMENT

1   These Regulations may be cited as the Registered Pension Schemes (Audited Accounts) (Specified Persons) Regulations 2005 and shall come into force on 6th April 2006.

SPECIFIED DESCRIPTIONS OF PERSONS IN RELATION TO THE AUDIT OF REGISTERED PENSION SCHEME ACCOUNTS

2   In relation to the audit of the accounts of a registered pension scheme, the following descriptions of person are specified namely–

(a)   a person specified in section 1212 of the Companies Act 2006 (individuals and firms: eligibility for appointment as a statutory auditor);

(b)   a person eligible for appointment as a scheme auditor under section 47(1) of the Pensions Act 1995 or Article 47(1) of the Pensions (Northern Ireland) Order 1995 (professional advisers).

This is subject to regulation 3.

History – Reg. 2(a) substituted by SI 2008/954, art. 56, with effect from 6 April 2008.

CIRCUMSTANCES IN WHICH A PERSON SPECIFIED UNDER REGULATION 2 IS NOT TO AUDIT SCHEME ACCOUNTS

3   Notwithstanding regulation 2, a person shall not be a registered pension scheme's auditor if he is–

(a)   a member of the scheme;

(b)   employed under a contract of service by the scheme administrator;

(c)   an employer in relation to the scheme; or

(d)   ineligible, by virtue of section 1214 of the Companies Act 2006, to audit the accounts of a company which is an employer in relation to the scheme.

History – In reg. 3 the words "section 1214 of the Companies Act 2006" substituted for "section 27 of the Companies Act 1989" by SI 2008/954, art. 57, with effect from 6 April 2008.

REGISTERED PENSION SCHEMES (RESTRICTION OF EMPLOYERS' RELIEF) REGULATIONS 2005

(SI 2005/3458)

Made on 14 December 2005 by the Commissioners for Her Majesty's Revenue and Customs, in exercise of the powers conferred by s. 196A(1) of the Finance Act 2004. Operative from 6 April 2006.

CITATION, COMMENCEMENT AND INTERPRETATION

1(1)   These Regulations may be cited as the Registered Pension Schemes (Restriction of Employers' Relief) Regulations 2005 and shall come into force on 6th April 2006.

1(2)   In these Regulations–

(a)   **"arrangement"** has the meaning in section 152(1);

(b)   **"period of account"** has the meaning in section 832(1) of the Income and Corporation Taxes Act 1988; and

(c)   references to a section (without more) are to that section of the Finance Act 2004.

SCOPE OF THESE REGULATIONS

2(1)   These Regulations apply in circumstances where–

(a)   subsection (2) or (3) of section 196A applies (or both do); and

(b)   the condition in paragraph (2) is not satisfied.

2(2)   The condition in this paragraph is that, in such of those subsections as apply–

(a)   the employer-financed retirement benefits scheme referred to is a recognised overseas pension scheme within the meaning in section 150(8); and

(b)   the individual referred to would be a relevant migrant member of that scheme by virtue of paragraph 4 of Schedule 33 to the Finance Act 2004, or regulations made under subparagraph (c) of that paragraph, modified as follows–

  (i)   in paragraph 4, in the words preceding sub-paragraph (a), omit "in relation to any contributions,";

  (ii)   in sub-paragraph (b) for "the time when the contributions are paid" substitute "the employer's period of account which is in question"; and

  (iii)   omit sub-paragraph (d).

RESTRICTION OF EMPLOYERS' RELIEF IN RESPECT OF CONTRIBUTIONS

3   Contributions paid by an employer under a registered pension scheme, where a member is an individual referred to in section 196A(2) or (3), shall be subject to the following restrictions on relief.

4   In respect of each arrangement relating to the individual under the scheme, calculate the individual's pension input amount (modified as follows) for the employer's period of account in which the contributions are paid, in accordance with regulations 5 to 8.

CASH BALANCE ARRANGEMENTS

5(1)   The individual's pension input amount for a period of account in respect of a cash balance arrangement shall be determined in accordance with sections 230 and 232, modified as follows.

5(2)   In both sections, for each of the references to the "pension input period" and the "pension input period of the arrangement that ends in the tax year" substitute references to the employer's period of account in question.

5(3)   In both section 230(4) and (5) at the end add "ignoring (if it be the case) the fact that payment of any benefits, or the amount of any recognised transfer, is subject to a contingency mentioned in section 196A(2) or (3)".

5(4)   In section 230(6) omit the reference to section 231.

5(5)   The amount of any relievable pension contributions paid by or on behalf of the individual under the arrangement during the period of account is to be subtracted from the closing value.

OTHER MONEY PURCHASE ARRANGEMENTS

6(1) The individual's pension input amount for a period of account in respect of a money purchase arrangement other than a cash balance arrangement shall be determined in accordance with section 233, modified as follows.

6(2) Omit section 233(1)(a) and the word "and" which follows it.

6(3) For the reference to the "pension input period of the arrangement that ends in the tax year" substitute a reference to the employer's period of account in question.

DEFINED BENEFITS ARRANGEMENTS

7(1) The individual's pension input amount for a period of account in respect of a defined benefits arrangement shall be determined in accordance with sections 234 and 236, modified as follows.

7(2) In both sections, for each of the references to the "pension input period" and the "pension input period of the arrangement that ends in the tax year" substitute references to the employer's period of account in question.

7(3) In section 234(4) and (5), in each of the definitions of PB, LSB, PE and LSE at the end add "ignoring (if it be the case) the fact that payment of any benefits, or the amount of any recognised transfer, is subject to a contingency mentioned in section 196A(2) or (3)".

7(4) In section 234(6) omit the reference to section 235.

7(5) The amount of any relievable pension contributions paid by or on behalf of the individual under the arrangement during the period of account is to be subtracted from the closing value.

HYBRID ARRANGEMENTS

8(1) The individual's pension input amount for a period of account in respect of a hybrid arrangement shall be determined in accordance with section 237, modified as follows.

8(2) Omit the references to sections 231 and 235.

8(3) Sections 230, 232 to 234 and 236 shall be modified in accordance with regulation 5, 6 or 7, as the case may be.

RESTRICTION OF RELIEF

9 Aggregate the pension input amounts for the period of account in question in respect of each arrangement relating to the individual under the scheme.

10 An amount equal to the aggregate pension input amount in respect of that individual for the period of account in question shall not be subject to relief within the meaning in section 196A(4).

REGISTERED PENSION SCHEMES (RELEVANT ANNUITIES) REGULATIONS 2006

(SI 2006/129, as amended by SI 2011/1751 and SI 2012/2940)

Made on 25 January 2006 by the Commissioners for Her Majesty's Revenue and Customs, in exercise of the powers conferred upon them by para. 14 of Sch. 28 to the Finance Act 2004. Operative from 6 April 2006.

CITATION, COMMENCEMENT AND INTERPRETATION

1(1) These Regulations may be cited as the Registered Pension Schemes (Relevant Annuities) Regulations 2006 and shall come into force on 6th April 2006.

1(2) In these Regulations **"the Act"** means the Finance Act 2004.

DEFINITION OF "RELEVANT ANNUITY"

2 For the purposes of Part 4 of the Act (pension schemes etc.) a **"relevant annuity"** is a level single life annuity without a guaranteed term.

DEFINITION OF "ANNUAL AMOUNT"

3(1) For the purposes of Part 4 of the Act the **"annual amount"** of a relevant annuity is the rate of annual income which the tables, published for this purpose by the Government Actuary's Department, show as available if–

(a)   a relevant annuity were purchased by the application of the sums and assets representing the member's or dependant's pension fund valued at the relevant date; and

(b)   the purchaser were male and the same age as the member or dependant (but in any case where that age is greater than 85, it shall be treated as 85).

3(2) For the purposes of paragraph (1) the **"relevant date"** in relation to drawdown pension years beginning on or before the member's or dependant's 75th birthday is–

(a)   for the first drawdown pension year falling within a reference period–

     (i)   the nominated date, as set out in paragraph 10(3) or 24(3) (as the case requires); or

     (ii)   if there has been an additional fund designation made during that year, the date on which that designation was made;

(b)   for each other drawdown pension year falling within a reference period, the date found in accordance with paragraph 10(4) or 24(4) (as the case requires).

3(3) For the purposes of paragraph (1) the **"relevant date"** in relation to drawdown pension years beginning after the member's or dependant's 75th birthday is–

(a)   the nominated date, as determined in accordance with paragraph 10A(3), (4) and (5) or 24A(3) (as the case requires); or

(b)   if there has been an additional fund designation during a drawdown pension year, the date on which that designation was made.

3(4) In paragraphs (2)(a)(i) and (b) and (3)(a), references to numbered paragraphs are to the paragraphs of Schedule 28 to the Act.

History – In reg. 3(1)(a), the words "member's or dependant's" substituted for the word "member's" by SI 2011/1751, reg. 6(2)(a), which came into force on 11 August 2011, with effect for the tax year 2011–12 and subsequent tax years.

Reg. 3(1)(b) substituted by SI 2012/2940, reg. 2(2), with effect in relation to: relevant dates (as defined in reg. 3(2) and 3(3)) falling on or after 21 December 2012; reference periods beginning on or after 21 December 2012, in relation to which the relevant date falls prior to that date; and drawdown pension years beginning on or after 21 December 2012 and after the member or dependant's 75th birthday, in relation to which the relevant date falls prior to 21 December 2012. Former reg. 3(1)(b) read as follows:

     "(b)   the purchaser were the same age and sex as the member or dependant (but in any case where that age is greater than 85, it shall be treated as 85).".

In reg. 3(2)(a)(i), the words "paragraph 10(3) or 24(3)" substituted for the words "paragraph 10(3)(a) or 24(3)(a)" by SI 2012/2940, reg. 2(3), with effect in relation to: relevant dates (as defined in reg. 3(2) and 3(3)) falling on or after 21 December 2012; reference periods beginning on or after 21 December 2012, in relation to which the relevant date falls prior to that date; and drawdown pension years beginning on or after 21 December 2012 and after the member or dependant's 75th birthday, in relation to which the relevant date falls prior to 21 December 2012.

In reg. 3(1)(b), "85" substituted for "75" in both places by SI 2011/1751, reg. 6(2)(b), which came into force on 11 August 2011, with effect for the tax year 2011–12 and subsequent tax years.

In reg. 3(2), the opening words and para. (a) substituted for the former wording by SI 2011/1751, reg. 6(2)(c), which came into force on 11 August 2011, with effect for the tax year 2011–12 and subsequent tax years. The former wording read as follows:

"**3(2)** For the purposes of paragraph (1) the **"relevant date"** is–
    (a)   for the first unsecured pension year falling within a reference period–
        (i)   the nominated date, as set out in paragraph 10(3)(a) or 24(3)(a) (as the case requires); or
        (ii)   if there has been an additional fund designation made during that year, the date on which that designation was made;".

In reg. 3(2)(b), the words "drawdown pension year" substituted for the words "unsecured pension year" by SI 2011/1751, reg. 6(2)(d), which came into force on 11 August 2011, with effect for the tax year 2011–12 and subsequent tax years.

Reg. 2(c) and (d) and the closing words of reg. 2 omitted by SI 2011/1751, reg. 6(2)(e), which came into force on 11 August 2011, with effect for the tax year 2011–12 and subsequent tax years. Former reg. 2(c) and (d) and closing words read as follows:

"(c)   for the first alternatively secured pension year, the date found in accordance with paragraph 13(1) or 27(1) (as the case requires); and

(d)   for each other alternatively secured pension year, the date found in accordance with paragraph 13(3) or 27(3) (as the case requires).

In sub-paragraphs (a)–(d) references to numbered paragraphs are to the paragraphs of Schedule 28 to the Act.".

Reg. 3(3) and (4) inserted by SI 2011/1751, reg. 6(2)(f), which came into force on 11 August 2011, with effect for the tax year 2011–12 and subsequent tax years.

REGISTERED PENSION SCHEMES (UPRATING PERCENTAGES FOR DEFINED BENEFITS ARRANGEMENTS AND ENHANCED PROTECTION LIMITS) REGULATIONS 2006

(SI 2006/130)

Made on 25 January 2006 by the Commissioners for Her Majesty's Revenue and Customs make the following Regulations in exercise of the powers conferred upon them by s. 235(3)(c) of, and para. 15(5)(b), 16(5A)(b) and 17(6)(b) of Sch. 36 to the Finance Act 2004. Operative from 6 April 2006.

CITATION, COMMENCEMENT AND INTERPRETATION

1(1) These Regulations may be cited as the Registered Pension Schemes (Uprating Percentages for Defined Benefits Arrangements and Enhanced Protection Limits) Regulations 2006 and shall come into force on 6th April 2006.

1(2) In these Regulations a reference to a numbered section or Schedule (without more) is a reference to the section of, or Schedule to, the Finance Act 2004 which bears that number.

1(3) In the application of these Regulations to Northern Ireland, a reference to an enactment applying only in Great Britain shall be construed as including a reference to any enactment having corresponding effect in Northern Ireland.

PERCENTAGE REFERRED TO FOR THE PURPOSES OF SECTION 235(3)(C)

2(1) For the purpose of section 235(3)(c) (defined benefits arrangements: uprating of opening value) the percentage to which these Regulations refer is the percentage found as follows.

2(2) In this regulation "the relevant percentage" is any of–

(a)   the percentage by which the individual's guaranteed minimum pension rights falls to be adjusted by virtue of one or more orders under section 148 of the Social Security Administration Act 1992;

(b)   the percentage by which the individual's earnings factors in respect of contracted-out employment by reference to the scheme shall be taken to be increased in accordance with section 16 of the Pension Schemes Act 1993 (revaluation of earnings factors);

(c)   the percentage by which the individual's occupational pension falls to be adjusted by virtue of the application of subsections (1) and (2) of section 84 of the Pension Schemes Act 1993 (which provide that the method of revaluation is to be the final salary method except where the trustees or managers otherwise provide); or

(d)   the percentage by which a pension, payment of which has been deferred until after normal pension age in accordance with the rules of the pension scheme in question, falls to be increased so that the scheme's trustees or managers can be reasonably satisfied that, when the member's benefit becomes payable, the total value of the benefits provided under regulation 8 of the Occupational Pension Schemes (Preservation of Benefit) Regulations 1991(early retirement or deferred retirement) is at least equal to the amount prescribed in regulation 11 of those Regulations (value of alternatives to short service benefit).

2(3) The percentage in a particular case is found as follows.

Step 1

Determine whether any of the relevant percentages applies to the defined benefit arrangement.

Step 2

If any of the relevant percentages applies to the arrangement, determine whether that percentage applies to the whole of the arrangement.

Step 3

If one relevant percentage applies to the whole of the arrangement, that is the percentage to which these Regulations refer.

Step 4

If different percentages apply to different parts of the arrangement, the percentage to which these Regulations refer is that found by the formula–

$$\left(RP1 \times \frac{P1}{W}\right) + \left(RP2 \times \frac{P2}{W}\right) + \left(RP3 \times \frac{P3}{W}\right) + \left(RP4 \times \frac{P4}{W}\right) + \left[SP \times \left(1 - \frac{PT}{W}\right)\right]$$

Here–

RP is the relevant percentage;

P is the amount of that part of the individual's rights under the arrangement to which the relevant percentage applies;

W is the whole amount of the individual's rights under the arrangement; and

SP is the greater of–

(a)   5%, or

(b)   the percentage (if any) by which the retail prices index for the month in which the pension input period ends is higher than it was for the month in which it began;

PT is the sum of the amounts of $P1$, $P2$, $P3$ and $P4$;

(c)   expressions with the suffix 1 refer to the percentage described in paragraph (2)(a);

(d)   expressions with the suffix 2 refer to the percentage described in paragraph (2)(b);

(e)   expressions with the suffix 3 refer to the percentage described in paragraph (2)(c);

(f)   expressions with the suffix 4 refer to the percentage described in paragraph (2)(d).

This step is subject to paragraph (4).

2(4) If–

(a)   any relevant percentage is a value less than the greater of–

     (i)   5%, or

     (ii)   the percentage (if any) by which the retail prices index for the month in which the pension input period ends is higher than it was for the month in which it began;

     the value shall instead be taken to be whichever is the greater of the two values given in this sub-paragraph;

(b)   two or more relevant percentages apply to the same part of the arrangement, the value of P1, P2, P3 or P4 (as the case may be) is found by determining which of those relevant percentages produces the greatest increase in the opening value in the pension input period in question.

PERCENTAGE INCREASES IN ENHANCED PROTECTION LIMITS

3(1) For the purposes of paragraph 15(5)(b) of Schedule 36 (relevant indexation percentage for the purposes of the appropriate limit in relation to a relevant event), the annual percentage rate referred to in these Regulations is found by the formula–

$$\left[\left(RP1 \times \frac{P1}{W}\right) + \left(RP2 \times \frac{P2}{W}\right) + \left(RP3 \times \frac{P3}{W}\right) + \left(RP4 \times \frac{P4}{W}\right) + \left(PP \times \left(1 - \frac{PT}{W}\right)\right)\right] \div \frac{MRE}{12}$$

3(2) In paragraph (1)–

     terms defined in regulation 2(3) bear the same meaning as they do there;

     MRE is the number of complete tax months which have elapsed since 6th April 2006 at the time when the relevant event occurs; and

     PP is the greater of–

     (a)   an annual rate of 5% for the period beginning on 6th April 2006 and ending with the last day of the tax month in which the relevant event occurs, or

     (b)   the percentage (if any) by which the retail prices index for the month in which the relevant event occurs is higher than it was for April 2006;

3(3) For the purposes of paragraphs 16(5A)(b) and 17(6)(b) of Schedule 36 (relevant indexation percentages for the purposes of limit on post-commencement earnings) the annual percentage rate referred to in these Regulations is that which would be found by the formula in paragraph (1) if–

(a)   for MRE there were substituted MBE, where MBE is the number of complete tax months between the date on which the appropriate three year period ends and the date of the first relevant event; and

(b)   in the definition of PP–

     (i)   in paragraph (a) for "6th April 2006" there were substituted "the first day of the tax month in which the appropriate period ends"; and

     (ii)   in paragraph (b) for "April 2006" there were substituted "the month in which the appropriate period ends".

3(4) In this regulation **"tax month"** means the period beginning on the 6th day of a calendar month and ending on the 5th day of the following calendar month.

REGISTERED PENSION SCHEMES (ENHANCED LIFETIME ALLOWANCE) REGULATIONS 2006

(SI 2006/131, as amended by SI 2006/3261, SI 2009/56 and SI 2010/651)

Made on 25 January 2006 by the Commissioners for Her Majesty's Revenue and Customs, in exercise of the powers conferred by s. 220(5), 221(6), 224(9), 251(1) and (6) and 256 of, and para. 7(1)(b), 12(1) and 18(6) of Sch. 36 to, the Finance Act 2004 and s. 113(1) of the Taxes Management Act 1970. Operative from 6 April 2006.

ARRANGEMENT OF REGULATIONS

PRELIMINARY

Citation and commencement

1 These Regulations may be cited as the Registered Pension Schemes (Enhanced Lifetime Allowance) Regulations 2006 and shall come into force on 6th April 2006.

2(1) In these Regulations–

"the closing date" is to be read in accordance with regulation 3(4), 3A(4), 4(4), 4A(4), 5(4), 6(4), 7(4) or 8(4) as the case may require;

"notification" is to be read in accordance with regulation 3(3), 3A(3), 4(3), 4A(3), 5(3), 6(3), 7(3) or 8(3) as the case may require;

"the Revenue and Customs" means Her Majesty's Revenue and Customs.

"relevant lump sum death benefit" shall be construed in accordance with paragraph 16 of Schedule 32 to the Finance Act 2004;

"**the specified regulations**" means regulations 3, 4, 5, 6, 7 and 8 of these Regulations.

"**tribunal**" means the First-tier Tribunal or, where determined by or under Tribunal Procedure Rules, the Upper Tribunal.

2(2) In these Regulations references to sections, without more, are references to sections of the Finance Act 2004, and references to provisions of Schedule 36 are references to provisions of Schedule 36 to that Act.

2(3) The expressions defined or otherwise explained in the list in section 280(2) have the same definitions or explanations in these Regulations as in Part 4 of the Finance Act 2004.

History – In reg. 2(1), the definition of "tribunal" inserted by SI 2009/56, art. 3(2) and Sch. 2, para. 148, operative from 1 April 2009 subject to transitional and saving provisions in SI 2009/56, Sch. 3.
In reg. 2, in the definition of "closing date" "3A(4), 4(4), 4A(4)," substituted for "4(4)," by SI 2006/3261, reg. 3(2) with effect from 28 December 2006.
In reg. 2, in the definition of "notification" "3A(3), 4(3), 4A(3)," substituted for "4(3)" by SI 2006/3261, reg. 3(3) with effect from 28 December 2006.
In reg. 2, at the end, the definitions of "relevant lump sum death benefit" and "the specified regulations" inserted by SI 2006/3261, reg. 3(4) with effect from 28 December 2006.

RELIANCE ON PROVISIONS OF THE FINANCE ACT 2004

Reliance on paragraph 7 of Schedule 36 (lifetime allowance enhancement: "primary protection")

3(1) This regulation applies if the amount of the relevant pre-commencement pension rights of an individual (determined in accordance with paragraph 7(5) of Schedule 36) exceeds £1,500,000.

3(2) The individual may give notice of intention to rely on paragraph 7 of Schedule 36 ("paragraph 7").

3(3) If the individual intends to rely on paragraph 7, the individual must give a notification to the Revenue and Customs on or before the closing date.

3(4) For the purposes of this regulation the closing date is 5th April 2009.

3(5) Paragraph (6) applies if–

(a) the individual gives the notification to the Revenue and Customs, and

(b) the Revenue and Customs issue a certificate to the individual in response to the giving of the notification.

3(6) The individual may rely on paragraph 7 during the period beginning on 6th April 2006 and ending on the day on which the Revenue and Customs–

(a) revoke the certificate, or

(b) issue an amended certificate to the individual.

3(7) Paragraph (8) applies if the Revenue and Customs–

(a) issue a certificate to which paragraph (6) applies to the individual, and

(b) later issue an amended certificate ("the subsequent certificate") to the individual.

3(8) The individual may rely on paragraph 7 during the period beginning on the day specified on the subsequent certificate and ending on the day on which the Revenue and Customs–

(a) revoke the subsequent certificate, or

(b) issue an amended certificate to the individual.

3(9) The day so specified must not be earlier than 6th April 2006.

Reliance on paragraph 11A of Schedule 36 (lifetime allowance enhancement: "primary protection": taking account of death benefit)

3A(1) This regulation applies if a person is paid a relevant lump sum death benefit in respect of an individual in the circumstances specified in paragraphs (a) and (b) of paragraph 11A(1) of Schedule 36.

3A(2) That person may give notice of intention to rely on paragraph 11A of Schedule 36 ("paragraph 11A").

3A(3) If that person intends to rely on paragraph 11A, that person must give a notification to the Revenue and Customs on or before the closing date.

3A(4) The closing date is the date specified by paragraph (5); but if paragraph (6) applies and specifies a later closing date, the closing date is the date specified in paragraph (6).

3A(5) The date specified by this paragraph is the date determined in accordance with the following rules.

First rule: Find the 31st January following the tax year in which the relevant lump sum death benefit is paid.

Second rule: Find the 31st January five years after that.

The date so found is the closing date.

3A(6) This paragraph applies if an assessment to income tax is made under section 217(2) on a person to whom a lump sum death benefit has been paid; and, if this paragraph applies, the closing date specified by this paragraph is 5th April in the tax year following the tax year in which the assessment is made.

History – Reg. 3A inserted by SI 2006/3261, reg. 4 with effect from 28 December 2006.

Reliance on paragraph 12 of Schedule 36 (lifetime allowances: "enhanced protection")

History – In reg. 7(1), the definition of "tribunal" inserted by SI 2009/56, art. 3(2) and Sch. 2, para. 148, operative from 28 December 2006.

4(1) This regulation applies in the case of an individual to whom paragraph 12(1) of Schedule 36 has applied at all times on and after 6th April 2006.

4(2) The individual may give notice of intention to rely on paragraph 12 of Schedule 36 ("paragraph 12").

4(3) If the individual intends to rely on paragraph 12, the individual must give a notification to the Revenue and Customs on or before the closing date.

4(4) For the purposes of this regulation the closing date is 5th April 2009.

4(5) Paragraph (6) applies if–

(a)   the individual gives the notification to the Revenue and Customs, and

(b)   the Revenue and Customs issue a certificate to the individual in response to the giving of the notification.

4(6) The individual may rely on paragraph 12 during the period beginning on 6th April 2006 and ending on the day on which the Revenue and Customs–

(a)   revoke the certificate,

(b)   issue an amended certificate to the individual, or

(c)   receive notice, given by the individual, that the individual no longer wishes to rely on paragraph 12.

4(7) Paragraph (8) applies if the Revenue and Customs–

(a)   issue a certificate to which paragraph (6) applies to the individual, and

(b)   later issue an amended certificate ("the subsequent certificate") to the individual.

4(8) The individual may rely on paragraph 12 during the period beginning on the day specified on the subsequent certificate and ending on the day on which the Revenue and Customs–

(a)   revoke the subsequent certificate,

(b)   issue an amended certificate to the individual, or

(c)   receive notice, given by the individual, that the individual no longer wishes to rely on paragraph 12.

4(9) The day so specified must not be earlier than 6th April 2006.

Reliance on paragraph 15A of Schedule 36 (lifetime allowances: "enhanced protection": taking account of death benefit)

4A(1) This regulation applies if a person is paid a relevant lump sum death benefit in respect of an individual under an arrangement in the circumstances specified in paragraph 15A(1)(a) of Schedule 36.

4A(2) That person may give notice of intention to rely on paragraph 15A of Schedule 36 ("paragraph 15A").

4A(3) If that person intends to rely on paragraph 15A, that person must give a notification to the Revenue and Customs on or before the closing date.

4A(4) The closing date is the date specified by paragraph (5); but if paragraph (6) applies and specifies a later closing date, the closing date is the date specified in paragraph (6).

4A(5) The date specified by this paragraph is the date determined in accordance with the following rules.

First rule: Find the 31st January following the tax year in which the relevant lump sum death benefit is paid.

Second rule: Find the 31st January five years after that.

The date so found is the closing date.

4A(6) This paragraph applies if an assessment to income tax is made under section 217(2) on a person to whom a lump sum death benefit has been paid; and, if this paragraph applies, the closing date specified by this paragraph is 5th April in the tax year following the tax year in which the assessment is made.

History – Reg. 4A inserted by SI 2006/3261, reg. 5 with effect from 28 December 2006.

Reliance on paragraph 18 of Schedule 36 (lifetime allowance enhancement: precommencement pension credits)

5(1) This regulation applies if a benefit crystallisation event occurs in relation to an individual in the circumstances specified in paragraph 18(1) of Schedule 36.

5(2) The individual may give notice of intention to rely on paragraph 18 of Schedule 36 ("paragraph 18").

5(3) If the individual intends to rely on paragraph 18, the individual must give a notification to the Revenue and Customs on or before the closing date.

5(4) For the purposes of this regulation the closing date is 5th April 2009.

5(5) Paragraph (6) applies if–

(a) the individual gives the notification to the Revenue and Customs, and

(b) the Revenue and Customs issue a certificate to the individual in response to the giving of the notification.

5(6) The individual may rely on paragraph 18 during the period beginning on 6th April 2006 and ending on the day on which the Revenue and Customs–

(a) revoke the certificate, or

(b) issue an amended certificate to the individual.

5(7) Paragraph (8) applies if the Revenue and Customs–

(a) issue a certificate to which paragraph (6) applies to the individual, and

(b) later issue an amended certificate ("the subsequent certificate") to the individual.

5(8) The individual may rely on paragraph 18 during the period beginning on the day specified on the subsequent certificate and ending on the day on which the Revenue and Customs–

(a) revoke the subsequent certificate, or

(b) issue an amended certificate to the individual.

5(9) The day so specified must not be earlier than 6th April 2006.

Reliance on section 220 (lifetime allowance enhancement: registration of pension credits)

6(1) This regulation applies if an individual acquires rights under a registered pension scheme in the circumstances specified in section 220(1).

6(2) The individual may give notice of intention to rely on section 220.

6(3) If the individual intends to rely on section 220, the individual must give a notification to the Revenue and Customs on or before the closing date.

6(4) For the purposes of this regulation use the rules in this paragraph to find the closing date.

First rule: Find the 31st January following the tax year in which the pension sharing order or provision takes effect.

Second rule: Find the 31st January five years after that.

The date so found is the closing date.

6(5) Paragraph (6) applies if–

(a) the individual gives the notification to the Revenue and Customs, and

(b) the Revenue and Customs issue a certificate to the individual in response to the giving of the notification.

6(6) The individual may rely on section 220 during the period beginning on the day on which the pension sharing order or provision takes effect and ending on the day on which the Revenue and Customs–

(a) revoke the certificate, or

(b) issue an amended certificate to the individual.

6(7) Paragraph (8) applies if the Revenue and Customs–

(a) issue a certificate to which paragraph (6) applies to the individual, and

(b)   later issue an amended certificate ("the subsequent certificate") to the individual.

6(8)   The individual may rely on section 220 during the period beginning on the day specified on the subsequent certificate and ending on the day on which the Revenue and Customs–

(a)   revoke the subsequent certificate, or

(b)   issue an amended certificate to the individual.

Reliance on section 221 (lifetime allowance enhancement: relevant overseas individuals)

7(1)   This regulation applies if, at any time on or after 6th April 2006, an individual is a relevant overseas individual during any part of a period that is the active membership period in relation to an arrangement relating to the individual.

7(2)   The individual may give notice of intention to rely on section 221.

7(3)   If the individual intends to rely on section 221, the individual must give a notification to the Revenue and Customs on or before the closing date.

7(4)   For the purposes of this regulation use the rules in this paragraph to find the closing date.

First rule: Find the 31st January following the tax year in which the accrual period ends (see paragraph (10)).

Second rule: Find the 31st January five years after that.

The date so found is the closing date.

7(5)   Paragraph (6) applies if–

(a)   the individual gives the notification to the Revenue and Customs, and

(b)   the Revenue and Customs issue a certificate to the individual in response to the giving of the notification.

7(6)   The individual may rely on section 221 during the period beginning on the accrual day (see paragraph (10)) and ending on the day on which the Revenue and Customs–

(a)   revoke the certificate, or

(b)   issue an amended certificate to the individual.

7(7)   Paragraph (8) applies if the Revenue and Customs–

(a)   issue a certificate to which paragraph (6) applies to the individual, and

(b)   later issue an amended certificate ("the subsequent certificate") to the individual.

7(8)   The individual may rely on section 221 during the period beginning on the day specified on the subsequent certificate and ending on the day on which the Revenue and Customs–

(a)   revoke the subsequent certificate, or

(b)   issue an amended certificate to the individual.

7(9)   The day so specified must not be earlier than the accrual day.

7(10)   For the purposes of this regulation–

(a)   the accrual period ends–

   (i)   when the individual ceases to be a relevant overseas individual,

   (ii)   immediately before a benefit crystallisation event occurring in relation to the arrangement relating to the individual, or

   (iii)   when benefits cease to accrue to or in respect of the individual under the arrangement, whichever is the earliest; and

(b)   **"the accrual day"** is the day on which the accrual period ends.

Reliance on section 224 (lifetime allowance enhancement: transfer from recognised overseas pension scheme)

8(1)   This regulation applies if, in relation to an individual, there is a recognised overseas scheme transfer in the circumstances specified in section 224(1).

8(2)   The individual may give notice of intention to rely on section 224.

8(3)   If the individual intends to rely on section 224, the individual must give a notification to the Revenue and Customs on or before the closing date.

8(4)   For the purposes of this regulation use the rules in this paragraph to find the closing date.

First rule: Find the 31st January following the tax year in which the recognised overseas scheme transfer takes place.

Second rule: Find the 31st January five years after that.

The date so found is the closing date.

8(5) Paragraph (6) applies if–

(a)   the individual gives the notification to the Revenue and Customs, and

(b)   the Revenue and Customs issue a certificate to the individual in response to the giving of the notification.

8(6) The individual may rely on section 224 during the period beginning on the day on which the recognised overseas scheme transfer takes place and ending on the day on which the Revenue and Customs–

(a)   revoke the certificate, or

(b)   issue an amended certificate to the individual.

8(7) Paragraph (8) applies if the Revenue and Customs–

(a)   issue a certificate to which paragraph (6) applies to the individual, and

(b)   later issue an amended certificate ("the subsequent certificate") to the individual.

8(8) The individual may rely on section 224 during the period beginning on the day specified on the subsequent certificate and ending on the day on which the Revenue and Customs–

(a)   revoke the subsequent certificate, or

(b)   issue an amended certificate to the individual.

LOSS OF ENHANCED PROTECTION

Loss of enhanced protection

9(1) This regulation applies if conditions A to F are met.

9(2) Condition A is that an individual has one or more relevant existing arrangements (within the meaning given by paragraph 12(4) of Schedule 36).

9(3) Condition B is that the lump sum condition specified in paragraph 24(2) of Schedule 36 is met in relation to the individual.

9(4) Condition C is that the first notice requirement condition specified in paragraph 24(5) of Schedule 36 is not met in relation to the individual.

9(5) Condition D is that the second notice requirement condition specified in paragraph 24(6) of Schedule 36 is met in relation to the individual.

9(6) Condition E is that the individual has a certificate issued under regulation 4 on which the individual may rely.

9(7) Condition F is that paragraph 12 of Schedule 36 has ceased to apply to the individual.

9(8) Paragraph 31 of Schedule 36 applies in relation to the individual and to a registered pension scheme which is a protected pension scheme.

9(9) In paragraph (8) **"protected pension scheme"** has the meaning given by paragraph 31 of Schedule 36.

NOTIFICATIONS

Form of notification: the specified regulations

10(1) This regulation applies if a notification is given under one of the specified regulations.

10(2) The notification must be in a form prescribed by the Commissioners for Her Majesty's Revenue and Customs.

10(3) The individual must sign and date the notification.

History – Reg. 10 and 10A substituted for reg. 10 by SI 2006/3261, reg. 6 with effect from 28 December 2006. Reg. 10 formerly read as follows:

> **"Form of notification**
>
> **10(1)**   A notification must be in a form prescribed by the Commissioners for Her Majesty's Revenue and Customs.
>
> **10(2)**   The individual must sign and date the notification.".

Form of notification: regulations 3A and 4A

10A(1) This regulation applies if a notification is given under regulation 3A or 4A.

10A(2) The notification must contain the following information–

(a)   the name and address of the person giving the notification;

(b)   the name of the deceased member in respect of whose death the person has received the relevant lump sum death benefit;

(c)   the name of the registered pension scheme under which that person was entitled to receive that relevant lump sum death benefit;

(d)   the name and address of the scheme administrator by whom the relevant lump sum death benefit was paid;

(e)   the amount of the relevant lump sum death benefit the person received; and

(f)   the date on which the relevant lump sum death benefit was paid.

10A(3)   The person who gives the notification must sign and date it.

History – Reg. 10 and 10A substituted for reg. 10 by SI 2006/3261, reg. 6 with effect from 28 December 2006.

Preservation of documents

11(1)   This regulation applies if–

(a)   an individual gives a notification to the Revenue and Customs, and

(b)   the Revenue and Customs issue a certificate to the individual in response to the giving of the notification.

11(2)   The individual must preserve all documents relating to the information given in the notification for a period of six years beginning with the day on which the individual gives the notification to the Revenue and Customs.

Late submission of notification

12(1)   This regulation applies if an individual–

(a)   gives a notification to the Revenue and Customs after the closing date,

(b)   had a reasonable excuse for not giving the notification on or before the closing date, and

(c)   gives the notification without unreasonable delay after the reasonable excuse ceased.

12(2)   If the Revenue and Customs are satisfied that paragraph (1) applies, they must consider the information provided in the notification.

12(3)   If there is a dispute as to whether paragraph (1) applies, the individual may require the Revenue and Customs to give notice of their decision to refuse to consider the information provided in the notification.

12(4)   If the Revenue and Customs gives notice of their decision to refuse to consider the information provided in the notification, the individual may appeal.

12(5)   [Omitted by SI 2009/56, art. 3(2) and Sch. 2, para. 149(3).]

12(6)   The notice of appeal must be given to the Revenue and Customs within 30 days after the day on which notice of their decision is given to the individual.

12(7)   On an appeal that is notified to the tribunal, the tribunal shall determine whether the individual gave the notification to the Revenue and Customs in the circumstances specified in paragraph (1).

12(8)   If the tribunal allows the appeal, the tribunal shall direct the Revenue and Customs to consider the information provided in the notification.

History – In reg. 12(4), the words "to the Commissioners", which appeared after "appeal", omitted by SI 2009/56, art. 3(2) and Sch. 2, para. 149(2), operative from 1 April 2009 subject to transitional and saving provisions in SI 2009/56, Sch. 3.
Reg. 12(5) omitted by SI 2009/56, art. 3(2) and Sch. 2, para. 149(3), operative from 1 April 2009 subject to transitional and saving provisions in SI 2009/56, Sch. 3. Former reg. 12(5) read as follows:

"**12(5)**   The appeal is to the General Commissioners, except that the individual may elect (in accordance with section 46(1) of the Taxes Management Act 1970) to bring the appeal before the Special Commissioners instead of the General Commissioners.".

In reg. 12(7), the words "appeal that is notified to the tribunal, the tribunal" substituted for the words "appeal, the Commissioners" by SI 2009/56, art. 3(2) and Sch. 2, para. 149(4), operative from 1 April 2009 subject to transitional and saving provisions in SI 2009/56, Sch. 3.
In reg. 12(8), the words "tribunal allows" substituted for the words "Commissioners allow" by SI 2009/56, art. 3(2) and Sch. 2, para. 149(5)(a), operative from 1 April 2009 subject to transitional and saving provisions in SI 2009/56, Sch. 3.
In reg. 12(8), the words "the tribunal" substituted for the word "they" by SI 2009/56, art. 3(2) and Sch. 2, para. 149(5)(b), operative from 1 April 2009 subject to transitional and saving provisions in SI 2009/56, Sch. 3.

PROCEDURE ON GIVING OF NOTIFICATIONS

Procedure on giving of notification: the specified provisions

13(1)   If an individual gives a notification to the Revenue and Customs under one of the specified provisions, and there are no obvious errors or omissions in the notification (whether errors of principle, arithmetical mistakes or otherwise), the Revenue and Customs must issue a certificate to the individual.

13(2) If an individual gives a notification to the Revenue and Customs under one of the specified provisions, and there are obvious errors or omissions in the notification (whether errors of principle, arithmetical mistakes or otherwise), the Revenue and Customs must return the notification to the individual.

History – Reg. 13 and 13A substituted for reg. 13 by SI 2006/3261, reg. 7 with effect from 28 December 2006. Formerly read as follows:

> "**Procedure on giving of notification to the Revenue and Customs**
>
> **13(1)** If an individual gives a notification to the Revenue and Customs, and there are no obvious errors or omissions in the notification (whether errors of principle, arithmetical mistakes or otherwise), the Revenue and Customs must issue a certificate to the individual.
>
> **13(2)** If an individual gives a notification to the Revenue and Customs, and there are obvious errors or omissions in the notification (whether errors of principle, arithmetical mistakes or otherwise), the Revenue and Customs must return the notification to the individual.".

Procedure on giving of notification: regulations 3A and 4A

13A(1) If a person gives a notification to the Revenue and Customs under regulation 3A or 4A, and there are no obvious errors or omissions in the notification (whether errors of principle, arithmetical mistakes or otherwise), the Revenue and Customs–

(a) must notify that person, in writing, that there are no obvious errors or omissions in the notification, and

(b) confirm that that person has given a valid notification of intention to rely on paragraph 11A or 15A (as the case may be).

13A(2) If a person gives a notification to the Revenue and Customs, and there are obvious errors or omissions in the notification (whether errors of principle, arithmetical mistakes or otherwise), the Revenue and Customs must return the notification to the individual.

History – Reg. 13 and 13A substituted for reg. 13 by SI 2006/3261, reg. 7 with effect from 28 December 2006.

Appeal against refusal to issue certificate

14(1) This regulation applies if there is a dispute as to whether the Revenue and Customs are entitled to take the view that there are obvious errors or omissions in a notification given under one of the specified regulations (whether errors of principle, arithmetical mistakes or otherwise).

14(2) The individual may require the Revenue and Customs to give notice of their decision to refuse to issue a certificate.

14(3) If the Revenue and Customs give notice of their decision to refuse to issue a certificate, the individual may appeal.

14(4) [Omitted by SI 2009/56, art. 3(2) and Sch. 2, para. 150(3).]

14(5) The notice of appeal must be given to the Revenue and Customs within 30 days after the day on which notice of their decision is given to the individual.

14(6) On an appeal that is notified to the tribunal, the tribunal shall determine whether the Revenue and Customs were entitled to take the view that there were obvious errors or omissions in the notification (whether errors of principle, arithmetical mistakes or otherwise).

14(7) If the tribunal allows the appeal, the tribunal may direct the Revenue and Customs to issue a certificate to the individual with effect from a date specified by the tribunal.

History – In reg. 14(1), the words "a notification given under one of the specified regulations" substituted for "the notification" by SI 2006/3261, reg. 8 with effect from 28 December 2006.

In reg. 14(3), the words "to the Commissioners", which appeared after "appeal", omitted by SI 2009/56, art. 3(2) and Sch. 2, para. 150(2), operative from 1 April 2009 subject to transitional and saving provisions in SI 2009/56, Sch. 3.

Reg. 14(4) omitted by SI 2009/56, art. 3(2) and Sch. 2, para. 150(3), operative from 1 April 2009 subject to transitional and saving provisions in SI 2009/56, Sch. 3. Former 14(4) read as follows:

> "**14(4)** The appeal is to the General Commissioners, except that the individual may elect (in accordance with section 46(1) of the Taxes Management Act 1970) to bring the appeal before the Special Commissioners instead of the General Commissioners.".

In reg. 14(6), the words "appeal that is notified to the tribunal, the tribunal" substituted for the words "appeal, the Commissioners" by SI 2009/56, art. 3(2) and Sch. 2, para. 150(4), operative from 1 April 2009 subject to transitional and saving provisions in SI 2009/56, Sch. 3.

In reg. 14(7), "tribunal allows" substituted for "Commissioners allow" by SI 2009/56, art. 3(2) and Sch. 2, para. 150(5)(a), operative from 1 April 2009 subject to transitional and saving provisions in SI 2009/56, Sch. 3.

In reg. 14(7), immediately before "may direct", "the tribunal" substituted for "they" by SI 2009/56, art. 3(2) and Sch. 2, para. 150(5)(b), operative from 1 April 2009 subject to transitional and saving provisions in SI 2009/56, Sch. 3.

In reg. 14(7), at the end, "tribunal" substituted for "Commissioners" by SI 2009/56, art. 3(2) and Sch. 2, para. 150(5)(c), operative from 1 April 2009 subject to transitional and saving provisions in SI 2009/56, Sch. 3.

APPEAL AGAINST REFUSAL TO CONFIRM VALIDITY OF NOTIFICATION

14A(1) This regulation applies if there is a dispute as to whether the Revenue and Customs are entitled to take the view that there are obvious errors or omissions in a notification given under regulation 3A or 4A (whether errors of principle, arithmetical mistakes or otherwise).

14A(2) The person may require the Revenue and Customs to give notice of their decision to refuse to confirm the validity of the notification.

14A(3) If the Revenue and Customs give notice of their decision to refuse to confirm the validity of the notification, the person may appeal.

14A(4) [Omitted by SI 2009/56, art. 3(2) and Sch. 2, para. 151(3).]

14A(5) The notice of appeal must be given to the Revenue and Customs within 30 days after the day on which notice of their decision is given to the person.

14A(6) On an appeal that is notified to the tribunal, the tribunal shall determine whether the Revenue and Customs were entitled to take the view that there were obvious errors or omissions in the notification (whether errors of principle, arithmetical mistakes or otherwise).

14A(7) If the tribunal allows the appeal, the tribunal may direct the Revenue and Customs to confirm the validity of the notification with effect from a date specified by the tribunal.

History – In reg. 14A(3), the words "to the Commissioners", which appeared after "appeal", omitted by SI 2009/56, art. 3(2) and Sch. 2, para. 151(2), operative from 1 April 2009 subject to transitional and saving provisions in SI 2009/56, Sch. 3.
Reg. 14A(4) omitted by SI 2009/56, art. 3(2) and Sch. 2, para. 151(3), operative from 1 April 2009 subject to transitional and saving provisions in SI 2009/56, Sch. 3. Former reg. 14A(4) read as follows:
"**14A(4)** The appeal is to the General Commissioners, except that the person may elect (in accordance with section 46(1) of the Taxes Management Act 1970) to bring the appeal before the Special Commissioners instead of the General Commissioners.".
In reg. 14A(6), the words "appeal that is notified to the tribunal, the tribunal" substituted for the words "appeal, the Commissioners" by SI 2009/56, art. 3(2) and Sch. 2, para. 151(4), operative from 1 April 2009 subject to transitional and saving provisions in SI 2009/56, Sch. 3.
In reg. 14A(7), "tribunal allows" substituted for "Commissioners allow" by SI 2009/56, art. 3(2) and Sch. 2, para. 151(5)(a), operative from 1 April 2009 subject to transitional and saving provisions in SI 2009/56, Sch. 3.
In reg. 14A(7), immediately before "may direct", "the tribunal" substituted for "they" by SI 2009/56, art. 3(2) and Sch. 2, para. 151(5)(b), operative from 1 April 2009 subject to transitional and saving provisions in SI 2009/56, Sch. 3.
In reg. 14A(7), at the end, "tribunal" substituted for "Commissioners" by SI 2009/56, art. 3(2) and Sch. 2, para. 151(5)(c), operative from 1 April 2009 subject to transitional and saving provisions in SI 2009/56, Sch. 3.
Reg. 14A inserted by SI 2006/3261, reg. 8 with effect from 28 December 2006.

CERTIFICATES

General

15(1) A certificate must be in a form prescribed by the Commissioners for Her Majesty's Revenue and Customs.

15(2) A certificate must have a unique reference number.

15(3) An individual to whom a certificate is issued must preserve the certificate until no further benefit crystallisation event can occur.

Aggregate certificates

16(1) This regulation applies if—

(a) an individual is a relevant overseas individual during any part of a period that is the active membership period in relation to an arrangement relating to an individual, and

(b) condition A, B or C is met.

16(2) Condition A is that—

(a) the individual has given a notification under regulation 7 to the Revenue and Customs in relation to a part of the active membership period, and

(b) the individual gives a further notification under regulation 7 to the Revenue and Customs in relation to a further part of the same active membership period.

16(3) Condition B is that—

(a) the Revenue and Customs have issued a certificate to an individual in response to a notification under regulation 7 given by the individual in relation to a part of the active membership period, and

(b) the individual gives a further notification under regulation 7 to the Revenue and Customs in relation to a further part of the same active membership period.

16(4)   Condition C is that–

(a)   the Revenue and Customs have issued a certificate to an individual in response to a notification under regulation 7 given by the individual in relation to a part of the active membership period, and

(b)   the Revenue and Customs issue a further certificate to the individual in response to a further notification under regulation 7 given by the individual in relation to a further part of the same active membership period.

16(5)   The individual may require the Revenue and Customs to issue a single certificate (an "aggregate certificate") to the individual.

16(6)   An aggregate certificate supersedes the certificates mentioned in paragraphs (3)(a) and (4).

16(7)   If the Revenue and Customs issue an aggregate certificate to an individual, paragraphs (6) to (10) of regulation 7 apply as if the aggregate certificate were the certificate referred to in paragraph (5)(b) of that regulation.

16(8)   Any notification mentioned in this regulation must be given on or before the closing date; and regulation 7 applies to find the closing date for a notification mentioned in this regulation in the same way as it applies to find the closing date for a notification given under that regulation.

Incorrect information given in connection with notification

17(1)   This regulation applies if–

(a)   after the giving of a notification, the Revenue and Customs have issued a certificate ("the first certificate") to an individual, and

(b)   either condition A or condition B is met.

17(2)   Condition A is that the individual informs the Revenue and Customs that information given in the notification was incorrect or has become incorrect.

17(3)   Condition B is that the individual informs the Revenue and Customs that information given in connection with the notification was incorrect or has become incorrect.

17(4)   The Revenue and Customs may revoke the first certificate and issue an amended certificate to the individual.

17(5)   The amended certificate supersedes the first certificate.

17(6)   If an individual realises that any information given in the notification, or given in connection with the notification, was incorrect or has become incorrect, the individual must inform the Revenue and Customs without undue delay.

17(7)   If condition A is met, the individual must inform the Revenue and Customs in a form prescribed by the Commissioners for Her Majesty's Revenue and Customs.

Incorrect information given in certificate

18(1)   This regulation applies if–

(a)   the Revenue and Customs have issued a certificate ("the first certificate") to an individual, and

(b)   the individual informs the Revenue and Customs that information given in the certificate was incorrect or has become incorrect.

18(2)   The Revenue and Customs may–

(a)   revoke the first certificate,

(b)   revoke the first certificate and issue an amended certificate to the individual, or

(c)   issue an additional certificate to the individual.

18(3)   The amended certificate supersedes the first certificate.

18(4)   This regulation is subject to regulation 16.

18(5)   If an individual realises that any information given in the certificate was incorrect or has become incorrect, the individual must inform the Revenue and Customs without undue delay.

Further supply of information given in certificate

19(1)   This regulation applies if, after the Revenue and Customs have issued a certificate to an individual, the individual no longer possesses information given in the certificate.

19(2)   The individual may require the Revenue and Customs to give the information to the individual.

COMPLIANCE

Review of notification after certificate issued

20(1) This regulation applies if–

(a) an individual has given a notification to the Revenue and Customs, and

(b) the Revenue and Customs have issued a certificate to the individual in response to the giving of the notification.

20(2) The Revenue and Customs may review any information given–

(a) in the notification, or

(b) in connection with the notification.

20(3) The Revenue and Customs may begin a review under this regulation at any time within a period of twelve months beginning with the day on which the notification was given to them.

20(4) [Omitted by SI 2010/651, reg. 2(2)(a).]

History – Reg. 20(4) omitted by SI 2010/651, reg. 2(2)(a), with effect from 1 April 2010 (but this amendment does not apply in relation to or in connection with a notice given before 1 April 2010 under reg. 22). Former reg. 20(4) read as follows:
"20(4) The procedure to be followed on the review is set out in regulation 22.".

Review of notification after receipt of further information

21(1) This regulation applies if–

(a) an individual has given a notification to the Revenue and Customs,

(b) the Revenue and Customs have issued a certificate to the individual in response to the giving of the notification, and

(c) after the certificate has been issued, the Revenue and Customs have reason to believe that information given in the notification, given in connection with the notification, or given in the certificate, either was incorrect or has become incorrect.

21(2) The Revenue and Customs may review any information given in the notification, in connection with the notification, or in the certificate.

21(3) The Revenue and Customs may begin a review under this regulation at any time.

21(4) [Omitted by SI 2010/651, reg. 2(2)(b).]

History – Reg. 21(4) omitted by SI 2010/651, reg. 2(2)(b), with effect from 1 April 2010 (but this amendment does not apply in relation to or in connection with a notice given before 1 April 2010 under reg. 22). Former reg. 21(4) read as follows:
"21(4) The procedure to be followed on the review is set out in regulation 22.".

Reviews of notifications: procedure to be followed

22 [Omitted by SI 2010/651, reg. 2(2)(c).]

History – Reg. 22 omitted by SI 2010/651, reg. 2(2)(c), with effect from 1 April 2010 (but this amendment does not apply in relation to or in connection with a notice given before 1 April 2010 under reg. 22). Former reg. 22 read as follows:
"22(1) This regulation applies if the Revenue and Customs decide to begin a review under regulation 20 or 21.
22(2) The Revenue and Customs must give notice to the individual requiring the individual to provide any information, particulars and documents specified in the notice which the Revenue and Customs may reasonably require.
22(3) A notice under this regulation must specify the period within which it is to be complied with; and that period may not end earlier than the period of 30 days beginning with the day on which the notice is given.
22(4) An individual may comply with a notice under this regulation requiring the production of a document by producing a copy of the document.
22(5) But where an individual produces a copy of a document in compliance with a notice under this regulation, the Revenue and Customs may by notice require the production of the original for inspection within a period specified in the notice; and that period may not end earlier than the period of 30 days beginning with the day on which the notice is given.
22(6) The Revenue and Customs may take copies of, or make extracts from, any document produced in compliance with a notice under this section.
22(7) A notice under this section does not require an individual–
(a) to produce or make available for inspection any document, or
(b) to provide any particulars,
relating to any pending appeal by the individual relating to tax.".

Appeals against notices under regulation 22

23 [Omitted by SI 2010/651, reg. 2(2)(d).]

History – Reg. 23 omitted by SI 2010/651, reg. 2(2)(d), with effect from 1 April 2010 (but this amendment does not apply in relation to or in connection with a notice given before 1 April 2010 under reg. 22). Former reg. 23 read as follows:
"23 Section 253 (appeal against notices) applies to a notice under regulation 22 as it applies to a notice under section 252(1).".

Revocation or amendment of certificate

24(1) The Revenue and Customs may revoke or amend a certificate at any time if–

(a)   after the certificate has been issued, the Revenue and Customs have reason to believe that any information given in the notification, given in connection with the notification, or given in the certificate, either was incorrect or has become incorrect, or

(b)   after notice has been given to an individual under paragraph 1 of Schedule 36 to the Finance Act 2008, the individual does not reply to the notice within the time specified in the notice.

24(2) If the Revenue and Customs revoke or amend a certificate, they must give notice to the individual of the revocation or amendment.

24(3) The individual may appeal against the revocation or amendment of the certificate.

24(4) [Omitted by SI 2009/56, art. 3(2) and Sch. 2, para. 152(3).]

24(5) The notice of appeal must be given to the Revenue and Customs within 30 days after the day on which notice of the revocation or amendment is given to the individual.

24(6) On an appeal that is notified to the tribunal, the tribunal shall determine whether the Revenue and Customs revoked or amended the certificate in the circumstances specified in paragraph (1).

24(7) If the tribunal allows the appeal, the tribunal may direct the Revenue and Customs to issue a certificate to the individual with effect from a date specified by the tribunal.

24(8) If the Revenue and Customs revoke a certificate and, on appeal, the tribunal determines that the certificate should have been amended, the tribunal shall order that the certificate shall be amended in such terms as the tribunal may specify.

24(9) If the Revenue and Customs amend a certificate and, on appeal, the tribunal determines that the certificate should have been amended in other terms, the tribunal shall order that the certificate shall be amended in such terms as the tribunal may specify.

History – In reg. 24(1)(b), the words "paragraph 1 of Schedule 36 to the Finance Act 2008" substituted for the words "regulation 22" by SI 2010/651, reg. 2(3), with effect from 1 April 2010 (but this amendment does not apply in relation to or in connection with a notice given before 1 April 2010 under reg. 22).
In reg. 24(3), the words "to the Commissioners", which appeared after "appeal", omitted by SI 2009/56, art. 3(2) and Sch. 2, para. 152(2), operative from 1 April 2009 subject to transitional and saving provisions in SI 2009/56, Sch. 3.
Reg. 24(4) omitted by SI 2009/56, art. 3(2) and Sch. 2, para. 152(3), operative from 1 April 2009 subject to transitional and saving provisions in SI 2009/56, Sch. 3. Former reg. 24(4) read as follows:
    "**24(4)** The appeal is to the General Commissioners, except that the individual may elect (in accordance with section 46(1) of the Taxes Management Act 1970) to bring the appeal before the Special Commissioners instead of the General Commissioners.".
In reg. 24(6), the words "appeal that is notified to the tribunal, the tribunal" substituted for the words "appeal, the Commissioners" by SI 2009/56, art. 3(2) and Sch. 2, para. 152(4), operative from 1 April 2009 subject to transitional and saving provisions in SI 2009/56, Sch. 3.
In reg. 24(7), "tribunal allows" substituted for "Commissioners allow" by SI 2009/56, art. 3(2) and Sch. 2, para. 152(5)(a), operative from 1 April 2009 subject to transitional and saving provisions in SI 2009/56, Sch. 3.
In reg. 24(7), immediately before "may direct", "the tribunal" substituted for "they" by SI 2009/56, art. 3(2) and Sch. 2, para. 152(5)(b), operative from 1 April 2009 subject to transitional and saving provisions in SI 2009/56, Sch. 3.
In reg. 24(7), at the end, "tribunal" substituted for "Commissioners" by SI 2009/56, art. 3(2) and Sch. 2, para. 152(5)(c), operative from 1 April 2009 subject to transitional and saving provisions in SI 2009/56, Sch. 3.
In reg. 24(8), the words "tribunal determines" substituted for the words "Commissioners determine" by SI 2009/56, art. 3(2) and Sch. 2, para. 152(6)(a), operative from 1 April 2009 subject to transitional and saving provisions in SI 2009/56, Sch. 3.
In reg. 24(8), "tribunal" substituted for "Commissioners" twice by SI 2009/56, art. 3(2) and Sch. 2, para. 152(6)(b), operative from 1 April 2009 subject to transitional and saving provisions in SI 2009/56, Sch. 3.
In reg. 24(9), the words "tribunal determines" substituted for the words "Commissioners determine" by SI 2009/56, art. 3(2) and Sch. 2, para. 152(7)(a), operative from 1 April 2009 subject to transitional and saving provisions in SI 2009/56, Sch. 3.
In reg. 24(9), "tribunal" substituted for "Commissioners" twice by SI 2009/56, art. 3(2) and Sch. 2, para. 152(7)(b), operative from 1 April 2009 subject to transitional and saving provisions in SI 2009/56, Sch. 3.

SUPPLEMENTARY

Special classes of individuals

25(1) If an individual is a person who is incapable, by reason of mental disorder, of managing and administering his property and affairs, anything under these Regulations which could have been done by the individual may be done–

(a)   in England and Wales or Northern Ireland, by the individual's attorney or receiver, or the person managing and administering the individual's property and affairs,

(b)   in Scotland, by the individual's guardian within the meaning of the Adults with Incapacity (Scotland) Act 2000, and

(c)   in a country or territory outside the United Kingdom, by a person authorised by a Court having jurisdiction, in that country or territory, to regulate the property and affairs of an individual to whom this paragraph applies.

25(2) If an individual is a person who is suffering from a physical disability, by reason of which that person has difficulty executing documents in respect of the management and administration of his property and affairs, anything under these Regulations which could have been done by the individual may be done–

(a)   in the United Kingdom, by a person having a power of attorney in relation to the individual's property and affairs, and

(b)   in a country or territory outside the United Kingdom, by a person authorised, under the laws of that country or territory, to execute documents in relation to the individual's property and affairs.

Personal representatives

26   If an individual dies, anything under these Regulations which could have been done by the individual may be done by the individual's personal representatives.

ARMED FORCES AND RESERVE FORCES (COMPENSATION SCHEME) (EXCLUDED BENEFITS FOR TAX PURPOSES) REGULATIONS 2006

(SI 2006/132)

Made on 25 January 2006 by the Commissioners for Her Majesty's Revenue and Customs, in exercise of the powers conferred upon them by s. 393B of the Income Tax (Earnings and Pensions) Act 2003. Operative from 6 April 2006.

CITATION AND COMMENCEMENT

1   These Regulations may be cited as the Armed Forces and Reserve Forces (Compensation Scheme) (Excluded Benefits for Tax Purposes) Regulations 2006 and shall come into force on 6th April 2006.

BENEFITS EXCLUDED FROM CHARGE UNDER CHAPTER 2 OF PART 6 OF ITEPA 2003

2   Any benefit provided under the Armed Forces and Reserve Forces (Compensation Scheme) Order 2005 is prescribed for the purposes of section 393B(3)(d) of the Income Tax Earnings and Pensions Act 2003 (prescribed benefits to be excluded benefits for the purposes of Chapter 2 of Part 6 of that Act).

REGISTERED PENSION SCHEMES (CO-OWNERSHIP OF LIVING ACCOMMODATION) REGULATIONS 2006

(SI 2006/133)

Made on 25 January 2006 by the Commissioners for Her Majesty's Revenue and Customs, in exercise of the powers conferred by s. 220(5), 221(6), 224(9), 251(1) and (6) and 256 of, and para. 7(1)(b), 12(1) and 18(6) of Sch. 36 to, the Finance Act 2004 and s. 113(1) of the Taxes Management Act 1970. Operative from 6 April 2006.

CITATION AND COMMENCEMENT

1 These Regulations may be cited as the Registered Pension Schemes (Co-ownership of Living Accommodation) Regulations 2006, and shall come into force on 6th April 2006.

CIRCUMSTANCES IN WHICH THESE REGULATIONS APPLY

2(1) These Regulations apply if, for the whole or part of a tax year, living accommodation is held–

(a) partly by persons for the purposes of a registered pension scheme, and

(b) partly by persons for other purposes.

2(2) In these Regulations–

an **"owner"** means a person for whom the living accommodation is held;

a **"pension scheme owner"** means a person who is an owner by virtue of paragraph (1)(a);

a **"scheme member"** means an individual who is a member of the registered pension scheme mentioned in paragraph (1)(a).

THE LIVING ACCOMMODATION BENEFIT

3(1) If these Regulations apply, a benefit is provided.

3(2) In these Regulations the benefit is called "the living accommodation benefit".

3(3) The amount of the living accommodation benefit is calculated in the same way as the cash equivalent of the benefit is calculated under Chapter 5.

3(4) For the purposes of the calculation required by paragraph (3)–

(a) references in Chapter 5 to the employee are to be treated as references to an individual for whom the living accommodation is provided,

(b) references in Chapter 5 to the employer are to be treated as references to the registered pension scheme, and

(c) references in Chapter 5 to the taxable period are to be treated as references to the period (consisting of the whole or part of a tax year) for which these Regulations apply.

3(5) In this regulation "Chapter 5" means Chapter 5 of Part 3 of the Income Tax (Employments and Pensions) Act 2003 (taxable benefits: living accommodation).

THE PENSION SCHEME OWNER'S BENEFIT

4(1) The amount of the living accommodation benefit must be apportioned among the owners according to their respective shares and interests.

4(2) In these Regulations, the amount of the living accommodation benefit so apportioned to a pension scheme owner is called "the pension scheme owner's benefit".

THE PRIVATE OWNER'S BENEFIT

5(1) The pension scheme owner's benefit must be apportioned.

5(2) If the living accommodation is used to provide a benefit for persons who consist of, or include–

(a) one particular scheme member, or

(b) a member of the scheme member's family or household,

the pension scheme owner's benefit is apportioned to the scheme member.

5(3) If the living accommodation is used to provide a benefit for persons who consist of, or include–

(a) a scheme member or a member of the scheme member's family or household, and

(b) another scheme member or a member of that other scheme member's family or household,

Statutory Instruments

the pension scheme owner's benefit is apportioned among those scheme members.

5(4) If paragraph (3)(b) applies in relation to more than one scheme member, the pension scheme owner's benefit is apportioned among all the scheme members in relation to whom paragraph (3)(a) or (3)(b) applies.

5(5) If paragraph (3) applies, the amount of the pension scheme benefit apportioned to any particular scheme member is to be such part of that benefit as is just and reasonable.

5(6) Section 721 of the Income Tax (Employments and Pensions) Act 2003 (definitions) applies for the purpose of determining the members of a scheme member's family or household.

5(7) In these Regulations the amount of the pension scheme owner's benefit apportioned under this regulation to a scheme member is called "the private owner's benefit".

UNAUTHORISED PAYMENTS TO MEMBERS OF REGISTERED PENSION SCHEMES

6(1) A pension scheme owner is to be treated as having made an unauthorised payment under section 173 of the Finance Act 2004 to a scheme member to whom regulation 5(7) applies.

6(2) The amount of the unauthorised payment is equal to the amount of the private owner's benefit.

REGISTERED PENSION SCHEMES (AUTHORISED PAYMENTS) (TRANSFERS TO THE PENSION PROTECTION FUND) REGULATIONS 2006

(SI 2006/134)

Made on 25 January 2006 by the Commissioners for Her Majesty's Revenue and Customs, in exercise of the powers conferred upon them by s. 164(f) of the Finance Act 2004. Operative from 6 April 2006.

CITATION AND COMMENCEMENT

1 These Regulations may be cited as the Registered Pension Schemes (Authorised Payments) (Transfers to the Pension Protection Fund) Regulations 2006 and shall come into force on 6th April 2006.

AUTHORISED PAYMENTS

2 For the purposes of section 164(f) of the Finance Act 2004 (authorised member payments), a transfer of the property, rights and liabilities of a registered pension scheme to the Board of the Pension Protection Fund is a payment of a description that is prescribed.

REGISTERED PENSION SCHEMES (MEANING OF PENSION COMMENCEMENT LUMP SUM) REGULATIONS 2006

(SI 2006/135 as amended by SI 2007/3533 and SI 2011/1751)

Made on 25 January 2006 by the Commissioners for Her Majesty's Revenue and Customs, in exercise of the powers conferred upon them by para. 1(6) of Sch. 29 to the Finance Act 2004. Operative from 6 April 2006.

CITATION AND COMMENCEMENT

1 These Regulations may be cited as the Registered Pension Schemes (Meaning of Pension Commencement Lump Sum) Regulations 2006, and shall come into force on 6th April 2006.

APPLICATION OF THESE REGULATIONS: GENERAL

2 These Regulations apply for the purposes of paragraph 1(6) of Schedule 29 to the Finance Act 2004 (regulations relating to meaning of "pension commencement lump sum").

CIRCUMSTANCES IN WHICH THESE REGULATIONS APPLY

3 The circumstances in which incorrect income tax has been paid by the scheme administrator in relation to the member by way of the lifetime allowance charge are circumstances in which–

(a) the scheme administrator has made an overpayment by way of the lifetime allowance charge in relation to the member, and

(b) Her Majesty's Revenue and Customs refund the overpayment to the scheme administrator.

4 The circumstances in which a lump sum subsequently paid to the member is to be treated as a pension commencement lump sum even though the condition in paragraph 1(1)(c) of Schedule 29 to the Finance Act 2004 is not met are circumstances in which–

(a) Her Majesty's Revenue and Customs refund an overpayment by way of the lifetime allowance charge in relation to the member to the scheme administrator, and

(b) the scheme administrator pays part or all of the overpayment to the member within the period of twelve months beginning with the day on which the scheme administrator receives the overpayment from Her Majesty's Revenue and Customs.

History – In reg. 4, the words "even though the condition in paragraph 1(1)(c) of Schedule 29 to the Finance Act 2004 is not met" substituted for the words "even though either or both of the conditions in paragraphs (a) and (c) of paragraph 1(1) of Schedule 29 to the Finance Act 2004 are not met" by SI 2011/1751, reg. 7(2), which came into force on 11 August 2011, with effect in relation to lump sums paid on or after 6 April 2011.

In reg. 4 the words "paragraphs (a) and (c)" substituted for "paragraphs (c) and (e)" and "twelve months" substituted for "three months" by SI 2007/3533. reg. 2, with effect from 7 January 2008.

Statutory Instruments

PENSION BENEFITS (INSURANCE COMPANY LIABLE AS SCHEME ADMINISTRATOR) REGULATIONS 2006

(SI 2006/136, as amended by SI 2011/702, SI 2011/1751 and SI 2013/1114)

Made on 25 January 2006 by the Commissioners for Her Majesty's Revenue and Customs, in exercise of the powers conferred upon them by s. 273A(1) and (2) of the Finance Act 2004. Operative from 6 April 2006.

CITATION AND COMMENCEMENT

1   These Regulations may be cited as the Pension Benefits (Insurance Company Liable as Scheme Administrator) Regulations 2005 and shall come into force on 6th April 2006.

INSURANCE COMPANY LIABLE AS SCHEME ADMINISTRATOR

2(1)   This regulation applies where an insurance company makes a payment of–

(a)   a pension protection lump sum death benefit,

(b)   an annuity protection lump sum death benefit, or

(c)   a drawdown pension fund lump sum death benefit

2(2)   The insurance company is to be treated as the scheme administrator for the purposes of the operation of section 206 (special lump sum death benefits charge) in relation to the lump sum death benefit.

2(3)   The insurance company is responsible for the discharge of the obligations imposed on the scheme administrator under subsections (1) to (7) of section 254 (accounting for tax by scheme administrators).

2(4)   The insurance company is liable to the penalties under–

(a)   Schedule 24 to the Finance Act 2007 (penalties for errors); and

(b)   Schedule 55 to the Finance Act 2009 (penalty for failure to make returns)

if it fails to comply with the obligations imposed by section 254(1) to (7) as applied to it by virtue of paragraphs (2) and (3).

History – Reg. 2(1)(c) substituted by SI 2011/1751, reg. 2(2), which came into force on 11 August 2011, with effect for the tax year 2011–12 and subsequent tax years. Former reg. 2(1)(c) read as follows:
   "(c)   an unsecured pension fund lump sum death benefit.".
Reg. 2(4) substituted by SI 2013/1114, art. 6(2), with effect from 1 June 2013. Former reg. 2(4) read as follows:
   "**2(4)**   The insurance company is liable to the penalties under–
   (a)   Schedule 55 to the Finance Act 2009 (penalty for failure to make returns) if it fails to comply with the obligations imposed by section 254(1) to (7) as applied to it by virtue of paragraph (2); and
   (b)   section 260(6) if it fraudulently or negligently makes an incorrect return under section 254(1) to (7) as so applied.".
In reg. 2(4)(a), the words "Schedule 55 to the Finance Act 2009 (penalty for failure to make returns)" substituted for the words "section 260(1) (accounting return)" by SI 2011/702, art. 17, with effect from 1 April 2011, but subject to SI 2011/702, art. 21, which provides that the substitution does not have effect in respect of a return period ending on or before 31 December 2010.

REGISTERED PENSION SCHEMES (AUTHORISED MEMBER PAYMENTS) REGULATIONS 2006

(SI 2006/137)

Made on 25 January 2006 by the Commissioners for Her Majesty's Revenue and Customs, in exercise of the powers conferred upon them by s. 164(f) of the Finance Act 2004. Operative from 6 April 2006.

CITATION AND COMMENCEMENT

1 These Regulations may be cited as the Registered Pension Schemes (Authorised Member Payments) Regulations 2006 and shall come into force on 6th April 2006.

AUTHORISED MEMBER PAYMENTS: DEMUTUALISATION OF INSURANCE COMPANIES AND MEMBERS OF QUALIFYING PENSION SCHEMES

2(1) Any payment made–

(a)   by a company to–

    (i)   a member of a qualifying pension scheme, or

    (ii)   a person who is the beneficiary under a qualifying annuity contract;

(b)   in connection with the demutualisation of an insurance company,

(c)   as compensation to that member or person, for the loss of his rights as a member of the insurance company, and

(d)   without reducing the total value of the sums and assets held for the purposes of the scheme, or the value or amount of the annuity, as the case may be,

is prescribed for the purposes of section 164 of the Finance Act 2004 (authorised member payments under registered pension schemes).

2(2) In this regulation–

"**the commencement date**" means 6th April 2006;

"**demutualisation**" means a transfer under an insurance business transfer scheme of the whole or any part of the business carried on by a mutual insurance company to one or more companies with a share capital;

"**insurance business transfer scheme**" means a scheme falling within section 105 FISMA 2000;

"**mutual insurance company**" means an insurance company not having a share capital;

"**qualifying annuity contract**" means an annuity contract made with an insurance company–

(a)

    (i)   by means of which benefits provided under a pension scheme which, at the time of the purchase of the annuity, fell within one of the categories set out in paragraphs (a) to (c) and (g) of paragraph 1(1) of Schedule 36 to the Finance Act 2004, have been secured, and

    (ii)   which, immediately before the commencement date, provided for the immediate payment of benefits; or

(b)   issued out of a trust scheme within section 620(5) of the Income and Corporation Taxes Act 1988, or

(c)   which is a lifetime annuity within the meaning in paragraph 3 of Schedule 28 to the Finance Act 2004, or a short term annuity within the meaning in paragraph 6 of that Schedule;

"**qualifying pension scheme**" means a registered pension scheme which is neither an occupational pension scheme nor a public service pension scheme; and

expressions defined in section 150, 151 or 280(1) of the Finance Act 2004 have the same meanings in this regulation as they have for the purposes of Part 4 of that Act.

PENSION SCHEMES (REDUCTION IN PENSION RATES) REGULATIONS 2006

(SI 2006/138, as amended by SI 2009/1311 and SI 2013/1111)

Made on 25 January 2006 by the Commissioners for Her Majesty's Revenue and Customs, in exercise of the powers conferred upon them by para. 2(4)(e) and (h) of Sch. 28 to the Finance Act 2004.
Operative from 6 April 2006.

CITATION, COMMENCEMENT AND INTERPRETATION

1(1) These Regulations may be cited as the Pension Schemes (Reduction in Pension Rates) Regulations 2006 and shall come into force on 6th April 2006.

1(2) In these Regulations a reference, without more, to a paragraph is a reference to a paragraph of Schedule 28 of the Finance Act 2004.

FORFEITURE OF ENTITLEMENT TO PENSION – PRESCRIBED CIRCUMSTANCES

2(1) For the purposes of paragraph 2(4)(e) (forfeiture of entitlement to pension) the prescribed circumstances are where forfeiture of a pension has been permitted–

(a)   under section 92(2) or 93 of the Pensions Act 1995 ("the 1995 Act") providing that the member meets the condition set out in sub-paragraph 2(2);

(b)   under section 92(4) or (5) of the 1995 Act;

(c)   under Article 90(4) or (5) or 91 of the Pensions (Northern Ireland) Order 1995;

(d)   in any of the circumstances prescribed by the Occupational Pension Schemes (Assignment, Forfeiture, Bankruptcy etc.) Regulations 1997 or the Occupational Pension Schemes (Assignment, Forfeiture, Bankruptcy etc.) Regulations (Northern Ireland) 1997.

2(2) The condition referred to in sub-paragraph 2(1)(a) is that the member is not connected with–

(a)   the sponsoring employer of the scheme in respect of which the scheme pension is payable ("the employer"); or

(b)   a person who is connected with the employer.

2(3) Section 839 of ICTA 1988 applies to determine whether persons are connected for the purposes of paragraph (2) of this regulation.

REDUCTION OF PENSION – PRESCRIBED CIRCUMSTANCES

3 The circumstances described in regulations 4, 4A and 5 are prescribed circumstances for the purpose of paragraph 2(4)(h) (scheme pension – other circumstances in which reduction does not breach condition in paragraph 2(3)).

History – In reg. 3 ", 4A" inserted by SI 2013/111, reg. 3(2), with effect from 6 April 2013.
Reg. 3–5 substituted for former reg. 3 by SI 2009/1311, reg. 2, coming into force on 1 July 2009 with effect from 6 April 2006. Former reg. 3 read as follows:

> "REDUCTION OF PENSION – PRESCRIBED CIRCUMSTANCES
>
> **3** For the purposes of paragraph 2(4)(h) (reduction of the pension in any other circumstances prescribed by regulations) the prescribed circumstances are where the amount of pension payable to a member has been reduced under any of the following provisions–
>
> (a)   section 138(2) of the Pensions Act 2004 (payment of scheme benefits);
>
> (b)   article 122(2) of the Pensions (Northern Ireland) Order 2005;
>
> (c)   paragraph 14(3) or 15(3) (guaranteed minimum pension etc) of Schedule 5 to the Gender Recognition Act 2004."

REDUCTION OF PENSION UNDER CERTAIN PROVISIONS

4 The circumstances are that the pension is reduced under any of the following provisions–

(a)   section 138(2) of the Pensions Act 2004 (payment of scheme benefits);

(b)   article 122(2) of the Pensions (Northern Ireland) Order 2005 (payment of scheme benefits);

(c)   paragraph 14(3) or 15(3) of Schedule 5 to the Gender Recognition Act 2004 (guaranteed minimum pension etc).

(d)   section 237E(1) of the Finance Act 2004 (consequential benefit adjustments to be reasonable etc)

History – Reg. 4(d) inserted by SI 2013/111, reg. 3(3), with effect from 6 April 2013.
Reg. 3–5 substituted for former reg. 3 by SI 2009/1311, reg. 2, coming into force on 1 July 2009 with effect from 6 April 2006.

Statutory Instruments

REDUCTION OF PENSION – VOLUNTARY SATISFACTION OF LIABILITY

4A   The circumstances are that the pension is reduced by reason of the satisfaction by the scheme administrator on a voluntary basis of all or part of a liability of a member arising under section 227(1) of the Finance Act 2004 (annual allowance charge).

History – Reg. 4A inserted by SI 2013/111, reg. 3(4), with effect from 6 April 2013.

REDUCTION OF PENSION DURING WINDING-UP

5(1)   The circumstances are that–

(a)   an occupational pension scheme reduces the pension while the scheme is being wound up; and

(b)   the reason for the reduction is that the sums or assets held for the purposes of the scheme are insufficient to pay the pension at the rate at which the pension was being paid at the relevant time.

5(2)   A reduction of pension is not within the circumstances described in this regulation if the reduction is part of avoidance arrangements.

5(3)   In this regulation, "avoidance arrangements" includes schemes, arrangements and understandings of any kind (whether or not legally enforceable) the main purpose, or one of the main purposes, of which is to increase the member's entitlement to a lump sum on which there is no liability to income tax.

History – Reg. 3–5 substituted for former reg. 3 by SI 2009/1311, reg. 2, coming into force on 1 July 2009 with effect from 6 April 2006.

PENSION SCHEMES (CATEGORIES OF COUNTRY AND REQUIREMENTS FOR OVERSEAS PENSION SCHEMES AND RECOGNISED OVERSEAS PENSION SCHEMES) REGULATIONS 2006

(SI 2006/206 as amended by SI 2007/1600, SI 2012/884, SI 2012/1221 and SI 2013/2259)

Made on 1 February 2006 by the Commissioners for Her Majesty's Revenue and Customs, in exercise of the powers conferred by s. 150(7) and (8) of the Finance Act 2004. Operative from 6 April 2006.

CITATION, COMMENCEMENT AND INTERPRETATION

1(1) These Regulations may be cited as the Pension Schemes (Categories of Country and Requirements for Overseas Pension Schemes and Recognised Overseas Pension Schemes) Regulations 2006 and shall come into force on 6 April 2006.

1(2) In these Regulations a reference, without more, to a numbered section or Schedule is a reference to the section of, or Schedule to, the Finance Act 2004 which is so numbered.

REQUIREMENTS OF AN OVERSEAS PENSION SCHEME

2(1) For the purposes of section 150(7) (meaning of overseas pension scheme) an overseas pension scheme must–

(a)   satisfy the requirements in paragraphs (2) and (3); or

(b)   be established (outside the United Kingdom) by an international organisation for the purpose of providing benefits for, or in respect of, past service as an employee of the organisation and satisfy the requirements in paragraph (4).

2(2) This paragraph is satisfied if–

(a)   the scheme is an occupational pension scheme and there is, in the country or territory in which it is established, a body–

    (i)   which regulates occupational pension schemes; and

    (ii)   which regulates the scheme in question; and

(b)   the scheme is not an occupational pension scheme and there is in the country or territory in which it is established, a body–

    (i)   which regulates pension schemes other than occupational pension schemes; and

    (ii)   which regulates the scheme in question; or

(c)   neither sub-paragraph (a) or (b) is satisfied by reason only that no such regulatory body exists in the country or territory and–

    (i)   the scheme is established in another member State, Norway, Iceland or Liechtenstein; or

    (ii)   the scheme's rules provide that at least 70% of a member's UK tax-relieved scheme funds will be designated by the scheme manager for the purpose of providing that individual with an income for life, and the pension benefits payable to the member under the scheme (and any lump sum associated with those benefits) are payable no earlier than they would be if pension rule 1 in section 165 applied.

2(3) This paragraph is satisfied if the scheme is recognised for tax purposes.

A scheme is "recognised for tax purposes" under the tax legislation of a country or territory in which it is established if it meets the following conditions.

Condition 1

The scheme is open to persons resident in the country or territory in which it is established.

Condition 2

The scheme is established in a country or territory where there is a system of taxation of personal income under which tax relief is available in respect of pensions and–

(a)   tax relief is not available to the member on contributions made to the scheme by the individual or, if the individual is an employee, by their employer, in respect of earnings to which benefits under the scheme relate;

(ab)   the scheme is liable to taxation on its income and gains and is of a kind specified in Schedule 1 to these Regulations; or

Statutory Instruments

(b)   all or most of the benefits paid by the scheme to members who are not in serious ill-health are subject to taxation.

For the purposes of this condition **"tax relief"** includes the grant of an exemption from tax.

Condition 3

The scheme is approved or recognised by, or registered with, the relevant tax authorities as a pension scheme in the country or territory in which it is established.

2(4)   In the case of an overseas pension scheme falling within paragraph (1)(b) the requirements are that—

(a)   the scheme rules must provide that at least 70% of a member's UK tax-relieved scheme funds will be designated by the scheme manager for the purpose of providing the member with an income for life, and

(b)   the pension benefits payable to the member under the scheme (and any lump sum associated with those benefits) under the scheme must be payable no earlier than they would be if pension rule 1 in section 165 applied.

2(5)   In this regulation—

   "international organisation" means an organisation to which section 1 of the International Organisations Act 1968 applies by virtue of an Order in Council under subsection (1) of that section;

   "occupational pension scheme" has the meaning given by section 150(5); and

   "UK tax-relieved scheme funds" means, in relation to a member, the sum of the member's UK tax-relieved fund and his relevant transfer fund, as defined respectively by regulations 2 and 3 of the Pension Schemes (Application of UK Provisions to Relevant Non-UK Schemes) Regulations 2006.

History – In reg. 2(3), the words "following conditions" substituted for the words "primary conditions and also meets one of Conditions A and B" by SI 2012/884, reg. 3(2)(a), with effect from 6 April 2012.
In reg. 2(3), the italic cross-headings "Condition 1", "Condition 2" and "Condition 3" substituted for the headings "Primary condition 1", "Primary condition 2" and "Condition A" respectively by SI 2012/884, reg. 3(2)(b), with effect from 6 April 2012.
In reg. 2(3), in Condition 2, in para. (ab) the words "Schedule 1" substituted for the words "the Schedule" by SI 2012/884, reg. 3(2)(c), with effect from 6 April 2012.
In reg. 2(3), Condition B omitted by SI 2012/884, reg. 3(2)(d), with effect from 6 April 2012.
In reg. 2(3), former Primary condition 2, para. (ab) inserted and the word "or" at the end of para. (a) omitted by SI 2007/1600, reg. 3 with effect from 1 July 2007.

RECOGNISED OVERSEAS PENSION SCHEMES: PRESCRIBED COUNTRIES OR TERRITORIES AND PRESCRIBED REQUIREMENTS

3(1)   For the purposes of section 150(8) (recognised overseas pension schemes), in addition to satisfying the requirements set out in regulation 2 above, the pension scheme must—

(a)   except where it falls within paragraph (1A), satisfy the requirement in paragraph (6); and

(b)   satisfy one or more of the following requirements—

   (i)   the requirement that the scheme must be established in a country or territory mentioned in paragraph (2),

   (ii)   the requirement in paragraph (4),

   (iii)   the requirement in paragraph (5).

3(1A)   A pension scheme falls within this paragraph if it is an overseas public service pension scheme or if it falls within regulation 2(1)(b).

3(1B)   A pension scheme is an **"overseas public service pension scheme"** for the purposes of paragraph (1A) if—

(a)   it is established in a country or territory outside the United Kingdom and is either—

   (i)   so established by or under the law of that country or territory, or

   (ii)   approved by the government of that country or territory; and

(b)   it is established for the purpose of providing benefits to individuals for or in respect of services rendered to that country or territory or any political subdivision or local authority thereof.

3(2)   The countries and territories referred to in paragraph (1)(b)(i) are—

(a)   the member States of the European Communities, other than the United Kingdom;

(b)   Iceland, Liechtenstein and Norway; and

(c)   any country or territory, other than New Zealand, in respect of which there is in force an Order in Council under section 788 of the Income and Corporation Taxes Act 1988 giving effect in the United Kingdom to an agreement which contains provision about–

    (i)   the exchange of information between the parties, and

    (ii)   non-discrimination.

3(3) For the purposes of paragraph (2)(c)(ii) an agreement "contains provision about nondiscrimination" if it provides that the nationals of a Contracting State shall not be subjected in the territory of the other Contracting State to any taxation, or any requirement connected to such taxation, which is other than, or more burdensome than, the taxation and connected requirements to which the nationals of the other State are or may be subjected in the same circumstances.

3(4) At the time of a transfer of sums or assets which would, subject to these Regulations, constitute a recognised transfer, a pension scheme must satisfy the condition in paragraph (4A) and the rules of that scheme must provide that–

(a)   at least 70% of the sums transferred will be designated by the scheme manager for the purpose of providing the member with an income for life;

(b)   the pension benefits (and any lump sum associated with those benefits) payable to the member under the scheme, to the extent that they relate to the transfer, are payable no earlier than they would be if pension rule 1 in section 165 applied; and

(c)   the scheme is open to persons resident in the country or territory in which it is established.

3(4A) Where the pension scheme–

(a)   is established in Guernsey, and

(b)   is an exempt pension contract or an exempt pension trust within the meaning of section 157E of the Income Tax (Guernsey) Law, 1975,

the scheme must not be open to non-residents of Guernsey.

3(5) At the time of a transfer of sums or assets which would, subject to these Regulations, constitute a recognised transfer the scheme must be of a kind specified in Schedule 2 to these Regulations.

3(6) Where tax relief in respect of benefits paid from the scheme is available to a member of the scheme who is not resident in the country or territory in which the scheme is established, the same or substantially the same tax relief must–

(a)   also be available to members of the scheme who are resident in the country or territory; and

(b)   apply regardless of whether the member was resident in the country or territory–

    (i)   when the member joined the scheme; or

    (ii)   for any period of time when they were a member of the scheme.

3(7) For the purposes of paragraph (6) **"tax relief"**–

(a)   is any tax relief that is available under the system of taxation of personal income in the country or territory in which the scheme is established; and

(b)   includes the grant of an exemption from tax other than an exemption which applies by virtue of double taxation arrangements.

3(8) In paragraph (7)(b) **"double taxation arrangements"** means arrangements made between the country or territory in which the scheme is established and another country or territory with a view to affording relief from double taxation.

History – In the heading to reg. 3, the word "requirements" substituted for the word "conditions" by SI 2012/1221, reg. 2(2)(a), with effect from 25 May 2012.

Reg. 3(1)–(1B) substituted for (1) by SI 2013/2259, reg. 8, operative from 14 October 2013 but with effect in relation to qualifying recognised overseas pension schemes (QROPS) in existence immediately before 6 April 2012 from that date, subject to transitional provisions in SI 2013/2259, reg. 6. Former reg. 3(1) read as follows:

"**3(1)** For the purposes of section 150(8) (recognised overseas pension schemes), in addition to satisfying the requirements set out in regulation 2 above, the pension scheme must satisfy–
(a)   the requirement in paragraph (6); and
(b)   one or more of the following requirements–
    (i)   the requirement that the scheme must be established in a country or territory mentioned in paragraph (2),
    (ii)   the requirement in paragraph (4),
    (iii)   the requirement in paragraph (5)."

In reg. 3(1), the words "the pension scheme must satisfy–" and para. (a) and (b) substituted for the former wording by SI 2012/884, reg. 4(a), with effect from 6 April 2012. The former wording read as follows:
"the pension scheme must–
(a)   be established in a country or territory mentioned in paragraph (2); or
(b)   satisfy the requirement in paragraph (4).".

In reg. 3(2), "paragraph (1)(b)(i)" substituted for "paragraph (1)(a)" by SI 2012/884, reg. 4(b)(i), with effect from 6 April 2012.

In reg. 3(2)(c), the words ", other than New Zealand," inserted by SI 2012/884, reg. 4(b)(ii), with effect from 6 April 2012.

Reg. 3(4) and (4A) substituted for former reg. 3(4) by SI 2012/1221, reg. 2(2)(b), with effect from 25 May 2012. Former reg. 3(4) read as follows:

> "**3(4)**   At the time of a transfer of sums or assets which would, subject to these Regulations, constitute a recognised transfer, the rules of the scheme must provide that–
>
> (a)   at least 70% of the sums transferred will be designated by the scheme manager for the purpose of providing the member with an income for life;
>
> (b)   the pension benefits (and any lump sum associated with those benefits) payable to the member under the scheme, to the extent that they relate to the transfer, are payable no earlier than they would be if pension rule 1 in section 165 applied; and
>
> (c)   the scheme is open to persons resident in the country or territory in which it is established.".

In former reg. 3(4), the words "The requirement is that," omitted from the beginning by SI 2012/884, reg. 4(c), with effect from 6 April 2012.

Reg. 3(5), (6), (7) and (8) inserted by SI 2012/884, reg. 4(d), with effect from 6 April 2012.

SCHEDULE 1

Regulation 2(3)

History – In the heading, "Schedule 1" substituted for "Schedule" by SI 2012/844, reg. 5, with effect from 6 April 2012.

SPECIFIED SCHEMES

A complying superannuation plan as defined in section 995-1 (definitions) of the Income Tax Assessment Act 1997 of Australia.

History – Schedule (now Sch. 1) inserted by SI 2007/1600, reg. 4 with effect from 1 July 2007.

SCHEDULE 2 – SPECIFIED SCHEMES

Regulation 3(5)

A pension scheme which is a KiwiSaver scheme as defined in section 4(1) (interpretation) of the KiwiSaver Act 2006 of New Zealand.

History – Sch. 2 inserted by SI 2012/844, reg. 6, with effect from 6 April 2012.

PENSIONS SCHEMES (APPLICATION OF UK PROVISIONS TO RELEVANT NON-UK SCHEMES) REGULATIONS 2006

(SI 2006/207, as amended by SI 2006/1960, SI 2007/493, SI 2009/2047, SI 2011/1751 and SI 2012/1795)

Made on 1 February 2006 by the Commissioners for Her Majesty's Revenue and Customs, in exercise of the powers conferred upon them by para. 3(2), (5) and (6), 4(2) and (4), 7, 12 and 19 of Sch. 34 to the Finance Act 2004. Operative from 6 April 2006.

PART 1 – INTRODUCTION

CITATION, COMMENCEMENT AND INTERPRETATION

1(1) These Regulations may be cited as the Pensions Schemes (Application of UK Provisions to Relevant Non-UK Schemes) Regulations 2006 and shall come into force on 6th April 2006.

1(2) In these Regulations–

"**the Act**" means the Finance Act 2004 any reference (without more) to a numbered section or Schedule is a reference, as the case requires, to the section of, or Schedule to, the Act which bears that number;

"**benefit crystallisation event 8**" means the event which constitutes benefit crystallisation event 8 in section 216;

"**recognised overseas pension scheme**" has the meaning given by section 150(8); and

"**relevant non-UK scheme**" has the same meaning given by paragraph 1(5) of Schedule 34.

"**taxable property**" has the meaning in Schedule 29A to the Act;

"**taxable property provisions**" has the meaning in paragraph 1(3) of that Schedule; and

"**transfer member**" of a scheme has the meaning in paragraph 1(8) of Schedule 34 to the Act.

History – In reg. 1(2), the definitions of "taxable property", "taxable property provisions" and "transfer member" inserted by SI 2006/1960, reg. 3, with effect from 6 April 2006.

PART 2 – APPLICATION AND COMPUTATION OF UK TAX CHARGES

COMPUTATION OF A MEMBER'S UK TAX-RELIEVED FUND UNDER A RELEVANT NON-UK SCHEME

2 The amount of a member's UK tax-relieved fund under a relevant non-UK scheme is the aggregate of–

(a)   the amounts which, for each tax year before that in which the computation falls to be made, would have been arrived at in relation to arrangements under the relevant non-UK scheme relating to the individual as pension input amounts under sections 230 to 238 of the Act (annual allowance) as they apply by virtue of paragraph 8 of Schedule 34 to the Act, and

(b)   the amount which would be so arrived at if the period beginning with 6 April of the tax year in which the computation falls to be made; and ending immediately before the making of the computation, were a tax year,

assuming that section 229(3) did not apply.

COMPUTATION OF A MEMBER'S RELEVANT TRANSFER FUND

3 The amount of a member's relevant transfer fund under a relevant non-UK scheme (that scheme being referred to here as "the RNUKS") is the sum of–

(a)   the amount crystallised by virtue of benefit crystallisation event 8 on the transfer from a UK registered scheme to the RNUKS; and

Statutory Instruments

(b)   so much of the member's UK tax-relieved fund under any other relevant non-UK scheme as has been transferred to the RNUKS but has not been subject to the unauthorised payments charge; and

(c)   so much of the member's relevant transfer fund under any other relevant non-UK scheme as has been transferred to the RNUKS–

    (i)   without being subject to the unauthorised payments charge;.

    (ii)   [omitted by SI 2006/1960, reg. 4.]

History – Reg. 3(c)(ii) and the word "and" which preceded it omitted by SI 2006/1960, reg. 4, with effect from 6 April 2006.

COMPUTATION OF A MEMBER'S TAXABLE ASSET TRANSFER FUND

3A(1)   The amount of a member's taxable asset transfer fund under a relevant non-UK scheme ("the RNUKS") is the sum of–

(a)   the amount crystallised by virtue of benefit crystallisation event 8 on the transfer from a UK registered pension scheme to the RNUKS; and

(b)   so much of the member's taxable asset transfer fund under any other relevant non- UK scheme as has been transferred to the RNUKS without being subject to the unauthorised payments charge.

3A(2)   Accordingly, the member's taxable asset transfer fund ("TATF") shall form part of the member's relevant transfer fund ("RTF"), except in a case where the member's RTF consists solely of a UK tax-relieved fund which has been transferred to the RNUKS.

History – Reg. 3A inserted by SI 2006/1960, reg. 5, with effect from 6 April 2006.

ATTRIBUTING PAYMENTS TO PARTICULAR FUNDS UNDER A RELEVANT NON-UK SCHEME

4(1)   This regulation applies to determine to which part of a relevant non-UK scheme a payment to, or in respect of, a member is referable.

4(2)   It shall be assumed that–

(a)   payments made by the scheme to or in respect of the member are made out of the member's UK tax-relieved fund in priority to any other fund under that scheme; and

(b)   the amount of the member's UK tax-relieved fund is reduced (but not below nil) by the amount paid out of the scheme.

4(3)   If the member's UK tax-relieved fund is nil, or has been reduced to nil, the following Rules apply (with an earlier Rule applying in preference to a later Rule).

Rule 1

Where an unauthorised payment is treated as made by the scheme to the transfer member by virtue of section 174A–

(a)   the payment shall be treated as made out of the member's RTF and TATF, but

(b)   the interest in taxable property, in respect of which the unauthorised payment is treated as made, shall represent the payment and form part of the member's RTF and TATF (an "appropriated asset"), up to an amount equal to the amount of that payment.

Rule 2

Accordingly, if a scheme transfers that appropriated asset (or an interest in a vehicle through which the scheme holds the interest in the taxable property indirectly), or part of it, to another pension scheme, that transfer shall be treated as a transfer of the whole or part, as the case may be, of the member's RTF and TATF (limited to the amount of the unauthorised payment) to that other scheme, falling (if appropriate) within regulation 3A(1)(b).

Rule 3

If a scheme disposes of (other than to another pension scheme) an appropriated asset (or an interest in a vehicle through which the scheme holds the interest in the taxable property indirectly), or part of it, any other property which directly or indirectly represents proceeds of either of those interests (limited to the amount of the unauthorised payment) shall form part of the member's RTF and TATF.

Rule 4

This Rule applies to payments made by the scheme to or in respect of the member, other than–

(a)   a transfer of an interest in taxable property or an interest in a vehicle through which the scheme holds the interest in the taxable property indirectly, and

(b)   payments treated as made by virtue of section 174A.

So far as the member's RTF and TATF are not represented by appropriated assets—

(a)   where the member has both an RTF and a TATF, and the amount of his RTF exceeds the amount of his TATF, such payments shall, to the extent of that excess, be treated as made out of his RTF (but not his TATF) and as reducing the RTF, and subject thereto

(b)   such payments are made out of the member's RTF and TATF in priority to any other fund under that scheme, and reduce (but not below nil) the amount of the RTF and TATF.

4(4)   In paragraph (3), references to payments made or treated as made by virtue of section 174A include references to payments treated as made by regulations under paragraph 37 of Schedule 29A, or paragraph 7A of Schedule 34, to the Act.

History – In reg. 4(2)(b) the words "(but not below nil)" inserted by SI 2006/1960, reg. 6, with effect from 6 April 2006. In reg. 4(3) the words from "(but not below nil)" to the end substituted by SI 2006/1960, reg. 7, with effect from 6 April 2006. Reg. 4(4) inserted by SI 2006/1960, reg. 8, with effect from 6 April 2006.

TAXABLE PROPERTY PROVISIONS TO APPLY TO A TRANSFER MEMBER OF A RELEVANT NON-UK SCHEME (TO PAYMENTS REFERABLE TO HIS TAXABLE ASSET TRANSFER FUND)

4A   The—

(a)   taxable property provisions, and

(b)   regulations made under paragraph 37 of Schedule 29A or paragraph 7A of Schedule 34,

apply to a transfer member of a relevant non-UK scheme, in relation to payments treated as made by those provisions or regulations which are referable to the member's taxable asset transfer fund under the scheme, but subject to the modifications in regulations 4B to 4D.

History – Reg. 4A inserted by SI 2006/1960, reg. 9, with effect from 6 April 2006.

UNAUTHORISED PAYMENTS CHARGE TO APPLY (IN LIEU OF SCHEME CHARGEABLE PAYMENT)

4B(1)   The scheme chargeable payment provisions in sections 185A to 185I shall not apply to a relevant non-UK scheme.

4B(2)   But, during such time as an appropriated asset forms the whole or part of a transfer member's TATF—

(a)   the scheme shall be treated as making unauthorised payments to that member equal in amount to the scheme chargeable payments (in respect of income and gains) which would have been computed in accordance with those sections, and

(b)   the transfer member shall be liable to pay the unauthorised payments charge in respect of such payments.

4B(3)   Where the scheme's interest in taxable property is not wholly referable to the transfer member's TATF, the amount of the unauthorised payment shall be proportionately reduced.

History – Reg. 4B inserted by SI 2006/1960, reg. 9, with effect from 6 April 2006.

MODIFICATION OF PARAGRAPH 15 OF SCHEDULE 29A

4C   Paragraph 15 of Schedule 29A applies to the transfer member of a relevant non-UK scheme as if "insurance company" included any person—

(a)   resident in a country or territory outside the European Economic Area,

(b)   whose business consists of, or includes, the effecting or carrying out of contracts of long-term insurance (within the meaning in Part 2 of Schedule 1 to the Financial Services and Markets Act 2000 (Regulated Activities) Order 2001), and

(c)   who is regulated in the conduct of that business by—

(i)   the government of that country or territory, or

(ii)   a body established under the law of that country or territory for the purpose of regulating such business.

History – Reg. 4C inserted by SI 2006/1960, reg. 9, with effect from 6 April 2006.

MODIFICATIONS OF PARAGRAPHS 29 AND 31 OF SCHEDULE 29A

4D(1)   This regulation applies where—

(a)   a relevant non-UK scheme acquires an interest in taxable property;

Statutory Instruments

(b)   the interest is acquired in the circumstances mentioned in paragraph 32(3), (5) (excluding paragraphs (a) and (b)) or (6) (excluding paragraphs (a) and (b)) of Schedule 29A; and

(c)   the whole or part of the consideration for the acquisition is rent.

4D(2)   The amount of the consideration (or the part that is rent) shall not be the relevant rental value of the property (as provided by paragraph 34(2) of Schedule 29A).

4D(3)   Each payment of rent (or the aggregate of such payments during a year, if there are more than one) shall be treated, for the purposes of the taxable property provisions, as if the pension scheme or other person who acquired the interest were being granted a lease for the period for which the rent is paid, in consideration of the rent (or aggregate) so paid.

History – Reg. 4D inserted by SI 2006/1960, reg. 9, with effect from 6 April 2006.

PART 3

MODIFICATIONS TO PART 4 OF THE FINANCE ACT 2004 IN RESPECT OF RELEVANT NON-UK SCHEMES

5   Part 4 of the Finance Act 2004 shall be modified in respect of relevant non-UK schemes, within the meaning of paragraph 1(5) of Schedule 34, in accordance with the following provisions of these Regulations.

MODIFICATION OF SECTION 165

6   In section 165 (pension rules)–

(a)   in subsection (1), in pension rule 4 omit from "but a scheme pension" to the end, and

(b)   in subsection (3A), for "scheme administrator" (in both places) substitute "scheme manager".

History – Reg. 6 substituted by SI 2012/1795, reg. 3, with effect for the tax year 2011–12 and subsequent tax years.

MODIFICATION OF SECTION 167

7   In section 167 (pension death benefit rules)–

(a)   in subsection (1), in pension death benefit rule 3 omit from "but a dependants' scheme pension" to the end, and

(b)   in subsection (2A), for "scheme administrator" (in both places) substitute "scheme manager".

History – Reg. 7 substituted by SI 2012/1795, reg. 4, with effect for the tax year 2011–12 and subsequent tax years.

MODIFICATION OF SECTION 227

8   [Omitted by SI 2011/1751, reg. 12(2).]

History – Reg. 8 omitted by SI 2011/1751, reg. 12(2), which came into force on 11 August 2011, with effect for the tax year 2011–12 and subsequent tax years. Former reg. 8 read as follows:
    "**8**   In section 227(3)(b) for "scheme administrator" substitute "scheme manager".".

MODIFICATION OF SECTION 231

9   In section 231–

(a)   in subsection (3) for "the consumer prices index" substitute "the relevant index"; and

(b)   at the end add–

    "**231(4)**   In this section **"the relevant index"** means–

        (a)   if there is an index of the movement of consumer prices maintained, or officially recognised, by the government of the country or territory in which the recognised overseas scheme is established, that index, or

        (b)   if there is no such index, the consumer prices index.".

History – Reg. 9(a) substituted by SI 2011/1751, reg. 12(3)(a), which came into force on 11 August 2011, with effect in relation to pension input periods ending in the tax year 2011–12 and subsequent tax years. Former reg. 9(a) read as follows:
    "(a)   in subsection (3)–
        (i)   in paragraph (b) for "the retail prices index" substitute "a relevant index";
        (ii)   omit paragraph (c); and".
In reg. 9(b), the inserted subsection (4) substituted by SI 2011/1751, reg. 12(3)(b), which came into force on 11 August 2011, with effect in relation to pension input periods ending in the tax year 2011–12 and subsequent tax years. The former inserted subsection (4) read as follows:
    "**231(4)**   In this section **"relevant index"** means–
    (a)   an index of the movement of retail prices maintained, or officially recognised, by the government of the country or territory in which the recognised overseas scheme is established; or
    (b)   if there is no such index as is mentioned in paragraph (a) of this definition, the retail prices index.".

MODIFICATION OF SECTION 235

10   In section 235–

(a)   in subsection (3) for "the consumer prices index" substitute "the relevant index"; and

(b)   at the end add–

"**235(4)**   In this section **"the relevant index"** means–

    (a)   if there is an index of the movement of consumer prices maintained, or officially recognised, by the government of the country or territory in which the recognised overseas scheme is established, that index, or

    (b)   if there is no such index, the consumer prices index.".

History – Reg. 10(a) substituted by SI 2011/1751, reg. 12(4)(a), which came into force on 11 August 2011, with effect in relation to pension input periods ending in the tax year 2011–12 and subsequent tax years. Former reg. 10(a) read as follows:

    "(a)   in subsection (3)–

       (i)   in paragraph (b) for "the retail prices index" substitute "a relevant index";

       (ii)   omit paragraph (c); and".

In reg. 10(b), the inserted subsection (4) substituted by SI 2011/1751, reg. 12(4)(b), which came into force on 11 August 2011, with effect in relation to pension input periods ending in the tax year 2011–12 and subsequent tax years. The former inserted subsection (4) read as follows:

    "**235(4)**   In this section **"relevant index"** means–

    (a)   an index of the movement of retail prices maintained, or officially recognised, by the government of the country or territory in which the recognised overseas scheme is established; or

    (b)   if there is no such index as is mentioned in paragraph (a) of this definition, the retail prices index.".

MODIFICATION OF SECTION 275

11(1)   In the heading of section 275 at the end add "and Non-EEA annuity provider".

11(2)   At the end of the section add–

"**275(3)**   In this Part **"non-EEA annuity provider"** means a person resident in a country or territory outside the European Economic Area–

(a)   whose normal business includes the provision of annuities; and

(b)   who is regulated in the conduct of that business–

    (i)   by the government of that country or territory; or

    (ii)   a body established under the law of that country or territory for the purpose of regulating such business.".

MODIFICATION OF SECTION 276

12   In section 276(2) for "scheme administrator" substitute "scheme manager".

MODIFICATION OF SECTION 279

13(1)   Section 279(1) shall be modified as follows.

13(2)   At the appropriate points in the alphabetical list insert–

""**applicable pension scheme"**, in relation to a pension sharing order in respect of a member's spouse, ex-spouse, civil partner or former civil partner, means a scheme which is–

(a)   a recognised overseas pension scheme within the meaning of this Part; or

(b)   a scheme which is recognised for tax purposes under the law of either the country or territory in which it is situate or that of the country or territory in which the pension sharing order is made;"; and

""**ex-spouse"**, in relation to a member, means the other party to a marriage with the member that has been dissolved or annulled;

"**former civil partner"**, in relation to a member means the other party to a civil partnership with the member that has been dissolved or annulled;";

13(3)   For the definitions of "pension credit" and "pension debit" substitute–

""**pension credit"** and **"pension debit"** mean respectively the amount by which–

(a)   the entitlement of a member's spouse, ex-spouse, civil partner or former civil partner under an applicable pension scheme, is increased; and

(b)   the entitlement of a member under a qualifying recognised overseas pension scheme is decreased,

pursuant to a pension sharing order;".

14,193   **Pensions Schemes (Application etc.) Regs 2006**   **SI 2006/207**

Statutory Instruments

13(4)   For the definition of "pension sharing order or provision" substitute–

""**pension sharing order**" means an order of a court, by virtue of which amounts are transferred from a recognised overseas pension scheme of a member to an applicable pension scheme of that member's spouse, ex-spouse, civil partner or former civil partner, in or in connection with proceedings relating to the dissolution or annulment of the marriage or civil partnership of the parties;".

History – In reg. 13(2) the words ", ex-spouse, civil partner or former civil partner" substituted for "or ex-spouse" by SI 2007/493, reg. 3(2)(a), with effect from 22 February 2007.
In reg. 13(2) the definition of "former civil partner" inserted by SI 2007/493, reg. 3(2)(b), with effect from 22 February 2007.
In reg. 13(3)(a) the words ", ex-spouse, civil partner or former civil partner" substituted for "or ex-spouse" by SI 2007/493, reg. 3(3), with effect from 22 February 2007.
In reg. 13(4) the words ", ex-spouse, civil partner or former civil partner" substituted for "or ex-spouse" by SI 2007/493, reg. 3(4)(a), with effect from 22 February 2007.
In reg. 13(4) the words "or civil partnership" inserted by SI 2007/493, reg. 3(4)(b), with effect from 22 February 2007.

MODIFICATION OF SCHEDULE 28

14(1)   Schedule 28 is modified as follows.

14(2)   In paragraph 1–

(a)   in sub-paragraph (a) after "registered medical practitioner" insert "or a recognised medical practitioner";

(b)   at the end of the paragraph add–

"In this paragraph **"recognised medical practitioner"** means a medical practitioner practising outside the United Kingdom who is authorised, licensed or registered to practise medicine in the country or territory, outside the United Kingdom, in which either the scheme or the member is resident.".

14(3)   In the following provisions for "scheme administrator" substitute "scheme manager".

The provisions are–

(a)   paragraph 1(a);

(b)   paragraph 2 (in each place where the expression occurs);

(c)   paragraph 10 (in each place where the expression occurs);

(ca)   paragraph 10A (in each place where the expression occurs);

(cb)   paragraph 10B (in each place where the expression occurs);

(d)   paragraph 13(3);

(da)   paragraph 14E(2);

(e)   paragraph 16(1) and (2);

(f)   paragraph 24 (in each place where the expression occurs);

(fa)   paragraph 24A (in each place where the expression occurs);

(fb)   paragraph 24B (in each place where the expression occurs);

(fc)   paragraph 24G(2);

(g)   paragraph 27(3).

14(4)   Omit paragraphs 3(1)(b), 6(1)(c), 17(1)(b) and 20(1)(c).

14(5)   In paragraph 15(2)(b) and (3) omit ", in the opinion of the scheme administrator".

14(6)   At the end of the Schedule add–

"Part 3 – Relevant Non UK Schemes – Interpretation

CONSTRUCTION OF REFERENCES TO INSURANCE COMPANIES

28(1)   In this Schedule, in its application to a scheme established in a country or territory outside the European Economic Area, any reference to an insurance company includes a non-EEA annuity provider.

28(2)   Section 275(3) defines "non-EEA annuity provider".".

History – Reg. 14(3)(c) substituted by SI 2012/1795, reg. 5(2), with effect for the tax year 2011–12 and subsequent tax years.
Reg. 14(3)(ca), (cb) inserted by SI 2012/1795, reg. 5(3), with effect for the tax year 2011–12 and subsequent tax years.
Reg. 14(3)(da) inserted by SI 2012/1795, reg. 5(4), with effect for the tax year 2011–12 and subsequent tax years.
Reg. 14(3)(f) substituted by SI 2012/1795 reg. 5(5), with effect for the tax year 2011–12 and subsequent tax years.
Reg. 14(3)(fa)–(fc) inserted by SI 2012/1795, reg. 5(6), with effect for the tax year 2011–12 and subsequent tax years.

MODIFICATION OF SCHEDULE 29

15(1)   Schedule 29 is modified as follows.

15(2)   In paragraph 1 after sub-paragraph (4) insert–

"**1(4A)**   In determining whether all or part of the member's lifetime allowance is available–

(a)   there shall be disregarded any amount treated as crystallising by virtue of a relevant BCE; but

(b)   the amount of the allowance available shall be reduced by the amount determined in accordance with sub-paragraph (4B) or (4C), as the case may require.

1(4B)   Where benefit crystallisation event 8 has occurred, the member's lifetime allowance that is available shall be reduced by the aggregate of–

(a)   the referable portion of any previous pension commencement lump sum paid to or in respect of the member by a recognised overseas pension scheme; and

(b)   the referable portion of the amount which would have crystallised by virtue of the member becoming entitled to a pension, had the scheme paying it been a registered pension scheme and disregarding paragraph 2 of Schedule 32.

1(4C)   Where the paragraph 15 BCE has occurred, the member's lifetime allowance that is available shall be reduced by the aggregate of–

(a)   the referable portion of any previous pension commencement lump sum to which the member became entitled under a relevant non-UK scheme since the paragraph 15 BCE occurred; and

(b)   in respect of any pension to which the member has become entitled since the paragraph 15 BCE occurred, the referable portion of the amount which would have crystallised by virtue of the member's becoming entitled to the pension, had the scheme paying it been a registered pension scheme and disregarding paragraph 2 of Schedule 32.".

15(3)   In paragraph 2–

(a)   in sub-paragraph (6) for the definition of AAC substitute–
"AAC is the aggregate of–

(a)   the amounts crystallised by each benefit crystallisation event (other than a relevant BCE) which has occurred in relation to the member before the member becomes entitled to the lump sum on each occasion on which entitlement to a pension arises, as adjusted under sub-paragraph (7); and

(b)   if a relevant BCE has occurred, RP.

RP is the referable portion of the amount which would have crystallised, had the scheme paying it been a registered pension scheme and disregarding paragraphs 2 and 15A of Schedule 32 , in respect of any previous pension commencement lump sum or pension to which the member became entitled since the relevant BCE occurred, as adjusted under sub-paragraph (7) (but excluding any amount included in paragraph (a)).";

(aa)   in sub-paragraph (7) for "the relevant amount" substitute "the amount which is, or would have, crystallised";

(b)   after sub-paragraph (7) insert–
"**2(7ZA)**   The member's becoming entitled to a pension commencement lump sum, or to a pension, as mentioned in the definition of RP in sub-paragraph (6) shall be treated as a benefit crystallisation event for the purposes of sub-paragraph (7).".

(c)   after sub-paragraph (7A) insert–
"**2(7B)**   But sub-paragraph (7A)(b) does not apply to anything which, but for paragraph 2 or 15A of Schedule 32 , would have constituted a relevant BCE."

15(3A)   In paragraph 3, after sub-paragraph (7) insert–
"**3(7ZA)**   Where a relevant BCE has occurred in relation to the member, sub-paragraph (6) has effect as if for the definition of "AC" in sub-paragraph (7) there were substituted–
""AC" is–

(a)   in a case where the member becomes entitled to the pension before reaching the age of 75, the referable portion of the amount that, had the scheme been a registered pension scheme, would have crystallised by reason of the member becoming entitled to the pension, disregarding paragraph 3 of Schedule 32, and

(b)   in a case where the member becomes entitled to the pension after reaching that age, the referable portion of the amount that would have been so crystallised (disregarding that paragraph) but for paragraph 2 of that Schedule, had the scheme been a registered pension scheme."'"

15(4)   In paragraph 4—

(a)   in sub-paragraph (1)(a) after "registered medical practitioner" insert "or a recognised medical practitioner";

(b)   at the end of the paragraph add—

"**4(4)**   In sub-paragraph (1) **"recognised medical practitioner"** means a medical practitioner practising outside the United Kingdom who is authorised, licensed or registered to practise medicine in the country or territory, outside the United Kingdom, in which either the scheme or the member is resident.

4(5)   In determining whether all or part of the member's lifetime allowance is available—

(a)   there shall be disregarded any amount treated as crystallising by virtue of a relevant BCE; but

(b)   the amount of the allowance available shall be reduced by the amount determined in accordance with sub-paragraph (6) or (7), as the case may require.

4(6)   Where benefit crystallisation event 8 has occurred, the member's lifetime allowance that is available shall be reduced by the aggregate of—

(a)   the referable portion of any previous pension commencement lump sum paid to or in respect of the member by a recognised overseas pension scheme; and

(b)   the referable portion of the amount which would have crystallised by virtue of the member becoming entitled to a pension, had the scheme paying it been a registered pension scheme and disregarding paragraph 2 of Schedule 32.

4(7)   Where the paragraph 15 BCE has occurred, the member's lifetime allowance that is available shall be reduced by the aggregate of—

(a)   the referable portion of any earlier pension commencement lump sum to which the member became entitled under a relevant non-UK scheme since the paragraph 15 BCE occurred; and

(b)   in respect of any pension to which the member has become entitled since the paragraph 15 BCE occurred, the referable portion of the amount which would have crystallised by virtue of the member's becoming entitled to the pension, had the scheme paying it been a registered pension scheme and disregarding paragraph 2 of Schedule 32.".

15(5)   In paragraph 5(1)(c) after "benefit crystallisation event" insert—

", other than an event which constitutes a relevant BCE,".

15(6)   At the end of paragraph 7 add—

"**7(6)**   In determining whether all or part of the member's lifetime allowance is available—

(a)   there shall be disregarded any amount treated as crystallising by virtue of a relevant BCE; but

(b)   the amount of the allowance available shall be reduced by the amount determined in accordance with sub-paragraph (7) or (8), as the case may require.

7(7)   Where benefit crystallisation event 8 has occurred, the member's lifetime allowance that is available shall be reduced by the aggregate of—

(a)   the referable portion of any previous pension commencement lump sum paid to or in respect of the member by a recognised overseas pension scheme; and

(b)   the referable portion of the amount which would have crystallised by virtue of the member becoming entitled to a pension, had the scheme paying it been a registered pension scheme and disregarding paragraph 2 of Schedule 32.

7(8)   Where the paragraph 15 BCE has occurred, the member's lifetime allowance that is available shall be reduced by the aggregate of—

(a)   the referable portion of any earlier pension commencement lump sum to which the member became entitled under a relevant non-UK scheme since the paragraph 15 BCE occurred; and

(b)   in respect of any pension to which the member has become entitled since the paragraph 15 BCE occurred, the referable portion of the amount which would have crystallised by virtue of the member's becoming entitled to the pension, had the scheme paying it been a registered pension scheme and disregarding paragraph 2 of Schedule 32.".

15(7) At the end of paragraph 10 add–

"**10(4)** In determining whether all or part of the member's lifetime allowance is available–

(a) there shall be disregarded any amount treated as crystallising by virtue of a relevant BCE; but

(b) the amount of the allowance available shall be reduced by the amount determined in accordance with sub-paragraph (5) or (6), as the case may require.

10(5) Where benefit crystallisation event 8 has occurred, the member's lifetime allowance that is available shall be reduced by the aggregate of–

(a) the referable portion of any previous pension commencement lump sum paid to or in respect of the member by a recognised overseas pension scheme; and

(b) the referable portion of the amount which would have crystallised by virtue of the member becoming entitled to a pension, had the scheme paying it been a registered pension scheme and disregarding paragraph 2 of Schedule 32.

10(6) Where the paragraph 15 BCE has occurred, the member's lifetime allowance that is available shall be reduced by the aggregate of–

(a) the referable portion of any earlier pension commencement lump sum to which the member became entitled under a relevant non-UK scheme since the paragraph 15 BCE occurred; and

(b) in respect of any pension to which the member has become entitled since the paragraph 15 BCE occurred, the referable portion of the amount which would have crystallised by virtue of the member's becoming entitled to the pension, had the scheme paying it been a registered pension scheme and disregarding paragraph 2 of Schedule 32.".

15(8) In paragraph 11 after sub-paragraph (b) insert–

"(bb) it is not paid from the relevant transfer fund of a qualifying recognised overseas pension scheme,

(bc) it is not paid from the UK tax-relieved fund of a relevant non-UK scheme,".

15(9) In paragraph 4(1)(a), and paragraph 19(1)(d) and (2)(e) for "scheme administrator" substitute "scheme manager".

15(9A) In paragraph 12 (interpretation of Part 1), after sub-paragraph (1A) insert–

"**12(1B)** But sub-paragraph (1A)(b) does not apply to anything which, but for paragraph 2 of Schedule 32, would have constituted a relevant BCE."

15(10) After paragraph 12 add–

"INTERPRETATION OF PART 1 – NON-UK SCHEMES

12A(1) The referable portion of a lump sum, pension or an amount which is or would have been crystallised is–

(a) in a case where benefit crystallisation event 8 has occurred, the extent to which it is referable to the member's relevant transfer fund; or

(b) in a case where the paragraph 15 BCE has occurred, the extent to which it is referable to the member's UK tax-relieved fund.

12A(2) In this Part–

"**the paragraph 15 BCE**" means the benefit crystallisation event treated as occurring by virtue of paragraph 15 of Schedule 34;

"**relevant BCE**" means–

(a) benefit crystallisation event 8; or

(b) the paragraph 15 BCE;

"**relevant transfer fund**" shall be construed in accordance with paragraph 4(2) of Schedule 34;

"**UK tax-relieved fund**" shall be construed in accordance with paragraph 3(2) of Schedule 34.".

History – In reg. 15(2), the inserted para. 1(4B)(b) the words "and disregarding paragraph 2 of Schedule 32" inserted by SI 2012/1795, reg. 6(2)(a), with effect in relation to any lump sum to which a person becomes entitled for the purposes of Part 4 of the Finance Act 2004 on or after 6 April 2011.

In reg. 15(2), the inserted para. 1(4C)(b) the words "and disregarding paragraph 2 of Schedule 32" inserted by SI 2012/1795, reg. 6(2)(b), with effect in relation to any lump sum to which a person becomes entitled for the purposes of Part 4 of the Finance Act 2004 on or after 6 April 2011.

In reg. 15(2), the inserted para. 1(4A), (4B) and (4C) substituted for the former inserted para. 1(4A) and (4B) by SI 2009/2047, reg. 3, with effect where there is a paragraph 15 BCE which is treated as occurring on a date ("the specified date") on or after 6 April 2006, and the member becomes entitled to a lump sum under a relevant non-UK scheme on or after the specified date. For this purpose "paragraph 15 BCE" means the benefit crystallisation event treated as occurring by virtue of FA 2004, Sch. 34, para. 15, and "relevant non-UK scheme" has the meaning given by FA 2004, Sch. 34, para. 1(5). The former inserted para. 1(4A) and (4B) read as follows:

"**1(4A)**   In determining whether all or part of the member's lifetime allowance is available–
  (a)   an amount treated as crystallising by virtue of benefit crystallisation event 8 shall be disregarded; and
  (b)   the amount of the allowance available shall be reduced by the aggregate of–
      (i)   the amount of any previous pension commencement lump sum paid to or in respect of the member by a recognised overseas pension scheme, to the extent that the lump sum is referable to the member's relevant transfer fund, and
      (ii)   the amount which would have crystallised by virtue of the member becoming entitled to a pension, had the scheme paying it been a registered pension scheme, to the extent that it is so referable.

1(4B)   For the purposes of sub-paragraph (4A) "the member's relevant transfer fund" has the meaning given in paragraph 4(2) of Schedule 34(a).".

In reg. 15(3)(a), the definition of "AAC" substituted by SI 2009/2047, reg. 4(a), with effect where there is a paragraph 15 BCE which is treated as occurring on a date ("the specified date") on or after 6 April 2006, and the member becomes entitled to a lump sum under a relevant non-UK scheme on or after the specified date. For this purpose "paragraph 15 BCE" means the benefit crystallisation event treated as occurring by virtue of FA 2004, Sch. 34, para. 15, and "relevant non-UK scheme" has the meaning given by FA 2004, Sch. 34, para. 1(5). The former definition read as follows:

"AAC is the aggregate of–
  (a)   the amounts crystallised by each benefit crystallisation event (other than benefit crystallisation event 8) which has occurred in relation to the member before the member becomes entitled to the lump sum (or treated as crystallised) on each occasion on which entitlement to a pension arises; and
  (b)   the amount which would have crystallised, had the scheme paying it been a registered pension scheme–
      (i)   on entitlement arising to any pension commencement lump sum, to the extent that the lump sum is referable to the member's relevant transfer fund, or
      (ii)   on entitlement arising to a pension, to the extent that it is so referable.".

In reg. 15(3)(a), the definition of "AAC" in para. (a) the words ", as adjusted under sub-paragraph (7)" inserted by SI 2012/1795, reg. 6(3)(a)(i), with effect in relation to any lump sum to which a person becomes entitled for the purposes of Part 4 of the Finance Act 2004 on or after 6 April 2011.

In reg. 15(3)(a), the definition of "RP" substituted by SI 2012/1795, reg. 6(3)(a)(ii), with effect in relation to any lump sum to which a person becomes entitled for the purposes of Part 4 of the Finance Act 2004 on or after 6 April 2011.

Reg. 15(3)(aa) inserted by SI 2012/1795, reg. 6(3)(b), with effect in relation to any lump sum to which a person becomes entitled for the purposes of Part 4 of the Finance Act 2004 on or after 6 April 2011.

Reg. 15(3)(b) the words "after sub-paragraph (7)" substituted for the words "after sub-paragraph (6)" by SI 2012/1795, reg. 6(3)(c)(i), with effect in relation to any lump sum to which a person becomes entitled for the purposes of Part 4 of the Finance Act 2004 on or after 6 April 2011.

In reg. 15(3)(b), the inserted para. 2(6A) renumbered as para. 2(7ZA) and the words "sub-paragraph (6)" therein substituted for the words "paragraph (6)" by SI 2012/1795, reg. 6(3)(c)(ii), (iii), with effect in relation to any lump sum to which a person becomes entitled for the purposes of Part 4 of the Finance Act 2004 on or after 6 April 2011.

In reg. 15(3)(b), in the inserted para. 2(6A), the words "the definition of RP" substituted for the words "paragraph (b) of the definition of AAC" by SI 2009/2047, reg. 4(b), with effect where there is a paragraph 15 BCE which is treated as occurring on a date ("the specified date") on or after 6 April 2006, and the member becomes entitled to a lump sum under a relevant non-UK scheme on or after the specified date. For this purpose "paragraph 15 BCE" means the benefit crystallisation event treated as occurring by virtue of FA 2004, Sch. 34, para. 15, and "relevant non-UK scheme" has the meaning given by FA 2004, Sch. 34, para. 1(5).

Reg. 15(3)(c) inserted by SI 2012/1795, reg. 6(3)(d), with effect in relation to any lump sum to which a person becomes entitled for the purposes of Part 4 of the Finance Act 2004 on or after 6 April 2011.

Reg. 15(3A) inserted by SI 2012/1795, reg. 6(4), with effect in relation to any lump sum to which a person becomes entitled for the purposes of Part 4 of the Finance Act 2004 on or after 6 April 2011.

In reg. 15(4), in inserted para. 4(5)(b), the words "sub-paragraph (6) or (7)" substituted for the words "sub-paragraph (5) or (6)" by SI 2012/1795, reg. 6(5)(b), with effect in relation to any lump sums paid on or after 6 April 2011.

In reg. 15(4), in inserted para. 4(6)(b), the words "and disregarding paragraph 2 of Schedule 32" inserted by SI 2012/1795, reg. 6(5)(c), with effect in relation to any lump sums paid on or after 6 April 2011.

In reg. 15(4), in inserted para. 4(7)(b), the words "and disregarding paragraph 2 of Schedule 32" inserted by SI 2012/1795, reg. 6(5)(d), with effect in relation to any lump sums paid on or after 6 April 2011.

In reg. 15(4), inserted para. 4(3)–(6) renumbered as para. 4(4)–(7) by SI 2012/1795, reg. 6(5)(a), with effect in relation to any lump sums paid on or after 6 April 2011.

In reg. 15(4)(b), former inserted para. 4(4), (5) and (6) substituted for former inserted para. 4(4) by SI 2009/2047, reg. 5, with effect where there is a paragraph 15 BCE which is treated as occurring on a date ("the specified date") on or after 6 April 2006, and the member becomes entitled to a lump sum under a relevant non-UK scheme on or after the specified date. For this purpose "paragraph 15 BCE" means the benefit crystallisation event treated as occurring by virtue of FA 2004, Sch. 34, para. 15, and "relevant non-UK scheme" has the meaning given by FA 2004, Sch. 34, para. 1(5). Former inserted para. 4(4) read as follows:

"**4(4)**   In determining whether all or part of the member's lifetime allowance is available–
  (a)   an amount crystallising by virtue of benefit crystallisation event 8 shall be disregarded; and
  (b)   the amount of the allowance available shall be reduced by the aggregate of–
      (i)   the amount of any previous pension commencement lump sum which has been paid to or in respect of the member by a recognised overseas pension scheme, to the extent that it is referable to the member's relevant transfer fund and
      (ii)   the amount which would have crystallised on the member becoming entitled to a pension, had the scheme paying it been a registered pension scheme, to the extent that it is so referable.".

In reg. 15(5), text inserted into para. 5(1)(c) substituted by SI 2009/2047, reg. 6, with effect where there is a paragraph 15 BCE which is treated as occurring on a date ("the specified date") on or after 6 April 2006, and the member becomes entitled to a lump sum under a relevant non-UK scheme on or after the specified date. For this purpose "paragraph 15 BCE" means the benefit crystallisation event treated as occurring by virtue of FA 2004, Sch. 34, para. 15, and "relevant non-UK scheme" has the meaning given by FA 2004, Sch. 34, para. 1(5). The former inserted text read as follows:

", other than an event which constitutes benefit crystallisation event 8".

In reg. 15(6), in inserted para. 7(7)(b), the words "and disregarding paragraph 2 of Schedule 32" inserted by SI 2012/1795, reg. 6(6)(a), with effect in relation to any lump sums paid on or after 6 April 2011.

In reg. 15(6), in inserted para. 7(8)(b), the words "and disregarding paragraph 2 of Schedule 32" inserted by SI 2012/1795, reg. 6(6)(b), with effect in relation to any lump sums paid on or after 6 April 2011.

In reg. 15(6), inserted para. 7(6), (7) and (8) substituted for former inserted para. 7(6) by SI 2009/2047, reg. 7, with effect where there is a paragraph 15 BCE which is treated as occurring on a date ("the specified date") on or after 6 April 2006, and the member becomes entitled to a lump sum under a relevant non-UK scheme on or after the specified date. For this purpose "paragraph 15 BCE" means the benefit crystallisation event treated as occurring by virtue of FA 2004, Sch. 34, para. 15, and "relevant non-UK scheme" has the meaning given by FA 2004, Sch. 34, para. 1(5). Former inserted para. 7(6) read as follows:

> "7(6)   In determining whether all or part of the member's lifetime allowance is available–
> (a)   an amount crystallising by virtue of benefit crystallisation event 8 shall be disregarded; and
> (b)   the amount of the allowance available shall be reduced by the aggregate of–
>   (i)   the amount of any previous pension commencement lump sum which has been paid to or in respect of the member by a recognised overseas pension scheme, to the extent that it is referable to the member's relevant transfer fund and
>   (ii)   the amount which would have crystallised on the member becoming entitled to a pension, had the scheme paying it been a registered pension scheme, to the extent that it is so referable.".

In reg. 15(7), in inserted para. 10(5)(b), the words "and disregarding paragraph 2 of Schedule 32" inserted by SI 2012/1795, reg. 6(7)(a), with effect in relation to any lump sums paid on or after 6 April 2011.

In reg. 15(7), in inserted para. 10(6)(b), the words "and disregarding paragraph 2 of Schedule 32" inserted by SI 2012/1795, reg. 6(7)(b), with effect in relation to any lump sums paid on or after 6 April 2011.

In reg. 15(7), inserted para. 10(4), (5) and (6) substituted for former inserted para. 10(4) by SI 2009/2047, reg. 8, with effect where there is a paragraph 15 BCE which is treated as occurring on a date ("the specified date") on or after 6 April 2006, and the member becomes entitled to a lump sum under a relevant non-UK scheme on or after the specified date. For this purpose "paragraph 15 BCE" means the benefit crystallisation event treated as occurring by virtue of FA 2004, Sch. 34, para. 15, and "relevant non-UK scheme" has the meaning given by FA 2004, Sch. 34, para. 1(5). Former inserted para. 10(4) read as follows:

> "10(4)   In determining whether all or part of the member's lifetime allowance is available–
> (a)   an amount crystallising by virtue of benefit crystallisation event 8 shall be disregarded; and
> (b)   the amount of the allowance available shall be reduced by the aggregate of–
>   (i)   the amount of any previous pension commencement lump sum which has been paid to or in respect of the member by a recognised overseas pension scheme, to the extent that the lump sum is referable to the member's relevant transfer fund, and
>   (ii)   the amount which would have crystallised on the member becoming entitled to a pension, had the scheme paying it been a registered pension scheme, to the extent that it is so referable.".

In reg. 15(8), inserted para. 11(bb) and (bc) substituted for former inserted para. 11(bb) by SI 2009/2047, reg. 9, with effect where there is a paragraph 15 BCE and the notice given under FA 2004, Sch. 34, para. 15 is given on or after 23 July 2009, and the member becomes entitled to a lump sum under a relevant non-UK scheme on or after the date on which the paragraph 15 BCE is treated as occurring. For this purpose "paragraph 15 BCE" means the benefit crystallisation event treated as occurring by virtue of FA 2004, Sch. 34, para. 15, and "relevant non-UK scheme" has the meaning given by FA 2004, Sch. 34, para. 1(5). Former inserted para. 11(bb) read as follows:

> "(bb)   it is not paid from the relevant transfer fund of a qualifying recognised overseas pension scheme,".

Reg. 15(9A) inserted by SI 2012/1795, reg. 6(8), with effect in relation to any lump sum to which a person becomes entitled for the purposes of Part 4 of the Finance Act 2004 on or after 6 April 2011.

Reg. 15(10) inserted by SI 2009/2047, reg. 10, with effect from 13 August 2009.

MODIFICATION OF SCHEDULE 32

16   In paragraph 11(6) of Schedule 32–

(a)   for "the retail prices index" (in both places) substitute "a relevant index"; and

(b)   at the end add–

"Here **"relevant index"** means–

(a)   an index of the movement of retail prices maintained, or officially recognised, by the government of the country or territory in which the recognised overseas scheme is established; or

(b)   if there is no such index as is mentioned in paragraph (a) of this definition, the retail prices index.".

MODIFICATION OF SCHEDULE 34

17   In Schedule 34 after paragraph 19 add–

"REVENUE AND CUSTOMS DISCRETION

19A(1)   Sub-paragraph (2) applies to–

(a)   the member payment provisions to a payment made (or treated by this Part as made) to or in respect of–
   (i)   a relieved member of a relevant non-UK scheme, or
   (ii)   a transfer member of such a scheme;

(b)   the annual allowance provisions in relation to an individual who is a currently relieved member of a currently-relieved non-UK scheme; and

(c)   the lifetime allowance provision charge in relation to an individual who is a relieved member of a relieved non-UK pension scheme.

19A(2) If it appears to an officer of Revenue and Customs that, by reason of some noncompliance with the requirements set out in this Part, which in the officer's view does not materially affect the nature of a payment, the payment, or the member in respect of whom it is payable, would be treated less favourably by the strict application of the provisions mentioned in paragraph (1) than in the officer's view is appropriate, sub-paragraph (3) applies.

19A(3) If this sub-paragraph applies, an officer of Revenue and Customs–

(a)   may decide, and

(b)   if requested to do so by a member falling within any of the descriptions in paragraphs (a) to (c) of sub-paragraph (1), shall decide,

whether, notwithstanding the non-compliance referred to in sub-paragraph (2), the treatment which, but for that non-compliance, would have applied under this Part should apply to the payment or the member (as the case may be).

This is subject to the qualification in sub-paragraph (4).

19A(4) An officer of Revenue and Customs shall not make a decision under sub-paragraph (3) that, notwithstanding the difference referred to in sub-paragraph (2), the provisions of this Part shall apply to the payment or the member unless–

(a)   it appears to the officer that the effect of the decision would be to reduce the total cumulative tax liability in respect of the charges mentioned in subparagraph (1) of the member whose tax liability would be affected by it, taking one year with another;

(b)   the officer has first given at least 28 days' notice of his intention to make the decision to the member whose tax liability would by affected by it; and

(c)   the member has–

     (i)   consented to the making of the decision; or

     (ii)   failed to respond to the notice within the period specified in paragraph (b).

19A(5) If an officer of Revenue and Customs decides under sub-paragraph (3) that–

(a)   the conditions for the exercise of his discretion under that paragraph are not met; or

(b)   the conditions for its exercise are met, but that it is otherwise inappropriate for him to exercise it in favour of the member,

the member may appeal against the decision.

19A(6) Subsections (3) to (5) of section 170 apply for the purposes of a decision by an officer of Revenue and Customs under sub-paragraph (3) as they apply to a decision under section 169(5).

19A(7) The Commissioners before whom an appeal under paragraph (5) is brought must consider–

(a)   whether the conditions for the exercise of the discretion of an officer of Revenue and Customs have been met; and

(b)   if they are satisfied that those conditions have been met, whether the discretion ought to have been exercised in favour of the member.

19A(8) If they decide that the conditions for the exercise of that discretion have not been met, they must dismiss the appeal.

19A(9) If they decide that the conditions for the exercise of that discretion have been met, they must decide whether the discretion ought to have been exercised in favour of the member.

19A(10) If they decide that although the conditions are met, the discretion ought not to have been exercised in favour of the member, they must dismiss the appeal.

19A(11) If they decide that the discretion ought to have been exercised in favour of the member they may so decide and the provisions of this Part shall apply accordingly to the member or the payment in question (as the case may be).

19A(12) A decision under sub-paragraph (8) or (10) is final but subject to any further appeal or any determination on, or in consequence of, a case stated.".

Statutory Instruments

PENSION SCHEMES (INFORMATION REQUIREMENTS – QUALIFYING OVERSEAS PENSION SCHEMES, QUALIFYING RECOGNISED OVERSEAS PENSIONS SCHEMES AND CORRESPONDING RELIEF) REGULATIONS 2006

(SI 2006/208, as amended by SI 2006/1961, SI 2012/884 and SI 2013/2259)

Made on 1 February 2006 by the Commissioners for Her Majesty's Revenue and Customs make the following Regulations in exercise of the powers conferred by s. 169 of, and para. 5(2) of Sch. 33 and para. 51(4) of Sch. 36 to, the Finance Act 2004. Operative from 6 April 2006.

CITATION, COMMENCEMENT AND INTERPRETATION

1(1) These Regulations may be cited as the Pension Schemes (Information Requirements for Qualifying Overseas Pension Schemes, Qualifying Recognised Overseas Pension Schemes and Corresponding Relief) Regulations 2006 and shall come into force on 6th April 2006.

1(2) In these Regulations–

"**the Act**" means the Finance Act 2004 and a reference to a numbered section or Schedule, without more, is a reference to the section of, or Schedule to, the Act bearing that number;

"**HMRC**" means the Commissioners for Her Majesty's Revenue and Customs;

"**tax identification number**" means–

(a) if the person is resident for tax purposes in the United Kingdom, the unique taxpayer reference (UTR) allocated to that person, and

(b) if the person is resident for tax purposes outside the United Kingdom, the unique taxpayer reference (UTR) allocated to that person or, if they do not have one, the reference number allocated to that person by the tax authority in the country or territory in which they are resident for tax purposes; and

"**tax year**" means a period beginning on 6th April of one year and ending on 5th April of the immediately following year.

History – In reg. 1(2), definitions of "HMRC" and "tax identification number" inserted (and the "and" after definition of "the Act" omitted) by SI 2013/2259, reg. 10, with effect from 14 October 2013.

INFORMATION – BENEFIT CRYSTALLISATION EVENTS IN RELATION TO RELEVANT MIGRANT MEMBERS AND INDIVIDUALS ENTITLED TO CORRESPONDING RELIEF

2(1) For the purposes of paragraph 5(2) of Schedule 33 and paragraph 51(4) of Schedule 36 (information about benefit crystallisation events in cases of relevant migrant members and individuals entitled to corresponding relief) the prescribed benefit crystallisation information is–

(a)   the name and address of the relevant migrant member or individual (as the case may be) in respect of whom there has been a benefit crystallisation event in the tax year; and

(b)   the date, amount and nature of the benefit crystallisation event.

2(2) The information must be provided by 31st January next following the end of the tax year in which the benefit crystallisation event occurs.

INFORMATION – QUALIFYING RECOGNISED OVERSEAS PENSION SCHEMES
Prospective amendments – Heading to reg. 3 substituted by SI 2013/2259, reg. 11, with effect in relation to five year periods ending on or after 1 April 2015.

3(1) For the purposes of section 169(4) (meaning of qualifying recognised overseas pension scheme), a qualifying recognised overseas pension scheme must provide to an officer of Revenue and Customs–

(a)   the name of the country or territory in which it is established;

(b)   in the case of a scheme falling within regulation 3(4) of the Pension Schemes (Categories of Country and Requirements for Overseas Pension Schemes and Recognised Overseas Pension Schemes) Regulations 2006, evidence demonstrating that it fulfils the requirement set out in that paragraph; and

(c)   any other evidence required in writing by the officer.

Statutory Instruments

3(2)   When a QROPS or former QROPS makes, or is treated under the relevant provisions as making, a payment in respect of a relevant member, the scheme manager of the QROPS or former QROPS must provide to HMRC–

(a)   the name, principal residential address, date of birth, contact details, the national insurance number or, if they do not have one, the tax identification number, if any, of the relevant member and if the relevant member has ceased to be resident for tax purposes in the United Kingdom, the date that residence ceased;

(b)   the name, address and contact details of the QROPS or former QROPS and of the scheme manager;

(c)   the date, amount and nature of the payment and if as a result of the payment no relevant transfer fund remains, a statement to that effect;

(d)   if the payment is made to a pension scheme, the name and address of the recipient and if the recipient is a registered pension scheme or a QROPS, the reference number allocated to that pension scheme by HMRC;

(e)   where the relevant member has died and the payment is made to an individual, the name, principal residential address, date of birth and the national insurance number or, if they do not have one, the tax identification number, if any, of that individual; and

(f)   where the relevant member has died and the payment is made to a person who is not an individual, the name and address of that person.

Here **"the relevant provisions"** means sections 172 to 174A, paragraph 2A of Schedule 28 and paragraph 3A of Schedule 29.

This paragraph is subject to the qualifications in paragraphs (3) and (4).

3(3)   No obligation arises under paragraph (2) if the following conditions are met–

(a)   at the date of the payment more than ten years has elapsed beginning with the date on which the relevant transfer fund in respect of the relevant member came into existence; and

(b)   the relevant member to whom the payment is made or treated as made is a person to whom the member payment provisions do not apply (see paragraph 2 of Schedule 34).

3(4)   In the case of a payment by way of a pension the obligation under paragraph (2) applies only to the first such payment.

3(5)   The information required by paragraph (2) must be provided–

(a)   within 90 days beginning with the day on which the payment is made or is treated as made; or

(b)   by such other time as may be agreed between an officer of Revenue and Customs and the scheme manager.

This paragraph is subject to regulation 4.

3(5A)   Where the scheme manager is a company it must provide the names and addresses of the directors of the company to an officer of Revenue and Customs if required to do so in writing, and within such time as may be specified, by the officer.

3(6)   For the purposes of this regulation and regulation 3C–

"payment" has the meaning given in section 161(2); and

"relevant member" means a member of a scheme in respect of whom there is a relevant transfer fund.

3(7)   For the purposes of this regulation, regulation 3B and regulation 3C **"relevant transfer fund"** has the meaning given in paragraph 4(2) of Schedule 34.

Prospective amendments – Reg. 3(1)–(1D) substituted for (1) by SI 2013/2259, reg. 11, with effect in relation to five year periods ending on or after 1 April 2015.

History – Reg. 3(2) substituted by SI 2013/2259, reg. 12, with effect in respect of information relating to payments that are made, or treated as made, on or after 14 October 2013 but in the case of a payment made by a former QROPS, does not have effect unless the former QROPS ceased to be a QROPS on or after 14 October 2013. Former reg. 3(2) read as follows:

"**3(2)**   When a qualifying recognised overseas pension scheme makes, or is treated under the relevant provisions as making, a payment in respect of a relevant member, it must provide to an officer of Revenue and Customs–
(a)   the name and principal residential address of the relevant member;
(aa)   the relevant member's national insurance number, if any; and
(b)   the date, amount and nature of that payment.

Here "the relevant provisions" means sections 172 to 174A(b) and paragraph 2A of Schedule 28 and 3A of Schedule 29.

This paragraph is subject to the qualifications in paragraphs (3) and (4).".

In former reg. 3(2)(a), the words "principal residential" inserted, and the word "and" omitted from the end, by SI 2012/884, reg. 8(2)(a) and (b), with effect in respect of information relating to payments that are made, or are treated as made, on or after 6 April 2012.

Former reg. 3(2)(aa) inserted by SI 2012/884, reg. 8(3), with effect in respect of information relating to payments that are made, or are treated as made, on or after 6 April 2012.

In former reg. 3(2), "174A(b)" substituted for "174" and the words "and 3A of Schedule 29" inserted by SI 2006/1961, reg. 5, with effect from 11 August 2006.

In reg. 3(3), the words "the following conditions are met–" and para. (a) and (b) substituted for the words "the relevant member to whom the payment is made or treated as made is a person to whom the member payment provisions do not apply (see paragraph 2 of Schedule 34)." by SI 2012/884, reg. 8(4), with effect in respect of information relating to payments that are made, or are treated as made, on or after 6 April 2012.

In reg. 3(5), the word "provided–" and para. (a) and (b) substituted for the words "provided by 31st January next following the tax year in which the payment is made or is treated as made." by SI 2012/884, reg. 8(5), with effect in respect of information relating to payments that are made, or are treated as made, on or after 6 April 2012.

Reg. 3(5A) inserted by SI 2012/884, reg. 8(6), with effect from 6 April 2012.

In reg. 3(6), the words "and regulation 3C" inserted by SI 2013/2259, reg. 13, with effect from 14 October 2013.

In reg. 3(6), in the definition of "relevant member", the words "within the meaning of the Pension Schemes (Application of UK Provisions to Relevant Non-UK Schemes) Regulations 2006" omitted from the end by SI 2012/884, reg. 8(7), with effect in respect of information relating to payments that are made, or are treated as made, on or after 6 April 2012.

In reg. 3(7), the words ", regulation 3B and regulation 3C" substituted for the words "and regulation 3B" by SI 2013/2259, reg. 14, with effect from 14 October 2013.

Reg. 3(7) inserted by SI 2012/884, reg. 8(8), with effect in respect of information relating to payments that are made, or are treated as made, on or after 6 April 2012.

INFORMATION – TRANSFER OF SUMS OR ASSETS TO A QROPS

3A(1)   For the purposes of section 169(4), where paragraph (2) applies the scheme manager of the QROPS (or former QROPS, if the scheme ceased to be a QROPS) must provide to HMRC such of the information specified in paragraph (3) as may be required in writing by an officer of Revenue and Customs.

3A(2)   This paragraph applies where there is a transfer to a QROPS of sums or assets which have at any time been held for the purposes of, or representing accrued rights under, a registered pension scheme from–

(a)   a registered pension scheme; or

(b)   another QROPS.

3A(3)   The information is–

(a)   the date of the transfer;

(b)   the name and address of any bank and details of any bank account which the scheme has used in relation to the transfer;

(c)   details of the sums or assets transferred;

(d)   where information is required from a scheme which is a transferee, the way that the sums or assets have been applied by the scheme;

(e)   where the transfer is from a registered pension scheme, the name and address of that scheme;

(f)   the name, principal residential address, date of birth and, if any, the national insurance number of the member who is connected with the sums or assets;

(g)   where the member referred to in sub-paragraph (f) is a person to whom the member payment provisions do not apply by virtue of paragraph 2 of Schedule 34, the date that the member ceased to be resident in the United Kingdom;

(h)   the name and address of the body that regulates the scheme and the reference number, if any, issued to the scheme by the regulator;

(i)   the name and address of the tax authority that administers the scheme and the reference number, if any, issued to the scheme by the authority;

(j)   evidence to show that the scheme met at the time of the transfer and continues to meet the requirements specified in regulations 2 and 3 of the Pension Schemes (Categories of Country and Requirements for Overseas Pension Schemes and Recognised Overseas Pension Schemes) Regulations 2006; and

(k)   any other evidence relating to the transfer as may be required by the officer of Revenue and Customs.

3A(4)   Information required in accordance with paragraph (1) must be provided–

(a)   within 90 days beginning with the day on which the requirement is notified by the officer of Revenue and Customs; or

(b)   by such other time as may be agreed between the officer and the scheme manager.

History – In heading, the word "QROPS" substituted for the words "qualifying recognised overseas pension scheme" by SI 2013/2259, reg. 15, with effect from 14 October 2013.

Reg. 3A(1) substituted by SI 2013/2259, reg. 16, with effect from 14 October 2013 but, so far as relating to former QROPS, only in relation to a scheme that ceased to be a QROPS on or after 14 October 2013. Former reg. 3A(1) read as follows:

Statutory Instruments

"**3A(1)**   For the purposes of section 169(4), where paragraph (2) applies a qualifying recognised overseas pension scheme ("the scheme") mentioned in that paragraph must provide to an officer of Revenue and Customs such of the information specified in paragraph (3) as may be required in writing by the officer.".

In reg. 3A(2), the word "QROPS" substituted for the words "qualifying recognised overseas pension scheme", in each place, by SI 2013/2259, reg. 17, with effect from 14 October 2013.

Reg. 3A inserted by SI 2012/884, reg. 9, with effect from 6 April 2012.

INFORMATION – CESSATION OF QROPS

3B   For the purposes of section 169(4), the scheme manager of a pension scheme which ceases to be a QROPS must within 30 days beginning with the day on which the cessation takes place ("the cessation date") provide to HMRC–

(za)   the name and address of the scheme and the date of and reason for the cessation; and

(a)   the value at the cessation date of the relevant transferred sums or assets pertaining to each relevant transfer fund under the scheme; and

(b)   the name, principal residential address, date of birth and the national insurance number or, if they do not have one, the tax identification number, if any, of each member in respect of whom there is a relevant transfer fund under the scheme at the cessation date.

History – In heading, the word "QROPS" substituted for the words "qualifying recognised overseas pension scheme" by SI 2013/2259, reg. 18, with effect from 14 October 2013.

In reg. 3B, the words "the scheme manager of" inserted, the word "QROPS" substituted for the words "qualifying overseas pension scheme" and the word "HMRC" substituted for the words "an officer of Revenue and Customs" by SI 2013/2259, reg. 19, with effect from 14 October 2013.

Reg. 3B(za) inserted by SI 2013/2259, reg. 19, with effect from 14 October 2013.

In reg. 3B(b), the words ", if any," which appeared after the words "national insurance number" omitted and the words "or, if they do not have one, the tax identification number, if any," inserted by SI 2013/2259, reg. 19, with effect from 14 October 2013.

Reg. 3B inserted by SI 2012/884, reg. 9, with effect from 6 April 2012.

INFORMATION – CHANGES, COMPLETION OR CORRECTION

3C(1)   For the purposes of section 169(4), if at any time after a QROPS or former QROPS has provided HMRC with information in accordance with regulation 3, 3A or 3B it becomes apparent to the QROPS or former QROPS that–

(a)   there is a material change affecting that information; or

(b)   the information is incomplete or contains a material inaccuracy,

the scheme manager of the QROPS or former QROPS must provide to HMRC details of the change, the complete information or correction of the inaccuracy ("the relevant obligation").

3C(2)   Where paragraph (1) applies the details of the change, the complete information or correction of the inaccuracy must be provided–

(a)   within 30 days beginning with the day on which the change, lack of completeness or inaccuracy becomes apparent to the QROPS or former QROPS; or

(b)   by such other time as may be agreed between an officer of Revenue and Customs and the scheme manager.

3C(3)   No obligation arises under paragraph (1) in respect of a former QROPS if at the time the relevant obligation arises–

(a)   the following conditions are met–

   (i)   more than ten years has elapsed beginning with the date on which the relevant transfer fund in respect of the relevant member came into existence; and

   (ii)   the relevant member to whom the payment is made or treated as made is a person to whom the member payment provisions do not apply (see paragraph 2 of Schedule 34); or

(b)   there is no relevant transfer fund.

History – Reg. 3C substituted by SI 2013/2259, reg. 20, with effect from 14 October 2013 but, so far as relating to a former QROPS, only in relation to a scheme that ceased to be a QROPS on or after 14 October 2013. Former reg. 3C read as follows:

"**3C**   For the purposes of section 169(4), if at any time after a pension scheme has provided an officer of Revenue and Customs with information in accordance with regulation 3, 3A or 3B it becomes apparent to the scheme that–

(a)   there is a material change affecting that information; or

(b)   the information is incomplete or contains a material inaccuracy,

the scheme must provide to an officer of Revenue and Customs details of the change, the complete information or correction of the inaccuracy without undue delay.".

Former reg. 3C inserted by SI 2012/884, reg. 9, with effect from 6 April 2012.

NOTICE IN CASES OF SERIOUS PREJUDICE TO PROPER ASSESSMENT OR COLLECTION OF TAX

4(1) If an officer of Revenue and Customs has reasonable grounds for believing that the pension scheme in question–

(a)   has failed or may fail to comply with any of the requirements imposed upon it under or by virtue of regulation 2, and

(b)   such failure is likely to have led or to lead to serious prejudice to the proper assessment or collection of tax,

paragraph (2) applies.

4(2) If this paragraph applies, the officer may notify the pension scheme that he requires such information to be provided within 30 days of the issue of that notice, notwithstanding the provisions set out in regulation 2.

History – In reg. 4(1)(a), the words "regulation 2" substituted for the words "these Regulations" by SI 2012/884, reg. 10(a), with effect from 6 April 2012.
In reg. 4(2), the words "regulation 2" substituted for the words "regulations 2 and 3" by SI 2012/884, reg. 10(b), with effect from 6 April 2012.

APPLICATION AND MODIFICATION OF THE PENALTY PROVISIONS IN PART 7 OF SCHEDULE 36 TO THE FINANCE ACT 2008

5(1) Where the scheme manager of a former QROPS is required to provide information under regulation 3(2), 3A(1) or 3C(1), Part 7 of Schedule 36 to the Finance Act 2008 (penalties) is to apply, with the modifications specified in paragraph (2), to the scheme manager as if–

(a)   that information had been required to be provided by an information notice given to the scheme manager under that Schedule; and

(b)   the information notice had specified that the information had to be provided by the time required under regulation 3, 3A or 3C, as the case may be.

5(2) The modifications of Part 7 of Schedule 36 to the Finance Act 2008 mentioned in paragraph (1) are as follows–

(a)   in paragraph 39, sub-paragraphs (1)(b) and (3) are omitted;

(b)   in paragraph 40, "or obstruction" is omitted wherever it appears;

(c)   in paragraph 40A(4)(b), "take reasonable steps to" is omitted and "within 30 days beginning with the date on which the inaccuracy becomes apparent" is inserted at the end;

(d)   paragraphs 42 and 43 are omitted;

(e)   in paragraph 45, in sub-paragraph (1) "or the obstruction of an officer of Revenue and Customs" is omitted, in sub-paragraph (2)(b) "or obstruction" is omitted and in sub-paragraph (2)(c) "or obstruction" and ", or the obstruction stops," are omitted;

(f)   in paragraph 46, in sub-paragraph (2) ", subject to sub-paragraph (3)" is omitted and sub-paragraph (3) is omitted;

(g)   in paragraph 49, in sub-paragraph (1)(a) and (b) "90 days" is substituted for "30 days";

(h)   in paragraph 49A, in sub-paragraph (1)(a) "an information notice" is substituted for "a notice under paragraph 5" and sub-paragraph (6) is omitted;

(i)   paragraphs 50 and 51 are omitted.

History – Reg. 5 inserted by SI 2013/2259, reg. 21, with effect from 14 October 2013.

REGISTERED PENSION SCHEMES (AUTHORISED PAYMENTS) REGULATIONS 2006

(SI 2006/209)

Made on 1 February 2006 by the Commissioners for Her Majesty's Revenue and Customs, in exercise of the powers conferred upon them by s. 164(f) of the Finance Act 2004. Operative from 6 April 2006.

CITATION AND COMMENCEMENT

1 These Regulations may be cited as the Registered Pension Schemes (Authorised Payments) Regulations 2006 and shall come into force on 6 April 2006.

PRESCRIBED PAYMENTS

2 For the purposes of section 164(f) of the Finance Act 2004 (authorised member payments), the following payments are prescribed–

(a) lump sum payments arising from the commutation of equivalent pension benefits pursuant to regulation 2(1A) of–

    (i) the Occupational Pension Schemes (Assignment, Forfeiture, Bankruptcy etc.) Regulations 1997, or

    (ii) the Occupational Pension Schemes (Assignment, Forfeiture, Bankruptcy etc.) Regulations (Northern Ireland) 1997,

(b) payments of state scheme premiums pursuant to–

    (i) section 55 of the Pension Schemes Act 1993, or

    (ii) section 51 of the Pension Schemes (Northern Ireland) Act 1993,

(c) payments of contributions equivalent premiums pursuant to–

    (i) section 55(2) of the Pension Schemes Act 1993, or

    (ii) [section 51(2) of the Pension Schemes (Northern Ireland) Act 1993; and]

(d) payments for restoring members' State scheme rights pursuant to–

    (i) paragraph 5(3B)(b) of Schedule 2 to the Pension Schemes Act 1993, or

    (ii) paragraph 5(3B)(b) of Schedule 1 to the Pension Schemes (Northern Ireland) Act 1993.

EMPLOYER-FINANCED RETIREMENT BENEFITS (EXCLUDED BENEFITS FOR TAX PURPOSES) REGULATIONS 2006

(SI 2006/210)

Made on 1 February 2006 by the Commissioners for Her Majesty's Revenue and Customs make the following regulations in exercise of the powers conferred by s. 393B(3)(d) of the Income Tax (Earnings and Pensions) Act 2003. Operative from 6 April 2006.

CITATION AND COMMENCEMENT

1　These Regulations may be cited as the Employer-Financed Retirement Benefits (Excluded Benefits for Tax Purposes) Regulations 2006 and come into force on 6 April 2006.

EXCLUDED BENEFIT

2(1)　For the purposes of section 393B(3)(d) of the Income Tax (Earnings and Pensions) Act 2003 (prescribed benefits to be excluded benefits for the purpose of Chapter 2 of Part 6 of that Act) a lump sum benefit which is–

(a)　in respect of the non-accidental death of an employee during service, and

(b)　already provided for under the rules of a scheme on 6 April 2006,

is prescribed.

2(2)　In paragraph (1) **"scheme"** means any scheme which, on 6 April 2006–

(a)　will be an employer-financed retirement benefits scheme, or

(b)　would be such a scheme but for the fact that it provides for a benefit which is an excluded benefit by virtue of this regulation.

2(3)　In paragraph (2) **"employer-financed retirement benefits scheme"** has the meaning given in section 393A of the Income Tax (Earnings and Pensions) Act 2003.

REGISTERED PENSION SCHEMES (SURRENDER OF RELEVANT EXCESS) REGULATIONS 2006
(SI 2006/211)

Made on 1 February 2006 by the Commissioners for Her Majesty's Revenue and Customs, in exercise of the powers conferred by s. 172A(5)(f) of, and para. 3(1) and 12(5) of Sch. 36 to, the Finance Act 2004. Operative from 6 April 2006.

CITATION, COMMENCEMENT AND INTERPRETATION

1(1) These Regulations may be cited as the Registered Pension Schemes (Surrender of Relevant Excess) Regulations 2006, and shall come into force on 6th April 2006.

1(2) In these Regulations, references to provisions are references to provisions of the Finance Act 2004.

1(3) In these Regulations, **"the relevant excess"** has the meaning given by paragraph 12(6) of Schedule 36(c).

RIGHTS REPRESENTING THE RELEVANT EXCESS

2 The rights that are to be treated as representing the relevant excess are rights that–

(a)   meet the qualification condition (see regulation 3), and

(b)   are valued in accordance with the computation condition (see regulation 4).

THE QUALIFICATION CONDITION

3(1) The rights that meet the qualification condition are all the individual's uncrystallised rights with the exception of excluded rights.

3(2) Rights are excluded rights if–

(a)   they are rights surrendered or transferred in any of the circumstances specified in paragraphs (a), (b), (c) and (e) of section 172A(5) (surrenders of benefits and rights), or

(b)   they are rights to which the individual has a prospective entitlement as a dependant of another individual.

THE COMPUTATION CONDITION

4(1) Rights are valued in accordance with the computation condition if the value of the rights surrendered–

(a)   is determined in accordance with section 212 (valuation of uncrystallised rights) on the date of the surrender, and

(b)   as so determined, is equal to the relevant excess.

4(2) If rights are surrendered on more than one occasion, the value of the rights surrendered–

(a)   is to be determined separately for each surrender, and

(b)   is the aggregate of the values as so determined.

SURRENDERS AND UNAUTHORISED PAYMENTS

5 Subsections (2) and (4) of section 172A (surrenders of benefits and rights) do not apply to a surrender of rights that are to be treated as representing the relevant excess to the extent that the value of the rights surrendered, determined in accordance with regulation 4, does not exceed the relevant excess.

MODIFICATION OF CONDITIONS OF PENSION SCHEMES

6 The rules of any pension scheme to which paragraph 1(1) of Schedule 36 (deemed registration of existing schemes) applies shall be modified so as to provide that a member may surrender rights that are to be treated as representing the relevant excess to the extent that the value of the rights surrendered, determined in accordance with regulation 4, does not exceed the relevant excess.

PENSION SCHEMES (RELEVANT MIGRANT MEMBERS) REGULATIONS 2006

(SI 2006/212)

Made on 1 February 2006 by the Commissioners for Her Majesty's Revenue and Customs, in exercise of the powers conferred by paragraph 4(c) of Schedule 33 to the Finance Act 2004. Operative from 6 April 2006.

CITATION AND COMMENCEMENT

1 These Regulations may be cited as the Pension Schemes (Relevant Migrant Members) Regulations 2006 and shall come into force on 6th April 2006.

ALTERNATIVE CONDITION FOR RELEVANT MIGRANT MEMBER RELIEF

2(1) For the purposes of paragraph 4(c) of Schedule 33 to the Finance Act 2004 (meaning of "relevant migrant member"), the prescribed condition, in relation to the individual is set out in paragraph (2).

2(2) The individual was at any time in the 10 years before the beginning of that period of residence, whether before or after the coming into force of these Regulations, entitled to tax relief in respect of contributions paid under the pension scheme under the law of the country or territory in which the individual was then resident.

Statutory Instruments

TONNAGE TAX (EXCEPTION OF FINANCIAL YEAR 2006) ORDER 2006

(SI 2006/333)

Made on 13 February 2006 by the Treasury in exercise of the powers conferred upon them by para. 22B(2) and 22C of Sch. 22 to the Finance Act 2000. Operative from 1 April 2006.

CITATION AND COMMENCEMENT

1   This Order may be cited as the Tonnage Tax (Exception of Financial Year 2006) Order 2006 and shall come into force on 1st April 2006.

PRESCRIBED THREE YEAR PERIOD AND OTHER DEFINITIONS

2   For the purposes of this Order–

(a)   the period prescribed for the purposes of paragraph 22C(1)(a) of Schedule 22 to the Finance Act 2000 (three year period to determine whether the percentage of the tonnage tax fleet which is Community-flagged has not decreased) is the period beginning on 2nd October 2002 and ending on 1st October 2005;

(b)   **"the tonnage tax fleet"** means qualifying ships operated by single companies or qualifying companies which are members of a tonnage tax group; and

(c)   **"the percentage of the tonnage tax fleet which is Community-flagged"** is–

$$\frac{CFT}{TT} \times 100$$

where–

CFT is the aggregate tonnage of qualifying ships registered in one of the Member States' registers,

TT is the aggregate tonnage of all qualifying ships, and

no qualifying ship is counted more than once in determining an aggregate.

EXCEPTION OF FINANCIAL YEAR 2006

3   The financial year 2006 is designated as one in relation to which paragraph 22A of Schedule 22 to the Finance Act 2000 is not to have effect.

REGISTERED PENSION SCHEMES (MODIFICATION OF THE RULES OF EXISTING SCHEMES) REGULATIONS 2006

(SI 2006/364)

Made on 16 February 2006 by the Commissioners for Her Majesty's Revenue and Customs in exercise of the powers conferred by para. 3 of Sch. 36 to the Finance Act 2004. Operative from 6 April 2006.

CITATION, COMMENCEMENT AND INTERPRETATION

1(1) These Regulations may be cited as the Registered Pension Schemes (Modification of the Rules of Existing Schemes) Regulations 2006 and shall come into force on 6th April 2006.

1(2) In these Regulations–

"**the Act**" means the Finance Act 2004 and a reference (without more) to a numbered provision is a reference to the provision of the Act bearing that number;

"**the commencement day**" means 6th April 2006;

"**existing scheme**" means a pension scheme to which paragraph 1(1) of Schedule 36 applies;

"**the permitted maximum**"–

(a)   in relation to times before the commencement day, has the meaning which it has by virtue of section 590C of the Income and Corporation Taxes Act 1988; and

(b)   in relation to times during the transitional period has the meaning which it would have had if–

     (i)   section 590C of the Income and Corporation Taxes Act 1988 (permitted maximum) had continued in force, and

     (ii)   the Treasury had made the orders required by that section, as it had effect immediately before its repeal, in respect of each tax year during that period;

"**rules**", in relation to an existing scheme, means the rules (whether contained in the governing instruments or otherwise) of an existing scheme;

"**the transitional period**", in relation to an existing scheme, means the period beginning with the commencement day and ending with the date on which, by virtue of paragraph 3(2) of Schedule 36, the modifications in these Regulations cease to have effect.

1(3) In the application of these Regulations to an annuity contract falling within paragraph 1(1)(d) of Schedule 36, references to the trustees or managers of a scheme are to be read as references to the insurance company with whom that contract is made.

1(4) For the purposes of these Regulations whether something would have prejudiced the approval of an existing scheme by the Inland Revenue or by Her Majesty's Revenue and Customs is to be determined–

(a)   in the case of an occupational pension scheme, in accordance with the publication IR 12(2001) (known as the Occupational Pension Scheme Practice Notes) published by the former Inland Revenue Pension Scheme Office on 23rd March 2001, and

(b)   in the case of a personal pension scheme, in accordance with the publication IR 76(2000) published by the former Inland Revenue Pension Scheme Office on 20th November 2000,

as each of those publications stood immediately before the making of these Regulations.

EXISTING SCHEMES TO WHICH THESE REGULATIONS APPLY

2   Each of the following provisions of these Regulations apply to existing schemes, unless–

(a)   before the commencement day amendments have been adopted, to have effect on and after that day, which have a corresponding effect to the modification contained in that provision; or

(b)   the rules of the scheme are framed in a way which means that no such amendment as is necessary.

SCHEMES RULES NOT TO REQUIRE THE MAKING OF UNAUTHORISED PAYMENTS

3(1) Any provision (however framed) in the rules of an existing scheme as they stood immediately before the commencement day, which would require the trustees or managers of the scheme–

(a) to make a payment which, by virtue of section 160 would be an unauthorised payment, or

(b) to make such a payment if the consent of the sponsoring employer or any other person was given for their doing so,

shall be construed, in respect of the transitional period, as conferring a discretion upon the trustees or managers to make that payment.

This is subject to the following qualification.

3(2) If, immediately before the commencement day, the consent of a sponsoring employer, or any other person, was required before the trustees or managers of a pension scheme could make any other discretionary payment under the scheme, then the discretion conferred by paragraph (1) may only be exercised with the consent of that person.

REFERENCES TO THE PERMITTED MAXIMUM

4(1) If the rules of an existing scheme, as they stood immediately before the commencement day, imposed a limit on a person's entitlement to any benefit, or liability to make any contribution, by reference to the permitted maximum (whether expressly or by necessary implication), paragraph (2) applies.

4(2) If this paragraph applies, the permitted maximum shall continue to apply in respect of the transitional period.

LIMITS ON AMOUNTS OF REMUNERATION TO BE TAKEN INTO ACCOUNT

5(1) This paragraph applies in the case of the rules of an existing scheme which becomes a registered pension scheme by virtue of paragraph 1(1)(a), (c) or (d) of Schedule 36–

(a) where the existing scheme came into existence before 14th March 1989, as regards an employee who became a member of that scheme on or after 1st June 1989;

(b) where the existing scheme came into existence on or after 14th March 1989, as regards any employee who is a member of that scheme (whenever he became a member).

This paragraph is subject to the following qualifications.

5(2) Paragraph (1) does not apply to the rules of an existing scheme in their application to an employee to whom paragraph 20 of Schedule 6 to the Finance Act 1989 did not apply, immediately before its repeal, by virtue of regulation 3(2), (3), (4), (6) or (8) or 3A(2) of the Continuation of Rights Regulations.

5(3) If, and to the extent that, paragraph (1) applies, paragraphs (4) to (7) have effect–

(a) in respect of the transitional period and

(b) regardless of anything contained in the rules of the existing scheme to the contrary.

5(4) In arriving at the employee's relevant annual remuneration for the purposes of calculating benefits, any excess of what would be the employee's relevant annual remuneration (apart from this paragraph) over the permitted maximum for the year of assessment in which his participation in the scheme ceases shall be disregarded.

5(5) In arriving at the employee's remuneration for the year 2006–07 or any subsequent year of assessment for the purposes of any restriction on the aggregate amount of contributions payable under the scheme by the employee and the employer, there shall be disregarded any excess of what would be his remuneration for the year (apart from this paragraph) over the permitted maximum for the year.

5(6) If–

(a) a transfer payment having been accepted by the existing scheme under its rules, the payment has been treated as entitling the employee to be regarded as having additional years of service (**"inserted years"**), and

(b) by virtue of the modification of paragraph 20 of Schedule 6 to the Finance Act 1989 contained in regulation 5 of the Continuation of Rights Regulations that paragraph did not apply to the inserted years, but did apply to the member's actual years of service,

paragraph (5) applies only to the computation of pension benefits so far as they are referable to the member's actual years of service.

5(7) The amount of contributions payable under the scheme by an employee in the year 2006–07 or any subsequent year of assessment shall be limited to 15 per cent of the employee's remuneration for the year in respect of the employment.

5(8) In this regulation **"the Continuation of Rights Regulations"** means the Retirement Benefits Schemes (Continuation of Rights of Members of Approved Schemes) Regulations 1990.

PAYMENTS NOT PREJUDICING HM REVENUE AND CUSTOMS APPROVAL

6(1) If the rules of an existing scheme–

(a)   provide for an absolute entitlement to the making of a transfer or the payment of a specified sum or rate of pension; and

(b)   refer (in whatever terms) to the possibility of making a transfer or a payment in any greater amount which would not prejudice approval of the scheme by–

    (i)   the Inland Revenue, or

    (ii)   Her Majesty's Revenue and Customs,

the following provisions of this regulation apply.

6(2) The scheme's rules shall be construed, in respect of the transitional period, as–

(a)   authorising the trustees or managers of the scheme to make transfers or payments falling within paragraph (1)(b) only to the extent that the payments would have been authorised by the rules immediately before the coming into force of these Regulations; and

(b)   to prohibit the making of transfers or payments which would not have been so authorised.

This is subject to the following qualification.

6(3) If, immediately before the commencement day, the consent of a sponsoring employer, or any other person except Her Majesty's Revenue and Customs, was required before the trustees or managers of a pension scheme could make a payment of the kind referred to in paragraph (1)(b), then the power conferred by paragraph (2)(a) may only be exercised with the consent of that person.

LIMITS ON PAYMENTS IN AMOUNTS "WHICH WOULD NOT PREJUDICE REVENUE APPROVAL"

7(1) If the rules of an existing scheme provide for an absolute entitlement to–

(a)   the making of a transfer, or

(b)   the payment of a specified sum or rate of pension,

in an amount which would not prejudice approval of the scheme by the Inland Revenue or Her Majesty's Revenue and Customs, paragraph (2) applies.

7(2) If this paragraph applies the rules of the existing scheme shall be construed, in respect of the transitional period, as prohibiting the trustees or managers of the scheme from making payments to the extent that they would not have been authorised by the rules immediately before the commencement day.

RECOVERY OF TAX IN RESPECT OF LIFETIME ALLOWANCE CHARGE

8(1) The rules of an existing scheme shall be modified, during the transitional period, so as to provide for the recovery, from present or future benefits or entitlement under the scheme in respect of a member, of an amount reflecting any liability of the scheme administrator in respect of the lifetime allowance charge under section 215 in respect of that member.

But this does not authorise the reduction of entitlement to a benefit which has not crystallised, except that in relation to which the lifetime allowance charge arises.

8(2) The methods of recovery authorised by virtue of paragraph (1) include reduction of benefits or entitlement determined in accordance with normal actuarial practice.

This paragraph does not limit the generality of paragraph (1).

REGISTERED PENSION SCHEMES (UNAUTHORISED PAYMENTS BY EXISTING SCHEMES) REGULATIONS 2006

(SI 2006/365)

Made on 16 February 2006 by the Commissioners for Her Majesty's Revenue and Customs make the following Regulations in exercise of the powers conferred upon them by s. 241(2)(e) of the Finance Act 2004. Operative from 6 April 2006.

CITATION, COMMENCEMENT AND INTERPRETATION

1   These Regulations may be cited as the Registered Pension Schemes (Unauthorised Payments by Existing Schemes) Regulations 2006 and shall come into force on 6th April 2006.

UNAUTHORISED MEMBER PAYMENTS NOT TO BE SCHEME CHARGEABLE

2(1)   An unauthorised member payment which–

(a)   is made in exercise of the discretion conferred by regulation 3(1) of the Registered Pension Schemes (Modification of the Rules of Existing Schemes) Regulations 2006, or

(b)   would be so made if that regulation applied to the scheme, or

(c)   would be so made if–

     (i)   those regulation applied to the scheme, and

     (ii)   the payment were made during the transitional period in relation to the scheme,

is a payment of a description prescribed for the purposes of section 241(2) (certain payments not to be scheme chargeable payments), but only to the extent that it is referable to subsisting rights which have accrued under defined benefits arrangements before the commencement day, or to contributions which have been paid to a scheme under money purchase arrangements before that day.

This is subject to the following qualification.

2(2)   In the case of an unauthorised member payment which comprises or includes a refund of additional voluntary contributions, so much of the refund payment as could have been used to provide pension benefits for the member and his dependants without prejudicing approval of the scheme, before the commencement day, by the Inland Revenue or Her Majesty's Revenue and Customs is not a payment of a description prescribed for the purposes of section 241(2).

2(3)   In this regulation–

"**the commencement day**" means 6th April 2006;

"**existing scheme**" means a pension scheme to which paragraph 1(1) of Schedule 36 applies;

"**subsisting rights**" shall be construed–

(a)   in Great Britain, in accordance with section 67A(6) of the Pensions Act 1995; and

(b)   in Northern Ireland, in accordance with Article 67A(6) of the Pensions (Northern Ireland) Order 1995; and

"**the transitional period**" means the period beginning with the commencement day and ending with the date on which, by virtue of paragraph 3(2) of Schedule 36, the modifications in Registered Pension Schemes (Modification of the Rules of Existing Schemes) Regulations 200 cease to have effect; and

a reference (without more) to a numbered provision is a reference to the provision of the Finance Act 2004 bearing that number.

2(4)   For the purposes of this regulation, whether something would have prejudiced the approval of an existing scheme by the Inland Revenue or by Her Majesty's Revenue and Customs is to be determined in the case of an occupational pension scheme, in accordance with the publication IR 12(2001) (known as the Occupational Pension Scheme Practice Notes) published by the former Inland Revenue Pension Scheme Office on 23rd March 2001 as that publication stood immediately before the coming into force of these Regulations.

TAXATION OF JUDICIAL PENSIONS (CONSEQUENTIAL PROVISIONS) ORDER 2006

(SI 2006/497)

Made on 28 February 2006 by the Treasury, in exercise of the powers conferred upon them by s. 281(2) and (3) of the Finance Act 2004. Operative from 6 April 2006.

CITATION AND COMMENCEMENT

1   This Order may be cited as the Taxation of Judicial Pensions (Consequential Provisions) Order 2006 and shall come into force on 6th April 2006.

INTERPRETATION

2   In this Order–

"**the 1993 Act**" means the Judicial Pensions and Retirement Act 1993,

"**the 1981 Act**" means the Judicial Pensions Act 1981,

"**the 1960 Act**" means the Resident Magistrates' Pensions Act (Northern Ireland) 1960,

"**the 1959 Act**" means the County Courts Act (Northern Ireland) 1959.

AMENDMENTS OF THE 1993 ACT

3(1)   Section 3 of the 1993 Act (the appropriate annual rate) is amended as follows.

3(2)   In subsection (3)–

(a)   in paragraph (a)(i) (definition of "pensionable pay") omit ", within the meaning of section 590C(1) of the Income and Corporation Taxes Act 1988 (earnings cap),";

(b)   in paragraph (b) (definition of "pension-capped salary") for the words from ", within the" to "assessment" substitute "does not exceed the permitted maximum for the tax year".

3(3)   After section (3) insert–

"**3(3A)**   In subsection (3)(b) above "**the permitted maximum**" means–

(a)   in relation to the tax year 2005–06 and any earlier tax year, the permitted maximum within the meaning of section 590C(1) of the Income and Corporation Taxes Act 1988 (earnings cap) as it had effect for the tax year, and

(b)   in relation to the tax year 2006–07 and any later tax year, the amount arrived at under subsection (3B) below.

3(3B)   The permitted maximum for the tax year 2006–07 and any later tax year is the permitted maximum for the previous tax year increased (if there is a relevant increase in the retail prices index for the tax year) by the appropriate percentage for the tax year.

3(3C)   There is a relevant increase in the retail prices index for a tax year if the retail prices index for the month of September before the tax year is higher than it was for the previous September.

3(3D)   And the appropriate percentage for the tax year is the same percentage as the percentage increase in the retail prices index.

3(3E)   But if the result of the application of subsection (3B) above in relation to a tax year would not be a multiple of £600, the permitted maximum for that tax year is what it would be apart from this subsection rounded up to the nearest amount which is such a multiple.".

3(4)   In subsection (6) (interpretation of section), insert at the end–

""**retail prices index**", in relation to a month, means–

(a)   the general index of retail prices (for all items) published by the Office for National Statistics for the month, or

(b)   if that index is not published for the month, any substituted index or index figures published by that Office for the month, and

"**tax year and the tax year 2006–2007**" (and corresponding expressions) have the meanings in section 279(1) of the Finance Act 2004.".

VOLUNTARY CONTRIBUTIONS

4(1) Section 10 of the 1993 Act (additional benefits from voluntary contributions) is amended as follows.

4(2) In subsection (4) (what regulations may not do or must do) in paragraph (b), (which refers to a limit fixed by or under section 594 of the Income and Corporation Taxes Act 1988), omit "either or both of the following, that is to say" and sub-paragraph (ii) and the word "or" before it.

4(3) In subsection (8) (interpretation)–

(a)   omit the definition of "relevant benefits",

(b)   in the definition of "retained benefits", omit "relevant" and for "has, or which may be expected to qualify for, tax-exemption or tax approval" substitute "is registered under Part 4 of the Finance Act 2004", and

(c)   omit the definitions of "tax-exemption" and "tax-approval".

CONTINUITY OF TAX TREATMENT

5 Section 18 of the 1993 Act (under which the scheme constituted by Part 1 of the 1993 Act is, for tax purposes, to be regarded as amendments of the statutory schemes constituted by or under the 1981 Act) shall cease to have effect.

SECTION 19 SCHEME

6 In section 19 of the 1993 Act (benefits in respect of earnings in excess of pension-capped salary), omit subsection (4) (tax treatment).

OTHER AMENDMENTS

7 The Schedule contains amendments of enactments other than the 1993 Act.

SCHEDULE

Article 7

1 The 1981 Act is amended as follows.

2 In section 33A (voluntary contributions)–

(a)   in subsection (2) (what regulations may not do or must do), in paragraph (b), (which refers to a limit fixed by or under section 594 of the Income and Corporation Taxes Act 1988), omit "either or both of the following, that is to say" and sub-paragraph (ii) and the word "or" before it; and

(b)   in subsection (9)–

(i)   omit the definition of "relevant benefits",

(ii)   in the definition of "retained benefits", omit "relevant" and for "has, or which may be expected to qualify for, tax-exemption or tax approval" substitute "is registered under Part 4 of the Finance Act 2004", and,

(iii)   omit the definitions of "tax-exemption" and "tax-approval".

3 The 1960 Act is amended as follows.

4 In section 9A (voluntary contributions)–

(a)   in subsection (2) (what regulations may not do), in paragraph (b), (which refers to a limit fixed by or under section 594 of the Income and Corporation Taxes Act 1988), omit "either or both of the following, that is to say" and sub-paragraph (ii) and the word "or" before it; and

(b)   in subsection (9)–

(i)   omit the definition of "relevant benefits",

(ii)   in the definition of "retained benefits", omit "relevant" and for "has, or which may be expected to qualify for, tax-exemption or tax approval" substitute "is registered under Part 4 of the Finance Act 2004", and,

(iii)   omit the definitions of "tax-exemption" and "tax-approval".

5 The 1959 Act is amended as follows.

6 In section 127A (voluntary contributions)–

(a)   in subsection (2) (what regulations may not do), in paragraph (b), (which refers to a limit fixed by or under section 594 of the Income and Corporation Taxes Act 1988), omit "either or both of the following, that is to say" and sub-paragraph (ii) and the word "or" before it; and

(b)   in subsection (9)–

(i)   omit the definition of "relevant benefits",

(ii)   in the definition of "retained benefits", omit "relevant" and for "has, or which may be expected to qualify for, tax-exemption or tax approval" substitute "is registered under Part 4 of the Finance Act 2004", and,

(iii)   omit the definitions of "tax-exemption" and "tax-approval".

Statutory Instruments

REGISTERED PENSION SCHEMES (BLOCK TRANSFERS) (PERMITTED MEMBERSHIP PERIOD) REGULATIONS 2006

(SI 2006/498 as amended by SI 2007/838)

Made on 28 February 2006 by the Commissioners for Her Majesty's Revenue and Customs, in exercise of the powers conferred by para. 22(6)(b) of Sch. 36 to the Finance Act 2004. Operative from 6 April 2006.

CITATION AND COMMENCEMENT

1 These Regulations may be cited as the Registered Pension Schemes (Block Transfers) (Permitted Membership Period) Regulations 2006, and shall come into force on 6th April 2006.

PERMITTED MEMBERSHIP PERIOD FOR BLOCK TRANSFERS

2(1) For the purposes of paragraph (b) of paragraph 22(6) of Schedule 36 to the Finance Act 2004 the period prescribed is a period of twelve months ending with the date on which the transfer is made ("the prescribed period").

2(2) But in calculating the prescribed period, any period preceding the period of twelve months ending with the date on which the transfer is made is ignored if conditions A and B are met.

2(3) Condition A is that immediately before 6th April 2006 the member was a member of a personal pension scheme approved under Chapter 4 of Part 14 of the Income and Corporation Taxes Act 1988 (personal pension schemes).

2(4) Condition B is that the member's rights under that scheme consist solely of rights referable to either or both of the following–

(a) amounts paid under the provisions mentioned in section 188(3)(c) of the Finance Act 2004;

(b) payments under the provisions mentioned in paragraph 14(2) of Schedule 36 to that Act.

History – In reg. 2(1) the words "("the prescribed period")" inserted by SI 2007/838, reg. 2(2), with effect from 6 April 2007. Reg. 2(2) substituted by SI 2007/838, reg. 2(3), with effect from 6 April 2007.

REGISTERED PENSION SCHEMES (TRANSFER OF SUMS AND ASSETS) REGULATIONS 2006

(SI 2006/499 as amended by SI 2008/1946, SI 2011/733, SI 2011/1790 and SI 2014/1449)

Made on 28 February 2006 by the Commissioners for Her Majesty's Revenue and Customs, in exercise of the powers conferred by s. 169(1B), (1C), (1D) and (1E) of, and para. 2(4)(h) and (6A), 3(2B) and (2C), 6(1B) and (1C), 16(2A) and (2B), 17(3) and (4) and 20(1B) and (1C) of Sch. 28 to, the Finance Act 2004. Operative from 6 April 2006.

CITATION AND COMMENCEMENT

1   These Regulations may be cited as the Registered Pension Schemes (Transfer of Sums and Assets) Regulations 2006 and shall come into force on 6th April 2006.

INTERPRETATION

2   In these Regulations **"Part"**, **"section"** or **"Schedule"**, without more, means a Part, section or Schedule of the Finance Act 2004.

SCHEME PENSION PAYABLE BY REGISTERED PENSION SCHEME – RECOGNISED TRANSFERS

3(1)   A transfer within section 169(1) or (1A) (recognised transfer) of sums or assets which represent rights in respect of a scheme pension to which a member of a registered pension scheme has become entitled ("the original scheme pension") is not a recognised transfer unless those sums and assets are, after the transfer, applied towards the provision of a scheme pension (a "new scheme pension").

3(2)   If the sums and assets are so applied, the new scheme pension is to be treated as if it were the original scheme pension for the purposes of Part 4 prescribed in table 1.

SCHEME PENSION PAYABLE BY INSURANCE COMPANY

4   If–

(a)   a scheme pension payable by an insurance company selected by the scheme administrator of a registered pension scheme ("the original scheme pension") ceases to be payable, and

(b)   in consequence of the transfer of sums or assets (or both) from the insurance company to another insurance company in connection with the original scheme pension ceasing to be payable, another scheme pension becomes payable by the other insurance company ("the new scheme pension"),

the new scheme pension is to be treated as if it were the original scheme pension for the purposes of Part 4 prescribed in table 1.

Table 1 – Prescribed purposes – scheme pensions

Provision	Purpose
Section 165(1), pension rule 1	To determine whether the individual has reached the normal minimum pension age by reference to the day on which the original scheme pension was first paid
Section 216(1), benefit crystallisation event 2 (benefit crystallisation event on becoming entitled to a scheme pension)	To determine whether the individual has become entitled to a scheme pension by reference to the original scheme pension (to prevent a benefit crystallisation event occurring in relation to the individual becoming entitled to the new scheme pension).
Section 216(1), benefit crystallisation event 3 (benefit crystallisation event on becoming entitled to a scheme pension at an increased rate)	To determine the rate at which the scheme pension was payable on the day on which the individual became entitled to it by reference to the rate payable in relation to the original scheme pension.

Provision	Purpose
Paragraph 2A(3) and (5) of Schedule 28 (unauthorised payments)	To determine— (i) the rate payable when the member became entitled to the pension and, (ii) the amount of any lump sum on which there is no liability to tax to which the member became entitled in conjunction with the pension, by reference to the original scheme pension.
Paragraph 1(1) and (3)(a) of Schedule 29 (pension commencement lump sum)	To determine whether the member has become entitled to a lump sum in connection with the member becoming entitled to the scheme pension by reference to the original scheme pension (to prevent a lump sum to which a member becomes entitled in connection with becoming entitled to the new scheme pension being a pension commencement lump sum).
Paragraph 14(3) of Schedule 29 (pension protection lump sum death benefit)	To determine— (i) the amount crystallised by reason of the member becoming entitled to the pension (AC) by reference to the member becoming entitled to the original scheme pension, (ii) the amount of pension paid (AP) as that paid in respect of the original scheme pension and the new scheme pension in respect of the period between the member becoming entitled to the original scheme pension and the member's death, (iii) the total amount of pension protection lump sum death benefit (TPLS) by reference to that paid in respect of the original scheme pension and the new scheme pension.
Paragraph 16(3) of Schedule 29 (annuity protection lump sum death benefit)	To determine— (i) the amount crystallised by reason of the member becoming entitled to the pension (AC) by reference to the member becoming entitled to the original scheme pension, (ii) the amount of pension paid (AP) as that paid in respect of the original scheme pension and the new scheme pension in respect of the period between the member becoming entitled to the original scheme pension and the member's death, and (iii) the total amount of annuity protection lump sum death benefit (TPLS) by reference to that paid in respect of the original scheme pension and the new scheme pension.
Paragraph 20(2), (3) and (5) of Schedule 36 (pre-commencement pensions)	To determine— (i) whether an individual has pre-commencement pension rights, (ii) whether an individual has a relevant existing pension.

History – In reg. 4, in Table 1 the entry relating to "Paragraph 20(2), (32) and (5) of Schedule 36" inserted by SI 2014/1449 in relation to transfers made on or after 6 April 2014.

In reg. 4, in Table 1, the entry relating to "section 165(1), pension rule 1" inserted by SI 2011/733, reg. 3(2), which came into force on 6 April 2011, with effect from 6 April 2010.

TERM AND REDUCTION IN THE RATE OF SCHEME PENSION

5 In a case within regulation 3 or 4 a reduction of the original scheme pension is a prescribed circumstance for the purposes of paragraph 2(4) of Schedule 28 (scheme pension: satisfying conditions) if–

(a) the rate of the pension payable under the new scheme pension on the day on which the member becomes entitled to it is not less than the rate payable under the original scheme pension immediately before the original scheme pension ceased to be payable save to the extent that any reduction reflects the reasonable administration costs of the transfer of sums or assets; and

(b) where the new scheme pension is payable until the later of the member's death and the end of a term certain, that term ends on or before the date on which the term certain under the original scheme pension would have ended.

LIFETIME ANNUITY – UNAUTHORISED PAYMENTS AND PRESCRIBED PURPOSES

6(1) In a case within paragraph 3(2B)(a) of Schedule 28 (transfer of sums or assets on cessation of lifetime annuity) where a new lifetime annuity becomes payable, the new lifetime annuity is to be treated as if it were the original lifetime annuity for the purposes of Part 4 prescribed in table 2 to the extent that the amount of the sums and the value of the assets applied to purchase the new lifetime annuity are equal to the amount of the sums and the value of the assets transferred.

6(2) In any other case within paragraph 3(2B), the relevant registered pension scheme is to be treated as making an unauthorised payment to the member of an amount equal to the aggregate of the amount of the sums and the market value of the assets transferred.

Table 2 – Prescribed purposes – lifetime annuities

Provision	*Purpose*
Section 165(1), pension rule 1	To determine whether the individual has reached the normal minimum pension age by reference to the day on which the original lifetime annuity was first paid.
Section 172A (surrender)	To determine for the purposes of section 172A(1) and (2) whether a surrender of (or agreement to surrender) rights to payments under a lifetime annuity has occurred.
Section 216(1), benefit crystallisation event 4 (benefit crystallisation event on becoming entitled to a lifetime annuity)	To determine whether the individual has become entitled to a lifetime annuity by reference to the original annuity (to prevent a benefit crystallisation event occurring in relation to the individual becoming entitled to the new lifetime annuity).
Paragraph 1(1) and (3)(a) of Schedule 29 (pension commencement lump sum)	To determine whether the member has become entitled to a lump sum in connection with the member becoming entitled to a lifetime annuity by reference to the original annuity (to prevent a lump sum to which a member becomes entitled in connection with becoming entitled to the new lifetime annuity being a pension commencement lump sum).
Paragraph 16(3) of Schedule 29 (annuity protection lump sum death benefit)	To determine– (i) the amount crystallised by reason of the member becoming entitled to the annuity (AC) by reference to the member becoming entitled to the original lifetime annuity, (ii) the amount of pension paid (AP) as that paid in respect of the original lifetime annuity and the new lifetime annuity in respect of the period between the member becoming entitled to the original lifetime annuity and the member's death, (iii) the total amount of annuity protection lump sum death benefit (TPLS) by reference to that paid in respect of the original lifetime annuity and the new lifetime annuity.

History – In reg. 6(2), in Table 2, the entry relating to "section 165(1), pension rule 1" inserted by SI 2011/733, reg. 4(2), which came into force on 6 April 2011, with effect from 6 April 2010.

In reg. 6(2), in Table 2, the entry relating to "section 172A" inserted by SI 2008/1946, reg. 2(2), which comes into force on 1 November 2008, with effect in relation to surrenders of and agreements to surrender rights to payments under lifetime annuities or dependants' annuities made on or after 10 October 2007.

SHORT-TERM ANNUITY – UNAUTHORISED PAYMENTS

7(1) In any case within paragraph 6(1B) of Schedule 28 (transfer of sums and assets on cessation of short-term annuity) except where a new short-term annuity becomes payable, the relevant registered pension scheme is to be treated as making an unauthorised payment to the member of an amount equal to the aggregate of the amount of the sums and the market value of the assets transferred.

7(2) In any case within paragraph 6(1B) where a new short-term annuity becomes payable, the new short-term annuity is to be treated as if it were the original short-term annuity for the purposes prescribed in paragraph (3).

7(3) The prescribed purposes are to determine, in relation to pension rule 1 in section 165(1), whether the individual has reached the normal minimum pension age by reference to the day on which the original short-term annuity was first paid.

History – Reg. 7 substituted by SI 2011/733, reg. 5, which came into force on 6 April 2011, with effect from 6 April 2010. Former reg. 7 read as follows:

"7   In any case within paragraph 6(1B) of Schedule 28 (short-term annuity payable by insurance company ceasing to be payable on transfer of sums or assets) except where a new short-term annuity becomes payable, the relevant registered pension scheme is to be treated as making an unauthorised payment to the member of an amount equal to the aggregate of the amount of the sums and the market value of the assets transferred.".

Statutory Instruments

DEPENDANTS' SCHEME PENSION PAYABLE BY REGISTERED PENSION SCHEME – RECOGNISED TRANSFERS

8 A transfer within section 169(1) or (1A) of sums or assets which represent rights in respect of a dependants' scheme pension to which a dependant of a member of a registered pension scheme has become entitled in respect of the member ("the original dependants' scheme pension") is not a recognised transfer unless those sums and assets are, after the transfer, applied towards the provision of a dependants' scheme pension (a "new dependants' scheme pension").

DEPENDANTS' SCHEME PENSION PAYABLE BY AN INSURANCE COMPANY – UNAUTHORISED PAYMENTS

9 In any case within paragraph 16(2A) of Schedule 28 (transfer of sums or assets on cessation of payment of a dependants' scheme pension by an insurance company) except where a new dependants' scheme pension becomes payable, the relevant registered pension scheme is to be treated as making an unauthorised payment in respect of the member of an amount equal to the aggregate of the amount of the sums and the market value of the assets transferred.

DEPENDANTS' ANNUITY – UNAUTHORISED PAYMENTS

10(1) In any case within paragraph 17(3) of Schedule 28 (transfer of sums or assets on cessation of dependants' annuity) where a new dependants' annuity becomes payable, the new dependants' annuity is to be treated as if it were the original dependants' annuity for the purposes of Part 4 prescribed in table 2A to the extent that the amount of the sums and the value of the assets applied to purchase the new dependants' annuity are equal to the amount of the sums and the value of the assets transferred.

10(2) In any other case within paragraph 17(3), except where a new dependants' annuity becomes payable, the relevant registered pension scheme is to be treated as making an unauthorised payment in respect of the member of an amount equal to the aggregate of the amount of the sums and the market value of the assets transferred.

Table 2A

Provision	*Purpose*
Section 172A (surrender)	To determine for the purposes of section 172A(1) and (2) whether a surrender of (or agreement to surrender) rights to payments under a lifetime annuity has occurred.

History – Reg. 10 substituted by SI 2008/1946, reg. 2(3), which comes into force on 1 November 2008, with effect in relation to surrenders of and agreements to surrender rights to payments under lifetime annuities or dependants' annuities made on or after 10 October 2007.

DEPENDANTS' SHORT-TERM ANNUITY – UNAUTHORISED PAYMENTS

11 In any case within paragraph 20(1B) of Schedule 28 (transfer of sums or assets on cessation of dependants' short-term annuity) except where a new dependant' short-term annuity becomes payable, the relevant registered pension scheme is to be treated as making an unauthorised payment in respect of the member of an amount equal to the aggregate of the amount of the sums and the market value of the assets transferred.

MEMBER'S DRAWDOWN PENSION FUND AND DEPENDANT'S DRAWDOWN PENSION FUND – RECOGNISED TRANSFERS AND PRESCRIBED PURPOSES

12(1) A transfer within section 169(1) of sums or assets which represent a member's drawdown pension fund or dependant's drawdown pension fund under an arrangement ("the old arrangement"), is not a recognised transfer unless all of those sums and assets become held under an arrangement under which no other sums or assets are held ("the new arrangement").

12(2) In a case where the sums and assets become so held, the sums and assets transferred are to be treated as remaining sums and assets held under the old arrangement for the purposes prescribed–

(a) in table 3 in the case of a member's drawdown pension fund, and

(b) in table 4 in the case of a dependant's drawdown pension fund.

Table 3 – Prescribed purposes – member's drawdown pension fund

Provision	Purpose
Section 165(1), pension rule 1 (normal minimum pension age)	To determine whether the individual has reached the normal minimum pension age by reference to the day on which, in the case of income withdrawal, the first payment of drawdown pension was made under the old arrangement.
Section 165(3A) (conditions for flexible drawdown arrangement)	To determine whether the limit in section 165(1), pension rule 5 (withdrawal limit for drawdown pension year) is disapplied by reference to whether the limit was disapplied in relation to the old arrangement (so that if the flexible drawdown conditions have been met in relation to the old arrangement, these conditions are treated as having been met in relation to the new arrangement).
Section 216(1), benefit crystallisation event 1 (benefit crystallisation event on designation of sums or assets held as available for payment of drawdown pension to the individual)	To determine whether there has been a designation of sums or assets held as available for payment of drawdown pension to the individual by reference to the designation of sums or assets held under the old arrangement (to prevent a benefit crystallisation event occurring in relation to the sums or assets becoming held under a new arrangement).
Paragraph 9(1)(a) of Schedule 28 (definition of drawdown pension year)	To determine the drawdown pension year for the purpose of paragraphs 9, 10 and 10A of Schedule 28 by reference to the day on which the member first became entitled to a drawdown pension in respect of the old arrangement, except where a determination has been made under paragraph 10B(3) in which case the drawdown pension year is to be determined by reference to that determination.
Paragraph 10(2) and (4)(a) of Schedule 28 (calculation of basis amount for drawdown pension year)	To determine, for the reference period in which the transfer is made, the annual amount of the relevant annuity which could have been purchased by the application of the sums and assets representing the member's drawdown pension fund on the nominated date, by reference to the sums and assets held under the old arrangement.
Paragraph 10A(2) of Schedule 28 (calculation of basis amount for drawdown pension year beginning after the member's 75th birthday)	To determine, for the drawdown pension year in which the transfer is made, the annual amount of the relevant annuity which could have been purchased by the application of the sums and assets representing the member's drawdown pension fund on the nominated date, by reference to the sums and assets held under the old arrangement.
Paragraph 1(1) and (3)(a) of Schedule 29 (pension commencement lump sum)	To determine whether the member has become entitled to a lump sum in connection with the member becoming entitled under an arrangement by reference to the old arrangement (to prevent a lump sum to which a member becomes entitled in connection with becoming entitled under the new arrangement being a pension commencement lump sum).

Table 4 – Prescribed purposes – dependant's drawdown pension fund

Provision	Purpose
Section 167(2A) (conditions for flexible drawdown arrangement)	To determine whether the limit in section 167(1), pension death benefit rule 4 (withdrawal limit for drawdown pension year) is disapplied by reference to whether the limit was disapplied in relation to the old arrangement (so that if the flexible drawdown conditions have been met in relation to the old arrangement, these conditions are treated as having been met in relation to the new arrangement).
Paragraph 23(1) of Schedule 28 (definition of drawdown pension year)	To determine the drawdown pension year for the purpose of paragraphs 23, 24 and 24A of Schedule 28 by reference to the day on which the dependant first became entitled to a dependant's drawdown pension in respect of the old arrangement, except where a determination has been made under paragraph 24B(3) in which case the drawdown pension year is to be determined by reference to that determination.

Provision	Purpose
Paragraph 24(2) and (4)(a) of Schedule 28 (calculation of basis amount for drawdown pension year)	To determine, for the reference period in which the transfer is made, the annual amount of the relevant annuity which could have been purchased by the application of the sums and assets representing the dependant's drawdown pension fund on the nominated date, by reference to the sums and assets held under the old arrangement.
Paragraph 24A(2) of Schedule 28 (calculation of basis amount for drawdown pension year beginning after the dependant's 75th birthday)	To determine, for the drawdown pension year in which the transfer is made, the annual amount of the relevant annuity which could have been purchased by the application of the sums and assets representing the dependant's drawdown pension fund on the nominated date, by reference to the sums and assets held under the old arrangement.

History – Reg. 12 substituted by SI 2011/1790, reg. 2(2), with effect from 11 August 2011 for the tax year 2011–12 and subsequent tax years.

REGISTERED PENSION SCHEMES (PROVISION OF INFORMATION) REGULATIONS 2006

(SI 2006/567, as amended by SI 2006/1961, SI 2008/720, SI 2010/581, SI 2011/301, SI 2011/1797, SI 2012/884 and FA 2014)

Made on 9 March 2006 by the Commissioners for Her Majesty's Revenue and Customs in exercise of the powers conferred upon them by s. 220(5), 221(6), 224(9), 251(1)(a) and (b), (4)(a) and (b), (5) and (6) and 256 of, and para. 7(1)(b), 12(1) and 18(6) of Sch. 36 to, the Finance Act 2004. Operative from 6 April 2006.

Cross references – SI 2010/1187, reg. 11: Financial Assistance Scheme: disapplication of SI 2006/567.

CITATION, COMMENCEMENT AND EFFECT

1   These Regulations may be cited as the Registered Pension Schemes (Provision of Information) Regulations 2006, shall come into force on 6th April 2006, and have effect in relation to any reportable event which takes place on or after 6th April 2006.

INTERPRETATION

2(1)   In these Regulations–

   "the Act" means the Finance Act 2004 and a reference, without more, to a numbered section or Schedule is a reference to the section of, or Schedule to the Act bearing that number;

   "associated company" has the meaning given by section 449 of the Corporation Tax Act 2010;

   "the Commissioners" means the Commissioners for Her Majesty's Revenue and Customs;

   "director" has the meaning given by section 67 of ITEPA 2003;

   "event report" means the report required by regulation 3(1);

   "fixed protection" means transitional protection provided for under paragraph 14 of Schedule 18 to the Finance Act 2011;

   "relevant lump sum death benefit" means a defined benefits lump sum death benefit or an uncrystallised funds lump sum death benefit;

   "reportable event" means an event in relation to which information is required to be provided by virtue of these Regulations;

   "reporting year" means the tax year to which an event report relates.

2(2)   Section 993 ITA 2007 applies for the purpose of determining whether a person is connected with another for the purposes of these Regulations.

2(3)   Expressions defined, or otherwise explained, in section 280, have the same meaning in these Regulations as they have in Part 4 of the Act.

History – In reg. 2(1), in the definition of "associated company", the words "section 449 of the Corporation Tax Act 2010" substituted for the words "section 416 of ICTA" by SI 2011/1797, reg. 3(2)(a), with effect from 11 August 2011.
In reg. 2(1), in the definition of "director", the words "section 67 of ITEPA 2003" substituted for the words "section 417 of ICTA" by SI 2011/1797, reg. 3(2)(b), with effect from 11 August 2011.
In reg. 2(1), the definition of "fixed protection" inserted by SI 2011/1797, reg. 3(2)(c), with effect from 11 August 2011.
In reg. 2(2), the words "Section 993 ITA 2007" substituted for the words "Section 839 of ICTA" by SI 2011/1797, reg. 3(3), with effect from 11 August 2011. Note that the amending provision quoted lower-case "section" in each case, and CCH have assumed that this was a drafting error and have corrected it accordingly.

PROVISION OF INFORMATION BY SCHEME ADMINISTRATOR TO THE COMMISSIONERS

3(1)   The scheme administrator of a registered pension scheme shall provide to the Commissioners an event report in respect of all of the reportable events specified in column (1) of the Table below which have occurred in respect of the scheme during the reporting year, containing the information specified in column (2).

Reportable event	*Information*
1. Unauthorised payments The scheme makes an unauthorised member payment or an unauthorised employer payment.	The name of the person to whom the payment was made, and– (a) where the person is an individual, the national insurance number, (b) where the person is a company, the company registration number, or (c) in any other case, an alternative number obtained from the Commissioners, together with the nature, amount and date of the payment.
2. Payments exceeding 50% of standard lifetime allowance The scheme makes a lump sum death benefit payment to a person in respect of the death of a member, and that payment, either alone or when aggregated with other such payments from that scheme, amounts to more than 50% of the standard lifetime allowance applicable at the time of the member's death.	The name and national insurance number of the deceased member, together with the name and national insurance number of the person to whom the payment was made, and the amount and date of the payment.
3. Early provision of benefits The scheme provides benefits to a member of the scheme who is under the normal minimum pension age and before the benefits were provided the member was, either in the year in which they were provided or any of the preceding six years– (a) in relation to the sponsoring employer, or an associated company of that employer, a director or a person connected with a director; (b) whether alone or with others, the sponsoring employer; or (c) a person connected with the sponsoring employer.	The name and national insurance number of the member, the nature, date and amount of the benefits provided, and reasons for those benefits having been provided under normal minimum pension age.
4. Serious ill-health lump sum A scheme pays a member of the scheme a serious ill-health lump sum and before the payment was made the member was, either in the year in which they were provided or any of the preceding six years– (a) in relation to the sponsoring employer, or an associated company of that employer, a director or a person connected with a director; or (b) whether alone or with others, the sponsoring employer; or (c) a person connected with the sponsoring employer.	The name and national insurance number of the member, and the date and amount of the payment.
5. Suspension of ill-health pension An ill-health pension which has been paid, pursuant to pension rule 1 in section 165(1), ceases to be paid for any reason other than the member's death.	The name and national insurance number of the member to whom the pension had been paid, the date on which the period of non-payment began and the annual rate of the pension, to which the member was entitled, immediately before that period began.

Reportable event

Information

6. Benefit crystallisation events and enhanced lifetime allowance, enhanced protection or fixed protection

A benefit crystallisation event occurs in relation to a member in respect of the scheme and–
(a) the amount crystallised by the event
(i) exceeds the standard lifetime allowance, or
(ii) together with amounts crystallised by other events in relation to that member, exceeds the standard lifetime allowance, for the year in which the event occurs; and
(b) in order to reduce or eliminate liability to the lifetime allowance charge the member relies on entitlement to–
(i) an enhanced lifetime allowance,
(ii) enhanced protection, or
(iii) fixed protection.

The name and national insurance number of the member, the amount crystallised by the event, the date of the event and the reference number given by the Commissioners under–
(a) the Registered Pension Schemes (Enhanced Lifetime Allowance) Regulations 2006 (where the member relies on an enhanced lifetime allowance or enhanced protection), or
(b) the Registered Pension Schemes (Lifetime Allowance Transitional Protection) Regulations 2011 (where the member relies on fixed protection).

7. Pension commencement lump sum

The scheme makes a pension commencement lump sum payment to a member which–
(a) exceeds 25% of the amount found by adding the amount of the payment to the entitlement amount; and
(b) is more than 7.5%, but less than 25%, of the standard lifetime allowance for the tax year in which the sum is paid.
For the purposes of this reportable event, "the entitlement amount" is–
(i) the amount crystallised by reason of the member becoming entitled to the pension with which the lump sum payment is associated, or
(ii) where a benefit crystallisation event did not occur by reason of the member becoming entitled to the pension with which the lump sum payment is associated, the amount that would have been so crystallised if the member had been under the age of 75 at the date the entitlement arose.

The name and national insurance number of the member, together with–
(a) the amount and date of payment of the lump sum; and
(b) the entitlement amount.

8. Pension commencement lump sum: primary and enhanced protection provisions of Schedule 36

The scheme makes a pension commencement lump sum payment to a member and the amount of the payment is an authorised payment by reason only of the application of paragraphs 24 to 30 of Schedule 36.

The name and national insurance number of the member, the amount and date of the payment, and the reference number given to the member by the Commissioners under the Registered Pension Schemes (Enhanced Lifetime Allowance) Regulations 2006.

Reportable event	Information

8A. Stand-alone lump sum

The scheme makes a stand-alone lump sum payment to a member where–
(a) circumstance A in article 25B(2) of the Taxation of Pension Schemes (Transitional Provisions) Order 2006 ("the 2006 Order") is met,
(b) circumstance B in article 25B(3) of the 2006 Order is met; or
(c) circumstance C in article 25B(4) of the 2006 Order is met and the payment is more than 7.5% of the standard lifetime allowance for the tax year in which the sum is paid.

(a) The name and national insurance number of the member;
(b) the amount and date of payment of the lump sum; and
(c) the reference number, if any, given by the Commissioners under the Registered Pension Schemes (Enhanced Lifetime Allowance) Regulations 2006.

9. Transfers to qualifying recognised overseas pension schemes

The scheme makes a recognised transfer to a qualifying recognised overseas pension scheme ("QROPS") which is not a registered pension scheme.

The name and national insurance number of the member, together with–
(a) the member's principal residential address and, where that address is not in the United Kingdom, the member's last principal residential address in the United Kingdom;
(b) the member's date of birth;
(c) the member's telephone number, if any, which the member has provided to the scheme administrator for use by the Commissioners in relation to the scheme;
(d) the acknowledgement mentioned in regulation 11BA(2)(b);
(e) the date of the recognised transfer;
(f) in the case of a transfer of sums, the amount of the sums;
(g) in the case of a transfer of assets, a description and valuation of each type of asset transferred including the value of any unquoted shares, quoted shares and real property;
(h) the name and address of the QROPS to which the sums or assets have been transferred;
(i) the country or territory under the law of which the QROPS is established and regulated; and
(j) the name, address, business telephone number and, where available, the electronic mail address of the manager of the QROPS.

10. Investment-regulated pension scheme

The scheme becomes, or ceases to be, an investment-regulated pension scheme.

(a) The date on which the scheme becomes, or ceases to be, an investment-regulated pension scheme; and
(b) whether all the investments held by the scheme comprise contracts or policies of insurance.

11. Changes in scheme rules

The scheme changes its rules to–
(a) entitle any person to require the making of unauthorised payments; or
(b) permit investment other than in contracts or policies of insurance.

The fact of the change and the date on which the change takes effect.

Reportable event	*Information*

12. Changes to rules of pre-commencement scheme treated as more than one scheme

The scheme, being one which immediately before 6 April 2006 was treated in accordance with section 611 of ICTA as two or more separate schemes, changes its rules in any way.   The fact of the change and the date on which the change takes effect.

13. Change in legal structure of scheme

The legal structure of the scheme changes from one of the following categories to another. The categories are–

(a) a single trust under which all of the assets are held for the benefit of all members of the scheme;

(b) [omitted]

(c) [omitted]

(d) an annuity contract;

(e) a body corporate; and

(f) other.

The date on which the change took effect, together with–

(a) the new category listed in column 1 which applies to the scheme; and

(b) in the case of a change falling within category (f), a brief description of the nature of the new category of legal structure of the scheme.

14. Change in number of members

The number of scheme members falls in a different band at the end of the tax year from that in which it fell at the end of the previous tax year. The bands are–

(a) 0 members;

(b) 1 to 10 members;

(c) 11 to 50 members;

(d) 51 to 10,000 members; and

(e) more than 10,000 members.

The new band applicable to the number of scheme members.

15. [Omitted by SI 2011/1797, reg. 4(7).]

16. [Omitted by SI 2008/720, reg. 3(d).]

17. [Omitted by SI 2011/1797, reg. 4(7).]

18. Scheme chargeable payment

The scheme is treated as having made a scheme chargeable payment under section 185A (income from taxable property) or section 185F (gains from taxable property).

The fact that the scheme is to be treated as having made a scheme chargeable payment.

19. Country or territory of establishment

The scheme changes the country or territory in which it is established.

The date of the change and the country or territory in which the scheme becomes established

20. Occupational pension scheme

The scheme becomes, or ceases to be, an occupational pension scheme.

The fact of the change and the date on which the change takes effect.

Reportable event	Information
21. Flexible drawdown arrangements	
Section 165(3A) or 167(2A) applies to an arrangement	The name and national insurance number of the member or dependant ("the member") who meets the flexible drawdown conditions together with the total amount of drawdown pension or dependant's drawdown pension ("drawdown pension") paid under the arrangement to the member during the reporting year and the country or territory where the sole or main address of the member was situated on the date– (i) the declaration under sections 165(3A)(b) or 167(2A)(b) was made in respect of the arrangement, or (ii) if later, the first payment of drawdown pension was made under the arrangement in the reporting year.

3(2) Where an individual provides the scheme administrator of a scheme with written confirmation that the individual does not qualify for a national insurance number, the scheme administrator must–

(a)   provide the Commissioners with the individual's date of birth and address in order to obtain an alternative number from them, and

(b)   provide this alternative number in place of the national insurance number (where the national insurance number is required by paragraph (1)).

3(2A) Paragraph (2B) applies to any amendment–

(a)   delivered on or after 6th April 2011 to an event report delivered before 6th April 2011, and

(b)   which relates to an individual whose details were included in respect of a reportable event in the event report which is being amended.

3(2B) Where paragraph (1) requires the scheme administrator of the scheme to provide the Commissioners with an individual's national insurance number and where the national insurance number is not known to the scheme administrator–

(a)   paragraph (2) does not apply, and

(b)   the scheme administrator may provide the date of birth in place of the national insurance number.

3(3) For the purposes of reportable event 3 "benefits" does not include a payment–

(a)   which is reportable as reportable event 1 or reportable event 4; or

(b)   which falls within paragraph 10 of Schedule 29.

3(4) Subject to paragraph (4A), in the tax year 2006–07 an event report is required by virtue of reportable event 10 where–

(a)   the scheme is an investment-regulated pension scheme, and

(b)   the scheme was registered on or after 6th April 2006 and did not state on the application that a member of the scheme, whether alone or with others, is able to control the way in which scheme assets are used to provide pension benefits.

3(4A) Paragraph (4) does not apply to a scheme treated as becoming a registered pension scheme on 6th April 2006 by virtue of paragraph 1(1) of Schedule 36 if the scheme is an investment-regulated pension scheme throughout the tax year.

3(5) No event report is required by virtue of reportable event 17–

(a)   if the same event constitutes reportable event 1; or

(b)   in respect of the payment of a life cover lump sum.

Here **"life cover lump sum"** has the same meaning as it has in the paragraph 21A treated as inserted into Part 2 of Schedule 29 by article 8(3) of the Taxation of Pension Schemes (Transitional Provisions) Order 2006.

3(6) The event report shall–

(a)   be in a form specified by the Commissioners, and

(b)   be delivered (subject to the qualification in paragraph (7) and regulation 4(3)) at any time which falls–

(i)   after the end of the end of the tax year to which the report relates, but

(ii)   no later than the 31st January following the tax year to which the report relates.

3(7)   An event report in respect of reportable event 9 must be delivered within 60 days beginning with the day of the transfer to which it relates.

History – In reg. 3(1), in the Table, in entry 1, in the second column, in sub-para. (c), "the Commissioners" substituted for "HMRC" by SI 2011/1797, reg. 4(2), with effect from 11 August 2011.

In reg. 3(1), in the Table, in entry 1, entry in second column substituted by SI 2011/301, reg. 3(a)(i), with effect from 6 April 2011. The former entry read: "The name, date of birth, last known address and national insurance number of the deceased member, together with the name and address of the person to whom the payment was made, and the amount and date of the payment.".

In reg. 3(1), in the Table, in entry 2, the words ", date of birth, last known address", which appeared after the words "The name", omitted, and the words "national insurance number" substituted for the word "address" (after the words "the name and") by SI 2011/301, reg. 3(a)(ii), with effect from 6 April 2011.

In reg. 3(1), in the Table, in entry 3, the words ", address, date of birth", which appeared after the words "The name", omitted by SI 2011/301, reg. 3(a)(iii), with effect from 6 April 2011.

In reg. 3(1), in the Table, in entry 4, the words ", address, date of birth", which appeared after the words "The name", omitted by SI 2011/301, reg. 3(a)(iii), with effect from 6 April 2011.

In reg. 3(1), in the Table, in entry 5, the words ", address, date of birth", which appeared after the words "The name", omitted by SI 2011/301, reg. 3(a)(iii), with effect from 6 April 2011.

In reg. 3(1) in the Table, in entry 5, the words "ceases to be paid for any reason other than the member's death" substituted for "is not now paid because the ill-health condition is no longer met" by SI 2008/720, reg. 3, with effect from 6 April 2008.

In reg. 3(1), in the Table, in entry 6, the heading "Benefit crystallisation events and enhanced lifetime allowance, enhanced protection or fixed protection" substituted for the former heading by SI 2011/1797, reg. 4(3)(a), with effect for the tax year 2012–13 and subsequent tax years.

In reg. 3(1), in the Table, in entry 6, in the first column, para. (b) substituted by SI 2011/1797, reg. 4(3)(b), with effect for the tax year 2012–13 and subsequent tax years.

In reg. 3(1), in the Table, in entry 6, the entry in the second column substituted by SI 2011/1797, reg. 4(3)(c), with effect for the tax year 2012–13 and subsequent tax years.

In reg. 3(1), in the Table, in entry 6, the words ", address, date of birth", which appeared after the words "The name", omitted by SI 2011/301, reg. 3(a)(iii), with effect from 6 April 2011.

In reg. 3(1), in the Table, in entry 7, the entry in the first column substituted by SI 2011/1797, reg. 4(4), with effect from 11 August 2011.

In reg. 3(1), in the Table, in entry 7, in the second column, in para. (b), the words "the entitlement amount" substituted for the words "the amount crystallised on the member becoming entitled to the pension, with which the lump sum is associated." by SI 2011/1797, reg. 4(5), with effect from 11 August 2011.

In reg. 3(1), in the Table, in entry 7, the words ", address, date of birth", which appeared after the words "The name", omitted by SI 2011/301, reg. 3(a)(iii), with effect from 6 April 2011.

In reg. 3(1), in the Table, in entry 8, the words ", address, date of birth", which appeared after the words "The name", omitted by SI 2011/301, reg. 3(a)(iii), with effect from 6 April 2011.

In reg. 3(1), in the Table, in entry 8A(a), the words ", address, date of birth", which appeared after the words "The name", omitted by SI 2011/301, reg. 3(a)(iii), with effect from 6 April 2011.

In reg. 3(1) in the Table, in entry 8A, (a)–(c) substituted for (a) and (b) by SI 2008/720, reg. 3, with effect from 6 April 2008.

In reg. 3(1), in the Table, entry 8A inserted, entry 10 substituted, in entry 11(b) the words "contracts or" inserted, entry 13 para. (b) and (c) omitted and entries 18, 19 and 20 inserted by SI 2006/1961, reg. 3(2), with effect from 11 August 2006.

In reg. 3(1), in the Table, in entry 9, in the first column, "("QROPS")" inserted by SI 2012/884, reg. 12(a)(i), with effect in relation to recognised transfers which are requested by the member on or after 6 April 2012.

In reg. 3(1), in the Table, in entry 9, in the second column, entries (a)–(j) substituted for former entries (a)–(d) by SI 2012/884, reg. 12(a)(ii), with effect in relation to recognised transfers which are requested by the member on or after 6 April 2012.

In reg. 3(1), in the Table, in entry 9, in the second column, in para. (a), the words "or territory" inserted, and the word "situated" substituted for the word "located" by SI 2011/1797, reg. 4(6), with effect from 11 August 2011.

In reg. 3(1), in the Table, in entry 9, entry in second column substituted by SI 2011/301, reg. 3(a)(iv), with effect from 6 April 2011. The former entry read: "The name, address, date of birth and national insurance number of the member, the amount of the sums or assets transferred, the date of the transfer together with the name of the qualifying recognised overseas pension scheme and the country or territory under the law of which it is established and regulated.".

In reg. 3(1), in the Table, entry 15 omitted by SI 2011/1797, reg. 4(7), with effect from 11 August 2011.

In reg. 3(1), in the Table, in former entry 15, column 1, substituted and in column 2 the words "such members and dependants in respect of whom the sums and assets have met the condition concerned for the first time during the reporting year falling" substituted for the words beginning with the word "members" and ending with the word "fall" by SI 2008/720, reg. 3, with effect from 6 April 2008.

In reg. 3(1), in the Table, entry 16 omitted by SI 2008/720, reg. 3, with effect from 6 April 2008.

In reg. 3(1), in the Table, entry 17 omitted by SI 2011/1797, reg. 4(7), with effect from 11 August 2011.

In reg. 3(1), in the Table, in former entry 17, the words ", date of birth, last known address", which appeared after the words "The name", omitted, and the words "national insurance number" substituted for the word "address" (after the words "the name and") by SI 2011/301, reg. 3(a)(ii), with effect from 6 April 2011.

In reg. 3(1), in the Table, in entry 18, in the first column, the words "section 181A (alternatively secured pensions: minimum level of payment);" omitted by SI 2011/1797, reg. 4(8), with effect from 11 August 2011.

In reg. 3(1), in the Table, in entry 18, in column 1, "section 181A (alternatively secured pensions: minimum level of payment)," inserted and the words "section 185F" substituted for "185F" and in column 2 "The fact that the scheme is to be treated as having made a scheme chargeable payment." substituted for "The fact of the payment." by SI 2008/720, reg. 3, with effect from 6 April 2008.

In reg. 3(1), in the Table, entry 21 inserted by SI 2011/1797, reg. 4(9), with effect for the tax year 2012–13 and subsequent tax years.

Reg. 3(2), (2A) and (2B) substituted for former reg. 3(2) by SI 2011/301, reg. 3(b), with effect from 6 April 2011. Former reg. 3(2) read as follows:

"**3(2)**   No obligation to report a national insurance number arises by virtue of paragraph (1) unless that number is known to the scheme administrator.".

Reg. 3(4) and (4A) substituted for former reg. 3(4) by SI 2006/1961, reg. 3(3), with effect from 11 August 2006.

In reg. 3(6)(b), the words "paragraph (7) and" inserted by SI 2012/884, reg. 12(b), with effect in relation to recognised transfers which are requested by the member on or after 6 April 2012.

Reg. 3(7) inserted by SI 2012/884, reg. 12(c), with effect in relation to recognised transfers which are requested by the member on or after 6 April 2012.

Cross references – SI 2013/2259, reg. 6(1): extension of time limit under reg. 3(7) in respect of the requirement to provide information in relation to transfers from Registered Pension Schemes to QROPS which were in existence immediately before 6 April 2012 and which would have ceased to meet the necessary conditions for QROPS status as at 6 April 2012 but for the coming into force of SI 2013/2259, reg. 7 and 8.

OTHER INFORMATION REQUIREMENTS

PROVISION OF INFORMATION IN RESPECT OF A PENSION SCHEME WHICH HAS BEEN WOUND-UP

4(1) The person who, immediately before the winding-up of a registered pension scheme, was the scheme administrator shall give notice to the Commissioners of the fact that the scheme has been wound up and the date on which the winding up was concluded.

4(2) No notice is required by virtue of paragraph (1) in respect of–

(a) an annuity contract or a trust scheme which is treated as a registered pension scheme by virtue of paragraph 1(1)(d), or (f) of Schedule 36, or article 27 of the Taxation of Pension Schemes (Transitional Provisions) Order 2006 (contracts approved under section 620 or 621 of the Income and Corporation Taxes Act 1988);

(b) a former approved superannuation fund within the meaning of paragraph 1(3) of Schedule 36;

(c) an annuity contract which is treated as a registered pension scheme by virtue of section 153(8) other than an annuity contract to which paragraph (2A) applies; or

(d) an annuity policy which is treated as a registered pension scheme by virtue of article 15(5) of the Pension Schemes (Transfers, Reorganisations and Winding Up) (Transitional Provisions) Order 2006 other than an annuity policy to which paragraph (2A) applies.

4(2A) This paragraph applies to an annuity contract or annuity policy–

(a) which has received a recognised transfer (within the meaning of section 169) subsequent to the one which led to–

   (i) the annuity contract becoming a registered pension scheme under section 153(8), or

   (ii) the annuity policy becoming a registered pension scheme under paragraph 1(1) of Schedule 36 by virtue of article 15(5) of the Pension Schemes (Transfers, Reorganisations and Winding Up) (Transitional Provisions) Order 2006;

(b) which has received–

   (i) relievable pension contributions as defined in section 188(2), or

   (ii) contributions paid by an employer,

   where the total of those contributions exceeds £10;

(c) where a declaration under section 270(2)(b) has been made by the scheme administrator to the Commissioners; or

(d) which is an investment-regulated pension scheme which directly or indirectly holds an interest in taxable property.

Here "taxable property" has the same meaning as in Part 2 of Schedule 29A and whether an interest in taxable property is held directly or indirectly shall be determined in accordance with Part 3 of that Schedule.

4(3) Where a pension scheme is wound up, the time prescribed in respect of any information required to be delivered under these Regulations (whether in the event report or otherwise) is any time on or before–

(a) the last day of the period of 3 months beginning with the day on which the winding up is completed, or

(b) the last day otherwise prescribed by these Regulations for the provision of that information,

whichever is the earlier.

History – In reg. 4(2), the word "or" at the end of para. (b) omitted and the word "; or" at the end of para. (c) inserted by SI 2010/581, reg. 3(1)(a), with effect from 6 April 2010.
Reg. 4(2)(d) inserted by SI 2010/581, reg. 3(1)(b), with effect from 6 April 2010.
In reg. 4(2)(a) the word "or" omitted at the end and in (b) the words
"; or
   (c) an annuity contract which is treated as a registered pension scheme by virtue of section 153(8) other than an annuity contract to which paragraph (2A) applies.".
inserted by SI 2008/720, reg. 4, with effect from 6 April 2008.
In reg. 4(2A), the words "or annuity policy" inserted after the words "annuity contract" by SI 2010/581, reg. 3(2)(a), with effect from 6 April 2010.

Reg. 4(2A)(a) substituted by SI 2010/581, reg. 3(2)(b), with effect from 6 April 2010.
Reg. 4(2A) inserted by SI 2008/720, reg. 4, with effect from 6 April 2008.

PROVISION OF INFORMATION BY EMPLOYER COMPANY TO THE COMMISSIONERS

5(1) Where a registered pension scheme makes an unauthorised employer payment to a company, the company shall provide the information specified in paragraph (2).

5(2) The information required is–

(a)   details of the scheme that made the payment;

(b)   the nature of the payment;

(c)   the amount of the payment; and

(d)   the date on which the payment was made.

5(3) This information shall be provided to the Commissioners no later than the 31st January following the tax year in which the payment is made.

UNAUTHORISED BORROWING: PROVISION OF INFORMATION BY SCHEME ADMINISTRATOR TO THE COMMISSIONERS

5A(1) Where a registered pension scheme is treated as having made a scheme chargeable payment ("the payment") by virtue of sections 183 (effect of unauthorised borrowing: money purchase arrangements) or 185 (effect of unauthorised borrowing: other arrangements), the scheme administrator shall provide the information specified in paragraph (2).

5A(2) The information required is–

(a)   the name and pension scheme tax reference number of the scheme that is treated as making the payment;

(b)   the name and address of the scheme administrator;

(c)   the tax year in which the payment is treated as having been made; and

(d)   the aggregate amount of payments treated as having been made by the scheme during that tax year.

5A(3) This information shall be provided to the Commissioners in an annual written report delivered at any time which falls–

(a)   after the end of the tax year in which the payment is treated as having been made, but

(b)   no later than the 31st January following that tax year.

History – Reg. 5A inserted by SI 2010/581, reg. 4, with effect from 6 April 2010.

MINIMUM INCOME REQUIREMENT: PROVISION OF INFORMATION BY SCHEME ADMINISTRATOR TO THE COMMISSIONERS FOR THE TAX YEAR 2011–12

5B(1) Where section 165(3A) or 167(2A) of the Finance Act 2004 applies to an arrangement ("the specified arrangement") the scheme administrator shall provide the information specified in paragraph (2) in the form of a written report.

5B(2) The information required is–

(a)   the name of the member or dependant ("the member") who meets the flexible drawdown conditions and the member's national insurance number or alternative number obtained in accordance with the procedure described in regulation 3(2)(c) (provision of information by scheme administrator to the Commissioners);

(b)   the country or territory where the member's sole or main address was situated on the date the declaration under section 165(3A)(b) or 167(2A)(b) was made in respect of the specified arrangement, and

(c)   the total amount of drawdown pension paid to the member under the specified arrangement for the tax year 2011–12.

5B(3) The information shall be provided to the Commissioners no later than the 31st January 2013.

History – Reg. 5B inserted by SI 2011/1797, reg. 5, with effect from 11 August 2011.

SCHEME ADMINISTRATION

6 The person who has been, but has ceased to be, the scheme administrator must notify the Commissioners of the termination of his appointment, together with the date on which the termination took effect, within 30 days.

PERCENTAGE OF STANDARD LIFETIME ALLOWANCE EXPENDED ON THE HAPPENING OF A BENEFIT CRYSTALLISATION EVENT

7(1) The percentage of standard lifetime allowance expended on the happening of each relevant benefit crystallisation event for the purposes of the provisions listed in paragraph (3) is found by the application of the formula–

$$\frac{AE}{RSLA} \times \frac{100}{1}$$

Here–

AE is the amount of lifetime allowance expended on the happening of the benefit crystallisation event; and

RSLA is the relevant standard lifetime allowance at the time of that event.

7(2) The amount of lifetime allowance expended on the happening of a benefit crystallisation event is the sum of AC and SFTP.

Here–

AC is the amount crystallised by the benefit crystallisation event; and

SFTP is the amount covered by a scheme-funded tax payment (within the meaning of section 215) in relation to that benefit crystallisation event.

7(3) The provisions to which this paragraph applies are–

(a)   regulation 8(2) and (3);

(b)   regulation 9(2);

(c)   regulation 14(3);

(d)   regulation 15(2);

(e)   regulation 16(2) and (3);

(f)   regulation 17(2), (3) (5) and (7).

7(4) The total percentage of standard lifetime allowance expended in relation to a member is the sum of the percentages found in accordance with paragraph (1) in respect of benefit crystallisation events in respect of the member.

DEATH: PROVISION OF INFORMATION BY SCHEME ADMINISTRATOR TO PERSONAL REPRESENTATIVES

8(1) The scheme administrator of a registered pension scheme shall provide to the personal representatives of a deceased member of that scheme, the information specified in paragraphs (2) and (3).

8(2) The information is the percentage of standard lifetime allowance expended by, and the amount and the date of payment of, a relevant lump sum death benefit by the scheme in relation to the member.

The information shall be provided no later than the last day of the period of 3 months beginning with the day on which the final such payment is made.

8(3) The information is the total percentage of standard lifetime allowance expended, at the date of the statement, by–

(a)   any benefit crystallisation event in respect of the deceased member's rights under the scheme to the extent that–

    (i)   the sums or assets subject to any such event; and

    (ii)   any sums or assets subsequently representing those sums or assets;

   have not been transferred to another registered pension scheme, and

(b)   where sums or assets have been transferred to the scheme from another registered pension scheme (whether directly or indirectly) in respect of the deceased member any benefit crystallisation event in connection with–

    (i)   those sums or assets; and

    (ii)   any other sums or assets held prior to the transfer which the sums and assets mentioned in sub-paragraph (i) represented,

but excluding from that percentage any amount in respect of any relevant lump sum death benefit payment in respect of the deceased member.

The information shall be provided no later than the last day of the period of 2 months beginning with the day on which a request for it is received from the member's personal representatives.

History – In reg. 8(1) the words "(within the meaning of section 279)" omitted by SI 2008/720, reg. 5, with effect from 6 April 2008.

DEATH: PROVISION OF INFORMATION BY INSURANCE COMPANY TO PERSONAL REPRESENTATIVES

9(1) Where–

(a)   an insurance company has paid a lifetime annuity or a scheme pension to an individual who has been a member of a registered pension scheme purchased with sums or assets held for the purposes of that scheme, and

(b)   the member to whom that annuity or pension was payable has died,

the insurance company shall, on request by the member's personal representatives, provide them with the information specified in paragraph (2).

9(2) The information is the total percentage of standard lifetime allowance expended, at the date of the statement, by–

(a)   any benefit crystallisation event in respect of the deceased member under the registered pension scheme to the extent that–

  (i)   the sums and assets subject to that event, or

  (ii)   sums and assets subsequently representing those sums and assets,

  have not been transferred to another such scheme, and

(b)   where sums or assets have been transferred to the scheme from another registered pension scheme (whether directly or indirectly) in respect of the deceased member's rights, any benefit crystallisation event in connection with–

  (i)   those sums or assets; and

  (ii)   any other sums or assets held prior to the transfer which the sums or assets mentioned in sub-paragraph (i) represented.

9(3) The information shall be provided no later than the last day of the period of 2 months beginning with the day on which the request was received.

DEATH: PROVISION OF INFORMATION BY PERSONAL REPRESENTATIVES TO THE COMMISSIONERS

10(1) Where–

(a)   a relevant lump sum death benefit is paid in respect of a deceased member of a registered pension scheme, and

(b)   that payment, of itself or together with any other relevant lump sum death benefit, results in a lifetime allowance charge,

the personal representatives of the member shall provide to the Commissioners the information specified in paragraph (2).

10(2) The information required is–

(a)   the name of the pension scheme from which, and the name and address of the scheme administrator by whom, the benefits were paid;

(b)   the name of the deceased member in respect of whom the benefits were paid;

(c)   the amount and date of payment of the benefits; and

(d)   the chargeable amount in respect of which a lifetime allowance charge is payable by virtue of the payments.

10(3) The information required shall be provided on or before the later of–

(a)   the end of the period of 13 months beginning with the death of the member; or

(b)   the end of the period of 30 days beginning with the date on which the personal representatives (or any of them) became aware that paragraph (1) applied to the deceased member.

10(4) Where a requirement to provide information under this regulation arises after the period specified in paragraph (3) has expired, the information shall be provided no later than the last day of the period of 30 months beginning with the death of the member.

10(5) If the personal representatives discover after the latest date for providing information under paragraph (4) any information required to be provided under paragraph (1), that information shall be provided no later than the last day of the period of 3 months beginning with the discovery of that information.

INFORMATION PROVIDED BY MEMBER TO SCHEME ADMINISTRATOR: ENHANCED LIFETIME ALLOWANCE, ENHANCED PROTECTION OR FIXED PROTECTION

11 If the member of a registered pension scheme intends to rely on entitlement to–

(a)   an enhanced lifetime allowance or enhanced protection by virtue of any provisions listed in section 256(1)(a), or

(b)   fixed protection by virtue of paragraph 14 of Schedule 18 to the Finance Act 2011

the member must give to the scheme administrator the reference number issued by the Commissioners under the Registered Pension Schemes (Enhanced Lifetime Allowance) Regulations 2006 or the Registered Pension Schemes (Lifetime Allowance Transitional Protection) Regulations 2011 in respect of that entitlement.

History – Reg. 11 substituted by SI 2011/1797, reg. 6, with effect for the tax year 2012–13 and subsequent tax years.

INFORMATION PROVIDED BY MEMBERS TO SCHEME ADMINISTRATORS: RECYCLING OF LUMP SUMS

11A Where a registered pension scheme is treated as making to a member of the scheme an unauthorised payment under paragraph 3A of Schedule 29 (recycling of lump sums), the member shall notify–

(a)   the date on which the unauthorised payment is treated as made, and

(b)   the amount of the payment,

to the scheme administrator within 30 days of the date on which the unauthorised payment is treated as made.

History – Reg. 11A inserted by SI 2006/1961, reg. 4, with effect from 11 August 2006.

INFORMATION PROVIDED BY MEMBERS TO SCHEME ADMINISTRATORS: PENSION COMMENCEMENT LUMP SUMS

11B Where–

(a)   a registered pension scheme intends to pay a pension commencement lump sum to a member of the scheme,

(b)   paragraph 2(5)(a) of Schedule 29 (available portion of the member's lump sum allowance) applies to determine the permitted maximum, and

(c)   a benefit crystallisation event has occurred previously in relation to the member in respect of a scheme pension that crystallised under a money purchase arrangement,

the member shall provide such information as will enable the scheme administrator to calculate the available portion of the member's lump sum allowance.

History – Reg. 11B inserted by SI 2006/1961, reg. 4, with effect from 11 August 2006.

INFORMATION PROVIDED BY MEMBERS TO SCHEME ADMINISTRATORS: RECOGNISED TRANSFERS

11BA(1) Paragraph (2) applies where a member of a registered pension scheme makes a request to the scheme administrator to make a recognised transfer ("transfer request") in respect of a qualifying recognised overseas pension scheme.

11BA(2) The member must provide to the scheme administrator–

(a)   the member's–

   (i)   name;

   (ii)   date of birth;

   (iii)   principal residential address and, where that address is not in the United Kingdom, the member's last principal residential address in the United Kingdom;

   (iv)   national insurance number or, where applicable, confirmation in writing that the member does not qualify for a national insurance number;

   (v)   telephone number, if any, which the member provides for use by the scheme administrator or the Commissioners in relation to the scheme;

   (vi)   the name and address of the qualifying recognised overseas pension scheme;

   (vii)   the country or territory under the law of which the qualifying recognised overseas pension scheme is established and regulated; and

(b)   the member's acknowledgement in writing that the member is aware that a transfer other than a recognised transfer to a qualifying recognised overseas pension scheme of sums or assets held for the purposes of, or representing accrued rights under, an arrangement under a registered pension scheme–

(i)   gives rise to a liability under section 208 (unauthorised payments charge); and

(ii)   may give rise to a liability under section 209 (unauthorised payments surcharge).

11BA(3)   The information specified in paragraph (2) must be provided within 60 days beginning with the day of the transfer request.

11BA(4)   The scheme administrator must send the member notification of the requirements specified in this regulation within 30 days beginning with the day of the transfer request.

History – Reg. 11BA inserted by SI 2012/884, reg. 13, with effect from 6 April 2012.

Cross references – SI 2013/2259, reg. 6(2) and (3): extension of time limits under reg. 11BA(3) and (4) in respect of the requirement to provide information in relation to transfers from Registered Pension Schemes to QROPS which were in existence immediately before 6 April 2012 and which would have ceased to meet the necessary conditions for QROPS status as at 6 April 2012 but for the coming into force of SI 2013/2259, reg. 7 and 8.

INFORMATION PROVIDED BY INDIVIDUALS TO SCHEME ADMINISTRATOR: NATIONAL INSURANCE NUMBER

11C(1)   Paragraph (2) applies where a scheme administrator needs an individual's national insurance number or to obtain an alternative number in respect of an individual in order to complete an event report, other than an event report in respect of reportable event 9, or a return under section 254.

11C(2)   The individual must provide the scheme administrator with the national insurance number or the information described in paragraph (3), as appropriate, within 60 days of the date on which the scheme administrator requests the individual to provide the information.

11C(3)   If the individual does not qualify for a national insurance number the individual must provide the scheme administrator with confirmation of this in writing, together with the individual's date of birth and address.

History – In reg. 11C(1) the words ", other than an event report in respect of reportable event 9," inserted by SI 2012/884, reg. 14, with effect from 6 April 2012.

Reg. 11C inserted by SI 2011/301, reg. 4, with effect from 6 April 2011.

INFORMATION ABOUT SCHEME ADMINISTRATOR'S LIABILITY FOR A LIFETIME ALLOWANCE CHARGE

12   If the scheme administrator of a registered pension scheme has made or intends to make a payment, on account of his liability to account for tax in respect of a lifetime allowance charge on a benefit crystallisation event, the scheme administrator shall within 3 months after the benefit crystallisation event provide the member with a notice stating–

(a)   the chargeable amount in respect of the benefit crystallisation event;

(b)   how that chargeable amount has been calculated;

(c)   the amount of the resulting charge to tax; and

(d)   whether the scheme administrator has accounted for the tax or intends to do so.

PROVISION OF INFORMATION ABOUT UNAUTHORISED PAYMENTS

13(1)   Where a registered pension scheme has made to a member of the scheme an unauthorised payment under section 173(1) (provision of benefits), the scheme administrator shall provide to the member before 7th July following the tax year in which the payment is made the information specified in paragraph (2).

13(2)   The information is–

(a)   the nature of the benefit provided;

(b)   the amount of the unauthorised payment which is treated as being made by the provision of the benefit; and

(c)   the date on which the benefit was provided.

INFORMATION PROVIDED TO MEMBERS BY SCHEME ADMINISTRATORS ABOUT BENEFIT CRYSTALLISATION EVENTS

14(1)   The scheme administrator shall provide a statement containing the information in paragraph (3) to each member of the scheme or, if the member has died, the member's personal representatives–

(a)   who has an actual (as opposed to prospective) entitlement to be paid a pension, at least once in each tax year, or

(b)   in respect of whom a benefit crystallisation event has occurred, within 3 months of that event.

This paragraph is subject to the following qualification.

14(2)　No obligation to provide a statement arises–

(a)　under paragraph (1) if a statement is required to be provided under regulation 16, 17 or 17A containing the same information as is required by paragraph (3);

(b)　under paragraph (1)(a) in relation to a relevant existing pension (within the meaning of paragraph 10(2) of Schedule 36) to which an individual has an actual (as opposed to prospective) entitlement to be paid a pension on 5th April 2006;

(ba)　under paragraph (1)(a) in a tax year following the tax year in which the member reaches the age of 75;

(c)　under paragraph (1)(b) if a statement is required to be provided under paragraph (1)(a) or under regulation 8(2).

14(3)　The information is the percentage of standard lifetime allowance expended by–

(a)　benefit crystallisation events in respect of the scheme, to the extent that the sums or assets subject to any such event have not been transferred to another registered pension scheme, and

(b)　where the first-mentioned scheme has received (whether directly or indirectly) a transfer in respect of the member, any benefit crystallisation event, prior to the transfer, in connection with–

　　(i)　the sums or assets represented by the transfer;

　　(ii)　sums and assets replaced by the sums or assets mentioned in paragraph (i).

History – In reg. 14(1) the words "or, if the member has died, the member's personal representatives" inserted by SI 2008/720, reg. 6, with effect from 6 April 2008.
Reg. 14(2)(ba) inserted by SI 2011/1797, reg. 7, with effect from 11 August 2011.
In reg. 14(2)(a) the words "16, 17 or 17A" substituted for "16 or 17" by SI 2008/720, reg. 6, with effect from 6 April 2008.

ANNUAL ALLOWANCE: ANNUAL PROVISION OF INFORMATION BY SCHEME ADMINISTRATOR TO MEMBER

14A(1)　Where–

(a)　an individual is a member ("the member") of a registered pension scheme for all or part of a pension input period ending in a tax year ("the relevant pension input period") who meets one of the conditions in paragraph (8), and

(b)　the aggregate of the pension input amounts for the relevant pension input period in respect of each arrangement under the registered pension scheme relating to the member exceeds the annual allowance for that tax year,

the scheme administrator must provide the member with a statement containing the information specified in paragraph (2) (the "pension savings statement").

14A(2)　The information is–

(a)　the aggregate of the pension input amounts for the relevant pension input period in respect of all the arrangements under the registered pension scheme relating to the member (see section 152),

(b)　the annual allowance for the tax year in which the relevant pension input period ends ("the relevant tax year"),

(c)　the aggregate of the pension input amounts in respect of all the arrangements under the registered pension scheme relating to the member for each of the pension input periods ending in the three tax years immediately preceding the relevant tax year (subject to paragraph (3)), and

(d)　the annual allowance for each of the three preceding tax years or where one or more of the three preceding tax years is the 2008–09, 2009–10 or 2010–11 tax year, the assumed annual allowance for that tax year pursuant to paragraph 30(3)(a) of Schedule 17 to the Finance Act 2011.

14A(3)　Where a pension input period in paragraph (2)(c) ends in the 2008–09, 2009–10 or 2010–11 tax year, the pension input amount for that pension input period must be determined on the basis that the assumptions in paragraph 30(3)(b) of Schedule 17 to the Finance Act 2011 apply to that pension input period.

14A(4)　The scheme administrator must provide the member with the pension savings statement no later than the 6th October following the relevant tax year. This paragraph is subject to paragraphs (5) and (6).

14A(5)　Where the relevant tax year is 2011–12, the scheme administrator must provide the member with the pension savings statement for that year no later than 6th October 2013.

14A(6) Where the scheme administrator has not been provided with the information concerning the member by the member's employer in respect of the relevant pension input period pursuant to regulation 15A, the scheme administrator must provide the pension savings statement–

(a)   within 3 months following receipt of that information, or

(b)   if later, on or before the date specified in paragraph (4) or (where the relevant tax year is 2011–12) paragraph (5).

14A(7) Where–

(a)   the member meets the conditions in paragraph (1)(a) and (b), and

(b)   paragraph 28 of Schedule 17 to the Finance Act 2011 applies (provision for a straddling pension input period),

the scheme administrator must provide the member with a pension savings statement containing the pension input amount in respect of the pre-announcement period and post-announcement period in addition to the information specified in paragraph (2).

Condition A

The individual is an active member of the registered pension scheme referred to in paragraph (1)

Condition B

The individual is a deferred member of the registered pension scheme referred to in paragraph (1) in relation to a cash balance arrangement and the condition in section 230(5B)(b) (cash balance arrangements) is not met in respect of the pension input amount for the relevant pension input period.

Condition C

The individual is a deferred member of the registered pension scheme referred to in paragraph (1) in relation to a defined benefits arrangement and the condition in section 234(5B)(b) (defined balance arrangements) is not met in respect of the pension input amount for the relevant pension input period.

History – Reg. 14A inserted by SI 2011/1797, reg. 8, with effect from 11 August 2011.

ANNUAL ALLOWANCE: PROVISION OF INFORMATION BY SCHEME ADMINISTRATOR TO MEMBER ON REQUEST

14B(1) Where a member or former member ("the member") of a registered pension scheme makes a written request to the scheme administrator of that scheme for any such information in respect of a pension input period ending in a tax year ("the relevant pension input period") as is referred to in regulations 14A(2) or (7), the scheme administrator must provide the member with the information requested–

(a)   within 3 months following receipt of the request, or

(b)   if later, on or before 6th October following the tax year ("the relevant tax year") in which the relevant pension input period ended.

This paragraph is subject to paragraphs (2) and (3).

14B(2) Where the relevant tax year is 2011–12, the scheme administrator must provide the member with the information requested under paragraph (1) for that tax year no later than 6th October 2013.

14B(3) Where the scheme administrator has not been provided with the information concerning the member by the member's employer in respect of the relevant pension input period pursuant to regulation 15A ("the regulation 15A information"), the scheme administrator must provide the information requested under paragraph (1)–

(a)   within 3 months following receipt of the regulation 15A information, or

(b)   if later, on or before–

       (i)   6th October following the relevant tax year, or

       (ii)   where the relevant tax year is 2011–12, the 6th October 2013.

History – Reg. 14B inserted by SI 2011/1797, reg. 8, with effect from 11 August 2011.

INFORMATION BETWEEN SCHEME ADMINISTRATORS

15(1) This regulation applies if, and to the extent that, a member's crystallised rights under one registered pension scheme ("Scheme A"), are transferred to another such scheme ("Scheme B").

15(2) The scheme administrator of Scheme A shall provide to the administrator of Scheme B, within 3 months of the transfer, a statement of the total percentage of the standard lifetime allowance expended, at the date of the statement, by–

(a)   benefit crystallisation events in respect of Scheme A in connection with the sums and assets represented by the transfer; and

(b)   where Scheme A has received (whether directly or indirectly) a transfer in respect of the member, any benefit crystallisation event prior to the occurrence of the transfer in connection with–

(i)   the sums or assets represented by the transfer; and

(ii)   sums and assets replaced by the sums and assets mentioned in paragraph (i).

ANNUAL ALLOWANCE: INFORMATION TO BE PROVIDED TO SCHEME ADMINISTRATORS BY CERTAIN PERSONS

15A(1)   Where–

(a)   an employer is a sponsoring employer of a registered pension scheme, and

(b)   an employee of that employer or a director is an active member of that scheme in relation to an arrangement under the scheme ("the arrangement") for all or part of a pension input period ending in a tax year,

the employer must provide to the scheme administrator such information as will enable the scheme administrator to calculate the pension input amount in respect of the arrangement for the pension input period ending in that tax year.

15A(2)   The information must be provided to the scheme administrator no later than the 6th July following the tax year in which the pension input period ends. This paragraph is subject to paragraph (3).

15A(3)   Where the pension input period ends in the tax year 2011–12, the employer must provide the information relating to the pension input period no later than 6th July 2013.

15A(4)   The employer must provide to the scheme administrator such information as will enable the scheme administrator to calculate the pension input amount for any of the pension input periods ending in the tax years 2008–09, 2009–10 and 2010–11, within 3 months following receipt of a written request from the scheme administrator or, (if later), on or before 6th July 2013.

15A(5)   Where–

(a)   regulation 14A(7) applies to a scheme administrator (obligation to provide information to a member where there is a straddling pension input period), and

(b)   a written request is made by the scheme administrator to the employer,

the employer must provide the scheme administrator with such information as will enable the scheme administrator to comply with the obligation contained in regulation 14A(7), such information to be supplied within three months of receipt of the written request or, (if later) on or before 6th July 2013.

15A(6)   The obligations contained in this regulation shall apply to a responsible person (see paragraph (7)) and for the purposes of applying this regulation to the responsible person, references to **"employer"** shall be read as referring to the responsible person.

15A(7)   For the purposes of this regulation **"responsible person"** means a person who is responsible for providing the scheme administrator of a registered pension scheme with 7 such information as will enable the scheme administrator to calculate the pension input amount in respect of a member where the member is an active member of that scheme in relation to an arrangement under the scheme for all or part of a pension input period ending in a tax year.

History – Reg. 15A inserted by SI 2011/1797, reg. 9, with effect from 11 August 2011.

PENSIONS AND ANNUITIES IN PAYMENT: INFORMATION PROVIDED TO AND BY INSURANCE COMPANIES

16(1)   This regulation applies if a registered pension scheme has provided an insurance company with funds, otherwise than from a drawdown pension fund, to secure the payment of–

(a)   a scheme pension, or

(b)   a lifetime annuity.

16(2)   The scheme administrator shall provide the insurance company, within 3 months of the date on which the recipient becomes entitled to the pension or annuity, with a statement of the total percentage of standard lifetime allowance expended, at the date of the statement by benefit crystallisation events in respect of that pension or annuity, and any pension commencement lump sum connected with that pension or annuity.

16(3)   The insurance company shall provide to each pensioner or annuitant, at least once in each tax year, a statement of the percentage of the standard lifetime allowance expended at the date of the statement, by benefit crystallisation events in respect of that pension or annuity and any pension commencement lump sum paid in connection with that pension or annuity.

16(4) No obligation to provide a statement arises—

(a)   under paragraph (2) in respect of any entitlement to a pension or annuity or pension commencement lump sum which does not give rise to a benefit crystallisation event;

(b)   under paragraph (3) in a tax year following the tax year in which the member reaches the age of 75.

History – In reg. 16(1), the words "a drawdown pension" substituted for the words "an unsecured pension" by SI 2011/1797, reg. 10(a), with effect from 11 August 2011.
Reg. 16(4) inserted by SI 2011/1797, reg. 10(b), with effect from 11 August 2011.

PAYMENTS TO INSURANCE COMPANIES FROM DRAWDOWN PENSION FUNDS

History – In the heading above reg. 17, the words "drawdown pension" substituted for the words "unsecured pension" by SI 2011/1797, reg. 11, with effect from 11 August 2011.

17(1) This regulation applies if a registered pension scheme has provided an insurance company with sums or assets from a drawdown pension fund, to secure the payment of—

(a)   a scheme pension, or

(b)   a lifetime annuity.

17(2) If the sums or assets provided comprise part of the member's drawdown pension fund, the scheme administrator shall provide the insurance company, within 3 months of the purchase of the pension or annuity, with a statement of the percentage of standard lifetime allowance expended by the member becoming entitled to the scheme pension or the lifetime annuity.

17(3) The insurance company shall provide to each pensioner or annuitant, at least once in each tax year, a statement of the percentage of the standard lifetime allowance expended at the date of the statement, in respect of that pension or annuity.

But no statement is required if the percentage expended is nil.

17(4) If the sums or assets provided comprise the whole of the member's drawdown pension fund, the scheme administrator shall provide the insurance company, within 3 months of the purchase of the pension or annuity, with a statement containing the information in paragraph (5).

17(5) The information is—

(a)   the sum of the percentages of standard lifetime allowance expended by—

   (i)   benefit crystallisation events in respect of the scheme referred to in paragraph (4) ("A"), to the extent that the sums and assets subject to those events have not been the subject of a transfer to another registered scheme; and

   (ii)   where A has received (whether directly or indirectly) a transfer in respect of that member, any benefit crystallisation event prior to the transfer in connection with the sums and assets represented by the transfer and sums and assets which were replaced by the sums and assets mentioned in paragraph (i), less

(b)   the sum of the percentages of standard lifetime allowance expended by benefit crystallisation events—

   (i)   which have been the subject of a statement under paragraph (2),

   (ii)   which have been the subject of a statement under regulation 16(2), or

   (iii)   which are referable to sums or assets which continue to be held by A.

17(6) The insurance company shall provide to the pensioner or annuitant, once in each tax year, a statement containing the information in paragraph (7).

17(7) The information is—

(a)   the sum of the percentages of standard lifetime allowance expended by—

   (i)   benefit crystallisation events in respect of the scheme referred to in paragraph (4) ("A"), to the extent that the sums and assets subject to those events have not been the subject of a transfer to another registered scheme;

   (ii)   benefit crystallisation events in respect of a scheme pension after the pensioner first became entitled to it; and

   (iii)   where A has received (whether directly or indirectly) a transfer in respect of that member, any benefit crystallisation event prior to the transfer in connection with the sums and assets represented by the transfer and sums and assets which were replaced by the sums and assets mentioned in paragraph (i), less

(b)   the sum of the percentages of standard lifetime allowance expended by benefit crystallisation events—

   (i)   which have been the subject of a statement under paragraph (2),

(ii)   which have been the subject of a statement under regulation 16(3), or

(iii)   which are referable to sums or assets which continue to be held by A.

17(8)   No obligation to provide a statement arises under paragraph (3) or (6) in a tax year following the tax year in which the pensioner or annuitant reaches the age of 75.

History – In reg. 17(1), the words "a drawdown pension" substituted for the words "an unsecured pension" by SI 2011/1797, reg. 12(a), with effect from 11 August 2011.
In reg. 17(2), the words "drawdown pension" substituted for the words "unsecured pension" by SI 2011/1797, reg. 12(b), with effect from 11 August 2011.
In reg. 17(4), the words "drawdown pension" substituted for the words "unsecured pension" by SI 2011/1797, reg. 12(b), with effect from 11 August 2011.
Reg. 17(8) inserted by SI 2011/1797, reg. 12(c), with effect from 11 August 2011.

TRANSFERS BETWEEN INSURANCE COMPANIES

17A(1)   This regulation applies if–

(a)   a scheme pension payable by an insurance company ("Insurer A") ceases to be payable and another scheme pension becomes payable by another insurance company ("Insurer B"), in the circumstances described in regulation 4 of the Registered Pension Schemes (Transfer of Sums and Assets) Regulations 2006 (scheme pension payable by insurance company) ("the Transfer Regulations"); or

(b)   a lifetime annuity payable by an insurance company ("Insurer A") ceases to be payable and a new lifetime annuity becomes payable by another insurance company ("Insurer B"), in the circumstances described in regulation 6 of the Transfer Regulations (lifetime annuity).

In the following provisions of this regulation "a relevant transfer" means a transfer which occurs in the circumstances described in regulation 4 or 6 of the Transfer Regulations.

17A(2)   If in connection with a relevant transfer–

(a)   Insurer A transfers funds to Insurer B; and

(b)   Insurer A was required to provide a statement under regulation 16(3),

Insurer A shall provide Insurer B, within 3 months of the transfer, with a statement containing the information specified in regulation 16(3).

17A(3)   After the relevant transfer the obligation imposed by regulation 16(3) shall be that of Insurer B.

17A(4)   Where in connection with a relevant transfer Insurer A transfers funds to Insurer B, and Insurer A was required to provide a statement under regulation 17(3) or 17(6)–

(a)   if the statement was provided under regulation 17(3), Insurer A must provide Insurer B, within 3 months of the transfer, with a statement containing the information specified in regulation 17(3); or

(b)   if the statement was provided under regulation 17(6), Insurer A must provide Insurer B, within 3 months of the transfer, with a statement containing the information specified in regulation 17(7).

17A(5)   Where paragraph (4)(a) applies, after the relevant transfer the obligation imposed by regulation 17(3) shall be that of Insurer B.

But no statement is required if the percentage expended is nil

17A(6)   Where paragraph (4)(b) applies, after the relevant transfer the obligation imposed by regulation 17(6) shall be that of Insurer B.

History – Reg. 17A inserted by SI 2008/720, reg. 7, with effect from 6 April 2008.

RECORD-KEEPING

RETENTION OF RECORDS

18(1)   The persons prescribed by paragraph (2) shall preserve any documents in their possession or under their control in relation to a registered pension scheme and relating to–

(a)   any monies received by or owing to the scheme;

(b)   any investments or assets held by the scheme;

(c)   any payments made by the scheme;

(d)   any contracts to purchase a lifetime annuity in respect of a member of the scheme; and

(e)   the administration of the scheme.

18(2)   In relation to a registered pension scheme the persons prescribed are–

(a)   any person who is or has been the scheme administrator;

(b)   any person who is or has been a trustee of the scheme;

(c)   any person who provides or has provided administrative services to the scheme; and

(d)   if the scheme is an occupational pension scheme, any person who is or has been a sponsoring employer or a director of an employer company.

This is subject to the following qualification.

18(3)   Any person who has ceased to act in relation to the scheme or ceased to provide administrative services to the scheme shall not be required to preserve documents where he has transferred all the documents to another person who has succeeded him in acting in relation to the scheme or providing administrative services to the scheme.

18(4)   Documents must be preserved for the tax year to which they relate and for a period of 6 years following that year.

MODIFIED OPERATION OF THESE REGULATIONS IN THE CASE OF CERTAIN PRE-6 APRIL 2015 LUMP SUMS

LUMP SUMS TO WHICH PARAGRAPH 1B OF SCHEDULE 29 APPLIES

19(1)   Regulations 3 to 18 have effect subject to the following provisions of this regulation.

19(2)   Paragraphs (3) to (8) apply if–

(a)   a lump sum is paid by a registered pension scheme ("the paying scheme") to a member of the scheme,

(b)   paragraph 1B of Schedule 29 applies to the lump sum, and

(c)   the member's becoming entitled to the actual pension mentioned in paragraph 1B(2)(h) of Schedule 29 has the effect that–

    (i)   the member also becomes entitled to the lump sum, and

    (ii)   the member's becoming entitled to the lump sum is a benefit crystallisation event.

19(3)   For the purposes of–

(a)   reportable event 6,

(b)   regulation 3 so far as applying by virtue of that event, and

(c)   obligations under regulation 14(1),

the benefit crystallisation event mentioned in paragraph (2)(c)(ii) is treated as occurring–

    (i)   in respect of the scheme to which the transfer mentioned in paragraph 1B(2)(g) of Schedule 29 was made ("the receiving scheme") and not in respect of the paying scheme, and

    (ii)   when the member becomes entitled to the actual pension or, if later, on 5 August 2014.

19(4)   For the purposes of regulations 15(2)(a) and 17(5)(a)(i) and (7)(a)(i), that benefit crystallisation event is treated as occurring in respect of the receiving scheme and not in respect of the paying scheme.

19(5)   For the purposes of–

(a)   reportable event 7 (but not its definition of "the entitlement amount"),

(b)   reportable event 8, and

(c)   regulation 3 so far as applying by virtue of either of those events,

the lump sum is treated as having been paid–

    (i)   by the receiving scheme and not by the paying scheme, and

    (ii)   when the member becomes entitled to the actual pension or, if later, on 5 August 2014.

19(6)   For the purposes of reportable event 7 **"the entitlement amount"** is the total of–

(a)   the sums held, at the time the lump sum is actually paid, for the purpose of providing the expected pension mentioned in paragraph 1B(2)(b) of Schedule 29, and

(b)   the market value at that time of the assets held at that time for that purpose.

19(7)   The scheme administrator of the paying scheme is to provide the scheme administrator of the receiving scheme with the following information–

(a)   the date the lump sum was paid,

(b)   the amount of the lump sum,

(c)   the total of–

    (i)   the sums held, at the time lump sum is paid, for the purpose of providing the expected pension mentioned in paragraph 1B(2)(b) of Schedule 29, and

    (ii)   the market value at that time of the assets held at that time for that purpose, and

(d)   a statement that no further pension commencement lump sum may be paid in connection with that expected pension.

19(8)   The scheme administrator of the paying scheme is to comply with its obligations under paragraph (7) before–

(a)   the end of 30 days beginning with the date of the transfer mentioned in paragraph 1B(2)(g) of Schedule 29, or

(b)   if later, the end of 3 September 2014.

History – Reg. 19 inserted by FA 2014, s. 43 and Sch. 5, para. 11(1), with effect from 19 March 2014.

LUMP SUMS TO WHICH PARAGRAPH 1B OF SCHEDULE 29 FAILS TO APPLY

20(1)   Regulations 3 to 18 have effect subject to the following provisions of this regulation.

20(2)   Paragraph (3) applies if–

(a)   a lump sum is paid by a registered pension scheme ("the paying scheme") to a member of the scheme,

(b)   paragraph 1B of Schedule 29 does not apply to the lump sum, but the conditions in paragraph 1B(2)(a) to (g) are met in the case of the lump sum, and

(c)   as at the end of 5 October 2015 it is the case that the lump sum is to be taken as having been an unauthorised member payment.

20(3)   For the purposes of reportable event 1, and regulation 3 so far as applying by virtue of that event, the lump sum is treated as having been paid–

(a)   by the receiving scheme and not by the paying scheme, and

(b)   on 6 October 2015.

History – Reg. 20 inserted by FA 2014, s. 43 and Sch. 5, para. 11(1), with effect from 19 March 2014.

REGISTERED PENSION SCHEMES (PRESCRIBED MANNER OF DETERMINING AMOUNT OF ANNUITIES) REGULATIONS 2006

(SI 2006/568, as amended by SI 2011/1751)

Made on 9 March 2006 by the Commissioners for Her Majesty's Revenue and Customs in exercise of the powers conferred by para. 3(1)(d), 6(1)(e), 17(1)(c) and 20(1)(e) of Sch. 28 to the Finance Act 2004. Operative from 6 April 2006.

CITATION, COMMENCEMENT AND INTERPRETATION

1(1) These Regulations may be cited as the Registered Pension Schemes (Prescribed Manner of Determining Amount of Annuities) Regulations 2006 and shall come into force on 6th April 2006.

1(2) In these Regulations a reference to a numbered section or Schedule (without more) is a reference to the section of, or Schedule to, the Finance Act 2004 bearing that number.

DETERMINING AMOUNT OF MEMBER'S LIFETIME ANNUITY

2(1) The annual amount of a member's lifetime annuity shall be determined in accordance with any of paragraphs (2) to (4).

2(2) The manner of determination prescribed by this paragraph is variation from year to year–

(a)   where the variation is in line with, or by a percentage which does not exceed, the percentage by which the amount would vary if it varied in line with, changes in–

     (i)   the retail prices index,

     (ii)   the market value of any freely marketable assets,

     (iii)   an index reflecting the value of freely marketable assets,

   after allowing for any contractual charges;

(b)   in accordance with an insurance company's published "Principles and Practices of Financial Management" in relation to with-profits business, as required under section 6.10 of the Financial Services Authority's Conduct of Business Sourcebook as it stood immediately before the coming into force of these Regulations; or

(c)   any combination of those factors.

2(3) The manner of determination prescribed by this paragraph is variation–

(a)   in line with, or by a percentage which does not exceed the percentage by which the amount would vary if it varied in line with, changes in any of the factors specified in paragraph (2) (or any combination of those factors); and

(b)   by reference to an assumed annual level of growth of between 0% and 5%, selected by the member, in the relevant factor or factors.

2(4) The manner of determination prescribed by this paragraph is determination in accordance with the following conditions.

Condition 1

The amount of the annuity payable is linked to any of the factors specified in sub-paragraphs (a) to (c) of paragraph (2) (or any combination of those factors).

Condition 2

A review is conducted, by the insurance company by whom the annuity is provided, at least once every 3 years of the value of the sums and assets which are applied towards the provision of the annuity.

Condition 3

At the time of the review, the maximum and minimum amount of income that may be drawn in each year until the next review is determined.

     The maximum amount of income which the annuitant may draw is 120% of the annual rate of a level annuity which could be purchased with the sums and assets which are applied to its provision for the member, for the term for which the annuity is provided.

     The minimum amount of income which the annuitant may draw is half of the annual rate of a level annuity which could be paid upon the assumptions in the preceding paragraph of this condition.

Statutory Instruments

2(5)   For the purposes of paragraph (4), the annual rate of an annuity which could be purchased with the sums and assets applied to its provision shall be assumed to be–

(a)   the freely marketable level annuity rate (if any) applicable in the case of the insurance company in question which could be purchased with those sums and assets; or

(b)   if the insurance company in question does not offer level annuities, the average of three current market annuity rates for a level annuity.

2(6)   For the purposes of paragraph (2)–

"**freely marketable assets**" means assets which are sold on the open market at a price not determined by the member;

"**the retail prices index**" has the meaning given in section 279(1).

History – In reg. 2(4), in condition 1, "(a) to (c)" substituted for "(a) to (d)" by SI 2011/1751, reg. 10(2)(a), which came into force on 11 August 2011, with effect for the tax year 2011–12 and subsequent tax years.
In reg. 2(4), in condition 2, "3" substituted for "5" by SI 2011/1751, reg. 10(2)(b), with effect for the tax year 2011–12 and subsequent tax years, subject to SI 2011/1751, reg. 11, which provides that where the amount of either a member's lifetime annuity or a dependant's annuity has been determined in accordance with SI 2006/568, reg. 2 or 3 before 11 August 2011, the amendment has effect from the date of the next review of the value of the sums and assets which are applied towards the provision of the annuity by the insurance company by whom the annuity is provided.

DETERMINING AMOUNT OF DEPENDANT'S ANNUITY

3(1)   The amount of a dependant's annuity shall be determined in the same manner as a member's lifetime annuity.

3(2)   For this purpose, paragraphs (2) to (6) of regulation 2 shall apply, but subject to the following modifications–

(a)   in paragraphs (2), (4) and (6) substitute "dependant" for "member" wherever it occurs, and

(b)   in paragraph (3)(b) for "member" substitute "member or dependant".

DETERMINING AMOUNT OF SHORT-TERM ANNUITIES

4(1)   The amount of a member's short-term annuity shall be determined in the same manner as a member's lifetime annuity in accordance with paragraph (2) or (3) of regulation 2.

4(2)   The amount of a dependant's short-term annuity shall be determined in the same manner as a member's short-term annuity, and for this purpose paragraphs (2), (3) and (6) of regulation 2 shall apply, but substituting "dependant" for "member" wherever it occurs.

REGISTERED PENSION SCHEMES (SPLITTING OF SCHEMES) REGULATIONS 2006

(SI 2006/569 as amended by SI 2007/793, SI 2011/702 and SI 2013/1114)

Made on 9 March 2006 by the Commissioners for Her Majesty's Revenue and Customs, in exercise of the powers conferred upon them by s. 274A of the Finance Act 2004. Operative from 6 April 2006.

CITATION, COMMENCEMENT AND INTERPRETATION

1(1) These Regulations may be cited as the Registered Pension Schemes (Splitting of Schemes) Regulations 2006 and shall come into force on 6th April 2006.

1(2) In these Regulations–

"group of employers" means two or more employers who are formally or informally linked to each other by reasons of common management, shareholding, staff or close business interests;

"HMRC" means the Commissioners for Her Majesty's Revenue and Customs;

"split scheme" means a registered pension scheme that is being treated, in accordance with regulation 2, as having been split into two or more sub-schemes;

"sub-scheme" means a scheme which forms part of a split scheme and which is being treated as a separate pension scheme under and for the purposes set out in these regulations;

"split scheme administrator" means a scheme administrator of a split scheme;

"sub-scheme administrator" means the scheme administrator of a sub-scheme appointed in accordance with the rules of the split scheme to be responsible for the discharge of the functions conferred or imposed on the sub-scheme administrator by or under these Regulations;

"section" without more, means a section of the Finance Act 2004;

"schedule" without more, means a schedule to the Finance Act 2004.

DESCRIPTION OF SCHEMES TO BE SPLIT

2(1) The following registered pension schemes shall be treated as split schemes for the purposes of these Regulations–

(a) the registered pension schemes listed in Schedule 1;

(b) a registered pension scheme which meets the conditions in paragraph (5);

(c) a successor scheme to any of the above schemes.

2(2) A successor scheme is a registered pension scheme established to take over some or all of the rights and obligations of a split scheme.

2(3) The scheme administrator of a successor scheme shall notify HMRC of any sub-schemes in respect of which he is assuming responsibility immediately following registration of the successor scheme.

The notification shall–

(a) be in a form specified by HMRC, and;

(b) contain any information reasonably required by HMRC.

2(4) Schedule 2 lists the schemes which, at the coming into force of these Regulations, are to be treated as sub-schemes of the split schemes referred to in sub-paragraph (1).

2(5) The conditions referred to in sub-paragraph (1)(b) are as follows.

Condition A

The pension scheme falls within Paragraph 1(1)(a) or (c) of Schedule 36 to the Finance Act 2004.

Condition B

The pension scheme provides benefits to or for the benefit of the employees of two or more employers.

Condition C

The rules of the pension scheme as at 28th February 2006 provided for the establishment of separate schemes for each of the participating employers or group of employers and for the administration of such schemes to be carried out by separate scheme administrators.

2(6) A successor sub-scheme is a scheme established to take over some or all of the rights and obligations of a sub-scheme.

2(7)   A successor sub-scheme is a scheme established to take over some or all of the rights and obligations of a sub-scheme.

The notification shall–

(a)   be in a form specified by HMRC, and

(b)   contain any information reasonably required, including the name and address of the scheme administrator.

RESPONSIBILITIES AND LIABILITIES OF SUB-SCHEME ADMINISTRATORS

3(1)   The sub-scheme administrator of a sub-scheme shall assume the liabilities and responsibilities set out in Schedule 3 to these Regulations in relation to that scheme.

3(2)   In the provisions referred to in that Schedule any reference to the scheme administrator shall be read as a reference to the sub-scheme administrator.

3(3)   The split scheme administrator shall cease to have responsibility or liability in relation to the matters referred to in paragraph (1) in respect of the sub-scheme.

3(4)   The provisions of section 270(2) and (3) (meaning of "scheme administrator") apply to the sub-scheme administrator and the references to the scheme administrator in those subsections shall be read as references to the sub-scheme administrator).

3(5)   Section 272 (trustees etc. liable as scheme administrator) applies to sub-scheme administrators with the following modifications–

(a)   in subsection (1) for "registered pension scheme"; substitute "sub-scheme";

(b)   in subsections (1)(a) to (c), (2)(a) and (b) for "scheme administrator" (in each place) substitute "sub-scheme administrator";

(c)   in subsections (1)(a) to (c) and (2), (3) and (5) for "pension scheme" (in each place) substitute "sub-scheme";

(d)   in subsection (2)–

  (i)   in paragraph (a) after "by virtue of this Part" insert "as applied by regulation 3 of the Registered Pensions (Splitting of Schemes) Regulations 2006"; and

  (ii)   in paragraph (b) after "by or under this Part." insert "as applied by the Registered Pensions (Splitting of Schemes) Regulations 2006"; and

(e)   in subsection (4) for "pension scheme" substitute "sub-scheme".

3(6)   Section 273 (members liable as scheme administrator) applies to members of a sub-scheme with the following modifications–

(a)   in subsection (1) for "registered pension scheme" substitute "sub-scheme";

(b)   in subsections (1)(a) and (b) for "pension scheme" substitute "sub-scheme";

(c)   in subsection (1)(a) after "(trustees, etc.)" add "(as modified by regulation 3 of the Registered Pensions (Splitting of Schemes) Regulations 2006)";

(d)   in subsection (1)(b) omit the words "or section 242 (de-registration charge)";

(e)   in subsections (2) and (4) for "pension scheme" substitute "sub-scheme";

(f)   in subsection (5)(a) for "the pension scheme" substitute "the split scheme";

(g)   in subsections (5)(b) and (d) for "the pension scheme" substitute "the sub-scheme";

(h)   in subsection (5)(c) after the words "that the pension scheme was" add "part of";

(i)   in subsection (10) for "the pension scheme" substitute "the sub-scheme".

3(7)   Section 274(2) (supplementary) applies to sub-scheme administrators with the following modifications–

(a)   for "scheme administrator" substitute "sub-scheme administrator"; and

(b)   for "registered pension scheme" substitute "sub-scheme".

4(1)   Section 209(5) (unauthorised payments surcharge) shall be modified as follows.

(a)   in paragraph (b) delete "and";

(b)   in paragraph (c) after "the scheme administrator" add "and";

(c)   after paragraph (c) add–

  "(d)   the sub-scheme administrator,".

5(1)   Paragraph 11 of Schedule 31 (insertion of chapter 15A into ITEPA 2003) shall be modified as follows.

5(2) After subsection (4) of the inserted section 636A insert–

"**636A(4A)** In the case of a registered pension scheme which is a split scheme for the purposes of the Registered Pensions Schemes (Splitting of Schemes) Regulations 2006, subsections (3) and (4) shall have effect as if the references to the scheme administrator were to the subscheme administrator (within the meaning of those Regulations).".

5(3) Paragraph 1 of Schedule 35 (consequential amendments to the Taxes Management Act 1970) shall be modified as follows.

(a)   in the substitution to section 9(1A) of the Taxes Management Act 1970, in sub-paragraph (a) delete "or"; and

(b)   after sub-paragraph (a) add–

"(ab)   is chargeable on the sub-scheme administrator of a sub-scheme under Part 4 of the Finance Act 2004 as modified by the Registered Pensions (Splitting of Schemes) Regulations 2006, or"

5(4) Paragraph 16 of Schedule 35 (consequential amendments to section 349B(3) of ICTA) shall be modified as follows.

5(5) After the substituted sub-paragraph (i) add–

"(ia)   the sub-scheme administrator of a sub-scheme which forms part of a split scheme pursuant to the Registered Pensions (Splitting of Schemes) Regulations 2006;"

5(6) Paragraph 33 of Schedule 35 (consequential amendments to section 824(9) of ICTA) shall be modified as follows.

5(7) After the insertion of the words "scheme administrators of registered pension schemes" add–

"sub-scheme administrators of sub-schemes which form part of a split scheme pursuant to the Registered Pensions (Splitting of Schemes) Regulations 2006".

SCHEDULE 1 – SCHEMES TO BE TREATED AS SPLIT SCHEMES PURSUANT TO REGULATION 2(1)(A)

Regulation 2(1)(a)

Name of scheme	Enabling legislation	Governing regulations
Police Pension Scheme	s. 1–8 Police Pensions Act 1982	The Police Pensions Regulations 1987 (SI 1987 No. 257) as amended
Firefighters Pension Scheme	s. 26 Fire Services Act 1947 and s. 34 Fire and Rescue Services Act 2004	The Firemen's Pension Scheme Order 1992 SI 1992 No. 129 as amended
Local Government Pension Scheme	s. 7 and s. 12 Superannuation Act 1972	The Local Government Pension Scheme Regulations 1997 SI 1997 No. 1612 as amended
Local Government Pension Scheme (Scotland)	s. 7 and s. 12 Superannuation Act 1972	The Local Government Pension Scheme (Scotland) Regulations 1998 SI 1998 No. 366 (s. 14) as amended
Electricity Supply Pension Scheme		

SCHEDULE 2 – SCHEMES TO BE TREATED AS SUB-SCHEMES PURSUANT TO REGULATION 2(4)

Regulation 2(4)

Name of sub-scheme	Split scheme to which it relates
Avon & Somerset Police Authority	Police Pension Scheme

Name of sub-scheme	*Split scheme to which it relates*
Bedfordshire Police Authority	
Cambridgeshire Police Authority	
Cheshire Police Authority	
City of London Police Authority	
Cleveland Police Authority	
Cumbria Police Authority	
Derbyshire Police Authority	
Devon & Cornwall Constabulary	
Dorset Police Force Headquarters	
Durham Police Authority	
Dyfed Powys Police Authority	
Essex Police Authority	
Gloucestershire Police Authority	
Greater Manchester Police Authority	
Gwent Police Authority Office	
Hampshire Police Authority	
Hertfordshire Police Authority	
Humberside Police Authority	
Kent Police Authority	
Lancashire Police Authority	
Leicestershire Police Authority	
Lincolnshire Police Headquarters	
Merseyside Police Authority	
Metropolitan Police Authority	
Norfolk Police Authority	
North Yorkshire Police Authority	
North Wales Police Authority	
Northamptonshire Police Authority	
Northumbria Police Authority	
Nottinghamshire Police Authority	
South Wales Police Authority	
South Yorkshire Police Authority	
Staffordshire Police Authority	
Suffolk Police Authority	
Surrey Police Authority	
Sussex Police	
Thames Valley Police Authority	
Warwickshire Police Authority	
West Mercia Police Authority	
West Midlands Police Authority	
West Yorkshire Police Authority	
Wilkshire Police Authority	
Central Scotland Joint Police Board	
Dumfries & Galloway Police Authority	
Fife Police Authority	
Grampian Joint Police Board	
Lothian and Borders Police Board	
Northern Joint Police Board	
Strathclyde Joint Police Fire Board	
Tayside Joint Police Board	
Avon Fire Authority	Firefighters Pension Scheme
Bedfordshire and Luton Combined Fire Authority	
Buckinghamshire and Milton Keynes Fire Authority	
Cambridgeshire and Peterborough Fire Authority	
Cheshire Fire Authority	

Name of sub-scheme	*Split scheme to which it relates*
Cleveland Fire Authority	
Cornwall Fire Authority	
County Durham and Darlington Fire and	
Rescue Authority	
Cumbria Fire Authority	
Derbyshire Fire Authority	
Devon Fire Authority	
Dorset Fire Authority	
East Sussex Fire Authority	
Essex Fire Authority	
Gloucestershire Fire Authority	
Greater Manchester Fire and Civil Defence	
Authority	
Hampshire Fire and Rescue Authority	
Hereford and Worcester Combined Fire	
Authority	
Hertfordshire Fire Authority	
Humberside Fire Authority	
Isle of Wight Fire Authority	
Kent and Medway Towns Fire Authority	
Lancashire Combined Fire Authority	
Leicester, Leicestershire and Rutland Combined	
Fire Authority	
Lincolnshire Fire Authority	
London Fire and Emergency Planning Authority	
Merseyside Fire and Civil Defence Authority	
Mid and West Wales Fire Authority	
Norfolk Fire Authority	
North Wales Fire Authority	
North Yorkshire Fire and Rescue Authority	
Northamptonshire Fire Authority	
Northumberland Fire Authority	
Nottinghamshire and City of Nottingham Fire	
Authority	
Oxfordshire Fire Authority	
Royal Berkshire Fire Authority	
Shropshire and Wrekin Fire Authority	
Somerset Fire Authority	
South Wales Fire Authority	
South Yorkshire Fire and Civil Defence	
Authority	
Stoke on Trent and Staffordshire Fire Authority	
Suffolk Fire Authority	
Surrey Fire Authority	
Tyne & Wear Fire and Civil Defence Authority	
Warwickshire Fire Authority	

Name of sub-scheme	*Split scheme to which it relates*
West Midlands Fire and Cvil Defence Authority	
West Sussex Fire Authority	
West Yorkshire Fire and Civil Defence Authority	
Wiltshire and Swindon Fire Authority	
Dumfries & Galloway Fire and Rescue Authority	
Highlands and Islands Fire Board	
Grampian Fire Board	
Lothian and Borders Fire Board	
Central Scotland Fire Board	
Fife Fire and Rescue Authority	
Strathclyde Fire Board	
Tayside Fire Board	
Bath & North East Somerset Council	Local Government Pension Scheme
Bedfordshire County Council	
Buckinghamshire County Council	
Cambridgeshire County Council	
Carmarthenshire County Council	
Cheshire County Council	
City and County of Cardiff Council	
City and County of Swansea	
City of London	
City of Bradford Metropolitan District Council	
Cornwall County Council	
Cumbria County Council	
Derbyshire County Council	
Devon County Council	
Dorset County Council	
Durham County Council	
East Riding of Yorkshire Council	
East Sussex County Council	
Environment Agency	
Essex County Council	
Flintshire County Council	
Gloucestershire County Council	
Gwynedd Council	
Hampshire County Council	
Hertforshire County Council	
Isle of Wight Council	
Kent County Council	
Lancashire County Council	
Leicestershire County Council	
Lincolnshire County Council	
London Borough of Barking and Dagenham	
London Borough of Barnet	
London Borough of Bexley	
London Borough of Brent	
London Borough of Bromley	
London Borough of Camden	
London Borough of Croydon	
London Borough of Ealing	
London Borough of Enfield	
London Borough of Greenwich	
London Borough of Hackney	

Name of sub-scheme	Split scheme to which it relates
London Borough of Hammersmith and Fulham	
London Borough of Haringey	
London Borough of Harrow	
London Borough of Havering	
London Borough of Hillingdon	
London Borough of Hounslow	
London Borough of Islington	
London Borough of Lambeth	
London Borough of Lewisham	
London Borough of Merton	
London Borough of Newham	
London Borough of Redbridge	
London Borough of Richmond Upon Thames	
London Borough of Southwark	Local Government Pension
London Borough of Sutton	
London Borough of Tower Hamlets	
London Borough of Waltham Forest	
London Borough of Wandsworth	
London Pensions Fund Authority	
Middlesbrough Borough Council	
Norfolk County Council	
North Yorkshire County Council	
Northamptonshire County Council	
Northumberland County Council	
Nottinghamshire County Council	
Oxfordshire County Council	
Powys County Council	
Rhondda-Cyon-Taff County Borough Council	
Royal Borough of Kensington & Chelsea	
Royal Borough of Kingston Upon Thames	
Royal Borough of Windsor and Maidenhead	
Shropshire County Council	
Somerset County Council	
South Tyneside Metropolitan Borough Council	
South Yorkshire Pensions Authority	
Stafforshire County Council	
Suffolk County Council	
Surrey County Council	
Tameside Metropolitan Borough Council	
Torfaen County Borough Council	
Warwickshire County Council	
Westminster City Council	
West Sussex County Council	
Wiltshire County Council	
Wirral District Council	
Wolvershampton City Council	
Worcestershire County Council	

Name of sub-scheme	*Split scheme to which it relates*
Aberdeen City Council	Local Government Pension Scheme (Scotland)
The City of Edinburgh Council	
The City of Glasgow Council	
Dumfries & Galloway Council	
Dundee City Council	
Falkirk Council	
Fife Council	
The Highland Council	
Orkney Islands Council	
Scottish Borders Council	
Shetland Islands Council	
Alfred McAlpine Group	Electricity Supply Pension Scheme
Areva Group	
British Energy Combined Group	
British Energy Generation Group	
Drax Power Group	
EA Technology Group	
EDF Energy Group	
Electricity Association Services Group	
E.ON UK Group	
First Hydro Group	
International Power Group	
Keadby Generation Group	
Magnox Electric Group	
Manweb Group	
National Grid Electricity Group	
Northern Electric Group	
RWE npower Group	
Southern Electric Group	
United Utilities Group	
Western Power Distribution Group	

History – In the first column of the table, at the start, the entries from "Avon and Somerset Police Authority" to "Merseyside Police Authority" inserted by SI 2007/793, reg. 2, with effect from 6 April 2007.

SCHEDULE 3 – RESPONSIBILITIES AND LIABILITIES OF SUB-SCHEME ADMINISTRATORS IN RESPECT OF A SUB-SCHEME

Regulation 3

Part 1 – Finance Act 2004

Statutory Reference	Subject matter
	Liabilities
Section 205	Short service refund lump sum charge
Section 206	Special lump sum death benefits charge
Section 207	Authorised surplus payments charge
Section 215(9)	Lifetime allowance charge – amount of charge
Section 217	Lifetime allowance charge (joint & several with the individual)
Section 227(3)	Annual allowance charge
Section 238(3) and (4)	Pension input period
Section 239	Scheme sanction charge
	Information
Section 250(1)	To make and deliver a registered pension scheme return
Section 254	Accounting for tax by scheme administrators
	Interest and penalties
Section 257	Penalty for failure to comply with a S250 notice
Section 258(1)	Penalty for failure to provide information within S251(1)(a)
Section 258(2)	Penalty for failure to comply with regulations within S251(1)(b)
Section 259(1)	Penalty for failure to comply with a notice under S252
Section 265(3)	Penalty for winding up a scheme to obtain a winding up lump sum
Section 266(2)	Penalty for transfers to "non" insured schemes (unauthorised transfer)
Section 266B	Scheme liability (inserted by Paragraph 4 Schedule 10 FA 2005)
Section 267	Discharge of lifetime allowance charge in the case of good faith.
Section 268	Unauthorised payment surcharge & scheme sanction charge
	Scheme administrator
Section 271	Liability of a scheme administrator
Section 272	Trustees etc. liable as scheme administrator
Section 273	Members liable as scheme administrator
Section 274	Supplementary provisions
Paragraph 1 of Schedule 28	Scheme administrator to receive evidence of member's ill health
Paragraph 15(2)(b) of Schedule 28	Scheme administrator to agree if a child is a dependant
Paragraph 15(3) of Schedule 28	Scheme administrator to decide whether someone is a dependant
Paragraph 4(1) of Schedule 29	Scheme administrator to consider evidence of serious ill health
Paragraph 19(1)(d) of Schedule 29	Scheme administrator to nominate arrangement for transfer lump sum benefit
Paragraph 19(2)(e) of Schedule 29	Scheme administrator to nominate arrangement for transfer lump sum benefit
Paragraph 9(2) of Schedule 32	Changes to benefit crystallisation event 2
Paragraph 9(3) of Schedule 32	Changes to benefit crystallisation event 2 (inserted by paragraph 43(4) of Schedule 10 to the Finance Act 2005)
Paragraph 13(4) and (5) of Schedule 32	Changes to benefit crystallisation event 3 (inserted by paragraph 43(5) of Schedule 10 to the Finance Act 2005)
Paragraph 14(1A) & (1B) of Schedule 32	Changes to benefit crystallisation event 5 (inserted by paragraph 43(7) of Schedule 10 to the Finance Act 2005)
Paragraph 5 of Schedule 34	Exemption for scheme administrator from s. 205 & s. 206 charges

Statutory Instruments

Statutory Reference	Subject matter
Paragraph 17 of Schedule 34	Omits reference to scheme administrator in s. 217
Paragraph 4(1), (2) and (3) of Schedule 36	Transitional provisions for deemed registered schemes
Paragraph 6 of Schedule 36	Pre-commencement liability of scheme administrator

History – In the table, entry relating to s. 260(6) omitted by SI 2013/1114, art. 7(2), with effect from 1 June 2013.
In the entry in the Table relating to s. 260, the words "(1), (4) and", which appeared after "260", omitted, and the words "Penalty for fraudulently or negligently making an incorrect return under S254" substituted for the words "Penalties for failure to make a return within S254", by SI 2011/702, art. 18(a)(i) and (ii) respectively, with effect from 1 April 2011, but subject to SI 2011/702, art. 21, which provides that these amendments do not have effect in respect of a return period ending on or before 31 December 2010.

Part 1A – Other Legislation

Statutory Reference	Subject-matter
Schedule 24 to the Finance Act 2007	Penalty for carelessly or deliberately making an incorrect return under section 254 of the Finance Act 2004
Schedule 55 to the Finance Act 2009	Penalty for failure to make returns

History – Table inserted by SI 2013/1114, art. 7(2)(b), with effect form 1 June 2013.
In Pt. 1A, the words "Schedule 55 to the Finance Act 2009 (penalty for failure to make returns)" omitted by SI 2013/1114, art. 7(2)(a), with effect from 1 June 2013.
Part 1A inserted by SI 2011/702, art. 18(b), with effect from 1 April 2011, but subject to SI 2011/702, art. 21, which provides that the insertion does not have effect in respect of a return period ending on or before 31 December 2010.

Part 2 – Secondary Legislation

The Pension Schemes (Discharge of Liabilities under Section 267 and 268 of the Finance Act 2004) Regulations 2005
The Registered Pension Schemes (Relief at Source) Regulations 2005
The Registered Pension Schemes (Minimum Contributions) Regulations 2006
The Registered Pension Schemes (Accounting and Assessment) Regulations 2005
The Registered Pension Schemes and Employer Financed Retirement Benefit Schemes (Information) (Prescribed Description of Person) Regulations 2005
The Registered Pension Schemes (Provision of Information) Regulations 2006
The Registered Pension Schemes (Modification of the Rules of Existing Schemes) Regulations 2006
The Pension Benefits (Insurance Company Liable as Scheme Administrator) Regulations 2006
The Registered Pension Schemes (Meaning of Pension Commencement Lump Sum) Regulations 2006
The Registered Pension Schemes and Overseas Pension Schemes (Electronic Communication of Returns and Information) Regulations 2006
The Taxes Management Act 1970 (Modification of Schedule 3 for Pension Schemes Appeals) Order 2005
The Registered Pension Schemes (Transfer of Sums and Assets) Regulations 2006
The Registered Pension Schemes (Unauthorised Payments by Existing Schemes) Regulations 2006

REGISTERED PENSION SCHEMES AND OVERSEAS PENSION SCHEMES (ELECTRONIC COMMUNICATION OF RETURNS AND INFORMATION) REGULATIONS 2006

(SI 2006/570, as amended by SI 2009/56, SI 2010/652, SI 2011/702, SI 2012/884 SI 2013/1114 and SI 2013/2259)

Made on 9 March 2006 by the Commissioners for Her Majesty's Revenue and Customs in exercise of the powers conferred by s. 132 and 133(2) of the Finance Act 1999 and s. 135 and 136 of the Finance Act 2002. Operative in accordance with reg. 1.

PART 1 – INTRODUCTION

CITATION AND COMMENCEMENT

1 These Regulations may be cited as the Registered Pension Schemes and Overseas Pension Schemes (Electronic Communication of Returns and Information) Regulations 2006 and shall come into force on such days or days as may be appointed by the Commissioners and specified in a notice in the London, Edinburgh and Belfast Gazettes.

INTERPRETATION

2(1) In these Regulations–

(a)   **"the Act"** means the Finance Act 2004;

(b)   **"Part 4"** means Part 4 of the Act; and

(c)   any reference to a numbered section or Schedule (without more) is a reference to the section or Schedule bearing that number in the Act.

2(2) In these Regulations, except where the context otherwise requires–

"approved method of electronic communications", in relation to the delivery of information in accordance with a provision of these Regulations, means a method of electronic communications which has been approved, by specific or general directions issued by the Commissioners, for the delivery of information of that kind under that provision;

"the Commissioners" means the Commissioners for Her Majesty's Revenue and Customs;

"the ELA Regulations" means the Pension Schemes (Enhanced Lifetime Allowance) Regulations 2006;

"electronic communications" has the meaning given in section 132(10) of the Finance Act 1999;

"official computer system" means a computer system maintained by or on behalf of the Commissioners or on behalf of an officer of Revenue and Customs;

"relevant information" means information which is required or authorised by virtue of these Regulations to be delivered to Revenue and Customs by an approved method of electronic communications;

"Revenue and Customs" means Her Majesty's Revenue and Customs; and

History – In reg. 2, the entry for "the tax appeal Commissioners" omitted by SI 2009/56, art. 3(2) and Sch. 2, para. 153(2), operative from 1 April 2009 subject to transitional and saving provisions in SI 2009/56, Sch. 3. The former entry read as follows: "**"the tax appeal Commissioners"** means, as the case requires, the General Commissioners or the Special Commissioners.".

INTRODUCTION

3(1) Part 2 of these Regulations makes provision about returns and information which must be delivered to Revenue and Customs by an approved method of electronic communications.

3(2) Part 3 of these Regulations makes provision about returns and information which may be delivered to Revenue and Customs by an approved method of electronic communications.

PART 2 – INFORMATION WHICH MUST BE DELIVERED BY ELECTRONIC COMMUNICATIONS

INFORMATION WHICH MUST BE DELIVERED BY ELECTRONIC COMMUNICATIONS

4(1) The information specified in Schedule 1 to these Regulations must be delivered to Revenue and Customs–

(a)   in a form approved for that purpose; and

(b)   by a method of electronic communications approved for that purpose.

4(2) The Commissioners may make a general or specific direction requiring a scheme administrator to deliver specified information to Revenue and Customs by a particular method of electronic communications.

4(3) Information specified in Schedule 1 which is delivered to Revenue and Customs in a form, or by a method, otherwise than that required by virtue of this regulation must be treated as not having been delivered.

PART 3 – INFORMATION WHICH MAY BE DELIVERED BY ELECTRONIC COMMUNICATIONS

INFORMATION WHICH MAY BE DELIVERED BY ELECTRONIC COMMUNICATIONS

5(1) Information specified in Schedule 2 to these Regulations may be delivered to Revenue and Customs, if–

(a)   it is in a form approved for that purpose;

(b)   it is sent by a method of electronic communications approved for that purpose; and

(c)   the sender is authorised by Revenue and Customs to use electronic communications for that purpose.

5(2) Information specified in Schedule 2 may be supplied by Revenue and Customs if–

(a)   the proposed recipient has consented to the use of electronic communications for the delivery of information by Revenue and Customs; and

(b)   that consent has not been withdrawn.

PART 4 – EVIDENTIAL PROVISIONS

WHETHER RELEVANT INFORMATION HAS BEEN DELIVERED ELECTRONICALLY

6(1) For the purposes of these Regulations, relevant information is to be taken to have been delivered to an official computer system by an approved method of electronic communications only if it is accepted by that official computer system.

This is subject to the following qualification.

6(2) Relevant information which is delivered to an official computer system must meet the standards of accuracy and completeness set by specific or general directions given by the Commissioners.

6(3) Relevant information which fails to meet those standards must be treated as not having been delivered.

PROOF OF CONTENT OF ELECTRONIC DELIVERY

7(1) A document certified by Revenue and Customs to be a printed-out version of information delivered by an approved method of electronic communications is evidence, unless the contrary is proved, that the information–

(a)   was delivered by an approved method of electronic communications on that occasion; and

(b)   constitutes everything which was delivered on that occasion.

7(2) A document which purports to be a certificate given in accordance with paragraph (1) is presumed to be such a certificate unless the contrary is proved.

PROOF OF IDENTITY OF PERSON SENDING OR RECEIVING ELECTRONIC DELIVERY

8 The identity of–

(a) the person sending any information delivered by an approved method of electronic communications to Revenue and Customs, or

(b) the person receiving any information delivered by an approved method of electronic communications by Revenue and Customs,

is presumed, unless the contrary is proved, to be the person recorded as such on an official computer system.

INFORMATION SENT ELECTRONICALLY ON BEHALF OF A PERSON

9(1) Any information delivered by an approved method of electronic communications–

(a) to Revenue and Customs, or

(b) to an official computer system,

on behalf of a person, is taken to have been delivered by that person.

9(2) But this does not apply if the person proves that the information was delivered without the person's knowledge or connivance.

PROOF OF INFORMATION SENT ELECTRONICALLY

10(1) The use of an approved method of electronic communications is presumed, unless the contrary is proved, to have resulted in the delivery of information–

(a) to Revenue and Customs, if the delivery of the information has been recorded on an official computer system;

(b) by Revenue and Customs, if the despatch of the information has been recorded on an official computer system.

10(2) The use of an approved method of electronic communications is presumed, unless the contrary is proved, not to have resulted in the delivery of relevant information–

(a) to Revenue and Customs, if the delivery of the information has not been recorded on an official computer system;

(b) by Revenue and Customs, if the despatch of the information has not been recorded on an official computer system.

10(3) The time of receipt or despatch of any relevant information delivered by an approved method of electronic communications is presumed, unless the contrary is proved, to be the time recorded on an official computer system.

This is subject to the following qualification.

10(4) The Commissioners may by a general or specific direction provide for information to be treated as delivered upon a different date (whether earlier or later) than that given by paragraph (3).

10(5) Information shall not be taken to have been delivered to an official computer system by means of electronic communications unless it is accepted by the system to which it is delivered.

AUTHENTICATION OF INFORMATION IN DOCUMENT OTHERWISE REQUIRED TO BE SIGNED

11 If–

(a) information specified in Schedule 2 to these Regulations is delivered to Revenue and Customs by a method of electronic communications; and

(b) the information is required to be signed by or on behalf of the person delivering it,

the requirement for a signature shall be treated as satisfied if the information is authenticated by or on behalf of the sender in such manner as may be approved by the Commissioners.

USE OF UNAUTHORISED METHOD OF ELECTRONIC COMMUNICATIONS

12(1) This regulation applies to information–

(a)   which is required to be delivered to Revenue and Customs under a provision of Part 2 of these Regulations; or

(b)   which is permitted to be delivered to Revenue and Customs under a provision of Part 3 of these Regulations.

12(2) The use of a method of electronic communications for the purpose of delivering such information is conclusively presumed not to have resulted in the delivery of that information, unless that method of electronic communications is for the time being approved for the delivery of information of that kind under that provision.

SCHEDULE 1 – INFORMATION WHICH MUST BE SUPPLIED TO REVENUE AND CUSTOMS BY AN APPROVED METHOD OF ELECTRONIC COMMUNICATIONS

Regulation 4

A form of application for the registration of a pension scheme under section 153 (registration of pension schemes).

A return under section 250(2) (registered pension scheme return) in response to a notice under section 250(1).

A return under section 254 (accounting for tax by scheme administrators), and any amendment of that return, which does not relate to a currently-relieved non-UK pension scheme.

A declaration under section 270 (scheme administrator's obligations).

An event report in respect of a reportable event specified in entries 1 to 8A and 10 to 21 in the table in paragraph (1) of regulation 3 of the Registered Pension Schemes (Provision of Information) Regulations 2006 (provision of information by scheme administrator to Revenue and Customs).

Information furnished under regulation 4 of the Registered Pension Schemes (Provision of Information) Regulations 2006 (information about a pension scheme which has been wound up).

A notice under regulation 6 of the Registered Pension Schemes (Provision of Information) Regulations 2006 (termination of scheme administrator's appointment).

History – In Sch. 1, in the entry relating to a return under section 254, the words ", which does not relate to a currently-relieved non-UK pension scheme" inserted by SI 2012/884, reg. 15(2)(a), with effect from 6 April 2012.

In Sch. 1, in the entry relating to an event report, the words "An event report in respect of a reportable event specified in entries 1 to 8A and 10 to 21 in the table in paragraph (1) of" substituted for the words "An event report under" inserted by SI 2012/884, reg. 15(2)(b), with effect from 6 April 2012.

SCHEDULE 2 – INFORMATION WHICH MAY BE SUPPLIED EITHER TO OR BY REVENUE AND CUSTOMS BY AN APPROVED METHOD OF ELECTRONIC COMMUNICATIONS

Regulation 5

A notification by Revenue and Customs under section 153(6) of a decision on an application to register a pension scheme under section 153(4).

A notification by Revenue and Customs under section 157(2) (withdrawal of registration) of withdrawal of the registration of a pension scheme under section 157(1).

A notification under section 169(2)(a) (recognised transfers) by a scheme manager (within the meaning of section 169(3)) that a scheme is a recognised overseas pension scheme.

An undertaking by the scheme manager under section 169(2)(b) that he will inform Revenue and Customs if the scheme ceases to be a recognised overseas pension scheme.

An undertaking by the scheme manager under section 169(2)(c) that he will comply with any prescribed information requirements.

A notification by Revenue and Customs of a decision under section 169(5), the effect of which is to exclude a recognised overseas pension scheme from being a qualifying recognised overseas pension scheme.

A notification by Revenue and Customs of a decision under section 169(7) that a recognised overseas pension scheme is to cease to be excluded from being a qualifying recognised overseas pension scheme.

A notice under section 250 requiring the scheme administrator of a registered pension scheme to deliver a return under that section.

An amendment to a return under section 250 by the scheme administrator.

A–

(a) taxpayer notice under paragraph 1 of Schedule 36 to the Finance Act 2008 (information and inspection powers),

(b) third party notice under paragraph 2 of that Schedule,

(c) notice under paragraph 5 of that Schedule

that relates to a registered pension scheme; and a notice of appeal against any such notice or against the imposition of a penalty in relation to any such notice.

An assessment made by Revenue and Customs under section 254 or 255 (assessments on scheme administrators and others under Part 4).

A notice issued by Revenue and Customs in respect of a penalty imposed under any of sections 257 to 266 (penalties for non-compliance with requirements to provide information or furnish returns).

An application–

(a) under section 267 for the discharge of the scheme administrator's liability to the lifetime allowance charge;

(b) under section 268 for the discharge of the scheme administrator's liability to the scheme sanction charge; or

(c) under that section for the discharge of a person's liability to the unauthorised payments surcharge

and a notification by Revenue and Customs of their decision upon that application.

An application by a former scheme administrator under section 271(5) (release of former scheme administrator) to be released from the liability as scheme administrator, and a notification by Revenue and Customs of their decision on that application.

A notification under paragraph 10(3) of Schedule 29 (winding up lump sum: employer's undertaking).

A notification, information or an undertaking provided by a scheme manager under paragraph 5(1) of Schedule 33 given for the purpose of securing that a pension scheme is a qualifying overseas pension scheme.

A notification by Revenue and Customs of their decision under paragraph 5(3) of Schedule 33 (exclusion of overseas pension scheme from being a qualifying overseas pension scheme).

A notification by Revenue and Customs of their decision under paragraph 5(5) of Schedule 33 (overseas pension scheme ceasing to be excluded from being a qualifying overseas pension scheme).

A notification by an individual under regulation 3, 4, 5, 6, 7 or 8 of the ELA Regulations.

A requirement by an individual under regulation 12 of the ELA Regulations that Revenue and Customs give notice of their decision to refuse to consider the information in a notification by the individual; the notice given of that decision; and a notice of appeal against that decision.

A requirement by an individual under regulation 14 of the ELA Regulations that Revenue and Customs give notice of their refusal to issue a certificate under those Regulations; the notice given of that refusal; and a notice of appeal against that refusal.

A requirement by an individual under regulation 16 of the ELA Regulations that Revenue and Customs issue an aggregate certificate.

A notice given by an individual under regulation 17 of the ELA Regulations that any information given in a notification, or in connection with a notification under those Regulations, was incorrect or has become incorrect.

A notice given by an individual under regulation 18 of the ELA Regulations that information given in a certificate issued by Revenue and Customs under those Regulations was incorrect or has become incorrect.

A notice by Revenue and Customs under regulation 24 of the ELA Regulations of the revocation or amendment of a certificate under those Regulations; and a notice of appeal against such a notice.

A certificate by Revenue and Customs under the ELA Regulations, and an amendment, under those Regulations, of such a certificate.

An amendment to an event report in respect of a reportable event specified in entries 1 to 8A and 10 to 21 in the table in paragraph (1) of regulation 3 of the Registered Pension Schemes (Provision of Information) Regulations 2006 (provision of information by scheme administrator to the Commissioners).

Information furnished by a company about an unauthorised employer payment under regulation 5 of the Registered Pension Schemes (Provision of Information) Regulations 2006.

Information furnished by personal representatives under regulation 10 of the Registered Pension Schemes (Provision of Information) Regulations 2006.

A notice of appeal against a decision by Revenue and Customs under section 153(6), 157(2), 169(5), 267, 268 or 271(6) or paragraph 5(3) of Schedule 33.

A notice of appeal against an assessment under regulation 4 of the Registered Pension Schemes (Accounting and Assessment) Regulations 2005) (assessment in respect of supplementary charges under Part 4).

Information required from qualifying overseas pension schemes, QROPS and former QROPS under regulations 2 to 3C of the Pension Schemes (Information Requirements – Qualifying Overseas Pension Schemes, Qualifying Recognised Overseas Pensions Schemes and Corresponding Relief) Regulations 2006).

A notice of appeal against the imposition of a penalty under–

(a)   section 98 of TMA 1970 by virtue of section 258 (penalties for failure to provide information required by regulations under section 251(1)(a) or (4) of the Finance Act 2004);

(b)   section 257 (scheme administrator failing to make a registered pension scheme return or negligently or fraudulently making an incorrect return or delivering incorrect documents);

(c)   [omitted by SI 2010/652, reg. 2(2);]

(d)   [omitted by SI 2013/1114, art. 8(2);]

(e)   section 261 (enhanced lifetime allowance regulations: documents and information);

(f)   section 262 (enhanced lifetime allowance regulations: failures to comply);

(g)   section 263 (lifetime allowance enhanced protection: benefit accrual);

(h)   section 264 (fraudulent or negligent misstatements, etc.);

(i)   section 265 (winding up wholly or mainly to facilitate payment of lump sums); or

(j)   section 266(2) (transfer of sums representing accrued rights to a registered pension scheme which is an insured scheme otherwise than to scheme administrator of the transferee scheme or an insurance company); or

(ja)   Schedule 24 to the Finance Act 2007 (penalties for errors) in respect of an error in a return under section 254 of the Finance Act 2004;

(k)   Schedule 55 to the Finance Act 2009 (penalty for failure to make returns).

History – In Sch. 2, in the penultimate para., the words ", QROPS and former QROPS under regulations 2 to 3C" substituted for the words "and qualifying recognised overseas pension schemes under regulations 2 and 3" by SI 2013/2259, reg. 22, with effect from 14 October 2013.

In Sch. 2, the entry relating to an amendment to a return under s. 250 inserted by SI 2012/884, reg. 15(3)(a), with effect from 6 April 2012.

In Sch. 2, the entry relating to an amendment to an event report inserted by SI 2012/884, reg. 15(3)(b), with effect from 6 April 2012.

In Sch. 2, in the last para., (d) omitted by SI 2013/1114, art. 8(2), with effect from 1 June 2013. Former (d) read as follows: "section 260 (fraudulently or negligently making an incorrect return);".

In Sch. 2, in the last para., in sub-para. (d), the words "(fraudulently or negligently making an incorrect return)" substituted for the words "(failure to deliver accounting return)" by SI 2011/702, art. 19(a), with effect from 1 April 2011, but subject to SI 2011/702, art. 21, which provides that the substitution does not have effect in respect of a return period ending on or before 31 December 2010.

In Sch. 2, in the last para., (ja) inserted by SI 2013/1114, art. 8(2), with effect from 1 June 2013.

In Sch. 2, in the last para., sub-para. (k) (and the "; or" at the end of sub-para. (j)) inserted by SI 2011/702, art. 19(b), with effect from 1 April 2011, but subject to SI 2011/702, art. 21, which provides that the insertion does not have effect in respect of a return period ending on or before 31 December 2010.

In Sch. 2, the following entries omitted by SI 2010/652, reg. 2(2), with effect from 1 April 2010 (but these amendments do not apply in relation to or in connection with a notice given before 1 April 2010 requiring the provision or production of documents):

"A notice under section 252 (notices requiring documents or particulars about registered pensions schemes, etc.) to a person of a description prescribed by the Registered Pension Schemes and Employer-Financed Retirement Benefits Schemes (Information) (Prescribed Descriptions of Persons) Regulations 2005 to produce or provide documents or particulars."

"A notice by Revenue and Customs under regulation 22 of the ELA Regulations requiring an individual to provide information, particulars or documents; and a notice of appeal to the tax appeal Commissioners against such a notice."

"A notice of appeal against a notice requiring the production of documents or the furnishing of particulars under section 252."

"(c) section 259 (failure to deliver documents or particulars required by notice);"

In Sch. 2, the following entry inserted by SI 2010/652, reg. 2(3), with effect from 1 April 2010 (but this amendment does not apply in relation to or in connection with a notice given before 1 April 2010 requiring the provision or production of documents):

"A–

(a)   taxpayer notice under paragraph 1 of Schedule 36 to the Finance Act 2008 (information and inspection powers),

(b)   third party notice under paragraph 2 of that Schedule,

(c)   notice under paragraph 5 of that Schedule

that relates to a registered pension scheme; and a notice of appeal against any such notice or against the imposition of a penalty in relation to any such notice.".

In Sch. 2, the words "to the tax appeal Commissioners", which appeared after "appeal", omitted in each place by SI 2009/56, art. 3(2) and Sch. 2, para. 153(3), operative from 1 April 2009 subject to transitional and saving provisions in SI 2009/56, Sch. 3.

REGISTERED PENSION SCHEMES (AUTHORISED MEMBER PAYMENTS) (NO. 2) REGULATIONS 2006

(SI 2006/571)

Made on 9 March 2006 by the Commissioners for Her Majesty's Revenue and Customs in exercise of the powers conferred upon them by s. 164(f) of the Finance Act 2004. Operative from 6 April 2006.

CITATION AND COMMENCEMENT

1 These Regulations may be cited as the Registered Pension Schemes (Authorised Member Payments) (No. 2) Regulations 2006 and shall come into force on 6th April 2006.

PAYMENTS WHICH ARE AUTHORISED MEMBER PAYMENTS

2 A payment which satisfies the conditions in article 39(1), 40(1), 41(1) or 42(1) of the Taxation of Pension Schemes (Transitional Provisions) Order 2006 is a payment which a registered pension scheme is authorised to make.

TAXATION OF PENSION SCHEMES (TRANSITIONAL PROVISIONS) ORDER 2006

(SI 2006/572, as amended by SI 2006/1962, SI 2006/2004, SI 2008/2990, SI 2009/1172, SI 2009/1989, SI 2011/732, SI 2011/1782 and FA 2014)

Made on 9 March 2006 by the Treasury, in exercise of the powers conferred upon them by s. 283(2) of the Finance Act 2004. Operative from 6 April 2006.

ARRANGEMENT OF REGULATIONS

REGULATION

CITATION AND COMMENCEMENT

1(1)   This Order may be cited as the Taxation of Pension Schemes (Transitional Provisions) Order 2006 and shall come into force on 6th April 2006.

1(2)   In this Order–

    "Revenue and Customs" means Her Majesty's Revenue and Customs (see section 4 of the Commissioners for Revenue and Customs Act 2005);

    "the 2004 Act" means the Finance Act 2004;

    "Part 4" means Part 4 of the Finance Act 2004;

    a reference to a numbered section or Schedule (without more) is a reference to the section or Schedule bearing that number in Part 4; and

    expressions which are defined, or are otherwise explained, in section 280 have the same meaning in this Order as they have in Part 4.

PAYMENTS MADE FROM ANNUITIES

2(1)   In its application to any pension scheme which by virtue of paragraph 1(1) of Schedule 36 (pension schemes: transitional provisions and savings)–

(a)   is to be treated as becoming a registered pension scheme on 6th April 2006;

(b)   would have been so treated had it not been wound up before that date; or

(c)   would have been so treated if the scheme administrator had not notified Revenue and Customs under paragraph 2 of Schedule 36 (opting out of deemed registration) that the pension scheme was not to become a registered pension scheme on that date,

section 161 (meaning of "payment" etc) is modified as follows.

2(2)   In subsection (3) after the words "of a registered pension scheme" add–

    "or, if the purchase took place before 6th April 2006, a pension scheme which at the time of purchase fell within one of the categories set out in paragraph 1(1)(a) to (g) of Schedule 36.".

2(3)   After subsection (3) add–

    "**161(3A)**   But subsection (4) does not apply to a payment made or benefit provided under or in connection with an annuity which fulfils the following conditions.

    Condition 1

    The annuity was purchased from an insurance company.

Condition 2

The annuity was purchased by a pension scheme which at the time of purchase fell within one of the categories set out in paragraph 1(1)(a) to (g) of Schedule 36.

Condition 3

The annuity was purchased in order to secure or provide benefits under the scheme referred to in Condition 2.

Condition 4

The terms of the annuity, or of any arrangement or agreement made in connection with that annuity do not permit a payment, the making of which would have given the Board(a) grounds for withdrawing approval of the pension scheme under section 591B of ICTA if it had been made before 6th April 2006.

Condition 5

The terms of the annuity contract have not been altered on or after 6th April 2006 to allow a payment that would be an unauthorised payment if it had been made by a registered pension scheme.".

2(4) In its application to any pension scheme which falls within sub-paragraph (1)(b) section 161(4) is modified as follows.

2(5) For the words "held for the purpose of the pension scheme" substitute "held for the purposes of a registered pension scheme".

COMMENCEMENT PROVISIONS FOR UNSECURED PENSION FUNDS

3 Part 4 of the 2004 Act shall be modified as set out in articles 4 and 5 in its application to any pension which–

(a) was paid by way of income withdrawal, income drawdown or annuity purchase deferral from a retirement benefits scheme, or a personal pension scheme approved under Part 14 of ICTA immediately before 6th April 2006; and

(b) on 6th April 2006 becomes an unsecured pension or a dependant's unsecured pension by virtue of a scheme which is treated as becoming a registered pension scheme on that date (see paragraph 1 of Schedule 36).

MODIFICATION OF SECTION 165

4(1) Section 165(1) (pension rules) shall be modified as follows.

4(2) In pension rule 5 after "basis amount for the unsecured pension year" add "or 100% of that amount during the first reference period as defined in paragraph 10(1A) of Schedule 28.".

4(3) Section 167(1) (pension death benefit rules) shall be modified as follows.

4(4) In pension death benefit rule 4 after "basis amount for the unsecured pension year" add "or 100% of that amount during the first reference period as defined in paragraph 24(1A) of Schedule 28.".

MODIFICATION OF SCHEDULE 28

5(1) Schedule 28 (registered pension schemes: authorised pensions – supplementary) shall be modified as follows.

5(2) In paragraph 10–

(a) in sub-paragraph (1) for "The period of five unsecured pension years" substitute "The first reference period as defined in sub-paragraph (1A) below";

(b) after sub-paragraph (1) insert a new sub-paragraph as follows–

"**10(1A)** The **"first reference period"** is the period commencing on 6th April 2006 and terminating on the earliest of–

(a) the day immediately before the day fixed by the scheme administrator on which to recalculate the basis amount;

(b) the day immediately before the day on which the basis amount was recalculated following an annuity purchase;

(c) 6th April 2008.";

(c) in sub-paragraph (2) for "sub-paragraph (5)" substitute "sub-paragraphs (2A) and (5).";

(d) after sub-paragraph (2) insert the following sub-paragraph–

"**10(2A)** For the first reference period as defined in sub-paragraph (1A), the basis amount is–

    (a)   the annual amount of the annuity calculated pursuant to section 630 of ICTA;

    (b)   the maximum annual pension calculated in accordance with the rules set out in Appendix XII Part I of the Occupational Pension Schemes Practice Notes (IR12) published by the Board on 22nd January 2001 ("the Notes");

    (c)   the annual amount of pension income which has been paid in accordance with paragraph 20.41 of the Notes in respect of a retirement benefits scheme approved for the purposes of Chapter 1 of Part 14 of ICTA, being paid as a small self-administered pension pursuant to the terms of Memorandum 119 issued on 6th May 1994 by the Board.

which could have been purchased by the application of the sums and assets which then represented the member's pension fund on the nominated date.";

(e)   in sub-paragraph (3)(a) for "the reference date" substitute "the applicable reference date";

(f)   after sub-paragraph (3) insert–

    "**10(3A)**   "**The applicable reference date**" is the date on which the pension fund was last valued–

    (a)   in the case of a personal pension fund, pursuant to section 634A of ICTA (income withdrawal by member),

    (b)   in the case of a retirement benefits scheme (other than one falling within paragraph (c) below), pursuant to the rules set out in the Notes, or

    (c)   in the case of a retirement benefits scheme referred to in sub-paragraph (2A)(c), the date of the scheme's last triennial report as required by paragraph 20.41 of the Notes.".

5(3)   In paragraph 24–

(a)   in sub-paragraph (1) for the words "The period of five unsecured pension years" substitute "The first reference period as defined in sub-paragraph (1A) below";

(b)   after sub-paragraph (1) insert a new sub-paragraph as follows–

    "**24(1A)**   The "**first reference period**" is the period commencing on 6th April 2006 and terminating on the earliest of–

    (a)   the day immediately before the day fixed by the scheme administrator on which to recalculate the basis amount;

    (b)   the day immediately before the day on which the basis amount was recalculated following an annuity purchase;

    (c)   6th April 2008.";

(c)   in sub-paragraph (2) for "sub-paragraph (5)" substitute "sub-paragraphs (2A) and (5).";

(d)   after sub-paragraph (2) insert the following sub-paragraph–

    "**24(2A)**   For the first reference period as defined in sub-paragraph (1A), the basis amount is–

    (a)   the annual amount of the annuity calculated pursuant to section 630 of ICTA,

    (b)   the maximum annual pension calculated in accordance with the rules set out in Appendix XII Part I of the Occupational Pension Schemes Practice Notes (IR12) published by the Board on 22nd January 2001 ("the Notes") or,

    (c)   the annual amount of pension income that has been paid in accordance with paragraph 20.41 of the Notes in respect of a retirement benefits scheme approved for the purposes of Chapter 1 of Part 14 of ICTA, being paid as a small selfadministered pension calculated pursuant to the terms of Memorandum 119 issued by the Board on 6 May 1994

which could have been purchased by the application of the sums and assets which then represented the member's pension fund on the nominated date.";

(e)   in sub-paragraph (3)(a) for "the reference date" substitute "the applicable reference date";

(f)   after sub-paragraph (3) insert–

    "**24(3A)**   "**The applicable reference date**" is the date on which the pension fund was last valued–

    (a)   in the case of a personal pension fund, pursuant to section 636A of ICTA (income withdrawal after the death of member),

    (b)   in the case of a retirement benefits scheme (other than one falling within paragraph (c) below), pursuant to the rules set out in the Notes, or

Statutory Instruments

(c)   in the case of a retirement benefits scheme referred to in sub-paragraph (2A)(c), the date of the scheme's last triennial report as required by paragraph 20.41 of the Notes.".

REDUCTION IN RATE OF PENSION

5A(1)   Part 4 of the 2004 Act shall be modified as set out in paragraph (2) in a case where the following conditions are satisfied–

(a)   the pension came into payment before 3rd July 2007;

(b)   the pension is paid to a person who was a member of the pension scheme on 5th April 2006;

(c)   on 5th April 2006 the rules of the pension scheme included provision that there shall or may be a reduction in the rate of the pension ("the rate reduction provisions");

(d)   the pension is paid at a rate required or permitted by the rate reduction provisions;

(e)   the rate reduction provisions would not have prejudiced the approval of the pension scheme by the Inland Revenue or by Her Majesty's Revenue and Customs;

(f)   the rate reduction provisions did not change in any material particular between 5th April 2006 and the date at which the pension became payable at the reduced rate.

5A(2)   In paragraph 2(4) of Schedule 28 to the 2004 Act insert after paragraph (d)–

"(da)   a reduction in respect of which an order made under section 283(2) and (3C) makes transitional provision,".

5A(3)   For the purposes of this article, whether something would have prejudiced the approval of the pension scheme by the Inland Revenue or by Her Majesty's Revenue and Customs is to be determined–

(a)   in the case of an occupational pension scheme approved for the purposes of Chapter 1 of Part 14 of ICTA, in accordance with the publication IR 12(2001) (known as the Occupational Pension Schemes Practice Notes) published by the former Inland Revenue Pension Schemes Office on 23rd March 2001, and

(b)   in the case of a personal pension scheme approved under Chapter 4 of Part 14 of ICTA, in accordance with the publication IR 76(2000) published by the former Inland Revenue Pension Schemes Office on 20th November 2000,

as each of those publications stood at 5th April 2006.

History – Art. 5A inserted by SI 2008/2990, art. 3, with effect from 1 January 2009, in respect of payments of pension made on or after 6 April 2006.

TRANSITIONAL PROTECTION FOR CONTINUED LIFE COVER (75+)

6   The modifications in articles 7 and 8 apply in the case of a member of a registered pension scheme who satisfies the following conditions.

Condition A

The registered pension scheme was, immediately before 6th April 2006, a retirement benefits scheme approved for the purposes of Chapter 1 of Part 14 of ICTA (retirement benefits schemes).

Condition B

The member had a right under the pension scheme to a life cover lump sum on 5th April 2006.

Condition C

The rules of the pension scheme on 10th December 2003 included provision conferring such a right on some or all of the persons who were then members of the pension scheme, and such a right was either then conferred on the member or would have been had the member been a member of the scheme on that date.

Condition D

The rules of the scheme in relation to life cover lump sums have not been changed since 10th December 2003.

Condition E

The member was–

(a)   in receipt of benefits from the scheme on or before 5th April 2006, or

(b)   entitled to one or more life cover lump sums, amounting in the aggregate, to £2,500 or less.

MODIFICATION OF SECTION 636A ITEPA 2003

7(1)   ITEPA 2003 is modified as follows.

7(2) In section 636A(1) (exemption for certain lump sums under registered pension schemes)–

(a)   at the end of paragraph (e) omit "or";

(b)   at the end of paragraph (f) add "or"; and

(c)   after paragraph (f) insert–

"(g)   a life cover lump sum.".

7(3) In section 636A(7) after "unsecured pension fund lump sum death benefit" insert "life cover lump sum".

MODIFICATION OF SECTION 168 AND SCHEDULE 29

8(1) The 2004 Act is modified as follows.

8(2) In section 168(1) (lump sum death benefit rule) after paragraph (i) insert–

"(j)   a life cover lump sum.".

8(3) In Part 2 of Schedule 29 (registered pension schemes: supplementary provisions about lump sums) after paragraph 21 insert–

"LIFE COVER LUMP SUM

21A For the purposes of this Part a lump sum death benefit is a life cover lump sum if–

(a) the member had reached the age of 75 before he died;

(b) payment of the sum would not have prejudiced approval of the scheme for the purposes of Chapter 1 of Part 14 of ICTA if it had been made on 5th April 2006.".

VALUATION OF "PRIMARY PROTECTION" – COMPENSATION FOR POORLY PERFORMING INVESTMENTS

9 Part 4 of 2004 Act shall be modified as set out in articles 10 and 11 in its application to any individual who has given notice of intention to rely on paragraph 7 Schedule 36 where the following conditions are met–

Condition A

The pension scheme in respect of which the individual has given notice is either–

(a)   a money purchase arrangement that is not a cash balance arrangement; or

(b)   a hybrid arrangement where the benefits that may be provided include money purchase benefits that are not cash balance benefits.

Condition B

An amount is paid into the pension scheme, or is determined as being so payable, between 6th April 2006 and 5th April 2009, in respect of compensation for the poor performance of an investment owned by that scheme.

Condition C

The investment in respect of which the compensation is payable was owned by the pension scheme at any time before 6th April 2006 and was offered for sale to the public on the open market.

Condition D

The amount of compensation paid, or determined as being so payable, is an amount which might reasonably have been expected to be paid between two parties in the same position as the payer and the scheme administrator acting at arm's length.

MODIFICATION OF SECTION 212

10(1) Section 212 (valuation of uncrystallised rights for the purposes of section 210) is modified, for the purposes of calculating the value of RR in paragraph 7(3) of Schedule 36, as follows.

10(2) In subsection (5) (valuation of money purchase arrangements other than cash balance arrangements) after paragraphs (a) and (b) add–

"together with the value, if any, of any relevant compensation on 5th April 2006.".

10(3) After subsection (5) add–

"**212(5A)** For the purposes of subsections (5) and (7) relevant compensation is the market value, calculated in accordance with section 278, of any compensation paid or payable in respect of the poor performance of an investment owned by the pension scheme on the earlier of the date of payment of the compensation or 5th April 2009.".

10(4) In subsection (7) (valuation of hybrid arrangements) after paragraphs (a) and (b) add– "together with any hybrid compensation as defined in subsection (7A) below.".

10(5) After subsection (7) add–

"**212(7A)** For the purposes of subsection (7) hybrid compensation is–

(a) any relevant compensation payable in respect of a money purchase arrangement which forms part of the hybrid arrangement calculated in accordance with subsection (5A); less

(b) the value of the hybrid arrangement calculated in accordance with subsection (7) less the value of any sums or assets representing other money purchase benefits calculated in accordance with subsection (5).

If this calculation results in a negative amount, the amount of relevant compensation to be added to the value of the member's uncrystallised rights under this subsection is nil.".

MODIFICATION OF PARAGRAPH 8 OF SCHEDULE 36

11(1) Part 2 of Schedule 36 (pre-commencement rights: lifetime allowance charge) is modified as follows.

11(2) In paragraph 8(5) after the words "(valuation of uncrystallised rights for the purposes of section 210)" add–

"(as modified by article 10 of The Taxation of Pension Schemes (Transitional Provisions) Order 2006)".

"PRIMARY PROTECTION" AND NON RESIDENTS

12(1) Part 4 of the 2004 Act shall have effect subject to the modifications set out in articles 13 and 14 below in its application to any individual to whom either paragraph (2) or (3) applies.

12(2) This paragraph applies if the following conditions are met–

Condition A

The individual has given the Inland Revenue a notice under section 221(6) of his intention to rely on that section where the active membership period in relation to the arrangement in respect of which the notice was given commenced on 6th April 2006

Condition B

The individual would have been a relevant overseas individual in the tax year 2005–06 pursuant to section 221(3) had that subsection been in force during that year.

Condition C

The individual gives or has already given notice to the Inland Revenue pursuant to paragraph 7(1)(b) of Schedule 36 that he intends to rely on that paragraph.

12(3) This paragraph applies if the following conditions are met–

Condition A

The individual has given the Inland Revenue a notice under paragraph 7(1)(b) of Schedule 36 of his intention to rely on that paragraph.

Condition B

The individual gives or has already given notice to the Inland Revenue pursuant to section 221(6) that he intends to rely on that section where the active membership period in relation to the arrangement in respect of which the notice was given commenced on 6th April 2006.

Condition C

The individual would have been a relevant overseas individual in the tax year 2005–06 pursuant to section 221(3) had that subsection been in force during that year.

MODIFICATION OF SECTION 222

13(1) In subsection 222(4) (non residence: money purchase arrangements) after "OV is" for the words "the opening value of the individual's rights under the arrangement" substitute "calculated in accordance with subsection (4A).".

13(2)   After subsection (4) add subsection (4A)–

"**222(4A)**   For the purposes of subsection (4)–

$$OV = OVA \times \frac{SLA}{CSLA}$$

Here–

OVA is the value of the individual's rights under the arrangement on 5th April 2006 calculated in accordance with subsection (5)(b).

SLA is the standard lifetime allowance at the time when the part of the active membership period referred to in subsection (4) ended and

CSLA is £1,500,000 (the lifetime allowance for the tax year 2006–07).".

13(3)   For subsection (5)(b) substitute–

"(b)   the value of the individual's rights under the arrangement on 5th April 2006 is the amount which would, on the valuation assumptions, be available for the provision of benefits to or in respect of the individual under the arrangement if the individual became entitled to the benefits on 5th April 2006.".

MODIFICATION OF SECTION 223

14(1)   Section 223 (non-residence: other arrangements) is modified as follows.

14(2)   In subsection (4) in the definitions of PB and LSB for "at the beginning of that part of that period" substitute "on 5th April 2006 indexed in accordance with subsection (4A).".

14(3)   After subsection (4) insert–

"**223(4A)**   PB and LSB shall be increased by multiplying the appropriate figure by–

$$\frac{SLA}{CSLA}$$

Here–

SLA is the standard lifetime allowance at the time when the part of the active membership period referred to in subsection (4) ended and

CSLA is £1,500,000 (the lifetime allowance for the tax year 2006–07).".

EMPLOYERS OR EMPLOYEES WITH PRE-COMMENCEMENT ENTITLEMENT TO CORRESPONDING RELIEF

15(1)   This article applies where Revenue and Customs allow contributions made between 1st April 2005 and 5th April 2006 by an employer under a pension scheme for the benefit of an employee (a "qualifying employee") to be deducted in accordance with section 76(6A) and (6C) of the Finance Act 1989–

(a)   for the purposes of Case I or Case II of Schedule D;

(b)   in respect of management expenses under section 75 of ICTA; or

(c)   in respect of the expenses of an insurance company under section 76 of ICTA;

(d)   in respect of profits of a trade, profession or vocation chargeable under section 5 of the Income Tax (Trading and Other Income) Act 2005.

15(2)   Where, at any time on or after 6th April 2006, the employer makes contributions under the pension scheme referred to in paragraph (1) for the benefit of the qualifying employee, Revenue and Customs may allow the contributions to be treated as if they were relevant migrant member contributions under paragraph 2 of Schedule 33 if–

(a)   they are satisfied that the conditions in paragraph (3) are met, and

(b)   the scheme manager complies with any prescribed benefit crystallisation information requirements imposed on the scheme manager.

15(3)   The conditions are that–

(a)   the contribution consists of the expenses of paying any sum, or of providing benefits, pursuant to a pension scheme which is established outside the United Kingdom; and

(b)   Revenue and Customs are satisfied that that scheme corresponds to such a scheme as is registered under Part 4 of the 2004 Act.

15(4)   For the purposes of this article and article 17, **"Prescribed benefit crystallisation information requirements"** means requirements imposed by regulation 2 of the Pension Schemes (Information Requirements – Qualifying Overseas Pension Schemes, Qualifying Recognised Overseas Pension Schemes and Corresponding Relief) Regulations 2006 ("the Overseas Information Requirements Regulations")."

For the purposes of this article, the provisions of regulation 2 of the Overseas Information Requirements Regulations shall apply to qualifying employees.

15(5)   The references in paragraphs (2), (3) and (4) to a pension scheme include a pension scheme to which there has been a block transfer on or after 6th April 2006 from a pension scheme to which paragraph (2) applies.

15(6)   In this article **"block transfer"** has the same meaning as in paragraph 22(6) of Schedule 36 but treating the references there to "the member" as references to the qualifying employee.

MODIFICATION OF SECTION 245

16(1)   In a case falling within article 15, section 245 (restriction of deduction for contributions by employer) is modified as follows.

16(2)   In subsection (5)–

(a)   after the words "(deductions to which Schedule does not apply)" insert "(a)"; and

(b)   after the words "relevant migrant member of the pension scheme in relation to the contributions," insert–
        "and

        (b)   after paragraph (g) insert–

        "(h)   in respect of contributions which have been given relief under section 196 as applied by paragraph 2 of Schedule 33 and modified by article 15 of The Taxation of Pension Schemes (Transitional Provisions) Order 2006.".".

APPLICATION OF 308A ITEPA 2003

17(1)   This article applies where–

(a)   Revenue and Customs allow an employee (an "exempt employee") to be exempted from income tax under section 390 ITEPA 2003 in relation to contributions made between 6th April 2005 and 5th April 2006 by his employer under a pension scheme; and

(b)   the conditions in paragraph (2) are met.

17(2)   The conditions are

Condition A

The scheme manager of the pension scheme referred to in paragraph (1)(a) complies with any prescribed benefit crystallisation information requirements imposed on the scheme manager.

Condition B

Revenue and Customs are satisfied that the pension scheme corresponds to such a scheme as is registered under Part 4 of this Act.

17(3)   For the purposes of this article, the provisions of regulation 2 of the Overseas Information Requirements Regulations shall apply to exempt employees.

17(4)   Section 308A of ITEPA 2003 (exemption of contributions to overseas pension scheme) shall apply in relation to any contributions made on or after 6th April 2006 for the benefit of the employee by an employer under the pension scheme as if–

(a)   the pension scheme were a qualifying overseas pension scheme, and

(b)   the contributions were relevant migrant member contributions.

17(5)   The references in paragraphs (1) and (2) to a pension scheme include a pension scheme to which there has been a block transfer on or after 6th April 2006 from a pension scheme to which paragraphs (1) and (2) apply.

17(6)   In this article **"block transfer"** has the same meaning as in paragraph 22(6) of Schedule 36 but treating the references there to "the member" as references to the exempt employee.

"ENHANCED PROTECTION" AND PENSION COMMENCEMENT LUMP SUMS

18   If (and for so long) as paragraph 27 or 29 of Schedule 36 applies in relation to an individual, paragraph 1(1) of Schedule 29 (supplementary provision about authorised lump sums: meaning of "pension commencement lump sum") shall have effect, in relation to that individual, with the omission of paragraph (b) (requirement that lump sum payable only when lifetime allowance available), and section 239 has effect in the case of a lump sum paid to that individual as if its subsection (3)(b) did not include a reference to paragraph 1(1)(b) of Schedule 29.

History – In art. 18 the words ", and section 239 has effect in the case of a lump sum paid to that individual as if its subsection (3)(b) did not include a reference to paragraph 1(1)(b) of Schedule 29" inserted by FA 2014, s. 43 and Sch. 5, para. 12(4), with effect from 19 March 2014.

PRE-COMMENCEMENT PENSION AND CALCULATION OF THE "PERMITTED MAXIMUM" PENSION COMMENCEMENT LUMP SUM

19(1)   In the case of an individual who falls within paragraph 20(1) of Schedule 36 (precommencement pensions) paragraph (2) applies.

19(2)   In paragraph 2(6) of Schedule 29 after the words "AAC is the aggregate of the amounts crystallised by each benefit crystallisation event which has occurred in relation to the member" insert "(including any pre-commencement pension rights valued under paragraph 20 of Schedule 36) and the amount of any lump sum deemed to have been crystallised under paragraph 1(1A) of Schedule 29)".

PRE-COMMENCEMENT LUMP SUM DEATH BENEFITS

20(1)   In the case of an individual who dies on or after 6th April 2006 and meets the conditions in paragraph (2) paragraph (3) applies.

20(2)   The conditions are–

Condition A

The individual had an actual right to one or more pre-commencement pensions immediately before his death.

Condition B

No benefit crystallisation event has occurred in relation to the individual before his death.

Condition C

After the individual's death a single benefit crystallisation event occurs in relation to that individual by reason of the payment of a lump sum death benefit in respect of that individual.

20(3)   Paragraph 20(2)(b) of Schedule 36 is to be treated as providing that the amount crystallised was the value of the individual's pre-commencement pension rights immediately before the individual's death.

TRANSFERS AND ENTITLEMENT TO LUMP SUMS EXCEEDING 25% OF UNCRYSTALLISED RIGHTS

21(1)   Articles 22 and 23 apply if–

(a)   a person was a member of a pension scheme–

    (i)   which was in existence on 5th April 2006; and

    (ii)   which is treated as becoming a registered pension scheme within Part 4 of the Finance Act 2004 on 6th April 2006 (see paragraph 1 of Schedule 36 to that Act); and

(b)   on or after 6th April 2006 sums and assets held for the purposes of, or representing accrued rights, under the registered pension scheme are transferred, otherwise than by a block transfer–

    (i)   to another registered pension scheme; or

    (ii)   to a registered pension scheme from a registered pension scheme which has received a block transfer of the sums and assets referred to in sub-paragraph 1(b) of this article.

21(2)   In this article "block transfer" has the meaning given in paragraph 31(8) of Schedule 36 (entitlement to lump sums exceeding 25% of uncrystallised rights).

MODIFICATION OF PARAGRAPH 31 OF SCHEDULE 36

22(1)   In a case to which this article applies, paragraph 31 of Schedule 36 is modified as follows.

22(2)   In sub-paragraph (1) for "sub-paragraph (2)" substitute "sub-paragraphs (2) and (2A)".

22(3)   After sub-paragraph (2) insert–

"**31(2A)**   Those provisions apply with the further modifications prescribed by Article 23 of the Taxation of Pension Schemes (Transitional Provisions) Order 2006 in the case of a person satisfying sub-paragraph (1) above–

(a)   who was a member of a pension scheme which–

(i) was in existence on 5th April 2006; and

(ii) is treated as becoming a registered pension scheme within Part 4 of the Finance Act 2004 on 6th April 2006 (see paragraph 1 of Schedule 36 to that Act); and

(b) in respect of whom sums and assets held for the purposes of, or representing accrued rights under, the registered pension scheme are transferred, otherwise than by a block transfer–

(i) to another registered pension scheme, or

(ii) to another registered pension scheme from a registered pension which has received a block transfer of the sums and assets referred to in paragraph (b) of this sub-paragraph.".

MODIFICATION OF PARAGRAPH 34 OF SCHEDULE 36

23(1) In a case to which this article applies, paragraph 34 of Schedule 36 is modified as follows.

23(2) In sub-paragraph (2) for the words from "pension scheme and for" to the end of the paragraph (7) (as substituted) substitute–

"pension scheme and for sub-paragraphs (5) to (8) there were substituted–

"2(5) If paragraph 2(2) does not apply, and there has been a transfer of part or all of the sums and assets held for the purposes of, or representing accrued rights under, the registered pension scheme in relation to the individual, the permitted maximum is the greater of–

$$\left(VULSR \times \left(\frac{ULA}{FSLA} \right) \right) + ALSA - \frac{TV}{4}$$

and nil.

2(6) [Omitted by SI 2008/2990, art. 4(b).]

2(7) In this paragraph–

VULSR is the value of the individual's uncrystallised lump sum rights under the pension scheme on 5th April 2006, calculated in accordance with paragraph 32 of Schedule 36,

ULA is the underpinned lifetime allowance,

FSLA is £1,500,000 (the standard lifetime allowance for the tax year 2006–07),

ALSA is the greater of the additional lump sum amount and nil; and

TV is the value of all sums and assets held for the purposes of, or representing accrued rights under the registered pension scheme transferred from the scheme on or after 6th April 2006.".".

History – In art. 23(2), in the sub-para. (5) treated as substituted, "ULA" substituted for "CLSA" by SI 2011/1782, art. 2(a)(i), with effect for the tax year 2012–13 and subsequent tax years.
In art. 23(2), in the sub-para. (5) treated as substituted, "FSLA" substituted for "FLSA" by SI 2011/1782, art. 2(a)(ii), with effect for the tax year 2012–13 and subsequent tax years.
In art. 23(2), in the sub-para. (7) treated as substituted, definition of "ULA" substituted for definition of "CSLA" by SI 2011/1782, art. 2(b), with effect for the tax year 2012–13 and subsequent tax years.
In art. 23(2), in the modified version of FA 2004, Sch. 36, para. 34(2) as it modifies FA 2004, Sch. 29, para. 2(5), the words "relevant benefit accrual has occurred in relation to the individual after 5th April 2006", which appeared after "does not apply,", omitted by SI 2008/2990, art. 4(a), with effect from 1 January 2009 in respect of lump sums paid on or after 6 April 2006.
In art. 23(2), in the modified version of FA 2004, Sch. 36, para. 34(2), the modified version of FA 2004, Sch. 29, para. 2(6) omitted by SI 2008/2990, art. 4(b), with effect from 1 January 2009 in respect of lump sums paid on or after 6 April 2006.

PENSION COMMENCEMENT LUMP SUMS WHERE NO PENSION IS PAID BEFORE DEATH

23ZA(1) Subject to articles 23ZD and 23ZE, in a case where an individual has received a pension commencement lump sum, or part of a pension commencement lump sum, but dies before becoming entitled to the pension in connection with the lump sum, Schedule 36 is modified as follows.

23ZA(2) For paragraph 31(3) (entitlement to lump sums exceeding 25% of uncrystallised rights – the pension condition) substitute–

"31(3) The pension condition is that, the scheme administrator considers that, had the individual not died, the individual would have become entitled to all of the pensions payable to the individual under arrangements under the pension scheme (to which the individual did not have an actual entitlement on or before 5th April 2006) on the same date.".

23ZA(3) In paragraph 34(2) (entitlement to lump sums exceeding 25% of uncrystallised rights – modifications to Schedule 29)–

(a)   in the substituted sub-paragraph (7A) for the definition of AC substitute–

"AC is the value of the individual's uncrystallised rights on the date of death under arrangements under the pension scheme in connection with which the lump sum is paid calculated in accordance with section 212 (but this is subject to sub-paragraphs (7B) and (7BA)) on the assumption that the individual became entitled to the present payment of benefits in respect of the rights on that date.".

(b)   omit substituted sub-paragraph (7AA); and

(c)   after the substituted sub-paragraph (7B) insert–

"**34(7BA)**   In determining AC, section 212 shall apply as if **"the value assumptions"** means the basis upon which the scheme administrator determined the amount of the lump sum to be paid.".

History – Art. 23ZA inserted by SI 2011/732, art. 3, which came into force on 6 April 2011, with effect in relation to any time on or after 6 April 2006.

PENSION COMMENCEMENT LUMP SUMS AND MULTIPLE PENSIONS

23ZB(1)   Article 23ZC applies where–

(a)   there is a single pension commencement lump sum;

(b)   the lump sum is paid in connection with at least two of the three types of pension listed in paragraph (4) from the same registered pension scheme; and

(c)   an individual becomes entitled to all of the pensions in connection with which the pension commencement lump sum is paid within the specified period.

23ZB(2)   Article 23ZD applies where–

(a)   there is a single pension commencement lump sum;

(b)   the scheme administrator anticipated that the lump sum would be paid in connection with at least two of the three types of pension listed in paragraph (4) from the same registered pension scheme;

(c)   an individual received the lump sum, or part of the lump sum, but died before becoming entitled to any of the pensions; and

(d)   the scheme administrator considers that, had the individual not died, the individual would have become entitled to all of the pensions in connection with the lump sum within the specified period.

23ZB(3)   Article 23ZE applies where–

(a)   there is a single pension commencement lump sum;

(b)   the scheme administrator anticipated that the lump sum would be paid in connection with at least two of the three types of pension listed in paragraph (4) from the same registered pension scheme;

(c)   an individual received the lump sum, or part of the lump sum, but died before the end of the specified period after becoming entitled to at least one but not all of the pensions; and

(d)   the scheme administrator considers that, had the individual not died, the individual would have become entitled to all of the pensions in connection with the lump sum within the specified period.

23ZB(4)   The three types of pension are–

(a)   a scheme pension under a defined benefits arrangement;

(b)   a scheme pension under a money purchase arrangement;

(c)   a lifetime annuity.

23ZB(5)   The **"specified period"** is the period of six months beginning with the earliest date on which the individual becomes entitled to any of the pensions or on which the scheme administrator considers, had the individual not died, that the individual would have become so entitled.

History – Art. 23ZB inserted by SI 2011/732, art. 3, which came into force on 6 April 2011, with effect in relation to any time on or after 6 April 2006.

INDIVIDUAL BECOMES ENTITLED TO THE PENSIONS

23ZC(1)   In a case to which this article applies, Part 4 is modified as follows.

23ZC(2)   For section 166(2)(a) (lump sum rule) substitute–

"(a)   in the case of a pension commencement lump sum, immediately before the person becomes entitled to the last of the pensions in connection with which it is paid, and".

Statutory Instruments

23ZC(3) In paragraph 31(3) of Schedule 36 for "on the same date" substitute "within a period of six months beginning with the earliest date on which the individual becomes entitled to any of the pensions".

History – Art. 23ZC inserted by SI 2011/732, art. 3, which came into force on 6 April 2011, with effect in relation to any time on or after 6 April 2006.

INDIVIDUAL DIES BEFORE BECOMING ENTITLED TO ANY OF THE PENSIONS

23ZD(1) In a case to which this article applies, Schedule 36 is modified as follows.

23ZD(2) For paragraph 31(3) substitute–

"**31(3)** The pension condition is that, the scheme administrator considers that, had the individual not died, the individual would have become entitled to all of the pensions payable to the individual under arrangements under the pension scheme (to which the individual did not have an actual entitlement on or before 5th April 2006) within a period of six months beginning with the earliest date on which the scheme administrator considers that the individual would have become entitled to any of the pensions.".

23ZD(3) In paragraph 34(2)–

(a) in the substituted sub-paragraph (7A) for the definition of AC substitute–
"AC is the value of the individual's uncrystallised rights on the date of death under arrangements under the pension scheme in connection with which the lump sum is paid calculated in accordance with section 212 (but this is subject to sub-paragraphs (7B) and (7BA)) on the assumption that the individual became entitled to the present payment of benefits in respect of the rights on that date.".

(b) omit sub-paragraph (7AA); and

(c) after the substituted sub-paragraph (7B) insert–
"**(7BA)** In determining AC, section 212 shall apply as if **"the value assumptions"** means the basis upon which the scheme administrator determined the amount of the lump sum to be paid.".

History – Art. 23ZD inserted by SI 2011/732, art. 3, which came into force on 6 April 2011, with effect in relation to any time on or after 6 April 2006.

INDIVIDUAL DIES AFTER BECOMING ENTITLED TO AT LEAST ONE BUT NOT ALL OF THE PENSIONS

23ZE(1) In a case to which this article applies, Part 4 is modified as follows.

23ZE(2) For section 166(2)(a) substitute–

"(a) in the case of a pension commencement lump sum, immediately before the latest time when the person becomes entitled to any of the pensions in connection with which it was anticipated that it would be paid, and".

23ZE(3) For paragraph 31(3) of Schedule 36 substitute–

"**31(3)** The pension condition is that, the scheme administrator considers that, had the individual not died, the individual would have become entitled to all of the pensions payable to the individual under arrangements under the pension scheme (to which the individual did not have an actual entitlement on or before 5th April 2006) within a period of six months beginning with the earliest date on which the individual became entitled to any of the pensions.".

23ZE(4) In paragraph 34(2) of Schedule 36–

(a) in the substituted sub-paragraph (7A) of paragraph 2 of Schedule 29, for the definition of AC substitute–
"AC is CB + UCB where–

CB is the amount crystallised, prior to death, on the individual becoming entitled to pensions in connection with which the lump sum is paid (see section 216) (but this is subject to sub-paragraphs (7AA) and (7B)), and

UCB is the value of the individual's uncrystallised rights on the date of death under arrangements under the pension scheme in connection with which the lump sum is paid calculated in accordance with section 212 (but this is subject to sub-paragraphs (7B) and (7BA)) on the assumption that the individual became entitled to the present payment of benefits in respect of the rights on that date.", and

(b)   after the substituted sub-paragraph (7B) of paragraph 2 of Schedule 29, insert–

"**34(7BA)**   In determining AC, section 212 shall apply as if **"the value assumptions"** means the basis upon which the scheme administrator determined the amount of the lump sum to be paid.".

History – Art. 23ZE inserted by SI 2011/732, art. 3, which came into force on 6 April 2011, with effect in relation to any time on or after 6 April 2006.

MODIFICATION OF TRIVIAL COMMUTATION LUMP SUM RULES

23A   Part 4 of the 2004 Act shall be modified as set out in articles 23B to 23D.

History – Art. 23A inserted by SI 2009/1172, art. 3, with effect from 1 June 2009.

Notes – Although reg. 23A states that the effects of reg. 23B–23D are modifications, they apply in all circumstances and are therefore in effect actual amendments.

23B(1)   [Substitutes FA 2004, s. 166(2).]

History – Art. 23B inserted by SI 2009/1172, art. 3, with effect from 1 June 2009.

Notes – Although reg. 23A states that the effects of reg. 23B–23D are modifications, they apply in all circumstances and are therefore in effect actual amendments.

23C(1)   Schedule 29 (registered pension schemes: authorised lump sums – supplementary) is modified as follows.

23C(2)   [Substitutes FA 2004, Sch. 29, para. 1(1)(aa).]

23C(3)   [Amends FA 2004, Sch. 29, para. 7(1).]

23C(4)   [Inserts FA 2004, Sch. 29, para. 7A.]

23C(5)   [Inserts FA 2004, Sch. 29, para. 9A.]

History – In art. 23C(4), in the inserted para. 7A(1)(a), "£10,000" substituted for "£2,000" by FA 2014, s. 42(5), with effect for lump sums paid on or after 27 March 2014.

In art. 23C(4), in the para. 7A(1)(b) inserted, the words ", but has not reached the age of 75" omitted by SI 2011/1782, art. 2(3), with effect in relation to lump sums paid on or after 6 April 2011.

Art. 23C inserted by SI 2009/1172, art. 3, with effect from 1 June 2009.

Notes – Although reg. 23A states that the effects of reg. 23B–23D are modifications, they apply in all circumstances and are therefore in effect actual amendments.

23D(1)   Schedule 36 (pension schemes etc: transitional provisions and savings) is modified as follows.

23D(2)   [Substitutes FA 2004, Sch. 36, para. 31(3).]

23D(3)   In the sub-paragraph (7A) of paragraph 2 of Schedule 29 that is substituted by paragraph 34(2) (modification of Schedule 29)–

(a)   [amends definition of "LS"; and]

(b)   [substitutes definition of "AC".]

History – Art. 23D inserted by SI 2009/1172, art. 3, with effect from 1 June 2009.

Notes – Although reg. 23A states that the effects of reg. 23B–23D are modifications, they apply in all circumstances and are therefore in effect actual amendments.

DEPENDANT'S SCHEME PENSION LIMIT

24(1)   Paragraph (2) applies where the member in respect of whom the dependant's scheme pension is payable was actually entitled to one or more relevant existing pensions (as defined in paragraph 10(2) of Schedule 36) on 5th April 2006.

24(2)   Paragraph 16A of Schedule 28 shall be modified as follows.

24(3)   After sub-paragraph (2) add–

"**16A(3)**   This paragraph shall not apply to a scheme pension where the member was actually entitled to that pension on 5th April 2006.".

STAND-ALONE LUMP SUMS: INTRODUCTORY AND DEFINITION

25(1)   This article and articles 25A to 25D deal with stand-alone lump sums.

25(2)   In those articles–

this article is introductory and sets out the definition of a stand-alone lump sum;

article 25A deals with the conditions that must be met before a lump sum may be classified as a stand-alone lump sum;

article 25B deals with the circumstances in which a stand-alone lump sum may be paid;

article 25C deals with the tax consequences;

and article 25D contains further provisions.

25(3) In this article and in articles 25A to 25D a "stand-alone lump sum" means a lump sum which–

(a)   meets all the conditions A to C set out in article 25A, and

(b)   is paid in one of the circumstances A to C set out in article 25B.

History – In art. 25(3)(a), "C" substituted for "D" by SI 2011/1782, art. 2(4), with effect in relation to lump sums paid on or after 6 April 2011.

Art. 25, 25A, 25B, 25C and 25D substituted for former art. 25 by SI 2006/2004, art. 3, with effect from 25 July 2006.

CONDITIONS TO BE MET BY STAND-ALONE SUMS

25A(1) This article sets out the conditions referred to in article 25(3)(a).

25A(2) Condition A is that, on or after 6th April 2006, the lump sum is paid to an individual under a registered pension scheme of which the individual is a member.

25A(3) Condition B is that the lump sum is paid in circumstances where all of the member's uncrystallised rights under the scheme come into payment on a single benefit crystallisation event.

25A(4) Condition C is that the lump sum is paid when the member has reached normal minimum pension age (or the ill-health condition is satisfied).

25A(5) [Omitted by SI 2011/1782, art. 2(5).]

History – Art. 25A(5) omitted by SI 2011/1782, art. 2(5), with effect in relation to lump sums paid on or after 6 April 2011.
Art. 25, 25A, 25B, 25C and 25D substituted for former art. 25 by SI 2006/2004, art. 3, with effect from 25 July 2006.

CIRCUMSTANCES IN WHICH STAND-ALONE SUMS ARE PAID

25B(1) This article sets out the circumstances referred to in article 25(3)(b).

25B(2) Circumstance A is where paragraph 28 of Schedule 36 (modification of paragraph 2 of Schedule 29 in the case of a member of a pension scheme to whom enhanced protection does not apply) applies in relation to the member.

25B(3) Circumstance B is where–

(a)   paragraph 29 of Schedule 36 (modification of applicable amount in the case of a member of a pension scheme to whom enhanced protection applies) applies in relation to the member, and

(b)   on 5th April 2006, and on the assumptions set out in paragraph (5), all of the member's rights under all of the member's pension schemes within paragraphs (a) to (g) of paragraph 1(1) of Schedule 36 could have been paid out to the member in the form of a lump sum.

25B(4) Circumstance C is where–

(a)   on 5th April 2006 the member was a member of a pension scheme within paragraphs (a) to (e) of paragraph 1(1) of Schedule 36 and relating to an employment (the "original pension scheme"),

(b)   on 5th April 2006, and on the assumptions set out in paragraph (5), all of the member's rights under the original pension scheme, and all of the member's rights under any other pension scheme within paragraphs (a) to (e) of paragraph 1(1) of Schedule 36 and relating to the same employment could have been paid out to the member in the form of a lump sum,

(c)   on and after 6th April 2006, relevant benefit accrual (as defined in paragraph 13 of Schedule 36) has not occurred under the original pension scheme in relation to the member,

(d)   on or after 6th April 2006 the member is paid a lump sum representing all of the member's rights (to which the member did not have an actual entitlement on or before 5th April 2006) under the original pension scheme,

(e)   the circumstances set out in paragraphs (2) and (3) (circumstances A and B) do not apply.

25B(5) The assumptions are that–

(a)   the member had retired on 5th April 2006;

(b)   the valuation assumptions apply (modified, if appropriate, in accordance with paragraph 25(7) of Schedule 36); and

(c)   the payment of the lump sum on 5th April 2006 (on the assumptions set out in paragraph 26(4) of Schedule 36) would not have given the Commissioners of Her Majesty's Revenue and Customs grounds for withdrawing the approval of the pension scheme.

History – Art. 25, 25A, 25B, 25C and 25D substituted for former art. 25 by SI 2006/2004, art. 3, with effect from 25 July 2006.

PAYMENT OF STAND-ALONE SUMS: TAX CONSEQUENCES

25C(1) In subsection (1) of section 166 (lump sum rule), the list of lump sums set out in the paragraphs of that subsection shall be treated as including a stand-alone lump sum.

25C(2)   In paragraph 15 of Schedule 32 (benefit crystallisation event 6: meaning of "relevant lump sum") the list of lump sums set out in the sub-paragraphs of that paragraph shall be treated as including a stand-alone lump sum.

25C(3)   In subsection (1) of section 636A of ITEPA 2003 (exemption for certain lump sums under registered pension schemes), the list of lump sums set out in the paragraphs of that subsection shall be treated as including a stand-alone lump sum.

History – Art. 25, 25A, 25B, 25C and 25D substituted for former art. 25 by SI 2006/2004, art. 3, with effect from 25 July 2006.

STAND-ALONE SUMS: FURTHER PROVISIONS

25D(1)   Paragraphs (2) and (3) apply if–

(a)   a stand-alone lump sum is paid to a member of a pension scheme in circumstances where article 25B(2) (circumstance A) applies, or

(b)   a stand-alone lump sum is paid to a member of a pension scheme, and a pension commencement lump sum is subsequently paid to the member (whether from the same pension scheme or from any other pension scheme) in circumstances where paragraph 28 of Schedule 36 applies to the payment of the pension commencement lump sum.

25D(2)   The stand-alone lump sum paid must not exceed the stand-alone lump sum maximum.

The **"stand-alone lump sum maximum"** means the amount given by the formula "VULSR – APCLS" in sub-paragraph (3) of paragraph 28 of Schedule 36, in the modified subparagraph (6) of paragraph 2 of Schedule 29 (as that formula is modified in accordance with paragraph (3)).

25D(3)   In sub-paragraph (3) of paragraph 28 of Schedule 36, in the modified sub-paragraph (6) of paragraph 2 of Schedule 29, the term **"APCLS"** shall be treated as referring to the aggregate of the amounts of each pension commencement lump sum and each stand-alone lump sum to which the individual has previously become entitled, as adjusted under subparagraph (7) (or, if the individual has not previously become entitled to a pension commencement lump sum or a stand-alone lump sum, is nil).

25D(4)   Paragraph (5) applies if–

(a)   an individual was a member of a pension scheme ("the original pension scheme"),

(b)   the original pension scheme was entitled to pay a stand-alone lump sum to the member which, if it had been paid, would have been a stand-alone lump sum paid in circumstances where article 25B(4) (circumstance C) applied,

(c)   the rights of the member under the original pension scheme are transferred to a new pension scheme (the "transferee pension scheme") as the result of a block transfer (within the meaning given by paragraph 22(6) of Schedule 36), and

(d)   the member had no rights under the transferee pension scheme before the block transfer.

25D(5)   The transferee pension scheme is treated as the same pension scheme as the original pension scheme (so that, accordingly, the transferee pension scheme may pay a stand-alone lump sum to the member in circumstances where article 25B(4) (circumstance C) applies).

25D(6)   Paragraphs (7) to (9) apply if–

(a)   an individual is a member of a pension scheme (a "stand-alone lump sum pension scheme") which is entitled to pay a stand-alone lump sum to the member in circumstances where article 25B(3) or (4) (circumstance B or C) applies;

(b)   on or after 6th April 2006 sums and assets are transferred in relation to the member by another pension scheme under which the member has rights (a "transferor scheme") to the stand-alone lump sum pension scheme; and

(c)   the stand-alone lump sum pension scheme subsequently makes a lump sum payment to the member.

25D(7)   The lump sum payment made by the stand-alone lump sum pension scheme to the member is not a stand-alone lump sum unless the lump sum is also made in the circumstances set out in paragraph (8).

25D(8)   The circumstances are that–

(a)   neither a stand-alone lump sum nor a pension commencement lump sum has previously been paid under the pension scheme to the member, and

(b)   the sums and assets transferred (or, if there is more than one transfer, all the sums and assets transferred), as specified in paragraph (6)(b), are stand-alone lump sum transfer sums.

25D(9) In paragraph (8)(b) **"stand-alone lump sum transfer sums"** means sums and assets transferred by the transferor scheme to the stand-alone lump sum pension scheme in the circumstances specified in paragraph (6)(b) which would have been a stand-alone lump sum on the assumptions that–

(a)   the sums and assets had been transferred not to the stand-alone lump sum pension scheme but to the member, and

(b)   the condition in article 25A(4) (condition C) is met."

History – Art. 25, 25A, 25B, 25C and 25D substituted for former art. 25 by SI 2006/2004, art. 3, with effect from 25 July 2006.

Cross references – SI 2010/1187, reg. 19: Financial Assistance Scheme: application of reg. 25D.

APPLICATION OF PARAGRAPH 31 OF SCHEDULE 36

26   [Omitted by SI 2006/2004, art. 4.]

History – Art. 26 omitted by SI 2006/2004, art. 3, with effect from 25 July 2006.

CONTRACTS APPROVED UNDER SECTION 621(1)(B) OF ICTA

27(1)   This article applies in the case of an individual who, immediately before 6th April 2006, had rights under a contract which had been approved under section 621(1)(b) of ICTA.

27(2)   Schedule 36 shall be modified as follows.

27(3)   In paragraph 1(1) (deemed registration of existing schemes) after paragraph (e) insert–

"(ea)   a contract approved under section 621(1)(b) of ICTA,".

27(4)   In paragraph 4 after sub-paragraph (4) add

"**4(4A)**   If the pension scheme is within paragraph 1(1)(ea) immediately before that date, the trustee or trustees of the pension scheme, or the insurance company which is party to the contract in which the pension scheme is comprised, is or are to be treated as becoming the scheme administrator.".

27(5)   In paragraph 40(3) (members' contributions to pre-commencement retirement annuity contracts) after paragraph (a) insert–

"(aa)   a contract approved under section 621(1)(b) of ICTA, where article 27(2) of the Taxation of Pension Schemes (Transitional Provisions) Order 2006 applies to the individual in question, or".

PRE-EXISTING ENTITLEMENT TO LUMP SUMS AND DEFERMENT

28(1)   In the case of an individual who meets the conditions set out in paragraph (2), paragraph (3) applies.

28(2)   The conditions are as follows.

Condition A

The individual is a member of a scheme which falls within paragraph 1(1)(a), (c), (d) or (e) of Schedule 36.

Condition B

The individual has become entitled to a tax-free lump sum under that scheme on or before 5th April 2006.

Condition C

The individual would but for an election to defer entitlement made on or after 27 July 2004, have been entitled to all or part of the pension to which the lump sum in Condition B relates on or before 5th April 2006.

Condition D

A benefit crystallisation event occurs on or after 6th April 2006 in relation to any of the rights, sums and assets of the scheme in relation to the individual.

28(3)   Paragraph 1 of Schedule 29 shall be modified, as follows.

(a)   After sub-paragraph (1) add–

"**1(1A)**   Where a member of a scheme has become entitled to a tax free lump sum on or before 5th April 2006, that lump sum is to be treated as if it were a pension commencement lump sum if–

(a)   the member who became entitled to the lump sum is a member of a scheme which falls within paragraph 1(1)(a), (c), (d) or (e) of Schedule 36,

(b)   the member has elected to defer entitlement to all or part of the pension to which the lump sum in sub-paragraph (a) relates until after 5th April 2006.

The lump sum shall be treated as if the member became entitled to it on 6th April 2006 and the amount to be treated as having been crystallised at that time shall be the amount of the lump sum to which the member became entitled.

1(1AA)   No lifetime allowance charge shall arise in respect of the amount deemed to have been crystallised in paragraph (1A).".

History – Art. 25, 25A, 25B, 25C and 25D substituted for former Art. 25 by SI 2010/0187, reg. 6, with effect from 6 April 2006.

Cross references – SI 2010/0187, reg. 19: Financial Assistance Scheme: application.

(b)   After sub-paragraph (3) add–

"**1(3A)**   But a pension–

(a)   which becomes payable under a scheme which falls within paragraph 1(1)(a), (c), (d) or (e) of Schedule 36 in respect of which entitlement to a lump sum has already arisen prior to 6th April 2006, and

(b)   entitlement to which has been deferred (in whole or in part) until after 5th April 2006, is not a relevant pension.

1(3B)   Sub-paragraph (3A) also applies to a pension payable under any registered pension scheme which has received, (whether directly or through one or more intermediate schemes), a transfer of the sums or assets held for the purposes of the scheme referred to in that sub-paragraph to the extent that the pension is payable in respect of those sums or assets and any investment growth that has been made on them.".

MEMBER'S UNSECURED PENSION FUNDS

29(1)   In the case of an individual who meets the conditions set out in paragraph (2), paragraphs (3) to (5) apply.

29(2)   The conditions are as follows.

Condition A

The individual had not reached the age of 75 on 6th April 2006.

Condition B

The individual is a member of a scheme which falls within paragraph 1(1) of Schedule 36.

Condition C

The individual was, on 5th April 2006 entitled to a pension which was not provided under a defined benefits arrangement and which–

(a)   took the form of income drawdown under a retirement benefits scheme approved for the purposes of Chapter 1 of Part 14 of ICTA; or

(b)   was paid from the resources of–

(i)   a small self-administered scheme as defined in the Retirement Benefits Schemes (Restriction on Discretion to Approve) (Small Self-Administered Schemes) Regulations 1991, or

(ii)   a small self-administered scheme that had been approved under section 590 of ICTA, and the rules of the scheme on 5th April 2006 did not require the purchase of an annuity in respect of the individual; or

(c)   took the form of income withdrawal under a personal pension scheme approved under Chapter 4 of Part 14 of ICTA pursuant to section 634A of that Act.

29(3)   Paragraph 8 of Schedule 28(c) (member's unsecured pension fund) is modified as follows–

(a)   for sub-paragraph (1A) substitute–

"**8(1A)**   For the purposes of this Part sums or assets held for the purposes of an arrangement are member-designated funds if they have at any time been applied to provide a pension which–

(a)   took the form of income drawdown under a retirement benefits scheme approved for the purposes of Chapter 1 of Part 14 of ICTA;

(b)   was paid from the resources of–

(i)   a small self-administered scheme as defined in the Retirement Benefits Schemes (Restriction on Discretion to Approve) (Small Self-administered Schemes) Regulations 1991, or

(ii)   a small self-administered scheme that had been approved under section 590 of ICTA;

and the rules of scheme on 5th April 2006 did not require the purchase of an annuity in respect of the individual; or

(c)   took the form of income withdrawal under a personal pension scheme approved under Chapter 4 of Part 14 of ICTA pursuant to section 634A of that Act.".

(b)   after sub-paragraph (1A) insert–

"**8(1AA)**   The sums or assets referred to in sub-paragraph (1A) shall be treated as comprising a separate arrangement and the deemed designation of those sums or assets does not constitute benefit crystallisation event 1.

8(1AB)   Any sums or assets transferred from an arrangement referred to in sub-paragraph (1AA) shall be treated as comprising a separate arrangement.".

29(4)   For paragraph 9(1) of Schedule 28 substitute–

"**9(1)**   "**Unsecured pension year**" in relation to an unsecured pension referred to in paragraph 8(1A), means–

(a)   the period beginning on 6th April 2006 and ending on the earlier of–

     (i)   5th April 2007, or

     (ii)   the date upon which the first reference period defined in paragraph 10(1A) treated as inserted by Article 5 of the Taxation of Pension Schemes (Transitional Provisions) Order 2006 terminates; and

(b)   each succeeding period of 12 months.".

29(5)   Section 216 (benefit crystallisation events and amounts crystallised) shall be modified as follows–

(a)   in BCE2, in column 1 of the table, after the words "under any of the relevant pension schemes" add–

"except to the extent that, the scheme pension was funded by the surrender of–

     (a)   sums or assets deemed to represent an arrangement pursuant to paragraph 8(1A) (a) to (c) of Schedule 28 as modified by article 29 of the Taxation of Pension Schemes (Transitional Provisions) Order 2006; or

     (b)   sums or assets which have been transferred from an arrangement referred to in subparagraph (a) to the extent that the scheme pension is payable in respect of those sums or assets and any investment growth that has been made on them.";

(b)   in BCE4, in column 1 of the table, after the words "under any of the relevant pension schemes" add–

"except to the extent that, the purchase of the lifetime annuity was funded by the surrender of–

     (a)   sums or assets deemed to represent an arrangement pursuant to paragraph 8(1A) (a) to (c) of Schedule 28 as modified by article 29 of the Taxation of Pension Schemes (Transitional Provisions) Order 2006; or

     (b)   sums or assets which have been transferred from an arrangement referred to in subparagraph (a) to the extent that the lifetime annuity is payable in respect of those sums or assets and any investment growth that has been made on them.";

(c)   in BCE8, in column 1 of the table, after the words "in connection with the individual's membership of that pension scheme" add–

"unless the sums or assets transferred were–

     (a)   deemed to represent an arrangement pursuant to paragraph 8(1A) (a) to (c) of Schedule 28 as modified by article 29 of the Taxation of Pension Schemes (Transitional Provisions) Order 2006; or

     (b)   sums or assets which had been transferred from an arrangement referred to in subparagraph (a).".

For the purposes of this paragraph references to "BCE" are references to a benefit crystallisation event as set out in section 216.

MEMBER'S UNSECURED PENSION FUNDS – FURTHER PROVISIONS

29A(1)   In the case of an individual who meets the conditions set out in paragraph (2), paragraph (3) applies.

29A(2)   The conditions are as follows.

Condition A

The individual is a member of a scheme which falls within paragraph 1(1) of Schedule 36.

Condition B

The individual was, on 5th April 2006, entitled to a pension which was not provided under a defined benefits arrangement and which–

(a)   took the form of income drawdown under a retirement benefits scheme approved for the purposes of Chapter 1 of Part 14 of ICTA; or

(b)   was paid from the resources of–

   (i)   a small self-administered scheme as defined in the Retirement Benefits Schemes (Restriction on Discretion to Approve) (Small Self-Administered Schemes) Regulations 1991, or

   (ii)   a small self-administered scheme that had been approved under section 590 of ICTA,

   the rules of which, on 5th April 2006, did not require the purchase of an annuity in respect of the individual; or

(c)   took the form of income withdrawal under a personal pension scheme approved under Chapter 4 of Part 14 of ICTA pursuant to section 634A of that Act.

29A(3) In section 216 (benefit crystallisation events and amounts crystallised) in benefit crystallisation event 5A, in column 1 of the table, after the words "available for the payment of unsecured pension to the individual" add–

   "except to the extent that, the sums and assets in the money purchase arrangement are sums or assets deemed to represent an arrangement pursuant to paragraph 8(1A) (a) to (c) of Schedule 28 as modified by article 29 of the Taxation of Pension Schemes (Transitional Provisions) Order 2006".

History – Reg. 29A inserted by SI 2006/1962, reg. 3, with effect in respect of death benefit lump sum payments made and benefit crystallisation events taking place on or after 6 April 2006.

DEPENDANT'S UNSECURED PENSION FUNDS

30(1) In the case of an individual who meets the conditions set out in paragraph (2), paragraphs (3) and (4) apply.

30(2) The conditions are as follows.

Condition A

The individual had not reached the age of 75 on the 6th April 2006.

Condition B

The individual is a dependant of a member who was a member of scheme which falls within paragraph 1(1) of Schedule 36.

Condition C

On 5th April 2006 the individual was, under an arrangement which was not a defined benefits arrangement–

(a)   entitled to a pension which took the form of income drawdown under a retirement benefits scheme approved for the purposes of Chapter 1 of Part 14 of ICTA;

(b)   entitled to a pension that was paid from the resources of–

   (i)   small self-administered scheme as defined in the Retirement Benefits Schemes (Restriction on Discretion to Approve) (Small Self-administered Schemes) Regulations 1991, or

   (ii)   a small self-administered scheme that had been approved under section 590 of ICTA, and the rules of the scheme on 5th April 2006 did not require the purchase of an annuity in respect of the individual;

(c)   entitled to a pension which took the form of income withdrawal under a personal pension scheme approved under Chapter 4 of Part 14 of ICTA pursuant to section 636A of that Act; or

(d)   prospectively entitled to an annuity payment of which has been deferred pursuant to section 636(5) of ICTA.

30(3) Paragraph 22 of Schedule 28 (dependant's unsecured pension fund) is modified as follows–

(a)   at the end of sub-paragraph (1)(a) omit word "and",

(b)   omit sub-paragraph (1)(b),

(c)   in sub-paragraph (2)–

   (i)   for paragraphs (a) and (b) substitute–

"(a)   have at any time been applied to provide a pension which – took the form of income drawdown under a retirement benefits scheme approved for the purposes of Chapter 1 of Part 14 of ICTA;

(b)   have at any time been applied to provide a pension which was paid from the resources of–

(i)   a small self-administered scheme as defined in the Retirement Benefits Schemes (Restriction on Discretion to Approve) (Small Self-administered Schemes) Regulations 1991, or

(ii)   a small self-administered scheme that had been approved under section 590 of ICTA

and the rules of scheme on 5th April 2006 did not require the purchase of an annuity in respect of the individual;

(c)   have at any time been applied to provide a pension which took the form of income withdrawal under a personal pension scheme approved under Chapter 4 of Part 14 of ICTA pursuant to section 636A of that Act; or

(d)   have, immediately before the coming into force of this Part, been held for the purpose of providing an annuity, payment of which has been deferred in accordance with section 636(5) of that Act.".

30(4)   For 23(1) (unsecured pension year and basis amount for unsecured pension year) of Schedule 28 substitute–

"**23(1)**   "**Unsecured pension year**", in relation to a dependant's unsecured pension referred to in paragraph 22(2) as modified by article 30 of the Taxation of Pension Schemes (Transitional Provisions) Order 2006, means–

(a)   the period beginning on 6th April 2006 and ending on the earlier of–

(i)   5th April 2007 or

(ii)   the date that the first reference period defined in paragraph 24(1A), as modified by article 5 of the 2006 Order, terminates, and

(b)   each succeeding period of 12 months.".

INDIVIDUALS OVER THE AGE OF 75 AND ALTERNATIVELY SECURED PENSION FUNDS

31(1)   In the case of an individual who meets the conditions set out in paragraph (2), paragraph (3) applies.

31(2)   The conditions are as follows.

Condition A

The individual had reached the age of 75 before 6th April 2006.

Condition B

The individual is a member of a scheme which falls within paragraphs 1(1)(a) to (d) of Schedule 36.

Condition C

The individual has a prospective right to receive a pension under that scheme on 5th April 2006.

31(3)   Paragraph 11 of Schedule 28 (member's alternatively secured pension fund) is modified as follows–

(a)   in sub-paragraph (1)(a) for "Condition A or Condition B" substitute "Condition A, Condition B or Condition C";

(b)   after sub-paragraph (3) add–

"**11(3A)**   Condition C is that immediately before the 6th April 2006–

(a)   the sums and assets were part of the member's pension fund which fell within subparagraphs 1(1)(a) to (d) of Schedule 36;

(b)   the member had a prospective right to receive a pension under that scheme, and

(c)   the member's pension fund was a money purchase arrangement that was not a cash balance arrangement immediately before 6th April 2006.".

31(4)   In the case of an individual who meets the conditions set out in paragraph (5), paragraph (6) applies.

31(5)   The conditions are as follows.

Condition A

The individual had reached the age of 75 before 6th April 2006.

Condition B

The individual is a member of a scheme which falls within sub-paragraph 1(1)(a) of Schedule 36.

Condition C

On 5th April 2006, the individual was entitled to a pension which–

(a)   was paid from the resources of–

   (i)   a small self-administered scheme as defined in regulation 2 of the Retirement Benefits Schemes (Restriction on Discretion to Approve) (Small self-administered Schemes) Regulations 1991, or

   (ii)   a small self-administered scheme that had been approved under section 590 of ICTA,

   and the rules of the scheme on 5th April 2006 did not require the purchase of an annuity in respect of the individual; and

(b)   is not provided under a defined benefits arrangement.

31(6)   Paragraph 11 of Schedule 28 (member's alternatively secured pension fund) shall be modified as follows–

(a)   after the words "held for the purposes of the arrangement as" add the words "meet condition A, B or C.";

(b)   omit sub-paragraphs (1)(a) and (b).

(c)   after sub-paragraph (3) add–

"**11(3A)**   Condition C is that immediately before the 6th April 2006–

   (a)   the sums and assets were part of the member's pension fund which fell within subparagraph 1(1)(a) of Schedule 36; and

   (b)   the member was drawing a pension payable from the resources of–

      (i)   a small self-administered scheme as defined in the Retirement Benefits Schemes (Restriction on Discretion to Approve) (Small Self-administered Schemes) Regulations 1991, or

      (ii)   a small self-administered scheme that had been approved under section 590 of ICTA,

   and the rules of scheme on 5th April 2006 did not require the purchase of an annuity in respect of the member.".

DEPENDANT'S ALTERNATIVELY SECURED PENSION FUNDS

32(1)   In the case of an individual who meets the conditions set out in paragraph (2), paragraph (3) applies.

32(2)   The conditions are as follows.

Condition A

The individual had reached the age of 75 before 6th April 2006.

Condition B

The individual is a dependant of a member who was a member of a scheme which falls within sub-paragraph 1(1)(a) of Schedule 36.

Condition C

The individual was, on 5th April 2006, entitled to a pension which was not provided under a defined benefits arrangement and was payable from the resources of–

(a)   a small self-administered scheme as defined in regulation 2 of the Retirement Benefits Schemes (Restriction on Discretion to Approve) (Small Self-administered Schemes) Regulations 1991, or

(b)   a small self-administered scheme that had been approved under section 590 of ICTA,

and the rules of the scheme on 5th April 2006 did not require the purchase of an annuity in respect of the individual.

32(3)   Paragraph 25(1) of Schedule 28 (dependant's alternatively secured pension fund) shall be modified as follows–

(a)   after the words "held for the purposes of the arrangement as" add the words "meet condition A, B or C.".

(b)   omit sub-paragraphs (1)(a) and (b).

(c)   after sub-paragraph (3) add—

"**25(3A)**   Condition C is that immediately before the 6th April 2006—

(a)   the sums and assets were part of the dependant's pension fund which fell within sub-paragraph 1(1)(a) of Schedule 36; and

(b)   the dependant was drawing a pension payable from the resources of—

(i)   a small self-administered scheme as defined in regulation 2 of the Retirement Benefits Schemes (Restriction on Discretion to Approve) (Small Self-administered Schemes) Regulations 1991, or

(ii)   a small self-administered scheme that had been approved under section 590 of ICTA,

and the rules of the scheme on 5th April 2006 did not require the purchase of an annuity in respect of the dependant.".

SERIOUS ILL-HEALTH LUMP SUMS, PENSION PROTECTION LUMP SUM DEATH BENEFITS AND ANNUITY PROTECTION LUMP SUM DEATH BENEFITS

33(1)   In the case of an individual who meets the conditions set out in paragraph (2), paragraphs (3), (4) and (5) apply.

33(2)   The conditions are as follows.

Condition A

The individual is a member of a scheme which falls within sub-paragraphs 1(1)(a) to (g) of Schedule 36.

Condition B

The individual has an actual (rather than a prospective) right to the payment of one or more relevant existing pensions under that scheme on 6th April 2006.

33(3)   In paragraph 4(2) of Schedule 29 (serious ill-health lump sum) for the words "there has been no previous benefit crystallisation event" substitute—

"the member has a prospective (rather than an actual) right to the payment of one or more relevant existing pensions.".

33(4)   In paragraph 14(3) of Schedule 29 (pension protection lump sum death benefit)—

(a)   for "AC is the amount crystallised by reason of the member becoming entitled to the pension (see section 216)" substitute—

"AC is the value of the individual's pre-commencement pension rights as defined in paragraph 20(3) to (5) of Schedule 36.".

(b)   in the definition of "AP" for the words after "paid in respect of the period" substitute—

"from the period from the 6th April 2006 and the date of the member's death.".

33(5)   In paragraph 16(3) of Schedule 29 (annuity protection lump sum death benefit)—

(a)   for "AC is the amount crystallised by reason of the member becoming entitled to the pension or annuity" substitute—

"AC is the value of the individual's pre-commencement pension rights as defined in paragraph 20(3) to (5) of Schedule 36.".

(b)   in the definition of "AP" for the words after "paid in respect of the period" substitute—

"from the period from the 6th April 2006 and the date of the member's death.".

PAYMENTS TO CHILDREN AGED 23 OR OVER

34(1)   Paragraph (2) applies to the payment of a pension death benefit by a pension scheme which falls within paragraph 1(1) of Schedule 36 where—

(a)   either of Conditions A and B is satisfied and the first scheme rules condition is satisfied; or

(b)   Condition C and the second scheme rules condition are satisfied.

34(2)   Paragraph 15(2) of Schedule 28 shall be modified as follows—

(a)   at the end of paragraph (a) omit the word "or"; and

(b)   after paragraph (b) insert—

"(c)   has reached that age and is in full time education or undertaking vocational training, or

(d)   on reaching that age or, if later, on ceasing full time education or vocational training is, in the opinion of the scheme administrator, suffering from physical or mental deterioration which is sufficiently serious to prevent the individual from following a normal employment or which would seriously impair his earning capacity."

34(3)   The Conditions A, B and C mentioned in paragraph (1) are:

Condition A

The pension was in payment to a child ("C") of the member ("M") on 5th April 2006 or M had died on or before that date and a pension was due to come into payment to C.

Condition B

The pension was in payment to M on 5th April 2006 and C was born on or before 5th April 2007.

Condition C

An election such as is described in the second scheme rules condition had been made by M and accepted by the scheme administrator on or before 5th April 2006.

34(4)   The scheme rules conditions mentioned in paragraph (1) are:

First scheme rules condition

The rules of the pension scheme allowed a pension to be paid to a child ("C") of the member ("M") following M's death until C ceased full-time education or vocational training.

Second scheme rules condition

The rules of the pension scheme on 10 December 2003 allowed an irrevocable election to be made designating part of the sums or assets representing M's rights as available for the payment of a pension to C following M's death until C ceased full-time education or vocational training.

34(5)   For the purpose of the first scheme rules condition, a rule that the pension would not be paid to C if or after C reached a specified age (even if that is before C ceased full-time education or vocational training) does not prevent the condition being satisfied.

34(6)   Paragraph (2) also applies to the payment of a pension death benefit by a qualifying transferee scheme (as to which see article 34B) where either–

(a)   paragraph (2) had applied to payment by the original pension scheme or another transferee pension scheme; or

(b)   paragraph (2) would have applied–

(i)   if there had been no block transfer on or after 6th April 2006, and

(ii)   if payment had been by the original pension scheme.

History – Reg. 34, 34A and 34B substituted for former reg. 34 by SI 2009/1989, art. 2(2), with effect in relation to payments of pension death benefit made on or after 6 April 2006.

PAYMENTS TO FINANCIALLY DEPENDENT CHILDREN AGED 23 OR OVER

34A(1)   Paragraph (2) applies to the payment of a pension death benefit by a pension scheme which falls within paragraph 1(1) of Schedule 36 where–

(a)   any of Conditions A to D is satisfied; and

(b)   the scheme rules condition is satisfied.

34A(2)   Paragraph 15(2) of Schedule 28 shall be modified as follows–

(a)   at the end of paragraph (a) omit the word "or"; and

(b)   after paragraph (b) insert–

"(c)   has reached that age and–

(i)   is financially dependent on the member at the date of the member's death, or

(ii)   the financial relationship with the member at the date of the member's death is one of mutual dependence."

34A(3)   The Conditions A to D mentioned in paragraph (1) are:

Condition A

The member's ("M's") pension was in payment on or before 1st July 2008.

Condition B

The pension death benefit was in payment on 1st July 2008.

Condition C

The entitlement to the pension death benefit arose before 1st July 2008.

Condition D

The entitlement to the pension death benefit was subject to the discretion of the trustees of the scheme and the discretion was capable of being exercised (in favour of the child having such an entitlement) so that the entitlement could have arisen before 1st July 2008.

34A(4) The scheme rules condition mentioned in paragraph (1) is:

Scheme rules condition

The rules of the pension scheme on 5th April 2006 allowed a pension to be paid to a child ("C") of the member ("M") following M's death if, at the date of M's death, C was financially dependent on M or C's financial relationship with M was one of mutual dependence.

34A(5) Paragraph (2) also applies to the payment of a pension death benefit by a qualifying transferee scheme (as to which see article 34B) where–

(a)   paragraph (2) had applied to payment by the original pension scheme or another transferee pension scheme; or

(b)   paragraph (2) would have applied–

     (i)   if there had been no block transfer on or after the relevant date, and

     (ii)   if payment had been by the original pension scheme.

34A(6) For the purposes of paragraph (5), the relevant date is–

(a)   in relation to Condition A, the later of–

     (i)   6th April 2006, and

     (ii)   the date on which the member's pension came into payment; and

(b)   in relation to Condition B, C or D, the later of–

     (i)   6th April 2006, and

     (ii)   the date of the member's death.

History – Reg. 34, 34A and 34B substituted for former reg. 34 by SI 2009/1989, art. 2(2), with effect in relation to payments of pension death benefit made on or after 6 April 2006.

MEANING OF "QUALIFYING TRANSFEREE SCHEME"

34B(1) A pension scheme is a qualifying transferee scheme for the purposes of articles 34 and 34A if it is a pension scheme to which there has been a relevant block transfer.

34B(2) A block transfer is relevant if any of Conditions A to C is satisfied as a result of–

(a)   a block transfer from a pension scheme within paragraph 1(1) of Schedule 36 ("the original pension scheme"); or

(b)   a block transfer to a pension scheme ("a transferee pension scheme") from a pension scheme that was a transferee pension scheme in relation to the original pension scheme by virtue of the previous application of sub-paragraph (a) or the previous application (on one or more occasions) of this sub-paragraph.

34B(3) The Conditions A to C mentioned in paragraph (2) are:

Condition A

The member became a member of the transferee pension scheme.

Condition B

The child is a pensioner member of the transferee pension scheme.

Condition C

An irrevocable election having been made designating part of the sums or assets representing the member's rights as available for the payment of a pension to the child, the child is entitled to such payment from the transferee pension scheme.

34B(4) In this article, "block transfer" has the meaning given by paragraph 22(6) of Schedule 36, but with the modification that for "as is prescribed" in paragraph (b) there is substituted "as has been prescribed".

History – Reg. 34, 34A and 34B substituted for former reg. 34 by SI 2009/1989, art. 2(2), with effect in relation to payments of pension death benefit made on or after 6 April 2006.

ENHANCED PROTECTION AND TRANSFERS MADE IN CONNECTION WITH THE WINDING UP OF A PENSION SCHEME

35(1) In the case of an individual who meets the conditions in paragraph (2), paragraph 12 of Schedule 36 (transitional provisions – "enhanced protection") is modified in accordance with paragraph (3).

35(2) The conditions are–

Condition A

The individual is one to whom paragraph 12 of Schedule 36 applies.

Condition B

The pension scheme of which the individual is a member makes a recognised transfer of sums or assets to an insurance company pursuant to section 169(1A) (permitted transfers).

Condition C

The transfer is made in connection with the winding up of the pension scheme from which the transfer is made.

35(3) Paragraph 12(8) is modified as follows–

(a)   after paragraph (a) delete the word "or"; and

(b)   after paragraph (b) add–
  "or;

    (c)   the transfer is a recognised transfer pursuant to section 169(1A).".

TRANSFER OF CRYSTALLISED RIGHTS WITH ENHANCED PROTECTION

36(1) In the case of an individual who meets the conditions in paragraph (2), paragraph 15 of Schedule 36 (definition of the "relevant crystallised amount") is modified in accordance with paragraph (3).

36(2) The conditions are–

Condition A

The individual is one to whom paragraph 12 of Schedule 36 applies.

Condition B

The individual is in receipt of a scheme pension.

Condition C

The pension scheme of which the individual is a member makes a recognised transfer of sums or assets in connection with the winding up of the pension scheme.

36(3) Paragraph 15 is modified as follows–

(a)   at the end of sub-paragraph (1) add–
  "This paragraph is subject to sub-paragraph (1A)."; and

(b)   after that sub-paragraph insert–

    "**15(1A)** If the relevant event is a transfer of sums or assets representing crystallised rights under a scheme pension and made in connection with the winding-up of the pension scheme under which the scheme pension is paid, the relevant crystallised amount shall be nil.".

MODIFICATION OF SECTION 636B ITEPA 2003

37(1) Section 636B of ITEPA 2003 (trivial commutation and winding-up lump sums) is modified as follows in relation to an equivalent pension benefits commutation lump sum pursuant to regulation 2(1A) of–

(a)   the Occupational Pension Schemes (Assignment, Forfeiture, Bankruptcy etc) Regulations 1997; or

(b)   the Occupational Pension Schemes (Assignment, Forfeiture, Bankruptcy etc) Regulations (Northern Ireland) 1997.

37(2) For the heading substitute–
  "Trivial commutation, winding-up lump sums etc."

37(3) In subsection (1)–

(a)   at the end of paragraph (a) omit "or";

(b)   at the end of paragraph (b) add "or"; and

(c)   after that paragraph insert the following paragraph–

    "(c)   an equivalent pension benefits commutation lump sum,"

37(4)   In subsection (4) after "In this section–" insert the following definition–

""**equivalent pension benefits commutation lump sum**" means a lump sum payment arising from the commutation of equivalent pension benefits pursuant to regulation 2(1A) of–

(a)   the Occupational Pension Schemes (Assignment, Forfeiture, Bankruptcy etc) Regulations 1997; or

(b)   the Occupational Pension Schemes (Assignment, Forfeiture, Bankruptcy etc) Regulations (Northern Ireland) 1997,".

LUMP SUM PAYMENTS – GENERAL

38(1)   This paragraph applies to a lump sum payment–

(a)   the entirety of which is made in accordance with the rules of the existing scheme as they stood immediately before the 6th April 2006;

(b)   which is made on or after the 6th April 2006 but before 6th July 2006;

(c)   to which the member became entitled before the 6th April 2006;

(d)   which would not have given the Commissioners grounds for withdrawing approval of the scheme had it been made before the 6th April 2006; and

(e)   which is not a lump sum paid in circumstances of the member's serious ill-health.

38(2)   In this article and articles 39, 40 and 41–

"**the 1995 Regulations**" means the Retirement Benefits Schemes (Information Powers) Regulations 1995;

"**the Commissioners**" means the Commissioners for Her Majesty's Revenue and Customs and, in relation to times before 18th April 2005, includes the Commissioners of Inland Revenue;

"**existing scheme**" means a scheme which becomes a registered pension scheme by virtue of paragraph 1(1) of Schedule 36 (pension schemes etc.: transitional provisions and savings – deemed registration of existing schemes);

"**lump sum paid in circumstances of the member's serious ill-health**" has the meaning given in article 39(3);

"**member**" means a member of an existing scheme;

38(3)   A payment to which paragraph (1) applies shall be chargeable to income tax in accordance with section 598, 599 or 599A of ICTA (which deal respectively with charges to tax on repayment of employee's contributions, on the commutation of the entire pension in special circumstances and on payments out of surplus funds), or Chapter 13 of Part 9 of ITEPA 2003 (return of employee's additional voluntary contributions) (as the case requires)–

(a)   to the same extent as it would have been if the provision in question had not been repealed; and

(b)   as if the references in section 598(2), 599(3) and section 599A(2)(b) of ICTA to the administrator of the scheme were instead references to the scheme administrator (within the meaning of section 270) of the registered pension scheme which is treated as coming into being by virtue of paragraph 1(1) of Schedule 36.

38(4)   For the purposes of a lump sum payment to which paragraph (1) applies, regulations 10 and 11 of the 1995 Regulations (reporting of chargeable events) shall continue to have effect, subject to the following modifications–

(a)   in paragraph (1) for the words preceding sub-paragraph (a) substitute–

"The scheme administrator of the registered pension scheme which, immediately before the coming into force of Part 4 of the Finance Act 2004, was both a retirement benefits scheme and–";

(b)   in paragraph (3) omit sub-paragraph (d); and

(c)   omit paragraph (4).

38(5)   In section 98(5) of the Taxes Management Act 1970 the entry in Table 1 relating to regulations under section 605(1A) of ICTA shall continue to have effect so far as it relates to regulations 10 and 11 of the 1995 Regulations as saved, with modifications, by paragraph (4).

LUMP SUMS – SERIOUS ILL-HEALTH

39(1)   This article applies to a lump sum–

(a)   paid to a member in circumstances of the member's serious ill-health; and

(b)   which satisfies the requirements set out in sub-paragraphs (a) to (d) of article 38(1).

39(2)   There is no charge to tax under Part 4 on a lump sum to which paragraph (1) applies.

39(3)   A lump sum is paid in circumstances of the member's serious ill-health if–

(a)   before it is paid the scheme administrator, or the administrator of the scheme which became a registered pension scheme on the 6th April 2006, received evidence from a registered medical practitioner that the member is expected to live for less than one year; and

(b)   all of the member's uncrystallised rights under the scheme making the payment, other than those which are–

   (i)   required to be maintained in order to meet contracted-out rights or safeguarded rights, or

   (ii)   retained by the scheme in accordance with its rules as they stood immediately before the 6th April 2006 to provide benefits for the member's dependants,

are paid out as a lump sum.

39(4)   In paragraph (3)(b)(i)–

"contracted-out rights" means–

(a)   entitlement to payment of, or accrued rights to–

   (i)   guaranteed minimum pensions within the meaning of section 8(2) of the Pension Schemes Act 1993; and

   (ii)   a pension in respect of protected rights within the meaning of section 10 of that Act;

(b)   section 9(2B) rights within the meaning of regulation 1(2) of the Occupational Pension Schemes (Contracting-Out) Regulations 1996, or

(c)   any of the rights in sub-paragraphs (a), (b) or (c) which themselves derive from any of those rights which have been the subject of a transfer payment; and

"safeguarded rights" have the same meaning as in section 68A of the Pension Schemes Act 1993.

39(5)   In the application of this article to Northern Ireland, a reference to a provision applying only in Great Britain shall be construed as a reference to any provision having corresponding effect in Northern Ireland.

LUMP SUM DEATH BENEFITS – DEATH OF MEMBER

40(1)   This paragraph applies to a lump sum paid–

(a)   in respect of the death, occurring before the 6th April 2006, of a member of a pension scheme;

(b)   within two years of the date upon which the administrator of the pension scheme could reasonably have known of the member's death;

(c)   by a scheme which is treated as becoming a registered pension scheme on the 6th April 2006 by virtue of paragraph 1(1) of Schedule 36;

(d)   in accordance with the rules of that scheme as they stood–

   (i)   immediately before the death; or

   (ii)   immediately before the 6th April 2006; and

(e)   in circumstances which would not have led to the Commissioners withdrawing the approval of the scheme.

40(2)   A lump sum to which paragraph (1) applies is not a relevant lump sum death benefit as defined in paragraph 16 of Schedule 32, and the payment of such a death benefit is to be disregarded for the purposes of benefit crystallisation event 7.

40(3)   A lump sum to which paragraph (1) applies shall be chargeable to income tax in accordance with section 648B of ICTA as if–

(a)   that section had not been repealed;

(b)   references in that section to the administrator of the scheme were references to the scheme administrator of the registered pension scheme which is treated as coming into being by virtue of paragraph 1(1)(g) of Schedule 36;

(c)   subsection (3) were omitted; and

(d)   the reference in subsection (4) to the rules of the scheme were a reference to the rules of the personal pension scheme as they stood immediately before the 6th April 2006.

40(4)   For the purposes of a lump sum payment to which paragraph (1) applies, regulation 5 of the Personal Pension Schemes (Information Powers) Regulations 2000 ("the 2000 Regulations") shall continue to have effect, subject to the following modifications—

(a)   references to the scheme administrator of the personal pension scheme are to be read as references to the scheme administrator of the registered pension scheme which is treated as coming into being by virtue of paragraph 1(1)(g) of Schedule 36; and

(b)   in paragraph (2) of that regulation for "an approved personal pension scheme" substitute "the registered pension scheme".

40(5)   In section 98(5) of the Taxes Management Act 1970 the entry in Table 1 relating to regulations under section 651A(1)(b) to (d) of ICTA shall continue to have effect, so far as it relates to regulation 5 of the 2000 Regulations as saved, with modifications, by paragraph (4).

History – In reg. 40(1)(b) the words "the date upon which the administrator of the pension scheme could reasonably have known of the member's death" substituted for the words "the member's death" by SI 2006/1962, reg. 4(a), with effect in respect of death benefit lump sum payments made and benefit crystalisation events taking place on or after 6 April 2006.
In reg. 40(1)(e) the words "led to the Commissioners withdrawing the approval of the scheme" substituted for the words "given the Commissioners grounds for withdrawing the approval of the scheme" by SI 2006/1962, reg. 4(b), with effect in respect of death benefit lump sum payments made and benefit crystalisation events taking place on or after 6 April 2006.

LUMP SUM DEATH BENEFITS – DEATH OF A DEPENDANT

41(1)   This paragraph applies to a lump sum paid—

(a)   in respect of the death, occurring before the 6th April 2006, of a dependant of a former member of a pension scheme;

(b)   by a scheme which is treated as becoming a registered pension scheme on the 6th April 2006 by virtue of paragraph 1(1)(g) of Schedule 36 (personal pension schemes);

(c)   within two years of the date upon which the administrator of the pension scheme could reasonably have known of the dependant's death;

(d)   in accordance with the rules of that scheme as they stood—

    (i)   immediately before the dependant's death; or

    (ii)   immediately before the 6th April 2006; and

(e)   in circumstances which would not have led to the Commissioners withdrawing the approval of the scheme.

41(2)   Paragraphs (3) to (5) of article 40 apply for the purposes of paragraph (1) as they apply for the purposes of paragraph (1) of that article.

History – In reg. 41(1)(c) the words "the date upon which the administrator of the pension scheme could reasonably have known of the dependant's death" substituted for the words "the dependant's death" by SI 2006/1962, reg. 5(a), with effect in respect of death benefit lump sum payments made and benefit crystalisation events taking place on or after 6 April 2006.
In reg. 41(1)(e) the words "led to the Commissioners withdrawing the approval of the scheme" substituted for the words "given the Commissioners grounds for withdrawing the approval of the scheme" by SI 2006/1962, reg. 5(b), with effect in respect of death benefit lump sum payments made and benefit crystalisation events taking place on or after 6 April 2006.

PROTECTED PENSION AGE AND MULTIPLE PENSIONS

42(1)   In the case of a member who has a protected pension age in connection with at least two of the three types of pension listed in paragraph (2) from the same registered pension scheme, Schedule 36 is modified in accordance with paragraph (3).

42(2)   The three types of pension are—

(a)   a scheme pension under a defined benefits arrangement;

(b)   a scheme pension under a money purchase arrangement;

(c)   a lifetime annuity.

42(3)   In paragraphs 22(7)(a) and 23(7) for "on the same date" substitute "within a period of six months beginning with the earliest date on which the individual becomes entitled to any of the benefits.".

History – Art. 42 inserted by SI 2011/732, art. 4, with effect in relation to any time on or after 6 April 2011.

PROTECTED PENSION AGE AND MULTIPLE PENSIONS – MEMBER DIES BEFORE RECEIVING ALL PENSIONS

43(1)   Schedule 36 is modified in accordance with paragraphs (3) and (4) where—

(a)   a member has a protected pension age in connection with at least two of the three types of pension listed in regulation 42(2) from the same registered pension scheme;

(b)   the member dies before the end of the specified period after becoming entitled to at least one but not all of the benefits in respect of the pensions; and

(c)   the scheme administrator considers that, had the individual not died, the individual would have become entitled to all of the benefits in respect of the pensions within the specified period.

43(2)   The **"specified period"** is the period of six months beginning with the earliest date on which the individual became entitled to any of the benefits in respect of the pensions.

43(3)   For paragraph 22(7)(a) substitute–

"(a)   the scheme administrator considers that, had the individual not died, the member would have become entitled to all the benefits payable to the member under arrangements under the pension scheme (to which the member did not have an actual entitlement on or before 5th April 2006) within a period of six months beginning with the earliest date on which the individual became entitled to any of the benefits, and".

43(4)   For paragraph 23(7) substitute–

"**23(7)**   The retirement condition is met in relation to the member and the pension scheme if the scheme administrator considers that, had the individual not died, the member would have become entitled to all the benefits payable to the member under arrangements under the pension scheme (to which the member did not have an actual entitlement on or before 5th April 2006) within a period of six months beginning with the earliest date on which the individual became entitled to any of the benefits.".

History – Art. 43 inserted by SI 2011/732, art. 4, with effect in relation to any time on or after 6 April 2011.

NORMAL MINIMUM PENSION AGE – MODIFICATION OF SECTION 165 (PAYMENT OF PENSION RULES)

44(1)   This article applies in the case of a member of a registered pension scheme where the primary condition in paragraph (2) and one of conditions in paragraph (3) are met.

44(2)   The primary condition is–

(a)   on 5th April 2010, the member was aged between 50 and 54 (inclusive); and

(b)   on or before that date, benefit crystallisation event 1 ("BCE1"), 2 ("BCE2") or 4 ("BCE4") had occurred in relation to that member.

44(3)   The conditions are–

Condition A

On or after 6th April 2010 some or all of the sums and assets held for the purposes of the arrangement in respect of which BCE1 had occurred are applied towards–

(a)   the purchase of a short-term annuity or a lifetime annuity ("the new annuity"); or

(b)   the provision of a scheme pension under the arrangement.

Condition B

On or after 6th April 2010 the first payment of pension by way of income withdrawal ("withdrawal pension") is made from some or all of the sums or assets held for the purposes of the arrangement in respect of which BCE1 had occurred.

Condition C

On or before 5th April 2010 some or all of the assets held for the purposes of the arrangement in respect of which BCE1 had occurred were applied towards the purchase of a short-term annuity ("the new annuity"), and the first payment of the new annuity is made on or after 6th April 2010.

Condition D

Where BCE2 or BCE4 had occurred in relation to the member on or before 5th April 2010, the first payment of scheme pension or lifetime annuity ("the new annuity") in respect of which BCE2 or BCE4 occurred, is made on or after 6th April 2010.

44(4)   For the purposes of determining whether pension rule 1 in section 165 (payment of pension rules) has been met in relation to a payment of the new annuity, scheme pension or withdrawal pension, the member is deemed to have reached the age of 55 immediately before the date on which the first payment of the new annuity, scheme pension or withdrawal pension is made. This paragraph is subject to paragraph (5).

44(5)   Where a member was chargeable to income tax at the additional rate for the tax year 2010–11, paragraph (4) shall only have effect in respect of 80% of the amount of any payment of the new annuity, scheme pension or withdrawal pension made in that tax year.

44(6)   For the purposes of this article **"sums or assets held for the purposes of the arrangement"** means sums or assets that–

(a)   on or before 5th April 2010, have been designated under the arrangement as available for the payment of unsecured pension; or

(b)   arise, or (directly or indirectly) derive from sums or assets which have been so designated or which so arise or derive.

History – Art. 44 inserted by SI 2011/732, art. 5, which came into force on 6 April 2011, with effect in relation to any time on or after 6 April 2010.

NORMAL MINIMUM PENSION AGE – MODIFICATION OF PARAGRAPH 1 OF SCHEDULE 29 (LUMP SUM RULE)

45(1)   This article applies in the case of a member of a registered pension scheme where the conditions in paragraph (2) are met.

45(2)   The conditions are that on 5th April 2010–

(a)   the member was aged between 50 and 54 (inclusive);

(b)   the member had become entitled to a lump sum ("the relevant lump sum") which would have been a pension commencement lump sum had it been paid on or before that date; and

(c)   no payment of the relevant lump sum had been made.

45(3)   For the purposes of determining whether the condition in paragraph 1(1)(d) of Schedule 29 (pension commencement lump sum) has been met in relation to a payment of the relevant lump sum made on or after 6th April 2010, the member is deemed to have reached the age of 55 immediately before the date on which the payment of the relevant lump sum is made.

History – Art. 45 inserted by SI 2011/732, art. 5, which came into force on 6 April 2011, with effect in relation to any time on or after 6 April 2010.

PENSION SCHEMES (TRANSFERS, REORGANISATIONS AND WINDING UP) (TRANSITIONAL PROVISIONS) ORDER 2006

(SI 2006/573, as amended by SI 2010/529)

Made on 9 March 2006 by the Treasury, in exercise of the powers conferred upon them by s. 283(2) of the Finance Act 2004. Operative from 6 April 2006.

GENERAL

Citation, commencement and interpretation

1(1) This Order may be cited as the Pension Schemes (Transfers, Reorganisations and Winding Up) (Transitional Provisions) Order 2006, and shall come into force on 6th April 2006.

1(2) In this Order, references to provisions of Schedule 36 are references to provisions of Schedule 36 to the Finance Act 2004.

1(3) In this Order–

"**normal minimum pension age**" has the meaning given in section 279(1) of the Finance Act 2004, and

"**the TUPE Regulations**" means the Transfer of Undertakings (Protection of Employment) Regulations 1981.

The original pension scheme condition

2(1) For the purposes of this Order the original pension scheme condition is met if conditions A and B are met.

2(2) Condition A is that on 10th December 2003 a pension scheme ("the original pension scheme") was either an approved scheme for the purposes of Chapter 1 of Part 14 of the Income and Corporation Taxes Act 1988 (see section 612(1) of that Act) or was a relevant statutory scheme for the purposes of that Chapter (see section 611A of that Act).

2(3) Condition B is that the original pension scheme was a scheme whose rules included provision conferring a right to retire before the normal minimum pension age on some or all of the persons who were then members of the scheme.

The employee condition

3(1) For the purposes of this Order the employee condition is met if either condition A or condition B is met.

3(2) Condition A is that, on 10th December 2003, a person ("the employee") was a person who had the right, under the original pension scheme, to retire before the normal minimum pension age.

3(3) Condition B is that the employee would have been a person who, on 10th December 2003, had the right, under the original pension scheme, to retire before the normal minimum pension age had the employee been a member of the scheme on that date.

TRANSFERS DURING PERIOD BEGINNING WITH 10TH DECEMBER 2003 AND ENDING WITH 5TH APRIL 2006

Conditions for application of article 8

4 Article 8 applies if the following conditions are met–

(a)   the original pension scheme condition (see article 2);

(b)   the employee condition (see article 3);

(c)   the transfer condition, either as it applies in the case of one transfer (see article 5), or as it applies in the case of two or more transfers (see article 6); and

(d)   the new pension scheme condition (see article 7).

The transfer condition as it applies in the case of one transfer

5(1) The transfer condition, as it applies in the case of one transfer, is met if conditions A to G are met.

5(2) Condition A is that, during the period beginning with 10th December 2003 and ending with 5th April 2006, there was one transfer of an undertaking, or part of an undertaking.

Statutory Instruments

5(3)   Condition B is that the TUPE Regulations applied to the transfer.

5(4)   Condition C is that by virtue of the transfer, the employee ceased to be employed by the transferor and became employed by the transferee.

5(5)   Condition D is that the transferor was the employer in relation to the original pension scheme.

5(6)   Condition E is that at the time immediately before the employee became employed by the transferee, the employee was a member of the original pension scheme.

5(7)   Condition E is that at the time immediately before the employee became employed by the transferee, the employee was a member of the original pension scheme.

(a)   was a member of a pension scheme in relation to which the transferee was the employer, or

(b)   was a member of one other pension scheme ("the new pension scheme") in relation to which the transferee was the employer.

5(8)   Condition G is that, as a result of the transfer, all the sums held for the purposes of, or representing the employee's accrued rights under, the original pension scheme have become held for the purposes of, or represented rights under, the new pension scheme.

5(9)   In paragraph (2) the reference to an undertaking or part of an undertaking has the same meaning as in the TUPE Regulations.

The transfer condition as it applies in the case of two or more transfers

6(1)   The transfer condition, as it applies in the case of two or more transfers, is met if conditions A to H are met.

6(2)   Condition A is that, during the period beginning with 10th December 2003 and ending with 5th April 2006, there were two or more transfers of an undertaking, or part of an undertaking.

6(3)   Condition B is that the TUPE Regulations applied to each transfer.

6(4)   Condition C is that by virtue of each transfer, the employee ceased to be employed by the transferor and became employed by the transferee.

6(5)   Condition D is that the transferor–

(a)   in the case of the first transfer, was the employer in relation to the original pension scheme, and

(b)   in the case of each subsequent transfer, was the employer in relation to the pension scheme of which the employee was a member immediately before the transfer.

6(6)   Condition E is that the employee–

(a)   in the case of the first transfer, was a member of the original pension scheme at the time immediately before the employee became employed by the transferee, and

(b)   in the case of each subsequent transfer, was a member of a pension scheme in relation to which the transferor was the employer at the time immediately before the employee became employed by the transferee.

6(7)   Condition F is that in the case of a transfer other than the final transfer, and from the time when he became employed by the transferee, the employee was a member of a pension scheme in relation to which the transferee was the employer.

6(8)   Condition G is that in the case of the final transfer, and from the time when he became employed by the transferee, the employee–

(a)   was a member of a pension scheme in relation to which the transferee was the employer, or

(b)   was a member of one other pension scheme ("the new pension scheme") in relation to which the transferee was the employer.

6(9)   Condition H is that, as a result of the transfers, all the sums held for the purposes of, or representing the employee's accrued rights under, the original pension scheme have become held for the purposes of, or represented rights under, the new pension scheme.

6(10) In paragraph (2) the reference to an undertaking or part of an undertaking has the same meaning as in the TUPE Regulations.

The new pension scheme condition

7(1)   The new pension scheme condition is met if conditions A and B are met.

7(2)   Condition A is that the new pension scheme was a scheme whose rules, at the time of the transfer (where article 5 applies), or at the time of the final transfer (where article 6 applies), included provision conferring a right on some or all of the persons who were then members of that scheme to retire before the normal minimum pension age.

7(3)   Condition B is that, on 6th April 2006, the new pension scheme was within any of paragraphs (a) to (e) of paragraph 1(1) of Schedule 36 (deemed registration of existing schemes) (and, accordingly, is treated as having become a registered pension scheme).

Rights to take benefit before normal minimum pension age

8(1)   For the purposes of paragraph 22 of Schedule 36 (rights to take benefit before normal minimum pension age), and in relation to the employee, the new pension scheme is a protected pension scheme.

8(2)   The employee has the right to retire at the age specified in paragraph (3) or (4), whichever is the greater.

8(3)   The age specified in this paragraph is the age at which—

(a)   immediately before the transfer, the employee had the right to retire under the original pension scheme (in a case where article 5 applies), or

(b)   immediately before the final transfer, the employee had the right to retire under the original pension scheme (in a case where article 6 applies).

8(4)   The age specified in this paragraph is the age at which, on 6th April 2006, the employee has the right to retire under the new pension scheme.

REORGANISATIONS DURING PERIOD BEGINNING WITH 10TH DECEMBER 2003 AND ENDING WITH 5TH APRIL 2006

Conditions for application of article 12

9   Article 12 applies if the following conditions are met—

(a)   the original pension scheme condition (see article 2);

(b)   the employee condition (see article 3);

(c)   the reorganisation condition (see article 10); and

(d)   the new pension scheme condition (see article 11).

The reorganisation condition

10(1)   The reorganisation condition is met if conditions A to C are met.

10(2)   Condition A is that, during the period beginning with 10th December 2003 and ending with 5th April 2006—

(a)   there was a transfer in a single transaction of all the sums and assets held for the purposes of, or representing the employee's accrued rights under, the original pension scheme to another pension scheme ("the new pension scheme"),

(b)   there was a transfer in a single transaction of all the sums and assets held for the purposes of, or representing the employee's accrued, non contracted-out rights under the original pension scheme to the new pension scheme, or

(c)   there were transfers of sums and assets held for the purposes of, or representing the employee's accrued rights under, the original pension scheme to the new pension scheme, and those transfers were made—

   (i)   in two separate transactions, and

   (ii)   in circumstances where paragraph (2A) applies.

10(2A)   This paragraph applies in circumstances where—

(a)   the employee's accrued rights under the original pension scheme included contracted-out rights;

(b)   all the sums and assets held for the purposes of, or representing accrued, non contracted-out rights under the original pension scheme were transferred to the new pension scheme in a single transaction; and

(c)   the sums and assets held for the purposes of, or representing contracted-out rights under the original pension scheme were transferred in a single transaction to—

   (i)   the new pension scheme referred to in sub-paragraph (b) of this paragraph, or

   (ii)   another pension scheme that satisfies the new pension scheme condition (see article 11).

10(3)   Condition B is that, immediately before the transfer mentioned in paragraph (2), the employee was an active member or a deferred member of the original pension scheme.

10(4)   Condition C is that, immediately before and after the transfer mentioned in paragraph (2), the employee was—

(a)   employed by a sponsoring employer of the new pension scheme,

(b)   employed by a sponsoring employer of the new pension scheme, or

(c)   a former employee of a former sponsoring employer of the original pension scheme in a case where the relevant sums and assets are transferred at the same time as the relevant sums and assets held for another employee or former employee who falls within sub-paragraphs (a) or (b).

10(5)   In this article–

"**active member**" has the meaning given by section 151(2) of the Finance Act 2004,

"**appropriate personal pension scheme**" means a scheme in respect of which an appropriate scheme certificate is in force under section 7 of the Pension Schemes Act 1993,

"**contracted-out rights**" means rights under or derived from an occupational pension scheme or an appropriate personal pension scheme which fell within the following categories–

(a)   entitlement to payment of, or accrued rights to, guaranteed minimum pensions;

(b)   protected rights; or

(c)   section 9(2B) rights.

"**deferred member**" has the meaning given by section 151(4) of that Act,

"**guaranteed minimum pensions**" has the meaning given by section 8 of the Pension Schemes Act 1993,

"**occupational pension scheme**" has the meaning given by section 1(1) of the Pension Schemes Act 1993,

"**protected rights**" has the meaning given by section 10 of the Pension Schemes Act 1993,

"**relevant sums and assets**", in relation to an employee or former employee, are the sums and assets held for the purposes of, or representing the accrued rights of the employee or former employee (as the case may be) under, the original pension scheme,

"**section 9(2B) rights**" has the meaning given by regulation 1(2) of the Protected Rights (Transfer Payment) Regulations 1996,

"**sponsoring employer**" has the meaning given by section 150(6) of that Act.

History – Art. 10(2) and (2A) substituted for former art. 10(2) by SI 2010/529, art. 3(2), with effect from 6 April 2006.
Art. 10(4)(c) inserted (and the "or" at the end of art. 10(4)(a) omitted and the "or" at the end of para. 10(4)(b) inserted) by SI 2010/529, art. 3(3), with effect from 6 April 2006.
In art. 10(5), definition of "appropriate personal pension scheme" inserted by SI 2010/529, art. 3(4)(a), with effect from 6 April 2006.
In art. 10(5), definition of "contracted-out rights" inserted by SI 2010/529, art. 3(4)(a), with effect from 6 April 2006.
In art. 10(5), definition of "guaranteed minimum pensions" inserted (and the "and" at the end of the definition of "deferred member" omitted) by SI 2010/529, art. 3(4)(b), with effect from 6 April 2006.
In art. 10(5), definition of "occupational pension scheme" inserted by SI 2010/529, art. 3(4)(b), with effect from 6 April 2006.
In art. 10(5), definition of "protected rights" inserted by SI 2010/529, art. 3(4)(b), with effect from 6 April 2006.
In art. 10(5), definition of "relevant sums and assets" inserted by SI 2010/529, art. 3(4)(b), with effect from 6 April 2006.
In art. 10(5), definition of "section 9(2B) rights" inserted by SI 2010/529, art. 3(4)(b), with effect from 6 April 2006.

The new pension scheme condition

11(1)   The new pension scheme condition is met if conditions A and B are met.

11(2)   Condition A is that the new pension scheme was a scheme whose rules, at the time of the transfer, included provision conferring a right on some or all of the persons who were then members of that scheme to retire before the normal minimum pension age,

11(3)   Condition B is that, on 6th April 2006, the new pension scheme was within either of paragraphs (a) or (c) of paragraph 1(1) of Schedule 36 (deemed registration of existing schemes) (and, accordingly, is treated as having become a registered pension scheme).

Rights to take benefit before normal minimum pension age

12   The employee has the right to retire–

(a)   at the age at which, immediately before the transfer mentioned in article 10(2), the employee had the right to retire under the original pension scheme, or

(b)   at the age at which, on 6th April 2006, the employee has the right to retire under the new pension scheme,

whichever is the greater.

WINDING UP OF ORIGINAL PENSION SCHEME

Conditions for application of article 16

13   Article 16 applies if the following conditions are met–

(a)   the winding up condition (see article 14); and

(b)   the annuity purchase condition (see article 15).

The winding up condition

14(1)   The winding up condition is met if the first or second condition is met.

(a)   [omitted by SI 2010/529, art. 4(2)(b).]

(b)   [omitted by SI 2010/529, art. 4(2)(b).]

(c)   [omitted by SI 2010/529, art. 4(2)(b).]

14(1A)   The first condition is met if–

(a)   a pension scheme ("the original pension scheme") is being wound up,

(b)   the original pension scheme is within any of paragraphs (a) to (d) of paragraph 1(1) of Schedule 36 (deemed registration of existing schemes), and

(c)   condition A, B or C is met as set out in paragraphs (2), (3) and (4).

14(1B)   The second condition is met if–

(a)   a registered pension scheme which is not within any of the paragraphs 1(1)(a) to (d) of paragraph 1(1) of Schedule 36 is being wound up, and

(b)   immediately before the commencement of the winding up, an individual member of that registered pension scheme has rights which are protected under paragraph 22 or 31 of Schedule 36 (or under both of those paragraphs).

14(2)   Condition A is that–

(a)   the winding up commences before 6th April 2006, and

(b)   immediately before the commencement of the winding up, an individual member of the original pension scheme would have had rights which were protected under paragraph 22 or 31 of Schedule 36 (or under both those paragraphs) if the winding up had commenced on or after 6th April 2006.

14(3)   Condition B is that–

(a)   the winding up commences before 6th April 2006,

(b)   an individual becomes a member of the original pension scheme after the commencement of the winding up but before 6th April 2006, and

(c)   on becoming a member of the original pension scheme, the individual would have had rights which were protected under paragraph 22 or 31 of Schedule 36 (or under both those paragraphs) if the winding up had commenced on or after 6th April 2006.

14(4)   Condition C is that–

(a)   the winding up commences on or after 6th April 2006, and

(b)   immediately before the commencement of the winding up, an individual member of the original pension scheme has rights which are protected under paragraph 22 or 31 of Schedule 36 (or under both those paragraphs).

History – In art. 14(1), the words "the first or second condition is met." inserted by SI 2010/529, art. 4(2)(a), with effect from 6 April 2006.
Art. 14(1)(a), (b) and (c) omitted by SI 2010/529, art. 4(2)(b), with effect from 6 April 2006.
Art. 14(1A) inserted by SI 2010/529, art. 4(3), with effect from 6 April 2006.
Art. 14(1B) inserted by SI 2010/529, art. 4(3), with effect from 6 April 2006.

The annuity purchase condition

15(1)   The annuity purchase condition is met if–

(a)   condition A is met in the case of an annuity policy that has been assigned, or

(b)   conditions A to C are met in the case of an annuity policy that has been purchased.

15(2)   Condition A is that all the rights of the member have been extinguished by–

(a)   purchasing one annuity policy which satisfies the requirements prescribed under section 74(3)(c) of the Pensions Act 1995 ("the prescribed requirements"), or

(b)   assigning one annuity policy which satisfies the prescribed requirements, to the member.

15(3)   Condition B is that the contract under which the annuity policy was purchased ("the annuity contract") does not authorise the making of any payment which would be an unauthorised payment within the meaning of Part 4 of the Finance Act 2004.

15(4)   Condition C is that the annuity contract does not provide for the immediate payment of benefits.

15(5)   If the annuity purchase condition is met, paragraph 1(1) of Schedule 36 shall be modified so as to provide in addition that–

(a)   in the case of an annuity policy within paragraph (2)(a), the annuity policy is treated as having become a registered pension scheme ("the new pension scheme") on the date on which the contract was made, and

(b)   in the case of an annuity policy within paragraph (2)(b), the annuity policy is treated as having become a registered pension scheme ("the new pension scheme") on the date the annuity policy was assigned.

History – Art. 15 substituted by SI 2010/529, art. 5(1), with effect from 6 April 2006.

Membership of the new pension scheme

16(1)   For the purposes of Part 3 of Schedule 36 (pension schemes: transitional provisions and savings: pre-commencement benefit rights) the member is to be treated as having become a member of the new pension scheme as the result of a block transfer to it.

16(2)   In paragraph (1) "block transfer" has the meaning given by paragraph 22(6) of Schedule 36.

Stand-alone lump sums

17(1)   Paragraph (6) applies if condition A, B or C is met.

17(2)   Condition A is that–

(a)   a pension scheme is being wound up ("the original pension scheme") and the winding up commenced before 6th April 2006,

(b)   the stand-alone lump sum condition (see paragraph (5)) would have been met immediately before the commencement of the winding up, if the pension scheme had commenced winding up on or after 6th April 2006, and

(c)   the annuity purchase condition set out in article 15 is met.

17(3)   Condition B is that–

(a)   the original pension scheme is being wound up and the winding up commenced before 6th April 2006,

(b)   an individual became a member of the original pension scheme before 6th April 2006 but after the commencement of the winding up,

(c)   the stand-alone lump sum condition would have been met immediately before the commencement of the winding up, if the pension scheme had commenced winding up on or after 6th April 2006, and

(d)   the annuity purchase condition set out in article 15 is met.

17(4)   Condition C is that–

(a)   the original pension scheme is being wound up and the winding up commenced on or after 6th April 2006,

(b)   the annuity purchase condition set out in article 15 is met, and

(c)   the stand-alone lump sum condition is met.

17(5)   The stand-alone lump sum condition is that a member of the original pension scheme was entitled to be paid, a stand-alone lump sum which, if it had been paid would have been a stand-alone lump sum paid in circumstances where article 25B(4) (circumstance C) of the Taxation of Pension Schemes (Transitional Provisions) Order 2006 ("the Transitional Provisions Order") applied.

17(6)   The new pension scheme (within the meaning of article 15(5)(a) or (b) as the case may be) is treated as the same pension scheme as the original pension scheme (so that accordingly, the new pension scheme may pay a stand-alone lump sum to the member in circumstances where Article 25B(4) (circumstance C) of the Transitional Provisions Order applies).

History – Art. 17 inserted by SI 2010/529, art. 6(1), with effect from 6 April 2006.

REGISTERED PENSION SCHEMES (AUTHORISED SURPLUS PAYMENTS) REGULATIONS 2006

(SI 2006/574, as amended by SI 2011/1751)

Made on 9 March 2006 by the Commissioners for Her Majesty's Revenue and Customs, in exercise of the powers conferred upon them by s. 177 of the Finance Act 2004. Operative from 6 April 2006.

CITATION, COMMENCEMENT AND INTERPRETATION

1(1) These Regulations may be cited as the Registered Pension Schemes (Authorised Surplus Payments) Regulations 2006 and shall come into force on 6th April 2006.

1(2) In these Regulations—

"**the 1995 Act**" means the Pensions Act 1995;

"**the 1988 Act**" means the Income and Corporation Taxes Act 1988;

"**controlling director**" means a director to whom subsection (5)(b) of section 417 of the 1988 Act (read with sections (3),(4) and (6) of that section) applies.

1(3) In the application of these Regulations to Northern Ireland, a reference to an enactment applying only in Great Britain shall be construed as a reference to the corresponding enactment in Northern Ireland.

PAYMENTS FALLING WITHIN SECTION 37 OR 76 OF THE PENSIONS ACT 1995

2(1) A payment is an authorised surplus payment if it satisfies either paragraph (2) or (3).

2(2) A payment satisfies this paragraph if it is made in compliance with the requirements contained in section 37 (payment of surplus to employer) of the 1995 Act.

This paragraph is subject to paragraph (4).

2(3) A payment satisfies this paragraph if—

(a) it is made in connection with the winding up of an occupational pension scheme and

(b) the scheme making it satisfies the requirements set out in section 76 (excess assets on winding up) of the 1995 Act.

This paragraph is subject to paragraph (4).

2(4) A payment made by an occupational pension scheme to a sponsoring employer solely in respect of the death of a member is an authorised surplus payment if—

(a) it satisfies the conditions in paragraphs (2) or (3), and

(b) the member was not connected to the sponsoring employer at the date of the member's death.

2(5) For the purposes of this regulation and regulation 3 a member is connected to a sponsoring employer if—

(a) the employer is a partnership and he is connected with—

(i) a partner in the partnership, or

(ii) a person who has been a partner in the partnership at any time during the preceding year, or

(b) the employer is a company and the member, or a person connected with him, is, or at any time during the preceding year has been, a controlling director of the company.

For the purposes of paragraph (5) any question whether a person is connected with another shall be determined in accordance with section 839(2) of the 1988 Act.

History – Reg. 2(4) substituted by SI 2011/1751, reg. 4, which came into force on 11 August 2011, with effect for the tax year 2011–12 and subsequent tax years. Former reg. 2(4) read as follows:

"**2(4)** A payment made by an occupational pension scheme to a sponsoring employer, solely in respect of the death of a member is an authorised surplus payment if it satisfies the conditions in paragraphs (2) or (3) and–
(a)   in a case where the deceased member's fund was an alternatively secured pension fund, it satisfies conditions A and B, and
(b)   in other cases, it satisfies condition B.
Condition A
The scheme administrator has been unable to identify any dependants of the deceased member.
Condition B
The member was not connected to the sponsoring employer at the date of his death.".

PAYMENTS FALLING OUTSIDE SECTION 37 OR 76 OF THE PENSIONS ACT 1995

3(1)   A payment made by an occupational pension scheme to a sponsoring employer which does not satisfy paragraph (2) or (3) of regulation 2 is an authorised surplus payment if it satisfies the following conditions.

Condition A

The rules of the scheme permit such a payment to be made.

Condition B

The rules of the scheme contain a limit, calculated other than by reference to the size of the member's fund, on the maximum amount of benefits that may be paid to, or in respect of, members of the scheme.

Condition C

If the scheme is being wound up, the liabilities of the scheme have been fully discharged including any tax that may be due and there is a surplus of assets over liabilities.

Condition D

If the scheme is not being wound up, the requirements set out in section 37 of the 1995 Act would have been met if the scheme had been one to which the section applied.

This paragraph is subject to paragraph (2).

3(2)   A payment made by an occupational pension scheme to a sponsoring employer solely in respect of the death of a member is an authorised surplus payment if–

(a)   it satisfies the conditions in paragraph (1), and

(b)   the member was not connected to the sponsoring employer at the date of the member's death.

History – Reg. 3(2) substituted by SI 2011/1751, reg. 5, which came into force on 11 August 2011, with effect for the tax year 2011–12 and subsequent tax years. Former reg. 3(2) read as follows:

> "**3(2)**   A payment made by an occupational pension scheme to a sponsoring employer solely in respect of the death of
> a member is an authorised surplus payment if it satisfies the conditions in paragraph (1) and–
> (a)   in a case where the deceased member's fund was an alternatively secured pension fund, it satisfies conditions E
> and F, and
> (b)   in other cases, it satisfies condition F.
> *Condition E*
> The scheme administrator has been unable to identify any dependants of the deceased member.
> *Condition F*
> The member was not connected to the sponsoring employer at the date of his death.".

PENSION PROTECTION FUND (TAX) REGULATIONS 2006

(SI 2006/575, as amended by SI 2013/1117)

Made on 9 March 2006 by the Treasury in exercise of the powers conferred upon them by s. 102 of the Finance Act 2005. Operative from 6 April 2006.

CITATION AND COMMENCEMENT

1 These Regulations may be cited as the Pension Protection Fund (Tax) Regulations 2006 and shall come into force on 6th April 2006.

INTERPRETATION

2(1) In this regulation–

(a) paragraph (2) gives the meaning of the abbreviated references to Acts and instruments used in these Regulations, and

(b) paragraph (3) deals with other expressions used in these Regulations.

2(2) In these Regulations–

"**FA 2004**" means the Finance Act 2004;

"**ICTA**" means the Income and Corporation Taxes Act 1988;

"**ITEPA 2003**" means the Income Tax (Earnings and Pensions) Act 2003;

"**P(No. 2)A(NI) 2008**" means the Pensions (No. 2) Act (Northern Ireland) 2008;

"**PA 2008**" means the Pensions Act 2008;

"**the Pensions Act**" (without more) means the Pensions Act 2004;

"**the Pensions Order**" means the Pensions (Northern Ireland) Order 2005;

"**TCGA 1992**" means the Taxation of Chargeable Gains Act 1992.

2(3) In these Regulations–

"**the Board of the Pension Protection Fund**" means the body corporate established under section 107 of the Pensions Act;

"**dependant**" is to be construed in accordance with paragraph 15 of Schedule 28 to FA 2004;

"**dependants' scheme pension**" is to be construed in accordance with paragraph 16 of Schedule 28 to FA 2004;

"**the Fraud Compensation Fund**" has the meaning given by regulation 3(1);

"**fraud compensation payment**"–

(a) in England, Wales and Scotland means a fraud compensation payment within the meaning of Part 2 of the Pensions Act (see section 182(1) of that Act), and

(b) Northern Ireland means a fraud compensation payment within the meaning of Part 3 of the Pensions Order (see Article 165(1) of that Order);

"**Part 4**" means Part 4 of FA 2004 (pension schemes);

"**the pension compensation provisions**"–

(a) in England, Wales and Scotland is to be construed in accordance with section 108 of PA 2008 (interpretation), and

(b) in Northern Ireland is to be construed in accordance with section 87 of P(No. 2)A(NI) 2008 (interpretation);

"**the Pension Protection Fund**" has the meaning given by regulation 3(1);

"**the Pensions Act Funds**" has the meaning given by regulation 3(1);

"**the Pensions Act levies**" means the levies specified in paragraph (2) or (3) of regulation 3, as the case may require;

"**periodic compensation**"–

(a) in England, Wales and Scotland is to be construed in accordance with Schedule 7 to the Pensions Act (pension compensation provisions) or, as the case may be, Schedule 5 to PA 2008 (pension compensation payable on discharge of pension compensation credit), and

(b)   in Northern Ireland is to be construed in accordance with Schedule 6 to the Pensions Order (pension compensation provisions) or, as the case may be, Schedule 4 to P(No. 2)A(NI) 2008 (pension compensation payable on discharge of pension compensation credit);

"PPF money purchase lump sum"

(a)   in England, Wales and Scotland has the meaning given by regulation 1(2) of the Pension Protection Fund (General and Miscellaneous Amendments) Regulations 2006 (citation, commencement and interpretation), and

(b)   in Northern Ireland has the meaning given by regulation 1(2) of the Pension Protection Fund (General and Miscellaneous Amendments) Regulations (Northern Ireland) 2006 (citation, commencement and interpretation).

"registered pension scheme" has the meaning given by section 832(1) of ICTA;

"Schedule 36" means Schedule 36 to FA 2004 (transitional provisions);

"scheme pension" is to be construed in accordance with paragraph 2 of Schedule 28 to FA 2004.

History – In reg. 2(2), definitions of "P(No. 2)A(NI) 2008" and "PA 2008" inserted by SI 2013/1117, reg. 3(1), with effect from 31 May 2013.

In reg. 2(3), in the definition of "the pension compensation provisions", (a) and (b) substituted by SI 2013/1117, reg. 3(2), with effect from 31 May 2013. Former (a) and (b) read as follows:

"(a)   in England, Wales and Scotland is to be construed in accordance with section 162(2) of the Pensions Act (the pension compensation provisions), and

(b)   in Northern Ireland is to be construed in accordance with Article 146(2) of the Pensions Order (the pension compensation provisions);".

In reg. 2(3), in the definition of "periodic compensation", in (a), the words "or, as the case may be, Schedule 5 to PA 2008 (pension compensation payable on discharge of pension compensation credit)" and in (b), the words "or, as the case may be, Schedule 4 to P(No. 2)A(NI) 2008 (pension compensation payable on discharge of pension compensation credit)" inserted by SI 2013/1117, reg. 3(3), with effect from 31 May 2013.

In reg. 2(3), definition of "PPF money purchase lump sum" inserted by SI 2013/1117, reg. 3(4), with effect from 31 May 2013.

MEANING OF "THE PENSION PROTECTION FUND" AND OTHER EXPRESSIONS

3(1)   In these Regulations–

"the Pension Protection Fund" means the Fund required to be held, managed and applied by the Board of the Pension Protection Fund under section 110(1)(a) of the Pensions Act;

"the Fraud Compensation Fund" means the Fund required to be held, managed and applied by the Board of the Pension Protection Fund under section 110(1)(b) of the Pensions Act;

"the Pensions Act Funds" means the Pension Protection Fund and the Fraud Compensation Fund.

3(2)   In England, Wales and Scotland **"the Pensions Act levies"** means–

(a)   the administration levy referred to in section 117(1) of the Pensions Act;

(b)   the risk-based pension protection levy referred to in section 175(1)(a) of that Act;

(c)   the scheme-based pension protection levy referred to in section 175(1)(b) of that Act;

(d)   the fraud compensation levy referred to in section 189(1) of that Act;

(e)   a levy in respect of eligible schemes imposed by regulations made under section 209(7) of that Act (the Ombudsman for the Board of the Pension Protection Fund).

3(3)   In Northern Ireland **"the Pensions Act levies"** means–

(a)   the administration levy referred to in Article 103(1) of the Pensions Order;

(b)   the risk-based pension protection levy referred to in Article 158(1)(a) of that Order;

(c)   the scheme-based pension protection levy referred to in Article 158(1)(b) of that Order;

(d)   the fraud compensation levy referred to in Article 171(1) of that Order;

(e)   a levy in respect of eligible schemes imposed by regulations made under Article 191(3) of that Order (the PPF Ombudsman).

APPLICATION OF THE TAX ACTS: GENERAL

4(1)   The Tax Acts apply in relation to the Pension Protection Fund in the same way as they apply in relation to a registered pension scheme.

4(2)   The general rule in paragraph (1) is subject to the further provisions contained in these Regulations.

APPLICATION OF PART 4 OF FA 2004: FURTHER PROVISIONS

5   Section 151 of FA 2004 (meaning of "member") applies as if, in Part 4, "member" in relation to the Pension Protection Fund, meant–

(a)   an individual in receipt of compensation from the Pension Protection Fund,

(b)   an individual who expects to receive such compensation following the assumption of responsibility, by the Board of the Pension Protection Fund, for a scheme of which that individual was a member, or

(c)   an individual who receives a PPF money purchase lump sum.

History – Reg. 5(c) (and the ", or" before it) inserted (and the "or" after (a) omitted) by SI 2013/1117, reg. 4, with effect from 31 May 2013.

6(1)   Section 152 of FA 2004 (meaning of "arrangement") applies as if, in Part 4, "arrangement", in relation to an individual specified in paragraph (2), meant an arrangement specified in paragraph (3).

6(2)   An individual is specified for the purposes of this paragraph if the individual–

(a)   is in receipt of compensation from the Pension Protection Fund,

(b)   expects to receive such compensation following the assumption of responsibility, by the Board of the Pension Protection Fund, for a scheme of which that individual was a member, or

(c)   receives a PPF money purchase lump sum.

6(3)   An arrangement is specified for the purposes of this paragraph if–

(a)   in relation to an individual falling within paragraph (2)(a) or (b), it is an arrangement under which the individual receives (or, as the case may be, expects to receive)–

   (i)   compensation paid under Schedule 7 to the Pensions Act or, as the case may be, Schedule 5 to PA 2008 (pension compensation provisions), or

   (ii)   compensation paid under Schedule 6 to the Pensions Order or, as the case may be, Schedule 4 to P(No. 2)A(NI) 2008 (pension compensation provisions), or

(b)   in relation to an individual falling within paragraph (2)(c), it is an arrangement under which the individual receives a PPF money purchase lump sum.

History – Reg. 6(2)(c) (and the ", or" before it) inserted (and the "or" after (a) omitted) by SI 2013/1117, reg. 5, with effect from 31 May 2013.
Reg. 6(3) substituted by SI 2013/1117, reg. 6, with effect from 31 May 2013. Former reg. 6(3) read as follows:

   "**6(3)**   An arrangement is specified for the purposes of this paragraph if it is an arrangement under which the individual receives (or, as the case may be, expects to receive)–
   (a)   compensation paid under Schedule 7 to the Pensions Act (pension compensation provisions), or
   (b)   compensation paid under Schedule 6 to the Pensions Order (pension compensation provisions).".

7   Chapter 2 of Part 4 (registration of pension schemes) does not apply in relation to the Pension Protection Fund.

8   Section 164 of FA 2004 (authorised member payments) applies as if it also provided that the Board of the Pension Protection Fund was authorised to make the following payments to or in respect of a member–

(a)   payments of an amount falling within section 166(2) of the Pensions Act (duty to pay scheme benefits unpaid at assessment date);

(b)   payments of an amount falling within Article 150(2) of the Pensions Order (duty to pay scheme benefits unpaid at assessment date);

(c)   a payment of a PPF money purchase lump sum.

History – Reg. 8(c) (and the semi-colon before it) inserted by SI 2013/1117, reg. 7, with effect from 31 May 2013.

9(1)   For the purposes of Part 4, payment of periodic compensation from the Pension Protection Fund to an individual is treated as payment of a scheme pension to a member of a registered pension scheme (see section 165 of FA 2004: pension rules).

9(2)   The payment of such compensation is treated as meeting the condition specified in paragraph 2(2)(a) of Schedule 28 to FA 2004 (condition relating to payer of scheme pension).

10(1)   This regulation applies if–

(a)   either condition A or B is met, and

(b)   condition C is met.

10(2)   Condition A is that the Board of the Pension Protection Fund is responsible for securing that compensation is (and has been) paid to an individual in accordance with the pension compensation provisions.

10(3)   Condition B is that the Board of the Pension Protection Fund is required to secure the discharge of liabilities to an individual in respect of benefits transferred to the Board under–

(a)   Chapter 3 of Part 2 of the Pensions Act (pension protection), or

(b)   Chapter 3 of Part 3 of the Pensions Order (pension protection).

10(4)   Condition C is that the Board of the Pension Protection Fund provides for the securing of–

(a)   the payment of compensation in the circumstances specified in condition A, or

(b)   the discharge of liabilities in the circumstances specified in condition B,

by the entry into an annuity contract or a number of such contracts.

10(5)   For the purposes of Part 4, payment of an annuity under an annuity contract mentioned in paragraph (4) is treated as payment of a scheme pension.

(6)   If this regulation applies, so much of Pension rule 4 in section 165(1) of FA 2004 (pension rules) as provides that a scheme pension may only be paid if the member had an opportunity to select a lifetime annuity instead is treated as omitted.

11(1)   Section 166 of FA 2004 (lump sum rule) and Part 1 of Schedule 29 to that Act (authorised lump sums: lump sum rule) apply with the following modifications to the payment of lump sums by the Pension Protection Fund to an individual.

11(2)   Section 166(2) of FA 2004 (time at which a person becomes entitled to a lump sum) applies as if the person becomes entitled to a lump sum when a person acquires an actual (rather than a prospective) right to receive the lump sum.

11(3)   In Schedule 29 to FA 2004, paragraph 5(1)(a) is treated as omitted.

12(1)   For the purposes of Part 4, payment of periodic compensation from the Pension Protection Fund to a dependant of an individual is treated as payment of a dependants' scheme pension in respect of a member of a registered pension scheme (see section 167 of FA 2004: pension death benefit rules).

12(2)   The payment of such compensation is treated as meeting the condition specified in paragraph 16(2)(a) of Schedule 28 to FA 2004(a) (condition relating to payer of dependants' scheme pension).

13(1)   This regulation applies if–

(a)   either condition A or B is met, and

(b)   condition C is met.

13(2)   Condition A is that the Board of the Pension Protection Fund is responsible for securing that compensation is (and has been) paid to a dependant of an individual in accordance with the pension compensation provisions.

13(3)   Condition B is that the Board of the Pension Protection Fund is required to secure the discharge of liabilities to a dependant of an individual in respect of benefits transferred to the Board under–

(a)   Chapter 3 of Part 2 of the Pensions Act (pension protection), or

(b)   Chapter 3 of Part 3 of the Pensions Order (pension protection).

13(4)   Condition C is that the Board of the Pension Protection Fund provides for the securing of–

(a)   the payment of compensation in the circumstances specified in condition A, or

(b)   the discharge of liabilities in the circumstances specified in condition B,

by the entry into an annuity contract or a number of such contracts.

13(5)   For the purposes of Part 4, payment of an annuity under an annuity contract mentioned in paragraph (4) is treated as payment of a dependants' scheme pension.

13(6)   If this regulation applies, so much of Pension death benefit rule 3 in section 167(1) of FA 2004 (pension death benefit rules) as provides that a dependants' scheme pension may only be paid if the member or dependant had an opportunity to select a dependants' annuity instead is treated as omitted.

14(1)   Section 168 of FA 2004 (lump sum death benefit rule) and Part 2 of Schedule 29 to that Act (authorised lump sums: lump sum death benefit rule) apply to the payment of lump sums by the Pension Protection Fund to a dependant of a qualifying individual.

14(2)   In paragraph (1) a **"qualifying individual"** means–

(a)   an individual who was a member of a scheme for which the Board of the Pension Protection Fund has assumed responsibility, or

(b)   an individual who was a transferee entitled to a pension compensation credit referred to in section 111(1) of PA 2008 or section 89(1) of P(No. 2)A(NI) 2008 (creation of pension compensation debits and credits).

History – Reg. 14(2) substituted by SI 2013/1117, reg. 8, with effect from 31 May 2013. Former reg. 14(2) read as follows:
    "**14(2)**   In paragraph (1) a **"qualifying individual"** means an individual who was a member of a scheme for which the Board of the Pension Protection Fund has assumed responsibility.".

15   Sections 175 to 181 of FA 2004 (authorised and unauthorised employer payments) do not apply in relation to the Pension Protection Fund.

16   Sections 182 to 185 of FA 2004 (borrowing) do not apply in relation to the Pension Protection Fund.

17(1)   Section 186 of FA 2004 (exemption from tax on certain types of income) applies in relation to each of the Pensions Act Funds as if in subsection (1) for the reference to income tax there were substituted a reference to corporation tax.

17(2)   The exemption provided by section 186(1) of FA 2004 (as modified by paragraph (1)) in relation to each of the Pensions Act Funds also applies in respect of–

(a)   any profit, gain or loss on a loan relationship within the meaning of Chapter 2 of Part 4 of the Finance Act 1996 (loan relationships), and

(b)   any amount received on account of the Pensions Act levies.

18(1)   Any amount recovered by an individual's employer on account of any of the Pensions Act levies is treated in the same way as relievable pension contributions paid during a tax year (see section 188 of FA 2004: relief for contributions).

18(2)   In paragraph (1) **"tax year"** has the meaning given by section 279(1) of FA 2004.

19   Relief on any amount recovered by an individual's employer on account of any of the Pensions Act levies may be given in accordance with section 193 of FA 2004 (relief under net pay arrangements).

20   Sections 197 and 198 of FA 2004 (spreading of relief) do not apply in relation to any sum paid by an employer on account of any of the Pensions Act levies.

21   Section 199 of FA 2004 (deemed contributions) applies in relation to any sum paid by an employer on account of any of the Pensions Act levies as it applies in relation to a sum paid by an employer in or towards the discharge of any liability of the employer under the enactments specified in subsection (1) of that section.

22   Section 213 of FA 2004 (surchargeable unauthorised employer payments) does not apply in relation to the Pension Protection Fund.

23(1)   For the purposes of benefit crystallisation event 2 (see the Table in section 216(1) of FA 2004) "P" is the amount of the periodic payments which will be payable to the individual in the period of 12 months beginning with the day on which the individual first becomes entitled to a periodic payment (assuming that it remains payable throughout that period at the rate at which it is payable on that day).

23(2)   Benefit crystallisation event 2 does not apply if–

(a)   an individual becomes entitled to a scheme pension under a relevant pension scheme,

(b)   the Board of the Pension Protection Fund assumes responsibility for that relevant pension scheme, and

(c)   the individual receives periodic compensation from the Pension Protection Fund under Schedule 7 to the Pensions Act or Schedule 6 to the Pensions Order (pension compensation provisions) in respect of the scheme pension mentioned in sub-paragraph (a).

23(3)   For the purposes of benefit crystallisation event 5 "DP" is the annual rate of periodic compensation to which the individual would be entitled if, on the date on which the individual reaches 75, the individual acquired an actual (rather than a prospective) right to receive it.

23(4)   Subject to the provisions of this regulation, section 216 of FA 2004 (benefit crystallisation events and amounts crystallised) applies to the payment, by the Board of the Pension Protection Fund, of any amount falling within section 166(2) of the Pensions Act or Article 150(2) of the Pensions Order (duty to pay scheme benefits unpaid at assessment date) in the same way as it would apply if that payment had been made by a registered pension scheme.

23(5)   Schedule 32 to FA 2004 (registered pension schemes: benefit crystallisation events: supplementary) applies to give the meaning of expressions used in this regulation as it applies to give the meaning of expressions used in the Table in section 216(1) of FA 2004 (benefit crystallisation events and amounts crystallised).

23A   Section 220 of FA 2004 (pension credits from previously crystallised rights) applies as if, in relation to the Pension Protection Fund–

(a)   in subsection (4) for "or Article 26(1) of WRP(NI)O 1999" here were substituted ", Article 26(1) of WRP(NI)O 1999, section 111(1) of the Pensions Act 2008 or section 89(1) of the Pensions (No. 2) Act (Northern Ireland) 2008",

(b)   in subsection (4A)(a) for "or Article 26(2) or (3)(b) of WRP(NI)O 1999" there were substituted ", Article 26(2) or (3)(b) of WRP(NI)O 1999, section 111(2)(a) or (b)(ii) of the Pensions Act 2008 or section 89(2)(a) or (b)(ii) of the Pensions (No. 2) Act (Northern Ireland) 2008", and

(c)   in subsection (4A)(b) for "or Article 26(3)(a) of WRP(NI)O 1999" there were substituted ", Article 26(3)(a) of WRP(NI)O 1999, section 111(2)(b)(i) of the Pensions Act 2008 or section 89(2)(b)(i) of the Pensions (No. 2) Act (Northern Ireland) 2008".

History – Reg. 23A inserted by SI 2013/1117, reg. 9, with effect from 31 May 2013.

24   Section 242 of FA 2004 (de-registration charge) does not apply in relation to the Pension Protection Fund.

25   Chapter 6 of Part 4 (schemes that are not registered pension schemes) does not apply in relation to the Pension Protection Fund.

26(1)   References in Part 4 to the scheme administrator, in relation to a pension scheme (see section 270 of FA 2004: meaning of "scheme administrator"), are to be treated as references to the scheme administrator of the Pension Protection Fund.

26(2)   For the purposes of paragraph (1) the **"scheme administrator of the Pension Protection Fund"** means the person appointed by the Board of the Pension Protection Fund to be responsible for the discharge of the functions conferred or imposed on the scheme administrator of the Pension Protection Fund by and under Part 4.

27(1)   If section 272 of FA 2004 (trustees etc. liable as scheme administrator) applies in relation to the Pension Protection Fund, the Board of the Pension Protection Fund assumes liability by reason of that section applying in relation to that Fund.

27(2)   For the purposes of section 272(4) of FA 2004 (specification of persons assuming liability) the Board of the Pension Protection Fund are treated as persons who assume liability by virtue of being specified under Head 2.

28   Section 273 of FA 2004 (members liable as scheme administrator) does not apply in relation to the Pension Protection Fund.

28A   Section 279(1) of FA 2004 (other definitions) applies as if, in relation to the Pension Protection Fund–

(a)   **"pension credit"** included any pension compensation credit mentioned in section 111(1)(b) of PA 2008 or section 89(1)(b) of P(No. 2)A(NI) 2008 (creation of pension compensation debits and credits),

(b)   **"pension debit"** included any pension compensation debit mentioned in section 111(1)(a) of PA 2008 or section 89(1)(a) of P(No. 2)A(NI) 2008 (creation of pension compensation debits and credits), and

(c)   **"pension sharing order or provision"** included any pension compensation sharing order or provision mentioned in section 109 of PA 2008 or section 88 of P(No. 2)A(NI) 2008 (activation of pension compensation sharing).

History – Reg. 28A inserted by SI 2013/1117, reg. 10, with effect from 31 May 2013.

29(1)   A lifetime allowance enhancement factor may operate in accordance with paragraph 7 of Schedule 36 (primary protection) in relation to all benefit crystallisation events occurring in relation to an individual in the circumstances specified in paragraph (2).

29(2)   The circumstances are where some or all of the individual's relevant pre-commencement rights are rights under a pension arrangement relating to that individual under a pension scheme for which the Board of the Pension Protection Fund assumes responsibility in accordance with–

(a)   Chapter 3 of Part 2 of the Pensions Act (pension protection), or

(b)   Chapter 3 of Part 3 of the Pensions Order (pension protection).

29(3)   This regulation is to be construed as one with paragraph 7 of Schedule 36.

30(1)   This regulation applies if there is a transfer to the Board of the Pension Protection Fund of all sums and assets held for the purposes of, or representing accrued rights under, an arrangement relating to an individual under a registered pension scheme.

30(2)   For the purposes of paragraph 12 of Schedule 36 (enhanced protection) the transfer is treated as a permitted transfer by virtue of sub-paragraph (8)(b) of that paragraph.

30(3)   This regulation is to be construed as one with paragraph 12 of Schedule 36.

31(1)   For the purposes of Part 3 of Schedule 36 (pre-commencement benefit rights), the transfer of the property, rights and liabilities of a scheme to the Board of the Pension Protection Fund in accordance with a relevant transfer notice is treated as a block transfer within the meaning given by paragraph 22(6) of Schedule 36.

31(2) But for the purposes of determining the compensation payable where the Board of the Pension Protection Fund assumes responsibility for a scheme in accordance with Chapter 3 of Part 2 of the Pensions Act or Chapter 3 of Part 3 of the Pensions Order (pension protection), paragraph (1) does not affect the application of–

(a)   Schedule 7 to the Pensions Act (pension compensation provisions) or regulations made under that Schedule, or

(b)   Schedule 6 to the Pensions Order (pension compensation provisions) or regulations made under that Schedule.

31(3) In paragraph (1) a **"relevant transfer notice"** means–

(a)   a transfer notice given under section 160 of the Pensions Act (transfer notice), or

(b)   a transfer notice given under Article 144 of the Pensions Order (transfer notice).

32 Paragraphs 35 and 36 of Schedule 36 (winding-up lump sums paid by former approved superannuation funds and right to payment of lump sum death benefit) do not apply in relation to the Pension Protection Fund.

APPLICATION OF THE INHERITANCE TAX ACT 1984: FURTHER PROVISIONS

33 Section 58 of the Inheritance Tax Act 1984 (relevant property) applies in relation to property which is held for the purposes of the Pension Protection Fund as it applies in relation to property which is held for the purposes of a registered pension scheme.

34 Section 151 of the Inheritance Tax Act 1984 (treatment of pension rights) applies in relation to an interest in or under the Pension Protection Fund as it applies in relation to an interest in or under a registered pension scheme.

APPLICATION OF ICTA: FURTHER PROVISIONS

35(1) Section 413(3) of ICTA (group relief: interpretation) applies as if it provided that two companies shall be deemed to be members of a group of companies if–

(a)   one company is the 75 per cent. subsidiary of the other and neither company is the Board of the Pension Protection Fund, or

(b)   both companies are 75 per cent. subsidiaries of the Board of the Pension Protection Fund.

This regulation is to be construed as one with Chapter 4 of Part 10 of ICTA (group relief).

36(1) If the Board of the Pension Protection Fund acquires more than half the ordinary share capital of a company (so that, accordingly, the condition in paragraph (a) of section 769(1) of ICTA is met), there is no change in the ownership of the company for the purposes of sections 767A to 768E of ICTA (change in ownership of company).

36(2) This regulation is to be construed as one with sections 767A to 768E of ICTA.

APPLICATION OF TCGA 1992: FURTHER PROVISIONS

37(1) For the purposes of section 170 of TCGA 1992 (groups of companies), none of the following may be a member of a group–

(a)   the Board of the Pension Protection Fund;

(b)   the Pension Protection Fund;

(c)   the Fraud Compensation Fund.

37(2) This regulation is to be construed as one with TCGA 1992.

38(1) For the purposes of TCGA 1992, any gain accruing to the Board of the Pension Protection Fund from its disposal of investments shall not be a chargeable gain if, or to the extent that, at the time of the disposal, those investments were held by the Board, or on its behalf, for the purposes of one of the Pensions Act Funds.

38(2) In paragraph (1) **"investments"** includes futures contracts and options contracts.

38(3) This regulation is to be construed as one with TCGA 1992.

APPLICATION OF ITEPA 2003: FURTHER PROVISIONS

39 Step 5 of section 54(1) of ITEPA 2003 (calculation of deemed employment payment under arrangements made by intermediaries) applies in relation to a payment, by the intermediary, of any sum in respect of any of the Pensions Act levies in the same way as it applies in relation to any contributions that may be deducted under that step.

40   Section 307 of ITEPA 2003 (exemption from employment income for death or retirement benefit provision made by employer) applies in relation to the payment of any sum in respect of any of the Pensions Act levies in the same way as it applies in respect of provision made by an employee's employer for a retirement or death benefit.

41   Section 579A of ITEPA 2003 (pensions) applies in relation to periodic compensation from the Pension Protection Fund as it applies to any pension under a registered pension scheme.

42   Unless it is a lump sum falling within any of paragraphs (a) to (c) of regulation 42A, a lump sum paid under any of the following provisions is treated as if it were a lump sum paid under a registered pension scheme to which section 636A of ITEPA 2003 (exemption for certain lump sums under registered pension schemes) applies–

(a)   Schedule 7 to the Pensions Act or Schedule 6 to the Pensions Order (pension compensation provisions), or

(b)   Schedule 5 to PA 2008 or Schedule 4 to P(No. 2)A(NI) 2008 (pension compensation provisions).

History – Reg. 42 substituted by SI 2013/1117, reg. 11, with effect from 31 May 2013. Former reg. 42 read as follows:
"**42**   A lump sum paid under Schedule 7 to the Pensions Act or Schedule 6 to the Pensions Order (pension compensation provisions) is treated as if it were a lump sum paid under a registered pension scheme to which subsection (1) of section 636A of ITEPA 2003 (exemption for certain lump sums under registered pension schemes) applied.".

42A   Each of the following is to be treated as if it were a lump sum, paid to a member under a registered pension scheme, in relation to which section 636B of ITEPA 2003 (trivial commutation and winding-up lump sums) applies–

(a)   a PPF money purchase lump sum,

(b)   a lump sum under paragraph 24 of Schedule 7 to the Pensions Act or paragraph 24 of Schedule 6 to the Pensions Order (commutation of periodic compensation), where the portion of periodic compensation commuted exceeds 25%, and

(c)   a lump sum under paragraph 9 of Schedule 5 to PA 2008 or paragraph 9 of Schedule 4 to P (No. 2)A(NI) 2008 (commutation of periodic compensation), where the portion of periodic compensation commuted exceeds 25%.

History – Reg. 42A inserted by SI 2013/1117, reg. 11, with effect from 31 May 2013.

APPLICATION OF THE FINANCE ACT 2003: FURTHER PROVISIONS

43(1)   Paragraph 8 of Schedule 4 to the Finance Act 2003 (debt as consideration) does not apply in relation to the Pension Protection Fund if–

(a)   the Board of the Pension Protection Fund acquires a chargeable interest as part of its assumption of responsibility for a scheme in accordance with Chapter 3 of Part 2 of the Pensions Act or Chapter 3 of Part 3 of the Pensions Order (pension protection), and

(b)   the chargeable interest is held by the Board of the Pension Protection Fund as an investment.

43(2)   Paragraph 1 of Schedule 7 to the Finance Act 2003 (group relief) applies in relation to a group of companies of which the Board of the Pension Protection Fund is a member as if, in the case of each reference to 75%, there were substituted a reference to 50%.

43(3)   For the purposes of paragraph 3(1) of Schedule 7 to the Finance Act 2003 (withdrawal of group relief) there is no withdrawal of group relief if the vendor is the Board of the Pension Protection Fund.

43(4)   This regulation is to be construed as one with Part 4 of the Finance Act 2003 (stamp duty land tax).

FRAUD COMPENSATION PAYMENTS AND OTHER RELATED PAYMENTS

44(1)   Receipt of a payment to which this regulation applies shall not be regarded as a disposal of an asset for the purposes of capital gains tax or for the purposes of corporation tax on chargeable gains.

44(2)   This regulation applies to–

(a)   a fraud compensation payment under section 185 of the Pensions Act;

(b)   an interim payment under section 186 of the Pensions Act;

(c)   a fraud compensation payment under Article 168 of the Pensions Order;

(d)   an interim payment under Article 169 of the Pensions Order;

(e) a payment made by the Board of the Pension Protection Fund under section 83 of the Pensions Act 1995;

(f) a payment in anticipation made by the Board of the Pension Protection Fund under section 84 of that Act;

(g) a payment made by the Board of the Pension Protection Fund under Article 81 of the Pensions (Northern Ireland) Order 1995;

(h) a payment in anticipation made by the Board of the Pension Protection Fund under Article 82 of that Order.

REGISTERED PENSION SCHEMES (AUTHORISED PAYMENTS – ARREARS OF PENSION) REGULATIONS 2006

(SI 2006/614)

Made on 9 March 2006 by the Commissioners for Her Majesty's Revenue and Customs, in exercise of the powers conferred by s. 164(f) of the Finance Act 2004. Operative from 6 April 2006.

CITATION AND COMMENCEMENT

1   These Regulations may be cited as the Registered Pension Schemes (Authorised Payments – Arrears of Pension) Regulations 2006 and shall come into force on 6th April 2006.

PAYMENT OF ARREARS OF PENSION TO BE AN AUTHORISED PAYMENT

2(1)   Where a registered pension scheme pays to a member of the scheme an amount representing accrued arrears of pension, paragraph (2) applies.

2(2)   Paragraph (3) applies to so much of the payment mentioned in paragraph (1) as–

(a)   does not exceed the amount accrued during the period–

   (i)   ending with the date on which he became entitled to the pension ("the actual start date"); and

   (ii)   beginning with the earliest date from which the member could, at the actual start date, have required the scheme administrator, in accordance with the rules of the scheme, to make a payment of arrears of pension; and

(b)   constitutes taxable pension income within section 579B of ITEPA 2003.

2(3)   The amount to which this paragraph applies is a payment of a prescribed description for the purposes of section 164(f).

2(4)   In this regulation–

"entitled" has the meaning given in section 165(3); and

a reference to a **numbered section**, without more, is a reference to the section of the Finance Act 2004 bearing that number.

FILMS (DEFINITION OF "BRITISH FILM") ORDER 2006

(SI 2006/643)

Made on 31 March 2006 by the Secretary of State, with the approval of Her Majesty's Treasury, in exercise of the powers conferred on her by para. 10(2) of Sch. 1 to the Films Act 1985.

CITATION, COMMENCEMENT AND INTERPRETATION

1(1) This Order may be cited as the Films (Definition of "British Film") Order 2006 and shall come into force on the day after the day on which it is made.

1(2) **"The Schedule"** means Schedule 1 to the Films Act 1985, and a reference to a numbered paragraph is a reference to the paragraph bearing that number in the Schedule.

TRANSITIONAL PROVISIONS

2(1) An application for certification under paragraph 2 which is made in relation to a film for which the first day of principal photography is on or after 1st April 2006 shall be determined by the Secretary of State in accordance with the Schedule as modified by this Order.

2(2) An application for certification under paragraph 2 which is made in relation to a film for which the first day of principal photography is before 1st April 2006 shall be determined by the Secretary of State in accordance with the Schedule as in force immediately before the commencement of this Order if production is completed before 1st January 2007; otherwise it shall be determined in accordance with the Schedule as modified by this Order.

2(3) For this purpose the production of a film is completed when the film is first in a form in which it can reasonably be regarded as ready for copies of it to be made and distributed for presentation to the general public.

MODIFICATION OF THE SCHEDULE

3 In paragraph 1(1) (preliminary) omit the definitions of "Commonwealth country" and "film production activity".

4 For paragraph 4 (British films for purposes of the Schedule) substitute–

"**4(1)** A film is a British film for the purposes of this Schedule if the requirements specified in sub-paragraphs (2) and (3) are met.

4(2) The first requirement is that throughout the period during which the film is being made the maker of the film is–

(a) a person ordinarily resident in a member State, or

(b) a company which is registered in a member State and of which the central management and control of business is exercised in a member State.

4(3) The second requirement is that the film passes the relevant cultural test (see paragraph 4A, 4B or 4C).

4(4) For the purposes of this paragraph and paragraphs 4A to 4D a state shall be treated as if it were a member State if–

(a) it is a party to an agreement under Article 310 of the Treaty establishing the European Community, and

(b) the agreement requires a maker of a film who is ordinarily resident or registered in that state to be treated for the purposes of this Schedule in the same way as a maker of a film who is ordinarily resident or registered in a member State.

4(5) Her Majesty may by Order in Council provide for films to be treated as British films for the purposes of this Schedule if they are made in accordance with the terms of any agreement between Her Majesty's Government in the United Kingdom and any other government, international organisation or authority.

4(6) This paragraph has effect subject to paragraph 5 (excluded films).

4A(1) The cultural test for a film other than a documentary (see paragraph 4B) or an animation (see paragraph 4C) is as follows.

4A(2) A film passes the cultural test if it is awarded at least 16 points in total.

Statutory Instruments

4A(3)   Up to 4 points shall be awarded in respect of the content of the film as follows–

(a)   1 point if at least 50% of the film is set in the United Kingdom;

(b)   1 point if at least one of the three principal characters depicted in the film (or, if there are three or fewer characters depicted in the film, any of them) is a British character;

(c)   1 point if the film depicts a British story;

(d)   1 point if at least 50% of the original dialogue is recorded in the English language or in a recognised regional or minority language.

4A(4)   Up to 15 points shall be awarded in respect of work carried out in the making of the film as follows–

(a)   up to 6 points depending on the percentage of principal photography that is carried out in the United Kingdom as follows–
  (i)   6 points for 75%,
  (ii)   5 points for 62.5%,
  (iii) 4 points for 50%,
  (iv)   3 points for 37.5%,
  (v)   2 points for 25%,
  (vi)   1 point for 10%;

(b)   up to 4 points depending on the percentage of the work on visual effects that is carried out in the United Kingdom as follows–
  (i)   4 points for 75%,
  (ii)   3 points for 50%,
  (iii) 2 points for 25%,
  (iv)   1 point for 10%;

(c)   1 point if at least 75% of the work on special effects is carried out in the United Kingdom;

(d)   up to 2 points depending on the percentage of the work on performing and recording the original music score created for the film that is carried out in the United Kingdom as follows–
  (i)   2 points for 75%,
  (ii)   1 point for 50%;

(e)   1 point if at least 75% of the work on audio post production is carried out in the United Kingdom;

(f)   1 point if at least 75% of the work on image processing is carried out in the United Kingdom.

4A(5)   Up to 13 points shall be awarded in respect of the personnel involved in the making of the film as follows–

(a)   2 points if the director (or, if there is more than one, the lead director) is a qualifying person;

(b)   up to 2 points depending on the number of the scriptwriters who are qualifying persons as follows–
  (i)   if there is only one scriptwriter, 2 points if he is a qualifying person,
  (ii)   if there are only two scriptwriters, 2 points if both of them are qualifying persons, 1 point if one of them is,
  (iii) if there are only three scriptwriters, 2 points if two or more of them are qualifying persons, 1 point if one of them is,
  (iv)   if there are more than three scriptwriters, 2 points if two or more of the three lead scriptwriters are qualifying persons, 1 point if one of the three lead scriptwriters is a qualifying person;

(c)   1 point if at least one of the producers (or, if there are more than three, of the three lead producers) is a qualifying person;

(d)   1 point if the composer (or, if there is more than one, the lead composer) is a qualifying person;

(e)   up to 2 points depending on the number of the actors who are qualifying persons as follows–
  (i)   if there are more than three actors, 2 points if two or more of the three lead actors are qualifying persons, 1 point if one of the three lead actors is a qualifying person,

(ii)   if there are only three actors, 2 points if two or more of them are qualifying persons, 1 point if one of them is,

(iii)   if there are only two actors, 2 points if both of them are qualifying persons, 1 point if one of them is,

(iv)   if there is only one actor, 2 points if he is a qualifying person;

(f)   1 point if at least 50% of the cast are qualifying persons;

(g)   up to 3 points depending on the number of the heads of department who are qualifying persons as follows–

     (i)   3 points for five or more,

     (ii)   2 points for three or four,

     (iii)   1 point for one or two;

(h)   1 point if at least 50% of the production crew are qualifying persons.

4B(1)   The cultural test for a documentary is as follows.

4B(2)   A film passes the cultural test if it is awarded at least 16 points in total.

4B(3)   Up to 4 points shall be awarded in respect of the content of the film as follows–

(a)   1 point if at least 50% of the film is set in the United Kingdom;

(b)   1 point if at least one of the three principal characters depicted in the film (or, if there are three or fewer characters depicted in the film, any of them) is a British character;

(c)   1 point if the film depicts a British story;

(d)   1 point if at least 50% of the original dialogue is recorded in the English language or in a recognised regional or minority language.

4B(4)   Up to 15 points shall be awarded in respect of work carried out in the making of the film as follows–

(a)   up to 6 points depending on the percentage of the work on shooting and visual effects that is carried out in the United Kingdom as follows–

     (i)   6 points for 75%,

     (ii)   5 points for 62.5%,

     (iii)   4 points for 50%,

     (iv)   3 points for 37.5%,

     (v)   2 points for 25%,

     (vi)   1 point for 10%;

(b)   up to 4 points depending on the percentage of the work on research and development that is carried out in the United Kingdom as follows–

     (i)   4 points for 75%,

     (ii)   3 points for 50%,

     (iii)   2 points for 25%,

     (iv)   1 point for 10%;

(c)   1 point if at least 75% of the work on special effects is carried out in the United Kingdom;

(d)   up to 2 points depending on the percentage of the work on performing and recording the original music score created for the film that is carried out in the United Kingdom as follows–

     (i)   2 points for 75%,

     (ii)   1 point for 50%;

(e)   1 point if at least 75% of the work on audio post production is carried out in the United Kingdom;

(f)   1 point if at least 75% of the work on image processing is carried out in the United Kingdom.

4B(5)   Up to 13 points shall be awarded in respect of the personnel involved in the making of the film as follows–

(a)   2 points if the director (or, if there is more than one, the lead director) is a qualifying person;

(b)   up to 2 points depending on the number of the scriptwriters who are qualifying persons as follows–

     (i)   if there is only one scriptwriter, 2 points if he is a qualifying person,

(ii)   if there are only two scriptwriters, 2 points if both of them are qualifying persons, 1 point if one of them is,

(iii)   if there are only three scriptwriters, 2 points if two or more of them are qualifying persons, 1 point if one of them is;

(iv)   if there are more than three scriptwriters, 2 points if two or more of the three lead scriptwriters are qualifying persons, 1 point if one of the three lead scriptwriters is a qualifying person;

(c)   1 point if at least one of the producers (or, if there are more than three, of the three lead producers) is a qualifying person;

(d)   1 point if the composer (or, if there is more than one, the lead composer) is a qualifying person;

(e)   up to 2 points depending on the number of the participants who are qualifying persons as follows–

     (i)   if there are more than three participants, 2 points if two or more of the three lead participants are qualifying persons, 1 point if one of the three lead participants is a qualifying person,

     (ii)   if there are only three participants, 2 points if two or more of them are qualifying persons, 1 point if one of them is,

     (iii)   if there are only two participants, 2 points if both of them are qualifying persons, 1 point if one of them is,

     (iv)   if there is only one participant, 2 points if he is a qualifying person;

(f)   1 point if at least 50% of all of the participants are qualifying persons;

(g)   up to 3 points depending on the number of the heads of department who are qualifying persons as follows–

     (i)   3 points for four,

     (ii)   2 points for three,

     (iii)   1 point for one or two;

(h)   1 point if at least 50% of the production crew are qualifying persons.

4C(1)   The cultural test for an animation is as follows.

4C(2)   A film passes the cultural test if it is awarded at least 16 points in total.

4C(3)   Up to 4 points shall be awarded in respect of the content of the film as follows–

(a)   1 point if at least 50% of the film is set in the United Kingdom;

(b)   1 point if at least one of the three principal characters depicted in the film (or, if there are three or fewer characters depicted in the film, any of them) is a British character;

(c)   1 point if the film depicts a British story;

(d)   1 point if at least 50% of the original dialogue is recorded in the English language or in a recognised regional or minority language.

4C(4)   Up to 15 points shall be awarded in respect of work carried out in the making of the film as follows–

(a)   up to 6 points depending on the percentage of the work on shooting, visual design, layout and storyboarding that is carried out in the United Kingdom as follows–

     (i)   6 points for 75%,

     (ii)   5 points for 62.5%,

     (iii)   4 points for 50%,

     (iv)   3 points for 37.5%,

     (v)   2 points for 25%,

     (vi)   1 point for 10%;

(b)   up to 4 points depending on the percentage of the work on visual effects that is carried out in the United Kingdom as follows–

     (i)   4 points for 75%,

     (ii)   3 points for 50%,

     (iii)   2 points for 25%,

     (iv)   1 point for 10%;

(c)   1 point if at least 75% of the work on special effects is carried out in the United Kingdom;

(d)   up to 2 points depending on the percentage of the work on performing and recording the original music score created for the film that is carried out in the United Kingdom as follows–
> (i)   2 points for 75%,
>
> (ii)   1 point for 50%;

(e)   1 point if at least 75% of the work on voice recording and audio post production is carried out in the United Kingdom;

(f)   1 point if at least 75% of the work on image processing is carried out in the United Kingdom.

4C(5)   Up to 13 points shall be awarded in respect of the personnel involved in the making of the film as follows–

(a)   2 points if the director (or, if there is more than one, the lead director) is a qualifying person;

(b)   up to 2 points depending on the number of the scriptwriters who are qualifying persons as follows–
> (i)   if there is only one scriptwriter, 2 points if he is a qualifying person,
>
> (ii)   if there are only two scriptwriters, 2 points if both of them are qualifying persons, 1 point if one of them is,
>
> (iii)   if there are only three scriptwriters, 2 points if two or more of them are qualifying persons, 1 point if one of them is,
>
> (iv)   if there are more than three scriptwriters, 2 points if two or more of the three lead scriptwriters are qualifying persons, 1 point if one of the three lead scriptwriters is a qualifying person;

(c)   1 point if at least one of the producers (or, if there are more than three, of the three lead producers) is a qualifying person;

(d)   1 point if the composer (or, if there is more than one, the lead composer) is a qualifying person;

(e)   up to 2 points depending on the number of the actors who are qualifying persons as follows–
> (i)   if there are more than three actors, 2 points if two or more of the three lead actors are qualifying persons, 1 point if one of the three lead actors is a qualifying person,
>
> (ii)   if there are only three actors, 2 points if two or more of them are qualifying persons, 1 point if one of them is,
>
> (iii)   if there are only two actors, 2 points if both of them are qualifying persons, 1 point if one of them is,
>
> (iv)   if there is only one actor, 2 points if he is a qualifying person;

(f)   1 point if at least 50% of the cast are qualifying persons;

(g)   up to 3 points depending on the number of the heads of department who are qualifying persons as follows–
> (i)   3 points for five or more,
>
> (ii)   2 points for three or four,
>
> (iii)   1 point for one or two;

4D(1)   In paragraphs 4A to 4C–

"cast" means all the actors and performers but not the extras who appear in a film;

"heads of department" has the meaning given by sub-paragraph (2);

"participant" means a presenter, narrator, subject or other person who participates and appears in a documentary;

"production crew" means all the persons directly involved in the production of a film who do not appear in the film;

"qualifying person" means a citizen of, or a person ordinarily resident in, a member State;

"recognised regional or minority language" means Welsh, Scottish-Gaelic, Irish, Scots, Ulster Scots or Cornish;

"special effects" means artificial techniques or processes, which are not visual effects, used to create an illusion in a film;

"visual effects" means digital alterations to a film's images.

4D(2)   **"Heads of department"** means–

(a)   in paragraph 4A, the lead cinematographer, the lead production designer, the lead costume designer, the lead editor, the lead sound designer, the lead visual effects supervisor and the lead hair and makeup supervisor;

(b)   in paragraph 4B, the lead cameraman, the lead sound recordist, the lead editor and the lead researcher;

(c)   in paragraph 4C, the lead layout supervisor, the lead production designer, the lead character designer, the lead editor, the lead sound designer, the lead visual effects supervisor and the lead modelling supervisor.

4D(3)   For the purposes of paragraphs 4A to 4C–

(a)   a film is set in the United Kingdom if it is set in a country which is now part of the United Kingdom; and

(b)   a film depicts a British story if the subject matter of the film or the underlying material on which the film is based is British.

4D(4)   The amount of work that is carried out in the United Kingdom or elsewhere shall be determined–

(a)   for the purposes of paragraph 4A(4)(a) (principal photography), by reference to the number of days spent on the work;

(b)   for the purposes of paragraphs 4A(4)(b) to (f), 4B(4)(a) to (f) and 4C(4)(a) to (f) (other matters), by reference to the amount of expenditure on the work.

4D(5)   No points shall be awarded under any provision of paragraph 4A(4), 4B(4) or 4C(4) (points awarded in respect of the making of the film) in respect of work the expenditure on which is, in the opinion of the Secretary of State, insignificant in relation to the expenditure on all the work carried out in the making of the film."

5   Omit paragraphs 6 (ascertainment of labour costs and playing time), 7 (determination of requisite amount of labour costs) and 8 (power of Secretary of State to direct alteration of labour costs).

LOAN RELATIONSHIPS AND DERIVATIVE CONTRACTS (DISREGARD AND BRINGING INTO ACCOUNT OF PROFITS AND LOSSES) REGULATIONS 2006

(SI 2006/843 as amended by SI 2006/936 and revoked by FA 2009, s. 43 and Sch. 21, para. 10)

Made on 21 March 2006 by the Treasury in exercise of the powers conferred upon them by s. 84A(3A) of the Finance Act 1996 and para. 16(3A) and 17C(1) of Sch. 26 to the Finance Act 2002. Operative from 22 March 2006.

Notes – SI 2006/843 revoked by FA 2009, s. 43 and Sch. 21, para. 10, with effect in relation to exchange gains and losses arising in accounting periods beginning on or after 22 April 2009 (subject to provisions of FA 2009, Sch. 21, para. 11(2)–(5). Former SI 2006/843 read as follows:

CITATION, COMMENCEMENT AND EFFECT

1(1) These Regulations may be cited as the Loan Relationships and Derivative Contracts (Disregard and Bringing into Account of Profits and Losses) Regulations 2006, and shall come into force on 22nd March 2006.

1(2) These Regulations have effect in relation to accounting periods ending on or after 22nd March 2006.

1(3) But these Regulations do not have effect where a company ceased to be party to a loan relationship or derivative contract before 22nd March 2006.

INTERPRETATION

2(1) In these Regulations–

"**for accounting purposes**" means for the purposes of accounts drawn up in accordance with generally accepted accounting practice, and "**generally accepted accounting practice**" has the meaning given by section 50 of the Finance Act 2004;

"**derivative contract**" has the same meaning as in Schedule 26 to the Finance Act 2002;

"**hedged item**" is to be construed in accordance with regulation 3;

"**hedging instrument**" is to be construed in accordance with regulation 3;

"**hedging relationship**" is to be construed in accordance with regulation 3;

"**underlying subject matter**" has the same meaning as in Schedule 26 to the Finance Act 2002.

2(2) In these Regulations "**designated**", "**effective hedge**", "**firm commitment**", "**forecast transaction**", "**foreign operation**" and "**net investment in a foreign operation**" have the same meaning as for accounting purposes.

2(3) For the purposes of these Regulations two companies are treated as being in the same group if there is a connection between the two companies within the meaning given by section 87 of the Finance Act 1996 (accounting method where parties have a connection).

INTERPRETATION OF "HEDGING RELATIONSHIP" AND RELATED EXPRESSIONS

3(1) For the purposes of these Regulations, a company has a hedging relationship between a derivative contract or a liability representing a loan relationship on the one hand ("the hedging instrument") and an asset, liability, receipt or expense on the other ("the hedged item") if and to the extent that–

(a)   the hedging instrument and the hedged item are designated by the company as a hedge; or

(b)   in any other case the hedging instrument is intended to act as a hedge of–

(i)   the exposure to changes in fair value of a hedged item which is a recognised asset or liability or an unrecognised firm commitment or an identified portion of such an asset, liability or commitment that is attributable to a particular risk and could affect profit or loss of the company;

Statutory Instruments

      (ii)   the exposure to variability in cash flows that is attributable to a particular risk associated with a hedged item that is a recognised asset or liability or a forecast transaction and could affect profit or loss of a company; or

      (iii) a net investment in a foreign operation of the company.

3(2) In these Regulations–

(a)   any reference to a hedging instrument includes a reference to part of an instrument; and

(b)   any reference to a hedged item includes a reference to part of a hedged item.

DISALLOWANCE OF CERTAIN EXCHANGE LOSSES WHERE OBLIGATIONS MAY BE SETTLED IN MORE THAN ONE CURRENCY

4(1) This regulation applies to an exchange loss arising to a company if–

(a)   the exchange loss arises–

      (i)   in relation to an asset or liability representing a loan relationship of the company, or

      (ii) in relation to a derivative contract whose underlying subject matter consists wholly or partly of currency, and

(b)   conditions A to D are met.

4(2) Condition A is that the company is party to one or more loan relationships or derivative contracts ("the specified instruments").

4(3) Condition B is that another company in the same group ("company Y") has a net investment in a foreign operation.

4(4) Condition C is that if the assets constituting the net investment were held instead by the company, it is likely that there would be a hedging relationship (with the specified instruments constituting the hedging instrument and the net investment constituting the hedged item).

4(5) Condition D is that there are arrangements in place such that–

(a)   the arrangements are represented by any combination of loan relationships and derivative contracts ("the arrangement instruments");

(b)   company Y is a party to at least one of the arrangement instruments; and

(c)   company Y, or another company that is party to the arrangements, can, by exercising an option included in the terms of any arrangement instrument or otherwise, determine that an exchange gain or loss that would arise, but for the company's ability to determine otherwise, does not arise.

4(6) For the purposes of section 84A(3A) of the Finance Act 1996 there is prescribed any exchange loss arising to the company in relation to any of the specified instruments representing a loan relationship of the company to the extent that existing unallowable purposes rules do not apply.

4(7) For the purposes of paragraph 16(3A) to Schedule 26 to the Finance Act 2002 there is prescribed any exchange loss arising to the company in relation to any derivative contract which is one of the specified instruments to the extent that existing unallowable purposes rules do not apply.

4(8) In this regulation **"existing unallowable purposes rules"** means the rules specified in–

(a)   paragraph 13 of Schedule 9 to the Finance Act 1996 (loan relationships for unallowable purposes), and

(b)   paragraph 23 of Schedule 26 to the Finance Act 2002 (derivative contracts for unallowable purposes).

DISALLOWANCE OF CERTAIN LOSSES ARISING ON DERIVATIVE CONTRACTS

5(1) This regulation applies if there is an arrangement where conditions A to D are met.

5(2) Condition A is that a company is party to two or more derivative contracts under the arrangement to hedge a currency risk.

5(3) Condition B is that those derivative contracts are intended, when taken together, to act as a hedge of that currency risk.

5(4) Condition C is that the arrangements are such that–

(a)   if a profit arises on at least one of those derivative contracts, that profit would fall within paragraph 16(3) of Schedule 26 to the Finance Act 2002, and

(b)   if a loss arises on at least one of those derivative contracts, that loss would not fall within paragraph 16(3) of Schedule 26 to the Finance Act 2002.

5(5) Condition D is that a loss to which paragraph (4)(b) applies arises under a derivative contract which is an option.

5(6) The amount of the loss arising on the derivative contract mentioned in paragraph (5) is not to be recognised in determining the company's profit or loss for any period.

History – Reg. 5 substituted by SI 2006/936, reg. 2, with effect in relation to accounting periods ending on or after 22 March 2006, in the case of accounting periods beginning on or after 1 January 2006, and in relation to accounting periods ending on or after 9 March 2006 in any other case.

AUTHORISED INVESTMENT FUNDS (TAX) REGULATIONS 2006

(SI 2006/964, as amended by SI 2006/3239, SI 2007/683, SI 2007/794, SI 2008/705, SI 2008/1463, SI 2008/3159, SI 2009/56, CTA 2009, SI 2009/2036, SI 2010/294, CTA 2010, SI 2010/1642, SI 2011/244, SI 2011/2192, SI 2012/519, SI 2012/1783, SI 2012/3043, 2013/1400, SI 2013/1411, SI 2013/1772, SI 2013/2819, SI 2013/2994, SI 2014/518 and SI 2014/685)

Made on 29 March 2006 by the Treasury, in exercise of the powers conferred upon them by s. 17(3) and 18 of the Finance (No. 2) Act 2005 and s. 152 of the Finance Act 1995. Operative from 1 April 2006.

ARRANGEMENT OF REGULATIONS

PART 2B – DIVERSELY OWNED AIFS

PART 3 – DISTRIBUTIONS MADE BY AUTHORISED INVESTMENT FUNDS

PART 4 – THE TREATMENT OF PARTICIPANTS IN AUTHORISED INVESTMENT FUNDS

REGULATION

PART 4A – PROPERTY AIFS

REGULATION

PART 1 – PRELIMINARY PROVISIONS AND INTERPRETATION

PRELIMINARY PROVISIONS

Citation, commencement and effect

1(1) These Regulations may be cited as the Authorised Investment Funds (Tax) Regulations 2006, and shall come into force on 1st April 2006.

1(2) These Regulations have effect–

Statutory Instruments

(a)　　for the purposes of income tax—

　　　(i)　　for the tax year 2006–07 and subsequent tax years, and

　　　(ii)　　for distributions made on or after 6th April 2006;

(b)　　for the purposes of corporation tax—

　　　(i)　　on income, for accounting periods beginning on or after 1st April 2006,

　　　(ii)　　on chargeable gains, in relation to disposals made on or after 1st April 2006, and

　　　(iii)　　for distributions made on or after 1st April 2006; and

(c)　　for the purposes of capital gains tax, in relation to disposals made on or after 6th April 2006.

1(3)　　[Revoked by SI 2007/794, reg. 8(a).]

History – Reg. 1(3) revoked by SI 2007/794, reg. 8(a), with effect from 6 April 2007.

Structure of these Regulations

2　　The structure of these Regulations is as follows—

　　this Part contains preliminary provisions and provides for interpretation;

　　Part 1A deals with the genuine diversity of ownership condition;

　　Part 2 deals with the tax treatment of authorised investment funds;

　　Part 2A deals with qualified investor schemes;

　　Part 2B deals with diversely owned AIFs;

　　Part 3 deals with distributions made by authorised investment funds;

　　Part 4 deals with the treatment of participants in authorised investment funds;

　　Part 4A deals with Property AIFs;

　　Part 4B deals with Tax Elected Funds;

　　Part 5 deals with compliance;

　　Part 6 contains further provisions relating to authorised investment funds;

　　Part 6A contains provisions relating to Funds Investing in Non-Reporting Offshore Funds (FINROFs);

　　Part 7 contains consequential amendments and modifications of enactments; and

　　Part 8 contains final provisions.

History – In reg. 2, the words "Part 6A contains provisions relating to Funds Investing in Non-Reporting Offshore Funds (FINROFs);" inserted by SI 2010/294, reg. 3, with effect from 6 March 2010.
In reg. 2, the words "Part 1A deals with the genuine diversity of ownership condition;" inserted by SI 2009/2036, reg. 3(a), with effect from 1 September 2009.
In reg. 2, the words "Part 2A deals with qualified investor schemes" inserted by SI 2008/3159, reg. 4, with effect from 1 January 2009, subject to the transitional rules in SI 2008/3159, reg. 1(2), 30 and 31.
In reg. 2, the words "Part 2B deals with diversely owned AIFs;" inserted by SI 2009/2036, reg. 3(b), with effect from 1 September 2009.
In reg. 2, the words "Part 4A deals with Property AIFs;" inserted by SI 2008/705, reg. 3, with effect from 6 April 2008.
In reg. 2, the words "Part 4B deals with Tax Elected Funds;" inserted by SI 2009/2036, reg. 3(c), with effect from 1 September 2009.

INTERPRETATION

Definition of "authorised investment funds"

3　　In these Regulations **"authorised investment funds"** means—

(a)　　open-ended investment companies, and

(b)　　authorised unit trust schemes.

Definition of "open-ended investment company"

4　　In these Regulations "open-ended investment company" means a company incorporated in the United Kingdom to which section 236 of FISMA 2000 applies.

Interpretation of expressions relating to authorised unit trust schemes

5(1)　　In these Regulations **"unit trust scheme"** has the meaning given by section 237 of FISMA 2000.

5(2)　　For the purposes of these Regulations a unit trust scheme is authorised in relation to an accounting period if an order under section 243 of FISMA 2000 is in force in relation to that scheme during the whole or part of that accounting period.

5(3)　　In these Regulations **"unit holder"** means a person entitled to a share of the investments subject to the trusts of a unit trust scheme.

Further definitions generally relevant for authorised investment funds

6(1) In these Regulations the **"legal owner"** means–

(a) in relation to an open-ended investment company, the open-ended investment company, and

(b) in relation to an authorised unit trust, the trustees of the trust.

6(2) In these Regulations the **"scheme property"** means–

(a) in relation to an open-ended investment company, the property subject to the collective investment scheme constituted by the company, and

(b) in relation to an authorised unit trust, the property subject to the collective investment scheme constituted by the trust.

6(3) In these Regulations the **"manager"** means–

(a) in relation to an open-ended investment company, the authorised corporate director, and

(b) in relation to an authorised unit trust, the person who is the manager of the trust for the purposes of Chapter 3 of Part 17 of FISMA 2000 (authorised unit trust schemes).

6(4) In these Regulations, unless a contrary intention appears, **"units"** means the rights or interests (however described) of the participants in the authorised investment fund.

6(5) In these Regulations **"accumulation unit"** means–

(a) in relation to an open-ended investment company, a share in the company in respect of which income is credited periodically to the capital part of the scheme property of the company, and

(b) in relation to an authorised unit trust, a unit in the trust in respect of which income is credited periodically to the capital part of the scheme property of the trust.

6(6) In these Regulations a **"participant"**, in relation to an authorised investment fund, means a beneficial owner of units in the fund, except where the units are held on trust (other than a bare trust) or are comprised in the estate of a deceased person, and in such a case the participant, in relation to the fund, means the trustees of the trust, or, as the case may be, the deceased's personal representatives.

6(7) In these Regulations **"instrument constituting the fund"** means–

(a) in relation to an open-ended investment company, the instrument of incorporation, and

(b) in relation to an authorised unit trust scheme, the trust deed.

6(8) In these Regulations **"genuine diversity of ownership condition"** has the meaning given by regulation 9A.

History – Reg. 6(7) inserted by SI 2009/2036, reg. 4, with effect from 1 September 2009.
Reg. 6(8) inserted by SI 2009/2036, reg. 4, with effect from 1 September 2009.

Umbrella companies and umbrella schemes: interpretation

7(1) In these Regulations **"umbrella company"** has the meaning given by section 468A(4) of ICTA, and a reference to a part of an umbrella company is to be construed in accordance with that provision.

7(2) For the purposes of these Regulations each of the parts of an umbrella company is regarded as an open-ended investment company and the umbrella company as a whole shall not be so regarded.

7(3) In relation to a part of an umbrella company, any reference–

(a) to investments or to scheme property of an open-ended investment company has effect as a reference to such of the investments or to such of the scheme property as under the arrangements form part of the separate pool to which that part of the umbrella company relates, and

(b) a person for the time being having rights in that part is regarded as the owner of shares in the open-ended investment company which that part is regarded as being by virtue of paragraph (2), and not as the owner of shares in the umbrella company itself.

7(4) In relation to a part of an umbrella company, any references in these Regulations to the instrument of incorporation or the prospectus in issue for the time being of an open-ended investment company have effect, for the purposes of these Regulations, as references to such parts of the instrument of incorporation or of that prospectus as apply to that part of the umbrella company.

7(5) In these Regulations **"umbrella scheme"** has the meaning given by section 468(8) of ICTA, and a reference to a part of an umbrella scheme is to be construed in accordance with that provision.

7(6) For the purposes of these Regulations each of the parts of an umbrella scheme is regarded as an authorised unit trust and the umbrella scheme as a whole is not regarded as an authorised unit trust or as any other form of collective investment scheme.

7(7) In relation to a part of an umbrella scheme, any reference–

(a)   to investments or to scheme property subject to the trusts of an authorised unit trust has effect as a reference to such of the investments or to such of the scheme property as under the arrangements form part of the separate pool to which that part of the umbrella scheme relates, and

(b)   to a unit holder, has effect as a reference to a person for the time being having rights in that separate pool.

7(8)   In relation to a part of an umbrella scheme, any references in these Regulations to the prospectus in issue for the time being of an authorised unit trust have effect, for the purposes of these Regulations, as references to such parts of that prospectus as apply to that part of the umbrella scheme.

History – In reg. 7(4), the words "(including any supplements to that prospectus)" omitted twice by SI 2010/294, reg. 23(1), with effect from 6 March 2010.

In reg. 7(8), the words "(including any supplements to that prospectus)" omitted twice by SI 2010/294, reg. 23(1), with effect from 6 March 2010.

General interpretation

8   In these Regulations–

"authorised corporate director", in relation to an open-ended investment company, means a corporate director of the company acting in the capacity as the director having responsibility for the management of its scheme property, being an authorised person within the meaning given by section 31(2) of FISMA 2000, or if there is no such director, the person for the time being having responsibility for the management of the scheme property of the company and acting in that capacity;

"collective investment scheme" has the meaning given by section 235 of FISMA 2000;

the **"Commissioners"** means the Commissioners for Revenue and Customs;

"connected person" has the meaning given in–

(a)   sections 993 and 994 of ITA 2007 (connected persons) in the case of a person chargeable to income tax, and

(b)   section 839 of ICTA (connected persons) in the case of a person chargeable to corporation tax;

"creditor relationship" has the meaning given by section 103(1) of FA 1996;

"derivative contract" means–

(a)   a contract which is a derivative contract within the meaning of Schedule 26 to FA 2002, or

(b)   a contract which is, in the accounting period in question, treated as if it were a derivative contract by virtue of paragraph 36 of that Schedule (contracts relating to holdings in unit trust schemes, open-ended investment companies and offshore funds);

"investments" do not include cash awaiting investment;

"net asset value" means the value of the assets of the authorised investment fund, after the deduction of specified liabilities;

"non-reporting fund" has the same meaning as in regulation 4(2) of the Offshore Funds Regulations;

"offshore fund" means a fund within the meaning of section 355 of the Taxation (International and Other Provisions) Act 2010;

"Offshore Funds Regulations" means the Offshore Funds (Tax) Regulations 2009;

"owner of shares", in relation to an open-ended investment company, means a beneficial owner of shares in the company, except where the shares are held on trust (other than a bare trust) or are comprised in the estate of a deceased person, and in such a case the owner of shares, in relation to the company, means the trustees of the trust, or, as the case may be, the deceased's personal representatives;

"prospectus" includes a proposed prospectus, supplements to a prospectus and supplements to a proposed prospectus;

"reportable income" has the same meaning as in Chapter 5 of Part 3 of the Offshore Funds Regulations;

"reporting date" means the final day of each annual and each half-yearly accounting period of the authorised investment fund;

"reporting fund" means an offshore fund to which Part 3 of the Offshore Funds Regulations applies;

"residence declaration" is to be construed in accordance with regulation 31;

"**Statement of Recommended Practice**" means, in relation to any accounting period for which it is required or permitted to be used, the Statement of Recommended Practice relating to authorised investment funds issued by the Investment Management Association in November 2008;

"**tax year**"–

(a) in relation to income tax, means a year of assessment within the meaning of ICTA (see section 832(1) of that Act), and

(b) in relation to capital gains tax, means a year of assessment within the meaning of TCGA 1992 (see section 288(1) of that Act).

"**tribunal**" means the First-tier Tribunal or, where determined by or under Tribunal Procedure Rules, the Upper Tribunal.

History – In reg. 8, definition of "connected person" inserted by SI 2009/2036, reg. 5, with effect from 1 September 2009.
In reg. 8, the definition of "non-reporting fund" inserted by SI 2011/244, reg. 3(2), with effect (subject to transitional provisions in SI 2011/244, reg. 8): for the purposes of corporation tax on income, for accounting periods ending on or after 6 March 2011; and for the purposes of corporation tax on chargeable gains and of capital gains tax, in relation to disposals made on or after 6 March 2011.
In reg. 8, the definition of "offshore fund" inserted by SI 2011/244, reg. 3(2), with effect (subject to transitional provisions in SI 2011/244, reg. 8): for the purposes of corporation tax on income, for accounting periods ending on or after 6 March 2011; and for the purposes of corporation tax on chargeable gains and of capital gains tax, in relation to disposals made on or after 6 March 2011.
In reg. 8, the definition of "Offshore Funds Regulations" inserted by SI 2011/244, reg. 3(2), with effect (subject to transitional provisions in SI 2011/244, reg. 8): for the purposes of corporation tax on income, for accounting periods ending on or after 6 March 2011; and for the purposes of corporation tax on chargeable gains and of capital gains tax, in relation to disposals made on or after 6 March 2011.
In reg. 8, the definition of "prospectus" inserted by SI 2010/294, reg. 4, with effect from 6 March 2010.
In reg. 8, the definition of "reportable income" inserted by SI 2011/244, reg. 3(3), with effect (subject to transitional provisions in SI 2011/244, reg. 8): for the purposes of corporation tax on income, for accounting periods ending on or after 6 March 2011; and for the purposes of corporation tax on chargeable gains and of capital gains tax, in relation to disposals made on or after 6 March 2011.
In reg. 8, the definition of "reporting fund" inserted by SI 2011/244, reg. 3(4), with effect (subject to transitional provisions in SI 2011/244, reg. 8): for the purposes of corporation tax on income, for accounting periods ending on or after 6 March 2011; and for the purposes of corporation tax on chargeable gains and of capital gains tax, in relation to disposals made on or after 6 March 2011.
In reg. 8, the definition of "Statement of Recommended Practice" inserted by SI 2010/294, reg. 4, with effect from 6 March 2010.
In reg. 8, definition of "tribunal" inserted by SI 2009/56, art. 3(2) and Sch. 2, para. 155, operative from 1 April 2009 subject to transitional and saving provisions in SI 2009/56, Sch. 3

Abbreviations and general index

9(1) The Schedule to these Regulations (which contains abbreviations and defined expressions that apply for the purposes of these Regulations) has effect.

9(2) Part 1 of the Schedule gives the meaning of the abbreviated references to Acts used in these Regulations.

9(3) Part 2 of the Schedule lists the places where expressions used in these Regulations are defined or otherwise explained–

(a) in these Regulations for the purposes of these Regulations, or

(b) in these Regulations for the purposes of a Part or Chapter of these Regulations.

PART 1A – THE GENUINE DIVERSITY OF OWNERSHIP CONDITION

History – Pt. 1A inserted by SI 2009/2036, reg. 6, with effect from 1 September 2009.

THE GENUINE DIVERSITY OF OWNERSHIP CONDITION

9A(1) For the purposes of these Regulations, the genuine diversity of ownership condition is as follows.

9A(2) The genuine diversity of ownership condition is that an authorised investment fund must–

(a) meet conditions A to C throughout the accounting period; or

(b) comply with paragraph (8).

9A(3) Condition A is that the fund documents–

(a) contain a statement that units in the fund will be widely available,

(b) specify the intended categories of investor, and

(c) specify that the manager of the fund must market and make available the units in the fund in accordance with paragraph 9A(6)(a).

9A(4) Condition B is that neither–

(a)   the specification of the intended categories of investor, nor

(b)   any other terms or conditions governing participation in the fund, whether or not specified in the fund documents,

have a limiting or deterring effect.

9A(5)   In paragraph (4) a limiting or deterring effect means an effect which–

(a)   limits investors to a limited number of specific persons or specific groups of connected persons, or

(b)   deters a reasonable investor within the intended categories of investor from investing in the fund.

9A(6)   Condition C is that–

(a)   units in the fund must be marketed and made available–

  (i)   sufficiently widely to reach the intended categories of investors, and

  (ii)   in a manner appropriate to attract those categories of investors; and

(b)   a person who is in an intended category of investor can, upon request to the manager of the fund, obtain information about that fund and acquire units in it.

Condition C is subject to paragraph (7).

9A(7)   Condition C shall be treated as being met even if at the relevant time the fund has no capacity to receive additional investments, unless–

(a)   the capacity of the fund to receive investments in it is fixed by the fund documents (or otherwise), and

(b)   a pre-determined number of specific persons or specific groups of connected persons make investments in the fund which collectively exhausts all, or substantially all, of that capacity.

9A(8)   An authorised investment fund also meets the genuine diversity of ownership condition if–

(a)   an investor in the fund is a unit trust scheme, an offshore fund or another authorised investment fund (a "feeder fund");

(b)   conditions A to C are met in relation to the authorised investment fund after taking into account–

  (i)   the fund documents relating to the feeder fund, and

  (ii)   the intended investors in the feeder fund; and

(c)   the authorised investment fund and the feeder fund have the same manager (or proposed manager).

9A(9)   In this Part **"fund documents"** means–

(a)   the instrument constituting the fund, and

(b)   the fund's prospectus in issue for the time being.

History – In reg. 9A(8), in the introductory wording, the words "which is a Property AIF", which appeared after "An authorised investment fund", omitted by SI 2011/2192, reg. 3(a), with effect: for the purposes of corporation tax on income, for accounting periods starting on or after 1 October 2011; and, for the purposes of corporation tax on chargeable gains or capital gains tax, in relation to disposals made on or after 1 October 2011.
In reg. 9A(8)(a), the words ", an offshore fund or another authorised investment fund" inserted by SI 2011/2192, reg. 3(b), with effect: for the purposes of corporation tax on income, for accounting periods starting on or after 1 October 2011; and, for the purposes of corporation tax on chargeable gains or capital gains tax, in relation to disposals made on or after 1 October 2011.
In reg. 9A(9)(b), the words "(including any supplements to the prospectus)" omitted by SI 2010/294, reg. 23(2), with effect from 6 March 2010.
Reg. 9A inserted by SI 2009/2036, reg. 6, with effect from 1 September 2009.

CLEARANCE IN RELATION TO THE GENUINE DIVERSITY OF OWNERSHIP CONDITION

9B(1)   An application for clearance that an authorised investment fund meets the genuine diversity of ownership condition (see regulation 9A) may be made in writing to the Commissioners by the manager (or proposed manager) of an authorised investment fund.

9B(2)   An application for clearance must be accompanied by the fund documents in the form in which it is proposed that those documents will apply at the beginning of the first accounting period of the fund for which clearance is sought.

9B(3)   If regulation 9A(2)(b) and (8) applies, an application for clearance by the authorised investment fund must be accompanied by–

(a)   the documents specified in paragraph (2), and

(b)   the fund documents of the feeder fund in the form in which it is proposed that those documents will apply at the beginning of the first accounting period of the fund for which clearance is sought.

9B(4)   The Commissioners may require the manager (or proposed manager) to provide further particulars if they believe that full particulars of the fund have not been provided.

9B(5)   The Commissioners must notify the applicant within 28 days of the receipt of the particulars (or, if paragraph (4) applies, of all further particulars required) that they–

(a)   give clearance that the fund meets the genuine diversity of ownership condition,

(b)   give that clearance subject to conditions, or

(c)   refuse to give that clearance.

9B(6)   An authorised investment fund (and investors in that fund) may not rely on a clearance given under this regulation if–

(a)   at the beginning of the first accounting period of the fund to which the clearance relates (and at the beginning of each subsequent accounting period), a relevant statement in the fund documents in issue for the time being is not in accordance with a relevant statement in the documents considered by the Commissioners before giving clearance,

(b)   the fund acts or is operated in contravention of a relevant statement in the fund documents,

(c)   the fund documents are materially amended, or

(d)   the fund is operated otherwise than in accordance with condition C of the genuine diversity of ownership condition (see regulation 9A(6)).

9B(7)   If regulation 9A(2)(b) and (8) applies an authorised investment fund (and investors in that fund) may not rely on a clearance given under this regulation if any of sub-paragraphs (a) to (d) of paragraph (6) apply in relation to either the authorised investment fund or the feeder fund.

9B(8)   Paragraph (6)(c) does not apply if the manager of the fund has obtained a clearance given under this regulation which applies to the amendment.

9B(9)   For the purposes of paragraph (6)(c), a material amendment is one that may reasonably be construed as causing, or likely to cause, the fund to fail to meet the genuine diversity of ownership condition in relation to any accounting period.

History – Reg. 9B inserted by SI 2009/2036, reg. 6, with effect from 1 September 2009.

PART 2 – THE TAX TREATMENT OF AUTHORISED INVESTMENT FUNDS

LOAN RELATIONSHIPS AND DERIVATIVE CONTRACTS: EXCLUSION OF CAPITAL PROFITS, GAINS OR LOSSES

General rule for loan relationships: exclusion of capital profits, gains or losses

10(1)   This regulation applies if any profits, gains or losses arising to an authorised investment fund from a creditor relationship in an accounting period are capital profits, gains or losses.

10(2)   For the purposes of Chapter 2 of Part 4 of FA 1996 (loan relationships) those profits, gains or losses must not be brought into account as credits or debits.

10(3)   Regulation 12 explains what is meant by "capital profits, gains or losses" in the case of an authorised investment fund that prepares accounts in accordance with UK generally accepted accounting practice.

10(4)   This regulation is subject to regulation 14B (tax treatment of qualified investor schemes.

History – Reg. 10(4) inserted by SI 2008/3159, reg. 5, with effect from 1 January 2009, subject to the transitional rules in SI 2008/3159, reg. 1(2), 30 and 31.

General rule for derivative contracts: exclusion of capital profits, gains or losses

11(1)   This regulation applies if any profits, gains or losses arising to an authorised investment fund from a derivative contract in an accounting period are capital profits, gains or losses.

11(2)   For the purposes of Schedule 26 to FA 2002 (derivative contracts) those profits, gains or losses must not be brought into account as credits or debits.

11(3)   Regulation 12 explains what is meant by "capital profits, gains or losses" in the case of an authorised investment fund that prepares accounts in accordance with UK generally accepted accounting practice.

11(4)　This regulation is subject to regulation 14B (tax treatment of qualified investor schemes).

History – Reg. 11(4) inserted by SI 2008/3159, reg. 6, with effect from 1 January 2009, subject to the transitional rules in SI 2008/3159, reg. 1(2), 30 and 31.

Accounts prepared in accordance with UK generally accepted accounting practice

12(1)　In the case of an authorised investment fund that prepares accounts in accordance with UK generally accepted accounting practice, capital profits, gains or losses arising from a creditor relationship in an accounting period, or capital profits, gains or losses arising from a derivative contract in an accounting period, are such profits, gains or losses as fall to be dealt with under the heading "net capital gains/losses"

in the statement of total return for the accounting period.

12(2)　For the purposes of paragraph (1), the statement of total return for an accounting period is the statement of total return which, in accordance with the Statement of Recommended Practice used for the accounting period, must be included in the accounts contained in the annual report of the authorised investment fund which deals with the accounting period.

12(3)　[Omitted by SI 2010/294, reg. 5.]

History – In reg. 12(1), the words "the heading "net capital gains/losses"" substituted for the former wording by SI 2008/3159, reg. 7, with effect from 1 January 2009, subject to the transitional rules in SI 2008/3159, reg. 1(2), 30 and 31. The former wording was:
　　　"(a)　the heading "net gains/losses on investments during the period", or
　　　(b)　the heading "other gains/losses",".
Reg. 12(3) omitted by SI 2010/294, reg. 5, with effect from 6 March 2010. Former reg. 12(3) read as follows:
　　　"**12(3)**　For the purposes of paragraph (2), **"Statement of Recommended Practice"** means–
　　　(a)　in relation to any accounting period for which it is required or permitted to be used, the Statement of Recommended Practice relating to authorised investment funds issued by the Investment Management Association in December 2005, as from time to time modified, amended or revised; or
　　　(b)　in relation to any accounting period for which it is required or permitted to be used, any subsequent Statement of Recommended Practice relating to authorised investment funds, as from time to time modified, amended or revised."
In former reg. 12(3)(a) the words "in December 2005" substituted for "on 21st November 2003" by SI 2008/705, reg. 4, with effect from 6 April 2008.

LOAN RELATIONSHIPS: TREATMENT OF INTEREST DISTRIBUTIONS AND DEFICITS

Treatment of interest distributions for purposes of loan relationships

13(1)　Chapter 2 of Part 4 of FA 1996 (loan relationships) has effect in relation to an authorised investment fund and to an interest distribution paid by that fund as it would have effect if the interest distribution were interest payable on a loan to the authorised investment fund and were, accordingly, interest under a loan relationship to which the authorised investment fund were a party.

13(1A)　But paragraph (1) only applies to the extent that the interest distribution is derived from income in respect of which the legal owner is charged to corporation tax.

13(2)　For the purposes of these Regulations, an interest distribution is treated as paid if it is credited to the capital part of the scheme property of an authorised investment fund on behalf of a participant in respect of the participant's accumulation units.

13(3)　This regulation is subject to regulation 14 and regulation 14B (tax treatment of qualified investor schemes).

13(4)　In this regulation an **"interest distribution"** includes a TEF distribution (non-dividend) (see regulation 69Z61(3)).

History – Reg 13(1A) substituted by SI 2012/519, reg. 3, with effect in relation to any distribution made at or after 1.30 p.m. on 27 February 2012. Former reg. 13(1A) read as follows:
　　　"**13(1A)**　But paragraph (1) does not apply to the extent that the interest distribution is derived from franked investment income.".
Former reg. 13(1A) inserted by SI 2010/1642, reg. 3, with effect in relation to distributions made at or after 1.45 p.m. on 22 June 2010.
Reg. 13(4) inserted by SI 2009/2036, reg. 7, with effect from 1 September 2009.
In reg. 13(3), the words "and regulation 14B (tax treatment of qualified investor schemes)" inserted by SI 2008/3159, reg. 8, with effect from 1 January 2009, subject to the transitional rules in SI 2008/3159, reg. 1(2), 30 and 31.

Treatment of deficits on loan relationships

14　Section 83(2)(c) of FA 1996 (carrying back of non-trading deficit on loan relationships) shall not have effect in relation to the loan relationships of an authorised investment fund (so that, accordingly, if for any accounting period there is a deficit on the loan relationships of the authorised investment fund, the deficit may not be carried back to be set off against profits for earlier accounting periods). This is subject to regulation 14B (tax treatment of qualified investor schemes).

History – In reg. 14, the words "This is subject to regulation 14B (tax treatment of qualified investor schemes)" inserted by SI 2008/3159, reg. 9, with effect from 1 January 2009, subject to the transitional rules in SI 2008/3159, reg. 1(2), 30 and 31.

AUTHORISED INVESTMENT FUNDS HAVING INTERESTS IN OFFSHORE NON-REPORTING FUNDS

Interests in offshore non-reporting funds: general

14ZA(1)   Regulation 14ZB applies if—

(a)   an authorised investment fund disposes of an asset which is an interest in a non-reporting fund ("the asset"); and

(b)   the conditions in paragraph (2) are satisfied for the period beginning with the date on which the authorised investment fund acquired the asset and ending on the date of the disposal.

14ZA(2)   The conditions are that—

(a)   the authorised investment fund has access to the accounts of the non-reporting fund,

(b)   the authorised investment fund had sufficient information about the non-reporting fund referred to in paragraph (1)(a) to enable it to prepare computations of reportable income for the non-reporting fund for every accounting period which, if the non-reporting fund were a reporting fund, would be a reporting period ending within the period mentioned in paragraph (1)(b),

(c)   the authorised investment fund has prepared such computations, and

(d)   any excess of the authorised investment fund's share of the reportable income of the non-reporting fund over the authorised investment fund's share of the distributions made by the non-reporting fund is included in the amount available for income allocation by the authorised investment fund for each reporting period of the authorised investment fund which falls within the period mentioned in paragraph (1)(b).

14ZA(3)   An authorised investment fund has an interest in a non-reporting fund if and to the extent that it has an interest in such a fund for the purposes of the Offshore Funds Regulations.

14ZA(4)   For the purposes of the computations mentioned in paragraph (2)(b), regulation 80 of the Offshore Funds Regulations applies if (and only if) the non-reporting fund is a UCITS fund.

14ZA(5)   In this regulation, **"UCITS fund"** has the same meaning as in regulation 12 of the Offshore Funds Regulations and **"reporting period"** has the same meaning as in regulation 91 of those Regulations.

History – Reg. 14ZA and the two headings before it inserted by SI 2011/244, reg. 4, with effect (subject to transitional provisions in SI 2011/244, reg. 8): for the purposes of corporation tax on income, for accounting periods ending on or after 6 March 2011; and for the purposes of corporation tax on chargeable gains and of capital gains tax, in relation to disposals made on or after 6 March 2011.

Treatment of disposal of interest in non-reporting fund

14ZB   No tax shall be charged on the authorised investment fund under regulation 17 of the Offshore Funds Regulations on the disposal by the authorised investment fund of an asset which is an interest in a non-reporting fund at the time of the disposal.

History – Reg. 14ZB and the heading before it inserted by SI 2011/244, reg. 4, with effect (subject to transitional provisions in SI 2011/244, reg. 8): for the purposes of corporation tax on income, for accounting periods ending on or after 6 March 2011; and for the purposes of corporation tax on chargeable gains and of capital gains tax, in relation to disposals made on or after 6 March 2011.

Treatment of interest in non-reporting fund: cases where the conditions in regulation 14ZA(2) would not be satisfied

14ZC(1)   This regulation applies in relation to an asset of an authorised investment fund ("the asset") which—

(a)   is an interest in a non-reporting fund, but

(b)   in relation to which the conditions in regulation 14ZA(2) would not (apart from this regulation) be satisfied for the whole of the period specified in regulation 14ZA(1)(b) in relation to the asset.

14ZC(2)   Paragraph (4) applies if the authorised investment fund, in relation to the asset, reasonably expects to satisfy the conditions in regulation 14ZA(2) for the period beginning with a date to be determined in accordance with paragraph (3) ("the deemed start date") and ending on the date of the disposal of the asset.

14ZC(3)   The deemed start date is a date to be determined by the authorised investment fund but which must not be earlier than 6th March 2011.

14ZC(4)   The authorised investment fund is treated for all purposes (including for the purposes of determining the beginning of the period mentioned in regulation 14ZA(1)(b)) as if it had, on the deemed start date, disposed of the asset (and not satisfied the conditions in regulation 14ZA(2)) and immediately reacquired the asset for a consideration equal to its market value on the deemed start date.

14ZC(5)   The authorised investment fund must notify the Commissioners of the deemed start date by making an appropriate entry in its tax return for the accounting period in which the deemed start date falls.

History – Reg. 14ZC and the heading before it inserted by SI 2011/244, reg. 4, with effect (subject to transitional provisions in SI 2011/244, reg. 8): for the purposes of corporation tax on income, for accounting periods ending on or after 6 March 2011; and for the purposes of corporation tax on chargeable gains and of capital gains tax, in relation to disposals made on or after 6 March 2011.

Index tracking funds

14ZD(1)   This regulation applies if–

(a)   an authorised investment fund has an interest in a non-reporting fund, and

(b)   the conditions in paragraph (2) are met throughout the relevant period.

14ZD(2)   The conditions are that–

(a)   in accordance with either the authorised investment fund's prospectus or the instrument constituting the authorised investment fund, the aim of the authorised investment fund's investment policy is to replicate the performance of a qualifying index,

(b)   the main purpose of the investment in the non-reporting fund is to represent the composition of the qualifying index, and

(c)   the capital and income returns of the authorised investment fund replicate as closely as practicable the returns of the investments comprised in the qualifying index.

14ZD(3)   For the purposes of paragraph (2) an index is a **"qualifying index"** if–

(a)   it is based solely on the value of securities listed on a recognised stock exchange or admitted to trading on a regulated market,

(b)   either a competent authority for the United Kingdom or an authority responsible for regulating offshore funds recognises the index on the basis that–

(i)   its composition is sufficiently diverse,

(ii)   it represents an adequate benchmark for the market to which it refers, and

(iii)   it is published in such a way that it is widely available, and

(c)   it is calculated and published by a body which is managed independently from the management of the authorised investment fund.

14ZD(4)   Regulation 17 of the Offshore Funds Regulations does not apply in respect of a disposal of the interest in the non-reporting fund by the authorised investment fund.

14ZD(5)   In this regulation **"the relevant period"** means the period–

(a)   starting on the day the authorised investment fund acquires the interest in the non-reporting fund (or any part of it), and

(b)   ending on the day of the disposal of the interest.

14ZD(6)   In this regulation–

(a)   a **"competent authority in the United Kingdom"** means the authority which is a competent authority for the United Kingdom for the purposes of Directive 2009/65/EC of the European Parliament and of the Council on the coordination of laws, regulations and administrative provisions relating to undertakings for collective investment in transferable securities (UCITS), and

(b)   **"regulated market"** has the same meaning as in Directive 2004/39/EC of the European Parliament and of the Council on markets in financial instruments (see article 4.1(14)).

History – Reg. 14ZD inserted by SI 2011/2192, reg. 4, with effect: for the purposes of corporation tax on income, for accounting periods starting on or after 1 October 2011; and, for the purposes of corporation tax on chargeable gains or capital gains tax, in relation to disposals made on or after 1 October 2011.

AUTHORISED INVESTMENT FUNDS WITH LIMITED INVESTMENT POWERS – STAMP DUTY RESERVE TAX

14A(1)   Where, for the relevant period–

(a)   an authorised investment fund is constituted as a unit trust scheme ("the scheme"); and

(b)   conditions A to D in this regulation are met,

paragraph 2 of Schedule 19 to the Finance Act 1999 ("FA 1999") shall not apply to a surrender to the scheme that would, but for this regulation, be taxable under Part II of that Schedule.

14A(2) Condition A is that the scheme must be dedicated to investment in the shares of a specified open-ended investment company to which Part 4A applies ("the PAIF").

14A(3) Condition B is that–

(a) the trust deed of the scheme must specify that the scheme may only invest in the PAIF; and

(b) the prospectus for the scheme must state that the scheme may only invest in the PAIF.

14A(4) Condition C is when an investment in the scheme is made, the scheme must (within one working day of that investment) invest in the PAIF an amount equal to the investment.

14A(5) Condition D is that when a withdrawal of investment from the scheme is made, the scheme must (within one working day of that withdrawal) withdraw from the PAIF an amount equal to the withdrawal.

14A(6) For the purposes of complying with conditions C and D, an investment in the scheme may not be set off against a withdrawal from the scheme.

14A(7) A scheme will not be dedicated to investment in the PAIF for the purpose of condition B if it has any assets other than shares in the PAIF and money.

14A(8) In this regulation–

"**relevant period**" means the relevant two-week period referred to in paragraph 4(2) of Schedule 19 to FA 1999.

"**surrender**" means a surrender within the meaning of paragraph 2 of Schedule 19 to FA 1999.

"**working day**" means a day other than–

(a) a Saturday, Sunday, Christmas Day or Good Friday; or

(b) a Bank Holiday in the United Kingdom under the Banking and Financial Dealings Act 1971.

"**money**" includes cash held on deposit but does not include securities of any kind.

History – Reg. 14A inserted by SI 2008/3159, reg. 10, with effect from 1 January 2009.

PART 2A – QUALIFIED INVESTOR SCHEMES

TAX TREATMENT OF QUALIFIED INVESTOR SCHEMES

14B(1) The provisions in paragraph (2) shall not apply to a qualified investor scheme in relation to an accounting period of the scheme unless the genuine diversity of ownership condition (see regulation 9A) is met in relation to that accounting period.

14B(2) The provisions referred to in paragraph (1) are–

(a) the provisions of Part 2 of these Regulations,

(aa) the provisions of Part 4 of these Regulations,

(b) the provisions of Part 4A of these Regulations,

(c) where the qualified investor scheme is an authorised unit trust scheme, section 468(1A) of ICTA,

(d) where the qualified investor scheme is an open-ended investment company, section 468A(1) of ICTA,

(e) in subsection (1) of section 99 of TCGA 1992 (as modified by these Regulations) the words "except that nothing in this section" to the end of that subsection, and

(f) section 100 of TCGA 1992.

14B(3) Where the genuine diversity of ownership condition is not met in relation to an accounting period of the scheme–

(a) section 13A of ICTA applies to the qualified investor scheme, whether or not that section would apply apart from this sub-paragraph; and

(b) the total amount available for income allocation to participants must only be allocated in accordance with paragraph (1)(b) of regulation 17 (allocation of income).

14B(4) In these Regulations a "**qualified investor scheme**" means a fund, authorised by the Financial Services Authority, in which a statement that the fund is a qualified investor scheme is included in the instrument constituting the scheme.

14B(5) [Omitted by SI 2009/2036, reg. 8(3).]

History – In reg. 14B(1), "9A" substituted for "14C" by SI 2009/2036, reg. 8(1), with effect from 1 September 2009. Reg. 14B(2)(aa) inserted by SI 2009/2036, reg. 8(2), with effect from 1 September 2009.

Reg. 14B(3)(b) substituted by SI 2010/294, reg. 6, with effect from 6 March 2010 (subject to the transitional provisions at SI 2010/294, reg. 24). Former reg. 14B(3)(b) read as follows:

"(b)   the total amount shown in the distribution accounts available for distribution to participants must only be shown as available for distribution in accordance with paragraph (1)(b) of regulation 17 (contents of distribution accounts)."

Reg. 14B(5) omitted by SI 2009/2036, reg. 8(3), with effect from 1 September 2009. Former reg. 14B(5) read as follows:

"**14B(5)**   For the purposes of these Regulations, in relation to a qualified investor scheme, the "**instrument constituting the scheme**" means–
(a)   in relation to an open-ended investment company, the instrument of incorporation, and
(b)   in relation to an authorised unit trust scheme, the trust deed.".

Reg. 14B inserted by SI 2008/3159, reg. 11, with effect from 1 January 2009, subject to the transitional rules in SI 2008/3159, reg. 1(2), 30 and 31.

THE GENUINE DIVERSITY OF OWNERSHIP CONDITION

14C   [Omitted by SI 2009/2036, reg. 9.]

History – Reg. 14C omitted by SI 2009/2036, reg. 9, with effect from 1 September 2009. Former reg. 14C read as follows:
"**14C(1)**   The genuine diversity of ownership condition is that the qualified investor scheme must–
(a)   meet Conditions A to D throughout the accounting period; or
(b)   comply with paragraph (9).

14C(2)   Condition A is that the scheme documents–
(a)   contain a statement that units in the scheme will be widely available,
(b)   specify the intended categories of investor, and
(c)   specify that the manager of the scheme must market and make available the units in the scheme in accordance with condition C.

14C(3)   Condition B is that neither–
(a)   the specification of the intended categories of investor referred to in paragraph (2)(b), nor
(b)   any other terms or conditions governing participation in the scheme, whether or not specified in the scheme documents,
have the effect of–
(i)   limiting investors to a limited number of specific persons or specific groups of connected persons, or
(ii)   deterring a reasonable investor within the intended categories of investor from investing in the scheme.

14C(4)   Condition C is that units in the scheme must be marketed and made available–
(a)   sufficiently widely to reach the intended categories of investors, and
(b)   in a manner appropriate to attract those categories of investors.

14C(5)   Condition C is subject to paragraph (8).

14C(6)   Condition D is that a person who is within one of the categories of intended investor in the scheme which have been specified in accordance with condition A may, upon request to the manager of the scheme, obtain information about the scheme and acquire units in it.

14C(7)   Condition D is subject to paragraph (8).

14C(8)   Conditions C and D shall be treated as being met even if at the relevant time the scheme has no capacity to receive additional investments, unless–
(a)   the capacity of the scheme to receive investments in it is fixed by the scheme documents (or otherwise); and
(b)   a pre-determined number of specific persons or specific groups of connected persons make investments in the scheme which collectively exhausts all, or substantially all, of that capacity.

14C(9)   The qualified investor scheme also meets the genuine diversity of ownership condition if–
(a)   an investor in the scheme is a unit trust scheme (a "feeder fund"),
(b)   paragraphs (2) to (8) are met in relation to the qualified investor scheme after taking into account the intended investors in the feeder fund, and
(c)   the qualified investor scheme and the feeder fund have the same manager (or proposed manager).

14C(10)   For the purposes of this regulation–
(a)   sections 993 and 994 of ITA 2007 (connected persons) apply in the case of a person chargeable to income tax, and
(b)   section 839 of ICTA (connected persons) applies in the case of a person chargeable to corporation tax.

14C(11)   In this regulation "**scheme documents**" means–
(a)   the instrument constituting the scheme, and
(b)   the scheme's prospectus in issue for the time being (including any supplements to the prospectus).".
Former reg. 14C inserted by SI 2008/3159, reg. 11, with effect from 1 January 2009, subject to the transitional rules in SI 2008/3159, reg. 1(2), 30 and 31.

CLEARANCE IN RELATION TO THE GENUINE DIVERSITY OF OWNERSHIP CONDITION

14D   [Omitted by SI 2009/2036, reg. 9.]

History – Reg. 14D omitted by SI 2009/2036, with effect from 1 September 2009. Former reg. 14D read as follows:
"**14D(1)**   An application for clearance that a qualified investor scheme meets the genuine diversity of ownership condition (see regulation 14C) may be made in writing to HM Revenue and Customs by the manager (or proposed manager) of a qualified investor scheme.

14D(2)   An application for clearance must be accompanied by the instrument constituting the scheme and its prospectus in the form in which it is proposed that those documents will apply at the beginning of the first accounting period of the scheme for which clearance is sought.

14D(3)   The Commissioners may require the manager (or proposed manager) to provide further particulars if they believe that full particulars of the scheme have not been provided.

14D(4)   The Commissioners must notify the applicant within 28 days of the receipt of the particulars (or, if paragraph (3) applies, of all further particulars required) that they–
(a)   give clearance that the scheme meets the genuine diversity of ownership condition;
(b)   give that clearance subject to conditions; or
(c)   refuse to give that clearance.

14D(5)   The qualified investor scheme (and investors in that scheme) may not rely on a clearance given under this regulation if–

(a)   at the beginning of the first accounting period of the scheme to which the clearance relates (and at the beginning of each subsequent accounting period), a relevant statement in the instrument constituting the scheme or in its prospectus in issue for the time being is not in accordance with a relevant statement in the documents considered by the Commissioners before giving clearance;

(b)   the scheme acts or is operated in contravention of a relevant statement in the instrument constituting the scheme or in its prospectus in issue for the time being;

(c)   the instrument constituting the scheme or the scheme's prospectus in issue for the time being is materially amended; or

(d)   the scheme is operated otherwise than in accordance with condition C or D of the genuine diversity of ownership condition.

14D(6)   But paragraph (5)(c) does not apply if the manager of the scheme has obtained a clearance given under this regulation which applies to the amendment.

14D(7)   For the purposes of paragraph (5)(c), a material amendment is one that may reasonably be construed as causing, or likely to cause, the scheme to fail to meets the genuine diversity of ownership condition in relation to any accounting period.".

Former reg. 14D inserted by SI 2008/3159, reg. 11, with effect from 1 January 2009, subject to the transitional rules in SI 2008/3159, reg. 1(2), 30 and 31.

PART 2B – DIVERSELY OWNED AIFS

History – Pt. 2B inserted by SI 2009/2036, reg. 10, with effect from 1 September 2009.

TAX TREATMENT OF DIVERSELY OWNED AIFS

14E(1)   This regulation applies to an authorised investment fund in respect of an accounting period if–

(a)   the fund carries out an investment transaction in that period, and

(b)   the fund meets the genuine diversity of ownership condition in relation to that period.

14E(2)   In these Regulations an authorised investment fund to which this regulation applies is referred to as a "diversely owned AIF".

14E(3)   If the profits or losses, as the case may be, arising from an investment transaction are capital profits, gains or losses, that investment transaction shall be treated as a non-trading transaction of the diversely owned AIF for the purposes of corporation tax.

14E(4)   Chapter 2 of Part 3 of CTA 2009 (income taxed as trade profits) does not apply to capital profits and losses arising from such an investment transaction.

14E(5)   For the purposes of these Regulations "investment transaction" means a transaction specified in regulation 2 of the Investment Transactions (Tax) Regulations 2014.

14E(6)   For the purposes of paragraphs (3) and (4) capital profits, gains or losses arising from an investment transaction in an accounting period are such profits, gains or losses as fall to be dealt with under the heading "net capital gains/losses" in the statement of total return for an accounting period.

14E(7)   For the purposes of paragraph (6), the **"statement of total return for an accounting period"** has the same meaning as in regulation 12(2).

History – In reg. 14E(5), the words "regulation 2 of the Investment Transactions (Tax) Regulations 2014" substituted for "regulation 14F" by SI 2014/685, reg. 7(2), with effect from transactions entered into on or after 8 April 2014.
Reg. 14E inserted by SI 2009/2036, reg. 10, with effect from 1 September 2009.

MEANING OF "INVESTMENT TRANSACTION"

14F   [Omitted by SI 2014/685, reg. 7(3).]

History – Reg. 14F and the heading immediately preceding it omitted by SI 2014/685, reg. 7(3), with effect from transactions entered into on or after 8 April 2014. Former reg. 14F read as follows:

"MEANING OF "INVESTMENT TRANSACTION"
14F(1)   For the purposes of these Regulations an **"investment transaction"** means–
(a)   any transaction in stocks and shares;
(b)   any transaction in a relevant contract (and see regulations 14G to 14K);
(c)   any transaction which results in a diversely owned AIF becoming a party to a loan relationship or a related transaction in respect of a loan relationship (and see regulation 14L);
(d)   any transaction in units in a collective investment scheme (and see regulation 14M);
(e)   any transaction in securities (and see paragraph (2));
(f)   any transaction consisting in the buying or selling of any foreign currency;
(g)   any transaction in a carbon emission trading product (and see regulation 14N).
14F(2)   In paragraph (1)(e) **"securities"** means securities of any description not falling within sub-paragraphs (a) to (d) of paragraph (1).
History – Former reg. 14F inserted by SI 2009/2036, reg. 10, with effect from 1 September 2009."

MEANING OF RELEVANT CONTRACTS: GENERAL

14G   [Omitted by SI 2014/685, reg. 7(3).]

History – Reg. 14G and the heading immediately preceding it omitted by SI 2014/685, reg. 7(3), with effect from transactions entered into on or after 8 April 2014. Former reg. 14G read as follows:

"MEANING OF RELEVANT CONTRACTS: GENERAL

14G(1) For the purposes of regulation 14F a **"relevant contract"** is–
(a) an option,
(b) a future, or
(c) a contract for differences.
14G(2) For the purposes of this regulation an option, a future or a contract for differences which relates to land will only be a relevant contract if the option, the future or the contract for differences uses an index referred to in regulation 14K(1)(b) and the index is–
(a) publicly accessible,
(b) comprised of a significant number of properties, and
(c) not maintained by–
    (i) the diversely owned AIF,
    (ii) the manager of the diversely owned AIF, or
    (iii) a person who is a connected person in relation to the diversely owned AIF or the manager of the diversely owned AIF.

History – Former reg. 14G inserted by SI 2009/2036, reg. 10, with effect from 1 September 2009."

MEANING OF RELEVANT CONTRACT: OPTIONS

14H [Omitted by SI 2014/685, reg. 7(3).]

History – Reg. 14H and the heading immediately preceding it omitted by SI 2014/685, reg. 7(3), with effect from transactions entered into on or after 8 April 2014. Former reg. 14H read as follows:

"MEANING OF RELEVANT CONTRACT: OPTIONS

14H(1) For the purposes of regulation 14G an **"option"** includes an instrument which entitles the holder to subscribe for shares in a company or assets representing a loan relationship of a company, and for these purposes it is immaterial whether the shares or assets to which the instrument relates exist or are identifiable.
14H(2) For the purposes of paragraph (1) the reference to a loan relationship of a company is to be construed in accordance with regulation 14L but with references in that regulation to **"diversely owned AIF"** treated as references to "company".

History – Former reg. 14H inserted by SI 2009/2036, reg. 10, with effect from 1 September 2009."

MEANING OF RELEVANT CONTRACT: FUTURES

14I [Omitted by SI 2014/685, reg. 7(3).]

History – Reg. 14I and the heading immediately preceding it omitted by SI 2014/685, reg. 7(3), with effect from transactions entered into on or after 8 April 2014. Former reg. 14I read as follows:

"MEANING OF RELEVANT CONTRACT: FUTURES

14I(1) For the purposes of regulation 14G a **"future"** is a contract for the sale of property under which delivery is to be made–
(a) at a future date agreed when the contract is made, and
(b) at a price so agreed.
14I(2) For the purposes of paragraph (1)(b) a price is taken to be agreed when the contract is made–
(a) notwithstanding that the price is left to be determined by reference to the price at which a contract is to be entered into on a market or exchange or could be entered into at a time and place specified in the contract, or
(b) in a case where the contract is expressed to be by reference to a standard lot and quality, notwithstanding that provision is made for a variation in the price to take account of any variation in quantity or quality on delivery.

History – Former reg. 14I inserted by SI 2009/2036, reg. 10, with effect from 1 September 2009."

MEANING OF RELEVANT CONTRACT: OPTIONS AND FUTURES – GENERAL PROVISIONS

14J [Omitted by SI 2014/685, reg. 7(3).]

History – Reg. 14J and the heading immediately preceding it omitted by SI 2014/685, reg. 7(3), with effect from transactions entered into on or after 8 April 2014. Former reg. 14J read as follows:

"MEANING OF RELEVANT CONTRACT: OPTIONS AND FUTURES – GENERAL PROVISIONS

14J(1) For the purposes of regulations 14H and 14I references to an option or a future do not include references to a contract whose terms provide–
(a) that, after setting off their obligations to each other under the contract, a cash payment is to be made by one party to the other in respect of the excess, if any, and do not provide for the delivery of any property,
(b) that each party is liable to make to the other party a cash payment in respect of all that party's obligations to the other under the contract and do not provide for the delivery of any property, or
(c) for the delivery of any property other than property a transaction in which would fall within regulation 14F(1) where the property is delivered.
14J(2) Nothing in paragraph (1) has effect to exclude, from references to a future or option, a future or option whose underlying subject matter is currency.
14J(3) In paragraph (1) **"underlying subject matter"** means–
(a) in relation to a future, the property which, if the future were to run to delivery, would fall to be delivered at the date and price agreed when the contract is made, and
(b) in relation to an option, the property which would fall to be delivered if the option were exercised."

History – Former reg. 14J inserted by SI 2009/2036, reg. 10, with effect from 1 September 2009."

MEANING OF RELEVANT CONTRACT: CONTRACT FOR DIFFERENCES

14K [Omitted by SI 2014/685, reg. 7(3).]

History – Reg. 14K and the heading immediately preceding it omitted by SI 2014/685, reg. 7(3), with effect from transactions entered into on or after 8 April 2014. Former reg. 14K read as follows:

"MEANING OF RELEVANT CONTRACT: CONTRACT FOR DIFFERENCES"

14K(1) For the purposes of regulation 14G a **"contract for differences"** is a contract the purpose or pretended purpose of which is to make a profit or avoid a loss by reference to fluctuations in–

(a) the value or price of property described in the contract, or

(b) an index or other factor designated in the contract.

14K(2) For the purposes of paragraph (1)(b) an index or factor may be determined by reference to any matter and, for these purposes, a numerical value may be attributed to any variation in a matter.

14K(3) For the purposes of regulation 14G none of the following is a contract for differences–

(a) an option,

(b) a future,

(c) a contract of insurance,

(d) a contract effected in the course of capital redemption business,

(e) a contract of indemnity,

(f) a guarantee,

(g) a warranty,

(h) a loan relationship.

14K(4) For the purposes of paragraph (3)–

"capital redemption business" means any business of a company carrying on insurance business in so far as it consists of the effecting on the basis of actuarial calculations, and the carrying out, of contracts under which, in return for one or more fixed payments, a sum or series of sums of a specified amount becomes payable at a future time or over a period;

"loan relationship" is to be construed in accordance with regulation 14L but with references to "diversely owned AIF" in that regulation treated as references to "company".

History – Former reg. 14K inserted by SI 2009/2036, reg. 10, with effect from 1 September 2009."

LOAN RELATIONSHIPS OR RELATED TRANSACTIONS

14L [Omitted by SI 2014/685, reg. 7(3).]

History – Reg. 14L and the heading immediately preceding it omitted by SI 2014/685, reg. 7(3), with effect from transactions entered into on or after 8 April 2014. Former reg. 14L read as follows:

"LOAN RELATIONSHIPS OR RELATED TRANSACTIONS"

14L(1) For the purposes of regulation 14F a diversely owned AIF has a **"loan relationship"** if that diversely owned AIF stands (whether by reference to a security or otherwise) in the position of a creditor or debtor as respects any money debt and either–

(a) that debt is one arising from a transaction for the lending of money; or

(b) that debt is not one which arose from a transaction for the lending of money but is one–

    (i) on which interest is payable to or by the diversely owned AIF, or

    (ii) in relation to which exchange gains or losses arise to the diversely owned AIF, or

    (iii) as respects which the conditions in paragraph (2) below are satisfied.

14L(2) The conditions referred to in paragraph (1)(b)(iii) are that–

(a) the diversely owned AIF stands in the position of creditor in relation to the money debt; and

(b) the money debt is one from which a discount (whether of an income or capital nature) arises to the diversely owned AIF.

14L(3) For the purposes of this regulation **"exchange gains or losses"** means profits or gains or losses which arise as a result of comparing at different times the expression in one currency of the whole or some part of the valuation put by the diversely owned AIF in another currency on an asset or liability of the diversely owned AIF.

14L(4) For the purposes of this regulation a **"money debt"** is a debt which is, or has at any time been, one that falls, or that may at the choice of the debtor or of the creditor fall, to be settled–

(a) by the payment of money,

(b) by the transfer of a right to settlement under a debt which is itself a money debt, or

(c) by the issue or transfer of shares in any company,

disregarding any other alternative exercisable by either party.

14L(5) Subject to paragraph (6), if an instrument is issued by any person for the purpose of representing security for, or the rights of a creditor in respect of, any money debt, then (whatever the circumstances of the issue of the instrument) that debt shall be taken for the purposes of this regulation to be a debt arising from a transaction for the lending of money.

14L(6) For the purposes of this regulation a debt shall not be taken to arise from a transaction for the lending of money to the extent that it is a debt arising from rights conferred by shares in a company.

14L(7) For the purposes of this regulation so far as relating to exchange gains or losses any currency held by the diversely owned AIF shall be treated as a money debt.

14L(8) For the purposes of this regulation **"money"** includes money expressed in a currency other than sterling.

14L(9) In this Part a **"related transaction"** in relation to a loan relationship means any disposal or acquisition (in whole or in part) of rights or liabilities under that relationship.

History – Former reg. 14L inserted by SI 2009/2036, reg. 10, with effect from 1 September 2009."

UNITS IN A COLLECTIVE INVESTMENT SCHEME

14M [Omitted by SI 2014/685, reg. 7(3).]

History – Reg. 14M and the heading immediately preceding it omitted by SI 2014/685, reg. 7(3), with effect from transactions entered into on or after 8 April 2014. Former reg. 14M read as follows:

"UNITS IN A COLLECTIVE INVESTMENT SCHEME"

14M(1) For the purposes of regulation 14F **"units"** in a collective investment scheme means the rights or interests (however described) of the participants in the collective investment scheme.

14M(2) For the purposes of this regulation **"participant"** has the same meaning as given by regulation 6(6) but with references to **"authorised investment fund"** and **"fund"** being read as references to "collective investment scheme".

History – Former reg. 14M inserted by SI 2009/2036, reg. 10, with effect from 1 September 2009."

CARBON EMISSION TRADING PRODUCTS

14N [Omitted by SI 2014/685, reg. 7(3).]

History – Reg. 14N and the heading immediately preceding it omitted by SI 2014/685, reg. 7(3), with effect from transactions entered into on or after 8 April 2014. Former reg. 14N read as follows:

"CARBON EMISSION TRADING PRODUCTS

14N(1) For the purposes of regulation 14F a carbon emission trading product is–
(a) a Community tradable emissions allowance, or
(b) a transferable unit issued pursuant to the Kyoto Protocol,
which does not otherwise fall within any other regulation of this Part.
14N(2) For the purpose of this regulation–
"Community tradable emissions allowance" means a transferable allowance which relates to the making of emissions of greenhouse gases which are allocated as part of a system made for the purpose of implementing any Community obligation of the United Kingdom relating to such emissions;
"the Kyoto Protocol" means the Kyoto Protocol to the United Nations Framework Convention on Climate Change signed at Kyoto on 11th December 1997;
"unit" includes an assigned amount unit, certified emission reductions, an emission reduction unit and a removal unit.
History – Former reg. 14N inserted by SI 2009/2036, reg. 10, with effect from 1 September 2009."

PART 3 – DISTRIBUTIONS MADE BY AUTHORISED INVESTMENT FUNDS

PRELIMINARY

Interpretation

15(1) In these Regulations–
(a) **"income allocation"** means the distribution of an amount to participants; and
(b) **"distribution"** includes the crediting of an amount to the capital part of the scheme property on behalf of a participant in respect of the participant's accumulation units.

15(2) In these Regulations **"distribution period"**, in relation to an authorised investment fund, means a period by reference to which the total amount available for income allocation to participants is ascertained.

15(3) [Omitted by SI 2010/294, reg. 7(4).]

15(4) In these Regulations the **"distribution date"** for a distribution period of an authorised investment fund means–
(a) the date specified by or in accordance with the terms of the trust or the instrument of incorporation of the company for any distribution for that distribution period, or
(b) if no date is specified, the last day of that distribution period.

History – Reg. 15(1) substituted by SI 2010/294, reg. 7(2), with effect from 6 March 2010 (subject to the transitional provisions at SI 2010/294, reg. 24). Former reg. 15(1) read as follows:

"**15(1)** In these Regulations a reference to a **"distribution"** includes crediting an amount to the capital part of the scheme property of an authorised investment fund on behalf of a participant in respect of the participant's accumulation units."

In reg. 15(2) the words "income allocation to participants" substituted for the words "distribution to participants" by SI 2010/294, reg. 7(3), with effect from 6 March 2010 (subject to the transitional provisions at SI 2010/294, reg. 24).
Reg. 15(3) omitted by SI 2010/294, reg. 7(4), with effect from 6 March 2010 (subject to the transitional provisions at SI 2010/294, reg. 24). Former reg. 15(3) read as follows:

"**15(3)** In these Regulations **"distribution accounts"**, in relation to an authorised investment fund, means accounts showing–
(a) the total amount available for distribution to participants, and
(b) how that total amount is computed."

Funds excluded from the ambit of this Part

16 This Part does not apply to an authorised investment fund if the fund–
(a) is a registered pension scheme within the meaning of Part 4 of the Finance Act 2004, or
(b) is treated, under paragraph 1(1) of Schedule 36 to that Act, as having become such a scheme.

Allocation of income

History – The heading to reg. 17 amended from "Contents of the distribution accounts" and the cross-heading "DISTRIBUTION ACCOUNTS: GENERAL", which immediately preceded reg. 17, omitted by SI 2010/294, reg. 8(2), with effect from 6 March 2010 (subject to the transitional provisions at SI 2010/294, reg. 24).

17(1) The total amount available for income allocation must be allocated in one of the following ways–
(a) for distribution as yearly interest (see regulations 18 to 21); or
(b) for distribution as dividends (see regulation 22).

17(1A)　Paragraph (1) does not apply in relation to an authorised investment fund to which Part 4A or 4B applies.

17(2)　Amounts chargeable to corporation tax in accordance with Part 4 of CTA 2009 or regulation 15 of the Unauthorised Unit Trusts (Tax) Regulations 2013 must not be included in any amount of income allocated for distribution as yearly interest.

History – Reg. 17(1) substituted by SI 2010/294, reg. 8(3), with effect from 6 March 2010 (subject to the transitional provisions at SI 2010/294, reg. 24). Former reg. 17(1) read as follows:

"**17(1)**　The total amount shown in the distribution accounts as available for distribution to participants must be shown as available for distribution in one of the following ways–
(a)　　it may be shown as available for distribution as yearly interest (see regulations 18 to 21 below); or
(b)　　it may be shown as available for distribution as dividends (see regulation 22 below)."

Reg. 17(1A) inserted by SI 2009/2036, reg. 11, with effect from 1 September 2009.

In reg. 17(2), the words "or regulation 15 of the Unauthorised Unit Trusts (Tax) Regulations 2013" inserted after the words "Part 4 of CTA 2009" by SI 2013/2819, reg. 42, with effect from 6 April 2014.

Reg. 17(2) substituted by SI 2010/294, reg. 8(4), with effect from 6 March 2010 (subject to the transitional provisions at SI 2010/294, reg. 24). Former reg. 17(2) read as follows:

"**17(2)**　The following may not be included in any amount shown in the distribution accounts as available for distribution as yearly interest–
(a)　　amounts chargeable to corporation tax under Schedule A;
(b)　　amounts chargeable to corporation tax as income of an overseas property business (see section 70A(4) of ICTA)."

INTEREST DISTRIBUTIONS

Interest distributions: general

18(1)　Paragraph (2) applies where the total amount available for income allocation is allocated for distribution as yearly interest.

18(2)　The Tax Acts shall have effect as if the total amount were payments of yearly interest made on the distribution date by the authorised investment fund to the participants in proportion to their rights.

18(3)　In these Regulations an **"interest distribution"** means a payment of yearly interest treated as made by virtue of paragraph (2) (including a payment of interest treated as made to a participant who is not chargeable to income tax).

18(4)　This regulation is subject to–

(a)　　regulation 19 (the qualifying investments test), and

(b)　　regulation 23 (treatment of de minimis amounts).

History – In reg. 18(1) the words "available for income allocation is allocated" substituted for the words "shown in the distribution accounts as available for distribution to participants is shown as available" by SI 2010/294, reg. 9, with effect from 6 March 2010 (subject to the transitional provisions at SI 2010/294, reg. 24).

The qualifying investments test

19(1)　No amount may be shown as available for distribution as yearly interest unless the authorised investment fund in question satisfies the qualifying investments test throughout the distribution period.

19(2)　An authorised investment fund satisfies the qualifying investments test throughout a distribution period (the "relevant period") if, at all times in that period, the market value of the qualifying investments exceeds 60% of the market value of all the investments of the fund.

19(3)　Regulations 20 and 21 deal with the meaning of the expression "qualifying investments".

Meaning of "qualifying investments"

20　In these Regulations **"qualifying investments"**, in relation to an authorised investment fund, means the investments of that fund which fall within any of the following categories (read, as appropriate, with any applicable provision in regulation 21)–

Category 1

Money placed at interest.

Category 2

Securities.

Category 3

Shares in a building society.

Category 4

Qualifying units in another authorised investment fund.

Category 4A

Qualifying units in an offshore fund.

Category 5

Derivative contracts whose underlying subject matter consists wholly of any one or more of the matters referred to in categories 1 to 4A and currency.

Category 6

Contracts for differences whose underlying subject matter consists wholly of any one or more of interest rates, creditworthiness and currency.

Category 7

Derivative contracts not within categories 5 or 6 where there is a hedging relationship between the derivative contract and an asset within categories 1 to 4A.

Category 8

Alternative finance arrangements.

History – In reg. 20, in Category 5 and Category 7, "4A" substituted for "4" by SI 2011/2192, reg. 5, with effect: for the purposes of corporation tax on income, for accounting periods starting on or after 1 October 2011; and, for the purposes of corporation tax on chargeable gains or capital gains tax, in relation to disposals made on or after 1 October 2011.
In reg. 20 the words "Category 4A Qualifying units in an offshore fund" inserted by SI 2010/294, reg. 10, with effect for accounting periods beginning on or after 6 March 2010.

Meaning of "qualifying investments": further provisions

21(1)   This regulation applies for the purposes of regulation 20.

21(2)   For the purposes of category 2 "securities" do not include shares in a company.

21(3)   For the purposes of category 4 units in another authorised investment fund are qualifying units at any time in the relevant period if, and only if, the other authorised investment fund would itself (on the relevant assumption) satisfy the qualifying investments test throughout that period.

21(4)   For the purposes of paragraph (3) the relevant assumption is that the only investments of the other authorised investment fund which are to be regarded as qualifying investments are those falling within categories 1 to 3 and 5 to 8.

21(5)   In paragraph (4) references to investments of an authorised investment fund–

(a)   in the case of an open-ended investment company are references to investments comprised in the scheme property of that company, but do not include references to cash awaiting investment, and

(b)   in the case of an authorised unit trust are references to investments subject to the trusts of that authorised unit trust, but do not include references to cash awaiting investment.

21(5A)   For the purpose of category 4A, units in an offshore fund are qualifying units at any time in the relevant period if, and only if, the offshore fund would itself (on the relevant assumption) satisfy the qualifying investments test throughout that period.

21(5B)   For the purposes of paragraph (5A), the relevant assumption is that the only investments of the offshore fund which are to be regarded as qualifying investments are those falling within categories 1 to 3 and 5 to 8.

21(5C)   In paragraph (5B), references to investments of an offshore fund–

(a)   in the case of an offshore fund which is a company, are references to investments which are the investments of the company, but do not include cash awaiting investment, and

(b)   in the case of any other offshore fund, are references to investments subject to the trust or other arrangements constituting the investments of the other offshore fund, but do not include cash awaiting investment.

21(6)   For the purposes of categories 5 and 6 **"underlying subject matter"** has the same meaning as in paragraph 11 of Schedule 26 to FA 2002.

21(7)   For the purposes of categories 5 and 6 underlying subject matter may consist of currency only if and to the extent that there is a hedging relationship between the contract and a qualifying investment falling within categories 1 to 4.

21(8)   In paragraph (7) **"hedging relationship"** has the meaning given by paragraph 12(14) of Schedule 26 to FA 2002.

21(9)   For the purposes of category 6 a **"contract for differences"** has the same meaning as in paragraph 12 of Schedule 26 to FA 2002.

21(10)   For the purposes of category 7 a fund has a hedging relationship between a derivative contract on the one hand ("the hedging instrument") and an asset on the other ("the hedged item") if and to the extent that–

(a)   the hedging instrument and the hedged item are designated by the fund as a hedge, or

(b)   in any other case the hedging instrument is intended to act as a hedge of the exposure to changes in fair value of a hedged item which is a recognised asset or an identified portion of such an asset that is attributable to a particular risk and could affect the total net return of the fund.

21(11)   For the purposes of category 8 **"alternative finance arrangements"** has the meaning given by section 46(1) of the Finance Act 2005.

History – Reg. 21(5A)–(5C) inserted by SI 2010/294, reg. 11, with effect for accounting periods beginning on or after 6 March 2010.

DIVIDEND DISTRIBUTIONS

Dividend distributions: general

22(1)   Paragraph (2) applies where the total amount available for income allocation is allocated for distribution as dividends.

22(2)   The Tax Acts shall have effect as if the total amount were dividends on shares paid on the distribution date by the authorised investment fund to the participants in proportion to their rights (but see regulation 96A (modification of CTA 2009)).

22(3)   In these Regulations a "dividend distribution" means a dividend treated as paid by virtue of paragraph (2) (including a dividend treated as paid to a participant who is not chargeable to corporation tax).

22(4)   This regulation is subject to regulation 23 (treatment of de minimis amounts).

History – In reg. 22(1) the words "available for income allocation is allocated" substituted for the words "shown in the distribution accounts as available for distribution to participants is shown as available" by SI 2010/294, reg. 12, with effect from 6 March 2010 (subject to the transitional provisions at SI 2010/294, reg. 24).
In reg. 22(2) the words "(but see regulation 96A (modification of CTA 2009))" inserted by SI 2012/519, reg. 4, with effect in relation to any distribution made at or after 1.30 p.m. on 27 February 2012.

DE MINIMIS AMOUNTS

Provisions applying if amounts available for distribution are de minimis

23(1)   An authorised investment fund is not treated as making a distribution for a distribution period if conditions A to D are met.

23(2)   Condition A is that, in accordance with rules made by the Financial Services Authority, the authorised investment fund has an agreed de minimis limit.

23(3)   Condition B is that the authorised investment fund–

(a)   has calculated that the total income available for income allocations is a de minimis amount, and

(b)   chooses to waive the allocation of that de minimis amount.

23(4)   Condition C is that the de minimis amount is carried forward to the next distribution period as an amount available for distribution to participants.

23(5)   Condition D is that none of the units of the authorised investment fund in issue on the distribution date are in bearer form.

23(6)   If this regulation applies, the authorised investment fund is not required to comply with the requirements of section 234A of ICTA (information relating to distributions) in respect of the de minimis amount for the distribution period in question.

23(7)   In this regulation–

the **"de minimis limit"**, in relation to an authorised investment fund, means an amount in respect of which a distribution of income of the fund is not required if the total amount available for income allocation to participants does not exceed that amount, and

"de minimis amount" means an amount falling within the de minimis limit.

History – Reg. 23(3)(a) and (b) substituted by SI 2010/294, reg. 13(2), with effect from 6 March 2010 (subject to the transitional provisions at SI 2010/294, reg. 24). Former reg. 23(3)(a) and (b) read as follows:
   "(a)   has prepared distribution accounts in which the amount shown as available for distribution to participants is a de minimis amount, and
   (b)   chooses to waive the distribution of that de minimis amount."
In reg. 23(7), the words "available for income allocation" substituted for the words "shown in the fund's distribution accounts as available for distribution" by SI 2010/294, reg. 13(3), with effect from 6 March 2010 (subject to the transitional provisions at SI 2010/294, reg. 24).

PART 4 – THE TREATMENT OF PARTICIPANTS IN AUTHORISED INVESTMENT FUNDS
Chapter 1 – Preliminary Provisions

STRUCTURE OF THIS PART

24   The structure of this Part of these Regulations is as follows–

this Chapter contains preliminary provisions;

Chapter 2 contains provisions relating to the tax treatment of participants chargeable to income tax;

Chapter 3 contains provisions relating to the tax treatment of participants chargeable to corporation tax.

History – In reg. 24, the words "Chapter 4 imposes a charge to tax on substantial QIS holdings in qualified investor schemes", which appeared at the end, omitted by SI 2008/3159, reg. 12, with effect from 1 January 2009, subject to the transitional rules in SI 2008/3159, reg. 1(2), 30 and 31.

FUNDS EXCLUDED FROM THE AMBIT OF THIS PART

25   This Part does not apply to an authorised investment fund if the fund–

(a)   is a registered pension scheme within the meaning of Part 4 of the Finance Act 2004, or

(b)   is treated, under paragraph 1(1) of Schedule 36 to that Act, as having become such a scheme.

Chapter 2 – Participants Chargeable to Income Tax

DEDUCTION OF TAX FROM INTEREST DISTRIBUTIONS: GENERAL
Deduction of tax where interest distributions made

26(1)   This regulation applies if an interest distribution is made for a distribution period to a participant chargeable to income tax.

26(2)   Any obligation to deduct a sum under section 874 of ITA 2007 is subject to the provisions of this regulation.

26(3)   In this Part the **"deduction obligation"** means the obligation specified in paragraph (2).

26(4)   The deduction obligation does not apply to the interest distribution if–

(a)   the participant is a company;

(b)   the participant consists of the trustees of a unit trust scheme;

(c)   the reputable intermediary condition is met with respect to a participant on the distribution date (see regulation 27);

(d)   the residence condition is met with respect to a participant on the distribution date (see regulation 30);

(e)   [Revoked by SI 2007/794, reg. 8(b), or

(f)   the offshore marketing condition is met with respect to the class of units in relation to which the distribution is made (see regulation 33A).

26(5)   But if the participant is a company which is the trustee of the trust to which (or under which) the interest distribution is made (or received), the deduction obligation is not excluded by virtue of paragraph (4)(a).

26(6)   In its application to an interest distribution to a participant in respect of accumulation units, the deduction obligation is an obligation to deduct a sum out of the amount being credited to scheme capital on the participant's behalf.

History – In reg. 26(2), the words "section 874 of ITA 2007" substituted for the words "section 349(2) of ICTA" by SI 2013/2994, reg. 3(a), with effect from 19 December 2013.
In reg. 26(4)(c) the word "or" inserted at the end by SI 2007/794, reg. 3, with effect from 6 April 2007.
Reg. 26(4)(e) and the word "or" before it, revoked by SI 2007/794, reg. 8(b), with effect from 6 April 2007.
Reg. 26(4)(f) (and the ", or" before it) inserted (and the "or" after (c) omitted) by SI 2013/2994, reg. 3(b), with effect in relation to units acquired on or after 19 December 2013.

THE REPUTABLE INTERMEDIARY CONDITION

The reputable intermediary condition

27(1)   The reputable intermediary condition is met with respect to a participant on the distribution date if conditions A to C are met.

27(2)   Condition A is that the interest distribution is paid on behalf of the participant to a company.

27(3)   Condition B is that the legal owner has reasonable grounds for believing that the participant is not resident in the United Kingdom.

27(4)   Condition C is that the company mentioned in paragraph (2)–

(a)   is subject to the EC Money Laundering Directive,

(b)   is subject to equivalent non-EC provisions, or

(c)   is a company which–

(i)   is resident in a regulating country or territory, and

(ii)   is an associated company of a company which is subject to paragraph (a) or (b).

History – In reg. 27(3), the word "ordinarily", which appeared before the word "resident", omitted by SI 2013/2994, reg. 7, with effect for the purposes of a person's liability to income tax for the tax year 2014–15 and any subsequent tax year.

The reputable intermediary condition: further provisions

28(1)   This regulation applies for the purposes of Condition C in regulation 27.

28(2)   A company is subject to the EC Money Laundering Directive if it is a credit institution or financial institution as defined by Article 1 of Directive 91/308/EEC, as amended by Directive 2001/97 /EC.

28(3)   A company is subject to equivalent non-EC provisions if it is required by the law of any country or territory which is not a member State to comply with requirements similar to those which, under Article 3 of that Directive (as so amended), member States must ensure are complied with by credit institutions and financial institutions.

28(4)   A country or territory is a regulating country or territory if it either is a member State or imposes requirements similar to those which, under Article 3 of that Directive (as so amended), member States must ensure are complied with by credit institutions and financial institutions.

28(5)   A company is to be treated as another's associated company if it would be so treated for the purposes of Part 11 of ICTA (close companies) (see section 416 of that Act).

Consequences of reasonable but incorrect belief

29(1)   This regulation applies if conditions A to D are met.

29(2)   Condition A is that an interest distribution is made to a participant.

29(3)   Condition B is that the legal owner, in reliance on the reputable intermediary condition being met with respect to the participant, does not comply with the deduction obligation in relation to the interest distribution.

29(4)   Condition C is that the deduction obligation would apply but for the reputable intermediary condition being met.

29(5)   Condition D is that (contrary to the belief of the legal owner) the participant is in fact resident in the United Kingdom.

29(6)   Section 350 of ICTA (charge to tax where payments made under section 349) and Schedule 16 to that Act (collection of income tax on company payments which are not distributions) have effect as if the deduction obligation applied.

History – In reg. 29(5), the word "ordinarily", which appeared before the word "resident", omitted by SI 2013/2994, reg. 8, with effect for the purposes of a person's liability to income tax for the tax year 2014–15 and any subsequent tax year.

THE RESIDENCE CONDITION

The residence condition

30(1)   The residence condition is met with respect to a participant on the distribution date if any of conditions A to E is met.

30(2)   Condition A is that, in relation to an interest distribution which is not made to or received under a trust, there is a valid declaration, made by the participant, that the participant is not resident in the United Kingdom.

30(3)   Condition B is–

(a)   that the participant holds the units as the personal representative of a deceased person, and

(b)   that the deceased, before his death, made a declaration, valid at the time of his death, that he was not resident in the United Kingdom.

30(4)   Condition C is–

(a)   that the participant holds the units as the personal representative of a deceased person, and

(b)   that the personal representative has made a declaration that the deceased, immediately before his death, was not resident in the United Kingdom.

30(5)   Condition D is that, in the case of an interest distribution made to or received under a trust where the whole of the income is, or falls to be treated as, or under any provision of the Tax Acts is deemed to be, the income of a person other than the trustees of that trust, there is a valid declaration, made by the person in question that the person is not resident in the United Kingdom.

30(6)   Condition E is that, in circumstances in which condition D does not apply and with respect to a participant in the case of an interest distribution made to or received under a trust, there is a valid declaration, made by the trustees of that trust that–

(a)   the trustees are not resident in the United Kingdom, and

(b)   each beneficiary of the trust is not resident in the United Kingdom.

History – In reg. 30(2), (3)(b) and (4)(b), the word "ordinarily", which appeared before the word "resident", omitted by SI 2013/2994, reg. 9(a), with effect in relation to the making of declarations on or after 6 April 2014. Any declarations made before that date continue to have effect in respect of interest distributions made on or after that date as if the amendment had not been made.
In reg. 30(5), the words "the person is" substituted for the words "he is either not ordinarily resident or, in the case of a company," by SI 2013/2994, reg. 9(b), with effect in relation to the making of declarations on or after 6 April 2014. Any declarations made before that date continue to have effect in respect of interest distributions made on or after that date as if the amendment had not been made.
In reg. 30(6)(b), the words "either not ordinarily resident or, in the case of a beneficiary which is a company,", which appeared before the words "not resident", omitted by SI 2013/2994, reg. 9(c), with effect in relation to the making of declarations on or after 6 April 2014. Any declarations made before that date continue to have effect in respect of interest distributions made on or after that date as if the amendment had not been made.

Residence declarations

31(1)   A declaration made for the purposes of regulation 30 must–

(a)   be in such form as may be required or authorised by the Commissioners;

(b)   be made in writing to the legal owner of the authorised investment fund in question; and

(c)   contain any details or undertakings required by paragraphs (2) to (4) below.

31(2)   A declaration made for the purposes of condition A or B in regulation 30 must contain–

(a)   the name and principal residential address of the person making it; and

(b)   an undertaking that he will notify the legal owner if he becomes resident in the United Kingdom.

31(3)   A declaration made for the purposes of condition C in regulation 30 must contain the name of the deceased and his principal residential address immediately before his death.

31(4)   A declaration made for the purposes of condition D or E in regulation 30 must contain–

(a)   the names and principal residential addresses of the trustees of the trust or, in the case of a trustee which is a company, the name of the company and the address of its registered or principal office;

(b)   the names and principal residential addresses of the beneficiaries of the trust or, in the case of a beneficiary which is a company, the name of the company and the address of its registered or principal office; and

(c)   an undertaking that the trustees of the trust will notify the legal owner of the authorised investment fund in question if–

(i)   they become resident in the United Kingdom,

(ii)   any beneficiary of the trust named in the declaration becomes resident in the United Kingdom, or

(iii)   any person who becomes a beneficiary of the trust after the making of the declaration either is at the time of becoming a beneficiary, or subsequently becomes, ordinarily resident or, in the case of a company, resident in the United Kingdom.

History – In reg. 31(2)(b), the word "ordinarily", which appeared before the word "resident", omitted by SI 2013/2994, reg. 10(a), with effect in relation to the making of declarations on or after 6 April 2014. Any declarations made before that date continue to have effect in respect of interest distributions made on or after that date as if the amendment had not been made. In reg. 31(4)(c)(ii), the words "ordinarily resident or, in the case of a company,", which appeared before the word "resident", omitted by SI 2013/2994, reg. 10(b), with effect in relation to the making of declarations on or after 6 April 2014. Any declarations made before that date continue to have effect in respect of interest distributions made on or after that date as if the amendment had not been made.

References to beneficiaries in regulations 30 and 31

32   In regulations 30 and 31 references to a beneficiary are references to any person who is known to the trustees of the trust to be either–

(a)   a person who is or will or may become, entitled to any income of the trust, whether in the form of income or not, or

(b)   a person to whom any such income may be paid, or for whose benefit any such income may be applied, whether in the form of income or not, in the exercise of a discretion by them.

Interest distributions: the position of the legal owner

33(1)   For the purposes of determining whether an interest distribution should be made with or without any deduction, the legal owner is entitled to treat a declaration made for the purposes of regulation 30 as valid.

33(2)   But the legal owner may not treat a declaration as valid if condition A or B is met.

33(3)   Condition A is that the legal owner receives a notification in compliance with an undertaking under regulation 31 that a person in question has become resident in the United Kingdom.

33(4)   Condition B is that the legal owner comes into possession of information by some other means which indicates that such a person is or may be resident or ordinarily resident in the United Kingdom.

History – In reg. 33(3), the words "or ordinarily resident", which appeared after the word "resident", omitted by SI 2013/2994, reg. 11, with effect in relation to the making of declarations on or after 6 April 2014. Any declarations made before that date continue to have effect in respect of interest distributions made on or after that date as if the amendment had not been made.

The offshore marketing condition

33A   The offshore marketing condition is met with respect to a class of units if–

(a)   marketing of units of that class is not directed to investors resident in the United Kingdom, and

(b)   before units of that class are acquired, information in relation to those units is available to investors to the effect that–

(i)   no sum representing income tax will be deducted from any interest distribution in relation to those units, and

(ii)   an investor must notify HM Revenue and Customs of any distribution in relation to such units if the investor is chargeable to income tax for the tax year in which the distribution date falls.

History – Reg. 33A inserted by SI 2013/2994, reg. 4, with effect in relation to units acquired on or after 19 December 2013.

THE NON-LIABILITY CONDITION

The non-liability condition

34   [Revoked by SI 2007/794, reg. 8(c).]

History – Reg. 34 revoked by SI 2007/794, reg. 8(c), with effect from 6 April 2007.

Qualifying certificates

35   [Revoked by SI 2007/794, reg. 8(c).]

History – Reg. 35 revoked by SI 2007/794, reg. 8(c), with effect from 6 April 2007.

The contents condition

36   [Revoked by SI 2007/794, reg. 8(c).]

History – Reg. 36 revoked by SI 2007/794, reg. 8(c), with effect from 6 April 2007.

The supplier condition

37   [Revoked by SI 2007/794, reg. 8(c).]

History – Reg. 37 revoked by SI 2007/794, reg. 8(c), with effect from 6 April 2007.

The time limit condition

38   [Revoked by SI 2007/794, reg. 8(c).]

History – Reg. 38 revoked by SI 2007/794, reg. 8(c), with effect from 6 April 2007.

The continuing validity condition

39   [Revoked by SI 2007/794, reg. 8(c).]

History – Reg. 39 revoked by SI 2007/794, reg. 8(c), with effect from 6 April 2007.

The qualifying circumstances condition

40   [Revoked by SI 2007/794, reg. 8(c).]

History – Reg. 40 revoked by SI 2007/794, reg. 8(c), with effect from 6 April 2007.

The joint holding condition

41 [Revoked by SI 2007/794, reg. 8(c).]

History – Reg. 41 revoked by SI 2007/794, reg. 8(c), with effect from 6 April 2007.

Qualifying certificates valid for only part of jointly held accounts: introductory

42 [Revoked by SI 2007/794, reg. 8(c).]

History – Reg. 42 revoked by SI 2007/794, reg. 8(c), with effect from 6 April 2007.

Qualifying certificates valid for only part of jointly held accounts: the general rule

43 [Revoked by SI 2007/794, reg. 8(c).]

History – Reg. 43 revoked by SI 2007/794, reg. 8(c), with effect from 6 April 2007.

Qualifying certificates valid for only part of jointly held accounts: further provisions

44 [Revoked by SI 2007/794, reg. 8(c).]

History – Reg. 44 revoked by SI 2007/794, reg. 8(c), with effect from 6 April 2007.

Consequences of notice under regulation 39(6)

45 [Revoked by SI 2007/794, reg. 8(c).]

History – Reg. 45 revoked by SI 2007/794, reg. 8(c), with effect from 6 April 2007.

Qualifying certificate not in writing

46 [Revoked by SI 2007/794, reg. 8(c).]

History – Reg. 46 revoked by SI 2007/794, reg. 8(c), with effect from 6 April 2007.

ANNUAL PAYMENTS TO NON-RESIDENTS

Annual Payments – duty to deduct income tax

46A(1) An annual payment made to a participant which meets the conditions in paragraphs (2) to (6) is not a qualifying annual payment for the purposes of Chapter 6 of Part 15 of ITA 2007 (deduction from annual payments and royalties).

46A(2) The payment must be charged to income tax under Chapter 7 of Part 5 of ITTOIA 2005 (annual payments not otherwise charged).

46A(3) The payment must be made in respect of the participant's interest in an authorised investment fund other than a Property AIF.

46A(4) The payment and the amount of the payment must be directly or indirectly referable to, and must not be more than, any management fees paid to the manager of the authorised investment fund in respect of the participant's interest in the fund.

46A(5) Any management fees must not exceed an amount representing a reasonable commercial amount in all the circumstances.

46A(6) At the time the payment is made, the person making the payment must have reasonable grounds for believing that–

(a) the participant is not resident in the United Kingdom, or

(b) the payment is made in respect of a class of units in relation to which of the offshore marketing condition in regulation 33A is met.

History – Reg. 46A(6)(a) and (b) (and the "that–" before them) substituted for the words "that the participant is not resident in the United Kingdom." by SI 2013/2994, reg. 5, with effect in relation to units acquired on or after 19 December 2013.
Reg. 46A inserted by SI 2013/1772, reg. 2(2), with effect in relation to annual payments made on or after 7 August 2013.

Consequences of reasonable but incorrect belief

46B(1) This regulation applies if–

(a) an annual payment is made to a participant without a sum representing income tax on the payment being deducted from it,

(b) at the time the payment is made, the condition in regulation 46A(6)(a) is met,

(c) the payment would be a qualifying annual payment but for that condition being met, and

(d) at the time the payment is made, the participant is resident in the United Kingdom.

46B(2) Section 900 (deduction from commercial payments made by individuals) and section 901 (deduction from annual payments made by other persons) of ITA 2007 apply as if the payment were a qualifying annual payment.

History – In reg. 46B(1)(b), the words "regulation 46A(6)(a)" substituted for the words "regulation 46A(6)" by SI 2013/2994, reg. 6, with effect in relation to units acquired on or after 19 December 2013.
Reg. 46B inserted by SI 2013/1772, reg. 2(2), with effect in relation to annual payments made on or after 7 August 2013.

Chapter 3 – Participants Chargeable to Corporation Tax

INTEREST DISTRIBUTIONS

The obligation to deduct tax

47(1) This regulation applies if an interest distribution is made for a distribution period to a participant chargeable to corporation tax.

47(2) The deduction obligation does not apply to the interest distribution.

47(3) But if the participant is a company which is the trustee of the trust to which (or under which) the interest distribution is made (or received), the deduction obligation is not excluded by virtue of paragraph (2).

47(4) In its application to an interest distribution to a participant in respect of accumulation units, the deduction obligation is an obligation to deduct a sum out of the amount being invested on the participant's behalf.

DIVIDEND DISTRIBUTIONS

General

48(1) Paragraph (2) applies if–

(a)   a dividend distribution for a distribution period is made to a participant by the legal owner of an authorised investment fund, and

(b)   on the distribution date for that distribution period the participant is within the charge to corporation tax.

48(2) Subject to paragraphs (2A), (2B) and (2BA), for the purpose of computing the corporation tax chargeable upon the participant, the unfranked part of the dividend distribution is treated–

(a)   as an annual payment and not as a dividend distribution or an interest distribution; and

(b)   as having been received by the participant after deduction of tax at a rate equal to the basic rate of income tax for the tax year in which the distribution date falls, from a corresponding gross amount.

48(2A) But paragraph (2) does not apply to a dividend distribution to which Chapter 2 of Part 3 of CTA 2009 applies unless the dividend distribution is made to–

(a)   an insurance company in respect of any non-BLAGAB long-term business carried on by it, or

(b)   an insurance special purpose vehicle that is not an insurance company in respect of any long-term business carried on by it that does not consist wholly of PHI business.

Expressions used in paragraph (a) or (b) have the same meaning as they have in Part 2 of FA 2012.

48(2B) If, on the distribution date, the participant is the manager of the authorised investment fund, paragraph (2) shall not apply to the extent that the rights in respect of which the dividend distribution is made are held by him in the ordinary course of the manager's business as manager of the fund.

48(2BA) Paragraph (2)(b) does not apply to so much of any dividend distribution as on a just and reasonable apportionment is attributable to an unallowable arrangement.

48(2BB) For the purposes of paragraph (2BA), an unallowable arrangement is an arrangement the main purpose or one of the main purposes of which is to secure that an amount of tax, or an increased amount of tax, is treated as deducted under paragraph (2)(b).

48(2BC) In paragraph (2BB), **"arrangement"** includes any arrangement, agreement, scheme, transaction, series of transactions or understanding (whether or not legally enforceable).

48(2C) Regulation 48A makes provision in relation to the unfranked part of the dividend distribution treated as an annual payment under paragraph (2)(a) and regulation 48B makes provision in relation to the tax treated as deducted under paragraph (2)(b).

48(3) Regulation 49 explains how to calculate the unfranked part of the dividend distribution.

48(4) This regulation does not apply in respect of a holding in a qualified investor scheme if the scheme has not met the genuine diversity of ownership condition in regulation 9A in relation to an accounting period.

History – In reg. 48(2), ", (2B) and (2BA)" substituted for "and (2B)" by SI 2012/519, reg. 5(2), with effect in relation to any distribution made at or after 1.30 p.m. on 27 February 2012.
In reg. 48(2)(b), the words "tax at a rate equal to the basic rate of income tax" substituted for the words "income tax at the basic rate" by SI 2010/1642, reg. 4(2), with effect in relation to distributions made at or after 1.45 p.m. on 22 June 2010.

Reg. 48(2A) amended and (2A)(a) and (b) inserted by SI 2012/3043, reg. 2(2), with effect in relation to dividend distributions (within the meaning given by reg. 22(3)) made on or after 1 January 2013.
Reg. 48(2BA), (2BB) and (2BC) inserted by SI 2012/519, reg. 5(3), with effect in relation to any distribution made at or after 1.30 p.m. on 27 February 2012.
Reg. 48(2C) inserted by SI 2010/1642, reg. 4(3), with effect in relation to distributions made at or after 1.45 p.m. on 22 June 2010.
In reg. 48(4), "9A" substituted for "14C" by SI 2009/2036, reg. 12, with effect from 1 September 2009.
In reg. 48(2), the words "Subject to paragraphs (2A) and (2B)," inserted by SI 2008/3159, reg. 13(2), with effect from 1 January 2009, subject to the transitional rules in SI 2008/3159, reg. 1(2), 30 and 31.
In reg. 48(2)(b) "basic rate" substituted for "lower rate", and "tax year" substituted for "year of assessment", by SI 2008/3159, reg. 13(3), with effect from 1 January 2009.
In reg. 48(2A), the words "Chapter 2 of Part 3 of CTA 2009" substituted for the words "section 95 of ICTA or section 219(4) of FA 1994" by SI 2010/294, reg. 14, with effect from 6 March 2010.
Reg. 48(2A) inserted by SI 2008/3159, reg. 13(4), with effect from 1 January 2009, subject to the transitional rules in SI 2008/3159, reg. 1(2), 30 and 31.
Reg. 48(2B) inserted by SI 2008/3159, reg. 13(4), with effect from 1 January 2009, subject to the transitional rules in SI 2008/3159, reg. 1(2), 30 and 31.
Reg. 48(4) inserted by SI 2008/3159, reg. 13(5), with effect from 1 January 2009, subject to the transitional rules in SI 2008/3159, reg. 1(2), 30 and 31.

Income treated as an annual payment treated as foreign income

48A   If there is a foreign element of the tax treated as deducted under regulation 48(2)(b) (see regulation 48B), a corresponding proportionate part of the distribution which is treated as an annual payment under regulation 48(2)(a) is treated as if it were income that—

(a)   arises in a territory of the kind mentioned in regulation 48B(3)(a), and

(b)   is income by reference to which the tax treated under that provision as payable was computed.

History – Reg. 48A inserted by SI 2010/1642, reg. 5, with effect in relation to distributions made at or after 1.45 p.m. on 22 June 2010.

Tax treated as deducted from a dividend distribution

48B(1)   The tax treated as deducted under regulation 48(2)(b) ("the deemed deduction") is treated as income tax.

48B(2)   But paragraph (1) does not apply to any foreign element of the deemed deduction.

48B(3)   Instead, for the purposes of the Tax Acts the foreign element of the deemed deduction is treated as if it were tax—

(a)   payable under the law of a territory outside the United Kingdom with which there are not in force any arrangements under section 2(1) of TIOPA 2010 (double taxation relief by agreement),

(b)   calculated by reference to income arising or any chargeable gain accruing, in the territory, and

(c)   corresponding to United Kingdom corporation tax.

48B(4)   The amount of the foreign element of the deemed deduction is the amount, if any, by which the participant's portion of the legal owner's liability to corporation tax in respect of the gross income is reduced by any relief which is given, or falls to be given by way of a credit under section 18 of TIOPA 2010 (entitlement to credit for foreign tax reduces UK tax by amount of the credit).

48B(5)   For the purposes of paragraph (4) the participant's portion shall be determined by reference to the proportions in which participants have rights in the authorised investment fund in the distribution period in question.

History – Reg. 48B inserted by SI 2010/1642, reg. 5, with effect in relation to distributions made at or after 1.45 p.m. on 22 June 2010.

Calculation of unfranked part of dividend distribution

49(1)   This is how to calculate the unfranked part of the dividend distribution—

$$U = \frac{A \times C}{D}$$

49(2)   In paragraph (1)—

U = the unfranked part of the dividend distribution to the participant;

A = the amount of the dividend distribution;

C = such amount of the gross income as derives from income in respect of which the legal owner is charged to corporation tax, as reduced by—

(a)   any amount carried forward from an earlier accounting period and allowed as a deduction in computing the legal owner's liability to corporation tax for the accounting period in which the last day of the distribution period falls, and

(b)   an amount equal to the legal owner's net liability to corporation tax in respect of the gross income.

D = the amount of the gross income, as reduced by an amount equal to the legal owner's net liability to corporation tax in respect of the gross income.

49(2A)   [Omitted by SI 2012/519, reg. 6(3).]

49(3)   Any reference in this regulation to the legal owner's net liability to corporation tax in respect of the gross income is a reference to the amount of the liability of the legal owner to corporation tax in respect of that gross income less the amount (if any) of any reduction of that liability which is given or falls to be given in accordance with any arrangements having effect by virtue of section 788 of ICTA (relief by agreement with other territories) or by way of a credit under section 790(1) of that Act (unilateral relief).

History – In reg. 49(2), the definition of "C" substituted by SI 2012/519, reg. 6(2), with effect in relation to any distribution made in respect of a distribution period ending at or after 1.30 p.m. on 27 February 2012. The former definition read as follows:
> "C = such amount of the gross income as does not derive from franked investment income, as reduced by an amount equal to the legal owner's net liability to corporation tax in respect of the gross income;".

Reg. 49(2A) omitted by SI 2012/519, reg. 6(3), with effect in relation to any distribution made in respect of a distribution period ending at or after 1.30 p.m. on 27 February 2012. Former reg. 49(2A) read as follows:
> "**49(2A)**   For the purpose of calculating the value of C in paragraph (1) in relation to a distribution made by an authorised investment fund ("AIF1") to a participant, the amount of any distribution from another authorised investment fund ("AIF2") which is treated by AIF1 as an annual payment by virtue of regulation 48(2)(a), shall be treated as not deriving from franked investment income arising to AIF2."

Former reg. 49(2A) inserted by SI 2008/3159, reg. 14, with effect from 1 January 2009, subject to the transitional rules in SI 2008/3159, reg. 1(2), 30 and 31.

References to gross income

50   For the purposes of this Chapter, references to gross income are references to the net revenue before taxation determined in accordance with the Statement of Recommended Practice.

History – Reg. 50 substituted by SI 2010/294, reg. 15, with effect from 6 March 2010 (subject to the transitional provisions at SI 2010/294, reg. 24). Former reg. 50 read as follows:
> "**50**   For the purposes of this Chapter the references to the gross income are references to the gross income entered in the distribution accounts for the purpose of computing the total amount available for distribution to participants for the distribution period in question."

Participants chargeable to corporation tax: holdings in qualified investor schemes where scheme does not meet the genuine diversity of ownership condition

51(1)   This regulation applies if–

(a)   a participant has a holding in a qualified investor scheme, and

(b)   the scheme has not met the genuine diversity of ownership condition in regulation 9A in relation to an accounting period.

51(2)   Section 212 of TCGA 1992 (annual deemed disposal of holdings of unit trusts etc.) does not apply to the participant in relation to that accounting period.

51(3)   Paragraph 4 of Schedule 10 to FA 1996 (company holdings in unit trusts and offshore funds) shall not apply to the participant in relation to that accounting period.

History – In reg. 51(1)(b), "9A" substituted for "14B" by SI 2009/2036, reg. 12, with effect from 1 September 2009. Reg. 51 substituted by SI 2008/3159, reg. 15, with effect from 1 January 2009, subject to the transitional rules in SI 2008/3159, reg. 1(2), 30 and 31. Former reg. 51 read as follows:
> "**Cases where participant is the manager of the fund**
> **51**   If on the distribution date the participant is the manager of the authorised investment fund, regulation 48(2) shall not apply in so far as the rights in respect of which the dividend distribution is made are held by him in the ordinary course of his business as manager of the fund.".

Repayments of tax

52   [Omitted by SI 2010/1642, reg. 6.]

History – Reg. 52 omitted by SI 2010/1642, reg. 6, with effect in relation to distributions made at or after 1.45 p.m. on 22 June 2010. Former reg. 52 read as follows:
> "**52(1)**   This regulation applies if, in relation to a dividend distribution, any tax is treated as having been deducted by virtue of regulation 48(2)(b).
> **52(2)**   The amount to which the participant is entitled by way of repayment of that tax must not exceed the amount of the participant's portion of the legal owner's net liability to corporation tax in respect of the gross income.
> **52(3)**   In calculating the amount to which the participant is entitled by way of repayment of that tax, tax treated as having been deducted by virtue of regulation 48(2)(b) is set off in priority to any other tax under section 7(2) of ICTA and under paragraph 5 of Schedule 16 to that Act.
> **52(4)**   For the purposes of paragraph (2) the participant's portion shall be determined by reference to the proportions in which participants have rights in the authorised investment fund in the distribution period in question.".

COMPANIES CARRYING ON GENERAL INSURANCE BUSINESS: TREATMENT OF CERTAIN AMOUNTS OF TAX AS FOREIGN TAX

52A   [Omitted by SI 2010/1642, reg. 7.]

History – Reg. 52A omitted by SI 2010/1642, reg. 7, with effect in relation to distributions made at or after 1.45 p.m. on 22 June 2010. Former reg. 52A read as follows:

"**52A(1)**   This regulation applies if conditions A to C are met.

52A(2)   Condition A is that–

(a)   an authorised investment fund makes a dividend distribution, to which regulation 48(2) applies, to a participant carrying on general insurance business, and

(b)   the distribution mentioned in sub-paragraph (a) falls to be brought into account as a trading receipt of that business.

52A(3)   Condition B is that there is some foreign tax suffered by the authorised investment fund in respect of which relief is given or falls to be given in accordance with any arrangements having effect by virtue of section 788 of ICTA (relief by agreement with other territories) or by way of a credit under section 790(1) of that Act (unilateral relief).

52A(4)   Condition C is that the participant–

(a)   owns units which represent rights to 10% or more of the net asset value of the authorised investment fund; and

(b)   does not own those units as a nominee or a bare trustee.

52A(5)   But, for the purposes of paragraph (4), rights in an authorised investment fund held as assets of a company's long-term insurance fund are not treated as held by the participant.

52A(6)   For the purposes of the specified provisions, an amount equal to the participant's portion of the foreign tax mentioned in paragraph (3) is treated as foreign tax and not as United Kingdom tax.

52A(7)   For the purposes of paragraph (6), the participant's portion shall be determined by reference to the proportions in which participants have rights in the authorised investment fund in the distribution period in question.

52A(8)   In paragraph (6), **"the specified provisions"** means–

(a)   section 804C of ICTA (insurance companies: allocation of expenses etc in computations under Case I of Schedule D), to the extent that it applies to business of a company which is not long-term business; and

(b)   regulation 48.

52A(9)   In this regulation–

"general insurance business" means the business of effecting and carrying out contracts of insurance falling within Part 1 of Schedule 1 to the Financial Services and Markets Act 2000 (Regulated Activities) Order 2001;

"long-term business" has the meaning given in section 431(2) of ICTA (interpretative provisions relating to insurance companies).

History – Reg. 52A substituted by SI 2008/3159, reg. 16, with effect from 1 January 2009, subject to the transitional rules in SI 2008/3159, reg. 1(2), 30 and 31. Former reg. 52A read as follows:

"BANKS AND OTHER FINANCIAL TRADERS: TREATMENT OF CERTAIN AMOUNTS OF TAX AS FOREIGN TAX

52A(1)   This regulation applies if–

(a)   conditions A to C are met, and

(b)   either condition D or E is met.

52A(2)   Condition A is that an authorised investment fund makes a dividend distribution to which regulation 48(2) applies.

52A(3)   Condition B is that there is some foreign tax suffered by the authorised investment fund in respect of which relief is given or falls to be given in accordance with any arrangements having effect by virtue of section 788 of ICTA (relief by agreement with other territories) or by way of a credit under section 790(1) of that Act (unilateral relief).

52A(4)   Condition C is that the dividend distribution is made to a participant carrying on–

(a)   a banking business, or

(b)   any other business where a distribution from an authorised investment fund is treated as a trading receipt.

52A(5)   Condition D is that the participant, either alone or together with connected persons (and otherwise than as a nominee or bare trustee), owns units which represent rights to 50% or more of the net asset value of the authorised investment fund.

52A(6)   But for the purposes of paragraph (5) rights in an authorised investment fund held as assets of a company's long-term insurance fund are not treated as held by the participant (either alone or together with connected persons) for the purposes of determining whether the participant owns units which represent rights to 50% or more of the net asset value of the authorised investment fund.

52A(6A)   Condition E is that the participant is a financial trader who–

(a)   owns units which represent rights to 10% or more of the net asset value of the authorised investment fund, and

(b)   does not own those units as a nominee or bare trustee.

52A(7)   Section 839 of ICTA (connected persons) applies for the purposes of this regulation.

52A(8)   For the purposes of the specified provisions, an amount equal to the participant's portion of the foreign tax mentioned in paragraph (3) is treated as foreign tax and not as United Kingdom tax.

52A(9)   For the purposes of paragraph (8) the participant's portion shall be determined by reference to the proportions in which participants have rights in the authorised investment fund in the distribution period in question.

52A(10) In paragraph (8) **"the specified provisions"** means–

(a)   section 798A of ICTA (limits for credit on foreign tax: corporation tax on trade income), and

(b)   section 804C of ICTA (insurance companies: allocation of expenses etc. in computations under Case I of Schedule D) to the extent that it applies to business of a company which is not long-term business.

52A(11) In this regulation **"financial trader"** means a participant who meets condition C (see paragraph (4));**"long-term business"** and **"long-term insurance fund"** have the same meanings as in Chapter 1 of Part 12 of ICTA (insurance companies etc.).".".

DIVERSELY OWNED AIFS AND FINANCIAL TRADERS: TREATMENT OF SHARES AND UNITS

52B(1)   This regulation and regulation 52C apply if a financial trader has held, or holds, shares or units in a diversely owned AIF.

52B(2)   In computing the trading profits or losses of the financial trader for the relevant period, the following amounts must be brought into account–

(a)   all distributions received by or credited to the financial trader in respect of such shares or units for the relevant period; and

(b)   any amount required to be brought into account under regulation 52C.

52B(3) In this regulation and in regulation 52D(2) references to distributions are subject to section 130 of CTA 2009 (insurers receiving distributions etc).

52B(4) In this regulation and in regulations 52C and 52D—

"**relevant period**" means—

(a)　in the case of a financial trader within the charge to corporation tax, an accounting period, and

(b)　in the case of a financial trader within the charge to income tax, a period of account;

"**financial trader**" has the meaning given by regulation 52E.

History – Reg. 52B inserted by SI 2009/2036, reg. 14, with effect from 1 September 2009.

FINANCIAL TRADERS: AMOUNTS TO BE BROUGHT INTO ACCOUNT IN RESPECT OF SHARES OR UNITS HELD IN DIVERSELY OWNED AIFS

52C(1) The only amounts that are to be brought into account in computing the trading profits or losses in respect of the shares or units in the diversely owned AIF for the relevant period are—

(a)　amounts that are brought into account in accordance with Cases 1 to 4, and

(b)　amounts within regulation 52B(2)(a).

This is subject to section 130 of CTA 2009 (insurers receiving distributions etc) and regulation 52D.

52C(2) Case 1 applies if the financial trader held the shares or units in a diversely owned AIF at the beginning of the relevant period and holds those shares or units throughout that period.

Where Case 1 applies, the amount to be brought into account is the difference between the market value of the shares or units at the end of the immediately preceding relevant period and the market value of those shares or units at the end of the relevant period.

52C(3) Case 2 applies if a financial trader acquired shares or units in a diversely owned AIF during the relevant period and retains those shares or units throughout the relevant period.

Where Case 2 applies, the amount to be brought into account is the difference between the market value of the shares or units at the end of the relevant period and the acquisition cost of those shares or units.

52C(4) Case 3 applies if the financial trader held shares or units in a diversely owned AIF at the beginning of the relevant period and disposes of those shares or units during that period.

Where Case 3 applies the amount to be brought into account is the difference between the market value of the shares or units at the end of the immediately preceding relevant period and the disposal value of the shares or units.

52C(5) Case 4 applies if the financial trader acquires shares or units in a diversely owned AIF during the relevant period and disposes of those shares or units during that period.

Where Case 4 applies the amount to be brought into account is the difference between the acquisition cost of the shares or units and the disposal value of those shares or units.

52C(6) In this regulation—

"**acquisition cost**" means the value of the consideration given for the acquisition of the shares or units;

"**disposal value**" means the value of the consideration received for the disposal of the shares or units;

"**market value**" means—

(a)　in the case of shares or units in a diversely owned AIF where both the buying and selling prices of units are published regularly by the manager of the fund, an amount equal to the buying price (that is the lower price) so published on any particular date or, if none were published on that date, on the latest date before;

(b)　in the case of shares or units in a diversely owned AIF where a single price is published regularly by the manager of the fund, the price so published on any particular date, or if none were published on that date, on the latest date before.

History – Reg. 52C inserted by SI 2009/2036, reg. 14, with effect from 1 September 2009.

SHARES AND UNITS NOT WITHIN REGULATION 52C

52D(1) Regulation 52C does not apply in respect of any shares or units in a diversely owned AIF in relation to which—

(a)　conditions A and B are both satisfied, or

(b)　condition C is satisfied.

52D(2)   Condition A is that the shares or units in the diversely owned AIF form part of the financial trader's stock in trade and all the profits and losses, including distributions, arising in relation to the shares or units in the diversely owned AIF are included in the computation of the financial trader's trading profits for the relevant period.

52D(3)   Condition B is that the shares or units in the diversely owned AIF are accounted for under generally accepted accounting practice on the basis of fair value accounting.

52D(4)   Condition C is that the shares or units in the diversely owned AIF are a relevant holding in respect of which the provisions of section 490 of CTA 2009 apply in relation to the financial trader.

52D(5)   In paragraph (4) **"relevant holding"** means–

(a)   any rights under a unit trust scheme;

(b)   an interest in an offshore fund; or

(c)   any shares in an open-ended investment company.

History – In reg. 52D(5)(b), the words "an interest" substituted for the words "a material interest" by SI 2013/1411, reg. 14(a), with effect from 28 June 2013.
Reg. 52D inserted by SI 2009/2036, reg. 14, with effect from 1 September 2009.

MEANING OF FINANCIAL TRADER

52E(1)   In regulations 52B, 52C and 52D **"financial trader"** means a person who is carrying on a business which is–

(a)   a banking business,

(b)   an insurance business, or

(c)   a business consisting wholly or in part of dealing in trading assets such that any profit on such assets would form part of the trading profits of that business.

This paragraph is subject to paragraphs (2) and (3).

52E(2)   **"An insurance business"** in paragraph (1)(b) does not include life assurance business carried on by an insurance company and in the event that such a company carries on both life assurance business and any other insurance business that company will not be a financial trader in respect of the life assurance business.

52E(3)   If–

(a)   a financial trader, "A", directly or indirectly transfers trading assets to a diversely owned AIF under or as part of an arrangement which has an unallowable purpose, and

(b)   a connected person, "B"–

    (i)   holds shares or units in that diversely owned AIF at the time of the transfer; or

    (ii)   directly or indirectly acquires shares or units in that diversely owned AIF at a later time,

B is treated as being a financial trader in relation to those shares or units.

52E(4)   In paragraphs (1) and (3) **"trading assets"** means–

(a)   stocks or shares;

(b)   a relevant contract within regulation 14G;

(c)   a loan relationship within regulation 14L;

(d)   units in a collective investment scheme within regulation 14M;

(e)   securities within regulation 14F;

(f)   foreign currency; or

(g)   a carbon emission trading product within regulation 14N,

a profit on the sale of which would form part of the trading profits of the financial trader.

52E(5)   An arrangement includes any scheme, understanding or transaction of any kind, whether or not legally enforceable and whether involving a single transaction or two or more transactions.

52E(6)   An arrangement has an unallowable purpose if the main purpose or one of the main purposes for either A or B being party to the arrangement is to obtain a tax advantage or an income tax advantage for any person.

52E(7)   In paragraph (6)–

    "tax advantage" has the meaning given by section of 840ZA of ICTA; and

    "income tax advantage" has the meaning given by section 683 of ITA 2007.

History – Reg. 52E inserted by SI 2009/2036, reg. 14, with effect from 1 September 2009.

Chapter 4 – Charge to Tax on Substantial QIS Holdings in Qualified Investor Schemes

History – Pt. 4, Ch. 4 omitted by SI 2008/3159, reg. 17, with effect from 1 January 2009, subject to the transitional rules in SI 2008/3159, reg. 1(2), 30 and 31. Former Pt. 4, Ch. 4 read as follows:

"Chapter 4 – Charge to Tax on Substantial QIS Holdings in Qualified Investor Schemes

GENERAL

Charge to tax under this Chapter

53(1)   A participant is charged to tax under this Chapter if the participant owns a substantial QIS holding in a qualified investor scheme.

53(2)   But a participant is excepted from the charge to tax under this Chapter if the participant is–
(a)   a charity within the meaning of section 506(1) of ICTA;
(b)   a registered pension scheme within the meaning of Part 4 of the Finance Act 2004;
(c)   a scheme which is treated, under paragraph 1(1) of Schedule 36 to the Finance Act 2004, as a registered pension scheme within the meaning of Part 4 of that Act;
(d)   an insurance company within the meaning of section 431(2) of ICTA holding the units in the qualified investor scheme as assets of its long-term insurance fund;
(e)   a friendly society within the meaning of section 466(2) of ICTA;
(f)   a person for whom any profit on a sale of the units in the qualified investor scheme would be treated as a trading profit of its trade; or
(g)   a qualified investor scheme.

53(3)   In these Regulations a **"qualified investor scheme"** means a fund, authorised by the Financial Services Authority, in which a statement that the fund is a qualified investor scheme is included in the instrument constituting the scheme.

53(4)   In paragraph (2)(d) **"long-term insurance fund"** has the meaning given by section 431(2) of ICTA.

Meaning of "substantial QIS holding"

54(1)   For the purposes of this Chapter a participant owns a substantial QIS holding in a qualified investor scheme if the participant, either alone or together with associates or connected persons, (and otherwise than as a nominee or a bare trustee) owns units which represent rights to 10% or more of the net asset value of the fund.

This is without prejudice to what is meant by "substantial" where the word appears in other contexts.

54(2)   Section 417 of ICTA applies for the purposes of this regulation to determine whether persons are associates.

54(3)   Section 839 of ICTA (connected persons) applies for the purposes of this regulation.

54(4)   A participant who owns a substantial QIS holding in a qualified investor scheme continues to own a substantial QIS holding in that scheme until the date on which the whole of that holding is disposed of (so that, accordingly, it does not matter that the holding no longer represents 10% or more of the net value of the qualified investor scheme).

54(5)   Paragraph (4) is subject to regulation 63 (cases where a participant's holding becomes substantial).

Amount charged to tax under this Chapter

55(1)   A participant is charged to tax under this Chapter by reference to the difference in value of a substantial QIS holding between two measuring dates (the "difference in value").

55(2)   The difference in value is the amount given by the formula–

VLMD – VEMD

55(3)   In paragraph (2)–

VLMD is the market value of the substantial QIS holding at the beginning of a chargeable measuring date (the "later measuring date"), and

VEMD is the market value of the substantial QIS holding at the end of the previous measuring date (the "earlier measuring date").

55(4)   In the case of units in a qualified investor scheme where both the buying and selling prices of units are published regularly by the manager of the scheme, **"market value"** means an amount equal to the buying price (that is the lower price) so published on any particular date, or if none were published on that date, on the latest date before.

55(5)   In the case of units in a qualified investor scheme where a single price is published regularly by the manager of the scheme, **"market value"** means the price so published on any particular date, or if none were published on that date, on the latest date before.

Measuring dates and meaning of "chargeable measuring date"

56(1)   Each of the following is a measuring date–
(a)   the first measuring date (see regulation 64);
(b)   in a case where a participant already owns a substantial QIS holding in a qualified investor scheme, the date on which the participant acquires additional units in the qualified investor scheme;
(c)   any reporting date;
(d)   the date on which there is a disposal of part of the substantial QIS holding (see regulation 67);
(e)   the date on which there is a disposal of the whole of the substantial QIS holding (see regulation 68);
(f)   the date of the participant's death.

56(2)   In this Chapter a **"chargeable measuring date"** means any measuring date other than the first measuring date.

How tax is charged under this Chapter: income tax

57(1)   This regulation applies in the case of a participant chargeable to income tax.

57(2)   The following amounts must be calculated–
(a)   the difference in value calculated by reference to each chargeable measuring date falling within a tax year; and
(b)   the aggregate amount of those differences in value.

Statutory Instruments

57(3)   If the aggregate amount is a positive amount, the participant is charged to income tax under Chapter 8 of Part 5 of ITTOIA 2005 (income not otherwise charged) on that aggregate amount for that tax year.

57(4)   If the aggregate amount is a negative amount, the participant is treated as if–
(a)   a loss of that aggregate amount had been sustained by the participant in a transaction, and
(b)   this regulation were listed in Part 3 of the Table in section 836B of ICTA.

How tax is charged under this Chapter: corporation tax

58(1)   This regulation applies in the case of a participant chargeable to corporation tax.

58(2)   The following amounts must be calculated–
(a)   the difference in value calculated by reference to each chargeable measuring date falling within an accounting period; and
(b)   the aggregate amount of those differences in value.

58(3)   If the aggregate amount is a positive amount, the participant is charged to corporation tax under Case VI of Schedule D on that aggregate amount for that accounting period.

58(4)   If the aggregate amount is a negative amount, the participant is treated as if a loss of that aggregate amount had been incurred by the participant in a transaction in respect of which the participant were within the charge to corporation tax under Case VI of Schedule D.

Further provisions

59(1)   In this Chapter **"disposal"** is to be construed in accordance with TCGA 1992, and cognate expressions are to be construed accordingly.

59(2)   The provisions of TCGA 1992 that apply to determine–
(a)   the time at which a disposal and acquisition is made, and
(b)   how assets disposed of are to be identified,
apply for the purposes of this Chapter in the same way as they apply for the purposes of that Act.

THE FIRST MEASURING DATE

The general rule

60(1)   The general rule is that on the first date on which a participant who is within the charge to tax under this Chapter owns a substantial QIS holding in a qualified investor scheme, the participant must value his own holding in that scheme as at that date.

60(2)   The general rule is modified if any of the following regulations apply–
(a)   regulation 61 (cases affected by the coming into force of these Regulations);
(b)   regulation 62 (cases involving the launch of qualified investor schemes);
(c)   regulation 63 (cases where a participant's holding becomes substantial).

Cases affected by the coming into force of these Regulations

61(1)   This regulation applies if–
(a)   a participant chargeable to income tax owns a substantial QIS holding in a qualified investor scheme on 6th April 2006, or
(b)   a participant chargeable to corporation tax owns a substantial QIS holding in a qualified investor scheme on 1st April 2006.

61(2)   If on the measuring date first occurring after 30th June 2006 the participant does not own a substantial QIS holding in the qualified investor scheme, the participant is not required to value his own holding in that scheme as at 1st or 6th April 2006 (as the case may be).

61(3)   If on the measuring date first occurring after 30th June 2006 the participant owns a substantial QIS holding in the qualified investor scheme and is chargeable to income tax, the participant must value his own holding in that scheme as at 6th April 2006.

61(4)   If on the measuring date first occurring after 30th June 2006 the participant owns a substantial QIS holding in the qualified investor scheme and is chargeable to corporation tax, the participant must value its own holding in that scheme as at 1st April 2006.

Cases involving the launch of qualified investor schemes

62(1)   This regulation applies if a qualified investor scheme is launched.

62(2)   If on the date immediately following the expiry of a period of twelve months beginning with the date of issue of the first prospectus of the scheme ("the qualification date") the participant does not own a substantial QIS holding in the qualified investor scheme, the participant is not required to value his own holding in that scheme as at that date or any earlier date.

62(3)   If on the qualification date the participant owns a substantial QIS holding in the qualified investor scheme, the participant must value his own holding in that scheme as at the date on which the participant first owned a substantial QIS holding in the scheme.

Cases where a participant's holding becomes substantial

63(1)   This regulation applies if, on any date, a participant owns a substantial QIS holding in a qualified investor scheme otherwise than as a result of the acquisition of units in that scheme.

63(2)   If on the next reporting date and the reporting date following it ("the second reporting date") the participant does not own a substantial QIS holding in the qualified investor scheme, the participant–
(a)   is not required to value his own holding in that scheme at any time, and
(b)   is not treated as owning a substantial QIS holding in the scheme on the second reporting date or at any earlier time.

63(3)   If on the second reporting date the participant owns a substantial QIS holding in the qualified investor scheme, the participant must value his own holding in that scheme as at the date mentioned in paragraph (1) and as at each subsequent measuring date.

Definition of the "first measuring date"

64   In this Chapter the **"first measuring date"** means the date on which, in accordance with regulation 60(1), 61(3) or (4), 62(3) or 63(3), the participant must value his own holding in the qualified investor scheme.

Calculation to be made on the first measuring date

65   On the first measuring date the participant must calculate the chargeable gain or loss that would have accrued for the purposes of tax in respect of chargeable gains if, on that date, the participant had disposed of the substantial QIS holding for a consideration equal to its market value at that time.

DISPOSALS OF HOLDINGS

Reorganisations etc.

66(1)   For the purposes of this Chapter, sections 116(10) and 127 of TCGA 1992 (reorganisations) do not apply to a substantial QIS holding in a qualified investor scheme; and a transaction which would otherwise have fallen within either of those provisions is treated as involving a disposal and subsequent acquisition of that holding.

66(2)   The consideration for the subsequent acquisition is a consideration equal to the market value of the holding immediately before the acquisition.

Disposal of part of a substantial QIS holding

67(1)   This regulation applies if a participant disposes of part of a substantial QIS holding.

67(2)   The date on which the participant disposes of the part of the substantial QIS holding is a chargeable measuring date.

67(3)   For the purposes of tax in respect of chargeable gains a corresponding part of the chargeable gain or loss specified in regulation 65 is treated as accruing on the disposal.

67(4)   Subject to paragraph (3) and for the purposes of tax in respect of chargeable gains, the participant is treated as making the disposal for a consideration of such amount as would secure that neither a gain nor a loss would accrue to the participant.

67(5)   For the purposes of tax in respect of chargeable gains, this regulation does not affect the treatment of the other party to the transaction involving the part of the substantial QIS holding of which there has been a disposal.

67(6)   This regulation is subject to regulation 69 (no gain/no loss disposals).

Disposal of the whole of a substantial QIS holding

68(1)   This regulation applies if a participant disposes of the whole of a substantial QIS holding.

68(2)   The date on which the participant disposes of the substantial QIS holding is a chargeable measuring date.

68(3)   For the purposes of tax in respect of chargeable gains–

(a)   in a case where regulation 67 has applied on any earlier disposal of part of the substantial QIS holding, the remaining part of the chargeable gain or loss specified in regulation 65 is treated as accruing on the disposal, and

(b)   in any other case, the whole of the chargeable gain or loss specified in regulation 65 is treated as accruing on the disposal.

68(4)   Subject to paragraph (3) and for the purposes of tax in respect of chargeable gains, the participant is treated as making the disposal for a consideration of such amount as would secure that neither a gain nor a loss would accrue to the participant.

68(5)   For the purposes of tax in respect of chargeable gains, this regulation does not affect the treatment of the other party to the transaction involving the substantial QIS holding.

68(6)   This regulation is subject to regulation 69 (no gain/no loss disposals).

No gain/no loss disposals

69(1)   This regulation applies if, for the purposes of tax in respect of chargeable gains, any disposal of the whole or part of a substantial QIS holding falls within any of the following provisions of TCGA 1992–

(a)   section 58(1) (transfers between spouses);

(b)   section 62(4) (acquisition as legatee);

(c)   section 139 (company reconstructions);

(d)   section 140A (transfers of a UK trade);

(e)   section 140E (merger leaving assets within the UK tax charge);

(f)   section 171(1) (transfers within a group).

69(2)   Regulation 67(3) or 68(3) (as the case may be) does not apply in relation to the disposal.

69(3)   On and after the date of the transfer, the transferee's holding in the qualified investor scheme is a substantial QIS holding in that scheme (whether or not the transferee's holding in that scheme (if any) was a substantial QIS holding in that scheme before that date).

69(4)   If the transferee disposes of the whole or, part, of the substantial QIS holding, the held-over gain or, as the case may be, a corresponding part of the held-over gain, is treated as accruing to the transferee on the disposal.

69(5)   In paragraph (4) **"the held-over gain"** means the chargeable gain or loss that would have accrued to the transferor if the disposal falling within paragraph (1) had been a disposal to which regulation 68(3) had applied."

PART 4A – PROPERTY AIFS

Chapter 1 – Preliminary Provisions

PROPERTY AIFS

History – Pt. 4A inserted by SI 2008/705, reg. 5, with effect from 6 April 2008.

69A(1)   This Part enables an open-ended investment company which meets the conditions in regulations 69D to 69O–

(a)   to benefit from the exemption from corporation tax in accordance with regulation 69Y(1), and

(b)   to have liabilities to tax imposed on the company and on participants in accordance with Chapters 3, 4 and 5 of this Part.

69A(2) In these Regulations an open-ended investment company to which this Part applies may be referred to as a "Property AIF".

STRUCTURE OF THIS PART

69B The structure of this Part of these Regulations is as follows—

This Chapter contains preliminary provisions;

Chapter 2 deals with entry into and membership of the Property AIF regime;

Chapter 3 deals with the tax treatment of Property AIFs;

Chapter 4 deals with distributions made by Property AIFs;

Chapter 5 deals with the treatment of participants in Property AIFs;

Chapter 6 deals with compliance in relation to the Property AIF regime; and

Chapter 7 contains provisions relating to an open-ended investment company's leaving the Property AIF regime.

KEY CONCEPTS

69C(1) In this Part **"entry"** means the time when this Part begins to apply to an open-ended investment company.

69C(2) In this Part **"cessation"** means the time when this Part ceases to apply to an open-ended investment company.

69C(3) In this Part, in relation to an open-ended investment company—

(a) **"F (pre-entry)"** means the open-ended investment company before this Part begins to apply to it,

(b) **"F (tax-exempt)"** means the open-ended investment company in so far as it carries on property investment business (within the meaning of regulation 69F) while this Part applies to it,

(c) **"F (residual)"** means the open-ended investment company in so far as it carries on business other than property investment business while this Part applies to it, and

(d) **"F (post-cessation)"** means the open-ended investment company after this Part has ceased to apply to it.

69C(4) In this Part, a **"dedicated feeder fund"** in relation to a property AIF means a fund which—

(a) is a unit trust scheme;

(b) is dedicated to investment in the property AIF for which it is a feeder fund (in accordance with its prospectus); and

(c) holds at least 85% of its assets in the form of shares in that property AIF.

History – Reg. 69C(4) inserted by SI 2012/1783, reg. 3, with effect for capital gains tax purposes in relation to disposals made on or after 1 August 2012 and for the purposes of corporation tax on chargeable gains in relation to disposals on or after 1 August 2012.

Chapter 2 – Entry Into and Membership of the Property AIF Regime

CONDITIONS OF MEMBERSHIP OF THE PROPERTY AIF REGIME

History – Pt. 4A inserted by SI 2008/705, reg. 5, with effect from 6 April 2008.

Conditions for this Part to apply to company

69D In order for this Part to apply to an open-ended investment company in respect of an accounting period, the following conditions must be met—

(a) the property investment business condition (see regulation 69E);

(b) the genuine diversity of ownership condition (see regulation 9A);

(c) the corporate ownership condition (see regulation 69K);

(d) the loan creditor condition (see regulation 69M);

(e) the balance of business conditions (see regulation 69N); and

(f) the notification condition (see regulation 69O).

History – In reg. 69D(b), "9A" substituted for "69J" by SI 2009/2036, reg. 15, with effect from 1 September 2009.

CONDITIONS FOR THIS PART TO APPLY TO A COMPANY WHERE THE COMPANY IS ALSO A QUALIFIED INVESTOR SCHEME

69DA   [Omitted by SI 2009/2036, reg. 15.]

History – Reg. 69DA omitted by SI 2009/2036, reg. 15, with effect from 1 September 2009. Former reg. 69DA read as follows:
> "**69DA**   Where an open-ended investment company–
>   (a)   is also a qualified investor scheme (see regulation 14C); and
>   (b)   meets the genuine diversity of ownership condition in regulation 14B for an accounting period,
> the company shall be treated as also meeting the genuine diversity of ownership condition in regulation 69J for the accounting period, even if it would not otherwise do so.".

Former reg. 69DA inserted by SI 2008/3159, reg. 18, with effect from 1 January 2009.

THE PROPERTY INVESTMENT BUSINESS CONDITION

The property investment business condition

69E(1)   The property investment business condition is that the open-ended investment company must meet conditions A and B throughout the accounting period.

69E(2)   Condition A is that the company's instrument of incorporation and its prospectus include a statement that the company's investment objectives are–

(a)   to carry on property investment business, and

(b)   to manage cash raised from investors for investment in the property investment business.

69E(3)   Condition B is that the company must carry on property investment business.

69E(4)   [Omitted by SI 2010/294, reg. 23(3).]

History – In reg. 69E(2), the words "(including any supplements to the prospectus)" omitted by SI 2010/294, reg. 23(2), with effect from 6 March 2010.
Reg. 69E(4) omitted by SI 2010/294, reg. 23(3), with effect from 6 March 2010. Former reg. 69E(4) read as follows:
> "**69E(4)**   In this Part **"prospectus"** includes any supplements to a prospectus."

Meaning of "property investment business"

69F(1)   In this Part **"property investment business"** means business consisting of any one or more of–

(a)   property rental business (see regulation 69H);

(b)   owning shares in UK-REITs; and

(c)   owning shares or units in an entity within section 528(4A)(j) of CTA 2010 (overseas equivalent to UK REIT).

69F(2)   In these Regulations **"UK-REIT"** has the meaning given in section 518(4) of CTA 2010.

69F(3)   [Omitted by SI 2014/518, reg. 3(2)(c).]

69F(4)   [Omitted by SI 2014/518, reg. 3(2)(c).]

69F(5)   [Omitted by SI 2014/518, reg. 3(2)(c).]

69F(6)   [Omitted by SI 2014/518, reg. 3(2)(c).]

69F(7)   [Omitted by SI 2011/2192, reg. 6.]

69F(8)   This regulation is subject to the further provisions in regulation 69G.

History – In reg. 69F(1)(c), the words "within section 528(4A)(j) of CTA 2010 (overseas equivalent to UK REIT)" substituted for "in circumstances in which conditions A to C are met" by SI 2014/518, reg. 3(2)(a), with effect from accounting periods beginning on or after 1 April 2014.
In reg. 69F(2), the words after "UK-REIT" substituted by SI 2014/518, reg. 3(2)(b), with effect from accounting periods beginning on or after 1 April 2014.
Reg. 69F(3)–(6) omitted by SI 2014/518, reg. 3(2)(c), with effect from accounting periods beginning on or after 1 April 2014.
Reg. 69F(7) omitted by SI 2011/2192, reg. 6, with effect: for the purposes of corporation tax on income, for accounting periods starting on or after 1 October 2011; and, for the purposes of corporation tax on chargeable gains or capital gains tax, in relation to disposals made on or after 1 October 2011. Former reg. 69F(7) read as follows:
> "**69F(7)**   In this regulation **"recognised stock exchange"** has the meaning given by section 1005(1) of ITA 2007.".

Property investment business: further provisions

69G(1)   If an open-ended investment company to which this Part applies receives a distribution from a UK-REIT–

(a)   the distribution is income of F (tax-exempt) to the extent that the distribution represents business of C (tax-exempt) carried on by the UK-REIT, and

(b)   the distribution is income of F (residual) to the extent that the distribution represents business other than business of C (tax-exempt) carried on by the UK-REIT.

69G(2)   In paragraph (1) **"C (tax-exempt)"** shall be construed in accordance with Part 4 of the Finance Act 2006.

69G(3) If an open-ended investment company to which this Part applies receives a distribution from an entity within regulation 69F(1)(c), the distribution is income of F (tax-exempt) except to the extent that the distribution is identified, at the time at which it is made, as arising from any activity of the entity that is not property rental business.

69G(4) For the purposes of this Part an asset is involved in property investment business if–

(a) it is an estate, interest or right in or over land by the exploitation of which property rental business is conducted;

(b) it consists of shares owned by the open-ended investment company in a UK-REIT; or

(c) it consists of shares or units owned by the open-ended investment company in an entity within regulation 69F(1)(c).

History – In reg. 69G(4)(c), the words "or units" inserted by SI 2008/3159, reg. 19, with effect from 1 January 2009.

Meaning of "property rental business"

69H(1) In this Part **"property rental business"** means–

(a) property rental business within the meaning given by section 104 of FA 2006, and

(b) the relevant business of an intermediate holding vehicle (see regulation 69I).

69H(2) For the purposes of paragraph (1)(b) the relevant business of an intermediate holding vehicle is its property rental business within the meaning given by section 104 of FA 2006, but disregarding subsection (1)(a) of that section.

69H(3) For the purposes of this Part an asset is involved in property rental business if–

(a) it is an estate, interest or right in or over land by the exploitation of which property rental business is conducted, or

(b) it consists of shares owned by the open-ended investment company in an intermediate holding vehicle.

Meaning of "intermediate holding vehicle"

69I(1) For the purposes of regulation 69H, an entity is an "intermediate holding vehicle" in an accounting period if it meets conditions A to F throughout the accounting period.

69I(2) Condition A is that the vehicle is a company, trust or partnership.

69I(3) Condition B is that the vehicle is not a collective investment scheme.

69I(4) Condition C is that the vehicle is wholly owned by the open-ended investment company (the "parent") or another intermediate holding vehicle or series of intermediate holding vehicles wholly owned by the parent, unless and to the extent that local legislation or regulations relating to the intermediate holding vehicle holding the property specified in paragraph (5) requires a proportion of local ownership.

69I(5) Condition D is that the function of the intermediate holding vehicle is solely to enable the holding, by the parent, of estates, interests or rights in or over land outside the United Kingdom by the exploitation of which property rental business is conducted.

69I(6) Condition E is that the intermediate holding vehicle has its accounts consolidated with those of the parent.

69I(7) Condition F is that all property rental income of the intermediate holding vehicle (or the full proportion of that income representing the interest of the parent in the intermediate holding vehicle) must be reflected in the distribution accounts of the parent at the same time as that income is reflected in the accounts of the intermediate holding vehicle.

THE GENUINE DIVERSITY OF OWNERSHIP CONDITION

69J [Omitted by SI 2009/2036, reg. 17.]

History – Reg. 69J omitted by SI 2009/2036, reg. 17, with effect from 1 September 2009. Former reg. 69J read as follows:

"**The genuine diversity of ownership condition**

69J(1) The genuine diversity of ownership condition is that the open-ended investment company must meet conditions A to F throughout the accounting period.

This is subject to paragraphs (8) and (9).

69J(2) Condition A is that the company's instrument of incorporation and prospectus in issue for the time being–
(a) contain a statement that shares in the company will be widely available, and
(b) specify the intended categories of investor.

69J(3) Condition B is that the specification of intended categories of investor referred to in paragraph (2)(b) does not have the effect of limiting the intended investors to a limited number of specific persons or specific groups of connected persons.

69J(4) Condition C is that shares in the company–

(a)   must be marketed and made available sufficiently widely to reach the intended categories of investors, and
(b)   must be marketed and made available in a manner appropriate to attract those categories of persons.

69J(5)   Condition D is–
(a)   that a person may easily acquire shares in the company, and may acquire the shares in the same way as a person may acquire shares or units in other authorised investment funds that are widely available, or
(b)   in the case of a qualified investor scheme, a person who is within one of the categories of intended investor in the scheme which have been specified in accordance with condition A may, upon request to the manager of the scheme, obtain information about the scheme and acquire units in it.

69J(6)   Condition E is that the minimum investment is not unreasonably high in view of the risk profile of the company or the intended categories of investors.

69J(7)   Condition F is that, in comparison with charges imposed on larger investors, charges imposed on smaller investors will not be greater than is commercially normal and reasonable.

69J(8)   The open-ended investment company meets the genuine diversity of ownership condition if–
(a)   an investor in the company is a unit trust scheme (a "feeder fund"), and
(b)   paragraphs (2) to (7) are met in relation to the company after taking into account the intended investors in the feeder fund.

69J(9)   If paragraph (8) applies–
(a)   the open-ended investment company and the feeder fund must have the same manager (or proposed manager),
(b)   a notice under regulation 69O must be accompanied by the feeder fund's trust deed and prospectus in issue, and
(c)   paragraphs (7) and (8) of regulation 69P apply in relation to the feeder fund's trust deed and prospectus as they apply to the open-ended investment company's instrument of incorporation and prospectus (or, as the case may be, to the proposed company's instrument of incorporation and prospectus).

69J(10)   For the purposes of this regulation–
(a)   sections 993 and 994 of ITA 2007 (connected persons) apply in the case of a person chargeable to income tax, and
(b)   section 839 of ICTA (connected persons) applies in the case of a person chargeable to corporation tax.".

Former reg. 69J(5)(b) substituted by SI 2008/3159, reg. 20, with effect from 1 January 2009.

THE CORPORATE OWNERSHIP CONDITION

The corporate ownership condition

69K(1)   The corporate ownership condition is that the open-ended investment company must meet conditions A to C and (if applicable) condition D at the time that this Part begins to apply to the company and throughout the accounting period.
This is subject to regulation 69L(1).

69K(2)   Condition A is that no body corporate is beneficially entitled (directly or indirectly) to 10% or more of the net asset value of the fund.

69K(3)   Condition A is treated as met if–
(a)   the company has taken reasonable steps to prevent a body corporate from acquiring a holding of 10% or more of the net asset value of the fund,
(b)   a body corporate has nevertheless acquired such a holding,
(c)   immediately upon becoming aware of the situation, the company has taken steps to ensure that the holding is reduced below 10% of the net asset value of the fund, and
(d)   the company has continued, with all reasonable speed, to take steps to ensure that the holding is so reduced.

69K(4)   Condition B is that the company's instrument of incorporation and its prospectus include provisions under which any body corporate which becomes a participant in the company–
(a)   must undertake not to acquire 10% or more of the share capital of the company, and
(b)   must undertake, on becoming aware that it has acquired 10% or more of the share capital of the company, to reduce its holding of that share capital below 10%.

69K(5)   Condition C is that the company's instrument of incorporation and its prospectus include provisions under which a body corporate acquiring shares in the company must give a certificate in accordance with paragraph (6) or (7).

69K(6)   The certificate is a certificate that the body corporate acquiring shares holds the shares as beneficial owner.

69K(7)   The certificate is a certificate that the body corporate acquiring shares holds some or all of those shares otherwise than as a beneficial owner, but that the body corporate–
(a)   holds less than 10% of the share capital of the company on behalf of itself or any one other corporate beneficial owner, and
(b)   has obtained the undertakings in the terms specified in sub-paragraphs (a) and (b) of paragraph (4) from every other body corporate on whose behalf it owns shares in the company otherwise than as a beneficial owner.

69K(8) Condition D is that, in a case in which the body corporate acquiring shares in the company gives a certificate in accordance with paragraph (7), the body corporate acquiring the shares has undertaken to disclose the following information to the manager of the company if the manager so requires–

(a) the names of any body corporate on whose behalf the body corporate owns shares in the company otherwise than as a beneficial owner, and

(b) the extent of the holding of that body corporate in the company.

History – In reg. 69K(4), "participant" substituted for "shareholder" by SI 2008/3159, reg. 21, with effect from 1 January 2009.

The corporate ownership condition: further provisions

69L(1) The open-ended investment company meets conditions B and C of the corporate ownership condition if it provides in its instrument of incorporation and its prospectus that a body corporate is prohibited from acquiring shares in the open-ended investment company.

69L(2) The open-ended investment company meets conditions B and C of the corporate ownership condition if–

(a) it provides in its instrument of incorporation and its prospectus that a body corporate is prohibited from acquiring shares as a participant in the open-ended investment company,

(b) a body corporate ("BC") acquires shares in the open-ended investment company,

(c) BC does not hold those shares as beneficial owner, and

(d) BC gives a certificate in accordance with paragraph (3).

69L(3) The certificate is a certificate–

(a) that BC does not hold any of the shares in the open-ended investment company as beneficial owner, and

(b) that none of the beneficial owners of BC's shares in the open-ended investment company is a body corporate.

69L(4) Paragraph (5) applies if the trustees of a unit trust scheme–

(a) hold shares in the open-ended investment company, and

(b) are chargeable, in the United Kingdom, either to income tax or to corporation tax in their capacity as trustees of that unit trust scheme.

69L(5) For the purposes of regulation 69K the unit trust scheme is treated as the beneficial owners of the shares; and a person holding units in the unit trust shall not be treated as beneficially entitled (directly or indirectly) to 10% or more of the net asset value of the open-ended investment company's fund by virtue of holding the units.

69L(6) In this Part **"body corporate"** means–

(a) a body corporate incorporated under the laws of any part of the United Kingdom or any other territory, or

(b) an entity which is treated as a body corporate for tax purposes–

(i) in accordance with the law of a territory outside the United Kingdom with which relevant arrangements have been entered into, or

(ii) in accordance with an international agreement containing relevant arrangements.

69L(7) In paragraph (6) "relevant arrangements" means arrangements which–

(a) have been entered into with a view to affording relief from double taxation, and

(b) have effect by virtue of an Order in Council under section 788 of ICTA.

History – In reg. 69L(2)(a), the words "as a participant" inserted by SI 2008/3159, reg. 22(2), with effect from 1 January 2009. In reg. 69L(5), the words "the unit trust scheme is treated" substituted for the words "the trustees are treated" by SI 2008/3159, reg. 22(3), with effect from 1 January 2009.

THE LOAN CREDITOR CONDITION

The loan creditor condition

69M(1) The loan creditor condition is that the open-ended investment company must meet conditions A to C throughout the accounting period in the case of any loan relationship to which the company is party as debtor.

69M(2) Condition A is that, in the case of a debtor relationship of the company, the person standing in the position of a creditor as respects the debt in question is not entitled to an amount by way of interest which depends to any extent on–

(a) the results of all or part of the open-ended investment company's business, or

(b) the value of any of the company's assets.

69M(3)   For the purposes of condition A, a loan shall not be treated as dependent on the results of the company's business by reason only that the terms of the loan provide—

(a)   for the interest to be reduced in the event of results improving, or

(b)   for the interest to be increased in the event of results deteriorating.

69M(4)   Condition B is that, in the case of a debtor relationship of the company, the person standing in the position of a creditor as respects the debt in question is not entitled to an amount by way of interest which exceeds a reasonable commercial return on the consideration lent.

69M(5)   Condition C is that, in the case of a debtor relationship of the company, the person standing in the position of a creditor as respects the debt in question is entitled on repayment to an amount which—

(a)   does not exceed the consideration lent, or

(b)   is reasonably comparable with the amount generally repayable (in respect of an equal amount of consideration) under the terms of issue of securities listed on a recognised stock exchange.

69M(6)   In this regulation **"loan relationship"** and **"debtor relationship"** shall be construed in accordance with Chapter 2 of Part 4 of FA 1996 (loan relationships).

THE BALANCE OF BUSINESS CONDITIONS

The balance of business conditions

69N(1)   The balance of business conditions are that conditions A and B must be met.

69N(2)   Condition A is that the net income of F (tax-exempt) for an accounting period (determined in accordance with regulation 69Z1) is—

(a)   at least 40% of the open-ended investment company's net income (as defined in regulation 69Z) where this Part applies to a newly qualified company in its first accounting period, or

(b)   at least 60% of the open-ended investment company's net income (as defined in regulation 69Z) where this Part applies to a company in an accounting period in any other circumstances.

69N(3)   Condition B is that the value of the assets involved in property investment business is—

(a)   at least 40% of the total value of the assets held by the open-ended investment company at the end of the accounting period where this Part applies to a newly qualified company in its first accounting period, or

(b)   at least 60% of the total value of the assets held by the open-ended investment company at the end of the accounting period where this Part applies to a company in an accounting period in any other circumstances.

69N(4)   For the purposes of condition B—

(a)   assets must be valued in accordance with generally accepted accounting practice,

(b)   where generally accepted accounting practice offers a choice of valuation between cost basis and fair value, fair value must be used, and

(c)   no account shall be taken of liabilities secured against or otherwise relating to assets (whether generally or specifically).

69N(5)   In this Part a **"newly qualified company"** means a company—

(a)   to which this Part applies immediately upon its authorisation, and

(b)   which has not been an authorised investment fund before that authorisation.

THE NOTIFICATION CONDITION

The notification condition

69O(1)   The notification condition is that conditions A and B must be met.

69O(2)   Condition A is—

(a)   that the manager of an existing open-ended investment company has given notice for this Part to apply to the company, or

(b)   if it is proposed to incorporate an open-ended investment company, that the person expected to become the manager of the open-ended investment company on its incorporation (the "applicant") has given notice for this Part to apply to the company.

69O(3)   Condition B is that the notice given under paragraph (2) has taken effect.

69O(4)   If notice is given under paragraph (2)(a), the company must obtain any necessary shareholder and regulatory approvals to its instrument of incorporation and prospectus before giving the notice.

69O(5) If notice is given under paragraph (2)(b), the terms of the proposed company's instrument of incorporation must be such that the proposed company, on its incorporation, will be required to meet–

(a) the property investment business condition (see regulation 69E), and

(b) the genuine diversity of ownership condition (see regulation 9A).

69O(6) In this Part–

the **"applicant"** means the person referred to in paragraph (2)(b),

an **"existing company notice"** means a notice given under paragraph (2)(a), and

a **"future company notice"** means a notice given under paragraph (2)(b).

History – In reg. 69O(5)(b), "9A" substituted for "69J" by SI 2009/2036, reg. 18, with effect from 1 September 2009.

Form and timing of notice under regulation 69O

69P(1) A notice under regulation 69O must be given in writing to the Commissioners.

69P(2) An existing company notice must be given at least 28 days before the beginning of the specified period.

This is subject to the following paragraphs of this regulation.

69P(3) A future company notice must be given at least 42 days before the date of the expected incorporation and authorisation.

This is subject to the following paragraphs of this regulation.

69P(4) A notice under regulation 69O may be withdrawn or amended at any time before it takes effect–

(a) by the manager (in the case of an existing company notice), or

(b) by the applicant (in the case of a future company notice).

69P(5) If a notice under regulation 69O is amended before it is due to take effect, regulation 69O shall apply to the amended notice.

69P(6) But if HM Revenue and Customs give notice that they are satisfied that the amended notice is valid, the amended notice shall take effect as if given on the date of the original notice.

69P(7) An existing company notice may be given at any time before the beginning of the specified period if–

(a) HM Revenue and Customs have given clearance under regulation 9B, and

(b) the manager of the open-ended investment company certifies that there have been no changes in substance between–

    (i) the form in which the company's instrument of incorporation and its prospectus were considered by HM Revenue and Customs before giving the clearance, and

    (ii) the form in which it is proposed that those documents will apply at the beginning of the specified period.

69P(8) A future company notice may be given at any time before the proposed company is authorised and incorporated if–

(a) HM Revenue and Customs have given clearance under regulation 9B, and

(b) the applicant certifies that there have been no changes in substance between–

    (i) the form in which the proposed company's instrument of incorporation and its prospectus were considered by HM Revenue and Customs before giving the clearance, and

    (ii) the form in which it is proposed that those documents will apply at the time when the proposed company is authorised.

History – In reg. 69P(7)(a), "9B" substituted for "69U" by SI 2009/2036, reg. 19(a), with effect from 1 September 2009.
In reg. 69P(8)(a), "9B" substituted for "69U" by SI 2009/2036, reg. 19(b), with effect from 1 September 2009.

Contents of notice under regulation 69O

69Q(1) This regulation applies if notice is given under regulation 69O.

69Q(2) An existing company notice must specify the accounting period from the beginning of which this Part is to apply to the company (the "specified accounting period").

69Q(3) An existing company notice must be accompanied by–

(a) a statement by the manager of the open-ended investment company that the conditions specified in regulation 9A and regulations 69E to 69N are reasonably expected to be met in respect of the company throughout the specified accounting period;

(b) the following documents relating to the company–

      (i)   its instrument of incorporation, and

      (ii) its prospectus;

(c)   a copy of the application to the Financial Services Authority for agreement to changes in the company's instrument of incorporation and its prospectus; and

(d)   copies of any documents accompanying the application mentioned in sub-paragraph (c) to the extent that those documents do not fall within sub-paragraphs (a) and (b).

69Q(4)   A future company notice must specify that this Part will apply to the proposed company from the date of its incorporation and authorisation.

69Q(5)   A future company notice must be accompanied by–

(a)   a statement by the applicant that the conditions specified in regulation 9A and regulations 69E to 69N are reasonably expected to be met in respect of the proposed company throughout its first accounting period;

(b)   the following documents relating to the proposed company–

      (i)   its proposed instrument of incorporation, and

      (ii) its prospectus;

(c)   a copy of the application to the Financial Services Authority for approval of the proposed company as an open-ended investment company; and

(d)   copies of any documents accompanying the application mentioned in sub-paragraph (c) to the extent that those documents do not fall within sub-paragraphs (a) and (b).

History – In reg. 69Q(3)(a), "regulation 9A and" inserted by SI 2009/2036, reg. 20(a), with effect from 1 September 2009.
In reg. 69Q(5)(b)(ii), the word "proposed" and the words "(including any supplements to the proposed prospectus)" omitted by SI 2010/294, reg. 23(4), with effect from 6 March 2010.
In reg. 69Q(5)(a), "regulation 9A and" inserted by SI 2009/2036, reg. 20(a), with effect from 1 September 2009.

PROCEDURAL MATTERS RELATING TO THE GIVING OF NOTICE FOR THIS PART TO APPLY

Notice: further provisions: quashing notices

69R(1)   This regulation applies if any of conditions A to C are met.

69R(2)   Condition A is that an existing company notice is given, but the notice is not accompanied by the documents specified in regulation 69Q(3)(b).

69R(3)   Condition B is that a future company notice is given, but the notice is not accompanied by the documents specified in regulation 69Q(5)(b).

69R(4)   Condition C is that a person gives a notice under regulation 69O in circumstances where the documents supplied do not demonstrate that the open-ended investment company (or the proposed open-ended investment company) will meet all the conditions of membership of the Property AIF regime.

69R(5)   HM Revenue and Customs may give a notice (a "quashing notice") quashing the notice given under regulation 69O–

(a)   to the manager of the open-ended investment company if an existing company notice has been given, or

(b)   to the applicant if a future company notice has been given.

Procedure relating to quashing notices

69S(1)   HM Revenue and Customs must not give a quashing notice until–

(a)   they have given a notice (a "preliminary notice") to the person giving the notice under regulation 69O specifying the reasons why the preliminary notice is given, and

(b)   they have given the person giving the notice under regulation 69O a period of 28 days to rectify the matters specified in the preliminary notice.

Paragraph (1)(b) is subject to paragraphs (7) to (9).

69S(2)   HM Revenue and Customs must give a preliminary notice within a period of 28 days beginning with the day on which they receive the notice given under regulation 69O.

69S(3)   HM Revenue and Customs must–

(a)   give a quashing notice, or

(b)   give notice to the manager of the open-ended investment company or to the applicant (as the case may be) that they are satisfied that the matters specified in the preliminary notice have been rectified, within a period of 28 days beginning on the day specified in paragraph (4).

69S(4) The day specified is whichever is the earlier to occur of–

(a) the day immediately following the expiry of the period specified in the preliminary notice, and

(b) the day on which HM Revenue and Customs receive notice from the manager of the open-ended investment company or from the applicant (as the case may be) that the manager or applicant thinks–

(i) that the matters specified in the preliminary notice have been rectified, or

(ii) that the original notice given under regulation 69O is valid.

69S(5) If HM Revenue and Customs give a preliminary notice, the open-ended investment company (or, as the case may be, the proposed open-ended investment company) in respect of which the notice is given may not enter the Property AIF regime until HM Revenue and Customs have notified the manager of the company (or, as the case may be, the applicant) that they are satisfied that the matters specified in the preliminary notice have been rectified.

69S(6) If HM Revenue and Customs give a quashing notice, and the person to whom the notice is given appeals, the open-ended investment company (or, as the case may be, the proposed open-ended investment company) in respect of which the notice is given may not enter the Property AIF regime until the appeal is determined.

69S(7) The period of 28 days mentioned in paragraph (1)(b) is replaced by the period referred to in paragraph (9) if, within that 28 day period, the conditions specified in paragraph (8) are met.

69S(8) The conditions are that–

(a) HM Revenue and Customs and the applicant are in agreement as to the changes needed to the notice or to the documents accompanying the notice (or to both),

(b) the applicant has given notice to HM Revenue and Customs stating that the changes referred to in sub-paragraph (a) will take a specified period (which is longer than 28 days) to effect, and

(c) HM Revenue and Customs have given notice to the applicant accepting the statement made in the notice given under sub-paragraph (b).

69S(9) The period is the specified period mentioned in paragraph (8)(b).

Appeal against quashing notice

69T(1) A person to whom a quashing notice is given may appeal.

69T(2) The notice of appeal must be given to HM Revenue and Customs within a period of 28 days beginning with the day on which the quashing notice is given.

69T(3) On an appeal that is notified to the tribunal, the tribunal shall determine whether it was just and reasonable for HM Revenue and Customs to give the quashing notice.

69T(4) If the tribunal allows the appeal–

(a) the tribunal may direct that this Part shall apply to the open-ended investment company (or, as the case may be to the proposed open-ended investment company), and

(b) the tribunal may specify the date from which this Part shall so apply.

69T(5) The date mentioned in paragraph (4)(b)–

(a) must not be earlier than the beginning of the specified accounting period if an existing company notice has been given, and

(b) must not be earlier than the date of incorporation and authorisation if a future company notice has been given.

History – In reg. 69T(1), the words "to the Special Commissioners", which appeared after "appeal", omitted by SI 2009/56, art. 3(2) and Sch. 2, para. 156(2), operative from 1 April 2009 subject to transitional and saving provisions in SI 2009/56, Sch. 3. In reg. 69T(3), the words "that is notified to the tribunal, the tribunal" substituted for the words "the Special Commissioners" by SI 2009/56, art. 3(2) and Sch. 2, para. 156(3), operative from 1 April 2009 subject to transitional and saving provisions in SI 2009/56, Sch. 3.
In reg. 69T(4), the words "tribunal allows" substituted for the words "Special Commissioners allow" by SI 2009/56, art. 3(2) and Sch. 2, para. 156(4)(a), operative from 1 April 2009 subject to transitional and saving provisions in SI 2009/56, Sch. 3.
In reg. 69T(4)(a) and (b), the words "the tribunal may" substituted for the words "they may" by SI 2009/56, art. 3(2) and Sch. 2, para. 156(4)(b), operative from 1 April 2009 subject to transitional and saving provisions in SI 2009/56, Sch. 3.

CLEARANCE APPLICATIONS

69U [Omitted by SI 2009/2036, reg. 21.]

History – Reg. 69U omitted by SI 2009/2036, reg. 21, with effect from 1 September 2009. Former reg. 69U read as follows:

"**Clearance in relation to the genuine diversity of ownership condition**

69U(1)   An application for clearance that an open-ended investment company meets the genuine diversity of ownership condition may be made in writing to HM Revenue and Customs–

(a)   by the manager of an open-ended investment company, or

(b)   if it is proposed to incorporate an open-ended investment company, by the applicant.

69U(2)   An application for clearance must be accompanied by the company's instrument of incorporation and its prospectus in the form in which it is proposed that those documents will apply at the beginning of the first accounting period in which this Part will apply to the open-ended investment company.

69U(3)   The officer of Revenue and Customs dealing with the application for clearance may require the manager of the company to provide further particulars if the officer thinks that full particulars of the company (or of the proposed company) have not been provided.

69U(4)   HM Revenue and Customs must notify the person making the application within 28 days of the receipt of the particulars (or, if paragraph (3) applies, of all further particulars required) that they–

(a)   give clearance that the company meets the genuine diversity of ownership condition;

(b)   give that clearance subject to conditions; or

(c)   refuse to give that clearance.

69U(5)   The company may not rely on a clearance given under this regulation if–

(a)   at the beginning of the first accounting period in which this Part applies to the company, a relevant statement in the company's instrument of incorporation or its prospectus is not in accordance with a relevant statement in the documents considered by HM Revenue and Customs before giving clearance,

(b)   the company acts in contravention of a relevant statement in its instrument of incorporation or prospectus in issue for the time being, or

(c)   the company amends a relevant statement in its instrument of incorporation or prospectus in issue for the time being.

69U(6)   But paragraph (5)(c) does not apply if the company has obtained a clearance given under this regulation which applies to the amendment.".

CONSEQUENCES OF ENTRY

Effects of entry

69V(1)   Property rental business of F (pre-entry) shall be treated for the purposes of corporation tax as ceasing at entry.

69V(2)   Assets which immediately before entry are involved in property rental business of F (pre-entry) shall be treated for the purposes of corporation tax as being sold by F (pre-entry) immediately before entry and reacquired by F (tax-exempt) immediately after entry.

69V(3)   For the purposes of corporation tax, on entry one accounting period of the open-ended investment company shall end and another shall begin.

69V(4)   On entry a new distribution period of the open-ended investment company shall begin.

69V(5)   The sale and reacquisition deemed under paragraph (2) shall not have effect for the purposes of tax in respect of chargeable gains.

69V(6)   For the purposes of CAA 2001, the sale and reacquisition deemed under paragraph (2)–

(a)   shall not give rise to allowances or charges, and

(b)   shall not make it possible to make an election under section 198 or 199 of that Act (apportionment).

69V(7)   For the purposes of CAA 2001, anything done by or to F (pre-entry) before entry in relation to an asset which is deemed under paragraph (2) to be sold and reacquired shall be treated after entry as having been done by or to F (tax-exempt).

Duration

69W   Once this Part has begun to apply to an open-ended investment company it shall continue to apply unless and until it ceases to apply in accordance with Chapter 7 of this Part.

Chapter 3 – The Tax Treatment of Property AIFS

History – Pt. 4A inserted by SI 2008/705, reg. 5, with effect from 6 April 2008.

CATEGORIES OF BUSINESS

Ring-fencing of tax-exempt business

69X(1)   For the purposes of corporation tax, the business of F (tax-exempt) shall be treated as a separate business (distinct from–

(a)   any business carried on by F (pre-entry),

(b)   any business carried on by F (residual), and

(c)   any business carried on by F (post-cessation)).

69X(2) For the purposes of corporation tax, F (tax-exempt) shall be treated as a separate company (distinct from–

(a)   F (pre-entry),

(b)   F (residual), and

(c)   F (post-cessation)).

69X(3) In particular–

(a)   a loss incurred by F (tax-exempt) may not be set off against the net income of F (residual),

(b)   a loss incurred in respect of F (residual) may not be set off against the net income of F (tax exempt),

(c)   a loss incurred in respect of F (pre-entry) may not be set off against the net income of F (tax-exempt) (but this regulation does not prevent a loss of that kind from being set off against profits of F (residual)),

(d)   a loss incurred by F (tax-exempt) may not be set off against profits arising to F (post-cessation) (in respect of business of any kind), and

(e)   receipts accruing after entry but relating to business of F (pre-entry) shall not be treated as receipts of F (tax-exempt).

69X(4) In paragraph (3) a reference to a loss includes a reference to a deficit, expense, charge or allowance.

69X(5) Section 392B of ICTA (ring-fencing of losses from overseas property business) shall not apply to business of F (tax-exempt).

69X(6) Paragraphs 5B and 5C of Schedule 28AA to ICTA (transfer pricing: exemption for small and medium enterprises) shall not apply to an open-ended investment company to which this Part applies (whether to F (tax-exempt) or to F (residual)).

CHARGEABILITY TO TAX

Chargeability to corporation tax

69Y(1) The net income of F (tax-exempt) (see regulation 69Z1) shall not be charged to corporation tax.

69Y(2) The net income of F (residual) (see regulation 69Z3) shall be charged to corporation tax at the rate applicable for open-ended investment companies (see section 468A(1) of ICTA).

Meaning of "net income"

69Z(1) In this Part the **"net income"** of an open-ended investment company for an accounting period means, in the case of an open-ended investment company that prepares accounts in accordance with UK generally accepted accounting practice, the amount falling to be dealt with under the heading "net revenue/(expense) before taxation" in the company's statement of total return for the accounting period.

69Z(2) In paragraph (1) **"the company's statement of total return for the accounting period"** is to be construed in accordance with regulation 12.

History – In reg. 692(1), the words , "net revenue/(expense) before taxation" substituted for the words "Net income/(expense) before taxation" by SI 2008/3159, reg. 23, with effect from 1 January 2009.

Calculation of net income of F (tax-exempt)

69Z1(1) This regulation applies to determine the net income of F (tax-exempt) for the purposes of this Part.

69Z1(2) Section 21A of ICTA (calculation of profits of Schedule A business) shall apply to income arising from the business of F (tax-exempt).

69Z1(3) Paragraph 2(3) of section 15(1) of ICTA (Schedule A: disregard of credits and debits from loan relationships and derivative contracts) shall not apply in respect of–

(a)   a loan relationship if or in so far as it relates to tax-exempt business,

(b)   a hedging derivative contract if or in so far as it relates to tax-exempt business, or

(c)   embedded derivatives if or in so far as the host contract is entered into for the purposes of tax-exempt business.

69Z1(4) For the purposes of paragraph (3)–

(a)   a derivative contract is hedging in relation to a company if or in so far as it is acquired as a hedge of risk in relation to an asset by the exploitation of which tax-exempt business is conducted,

(b)   a derivative contract is hedging in relation to a company if or in so far as it is acquired as a hedge of risk in relation to a liability incurred in connection with tax-exempt business,

(c)   a designation of a contract as wholly or partly hedging for the purposes of a company's accounts shall be conclusive, and

(d)   **"embedded derivatives"** and **"host contract"** shall be construed–

     (i)   in accordance with section 94A of FA 1996 in relation to loan contracts with embedded derivatives,

     (ii)   in accordance with paragraph 2A of Schedule 26 to FA 2002 in relation to non-financial contracts with embedded derivatives,

     (iii)   in accordance with paragraph 2B of Schedule 26 to FA 2002 in relation to hybrid derivatives.

69Z1(5)   In paragraph (4)(a) the reference to an asset includes a reference to–

(a)   the value of an asset, and

(b)   profits attributable to it.

69Z1(6)   Net income shall be computed without regard to items giving rise to credits or debits which would be within Schedule 26 to FA 2002 (derivative contracts) but for paragraph 4(2)(b) of that Schedule (exclusion of share-based and unit-trust-based contracts).

69Z1(7)   Income and expenditure relating partly to tax-exempt business and partly to non-tax-exempt business shall be apportioned reasonably.

69Z1(8)   Section 3(1) of CAA 2001 (claims for capital allowances) shall not apply; and any allowance which the company could claim under that section shall be made automatically and reflected in the calculation of net income.

Components of income arising to F (residual)

69Z2(1)   For the purposes of this Part the income arising to F (residual) consists of–

(a)   distributions qualifying for exemption under section 208 of ICTA, and

(b)   income arising from the business of F (residual).

69Z2(2)   Section 21A of ICTA (calculation of profits of Schedule A business) shall apply to income arising from the business of F (residual) if and to the extent that income arising from the business of F (residual) is chargeable to corporation tax under Schedule A.

Calculation of net income of F (residual)

69Z3   Use this regulation to determine the net income of F (residual) for the purposes of this Part.

First rule

Determine the amount of the income arising to F (residual).

Second rule

Deduct any amounts whose deduction is required or allowed under the Corporation Tax Acts (including any distributions qualifying for exemption under section 208 of ICTA).

In this Part the amount so found is called the "pre-distribution amount".

Third rule

Deduct the amount attributed to PAIF distributions (interest) under regulation 69Z14(b).

The result is the net income of F (residual).

BREACHES OF CONDITIONS

Breach of the genuine diversity of ownership condition

69Z4(1)   This regulation applies if an open-ended investment company to which this Part applies is in breach of the genuine diversity of ownership condition.

69Z4(2)   Within 28 days of becoming aware of the breach, the company must provide the following information to the Commissioners–

(a)   the date on which the condition first ceased to be met;

(b)   the date on which the company became aware of the breach;

(c)   details of the condition that was breached;

(d)   the nature of the breach;

(e)   the steps the company proposes to take to rectify the breach; and

(f)   the date by which the company proposes to rectify the breach.

69Z4(3)   The date referred to in paragraph (2)(f) must be the earliest date by which the objective of complying with the genuine diversity of ownership condition may reasonably be achieved.

69Z4(4)   The Commissioners may give a termination notice to the company if–

(a)   the steps that the company proposes to take will not rectify the breach, or

(b)   the date by which the company proposes to rectify the breach is not the earliest date by which the objective of remedying the genuine diversity ownership condition may reasonably be achieved.

69Z4(5)   If there are three different breaches of the genuine diversity of ownership condition in three different accounting periods in a period of ten years beginning with the first day of the accounting period in which the company becomes aware of the first of those breaches, the Commissioners may give a termination notice to the company.

Breach of the corporate ownership condition

69Z5(1)   This regulation applies if an open-ended investment company to which this Part applies is in breach of the corporate ownership condition.

69Z5(2)   If there is a breach which is caused by the action of a shareholder in the company and the company has not taken reasonable steps to prevent the breach (so that, accordingly, there is a charge to corporation tax under regulation 69Z12) (a "specified breach"), this Part shall continue to apply to the company despite the breach (but see paragraph (3) and regulation 69Z8).

69Z5(3)   If there are three specified breaches in a period of ten years beginning with the first day of the accounting period in which the first specified breach occurs, the Commissioners may give a termination notice to the company.

Breach of the loan creditor condition

69Z6(1)   This regulation applies if an open-ended investment company to which this Part applies is in breach of the loan creditor condition.

69Z6(2)   If the company is inadvertently in breach of the loan creditor condition but rectifies the breach within a period of 28 days beginning with the day on which the company first becomes aware of the breach, this Part shall continue to apply to the company despite the breach (but see paragraphs (5) and (6) and regulation 69Z8).

69Z6(3)   If the company is inadvertently in breach of the loan creditor condition but does not rectify the breach within a period of 28 days beginning with the day on which the company first becomes aware of the breach, the Commissioners may give a termination notice to the company.

69Z6(4)   If the company is intentionally or negligently in breach of the loan creditor condition, the Commissioners may give a termination notice to the company.

69Z6(5)   If the company is in breach of the same condition specified in paragraphs (2) to (5) of regulation 69M in two different accounting periods in a period of ten years beginning with the first day of the accounting period in which the company becomes aware of the first of those breaches, the Commissioners may give a termination notice to the company.

69Z6(6)   If the company is in breach of the conditions specified in paragraphs (2) to (5) of regulation 69M in three different accounting periods in a period of ten years beginning with the first day of the accounting period in which the company becomes aware of the first of those breaches, the Commissioners may give a termination notice to the company.

Breach of balance of business conditions

69Z7(1)   Paragraph (2) applies if a newly qualified company–

(a)   is in breach of condition A set out in regulation 69N(2)(a) in its first accounting period, or

(b)   is in breach of condition B set out in regulation 69N(3)(a) at the end of its first accounting period.

69Z7(2)   This Part shall cease to apply to the company at the end of its first accounting period and regulation 69Z41 shall apply.

69Z7(3)   Paragraphs (4) to (7) apply if an open-ended-investment company to which this Part applies–

(a)   is in breach of condition A set out in regulation 69N(2)(b) in an accounting period, or

(b)   is in breach of condition B set out in regulation 69N(3)(b) at the end of an accounting period.

69Z7(4)   If the conditions specified in paragraph (6) are met, this Part shall continue to apply to the company despite the breach (but see paragraph (7) and regulation 69Z8).

69Z7(5) If the conditions specified in paragraph (6) are not met, the Commissioners may give a termination notice to the company.

69Z7(6) The conditions are that—

(a) property investment business is at least 50% of the company's net income in the accounting period,

(b) the value of the assets involved in property investment business is at least 50% of the total value of assets held by the company at the end of the accounting period.

69Z7(7) If this regulation applies to a company in three different accounting periods in a period of ten years beginning with the first day of the accounting period in which the company becomes aware of the first of those breaches, the Commissioners may give a termination notice to the company.

Multiple breaches of separate conditions

69Z8(1) This regulation applies in relation to an open-ended investment company to which this Part applies if—

(a) there has been a breach of at least two of the conditions in regulation 9A or regulations 69E to 69N,

(b) at least one of the conditions breached is contained in a different regulation from that containing another of those breached, and

(c) there have been five breaches in a period of ten years beginning with the first day of the accounting period in which the first breach occurs.

69Z8(2) The Commissioners may give a termination notice to the company.

History – In reg. 69Z8(1)(a), the words "regulation 9A or" inserted by SI 2009/2036, reg. 22, with effect from 1 September 2009.

FURTHER PROVISIONS

Profit/financing costs in the case of a Property AIF that is a qualified investor scheme

69Z9(1) This regulation applies if conditions A and B are met.

69Z9(2) Condition A is that an open-ended investment company to which this Part applies is a qualified investor scheme.

69Z9(3) Condition B is that the result of the following calculation is less than 1.25 in respect of an accounting period—

$$\frac{Income}{Financing\ Costs}$$

69Z9(4) In paragraph (3)—

"**Income**" means the amount of the net income of F (tax-exempt) arising in the accounting period (before the offset of capital allowances, of losses from a previous accounting period, and of amounts taken into account under regulation 69Z1(3)), and

"**Financing Costs**" means the amount of the financing costs incurred in that period in respect of the business of F (tax-exempt).

69Z9(5) An amount shall be charged to corporation tax.

69Z9(6) That amount is determined as follows—

Step One

Determine the financing costs which, given the actual income, would produce the result of 1.25 in the calculation specified in paragraph (3) (the "theoretical financing costs").

Step Two

Determine the amount by which the actual financing costs exceed the theoretical financing costs ("the excess financing cost").

Step Three

Divide the main rate at which corporation tax is charged for the accounting period by the rate at which corporation tax is charged on an open-ended investment company for the accounting period (see section 468A(1) of ICTA) to determine the multiplier.

Step Four

Multiply the excess financing cost by the multiplier.

The result is the amount charged to tax.

69Z9(7)   For the purposes of paragraphs (3) and (4) **"financing costs"** are the costs of debt finance; and in calculating the costs of debt finance in respect of an accounting period the matters to be taken into account include–

(a)   costs giving rise to debits in respect of debtor relationships of the company under Chapter 2 of Part 4 of FA 1996 (loan relationships), other than debits in respect of exchange losses from such relationships (within the meaning of section 103(1A) and (1B) of that Act),

(b)   any exchange gain or loss from a debtor relationship within the meaning of that Chapter in relation to debt finance,

(c)   any credit or debit falling to be brought into account under Schedule 26 to FA 2002 (derivative contracts) in relation to debt finance,

(d)   the financing cost implicit in a payment under a finance lease, and

(e)   any other costs arising from what would be considered, in accordance with generally accepted accounting practice, to be a financing transaction.

69Z9(8)   No loss, deficit, expense or allowance may be set off against the amount charged to tax by paragraph (5).

Cancellation of tax advantage

69Z10(1)   This regulation applies if a company to which this Part applies has tried to obtain a tax advantage for itself or another person.

69Z10(2)   The Commissioners may give a notice to the company specifying the tax advantage.

69Z10(3)   If the Commissioners give a notice to the company under paragraph (2) a tax advantage obtained by the company shall be counteracted, in accordance with the notice, by an adjustment by way of–

(a)   an assessment;

(b)   the cancellation of a right of repayment;

(c)   a requirement to return a repayment already made; or

(d)   the computation or recomputation of profits or gains, or liability to tax, on a basis specified by the Commissioners in the notice.

69Z10(4)   The Commissioners may (in addition to the adjustment under paragraph (3)) assess the company to such additional amount of income tax under Case VI of Schedule D as they think is equivalent to the value of the tax advantage.

69Z10(5)   For the purposes of this regulation **"tax advantage"** has the meaning given by section 709 of ICTA.

69Z10(6)   But a company does not obtain a tax advantage by reason only of this Part applying to it, unless it does anything (whether before or during the application of this Part) which is wholly or principally designed to create or inflate or apply a loss, deduction or expense (whether or not suffered or incurred by the company).

Appeal against notice under regulation 69Z10

69Z11(1)   If a notice is given to a company under regulation 69Z10, the company may appeal.

69Z11(2)   The notice of appeal must be given to HM Revenue and Customs within a period of 28 days beginning with the day on which the notice under regulation 69Z10 is given.

69Z11(3)   On an appeal that is notified to the tribunal, the tribunal may–

(a)   affirm, vary or cancel the notice, and

(b)   affirm, vary or quash an assessment made under regulation 69Z10(4).

History – In reg. 69Z11(1), the words "to the Special Commissioners", which appeared after "appeal", omitted by SI 2009/56, art. 3(2) and Sch. 2, para. 157(2), operative from 1 April 2009 subject to transitional and saving provisions in SI 2009/56, Sch. 3. In reg. 69Z11(3), the words "that is notified to the tribunal, the tribunal" substituted for the words "the Special Commissioners" by SI 2009/56, art. 3(2) and Sch. 2, para. 157(3), operative from 1 April 2009 subject to transitional and saving provisions in SI 2009/56, Sch. 3.

Distribution to holder of excessive rights: charge to tax

69Z12(1)   This regulation applies if an open-ended investment company to which this Part applies–

(a)   makes a distribution to, or in respect of, a holder of excessive rights (see regulation 69Z13), and

(b)   the company has not taken reasonable steps to prevent the possibility of such a distribution being made.

69Z12(2)   The company is treated as having received an amount of income calculated in accordance with paragraph (3).

69Z12(3) The amount of the income is determined by the formula—

$$I \times P$$

69Z12(4) In paragraph (3)—

I is the net income of F (tax-exempt) distributable in accordance with regulation 69Z14(a);

P is the percentage of the rights to the net asset value of the company held by, or on behalf of, the holder of excessive rights.

69Z12(5) The amount determined in accordance with paragraph (3) shall be charged to corporation tax as if it were income of F (residual) chargeable under Case VI of Schedule D arising in the accounting period in which the distribution mentioned in paragraph (1) was made by the company.

69Z12(6) No loss, deficit, expense or allowance may be set off against the amount charged to tax by paragraph (5).

Meaning of "holder of excessive rights"

69Z13(1) In this Part a **"holder of excessive rights"** means a body corporate which—

(a) is a participant in an open-ended investment company to which this Part applies, and

(b) is beneficially entitled to shares representing rights to 10% or more of the net asset value of the company.

69Z13(2) Paragraphs (4) and (5) of regulation 69L apply for the purposes of paragraph (1) as they apply for the purposes of regulation 69K.

69Z13(3) In this Part an "excessive holding" means the holding of a holder of excessive rights.

Chapter 4 – Distributions Made by Property AIFS

History – Pt. 4A inserted by SI 2008/705, reg. 5, with effect from 6 April 2008.

ALLOCATION OF INCOME

History – The heading to reg. 69Z14 changed from "ATTRIBUTION OF DISTRIBUTIONS" by SI 2010/294, reg. 16(2), with effect from 6 March 2010 (subject to the transitional provisions at SI 2010/294, reg. 24).

69Z14 The total amount available for income allocation in an open-ended investment company to which this Part applies shall be attributed—

(a) first, to property income distributions up to the amount of the net income of F (tax-exempt) (determined in accordance with regulation 69Z1),

(b) secondly, to PAIF distributions (interest) up to the pre-distribution amount (determined in accordance with regulation 69Z3), and

(c) finally, to PAIF distributions (dividends).

History – In reg. 69Z14, the words "the total amount available for income allocation in an open-ended investment company to which this Part applies shall be attributed" substituted for the words "The total amount shown in the distribution accounts of an open-ended investment company to which this Part applies as available for distribution to participants shall be attributed" by SI 2010/294, reg. 16(3), with effect from 6 March 2010 (subject to the transitional provisions at SI 2010/294, reg. 24).

PROPERTY INCOME DISTRIBUTIONS

69Z15(1) This regulation applies if—

(a) an open-ended investment company to which this Part applies makes a distribution, and

(b) the amount distributed includes sums attributed to property income distributions.

69Z15(2) The Tax Acts shall have effect as if the sums were payments made on the distribution date by the company to the participants in proportion to their rights.

69Z15(3) Regulation 69Z18 (property income distributions: liability to tax of participants) explains how a property income distribution received by a participant is treated.

69Z15(4) In these Regulations a "property income distribution" means a sum attributed to property income distributions which is distributed (including a payment made to a participant who is not chargeable to income tax or corporation tax).

PAIF DISTRIBUTIONS (INTEREST)

69Z16(1) This regulation applies if—

(a) an open-ended investment company to which this Part applies makes a distribution, and

(b) the amount distributed includes sums attributed to PAIF distributions (interest).

69Z16(2)   The Tax Acts shall have effect as if the sums were payments of yearly interest made on the distribution date by the company to the participants in proportion to their rights.

69Z16(3)   In this Part a **"PAIF distribution (interest)"** means a sum attributed to PAIF distributions (interest) which is distributed (including a payment made to a participant who is not chargeable to income tax).

PAIF DISTRIBUTIONS (DIVIDENDS)

69Z17(1)   This regulation applies if–

(a)   an open-ended investment company to which this Part applies makes a distribution, and

(b)   the amount distributed includes sums attributed to PAIF distributions (dividends).

69Z17(2)   The Tax Acts shall have effect as if the sums were dividends on shares paid on the distribution date by the company to the participants in proportion to their rights.

69Z17(3)   In this Part a **"PAIF distribution (dividends)"** means a sum attributed to PAIF distributions (dividends) which is distributed (including a dividend treated as paid to a participant who is not chargeable to corporation tax).

Chapter 5 – The Treatment of Participants in Property AIFS

History – Pt. 4A inserted by SI 2008/705, reg. 5, with effect from 6 April 2008.

TREATMENT OF DISTRIBUTIONS: LIABILITY TO TAX OF PARTICIPANTS

Property income distributions: liability to tax of participants

69Z18(1)   A property income distribution received by a participant in an open-ended investment company to which this Part applies shall be treated–

(a)   in the case of a participant within the charge to corporation tax, as profits of a Schedule A business, and

(b)   in the case of a participant within the charge to income tax, as the profits of a UK property business (within the meaning of section 264 of ITTOIA 2005).

69Z18(2)   A distribution received by a participant who is not resident in the United Kingdom–

(a)   if the participant is a company within the charge to corporation tax, shall be chargeable to tax as profits of a Schedule A business,

(b)   if the participant is a person other than a company within the charge to corporation tax, shall be chargeable to tax as profits of a UK property business (within the meaning of section 264 of ITTOIA 2005), and

(c)   in either case shall not be chargeable to tax by virtue of sections 971 and 972 of ITA 2007 (non-resident landlords).

69Z18(3)   Paragraph (1) shall not apply in relation to a participant if and in so far as the participant–

(a)   is a dealer in respect of distributions (within the meaning of section 95 of ICTA),

(b)   is a dealer in securities who is charged to tax under Part 2 of ITTOIA 2005 (trading income) in respect of distributions made by companies,

(c)   is an individual member of Lloyd's (within the meaning given by section 184(1) of FA 1993) and the distribution is made in respect of assets forming part of–

(i)   a premium trust fund of his (within the meaning given by section 174 of FA 1993), or

(ii)   an ancillary trust fund of his (within the meaning given by section 176 of FA 1993), or

(d)   is a corporate member of Lloyd's (within the meaning given by section 230(1) of FA 1994) and the distribution is made in respect of assets forming part of–

(i)   a premium trust fund of his (within the meaning given by section 222 of FA 1994), or

(ii)   an ancillary trust fund of his (within the meaning given by section 223 of FA 1994).

69Z18(4)   Section 114(1)(a) of ICTA (partnerships with companies as members) does not disapply paragraph (1).

69Z18(5)   Sections 231 of ICTA and 397 of ITTOIA 2005 (tax credits in respect of qualifying distributions) shall not apply to property income distributions.

69Z18(6)   Property income distributions received by one participant acting in one capacity shall be treated, for the purposes of paragraph (1), as the profits of a single business which is separate from–

(a) any other Schedule A business carried on by the participant,

(b) any other UK property business (within the meaning of section 264 of ITTOIA 2005) carried on by the participant,

(c) any overseas property business (within the meaning of section 70A(4) of ICTA) carried on by the participant, and

(d) any overseas property business (within the meaning of section 265 of ITTOIA 2005) carried on by the participant.

69Z18(7) In the case of a participant which is a partnership, paragraph (6) applies to receipts by a partner of a share of any distribution as it applies to receipts by a participant.

PAIF distributions (interest): liability to tax of participants

69Z19(1) A PAIF distribution (interest) received by a participant in an open-ended investment company to which this Part applies shall be treated–

(a) in the case of a participant within the charge to corporation tax, as if it were interest arising from a loan relationship; and

(b) in the case of a participant within the charge to income tax, as if it were a payment of yearly interest falling within Chapter 2 of Part 4 of ITTOIA 2005.

69Z19(2) Sections 231 of ICTA and 397 of ITTOIA 2005 (tax credits in respect of qualifying distributions) shall not apply to PAIF distributions (interest).

History – Reg. 69Z19(1) substituted by SI 2008/3159, reg. 24, with effect from 1 January 2009. Former reg. 69Z19(1) read as follows:

> "**69Z19(1)** A PAIF distribution (interest) received by a participant in an open-ended investment company to which this Part applies shall be treated as if it were a payment of yearly interest.".

Property distributions (dividends): liability to tax of participants

69Z20(1) A PAIF distribution (dividends) received by a participant in an open-ended investment company to which this Part applies shall be treated as if it were a dividend on shares.

69Z20(2) If a PAIF distribution (dividends) is made for a distribution period to a participant chargeable to corporation tax, regulations 48 to 52A) shall not apply to the distribution.

Distributions made after cessation

69Z21(1) This regulation applies if an open-ended investment company–

(a) is a company to which this Part applies in respect of an accounting period,

(b) makes a distribution in respect of that accounting period, and

(c) the distribution is made after cessation.

69Z21(2) Regulations 69Z18 to 69Z20 apply in relation to the distribution.

DEDUCTION OF TAX FROM DISTRIBUTIONS

Deduction of tax from property income distributions

69Z22(1) On making a property income distribution, an open-ended investment company to which this Part applies must deduct a sum representing income tax at the basic rate in force for the tax year in which the distribution date falls.

69Z22(2) A property income distribution shall be treated as having been received by the participant after deduction of income tax at the basic rate for the year of assessment in which the distribution date falls, from a corresponding gross amount.

69Z22(3) The sum is accordingly taken into account under sections 59B and 59D of TMA 1970 (see also paragraph 8 of Schedule 18 to the Finance Act 1998) in determining the income tax or corporation tax payable by, or repayable to, the participant.

69Z22(4) This regulation is subject to regulation 69Z24 (distribution payments to be made without deduction of tax).

Deduction of tax from PAIF distributions (interest)

69Z23(1) On making a PAIF distribution (interest), an open-ended investment company to which this Part applies must deduct a sum representing income tax at the basic rate in force for the tax year in which the PAIF distribution (interest) is made.

69Z23(2) Accordingly, the sum is one to which section 874 of ITA 2007 applies.

69Z23(3) [Omitted by SI 2008/3159, reg. 25(b).]

69Z23(4)   This regulation is subject to regulation 69Z24 (distribution payments to be made without deduction of tax).

History – In reg. 69Z23(1), "basic rate" substituted for "savings rate" by SI 2008/3159, reg. 25(a), with effect from 1 January 2009.

Reg. 69Z23(3) omitted by SI 2008/3159, reg. 25(b), with effect from 1 January 2009.

Distribution payments to be made without deduction of tax

69Z24(1)   Subject to paragraphs (3A) and (3B), on making a distribution, an open-ended investment company to which this Part applies must not deduct any sum representing income tax if the company reasonably believes that conditions A and B are met.

69Z24(2)   Condition A is that if the distribution were made by a UK-REIT out of the profits of C (tax-exempt), the distribution would be required to be made without any deduction representing income tax.

69Z24(3)   Condition B is that if the distribution were a distribution of yearly interest, the distribution would be required to be made without any deduction representing income tax.

69Z24(3A)   But neither condition A nor condition B is met, in relation to a unit trust scheme, where–

(a)   the distribution is made to the trustee of the scheme;

(b)   the trustee is chargeable to corporation tax or income tax on the distribution in the United Kingdom; and

(c)   the trustee has made a request in writing to the Property AIF that the Property AIF should deduct tax from the distribution.

69Z24(3B)   The Property AIF must not specify that the trustee of any unit trust scheme seeking to acquire shares in the Property AIF must have tax deducted from any distribution.

69Z24(4)   If at the time it makes a distribution the company reasonably believes that conditions A and B are met, but in fact those conditions are not both met, these Regulations shall apply to the distribution as if it were never one which could be made without deduction of tax.

69Z24(5)   In paragraph (2) **"profits of C (tax-exempt)"** shall be construed in accordance with Part 4 of FA 2006.

History – In reg. 69Z24(1), the words "Subject to paragraphs (3A) and (3B)," inserted by SI 2008/3159, reg. 26(a), with effect from 1 January 2009.

Reg. 69Z24(3A) inserted by SI 2008/3159, reg. 26(b), with effect from 1 January 2009.

Reg. 69Z24(3B) inserted by SI 2008/3159, reg. 26(b), with effect from 1 January 2009.

MANUFACTURED DIVIDENDS REPRESENTING PROPERTY INCOME DISTRIBUTIONS

69Z24A(1)   This regulation applies to the extent that a manufactured dividend which is paid by a dividend manufacturer is representative of property income distributions to which regulation 69Z15 applies.

69Z24A(2)   The amount of the manufactured dividend falling within paragraph (1) is referred to in this regulation as "the manufactured PID amount".

69Z24A(3)   The recipient of the manufactured PID amount is treated as having received a distribution to which regulation 69Z18 applies.

69Z24A(4)   In relation to the dividend manufacturer–

(a)   if the dividend manufacturer is a company and the manufactured dividend is paid in the course of a trade carried on in the United Kingdom, the manufactured PID amount shall be treated as an expense of the trade;

(b)   if the manufactured dividend is paid in connection with investment business, the manufactured PID amount shall be treated for the purposes of section 75 of ICTA as expenses of management; and

(c)   in the case of a company carrying on life assurance business, so much of the manufactured PID amount as would be referable by virtue of section 432A of ICTA to basic life assurance and general annuity business if it were received by the company shall be treated for the purposes of section 76 of ICTA as if it were an expense payable falling to be brought into account at step 3 of section 76(7).

69Z24A(5)   Regulations 69Z22, 69Z24 and 69Z29 to 69Z35 apply to the dividend manufacturer as if–

(a)   the dividend manufacturer were an open-ended investment company to which this Part applies; and

(b)   the manufactured PID amount were a distribution to which those regulations apply.

History – Reg. 69Z24A inserted by SI 2008/3159, reg. 27, with effect in relation to manufactured dividends paid on or after 1 January 2009.

MANUFACTURED DIVIDENDS REPRESENTING PAIF DISTRIBUTIONS (INTEREST)

69Z24B(1) This regulation applies to the extent that a manufactured dividend which is paid by a dividend manufacturer is representative of a PAIF distribution (interest) to which regulation 69Z16 applies.

69Z24B(2) The amount of the manufactured dividend to which this regulation applies is referred to in this regulation as the "manufactured PAIF interest amount".

69Z24B(3) If the recipient of the manufactured dividend is a company within the charge to corporation tax it is treated as having received, in relation to the manufactured PAIF interest amount, an amount to which section 97 of FA 1996 applies.

69Z24B(4) If the recipient of the manufactured dividend is within the charge to income tax it is treated as having received, in relation to the manufactured PAIF interest amount, an amount to which regulation 69Z19 applies.

69Z24B(5) If the dividend manufacturer is a company within the charge to corporation tax, section 97 of FA 1996 is treated as applying to the manufactured PAIF interest amount.

69Z24B(6) Regulations 69Z23, 69Z24 and 69Z29 to 69Z35 apply to the dividend manufacturer in relation to the manufactured PAIF interest amount as if the dividend manufacturer were an open-ended investment company to which this Part applies.

History – Reg. 69Z24B inserted by SI 2008/3159, reg. 27, with effect in relation to manufactured dividends paid on or after 1 January 2009.

MANUFACTURED DIVIDENDS – PAIF DISTRIBUTIONS (DIVIDENDS)

69Z24C(1) This regulation applies to the extent that a manufactured dividend which is paid by a dividend manufacturer is representative of a PAIF distribution (dividends) to which regulation 69Z17 applies.

69Z24C(2) The recipient of the manufactured dividend is treated as having received, to that extent, an amount to which regulation 69Z20 applies.

69Z24C(3) If the dividend manufacturer is a company, paragraph 2(2)(b) of Schedule 23A to ICTA has effect in relation to the amount of the manufactured dividend to which paragraph (1) applies.

History – Reg. 69Z24C inserted by SI 2008/3159, reg. 27, with effect in relation to manufactured dividends paid on or after 1 January 2009.

INTERPRETATION

69Z24D In regulations 69Z24A to 69Z24C, "manufactured dividend" and "dividend manufacturer" have the meanings given by Schedule 23A to ICTA.

History – Reg. 69Z24D inserted by SI 2008/3159, reg. 27, with effect in relation to manufactured dividends paid on or after 1 January 2009.

CONVERSIONS AND EXCHANGES

Conversion to property AIF

69Z24E(1) This regulation applies if–

(a)   a fund ("the pre-conversion fund") which is not a property AIF becomes, or intends to become, a property AIF,

(b)   the unit-holders in the pre-conversion fund dispose of the units which they hold in that fund ("the original units") and, as part of an arrangement, acquire units of the same, or substantially the same, value as the original units in the fund which is, or is intended to become, the dedicated feeder fund for the property AIF, and

(c)   the further requirement of regulation 69Z24G is met.

69Z24E(2) Sections 127 to 131 of TCGA apply in relation to the disposal and subsequent acquisition of units specified in this regulation.

69Z24E(3) A fund converting to a property AIF in accordance with this regulation shall be treated as meeting condition A in regulation 69K (the corporate ownership condition) where the conditions in paragraph (4) are met, notwithstanding that the holding of a body corporate in the property AIF may exceed the percentage mentioned in regulation 69K(3)(a) during the relevant period.

69Z24E(4) The conditions in this paragraph are that–

(a) during the relevant period, no distributions are declared or made,

(b) any distribution which was declared before the beginning of the relevant period is paid before the beginning of that period, and

(c) the units held by the body corporate in the property AIF are exchanged for units in the dedicated feeder fund as soon as reasonably practicable.

69Z24E(5) In this regulation, **"the relevant period"** is the period beginning with the time at which the fund becomes a property AIF and ending with the time at which the units in the dedicated feeder fund for the property AIF are issued to a participant which is a body corporate.

History – Reg. 69Z24E inserted by SI 2012/1783, reg. 4, with effect for capital gains tax purposes in relation to disposals made on or after 1 August 2012 and for the purposes of corporation tax on chargeable gains in relation to disposals on or after 1 August 2012.

Exchange of units

69Z24F(1) This regulation applies if–

(a) there is–

  (i) an exchange of units in a dedicated feeder fund for shares in the property AIF for which that fund is the dedicated feeder fund, or

  (ii) an exchange of shares in a property AIF for units in the dedicated feeder fund for that property AIF, and

(b) the further requirement of regulation 69Z24G is met.

69Z24F(2) The units to be exchanged in accordance with either paragraph (1)(a) or (b) must represent the same, or substantially the same, share of the net asset value of the property AIF as the units which are held immediately after the exchange.

69Z24F(3) Sections 127 to 131 of TCGA 1992 apply in relation to a disposal or acquisition of units or shares specified in paragraph (1).

History – Reg. 69Z24F inserted by SI 2012/1783, reg. 4, with effect for capital gains tax purposes in relation to disposals made on or after 1 August 2012 and for the purposes of corporation tax on chargeable gains in relation to disposals on or after 1 August 2012.

Further requirement

69Z24G The further requirement is that if a transaction involves the acquisition of units in a dedicated feeder fund, that it is undertaken with the agreement of the manager of the property AIF.

History – Reg. 69Z24G inserted by SI 2012/1783, reg. 4, with effect for capital gains tax purposes in relation to disposals made on or after 1 August 2012 and for the purposes of corporation tax on chargeable gains in relation to disposals on or after 1 August 2012.

Application of section 137 of TCGA

69Z24H Section 137 of TCGA (restriction on application of tax treatment) applies to any transaction specified in regulations 69Z24E or 69Z24F in the circumstances mentioned in that section.

History – Reg. 69Z24H inserted by SI 2012/1783, reg. 4, with effect for capital gains tax purposes in relation to disposals made on or after 1 August 2012 and for the purposes of corporation tax on chargeable gains in relation to disposals on or after 1 August 2012.

Chapter 6 – Compliance in Relation to the Property AIF Regime

History – Pt. 4A inserted by SI 2008/705, reg. 5, with effect from 6 April 2008.

COMPANY TAX RETURN

Documents to be included with company tax return

69Z25(1) An open-ended investment company to which this Part applies must include documents A and B in its company tax return.

69Z25(2) Document A is a calculation of the net income of F(tax-exempt) and F(residual) in accordance with regulations 69Z1 to 69Z3.

69Z25(3) Document B is a reconciliation between–

(a) the net income of the company (see regulation 69Z), and

(b) the total amount available for income allocation as attributed in accordance with regulation 69Z14.

69Z25(4) In paragraph (1) **"company tax return"** means the return required to be delivered pursuant to a notice under paragraph 3 of Schedule 18 to the Finance Act 1998, as read with paragraph 4 of that Schedule.

69Z25(5) Section 98 of TMA 1970 applies to any failure to furnish any information, give any certificate or produce any document or record in accordance with any provision of this Chapter as it applies to any such failure in the case of any provision specified in the second column of the Table below that section.

History – In reg. 69Z25(3)(b), the words "the total amount available for income allocation" substituted for the words "the total income shown in the distribution accounts" by SI 2010/294, reg. 17, with effect from 6 March 2010 (subject to the transitional provisions at SI 2010/294, reg. 24).

BREACHES OF CONDITIONS IN CHAPTER 2

Information to be provided by company to which this Part applies

69Z26(1) This regulation applies if an open-ended investment company to which this Part applies–

(a) does not meet a condition set out in Chapter 2 of this Part (entry into and membership of the Property AIF regime), and

(b) becomes aware that it does not meet the condition.

69Z26(2) As soon as reasonably practicable, the company must provide the following information to the Commissioners–

(a) the date on which the condition first ceased to be met and the date (if any) on which the condition was satisfied again;

(b) details of the condition that was breached;

(c) the nature of the breach; and

(d) what (if anything) the company has done to prevent the breach recurring.

69Z26(3) This regulation does not apply if the breach of condition is one to which regulation 69Z27 applies.

HOLDERS OF EXCESSIVE RIGHTS

Information relating to holders of excessive rights

69Z27(1) This regulation applies if an open-ended investment company to which this Part applies becomes aware that it has made a distribution to, or in respect of, a holder of excessive rights.

69Z27(2) As soon as reasonably practicable, the company must provide the following information to the Commissioners–

(a) the name of every person to whom, or in respect of whom, the distribution specified in paragraph (1) was made;

(b) the address of every such person;

(c) the amount or value of the distribution;

(d) particulars of those persons' interests in the company, including details of the percentage of rights to the net asset value of the company represented by the shares held by those persons;

(e) the steps the company took to prevent the acquisition of any excessive holding; and

(f) the steps the company has taken, or is taking, to ensure that there is no longer any excessive holding in the company.

INFORMATION ABOUT POSSIBLE BREACHES OF CONDITIONS OF MEMBERSHIP OF PROPERTY AIF REGIME

Information to be provided to officers of Revenue and Customs

69Z28(1) This regulation applies if an officer of Revenue and Customs thinks that an open-ended investment company to which this Part applies–

(a) does not meet, or may not meet, a condition specified in Chapter 2 of this Part, or

(b) has not rectified a breach of such a condition.

69Z28(2) The officer may serve a notice on the manager of the company.

69Z28(3) The notice may require the manager to provide any of the information specified in regulation 69Z26(2) or, as the case may be, regulation 69Z27(2).

69Z28(4) The manager must comply with the notice within a period of 28 days beginning with the day on which the notice is served.

ACCOUNTING FOR TAX DEDUCTED FROM PROPERTY INCOME DISTRIBUTIONS

Payments in an accounting period

69Z29(1) This regulation applies if–

(a) an open-ended investment company to which this Part applies makes a distribution in an accounting period of the company, and

(b) the distribution includes sums attributed to property income distributions or to PAIF distributions (interest) (or to both) (referred to in this Chapter as a "relevant distribution").

69Z29(2) The company must deliver a return to an officer of Revenue and Customs for each return period–

(a) which falls within the accounting period, and

(b) in which the company makes a relevant distribution.

69Z29(3) The return periods are–

(a) the quarters ending on 31st March, 30th June, 30th September and 31st December (the "quarter days"); and

(b) any shorter period which–

    (i) starts on the first day of an accounting period and ends with the first or only quarter day in that accounting period;

    (ii) begins immediately after the last or only quarter day in that accounting period and ends on the last day of that accounting period; or

    (iii) is an accounting period which starts and ends within a quarter.

69Z29(4) The company must deliver the return during a period of 14 days beginning with the day immediately following the end of the return period.

69Z29(5) The return must show the amount of–

(a) any relevant distributions made by the company in the return period, and

(b) the tax (if any) payable by the company in respect of those payments.

69Z29(6) The company must deliver, with the return for the return period which ends on the last day of an accounting period, a reconciliation statement showing, in relation to any distribution made during the accounting period, the amounts (if any) which are attributable to each of paragraphs (a) to (c) of regulation 69Z14 (attribution of distributions).

Collection and payment of tax

69Z30(1) Tax in respect of a relevant distribution is due at the time by which the return on which the distribution must be included is required to be delivered.

69Z30(2) The tax due is equal to the sum which the company is required to deduct from the relevant distribution under–

(a) regulation 69Z22(1) (deduction of tax from property income distributions), and

(b) regulation 69Z23(1) (deduction of tax from PAIF distributions (interest)).

69Z30(3) The tax is due from the company making the relevant distribution.

69Z30(4) The tax is payable without an officer of Revenue and Customs making any assessment.

Assessments where relevant distribution included in return

69Z31(1) This regulation applies if any tax in respect of a relevant distribution which is included in a return under this Chapter has not been paid at or before the time mentioned in regulation 69Z30.

69Z31(2) An officer of Revenue and Customs may make an assessment on the person who made the relevant distribution.

69Z31(3) Tax may be assessed under this regulation whether or not it has been paid when the assessment is made.

Assessments in other cases

69Z32(1) This regulation applies if an officer of Revenue and Customs thinks–

(a) that there is a relevant distribution which should have been included in a return under this Chapter and which has not been so included, or

(b) that a return under this Chapter is otherwise incorrect.

69Z32(2)   An officer of Revenue and Customs may make an assessment on the person who made the relevant distribution to the best of the officer's judgement.

Application of Income Tax Acts provisions about time limits for assessments

69Z33(1)   The provisions of the Income Tax Acts about the time within which an assessment may be made apply to assessments under this Chapter, so far as those provisions refer or relate to–

(a)   the tax year for which an assessment is made, or

(b)   the year to which an assessment relates.

69Z33(2)   Paragraph (1) applies despite the fact that an assessment under this Chapter may relate to a return period which is not a tax year.

69Z33(3)   The provisions of section 36 of TMA 1970 (fraudulent or negligent conduct) about the circumstances in which an assessment may be made out of time apply accordingly on the basis that any such assessment relates to the tax year in which the return period ends.

69Z33(4)   Section 87 of TMA 1970 (interest on overdue income tax deducted at source) applies for the purposes of a payment due under regulation 69Z30 or an assessment made under regulation 69Z31 or 69Z32.

Certificates of deduction of tax

69Z34(1)   A company making a relevant distribution which is subject to deduction of tax by virtue of regulation 69Z22(1) must furnish the recipient with a statement that complies with condition A or B. This is subject to paragraph (5).

69Z34(2)   The duty imposed by paragraph (1) is enforceable at the suit or instance of the recipient.

69Z34(3)   Condition A is that the statement is in writing showing–

(a)   the gross amount of the payment,

(b)   the amount of tax deducted, and

(c)   the actual amount paid.

69Z34(4)   Condition B is that the statement is in writing–

(a)   showing–

   (i)   the gross amount of the distribution made to the participant,

   (ii)   the number and class of units held by the participant in respect of which the distribution is made,

   (iii)   the net amount of the distribution per unit,

   (iv)   whether any tax has been deducted from the distribution, and

   (v)   the date the distribution was made;

(b)   providing details to allow the participant to access an electronic means of calculating the amounts that would be shown in a statement provided in accordance with condition A; and

(c)   providing the participant with an alternative method of obtaining the details of those amounts without recourse to electronic means.

69Z34(5)   If an appropriate statement for the purposes of section 234A of ICTA is provided by the company in accordance with regulation 70(4) and (5)–

(a)   condition A does not apply, and

(b)   the statement required by condition B must be included in the appropriate statement.

69Z34(6)   Where paragraph (5) applies, **"distribution"** in regulation 70(4) and (5) shall be taken to include the property income distribution and the statement must show the percentage of the gross distribution attributable to the property income distribution.

History – Reg. 69Z34 substituted by SI 2009/2036, reg. 23, with effect from 1 September 2009. Former reg. 69Z34 read as follows:

  "**69Z34(1)**   A company making a relevant distribution which is subject to deduction of tax by virtue of regulation 69Z22(1) must furnish the recipient with a statement in writing showing–
    (a)   the gross amount of the payment,
    (b)   the amount of tax deducted, and
    (c)   the actual amount paid.
  69Z34(2)   The duty imposed by subsection (1) is enforceable at the suit or instance of the recipient.".

Company's duty to deliver amended return

69Z35(1)   This regulation applies if an open-ended investment company to which this Part applies makes a distribution, and then becomes aware that–

Statutory Instruments

(a)   anything which should have been included in a return delivered by the company under these Regulations has not been so included,

(b)   anything which should not have been included in a return delivered by the company under these Regulations has been so included, or

(c)   any other error has occurred in a return delivered by the company under these Regulations.

69Z35(2)   The company must deliver an amended return correcting the error to an officer of Revenue and Customs without delay.

69Z35(3)   If the company delivers an amended return such assessments, adjustments, setoffs or payments or repayments of tax as are necessary for achieving the objective mentioned in paragraph (4) must be made.

69Z35(4)   The objective is that the resulting liabilities to income and corporation tax (including interest on unpaid or overpaid tax) of the company or any other person are the same as they would have been if a correct return had been delivered.

Chapter 7 – Leaving the Property AIF Regime

History – Pt. 4A inserted by SI 2008/705, reg. 5, with effect from 6 April 2008.

TERMINATION BY NOTICE: COMPANY

69Z36(1)   This regulation applies if an open-ended investment company to which this Part applies gives a notice under this regulation specifying a date at the end of which this Part is to cease to apply to the company.

69Z36(2)   This Part shall cease to apply to the company at the end of that date.

69Z36(3)   A notice under paragraph (1) must be given in writing to the Commissioners.

69Z36(4)   The date specified under paragraph (1) must be after the date on which the Commissioners receive the notice.

TERMINATION BY NOTICE: COMMISSIONERS

69Z37(1)   This regulation applies if the Commissioners give a notice in writing under this paragraph to an open-ended investment company to which this Part applies (a "termination notice").

69Z37(2)   This Part shall cease to apply to the company.

69Z37(3)   The Commissioners may give a termination notice only if–

(a)   a provision contained in this Part provides that the Commissioners may give a termination notice,

(b)   there is an intentional or negligent breach of a condition in Chapter 2, or

(c)   there is an attempt to gain a tax advantage to which regulation 69Z10 applies.

69Z37(4)   A termination notice must state the reason for it.

69Z37(5)   If a termination notice is given to an open-ended investment company, this Part shall be taken to have ceased to apply to the open-ended investment company at the end of the accounting period before the accounting period during which the event occurs (or the last event occurs) which caused the Commissioners to give the notice.

APPEAL AGAINST TERMINATION NOTICE

69Z38(1)   An open-ended investment company to which a termination notice is given may appeal.

69Z38(2)   The notice of appeal must be given to HM Revenue and Customs within a period of 28 days beginning with the day on which the termination notice is given.

69Z38(3)   On an appeal that is notified to the tribunal, the tribunal shall determine whether it was just and reasonable for HM Revenue and Customs to give the termination notice.

69Z38(4)   If the tribunal decides that it was, the tribunal must confirm the notice.

69Z38(5)   If the tribunal decides that it was not, the tribunal must set aside the notice.

History – In reg. 69Z38(1), the words "to the Special Commissioners", which appeared after "appeal", omitted by SI 2009/56, art. 3(2) and Sch. 2, para. 158(2), operative from 1 April 2009 subject to transitional and saving provisions in SI 2009/56, Sch. 3. In reg. 69Z38(3), the words "that is notified to the tribunal, the tribunal" substituted for the words "the Special Commissioners" by SI 2009/56, art. 3(2) and Sch. 2, para. 158(3), operative from 1 April 2009 subject to transitional and saving provisions in SI 2009/56, Sch. 3.

In reg. 69Z38(4), the words "the tribunal decides" and "the tribunal must" substituted for the words "they decide" and "they must" respectively by SI 2009/56, art. 3(2) and Sch. 2, para. 158(4), operative from 1 April 2009 subject to transitional and saving provisions in SI 2009/56, Sch. 3.

In reg. 69Z38(5), the words "the tribunal decides" and "the tribunal must" substituted for the words "they decide" and "they must" respectively by SI 2009/56, art. 3(2) and Sch. 2, para. 158(4), operative from 1 April 2009 subject to transitional and saving provisions in SI 2009/56, Sch. 3.

COMPANY CEASING TO BE AUTHORISED ETC.

69Z39(1) This regulation applies if an open-ended investment company to which this Part applies–

(a)   ceases to be authorised by the Financial Services Authority,

(b)   ceases to be an open-ended investment company, or

(c)   ceases to carry on property investment business.

69Z39(2) This Part shall cease to apply to the company at the end of the date on which the company ceases to be authorised by the Financial Services Authority, to be an open-ended investment company, or to carry on property investment business (as the case may be).

MERGERS

69Z40(1) This regulation applies if an open-ended investment company to which this Part applies–

(a)   is party to a merger or takeover, and

(b)   as a result, ceases to meet one or more of the conditions for this Part to apply.

69Z40(2) On the occurrence of the merger or takeover–

(a)   an accounting period of the company shall end at the end of the date of the merger or takeover, and

(b)   this Part shall cease to apply to the company at the end of that date.

EFFECTS OF CESSATION

69Z41(1) The business of F (tax-exempt) shall be treated for the purposes of corporation tax as ceasing immediately before cessation.

69Z41(2) Assets which immediately before cessation are involved in the business of F (tax-exempt) shall be treated for the purposes of corporation tax as being sold by F (tax-exempt) immediately before cessation and reacquired immediately after cessation by F (post-cessation).

69Z41(3) For the purposes of corporation tax, on cessation one accounting period of F (residual) shall end and an accounting period of F (post-cessation) shall begin.

69Z41(4) The sale and reacquisition deemed under paragraph (2) shall not have effect for the purposes of tax in respect of chargeable gains.

69Z41(5) For the purposes of CAA 2001, the sale and re-acquisition deemed under paragraph (2)–

(a)   shall not give rise to allowances or charges, and

(b)   shall not make it possible to make an election under section 198 or 199 of that Act (apportionment).

69Z41(6) For the purposes of CAA 2001, anything done by or to F (tax-exempt) before cessation in relation to an asset which is deemed under paragraph (2) to be sold and re-acquired shall be treated after cessation as having been done by or to F (post-cessation).

PART 4B – TAX ELECTED FUNDS

History – Pt. 4B inserted by SI 2009/2036, reg. 24, with effect from 1 September 2009.

Chapter 1 – Preliminary Provisions

TAX ELECTED FUNDS

69Z42(1) This Part makes provision in relation to an authorised investment fund which meets the conditions in regulations 69Z45 to 69Z48.

69Z42(2) In these Regulations an authorised investment fund to which this Part applies may be referred to as a **"Tax Elected Fund"**.

History – Reg. 69Z42 inserted by SI 2009/2036, reg. 24, with effect from 1 September 2009.

STRUCTURE OF THIS PART

69Z43   The structure of this Part is as follows–

this Chapter contains preliminary provisions;

Chapter 2 deals with entry into and membership of the Tax Elected Funds regime;

Chapter 3 deals with the tax treatment of Tax Elected Funds;

Chapter 4 deals with distributions made by Tax Elected Funds;

Chapter 5 deals with the treatment of participants in Tax Elected Funds;

Chapter 6 deals with compliance in relation to the Tax Elected Funds regime; and

Chapter 7 contains provisions relating to an authorised investment fund's leaving the Tax Elected Funds regime.

History – Reg. 69Z43 inserted by SI 2009/2036, reg. 24, with effect from 1 September 2009.

INTERPRETATION

69Z44   In this Part–

"entry" means the time when this Part begins to apply to an authorised investment fund;

"cessation" means the time when this Part ceases to apply to an authorised investment fund;

"overseas property business" has the meaning given in section 206 of CTA 2009;

"UK property business" has the meaning given in section 205 of CTA 2009.

History – Reg. 69Z44 inserted by SI 2009/2036, reg. 24, with effect from 1 September 2009.

Chapter 2 – Entry into and Membership of the Tax Elected Funds Regime

CONDITIONS OF MEMBERSHIP OF THE TAX ELECTED FUNDS REGIME

Conditions for this Part to apply to fund

69Z45   In order for this Part to apply to an authorised investment fund in respect of an accounting period–

(a)   the following conditions (the "TEF conditions") must be met–

    (i)   the property condition (see regulation 69Z46);

    (ii)   the genuine diversity of ownership condition (see regulation 9A);

    (iii)   the loan creditor condition (see regulation 694Z47); and

    (iv)   the scheme documentation condition (see regulation 69Z48); and

(b)   an application for this Part to apply must be accepted by HM Revenue and Customs (see regulations 69Z49 to 69Z53).

History – Reg. 69Z45 inserted by SI 2009/2036, reg. 24, with effect from 1 September 2009.

THE TEF CONDITIONS

The property condition

69Z46   The property condition is that the authorised investment fund does not have a UK property business or an overseas property business.

History – Reg. 69Z46 inserted by SI 2009/2036, reg. 24, with effect from 1 September 2009.

The loan creditor condition

69Z47(1)   The loan creditor condition is that the authorised investment fund must meet conditions A to C throughout the accounting period in the case of any loan relationship to which the fund is party as a debtor.

69Z47(2)   Condition A is that, in the case of a debtor relationship of the fund, the person standing in the position of a creditor as respects the debt in question is not entitled to an amount by way of interest which depends to any extent on–

(a)   the results of all or part of the authorised investment fund's business, or

(b)   the value of any of the fund's assets.

69Z47(3) For the purposes of condition A, a loan shall not be treated as dependent on the results of the fund's business by reason only that the terms of the loan provide–

(a)   for the interest to be reduced in the event of results improving, or

(b)   for the interest to be increased in the event of results deteriorating.

69Z47(4) Condition B is that, in the case of a debtor relationship of the fund, the person standing in the position of a creditor as respects the debt in question is not entitled to an amount by way of interest which exceeds a reasonable commercial return on the consideration lent.

69Z47(5) Condition C is that, in the case of a debtor relationship of the fund, the person standing in the position of a creditor as respects the debt in question is entitled on repayment to an amount which–

(a)   does not exceed the consideration lent, or

(b)   is reasonably comparable with the amount generally repayable (in respect of an equal amount of consideration) under the terms of issue of securities listed on a recognised stock exchange.

69Z47(6) In this regulation **"loan relationship"** and **"debtor relationship"** shall be construed in accordance with Part 5 of CTA 2009 (loan relationships).

History – Reg. 69Z47 inserted by SI 2009/2036, reg. 24, with effect from 1 September 2009.

The scheme documentation condition

69Z48 The scheme documentation condition is that the instrument constituting the authorised investment fund and its prospectus must include provisions which require the fund to meet the property condition and the loan creditor condition on entry and throughout the accounting period.

History – Reg. 69Z48 inserted by SI 2009/2036, reg. 24, with effect from 1 September 2009.

APPLICATION FOR THIS PART TO APPLY
Application process

69Z49(1) An application for this Part to apply to an authorised investment fund may be made by–

(a)   the manager of an existing authorised investment fund, or

(b)   if it is proposed to establish an authorised investment fund, the person expected to become the manager of the fund once established (the "applicant").

69Z49(2) Before making an application in relation to an existing authorised investment fund, the fund must obtain any necessary shareholder or unit holder approval and must have applied for any necessary regulatory approval in respect of the instrument constituting the fund and the prospectus.

69Z49(3) The manager or applicant must notify HM Revenue and Customs when any necessary regulatory authorisation has been given.

69Z49(4) Where in relation to an existing authorised investment fund this Part has previously applied to the fund–

(a)   no application may be made if a termination notice was issued in relation to the fund, or

(b)   if an election was made under regulation 69Z70 that this Part should cease to apply, no application can be made in relation to any accounting period which begins within six years of the cessation.

69Z49(5) In this Part–

"applicant" means the person referred to in paragraph (1)(b);

"application" means an application under this regulation;

"existing fund application" means an application made under paragraph (1)(a); and

"future fund application" means an application made under paragraph (1)(b).

History – Reg. 69Z49 inserted by SI 2009/2036, reg. 24, with effect from 1 September 2009.

Form and timing of application under regulation 69Z49

69Z50(1) An application must be made in writing to the Commissioners.

69Z50(2) An existing fund application must be received by HM Revenue and Customs at least 28 days before the beginning of the specified accounting period (see regulation 69Z51(2)).

This is subject to paragraph (8).

69Z50(3) A future fund application must be received by HM Revenue and Customs at least 42 days before the date the fund is expected to be established and authorisation given.

This is subject to paragraph (9).

69Z50(4) Within a period of 28 days (or 14 days in the case of an application within paragraph (8) or (9)) beginning on the day on which the application is received, HM Revenue and Customs must–

Statutory Instruments

(a)   notify the manager or applicant that the application is accepted, or

(b)   issue a refusal notice.

69Z50(5)   An application may be withdrawn or amended at any time before it is accepted–

(a)   by the manager (in the case of an existing fund application), or

(b)   by the applicant (in the case of a future fund application).

69Z50(6)   If an application is amended before it is accepted, regulation 69Z49 shall apply to the amended application.

69Z50(7)   But if HM Revenue and Customs give notice that they are satisfied that the amended application is valid, the amended application shall take effect as if made on the date of the original application.

69Z50(8)   An existing fund application may be received by HM Revenue and Customs at least 14 days before the beginning of the specified accounting period if–

(a)   HM Revenue and Customs have given clearance under regulation 9B, and

(b)   the manager of the authorised investment fund certifies that there have been no changes in substance between–

   (i)   the form in which the instrument constituting the fund and its prospectus were considered by HM Revenue and Customs before giving the clearance, and

   (ii)   the form in which it is proposed that those documents will apply at the beginning of the specified accounting period.

69Z50(9)   A future fund application may be received by HM Revenue and Customs at least 14 days before the proposed fund is authorised and established if–

(a)   HM Revenue and Customs have given clearance under regulation 9B, and

(b)   the applicant certifies that there have been no changes in substance between–

   (i)   the form in which the instrument constituting the fund and its prospectus were considered by HM Revenue and Customs before giving the clearance, and

   (ii)   the form in which it is proposed that those documents will apply at the time when the proposed fund is authorised.

History – Reg. 69Z50 inserted by SI 2009/2036, reg. 24, with effect from 1 September 2009.

Contents of application under regulation 69Z49

69Z51(1)   An application must include the following information.

69Z51(2)   An existing fund application must specify the accounting period from the beginning of which the application seeks to apply this Part to the fund (the "specified accounting period").

69Z51(3)   An existing fund application must be accompanied by–

(a)   a statement by the manager of the authorised investment fund that the TEF conditions are reasonably expected to be met in respect of the fund throughout the specified accounting period;

(b)   the following documents relating to the fund–

   (i)   the instrument constituting the fund, and

   (ii)   its prospectus;

(c)   a statement by the manager as to whether or not this Part has previously applied to the fund and where this Part has previously applied that statement must include–

   (i)   the dates of entry and cessation, and

   (ii)   a statement by the manager that a termination notice has never been issued in respect of the fund;

(d)   a statement by the manager that either–

   (i)   shareholder or unit holder consent to the application is not required, or

   (ii)   shareholder or unit holder consent has been given, in which case the statement must specify the date of the shareholder or unit holder resolution giving consent;

(e)   a copy of the application to the Financial Services Authority for approval for any changes in the instrument constituting the fund and its prospectus; and

(f)   copies of any documents accompanying the application mentioned in subparagraph (e) to the extent that those documents do not fall within sub-paragraphs (a) to (d).

69Z51(4)   A future fund application must specify the date it is expected the fund will be established and authorisation given and seek to apply this Part to the proposed fund from that date.

69Z51(5) A future fund application must be accompanied by–

(a)   a statement by the applicant that the TEF conditions are reasonably expected to be met in respect of the proposed fund throughout its first accounting period;

(b)   the following documents relating to the proposed fund–

     (i)   the proposed instrument constituting the fund, and

     (ii)   its prospectus;

(c)   a copy of the application to the Financial Services Authority for authorisation of the proposed fund as an authorised investment fund; and

(d)   copies of any documents accompanying the application mentioned in subparagraph (c) to the extent that those documents do not fall within sub-paragraphs (a) and (b).

History – In reg. 69Z51(5)(b)(ii), the word "proposed" and the words "(including any supplements to the proposed prospectus)" omitted by SI 2010/294, reg. 23(4), with effect from 6 March 2010.
Reg. 69Z51 inserted by SI 2009/2036, reg. 24, with effect from 1 September 2009.

PROCEDURAL MATTERS RELATING TO THE MAKING OF APPLICATIONS FOR THIS PART TO APPLY

Refusing an application: refusal notice

69Z52(1) If any of conditions A to C are met HM Revenue and Customs must refuse the application and give a notice (a "refusal notice")–

(a)   to the manager of the authorised investment fund if an existing fund application has been made, or

(b)   to the applicant if a future fund application has been made.

69Z52(2) Condition A is that–

(a)   the documents supplied do not demonstrate that the authorised investment fund (or the proposed authorised investment fund) will meet all the TEF conditions, or

(b)   the statement given in accordance with regulation 69Z51(3)(a) or (5)(a) does not demonstrate that the fund (or proposed fund) can reasonably be expected to meet all the TEF conditions throughout the specified accounting period or the first accounting period.

69Z52(3) Condition B is that the application is not accompanied by the documents and statements specified in regulation 69Z51(3) in the case of an existing fund application or regulation 69Z51(5) in the case of a future fund application.

69Z52(4) Condition C is that any necessary shareholder, unit holder or regulatory authorisation or approval has not been given.

69Z52(5) A refusal notice must specify the reason for refusing the application.

History – Reg. 69Z52 inserted by SI 2009/2036, reg. 24, with effect from 1 September 2009.

Appeal against refusal notice

69Z53(1) A person to whom a refusal notice is given may appeal.

69Z53(2) The notice of appeal must be given to HM Revenue and Customs within a period of 28 days beginning with the day on which the refusal notice is given.

69Z53(3) On an appeal that is notified to the tribunal, the tribunal shall determine whether it was just and reasonable for HM Revenue and Customs to give the refusal notice.

69Z53(4) If the tribunal allow the appeal–

(a)   they may direct that this Part shall apply to the authorised investment fund (or, as the case may be, to the proposed authorised investment fund), and

(b)   they may specify the date from which this Part shall so apply.

69Z53(5) The date mentioned in paragraph (4)(b)–

(a)   must not be earlier than the beginning of the specified accounting period if an existing fund application has been made, and

(b)   must not be earlier than the date of authorisation by the Financial Services Authority if a future fund application has been made.

History – Reg. 69Z53 inserted by SI 2009/2036, reg. 24, with effect from 1 September 2009.

CONSEQUENCES OF ENTRY

Effects of entry

69Z54   On entry a new distribution period of the authorised investment fund shall begin.

History – Reg. 69Z54 inserted by SI 2009/2036, reg. 24, with effect from 1 September 2009.

Duration

69Z55   Once this Part has begun to apply to an authorised investment fund it shall continue to apply unless and until it ceases to apply in accordance with Chapter 7 of this Part.

History – Reg. 69Z55 inserted by SI 2009/2036, reg. 24, with effect from 1 September 2009.

Chapter 3 – The Tax Treatment of Tax Elected Funds

COMPONENTS OF INCOME

69Z56(1)   For the purposes of corporation tax, the income arising to a Tax Elected Fund consists of–

(a)   dividend income;

(b)   property investment income, being–

     (i)   distributions of profits of C (tax-exempt) in relation to shares held in a UKREIT, and

     (ii)   property income distributions in relation to shares held in a Property AIF;

(c)   property business income (arising on a breach of the property condition), being–

     (i)   profits of a UK property business that are not within sub-paragraph (b), and

     (ii)   income from an overseas property business; and

(d)   other income.

69Z56(2)   In this regulation, **"C (tax-exempt)"** shall be construed in accordance with Part 4 of FA 2006.

History – Reg. 69Z56 inserted by SI 2009/2036, reg. 24, with effect from 1 September 2009.

TREATMENT OF PROPERTY INVESTMENT INCOME

69Z57(1)   Section 7(2) of ICTA (treatment of certain payments and repayments of income tax: set off of tax) shall not apply to payments of property investment income.

69Z57(2)   Property investment income arising to a Tax Elected Fund shall be treated for the purposes of the Tax Acts as a distribution that is exempt for the purposes of Part 9A of CTA 2009 (company distributions) but shall not be treated as franked investment income.

History – Reg. 69Z57 inserted by SI 2009/2036, reg. 24, with effect from 1 September 2009.

TREATMENT OF DISTRIBUTIONS

69Z58   Section 931R of CTA 2009 (election that distribution should not be exempt) shall not apply in relation to distributions received by a Tax Elected Fund.

History – Reg. 69Z58 inserted by SI 2009/2036, reg. 24, with effect from 1 September 2009.

Chapter 4 – Distributions Made by Tax Elected Funds

ALLOCATION OF INCOME

History – The heading to reg. 69Z14 changed from "ATTRIBUTION OF DISTRIBUTIONS" by SI 2010/294, reg. 18(2), with effect from 6 March 2010 (subject to the transitional provisions at SI 2010/294, reg. 24).

69Z59(1)   The total amount available for income allocation in a Tax Elected Fund shall be attributed as follows.

69Z59(2)   There shall be attributed to TEF distributions (dividends)–

(a)   dividend income,

(b)   property investment income, and

(c)   property business income.

69Z59(3)   Other income shall be attributed to TEF distributions (non-dividend).

History – Reg. 69Z59(1) substituted by SI 2010/294, reg. 18(3), with effect from 6 March 2010 (subject to the transitional provisions at SI 2010/294, reg. 24). Former reg. 69Z59(1) read as follows:

    "**69Z59(1)**   The total amount shown in the distribution accounts of a Tax Elected Fund as available for distribution to participants shall be attributed as follows."

Reg. 69Z59 inserted by SI 2009/2036, reg. 24, with effect from 1 September 2009.

TEF DISTRIBUTIONS (DIVIDENDS)

69Z60(1)   This regulation applies if–

(a)   a Tax Elected Fund makes a distribution, and

(b)   the amount distributed includes sums attributed to TEF distributions (dividends).

69Z60(2)   The Tax Acts shall have effect as if the sums were dividends on shares paid on the distribution date by the fund to the participants in proportion to their rights.

69Z60(3)   In this Part a **"TEF distribution (dividend)"** means a sum attributed to TEF distributions (dividends) which is distributed (including a dividend treated as paid to a participant who is not chargeable to corporation tax).

69Z60(4)   This regulation is subject to regulation 23 (treatment of de minimis amounts).

History – Reg. 69Z60 inserted by SI 2009/2036, reg. 24, with effect from 1 September 2009.

TEF DISTRIBUTIONS (NON-DIVIDEND)

69Z61(1)   This regulation applies if–

(a)   a Tax Elected Fund makes a distribution, and

(b)   the amount distributed includes sums attributed to TEF distributions (non-dividend).

69Z61(2)   The Tax Acts shall have effect as if the sums were payments of yearly interest made on the distribution date by the fund to the participants in proportion to their rights.

69Z61(3)   In these Regulations a **"TEF distribution (non-dividend)"** means a sum attributed to TEF distributions (non-dividend) which is distributed (including a payment made to a participant who is not chargeable to income tax).

69Z61(4)   This regulation is subject to regulation 23 (treatment of de minimis amounts).

History – Reg. 69Z61 inserted by SI 2009/2036, reg. 24, with effect from 1 September 2009.

Chapter 5 – The Treatment of Participants in Tax Elected Funds

TEF DISTRIBUTION (DIVIDEND)
Participants chargeable to corporation tax

69Z62(1)   If a TEF distribution (dividend) is made for a distribution period to a participant within the charge to corporation tax, regulations 48 to 52A (dividend distributions) shall apply with the modifications specified in paragraph (2).

69Z62(2)   The specified modifications are–

(a)   for "dividend distribution" in each place it occurs there shall be substituted "TEF distribution (dividend)";

(b)   in regulation 50 (references to gross income) for "the net revenue before taxation shall be determined in accordance with the Statement of Recommended Practice" there shall be substituted "the amount attributed to TEF distributions (dividends) in accordance with regulation 69Z59 (allocation of income);".

(c)   for "an authorised investment fund" in each place it occurs there shall be substituted "a Tax Elected Fund"; and

(d)   for "the authorised investment fund" in each place it occurs there shall be substituted "the Tax Elected Fund".

History – Reg. 69Z62(2)(b) substituted by SI 2010/294, reg. 19, with effect from 6 March 2010 (subject to the transitional provisions at SI 2010/294, reg. 24). Former reg. 69Z62(2)(b) read as follows:
    "(b)   in regulation 50 (references to gross income) for "distribution accounts" there shall be substituted "TEF distributions (dividends) account";"
Reg. 69Z62 inserted by SI 2009/2036, reg. 24, with effect from 1 September 2009.

TEF DISTRIBUTIONS (NON-DIVIDEND)
Obligation to deduct tax from TEF distributions (non-dividend)

69Z63(1)   If a TEF distribution (non-dividend) is made for a distribution period to a participant within the charge to income tax, regulations 26 to 33 (deduction of tax from interest distributions: general) shall apply with the modification specified in paragraph (3).

69Z63(2)   If a TEF distribution (non-dividend) is made for a distribution period to a participant within the charge to corporation tax, regulation 47 (the obligation to deduct tax) shall apply with the modification specified in paragraph (3).

69Z63(3)   The modification specified is that for "interest distribution" in each place it occurs there shall be substituted "TEF distribution (non-dividend)".

History – Reg. 69Z63 inserted by SI 2009/2036, reg. 24, with effect from 1 September 2009.

Modification of section 490 of CTA 2009

69Z64(1)   Section 490 of CTA 2009 (holdings in OEICs, unit trusts and offshore funds treated as creditor relationship rights) shall apply to a participant in a TEF as if in subsections (4) and (5) for "interest distribution" there were substituted "TEF distribution (non-dividend)".

History – Reg. 69Z64 inserted by SI 2009/2036, reg. 24, with effect from 1 September 2009.

Chapter 6 – Compliance in Relation to the Tax Elected Funds Regime

BREACHES OF TEF CONDITIONS

Breach of conditions: general

69Z65(1)   This regulation applies if a Tax Elected Fund–

(a)   does not meet one of the TEF conditions, and

(b)   becomes aware that it does not meet the condition.

69Z65(2)   Within 28 days of becoming aware of the breach, the fund must provide the following information to the Commissioners–

(a)   the date on which the condition first ceased to be met;

(b)   the date on which the fund became aware of the breach;

(c)   details of the condition that was breached;

(d)   the nature of the breach;

(e)   the steps the fund proposes to take to rectify the breach;

(f)   the date by which the fund proposes to rectify the breach; and

(g)   where there has been a previous breach of the TEF conditions, details of the condition that was breached on that occasion, the date of that breach and the date that breach was rectified.

69Z65(3)   The date referred to in paragraph (2)(f) must be the earliest date by which the objective of complying with the relevant condition may reasonably be achieved.

69Z65(4)   The Commissioners must give a termination notice to the fund if–

(a)   the steps that the fund proposes to take will not rectify the breach;

(b)   the date by which the fund proposes to rectify the breach is not the earliest date by which the objective of remedying the relevant condition may reasonably be achieved;

(c)   the fund is intentionally or negligently in breach of a condition; or

(d)   there are three breaches of the same TEF condition in a period of ten years beginning with the first day of the accounting period in which the fund becomes aware of the first of those breaches.

History – Reg. 69Z65 inserted by SI 2009/2036, reg. 24, with effect from 1 September 2009.

Breach of the property condition, genuine diversity of ownership condition or scheme documentation condition

69Z66(1)   This regulation applies if a Tax Elected Fund is in breach of the property condition, genuine diversity of ownership condition or scheme documentation condition.

69Z66(2)   If the fund is inadvertently in breach but rectifies the breach within a reasonable time of the fund becoming aware of the breach, this Part shall continue to apply to the fund despite the breach (but see regulations 69Z65(4)(d) and 69Z68).

69Z66(3)   If the fund is inadvertently in breach but does not rectify the breach within a reasonable time of the fund first becoming aware of the breach, the Commissioners must give a termination notice to the fund.

History – Reg. 69Z66 inserted by SI 2009/2036, reg. 24, with effect from 1 September 2009.

Breach of the loan creditor condition

69Z67(1) This regulation applies if a Tax Elected Fund is in breach of the loan creditor condition.

69Z67(2) If the fund is inadvertently in breach but rectifies the breach within a period of 28 days beginning with the day on which the fund first becomes aware of the breach, this Part shall continue to apply to the fund despite the breach (but see paragraph (4) and regulations 69Z65(4)(d) and 69Z68).

69Z67(3) If the fund is inadvertently in breach but does not rectify the breach within a period of 28 days beginning with the day on which the fund first becomes aware of the breach, the Commissioners must give a termination notice to the fund.

69Z67(4) If the fund is in breach of the same condition specified in paragraphs (2) to (5) of regulation 69Z47 in two different accounting periods in a period of ten years beginning with the first day of the accounting period in which the fund becomes aware of the first of those breaches, the Commissioners must give a termination notice to the fund.

History – Reg. 69Z67 inserted by SI 2009/2036, reg. 24, with effect from 1 September 2009.

Multiple breaches of separate conditions

69Z68 The Commissioners must give a termination notice to a Tax Elected Fund if–

(a) there has been a breach of at least two of the TEF conditions, and

(b) there have been four breaches in a period of ten years beginning with the first day of the accounting period in which the first breach occurs.

History – Reg. 69Z68 inserted by SI 2009/2036, reg. 24, with effect from 1 September 2009.

INFORMATION ABOUT POSSIBLE BREACHES OF THE TEF CONDITIONS

Information to be provided to officers of Revenue and Customs

69Z69(1) This regulation applies if an officer of Revenue and Customs thinks that a Tax Elected Fund–

(a) does not meet, or may not meet, one of the TEF conditions, or

(b) has not rectified a breach of such a condition.

69Z69(2) The officer may serve a notice (an "information notice") on the manager of the fund requiring the manager to provide any of the information specified in regulation 69Z65(2) within a specified period.

69Z69(4) If the manager does not comply with the information notice within the specified period the Commissioners must give a termination notice.

69Z69(5) In this regulation the specified period is a period of 28 days beginning with the day on which the notice is served or, on an application by the manager, such longer period as the officer of Revenue and Customs thinks is reasonable.

History – Reg. 69Z69 inserted by SI 2009/2036, reg. 24, with effect from 1 September 2009.

Chapter 7 – Leaving the Tax Elected Funds Regime

TERMINATION BY ELECTION: AUTHORISED INVESTMENT FUND

69Z70(1) This regulation applies if a Tax Elected Fund gives a notice under this regulation electing that this Part is to cease to apply to the fund at the end of a specified accounting period.

69Z70(2) This Part shall cease to apply to the fund at the end of that accounting period.

69Z70(3) A notice under paragraph (1) must–

(a) be given in writing to the Commissioners,

(b) be given before the end of the accounting period specified in paragraph (1), and

(c) give the reasons for the fund leaving the TEF regime.

History – Reg. 69Z70 inserted by SI 2009/2036, reg. 24, with effect from 1 September 2009.

TERMINATION BY NOTICE: COMMISSIONERS

69Z71(1) This regulation applies if the Commissioners give a notice in writing under this paragraph to a Tax Elected Fund (a "termination notice").

69Z71(2) This Part shall cease to apply to the fund.

69Z71(3) The Commissioners may give a termination notice only if a provision contained in this Part provides that the Commissioners must give a termination notice.

69Z71(4)   A termination notice must state the reason for it.

69Z71(5)   If a termination notice is given to an authorised investment fund, this Part shall be taken to have ceased to apply to the fund at the end of the accounting period immediately preceding the accounting period in which the notice was given.

69Z71(6)   But regulations 13 (treatment of interest distributions for the purpose of loan relationships), 69Z61 (TEF distributions (non-dividend)) and 69Z63 (obligation to deduct tax from TEF distributions (non-dividend)) shall apply in relation to any TEF distribution (non-dividend) made before the notice was given.

History – Reg. 69Z71 inserted by SI 2009/2036, reg. 24, with effect from 1 September 2009.

APPEAL AGAINST TERMINATION NOTICE

69Z72(1)   An authorised investment fund to which a termination notice is given may appeal.

69Z72(2)   The notice of appeal must be given to HM Revenue and Customs within a period of 28 days beginning with the day on which the termination notice is given.

69Z72(3)   On an appeal that is notified to the tribunal, the tribunal shall determine whether it was just and reasonable for HM Revenue and Customs to give the termination notice.

69Z72(4)   If they decide that it was, they must confirm the notice.

69Z72(5)   If they decide that it was not, they must set aside the notice.

History – Reg. 69Z72 inserted by SI 2009/2036, reg. 24, with effect from 1 September 2009.

MERGERS

69Z73(1)   This regulation applies if a Tax Elected Fund–

(a)   is party to a merger or takeover, and

(b)   as a result, ceases to meet one or more of the TEF conditions.

69Z73(2)   On the occurrence of the merger or takeover–

(a)   an accounting period of the fund shall end at the end of the date of the merger or takeover, and

(b)   this Part shall cease to apply to the fund at the end of that date.

History – Reg. 69Z73 inserted by SI 2009/2036, reg. 24, with effect from 1 September 2009.

PART 5 – COMPLIANCE

INFORMATION RELATING TO DISTRIBUTIONS

Application of section 234A of ICTA

70(1)   Section 234A of ICTA (information relating to distributions) applies in relation to an authorised investment fund with any necessary modifications.

70(2)   In the appropriate statement sent under that section to a participant within the charge to corporation tax, the legal owner of the authorised investment fund must include a statement showing the legal owner's net liability to corporation tax in respect of the gross income.

70(3)   In paragraph (2)–

"**gross income**" has the same meaning as in regulation 50, and

"**net liability to corporation tax**" is to be construed in accordance with regulation 49(3).

70(4)   In the case of a Property AIF and a Tax Elected Fund, an appropriate statement for the purposes of section 234A of ICTA includes a written statement–

(a)   showing the details specified in paragraph (5),

(b)   providing details to allow the participant to access an electronic means of calculating the amounts that would be shown in a written statement that would, apart from this paragraph, be provided in accordance with subsection (6) (in the case of a PAIF distribution (interest) or a TEF distribution (non-dividend)) or subsection (7) (in the case of a PAIF distribution (dividends) or a TEF distribution (dividend)) of section 234A, and

(c)   providing the participant with an alternative method of obtaining the details of those amounts without recourse to electronic means.

70(5)   The specified details are–

(a)   the gross amount of the distribution made to the participant,

(b)   the number and class of units held by the participant in respect of which the distribution is made,

(c)   the net amount of the distribution per unit,

(d)   whether any tax has been deducted from the distribution,

(e)   the date the distribution was made, and

(f)   the percentage of the gross distribution attributable–

     (i)   in the case of a Property AIF, to PAIF distribution (interest) and to PAIF distribution (dividends), or

     (ii)   in the case of a Tax Elected Fund, to TEF distribution (dividend) and to TEF distribution (non-dividend).

History – Reg. 70(4) inserted by SI 2009/2036, reg. 25, with effect from 1 September 2009.
Reg. 70(5) inserted by SI 2009/2036, reg. 25, with effect from 1 September 2009.

INTEREST DISTRIBUTIONS AND TEF DISTRIBUTIONS (NON-DIVIDEND)

History – In the heading before reg. 71, the words "and TEF distributions (non-dividend)" inserted by SI 2009/2036, reg. 26, with effect from 1 September 2009.

Notification of interest distributions and TEF distributions (non-dividend) made without deduction of tax

History – In the heading to reg. 71, the words "and TEF distributions (non-dividend)" inserted by SI 2009/2036, reg. 26, with effect from 1 September 2009.

71(1)   If, during a tax year, an authorised investment fund has made interest distributions and TEF distributions (non-dividend) without deduction of tax, the legal owner must give notice of that fact to the Commissioners within 14 days of the end of that tax year.

71(2)   Notice given under paragraph (1)–

(a)   must be in writing, and

(b)   has effect for the tax year in which it is given and for subsequent tax years until the notice is withdrawn.

71(3)   An authorised investment fund that fails to comply with paragraph (1) is liable to a penalty not exceeding £3,000 determined in accordance with section 100 of TMA 1970.

71(4)   Sections 100A, 100B, 102, 103(4) and 118(2) of TMA 1970 apply to a penalty determined in accordance with paragraph (3).

History – In reg. 71(1), the words "and TEF distributions (non-dividend)" inserted by SI 2009/2036, reg. 27, with effect from 1 September 2009.

Information about interest distributions and TEF distributions (non-dividend) made without deduction of tax

History – In the heading to reg. 72, the words "and TEF distributions (non-dividend)" inserted by SI 2009/2036, reg. 26, with effect from 1 September 2009.

72(1)   The Commissioners may by notice require a person specified in paragraph (2) to provide them with such information as they may reasonably require for the purpose of determining whether interest distributions and TEF distributions (non-dividend) were properly made by that person without deduction of tax.

72(2)   The persons specified are–

(a)   an open-ended investment company;

(b)   the authorised corporate director of an open-ended investment company;

(c)   a trustee of an authorised unit trust.

72(3)   The information to be provided may include copies of any relevant books, documents or other records.

72(4)   The information must be provided within such time (not being less than 14 days) as may be specified in the notice.

History – In reg. 72(1), the words "and TEF distributions (non-dividend)" inserted by SI 2009/2036, reg. 28, with effect from 1 September 2009.

Inspection of records

73(1)   A person specified in regulation 72(2) must, whenever required to do so, make available for inspection by an officer of the Commissioners authorised for that purpose, at such time as that officer may reasonably require, all such copies of books, documents or other records in their possession or under their control as may be required by the Commissioners under regulation 72.

73(2)   Every qualifying certificate supplied to a legal owner under Chapter 2 of Part 4 (participants chargeable to income tax) must be preserved by the legal owner in such manner as may be approved by the Commissioners for two years after it has ceased to be otherwise required under the provisions of these Regulations.

Use of information

74(1)   Information obtained by the Commissioners under regulation 72 or 73–

(a)   must not be used for the purpose of ascertaining the tax liability (if any) of any person other than the persons specified in paragraph (2), and

(b)   must otherwise be used only for the purposes of these Regulations.

74(2)   The persons specified in this paragraph are–

(a)   the open-ended investment company in question;

(b)   the trustees of the authorised unit trust in question;

(c)   a participant who is beneficially entitled to an interest distribution or a TEF distribution (non-dividend) made without deduction of tax to whom the information obtained relates;

(d)   where the whole of an interest distribution or a TEF distribution (non-dividend) made to or received under a trust without deduction of tax is, or falls to be treated as, or under any provision of the Tax Acts is deemed to be, the income of a person other than the trustees of that trust, that person in so far as the information obtained relates to him; and

(e)   where an interest distribution or a TEF distribution (non-dividend) is made to or received under a trust without deduction of tax and sub-paragraph (d) does not apply, the trustees of that trust and any beneficiary of the trust to whom the information obtained relates.

74(3)   In paragraph (2)(e) **"any beneficiary of the trust"** means–

(a)   any person who is, or will or may become, entitled to any income of the trust, whether in the form of income or not, and

(b)   any person to whom any such income may be paid, or for whose benefit any such income may be applied, whether in the form of income or not, in the exercise of a discretion by the trustees of the trust.

74(4)   Paragraph (1) does not prevent any disclosure of information authorised under section 182(5) of the Finance Act 1989.

History – In reg. 74(2)(c), the words "or a TEF distribution (non-dividend)" inserted by SI 2009/2036, reg. 29, with effect from 1 September 2009.
In reg. 74(2)(d), the words "or a TEF distribution (non-dividend)" inserted by SI 2009/2036, reg. 29, with effect from 1 September 2009.
In reg. 74(2)(e), the words "or a TEF distribution (non-dividend)" inserted by SI 2009/2036, reg. 29, with effect from 1 September 2009.

RESIDENCE DECLARATIONS

Inspection of residence declarations

75(1)   The legal owner of an authorised investment fund must, on being required to do so by a notice given by an officer of the Commissioners, make available for inspection by such an officer–

(a)   any residence declarations made to the authorised investment fund under Chapter 2 of Part 4 (participants chargeable to income tax), or

(b)   any specified declaration or description of declarations.

75(2)   If a notice has been given to the legal owner under paragraph (1), the declarations shall be made available within such time as may be specified in the notice and the person carrying out the inspection may take copies of or extracts from them.

PART 6 – FURTHER PROVISIONS RELATING TO AUTHORISED INVESTMENT FUNDS

Chapter 1 – General

OWNERSHIP OF SHARES OF DIFFERENT DENOMINATIONS IN OPEN-ENDED INVESTMENT COMPANIES

76(1)   This regulation applies if conditions A and B are met.

76(2) Condition A is that in respect of a given class of shares specified in the instrument of incorporation of an open-ended investment company, shares issued of that class consist of both smaller denomination shares and larger denomination shares.

76(3) Condition B is that a participant owns both smaller denomination shares and larger denomination shares of that class.

76(4) For the purposes of the provisions relating to ownership of shares in a company contained in the Tax Acts and TCGA 1992, the shares owned by the participant are treated as securities of the same class.

76(5) Each larger denomination share is to be treated for those purposes as if it were comprised of the relevant number of smaller denomination shares.

76(6) The market value of each smaller denomination share is to be taken for those purposes to be the relevant proportion of the market value of each larger denomination share.

76(7) In this regulation–

"smaller denomination shares" means shares to which are attached rights specified in the company's instrument of incorporation that are expressed in the smaller of two denominations;

"larger denomination shares" means shares to which are attached rights so specified that are expressed in the larger of two denominations;

"relevant number" means the number calculated by reference to the relevant proportion; and

"relevant proportion" means the proportion, determined by the company's instrument of incorporation, which the rights attaching to each smaller denomination share bear to the rights attaching to each larger denomination share.

NON-DISCRIMINATION IN RESPECT OF DIFFERENT CLASSES OF SHARES

77(1) This regulation applies if there is an amount available for income allocation.

77(2) There must not be any discrimination between participants in respect of different classes of shares.

77(3) There is no such discrimination if condition A and either condition B or C is met.

77(4) Condition A is that the differences are wholly attributable to differences between the amounts or treatment for accounting purposes of the charges or expenses which–

(a)   are permitted by the instrument of incorporation of the open-ended investment company concerned or the prospectus in issue for the time being of that company or by the trust deed under which the authorised unit trust is constituted, and

(b)   are payable out of the scheme property of that authorised investment fund in respect of the shares of those classes.

77(5) Condition B is that the authorised investment fund is able to show that the differences between the amounts or treatment for accounting purposes of the charges or expenses referred to in condition A apply for bona fide commercial reasons.

77(6) Condition C is that the differences are not such as to enable the participants in any one of those classes to obtain a tax advantage which they would not obtain if there were no differences between the amounts or treatment for accounting purposes of those charges or expenses.

77(7) In paragraph (6) "tax advantage" has the same meaning as in Chapter 1 of Part 17 of ICTA (cancellation of tax advantages from transactions in securities).

History – Reg. 77(1) substituted by SI 2010/294, reg. 20, with effect from 6 March 2010 (subject to the transitional provisions at SI 2010/294, reg. 24). Former reg. 77(1) read as follows:

"**77(1)** This regulation applies if the distribution accounts show an amount as available for distribution to participants."

In reg. 77(4)(a), the words "(including any supplements to that prospectus)" omitted by SI 2010/294, reg. 23(1), with effect from 6 March 2010.

Chapter 2 – Amalgamation of an Authorised Unit Trust with, and Conversion of an Authorised Unit Trust to, an Open-Ended Investment Company

CIRCUMSTANCES IN WHICH THIS CHAPTER APPLIES

78(1)   This Chapter applies if, in connection with a scheme of reorganisation, conditions A to E are met.

78(2)   Condition A is that the whole of the scheme property of an authorised unit trust that is available for transfer is transferred on a given date under an arrangement to an open-ended investment company.

78(3)   Condition B is that the consideration under the arrangement consists of or includes the issue, on the transfer date, of shares in the acquiring company to the holders of units in the target trust in exchange for those units.

78(4)   Condition C is that the consideration shares are issued to the holders of units in proportion to their holdings of the exchanged units.

78(5)   Condition D is that the consideration under the arrangement does not include anything else in addition to the issue of the consideration shares, other than (where applicable) the assumption or discharge by the acquiring company of liabilities of the trustees of the target trust.

78(6)   Condition E is that under the arrangement all the units in the target trust are extinguished.

78(7)   In this Chapter–

the **"target trust"** means the authorised unit trust mentioned in paragraph (2);

the **"transfer date"** means the given date mentioned in paragraph (2);

the **"acquiring company"** means the open-ended investment company mentioned in paragraph (2); and

"the whole of the scheme property of an authorised unit trust that is available for transfer" means the whole of the property subject to the trusts of the target trust, other than any property which is retained for the purpose of discharging liabilities of the trustees of the target trust;

the **"consideration shares"** means the shares in the acquiring company mentioned in paragraph (4); and

the **"exchanged units"** means the units in the target trust mentioned in paragraph (4).

ENDING OF ACCOUNTING PERIOD OF THE TARGET TRUST

79(1)   An accounting period of the target trust (the "pre-transfer accounting period") ends immediately before the transfer date; and, for the purposes of the Corporation Tax Acts, the whole of the scheme property of the target trust that is available for transfer is treated as having been transferred immediately after the end of that accounting period.

79(2)   This regulation applies despite anything in section 12(1) to (7) of ICTA (periods of assessment for corporation tax).

CARRYING FORWARD OF EXCESS MANAGEMENT EXPENSES

80(1)   This regulation applies if condition A or B is met.

80(2)   Condition A is that, in respect of the pre-transfer accounting period of the target trust, the trustees are entitled, under section 75(9) of ICTA (carry forward of management expenses and sums treated as management expenses), to carry forward an excess amount to the next accounting period of the trust.

80(3)   Condition B is that–

(a)   the pre-transfer accounting period is the final accounting period of the target trust, and

(b)   the trustees are entitled, under section 75(9) of ICTA, to carry forward an excess amount to what would have been the next accounting period of the trust were the trust to have an accounting period beginning on the transfer date.

80(4)   With effect from the transfer date, the entitlement is translated into a right in the acquiring company to treat the amount as if it had been carried forward under section 75(9) of ICTA to the first of its accounting periods to end on or after the transfer date.

DISTRIBUTIONS BY AUTHORISED UNIT TRUST AFTER THE END OF ITS PRE-TRANSFER ACCOUNTING PERIOD

81(1)   This regulation applies if, in respect of any post-transfer distribution date of the target trust, there is an amount which falls to be treated, in accordance with regulation 22 (dividend distributions: general), as dividends on shares paid on that distribution date by the target trust to its participants in proportion to their rights.

81(2)   The amount shall instead be treated as dividends on shares paid on that date by the acquiring company to those persons in proportion to their rights.

81(3)   In this regulation "post-transfer distribution date" of a target trust means a distribution date of that trust which—

(a)   occurs on or after the transfer date, and

(b)   is the distribution date for a distribution period of the trust ending before the transfer date.

History – In reg. 81(1) figure "22" substituted for "3.1.4" by SI 2007/794, reg. 4, with effect from 6 April 2007.

CONTINUING VALIDITY OF RESIDENCE DECLARATIONS

82(1)   This regulation applies if—

(a)   before the transfer date, a unit holder has made a residence declaration to the trustees of the target trust, and

(b)   immediately before the transfer date, the trustees of the target trust treated the residence declaration as valid.

82(2)   The acquiring company may treat the residence declaration as valid.

POWERS OF THE ACQUIRING COMPANY

83(1)   On and after the transfer date, the acquiring company has the powers set out in paragraphs (2) and (3).

83(2)   The acquiring company may continue anything which—

(a)   immediately before the transfer date was in the process of being done by the trustees of the target trust for the purposes of tax in relation to accounting periods of the target trust ending before that date, and

(b)   is not continued by those trustees on or after the transfer date.

83(3)   The acquiring company may do anything which—

(a)   immediately before the transfer date was not in the process of being done by the trustees of the target trust for the purposes of tax in relation to accounting periods of the target trust ending before that date and is not done by them for those purposes, and

(b)   might reasonably have been expected to be done by those trustees for those purposes had the scheme of reorganisation not taken place.

ASSESSMENTS MADE ON DISCOVERY

84   The provisions of this Chapter do not affect any enactment in the Tax Acts which provides for assessments to be made where an officer of the Commissioners discovers that a set-off, matching, repayment of tax, or payment of tax credit or provision for relief in any other form ought not to have been made, given or otherwise allowed, or is or has become excessive.

PREVENTION OF DOUBLE RELIEF

85   For the purposes of the Tax Acts, nothing in this Chapter has the effect of enabling—

(a)   any set-off or matching of an amount to be made,

(b)   any repayment of an amount of tax or payment of an amount of tax credit to be made, or

(c)   any other relief to be given,

more than once in respect of the same amount or relief.

PART 6A – FUNDS INVESTING IN NON-REPORTING OFFSHORE FUNDS

History – Pt. 6A inserted by SI 2010/294, reg. 21, with effect from 6 March 2010 (subject to the transitional provisions at SI 2010/294, reg. 25 and 26).

Chapter 1 – Preliminary Provisions

History – Pt. 6A inserted by SI 2010/294, reg. 21, with effect from 6 March 2010 (subject to the transitional provisions at SI 2010/294, reg. 25 and 26).

FINROFS

85A(1)　This Part applies to–

(a)　an authorised investment fund which meets the investment condition in regulation 85D (the investment condition);

(b)　an authorised investment fund in respect of which an election has been made in accordance with regulation 85F (elective FINROFs);

(c)　a participant in a fund mentioned in paragraph (a) or (b); and

(d)　a participant in a fund which has left the FINROF regime, where the participant has not made a valid election under regulation 85Z11 (participant's power to elect for deemed disposal).

85A(2)　A fund to which this Part applies shall be known as a Fund Investing in Non- Reporting Offshore Funds ("FINROF").

STRUCTURE OF THIS PART

85B　The structure of this Part is as follows–

This Chapter contains preliminary provisions;

Chapter 2 deals with entry into the Funds Investing in Non-Reporting Offshore Funds regime ("FINROF regime");

Chapter 3 deals with the tax treatment of FINROFs and of participants in FINROFs;

Chapter 4 deals with exceptions, etc from the charge to tax;

Chapter 5 deals with disposal of units in FINROFs;

Chapter 6 deals with income gains and computation of income gains;

Chapter 7 deals with deduction of income gains in computing chargeable gains;

Chapter 8 deals with leaving the FINROF regime.

INTERPRETATION

85C　In this Part–

"**gross asset value**" means the value of the investments comprising the scheme property of the authorised investment fund before the deduction of specified liabilities, but does not include cash awaiting investment.

History – In reg. 85C, the entries relating to "non-reporting fund", "offshore fund", "Offshore Funds Regulations" and "reporting fund" omitted by SI 2011/244, reg. 9(1), with effect (subject to transitional provisions in SI 2011/244, reg. 8): for the purposes of corporation tax on income, for accounting periods ending on or after 6 March 2011; and for the purposes of corporation tax on chargeable gains and of capital gains tax, in relation to disposals made on or after 6 March 2011. The omitted entries read as follows:

"**"non-reporting fund"** has the same meaning as in the Offshore Funds Regulations;

"offshore fund" means a fund within the meaning of section 40A(2) of the Finance Act 2008;

"Offshore Funds Regulations" means the Offshore Funds (Tax) Regulations 2009;

"reporting fund" has the same meaning as in regulation 50 of the Offshore Funds Regulations.".

THE INVESTMENT CONDITION

85D(1)　The investment condition is met in relation to an authorised investment fund if the total amount invested in non-reporting funds or FINROFs is more than 50% of the gross asset value of the authorised investment fund.

85D(2)　This regulation is subject to regulation 85E.

History – In reg. 85D(1), "50%" substituted for "20%" by SI 2011/244, reg. 5, with effect (subject to transitional provisions in SI 2011/244, reg. 8): for the purposes of corporation tax on income, for accounting periods ending on or after 6 March 2011; and for the purposes of corporation tax on chargeable gains and of capital gains tax, in relation to disposals made on or after 6 March 2011.

INTERESTS IN FUNDS TREATED AS NOT BEING INTERESTS IN NON-REPORTING FUNDS

85E(1)　For the purposes of regulation 85D(1) the interests specified in paragraph (2) shall not be regarded as interests in non-reporting funds.

85E(2)   The interests specified are–

(a)   any interest in an offshore fund in respect of which, by virtue of regulation 29 or 30 of the Offshore Funds Regulations, no liability to tax would arise under regulation 17 of those Regulations on a disposal of that interest; and

(b)   any interest of an authorised investment fund in a non-reporting fund which meets the conditions in regulation 14ZA(2).

History – Reg. 85E(2) substituted by SI 2011/244, reg. 6(2), with effect (subject to transitional provisions in SI 2011/244, reg. 8): for the purposes of corporation tax on income, for accounting periods ending on or after 6 March 2011; and for the purposes of corporation tax on chargeable gains and of capital gains tax, in relation to disposals made on or after 6 March 2011. Former reg. 85E(2) read as follows:

"**85E(2)**   The interests specified are–
(a)   any interest in an offshore fund in respect of which, by virtue of regulation 29 of the Offshore Funds Regulations (interests in transparent funds), no liability to tax would arise under regulation 17 of those Regulations (the charge to tax) on a disposal of that interest, and
(b)   any interest in an offshore fund that is treated as creditor relationship rights under section 490 of CTA 2009.".

ELECTIVE FINROFS

85F(1)   An authorised investment fund which does not meet the investment condition may elect to be treated as a FINROF (an "elective FINROF").

This is subject to paragraph (4).

85F(2)   An election under paragraph (1) must–

(a)   be made in writing to HM Revenue and Customs by the manager; and

(b)   specify the date from which the fund is to be so treated.

85F(3)   But the manager must not specify a date which is more than 3 months before the date of the election mentioned in paragraph (2).

85F(4)   Before making an election, the fund must have obtained any necessary regulatory approval in respect of the instrument constituting the fund and the prospectus.

Chapter 2 – Entry into Funds Investing in Non-Reporting Offshore Fund ("FINROF") regime

History – Pt. 6A inserted by SI 2010/294, reg. 21, with effect from 6 March 2010 (subject to the transitional provisions at SI 2010/294, reg. 25 and 26).

ENTRY INTO FINROF REGIME: THE BASIC RULE

85G   This Part applies to an authorised investment fund from–

(a)   the date on which the fund first met the condition in regulation 85D (the investment condition); or

(b)   the date specified in the notice given under regulation 85F (elective FINROFs), whichever is the earlier.

THE REQUIREMENT TO NOTIFY WHERE REGULATION 85D IS SATISFIED

85H(1)   The legal owner of an authorised investment fund which is a FINROF by virtue of regulation 85D must notify HM Revenue and Customs of the date on which the fund first met the investment condition within a period of 3 months beginning with the date on which the fund first met that condition.

85H(2)   For the purposes of paragraph (1), no account shall be taken of the period before the date of any previous valid election under regulation 85Z9 (leaving the FINROF regime).

85H(3)   An authorised investment fund that fails to comply with this regulation is liable to a penalty not exceeding £3,000 determined in accordance with section 100 of TMA 1970.

85H(4)   Sections 100A, 100B, 102, 103(4) and 118(2) of TMA 1970 apply to a penalty determined in accordance with paragraph (3).

85H(5)   This regulation is subject to regulation 85J (inadvertent fulfilment of investment condition).

THE REQUIREMENT TO NOTIFY PARTICIPANTS WHEN A FUND ENTERS THE FINROF REGIME

85I(1) The legal owner must notify the participants in a fund that the fund has entered the FINROF regime and inform them that any gains made on the disposal of units in the fund shall be treated as an income gain rather than a capital gain, in accordance with Chapter 3 of this Part.

85I(2) The notification under paragraph (1) must be given within a period of 3 months beginning with the date on which this Part first applied to the fund.

85I(3) For the purposes of paragraph (2), no account shall be taken of the period before the date of any previous valid election under regulation 85Z9 (leaving the FINROF regime).

85I(4) An authorised investment fund that fails to comply with this regulation is liable to a penalty not exceeding £3,000 determined in accordance with section 100 of TMA 1970.

85I(5) Sections 100A, 100B, 102, 103(4) and 118(2) of TMA 1970 apply to a penalty determined in accordance with paragraph (4).

85I(6) This regulation is subject to regulation 85J.

INADVERTENT FULFILMENT OF INVESTMENT CONDITION

85J(1) If this regulation applies a fund shall be treated as if it had never met the investment condition and consequently none of the provisions of this Part (including the penalty provisions in regulations 85H and 85I) apply to the fund.

85J(2) This regulation applies where–

(a) an authorised investment fund meets the investment condition but as soon as possible after becoming aware that the condition is met, the legal owner gives notice in writing to HM Revenue and Customs of the steps that the fund has taken, or proposes to take, to ensure that the fund no longer meets that condition,

(b) the fund ceases the meet the investment condition before the end of a 4 month period beginning with the date that the fund first met the condition and the legal owner gives notice in writing to HM Revenue and Customs that the fund no longer meets the condition, and

(c) HM Revenue and Customs issue a notice in writing that this regulation applies.

85J(3) HM Revenue and Customs must, within a period of 28 days beginning with the date on which they receive notice from the legal owner that the fund no longer meets the investment condition, issue a notice in writing to the legal owner that–

(a) this regulation applies, or

(b) this regulation does not apply as HM Revenue and Customs are not satisfied that the conditions in sub-paragraphs (a) and (b) of paragraph (2) are met for the reasons specified in the notice.

APPEAL AGAINST REFUSAL TO PROVIDE WRITTEN NOTICE

85K(1) A legal owner to whom a notice is issued under paragraph (3)(b) of regulation 85J (a "refusal notice") may appeal.

85K(2) The notice of appeal must be given to HM Revenue and Customs within a period of 28 days beginning with the day on which HM Revenue and Customs issued the refusal notice.

85K(3) On an appeal that is notified to the tribunal, the tribunal shall determine whether it was just and reasonable for HM Revenue and Customs to issue the refusal notice.

85K(4) If the tribunal determine that it was just and reasonable for HM Revenue and Customs to issue the refusal notice, this Part applies to the fund from the date on which it first met the investment condition and the legal owner must notify the participants in the fund in accordance with regulation 85I.

85K(5) If the tribunal determine that it was not just and reasonable for HM Revenue and Customs to issue the refusal notice, paragraph (1) of regulation 85J shall apply.

DISPOSAL OF AN INTEREST IN AN AUTHORISED INVESTMENT FUND PRIOR TO ITS BECOMING A FINROF

85L(1) This regulation applies if an authorised investment fund either meets the investment condition or becomes an elective FINROF in accordance with regulation 85F.

85L(2) A participant in the fund may make an election to be treated for the purposes of TCGA 1992–

(a) as disposing of all the units that they hold in the authorised investment fund on the deemed disposal date, and

(b)   as immediately upon that disposal, acquiring units in the FINROF.

85L(3)   The disposal referred to in paragraph (2)(a) is treated as made for a consideration equal to the market value of the participant's holding of units in the fund on the deemed disposal date.

85L(4)   The acquisition referred to in paragraph (2)(b) is treated as made for a consideration equal to the consideration for the disposal referred to in paragraph (2)(a).

85L(5)   If the participant is chargeable to income tax, the election mentioned in paragraph (2) must be made by being included in a return made for the tax year which includes the deemed disposal date.

85L(6)   If the participant is chargeable to corporation tax, the election mentioned in paragraph (2) must be made by being included in the participant's company tax return for the accounting period which includes the deemed disposal date.

85L(7)   In this regulation–

(a)   **"company tax return"** has the same meaning as in Schedule 18 to the Finance Act 1998, and

(b)   **"deemed disposal date"** means the date on which this Part begins to apply to the authorised investment fund.

Chapter 3 – Tax treatment of FINROFs and of participants in FINROFs

History – Pt. 6A inserted by SI 2010/294, reg. 21, with effect from 6 March 2010 (subject to the transitional provisions at SI 2010/294, reg. 25 and 26).

THE CHARGE TO TAX

The charge to tax: general provisions

85M(1)   There is a charge to tax if–

(a)   a person disposes of an asset,

(b)   either condition A or condition B is met, and

(c)   as a result of the disposal, an income gain (see regulation 85Z) arises to the person making the disposal.

85M(2)   Condition A is that the asset consists of units in a FINROF at the time of the disposal.

85M(3)   Condition B is that–

(a)   the asset consists of units in an authorised investment fund that had been a FINROF for some of the material period; and

(b)   no valid election under regulation 85Z11 (participant's power to elect for deemed disposal) was made in relation to the asset.

85M(4)   In paragraph (3) **"the material period"** means a period beginning with the date of acquisition of the asset and ending with the date of the disposal.

The charge to tax: further provisions

85N(1)   The income gain arising is treated for all purposes of the Tax Acts as income which arises at the time of the disposal to the person making the disposal (or treated as making the disposal).

85N(2)   The tax is charged on the person making the disposal (or treated as making the disposal).

85N(3)   In the case of a person chargeable to income tax, tax is charged under Chapter 8 of Part 5 of ITTOIA 2005 (miscellaneous income: income not otherwise charged) for the year of assessment in which the disposal is made, but sections 688(1) (income charged) and 689 (person liable) of ITTOIA 2005 do not apply.

85N(4)   In the case of a person chargeable to corporation tax, tax is charged under Chapter 8 of Part 10 of CTA 2009 (miscellaneous income: income not otherwise charged) for the accounting period in which the disposal is made.

Application of certain provisions of TCGA 1992

85O   The following enactments have effect in relation to income tax or corporation tax in respect of income gains as they have effect in relation to capital gains tax or corporation tax in respect of chargeable gains–

(a)   section 2(1) of TCGA 1992 (persons chargeable to capital gains tax);

(b)   section 10 of TCGA 1992 (non-resident with a United Kingdom branch or agency);

(c)   section 10B of TCGA 1992 (non-resident company with United Kingdom permanent establishment).

Application of section 10A of TCGA 1992

85P(1)   Section 10A of TCGA 1992 (temporary non-residence) applies for the purposes of this Part with the following modifications.

85P(2)   The section applies as if, in subsection (2)–

(a)   the reference to section 86A were omitted;

(b)   for the reference to capital gains tax there were substituted a reference to income tax;

(c)   in paragraph (a), for the reference to chargeable gains and losses there were substituted a reference to income gains;

(d)   paragraphs (b) and (c) were omitted; and

(e)   for the references to gains or losses there were substituted a reference to income gains.

85P(3)   The section applies as if, in subsection (3)–

(a)   for the reference to gains and losses there were substituted a reference to income gains; and

(b)   for the reference to any gain or loss there were substituted a reference to any income gains.

85P(4)   The section applies as if, in subsection (4) were omitted.

85P(5)   The section applies as if, in subsection (5)–

(a)   for the reference to gains and losses there were substituted a reference to income gains;

(b)   for the reference to any chargeable gain or allowable loss there were substituted a reference to an any income gain; and

(c)   for the reference to section 10 or 16(3) there were substituted a reference to regulation 85O(b) (application of certain provisions of TCGA).

85P(6)   The section applies as if, in subsection (6) were omitted.

85P(7)   The section applies as if, in subsection (7), for the reference to capital gains tax there were substituted a reference to income tax.

85P(8)   The section applies as if, in subsection (9C)–

(a)   for the reference to capital gains tax there were substituted a reference to income tax; and

(b)   for the reference to chargeable gains there were substituted a reference to income gains.

Chapter 4 – Exceptions, etc from the charge to tax

History – Pt. 6A inserted by SI 2010/294, reg. 21, with effect from 6 March 2010 (subject to the transitional provisions at SI 2010/294, reg. 25 and 26).

EXCEPTIONS FROM THE CHARGE TO TAX

85Q(1)   No liability to tax arises under regulation 85M (the charge to tax: general provisions) if condition A or B is met.

85Q(2)   Condition A is that the participant is required to treat units in the FINROF as a loan relationship to which the provisions of Chapter 3 of Part 6 of CTA 2009 apply.

85Q(3)   Condition B is that the participant is required to treat units in the FINROF as a derivative contract to which the provisions of Part 7 of CTA 2009 apply.

TRADING STOCK ETC.

85R(1)   No liability to tax arises under regulation 85M if condition A or B is met.

85R(2)   Condition A is that the units in the fund are held as trading stock.

85R(3)   Condition B is that the disposal of the units is taken into account in computing the profits of a trade.

LONG-TERM INSURANCE FUNDS OF INSURANCE COMPANIES

85S(1)   No liability to tax arises under regulation 85M in respect of disposals of units of an insurance company's long-term insurance fund.

85S(2)   In paragraph (1) **"insurance company"** and **"long-term insurance fund"** have the same meaning as is section 431(2) of ICTA.

CHARITABLE COMPANIES AND CHARITABLE TRUSTS

85T(1)   A charitable company shall be exempt from corporation tax in respect of an income gain if the gain is applicable and is applied for charitable purposes.

85T(2)   A charitable trust shall be exempt from income tax in respect of an income gain if the gain is applicable and is applied for charitable purposes.

85T(3)   Paragraphs (4) and (5) apply if–

(a)   property held on charitable trusts ceases to be subject to charitable trusts, and

(b)   that property represents directly or indirectly an income gain.

85T(4)   The trustees are treated as if they had disposed of and immediately reacquired that property for a consideration equal to its market value.

85T(5)   An income gain accruing on the disposal arising under paragraph (4) is treated as an income gain not accruing to a charity.

85T(6)   In this regulation **"charity"** and **"charitable company"** have the same meaning as in section 506 of ICTA.

Chapter 5 – Disposal of units in FINROFs

History – Pt. 6A inserted by SI 2010/294, reg. 21, with effect from 6 March 2010 (subject to the transitional provisions at SI 2010/294, reg. 25 and 26).

APPLICATION OF THIS CHAPTER

85U   This Chapter applies if a participant disposes of an asset and at the time of the disposal–

(a)   the asset consists of units in a FINROF, or

(b)   the asset consists of units in an authorised investment fund that is not a FINROF and the requirements specified in paragraph (3) of regulation 85M are met.

DISPOSAL OF AN ASSET: THE BASIC RULE

85V(1)   There is a disposal of an asset for the purposes of this Part if there would be a disposal of an asset for the purposes of TCGA 1992.

85V(2)   Paragraph (1) is subject to the following regulations in this Chapter.

PROVISIONS APPLICABLE ON DEATH

85W(1)   Notwithstanding anything in paragraph (b) of subsection (1) of section 62 of TCGA 1992 (general provisions applicable on death: no deemed disposal by the deceased), where a person dies and the assets of which the deceased was competent to dispose at the time of death include units in a FINROF, then, for the purposes of these Regulations–

(a)   immediately before the acquisition referred to in paragraph (a) of that subsection, those units shall be deemed to be disposed of by the deceased for such a consideration as is mentioned in that subsection; but

(b)   nothing in this regulation affects the determination, in accordance with regulation 85U, of the question whether that deemed disposal is one to which this Chapter applies.

85W(2)   Subject to paragraph (1), section 62 of TCGA 1992 applies for the purposes of these Regulations as it applies for the purposes of that Act, and the reference in that paragraph to the assets of which a deceased person was competent to dispose are to be construed in accordance with subsection (10) of that section.

APPLICATION OF SECTION 135 OF TCGA 1992

85X(1)   Section 135 of TCGA 1992 (exchange of securities for those in another company treated as not involving a disposal) does not apply for the purposes of this Part to the extent that–

(a)   the interest in the entity that is company A for the purposes of that section that is exchanged is units in a FINROF, and

(b)   the interest in the entity that is company B for those purposes that is exchanged is not units in such a fund.

85X(2) In a case where section 135 of TCGA 1992 would apply apart from paragraph (1), the exchange in question shall for the purposes of this Part constitute a disposal of units in the FINROF for a consideration equal to their market value at the time of the exchange.

APPLICATION OF SECTION 136 OF TCGA 1992

85Y(1) Section 136 of TCGA 1992 (scheme of reconstruction involving issue of securities treated as exchange not involving disposal) does not apply for the purposes of this Part to the extent that–

(a)   the interest in the entity that is company A for the purposes of that section that is exchanged is units in a FINROF, and

(b)   the interest in the entity that is company B for those purposes that is exchanged is not units in such a fund.

85Y(2) In a case where section 136 of TCGA 1992 would apply apart from paragraph (1), the deemed exchange in question shall for the purposes of this Part constitute a disposal of units in the FINROF for a consideration equal to their market value at the time of the deemed exchange.

Chapter 6 – Income gains and computation of income gains

History – Pt. 6A inserted by SI 2010/294, reg. 21, with effect from 6 March 2010 (subject to the transitional provisions at SI 2010/294, reg. 25 and 26).

GENERAL PROVISIONS

85Z(1) An income gain arises to a person on the disposal of an asset if a basic gain arises on the disposal.

85Z(2) The disposal gives rise to an income gain of an amount equal to the basic gain on the disposal.

85Z(3) The following provisions of this Chapter explain how the basic gain is computed.

THE BASIC GAIN AND ITS COMPUTATION

85Z1(1) In the case of a participant chargeable to income tax, the basic gain is a gain of the amount which would be the gain on that disposal for the purposes of TCGA 1992 if the gain were computed without regard to any charge to income tax arising under this Part.

85Z1(2) In the case of a participant chargeable to corporation tax, the basic gain is a gain of the amount which would be the gain on that disposal for the purposes of TCGA 1992 if the gain were computed–

(a)   without regard to any charge to corporation tax arising under this Part, and

(b)   without regard to any indexation allowance on the disposal under TCGA 1992.

85Z1(3) The computation of the basic gain is subject to–

(a)   regulation 85W (provisions applicable on death);

(b)   regulation 85X (application of section 135 of TCGA 1992);

(c)   regulation 85Y (application of section 136 of TCGA 1992);

(d)   regulation 85Z2 (earlier disposal to which the no gain/no loss basis applies);

(e)   regulation 85Z3 (modifications of TCGA 1992); and

(f)   regulation 85Z4 (losses).

EARLIER DISPOSAL TO WHICH THE NO GAIN/NO LOSS BASIS APPLIES

85Z2(1) This regulation applies if–

(a)   a participant is chargeable to corporation tax, and

(b)   the amount of any chargeable gain or allowable loss which would arise on the disposal would fall to be computed in a way which, in whole or in part, would take account of the indexation allowance on an earlier disposal to which section 56(2) of TCGA 1992 (disposals on a no gain/no loss basis) applies.

85Z2(2) The basic gain on the disposal is computed as if–

(a)   no indexation allowance had been available on any such earlier disposal, and

(b)   subject to that, neither a gain nor a loss had arisen to the person making such an earlier disposal.

MODIFICATIONS OF TCGA 1992

85Z3(1)   If the disposal forms part of a transfer to which section 162 of TCGA 1992 (roll-over relief on transfer of business) applies, the basic gain arising on the disposal is computed without regard to any deduction which falls to be made under that section in computing a chargeable gain.

85Z3(2)   If the disposal is made otherwise than under a bargain at arm's length and a claim for relief is made in respect of that disposal under section 165 or 260 of TCGA 1992 (relief for gifts), the claim does not affect the computation of the basic gain arising on the disposal.

LOSSES

85Z4(1)   If the effect of any computation under regulations 85Z1 to 85Z3 would be to produce a loss, the basic gain on the disposal is nil.

85Z4(2)   Paragraph (1) applies notwithstanding section 16 of TCGA 1992 (losses determined in like manner as gains).

85Z4(3)   Accordingly, for the purposes of these Regulations, no loss is to be treated as arising on the disposal.

Chapter 7 – Deduction of income gains in computing chargeable gains

History – Pt. 6A inserted by SI 2010/294, reg. 21, with effect from 6 March 2010 (subject to the transitional provisions at SI 2010/294, reg. 25 and 26).

SCOPE OF THIS CHAPTER

85Z5(1)   This Chapter applies if–

(a)   a disposal gives rise to an income gain, and

(b)   that disposal also constitutes the disposal of the units concerned for the purposes of TCGA 1992

85Z5(2)   In this Chapter, the disposal specified in paragraph (1)(b) is called the "TCGA disposal".

TREATMENT OF THE TCGA DISPOSAL: GENERAL RULES

85Z6(1)   This regulation applies for the purposes of the computation of the chargeable gain arising on the TCGA disposal.

85Z6(2)   The provisions of this regulation have effect in relation to the TCGA disposal in substitution for section 37(1) of TCGA 1992 (deduction of consideration chargeable to tax on income).

85Z6(3)   In the computation of the gain arising on the TCGA disposal, a sum equal to the income gain shall be deducted from the sum which would otherwise constitute the amount or value of the consideration for the disposal.

85Z6(4)   Paragraph (3) is subject to the following provisions of this Chapter.

85Z6(5)   Paragraph (6) applies if the TCGA disposal is of such a nature that, by virtue of section 42 of TCGA (part disposal), an apportionment falls to be made of certain expenditure.

85Z6(6)   No deduction is to be made by virtue of paragraph (3) in determining the amount or value of the consideration for the purpose of the fraction in section 42(2) of TCGA 1992.

MODIFICATION OF SECTION 162 TCGA 1992

85Z7(1)   This regulation applies if the TCGA disposal forms part of a transfer to which section 162 of TCGA applies (roll-over relief on transfer of business in exchange wholly or partly for shares).

85Z7(2)   For the purposes of subsection (4) of section 162 of TCGA 1992 (determination of the amount of the deduction from the gain on the old assets) "B" in the fraction in that subsection (the value of the whole of the consideration received by the transferor in exchange for the business) is to be taken to be what it would be if the value of the consideration other than shares so received by the transferor were reduced by an amount equal to the income gain.

APPLICATION OF SECTION 128 OF TCGA 1992

85Z8(1)   This regulation applies if there is a disposal to which this Part applies by virtue of–

(a)   regulation 85X (application of section 135 of TCGA 1992), and

(b)   regulation 85Y (application of section 136 of TCGA 1992).

85Z8(2) TCGA 1992 has effect as if an amount equal to the income gain to which that disposal gives rise were given (by the person making the exchange) as consideration for the new holding (within the meaning of section 128 of that Act (consideration given or received for new holding on a reorganisation)).

Chapter 8 – Leaving the FINROF regime

History – Pt. 6A inserted by SI 2010/294, reg. 21, with effect from 6 March 2010 (subject to the transitional provisions at SI 2010/294, reg. 25 and 26).

LEAVING THE FINROF REGIME

85Z9(1) The provisions of this Part apply to a FINROF until the date specified in an election under this regulation made by the manager.

85Z9(2) An election under this regulation must be made to HM Revenue and Customs in writing and must comply with the following provisions of this regulation.

85Z9(3) An election may only be made in respect of a FINROF if–

(a)   the FINROF does not meet the investment condition–

(i)   at the date specified in the election, and

(ii)   at the date on which the election is made,

(b)   the FINROF has been subject to this Part for at least one complete accounting period, and

(c)   the fund has obtained any necessary regulatory approval of the instrument constituting the fund and the prospectus.

85Z9(4) An election under this regulation must specify the date from which this Part ceases to apply to the FINROF.

85Z9(5) But the date specified in paragraph (4) must not be earlier than the date which is 3 months before the date on which the election is made.

REQUIREMENT TO NOTIFY PARTICIPANTS WHEN A FUND LEAVES THE FINROF REGIME

85Z10(1) If an election is made under regulation 85Z9, the legal owner must notify the participants in a fund that this Part no longer applies to the fund but continues to apply to a participant unless an election is made in accordance with regulation 85Z11.

85Z10(2) The notification under paragraph (1) must be made within a period of 3 months beginning with the date mentioned in regulation 85Z9(5).

85Z10(3) An authorised investment fund which fails to comply with this regulation is liable to a penalty not exceeding £3,000 determined in accordance with section 100 of TMA 1970.

85Z10(4) Sections 100A, 100B, 102, 103(4) and 118(2) of TMA 1970 apply to a penalty determined in accordance with paragraph (3).

PARTICIPANT'S POWER TO ELECT FOR DEEMED DISPOSAL

85Z11(1) Notwithstanding an election made under regulation 85Z9, this Part continues to apply to a participant in a FINROF unless the participant makes an election in accordance with paragraph (2).

85Z11(2) A participant in the fund may make an election to be treated–

(a)   as disposing of the units owned by the participant in the FINROF at their market value on the deemed disposal date, and

(b)   as acquiring units in the authorised investment fund on the deemed disposal date.

85Z11(3) The income gain arising on the deemed disposal referred to in paragraph (2)(a) shall be determined in accordance with Chapter 6 of this Part.

85Z11(4) The acquisition referred to in paragraph (2)(b) is treated as made for a consideration equal to the consideration for the disposal referred to in paragraph (2)(a).

85Z11(5) An election may not be made under paragraph (2) unless the income gain arising on the disposal referred to in paragraph (2)(a) (determined in accordance with Chapter 6 of this Part) is greater than zero.

85Z11(6) If the participant is chargeable to income tax, the election mentioned in paragraph (2) must be made by being included in a return made for the tax year which includes the deemed disposal date.

85Z11(7) If the participant is chargeable to corporation tax, the election mentioned in paragraph (2) must be made by being included in the participant's company tax return for the accounting period which includes the deemed disposal date.

85Z11(8) In this regulation–

"**company tax return**" has the same meaning as in Schedule 18 to the Finance Act 1998; and

the "**deemed disposal date**" means the date on which, in accordance with regulation 85Z9, the fund ceases to be a FINROF.

PART 7 – CONSEQUENTIAL AMENDMENTS AND MODIFICATIONS OF ENACTMENTS

Chapter 1 – Amendments of References to Repealed Enactments

INTRODUCTION

86 Regulations 87 to 92–

(a) amend references in enactments to provisions repealed by section 17(1) of the Finance (No. 2) Act 2005, and

(b) make incidental, consequential and supplemental provision.

AMENDMENTS OF TMA 1970

87(1) TMA 1970 is amended as follows.

87(2) [Amends TMA 1970, s. 98.]

AMENDMENT OF ICTA

88 [Repealed by CTA 2010, s. 1181 and Sch. 3, Pt. 1.]

History – Reg. 88 repealed by CTA 2010, s. 1181 and Sch. 3, Pt. 1, with effect for corporation tax purposes for accounting periods ending on or after 1 April 2010, and for income tax and capital gains tax purposes for the tax year 2010–11 and subsequent tax years. Former reg. 88 amended ICTA 1988, s. 468(1).

AMENDMENT OF TCGA 1992

89(1) TCGA 1992 is amended as follows.

89(2) [Amends TCGA 1992, s. 99B(3).]

AMENDMENT OF FA 1996

90(1) FA 1996 is amended as follows.

90(2) [Amends FA 1996, Sch. 10, para. 4(4).]

AMENDMENTS OF ITTOIA 2005

91(1) ITTOIA 2005 is amended as follows.

91(2) [Amends ITTOIA 2005, s. 373(2).]

91(3) [Amends ITTOIA 2005, s. 376(2).]

AMENDMENT OF THE FINANCE ACT 2005

92(1) The Finance Act 2005 is amended as follows.

92(2) [Omits FA 2005, Sch. 2, para. 4.]

Chapter 2 – Modifications of the Tax Acts

INTRODUCTION

93 In their application in relation to–

(a) authorised investment funds,

(b)   shareholders or unit holders in authorised investment funds, and

(c)   transactions involving authorised investment funds,

the Tax Acts have effect with the modifications specified in regulations 94 to 96A.

History – In reg. 93, "96A" substituted for "96" by SI 2012/519, reg. 7, with effect in relation to any distribution made at or after 1.30 p.m. on 27 February 2012.

MODIFICATIONS OF ICTA

94(1)   ICTA is modified as follows.

94(2)   In section 402 (surrender of relief between members of groups and consortia) after subsection (3) the following subsection is treated as inserted–

"**402(3AA)**   For the purposes of this Chapter–

(a)   an open-ended investment company cannot be either the surrendering company or the claimant company, and

(b)   an authorised unit trust shall not be regarded as a company.".

94(3)   In section 413 (interpretation of Chapter 4), in subsection (2), the following definitions are treated as inserted at the appropriate places–

"**authorised unit trust**" has the meaning given by section 468(6);

"**open-ended investment company**" has the meaning given by section 468A(2);".

94(4)   In section 413 after subsection (3) the following subsection is treated as inserted–

"**413(3A)**   For the purposes of paragraph (a) of subsection (3) above an open-ended investment company cannot be the third company mentioned in that paragraph.".

94(4A)   After paragraph (b) of section 432A(1ZA) of ICTA (apportionment of income and gains), there is treated as inserted–

"(ba)   income from property income distributions to which regulation 69Z15 of the Authorised Investment Funds (Tax) Regulations 2006 apply (property income distributions by an open-ended investment company."

94(5)   In section 832 (interpretation of the Tax Acts) after subsection (2) the following subsection is treated as inserted–

"**832(2A)**   The definition of "ordinary share capital" does not include the issued share capital of an open-ended investment company.".

94(6)   In section 834 (interpretation of the Corporation Tax Acts), in subsection (3), the words "except in so far as regulations made under section 17(3) of the Finance (No. 2) Act 2005 make other provision for dividends treated as paid by virtue of those Regulations" are treated as substituted for the words from "except in so far as" to the end.

94(7)   In Schedule 20 (charities: qualifying investments and loans) after paragraph 6 the following paragraph is treated as inserted–

"**6A**   Shares in an open-ended investment company.".

History – Reg. 94(4A) inserted by SI 2008/3159, reg. 28, with effect in relation to property income distributions paid on or after 1 January 2009.

In reg. 94(5) the words "the following subsection is treated as inserted" substituted for "he following subsection is treated as insert" by SI 2007/794, reg. 6, with effect from 6 April 2007.

MODIFICATIONS OF FA 1996

95   [Repealed by CTA 2009, s. 1326 and Sch. 3, Pt. 1.]

History – Reg. 95 (described as relating to modifications of CTA 2009) amended by SI 2009/2036, reg. 30, with effect from 1 September 2009, in error. SI 2009/2036 was revoked with effect from 31 August 2009 by SI 2009/2199, reg. 2(2), so that SI 2009/2036, reg. 30 did not ever come into effect.

Reg. 95 repealed by CTA 2009, s. 1326 and Sch. 3, Pt. 1, with effect for corporation tax purposes for accounting periods ending on or after 1 April 2009, and for income tax and capital gains tax purposes for the tax year 2009–10 and subsequent tax years. Former reg. 95 read as follows:

"**95(1)**   FA 1996 is modified as follows.

95(2)   In paragraph 4 of Schedule 10 (loan relationships: collective investment schemes: company holdings in unit trusts and offshore funds)–

(a)   in sub-paragraph (1)(a) the words ", open-ended investment company" are treated as inserted after the words "unit trust scheme",

(b)   in sub-paragraph (1)(b) the word ", company" is treated as inserted after the word "scheme",

(c)   in sub-paragraph (4) the words "or open-ended investment company" are treated as inserted after the words "authorised unit trust",

(d)   in sub-paragraph (5) the words "scheme, fund or open-ended investment company" are treated as substituted for the words "scheme or fund", and

(e)   the following sub-paragraph is treated as inserted at the end–

"**4(7)** In this paragraph "**open-ended investment company**" has the same meaning as in sub-paragraph (7A)(b) of paragraph 8 below; and sub-paragraphs (7A) to (7D) of that paragraph apply for the purposes of this paragraph as they apply for the purposes of paragraph 8.".

95(3) In paragraph 8 of Schedule 10 (loan relationships: collective investment schemes: non-qualifying investments test)—

(a) in sub-paragraph (1)—

    (i) the words ", open-ended investment company" are treated as inserted after the words "unit trust scheme", and

    (ii) the word ", company" is treated as inserted after the words "investments of the scheme";

(b) in sub-paragraph (2)—

    (i) the words ", open-ended investment company" are treated as inserted after the words "unit trust scheme", and

    (ii) the word ", company" is treated as inserted after the words "investments of the scheme".".

Former reg. 95 substituted by SI 2008/1463, reg. 2, with effect from 30 June 2008.

MODIFICATIONS OF ITTOIA 2005

96(1) ITTOIA 2005 is modified as follows.

96(1A) In the application of the provisions specified in paragraph (1B) in relation to a Property AIF and a Tax Elected Fund—

(a) for "the total" substitute "an", and

(b) the amount available for distribution as PAIF distribution (interest) or TEF distribution (non-dividend), as the case may be, shall be treated as the amount available for distribution as yearly interest.

96(1B) The specified provisions are—

(a) section 373(1) (open-ended investment company interest distributions), and

(b) section 376(1) (authorised unit trust interest distributions).

96(2) The words ", except in so far as regulations made under section 17(3) of the Finance (No. 2) Act 2005 make other provision for dividends treated as paid by virtue of those regulations" are treated as inserted at the end of each of the provisions specified in paragraph (3).

96(3) The provisions specified are—

(a) section 374(1) (date when open-ended investment company interest distributions made),

(b) section 377(1) (date when authorised unit trust interest distributions made),

(c) section 387(1) (date when open-ended investment company dividend distributions made), and

(d) section 390(1) (date when authorised unit trust dividend distributions made).

96(4) In sections 375(1) (interpretation of sections 373 and 374) and 388(1) (interpretation of sections 386 and 387) the definition of "the OEIC Regulations" is treated as omitted.

96(5) In those provisions, the following definitions are treated as substituted for the definitions of "open-ended investment company", "owner of shares" and "umbrella company"—

    "**open-ended investment company**" means a company incorporated in the United Kingdom to which section 236 of FISMA 2000 applies,

    "**owner of shares**", in relation to an open-ended investment company, has the meaning given in regulations made under section 17(3) of the Finance (No. 2) Act 2005.".

96(6) In sections 375(3) and 388(3) the words "regulations under section 17(3) of the Finance (No. 2) Act 2005 (as at 1st April 2006, see regulation 6(2) of the Authorised Investment Funds (Tax) Regulations 2006 (S.I. 2006/964))" are treated as substituted for the words from "Chapter 3 of Part 12 of ICTA" to the end.

History – Reg. 96(1A) inserted by SI 2009/2036, reg. 31(2), with effect from 1 September 2009.
Reg. 96(1B) inserted by SI 2009/2036, reg. 31(2), with effect from 1 September 2009.
In reg. 96(3)(b), "377(1)" substituted for "376(1)" by SI 2009/2036, reg. 31(2), with effect from 1 September 2009.
In reg. 96(5), the definition of "umbrella company", and the "and" before it, repealed by CTA 2010, s. 1181 and Sch. 3, Pt. 1, with effect for corporation tax purposes for accounting periods ending on or after 1 April 2010, and for income tax and capital gains tax purposes for the tax year 2010–11 and subsequent tax years. Former definition read as follows:
    "**umbrella company**" has the meaning given by section 468A of ICTA.".

MODIFICATION OF CTA 2009

96A(1) CTA 2009 is modified as follows.

96A(2) In section 490 (holdings in OEICs, unit trusts and offshore funds treated as creditor relationship rights)—

(a) for subsection (2) the following subsection is treated as substituted—

    "**490(2)** The Corporation Tax Acts have effect for the accounting period in accordance with subsections (3) and (3A) as if—

    (a)   the relevant holding were rights under a creditor relationship of the company, and

    (b)   any distribution in respect of the relevant holding were not a distribution (and accordingly is within Part 5).";

(b)   after subsection (3) the following subsections are treated as inserted—

    "**490(3A)**   To the extent that any distribution to which subsection (2)(b) applies relates to an unfranked part of a dividend distribution—

    (a)   regulation 48(2)(b) of the Authorised Investment Funds (Tax) Regulations 2006 applies to determine the amount of the distribution and any tax treated as deducted from that distribution, and

    (b)   regulations 48A and 48B of those Regulations apply to determine the amount of any foreign income and the foreign element of the tax treated as deducted.

    490(3B)   For the purposes of subsection (3A)—

    (a)   **"dividend distribution"** has the meaning given by regulation 22(3) of the Authorised Investment Funds (Tax) Regulations 2006, and

    (b)   regulation 49 of those Regulations explains how to calculate the unfranked part of the dividend distribution."; and

(c)   subsections (4) and (5) are treated as omitted.

History – Reg. 96A inserted by SI 2012/519, reg. 8, with effect in relation to any distribution made at or after 1.30 p.m. on 27 February 2012.

Chapter 3 – Modifications of TCGA 1992

PRELIMINARY

Introduction

97   In its application in relation to–

(a)   authorised investment funds,

(b)   shareholders or unit holders in authorised investment funds, and

(c)   transactions involving authorised investment funds

TCGA 1992 has effect with the modifications specified in regulations 98 to 110.

GENERAL

Application of TCGA 1992: general

98(1)   TCGA 1992 has effect in relation to–

(a)   open-ended investment companies,

(b)   holdings in, and the assets of, such companies, and

(c)   transactions involving such companies,

in like manner as the manner in which it has effect in relation to authorised unit trusts, to rights under, and the assets subject to, such trusts and to transactions for purposes connected with such trusts.

98(2)   References in TCGA 1992 to companies, to holdings in, and the assets of, companies and to transactions involving companies accordingly have effect (or do not have effect as the case may be) in relation to open-ended investment companies, to holdings in, and the assets of, such companies, and to transactions involving such companies, in like manner as the manner in which they have effect (or do not have effect) in relation to authorised unit trusts, to rights under, and the assets subject to, such trusts, and to transactions for purposes connected with such trusts.

98(3)   This regulation has effect subject to the other modifications contained in this Chapter.

GENERAL MODIFICATIONS OF TCGA 1992

General modifications: introduction

99   The modifications specified in regulations 100 to 104 have effect subject to the modifications specified in regulations 105 to 110.

General modification: authorised unit trust

100(1)   The modifications specified in this regulation are that references, however expressed, in TCGA 1992 to–

(a)   an authorised unit trust (other than references in a definition of an authorised unit trust, an unauthorised unit trust or a unit trust scheme),

(b)   a unit trust scheme as denoting or including (whether expressly or by implication) an authorised unit trust (other than references in a definition of an authorised unit trust, an unauthorised unit trust or a unit trust scheme),

(c)   the trustees of an authorised unit trust within sub-paragraph (a) or of a unit trust scheme within sub-paragraph (b),

have effect as if they included references to an open-ended investment company.

100(2)   Paragraph (1) does not apply–

(a)   to references in any of the provisions specified in paragraph (3), or

(b)   to references to provisions which include reference, whether made expressly or by implication, to an open-ended investment company.

100(3)   The provisions specified are–

(a)   section 99(1) (application of Act to unit trust scheme),

(b)   [omitted by SI 2013/1400, reg. 14(a),]

(c)   section 100(2) (exemption for units in unit trust scheme), and

(d)   section 272(5) (valuation of rights of unit holders).

History – Reg. 100(3)(b) omitted by SI 2013/1400, reg. 14(a), with effect in relation to disposals on or after 8 June 2013. Former reg. 100(3)(b) read as follows:
        "(b)   section 99A (authorised unit trusts: treatment of umbrella schemes),".

General modification: manager of authorised unit trust

101(1)   The modifications specified in this regulation are that references, however expressed, in TCGA 1992 to the manager of an authorised unit trust or of a unit trust scheme within regulation 100(1)(b) have effect as if they included references to the authorised corporate director of the open-ended investment company concerned.

101(2)   Paragraph (1) does not apply–

(a)   to section 272(5) (valuation of rights of unit holders), or

(b)   to references in provisions which include reference, whether made expressly or by implication, to the authorised corporate director of an open-ended investment company.

General modification: unit in authorised unit trust

102(1)   The modifications specified in this regulation are that references, however expressed, in TCGA 1992 to–

(a)   a unit or an interest in, or rights under, an authorised unit trust,

(b)   a unit or an interest in, or rights under, a unit trust scheme within regulation 100(1)(b), or

(c)   an entitlement to a share of, or in, the investments subject to the trusts of an authorised unit trust or a unit trust scheme within regulation 100(1)(b),

have effect as if they included references to a share in the open-ended investment company concerned.

102(2)   Paragraph (1) does not apply–

(a)   to section 99(1) (application of Act to unit trust scheme),

(b)   [omitted by SI 2013/1400, reg. 14(b),]

(c)   to section 272(5) (valuation of rights of unit holders), or

(d)   to references in provisions which include reference, whether made expressly or by implication, to shares in, or an owner of shares in, an open-ended investment company.

History – Reg. 102(2)(b) omitted by SI 2013/1400, reg. 14(b), with effect in relation to disposals on or after 8 June 2013. Former reg. 102(2)(b) read as follows:
        "(b)   to section 99A (authorised unit trusts: treatment of umbrella schemes),".

General modification: accumulation units in authorised unit trusts

103(1)   The modifications specified in this regulation are that references, however expressed, in TCGA 1992 to accumulation units in an authorised unit trust or in a unit trust scheme within regulation 100(1)(b) have effect as if they included references to accumulation shares in an openended investment company.

103(2)   In paragraph (1) **"accumulation shares in an open-ended investment company"** means shares in the company in respect of which income is credited periodically to the capital part of the scheme property of the company.

Statutory Instruments

General modification: accumulation units in authorised unit trusts

104(1) The modifications specified in this regulation are that references, however expressed, in TCGA 1992 to the holder of a unit within regulation 102(1) (other than references in a definition of a unit holder) have effect as if they included references to the owner of a share in the open-ended investment company concerned.

104(2) Paragraph (1) does not apply–

(a)   to section 99(1) (application of Act to unit trust scheme),

(b)   [omitted by SI 2013/1400, reg. 14(c),]

(c)   to section 272(5) (valuation of rights of unit holders), or

(d)   to references in provisions which include reference, whether made expressly or by implication, to shares in, or an owner of shares in, an open-ended investment company.

History – Reg. 104(2)(b) omitted by SI 2013/1400, reg. 14(c), with effect in relation to disposals on or after 8 June 2013. Former reg. 104(2)(b) read as follows:

   "(b)   to section 99A (authorised unit trusts: treatment of umbrella schemes),".

SPECIFIC MODIFICATIONS OF TCGA 1992

Modification of section 99 of TCGA 1992

105 In section 99 of TCGA 1992 (application of Act to unit trust schemes), in subsection (2), the words "sections 99A and 99AA" are treated as substituted for "section 99A".

Insertion of section 99AA of TCGA 1992

106 [Omitted by SI 2013/1400, reg. 14(d).]

History – Reg. 106 omitted by SI 2013/1400, reg. 14(d), with effect in relation to disposals on or after 8 June 2013. Former reg. 106 read as follows:

   "**106** After section 99A of TCGA 1992 the following section is treated as inserted–

           "Open-ended investment companies: treatment of umbrella companies

99AA(1) In this section an "umbrella company" has the meaning given by section 468A(4) of the Taxes Act, and a reference to a part of an umbrella company is to be construed in accordance with that provision.

99AA(2) For the purposes of this Act (except subsection (1))–

(a)   each of the parts of an umbrella company shall be regarded as an open-ended investment company, and

(b)   the umbrella company as a whole shall not be so regarded (and shall not, unless express provision is made otherwise, be regarded as a company).

99AA(3) In this Act, in relation to a part of an umbrella company, any reference, however expressed, to an owner of shares in an open-ended investment company is to a person for the time being having rights in the separate pool to which the part of the umbrella company relates.

99AA(4) Nothing in subsection (2) or (3) shall prevent–

(a)   gains accruing to an umbrella company being regarded as gains accruing to an open-ended investment company for the purposes of section 100(1) (exemption for authorised unit trusts etc);

(b)   a transfer of business to an umbrella company being regarded as a transfer to an open-ended investment company for the purposes of section 139(4) (exclusion of transfers to authorised unit trusts etc).".".

Modification of section 170 of TCGA 1992

107 In section 170 of TCGA 1992 (groups of companies: interpretation), after subsection (4), the following subsection is treated as inserted–

   "**170(4A)** An open-ended investment company cannot be the principal company of a group.".

Modifications of section 272 of TCGA 1992

108(1) Section 272 of TCGA 1992 (valuation: general) is modified as follows.

108(2) In subsection (3)(a) the words "where a single price is shown in the quotations for the shares or securities in The Stock Exchange Daily Official List on the relevant date, that price, or" are treated as inserted after "2 figures, or".

108(3) After subsection (5) the following subsection is treated as inserted–

   "**272(5AA)** In this Act **"market value"** in relation to shares of a given class in an open-ended investment company the prices of which are published regularly by the authorised corporate director of that company (whether or not those shares are also quoted in The Stock Exchange Daily Official List) shall mean an amount equal to the price so published on the relevant date, or if no price was published on that date, on the latest date before that date.".

Modifications of section 288 of TCGA 1992

109(1) Section 288 of TCGA 1992 (interpretation) is modified as follows.

109(2) In subsection (1)–

(a)   [omitted by SI 2013/1400, reg. 14(e),]

(b)   the following definitions are treated as inserted at the appropriate places in alphabetical order–

""**authorised corporate director**" has the meaning given in regulations made under section 17(3) of the Finance (No. 2) Act 2005 (as at 1st April 2006, see regulation 8 of the Authorised Investment Funds (Tax) Regulations 2006 (S.I. 2006/964));"

""**open-ended investment company**" has the meaning given in regulations made under section 17(3) of the Finance (No. 2) Act 2005 (as at 1st April 2006, see regulation 4 of the Authorised Investment Funds (Tax) Regulations 2006 (S.I. 2006/964));"

""**owner of shares**" has the meaning given in regulations made under section 17(3) of the Finance (No. 2) Act 2005 (as at 1st April 2006, see regulation 8 of the Authorised Investment Funds (Tax) Regulations 2006 (S.I. 2006/964));".

History – Reg. 109(2)(a) (and the "and" at the end) omitted by SI 2013/1400, reg. 14(e), with effect in relation to disposals on or after 8 June 2013. Former reg. 109(2)(a) read as follows:

     "(a)   in the definition of "collective investment scheme", the words "sections 99A and 99AA" are treated as substituted for "section 99A", and".

Modification of Schedule A1 to TCGA 1992

110   In Schedule A1 to TCGA 1992 (application of taper relief), in paragraph 16(2) (special rules for postponed gains), at the end of paragraph (f) the word ", or" is treated as added and the following paragraph is then also treated as added–

     "(g)   regulations 67(4) and 68(4) of the Authorised Investment Funds (Tax) Regulations 2006.".

PART 8 – FINAL PROVISIONS

INSTRUMENTS REVOKED

111   The following statutory instruments are revoked–

     The Open-ended Investment Companies (Tax) Regulations 1997;

     The Open-ended Investment Companies (Tax) (Amendment) Regulations 1997;

     The Open-ended Investment Companies (Tax) (Amendment) Regulations 2002;

     The Open-ended Investment Companies (Tax) (Amendment) Regulations 2003.

SCHEDULE – ABBREVIATIONS AND DEFINED EXPRESSIONS

Part 1 – Abbreviations of Acts

TMA 1970	The Taxes Management Act 1970 (c. 9)
ICTA	The Income and Corporation Taxes Act 1988 (c. 1)
TCGA 1992	The Taxation of Chargeable Gains Act 1992 (c. 12)
FA 1993	The Finance Act 1993 (c. 34)
FA 1994	The Finance Act 1994 (c. 9)
FA 1996	The Finance Act 1996 (c. 8)
FISMA 2000	The Financial Services and Markets Act 2000 (c. 8)
FA 2002	The Finance Act 2002 (c. 23)
ITEPA 2003	The Income Tax (Earnings and Pensions) Act 2003 (c. 1)
ITTOIA 2005	The Income Tax (Trading and Other Income) Act 2005 (c. 5)
FA 2006	The Finance Act 2006 (c. 25)
ITA 2007	The Income Tax Act 2007 (c. 3)
CTA 2009	The Corporation Tax Act 2009 (c. 4)
CTA 2010	The Corporation Tax Act 2010 (c. 4)
TIOPA 2010	The Taxation (International and Other Provisions) Act 2010 (c. 8)
FA 2012	The Finance Act 2012 (c. 14)

History – In Schedule, Pt. 1, entries for "FA 1993", "FA 1994", "FA 2006" and "ITA 2007" inserted by SI 2008/705, reg. 6, with effect from 6 April 2008.

In Schedule, Pt. 1, entry for "CTA 2009" inserted by SI 2009/2036, reg. 32(2), with effect from 1 September 2009.

In Schedule, Pt. 1, entry for "CTA 2010" inserted by SI 2014/518, reg. 3(3), with effect from accounting periods beginning on or after 1 April 2014.

In Schedule, Pt. 1, entry for "TIOPA 2010" inserted by SI 2010/1642, reg. 8, with effect in relation to distributions made at or after 1.45 p.m. on 22 June 2010.

In Schedule, Pt. 1, entry for "FA 2012" inserted by SI 2012/3043, reg. 2(3), with effect in relation to dividend distributions (within the meaning given by reg. 22(3)) made on or after 1 January 2013.

Part 2 – Index of Expressions Defined or Otherwise Explained in These Regulations

Unit holder	Regulation 5(3)
Unit trust scheme	Regulation 5(1)
Units	Regulation 6(4)
The whole of the scheme property of an authorised unit trust that is available for transfer (in Chapter 2 of Part 6)	Regulation 78(7)

History – In Schedule, Pt. 2, the entry relating to "investment transaction" omitted by SI 2014/685, reg. 7(4), with effect from transactions entered into on or after 8 April 2014.

In Schedule, Pt. 2, the entry relating to "Dedicated feeder fund" inserted by SI 2012/1783, reg. 5, with effect for capital gains tax purposes in relation to disposals made on or after 1 August 2012 and for the purposes of corporation tax on chargeable gains in relation to disposals on or after 1 August 2012.

In Schedule, Pt. 2, the entries relating to "non-reporting fund (in Part 6A)", "offshore fund (in Part 6A)", "Offshore Funds Regulations (in Part 6A)" and "reporting fund (in Part 6A)" omitted by SI 2011/244, reg. 7(2)(a), with effect (subject to transitional provisions in SI 2011/244, reg. 8): for the purposes of corporation tax on income, for accounting periods ending on or after 6 March 2011; and for the purposes of corporation tax on chargeable gains and of capital gains tax, in relation to disposals made on or after 6 March 2011. The omitted entries read as follows:

"Non-reporting fund (in Part 6A): Regulation 85C
Offshore fund (in Part 6A): Regulation 85C
Offshore Funds Regulations (In Part 6A): Regulation 85C
Reporting fund (in Part 6A): Regulation 85C".

In Schedule, Pt. 2, the entries relating to "non-reporting fund", "offshore fund", "Offshore Funds Regulations", "reportable income" inserted by SI 2011/244, reg. 7(2)(b), with effect (subject to transitional provisions in SI 2011/244, reg. 8): for the purposes of corporation tax on income, for accounting periods ending on or after 6 March 2011; and for the purposes of corporation tax on chargeable gains and of capital gains tax, in relation to disposals made on or after 6 March 2011.

In Schedule, Pt. 2 the entries relating to "Distribution", "Elective FINROF (in Part 6A)", "FINROF (in Part 6A)", "Gross asset value (in Part 6A)", "Income allocation", "Investment condition (in Part 6A)", "Non-reporting fund (in Part 6A)", "Offshore fund (in Part 6A)", "Offshore Funds Regulations (in Part 6A)", "Prospectus", "Reporting fund (in Part 6A)" and "Statement of Recommended Practice" inserted by SI 2010/294, reg. 22(2)(b), with effect from 6 March 2010.

In Schedule, Pt. 2 the entries relating to "Prospectus (in Part 4A)", "Distribution" and "Distribution accounts" omitted by SI 2010/294, reg. 22(2)(a), with effect from 6 March 2010. The omitted entries read as follows:

"Prospectus (in Part 4A) Regulation 69E(4)
Distribution Regulation 15(1)
Distribution accounts Regulation 15(3)"

In Schedule, Pt. 2, in the entry relating to "genuine diversity of ownership condition", the words "(in Part 4A)" omitted, and "9A" substituted for "69J", by SI 2009/2036, reg. 32(3)(a), with effect from 1 September 2009.

In Schedule, Pt. 2, in the entry relating to "instrument constituting the scheme", "6(7)" substituted for "14B" by SI 2009/2036, reg. 32(3)(b), with effect from 1 September 2009.

In Schedule, Pt. 2, entries relating to the following inserted by SI 2009/2036, reg. 32(3)(c), with effect from 1 September 2009: "Applicant (in Part 4B)", "Application (in Part 4B)", "Cessation (in Part 4B)", "Distribution income (in Part 4B)", "Diversely owned AIF", "Entry (in Part 4B)", "Existing fund application (in Part 4B)", "Fund documents", "Future fund application (in Part 4B)", "Information notice (in Part 4B)", "Instrument constituting the fund", "Investment transaction", "Loan creditor condition (in Part 4B)", "Property condition (in Part 4B)", "Property business income (in Part 4B)", "Property investment income (in Part 4B)", "Refusal notice (in Part 4B)", "Specified accounting period (in Part 4B)", "Tax Elected Fund", "TEF conditions (in Part 4B)", "TEF distribution (dividend) (in Part 4B)", "TEF distribution (non-dividend)", "Termination notice (in Part 4B)", .

In Schedule, Pt. 2, entry relating to "instrument constituting the scheme" inserted by SI 2008/3159, with effect from 1 January 2009.

In Schedule, Pt. 2, in the entry relating to "Qualified investor scheme", "14B(4)" substituted for "53(3)" by SI 2008/3159, with effect from 1 January 2009.

In Schedule, Pt. 2, the entries relating to the following omitted by SI 2008/3159, reg. 29(a), with effect from 1 January 2009: "Chargeable measuring date (in Chapter 4 of Part 4)"; "Difference in value (in Chapter 4 of Part 4)"; "Disposal (in Chapter 4 of Part 4)"; "Earlier measuring value (in Chapter 4 of Part 4)"; "First measuring value (in Chapter 4 of Part 4)"; "Later measuring value (in Chapter 4 of Part 4)"; "Market value (in Chapter 4 of Part 4)"; "Measuring date (in Chapter 4 of Part 4)"; and "Substantial QIS holding (in Chapter 4 of Part 4)".

In Schedule, Pt. 2 the entries relating to "Reputable intermediary condition" and "residence condition" inserted by SI 2007/794, reg. 7, with effect from 6 April 2007.

In Schedule, Pt. 2, references to the following inserted by SI 2008/705, reg. 7, with effect from 6 April 2008: "Applicant (in Part 4A)", "Balance of business conditions (in Part 4A)", "Body corporate (in Part 4A)", "Cessation (in Part 4A)", "Corporate ownership condition (in Part 4A)", "Entry (in Part 4A)", "Excessive holding (in Part 4A)", "Existing company notice (in Part 4A)", "Future company notice (in Part 4A)", "F (post-cessation) (in Part 4A)", "F (pre-entry) (in Part 4A)", "F (residual) (in Part 4A)", "F (tax-exempt) (in Part 4A)", "Genuine diversity of ownership condition (in Part 4A)", "Holder of excessive rights (in Part 4A)", "Loan creditor condition (in Part 4A)", "Net income (in Part 4A)", "Net income of F (residual) (in Part 4A)", "Net income of F (tax-exempt) (in Part 4A)", "Newly qualified company (in Part 4A)", "PAIF distribution (dividends) (in Part 4A)", "PAIF distribution (interest) (in Part 4A)", "Pre-distribution amount (in Part 4A)", "Property AIF", "Property income distribution", "Property investment business (in Part 4A)", "Property rental business (in Part 4A)", "Prospectus (in Part 4A)", "Relevant distribution (in Chapter 6 of Part 4A)", "Specified accounting period (in Part 4A)", "Termination notice (in Part 4A)" and "UK-REIT".

PROCEEDS OF CRIME ACT 2002 (MONEY LAUNDERING: EXCEPTIONS TO OVERSEAS CONDUCT DEFENCE) ORDER 2006

(SI 2006/1070)

Made on 5 April 2006 by the Secretary of State, in exercise of the powers conferred upon him by s. 327(2A)(b)(ii), 328(3)(b)(ii) and 329(2A)(b)(ii) of the Proceeds of Crime Act 2002. Operative from 15 May 2006.

1 This Order may be cited as the Proceeds of Crime Act 2002 (Money Laundering: Exceptions to Overseas Conduct Defence) Order 2006 and shall come into force on 15 May 2006.

2(1) Relevant criminal conduct of a description falling within paragraph (2) is prescribed for the purposes of sections 327(2A)(b)(ii), 328(3)(b)(ii) and 329(2A)(b)(ii) of the Proceeds of Crime Act 2002 (exceptions to defence where overseas conduct is legal under local law).

2(2) Such relevant criminal conduct is conduct which would constitute an offence punishable by imprisonment for a maximum term in excess of 12 months in any part of the United Kingdom if it occurred there other than—

(a)   an offence under the Gaming Act 1968;

(b)   an offence under the Lotteries and Amusements Act 1976, or

(c)   an offence under section 23 or 25 of the Financial Services and Markets Act 2000.

Statutory Instruments

REGISTERED PENSION SCHEMES (AUTHORISED REDUCTIONS) REGULATIONS 2006

(SI 2006/1465)

Made on 6 June 2006 by the Commissioners for Her Majesty's Revenue and Customs in exercise of the powers conferred upon them by para. 2(4)(h), (4A) and (8) of Sch. 28 to the Finance Act 2004. Operative from 27 June 2006.

CITATION, COMMENCEMENT AND EFFECT

1 These Regulations may be cited as the Registered Pension Schemes (Authorised Reductions) Regulations 2006, shall come into force on 27th June 2006 and shall have effect in relation to all times on and after 6th April 2006.

EFFECT OF CESSATION OF PENSION IN CONNECTION WITH ADMISSION TO CHELSEA HOSPITAL

2 The reduction of a scheme pension upon the admission of the pensioner to Royal Hospital at Chelsea in accordance with section 24 of the Chelsea and Kilmainham Hospitals Act 1826 (pension forfeited upon becoming an in-pensioner at Chelsea) does not prevent that pension from satisfying the condition in sub-paragraph (3) of paragraph 2 of Schedule 28 to the Finance Act 2004 (pension payable in any relevant 12 month period to be not less than that for the previous such period).

TAX AVOIDANCE SCHEMES (PRESCRIBED DESCRIPTIONS OF ARRANGEMENTS) REGULATIONS 2006

(SI 2006/1543, as amended by SI 2007/2484, SI 2009/1890, SI 2009/2033, SI 2010/2834 and SI 2013/2595)

Made on 15 June 2006 by the Treasury in exercise of the powers conferred upon them by s. 306(1)(a) and (b) of the Finance Act 2004. Operative from 1 August 2006.

PART 1 – PRELIMINARY

CITATION, COMMENCEMENT AND EFFECT

Cross references – SI 2007/785, reg. 16: modification of SI 2006/1543 so that any reference to s. 306–313 shall be construed as a reference to the corresponding provision within SI 2007/785.

1(1)   These Regulations may be cited as the Tax Avoidance Schemes (Prescribed Descriptions of Arrangements) Regulations 2006, and shall come into force on 1st August 2006.

1(2)   These Regulations do not have effect–

(a)   for the purposes of section 308(1) of FA 2004 (duties of promoter relating to any notifiable proposal), if the relevant date falls before 1st August 2006;

(b)   for the purposes of section 308(3) of FA 2004 (duties of promoter relating to any notifiable arrangements), if the date on which the promoter first becomes aware of any transaction forming part of notifiable arrangements falls before 1st August 2006;

(c)   for the purposes of section 309(1) of FA 2004 (duty of person dealing with promoter outside United Kingdom), and of section 310 of that Act (duty of parties to notifiable arrangements not involving promoter) if the date on which any transaction forming part of notifiable arrangements is entered into falls before 1st August 2006.

1(3)   In paragraph (2)(a) **"the relevant date"** has the meaning given by section 308(2) of FA 2004.

Cross references – SI 2007/785, reg. 16(2): modification of reg. 1, omitting para. (2) and (3).

INTERPRETATION: GENERAL

2(1)   This paragraph gives the meaning of the abbreviated references to Acts used in these Regulations–

"CAA 2001" means the Capital Allowances Act 2001;

"FA 2004 " means the Finance Act 2004;

"ICTA 1988" means the Income and Corporation Taxes Act 1988

"ITEPA 2003" means the Income Tax (Earnings and Pensions) Act 2003;

"ITTOIA 2005" means the Income Tax (Trading and Other Income) Act 2005;

"TCGA 1992" means the Taxation of Chargeable Gains Act 1992.

2(2)   In these Regulations–

"business" has the meaning given by regulation 3;

"HMRC" means Her Majesty's Revenue and Customs;

"the Information Regulations" means the Tax Avoidance Schemes (Information) Regulations 2004;

"the material date" means whichever of the following is applicable–

(a)   for a proposal notifiable under section 308(1) of FA 2004, the relevant date (as defined in section 308(2) of FA 2004);

(b)   for arrangements notifiable under section 308(3) of FA 2004, the date the promoter first becomes aware of any transaction forming part of the notifiable arrangements; or

(c)   for arrangements notifiable under section 309 or 310 of FA 2004, the date the person enters into any transaction forming part of the notifiable arrangements;

"plant or machinery lease" has the meaning given by section 70K CAA 2001;

"the Promoters Regulations" means the Tax Avoidance Schemes (Promoters and Prescribed Circumstances) Regulations 2004;

Statutory Instruments

"small or medium-sized enterprise" has the meaning given by regulation 4;.

2(3) For the purposes of these Regulations section 839 of ICTA 1988 applies to determine whether persons are connected.

History – In reg. 2(2), definition of "HMRC" inserted by SI 2010/2834, reg. 3(2), with effect from 1 January 2011.
In reg. 2(2), definition of "the material date" inserted by SI 2010/2834, reg. 3(3), with effect from 1 January 2011.
In reg. 2(2), definition of ""lease", "lessor" and "lessee"" omitted by SI 2010/2834, reg. 3(4), with effect from 1 January 2011. The former definition read as follows:
"'**lease**",
"'**lessor**" and
"'**lessee**" are to be construed in accordance with regulation 14(1);".
In reg. 2(2), in the description of "plant or machinery lease", the words "section 70K CAA 2001" substituted for the words "regulation 14" by SI 2010/2834, reg. 3(5), with effect from 1 January 2011.

MEANING OF "BUSINESS"

3 In these Regulations **"business"** means–

(a) a company;

(b) a partnership; or

(c) any person whose profits are charged to income tax, otherwise than by virtue of his being a partner

    (i) as trading income under Part 2 of ITTOIA 2005 (trading income), or

    (ii) as property income under section 268 of ITTOIA 2005 (charge to tax on profits of a property business).

MEANING OF "SMALL OR MEDIUM-SIZED ENTERPRISE"

4(1) For the purposes of these Regulations a "small or medium-sized enterprise" means a micro, small or medium-sized enterprise as defined in the Recommendation.

4(2) In this regulation–

"the Recommendation" means the Commission Recommendation of 6th May 2003, and

"the Annex" means the Annex to the Recommendation.

4(3) Paragraph (1) is subject to the following provisions.

4(4) If a company ("C") is a micro, small or medium-sized enterprise, disregarding any partner enterprise or linked enterprise, and, taken alone, it would satisfy the employee limit and at least one of the financial limits, but–

(a) the number of employees, annual turnover or annual balance sheet total (as the case may be) of a partner enterprise or linked enterprise to which it is related has been taken into account in determining whether the employee limits or the financial limits have been exceeded, and

(b) a partner enterprise or linked enterprise to which C is related would, disregarding the number of employees, and the annual turnover and annual balance sheet totals of C, exceed the employee limit, or either of the financial limits,

Article 4(2) of the Annex is to be disregarded in determining whether C is a small or mediumsized enterprise for an accounting period in which it exceeds the employee or financial limits.

In this paragraph references to the employee limit and the financial limits are to the limits respectively on the number of employees, and the annual turnover and balance sheet totals, contained in Article 2(1) of the Annex.

PART 2 – GENERAL

PRESCRIBED DESCRIPTIONS OF ARRANGEMENTS

5(1) Any arrangements which fall within any description specified in a provision of these Regulations listed in paragraph (2) are prescribed for the purposes of Part 7 of the Finance Act 2004 (disclosure of tax avoidance schemes) in relation to income tax, corporation tax and capital gains tax.

5(2) The provisions are–

(a) regulation 6 (description 1: confidentiality in cases involving a promoter);

(b) regulation 7 (description 2: confidentiality in cases not involving a promoter);

(c) regulation 8 (description 3: premium fee);

(d) [omitted by SI 2010/2834, reg. 4;]

(e)   regulation 10 (description 5: standardised tax products);

(f)   regulation 12 (description 6: loss schemes);

(g)   regulation 13 (description 7: leasing arrangements), and

(h)   regulation 18 (description 8: employment income provided through third parties).

5(3)   For the purpose only of determining whether arrangements are prescribed by regulations 6, 7, 8 and 13 of these Regulations, regulation 6 of the Promoters Regulations (persons not to be treated as promoters: legal professional privilege) shall be disregarded.

History – Reg. 5(2)(d) omitted by SI 2010/2834, reg. 4, with effect from 1 January 2011. Former reg. 5(2)(d) read: "regulation 9 (description 4: off market terms);".
In reg. 5(2)(f), the word "and" at the end omitted by SI 2009/2033, reg. 2(2)(a), with effect from 1 September 2009, subject to transitional rules in SI 2009/2033, reg. 3.
In reg. 5(2)(g), the word ", and" substituted for the full stop at the end by SI 2009/2033, reg. 2(2)(b), with effect from 1 September 2009, subject to transitional rules in SI 2009/2033, reg. 3.
Reg. 5(2)(h) substituted by SI 2013/2595, reg. 9, with effect from 4 November 2013 (but the amendments do not have effect for the purposes of FA 2004, s. 308(1) if the relevant date falls before 4 November 2004 or for the purposes of FA 2004, s. 308(3) if the date on which the promoter first becomes aware of any transaction forming part of notifiable arrangements falls before 4 November 2013). Former reg. 5(2)(h) read as follows:
    "(h)   regulation 17A (description 8: pensions).".
Reg. 5(2)(h) inserted by SI 2009/2033, reg. 2(2)(c), with effect from 1 September 2009, subject to transitional rules in SI 2009/2033, reg. 3.
Cross references – SI 2007/785, reg. 16(3): modification of reg. 5.

PART 3 – PRESCRIBED ARRANGEMENTS

DESCRIPTION 1: CONFIDENTIALITY WHERE PROMOTER INVOLVED

Cross references – SI 2007/785, reg. 16(4): modification of Pt. 3, substituting the word "advantage" for "tax advantage", and "an advantage" for "a tax advantage", throughout.

6(1)   Arrangements are prescribed if–

(a)   any element of the arrangements (including the way in which the arrangements are structured) gives rise to the tax advantage expected to be obtained under the arrangements; and

(b)   it might reasonably be expected that a promoter would wish the way in which that element of those arrangements secures, or might secure, a tax advantage to be kept confidential from any other promoter at any time following the material date.

6(2)   Arrangements are prescribed if it might reasonably be expected that a promoter would, but for the requirements of these Regulations, wish to keep the way in which any element of those arrangements (including the way in which the arrangements are structured) that secures, or might secure, the tax advantage confidential from HMRC at any time following the material date, and a reason for doing so is to facilitate repeated or continued use of the same element, or substantially the same element, in the future.

6(2A)   Cases where arrangements will be prescribed under paragraph (2) include, but are not limited to, where–

(a)   a promoter does not provide to the user of the arrangements ("the user"), or prevents or discourages the user from retaining, any promotional materials, data or written professional advice relating to those arrangements; and

(b)   it might reasonably be expected that the reason for doing so is to keep the arrangements confidential from HMRC in order to facilitate repeated or continued use of any element of those arrangements.

6(3)   In a case where–

(a)   by virtue of regulation 6 of the Promoters Regulations (persons not to be treated as promoters: legal professional privilege), no person is to be treated as the promoter in relation to the arrangements; or

(b)   by virtue of section 309(1) of FA 2004 (duty of person dealing with promoter outside United Kingdom), a user of the arrangements has a duty to provide prescribed information,

for paragraph (2) substitute–

"**6(2)**   Arrangements are prescribed if it might reasonably be expected that the user of the arrangements would, but for the requirements of these regulations, wish to keep the way in which any element of those arrangements (including the way in which the arrangements are structured) that secures the tax advantage confidential from HMRC at any time following the material date."

Statutory Instruments

History – In reg. 6(2), the words "if it might reasonably be expected that a promoter would" substituted for the words "if the promoter would" and the words "the way in which any element of those arrangements (including the way in which the arrangements are structured)" substituted for the words "the way in which the element of these arrangements" by SI 2013/2595, reg. 3, with effect from 4 November 2013 (but the amendments do not have effect for the purposes of FA 2004, s. 308(1) if the relevant date falls before 4 November 2004 or for the purposes of FA 2004, s. 308(3) if the date on which the promoter first becomes aware of any transaction forming part of notifiable arrangements falls before 4 November 2013).

Reg. 6(2A) inserted by SI 2013/2595, reg. 4, with effect from 4 November 2013 (but the amendments do not have effect for the purposes of FA 2004, s. 308(1) if the relevant date falls before 4 November 2004 or for the purposes of FA 2004, s. 308(3) if the date on which the promoter first becomes aware of any transaction forming part of notifiable arrangements falls before 4 November 2013).

In reg. 6(3), substituted para. (2) substituted by SI 2013/2595, reg. 5, with effect from 4 November 2013 (but the amendments do not have effect for the purposes of FA 2004, s. 308(1) if the relevant date falls before 4 November 2004 or for the purposes of FA 2004, s. 308(3) if the date on which the promoter first becomes aware of any transaction forming part of notifiable arrangements falls before 4 November 2013). Former substituted para. (2) read as follows:

"**6(2)**   Arrangements are prescribed if the user of the arrangements wishes to keep the way in which the element that secures the tax advantage confidential from HMRC at any time following the material date.".

Reg. 6 substituted by SI 2010/2834, reg. 5, with effect from 1 January 2011.

DESCRIPTION 2: CONFIDENTIALITY WHERE NO PROMOTER INVOLVED

7(1)   Arrangements are prescribed if–

(a)   no person is a promoter in relation to them;

(b)   the intended user of the arrangements is a business which is not a small or medium-sized enterprise;

(c)   any element of the arrangements (including the way in which the arrangements are structured) gives rise to the tax advantage expected to be obtained under the arrangements;

(d)   it might reasonably be expected that a user would, but for the requirements of these Regulations, wish to keep the way in which that element secures the advantage confidential from HMRC at any time following the material date; and

(e)   a reason for the user's wishing to keep the element confidential from HMRC is–

    (i)   to facilitate repeated or continued use of the same element, or substantially the same element, in the future; or

    (ii)   to reduce the risk of HMRC using that information to open an enquiry into any return or account which a person is required by or under any enactment to deliver to HMRC; or

    (iii)   to reduce the risk of HMRC using that information to withhold payment of all or part of an amount claimed separately from a return under–

        (aa)   section 261B of the Taxation of Chargeable Gains Act 1992 (treating trade loss etc as CGT loss); or

        (bb)   Part 4 of the Income Tax Act 2007 (loss relief).

7(2)   Arrangements are also prescribed if–

(a)   paragraphs (1)(a) to (c) are met; and

(b)   if there had been a promoter in relation to the arrangements, it might reasonably have been expected that they would, but for the requirements of these Regulations, wish to have kept the way in which any element of the arrangements (including the way in which the arrangements were structured) that secured the tax advantage confidential from HMRC at any time following the material date, and a reason for doing so would be to facilitate repeated or continued use of the same element, or substantially the same element, in the future.

History – Reg. 7(1) renumbered by SI 2013/2595, reg. 6, with effect from 4 November 2013 (but the amendments do not have effect for the purposes of FA 2004, s. 308(1) if the relevant date falls before 4 November 2004 or for the purposes of FA 2004, s. 308(3) if the date on which the promoter first becomes aware of any transaction forming part of notifiable arrangements falls before 4 November 2013).

In reg. 7(1)(d), the words "it might reasonably be expected that a user would" substituted for the words "the user would" by SI 2013/2595, reg. 7, with effect from 4 November 2013 (but the amendments do not have effect for the purposes of FA 2004, s. 308(1) if the relevant date falls before 4 November 2004 or for the purposes of FA 2004, s. 308(3) if the date on which the promoter first becomes aware of any transaction forming part of notifiable arrangements falls before 4 November 2013).

Reg. 7(1)(d) (as renumbered from reg. 7(d)) substituted by SI 2010/2834, reg. 6(2), with effect from 1 January 2011.

Reg. 7(1)(e) (as renumbered from reg. 7(e)) substituted by SI 2010/2834, reg. 6(3), with effect from 1 January 2011.

Reg. 7(2) inserted by SI 2013/2595, reg. 8, with effect from 4 November 2013 (but the amendments do not have effect for the purposes of FA 2004, s. 308(1) if the relevant date falls before 4 November 2004 or for the purposes of FA 2004, s. 308(3) if the date on which the promoter first becomes aware of any transaction forming part of notifiable arrangements falls before 4 November 2013).

DESCRIPTION 3: PREMIUM FEE

8(1)   Arrangements are prescribed if they are such that it might reasonably be expected that a promoter or a person connected with a promoter of arrangements that are the same as, or substantially similar to, the arrangements in question, would, but for the requirements of these Regulations, be able to obtain a premium fee from a person experienced in receiving services of the type being provided.

But arrangements are not prescribed by this regulation if–

(a)   no person is a promoter in relation to them; and

(b)   the tax advantage which may be obtained under the arrangements is intended to be obtained by an individual or a business which is a small or medium-sized enterprise.

8(2)   For the purposes of paragraph (1), and in relation to any arrangements, a **"premium fee"** is a fee chargeable by virtue of any element of the arrangements (including the way in which they are structured) from which the tax advantage expected to be obtained arises, and which is–

(a)   to a significant extent attributable to that tax advantage, or

(b)   to any extent contingent upon the obtaining of that tax advantage as a matter of law.

History – In reg. 8(1) the word "of" substituted for the words "to disclose information under" by SI 2010/2834, reg. 7(2), with effect from 1 January 2011.
In reg. 8(2)(b) the words "as a matter of law" inserted by SI 2010/2834, reg. 7(3), with effect from 1 January 2011.

9   [Omitted by SI 2010/2834, reg. 8.]

History – Reg. 9 and the heading before it omitted by SI 2010/2834, reg. 8, with effect from 1 January 2011. Former reg. 9 and its heading read as follows:

"DESCRIPTION 4: OFF MARKET TERMS

9(1)   Arrangements are prescribed if–
(a)   the tax advantage expected to be obtained under the arrangements arises, to more than an incidental degree, from the inclusion in those arrangements of one or more financial products;
(b)   a promoter, or a person connected with the promoter, becomes party to one or more of those financial products; and
(c)   the price of the financial product or products differs significantly from that which might reasonably be expected to apply in the open market upon its being, or their being, made available to the other party when compared with a product that is, or products that are, the same as, or substantially similar to, the product or products in question.
9(2)   For the purpose of paragraph (1) a financial product is–
(a)   a loan;
(b)   a contract which–
    (i)   is a derivative contract for the purposes of Schedule 26 to the Finance Act 2002;
    (ii)   would be such a derivative contract if paragraph 4 of that Schedule (contracts which are excluded by virtue of their underlying subject matter) were omitted; or
    (iii)   would be a derivative contract falling within sub-paragraph (i) or (ii) if it were a contract of a company;
(c)   an agreement for the sale and repurchase of securities of the kind described in paragraphs (a) to (c) of subsection (1) of section 730A of ICTA 1988;
(ca)   an arrangement which is a debtor repo, a debtor quasi-repo, a creditor repo or a creditor quasi-repo (within the meanings given by Schedule 13 to the Finance Act 2007);
(d)   a stock lending arrangement within the meaning given by section 263B(1) of the Taxation of Chargeable Gains Act 1992;
(e)   a share; or
(f)   a contract, not being one of the above, which, whether alone or in combination with one or more other contracts (including any of the above), in substance represents the making of a loan, or the advancing or depositing of money, whatever its form and falls to be accounted for on that basis.
This paragraph is subject to the following qualifications.
9(3)   This regulation does not apply if the only financial products involved in the arrangements are assets held within an account which satisfies the conditions in the Individual Savings Account Regulations 1998.
9(4)   For the purposes of this regulation a contract, or a combination of contracts, falls to be accounted for as a loan, or as the advancing or depositing of money, if the person entering into the arrangements–
(a)   is, in accordance with generally accepted accounting practice, required to treat the contract, or the combination of contracts, as a loan, deposit or other financial asset or obligation, or
(b)   would be so required if the person were a company to which the Companies Act 2006 applied.
This is subject to the following qualification.
9(5)   Anything which is a finance lease for the purposes of generally accepted accounting practice does not fall to be accounted for as a loan for the purposes of this regulation.
9(6)   In this regulation **"generally accepted accounting practice"** has the meaning given by section 50 of the Finance Act 2004.".

DESCRIPTION 5: STANDARDISED TAX PRODUCTS

10(1)   Arrangements are prescribed if the arrangements are a standardised tax product.

But arrangements are excepted from being prescribed under this regulation if they are specified in regulation 11.

10(2)   For the purposes of paragraph (1) arrangements are a product if–

(a)   the arrangements have standardised, or substantially standardised, documentation–

    (i)   the purpose of which is to enable the implementation, by the client, of the arrangements; and

    (ii)   the form of which is determined by the promoter, and not tailored, to any material extent, to reflect the circumstances of the client;

(b)   a client must enter into a specific transaction or series of transactions; and

(c)   that transaction or that series of transactions are standardised, or substantially standardised in form.

10(3)   For the purpose of paragraph (1) arrangements are a tax product if it would be reasonable for an informed observer (having studied the arrangements) to conclude that the main purpose of the arrangements was to enable a client to obtain a tax advantage.

10(4)   For the purpose of paragraph (1) arrangements are standardised if a promoter makes the arrangements available for implementation by more than one other person.

Cross references – SI 2007/785, reg. 16(5): modification of reg. 10.

ARRANGEMENTS EXCEPTED FROM DESCRIPTION 5

11(1)   The arrangements specified in this regulation are–

(a)   those described in paragraph (2); and

(b)   those which are of the same, or substantially the same, description as arrangements which were first made available for implementation before 1st August 2006.

11(2)   The arrangements referred to in paragraph (1)(a) are–

(a)   arrangements which consist solely of one or more plant or machinery leases;

(b)   an enterprise investment scheme (Chapter 3 of Part 7 of ICTA 1988 and Schedules 5B and 5BA to TCGA 1992);

(c)   arrangements using a venture capital trust (see section 842AA of, and Schedule 15B to, ICTA 1988 and Schedule 5C to TCGA 1992);

(d)   arrangements qualifying under the corporate venturing scheme (see Schedule 15 to the Finance Act 2000);

(e)   arrangements qualifying for community investment tax relief (see Schedules 16 and 17 to the Finance Act 2002);

(f)   an account which satisfies the conditions in the Individual Savings Account Regulations 1998;

(g)   an approved share incentive plan (see Chapter 6 of Part 7 of, and Schedule 2 to, ITEPA 2003);

(h)   an approved share option scheme (see Chapter 7 of Part 7 of, and Schedule 3 to, ITEPA 2003);

(i)   an approved CSOP scheme (see Chapter 8 of Part 7 of, and Schedule 4 to, ITEPA 2003);

(j)   the grant of one or more qualifying options which meet the requirements of Schedule 5 to ITEPA 2003 (enterprise management incentives)–

    (i)   together only with such other steps as are reasonably necessary in all the circumstances for the purposes of facilitating it, or

    (ii)   which fall to be notified to the Board in accordance with Part 7 of that Schedule;

(k)   a registered pension scheme (see section 150(2) of FA 20044);

(l)   an overseas pension scheme in respect of which tax relief is granted in the United Kingdom under section 615 of ICTA 1988 (exemption from tax for superannuation payments in respect of persons not resident in the United Kingdom or in respect of trades carried on wholly or partly outside the United Kingdom);

(m)   a pension scheme which is a relevant non-UK pension scheme within the meaning given by paragraph 1(5) of Schedule 34 to FA 2004;

(n)   a scheme to which section 731 of ITTOIA 2005 applies (periodical payments of personal injury damages).

History – In reg. 11(2)(a), the words "(see regulation 14)", which appeared at the end, omitted by SI 2010/2834, reg. 9, with effect from 1 January 2011.

DESCRIPTION 6: LOSS SCHEMES

12   Arrangements are prescribed if–

(a)   the promoter expects more than one individual to implement the same, or substantially the same, arrangements; and

(b)   the arrangements are such that an informed observer (having studied them) could reasonably conclude–

    (i)   that the main benefit of those arrangements which could be expected to accrue to some or all of the individuals participating in them is the provision of losses, and

    (ii)   that those individuals would be expected to use those losses to reduce their liability to income tax or capital gains tax.

Cross references – SI 2007/785, reg. 16(6): modification omitting reg. 12.

DESCRIPTION 7: LEASING ARRANGEMENTS

13(1)   Arrangements are prescribed if–

(a)   the arrangements include a plant or machinery lease;

(b)   one of the additional conditions is met (see regulation 15);

(c)   the relevant value condition is met (see regulation 16); and

(d)   the lease is not a short-term lease (see regulation 17).

13(2)   But arrangements are not prescribed by this regulation if–

(a)   no person is a promoter in relation to them; and

(b)   the tax advantage which may be obtained under the arrangements is intended to be obtained by an individual or a business which is a small or medium-sized enterprise.

History – In reg. 13(1)(a), the words "(see regulation 14)", which appeared at the end, omitted by SI 2010/2834, reg. 10, with effect from 1 January 2011.

Cross references – SI 2007/785, reg. 16(6): modification omitting reg. 13.

MEANING OF "PLANT OR MACHINERY LEASE"

14   [Omitted by SI 2010/2834, reg. 11.]

History – Reg. 14 omitted by SI 2010/2834, reg. 11, with effect from 1 January 2011. Former reg. 14 read as follows:
> **"14(1)**   A **"plant or machinery lease"** is any of the following–
>> (a)   any agreement or arrangement to which paragraph (2) applies,
>> (b)   any other agreement or arrangement to the extent that paragraph (3) applies to it,
>> (c)   where plant or machinery is the subject of a sale and finance leaseback, as defined in section 221 of CAA 2001, the finance lease mentioned in subsection (1)(c) of that section;
>
> and in these Regulations "lease", "lessor" and "lessee" are to be construed accordingly.
> **14(2)**   This paragraph applies to an agreement or arrangement–
>> (a)   under which a person (the lessor) grants to another person (the lessee) the right to use plant or machinery for a period, and
>> (b)   which, in accordance with generally accepted accounting practice, falls (or would fall) to be treated as a lease.
> **14(3)**   This paragraph applies to an agreement or arrangement to the extent that–
>> (a)   in accordance with generally accepted accounting practice, it falls (or would fall) to be treated as a lease, and
>> (b)   it meets the conditions in paragraph (4).
> **14(4)**   The conditions are that, for the purposes of generally accepted accounting practice,–
>> (a)   the agreement or arrangement conveys, or falls (or would fall) to be regarded as conveying, the right to use an asset, and
>> (b)   the asset is plant or machinery.
> **14(5)**   In the case of an agreement or arrangement that falls (or would fall) within paragraph (2) or (3) immediately after the commencement of the term of the lease, the condition in paragraph (2)(b) or (3)(a) (as the case may be) is to be taken to be met as respects any time in the pre-commencement period.
> **14(6)**   For the purposes of paragraph (5), the **"pre-commencement period"** is the period that–
>> (a)   begins with the inception of the lease, and
>> (b)   ends with the commencement of the term of the lease.
> **14(7)**   In paragraph (6)(a), **"inception"**, in relation to a plant or machinery lease, means the earliest date on which all of the following conditions are met–
>> (a)   there is a contract in writing for the lease between the lessor and the lessee;
>> (b)   the contract is unconditional, or (if the contract is conditional) the conditions have been met; and
>> (c)   no terms remain to be agreed.".

THE ADDITIONAL CONDITIONS

15(1)   The first additional condition is that the arrangements are designed in such a way that one or more of the plant or machinery leases, comprised in the arrangements, are or would be entered into by–

(a)   one party who has or would have a right or entitlement to claim capital allowances under Part 2 of CAA 2001 (plant and machinery allowances) in respect of the expenditure incurred on the plant or machinery, and

(b)   another party who is not, or would not be, within the charge to corporation tax.

15(2)   A lease satisfies this condition if sub-paragraphs (a) and (b) of paragraph (1) are met, regardless of whether there are or would be (in addition to the parties mentioned in those subparagraphs) other parties to the lease who satisfy neither of those conditions.

15(3)   A party who acts merely as a guarantor under the lease is to be disregarded for the purposes of paragraph (1)(b).

15(4)   The second additional condition is that the arrangements include provision designed to–

(a)   remove from the lessor the whole, or the greater part, of any risk, which would otherwise fall directly or indirectly upon the lessor, of sustaining a loss if payments due under the lease are not made in accordance with its terms, and

(b)   do so by the provision of money or a money debt.

For the purposes of this paragraph **"money"** and **"money debt"** have the same meanings as they have in section 702(6) of ITEPA 2003.

15(5) The third additional condition is that the arrangements are designed to consist of, or include–

(a) a sale and finance leaseback arrangement (within the meaning of section 221 of CAA 2001), or

(b) a lease and finance leaseback (within the meaning of section 228A(2) of CAA 2001).

The third additional condition is subject to the following paragraphs of this regulation.

15(6) In a case falling within paragraph (5)(a) the third additional condition does not apply if the arrangements are designed in such a way that–

(a) the assets leased or to be leased under the sale and finance leaseback are or will be unused and not second-hand at the time when the assets are acquired or created; and

(b) the interval between the acquisition or creation of the asset and the sale of the asset under the sale and finance leaseback arrangement is not more than four months.

15(7) The third additional condition does not apply if plant or machinery which is, or which the promoter expects to become, a fixture, is leased with relevant land, unless the plant or machinery is used for storage or production.

Here **"used for storage or production"** means used for the purposes of–

(a) storing, moving or displaying goods to be sold in the course of a trade;

(b) manufacturing goods or materials;

(c) subjecting goods or materials to a process;

(d) storing goods or materials–

　　(i) which are to be used in the manufacture of other goods or materials;

　　(ii) which are to be subjected to a process in the course of a trade;

　　(iii) which having been subjected in the course of a trade to process, manufactured or produced, have not yet been delivered to a purchaser; or

　　(iv) upon their arrival in the United Kingdom from a place outside it.

15(8) But paragraph (7) does not apply (so that, accordingly, the third additional condition is met) if the arrangements are designed in such a way that–

(a) the qualifying expenditure incurred on the fixture referred to in paragraph (7) amounts or will amount to more than 50% of the aggregate value of the assets subject to the lease, and

(b) the rent payable under the lease is directly or indirectly dependent on the availability of capital allowances under Part 2 of CAA 2001 in respect of expenditure on any plant or machinery comprised in the lease.

15(9) In determining the value of the assets comprised in the lease the following rules apply.

Rule 1

The value of the land subject to the lease is the market value of the lessor's interest.

Rule 2

The value of the plant or machinery subject to the lease is to be determined in the same manner as for the purposes of regulation 16(1).

15(10) In this regulation–

　　"fixture" has the meaning given by section 173(1) of CAA 2001;

　　"relevant land" has the meaning given by section 173(2) of CAA 2001.

History – In reg. 15(5)(b), "228A(2)" substituted for "228F(5)" by SI 2010/2834, reg. 12, with effect from 1 January 2011.

Cross references – SI 2007/785, reg. 16(6): modification omitting reg. 15.

THE RELEVANT VALUE CONDITION

16(1) The relevant value condition is met if–

(a) the lower of the cost to the lessor, or the market value, of any one asset forming part of the plant and machinery leased or to be leased under the arrangements is at least £10,000,000; or

(b) the aggregate of the lower of the costs to the lessor, or the market values, of all of the assets forming part of the plant and machinery leased or to be leased under the arrangements is at least £25,000,000.

16(2) For the purposes of paragraph (1) the market value of plant or machinery leased or to be leased under the arrangements is to be determined on the assumption of a disposal–

(a) by an absolute owner;

(b)   free from all encumbrances; and

(c)   in the open market.

16(3)   **"Absolute owner"** in the application of paragraph (2)(a) to Scotland, means the owner.

Cross references – SI 2007/785, reg. 16(6): modification omitting reg. 16.

SHORT-TERM LEASES

17(1)   For the purposes of regulation 13(1)(d) a lease whose term is 2 years or less is a short-term lease. But a lease is not a short-term lease if any of the following Conditions apply.

In those Conditions "L" is the lessee.

17(2)   Condition A is that the lease contains an option exercisable by L to extend the term so that the total term exceeds 2 years.

17(3)   Condition B is that at the time of the inception of the lease, other arrangements have been entered into which contemplate the extension of the lease to L which, if carried out, would extend the term of the lease so that it exceeds 2 years.

17(4)   Condition C is that–

(a)   a person leases an asset to L under a lease that would, apart from this paragraph, be a short-term lease,

(b)   the inception of that lease is on or after the date on which these Regulations come into force,

(c)   at or about the time of the inception of that lease, arrangements are entered into for the asset to be leased to one or more other persons under one or more other leases, and

(d)   in the aggregate, the term of the lease to L and the terms of the leases to such of those other persons as are connected with L exceed 2 years.

17(5)   In this regulation **"inception"** has the meaning given by section 70YI CAA 2001.

History – Reg. 17(5) inserted by SI 2010/2834, reg. 13, with effect from 1 January 2011.

Cross references – SI 2007/785, reg. 16(6): modification omitting reg. 17.

DESCRIPTION 8: EMPLOYMENT INCOME PROVIDED THROUGH THIRD PARTIES

18(1)   Arrangements are prescribed if–

(a)   Conditions 1 and 2 are met and Condition 3 is not met; or

(b)   Conditions 1, 2 and 3 are met and at least one of Conditions 4 and 5 is met.

18(2)   Condition 1 is met if the arrangements involve at least one of the following–

(a)   a relevant third person taking a relevant step under section 554B;

(b)   any person taking a relevant step under section 554C or 554D; or

(c)   B taking a step under section 554Z18 or 554Z19.

18(3)   Condition 2 is met if the main benefit, or one of the main benefits, of the arrangements is that an amount that would otherwise count as employment income under section 554Z2(1) is reduced or eliminated.

18(4)   Condition 3 is met if, by reason of at least one of sections 554E to 554X or regulations made under section 554Y, Chapter 2 of Part 7A does not apply.

18(5)   Condition 4 is met if the arrangements involve one or more contrived or abnormal steps without which the main benefit in paragraph (3) would not be obtained.

18(6)   Condition 5 is met if the arrangements involve–

(a)   a relevant step being treated as taking place; and

(b)   Chapter 2 of Part 7A applying as a consequence of sub-paragraph (a).

18(7)   In this regulation–

(a)   references to sections or Parts are to those in ITEPA unless otherwise stated;

(b)   **"B"** has the meaning given for Part 7A by sections 554A(1)(a) and 554Z17(7) read together;

(c)   **"contrived or abnormal"** has the same meaning as in section 207 of the Finance Act 2013; and

(d)   **"relevant third person"** has the same meaning as in section 554A(7).

History – Reg. 18 (and the heading before it) substituted for reg. 17A (and the heading before it) by SI 2013/2595, reg. 10(2), with effect from 4 November 2013 (but the amendments do not have effect for the purposes of FA 2004, s. 308(1) if the relevant date falls before 4 November 2004 or for the purposes of FA 2004, s. 308(3) if the date on which the promoter first becomes aware of any transaction forming part of notifiable arrangements falls before 4 November 2013). Former reg. 17A (and the heading before it) read as follows:

Statutory Instruments

"DESCRIPTION 8: PENSIONS

17A　Arrangements are prescribed if—

(a)　they involve the accrual or expected accrual of benefits in a pension scheme (within the meaning of section 150 of the Finance Act 2004) to or in respect of a person; and

(b)　the main benefit of those arrangements is that—

　　(i)　the person would not be subject to the special annual allowance charge provided under Schedule 35 to the Finance Act 2009; or

　　(ii)　the person incurs the special annual allowance charge but at a lesser amount than would have been incurred if the arrangements had not been entered into.".

Former reg. 17A inserted by SI 2009/2033, reg. 2(3), with effect from 1 September 2009, subject to transitional rules in SI 2009/2033, reg. 3.

PART 4 – FURTHER PROVISIONS

History – Pt. 4 repealed by SI 2013/2595, reg. 10(1), with effect from 4 November 2013 (but the amendments do not have effect for the purposes of FA 2004, s. 308(1) if the relevant date falls before 4 November 2004 or for the purposes of FA 2004, s. 308(3) if the date on which the promoter first becomes aware of any transaction forming part of notifiable arrangements falls before 4 November 2013). Former Pt. 4 revoked SI 2004/1863 and SI 2004/2429.

PARTNERSHIPS (RESTRICTIONS ON CONTRIBUTIONS TO A TRADE) REGULATIONS 2006

(SI 2006/1639, as amended by ITA 2007)

Made on 21 June 2006 by the Commissioners for Her Majesty's Revenue and Customs in exercise of the powers conferred by s. 122A(2)–(4) of the Finance Act 2004 [ITA 2007, s. 802]. Operative from 22 June 2006.

CITATION, COMMENCEMENT AND EFFECT

1(1)   These Regulations may be cited as the Partnerships (Restrictions on Contributions to a Trade) Regulations 2006 and shall come into force on the day after the day on which they are made.

1(2)   These Regulations shall have effect from 20th December 2005.

INTERPRETATION

2   In these Regulations–

"**ITA 2007**" means the Income Tax Act 2007;

"**ITTOIA**" means the Income Tax (Trading and Other Income) Act 2005;

"**relevant individual**" means–

(a)   a limited partner (within the meaning given by section 106 of ITA 2007),

(b)   a member of a limited liability partnership, and

(c)   a non-active partner (within the meaning given by section 112 of ITA 2007),

where the partnership carries on a trade in which the individual makes a film-related loss (as defined in section 800(2) of ITA 2007) for which the individual makes a claim as mentioned in section 802(1) of that Act; and

"**profit-sharing arrangements**" has the meaning in section 850(6) of ITTOIA.

History – In reg. 2, the definition of "ITA 2007" substituted by ITA 2007, s. 1031 and Sch. 2, para. 148(3)(a), with effect, for income tax purposes, from 6 April 2007, and, for corporation tax purposes, for accounting periods ending after 5 April 2007. In reg. 2, the definition of "relevant individual" substituted by ITA 2007, s. 1031 and Sch. 2, para. 148(3)(b), with effect, for income tax purposes, from 6 April 2007, and, for corporation tax purposes, for accounting periods ending after 5 April 2007.

SCOPE OF THESE REGULATIONS

3   These Regulations apply where (and if there are successive events, in each case where)–

(a)   a relevant individual disposes of his right to profits arising from a firm's trade (within the meaning in section 799 of ITA 2007),

(b)   the result of the disposal is that his share of the profits (or any part of the profits) arising from the trade is reduced or extinguished, or his share of the losses (or any part of the losses) arising from the trade is increased,

(c)   another person ("the new partner") becomes a partner in the firm, and

(d)   the new partner contributes or agrees to contribute an amount as capital to the partnership.

History – In reg. 3(a), the words "section 799 of ITA 2007" substituted for the words "section 120 of the Finance act 2004" by ITA 2007, s. 1031 and Sch. 2, para. 148(4), with effect, for income tax purposes, from 6 April 2007, and, for corporation tax purposes, for accounting periods ending after 5 April 2007.

EXCLUSION WHEN COMPUTING THE AMOUNT OF THE RELEVANT INDIVIDUAL'S CONTRIBUTION TO THE TRADE

4   Where these Regulations apply–

(a)   apportion the amount referred to in regulation 3(d) between the partners in the firm immediately before the new partner becomes a partner, according to their profit-sharing arrangements at that time,

(b)   the amount apportioned to the relevant individual under paragraph (a) shall be excluded when computing the amount of that individual's capital contribution (but not so as to produce a contribution less than nil), at the time of whichever of the events referred to in regulation 3 is the latest to occur, for the purposes of section 797(2)(b) of ITA 2007, and

(c)   accordingly, recalculate that individual's capital contribution, as at the time of that event, for the purposes of determining–

(i)   whether that event is an exit event within the meaning of section 797(2)(b) of ITA 2007, and

(ii)   the amount of income treated as received in accordance with section 797(5) of that Act.

History – In reg. 4, the words "capital contribution" substituted for the words "contribution to the trade" (twice), the words "section 797(2)(b) of ITA 2007" substituted for the words "section 119(2)(b) or (c) of the Finance Act 2004" (twice) and (c)(ii) substituted by ITA 2007, s. 1031 and Sch. 2, para. 148(4), with effect, for income tax purposes, from 6 April 2007, and, for corporation tax purposes, for accounting periods ending after 5 April 2007.

REGISTERED PENSION SCHEMES (EXTENSION OF MIGRANT MEMBER RELIEF) REGULATIONS 2006

(SI 2006/1957)

Made on 20 July 2006 by the Commissioners for Her Majesty's Revenue and Customs in exercise of the powers conferred upon them by para. 4(2) and (3) of Sch. 33 to the Finance Act 2004. Operative from 11 August 2006.

CITATION, COMMENCEMENT, EFFECT AND INTERPRETATION

1(1)   These Regulations may be cited as the Registered Pension Schemes (Extension of Migrant Member Relief) Regulations 2006, shall come into force on 11th August 2006 and shall have effect in relation to all times on or after 6th April 2006.

1(2)   In these Regulations–

"**the Act**" means the Finance Act 2004;

"**block transfer**" has the same meaning as it has in paragraph 22(6) of Schedule 36;

"**the receiving scheme**" means the scheme referred to in the relevant provisions;

"**the relevant provisions**" means paragraphs (a), (b) and (c) of paragraph 4(1) of Schedule 33 (meaning of relevant migrant member); and

"**Schedule**" means a Schedule to the Act.

REFERENCES IN RELEVANT PROVISIONS TREATED AS INCLUDING REFERENCES TO OTHER SCHEMES

2(1)   Paragraphs (2) to (4) prescribe circumstances in which references in the relevant provisions to the pension scheme are to be read as including other schemes.

2(2)   The circumstance prescribed by this paragraph is that there has been a block transfer to the receiving scheme on or after 6th April 2006.

In the circumstance prescribed by this paragraph, references in the relevant provisions to the pension scheme are to either the receiving scheme or to the scheme from which the block transfer takes place.

2(3)   The circumstance prescribed by this paragraph is that there has been a series of transfers, all of which were block transfers from one overseas pension scheme to another and the last of which was a transfer to the receiving scheme occurring on or after 6th April 2006.

In the circumstance prescribed by this paragraph, references in the relevant provisions to the pension scheme are to either the receiving scheme or to any of the overseas pension schemes from which a block transfer, which forms part of the series, has taken place.

2(4)   The circumstance prescribed by this paragraph is that–

(a)   under the rules of a pension scheme ("the original scheme") on and after a specified date it is no longer possible for further accruals to occur;

(b)   a further pension scheme ("the new scheme") has been established to provide benefits in respect of rights accruing to members of the original scheme after the specified date;

(c)   more than one member of the original scheme has become a member of the new scheme in relation to all rights accruing after the specified date;

(d)   rights do not accrue to any member of the new scheme after the specified date under the original scheme.

In the circumstance prescribed by this paragraph references in the relevant provisions to the pension scheme are to either the new scheme or the original scheme.

PENSIONS SCHEMES (TAXABLE PROPERTY PROVISIONS) REGULATIONS 2006

(SI 2006/1958 as amended by SI 2013/605 and SI 2013/1810)

Made on 20 July 2006 by the Treasury, in exercise of the powers conferred upon them by s. 273ZA of, and para. 33(4), 34(4), 36 and 37 of Sch. 29A to, the Finance Act 2004. Operative from 11 August 2006.

CITATION, COMMENCEMENT AND EFFECT

1(1) These Regulations may be cited as the Pensions Schemes (Taxable Property Provisions) Regulations 2006 and shall come into force on 11th August 2006.

1(2) These Regulations shall have effect from 6th April 2006.

INTERPRETATION

2 In these Regulations–

"**taxable property**" has the meaning in Schedule 29A;

"**taxable property provisions**" has the meaning in paragraph 1(3) of that Schedule; and any reference (without more) to a numbered section or Schedule is a reference to that section of, or Schedule to, the Finance Act 2004.

PROVISIONS SUPPLEMENTING SCHEDULE 29A

3 Paragraphs 33 and 34 of Schedule 29A shall apply to land outside the United Kingdom as if–

(a) "chargeable interest" (in section 48(1) of the Finance Act 2003(b)) applied to such land, and

(b) in relation to such land, the meaning of "**lease**" in paragraphs 1 and 19 of Schedule 17A to the Finance Act 2003(c), included any interest corresponding to a lease,

and "rent" and "tenant" shall be construed accordingly.

4 Paragraph 32 of Schedule 29A (and the remainder of the taxable property provisions excepting paragraph 34 of that Schedule) shall apply to–

(a) a licence to use or occupy residential property (for a consideration which is wholly or partly rent), and

(b) the right to use, or participate in arrangements relating to the use of, taxable property or a description of taxable property to which the property in question belongs (for a consideration which is wholly or partly rent),

as if each payment of rent represented the grant, to the pension scheme or other person who acquired the interest in taxable property, of a lease of the taxable property for the period for which the rent is paid, and in consideration of the rent so paid.

5 Paragraph 33 of Schedule 29A shall apply to–

(a) tangible moveable property,

(b) a licence to use or occupy residential property (for a consideration wholly or partly other than rent), and

(c) the right to use, or participate in arrangements relating to the use of, taxable property or a description of taxable property to which the property in question belongs (for a consideration wholly or partly other than rent),

as they apply to a chargeable interest in property.

6 Paragraph 34 of Schedule 29A shall apply to tangible moveable property.

APPLICATION OF PARAGRAPHS 3 AND 4 OF SCHEDULE 17A TO THE FINANCE ACT 2003

7(1) The following provisions–

(a) paragraph 3(1) and (2) of Schedule 17A to the Finance Act 2003 (leases that continue after a fixed term), and

(b) paragraph 4(1), (2) and (5) of that Schedule (treatment of leases for indefinite term), apply for the purposes of paragraph 34(2) of Schedule 29A, for determining the amount of rent payable, with the following modifications.

7(2) Each extension of the original fixed term by paragraph 3(2) or 4(1) of Schedule 17A shall be treated as the grant of a new lease for the period of the extension.

7(3) Accordingly, an investment-regulated pension scheme is to be treated as making an unauthorised payment within section 174A(1)(a) to a member of the scheme, on the occasion of each such extension.

APPLICATION OF PARAGRAPH 8 OF SCHEDULE 17A TO THE FINANCE ACT 2003

8(1) Paragraph 8(1) and (2) of Schedule 17A to the Finance Act 2003 (adjustment where rent ceases to be uncertain) shall apply for the purposes of paragraph 34(2) of Schedule 29A, for determining the amount of rent payable, with the following modifications.

8(2) If the result of the recalculation as at the date referred to in paragraph 8(1)(a) or (b) of Schedule 17A is that the rent paid or payable in respect of the first five years of the term is greater than the rent originally calculated, an investment-regulated pension scheme is to be treated as making an unauthorised payment within section 174A(1) to a member of the scheme, based on the difference between the two calculations.

VARIATION OF A LEASE TO GIVE RISE TO AN ADDITIONAL UNAUTHORISED PAYMENT

9(1) An investment-regulated pension scheme is to be treated as making an unauthorised payment within section 174A(1) to a member of the pension scheme, if–

(a)   a lease of taxable property is varied (whether or not in pursuance of a provision in the lease) so as to increase the amount of the rent; and

(b)   the increase falls to be regarded as abnormal (within the meaning of paragraph 15 of Schedule 17A to the Finance Act 2003).

The variation shall be treated for the purposes of the taxable property provisions as if it were the grant of a lease in consideration of the additional rent made payable by the variation.

SCHEME CHARGEABLE PAYMENT ON INCOME AND GAINS FROM NON-U.K. TAXABLE PROPERTY

10(1) This regulation applies to a registered pension scheme which–

(a)   is for the time being established in a country or territory outside the United Kingdom, and

(b)   falls within the circumstances mentioned in section 273ZA(1)(a) and (c).

10(2) Liability to pay the scheme sanction charge so far as relating to a scheme chargeable payment treated as made by the pension scheme–

(a)   under section 185A (income from taxable property) by virtue of the pension scheme holding an interest in the property, or

(b)   under section 185F (gains from taxable property) by virtue of a gain treated as accruing to the pension scheme in respect of an interest in the property,

("the property enjoyment scheme sanction charge") shall be determined under this regulation and not under section 239 (see section 239(6)(c)).

10(3) Any member of the pension scheme resident in the United Kingdom, for the purposes of whose arrangement the interest in taxable property referred to in section 273ZA(1)(a) is held, is liable to pay the property enjoyment scheme sanction charge, subject to paragraphs (4) and (5).

10(4) Where the interest in taxable property is held by the pension scheme for the purposes of more than one arrangement, the property enjoyment scheme sanction charge shall be apportioned between the members whose arrangements they are, on a just and reasonable basis.

10(5) Where a member is temporarily non-resident at a time when a scheme chargeable payment would, but for this regulation, be treated as made by virtue of section 185F, that member shall be liable to the property enjoyment scheme sanction charge so far as relating to that scheme chargeable payment, as if that scheme chargeable payment were treated as made in the period of return.

10(6) [Omitted by SI 2013/1810, reg. 3(2)(c).]

10(7) Where paragraph (5) applies, nothing in any enactment imposing any limit on the time within which an assessment to tax may be made shall prevent an assessment to the property enjoyment scheme sanction charge from being made on the member at any time before the end of two years after the 31st January next following the tax year in which the period of return falls.

Statutory Instruments

10(8)   In this regulation–

(a)   **"period of return"** has the meaning given in paragraph 115 of Schedule 45 to the Finance Act 2013(statutory residence test: anti-avoidance),

(b)   **"temporarily non-resident"** has the meaning given in paragraph 110 of that Schedule.

History – In reg. 10(3), the words "subject to paragraphs (4) and (5)" substituted for the words "subject to paragraphs (4) to (6)" by SI 2013/1810, reg. 3(2)(a), with effect in relation to a scheme chargeable payment treated as made in the tax year 2013–14 and any subsequent tax year.

In reg. 10(3), the words "or ordinarily resident" omitted by SI 2013/605, reg. 5, with effect in relation to a scheme chargeable payment treated as made in the tax year 2013–14 or any subsequent tax years.

Reg. 10(5) substituted by SI 2013/1810, reg. 3(2)(b), with effect in relation to a scheme chargeable payment treated as made in the tax year 2013–14 and any subsequent tax year. Former reg. 10(5) read as follows:

> **"10(5)**   A member shall be liable to the property enjoyment scheme sanction charge (so far as relating to a scheme chargeable payment treated as made under section 185F) as if any scheme chargeable payment mentioned in Condition 2 were treated as made in the renewed residence period, if the following conditions apply, subject to paragraph (6).
>
> *Condition 1*
>
> The member has, for four out of the seven tax years immediately preceding the tax year in which the time of departure falls (see Condition 4), been resident in the United Kingdom during any part of the year, or ordinarily resident in the United Kingdom during the year ("the original residence period").
>
> *Condition 2*
>
> A scheme chargeable payment would otherwise be treated as made under section 185F, in any part of a tax year or tax year–
>
> (a)   later than the time of departure, and
> (b)   during which the member is resident outside the United Kingdom, and ordinarily resident outside the United Kingdom ("the non-resident period").
>
> *Condition 3*
>
> There is a later part of a tax year, or tax year, during which he becomes resident in the United Kingdom or ordinarily resident in the United Kingdom ("the renewed residence period").
>
> *Condition 4*
>
> There are fewer than five tax years falling between–
>
> (a)   the time after the original residence period, when he ceased to be resident or ordinarily resident in the United Kingdom ("the time of departure"), and
> (b)   the renewed residence period.".

Reg. 10(6) omitted by SI 2013/1810, reg. 3(2)(c), with effect in relation to a scheme chargeable payment treated as made in the tax year 2013–14 and any subsequent tax year. Former reg. 10(6) read as follows:

> **"10(6)**   Where–
>
> (a)   the member is resident or ordinarily resident in the United Kingdom during only part of a tax year, and for a later part of that tax year is not so resident or ordinarily resident, and
> (b)   a gain or loss is treated as accruing to the pension scheme under section 185F(3) at a time during that year when the member is so resident or ordinarily resident,
>
> any such gain (in so far as it exceeds any such loss) shall be treated as giving rise to a separate scheme chargeable payment under section 185F made by the scheme as at that time, and liability to the scheme sanction charge on that payment shall be determined under paragraph (3), not (5).".

In reg. 10(7), the words "period of return" substituted for the words "renewed residence period" by SI 2013/1810, reg. 3(2)(d), with effect in relation to a scheme chargeable payment treated as made in the tax year 2013–14 and any subsequent tax year.

Reg. 10(8) inserted by SI 2013/1810, reg. 3(2)(e), with effect in relation to a scheme chargeable payment treated as made in the tax year 2013–14 and any subsequent tax year.

INVESTMENT-REGULATED PENSION SCHEMES (EXCEPTION OF TANGIBLE MOVEABLE PROPERTY) ORDER 2006

(SI 2006/1959)

Made on 20 July 2006 by the Treasury, in exercise of the powers conferred upon them by para. 11 of Sch. 29A to the Finance Act 2004. Operative from 11 August 2006.

CITATION, COMMENCEMENT, EFFECT AND INTERPRETATION

1(1) This Order may be cited as the Investment-regulated Pension Schemes (Exception of Tangible Moveable Property) Order 2006 and shall come into force on 11th August 2006.

1(2) This Order has effect from 6th April 2006.

1(3) In these Regulations–

"**market value**" is to be determined in accordance with section 272 of the Taxation of Chargeable Gains Act 1992; and

"**connected persons**" (and cognate expressions) have the meaning in section 839 of the Income and Corporation Taxes Act 1988.

EXCLUSIONS FROM TANGIBLE MOVEABLE PROPERTY

2 The following property shall not be regarded as taxable property for the purposes of the taxable property provisions (within the meaning in paragraph 1(3) of Schedule 29A to the Finance Act 2004)–

(a)   gold bullion (that is, gold of a purity not less than 995 thousandths, which is in the form of a bar, or of a wafer, of a weight accepted by the bullion markets);

(b)   any item of tangible moveable property (whose market value does not exceed £6,000)–

    (i)   held by a vehicle (within the meaning in paragraph 20(2) of Schedule 29A to the Finance Act 2004) solely for the purposes of the administration or management of the vehicle;

    (ii)   in which the relevant investment-regulated pension scheme does not hold an interest directly; and

    (iii)   where a member of the pension scheme or a person connected with such a member does not occupy or use, or have any right to occupy or use, the property.

Statutory Instruments

EUROPEAN CONVENTION ON CINEMATOGRAPHIC CO-PRODUCTION ORDER 2006

(SI 2006/2656)

Made on 10 October 2006 by Her Majesty, in exercise of the powers conferred upon Her by paragraph 4(5) of Schedule 1 to the Films Act 1985. Operative from 11 October 2006.

CITATION, COMMENCEMENT AND INTERPRETATION

1(1) This Order may be cited as the European Convention on Cinematographic Co-production Order 2006 and shall come into force on 11th October 2006.

1(2) In this Order **"Convention"** means the European Convention on Cinematographic Co-production.

1(3) For the purposes of this Order a State is a Contracting Party to the Convention if–

(a)   under Article 16 of that Convention, that State has ratified, accepted or approved that Convention, or

(b)   under Article 18 of that Convention, that State has acceded to it,

and the Convention is in force in relation to that State.

TREATMENT AS A BRITISH FILM

2 A film shall be treated as a British film for the purposes of Schedule 1 to the Films Act 1985 if it is made in accordance with the terms of the Convention and if–

(a)   where there are two co-producers, one is established in the United Kingdom and the other is established in a State which is a Contracting Party to the Convention, or

(b)   where there are three or more co-producers, one is established in the United Kingdom and at least two others are established in different States each of which is a Contracting Party to the Convention.

REVOCATION

3 The Orders specified in the Schedule are revoked.

SCHEDULE

Article 3

REVOCATIONS

1 The European Convention on Cinematographic Co-production Order 1994 (No.1065).

2 The European Convention on Cinematographic Co-production (Amendment) Order 1994 (No. 1904).

3 The European Convention on Cinematographic Co-production (Amendment) (No. 2) Order 1994 (No. 3218).

4 The European Convention on Cinematographic Co-production (Amendment) Order 1995 (No. 1298).

5 The European Convention on Cinematographic Co-production (Amendment) (No. 2) Order 1995 (No. 1963).

6 The European Convention on Cinematographic Co-production (Amendment) (No. 3) Order 1995 (No. 2730).

7 The European Convention on Cinematographic Co-production (Amendment) Order 1996 (No. 2600).

8 The European Convention on Cinematographic Co-production (Amendment) (No. 2) Order 1996 (No. 3169).

9 The European Convention on Cinematographic Co-production (Amendment) Order 1997 (No. 870).

10 The European Convention on Cinematographic Co-production (Amendment) (No. 2) Order 1997 (No. 1319).

11   The European Convention on Cinematographic Co-production (Amendment) (No. 3) Order 1997 (No. 1743).

12   The European Convention on Cinematographic Co-production (Amendment) Order 1999 (No. 3131).

13   The European Convention on Cinematographic Co-production (Amendment) Order 2000 (No. 1555).

14   The European Convention on Cinematographic Co-production (Amendment) Order 2001 (No. 411).

15   The European Convention on Cinematographic Co-production (Amendment) (No. 2) Order 2001 (No. 3931).

16   The European Convention on Cinematographic Co-production (Amendment) Order 2002 (No. 1398).

17   The European Convention on Cinematographic Co-production (Amendment) (No. 2) Order 2002 (No. 2635).

18   The European Convention on Cinematographic Co-production (Amendment) Order 2003 (No. 828).

19   The European Convention on Cinematographic Co-production (Amendment) (No. 2) Order 2003 (No. 2630).

20   The European Convention on Cinematographic Co-production (Amendment) Order 2004 (No. 724).

21   The European Convention on Cinematographic Co-production (Amendment) (No. 2) Order 2004 (No. 2031).

22   The European Convention on Cinematographic Co-production (Amendment) (No. 3) Order 2004 (No. 3043)

23   The European Convention on Cinematographic Co-production (Amendment) Order 2005 (No. 247).

24   The European Convention on Cinematographic Co-production (Amendment) (No. 2) Order 2005 (No. 1464).

REAL ESTATE INVESTMENT TRUSTS (BREACH OF CONDITIONS) REGULATIONS 2006

(SI 2006/2864 as amended by SI 2007/3540 and CTA 2010)

Made on 1 November 2006 by the Treasury in exercise of the powers conferred by s. 114 to 116, 122, 129(2) (a) and (b), 134(1) and 144 of the Finance Act 2006. Operative from 1 January 2007.

CITATION AND COMMENCEMENT AND INTERPRETATION

1(1) These Regulations may be cited as the Real Estate Investment Trust (Breach of Conditions) Regulations 2006 and shall come into force on 1st January 2007.

1(1A) In these Regulations–

(a)   a reference to Part 4 is a reference to Part 4 of the Finance Act 2006,

(b)   a reference to a section (without more) is a reference to that section of the Finance Act 2006, and

(c)   a reference to a paragraph of Schedule 17 is a reference to that paragraph of Schedule 17 to the Finance Act 2006.

1(2) In these Regulations–

"**the Commissioners**" means the Commissioners for Her Majesty's Revenue and Customs;

"**the holder of excessive rights**" means a person falling within section 114(1)(a), (b) or (c) being–

(a)   a company as defined in section 832(1) of the Income and Corporation Taxes Act 1988; or

(b)   an entity which is treated as a body corporate for tax purposes–

     (i)   in accordance with the law of a territory outside the United Kingdom with which arrangements have been entered into to provide relief from double taxation; or

     (ii)   in accordance with an international agreement containing such arrangements;

where those arrangements have effect by virtue of an Order in Council under section 788 of the Income and Corporation Taxes Act 1988;

"**JV Regulations**" means the Real Estate Investment Trusts (Joint Ventures) Regulations 2006;

"**JVG Regulations**" means the Real Estate Investment Trusts (Joint Venture Groups) Regulations 2007;

"**MCT**" means–

(a)   in relation to a company to which Part 4 applies, the rate of tax applicable to the company under section 119(2) (rate of corporation tax: profits of C (residual)); and

(b)   in relation to a group to which Part 4 applies, the rate of tax applicable to the members of the group under section 119(2) as modified by virtue of paragraph 17 of Schedule 17;

"**specified accounting period**" means the accounting period referred to in regulation 7(1)(a);

"**UK property rental business**" means the property rental business of a UK resident company or the property rental business in the United Kingdom of a company which is not a UK resident company; and

"**UK resident company**" means a company which is resident in the United Kingdom, and is not resident in another place in accordance with the law of that place relating to taxation.

1(3) The following provisions of these Regulations, other than regulations 10 and 12, apply to groups to which Part 4 applies as they apply to companies to which that Part applies, and for that purpose references in the following regulations to the company are to the principal company save that the references in regulations 6, 7, 7A, 7B, 8 and 9 are to be read as references to the group.

History – Reg. 1(1A) inserted by SI 2007/3540, reg. 3(2) with effect from 7 January 2008, in relation to accounting periods beginning on or after 1 January 2007.

In reg. 1(2) in the definition of "MCT" the word "and" omitted at the end of para. (b), and the words "a reference (without more) to a numbered provision of the Finance Act 2006, is a reference to the provision bearing that number." omitted by SI 2007/3540, reg. 3(3) with effect from 7 January 2008, in relation to accounting periods beginning on or after 1 January 2007.

In reg. 1(2) definitions of "JV Regulations", "JVG Regulations", "specified accounting period", "UK property rental business" and "UK resident company" inserted by SI 2007/3540, reg. 3(3) with effect from 7 January 2008, in relation to accounting periods beginning on or after 1 January 2007.

In reg. 1(3) the reference to "7, 7A, 7B," inserted by SI 2007/3540, reg. 3(4) with effect from 7 January 2008, in relation to accounting periods beginning on or after 1 January 2007.

BREACH OF CONDITIONS IN SECTION 106

Breach of Conditions for Company – Take-Overs and Demergers

2   [Repealed by CTA 2010, s. 1181 and Sch. 3, Pt. 1.]

History – Reg. 2 repealed by CTA 2010, s. 1181 and Sch. 3, Pt. 1, with effect for corporation tax purposes for accounting periods ending on or after 1 April 2010, and for income tax and capital gains tax purposes for the tax year 2010–11 and subsequent tax years. Former reg. 2 read as follows:

"**2(1)**   This regulation applies if a company to which Part 4 applies breaches Conditions 3 and 4 in section 106 in consequence of its becoming a member of a group (or another group) to which that Part applies.

2(2)   Part 4 shall continue to apply despite the breach.".

Notes – Reg. 2 rewritten as follows:
Reg. 2(1): CTA 2010, s. 562(1), (2).
Reg. 2(2): CTA 2010, s. 562(2).

Breach of Condition for Company – Actions of Others

3   [Repealed by CTA 2010, s. 1181 and Sch. 3, Pt. 1.]

History – Reg. 3 repealed by CTA 2010, s. 1181 and Sch. 3, Pt. 1, with effect for corporation tax purposes for accounting periods ending on or after 1 April 2010, and for income tax and capital gains tax purposes for the tax year 2010–11 and subsequent tax years. Former reg. 3 read as follows:

"**3(1)**   This regulation applies if a company to which Part 4 applies breaches Condition 4 in section 106 where the breach is caused by someone other than the company.

3(2)   Part 4 shall continue to apply to the company, despite the breach, provided that the breach is remedied not later than the end of the accounting period following that in which it began.

3(3)   But if the breach is not remedied before the end of the accounting period following that in which it began, Part 4 shall be taken to have ceased to apply to the company at the end of the accounting period in which the breach began.".

Notes – Reg. 3 rewritten as follows:
Reg. 3(1): CTA 2010, s. 562(1), (3).
Reg. 3(2): CTA 2010, s. 562(3).
Reg. 3(3): CTA 2010, s. 562(4).

Breach of Condition for Company – Other

4   [Repealed by CTA 2010, s. 1181 and Sch. 3, Pt. 1.]

History – Reg. 4 repealed by CTA 2010, s. 1181 and Sch. 3, Pt. 1, with effect for corporation tax purposes for accounting periods ending on or after 1 April 2010, and for income tax and capital gains tax purposes for the tax year 2010–11 and subsequent tax years. Former reg. 4 read as follows:

"**4(1)**   This regulation applies if a company to which Part 4 applies breaches Condition 3 or 4 in section 106 in respect of an accounting period where the breach arises in circumstances other than those specified in regulations 2 and 3.

4(2)   Part 4 shall be taken to have ceased to apply to the company at the end of the previous accounting period.".

Notes – Reg. 4 rewritten as follows:
Reg. 4(1): CTA 2010, s. 562(1), (5).
Reg. 4(2): CTA 2010, s. 562(5).

BREACH OF CONDITIONS IN SECTION 107

Breach of Requirements as to Properties

5   [Repealed by CTA 2010, s. 1181 and Sch. 3, Pt. 1.]

History – Reg. 5 repealed by CTA 2010, s. 1181 and Sch. 3, Pt. 1, with effect for corporation tax purposes for accounting periods ending on or after 1 April 2010, and for income tax and capital gains tax purposes for the tax year 2010–11 and subsequent tax years. Former reg. 5 read as follows:

"**5(1)**   This regulation applies in relation to breaches of Condition 1 (minimum number of properties) or Condition 2 (individual property not to represent more than 40 per cent of the total value of the property value business) in section 107.

5(2)   For the purposes of section 129(2)(a) (number of breaches during a specified period which are to be disregarded)–

(a)   the number of occasions on which the company can rely on this regulation in respect of a breach of either Condition 1 or Condition 2 in an accounting period is two; and

(b)   the specified period is the ten year period beginning on the day on which the company first failed to satisfy one of those condition and ending immediately before the tenth anniversary of that day.

5(3)   Any breach of Condition 2 which is a necessary consequence of a contemporaneous breach of Condition 1 shall be disregarded in computing the number of breaches of–

(a)   Condition 2; and

(b)   the total number of breaches;

during any ten year period.

But the breach of Condition 1 giving rise to the breach of Condition 2 shall not be so disregarded.
This is subject to the following qualifications.

5(4)   If a breach of Condition 1 or 2 lasts for more than one, but not more than two, accounting periods, it constitutes only one breach for the purposes of paragraph (2).

5(5)   If in any three consecutive accounting periods a company fails to satisfy at least one of Conditions 1 and 2 the breach is not to be considered as minor and the company may not rely upon this regulation for the purposes of section 129(2)(a).".

Notes – Reg. 5 rewritten as follows:
Reg. 5(1): CTA 2010, s. 563(1).
Reg. 5(2): CTA 2010, s. 563(1), (2), 575(2), (3).
Reg. 5(3): CTA 2010, s. 575(4).
Reg. 5(4): CTA 2010, s. 575(4).
Reg. 5(5): CTA 2010, s. 575(1).

Breach of Distribution Condition

6 [Repealed by CTA 2010, s. 1181 and Sch. 3, Pt. 1.]

History – Reg. 6 repealed by CTA 2010, s. 1181 and Sch. 3, Pt. 1, with effect for corporation tax purposes for accounting periods ending on or after 1 April 2010, and for income tax and capital gains tax purposes for the tax year 2010–11 and subsequent tax years. Former reg. 6 read as follows:

> "**6(1)** This regulation applies to a company which has not satisfied (to the extent required) Condition 4 in section 107 for an accounting period.
>
> **6(2)** Part 4 shall continue to apply to the company despite the failure.
> But this is subject to the rest of this regulation.
>
> **6(3)** Where a company has not satisfied Condition 4 in section 107 the amount computed in accordance with paragraph (4) shall be charged to corporation tax as if it were income of C (residual) chargeable to tax under Case VI of Schedule D at MCT.
>
> **6(4)** The amount is—
>
> $$P - D$$
>
> Here—
> P is 90 per cent of the profits of the property rental business arising in the accounting period referred to in section 107(8); and
>
> D is the gross amount of profits of the property rental business distributed in respect of the accounting period on or before the date set out in section 107(8)(b) or on any later date that the Commissioners may specify.
>
> **6(5)** No tax shall be charged if—
> (a) the company declares and pays an additional dividend within 3 months following the date on which the profits of the property rental business as calculated in accordance with section 120 can no longer be altered; and
> (b) the payment of the additional dividend results in the total amount of profits distributed in respect of the accounting period being 90 per cent or more of the profits of the property rental business in that accounting period.
>
> **6(6)** Any additional dividend declared and paid by the company which is taken into account under this regulation must be disregarded for the purposes of determining whether or not the company has met Condition 4 in section 107 in respect of another accounting period.
>
> **6(7)** Profits relating to a different accounting period shall not be taken into account when calculating whether the condition in section 107(8) has been met.
>
> **6(8)** No loss, deficit, expense or allowance may be set off against the amount charged to tax by paragraph (3).".

Notes – Reg. 6 rewritten as follows:
Reg. 6(1): CTA 2010, s. 564(1).
Reg. 6(2): CTA 2010, s. 564(2).
Reg. 6(3): CTA 2010, s. 564(2), (3), (4).
Reg. 6(4): CTA 2010, s. 565(1), (2), (3).
Reg. 6(5): CTA 2010, s. 564(5), (6).
Reg. 6(6): CTA 2010, s. 564(7).
Reg. 6(7): CTA 2010, s. 564(8).
Reg. 6(8): CTA 2010, s. 564(9).

INITIAL BREACH OF CONDITION 2 IN SECTION 108(3)

7 [Repealed by CTA 2010, s. 1181 and Sch. 3, Pt. 1.]

History – Reg. 7 repealed by CTA 2010, s. 1181 and Sch. 3, Pt. 1, with effect for corporation tax purposes for accounting periods ending on or after 1 April 2010, and for income tax and capital gains tax purposes for the tax year 2010–11 and subsequent tax years. Former reg. 7 read as follows:

> "**7(1)** This regulation applies to a company if—
> (a) the company gives a notice under section 109 specifying an accounting period from the beginning of which Part 4 is to apply to the company (the "specified accounting period"), and
> (b) at the beginning of the specified accounting period, the company is in breach of Condition 2 in section 108(3).
>
> **7(2)** Part 4 shall apply to the company from the beginning of the specified accounting period if, at the beginning of the following accounting period, the company satisfies the requirements of Condition 2 in section 108(3).
>
> **7(3)** If paragraph (2) applies, the company's breach of Condition 2 in section 108(3) at the beginning of the specified accounting period shall not be taken into account for the purposes of paragraphs (4) and (5) of regulation 7B.
>
> **7(4)** Part 4 ceases to apply if—
> (a) the company does not satisfy the requirements of Condition 2 in section 108(3) at the beginning of the following accounting period, and
> (b) the Commissioners think, for the purposes of section 129(2)(c), that a breach of that requirement is so serious that Part 4 should cease to apply to the company.
>
> **7(5)** For the purposes of paragraph (4), section 129 shall be modified by substituting for subsection (5)–
> "**129(5)** Where a notice is given to a company in respect of an event occurring during the accounting period specified in the company's section 109 notice, this Part shall be taken to have ceased to apply to the company on the first day of that accounting period.".".

Notes – Reg. 7 rewritten as follows:
Reg. 7(1): CTA 2010, s. 566(1).
Reg. 7(2): CTA 2010, s. 566(1), (2).
Reg. 7(3): CTA 2010, s. 576(6).
Reg. 7(4): CTA 2010, s. 574(2).
Reg. 7(5): CTA 2010, s. 574(3).

TAX CHARGE FOR SPECIFIED ACCOUNTING PERIOD

7A [Repealed by CTA 2010, s. 1181 and Sch. 3, Pt. 1.]

History – Reg. 7A repealed by CTA 2010, s. 1181 and Sch. 3, Pt. 1, with effect for corporation tax purposes for accounting periods ending on or after 1 April 2010, and for income tax and capital gains tax purposes for the tax year 2010–11 and subsequent tax years. Former reg. 7A read as follows:

7A(1)   This regulation applies if regulation 7(1) and (2) apply.

7A(2)   A company to which this regulation applies shall be chargeable to corporation tax under Case VI of Schedule D on an amount of notional income calculated in accordance with this regulation.

7A(3)   The notional income shall be treated as arising at the end of the specified accounting period–
(a)   to C (residual), or
(b)   to the company as a member of G (residual).

7A(4)   The notional income is–

$$\left(\frac{\text{Market Value of Assets}}{\text{Tax Rate}} \right) \times 2\% - \text{Entry Charge Notional Income}$$

7A(5)   In paragraph (4)–
"Market Value of Assets" means–
(a)   the aggregate market value of assets involved in the UK property rental business of C (tax exempt), or
(b)   if the company is a member of a group to which Part 4 applies, the aggregate market value of assets involved in the UK property rental business of G (property rental business),
together with–
(c)   if the company is a venturing company or the principal company of a venturing group to which the JV Regulations apply, the value representing the proportion of the beneficial interest which that company has in the aggregate market value of the assets of the UK property rental business of the joint venture company, or
(d)   if the company is a venturing company or the principal company of a venturing group to which the JVG Regulations apply, the value representing the proportion of the beneficial interest which that company has in the aggregate market value of the assets of the UK property rental business of JVG (property rental business),
and for the purposes of this definition, the market value of assets is to be determined as at the end of the specified accounting period (ignoring any asset of negative market value);
"Tax Rate" means–
(a)   the percentage rate at which C (residual) is chargeable to tax on profits, or
(b)   the percentage rate at which the company, as a member of G (residual), is chargeable to tax on profits; and
"Entry Charge Notional Income" means–
(a)   the notional income calculated in accordance with section 112(3) which is chargeable on the company, or
(b)   the notional income calculated in accordance with section 112(3) as modified by paragraph 11(1)(c) of Schedule 17 which is chargeable on the members of the group,
together with–
(c)   if the company is a venturing company or the principal company of a venturing group to which the JV Regulations apply, the notional income calculated in accordance with section 112(3) as modified by regulation 7(3) or 13(4) of the JV Regulations, which is chargeable on the joint venture company, or
(d)   if the company is a venturing company or the principal company of a venturing group to which the JVG Regulations apply, the notional income calculated in accordance with section 112(3) as modified by the JVG Regulations, which is chargeable on the members of the joint venture group.

7A(6)   If the company holds an asset at the beginning of the specified accounting period but disposes of that asset during that accounting period, the Entry Charge Notional Income shall be reduced by an amount calculated as follows–

$$\left(\frac{\text{Asset Market Value}}{\text{Aggregate Market Value}} \right) \times \text{Entry Charge Notional Income}$$

7A(7)   In paragraph (6)–
"Asset Market Value" means the market value of the asset at the beginning of the specified accounting period;
"Aggregate Market Value" means the aggregate market value of assets treated as sold and reacquired under section 111(2), or section 111(2) as modified by paragraph 9(2) of Schedule 17, (ignoring any asset of negative market value); and
"Entry Charge Notional Income" has the same meaning as in paragraph (4).

7A(8)   No loss, deficit, expense or allowance may be set off against notional income or tax arising under this regulation.".

Notes – Reg. 7A rewritten as follows:
Reg. 7A(1): CTA 2010, s. 566(2).
Reg. 7A(2): CTA 2010, s. 566(2), (5).
Reg. 7A(3): CTA 2010, s. 566(2), (4), (5).
Reg. 7A(4): CTA 2010, s. 567(1), (2), (6).
Reg. 7A(5): CTA 2010, s. 567(3), (4), (5), (7).
Reg. 7A(6): CTA 2010, s. 567(8), (9).
Reg. 7A(7): CTA 2010, s. 567(9).
Reg. 7A(8): CTA 2010, s. 566(6).

BREACH OF BALANCE OF BUSINESS CONDITIONS

7B   [Repealed by CTA 2010, s. 1181 and Sch. 3, Pt. 1.]

History – Reg. 7B repealed by CTA 2010, s. 1181 and Sch. 3, Pt. 1, with effect for corporation tax purposes for accounting periods ending on or after 1 April 2010, and for income tax and capital gains tax purposes for the tax year 2010–11 and subsequent tax years. Former reg. 7B read as follows:

"**7B(1)**   This regulation applies to a company if–
(a)   Part 4 applies to the company, and
(b)   the company does not satisfy the requirements of Condition 1 in section 108(2)(a) or Condition 2 in section 108(3) in respect of any accounting period subsequent to the specified accounting period.

7B(2)   If the company does not satisfy the requirements of Condition 1 in section 108(2), but the profits arising from the tax-exempt business referred to in that condition are not less than 50% of the company's total profits for that accounting period, Part 4 shall continue to apply to the company.

7B(3)   If the company does not satisfy the requirements of Condition 2 in section 108(3), but the value of the assets involved in the tax-exempt business referred to in that condition has not fallen below 50% of the total value of assets held by the company, Part 4 shall continue to apply to the company.

7B(4) But, if the company does not satisfy the requirements of Condition 1 in section 108(2) or Condition 2 in section 108(3) in any three consecutive accounting periods, the breach is not to be considered as minor and the company may not rely upon this regulation for the purposes of section 129(2)(a).

7B(5) Subject to paragraph (4), if a breach of Condition 1 in section 108(2) or Condition 2 in section 108(3) lasts for more than one, but not more than two, consecutive accounting periods, it constitutes only one breach for the purposes of paragraph (7).

7B(6) The specified accounting period is not to be taken into account in reckoning the consecutive accounting periods mentioned in paragraph (4) and in paragraph (5).

7B(7) For the purposes of section 129(2)(a)–

(a)   the specified number of occasions on which the company can rely on this regulation is–
     (i)   two in respect of a breach of Condition 1 in section 108(2), and
     (ii)   two in respect of a breach of Condition 2 in section 108(3); and

(b)   the specified period is the ten year period beginning on the day on which the company first failed to satisfy Condition 1 in section 108(2) or Condition 2 in section 108(3) and ending immediately before the tenth anniversary of that day; and

(c)   for the purposes of paragraph (b), the company shall be treated as having first failed to satisfy Condition 1 in section 108(2) on the last day of the accounting period in which its profits are assessed for the purposes of that condition.".

Notes – Reg. 7B rewritten as follows:
Reg. 7B(1): CTA 2010, s. 568(1), (2).
Reg. 7B(2): CTA 2010, s. 568(1).
Reg. 7B(3): CTA 2010, s. 568(2).
Reg. 7B(4): CTA 2010, s. 576(1).
Reg. 7B(5): CTA 2010, s. 576(5).
Reg. 7B(6): CTA 2010, s. 576(6).
Reg. 7B(7): CTA 2010, s. 576(2), (3), (4).

GENERAL PROVISIONS ABOUT BREACHES UNDER SECTIONS 106 TO 108

Multiple Breaches of Separate Conditions

8   [Repealed by CTA 2010, s. 1181 and Sch. 3, Pt. 1.]

History – Reg. 8 repealed by CTA 2010, s. 1181 and Sch. 3, Pt. 1, with effect for corporation tax purposes for accounting periods ending on or after 1 April 2010, and for income tax and capital gains tax purposes for the tax year 2010–11 and subsequent tax years. Former reg. 8 read as follows:

"**8(1)** This regulation applies in relation to a company to which Part 4 applies where–
(a)   there has been a breach of at least two of the conditions in sections 106 to 108; and
(b)   at least one of the conditions breached is contained in a different section from that containing another of those breached.

8(2) For the purposes of section 129(2)(a), the specified number of occasions on which the company can rely on regulation 2, 3, 5 or 7B of these Regulations is four.

8(3) In reckoning the number of breaches of sections 106 to 108 the following are not to be taken into account–
(a)   breaches of Condition 3 in section 106(5) or Condition 4 in section 106(6) in consequence of a company to which Part 4 applies becoming part of a group (or of another group) to which Part 4 applies;
(b)   breaches of Condition 3 in section 106(5) or Condition 4 in section 106(6) in respect of which a company has relied upon section 109(3), (4) and (5);
(c)   breaches of Condition 1 in section 108(2) in the specified accounting period; and
(d)   breaches of Condition 2 in section 108(3) at the beginning of the specified accounting period.

8(4) For the purposes of section 129(2)(a) the specified period is the ten year period beginning on the day on which the company first failed to satisfy any of the conditions set out in section 106(5) or (6), 107 or 108 and ending immediately before the tenth anniversary of that day.

8(5) For the purposes of paragraph (4), the company shall be treated as having first failed to satisfy Condition 1 in section 108(2) on the last day of the accounting period in which its profits are assessed for the purposes of that condition.

8(6) Any breach of Condition 1 in section 108(2) in the specified accounting period, or any breach of Condition 2 in section 108(3) at the beginning of the specified accounting period, shall be disregarded in determining the day on which the ten year period begins.".

Notes – Reg. 8 rewritten as follows:
Reg. 8(1): CTA 2010, s. 577(2), (3), (5).
Reg. 8(2): CTA 2010, s. 577(4), (5).
Reg. 8(3): CTA 2010, s. 577(7).
Reg. 8(4): CTA 2010, s. 577(2), (5).
Reg. 8(5): CTA 2010, s. 577(6).
Reg. 8(6): CTA 2010, s. 577(7).

Breach of Condition – Information Requirements

9   [Repealed by CTA 2010, s. 1181 and Sch. 3, Pt. 1.]

History – Reg. 9 repealed by CTA 2010, s. 1181 and Sch. 3, Pt. 1, with effect for corporation tax purposes for accounting periods ending on or after 1 April 2010, and for income tax and capital gains tax purposes for the tax year 2010–11 and subsequent tax years. Former reg. 9 read as follows:

"**9(1)** This regulation applies if a company fails to satisfy a requirement set out in section 106(5) or (6), 107 or 108 ("a relevant failure").

9(2) Once a company becomes aware of a relevant failure it must provide the Commissioners as soon as reasonably practicable with the following information–
(a)   the date on which the requirement first ceased to be met and the date (if any) on which the requirement was satisfied again;
(b)   details of the requirement that was breached;
(c)   the nature of the breach; and
(d)   what (if anything) the company has done to avoid the breach recurring.".

Notes – Reg. 9 rewritten as follows:
Reg. 9(1): CTA 2010, s. 561(4).
Reg. 9(2): CTA 2010, s. 561(4).

BREACH OF SECTION 114: MAXIMUM SHAREHOLDING

Distribution to a Person With More Than the Maximum Shareholding: Charge to Tax

10   [Repealed by CTA 2010, s. 1181 and Sch. 3, Pt. 1.]

History – Reg. 10 repealed by CTA 2010, s. 1181 and Sch. 3, Pt. 1, with effect for corporation tax purposes for accounting periods ending on or after 1 April 2010, and for income tax and capital gains tax purposes for the tax year 2010–11 and subsequent tax years. Former reg. 10 read as follows:

"**10(1)**   If–

(a)   a company to which Part 4 applies, or the principal company of a group to which Part 4 applies, ("the distributor") makes a distribution to, or in respect of, the holder of excessive rights, and

(b)   the distributor has not taken reasonable steps to prevent the possibility of such a distribution being made,

the distributor is to be treated as having received an amount of income computed in accordance with paragraph (2).

10(2)   The amount is that found by the formula–

$$\left(DO \times SO \times \left(\frac{BRT}{MCT} \right) \right) + \left(DP \times SP \times \left(\frac{BRT}{MCT} \right) \right)$$

Here–
DO is the total amount of the profits of C (tax-exempt) distributed in respect of ordinary shares;
SO is the lesser of the percentage of rights–
     (a)   in respect of those ordinary shares held by the holder of excessive rights; and
     (b)   held by the recipient of the distribution;
in respect of which a distribution is made;
BRT is the basic rate of tax in force at the time the distributor distributed the income;
DP is the total amount of profits of C (tax-exempt) distributed by the distributor in respect of preference shares; and
SP is the lesser of the percentage of rights–
     (a)   in respect of preference shares held by the holder of excessive rights; and
     (b)   held by the recipient of the distribution;
in respect of which a distribution is made.

10(3)   The amount specified in paragraph (2) shall be charged to corporation tax as if it were income of C (residual) chargeable under Case VI of Schedule D arising in the accounting period in which the distributions referred to in paragraph (2) were made by the company.

10(4)   The rate of tax applicable to that amount is MCT.

10(5)   No loss, deficit, expense or allowance may be set off against the amount charged to tax by paragraph (3).".

Notes – Reg. 10 rewritten as follows:
Reg. 10(1): CTA 2010, s. 551(1), (2), (3), 552(1).
Reg. 10(2): CTA 2010, s. 552(2), (3), (4).
Reg. 10(3): CTA 2010, s. 551(4), (5).
Reg. 10(4): CTA 2010, s. 551(6).
Reg. 10(5): CTA 2010, s. 551(7).

Distribution to Holder of Excessive Rights: Information

11(1)   This regulation applies if a company to which Part 4 applies makes a distribution to, or in respect of, a holder of excessive rights.

11(2)   When the company makes its return under regulation 4 of the Real Estate Investment Trusts (Assessment and Recovery of Tax) Regulations 2006 for the quarter in which the date of any distribution falls, the company must provide the Commissioners with the following information–

(a)   the name and address of every person to, or in respect of, whom the distribution was made;

(b)   the amount or value of the distribution;

(c)   particulars of those persons' interests in the company including details of the percentages they form of the total issued share capital, ordinary share capital or any other share capital of the company;

(d)   particulars of the transaction giving rise to the distribution; and

(e)   what (if anything) the company has done to avoid the possibility of such a distribution being made.

BREACH OF SECTION 115(2) – PROFIT: FINANCING COSTS RATIO

Charge to Tax Where Profit: Financing-Cost Ratio Less Than 1.25 – Real Estate Investment Trusts which are not Group Real Estate Investment Trusts

12   [Repealed by CTA 2010, s. 1181 and Sch. 3, Pt. 1.]

History – Reg. 12 repealed by CTA 2010, s. 1181 and Sch. 3, Pt. 1, with effect for corporation tax purposes for accounting periods ending on or after 1 April 2010, and for income tax and capital gains tax purposes for the tax year 2010–11 and subsequent tax years. Former reg. 12 read as follows:

"**12(1)**   This regulation applies in the case of a company to which Part 4 applies, if the result of the sum specified in section 115(2) is less than 1,25 in respect of an accounting period.

12(2)   The amount by which–

(a)   the company's financing costs (as defined in section 115(2)(a)) exceeds

(b)   the amount of those costs which would cause the sum specified in section 115(2) to equal 1.25

shall be chargeable to tax as income of C(residual) on which corporation tax is chargeable under Case VI of Schedule D for the accounting period in which the excess arises.

12(3)   The amount charged to tax by paragraph (2) shall be charged at MCT.

12(4)   No loss, deficit, expense or allowance may be set off against the amount charged to tax by paragraph (2).".

Notes – Reg. 12 rewritten as follows:

Reg. 12(1): CTA 2010, s. 543(1).

Reg. 12(2): CTA 2010, s. 543(3), (4).

Reg. 12(3): CTA 2010, s. 543(5).

Reg. 12(4): CTA 2010, s. 543(6).

CHARGE TO TAX WHERE PROFIT: FINANCING-COST RATIO – GROUP REAL ESTATE INVESTMENT TRUSTS

13   [Repealed by CTA 2010, s. 1181 and Sch. 3, Pt. 1.]

History – Reg. 13 repealed by CTA 2010, s. 1181 and Sch. 3, Pt. 1, with effect for corporation tax purposes for accounting periods ending on or after 1 April 2010, and for income tax and capital gains tax purposes for the tax year 2010–11 and subsequent tax years. Former reg. 13 read as follows:

"**13(1)**   This regulation applies in the case of a group to which Part 4 applies if the result of the sum specified in section 115(2), as substituted by paragraph 14 of Schedule 17, is less than 1.25 in respect of an accounting period.

13(2)   The amount by which–

(a)   Financing Costs (External) (as defined in section 115(2)(c) as substituted by paragraph 14 of Schedule 17) exceeds

(b)   the amount of those costs which would cause the sum specified in section 115(2) to equal 1.25

shall be chargeable under Case VI of Schedule D as income of the residual part of the principal company of the group to which Part 4 applies for the accounting period in which the excess arises.

13(3)   The amount charged to tax by paragraph (2) shall be charged at MCT.

13(4)   No loss, deficit, expense or allowance may be set off against the amount charged to tax by paragraph (2).".

Notes – Reg. 13 rewritten as follows:

Reg. 13(1): CTA 2010, s. 543(1).

Reg. 13(2): CTA 2010, s. 543(3), (4).

Reg. 13(3): CTA 2010, s. 543(5).

Reg. 13(4): CTA 2010, s. 543(6).

TERMINATION BY NOTICE AFTER SERVICE OF NOTICES CANCELLING TAX ADVANTAGE

Termination by Notice – Specified Number of Section 117 Notices

14   [Repealed by CTA 2010, s. 1181 and Sch. 3, Pt. 1.]

History – Reg. 14 repealed by CTA 2010, s. 1181 and Sch. 3, Pt. 1, with effect for corporation tax purposes for accounting periods ending on or after 1 April 2010, and for income tax and capital gains tax purposes for the tax year 2010–11 and subsequent tax years. Former reg. 14 read as follows:

"**14**   For the purposes of section 129(2)(b) (specified number of notices under section 117)–

(a)   the specified number of notices is two; and

(b)   the specified period is the period commencing with the day on which the first notice was issued and ending immediately before the tenth anniversary of that day.".

Notes – Reg. 14 rewritten in CTA 2010, s. 573(2), (3), (4).

REAL ESTATE INVESTMENT TRUSTS (FINANCIAL STATEMENTS OF GROUP REAL ESTATE INVESTMENT TRUSTS) REGULATIONS 2006

(SI 2006/2865 as amended by SI 2007/3536)

Made on 1 November 2006 by the Commissioners for Her Majesty's Revenue and Customs in exercise of the powers conferred by s. 144 of, and para. 31(7) of Sch. 17 to, the Finance Act 2006. Operative from 1 January 2007.

PRELIMINARY

CITATION, COMMENCEMENT AND EFFECT

1(1) These Regulations may be cited as the Real Estate Investment Trusts (Financial Statements of Group Real Estate Investment Trusts) Regulations 2006, and shall come into force on 1st January 2007.

1(2) These Regulations have effect in relation to accounting periods beginning on and after 1st January 2007.

INTERPRETATION

2(1) In these Regulations—

(a) a reference to Part 4 is a reference to Part 4 of the Finance Act 2006,

(b) a reference to a section (without more) is a reference to that section of the Finance Act 2006,

(c) a reference to Schedule 17 is a reference to Schedule 17 to the Finance Act 2006, and

(d) a reference to paragraph 31 (however expressed) is a reference to paragraph 31 of Schedule 17.

2(2) In these Regulations—

"**financing costs**" has the meaning given by section 115(4);

"**G (property rental business)**" has the meaning given by paragraph 2(b) of Schedule 17;

"**G (residual)**" has the meaning given by paragraph 2(c) of Schedule 17;

"**the Joint Ventures Regulations**" means the Real Estate Investment Trusts (Joint Ventures) Regulations 2006;

"**open-ended investment company**" has the meaning given by section 17(4)(e) of the Finance (No. 2) Act 2005;

"**the principal company**" is to be construed in accordance with section 134(2);

"**significant influence**" is to be construed in accordance with regulation 3(1);

"**UK business**" is to be construed in accordance with paragraph 3(3) of Schedule 17.

2(3) In these Regulations—

"**for accounting purposes**" means for the purposes of accounts drawn up in accordance with generally accepted accounting practice;

"**fair value accounting**" means a basis of accounting under which assets or liabilities are shown in the company's balance sheet at their fair value

"**generally accepted accounting practice**" has the meaning given by section 50 of the Finance Act 2004;

"**joint venture**" and "**venturer**" have the same meaning as for accounting purposes.

SIGNIFICANT INFLUENCE AND PROFITS AVAILABLE FOR DISTRIBUTION TO EQUITY HOLDERS

3(1) For the purposes of these Regulations a member of a group has significant influence over another entity if—

(a) the member holds a percentage of the beneficial interest in the other entity, and

(b) the members of the group hold more than 20 per cent of the beneficial interest in that other entity.

3(2) For the purposes of these Regulations percentages of beneficial interest in an entity must be determined by reference to entitlement to profits available for distribution to equity holders.

3(3) Profits available for distribution to equity holders do not include any profits or assets available to equity holders otherwise than as equity holders.

3(4) For the purpose of determining profits available for distribution to equity holders in relation to an entity other than a company these Regulations have effect as if–

(a)   the entity were a company resident in the United Kingdom, and

(b)   the rights of persons in the entity were shares in the company.

GENERAL

SCOPE OF THESE REGULATIONS

4(1) These Regulations apply in respect of a group to which Part 4 applies in relation to an accounting period of the principal company.

4(2) In accordance with Schedule 17 the principal company must prepare–

(a)   a financial statement for G (property rental business) for the accounting period (see paragraph 31(2)(a)),

(b)   a financial statement for G (residual) for the accounting period (see paragraph 31(2)(c)), and

(c)   a financial statement for G (property rental business) in respect of its UK business (see paragraph 31(2)(b)).

4(3) In these Regulations–

(a)   regulations 5 to 11 make further provision relating to the content of–

    (i)   a financial statement for G (property rental business) for an accounting period, and

    (ii)   a financial statement for G (residual) for an accounting period;

(b)   regulation 12 makes further provision relating to the content of a financial statement for G (property rental business) in respect of its UK business; and

(c)   regulation 13 contains further provisions.

FINANCIAL STATEMENTS FOR G (PROPERTY RENTAL BUSINESS) AND G (RESIDUAL)

GENERAL

5(1) In accordance with paragraph 31(3), a financial statement for G (property rental business) for an accounting period and a financial statement for G (residual) for an accounting period must specify–

(a)   income (in the manner specified in paragraph 31(3)(a)),

(b)   expenses (in the manner specified in paragraph 31(3)(b)),

(c)   profits before tax (in the manner specified in paragraph 31(3)(c)), and

(d)   assets valued (in the manner specified in paragraph 31(3)(d)).

5(2) The financial statement for G (property rental business) for an accounting period and the financial statement for G (residual) for an accounting period must exclude the following items–

(a)   transactions between one member of the group and another member of the group;

(b)   income and expenses payable between one member of the group and another member of the group;

(c)   the value of holdings of one member of the group in another member of the group; and

(d)   any balances held by one member of the group that relate to another member of the group.

5(3) In accordance with paragraph 31(5), where a non-member of the group holds a percentage of the beneficial interest in a member (other than the principal company), the financial statement for G (property rental business) for an accounting period and the financial statement for G (residual) for an accounting period must exclude that percentage of income, expenses, gains, losses, assets and liabilities of the member.

5(4) A reconciliation must be provided between–

(a)   the financial statement for G (property rental business) for an accounting period and the financial statement for G (residual) for that accounting period, and

(b)   the audited financial statements of the group for that accounting period (whether in the form of consolidated statements or of statements of individual members of the group).

5(5) The expenses must show the following amounts separately–

(a)   financing costs, and

(b)   all other expenses.

5(6) Financing costs–

(a)   in the case of the financial statement for G (property rental business) for an accounting period, must include Financing Costs (external) (see regulation 6), and

(b)   in the case of the financial statement for G (residual) for an accounting period, must include financing costs payable by a member of the group in respect of financing used inthe business of G (residual).

FINANCING COSTS (EXTERNAL)

6(1) In the case of the financial statement for G (property rental business) for an accounting period, the amount of Financing Costs (external) is determined as follows–

Step 1

Determine the amount of the financing costs incurred in respect of the property rental business of G (property rental business) owed by group entities to non-group entities (the "outside financing costs").

Step 2

Determine the percentages of the outside financing costs incurred in respect of–

(a)   the UK business of G (property rental business), and

(b)   other matters.

The amount of Financing Costs (external) is the percentage of the outside financing costs incurred in respect of the UK business of G (property rental business).

6(2) If the outside financing costs are owed by a group entity (other than the principal company) and a non-group entity holds a percentage of the beneficial interest in that group entity, the outside financing costs must exclude that percentage of those costs.

6(3) For the purposes of paragraph (2), percentages of beneficial interest must be determined by reference to beneficial entitlement to profits available for distribution to equity holders.

6(4) In this regulation–

    "group entity" means–

    (a)   a member of the group, or

    (b)   an entity which, under these Regulations, is treated as a member of the group for accounting purposes and for the purposes of the financial statements specified in regulation 4(2) (see regulations 9 to 11); and

    "non-group entity" means an entity which is not a group entity.

TREATMENT OF CERTAIN EXCEPTIONAL ITEMS

7(1) This regulation applies to the items specified in sub-paragraphs (ii) and (iii) of section 108(2)(b) (the "specified items").

7(2) The financial statement for G (property rental business) for an accounting period and the financial statement for G (residual) for an accounting period must show the specified items.

7(3) For the purposes of paragraph 7 of Schedule 17 (which modifies section 108 (conditions for balance of business)), the specified items are excluded from–

(a)   the amount of the income, expenses and profits accruing from any business, and

(b)   the amount of the assets involved in any business.

History – Reg. 7 substituted by SI 2007/3536, reg. 3, with effect in relation to accounting periods beginning on or after 1 January 2008 and ending on or after 7 January 2008.

BENEFICIAL INTERESTS IN ENTITIES OTHER THAN GROUP COMPANIES

8(1) This regulation applies if–

(a)   a member of a group holds a percentage of the beneficial interest in another entity, and

(b)   that other entity is not a member of the group.

8(2) The member of the group must account for income received from that other entity–

(a)   on the basis that the beneficial interest is held as an investment, and

(b)   in accordance with generally accepted accounting practice.

8(3) The financial statement for G (residual) must–

(a)   show the beneficial interest in that other entity as an asset of the member of the group, and

(b)   account for that beneficial interest in accordance with fair value accounting.

8(4) The general rules in paragraphs (2) and (3) are subject to further provisions relating to–

(a)   a joint venture (see regulation 9),

(b)   an open-ended investment company (see regulation 10), and

(c)   certain other non-corporate entities (see regulation 11).

JOINT VENTURES

9(1) This regulation applies if–

(a)   a member of a group (the "venturing group") is a venturer in a joint venture, and

(b)   notice has been given–

    (i)   in accordance with the Joint Ventures Regulations for those Regulations to apply to the joint venture, or

    (ii)   in accordance with the Real Estate Investment Trusts (Joint Venture Groups) Regulations 2007 for those Regulations to apply to the joint venture.

9(2) If the joint venture takes the form of a company, the joint venture must be treated, for accounting purposes, as a member of the venturing group for the purposes of the financial statements specified in regulation 4(2).

9(3) If the joint venture takes the form of another group ("the joint venture group"), the principal company of the venturing group must reflect the relevant information in its financial statements.

9(4) In paragraph (3) the **"relevant information"** means the information specified in sub-paragraphs (3) and (4) of paragraph 31 as set out in the financial statements of the principal company of the joint venture group.

History – Reg. 9 substituted by SI 2007/3536, reg. 4, with effect in relation to accounting periods beginning on or after 1 January 2008 and ending on or after 7 January 2008.

OPEN-ENDED INVESTMENT COMPANIES

10(1) This regulation applies if a member of a group has significant influence over an open-ended investment company.

10(2) For the purposes of the financial statements specified in regulation 4(2), the open-ended investment company must be treated, for accounting purposes, as a member of the group.

OTHER NON-CORPORATE ENTITIES

11(1) This regulation applies if a member of a group has significant influence over a noncorporate entity.

11(2) For the purposes of the financial statements specified in regulation 4(2), that other entity must be treated, for accounting purposes, as a member of the group.

FINANCIAL STATEMENTS FOR G (PROPERTY RENTAL BUSINESS) IN RESPECT OF ITS UK BUSINESS

CONTENTS OF THE FINANCIAL STATEMENT

12(1) In accordance with paragraph 31(4), a financial statement for G (property rental business) in respect of its UK business must specify profits calculated in accordance with section 120 in relation to each member of the group.

12(2) In accordance with paragraph 31(5), where a non-member of the group holds a percentage of the beneficial interest in a member (other than the principal company), the financial statement for G (property rental business) in respect of its UK business must exclude that percentage of income, expenses, gains, losses, assets and liabilities of the member.

12(3) The financial statement must also show the following amounts separately—

(a) capital allowances, and

(b) financing costs.

FURTHER PROVISIONS

TIME BY WHICH FINANCIAL STATEMENTS MUST BE SUPPLIED

13(1) The financial statements specified in regulation 4(2) must be supplied with the company tax return for the relevant accounting period.

13(2) Accordingly, the filing date for those financial statements must be determined in accordance with paragraph 14 of Schedule 18 to the Finance Act 1998.

REAL ESTATE INVESTMENT TRUSTS (ASSESSMENT AND RECOVERY OF TAX) REGULATIONS 2006

(SI 2006/2867 as amended by SI 2006/3222 and SI 2009/2036)

Made on 1 November 2006 by the Treasury in exercise of the powers conferred by s. 122 and para. 4 and 19 of Sch. 17 to the Finance Act 2006. Operative from 1 January 2007.

PART 1 – INTRODUCTORY

CITATION, COMMENCEMENT AND INTERPRETATION

1(1) These Regulations may be cited as the Real Estate Investment Trusts (Assessment and Recovery of Tax) Regulations 2006 and shall come into force on 1st January 2007.

1(2) In these Regulations–

(a) **"ICTA"** means the Income and Corporation Taxes Act 1988;

(b) **"FA 2006"** means the Finance Act 2006;

(c) **"TMA"** means the Taxes Management Act 1970;

(d) **"TCGA"** means the Taxation of Chargeable Gains Act 1992;

(e) a reference to a numbered section or Schedule (without more) is a reference to a section of, or Schedule to, FA 2006 bearing that number.

1(3) In these Regulations–

"C (residual)" has the meaning given by section 105(3)(c);

"C (post-cessation)" has the meaning given by section 105(3)(d);

"C (tax-exempt)" has the meaning given by section 105(3)(b);

"G (post-cessation)" has the meaning given by paragraph 2(d) of Schedule 17;

"G (property rental business)" has the meaning given by paragraph 3(2)(b) of that Schedule;

"profits" means income and gains; and

"UK profits" shall be construed in accordance with paragraph 3(2) of Schedule 17.

INTRODUCTION

2(1) These Regulations provide for the deduction of sums representing tax–

(a) where a company to which Part 4 of FA 2006 applies makes a distribution of profits of C (tax-exempt) or,

(b) in a case where Part 4 of FA 2006 applies to a group by virtue of section 134(1), where the principal company makes a distribution out of the UK profits of G (property rental business).

2(2) Part 2 of these Regulations applies in the case of a company to which Part 4 of FA 2006 applies but which is not part of a group to which that Part applies.

2(3) Part 3 of these Regulations modifies Part 2 of these Regulations in the case of–

(a) C (post-cessation) where the company to which Part 4 of FA 2006 applied was not part of a group to which that Part applied;

(b) a group to which Part 4 of FA 2006 applies; and

(c) each UK resident company which is a member of G (post-cessation).

PART 2 – COMPANIES TO WHICH PART 4 OF FA 2006 APPLIES, BUT WHICH ARE NOT PART OF A GROUP

DEDUCTION OF TAX

3(1) This regulation applies if a company to which Part 4 of FA 2006 applies, and which is not part of a group to which that Part applies, makes a distribution of profits of C (tax-exempt) ("a relevant distribution").

3(2) The company must, on making a relevant distribution, deduct from it a sum representing tax at the basic rate in force for the year in which it is made, unless (or to the extent that) regulation 7 authorises the distribution to be made without deduction of tax.

PAYMENTS IN AN ACCOUNTING PERIOD

4(1) This regulation applies if the company makes a relevant distribution in an accounting period of the company.

4(2) The company must deliver a return to an officer of Revenue and Customs for each return period in which the company makes a relevant distribution and which falls within the accounting period.

4(3) The return periods are–

(a) the quarters ending upon 31st March, 30th June, 30th September and 31st December ("the quarter days"); and

(b) any shorter period which–

(i) starts on the first day of an accounting period and ends with the first or only quarter day in that accounting period;

(ii) begins immediately after the last or only quarter day in that accounting period and ends on the last day of that accounting period; or

(iii) is an accounting period which starts and ends within a quarter.

4(4) The company must deliver the return within 14 days after the end of the return period.

4(5) The return must show the amount of–

(a) any relevant distributions made by the company in the return period, and

(b) the tax (if any) payable by the company in respect of those payments.

4(6) The company must deliver, with the return for the return period which ends on the last day of an accounting period, a reconciliation statement showing, in relation to any distribution made during the accounting period, the amounts (if any) which are attributable to each of paragraphs (a) to (e) of section 123.

COLLECTION AND PAYMENT OF TAX

5(1) Tax in respect of a relevant distribution is due, from the company making it, at the time by which the return on which the distribution must be included is required to be delivered.

5(2) The tax due is equal to the sum which the company is required to deduct from the relevant distribution under regulation 3(2).

5(3) The tax is payable without an officer of Revenue and Customs making any assessment.

CERTIFICATES OF DEDUCTION OF TAX

6(1) A company making a relevant distribution which is subject to deduction of tax by virtue of section 122 must furnish the recipient with a statement in writing showing–

(a) the gross amount of the payment,

(b) the amount of tax deducted, and

(c) the actual amount paid.

6(2) The duty imposed by paragraph (1) is enforceable at the suit or instance of the recipient.

GROSS PAYMENT OF DISTRIBUTIONS

7(1) A payment of a relevant distribution must be made without deduction of income tax if the company reasonably believes that–

(a) the person beneficially entitled to the payment is a person or body to which one of paragraphs (2) and (3) applies;

(b) the recipient is a person or body to which paragraph (4) applies, and the payment satisfies the condition in paragraph (5);

(c) the recipient is a partnership to which paragraph (6) applies; or

(d) the distribution arises in respect of shares held as investments of the Overseas Service Pension Fund established pursuant to section 7(1) of the Overseas Aid Act 1966.

This paragraph is subject to the qualifications in paragraphs (7) and (8).

7(2) This paragraph applies to–

Statutory Instruments

(a)   a company resident in the United Kingdom for corporation tax purposes; and

(b)   a company that—

    (i)   is not resident in the United Kingdom;

    (ii)   carries on a trade in the United Kingdom through a permanent establishment; and

    (iii)   is required to bring the relevant distribution into account in computing the chargeable profits (within the meaning of section 11(2) of ICTA).

7(2A)   But paragraph (2) does not apply to a Tax Elected Fund.

7(2B)   In paragraph (2A) **"Tax Elected Fund"** has the meaning given by regulation 69Z42(2) of the Authorised Investment Funds (Tax) Regulations 2006.

7(3)   This paragraph applies to—

(a)   a local authority;

(b)   a health service body within the meaning of section 519A(2) of ICTA;

(c)   a public office or department of the Crown to which section 829(1) of that Act applies;

(d)   a charity within the meaning of section 506(1) of that Act;

(e)   a body for the time being mentioned in section 507(1) of that Act (bodies which are allowed the same exemption from tax as charities the whole income of which is applied to charitable purposes);

(f)   an Association of a description specified in section 508 of that Act (scientific research organisations); and

(g)   the European Investment Fund.

7(4)   This paragraph applies to a payment which is made to—

(a)   the trustees of a scheme entitled to exemption under section 613(4) of that Act (Parliamentary pension funds);

(b)   the scheme administrator of a registered pension scheme;

(c)   the sub-scheme administrator of a sub-scheme which forms part of a split scheme pursuant to the Registered Pension Schemes (Splitting of Schemes) Regulations 2006;

(d)   the account provider for a child trust fund within the meaning of section 1(2) of the Child Trust Funds Act 2004 or the nominee of the account provider;

(e)   the account manager of an account within the meaning of regulation 4(1) of the Individual Savings Account Regulations 1998 or the nominee of the account manager;

(f)   the plan manager of a plan within the meaning of regulation 4(1) of the Personal Equity Plan Regulations 1989 or the nominee of the plan manager;

and satisfies the condition in paragraph (5).

7(5)   The condition is that the payment is to be applied for the purposes of the fund, scheme, account or plan mentioned in paragraph (4) in respect of which the recipient has duties.

7(6)   This paragraph applies to a partnership each member of which is a person or body mentioned in paragraph (2), (3), or (4), provided that, in the case of a person or body mentioned in paragraph (4) its share of the partnership profits are to be applied for the purposes of the fund, scheme, account or plan in respect of which that person or body has duties.

7(7)   If the owner of securities in a company that is a Real Estate Investment Trust has sold or transferred the right to receive a relevant distribution (whether before or after the sale or transfer), without selling or transferring those securities, the company must deduct tax at the basic rate.

7(8)   If the company reasonably believes, at the time that it makes a payment without deduction of tax, that paragraph (2), (3), (4) or (6) applies, but in fact none of those paragraphs applies, these Regulations shall apply to the payment as if it were never one which could be made without deduction of tax.

7(9)   Upon discovering that the payment mentioned in paragraph (8) is one from which tax should have been deducted, the company making it must deliver an amended return in accordance with regulation 11.

History – Reg. 7(2A) inserted by SI 2009/2036, reg. 33(2), with effect from 1 September 2009.
Reg. 7(2B) inserted by SI 2009/2036, reg. 33(2), with effect from 1 September 2009.

ASSESSMENTS WHERE RELEVANT DISTRIBUTION INCLUDED IN RETURN

8(1)   This regulation applies if any tax in respect of a relevant distribution which is included in a return under these Regulations has not been paid at or before the time mentioned in regulation 5.

8(2)   An officer of Revenue and Customs may make an assessment on the person who made the relevant distribution.

8(3)   Tax may be assessed under this regulation whether or not it has been paid when the assessment is made.

ASSESSMENTS IN OTHER CASES

9(1)   This regulation applies if an officer of Revenue and Customs thinks—

(a)   that there is a relevant distribution which should have been included in a return under these Regulations and which has not been so included, or

(b)   that a return under these Regulations is otherwise incorrect.

9(2)   An officer of Revenue and Customs may make an assessment on the person who made the relevant distribution to the best of the officer's judgement.

APPLICATION OF INCOME TAX ACTS PROVISIONS ABOUT TIME LIMITS FOR ASSESSMENTS

10(1)   The provisions of the Income Tax Acts about the time within which an assessment may be made apply to assessments under these Regulations, so far as those provisions refer or relate to—

(a)   the tax year for which an assessment is made, or

(b)   the year to which an assessment relates.

10(2)   Paragraph (1) applies despite the fact that an assessment under these Regulations may relate to a return period which is not a tax year.

10(3)   The provisions of section 36 of TMA (fraudulent or negligent conduct) about the circumstances in which an assessment may be made out of time apply accordingly on the basis that any such assessment relates to the tax year in which the return period ends.

10(4)   Section 87 of TMA (late payments of tax on assessments made or payments due under Schedule 16 to ICTA) applies for the purposes of a payment due under regulation 4 or an assessment made under regulation 8 or 9.

COMPANY'S DUTY TO DELIVER AMENDED RETURN

11(1)   This regulation applies if a company which has made a relevant distribution becomes aware that—

(a)   anything which should have been included in a return delivered by the company under these Regulations has not been so included,

(b)   anything which should not have been included in a return delivered by the company under these Regulations has been so included, or

(c)   any other error has occurred in a return delivered by the company under these Regulations.

11(2)   The company must deliver an amended return correcting the error to an officer of Revenue and Customs without delay.

11(3)   If the company delivers an amended return such assessments, adjustments, set-offs or payments or repayments of tax as are necessary for achieving the objective mentioned in paragraph (4) must be made.

11(4)   The objective is that the resulting liabilities to income and corporation tax (including interest on unpaid or overpaid tax) of the company or any other person are the same as they would have been if a correct return had been delivered.

PART 3 – COMPANY TO WHICH PART 4 OF FA 2006 FORMERLY APPLIED, AND GROUPS

12(1)   Part 2 of these Regulations applies—

(a)   to a group to which Part 4 of FA 2006 applies;

(b)   to a company to which Part 4 of FA 2006 formerly applied, but which was not part of a group to which that Part applied, and

(c)   to a group to which Part 4 of FA 2006 formerly applied

with the following modifications.

12(2) In a case falling within paragraph (1)(a) the modifications are that–

(a)   references to the company shall be read as references to the principal company;

(b)   references to a relevant distribution shall be read as references to a distribution out of amounts shown in the financial statements of G (property rental business) as–

     (i)   the profits of the UK-resident members of the group; and

     (ii)   gains accruing to UK-resident members of the group.

12(3) In a case falling within paragraph (1)(b) references to company shall be read as references to a company to which Part 4 formerly applied.

12(4) In a case falling within paragraph (1)(c)–

(a)   references to company shall be read as references to the principal company of G (post-cessation); and

(b)   references to relevant distribution are to be read as references to a distribution out of amounts shown in the financial statements of G (property rental business) as–

     (i)   the profits of the UK-resident members of the group; and

     (ii)   gains accruing to UK-resident members of the group.

12(5) [Omitted by SI 2006/3222, reg. 2.]

History – Reg. 12(5) omitted by SI 2006/3222, reg. 2 with effect from 26 December 2006. Former reg. 12(5) appears to have a been a mistake as it read:

     "**12(5)** In this regulation–"

LLOYD'S UNDERWRITERS (DOUBLE TAXATION RELIEF) (CORPORATE MEMBERS) REGULATIONS 2006

(SI 2006/3262)

Made on 6 December 2006 by the Commissioners for Her Majesty's Revenue and Customs in exercise of the powers conferred upon them by s. 229 of the Finance Act 1994. Operative from 31 December 2006.

PRELIMINARY

Citation, commencement and effect

1(1) These Regulations may be cited as the Lloyd's Underwriters (Double Taxation Relief) (Corporate Members) Regulations 2006 and shall come into force on 31st December 2006.

1(2) These Regulations shall have effect in relation to accounting periods ending on or after the date on which these Regulations come into force.

Interpretation

2(1) This paragraph gives the meaning of abbreviated references to legislation used in these Regulations–

"**ICTA**" means the Income and Corporation Taxes Act 1988;

"**Chapter 2 of Part 18**" means Chapter 2 of Part 18 of ICTA (rules governing relief by way of credit).

2(2) In these Regulations–

"**foreign amount of tax**" has the meaning given by regulation 5(4);

"**foreign tax**" means tax chargeable under the law of a territory outside the United Kingdom.

GENERAL SCOPE OF THESE REGULATIONS

General provisions

3(1) These Regulations make provision for giving credit for foreign tax payable in respect of profits or losses arising from a corporate member's underwriting business in an accounting period.

3(2) Relief from corporation tax shall be given under Chapters 1 and 2 of Part 18 of ICTA in respect of the foreign tax payable by allowing the amount of the pool of adjusted sums of foreign tax for an accounting period as a credit against the corporation tax payable on the profits arising from the corporate member's underwriting business.

3(3) In these Regulations–

(a) regulations 5 to 10 apply to determine how the amount of the pool of adjusted sums of foreign tax for an accounting period is ascertained, and

(b) regulation 11 explains how the amount of the pool of adjusted sums of foreign tax for an accounting period is allowed as a credit against the corporation tax payable on the profits arising from the corporate member's underwriting business.

Application of sections in Chapter 2 of Part 18

4 The following sections of Chapter 2 of Part 18 apply for the purposes of these Regulations–

section 792 (interpretation of credit code);

sections 793 to 795A (general rules);

sections 797 to 798C (the measure of the foreign income);

sections 805 and 806 (elections and claims).

THE POOL OF ADJUSTED SUMS OF FOREIGN TAX

Allocation of foreign tax to accounting periods

5(1) The amount of the pool of adjusted sums of foreign tax for an accounting period is calculated by reference to the foreign tax payable for the corresponding foreign period of accounting.

5(2) Adjusted sums of foreign tax must be calculated separately for each relevant territory outside the United Kingdom.

5(3) For the purposes of these Regulations an accounting period corresponds to a foreign period of accounting if the foreign period of accounting ends in the period of twelve months immediately preceding the beginning of the accounting period.

5(4) In these Regulations an amount of foreign tax payable for a corresponding foreign period of accounting is called a foreign amount of tax.

Further provisions relating to accounting periods and to foreign periods of accounting

6(1) If a foreign period of accounting is more than twelve months–

(a) the period must be split into successive periods of twelve months and a final period not exceeding twelve months, and

(b) the profit of the corporate member's underwriting business and the amount of foreign tax must be apportioned rateably.

6(2) If a foreign period of accounting is less than twelve months and more than one such period ends in the period of twelve months immediately preceding the beginning of the accounting period, the accounting period corresponds to all those foreign periods of accounting.

6(3) If a foreign period of accounting ends at a time which is within the immediately preceding twelve months period of more than one accounting period, the accounting period to which the foreign period of accounting corresponds is the first accounting period to begin after the foreign period of accounting ends.

6(4) In paragraph (3) **"the immediately preceding twelve months period"** means the period of twelve months immediately preceding an accounting period.

Adjustments of foreign amounts of tax

7(1) If necessary, foreign amounts of tax must be adjusted in accordance with the provisions of this regulation to determine the adjusted sums of foreign tax.

7(2) The effective rate of foreign tax must be determined in accordance with the equation–

$$ERFT = \frac{F}{P} \times 100$$

7(3) In this regulation–

ERFT = the effective rate of foreign tax;

F = the foreign tax payable for the corresponding foreign period of accounting;

P = the profit of the corporate member's underwriting business arising in the relevant territory outside the United Kingdom for the foreign period of accounting in respect of which the foreign tax is payable.

7(4) If the effective rate of foreign tax for a corresponding foreign period of accounting is less than, or equal to, the average rate of corporation tax fixed for companies generally for the accounting period corresponding to the foreign period of accounting, the amount of the adjusted sum of foreign tax is the foreign amount of tax.

7(5) If the effective rate of foreign tax for a corresponding foreign period of accounting is greater than the average rate of corporation tax fixed for companies generally for the accounting period corresponding to the foreign period of accounting, the amount of the adjusted sum of foreign tax is determined in accordance with the equation–

$$ASFT = \frac{CTR}{ERFT} \times FT$$

7(6) In paragraph (5)–

ASFT = the amount of the adjusted sum of foreign tax;

CTR = the average rate of corporation tax fixed for companies generally for the accounting period corresponding to the foreign period of accounting;

FT = the foreign amount of tax.

Calculation of amount of pool of adjusted sums of foreign tax

8(1) The amount of the pool of adjusted sums of foreign tax for an accounting period is determined in accordance with the equation–

PASFT = AASFT + ATA + BFA

8(2) In paragraph (1)–

PASFT = the amount of the pool of adjusted sums of foreign tax;

AASFT = the aggregate amount of adjusted sums of foreign tax;

ATA = an additional transitional amount (see regulation 9(2));

BFA = the amount brought forward from the previous accounting period (see regulation 11(2)).

8(3) If regulation 10 applies, the amount of an adjusted sum of foreign tax must be determined in accordance with that regulation.

Transitional provision

9(1) This regulation applies if, for the first accounting period for which these Regulations apply–

(a) a corporate member has an amount of tax chargeable under the law of a territory outside the United Kingdom for which relief has not been given, and

(b) that amount of tax relates to foreign periods of accounting earlier than the period to which the first accounting period corresponds.

9(2) If the corporate member so chooses, that amount of tax may be added to the pool of adjusted sums of foreign tax for that first accounting period.

9(3) If paragraph (2) applies, the amount of tax must be adjusted in accordance with the provisions of regulation 7 if necessary.

9(4) In any other case, relief must be given for that amount of tax before relief is given under these Regulations.

Refunds of foreign tax

10(1) This regulation applies if–

(a) relief for foreign tax paid is given by way of credit against United Kingdom tax on profits arising from a corporate member's underwriting business, and

(b) an amount of that foreign tax ("the repaid amount") is subsequently repaid to the member.

10(2) For the purposes of regulations 5 to 8 the repaid amount must be dealt with in accordance with paragraphs (3) and (4).

10(3) For the purposes of regulation 7–

(a) the repaid amount is to be treated as if it were a foreign amount of tax repayable for the corresponding foreign period of accounting, and

(b) the following are to be adjusted by deducting the repaid amount–

   (i) the foreign tax payable for the corresponding foreign period of accounting (see paragraphs (2) and (3) of regulation 7), and

   (ii) the foreign amount of tax (see paragraphs (5) and (6) of regulation 7).

10(4) For the purposes of regulation 8 the repaid amount (adjusted, if necessary, under paragraph (3)) must be deducted from the amount AASFT.

10(5) Paragraph (6) applies if–

(a) any credit for foreign tax has been allowed to a corporate member under any arrangements, and

(b) the amount of that credit is subsequently rendered excessive by reason of an adjustment of the amount of any tax payable under the laws of a territory outside the United Kingdom.

10(6) The corporate member shall give notice in writing to an Officer of Revenue and Customs that an adjustment has been made that has rendered the amount of the credit excessive.

10(7) A notice under paragraph (6) must be given within one year from the time of the making of the adjustment.

10(8) A corporate member which fails to comply with the requirements imposed by paragraphs (6) and (7) in relation to any adjustment shall be liable to a penalty of an amount not exceeding the amount by which the credit allowed has been rendered excessive by reason of the adjustment.

10(9) If the condition in paragraph (10) is met, any assessments may be made as are necessary to ensure that the total amount of the corporate member's income or chargeable gains is assessed, and the proper credit, if any, is given in respect of that income or those gains.

10(10) The condition is that it appears that the assessment to corporation tax made on the corporate member in respect of the income or chargeable gains–

(a) is not made in respect of the full amount of that income or those gains, or

(b) is incorrect having regard to the repaid amount.

10(11) Where the income is, or the chargeable gains are, entrusted to any person in the United Kingdom for payment, any such assessment may be made on the recipient of the income or gains; and, in the case of an assessment to corporation tax in respect of the income, may be assessed under Case VI of Schedule D.

DOUBLE TAXATION RELIEF GIVEN

How relief is given

11(1) Relief from corporation tax for an accounting period in respect of foreign tax shall be given by allowing the amount of the pool of adjusted sums of foreign tax for that accounting period as a credit against corporation tax payable on the profits arising from a corporate member's underwriting business—

(a)   in that accounting period, or

(b)   in such one or more preceding accounting periods, beginning not more than three years before the accounting period mentioned in sub-paragraph (a),

or partly in the one way and partly in the other as the corporate member may choose.

11(2) Any amount in the pool of adjusted sums of foreign tax for an accounting period that is not allowed as a credit against corporation tax in accordance with paragraph (1) shall be carried forward and added to the pool of adjusted sums of foreign tax for the next accounting period (see regulation 8(1)).

OVERSEAS LIFE INSURANCE COMPANIES REGULATIONS 2006

(SI 2006/3271, as amended by SI 2007/2146, SI 2007/3449 and SI 2008/1924)

Made on 7 December 2006 by the Treasury in exercise of the powers conferred upon them by s. 156 of the Finance Act 2003. Operative from 31 December 2006.

CITATION, COMMENCEMENT AND EFFECT

1 These Regulations may be cited as the Overseas Life Insurance Companies Regulations 2006, shall come into force on 31st December 2006 and shall have effect in relation to periods of account (whenever beginning) which end on or after that day.

2 In these Regulations–

"overseas life insurance company" has the meaning given in section 156(5) of the Finance Act 2003;

"period of account" has the meaning given in section 832(1) of the Income and Corporation Taxes Act 1988.

MODIFICATIONS OF THE INCOME AND CORPORATION TAXES ACT

3 In relation to an overseas life insurance company, the Income and Corporation Taxes Act 1988 shall have effect as if it were subject to the following modifications.

4 [Omitted by SI 2007/2146, reg. 3.]

History – Reg. 4 omitted by SI 2007/2146, reg. 3, with effect in relation to periods of account beginning on or after 1 January 2007 which end on or after 14 August 2007.

5(1) Modify section 76 (expenses of insurance companies) as follows.

5(2) For subsection (3) substitute–

"76(3) For the purposes of this section **"expenses payable"** means–

(a) where the company is a UK-authorised firm, expenses brought into account in the periodical return of the company for a period of account in line 12, 22 or 25 of Form 40 (the revenue account) in relation to the long-term business carried on by the company at a permanent establishment in the United Kingdom;

(b) where the company is an EEA firm or a Treaty firm–

(i) so much of the expenses included in item II.8 or 9(a) of the long-term business technical account included in IAD accounts as are attributable to a permanent establishment in the United Kingdom through which the company carries on life assurance business; or

(ii) so much of the expenses included in the income statement included in IAS accounts as are equivalent to expenses that would be included in item II.8 or 9(a) of the long-term business technical account included in any IAD accounts and are so attributable;

but does not include any of the amounts falling within subsections (4), (5) or (6).".

5(3) In subsection (7), in Step 2–

(a) in paragraph (c) omit "or", and

(b) at the end insert–
", or

(e) equal to the amount–

$$S1 = \frac{FOTRA}{TBLAGAB}$$

where–

S1 is the amount given by Step 1,

FOTRA is the amount of any profits and gains arising from a FOTRA security, or from any loan relationship represented by it (after applying the provisions of section 154(2) to (7) of the Finance Act 1996), excluded by virtue of the tax exemption condition of that security,

TBLAGAB means the income from the investments of an overseas life insurance company referable in accordance with section 432A to the basic life assurance and general annuity business of the permanent establishment in the United Kingdom through which the company carries on life assurance business, and

"FOTRA security" and **"tax exemption condition"** have the same meaning as in section 154(8) of the Finance Act 1996.".

5(4)   [Omitted by SI 2007/2146, reg. 4(3).]

5(5)   In subsection (15), after the definition of "expenses payable" insert–

"**"long-term business technical account"** means the technical account for life-assurance business included in IAD accounts, or where the technical account included in the IAD accounts for non-life-insurance business of the company is used for all business, such part of that account as relates to the long-term business of the company;".

History – In reg. 5(2) in the substituted subsection (3)(b)(i) and (ii) the words "long-term business technical account" substituted for "profit and loss account" by SI 2007/3449, reg. 3(2), with effect from 28 December 2007 in relation to periods of account which begin on or after 1 January 2008.
In reg. 5(2), in the substituted subsection (3), para. (b) substituted by SI 2007/2146, reg. 4(2), with effect in relation to periods of account beginning on or after 1 January 2007 which end on or after 14 August 2007.
In reg. 5(3)(a) "(c)" substituted for "(b)" and in reg. 5(3)(b) the inserted paragraph renumbered from "(d)" to "(e)" by SI 2008/1924, reg. 3, with effect in relation to periods of account beginning on or after 1 January 2008 which end on or after 12 August 2008.
Reg. 5(4) omitted by SI 2007/2146, reg. 4(3), with effect in relation to periods of account beginning on or after 1 January 2007 which end on or after 14 August 2007.
Reg. 5(5) inserted by SI 2007/3449, reg. 3(3), with effect from 28 December 2007 in relation to periods of account which begin on or after 1 January 2008.

6(1)   Modify section 431 (interpretative provisions relating to insurance companies) as follows.

6(1ZA)   Modify subsection (2) in accordance with paragraphs (1A) to (5).

6(1A)   In the definition of "foreign business assets" omit–

(a)   "either",

(b)   "or" at the end of paragraph (a), and

(c)   paragraph (b).

6(2)   In the definition of "insurance company"–

(a)   in paragraph (a), after "contracts of insurance" insert "(a "UK-authorised firm")", and

(b)   in paragraph (b)–

(i)   for "paragraph 5(d) of Schedule 3 to that Act" substitute "sub-paragraph (d) or (da) of paragraph 5 of Schedule 3 to that Act (an "EEA firm");",

(ii)   after "Schedule 4 to that Act" insert "(a "Treaty firm")", and

(iii)   in sub-paragraph (ii) for "branch or agency" substitute "permanent establishment".

6(2A)   In the case of an EEA firm or a Treaty firm, for the definition of "liabilities" substitute–

"**"liabilities"**, where the company concerned is an EEA firm or a Treaty firm–

(a)   does not include liabilities that have been reinsured, but

(b)   subject to that, means liabilities (including those which arise from deposit back arrangements) as determined in accordance with actuarial principles for the purposes of any return equivalent to a periodical return and required to be made by the company under the law of the territory in which the company is resident;".

6(3)   In the definition of "overseas life insurance company" for "branch or agency" substitute "permanent establishment".

6(4)   Substitute the following definitions in the appropriate places–

"**"value"**, in relation to assets and where the company concerned is an overseas life insurance company, means–

(a)   their value as taken into account for the purposes of the company's periodical return, or

(b)   where their value is not taken into account for the purposes of such a periodical return, their value as taken into account for the purposes of any return equivalent to a periodical return and required to be made by the company under the law of the territory in which the company is resident;";

"**"insurance business transfer scheme"** means a scheme falling within section 105 of the Financial Services and Markets Act 2000 and includes a reference to–

(a)   an excluded scheme falling within Case 2, 3, 4 or 5 of subsection (3) of that section; and

(b)   a qualifying overseas transfer;".

6(5)   Insert the following definitions in the appropriate places–

    ""free assets amount", in relation to an overseas life insurance company, means the excess of the value of the relevant assets over the relevant liabilities, and for the purposes of this definition–

    (a)   relevant assets are such assets of the company's long-term insurance fund as fall to be attributed, for the purposes of section 11AA(2), to the permanent establishment in the United Kingdom through which the company carries on long-term business; and

    (b)   relevant liabilities are–

        (i)   such liabilities of the long-term business as fall to be attributed, for the purposes of section 11AA(2), to the permanent establishment; and

        (ii)   any money debts (within the meaning of Chapter 2 of Part 4 of the Finance Act 1996) of the company which are not within sub-paragraph (i) above but which are owed in respect of that business and fall to be attributed, for the purposes of section 11AA(2), to the permanent establishment; and

    (c)   [omitted by SI 2008/1924, reg. 4(7);]";

    ""IAD accounts" means the accounts drawn up in accordance with the Council Directive of 19th December 1991 on the annual accounts and consolidated accounts of insurance undertakings (No. 91/674/EEC);";

    ""IAS accounts" means accounts prepared in accordance with international accounting standards;";

    ""long-term insurance fund", in the case of an overseas life insurance company where the company is an EEA firm or a Treaty firm, means–

    (a)   the technical account for life-assurance business of the company included in the IAD accounts; or

    (b)   where the technical account included in the IAD accounts for non-life-insurance business of the company is used for all business, such part of that account as relates to the long-term business of the company; or

    (c)   such part of the income statement the life assurance business of the company included in the IAS accounts;

    and references to assets of the long-term insurance fund shall be read as references to assets from which any income or gain is or would be included in either that technical account or that part of the technical account or that part of the income statement";

    ""periodical return" means, in relation to an overseas life insurance company, where the company is an EEA firm or a Treaty firm, the IAD accounts or the IAS accounts;";

    ""qualifying overseas transfer" means so much of any transfer of the whole or any part of the business of an overseas life insurance company carried on through a permanent establishment in the United Kingdom as takes place in accordance with any authorisation granted outside the United Kingdom for the purposes of Article 14 of the Council Directive of 5th November 2002 concerning life assurance (No. 2002/83/EC);".

6(6)   In subsection (2YC), at the end insert–

    "so far as that income and those gains fall to be attributed, for the purposes of section 11AA(2), to the permanent establishment in the United Kingdom through which the company carries on life assurance business.".

6(7)   In subsection (2YD), at the end insert–

    "so far as those amounts and that deduction fall to be attributed, for the purposes of section 11AA(2), to the permanent establishment in the United Kingdom through which the company carries on life assurance business.".

History – In reg. 6(1) "(2)" which appeared after "431" omitted by SI 2008/1924, reg. 4(2), with effect in relation to periods of account beginning on or after 1 January 2008 which end on or after 12 August 2008.
Reg. 6(1ZA) inserted by SI 2008/1924, reg. 4(3), with effect in relation to periods of account beginning on or after 1 January 2008 which end on or after 12 August 2008.
Reg. 6(1A) substituted by SI 2008/1924, reg. 4(4), with effect in relation to periods of account beginning on or after 1 January 2008 which end on or after 12 August 2008.
Former reg. 6(1A) inserted by SI 2007/2146, reg. 5(2), with effect in relation to periods of account beginning on or after 1 January 2007 which end on or after 14 August 2007.
In reg. 6(5), definition of "IAS accounts" inserted by SI 2007/2146, reg. 5(3)(a), with effect in relation to periods of account beginning on or after 1 January 2007 which end on or after 14 August 2007.
Reg. 6(2)(b)(i) substituted by SI 2007/3449, reg. 4(2), with effect from 28 December 2007 in relation to periods of account which begin on or after 1 January 2008.
Reg. 6(2A) inserted by SI 2008/1924, reg. 4(5), with effect in relation to periods of account beginning on or after 1 January 2008 which end on or after 12 August 2008.

In reg. 6(4) the inserted definition of "liabilities" omitted and in the inserted definition of "insurance business transfer scheme" the words ", 4 or 5" substituted for "or 4" omitted by SI 2008/1924, reg. 4(6), with effect in relation to periods of account beginning on or after 1 January 2008 which end on or after 12 August 2008. Former definition of "liabilities" read as follows: ""**liabilities**", where the company concerned is an overseas life insurance company, does not include liabilities that have been reinsured, and (subject to that) means–

    "(a) the long-term liabilities of the company determined for the purposes of the company's periodical return on actuarial principles in accordance with section 5.6 of the Prudential Sourcebook (Insurers), or

    (b) in the case of liabilities not determined for the purposes of such a periodical return, liabilities as determined in accordance with actuarial principles for the purposes of any return equivalent to a periodical return and required to be made by the company under the law of the territory in which the company is resident;"

In reg. 6(5) in the inserted definition of "free assets amount" the words "relevant liabilities" substituted for the words "aggregate of the relevant liabilities and the amount of the shareholders' excess assets", the word and at end of para. (a) inserted and para. (c) omitted by SI 2008/1924, reg. 4(7), with effect in relation to periods of account beginning on or after 1 January 2008 which end on or after 12 August 2008.

In reg. 6(5) in the inserted definition of "long-term insurance fund", "life-assurance" substituted for "life assurance" by SI 2007/3449, reg. 4(3), with effect from 28 December 2007 in relation to periods of account which begin on or after 1 January 2008.

Reg. 6(5)(aa) inserted by SI 2007/3449, reg. 4(3), with effect from 28 December 2007 in relation to periods of account which begin on or after 1 January 2008.

In reg. 6(5)(b) the words "as relates to" omitted following "statement" and the words "either that technical account or that part of the technical account or that part of the income statement" substituted for "that technical account or income statement" by SI 2007/3449, reg. 4(3), with effect from 28 December 2007 in relation to periods of account which begin on or after 1 January 2008.

In reg. 6(5), in the definition of "long-term insurance fund" words from "means–" onwards substituted for the words "means the technical account for life assurance business of the company included in the IAD accounts, and references to assets of the long-term insurance fund shall be read as references to assets from which any income or gain is or would be included in the technical account" inserted by SI 2007/2146, reg. 5(3)(b), with effect in relation to periods of account beginning on or after 1 January 2007 which end on or after 14 August 2007.

In reg. 6(5), in the definition of "periodical return" the words "or the IAS accounts" inserted by SI 2007/2146, reg. 5(3)(c), with effect in relation to periods of account beginning on or after 1 January 2007 which end on or after 14 August 2007.

Reg. 6(6) inserted by SI 2008/1924, reg. 4(8), with effect in relation to periods of account beginning on or after 1 January 2008 which end on or after 12 August 2008.

Reg. 6(7) inserted by SI 2008/1924, reg. 4(8), with effect in relation to periods of account beginning on or after 1 January 2008 which end on or after 12 August 2008.

7   In section 431D (meaning of "overseas life assurance business"), in subsection (1), after "means life assurance business" insert "carried on through a permanent establishment in the United Kingdom by an overseas life insurance company".

7A(1)   Modify section 431G (company carrying on life assurance business) as follows.

7A(2)   In subsection (1) after "life assurance business" insert "through a permanent establishment in the United Kingdom".

7A(2)   In subsections (2) and (3)(a) and (b), after "life assurance business" insert "carried on through a permanent establishment in the United Kingdom".

History – Reg. 7A inserted by SI 2007/2146, reg. 6, with effect in relation to periods of account beginning on or after 1 January 2007 which end on or after 14 August 2007.

7B   In section 431H (company carrying on life assurance business and other insurance business), in subsection (1), after "any other kind" insert "through a permanent establishment in the United Kingdom".

History – Reg. 7B inserted by SI 2007/2146, reg. 6, with effect in relation to periods of account beginning on or after 1 January 2007 which end on or after 14 August 2007.

8(1)   Modify section 432A (apportionment of income and gains) as follows.

8(2)   [Omitted by SI 2008/1924, reg. 5.]

8(3)   After subsection (9A) insert–

"**432A(9AA)** In this section–

    "**assets**" means those assets that fall to be attributed, for the purposes of section 11AA(2), to the permanent establishment in the United Kingdom through which the company carries on life assurance business;

    "**liabilities**" means those liabilities that fall to be attributed, for the purposes of section 11AA(2), to the permanent establishment in the United Kingdom through which the company carries on life assurance business.".

History – Reg. 8(2) omitted by SI 2008/1924, reg. 5, with effect from 12 August 2008.

Former reg. 8(2) substituted by SI 2007/2146, reg. 7, with effect in relation to periods of account beginning on or after 1 January 2007 which end on or after 14 August 2007.

9(1)   Modify section 432B (apportionment of receipts brought into account) as follows.

9(2)   In subsection (3) after "business" insert (in the first place) "of the permanent establishment in the United Kingdom through which the company carries on life assurance business".

9(3)   [Omitted by SI 2008/1924, reg. 6.]

History – In reg. 9(2) the words "(in the first place" substituted for the words "in (both places" by SI 2007/2146, reg. 8(2), with effect in relation to periods of account beginning on or after 1 January 2007 which end on or after 14 August 2007.
Reg. 9(3) omitted by SI 2008/1924, reg. 6, with effect from 12 August 2008.
In former reg. 9(3)(a) substituted for reg. 9(3)(a) and (b) by SI 2007/2146, reg. 8(3), with effect in relation to periods of account beginning on or after 1 January 2007 which end on or after 14 August 2007.

10   After section 434A (computation of losses and limitation on relief) insert–

"Treatment of annuities

434AA   An overseas life insurance company shall not be entitled to treat as paid out of profits or gains brought into charge to income tax any part of the annuities paid by the company which is referable to its life assurance business.".

11(1)   Modify section 440 (transfers of assets etc) as follows.

11(2)   In subsection (2), in paragraph (b), for is "within another of those categories" substitute "is not within the corresponding category".

11(3)   In subsection (4)–

(a)   in paragraphs (a) and (d) to (f) before "assets" insert "UK", and

(b)   at the end insert–

     "(h)   assets of the company which are not UK assets.".

11(4)   After subsection (4) insert–

     "**440(4AA)**   Section 13 of the Capital Allowances Act 2001 (use for qualifying activity of plant or machinery provided for other purposes) shall apply in relation to any case in which an asset or part of an asset held by an overseas life insurance company–

     (a)   ceases to be within the category set out in paragraph (h) of subsection (4) above; and

     (b)   at the same time comes within another of the categories set out in that subsection.".

     "**440(4AB)**   Where goodwill is acquired by an EEA firm or a Treaty firm ("the transferee") as a result of an insurance business transfer scheme which has effect to transfer long-term business from any person who is not such a firm to the transferee–

     (a)   if the goodwill (or part of it) was within the category set out in paragraph (e) of subsection (4) above immediately before the acquisition, the goodwill (or part) shall for the purposes of subsections (2) and (3) above be treated as being within that category immediately afterwards, and

     (b)   if the goodwill (or part of it) was within the category set out in paragraph (f) of subsection (4) above immediately before the acquisition, the goodwill (or part) shall for the purposes of subsections (2) and (3) above be treated as being within that category immediately afterwards.".

11(5)   At the end insert–

     "**440(7)**   For the purposes of this section UK assets are assets which fall to be attributed, for the purposes of section 11AA(2), to the permanent establishment in the United Kingdom through which the company carries on life assurance business.

     440(8)   Where the transferor company mentioned in subsection (2) is an overseas life insurance company, this section shall have effect, as regards the time immediately before the acquisition.

     440(9)   Where the acquiring company mentioned in subsection (2) is an overseas life insurance company, this section shall have effect as regards the time immediately after the acquisition.".

History – In reg. 11(3)(a) the words "and (d) to (f)" substituted for the words "to (f)" by SI 2007/2146, reg. 9, with effect in relation to periods of account beginning on or after 1 January 2007 which end on or after 14 August 2007.
In reg. 11(4), in the inserted (4AA), the reference to "2001" inserted after "Act" by SI 2007/3449, reg. 5, with effect from 28 December 2007 in relation to periods of account which begin on or after 1 January 2008.
In reg. 11(4), the inserted (4AB) inserted by SI 2007/3449, reg. 5, with effect from 28 December 2007 in relation to periods of account which begin on or after 1 January 2008.

12(1)   Modify section 440A (securities) as follows.

12(2)   In subsection (2)–

(a)   in paragraph (a) before "securities" in the first place where it occurs insert "UK",

(b)   in paragraphs (d) and (e) before "securities" insert "UK",

(c)   in paragraph (d) omit "and", and

(d)   at the end insert

     ", and

Statutory Instruments

(g)　the non-UK securities shall be treated for those purposes as a separate holding which is not of any of the descriptions mentioned in the preceding paragraphs.".

12(3)　After subsection (6) insert–

"**440A(6A)**　For the purposes of this section–

(a)　UK securities are such securities as are assets which fall to be attributed, for the purposes of section 11AA(2), to the permanent establishment in the United Kingdom through which the company carries on life assurance business; and

(b)　non-UK securities are securities which are not UK securities.".

History – In reg. 12(2)(b) the words "(d) and" substituted for the words "(c) to" by SI 2007/2146, reg. 10, with effect in relation to periods of account beginning on or after 1 January 2007 which end on or after 14 August 2007.

13　In section 440B (modifications where tax charged under Case I of Schedule D)–

(a)　for subsection (3) substitute–

"**440B(3)**　Subsection (1) of section 440 has effect as if the only categories specified in subsection (4) of that section were–

(a)　UK assets of the long-term insurance fund,

(b)　other UK assets, and

(c)　assets of the company which are not UK assets,

and UK assets has the meaning given by section 440(7).", and

(b)　for subsection (4) substitute–

"**440B(4)**　Section 440A applies as if for paragraphs (a), (d) and (e) of subsection (2) there were substituted–

"(a)　so many of the UK securities as are included in the company's long-term insurance fund shall be treated for the purposes of corporation tax as a separate holding which is an asset of that fund,

(b)　any remaining UK securities shall be treated for those purposes as a separate holding which is not of the description mentioned in the preceding paragraph, and

(c)　the non-UK securities shall be treated for those purposes as a separate holding which is not of any of the descriptions mentioned in the preceding paragraphs.".".

History – In reg. 13(a), in the substituted subsection (3), the words "Subsection (1) of section 440 has" substituted for the words "Section 440(1) and (2) have" by SI 2007/2146, reg. 11(2), with effect in relation to periods of account beginning on or after 1 January 2007 which end on or after 14 August 2007.
In reg. 13(b), in the substituted subsection (4), the words ", (d) and (e)" substituted for the words "to (e)" and para. (a) substituted by SI 2007/2146, reg. 11(3), with effect in relation to periods of account beginning on or after 1 January 2007 which end on or after 14 August 2007.

14　In section 442A (taxation of investment return where risk reinsured) after subsection (6) insert–

"**442A(7)**　In the case of an overseas life insurance company, the investment return treated as accruing under this section in any accounting period in relation to a policy or contract shall be treated as chargeable profits within section 11(2) of the Taxes Act 1988 where the policy or contract is one which in that accounting period gives rise, or but for the reinsurance arrangement would give rise, to such profits.".

14ZA　In section 444AA (transfers of business: deemed periodical returns), in subsection (5), in a case where the transferor is an EEA firm or a Treaty firm, for paragraphs (a) and (b) substitute–

"(a)　in respect of the amount of the relevant long-term business provisions immediately before the transfer, and

(b)　in respect of the value, immediately before the transfer, of the assets transferred.".

History – Reg. 14ZA inserted by SI 2008/1924, reg. 7, with effect in relation to periods of account beginning on or after 1 January 2008 which end on or after 12 August 2008 but only in relation to transfers of business taking place on or after 1 July 2008.

14ZB　In section 444ABA (relevant non-transferred assets), in subsection (1), in a case where the transferor is an EEA firm or a Treaty firm, for the definition of BTO substitute–

"BTO is the lesser of VA and APL, where–

(a)　VA is the value of the assets transferred by the insurance business transfer scheme shown (or treated as shown) in the periodical return of the transferor for the period of account of the transferor including the transfer date, and

(b)　APL is the amount of the profit or loss for the financial year shown in the balance sheet in the periodical return for the last period of account of the transferor ending before the transfer date, together with–

(i) in the case of IAD accounts, the amount of profit or loss shown as being brought forward in that balance sheet, and

(ii) in the case of IAS accounts, the amount of retained earnings shown as being brought forward in that balance sheet.".

History – Reg. 14ZB inserted by SI 2008/1924, reg. 7, with effect in relation to periods of account beginning on or after 1 January 2008 which end on or after 12 August 2008 but only in relation to transfers of business taking place on or after 1 July 2008.

14ZC(1)   In a case where the transferor is an EEA or a Treaty firm, modify section 444ABB (retained assets) as follows.

14ZC(2)   In subsection (1)–

(a)   for "RL13" (in both places) substitute "RL"; and

(b)   in the definition of RL13, for "AL13" substitute "APL".

14ZC(3)   In subsection (1A) for paragraphs (a) to (c) substitute–

"(a)   APL is the amount of the profit or loss for the financial year shown in the balance sheet in the periodical return for the last period of account of the transferor ending before the transfer date, together with–

(i) in the case of IAD accounts, the amount of profit or loss shown as brought forward in that balance sheet, and

in the case of IAS accounts, the amount of retained earnings shown as brought forward in that balance sheet;

(b)   VE is the amount (if any) by which VA exceeds VTL where–

(i) VA is the value of the assets transferred by the insurance business transfer scheme shown (or treated as shown) in the periodical return of the transferor for the period of account of the transferor including the transfer date, and

(ii) VTL is the value of the liabilities transferred by the insurance business transfer scheme (but excluding those which arise from deposit back arrangements); and

(c)   relevant retained liabilities are any liabilities of the company's long-term business which are owed by the company immediately after the transfer date and are shown (or treated as shown) as entries–

(i) at items C3 (net of reinsurance) and G in IAD accounts, or

at equivalent items in the balance sheet in IAS accounts.".

History – Reg. 14ZC inserted by SI 2008/1924, reg. 7, with effect in relation to periods of account beginning on or after 1 January 2008 which end on or after 12 August 2008 but only in relation to transfers of business taking place on or after 1 July 2008.

14A(1)   In a case where the transferor is an EEA firm or a Treaty firm, modify section 444ABD (transferor's period of account including transfer) as follows.

14A(2)   In subsection (1), for paragraphs (a) and (b) substitute–

"(a)   the value of the liabilities transferred by the insurance business transfer scheme (but excluding those which arise from deposit back arrangements), exceeds

(b)   the value, immediately before the transfer, of the assets transferred by the insurance business transfer scheme,".

History – Reg. 14A substituted by SI 2008/1924, reg. 8, with effect in relation to periods of account beginning on or after 1 January 2008 which end on or after 12 August 2008. Former reg. 14A read as follows:
"**14A**   In section 444ABD (transferor's period of account including transfer), in subsection (1)(b), in a case where the transferor is an EEA firm or a Treaty firm, omit "line 32 of".

History – Reg. 14A inserted by SI 2007/2146, reg. 12, with effect in relation to periods of account beginning on or after 1 January 2007 which end on or after 14 August 2007."

14A(3)   In subsection (1E) for "amount" (in the first place) substitute "value".

15(1)   In a case where the transferor is an EEA firm or a Treaty firm, modify section 444AC (transfer schemes: reduction of income of transferee) as follows.

15(2)   In subsection (4) for the words from "lesser of" to the end substitute–

"the amount of the profit or loss for the financial year shown in the balance sheet in the periodical return for the last period of account of the transferor ending before the transfer date, together with–

(a)   in the case of IAD accounts, the amount of profit or loss shown as being brought forward in that balance sheet, and

(b)   in the case of IAS accounts, the amount of retained earnings shown as being brought forward in that balance sheet.".

15(3) Omit subsection (5).

History – Reg. 15 substituted by SI 2008/1924, reg. 9, with effect in relation to periods of account beginning on or after 1 January 2008 which end on or after 12 August 2008 but only in relation to transfers of business taking place on or after 1 July 2008. Former reg. 15 read as follows:

"**15(1)** Modify section 444AC (transfers of business: excess of assets or liabilities) as follows.

15(2) In subsections (2)(a), (2A)(b) and (5)(b), in a case where the transferee is an EEA firm or a Treaty firm, for "transferee's line 31 amount in relation to the transfer" substitute "value of the assets transferred to the transferee's long-term insurance fund in consideration of the assumption by the transferee of the liabilities to policy holders and annuitants".

15(3) In subsection (5A), in a case where the transferor is an EEA firm or a Treaty firm–

(a) for the words from "means–" to "other" substitute "means, in relation to an overseas life insurance company where the company is an EEA firm or a Treaty firm,"; and

(b) omit "(in either case)".

History – Reg. 15 substituted by SI 2007/3449, reg. 6, with effect from 28 December 2007 in relation to periods of account which begin on or after 1 January 2008."

15A [Omitted by SI 2008/1924, reg. 10.]

History – Reg. 15A omitted by SI 2008/1924, reg. 10, with effect in relation to periods of account beginning on or after 1 January 2008 which end on or after 12 August 2008 but only in relation to transfers of business taking place on or after 1 July 2008.

15B In a case where the transferor or the transferee is an EEA firm or a Treaty firm (or both are), omit section 444AE (transfers of business: FAFTS).

History – Reg. 15B inserted by SI 2008/1924, reg. 11, with effect in relation to periods of account beginning on or after 1 January 2008 which end on or after 12 August 2008.

15C In section 444AEA (transfer schemes: anti-avoidance rule), in subsection (6), in the definition of "surplus-increasing transfer of assets", in a case where the transferor is an EEA firm or a Treaty firm, for "increases the amount of total surplus shown in line 39 of Form 58" substitute "gives rise to an amount that increases the profits or reduces the losses shown".

History – Reg. 15C inserted by SI 2008/1924, reg. 12, with effect in relation to periods of account beginning on or after 1 January 2008 which end on or after 12 August 2008 but only in relation to transfers of business taking place on or after 1 July 2008.

16 In section 444AL (interpretation of sections 444AF to 444AK), in subsection (3), in a case where the transferor is an EEA firm or a Treaty firm–

(a) for "insurance company" substitute "overseas life insurance company where the company is an EEA firm or a Treaty firm", and

(b) for "surplus on valuation as shown in the periodical return" substitute "balance on the technical account – long-term business, so far as it relates to life assurance business carried on in the United Kingdom through a permanent establishment".

17 In section 460(10A) (exemption from tax in respect of life or endowment business) after "scheme" insert "or a qualifying overseas transfer".

18 [Omitted by SI 2007/2146, reg. 13.]

History – Reg. 18 omitted by SI 2007/2146, reg. 13, with effect in relation to periods of account beginning on or after 1 January 2007 which end on or after 14 August 2007. Former reg. 18 read as follows:

"**18(1)** In Schedule 19AA (overseas life assurance fund)–

(a) omit paragraph 5(5)(c) (and the reference to it in paragraph 2(3) of that Schedule),

(b) at the end insert–

"6 In its application to an overseas life insurance company this Schedule shall have effect as if–

(a) the references in paragraphs 2 and 3 to assets of the long-term insurance fund were to such of those assets as fall to be attributed, for the purposes of section 11AA(2), to the permanent establishment in the United Kingdom through which the company carries on life assurance business; and

(b) the references in paragraphs 2 and 4 to the liabilities of the company's long-term business were to such of those liabilities as are attributable to the permanent establishment; and

(c) the references in paragraph 4(1) and (2) to liabilities of the company's long-term insurance fund which represent a money debt, and the reference in paragraph 4(5)(b) to money debts of the company, were references to such of those liabilities or debts as fall to be attributed, for the purposes of section 11AA(2), to the permanent establishment."."

MODIFICATIONS OF THE FINANCE ACT 1989

19 In relation to an overseas life insurance company, the Finance Act 1989 shall have effect as if it were subject to the following modifications.

20 In section 82 (calculation of profits: bonuses etc), in subsection (2) at the end insert "to the extent that such amounts fall to be attributed, for the purposes of section 11AA(2) of the Taxes Act 1988, to the permanent establishment in the United Kingdom through which the company carries on life assurance business".

21 In section 82A (calculation of profits: policy holders' tax), in subsection (1) at the end insert "and that such tax falls to be attributed, for the purposes of section 11AA(2) of the Taxes Act 1988, to the permanent establishment in the United Kingdom through which the company carries on life assurance business".

22(1) Modify section 83 (receipts to be taken into account) as follows.

22(2)   In subsection (2)(a) and (d) after "income" insert–

"so far as such income falls to be attributed, for the purposes of section 11AA(2) of the Taxes Act 1988, to the permanent establishment in the United Kingdom through which the company carries on life assurance business".

22(2A)   In subsection (2A), in the case of an EEA firm or a Treaty firm, omit paragraph (ac).

22(3)   [Omitted by SI 2007/2146, reg. 14.]

22(4)   [Omitted by SI 2007/2146, reg. 14.]

22(5)   In subsection (8) after the definition of "add" insert–

""**assets**" means those assets that fall to be attributed, for the purposes of section 11AA(2), to the permanent establishment in the United Kingdom through which the company carries on life assurance business;".

History – Reg. 22(2A) inserted by SI 2008/1924, reg. 13, with effect in relation to periods of account beginning on or after 1 January 2008 which end on or after 12 August 2008.
Reg. 22(3) and (4) omitted by SI 2007/2146, reg. 14, with effect in relation to periods of account beginning on or after 1 January 2007 which end on or after 14 August 2007, but only where the transfer of business or demutualisation concerned took place before 21 March 2007.

22A   In section 83XA (structural assets), in subsection (3), in the case of an EEA firm or a Treaty firm, for paragraph (a) substitute–

"(a)   assets listed under 1 and 2 in C(ii) in Article 6 of the Council Directive of 19th December 1991 on the annual accounts and consolidated accounts of insurance undertakings (no. 91/674/EEC), and".

History – Reg. 22A inserted by SI 2007/2146, reg. 15, with effect in relation to periods of account beginning on or after 1 January 2007 which end on or after 14 August 2007.

22B   In the case of an EEA firm or a Treaty firm, omit section 83YC to 83YF (financing-arrangement-funded transfers).

History – Reg. 22B inserted by SI 2008/1924, reg. 14, with effect in relation to periods of account beginning on or after 1 January 2008 which end on or after 12 August 2008. The heading to reg. 14 suggests that there is a reg. 22C also to be inserted but no reg. 22C is provided.

23   [Omitted by SI 2008/1924, reg. 15.]

History – Reg. 23 omitted by SI 2008/1924, reg. 15, with effect in relation to periods of account beginning on or after 1 January 2008 which end on or after 12 August 2008.

24(1)   Modify section 83A (meaning of "brought into account"), as follows.

24(2)   After subsection (2) insert–

"**83A(2A)**   In the case of an EEA firm or a Treaty firm, subject to the following provisions of this section, the accounts recognised for the purposes of those sections are–

(a)   such technical accounts (or such parts of those accounts) included in the IAD accounts, or

(b)   such parts of the income statements included in the IAS accounts,

as relate to the whole of the company's long-term business or such of that business as is carried on through the permanent establishment in the United Kingdom through which the company carries on life assurance business.".

24(3)   At the end insert–

"**83A(7)**   In the case of a UK-authorised firm references in this section to the company's long-term business shall be treated as references to the whole of that business or to the whole of that business other than business in respect of which preparation of a revenue account for the purposes of Chapter 9 of the Prudential Sourcebook (Insurers) is not required.".

History – In reg. 24(2), in the inserted subsection (2A), the words ", or the income statement included in the IAS accounts," inserted by SI 2007/2146, reg. 16, with effect in relation to periods of account beginning on or after 1 January 2007 which end on or after 14 August 2007.
In reg. 24(2), in the inserted (2A) the words from "are–" to the end substituted by SI 2007/3449, reg. 7, with effect from 28 December 2007 in relation to periods of account which begin on or after 1 January 2008.

24A   In section 85A(6) (excess adjusted Case I profits)–

(a)   in paragraph (a), at the end insert "to the extent such income falls to be attributed, for the purposes of section 11AA(2) of that Act, to the permanent establishment in the United Kingdom through which the company carries on life assurance business",

(b)   in paragraph (b), at the end insert "to the extent such gains fall to be attributed, for the purposes of section 11AA(2) of that Act, to the permanent establishment in the United Kingdom through which the company carries on life assurance business".

History – Reg. 24A inserted by SI 2007/2146, reg. 17, with effect in relation to periods of account beginning on or after 1 January 2007 which end on or after 14 August 2007.

25 [Omitted by SI 2008/1924, reg. 16.]

History – Reg. 25 omitted by SI 2008/1924, reg. 16, with effect in relation to periods of account beginning on or after 1 January 2008 which end on or after 12 August 2008. Former reg. 25 read as follows:

"**25** In section 88 (corporation tax: policy holders' fraction of profits), in subsection (3)–

    (a)   after "business" insert "so far as that income and those gains fall to be attributed, for the purposes of section 11AA(2) of the Taxes Act 1988, to the permanent establishment in the United Kingdom through which the company carries on life assurance business", and

    (b)   at the end insert–

"so far as those amounts and that deduction fall to be attributed, for the purposes of section 11AA(2) of the Taxes Act 1988, to that permanent establishment"."

26(1) Modify section 89 (policy holders' share of profits) as follows.

26(2) [Omitted by SI 2008/1924, reg. 17.]

26(3) In subsection (2), in paragraph (b), after "distributions" insert–

", so far as those distributions fall to be attributed, for the purposes of section 11AA(2) of the Taxes Act 1988, to the permanent establishment in the United Kingdom through which the company carries on life assurance business,".

26(4) In subsection (5) after "business" insert "carried on at a permanent establishment in the United Kingdom".

26(5) In subsection (6) after "provide" insert "and subject to subsection (6A)".

26(6) After subsection (6) insert–

"**89(6A)** In the case of an EEA firm or a Treaty firm, in this section "brought into account" means brought into account–

    (a)   in such technical accounts (or such parts of those accounts) included in the IAD accounts, or

    (b)   in such parts of the income statements included in the IAS accounts,

as relate to the whole of the company's long-term business or such of that business as is carried on through the permanent establishment in the United Kingdom through which the company carries on life assurance business.".

History – Reg. 26(2) omitted by SI 2008/1924, reg. 17, with effect in relation to periods of account beginning on or after 1 January 2008 which end on or after 12 August 2008.

In reg. 26(6), in the inserted subsection (6A), the words from "means" to the end substituted by SI 2007/3449, reg. 8, with effect from 28 December 2007 in relation to periods of account which begin on or after 1 January 2008.

In reg. 26(6), in the inserted subsection (6A), the words ", or the income statement included in the IAS accounts," inserted by SI 2007/2146, reg. 18, with effect in relation to periods of account beginning on or after 1 January 2007 which end on or after 14 August 2007.

MODIFICATION OF THE TAXATION OF CHARGEABLE GAINS ACT 1992

27 In relation to an overseas life insurance company, the Taxation of Chargeable Gains Act 1992 shall have effect as if it were subject to the following modifications.

28 In section 10B (non-resident company with United Kingdom permanent establishment), in subsection (1)(b) omit "situated in the United Kingdom and".

29 In section 185 (deemed disposal of assets on company ceasing to be resident in UK), in subsection (4)–

(a)   in paragraph (a) omit "are situated in the United Kingdom and", and

(b)   in paragraph (b) omit "are so situated and".

30 In section 212 (annual deemed disposal of holdings of unit trusts etc) after subsection (5) insert–

"**212(5A)** In its application to an overseas life insurance company, this section shall have effect as if the references in subsections (1) and (2) to assets were to such of the assets concerned as fall to be attributed, for the purposes of section 11AA(2) of the Taxes Act, to the permanent establishment in the United Kingdom through which the company carries on life assurance business.".

31 In section 213 (spreading of gains and losses under section 212), in subsection (4) after "long-term business" insert "in the United Kingdom through a permanent establishment".

32 In Schedule 7A (restriction on set-off of pre-entry losses), after paragraph 1(4) insert–

"**1(4A)** Where–

    (a)   an asset is held by an overseas life insurance company, and

    (b)   section 440 of the Taxes Act applies at any time in relation to the asset,

the asset shall not be treated for the purposes of sub-paragraph (3A)(b) above as having become a chargeable asset at that time.".

MODIFICATION OF THE FINANCE (NO. 2) ACT 1992

33 [Omitted by SI 2007/2146, reg. 19.]

History – Reg. 33 omitted by SI 2007/2146, reg. 19, with effect in relation to periods of account beginning on or after 1 January 2007 which end on or after 14 August 2007.

MODIFICATION OF THE FINANCE ACT 1995

34(1) In relation to an overseas life insurance company, the Finance Act 1995 shall have effect as if it were subject to the following modifications.

34(2) In Schedule 8, in paragraph 55(1)–

(a) for "33, 37, 38 and 45(1) and (3)" substitute "33 and 37", and

(b) omit the words from "paragraph 46" to the end.

MODIFICATION OF THE FINANCE ACT 1996

35(1) In relation to an overseas life insurance company, the Finance Act 1996 shall have effect as if it were subject to the following modifications.

35(2) In Schedule 9, in paragraph 12 (continuity of treatment: groups etc), in subsection (1)(d) omit the words from "within the meaning" to "overseas life insurance company)".

History – In reg. 35(2) the words "the words from "within the meaning" to "overseas life insurance company)"" substituted for the words ""by paragraph 6(9) of Schedule 19AC to that Act"" by SI 2007/2146, reg. 20, with effect in relation to periods of account beginning on or after 1 January 2007 which end on or after 14 August 2007.

MODIFICATION OF THE CAPITAL ALLOWANCES ACT 2001

36(1) In relation to an overseas life insurance company, the Capital Allowances Act 2001 shall have effect as if it were subject to the following modifications.

36(2) In section 255 (apportionment of allowances and charges), after subsection (1B) insert–

"(2) In its application to an overseas life insurance company, subsection (1A) has effect as if the references to liabilities were only to such liabilities as are attributable to the permanent establishment in the United Kingdom through which the company carries on the business concerned."

History – Reg. 36(2) substituted by SI 2007/2146, reg. 21, with effect in relation to periods of account beginning on or after 1 January 2007 which end on or after 14 August 2007.

MODIFICATION OF THE FINANCE ACT 2002

37 In relation to an overseas life insurance company, the Finance Act 2002 shall have effect as if it were subject to the following modifications.

38 [Omitted by SI 2007/2146, reg. 22(a).]

History – Reg. 38 omitted by SI 2007/2146, reg. 22(a), with effect in relation to periods of account beginning on or after 1 January 2007 which end on or after 14 August 2007.

39 [Omitted by SI 2007/2146, reg. 22(b).]

History – Reg. 39 omitted by SI 2007/2146, reg. 22(b), with effect in relation to periods of account beginning on or after 1 January 2007 which end on or after 14 August 2007.

40 In Schedule 26–

(a) in the case of an EEA firm or a Treaty firm, in paragraph 4 (contracts excluded by virtue of their underlying subject matter), in sub-paragraph (2A)–

after paragraph (a) insert–

"(aa) the company is an EEA firm or a Treaty firm within the meaning of Chapter 1 Part 12 of ICTA;", and

in paragraph (b) for the words "is an approved derivative for the purposes of Rule 3.2.5 of the Insurance Prudential Sourcebook" substitute "is a derivative instrument falling within article 23.3 of the EC Consolidated Life Directive (EC/2002/83)".

(b) in paragraph 28 (transactions within groups), in sub-paragraph (2)(d) omit the words from "within the meaning" to the end.

History – In reg. 40(a)(ii) the words "3.2.5 of the Insurance" substituted for the words "4.3.5 of the Integrated" by SI 2007/2146, reg. 23(2), with effect in relation to periods of account beginning on or after 1 January 2007 which end on or after 14 August 2007.
In reg. 40(b) the words "the words from "within the meaning" to the end" substituted for the words ""by paragraph 6(9) of Schedule 19AC to that Act"" by SI 2007/2146, reg. 23(3), with effect in relation to periods of account beginning on or after 1 January 2007 which end on or after 14 August 2007.

41 In Schedule 29, in paragraph 89 (transfer of life assurance business), in sub-paragraph (1)(b) omit the words from "within the meaning" to "overseas life insurance company)".

History – In reg. 41(2) the words "the words from "within the meaning" to "overseas life insurance company)"" substituted for the words ""by paragraph 6(9) of Schedule 19AC to that Act"" by SI 2007/2146, reg. 23(3), with effect in relation to periods of account beginning on or after 1 January 2007 which end on or after 14 August 2007.

MODIFICATION OF THE INSURANCE COMPANIES (OVERSEAS LIFE ASSURANCE BUSINESS) (COMPLIANCE) REGULATIONS 1995

42(1) In relation to an overseas life insurance company, the Insurance Companies (Overseas Life Assurance Business) (Compliance) Regulations 1995 shall have effect as if they were subject to the following modifications.

42(2) In paragraph 2(1), in the definition of "relevant business", for "branch or agency" substitute "permanent establishment".

REPEALS AND REVOCATIONS

43(1) The enactments specified in Part 1 of the Schedule are repealed to the extent specified.

43(2) The instruments specified in Part 2 of the Schedule are revoked to the extent specified.

SCHEDULE – REPEALS AND REVOCATION

Regulation 41

PART 1

Enactment	Extent of Repeal
Income and Corporation Taxes Act 1988 (c. 1)	Section 444B. Schedule 19AC.
Finance Act 1989 (c. 26)	Section 89A. Schedule 8A.
Taxation of Chargeable Gains Act 1992 (c. 12)	Section 214B. Schedule 7B.
Finance Act 1993 (c. 34)	Section 97. Section 98. Section 101. Section 102. Schedule 9. Schedule 10. Schedule 11.
Finance Act 1995 (c. 4)	In Schedule 8, in paragraph 55(1) the words from 'paragraph 46' to the end. In Schedule 8, paragraphs 35, 38, 39, 40, 42, 44, 45, 46, 48 and 49. In Schedule 9, paragraphs 2 and 6.
Finance Act 1996 (c. 8)	Section 164(3). In Schedule 28, paragraph 5. In Schedule 31, paragraph 8(4) and (5).
Finance Act 1997 (c. 16)	Section 67(5).
Finance (No. 2) Act 1997 (c. 58)	In Schedule 3, paragraph 13.
Finance Act 2000 (c. 17)	Section 75(4). In section 75(6), the words 'In this section–' and paragraph (a). In Schedule 29, paragraph 39.
Capital Allowances Act 2001 (c. 2)	In Schedule 2, paragraph 64(2).

PART 2

Instrument	Extent of Revocation
The Manufactured Dividends (Tax) Regulations 1997 (S.I. 1997/993)	Regulation 2(3)(a).
The Insurance Companies (Capital Redemption Business) (Modification of the Corporation Tax Acts) Regulations 1999 (S.I. 1999/498)	Regulation 8.
The Individual Savings Account (Insurance Companies) (Amendment) Regulations 2000 (S.I. 2000/2075)	Regulation 1A.
The Overseas Life Assurance Fund (Amendment) Order 2000 (S.I. 2000/2188)	Regulation 5.
The Financial Services and Markets Act 2000 (Consequential Amendments) (Taxes) Order 2001 (S.I. 2001/3629)	Article 49. Article 52(1)(l) and (2)(o). Article 59. Article 60(1)(d) and (2)(b). Article 72. Article 73(1)(b) and (2)(b).
The Overseas Life Insurance Companies Regulations 2004 (S.I. 2004/2200)	The whole instrument.
The Finance Act 2004, Sections 38 to 40 and 45 and Schedule 6 (Consequential Amendment of Enactments) Order 2004 (S.I. 2004/2310)	Paragraph 36 of the Schedule.
The Overseas Life Insurance Companies (Amendment) Regulations 2005 (S.I. 2005/3375)	The whole instrument.

FILMS (CERTIFICATION) REGULATIONS 2006

(SI 2006/3281, as amended by SI 2007/3478)

Made on 7 December 2006, by the Secretary of State in exercise of the powers conferred by para. 10(1)
of Sch. 1 to the Films Act 1985. Operative in accordance with reg. 1.

CITATION AND COMMENCEMENT

1(1) These Regulations may be cited as the Films (Certification) Regulations 2006.

1(2) This Order shall come into force only if the Films (Definition of "British Film") (No. 2) Order 2006 comes into force, and shall do so on the day that Order comes into force.

1(3) If the Films (Definition of "British Film") (No. 2) Order 2006 does not come into force before 31st March 2007, this Order is revoked with effect from that date.

INTERPRETATION

2 In the Regulations–

    "the Act" means the Films Act 1985;

    "co-production film" means a film which by virtue of any Order in Council made under paragraph 4(5) of Schedule 1 to the Act is to be treated as if it is a British film for the purposes of Schedule 1 to the Act;

    "core expenditure" has the same meaning as in section 34(1) of the Finance Act 2006;

    "film production company" has the same meaning as in section 32 of the Finance Act 2006;

    "group of companies" means a company and all other companies which are its subsidiaries within the meaning of section 736 of the Companies Act 1985;

    "other expenditure" means all the expenditure on the work carried out in the making of the film which is not core expenditure;

    "producer" means the person by whom the arrangements necessary for the making of the film are undertaken;

    "theatrical release" means exhibition to the paying public at the commercial cinema;

    "UK expenditure" has the same meaning as in section 35(1) of the Finance Act 2006. Applications

APPLICATIONS

3 An application under paragraph 2(1) of Schedule 1 to the Act for the certification of a film as a British film, other than a co-production film, shall be made in writing to the Secretary of State.

PARTICULARS

4 The application shall set out the particulars of the film described in the Schedule.

EVIDENCE

5(1) The application shall be accompanied by a statutory declaration made by the applicant as to the truth of the particulars given in the application.

5(2) A statutory declaration shall be deemed to be properly made by the applicant if it has been made on behalf of the company by the Secretary or one of the directors of the company or a by any person duly authorised by the company to make the declaration on its behalf.

6(1) Where an application for final certification seeks to rely on any point that may be awarded under paragraph 4A(5), 4B(5), 4C(5), 4A(6), 4B(6) or 4C(6) of Schedule 1 to the Act, the application shall be accompanied by a report prepared by a person referred to in paragraph (2) verifying the particulars in paragraphs 18 to 20 of the Schedule.

6(2) The person referred to in this paragraph is a person who is eligible for appointment as a company auditor under section 25 of the Companies Act 1989 and is not and was not at any time while the film was being made–

(a) in partnership with the applicant or any officer or servant of the applicant;

(b) in the employment of the applicant or any officer or servant of the applicant; or

(c)   an officer or servant of the applicant or, if the applicant is a member of a group of companies, of any other company in that group.

History – Reg. 6(1) substituted by SI 2007/3478, reg. 2, with effect from 1 January 2008.

TRANSITIONAL PROVISIONS

7(1)   Subject to paragraphs (2) and (3), the following Regulations are revoked–

(a)   the Films (Certification) Regulations 1985 (No. 994);

(b)   the Films (Certification) (Amendment) Regulations 1999 (No. 2224);

(c)   the Films (Certification) (Amendment) (No. 2) Regulations 1999 (No. 2334);

(d)   the Films (Certification) (Amendment) Regulations 2006 (No. 642).

7(2)   If an application falls to be determined by the Secretary of State in accordance with Schedule 1 to the Act as in force immediately before 1st April 2006 the Films (Certification) Regulations 1985 shall continue to have effect to the application as if the Films (Certification) (Amendment) Regulations 2006 and these Regulations had not been made.

7(3)   If an application falls to be determined by the Secretary of State in accordance with Schedule 1 to the Act as in force immediately before the commencement of these Regulations the Films (Certification) Regulations 1985 shall continue to have effect to the application as if these Regulations had not been made.

History – In reg. 7(2), the words "and these Regulations" inserted by SI 2007/3478, reg. 3, with effect from 1 January 2008.

SCHEDULE

Regulation 4

1   Title of the film or, in the case of a series of films or a part thereof, the title of the series or part.

2   Total playing time in minutes and seconds of the film, including credits and titles.

3   Whether the application is for interim or final certification.

4   Whether the film is intended for theatrical release.

5   Name of the applicant.

6   Address of the applicant's principal place of business.

7   Address of the applicant's registered office.

8   Registered number of the applicant.

9   Date of registration of the applicant.

10   Date of the first day of principal photography.

11   Date on which the film was completed for the purposes of Schedule 1 to the Act.

12   If the applicant seeks treatment of a series of films as a single film in reliance upon paragraph 1(2) of Schedule 1 to the Act–

(a)   the number of parts in the series;

(b)   the combined playing time in minutes and seconds of those parts, including credits and titles, and

(c)   the reasons why the series constitutes a self-contained work or is series of documentaries with a common theme.

13   Type of film: documentary, animation or standard.

14   If the film is a documentary, the reasons why the film should be considered to be a documentary.

15   If the film is an animation, the reasons why the film should be considered to be an animation.

16   The reasons why any point should be awarded under paragraphs 4A(3), 4B(3) or 4C(3) of Schedule 1 to the Act.

17   The reasons why any point should be awarded under paragraphs 4A(4), 4B(4) or 4C(4) of Schedule 1 to the Act.

18   If the applicant seeks to rely on paragraph 4A(5)(a)(i) of Schedule 1 to the Act, the total number of days of principal photography and the number of days of principal photography carried out in the United Kingdom.

19   If the applicant seeks to rely on the rest of paragraph 4A(5), 4B(5) and 4C(5), the total expenditure of the work in relation to which the applicant is applying for points to be awarded and the expenditure of such work carried out in the United Kingdom.

20   The nationality or ordinary residence of all the persons mentioned in paragraphs 4A(6), 4B(6) or 4C(6) of Schedule 1 to the Act in relation to whom the applicant is applying for a point to be awarded.

History – In para. 20, the word "or" substituted for the word "and" by SI 2007/3478, reg. 4, with effect from 1 January 2008.

21   Total core expenditure.

22   Total UK expenditure.

23   Total non-UK expenditure by each country the expenditure is carried out in.

24   Other expenditure on the work carried out in the making of the film which is not core expenditure.

25   Shooting script in the English language.

26   A complete synopsis or treatment of the screenplay in the English language.

27   Shooting schedule.

28   Production budget.

29   Copy of the chain of tile.

30   If any part of the film is derived from any previous film ("the previous film")–

(a)   for each part of the film so derived and in respect of which–

     (i)   the two films do not have the same film production company or producer, and

     (ii)   the previous film has not been certified under Schedule 1 to the Act, the playing time in minutes and seconds of that part;

(b)   the combined playing time in minutes and seconds of all the parts referred to in sub-paragraph (a); and

(c)   if the applicant seeks to rely on paragraph 5(2) of Schedule 1 to the Act the reasons why the subject matter of the film makes it appropriate for paragraph 5(1) of Schedule 1 to the Act not to be applied.

TAXATION OF SECURITISATION COMPANIES REGULATIONS 2006

(SI 2006/3296, amended by SI 2007/3339 and SI 2007/3401)

Made on 11 December 2006 by the Treasury in exercise of the powers conferred upon them by s. 84 of the Finance Act 2005. Operative in accordance with reg. 1.

PRELIMINARY

Citation, commencement and effect

1(1) These Regulations may be cited as the Taxation of Securitisation Companies Regulations 2006 and shall come into force on the day after the day on which they are made.

1(2) These Regulations have effect for periods of account beginning on or after 1st January 2007.

Interpretation

2(1) In these Regulations–

"asset-holding company" has the meaning given by regulation 6;

"capital market arrangement" and **"capital market investment"** have the same meaning as in section 72B(1) of the Insolvency Act 1986 (see paragraphs 1, 2 and 3 of Schedule 2A to that Act);

"commercial paper funded company" has the meaning given by regulation 9;

"financial asset" has the meaning it has for generally accepted accounting practice (subject to paragraph (2)) but–

(a) subject to paragraph (b)(ii) includes derivative contracts as defined for the purposes of Schedule 26 to the Finance Act 2002 (see paragraph 2 (1) of that Schedule) whether otherwise constituting an asset or a liability, and

(b) does not include–

   (i) shares (other than shares in a securitisation company which is party to the capital market arrangement);

   (ii) derivative contracts as defined for the purposes of Schedule 26 to the Finance Act 2002 where the underlying subject matter is or includes shares (other than shares in a securitisation company which is party to the capital market arrangement) or land;

   (iii) loan relationships with embedded derivatives within section 94A(1) of the Finance Act 1996 (loan relationships with embedded derivatives) where the underlying subject matter of the embedded derivative is or includes shares or land;

   (iv) relevant assets within paragraph 7(1) of Schedule 6 to the Finance (No. 2) Act 2005 (loan relationships with embedded derivatives) where the underlying subject matter of any embedded derivative is or includes shares or land.

"ICTA" means the Income and Corporation Taxes Act 1988;

"independent persons" means persons who are not connected with a company (and see paragraph (3));

"insurance special purpose vehicle" has the same meaning as in section 431(2) of ICTA;

"intermediate borrowing company" has the meaning given by regulation 7;

"note-issuing company" has the meaning given by regulation 5;

"related transaction" is to be construed in accordance with paragraphs (4) and (5);

"retained profit" is to be construed in accordance with regulation 10;

"securitisation company" has the meaning given by regulation 4;

"specified regulations" means regulations 14 (corporation tax charge) and 16 to 20 (application, modification and non-application of provisions of the Corporation Tax Acts);

"warehouse company" has the meaning given by regulation 8.

2(2) For the purposes of these Regulations whether an asset acquired, held or managed by a company is a financial asset shall be determined at the time that asset is first acquired, held or managed by that company.

2(3) Section 839 of ICTA (connected persons) applies for the purposes of the definition of "independent persons", except that in applying the definition of "control" in that section a person is not to be treated as a participator in a company by reason only that he is a loan creditor of the company.

2(4) For the purpose of these Regulations one or more transactions are to be regarded as related transactions, in the case of any arrangements, if it would be reasonable to assume, from either or both of–

(a)   the likely effect of the transactions, and

(b)   the circumstances in which the transactions are entered into or effected,

that none of the transactions would have been entered into or effected independently of the arrangements.

2(5) Transactions are not prevented from being related transactions, in the case of any arrangements, just because the transactions–

(a)   are not between the same parties, or

(b)   are not between the parties to the capital market arrangements.

History – In reg. 2(1), in the definition of "financial asset", the words "subject to paragraph (b)(ii)" inserted and para. (b) substituted by SI 2007/3339, reg. 2(2), operative from 27 December 2007, with effect from the beginning of periods of account beginning on or after 1 January 2007 and current on 3 December 2007, but not in relation to a company to which SI 2006/3296 applies in relation to a capital market arrangement in existence on 3 December 2007, SI 2007/3339, reg. 1(3).
In reg. 2(1) the definition of "insurance special purpose vehicle" inserted by SI 2007/3401, reg. 2(2), with effect from the beginning of periods of account beginning on or after 1 January 2007 and current on 4 December 2007.

Scope of these Regulations

3(1) These Regulations make provision as to the application of the Corporation Tax Acts in relation to a securitisation company.

3(2) The Regulations deal with the following matters–

(a)   they define "securitisation company" and related expressions (see regulations 4 to 10);

(b)   they specify securitisation companies to which specified regulations do not apply (see regulations 11 to 12);

(c)   they specify companies to which these Regulations do not apply (see regulations 13 and 13A);

(d)   they make provision as to profit of a securitisation company to be brought into account for an accounting period for corporation tax purposes (see regulation 14);

(e)   they make supplementary provision (see regulations 15 to 21).

History – In reg. 3(2)(c), the words "regulations 13 and 13A" substituted for "regulation 13" by SI 2007/3339, reg. 2(3), operative from 27 December 2007, with effect from the beginning of periods of account beginning on or after 1 January 2007 and current on 3 December 2007.

MEANING OF "SECURITISATION COMPANY" AND RELATED EXPRESSIONS

Meaning of "securitisation company"

4(1) For the purposes of these Regulations a **"securitisation company"** means a company that meets conditions A and B.

4(2) Condition A is that the company is–

(a)   a note-issuing company (see regulation 5),

(b)   an asset-holding company (see regulation 6),

(c)   an intermediate borrowing company (see regulation 7),

(d)   a warehouse company (see regulation 8), or

(e)   a commercial paper funded company (see regulation 9).

4(3) Condition B is that the company has a retained profit (see regulation 10).

Meaning of "note-issuing company"

5(1) For the purposes of these Regulations a **"note-issuing company"** means a company that meets conditions A to D.

5(2) Condition A is that the company is within section 84(2)(a) of the Finance Act 2005.

5(3) Condition B is that the securities that represent the capital market investment referred to in section 84(2)(a)(ii) of that Act are issued wholly or mainly to independent persons.

5(4) Condition C is that the total value of the capital market investments made under the capital market arrangement referred to in section 84(2)(a)(iii) of that Act is at least £10 million.

5(5) Condition D is that the company's only business apart from the activity mentioned in section 84(2)(a)(i) of that Act (being party as debtor to a capital market investment), and apart from any incidental activities, consists in—

(a)   one

     (i)   acquiring, holding and managing financial assets forming the whole or part of the security for the capital market arrangement; or

     (ii)   acting as guarantor in respect of loan relationships, derivative contracts, finance leases or other liabilities of other companies where the whole, or substantially the whole, of the company's rights in respect of the guarantee (including any right of subrogation) form the whole or part of the security for the capital market arrangement; or

(b)   being party to a creditor relationship with an insurance special purpose vehicle.

History – In reg. 5(5) the words
    ""consists in –"
    "(a)   one";"
substituted for "consists in one", paras. (a) and (b) renumbered as (i) and (ii), and a new para. (b) inserted with the word "; or" preceding it, by SI 2007/3401, reg. 2(3), with effect from the beginning of periods of account beginning on or after 1 January 2007 and current on 4 December 2007. It is presumed that the original words following "consists in one" which read "or both of the following activities–" are also omitted and have not been referred to due to an oversight.

Meaning of "asset-holding company"

6(1) For the purposes of these Regulations an **"asset-holding company"** means a company that meets conditions A and B.

6(2) Condition A is that the company's business, apart from any incidental activities, consists in acquiring, holding and managing financial assets forming the whole or part of the security for a capital market arrangement entered into by a note-issuing company.

6(3) Condition B is that the company's initial liabilities representing debtor relationships are owed wholly or mainly to a note-issuing company or intermediate borrowing company.

History – In reg. 6(3), the word "initial" inserted by SI 2007/3339, reg. 2(4), operative from 27 December 2007, with effect from the beginning of periods of account beginning on or after 1 January 2007 and current on 3 December 2007.

Meaning of "intermediate borrowing company"

7(1) For the purposes of these Regulations an **"intermediate borrowing company"** means a company that meets conditions A and B.

7(2) Condition A is that the company's only business, apart from any incidental activities, is to enter into and be a party to creditor relationships with—

(a)   an asset-holding company,

(aa)   a partnership that would be an asset-holding company if it were a company,

(b)   a company that would be an asset-holding company if the assets forming the security for the capital market arrangement were financial assets,

(c)   a partnership that would be an asset-holding company if it were a company and the assets forming the security for the capital market arrangement were financial assets,

(d)   another intermediate borrowing company, or

(e)   an insurance special purpose vehicle.

7(3) Condition B is that the company's liabilities representing debtor relationships are owed wholly or mainly to a note-issuing company or another intermediate borrowing company.

History – Reg. 7(2)(aa) inserted by SI 2007/3339, reg. 2(5), operative from 27 December 2007, with effect from the beginning of periods of account beginning on or after 1 January 2007 and current on 3 December 2007.
In reg. 7(2) the word "or" omitted in para. (c), and the word ", or " and para. (e) inserted at the end by SI 2007/3401, reg. 2(4), with effect from the beginning of periods of account beginning on or after 1 January 2007 and current on 4 December 2007.

Meaning of "warehouse company"

8(1) For the purposes of these Regulations a **"warehouse company"** means a company whose business, apart from any incidental activities, consists in acquiring and holding financial assets for the purpose–

(a)   of transferring them to a company (whether or not yet in existence) that at the time of the transfer is, or as a result of the transfer will become, an asset-holding or note-issuing company, or

(b)   of itself becoming an asset-holding or note-issuing company.

8(2) For the purposes of these Regulations the business of a warehouse company described in paragraph (1) shall be referred to as a "warehouse arrangement".

History – Reg. 8 renumbered as reg. 8(1) and reg. 8(2), inserted by SI 2007/3339, reg. 2(6), operative from 27 December 2007, with effect from the beginning of periods of account beginning on or after 1 January 2007 and current on 3 December 2007.

Meaning of "commercial paper funded company"

9 For the purposes of these Regulations a **"commercial paper funded company"** means–

(a)   a company that was an asset-holding company but whose obligations under debtor relationships to a note-issuing company or intermediate borrowing company–

    (i)   have been transferred to, or

    (ii)   have been replaced by obligations under debtor relationships to,

one or more companies carrying on a business of banking, or

(b)   a company that was an intermediate borrowing company but whose obligations under debtor relationships to a note-issuing company–

    (i)   have been transferred to, or

    (ii)   have been replaced by obligations under debtor relationships to,

one or more companies carrying on a business of banking.

Meaning of "retained profit"

10(1)   For the purposes of these Regulations the **"retained profit"** of a securitisation company for an accounting period is the amount required by the capital market arrangement, a related transaction or a warehouse arrangement to be retained, made available to be retained, or designated as profits of the securitisation company (however described).

10(2)   If retained profit relates to two or more accounting periods, it shall be apportioned on a just and reasonable basis between them.

10(3)   If in an accounting period the securitisation company has insufficient funds available to meet the retained profit required by the capital market arrangement or a related transaction–

(a)   the amount of the retained profit for the purposes of these Regulations is the amount actually retained as profit for that accounting period, and

(b)   in a later accounting period the amount of the retained profit may be increased by up to the amount of the shortfall in the earlier period.

History – In reg. 10(1), the word ", a" substituted for "or a" and "or a warehouse arrangement" inserted by SI 2007/3339, reg. 2(7), operative from 27 December 2007, with effect from the beginning of periods of account beginning on or after 1 January 2007 and current on 3 December 2007.

COMPANIES TO WHICH SPECIFIED REGULATIONS DO NOT APPLY

Securitisation companies that do not meet the payments condition

11(1)   The specified regulations do not apply to a securitisation company that–

(a)   does not meet the payments condition, or

(b)   at any time has not met the payments condition.

11(2)   The payments condition is that in any accounting period R is equal to or less than the sum of P + RA + RP

11(3)   In paragraph (2)–

R is, subject to paragraph (6), the aggregate of–

(a)   amounts received by the securitisation company in the accounting period, and

(b)   amounts which have been–

    (i)   retained as RA in that accounting period, or

    (ii)   taken into account as RA for the purposes of this regulation in a previous accounting period,

where those amounts are no longer reasonably required to be retained as RA;

P is the aggregate amount of–

(a)   payments made by the securitisation company in the accounting period and the following 18 months except payments which have already been taken into account for the purposes of this regulation for a previous accounting period, and

(b)   payments made by the securitisation company in the previous accounting period but not taken into account for the purposes of this regulation;

RA is the aggregate of amounts retained by the securitisation company in the accounting period, which have not already been taken into account for the purposes of this regulation in a previous accounting period, which are reasonably required to–

(a)   provide for losses or expenses arising from the company's business, or

(b)   maintain or enhance the company's creditworthiness; and

RP is the amount of the retained profit of the securitisation company in the accounting period.

11(4)   If a securitisation company receives amounts or makes payments of amounts in a currency other than its functional currency, that amount shall be translated into the functional currency by reference to the appropriate exchange rate for the last day of the accounting period.

11(5)   For the purposes of this regulation the aggregate amount of payments made includes any payment which was not made but which would have been made but for—

(a)   a legal prohibition, or

(b)   a reasonable excuse for failing to make that payment,

but if any such payment is subsequently made it shall be disregarded.

11(6)   In the case of a company which has elected in accordance with regulation 13(2) that these Regulations shall apply—

(a)   in the first accounting period to which these Regulations apply, R includes an amount that would be given by the formula—

$$R - P - RA - RP$$

in relation to the previous accounting period ("the relevant accounting period");

(b)   sub-paragraph (b)(ii) of the definition of R in paragraph (3) shall apply as if there were included in those amounts the aggregate of amounts retained by the company in previous accounting periods, in which these Regulations did not apply, which were reasonably required to—

(i)   provide for losses or expenses arising from the company's business, or

(ii)   maintain or enhance the company's creditworthiness.

11(7)   For the purposes of the formula in paragraph (6)(a)—

R is the aggregate of amounts received by the company in the relevant accounting period;

P is the aggregate amount of payments made by the company in the relevant accounting period;

RA is the aggregate of amounts retained by the company for the relevant accounting period which were reasonably required to—

(a)   provide for losses or expenses arising from the company's business, or

(b)   maintain or enhance the company's creditworthiness; and

RP is the amount that would be the retained profit of the company in the relevant accounting period if these Regulations applied.

11(8)   In this regulation—

"appropriate exchange rate" has the meaning given in section 92D(2)(b) of the Finance Act 1993;

"functional currency" has the meaning given in section 92E(3) of the Finance Act 1993;

"payment" includes part of a payment.

Securitisation companies that have an unallowable purpose

12(1)   The specified regulations do not apply to a securitisation company that—

(a)   has an unallowable purpose, or

(b)   at any time has had an unallowable purpose.

12(2)   For the purpose of these Regulations a securitisation company has an unallowable purpose if the purpose for which the securitisation company is a party to—

(a)   the capital market arrangement,

(b)   any related transaction, or

(c)   any transaction in pursuance of the capital market arrangement,

includes a purpose which is not amongst the business or other commercial purposes of the securitisation company.

12(3)   If one of the purposes for which a securitisation company is at any time a party to—

(a)   any capital market arrangement,

(b)   any related transaction in the case of any capital market arrangement, or

(c)   any transaction in pursuance of any capital market arrangement, is a tax avoidance purpose, that purpose shall be taken to be a business or other commercial purpose of the securitisation company only where it is not the main purpose, or one of the main purposes, for which the company is party to the arrangements or transaction at that time.

12(4) In this regulation–

"**tax avoidance purpose**" means any purpose that consists in securing a tax advantage for any other person;

"**tax advantage**" has the same meaning as in section 840ZA of ICTA (tax avoidance).

History – In reg. 12(4), the words "section 840ZA" substituted for "section 709(1)" by SI 2007/3339, reg. 2(8), operative from 27 December 2007, with effect from the beginning of periods of account beginning on or after 1 January 2007 and current on 3 December 2007.

COMPANIES TO WHICH THESE REGULATIONS DO NOT APPLY

Securitisation companies on 1st January 2007

13(1) These Regulations do not apply to a company which before the start of the first accounting period of the company beginning on or after 1st January 2007–

(a) is a securitisation company within section 83 of the Finance Act 2005 (application of accounting standards to securitisation companies), or

(b) is a company in relation to which the following conditions are met–

(i) it is party as debtor to a capital market investment,

(ii) securities representing that capital market investment are issued, and

(iii) the capital market investment is part of a capital market arrangement.

This is subject to paragraph (2).

13(2) The company may elect by notice in writing to Her Majesty's Revenue and Customs, within 18 months of the end of that period, that these Regulations shall apply.

13(3) An election under paragraph (2) is irrevocable.

SECURITISATION COMPANIES TO WHICH SECTION 83 OF THE FINANCE ACT 2005 DOES NOT APPLY

13A These Regulations do not apply to a company in a case where–

(a) section 83(1) of the Finance Act 2005 does not apply by virtue of an election under regulation 2 of the Securitisation Companies (Application of Section 83(1) of the Finance Act 2005: Accounting Standards) Regulations 2007, and

(b) the company continues to be party to the arrangement or transaction referred to in paragraph (1)(b) of regulation 2 of those Regulations.

History – Reg. 13A inserted by SI 2007/3339, reg. 2(9), operative from 27 December 2007, with effect from the beginning of periods of account beginning on or after 1 January 2007 and current on 3 December 2007.

APPLICATION OF THE CORPORATION TAX ACTS

Corporation tax charge

14(1) The profit of a securitisation company to be brought into account for an accounting period for corporation tax purposes is the aggregate of–

(a) the greater of–

(i) nil; and

(ii) the amount given by the formula–

$$RP - DS + D, and$$

(b) the amount specified in paragraph (3).

14(2) In paragraph (1)–

RP is the amount of the retained profit of the securitisation company for the accounting period;

DS is the amount of any distribution received in that accounting period from another securitisation company which is party to the capital market arrangement where the distribution is made from that company's retained profit;

D is the greater of–

(a) the amount equal to the aggregate of any dividends paid by the securitisation company in that and any previous accounting period, less–

(i) RP for the accounting period,

      (ii)   the aggregate of profits calculated under this regulation for previous accounting periods,

      (iii) the aggregate of DS calculated under this regulation for previous accounting periods, and

      (iv) the amount of any dividends paid out of profits arising in any previous accounting period in which these Regulations did not apply; and

  (b)   nil.

14(3) The specified amount is any credit that would be brought into account by the securitisation company in the accounting period in consequence of paragraph 12A of Schedule 9 to the Finance Act 1996 (transferee leaving group after replacing transferor as party to loan relationship) or paragraph 30A of Schedule 26 to the Finance Act 2002 (transferee leaving group after replacing transferor as party to derivative contract).

14(4) The amount of profit calculated under this regulation shall be brought into account for corporation tax purposes instead of any other amount that would fall to be brought into account.

SUPPLEMENTARY PROVISION

Application, modification and non-application of provisions of the Corporation Tax Acts

15(1) In relation to a securitisation company, ICTA has effect as if it were subject to the following modification.

15(2) In section 12 (basis of, and periods for, assessment)(a), in subsection (3) after paragraph (e) insert–

    "(f)   the company becoming or ceasing to be a securitisation company to which regulation 14 of the Taxation of Securitisation Companies Regulations 2006 applies.".

16 Paragraphs (b) to (f) in section 209(2) (meaning of distribution) of ICTA shall not apply in relation to any interest paid or other distribution made by a securitisation company.

17 For the purposes of Chapter 4 of Part 10 (group relief) of ICTA, a securitisation company shall not be treated as the member of any group or consortium.

18(1) Section 171 (transfers within a group: general provisions) of the Taxation of Chargeable Gains Act 1992 shall not apply if "company B" in subsection (1) of that section is a securitisation company.

18(2) Section 179A (reallocation within group of gain or loss accruing under section 179) of that Act shall not apply if "company C" in that section is a securitisation company.

19(1) Paragraph 2 of Schedule 9 to the Finance Act 1996 (loan relationships: special computational provisions: late interest) shall not apply if the person standing in the position of a creditor as respects a loan relationship within that paragraph is a securitisation company.

19(2) Paragraph 12 of that Schedule (continuity of treatment: groups etc) shall not apply if the "transferee company" or "transferor company" in subparagraph (1) of that paragraph is a securitisation company.

19(3) Paragraph 17 of that Schedule (deeply discounted securities where companies have a connection) shall not apply if the person standing in the position of a creditor as respects a security within that paragraph is a securitisation company.

19(4) Paragraph 18 of that Schedule (deeply discounted securities of close companies) shall not apply if the person standing in the position of a creditor as respects a security within that paragraph is a securitisation company.

History – Reg. 19(3) and (4) inserted by SI 2007/3339, reg. 2(10), operative from 27 December 2007, with effect from the beginning of periods of account beginning on or after 1 January 2007 and current on 3 December 2007.

20 Paragraph 28 of Schedule 26 to the Finance Act 2002 (derivative contracts: transactions within groups) shall not apply if the "transferee company" or "transferor company" in subparagraph (1) of that paragraph is a securitisation company.

21 Section 83 of the Finance Act 2005 (application of accounting standards to securitisation companies) shall not apply to a securitisation company.

Statutory Instruments

FILMS (DEFINITION OF "BRITISH FILM") (NO. 2) ORDER 2006

(SI 2006/3430)

Made on 18 December 2006 by the Secretary of State, with the approval of the Treasury, in exercise of the powers conferred on her by paragraph 10(2) of Schedule 1 to the Films Act 1985. Operative from 1 January 2007.

CITATION, COMMENCEMENT AND INTERPRETATION

1(1)   This Order may be cited as the Films (Definition of "British Film") (No. 2) Order 2006 and shall come into force on 1st January 2007 or, if later, the day after the day on which it is made.

1(2)   "The Schedule" means Schedule 1 to the Films Act 1985, and a reference to a numbered paragraph is a reference to the paragraph bearing that number in the Schedule.

TRANSITIONAL PROVISION

2   An application for certification under paragraph 2 which is made in relation to a film for which the first day of principal photography is on or after the day this Order comes into force shall be determined by the Secretary of State in accordance with the Schedule as modified by this Order.

MODIFICATION OF THE SCHEDULE

3   For paragraphs 4A to 4C (British films for purposes of the Schedule) substitute–

"**4A(1)**   The cultural test for a film other than a documentary (see paragraph 4B) or an animation (see paragraph 4C) is as follows.

4A(2)   Subject to sub-paragraph (7), a film passes the cultural test if it is awarded at least 16 points in total.

4A(3)   Up to 16 points shall be awarded in respect of the content of the film as follows–

(a)   up to 4 points depending on the percentage of the film that is set in the United Kingdom as follows–

    (i)   4 points for at least 75%;

    (ii)   3 points for at least 66%;

    (iii)   2 points for at least 50%;

    (iv)   1 point for at least 25%;

(b)   up to 4 points depending on the number of the characters depicted in the film that are British as follows–

    (i)   if there are more than three characters depicted in the film, 4 points if two or three of the three lead characters are British or, if only one of the three lead characters is British, 2 points if he is the first or second lead, 1 point if he is the third lead;

    (ii)   if there are only three characters depicted in the film, 4 points if two or three of them are British or, if only one of them is British, 2 points if he is the first or second lead, 1 point if he is the third lead;

    (iii)   if there are only two characters depicted in the film, 4 points if both of them are British, 2 points if one of them is;

    (iv)   if there is only one character depicted in the film, 4 points if he is British;

(c)   4 points if the film depicts a British story;

(d)   up to 4 points depending on the percentage of the original dialogue that is recorded in the English language or in a recognised regional or minority language as follows–

    (i)   4 points for at least 75%;

    (ii)   3 points for at least 66%;

    (iii)   2 points for at least 50%;

    (iv)   1 point for at least 25%.

4A(4)   Up to 4 points may be awarded in respect of the contribution of the film to the promotion, development and enhancement of British culture.

4A(5)   Up to 3 points shall be awarded in respect of work carried out in the making of the film as follows–

  (a)   2 points if at least 50% of the work carried out on any of the following is carried out in the United Kingdom–

      (i)   principal photography;

      (ii)   visual effects;

      (iii)   special effects;

  (b)   1 point if at least 50% of the work carried out on any of the following is carried out in the United Kingdom–

      (i)   performing and recording the music score created for the film;

      (ii)   audio post production;

      (iii)   picture post production.

4A(6)   Up to 8 points shall be awarded in respect of the personnel involved in the making of the film as follows–

  (a)   1 point if the director (or, if there is more than one, the lead director) is a qualifying person;

  (b)   1 point if at least one of the scriptwriters (or, if there are more than three, of the three lead scriptwriters) is a qualifying person;

  (c)   1 point if at least one of the producers (or, if there are more than three, of the three lead producers) is a qualifying person;

  (d)   1 point if the composer (or, if there is more than one, the lead composer) is a qualifying person;

  (e)   1 point if at least one of the actors (or, if there are more than three, of the three lead actors) is a qualifying person;

  (f)   1 point if at least 50% of the cast are qualifying persons;

  (g)   1 point if at least one of the heads of department is a qualifying person;

  (h)   1 point if at least 50% of the production crew are qualifying persons.

4A(7)   A film that is awarded all the points available under sub-paragraphs (3)(d) (language), (5) (where work carried out) and (6) (personnel) does not pass the cultural test unless–

  (a)   it is awarded at least 2 points under sub-paragraph (3)(a) (setting),

  (b)   it is awarded at least 2 points under sub-paragraph (3)(b) (characters), or

  (c)   it is awarded 4 points under sub-paragraph (3)(c) (story).

4B(1)   The cultural test for a documentary is as follows.

4B(2)   Subject to sub-paragraph (7), a film passes the cultural test if it is awarded at least 16 points in total.

4B(3)   Up to 16 points shall be awarded in respect of the content of the film as follows–

  (a)   up to 4 points depending on the percentage of the film that is set in the United Kingdom as follows–

      (i)   4 points for at least 75%;

      (ii)   3 points for at least 66%;

      (iii)   2 points for at least 50%;

      (iv)   1 point for at least 25%;

  (b)   up to 4 points depending on the number of the characters depicted in the film that are British as follows–

      (i)   if there are more than three characters depicted in the film, 4 points if two or three of the three lead characters are British or, if only one of the three lead characters is British, 2 points if he is the first or second lead, 1 point if he is the third lead;

      (ii)   if there are only three characters depicted in the film, 4 points if two or three of them are British or, if only one of them is British, 2 points if he is the first or second lead, 1 point if he is the third lead;

      (iii)   if there are only two characters depicted in the film, 4 points if both of them are British, 2 points if one of them is;

      (iv)   if there is only one character depicted in the film, 4 points if he is British;

  (c)   4 points if the film depicts a British story;

  (d)   up to 4 points depending on the percentage of the original dialogue that is recorded in the English language or in a recognised regional or minority language as follows–

      (i)   4 points for at least 75%;

      (ii)   3 points for at least 66%;

           (iii)   2 points for at least 50%;

           (iv)   1 point for at least 25%.

4B(4)   Up to 4 points may be awarded in respect of the contribution of the film to the promotion, development and enhancement of British culture.

4B(5)   Up to 3 points shall be awarded in respect of work carried out in the making of the film as follows—

     (a)   2 points if at least 50% of the work carried out on any of the following is carried out in the United Kingdom—

           (i)   shooting;

           (ii)   visual effects;

           (iii)   research and development;

           (iv)   special effects;

     (b)   1 point if at least 50% of the work carried out on any of the following is carried out in the United Kingdom—

           (i)   performing and recording the music score created for the film;

           (ii)   audio post production;

           (iii)   picture post production.

4B(6)   Up to 8 points shall be awarded in respect of the personnel involved in the making of the film as follows—

     (a)   1 point if the director (or, if there is more than one, the lead director) is a qualifying person;

     (b)   1 point if at least one of the scriptwriters (or, if there are more than three, of the three lead scriptwriters) is a qualifying person;

     (c)   1 point if at least one of the producers (or, if there are more than three, of the three lead producers) is a qualifying person;

     (d)   1 point if the composer (or, if there is more than one, the lead composer) is a qualifying person;

     (e)   1 point if at least one of the participants (or, if there are more than three, of the three lead participants) is a qualifying person;

     (f)   1 point if at least 50% of the participants are qualifying persons;

     (g)   1 point if at least one of the heads of department is a qualifying person;

     (h)   1 point if at least 50% of the production crew are qualifying persons.

4B(7)   A film that is awarded all the points available under sub-paragraphs (3)(d) (language), (5) (where work carried out) and (6) (personnel) does not pass the cultural test unless—

     (a)   it is awarded at least 2 points under sub-paragraph (3)(a) (setting),

     (b)   it is awarded at least 2 points under sub-paragraph (3)(b) (characters), or

     (c)   it is awarded 4 points under sub-paragraph (3)(c) (story).

4C(1)   The cultural test for an animation is as follows.

4C(2)   Subject to sub-paragraph (7), a film passes the cultural test if it is awarded at least 16 points in total.

4C(3)   Up to 16 points shall be awarded in respect of the content of the film as follows—

     (a)   up to 4 points depending on the percentage of the film that is set in the United Kingdom as follows—

           (i)   4 points for at least 75%;

           (ii)   3 points for at least 66%;

           (iii)   2 points for at least 50%;

           (iv)   1 point for at least 25%;

     (b)   up to 4 points depending on the number of the characters depicted in the film that are British as follows—

           (i)   if there are more than three characters depicted in the film, 4 points if two or three of the three lead characters are British or, if only one of the three lead characters is British, 2 points if he is the first or second lead, 1 point if he is the third lead;

           (ii)   if there are only three characters depicted in the film, 4 points if two or three of them are British or, if only one of them is British, 2 points if he is the first or second lead, 1 point if he is the third lead;

    (iii)   if there are only two characters depicted in the film, 4 points both of them are British, 2 points if one of them is;

    (iv)   if there is only one character depicted in the film, 4 points if he is British;

  (c)   4 points if the film depicts a British story;

  (d)   up to 4 points depending on the percentage of the original dialogue that is recorded in the English language or in a recognised regional or minority language as follows—

    (i)   4 points for at least 75%;

    (ii)   3 points for at least 66%;

    (iii)   2 points for at least 50%;

    (iv)   1 point for at least 25%.

4C(4)   Up to 4 points may be awarded in respect of the contribution of the film to the promotion, development and enhancement of British culture.

4C(5)   Up to 3 points shall be awarded in respect of work carried out in the making of the film as follows—

  (a)   2 points if at least 50% of the work carried out on any of the following is carried out in the United Kingdom—

    (i)   shooting,

    (ii)   visual design,

    (iii)   layout and storyboarding;

    (iv)   visual effects;

    (v)   special effects;

  (b)   1 point if at least 50% of the work carried out on any of the following is carried out in the United Kingdom—

    (i)   performing and recording the music score created for the film;

    (ii)   voice recording;

    (iii)   audio post production;

    (iv)   picture post production.

4C(6)   Up to 8 points shall be awarded in respect of the personnel involved in the making of the film as follows—

  (a)   1 point if the director (or, if there is more than one, the lead director) is a qualifying person;

  (b)   1 point if at least one of the scriptwriters (or, if there are more than three, of the three lead scriptwriters) is a qualifying person;

  (c)   1 point if at least one of the producers (or, if there are more than three, of the three lead producers) is a qualifying person;

  (d)   1 point if the composer (or, if there is more than one, the lead composer) is a qualifying person;

  (e)   1 point if at least one of the actors (or, if there are more than three, of the three lead actors) is a qualifying person;

  (f)   1 point if at least 50% of the cast are qualifying persons;

  (g)   1 point if at least one of the heads of department is a qualifying person;

  (h)   1 point if at least 50% of the production crew are qualifying persons.

4C(7)   A film that is awarded all the points available under sub-paragraphs (3)(d) (language), (5) (where work carried out) and (6) (personnel) does not pass the cultural test unless—

  (a)   it is awarded at least 2 points under sub-paragraph (3)(a) (setting),

  (b)   it is awarded at least 2 points under sub-paragraph (3)(b) (characters), or

  (c)   it is awarded 4 points under sub-paragraph (3)(c) (story)."

4(1)   Paragraph 4D of the Schedule shall be amended as follows.

4(2)   In sub-paragraph (4)(a) for "paragraph 4A(4)(a)" substitute "paragraph 4A(5)(a)(i)".

4(3)   For sub-paragraph (4)(b) substitute—

"(b) for the purposes of the rest of paragraph 4A(5) and paragraphs 4B(5) and 4C(5) (other matters), by reference to the amount of expenditure on the work."

4(4)   In sub-paragraph (5) for "paragraph 4A(4), 4B(4) or 4C(4) (points awarded in respect of the making of the film)" substitute "paragraph 4A(5), 4B(5) or 4C(5) (where work carried out)".

FINANCE ACT 2004, SECTION 61(2), (RELEVANT PERCENTAGE) ORDER 2007

(SI 2007/46)

Made on 11 January 2007 by the Treasury in exercise of the powers conferred upon them by s. 61(2) of the Finance Act 2004. Operative from 1 February 2007.

1 This Order may be cited as the Finance Act 2004, Section 61(2), (Relevant Percentage) Order 2007 and shall come into force on 1st February 2007.

2 For the purposes of section 61(1) of the Finance Act 2004 (deductions on account of tax from contract payments) the relevant percentage is–

(a)   20% if the person for whose labour (or for whose employees' or officers' labour) the payment in question is made is registered for payment under deduction, or

(b)   30% if that person is not so registered.

Statutory Instruments

ASSISTED AREAS ORDER 2007
(SI 2007/107)

Made on 22 January 2007 by the Secretary of State in exercise of the powers conferred upon him by s. 1(1), (3), (4) and (7) of the Industrial Development Act 1982. Operative from 13 February 2007.

COMMENCEMENT

1 The Order may be cited as the Assisted Areas Order 2007 and shall come into force on 13th February 2007.

INTERPRETATION

2(1) In this Order–

    "the 1982 Act" means the Industrial Development Act 1982; and

    "the 2000 Order" means the Assisted Areas Order 2000.

2(2) In Schedule 1–

(a) any reference to a local authority area in England and Wales shall be a reference to that area as it existed on 21 June 2003;

(b) any reference to a local government area in Scotland shall be a reference to that area as it existed on 21 June 2003; and

(c) any reference to a parish or a former district council in Scotland shall be a reference to that area as it existed on 31 December 1993.

2(3) In Schedule 2–

(a) any reference to a ward shall be a reference to the Census Area Statistic ward relating to the 2001 Census; and

(b) any reference to a local authority area shall be a reference to that area as it existed on 21 June 2003.

SPECIFICATION

3(1) In this Order the specification of an area as a development area is for the purposes of the 1982 Act and section 1 of the Derelict Land Act 1982.

3(2) On and after 13th February 2007 the areas described in Schedules 1 and 2 shall be development areas.

3(3) The area in Scotland in Schedule 1 shall be a development area until 31st December 2010.

REVOCATION

4 The 2000 Order is revoked.

SCHEDULE 1 – DEVELOPMENT AREAS

Article 3

TIER 1 AREAS

ENGLAND

The local authority areas of–

    Caradon

    Carrick

    Isles of Scilly

    Kerrier

    North Cornwall

    Penwith

    Restormel

Statutory Instruments

WALES

The local authority areas of–

Blaenau Gwent

Bridgend

Caerphilly

Carmarthenshire

Ceredigion

Conwy

Denbighshire

Gwynedd

Isle of Anglesey

Merthyr Tydfil

Neath Port Talbot

Pembrokeshire

Rhondda Cynon Taff

Swansea

Torfaen

SCOTLAND

The local government areas of–

Highland

Western Isles

Orkney Islands

Shetland Islands

Part of Argyll and Bute, namely–

the former Argyll and Bute District Council

Part of Moray, namely the parishes of–

Aberlour

Cabrach

Dallas

Dyke

Edinkillie

Forres

Inveravon

Kinloss

Kirkmichael

Knockando

Mortlach

Rafford

Rothes

The islands of–

Arran

Great Cumbrae

Little Cumbrae

SCHEDULE 2 – DEVELOPMENT AREAS

Article 3

TIER 2 AREAS

ENGLAND

North East

The following wards in the local authority area of Blyth Valley–

Cowpen
Cramlington East
Cramlington Eastfield with East Hartford
Cramlington North
Cramlington Parkside
Cramlington South East
Cramlington Village
Cramlington West
Croft
Hartley
Holywell
Isabella
Kitty Brewster
Newsham and New Delaval
Plessey
Seaton Delaval
Seghill
South Beach
South Newsham
Wensleydale

The following wards in the local authority area of Castle Morpeth–

Ellington
Hebron, Hepscott and Mitford
Lynemouth
Stannington

The following wards in the local authority area of Chester-le-Street–

Chester North
North Lodge

The following wards in the local authority area of Darlington UA–

Faverdale
Lingfield
Middleton St George
Sadberge and Whessoe

The following wards in the local authority area of Derwentside–

Annfield Plain
Blackhill
Burnopfield
Castleside
Catchgate
Consett East
Consett North
Consett South

Delves Lane
Dipton
Havannah
Leadgate
South Moor
Stanley Hall
Tanfield

The following wards in the local authority area of Durham–

Belmont
Brancepeth, Langley Moor and Meadowfield
Carrville and Gilesgate Moor
Cassop-cum-Quarrington
Coxhoe
Pelaw and Gilesgate
Shadforth and Sherburn
Shincliffe

The following wards in the local authority area of Easington–

Acre Rigg
Blackhalls
Dawdon
Dene House
Deneside
Easington Colliery
Easington Village and South Hetton
Eden Hill
Haswell and Shotton
Horden North
Horden South
Howletch
Hutton Henry
Murton East
Murton West
Passfield
Seaham Harbour
Seaham North
Thornley and Wheatley Hill
Wingate

The following wards in the local authority area of Gateshead–

Bede
Bensham
Birtley
Chowdene
Deckham
Dunston
Felling
High Fell
Lamesley
Leam
Low Fell
Pelaw and Heworth

Saltwell

Teams

Wrekendyke

The following wards in the local authority area of Hartlepool UA–

Brinkburn

Brus

Dyke House

Elwick

Fens

Grange

Greatham

Hart

Jackson

Owton

Park

Rift House

Rossmere

Seaton

St. Hilda

Stranton

Throston

The following wards in the local authority area of Middlesbrough UA–

Ayresome

Beechwood

Clairville

Gresham

Linthorpe

Middlehaven

North Ormesby and Brambles Farm

Pallister

Park

Thorntree

University

The following wards in the local authority area of Newcastle upon Tyne–

Benwell

Byker

Castle

Lemington

Monkchester

Sandyford

Scotswood

Walker

Walkergate

West City

The following wards in the local authority area of North Tyneside–

Chirton

Collingwood

Longbenton

Riverside

Wallsend

Weetslade

The following wards in the local authority area of Redcar and Cleveland UA–

Brotton

Coatham

Dormanstown

Grangetown

Guisborough

Kirkleatham

Loftus

Longbeck

Newcomen

Saltburn

Skelton

South Bank

St. Germain's

West Dyke

Zetland

The following wards in the local authority area of Sedgefield–

Bishop Middleham and Cornforth

Broom

Byerley

Chilton

Ferryhill

Fishburn and Old Trimdon

Greenfield Middridge

Low Spennymoor and Tudhoe Grange

Middlestone

Neville and Simpasture

New Trimdon and Trimdon Grange

Sedgefield

Shafto St. Marys

Spennymoor

Sunnydale

Thickley

Tudhoe

West

Woodham

The following wards in the local authority area of South Tyneside–

All Saints

Beacon and Bents

Bede

Biddick Hall

Boldon Colliery

Cleadon and East Boldon

Cleadon Park

Fellgate and Hedworth

Harton

Hebburn Quay

Hebburn South

Horsley Hill

Monkton

Primrose

Rekendyke

Tyne Dock and Simonside

West Park

Westoe

Whitburn and Marsden

Whiteleas

The following wards in the local authority area of Stockton-on-Tees UA–

Bishopsgarth

Blue Hall

Charltons

Elm Tree

Fairfield

Glebe

Grange

Grangefield

Hardwick

Hartburn

Mandale

Marsh House

Mile House

Newtown

Northfield

Norton

Parkfield

Portrack and Tilery

Preston

Roseworth

St. Aidan's

St. Cuthbert's

Stainsby

Victoria

Village

Whitton

Wolviston

The following wards in the local authority area of Sunderland–

Castletown

Central

Colliery

Eppleton

Fulwell

Grindon

Hendon

Hetton

Houghton

Pallion

Ryhope

Shiney Row

Silksworth

South Hylton

Southwick

St. Chad's

St. Michael's

St. Peter's

Thorney Close

Thornholme

Town End Farm

Washington East

Washington North

Washington South

Washington West

The following wards in the local authority area of Teesdale–

Etherley

Evenwood, Ramshaw and Lands

The following wards in the local authority area of Wansbeck–

Bedlington Central

Bedlington East

Bedlington West

Bothal

Central

Choppington

College

Guide Post

Haydon

Hirst

Newbiggin East

Newbiggin West

Park

Seaton

Sleekburn

Stakeford

The following wards in the local authority area of Wear Valley–

Bishop Auckland Town

Cockton Hill

Coundon

Crook South

Dene Valley

Henknowle

Howden

West Auckland

Wheatbottom and Helmington Row

Willington Central

Willington West End

Woodhouse Close

North West

The following wards in the local authority area of Allerdale–

Ewanrigg

Flimby

Harrington
Moorclose
Moss Bay
Netherhall
Seaton
St. John's
St. Michael's

The following wards in the local authority area of Barrow-in-Furness–

Barrow Island
Central
Dalton North
Dalton South
Hawcoat
Hindpool
Newbarns
Ormsgill
Parkside
Risedale
Roosecote
Walney North
Walney South

The following wards in the local authority area of Blackburn with Darwen UA–

Audley
Bastwell
Corporation Park
Earcroft
East Rural
Ewood
Fernhurst
Higher Croft
Little Harwood
Marsh House
Meadowhead
Mill Hill
Queen's Park
Roe Lee
Shadsworth with Whitebirk
Shear Brow
Sudell
Sunnyhurst
Wensley Fold
Whitehall

The following wards in the local authority area of Bolton–

Blackrod
Central
Daubhill
Derby
Farnworth
Halliwell
Harper Green

Kearsley

The following wards in the local authority area of Burnley–

Gawthorpe

Hapton with Park

The following wards in the local authority area of Copeland–

Arlecdon

Beckermet

Bootle

Bransty

Cleator Moor North

Cleator Moor South

Distington

Egremont North

Egremont South

Ennerdale

Frizington

Gosforth

Harbour

Haverigg

Hensingham

Hillcrest

Holborn Hill

Kells

Millom Without

Mirehouse

Moresby

Newtown

Sandwith

Seascale

St. Bees

The following wards in the local authority area of Hyndburn–

Altham

Clayton-le-Moors

Rishton

The following wards in the local authority area of Knowsley–

Cantril Farm

Cherryfield

Halewood East

Halewood South

Halewood West

Kirkby Central

Knowsley Park

Longview

Northwood

Page Moss

Park

Prescot East

Prescot West

Princess

Roby

St. Gabriels
St. Michaels
Swanside
Tower Hill
Whiston North
Whiston South
Whitefield

The following wards in the local authority area of Liverpool–

Abercromby
Aigburth
Allerton
Anfield
Arundel
Breckfield
Broadgreen
Childwall
Church
Clubmoor
County
Croxteth
Dingle
Dovecot
Everton
Fazakerley
Gillmoss
Granby
Grassendale
Kensington
Melrose
Netherley
Old Swan
Picton
Pirrie
Smithdown
Speke
St. Mary's
Tuebrook
Valley
Vauxhall
Warbreck
Woolton

The following wards in the local authority area of Oldham–

Alexandra
Chadderton Central
Chadderton North
Chadderton South
Coldhurst
Crompton
Failsworth East
Hollinwood

> Lees
> Royton North
> Royton South
> Shaw
> St. James
> St. Marys
> Waterhead
> Werneth

The following wards in the local authority area of Rochdale–

> Balderstone
> Castleton
> Central and Falinge
> Middleton Central
> Middleton North
> Middleton West
> Milnrow
> Newbold
> Smallbridge and Wardleworth

The following wards in the local authority area of Sefton–

> Church
> Derby
> Ford
> Linacre
> Litherland
> Molyneux
> Netherton and Orrell
> St. Oswald
> Victoria

The following wards in the local authority area of South Lakeland–

> Broughton
> Crake Valley
> Low Furness & Swarthmoor
> Ulverston Central
> Ulverston East
> Ulverston North
> Ulverston South
> Ulverston Town
> Ulverston West

The following wards in the local authority area of St. Helens–

> Billinge and Seneley Green
> Blackbrook
> Broad Oak
> Eccleston
> Grange Park
> Haydock
> Marshalls Cross
> Moss Bank
> Newton East
> Newton West
> Parr and Hardshaw

Queen's Park
Rainford
Rainhill
Sutton and Bold
Thatto Heath
West Sutton
Windle

The following wards in the local authority area of West Lancashire–

Bickerstaffe
Birch Green
Digmoor
Moorside
Skelmersdale North
Skelmersdale South
Tanhouse
Up Holland

The following wards in the local authority area of Wigan–

Abram
Ashton-Golborne
Aspull-Standish
Atherton
Beech Hill
Bryn
Hindley
Hindley Green
Hindsford
Hope Carr
Ince
Leigh Central
Leigh East
Lightshaw
Newtown
Norley
Orrell
Swinley
Whelley
Winstanley
Worsley Mesnes

The following wards in the local authority area of Wirral–

Bidston
Birkenhead
Bromborough
Claughton
Eastham
Egerton
Leasowe
Liscard
New Brighton
Oxton
Prenton

    Seacombe
    Tranmere
    Upton
    Wallasey

Yorkshire and the Humber

The following wards in the local authority area of Barnsley–
    Ardsley
    Athersley
    Brierley
    Central
    Cudworth
    Darfield
    Darton
    Dearne South
    Dearne Thurnscoe
    Dodworth
    Hoyland East
    Hoyland West
    Monk Bretton
    North West
    Park
    Penistone East
    Royston
    South West
    Wombwell North
    Wombwell South
    Worsbrough

The following wards in the local authority area of Doncaster–
    Adwick
    Armthorpe
    Askern
    Balby
    Bentley Central
    Bentley North Road
    Bessacarr
    Central
    Conisbrough
    Edlington and Warmsworth
    Hatfield
    Intake
    Mexborough
    Richmond
    Rossington
    South East
    Southern Parks
    Stainforth
    Thorne
    Town Field
    Wheatley

Statutory Instruments

The following wards in the local authority area of East Riding of Yorkshire UA–
    Hessle
    South Hunsley
    South West Holderness

The following wards in the local authority area of Kingston upon Hull; City of UA–
    Drypool
    Holderness
    Marfleet
    Myton
    Newland
    Pickering
    Southcoates West
    St. Andrew's

The following wards in the local authority area of North East Lincolnshire UA–
    Croft Baker
    East Marsh
    Freshney
    Heneage
    Immingham
    Sidney Sussex
    West Marsh
    Wolds
    Yarborough

The following ward in the local authority area of North Lincolnshire UA–
    Ferry

The following wards in the local authority area of Rotherham–
    Anston and Woodsetts
    Aston, Orgreave and Ulley
    Boston
    Bramley, Ravenfield and Wickersley
    Brampton, Melton and Wentworth
    Brinsworth, Catcliffe and Treeton
    Broom
    Central
    Dalton, Hooton Roberts and Thrybergh
    Greasbrough
    Herringthorpe
    Kimberworth
    Kiveton Park
    Maltby
    Park
    Rawmarsh East
    Rawmarsh West
    St. John's
    Swinton
    Thorpe Hesley
    Thurcroft and Whiston
    Wath

The following ward in the local authority area of Selby–
    Whitley

The following wards in the local authority area of Sheffield–
- Brightside
- Burngreave
- Castle
- Darnall
- Firth Park
- Handsworth
- Manor
- Mosborough
- Nether Shire
- Netherthorpe
- Owlerton
- Park
- Sharrow
- Southey Green

The following wards in the local authority area of Wakefield–
- Castleford Glasshoughton
- Castleford Whitwood
- Crofton and Ackworth
- Featherstone
- Hemsworth
- Normanton and Sharlston
- Pontefract South
- South Elmsall
- South Kirkby

East Midlands

The following ward in the local authority area of Amber Valley–
- Somercotes

The following wards in the local authority area of Ashfield–
- Hucknall Central
- Hucknall East
- Hucknall North
- Hucknall West
- Kirkby in Ashfield Central
- Kirkby in Ashfield East
- Kirkby in Ashfield West
- Sutton in Ashfield Central
- Sutton in Ashfield East
- Sutton in Ashfield North
- Sutton in Ashfield West
- Woodhouse

The following wards in the local authority area of Bassetlaw–
- Welbeck
- Worksop East
- Worksop North
- Worksop North East
- Worksop North West
- Worksop South
- Worksop South East

The following wards in the local authority area of Bolsover–
- Barlborough
- Blackwell
- Bolsover North West
- Bolsover South
- Bolsover West
- Clowne North
- Clowne South
- Elmton-with-Creswell
- Pinxton
- Pleasley
- Scarcliffe
- Shirebrook East
- Shirebrook Langwith
- Shirebrook North West
- Shirebrook South East
- Shirebrook South West
- South Normanton East
- South Normanton West
- Whitwell

The following wards in the local authority area of Chesterfield–
- Barrow Hill and New Whittington
- Brimington North
- Brimington South
- Dunston
- Hasland
- Hollingwood and Inkersall
- Lowgates and Woodthorpe
- Middlecroft and Poolsbrook
- Moor
- Old Whittington
- St. Helen's
- St. Leonard's

The following ward in the local authority area of Gedling–
- Newstead

The following wards in the local authority area of Mansfield–
- Berry Hill
- Birklands
- Broomhill
- Cumberlands
- Eakring
- Forest Town East
- Forest Town West
- Grange Farm
- Ladybrook
- Leeming
- Lindhurst
- Meden
- Oak Tree
- Pleasley Hill

Portland
Priory
Ravensdale
Robin Hood
Sherwood

The following wards in the local authority area of Newark and Sherwood–
Bilsthorpe
Blidworth
Boughton
Clipstone
Edwinstowe
Ollerton
Rainworth

The following wards in the local authority area of North East Derbyshire–
Clay Cross North
Clay Cross South
Grassmoor
Holmewood and Heath
North Wingfield Central
Sutton
Tupton

The following wards in the local authority area of Nottingham UA–
Basford
Bulwell

West Midlands

The following wards in the local authority area of Birmingham–
Acock's Green
Aston
Edgbaston
Fox Hollies
Handsworth
Hodge Hill
Kingsbury
Ladywood
Longbridge
Nechells
Northfield
Perry Barr
Selly Oak
Shard End
Sheldon
Small Heath
Soho
Sparkbrook
Washwood Heath
Yardley

The following wards in the local authority area of Bromsgrove–
Hillside
Uffdown

The following wards in the local authority area of Coventry–
- Bablake
- Binley and Willenhall
- Cheylesmore
- Foleshill
- Henley
- Holbrook
- Longford
- Lower Stoke
- Radford
- Sherbourne
- St. Michael's
- Upper Stoke
- Westwood
- Whoberley
- Woodlands

The following wards in the local authority area of Dudley–
- Amblecote
- Belle Vale and Hasbury
- Brierley Hill
- Brockmoor and Pensnett
- Castle and Priory
- Coseley East
- Coseley West
- Gornal
- Halesowen North
- Halesowen South
- Kingswinford North and Wall Heath
- Lye and Wollescote
- Netherton and Woodside
- Quarry Bank and Cradley
- St. Andrews
- St. James's
- St. Thomas's

The following wards in the local authority area of Newcastle-under-Lyme–
- Bradwell
- Butt Lane
- Chesterton
- Cross Heath
- Holditch
- Keele
- Knutton and Silverdale
- Madeley
- May Bank
- Porthill
- Ravenscliffe
- Silverdale and Parksite
- Thistleberry
- Town
- Wolstanton

The following wards in the local authority area of Sandwell–
    Abbey
    Blackheath
    Bristnall
    Cradley Heath and Old Hill
    Friar Park
    Great Bridge
    Greets Green and Lyng
    Hateley Heath
    Langley
    Old Warley
    Oldbury
    Princes End
    Rowley
    Smethwick
    Soho and Victoria
    St. Pauls
    Tipton Green
    Tividale
    Wednesbury North
    Wednesbury South
    West Bromwich Central

The following wards in the local authority area of Solihull–
    Bickenhill
    Elmdon
    Lyndon
    Silhill

The following wards in the local authority area of South Staffordshire–
    Bilbrook
    Brewood and Coven
    Essington
    Featherstone and Shareshill

The following wards in the local authority area of Stoke-on-Trent UA–
    Bentilee and Townsend
    Berryhill and Hanley East
    Blurton
    Burslem South
    Chell and Packmoor
    Fenton
    Hanley West and Shelton
    Hartshill and Penkhull
    Longton North
    Longton South
    Meir Park and Sandon
    Stoke and Trent Vale
    Trentham and Hanford
    Tunstall

The following wards in the local authority area of Walsall–
    Bentley and Darlaston North
    Birchills Leamore

Blakenall
Bloxwich East
Bloxwich West
Brownhills
Darlaston South
Hatherton Rushall
Palfrey
Pelsall
Pleck
Short Heath
St. Matthew's
Willenhall North
Willenhall South

The following wards in the local authority area of Wolverhampton–

Bilston East
Bilston North
Blakenhall
Bushbury
East Park
Ettingshall
Fallings Park
Graiseley
Heath Town
Low Hill
Oxley
Spring Vale
St. Peter's
Wednesfield North
Wednesfield South

East of England

The following wards in the local authority area of Luton UA–

Biscot
Challney
Crawley
Dallow
High Town
Lewsey
Round Green
Saints
South
Stopsley
Wigmore

The following wards in the local authority area of South Bedfordshire–

Houghton Hall
Icknield
Parkside
Tithe Farm

London

The following wards in the local authority area of Barking and Dagenham–
  River
  Thames

The following ward in the local authority area of Bexley–
  Thamesmead East

The following wards in the local authority area of Greenwich–
  Glyndon
  Thamesmead Moorings
  Woolwich Riverside

The following ward in the local authority area of Havering–
  South Hornchurch

The following wards in the local authority area of Newham–
  Beckton
  Custom House
  East Ham South
  Royal Docks

South East

The following wards in the local authority area of Dover–
  Eastry
  Sandwich
  Whitfield

The following wards in the local authority area of Thanet–
  Beacon Road
  Birchington North
  Birchington South
  Bradstowe
  Central Harbour
  Cliffsend and Pegwell
  Cliftonville East
  Cliftonville West
  Dane Valley
  Eastcliff
  Garlinge
  Kingsgate
  Margate Central
  Nethercourt
  Newington
  Northwood
  Salmestone
  Sir Moses Montefiore
  St. Peters
  Thanet Villages
  Viking
  Westbrook
  Westgate-on-Sea

South West

The following wards in the local authority area of Plymouth UA–
     Budshead
     Devonport
     Drake
     Eggbuckland
     Ham
     Honicknowle
     Moor View
     Southway
     St. Budeaux
     St. Peter and the Waterfront
     Stoke
     Sutton and Mount Gould

The following wards in the local authority area of South Hams–
     Bickleigh and Shaugh
     Cornwood and Sparkwell

WALES

The following wards in the local authority area of Cardiff–
     Creigiau/St. Fagans
     Pentyrch
     Pontprennau/Old St. Mellons
     Trowbridge

The following wards in the local authority area of Flintshire–
     Aston
     Bagillt East
     Bagillt West
     Broughton North East
     Broughton South
     Brynford
     Buckley Mountain
     Caerwys
     Cilcain
     Connah's Quay Central
     Connah's Quay Golftyn
     Connah's Quay South
     Connah's Quay Wepre
     Ewloe
     Ffynnongroyw
     Flint Castle
     Flint Coleshill
     Flint Oakenholt
     Flint Trelawny
     Greenfield
     Gronant
     Halkyn
     Hawarden
     Holywell Central
     Holywell East
     Holywell West

    Mancot
    Mostyn
    Northop
    Northop Hall
    Queensferry
    Sealand
    Shotton East
    Shotton Higher
    Shotton West
    Trelawnyd and Gwaenysgor
    Whitford

The following wards in the local authority area of Newport–
    Gaer
    Graig
    Liswerry
    Llanwern
    Marshfield
    Pillgwenlly
    Tredegar Park

The following wards in the local authority area of Powys–
    Aber-craf
    Cwm-twrch
    Ynyscedwyn
    Ystradgynlais

SCOTLAND

The following wards in the local authority area of Clackmannanshire–
    Alloa East
    Alloa Mar
    Alloa West
    Clackmannan
    Delph and Cambus
    Devon and Clackmannan North
    Gartmorn
    Tillicoultry East
    Tillicoultry West

The following wards in the local authority area of Dundee City–
    Ardler
    Balgay
    Balgillo
    Baxter Park
    Bowbridge
    Camperdown
    Claverhouse
    Craigiebank
    Douglas
    East Port
    Fairmuir
    Hilltown
    Law
    Lochee East

Lochee West
Logie
Longhaugh
Ninewells
Pitkerro
Riverside
Stobswell
Tay Bridges
Whitfield

The following wards in the local authority area of East Ayrshire—

Altonhill, Hillhead and Longpark
Auchinleck
Bellfield
Crookedholm, Moscow, Galston West and Hurlford North
Crosshouse, Gatehead and Knockentiber
Cumnock West
Drongan, Stair and Rankinston
Galston East
Grange/Howard
Hurlford
Kilmarnock Central East
Kilmarnock Central South
Kilmarnock Central West
Newmilns
North Kilmarnock, Fenwick and Waterside
North New Farm Loch and Dean
Ochiltree, Skares, Netherthird and Craigens
Riccarton
Shortlees
South New Farm Loch

The following wards in the local authority area of East Dunbartonshire—

Cadder/Langbrae
Hillhead and Broomhill
Kirkintilloch Central
Lenzie

The following wards in the local authority area of Falkirk—

Camelon
Carrongrange
Dawson
Dundas/Kerse
Forthside
Herbertshire
Inchyra
Kinnaird
Larbert
Middlefield
Summerford
Tryst
Zetland

The following wards in the local authority area of Fife–

    Aberdour and Burntisland West

    Auchmuty and Woodside West

    Auchtertool and Burntisland East

    Bennochy and Valley

    Brucefield and Nethertown

    Buckhaven and Denbeath

    Cadham, Pitcoudie and Balfarg

    Cardenden, Cluny and Chapel

    Caskieberran and Rimbleton

    Crossgates and Mossside

    Dalgety Bay East

    Dalgety Bay West and Hillend

    Dunnikier

    Dysart and Gallatown

    Glebe Park, Pathhead and Sinclairtown

    Halbeath, Hill of Beath and Kingseat

    Hayfield and Balsusney

    Inverkeithing East and North Queensferry

    Inverkeithing West and Rosyth South

    Kinghorn and Invertiel

    Kinglassie, Bowhill and Dundonald

    Leven West and Kirkland

    Limekilns and Pitreavie

    Linburn

    Linktown and Kirkcaldy Central

    Methil

    Methilhill

    Pitcorthie

    Pitteuchar and Finglassie North

    Raith and Longbraes

    Rosyth East

    Rosyth West

    Smeaton and Overton

    Templehall East

    Templehall West

    Thornton, Stenton and Finglassie South

    Wemyss and Muiredge

    Woodmill

The following wards in the local authority area of Glasgow City–

    Anderston

    Baillieston

    Barlanark

    Braidfauld

    Bridgeton/Dalmarnock

    Calton

    Carmunnock

    Carntyne

    Cowlairs

    Dennistoun

Drumoyne
Drumry
Easterhouse
Firhill
Garrowhill
Gartcraig
Garthamlock
Glenwood
Govan
Govanhill
Greenfield
Hayburn
Hutchesontown
Ibrox
Kelvingrove
Keppochhill
Kingston
Merchant City
Milnbank
Mount Vernon
North Cardonald
Parkhead
Partick
Queenslie
Robroyston
Royston
Scotstoun
Shettleston
Tollcross Park
Victoria Park
Yoker

The following wards in the local authority area of Inverclyde–
Ward 10
Ward 11
Ward 12
Ward 13
Ward 14
Ward 15
Ward 16
Ward 17
Ward 18
Ward 19
Ward 2
Ward 3
Ward 4
Ward 5
Ward 6
Ward 7
Ward 8
Ward 9

The following wards in the local authority area of North Ayrshire–

    Ardrossan North
    Ardrossan South
    Bourtreehill
    Dalry
    Dreghorn
    Irvine Landward
    Irvine North
    Irvine Townhead
    Irvine Vineburgh and Woodlands South
    Irvine West
    Kilbirnie South
    Kilwinning East
    Kilwinning South
    Kilwinning West
    Largs South and Fairlie
    Saltcoats East
    Saltcoats North
    South Beach
    Stevenston North
    Stevenston South
    West Kilbride
    Woodlands North and Girdle Toll

The following wards in the local authority area of North Lanarkshire–

    Academy
    Airdrie Central
    Bargeddie and Langloan
    Belhaven
    Bellshill North
    Benhar
    Blairpark
    Calder Valley
    Calderbank
    Carbrain East
    Carbrain West and Greenfaulds
    Chapelhall
    Chryston and Auchinloch
    Clarkston
    Cleland
    Coatbridge Central
    Coltness
    Condorrat Central
    Condorrat North and Westfield
    Craigneuk
    Craigneuk and Petersburn
    Dykehead
    Fallside
    Forgewood
    Garrion
    Hattonrig

Holytown
Kirkshaws
Kirkwood
Knowetop
Moodiesburn East and Blackwood West
Moodiesburn West and Gartcosh
Mossend East and New Stevenston North
Mossend West and Thorndean
Muirhouse and Netherton
New Stevenston and Carfin
Newarthill
North Cairnhill and Coatdyke
North Central and Glenboig
North Motherwell
Old Monkland
Orbiston
Pather and Gowkthrapple
Salsburgh
Seafar and The Village
Shawhead
Sikeside and Carnbroe
South East Cairnhill and Gartlea
Stepps
Stewarton
Tannochside
Townhead
Viewpark
Watsonville
Westerwood, Carrickstone and Dullatur
Whinhall

The following wards in the local authority area of Renfrewshire–

Arkleston and Newmains
Bishopton
Blackhall and Hawkhead
Blythswood
Deanside
Erskine Central
Erskine S.E. and Inchinnan
Erskine West
Ferguslie
Gallowhill and Whitehaugh
Houston and Langbank
Linwood East
Moorpark
Paisley Central
Parkmains
Sandyford
Seedhill
Shortroods
St. James

Townhead

The following wards in the local authority area of South Ayrshire–

Annbank Mossblown St Quivox

Dundonald and Loans

Prestwick St Cuthbert's and Monkton

Prestwick St Nicholas'

Tarbolton Symington Craigie

Troon East

Troon North

Troon South

Troon West

The following wards in the local authority area of South Lanarkshire–

Avondale North

Blantyre West

Bothwell South

Burgh

Burnbank/Blantyre

Cairns

Cambuslang Central

Coatshill/Low Blantyre

Earnock

Eastfield

Hallside

Hamilton Centre North

Heatheryknowe

High Blantyre

Hillhouse

Kirkhill/Whitlawburn

Long Calderwood

Low Waters

Mossneuk/Kittoch

Stewartfield

Uddingston

Uddingston South/Bothwell

Udston

Wellhall/Earnock

Whitehill

Whitehills

The following wards in the local authority area of Stirling–

Argyll

Logie

Polmaise

Raploch

Sauchenford

The following wards in the local authority area of West Dunbartonshire–

Alexandria North/Tullichewan

Barloan/Overtoun

Bowling/Milton/Old Kilpatrick

Dalmuir/Central

Dumbarton Central

Dumbarton East
Kilbowie
Kilbowie West
Linnvale/Drumry
Mountblow
Parkhall
Renton/Alexandria South
Riverside
Whitecrook

CAPITAL ALLOWANCES (LEASES OF BACKGROUND PLANT OR MACHINERY FOR A BUILDING) ORDER 2007

(SI 2007/303)

Made on 6 February 2007 by the Treasury in exercise of the powers conferred upon them by s. 70T of the Capital Allowances Act 2001. Operative from 28 February 2007.

Statutory Instruments

CITATION, COMMENCEMENT AND EFFECT

1(1)   This Order may be cited as the Capital Allowances (Leases of Background Plant or Machinery for a Building) Order 2007 and comes into force on 28th February 2007.

1(2)   This Order has effect in relation to times on and after 1st April 2006.

EXAMPLES OF BACKGROUND PLANT OR MACHINERY

2(1)   The descriptions of plant or machinery in paragraph (2) are prescribed examples of the kinds of plant or machinery that may be regarded as falling within the definition of background plant or machinery for a building in determining whether any particular plant or machinery does or does not fall within that definition.

2(2)   The descriptions of plant or machinery are–

(a)   heating and air conditioning installations,

(b)   ceilings which are part of an air conditioning system,

(c)   hot water installations,

(d)   electrical installations that provide power to a building, such as high and low voltage switchgear, all sub-mains distribution systems and standby generators,

(e)   mechanisms, including automatic control systems, for opening and closing doors, windows and vents,

(f)   escalators and passenger lifts,

(g)   window cleaning installations,

(h)   fittings such as fitted cupboards, blinds, curtains and associated mechanical equipment,

(i)   demountable partitions,

(j)   protective installations such as lightning protection, sprinkler and other equipment for containing or fighting fires, fire alarm systems and fire escapes, and

(k)   building management systems.

2(3)   This article is subject to article 4.

PLANT OR MACHINERY DEEMED TO BE BACKGROUND PLANT OR MACHINERY

3(1)   The following descriptions of plant or machinery are deemed to be background plant or machinery.

3(2)   The descriptions of plant or machinery are–

(a)   lighting installations including all fixed light fittings and emergency lighting systems,

(b)   telephone, audio-visual and data installations incidental to the occupation of the building,

(c)   computer networking facilities incidental to the occupation of the building,

(d)   sanitary appliances and other bathroom fittings including hand driers, counters, partitions, mirrors, shower and locker facilities,

(e)   kitchen and catering facilities for producing and storing food and drink for the occupants of the building,

(f)   fixed seating,

(g)   signs,

(h)   public address systems, and

(i)   intruder alarm systems and other security equipment including surveillance equipment.

PLANT OR MACHINERY DEEMED NOT TO BE BACKGROUND PLANT OR MACHINERY

4(1)   The following descriptions of plant or machinery are deemed not to be background plant or machinery.

4(2)   The descriptions of plant or machinery are plant or machinery used for any of the purposes in paragraph (3).

4(3)   The purposes are–

(a)   storing, moving or displaying goods to be sold in the course of a trade, whether wholesale or retail,

(b)   manufacturing goods or materials,

(c)   subjecting goods or materials to a process,

(d)   storing goods or materials–

    (i)   which are to be used in the manufacture of other goods or materials,

    (ii)   which are to be subjected, in the course of a trade, to a process,

    (iii)   which, having been manufactured or produced or subjected in the course of a trade to a process, have not yet been delivered to any purchaser, or

    (iv)   on their arrival in the United Kingdom from a place outside the United Kingdom.

4(4)   This article is subject to article 3.

LONG FUNDING LEASES (ELECTIONS) REGULATIONS 2007

(SI 2007/304)

Made on 6 February 2007 by the Treasury in exercise of the powers conferred upon them by para. 16 of Sch. 8 to the Finance Act 2006. Operative from 28 February 2007.

CITATION, COMMENCEMENT, INTERPRETATION AND EFFECT

1(1) These Regulations may be cited as the Long Funding Leases (Elections) Regulations 2007, shall come into force on 28th February 2007 and shall have effect in respect of leases finalised on or after 1st April 2006.

1(2) In these Regulations–

"**CAA**" means the Capital Allowances Act 2001; and

"**TMA**" means the Taxes Management Act 1970.

1(3) In these Regulations–

"**eligible lease**" has the meaning given by regulation 3;

"**lessor**" has the meaning given in section 70YI of CAA;

"**qualifying incidental lease**" has the meaning given by regulation 4; and

other terms defined or otherwise explained in Chapter 6A of CAA have the same meaning in these Regulations as they have there.

ELECTION

2(1) A lessor may make an election ("a long funding lease election") in respect of all his eligible leases and qualifying incidental leases.

In these Regulations "**electing lessor**" means a lessor who makes such an election.

2(2) A long-funding lease election–

(a) must be made within the permitted time;

(b) must be made in the return for the relevant chargeable period or for the year of assessment to which the election relates, either by inclusion in the return as originally made or by an amendment to that return;

(c) must specify the date from which it is to take effect ("the effective date"); and

(d) may be withdrawn by amending that return within the permitted time (but is otherwise irrevocable).

Sub-paragraph (c) is subject to the qualification in paragraph (4).

2(3) The permitted time is–

(a) for income tax purposes, the period beginning with the end of the year of assessment to which the election relates, and ending 12 months after the 31st January next following that year of assessment;

(b) for corporation tax purposes, the period beginning with the time when the relevant chargeable period ends and ending with the second anniversary of that time.

2(4) The effective date may not be earlier than the later of–

(a) 1st April 2006; and

(b) the beginning of the relevant chargeable period or the year of assessment to which the election relates (as the case requires).

2(5) If a long funding lease election has been made, the electing lessor shall be treated as if all the electing lessor's eligible and qualifying incidental leases finalised on or after the effective date (including those finalised in subsequent chargeable periods or years of assessment) had been long funding leases for the purposes of Part 2 of CAA since they were finalised.

2(6) For the purposes of this regulation–

"**chargeable period**" has the meaning given by section 6 of CAA;

"**relevant chargeable period**" means the chargeable period in which the effective date falls; and

"**the year of assessment to which the election relates**" means the tax year in which ends the basis period in which falls the effective date.

ELIGIBLE LEASES

3 An eligible lease is one which meets the following conditions.

Condition A

The lease is a plant or machinery lease.

Condition B

The lease is not, apart from the provisions of these Regulations, a long funding lease.

Condition C

The lease was finalised, as defined in paragraph 23 of Schedule 8 of the Finance Act 2006, on or after 1 April 2006.

Condition D

The term of the lease is 12 months or more.

Condition E

The plant or machinery made available under the lease–

(a)   was unused and not second-hand at the commencement of the term of the lease;

(b)   if leased previously, was last leased under a long funding lease (under the provisions of Part 2 of CAA or pursuant to these Regulations) before the commencement of the term of the lease;

(c)   was the subject of a valid election under section 227 of CAA before the electing lessor made a return for the period in which the commencement of the term of the lease occurred; or

(d)   replaces (whether by one or more substitutions) plant or machinery of the same type and quantity previously made available by the electing lessor to the lessee under a lease which is an eligible lease by virtue of one of the preceding paragraphs of this condition.

Condition F

The lease is not a lease for the provision of a car as defined in section 81 of CAA.

Condition G

The lease does not provide for the leasing of any asset whose market value is more than £10 million at its commencement.

Condition H

The lease is not one to which section 70R or section 70U of CAA applies.

Condition I

If the original lessor's interest under the lease has been assigned–

(a)   the assignment, or where there is more than one assignment, both or all of them, must have occurred within 4 months of the commencement of the term of the lease; and

(b)   the original lessor, and any person later owning the leased assets and through whom the lessor making the long funding lease election derives title to them, must not claim, or have claimed, capital allowances at any time in respect of those assets.

QUALIFYING INCIDENTAL LEASES

4 A qualifying incidental lease is a lease of plant or machinery which–

(a)   is wholly incidental to an eligible lease; and

(b)   disregarding Condition D in regulation 3, would have been an eligible lease.

Statutory Instruments

REGISTERED PENSION SCHEMES (STANDARD LIFETIME AND ANNUAL ALLOWANCES) ORDER 2007

(SI 2007/494)

Made on 21 February 2007 by the Treasury in exercise of the powers conferred upon them by s. 218(3) and 228(2) of the Finance Act 2004. Operative from 6 April 2007.

CITATION AND COMMENCEMENT

1 This Order may be cited as the Registered Pension Schemes (Standard Lifetime and Annual Allowances) Order 2007 and shall come into force on 6th April 2007.

STANDARD LIFETIME ALLOWANCE

2 The standard lifetime allowance–
(a)　for the tax year 2007–08 is £1,600,000;
(b)　for the tax year 2008–09 is £1,650,000;
(c)　for the tax year 2009–10 is £1,750,000;
(d)　for the tax year 2010–11 is £1,800,000.

ANNUAL ALLOWANCE

3 The annual allowance–
(a)　for the tax year 2007–08 is £225,000;
(b)　for the tax year 2008–09 is £235,000;
(c)　for the tax year 2009–10 is £245,000;
(d)　for the tax year 2010–11 is £255,000.

CORPORATION TAX (SURRENDER OF TERMINAL LOSSES ON FILMS AND CLAIMS FOR RELIEF) REGULATIONS 2007

(SI 2007/678)

Made on 5 March 2007 by the Treasury in exercise of the powers conferred upon them by s. 45(5) of the Finance Act 2006. Operative from 27 March 2007.

CITATION AND COMMENCEMENT

1 These Regulations may be cited as the Corporation Tax (Surrender of Terminal Losses on Films and Claims for Relief) Regulations 2007 and shall come into force on 27th March 2007.

INTERPRETATION

2 In these Regulations–

"**FA**" followed by a year means the Finance Act of that year;

"**TMA**" means the Taxes Management Act 1970; and

"**Part 8**" means Part 8 of Schedule 18 to FA 1998 (claims for group relief).

PROVISION CORRESPONDING TO PART 8 OF SCHEDULE 18 TO FA 1998

3 The provision made by regulations 4 to 15 corresponds to the provision made by Part 8.

The Table below shows the correspondence between those regulations and the paragraphs of Part 8.

TABLE

Regulation	Paragraph of Part 8 to which the regulation corresponds
4	66 (introduction)
5	67 (claims to be included in company tax return)
6	68 (content of claims)
7	69 (claims for more or less than the amount available for surrender)
8	70 (consent to surrender)
9	71 (notice of consent)
10	72 (notice of consent requiring amendment of return)
11	73 (withdrawal or amendment of claim)
12	74 (time limit for claims)
13	75 (reduction in amount available for surrender)
14	75A (assessment on other claimant companies)
15	76 (assessment to recover excessive group relief)

INTRODUCTION OF PROVISIONS ON CLAIMS FOR RELIEF IN RESPECT OF TERMINAL LOSSES

4 Regulations 5 to 16 apply to claims for relief made by virtue of section 45(3) of FA 2006 (terminal losses of company A may be surrendered to company B and treated as a loss of company B).

CLAIM TO BE INCLUDED IN COMPANY B'S RETURN

5(1) A claim to treat the terminal loss surrendered by company A as if it were a loss brought forward by company B must be included in company B's tax return for the accounting period for which the claim is made.

5(2) It may be included in the return originally made or by amendment.

CONTENT OF CLAIMS

6(1) A claim to treat the terminal loss surrendered by company A as if it were a loss brought forward by company B must specify–

(a)　　the amount of relief claimed, and

(b)　　the name of company A.

6(2)　　The amount specified must be an amount which is quantified at the time the claim is made.

6(3)　　A claim to treat the terminal loss surrendered by company A as if it were a loss brought forward by company B must also state whether or not there is a company mentioned in paragraph (4) that was not resident in the United Kingdom in either or both of the following periods–

(a)　　the accounting period of company A to which the surrender relates,

(b)　　the corresponding accounting period of company B.

6(4)　　Those companies are company A, company B and any other company by reference to which company A or company B are members of the same group.

CLAIMS FOR MORE OR LESS THAN THE TERMINAL LOSS AVAILABLE FOR SURRENDER

7(1)　　A claim to treat the terminal loss surrendered by company A as if it were a loss brought forward by company B may be made for less than the amount available for surrender at the time the claim is made.

7(2)　　A claim is ineffective if the amount claimed exceeds the terminal loss available for surrender at the time the claim is made.

7(3)　　For these purposes the terminal loss available for surrender is calculated as follows, subject to paragraphs (4) and (5).

First step

Determine the total amount available for surrender under section 45 of FA 2006–

(a)　　on the basis of the information in company A's company tax return, and

(b)　　disregarding any amendments whose effect is deferred under paragraph 31(3) of Schedule 18 to FA 1998.

Second step

Then deduct the total of all amounts for which notices of consent have been given by company A and not withdrawn.

7(4)　　Where one or more claims are withdrawn on the same day as one or more claims are made, the withdrawals are given effect first.

7(5)　　Where more than one claim is made on the same day, and the claims together take the amount claimed over the limit of what is available for surrender, an officer of Revenue and Customs may determine which of the claims is to be ineffective.

CONSENT TO SURRENDER

8(1)　　A claim for terminal loss surrendered by company A as if it were a loss brought forward by company B requires the consent of company A.

8(2)　　The necessary consent must be given–

(a)　　by notice in writing,

(b)　　to the officer of Revenue and Customs to whom company A makes its company tax returns,

(c)　　at or before the time the claim is made.

Otherwise the claim is ineffective.

8(3)　　A claim to treat the terminal loss surrendered by company A as if it were a loss brought forward by company B is ineffective unless it is accompanied by a copy of the notice of consent to surrender given by company A.

NOTICE OF CONSENT

9(1)　　Notice of consent by company A must contain all of the following details–

(a)　　the name of company A;

(b)　　the name of company B;

(c)　　the amount of the terminal loss being surrendered;

(d)　　the accounting period of company A to which the surrender relates;

(e)　　the tax district references of company A and company B.

Otherwise the notice is ineffective.

9(2)   A notice of consent may not be amended, but it may be withdrawn and replaced by another notice of consent.

9(3)   A notice of consent may be withdrawn by notice to the officer of Revenue and Customs to whom the notice of consent was given.

9(4)   Except where the consent is withdrawn under regulation 13 (withdrawal in consequence of reduction of the amount available for surrender), the notice of withdrawal must be accompanied by a notice signifying the consent of company B to the withdrawal.

Otherwise the notice is ineffective.

9(5)   Company B must, so far as it may do so, amend its company tax return for the accounting period for which the claim was made so as to reflect the withdrawal of consent.

NOTICE OF CONSENT REQUIRING AMENDMENT OF RETURN

10(1)   Where notice of consent by company A is given after that company has made a company tax return for the period to which the surrender relates, company A must at the same time amend its return so as to reflect the notice of consent.

10(2)   Where a notice of consent given by company A relates to a loss in respect of which relief has been given to company A, company A must at the same time amend its tax return for the period or, if more than one, each of the periods in which relief for that loss has been given in accordance with section 45(2) of FA 2006 so as to reflect the new notice of consent.

10(3)   The time limits otherwise applicable to amendment of a company tax return do not prevent an amendment being made under paragraph (1) or (2).

10(4)   But if company A fails to comply with paragraph (1) or (2), the notice of consent is ineffective.

WITHDRAWAL OR AMENDMENT OF CLAIM

11(1)   A claim to treat the terminal loss surrendered by company A as if it were a loss brought forward by company B may be withdrawn by company B only by amending its company tax return.

11(2)   A claim to treat the terminal loss surrendered by company A as if it were a loss brought forward by company B may not be amended by company B, but must be withdrawn and replaced by another claim.

TIME LIMIT FOR CLAIMS

12(1)   A claim to treat the terminal loss surrendered by company A as if it were a loss brought forward by company B may be withdrawn by company B at any time up to whichever is the last of the following dates–

(a)   the first anniversary of the filing date for the company tax return of company B for the accounting period for which the claim is made;

(b)   if notice of enquiry is given into that return, 30 days after the enquiry is completed;

(c)   if after such an enquiry an officer of Revenue and Customs amends the return under paragraph 34(2) of Schedule 18 to FA 1998, 30 days after the date on which the amendment is issued;

(d)   if an appeal is brought against such an amendment, 30 days after the date on which the appeal is finally determined.

12(2)   A claim to treat the terminal loss surrendered by company A as if it were a loss brought forward by company B may be made or withdrawn at a later time if an officer of Revenue and Customs allows it.

12(3)   The time limits otherwise applicable to amendment of a company tax return do not apply to an amendment to the extent that it makes or withdraws a claim to treat the terminal loss surrendered by company A as if it were a loss brought forward by company B within the time allowed by this regulation.

12(4)   The references in paragraph (1) to an enquiry into a company tax return do not include an enquiry restricted to a previous amendment making or withdrawing a claim to treat the terminal loss surrendered by company A as if it were a loss brought forward by company B.

An enquiry is so restricted if–

(a)   the scope of the enquiry is limited as mentioned in paragraph 25(2) of Schedule 18 to FA 1998 (limiting scope of enquiry into a company tax return);

(b)   the amendment giving rise to the enquiry consisted of the making or withdrawal of a claim to treat the terminal loss surrendered by company A as if it were a loss brought forward by company B.

REDUCTION IN AMOUNT AVAILABLE FOR SURRENDER

13(1)   This regulation applies if, after company A has given one or more notices of consent to a claim by company B to treat the terminal loss surrendered by company A as if it were a loss brought forward by company B, the total available to be so treated is reduced to less than the amount stated in the notice, or the total amount of the amounts stated in the notices, as being available to be so treated.

13(2)   Company A must within 30 days withdraw the notice of consent, or as many of the notices as is necessary to bring the total amount surrendered within the new total amount available to be treated as a loss carried forward by company B, and may give one or more new notices of consent.

13(3)   Company A must give notice in writing of the withdrawal of consent, and send a copy of any new notice of consent—

(a)   to each of the companies affected; and

(b)   to an officer of Revenue and Customs.

13(4)   If company A fails to act in accordance with paragraph (2) an officer of Revenue and Customs may by notice to company A give such directions as he thinks fit as to which notice or notices are to be ineffective or are to have effect in a lesser amount.

The power shall not be exercised to any greater extent than is necessary to secure that the total amount stated in the notice or notices is consistent with the total amount available to be treated as a loss carried forward by company B by virtue of section 45 of FA 2006.

13(5)   An officer of Revenue and Customs must at the same time send a copy of the notice to company B.

13(6)   Company B upon receipt of—

(a)   a notice of the withdrawal of consent, or a copy of a new notice of consent under paragraph (3), or

(b)   a copy of a notice containing directions by an officer of Revenue and Customs under paragraph (4),

must, so far as it may do so, amend its company tax return for the accounting period for which the claim is made so that it is consistent with the new position with regard to consent to surrender.

13(7)   Company A may appeal against any directions given by an officer of Revenue and Customs under paragraph (4).

13(8)   Notice of appeal must be given—

(a)   in writing,

(b)   within 30 days after the notice containing the directions was issued,

(c)   to the officer of Revenue and Customs by whom the notice was given.

ASSESSMENT ON OTHER CLAIMANT COMPANIES

14(1)   This regulation applies where, after company A has given notice of consent to surrender, company B has become liable to tax in consequence of receiving—

(a)   notice of the withdrawal of consent, or a copy of a new notice of consent under regulation 13(3); or

(b)   a copy of a notice containing directions by an officer of Revenue and Customs under regulation 13(4).

14(2)   If any of the tax is unpaid six months after company B's time limit for claims, an officer of Revenue and Customs may make an assessment to tax in the name of company B on any other company which has obtained relief as a result of the surrender.

14(3)   The assessment must not be made more than two years after that time limit.

14(4)   The amount of the assessment must not exceed—

(a)   the amount of the unpaid tax, or

(b)   if less, the amount of tax which the other company saves by virtue of the surrender.

14(5)   A company assessed to an amount of tax under paragraph (2) is entitled to recover from company B—

(a)   a sum equal to that amount, and

(b)   any interest on that amount which it has paid under section 87A of TMA (interest on unpaid corporation tax).

14(6) For the purposes of this regulation company B's time limit for claims is the last of the dates mentioned in regulation 12(1) on which company B could make or withdraw a claim to treat the terminal loss surrendered by company A as if it were a loss brought forward by company B.

ASSESSMENT TO RECOVER EXCESS RELIEF

15(1) If an officer of Revenue and Customs discovers that any relief given in respect of a claim by company B to treat the terminal loss surrendered by company A as if it were a loss brought forward by company B is or has become excessive, he may make an assessment to tax which in his opinion ought to be charged.

15(2) This power—

(a)   is in addition to the power to make a discovery assessment under paragraph 41(1) of Schedule 18 to FA 1998; and

(b)   does not prevent the making of such adjustments by way of discharge or repayment of tax or otherwise as may be required where company B has obtained too much relief, or company A has forgone relief in respect of a corresponding amount.

15(3) If an assessment under this regulation is made because company B fails, or is unable, to amend its company tax return under regulation 13(6), the assessment is not out of time if it is made within one year from—

(a)   the date on which company A gives notice of the withdrawal of consent, or (if later) sends a new notice of consent, to company B under regulation 13(3), or

(b)   the date on which an officer of Revenue and Customs sends the company B a copy of a notice containing his directions under regulation 13(4).

TRANSFER OF THE NORTHERN IRELAND WATER SERVICE (TAX) REGULATIONS 2007

(SI 2007/766)

Made on 8 March 2007 by the Treasury, in exercise of the powers conferred by s. 67 of the Finance (No. 2) Act 2005. Operative from 1 April 2007.

CITATION AND COMMENCEMENT

1 These Regulations may be cited as the Transfer of the Northern Ireland Water Service (Tax) Regulations 2007 and come into force on 1st April 2007.

INTERPRETATION

2 In these Regulations—

"**CAA**" means the Capital Allowances Act 2001;

"**TCGA**" means the Taxation of Chargeable Gains Act 1992;

"**relevant transfer**" has the meaning given in section 67(1) of the Finance (No.2) Act 2005;

"**successor company**" has the meaning given in Article 269 of the Water and Sewerage Services (Northern Ireland) Order 2006;

"**transferor**" means the Department for Regional Development;

"**wholly owned subsidiary**" has the meaning given in Article 4 of the Companies (Northern Ireland) Order 1986.

CAPITAL ALLOWANCES: TRANSFER OF PLANT OR MACHINERY

3(1) This regulation applies where—

(a) there is a relevant transfer of plant or machinery; and

(b) the plant or machinery would have been treated for the purposes of CAA (had the transferor incurred expenditure qualifying for allowances under Part 2 of that Act on the provision of the plant or machinery) as disposed of by the transferor to the successor company on the transfer taking effect.

3(2) Where this regulation applies, the Secretary of State may determine the amount which is to be taken for the purposes of Part 2 of CAA to be the amount of capital expenditure incurred by the successor company on the provision of plant or machinery.

3(3) A determination referred to in paragraph (2) may only be made with the consent of the Treasury.

3(4) Expressions used in this regulation and in Part 2 of CAA have the same meanings in this regulation as in that Part.

CAPITAL ALLOWANCES: DETERMINATION OF CAPITAL VALUE OF INDUSTRIAL BUILDINGS ETC.

4(1) This regulation applies where there is a relevant transfer of a relevant interest in an industrial building or structure.

4(2) Where this regulation applies the Secretary of State may determine—

(a) the amount to be taken as the amount of the residue of qualifying expenditure immediately after the transfer; and

(b) the period to be taken as the period from the date of the transfer to the end of the period of 25 years beginning with the day on which the building or structure was first used.

4(3) A determination referred to in paragraph (2) may only be made with the consent of the Treasury.

4(4) Expressions used in this regulation and in Part 3 of CAA have the same meanings in this regulation as in that Part.

AMENDMENT OF COMPANY TAX RETURN FOLLOWING DETERMINATION BY SECRETARY OF STATE

5(1) Where the Secretary of State makes a determination in accordance with regulations 3(2) or 4(2) the successor company—

(a)   may amend its company tax return where necessary in accordance with paragraph 15(4) of Schedule 18 to the Finance Act 1998; or

(b)   shall amend its company tax return not more than twelve months after the end of the accounting period in which the determination occurred where the date of the determination makes it impossible to comply with the time limits set out in paragraph 15(4) of Schedule 18 to that Act.

5(2) Where a company does not make an amended return in accordance with sub-paragraph (b), an officer of Revenue and Customs may make an assessment or determination–

(a)   in accordance with paragraph 46 of Schedule 18 to the Finance Act 1998; or

(b)   not later than two years after the end of the accounting period in which the determination occurred,

whichever is the later.

CHARGEABLE GAINS: TRANSFER VALUES

6 Where there is a relevant transfer, to the extent that section 171 of TCGA would otherwise apply to the transfer, that section shall not apply.

CHARGEABLE GAINS: DEGROUPING CHARGES

7(1) This regulation applies if the successor company acquires an asset from the transferor by way of a relevant transfer at a time when both are members of the same group of companies.

7(2) Where paragraph (1) applies the successor company shall not be treated as having acquired the asset from the transferor for the purposes of section 179 of TCGA (company ceasing to be member of group).

7(3) Expressions used in this regulation and in section 179 of TCGA have the same meanings in this regulation as in that section.

OWNERSHIP OF SUCCESSOR COMPANY: ISSUE OF SECURITIES

8 Any security (other than a share) issued by the successor company or its wholly owned subsidiary pursuant to Article 271 of the Water and Sewerage Services (Northern Ireland) Order 2006 shall be treated for the purposes of the Corporation Tax Acts as if it had been issued for new consideration, such new consideration being equal to the principal sum payable under the security.

MODIFICATION OF TRANSFER SCHEMES

9(1) Where a transfer scheme is treated as modified under, or by an order made under paragraph 3 of Schedule 11 to the Water and Sewerage Services (Northern Ireland) Order 2006 the successor company–

(a)   may amend its company tax return in accordance with paragraph 15(4) of Schedule 18 to the Finance Act 1998; or

(b)   shall amend its company tax return not more than twelve months after the end of the accounting period in which the modification occurred where the date of the modification makes it impossible to comply with the time limits set out in paragraph 15(4) of Schedule 18 to that Act.

9(2) Where a company does not make an amended return in accordance with sub-paragraph (b), an officer of Revenue and Customs may make an assessment or determination–

(a)   in accordance with paragraph 46 of Schedule 18 to the Finance Act 1998; or

(b)   not later than two years after the end of the accounting period in which the modification occurred, whichever is the later.

EMPLOYEE SHARE SCHEMES (ELECTRONIC COMMUNICATION OF RETURNS AND INFORMATION) REGULATIONS 2007

(SI 2007/792)

Made on 12 March 2007 by the Commissioners for Her Majesty's Revenue and Customs in exercise of the powers conferred upon them by s. 132 and 133(2) of the Finance Act 1999. Operative from 6 April 2007.

History – SI 2007/792 revoked by FA 2014, s. 51 and Sch. 8, para. 88, with effect from 6 April 2014 (subject to the provisions of Sch. 8, para. 90–96).

PART 1 – INTRODUCTION

CITATION AND COMMENCEMENT

1   These Regulations may be cited as the Employee Share Schemes (Electronic Communication of Returns and Information) Regulations 2007 and shall come into force on 6th April 2007.

INTERPRETATION

2(1)   In these Regulations–
(a)   "**the Act**" means the Income Tax (Earnings and Pensions) Act 2003; and
(b)   any reference to a numbered section or Schedule (without more) is a reference to the section or Schedule bearing that number in the Act.
2(2)   In these Regulations–
"**approved method of electronic communications**", in relation to the delivery of information in accordance with a provision of these Regulations, means a method of electronic communications which has been approved, by specific or general directions issued by the Commissioners, for the delivery of information of that kind under that provision;
"**the Commissioners**" means the Commissioners for Her Majesty's Revenue and Customs;
"**electronic communications**" has the meaning given in section 132(10) of the Finance Act 1999;
"**official computer system**" means a computer system maintained by or on behalf of the Commissioners or on behalf of an officer of Revenue and Customs–
(a)   to send or receive information, or
(b)   to process or store information;
"**relevant information**" means information which is authorised by virtue of these Regulations to be delivered to or dispatched by Revenue and Customs by an approved method of electronic communications;
"**Revenue and Customs**" means Her Majesty's Revenue and Customs.

PART 2 – INFORMATION WHICH MAY BE DELIVERED BY ELECTRONIC COMMUNICATIONS

INFORMATION WHICH MAY BE DELIVERED BY ELECTRONIC COMMUNICATIONS UNDER THESE REGULATIONS

3(1)   Information specified in the Schedule to these Regulations may be delivered to Revenue and Customs if–
(a)   it is sent by an approved method of electronic communications, and
(b)   the sender is authorised by Revenue and Customs to use electronic communications for that purpose.
3(2)   Revenue and Customs may dispatch an acknowledgement to confirm receipt of any information specified in the Schedule to these Regulations.

PART 3 – EVIDENTIAL PROVISIONS

WHETHER RELEVANT INFORMATION HAS BEEN DELIVERED ELECTRONICALLY

4(1)   For the purposes of these Regulations, relevant information is to be taken to have been delivered to an official computer system by an approved method of electronic communications only if it is accepted by that official computer system.

This is subject to the following qualification.
4(2)   Relevant information which is delivered to an official computer system must meet the standards of accuracy and completeness set by specific or general directions given by the Commissioners.
4(3)   Relevant information which fails to meet those standards must be treated as not having been delivered.

PROOF OF CONTENT OF ELECTRONIC DELIVERY

5(1) A document certified by Revenue and Customs to be a printed-out version of information delivered by an approved method of communications is evidence, unless the contrary is proved, that the information–

(a)   was delivered by an approved method of electronic communications on that occasion, and

(b)   constitutes everything which was delivered on that occasion.

5(2) A document which purports to be a certificate given in accordance with paragraph (1) is presumed to be such a certificate unless the contrary is proved.

PROOF OF IDENTITY OF PERSON SENDING OR RECEIVING ELECTRONIC DELIVERY

6 The identity of–

(a)   the person sending any information delivered by an approved method of electronic communications to Revenue and Customs, or

(b)   the person receiving any information delivered by an approved method of electronic communications by Revenue and Customs,

is presumed, unless the contrary is proved, to be the person recorded as such on an official computer system.

INFORMATION SENT ELECTRONICALLY ON BEHALF OF A PERSON

7(1) Any information delivered by an approved method of electronic communications–

(a)   to Revenue and Customs, or

(b)   to an official computer system,

on behalf of a person, is presumed to have been delivered by that person.

7(2) But this does not apply if the person proves that the information was delivered without the person's knowledge or connivance.

PROOF OF INFORMATION SENT ELECTRONICALLY

8(1) The use of an approved method of electronic communications is presumed, unless the contrary is proved, to have resulted in the delivery of information–

(a)   to Revenue and Customs, if the delivery of the information has been recorded on an official computer system;

(b)   by Revenue and Customs, if the dispatch of the information has been recorded on an official computer system.

8(2) The use of an approved method of electronic communications is presumed, unless the contrary is proved, not to have resulted in the delivery of relevant information–

(a)   to Revenue and Customs, if the delivery of the information has not been recorded on an official computer system;

(b)   by Revenue and Customs, if the dispatch of the information has not been recorded on an official computer system.

8(3) The time of receipt or dispatch of any relevant information delivered by an approved method of electronic communications is presumed, unless the contrary is proved, to be the time recorded on an official computer system.

This is subject to the following qualification.

8(4) The Commissioners may, by a general or specific direction, provide for information to be treated as delivered upon a different date (whether earlier or later) than that given by paragraph (3).

8(5) Information shall not be taken to have been delivered to an official computer system by means of electronic communications unless it is accepted by the system to which it is delivered.

AUTHENTICATION OF INFORMATION IN DOCUMENT OTHERWISE REQUIRED TO BE SIGNED

9(1) This regulation applies if–

(a)   information specified in the Schedule to these Regulations is delivered to Revenue and Customs by a method of electronic communications, and

(b)   the information is required to be signed by or on behalf of the person delivering it.

9(2) The requirement for a signature shall be treated as satisfied if the information is authenticated by or on behalf of the sender in such manner as may be approved by the Commissioners.

USE OF UNAUTHORISED METHOD OF ELECTRONIC COMMUNICATIONS

10(1) This regulation applies if–

(a)   a method of electronic communications is used for the purpose of delivering information under Part 2 of these Regulations, and

(b)   that method of electronic communications is not for the time being approved for the delivery of information of that kind under that Part.

10(2) The use of that method of electronic communications is conclusively presumed not to have resulted in the delivery of the information.

SCHEDULE

Regulation 3

INFORMATION WHICH MAY BE SUPPLIED TO REVENUE AND CUSTOMS BY AN APPROVED METHOD OF ELECTRONIC COMMUNICATIONS

1   Information required under section 421J(3) (particulars of any reportable events under section 421K(3)).

2   Information pursuant to a notice given under section 421J(4) requiring a person to provide an officer of Revenue and Customs with particulars of any reportable events under section 421K(3) or, if there are none, a statement of that fact.

3   Information pursuant to a notice given under paragraph 93 of Schedule 2 requiring a person to provide an officer of Revenue and Customs with any information that officer reasonably requires under the SIP code (see section 488(3)).

4   Information pursuant to a notice given under paragraph 45 of Schedule 3 requiring a person to provide an officer of Revenue and Customs with any information that officer reasonably requires under the SAYE code (see section 516(3)).

5   Information pursuant to a notice given under paragraph 33 of Schedule 4 requiring a person to provide an officer of Revenue and Customs with any information that officer reasonably requires under the CSOP code (see section 521(3)).

REGISTERED PENSION SCHEMES (BRIDGING PENSIONS) REGULATIONS 2007

(SI 2007/826)

Made on 13 March 2007 by the Treasury in exercise of the powers conferred upon them by para. 2(5) and 2(8) of Sch. 28 to the Finance Act 2004. Operative from 6 April 2007.

CITATION, COMMENCEMENT AND EFFECT

1(1) These Regulations may be cited as the Registered Pension Schemes (Bridging Pensions) Regulations 2007 and shall come into force on 6th April 2007.

1(2) These Regulations have effect in relation to payments of scheme pensions made on or after 6th April 2006.

PRESCRIBED PERCENTAGE OF THE BASIC PENSION RATE

2(1) The prescribed percentage of the rate of the basic pension under paragraph 2(5)(c) of Schedule 28 to the Finance Act 2004 is that found by the formula–

$$125 + \left(125\frac{A}{B}\right)$$

Here–

A is the total number of years of a member's employment to which the pension scheme relates which is not or has not been contracted-out employment, and

B is the total number of years of a member's employment to which the pension scheme relates.

2(2) In paragraph (1) **"the basic pension"** and **"contracted-out employment"** have the meanings given by paragraph 2(5A) of Schedule 28 to the Finance Act 2004.

TONNAGE TAX (EXCEPTION OF FINANCIAL YEAR 2007) ORDER 2007

(SI 2007/850)

Made on 14 March 2007 by the Treasury in exercise of the powers conferred upon them by para. 22B(2) and 22C(1) of Sch. 22 to the Finance Act 2000. Operative from 1 April 2007.

CITATION AND COMMENCEMENT

1   This Order may be cited as the Tonnage Tax (Exception of Financial Year 2007) Order 2007 and shall come into force on 1st April 2007.

PRESCRIBED THREE YEAR PERIOD AND OTHER DEFINITIONS

2   For the purposes of this Order–

(a)   the period prescribed for the purposes of paragraph 22C(1)(a) of Schedule 22 to the Finance Act 2000 (three year period to determine whether the percentage of the tonnage tax fleet which is Community-flagged has not decreased) is the period beginning on 2nd October 2003 and ending on 1st October 2006;

(b)   **"the tonnage tax fleet"** means qualifying ships operated by single companies or qualifying companies which are members of a tonnage tax group; and

(c)   **"the percentage of the tonnage tax fleet which is Community-flagged"** is–

$$\frac{CFT}{TT} \times 100$$

where–
CFT is the aggregate tonnage of qualifying ships registered in one of the Member States' registers,
TT is the aggregate tonnage of all qualifying ships, and
no qualifying ship is counted more than once in determining an aggregate.

EXCEPTION OF FINANCIAL YEAR 2007

3   The financial year 2007 is designated as one in relation to which paragraph 22A of Schedule 22 to the Finance Act 2000 is not to have effect.

BUSINESS PREMISES RENOVATION ALLOWANCES REGULATIONS 2007

(SI 2007/945, as amended by SI 2012/868)

Made on 21 March 2007 by the Treasury in exercise of the powers conferred by s. 360C(2)(a) and (3) and 360D(4) of the Capital Allowances Act 2001. Operative from 11 April 2007.

CITATION AND COMMENCEMENT

1 These Regulations may be cited as the Business Premises Renovation Allowances Regulations 2007 and shall come into force on 11th April 2007.

INTERPRETATION

2 In these Regulations **"the Act"** means the Capital Allowances Act 2001.

EXPIRY DATE FOR INCURRING QUALIFYING EXPENDITURE

2A For the purposes of Part 3A of the Act, **"the expiry date"** is prescribed as–

(a)　1 April 2017, for corporation tax purposes; and

(b)　6 April 2017, for income tax purposes.

History – Reg. 2A inserted by SI 2012/868, reg. 3, with effect from 11 April 2012.

DESIGNATION OF AREAS AS DISADVANTAGED AREAS

3 The following areas are designated as disadvantaged areas for the purposes of section 360C of the Act (meaning of **"qualifying building"**)–

(a)　areas specified as development areas by the Assisted Areas Order 2007;

(b)　Northern Ireland.

MEANING OF "QUALIFYING BUSINESS PREMISES"

4(1) For the purposes of Part 3A of the Act (business premises renovation allowances) premises are not qualifying business premises where–

(a)　the person entitled to the relevant interest in the premises is carrying on a relevant trade; or

(b)　the premises are used, or used in part, for the purposes of such a trade.

4(2) In this regulation–

"relevant interest" has the meaning given by Chapter 4 of Part 3A of the Act (the relevant interest in the qualifying building);

"relevant trade" means a trade–

(a)　in any sector in relation to which Commission Regulation (EC) No 800/2008 declaring certain categories of aid compatible with the common market in the application of Articles 87 and 88 of the Treaty (General block exemption Regulation) does not apply by virtue of paragraph 3 of Article 1 of that Regulation; or

(b)　carried on by any undertaking which–

　(i)　is subject to an outstanding recovery order made by virtue of Article 108(2) of the Treaty on the Functioning of the European Union; or

　(ii)　it is reasonable to assume would be regarded as a firm in difficulty for the purposes of the Community Guidelines on State Aid for Rescuing and Restructuring Firms in Difficulty.

4(3) This regulation applies in relation to part of a trade as it applies in relation to a trade.

4(4) In this regulation **"undertaking"** has the same meaning as it has for the purposes of section 45DB (exclusions from allowances under section 45DA) of the Act.

History – In reg. 4(2), definition of "relevant trade" substituted by SI 2012/868, reg. 4(1), with effect in relation to expenditure incurred on or after 11 April 2012. The former definition read: "'relevant trade" means a trade in any sector in relation to which Commission Regulation (EC) No 1628/2006 on the application of Articles 87 and 88 of the Treaty to national regional investment aid does not apply by virtue of paragraph 2 of Article 1 of that Regulation.".
Reg. 4(4) inserted by SI 2012/868, reg. 4(2), with effect in relation to expenditure incurred on or after 11 April 2012.

MEANING OF "QUALIFYING EXPENDITURE"

5(1)   For the purposes of Part 3A of the Act, expenditure is not qualifying expenditure if the expenditure is incurred on or in connection with a qualifying building and the building is not in a disadvantaged area on the date the expenditure is incurred.

5(2)   For the purposes of Part 3A of the Act, expenditure is not qualifying expenditure if, and to the extent that,–

(a)   the amount of the expenditure ("current expenditure"); or

(b)   the current expenditure and the aggregate amount of the single project investment expenditure in respect of which allowances under Part 3A of the Act have previously been made,

exceeds 20 million euros.

5(3)   In this regulation **"single project investment expenditure"** means expenditure–

(a)   incurred by any person within a period of three years prior to the date on which the current expenditure is incurred; and,

(b)   which, together with the current expenditure, would be treated as incurred in an economically indivisible way for the purposes of Article 13(10) of Commission Regulation (EC) No 800/2008 declaring certain categories of aid compatible with the common market in application of Articles 87 and 88 of the Treaty (General block exemption Regulation).

5(4)   In this regulation **"disadvantaged area"** has the same meaning as that which applies for the purposes of section 360C of the Act.

5(5)   For the purposes of this regulation, expenditure incurred in a currency other than the euro is to be converted into its equivalent in euros using the spot rate of exchange for the day on which the expenditure is incurred.

History – Reg. 5 inserted by SI 2012/868, reg. 5, with effect in relation to expenditure incurred on or after 11 April 2012.

FINANCE ACT 1995, SECTION 127(12), (DESIGNATED TRANSACTIONS) REGULATIONS 2007

(SI 2007/963)

Made on 22 March 2007 by the Treasury in exercise of the powers conferred by s. 127(12)(c) of the Finance Act 1995. Operative from 12 April 2007.

CITATION AND COMMENCEMENT

1 These Regulations may be cited as the Finance Act 1995, Section 127(12), (Designated Transactions) Regulations 2007 and shall come into force on 12th April 2007.

TRANSACTION DESIGNATED AS AN INVESTMENT TRANSACTION

2(1) A transaction is designated as an investment transaction for the purposes of section 127 of the Finance Act 1995 (persons not treated as United Kingdom representatives) if conditions A to C are met.

2(2) Condition A is that the transaction is a transaction–

(a)   in Community tradeable emissions allowances, or

(b)   in transferable units issued pursuant to the Kyoto Protocol.

2(3) Condition B is that the transaction does not give rise to a chargeable gain falling within section 10 of the Taxation of Chargeable Gains Act 1992 (non-resident with United Kingdom branch or agency).

2(4) Condition C is that the transaction does not otherwise fall within section 127(12).

2(5) For the purposes of this regulation–

"Community tradeable emissions allowances" are transferable allowances which relate to the making of emissions of greenhouse gases, and are allocated as part of a system made for the purpose of implementing any Community obligation of the United Kingdom relating to such emissions;

"Kyoto Protocol" means the Kyoto Protocol to the United Nations Framework Convention on Climate Change signed at Kyoto on 11th December 1997;

"section 127(12)" means section 127(12) of the Finance Act 1995 (meaning of "investment transaction" for the purposes of determining whether a person is capable of being the UK representative of a non-resident taxpayer); and

"units" include assigned amount units, certified emission reductions, emission reduction units and removal units.

Statutory Instruments

FINANCE ACT 2003, PARAGRAPH 3(3) OF SCHEDULE 26, (DESIGNATED TRANSACTIONS) REGULATIONS 2007

(SI 2007/964)

Made on 22 March 2007 by the Treasury in exercise of the powers conferred upon them by para. 3(3)(c) of Sch. 26 to the Finance Act 2003. Operative from 12 April 2007

CITATION AND COMMENCEMENT

1   These Regulations may be cited as the Finance Act 2003, Paragraph 3(3) of Schedule 26, (Designated Transactions) Regulations 2007 and shall come into force on 12th April 2007.

TRANSACTION DESIGNATED AS AN INVESTMENT TRANSACTION

2(1)   A transaction is designated as an investment transaction for the purposes of Schedule 26 to the Finance Act 2003 (non-resident companies: transactions through investment manager and others) if conditions A to C are met.

2(2)   Condition A is that the transaction is a transaction–

(a)   in Community tradeable emissions allowances, or

(b)   in transferable units issued pursuant to the Kyoto Protocol.

2(3)   Condition B is that the transaction does not give rise to a chargeable gain falling within section 10B of the Taxation of Chargeable Gains Act 1992 (non-resident company with United Kingdom permanent establishment) (and accordingly taken into account for the purposes of section 11(2A) of the Income and Corporation Taxes Act 1988 (profits attributable to a permanent establishment)).

2(4)   Condition C is that the transaction does not otherwise fall within paragraph 3(3).

2(5)   For the purposes of this regulation–

  "Community tradeable emissions allowances" are transferable allowances which relate to the making of emissions of greenhouse gases, and are allocated as part of a system made for the purpose of implementing any Community obligation of the United Kingdom relating to such emissions;

  "Kyoto Protocol" means the Kyoto Protocol to the United Nations Framework Convention on Climate Change signed at Kyoto on 11th December 1997;

  "paragraph 3(3)" means paragraph 3(3) of Schedule 26 to the Finance Act 2003 (meaning of "investment transaction" for the purposes of determining whether a person is an agent of independent status in respect of investment transactions);

  "units" include assigned amount units, certified emission reductions, emission reduction units and removal units.

CORPORATION TAX (TAXATION OF FILMS) (TRANSITIONAL PROVISIONS) REGULATIONS 2007

(SI 2007/1050)

Made on 28 March 2007 by the Treasury in exercise of the powers conferred upon them by s. 52 of the Finance Act 2006 [CTA 2009, Sch. 2, para. 130]. Operative in accordance with regulation 1.

Cross references – CTA 2009, Sch. 2, para. 131: modification of SI 2007/1050.

PRELIMINARY

Citation, commencement and effect

1(1) These Regulations may be cited as the Corporation Tax (Taxation of Films) (Transitional Provisions) Regulations 2007 and shall come into force on the day after the day on which they are made.

1(2) The provisions of Chapter 3 of Part 3 of the Finance Act 2006 (films and sound recordings) applied by these Regulations shall have effect as if they had been in force at all material times.

Cross references – CTA 2009, Sch. 2, para. 131(3): modification of SI 2007/1050, reg. 1.

Interpretation

2 In these Regulations a reference to a "Chapter", "Part", "section" or "Schedule" without more is a reference to a Chapter, Part, section or Schedule of the Finance Act 2006, unless the context otherwise requires.

Cross references – CTA 2009, Sch. 2, para. 131(4): modification of SI 2007/1050, reg. 2.

Application of enactments

3 The provisions of Chapter 3 of Part 3, the enactments amended by that Chapter and the Corporation Tax Acts apply with the modifications provided in regulations 4 to 12 in relation to films that commenced principal photography before 1st January 2007 but are not completed before that date.

Cross references – CTA 2009, Sch. 2, para. 131(5): modification of SI 2007/1050, reg. 3.

MODIFICATIONS TO THE FINANCE ACT 2006

Modification of section 32 (meaning of "film production company")

4 In section 32 (meaning of "film production company"), in subsection (3), in relation to a film that commenced principal photography before 1st April 2006, omit "pre-production," in both places.

Cross references – CTA 2009, Sch. 2, para. 131(6): modification of SI 2007/1050, reg. 4.

Modification of section 40 (conditions of relief: British film)

5 In section 40 (conditions of relief: British film) at the end insert "for the purposes of film tax relief".

Cross references – CTA 2009, Sch. 2, para. 131(7): modification of SI 2007/1050, reg. 5.

Modification of section 46 (films: withdrawal of existing reliefs (corporation tax))

6(1) Modify section 46 (films: withdrawal of existing reliefs (corporation tax)) as follows.

6(2) In the provisions listed below for the words "commences principal photography on or after 1st January 2007" substitute "is certified by the Secretary of State under Schedule 1 to the Films Act 1985 as a British film for the purposes of film tax relief and is intended for theatrical release at the time the film commences principal photography".

The provisions are–

    subsection (1)(a);

    subsection (1)(b)(i);

    subsection (3)(a); and

    subsection (3)(b)(i).

6(3) In subsections (1)(b)(ii) and (3)(b)(ii) for "1st October 2007" substitute "31st March 2008".

Cross references – CTA 2009, Sch. 2, para. 131(8): modification of SI 2007/1050, reg. 6.

Modification of section 47 (films: withdrawal of existing reliefs (income tax))

7(1) Modify section 47 (films: withdrawal of existing reliefs (income tax)) as follows.

7(2) In the provisions listed below for the words "commences principal photography on or after 1st January 2007" substitute "is certified by the Secretary of State under Schedule 1 to the Films Act

1985 as a British film for the purposes of film tax relief and is intended for theatrical release at the time the film commences principal photography".

The provisions are—

     subsection (1)(a);

     subsection (1)(b)(i);

     subsection (3)(a); and

     subsection (3)(b)(i).

7(3)   In subsections (1)(b)(ii) and (3)(b)(ii) for "1st October 2007" substitute "31st March 2008".

Cross references – CTA 2009, Sch. 2, para. 131(9): modification of SI 2007/1050, reg. 7.

Modification of section 51 (supplementary provisions)

8(1)   In the substitution made by section 51(1) (supplementary provisions) for paragraph 80 (exclusion of films and sound recordings) of Schedule 29 to the Finance Act 2002 (corporation tax: gains and losses from intangible fixed assets) modify substituted paragraph 80A(2) as follows.

8(2)   In paragraphs (a) and (b) for the words "that commenced principal photography before 1st January 2007" substitute "to which Schedule 4 of the Finance Act 2006 does not apply".

8(3)   In paragraph (b) for "1st October 2007" substitute "31st March 2008".

Cross references – CTA 2009, Sch. 2, para. 131(10): modification of SI 2007/1050, reg. 8.

Modification of Schedule 4 (taxation of activities of film production company)

9   In Schedule 4 (taxation of activities of film production company), in paragraph 1 (films to which this Schedule applies) for the words "commence principal photography on or after 1st January 2007" substitute "are certified by the Secretary of State under Schedule 1 to the Films Act 1985 as British films for the purposes of film tax relief and are intended for theatrical release at the time principal photography commences".

Cross references – CTA 2009, Sch. 2, para. 131(11): modification of SI 2007/1050, reg. 9

Modifications of Schedule 5 (film tax relief: further provisions)

10(1)   Modify Schedule 5 (film tax relief: further provisions) as follows.

10(2)   In paragraph 1(1) omit the words from ", and" to the end.

10(3)   After paragraph 15 insert—

     "**15A**   After section 6 of that Act insert–

     "**6A**   Where the Secretary of State refuses an application for interim or final certification of a film as a British film for the purposes of film tax relief, Schedule 1A to this Act has effect with respect to the certification by the Secretary of State of a master negative, tape or disc of a film as a qualifying film, tape or disc for the purposes of section 40D of the Finance (No. 2) Act 1992 (election for sections 40A and 40B not to apply) or Chapter 9 of Part 2 of the Income Tax (Trading and Other Income) Act 2005 (election relating to tax treatment of films expenditure).".".

10(4)   In paragraph 17, in the substituted paragraph 1 of Schedule 1 to the Films Act 1985 after "Schedule" insert "and Schedule 1A" in each place.

10(5)   In paragraph 19, in the substituted paragraph 3 of Schedule 1 to the Films Act 1985, in subparagraph (4) after "otherwise" insert "and except in relation to sections 46 and 47 (films: withdrawal of existing reliefs) of, and paragraph 1 of Schedule 4 (taxation of activities of film production company) to, the Finance Act 2006".

10(6)   After paragraph 20 insert–

     "**20A**   For paragraphs 4A to 4C of that Schedule substitute–

     "**4A(1)**   The cultural test for a film other than a documentary (see paragraph 4B) or an animation (see paragraph 4C) is as follows.

     4A(2)   Subject to sub-paragraph (7), a film passes the cultural test if it is awarded at least 16 points in total.

     4A(3)   Up to 16 points shall be awarded in respect of the content of the film as follows–

         (a)   up to 4 points depending on the percentage of the film that is set in the United Kingdom as follows–

            (i)   4 points for at least 75%;

            (ii)   3 points for at least 66%;

            (iii)   2 points for at least 50%;

            (iv)   1 point for at least 25%;

(b)   up to 4 points depending on the number of the characters depicted in the film that are British as follows–

    (i)   if there are more than three characters depicted in the film, 4 points if two or three of the three lead characters are British or, if only one of the three lead characters is British, 2 points if he is the first or second lead, 1 point if he is the third lead;

    (ii)   if there are only three characters depicted in the film, 4 points if two or three of them are British or, if only one of them is British, 2 points if he is the first or second lead, 1 point if he is the third lead;

    (iii)   if there are only two characters depicted in the film, 4 points if both of them are British, 2 points if one of them is;

    (iv)   if there is only one character depicted in the film, 4 points if he is British;

(c)   4 points if the film depicts a British story;

(d)   up to 4 points depending on the percentage of the original dialogue that is recorded in the English language or in a recognised regional or minority language as follows–

    (i)   4 points for at least 75%;

    (ii)   3 points for at least 66%;

    (iii)   2 points for at least 50%;

    (iv)   1 point for at least 25%.

4A(4)   Up to 4 points may be awarded in respect of the contribution of the film to the promotion, development and enhancement of British culture.

4A(5)   Up to 3 points shall be awarded in respect of work carried out in the making of the film as follows–

(a)   2 points if at least 50% of the work carried out on any of the following is carried out in the United Kingdom–

    (i)   principal photography;

    (ii)   visual effects;

    (iii)   special effects;

(b)   1 point if at least 50% of the work carried out on any of the following is carried out in the United Kingdom–

    (i)   performing and recording the music score created for the film;

    (ii)   audio post production;

    (iii)   picture post production.

4A(6)   Up to 8 points shall be awarded in respect of the personnel involved in the making of the film as follows–

(a)   1 point if the director (or, if there is more than one, the lead director) is a qualifying person;

(b)   1 point if at least one of the scriptwriters (or, if there are more than three, of the three lead scriptwriters) is a qualifying person;

(c)   1 point if at least one of the producers (or, if there are more than three, of the three lead producers) is a qualifying person;

(d)   1 point if the composer (or, if there is more than one, the lead composer) is a qualifying person;

(e)   1 point if at least one of the actors (or, if there are more than three, of the three lead actors) is a qualifying person;

(f)   1 point if at least 50% of the cast are qualifying persons;

(g)   1 point if at least one of the heads of department is a qualifying person;

(h)   1 point if at least 50% of the production crew are qualifying persons.

4A(7)   A film that is awarded all the points available under sub-paragraphs (3)(d) (language), (5) (where work carried out) and (6) (personnel) does not pass the cultural test unless–

(a)   it is awarded at least 2 points under sub-paragraph (3)(a) (setting),

(b)   it is awarded at least 2 points under sub-paragraph (3)(b) (characters), or

(c)   it is awarded 4 points under sub-paragraph (3)(c) (story).

4B(1)   The cultural test for a documentary is as follows.

Statutory Instruments

4B(2) Subject to sub-paragraph (7), a film passes the cultural test if it is awarded at least 16 points in total.

4B(3) Up to 16 points shall be awarded in respect of the content of the film as follows–

(a)   up to 4 points depending on the percentage of the film that is set in the United Kingdom as follows–

      (i)   4 points for at least 75%;

      (ii)   3 points for at least 66%;

      (iii) 2 points for at least 50%;

      (iv) 1 point for at least 25%;

(b)   up to 4 points depending on the number of the characters depicted in the film that are British as follows–

      (i)   if there are more than three characters depicted in the film, 4 points if two or three of the three lead characters are British or, if only one of the three lead characters is British, 2 points if he is the first or second lead, 1 point if he is the third lead;

      (ii)   if there are only three characters depicted in the film, 4 points if two or three of them are British or, if only one of them is British, 2 points if he is the first or second lead, 1 point if he is the third lead;

      (iii) if there are only two characters depicted in the film, 4 points if both of them are British, 2 points if one of them is;

      (iv) if there is only one character depicted in the film, 4 points if he is British;

(c)   4 points if the film depicts a British story;

(d)   up to 4 points depending on the percentage of the original dialogue that is recorded in the English language or in a recognised regional or minority language as follows–

      (i)   4 points for at least 75%;

      (ii)   3 points for at least 66%;

      (iii) 2 points for at least 50%;

      (iv) 1 point for at least 25%.

4B(4) Up to 4 points may be awarded in respect of the contribution of the film to the promotion, development and enhancement of British culture.

4B(5) Up to 3 points shall be awarded in respect of work carried out in the making of the film as follows–

(a)   2 points if at least 50% of the work carried out on any of the following is carried out in the United Kingdom–

      (i)   shooting;

      (ii)   visual effects;

      (iii) research and development;

      (iv) special effects;

(b)   1 point if at least 50% of the work carried out on any of the following is carried out in the United Kingdom–

      (i)   performing and recording the music score created for the film;

      (ii)   audio post production;

      (iii) picture post production.

4B(6) Up to 8 points shall be awarded in respect of the personnel involved in the making of the film as follows–

(a)   1 point if the director (or, if there is more than one, the lead director) is a qualifying person;

(b)   1 point if at least one of the scriptwriters (or, if there are more than three, of the three lead scriptwriters) is a qualifying person;

(c)   1 point if at least one of the producers (or, if there are more than three, of the three lead producers) is a qualifying person;

(d)   1 point if the composer (or, if there is more than one, the lead composer) is a qualifying person;

(e)   1 point if at least one of the participants (or, if there are more than three, of the three lead participants) is a qualifying person;

(f)   1 point if at least 50% of the participants are qualifying persons;

(g)   1 point if at least one of the heads of department is a qualifying person;

(h)   1 point if at least 50% of the production crew are qualifying persons.

4B(7) A film that is awarded all the points available under sub-paragraphs (3)(d) (language), (5) (where work carried out) and (6) (personnel) does not pass the cultural test unless–

(a) it is awarded at least 2 points under sub-paragraph (3)(a) (setting),

(b) it is awarded at least 2 points under sub-paragraph (3)(b) (characters), or

(c) it is awarded 4 points under sub-paragraph (3)(c) (story).

4C(1) The cultural test for an animation is as follows.

4C(2) Subject to sub-paragraph (7), a film passes the cultural test if it is awarded at least 16 points in total.

4C(3) Up to 16 points shall be awarded in respect of the content of the film as follows–

(a) up to 4 points depending on the percentage of the film that is set in the United Kingdom as follows–
    (i) 4 points for at least 75%;
    (ii) 3 points for at least 66%;
    (iii) 2 points for at least 50%;
    (iv) 1 point for at least 25%;

(b) up to 4 points depending on the number of the characters depicted in the film that are British as follows–
    (i) if there are more than three characters depicted in the film, 4 points if two or three of the three lead characters are British or, if only one of the three lead characters is British, 2 points if he is the first or second lead, 1 point if he is the third lead;
    (ii) if there are only three characters depicted in the film, 4 points of two or three of them are British or, if only one of them is British, 2 points if he is the first or second lead, 1 point if he is the third lead;
    (iii) if there are only two characters depicted in the film, 4 points both of them are British, 2 points if one of them is;
    (iv) if there is only one character depicted in the film, 4 points if he is British;

(c) 4 points if the film depicts a British story;

(d) up to 4 points depending on the percentage of the original dialogue that is recorded in the English language or in a recognised regional or minority language as follows–
    (i) 4 points for at least 75%;
    (ii) 3 points for at least 66%;
    (iii) 2 points for at least 50%;
    (iv) 1 point for at least 25%.

4C(4) Up to 4 points may be awarded in respect of the contribution of the film to the promotion, development and enhancement of British culture.

4C(5) Up to 3 points shall be awarded in respect of work carried out in the making of the film as follows–

(a) 2 points if at least 50% of the work carried out on any of the following is carried out in the United Kingdom–
    (i) shooting;
    (ii) visual design;
    (iii) layout and storyboarding;
    (iv) visual effects;
    (v) special effects;

(b) 1 point if at least 50% of the work carried out on any of the following is carried out in the United Kingdom–
    (i) performing and recording the music score created for the film;
    (ii) voice recording;
    (iii) audio post production;
    (iv) picture post production.

4C(6) Up to 8 points shall be awarded in respect of the personnel involved in the making of the film as follows–

(a) 1 point if the director (or, if there is more than one, the lead director) is a qualifying person;

(b) 1 point if at least one of the scriptwriters (or, if there are more than three, of the three lead scriptwriters) is a qualifying person;

(c)   1 point if at least one of the producers (or, if there are more than three, of the three lead producers) is a qualifying person;

(d)   1 point if the composer (or, if there is more than one, the lead composer) is a qualifying person;

(e)   1 point if at least one of the actors (or, if there are more than three, of the three lead actors) is a qualifying person;

(f)   1 point if at least 50% of the cast are qualifying persons;

(g)   1 point if at least one of the heads of department is a qualifying person;

(h)   1 point if at least 50% of the production crew are qualifying persons.

4C(7)   A film that is awarded all the points available under sub-paragraphs (3)(d) (language), (5) (where work carried out) and (6) (personnel) does not pass the cultural test unless–

(a)   it is awarded at least 2 points under sub-paragraph (3)(a) (setting),

(b)   it is awarded at least 2 points under sub-paragraph (3)(b) (characters), or

(c)   it is awarded 4 points under sub-paragraph (3)(c) (story).".

20B   In paragraph 4D of that Schedule–

20B(a)   in sub-paragraph (4)(a) for "paragraph 4A(4)(a)" substitute "paragraph 4A(5)(a)(i)";

20B(b)   for sub-paragraph (4)(b) substitute–

" (b)   for the purposes of the rest of paragraph 4A(5) and paragraphs 4B(5) and 4C(5) (other matters), by reference to the amount of expenditure on the work.";

20B(c)   in sub-paragraph (5) for "paragraph 4A(4), 4B(4) or 4C(4) (points awarded in respect of the making of the film)" substitute "paragraph 4A(5), 4B(5) or 4C(5) (where work carried out)".".

10(7)   After paragraph 25 insert–

"PART 2A – CERTIFICATION OF MASTER NEGATIVE, TAPE OR DISC OF A FILM AS A QUALIFYING FILM, TAPE OR DISC FOR THE PURPOSES OF SECTION 40D OF THE FINANCE (NO. 2) ACT 1992 OR CHAPTER 9 OF PART 2 OF ITTOIA 2005

25A   After Schedule 1 to the Films Act 1985 insert–

"SCHEDULE 1A – CERTIFICATION OF MASTER NEGATIVE, TAPE OR DISC OF A FILM AS A QUALIFYING FILM, TAPE OR DISC FOR THE PURPOSES OF SECTION 40D OF THE FINANCE (NO. 2) ACT 1992 OR CHAPTER 9 OF PART 2 OF THE INCOME TAX (TRADING AND OTHER INCOME) ACT 2005

Section 6A

PRELIMINARY

1(1)   In this Schedule–

"maker", in relation to a film, means the person by whom the arrangements necessary for the making of the film are undertaken;

"master disc", in relation to a film, means the original master film disc or the original master audio disc of the film;

"master negative", in relation to a film, means the original master negative of the film and its soundtrack (if any);

"master tape", in relation to a film, means the original master film tape or the original master audio tape of the film;

1(2) Any reference in this Schedule to a master negative, tape or disc certified under paragraph 3(1) or to a certificate issued under that provision includes a reference to a master negative, tape or disc certified in pursuance of section 72(7)(b) of the Finance Act 1982 as originally enacted or to a certificate issued in pursuance of that provision.

Applications for certification of master negatives, tapes and discs

2(1) An application for the certification by the Secretary of State of a master negative, master tape or master disc of a film as a qualifying film, qualifying tape or qualifying disc for the purposes of section 40D of the Finance (No 2) Act 1992, or Chapter 9 of Part 2 of the Income Tax (Trading and Other Income) Act 2005, may be made by any person who has incurred expenditure on the production or acquisition of that negative, tape, or disc.

2(2) In sub-paragraph (1) the reference to the acquisition of a master negative, tape or disc includes a reference to the acquisition of any description of rights in it.

2(3) On an application under this paragraph for the certification of a master negative, tape or disc the applicant shall—

(a)   produce to the Secretary of State such books and other documents relating to it; and

(b)   furnish to the Secretary of State such other information with respect to it,

as the Secretary of State may require for the purpose of determining the application.

2(4) Any information furnished for the purposes of sub-paragraph (3) shall, if the Secretary of State so directs, be accompanied by a statutory declaration as to the truth of the information made by the person furnishing it.

Certification by Secretary of State of master negatives, tapes and discs

3(1) If the Secretary of State is satisfied that a master negative, tape or disc with respect to which an application is made under paragraph 2 is a master negative, tape or disc of a film which, in his opinion, is a British film for the purposes of this Schedule, he shall certify that negative, tape or disc as a qualifying film, qualifying tape or qualifying disc for the purposes of section 40D of the Finance (No 2) Act 1992 or, as the case may be, Chapter 9 of Part 2 of the Income Tax (Trading and Other Income) Act 2005.

3(2) If the Secretary of State is for any reason not satisfied as mentioned in sub-paragraph (1) he shall refuse the application.

3(3) If it appears to the Secretary of State that any negative, tape or disc certified by him under sub-paragraph (1) ought for any reason not to have been so certified he shall revoke its certification.

3(4) Where an application is made under paragraph 2 in relation to a negative, tape or disc of a film which has already been certified by the Secretary of State under sub-paragraph (1) on a prior application, the Secretary of State may issue the applicant with a duplicate or copy of the certificate issued on that prior application.

British films for purposes of the Schedule

4(1) A film is a British film for the purposes of this Schedule if it passes the relevant cultural test (see paragraph 4A, 4B or 4C).

4(2) For the purposes of this paragraph and paragraphs 4A to 4D a state shall be treated as if it were a member State if—

(a)   it is a party to an agreement under Article 310 of the Treaty establishing the European Community, and

(b)   the agreement requires a maker of a film who is ordinarily resident or registered in that state to be treated for the purposes of this Schedule in the same way as a maker of a film who is ordinarily resident or registered in a member State.

4(3) This paragraph has effect subject to paragraph 5 (excluded films).

4A(1) The cultural test for a film other than a documentary (see paragraph 4B) or an animation (see paragraph 4C) is as follows.

4A(2) A film passes the cultural test if it is awarded at least 16 points in total.

4A(3) Up to 4 points shall be awarded in respect of the content of the film as follows—

(a)   1 point if at least 50% of the film is set in the United Kingdom;

(b)   1 point if at least one of the three principal characters depicted in the film (or, if there are three or fewer characters depicted in the film, any of them) is a British character;

(c)   1 point if the film depicts a British story;

(d)   1 point if at least 50% of the original dialogue is recorded in the English language or in a recognised regional or minority language.

4A(4)   Up to 15 points shall be awarded in respect of work carried out in the making of the film as follows–

(a)   up to 6 points depending on the percentage of principal photography that is carried out in the United Kingdom as follows–

     (i)   6 points for 75%,

     (ii)   5 points for 62.5%,

     (iii)   4 points for 50%,

     (iv)   3 points for 37.5%,

     (v)   2 points for 25%,

     (vi)   1 point for 10%;

(b)   up to 4 points depending on the percentage of the work on visual effects that is carried out in the United Kingdom as follows–

     (i)   4 points for 75%,

     (ii)   3 points for 50%,

     (iii)   2 points for 25%,

     (iv)   1 point for 10%;

(c)   1 point if at least 75% of the work on special effects is carried out in the United Kingdom;

(d)   up to 2 points depending on the percentage of the work on performing and recording the original music score created for the film that is carried out in the United Kingdom as follows–

     (i)   2 points for 75%,

     (ii)   1 point for 50%;

(e)   1 point if at least 75% of the work on audio post production is carried out in the United Kingdom;

(f)   1 point if at least 75% of the work on image processing is carried out in the United Kingdom.

4A(5)   Up to 13 points shall be awarded in respect of the personnel involved in the making of the film as follows–

(a)   2 points if the director (or, if there is more than one, the lead director) is a qualifying person;

(b)   up to 2 points depending on the number of the scriptwriters who are qualifying persons as follows–

     (i)   if there is only one scriptwriter, 2 points if he is a qualifying person,

     (ii)   if there are only two scriptwriters, 2 points if both of them are qualifying persons, 1 point if one of them is,

     (iii)   if there are only three scriptwriters, 2 points if two or more of them are qualifying persons, 1 point if one of them is,

     (iv)   if there are more than three scriptwriters, 2 points if two or more of the three lead scriptwriters are qualifying persons, 1 point if one of the three lead scriptwriters is a qualifying person;

(c)   1 point if at least one of the producers (or, if there are more than three, of the three lead producers) is a qualifying person;

(d)   1 point if the composer (or, if there is more than one, the lead composer) is a qualifying person;

(e)   up to 2 points depending on the number of the actors who are qualifying persons as follows–

     (i)   if there are more than three actors, 2 points if two or more of the three lead actors are qualifying persons, 1 point if one of the three lead actors is a qualifying person,

    (ii) if there are only three actors, 2 points if two or more of them are qualifying persons, 1 point if one of them is;

    (iii) if there are only two actors, 2 points if both of them are qualifying persons, 1 point if one of them is;

    (iv) if there is only one actor, 2 points if he is a qualifying person;

(f) 1 point if at least 50% of the cast are qualifying persons;

(g) up to 3 points depending on the number of the heads of department who are qualifying persons as follows—

    (i) 3 points for five or more,

    (ii) 2 points for three or four,

    (iii) 1 point for one or two;

(h) 1 point if at least 50% of the production crew are qualifying persons.

4B(1) The cultural test for a documentary is as follows.

4B(2) A film passes the cultural test if it is awarded at least 16 points in total.

4B(3) Up to 4 points shall be awarded in respect of the content of the film as follows—

(a) 1 point if at least 50% of the film is set in the United Kingdom;

(b) 1 point if at least one of the three principal characters depicted in the film (or, if there are three or fewer characters depicted in the film, any of them) is a British character;

(c) 1 point if the film depicts a British story;

(d) 1 point if at least 50% of the original dialogue is recorded in the English language or in a recognised regional or minority language.

4B(4) Up to 15 points shall be awarded in respect of work carried out in the making of the film as follows—

(a) up to 6 points depending on the percentage of the work on shooting and visual effects that is carried out in the United Kingdom as follows—

    (i) 6 points for 75%,

    (ii) 5 points for 62.5%,

    (iii) 4 points for 50%,

    (iv) 3 points for 37.5%,

    (v) 2 points for 25%,

    (vi) 1 point for 10%;

(b) up to 4 points depending on the percentage of the work on research and development that is carried out in the United Kingdom as follows—

    (i) 4 points for 75%,

    (ii) 3 points for 50%,

    (iii) 2 points for 25%,

    (iv) 1 point for 10%;

(c) 1 point if at least 75% of the work on special effects is carried out in the United Kingdom;

(d) up to 2 points depending on the percentage of the work on performing and recording the original music score created for the film that is carried out in the United Kingdom as follows—

    (i) 2 points for 75%,

    (ii) 1 point for 50%;

(e) 1 point if at least 75% of the work on audio post production is carried out in the United Kingdom;

(f) 1 point if at least 75% of the work on image processing is carried out in the United Kingdom.

4B(5) Up to 13 points shall be awarded in respect of the personnel involved in the making of the film as follows—

(a) 2 points if the director (or, if there is more than one, the lead director) is a qualifying person;

(b) up to 2 points depending on the number of the scriptwriters who are qualifying persons as follows—

    (i) if there is only one scriptwriter, 2 points if he is a qualifying person,

(ii) if there are only two scriptwriters, 2 points if both of them are qualifying persons, 1 point if one of them is,

(iii) if there are only three scriptwriters, 2 points if two or more of them are qualifying persons, 1 point if one of them is,

(iv) if there are more than three scriptwriters, 2 points if two or more of the three lead scriptwriters are qualifying persons, 1 point if one of the three lead scriptwriters is a qualifying person;

(c) 1 point if at least one of the producers (or, if there are more than three, of the three lead producers) is a qualifying person;

(d) 1 point if the composer (or, if there is more than one, the lead composer) is a qualifying person;

(e) up to 2 points depending on the number of the participants who are qualifying persons as follows—

(i) if there are more than three participants, 2 points if two or more of the three lead participants are qualifying persons, 1 point if one of the three lead participants is a qualifying person,

(ii) if there are only three participants, 2 points if two or more of them are qualifying persons, 1 point if one of them is,

(iii) if there are only two participants, 2 points if both of them are qualifying persons, 1 point if one of them is,

(iv) if there is only one participant, 2 points if he is a qualifying person;

(f) 1 point if at least 50% of all of the participants are qualifying persons;

(g) up to 3 points depending on the number of the heads of department who are qualifying persons as follows—

(i) 3 points for four,

(ii) 2 points for three,

(iii) 1 point for one or two;

(h) 1 point if at least 50% of the production crew are qualifying persons.

4C(1) The cultural test for an animation is as follows.

4C(2) A film passes the cultural test if it is awarded at least 16 points in total.

4C(3) Up to 4 points shall be awarded in respect of the content of the film as follows—

(a) 1 point if at least 50% of the film is set in the United Kingdom;

(b) 1 point if at least one of the three principal characters depicted in the film (or, if there are three or fewer characters depicted in the film, any of them) is a British character;

(c) 1 point if the film depicts a British story;

(d) 1 point if at least 50% of the original dialogue is recorded in the English language or in a recognised regional or minority language.

4C(4) Up to 15 points shall be awarded in respect of work carried out in the making of the film as follows—

(a) up to 6 points depending on the percentage of the work on shooting, visual design, layout and storyboarding that is carried out in the United Kingdom as follows—

(i) 6 points for 75%,

(ii) 5 points for 62.5%,

(iii) 4 points for 50%,

(iv) 3 points for 37.5%,

(v) 2 points for 25%,

(vi) 1 point for 10%;

(b) up to 4 points depending on the percentage of the work on visual effects that is carried out in the United Kingdom as follows—

(i) 4 points for 75%,

(ii) 3 points for 50%,

(iii) 2 points for 25%,

(iv) 1 point for 10%;

(c) 1 point if at least 75% of the work on special effects is carried out in the United Kingdom;

   (d)   up to 2 points depending on the percentage of the work on performing and recording the original music score created for the film that is carried out in the United Kingdom as follows–

        (i)   2 points for 75%,

        (ii)   1 point for 50%;

   (e)   1 point if at least 75% of the work on voice recording and audio post production is carried out in the United Kingdom;

   (f)   1 point if at least 75% of the work on image processing is carried out in the United Kingdom.

4C(5) Up to 13 points shall be awarded in respect of the personnel involved in the making of the film as follows–

   (a)   2 points if the director (or, if there is more than one, the lead director) is a qualifying person;

   (b)   up to 2 points depending on the number of the scriptwriters who are qualifying persons as follows–

        (i)   if there is only one scriptwriter, 2 points if he is a qualifying person,

        (ii)   if there are only two scriptwriters, 2 points if both of them are qualifying persons, 1 point if one of them is,

        (iii)   if there are only three scriptwriters, 2 points if two or more of them are qualifying persons, 1 point if one of them is,

        (iv)   if there are more than three scriptwriters, 2 points if two or more of the three lead scriptwriters are qualifying persons, 1 point if one of the three lead scriptwriters is a qualifying person;

   (c)   1 point if at least one of the producers (or, if there are more than three, of the three lead producers) is a qualifying person;

   (d)   1 point if the composer (or, if there is more than one, the lead composer) is a qualifying person;

   (e)   up to 2 points depending on the number of the actors who are qualifying persons as follows–

        (i)   if there are more than three actors, 2 points if two or more of the three lead actors are qualifying persons, 1 point if one of the three lead actors is a qualifying person,

        (ii)   if there are only three actors, 2 points if two or more of them are qualifying persons, 1 point if one of them is,

        (iii)   if there are only two actors, 2 points if both of them are qualifying persons, 1 point if one of them is,

        (iv)   if there is only one actor, 2 points if he is a qualifying person;

   (f)   1 point if at least 50% of the cast are qualifying persons;

   (g)   up to 3 points depending on the number of the heads of department who are qualifying persons as follows–

        (i)   3 points for five or more,

        (ii)   2 points for three or four,

        (iii)   1 point for one or two;

   (h)   1 point if at least 50% of the production crew are qualifying persons.

4D(1) In paragraphs 4A to 4C–

"cast" means all the actors and performers but not the extras who appear in a film;

"heads of department" has the meaning given by sub-paragraph (2);

"participant" means a presenter, narrator, subject or other person who participates and appears in a documentary;

"production crew" means all the persons directly involved in the production of a film who do not appear in the film;

"qualifying person" means a citizen of, or a person ordinarily resident in, a member State;

"recognised regional or minority language" means Welsh, Scottish-Gaelic, Irish, Scots, Ulster Scots or Cornish;

"special effects" means artificial techniques or processes, which are not visual effects, used to create an illusion in a film;

"visual effects" means digital alterations to a film's images.

4D(2) **"Heads of department"** means–

(a)   in paragraph 4A, the lead cinematographer, the lead production designer, the lead costume designer, the lead editor, the lead sound designer, the lead visual effects supervisor and the lead hair and makeup supervisor;

(b)   in paragraph 4B, the lead cameraman, the lead sound recordist, the lead editor and the lead researcher;

(c)   in paragraph 4C, the lead layout supervisor, the lead production designer, the lead character designer, the lead editor, the lead sound designer, the lead visual effects supervisor and the lead modelling supervisor.

4D(3) For the purposes of paragraphs 4A to 4C–

(a)   a film is set in the United Kingdom if it is set in a country which is now part of the United Kingdom; and

(b)   a film depicts a British story if the subject matter of the film or the underlying material on which the film is based is British.

4D(4) The amount of work that is carried out in the United Kingdom or elsewhere shall be determined–

(a)   for the purposes of paragraph 4A(4)(a) (principal photography), by reference to the number of days spent on the work;

(b)   for the purposes of paragraphs 4A(4)(b) to (f), 4B(4)(a) to (f) and 4C(4)(a) to (f) (other matters), by reference to the amount of expenditure on the work.

4D(5) No points shall be awarded under any provision of paragraph 4A(4), 4B(4) or 4C(4) (points awarded in respect of the making of the film) in respect of work the expenditure on which is, in the opinion of the Secretary of State, insignificant in relation to the expenditure on all the work carried out in the making of the film.

EXCLUDED FILMS

5(1) Subject to sub-paragraph (2), a film is not a British film for the purposes of this Schedule by virtue of paragraph 4(1) if parts of the film are derived from–

(a)   any film of which the master negative, tape or disc is certified under paragraph 3(1), or

(b)   any film not made by the same maker as the first-mentioned film, and the playing time of those parts exceeds 10 per cent of the total playing time of the film.

5(2) The Secretary of State may direct that sub-paragraph (1) shall not apply in relation to a film if in his opinion–

(a)   it is a documentary; and

(b)   its subject matter makes it appropriate for sub-paragraph (1) not to be applied.

DETERMINATION OF DISPUTES

6(1) Any person who is aggrieved by any decision of the Secretary of State to refuse an application under paragraph 2 or to revoke any certification under paragraph 3(1) may, subject to rules of court, apply to the High Court, and the decision of that Court shall be final.

6(2) In relation to any person whose principal place of business is in Scotland, sub-paragraph (1) shall have effect as if for any reference to the High Court there were substituted a reference to the Court of Session.

APPLICATION FOR CERTIFICATION

7(1) The Films (Certification) Regulations 1985 shall apply to an application for certification under paragraph 2 as if a reference to Schedule 1 in those Regulations were a reference to this Schedule.

7(2) For the purposes of subparagraph (1) the application under paragraph 2 shall be treated as an application to be determined by the Secretary of State in accordance with Schedule 1 as in force immediately before the commencement of the Films (Certification) Regulations 2006".".

Cross references – CTA 2009, Sch. 2, para. 131(12)–(14): modification of SI 2007/1050, reg. 10.

MODIFICATION OF OTHER ENACTMENTS

Modification of the Finance (No. 2) Act 1992

11(1)   Modify the Finance (No. 2) Act 1992 as follows.

11(2)   In section 40D (election for sections 40A and 40B not to apply), in subsection (2)(b)–

(a)   for "Schedule 1" substitute "Schedule 1A"; and

(b)   at the end insert "or certified by the Secretary of State under paragraph 3 of Schedule 1 to that Act as a British film for the purposes of film tax relief".

11(3)   In section 43 (interpretation of sections 41 and 42), in subsection (1), in the definitions of "qualifying disc", "qualifying film" and "qualifying tape"–

(a)   for "Schedule 1" substitute "Schedule 1A"; and

(b)   at the end insert "or certified by the Secretary of State under paragraph 3 of Schedule 1 to that Act as a British film for the purposes of film tax relief".

Modification of ITTOIA 2005

12   In section 132 (meaning of "original master version" and "certified master version") of ITTOIA 2005, in subsection (3)–

(a)   for "Schedule 1" substitute "Schedule 1A"; and

(b)   at the end insert "or certified by the Secretary of State under paragraph 3 of Schedule 1 to that Act as a British film for the purposes of film tax relief".

CONSEQUENTIAL PROVISION

Returns, amendments to returns and assessments

13(1)   Where the provisions of Chapter 3 of Part 3, of the enactments amended by that Chapter and the Corporation Tax Acts apply in accordance with these Regulations, returns must be made or amended, and assessments may be made in relation to past accounting periods or tax years (whether before or after the commencement of that Chapter) in accordance with those provisions as modified by these Regulations.

13(2)   Any return, amendment or assessment necessary to give effect to paragraph (1) may be made notwithstanding any limitation on the time within which a return, amendment or assessment may normally be made.

Cross references – CTA 2009, Sch. 2, para. 131(15): modification of SI 2007/1050, reg. 13.

Statutory Instruments

INTERNATIONAL MUTUAL ADMINISTRATIVE ASSISTANCE IN TAX MATTERS ORDER 2007

(SI 2007/2126)

Made on 25 July 2007 by Her Majesty in exercise of the powers conferred by s. 173(1) to (3) of the Finance Act 2006, by and with the advice of Her Privy Council. A draft of this Order was laid before the House of Commons in accordance with s. 173(7) of the Finance Act 2006 and approved by a resolution of that House.

CITATION

1 This Order may be cited as the International Mutual Administrative Assistance in Tax Matters Order 2007.

MUTUAL ADMINISTRATIVE ASSISTANCE ARRANGEMENTS TO HAVE EFFECT

2 It is declared that—

(a) arrangements relating to international tax enforcement that fall within the joint Council of Europe/Organisation for Economic Co-operation and Development Convention on Mutual Administrative Assistance in Tax Matters, signed on behalf of the United Kingdom on 24th May 2007, have been made in relation to the other signatory territories, and

(b) it is expedient that those arrangements have effect.

INSURANCE COMPANIES (TAX EXEMPT BUSINESS) REGULATIONS 2007

(SI 2007/2145)

Made 23 July 2007 by the Treasury in exercise of the powers conferred upon them by s. 460(15) and (16), 461(12) and (13) and 461B(8) and (9) of the Income and Corporation Taxes Act 1988. Operative from 14 August 2007.

History – SI 2007/2145 revoked by SI 2012/3008, reg. 16, with effect in relation to accounting periods beginning on or after 1 January 2013. The text of former SI 2007/2145 read as follows:

"CITATION, COMMENCEMENT AND EFFECT

1(1) These Regulations may be cited as the Insurance Companies (Tax Exempt Business) Regulations 2007 and shall come into force on 14th August 2007.

1(2) Subject to paragraph (3), these Regulations have effect for periods of account ending on or after the date on which these Regulations come into force.

1(3) Where any part of a company's business is exempt from corporation tax by virtue of section 460(11), 461(4) or 461B(5) of the Taxes Act 1988, these Regulations have effect for periods of account beginning on or after 1st January 2007 (whenever ending).

INTERPRETATION

2 In these Regulations–
"the Taxes Act 1988" means the Income and Corporation Taxes Act 1988;
"tax exempt business" means business which is exempt from corporation tax by virtue of any of the following provisions of the Taxes Act 1988–
(a)   section 460(11) or (12);
(b)   section 461(4) or (4A); and
(c)   section 461B(5) or (6A).

MODIFICATIONS OF THE TAXES ACT 1988

3 Where any part of the business of a company is tax exempt business, the Taxes Act 1988 has effect subject to the following modifications.

MODIFICATION OF SECTION 431

4(1) Section 431 (interpretative provisions relating to insurance companies) is modified as follows.
4(2) In subsection (2), insert at the appropriate places–
""tax exempt life assurance business" has the meaning given by section 431FA; and"; and
""tax exempt other business" has the meaning given by section 431FB;".

INSERTION OF SECTIONS 431FA AND 431FB

5 After section 431F (meaning of "basic life assurance and general annuity business") insert–

"Meaning of "tax exempt life assurance business"

431FA(1) In this Chapter **"tax exempt life assurance business"** means business which is exempt from corporation tax by virtue of section 460(11) or (12).
431FA(2) For the purposes of this Chapter, tax exempt life assurance business shall be treated as not being life assurance business.

Meaning of "tax exempt other business"

431FB(1) In this Chapter **"tax exempt other business"** means business which is exempt from corporation tax by virtue of section 461(4) or (4A) or 461B(5) or (6A).
431FB(2) For the purposes of this Chapter, tax exempt other business shall be treated as being neither PHI business nor general insurance business."

MODIFICATIONS OF SECTION 431H

6(1) Section 431H (company carrying on life assurance business and other insurance business) is modified as follows.
6(2) For subsection (1) substitute–
"431H(1) This section applies in relation to an insurance company which carries on two or more of the following–
(a)   life assurance business,
(b)   tax exempt life assurance business,
(c)   tax exempt other business, and
(d)   insurance business of any other kind."
6(3) In subsection (2)–
(a)   omit the word "and" immediately following paragraph (a),
(b)   after paragraph (a) insert–
"(aa)   tax exempt life assurance
(ab)   tax exempt other business, and", and
(c)   in paragraph (b), for "the" substitute "any".

MODIFICATIONS OF SECTION 432A

7(1) Section 432A (apportionment of income and gains)(a) is modified as follows.
7(2) In subsection (2)–
(a)   omit the word "and" immediately following paragraph (b), and
(b)   for paragraph (c) substitute–
"(c)   PHI business,
(d)   tax exempt life assurance business, and
(e)   tax exempt other business."

7(3)   In subsection (6)–
(a)   in the fraction, for the denominator "$A + B + C$" substitute "$A + B + C + D + E$",
(b)   omit the word "and" immediately following the definition of B, and
(c)   after the definition of C insert–
"D is the aggregate of–
(a)   the mean of the opening and closing liabilities of the tax exempt life assurance business (but taking that mean to be nil if it would otherwise be below nil), and
(b)   the mean of the appropriate parts (that is, the parts relating to that category) of the opening and closing amounts of the free assets amounts,
reduced (but not below nil) by the mean of the opening and closing net values of any assets directly referable to that category; and
E is the aggregate of–
(a)   the mean of the opening and closing liabilities of the tax exempt other business (but taking that mean to be nil if it would otherwise be below nil), and
(b)   the mean of the appropriate parts (that is, the parts relating to that category) of the opening and closing amounts of the free assets amounts,
reduced (but not below nil) by the mean of the opening and closing net values of any assets directly referable to that category."
7(4)   In subsection (6A)–
(a)   in the fraction, for the denominator "$A + B + C$" substitute "$A + B + C + D + E$", and
(b)   for "and C" substitute ", C, D and E".
7(5)   In subsection (6B)–
(a)   in the fraction, for the denominator "$A + B + C$" substitute "$A + B + C + D + E$", and
(b)   for "and C" substitute ", C, D and E".
7(6)   After subsection (6B) insert–
"**432A(6BA)**   For the purposes of subsection (5) above "the relevant fraction", in relation to tax exempt life assurance business, is–

$$\frac{D}{A + B + C + D + E}$$

where A, B, C, D and E have the same meaning as in subsection (6) above.
432A(6BB)   For the purposes of subsection (5) above "the relevant fraction", in relation to tax exempt other business, is–

$$\frac{E}{A + B + C + D + E}$$

where A, B, C, D and E have the same meaning as in subsection (6) above."
7(7)   In subsection (6C), for "or (6B)" substitute ", (6B), (6BA) or (6BB)".
7(8)   In subsection (7), for "and (6B)" substitute ", (6B), (6BA) and (6BB)".
7(9)   In subsection (8ZA), for "and C" substitute ", C, D and E".

MODIFICATIONS OF SECTION 432AA
8(1)   Section 432AA (Schedule A business or overseas property business) is modified as follows.
8(2)   In subsection (4)–
(a)   omit the word "and" immediately following paragraph (b), and
(b)   after paragraph (c) insert–
"(d)   tax exempt life assurance business; and
(e)   tax exempt other business."

MODIFICATIONS OF SECTION 432C
9(1)   Section 432C (section 432B apportionment: non-participating funds) is modified as follows.
9(2)   In subsection (5), in the definition of B, after "PHI business" (in both places) insert ", tax exempt life assurance business or tax exempt other business".
9(3)   In subsection (9), in the definition of D–
(a)   for "or PHI business" substitute ", PHI business, tax exempt life assurance business or tax exempt other business", and
(b)   for "either" substitute "any".

MODIFICATIONS OF SECTION 440
10(1)   Section 440 (transfers of assets etc) is modified as follows.
10(2)   In subsection (4)–
(a)   after paragraph (a) insert–
"(b)   assets which are linked solely to tax exempt life assurance business;", and
(b)   in paragraph (e), for "either" substitute "any".

MODIFICATION OF SECTION 440A
11(1)   Section 440A (securities) is modified as follows.
11(2)   In subsection (2)(a)–
(a)   omit the word "or" immediately following sub-paragraph (i), and
(b)   after sub-paragraph (ii) insert–
"(iii)   tax exempt life assurance business, or
(iv)   tax exempt other business,".

MODIFICATIONS OF SECTION 755A
12(1)   Section 755A (treatment of chargeable profits and creditable tax apportioned to company carrying on life assurance business) is modified as follows.
12(2)   In subsection (4), for the words from "as is referable" to the end substitute–
"as is referable to–
(a)   gross roll-up business,
(b)   tax exempt life assurance business, or
(c)   tax exempt other business,
carried on by the UK company."

In subsection (6)(c), for "gross roll-up business" substitute "a category of business specified in paragraphs (a) to (c) of subsection (4) above".

12(4) In subsection (13)–

(a)   omit the word "or" immediately following paragraph (a), and

(b)   after paragraph (ba) insert–

"(bb)   tax exempt life assurance business, or

(bc)   tax exempt other business,".

MODIFICATION OF SECTION 212 OF THE TAXATION OF CHARGEABLE GAINS ACT 1992

13(1) Where any part of the business of a company is tax exempt life assurance business, section 212 of the Taxation of Chargeable Gains Act 1992 (annual deemed disposal of holdings of unit trusts) is modified as follows.

13(2) In subsection (2), after "gross roll-up business" insert "or tax exempt life assurance business".

MODIFICATION OF PARAGRAPH 3A OF SCHEDULE 11 TO THE FINANCE ACT 1996

14(1) Where any part of the business of a company is tax exempt business, paragraph 3A of Schedule 11 to the Finance Act 1996 (loan relationships: special provisions for insurers) is modified as follows.

14(2) In sub-paragraph (5), after "(6B)" insert ", (6BA), (6BB)".

MODIFICATION OF SECTION 255 OF THE CAPITAL ALLOWANCES ACT 2001

15(1) Where any part of the business of a company is tax exempt business, section 255 of the Capital Allowances Act 2001 (apportionment of allowances and charges) is modified as follows.

15(2) In subsection (1), for "and PHI business" substitute ", PHI business, tax exempt life assurance business and tax exempt other business".".

MONEY LAUNDERING REGULATIONS

(SI 2007/2157, as amended by SI 2007/3299, SI 2009/56, SI 2009/209, SI 2010/22, SI 2011/99, SI 2011/1265, SI 2011/1781, SI 2011/2699, SI 2011/2833, SI 2012/2298, SI 2013/429, SI 2013/1881, SI 2013/3115, SI 2014/506 and SI 2014/1264)

Made on 24 July 2007 by the Treasury, in exercise of the powers conferred on them by the European Communities Act 1972, s. 2(2) and by the Financial Services and Markets Act 2000, s. 168(4)(b), s. 417(1) and s. 428(3).

Official publications – Notice MLR 8: "Preventing Money Laundering and Terrorist Activity".
Notice MLR 9: "Money Laundering Regulations 2007 Registration".
Notice MLR 9a: "Registration guide for Money Service Businesses".
Notice MLR 9b: "Registration Guide for High Value Dealers".
Notice MLR 9c: "Registration Guide for Trust or Company Service Providers".
Notice MLR 9d: "Registration Guide for Accountancy Service Providers".

Other material – HM Treasury advisory notice on money laundering and terrorist financing controls in overseas countries is available at http://www.hmrc.gov.uk/news/mlr-controls-overseas.htm .
Code of Practice 28 (COP 28): "Money Laundering Regulations 2007"

ARRANGEMENT OF REGULATIONS

REGULATION

PART 1 – GENERAL

PART 2 – CUSTOMER DUE DILIGENCE

PART 3 – RECORD-KEEPING, PROCEDURES AND TRAINING

PART 4 – SUPERVISION AND REGISTRATION

PART 5 – ENFORCEMENT

PART 6 – MISCELLANEOUS

SCHEDULES

PART 1 – GENERAL

CITATION, COMMENCEMENT, ETC

1(1) These Regulations may be cited as the Money Laundering Regulations 2007 and come into force on 15th December 2007.

1(2) These Regulations are prescribed for the purposes of sections 168(4)(b) (appointment of persons to carry out investigations in particular cases) and 402(1)(b) (power of the Authority to institute proceedings for certain other offences) of the 2000 Act.

1(3) The Money Laundering Regulations 2003 are revoked.

INTERPRETATION

2(1) In these regulations–

"**the 2000 Act**" means the Financial Services and Markets Act 2000;

"**Annex I financial institution**" has the meaning given to it by regulation 22(1);

"**auction platform**" has the meaning given by regulation 3(13A);

"**auditor**" except in regulation 17(2)(c) and (d), has the meaning given by regulation 3(4) and (5);

"**authorised person**" means a person who is authorised for the purposes of the 2000 Act;

"**the Authority**" means the Financial Services Authority;

"**beneficial owner**" has the meaning given by regulation 6;

"**bill payment service provider**" means an undertaking which provides a payment service enabling the payment of utility and other household bills;

"**business relationship**" means a business, professional or commercial relationship between a relevant person and a customer, which is expected by the relevant person, at the time when contact is established, to have an element of duration;

"**the capital requirements directive**" means Directive 2013/36/EU of the European Parliament and of the Council of 26 June 2013 relating to the activity of credit institutions and the prudential supervision of credit institutions and investment firms, amending Directive 2002/87/EC and repealing Directives 2006/48/EC and 2006/49/EC;

"**the capital requirements regulation**" means Regulation (EU) 575/2013 of the European Parliament and of the Council of 26 June 2013 on prudential requirements for credit institutions and investment firms and amending Regulation (EU) No 648/2012;

"**cash**" means notes, coins or travellers' cheques in any currency;

"**casino**" has the meaning given by regulation 3(13);

"**the Commissioners**" means the Commissioners for Her Majesty's Revenue and Customs;

"**credit institution**" has the meaning given by regulation 3(2);

"**customer due diligence measures**" has the meaning given by regulation 5;

"**DETI**" means the Department of Enterprise, Trade and Investment in Northern Ireland;

"**the electronic money directive**" means Directive 2009/110/EC of the European Parliament and of the Council of 16th September 2009 on the taking up, pursuit and prudential supervision of the business of electronic money institutions;

"**electronic money institution**" has the meaning given by regulation 2(1) of the Electronic Money Regulations 2011;

"**the emission allowance auctioning regulation**" means Commission Regulation (EU) No. 1031/2010 of 12 November 2010 on the timing, administration and other aspects of auctioning of greenhouse gas emission allowances pursuant to Directive 2003/87/EC of the European Parliament and of the Council establishing a scheme for greenhouse gas emission allowances trading within the Community;

"**estate agent**" has the meaning given by regulation 3(11);

"**external accountant**" has the meaning given by regulation 3(7);

"**financial institution**" has the meaning given by regulation 3(3)

"**firm**" means any entity, whether or not a legal person, that is not an individual and includes a body corporate and a partnership or other unincorporated association;

"**high value dealer**" has the meaning given by regulation 3(12);

"**the implementing measures directive**" means Commission Directive 2006/70/EC of 1st August 2006 laying down implementing measures for the money laundering directive;

"**independent legal professional**" has the meaning given by regulation 3(9);

"**insolvency practitioner**", except in regulation 17(2)(c) and (d), has the meaning given by regulation 3(6);

"**the life assurance consolidation directive**" means Directive 2002/83/EC of the European Parliament and of the Council of 5th November 2002 concerning life assurance;

"**local weights and measures authority**" has the meaning given by section 69 of the Weights and Measures Act 1985 (local weights and measures authorities);

"**the markets in financial instruments directive**" means Directive 2004/39/EC of the European Parliament and of the Council of 12th April 2004 on markets in financial instruments;

"**money laundering**" means an act which falls within section 340(11) of the Proceeds of Crime Act 2002;

"**the money laundering directive**" means Directive 2005/60/EC of the European Parliament and of the Council of 26th October 2005 on the prevention of the use of the financial system for the purpose of money laundering and terrorist financing;

"**money service business**" means an undertaking which by way of business operates a currency exchange office, transmits money (or any representations of monetary value) by any means or cashes cheques which are made payable to customers;

"**nominated officer**" means a person who is nominated to receive disclosures under Part 7 of the Proceeds of Crime Act 2002 (money laundering) or Part 3 of the Terrorism Act 2000 (terrorist property);

"**non-EEA state**" means a state that is not an EEA state;

"**notice**" means a notice in writing;

"**occasional transaction**" means a transaction (carried out other than as part of a business relationship) amounting to 15,000 euro or more, whether the transaction is carried out in a single operation or several operations which appear to be linked;

"**ongoing monitoring**" has the meaning given by regulation 8(2);

"**payment services**" has the meaning given by regulation 2(1) of the Payment Services Regulations 2009;

"**regulated market**"–

(a) within the EEA, has the meaning given by point 14 of Article 4(1) of the markets in financial instruments directive; and

(b) outside the EEA, means a regulated financial market which subjects companies whose securities are admitted to trading to disclosure obligations which are contained in international standards and are equivalent to the specified disclosure obligations;

"**relevant person**" means a person to whom, in accordance with regulations 3 and 4, these Regulations apply;

"**the specified disclosure obligations**" means disclosure requirements consistent with–

(a) Article 6(1) to (4) of Directive 2003/6/EC of the European Parliament and of the Council of 28th January 2003 on insider dealing and market manipulation;

(b) Articles 3, 5, 7, 8, 10, 14 and 16 of Directive 2003/71/EC of the European Parliament and of the Council of 4th November 2003 on the prospectuses to be published when securities are offered to the public or admitted to trading;

(c) Articles 4 to 6, 14, 16 to 19 and 30 of Directive 2004/109/EC of the European Parliament and of the Council of 15th December 2004 relating to the harmonisation of transparency requirements in relation to information about issuers whose securities are admitted to trading on a regulated market; or

(d) Community legislation made under the provisions mentioned in sub-paragraphs (a) to (c);

"**supervisory authority**" in relation to any relevant person means the supervisory authority specified for such a person by regulation 23;

"**tax adviser**" (except in regulation 11(3)) has the meaning given by regulation 3(8);

"**telecommunication, digital and IT payment service provider**" means an undertaking which provides payment services falling within paragraph 1(g) of Schedule 1 to the Payment Services Regulations 2009;

"**terrorist financing**" means an offence under–

(a) section 15 (fund-raising), 16 (use and possession), 17 (funding arrangements), 18 (money laundering) or 63 (terrorist finance: jurisdiction) of the Terrorism Act 2000;

(b) paragraph 7(2) or (3) of Schedule 3 to the Anti-Terrorism, Crime and Security Act 2001 (freezing orders);

　　　(c)　article 7, 8 or 10 of the Terrorism (United Nations Measures) Order 2006; or

　　　(d)　article 7, 8 or 10 of the Al-Qaida and Taliban (United Nations Measures) Order 2006;

"trust or company service provider" has the meaning given by regulation 3(10).

2(2)　In these Regulations, references to amounts in euro include references to equivalent amounts in another currency.

2(3)　Unless otherwise defined, expressions used in these Regulations and the money laundering directive have the same meaning as in the money laundering directive and expressions used in these Regulations and in the implementing measures directive have the same meaning as in the implementing measures directive.

History – In reg. 2(1), definitions of "consumer credit financial institution" and "the OFT" omitted by SI 2013/1881, art. 28 and Schedule, para. 31(2), with effect from 1 April 2014.
In reg. 2(1), the definition of "auction platform" inserted by SI 2011/2699, reg. 11(2), with effect from 12 December 2011.
In reg. 2(1), the definition of "the banking consolidation directive" omitted by SI 2013/3115, Sch. 2, para. 68(2)(a), with effect from 1 January 2014.
In reg. 2(1), the definition of "bill payment service provider" inserted by SI 2009/209, reg. 126 and Sch. 6, para. 6(a)(i), with effect from 1 November 2009.
In reg. 2(1), the definitions of "the capital requirements directive" and "the capital requirements regulation" inserted by SI 2013/3115, Sch. 2, para. 68(2)(b), with effect from 1 January 2014.
In reg. 2(1), the definitions of "the electronic money directive" and "electronic money institution" substituted for the former definition of "the electronic money directive" by SI 2011/99, reg. 79 and Sch. 4, para. 19(a), with effect from 30 April 2011.
In reg. 2(1), the definition of "the emission allowance auctioning regulation" inserted by SI 2011/2699, reg. 11(2), with effect from 12 December 2011.
In reg. 2(1), the definition of "payment services" inserted by SI 2009/209, reg. 126 and Sch. 6, para. 6(a)(ii), with effect from 1 November 2009.
In reg. 2(1), the definition of "telecommunication, digital and IT payment service provider" inserted by SI 2009/209, reg. 126 and Sch. 6, para. 6(a)(iii), with effect from 1 November 2009.

APPLICATION OF THE REGULATIONS

3(1)　Subject to regulation 4, these Regulations apply to the following persons acting in the course of business carried on by them in the United Kingdom ("relevant persons")–

　　(a)　credit institutions;

　　(b)　financial institutions;

　　(c)　auditors, insolvency practitioners, external accountants and tax advisers;

　　(d)　independent legal professionals

　　(e)　trust or company service providers;

　　(f)　estate agents;

　　(g)　high value dealers;

　　(h)　casinos.

3(1A)　Regulations 2, 20, 21, 23, 24, 35 to 42, and 44 to 48 apply to an auction platform acting in the course of business carried on by it in the United Kingdom, and such an auction platform is a relevant person for the purposes of those provisions.

3(2)　**"Credit institutions"** means–

　　(a)　a credit institution as defined in Article 4(1)(1) of the capital requirements regulation; or

　　(b)　a branch (within the meaning of Article 4(1)(17) of that regulation) located in an EEA state of an institution falling within sub-paragraph (a) (or an equivalent institution whose head office is located in a non-EEA state) wherever its head office is located,

when it accepts deposits or other repayable funds from the public or grants credits for its own account (within the meaning of the banking consolidation directive).

3(3)　**"Financial institution"** means–

　　(a)　an undertaking, including a money service business, when it carries out one or more of the activities listed in points 2 to 12, 14 and 15 of Annex 1 to the capital requirements directive (the relevant text of which is set out in Schedule 1 to these Regulations), other than–

　　　　(i)　a credit institution;

　　　　(ii)　an undertaking whose only listed activity is as a creditor under an agreement which–

　　　　　　(aa)　falls within section 12(a) of the Consumer Credit Act 1974 (debtor-creditor-supplier agreements),

　　　　　　(bb)　provides fixed sum credit (within the meaning given in section 10 of the Consumer Credit Act 1974 (running-account credit and fixed-sum credit)) in relation to the provision of services, and (cc)   provides financial accommodation by way of deferred payment or payment by instalments over a period not exceeding 12 months;

(iii)   an undertaking whose only listed activity is trading for own account in one or more of the products listed in point 7 of Annex 1 to the capital requirements directive where the undertaking does not have a customer,

and, for this purpose, **"customer"** means a third party which is not a member of the same group as the undertaking;

(b)   an insurance company duly authorised in accordance with the life assurance consolidation directive, when it carries out activities covered by that directive;

(c)   a person whose regular occupation or business is the provision to other persons of an investment service or the performance of an investment activity on a professional basis, when providing or performing investment services or activities (within the meaning of the markets in financial instruments directive), other than a person falling within Article 2 of that directive;

(d)   a collective investment undertaking, when marketing or otherwise offering its units or shares;

(e)   an insurance intermediary as defined in Article 2(5) of Directive 2002/92/EC of the European Parliament and of the Council of 9th December 2002 on insurance mediation, with the exception of a tied insurance intermediary as mentioned in Article 2(7) of that Directive, when it acts in respect of contracts of long-term insurance within the meaning given by article 3(1) of, and Part II of Schedule 1 to, the Financial Services and Markets Act 2000 (Regulated Activities) Order 2001;

(f)   a branch located in an EEA state of a person referred to in sub-paragraphs (a) to (e) (or an equivalent person whose head office is located in a non-EEA state), wherever its head office is located, when carrying out any activity mentioned in sub-paragraphs (a) to (e);

(g)   the National Savings Bank;

(h)   the Director of Savings, when money is raised under the auspices of the Director under the National Loans Act 1968.

3(4)   **"Auditor"** means any firm or individual who is a statutory auditor within the meaning of Part 42 of the Companies Act 2006 (statutory auditors), when carrying out statutory audit work within the meaning of section 1210 of that Act.

3(5)   Before the entry into force of Part 42 of the Companies Act 2006 the reference in paragraph (4) to–

(a)   a person who is a statutory auditor shall be treated as a reference to a person who is eligible for appointment as a company auditor under section 25 of the Companies Act 1989 (eligibility for appointment) or article 28 of the Companies (Northern Ireland) Order 1990; and

(b)   the carrying out of statutory audit work shall be treated as a reference to the provision of audit services.

3(6)   **"Insolvency practitioner"** means any person who acts as an insolvency practitioner within the meaning of section 388 of the Insolvency Act 1986 (meaning of "act as insolvency practitioner") or article 3 of the Insolvency (Northern Ireland) Order 1989.

3(7)   **"External accountant"** means a firm or sole practitioner who by way of business provides accountancy services to other persons, when providing such services.

3(8)   **"Tax adviser"** means a firm or sole practitioner who by way of business provides advice about the tax affairs of other persons, when providing such services.

3(9)   **"Independent legal professional"** means a firm or sole practitioner who by way of business provides legal or notarial services to other persons, when participating in financial or real property transactions concerning–

(a)   the buying and selling of real property or business entities;

(b)   the managing of client money, securities or other assets;

(c)   the opening or management of bank, savings or securities accounts;

(d)   the organisation of contributions necessary for the creation, operation or management of companies; or

(e)   the creation, operation or management of trusts, companies or similar structures,

and, for this purpose, a person participates in a transaction by assisting in the planning or execution of the transaction or otherwise acting for or on behalf of a client in the transaction.

3(10)   **"Trust or company service provider"** means a firm or sole practitioner who by way of business provides any of the following services to other persons–

(a)   forming companies or other legal persons;

(b)   acting, or arranging for another person to act–

       (i)   as a director or secretary of a company;

       (ii)   as a partner of a partnership; or

       (iii)   in a similar position in relation to other legal persons;

(c)   providing a registered office, business address, correspondence or administrative address or other related services for a company, partnership or any other legal person or arrangement;

(d)   acting, or arranging for another person to act, as–

       (i)   a trustee of an express trust or similar legal arrangement; or

       (ii)   a nominee shareholder for a person other than a company whose securities are listed on a regulated market,

      when providing such services.

3(11)   **"Estate agent"** means–

(a)   a firm; or

(b)   sole practitioner,

who, or whose employees, carry out estate agency work, when in the course of carrying out such work.

3(11A)   For the purposes of paragraph (11) **"estate agency work"** is to be read in accordance with section 1 of the Estate Agents Act 1979 (estate agency work), but for those purposes references in that section to disposing of or acquiring an interest in land are (despite anything in section 2 of that Act) to be taken to include references to disposing of or acquiring an estate or interest in land outside the United Kingdom where that estate or interest is capable of being owned or held as a separate interest.

3(12)   **"High value dealer"** means a firm or sole trader who by way of business trades in goods (including an auctioneer dealing in goods), when he receives, in respect of any transaction, a payment or payments in cash of at least 15,000 euros in total, whether the transaction is executed in a single operation or in several operations which appear to be linked.

3(13)   **"Casino"** means the holder of a casino operating licence and, for this purpose, a **"casino operating licence"** has the meaning given by section 65(2) of the Gambling Act 2005 (nature of licence).

3(13A)   **"Auction platform"** means a platform which auctions two-day spot or five-day futures, within the meanings given by Article 3(4) and (5) of the emission allowance auctioning regulation, when it carries out activities covered by that regulation.

3(14)   In the application of this regulation to Scotland, for "real property" in paragraph (9) substitute "heritable property".

History – Reg. 3(1A) inserted by SI 2011/2699, reg. 3(a), with effect from 12 December 2011.
In reg. 3(2)(a), "Article 4(1)(1) of the capital requirements regulation" substituted for "Article 4(1) of the banking consolidated directive" by SI 2013/3115, Sch. 2, para. 68(3)(a), with effect from 1 January 2014.
In reg. 3(2)(a), "Article 4(1)" substituted for "Article 4(1)(a)" by SI 2011/99, reg. 79 and Sch. 4, para. 19(b)(i), with effect from 30 April 2011.
In reg. 3(2)(b), "Article 4(1)(17) of that regulation" substituted for "Article 4(3) of that directive" by SI 2013/3115, Sch. 2, para. 68(3)(b), with effect from 1 January 2014.
In reg. 3(3)(a), ", 14 and 15" substituted for "and 14" by SI 2011/99, reg. 79 and Sch. 4, para. 19(b)(ii), with effect from 30 April 2011.
In reg. 3(3)(a) and (a)(iii), the words "banking consolidated directive" substituted for "capital requirements directive" by SI 2013/3115, Sch. 2, para. 68(3)(c), with effect from 1 January 2014.
Reg. 3(3)(a)(ii) inserted (and former (ii) renumbered as (iii)) by SI 2012/2298, reg. 3(a), with effect from 1 October 2012.
In reg. 3(11), the words "(within the meaning given by section 1 of the Estate Agents Act 1979 (estate agency work))" omitted by SI 2012/2298, reg. 3(b), with effect from 1 October 2012.
Reg. 3(11A) inserted by SI 2012/2298, reg. 3(c), with effect from 1 October 2012.
Reg. 3(13A) inserted by SI 2011/2699, reg. 3(b), with effect from 12 December 2011.

EXCLUSIONS

4(1)   These Regulations do not apply to the following persons when carrying out any of the following activities–

(a)   a society registered under the Industrial and Provident Societies Act 1965, when it–

       (i)   issues withdrawable share capital within the limit set by section 6 of that Act (maximum shareholding in society); or

       (ii)   accepts deposits from the public within the limit set by section 7(3) of that Act (carrying on of banking by societies);

(b)   a society registered under the Industrial and Provident Societies Act (Northern Ireland) 1969, when it–

     (i)   issues withdrawable share capital within the limit set by section 6 of that Act (maximum shareholding in society); or

     (ii)   accepts deposits from the public within the limit set by section 7(3) of that Act (carrying on of banking by societies);

(c)   a person who is (or falls within a class of persons) specified in any of paragraphs 2 to 23, 25 to 38 or 40 to 49 of the Schedule to the Financial Services and Markets Act 2000 (Exemption) Order 2001, when carrying out any activity in respect of which he is exempt;

(ca)   a local authority within the meaning given in article 3 of the Financial Services and Markets Act 2000 (Regulated Activities) Order 2001, when carrying on an activity which would be a regulated activity for the purposes of the Financial Services and Markets Act 2000 but for article 72G of that Order;

(d)   a person who was an exempted person for the purposes of section 45 of the Financial Services Act 1986 (miscellaneous exemptions) immediately before its repeal, when exercising the functions specified in that section;

(e)   a person whose main activity is that of a high value dealer, when he engages in financial activity on an occasional or very limited basis as set out in paragraph 1 of Schedule 2 to these Regulations; or

(f)   a person, when he prepares a home report.

4(2)   These Regulations do not apply to a person who falls within regulation 3 solely as a result of his engaging in financial activity on an occasional or very limited basis as set out in paragraph 1 of Schedule 2 to these Regulations.

4(3)   Parts 2 to 5 of these Regulations do not apply to–

(a)   the Auditor General for Scotland;

(b)   the Auditor General for Wales;

(c)   the Bank of England;

(d)   the Comptroller and Auditor General;

(e)   the Comptroller and Auditor General for Northern Ireland;

(f)   the Official Solicitor to the Supreme Court, when acting as trustee in his official capacity;

(g)   the Treasury Solicitor.

4(4)   In paragraph (1)(f), **"home report"** means the documents prescribed for the purposes of section 98, 99(1) or 101(2) of the Housing (Scotland) Act 2006.

History – Reg. 4(1)(ca) inserted by SI 2014/506, art. 4, with effect from 1 April 2014.
Reg. 4(1)(f) substituted by SI 2012/2298, reg. 4(a), with effect from 1 October 2012. Former reg. 4(1)(f) read as follows:
     "(f)   a person, when he prepares a home information pack or a document or information for inclusion in a home information pack.".
Reg. 4(4) substituted by SI 2012/2298, reg. 4(b), with effect from 1 October 2012. Former reg. 4(4) read as follows:
     "**4(4)**   In paragraph (1)(f), **"home information pack"** has the same meaning as in Part 5 of the Housing Act 2004 (home information packs).".

PART 2 – CUSTOMER DUE DILIGENCE

MEANING OF CUSTOMER DUE DILIGENCE

5   **"Customer due diligence measures"** means–

(a)   identifying the customer and verifying the customer's identity on the basis of documents, data or information obtained from a reliable and independent source;

(b)   identifying, where there is a beneficial owner who is not the customer, the beneficial owner and taking adequate measures, on a risk-sensitive basis, to verify his identity so that the relevant person is satisfied that he knows who the beneficial owner is, including, in the case of a legal person, trust or similar legal arrangement, measures to understand the ownership and control structure of the person, trust or arrangement; and

(c)   obtaining information on the purpose and intended nature of the business relationship.

MEANING OF BENEFICIAL OWNER

6(1) In the case of a body corporate, **"beneficial owner"** means any individual who–

(a)   as respects any body other than a company whose securities are listed on a regulated market, ultimately owns or controls (whether through direct or indirect ownership or control, including through bearer share holdings) more than 25% of the shares or voting rights in the body; or

(b)   as respects any body corporate, otherwise exercises control over the management of the body.

6(2) In the case of a partnership (other than a limited liability partnership), **"beneficial owner"** means any individual who–

(a)   ultimately is entitled to or controls (whether the entitlement or control is direct or indirect) more than a 25% share of the capital or profits of the partnership or more than 25% of the voting rights in the partnership; or

(b)   otherwise exercises control over the management of the partnership.

6(3) In the case of a trust, **"beneficial owner"** means–

(a)   any individual who is entitled to a specified interest in at least 25% of the capital of the trust property;

(b)   as respects any trust other than one which is set up or operates entirely for the benefit of individuals falling within sub-paragraph (a), the class of persons in whose main interest the trust is set up or operates;

(c)   any individual who has control over the trust.

6(4) In paragraph (3)–

    "specified interest" means a vested interest which is–

      (a)   in possession or in remainder or reversion (or, in Scotland, in fee); and

      (b)   defeasible or indefeasible;

    "control" means a power (whether exercisable alone, jointly with another person or with the consent of another person) under the trust instrument or by law to–

      (a)   dispose of, advance, lend, invest, pay or apply trust property;

      (b)   vary the trust;

      (c)   add or remove a person as a beneficiary or to or from a class of beneficiaries;

      (d)   appoint or remove trustees;

      (e)   direct, withhold consent to or veto the exercise of a power such as is mentioned in sub-paragraph (a), (b), (c) or (d).

6(5) For the purposes of paragraph (3)–

(a)   where an individual is the beneficial owner of a body corporate which is entitled to a specified interest in the capital of the trust property or which has control over the trust, the individual is to be regarded as entitled to the interest or having control over the trust; and

(b)   an individual does not have control solely as a result of–

      (i)   his consent being required in accordance with section 32(1)(c) of the Trustee Act 1925 (power of advancement);

      (ii)   any discretion delegated to him under section 34 of the Pensions Act 1995 (power of investment and delegation);

      (iii)   the power to give a direction conferred on him by section 19(2) of the Trusts of Land and Appointment of Trustees Act 1996 (appointment and retirement of trustee at instance of beneficiaries); or

      (iv)   the power exercisable collectively at common law to vary or extinguish a trust where the beneficiaries under the trust are of full age and capacity and (taken together) absolutely entitled to the property subject to the trust (or, in Scotland, have a full and unqualified right to the fee).

6(6) In the case of a legal entity or legal arrangement which does not fall within paragraph (1), (2) or (3), **"beneficial owner"** means–

(a)   where the individuals who benefit from the entity or arrangement have been determined, any individual who benefits from at least 25% of the property of the entity or arrangement;

(b)   where the individuals who benefit from the entity or arrangement have yet to be determined, the class of persons in whose main interest the entity or arrangement is set up or operates;

(c)   any individual who exercises control over at least 25% of the property of the entity or arrangement.

6(7)   For the purposes of paragraph (6), where an individual is the beneficial owner of a body corporate which benefits from or exercises control over the property of the entity or arrangement, the individual is to be regarded as benefiting from or exercising control over the property of the entity or arrangement.

6(8)   In the case of an estate of a deceased person in the course of administration, **"beneficial owner"** means–

(a)   in England and Wales and Northern Ireland, the executor, original or by representation, or administrator for the time being of a deceased person;

(b)   in Scotland, the executor for the purposes of the Executors (Scotland) Act 1900.

6(9)   In any other case, **"beneficial owner"** means the individual who ultimately owns or controls the customer or on whose behalf a transaction is being conducted.

6(10)   In this regulation–

> **"arrangement,"**"**entity"** and **"trust"** means an arrangement, entity or trust which administers and distributes funds;

> **"limited liability partnership"** has the meaning given by the Limited Liability Partnerships Act 2000.

APPLICATION OF CUSTOMER DUE DILIGENCE

7(1)   Subject to regulations 9, 10, 12, 13, 14, 16(4) and 17, a relevant person must apply customer due diligence measures when he–

(a)   establishes a business relationship;

(b)   carries out an occasional transaction;

(c)   suspects money laundering or terrorist financing;

(d)   doubts the veracity or adequacy of documents, data or information previously obtained for the purposes of identification or verification.

7(2)   Subject to regulation 16(4), a relevant person must also apply customer due diligence measures at other appropriate times to existing customers on a risk-sensitive basis.

7(3)   A relevant person must–

(a)   determine the extent of customer due diligence measures on a risk-sensitive basis depending on the type of customer, business relationship, product or transaction; and

(b)   be able to demonstrate to his supervisory authority that the extent of the measures is appropriate in view of the risks of money laundering and terrorist financing.

7(4)   Where–

(a)   a relevant person is required to apply customer due diligence measures in the case of a trust, legal entity (other than a body corporate) or a legal arrangement (other than a trust); and

(b)   the class of persons in whose main interest the trust, entity or arrangement is set up or operates is identified as a beneficial owner,

the relevant person is not required to identify all the members of the class.

7(5)   Paragraph (3)(b) does not apply to the National Savings Bank or the Director of Savings.

ONGOING MONITORING

8(1)   A relevant person must conduct ongoing monitoring of a business relationship.

8(2)   **"Ongoing monitoring"** of a business relationship means–

(a)   scrutiny of transactions undertaken throughout the course of the relationship (including, where necessary, the source of funds) to ensure that the transactions are consistent with the relevant person's knowledge of the customer, his business and risk profile; and

(b)   keeping the documents, data or information obtained for the purpose of applying customer due diligence measures up-to-date.

8(3)   Regulation 7(3) applies to the duty to conduct ongoing monitoring under paragraph (1) as it applies to customer due diligence measures.

TIMING OF VERIFICATION

9(1) This regulation applies in respect of the duty under regulation 7(1)(a) and (b) to apply the customer due diligence measures referred to in regulation 5(a) and (b).

9(2) Subject to paragraphs (3) to (5) and regulation 10, a relevant person must verify the identity of the customer (and any beneficial owner) before the establishment of a business relationship or the carrying out of an occasional transaction.

9(3) Such verification may be completed during the establishment of a business relationship if–

(a)   this is necessary not to interrupt the normal conduct of business; and

(b)   there is little risk of money laundering or terrorist financing occurring,

provided that the verification is completed as soon as practicable after contact is first established.

9(4) The verification of the identity of the beneficiary under a life insurance policy may take place after the business relationship has been established provided that it takes place at or before the time of payout or at or before the time the beneficiary exercises a right vested under the policy.

9(5) The verification of the identity of a bank account holder may take place after the bank account has been opened provided that there are adequate safeguards in place to ensure that–

(a)   the account is not closed; and

(b)   transactions are not carried out by or on behalf of the account holder (including any payment from the account to the account holder),

before verification has been completed.

CASINOS

10(1) A casino must establish and verify the identity of-

(a)   all customers to whom the casino makes facilities for gaming available–

     (i)   before entry to any premises where such facilities are provided; or

     (ii)   where the facilities are for remote gaming, before access is given to such facilities; or

(b)   if the specified conditions are met, all customers who, in the course of any period of 24 hours–

     (i)   purchase from, or exchange with, the casino chips with a total value of 2,000 euro or more;

     (ii)   pay the casino 2,000 euro or more for the use of gaming machines; or

     (iii)   pay to, or stake with, the casino 2,000 euro or more in connection with facilities for remote gaming.

10(2) The specified conditions are–

(a)   the casino verifies the identity of each customer before or immediately after such purchase, exchange, payment or stake takes place, and

(b)   the Gambling Commission is satisfied that the casino has appropriate procedures in place to monitor and record–

     (i)   the total value of chips purchased from or exchanged with the casino;

     (ii)   the total money paid for the use of gaming machines; or

     (iii)   the total money paid or staked in connection with facilities for remote gaming,

   by each customer.

10(3) In this regulation–

   "gaming", **"gaming machine"**, **"remote operating licence"** and **"stake "** have the meanings given by, respectively, sections 6(1) (gaming & game of chance), 235 (gaming machine), 67 (remote gambling) and 353(1) (interpretation) of the Gambling Act 2005;

   "premises" means premises subject to–

     (a)   a casino premises licence within the meaning of section 150(1)(a) of the Gambling Act 2005 (nature of licence); or

     (b)   a converted casino premises licence within the meaning of paragraph 65 of Part 7 of Schedule 4 to the Gambling Act 2005 (Commencement No. 6 and Transitional Provisions) Order 2006;

   "remote gaming" means gaming provided pursuant to a remote operating licence.

History – In reg. 10(1)(b)(ii) the word "euro" inserted by SI 2007/3299, reg. 2(a), with effect from 15 December 2007.

REQUIREMENT TO CEASE TRANSACTIONS ETC

11(1) Where, in relation to any customer, a relevant person is unable to apply customer due diligence measures in accordance with the provisions of this Part, he—

(a)   must not carry out a transaction with or for the customer through a bank account;

(b)   must not establish a business relationship or carry out an occasional transaction with the customer;

(c)   must terminate any existing business relationship with the customer;

(d)   must consider whether he is required to make a disclosure by Part 7 of the Proceeds of Crime Act 2002 or Part 3 of the Terrorism Act 2000.

11(2) Paragraph (1) does not apply where a lawyer or other professional adviser is in the course of ascertaining the legal position for his client or performing his task of defending or representing that client in, or concerning, legal proceedings, including advice on the institution or avoidance of proceedings.

11(3) In paragraph (2), **"other professional adviser"** means an auditor, accountant or tax adviser who is a member of a professional body which is established for any such persons and which makes provision for—

(a)   testing the competence of those seeking admission to membership of such a body as a condition for such admission; and

(b)   imposing and maintaining professional and ethical standards for its members, as well as imposing sanctions for non-compliance with those standards.

EXCEPTION FOR TRUSTEES OF DEBT ISSUES

12(1) A relevant person—

(a)   who is appointed by the issuer of instruments or securities specified in paragraph (2) as trustee of an issue of such instruments or securities; or

(b)   whose customer is a trustee of an issue of such instruments or securities,

is not required to apply the customer due diligence measure referred to in regulation 5(b) in respect of the holders of such instruments or securities.

12(2) The specified instruments and securities are—

(a)   instruments which fall within article 77 of the Financial Services and Markets Act 2000 (Regulated Activities) Order 2001; and

(b)   securities which fall within article 78 of that Order.

SIMPLIFIED DUE DILIGENCE

13(1) A relevant person is not required to apply customer due diligence measures in the circumstances mentioned in regulation 7(1)(a), (b) or (d) where he has reasonable grounds for believing that the customer, transaction or product related to such transaction, falls within any of the following paragraphs.

13(2) The customer is—

(a)   a credit or financial institution which is subject to the requirements of the money laundering directive; or

(b)   a credit or financial institution (or equivalent institution) which—

     (i)   is situated in a non-EEA state which imposes requirements equivalent to those laid down in the money laundering directive; and

     (ii)   is supervised for compliance with those requirements.

13(3) The customer is a company whose securities are listed on a regulated market subject to specified disclosure obligations.

13(4) The customer is an independent legal professional and the product is an account into which monies are pooled, provided that—

(a)   where the pooled account is held in a non-EEA state—

     (i)   that state imposes requirements to combat money laundering and terrorist financing which are consistent with international standards; and

     (ii)   the independent legal professional is supervised in that state for compliance with those requirements; and

(b)   information on the identity of the persons on whose behalf monies are held in the pooled account is available, on request, to the institution which acts as a depository institution for the account.

13(5)   The customer is a public authority in the United Kingdom.

13(6)   The customer is a public authority which fulfils all the conditions set out in paragraph 2 of Schedule 2 to these Regulations.

13(7)   The product is–

(a)   a life insurance contract where the annual premium is no more than 1,000 euro or where a single premium of no more than 2,500 euro is paid;

(b)   an insurance contract for the purposes of a pension scheme where the contract contains no surrender clause and cannot be used as collateral;

(c)   a pension, superannuation or similar scheme which provides retirement benefits to employees, where contributions are made by an employer or by way of deduction from an employee's wages and the scheme rules do not permit the assignment of a member's interest under the scheme (other than an assignment permitted by section 44 of the Welfare Reform and Pensions Act 1999 (disapplication of restrictions on alienation) or section 91(5)(a) of the Pensions Act 1995 (inalienability of occupational pension)); or

(d)   electronic money, within the meaning of Article 1(3)(b) of the electronic money directive, where–

     (i)   if the device cannot be recharged, the maximum amount stored in the device is no more than 250 euro or, in the case of electronic money used to carry out payment transactions within the United Kingdom, 500 euro; or

     (ii)   if the device can be recharged, a limit of 2,500 euro is imposed on the total amount transacted in a calendar year, except when an amount of 1,000 euro or more is redeemed in the same calendar year by the electronic money holder (within the meaning of Article 11 of the electronic money directive).

13(8)   The product and any transaction related to such product fulfils all the conditions set out in paragraph 3 of Schedule 2 to these Regulations.

13(9)   The product is a child trust fund within the meaning given by section 1(2) of the Child Trust Funds Act 2004.

13(10)   The product is a junior ISA within the meaning given by regulation 2B of the Individual Savings Account Regulations 1998.

History – In reg. 13(7)(d), in the opening words, "Article 2(2)" substituted for "Article 1(3)(b)" by SI 2011/99, reg. 79 and Sch. 4, para. 19(c)(i), with effect from 30 April 2011.
In reg. 13(7)(d)(i), the words "250 euro or, in the case of electronic money used to carry out payment transactions within the United Kingdom, 500 euro" substituted for "150 euro" by SI 2011/99, reg. 79 and Sch. 4, para. 19(c)(ii), with effect from 30 April 2011.
In reg. 13(7)(d)(ii), the words "by the electronic money holder (within the meaning of Article 11 of the electronic money directive)." substituted for the words "by the bearer (within the meaning of Article 3 of the electronic money directive)." by SI 2011/99, reg. 79 and Sch. 4, para. 19(c)(iii), with effect from 30 April 2011.
Reg. 13(10) inserted by SI 2011/1781, reg. 2, with effect from 1 November 2011.

ENHANCED CUSTOMER DUE DILIGENCE AND ONGOING MONITORING

14(1)   A relevant person must apply on a risk-sensitive basis enhanced customer due diligence measures and enhanced ongoing monitoring–

(a)   in accordance with paragraphs (2) to (4);

(b)   in any other situation which by its nature can present a higher risk of money laundering or terrorist financing.

14(2)   Where the customer has not been physically present for identification purposes, a relevant person must take specific and adequate measures to compensate for the higher risk, for example, by applying one or more of the following measures–

(a)   ensuring that the customer's identity is established by additional documents, data or information;

(b)   supplementary measures to verify or certify the documents supplied, or requiring confirmatory certification by a credit or financial institution which is subject to the money laundering directive;

(c)   ensuring that the first payment is carried out through an account opened in the customer's name with a credit institution.

14(3) A credit institution ("the correspondent") which has or proposes to have a correspondent banking relationship with a respondent institution ("the respondent") from a non-EEA state must–

(a)   gather sufficient information about the respondent to understand fully the nature of its business;

(b)   determine from publicly-available information the reputation of the respondent and the quality of its supervision;

(c)   assess the respondent's anti-money laundering and anti-terrorist financing controls;

(d)   obtain approval from senior management before establishing a new correspondent banking relationship;

(e)   document the respective responsibilities of the respondent and correspondent; and

(f)   be satisfied that, in respect of those of the respondent's customers who have direct access to accounts of the correspondent, the respondent–

     (i)   has verified the identity of, and conducts ongoing monitoring in respect of, such customers; and

     (ii)   is able to provide to the correspondent, upon request, the documents, data or information obtained when applying customer due diligence measures and ongoing monitoring.

14(4) A relevant person who proposes to have a business relationship or carry out an occasional transaction with a politically exposed person must–

(a)   have approval from senior management for establishing the business relationship with that person;

(b)   take adequate measures to establish the source of wealth and source of funds which are involved in the proposed business relationship or occasional transaction; and

(c)   where the business relationship is entered into, conduct enhanced ongoing monitoring of the relationship.

14(5) In paragraph (4), **"a politically exposed person"** means a person who is–

(a)   an individual who is or has, at any time in the preceding year, been entrusted with a prominent public function by–

     (i)   a state other than the United Kingdom;

     (ii)   a Community institution; or

     (iii)   an international body,

     including a person who falls in any of the categories listed in paragraph 4(1)(a) of Schedule 2;

(b)   an immediate family member of a person referred to in sub-paragraph (a), including a person who falls in any of the categories listed in paragraph 4(1)(c) of Schedule 2; or

(c)   a known close associate of a person referred to in sub-paragraph (a), including a person who falls in either of the categories listed in paragraph 4(1)(d) of Schedule 2.

14(6) For the purpose of deciding whether a person is a known close associate of a person referred to in paragraph (5)(a), a relevant person need only have regard to information which is in his possession or is publicly known.

BRANCHES AND SUBSIDIARIES

15(1) A credit or financial institution must require its branches and subsidiary undertakings which are located in a non-EEA state to apply, to the extent permitted by the law of that state, measures at least equivalent to those set out in these Regulations with regard to customer due diligence measures, ongoing monitoring and record-keeping.

15(2) Where the law of a non-EEA state does not permit the application of such equivalent measures by the branch or subsidiary undertaking located in that state, the credit or financial institution must–

(a)   inform its supervisory authority accordingly; and

(b)   take additional measures to handle effectively the risk of money laundering and terrorist financing.

15(3) In this regulation **"subsidiary undertaking"**–

(a)   except in relation to an incorporated friendly society, has the meaning given by section 1162 of the Companies Act 2006 (parent and subsidiary undertakings) and, in relation to a body corporate in or formed under the law of an EEA state other than the United Kingdom, includes an undertaking which is a subsidiary undertaking within the meaning of any rule of law in force in that state for purposes connected with implementation of the European Council Seventh Company Law Directive 83/349/EEC of 13th June 1983 on consolidated accounts;

(b) in relation to an incorporated friendly society, means a body corporate of which the society has control within the meaning of section 13(9)(a) or (aa) of the Friendly Societies Act 1992 (control of subsidiaries and other bodies corporate).

15(4) Before the entry into force of section 1162 of the Companies Act 2006 the reference to that section in paragraph (3)(a) shall be treated as a reference to section 258 of the Companies Act 1985 (parent and subsidiary undertakings).

SHELL BANKS, ANONYMOUS ACCOUNTS ETC

16(1) A credit institution must not enter into, or continue, a correspondent banking relationship with a shell bank.

16(2) A credit institution must take appropriate measures to ensure that it does not enter into, or continue, a corresponding banking relationship with a bank which is known to permit its accounts to be used by a shell bank.

16(3) A credit or financial institution carrying on business in the United Kingdom must not set up an anonymous account or an anonymous passbook for any new or existing customer.

16(4) As soon as reasonably practicable on or after 15th December 2007 all credit and financial institutions carrying on business in the United Kingdom must apply customer due diligence measures to, and conduct ongoing monitoring of, all anonymous accounts and passbooks in existence on that date and in any event before such accounts or passbooks are used.

16(5) A **"shell bank"** means a credit institution, or an institution engaged in equivalent activities, incorporated in a jurisdiction in which it has no physical presence involving meaningful decision-making and management, and which is not part of a financial conglomerate or third-country financial conglomerate.

16(6) In this regulation, **"financial conglomerate"** and **"third-country financial conglomerate"** have the meanings given by regulations 1(2) and 7(1) respectively of the Financial Conglomerates and Other Financial Groups Regulations 2004.

RELIANCE

17(1) A relevant person may rely on a person who falls within paragraph (2) (or who the relevant person has reasonable grounds to believe falls within paragraph (2)) to apply any customer due diligence measures provided that—

(a) the other person consents to being relied on; and

(b) notwithstanding the relevant person's reliance on the other person, the relevant person remains liable for any failure to apply such measures.

17(2) The persons are—

(a) a credit or financial institution which is an authorised person;

(aa) [omitted by SI 2013/1881, art. 28 and Schedule, para. 31(3);]

(b) a relevant person who is—

    (i) an auditor, insolvency practitioner, external accountant, tax adviser or independent legal professional; and

    (ii) supervised for the purposes of these Regulations by one of the bodies listed in Schedule 3;

(c) a person who carries on business in another EEA state who is—

    (i) a credit or financial institution, auditor, insolvency practitioner, external accountant, tax adviser or independent legal professional;

    (ii) subject to mandatory professional registration recognised by law; and

    (iii) supervised for compliance with the requirements laid down in the money laundering directive in accordance with section 2 of Chapter V of that directive; or

(d) a person who carries on business in a non-EEA state who is—

    (i) a credit or financial institution (or equivalent institution), auditor, insolvency practitioner, external accountant, tax adviser or independent legal professional;

    (ii) subject to mandatory professional registration recognised by law;

(iii)   subject to requirements equivalent to those laid down in the money laundering directive; and

(iv)   supervised for compliance with those requirements in a manner equivalent to section 2 of Chapter V of the money laundering directive.

17(3)   In paragraph (2)(c)(i) and (d)(i), **"auditor"** and **"insolvency practitioner"** includes a person situated in another EEA state or a non-EEA state who provides services equivalent to the services provided by an auditor or insolvency practitioner.

17(4)   Nothing in this regulation prevents a relevant person applying customer due diligence measures by means of an outsourcing service provider or agent provided that the relevant person remains liable for any failure to apply such measures.

17(5)   In this regulation, **"financial institution"** excludes—

(a)   any money service business;

(b)   any authorised payment institution, EEA authorised payment institution or small payment institution (within the meaning of the Payment Services Regulations 2009) which provides payment services mainly falling within paragraph 1(f) of Schedule 1 to those Regulations; and

(c)   any electronic money institution or EEA authorised electronic money institution (within the meaning of the Electronic Money Regulations 2011) which provides payment services mainly falling within paragraph 1(f) of Schedule 1 to the Payment Services Regulations 2009.

History – Reg. 17(2)(aa) omitted by SI 2013/1881, art. 28 and Schedule, para. 31(3), with effect from 1 April 2014.
Reg. 17(2)(aa) inserted by SI 2012/2298, reg. 5(a), with effect from 1 October 2012.
In reg. 17(2)(b)(ii), the words "Part 1 of" omitted by SI 2012/2298, reg. 5(b), with effect from 1 October 2012.
Reg. 17(5)(c) (and the "and" preceding it) inserted by SI 2011/99, reg. 79 and Sch. 4, para. 19(d), with effect from 30 April 2011.
Reg. 17(5) substituted by SI 2009/209, reg. 126 and Sch. 6, para. 6(b), with effect from 1 November 2009.

DIRECTIONS WHERE FINANCIAL ACTION TASK FORCE APPLIES COUNTERMEASURES

18   [Omitted by SI 2012/2298, reg. 6.]

History – Reg. 18 omitted by SI 2012/2298, reg. 6, with effect from 1 October 2012. Former reg. 18 read as follows:
"**18**   The Treasury may direct any relevant person–
        (a)   not to enter into a business relationship;
        (b)   not to carry out an occasional transaction; or
        (c)   not to proceed any further with a business relationship or occasional transaction,
with a person who is situated or incorporated in a non-EEA state to which the Financial Action Task Force has decided to apply counter-measures.".

PART 3 – RECORD-KEEPING, PROCEDURES AND TRAINING

RECORD-KEEPING

19(1)   Subject to paragraph (4), a relevant person must keep the records specified in paragraph (2) for at least the period specified in paragraph (3).

19(2)   The records are–

(a)   a copy of, or the references to, the evidence of the customer's identity obtained pursuant to regulation 7, 8, 10, 14 or 16(4);

(b)   the supporting records (consisting of the original documents or copies) in respect of a business relationship or occasional transaction which is the subject of customer due diligence measures or ongoing monitoring.

19(3)   The period is five years beginning on–

(a)   in the case of the records specified in paragraph (2)(a), the date on which—

        (i)   the occasional transaction is completed; or

        (ii)   the business relationship ends; or

(b)   in the case of the records specified in paragraph (2)(b)–

        (i)   where the records relate to a particular transaction, the date on which the transaction is completed;

        (ii)   for all other records, the date on which the business relationship ends.

19(4) A relevant person who is relied on by another person must keep the records specified in paragraph (2)(a) for five years beginning on the date on which he is relied on for the purposes of regulation 7, 10, 14 or 16(4) in relation to any business relationship or occasional transaction.

19(5) A person referred to in regulation 17(2)(a) or (b) who is relied on by a relevant person must, if requested by the person relying on him within the period referred to in paragraph (4)–

(a) as soon as reasonably practicable make available to the person who is relying on him any information about the customer (and any beneficial owner) which he obtained when applying customer due diligence measures; and

(b) as soon as reasonably practicable forward to the person who is relying on him copies of any identification and verification data and other relevant documents on the identity of the customer (and any beneficial owner) which he obtained when applying those measures.

19(6) A relevant person who relies on a person referred to in regulation 17(2)(c) or (d) (a "third party") to apply customer due diligence measures must take steps to ensure that the third party will, if requested by the relevant person within the period referred to in paragraph (4)–

(a) as soon as reasonably practicable make available to him any information about the customer (and any beneficial owner) which the third party obtained when applying customer due diligence measures; and

(b) as soon as reasonably practicable forward to him copies of any identification and verification data and other relevant documents on the identity of the customer (and any beneficial owner) which the third party obtained when applying those measures.

19(7) Paragraphs (5) and (6) do not apply where a relevant person applies customer due diligence measures by means of an outsourcing service provider or agent.

19(8) For the purposes of this regulation, a person relies on another person where he does so in accordance with regulation 17(1).

POLICIES AND PROCEDURES

20(1) A relevant person must establish and maintain appropriate and risk-sensitive policies and procedures relating to–

(a) customer due diligence measures and ongoing monitoring;

(b) reporting;

(c) record-keeping;

(d) internal control;

(e) risk assessment and management;

(f) the monitoring and management of compliance with, and the internal communication of, such policies and procedures,

in order to prevent activities related to money laundering and terrorist financing.

20(2) The policies and procedures referred to in paragraph (1) include policies and procedures–

(a) which provide for the identification and scrutiny of–

(i) complex or unusually large transactions;

(ii) unusual patterns of transactions which have no apparent economic or visible lawful purpose; and

(iii) any other activity which the relevant person regards as particularly likely by its nature to be related to money laundering or terrorist financing;

(b) which specify the taking of additional measures, where appropriate, to prevent the use for money laundering or terrorist financing of products and transactions which might favour anonymity;

(c) to determine whether a customer is a politically exposed person;

(d) under which–

(i) an individual in the relevant person's organisation is a nominated officer under Part 7 of the Proceeds of Crime Act 2002 and Part 3 of the Terrorism Act 2000;

(ii) anyone in the organisation to whom information or other matter comes in the course of the business as a result of which he knows or suspects or has reasonable grounds for knowing or suspecting that a person is engaged in money laundering or terrorist financing is required to comply with Part 7 of the Proceeds of Crime Act 2002 or, as the case may be, Part 3 of the Terrorism Act 2000; and

(iii) where a disclosure is made to the nominated officer, he must consider it in the light of any relevant information which is available to the relevant person and determine whether it gives rise to knowledge or suspicion or reasonable grounds for knowledge or suspicion that a person is engaged in money laundering or terrorist financing.

20(3) Paragraph (2)(d) does not apply where the relevant person is an individual who neither employs nor acts in association with any other person.

20(4) A credit or financial institution and an auction platform must establish and maintain systems which enable it to respond fully and rapidly to enquiries from financial investigators accredited under section 3 of the Proceeds of Crime Act 2002 (accreditation and training), persons acting on behalf of the Scottish Ministers in their capacity as an enforcement authority under that Act, officers of Revenue and Customs or constables as to–

(a) whether it maintains, or has maintained during the previous five years, a business relationship with any person; and

(b) the nature of that relationship.

20(5) A credit or financial institution and an auction platform must communicate where relevant the policies and procedures which it establishes and maintains in accordance with this regulation to its branches and subsidiary undertakings which are located outside the United Kingdom.

20(5A) A relevant person who is an issuer of electronic money must appoint an individual to monitor and manage compliance with, and the internal communication of, the policies and procedures relating to the matters referred to in paragraph (1)(a) to (e), and in particular to–

(a) identify any situations of higher risk of money laundering or terrorist financing;

(b) maintain a record of its policies and procedures, risk assessment and risk management including the application of such policies and procedures;

(c) apply measures to ensure that such policies and procedures are taken into account in all relevant functions including in the development of new products, dealing with new customers and in changes to business activities; and

(d) provide information to senior management about the operation and effectiveness of such policies and procedures at least annually.

20(6) In this regulation–

"politically exposed person" has the same meaning as in regulation 14(4);

"subsidiary undertaking" has the same meaning as in regulation 15.

History – In reg. 20(4) and (5), the words "and an auction platform" inserted by SI 2011/2699, reg. 4, with effect from 12 December 2011.
Reg. 20(5A) inserted by SI 2011/99, reg. 79 and Sch. 4, para. 19(e), with effect from 30 April 2011.

TRAINING

21 A relevant person must take appropriate measures so that all relevant employees of his are–

(a) made aware of the law relating to money laundering and terrorist financing; and

(b) regularly given training in how to recognise and deal with transactions and other activities which may be related to money laundering or terrorist financing.

PART 4 – SUPERVISION AND REGISTRATION

INTERPRETATION

INTERPRETATION

22(1) In this Part–

"Annex I financial institution" means any undertaking which falls within regulation 3(3)(a) other than–

(a) [omitted by SI 2013/1881, art. 28 and Schedule, para. 31(4)(a);]

(b) a money service business;

(c) an authorised person;

(d) a bill payment service provider; or

(e) a telecommunication, digital and IT payment service provider;

"**recognised investment exchange**" has the same meaning as in section 285 of the 2000 Act (exemption for recognised investment exchanges and clearing houses).

22(2)   [Omitted by SI 2013/1881, art. 28 and Schedule, para. 31(4)(b).]

History – In reg. 22(1), in the definition of "Annex 1 financial institution", para. (a) omitted by SI 2013/1881, art. 28 and Schedule, para. 31(4)(a), with effect from 1 April 2014.
Reg. 22(1), in the definition of "Annex I financial institution", para. (d) and (e) inserted (and the "or" at the end of para. (b) omitted) by SI 2009/209, reg. 126 and Sch. 6, para. 6(c)(i), with effect from 1 November 2009.
In reg. 22(1), definition of "consumer credit financial institution" omitted by SI 2013/1881, art. 28 and Schedule, para. 31(4)(a), with effect from 1 April 2014.
Reg. 22(1), in the definition of "consumer credit financial institution", para. (d) and (e) inserted (and the "or" at the end of para. (b) omitted) by SI 2009/209, reg. 126 and Sch. 6, para. 6(c)(ii), with effect from 1 November 2009.
In reg. 22(1), the definition of "recognised investment exchange" inserted by SI 2012/2298, reg. 7, with effect from 1 October 2012.
Reg. 22(2) omitted by SI 2013/1881, art. 28 and Schedule, para. 31(4)(b), with effect from 1 April 2014.

SUPERVISION

SUPERVISORY AUTHORITIES

23(1)   Subject to paragraph (2), the following bodies are supervisory authorities–

(a)   the Authority is the supervisory authority for–

     (i)   credit and financial institutions which are authorised persons but not excluded money service businesses;

     (ii)   trust or company service providers which are authorised persons;

     (iii)   Annex I financial institutions;

     (iv)   electronic money institutions;

     (v)   auction platforms;

     (vi)   credit unions in Northern Ireland;

     (vii)   recognised investment exchanges;

(b)   [omitted by SI 2013/1881, art. 28 and Schedule, para. 31(5)(a);]

(c)   each of the professional bodies listed in Schedule 3 is the supervisory authority for relevant persons who are regulated by it;

(d)   the Commissioners are the supervisory authority for–

     (i)   high value dealers;

     (ii)   money service businesses which are not supervised by the Authority;

     (iii)   trust or company service providers which are not supervised by the Authority or one of the bodies listed in Schedule 3;

     (iv)   auditors, external accountants and tax advisers who are not supervised by one of the bodies listed in Schedule 3.

     (v)   bill payment service providers which are not supervised by the Authority;

     (vi)   telecommunication, digital and IT payment service providers which are not supervised by the Authority;

(e)   the Gambling Commission is the supervisory authority for casinos;

(f)   DETI is the supervisory authority for–

     (i)   [omitted by SI 2011/2833, reg. 2(a)(i).]

     (ii)   insolvency practitioners authorised by it under article 351 of the Insolvency (Northern Ireland) Order 1989;

(g)   the Secretary of State is the supervisory authority for insolvency practitioners authorised by him under section 393 of the Insolvency Act 1986 (grant, refusal and withdrawal of authorisation).

23(2)   Where under paragraph (1) there is more than one supervisory authority for a relevant person, the supervisory authorities may agree that one of them will act as the supervisory authority for that person.

23(3)   Where an agreement has been made under paragraph (2), the authority which has agreed to act as the supervisory authority must notify the relevant person or publish the agreement in such manner as it considers appropriate.

23(4)   Where no agreement has been made under paragraph (2), the supervisory authorities for a relevant person must cooperate in the performance of their functions under these Regulations.

23(5) For the purposes of this regulation, a money service business is an **"excluded money service business"** if it is an authorised person who has permission under the 2000 Act which relates to or is connected with a contract of the kind mentioned in paragraph 23 or paragraph 23B of Schedule 2 to that Act (credit agreements and contracts for hire of goods) but does not have permission to carry on any other kind of regulated activity.

23(6) Paragraph (5) must be read with—

(a)   section 22 of the 2000 Act,

(b)   any relevant order under that section, and

(c)   Schedule 2 to that Act.

History – In reg. 23(1)(a)(i), the words "but not excluded money service businesses" inserted at the end by SI 2013/1881, art. 28 and Schedule, para. 31(5)(a), with effect from 1 April 2014.
Reg. 23(1)(a)(iv) inserted by SI 2011/99, reg. 79 and Sch. 4, para. 19(f), with effect from 30 April 2011.
Reg. 23(1)(a)(v) inserted by SI 2011/2699, reg. 5, with effect from 12 December 2011.
Reg. 23(1)(a)(vi) inserted by SI 2011/2833, reg. 2(a)(i), with effect from 31 March 2012.
Reg. 23(1)(a)(vii) inserted by SI 2012/2298, reg. 8, with effect from 1 October 2012.
Reg. 23(1)(b) omitted by SI 2013/1881, art. 28 and Schedule, para. 31(5)(a), with effect from 1 April 2014.
Reg. 23(1)(d)(v) and (vi) inserted by SI 2009/209, reg. 126 and Sch. 6, para. 6(d), with effect from 1 November 2009.
Reg. 23(1)(f)(i) omitted by SI 2011/2833, reg. 2(a)(ii), with effect from 31 March 2012.
Reg. 23(5) and (6) inserted by SI 2013/1881, art. 28 and Schedule, para. 31(5)(b), with effect from 1 April 2014.

DUTIES OF SUPERVISORY AUTHORITIES

24(1) A supervisory authority must effectively monitor the relevant persons for whom it is the supervisory authority and take necessary measures for the purpose of securing compliance by such persons with the requirements of these Regulations.

24(1A) The Authority, when carrying out its supervisory functions in relation to an auction platform—

(a)   must effectively monitor the auction platform's compliance with—

    (i)   the customer due diligence requirements of Articles 19 and 20(6) of the emission allowance auctioning regulation;

    (ii)   the monitoring and record keeping requirements of Article 54 of the emission allowance auctioning regulation; and

    (iii)   the notification requirements of Article 55(2) and (3) of the emission allowance auctioning regulation; and

(b)   may monitor the auction platform's compliance with regulations 20 and 21 of these Regulations.

24(2) A supervisory authority which, in the course of carrying out any of its functions under these Regulations, knows or suspects that a person is or has engaged in money laundering or terrorist financing must promptly inform the Serious Organised Crime Agency.

24(3) A disclosure made under paragraph (2) is not to be taken to breach any restriction, however imposed, on the disclosure of information.

24(4) The functions of the Authority under these Regulations shall be treated for the purposes of Parts 1, 2 and 4 of Schedule 1 to the 2000 Act (the Financial Services Authority) as functions conferred on the Authority under that Act.

History – Reg. 24(1A) inserted by SI 2011/2699, reg. 6, with effect from 12 December 2011.

DISCLOSURE BY SUPERVISORY AUTHORITIES

24A(1) A supervisory authority may disclose to another supervisory authority information it holds relevant to its functions under these Regulations, provided the disclosure is made for purposes connected with the effective exercise of the functions of either supervisory authority under these Regulations.

24A(2) Information disclosed to a supervisory authority under paragraph (1) may not be further disclosed by that authority, except—

(a)   in accordance with paragraph (1);

(b)   with a view to the institution of, or otherwise for the purposes of, any criminal or other enforcement proceedings; or

(c)   as otherwise required by law.

History – Reg. 24A (and the heading before it) inserted by SI 2012/2298, reg. 9, with effect from 1 October 2012.

REGISTRATION OF HIGH VALUE DEALERS, MONEY SERVICE BUSINESSES AND TRUST OR COMPANY SERVICE PROVIDERS

DUTY TO MAINTAIN REGISTERS

25(1) The Commissioners must maintain registers of–

(a) high value dealers;

(b) money service businesses for which they are the supervisory authority;

(c) trust or company service providers for which they are the supervisory authority;

(d) bill payment service providers for which they are the supervisory authority; and

(e) telecommunication, digital and IT payment service providers for which they are the supervisory authority.

25(2) The Commissioners may keep the registers in any form they think fit.

25(3) The Commissioners may publish or make available for public inspection all or part of a register maintained under this regulation.

History – Reg. 25(1)(d) and (e) inserted (and the "and" at the end of reg. 25(1)(b) omitted) by SI 2009/209, reg. 126 and Sch. 6, para. 6(e), with effect from 1 November 2009.

REQUIREMENT TO BE REGISTERED

26(1) A person in respect of whom the Commissioners are required to maintain a register under regulation 25 must not act as a–

(a) high value dealer;

(b) money service business;

(c) trust or company service provider;

(d) bill payment service provider; or

(e) telecommunication, digital and IT payment service provider,

unless he is included in the register.

26(2) Paragraph (1) and regulation 29 are subject to the transitional provisions set out in regulation 50.

History – Reg. 26(1)(d) and (e) inserted (and the "or" at the end of reg. 26(1)(b) omitted) by SI 2009/209, reg. 126 and Sch. 6, para. 6(f), with effect from 1 November 2009.

APPLICATIONS FOR REGISTRATION IN A REGISTER MAINTAINED UNDER REGULATION 25

27(1) An applicant for registration in a register maintained under regulation 25 must make an application in such manner and provide such information as the Commissioners may specify.

27(2) The information which the Commissioners may specify includes–

(a) the applicant's name and (if different) the name of the business;

(b) the nature of the business;

(c) the name of the nominated officer (if any);

(d) in relation to a money service business or trust or company service provider–

    (i) the name of any person who effectively directs or will direct the business and any beneficial owner of the business; and

    (ii) information needed by the Commissioners to decide whether they must refuse the application pursuant to regulation 28.

27(3) At any time after receiving an application and before determining it, the Commissioners may require the applicant to provide, within 21 days beginning with the date of being requested to do so, such further information as they reasonably consider necessary to enable them to determine the application.

27(4) If at any time after the applicant has provided the Commissioners with any information under paragraph (1) or (3)–

(a) there is a material change affecting any matter contained in that information; or

(b) it becomes apparent to that person that the information contains a significant inaccuracy,

he must provide the Commissioners with details of the change or, as the case may be, a correction of the inaccuracy within 30 days beginning with the date of the occurrence of the change (or the discovery of the inaccuracy) or within such later time as may be agreed with the Commissioners.

27(5) The obligation in paragraph (4) applies also to material changes or significant inaccuracies affecting any matter contained in any supplementary information provided pursuant to that paragraph.

27(6) Any information to be provided to the Commissioners under this regulation must be in such form or verified in such manner as they may specify.

FIT AND PROPER TEST

28(1) The Commissioners must refuse to register an applicant as a money service business or trust or company service provider if they are satisfied that—

(a)   the applicant;

(b)   a person who effectively directs, or will effectively direct, the business or service provider;

(c)   a beneficial owner of the business or service provider; or

(d)   the nominated officer of the business or service provider,

is not a fit and proper person with regard to the risk of money laundering or terrorist financing.

28(2) [Omitted by SI 2012/2298, reg. 10(b).]

28(3) [Omitted by SI 2012/2298, reg. 10(b).]

History – In reg. 28(1), the words "with regard to the risk of money laundering or terrorist financing" inserted by SI 2012/2298, reg. 10(a), with effect from 1 October 2012.
Reg. 28(2) and (3) omitted by SI 2012/2298, reg. 10(b), with effect from 1 October 2012.

DETERMINATION OF APPLICATIONS UNDER REGULATION 27

29(1) Subject to regulation 28, the Commissioners may refuse to register an applicant for registration in a register maintained under regulation 25 only if—

(a)   any requirement of, or imposed under, regulation 27 has not been complied with;

(b)   it appears to the Commissioners that any information provided pursuant to regulation 27 is false or misleading in a material particular; or

(c)   the applicant has failed to pay a charge imposed by them under regulation 35(1).

29(2) The Commissioners must within 45 days beginning either with the date on which they receive the application or, where applicable, with the date on which they receive any further information required under regulation 27(3), give the applicant notice of—

(a)   their decision to register the applicant; or

(b)   the following matters—

    (i)   their decision not to register the applicant;

    (ii)   the reasons for their decision;

    (iii)   the right to a review under regulation 43A; and

    (iv)   the right to appeal under regulation 43.

29(3) The Commissioners must, as soon as practicable after deciding to register a person, include him in the relevant register.

History – Reg. 29(2)(b)(iii) substituted by SI 2009/56, art. 3(2) and Sch. 2, para. 169(2), operative from 1 April 2009 subject to transitional and saving provisions in SI 2009/56, Sch. 3. Former reg. 29(2)(b)(iiii) read as follows:
    "(iii)   the right to require a review under regulation 43; and".
In reg. 29(2)(b)(iv), "43" substituted for "44(1)(a)" by SI 2009/56, art. 3(2) and Sch. 2, para. 169(3), operative from 1 April 2009 subject to transitional and saving provisions in SI 2009/56, Sch. 3.

CANCELLATION OF REGISTRATION IN A REGISTER MAINTAINED UNDER REGULATION 25

30(1) The Commissioners must cancel the registration of a money service business or trust or company service provider in a register maintained under regulation 25(1) if, at any time after registration, they are satisfied that he or any person mentioned in regulation 28(1)(b), (c) or (d) is not a fit and proper person within the meaning of regulation 28.

30(2) The Commissioners may cancel a person's registration in a register maintained by them under regulation 25 if, at any time after registration—

(a)   it appears to them that that any condition in regulation 29(1) is met; or

(b)   the person has failed to comply with any requirement of a notice given under regulation 37.

30(3) Where the Commissioners decide to cancel a person's registration they must give him notice of—

(a)   their decision and, subject to paragraph (4), the date from which the cancellation takes effect;

(b)   the reasons for their decision;

(c)   the right to a review under regulation 43A; and

(d)   the right to appeal under regulation 43

30(4)   If the Commissioners—

(a)   consider that the interests of the public require the cancellation of a person's registration to have immediate effect; and

(b)   include a statement to that effect and the reasons for it in the notice given under paragraph (3),

the cancellation takes effect when the notice is given to the person.

History – In reg. 30(1), "28" substituted for "28(2)" by SI 2012/2298, reg. 11(a), with effect from 1 October 2012.
Reg. 30(2) substituted by SI 2012/2298, reg. 11(b), with effect from 1 October 2012.
Reg. 30(3)(c) substituted by SI 2009/56, art. 3(2) and Sch. 2, para. 170(2), operative from 1 April 2009 subject to transitional and saving provisions in SI 2009/56, Sch. 3. Former reg. 30(3)(c) read as follows:
    "(c)   the right to require a review under regulation 43; and".
In reg. 30(3)(d), "43" substituted for "44(1)(a)" by SI 2009/56, art. 3(2) and Sch. 2, para. 170(3), operative from 1 April 2009 subject to transitional and saving provisions in SI 2009/56, Sch. 3.

REQUIREMENT TO INFORM THE AUTHORITY

REQUIREMENT ON AUTHORISED PERSON TO INFORM THE AUTHORITY

31(1)   An authorised person whose supervisory authority is the Authority must, before acting as a money service business or a trust or company service provider or within 28 days of so doing, inform the Authority that he intends, or has begun, to act as such.

31(2)   Paragraph (1) does not apply to an authorised person who—

(a)   immediately before 15th December 2007 was acting as a money service business or a trust or company service provider and continues to act as such after that date; and

(b)   before 15th January 2008 informs the Authority that he is or was acting as such.

31(3)   Where an authorised person whose supervisory authority is the Authority ceases to act as a money service business or a trust or company service provider, he must immediately inform the Authority.

31(4)   Any requirement imposed by this regulation is to be treated as if it were a requirement imposed by or under the 2000 Act.

31(5)   Any information to be provided to the Authority under this regulation must be in such form or verified in such manner as it may specify.

REGISTRATION OF ANNEX I FINANCIAL INSTITUTIONS, ESTATE AGENTS, ETC.

POWER TO MAINTAIN REGISTERS

32(1)   The supervisory authorities mentioned in paragraph (2), (3) or (4) may, in order to fulfil their duties under regulation 24, maintain a register under this regulation.

32(2)   The Authority may maintain a register of Annex I financial institutions.

32(3)   [Omitted by SI 2013/1881, art. 28 and Schedule, para. 31(6).]

32(4)   The Commissioners may maintain registers of—

(a)   auditors;

(b)   external accountants; and

(c)   tax advisers,

who are not supervised by the Secretary of State, DETI or any of the professional bodies listed in Schedule 3.

32(5)   Where a supervisory authority decides to maintain a register under this regulation, it must take reasonable steps to bring its decision to the attention of those relevant persons in respect of whom the register is to be established.

32(6)   A supervisory authority may keep a register under this regulation in any form it thinks fit.

32(7)   A supervisory authority may publish or make available to public inspection all or part of a register maintained by it under this regulation.

History – Reg. 32(3) omitted by SI 2013/1881, art. 28 and Schedule, para. 31(6), with effect from 1 April 2014.

REQUIREMENT TO BE REGISTERED

33   Where a supervisory authority decides to maintain a register under regulation 32 in respect of any description of relevant persons and establishes a register for that purpose, a relevant person of that description may not carry on the business or profession in question for a period of more than six months beginning on the date on which the supervisory authority establishes the register unless he is included in the register.

APPLICATIONS FOR AND CANCELLATION OF REGISTRATION IN A REGISTER MAINTAINED UNDER REGULATION 32

34(1) Regulations 27, 29 (with the omission of the words "Subject to regulation 28" in regulation 29(1)) and 30(2), (3) and (4) apply to registration in a register maintained by the Commissioners under regulation 32 as they apply to registration in a register maintained under regulation 25.

34(2) Regulation 27 applies to registration in a register maintained by the Authority under regulation 32 as it applies to registration in a register maintained under regulation 25 and, for this purpose, references to the Commissioners are to be treated as references to the Authority.

34(3) The Authority may refuse to register an applicant for registration in a register maintained under regulation 32 only if—

(a)   any requirement of, or imposed under, regulation 27 has not been complied with;

(b)   it appears to the Authority that any information provided pursuant to regulation 27 is false or misleading in a material particular; or

(c)   the applicant has failed to pay a charge imposed by the Authority under regulation 35(1).

34(4) The Authority must, within 45 days beginning either with the date on which it receives an application or, where applicable, with the date on which it receives any further information required under regulation 27(3), give the applicant notice of—

(a)   its decision to register the applicant; or

(b)   the following matters—

     (i)   that it is minded not to register the applicant;

     (ii)   the reasons for being minded not to register him; and

     (iii)   the right to make representations to it within a specified period (which may not be less than 28 days).

34(5) The Authority must then decide, within a reasonable period, whether to register the applicant and it must give the applicant notice of—

(a)   its decision to register the applicant; or

(b)   the following matters—

     (i)   its decision not to register the applicant;

     (ii)   the reasons for its decision; and

     (iii)   the right to appeal under regulation 44(1)(b).

34(6) The Authority must, as soon as reasonably practicable after deciding to register a person, include him in the relevant register.

34(7) The Authority may cancel a person's registration in a register maintained by them under regulation 32 if, at any time after registration—

(a)   it appears to them that any condition in paragraph (3) is met; or

(b)   the person has failed to comply with any requirement of a notice given under regulation 37.

34(8) Where the Authority proposes to cancel a person's registration, it must give him notice of—

(a)   its proposal to cancel his registration;

(b)   the reasons for the proposed cancellation; and

(c)   the right to make representations to it within a specified period (which may not be less than 28 days).

34(9) The Authority must then decide, within a reasonable period, whether to cancel the person's registration and it must give him notice of—

(a)   its decision not to cancel his registration; or

(b)   the following matters—

     (i)   its decision to cancel his registration and, subject to paragraph (10), the date from which cancellation takes effect;

     (ii)   the reasons for its decision; and

     (iii)   the right to appeal under regulation 44(1)(b).

34(10) If the Authority—

(a)   considers that the interests of the public require the cancellation of a person's registration to have immediate effect; and

Statutory Instruments

(b)   includes a statement to that effect and the reasons for it in the notice given under paragraph (9)(b),

the cancellation takes effect when the notice is given to the person.

34(11)   In paragraphs (3) and (4), references to regulation 27 are to be treated as references to that paragraph as applied by paragraph (2) of this regulation.

History – In reg. 34(2), the words "or the OFT" and the words "or the OFT, as the case may be,", which appeared after the word "Authority" (in the first and second place respectively), omitted by SI 2013/1881, art. 28 and Schedule, para. 31(7), with effect from 1 April 2014.
In reg. 34(3), the words "and the OFT", which appeared after the word "Authority" (in the first place it appears), omitted by SI 2013/1881, art. 28 and Schedule, para. 31(7)(b), with effect from 1 April 2014.
In reg. 34(3)(b) and (c), the words "or the OFT, as the case may be,", which appeared after the word "Authority", omitted by SI 2013/1881, art. 28 and Schedule, para. 31(7)(c), with effect from 1 April 2014.
In reg. 34(4), (5) and (6), the words "or the OFT, as the case may be,", which appeared after the word "Authority", omitted by SI 2013/1881, art. 28 and Schedule, para. 31(7)(c), with effect from 1 April 2014.
In reg. 34(7), the words "or the OFT", which appeared after the word "Authority", omitted by SI 2013/1881, art. 28 and Schedule, para. 31(7)(a), with effect from 1 April 2014.
Reg. 34(7) substituted by SI 2012/2298, reg. 12, with effect from 1 October 2012.
In reg. 34(8), the words "or the OFT", which appeared after the word "Authority", omitted by SI 2013/1881, art. 28 and Schedule, para. 31(7)(a), with effect from 1 April 2014.
In reg. 34(9) and (10), the words "or the OFT, as the case may be,", which appeared after the word "Authority", omitted by SI 2013/1881, art. 28 and Schedule, para. 31(7)(c), with effect from 1 April 2014.

FINANCIAL PROVISIONS

COSTS OF SUPERVISION

35(1)   The Authority and the Commissioners may impose charges–

(a)   on applicants for registration;

(b)   on relevant persons supervised by them.

35(2)   Charges levied under paragraph (1) must not exceed such amount as the Authority, the OFT or the Commissioners (as the case may be) consider will enable them to meet any expenses reasonably incurred by them in carrying out their functions under these Regulations or for any incidental purpose.

35(3)   Without prejudice to the generality of paragraph (2), a charge may be levied in respect of each of the premises at which a person carries on (or proposes to carry on) business.

35(4)   The Authority must pay to the Treasury any amounts received by the Financial Services Authority during the financial year beginning with 1st April 2012 year by way of penalties imposed under regulation 42 after deducting any amounts the Financial Services Authority has, prior to 1st April 2013, applied towards expenses incurred by it in carrying out its functions under these Regulations or for any incidental purpose.

35(4A)   The Authority must in respect of the financial year beginning with 1st April 2013 and each subsequent financial year pay to the Treasury any amounts received by it during the year by way of penalties imposed under regulation 42.

35(4B)   The Treasury may give directions to the Authority as to how the Authority is to comply with its duties under paragraphs (4) and (4A).

35(4C)   The directions may in particular–

(a)   specify the time when any payment is required to be made to the Treasury, and

(b)   require the Authority to provide the Treasury at specified times with information relating to penalties that the Authority has imposed under regulation 42.

35(4D)   The Treasury must pay into the Consolidated Fund any sums received by them under this regulation.

35(5)   In paragraph (2), **"expenses"** in relation to the Authority includes expenses incurred by a local weights and measures authority or DETI pursuant to arrangements made for the purposes of these Regulations with the Authority–

(a)   by or on behalf of the authority; or

(b)   by DETI.

History – In reg. 35(1) and (2), the words ", the OFT", which appeared after the word "Authority", omitted by SI 2013/1881, art. 28 and Schedule, para. 31(8)(a), with effect from 1 April 2014.
Reg. 35(4) to (4D) substituted for (4) by SI 2013/429, reg. 2(1), with effect from 1 April 2013.
In reg. 35(5), the word "Authority" substituted for the word "OFT", in each place, by SI 2013/1881, art. 28 and Schedule, para. 31(8)(b), with effect from 1 April 2014.

PART 5 – ENFORCEMENT

POWERS OF DESIGNATED AUTHORITIES
INTERPRETATION

36   In this Part–

"designated authority" means–

(a)   the Authority; and

(b)   the Commissioners;

(c)   [omitted by SI 2013/1881, art. 28 and Schedule, para. 31(9)(a);]

(d)   [omitted by SI 2011/2833, reg. 2(b);]

"officer", except in regulations 40(3), 41 and 47 means–

(a)   an officer of the Authority, including a member of the Authority's staff or an agent of the Authority;

(b)   an officer of Revenue and Customs; or

(c)   [omitted by SI 2013/1881, art. 28 and Schedule, para. 31(9)(b);]

(d)   a relevant officer;

(e)   [omitted by SI 2011/2833, reg. 2(c);]

"recorded information" includes information recorded in any form and any document of any nature;

"relevant officer" means

(a)   in Great Britain, an officer of a local weights and measures authority;

(b)   in Northern Ireland, an officer of DETI acting pursuant to arrangements made with the Authority for the purposes of these Regulations.

History – In reg. 36, in the definition of "designated authority", para. (c) (and the "and" before it) omitted (and the "and" at the end of (a) inserted) by SI 2013/1881, art. 28 and Schedule, para. 31(9)(a), with effect from 1 April 2014.
In reg. 36, in the definition of "designated authority", para. (d) omitted (and the "and" at the end of para. (c) omitted, and the "and" at the end of para. (b) inserted) by SI 2011/2833, reg. 2(b), with effect from 31 March 2012.
In reg. 36, in the definition of "officer", para. (c) omitted (and the "or" at the end of (b) inserted) by SI 2013/1881, art. 28 and Schedule, para. 31(9)(b), with effect from 1 April 2014.
In reg. 36, in the definition of "officer", para. (e) omitted (and the "or" at the end of para. (d) omitted, and the "or" at the end of para. (c) inserted) by SI 2011/2833, reg. 2(c), with effect from 31 March 2012.
In reg. 36, in the definition of "relevant officer", in para. (b), the word "Authority" substituted for the word "OFT" by SI 2013/1881, art. 28 and Schedule, para. 31(9)(c), with effect from 1 April 2014.

POWER TO REQUIRE INFORMATION FROM, AND ATTENDANCE OF, RELEVANT AND CONNECTED PERSONS

37(1)   An officer may, by notice to a relevant person or to a person connected with a relevant person, require the relevant person or the connected person, as the case may be–

(a)   to provide such information as may be specified in the notice;

(b)   to produce such recorded information as may be so specified; or

(c)   to attend before an officer at a time and place specified in the notice and answer questions.

37(2)   For the purposes of paragraph (1)–

(a)   **"relevant person"** includes a person whom a designated authority believes, or has reasonable grounds to suspect, is or has at any time been a relevant person; and

(b)   a person is connected with a relevant person if the person is, or has at any time been, in relation to the relevant person, a person listed in Schedule 4 to these Regulations.

37(3)   An officer may exercise powers under this regulation only if the information sought to be obtained as a result is reasonably required in connection with the exercise by the designated authority for whom he acts of its functions under these Regulations.

37(4)   Where an officer requires information to be provided or produced pursuant to paragraph (1)(a) or (b)–

(a)   the notice must set out the reasons why the officer requires the information to be provided or produced; and

(b)   such information must be provided or produced–

(i)   before the end of such reasonable period as may be specified in the notice; and

(ii)   at such place as may be so specified.

Statutory Instruments

37(5) In relation to information recorded otherwise than in legible form, the power to require production of it includes a power to require the production of a copy of it in legible form or in a form from which it can readily be produced in visible and legible form.

37(6) The production of a document does not affect any lien which a person has on the document.

37(7) A person may not be required under this regulation to provide or produce information or to answer questions which he would be entitled to refuse to provide, produce or answer on grounds of legal professional privilege in proceedings in the High Court, except that a lawyer may be required to provide the name and address of his client.

37(8) Subject to paragraphs (9) and (10), a statement made by a person in compliance with a requirement imposed on him under paragraph (1)(c) is admissible in evidence in any proceedings, so long as it also complies with any requirements governing the admissibility of evidence in the circumstances in question.

37(9) In criminal proceedings in which a person is charged with an offence to which this paragraph applies—

(a)   no evidence relating to the statement may be adduced; and

(b)   no question relating to it may be asked,

by or on behalf of the prosecution unless evidence relating to it is adduced, or a question relating to it is asked, in the proceedings by or on behalf of that person.

37(10) Paragraph (9) applies to any offence other than one under—

(a)   section 5 of the Perjury Act 1911 (false statements without oath);

(b)   section 44(2) of the Criminal Law (Consolidation) (Scotland) Act 1995 (false statements and declarations); or

(c)   Article 10 of the Perjury (Northern Ireland) Order 1979 (false unsworn statements).

37(11) In the application of this regulation to Scotland, the reference in paragraph (7) to—

(a)   proceedings in the High Court is to be read as a reference to legal proceedings generally; and

(b)   an entitlement on grounds of legal professional privilege is to be read as a reference to an entitlement on the grounds of confidentiality of communications—

(i)   between a professional legal adviser and his client; or

(ii)   made in connection with or in contemplation of legal proceedings and for the purposes of those proceedings.

History – Reg. 37(2) substituted by SI 2012/2298, reg. 13, with effect from 1 October 2012.
In reg. 37(11) the words following "communications" inserted by SI 2007/3299, reg. 2(b), with effect from 15 December 2007.

ENTRY, INSPECTION WITHOUT A WARRANT ETC.

38(1) Where an officer has reasonable cause to believe that any premises are being used by a relevant person in connection with his business or professional activities, he may on producing evidence of his authority at any reasonable time—

(a)   enter the premises;

(b)   inspect the premises;

(c)   observe the carrying on of business or professional activities by the relevant person;

(d)   inspect any recorded information found on the premises;

(e)   require any person on the premises to provide an explanation of any recorded information or to state where it may be found;

(f)   in the case of a money service business or a high value dealer, inspect any cash found on the premises.

38(2) An officer may take copies of, or make extracts from, any recorded information found under paragraph (1).

38(3) Paragraphs (1)(d) and (e) and (2) do not apply to recorded information which the relevant person would be entitled to refuse to disclose on grounds of legal professional privilege in proceedings in the High Court, except that a lawyer may be required to provide the name and address of his client and, for this purpose, regulation 37(11) applies to this paragraph as it applies to regulation 37(7).

38(4) An officer may exercise powers under this regulation only if the information sought to be obtained as a result is reasonably required in connection with the exercise by the designated authority for whom he acts of its functions under these Regulations.

38(5) In this regulation, **"premises"** means any premises other than premises used only as a dwelling.

ENTRY TO PREMISES UNDER WARRANT

39(1)   A justice may issue a warrant under this paragraph if satisfied on information on oath given by an officer that there are reasonable grounds for believing that the first, second or third set of conditions is satisfied.

39(2)   The first set of conditions is–

(a)   that there is on the premises specified in the warrant recorded information in relation to which a requirement could be imposed under regulation 37(1)(b); and

(b)   that if such a requirement were to be imposed–

     (i)   it would not be complied with; or

     (ii)   the recorded information to which it relates would be removed, tampered with or destroyed.

39(3)   The second set of conditions is–

(a)   that a person on whom a requirement has been imposed under regulation 37(1)(b) has failed (wholly or in part) to comply with it; and

(b)   that there is on the premises specified in the warrant recorded information which has been required to be produced.

39(4)   The third set of conditions is–

(a)   that an officer has been obstructed in the exercise of a power under regulation 38; and

(b)   that there is on the premises specified in the warrant recorded information or cash which could be inspected under regulation 38(1)(d) or (f).

39(5)   A justice may issue a warrant under this paragraph if satisfied on information on oath given by an officer that there are reasonable grounds for suspecting that–

(a)   an offence under these Regulations has been, is being or is about to be committed by a relevant person; and

(b)   there is on the premises specified in the warrant recorded information relevant to whether that offence has been, or is being or is about to be committed.

39(6)   A warrant issued under this regulation shall authorise an officer–

(a)   to enter the premises specified in the warrant;

(b)   to search the premises and take possession of any recorded information or anything appearing to be recorded information specified in the warrant or to take, in relation to any such recorded information, any other steps which may appear to be necessary for preserving it or preventing interference with it;

(c)   to take copies of, or extracts from, any recorded information specified in the warrant;

(d)   to require any person on the premises to provide an explanation of any recorded information appearing to be of the kind specified in the warrant or to state where it may be found;

(e)   to use such force as may reasonably be necessary.

39(7)   Where a warrant is issued by a justice under paragraph (1) or (5) on the basis of information on oath given by an officer of the Authority, for "an officer" in paragraph (6) substitute "a constable".

39(8)   In paragraphs (1), (5) and (7), **"justice"** means–

(a)   in relation to England and Wales, a justice of the peace;

(b)   in relation to Scotland, a justice within the meaning of section 307 of the Criminal Procedure (Scotland) Act 1995 (interpretation);

(c)   in relation to Northern Ireland, a lay magistrate.

39(9)   In the application of this regulation to Scotland, the references in paragraphs (1), (5) and (7) to information on oath are to be read as references to evidence on oath.

History – In reg. 39(7) the words "on oath" inserted by SI 2007/3299, reg. 2(c)(i), with effect from 15 December 2007.
In reg. 39(9) the words "(1), (5) and (7)" substituted for "(1) and (5)" by SI 2007/3299, reg. 2(c)(ii), with effect from 15 December 2007.

FAILURE TO COMPLY WITH ENFORCEMENT REQUIREMENT

40(1)   If, on an application made by–

(a)   a designated authority; or

(b)   a local weights and measures authority or DETI pursuant to arrangements made with the Authority–

     (i)   by or on behalf of the authority; or

     (ii)   by DETI,

it appears to the court that a person (the "information defaulter") has failed to do something that he was required to do under regulation 37(1), the court may make an order under this regulation.

40(2)   An order under this regulation may require the information defaulter–

(a)   to do the thing that he failed to do within such period as may be specified in the order;

(b)   otherwise to take such steps to remedy the consequences of the failure as may be so specified.

40(3)   If the information defaulter is a body corporate, a partnership or an unincorporated body of persons which is not a partnership, the order may require any officer of the body corporate, partnership or body, who is (wholly or partly) responsible for the failure to meet such costs of the application as are specified in the order.

40(4)   In this regulation, **"court"** means–

(a)   in England and Wales and Northern Ireland, the High Court or the county court;

(b)   in Scotland, the Court of Session or the sheriff court.

History – In reg. 40(1)(b), the word "Authority" substituted for the word "OFT" by SI 2013/1881, art. 28 and Schedule, para. 31(10), with effect from 1 April 2014.
In reg. 40(4)(b) the word "court" inserted by SI 2007/3299, reg. 2(d), with effect from 15 December 2007.

POWERS OF RELEVANT OFFICERS

41(1)   A relevant officer may only exercise powers under regulations 37 to 39 pursuant to arrangements made with the Authority–

(a)   by or on behalf of the local weights and measures authority of which he is an officer ("his authority"); or

(b)   by DETI.

41(2)   Anything done or omitted to be done by, or in relation to, a relevant officer in the exercise or purported exercise of a power in this Part shall be treated for all purposes as having been done or omitted to be done by, or in relation to, an officer of the Authority.

41(3)   Paragraph (2) does not apply for the purposes of any criminal proceedings brought against the relevant officer, his authority, DETI or the Authority, in respect of anything done or omitted to be done by the officer.

41(4)   A relevant officer shall not disclose to any person other than the Authority and his authority or, as the case may be, DETI information obtained by him in the exercise of such powers unless–

(a)   he has the approval of the Authority to do so; or

(b)   he is under a duty to make the disclosure.

History – In reg. 41, the word "Authority" substituted for the word "OFT" in each place by SI 2013/1881, art. 28 and Schedule, para. 31(11), with effect from 1 April 2014.

CIVIL PENALTIES, REVIEW AND APPEALS

POWER TO IMPOSE CIVIL PENALTIES

42(1)   A designated authority may impose a penalty of such amount as it considers appropriate on a person (except an auction platform) who fails to comply with any requirement in regulation 7(1), (2) or (3), 8(1) or (3), 9(2), 10(1), 11(1), 14(1), 15(1) or (2), 16(1), (2), (3) or (4), 19(1), (4), (5) or (6), 20(1), (4) or (5), 21, 26, 27(4) or 33.

42(1A)   A designated authority may impose a penalty of such amount as it considers appropriate on an auction platform which fails to comply with–

(a)   the customer due diligence requirements of Article 19 or 20(6) of the emission allowance auctioning regulation;

(b)   the monitoring and record keeping requirements of Article 54 of the emission allowance auctioning regulation; or

(c)   regulation 20(1), (4) or (5) or 21 of these Regulations.

42(1B)   A designated authority may impose a penalty of such amount as it considers appropriate on a person who fails to comply with any requirement of a notice given under regulation 37(1).

42(1C)   In paragraphs (1), (1A) and (1B), **"appropriate"** means effective, proportionate and dissuasive.

42(2)   The designated authority must not impose a penalty on a person under paragraph (1), (1A) or (1B) where there are reasonable grounds for it to be satisfied that the person took all reasonable steps and exercised all due diligence to ensure that the requirement would be complied with.

42(3) In deciding whether a person has failed to comply with a requirement of these Regulations, the designated authority must consider whether he followed any relevant guidance which was at the time–

(a) issued by a supervisory authority or any other appropriate body;

(b) approved by the Treasury; and

(c) published in a manner approved by the Treasury as suitable in their opinion to bring the guidance to the attention of persons likely to be affected by it.

42(4) In paragraph (3), an **"appropriate body"** means any body which regulates or is representative of any trade, profession, business or employment carried on by the person.

42(5) Where the Commissioners decide to impose a penalty under this regulation, they must give the person notice of–

(a) their decision to impose the penalty and its amount;

(b) the reasons for imposing the penalty;

(c) the right to a review under regulation 43A; and

(d) the right to appeal under regulation 43.

42(6) Where the Authority or DETI proposes to impose a penalty under this regulation, it must give the person notice of–

(a) its proposal to impose the penalty and the proposed amount;

(b) the reasons for imposing the penalty; and

(c) the right to make representations to it within a specified period (which may not be less than 28 days).

42(7) The Authority or DETI, as the case may be, must then decide, within a reasonable period, whether to impose a penalty under this regulation and it must give the person notice of–

(a) its decision not to impose a penalty; or

(b) the following matters–

    (i) its decision to impose a penalty and the amount;

    (ii) the reasons for its decision; and

    (iii) the right to appeal under regulation 44(1)(b).

42(8) A penalty imposed under this regulation is payable to the designated authority which imposes it.

History – In reg. 42(1), the word "relevant" and the words "or a direction made under regulation 18 and, for this purpose, **"appropriate"** means effective, proportionate and dissuasive" omitted by SI 2012/2298, reg. 14(a), with effect from 1 October 2012.
In reg. 42(1), the words "(except an auction platform)" inserted by SI 2011/2699, reg. 7(a), with effect from 12 December 2011.
In reg. 42(1A), the words "and, for this purpose, "appropriate" means effective, proportionate and dissuasive." omitted by SI 2012/2298, reg. 14(b), with effect from 1 October 2012.
Reg. 42(1A) inserted by SI 2011/2699, reg. 7(b), with effect from 12 December 2011.
Reg. 42(1B) and (1C) inserted by SI 2012/2298, reg. 14(c), with effect from 1 October 2012.
In reg. 42(2), the words ", (1A) or (1B)" substituted for the words "or (1A)" by SI 2012/2298, reg. 14(d), with effect from 1 October 2012.
In reg. 42(2), the words "or (1A)" inserted by SI 2011/2699, reg. 7(c), with effect from 12 December 2011.
In reg. 42(4) the word "person" substituted for "alleged offender" by SI 2007/3299, reg. 2(e), with effect from 15 December 2007.
In reg. 42(5)(c), "43A" substituted for "43" by SI 2009/56, art. 3(2) and Sch. 2, para. 171(2), operative from 1 April 2009 subject to transitional and saving provisions in SI 2009/56, Sch. 3.
In reg. 42(5)(d), "43" substituted for "44(1)(a)" by SI 2009/56, art. 3(2) and Sch. 2, para. 171(3), operative from 1 April 2009 subject to transitional and saving provisions in SI 2009/56, Sch. 3.
In reg. 42(6) and (7), the words ", the OFT" omitted by SI 2013/1881, art. 28 and Schedule, para. 31(12), with effect from 1 April 2014.

APPEALS AGAINST DECISIONS OF THE COMMISSIONERS

43(1) This regulation applies to decisions of the Commissioners made under–

(za) regulation 28, to the effect that a person is not a fit and proper person;

(a) regulation 29, to refuse to register an applicant;

(b) regulation 30, to cancel the registration of a registered person; and

(c) regulation 42, to impose a penalty.

43(2) Any person who is the subject of a decision to which this regulation applies may appeal to the tribunal in accordance with regulation 43F.

43(3) The provisions of Part 5 of the Value Added Tax Act 1994 (appeals), subject to the modifications set out in paragraph 1 of Schedule 5 to these Regulations, apply in respect of appeals to a tribunal made under this regulation as they apply in respect of appeals made to the tribunal under section 83 (appeals) of that Act.

43(4) A tribunal hearing an appeal under paragraph (2) has the power to–

(a) quash or vary any decision of the supervisory authority, including the power to reduce any penalty to such amount (including nil) as it thinks proper, and

(b) substitute its own decision for any decision quashed on appeal.

43(5) The modifications in Schedule 5 have effect for the purposes of appeals made under this regulation.

43(6) For the purposes of appeals under this regulation, the meaning of **"tribunal"** is as defined in section 82 of the Value Added Tax Act 1994.

History – The heading to reg. 43 substituted by SI 2009/56, art. 3(2) and Sch. 2, para. 172(2), operative from 1 April 2009 subject to transitional and saving provisions in SI 2009/56, Sch. 3. The former heading was "Review procedure".
Reg. 43(1)(za) inserted by SI 2012/2298, reg. 15, with effect from 1 October 2012.
In reg. 43(2), the words "appeal to the tribunal in accordance with regulation 43F" substituted for the words "by notice to the Commissioners require them to review that decision" by SI 2009/56, art. 3(2) and Sch. 2, para. 172(3), operative from 1 April 2009 subject to transitional and saving provisions in SI 2009/56, Sch. 3.
Reg. 43(3), (4), (5) and (6) substituted for former reg. 43(3)–(5) by SI 2009/56, art. 3(2) and Sch. 2, para. 172(4), operative from 1 April 2009 subject to transitional and saving provisions in SI 2009/56, Sch. 3. Former reg. 43(3)–(5) read as follows:

> "**43(3)** The Commissioners need not review any decision unless the notice requiring the review is given within 45 days beginning with the date on which they first gave notice of the decision to the person requiring the review.
>
> **43(4)** Where the Commissioners are required under this regulation to review any decision they must either–
> (a) confirm the decision; or
> (b) withdraw or vary the decision and take such further steps (if any) in consequence of the withdrawal or variation as they consider appropriate.
>
> **43(5)** Where the Commissioners do not, within 45 days beginning with the date on which the review was required by a person, give notice to that person of their determination of the review, they are to be taken for the purposes of these Regulations to have confirmed the decision.".

OFFER OF REVIEW

43A(1) The Commissioners must offer a person (P) a review of a decision that has been notified to P if an appeal lies under regulation 43 in respect of the decision.

43A(2) The offer of the review must be made by notice given to P at the same time as the decision is notified to P.

43A(3) This regulation does not apply to the notification of the conclusions of a review.

History – Reg. 43A inserted by SI 2009/56, art. 3(2) and Sch. 2, para. 173, operative from 1 April 2009 subject to transitional and saving provisions in SI 2009/56, Sch. 3.

REVIEW BY THE COMMISSIONERS

43B(1) The Commissioners must review a decision if–

(a) they have offered a review of the decision under regulation 43A, and

(b) P notifies the Commissioners accepting the offer within 30 days from the date of the document containing the notification of the offer.

43B(2) But P may not notify acceptance of the offer if P has already appealed to the tribunal under regulation 43F.

43B(3) The Commissioners shall not review a decision if P has appealed to the tribunal under regulation 43F in respect of the decision.

History – Reg. 43B inserted by SI 2009/56, art. 3(2) and Sch. 2, para. 173, operative from 1 April 2009 subject to transitional and saving provisions in SI 2009/56, Sch. 3.

EXTENSIONS OF TIME

43C(1) If under regulation 43A, the Commissioners have offered P a review of a decision, the Commissioners may within the relevant period notify P that the relevant period is extended.

43C(2) If notice is given the relevant period is extended to the end of 30 days from–

(a) the date of the notice, or

(b) any other date set out in the notice or a further notice.

43C(3) In this regulation **"relevant period"** means–

(a) the period of 30 days referred to in regulation 43B(1)(b), or

(b) if notice has been given under paragraph (1) that period as extended (or as most recently extended) in accordance with paragraph (2).

History – Reg. 43C inserted by SI 2009/56, art. 3(2) and Sch. 2, para. 173, operative from 1 April 2009 subject to transitional and saving provisions in SI 2009/56, Sch. 3.

REVIEW OUT OF TIME

43D(1) This regulation applies if–

(a) the Commissioners have offered a review of a decision under regulation 43A, and

(b)   P does not accept the offer within the time allowed under regulation 43B(1)(b) or 43C(2).

43D(2)   The Commissioners must review the decision under regulation 43B if–

(a)   after the time allowed, P notifies the Commissioners in writing requesting a review out of time,

(b)   the Commissioners are satisfied that P had a reasonable excuse for not accepting the offer or requiring review within the time allowed, and

(c)   the Commissioners are satisfied that P made the request without unreasonable delay after the excuse had ceased to apply.

43D(3)   The Commissioners shall not review a decision if P has appealed to the tribunal under regulation 43F in respect of the decision.

History – Reg. 43D inserted by SI 2009/56, art. 3(2) and Sch. 2, para. 173, operative from 1 April 2009 subject to transitional and saving provisions in SI 2009/56, Sch. 3.

NATURE OF REVIEW ETC

43E(1)   This regulation applies if the Commissioners are required to undertake a review under regulation 43B or 43D.

43E(2)   The nature and extent of the review are to be such as appear appropriate to the Commissioners in the circumstances.

43E(3)   For the purpose of paragraph (2), the Commissioners must, in particular, have regard to steps taken before the beginning of the review–

(a)   by the Commissioners in reaching the decision, and

(b)   by any person in seeking to resolve disagreement about the decision.

43E(4)   The review must take account of any representations made by P at a stage which gives the Commissioners a reasonable opportunity to consider them.

43E(5)   The review may conclude that the decision is to be–

(a)   upheld,

(b)   varied, or

(c)   cancelled.

43E(6)   The Commissioners must give P notice of the conclusions of the review and their reasoning within–

(a)   a period of 45 days beginning with the relevant date, or

(b)   such other period as the Commissioners and P may agree.

43E(7)   In paragraph (6) **"relevant date"** means–

(a)   the date the Commissioners received P's notification accepting the offer of a review (in a case falling within regulation 43A), or

(b)   the date on which the Commissioners decided to undertake the review (in a case falling within 43D).

43E(8)   Where the Commissioners are required to undertake a review but do not give notice of the conclusions within the time period specified in paragraph (6), the review is to be treated as having concluded that the decision is upheld.

43E(9)   If paragraph (8) applies, the Commissioners must notify P of the conclusion which the review is treated as having reached.

History – Reg. 43E inserted by SI 2009/56, art. 3(2) and Sch. 2, para. 173, operative from 1 April 2009 subject to transitional and saving provisions in SI 2009/56, Sch. 3.

BRINGING OF APPEALS AGAINST DECISIONS OF THE COMMISSIONERS

43F(1)   An appeal under regulation 43 is to be made to the tribunal before–

(a)   the end of the period of 30 days beginning with the date of the document notifying the decision to which the appeal relates, or

(b)   if later, the end of the relevant period (within the meaning of regulation 43C).

43F(2)   But that is subject to paragraphs (3) to (5).

43F(3)   In a case where the Commissioners are required to undertake a review under regulation 43B–

(a)   an appeal may not be made until the conclusion date, and

(b)   any appeal is to be made within the period of 30 days beginning with the conclusion date.

43F(4)   In a case where the Commissioners are requested to undertake a review in accordance with regulation 43D–

(a)   an appeal may not be made–

   (i)   unless the Commissioners have notified P as to whether or not a review will be undertaken, and

   (ii)   if the Commissioners have notified P that a review will be undertaken, until the conclusion date;

(b)   any appeal where sub-paragraph (a)(ii) applies is to be made within the period of 30 days beginning with the conclusion date;

(c)   if the Commissioners have notified P that a review will not be undertaken, an appeal may be made only if the tribunal gives permission to do so.

43F(5)   In a case where regulation 43E(8) applies, an appeal may be made at any time from the end of the period specified in regulation 43E(6) to the date 30 days after the conclusion date.

43F(6)   An appeal may be made after the end of the period specified in paragraph (1), (3)(b), (4)(b) or (5) if the tribunal gives permission to do so.

43F(7)   In this regulation **"conclusion date"** means the date of the document notifying the conclusions of the review.

History – Reg. 43F(4) substituted by SI 2014/1264, art. 11, with effect from 1 June 2014 in relation to requests for a review out of time notified to HMRC on or after that date. Former reg. 43F(4) read as follows:

"**43F(4)**   In a case where the Commissioners are requested to undertake a review in accordance with regulation 43D–
  (a)   an appeal may not be made–
      (i)   unless the Commissioners have decided whether or not to undertake a review, and
      (ii)   if the Commissioners decide to undertake a review, until the conclusion date; and
  (b)   any appeal is to be made within the period of 30 days beginning with–
      (i)   the conclusion date (if the Commissioners decide to undertake a review), or
      (ii)   the date on which the Commissioners decide not to undertake a review.".

Reg. 43F inserted by SI 2009/56, art. 3(2) and Sch. 2, para. 173, operative from 1 April 2009 subject to transitional and saving provisions in SI 2009/56, Sch. 3.

APPEALS

44(1)   A person may appeal from a decision by–

(a)   [Omitted by SI 2009/56, art. 3(2) and Sch. 2, para. 174(2).]

(b)   the Authority or DETI under regulation 34 or 42.

44(2)   An appeal from a decision by–

(a)   [omitted by SI 2009/56, art. 3(2) and Sch. 2, para. 174(2);]

(b)   the Authority is to the Upper Tribunal;

(c)   [omitted by SI 2013/1881, art. 28 and Schedule, para. 31(13)(b);]

(d)   DETI is to the High Court.

44(3)   [Omitted by SI 2009/56, art. 3(2) and Sch. 2, para. 174(3).]

44(4)   The provisions of Part 9 of the 2000 Act (hearings and appeals), subject to the modifications set out in paragraph 2 of Schedule 5, apply in respect of appeals to the Upper Tribunal made under this regulation as they apply in respect of references made to that Tribunal under that Act.

44(5)   Sections 40A (the Consumer Credit Appeals Tribunal), 41 (appeals to the Secretary of State under Part 3) and 41A (appeals from the Consumer Credit Appeals Tribunal) of the Consumer Credit Act 1974 apply in respect of appeals to the Consumer Credit Appeal Tribunal made under this regulation as they apply in respect of appeals made to that Tribunal under section 41 of that Act.

44(6)   [Omitted by SI 2009/56, art. 3(2) and Sch. 2, para. 174(4).]

44(7)   [Omitted by SI 2013/1881, art. 28 and Schedule, para. 31(13)(c).]

44(8)   The modifications in Schedule 5 have effect for the purposes of appeals made under this regulation.

History – Reg. 44(1)(a) omitted by SI 2009/56, art. 3(2) and Sch. 2, para. 174(2), operative from 1 April 2009 subject to transitional and saving provisions in SI 2009/56, Sch. 3.
In reg. 44(1)(b), the words ", the OFT", which appeared after the word "Authority", omitted by SI 2013/1881, art. 28 and Schedule, para. 31(13)(a), with effect from 1 April 2014.
Reg. 44(2)(a) omitted by SI 2009/56, art. 3(2) and Sch. 2, para. 174(2), operative from 1 April 2009 subject to transitional and saving provisions in SI 2009/56, Sch. 3.
In reg. 44(2)(b), the words "Upper Tribunal" substituted for the words "Financial Services and Markets Tribunal" by SI 2010/22, art. 5(2) and Sch. 3, para. 141, with effect from 6 April 2010, subject to transitional rules in SI 2010/22, Sch. 5.
Reg. 44(2)(c) omitted by SI 2013/1881, art. 28 and Schedule, para. 31(13)(b), with effect from 1 April 2014.
Reg. 44(3) omitted by SI 2009/56, art. 3(2) and Sch. 2, para. 174(3), operative from 1 April 2009 subject to transitional and saving provisions in SI 2009/56, Sch. 3.
In reg. 44(4), the words "Upper Tribunal" substituted for the words "Financial Services and Markets Tribunal" by SI 2010/22, art. 5(2) and Sch. 3, para. 1, with effect from 6 April 2010, subject to transitional rules in SI 2010/22, Sch. 5.
Reg. 44(6) omitted by SI 2009/56, art. 3(2) and Sch. 2, para. 174(4), operative from 1 April 2009 subject to transitional and saving provisions in SI 2009/56, Sch. 3.
Reg. 44(7) omitted by SI 2013/1881, art. 28 and Schedule, para. 31(13)(c), with effect from 1 April 2014.

CRIMINAL OFFENCES
OFFENCES

45(1)   A person (except an auction platform) who fails to comply with any requirement in regulation 7(1), (2) or (3), 8(1) or (3), 9(2), 10(1), 11(1)(a), (b) or (c), 14(1), 15(1) or (2), 16(1), (2), (3) or (4), 19(1), (4), (5) or (6), 20(1), (4) or (5), 21, 26, 27(4) or 33 is guilty of an offence and liable–

(a)   on summary conviction, to a fine not exceeding the statutory maximum;

(b)   on conviction on indictment, to imprisonment for a term not exceeding two years, to a fine or to both.

45(1A)   An auction platform which fails to comply with the customer due diligence requirements of Article 19 or 20(6) of the emission allowance auctioning regulation, the monitoring and record keeping requirements of Article 54 of that regulation, or regulation 20(1), (4) or (5) or 21 of these Regulations, is guilty of an offence and liable–

(a)   on summary conviction, to a fine not exceeding the statutory maximum;

(b)   on conviction on indictment, to imprisonment for a term not exceeding two years, to a fine or to both.

45(2)   In deciding whether a person has committed an offence under paragraph (1) or (1A), the court must consider whether he followed any relevant guidance which was at the time–

(a)   issued by a supervisory authority or any other appropriate body;

(b)   approved by the Treasury; and

(c)   published in a manner approved by the Treasury as suitable in their opinion to bring the guidance to the attention of persons likely to be affected by it.

45(3)   In paragraph (2), an **"appropriate body"** means any body which regulates or is representative of any trade, profession, business or employment carried on by the alleged offender.

45(4)   A person is not guilty of an offence under this regulation if he took all reasonable steps and exercised all due diligence to avoid committing the offence.

45(5)   Where a person is convicted of an offence under this regulation, he shall not also be liable to a penalty under regulation 42.

History – In reg. 45(1), the words ", or a direction made under regulation 18," omitted by SI 2012/2298, reg. 16, with effect from 1 October 2012.
In reg. 45(1), the words "(except an auction platform)" inserted by SI 2011/2699, reg. 8(a), with effect from 12 December 2011. Reg. 45(1A) inserted by SI 2011/2699, reg. 8(b), with effect from 12 December 2011.
In reg. 45(2), the words "or (1A)" inserted by SI 2011/2699, reg. 8(c), with effect from 12 December 2011.

PROSECUTION OF OFFENCES

46(1)   Proceedings for an offence under regulation 45 may be instituted by–

(a)   the Director of Revenue and Customs Prosecutions or by order of the Commissioners;

(b)   [omitted by SI 2013/1881, art. 28 and Schedule, para. 31(14)(a);]

(c)   a local weights and measures authority;

(d)   DETI;

(e)   the Director of Public Prosecutions; or

(f)   the Director of Public Prosecutions for Northern Ireland.

46(2)   Proceedings for an offence under regulation 45 may be instituted only against a relevant person or, where such a person is a body corporate, a partnership or an unincorporated association, against any person who is liable to be proceeded against under regulation 47.

46(3)   Where proceedings under paragraph (1) are instituted by order of the Commissioners, the proceedings must be brought in the name of an officer of Revenue and Customs.

46(4)   [Omitted by SI 2013/1881, art. 28 and Schedule, para. 31(14)(b).]

46(5)   [Omitted by SI 2013/1881, art. 28 and Schedule, para. 31(14)(b).]

46(6)   A local weights and measures authority must, whenever the Authority requires, report in such form and with such particulars as the Authority requires on the exercise of its functions under these Regulations.

46(7)   Where the Commissioners investigate, or propose to investigate, any matter with a view to determining–

(a)   whether there are grounds for believing that an offence under regulation 45 has been committed by any person; or

(b)   whether such a person should be prosecuted for such an offence,

that matter is to be treated as an assigned matter within the meaning of section 1(1) of the Customs and Excise Management Act 1979.

46(8)   Paragraphs (1) and (3) to (6) do not extend to Scotland.

46(9)   In its application to the Commissioners acting in Scotland, paragraph (7)(b) shall be read as referring to the Commissioners determining whether to refer the matter to the Crown Office and Procurator Fiscal Service with a view to the Procurator Fiscal determining whether a person should be prosecuted for such an offence.

History – Reg. 46(1)(b) omitted by SI 2013/1881, art. 28 and Schedule, para. 31(14)(a), with effect from 1 April 2014.
Reg. 46(4) and (5) omitted by SI 2013/1881, art. 28 and Schedule, para. 31(14)(b), with effect from 1 April 2014.
In reg. 46(6), the word "Authority" substituted for the word "OFT" in each place by SI 2013/1881, art. 28 and Schedule, para. 31(14)(c), with effect from 1 April 2014.
Reg. 46(9) inserted by SI 2007/3299, reg. 2(f), with effect from 15 December 2007.

OFFENCES BY BODIES CORPORATE, ETC.

47(1)   If an offence under regulation 45 committed by a body corporate is shown–

(a)   to have been committed with the consent or the connivance of an officer of the body corporate; or

(b)   to be attributable to any neglect on his part,

the officer as well as the body corporate is guilty of an offence and liable to be proceeded against and punished accordingly.

47(2)   If an offence under regulation 45 committed by a partnership is shown–

(a)   to have been committed with the consent or the connivance of a partner; or

(b)   to be attributable to any neglect on his part,

the partner as well as the partnership is guilty of an offence and liable to be proceeded against and punished accordingly.

47(3)   If an offence under regulation 45 committed by an unincorporated association (other than a partnership) is shown–

(a)   to have been committed with the consent or the connivance of an officer of the association; or

(b)   to be attributable to any neglect on his part,

that officer as well as the association is guilty of an offence and liable to be proceeded against and punished accordingly.

47(4)   If the affairs of a body corporate are managed by its members, paragraph (1) applies in relation to the acts and defaults of a member in connection with his functions of management as if he were a director of the body.

47(5)   Proceedings for an offence alleged to have been committed by a partnership or an unincorporated association must be brought in the name of the partnership or association (and not in that of its members).

47(6)   A fine imposed on the partnership or association on its conviction of an offence is to be paid out of the funds of the partnership or association.

47(7)   Rules of court relating to the service of documents are to have effect as if the partnership or association were a body corporate.

47(8)   In proceedings for an offence brought against the partnership or association–

(a)   section 33 of the Criminal Justice Act 1925 (procedure on charge of offence against corporation) and Schedule 3 to the Magistrates' Courts Act 1980 (corporations) apply as they do in relation to a body corporate;

(b)   section 70 (proceedings against bodies corporate) of the Criminal Procedure (Scotland) Act 1995 applies as it does in relation to a body corporate;

(c)   section 18 of the Criminal Justice (Northern Ireland) Act 1945 (procedure on charge) and Schedule 4 to the Magistrates' Courts (Northern Ireland) Order 1981 (corporations) apply as they do in relation to a body corporate.

47(9)   In this regulation–

"officer"

(a)   in relation to a body corporate, means a director, manager, secretary, chief executive, member of the committee of management, or a person purporting to act in such a capacity; and

(b) in relation to an unincorporated association, means any officer of the association or any member of its governing body, or a person purporting to act in such capacity; and

"partner" includes a person purporting to act as a partner.

PART 6 – MISCELLANEOUS

RECOVERY OF CHARGES AND PENALTIES THROUGH THE COURT

48 Any charge or penalty imposed on a person by a supervisory authority under regulation 35(1) or 42(1) is a debt due from that person to the authority, and is recoverable accordingly.

OBLIGATIONS ON PUBLIC AUTHORITIES

49(1) The following bodies and persons must, if they know or suspect or have reasonable grounds for knowing or suspecting that a person is or has engaged in money laundering or terrorist financing, as soon as reasonably practicable inform the Serious Organised Crime Agency–

(a) the Auditor General for Scotland;

(b) the Auditor General for Wales;

(c) the Authority;

(d) the Bank of England;

(e) the Comptroller and Auditor General;

(f) the Comptroller and Auditor General for Northern Ireland;

(g) the Gambling Commission;

(h) [omitted by SI 2013/1881, art. 28 and Schedule, para. 31(15);]

(i) the Official Solicitor to the Supreme Court;

(j) the Pensions Regulator;

(k) the Public Trustee;

(l) the Secretary of State, in the exercise of his functions under enactments relating to companies and insolvency;

(m) the Treasury, in the exercise of their functions under the 2000 Act;

(n) the Treasury Solicitor;

(o) a designated professional body for the purposes of Part 20 of the 2000 Act (provision of financial services by members of the professions);

(p) a person or inspector appointed under section 65 (investigations on behalf of Authority) or 66 (inspections and special meetings) of the Friendly Societies Act 1992;

(q) an inspector appointed under section 49 of the Industrial and Provident Societies Act 1965 (appointment of inspectors) or section 18 of the Credit Unions Act 1979 (power to appoint inspector);

(r) an inspector appointed under section 431 (investigation of a company on its own application), 432 (other company investigations), 442 (power to investigate company ownership) or 446D (appointment of replacement inspectors) of the Companies Act 1985;

(s) a person or inspector appointed under section 55 (investigations on behalf of Authority) or 56 (inspections and special meetings) of the Building Societies Act 1986;

(t) a person appointed under section 167 (appointment of persons to carry out investigations), 168(3) or (5) (appointment of persons to carry out investigations in particular cases), 169(1)(b) (investigations to support overseas regulator) or 284 (power to investigate affairs of a scheme) of the 2000 Act, or under regulations made under section 262(2)(k) (open-ended investment companies) of that Act, to conduct an investigation; and

(u) a person authorised to require the production of documents under section 447 of the Companies Act 1985 (Secretary of State's power to require production of documents), Article 440 of the Companies (Northern Ireland) Order 1986 or section 84 of the Companies Act 1989 (exercise of powers by officer).

49(2) A disclosure made under paragraph (1) is not to be taken to breach any restriction on the disclosure of information however imposed.

History – Reg. 49(1)(h) omitted by SI 2013/1881, art. 28 and Schedule, para. 31(15), with effect from 1 April 2014.

In reg. 49(1)(r), the words "446D (appointment of replacement inspectors)" substituted for the words "446 (investigation of share dealings)" by SI 2011/1265, art. 30, with effect from 12 May 2011.

In reg. 49(1)(r), the words "or under Article 424, 425, 435 or 439 of the Companies (Northern Ireland) Order 1986", which appeared at the end, omitted by SI 2011/1265, art. 30, with effect from 12 May 2011.

DISCLOSURE BY THE COMMISSIONERS

49A(1) The Commissioners may disclose to the Authority information held in connection with their functions under these Regulations if the disclosure is made for the purpose of enabling or assisting the Authority to discharge any of its functions under the Payment Services Regulations 2009 or the Electronic Money Regulations 2011.

49A(2) Information disclosed to the Authority under subsection (1) may not be disclosed by the Authority or any person who receives the information directly or indirectly from the Authority except–

(a)   to, or in accordance with authority given by, the Commissioners;

(b)   with a view to the institution of, or otherwise for the purposes of, any criminal proceedings;

(c)   with a view to the institution of any other proceedings by the Authority, for the purposes of any such proceedings instituted by the Authority, or for the purposes of any reference to the Tribunal under the Payment Services Regulations 2009; or

(d)   in the form of a summary or collection of information so framed as not to enable information relating to any particular person to be ascertained from it.

49A(3) Any person who discloses information in contravention of subsection (2) is guilty of an offence and liable–

(a)   on summary conviction, to imprisonment for a term not exceeding three months, to a fine not exceeding the statutory maximum, or to both;

(b)   on conviction on indictment, to imprisonment for a term not exceeding two years to a fine, or to both.

49A(4) It is a defence for a person charged with an offence under this regulation of disclosing information to prove that they reasonably believed

(a)   that the disclosure was lawful; or

(b)   that the information had already and lawfully been made available to the public.

History – In reg. 49A(1), the words "or the Electronic Money Regulations 2011" inserted by SI 2011/99, reg. 79 and Sch. 4, para. 19(g), with effect from 30 April 2011.

Reg. 49A inserted by SI 2009/209, reg. 126 and Sch. 6, para. 6(g), with effect from 1 November 2009.

TRANSITIONAL PROVISIONS; REQUIREMENT TO BE REGISTERED

50(1) Regulation 26 does not apply to an existing money service business, an existing trust or company service provider , an existing high value dealer, an existing bill payment service provider or an existing telecommunication, digital and IT payment service provider until–

(a)   where it has applied in accordance with regulation 27 before the specified date for registration in a register maintained under regulation 25(1) (a "new register")–

     (i)   the date it is included in a new register following the determination of its application by the Commissioners; or

     (ii)   where the Commissioners give it notice under regulation 29(2)(b) of their decision not to register it, the date on which the Commissioners state that the decision takes effect or, where a statement is included in accordance with paragraph (3)(b), the time at which the Commissioners give it such notice;

(b)   in any other case, the specified date.

50(2) The specified date is–

(a)   in the case of an existing money service business, 1st February 2008;

(b)   in the case of an existing trust or company service provider, 1st April 2008;

(c)   in the case of an existing high value dealer, the first anniversary which falls on or after 1st January 2008 of the date of its registration in a register maintained under regulation 10 of the Money Laundering Regulations 2003;

(d)   in the case of an existing bill payment service provider or an existing telecommunication, digital and IT payment service provider, 1st March 2010.

50(3) In the case of an application for registration in a new register made before the specified date by an existing money service business, an existing trust or company service provider, an existing high value dealer, an existing bill payment service provider or an existing telecommunication, digital and IT payment service provider, the Commissioners must include in a notice given to it under regulation 29(2)(b)–

(a)   the date on which their decision is to take effect; or

(b)   if the Commissioners consider that the interests of the public require their decision to have immediate effect, a statement to that effect and the reasons for it.

50(4)   In the case of an application for registration in a new register made before the specified date by an existing money services business or an existing trust or company service provider, the Commissioners must give it a notice under regulation 29(2) by–

(a)   in the case of an existing money service business, 1st June 2008;

(b)   in the case of an existing trust or company service provider, 1st July 2008; or

(c)   where applicable, 45 days beginning with the date on which they receive any further information required under regulation 27(3).

50(5)   In this regulation–

    "existing bill payment service provider" and an **"existing telecommunication, digital and IT payment service provider"** mean a bill payment service provider or a telecommunication, digital and IT payment service provider carrying on business in the United Kingdom immediately before 1st November 2009;

    "existing money service business" and an **"existing high value dealer"** mean a money service business or a high value dealer which, immediately before 15th December 2007, was included in a register maintained under regulation 10 of the Money Laundering Regulations 2003;

    "existing trust or company service provider" means a trust or company service provider carrying on business in the United Kingdom immediately before 15th December 2007.

History – In reg. 50(1), the words ", an existing high value dealer, an existing bill payment service provider or an existing telecommunication, digital and IT payment service provider" substituted for the words "or an existing high value dealer" by SI 2009/209, reg. 126 and Sch. 6, para. 6(h)(i), with effect from 1 November 2009.
Reg. 50(2)(d) inserted by SI 2009/209, reg. 126 and Sch. 6, para. 6(h)(ii), with effect from 1 November 2009.
In reg. 50(3), the words ", an existing high value dealer, an existing bill payment service provider or an existing telecommunication, digital and IT payment service provider" substituted for the words "or an existing high value dealer" by SI 2009/209, reg. 126 and Sch. 6, para. 6(h)(iii), with effect from 1 November 2009.
In reg. 50(5), the definitions of "existing bill payment service provider" and "existing telecommunication, digital and IT payment service provider" inserted by SI 2009/209, reg. 126 and Sch. 6, para. 6(h)(iv), with effect from 1 November 2009.

MINOR AND CONSEQUENTIAL AMENDMENTS

51   Schedule 6, which contains minor and consequential amendments to primary and secondary legislation, has effect.

SCHEDULES

SCHEDULE 1 – ACTIVITIES LISTED IN POINTS 2 TO 12, 14 AND 15 OF ANNEX 1 TO THE CAPITAL REQUIREMENTS DIRECTIVE

Regulation 3(3)(a)

History – Sch. 1 heading substituted by SI 2013/3115, Sch. 2, para. 68(4), with effect from 1 January 2014.
In the former heading to Sch. 1, ", 14 and 15" substituted for "and 14" by SI 2011/99, reg. 79 and Sch. 4, para. 19(h)(i), with effect from 30 April 2011.

2   Lending including, inter alia: consumer credit, mortgage credit, factoring, with or without recourse, financing of commercial transactions (including forfeiting).

3   Financial leasing.

4   Payment services as defined in Article 4(3) of Directive 2007/64/EC of the European Parliament and of the Council of 13 November 2007 on payment services in the internal market.

History – Para. 4 substituted by SI 2009/209, reg. 126 and Sch. 6, para. 6(i), with effect from 1 November 2009.

5   Issuing and administering other means of payment (including travellers' cheques and bankers' drafts) insofar as this activity is not covered by point 4.

History – Para. 5 substituted by SI 2009/209, reg. 126 and Sch. 6, para. 6(i), with effect from 1 November 2009.

6   Guarantees and commitments.

7   Trading for own account or for account of customers in:

(a)   money market instruments (cheques, bills, certificates of deposit, etc.);

(b)   foreign exchange;

(c)   financial futures and options;

(d)   exchange and interest-rate instruments; or

(e)   transferable securities.

8   Participation in securities issues and the provision of services related to such issues.

9   Advice to undertakings on capital structure, industrial strategy and related questions and advice as well as services relating to mergers and the purchase of undertakings.

10   Money broking.

11   Portfolio management and advice.

12   Safekeeping and administration of securities.

14   Safe custody services.

15   Issuing electronic money.

History – Para. 15 inserted by SI 2011/99, reg. 79 and Sch. 4, para. 19(h)(ii), with effect from 30 April 2011.

SCHEDULE 2 – FINANCIAL ACTIVITY, SIMPLIFIED DUE DILIGENCE AND POLITICALLY EXPOSED PERSONS

Regulations 4(1)(e) and (2), 13(6) and (8) and 14(5).

FINANCIAL ACTIVITY ON AN OCCASIONAL OR VERY LIMITED BASIS

1   For the purposes of regulation 4(1)(e) and (2), a person is to be considered as engaging in financial activity on an occasional or very limited basis if all the following conditions are fulfilled–

(a)   the person's total annual turnover in respect of the financial activity does not exceed £64,000;

(b)   the financial activity is limited in relation to any customer to no more than one transaction exceeding 1,000 euro, whether the transaction is carried out in a single operation, or a series of operations which appear to be linked;

(c)   the financial activity does not exceed 5% of the person's total annual turnover;

(d)   the financial activity is ancillary and directly related to the person's main activity;

(e)   the financial activity is not the transmission or remittance of money (or any representation of monetary value) by any means;

(f)   the person's main activity is not that of a person falling within regulation 3(1)(a) to (f) or (h);

(g)   the financial activity is provided only to customers of the person's main activity and is not offered to the public.

SIMPLIFIED DUE DILIGENCE

2   For the purposes of regulation 13(6), the conditions are–

(a)   the authority has been entrusted with public functions pursuant to the Treaty on the European Union, the Treaties on the European Communities or Community secondary legislation;

(b)   the authority's identity is publicly available, transparent and certain;

(c)   the activities of the authority and its accounting practices are transparent;

(d)   either the authority is accountable to a Community institution or to the authorities of an EEA state, or otherwise appropriate check and balance procedures exist ensuring control of the authority's activity.

3   For the purposes of regulation 13(8), the conditions are–

(a)   the product has a written contractual base;

(b)   any related transaction is carried out through an account of the customer with a credit institution which is subject to the money laundering directive or with a credit institution situated in a non-EEA state which imposes requirements equivalent to those laid down in that directive;

(c)   the product or related transaction is not anonymous and its nature is such that it allows for the timely application of customer due diligence measures where there is a suspicion of money laundering or terrorist financing;

(d)   the product is within the following maximum threshold–

     (i)   in the case of insurance policies or savings products of a similar nature, the annual premium is no more than 1,000 euro or there is a single premium of no more than 2,500 euro;

     (ii)   in the case of products which are related to the financing of physical assets where the legal and beneficial title of the assets is not transferred to the customer until the termination of the contractual relationship (whether the transaction is carried out in a single operation or in several operations which appear to be linked), the annual payments do not exceed 15,000 euro;

     (iii)   in all other cases, the maximum threshold is 15,000 euro;

(e)   the benefits of the product or related transaction cannot be realised for the benefit of third parties, except in the case of death, disablement, survival to a predetermined advanced age, or similar events;

(f)   in the case of products or related transactions allowing for the investment of funds in financial assets or claims, including insurance or other kinds of contingent claims–

     (i)   the benefits of the product or related transaction are only realisable in the long term;

     (ii)   the product or related transaction cannot be used as collateral; and

     (iii)   during the contractual relationship, no accelerated payments are made, surrender clauses used or early termination takes place.

POLITICALLY EXPOSED PERSONS

4(1)   For the purposes of regulation 14(5)–

(a)   individuals who are or have been entrusted with prominent public functions include the following–

     (i)   heads of state, heads of government, ministers and deputy or assistant ministers;

     (ii)   members of parliaments;

     (iii)   members of supreme courts, of constitutional courts or of other high-level judicial bodies whose decisions are not generally subject to further appeal, other than in exceptional circumstances;

     (iv)   members of courts of auditors or of the boards of central banks;

     (v)   ambassadors, chargés d'affaires and high-ranking officers in the armed forces; and

     (vi)   members of the administrative, management or supervisory bodies of state-owned enterprises;

(b)   the categories set out in paragraphs (i) to (vi) of sub-paragraph (a) do not include middle-ranking or more junior officials;

(c)   immediate family members include the following–

     (i)   a spouse;

     (ii)   a partner;

     (iii)   children and their spouses or partners; and

     (iv)   parents;

(d)   persons known to be close associates include the following–

     (i)   any individual who is known to have joint beneficial ownership of a legal entity or legal arrangement, or any other close business relations, with a person referred to in regulation 14(5)(a); and

     (ii)   any individual who has sole beneficial ownership of a legal entity or legal arrangement which is known to have been set up for the benefit of a person referred to in regulation 14(5)(a).

4(2)   In paragraph (1)(c), **"partner"** means a person who is considered by his national law as equivalent to a spouse.

SCHEDULE 3 – PROFESSIONAL BODIES

Regulations 17(2)(b), 23(1)(c) and 32(4)

1   Association of Accounting Technicians
2   Association of Chartered Certified Accountants
3   Association of International Accountants
4   Association of Taxation Technicians
5   Chartered Institute of Management Accountants
6   Chartered Institute of Public Finance and Accountancy
7   Chartered Institute of Taxation
8   Council for Licensed Conveyancers
9   Faculty of Advocates
10   Faculty Office of the Archbishop of Canterbury
11   General Council of the Bar
12   General Council of the Bar of Northern Ireland
13   Insolvency Practitioners Association
14   Institute of Certified Bookkeepers
15   Institute of Chartered Accountants in England and Wales
16   Institute of Chartered Accountants in Ireland
17   Institute of Chartered Accountants of Scotland
18   Institute of Financial Accountants
19   International Association of Book-keepers
20   Law Society
21   Law Society of Northern Ireland
22   Law Society of Scotland

History – Sch. 3 substituted by SI 2012/2298, reg. 17, with effect from 1 October 2012.

SCHEDULE 4 – CONNECTED PERSONS

Regulation 37(2)

CORPORATE BODIES

1   If the relevant person is a body corporate ("BC"), a person who is or has been–
(a)   an officer or manager of BC or of a parent undertaking of BC;
(b)   an employee of BC;
(c)   an agent of BC or of a parent undertaking of BC.

PARTNERSHIPS

2   If the relevant person is a partnership, a person who is or has been a member, manager, employee or agent of the partnership.

UNINCORPORATED ASSOCIATIONS

3   If the relevant person is an unincorporated association of persons which is not a partnership, a person who is or has been an officer, manager, employee or agent of the association.

INDIVIDUALS

4   If the relevant person is an individual, a person who is or has been an employee or agent of that individual.

SCHEDULE 5 – MODIFICATIONS IN RELATION TO APPEALS

Regulation 44(8)

Part 1 – Primary Legislation

THE VALUE ADDED TAX ACT 1994 (C. 23)

1   Part 5 of the Value Added Tax Act 1994 (appeals) is modified by omitting sections 83A to 84, 85A and 85B.

History – Para. 1 substituted by SI 2009/56, art. 3(2) and Sch. 2, para. 175, operative from 1 April 2009 subject to transitional and saving provisions in SI 2009/56, Sch. 3. Former para. 1 read as follows:
> "**1**   Part 5 of the Value Added Tax Act 1994 (appeals) is modified as follows–
> (a)   omit section 84; and
> (b)   in paragraphs (1)(a), (2)(a) and (3)(a) of section 87, omit ", or is recoverable as, VAT".".

THE FINANCIAL SERVICES AND MARKETS ACT 2000 (C. 8)

2   Part 9 of the 2000 Act (hearings and appeals) is modified as follows–

(a)   in the application of sections 133 to 133B to any appeal commenced before the coming into force of section 55 of the Consumer Credit Act 2006, for all the references to "the Authority", substitute "the Authority or the OFT (as the case may be)";

(b)   [omitted by SI 2010/22, art. 5(2) and Sch. 3, para. 142(a)(ii);]

(c)   in section 133A omit subsections (1), (2), (3) and (5); and

(d)   in section 133A(4) for "decision notice" in both places where it occurs substitute "notice under regulation 34(5) or (9) or 42(7) of the Money Laundering Regulations 2007".

History – In para. 2(a), "sections 133 to 133B" substituted for "section 133 and Schedule 13" by SI 2010/22, art. 5(2) and Sch. 3, para. 142(a)(i), with effect from 6 April 2010, subject to transitional rules in SI 2010/22, Sch. 5.
Para. 2(b) omitted by SI 2010/22, art. 5(2) and Sch. 3, para. 142(a)(ii), with effect from 6 April 2010, subject to transitional rules in SI 2010/22, Sch. 5. Former para. 2(b) read as follows:
> "(b)   in section 133(1)(a) for "decision notice or supervisory notice in question" substitute "notice under regulation 34(5) or (9) or 42(7) of the Money Laundering Regulations 2007";".
Para. 2(c) substituted by SI 2010/22, art. 5(2) and Sch. 3, para. 142(a)(iii), with effect from 6 April 2010, subject to transitional rules in SI 2010/22, Sch. 5. Former para. 2(c) read as follows:
> "(c)   in section 133 omit subsections (6), (7), (8) and (12); and".
In para. 2(d), "section 133A(4)" substituted for "section 133(9)" by SI 2010/22, art. 5(2) and Sch. 3, para. 142(a)(iv), with effect from 6 April 2010, subject to transitional rules in SI 2010/22, Sch. 5.

Part 2 – Secondary Legislation

[Omitted by SI 2010/22, art. 5(2) and Sch. 3, para. 142(b).]

History – Pt. 2 omitted by SI 2010/22, art. 5(2) and Sch. 3, para. 142(b), with effect from 6 April 2010, subject to transitional rules in SI 2010/22, Sch. 5. Former Pt. 2 read as follows:
> **"PART 2 – SECONDARY LEGISLATION**
>
> THE FINANCIAL SERVICES AND MARKETS TRIBUNAL RULES 2001
> **3**   In the application of the Financial Services and Markets Tribunal Rules 20019 to any appeal commenced before the coming into force of section 55 of the Consumer Credit Act 2006, for all the references to "the Authority" substitute "the Authority or the OFT (as the case may be)".".

FINANCE ACT 2007 (SCHEDULES 13 AND 14) ORDER 2007

(SI 2007/2483)

Made on 30 August 2007 by the Treasury in exercise of the powers conferred by s 47(4) and (5) of the Finance Act 2007.

CITATION

1 This Order may be cited as the Finance Act 2007 (Schedules 13 and 14) Order 2007.

SCHEDULE 13 TO THE FINANCE ACT 2007

2 Schedule 13 to the Finance Act 2007 (sale and repurchase of securities) shall have effect in relation to an arrangement that comes into force on or after 1st October 2007.

SCHEDULE 14 TO THE FINANCE ACT 2007

3 The amendments made by Schedule 14 to the Finance Act 2007 (sale and repurchase of securities: minor and consequential amendments), with the exception of the amendments made by paragraphs 10 and 18 of that Schedule, shall have effect in relation to an arrangement that comes into force on or after 1st October 2007.

4(1) The amendments made by paragraph 10 of Schedule 14 to the Finance Act 2007 shall have effect as follows.

4(2) In a case where there is a debtor repo within the meaning of paragraph 2 of Schedule 13 to the Finance Act 2007, the amendments shall have effect in relation to an arrangement that comes into force on or after 1st October 2007.

4(3) In a case where there is a stock lending arrangement within the meaning of section 263B(1) of the Taxation of Chargeable Gains Act 1992, the amendments shall have effect in relation to an arrangement under which the lender transfers securities to the borrower otherwise than by way of sale on or after 1st October 2007.

5(1) The amendments made by paragraph 18 of Schedule 14 to the Finance Act 2007 shall have effect as follows.

5(2) In a case where there is an arrangement to which Schedule 13 to the Finance Act 2007 applies, the amendments shall have effect in relation to an arrangement that comes into force on or after 1st October 2007.

5(3) In a case where there is a stock lending arrangement within the meaning of section 263B(1) of the Taxation of Chargeable Gains Act 1992, the amendments shall have effect in relation to an arrangement under which the lender transfers securities to the borrower otherwise than by way of sale on or after 1st October 2007.

5(4) In any other case, the amendments shall have effect in relation to disposals on or after 1st October 2007.

INTERPRETATION

6 Paragraph 14(6) of Schedule 13 to the Finance Act 2007 applies for the purpose of determining the times at which an arrangement is in force.

SALE AND REPURCHASE OF SECURITIES (MODIFICATION OF SCHEDULE 13 TO THE FINANCE ACT 2007) REGULATIONS 2007

(SI 2007/2485)

Made on 30 August 2007 by the Treasury in exercise of the powers conferred by para. 15 of Sch. 13 to the Finance Act 2007. Operative from 1 October 2007.

CITATION, COMMENCEMENT AND INTERPRETATION

1(1) These Regulations may be cited as the Sale and Repurchase of Securities (Modification of Schedule 13 to the Finance Act 2007) Regulations 2007, shall come into force on 1st October 2007, and shall have effect in relation to arrangements that come into force on or after that day.

1(2) Paragraph 14(6) of Schedule 13 to the Finance Act 2007 applies for the purpose of determining the time at which an arrangement is in force.

1(3) In these Regulations–

> **"non-standard repo case"** shall be construed in accordance with paragraph 15(2) of Schedule 13;
>
> **"redemption arrangements"** shall be construed in accordance with paragraph 15(6) of Schedule 13;
>
> **"Schedule 13"** means Schedule 13 to the Finance Act 2007.

NON-STANDARD REPO CASES: SUBSTITUTION OF SECURITIES

2(1) In a non-standard repo case where–

(a) condition B is met in relation to the repo (see paragraph 15(4) of Schedule 13), and

(b) securities ("the substituted securities") are substituted for other securities,

Schedule 13 applies with the modifications specified in paragraph (2).

2(2) Paragraphs 2 (meaning of debtor repo), 6 (ignoring sale and subsequent purchase for purposes of chargeable gains: debtor repos), 7 (meaning of creditor repo) and 11 (ignoring purchase and subsequent sale for purposes of chargeable gains: creditor repos) of Schedule 13 apply as if any references in any of those paragraphs to "securities or similar securities" (however expressed) included a reference to the substituted securities.

REDEMPTION ARRANGEMENTS: MODIFICATIONS OF SCHEDULE 13

3(1) In a case involving redemption arrangements–

(a) paragraphs 2 (meaning of debtor repo) and 3 (meaning of debtor quasi-repo) of Schedule 13 apply with the modifications specified in paragraphs (2) and (3), and

(b) paragraphs 7 (meaning of creditor repo) and 8 (meaning of creditor quasi-repo) of Schedule 13 apply with the modifications specified in paragraphs (4) and (5).

3(2) Any reference in paragraphs 2 and 3 to an arrangement that makes provision conferring a right or imposing an obligation on the borrower to buy securities at any subsequent time shall be treated as if it included a reference to an arrangement under which the borrower has the right or obligation to receive an amount equivalent to the proceeds of redemption of the securities.

3(3) Any reference in paragraphs 2 and 3 to the buying of securities extinguishing the financial liability in respect of the advance recorded in the accounts of the borrower in accordance with generally accepted accounting practice shall be treated as if it included a reference to a payment of an amount equivalent to the proceeds of redemption of the securities extinguishing the financial liability in respect of the advance recorded in the accounts of the borrower in accordance with generally accepted accounting practice.

3(4) Any reference in paragraphs 7 and 8 to an arrangement that makes provision conferring a right or imposing an obligation on the lender to sell securities at any subsequent time shall be treated as if it included a reference to an arrangement under which the lender has the right or obligation to pay the proceeds of redemption of the securities to any person.

3(5) Any reference in paragraphs 7 and 8 to the subsequent sale of securities extinguishing the financial asset in respect of the advance recorded in the accounts of the lender in accordance with

Statutory Instruments

generally accepted accounting practice shall be treated as if it included a reference to the payment of an amount equivalent to the proceeds of redemption of the securities extinguishing the financial asset in respect of the advance recorded in the accounts of the lender in accordance with generally accepted accounting practice.

REDEMPTION ARRANGEMENTS: CONSEQUENCES FOR TAX IN RESPECT OF CHARGEABLE GAINS

4(1) In a case where paragraph 2 of Schedule 13 applies with the modifications specified in regulation 3, sub-paragraphs (3) to (5) of paragraph 6 of Schedule 13 apply as if those sub-paragraphs provided that, in such a case, the borrower shall be treated for the purposes of tax in respect of chargeable gains as having disposed of the securities transferred by him to the lender under the arrangement–

(a)   on the occasion of the redemption of the securities, and

(b)   for an amount equivalent to the proceeds of redemption.

4(2) In a case where paragraph 7 of Schedule 13 applies with the modifications specified in regulation 3, sub-paragraphs (3) to (5) of paragraph 11 of Schedule 13 apply as if those sub-paragraphs provided that, in such a case, the lender shall be treated for the purposes of tax in respect of chargeable gains as having acquired the securities transferred to him under the arrangement–

(a)   on the occasion of the redemption of the securities, and

(b)   for an amount equivalent to the proceeds of redemption.

SALE AND REPURCHASE OF SECURITIES (MODIFICATION OF ENACTMENTS) REGULATIONS 2007

(SI 2007/2486)

Made on 30 August 2007 by the Treasury in exercise of the powers conferred by s. 612, 613 and 614 of the Income Tax Act 2007 and s. 263F, 263G and 263H of the Taxation of Chargeable Gains Act 1992. Operative from 1 October 2007.

CITATION, COMMENCEMENT AND INTERPRETATION

1(1) These Regulations may be cited as the Sale and Repurchase of Securities (Modification of Enactments) Regulations 2007 and shall come into force on 1st October 2007.

1(2) These Regulations shall have effect in relation to arrangements where the transfer of securities referred to in section 607(1)(b) of ITA 2007 takes place on or after 1st October 2007.

1(3) In these Regulations–

"**ITA 2007**" means the Income Tax Act 2007;

"**non-standard repo case**" shall be construed in accordance with section 612(2) of ITA 2007;

"**redemption arrangements**" shall be construed in accordance with section 613(2) of ITA 2007;

"**TCGA 1992**" means the Taxation of Chargeable Gains Act 1992.

NON-STANDARD REPO CASES: SUBSTITUTION OF SECURITIES

2(1) This regulation applies in a non-standard repo case where–

(a)   condition B is met in relation to the repo (see section 612(4) of ITA 2007), and

(b)   securities ("the substituted securities") are substituted for other securities.

2(2) Sections 601 to 610 of ITA 2007 (repos) and section 263A of TCGA 1992 (agreements for sale and repurchase of securities) apply as if any references in any of those sections to "securities or similar securities" (however expressed) included a reference to the substituted securities.

REDEMPTION ARRANGEMENTS: MODIFICATIONS OF ENACTMENTS RELATING TO INCOME TAX

3(1) In a case involving redemption arrangements, sections 601 to 610 of ITA 2007 apply with the modifications specified in paragraph (2).

3(2) Sections 601 to 610 apply as if any references in any of those sections to the repurchase of the securities (however expressed) included a reference to an arrangement under which the borrower has the right or obligation to receive an amount equivalent to the proceeds of redemption of the securities.

REDEMPTION ARRANGEMENTS: MODIFICATIONS OF ENACTMENTS RELATING TO CAPITAL GAINS TAX

4(1) In a case involving redemption arrangements, section 263A of TCGA 1992 applies with the following modifications.

4(2) Subsection (1A) applies as if it provided that the interim holder shall be treated for the purposes of capital gains tax as acquiring the securities–

(a)   on the occasion of the redemption of the securities, and

(b)   for an amount equivalent to the proceeds of redemption.

4(3) Subsection (1B) applies as if it provided that the original owner shall be treated for the purposes of capital gains tax as disposing of the securities–

(a)   on the occasion of the redemption of the securities, and

(b)   for an amount equivalent to the proceeds of redemption.

14,603   **Administrative Justice etc. Order 2007**   **SI 2007/2951**

Statutory Instruments

ADMINISTRATIVE JUSTICE AND TRIBUNALS COUNCIL (LISTED TRIBUNALS) ORDER 2007

(SI 2007/2951, as amended by SI 2008/2683, SI 2009/1307, SI 2010/22, SI 2013/1881 and revoked by SI 2013/2042)

Made on 9 October 2007 by the Lord Chancellor in exercise of the powers conferred by para. 25(2) of Sch. 7 to the Tribunals, Courts and Enforcement Act 2007. Operative from 1 November 2007.

History – SI 2007/2951 revoked by SI 2013/2042, art. 67, with effect from 19 August 2013. Former SI 2007/2951 read as follows:

"CITATION AND COMMENCEMENT

1 This Order may be cited as the Administrative Justice and Tribunals Council (Listed Tribunals) Order 2007 and shall come into force on 1st November 2007.

LIST OF TRIBUNALS

2 The following are listed tribunals for the purposes of Schedule 7 to the Tribunals, Courts and Enforcement Act 2007–

Tribunal	*Legislation*
Adjudicator to Her Majesty's Land Registry	Section 107 of the Land Registration Act 2002 (c.9)
Adjudicators	Section 25 of the School Standards and Framework Act 1998 (c.31)
Adjudicators	Section 81 of the Traffic Management Act 2004 (c.18)
Admission Appeal Panels in England	Section 94(5) or 95(3) of the School Standards and Framework Act 1998 (c.31)
Agricultural Land Tribunals	Section 73 of the Agriculture Act 1947 (c.48)
Aircraft and Shipbuilding Industries Arbitration Tribunal, except for its functions in respect of Northern Ireland	Section 42 of the Aircraft and Shipbuilding Industries Act 1977 (c.3)
Antarctic Act Tribunal, except for its functions in respect of Northern Ireland	Regulation 11 of the Antarctic Regulations 1995 (S.I. 1995/490)
Appeal Tribunals	Part 2 of Schedule 9 to the Scheme set out in Schedule 2 to the Firefighters' Pension Scheme Order 1992 (S.I. 1992/129)
Appeal Tribunals	Section 4 of the Social Security Act 1998 (c.14)
Appeal Tribunals appointed for England and Wales	Regulation H6(3) of the Police Pensions Regulations 1987 (S.I. 1987/257)
Appeals Tribunals	Regulation 10 of the Local Authorities (Code of Conduct) (Local Determination) Regulations 2003 (S.I. 2003/1483)
Arbitrators (unless appointed by agreement)	Section 84 of the Agricultural Holdings Act 1986 (c.5)
Asylum and Immigration Tribunal	Section 81 of the Nationality, Immigration and Asylum Act 2002 (c.41)
Board of the Pension Protection Fund in respect of functions under or by virtue of section 207 of the Pensions Act 2004 (c.35)	Section 107 of the Pensions Act 2004 (c.35)
Bus Lane Adjudicators	Regulation 11 of the Bus Lane Contraventions (Penalty Charges, Adjudication and Enforcement) (England) Regulations 2005 (S.I. 2005/2757)
Charity Tribunal	Section 2A of the Charities Act 1993 (c.10)
Child Support Commissioners and any tribunal of Commissioners under paragraph 5 of Schedule 4 to the Child Support Act 1991 (c.48)	Section 22 of the Child Support Act 1991 (c.48)
Civil Aviation Authority in respect of its functions prescribed for the purposes of section 7(2) of the Civil Aviation Act 1982 (c.16), except functions in respect of Northern Ireland	Section 2 of the Civil Aviation Act 1982 (c.16)
Committees for England	Section 27 of the Forestry Act 1967 (c.10)
Committees of Primary Care Trusts in England	Regulation 3 of the National Health Service (Service Committees and Tribunal) Regulations 1992 (S.I. 1992/664)
Competition Appeal Tribunal, except for its functions in respect of Northern Ireland	Section 12 of the Enterprise Act 2002 (c.40)
Comptroller in respect of non-executive functions, including any delegation of those functions under section 62(3) of the Patents and Designs Act 1907 (c.29), except functions in respect of Northern Ireland	Section 62(2) of the Patents and Designs Act 1907 (c.29)
Consumer Credit Appeals Tribunal, except for its functions in respect of Northern Ireland	Section 40A of the Consumer Credit Act 1974 (c.39)
Controller of Plant Variety Rights in respect of non-executive functions, including any delegation of those functions under paragraph 3 of Schedule 1 to the Plant Varieties Act 1997 (c.66), except functions in respect of Northern Ireland	Section 2(1) of the Plant Varieties Act 1997 (c.66)

Tribunal	Legislation
Conveyancing Appeal Tribunals	Section 41 of the Courts and Legal Services Act 1990 (c.41)
Copyright Tribunal, except for its functions in respect of Northern Ireland	Section 145 of the Copyright, Designs and Patents Act 1988 (c.48)
Employment Tribunals	Section 1(1) of the Employment Tribunals Act 1996 (c.17)
Exclusion Appeal Panels in England	Paragraph 2 of the Schedule to the Education (Pupil Exclusions and Appeals) (Maintained Schools) (England) Regulations 2002 (S.I. 2002/3178)
Foreign Compensation Commission in respect of its non-executive functions	Section 1(1) of the Foreign Compensation Act 1950 (c.12)
Gender Recognition Panels, except for their functions in respect of Northern Ireland	Section 1(3) to the Gender Recognition Act 2004 (c.7)
Horserace Betting Levy Appeal Tribunals for England and Wales	Section 29 of the Betting, Gaming and Lotteries Act 1963 (c.2)
Information Commissioner in respect of non-executive functions, except functions in respect of Northern Ireland	Section 6(1) of the Data Protection Act 1998 (c.29)
Insolvency Practitioners Tribunal	Section 396(1) of the Insolvency Act 1986 (c.45)
Mental Health Review Tribunal for Wales	Section 65 of the Mental Health Act 1983 (c.20)
National Lottery Commission in respect of its functions under sections 10 and 10A of, and Schedule 3 to, the National Lottery etc. Act 1993 (c.39), including any delegation under paragraph 8 of Schedule 2A to that Act, except for its functions in respect of Northern Ireland	Section 3A of the National Lottery etc. Act 1993 (c.39)
Ombudsman for the Board of the Pension Protection Fund in respect of functions under or by virtue of section 213 of the Pensions Act 2004 (c.35)	Section 209 of the Pensions Act 2004 (c.35)
Parking Adjudicators in England	Section 73 of the Road Traffic Act 1991 (c.40)
Pensions Ombudsman, and any Deputy Pensions Ombudsman, in respect of functions under section 146(1)(c) and (d) of the Pensions Schemes Act 1993 (c.48)	Sections 145(1) and 145A(1) of the Pensions Schemes Act 1993 (c.48)
Pensions Regulator in respect of regulatory functions under section 93(2) of the Pensions Act 2004 (c.35)	Section 1 of the Pensions Act 2004 (c.35)
Pensions Regulator Tribunal in respect of functions under sections 103 and 105 of the Pensions Act 2004 (c.35)	Section 102 of the Pensions Act 2004 (c.35)
Plant Varieties and Seeds Tribunal, except for its functions in respect of Northern Ireland	Section 42(1) of the Plant Varieties Act 1997 (c.66)
Police Appeals Tribunals	Section 85 of the Police Act 1996 (c.16)
Primary Care Trusts in England in respect of their functions under the National Health Service (Service Committees and Tribunal) Regulations 1992 (S.I. 1992/664)	Section 18 of the National Health Service Act 2006 (c.41)
Referees	Regulation 3 of the Industrial Training (Levy Exemption References) Regulations 1974 (S.I. 1974/1335)
Reinstatement Committees	Paragraph 1 of Schedule 2 to the Reserve Forces (Safeguard of Employment) Act 1985 (c.17)
Rent Assessment Committees in England	Section 65 of the Rent Act 1977 (c.42)
Reserve Forces Appeal Tribunals	Section 88 of the Reserve Forces Act 1996 (c.14)
Road User Charging Adjudicators	Regulation 3 of the Road User Charging (Enforcement and Adjudication) (London) Regulations 2001 (S.I. 2001/2313)
Sea Fish Licence Tribunal, except for its functions in respect of Northern Ireland	Section 4AA of the Sea Fish (Conservation) Act 1967 (c.84)
Social Security Commissioners and any tribunal presided over by such a Commissioner	Schedule 4 to the Social Security Act 1998 (c.14)
The Office of Fair Trading and any member of its staff authorised to exercise its relevant functions, except functions in respect of Northern Ireland	Functions of the Office of Fair Trading under the Consumer Credit Act 1974 (c.39) and the Estate Agents Act 1979 (c.38), not being executive functions
Traffic Commissioners for areas in England and Wales	Section 4 of the Public Passenger Vehicle Act 1981 (c.14)
Transport Tribunal	Schedule 4 to the Transport Act 1985 (c.67)
Tribunal, except for its functions in respect of Northern Ireland	Health Service Medicines (Price Control Appeals) Regulations 2000 (S.I. 2000/124)
Tribunal, except for its functions in respect of Northern Ireland	Schedule 3 to the Industry Act 1975 (c.68)
Tribunals	Rule 6 of the model provisions with respect to appeals as modified by the Chemical Weapons (Licence Appeal Provisions) Order 1996 (S.I. 1996/3030)
Tribunals	Section 150(3) of the Mines and Quarries Act 1954 (c.70)
Tribunals for England and Wales	Section 14 of the Misuse of Drugs Act 1971 (c.38)
Tribunals of Appeal	Section 109 of the London Building Acts (Amendment) Act 1939 (c. xcvii)

Tribunal	Legislation
Umpire and any Deputy Umpires	Paragraph 5 of Schedule 2 to the Reserve Forces (Safeguard of Employment) Act 1985 (c.17)
Valuation Tribunals in England	Regulations under Schedule 11 to the Local Government Finance Act 1988 (c.41)

History – In art. 2, entry relating to the Financial Services and Markets Tribunal omitted by SI 2010/22, art. 5(2) and Sch. 3, para. 143(d), with effect from 6 April 2010, subject to transitional provisions in SI 2010/22, Sch. 5. The former entry read as follows:

"Financial Services and Markets Tribunal, except for its functions in respect of Northern Ireland – Section 132 of the Financial Services and Markets Act 2000 (c 8)".

In art. 2, the following entries omitted by SI 2010/22, art. 5(2) and Sch. 3, para. 143, with effect from 18 January 2010, subject to transitional provisions in SI 2010/22, Sch. 5:

- Case Tribunals, or Interim Case Tribunals, drawn from the Adjudication Panel for England – Section 76 of the Local Government Act 2000 (c.22)
- Claims Management Services Tribunal – Section 12 of the Compensation Act 2006 (c.29)
- Family Health Services Appeal Authority in respect of its non-executive functions – Section 169 of the National Health Service Act 2006 (c.41)
- Gambling Appeals Tribunal – Section 140 of the Gambling Act 2005 (c. 19)
- Immigration Services Tribunal – Section 87 of the Immigration and Asylum Act 1999 (c.33)
- Information Tribunal except in respect of appeals relating to national security and its functions in respect of Northern Ireland – Section 6(3) of the Data Protection Act 1998 (c.29)

In art. 2, the following entries omitted by SI 2009/1307, art. 5(1) and (3) and Sch. 2, para. 121, with effect from 1 June 2009 (subject to transitional and savings at SI 2009/1307, Sch. 5):

- Commissioners for the general purposes of the income tax for England and Wales – Section 2 of the Taxes Management Act 1970 (c.9)
- Commissioners for the special purposes of the Income Tax Acts – Section 4 of the Taxes Management Act 1970 (c.9)
- Lands Tribunal – Section 1(1)(b) of the Lands Tribunal Act 1949 (c.42)
- Tribunal – Section 706 of the Income and Corporation Taxes Act 1988 (c.1)
- Tribunal – Section 704 of the Income Tax Act 2007 (c.3)
- VAT and Duties Tribunals for England, Wales and Northern Ireland – Schedule 12 to the Value Added Tax Act 1994 (c.23)

In art. 2, the words "Mental Health Review Tribunal for Wales" substituted for the words "Mental Health Review Tribunals for England and Wales" by SI 2008/2683, art. 6 and Sch. 1, para. 331(b), with effect from 3 November 2008.".

INCOME TAX (BENEFITS RECEIVED BY FORMER OWNER OF PROPERTY) (ELECTION FOR INHERITANCE TAX TREATMENT) REGULATIONS 2007

(SI 2007/3000)

Made on 19 October 2007 by the Treasury, in exercise of the power conferred by para. 23(2) of Sch. 15 to the Finance Act 2004. Operative from 14 November 2007.

CITATION AND COMMENCEMENT

1 These Regulations may be cited as the Income Tax (Benefits Received by Former Owner of Property) (Election for Inheritance Tax Treatment) Regulations 2007 and shall come into force on 14th November 2007.

MANNER IN WHICH ELECTION TO BE MADE

2 An election under paragraph 21 or 22 of Schedule 15 to the Finance Act 2004 (power to elect for inheritance tax treatment of pre-owned assets) is to be made in writing on the form designated IHT 500 in the Schedule to these Regulations.

SCHEDULE – FORM IHT 500

Regulation 2

HM Revenue & Customs

Election for Inheritance Tax to apply to asset previously owned

Fill in this form if you are chargeable to Income Tax on the benefit you receive from property you previously owned but want to elect for the property to be treated as part of your estate for Inheritance Tax purposes.

You should read the notes IHT501 as you fill in this form. Please provide information for all sections, inserting 'not applicable' where appropriate.

About the person making the election

Title

Unique Taxpayer Reference (UTR)

Surname

National Insurance number

First name(s)

Address

Date of birth *DD MM YYYY*

Postcode

HMRC Income Tax office

HMRC Income Tax office reference

About the property subject to the election

The property is:

an interest in land ☐   a chattel ☐   intangible property ☐

Description of the property

Name(s) of the legal owners of the property

Details of disposal(s) or contribution(s)

What is the nature and extent of your interest in the property?

Is the property conditionally exempt from Inheritance Tax or Capital Gains Tax on an earlier event?

Yes ☐   No ☐

If 'Yes', please provide details

Name(s) of anyone else who receives a benefit from the property

The election

I elect that the property specified above is to form part of my estate for Inheritance Tax purposes under the provisions of paragraphs 21 to 23, Schedule 15 to the Finance Act 2004.

Signature of person making the election

Date *DD MM YYYY*

Capacity

The election applies from the year of Assessment beginning on

6 April

When you have completed this form send it to:

Pre-owned Assets Section
HMRC Inheritance Tax
PO Box 38
Castle Meadow Road
Nottingham
NG2 1BB

Document Exchange: DX 701201 Nottingham 4.

Probate and Inheritance Tax helpline:
0845 30 20 900.

For further guidance go to:
www.hmrc.gov.uk/poa/index.htm

Statutory Instruments

TAX AVOIDANCE SCHEMES (PENALTY) REGULATIONS 2007

(SI 2007/3104, as amended by SI 2010/2743)

Made on 30 October 2007 by the Treasury, in exercise of the powers conferred by s. 98C(2A)–(2C)(a) of the Taxes Management Act 1970. Operative in accordance with regulation 1.

CITATION AND COMMENCEMENT

1 These Regulations may be cited as the Tax Avoidance Schemes (Penalty) Regulations 2007 and shall come into force 21 days after they are made.

INTERPRETATION

2 In these Regulations–

"**FA 2004**" means the Finance Act 2004; and

"**TMA 1970**" means the Taxes Management Act 1970.

INCREASED PENALTY FOLLOWING THE MAKING OF AN ORDER UNDER SECTION 306A OF FA 2004

3 For the purposes of section 98C(2A) of TMA 1970, the prescribed sum is £5,000.

History – Reg. 3 substituted by SI 2010/2743, reg. 3, with effect from 1 January 2011. Former reg. 3 read as follows: "**3** Where a penalty is imposed under section 98C(1) of TMA 1970 following the making of an order under section 306A of FA 2004, the amount specified in section 98C(1)(b) of TMA 1970 (daily penalty) is increased to £5,000.".

INCREASED PENALTY FOLLOWING THE MAKING OF AN ORDER UNDER SECTION 314A OF FA 2004

4 For the purposes of section 98C(2B) of TMA 1970, the prescribed sum is £5,000.

History – Reg. 4 substituted by SI 2010/2743, reg. 4, with effect from 1 January 2011. Former reg. 4 read as follows: "**4** Where a penalty is imposed under section 98C(1) of TMA 1970 following the making of an order under section 314A of FA 2004, the amount specified in section 98C(1)(b) of TMA 1970 is increased to £5,000.".

POLICE AND CRIMINAL EVIDENCE ACT 1984 (APPLICATION TO REVENUE AND CUSTOMS) ORDER 2007

(SI 2007/3175, as amended by SI 2010/360)

Made on 8 November 2007 by the Treasury in exercise of the powers conferred by s. 114 (2) and (3) of the Police and Criminal Evidence Act 1984. Operative from 1 December 2007.

CITATION AND COMMENCEMENT

1 This Order may be cited as the Police and Criminal Evidence Act 1984 (Application to Revenue and Customs) Order 2007 and shall come into force on 1st December 2007.

INTERPRETATION

2(1) In this Order–

"the Act" means the Police and Criminal Evidence Act 1984;

"the Commissioners" means the Commissioners for Her Majesty's Revenue and Customs;

"the customs and excise Acts" has the meaning given to it by section 1 of the Customs and Excise Management Act 1979;

"former Inland Revenue matter" means a matter specified in section 54(4) (b) or (f) of, or in paragraphs 3, 7, 10, 14, 15, 19 or 24 to 29 of Schedule 1 to, the Commissioners for Revenue and Customs Act 2005;

"office of Revenue and Customs" means premises wholly or partly occupied by Her Majesty's Revenue and Customs;

"relevant indictable offence" means an indictable offence which relates to a matter in relation to which Her Majesty's Revenue and Customs have functions apart from a former Inland Revenue matter;

"relevant investigation" means a criminal investigation conducted by officers of Revenue and Customs which relates to a matter in relation to which Her Majesty's Revenue and Customs have functions apart from a former Inland Revenue matter.

2(2) A person is in Revenue and Customs detention for the purpose of this Order if–

(a) he has been taken to an office of Revenue and Customs after being arrested for an offence; or

(b) he is arrested at an office of Revenue and Customs after attending voluntarily at the office or accompanying an officer of Revenue and Customs to it,

and is detained there or detained elsewhere in the charge of an officer of Revenue and Customs, and nothing shall prevent a detained person from being transferred between Revenue and Customs detention and police detention.

History – In art. 2(1), in the definition of "former Inland Revenue matter", "14, 15" substituted for "13 to 15" by SI 2010/360, art. 2(2), with effect from 19 March 2010.

APPLICATION

3(1) The provisions of the Act contained in Schedule 1 to this Order which relate to investigations of offences conducted by police officers or to persons detained by the police shall apply to relevant investigations conducted by officers of Revenue and Customs and to persons detained by such officers.

This is subject to the modifications in paragraphs (2) and (3) and articles 4 to 19 and Schedule 2.

3(2) The Act shall have effect as if the words and phrases in Column 1 of Part 1 of Schedule 2 to this Order were replaced by the substitute words and phrases in Column 2 of that Part.

3(3) Where in the Act any act or thing is to be done by a constable of a specified rank, that act or thing shall be done by an officer of Revenue and Customs of at least the grade specified in Column 2 of Part 2 of Schedule 2 to this Order, and the Act shall be construed accordingly.

EXCEPTIONS

4 Nothing in the application of the Act to Revenue and Customs confers on an officer of Revenue and Customs any power–

(a) to charge a person with any offence;

(b)   to release a person on bail; or

(c)   to detain a person for an offence after he has been charged with that offence.

SEIZURE AND RETENTION OF THINGS FOUND UPON SEARCH

5(1)   Where in the Act a constable is given power to seize and retain any thing found upon a lawful search of person or premises, an officer of Revenue and Customs shall have the same power notwithstanding that the thing found is not evidence of an offence which relates to a matter in relation to which Her Majesty's Revenue and Customs have functions.

5(2)   Nothing in the application of the Act to Revenue and Customs prevents any thing lawfully seized by a person under any enactment from being accepted and retained by an officer of Revenue and Customs.

5(3)   Section 21 of the Act (access and copying) shall not apply to any thing seized as liable to forfeiture under the customs and excise Acts.

EXCLUDED AND SPECIAL PROCEDURE MATERIAL

6   In its application by virtue of article 3 above the Act shall have effect as if the following section were inserted after section 14—

> **"14A   Exception for Revenue and Customs**
>
> **14A**   Material in the possession of a person who acquired or created it in the course of any trade, business, profession or other occupation or for the purpose of any paid or unpaid office and which relates to a matter in relation to which Her Majesty's Revenue and Customs have functions, is neither excluded material nor special procedure material for the purposes of any enactment such as is mentioned in section 9(2) above.".

RESTRICTION ON OTHER POWERS TO APPLY FOR PRODUCTION OF DOCUMENTS

7   In its application by virtue of article 3 above the Act shall have effect as if the following section were inserted after section 14A—

> **"14B   Revenue and Customs: restriction on other powers to apply for production of documents**
>
> **14B(1)**   An officer of Revenue and Customs may make an application for the delivery of, or access to, documents under a provision specified in subsection (3) only if the condition in subsection (2) is satisfied.
>
> **14B(2)**   The condition is that the officer thinks that an application under Schedule 1 would not succeed because the material required does not consist of or include special procedure material.
>
> **14B(3)**   The provisions are—
>
> (a)   section 20BA and Schedule 1AA of the Taxes Management Act 1970 (serious tax fraud);
>
> (b)   paragraph 11 of Schedule 11 to the Value Added Tax Act 1994 (VAT);
>
> (c)   paragraph 4A of Schedule 7 to the Finance Act 1994 (insurance premium tax);
>
> (d)   paragraph 7 of Schedule 5 to the Finance Act 1996 (landfill tax);
>
> (e)   paragraph 131 of Schedule 6 to the Finance Act 2000 (climate change levy);
>
> (f)   paragraph 8 of Schedule 7 to the Finance Act 2001 (aggregates levy);
>
> (g)   Part 6 of Schedule 13 to the Finance Act 2003 (stamp duty land tax).".

MODIFICATION OF SECTION 18 OF THE ACT (ENTRY AND SEARCH AFTER ARREST)

8(1)   Section 18 of the Act (entry and search after arrest) is modified as follows.

8(2)   For subsection 18 (1) substitute—

> **"18(1)**   Subject to the following provisions of this section, an officer of Revenue and Customs may enter and search any premises occupied or controlled by a person who is under arrest for any relevant indictable offence if he has reasonable grounds for suspecting that there is on the premises evidence, other than items subject to legal privilege, that relates—
>
> (a)   to that offence; or

(b)   to some other indictable offence which is connected with or similar to that offence.".

MODIFICATION OF SECTION 35 OF THE ACT (DESIGNATED POLICE STATIONS)

9(1)   Section 35 of the Act (designated police stations) is modified as follows.

9(2)   For subsection 35(1) substitute–

"**35(1)**   The Director of Detection shall designate offices of Revenue and Customs which, subject to sections 30(3) and (5), are to be the offices to be used for the purposes of detaining arrested persons."

9(3)   For subsection 35(2) substitute–

"**35(2)**   The Director of Detection's duty under subsection (1) above is to designate offices of Revenue and Customs appearing to him to provide enough accommodation for that purpose.".

9(4)   For subsection 35(3) substitute–

"**35(3)**   Without prejudice to section 12 of the Interpretation Act 1978 (continuity of duties) the Director of Detection–

(a)   may designate an office which was not previously designated; and

(b)   may direct that a designation of an office previously made shall cease to operate.".

MODIFICATION OF SECTION 36 OF THE ACT (CUSTODY OFFICERS AT POLICE STATIONS)

10(1)   Section 36 of the Act (custody officers at police stations) is modified as follows.

10(2)   For subsection (2) substitute–

"**36(2)**   A custody officer for an office of Revenue and Customs designated under section 35(1) above shall be appointed–

(a)   by the Director of Detection; or

(b)   by such other officer of Revenue and Customs as the Director of Detection may direct.".

MODIFICATION OF SECTION 41 OF THE ACT (LIMITS ON PERIOD OF DETENTION WITHOUT CHARGE)

11(1)   Section 41 of the Act (limits on period of detention without charge) is modified as follows.

11(2)   For subsection (2)(b) substitute–

"(b)   in the case of a person arrested outside England and Wales, shall be–

(i)   the time at which that person arrives at the office of Revenue and Customs in England and Wales in which the offence for which he was arrested is being investigated; or

(ii)   the time 24 hours after the time of that person's entry into England and Wales.".

MODIFICATION OF SECTION 50 OF THE ACT (RECORDS OF DETENTION)

12(1)   Section 50 of the Act (records of detention) is modified as follows.

12(2)   For subsection (1) substitute–

"**50(1)**   The Commissioners shall keep written records showing on an annual basis–

(a)   the number of persons kept in Revenue and Customs detention for more than 24 hours and subsequently released without charge;

(b)   the number of applications for warrants of further detention and the results of the applications; and

(c)   in relation to each warrant of further detention–

(i)   the period of further detention authorised by it;

(ii)   the period which the person named in it spent in Revenue and Customs detention on its authority; and

(iii)   whether he was charged or released without charge."

12(3)   For subsection (2) substitute–

"**50(2)**   Every annual report made by the Commissioners shall contain information about the matters mentioned in subsection (1) above in respect of the period to which the report relates.".

MODIFICATION OF SECTION 55 OF THE ACT (INTIMATE SEARCHES)

13(1)   Section 55 of the Act (intimate searches) shall have effect as if it related only to things such as are mentioned in subsection (1)(a) of that section.

13(2)   The annual report of the Commissioners shall contain information about searches under section 55 which have been carried out during the period to which the report relates.

MODIFICATION OF SECTION 64 OF THE ACT (DESTRUCTION OF FINGERPRINTS AND SAMPLES)

14(1)   Section 64 of the Act (destruction of fingerprints and samples) is modified as follows.

14(2)   For subsection (5)(b) substitute–

"(b)   the Director of Risk and Intelligence shall make access to the data impossible, as soon as it is practicable to do so.".

14(3)   For subsection (6A) substitute–

"**64(6A)**   If–

(a)   subsection (5)(b) above falls to be complied with; and

(b)   the person to whose fingerprints or impressions of footwear the data relates asks for a certificate that it has been complied with,

such a certificate shall be issued to him, not later than the end of the period of three months beginning with the day on which he asks for it, by the Director of Risk and Intelligence or a person authorised by him or on his behalf for the purposes of this section."

MODIFICATION OF SECTION 77 OF THE ACT (DEFINITION OF INDEPENDENT PERSON)

15   Section 77(3) of the Act (definition of independent person) shall be modified to the extent that the definition of "independent person" shall, in addition to the persons mentioned therein, also include an officer of Revenue and Customs or any other person acting under the authority of the Commissioners.

USE OF REASONABLE FORCE

16   Where any provision of the Act as applied to Revenue and Customs–

(a)   confers a power on an officer of Revenue and Customs, and

(b)   does not provide that the power may only be exercised with the consent of some person other than that officer,

the officer may use reasonable force, if necessary, in the exercise of the power.

ARREST WITHOUT WARRANT

17   Section 24(2) of the Act (arrest without warrant) does not limit–

(a)   section 138(1) of the Customs and Excise Management Act 1979;

(b)   section 20 and paragraph 4 of Schedule 3 to the Criminal Justice (International Co-operation) Act 1990;

(c)   any other enactment, including any enactment contained in subordinate legislation, for the time being in force which confers upon officers of Revenue and Customs the power to arrest or detain persons.

SEARCH OF PERSONS

18   Where an officer of Revenue and Customs searches premises in reliance on a warrant under section 8 of, or paragraph 12 of Schedule 1 to, the Act (power of justice of the peace to authorise entry and search of premises), he may search any person found on the premises–

(a)   where he has reasonable cause to believe that person to be in possession of material which is likely to be of substantial value (whether by itself or together with other material) to the investigation of the offence;

(b)   but no person should be searched except by a person of the same sex.

AUTHORISATION

19 Powers and functions in the provisions of the Act contained in Schedule 1 to this Order may be exercised only by officers of Revenue and Customs acting with the authority (which may be general or specific) of the Commissioners.

REVOCATION

20 The following instruments are revoked—

(a)   the Police and Criminal Evidence Act 1984 (Application to Customs and Excise) Order 1981;

(b)   the Police and Criminal Evidence Act 1984 (Application to Customs and Excise) Order 1987;

(c)   the Police and Criminal Evidence Act 1984 (Application to Customs and Excise) (Amendment) Order 1995; and

(d)   the Police and Criminal Evidence Act 1984 (Application to Customs and Excise) (Amendment) Order 1996.

SCHEDULES

SCHEDULE 1 – PROVISIONS OF THE ACT APPLIED TO REVENUE AND CUSTOMS

Article 3(1)

Section 8 (power of justice of the peace to authorise entry and search of premises)

Section 9 (special provisions as to access) and Schedule 1 (special procedure)

Section 15 (search warrants-safeguards)

Section 16 (execution of warrants)

Section 17(1)(a)(i), (1)(b), (1)(cb), (1)(d), (2), (4)(c) (entry for purpose of arrest etc.)

Section 18 (entry and search after arrest) (subject to the modification in article 8)

Section 19 (general power of seizure etc.)

Section 20 (extension of powers of seizure to computerised information)

Section 21 (access and copying) (subject to the modification in article 5)

Section 22(1) to (4) and (7) (retention)

Section 24(2), (4), (5) (arrest without warrant: constables) (subject to the modification in article 17)

Section 28 (information to be given on arrest)

Section 29 (voluntary attendance at police station etc.)

Section 30(1) to (4) (a) and (5) to (11) (arrest elsewhere than at police station)

Section 31 (arrest for further offence)

Section 32(1) to (9) (search upon arrest) (subject to the modifications in article 5)

Section 34(1) to (5) (limitations on police detention)

Section 35(1), (2), (3) and (4) (designated police stations) (subject to the modification in article 9)

Section 36(1), (2), (3), (4), (5), (6), (7), (8), (9) and (10) (custody officers at police stations) (subject to the modification in article 10)

Section 37 (duties of custody officer before charge)

Section 39 (responsibilities in relation to persons detained)

Section 40 (review of police detention)

Section 41(1), (2), (4) and (6) to (9) (limits on period of detention without charge) (subject to the modification in article 11)

Section 42(1), (2) and (4) to (11) (authorisation of continued detention)

Section 43(1) to (12) and (14) to (19) (warrants of further detention)

Section 44 (extension of warrants of further detention)

Section 50 (records of detention) (subject to the modification in article 12)

Section 51(d) (savings)

Section 54 (searches of detained persons)

Section 55 (intimate searches) (subject to the modifications in articles 5 and 13)

Statutory Instruments

Section 56(1) to (9) (right to have someone informed when arrested)

Section 57 (additional rights of children and young persons)

Section 58(1) to (11) (access to legal advice)

Section 62 (intimate samples)

Section 63 (other samples)

Section 64, except (6B), (destruction of fingerprints and samples) (subject to the modification in article 14)

Section 66 (codes of practice)

Section 67 (codes of practice-supplementary)

Section 77 (confessions by mentally handicapped persons) (subject to the modification in article 15)

Section 107 (police officers performing duties of higher rank)

History – In Sch. 1, the words "Section 17(1)(a)(i), (1)(b), (1)(cb), (1)(d), (2), (4)(c)" substituted for "Section 17(1)(b), (2), (4)" by SI 2010/360, art. 2(3)(a), with effect from 19 March 2010.
In Sch. 1, the words "Section 22(1) to (4) and (7)" substituted for "Section 22(1) to (4)" by SI 2010/360, art. 2(3)(b), with effect from 19 March 2010.
In Sch. 1, the words "Section 24(2), (4), (5)" substituted for "Section 24(2)" by SI 2010/360, art. 2(3)(c), with effect from 19 March 2010.

SCHEDULE 2

Article 3(2)

Part 1 – Substitution of Equivalent Words and Phrases in the Act

Where in the Act a word or phrase specified in Column 1 is used, in the application of the Act to Revenue and Customs, there shall be substituted the equivalent word or phrase in column 2–

Column 1	Column 2
WORDS AND PHASES USED IN THE ACT	*SUBSTITUTED WORDS AND PHRASES*
chief officer of police	director
constable	officer of Revenue and Customs
designated police station	designated office of Revenue and Customs
officer of a force maintained by a police authority	officer of Revenue and Customs
Police detention (except in section 118 and in section 39(1)(a) the second time the words occur)	Revenue and Customs detention
Police officer	Officer of Revenue and Customs
Police station	Office of Revenue and Customs
rank	Grade
station	Office of Revenue and Customs
The police	Her Majesty's Revenue and Customs

Part 2 – Equivalent Titles of Officers

Where in the Act an act or thing is to be done by a constable of the rank specified in Column 1, that same act or thing shall, in the application of the Act to Revenue and Customs, be done by an officer of Revenue and Customs of at least an equivalent grade specified in Column 2–

Column 1	Column 2
RANK OF CONSTABLE	GRADE OF OFFICER
Sergeant	Officer
Inspector	Higher officer
Chief Inspector	Higher officer
Superintendent	Senior officer

ENERGY-SAVING ITEMS (INCOME TAX) REGULATIONS 2007

(SI 2007/3278)

Made on 15 November 2007 by the Treasury, in exercise of the powers conferred by s. 312 and 314 of the Income Tax (Trading and Other Income) Act 2005. Operative from 6 December 2007.

CITATION, COMMENCEMENT AND INTERPRETATION

1(1) These Regulations may be cited as the Energy-Saving Items (Income Tax) Regulations 2007, shall come into force on 6th December 2007, and shall have effect in respect of expenditure incurred on or after 6th April 2007.

1(2) In these Regulations–

"**ITTOIA 2005**" means the Income Tax (Trading and Other Income) Act 2005;

"**deduction**" means a deduction allowed under section 312 of ITTOIA 2005 (deduction for expenditure on energy-saving items);

"**maximum amount**" shall be construed in accordance with regulation 3(1);

"**relevant expenditure**" means–

(a)   expenditure incurred in acquiring and installing an energy-saving item in a dwelling-house, or

(b)   in so far as it is for the benefit of a dwelling-house, expenditure incurred in acquiring and installing an energy-saving item in a building containing that dwelling-house.

ITEMS OF AN ENERGY-SAVING NATURE

2 The following descriptions of items of an energy-saving nature are specified for the purposes of section 312(5)(c) of ITOIA 2005–

(a)   hot water system insulation;

(b)   draught proofing;

(c)   solid wall insulation; and

(d)   floor insulation.

RESTRICTIONS ON RELEVANT EXPENDITURE TO BE TAKEN INTO ACCOUNT: GENERAL

3(1) The maximum amount of the relevant expenditure which may be taken into account in calculating the deduction is £1,500 per dwelling-house.

3(2) Paragraph (1) applies irrespective of the number of persons incurring relevant expenditure or entitled to a deduction in respect of a dwelling-house.

3(3) If the person entitled to the deduction has received a contribution from any other person towards the relevant expenditure incurred, that contribution shall be excluded in calculating the relevant expenditure incurred by the person entitled to the deduction.

3(4) Further rules (to be applied in the order stated) are set out in–

(a)   regulation 4 (first further rule: apportionment of relevant expenditure benefiting more than one property);

(b)   regulation 5 (second further rule: restriction of relevant expenditure to the maximum amount);

(c)   regulation 6 (third further rule: apportionment of relevant expenditure if a dwelling-house or building is owned jointly or in common or is subject to differing estates or interests).

FIRST FURTHER RULE: APPORTIONMENT OF RELEVANT EXPENDITURE BENEFITING MORE THAN ONE PROPERTY

4(1) This regulation applies to relevant expenditure which is incurred in acquiring and installing an energy-saving item–

(a)   in more than one dwelling-house,

(b)   in a building containing more than one dwelling-house, or

(c)   in a building containing one or more dwelling-houses and one or more properties which are not dwelling-houses.

4(2)   The relevant expenditure must be apportioned on a just and reasonable basis to all the properties which benefit from it.

4(3)   The amount of the relevant expenditure for which a deduction is allowable in respect of a dwelling-house shall not exceed the amount which is apportioned to that dwelling-house.

SECOND FURTHER RULE: RESTRICTION OF RELEVANT EXPENDITURE TO THE MAXIMUM AMOUNT

5(1)   This regulation applies if the relevant expenditure benefiting a particular dwelling-house (including any relevant expenditure apportioned to the dwelling-house under regulation 4) exceeds the maximum amount.

5(2)   The relevant expenditure must be restricted to the maximum amount.

THIRD FURTHER RULE: APPORTIONMENT OF RELEVANT EXPENDITURE IF A DWELLING-HOUSE OR BUILDING IS OWNED JOINTLY OR IN COMMON OR IS SUBJECT TO DIFFERING ESTATES OR INTERESTS

6(1)   This regulation applies if relevant expenditure is incurred benefiting a dwelling-house and the dwelling-house or the building containing it–

(a)   is owned jointly or in common by the person entitled to the deduction and by other persons, or

(b)   is subject to differing estates or interests.

6(2)   The relevant expenditure (restricted if necessary to the maximum amount) must be apportioned on a just and reasonable basis.

6(3)   The amount of the deduction to which the person entitled to it is entitled shall not exceed the amount apportioned to that person in accordance with paragraph (2).

FURTHER PROVISIONS

7(1)   This regulation applies if any question arises under regulations 3(3) or 4 to 6 as to the amount of the deduction to which a person may be entitled.

7(2)   The amount shall be treated as if it were an amount specified in a paragraph of subsection (1) of section 42 of ICTA 1988 (appeals against determinations under sections 34 to 36 or Chapter 4 of Part 3 of the Income Tax (Trading and Other Income) Act 2005), and the procedure set out in that section shall apply accordingly.

REVOCATION OF THE ENERGY-SAVING ITEMS REGULATIONS 2007 (S.I. 2007/831)

8   The Energy-Saving Items Regulations 2007 (S.I. 2007/831) are revoked.

SECURITISATION COMPANIES (APPLICATION OF SECTION 83(1) OF THE FINANCE ACT 2005: ACCOUNTING STANDARDS) REGULATIONS 2007

(SI 2007/3338)

Made on 3 December 2007 by the Treasury in exercise of the powers conferred by s. 83(7A) and (7B) of the Finance Act 2005. Operative from 27 December 2007.

CITATION AND COMMENCEMENT

1 These Regulations may be cited as the Securitisation Companies (Application of Section 83(1) of the Finance Act 2005: Accounting Standards) Regulations 2007 and shall come into force on 27th December 2007.

APPLICATION OF SECTION 83(1) OF THE FINANCE ACT 2005: ACCOUNTING STANDARDS

2(1) This regulation applies where–

(a) subsection (1) of section 83 of the Finance Act 2005 (application of accounting standards to securitisation companies) applies to a company in relation to a period of account ending before 1st January 2008, and

(b) the company–

    (i) became party to a capital market arrangement referred to in subsection (3)(c) of that section or a related transaction before 1st January 2008 and continues to be party to that arrangement or transaction, or

    (ii) is a warehouse company where any of the financial assets referred to in subsection (6) of that section were acquired before 1st January 2008.

2(2) Subsection (1) of section 83 of the Finance Act 2005 shall apply in relation to periods of account ending on or after 1st January 2008 but before 1st January 2017.

This is subject to paragraph (3).

2(3) Paragraph (2) shall not apply to a company that elects that the paragraph shall not apply to it.

2(4) An election under paragraph (3)–

(a) must be made in writing to Her Majesty's Revenue and Customs,

(b) must be made before the end of the first accounting period ending on or after 1st January 2008, and

(c) is irrevocable.

MODIFICATION OF PROVISIONS OF, AND MADE UNDER, THE CORPORATION TAX ACTS

3(1) This regulation applies in relation to the first period of account of a securitisation company in the case of which section 83(1) of the Finance Act 2005 does not apply by virtue of that section itself or regulation 2 ("the first period") where–

(a) the company continues to be party to a capital market arrangement or a related transaction, or

(b) the company would continue to be a warehouse company if that section continued to apply.

3(2) Where this regulation applies–

(a) there shall be treated as arising any adjustment that would have been made in accordance with section 64 of the Finance Act 2002 (adjustment on change of basis) in any previous period of account had section 83 of the Finance Act 2005 not applied to that period;

(b) in relation to the Loan Relationships and Derivative Contracts (Change of Accounting Practice) Regulations 2004–

    (i) the prescribed period in regulation 3A shall be treated as beginning with the first period, and

    (ii) there shall be treated as prescribed by regulation 4 any debit or credit that would have been brought into account in accordance with regulation 3 in any previous period had section 83 of the Finance Act 2005 not applied to that period.

This is subject to paragraph (3).

Statutory Instruments

3(3) Any amount brought into account on the application of this regulation must be just and reasonable in the circumstances and with regard to whether as a result any amounts cease to be brought into account or are brought into account more than once.

INTERPRETATION

4 For the purposes of these Regulations—

(a)　"party" to a capital market arrangement or a related transaction includes a party to an agreement which—

　　(i)　forms part of the arrangement,

　　(ii)　provides for the raising of finance as part of the arrangement, or

　　(iii)　is necessary for the purposes of implementing the arrangement;

(b)　one or more transactions are to be regarded as related transactions, in the case of any capital market arrangement, if it would be reasonable to assume, from either or both of—

　　(i)　the likely effect of the transactions, and

　　(ii)　the circumstances in which the transactions are entered into or effected,

　　that none of the transactions would have been entered into or effected independently of the arrangement;

(c)　transactions are not prevented from being related transactions, in the case of any capital market arrangement, just because the transactions—

　　(i)　are not between the same parties, or

　　(ii)　are not between the parties to the capital market arrangement.

TAXATION OF INSURANCE SECURITISATION COMPANIES REGULATIONS 2007

(SI 2007/3402)

Made on 4 December 2007 by the Treasury in exercise of the power conferred by s. 84 of the Finance Act 2005. Operative from 28 December 2007.

PRELIMINARY

Citation, commencement and effect

1(1) These Regulations may be cited as the Taxation of Insurance Securitisation Companies Regulations 2007 and shall come into force on 28th December 2007 immediately after the coming into force of the Taxation of Securitisation Companies (Amendment No. 2) Regulations 2007.

1(2) These Regulations have effect from the beginning of periods of account beginning on or after 1st January 2007 and current on 4th December 2007.

Interpretation

2(1) In these Regulations–

"**capital market arrangement**" and "**capital market investment**" have the same meaning as in section 72B(1) of the Insolvency Act 1986 (see paragraphs 1, 2 and 3 of Schedule 2A to that Act);

"**ICTA**" means the Income and Corporation Taxes Act 1988;

"**independent persons**" means persons who are not connected with a company (and see paragraph (3));

"**insurance special purpose vehicle**" and "**Insurance Prudential Sourcebook**" have the same meanings as in section 431(2) of ICTA.

2(2) Section 839 of ICTA (connected persons) applies for the purposes of the definition of "**independent persons**", except that in applying the definition of "**control**" in that section a person is not to be treated as a participator in a company by reason only that he is a loan creditor of the company.

Scope of these Regulations

3(1) These Regulations make provision as to the application of the Corporation Tax Acts in relation to an insurance securitisation company.

3(2) The Regulations deal with the following matters–

(a)   they define "**insurance securitisation company**" (see regulation 4);

(b)   they provide that the Regulations do not apply if an insurance securitisation company has an unallowable purpose (see regulation 5);

(c)   they make provision for the application of accounting standards to an insurance securitisation company (see regulation 6);

(d)   they make supplementary provision in relation to the application, modification and non-application of provisions of the Corporation Tax Acts (see regulations 7 to 11).

INSURANCE SECURITISATION COMPANIES

Meaning of insurance securitisation company

4(1) For the purposes of these Regulations an "**insurance securitisation company**" means a company that is an insurance special purpose vehicle and–

(a)   meets conditions A to C, or

(b)   whose liabilities representing debtor relationships are owed wholly or mainly to a note-issuing company or intermediate borrowing company within the Taxation of Securitisation Companies Regulations 2006.

4(2) Condition A is that the company is within section 84(2)(a) of the Finance Act 2005.

4(3) Condition B is that the securities that represent the capital market investment referred to in section 84(2)(a)(ii) of that Act are issued wholly or mainly to independent persons.

4(4) Condition C is that the total value of the capital market investments made under the capital market arrangement referred to in section 84(2)(a)(iii) of that Act is at least £10 million.

Insurance securitisation companies that have an unallowable purpose

5(1) These Regulations do not apply or will cease to apply to an insurance securitisation company that—

(a)   has an unallowable purpose, or

(b)   at any time has had an unallowable purpose.

5(2) Where these Regulations cease to apply by virtue of this regulation the accounting period of the company shall end.

5(3) For the purpose of these Regulations an insurance securitisation company has an unallowable purpose if the purpose for which the company is a party to—

(a)   the capital market arrangement,

(b)   any related transaction, or

(c)   any transaction in pursuance of the capital market arrangement,

includes a purpose which is not amongst the business or other commercial purposes of the company.

5(4) If one of the purposes for which an insurance securitisation company is at any time a party to—

(a)   any capital market arrangement,

(b)   any related transaction in the case of any capital market arrangement, or

(c)   any transaction in pursuance of any capital market arrangement,

is a tax avoidance purpose, that purpose shall be taken to be a business or other commercial purpose of the company only where it is not the main purpose, or one of the main purposes, for which the company is party to the arrangements or transaction at that time.

5(5) For the purpose of this regulation—

(a)   one or more transactions are to be regarded as related transactions, in the case of any arrangements, if it would be reasonable to assume, from either or both of—

    (i)   the likely effect of the transactions, and

    (ii)   the circumstances in which the transactions are entered into or effected,

that none of the transactions would have been entered into or effected independently of the arrangements; and

(b)   transactions are not prevented from being related transactions, in the case of any arrangements, just because the transactions—

    (i)   are not between the same parties, or

    (ii)   are not between the parties to the capital market arrangements.

5(6) In this regulation—

"**tax avoidance purpose**" means any purpose that consists in securing a tax advantage for any other person;

"**tax advantage**" has the same meaning as in section 840ZA of ICTA (tax avoidance).

Application of accounting standards to insurance securitisation companies

6 For the purposes of the Corporation Tax Acts as they apply to an insurance securitisation company, generally accepted accounting practice shall be taken to be UK generally accepted accounting practice as it applied for a period of account ending on 31 December 2006 but excluding the application of Financial Reporting Standard 26 issued in December 2004 by the Accounting Standards Board.

SUPPLEMENTARY PROVISIONS

Application, modification and non-application of provisions of the Corporation Tax Acts

7 In relation to an insurance securitisation company the provisions of the Corporation Tax Acts have effect in accordance with regulations 8 to 11.

ICTA

8(1) ICTA has effect as follows.

8(2) In section 209(2) (meaning of distribution) paragraphs (b) to (f) shall not apply in relation to any interest paid or other distribution made by an insurance securitisation company.

8(3) For the purposes of Chapter 4 of Part 10 (group relief) an insurance securitisation company shall not be treated as the member of any group or consortium.

The Taxation of Chargeable Gains Act 1992

9(1)   Taxation of Chargeable Gains Act 1992 has effect as follows.

9(2)   Section 171 (transfers within a group: general provisions) shall not apply if **"company B"** in subsection (1) of that section is an insurance securitisation company.

9(3)   Section 179A (reallocation within group of gain or loss accruing under section 179) shall not apply if **"company C"** in that section is an insurance securitisation company.

The Finance Act 1996

10(1)   The Finance Act 1996 has effect as follows.

10(2)   In Schedule 9 (loan relationships: special computational provisions)–

(a)   paragraph 2 (late interest) shall not apply if the person standing in the position of a creditor as respects a loan relationship within that paragraph is an insurance securitisation company;

(b)   paragraph 12 (continuity of treatment: groups etc) shall not apply if the **"transferee company"** or **"transferor company"** in subparagraph (1) of that paragraph is an insurance securitisation company;

(c)   paragraph 17 (deeply discounted securities where companies have a connection) shall not apply if the **"issuing company"** or the company standing in the position of a creditor in subparagraph (1) of that paragraph is an insurance securitisation company;

(d)   paragraph 18 (deeply discounted securities of companies) shall not apply if the **"issuing company"** or the company standing in the position of a creditor in subparagraph (1) of that paragraph is an insurance securitisation company.

The Finance Act 2002

11(1)   The Finance Act 2002 has effect as follows.

11(2)   Paragraph 28 of Schedule 26 (derivative contracts: transactions within groups) shall not apply if the **"transferee company"** or **"transferor company"** in subparagraph (1) of that paragraph is an insurance securitisation company.

SCIENTIFIC RESEARCH ORGANISATIONS REGULATIONS 2007

(SI 2007/3426)

Made on 5 December 2007 by the Treasury in exercise of the powers conferred by s. 508(1A) and (1B) of the Income and Corporation Taxes Act 1988. Operative from 1 January 2008.

PART 1 – INTRODUCTION

CITATION, COMMENCEMENT AND EFFECT

1(1)   These Regulations may be cited as the Scientific Research Organisations Regulations 2007 and shall come into force on 1st January 2008.

1(2)   These Regulations have effect in relation to accounting periods that begin on or after that date.

INTERPRETATION

2(1)   In these Regulations a reference to a section without more is a reference to that section of the Income and Corporation Taxes Act 1988.

2(2)   In these Regulations–

"constitutional document" means the memorandum of association, articles of association or other similar instrument regulating the functions of the Association;

"intellectual property" has the meaning it has in paragraph 2(2) of Schedule 29 to the Finance Act 2002;

"relevant income" means the amount determined in accordance with regulation 7 (relevant income of an accounting period); and

"100% subsidiary company" means a company–

(a)   the entire ordinary share capital of which is beneficially owned directly or indirectly by the Association, or

(b)   which is one limited by guarantee and of which the Association is the only member.

2(3)   Section 838 (subsidiaries) shall apply for the purpose of determining whether a company is a 100% subsidiary company of an Association but construing references in section 838(1)(b) to 75 per cent as to 100%.

PART 2 – ASSOCIATIONS, OBJECT AND PROFITS

ASSOCIATIONS FOR THE PURPOSES OF SECTION 508

3   The following shall be deemed to be an Association for the purposes of section 508(1)(a)–

(a)   a body formed by the combining of two or more persons for a purpose common to those persons, or

(b)   a body corporate comprised of two or more members.

ASSOCIATION'S OBJECT

4(1)   In relation to an accounting period, an Association shall be deemed to have as its object the undertaking of research and development which may lead to or facilitate an extension of any class or classes of trade if–

(a)   the Association's constitutional document states that the object of the Association is the undertaking of research and development which may lead to or facilitate an extension of any class or classes of trade;

(b)   the stated object is the only object of the Association;

(c)   the Association satisfies the income spending condition in regulation 5;

(d)   regulation 6 (breach of income spending condition) does not apply;

(e)   regulation 15 (breach of arrangements for disseminating the results of research and development) does not apply; and

(f)   regulation 17 (breach of intellectual property requirements) does not apply.

This paragraph is subject to paragraph (2).

4(2)   Where an Association's constitutional document does not satisfy sub-paragraph (b) of paragraph (1) that sub-paragraph shall be deemed to be satisfied if–

(a)   in relation to the accounting period immediately preceding the first accounting period in relation to which these Regulations have effect, an Association is approved by the Secretary of State for the purposes of section 508, and

(b)   the object or objects stated in the constitutional document in relation to the accounting period for which the approval was given has not or have not in any way been altered or replaced.

INCOME SPENDING CONDITION

5(1)   The income spending condition in relation to an accounting period is that the Association must apply, or intend to apply, at least 75% of the amount of its relevant income of the accounting period to activities that are treated as research and development which may lead to or facilitate an extension of any class or classes of trade.

This is subject to paragraphs (2) and (3).

5(2)   Paragraph (3) applies in a case where an Association–

(a)   intends to apply an amount of its relevant income of an accounting period to activities that are treated as research and development, and

(b)   intends to so apply the amount after the accounting period in which the relevant income arose.

5(3)   Where this paragraph applies–

(a)   the activities, to which the amount referred to in paragraph (2) is to be applied, must be planned or programmed to be undertaken by or on behalf of the Association; and

(b)   the plan or programme of activities must have been prepared on or before the last day of the accounting period.

BREACH OF INCOME SPENDING CONDITION

6(1)   This regulation applies where an Association fails to apply the amount (or any part of it) referred to in regulation 5(2) to the planned or programmed activities referred to in regulation 5(3) before the fifth anniversary of the last day of the accounting period in which the relevant income arose.

6(2)   Where this regulation applies the Association shall be deemed not to have complied with the condition in section 508(1)(a) in relation to any accounting period which falls in whole or in part in the calendar year that ends on the sixth anniversary of the last day of the accounting period in which the relevant income arose.

RELEVANT INCOME OF AN ACCOUNTING PERIOD

7   For the purposes of regulation 5, the amount of an Association's relevant income of an accounting period is the amount of its gross income of the accounting period less any amount paid by the Association in the accounting period in respect of pension deficit funding.

GROSS INCOME OF AN ACCOUNTING PERIOD

8(1)   For the purposes of regulation 7, the gross income of an accounting period shall be determined in accordance with generally accepted accounting practice but subject to paragraphs (2) to (4).

8(2)   The amount of the gross income of an accounting period is the amount of–

(a)   the revenue of the period, and

(b)   subject to paragraph (4), any chargeable gains arising to the Association in the period.

8(3)   For the purposes of paragraph (2) the revenue of the period includes in particular–

(a)   gross investment income;

(b)   interest;

(c)   dividends;

(d)   royalties;

(e)   grants of funding for the undertaking of research and development;

Statutory Instruments

(f)   grants from public funds;

(g)   any payment of a sum of money received by the Association which, if the Association were a charity, would be a qualifying donation received by it within the meaning of–

    (i)   section 339 (charges on income: donations to charity), or

    (ii)   section 25 of the Finance Act 1990 (donations to charity by individuals), and

(h)   any other amounts received by the Association which, if the Association were a charity, would be treated for the purposes of the Tax Acts in relation to the Association as a donation to it.

8(4)   Where in an accounting period an Association sells or otherwise disposes of real property to a 100% subsidiary company of the Association any chargeable gain arising to the Association on the sale or disposal of the real property shall not be included in the determination of the gross income of the accounting period.

8(5)   In paragraph (1) **"generally accepted accounting practice"** has the meaning it has in section 50(1) of the Finance Act 2004.

PENSION DEFICIT FUNDING

9(1)   For the purposes of regulation 7, an amount is paid in respect of pension deficit funding if–

(a)   it is paid directly or indirectly to the trustees or managers of an occupational pension scheme to which Part 3 of the Pensions Act 2004 applies;

(b)   the amount paid–

    (i)   is recommended by an actuary, or

    (ii)   made in compliance with a direction, notice or order of the Pensions Regulator made under the Pensions Act 2004;

(c)   the amount paid discharges, in whole or part, an obligation of the Association to make good any deficiency in the assets of the scheme required to meet the scheme's liabilities;

(d)   the obligation discharged by the amount paid is in respect of only those of the scheme's liabilities which arise before the first day of the first accounting period in relation to which these Regulations have effect; and

(e)   the obligation discharged by the amount paid is in respect of only those of the scheme's liabilities to beneficiaries who undertook scientific research the purpose of which was to facilitate an extension of any class or classes of trade.

9(2)   In paragraph (1) **"scientific research"** means any activities in the fields of natural or applied science for the extension of knowledge.

RELEVANT INCOME OF AN EARLIER ACCOUNTING PERIOD APPLIED IN A LATER ACCOUNTING PERIOD

10   For the purposes of regulation 5, in determining the percentage of the amount of the relevant income of an accounting period ("the relevant period") applied, or intended to be applied, to activities treated as research and development, any amount which–

(a)   arose in an earlier accounting period, and

(b)   is applied, or intended to be applied, in the relevant period,

shall not be taken into account.

NON-DISTRIBUTION OF PROFITS

11(1)   In relation to an accounting period, an Association shall be deemed not to have complied with the condition in section 508(1)(b) if in the accounting period the Association directly or indirectly distributes, or intends to so distribute, in any manner or form any of its profits of that accounting period or any other accounting period to any of its members, subscribers or shareholders.

This is subject to paragraph (2).

11(2)   Payments made by an Association to a member, subscriber or shareholder–

(a)   of reasonable remuneration for goods, labour, power supplied or services rendered,

(b)   of reasonable interest for money lent, or

(c)   of reasonable rent for any premises,

shall be treated as not being a distribution of profits for the purposes of paragraph (1) if such payments are not prohibited by the Association's constitutional document.

PART 3 – RESEARCH AND DEVELOPMENT CAPABLE OF EXTENDING TRADE

UNDERTAKING OF RESEARCH AND DEVELOPMENT LEADING TO OR FACILITATING AN EXTENSION OF A CLASS OF TRADE

12   In relation to an accounting period, the undertaking of research and development is deemed to be capable of leading to or facilitating an extension of a class of trade if–

(a)   the research and development is undertaken in accordance with regulation 13;

(b)   the results of any research and development are or will be disseminated in accordance with regulation 14; and

(c)   the intellectual property requirements in regulation 16 are satisfied.

MANNER OF UNDERTAKING RESEARCH AND DEVELOPMENT

13   Research and development is undertaken in accordance with this regulation if–

(a)   the Association directly undertakes by using its own facilities activities that are treated as research and development;

(b)   a person under the terms of a contract with the Association undertakes on behalf of the Association activities that are treated as research and development; or

(c)   a 100% subsidiary company of the Association undertakes on behalf of the Association activities that are treated as research and development.

ARRANGEMENTS FOR DISSEMINATING THE RESULTS OF RESEARCH AND DEVELOPMENT

14(1)   For the purposes of regulation 12, the Association must disseminate the results of any research and development in accordance with the arrangements referred to in paragraph (2).

14(2)   The arrangements for the dissemination of the results of any research and development must be made, on or before the last day of the accounting period, and must ensure that the results of any research and development undertaken in the accounting period are to be–

(a)   made available upon request and without charge, subject to paragraph (3);

(b)   made available, subject to paragraph (4)–

   (i)   to all the members and shareholders of, and all the subscribers to, the Association who undertake the class of trade that may be facilitated or extended by the research and development; or

   (ii)   to all the members and shareholders of, and all the subscribers to, the Association; or

   (iii)   generally to the public; and

(c)   made available not later than one year after the completion of the research and development.

14(3)   Paragraph (2)(a) does not prevent an Association from recovering from a recipient of the results of any research and development the reasonable costs of publishing or distributing the results to the recipient.

14(4)   Where any member or shareholder of, or subscriber to, the Association is connected with the Association paragraph (2)(b) does not apply and instead the arrangements must ensure that the results of any research and development undertaken in the accounting period are made available–

(a)   generally to the public, or

(b)   to any person who undertakes the class of trade that may be facilitated or extended by the research and development whether or not the person is or is not a member or shareholder of, or subscriber to, the Association.

Section 839 (connected persons) shall apply for the purpose of determining whether a member, shareholder or subscriber is connected with the Association.

BREACH OF ARRANGEMENTS FOR DISSEMINATING THE RESULTS OF RESEARCH AND DEVELOPMENT

15(1)   This regulation applies where–

(a)   the arrangements referred to in paragraph (2) of regulation 14 are altered or replaced after the end of an accounting period in respect of which a claim under section 508 is made with the effect that the requirements of that paragraph cease to met in relation to research and development undertaken in that accounting period; or

(b)   any results of any research and development undertaken in an accounting period in respect of which a claim under section 508 is made are disseminated other than in accordance with the arrangements referred to in that paragraph.

15(2)   Where this regulation applies the Association shall be deemed not to have satisfied the condition in section 508(1)(a) in relation to the accounting period in which the alteration or replacement occurs or in which the dissemination occurs.

INTELLECTUAL PROPERTY REQUIREMENTS

16   For the purposes of regulation 12, the intellectual property requirements are that any intellectual property from any research and development undertaken by or on behalf of an Association in an accounting period–

(a)   must be solely and beneficially owned by the Association for a period of not less than one year from the date on which the accounting period ends;

(b)   in a case where the intellectual property is sold, transferred, assigned, licensed or otherwise made available by an Association to any person–

      (i)   in the accounting period, or

      (ii)   in the period that ends one year from the date on which the accounting period ends,

    the intellectual property must also be made available by the Association to all the members and shareholders of, and all the subscribers to, the Association; or

(c)   in a case where the funding of the research and development is–

      (i)   shared by the Association and another person or body ("shared funding"), and

      (ii)   as a consequence of the shared funding the Association is unable to secure sole beneficial ownership of any intellectual property from the research and development,

    the Association must secure in the accounting period a right to use or exploit any intellectual property from the research and development for a period of not less than one year from the date on which the accounting period ends.

BREACH OF INTELLECTUAL PROPERTY REQUIREMENTS

17(1)   This regulation applies where in respect of any intellectual property from research and development undertaken by or on behalf of an Association in an accounting period in respect of which a claim under section 508 is made the circumstances are such that none of the requirements in regulation 16(a), (b) or (c) is satisfied in relation to the intellectual property.

17(2)   Where this regulation applies at any time in an accounting period, the Association shall be deemed not to have satisfied the condition in section 508(1)(a) in relation to that accounting period (whether or not the intellectual property involved arose in or existed in that accounting period or in an earlier accounting period).

RECOVERY OF FOREIGN TAXES REGULATIONS 2007

(SI 2007/3507, as amended by SI 2010/794)

Made on 12 December 2007 by the Treasury, in exercise of the powers conferred by s. 175(1) of the Finance Act 2006. Operative from 3 January 2008.

CITATION AND COMMENCEMENT

1   These Regulations may be cited as the Recovery of Foreign Taxes Regulations 2007 and shall come into force on 3rd January 2008.

INTERPRETATION

2   In these Regulations–

"applicant authority" means an authority in a foreign territory which makes a request for recovery in accordance with arrangements having effect by virtue of section 173 of the Finance Act 2006;

"the Commissioners" means the Commissioners for Her Majesty's Revenue and Customs, or an officer of Her Majesty's Revenue and Customs;

"a contested claim" is one which is subject to action challenging either the foreign claim or the instrument permitting enforcement brought by an interested party before the competent body of the foreign territory in which the applicant authority is situated in accordance with the laws in force there;

"enforcement action" means action to enforce a foreign claim by way of legal proceedings, distress, diligence or other process which might be taken to enforce a United Kingdom claim for income tax of the same amount;

"a final decision" is one against which no appeal lies or against which an appeal lies within a period that has expired without an appeal having been brought by either party to the proceedings;

"a foreign claim" means a debt relating to any relevant foreign tax;

"instrument permitting enforcement" means–

(a)   any instrument issued by an applicant authority in a foreign territory in relation to a sum claimed by that authority within the jurisdiction of that territory; or

(b)   a decision on that claim given in favour of that authority by a court or tribunal or other competent body in that territory which permits recovery of that claim in that territory or part thereof;

"request for recovery" means a request for recovery of a foreign claim by an applicant authority;

"the Taxes Acts" has the meaning given in section 118(1) of the Taxes Management Act 1970;

"transmission by electronic means" includes transmission by means of an electronic communications system (and cognate expressions shall be construed accordingly).

History – In reg. 2, in the definition of "applicant authority", the words "arrangements having effect by virtue of section 173 of the Finance Act 2006" substituted for the words "these Regulations" by SI 2010/794, reg. 3(2), with effect from 6 April 2010.
In reg. 2, the definition of "a foreign claim" inserted by SI 2010/794, reg. 3(3), with effect from 6 April 2010.
In reg. 2, in the definition of "request for recovery", the words "foreign claim" substituted for the words "relevant foreign tax" by SI 2010/794, reg. 3(4), with effect from 6 April 2010.

RELEVANT FOREIGN TAX CLAIM

3(1)   For the purposes of these Regulations a foreign claim shall be treated as if it were a claim for income tax under the Taxes Acts subject to what follows.

3(2)   The Commissioners may take such enforcement action in relation to a foreign claim as they would for a claim for income tax under the Taxes Acts in the same amount.

History – In reg. 3(1), the words "foreign claim" substituted for the words "claim for a relevant foreign tax by an applicant authority" by SI 2010/794, reg. 4(2), with effect from 6 April 2010.
In reg. 3(1), the words "in relation to a foreign claim" inserted by SI 2010/794, reg. 4(3), with effect from 6 April 2010.

Statutory Instruments

REQUESTS FOR RECOVERY

4(1) A request for recovery shall be in writing.

4(2) A request for recovery shall give the sterling equivalent of the amount of the foreign claim, using the latest selling rate for sterling recorded on the most representative exchange market or markets of the territory in which the applicant authority is situated on the date when the request for recovery is made.

History – Reg. 4 substituted by SI 2010/794, reg. 5, with effect from 6 April 2010.

PROCEDURE ON RECEIPT OF REQUEST

5 When the Commissioners receive a request for recovery they–

(a)   shall acknowledge receipt of the request in writing to the applicant authority, and

(b)   may request additional information or documentation from the applicant authority if the agreed information and documentation has not been supplied in accordance with regulation 4(1)(b).

REQUESTS FOR RECOVERY – FURTHER PROVISIONS

6 For the purposes of these Regulations–

(a)   a request for recovery made by an applicant authority shall be taken to be duly made in accordance with arrangements relating to international tax enforcement unless the contrary is proved, and

(b)   except as set out in regulations 9, 10 and 11, no question may be raised as to a person's liability on the foreign claim.

COMMUNICATION OF INFORMATION

7 Information sent to the Commissioners as part of a request for recovery may only be communicated by them to–

(a)   the person mentioned in the request for assistance;

(b)   those persons and authorities responsible for the recovery of the claims, and solely for that purpose, or

(c)   the judicial authorities dealing with matters concerning the recovery of claims.

ADJUSTMENT OF A FOREIGN CLAIM

8(1) This regulation applies where the amount of a foreign claim is amended for any reason.

8(2) Where the amendment leads to a reduction in the amount of the foreign claim the following rules apply.

Rule 1

The Commissioners shall continue the action which they have undertaken with a view to recovery but that action shall be limited to the amount still outstanding.

Rule 2

If at the time the Commissioners are informed of the reduction in the amount of the foreign claim, an amount exceeding the amount still outstanding has already been recovered by them, but this amount has not yet been transferred to the applicant authority, the Commissioners shall repay the excess to the person who appears to them to be entitled to it.

8(3) Where the amendment leads to an increase in the amount of the foreign claim the following rules apply.

Rule 1

The additional request shall as far as possible be dealt with by the Commissioners at the same time as the original request.

Rule 2

Where, in view of the state of progress of the existing recovery procedure, consolidation of the additional request with the original request is not possible, the Commissioners shall treat that request as a new claim but shall be required to comply with it only if it concerns an amount not less than the minimum amount referred to in regulation 4(3).

CANCELLATION OR PAYMENT OF A CLAIM

9 In any case where the Commissioners take enforcement action in relation to a foreign claim, and upon receipt of notice in writing by the applicant authority that–

(a)   the taxpayer has made payment in satisfaction of that claim; or

(b)   the claim has been terminated or cancelled for some other reason;

they shall cease any enforcement action in relation to that claim.

DISPUTED CLAIMS

10(1) No enforcement action under these Regulations shall be taken against a person if he shows that proceedings relevant to his liability on the foreign claim are pending, or are about to be instituted, before a court, tribunal or other competent body in the foreign territory in question.

10(2) For this purpose proceedings relevant to a person's liability on a foreign claim are pending until a final decision is made.

CLAIMS DETERMINED IN TAXPAYER'S FAVOUR

11(1) No enforcement action under these Regulations shall be taken against a person if a final decision on the foreign claim has been given in his favour by a court, tribunal or other competent body in the foreign territory in question.

11(2) If a person shows that such a decision has been given in respect of part of the claim, no enforcement action under these Regulations shall be taken in relation to that part.

LIMITATION

12(1) The period of limitation or prescription in relation to any issue arising on the recovery of any foreign claim shall be that applicable under the laws in force in the foreign territory in which the applicant authority is situated.

12(2) For the purposes of paragraph (1) any step taken by the Commissioners in recovery of a foreign claim in pursuance of a request for assistance shall be deemed to have been taken in the foreign territory in which the applicant authority is situated where that step, if it had been taken by that applicant authority, would have had the effect of suspending or interrupting the period of limitation or prescription in accordance with the laws in force in that territory.

INTEREST

13(1) A foreign claim carries interest in respect of the relevant foreign tax and any penalty claimed if arrangements having effect by virtue of section 173 of the Finance Act 2006 so provide.

13(2) Where the arrangements provide that the rate of interest is that which applies under the law of the territory in which the applicant authority is situated, the claim carries interest at that rate for the period determined in accordance with those laws.

13(3) Where paragraph (2) applies, the applicant authority must provide details to the Commissioners–

(a)   of the daily rate of interest to be applied, and

(b)   of the period for which interest runs.

13(4) Where the arrangements provide that the rate of interest is that which applies in respect of any tax or duty imposed under the domestic law of the United Kingdom, the claim carries interest at the rate applicable to income tax under section 178 of the Finance Act 1989 from the date of recognition until payment.

13(5) In paragraph (4), **"the date of recognition"** means the earlier of–

(a)   the day following the expiry of three months from the date of receipt by the Commissioners of the request for recovery of the foreign claim, and

(b)   the date the receipt of the request for recovery is acknowledged in writing by the Commissioners to the applicant authority.

13(6) Paragraph (4) applies even if the date of recognition is a non-business day within the meaning of section 92 of the Bills of Exchange Act 1882.

13(7) Interest is payable under this regulation without any deduction of income tax.

13(8) For the purposes of this regulation, where–

(a)   any payment is made by cheque to Her Majesty's Revenue and Customs, and

(b)   the cheque is paid on its first presentation to the banker on whom it is drawn;

the payment shall be treated as made on the day on which the cheque is received by the Commissioners.

13(9)   Interest charged under this regulation shall be recoverable as if it were interest charged under a provision of the Taxes Management Act 1970.

History – Reg. 13 substituted by SI 2010/794, reg. 6, with effect from 6 April 2010.

EVIDENCE

14(1)   An instrument permitting enforcement of a foreign claim recognised by the Commissioners as an instrument authorising enforcement of the claim in the United Kingdom, together with a certificate of an officer of Revenue and Customs that payment of the claim has not been made to him, or to the best of his knowledge and belief, to any other officer, or to any person acting on his behalf, or on behalf of another officer, or to the applicant authority, is sufficient evidence that the sum mentioned in the instrument is unpaid and is due to the applicant authority.

14(2)   A certificate of an officer of Revenue and Customs that interest is payable under either regulation 13(2) or 13(3) and that payment of the interest has not been made to him, or, to the best of his knowledge and belief, to any other officer, or to any person acting on his behalf or on behalf of another officer, or to the applicant authority, is sufficient evidence that the interest is unpaid and due to the applicant authority.

14(3)   For the purposes of this regulation, any document purporting to be such a certificate as is mentioned in paragraphs (1) and (2) is deemed to be such a certificate unless the contrary is proved.

ENFORCEMENT IN SCOTLAND

15(1)   For the purposes of enforcement in Scotland, an original, official or certified copy of a final decision on a foreign claim by a court, tribunal or other competent body in the foreign territory in which the applicant authority is situated shall be of the same force and effect as an extract of a decree of the Court of Session for the payment of money bearing a warrant for execution.

15(2)   For the purposes of paragraph (1), a final decision on a foreign claim is a final decision on a foreign claim which permits recovery of that claim in the foreign territory in which the applicant authority is situated or in part thereof.

REGISTERED PENSION SCHEMES (AUTHORISED MEMBER PAYMENTS) REGULATIONS 2007

(SI 2007/3532)

Made on 14 December 2007 by the Commissioners for Her Majesty's Revenue and Customs, in exercise of the powers conferred by s. 164(f) of the Finance Act 2004 and now exercisable by them. Operative from 7 January 2008.

CITATION AND COMMENCEMENT

1 These Regulations may be cited as the Registered Pension Schemes (Authorised Member Payments) Regulations 2007 and shall come into force on 7th January 2008.

PRESCRIBED AUTHORISED MEMBER PAYMENT RELATING TO INHERITED ESTATE ON REATTRIBUTION

2(1) For the purposes of section 164(f) of the Finance Act 2004 (authorised member payments) a payment made by a registered pension scheme to or in respect of a person who is or has been a member of the pension scheme is of a description that is prescribed if the payment meets conditions A, B and C.

2(2) Condition A is that the payment is made as part of a scheme which–

(a)   makes a reattribution of the inherited estate of a person who carries on with-profits business, and

(b)   is made or sanctioned by a court of competent jurisdiction.

2(3) Condition B is that the payment is made to or in respect of the registered pension scheme's with-profits policyholders in exchange for giving up rights and interests over the inherited estate.

2(4) Condition C is that the payment does not reduce the total value of the sums and assets held for the purposes of the registered pension scheme.

2(5) In this regulation–

"**inherited estate**" has the same meaning as in the Conduct of Business sourcebook issued by the Financial Services Authority;

a "**reattribution**" means a redefinition of rights and interests of the with-profits policyholders mentioned in paragraph (3) over the inherited estate; and

"**with-profits business**" has the same meaning as in the Conduct of Business sourcebook issued by the Financial Services Authority.

14,633   **Employer-Financed Retirement Benefits etc. Regs 2007**   **SI 2007/3537**

Statutory Instruments

EMPLOYER-FINANCED RETIREMENT BENEFITS (EXCLUDED BENEFITS FOR TAX PURPOSES) REGULATIONS 2007

(SI 2007/3537, as amended by SI 2009/2886 and SI 2011/2281)

Made on 14 December 2007 by the Commissioners for Her Majesty's Revenue and Customs in exercise of the powers conferred by s. 393B(3)(d) and (4A) of the Income Tax (Earnings and Pensions) Act 2003. Operative from 8 January 2008.

CITATION AND COMMENCEMENT

1(1) These Regulations may be cited as the Employer-Financed Retirement Benefits (Excluded Benefits for Tax Purposes) Regulations 2007 and come into force on 8th January 2008.

1(2) Subject to paragraph (3), these Regulations have effect for the tax year 2006–07 and subsequent tax years.

1(3) These Regulations have effect–

(a)   so far as they relate to tuition fees, as described in paragraph 18 of the Schedule, for the tax year 2009–2010 and subsequent tax years; and

(b)   so far as they relate to resettlement commutation, resettlement grants, gratuity earnings and the provision of independent inquest advice, as described in paragraphs 19, 20 and 21 of the Schedule, for the tax year 2010–2011 and subsequent tax years.

History – In reg. 1(2) the words "Subject to paragraph (3), these" substituted for the word "These" by SI 2011/2281, reg. 3, with effect from 7 October 2011.
Reg. 1(3) inserted by SI 2011/2281, reg. 4, with effect from 7 October 2011.

INTERPRETATION

2(1) In these Regulations–

    "armed forces" means the regular forces and the reserve forces as defined in section 374 of the Armed Forces Act 2006 and former members of both;

    "employee" includes a former employee;

    "employer" includes–

    (a)   a former employer; and

    (b)   a person who has assumed the responsibility for providing a benefit in place of the person who employed the employee;

    "ill-health" means physical or mental impairment;

    "ITEPA 2003" means the Income Tax (Earnings and Pensions) Act 2003;

    "medical discharge" means the discharge from service of a member of the armed forces because the member is medically unfit to continue in service due to injury or illness caused or worsened by service in the armed forces;

    "relevant benefit" means a benefit to which Chapter 2 of Part 6 of ITEPA 2003 applies.

2(2) References to a member of a person's family shall be construed in accordance with section 721(4) of ITEPA 2003, but this is subject to regulation 3(4).

History – In reg. 2(1), definition of "armed forces" inserted by SI 2011/2281, reg. 5, with effect from 7 October 2011.
In reg. 2(1), definition of "medical discharge" inserted by SI 2011/2281, reg. 5, with effect from 7 October 2011.

EXCLUDED BENEFITS

3(1) A relevant benefit–

(a)   that is provided (or to be provided) in any of the circumstances mentioned in paragraphs (a) to (c) of section 393B(1) of ITEPA 2003;

(b)   that is described in the Schedule; and

(c)   that is provided to a qualifying person,

is an excluded benefit for the purposes of section 393B(3)(d) of ITEPA 2003.

3(2) The following are qualifying persons for the purposes of paragraph (1)–

(a)   in the case of the benefits described in the following paragraphs of the Schedule, the employee: paragraph 2 (accommodation provided for performance of duties – employees), paragraph 16 (equipment for disabled employees) and paragraph 17 (health-screening and medical check-ups),

(b) in the case of the benefit described in paragraph 3 of the Schedule (accommodation provided for performance of duties – members of employees' families), a member of the employee's family,

(c) in the case of any other benefit described in Part 1 of the Schedule–

   (i) the employee, and

   (ii) after any of the events specified in paragraph (3), a member of the employee's family,

(ca) in the case of the benefits described in paragraph 18 (tuition fees for armed forces personnel) of Part 3 of the Schedule (other benefits)–

   (i) a member of the armed forces, and

   (ii) after the death or medical discharge of a member of the armed forces, a member of his or her family,

(cb) in the case of the benefits described in paragraph 19 (armed forces resettlement commutation and resettlement grants schemes) of the Schedule, a member of the armed forces, and

(cc) in the case of the benefits described in paragraph 20 (the armed forces gratuity earnings scheme) of the Schedule–

   (i) a member of the armed forces, and

   (ii) after the death of a member of the armed forces, a member of his or her family or the personal representatives of the member of the armed forces, and

(cd) in the case of the benefits described in paragraph 21 (independent inquest advice service) of the Schedule–

   (i) a member of the family of the armed forces member, or

   (ii) a brother or sister of the member of the armed forces.

(d) in the case of any other benefit described in Part 3 of the Schedule–

   (i) the employee, and

   (ii) after the employee's death, a member of the employee's family.

3(3) The events mentioned in paragraph (2)(c)(ii) are–

(a) the employee's death;

(b) the employee's taking up residence elsewhere (than in the living accommodation concerned) as a result of ill-health;

(c) the employee's taking up residence elsewhere (than in the living accommodation concerned) following–

   (i) a separation,

   (ii) the annulment or divorce of a marriage, or

   (iii) the nullity or dissolution of a civil partnership.

3(4) Where the event mentioned in paragraph (3)(c)(ii) or (iii) has occurred, the ex-spouse or ex-civil partner shall be treated as a member of the employee's family.

History – Reg. 3(2)(a) substituted by SI 2009/2886, reg. 3, which came into force on 1 December 2009, with effect for the tax year 2006–07 and subsequent tax years.
Reg. 3(2)(ca), (cb), (cc) and (cd) inserted by SI 2011/2281, reg. 6, with effect from 7 October 2011.

SCHEDULE

Regulation 3

Part 1 – Living Accommodation and Related Benefits

ACCOMMODATION PROVIDED BY LOCAL AUTHORITY

1 Living accommodation if–

(a) it is provided by a local authority, and

(b) Chapter 5 of Part 3 of ITEPA 2003 (taxable benefits: living accommodation) would not have applied to the provision of that accommodation by virtue of section 98 of that Act (accommodation provided by local authority) if the employee had remained in that employment.

ACCOMMODATION PROVIDED FOR PERFORMANCE OF DUTIES – EMPLOYEES

2(1) Living accommodation if–

(a)   the employee had been in continuous occupation of the same or similar living accommodation during the five years immediately preceding the employee's retirement,

(b)   throughout that period of five years–

    (i)   Chapter 5 of Part 3 of ITEPA 2003 did not apply to the provision of that accommodation by virtue of section 99 of that Act (accommodation provided for performance of duties), and

    (ii)   for any tax year before 2003–04, the accommodation attracted similar treatment for tax purposes by virtue of an enactment that was restated by section 99,

(c)   the employee continued to occupy the same or similar accommodation after retirement.

2(2) In determining whether the occupation of living accommodation is continuous, the following breaks in occupation shall be disregarded–

(a)   any one break not exceeding six months,

(b)   breaks not exceeding one month each,

(c)   breaks (of any duration) resulting from the employee's ill health.

2(3) Living accommodation is not within this paragraph if it is improved property.

ACCOMMODATION PROVIDED FOR PERFORMANCE OF DUTIES – MEMBERS OF EMPLOYEES' FAMILIES

3(1) Living accommodation provided to a member of the employee's family after the employee's death if–

(a)   the employee died before retirement and Condition A is satisfied; or

(b)   the employee died after retirement and Condition B is satisfied.

3(2) Condition A is that–

(a)   the employee had been in occupation of the same or similar living accommodation at any time during the five years immediately preceding the employee's death,

(b)   at any time during that period of five years–

    (i)   Chapter 5 of Part 3 of ITEPA 2003 did not apply to the provision of that accommodation by virtue of section 99 of that Act, or

    (ii)   for a tax year before 2003–04, the accommodation attracted similar treatment for tax purposes by virtue of an enactment that was restated by section 99,

3(3) Condition B is that the living accommodation was living accommodation described in paragraph 2 immediately before the employee's death.

3(4) In determining whether the occupation of living accommodation is continuous, the breaks in occupation mentioned in paragraph 2(2) shall be disregarded.

3(5) Living accommodation is not within this paragraph if it is improved property.

ACCOMMODATION PROVIDED FOR MINISTERS OF RELIGION

4(1) Living accommodation if–

(a)   the employee had been employed as a minister of a religious denomination–

    (i)   for the period of five years immediately preceding the employee's retirement,

    (ii)   immediately preceding the employee's death, or

    (iii)   if the employee retired immediately after a period of ill-health, immediately preceding the beginning of that period, and

(b)   at any time while the employee had been a minister, either–

    (i)   Chapter 5 of Part 3 of ITEPA 2003 did not apply to the provision of that or some other living accommodation provided to the employee by the employer by virtue of section 99 of that Act, or

    (ii)   for a tax year before 2003–04, such accommodation attracted similar treatment for tax purposes by virtue of an enactment that was restated by section 99.

4(2) The condition in sub-paragraph (1)(a)(iii) is not satisfied unless and until the employer has received evidence from a registered medical practitioner that the employee is incapable of carrying on the occupation.

ACCOMMODATION PROVIDED AS RESULT OF SECURITY THREAT

5   Living accommodation if–

(a)   at any time before the employee's retirement or death–

  (i)   Chapter 5 of Part 3 of ITEPA 2003 did not apply to the provision of that or similar accommodation provided to the employee by the employer by virtue of section 100 of that Act (accommodation provided as result of security threat), and

  (ii)   for any tax year before 2003–04, such accommodation attracted similar treatment for tax purposes by virtue of an enactment that was restated by section 100,

(b)   except that the employment has been terminated, the conditions set out in paragraphs (a) to (c) of section 100 continue to be satisfied.

REMOVAL EXPENSES

6(1)   A benefit provided by the employer in connection with a change of residence if–

(a)   it is a benefit of a description within section 280 of ITEPA 2003;

(b)   there would have been no liability to income tax by virtue of section 271 of ITEPA 2003 if–

  (i)   the benefit had been provided in the course of the employment,

  (ii)   the change of residence had met the conditions in section 273 of ITEPA 2003,

  (iii)   the last day of the tax year after that in which the change of residence occurred had constituted the limitation day;

(c)   the former residence is living accommodation described in this Part.

6(2)   If the cash equivalent of the benefit determined in accordance with the rules in section 203 of ITEPA 2003 exceeds £8,000–

(a)   the excess is not within the description in this paragraph; and

(b)   in determining whether there would have been no liability to income tax by virtue of section 271 of ITEPA 2003 for the purposes of sub-paragraph (1)(b), the excess shall be disregarded.

REPAIRS AND ALTERATIONS TO LIVING ACCOMMODATION

7   Works–

(a)   in respect of which there would have been no liability to income tax by virtue of section 313 of ITEPA 2003 if they had been carried out in relation to living accommodation provided by reason of the employee's employment;

(b)   that are carried out in relation to living accommodation described in this Part; and

(c)   that do not have the effect of the living accommodation becoming improved property.

COUNCIL TAX ETC.PAID FOR LIVING ACCOMMODATION

8   Payments or reimbursements if–

(a)   they are of a description within section 314(2) of ITEPA 2003;

(b)   section 314 would have applied to them if the living accommodation had been of a description within subsection (1) of that section;

(c)   they are in respect of living accommodation described in this Part.

Part 2 – Interpretation of Part 1

SIMILAR ACCOMMODATION

9(1)   All living accommodation is similar to other living accommodation unless, at the time the employee or member of the employee's family starts to occupy the new accommodation, its market value exceeds that of the accommodation occupied immediately prior to it by more than 20%.

9(2)   Where the living accommodation is not capable of being sold separately (whether because it forms part of larger premises in multiple occupation or otherwise), its market value shall be taken to be such amount as would be obtained if the factors that prevented its separate sale were disregarded.

IMPROVED PROPERTY

10(1)   Living accommodation is improved property if works have been carried out to it which–

(a)   materially improve it; and

(b) are not carried out wholly for the purposes of complying with a statutory requirement or a requirement imposed by a government department, a statutory body or a person holding a statutory office.

10(2) For the purposes of sub-paragraph (1), a property is materially improved by works if—

(a) its market value on the date the works are substantially completed ("MVW") exceeds what would have been its market value on that date if the works had not been carried out ("MV"); and

(b) the amount by which MVW exceeds MV is greater than 20% of MV.

10(3) Where the living accommodation is not capable of being sold separately (whether because it forms part of larger premises in multiple occupation or otherwise), both MVW and MV shall be taken to be such amount as would be obtained if the factors that prevented its separate sale were disregarded.

10(4) For the purposes of sub-paragraph (1)(b)—

"**statutory body**" means a body set up by or under an enactment (including an enactment comprised in, or an instrument made under, an Act of the Scottish Parliament);

"**statutory office**" means a body set up by or under such an enactment; and

"**statutory requirement**" means a requirement imposed by provision made by or under such an enactment.

Part 3 – Other Benefits

NON-CASH BENEFITS RECEIVED BEFORE 6TH APRIL 1998

11 The provision of a non-cash benefit if—

(a) it was received in connection with the termination of the employee's employment,

(b) that termination took place before 6th April 1998.

WELFARE COUNSELLING

12 The provision of welfare counselling which would have been exempted by virtue of the Income Tax (Benefits in Kind) (Exemption for Welfare Counselling) Regulations 2000 if it had been provided in the course of the employee's employment.

RECREATIONAL BENEFITS

13 The provision of recreational benefits if no liability to income tax would have arisen by virtue of section 261 of ITEPA 2003 if it had been provided in the course of the employee's employment.

ANNUAL PARTIES AND SIMILAR FUNCTIONS

14 The provision of an annual party or similar annual function if no liability to income tax would have arisen by virtue of section 264 of ITEPA 2003 if it had been provided in the course of the employee's employment.

WRITING OF WILLS ETC.

15 The provision of a service for the writing of a will or similar testamentary document if the cash equivalent of the benefit determined in accordance with the rules in section 203 of ITEPA 2003 does not exceed £150.

EQUIPMENT FOR DISABLED EMPLOYEES

16(1) The provision of a benefit which—

(a) was first provided in the course of the employee's employment; and

(b) satisfied Conditions 1 to 5 of regulation 3 of the Income Tax (Benefits in Kind) (Exception for Employment Costs resulting from Disability) Regulations 2002 ("the 2002 Regulations") at that time.

16(2) The replacement, whenever provided, for a hearing aid or other equipment, services or facilities mentioned in Condition 3 of the 2002 Regulations where the aid, equipment, services or facilities are no longer usable or appropriate to the needs of the employee.

HEALTH-SCREENING AND MEDICAL CHECK-UPS

17(1) The provision of a health-screening assessment or medical check-up if–

(a) no liability to income tax would have arisen by virtue of section 320B of ITEPA 2003 if it had been provided in the course of the employee's employment; and

(b) at least one health-screening assessment or medical check-up (as defined in that section) had been provided to the employee in the course of the employee's employment.

17(2) A health-screening assessment or medical check-up that was provided during the tax year 2006–07, 2007–08 or 2008–09 shall be taken to satisfy the condition in sub-paragraph (1)(a) if it would have satisfied that condition if section 320B of ITEPA 2003 had had effect for the tax year concerned.

History – Para. 17 inserted by SI 2009/2886, reg. 4, which came into force on 1 December 2009, with effect for the tax year 2006–07 and subsequent tax years.

TUITION FEES FOR ARMED FORCES PERSONNEL

18(1) The payment of tuition fees for higher level learning and qualification level learning.

18(2) For the purposes of this paragraph–

"higher level learning" means full or part time study towards the achievement of a higher level learning qualification;

"higher level learning qualification" means a qualification at Level 3 or above on the Qualifications and Credit Framework or such other equivalent qualification in respect of which qualifying persons may claim tuition fees;

"qualification level learning" means a first qualification at Level 3 or above on the Qualifications and Credit Framework, a first vocational qualification which is the equivalent of the preceding qualification, a first undergraduate degree (including a foundation degree), a first Higher National Certificate, a first Higher National Diploma or such other equivalent qualifications in respect of which qualifying persons may claim tuition fees;

"the Qualifications and Credit Framework" is a national framework which accommodates qualifications and operates across England, Wales and Northern Ireland;

"tuition fees" means the fees charged by the provider of a course of study leading to a higher level learning qualification or to qualification level learning and such fees may include registration, examination and accreditation fees.

History – Para. 18 inserted by SI 2011/2281, reg. 7, with effect from 7 October 2011.

ARMED FORCES RESETTLEMENT COMMUTATION AND RESETTLEMENT GRANTS SCHEMES

19 The provision of a lump sum in connection with resettlement commutation or resettlement grants of the description given in the Armed Forces (Redundancy, Resettlement and Gratuity Earnings Schemes) (No. 2) Order 2010.

History – Para. 19 inserted by SI 2011/2281, reg. 7, with effect from 7 October 2011.

ARMED FORCES GRATUITY EARNINGS SCHEME

20 The provision of gratuity earnings of the description given in the Armed Forces (Redundancy, Resettlement and Gratuity Earnings Schemes) (No. 2) Order 2010.

History – Para. 20 inserted by SI 2011/2281, reg. 7, with effect from 7 October 2011.

INDEPENDENT INQUEST ADVICE SERVICE

21 The provision of independent inquest advice in connection with the death in service of a member of the armed forces.

History – Para. 21 inserted by SI 2011/2281, reg. 7, with effect from 7 October 2011.

Statutory Instruments

SERIOUS CRIME ACT 2007 (DISCLOSURE OF INFORMATION BY REVENUE AND CUSTOMS) ORDER 2008

(SI 2008/403)

Made on 19 February 2008 by the Treasury in exercise of the powers conferred by s. 85(7) and 89(1) of the Serious Crime Act 2007. Operative from 11 March 2008.

CITATION AND COMMENCEMENT

1 This Order may be cited as the Serious Crime Act 2007 (Disclosure of Information by Revenue and Customs) Order 2008 and shall come into force on 11th March 2008.

INTERPRETATION

2 In this Order **"the CAB"** means the Criminal Assets Bureau in Ireland established under section 3(1) of the Criminal Assets Bureau Act 1996.

DISCLOSURE OF INFORMATION BY REVENUE AND CUSTOMS

3 The following persons are specified in relation to the CAB for the purposes of section 85(7) of the Serious Crime Act 2007 (disclosure of information by Revenue and Customs)—

(a)   the Chief Bureau Officer;

(b)   the bureau legal officer; and

(c)   any person appointed as a bureau officer under section 8 of the Criminal Assets Bureau Act 1996.

INCOME TAX (PURCHASED LIFE ANNUITIES) REGULATIONS 2008

(SI 2008/562, as amended by SI 2008/1481, SI 2009/56 and SI 2012/2902)

Made on 5 March 2008 by the Commissioners of Her Majesty's Revenue and Customs in exercise of the powers conferred by s. 658(3) of the Income and Corporation Taxes Act 1988 and s. 724 of the Income Tax (Trading and Other Income) Act 2005. Operative from 6 April 2008.

PART 1 – INTRODUCTION

CITATION, COMMENCEMENT AND APPLICATION

1(1) These Regulations may be cited as The Income Tax (Purchased Life Annuities) Regulations 2008 and come into force on 6th April 2008.

1(2) These Regulations apply to an annuity under which the first payment to the annuitant is made on or after 6th April 2008, subject to the transitional provision in regulation 27.

INTERPRETATION

2 In these Regulations–

"**the 1956 Regulations**" means the Income Tax (Purchased Life Annuities) Regulations 1956;

"**the 2005 Act**" means the Income Tax (Trading and Other Income) Act 2005;

"**annuitant**" means the person beneficially entitled for the time being to the payments on account of an annuity;

"**annuity**" means a purchased life annuity within the meaning of section 423 of the 2005 Act;

"**the Commissioners**" means the Commissioners for Her Majesty's Revenue and Customs;

"**insurer**" means a United Kingdom insurer or a non-United Kingdom insurer, as the case may be;

"**non-United Kingdom insurer**" means any person carrying on life annuity business and who–

(a) is resident outside the United Kingdom; and

(b) does not carry on such business through a permanent establishment in the United Kingdom;

"**relevant EEA State**" means an EEA State, other than the United Kingdom;

"**relevant person**" means–

(a) a United Kingdom insurer; or

(b) a tax representative appointed in accordance with Part 3; or

(c) a person appointed in accordance with arrangements made under regulation 18;

"**relevant records**" means the records referred to in regulation 21(1);

"**tax representative**" means the person appointed in accordance with Part 3 to act as such for a non-United Kingdom insurer;

"**the partial tax exemption**" means the exemption provided by Chapter 7 of Part 6 of the 2005 Act; and

"**United Kingdom insurer**" means–

(a) any person resident in the United Kingdom carrying on life annuity business; or

(b) any person not so resident who carries on life annuity business through a permanent establishment in the United Kingdom.

PART 2 – PROCEDURE WHERE ANNUITY IS PURCHASED

APPLICATION OF THIS PART

3 This Part applies where—

(a)   an annuitant purchases an annuity from a United Kingdom insurer;

(b)   a tax representative is appointed in accordance with Part 3; or

(c)   a person is appointed in accordance with arrangements made under regulation 18.

INITIAL STEPS

4(1) The relevant person must provide the annuitant with the form on which the annuitant is to make the declaration in accordance with regulation 5, within such time as is reasonable to enable the annuitant to comply with this Part before the first annuity payment becomes due and payable.

4(2) The form mentioned in paragraph (1) must include such of the following information as is known (at the appropriate place in each case) before it is provided to the annuitant—

(a)   the name of the insurer;

(b)   the insurer's life office reference number;

(c)   a reference number for the quotation that relates to the annuity in question or the policy number for that annuity, if the latter is available;

(d)   the name or names of the person or persons on whose life or lives the annuity depends;

(e)   the gross amount of each payment to be made under the annuity;

(f)   the frequency of the payment referred to in sub-paragraph (e); and

(g)   the date on which the first payment under the annuity is to be made.

4(3) Where the relevant person is either—

(a)   a tax representative appointed in accordance with Part 3; or

(b)   a person appointed in accordance with arrangements made under regulation 18;

that person must comply with the requirements of paragraphs (1) and (2) within 30 days of the date of the first payment being made under the annuity.

ANNUITANT TO PROVIDE INFORMATION AND MAKE DECLARATION

5(1) The annuitant must, upon receipt of the form referred to in regulation 4–

(a)   provide, at the appropriate part of the form in each case, the information specified in paragraph (2); and

(b)   make a declaration–

(i)   as to whether the annuity is a purchased life annuity which is eligible for the partial tax exemption; and

(ii)   confirming the accuracy of the other information provided on the form.

5(2) The information specified is–

(a)   the full name and home address (including the postal code) of each annuitant;

(b)   the national insurance number for each annuitant; and

(c)   the name, address and reference of the office of Her Majesty's Revenue and Customs to which each annuitant sends their tax return, or to which the last claim for an exemption under the 1956 Regulations was submitted.

5(3) Where there is more than one annuitant, any of them may make the declaration referred to in paragraph (1)(b), provided that the declaration properly reflects all the material facts about the annuity.

FORM TO BE RETURNED ON COMPLETION

6(1) The annuitant must–

(a)   complete the form and make the declaration in accordance with regulation 5; and

(b)   return the form to the person who provided it, together with any other information and documents that are required to accompany it.

6(2) Until the annuitant complies with paragraph (1), the annuity must be treated as one for which no part of the payments are eligible for the partial tax exemption.

WHAT MUST BE DONE ON RECEIPT OF THE COMPLETED FORM

7(1) This regulation applies where the annuitant has complied with regulations 5 and 6(1).

7(2) The relevant person must calculate the exempt capital element of the annuity in accordance with the mortality table which, at the time when the annuity payments become due and payable, is prescribed in paragraph (3).

7(3) The mortality table prescribed for the purposes of sections 720(4) and 721(4) of the 2005 Act is the table which specifies mortality rates according to "lives" and which is comprised in Table A11 set out in Appendix A on pages 181 to 183 of the booklet entitled "Continuous Mortality Investigation Reports Number 17", published by the Institute of Actuaries and the Faculty of Actuaries in 1999.

7(4) For the purposes of this regulation the relevant person must assume that the information provided by the annuitant on the form referred to in regulation 6 is correct unless there are reasonable grounds to believe otherwise.

7(5) When calculating the exempt capital element, the relevant person must–

(a) if the annuity is one to which section 720 of the 2005 Act applies, calculate the exempt proportion; or

(b) if the annuity is one to which section 721 of the 2005 Act applies, calculate the amount of the exempt sum.

7(6) If the annuitant has made a declaration under regulation 5(1)(b) that would lead the relevant person to reasonably conclude that the annuity is ineligible for the partial tax exemption, the insurer must make a statement, on the appropriate part of the form, that the annuity has no exempt capital element.

7(7) The relevant person must state, on the appropriate parts of the form–

(a) if paragraph (5)(a) applies, the exempt proportion, or

(b) if paragraph (5)(b) applies, the exempt sum and

notify the annuitant of the amount so calculated.

7(8) The relevant person must complete the appropriate parts of the form in accordance with this regulation, and must–

(a) sign and date the form; and

(b) state the business address and position in the organisation of the individual who completes the form.

7(9) The relevant person must send the form fully completed with the information required by regulation 4(2) (including the reference number for the annuity) to the annuitant.

7(10) The relevant person must comply with paragraphs (1) to (9) within 30 days beginning with–

(a) the date of receipt of the form referred to in regulation 5 (or, if the declaration and the other information required by the form are received on different dates, the date of receipt of the latter); or

(b) the date of the first payment under the annuity.

7(11) The relevant person must send a true photostat copy of the form referred to in paragraph (9) to such office of Her Majesty's Revenue and Customs as the Commissioners may from time to time specify, within 3 months of the date of first payment under the annuity.

History – In reg. 7(2), the word "table" substituted for the word "tables" and the words "is prescribed" substituted for the words "are prescribed" by SI 2012/2902, reg. 2(2), with effect in relation to any annuity the contract for which is made on or after 21 December 2012. In the case of any annuity contract made before 21 December 2012 under which the first annuity payment becomes due and payable on or after that date, the relevant person is entitled to comply with reg. 7 of the Income Tax (Purchased Life Annuities) Regulations 2008 as if this amendment had effect.
Reg. 7(3) substituted by SI 2012/2902, reg. 2(3), with effect in relation to any annuity the contract for which is made on or after 21 December 2012. In the case of any annuity contract made before 21 December 2012 under which the first annuity payment becomes due and payable on or after that date, the relevant person is entitled to comply with reg. 7 of the Income Tax (Purchased Life Annuities) Regulations 2008 as if this amendment had effect. Former reg. 7(3) read as follows:

> "**7(3)** The mortality tables prescribed for the purposes of sections 720(4) and 721(4) of the 2005 Act are those which specify mortality rates according to "lives" and which are comprised in Table A11 and Table A12 set out in Appendix A on pages 181 to 186 of the booklet entitled "Continuous Mortality Investigation Reports Number 17", published by the Institute of Actuaries and the Faculty of Actuaries in 1999.".

Statutory Instruments

WHAT THE RELEVANT PERSON MUST DO IF NO COMPLETED FORM IS RECEIVED

8(1) If the annuitant does not send a completed form to the relevant person in accordance with regulation 6 the latter must send, to such office of Her Majesty's Revenue and Customs as the Commissioners may from time to time specify, such details of the annuity policy specified in regulation 4 as are known to the relevant person.

8(2) The relevant person must comply with this regulation within 3 months of the end of the month in which the first payment under the annuity is due and payable.

PART 3 – ADDITIONAL REQUIREMENTS WHERE ANNUITY IS PURCHASED FROM A NON-UNITED KINGDOM INSURER

APPLICATION OF THIS PART

9 This Part applies where an annuitant has purchased an annuity from a non-United Kingdom insurer.

NOMINATION OF A TAX REPRESENTATIVE

10(1) Subject to regulations 17 and 18, a non-United Kingdom insurer who sells or intends to sell annuities to annuitants in the United Kingdom, must nominate a United Kingdom resident tax representative.

10(2) A person shall not be a tax representative unless–

(a)   if an individual, that person is resident in the United Kingdom and has a fixed place of residence there; or

(b)   if not an individual, that person has a business establishment in the United Kingdom; and

(c)   there has been a nomination approved by the Commissioners in accordance with regulation 11.

PROCEDURE FOR NOMINATION

11(1) A nomination to the Commissioners of a tax representative by a non-United Kingdom insurer must be made in writing and must contain the following information–

(a)   the full name or title under which the non-United Kingdom insurer is registered in the country in which his principal place of business is situated and the address in that country of the principal place of business;

(b)   the business address of any permanent establishment which the non-United Kingdom insurer has in the United Kingdom;

(c)   the name of the person nominated as a tax representative, and–

    (i)   if an individual, the address of that person's fixed place of residence in the United Kingdom; or

    (ii)   if not an individual, the address of that person's business establishment in the United Kingdom; and

(d)   the office of Her Majesty's Revenue and Customs to which, and the tax reference under which, the person nominated submits tax returns.

11(2) A nomination under this regulation must be accompanied by a declaration that the person nominated is willing and able to secure that the relevant duties are discharged by or on behalf of the non-United Kingdom insurer, signed–

(a)   if the person nominated is an individual, by that individual; or

(b)   if the person nominated is not an individual–

    (i)   by a proper officer as defined by section 108(3) of the Taxes Management Act 1970 in the case of a company; and

    (ii)   by any partner who is an individual in the case of a partnership.

11(3) The insurer must make a nomination under this regulation within 3 months of the first instance on which payments under an annuity commence.

DECISION AS TO NOMINATION

12(1) Within the period of 30 days beginning with the date of receipt of a nomination under regulation 11, the Commissioners must give notice to the non-United Kingdom insurer and the person nominated that they—

(a) approve the person nominated by the non-United Kingdom insurer as the insurer's tax representative;

(b) refuse to approve the person nominated by the non-United Kingdom insurer as the insurer's tax representative on one or more of the grounds specified in paragraph (4); or

(c) require the non-United Kingdom insurer or the person nominated, or both, to supply within the period of 30 days beginning with the date on which the notice in paragraph (1) was received, such further information as they may reasonably require in order to satisfy the Commissioners that the person nominated is a fit and proper person to be a tax representative.

12(2) A notice under paragraph (1)(c) must specify the further information that the Commissioners require.

12(3) Where the non-United Kingdom insurer or the person nominated, supplied, or both of them supply, information pursuant to a notice under paragraph (1)(c), the Commissioners must within the period of 30 days beginning with the date on which the information is received—

(a) give notice to the non-United Kingdom insurer and the person nominated—

    (i) that they approve the person nominated; or

    (ii) that they refuse to approve the person nominated, stating on which of the grounds specified in paragraph (4) they rely, or

(b) give further notice under paragraph (1)(c).

12(4) The grounds on which the Commissioners may refuse to approve the person nominated by the non-United Kingdom insurer are that—

(a) the requirements of regulation 11 have not been complied with; or

(b) the Commissioners have reasonable grounds to believe that the nominated person is unwilling or unable to assume any of the obligations that are prescribed in these Regulations.

12(5) Where the Commissioners refuse to approve the person nominated they must give the insurer notice in writing to that effect, stating the reason for the refusal.

12(6) Where the Commissioners refuse to approve the person nominated on the ground set out in paragraph (4)(a), the insurer must—

(a) submit a further nomination for that person; or

(b) nominate another person as tax representative,

within 30 days beginning with the date of receipt of the notice under paragraph (5).

12(7) Where the Commissioners refuse to approve the person nominated on the ground set out in paragraph (4)(b), the insurer must nominate another person in accordance with regulation 11 within 3 months beginning with the date of receipt of the notice under paragraph (5).

12(8) A nomination made under paragraph (6) or (7) must contain the information required by regulation 11 and the Commissioners must give their decision on that nomination in accordance with this regulation.

NOTIFICATION OF CHANGES

13 The insurer must notify the Commissioners of any changes to the information that was provided in the nomination made under regulation 11 as soon as practicable.

TERMINATION OF APPOINTMENT OF A TAX REPRESENTATIVE – OTHER THAN DEATH OR BANKRUPTCY, ETC

14(1) The appointment of a tax representative may be terminated at any time, either by the insurer or the tax representative, or by the Commissioners' withdrawing their approval of the tax representative's nomination.

14(2) Where the Commissioners withdraw their approval of the nomination, they must state on which of the grounds specified in paragraph (3) they rely and send notice in writing of the withdrawal to the insurer and the tax representative.

14(3) The grounds on which the Commissioners may withdraw approval of the appointment are where they have reason to believe that the tax representative—

(a)   has failed to fulfil any obligations under these Regulations;

(b)   no longer satisfies the requirements of regulation 10(2); or

(c)   for some other reason is not fit to act as such.

14(4)   The tax representative or the non-United Kingdom insurer may terminate the appointment on any ground whatsoever.

14(5)   Where the appointment is terminated under paragraph (4) the person terminating the appointment must send notice in writing of the termination to the other party to the appointment and to the Commissioners.

14(6)   Where the appointment is terminated under this regulation the insurer must, within 3 months starting with the date on which notice of the termination under paragraph (5) was given–

(a)   nominate another person as tax representative;

(b)   make an application under regulation 17 to be released from the requirement to nominate a tax representative; or

(c)   make other arrangements with the Commissioners in accordance with regulation 18.

14(7)   Where a nomination is made under paragraph (6)(a), that nomination must contain the information required by regulation 11 and the Commissioners must give their decision on the nomination in accordance with regulation 12.

TERMINATION OF APPOINTMENT OF A TAX REPRESENTATIVE – DEATH OR BANKRUPTCY, ETC

15(1)   Where the person nominated as a tax representative–

(a)   is an individual who–

    (i)   becomes bankrupt or in Scotland, whose estate is sequestered;

    (ii)   makes any arrangement or composition with their creditors generally; or

    (iii)   dies, or

(b)   is a company or partnership which is dissolved or wound up,

the appointment ceases and the non-United Kingdom insurer must comply with paragraphs (2) and (3).

15(2)   The insurer must–

(a)   nominate another person as tax representative;

(b)   make an application under regulation 17 to be released from the requirement to nominate a tax representative; or

(c)   make other arrangements with the Commissioners in accordance with regulation 18,

within the period of 3 months beginning with the date of the event in question.

15(3)   Where a nomination is made under paragraph (2)(a), that nomination must contain the information required by regulation 11 and the Commissioners must give their decision on the nomination in accordance with regulation 12.

TAX REPRESENTATIVE TO REMAIN IN POST UNTIL SUCCESSOR APPOINTED

16   Where a tax representative's appointment is terminated in accordance with regulation 14, the representative must continue to act as tax representative until a successor's nomination is approved by the Commissioners.

RELEASE OF NON-UNITED KINGDOM INSURER FROM REQUIREMENT TO NOMINATE A TAX REPRESENTATIVE

17(1)   Where the non-United Kingdom insurer makes a declaration that the insurer will conduct life annuity business in accordance with the law applicable in the United Kingdom (including these Regulations), the Commissioners may agree to release the insurer from the requirement to have a tax representative.

17(2)   Paragraph (1) is subject to paragraph (3) and regulation 4(3).

17(3)   Where the insurer–

(a)   is resident in a relevant EEA State; and

(b)   the disclosure by that person to the Commissioners of information with respect to holders of annuities is a criminal offence under the law of that State,

the insurer is not bound by the requirements of regulation 7(11).

17(4)   The Commissioners may at any time give notice to the non-United Kingdom insurer of their decision to withdraw their agreement to release the insurer from the requirement that there be a tax representative, other than where the circumstances described in paragraph (3) exist.

17(5)   An application by a non-United Kingdom insurer to be released from the requirement to have a tax representative must be made in writing to the Commissioners within the period specified in regulation 11(3).

17(6)   The Commissioners must, within the period of 30 days beginning with the date on which an application under paragraph (5) was received, give notice to the insurer that they—

(a)   agree to release the insurer from the requirement to have a tax representative;

(b)   refuse to agree to release the insurer from that requirement; or

(c)   require the insurer to supply, within the period of 30 days beginning with the date of the notice, such information as they may reasonably require to enable them to determine whether there are sufficient grounds to release the insurer from that requirement.

17(7)   A notice under paragraph (6)(c) must specify the information that the Commissioners require.

17(8)   Where the insurer supplies information required by a notice under paragraph (6)(c) the Commissioners must, within the period of 30 days beginning with the date on which that information was received—

(a)   give notice to the insurer that they agree to release the insurer from the requirement that there be a tax representative;

(b)   give notice to the insurer that they refuse to do so; or

(c)   give a further notice under paragraph (6)(c).

17(9)   Where—

(a)   the Commissioners give notice that they refuse to release the insurer from the requirement that there be a tax representative;

(b)   it ceases to be a criminal offence under the law of the relevant EEA State in which the non-United Kingdom insurer is resident for that person to disclose to the Commissioners information with respect to the holders of annuities; or

(c)   the Commissioners give notice to the non-United Kingdom insurer of their decision to withdraw their agreement to release the insurer from the requirement that there be a tax representative,

paragraph (10) applies.

17(10)   If this paragraph applies, the non-United Kingdom insurer must either nominate a person as a tax representative, or make other arrangements with the Commissioners in accordance with regulation 18, within the period of 3 months beginning with either—

(i)   the date of the notice; or

(ii)   the date on which disclosure to the Commissioners ceased to be a criminal offence,

as the case may be.

17(11)   Where the non-United Kingdom insurer nominates a person as a tax representative in accordance with paragraph (10), that nomination must contain the information required by regulation 11 and the Commissioners must give their decision on that nomination in accordance with regulation 12.

OTHER ARRANGEMENTS

18(1)   A non-United Kingdom insurer may make other arrangements with the Commissioners for the purpose of securing the discharge by the insurer or on the insurer's behalf of the obligations under United Kingdom law.

18(2)   A non-United Kingdom insurer must, within the period specified in regulation 11(3), give notice in writing to the Commissioners applying to—

(a)   make arrangements for the purpose specified in paragraph (1); and

(b)   be released from the duty to either nominate a tax representative or the requirement to nominate a tax representative.

18(3)   The notice referred to in paragraph (2) must—

(a)   set out the other arrangements that the non-United Kingdom insurer wishes to make with the Commissioners; and

(b)   give reasons why the requirement either to nominate a tax representative or have to apply to be released from the requirement to nominate a tax representative, should not apply.

18(4) The Commissioners must, within the period of 30 days beginning with the date on which an application under paragraph (2) was received, give notice to the insurer that they–

(a)   agree to the proposed arrangements, with such modification as they may specify;

(b)   refuse to agree to those arrangements; or

(c)   require the insurer to supply, within the period of 30 days beginning with the date of the notice, such information as they may reasonably require to enable them to determine whether they should agree to those arrangements.

18(5) A notice under paragraph (4)(a) must specify the modifications to the arrangements that the Commissioners require.

18(6) A notice under paragraph (4)(c) must specify the further information that the Commissioners require.

18(7) Where the non-United Kingdom insurer indicates the ability to comply with the modifications required by the Commissioners, or supplies information pursuant to a notice under paragraph (4)(c) as the case may be, the Commissioners must, within the period of 30 days beginning with the date on which the indication or the information is received–

(a)   give notice to the insurer–

    (i)   that they approve the arrangement set out in the application;

    (ii)   that they refuse to approve the arrangement, stating the reason for the refusal; or

(b)   give further notice under paragraph (4)(c).

18(8) If the Commissioners have reason to believe that any arrangements which have been made under this regulation do not secure the discharge by the non-United Kingdom insurer or on the insurer's behalf of the obligations under United Kingdom law, they must give notice to the insurer that those arrangements are no longer in force with effect from the date of the notice.

18(9) Where notice is given by the Commissioners in accordance with paragraph (8)–

(a)   subject to compliance with any modifications specified under paragraph (5), the non-United Kingdom insurer must nominate a person as a tax representative within the period of 3 months from the date of the notice;

(b)   that nomination must contain the information specified in regulation 11; and

(c)   the Commissioners must give their decision on that nomination in accordance with regulation 12.

APPOINTMENT BY THE COMMISSIONERS OF A NON-UNITED KINGDOM INSURER'S TAX REPRESENTATIVE

19(1) Where the non-United Kingdom insurer has failed–

(a)   to nominate a person as tax representative in accordance with regulations 10 and 11;

(b)   following the refusal of the Commissioners to approve a person so nominated, to nominate another person as tax representative in accordance with regulation 12(6)(b) or (7);

(c)   following the withdrawal by the Commissioners of their approval of a person nominated, to nominate another person as tax representative in accordance with regulation 14(6);

(d)   following–

    (i)   the termination of the appointment of the insurer's tax representative under regulation 14(4); or

    (ii)   the occurrence of one of the events described in regulation 15(1),

(e)   following the giving of a notice by the Board in accordance with regulation 18(8), to nominate a person as tax representative in accordance with regulation 18(9);

(f)   following–

    (i)   the refusal of the Commissioners to agree to release the insurer from the requirement that there be a tax representative;

    (ii)   the disclosure to the Commissioners of information with respect to relevant annuities ceasing to be a criminal offence under the law of the relevant EEA State in which the insurer is resident; or

    (iii) the giving of a notice by the Commissioners of their intention to withdraw from their agreement to release the insurer from the requirement that there be a tax representative,

to nominate a person as tax representative in accordance with regulation 17(10);

(g) following the termination of the appointment of a person under this paragraph, to nominate another person in accordance with paragraph (2) of this regulation;

the Commissioners may appoint a person who satisfies the requirements of paragraphs (2) and (3) to be the non-United Kingdom insurer's tax representative.

19(2) A person appointed by the Commissioners to be the tax representative of a non-United Kingdom insurer must be a person who has a significant business or economic connection with the non-United Kingdom insurer and may in particular be–

(a) a company which is connected within the meaning of section 839 of the Income and Corporation Taxes Act 1988; or

(b) the permanent establishment in the United Kingdom of any such company.

19(3) Before being appointed under this regulation, the person must make a declaration to the Commissioners in similar terms to the declaration specified in regulation 11(2).

19(4) The Commissioners must give notice in writing of their decision to the person appointed under this regulation and to the non-United Kingdom insurer and, subject to regulation 20(6), the date of the appointment is the date of the notice.

19(5) The Commissioners may at any time terminate the appointment of the person appointed by them as the tax representative under this regulation by giving notice in writing to the person appointed and to the non-United Kingdom insurer.

19(6) If the Commissioners terminate an appointment under paragraph (5), the non-United Kingdom insurer must nominate another person as tax representative within the period of 3 months beginning with the date on which that notice is given.

19(7) The non-United Kingdom insurer may at any time nominate a person as tax representative in place of the person appointed by the Commissioners and, if the Commissioners approve the nomination of that person, at the same time as the Commissioners give notice of their decision approving it they must give notice in writing to the person appointed by them that the latter's appointment ceased on the date of the appointment of the substitute.

19(8) If the non-United Kingdom insurer nominates another person in accordance with paragraph (7), that nomination must contain the information required by regulation 11 and the Commissioners must give their decision on that nomination in accordance with regulation 12.

History – Reg. 19(1)(d) substituted by SI 2008/1481, reg. 2(2), with effect from 1 July 2008.

APPEALS AGAINST DECISIONS OF THE COMMISSIONERS

20(1) A non-United Kingdom insurer to whom notice has been given of a decision of the Commissioners–

(a) refusing to approve a person nominated as tax representative;

(b) withdrawing their approval of a person nominated as tax representative;

(c) appointing a person as tax representative;

(d) that arrangements made under regulation 18 are no longer in force;

(e) refusing to agree to release the insurer from the requirement that there be a tax representative; or

(f) to withdraw from their agreement to release the insurer from the requirement to have a tax representative,

may appeal against the decision contained in that notice by giving notice in writing to the Commissioners within the period of 30 days after the date of the notice of the decision in question.

20(2) A person who has been appointed to be the tax representative of a non-United Kingdom insurer under regulation 12(1) may appeal against the decision contained in that notice by giving notice to the Commissioners within the period of 30 days after the date of the notice of the decision sought to be appealed.

20(3) [Omitted by SI 2009/56, art. 3(2) and Sch. 2, para. 183(2).]

20(4) The provisions in Part 5 of the Taxes Management Act 1970 (appeals and other proceedings) apply to an appeal under this regulation and on an appeal that is notified to the tribunal, the tribunal must confirm the decision contained in the notice unless satisfied that it ought to be quashed.

20(5) Where a non-United Kingdom insurer appeals against a decision of the Commissioners referred to in paragraph (1)(a), (b), (d), (e) or (f), and the decision is confirmed on appeal, the period of 3 months within which another person must be nominated as tax representative does not begin to run until such time as there is no possibility of a further appeal against that decision.

20(6) Where a non-United Kingdom insurer appeals against a decision of the Commissioners appointing a person as tax representative, or the person appointed by the Commissioners to be the tax representative of a non-United Kingdom insurer appeals against the decision to appoint, the date of the appointment of that person is the first date on which there is no possibility of a further appeal against that decision.

20(7) Where a non-United Kingdom insurer appeals against a decision of the Commissioners referred to in paragraph (1)(a) and the decision of the Commissioners is quashed on appeal, the date of the appointment of the person nominated as the tax representative of the non-United Kingdom insurer is the first date on which there is no possibility of a further appeal against the decision quashing the decision of the Commissioners.

History – Reg. 20(3) omitted by SI 2009/56, art. 3(2) and Sch. 2, para. 183(2), operative from 1 April 2009 subject to transitional and saving provisions in SI 2009/56, Sch. 3. Former reg. 20(3) read as follows:

"**20(3)** An appeal under paragraph (1) or (2) is to the Special Commissioners.".

In reg. 20(4), the words "and in regulations made under sections 56B to 56D of that Act", which appeared after "proceedings)", omitted by SI 2009/56, art. 3(2) and Sch. 2, para. 183(3)(a), operative from 1 April 2009 subject to transitional and saving provisions in SI 2009/56, Sch. 3.

In reg. 20(4), the words "on an appeal that is notified to the tribunal, the tribunal must" substituted for the words "the Special Commissioners must, on appeal to them," by SI 2009/56, art. 3(2) and Sch. 2, para. 183(3)(b) operative from 1 April 2009 subject to transitional and saving provisions in SI 2009/56, Sch. 3.

In reg. 20(4), the words "they are", which appeared before "satisfied", omitted by SI 2009/56, art. 3(2) and Sch. 2, para. 183(3)(c), operative from 1 April 2009 subject to transitional and saving provisions in SI 2009/56, Sch. 3.

PART 4 – RECORD-KEEPING AND PROVISION OF INFORMATION

OBLIGATION TO KEEP PROPER RECORDS

21 A relevant person shall, in respect of each annuity, keep relevant records to enable the Commissioners to ascertain the terms of the annuity and to whether there has been or is likely to be any contravention of the requirements of Chapter 7 of Part 6 of the 2005 Act or these Regulations.

INFORMATION TO BE PROVIDED TO THE COMMISSIONERS

22(1) The Commissioners may by notice require any person to whom premiums under an annuity are or have at any time been payable, within such period as may be specified in the notice, to furnish them with such information as they may reasonably require to enable them to ascertain or verify any of the matters mentioned in regulation 21.

22(2) The period specified in a notice given under paragraph (1) shall be not less than 30 days beginning with the date on which the notice is given.

INSPECTION OF RECORDS

23(1) The Commissioners may by notice require any person to whom premiums under an annuity are or have at any time been payable, to make available for inspection by an officer duly authorised for that purpose, at such a time as that officer may reasonably require, any documents (in any format) that–

(a) are in that person's possession or control; and

(b) are relevant records.

23(2) The period specified in a notice given under paragraph (1) shall be not less than 30 days beginning with the date on which the notice was given.

PERIOD FOR WHICH RECORDS TO BE KEPT

24 An insurer must, in respect of each annuity, keep the relevant records for a period of three years beginning with the date on which the contract for the annuity was terminated.

TRANSFER OF RECORDS

25(1) This regulation applies in any case where the obligations under any annuity of the person that issued, entered into or effected it ("the original relevant person") are at any time the obligations of another person ("the transferee") to whom there has been a transfer of the whole or part of a business previously carried on by the original relevant person.

25(2) The original relevant person must, in respect of that annuity, deliver to the transferee the records that it was required to keep under regulation 21, within the period of three months beginning with the date of the transfer.

PART 5 – MISCELLANEOUS

PENALTIES

26(1) The Table in section 98 of the Taxes Management Act 1970 is modified in accordance with this regulation.

26(2) In column 1, there shall be treated as having been added at the end–
"Regulations 21 and 22 of the Income Tax (Purchased Life Annuities) Regulations 2007."

26(3) In column 2, there shall be treated as having been added–
"Regulations 7, 23 and 25 of the Income Tax (Purchased Life Annuities) Regulations 2007."

TRANSITIONAL PROVISION

27 In the case of an annuity–

(a)   the contract for which was made during the period beginning with 6th April 2007 and ending with (and including) 5th April 2008;

(b)   under which the payments by the insurer to the annuitant are made in arrears; and

(c)   under which the first payment to the annuitant is made on or after 6th April 2008,

the mortality tables applicable shall be the ones which were in force when the annuity was made and not those prescribed by regulation 7(3).

REVOCATIONS

28 The following instruments are revoked–

(a)   the Income Tax (Purchased Life Annuities) Regulations 1956;

(b)   the Income Tax (Purchased Life Annuities) (Amendment) Regulations 1960;

(c)   the Income Tax (Purchased Life Annuities) (Amendment) Regulations 1990; and

(d)   the Income Tax (Purchased Life Annuities) (Amendment) Regulations 1991.

PROCEEDS OF CRIME ACT 2002 (CASH SEARCHES: CODE OF PRACTICE) ORDER 2008

(SI 2008/947)

Made on 31 March 2008 by the Secretary of State in exercise of the powers conferred by s. 292(4) and (5) and 459(2)(b) of the Proceeds of Crime Act 2002. Operative from 6 April 2008.

CITATION AND COMMENCEMENT

1 This Order may be cited as the Proceeds of Crime Act 2002 (Cash Searches: Code of Practice) Order 2008 and shall come into force on 6th April 2008.

REVISED CODE OF PRACTICE

2 Subject to article 3, the revised code of practice entitled "Code of Practice issued under section 292 of the Proceeds of Crime Act 2002" laid in draft before Parliament on 18th February 2008 shall come into operation on 6th April 2008.

EXERCISE OF POWERS AT TIME OF COMING INTO OPERATION

3 The revised code of practice referred to in article 2 shall apply to the exercise of any power conferred by virtue of section 289 of the Proceeds of Crime Act 2002 by an officer of Revenue and Customs or (in relation to England and Wales and Northern Ireland) a constable or an accredited financial investigator after midnight on 5th April 2008 notwithstanding that the exercise of the power may have begun before that time.

Statutory Instruments

MEMBERSHIP OF THE TRIBUNAL PROCEDURE COMMITTEE TRANSITIONAL ORDER 2008

(SI 2008/1149)

Made on 18 April 2008 by the Lord Chancellor in exercise of the powers conferred by para. 2 of Sch. 9 to the Tribunals, Courts and Enforcement Act 2007. Operative from 19 May 2008.

CITATION, COMMENCEMENT AND INTERPRETATION

1(1) This Order may be cited as the Membership of the Tribunal Procedure Committee Transitional Order 2008 and shall come into force on 19th May 2008.

1(2) In this Order **"the Act"** means the Tribunals, Courts and Enforcement Act 2007.

LORD CHIEF JUSTICE'S APPOINTEES TO THE TRIBUNAL PROCEDURE COMMITTEE

2(1) The person listed as entry number 1 in the first column of the Table, being appointed as a legal member of the scheduled tribunal in the corresponding entry in the second column of the Table, shall be treated as falling within the sub-paragraph of paragraph 22 of Schedule 5 to the Act in the corresponding entry in the third column of the Table.

2(2) The persons listed as entries number 2 and 3 of the first column of the Table, being appointed as the scheduled tribunal in the corresponding entry in the second column of the Table, shall be treated as falling within the sub-paragraph of paragraph 22 of Schedule 5 to the Act in the corresponding entry in the third column of the Table.

Appointee	Scheduled tribunal	Relevant sub-paragraph of paragraph 22 of Schedule 5
1. Nicolas Warren	Appeal Tribunal established under Chapter 1 of Part 1 of the Social Security Act 1998 (c.14)	sub-paragraph (1)(a)
2. Mark Rowland	Child Support Commissioner appointed under section 22 of the Child Support Act 1991 (c.48)	sub-paragraph (1)(b)
3. Lesley Clare	Adjudicator appointed under section 5 of the Criminal Injuries Compensation Act 1995 (c.53)	sub-paragraph (1)(c)

TAXATION OF BENEFITS UNDER GOVERNMENT PILOT SCHEMES (UP-FRONT CHILDCARE FUND) ORDER 2008

(SI 2008/1464)

Made on 9 June 2008 by the Treasury in exercise of the powers conferred by s. 151(1)(a) and (7)(a) of the Finance Act 1996. Operative from 1 July 2008.

CITATION AND COMMENCEMENT

1 This Order may be cited as the Taxation of Benefits under Government Pilot Schemes (Up-Front Childcare Fund) Order 2008 and shall come into force on 1st July 2008.

INCOME TAX EXEMPTION UNDER PART 2 OF THE INCOME TAX (EARNINGS AND PENSIONS) ACT 2003

2 The Income Tax Acts shall have effect in relation to any amount of benefit payable by virtue of the Government pilot scheme known as the Up-Front Childcare Fund as if it was exempt from income tax as employment income under Part 2 of the Income Tax (Earnings and Pensions) Act 2003.

Statutory Instruments

ENERGY-SAVING ITEMS (CORPORATION TAX) REGULATIONS 2008

(SI 2008/1520)

Made on 11 June 2008 by the Treasury in exercise of the powers conferred by s. 31ZA and 31ZC of the Income and Corporation Taxes Act 1988. Operative from 7 July 2008.

CITATION, COMMENCEMENT AND INTERPRETATION

1(1) These Regulations may be cited as the Energy-Saving Items (Corporation Tax) Regulations 2008, shall come into force on 7th July 2008, and shall have effect in respect of expenditure incurred on or after 8th July 2008.

1(2) In these Regulations–

"**ICTA 1988**" means the Income and Corporation Taxes Act 1988;

"**deduction**" means a deduction allowed under section 31ZA of ICTA 1988 (deduction for expenditure on energy-saving items);

"**maximum amount**" shall be construed in accordance with regulation 3(1);

"**relevant expenditure**" means–

(a)   expenditure incurred in acquiring and installing an energy-saving item in a dwelling-house, or

(b)   in so far as it is for the benefit of a dwelling-house, expenditure incurred in acquiring and installing an energy-saving item in a building containing that dwelling-house.

ITEMS OF AN ENERGY-SAVING NATURE

2   The following descriptions of items of an energy-saving nature are specified for the purposes of section 31ZA(5) of ICTA 1988–

(a)   hot water system insulation;

(b)   draught proofing;

(c)   cavity wall insulation;

(d)   solid wall insulation;

(e)   floor insulation; and

(f)   loft insulation.

RESTRICTIONS ON RELEVANT EXPENDITURE TO BE TAKEN INTO ACCOUNT: GENERAL

3(1) The maximum amount of the relevant expenditure which may be taken into account in calculating the deduction is £1,500 per dwelling-house.

3(2) Paragraph (1) applies irrespective of the number of persons incurring relevant expenditure or entitled to a deduction in respect of a dwelling-house.

3(3) If the company entitled to the deduction has received a contribution from any other person towards the relevant expenditure incurred, that contribution shall be excluded in calculating the relevant expenditure incurred by the company entitled to the deduction.

3(4) Further rules (to be applied in the order stated) are set out in–

(a)   regulation 4 (first further rule: apportionment of relevant expenditure benefiting more than one property);

(b)   regulation 5 (second further rule: restriction of relevant expenditure to the maximum amount);

(c)   regulation 6 (third further rule: apportionment of relevant expenditure if a dwelling-house or building is owned jointly or in common or is subject to differing estates or interests).

FIRST FURTHER RULE: APPORTIONMENT OF RELEVANT EXPENDITURE BENEFITING MORE THAN ONE PROPERTY

4(1) This regulation applies to relevant expenditure which is incurred in acquiring and installing an energy-saving item–

(a)   in more than one dwelling-house,

(b)   in a building containing more than one dwelling-house, or

(c)   in a building containing one or more dwelling-houses and one or more properties which are not dwelling-houses.

4(2)   The relevant expenditure must be apportioned on a just and reasonable basis to all the properties which benefit from it.

4(3)   The amount of the relevant expenditure for which a deduction is allowable in respect of a dwelling-house shall not exceed the amount which is apportioned to that dwelling-house.

SECOND FURTHER RULE: RESTRICTION OF RELEVANT EXPENDITURE TO THE MAXIMUM AMOUNT

5(1)   This regulation applies if the relevant expenditure benefiting a particular dwelling-house (including any relevant expenditure apportioned to the dwelling-house under regulation 4) exceeds the maximum amount.

5(2)   The relevant expenditure must be restricted to the maximum amount.

THIRD FURTHER RULE: APPORTIONMENT OF RELEVANT EXPENDITURE IF A DWELLING-HOUSE OR BUILDING IS OWNED JOINTLY OR IN COMMON OR IS SUBJECT TO DIFFERING ESTATES OR INTERESTS

6(1)   This regulation applies if relevant expenditure is incurred benefiting a dwelling-house and the dwelling-house or the building containing it–

(a)   is owned jointly or in common by the company entitled to the deduction and by other persons, or

(b)   is subject to differing estates or interests.

6(2)   The relevant expenditure (restricted if necessary to the maximum amount) must be apportioned on a just and reasonable basis.

6(3)   The amount of the deduction to which the company entitled to it is entitled shall not exceed the amount apportioned to that company in accordance with paragraph (2).

FURTHER PROVISIONS

7(1)   This regulation applies if any question arises under regulations 3(3) or 4 to 6 as to the amount of the deduction to which a company may be entitled.

7(2)   The amount shall be treated as if it were an amount specified in a paragraph of subsection (1) of section 42 of ICTA 1988 (appeals against determinations under sections 34 to 36 or Chapter 4 of Part 3 of the Income Tax (Trading and Other Income) Act 2005), and the procedure set out in that section shall apply accordingly.

TRIBUNALS, COURTS AND ENFORCEMENT ACT 2007 (COMMENCEMENT NO. 5 AND TRANSITIONAL PROVISIONS) ORDER 2008

(SI 2008/1653)

Made on 23 June 2008 by the Lord Chancellor in exercise of the powers conferred by s. 145 and 148(5) and (6) of the Tribunals, Courts and Enforcement Act 2007. Operative from 21 July 2008.

CITATION AND COMMENCEMENT

1 This Order may be cited as the Tribunals, Courts and Enforcement Act 2007 (Commencement No. 5 and Transitional Provisions) Order 2008.

2 The following provisions of the Tribunals, Courts and Enforcement Act 2007 come into force on 21st July 2008–

(a)   section 48(1) partially and the repeal in paragraph 27 of Schedule 8 in so far as it applies to the powers of a Minister;

(b)   sections 50, 51 and 52 in so far as they are not already in force;

(c)   paragraph 24 of Schedule 7; and

(d)   Schedule 10.

TRANSITIONAL PROVISIONS

3 Where a process to select a person for appointment to an office or other position–

(a)   would be affected by the commencement provisions in article 2; and

(b)   has been started but the appointment has not been made by 31 July 2008;

then the process may be completed and the appointment made as if the commencement provisions in article 2 were not yet effective.

4 A selection process has been started for the purpose of article 3 if the Lord Chancellor has–

(a)   made a request for selection under section 87 of the Constitutional Reform Act 2005 (the "2005 Act");

(b)   given the Judicial Appointments Commission notice in accordance with section 94 of the 2005 Act of a request he expects to make under section 87 of that Act; or

(c)   requested assistance under section 98 of the 2005 Act in connection with an appointment.

Statutory Instruments

FINANCING-ARRANGEMENT-FUNDED TRANSFERS TO SHAREHOLDERS REGULATIONS 2008

(SI 2008/1926)

Made on 22 July 2008 by the Treasury in exercise of the powers conferred by s. 83YE(1) and (4) of the Finance Act 1989. Operative from 12 August 2008.

PRELIMINARY

Citation, commencement and effect

1(1) These Regulations may be cited as the Financing-Arrangement-Funded Transfers to Shareholders Regulations 2008 and shall come into force on 12th August 2008.

1(2) These Regulations have effect in relation to periods of account beginning on or after 1st January 2008.

Interpretation

2 In these Regulations—

a **"relevant financing arrangement"** means a relevant financing arrangement in relation to a non-profit fund within section 83YC(4) of the Finance Act 1989;

a **"section 83YC(3) amount"** means an amount within section 83YC(3) of the Finance Act 1989;

a **"section 83YC(3) period of account"** means a period of account for which there is a section 83YC(3) amount;

a **"section 83YD arrangement"** means a relevant financing arrangement in respect of which there is a section 83YD(2) amount;

a **"section 83YD(2) amount"** means an amount within section 83YD(2) of the Finance Act 1989;

a **"section 83YD(2) period of account"** means a period of account for which there is a section 83YD(2) amount.

THE TREATMENT OF SECTION 83YC(3) AMOUNTS

Amounts wholly attributable to life assurance business or to gross roll-up business

3(1) This regulation applies if, at the end of a section 83YC(3) period of account, each relevant financing arrangement of an insurance company has as a condition of the arrangement that—

(a) in the case of a loan, any repayment may only be made if the company has an amount of surplus from carrying on life assurance business or gross roll-up business and the repayment is made from that surplus, or

(b) in the case of a financial reinsurance arrangement, any recapture of liabilities may only be made if the company has an amount of surplus from carrying on life assurance business or gross roll-up business.

3(2) The section 83YC(3) amount is wholly referable to life assurance business or to gross roll-up business (as the case may be).

Other cases where relevant financing arrangements meet the loan condition only: life assurance business and PHI business

4(1) This regulation applies if, in a section 83YC(3) period of account–

(a) an insurance company carries on both life assurance business and PHI business, and

(b) each relevant financing arrangement of the company in force in that period of account meets the loan condition (and not the reinsurance condition).

4(2) The part of the section 83YC(3) amount referable to life assurance business is–

$$\frac{LABL}{LABL + PHIL}$$

where–

"LABL" is the mean of the opening and closing liabilities of the company's life assurance business relating to the non-profit fund for the section 83YC(3) period of account, and

"**PHIL**" is the mean of the opening and closing liabilities of the company's PHI business relating to the non-profit fund for that period of account.

Other cases where relevant financing arrangements meet the loan condition only: gross roll-up business and basic life assurance and general annuity business

5(1) This regulation applies if, in a section 83YC(3) period of account–

(a) an insurance company carries on both gross roll-up business and basic life assurance and general annuity business, and

(b) each relevant financing arrangement of the company in force in that period of account meets the loan condition (and not the reinsurance condition).

5(2) The part of the section 83YC(3) amount referable to gross roll-up business is–

$$\frac{GRBL}{LABL + PHIL}$$

where–

"**GRBL**" is the mean of the opening and closing liabilities of the company's gross roll-up business relating to the non-profit fund for the section 83YC(3) period of account, and

"**LABL**" and "**PHIL**" each have the same meaning as in regulation 4(2).

Other cases where relevant financing arrangements meet the reinsurance condition only: life assurance business and PHI business

6(1) This regulation applies if, in a section 83YC(3) period of account–

(a) an insurance company carries on both life assurance business and PHI business, and

(b) each relevant financing arrangement of the company in force in that period of account meets the reinsurance condition (and not the loan condition).

6(2) The part of the section 83YC(3) amount referable to life assurance business is–

$$\frac{LABL + LFRAL}{LABL + PHIL + TFRAL}$$

where–

"**LFRAL**" is the mean of the opening and closing life assurance liabilities reinsured under relevant financing arrangements relating to the non-profit fund for that period of account,

"**TFRAL**" is the mean of the total opening and closing liabilities reinsured under relevant financing arrangements relating to the non-profit fund for that period of account, and

"**LABL**" and "**PHIL**" each have the same meaning as in regulation 4(2).

Other cases where relevant financing arrangements meet the reinsurance condition only: gross roll-up business and basic life assurance and general annuity business

7(1) This regulation applies if, in a section 83YC(3) period of account–

(a) an insurance company carries on both gross roll-up business and basic life assurance and general annuity business, and

(b) each relevant financing arrangement of the company in force in that period of account meets the reinsurance condition (and not the loan condition).

7(2) The part of the section 83YC(3) amount referable to gross roll-up business is–

$$\frac{GRBL + GFRAL}{LABL + PHIL + TFRAL}$$

where–

"**GFRAL**" is the mean of the opening and closing gross roll-up business liabilities reinsured under relevant financing arrangements relating to the non-profit fund for that period of account,

"**GRBL**" has the same meaning as in regulation 5(2),

"**LABL**" and "**PHIL**" each have the same meaning as in regulation 4(2), and

"**TFRAL**" has the same meaning as in regulation 6(2).

Relevant financing arrangements of more than one type

8(1) This regulation applies if, in a section 83YC(3) period of account–

(a) an insurance company carries on–

      (i)   both life assurance business and PHI business, or

      (ii)   both gross roll-up business and basic life assurance and general annuity business; and

(b)   the relevant financing arrangements of the company in force in that period of account include–

      (i)   at least one arrangement that meets the loan condition (and not the reinsurance condition), and

      (ii)   at least one arrangement that meets the reinsurance condition (and not the loan condition).

8(2)   The part of the section 83YC(3) amount referable to life assurance business is determined in accordance with regulation 6(2).

8(3)   The part of the section 83YC(3) amount referable to gross roll-up business is determined in accordance with regulation 7(2).

THE TREATMENT OF SECTION 83YD(2) AMOUNTS

Amounts wholly attributable to life assurance business or to gross roll-up business

9(1)   This regulation applies if, at the beginning of a section 83YD(2) period of account, each relevant financing arrangement of an insurance company has as a condition of the arrangement that–

(a)   in the case of a loan, any repayment may only be made if the company has an amount of surplus from carrying on life assurance business or gross roll-up business and the repayment is made from that surplus, or

(b)   in the case of a financial reinsurance arrangement, any recapture of liabilities may only be made if the company has an amount of surplus from carrying on life assurance business or gross roll-up business.

9(2)   The section 83YD(2) amount is wholly referable to life assurance business or to gross roll-up business (as the case may be).

Other cases where relevant financing arrangements meet the loan condition only: life assurance business and PHI business

10(1)   This regulation applies if, in a section 83YD(2) period of account–

(a)   an insurance company carries on both life assurance business and PHI business,

(b)   each relevant financing arrangement of the company in force in that period of account meets the loan condition (and not the reinsurance condition), and

(c)   there has been only one section 83YC(3) amount in that period of account and all preceding periods of account.

10(2)   The part of the section 83YD(2) amount referable to life assurance business is a fraction of that amount, determined in accordance with regulation 4(2), for the period of account in which the section 83YC(3) amount arose in respect of the section 83YD arrangement.

Other cases where relevant financing arrangements meet the loan condition only: gross roll-up business and basic life assurance and general annuity business

11(1)   This regulation applies if, in a section 83YD(2) period of account–

(a)   an insurance company carries on both gross roll-up business and basic life assurance and general annuity business,

(b)   each relevant financing arrangement of the company in force in that period of account meets the loan condition (and not the reinsurance condition), and

(c)   there has been only one section 83YC(3) amount in that period of account and all preceding periods of account.

11(2)   The part of the section 83YD(2) amount referable to gross roll-up business is a fraction of that amount, determined in accordance with regulation 5(2), for the period of account in which the section 83YC(3) amount arose in respect of the section 83YD arrangement.

Other cases where relevant financing arrangements meet the reinsurance condition: life assurance business and PHI business

12(1)   This regulation applies if, in a section 83YD(2) period of account–

(a)   an insurance company carries on both life assurance business and PHI business,

(b)   each relevant financing arrangement of the company in force in that period of account–

      (i)   meets the reinsurance condition (and not the loan condition), or

      (ii)   meets both the reinsurance condition and the loan condition, and

(c)   there has been only one section 83YC(3) amount in that period of account and all preceding periods of account.

12(2)   The part of the section 83YD(2) amount referable to life assurance business is a fraction of that amount, determined in accordance with regulation 6(2), for the period of account in which the section 83YC(3) amount arose in respect of the section 83YD arrangement.

Other cases where relevant financing arrangements meet the reinsurance condition: gross roll-up business and basic life assurance and general annuity business

13(1)   This regulation applies if, in a section 83YD(2) period of account—

(a)   an insurance company carries on both gross roll-up business and basic life assurance and general annuity business,

(b)   each relevant financing arrangement of the company in force in that period of account—

      (i)   meets the reinsurance condition (and not the loan condition), or

      (ii)   meets both the reinsurance condition and the loan condition, and

(c)   there has been only one section 83YC(3) amount in that period of account and all preceding periods of account.

13(2)   The part of the section 83YD(2) amount referable to gross roll-up business is a fraction of that amount, determined in accordance with regulation 7(2), for the period of account in which the section 83YC(3) amount arose in respect of the section 83YD arrangement.

Cases involving more than one section 83YC(3) amount

14(1)   This regulation applies if—

(a)   there has been more than one section 83YC(3) amount for a period of account (or for more than one period of account),

(b)   that period of account is (or those periods of account are) earlier than the section 83YD(2) period of account, and

(c)   regulation 9 does not apply.

14(2)   The insurance company may claim that the section 83YD(2) amount is such a fraction of the amount determined under section 83YD(4) of the Finance Act 1989 as is just and reasonable in the circumstances.

FINANCE ACT 2008 SECTION 135 (DISASTER OR EMERGENCY) ORDER 2008

(SI 2008/1936)

Made on 22 July 2008 by the Treasury in exercise of the powers conferred by s. 135 of the Finance Act 2008. Operative from 13 August 2008.

CITATION, COMMENCEMENT AND INTERPRETATION

1 This order may be cited as the Finance Act 2008 Section 135 (Disaster or Emergency) Order 2008 and comes into force on 13th August 2008.

SPECIFICATION OF DISASTER

2 For the purposes of section 135 of the Finance Act 2008 (interest on unpaid tax in case of disaster etc of national significance), floods, caused by weather conditions, which occurred in the United Kingdom in June and July 2007 are a disaster.

SPECIFIED DATE

3 For the purposes of section 135(4)(a) of the Finance Act 2008 (relief period), the date specified is 1st June 2007.

FRIENDLY SOCIETIES (TRANSFERS OF OTHER BUSINESS) (MODIFICATION OF THE CORPORATION TAX ACTS) REGULATIONS 2008

(SI 2008/1942)

Made on 22 July 2008 by the Treasury in exercise of the powers conferred by s. 461D(4) and (5) of the Income and Corporation Taxes Act 1988. Operative from 12 August 2008.

History – SI 2008/1942 revoked by SI 2012/3008, reg. 16, with effect in relation to accounting periods beginning on or after 1 January 2013. The text of former SI 2008/1942 read as follows:

"CITATION, COMMENCEMENT AND EFFECT

1(1) These Regulations may be cited as the Friendly Societies (Transfers of Other Business) (Modification of the Corporation Tax Acts) Regulations 2008 and shall come into force on 12th August 2008.

1(2) These Regulations shall have effect in relation transfers of engagements and amalgamations taking place on or after 21st July 2008.

MODIFICATION OF THE CORPORATION TAX ACTS

2 Where in any accounting period in which a friendly society carries on business other than life or endowment business–

(a) any business of the society is exempt from corporation tax by virtue of section 461D(1) of the Income and Corporation Taxes Act 1988 (transfers of other business: exempt from tax), or

(b) any business of the society is not exempt from corporation tax by virtue of section 461D(3) of the Income and Corporation Taxes Act 1988 (transfers of other business: not exempt from tax),

the Corporation Tax Acts shall have effect for the period as if they were subject to the following modifications.

MODIFICATION OF THE INCOME AND CORPORATION TAXES ACT 1988

3 Modify the Income and Corporation Taxes Act 1988 as follows.

MODIFICATION OF SECTION 432ZA (LINKED ASSETS)

4(1) Modify section 432ZA (linked assets) as follows.

4(2) In subsection (1)–

(a) after "Chapter" insert "and section 461F", and

(b) after "insurance company" insert "or, as the case may be, a friendly society".

4(3) In subsection (5), after "432E" insert "or, as the case may be, section 461F".

MODIFICATION OF SECTION 461 (TAXATION IN RESPECT OF OTHER BUSINESS)

5(1) Modify section 461 (taxation in respect of other business) as follows.

5(2) In subsection (3) after "applies" insert ", or a transferee within subsection (3ZB) below,".

5(3) After subsection (3) insert–

"**461(3ZA)** But where there has been a transfer of other business within section 461D(1), subsection (3) above shall not apply to a payment made by the transferee if–

(a) the transferor was a society to which subsection (2) above did not apply, and

(b) the member to whom the payment is made was a member of the transferor.

461(3ZB) And where there has been a transfer of other business within section 461D(3), subsection (3) above shall apply to a payment made by the transferee if–

(a) the transferor was a society to which subsection (2) above applied, and

(b) the member to whom the payment is made was a member of the transferor.

461(3ZC) Where subsection (3ZB) above applies, for the purposes of subsection (3) above–

(a) any payment of sums by a member to the society by way of contributions or deposits shall be treated as including any payment to the transferor, and

(b) any payment or repayment of sums to a member by the society within subsection (3)(a) or (b) shall be treated as including any payment or repayment made by the transferor.

461(3ZD) In subsections (3) to (3ZD) above "transferee" and "transferor" shall be construed in accordance with section 461D.".

MODIFICATION OF SECTION 461B (TAXATION IN RESPECT OF OTHER BUSINESS: INCORPORATED FRIENDLY SOCIETIES ETC)

6(1) Modify section 461B (taxation in respect of other business: incorporated friendly societies etc) as follows.

6(2) In subsection (3) after "qualifying society" insert ", or a transferee within subsection (3B) below,".

6(3) After subsection (3) insert–

"**461B(3A)** But where there has been a transfer of other business within section 461D(1), subsection (3) above shall not apply to a payment made by the transferee if–

(a) the transferor was a society to which subsection (2) above did not apply, and

(b) the member to whom the payment is made was a member of the transferor.

461B(3B) And where there has been a transfer of other business within section 461D(3), subsection (3) above shall apply to a payment made by the transferee if–

(a) the transferor was a society to which subsection (2) above applied, and

(b) the member to whom the payment is made was a member of the transferor.

461B(3C) Where subsection (3B) above applies, for the purposes of subsection (3) above–

(a) any payment of sums by a member to the society by way of contributions or deposits shall be treated as including any payment to the transferor, and

(b) any payment or repayment of sums to a member by the society within subsection (3)(a) or (b) shall be treated as including any payment or repayment made by the transferor.

461B(3D) In subsections (3) to (3D) above "transferee" and "transferor" shall be construed in accordance with section 461D.".

INSERTION OF REGULATIONS 461E TO 461G (APPORTIONMENT)

7. After section 461D insert–

"*Apportionments following transfer of other business*

461E(1) Where a friendly society carries on tax exempt other business and taxable other business sections 461F and 461G shall apply.

461E(2) In subsection (1)–

"**tax exempt other business**" means any business, other than long-term business, the profits arising from which are exempt from corporation tax by virtue of section 461(1), 461B(1) or 461D(1);

"**taxable other business**" means any business, other than long-term business, the profits arising from which are not exempt from corporation tax by virtue of section 461(1), 461B(1) or 461D(1).

Apportionment of income and gains

461F(1) This section has effect for determining for the purposes of the Corporation Tax Acts what parts of–

(a) income or losses arising from the assets of the friendly society, or

(b) gains or losses accruing on the disposal of such assets in accordance with the provisions of the Taxation of Chargeable Gains Act 1992,

are referable to each category of business referred to in section 461E.

461F(2) In subsection (1)(a)–

"**income**" has the meaning given in subsection (1ZA) of section 432A (apportionment of income and gains), and "**losses**" has the meaning given in subsection (1ZB) of that section.

461F(3) Income and losses arising from, and gains and losses accruing on the disposal of, assets linked ("linked assets") to either category of business are referable to that category of business.

461F(4) For the purposes of subsection (3), "linked assets" shall be construed in accordance with section 432ZA.

461F(5) There is referable to each category of business the relevant fraction of any income and losses referred to in paragraph (a) of subsection (1), and any gains and losses referred to in paragraph (b) of that subsection, not directly referable to the other category of business.

461F(6) For the purposes of subsection (5), "the relevant fraction" in relation to each category of business is–

$$\frac{A}{A + B}$$

where–

A is the mean of the opening and closing liabilities of that category of business (but taking that mean to be nil if it would otherwise be below nil), reduced (but not below nil) by the mean of the opening and closing net values of any assets directly referable to that category of business; and

B is the mean of the opening and closing liabilities of the other category of business which is carried on by the society (but taking that mean to be nil if it would otherwise be below nil), reduced (but not below nil) by the mean of the opening and closing net values of any assets directly referable to that category of business.

461F(7) But if the denominator found in accordance with subsection (6) is nil the relevant fraction for the purpose of subsection (5) in relation to each category of business is such fraction as is just and reasonable.

461F(8) In subsection (6) "**liabilities**" means the technical provisions determined in accordance with Part 6 of Schedule 6 to the Friendly Societies (Accounts and Related Provisions) Regulations 1994.

461F(9) In subsection (8) "**the Insurance Prudential Sourcebook**" has the same meaning as in section 431(2).

Apportionment of expenses

461G(1) This section has effect for determining for the purposes of the Corporation Tax Acts the deduction for expenses in relation to each category of business referred to in section 461E.

461G(2) In subsection (1) "**the deduction for expenses**" means either–

(a) a deduction for expenses in computing profits in accordance with the provisions of Case I of Schedule D, or

(b) a deduction for management expenses under section 75.

461G(3) The expenses attributable to each category of business are the expenses attributable to that business in accordance with proper internal accounting practice.

461G(4) In subsection (3) "**proper internal accounting practice**" means the practice of friendly societies in allocating all the expenses of the society to each category of business in accordance with any applicable requirements of–

(a) generally accepted accounting practice,

(b) the Prudential Sourcebook (Friendly Societies), or

(c) the Insurance Prudential Sourcebook.

461G(5) In subsection (4)–

"**the Prudential Sourcebook (Friendly Societies)**" means the Interim Prudential Sourcebook for Friendly Societies made by the Financial Services Authority under the Financial Services and Markets Act 2000;

"**the Insurance Prudential Sourcebook**" has the same meaning as in section 431(2).".

MODIFICATION OF THE CAPITAL ALLOWANCES ACT 2001

8(1) Modify the Capital Allowances Act 2001 as follows.

8(2) After section 257 insert–

"FRIENDLY SOCIETIES

Apportionment of allowances and charges

257A(1) Where a friendly society carries on tax exempt other business and taxable other business and is entitled or liable to any allowance or charge for a chargeable period in respect of plant or machinery provided for use, or used, for the management of that business, that allowance or charge must be apportioned between each category of business in accordance with this section.

257A(2) There shall be apportioned to each category of business the relevant fraction of any allowance or charge.

257A(3) For the purposes of subsection (2) "**the relevant fraction**" in relation to each category of business is–

$$\frac{A}{A + B}$$

where–

A is the mean of the opening and closing liabilities of that category of business (but taking that mean to be nil if it would otherwise be below nil); and

B is the mean of the opening and closing liabilities of the other category of business which is carried on by the society (but taking that mean to be nil if it would otherwise be below nil).

257A(4) But if the denominator found in accordance with subsection (3) is nil the relevant fraction for the purpose of subsection (2) in relation to each category of business is such fraction as is just and reasonable.

257A(5) For the purposes of this section, the management of a business, or a category of business, consists of pursuing those purposes expenditure on which falls to be regarded as expenses payable for the purposes of section 461G of ICTA.

257A(6) In this section–

"**friendly society**" has the same meaning as in section 466(2) of ICTA;

"**the Insurance Prudential Sourcebook**" has the same meaning as in section 431(2) of ICTA;

"**liabilities**" means the technical provisions determined in accordance with Part 6 of Schedule 6 to the Friendly Societies (Accounts and Related Provisions) Regulations 1994;

"**long-term business**" shall be construed in accordance with section 431(2) of ICTA;

"**tax exempt other business**" and "**taxable other business**" have the same meanings as in section 461E of ICTA.".".

TAXES (FEES FOR PAYMENT BY TELEPHONE) REGULATIONS 2008

(SI 2008/1948)

Made on 22 July 2008 by the Commissioners for Her Majesty's Revenue and Customs in exercise of the powers conferred by s. 136(1) and (3) of the Finance Act 2008. Operative from 13 August 2008.

CITATION AND COMMENCEMENT

1 These Regulations may be cited as the Taxes (Fees for Payment by Telephone) Regulations 2008 and shall come into force on 13th August 2008.

FEE PAYABLE FOR TELEPHONE PAYMENTS BY CREDIT CARD

2(1) Since the Commissioners expect that they will be required to pay a fee in connection with amounts paid by using a credit card, a person who–

(a) makes a payment to the Commissioners or a person authorised by the Commissioners, and

(b) gives telephone authorisation to make the payment by credit card,

must also pay a fee of 0.91% of the payment.

2(2) The fee must be paid by being added to the payment (so that, accordingly, the person must make a single overall payment, consisting of the payment and the fee).

2(3) In these Regulations **"credit card"** means a card which–

(a) is a credit-token falling within section 14(1)(b) of the Consumer Credit Act 1974, or

(b) would be a credit-token falling within that enactment were the card to be given to an individual.

SERIOUS CRIME ACT 2007 (SPECIFIED ANTI-FRAUD ORGANISATIONS) ORDER 2008

(SI 2008/2353)

Made on 2 September 2008 by the Secretary of State, in exercise of the powers conferred by s. 68(8) of the Serious Crime Act 2007. Operative from 1 October 2008.

CITATION AND COMMENCEMENT

1 This Order may be cited as the Serious Crime Act 2007 (Specified Anti-fraud Organisations) Order 2008 and shall come into force on 1st October 2008.

SPECIFIED ANTI-FRAUD ORGANISATIONS

2 The following anti-fraud organisations are specified pursuant to section 68 of the Serious Crime Act 2007–

(a)   CIFAS;

(b)   Experian Limited;

(c)   Insurance Fraud Investigators Group;

(d)   N Hunter Limited;

(e)   The Insurance Fraud Bureau;

(f)   The Telecommunications United Kingdom Fraud Forum Limited.

TAXATION OF BENEFITS UNDER GOVERNMENT PILOT SCHEMES (BETTER OFF IN WORK CREDIT) ORDER 2008

(SI 2008/2603)

Made on 6 October 2008 by the Treasury in exercise of the powers conferred by s. 151(1)(a) and (7)(a) of the Finance Act 1996. Operative from 27 October 2008.

CITATION AND COMMENCEMENT

1 This Order may be cited as the Taxation of Benefits under Government Pilot Schemes (Better off in Work Credit) Order 2008 and shall come into force on 27th October 2008.

INTERPRETATION

2 In this Order, **"Better off in Work Credit"** means benefit payable by virtue of the Government pilot scheme known by that name.

EXEMPTION FROM INCOME TAX

3 The Income Tax Acts shall have effect in relation to any amount of Better off in Work Credit as if it was wholly exempt from income tax and accordingly to be disregarded in computing the amount of any receipts brought into account for income tax purposes.

GROUP RELIEF FOR OVERSEAS LOSSES (MODIFICATION OF THE CORPORATION TAX ACTS FOR NON-RESIDENT INSURANCE COMPANIES) REGULATIONS 2008

(SI 2008/2646)

Made on 7 October 2008 by the Treasury in exercise of the powers conferred by para. 16(2)–(4) of Sch. 18A to the Income and Corporation Taxes Act 1988. Operative from 28 October 2008.

CITATION, COMMENCEMENT AND EFFECT

1(1) These Regulations may be cited as the Group Relief for Overseas Losses (Modification of the Corporation Tax Acts for Non-resident Insurance Companies) Regulations 2008 and shall come into force on 28th October 2008.

1(2) These Regulations shall have effect for accounting periods beginning on or after 28th October 2008.

MODIFICATION OF THE CORPORATION TAX ACTS

2(1) For the purposes of Part 2 of Schedule 18A to the Income and Corporation Taxes Act 1988, the Corporation Tax Acts, and provisions made under them, shall have effect with the modifications–

(a) in regulation 3, in relation to EEA life insurance companies, and

(b) in regulation 4, in relation to EEA general insurers.

2(2) For the purposes of these Regulations–

"EEA general insurer" means an EEA company whose business consists of, or includes, the effecting or carrying out of contracts falling within Part 1 of Schedule 1 to the Financial Services and Markets Act 2000 (Regulated Activities) Order 2001; and

"EEA life insurance company" means an EEA company whose business consists of, or includes, the effecting or carrying out of contracts falling within Part 2 of Schedule 1 to the Financial Services and Markets Act 2000 (Regulated Activities) Order 2001.

2(3) In paragraph (2)–

"EEA company" means a non-resident company–

(a) which is resident in an EEA territory; or

(b) which is not so resident but which carries on a trade in an EEA territory through a permanent establishment.

2(4) In paragraph (3)–

"EEA territory" has the meaning given in section 413(2) of the Income and Corporation Taxes Act 1988, and

"non-resident" means a company which is not resident in the United Kingdom.

MODIFICATION OF SECTION 431(2) OF THE INCOME AND CORPORATION TAXES ACT 1988

3(1) It shall be assumed that the definition of "insurance special purpose vehicle" in section 413(2) of the Income and Corporation Taxes Act 1988 includes an EEA life insurance company but does not include an insurance special purpose vehicle treated as a BLAGAB group reinsurer.

3(2) In paragraph (1) "BLAGAB group reinsurer" has the meaning given in paragraph 1 of Schedule 19ABA to the Income and Corporation Taxes Act 1988.

MODIFICATION OF THE INSURANCE COMPANIES (RESERVES) (TAX) REGULATIONS 1996

4 It shall be assumed that regulation 8 of the Insurance Companies (Reserves) (Tax) Regulations 1996 applies to an EEA general insurer.

REVOCATIONS

5 The following instruments are hereby revoked–

(a)   [Revokes SI 2006/3389;]

(b)   [Revokes SI 2007/2147.]

INCOME TAX (DEPOSIT-TAKERS AND BUILDING SOCIETIES) (INTEREST PAYMENTS) REGULATIONS 2008

(SI 2008/2682, as amended by SI 2011/22)

Made on 9 October 2008 by the Commissioners for Her Majesty's Revenue and Customs in exercise of the powers conferred by s. 852 and 871 of the Income Tax Act 2007. Operative from 31 October 2008.

PART 1 – INTRODUCTION

CITATION, COMMENCEMENT AND EFFECT

1(1) These Regulations may be cited as the Income Tax (Deposit-takers and Building Societies) (Interest Payments) Regulations 2008 and shall come into force on 31st October 2008.

1(2) These Regulations shall have effect in relation to payments of interest made on or after 31st October 2008.

INTERPRETATION

2 In these Regulations–

"**certificate**" means a certificate of non-liability to tax given in accordance with regulation 5;

"**the Commissioners**" means the Commissioners for Her Majesty's Revenue and Customs;

"**electronic communication**" includes any communication conveyed by means of an electronic communications network;

"**electronic signature**" has the meaning given by section 7(2) of the Electronic Communications Act 2000;

"**ITA 2007**" means the Income Tax Act 2007;

"**ITTOIA 2005**" means the Income Tax (Trading and Other Income) Act 2005;

"**notice**" means notice in writing;

"**officer**" means an officer of Revenue and Customs;

"**relevant dormant account**" has the meaning given in section 39(2) of the Finance Act 2008;

"**relevant financial institution**" means a deposit-taker or building society as the case requires;

"**repayment claim**" means a repayment claim mentioned in section 5(6) of the Dormant Bank and Building Society Accounts Act 2008, and other terms used in regulations 4A and 4B and in that Act have the same meaning in those regulations as in that Act;

"**section 851**" means section 851 of ITA 2007 (duty to deduct sums representing income tax);

"**tax year**" means a year beginning with 6th April in any year and ending with 5th April in the following year.

History – In reg. 2, the definition of "relevant dormant account" inserted by SI 2011/22, reg. 6, with effect in relation to interest paid or credited on or after 1 February 2011.
In reg. 2, the definition of "repayment claim" inserted by SI 2011/22, reg. 6, with effect in relation to interest paid or credited on or after 1 February 2011.

SCOPE OF THESE REGULATIONS

3(1) These Regulations make the following provisions.

3(2) Part 2 makes provision in respect of payments of interest by relevant financial institutions relating to relevant investments (regulations 4 to 13).

3(3) Part 3 makes provision in respect of payments of interest by relevant financial institutions relating to investments which are not relevant investments (regulation 14).

3(4) Part 4 makes provision in relation to information requirements (regulations 15 to 18).

3(5) Part 5 makes general provisions relating to continuity of certificates and declarations, consequential amendments, savings and revocations (regulations 19 to 20).

PART 2 – PAYMENTS OF INTEREST IN RELATION TO RELEVANT INVESTMENTS

GROSS PAYMENTS

4(1)   Section 851 does not apply in relation to–

(a)   a payment of interest, or

(b)   part of a payment of interest within regulation 13(2)(a) (joint accounts),

where, in respect of the person beneficially entitled to the payment or the part of the payment, a certificate has been supplied (see regulation 5) and has not ceased to be valid (see regulation 11). This is subject to regulation 13(3).

4(2)   But paragraph (1) does not apply if–

(a)   the provisions of section 629 of ITTOIA 2005 (income paid to relevant children of settlor) apply to the payment; or

(b)   a notice of deduction under regulation 12 has been issued in relation to the payment and it has not been cancelled.

4(3)   Where a certificate has been supplied and it has not ceased to be valid, a relevant financial institution which operates a system which refunds an amount corresponding to tax deducted from payments of interest made previously in the tax year shall–

(a)   refund any such amount in relation to the investment to which the certificate relates, and

(b)   recover an amount corresponding to the amount refunded on a written application to the Commissioners.

This is subject to paragraph (4).

4(4)   Paragraph (3) shall not apply where a relevant financial institution has given a statement under section 975 of ITA 2007 (statements about deduction of income tax), if–

(a)   the statement relates to the tax year in which the certificate was given; and

(b)   the statement was given prior to the receipt of the certificate.

DORMANT ACCOUNTS – POSTPONEMENT OF OBLIGATION TO DEDUCT SUM REPRESENTING INCOME TAX

4A(1)   Section 851 does not apply to a payment of interest in respect of a relevant dormant account before the time (if any) at which the balance of the account is paid out to the holder of the relevant dormant account following a repayment claim (such payment being referred to in this regulation as the repayment claim being "settled"), subject to paragraph (4).

4A(2)   In paragraph (3) and regulation 4B, the period between–

(a)   the time when a dormant account first becomes a relevant dormant account, and

(b)   the time at which a repayment claim to the balance of the account is settled,

is referred to, in relation to the account, as the "relevant dormant period".

4A(3)   Where a repayment claim to the balance of a dormant account is settled, all interest paid or credited to the account, or included in the balance of the account, during and at the end of the relevant dormant period, shall be treated for the purposes of section 851–

(a)   as paid at the time the repayment claim is settled; and

(b)   as if the account were at that time an investment, and a relevant investment for the purposes of Chapter 2 of Part 15 of ITA 2007 (deduction by deposit-takers and building societies).

4A(4)   Section 851 does not apply to a payment of interest in respect of a relevant dormant account which, at the time it first became a relevant dormant account, was a plan provided for by regulations made under Chapter 3 of Part 6 of ITTOIA 2005 (individual investment plans).

History – Reg. 4A and the heading before it inserted by SI 2011/22, reg. 7, with effect in relation to interest paid or credited on or after 1 February 2011.

4B   The duty to deduct a sum representing income tax under section 874 of ITA 2007 (duty to deduct from certain payments of yearly interest) does not apply to a payment of interest in respect of a relevant dormant account, made by or through a reclaim fund, deposit-taker or building society, during or at the end of the relevant dormant period for the account.

History – Reg. 4B inserted by SI 2011/22, reg. 7, with effect in relation to interest paid or credited on or after 1 February 2011.

CERTIFICATE OF NON-LIABILITY TO TAX

5   A certificate of non-liability to tax must—

(a)   certify that the person beneficially entitled to a payment of interest or, where regulation 13 (joint accounts) applies, to part of a payment of interest, is unlikely to be liable to pay any amount by way of income tax for the tax year in which that payment is made,

(b)   be supplied by a prescribed person (regulation 6),

(c)   be supplied to the relevant financial institution within the prescribed time limit (regulation 7),

(d)   be in the prescribed form (regulation 8), and

(e)   contain the prescribed contents (regulation 9).

PRESCRIBED PERSONS

6(1)   A prescribed person is—

(a)   a person—

    (i)   in whose name an investment is held,

    (ii)   who is beneficially entitled to a payment of interest on that investment, and

    (iii)   who was aged 16 or over at the beginning of the tax year in which the payment is made;

(b)   the parent or guardian of a person who is beneficially entitled to a payment of interest where that person is under the age of 16 at the beginning of the tax year in which the payment is made;

(c)   a person—

    (i)   who is beneficially entitled to a payment of interest, and

    (ii)   who is under the age of 16 at the beginning of the tax year in which the payment is made but who will become 16 during that tax year;

(d)   the donee of a power of attorney authorising the donee to administer the financial affairs of a person beneficially entitled to a payment of interest;

(e)   a parent, guardian, spouse, civil partner, daughter or son of a person suffering from mental disorder who is beneficially entitled to a payment of interest;

(f)   a receiver or other person appointed by any court in the United Kingdom to act in relation to the property and affairs of a person beneficially entitled to a payment of interest who is incapable, by reason of mental disorder, of managing and administering their property and affairs; or

(g)   a person appointed by the Secretary of State under—

    (i)   paragraph (1) of regulation 33 of the Social Security (Claims and Payments) Regulations 1987 (persons unable to act), whose appointment has not been revoked or terminated, or who has not resigned, under paragraph (2) of that regulation; or

    (ii)   paragraph (2) of regulation 28 of the Child Benefit and Guardian's Allowance (Administration) Regulations 2003 (appointment of persons to act on behalf of those unable to act), whose appointment has not been revoked, or who has not resigned, under paragraph (3) of that regulation, or whose appointment has not been terminated under paragraph (4) of that regulation.

6(2)   In this regulation—

"**daughter or son**" means a daughter or son aged 16 or over and includes a stepdaughter or stepson and an adopted or illegitimate daughter or son; and

"**mental disorder**" has the meaning given by—

(a)   section 1(2) of the Mental Health Act 1983 (application of Act: "mental disorder") in England and Wales,

(b)   section 328 of the Mental Health (Care and Treatment) (Scotland) Act 2003 (meaning of "mental disorder") in Scotland, and

(c)   Article 3 of the Mental Health (Northern Ireland) Order 1986 (definition of "mental disorder" and related expressions) in Northern Ireland.

SUPPLY WITHIN PRESCRIBED TIME LIMIT

7(1)   A certificate is treated as supplied to the relevant financial institution on the date it is given to the relevant financial institution or recorded by the relevant financial institution in accordance with paragraph (1)(b) of regulation 8 and nothing in paragraphs (2) or (3) of that regulation affects that date.

7(2)   The prescribed time limit is—

(a)   where regulation 6(1)(c) applies, before the end of the tax year in which the person beneficially entitled to the payment attains the age of 16; and

(b)   in any other case, before the end of the tax year in which the payment is made.

PRESCRIBED FORM OF A CERTIFICATE

8(1)   A certificate must be–

(a)   in writing, signed by a prescribed person, or

(b)   if not in writing, recorded in writing by the relevant financial institution on behalf of a prescribed person.

8(2)   If the relevant financial institution operates a record system under which the original certificate is not retained, the relevant financial institution must make a record of the certificate.

8(3)   Where paragraph (1)(b) or (2) applies–

(a)   a copy of the record of the certificate must be sent by the relevant financial institution to the prescribed person within 30 days of that record being made;

(b)   the prescribed person must notify the relevant financial institution of any corrections required within 30 days from the date the copy is sent; and

(c)   the relevant financial institution must incorporate any such corrections in a revised record which must be sent to the prescribed person as soon as possible.

8(4)   A certificate shall be regarded as being in writing if it was supplied–

(a)   by telephonic facsimile transmission; or

(b)   by electronic communication containing an electronic signature of the prescribed person.

8(5)   A certificate or a record of a certificate must be retained by a relevant financial institution in such manner as may be approved by the Commissioners for two years after the relevant financial institution has ceased to pay interest without deduction of a sum representing income tax in relation to a relevant investment.

PRESCRIBED CONTENTS OF A CERTIFICATE

9(1)   A certificate must contain–

(a)   the information prescribed in paragraphs (2) and (4); and

(b)   the undertaking prescribed in paragraph (5).

9(2)   In relation to the person beneficially entitled to the payment of interest, the prescribed information is that person's–

(a)   name,

(b)   permanent residential address (including post code),

(c)   date of birth, and

(d)   national insurance number if the circumstances in paragraph (3) apply, except where, in a particular case, an officer has indicated that this information is not required.

9(3)   The circumstances referred to in paragraph (2)(d) are that the person beneficially entitled to the payment of interest–

(a)   was aged 16 or over at the beginning of the tax year in which the payment was made, and

(b)   was liable to pay Class 1 or Class 2 contributions within the meaning of section 1(2) of the Social Security Contributions and Benefits Act 1992, at any time within the period of three years ending with the date on which the certificate is signed.

9(4)   In relation to the investment to which the certificate relates, the prescribed information is–

(a)   the name of the relevant financial institution,

(b)   the account number, and

(c)   the branch, sort code or roll number as appropriate, of the relevant financial institution where the account is held, if the account cannot otherwise be identified.

9(5)   The prescribed person must undertake to notify the relevant financial institution that if–

(a)   that person, being the person beneficially entitled to the payment of interest, or

(b)   the person so entitled,

becomes liable to pay any amount by way of income tax for the tax year in which the payment is made, that person will notify the relevant financial institution in accordance with regulation 10.

NOTIFICATION OF LIABILITY TO INCOME TAX IN ACCORDANCE WITH REGULATION 9(5)

10   A notification given in accordance with the undertaking in regulation 9(5) must contain details of the investment to which the certificate relates, including the account number and where necessary for identifying the account, the branch, sort code or roll number as appropriate, of the relevant financial institution.

CERTIFICATE CEASING TO BE VALID

11(1)   A certificate ceases to be valid in any of the circumstances specified in paragraph (2).

11(2)   The circumstances specified in this paragraph are—

(a)   the receipt by the relevant financial institution of a notification under regulation 10 that the person beneficially entitled to a payment of interest arising on an account specified in the notification has become liable to pay an amount by way of income tax for the tax year in which the payment is made;

(b)   in the case of a certificate supplied by a prescribed person within regulation 6(1)(b), the ending of the tax year in which the person beneficially entitled to the payment of interest reaches the age of 16;

(c)   the failure by a person who has given a certificate under regulation 6(1)(c) to become the holder of the investment to which the certificate relates before the first payment of interest after the end of the tax year in which the age of 16 is reached;

(d)   the issue of a notice of deduction under regulation 12;

(e)   the notification of the relevant financial institution that the person beneficially entitled to the payment of interest in respect of whom the certificate was given has died.

NOTICE OF DEDUCTION

12(1)   If an officer thinks that a person beneficially entitled to a payment of interest is or has become liable to pay an amount by way of income tax the officer must notify the prescribed person accordingly.

12(2)   If the prescribed person does not satisfy the officer within 30 days of the notification under paragraph (1) that the person beneficially entitled to the payment is not, or has not become, liable to pay an amount by way of income tax, the officer shall issue a notice of deduction to the relevant financial institution.

12(3)   A notice of deduction must—

(a)   give the name of the person beneficially entitled to the payment of interest;

(b)   give the account number of the account in respect of which the payment of interest is made;

(c)   give the branch, sort code or roll number as appropriate, of the relevant financial institution where the account is held, if the account cannot otherwise be identified; and

(d)   require a sum representing income tax to be deducted under section 851.

12(4)   Following the issue of a notice of deduction under this regulation no further certificate shall be accepted from or in respect of the person beneficially entitled to the payment of interest relating to the account specified in the notice.

This is subject to paragraph (7).

12(5)   A sum representing income tax shall be deducted under section 851 as soon as it is reasonably practicable to do so and in any event not later than 30 days following the date of issue of the notice.

12(6)   Where an officer is satisfied that the person referred to in the notice was not liable at the date of the notice and has not since become liable, or is no longer liable, to tax, the notice of deduction must be cancelled and notice of the cancellation must be given to that person and to the relevant financial institution.

12(7)   Where notice of the cancellation is given by an officer under paragraph (6) a further certificate may be supplied by or in respect of the person beneficially entitled to the payment of interest.

JOINT ACCOUNTS

13(1)   Where—

(a)   more than one person is beneficially entitled to a payment of interest on a relevant investment, and

(b)   a certificate is given by or in respect of—

 (i) one or more (but not all) of the persons beneficially entitled to the payment of interest, or

 (ii) each person beneficially entitled to the payment of interest but one or more of the certificates has ceased to be valid at any time due to the occurrence of one of the circumstances specified in sub-paragraphs (a), (b), (c), or (d) of regulation 11(2) (circumstances in which a certificate ceases to be valid),

for the purposes of these Regulations and section 851, it shall be assumed that those persons are beneficially entitled to the payment of interest in equal shares.

13(2) Where paragraph (1) applies, payment of–

(a) so much of the interest as corresponds to the share of any person by, or in respect of whom, a certificate was supplied and has not ceased to be valid shall be made without deduction of tax under regulation 4, and

(b) the remainder of the interest–

 (i) must be made under deduction of tax in accordance with section 851, and

 (ii) the amount so deducted must be treated as income tax paid by the person or persons to whom the payment is treated as being made for all purposes of the Income Tax Acts.

This is subject to paragraph (4).

13(3) Where paragraph (2)(b) applies, in the case of a certificate which ceases to be valid the deduction of tax pursuant to section 851 must be made–

(a) as soon as the certificate has ceased to be valid, or

(b) where regulation 12 (notice of deduction) applies, in accordance with paragraph (5) of that regulation.

13(4) Where paragraph (1) applies–

(a) a relevant financial institution may by notice inform an officer that the whole of the payment of interest referred to in the notice shall be made under deduction of tax in accordance with section 851; and

(b) an amount representing income tax shall accordingly be deducted by the relevant financial institution from the payment to which the notice relates and which is made after the date of the notice.

13(5) A relevant financial institution may by notice to an officer ("the cancellation notice")–

(a) cancel a notice given under paragraph (4), and

(b) where a notice is so cancelled, paragraph (2) shall apply to any payment of interest to which the notice formerly related and which is made after the date of the cancellation notice.

PART 3 – DECLARATIONS OF NON-UK RESIDENCE (INVESTMENTS WHICH ARE NOT RELEVANT INVESTMENTS)

PRESCRIBED FORM OF A DECLARATION

14(1) A declaration made under any of sections 858 to 861 of ITA 2007 must be–

(a) in writing signed by an appropriate person, or

(b) if not in writing, recorded in writing by the relevant financial institution, on behalf of an appropriate person.

14(2) If the relevant financial institution operates a record system under which the original declaration is not retained, the relevant financial institution must make a record of the declaration.

14(3) Where paragraph (1)(b) or (2) applies–

(a) a copy of the record of the declaration must be sent by the relevant financial institution to the appropriate person within 30 days of that record being made;

(b) the appropriate person must notify the relevant financial institution of any corrections required within 30 days from the date the copy is sent; and

(c) the relevant financial institution must incorporate any such corrections in a revised record which must be sent to the appropriate person as soon as possible.

14(4) The declaration has effect at the later of the date on which–

(a) it was given to the relevant financial institution,

(b)   a copy of the record in paragraph (3)(a) was sent, or

(c)   a revised copy of the record in paragraph (3)(c) was sent.

14(5)   A declaration shall be regarded as being in writing if it was made–

(a)   by telephonic facsimile transmission, or

(b)   by electronic communication containing an electronic signature of the appropriate person.

14(6)   A declaration or record of a declaration must be retained by a relevant financial institution in such manner as may be approved by the Commissioners for two years after the investment has been repaid or has become a relevant investment.

PART 4 – INFORMATION REQUIREMENTS

INFORMATION TO BE PROVIDED TO AN OFFICER – (RELEVANT INVESTMENTS)

15(1)   This regulation applies to payments of interest made by relevant financial institutions in respect of relevant investments.

15(2)   An officer may by notice require a relevant financial institution to provide such information (including copies of any relevant books, documents and other records) as that officer may reasonably require for the purposes of these Regulations and, in particular, in relation to the matters covered in paragraph (3).

15(3)   The matters are–

(a)   verifying payments of interest made without deduction of tax in accordance with these Regulations;

(b)   determining whether a certificate has been supplied in accordance with Part 2;

(c)   verifying amounts of interest paid by the relevant financial institution to which this regulation applies; and

(d)   verifying amounts representing income tax deducted by the relevant financial institution from such payments in accordance with section 851.

15(4)   The information required must be provided within such time (not being less than 14 days) as stated in the notice.

INFORMATION TO BE PROVIDED TO AN OFFICER – (INVESTMENTS WHICH ARE NOT RELEVANT INVESTMENTS)

16(1)   This regulation applies to payments of interest made without deduction of tax by relevant financial institutions in respect of investments which are not relevant investments.

16(2)   Where this regulation applies, an officer may by notice require a relevant financial institution to provide such information (including copies of any relevant books, documents and other records) as that officer may reasonably require for the purposes of determining whether payments of interest by that relevant financial institution were properly made without deduction of tax.

16(3)   The information required must be provided within such time (not being less than 14 days) as may be provided by the notice.

INSPECTION OF RECORDS

17(1)   An officer may require a relevant financial institution to produce all books, documents and other records, or such of these as may be specified, either in the possession of or under the control of the relevant financial institution, for inspection at such time and place as that officer may reasonably require under this Part.

17(2)   Where records are maintained by computer the person required to make them available for inspection shall provide the officer making the inspection with all the facilities necessary for obtaining information from these.

USE OF INFORMATION

18(1)   Subject to paragraph (2), information obtained by an officer under this Part–

(a)   must not be used for the purpose of ascertaining the tax liability (if any) of any person other than–

    (i)   a person beneficially entitled to a payment of interest specified in regulation 15(1) or 16(1) to whom the information obtained relates, and

    (ii)   the relevant financial institution; and

(b)   must otherwise be used only for the purposes of these Regulations.

18(2)   Paragraph (1) shall not be construed as preventing any disclosure of information within section 182(5) of the Finance Act 1989.

PART 5 – GENERAL PROVISIONS

CONTINUITY OF CERTIFICATES AND DECLARATIONS OF NON-UK RESIDENCE FOLLOWING TRANSFER OF BUSINESS

19   Where a relevant financial institution ("the original institution") transfers the whole or part of its business to another relevant financial institution ("the successor institution")–

(a)   a certificate under regulation 5, or

(b)   a declaration made under any of sections 858 to 861 of ITA 2007 (declaration of non-UK residence),

supplied to the original institution in relation to an investment shall be treated as supplied to the successor institution.

CONSEQUENTIAL AMENDMENTS, SAVINGS AND REVOCATION

20(1)   Schedule 1 (consequential amendments) and Schedule 2 (transitional provisions and savings) have effect.

20(2)   The Regulations listed in column 1 of Schedule 3 are revoked.

20(3)   Paragraph (2) is subject to Schedule 2.

SCHEDULE 1 – CONSEQUENTIAL AMENDMENTS

Regulation 20

1   Regulation 16 of the Reporting of Savings Income Information Regulations 2003 (audit and related issues) is amended as follows.

2   [Amends SI 2003/3297, reg. 16(5).]

3   [Amends SI 2003/3297, reg. 16(6).]

SCHEDULE 2 – TRANSITIONAL PROVISIONS AND SAVINGS

Regulation 20

Part 1 – General Provisions

CONTINUITY OF THE LAW

1   The revocation of provisions and their making in a rewritten form by these Regulations does not affect the continuity of the law.

2   Paragraph 1 does not apply to any change in the law made by these Regulations.

3   Anything which–

(a)   has been done, or has effect as if done, under or for the purposes of a provision of the revoked Regulations, and

(b)   is in force or effective immediately before the commencement of these Regulations,

has effect after that commencement as if done under or for the purposes of the corresponding provision of these Regulations.

4   Any reference (express or implied) in these Regulations or any document made under these Regulations to–

(a)   a provision of these Regulations, or

(b)   things done or falling to be done under or for the purposes of a provision of these Regulations, is to be read as including, in relation to times, circumstances or purposes in relation to which any corresponding provision of the revoked Regulations had effect, a reference to the provision of the revoked Regulations or to things done or falling to be done under or for the purposes of the provision of the revoked Regulations.

5 Any reference (express or implied) in these Regulations to—

(a) a provision of ITA 2007, or

(b) things done or falling to be done under or for the purposes of a provision of ITA 2007,

is to be read as including, in relation to times, circumstances or purposes in relation to which any corresponding provision repealed by that Act had effect, a reference to the repealed provision or to things done or falling to be done under or for the purposes of the repealed provision.

6 Paragraphs 4 and 5 apply only so far as the context permits.

7 Paragraphs 1 to 5 have effect instead of paragraph (b) of section 17(2) of the Interpretation Act 1978.

GENERAL SAVING FOR OLD SAVINGS

8(1) The revocation by these Regulations of a provision previously revoked subject to savings does not affect the continued operation of those savings.

8(2) The revocation by these Regulations of a saving on the previous revocation of a provision does not affect the operation of the saving in so far as it is not specifically reproduced in these Regulations but remains capable of having effect.

Part 2 – Specific Provisions

9(1) Declarations made under regulation 11 of the Income Tax (Building Societies) (Dividends and Interest) Regulations 1990 or treated as having effect as if made under that provision shall have effect as if made under section 858(3), 859(3), 860(3) or 861(3) of ITA 2007.

9(2) Declarations within paragraph (1) shall be preserved by a building society for two years after the investment has been repaid or become a relevant investment.

SCHEDULE 3 – REVOCATIONS

Regulation 20

[Revokes SI 1990/2231, SI 1992/11, SI 1992/2915, SI 1994/296, SI 1995/1184, SI 1996/223, SI 2001/404, SI 2005/3474, SI 1990/2232, SI 1992/13, SI 1994/295, SI 2001/406, SI 1992/10, SI 1992/12 and SI 1992/14.]

TRIBUNAL PROCEDURE (FIRST-TIER TRIBUNAL) (SOCIAL ENTITLEMENT CHAMBER) RULES 2008

(SI 2008/2685, as amended by SI 2009/274, SI 2009/1975, SI 2010/43, SI 2010/2653, SI 2011/651, SI 2012/500, SI 2012/2007, SI 2013/477, SI 2013/2067 and SI 2014/514)

Made on 9 October 2008 by the Tribunal Procedure Committee in exercise of the powers conferred by s. 20(2) and (3) of the Social Security Act 1998 and s. 9(3), 22 and 29(3) of, and Sch. 5 to, the Tribunals, Courts and Enforcement Act 2007. Operative from 3 November 2008.

PART 1 – INTRODUCTION

CITATION, COMMENCEMENT, APPLICATION AND INTERPRETATION

1(1) These Rules may be cited as the Tribunal Procedure (First-tier Tribunal) (Social Entitlement Chamber) Rules 2008 and come into force on 3rd November 2008.

1(2) These Rules apply to proceedings before the Social Entitlement Chamber of the First-tier Tribunal.

1(3) In these Rules–

"**the 2007 Act**" means the Tribunals, Courts and Enforcement Act 2007;

"**appeal**" includes an application under section 19(9) of the Tax Credits Act 2002;

"**appellant**" means a person who makes an appeal to the Tribunal, or a person substituted as an appellant under rule 9(1) (substitution of parties);

"**asylum support case**" means proceedings concerning the provision of support for an asylum seeker, a failed asylum seeker or a person designated under section 130 of the Criminal Justice and Immigration Act 2008 (designation), or the dependants of any such person;

"**criminal injuries compensation case**" means proceedings concerning the payment of compensation under a scheme made under the Criminal Injuries Compensation Act 1995 or section 47 of the Crime and Security Act 2010;

"**decision maker**" means the maker of a decision against which an appeal has been brought;

"**dispose of proceedings**" includes, unless indicated otherwise, disposing of a part of the proceedings;

"**document**" means anything in which information is recorded in any form, and an obligation under these Rules to provide or allow access to a document or a copy of a document for any purpose means, unless the Tribunal directs otherwise, an obligation to provide or allow access to such document or copy in a legible form or in a form which can be readily made into a legible form;

"**hearing**" means an oral hearing and includes a hearing conducted in whole or in part by video link, telephone or other means of instantaneous two-way electronic communication;

"**legal representative**" means a person who, for the purposes of the Legal Services Act 2007, is an authorised person in relation to an activity which constitutes the exercise of a right of audience or the conduct of litigation within the meaning of that Act, an advocate or solicitor in Scotland or a barrister or solicitor in Northern Ireland;

"**party**" means–

(a)   a person who is an appellant or respondent in proceedings before the Tribunal;

(b)   a person who makes a reference to the Tribunal under section 28D of the Child Support Act 1991;

(c)   a person who starts proceedings before the Tribunal under paragraph 3 of Schedule 2 to the Tax Credits Act 2002; or

(d)   if the proceedings have been concluded, a person who was a party under paragraph (a), (b) or (c) when the Tribunal finally disposed of all issues in the proceedings;

"**practice direction**" means a direction given under section 23 of the 2007 Act;

"**respondent**" means–

(a) in an appeal against a decision, the decision maker and any person other than the appellant who had a right of appeal against the decision;

(b) in a reference under section 28D of the Child Support Act 1991–

    (i) the absent parent or non-resident parent;

    (ii) the person with care; and

    (iii) in Scotland, the child if the child made the application for a departure direction or a variation;

(c) in proceedings under paragraph 3 of Schedule 2 to the Tax Credits Act 2002, a person on whom it is proposed that a penalty be imposed; or

(d) a person substituted or added as a respondent under rule 9 (substitution and addition of parties);

"social security and child support case" means any case allocated to the Social Entitlement Chamber of the First-tier Tribunal except an asylum support case or a criminal injuries compensation case;

"Tribunal" means the First-tier Tribunal.

History – R. 1(2) substituted by SI 2010/2653, r. 5(2), with effect from 29 November 2010.
In r. 1(3), in the definition of "asylum support case", the words ", a failed asylum seeker or a person designated under section 130 of the Criminal Justice and Immigration Act 2008 (designation), or the dependants of any such person" substituted for the words "or his or her dependants" by SI 2009/274, r. 2, with effect from 1 April 2009.
In r. 1(3), in the definition of "criminal injuries compensation case", the words "or section 47 of the Crime and Security Act 2010" inserted by SI 2013/477, r. 23, with effect from 8 April 2013.
In r. 1(3), in the definition of "legal representative", the words "a person who, for the purposes of the Legal Services Act 2007, is an authorised person in relation to an activity which constitutes the exercise of a right of audience or the conduct of litigation within the meaning of that Act" substituted for the words "an authorised advocate or authorised litigator as defined by section 119(1) of the Courts and Legal Services Act 1990" by SI 2010/43, r. 3, with effect from 18 January 2010.
In r. 1(3), definition of "Social Entitlement Chamber" omitted by SI 2011/651, r. 4(2)(a), with effect from 1 April 2011.
In r. 1(3), in the definition of "social security and child support case", the words "of the First-tier Tribunal" inserted by SI 2011/651, r. 4(2)(b), with effect from 1 April 2011.

OVERRIDING OBJECTIVE AND PARTIES' OBLIGATION TO CO-OPERATE WITH THE TRIBUNAL

2(1) The overriding objective of these Rules is to enable the Tribunal to deal with cases fairly and justly.

2(2) Dealing with a case fairly and justly includes–

(a) dealing with the case in ways which are proportionate to the importance of the case, the complexity of the issues, the anticipated costs and the resources of the parties;

(b) avoiding unnecessary formality and seeking flexibility in the proceedings;

(c) ensuring, so far as practicable, that the parties are able to participate fully in the proceedings;

(d) using any special expertise of the Tribunal effectively; and

(e) avoiding delay, so far as compatible with proper consideration of the issues.

2(3) The Tribunal must seek to give effect to the overriding objective when it–

(a) exercises any power under these Rules; or

(b) interprets any rule or practice direction.

2(4) Parties must–

(a) help the Tribunal to further the overriding objective; and

(b) co-operate with the Tribunal generally.

ALTERNATIVE DISPUTE RESOLUTION AND ARBITRATION

3(1) The Tribunal should seek, where appropriate–

(a) to bring to the attention of the parties the availability of any appropriate alternative procedure for the resolution of the dispute; and

(b) if the parties wish and provided that it is compatible with the overriding objective, to facilitate the use of the procedure.

3(2) Part 1 of the Arbitration Act 1996 does not apply to proceedings before the Tribunal.

PART 2 – GENERAL POWERS AND PROVISIONS

DELEGATION TO STAFF

4(1) Staff appointed under section 40(1) of the 2007 Act (tribunal staff and services) may, with the approval of the Senior President of Tribunals, carry out functions of a judicial nature permitted or required to be done by the Tribunal.

4(2) The approval referred to at paragraph (1) may apply generally to the carrying out of specified functions by members of staff of a specified description in specified circumstances.

4(3) Within 14 days after the date on which the Tribunal sends notice of a decision made by a member of staff under paragraph (1) to a party, that party may apply in writing to the Tribunal for that decision to be considered afresh by a judge.

CASE MANAGEMENT POWERS

5(1) Subject to the provisions of the 2007 Act and any other enactment, the Tribunal may regulate its own procedure.

5(2) The Tribunal may give a direction in relation to the conduct or disposal of proceedings at any time, including a direction amending, suspending or setting aside an earlier direction.

5(3) In particular, and without restricting the general powers in paragraphs (1) and (2), the Tribunal may–

(a)   extend or shorten the time for complying with any rule, practice direction or direction;

(aa)   extend the time within which an appeal must be brought under regulation 28(1) of the Child Benefit and Guardian's Allowance (Decisions and Appeals) Regulations 2003

(b)   consolidate or hear together two or more sets of proceedings or parts of proceedings raising common issues, or treat a case as a lead case (whether in accordance with rule 18 (lead cases) or otherwise);

(c)   permit or require a party to amend a document;

(d)   permit or require a party or another person to provide documents, information, evidence or submissions to the Tribunal or a party;

(e)   deal with an issue in the proceedings as a preliminary issue;

(f)   hold a hearing to consider any matter, including a case management issue;

(g)   decide the form of any hearing;

(h)   adjourn or postpone a hearing;

(i)   require a party to produce a bundle for a hearing;

(j)   stay (or, in Scotland, sist) proceedings;

(k)   transfer proceedings to another court or tribunal if that other court or tribunal has jurisdiction in relation to the proceedings and–

     (i)   because of a change of circumstances since the proceedings were started, the Tribunal no longer has jurisdiction in relation to the proceedings; or

     (ii)   the Tribunal considers that the other court or tribunal is a more appropriate forum for the determination of the case; or

(l)   suspend the effect of its own decision pending the determination by the Tribunal or the Upper Tribunal of an application for permission to appeal against, and any appeal or review of, that decision.

History – R. 5(3)(aa) inserted by SI 2013/2067, r. 23, with effect from 1 November 2013.

PROCEDURE FOR APPLYING FOR AND GIVING DIRECTIONS

6(1) The Tribunal may give a direction on the application of one or more of the parties or on its own initiative.

6(2) An application for a direction may be made–

(a)   by sending or delivering a written application to the Tribunal; or

(b)   orally during the course of a hearing.

6(3) An application for a direction must include the reason for making that application.

6(4)   Unless the Tribunal considers that there is good reason not to do so, the Tribunal must send written notice of any direction to every party and to any other person affected by the direction.

6(5)   If a party or any other person sent notice of the direction under paragraph (4) wishes to challenge a direction which the Tribunal has given, they may do so by applying for another direction which amends, suspends or sets aside the first direction.

FAILURE TO COMPLY WITH RULES ETC.

7(1)   An irregularity resulting from a failure to comply with any requirement in these Rules, a practice direction or a direction, does not of itself render void the proceedings or any step taken in the proceedings.

7(2)   If a party has failed to comply with a requirement in these Rules, a practice direction or a direction, the Tribunal may take such action as it considers just, which may include–

(a)   waiving the requirement;

(b)   requiring the failure to be remedied;

(c)   exercising its power under rule 8 (striking out a party's case); or

(d)   exercising its power under paragraph (3).

7(3)   The Tribunal may refer to the Upper Tribunal, and ask the Upper Tribunal to exercise its power under section 25 of the 2007 Act in relation to, any failure by a person to comply with a requirement imposed by the Tribunal–

(a)   to attend at any place for the purpose of giving evidence;

(b)   otherwise to make themselves available to give evidence;

(c)   to swear an oath in connection with the giving of evidence;

(d)   to give evidence as a witness;

(e)   to produce a document; or

(f)   to facilitate the inspection of a document or any other thing (including any premises).

STRIKING OUT A PARTY'S CASE

8(1)   The proceedings, or the appropriate part of them, will automatically be struck out if the appellant has failed to comply with a direction that stated that failure by a party to comply with the direction would lead to the striking out of the proceedings or that part of them.

8(2)   The Tribunal must strike out the whole or a part of the proceedings if the Tribunal–

(a)   does not have jurisdiction in relation to the proceedings or that part of them; and

(b)   does not exercise its power under rule 5(3)(k)(i) (transfer to another court or tribunal) in relation to the proceedings or that part of them.

8(3)   The Tribunal may strike out the whole or a part of the proceedings if–

(a)   the appellant has failed to comply with a direction which stated that failure by the appellant to comply with the direction could lead to the striking out of the proceedings or part of them;

(b)   the appellant has failed to co-operate with the Tribunal to such an extent that the Tribunal cannot deal with the proceedings fairly and justly; or

(c)   the Tribunal considers there is no reasonable prospect of the appellant's case, or part of it, succeeding.

8(4)   The Tribunal may not strike out the whole or a part of the proceedings under paragraph (2) or (3)(b) or (c) without first giving the appellant an opportunity to make representations in relation to the proposed striking out.

8(5)   If the proceedings, or part of them, have been struck out under paragraph (1) or (3)(a), the appellant may apply for the proceedings, or part of them, to be reinstated.

8(6)   An application under paragraph (5) must be made in writing and received by the Tribunal within 1 month after the date on which the Tribunal sent notification of the striking out to the appellant.

8(7)   This rule applies to a respondent as it applies to an appellant except that–

(a)   a reference to the striking out of the proceedings is to be read as a reference to the barring of the respondent from taking further part in the proceedings; and

(b)   a reference to an application for the reinstatement of proceedings which have been struck out is to be read as a reference to an application for the lifting of the bar on the respondent from taking further part in the proceedings.

Statutory Instruments

8(8)   If a respondent has been barred from taking further part in proceedings under this rule and that bar has not been lifted, the Tribunal need not consider any response or other submission made by that respondent and may summarily determine any or all issues against that respondent.

History – In r. 8(8), the words "and may summarily determine any or all issues against that respondent" inserted by SI 2010/2653, r. 5(3), with effect from 29 November 2010.

SUBSTITUTION AND ADDITION OF PARTIES

9(1)   The Tribunal may give a direction substituting a party if–

(a)   the wrong person has been named as a party; or

(b)   the substitution has become necessary because of a change in circumstances since the start of proceedings.

9(2)   The Tribunal may give a direction adding a person to the proceedings as a respondent.

9(3)   If the Tribunal gives a direction under paragraph (1) or (2) it may give such consequential directions as it considers appropriate.

NO POWER TO AWARD COSTS

10   The Tribunal may not make any order in respect of costs (or, in Scotland, expenses).

REPRESENTATIVES

11(1)   A party may appoint a representative (whether a legal representative or not) to represent that party in the proceedings.

11(2)   Subject to paragraph (3), if a party appoints a representative, that party (or the representative if the representative is a legal representative) must send or deliver to the Tribunal written notice of the representative's name and address.

11(3)   In a case to which rule 23 (cases in which the notice of appeal is to be sent to the decision maker) applies, if the appellant (or the appellant's representative if the representative is a legal representative) provides written notification of the appellant's representative's name and address to the decision maker before the decision maker provides its response to the Tribunal, the appellant need not take any further steps in order to comply with paragraph (2).

11(4)   If the Tribunal receives notice that a party has appointed a representative under paragraph (2), it must send a copy of that notice to each other party.

11(5)   Anything permitted or required to be done by a party under these Rules, a practice direction or a direction may be done by the representative of that party, except signing a witness statement.

11(6)   A person who receives due notice of the appointment of a representative–

(a)   must provide to the representative any document which is required to be provided to the represented party, and need not provide that document to the represented party; and

(b)   may assume that the representative is and remains authorised as such until they receive written notification that this is not so from the representative or the represented party.

11(7)   At a hearing a party may be accompanied by another person whose name and address has not been notified under paragraph (2) or (3) but who, with the permission of the Tribunal, may act as a representative or otherwise assist in presenting the party's case at the hearing.

11(8)   Paragraphs (2) to (6) do not apply to a person who accompanies a party under paragraph (7).

CALCULATING TIME

12(1)   Except in asylum support cases, an act required by these Rules, a practice direction or a direction to be done on or by a particular day must be done by 5pm on that day.

12(2)   If the time specified by these Rules, a practice direction or a direction for doing any act ends on a day other than a working day, the act is done in time if it is done on the next working day.

12(3)   In this rule **"working day"** means any day except a Saturday or Sunday, Christmas Day, Good Friday or a bank holiday under section 1 of the Banking and Financial Dealings Act 1971.

SENDING AND DELIVERY OF DOCUMENTS

13(1)   Any document to be provided to the Tribunal under these Rules, a practice direction or a direction must be–

(a)   sent by pre-paid post or delivered by hand to the address specified for the proceedings;

(b)   sent by fax to the number specified for the proceedings; or

(c)   sent or delivered by such other method as the Tribunal may permit or direct.

13(2)   Subject to paragraph (3), if a party provides a fax number, email address or other details for the electronic transmission of documents to them, that party must accept delivery of documents by that method.

13(3)   If a party informs the Tribunal and all other parties that a particular form of communication (other than pre-paid post or delivery by hand) should not be used to provide documents to that party, that form of communication must not be so used.

13(4)   If the Tribunal or a party sends a document to a party or the Tribunal by email or any other electronic means of communication, the recipient may request that the sender provide a hard copy of the document to the recipient. The recipient must make such a request as soon as reasonably practicable after receiving the document electronically.

13(5)   The Tribunal and each party may assume that the address provided by a party or its representative is and remains the address to which documents should be sent or delivered until receiving written notification to the contrary.

USE OF DOCUMENTS AND INFORMATION

14(1)   The Tribunal may make an order prohibiting the disclosure or publication of–

(a)   specified documents or information relating to the proceedings; or

(b)   any matter likely to lead members of the public to identify any person whom the Tribunal considers should not be identified.

14(2)   The Tribunal may give a direction prohibiting the disclosure of a document or information to a person if–

(a)   the Tribunal is satisfied that such disclosure would be likely to cause that person or some other person serious harm; and

(b)   the Tribunal is satisfied, having regard to the interests of justice, that it is proportionate to give such a direction.

14(3)   If a party ("the first party") considers that the Tribunal should give a direction under paragraph (2) prohibiting the disclosure of a document or information to another party ("the second party"), the first party must–

(a)   exclude the relevant document or information from any documents that will be provided to the second party; and

(b)   provide to the Tribunal the excluded document or information, and the reason for its exclusion, so that the Tribunal may decide whether the document or information should be disclosed to the second party or should be the subject of a direction under paragraph (2).

14(4)   The Tribunal must conduct proceedings as appropriate in order to give effect to a direction given under paragraph (2).

14(5)   If the Tribunal gives a direction under paragraph (2) which prevents disclosure to a party who has appointed a representative, the Tribunal may give a direction that the documents or information be disclosed to that representative if the Tribunal is satisfied that–

(a)   disclosure to the representative would be in the interests of the party; and

(b)   the representative will act in accordance with paragraph (6).

14(6)   Documents or information disclosed to a representative in accordance with a direction under paragraph (5) must not be disclosed either directly or indirectly to any other person without the Tribunal's consent.

EVIDENCE AND SUBMISSIONS

15(1)   Without restriction on the general powers in rule 5(1) and (2) (case management powers), the Tribunal may give directions as to–

(a)   issues on which it requires evidence or submissions;

(b)   the nature of the evidence or submissions it requires;

(c)   whether the parties are permitted or required to provide expert evidence;

(d)   any limit on the number of witnesses whose evidence a party may put forward, whether in relation to a particular issue or generally;

(e)   the manner in which any evidence or submissions are to be provided, which may include a direction for them to be given–

    (i)   orally at a hearing; or

    (ii)   by written submissions or witness statement; and

(f)   the time at which any evidence or submissions are to be provided.

15(2)   The Tribunal may–

(a)   admit evidence whether or not–

    (i)   the evidence would be admissible in a civil trial in the United Kingdom; or

    (ii)   the evidence was available to a previous decision maker; or

(b)   exclude evidence that would otherwise be admissible where–

    (i)   the evidence was not provided within the time allowed by a direction or a practice direction;

    (ii)   the evidence was otherwise provided in a manner that did not comply with a direction or a practice direction; or

    (iii)   it would otherwise be unfair to admit the evidence.

15(3)   The Tribunal may consent to a witness giving, or require any witness to give, evidence on oath, and may administer an oath for that purpose.

SUMMONING OR CITATION OF WITNESSES AND ORDERS TO ANSWER QUESTIONS OR PRODUCE DOCUMENTS

16(1)   On the application of a party or on its own initiative, the Tribunal may–

(a)   by summons (or, in Scotland, citation) require any person to attend as a witness at a hearing at the time and place specified in the summons or citation; or

(b)   order any person to answer any questions or produce any documents in that person's possession or control which relate to any issue in the proceedings.

16(2)   A summons or citation under paragraph (1)(a) must–

(a)   give the person required to attend 14 days' notice of the hearing or such shorter period as the Tribunal may direct; and

(b)   where the person is not a party, make provision for the person's necessary expenses of attendance to be paid, and state who is to pay them.

16(3)   No person may be compelled to give any evidence or produce any document that the person could not be compelled to give or produce on a trial of an action in a court of law in the part of the United Kingdom where the proceedings are due to be determined.

16(4)   A summons, citation or order under this rule must–

(a)   state that the person on whom the requirement is imposed may apply to the Tribunal to vary or set aside the summons, citation or order, if they have not had an opportunity to object to it; and

(b)   state the consequences of failure to comply with the summons, citation or order.

WITHDRAWAL

17(1)   Subject to paragraph (2), a party may give notice of the withdrawal of its case, or any part of it–

(a)   by sending or delivering to the Tribunal a written notice of withdrawal; or

(b)   orally at a hearing.

17(2)   In the circumstances described in paragraph (3), a notice of withdrawal will not take effect unless the Tribunal consents to the withdrawal.

17(3)   The circumstances referred to in paragraph (2) are where a party gives notice of withdrawal–

(a)   in a criminal injuries compensation case; or

(b)   in a social security and child support case where the Tribunal has directed that notice of withdrawal shall take effect only with the Tribunal's consent; or

(c)   at a hearing.

17(4)   A party who has withdrawn their case may apply to the Tribunal for the case to be reinstated.

17(5)   An application under paragraph (4) must be made in writing and be received by the Tribunal within 1 month after–

(a)   the date on which the Tribunal received the notice under paragraph (1)(a); or

(b)   the date of the hearing at which the case was withdrawn orally under paragraph (1)(b).

17(6)   The Tribunal must notify each party in writing that a withdrawal has taken effect under this rule.

History – In r. 17(1)(a), the words "at any time before a hearing to consider the disposal of the proceedings (or, if the Tribunal disposes of the proceedings without a hearing, before that disposal)," at the beginning omitted by SI 2013/477, r. 24(a), with effect from 8 April 2013.
In r. 17(3)(a), the words "under paragraph (1)(a)" at the beginning omitted and r. 17(b) and (c) substituted for former r. 17(3)(b) by SI 2013/477, r. 24(b) and (c), with effect from 8 April 2013. Former r. 17(3)(b) read as follows:
"(b)   under paragraph (1)(b)."
In r. 17(6), the words "that a withdrawal has taken effect" substituted for the words "of an withdrawal" by SI 2013/477, r. 24(d), with effect from 8 April 2013.

LEAD CASES

18(1)   This rule applies if–

(a)   two or more cases have been started before the Tribunal;

(b)   in each such case the Tribunal has not made a decision disposing of the proceedings; and

(c)   the cases give rise to common or related issues of fact or law.

18(2)   The Tribunal may give a direction–

(a)   specifying one or more cases falling under paragraph (1) as a lead case or lead cases; and

(b)   staying (or, in Scotland, sisting) the other cases falling under paragraph (1) ("the related cases").

18(3)   When the Tribunal makes a decision in respect of the common or related issues–

(a)   the Tribunal must send a copy of that decision to each party in each of the related cases; and

(b)   subject to paragraph (4), that decision shall be binding on each of those parties.

18(4)   Within 1 month after the date on which the Tribunal sent a copy of the decision to a party under paragraph (3)(a), that party may apply in writing for a direction that the decision does not apply to, and is not binding on the parties to, a particular related case.

18(5)   The Tribunal must give directions in respect of cases which are stayed or sisted under paragraph (2)(b), providing for the disposal of or further directions in those cases.

18(6)   If the lead case or cases lapse or are withdrawn before the Tribunal makes a decision in respect of the common or related issues, the Tribunal must give directions as to–

(a)   whether another case or other cases are to be specified as a lead case or lead cases; and

(b)   whether any direction affecting the related cases should be set aside or amended.

CONFIDENTIALITY IN CHILD SUPPORT OR CHILD TRUST FUND CASES

19(1)   Paragraph (3) applies to proceedings under the Child Support Act 1991 in the circumstances described in paragraph (2), other than an appeal against a reduced benefit decision (as defined in section 46(10)(b) of the Child Support Act 1991, as that section had effect prior to the commencement of section 15(b) of the Child Maintenance and Other Payments Act 2008).

19(2)   The circumstances referred to in paragraph (1) are that the absent parent, non-resident parent or person with care would like their address or the address of the child to be kept confidential and has given notice to that effect–

(a)   in the notice of appeal or when notifying the Secretary of State or the Tribunal of any subsequent change of address; or

(b)   within 14 days after an enquiry is made by the recipient of the notice of appeal or the notification referred to in sub-paragraph (a).

19(3)   Where this paragraph applies, the Secretary of State and the Tribunal must take appropriate steps to secure the confidentiality of the address, and of any information which could reasonably be expected to enable a person to identify the address, to the extent that the address or that information is not already known to each other party.

19(4)   Paragraph (6) applies to proceedings under the Child Trust Funds Act 2004 in the circumstances described in paragraph (5).

19(5)   The circumstances referred to in paragraph (4) are that a relevant person would like their address or the address of the eligible child to be kept confidential and has given notice to that effect, or a local authority with parental responsibility in relation to the eligible child would like the address of the eligible child to be kept confidential and has given notice to that effect–

(a)   to HMRC in the notice of appeal or when notifying any subsequent change of address;

(b)   to HMRC within 14 days after an enquiry by HMRC; or

(c)   to the Tribunal when notifying any change of address.

19(6)   Where this paragraph applies, HMRC and the Tribunal must take appropriate steps to secure the confidentiality of the address, and of any information which could reasonably be expected to enable a person to identify the address, to the extent that the address or that information is not already known to each other party.

19(7)   In this rule–

"**eligible child**" has the meaning set out in section 2 of the Child Trust Funds Act 2004;

"**HMRC**" means Her Majesty's Revenue and Customs;

"**non-resident parent**" and "**parent with care**" have the meanings set out in section 54 of the Child Support Act 1991;

"**parental responsibility**" has the meaning set out in section 3(9) of the Child Trust Funds Act 2004; and

"**relevant person**" has the meaning set out in section 22(3) of the Child Trust Funds Act 2004.

History – R. 19(2)(a) and (b) substituted for (a)–(c) by SI 2013/2067, r. 24, with effect from 1 November 2013. Former r. 19(2)(a)–(c) read as follows:
>   "(a)   to the Secretary of State in the notice of appeal or when notifying any subsequent change of address;
>   (b)   to the Secretary of State within 14 days after an enquiry is made; or
>   (c)   to the Tribunal when notifying any change of address.".

In r. 19(2)(a), the words "or the Child Maintenance and Enforcement Commission" omitted by SI 2012/2007, art. 117(a), with effect from 31 July 2012.
In r. 19(2)(b), the words "or the Child Maintenance and Enforcement Commission, whichever has made enquiry" omitted by SI 2012/2007, art. 117(b), with effect from 31 July 2012.
In r. 19(3), the words "the Child Maintenance and Enforcement Commission" omitted by SI 2012/2007, art. 117(c), with effect from 31 July 2012.

EXPENSES IN CRIMINAL INJURIES COMPENSATION CASES

20(1)   This rule applies only to criminal injuries compensation cases.

20(2)   The Tribunal may meet reasonable expenses–

(a)   incurred by the appellant, or any person who attends a hearing to give evidence, in attending the hearing; or

(b)   incurred by the appellant in connection with any arrangements made by the Tribunal for the inspection of the appellant's injury.

EXPENSES IN SOCIAL SECURITY AND CHILD SUPPORT CASES

21(1)   This rule applies only to social security and child support cases.

21(2)   The Secretary of State may pay such travelling and other allowances (including compensation for loss of remunerative time) as the Secretary of State may determine to any person required to attend a hearing in proceedings under section 20 of the Child Support Act 1991, section 12 of the Social Security Act 1998 or paragraph 6 of Schedule 7 to the Child Support, Pensions and Social Security Act 2000.

PART 3 – PROCEEDINGS BEFORE THE TRIBUNAL
Chapter 1 – Before the Hearing

CASES IN WHICH THE NOTICE OF APPEAL IS TO BE SENT TO THE TRIBUNAL

22(1)   This rule applies to all cases except those to which–

(a)   rule 23 (cases in which the notice of appeal is to be sent to the decision maker), or

(b)   rule 26 (social security and child support cases started by reference or information in writing), applies.

22(2)   An appellant must start proceedings by sending or delivering a notice of appeal to the Tribunal so that it is received–

(a)   in asylum support cases, within 3 days after the date on which the appellant received written notice of the decision being challenged;

(b)   in criminal injuries compensation cases, within 90 days after the date of the decision being challenged;

(c)   in appeals under the Vaccine Damage Payments Act 1979, at any time;

(d)   in other cases—

    (i)   if mandatory reconsideration applies, within 1 month after the date on which the appellant was sent notice of the result of mandatory reconsideration;

    (ii)   if mandatory reconsideration does not apply, within the time specified in Schedule 1 to these Rules (time specified for providing notices of appeal).

22(3) The notice of appeal must be in English or Welsh, must be signed by the appellant and must state—

(a)   the name and address of the appellant;

(b)   the name and address of the appellant's representative (if any);

(c)   an address where documents for the appellant may be sent or delivered;

(d)   the name and address of any respondent other than the decision maker; and

(e)   [omitted by SI 2013/477, r. 25(c);]

(f)   the grounds on which the appellant relies.

22(4) The appellant must provide with the notice of appeal—

(a)   a copy of—

    (i)   the notice of the result of mandatory reconsideration, in any social security and child support case to which mandatory reconsideration applies;

    (ii)   the decision being challenged, in any other case;

(b)   any statement of reasons for that decision that the appellant has; and

(c)   any documents in support of the appellant's case which have not been supplied to the respondent.

(d)   [omitted by SI 2013/477, r. 25(d).]

22(5) In asylum support cases the notice of appeal must also—

(a)   state whether the appellant will require an interpreter at any hearing, and if so for which language or dialect; and

(b)   state whether the appellant intends to attend or be represented at any hearing.

22(6) If the appellant provides the notice of appeal to the Tribunal later than the time required by paragraph (2) or by an extension of time allowed under rule 5(3)(a) (power to extend time)—

(a)   the notice of appeal must include a request for an extension of time and the reason why the notice of appeal was not provided in time; and

(b)   subject to paragraph (8) unless the Tribunal extends time for the notice of appeal under rule 5(3)(a) (power to extend time) the Tribunal must not admit the notice of appeal.

22(7) The Tribunal must send a copy of the notice of appeal and any accompanying documents to each other party—

(a)   in asylum support cases, on the day that the Tribunal receives the notice of appeal, or (if that is not reasonably practicable) as soon as reasonably practicable on the following day;

(b)   in all other, as soon as reasonably practicable after the Tribunal receives the notice of appeal.

22(8) Where an appeal in a social security and child support case is not made within the time specified in paragraph (2)—

(a)   it will be treated as having been made in time, unless the Tribunal directs otherwise, if it is made within not more than 12 months of the time specified and neither the decision maker nor any other respondent objects;

(b)   the time for bringing the appeal may not be extended under rule 5(3)(a) by more than 12 months.

22(9) For the purposes of this rule, mandatory reconsideration applies where the notice of the decision being challenged includes a statement to the effect that there is a right of appeal in relation to the decision only if the decision-maker has considered an application for the revision, reversal, review or reconsideration (as the case may be) of the decision being challenged.

History – R. 22(1) substituted by SI 2013/477, r. 25(a), with effect from 8 April 2013. Former r. 22(1) read as follows:

    "**22(1)**   This rule applies to asylum support cases and criminal injuries compensation cases."

R. 22(2)(c) and (d) inserted by SI 2013/477, r. 25(b), with effect from 8 April 2013.

In r. 22(3)(d) the words "other than the decision maker" inserted and r. 22(3)(e) omitted by SI 2013/477, r. 25(c), with effect from 8 April 2013. Former r. 22(3)(e) read as follows:

    "(e)   details (including the full reference) of the decision being appealed; and"

R. 22(4)(a) substituted, in r. 22(4)(b) the words "; and" substituted for the words "or can reasonably obtain" and r. 22(4)(d) and the word "; and" at the end of r. 22(4)(c) omitted by SI 2013/477, r. 25(d), with effect from 8 April 2013. Former r. 22(4)(a) read as follows:

"(a)   a copy of any written record of the decision being challenged;"
and former r. 22(4)(d) read as follows;
"(d)   any further information or documents required by an applicable practice direction."
In r. 22(6), the words "or (aa)" omitted (in both places) by SI 2014/514, r. 22, with effect from 6 April 2014.
In r. 22(6), the former words "or (aa)" inserted (in both places) by SI 2013/2067, r. 25, with effect from 1 November 2013.
In r. 22(6)(b) the words "subject to paragraph (8)" inserted by SI 2013/477, r. 25(e), with effect from 8 April 2013.
In r. 22(7)(b) the words "all other" substituted for the words "criminal injuries compensation cases" by SI 2013/477, r. 25(f), with effect from 8 April 2013.
R. 22(8) inserted by SI 2013/477, r. 25(g), with effect from 8 April 2013.
R. 22(9) inserted by SI 2013/477, r. 25(g), with effect from 8 April 2013.

CASES IN WHICH THE NOTICE OF APPEAL IS TO BE SENT TO THE DECISION MAKER

23(1)   This rule applies to social security and child support cases in which the notice of decision being challenged informs the appellant that any appeal must be sent to the decision maker.

23(2)   An appellant must start proceedings by sending or delivering a notice of appeal to the decision maker so that it is received within the time specified in Schedule 1 to these Rules (time limits for providing notices of appeal to the decision maker).

23(3)   If the appellant provides the notice of appeal to the decision maker later than the time required by paragraph (2) the notice of appeal must include the reason why the notice of appeal was not provided in time.

23(4)   Subject to paragraph (5), where an appeal is not made within the time specified in Schedule 1, it will be treated as having been made in time if neither the decision maker nor any other respondent objects.

23(5)   No appeal may be made more than 12 months after the time specified in Schedule 1.

23(6)   The notice of appeal must be in English or Welsh, must be signed by the appellant and must state–

(a)   the name and address of the appellant;

(b)   the name and address of the appellant's representative (if any);

(c)   an address where documents for the appellant may be sent or delivered;

(d)   details of the decision being appealed; and

(e)   the grounds on which the appellant relies.

23(7)   The decision maker must refer the case to the Tribunal immediately if—

(a)   the appeal has been made after the time specified in Schedule 1 and the decision maker or any other respondent objects to it being treated as having been made in time; or

(b)   the decision maker considers that the appeal has been made more than 12 months after the time specified in Schedule 1.

23(8)   Notwithstanding rule 5(3)(a) or (aa) (case management powers) and rule 7(2) (failure to comply with rules etc.), the Tribunal must not extend the time limit in paragraph (5).

History – R. 23(1) substituted by SI 2013/477, r. 26, with effect from 8 April 2013. Former r. 23(1) read as follows:
"**23(1)**   This rule applies to social security and child support cases (except references under the Child Support Act 1991 and proceedings under paragraph 3 of Schedule 2 to the Tax Credits Act 2002)."
In r. 23(4), the words "if neither the decision maker nor any other respondent objects" substituted for the words "if the decision maker does not object" by SI 2012/500, r. 4(2), with effect from 6 April 2012.
In r. 23(7), the words "or any other respondent" inserted by SI 2012/500, r. 4(2), with effect from 6 April 2012.
In r. 23(8), the words "or (aa)" inserted by SI 2013/2067, r. 26, with effect from 1 November 2013.
R. 23(8) inserted by SI 2009/1975, r. 3, with effect from 1 September 2009.

RESPONSES AND REPLIES

24(1)   When a decision maker receives a copy of a notice of appeal from the Tribunal under rule 22(7), the decision maker must send or deliver a response to the Tribunal–

(a)   in asylum support cases, so that it is received within 3 days after the date on which the Tribunal received the notice of appeal;

(b)   in–

    (i)   criminal injuries compensation cases,

    (ii)   appeals under the Child Support Act 1991, or

    (iii)   appeals under the Child Trust Funds Act 2004,

within 42 days after the date on which the decision maker received the copy of the notice of appeal; and

(c)   in other cases, within 28 days after the date on which the decision maker received the copy of the notice of appeal.

24(1A)   Where a decision maker receives a notice of appeal from an appellant under rule 23(2), the decision maker must send or deliver a response to the Tribunal so that it is received as soon as reasonably practicable after the decision maker received the notice of appeal.

24(2)   The response must state–

(a)   the name and address of the decision maker;

(b)   the name and address of the decision maker's representative (if any);

(c)   an address where documents for the decision maker may be sent or delivered;

(d)   the names and addresses of any other respondents and their representatives (if any);

(e)   whether the decision maker opposes the appellant's case and, if so, any grounds for such opposition which are not set out in any documents which are before the Tribunal; and

(f)   any further information required by a practice direction or direction.

24(3)   The response may include a submission as to whether it would be appropriate for the case to be disposed of without a hearing.

24(4)   The decision maker must provide with the response–

(a)   a copy of any written record of the decision under challenge, and any statement of reasons for that decision, if they were not sent with the notice of appeal;

(b)   copies of all documents relevant to the case in the decision maker's possession, unless a practice direction or direction states otherwise; and

(c)   in cases to which rule 23 (cases in which the notice of appeal is to be sent to the decision maker) applies, a copy of the notice of appeal, any documents provided by the appellant with the notice of appeal and (if they have not otherwise been provided to the Tribunal) the name and address of the appellant's representative (if any).

24(5)   The decision maker must provide a copy of the response and any accompanying documents to each other party at the same time as it provides the response to the Tribunal.

24(6)   The appellant and any other respondent may make a written submission and supply further documents in reply to the decision maker's response.

24(7)   Any submission or further documents under paragraph (6) must be provided to the Tribunal within 1 month after the date on which the decision maker sent the response to the party providing the reply, and the Tribunal must send a copy to each other party.

History – R. 24(1) and (1A) substituted for former r. 24(1) by SI 2013/477, r. 27, with effect from 1 October 2014. Former r. 24(1) and (1A) read as follows:

"**24(1)**   When a decision maker receives the notice of appeal or a copy of it, the decision maker must send or deliver a response to the Tribunal–

(a)   in asylum support cases, so that it is received within 3 days after the date on which the Tribunal received the notice of appeal;

(aa)   in criminal injuries compensation cases, so that it is received within 42 days after the date on which the decision maker received the notice of appeal; and

(b)   in other cases, as soon as reasonably practicable after the decision maker received the notice of appeal."

In r. 24(2)(f) the words "or documents" omitted by SI 2013/477, r. 27, with effect from 1 October 2014.
Former r. 24(1)(aa) inserted (and the "and" at the end of r. 24(1)(a) omitted) by SI 2011/651, r. 4(3), with effect from 1 April 2011.

MEDICAL AND PHYSICAL EXAMINATION IN APPEALS UNDER SECTION 12 OF THE SOCIAL SECURITY ACT 1998

25(1)   This rule applies only to appeals under section 12 of the Social Security Act 1998.

25(2)   At a hearing an appropriate member of the Tribunal may carry out a physical examination of a person if the case relates to–

(a)   the extent of that person's disablement and its assessment in accordance with section 68(6) of and Schedule 6 to, or section 103 of, the Social Security Contributions and Benefits Act 1992; or

(b)   diseases or injuries prescribed for the purpose of section 108 of that Act.

25(3)   If an issue which falls within Schedule 2 to these Rules (issues in relation to which the Tribunal may refer a person for medical examination) is raised in an appeal, the Tribunal may exercise its power under section 20 of the Social Security Act 1998 to refer a person to a health care professional approved by the Secretary of State for–

(a)   the examination of that person; and

(b)   the production of a report on the condition of that person.

25(4)   Neither paragraph (2) nor paragraph (3) entitles the Tribunal to require a person to undergo a physical test for the purpose of determining whether that person is unable to walk or virtually unable to do so.

SOCIAL SECURITY AND CHILD SUPPORT CASES STARTED BY REFERENCE OR INFORMATION IN WRITING

26(1) This rule applies to proceedings under section 28D of the Child Support Act 1991 and paragraph 3 of Schedule 2 to the Tax Credits Act 2002.

26(2) A person starting proceedings under section 28D of the Child Support Act 1991 must send or deliver a written reference to the Tribunal.

26(3) A person starting proceedings under paragraph 3 of Schedule 2 to the Tax Credits Act 2002 must send or deliver an information in writing to the Tribunal.

26(4) The reference or the information in writing must include—

(a) an address where documents for the person starting proceedings may be sent or delivered;

(b) the names and addresses of the respondents and their representatives (if any); and

(c) a submission on the issues that arise for determination by the Tribunal.

26(5) Unless a practice direction or direction states otherwise, the person starting proceedings must also provide a copy of each document in their possession which is relevant to the proceedings.

26(6) Subject to any obligation under rule 19(3) (confidentiality in child support cases), the person starting proceedings must provide a copy of the written reference or the information in writing and any accompanying documents to each respondent at the same time as they provide the written reference or the information in writing to the Tribunal.

26(7) Each respondent may send or deliver to the Tribunal a written submission and any further relevant documents within one month of the date on which the person starting proceedings sent a copy of the written reference or the information in writing to that respondent.

Chapter 2 – Hearings

DECISION WITH OR WITHOUT A HEARING

27(1) Subject to the following paragraphs, the Tribunal must hold a hearing before making a decision which disposes of proceedings unless—

(a) each party has consented to, or has not objected to, the matter being decided without a hearing; and

(b) the Tribunal considers that it is able to decide the matter without a hearing.

27(2) This rule does not apply to decisions under Part 4.

27(3) The Tribunal may in any event dispose of proceedings without a hearing under rule 8 (striking out a party's case).

27(4) In a criminal injuries compensation case—

(a) the Tribunal may make a decision which disposes of proceedings without a hearing; and

(b) subject to paragraph (5), if the Tribunal makes a decision which disposes of proceedings without a hearing, any party may make a written application to the Tribunal for the decision to be reconsidered at a hearing.

27(5) An application under paragraph (4)(b) may not be made in relation to a decision—

(a) not to extend a time limit;

(b) not to set aside a previous decision;

(c) not to allow an appeal against a decision not to extend a time limit; or

(d) not to allow an appeal against a decision not to reopen a case.

27(6) An application under paragraph (4)(b) must be received within 1 month after the date on which the Tribunal sent notice of the decision to the party making the application.

ENTITLEMENT TO ATTEND A HEARING

28 Subject to rule 30(5) (exclusion of a person from a hearing), each party to proceedings is entitled to attend a hearing.

NOTICE OF HEARINGS

29(1) The Tribunal must give each party entitled to attend a hearing reasonable notice of the time and place of the hearing (including any adjourned or postponed hearing) and any changes to the time and place of the hearing.

29(2) The period of notice under paragraph (1) must be at least 14 days except that—

(a) in an asylum support case the Tribunal must give at least 1 day's and not more than 5 days' notice; and

(b) the Tribunal may give shorter notice—

(i) with the parties' consent; or

(ii) in urgent or exceptional circumstances.

PUBLIC AND PRIVATE HEARINGS

30(1) Subject to the following paragraphs, all hearings must be held in public.

30(2) A hearing in a criminal injuries compensation case must be held in private unless—

(a) the appellant has consented to the hearing being held in public; and

(b) the Tribunal considers that it is in the interests of justice for the hearing to be held in public.

30(3) The Tribunal may give a direction that a hearing, or part of it, is to be held in private.

30(4) Where a hearing, or part of it, is to be held in private, the Tribunal may determine who is permitted to attend the hearing or part of it.

30(5) The Tribunal may give a direction excluding from any hearing, or part of it—

(a) any person whose conduct the Tribunal considers is disrupting or is likely to disrupt the hearing;

(b) any person whose presence the Tribunal considers is likely to prevent another person from giving evidence or making submissions freely;

(c) any person who the Tribunal considers should be excluded in order to give effect to a direction under rule 14(2) (withholding information likely to cause harm); or

(d) any person where the purpose of the hearing would be defeated by the attendance of that person.

30(6) The Tribunal may give a direction excluding a witness from a hearing until that witness gives evidence.

HEARINGS IN A PARTY'S ABSENCE

31 If a party fails to attend a hearing the Tribunal may proceed with the hearing if the Tribunal—

(a) is satisfied that the party has been notified of the hearing or that reasonable steps have been taken to notify the party of the hearing; and

(b) considers that it is in the interests of justice to proceed with the hearing.

Chapter 3 – Decisions

CONSENT ORDERS

32(1) The Tribunal may, at the request of the parties but only if it considers it appropriate, make a consent order disposing of the proceedings and making such other appropriate provision as the parties have agreed.

32(2) Notwithstanding any other provision of these Rules, the Tribunal need not hold a hearing before making an order under paragraph (1), or provide reasons for the order.

NOTICE OF DECISIONS

33(1) The Tribunal may give a decision orally at a hearing.

33(2) Subject to rule 14(2) (withholding information likely to cause harm), the Tribunal must provide to each party as soon as reasonably practicable after making a decision (other than a decision under Part 4) which finally disposes of all issues in the proceedings or of a preliminary issue dealt with following a direction under rule 5(3)(e)—

(a) a decision notice stating the Tribunal's decision;

(b) where appropriate, notification of the right to apply for a written statement of reasons under rule 34(3); and

(c)   notification of any right of appeal against the decision and the time within which, and the manner in which, such right of appeal may be exercised.

33(3)   In asylum support cases the notice and notifications required by paragraph (2) must be provided at the hearing or sent on the day that the decision is made.

History – In r. 33(2) the words "a decision (other than a decision under Part 4) which finally disposes of all issues in the proceedings or of a preliminary issue dealt with following a direction under rule 5(3)(e)" substituted for the words "a decision which finally disposes of all issues in the proceedings (except a decision under Part 4)" by SI 2013/477, r. 28, with effect from 8 April 2013.

REASONS FOR DECISIONS

34(1)   In asylum support cases the Tribunal must send a written statement of reasons for a decision which disposes of proceedings (except a decision under Part 4) to each party–

(a)   if the case is decided at a hearing, within 3 days after the hearing; or

(b)   if the case is decided without a hearing, on the day that the decision is made.

34(2)   In all other cases the Tribunal may give reasons for a decision which disposes of proceedings (except a decision under Part 4)–

(a)   orally at a hearing; or

(b)   in a written statement of reasons to each party.

34(3)   Unless the Tribunal has already provided a written statement of reasons under paragraph (2)(b), a party may make a written application to the Tribunal for such statement following a decision which finally disposes of–

(a)   all issues in the proceedings; or

(b)   a preliminary issue dealt with following a direction under rule 5(3)(e).

34(4)   An application under paragraph (3) must be received within 1 month of the date on which the Tribunal sent or otherwise provided to the party a decision notice relating to the decision.

34(5)   If a party makes an application in accordance with paragraphs (3) and (4) the Tribunal must, subject to rule 14(2) (withholding information likely to cause harm), send a written statement of reasons to each party within 1 month of the date on which it received the application or as soon as reasonably practicable after the end of that period.

History – In r. 34(3) the words from "which finally disposes of–" to the end of para. (b) substituted for the words "which finally disposes of all issues in the proceedings" by SI 2013/477, r. 29(a), with effect from 8 April 2013.
In r. 34(4) the words "which finally disposes of all issues in the proceedings" omitted by SI 2013/477, r. 29(b), with effect from 8 April 2013.

PART 4 – CORRECTING, SETTING ASIDE, REVIEWING AND APPEALING TRIBUNAL DECISIONS

INTERPRETATION

35 In this Part–

"**appeal**" means the exercise of a right of appeal–

(a)   under paragraph 2(2) or 4(1) of Schedule 2 to the Tax Credits Act 2002;

(b)   under section 21(10) of the Child Trust Funds Act 2004; or

(c)   on a point of law under section 11 of the 2007 Act; and

"**review**" means the review of a decision by the Tribunal under section 9 of the 2007 Act.

CLERICAL MISTAKES AND ACCIDENTAL SLIPS OR OMISSIONS

36 The Tribunal may at any time correct any clerical mistake or other accidental slip or omission in a decision, direction or any document produced by it, by–

(a)   sending notification of the amended decision or direction, or a copy of the amended document, to all parties; and

(b)   making any necessary amendment to any information published in relation to the decision, direction or document.

SETTING ASIDE A DECISION WHICH DISPOSES OF PROCEEDINGS

37(1)   The Tribunal may set aside a decision which disposes of proceedings, or part of such a decision, and re-make the decision, or the relevant part of it, if–

(a)   the Tribunal considers that it is in the interests of justice to do so; and

(b)   one or more of the conditions in paragraph (2) are satisfied.

37(2)   The conditions are–

(a)   a document relating to the proceedings was not sent to, or was not received at an appropriate time by, a party or a party's representative;

(b)   a document relating to the proceedings was not sent to the Tribunal at an appropriate time;

(c)   a party, or a party's representative, was not present at a hearing related to the proceedings; or

(d)   there has been some other procedural irregularity in the proceedings.

37(3)   A party applying for a decision, or part of a decision, to be set aside under paragraph (1) must make a written application to the Tribunal so that it is received no later than 1 month after the date on which the Tribunal sent notice of the decision to the party.

APPLICATION FOR PERMISSION TO APPEAL

38(1)   This rule does not apply to asylum support cases or criminal injuries compensation cases.

38(2)   A person seeking permission to appeal must make a written application to the Tribunal for permission to appeal.

38(3)   An application under paragraph (2) must be sent or delivered to the Tribunal so that it is received no later than 1 month after the latest of the dates that the Tribunal sends to the person making the application–

(za)   the relevant decision notice;

(a)   written reasons for the decision, if the decision disposes of–

(i)   all issues in the proceedings; or

(ii)   subject to paragraph (3A), a preliminary issue dealt with following a direction under rule 5(3)(e);

(b)   notification of amended reasons for, or correction of, the decision following a review; or

(c)   notification that an application for the decision to be set aside has been unsuccessful.

38(3A)   The Tribunal may direct that the 1 month within which a party may send or deliver an application for permission to appeal against a decision that disposes of a preliminary issue shall run from the date of the decision that disposes of all issues in the proceedings.

38(4)   The date in paragraph (3)(c) applies only if the application for the decision to be set aside was made within the time stipulated in rule 37 (setting aside a decision which disposes of proceedings) or any extension of that time granted by the Tribunal.

38(5)   If the person seeking permission to appeal sends or delivers the application to the Tribunal later than the time required by paragraph (3) or by any extension of time under rule 5(3)(a) (power to extend time)–

(a)   the application must include a request for an extension of time and the reason why the application was not provided in time; and

(b)   unless the Tribunal extends time for the application under rule 5(3)(a) (power to extend time) the Tribunal must not admit the application.

38(6)   An application under paragraph (2) must–

(a)   identify the decision of the Tribunal to which it relates;

(b)   identify the alleged error or errors of law in the decision; and

(c)   state the result the party making the application is seeking.

38(7)   If a person makes an application under paragraph (2) in respect of a decision that disposes of proceedings or of a preliminary issue dealt with following a direction under rule 5(3)(e) when the Tribunal has not given a written statement of reasons for its decision–

(a)   if no application for a written statement of reasons has been made to the Tribunal, the application for permission must be treated as such an application;

(b)   unless the Tribunal decides to give permission and directs that this sub-paragraph does not apply, the application is not to be treated as an application for permission to appeal; and

Statutory Instruments

(c)   if an application for a written statement of reasons has been, or is, refused because of a delay in making the application, the Tribunal must only admit the application for permission if the Tribunal considers that it is in the interests of justice to do so.

History – R. 38(3)(za) inserted by SI 2013/477, r. 30(a), with effect from 8 April 2013.
In r. 38(3)(a) the words from ", if the decision disposes of–" to the end inserted by SI 2013/477, r. 30(b), with effect from 8 April 2013.
R. 38(3A) inserted by SI 2013/477, r. 30(c), with effect from 8 April 2013.
In r. 38(7) the words "in respect of a decision that disposes of proceedings or of a preliminary issue dealt with following a direction under rule 5(3)(e)" inserted by SI 2013/477, r. 30(d), with effect from 8 April 2013.

TRIBUNAL'S CONSIDERATION OF APPLICATION FOR PERMISSION TO APPEAL

39(1)   On receiving an application for permission to appeal the Tribunal must first consider, taking into account the overriding objective in rule 2, whether to review the decision in accordance with rule 40 (review of a decision).

39(2)   If the Tribunal decides not to review the decision, or reviews the decision and decides to take no action in relation to the decision, or part of it, the Tribunal must consider whether to give permission to appeal in relation to the decision or that part of it.

39(3)   The Tribunal must send a record of its decision to the parties as soon as practicable.

39(4)   If the Tribunal refuses permission to appeal it must send with the record of its decision–

(a)   a statement of its reasons for such refusal; and

(b)   notification of the right to make an application to the Upper Tribunal for permission to appeal and the time within which, and the method by which, such application must be made.

39(5)   The Tribunal may give permission to appeal on limited grounds, but must comply with paragraph (4) in relation to any grounds on which it has refused permission.

REVIEW OF A DECISION

40(1)   This rule does not apply to asylum support cases or criminal injuries compensation cases.

40(2)   The Tribunal may only undertake a review of a decision–

(a)   pursuant to rule 39(1) (review on an application for permission to appeal); and

(b)   if it is satisfied that there was an error of law in the decision.

40(3)   The Tribunal must notify the parties in writing of the outcome of any review, and of any right of appeal in relation to the outcome.

40(4)   If the Tribunal takes any action in relation to a decision following a review without first giving every party an opportunity to make representations, the notice under paragraph (3) must state that any party that did not have an opportunity to make representations may apply for such action to be set aside and for the decision to be reviewed again.

POWER TO TREAT AN APPLICATION AS A DIFFERENT TYPE OF APPLICATION

41   The Tribunal may treat an application for a decision to be corrected, set aside or reviewed, or for permission to appeal against a decision, as an application for any other one of those things.

SCHEDULE 1 – TIME LIMITS FOR PROVIDING NOTICES OF APPEAL

Rule 23

History – In the heading the words "to the decision maker" omitted by SI 2013/477, r. 31(a), with effect from 8 April 2013.

Type of proceedings	Time for providing notice of appeal
cases other than those listed below	the latest of– (a) one month after the date on which notice of the decision being challenged was sent to the appellant;

Type of proceedings	Time for providing notice of appeal
	(b) if a written statement of reasons for the decision was requested within that month, 14 days after the later of–
	(i) the end of that month; or
	(ii) the date on which the written statement of reasons was provided; or
	(c) if the appellant made an application for revision of the decision under–
	(i) regulation 14 of the Child Support Maintenance Calculation Regulations 2012;
	(ii) regulation 3(1) or (3) of the Social Security and Child Support (Decision and Appeals) Regulations 1999;
	(iii) regulation 4 of the Housing Benefit and Council Tax Benefit (Decisions and Appeals) Regulations 2001;
	(iv) regulation 17(1)(a) of the Child Support (Maintenance Assessment Procedure) Regulations 1992 (where still applicable to the particular case); or
	(v) regulation 3A(1) of the Social Security and Child Support (Decisions and Appeals) Regulations 1999 (where still applicable to the particular case),
	and that application was unsuccessful, 1 month after the date on which notice that the decision would not be revised was sent to the appellant.
appeal against a certificate of NHS charges under section 157(1) of the Health and Social Care (Community Health and Standards) Act 2003	(a) 3 months after the latest of–
	(i) the date on the certificate;
	(ii) the date on which the compensation payment was made;
	(iii) if the certificate has been reviewed, the date the certificate was confirmed or a fresh certificate was issued; or
	(iv) the date of any agreement to treat an earlier compensation payment as having been made in final discharge of a claim made by or in respect of an injured person and arising out of the injury or death; or
	(b) if the person to whom the certificate has been issued makes an application under section 157(4) of the Health and Social Care (Community Health and Standards) Act 2003, one month after–
	(i) the date of the decision on that application; or
	(ii) if the person appeals against that decision under section 157(6) of that Act, the date on which the appeal is decided or withdrawn
appeal against a waiver decision under section 157(6) of the Health and Social Care (Community Health and Standards) Act 2003	one month after the date of the decision
appeal against a certificate of NHS charges under section 7 of the Road Traffic (NHS Charges) Act 1999	3 months after the latest of–
	(a) the date on which the liability under section 1(2) of the Road Traffic (NHS Charges) Act 1999 was discharged;
	(b) if the certificate has been reviewed, the date the certificate was confirmed or a fresh certificate was issued; or
	(c) the date of any agreement to treat an earlier compensation payment as having been made in final discharge of a claim made by or in respect of a traffic casualty and arising out of the injury or death

Type of proceedings	Time for providing notice of appeal
appeal against a certificate of recoverable benefits under section 11 of the Social Security (Recovery of Benefits) Act 1997	one month after the latest of— (a) the date on which any payment to the Secretary of State required under section 6 of the Social Security (Recovery of Benefits) Act 1997 was made; (b) if the certificate has been reviewed, the date the certificate was confirmed or a fresh certificate was issued; or (c) the date of any agreement to treat an earlier compensation payment as having been made in final discharge of a claim made by or in respect of an injured person and arising out of the accident, injury or disease
appeal under the Vaccine Damage Payments Act 1979	no time limit
appeal under the Tax Credits Act 2002	as set out in the Tax Credits Act 2002
appeal under the Child Trust Funds Act 2004	as set out in the Child Trust Funds Act 2004
appeal against a decision in respect of a claim for child benefit or guardian's allowance under section 12 of the Social Security Act 1998	as set out in regulation 28 of the Child Benefit and Guardian's Allowance (Decisions and Appeals) Regulations 2003

History – In the Table, in the former first entry, in the second column, para. (c) substituted by SI 2013/477, r. 31(b) with effect from 8 April 2013. Former para. (c) read as follows).

"(c) if the appellant made an application for revision of the decision under–
(i) regulation 17(1)(a) of the Child Support (Maintenance Assessment Procedure) Regulations 1992,
(ii) regulation 3(1) or (3) or 3A(1) of the Social Security and Child Support (Decision and Appeals) Regulations 1999, or
(iii) regulation 4 of the Housing Benefit and Council Tax Benefit (Decisions and Appeals) Regulations 2001,
and that application was unsuccessful, one month after the date on which notice that the decision would not be revised was sent to the appellant."

In the Table, the first entry substituted by SI 2010/2653, r. 5(4), with effect from 29 November 2010.
In the Table, in the former first entry, in the second column, para (c) substituted by SI 2009/1975, r. 4, with effect from 1 September 2009.

SCHEDULE 2 – ISSUES IN RELATION TO WHICH THE TRIBUNAL MAY REFER A PERSON FOR MEDICAL EXAMINATION UNDER SECTION 20(2) OF THE SOCIAL SECURITY ACT 1998

Rule 25(3)

An issue falls within this Schedule if the issue–

(a) is whether the claimant satisfies the conditions for entitlement to–

   (i) an attendance allowance specified in section 64 and 65(1) of the Social Security Contributions and Benefits Act 1992;

   (ii) severe disablement allowance under section 68 of that Act;

   (iii) the care component of a disability living allowance specified in section 72(1) and (2) of that Act;

   (iv) the mobility component of a disability living allowance specified in section 73(1), (8) and (9) of that Act;

   (v) a disabled person's tax credit specified in section 129(1)(b) of that Act.

   (vi) the daily living component of personal independence payment specified in section 78 of the Welfare Reform Act 2012; or

   (vii) the mobility component of personal independence payment specified in section 79 of the Welfare Reform Act 2012.

(b)   relates to the period throughout which the claimant is likely to satisfy the conditions for entitlement to an attendance allowance or a disability living allowance;

(c)   is the rate at which an attendance allowance is payable;

(d)   is the rate at which the care component or the mobility component of a disability living allowance is payable;

(e)   is whether a person is incapable of work for the purposes of the Social Security Contributions and Benefits Act 1992;

(f)   relates to the extent of a person's disablement and its assessment in accordance with Schedule 6 to the Social Security Contributions and Benefits Act 1992;

(g)   is whether the claimant suffers a loss of physical or mental faculty as a result of the relevant accident for the purposes of section 103 of the Social Security Contributions and Benefits Act 1992;

(h)   relates to any payment arising under, or by virtue of a scheme having effect under, section 111 of, and Schedule 8 to, the Social Security Contributions and Benefits Act 1992 (workmen's compensation);

(i)   is whether a person has limited capability for work or work-related activity for the purposes of the Welfare Reform Act 2007.

(j)   is the rate at which the daily living component or mobility component of personal independence payment is payable.

History – In para. (a) the word "or" at end of para. (a)(iv) omitted and para. (a)(vi) and (vii) inserted by SI 2013/477, r. 32(a) and (b), with effect from 8 April 2013.
Para. (j) inserted by SI 2013/477, r. 32(c), with effect from 8 April 2013.

QUALIFICATIONS FOR APPOINTMENT OF MEMBERS TO THE FIRST-TIER TRIBUNAL AND UPPER TRIBUNAL ORDER 2008

(SI 2008/2692, as amended by SI 2009/1592, SI 2012/897 and SI 2013/1185)

Made on 15 October 2008 by The Lord Chancellor, with the concurrence of the Senior President of Tribunals, in exercise of the powers conferred by para. 2(2) of Sch. 2 and para. 2(2) of Sch. 3 to the Tribunals, Courts and Enforcement Act 2007. Operative from 3 November 2008.

1   This Order may be cited as the Qualifications for Appointment of Members to the First-tier Tribunal and Upper Tribunal Order 2008 and shall come into force on 3rd November 2008.

Prospective amendments – Art. 1 to become art. 1(1) and art. 1(2) inserted by SI 2009/1592, art. 3, with effect from the day on which SI 2002/3135, Sch. 1, para. 10 comes into effect. New art. 1(2) reads as follows:

> "**1(2)**   In this Order "registered medical practitioner" means a fully registered person within the meaning of the Medical Act 1983 whether or not they hold a licence to practise under that Act."

2(1)   A person is eligible for appointment as a member of the First-tier Tribunal or the Upper Tribunal who is not a judge of those tribunals if paragraph (2), (3) or (4) applies.

2(2)   This paragraph applies to a person who is–

(a)   a registered medical practitioner;

(b)   a registered nurse;

(c)   a registered dentist;

(ca)   a registered optometrist;

(d)   a clinical psychologist;

(e)   an educational psychologist;

(f)   a pharmacologist;

(g)   a veterinary surgeon or a veterinary practitioner registered under the Veterinary Surgeons Act 1966;

(h)   a Member or Fellow of the Royal Institution of Chartered Surveyors; or

(i)   an accountant who is a member of–

    (i)   the Institute of Chartered Accountants in England and Wales;

    (ii)   the Institute of Chartered Accountants in Scotland;

    (iii)   the Institute of Chartered Accountants in Ireland;

    (iv)   the Institute of Certified Public Accountants in Ireland;

    (v)   the Association of Chartered Certified Accountants;

    (vi)   the Chartered Institute of Management Accountants; or

    (vii)   the Chartered Institute of Public Finance and Accountancy.

2(3)   This paragraph applies to a person who is experienced in dealing with the physical or mental needs of disabled persons because they–

(a)   work with disabled persons in a professional or voluntary capacity; or

(b)   are themselves disabled.

2(3A)   A person is not eligible for appointment under paragraph (3) if they are a registered medical practitioner.

2(4)   This paragraph applies to a person who has substantial experience–

(a)   of service in Her Majesty's naval, military, or air forces;

(b)   of educational, child care, health, or social care matters;

(c)   of dealing with victims of violent crime;

(d)   in transport operations and its law and practice;

(e)   in the regulatory field;

(f)   in consumer affairs;

(g)   in an industry, trade or business sector and the matters that are likely to arise as issues in the course of disputes with regulators of such industries, trades or businesses;

(h)   in tax matters and related tax procedures;

(i)   in a business, trade, charity or not-for-profit organisation.

(j)   in immigration services or the law and procedure relating to immigration;

(k)   of data protection;

(l)   of freedom of information (including environmental information) rights;

(m)   of service as a Member or Senior Officer of a local authority in England.

(n)   in environmental matters;

(o)   in the drainage of land;

(p)   in farming and the ownership or management of agricultural property;

(q)   in relation to housing or housing conditions;

(r)   in matters relating to landlord and tenant relationships;

(s)   in valuation.

History – Art. 2(2)(ca) inserted by SI 2009/1592, art. 4(a), with effect from 1 September 2009.
In art. 2(3) the words", other than a registered medical practitioner," omitted by SI 2009/1592, art. 4(b), with effect from 1 September 2009.
Art. 2(3A) inserted by SI 2009/1592, art. 4(c), with effect from 1 September 2009.
Art. 2(4)(o)–(s) inserted by SI 2013/1185, art. 3, with effect from 1 July 2013.
In art. 2(4)(i) the words", charity" inserted by SI 2009/1592, art. 4(d), with effect from 1 September 2009.
Art. 2(4)(j)–(m) inserted by SI 2009/1592, art. 4(e), with effect from 1 September 2009.
Art. 2(4)(n) inserted by SI 2012/897, with effect from 16 April 2012.

TRIBUNALS, COURTS AND ENFORCEMENT ACT 2007 (COMMENCEMENT NO. 6 AND TRANSITIONAL PROVISIONS) ORDER 2008

(SI 2008/2696)

Made on 9 October 2008 by the Lord Chancellor in exercise of the powers conferred by s. 31(9) and 148(5) of the Tribunals, Courts and Enforcement Act 2007. Operative in accordance with art. 2.

CITATION AND COMMENCEMENT

1 This Order may be cited as the Tribunals, Courts and Enforcement Act 2007 (Commencement No. 6 and Transitional Provisions) Order 2008.

2 Articles 4 and 6 come into force on 1st April 2009. All other provisions come into force on 3rd November 2008.

TRANSITIONAL AND SAVINGS PROVISIONS

3 Staff appointed to the following tribunals before the 3rd November 2008 are to be treated, for the purpose of any enactment, as if they had been appointed by the Lord Chancellor under section 40(1) of the Tribunals, Courts and Enforcement Act 2007 (tribunal staff and services)—

(a) a tribunal listed under Schedule 6 to the Tribunals, Courts and Enforcement Act 2007 whose functions are transferred to the First-tier Tribunal or Upper Tribunal by order under section 30(1) of that Act on 3rd November 2008;

(b) the Employment Appeal Tribunal;

(c) the employment tribunals; and

(d) the Asylum and Immigration Tribunal.

4 Sections 2 to 3A of the Taxes Management Act 1970 shall continue to apply for the purpose of section 56 of the 1970 Act (statement of case for opinion of the High Court) arising from a decision of the General Commissioners made before 1st of April 2009 as if article 6(b)(i) and (c)(i) had not been commenced.

PROVISIONS COMING INTO FORCE ON 3RD NOVEMBER 2008

5 The following provisions of the Tribunals, Courts and Enforcement Act 2007 come into force on 3rd November 2008–

(a) sections 3 to 6, 7(2) to (8), 8, 9(1), (2) and (4) to (11), 10(1), (2) and (4) to (9), 11(1) to (4) and (5)(a) to (e), 12, 13(1) to (5), (7), (8)(a) to (e) and (11) to (13), 14 to 17, 18(1) to (9) and (12) 19, 20(1), (2), (4), (5) and (8), 21(1) to (5), 23 to 26, 28, 29, 43 and 47;

(b) section 46 to the extent that it is not already in force;

(c) section 48(1) to the extent that it relates to the following paragraphs of Schedule 8–

    (i) paragraphs 6, 16, 28, 31(4) to (6), 33(3), 40, 41, 42, 44 to 48, 54, 64(b), and 66;

    (ii) paragraph 25 to the extent that it relates to paragraph 7(b) of Schedule 1 of the Tribunals and Inquiries Act 1992;

    (iii) paragraphs 4 and 5 to the extent that they are not already in force; and

    (iv) paragraph 65(3) to the extent that it is not already in force;

(d) section 48(2) to the extent it relates to paragraphs 3 to 11, 12(1) and (3) to (7), and 13 to 19 of Schedule 9;

(e) paragraphs 12 to 14 of Schedule 1;

(f) Schedule 2;

(g) Schedule 3;

(h) paragraphs 1 to 14 of Schedule 4; and

(i) in Part 1 of Schedule 23, the entries relating to–

    (i) the Consumer Credit Act 1974;

    (ii) the Judicial Pensions and Retirement Act 1993;

    (iii) the Employment Tribunals Act 1996;

(iv)   the Justice (Northern Ireland) Act 2002;
(v)   the Nationality, Immigration and Asylum Act 2002;
(vi)   Schedule 4 of the Constitutional Reform Act 2005; and
(vii)   the Tribunals, Courts and Enforcement Act 2007; and
(j)   Part 2 of Schedule 23.

PROVISIONS COMING INTO FORCE ON 1ST APRIL 2009

6 The following provisions of the Tribunals, Courts and Enforcement Act 2007 come into force on 1st April 2009–

(a)   sections 27(1) to (4) and 142;

(b)   section 48(1) to the extent that it relates the following paragraphs of Schedule 8–
    (i)   paragraph 1; and
    (ii)   paragraphs 43 and 55; and

(c)   in Part 1 of Schedule 23 the entries relating to–
    (i)   the Taxes Management Act 1970;
    (ii)   the Superannuation Act 1972;
    (iii)   the Finance Act 1972;
    (iv)   the Finance Act 1988;
    (v)   the Finance (No. 2) Act 1992;
    (vi)   the Social Security Contributions (Transfer of Functions, etc.) Act 1999;
    (vii)   the Access to Justice Act 1999;
    (viii)   the Social Security Contributions (Transfer of Functions, Etc.) (Northern Ireland) Order 1999;
    (ix)   the Scotland Act 1998 (Transfer of Functions to the Scottish Ministers etc.) Order 1999; and
    (x)   Schedule 12 and Part 2 of Schedule 14 of the Constitutional Reform Act 2005.

Statutory Instruments

TRIBUNAL PROCEDURE (UPPER TRIBUNAL) RULES 2008

(SI 2008/2698, as amended by SI 2009/274, SI 2009/1975, SI 2010/43, SI 2010/44, SI 2010/747, SI 2010/2653, SI 2011/651, SI 2012/500, SI 2012/1363, SI 2012/2007, SI 2012/2890, SI 2013/477, SI 2013/606, SI 2013/2067, SI 2014/514 and SI 2014/1505)

Made on 9 October 2008 by the Tribunal Procedure Committee in exercise of the power conferred by s. 10(3), 16(9), 22 and 29(3) and (4) of, and Sch. 5 to the Tribunals, Courts and Enforcement Act 2007. Operative from 3 November 2008.

PART 1 – INTRODUCTION

CITATION, COMMENCEMENT, APPLICATION AND INTERPRETATION

1(1) These Rules may be cited as the Tribunal Procedure (Upper Tribunal) Rules 2008 and come into force on 3rd November 2008.

1(2) These Rules apply to proceedings before the Upper Tribunal except proceedings in the Lands Chamber.

1(3) In these Rules–

"**the 2007 Act**" means the Tribunals, Courts and Enforcement Act 2007;

"**appellant**" means–

(a) a person who makes an appeal, or applies for permission to appeal, to the Upper Tribunal;

(b) in proceedings transferred or referred to the Upper Tribunal from the First-tier Tribunal, a person who started the proceedings in the First-tier Tribunal; or

(c) a person substituted as an appellant under rule 9(1) (substitution and addition of parties);

"**applicant**" means–

(a) a person who applies for permission to bring, or does bring, judicial review proceedings before the Upper Tribunal and, in judicial review proceedings transferred to the Upper Tribunal from a court, includes a person who was a claimant or petitioner in the proceedings immediately before they were transferred; or

(b) a person who refers a financial services case or a wholesale energy case to the Upper Tribunal;

"**appropriate national authority**" means, in relation to an appeal, the Secretary of State, the Scottish Ministers, the Department of the Environment in Northern Ireland or the Welsh Ministers, as the case may be;

"**asylum case**" means proceedings before the Upper Tribunal on appeal against a decision in proceedings under section 82, 83 or 83A of the Nationality, Immigration and Asylum Act 2002 in which a person claims that removal from, or a requirement to leave, the United Kingdom would breach the United Kingdom's obligations under the Convention relating to the Status of Refugees done at Geneva on 28 July 1951 and the Protocol to the Convention;

"**authorised person**" means–

(a) an examiner appointed by the Secretary of State under section 66A of the Road Traffic Act 1988;

(b) an examiner appointed by the Department of the Environment in Northern Ireland under Article 74 of the Road Traffic (Northern Ireland) Order 1995; or

(c) any person authorised in writing by the Department of the Environment in Northern Ireland for the purposes of the Goods Vehicles (Licensing of Operators) Act (Northern Ireland) 2010;

and includes a person acting under the direction of such an examiner or other authorised person, who has detained the vehicle to which an appeal relates;

"**dispose of proceedings**" includes, unless indicated otherwise, disposing of a part of the proceedings;

"**document**" means anything in which information is recorded in any form, and an obligation under these Rules or any practice direction or direction to provide or allow access to a document or a copy of a document for any purpose means, unless the Upper Tribunal directs otherwise, an obligation to provide or allow access to such document or copy in a legible form or in a form which can be readily made into a legible form;

"**fast-track case**" means an asylum case or an immigration case where the person who appealed to the First-tier Tribunal–

(a)   was detained under the Immigration Acts at a place specified in Schedule 2 to the Asylum and Immigration Tribunal (Fast Track Procedure) Rules 2005 when the notice of decision that was the subject of the appeal to the First-tier Tribunal was served on the appellant;

(b)   remains so detained; and

(c)   the First-tier Tribunal or the Upper Tribunal has not directed that the case cease to be treated as a fast-track case;

"**financial services case**" means a reference to the Upper Tribunal in respect of–

(a)   a decision of the Financial Conduct Authority;

(aa)   a decision of the Prudential Regulation Authority;

(b)   a decision of the Bank of England;

(c)   a decision of the Pensions Regulator;

(d)   a decision of a person relating to the assessment of any compensation or consideration under the Banking (Special Provisions) Act 2008 or the Banking Act 2009; or

(e)   any determination, calculation or dispute which may be referred to the Upper Tribunal under the Financial Services and Markets Act 2000 (Contribution to Costs of Special Resolution Regime) Regulations 2010 (and in these Rules a decision in respect of which a reference has been made to the Upper Tribunal in a financial services case includes any such determination, calculation or, except for the purposes of rule 5(5), dispute relating to the making of payments under the Regulations);

"**hearing**" means an oral hearing and includes a hearing conducted in whole or in part by video link, telephone or other means of instantaneous two-way electronic communication;

"**immigration case**" means proceedings before the Upper Tribunal on appeal against a decision in proceedings under section 40A of the British Nationality Act 1981, section 82 of the Nationality, Immigration and Asylum Act 2002, or regulation 26 of the Immigration (European Economic Area) Regulations 2006 that are not an asylum case;

"**immigration judicial review proceedings**" means judicial review proceedings which are designated as an immigration matter–

(a)   in a direction made in accordance with Part 1 of Schedule 2 to the Constitutional Reform Act 2005 specifying a class of case for the purposes of section 18(6) of the 2007 Act; or

(b)   in an order of the High Court in England and Wales made under section 31A(3) of the Senior Courts Act 1981, transferring to the Upper Tribunal an application of a kind described in section 31A(1) of that Act;

"**interested party**" means–

(a)   a person who is directly affected by the outcome sought in judicial review proceedings, and has been named as an interested party under rule 28 or 29 (judicial review), or has been substituted or added as an interested party under rule 9 (addition, substitution and removal of parties);

(b)   in judicial review proceedings transferred to the Upper Tribunal under section 25A(2) or (3) of the Judicature (Northern Ireland) Act 1978 or section 31A(2) or (3) of the Supreme Court Act 1981, a person who was an interested party in the proceedings immediately before they were transferred to the Upper Tribunal; and

(c)   in a financial services case or a wholesale energy case, any person other than the applicant who could have referred the case to the Upper Tribunal and who has been added or substituted as an interested party under rule 9 (addition, substitution and removal of parties);

"**judicial review proceedings**" means proceedings within the jurisdiction of the Upper Tribunal pursuant to section 15 or 21 of the 2007 Act, whether such proceedings are started in the Upper Tribunal or transferred to the Upper Tribunal;

Statutory Instruments

"mental health case" means proceedings before the Upper Tribunal on appeal against a decision in proceedings under the Mental Health Act 1983 or paragraph 5(2) of the Schedule to the Repatriation of Prisoners Act 1984;

"national security certificate appeal" means an appeal under section 28 of the Data Protection Act 1998 or section 60 of the Freedom of Information Act 2000 (including that section as applied and modified by regulation 18 of the Environmental Information Regulations 2004);

"party" means a person who is an appellant, an applicant, a respondent or an interested party in proceedings before the Upper Tribunal, a person who has referred a question or matter to the Upper Tribunal or, if the proceedings have been concluded, a person who was an appellant, an applicant, a respondent or an interested party when the Upper Tribunal finally disposed of all issues in the proceedings;

"permission" includes leave in cases arising under the law of Northern Ireland;

"practice direction" means a direction given under section 23 of the 2007 Act;

"reference", in a financial services case, includes an appeal;

"relevant minister" means the Minister or designated person responsible for the signing of the certificate to which a national security certificate appeal relates;

"respondent" means–

(a)   in an appeal, or application for permission to appeal, against a decision of another tribunal, any person other than the appellant who–

    (i)   [omitted by SI 2009/274, r. 5(d)(i);]

    (ii)   could (if they had been notified of the proceedings) have been a party before that other tribunal; or

    (iii)   otherwise has a right of appeal against the decision of the other tribunal and has given notice to the Upper Tribunal that they wish to be a party to the appeal;

(b)   in an appeal other than a road transport case, the person who made the decision;

(c)   in judicial review proceedings–

    (i)   in proceedings started in the Upper Tribunal, the person named by the applicant as the respondent;

    (ii)   in proceedings transferred to the Upper Tribunal under section 25A(2) or (3) of the Judicature (Northern Ireland) Act 1978 or section 31A(2) or (3) of the Supreme Court Act 1981, a person who was a defendant in the proceedings immediately before they were transferred;

    (iii)   in proceedings transferred to the Upper Tribunal under section 20(1) of the 2007 Act, a person to whom intimation of the petition was made before the proceedings were transferred, or to whom the Upper Tribunal has required intimation to be made.

(ca)   in proceedings transferred or referred to the Upper Tribunal from the First-tier Tribunal, a person who was a respondent in the proceedings in the First-tier Tribunal;

(d)   in a reference under the Forfeiture Act 1982, the person whose eligibility for a benefit or advantage is in issue;

(da)   in a financial services case–

    (i)   where the case is a multiple regulator case, both the primary and secondary regulator as defined in Schedule 3 to these rules (but subject to the operation of paragraph 4A(3) of that Schedule);

    (ii)   where the case is a single regulator case, the maker of the decision in respect of which a reference has been made; or

(db)   in a wholesale energy case, in relation to Great Britain, the Gas and Electricity Markets Authority or, in relation to Northern Ireland, the Northern Ireland Authority for Utility Regulation; or

(e)   a person substituted or added as a respondent under rule 9 (substitution and addition of parties);

"road transport case" means an appeal against a decision of a traffic commissioner or the Department of the Environment in Northern Ireland;

"tribunal" does not include a traffic commissioner;

"wholesale energy case" means a reference to the Upper Tribunal in respect of a decision of–

(a)   in relation to Great Britain, the Gas and Electricity Markets Authority under the Electricity and Gas (Market Integrity and Transparency) (Enforcement etc.) Regulations 2013; or

(b)   in relation to Northern Ireland, the Northern Ireland Authority for Utility Regulation under the Electricity and Gas (Market Integrity and Transparency) (Enforcement etc.) Regulations (Northern Ireland) 2013;

"working day" means any day except a Saturday or Sunday, Christmas Day, Good Friday or a bank holiday under section 1 of the Banking and Financial Dealings Act 1971.

History – In r. 1(2), the words "except proceedings in the Lands Chamber" inserted by SI 2009/1975, r. 8(a), with effect from 1 September 2009.
In r. 1(3), in the definition of "applicant", the words "or a wholesale energy case" in para. (b) inserted by SI 2014/514, r. 4(a), with effect from 6 April 2014.
In r. 1(3), in the definition of "financial services case", the word "or" at the end of para. (c) omitted by SI 2014/514, r. 4(b), with effect from 6 April 2014.
In r. 1(3), in the definition of "interested party", the words "or a wholesale energy case" in para. (c) inserted by SI 2014/514, r. 4(c), with effect from 6 April 2014.
In r. 1(3), in the definition of "respondent", para. (db) inserted by SI 2014/514, r. 4(d), with effect from 6 April 2014.
In r. 1(3), the definition of "wholesale energy case" inserted by SI 2014/514, r. 4(e), with effect from 6 April 2014.
In r. 1(3), definition of "applicant" substituted by SI 2010/747, r. 4(a), with effect from 6 April 2010. The former definition read as follows:
  ""applicant" means a person who applies for permission to bring, or does bring, judicial review proceedings before the Upper Tribunal and, in judicial review proceedings transferred to the Upper Tribunal from a court, includes a person who was a claimant or petitioner in the proceedings immediately before they were transferred;".
In r. 1(3), in the definition of "appropriate national authority", the words ", the Department of the Environment in Northern Ireland" inserted by SI 2012/1363, r. 5(a), with effect from 1 July 2012.
In r. 1(3), definition of "appropriate national authority" inserted by SI 2009/1975, r. 8(b)(i), with effect from 1 September 2009.
In r. 1(3), definition of "asylum case" inserted by SI 2010/44, r. 3(a), with effect from 15 February 2010.
In r. 1(3), definition of "authorised person" substituted by SI 2012/1363, r. 5(b), with effect from 1 July 2012.
In r. 1(3), definition of "authorised person" inserted by SI 2009/1975, r. 8(b)(i), with effect from 1 September 2009.
In r. 1(3), definition of "fast-track case" inserted by SI 2010/44, r. 3(c), with effect from 15 February 2010.
In r. 1(3), in the definition of "financial services case", sub-para. (a) substituted and (aa) inserted by SI 2013/606, r. 2(2)(a), with effect from 1 April 2013.
In r. 1(3), in the definition of "financial services case", sub-para. (e) (and the "or" at the end of sub-para. (d)) inserted by SI 2011/651, r. 8(2), with effect from 1 April 2011.
In r. 1(3), definition of "financial services case" inserted by SI 2010/747, r. 4(b), with effect from 6 April 2010.
In r. 1(3), definition of "fresh claim proceedings" omitted by SI 2013/2067, r. 4(a), with effect from 1 November 2013. Former definition read as follows:
  ""fresh claim proceedings" means judicial review proceedings which call into question a decision of the Secretary of State not to treat submissions as an asylum claim or a human rights claim within the meaning of Part 5 of the Nationality, Immigration and Asylum Act 2002 wholly or partly on the basis that they are not significantly different from material that has previously been considered, and which have been begun in or transferred to the Upper Tribunal pursuant to a direction made by the Lord Chief Justice of England and Wales for the purposes of section 18(6) of the 2007 Act;".
In r. 1(3), definition of "fresh claim proceedings" inserted by SI 2011/2343, r. 4, with effect from 17 October 2011.
In r. 1(3), definition of "immigration case" inserted by SI 2010/44, r. 3(b), with effect from 15 February 2010.
In r. 1(3), definition of "immigration judicial review proceedings" inserted by SI 2013/2067, r. 4(b), with effect from 1 November 2013.
In r. 1(3), in the definition of "interested party", in sub-para. (a), the words "(addition, substitution and removal of parties)" substituted for the words "(substitution and addition of parties)" by SI 2010/747, r. 4(c)(i), with effect from 6 April 2010.
In r. 1(3), in the definition of "interested party", in sub-para. (a), the word "and" at the end omitted by SI 2010/747, r. 4(c)(ii), with effect from 6 April 2010.
In r. 1(3), in the definition of "interested party", sub-para. (c) (and the "and" at the end of sub-para. (b)) inserted by SI 2010/747, r. 4(c)(iii), with effect from 6 April 2010.
In r. 1(3), definition of "national security certificate appeal" inserted by SI 2010/43, r. 6(a), with effect from 18 January 2010.
In r. 1(3), in the definition of "party", the word "Upper" inserted before the words "Tribunal finally" by SI 2013/2067, r. 4(c), with effect from 1 November 2013.
In r. 1(3), in the definition of "party", the words "or matter" inserted by SI 2010/747, r. 4(d), with effect from 6 April 2010.
In r. 1(3), definition of "reference" inserted by SI 2010/747, r. 4(e), with effect from 6 April 2010.
In r. 1(3), definition of "relevant minister" inserted by SI 2010/43, r. 6(b), with effect from 18 January 2010.
In r. 1(3), in the definition of "respondent", sub-para. (da) substituted by SI 2013/606, r. 2(2)(b), with effect from 1 April 2013.
In r. 1(3), in the definition of "respondent", in sub-para. (b), the words "other than a road transport case" substituted for the words "against any other decision except a decision of a traffic commissioner" by SI 2012/1363, r. 5(c), with effect from 1 July 2012.
In r. 1(3), in the definition of "respondent", sub-para. (da) (and the "or" at the end of sub-para. (d)) inserted by SI 2010/747, r. 4(f), with effect from 6 April 2010.
In r. 1(3), in the definition of "respondent", in para. (b), the words "except a decision of a traffic commissioner" inserted by SI 2009/1975, r. 8(b)(ii), with effect from 1 September 2009.
In r. 1(3), definition of "road transport case" inserted by SI 2012/1363, r. 5(d), with effect from 1 July 2012.
In r. 1(3), definition of "tribunal" inserted by SI 2009/1975, r. 8(b)(iii), with effect from 1 September 2009.
In r. 1(3), definition of "appellant" substituted by SI 2009/274, r. 5(a), with effect from 1 April 2009.

OVERRIDING OBJECTIVE AND PARTIES' OBLIGATION TO CO-OPERATE WITH THE UPPER TRIBUNAL

2(1)   The overriding objective of these Rules is to enable the Upper Tribunal to deal with cases fairly and justly.

2(2)   Dealing with a case fairly and justly includes–

(a) dealing with the case in ways which are proportionate to the importance of the case, the complexity of the issues, the anticipated costs and the resources of the parties;

(b) avoiding unnecessary formality and seeking flexibility in the proceedings;

(c) ensuring, so far as practicable, that the parties are able to participate fully in the proceedings;

(d) using any special expertise of the Upper Tribunal effectively; and

(e) avoiding delay, so far as compatible with proper consideration of the issues.

2(3) The Upper Tribunal must seek to give effect to the overriding objective when it–

(a) exercises any power under these Rules; or

(b) interprets any rule or practice direction.

2(4) Parties must–

(a) help the Upper Tribunal to further the overriding objective; and

(b) co-operate with the Upper Tribunal generally.

ALTERNATIVE DISPUTE RESOLUTION AND ARBITRATION

3(1) The Upper Tribunal should seek, where appropriate–

(a) to bring to the attention of the parties the availability of any appropriate alternative procedure for the resolution of the dispute; and

(b) if the parties wish and provided that it is compatible with the overriding objective, to facilitate the use of the procedure.

3(2) Part 1 of the Arbitration Act 1996 does not apply to proceedings before the Upper Tribunal.

PART 2 – GENERAL POWERS AND PROVISIONS

DELEGATION TO STAFF

4(1) Staff appointed under section 40(1) of the 2007 Act (tribunal staff and services) may, with the approval of the Senior President of Tribunals, carry out functions of a judicial nature permitted or required to be done by the Upper Tribunal.

4(2) The approval referred to at paragraph (1) may apply generally to the carrying out of specified functions by members of staff of a specified description in specified circumstances.

4(3) Within 14 days after the date on which the Upper Tribunal sends notice of a decision made by a member of staff under paragraph (1) to a party, that party may apply in writing to the Upper Tribunal for that decision to be considered afresh by a judge.

CASE MANAGEMENT POWERS

5(1) Subject to the provisions of the 2007 Act and any other enactment, the Upper Tribunal may regulate its own procedure.

5(2) The Upper Tribunal may give a direction in relation to the conduct or disposal of proceedings at any time, including a direction amending, suspending or setting aside an earlier direction.

5(3) In particular, and without restricting the general powers in paragraphs (1) and (2), the Upper Tribunal may

(a) extend or shorten the time for complying with any rule, practice direction or direction;

(b) consolidate or hear together two or more sets of proceedings or parts of proceedings raising common issues, or treat a case as a lead case;

(c) permit or require a party to amend a document;

(d) permit or require a party or another person to provide documents, information, evidence or submissions to the Upper Tribunal or a party;

(e) deal with an issue in the proceedings as a preliminary issue;

(f) hold a hearing to consider any matter, including a case management issue;

(g) decide the form of any hearing;

(h) adjourn or postpone a hearing;

(i) require a party to produce a bundle for a hearing;

(j) stay (or, in Scotland, sist) proceedings;

(k) transfer proceedings to another court or tribunal if that other court or tribunal has jurisdiction in relation to the proceedings and–

 (i) because of a change of circumstances since the proceedings were started, the Upper Tribunal no longer has jurisdiction in relation to the proceedings; or

 (ii) the Upper Tribunal considers that the other court or tribunal is a more appropriate forum for the determination of the case;

(l) suspend the effect of its own decision pending an appeal or review of that decision;

(m) in an appeal, or an application for permission to appeal, against the decision of another tribunal, suspend the effect of that decision pending the determination of the application for permission to appeal, and any appeal;

(n) require any person, body or other tribunal whose decision is the subject of proceedings before the Upper Tribunal to provide reasons for the decision, or other information or documents in relation to the decision or any proceedings before that person, body or tribunal.

5(4) The Upper Tribunal may direct that a fast-track case cease to be treated as a fast-track case if–

(a) all the parties consent;

(b) the Upper Tribunal is satisfied that there are exceptional circumstances which suggest that the appeal or application could not be justly determined if it were treated as a fast-track case; or

(c) the Secretary of State for the Home Department has failed to comply with a provision of these Rules or a direction of the First-tier Tribunal or the Upper Tribunal, and the Upper Tribunal is satisfied that the other party would be prejudiced if the appeal or application were treated as a fast-track case.

5(5) In a financial services case, the Upper Tribunal may direct that the effect of the decision in respect of which the reference has been made is to be suspended pending the determination of the reference, if it is satisfied that to do so would not prejudice–

(a) the interests of any persons (whether consumers, investors or otherwise) intended to be protected by that notice;

(b) the smooth operation or integrity of any market intended to be protected by that notice; or

(c) the stability of the financial system of the United Kingdom.

5(6) Paragraph (5) does not apply in the case of a reference in respect of a decision of the Pensions Regulator.

5(7) In a wholesale energy case, the Upper Tribunal may direct that the effect of the decision in respect of which the reference has been made is to be suspended pending the determination of the reference.

History – R. 5(3)(n) substituted by SI 2009/1975, r. 9, with effect from 1 September 2009. Former r. 5(3)(n) read as follows:
 "(n) require any other tribunal whose decision is the subject of proceedings before the Upper Tribunal to provide reasons for the decision, or other information or documents in relation to the decision or the proceedings in that tribunal.".
R. 5(4) inserted by SI 2010/44, r. 4, with effect from 15 February 2010.
R. 5(5)(c) (and the "; or" before it) inserted (and the "or" after (a) omitted) by SI 2013/606, r. 2(3), with effect from 1 April 2013.
R. 5(5) and (6) inserted by SI 2010/747, r. 5, with effect from 6 April 2010.
R. 5(7) inserted by SI 2014/514, r. 5, with effect from 6 April 2014.

PROCEDURE FOR APPLYING FOR AND GIVING DIRECTIONS

6(1) The Upper Tribunal may give a direction on the application of one or more of the parties or on its own initiative.

6(2) An application for a direction may be made–

(a) by sending or delivering a written application to the Upper Tribunal; or

(b) orally during the course of a hearing.

6(3) An application for a direction must include the reason for making that application.

6(4) Unless the Upper Tribunal considers that there is good reason not to do so, the Upper Tribunal must send written notice of any direction to every party and to any other person affected by the direction.

6(5) If a party or any other person sent notice of the direction under paragraph (4) wishes to challenge a direction which the Upper Tribunal has given, they may do so by applying for another direction which amends, suspends or sets aside the first direction.

FAILURE TO COMPLY WITH RULES ETC.

7(1) An irregularity resulting from a failure to comply with any requirement in these Rules, a practice direction or a direction, does not of itself render void the proceedings or any step taken in the proceedings.

7(2) If a party has failed to comply with a requirement in these Rules, a practice direction or a direction, the Upper Tribunal may take such action as it considers just, which may include–

(a) waiving the requirement;

(b) requiring the failure to be remedied;

(c) exercising its power under rule 8 (striking out a party's case); or

(d) except in a mental health case, an asylum case or an immigration case, restricting a party's participation in the proceedings.

7(3) Paragraph (4) applies where the First-tier Tribunal has referred to the Upper Tribunal a failure by a person to comply with a requirement imposed by the First-tier Tribunal–

(a) to attend at any place for the purpose of giving evidence;

(b) otherwise to make themselves available to give evidence;

(c) to swear an oath in connection with the giving of evidence;

(d) to give evidence as a witness;

(e) to produce a document; or

(f) to facilitate the inspection of a document or any other thing (including any premises).

7(4) The Upper Tribunal may exercise its power under section 25 of the 2007 Act (supplementary powers of the Upper Tribunal) in relation to such non-compliance as if the requirement had been imposed by the Upper Tribunal.

History – In r. 7(2)(d), the words "a mental health case, an asylum case or an immigration case" substituted for the words "mental health cases" by SI 2010/44, r. 5, with effect from 15 February 2010.

STRIKING OUT A PARTY'S CASE

8(1A) Except for paragraph (2), this rule does not apply to an asylum case or an immigration case.

8(1) The proceedings, or the appropriate part of them, will automatically be struck out–

(a) if the appellant or applicant has failed to comply with a direction that stated that failure by the appellant or applicant to comply with the direction would lead to the striking out of the proceedings or part of them; or

(b) in immigration judicial review proceedings, when a fee has not been paid, as required, in respect of an application under rule 30(4) or upon the grant of permission.

8(2) The Upper Tribunal must strike out the whole or a part of the proceedings if the Upper Tribunal–

(a) does not have jurisdiction in relation to the proceedings or that part of them; and

(b) does not exercise its power under rule 5(3)(k)(i) (transfer to another court or tribunal) in relation to the proceedings or that part of them.

8(3) The Upper Tribunal may strike out the whole or a part of the proceedings if–

(a) the appellant or applicant has failed to comply with a direction which stated that failure by the appellant or applicant to comply with the direction could lead to the striking out of the proceedings or part of them;

(b) the appellant or applicant has failed to co-operate with the Upper Tribunal to such an extent that the Upper Tribunal cannot deal with the proceedings fairly and justly; or

(c) in proceedings which are not an appeal from the decision of another tribunal or judicial review proceedings, the Upper Tribunal considers there is no reasonable prospect of the appellant's or the applicant's case, or part of it, succeeding.

8(4) The Upper Tribunal may not strike out the whole or a part of the proceedings under paragraph (2) or (3)(b) or (c) without first giving the appellant or applicant an opportunity to make representations in relation to the proposed striking out.

8(5) If the proceedings have been struck out under paragraph (1) or (3)(a), the appellant or applicant may apply for the proceedings, or part of them, to be reinstated.

8(6) An application under paragraph (5) must be made in writing and received by the Upper Tribunal within 1 month after the date on which the Upper Tribunal sent notification of the striking out to the appellant or applicant.

8(7) This rule applies to a respondent or an interested party as it applies to an appellant or applicant except that–

(a) a reference to the striking out of the proceedings is to be read as a reference to the barring of the respondent or interested party from taking further part in the proceedings; and

(b) a reference to an application for the reinstatement of proceedings which have been struck out is to be read as a reference to an application for the lifting of the bar on the respondent or interested party from taking further part in the proceedings.

8(8) If a respondent or an interested party has been barred from taking further part in proceedings under this rule and that bar has not been lifted, the Upper Tribunal need not consider any response or other submission made by that respondent or interested party, and may summarily determine any or all issues against that respondent or interested party.

History – R. 8(1A) inserted (before r. 8(1)) by SI 2010/44, r. 6, with effect from 1 February 2010.
R. 8(1) substituted by SI 2011/2343, r. 5, with effect from 17 October 2011.
R. 8(1)(b) substituted by SI 2013/2067, r. 5, with effect from 1 November 2013. Former r. 8(1)(b) read as follows:
    "(b)   when a fee has not been paid upon the grant of permission in fresh claim proceedings as required.".
In r. 8(7), the words "or an interested party" inserted by SI 2009/274, r. 6(2)(a), with effect from 1 April 2009.
In r. 8(7)(a), the words "or interested party" inserted by SI 2009/274, r. 6(2)(b), with effect from 1 April 2009.
In r. 8(7)(b), the words "or interested party" inserted by SI 2009/274, r. 6(2)(b), with effect from 1 April 2009.
In r. 8(7)(b), the word "from", which appeared before the word "taking", inserted by SI 2009/274, r. 6(2)(c), with effect from 1 April 2009.
In r. 8(8), the words "or an interested party" inserted by SI 2009/274, r. 6(3)(a), with effect from 1 April 2009.
In r. 8(8), the words "or interested party, and may summarily determine any or all issues against that respondent or interested party" inserted by SI 2009/274, r. 6(3)(b), with effect from 1 April 2009.

ADDITION, SUBSTITUTION AND REMOVAL OF PARTIES

9(1) The Upper Tribunal may give a direction adding, substituting or removing a party as an appellant, a respondent or an interested party.

9(2) If the Upper Tribunal gives a direction under paragraph (1) it may give such consequential directions as it considers appropriate.

9(3) A person who is not a party may apply to the Upper Tribunal to be added or substituted as a party.

9(4) If a person who is entitled to be a party to proceedings by virtue of another enactment applies to be added as a party, and any conditions applicable to that entitlement have been satisfied, the Upper Tribunal must give a direction adding that person as a respondent or, if appropriate, as an appellant.

9(5) In an asylum case, the United Kingdom Representative of the United Nations High Commissioner for Refugees ("the United Kingdom Representative") may give notice to the Upper Tribunal that the United Kingdom Representative wishes to participate in the proceedings.

9(6) If the United Kingdom Representative gives notice under paragraph (5)–

(i) the United Kingdom Representative is entitled to participate in any hearing; and

(ii) all documents which are required to be sent or delivered to parties must be sent or delivered to the United Kingdom Representative.

History – R. 9(5) inserted by SI 2010/44, r. 7, with effect from 15 February 2010.
R. 9(6) inserted by SI 2010/44, r. 7, with effect from 15 February 2010.
R. 9 substituted by SI 2009/1975, r. 10, with effect from 1 September 2009. Former r. 9 read as follows:

    "SUBSTITUTION AND ADDITION OF PARTIES
    9(1)   The Upper Tribunal may give a direction substituting a party if–
    (a)   the wrong person has been named as a party; or
    (b)   the substitution has become necessary because of a change in circumstances since the start of proceedings.
    9(2)   The Upper Tribunal may give a direction adding a person to the proceedings as a respondent or, in judicial review proceedings, as an interested party.
    9(3)   If the Upper Tribunal gives a direction under paragraph (1) or (2) it may give such consequential directions as it considers appropriate.".

ORDERS FOR COSTS

10(1) The Upper Tribunal may not make an order in respect of costs (or, in Scotland, expenses) in proceedings transferred or referred by, or on appeal from, another tribunal except–

(aa) in a national security certificate appeal, to the extent permitted by paragraph (1A);

(a) in proceedings transferred by, or on appeal from, the Tax Chamber of the First-tier Tribunal; or

(b) to the extent and in the circumstances that the other tribunal had the power to make an order in respect of costs (or, in Scotland, expenses).

10(1A) In a national security certificate appeal–

(a)   the Upper Tribunal may make an order in respect of costs or expenses in the circumstances described at paragraph (3)(c) and (d);

(b)   if the appeal is against a certificate, the Upper Tribunal may make an order in respect of costs or expenses against the relevant Minister and in favour of the appellant if the Upper Tribunal allows the appeal and quashes the certificate to any extent or the Minister withdraws the certificate;

(c)   if the appeal is against the application of a certificate, the Upper Tribunal may make an order in respect of costs or expenses–

    (i)   against the appellant and in favour of any other party if the Upper Tribunal dismisses the appeal to any extent; or

    (ii)   in favour of the appellant and against any other party if the Upper Tribunal allows the appeal to any extent.

10(2)   The Upper Tribunal may not make an order in respect of costs or expenses under section 4 of the Forfeiture Act 1982.

10(3)   In other proceedings, the Upper Tribunal may not make an order in respect of costs or expenses except–

(a)   in judicial review proceedings;

(b)   [omitted by SI 2009/1975, r. 11(b).]

(c)   under section 29(4) of the 2007 Act (wasted costs) and costs incurred in applying such costs;

(d)   if the Upper Tribunal considers that a party or its representative has acted unreasonably in bringing, defending or conducting the proceedings; or

(e)   if, in a financial services case or a wholesale energy case, the Upper Tribunal considers that the decision in respect of which the reference was made was unreasonable.

10(4)   The Upper Tribunal may make an order for costs (or, in Scotland, expenses) on an application or on its own initiative.

10(5)   A person making an application for an order for costs or expenses must–

(a)   send or deliver a written application to the Upper Tribunal and to the person against whom it is proposed that the order be made; and

(b)   send or deliver with the application a schedule of the costs or expenses claimed sufficient to allow summary assessment of such costs or expenses by the Upper Tribunal.

10(6)   An application for an order for costs or expenses may be made at any time during the proceedings but may not be made later than 1 month after the date on which the Upper Tribunal sends–

(a)   a decision notice recording the decision which finally disposes of all issues in the proceedings; or

(b)   notice under rule 17(5) that a withdrawal which ends the proceedings has taken effect.

10(7)   The Upper Tribunal may not make an order for costs or expenses against a person (the "paying person") without first–

(a)   giving that person an opportunity to make representations; and

(b)   if the paying person is an individual and the order is to be made under paragraph (3)(a), (b) or (d), considering that person's financial means.

10(8)   The amount of costs or expenses to be paid under an order under this rule may be ascertained by–

(a)   summary assessment by the Upper Tribunal;

(b)   agreement of a specified sum by the paying person and the person entitled to receive the costs or expenses ("the receiving person"); or

(c)   assessment of the whole or a specified part of the costs or expenses, including the costs or expenses of the assessment incurred by the receiving person, if not agreed.

10(9)   Following an order for assessment under paragraph (8)(c), the paying person or the receiving person may apply–

(a)   in England and Wales, to the High Court or the Costs Office of the Supreme Court (as specified in the order) for a detailed assessment of the costs on the standard basis or, if specified in the order, on the indemnity basis; and the Civil Procedure Rules 1998 shall apply, with necessary modifications, to that application and assessment as if the proceedings in the tribunal had been proceedings in a court to which the Civil Procedure Rules 1998 apply;

(b) in Scotland, to the Auditor of the Court of Session for the taxation of the expenses according to the fees payable in that court; or

(c) in Northern Ireland, to the Taxing Office of the High Court of Northern Ireland for taxation on the standard basis or, if specified in the order, on the indemnity basis.

10(10) Upon making an order for the assessment of costs, the Upper Tribunal may order an amount to be paid on account before the costs or expenses are assessed.

History – In r. 10(1), the words "transferred or referred by, or on appeal from," substituted for the words "referred by or on appeal from" by SI 2009/1975, r. 11(a)(i), with effect from 1 September 2009.
R. 10(1)(aa) inserted by SI 2010/43, r. 7(a), with effect from 18 January 2010.
In r. 10(1)(a), the words "transferred by, or on appeal from," substituted for the words "on appeal from" by SI 2009/1975, r. 11(a)(ii), with effect from 1 September 2009.
R. 10(1A) inserted by SI 2010/43, r. 7(b), with effect from 18 January 2010.
In r. 10(3) the words "and costs incurred in applying such costs" inserted by SI 2013/477, r. 50, with effect from 1 April 2013.
R. 10(3)(b) omitted by SI 2009/1975, r. 11(b), with effect from 1 September 2009. Former r. 10(3)(b) read as follows:
    "(b)   in proceedings transferred from the Tax Chamber of the First-tier Tribunal;".
In r. 10(3)(c), the "or" at the end omitted by SI 2010/747, r. 6(a), with effect from 6 April 2010.
In r. 10(3)(e), the words "or a wholesale energy case" inserted by SI 2014/514, r. 6, with effect from 6 April 2014.
R. 10(3)(e) (and the "or" at the end of s. 10(3)(d)) inserted by SI 2010/747, r. 6(b), with effect from 6 April 2010.
R. 10(3)(b) substituted by SI 2013/477, r. 51, with effect from 1 April 2013. Former r. 10(3)(b) read as follows:
    "(b)   notice of a withdrawal under rule 17 which ends the proceedings."
In r. 10(8)(c) the words ", including the costs or expenses of the assessment" inserted by SI 2013/477, r. 52, with effect from 1 April 2013.
In r. 10(10), the word "Upper" inserted by SI 2013/2067, r. 6, with effect from 1 November 2013.
R. 10(10) inserted by SI 2013/477, r. 53, with effect from 1 April 2013.
R. 10 substituted by SI 2009/274, r. 7, with effect from 1 April 2009.

REPRESENTATIVES

11(1) Subject to paragraph (5A), a party may appoint a representative (whether a legal representative or not) to represent that party in the proceedings save that a party in an asylum or immigration case may not be represented by any person prohibited from representing by section 84 of the Immigration and Asylum Act 1999.

11(2) If a party appoints a representative, that party (or the representative if the representative is a legal representative) must send or deliver to the Upper Tribunal written notice of the representative's name and address.

11(2A) If the Upper Tribunal receives notice that a party has appointed a representative under paragraph (2), it must send a copy of that notice to each other party.

11(3) Anything permitted or required to be done by a party under these Rules, a practice direction or a direction may be done by the representative of that party, except signing a witness statement.

11(4) A person who receives due notice of the appointment of a representative–

(a) must provide to the representative any document which is required to be provided to the represented party, and need not provide that document to the represented party; and

(b) may assume that the representative is and remains authorised as such until they receive written notification that this is not so from the representative or the represented party.

11(5) Subject to paragraph (5B), at a hearing a party may be accompanied by another person whose name and address has not been notified under paragraph (2) but who, subject to paragraph (8) and with the permission of the Upper Tribunal, may act as a representative or otherwise assist in presenting the party's case at the hearing.

11(5A) In immigration judicial review proceedings, a party may appoint as a representative only a person authorised under the Legal Services Act 2007 to undertake the conduct of litigation in the High Court.

11(5B) At a hearing of immigration judicial review proceedings, rights of audience before the Upper Tribunal are restricted to persons authorised to exercise those rights in the High Court under the Legal Services Act 2007.

11(6) Paragraphs (2) to (4) do not apply to a person who accompanies a party under paragraph (5).

11(7) In a mental health case if the patient has not appointed a representative the Upper Tribunal may appoint a legal representative for the patient where–

(a) the patient has stated that they do not wish to conduct their own case or that they wish to be represented; or

(b) the patient lacks the capacity to appoint a representative but the Upper Tribunal believes that it is in the patient's best interests for the patient to be represented.

11(8) In a mental health case a party may not appoint as a representative, or be represented or assisted at a hearing by–

Statutory Instruments

(a)　　a person liable to be detained or subject to guardianship or after-care under supervision, or who is a community patient, under the Mental Health Act 1983; or

(b)　　a person receiving treatment for mental disorder at the same hospital or home as the patient.

11(9)　In this rule **"legal representative"** means a person who, for the purposes of the Legal Services Act 2007, is an authorised person in relation to an activity which constitutes the exercise of a right of audience or the conduct of litigation within the meaning of that Act, a qualified person as defined in section 84(2) of the Immigration and Asylum Act 1999, an advocate or solicitor in Scotland or a barrister or solicitor in Northern Ireland.

11(10)　In an asylum case or an immigration case, an appellant's representative before the First-tier Tribunal will be treated as that party's representative before the Upper Tribunal, unless the Upper Tribunal receives notice–

(a)　　of a new representative under paragraph (2) of this rule; or

(b)　　from the appellant stating that they are no longer represented.

History – In r. 11(1), the words "Subject to paragraph (5A)," inserted by SI 2011/2343, r. 6(a), with effect from 17 October 2011. In r. 11(1), the words "save that a party in an asylum or immigration case may not be represented by any person prohibited from representing by section 84 of the Immigration and Asylum Act 1999" inserted by SI 2010/44, r. 8(a), with effect from 15 February 2010.
In r. 11(2), the words "and to each other party", which appeared after "Upper Tribunal", omitted by SI 2009/274, r. 8(a), with effect from 1 April 2009.
R. 11(2A) inserted by SI 2009/274, r. 8(b), with effect from 1 April 2009.
In r. 11(5), the words "Subject to paragraph (5B)," inserted by SI 2011/2343, r. 6(b), with effect from 17 October 2011.
In r. 11(5A) and (5B), the words "immigration judicial review" substituted for the words "fresh claim" by SI 2013/2067, r. 7, with effect from 1 November 2013.
R. 11(5A) and (5B) inserted by SI 2011/2343, r. 6(c), with effect from 17 October 2011.
In r. 11(8)(b), the word "or" inserted by SI 2009/1975, r. 12, with effect from 1 September 2009.
In r. 11(9), the words "a qualified person as defined in section 84(2) of the Immigration and Asylum Act 1999," inserted by SI 2010/44, r. 8(b), with effect from 15 February 2010.
In r. 11(9), the words "a person who, for the purposes of the Legal Services Act 2007, is an authorised person in relation to an activity which constitutes the exercise of a right of audience or the conduct of litigation within the meaning of that Act" substituted for the words "an authorised advocate or authorised litigator as defined by section 119(1) of the Courts and Legal Services Act 1990" by SI 2010/43, r. 8, with effect from 18 January 2010.
R. 11(9) inserted by SI 2009/274, r. 8(c), with effect from 1 April 2009.
R. 11(10) inserted by SI 2010/44, r. 8(c), with effect from 15 February 2010.

CALCULATING TIME

12(1)　An act required by these Rules, a practice direction or a direction to be done on or by a particular day must be done by 5pm on that day.

12(2)　If the time specified by these Rules, a practice direction or a direction for doing any act ends on a day other than a working day, the act is done in time if it is done on the next working day.

12(3)　In a special educational needs case or a disability discrimination in schools case, the following days must not be counted when calculating the time by which an act must be done–

(a)　　25th December to 1st January inclusive; and

(b)　　any day in August.

12(3A)　In an asylum case or an immigration case, when calculating the time by which an act must be done, in addition to the days specified in the definition of "working days" in rule 1 (interpretation), the following days must also not be counted as working days–

(a)　　27th to 31st December inclusive; and

(b)　　in a fast-track case, 24th December, Maundy Thursday, or the Tuesday after the last Monday in May.

12(4)　Paragraph (3) or (3A) does not apply where the Upper Tribunal directs that an act must be done by or on a specified date.

12(5)　In this rule–

"disability discrimination in schools case" means proceedings concerning disability discrimination in the education of a child or related matters; and

"special educational needs case" means proceedings concerning the education of a child who has or may have special educational needs.

History – R. 12(3A) inserted by SI 2010/44, r. 9(a), with effect from 15 February 2010.
In r. 12(4), "or (3A)" inserted by SI 2010/44, r. 9(b), with effect from 15 February 2010.
R. 12(5) inserted by SI 2009/274, r. 9, with effect from 1 April 2009.

SENDING AND DELIVERY OF DOCUMENTS

13(1) Any document to be provided to the Upper Tribunal under these Rules, a practice direction or a direction must be—

(a) sent by pre-paid post or by document exchange, or delivered by hand, to the address specified for the proceedings;

(b) sent by fax to the number specified for the proceedings; or

(c) sent or delivered by such other method as the Upper Tribunal may permit or direct.

13(2) Subject to paragraph (3), if a party provides a fax number, email address or other details for the electronic transmission of documents to them, that party must accept delivery of documents by that method.

13(3) If a party informs the Upper Tribunal and all other parties that a particular form of communication, other than pre-paid post or delivery by hand, should not be used to provide documents to that party, that form of communication must not be so used.

13(4) If the Upper Tribunal or a party sends a document to a party or the Upper Tribunal by email or any other electronic means of communication, the recipient may request that the sender provide a hard copy of the document to the recipient. The recipient must make such a request as soon as reasonably practicable after receiving the document electronically.

13(5) The Upper Tribunal and each party may assume that the address provided by a party or its representative is and remains the address to which documents should be sent or delivered until receiving written notification to the contrary.

13(6) Subject to paragraph (7), if a document submitted to the Upper Tribunal is not written in English, it must be accompanied by an English translation.

13(7) In proceedings that are in Wales or have a connection with Wales, a document or translation may be submitted to the Upper Tribunal in Welsh.

History – In r. 13(1)(a), the words "by document exchange, or delivered by hand," substituted for the words "delivered by hand" by SI 2009/274, r. 10, with effect from 1 April 2009.
R. 13(6) inserted by SI 2010/44, r. 10, with effect from 15 February 2010.
In r. 13(7), the word "Upper" inserted by SI 2013/2067, r. 8, with effect from 1 November 2013.
R. 13(7) inserted by SI 2010/44, r. 10, with effect from 15 February 2010.

USE OF DOCUMENTS AND INFORMATION

14(1) The Upper Tribunal may make an order prohibiting the disclosure or publication of—

(a) specified documents or information relating to the proceedings; or

(b) any matter likely to lead members of the public to identify any person whom the Upper Tribunal considers should not be identified.

14(2) The Upper Tribunal may give a direction prohibiting the disclosure of a document or information to a person if—

(a) the Upper Tribunal is satisfied that such disclosure would be likely to cause that person or some other person serious harm; and

(b) the Upper Tribunal is satisfied, having regard to the interests of justice, that it is proportionate to give such a direction.

14(3) If a party ("the first party") considers that the Upper Tribunal should give a direction under paragraph (2) prohibiting the disclosure of a document or information to another party ("the second party"), the first party must—

(a) exclude the relevant document or information from any documents that will be provided to the second party; and

(b) provide to the Upper Tribunal the excluded document or information, and the reason for its exclusion, so that the Upper Tribunal may decide whether the document or information should be disclosed to the second party or should be the subject of a direction under paragraph (2).

14(4) [Omitted by SI 2009/1975, r. 13(a).]

14(5) If the Upper Tribunal gives a direction under paragraph (2) which prevents disclosure to a party who has appointed a representative, the Upper Tribunal may give a direction that the documents or information be disclosed to that representative if the Upper Tribunal is satisfied that—

(a) disclosure to the representative would be in the interests of the party; and

(b) the representative will act in accordance with paragraph (6).

Statutory Instruments

14(6)   Documents or information disclosed to a representative in accordance with a direction under paragraph (5) must not be disclosed either directly or indirectly to any other person without the Upper Tribunal's consent.

14(7)   Unless the Upper Tribunal gives a direction to the contrary, information about mental health cases and the names of any persons concerned in such cases must not be made public.

14(8)   The Upper Tribunal may, on its own initiative or on the application of a party, give a direction that certain documents or information must or may be disclosed to the Upper Tribunal on the basis that the Upper Tribunal will not disclose such documents or information to other persons, or specified other persons.

14(9)   A party making an application for a direction under paragraph (8) may withhold the relevant documents or information from other parties until the Upper Tribunal has granted or refused the application.

14(10)   In a case involving matters relating to national security, the Upper Tribunal must ensure that information is not disclosed contrary to the interests of national security.

14(11)   The Upper Tribunal must conduct proceedings and record its decision and reasons appropriately so as not to undermine the effect of an order made under paragraph (1), a direction given under paragraph (2) or (8) or the duty imposed by paragraph (10).

History – R. 14(4) omitted by SI 2009/1975, r. 13(a), with effect from 1 September 2009. Former r. 14(4) read as follows:
"**14(4)**   The Upper Tribunal must conduct proceedings as appropriate in order to give effect to a direction given under paragraph (2).".
R. 14(8) inserted by SI 2009/1975, r. 13(b), with effect from 1 September 2009.
R. 14(9) inserted by SI 2009/1975, r. 13(b), with effect from 1 September 2009.
R. 14(10) inserted by SI 2009/1975, r. 13(b), with effect from 1 September 2009.
R. 14(11) inserted by SI 2009/1975, r. 13(b), with effect from 1 September 2009.

EVIDENCE AND SUBMISSIONS

15(1)   Without restriction on the general powers in rule 5(1) and (2) (case management powers), the Upper Tribunal may give directions as to–

(a)   issues on which it requires evidence or submissions;

(b)   the nature of the evidence or submissions it requires;

(c)   whether the parties are permitted or required to provide expert evidence, and if so whether the parties must jointly appoint a single expert to provide such evidence;

(d)   any limit on the number of witnesses whose evidence a party may put forward, whether in relation to a particular issue or generally;

(e)   the manner in which any evidence or submissions are to be provided, which may include a direction for them to be given–

(i)   orally at a hearing; or

(ii)   by written submissions or witness statement; and

(f)   the time at which any evidence or submissions are to be provided.

15(2)   The Upper Tribunal may–

(a)   admit evidence whether or not–

(i)   the evidence would be admissible in a civil trial in the United Kingdom; or

(ii)   the evidence was available to a previous decision maker; or

(b)   exclude evidence that would otherwise be admissible where–

(i)   the evidence was not provided within the time allowed by a direction or a practice direction;

(ii)   the evidence was otherwise provided in a manner that did not comply with a direction or a practice direction; or

(iii)   it would otherwise be unfair to admit the evidence.

15(2A)   In an asylum case or an immigration case–

(a)   if a party wishes the Upper Tribunal to consider evidence that was not before the First-tier Tribunal, that party must send or deliver a notice to the Upper Tribunal and any other party–

(i)   indicating the nature of the evidence; and

(ii)   explaining why it was not submitted to the First-tier Tribunal; and

(b) when considering whether to admit evidence that was not before the First-tier Tribunal, the Upper Tribunal must have regard to whether there has been unreasonable delay in producing that evidence.

15(3) The Upper Tribunal may consent to a witness giving, or require any witness to give, evidence on oath, and may administer an oath for that purpose.

History – R. 15(2A) inserted by SI 2010/44, r. 11, with effect from 15 February 2010.

SUMMONING OR CITATION OF WITNESSES AND ORDERS TO ANSWER QUESTIONS OR PRODUCE DOCUMENTS

16(1) On the application of a party or on its own initiative, the Upper Tribunal may–

(a) by summons (or, in Scotland, citation) require any person to attend as a witness at a hearing at the time and place specified in the summons or citation; or

(b) order any person to answer any questions or produce any documents in that person's possession or control which relate to any issue in the proceedings.

16(2) A summons or citation under paragraph (1)(a) must–

(a) give the person required to attend 14 days' notice of the hearing or such shorter period as the Upper Tribunal may direct; and

(b) where the person is not a party, make provision for the person's necessary expenses of attendance to be paid, and state who is to pay them.

16(3) No person may be compelled to give any evidence or produce any document that the person could not be compelled to give or produce on a trial of an action in a court of law in the part of the United Kingdom where the proceedings are due to be determined.

16(4) A person who receives a summons, citation or order may apply to the Upper Tribunal for it to be varied or set aside if they did not have an opportunity to object to it before it was made or issued.

16(5) A person making an application under paragraph (4) must do so as soon as reasonably practicable after receiving notice of the summons, citation or order.

16(6) A summons, citation or order under this rule must–

(a) state that the person on whom the requirement is imposed may apply to the Upper Tribunal to vary or set aside the summons, citation or order, if they did not have an opportunity to object to it before it was made or issued; and

(b) state the consequences of failure to comply with the summons, citation or order.

History – R. 16(4), (5) and (6) substituted for former r. 16(4) by SI 2009/274, r. 11, with effect from 1 April 2009.

WITHDRAWAL

17(1) Subject to paragraph (2), a party may give notice of the withdrawal of its case, or any part of it–

(a) by sending or delivering to the Upper Tribunal a written notice of withdrawal; or

(b) orally at a hearing.

17(2) Notice of withdrawal will not take effect unless the Upper Tribunal consents to the withdrawal except in relation to an application for permission to appeal.

17(3) A party which has withdrawn its case may apply to the Upper Tribunal for the case to be reinstated.

17(4) An application under paragraph (3) must be made in writing and be received by the Upper Tribunal within 1 month after–

(a) the date on which the Upper Tribunal received the notice under paragraph (1)(a); or

(b) the date of the hearing at which the case was withdrawn orally under paragraph (1)(b).

17(5) The Upper Tribunal must notify each party in writing that a withdrawal has taken effect under this rule.

17(6) Paragraph (3) does not apply to a financial services case other than a reference against a penalty.

History – In r. 17(1)(a) the words "at any time before a hearing to consider the disposal of the proceedings (or, if the Upper Tribunal disposes of the proceedings without a hearing, before that disposal)," omitted by SI 2013/477, r. 54, with effect from 1 April 2013.
In r. 17(5) the words "that a withdrawal has taken effect" substituted for the words "of a withdrawal" by SI 2013/477, r. 54, with effect from 1 April 2013.
R. 17(6) inserted by SI 2010/747, r. 7, with effect from 6 April 2010.

APPEAL TREATED AS ABANDONED OR FINALLY DETERMINED IN AN ASYLUM CASE OR AN IMMIGRATION CASE

17A(1)   A party to an asylum case or an immigration case before the Upper Tribunal must notify the Upper Tribunal if they are aware that–

(a)   the appellant has left the United Kingdom;

(b)   the appellant has been granted leave to enter or remain in the United Kingdom;

(c)   a deportation order has been made against the appellant; or

(d)   a document listed in paragraph 4(2) of Schedule 2 to the Immigration (European Economic Area) Regulations 2006 has been issued to the appellant.

17A(2)   Where an appeal is treated as abandoned pursuant to section 104(4) or (4A) of the Nationality, Immigration and Asylum Act 2002 or paragraph 4(2) of Schedule 2 to the Immigration (European Economic Area) Regulations 2006, or as finally determined pursuant to section 104(5) of the Nationality, Immigration and Asylum Act 2002, the Upper Tribunal must send the parties a notice informing them that the appeal is being treated as abandoned or finally determined.

17A(3)   Where an appeal would otherwise fall to be treated as abandoned pursuant to section 104(4A) of the Nationality, Immigration and Asylum Act 2002, but the appellant wishes to pursue their appeal, the appellant must send or deliver a notice, which must comply with any relevant practice directions, to the Upper Tribunal and the respondent so that it is received within thirty days of the date on which the notice of the grant of leave to enter or remain in the United Kingdom was sent to the appellant.

17A(4)   Where a notice of grant of leave to enter or remain is sent electronically or delivered personally, the time limit in paragraph (3) is twenty eight days.

17A(5)   Notwithstanding rule 5(3)(a) (case management powers) and rule 7(2) (failure to comply with rules etc.), the Upper Tribunal must not extend the time limits in paragraph (3) and (4).

History – In r. 17A(1), the word "Upper" inserted before the words "Tribunal if" by SI 2013/2067, r. 9, with effect from 1 November 2013.

R. 17A inserted by SI 2010/44, r. 12, with effect from 15 February 2010.

NOTICE OF FUNDING OF LEGAL SERVICES

18   If a party is granted funding of legal services at any time, that party must as soon as practicable–

(a)

(i)   if civil legal services (within the meaning of section 8 of the Legal Aid, Sentencing and Punishment of Offenders Act 2012) are provided under arrangements made for the purposes of Part 1 of that Act or by the Northern Ireland Legal Services Commission, send a copy of the certificate or funding notice to the Upper Tribunal; or

(ii)   if funding is granted by the Scottish Legal Aid Board, send a copy of the legal aid certificate to the Upper Tribunal; and

(b)   notify every other party in writing that funding has been granted.

History – In r. 18(a)(i) the words "civil legal services (within the meaning of section 8 of the Legal Aid, Sentencing and Punishment of Offenders Act 2012) are provided under arrangements made for the purposes of Part 1 of that Act or by" substituted for the words "funding is granted by the Legal Services Commission or" and the words "certificate or" inserted by SI 2013/477, r. 55 with effect from 1 April 2013.

CONFIDENTIALITY IN CHILD SUPPORT OR CHILD TRUST FUND CASES

19(1)   Paragraph (3) applies to an appeal against a decision of the First-tier Tribunal in proceedings under the Child Support Act 1991 in the circumstances described in paragraph (2), other than an appeal against a reduced benefit decision (as defined in section 46(10)(b) of the Child Support Act 1991, as that section had effect prior to the commencement of section 15(b) of the Child Maintenance and Other Payments Act 2008).

19(2)   The circumstances referred to in paragraph (1) are that–

(a)   in the proceedings in the First-tier Tribunal in respect of which the appeal has been brought, there was an obligation to keep a person's address confidential; or

(b)   a person whose circumstances are relevant to the proceedings would like their address (or, in the case of the person with care of the child, the child's address) to be kept confidential and has given notice to that effect–

(i)   to the Upper Tribunal in an application for permission to appeal or notice of appeal;

(ii)   to the Upper Tribunal within 1 month after an enquiry by the Upper Tribunal; or

    (iii)   to the Secretary of State or the Upper Tribunal when notifying a change of address after proceedings have been started.

19(3)   Where this paragraph applies, the Secretary of State and the Upper Tribunal must take appropriate steps to secure the confidentiality of the address, and of any information which could reasonably be expected to enable a person to identify the address, to the extent that the address or that information is not already known to each other party.

19(4)   Paragraph (6) applies to an appeal against a decision of the First-tier Tribunal in proceedings under the Child Trust Funds Act 2004 in the circumstances described in paragraph (5).

19(5)   The circumstances referred to in paragraph (4) are that—

(a)   in the proceedings in the First-tier Tribunal in respect of which the appeal has been brought, there was an obligation to keep a person's address confidential; or

(b)   a person whose circumstances are relevant to the proceedings would like their address (or, in the case of the person with care of the eligible child, the child's address) to be kept confidential and has given notice to that effect—

    (i)   to the Upper Tribunal in an application for permission to appeal or notice of appeal;

    (ii)   to the Upper Tribunal within 1 month after an enquiry by the Upper Tribunal; or

    (iii)   to HMRC or the Upper Tribunal when notifying a change of address after proceedings have been started.

19(6)   Where this paragraph applies, HMRC and the Upper Tribunal must take appropriate steps to secure the confidentiality of the address, and of any information which could reasonably be expected to enable a person to identify the address, to the extent that the address or that information is not already known to each other party.

19(7)   In this rule—

    "eligible child" has the meaning set out in section 2 of the Child Trust Funds Act 2004; and

    "HMRC" means Her Majesty's Revenue and Customs.

History – In r. 19(2)(b)(iii), the words ", the Child Maintenance and Enforcement Commission" omitted by SI 2012/2007, art. 118(a), with effect from 31 July 2012.
In r. 19(3), the words ", the Child Maintenance and Enforcement Commission" omitted by SI 2012/2007, art. 118(b), with effect from 31 July 2012.

POWER TO PAY EXPENSES AND ALLOWANCES

20(1)   In proceedings brought under section 4 of the Safeguarding Vulnerable Groups Act 2006, the Secretary of State may pay such allowances for the purpose of or in connection with the attendance of persons at hearings as the Secretary of State may, with the consent of the Treasury, determine.

20(2)   Paragraph (3) applies to proceedings on appeal from a decision of—

(a)   the First-tier Tribunal in proceedings under the Child Support Act 1991, section 12 of the Social Security Act 1998 or paragraph 6 of Schedule 7 to the Child Support, Pensions and Social Security Act 2000;

(b)   the First-tier Tribunal in a war pensions and armed forces case (as defined in the Tribunal Procedure (First-tier Tribunal) (War Pensions and Armed Forces Compensation Chamber) Rules 2008); or

(c)   a Pensions Appeal Tribunal for Scotland or Northern Ireland.

20(3)   The Lord Chancellor (or, in Scotland, the Secretary of State) may pay to any person who attends any hearing such travelling and other allowances, including compensation for loss of remunerative time, as the Lord Chancellor (or, in Scotland, the Secretary of State) may determine.

History – In r. 20(1), the words "which are not an appeal from the decision of another tribunal or judicial review proceedings", which appeared after "section 4 of the Safeguarding Vulnerable Groups Act 2006", omitted by SI 2009/274, r. 12, with effect from 1 April 2009.

PROCEDURE FOR APPLYING FOR A STAY OF A DECISION PENDING AN APPEAL

20A(1)   This rule applies where another enactment provides in any terms for the Upper Tribunal to stay or suspend, or to lift a stay or suspension of, a decision which is or may be the subject of an appeal to the Upper Tribunal ("the substantive decision") pending such appeal.

20A(2)   A person who wishes the Upper Tribunal to decide whether the substantive decision should be stayed or suspended must make a written application to the Upper Tribunal which must include—

(a)   the name and address of the person making the application;

(b)   the name and address of any representative of that person;

(c)   the address to which documents for that person should be sent or delivered;

(d)   the name and address of any person who will be a respondent to the appeal;

(e)   details of the substantive decision and any decision as to when that decision is to take effect, and copies of any written record of, or reasons for, those decisions; and

(f)   the grounds on which the person making the application relies.

20A(3)   In the case of an application under paragraph (2) in a road transport case–

(a)   the person making the application must notify the decision maker when making the application;

(b)   within 7 days of receiving notification of the application the decision maker must send or deliver written reasons for refusing or withdrawing the stay–

     (i)   to the Upper Tribunal; and

     (ii)   to the person making the application, if the decision maker has not already done so.

20A(4)   If the Upper Tribunal grants a stay or suspension following an application under this rule–

(a)   the Upper Tribunal may give directions as to the conduct of the appeal of the substantive decision; and

(b)   the Upper Tribunal may, where appropriate, grant the stay or suspension subject to conditions.

20A(5)   Unless the Upper Tribunal considers that there is good reason not to do so, the Upper Tribunal must send written notice of any decision made under this rule to each party.

History – In r. 20A(3), the words "in a road transport case" substituted for the words "for a stay of a decision of a traffic commissioner" by SI 2012/1363, r. 6(a), with effect from 1 July 2012.

In r. 20A(3)(a) and (b), the words "decision maker" substituted for the words "traffic commissioner" by SI 2012/1363, r. 6(b), with effect from 1 July 2012.

R. 20A inserted by SI 2009/1975, r. 14, with effect from 1 September 2009.

PART 3 – PROCEDURE FOR CASES IN THE UPPER TRIBUNAL

History – In the heading to Part 3, the words "Procedure for cases in" substituted for the words "Appeals and references to" by SI 2009/274, r. 12, with effect from 1 April 2009.

APPLICATION TO THE UPPER TRIBUNAL FOR PERMISSION TO APPEAL

21(1)   [Omitted by SI 2009/1975, r. 15.]

21(2)   A person may apply to the Upper Tribunal for permission to appeal to the Upper Tribunal against a decision of another tribunal only if–

(a)   they have made an application for permission to appeal to the tribunal which made the decision challenged; and

(b)   that application has been refused or has not been admitted or has been granted only on limited grounds.

21(3)   An application for permission to appeal must be made in writing and received by the Upper Tribunal no later than–

(a)   in the case of an application under section 4 of the Safeguarding Vulnerable Groups Act 2006, 3 months after the date on which written notice of the decision being challenged was sent to the appellant;

(aa)   subject to paragraph (3A), in an asylum case or an immigration case where the appellant is in the United Kingdom at the time that the application is made–

     (i)   seven working days after the date on which notice of the First-tier Tribunal's refusal of permission was sent to the appellant; or

     (ii)   if the case is a fast-track case, four working days after the date on which notice of the First-tier Tribunal's refusal of permission was sent to the appellant;

(ab)   subject to paragraph (3A), in an asylum case or an immigration case where the appellant is outside the United Kingdom at the time that the application is made, fifty six days after the date on which notice of the First-tier Tribunal's refusal of permission was sent to the appellant; or

(b)   otherwise, a month after the date on which the tribunal that made the decision under challenge sent notice of its refusal of permission to appeal, or refusal to admit the application for permission to appeal, to the appellant.

21(3A)　Where a notice of decision is sent electronically or delivered personally, the time limits in paragraph (3)(aa) and (ab) are—

(a)　in sub-paragraph (aa)(i), five working days;

(b)　in sub-paragraph (aa)(ii), two working days; and

(c)　in sub-paragraph (ab), twenty eight days.

21(4)　The application must state—

(a)　the name and address of the appellant;

(b)　the name and address of the representative (if any) of the appellant;

(c)　an address where documents for the appellant may be sent or delivered;

(d)　details (including the full reference) of the decision challenged;

(e)　the grounds on which the appellant relies; and

(f)　whether the appellant wants the application to be dealt with at a hearing.

21(5)　The appellant must provide with the application a copy of—

(a)　any written record of the decision being challenged;

(b)　any separate written statement of reasons for that decision; and

(c)　if the application is for permission to appeal against a decision of another tribunal, the notice of refusal of permission to appeal, or notice of refusal to admit the application for permission to appeal, from that other tribunal.

21(6)　If the appellant provides the application to the Upper Tribunal later than the time required by paragraph (3) or by an extension of time allowed under rule 5(3)(a) (power to extend time)—

(a)　the application must include a request for an extension of time and the reason why the application was not provided in time; and

(b)　unless the Upper Tribunal extends time for the application under rule 5(3)(a) (power to extend time) the Upper Tribunal must not admit the application.

21(7)　If the appellant makes an application to the Upper Tribunal for permission to appeal against the decision of another tribunal, and that other tribunal refused to admit the appellant's application for permission to appeal because the application for permission or for a written statement of reasons was not made in time—

(a)　the application to the Upper Tribunal for permission to appeal must include the reason why the application to the other tribunal for permission to appeal or for a written statement of reasons, as the case may be, was not made in time; and

(b)　the Upper Tribunal must only admit the application if the Upper Tribunal considers that it is in the interests of justice for it to do so.

21(8)　In this rule, a reference to notice of a refusal of permission to appeal is to be taken to include a reference to notice of a grant of permission to appeal on limited grounds.

History – R. 21(1) omitted by SI 2009/1975, r. 15, with effect from 1 September 2009. Former r. 21(1) read as follows:

"**21(1)**　This rule applies to an application for permission to appeal to the Upper Tribunal against any decision.".

In r. 21(2)(b), the words "or has been granted only on limited grounds" inserted by SI 2014/514, r. 7(a), with effect from 6 April 2014.

R. 21(3)(aa) and (ab) inserted (and the "or" at the end of r. 21(3)(a) omitted) by SI 2010/44, r. 13(a), with effect from 15 February 2010.

R. 21(3A) inserted by SI 2010/44, r. 13(b), with effect from 15 February 2010.

R. 21(8) inserted by SI 2014/514, r. 7(b), with effect from 6 April 2014.

DECISION IN RELATION TO PERMISSION TO APPEAL

22(1)　Subject to rule 40A, if the Upper Tribunal refuses permission to appeal or refuses to admit a late application for permission, it must send written notice of the refusal and of the reasons for the refusal to the appellant.

22(2)　If the Upper Tribunal gives permission to appeal—

(a)　the Upper Tribunal must send written notice of the permission, and of the reasons for any limitations or conditions on such permission, to each party;

(b)　subject to any direction by the Upper Tribunal, the application for permission to appeal stands as the notice of appeal and the Upper Tribunal must send to each respondent a copy of the application for permission to appeal and any documents provided with it by the appellant; and

(c)　the Upper Tribunal may, with the consent of the appellant and each respondent, determine the appeal without obtaining any further response.

22(3)   Paragraph (4) applies where the Upper Tribunal, without a hearing, determines an application for permission to appeal—

(a)   against a decision of—

    (i)   the Tax Chamber of the First-tier Tribunal;

    (ii)   the Health, Education and Social Care Chamber of the First-tier Tribunal;

    (iia)   the General Regulatory Chamber of the First-tier Tribunal;

    (iib)   the Property Chamber of the First-tier Tribunal;

    (iii)   the Mental Health Review Tribunal for Wales; or

    (iv)   the Special Educational Needs Tribunal for Wales; or

(b)   under section 4 of the Safeguarding Vulnerable Groups Act 2006.

22(4)   In the circumstances set out at paragraph (3) the appellant may apply for the decision to be reconsidered at a hearing if the Upper Tribunal—

(a)   refuses permission to appeal or refuses to admit a late application for permission; or

(b)   gives permission to appeal on limited grounds or subject to conditions.

22(5)   An application under paragraph (4) must be made in writing and received by the Upper Tribunal within 14 days after the date on which the Upper Tribunal sent written notice of its decision regarding the application to the appellant.

History – In r. 22(1) the words "Subject to rule 40A," inserted by SI 2014/1505, reg. 3, with effect from 30 June 2014.
In r. 22(1), the words "or refuses to admit a late application for permission" inserted by SI 2014/514, r. 8(a), with effect from 6 April 2014.
R. 22(3)(a)(iia) inserted by SI 2009/1975, r. 16, with effect from 1 September 2009.
R. 22(3)(a)(iib) inserted by SI 2014/514, r. 8(b), with effect from 6 April 2014.
R. 22(3) substituted by SI 2009/274, r. 14, with effect from 1 April 2009.
In r. 22(4)(a), the words "or refuses to admit a late application for permission" inserted by SI 2014/514, r. 8(c), with effect from 6 April 2014.

NOTICE OF APPEAL

23(1)   This rule applies—

(a)   to proceedings on appeal to the Upper Tribunal for which permission to appeal is not required, except proceedings to which rule 26A or 26B applies;

(b)   if another tribunal has given permission for a party to appeal to the Upper Tribunal; or

(c)   subject to any other direction by the Upper Tribunal, if the Upper Tribunal has given permission to appeal and has given a direction that the application for permission to appeal does not stand as the notice of appeal.

23(1A)   In an asylum case or an immigration case in which the First-tier Tribunal has given permission to appeal, subject to any direction of the First-tier Tribunal or the Upper Tribunal, the application for permission to appeal sent or delivered to the First-tier Tribunal stands as the notice of appeal and accordingly paragraphs (2) to (6) of this rule do not apply.

23(2)   The appellant must provide a notice of appeal to the Upper Tribunal so that it is received within 1 month after—

(a)   the date that the tribunal that gave permission to appeal sent notice of such permission to the appellant; or

(b)   if permission to appeal is not required, the date on which notice of decision to which the appeal relates was sent to the appellant.

23(3)   The notice of appeal must include the information listed in rule 21(4)(a) to (e) (content of the application for permission to appeal) and, where the Upper Tribunal has given permission to appeal, the Upper Tribunal's case reference.

23(4)   If another tribunal has granted permission to appeal, the appellant must provide with the notice of appeal a copy of—

(a)   any written record of the decision being challenged;

(b)   any separate written statement of reasons for that decision; and

(c)   the notice of permission to appeal.

23(5)   If the appellant provides the notice of appeal to the Upper Tribunal later than the time required by paragraph (2) or by an extension of time allowed under rule 5(3)(a) (power to extend time)—

(a)   the notice of appeal must include a request for an extension of time and the reason why the notice was not provided in time; and

(b)   unless the Upper Tribunal extends time for the notice of appeal under rule 5(3)(a) (power to extend time) the Upper Tribunal must not admit the notice of appeal.

23(6)   When the Upper Tribunal receives the notice of appeal it must send a copy of the notice and any accompanying documents–

(a)   to each respondent; or

(b)   in a road transport case, to–

    (i)   the decision maker;

    (ii)   the appropriate national authority; and

    (iii)   in a case relating to the detention of a vehicle, the authorised person

History – In r. 23(1)(a), "or 26B" inserted by SI 2010/747, r. 8, with effect from 6 April 2010.
R. 23(1) substituted by SI 2009/1975, r. 17(a), with effect from 1 September 2009.
R. 23(1A) inserted by SI 2010/44, r. 14, with effect from 15 February 2010.
R. 23(6) substituted by SI 2009/1975, r. 17(a), with effect from 1 September 2009.
R. 23(6)(b) substituted by SI 2012/1363, r. 7, with effect from 1 July 2012.
R. 23(6) substituted by SI 2009/1975, r. 17(b), with effect from 1 September 2009.

RESPONSE TO THE NOTICE OF APPEAL

24(1)   This rule and rule 25 do not apply to a road transport case, in respect of which Schedule 1 makes alternative provision.

24(1A)   Subject to any direction given by the Upper Tribunal, a respondent may provide a response to a notice of appeal.

24(2)   Any response provided under paragraph (1A) must be in writing and must be sent or delivered to the Upper Tribunal so that it is received–

(a)   if an application for permission to appeal stands as the notice of appeal, no later than one month after the date on which the respondent was sent notice that permission to appeal had been granted;

(aa)   in a fast-track case, one day before the hearing of the appeal; or

(b)   in any other case, no later than 1 month after the date on which the Upper Tribunal sent a copy of the notice of appeal to the respondent.

24(3)   The response must state–

(a)   the name and address of the respondent;

(b)   the name and address of the representative (if any) of the respondent;

(c)   an address where documents for the respondent may be sent or delivered;

(d)   whether the respondent opposes the appeal;

(e)   the grounds on which the respondent relies, including (in the case of an appeal against the decision of another tribunal) any grounds on which the respondent was unsuccessful in the proceedings which are the subject of the appeal, but intends to rely in the appeal; and

(f)   whether the respondent wants the case to be dealt with at a hearing.

24(4)   If the respondent provides the response to the Upper Tribunal later than the time required by paragraph (2) or by an extension of time allowed under rule 5(3)(a) (power to extend time), the response must include a request for an extension of time and the reason why the response was not provided in time.

24(5)   When the Upper Tribunal receives the response it must send a copy of the response and any accompanying documents to the appellant and each other party.

History – In r. 24(1), the words "a road transport case" substituted for the words "an appeal against a decision of a traffic commissioner" by SI 2012/1363, r. 8, with effect from 1 July 2012.
R. 24(1) and (1A) substituted for former r. 24(1) by SI 2009/1975, r. 18(a), with effect from 1 September 2009. Former r. 24(1) read as follows:
    "**24(1)**   Subject to any direction given by the Upper Tribunal, a respondent may provide a response to the notice of appeal.".
In r. 24(2), "(1A)" substituted for "(1)" by SI 2010/43, r. 9, with effect from 18 January 2010.
R. 24(2)(a) substituted by SI 2010/44, r. 15(a) with effect from 15 February 2010. Former r. 24(2)(a) read as follows:
    "(a)   if an application for permission to appeal stands as the notice of appeal, no later than 1 month after the date on which the Upper Tribunal sent notice that it had granted permission to appeal to the respondent; or".
In former r. 24(2)(a), the words "if an application for permission to appeal" substituted for the words "if the application for permission" by SI 2009/1975, r. 18(b), with effect from 1 September 2009.
R. 24(2)(aa) inserted (and the "and" after the end of r. 24(2)(a) omitted) by SI 2010/44, r. 15(b) and (c), with effect from 15 February 2010.
In r. 24(3)(e), the words "(in the case of an appeal against the decision of another tribunal)" inserted SI 2009/1975, r. 18(c), with effect from 1 September 2009.
In r. 24(4), "response" substituted for "notice" by SI 2009/274, r. 15, with effect from 1 April 2009.

Statutory Instruments

APPELLANT'S REPLY

25(1) Subject to any direction given by the Upper Tribunal, the appellant may provide a reply to any response provided under rule 24 (response to the notice of appeal).

25(2) Subject to paragraph (2A), any reply provided under paragraph (1) must be in writing and must be sent or delivered to the Upper Tribunal so that it is received within one month after the date on which the Upper Tribunal sent a copy of the response to the appellant.

25(2A) In an asylum case or an immigration case, the time limit in paragraph (2) is–

(a)   one month after the date on which the Upper Tribunal sent a copy of the response to the appellant, or five days before the hearing of the appeal, whichever is the earlier; and

(b)   in a fast-track case, the day of the hearing.

25(3) When the Upper Tribunal receives the reply it must send a copy of the reply and any accompanying documents to each respondent.

History – In r. 25(2), the words "Subject to paragraph (2A), any" substituted for the word "Any" by SI 2010/44, r. 16(a), with effect from 15 February 2010.
R. 25(2A) inserted by SI 2010/44, r. 16(b), with effect from 15 February 2010.

REFERENCES UNDER THE FORFEITURE ACT 1982

26(1) If a question arises which is required to be determined by the Upper Tribunal under section 4 of the Forfeiture Act 1982, the person to whom the application for the relevant benefit or advantage has been made must refer the question to the Upper Tribunal.

26(2) The reference must be in writing and must include–

(a)   a statement of the question for determination;

(b)   a statement of the relevant facts;

(c)   the grounds upon which the reference is made; and

(d)   an address for sending documents to the person making the reference and each respondent.

26(3) When the Upper Tribunal receives the reference it must send a copy of the reference and any accompanying documents to each respondent.

26(4) Rules 24 (response to the notice of appeal) and 25 (appellant's reply) apply to a reference made under this rule as if it were a notice of appeal.

CASES TRANSFERRED OR REFERRED TO THE UPPER TRIBUNAL, APPLICATIONS MADE DIRECTLY TO THE UPPER TRIBUNAL AND PROCEEDINGS WITHOUT NOTICE TO A RESPONDENT

26A(1) Paragraphs (2) and (3) apply to–

(a)   a case transferred or referred to the Upper Tribunal from the First-tier Tribunal; or

(b)   a case, other than an appeal or a case to which rule 26 (references under the Forfeiture Act 1982) applies, which is started by an application made directly to the Upper Tribunal.

26A(2) In a case to which this paragraph applies–

(a)   the Upper Tribunal must give directions as to the procedure to be followed in the consideration and disposal of the proceedings;

(aa)   in a reference under Schedule 1D of the Charities Act 1993, the Upper Tribunal may give directions providing for an application to join the proceedings as a party and the time within which it may be made; and

(b)   the preceding rules in this Part will only apply to the proceedings to the extent provided for by such directions.

26A(3) If a case or matter to which this paragraph applies is to be determined without notice to or the involvement of a respondent–

(a)   any provision in these Rules requiring a document to be provided by or to a respondent; and

(b)   any other provision in these Rules permitting a respondent to participate in the proceedings

does not apply to that case or matter.

26A(4) Schedule 2 makes further provision for national security certificate appeals transferred to the Upper Tribunal.

History – R. 26A(1) substituted by SI 2009/1975, r. 19, with effect from 1 September 2009.
R. 26A(2)(aa) inserted (and the "and" after (a) omitted) by SI 2012/500, r. 5, with effect from 6 April 2012.
R. 26A(4) inserted by SI 2010/43, r. 10, with effect from 18 January 2010.
R. 26A inserted by SI 2009/274, r. 16, with effect from 1 April 2009.

FINANCIAL SERVICES CASES AND WHOLESALE ENERGY CASES

History – In r. 26B heading, the words "and wholesale energy cases" inserted by SI 2014/514, r. 9, with effect from 6 April 2014.

26B   Schedule 3 makes provision for financial services cases and wholesale energy cases.

History – In r. 26B, the words "and wholesale energy cases" inserted by SI 2014/514, r. 10, with effect from 6 April 2014. R. 26B and the heading before it inserted by SI 2010/747, r. 9, with effect from 6 April 2010.

PART 4 – JUDICIAL REVIEW PROCEEDINGS IN THE UPPER TRIBUNAL

APPLICATION OF THIS PART TO JUDICIAL REVIEW PROCEEDINGS TRANSFERRED TO THE UPPER TRIBUNAL

27(1)   When a court transfers judicial review proceedings to the Upper Tribunal, the Upper Tribunal–

(a)   must notify each party in writing that the proceedings have been transferred to the Upper Tribunal; and

(b)   must give directions as to the future conduct of the proceedings.

27(2)   The directions given under paragraph (1)(b) may modify or disapply for the purposes of the proceedings any of the provisions of the following rules in this Part.

27(3)   In proceedings transferred from the Court of Session under section 20(1) of the 2007 Act, the directions given under paragraph (1)(b) must–

(a)   if the Court of Session did not make a first order specifying the required intimation, service and advertisement of the petition, state the Upper Tribunal's requirements in relation to those matters;

(b)   state whether the Upper Tribunal will consider summary dismissal of the proceedings; and

(c)   where necessary, modify or disapply provisions relating to permission in the following rules in this Part.

APPLICATIONS FOR PERMISSION TO BRING JUDICIAL REVIEW PROCEEDINGS

28(1)   A person seeking permission to bring judicial review proceedings before the Upper Tribunal under section 16 of the 2007 Act must make a written application to the Upper Tribunal for such permission.

28(2)   Subject to paragraph (3), an application under paragraph (1) must be made promptly and, unless any other enactment specifies a shorter time limit, must be sent or delivered to the Upper Tribunal so that it is received no later than 3 months after the date of the decision, action or omission to which the application relates.

28(3)   An application for permission to bring judicial review proceedings challenging a decision of the First-tier Tribunal may be made later than the time required by paragraph (2) if it is made within 1 month after the date on which the First-tier Tribunal sent–

(a)   written reasons for the decision; or

(b)   notification that an application for the decision to be set aside has been unsuccessful, provided that that application was made in time.

28(4)   The application must state–

(a)   the name and address of the applicant, the respondent and any other person whom the applicant considers to be an interested party;

(b)   the name and address of the applicant's representative (if any);

(c)   an address where documents for the applicant may be sent or delivered;

(d)   details of the decision challenged (including the date, the full reference and the identity of the decision maker);

(e)   that the application is for permission to bring judicial review proceedings;

(f)   the outcome that the applicant is seeking; and

(g)   the facts and grounds on which the applicant relies.

28(5)   If the application relates to proceedings in a court or tribunal, the application must name as an interested party each party to those proceedings who is not the applicant or a respondent.

Statutory Instruments

28(6) The applicant must send with the application—

(a) a copy of any written record of the decision in the applicant's possession or control; and

(b) copies of any other documents in the applicant's possession or control on which the applicant intends to rely.

28(7) If the applicant provides the application to the Upper Tribunal later than the time required by paragraph (2) or (3) or by an extension of time allowed under rule 5(3)(a) (power to extend time)—

(a) the application must include a request for an extension of time and the reason why the application was not provided in time; and

(b) unless the Upper Tribunal extends time for the application under rule 5(3)(a) (power to extend time) the Upper Tribunal must not admit the application.

28(8) Except where rule 28A(2)(a) (special provisions for immigration judicial review proceedings) applies, when the Upper Tribunal receives the application it must send a copy of the application and any accompanying documents to each person named in the application as a respondent or interested party.

History – In r. 28(2), the words ", action or omission" inserted by SI 2009/274, r. 17, with effect from 1 April 2009.
In r. 28(8), the words "immigration judicial review" substituted for the words "fresh claim" by SI 2013/2067, r. 10, with effect from 1 November 2013.
In r. 28(8), the words "Except where rule 28A(2)(a) (special provisions for fresh claim proceedings) applies," inserted by SI 2011/2343, r. 7, with effect from 17 October 2011.

SPECIAL PROVISIONS FOR IMMIGRATION JUDICIAL REVIEW PROCEEDINGS

28A(1) The Upper Tribunal must not accept an application for permission to bring immigration judicial review proceedings unless it is either accompanied by any required fee or the Upper Tribunal accepts an undertaking that the fee will be paid.

28A(2) Within 9 days of making an application referred to in paragraph (1), an applicant must provide—

(a) a copy of the application and any accompanying documents to each person named in the application as a respondent or an interested party; and

(b) the Upper Tribunal with a written statement of when and how this was done.

History – In the heading, the words "immigration judicial review" substituted for the words "fresh claim" by SI 2013/2067, r. 11(a), with effect from 1 November 2013.
In r. 28A(1), the words "immigration judicial review" substituted for the words "fresh claim" by SI 2013/2067, r. 11(b), with effect from 1 November 2013.
R. 28A inserted by SI 2011/2343, r. 8, with effect from 17 October 2011.

ACKNOWLEDGMENT OF SERVICE

29(1) A person who is sent or provided with a copy of an application for permission under rule 28(8) (application for permission to bring judicial review proceedings) or rule 28A(2)(a) (special provisions for immigration judicial review proceedings) and wishes to take part in the proceedings must provide to the Upper Tribunal an acknowledgment of service so that it is received no later than 21 days after the date on which the Upper Tribunal sent, or in immigration judicial review proceedings the applicant provided, a copy of the application to that person.

29(2) An acknowledgment of service under paragraph (1) must be in writing and state—

(a) whether the person intends to support or oppose the application for permission;

(b) their grounds for any support or opposition under sub-paragraph (a), or any other submission or information which they consider may assist the Upper Tribunal; and

(c) the name and address of any other person not named in the application as a respondent or interested party whom the person providing the acknowledgment considers to be an interested party.

29(2A) In immigration judicial review proceedings, a person who provides an acknowledgement of service under paragraph (1) must also provide a copy to—

(a) the applicant; and

(b) any other person named in the application under rule 28(4)(a) or acknowledgement of service under paragraph (2)(c)

no later than the time specified in paragraph (1).

29(3) A person who is provided with a copy of an application for permission under rule 28(8) or 28A(2)(a) but does not provide an acknowledgment of service to the Upper Tribunal may not take part in the application for permission unless allowed to do so by the Upper Tribunal, but may take part in the subsequent proceedings if the application is successful.

History – In r. 29(1), the words "immigration judicial review" substituted for the words "fresh claim" (in both places) by SI 2013/2067, r. 12(a), with effect from 1 November 2013.

In r. 29(1), the words "or provided with", the words "or rule 28A(2)(a) (special provisions for fresh claim proceedings)" and the words ", or in fresh claim proceedings the applicant provided," inserted, and the word "provide" substituted for the words "send or deliver" by SI 2011/2343, r. 9(a), with effect from 17 October 2011.

In r. 29(2), the words "immigration judicial review" substituted for the words "fresh claim" by SI 2013/2067, r. 12(b), with effect from 1 November 2013.

In r. 29(2)(a), the words "support or" inserted by SI 2009/274, r. 18(a), with effect from 1 April 2009.

In r. 29(2)(b), the words "support or" inserted by SI 2009/274, r. 18(b), with effect from 1 April 2009.

R. 29(2A) inserted by SI 2011/2343, r. 9(b), with effect from 17 October 2011.

In r. 29(3), the words "provided with" substituted for the word "sent" and the words "or 28A(2)(a)" and the words "to the Upper Tribunal" inserted by SI 2011/2343, r. 9(c), with effect from 17 October 2011.

In r. 29(3), the words "unless allowed to do so by the Upper Tribunal" inserted by SI 2011/651, r. 8(3), with effect from 1 April 2011.

DECISION ON PERMISSION OR SUMMARY DISMISSAL, AND RECONSIDERATION OF PERMISSION OR SUMMARY DISMISSAL AT A HEARING

30(1) The Upper Tribunal must send to the applicant, each respondent and any other person who provided an acknowledgment of service to the Upper Tribunal, and may send to any other person who may have an interest in the proceedings, written notice of–

(a)   its decision in relation to the application for permission; and

(b)   the reasons for any–

     (i)   refusal of the application or refusal to admit the late application, or

     (ii)   limitations or conditions on permission.

30(2) In proceedings transferred from the Court of Session under section 20(1) of the 2007 Act, where the Upper Tribunal has considered whether summarily to dismiss of the proceedings, the Upper Tribunal must send to the applicant and each respondent, and may send to any other person who may have an interest in the proceedings, written notice of–

(a)   its decision in relation to the summary dismissal of proceedings; and

(b)   the reasons for any decision summarily to dismiss part or all of the proceedings, or any limitations or conditions on the continuation of such proceedings.

30(3) Paragraph (4) applies where the Upper Tribunal, without a hearing–

(a)   determines an application for permission to bring judicial review proceedings by–

     (i)   refusing permission or refusing to admit the late application, or

     (ii)   giving permission on limited grounds or subject to conditions

(b)   in proceedings transferred from the Court of Session, summarily dismisses part or all of the proceedings, or imposes any limitations or conditions on the continuation of such proceedings.

30(4) Subject to paragraph (4A), in the circumstances specified in paragraph (3) the applicant may apply for the decision to be reconsidered at a hearing.

30(4A) Where the Upper Tribunal refuses permission to bring immigration judicial review proceedings or refuses to admit a late application for permission to bring such proceedings and considers the application to be totally without merit, it shall record that fact in its decision and, in those circumstances, the applicant may not request the decision to be reconsidered at a hearing.

30(5) An application under paragraph (4) must be made in writing and must be sent or delivered to the Upper Tribunal so that it is received within 14 days, or in immigration judicial review proceedings 9 days, after the date on which the Upper Tribunal sent written notice of its decision regarding the application to the applicant.

History – R. 30(1)(b) substituted by SI 2014/514, r. 11(a), with effect from 6 April 2014. Former r. 30(1)(b) read as follows:

     "(b)   the reasons for any refusal of the application, or any limitations or conditions on permission."

R. 30(3)(a) substituted by SI 2014/514, r. 11(b), with effect from 6 April 2014. Former r. 30(3)(a) read as follows:

     "(a)   determines an application for permission to bring judicial review proceedings and either refuses permission or gives permission on limited grounds or subject to conditions; or"

In r. 30(4), the words "Subject to paragraph (4A), in" substituted for the word "In" by SI 2013/2067, r. 13(a), with effect from 1 November 2013 (but the amendments do not apply to fresh claim proceedings (within the meaning in r. 1(3) as it was in force immediately before 1 November 2013) where (a) an application for permission to bring judicial review proceedings was issued in the Upper Tribunal before 1 November 2013; or (b) an application for permission to apply for judicial review was transferred to the Upper Tribunal by the High Court under section 31A of the Senior Courts Act 1981 before 1 November 2013).

In r. 30(4A), the words "or refuses to admit a late application for permission to bring such proceedings" inserted by SI 2014/514, r. 11(c), with effect from 6 April 2014.

R. 30(4A) inserted by SI 2013/2067, r. 13(b), with effect from 1 November 2013 (but the amendments do not apply to fresh claim proceedings (within the meaning in r. 1(3) as it was in force immediately before 1 November 2013) where (a) an application for

Statutory Instruments

permission to bring judicial review proceedings was issued in the Upper Tribunal before 1 November 2013; or (b) an application for permission to apply for judicial review was transferred to the Upper Tribunal by the High Court under section 31A of the Senior Courts Act 1981 before 1 November 2013).

In r. 30(5), the words "immigration judicial review" substituted for the words "fresh claim" by SI 2013/2067, r. 13(c), with effect from 1 November 2013.

In r. 30(5), the words ", or in fresh claim proceedings 9 days," inserted by SI 2011/2343, r. 10, with effect from 17 October 2011.

RESPONSES

31(1) Any person to whom the Upper Tribunal has sent notice of the grant of permission under rule 30(1) (notification of decision on permission), and who wishes to contest the application or support it on additional grounds, must provide detailed grounds for contesting or supporting the application to the Upper Tribunal.

31(2) Any detailed grounds must be provided in writing and must be sent or delivered to the Upper Tribunal so that they are received not more than 35 days after the Upper Tribunal sent notice of the grant of permission under rule 30(1).

APPLICANT SEEKING TO RELY ON ADDITIONAL GROUNDS

32 The applicant may not rely on any grounds, other than those grounds on which the applicant obtained permission for the judicial review proceedings, without the consent of the Upper Tribunal.

RIGHT TO MAKE REPRESENTATIONS

33 Each party and, with the permission of the Upper Tribunal, any other person, may–

(a) submit evidence, except at the hearing of an application for permission;

(b) make representations at any hearing which they are entitled to attend; and

(c) make written representations in relation to a decision to be made without a hearing.

AMENDMENTS AND ADDITIONAL GROUNDS RESULTING IN TRANSFER OF PROCEEDINGS TO THE HIGH COURT IN ENGLAND AND WALES

33A(1) This rule applies only to judicial review proceedings arising under the law of England and Wales.

33A(2) In relation to such proceedings–

(a) the powers of the Upper Tribunal to permit or require amendments under rule 5(3)(c) extend to amendments which would, once in place, give rise to an obligation or power to transfer the proceedings to the High Court in England and Wales under section 18(3) of the 2007 Act or paragraph (3);

(b) except with the permission of the Upper Tribunal, additional grounds may not be advanced, whether by an applicant or otherwise, if they would give rise to an obligation or power to transfer the proceedings to the High Court in England and Wales under section 18(3) of the 2007 Act or paragraph (3).

33A(3) Where the High Court in England and Wales has transferred judicial review proceedings to the Upper Tribunal under any power or duty and subsequently the proceedings are amended or any party advances additional grounds–

(a) if the proceedings in their present form could not have been transferred to the Upper Tribunal under the relevant power or duty had they been in that form at the time of the transfer, the Upper Tribunal must transfer the proceedings back to the High Court in England and Wales;

(b) subject to sub-paragraph (a), where the proceedings were transferred to the Upper Tribunal under section 31A(3) of the Senior Courts Act 1981 (power to transfer judicial review proceedings to the Upper Tribunal), the Upper Tribunal may transfer proceedings back to the High Court in England and Wales if it appears just and convenient to do so.

History – R. 33A inserted by SI 2011/2343, r. 11, with effect from 17 October 2011.

PART 5 – HEARINGS

DECISION WITH OR WITHOUT A HEARING

34(1) Subject to paragraphs (2) and (3), the Upper Tribunal may make any decision without a hearing.

34(2) The Upper Tribunal must have regard to any view expressed by a party when deciding whether to hold a hearing to consider any matter, and the form of any such hearing.

34(3) In immigration judicial review proceedings, the Upper Tribunal must hold a hearing before making a decision which disposes of proceedings.

34(4) Paragraph (3) does not affect the power of the Upper Tribunal to—

(a) strike out a party's case, pursuant to rule 8(1)(b) or 8(2);

(b) consent to withdrawal, pursuant to rule 17;

(c) determine an application for permission to bring judicial review proceedings, pursuant to rule 30; or

(d) make a consent order disposing of proceedings, pursuant to rule 39,

without a hearing.

History – In r. 34(1), the words "paragraphs (2) and (3)" substituted for the words "paragraph (2)" by SI 2013/2067, r. 14(a), with effect from 1 November 2013.
R. 34(3) and (4) inserted by SI 2013/2067, r. 14(b), with effect from 1 November 2013.

ENTITLEMENT TO ATTEND A HEARING

35(1) Subject to rule 37(4) (exclusion of a person from a hearing), each party is entitled to attend a hearing.

35(2) In a national security certificate appeal the relevant Minister is entitled to attend any hearing.

History – R. 35(2) inserted (and existing text of r.35 redesignated as r. 35(1)) by SI 2010/43, r. 11, with effect from 18 January 2010.

NOTICE OF HEARINGS

36(1) The Upper Tribunal must give each party entitled to attend a hearing reasonable notice of the time and place of the hearing (including any adjourned or postponed hearing) and any change to the time and place of the hearing.

36(2) The period of notice under paragraph (1) must be at least 14 days except that—

(a) in applications for permission to bring judicial review proceedings, the period of notice must be at least 2 working days;

(aa) in a fast-track case the period of notice must be at least one working day; and

(b) in any case other than a fast-track case the Upper Tribunal may give shorter notice–

(i) with the parties' consent; or

(ii) in urgent or exceptional cases.

History – R. 36(2)(aa) inserted (and the "and" after r. 36(2)(a) omitted) by SI 2010/44, r. 17(a), with effect from 15 February 2010.
In r. 36(2)(b), the words "in any case other than a fast-track case" inserted by SI 2010/44, r. 17(b), with effect from 15 February 2010.

SPECIAL TIME LIMITS FOR HEARING AN APPEAL IN A FAST-TRACK CASE

36A(1) Subject to rule 36(2)(aa) (notice of hearings) and paragraph (2) of this rule, where permission to appeal to the Upper Tribunal has been given in a fast-track case, the Upper Tribunal must start the hearing of the appeal not later than–

(a) four working days after the date on which the First-tier Tribunal or the Upper Tribunal sent notice of its grant of permission to appeal to the appellant; or

(b) where the notice of its grant of permission to appeal is sent electronically or delivered personally, two working days after the date on which the First-tier Tribunal or the Upper Tribunal sent notice of its grant of permission to appeal to the appellant.

36A(2) If the Upper Tribunal is unable to arrange for the hearing to start within the time specified in paragraph (1), it must set a date for the hearing as soon as is reasonably practicable.

History – R. 36A inserted by SI 2010/44, r. 18, with effect from 15 February 2010.

PUBLIC AND PRIVATE HEARINGS

37(1) Subject to the following paragraphs, all hearings must be held in public.

37(2) The Upper Tribunal may give a direction that a hearing, or part of it, is to be held in private.

37(2A) In a national security certificate appeal, the Upper Tribunal must have regard to its duty under rule 14(10) (no disclosure of information contrary to the interests of national security) when considering whether to give a direction that a hearing, or part of it, is to be held in private.

37(3) Where a hearing, or part of it, is to be held in private, the Upper Tribunal may determine who is entitled to attend the hearing or part of it.

Statutory Instruments

37(4)   The Upper Tribunal may give a direction excluding from any hearing, or part of it–

(a)   any person whose conduct the Upper Tribunal considers is disrupting or is likely to disrupt the hearing;

(b)   any person whose presence the Upper Tribunal considers is likely to prevent another person from giving evidence or making submissions freely;

(c)   any person who the Upper Tribunal considers should be excluded in order to give effect to the requirement at rule 14(11) (prevention of disclosure or publication of documents and information);

(d)   any person where the purpose of the hearing would be defeated by the attendance of that person; or

(e)   a person under the age of eighteen years.

37(5)   The Upper Tribunal may give a direction excluding a witness from a hearing until that witness gives evidence.

History – R. 37(2A) inserted by SI 2010/43, r. 12, with effect from 18 January 2010.

In r. 37(4)(c), the words "the requirement at rule 14(11) (prevention of disclosure or publication of documents and information)" substituted for the words "a direction under rule 14(2) (withholding information likely to cause harm)" by SI 2009/1975, r. 20, with effect from 1 September 2009.

R. 37(4)(e) inserted, the word "or" at the end of r. 37(4)(c) omitted, and the word "or" at the end of r. 37(4)(d) inserted, by SI 2009/274, r. 19, with effect from 1 April 2009.

HEARINGS IN A PARTY'S ABSENCE

38   If a party fails to attend a hearing, the Upper Tribunal may proceed with the hearing if the Upper Tribunal–

(a)   is satisfied that the party has been notified of the hearing or that reasonable steps have been taken to notify the party of the hearing; and

(b)   considers that it is in the interests of justice to proceed with the hearing.

PART 6 – DECISIONS

CONSENT ORDERS

39(1)   The Upper Tribunal may, at the request of the parties but only if it considers it appropriate, make a consent order disposing of the proceedings and making such other appropriate provision as the parties have agreed.

39(2)   Notwithstanding any other provision of these Rules, the Upper Tribunal need not hold a hearing before making an order under paragraph (1).

History – In r. 39(2), the word "Upper" inserted by SI 2013/2067, r. 15, with effect from 1 November 2013.

In r. 39(2), the words ", or provide reasons for the order", which appeared after "paragraph (1)", omitted by SI 2009/274, r. 20, with effect from 1 April 2009.

DECISIONS

40(1)   The Upper Tribunal may give a decision orally at a hearing.

40(1A)   Subject to paragraph (1B), in immigration judicial review proceedings, a decision which disposes of proceedings shall be given at a hearing.

40(1B)   Paragraph (1A) does not affect the power of the Upper Tribunal to–

(a)   strike out a party's case, pursuant to rule 8(1)(b) or 8(2);

(b)   consent to withdrawal, pursuant to rule 17;

(c)   determine an application for permission to bring judicial review proceedings pursuant to rule 30; or

(d)   make a consent order disposing of proceedings, pursuant to rule 39,

without a hearing.

40(2)   Except where rule 40A (special procedure for providing notice of a decision relating to an asylum case) applies, the Upper Tribunal must provide to each party as soon as reasonably practicable after making a decision (other than a decision under Part 7) which finally disposes of all issues in the proceedings or of a preliminary issue dealt with following a direction under rule 5(3)(e)–

(a)   a decision notice stating the Upper Tribunal's decision; and

(b)   notification of any rights of review or appeal against the decision and the time and manner in which such rights of review or appeal may be exercised.

40(3)   Subject to rule 14(11) (prevention of disclosure or publication of documents and information), the Upper Tribunal must provide written reasons for its decision with a decision notice provided under paragraph (2)(a) unless–

(a)   the decision was made with the consent of the parties; or

(b)   the parties have consented to the Upper Tribunal not giving written reasons.

40(4)   The Upper Tribunal may provide written reasons for any decision to which paragraph (2) does not apply.

40(5)   In a national security certificate appeal, when the Upper Tribunal provides a notice or reasons to the parties under this rule, it must also provide the notice or reasons to the relevant Minister and the Information Commissioner, if they are not parties.

History – R. 40(1A) and (1B) inserted by SI 2013/2067, r. 16, with effect from 1 November 2013.
In r. 40(2) the words "a decision (other than a decision under Part 7) which finally disposes of all issues in the proceedings or of a preliminary issue dealt with following a direction under rule 5(3)(e)" substituted for the words "a decision which finally disposes of all issues in the proceedings (except a decision under Part 7)" and the words "Upper" inserted by SI 2013/477, r. 56 with effect from 1 April 2013.
In r. 40(2), the words "Except where rule 40A (special procedure for providing notice of a decision relating to an asylum case) applies," inserted by SI 2010/44, r. 19, with effect from 15 February 2010.
In r. 40(2), the words "Subject to rule 14(2) (withholding harmful information),", which appeared at the beginning, omitted by SI 2009/274, r. 21(a), with effect from 1 April 2009.
In r. 40(3), the words "14(11) (prevention of disclosure or publication of documents and information)" substituted for the words "14(2) (withholding harmful information)" by SI 2009/1975, r. 21(a), with effect from 1 September 2009.
In r. 40(3), the words "Subject to rule 14(2) (withholding harmful information)," inserted by SI 2009/274, r. 21(b), with effect from 1 April 2009.
In r. 40(4), the word "Upper" inserted by SI 2009/1975, r. 21(b), with effect from 1 September 2009.
R. 40(5) inserted by SI 2010/43, r. 13, with effect from 18 January 2010.

SPECIAL PROCEDURE FOR PROVIDING NOTICE OF A DECISION RELATING TO AN ASYLUM CASE

40A(1)   This rule applies to a decision of the Upper Tribunal in an asylum case–

(a)   to refuse (or not to admit) an application for permission to appeal to the Upper Tribunal made by the person who appealed to the First-tier Tribunal; or

(b)   on an appeal under section 11 of the 2007 Act,

    where–

      (i)   at the time the application or appeal (as the case may be) is made the person who appealed to the First-tier Tribunal is in the United Kingdom; and

      (ii)   the decision is not made in a fast track case.

40A(2)   The Upper Tribunal must provide to the Secretary of State for the Home Department as soon as reasonably practicable–

(a)   a decision notice stating the Upper Tribunal's decision; and

(b)   a statement of any right of appeal against the decision and the time and manner in which such a right of appeal may be exercised.

40A(3)   The Secretary of State must, subject to paragraph (5)–

(a)   send the documents listed in paragraph (2) to the other party not later than 30 days after the Upper Tribunal sent them to the Secretary of State for the Home Department; and

(b)   as soon as practicable after sending the documents listed in paragraph (2), notify the Upper Tribunal on what date and by what means they were sent.

40A(4)   If the Secretary of State does not notify the Upper Tribunal under paragraph (3)(b) within 31 days after the documents listed in paragraph (2) were sent, the Upper Tribunal must send the notice of decision to the other party as soon as reasonably practicable.

40A(5)   If the Secretary of State applies for permission to appeal under section 13 of the 2007 Act, the Secretary of State must send the documents listed in paragraph (2) to the other party no later than the date on which the application for permission is sent to the Upper Tribunal.

History – R. 40A(1) substituted y SI 2014/1505, reg. 4, with effect from 30 June 2014. Former r. 40A(1) read as follows:

"**40A(1)**   This rule applies to an appeal before the Upper Tribunal under section 11 of the 2007 Act in an asylum case where–
(a)   the person who appealed to the First-tier Tribunal is in the United Kingdom; and
(b)   the case is not a fast-track case."
R. 40A inserted by SI 2010/44, r. 20, with effect from 15 February 2010.

PART 7 – CORRECTING, SETTING ASIDE, REVIEWING AND APPEALING DECISIONS OF THE UPPER TRIBUNAL

INTERPRETATION

41   In this Part–

"**appeal**", except in rule 44(2) (application for permission to appeal), means the exercise of a right of appeal under section 13 of the 2007 Act; and

"**review**" means the review of a decision by the Upper Tribunal under section 10 of the 2007 Act.

History – In r. 41, in the definition of "appeal", the words ", except in rule 44(2) (application for permission to appeal)," inserted by SI 2009/274, r. 22, with effect from 1 April 2009.

CLERICAL MISTAKES AND ACCIDENTAL SLIPS OR OMISSIONS

42   The Upper Tribunal may at any time correct any clerical mistake or other accidental slip or omission in a decision or record of a decision by–

(a)   sending notification of the amended decision, or a copy of the amended record, to all parties; and

(b)   making any necessary amendment to any information published in relation to the decision or record.

SETTING ASIDE A DECISION WHICH DISPOSES OF PROCEEDINGS

43(1)   The Upper Tribunal may set aside a decision which disposes of proceedings, or part of such a decision, and re-make the decision or the relevant part of it, if–

(a)   the Upper Tribunal considers that it is in the interests of justice to do so; and

(b)   one or more of the conditions in paragraph (2) are satisfied.

43(2)   The conditions are–

(a)   a document relating to the proceedings was not sent to, or was not received at an appropriate time by, a party or a party's representative;

(b)   a document relating to the proceedings was not sent to the Upper Tribunal at an appropriate time;

(c)   a party, or a party's representative, was not present at a hearing related to the proceedings; or

(d)   there has been some other procedural irregularity in the proceedings.

43(3)   Except where paragraph (4) applies, a party applying for a decision, or part of a decision, to be set aside under paragraph (1) must make a written application to the Upper Tribunal so that it is received no later than 1 month after the date on which the Upper Tribunal sent notice of the decision to the party.

43(4)   In an asylum case or an immigration case, the written application referred to in paragraph (3) must be sent or delivered so that it is received by the Upper Tribunal–

(a)   where the person who appealed to the First-tier Tribunal is in the United Kingdom at the time that the application is made, no later than twelve days after the date on which the Upper Tribunal or, as the case may be in an asylum case, the Secretary of State for the Home Department, sent notice of the decision to the party making the application; or

(b)   where the person who appealed to the First-tier Tribunal is outside the United Kingdom at the time that the application is made, no later than thirty eight days after the date on which the Upper Tribunal sent notice of the decision to the party making the application.

43(5)   Where a notice of decision is sent electronically or delivered personally, the time limits in paragraph (4) are ten working days.

History – In r. 43(3), the word "Upper" inserted before the words "Tribunal sent" by SI 2013/2067, r. 17, with effect from 1 November 2013.

In r. 43(3), the words "Except where paragraph (4) applies," inserted by SI 2010/44, r. 21(a), with effect from 15 February 2010.

R. 43(4) inserted by SI 2010/44, r. 21(b), with effect from 15 February 2010.

R. 43(5) inserted by SI 2010/44, r. 21(b), with effect from 15 February 2010.

APPLICATION FOR PERMISSION TO APPEAL

44(1)   Subject to paragraphs (4A) and (4B), a person seeking permission to appeal must make a written application to the Upper Tribunal for permission to appeal.

44(2)   Paragraph (3) applies to an application under paragraph (1) in respect of a decision–

(a)   on an appeal against a decision in a social security and child support case (as defined in the Tribunal Procedure (First-tier Tribunal) (Social Entitlement Chamber) Rules 2008);

(b)   on an appeal against a decision in proceedings in the War Pensions and Armed Forces Compensation Chamber of the First-tier Tribunal;

(ba)   on an appeal against a decision of a Pensions Appeal Tribunal for Scotland or Northern Ireland; or

(c)   in proceedings under the Forfeiture Act 1982.

44(3)   Where this paragraph applies, the application must be sent or delivered to the Upper Tribunal so that it is received within 3 months after the date on which the Upper Tribunal sent to the person making the application–

(a)   written notice of the decision;

(b)   notification of amended reasons for, or correction of, the decision following a review; or

(c)   notification that an application for the decision to be set aside has been unsuccessful.

44(3A)   An application under paragraph (1) in respect of a decision in an asylum case or an immigration case must be sent or delivered to the Upper Tribunal so that it is received within the appropriate period after the Upper Tribunal or, as the case may be in an asylum case, the Secretary of State for the Home Department, sent any of the documents in paragraph (3) to the party making the application.

44(3B)   The appropriate period referred to in paragraph (3A) is as follows–

(a)   where the person who appealed to the First-tier Tribunal is in the United Kingdom at the time that the application is made–

     (i)   twelve working days; or

     (ii)   if the party making the application is in detention under the Immigration Acts, seven working days; and

(b)   where the person who appealed to the First-tier Tribunal is outside the United Kingdom at the time that the application is made, thirty eight days.

44(3C)   Where a notice of decision is sent electronically or delivered personally, the time limits in paragraph (3B) are–

(a)   in sub-paragraph (a)(i), ten working days;

(b)   in sub-paragraph (a)(ii), five working days; and

(c)   in sub-paragraph (b), ten working days.

44(3D)   An application under paragraph (1) in respect of a decision in a financial services case must be sent or delivered to the Upper Tribunal so that it is received within 14 days after the date on which the Upper Tribunal sent to the person making the application–

(a)   written notice of the decision;

(b)   notification of amended reasons for, or correction of, the decision following a review; or

(c)   notification that an application for the decision to be set aside has been unsuccessful.

44(4)   Where paragraph (3), (3A), (3D) or (4C) does not apply, an application under paragraph (1) must be sent or delivered to the Upper Tribunal so that it is received within 1 month after the latest of the dates on which the Upper Tribunal sent to the person making the application–

(a)   written reasons for the decision;

(b)   notification of amended reasons for, or correction of, the decision following a review; or

(c)   notification that an application for the decision to be set aside has been unsuccessful.

44(4A)   Where a decision that disposes of immigration judicial review proceedings is given at a hearing, a party may apply at that hearing for permission to appeal, and the Upper Tribunal must consider at the hearing whether to give or refuse permission to appeal.

44(4B)   Where a decision that disposes of immigration judicial review proceedings is given at a hearing and no application for permission to appeal is made at that hearing–

(a)   the Upper Tribunal must nonetheless consider at the hearing whether to give or refuse permission to appeal; and

Statutory Instruments

(b)   if permission to appeal is given to a party, it shall be deemed for the purposes of section 13(4) of the 2007 Act to be given on application by that party.

44(4C)   Where a decision that disposes of immigration judicial review proceedings is given pursuant to rule 30 and the Upper Tribunal records under rule 30(4A) that the application is totally without merit, an application under paragraph (1) must be sent or delivered to the Upper Tribunal so that it is received within 7 days after the later of the dates on which the Upper Tribunal sent to the applicant–

(a)   written reasons for the decision; or

(b)   notification of amended reasons for, or correction of, the decision following a review.

44(5)   The date in paragraph (3)(c) or (4)(c) applies only if the application for the decision to be set aside was made within the time stipulated in rule 43 (setting aside a decision which disposes of proceedings) or any extension of that time granted by the Upper Tribunal.

44(6)   If the person seeking permission to appeal provides the application to the Upper Tribunal later than the time required by paragraph (3), (3A), (3D) or (4), or by any extension of time under rule 5(3)(a) (power to extend time)–

(a)   the application must include a request for an extension of time and the reason why the application notice was not provided in time; and

(b)   unless the Upper Tribunal extends time for the application under rule 5(3)(a) (power to extend time) the Upper Tribunal must refuse the application.

44(7)   An application under paragraph (1) or (4A)(a) must–

(a)   identify the decision of the Upper Tribunal to which it relates;

(b)   identify the alleged error or errors of law in the decision; and

(c)   state the result the party making the application is seeking.

History – In r. 44(1), the words "paragraphs (4A) and (4B)" substituted for the words "paragraph (4A)" by SI 2013/2067, r. 18(a), with effect from 1 November 2013.
In r. 44(1), the words "Subject to paragraph (4A)," inserted by SI 2012/2890, r. 3(a), with effect from 11 December 2012.
R. 44(2)(ba) inserted, and the "or" at the end of r. 44(2)(b) omitted, by SI 2009/274, r. 23, with effect from 1 April 2009.
R. 44(3A) inserted by SI 2010/44, r. 22(2), with effect from 15 February 2010.
In r. 44(3B)(a)(i), the words "twelve working days" substituted for the words "twelve days" by SI 2011/651, r. 8(4), with effect from 1 April 2011.
R. 44(3B) inserted by SI 2010/44, r. 22(2), with effect from 15 February 2010.
R. 44(3C) inserted by SI 2010/44, r. 22(2), with effect from 15 February 2010.
R. 44(3D) inserted by SI 2010/747, r. 10(a), with effect from 6 April 2010.
In r. 44(4), ", (3D) or (4C)" substituted for "or (3D)" by SI 2013/2067, r. 18(b), with effect from 1 November 2013.
In r. 44(4), ", (3A) or (3D)" substituted for "or (3A)" by SI 2010/747, r. 10(b), with effect from 6 April 2010.
In r. 44(4), "or (3A)" inserted by SI 2010/44, r. 22(3), with effect from 15 February 2010.
R. 44(4A)–(4C) substituted for (4A) by SI 2013/2067, r. 18(c), with effect from 1 November 2013. Former r. 44(4A) read as follows:

> "**44(4A)**   Where, in judicial review proceedings in the Immigration and Asylum Chamber of the Upper Tribunal, a decision is given orally at a hearing, a person may apply to the Tribunal for permission to appeal–
> (a)   orally at that hearing; or
> (b)   in writing, before the commencement or the expiry of the relevant period determined by reference to paragraph (4).".

R. 44(4A) inserted by SI 2012/2890, r. 3(b), with effect from 11 December 2012.
In r. 44(6), ", (3D)" inserted by SI 2010/747, r. 10(c), with effect from 6 April 2010.
In r. 44(6), ", (3A)" inserted by SI 2010/44, r. 22(4), with effect from 15 February 2010.
In r. 44(7), the word "Upper" inserted by SI 2013/2067, r. 18(d), with effect from 1 November 2013.
In r. 44(7), the words "or (4A)(a)" inserted by SI 2012/2890, r. 3(c), with effect from 11 December 2012.

UPPER TRIBUNAL'S CONSIDERATION OF APPLICATION FOR PERMISSION TO APPEAL

45(1)   On receiving an application for permission to appeal the Upper Tribunal may review the decision in accordance with rule 46 (review of a decision), but may only do so if–

(a)   when making the decision the Upper Tribunal overlooked a legislative provision or binding authority which could have had a material effect on the decision; or

(b)   since the Upper Tribunal's decision, a court has made a decision which is binding on the Upper Tribunal and which, had it been made before the Upper Tribunal's decision, could have had a material effect on the decision.

45(2)   If the Upper Tribunal decides not to review the decision, or reviews the decision and decides to take no action in relation to the decision or part of it, the Upper Tribunal must consider whether to give permission to appeal in relation to the decision or that part of it.

45(3)   The Upper Tribunal must provide a record of its decision to the parties as soon as practicable.

45(4)   If the Upper Tribunal refuses permission to appeal it must provide with the record of its decision–

(a)   a statement of its reasons for such refusal; and

(b)   notification of the right to make an application to the relevant appellate court for permission to appeal and the time within which, and the method by which, such application must be made.

45(5)   The Upper Tribunal may give permission to appeal on limited grounds, but must comply with paragraph (4) in relation to any grounds on which it has refused permission.

History – In r. 45(3) and (4), the word "provide" substituted for the word "send" by SI 2013/2067, r. 19, with effect from 1 November 2013.

REVIEW OF A DECISION

46(1)   The Upper Tribunal may only undertake a review of a decision pursuant to rule 45(1) (review on an application for permission to appeal).

46(2)   The Upper Tribunal must notify the parties in writing of the outcome of any review and of any rights of review or appeal in relation to the outcome.

46(3)   If the Upper Tribunal decides to take any action in relation to a decision following a review without first giving every party an opportunity to make representations, the notice under paragraph (2) must state that any party that did not have an opportunity to make representations may apply for such action to be set aside and for the decision to be reviewed again.

History – R. 46(1) substituted by SI 2011/2343, r. 12, with effect from 17 October 2011.

SETTING ASIDE A DECISION IN PROCEEDINGS UNDER THE FORFEITURE ACT 1982

47(1)   A person who referred a question to the Upper Tribunal under rule 26 (references under the Forfeiture Act 1982) must refer the Upper Tribunal's previous decision in relation to the question to the Upper Tribunal if they–

(a)   consider that the decision should be set aside and re-made under this rule; or

(b)   have received a written application for the decision to be set aside and re-made under this rule from the person to whom the decision related.

47(2)   The Upper Tribunal may set aside the decision, either in whole or in part, and re-make it if–

(a)   [omitted by SI 2011/2343, r. 13(e);]

(b)   the decision was made in ignorance of, or was based on a mistake as to, some material fact; or

(c)   there has been a relevant change in circumstances since the decision was made.

47(3)   Rule 26(2) to (4), Parts 5 and 6 and this Part apply to a reference under this rule as they apply to a reference under rule 26(1).

History – In the heading, the words "Setting aside" substituted for the words "Review of" by SI 2011/2343, r. 13(a), with effect from 17 October 2011.
In r. 47(1)(a), the words "set aside and re-made under this rule" substituted for the word "reviewed" by SI 2011/2343, r. 13(b), with effect from 17 October 2011.
In r. 47(1)(b), the words "set aside and re-made under this rule" substituted for the word "reviewed" by SI 2011/2343, r. 13(c), with effect from 17 October 2011.
In r. 47(2), the words "set aside the decision, either in whole or in part, and re-make it" substituted for the words "review the decision" by SI 2011/2343, r. 13(d), with effect from 17 October 2011.
R. 47(2)(a), omitted by SI 2011/2343, r. 13(e), with effect from 17 October 2011.
R. 47(3) substituted for (3) to (5), by SI 2011/2343, r. 13(f), with effect from 17 October 2011.

POWER TO TREAT AN APPLICATION AS A DIFFERENT TYPE OF APPLICATION

48   The Upper Tribunal may treat an application for a decision to be corrected, set aside or reviewed, or for permission to appeal against a decision, as an application for any other one of those things.

History – In r. 48, the word "Upper" inserted by SI 2013/2067, r. 20, with effect from 1 November 2013.
R. 48 inserted by SI 2010/2653, r. 8(2), with effect from 29 November 2010.

SCHEDULES

SCHEDULE 1 – PROCEDURE AFTER THE NOTICE OF APPEAL IN ROAD TRANSPORT CASES

Rule 24(1)

History – In the heading, the words "road transport cases" substituted for the words "appeals against decisions of traffic commissioners" by SI 2012/1363, r. 9(a), with effect from 1 July 2012.
Sch. 1 inserted by SI 2009/1975, r. 22, with effect from 1 September 2009.

1   This Schedule applies to road transport cases.

2 The only parties to the appeal are the appellant and any person added as a party under rule 9 (addition, substitution and removal of parties).

History – In para. 1, the words "road transport cases" substituted for the words "an appeal against the decision of a traffic commissioner" by SI 2012/1363, r. 9(b), with effect from 1 July 2012.

In para. 2, the words "(addition, substitution and removal of parties)" substituted for the words "(substitution and addition of parties)" by SI 2010/747, r. 11, with effect from 6 April 2010.

3 On receipt of a copy of a notice of appeal under rule 23(6)(b), the decision maker must send to the Upper Tribunal a copy (and, on request, further copies) of–

(a)   a written record of the decision appealed against and reasons for the decision;

(b)   all documents produced to the decision maker in connection with the decision;

(c)   if a public inquiry was held, the transcript of the inquiry or, if no such transcript was produced, the decision maker's note of the inquiry; and

(d)   in an appeal under–

     (i)   section 50 of the Public Passenger Vehicles Act 1981 or section 37 of the Goods Vehicles (Licensing of Operators) Act 1995, or

     (ii)   section 35 of the Goods Vehicles (Licensing of Operators) Act (Northern Ireland) 2010,

a list of the names and addresses of objectors and representors.

History – In para. 3, the words "decision maker" substituted for the words "traffic commissioner" and the words "decision maker's" substituted for the words "traffic commissioner's" by SI 2012/1363, r. 9(c), with effect from 1 July 2012. Para. 3(d) substituted by SI 2012/1363, r. 9(d), with effect from 1 July 2012.

4 On receipt of a list under paragraph 3(d) the Upper Tribunal must send a copy of the notice of appeal–

(a)   where the appellant had applied for, or for the variation of, an operator's licence, to each person who made an objection to the application;

(b)   where the appellant had made an objection to an application for, or (in the case of a goods vehicle operator's licence) for the variation of, an operator's licence, to the person who made the application and to every other person who made an objection to the application;

(c)   in an appeal under section 37(5) of the Goods Vehicles (Licensing of Operators) Act 1995, to each person who made representations under section 12(4) or 19(2) of that Act against the application for, or for the variation of, the operator's licence in question.

(d)   in an appeal under section 35(5) of the Goods Vehicles (Licensing of Operators) Act (Northern Ireland) 2010, to each person who made representations under section 11(4) or 18(2) of that Act.

History – In para. 4(b), the word "and" omitted by SI 2012/1363, r. 9(e)(i), with effect from 1 July 2012.

In para. 4(c) the word "to" inserted by SI 2013/477, r. 57(a) with effect from 1 April 2013.

In para. 4(c), the word "to" before "each" inserted by SI 2012/1363, r. 9(e)(i), with effect from 1 July 2012. Note: the destination for the insertion of the word "to" is stated in r. 9(e)(i) as para. 4(b). It is assumed that this is a drafting error and that the insertion of the word "to" was intended for para. 4(c).

Para. 4(d) inserted by SI 2012/1363, r. 9(e)(ii), with effect from 1 July 2012.

5 The appropriate national authority and any person to whom the Upper Tribunal has sent a copy of the notice of appeal under paragraph 4 may apply for a direction under rule 9(2) adding them as a respondent.

6 An application under paragraph 5 must be sent or delivered to the Upper Tribunal so that it is received within 14 days of the date that the Upper Tribunal sent a copy of the notice of appeal to the person making the application.

7 If a person makes an application in accordance with paragraphs 5 and 6, the Upper Tribunal must give a direction under rule 9(2) adding that person as a respondent.

History – In para. 7 the words "specified in paragraph 8" omitted by SI 2013/477, r. 57(b) with effect from 1 April 2013.

8 [Omitted by SI 2013/477, r. 57(b).]

History – Para. 8 omitted by SI 2013/477, r. 57(c) with effect from 1 April 2013. Former para. 8 read as follows:

"**8**   The persons specified for the purposes of paragraph 7 are–

     (a)   the appropriate national authority;

     (b)   an objector who was sent a copy of the notice of appeal under paragraph 4(a) or (b); and

     (c)   a person who made an application and was sent a copy of the notice of appeal under paragraph 4(b)."

9 The Upper Tribunal must notify each other party of any application under paragraph 3 and the Upper Tribunal's decision in respect of each such application.

10 Any party may make a request to the Upper Tribunal for copies of specified documents provided by the decision maker under paragraph 3.

History – In para. 10, the words "decision maker" substituted for the words "traffic commissioner" by SI 2012/1363, r. 9(f), with effect from 1 July 2012.

11 On receiving a request under paragraph 9 the Upper Tribunal–

(a)   must provide the requested copies unless it considers the request unreasonable; and

(b)   if it considers the request unreasonable, give details of why it considers the request unreasonable.

SCHEDULE 2 – ADDITIONAL PROCEDURE IN NATIONAL SECURITY CERTIFICATE CASES

Rule 26A(4)

History – Sch. 2 inserted by SI 2010/43, r. 14, with effect from 18 January 2010.

1   This Schedule applies only to national security certificate appeals.

2   Following the transfer of the appeal from the First-tier Tribunal, the Upper Tribunal must provide a copy of the notice of appeal to the respondent, the relevant Minister and the Information Commissioner.

3   The relevant Minister must send or deliver to the Upper Tribunal a copy of the certificate to which the appeal relates, and a response to the notice of appeal, not later than 42 days after the date on which the relevant Minister received a copy of the notice of appeal.

4   In an appeal under section 28(4) of the Data Protection Act 1998 or section 60(1) of the Freedom of Information Act 2000 (including that subsection as applied and modified by regulation 18 of the Environmental Information Regulations 2004), the relevant Minister's response must state whether the relevant Minister intends to oppose the appeal and, if so set out–

(a)   a summary of the circumstances relating to the issue of the certificate;

(b)   the reason for the issue of the certificate;

(c)   the grounds on which the relevant Minister relies in opposing the appeal; and

(d)   a statement of the evidence on which the relevant Minister relies in support of those grounds.

5   In an appeal under section 28(6) of the Data Protection Act 1998 or section 60(4) of the Freedom of Information Act 2000 (including that subsection as applied and modified by regulation 18 of the Environmental Information Regulations 2004), the relevant Minister's response must state whether the relevant Minister intends to make representations in relation to the appeal and, if so set out–

(a)   the extent to which the relevant Minister intends to support or oppose the appeal;

(b)   the grounds on which the relevant Minister relies in supporting or opposing the appeal; and

(c)   a statement of the evidence on which the relevant Minister relies in support of those grounds.

6   The Upper Tribunal must–

(a)   subject to paragraph 11, provide the relevant Minister's response and any other response to the appellant, the Information Commissioner and any respondent; and

(b)   send a copy of any other response to the relevant Minister.

7   On grounds of the need to ensure that information is not disclosed contrary to the interests of national security, the relevant Minister may–

(a)   object to the disclosure of the relevant Minister's response to the appellant, the Information Commissioner or any respondent, by sending a notice to the Upper Tribunal with the response; or

(b)   object to the disclosure of any other response to the Information Commissioner or any respondent, by sending a notice to the Upper Tribunal within 42 days of the date on which the relevant Minister received a copy of the response.

8   A notice under paragraph 7 must–

(a)   state the reason for the objection; and

(b)   in the case of a notice under paragraph 7(a) and to the extent that it is possible to do so, be accompanied by a version of the relevant Minister's response in a form that can be shown to the appellant, the Commissioner or, as the case may be, a respondent

9   Before the Upper Tribunal gives a direction, issues a summons or citation, or produces or publishes a written record of, or reasons for, a decision–

(a)   the Upper Tribunal must notify the relevant Minister of the proposed action; and

(b)   if the relevant Minister considers that the proposal would cause information that is or would be exempt by virtue of a provision in Part 2 of the Freedom of Information Act 2000 to be disclosed, the relevant Minister may object to the proposal by sending a notice to the Upper Tribunal so that the Upper Tribunal receives the notice within 14 days of the date that the Minister received notice of the proposal.

History – In para. 9(b), the words "so that the Upper Tribunal receives the notice within 14 days of the date that the Minister received notice of the proposal" inserted by SI 2010/747, r. 12, with effect from 6 April 2010.

Statutory Instruments

10 When deciding whether to uphold an objection made by the relevant Minister–

(a) any hearing must take place in the absence of the parties;

(b) if the Upper Tribunal is minded to overrule the relevant Minister's objection, or to require the relevant Minister to provide a version of the relevant Minister's response in a form other than one provided under paragraph 8(b) above, the Upper Tribunal must invite the relevant Minister to make representations; and

(c) if the Upper Tribunal overrules an objection in relation to the disclosure of a response, the Upper Tribunal must not disclose, or require the relevant Minister to disclose, any material the subject of the objection unless the relevant Minister relies upon that material in opposing the appeal.

History – In para. 10(c), the word "Upper" inserted before the words "Tribunal must" by SI 2013/2067, r. 21(a), with effect from 1 November 2013.

11 Where the relevant Minister may object to the disclosure of a response or proposed action by the Upper Tribunal, the Upper Tribunal may not proceed with that disclosure or that proposed action unless–

(a) the time for the relevant Minister to object has expired; and

(b) the relevant Minister has not objected, or the Upper Tribunal has overruled the relevant Minister's objection and, in the case of the disclosure of a response, may proceed with the disclosure under paragraph 10(c).

History – In para. 11(b), the word "Upper" inserted by SI 2013/2067, r. 21(b), with effect from 1 November 2013.

SCHEDULE 3 – PROCEDURE IN FINANCIAL SERVICES CASES AND WHOLESALE ENERGY CASES

Rule 26B

History – In Sch. 3 heading, the words "and Wholesale Energy Cases" inserted by SI 2014/514, r. 12, with effect from 6 April 2014.
Sch. 3 inserted by SI 2010/747, r. 13, with effect from 6 April 2010.

INTERPRETATION

1 In this Schedule–

"further material" means–

(a) in a single regulator case, documents which–

   (i) were considered by the respondent in reaching or maintaining the decision to give the notice in respect of which the reference has been made; or

   (ii) were obtained by the respondent in connection with the matter to which that notice relates (whether they were obtained before or after giving the notice) but which were not considered by it in reaching or maintaining that decision;

   but does not include documents on which the respondent relies in support of the referred action;

(b) in a multiple regulator case–

   (i) in relation to a respondent who is the primary regulator, documents which–

      (aa) were considered by that regulator in reaching or maintaining its decision to give the notice in respect of which the reference has been made; or

      (bb) were obtained by that regulator in connection with the matter to which that notice relates (whether they were obtained before or after the notice was given) but which were not considered by that regulator in reaching or maintaining its decision;

   (ii) in relation to a respondent who is the secondary regulator, documents which–

      (aa) were considered by that regulator in reaching or maintaining its decision to take the secondary regulator action in relation to the notice in respect of which the reference has been made; or

      (bb) were obtained by that regulator in connection with the matter to which that notice relates (whether they were obtained before or after the notice was given) but which were not considered by that regulator in reaching or maintaining its decision;

   but does not include documents on which either the primary regulator or the secondary regulator relies;

"multiple regulator case" means a case where–

(a)   any of the Financial Conduct Authority, the Prudential Regulation Authority or the Bank of England has given the notice in respect of which the reference has been made; and

(b)   such notice stated that another of those regulators had decided to take one of the following actions–

     (i)   to refuse a consent where such consent is required under the 2000 Act;

     (ii)   to give a conditional consent under the 2000 Act; or

     (iii)   to direct another regulator to take an action or not to take an action under the 2000 Act;

"primary regulator" means, in a multiple regulator case, the regulator giving the notice;

"reference notice" means the written notice required in making a reference in a financial services case or a wholesale energy case;

"referred action" means–

(a)   in a single regulator case, the act (or proposed act) on the part of the respondent that gave rise to the reference; and

(b)   in a multiple regulator case, the act (or proposed act) on the part of the primary regulator that gave rise to the reference;

"secondary regulator action" means an action taken by a secondary regulator, as stated in the notice given by the primary regulator;

"secondary regulator" means, in a multiple regulator case, a regulator specified in the notice other than the primary regulator;

"single regulator case" means a case that is not a multiple regulator case;

"the 2000 Act" means the Financial Services and Markets Act 2000;

"the 2013 Regulations" means the Electricity and Gas (Market Integrity and Transparency) (Enforcement etc.) Regulations 2013;

"the 2013 (NI) Regulations" means the Electricity and Gas (Market Integrity and Transparency) (Enforcement etc.) Regulations (Northern Ireland) 2013.

History – In para. 1, in the definition of "reference notice", the words "or a wholesale energy case" inserted by SI 2014/514, r. 13(a), with effect from 6 April 2014.
In para. 1, the definitions of "the 2013 Regulations" and "the 2013 (NI) Regulations" inserted by SI 2014/514, r. 13(b), with effect from 6 April 2014.
In para. 1, definition of "further material" substituted by SI 2013/606, r. 2(4)(b), with effect from 1 April 2013.
In para. 1, definitions of "multiple regulator case", "primary regulator", "secondary regulator action", "secondary regulator" and "single regulator case" inserted by SI 2013/606, r. 2(4)(a), with effect from 1 April 2013.
In para. 1, definition of "referred action" substituted by SI 2013/606, r. 2(4)(c), with effect from 1 April 2013.

REFERENCE NOTICE

2(1)   A reference notice must be signed by or on behalf of the applicant and sent or delivered by the applicant to the Upper Tribunal.

2(2)   A reference notice must be received by the Upper Tribunal no later than 28 days after notice was given of the decision in respect of which the reference is made.

2(3)   The reference notice must state–

(a)   the name and address of the applicant;

(b)   the name and address of the applicant's representative (if any);

(c)   if no representative is named under sub-paragraph (b), an address where documents for the applicant may be sent or delivered; and

(d)   the issues that the applicant wishes the Upper Tribunal to consider.

2(4)   The applicant must send or deliver to the Upper Tribunal with the reference notice a copy of the notice of the decision in respect of which the reference has been made.

2(5)   At the same time the applicant must send a copy of the reference notice–

(a)   in a single regulator case, to the respondent; and

(b)   in a multiple regulator case, to each of the primary and secondary regulators.

History – Para. 2(5) substituted by SI 2013/606, r. 2(5), with effect from 1 April 2013.

Statutory Instruments

REGISTER OF REFERENCES AND DECISIONS

3(1) The Upper Tribunal must keep a register of references and decisions in financial services cases and wholesale energy cases.

3(2) The register must be open to inspection by any person without charge and at all reasonable hours.

3(3) The Upper Tribunal may direct that the register is not to include particulars of a reference if it is satisfied that it is necessary to do so having regard in particular to–

(a)   any unfairness to the applicant or, except as regards a reference in respect of a decision of the Prudential Regulation Authority, any prejudice to the interests of consumers that might otherwise result;

(b)   as regards a reference in respect of a decision of the Financial Conduct Authority, any detriment to the stability of the UK financial system;

(c)   as regards a reference in respect of a decision of the Prudential Regulation Authority, any prejudice to the safety and soundness of persons authorised by it, or where section 2C of the 2000 Act applies, any prejudice to securing the appropriate degree of protection for policy holders; or

(d)   as regards a reference under the 2013 Regulations or the 2013 (NI) Regulations any detriment to the stability of the wholesale energy market as defined in those Regulations.

3(4) Upon receiving a reference notice, the Upper Tribunal must–

(a)   subject to any direction given under sub-paragraph (3), enter particulars of the reference in the register; and

(b)   notify the parties either that it has done so or that it will not include particulars in the register, as the case may be.

3(5) In a multiple regulator case, notification under sub-paragraph (4)(b) must be given to each of the primary and secondary regulators.

History – In para. 3(1), the words "and wholesale energy cases" inserted by SI 2014/514, r. 13(c)(i), with effect from 6 April 2014. In para. 3(3), the words "in particular to" to the end, substituted by SI 2014/514, r. 13(c)(ii), with effect from 6 April 2014. Para. 3(5) inserted by SI 2013/606, r. 2(6), with effect from 1 April 2013.

RESPONDENT'S STATEMENT OF CASE IN A SINGLE REGULATOR CASE

4(1) The respondent in a single regulator case must send or deliver a written statement ("a statement of case") in support of the referred action so that it is received by the Upper Tribunal no later than 28 days after the day on which the respondent received from the Upper Tribunal the notification required by paragraph 3(4)(b).

4(2) The statement of case must–

(a)   identify the statutory provisions providing for the referred action;

(b)   state the reasons for the referred action; and

(c)   set out all the matters and facts upon which the respondent relies to support the referred action.

4(3) The respondent must provide with the statement of case a list of–

(a)   any documents on which the respondent relies in support of the referred action; and

(b)   any further material which in the opinion of the respondent might undermine the decision to take that action.

4(4) At the same time as it sends or delivers the statement of case, the respondent must send to the applicant a copy of the statement of case and of the list referred to in sub-paragraph (3).

History – Heading to para. 4 substituted by SI 2013/606, r. 2(7)(a), with effect from 1 April 2013. In para. 4(1), the words "in a single regulator case" inserted by SI 2013/606, r. 2(7)(b), with effect from 1 April 2013.

RESPONDENTS' STATEMENTS OF CASE IN A MULTIPLE REGULATOR CASE

4A(1) This paragraph applies in a multiple regulator case.

4A(2) The primary regulator must send or deliver either–

(a)   a written statement (a "statement of case") in support of the referred action; or

(b)   a written notification that it does not itself advance a case in support of the referred action,

so that it is received by the Upper Tribunal no later than 28 days after the day on which the primary regulator received from the Upper Tribunal the notification required by paragraph 3(4)(b).

4A(3) A primary regulator providing a written notification under sub-paragraph (2)(b) must send or deliver a copy to the secondary regulator and the applicant and upon so doing–

(a)   the primary regulator shall not be required to take further steps in the proceedings unless the Upper Tribunal gives a direction to the contrary under rule 6; and

(b)   the respondent shall be the secondary regulator unless the Upper Tribunal orders otherwise.

4A(4)   The secondary regulator must send or deliver a written statement ("a statement of case") in support of its decision to take the secondary regulator action so that it is received by the Upper Tribunal no later than 28 days after the day on which the secondary regulator received from the Upper Tribunal the notification required by paragraph 3(4)(b).

4A(5)   A statement of case must–

(a)   identify the statutory provisions providing for the referred action;

(b)   state the reasons in support for the referred action; and

(c)   set out all the matters and facts upon which the regulator relies to support the referred action.

4A(6)   A regulator must provide with the statement of case a list of–

(a)   all documents on which it relies in support of the referred action;

(b)   any further material which, in the opinion of the regulator, might undermine its decision to–

       (i)   in the case of a primary regulator; take the referred action; and

       (ii) in the case of a secondary regulator; take the secondary regulator action.

4A(7)   The primary regulator and the secondary regulator must send to the applicant and the other regulator a copy of any statement of case required by sub-paragraphs (2) and (4) above and of the list referred to in sub-paragraph (6).

History – Para. 4A inserted by SI 2013/606, r. 2(8), with effect from 1 April 2013.

APPLICANT'S REPLY

5(1)   The applicant must send or deliver a written reply so that it is received by the Upper Tribunal no later than 28 days after–

(a)   in a single regulator case, on the date on which the applicant received a copy of the statement of case;

(aa) in a multiple regulator case, on the first date on which the applicant was in receipt of all the statements and, where relevant, notifications required under paragraphs 4A(2) and 4A(4); or

(b)   if a respondent amends its statement of case, the date on which the applicant received a copy of the amended statement of case.

5(2)   The reply must–

(a)   state the grounds on which the applicant relies in the reference;

(b)   identify all matters contained in the respondent's statement of case (or, where applicable, respondents' statements of case) which are disputed by the applicant;

(c)   state the applicant's reasons for disputing them.

5(3)   The applicant must send with the reply a list of all the documents on which the applicant relies in support of his case.

5(4)   At the same time the applicant must send to all other parties a copy of the reply and of the list referred to in sub-paragraph (3).

5(5)   Where the primary regulator has provided a written notification under paragraph 4A(2)(b), if the applicant wishes the Tribunal to direct that further steps in the proceedings be taken by the primary regulator, an application must be made at the time of sending the reply.

History – Para. 5(1)(a) and (aa) substituted for (a) by SI 2013/606, r. 2(9)(a)(i), with effect from 1 April 2013.
In para. 5(1)(b), the words "a respondent" substituted for the words "the respondent" by SI 2013/606, r. 2(9)(a)(ii), with effect from 1 April 2013.
In para. 5(2)(b), the words "the respondent's statement of case (or, where applicable, respondents' statements of case)" substituted for the words "the statement of case" (and the "and" at the end omitted) by SI 2013/606, r. 2(9)(b), with effect from 1 April 2013.
In para. 5(4), the words "all other parties" substituted for the words "the respondent" by SI 2013/606, r. 2(9)(c), with effect from 1 April 2013.
Para. 5(5) inserted by SI 2013/606, r. 2(9)(d), with effect from 1 April 2013.

SECONDARY DISCLOSURE BY A RESPONDENT

6(1)   After the applicant's reply has been sent or delivered, if there is any further material which might reasonably be expected to assist the applicant's case as disclosed by the applicant's reply and which is not listed in the list (or lists) provided in accordance with paragraph 4(3) (or paragraph 4A(6) where applicable), the respondent (or the respondents) must send or deliver to the Upper Tribunal a list (or lists) of such further material.

Statutory Instruments

6(2) Any list required to be sent or delivered by sub-paragraph (1) must be sent or delivered so that it is received no later than 14 days after the day on which the respondent in question received the applicant's reply.

6(3) At the same time as it sends or delivers any list required by sub-paragraph (1) a respondent must send a copy to the applicant (and where applicable the other parties).

History – Heading to para. 6 substituted by SI 2013/606, r. 2(10)(a), with effect from 1 April 2013.
In para. 6(1), the words "(or lists)" (in both places), the words "(or paragraph 4A(6) where applicable)" and the words "(or the respondents)" inserted by SI 2013/606, r. 2(10)(b), with effect from 1 April 2013.
In para. 6(2), the words "in question" inserted by SI 2013/606, r. 2(10)(c), with effect from 1 April 2013.
In para. 6(3), the words "a respondent must send a copy to the applicant (and where applicable the other parties)" inserted by SI 2013/606, r. 2(10)(d), with effect from 1 April 2013.

EXCEPTIONS TO DISCLOSURE

7(1) A list provided in accordance with paragraph 4(3), 4A(6) or 6(1) need not include any document that relates to a case involving a person other than the applicant which was taken into account by the respondent providing the list in the applicant's case only for the purposes of comparison with other cases.

7(2) A list provided in accordance with paragraph 4(3), 4A(6), 5(3) or 6(1) need not include any document that is material the disclosure of which for the purposes of or in connection with any legal proceedings is prohibited by section 17 of the Regulation of Investigatory Powers Act 2000.

7(3) A list provided in accordance with paragraph 4(3), 4A(6), 5(3) or 6(1) need not include any document in respect of which an application has been or is being made under sub-paragraph (4).

7(4) A party may apply to the Upper Tribunal (without giving notice to any other party) for a direction authorising the party making the application not to include in the list required by paragraph 4(3), 4A(6), 5(3) or 6(1) a document on the ground that disclosure of the document–

(a) would not be in the public interest; or

(b) would not be fair, having regard to–

   (i) the likely significance of the document to the applicant in relation to the matter referred to the Upper Tribunal; and

   (ii) the potential prejudice to the commercial interests of a person other than the applicant which would be caused by disclosure of the document.

7(5) For the purpose of deciding an application by a party under sub-paragraph (4), the Upper Tribunal may–

(a) require the document to be produced to the Upper Tribunal together with a statement of the reasons why its inclusion in the list would–

   (i) in the case of an application under sub-paragraph (4)(a), not be in the public interest; or

   (ii) in the case of an application under sub-paragraph (4)(b), not be fair; and

(b) invite any other party to make representations.

7(6) If the Upper Tribunal refuses an application under sub-paragraph (4), it must direct the party–

(a) to revise its list so as to include the document; and

(b) to send or deliver a copy of the revised list to the Upper Tribunal and to any other party.

7(7) A party ("P") who has sent or delivered a list under paragraph 4(3), 4A(6), 5(3) or 6(1) must, upon the request of another party, provide that other party with a copy of any document which P has which is specified in the list, or make it available for inspection or copying, and if P does not have it, tell the other party where to the best of P's knowledge and belief it may be found.

7(8) A party who has sent or delivered a list under paragraph 4(3), 5(3) or 6(1) must, upon the request of another party, provide that other party with a copy of any document specified in the list or make any such document available to that party for inspection or copying.

7(9) In this paragraph **"protected item"** has the meaning provided by section 413 of the 2000 Act, section 311(2) of the Pensions Act 2004 or article 283(2) of the Pensions (Northern Ireland) Order 2005 or regulation 52(2) of the 2013 Regulations or regulation 51(2) of the 2013 (NI) Regulations.

History – In para. 7(1), the words ", 4A(6)" and the words "providing the list" inserted by SI 2013/606, r. 2(11)(a), with effect from 1 April 2013.
In para. 7(2), (3) and (4), the words ", 4A(6)" inserted by SI 2013/606, r. 2(11), with effect from 1 April 2013.
Para. 7(7) substituted by SI 2013/606, r. 2(11)(e), with effect from 1 April 2013.
In para. 7(9), the words "or regulation 52(2) of the 2013 Regulations or regulation 51(2) of the 2013 (NI) Regulations" inserted by SI 2014/514, r. 13(d), with effect from 6 April 2014.

SUBSEQUENT NOTICES IN RELATION TO THE REFERRED ACTION

8   Where, after a reference notice has been sent or delivered, a respondent gives the applicant any further, amended or supplementary notice in relation to the referred action, that respondent must without delay send or deliver a copy of that notice to the Upper Tribunal.

History – In para. 8, the words "a respondent" substituted for the words "the respondent" and the words "that respondent" substituted for the words "the respondent" by SI 2013/606, r. 2(12), with effect from 1 April 2013.

REFERENCES BY THIRD PARTIES

9(1)   In the case of any reference made by an applicant under section 393 of the 2000 Act, regulation 40 of the 2013 Regulations or regulation 40 of the 2013 (NI) Regulations (third party rights) these rules apply subject to the modifications set out in this paragraph.

9(2)   In this paragraph–

(a)   if the reference was made under section 393(9) of the 2000 Act, regulation 40(9) of the 2013 Regulations or regulation 40(9) of the 2013 (NI) Regulations (reference to the Upper Tribunal by a third party to whom a decision notice was copied), the notice of the decision in respect of which the reference has been made is the decision notice which was copied to the applicant by the respondent that gave the notice; and

(b)   if the reference was made under section 393(11) of the 2000 Act, regulation 40(11) of the 2013 Regulations or regulation 40(11) of the 2013 (NI) Regulations (reference to the Upper Tribunal by a third party who alleges that they were not given a copy of a decision notice), the notice of the decision in respect of which the reference has been made is the decision notice which the applicant alleges was not copied to them.

9(3)   If the reference was made under section 393(11) of the 2000 Act, regulation 40(11) of the 2013 Regulations or regulation 40(11) of the 2013 (NI) Regulations, paragraph 2(4) does not apply.

9(4)   The duties of a respondent to–

(a)   set out information under paragraphs 4(2), 4A(2), 4A(4) or 4A(5); or

(b)   list material under paragraphs 4(3), 4A(6) or 6(1);

apply only to information or material which relate to the matters referred to the Upper Tribunal in accordance with section 393(9) or (as the case may be) section 393(11) of the 2000 Act, regulation 40(9) or, as the case may be, regulation 40(11) of the 2013 Regulations, or regulation 40(9) or, as the case may be, regulation 40(11) of the 2013 (NI) Regulations.

History – In para. 9(1), the words ", regulation 40 of the 2013 Regulations or regulation 40 of the 2013 (NI) Regulations" inserted by SI 2014/514, r. 13(e)(i), with effect from 6 April 2014.
In para. 9(2)(a), the words ", regulation 40(9) of the 2013 Regulations or regulation 40(9) of the 2013 (NI) Regulations" inserted by SI 2014/514, r. 13(e)(ii), with effect from 6 April 2014.
In para. 9(2)(a), the words "that gave the notice" inserted by SI 2013/606, r. 2(13)(a), with effect from 1 April 2013.
In para. 9(2)(b), the words ", regulation 40(11) of the 2013 Regulations or regulation 40(11) of the 2013 (NI) Regulations" inserted by SI 2014/514, r. 13(e)(iii), with effect from 6 April 2014.
In para. 9(3), the words ", regulation 40(11) of the 2013 Regulations or regulation 40(11) of the 2013 (NI) Regulations" inserted by SI 2014/514, r. 13(e)(iv), with effect from 6 April 2014.
In para. 9(4), the words ", regulation 40(9) or, as the case may be, regulation 40(11) of the 2013 Regulations, or regulation 40(9) or, as the case may be, regulation 40(11) of the 2013 (NI) Regulations" inserted by SI 2014/514, r. 13(e)(v), with effect from 6 April 2014.
Para. 9(4) substituted by SI 2013/606, r. 2(13)(b), with effect from 1 April 2013.

TRANSFER OF TRIBUNAL FUNCTIONS ORDER 2008
(SI 2008/2833)

Made on 29 October 2008 by the Lord Chancellor in exercise of the powers conferred by s. 30(1) and (4), 31(1), (2) and (9), 32(3) and (5), 33(2) and (3), 34(2) and (3), 37(1), 38 and 145 of, and para. 30 of Sch. 5 to, the Tribunals, Courts and Enforcement Act 2007. Operative from 3 November 2008.

CITATION, COMMENCEMENT, INTERPRETATION AND EXTENT

1(1)　This Order may be cited as the Transfer of Tribunal Functions Order 2008 and comes into force on 3rd November 2008.

1(2)　A reference in this Order to a Schedule by a number alone is a reference to the Schedule so numbered in this Order.

1(3)　Subject as follows, this Order extends to England and Wales, Scotland and Northern Ireland.

1(4)　Except as provided by paragraph (5) or (6), an amendment, repeal or revocation of any enactment by any provision of Schedule 3 extends to the part or parts of the United Kingdom to which the enactment extends.

1(5)　[Not relevant to income tax, corporation tax or capital gains tax.]

1(6)　[Not relevant to income tax, corporation tax or capital gains tax.]

ADDITIONS TO THE LIST OF TRIBUNALS IN SCHEDULE 6

2　In Part 4 of Schedule 6 to the Tribunals, Courts and Enforcement Act 2007 (tribunals for the purposes of section 30), insert the following entries at the appropriate places–

[Inserts entries for "Claims Management Services Tribunal", for "Gender Recognition Panel", and for "Tribunal" (under ITA 2007, s. 704).]

MINOR, CONSEQUENTIAL AND TRANSITIONAL PROVISIONS

9(1)　Schedule 3 contains minor, consequential and supplemental amendments, and repeals and revocations as a consequence of those amendments.

9(2)　Schedule 4 contains transitional provisions.

SCHEDULE 3 – MINOR, CONSEQUENTIAL AND SUPPLEMENTAL PROVISIONS

Article 6

CHILD TRUST FUNDS ACT 2004

202(1)　Section 24 of the Child Trust Funds Act 2004 (temporary modifications) is amended as follows.

202(2)　In subsection (2)–

(a)　[amends CTFA 2004, s. 24(2),]

(b)　[amends CTFA 2004, s. 24(2),]

(c)　[amends CTFA 2004, s. 24(2).]

202(3)　In subsection (3)–

(a)　[amends CTFA 2004, s. 24(3),]

(b)　[amends CTFA 2004, s. 24(3).]

202(4)　[Amends CTFA 2004, s. 24(4).]

202(5)　In subsection (5)–

(a)　[amends CTFA 2004, s. 24(5),]

(b)　[amends CTFA 2004, s. 24(5).]

202(6)　[Substitutes CTFA 2004, s. 24(6).]

202(7)　[Amends CTFA 2004, s. 24(7).]

Statutory Instruments

SCHEDULE 4 – TRANSITIONAL PROVISIONS

Article 6

TRANSITIONAL PROVISIONS

1 Subject to article 3(3)(a) any proceedings before a tribunal listed in Table 1 of Schedule 1 which are pending immediately before 3rd November 2008 shall continue on and after 3rd November 2008 as proceedings before the First-tier Tribunal.

2 Subject to article 3(3)(b) any proceedings before a tribunal listed in Table 2 of Schedule 1 which are pending immediately before 3rd November 2008 shall continue on and after 3rd November 2008 as proceedings before the Upper Tribunal.

3(1) The following sub-paragraphs apply where proceedings are continued in the First-tier Tribunal or Upper Tribunal by virtue of paragraph 1 or 2.

3(2) Where a hearing began before 3rd November 2008 but was not completed by that date, the First-tier Tribunal or the Upper Tribunal, as the case may be, must be comprised for the continuation of that hearing of the person or persons who began it.

3(3) The First-tier Tribunal or Upper Tribunal, as the case may be, may give any direction to ensure that proceedings are dealt with fairly and, in particular, may–

(a)   apply any provision in procedural rules which applied to the proceedings before 3rd November 2008; or

(b)   disapply provisions of Tribunal Procedure Rules.

3(4) In sub-paragraph (3) "procedural rules" means provision (whether called rules or not) regulating practice or procedure before a tribunal.

3(5) Any direction or order given or made in proceedings which is in force immediately before 3rd November 2008 remains in force on and after that date as if it were a direction or order of the First-tier Tribunal or Upper Tribunal, as the case may be.

3(6) A time period which has started to run before 3rd November 2008 and which has not expired shall continue to apply.

3(7) An order for costs may only be made if, and to the extent that, an order could have been made before 3rd November 2008.

4 Subject to article 3(3)(a) and (b) where an appeal lies to a Child Support or Social Security Commissioner from any decision made before 3rd November 2008 by a tribunal listed in Table 1 of Schedule 1, section 11 of the 2007 Act (right to appeal to Upper Tribunal) shall apply as if the decision were a decision made on or after 3rd November 2008 by the First-tier Tribunal.

5 Subject to article 3(3)(b) where an appeal lies to a court from any decision made before 3rd November 2008 by a Child Support or Social Security Commissioner, section 13 of the 2007 Act (right to appeal to Court of Appeal etc.) shall apply as if the decision were a decision made on or after 3rd November 2008 by the Upper Tribunal.

6 Subject to article 3(3)(a) and (b) any case to be remitted by a court on or after 3rd November 2008 in relation to a tribunal listed in Schedule 1 shall be remitted to the First-tier Tribunal or Upper Tribunal as the case may be.

Statutory Instruments

APPEALS FROM THE UPPER TRIBUNAL TO THE COURT OF APPEAL ORDER 2008

(SI 2008/2834)

Made on 29 October 2008 by The Lord Chancellor in exercise of the power conferred by s. 13(6) of the Tribunals, Courts and Enforcement Act 2007. Operative in accordance with art. 1.

Cross references – The Tribunals (Scotland) Act 2014 prospectively creates a new structure for tribunals dealing with devolved matters under the judicial leadership of the Lord President of the Court of Session as head of the Scottish Tribunals including the creation of a first-tier tribunal and an upper tribunal.

1 This Order may be cited as the Appeals from the Upper Tribunal to the Court of Appeal Order 2008 and shall come into force on 3rd November 2008.

2 Permission to appeal to the Court of Appeal in England and Wales or leave to appeal to the Court of Appeal in Northern Ireland shall not be granted unless the Upper Tribunal or, where the Upper Tribunal refuses permission, the relevant appellate court, considers that–

(a)   the proposed appeal would raise some important point of principle or practice; or

(b)   there is some other compelling reason for the relevant appellate court to hear the appeal.

FIRST-TIER TRIBUNAL AND UPPER TRIBUNAL (COMPOSITION OF TRIBUNAL) ORDER 2008

(SI 2008/2835)

Made on 29 October 2008 by the Lord Chancellor in exercise of the powers conferred by s. 145(1) of, and para. 15 of Sch. 4 to, the Tribunals, Courts and Enforcement Act 2007. Operative from 3 November 2008.

Cross references – The Tribunals (Scotland) Act 2014 prospectively creates a new structure for tribunals dealing with devolved matters under the judicial leadership of the Lord President of the Court of Session as head of the Scottish Tribunals including the creation of a first-tier tribunal and an upper tribunal.

CITATION AND COMMENCEMENT

1 This Order may be cited as the First-tier Tribunal and Upper Tribunal (Composition of Tribunal) Order 2008 and comes into force on 3rd November 2008.

NUMBER OF MEMBERS OF THE FIRST-TIER TRIBUNAL

2(1) The number of members of the tribunal who are to decide any matter that falls to be decided by the First-tier Tribunal must be determined by the Senior President of Tribunals in accordance with paragraph (2).

2(2) The Senior President of Tribunals must have regard to–

(a)   where the matter which falls to be decided by the tribunal fell to a tribunal in a list in Schedule 6 to the Tribunals, Courts and Enforcement Act 2007 before its functions were transferred by order under section 30(1) of that Act, any provision made by or under any enactment for determining the number of members of that tribunal; and

(b)   the need for members of tribunals to have particular expertise, skills or knowledge.

NUMBER OF MEMBERS OF THE UPPER TRIBUNAL

3(1) The number of members of the tribunal who are to decide any matter that falls to be decided by the Upper Tribunal is one unless determined otherwise under paragraph (2).

3(2) The tribunal may consist of two or three members if the Senior President of Tribunals so determines.

TRIBUNAL CONSISTING OF SINGLE MEMBER

4(1) Where a matter is to be decided by a single member of a tribunal, it must be decided by a judge of the tribunal unless paragraph (2) applies.

4(2) The matter may be decided by one of the other members of the tribunal if the Senior President of Tribunals so determines.

TRIBUNAL CONSISTING OF TWO OR MORE MEMBERS

5 The following articles apply where a matter is to be decided by two or more members of a tribunal.

6 The number of members who are to be judges of the tribunal and the number of members who are to be other members of the tribunal must be determined by the Senior President of Tribunals.

7 The Senior President of Tribunals must select one of the members (the "presiding member") to chair the tribunal.

8 If the decision of the tribunal is not unanimous, the decision of the majority is the decision of the tribunal; and the presiding member has a casting vote if the votes are equally divided.

Statutory Instruments

AUTHORISED INVESTMENT FUNDS (TAX) (AMENDMENT NO. 3) REGULATIONS 2008

(SI 2008/3159, as amended by SI 2012/519)

Made on 10 December 2008 by the Treasury in exercise of the powers conferred by s. 17(3) and 18 of the Finance (No. 2) Act 2005. Operative from 1 January 2009.

CITATION, COMMENCEMENT AND EFFECT

1(1)   These Regulations may be cited as the Authorised Investment Funds (Tax) (Amendment No. 3) Regulations 2008 and shall come into force on 1st January 2009.

1(2)   In relation to a qualified investor scheme authorised by the Financial Services Authority before 1st January 2009, these regulations have effect subject to regulation 31.

1(3)   Regulation 27 of these Regulations (inserted regulations 69Z24A to 69Z24D) has effect in relation to manufactured dividends paid on or after 1st January 2009.

1(4)   Regulation 28 of these Regulations (amendment of regulation 94 of the principal Regulations) has effect in relation to property income distributions paid on or after 1st January 2009.

History – In reg. 1(2), the word "regulation" substituted for the words "regulations 30 and" by SI 2012/519, reg. 9(2), with effect in relation to accounting periods starting at or after 1.30 p.m. on 27 February 2012.

INTERPRETATION

2   In these Regulations–

"**qualified investor scheme**" has the same meaning as regulation 14B(4) (inserted by regulation 11 of these Regulations);

"**tax year**"–

(a)   in relation to income tax, means a year of assessment within the meaning of ICTA (see section 832(1) of that Act); and

(b)   in relation to capital gains tax, means a year of assessment within the meaning of TCGA 1992 (see section 288(1) of that Act);

"**the principal Regulations**" means the Authorised Investment Funds (Tax) Regulations 2006.

AMENDMENT OF THE PRINCIPAL REGULATIONS

3   The principal Regulations are amended as follows.

AMENDMENT OF REGULATION 2

4   [Amends SI 2006/964, reg. 2.]

AMENDMENT OF REGULATION 10

5   [Amends SI 2006/964, reg. 10.]

AMENDMENT OF REGULATION 11

6   [Amends SI 2006/964, reg. 11.]

AMENDMENT OF REGULATION 12

7   [Amends SI 2006/964, reg. 12.]

AMENDMENT OF REGULATION 13

8   [Amends SI 2006/964, reg. 13.]

AMENDMENT OF REGULATION 14

9   [Amends SI 2006/964, reg. 14.]

INSERTION OF REGULATION 14A

10   [Inserts SI 2006/964, reg. 14A.]

INSERTION OF PART 2A

11 [Inserts SI 2006/964, Pt. 2A.]

AMENDMENT OF REGULATION 24

12 [Amends SI 2006/964, reg. 24.]

AMENDMENT OF REGULATION 48

13(1) Regulation 48 (dividend distributions: general) is amended as follows.

13(2) [Amends SI 2006/964, reg. 48.]

13(3) [Amends SI 2006/964, reg. 48.]

13(4) [Inserts SI 2006/964, reg. 48(2A) and (2B).]

13(5) [Inserts SI 2006/964, reg. 48(4).]

AMENDMENT OF REGULATION 49

14 [Inserts SI 2006/964, reg. 49(2A).]

SUBSTITUTION OF REGULATION 51

15 [Substitutes SI 2006/964, reg. 51.]

SUBSTITUTION OF REGULATION 52A

16 [Substitutes SI 2006/964, reg. 52A.]

OMISSION OF CHAPTER 4 OF PART 4

17(1) [Omits SI 2006/964, Pt. 4, Ch. 4.]

17(2) Paragraph (1) is subject to regulation 31 of these Regulations.

History – In reg. 17(2), the word "regulation" substituted for the words "regulations 30 and" by SI 2012/519, reg. 9(3), with effect in relation to accounting periods starting at or after 1.30 p.m. on 27 February 2012.

INSERTION OF REGULATION 69DA

18 [Inserts SI 2006/964, reg. 69DA.]

AMENDMENT OF REGULATION 69G

19 [Amends SI 2006/964, reg. 69G.]

AMENDMENT OF REGULATION 69J

20 [Amends SI 2006/964, reg. 69J.]

AMENDMENT OF REGULATION 69K

21 In paragraph (4) of regulation 69K (the corporate ownership condition), for "shareholder" substitute "participant".

AMENDMENT OF REGULATION 69L

22(1) Regulation 69L (the corporate ownership condition: further provisions) is amended as follows.

22(2) [Amends SI 2006/964, reg. 69L(2)(a).]

22(3) [Amends SI 2006/964, reg. 69L(5).]

AMENDMENT OF REGULATION 69Z

23 [Amends SI 2006/964, reg. 69Z(1).]

AMENDMENT OF REGULATION 69Z19

24 [Substitutes SI 2006/964, reg. 69Z19(1).]

AMENDMENT OF REGULATION 69Z23

25 Regulation 69Z23 (deduction of tax from PAIF distributions (interest)) is amended as follows–

(a)   [Amends SI 2006/964, reg. 69Z23(1).]

(b)   [Omits SI 2006/964, reg. 69Z23(3).]

AMENDMENT OF REGULATION 69Z24

26 Regulation 69Z24 (distribution payments to be made without deduction of tax) is amended as follows–

(a)   [Amends SI 2006/964, reg. 69Z24(1).]

(b)   [Inserts SI 2006/964, reg. 69Z24(3A) and (3B).]

INSERTION OF REGULATIONS 69Z24A TO 69Z24D

27 [Inserts SI 2006/964, reg. 69Z24A to 69Z24D.]

AMENDMENT OF REGULATION 94

28 [Inserts SI 2006/964, reg. 94(4A).]

AMENDMENTS TO PART 2 OF THE SCHEDULE

29 In Part 2 of the Schedule (index of expressions defined or otherwise explained in these regulations)–

(a)   omit the entries in the index for the following expressions–

(i)   [Omits entries for: "Chargeable measuring date (in Chapter 4 of Part 4)"; "Difference in value (in Chapter 4 of Part 4)"; "Disposal (in Chapter 4 of Part 4)"; "Earlier measuring value (in Chapter 4 of Part 4)"; "First measuring value (in Chapter 4 of Part 4)"; "Later measuring value (in Chapter 4 of Part 4)"; "Market value (in Chapter 4 of Part 4)"; "Measuring date (in Chapter 4 of Part 4)"; and "Substantial QIS holding (in Chapter 4 of Part 4)".]

(b)   [Amends the entry relating to "Qualified investor scheme".]

(c)   [Inserts the entry relating to "instrument constituting the scheme".]

TRANSITORY PROVISION

Schemes authorised before 1st January 2009 – genuine diversity of ownership condition

30 [Omitted by SI 2012/519, reg. 9(4).]

History – Reg. 30 omitted by SI 2012/519, reg. 9(4), with effect in relation to accounting periods starting at or after 1.30 p.m. on 27 February 2012. Former reg. 30 read as follows:

"**30** Where a qualified investor scheme is authorised by the Financial Services Authority before 1st January 2009, the scheme shall be deemed to have met the genuine diversity of ownership condition in the inserted regulation 14C (regulation 11 of these Regulations) for the period–
(a)   beginning on 1st January 2009; and
(b)   ending on the date on which the scheme's first accounting period beginning on or after 1st January 2009 ends.".

Schemes authorised before 1st January 2009 - continuation of provisions in Chapter 4 of Part 4 of the principal Regulations

31(1) Regulations 55 (amount charged to tax under this Chapter) and 56 (measuring date and meaning of "chargeable measuring date") continue to have effect in relation to qualified investor schemes authorised by the Financial Services Authority before 1st January 2009, with the amendments specified in this regulation.

31(2) For paragraph (1) of regulation 55 substitute–

"**55(1)** A participant in a qualified investor scheme authorised by the Financial Services Authority before 1st January 2009 is charged to tax under Chapter 4 of Part 4 by reference to the difference in value of a substantial QIS holding between the two measuring dates specified in regulation 56 ("the difference in value")."

31(3) For paragraph (1) of regulation 56 substitute–

"**56(1)** For the purposes of regulation 55–

(a)   the earlier measuring date is the date that was the later measuring date on the last occasion that the value was calculated in accordance with this Chapter; and

(b)   the later measuring date is 31st December 2008.".

31(4) For the purposes of regulations 55 and 56 (as amended by this regulation), the remaining provisions of Chapter 4 of Part 4 of the principal Regulations continue to have effect.

AMENDMENT OF REGULATION 69ZZA

25 Regulation 69ZZA (deduction of tax from PAIF distributions (interest)) is amended as follows—

(a) [Amends SI 2006/964, reg. 69ZZA(1).]

(b) [Omits SI 2006/964, reg. 69ZZA(3).]

AMENDMENT OF REGULATION 69ZZB

26 Regulation 69ZZB (distribution payments to be made without deduction of tax) is amended as follows—

(a) [Amends SI 2006/964, reg. 69ZZB(1).]

(b) [Inserts SI 2006/964, reg. 69ZZB(3A) and (3B).]

INSERTION OF REGULATIONS 69ZZBA TO 69ZZBD

27 [Inserts SI 2006/964 reg. 69ZZBA to 69ZZBD.]

AMENDMENT OF REGULATION 94

28 [Inserts SI 2006/964 reg. 94(4A).]

AMENDMENTS TO PART 2 OF THE SCHEDULE

29 In Part 2 of the Schedule (index of expressions defined or otherwise explained in these regulations)—

(a) omit the entries in the index for the following expressions—

(i) [Omits entries for: "Chargeable measuring date (in Chapter 4 of Part 4)"; "Difference in value (in Chapter 4 of Part 4)"; "Disposal (in Chapter 4 of Part 4)"; "Earlier measuring value (in Chapter 4 of Part 4)"; "First measuring value (in Chapter 4 of Part 4)"; "Later measuring value (in Chapter 4 of Part 4)"; "Market value (in Chapter 4 of Part 4)"; "Measuring date (in Chapter 4 of Part 4)"; and "Substantial QIS holding (in Chapter 4 of Part 4)".]

(b) [Amends the entry relating to "Qualified investor scheme".]

(c) [Inserts the entry relating to "instrument constituting the scheme".]

TRANSITORY PROVISION

Schemes authorised before 1st January 2009 – genuine diversity of ownership condition

30 [Omitted by SI 2012/519, reg 9(4).]

History – Reg. 30 omitted by SI 2012/519, reg. 9(4), with effect in relation to accounting periods starting or in effect at 30 p.m. on 27 February 2012. Former reg. 30 read as follows:

"30 Where a qualified investor scheme is authorised by the Financial Services Authority before 1st January 2009, the scheme shall be deemed to have met the genuine diversity of ownership condition in the intended regulation 14C (regulation 11) of these Regulations), for the period—

(a) beginning on 1st January 2009; and

(b) ending on the date on which the scheme's first accounting period beginning on or after 1st January 2009 ends.

Schemes authorised before 1st January 2009 – continuation of provisions in Chapter 4 of Part 4 of the principal Regulations

31(1) Regulations 55 (amount charged to tax under this Chapter) and 56 (measuring date and meaning of "chargeable measuring date") continue to have effect in relation to qualified investor schemes authorised by the Financial Services Authority before 1st January 2009, with the amendments specified in this regulation.

31(2) For paragraph (1) of regulation 55 substitute—

"55(1) A participant in a qualified investor scheme authorised by the Financial Services Authority before 1st January 2009 is charged to tax under Chapter 4 of Part 4 by reference to the difference in value of a substantial QIS holding between the two measuring dates specified in regulation 56 ("the difference in value").

31(3) For paragraph (1) of regulation 56 substitute—

"56(1) For the purposes of regulation 55—

(a) the earlier measuring date is the date that was the later measuring date on the last occasion that the value was calculated in accordance with this Chapter; and

(b) the later measuring date is 31st December 2008.".

31(4) For the purposes of regulations 55 and 56 (as amended by this regulation), the remaining provisions of Chapter 4 of Part 4 of the principal Regulations continue to have effect.

INVESTMENT MANAGER (SPECIFIED TRANSACTIONS) REGULATIONS 2009

(2009/May)

Made by the Commissioners for Her Majesty's Revenue and Customs in exercise of the powers conferred on them by s. 127(12) and (13) of the Finance Act 1995, para. 3(3) and (4) of Sch. 26 to the Finance Act 2003 and s. 827(2) and (3) of the Income Tax Act 2007.

CITATION, COMMENCEMENT AND EFFECT

1(1)   These Regulations may be cited as the Investment Manager (Specified Transactions) Regulations 2009 and come into force on 12 May 2009.

1(2)   These Regulations have effect–

(a)   for income tax purposes for the tax year 2009–10 and subsequent tax years; and

(b)   for corporation tax purposes in relation to accounting periods ending on or after 12 May 2009.

INTERPRETATION

2   In these Regulations–

"**loan relationship**" has the meaning given by regulation 7; and

"**non-resident person**" means a person who is not resident in the United Kingdom.

SPECIFIED TRANSACTIONS

3   Any transaction falling within any of regulations 4 to 6 and 8 to 11 is of a description specified for the purposes of–

(a)   section 127 of the Finance Act 1995 (persons not treated as UK representatives);

(b)   paragraph 3 of Schedule 26 to the Finance Act 2003 (investment managers); and

(c)   section 827 of the Income Tax Act 2007 (meaning of "investment manager" and "investment transaction").

TRANSACTIONS IN STOCKS OR SHARES

4   Any transaction in stocks or shares falls within this regulation.

TRANSACTIONS IN RELEVANT CONTRACTS

5(1)   Any transaction in a relevant contract falls within this regulation.

5(2)   For the purposes of this regulation a "**relevant contract**" is–

(a)   an option;

(b)   a future; or

(c)   a contract for differences.

5(3)   For the purposes of paragraph (2) an "**option**" includes an instrument which entitles the holder to subscribe for shares in a company or assets representing a loan relationship of a company; and for these purposes it is immaterial whether the shares or assets to which the instrument relates exist or are identifiable.

5(4)   For the purposes of paragraph (3) the reference to a loan relationship of a company is to be construed in accordance with regulation 7 but with references in that regulation to "the non-resident person" treated as references to the company.

5(5)   For the purposes of paragraph (2) a "**future**" is a contract for the sale of property under which delivery is to be made–

(a)   at a future date agreed when the contract is made, and

(b)   at a price so agreed.

5(6)   For the purposes of paragraph (5)(b) a price is taken to be agreed when the contract is made–

(a)   notwithstanding that the price is left to be determined by reference to the price at which a contract is to be entered into on a market or exchange or could be entered into at a time and place specified in the contract; or

(b)   in a case where the contract is expressed to be by reference to a standard lot and quality notwithstanding that provision is made for a variation in the price to take account of any variation in quantity or quality on delivery.

5(7)   For the purposes of paragraph (2) and (5) references to an option or a future do not include references to a contract whose terms provide–

(a)   that, after setting off their obligations to each other under the contract, a cash payment is to be made by one party to the other in respect of the excess, if any, and do not provide for the delivery of any property;

(b)   that each party is liable to make to the other party a cash payment in respect of all that party's obligations to the other under the contract and do not provide for the delivery of any property; or

(c)   for the delivery of any property other than property a transaction in which would fall within any of regulations 4 to 6 and 8 to 11 of these Regulations where the property is delivered.

Nothing in this paragraph has effect to exclude from references to an option or a future, an option or a future whose underlying subject matter is currency.

5(8)   In paragraph (7) **"underlying subject matter"** means–

(a)   in relation to an option, the property which would fall to be delivered if the option were exercised, and

(b)   in relation to a future, the property which, if the future were to run to delivery, would fall to be delivered at the date and price agreed when the contract is made.

5(9)   For the purposes of paragraph (2) **"a contract for differences"** is a contract the purpose or pretended purpose of which is to make a profit or avoid a loss by reference to fluctuations in–

(a)   the value or price of property described in the contract, or

(b)   an index or other factor designated in the contract.

5(10)   For the purposes of paragraph (9)(b) an index or other factor may be determined by reference to any matter and, for these purposes, a numerical value may be attributed to any variation in a matter.

5(11)   For the purposes of paragraph (2) none of the following is a contract for differences–

(a)   an option;

(b)   a future;

(c)   a contract of insurance;

(d)   a contract effected in the course of capital redemption business;

(e)   a contract of indemnity;

(f)   a guarantee;

(g)   a warranty;

(h)   a loan relationship.

5(12)   For the purposes of paragraph (11)–

(a)   **"capital redemption business"** means any business of a company carrying on insurance business in so far as it consists of the effecting on the basis of actuarial calculations, and the carrying out, of contracts under which, in return for one or more fixed payments, a sum or series of sums of a specified amount become payable at a future time or over a period; and

(b)   **"loan relationship"** is to be construed in accordance with regulation 8 but with references to **"the non-resident person"** in that regulation treated as including references to a UK resident company.

5(13)   For the purposes of this regulation where an option, a future or a contract for differences relates to land , such option, future or contract for differences will not be a relevant contract except in cases where the option, the future or the contract for differences uses an index referred to in paragraph (9)(b) and the index is–

(a)   publicly accessible;

(b)   comprised of a significant number of properties; and

(c)   not maintained by–

    (i)   the non-resident person;

    (ii)   the investment manager of the non-resident person; or

    (iii)   a person or persons connected with the non-resident person or the investment manager of the non-resident person.

5(14) In paragraph (13) **"investment manager"** means a person providing investment or asset management services in the United Kingdom to a non-resident person.

5(15) For the purposes of this regulation–

(a)   sections 993 and 994 of the Income Tax Act 2007 (connected persons and the meaning of control) apply in the case of a person chargeable to income tax; and

(b)   section 839 of the Income and Corporation Taxes Act 1988 (connected persons and the meaning of control) apply in the case of a person chargeable to corporation tax.

TRANSACTIONS INVOLVING LOAN RELATIONSHIPS OR RELATED TRANSACTIONS

6   Any transaction which results in a non-resident person becoming a party to a loan relationship or a related transaction in respect of a loan relationship falls within this regulation.

LOAN RELATIONSHIPS: SUPPLEMENTAL PROVISIONS

7(1)   For the purposes of regulation 7 a non-resident person has a **"loan relationship"** where that person stands (whether by reference to a security or otherwise) in the position of a creditor or debtor as respects any money debt and either–

(a)   that debt is one arising from a transaction for the lending of money; or

(b)   that debt is not one which arose from a transaction for the lending of money but is one–

     (i)   on which interest is payable to or by the non-resident person;

     (ii)   in relation to which exchange gains or losses arise to the non-resident person; or

     (iii)   as respects which the conditions in paragraph (2) are satisfied.

7(2)   The conditions referred to in paragraph (1)(b)(iii) are that–

(a)   the non-resident person stands in the position of creditor in relation to the money debt; and

(b)   the money debt is one from which a discount (whether of an income or capital nature) arises to the non-resident.

7(3)   In this regulation **"exchange gains or losses"** means–

(a)   profits or gains, or

(b)   losses,

which arise as a result of comparing at different times the expression in one currency of the whole or some part of the valuation put by the non-resident person in another currency on an asset or liability of the non-resident person.

7(4)   For the purposes of this regulation a **"money debt"** is a debt which is, or has at any time been, one that falls, or that may at the choice of the debtor or of the creditor fall, to be settled–

(a)   by the payment of money,

(b)   by the transfer of a right to settlement under a debt which is itself a money debt, or

(c)   by the issue or transfer of shares in any company,

disregarding any other alternative exercisable by either party.

7(5)   Subject to paragraph (6), where an instrument is issued by any person for the purpose of representing security for, or the rights of a creditor in respect of, any money debt, then (whatever the circumstances of the issue of the instrument) that debt shall be taken for the purposes of these Regulations to be a debt arising from a transaction for the lending of money.

7(6)   For the purposes of these Regulations a debt shall not be taken to arise from a transaction for the lending of money to the extent that it is a debt arising from rights conferred by shares in a company.

7(7)   For the purposes of this regulation so far as relating to exchange gains and losses, any currency held by the company shall be treated as a money debt.

7(8)   For the purposes of this regulation **"money"** includes money expressed in a currency other than sterling.

7(9)   For the purposes of regulation 6 a **"related transaction"** in relation to a loan relationship means any disposal or acquisition (in whole or in part) of rights or liabilities under that relationship.

TRANSACTIONS IN UNITS IN COLLECTIVE INVESTMENT SCHEMES

8(1)   Any transaction in units in a collective investment scheme falls within this regulation.

8(2)   In this regulation–

(a)   **"collective investment scheme"** means any arrangements with respect to property of any description, including money, the purpose or effect of which is to enable persons taking part in the arrangements (whether by becoming owners of the property or any part of it or otherwise) to participate in or receive profits or income arising from the acquisition, holding, management or disposal of the property or sums paid out of such profits or income; and

(b)   **"units"** means the rights or interests (however described) of the persons who are to participate in a collective investment scheme.

8(3)   The arrangements must be such that the persons who are to participate ("participants") do not have day-to-day control over the management of the property, whether or not they have the right to be consulted or to give directions.

8(4)   The arrangements must also have either of the following characteristics–

(a)   the contributions of the participants and the profits or income out of which payments are to be made to them are pooled; or

(b)   the property is managed as a whole by or on behalf of the operator of the collective investment scheme.

8(5)   If arrangements provide for such pooling as is mentioned in paragraph (4)(a) in relation to separate parts of the property, the arrangements are not to be regarded as constituting a single collective investment scheme unless the participants are entitled to exchange rights in one part for rights in another.

TRANSACTIONS IN SECURITIES

9(1)   Any transaction in securities falls within this regulation.

9(2)   For the purposes of this regulation a **"transaction in securities"** is any transaction in securities of any description not falling within regulations 4 to 6 and 8.

TRANSACTIONS IN BUYING OR SELLING FOREIGN CURRENCY

10   Any transaction consisting in the buying or selling of any foreign currency falls within this regulation.

TRANSACTIONS IN CARBON EMISSION TRADING PRODUCTS

11(1)   Any transaction in a carbon emission trading product falls within this regulation.

11(2)   For the purposes of this regulation a **"transaction in a carbon emission trading product"** is any transaction which meets conditions A to C.

11(3)   Condition A is that the transaction is a transaction–

(a)   in Community tradable emissions allowances, or

(b)   in transferable units issued pursuant to the Kyoto Protocol.

11(4)   Condition B is that the transaction is not one which gives rise to either–

(a)   a chargeable gain falling within section 10 of the Taxation of Chargeable Gains Act 1992 (non-resident with United Kingdom branch or agency), or

(b)   a chargeable gain falling within section 10B of that Act (non-resident company with United Kingdom permanent establishment) (and accordingly taken into account for the purposes of section 11(2A) of the Income and Corporation Taxes Act 1988 (profits attributable to a permanent establishment)).

11(5)   Condition C is that the transaction does not otherwise fall within any other regulation of these Regulations.

11(6)   In this regulation–

"Community tradable emissions allowances" means transferable allowances which relate to the making of emissions of greenhouse gases, and are allocated as part of a system made for the purpose of implementing any community obligation of the United Kingdom relating to such emissions;

"the Kyoto Protocol" means the Kyoto Protocol to the United Nations Framework Convention on Climate Change signed at Kyoto on 11th December 1997; and

"units" includes assigned amount units, certified emission reductions, emission reduction units and removal units.

TRANSFER OF TRIBUNAL FUNCTIONS AND REVENUE AND CUSTOMS APPEALS ORDER 2009

(SI 2009/56, as amended by SI 2009/777, CTA 2010, TIOPA 2010 and SI 2010/466)

Made on 18 January 2009 by the Lord Chancellor and the Treasury in exercise of the powers conferred by s. 30(1) and (4), 31(1), (2) and (9) and 38 of, and para. 30 of Sch. 5 to, the Tribunals, Courts and Enforcement Act 2007 and s. 124(1)–(7) of the Finance Act 2008. Operative from 1 April 2009.

CITATION AND COMMENCEMENT

1(1) This Order may be cited as the Transfer of Tribunal Functions and Revenue and Customs Appeals Order 2009.

1(2) This Order comes into force on 1st April 2009.

THE EXISTING TRIBUNALS

2 In this Order **"existing tribunals"** means–

(a) the Commissioners for the general purposes of the income tax established under section 2 of the Taxes Management Act 1970;

(b) the Commissioners for the special purposes of the Income Tax Acts established under section 4 of the Taxes Management Act 1970;

(c) the VAT and duties tribunals established under Schedule 12 to the Value Added Tax Act 1994;

(d) the tribunal established under section 706 of the Income and Corporation Taxes Act 1988; and

(e) the tribunal established under section 704 of the Income Tax Act 2007.

TRANSFER OF FUNCTIONS, CONSEQUENTIAL AND OTHER AMENDMENTS

3(1) Schedule 1 contains amendments to primary legislation which–

(a) transfer functions of existing tribunals, and

(b) make consequential and other provision (including provision about reviews of decisions by Her Majesty's Revenue and Customs).

3(2) Schedule 2 contains amendments to secondary legislation which–

(a) transfer functions of existing tribunals, and

(b) make consequential and other provision (including provision about reviews of decisions by Her Majesty's Revenue and Customs).

ABOLITION OF EXISTING TRIBUNALS

4 The existing tribunals (apart from the Commissioners for the general purposes of the income tax) are abolished.

TRANSFER OF MEMBERS OF EXISTING TRIBUNALS

5 A person who, immediately before this Order comes into force, holds an office listed in column 1 of any of the following tables is to hold the office or offices listed in the corresponding entry in column 2 of that table–

THE SPECIAL COMMISSIONERS

1. Office held	2. Office or offices to be held
Commissioner for the special purposes of the Income Tax Acts appointed under section 4 of the Taxes Management Act 1970	Transferred-in judge of the Upper Tribunal
Deputy Commissioner for the special purposes of the Income Tax Acts appointed under section 4A of the Taxes Management Act 1970	Transferred-in judge of the First-tier Tribunal and deputy judge of the Upper Tribunal

Statutory Instruments

TRIBUNAL ESTABLISHED UNDER SECTION 706 ICTA 1988

1. Office held

Chairman of the tribunal appointed under section 706(1)(a) of the Income and Corporation Taxes Act 1988

Other member of the tribunal appointed under section 706(1)(b) of the Income and Corporation Taxes Act 1988

2. Office or offices to be held

Transferred-in judge of the Upper Tribunal

Transferred-in other member of the First-tier Tribunal

TRIBUNAL ESTABLISHED UNDER SECTION 704 ITA 2007

1. Office held

Chairman of the tribunal appointed under section 704(1)(a) of the Income Taxes Act 2007

Other member of the tribunal appointed under section 704(1)(b) of the Income Taxes Act 2007

2. Office or offices to be held

Transferred-in judge of the Upper Tribunal

Transferred-in other member of the First-tier Tribunal

TRANSITIONALS AND SAVINGS

6   Schedule 3 contains–

(a)   transitional provision, and

(b)   saving provision.

SCHEDULES

SCHEDULE 1 – CONSEQUENTIAL AMENDMENTS AND SUPPLEMENTAL PROVISIONS – PRIMARY LEGISLATION

Article 3

TAXES MANAGEMENT ACT 1970

5   The Taxes Management Act 1970 is amended as follows.

6   [Omits TMA 1970, s. 4, TMA 1970, s. 4A, TMA 1970, s. 5, TMA 1970, s. 6(1) and (5).]

7   [Amends TMA 1970, s. 12B(4).]

8   [Amends TMA 1970, s. 19A.]

9   [Amends TMA 1970, s. 20.]

10   [Amends TMA 1970, s. 20B.]

11   [Amends TMA 1970, s. 20BB(2)(a).]

12   [Amends TMA 1970, s. 28ZA.]

13   [Amends TMA 1970, s. 28ZB.]

14   [Omits TMA 1970, s. 28ZC.]

15   [Amends TMA 1970, s. 28ZD(3)(a).]

16   [Amends TMA 1970, s. 28ZE(1).]

17   [Amends TMA 1970, s. 28A.]

18   [Amends TMA 1970, s. 28B.]

19   [Amends TMA 1970, s. 31(2).]

20   [Omits TMA 1970, s. 31A(6).]

21   [Amends TMA 1970, s. 31B–31D.]

22   [Substitutes TMA 1970, s. 32(2).]

23   [Substitutes TMA 1970, s. 33(4).]

24   [Amends TMA 1970, s. 33A.]

25 [Omits TMA 1970, s. 44–46C.]

26 [Amends the heading preceding TMA 1970, s. 48.]

27 [Inserts TMA 1970, s. 47C.]

28 [Substitutes TMA 1970, s. 48.]

29 [Substitutes TMA 1970, s. 49.]

30 [Inserts TMA 1970, s. 49A–49I.]

31 [Amends TMA 1970, s. 50.]

32 [Omits TMA 1970, s. 53.]

33 [Amends TMA 1970, s. 54(1).]

34 [Amends TMA 1970, s. 55.]

36 [Omits TMA 1970, s. 56A–56D.]

37 [Amends TMA 1970, s. 57.]

38 [Amends TMA 1970, s. 58.]

39 [Amends TMA 1970, s. 59C(9).]

40 [Amends TMA 1970, s. 59DA.]

41 [Amends TMA 1970, s. 93.]

42 [Amends TMA 1970, s. 93A.]

43 [Amends TMA 1970, s. 97AA(2)(b).]

44 [Amends TMA 1970, s. 98B(2B).]

45 [Amends TMA 1970, s. 100B.]

46 [Amends TMA 1970, s. 100C.]

47 [Amends TMA 1970, s. 101.]

48 [Amends TMA 1970, s. 103(1) and (4).]

49 [Amends TMA 1970, s. 112.]

50 [Amends TMA 1970, s. 115.]

51 [Amends TMA 1970, s. 118.]

52 [Omits TMA 1970, Sch. 1.]

53 Schedule 1A (claims etc not included in returns) is amended as follows.

54 [Amends TMA 1970, Sch. 1A, para. 2A(3).]

55 [Amends TMA 1970, Sch. 1A, para. 6A.]

56 [Amends TMA 1970, Sch. 1A, para. 7.]

57 [Amends TMA 1970, Sch. 1A, para. 9.]

58 [Omits TMA 1970, Sch. 1A, para. 10 and 11.]

59 [Omits TMA 1970, Sch. 3.]

60 Schedule 3A (electronic lodgement of tax returns etc) is amended as follows.

61 [Amends TMA 1970, Sch. 3A, para. 4.]

62 [Amends TMA 1970, Sch. 3A, para. 11.]

FINANCE ACT 1973

64 The Finance Act 1973 is amended as follows.

65 [Omits FA 1973, s. 41.]

FINANCE ACT 1975

66 The Finance Act 1975 is amended as follows.

67 [Omits FA 1975, s. 57.]

FINANCE ACT 1984

106   [Omits FA 1984, s. 127.]

107   [Omits FA 1984, Sch. 22.]

INCOME AND CORPORATION TAXES ACT 1988

132   The Income and Corporation Taxes Act 1988 is amended as follows.

133(1)   Section 42 (appeals against determinations under sections 34 to 36 etc) is amended as follows.

133(2)   [Amends ICTA 1988, s. 42(4).]

133(3)   [Repealed by TIOPA 2010, s. 378 and Sch. 10, Pt. 12.]

History – Para. 133(3) repealed by TIOPA 2010, s. 378 and Sch. 10, Pt. 12, with effect for corporation tax purposes for accounting periods ending on or after 1 April 2010, for income tax and capital gains tax purposes for the tax year 2010–11 and subsequent tax years, and for petroleum revenue tax purposes for chargeable periods beginning on or after 1 July 2010. Former para. 133(3) amended ICTA 1988, s. 42(5).

134   [Substitutes ICTA 1988, s. 102(1).]

135(1)   Section 152 (notification of taxable amount of certain benefits) is amended as follows.

135(2)   [Repealed by TIOPA 2010, s. 378 and Sch. 10, Pt. 12.]

135(3)   [Omits ICTA 1988, s. 152(5)(i) and (ii).]

History – Para. 135(2) repealed by TIOPA 2010, s. 378 and Sch. 10, Pt. 12, with effect for corporation tax purposes for accounting periods ending on or after 1 April 2010, for income tax and capital gains tax purposes for the tax year 2010–11 and subsequent tax years, and for petroleum revenue tax purposes for chargeable periods beginning on or after 1 July 2010. Former para. 135(2) amended ICTA 1988, s. 152(5).

136   [Amends ICTA 1988, s. 215(7) and (8).]

137   [Amends ICTA 1988, s. 343(10).]

138   [Amends ICTA 1988, s. 376A(6).]

139   [Amends ICTA 1988, s. 378(3).]

140   [Amends ICTA 1988, s. 444A(6).]

141   [Amends ICTA 1988, s. 444AZA(5).]

142   [Amends ICTA 1988, s. 444AZB(5).]

143   [Amends ICTA 1988, s. 444AED.]

144   [Amends ICTA 1988, s. 461(8).]

145   [Amends ICTA 1988, s. 461C(5).]

146   [Amends ICTA 1988, s. 465(5).]

147   [Amends ICTA 1988, s. 506C(8).]

148   [Amends ICTA 1988, s. 552A(9)(k).]

149   [Omits ICTA 1988, s. 584(9).]

150   [Repealed by CTA 2010, s. 1181 and Sch. 3, Pt. 1.]

History – Para. 150 repealed by CTA 2010, s. 1181 and Sch. 3, Pt. 1, with effect for corporation tax purposes for accounting periods ending on or after 1 April 2010, and for income tax and capital gains tax purposes for the tax year 2010–11 and subsequent tax years. Former para. 150 amended ICTA 1988, s. 703(10)(b).

151   [Repealed by CTA 2010, s. 1181 and Sch. 3, Pt. 1.]

History – Para. 151 repealed by CTA 2010, s. 1181 and Sch. 3, Pt. 1, with effect for corporation tax purposes for accounting periods ending on or after 1 April 2010, and for income tax and capital gains tax purposes for the tax year 2010–11 and subsequent tax years. Former para. 151 amended ICTA 1988, s. 705.

152   [Repealed by CTA 2010, s. 1181 and Sch. 3, Pt. 1.]

History – Para. 152 repealed by CTA 2010, s. 1181 and Sch. 3, Pt. 1, with effect for corporation tax purposes for accounting periods ending on or after 1 April 2010, and for income tax and capital gains tax purposes for the tax year 2010–11 and subsequent tax years. Former para. 152 omitted ICTA 1988, s. 705A, ICTA 1988, s. 705B and ICTA 1988, s. 706.

153   [Repealed by CTA 2010, s. 1181 and Sch. 3, Pt. 1.]

History – Para. 153 repealed by CTA 2010, s. 1181 and Sch. 3, Pt. 1, with effect for corporation tax purposes for accounting periods ending on or after 1 April 2010, and for income tax and capital gains tax purposes for the tax year 2010–11 and subsequent tax years. Former para. 153 amended ICTA 1988, s. 709(4).

154   [Amends ICTA 1988, s. 751B.]

155 [Amends ICTA 1988, s. 754.]

156(1) [Amends ICTA 1988, s. 783(9).]

156(2) [Repealed by CTA 2010, s. 1181 and Sch. 3, Pt. 2; also repealed by TIOPA 2010, s. 378 and Sch. 10, Pt. 9.]

History – Para. 156(2) repealed by CTA 2010, s. 1181 and Sch. 3, Pt. 2, for corporation tax purposes only, with effect for accounting periods ending on or after 1 April 2010. Para. 156(2) also repealed by TIOPA 2010, s. 378 and Sch. 10, Pt. 9, with effect for corporation tax purposes for accounting periods ending on or after 1 April 2010, for income tax and capital gains tax purposes for the tax year 2010–11 and subsequent tax years, and for petroleum revenue tax purposes for chargeable periods beginning on or after 1 July 2010. Former para. 156(2) omitted ICTA 1988, s.783(9)(a), (b), (c) and the words following ICTA 1988, s. 789(c).

157 [Amends ICTA 1988, s. 832.]

158 [Amends ICTA 1988, Sch. 9, para. 5.]

159 [Amends ICTA 1988, Sch. 15, para. 21(3).]

160 [Amends ICTA 1988, Sch. 17, para. 7.]

161 [Amends ICTA 1988, Sch. 27.]

162(1) Paragraph 12 of Schedule 28AA (provision not at arm's length) is amended as follows.

162(2) [Repealed by TIOPA 2010, s. 378 and Sch. 10, Pt. 2.]

162(3) [Omits ICTA 1988, Sch. 28AA, para. 12(3).]

162(4) [Repealed by TIOPA 2010, s. 378 and Sch. 10, Pt. 2.]

History – Para. 162(2) and (4) repealed by TIOPA 2010, s. 378 and Sch. 10, Pt. 2, with effect for corporation tax purposes for accounting periods ending on or after 1 April 2010, for income tax and capital gains tax purposes for the tax year 2010–11 and subsequent tax years, and for petroleum revenue tax purposes for chargeable periods beginning on or after 1 July 2010. Former para. 162(2) substituted ICTA 1988, Sch. 28AA, para. 12(1). Former para. 162(4) amended ICTA 1988, Sch. 28AA, para. 12(4).

FINANCE ACT 1988

163 The Finance Act 1988 is amended as follows.

164 [Repealed by TIOPA 2010, s. 378 and Sch. 10, Pt. 12.]

History – Para. 164 repealed by TIOPA 2010, s. 378 and Sch. 10, Pt. 12, with effect for corporation tax purposes for accounting periods ending on or after 1 April 2010, for income tax and capital gains tax purposes for the tax year 2010–11 and subsequent tax years, and for petroleum revenue tax purposes for chargeable periods beginning on or after 1 July 2010. Former para. 164 amended FA 1988, s. 130(4).

165 [Omits FA 1988, s. 133–135.]

FINANCE ACT 1989

166 The Finance Act 1989 is amended as follows.

167 [Amends FA 1989, s. 182.]

TAXATION OF CHARGEABLE GAINS ACT 1992

177 The Taxation of Chargeable Gains Act 1992 is amended as follows.

178 [Omits TCGA 1992, s. 13(15).]

179 [Amends TCGA 1992, s. 138.]

180 [Amends TCGA 1992, s. 211ZA(9).]

181 [Amends TCGA 1992, s. 213(8).]

182 [Amends TCGA 1992, s. 261B(4)(a).]

183 [Amends TCGA 1992, s. 261C(3)(a).]

184 [Amends TCGA 1992, s. 288(1).]

FINANCE (NO 2) ACT 1992

185 The Finance (No 2) Act 1992 is amended as follows.

186 [Omits the heading before F(No. 2)A 1992, s. 75, F(No. 2)A 1992, s. 75, F(No. 2)A 1992, s. 76 and F(No. 2)A 1992, Sch. 16.]

187 [Amends F(No. 2)A 1992, Sch. 17, para. 8.]

FINANCE ACT 1994

196   The Finance Act 1994 is amended as follows.

210   Schedule 22 (supplementary provisions as to elections by reference to pipe-line usage) is amended as follows.

211   [Amends FA 1994, Sch. 22, para. 4.]

212   [Amends FA 1994, Sch. 22, para. 7(5)(b).]

213   [Amends FA 1994, Sch. 22, para. 8.]

FINANCE ACT 1996

232   The Finance Act 1996 is amended as follows.

FINANCE (NO 2) ACT 1997

245   The Finance (No 2) Act 1997 is amended as follows.

246   [Amends F(No. 2)A 1997, s. 35(9).]

FINANCE ACT 1998

251   The Finance Act 1998 is amended as follows.

252   [Repealed by TIOPA 2010, s. 378 and Sch. 10, Pt. 2.]

History – Para. 252 repealed by TIOPA 2010, s. 378 and Sch. 10, Pt. 2, with effect for corporation tax purposes for accounting periods ending on or after 1 April 2010, for income tax and capital gains tax purposes for the tax year 2010–11 and subsequent tax years, and for petroleum revenue tax purposes for chargeable periods beginning on or after 1 July 2010. Former para. 252 amended FA 1998, s. 111(5)(c).

253   Schedule 18 (company tax returns, assessments and related matters) is amended as follows.

254   [Amends FA 1998, Sch. 18, para. 27(5)(b).]

255   [Amends FA 1998, Sch. 18, para. 28.]

256   [Amends FA 1998, Sch. 18, para. 29(2)(b).]

257   [Substitutes FA 1998, Sch. 18, para. 30(5).]

258   [Amends FA 1998, Sch. 18, para. 31A.]

259   [Amends FA 1998, Sch. 18, para. 31B.]

260   [Amends FA 1998, Sch. 18, para. 31C(3)(a).]

261   [Amends FA 1998, Sch. 18, para. 31D(1).]

262   [Amends FA 1998, Sch. 18, para. 33.]

263   [Amends FA 1998, Sch. 18, para. 50(3).]

264   [Amends FA 1998, Sch. 18, para. 51.]

265   [Amends FA 1998, Sch. 18, para. 89(1)(b).]

266   [Omits FA 1998, Sch. 18, para. 92(3).]

267   [Omits FA 1998, Sch. 18, para. 93 and 94.]

FINANCE ACT 1999

276   The Finance Act 1999 is amended as follows.

277   [Omits FA 1999, Sch. 11, para. 9.]

FINANCE ACT 2000

285   The Finance Act 2000 is amended as follows.

294   [Amends FA 2000, Sch. 22.]

295   [Amends FA 2000, Sch. 38, para. 4(3).]

FREEDOM OF INFORMATION ACT 2000

296   [Amends FIA 2000, Sch. 1, Pt. VI and VII.]

CAPITAL ALLOWANCES ACT 2001

297   The Capital Allowances Act 2001 is amended as follows.

298   [Amends CAA 2001, s. 204.]

299   [Amends CAA 2001, s. 563.]

300   [Omits CAA 2001, Sch. 2, para. 5.]

301   [Amends CAA 2001, Sch. 3, para. 91.]

FINANCE ACT 2001

302   The Finance Act 2001 is amended as follows.

310   [Omits FA 2001, Sch. 24, para. 2.]

311   [Omits FA 2001, Sch. 29, para. 27 and 28.]

FINANCE ACT 2002

326   The Finance Act 2002 is amended as follows.

327   [Amends FA 2002, Sch. 18.]

328   [Amends FA 2002, Sch. 29, para. 88.]

PROCEEDS OF CRIME ACT 2002

333   [Omits PCA 2002, s. 320.]

INCOME TAX (EARNINGS AND PENSIONS) ACT 2003

334   The Income Tax (Earnings and Pensions) Act 2003 is amended as follows.

335   [Amends ITEPA 2003, s. 43.]

336   [Amends ITEPA 2003, s. 111.]

337   [Amends ITEPA 2003, s. 345(2).]

338   [Amends ITEPA 2003, s. 684(5).]

339   [Amends ITEPA 2003, s. 715(3)(b).]

340   [Amends ITEPA 2003, Sch. 1. Pt. 2.]

341   [Amends ITEPA 2003, Sch. 2, para. 82.]

342   [Amends ITEPA 2003, Sch. 2, para. 85(2).]

343   [Amends ITEPA 2003, Sch. 2, para. 100.]

344   Schedule 3 (approved SAYE option schemes) is amended as follows.

345   [Amends ITEPA 2003, Sch. 3, para. 41.]

346   [Amends ITEPA 2003, Sch. 3, para. 44(2).]

347   [Amends ITEPA 2003, Sch. 3, para. 49.]

348   Schedule 4 (approved CSOP schemes) is amended as follows.

349   [Amends ITEPA 2003, Sch. 4, para. 29.]

350   [Amends ITEPA 2003, Sch. 4, para. 32(2).]

351   [Amends ITEPA 2003, Sch. 4, para. 37.]

352   Schedule 5 (enterprise management incentives) is amended as follows.

353   [Amends ITEPA 2003, Sch. 5, para. 48.]

354   [Omits ITEPA 2003, Sch. 5, para. 50(4).]

355   [Amends ITEPA 2003, Sch. 5, para. 56.]

356   [Omits ITEPA 2003, Sch. 5, para. 57(3).]

357   [Amends ITEPA 2003, Sch. 5, para. 59.]

358   [Amends ITEPA 2003, Sch. 6, para. 129 and 142.]

CHILD TRUST FUNDS ACT 2004

414   The Child Trust Funds Act 2004 is amended as follows.

415 [Amends CTFA 2004, s. 21.]

416 [Amends CTFA 2004, s. 23.]

417 [Omits CTFA 2004, s. 24.]

418 [Amends CTFA 2004, s. 29.]

FINANCE ACT 2004

419 The Finance Act 2004 is amended as follows.

420 [Amends FA 2004, s. 59(4)(b).]

421 [Amends FA 2004, s. 67.]

422(1) Section 114 (refusal to issue certificate and appeal against refusal) is amended as follows.

422(2) [Amends FA 2004, s. 114(4).]

422(3) [Repealed by TIOPA 2010, s. 378 and Sch. 10, Pt. 1.]

History – Para. 422(3) repealed by TIOPA 2010, s. 378 and Sch. 10, Pt. 1, with effect for corporation tax purposes for accounting periods ending on or after 1 April 2010, for income tax and capital gains tax purposes for the tax year 2010–11 and subsequent tax years, and for petroleum revenue tax purposes for chargeable periods beginning on or after 1 July 2010. Former para. 422(3) amended FA 2004, s. 114(4).

423 [Amends FA 2004, s. 156.]

424 [Amends FA 2004, s. 159.]

425 [Amends FA 2004, s. 170.]

426 [Amends FA 2004, s. 253.]

427 [Amends FA 2004, s. 269.]

428 [Amends FA 2004, s. 271.]

429 [Amends FA 2004, s. 306(1A) and (3).]

430 [Amends FA 2004, s. 308A(2) and (3).]

431 [Amends FA 2004, s. 313B(1).]

432 [Amends FA 2004, s. 314A(1) and (3).]

433 [Omits FA 2004, s. 317A.]

434 [Amends FA 2004, s. 318(1).]

435 [Amends FA 2004, Sch. 33, para. 6.]

INCOME TAX (TRADING AND OTHER INCOME) ACT 2005

437 The Income Tax (Trading and Other Income) Act 2005 is amended as follows.

438 [Amends ITTOIA 2005, s. 54(2).]

439 [Amends ITTOIA 2005, s. 186.]

440 [Amends ITTOIA 2005, s. 218.]

441 [Amends ITTOIA 2005, s. 646(7).]

442 [Amends ITTOIA 2005, s. 869.]

443 [Omits ITTOIA 2005, Sch. 1, para. 373–375 and 383.]

444 [Omits ITTOIA 2005, Sch. 2, para. 153(3) and (4).]

FINANCE ACT 2005

445 [Amends FA 2005, s. 40(4).]

FINANCE ACT 2006

446 [Repealed by CTA 2010, s. 1181 and Sch. 3, Pt. 1.]

History – Para. 446 repealed by CTA 2010, s. 1181 and Sch. 3, Pt. 1, with effect for corporation tax purposes for accounting periods ending on or after 1 April 2010, and for income tax and capital gains tax purposes for the tax year 2010–11 and subsequent tax years. Former para. 446 read: "The Finance Act 2006 is amended as follows.".

447 [Repealed by CTA 2010, s. 1181 and Sch. 3, Pt. 1.]

History – Para. 447 repealed by CTA 2010, s. 1181 and Sch. 3, Pt. 1, with effect for corporation tax purposes for accounting periods ending on or after 1 April 2010, and for income tax and capital gains tax purposes for the tax year 2010–11 and subsequent tax years. Former para. 447 amended FA 2006, s. 117.

448   [Repealed by CTA 2010, s. 1181 and Sch. 3, Pt. 1.]

History – Para. 448 repealed by CTA 2010, s. 1181 and Sch. 3, Pt. 1, with effect for corporation tax purposes for accounting periods ending on or after 1 April 2010, and for income tax and capital gains tax purposes for the tax year 2010–11 and subsequent tax years. Former para. 448 amended FA 2006, s. 129(6).

449   [Repealed by CTA 2010, s. 1181 and Sch. 3, Pt. 1.]

History – Para. 449 repealed by CTA 2010, s. 1181 and Sch. 3, Pt. 1, with effect for corporation tax purposes for accounting periods ending on or after 1 April 2010, and for income tax and capital gains tax purposes for the tax year 2010–11 and subsequent tax years. Former para. 449 amended FA 2006, s. 133.

INCOME TAX ACT 2007

450   The Income Tax Act 2007 is amended as follows.

451   [Amends ITA 2007, s. 341(3)(a).]

452   [Omits ITA 2007, s. 538(4).]

453   [Amends ITA 2007, s. 557(2).]

454   [Substitutes ITA 2007, s. 674(7).]

455   [Amends ITA 2007, s. 692(2).]

456   [Amends ITA 2007, s. 697(2).]

457   [Amends ITA 2007, s. 698(1)(b).]

458   [Omits ITA 2007, s. 704.]

459   [Amends ITA 2007, s. 705.]

460   [Omits ITA 2007, s. 706–711.]

461   [Amends ITA 2007, s. 751.]

462   [Amends ITA 2007, s. 989.]

463   [Omits ITA 2007, Sch. 1, para. 243, ITA 2007, Sch. 1, para. 250, ITA 2007, Sch. 1, para. 255, ITA 2007, Sch. 1, para. 256, ITA 2007, Sch. 1, para. 267 and ITA 2007, Sch. 1, para. 351.]

FINANCE ACT 2007

464   The Finance Act 2007 is amended as follows.

465   [Omits FA 2007, s. 108(10)(a).]

466   [Substitutes FA 2007, Sch. 24, para. 16.]

467   [Amends FA 2007, Sch. 24, para. 17.]

FINANCE ACT 2008

468   The Finance Act 2008 is amended as follows.

469   [Omits FA 2008, s. 119(12)(a)(i) and (ii).]

470   [Omits FA 2008, Sch. 7, para. 161.]

471   [Amends FA 2008, Sch. 36.]

472   [Omits FA 2008, Sch. 40, para. 14.]

473   [Amends FA 2008, Sch. 41.]

SCHEDULE 2 – CONSEQUENTIAL AMENDMENTS AND SUPPLEMENTAL PROVISIONS – SECONDARY LEGISLATION

Article 3

CAPITAL GAINS TAX REGULATIONS 1967

1   The Capital Gains Tax Regulations 1967 are amended as follows.

2   [Amends SI 1967/149, reg. 2(1).]

3   [Amends SI 1967/149, reg. 8.]

4   [Amends SI 1967/149, reg. 9.]

5   [Amends SI 1967/149, reg. 12.]

6 [Omits SI 1967/149, reg. 17.]

INCOME TAX (LIFE ASSURANCE PREMIUM RELIEF) REGULATIONS 1978

7 [Amends SI 1978/1159, reg. 10.]

INCOME TAX (INTEREST RELIEF) REGULATIONS 1982

9 The Income Tax (Interest Relief) Regulations 1982 are amended as follows

10 [Amends SI 1982/1236, reg. 14.]

11 [Amends SI 1982/1236, reg. 19.]

CHARITABLE DEDUCTIONS (APPROVED SCHEMES) REGULATIONS 1986

22 [Amends SI 1986/2211, reg. 8.]

VENTURE CAPITAL TRUST REGULATIONS 1995

23 The Venture Capital Trust Regulations 1995 are amended as follows.

24 [Amends SI 1995/1979, reg. 4(4).]

25 [Amends SI 1995/1979, reg. 5(3).]

26 [Amends SI 1995/1979, reg. 6(3).]

27 [Amends SI 1995/1979, reg. 7.]

TAXATION OF INCOME FROM LAND (NON-RESIDENTS) REGULATIONS 1995

28 The Taxation of Income from Land (Non-residents) Regulations 1995 are amended as follows.

29 [Amends SI 1995/2902, reg. 6.]

30 [Amends SI 1995/2902, reg. 9(8).]

31 [Amends SI 1995/2902, reg. 17.]

32 [Amends SI 1995/2902, reg. 19.]

INDIVIDUAL SAVINGS ACCOUNT REGULATIONS 1998

45 The Individual Savings Account Regulations 1998 are amended as follows.

46 [Amends SI 1998/1871, reg. 18.]

47 [Amends SI 1998/1871, reg. 27.]

CORPORATION TAX (INSTALMENT PAYMENTS) REGULATIONS 1998

48 The Corporation Tax (Instalment Payments) Regulations 1998 are amended as follows.

49 [Amends SI 1998/3175, reg. 6.]

OVERSEAS INSURERS (TAX REPRESENTATIVES) REGULATIONS 1999

57 The Overseas Insurers (Tax Representatives) Regulations 1999 are amended as follows.

58 [Amends SI 1999/881, reg. 13.]

EDUCATION (STUDENT LOANS) (REPAYMENT) REGULATIONS 2000

73(1) The Education (Student Loans) (Repayment) Regulations 2000 are amended as follows.

73(2) [Amends SI 2000/944, reg. 7.]

73(3) [Amends SI 2000/944, reg. 45(5).]

COMMUNITY INVESTMENT TAX RELIEF (ACCREDITATION OF COMMUNITY DEVELOPMENT FINANCE INSTITUTIONS) REGULATIONS 2003

83 [Amends SI 2003/96, reg. 16.]

INCOME TAX (INCENTIVE PAYMENTS FOR VOLUNTARY ELECTRIC COMMUNICATION OF PAYE RETURNS) REGULATIONS 2003

91(1) The Income Tax (Incentive Payments for Voluntary Electric Communication of PAYE Returns) Regulations 2003 are amended as follows.

91(2) [Substitutes SI 2003/2495, reg. 3.]

INCOME TAX (PAY AS YOU EARN) REGULATIONS 2003

92 The Income Tax (Pay As You Earn) Regulations 2003 are amended as follows.

93 [Amends SI 2003/2682, reg. 2.]

94 [Amends SI 2003/2682, reg. 18.]

95 [Amends SI 2003/2682, reg. 19(1).]

96 [Amends SI 2003/2682, reg. 72A(6).]

97 [Amends SI 2003/2682, reg. 72B(3).]

98 [Amends SI 2003/2682, reg. 72C(3).]

99 [Amends SI 2003/2682, reg. 72D.]

100 [Amends SI 2003/2682, reg. 72G(3).]

101 [Amends SI 2003/2682, reg. 80.]

102 [Amends SI 2003/2682, reg. 81A(3).]

103 [Amends SI 2003/2682, reg. 97G(5).]

104 [Amends SI 2003/2682, reg. 97H.]

105 [Amends SI 2003/2682, reg. 97J.]

106 [Amends SI 2003/2682, reg. 110(5).]

107 [Amends SI 2003/2682, reg. 126(7).]

108 [Amends SI 2003/2682, reg. 127.]

109 [Amends SI 2003/2682, reg. 128(1).]

110 [Omitted by SI 2010/466, art. 4(4).]

History – Para. 110 omitted by SI 2010/466, art. 4(4), with effect from 6 April 2010.

111 [Amends SI 2003/2682, reg. 217.]

CHILD TRUST FUNDS REGULATIONS 2004

127 [Amends SI 2004/1450, reg. 28.]

VENTURE CAPITAL TRUST (WINDING UP AND MERGERS) (TAX) REGULATIONS 2004

128 The Venture Capital Trust (Winding up and Mergers) (Tax) Regulations 2004 are amended as follows.

129 [Amends SI 2004/2199, reg. 10.]

EXEMPTION FROM TAX FOR CERTAIN INTEREST PAYMENTS REGULATIONS 2004

130 [Amends SI 2004/2622, reg. 9.]

CHILD TRUST FUNDS (NON-TAX APPEALS) REGULATIONS 2005

131 The Child Trust Funds (Non-tax Appeals) Regulations 2005 are amended as follows.

132 [Omits SI 2005/191, reg. 1(2).]

133 [Amends SI 2005/191, reg. 4(2).]

134 [Omits SI 2005/191, reg. 14.]

CHILD TRUST FUNDS (APPEALS) REGULATIONS 2005

136 [Omits SI 2005/990, reg. 1(2).]

INCOME TAX (CONSTRUCTION INDUSTRY SCHEME) REGULATIONS 2005

137 The Income Tax (Construction Industry Scheme) Regulations 2005 are amended as follows.

138 [Amends SI 2005/2045, reg. 2.]

139 [Amends SI 2005/2045, reg. 9(9).]

140 [Amends SI 2005/2045, reg. 13.]

141 [Omits SI 2005/2045, reg. 25(6).]

142 [Amends SI 2005/2045, reg. 59.]

REGISTERED PENSION SCHEMES (RELIEF AT SOURCE) REGULATIONS 2005

143 The Registered Pension Schemes (Relief at Source) Regulations 2005 are amended as follows.

144 [Amends SI 2005/3448, reg. 2(2).]

145 [Amends SI 2005/3448, reg. 12.]

REGISTERED PENSION SCHEMES (ENHANCED LIFETIME ALLOWANCE) REGULATIONS 2006

147 The Registered Pension Schemes (Enhanced Lifetime Allowance) Regulations 2006 are amended as follows.

148 [Amends SI 2006/131, reg. 2(1).]

149 [Amends SI 2006/131, reg. 12.]

150 [Amends SI 2006/131, reg. 14.]

151 [Amends SI 2006/131, reg. 14A.]

152 [Amends SI 2006/131, reg. 24.]

REGISTERED PENSION SCHEMES AND OVERSEAS PENSIONS SCHEMES (ELECTRONIC COMMUNICATIONS OF RETURNS AND INFORMATION) REGULATIONS 2006

153(1) The Registered Pension Schemes and Overseas Pensions Schemes (Electronic Communications of Returns and Information) Regulations 2006 are amended as follows.

153(2) [Amends SI 2006/570, reg. 2.]

153(3) [Amends SI 2006/570, Sch. 2.]

AUTHORISED INVESTMENT FUNDS (TAX) REGULATIONS 2006

154 The Authorised Investment Funds (Tax) Regulations 2006 are amended as follows.

155 [Amends SI 2006/964, reg. 8.]

156 [Amends SI 2006/964, reg. 69T.]

157 [Amends SI 2006/964, reg. 69Z11.]

158 [Amends SI 2006/964, reg. 69Z38.]

MONEY LAUNDERING REGULATIONS 2007

168 The Money Laundering Regulations 2007 are amended as follows.

169 [Amends SI 2007/2157, reg. 29.]

170 [Amends SI 2007/2157, reg. 30.]

171 [Amends SI 2007/2157, reg. 42.]

172 [Amends SI 2007/2157, reg. 43.]

173 [Inserts SI 2007/2157, reg. 43A–43E.]

174 [Amends SI 2007/2157, reg. 44.]

175 [Amends SI 2007/2157, Sch. 5, para. 1.]

INCOME TAX (PURCHASED LIFE ANNUITIES) REGULATIONS 2008

182 The Income Tax (Purchased Life Annuities) Regulations 2008 are amended as follows.

183 [Amends SI 2008/562, reg. 20.]

THE TRANSFER OF TRIBUNAL FUNCTIONS ORDER 2008

186   [Amends SI 2008/2833, Sch. 3, para. 191(2)–(7).]

REVOCATIONS

187   The following instruments are revoked–

(e)   The Special Commissioners (Jurisdiction and Procedure) Regulations 1994.

(f)   The General Commissioners (Jurisdiction and Procedure) Regulations 1994.

(h)   The Retirement Age of General Commissioners Order 1995.

(i)   The Special Commissioners (Jurisdiction and Procedure) (Amendment) Regulations 1999.

(j)   The General Commissioners (Jurisdiction and Procedure) (Amendment) Regulations 1999.

(k)   The Special Commissioners (Amendment of the Taxes Management Act 1970) Regulations 1999.

(l)   The Special Commissioners (Jurisdiction and Procedure) (Amendment) Regulations 2000.

(m)   The General Commissioners of Income Tax (Costs) Regulations 2001.

(o)   The Referrals to the Special Commissioners Regulations 2001.

(p)   The General Commissioners and Special Commissioners (Jurisdiction and Procedure) (Amendment) Regulations 2002.

(q)   The Special Commissioners (Jurisdiction and Procedure) (Amendment) Regulations 2003.

(s)   The General Commissioners (Jurisdiction and Procedure) (Amendment) Regulations 2005.

(t)   The Special Commissioners (Jurisdiction and Procedure) (Amendment) Regulations 2005.

(u)   The Taxes Management Act 1970 (Modifications to Schedule 3 for Pensions Scheme Appeals) Order 2005.

(v)   The General Commissioners and Special Commissioners (Jurisdiction and Procedure) (Amendment) Regulations 2007.

SCHEDULE 3 – TRANSITIONAL AND SAVING PROVISIONS

Article 6

GENERAL

1(1)   In this Schedule–

"commencement date" means the date on which this Order comes into force;

"enactment" includes subordinate legislation (within the meaning of the Interpretation Act 1978);

"HMRC" means Her Majesty's Revenue and Customs;

"tribunal" means the First-tier Tribunal or, where determined by or under Tribunal Procedure Rules, the Upper Tribunal.

1(2)   For the purposes of this Schedule there are "current proceedings" if, before the commencement date–

(a)   any party has served notice on an existing tribunal for the purpose of beginning proceedings before the existing tribunal, and

(b)   the existing tribunal has not concluded proceedings arising by virtue of that notice.

FORMER VAT AND DUTIES TRIBUNALS MATTERS (EXCEPT VAT)

2(1)   This paragraph applies in relation to the following decisions–

(a)   any relevant decision which HMRC notify before the commencement date, unless–

    (i)   the period to require a review of the decision has expired before that date, or

    (ii)   a review of the decision has been required before that date;

(b)   any relevant review decision which HMRC notify before the commencement date unless–

    (i)   the period to serve notice of appeal against the decision on an existing tribunal has expired before that date, or

    (ii)   notice of appeal against the decision has been served on an existing tribunal before that date.

2(2) On and after the commencement date, the following enactments continue to apply (subject to sub-paragraphs (3) and (4)) as they applied immediately before that date–

(a) the review and appeal provisions,

(b) rule 4(2) of the Value Added Tax Tribunals Rules 1986, and

(c) any other enactments that apply in relation to relevant decisions or relevant review decisions.

2(3) Those enactments apply subject to Tribunal Procedure Rules.

2(4) Any reference to an existing tribunal is to be substituted with a reference to the tribunal.

2(5) Any time period which has started to run before the commencement date and has not expired will continue to apply.

2(6) In this paragraph–

"relevant decision" means a decision to which a review and appeal provision applies (apart from a relevant review decision);

"relevant review decision" means a decision–

(a) that is made on a review of a relevant decision, and

(b) to which a review and appeal provision applies,

and includes a relevant decision that is treated as having been confirmed under a review and appeal provision.

"review and appeal provisions" means–

(a) sections 14 to 16 of the Finance Act 1994,

(b) sections 59 and 60 of the Finance Act 1994,

(c) sections 54 to 56 of the Finance Act 1996,

(d) paragraphs 121 to 123 of Schedule 6 to the Finance Act 2000,

(e) sections 40 to 42 of the Finance Act 2001,

(f) sections 33 to 37 of the Finance Act 2003,

(g) regulations 9 to 13 of the Export (Penalty) Regulations 2003,

(h) regulations 4 to 7 of the Control of Cash (Penalties) Regulations 2007,

(i) regulations 43 and 44 of the Money Laundering Regulations 2007, and

(j) regulations 12 and 13 of the Transfer of Funds (Information on the Payer) Regulations 2007.

3(1) This paragraph applies in relation to a relevant decision if, before the commencement date–

(a) HMRC have notified the relevant decision, and

(b) a review of the decision has begun under a review and appeal provision (whether or not a relevant review decision has been notified).

3(2) On and after the commencement date the following enactments continue to apply (subject to sub-paragraphs (3) and (4)), as they applied immediately before that date–

(a) the review and appeal provisions,

(b) rule 4(2) of the VAT Tribunals Rules 1986, and

(c) any other enactments that apply in relation to relevant decisions or relevant review decisions.

3(3) Those enactments apply subject to Tribunal Procedure Rules.

3(4) Any reference to an existing tribunal is to be substituted with a reference to the tribunal.

3(5) Any time period which has started to run before the commencement date and has not expired will continue to apply.

3(6) On and after the commencement date, no notification offering or requiring a review may be given under any review and appeal provision or any other enactments that are applicable to the decision as they apply after that date.

3(7) In this paragraph **"review and appeal provision"**, **"relevant decision"** and **"relevant review decision"** have the same meaning as in paragraph 2.

FORMER VAT AND DUTIES TRIBUNALS MATTERS: VAT

4(1) This paragraph applies if, before the commencement date–

(a) HMRC have notified a decision relating to a matter to which section 83 of the Value Added Tax Act 1994 applies, and

(b) no party has served notice on a VAT and duties tribunal for the purpose of beginning proceedings before such a tribunal in relation to that decision.

4(2) On and after the commencement date, the following enactments continue to apply (subject to sub-paragraphs (3) and (4)) as they applied immediately before that date–

(a) the Value Added Tax Act 1994,

(b) rule 4(2) of the VAT Tribunals Rules 1986, and

(c) any other enactments that are applicable to the decision.

4(3) Those enactments apply subject to Tribunal Procedure Rules.

4(4) Any reference to an existing tribunal is to be substituted with a reference to the tribunal.

4(5) Any time period which has started to run before the commencement date and has not expired will continue to apply.

MATTERS FORMERLY HEARD BY EXISTING TRIBUNALS
(EXCEPT VAT AND DUTIES TRIBUNALS)

5(1) This paragraph applies if, before the commencement date–

(a) a notice of appeal has been given to HMRC; but

(b) no party has served notice on an existing tribunal for the purpose of beginning proceedings before the existing tribunal in relation to that appeal.

5(2) Where the date on which a review is required or offered falls on or before 31 March 2010, the period for HMRC to give notice of their conclusions for the purposes of the relevant provision is to be 90 days (but without prejudice to any power to agree to a different period).

5(3) In this paragraph–

"review" means a review under–

(a) section 49B or 49C of the Taxes Management Act 1970, or

(b) any other enactment which, as amended by this Order, contains provisions corresponding to section 49B or 49C for review to be required or offered;

"relevant provision" means–

(a) in the case of a review under section 49B or 49C of the Taxes Management Act 1970, section 49E(6) of that Act, or

(b) in the case of a review under any other enactment amended by this Order, the provision that corresponds to section 49E(6) of the Taxes Management Act 1970 in relation to that review.

CURRENT PROCEEDINGS

6 Any current proceedings are to continue on and after the commencement date as proceedings before the tribunal.

7(1) This paragraph applies to current proceedings that are continued before the tribunal by virtue of paragraph 6.

7(2) Where a hearing before an existing tribunal (except for the Commissioners for the general purposes of the income tax) began before the commencement date but was not completed by that date, the tribunal must be comprised for the continuation of that hearing of the person or persons who began it.

7(3) The tribunal may give any direction to ensure that proceedings are dealt with fairly and justly and, in particular, may–

(a) apply any provision in procedural rules which applied to the proceedings before the commencement date; or

(b) disapply any provision of Tribunal Procedure Rules.

7(4) In sub-paragraph (3) "procedural rules" means any provision (whether called rules or not) regulating practice or procedure before an existing tribunal.

7(5) Any direction or order made or given in proceedings which is in force immediately before the commencement date remains in force on and after that date as if it were a direction or order of the tribunal relating to proceedings before that tribunal.

7(6) A time period which has started to run before the commencement date and which has not expired will continue to apply.

7(7)   An order for costs may only be made if, and to the extent that, an order could have been made before the commencement date (on the assumption, in the case of costs actually incurred after that date, that they had been incurred before that date).

CASES TO BE REMITTED BY COURTS

8   Any case to be remitted by a court on or after the commencement date in relation to an existing tribunal shall be remitted to the tribunal.

DECISIONS OF VAT AND DUTIES TRIBUNALS AND COURTS: INTEREST AND PAYMENT

9(1)   This paragraph applies in relation to any decision of a VAT and duties tribunal made before the commencement date.

9(2)   On and after that date, the following provisions continue to apply as they applied immediately before that date–

(a)   section 84(8) of the Value Added Tax Act 1994 (VAT),

(b)   section 60(6) to (8) of the Finance Act 1994 (insurance premium tax),

(c)   paragraphs 8 and 10 of Schedule 6 to the Finance Act 1994 (air passenger duty),

(d)   section 56(3) to (5) of the Finance Act 1996 (landfill tax),

(e)   paragraph 123(4) to (6) of Schedule 6 to the Finance Act 2000 (climate change levy),

(f)   section 42(4) to (6) of the Finance Act 2001 (aggregates levy),

(g)   paragraph 14(4) of Schedule 3 to the Finance Act 2001 (excise and customs).

10(1)   This paragraph applies if an appeal from a decision of a VAT and duties tribunal, or from a court, is made before the commencement date.

10(2)   Section 85B of the Value Added Tax Act 1994 does not apply in relation to that decision.

DECISIONS OF EXISTING TRIBUNALS: RIGHTS OF APPEAL, REVIEWS AND IRREGULARITIES

11(1)   This paragraph applies to a decision of an existing tribunal if, immediately before the commencement date–

(a)   an appeal lies to a court from that decision,

(b)   an application may be or has been made to an existing tribunal seeking a review of that decision, or

(c)   the existing tribunal wishes to correct an irregularity.

11(2)   Except as provided for in sub-paragraph (3), on and after the commencement date such rights of appeal shall lie from the decision as would lie from a decision of the First-tier Tribunal made on or after that date.

11(3)   Subject to the modifications specified in sub-paragraphs (4) and (5) the following enactments continue to apply for the purposes of a case to be stated, a review, or for correcting an irregularity in respect of any decision of the Commissioners for the general purposes of the income tax made before the commencement date, as if the amendments in this Order had not been made–

(a)   sections 56 and 58 of the Taxes Management Act 1970,

(b)   regulations 17 and 20 to 24 of the General Commissioners (Jurisdiction and Procedure) Regulations 1994, and

(c)   the General Commissioners of Income Tax (Costs) Regulations 2001.

11(4)   Section 56(6) of the Taxes Management Act 1970 is modified so that for "the Commissioners" there is substituted "the tribunal".

11(5)   Section 58 of the Taxes Management Act 1970 is modified as follows–

(a)   omit subsection (2B); and

(b)   in subsection (2C) omit "or on an appeal under section 56A of this Act".

11(6)   In article 4 of the Tribunals, Courts and Enforcement Act 2007 (Commencement No. 6 and Transitional Provisions) Order 2008–

(a)   for "section 56 of the 1970 Act (statement of case for opinion of the High Court)" substitute " sections 56(3) and (11) and 58 of the 1970 Act (statement of case for opinion of the High Court) and regulations 17 and 20 to 24 of the General Commissioners (Jurisdiction and Procedure)

Regulations 1994 (review of tribunal's final determination, stated case procedures and correction of irregularities)"; and

(b)   after "commenced" insert ", and the amendments to the 1970 Act and the revocation of the General Commissioners (Jurisdiction and Procedure) Regulations 1994, the General Commissioners (Jurisdiction and Procedure) (Amendment) Regulations 1999, the General Commissioners (Jurisdiction and Procedure) (Amendment) Regulations 2005 and the General Commissioners and Special Commissioners (Jurisdiction and Procedure) (Amendment) Regulations 2007 (as they relate to the General Commissioners) in the Transfer of Tribunal Functions and Revenue and Customs Appeals Order 2009 had not been made".

EXISTING TRIBUNALS – STAFF

12   Staff appointed to the existing tribunals (except to the Commissioners for the general purposes of the income tax) before the commencement date are, on and after that date, to be treated, for the purpose of any enactment, as if they had been appointed by the Lord Chancellor under section 40(1) of the Tribunals, Courts and Enforcement Act 2007 (tribunal staff and services).

TRANSITIONAL: GENERAL

13(1)   In so far as appropriate in consequence of this Order, a reference in an enactment, instrument or other document to an existing tribunal, or a member or official of an existing tribunal (however expressed) is to be taken to be a reference to the tribunal.

13(2)   Sub-paragraph (1) does not apply to any reference that is amended by Schedule 1 or 2.

CONTRACTING OUT (ADMINISTRATIVE WORK OF TRIBUNALS) ORDER 2009

(SI 2009/121)

Made on 22 January 2009 by the Lord Chancellor in exercise of the powers conferred by s. 40(4) and 145(1) of the Tribunals, Courts and Enforcement Act 2007 Operative from 2 March 2009.

1 This Order may be cited as the Contracting Out (Administrative Work of Tribunals) Order 2009 and comes into force on 2nd March 2009.

2 The Lord Chancellor may enter into such contracts with other persons for the provision, by them or their sub-contractors, of staff to carry out the administrative work of—

(a)   the First-tier Tribunal;

(b)   the Upper Tribunal;

(c)   employment tribunals;

(d)   the Employment Appeal Tribunal; and

(e)   the Asylum and Immigration Tribunal.

3 [Not relevant.]

FIRST-TIER TRIBUNAL AND UPPER TRIBUNAL (CHAMBERS) (AMENDMENT) ORDER 2009

(SI 2009/196, revoked by SI 2010/2655)

Made on 9 February 2009 by the Lord Chancellor, with the concurrence of the Senior President of Tribunals, in exercise of the power conferred by s. 7(1) and (9) and 145 of the Tribunals, Courts and Enforcement Act 2007. Operative from 1 April 2009.

History – SI 2009/196 revoked by SI 2010/2655, Schedule, with effect from 29 November 2010, except for the purposes of SI 2009/196, art. 9 (transitional provision).

CITATION AND COMMENCEMENT

1 [Revoked by SI 2010/2655, Schedule.]

History – SI 2009/196 revoked by SI 2010/2655, Schedule, with effect from 29 November 2010, except for the purposes of SI 2009/196, art. 9 (transitional provision). Former art. 1 read as follows:
  "**1** This order may be cited as the First-tier Tribunal and Upper Tribunal (Chambers) (Amendment) Order 2009 and comes into force on 1st April 2009.".

AMENDMENTS TO THE FIRST-TIER TRIBUNAL AND UPPER TRIBUNAL (CHAMBERS) ORDER 2008

2-8 [Revoked by SI 2010/2655, Schedule.]

History – SI 2009/196 revoked by SI 2010/2655, Schedule, with effect from 29 November 2010, except for the purposes of SI 2009/196, art. 9 (transitional provision). Former art. 2–8 amended SI 2008/2684 (SI 2008/2684 also revoked by SI 2010/2655).

TRANSITIONAL PROVISION

9(1) This article applies to an appeal which lies to the to the Upper Tribunal by virtue of paragraph 11(2) of Schedule 3 to the Transfer of Tribunal Functions and Revenue and Customs Appeals Order 2009 (transitional provisions) against a decision of–

(a)   the Commissioners for the general purposes of the income tax established under section 2 of the Taxes Management Act 1970;

(b)   the Commissioners for the special purposes of the Income Tax Acts established under section 4 of the Taxes Management Act 1970;

(c)   the VAT and duties tribunals established under Schedule 12 to the Value Added Tax Act 1994;

(d)   the tribunal established under section 706 of the Income and Corporation Taxes Act 1988; or

(e)   the tribunal established under section 704 of the Income Tax Act 2007.

9(2) In rule 21(2)(a) of the Tribunal Procedure (Upper Tribunal) Rules 2008 (application to the Upper Tribunal for permission to appeal) the reference to the tribunal which made the decision challenged is to be read as a reference to the First-tier Tribunal.

TRIBUNAL PROCEDURE (FIRST-TIER TRIBUNAL) (TAX CHAMBER) RULES 2009

(SI 2009/273, as amended by SI 2010/43, SI 2010/273, SI 2011/651 and SI 2013/477)

Made on 5 February 2009 in accordance with para. 28(1) of Sch. 5 to the Tribunals, Courts and Enforcement Act 2007 by the Tribunal Procedure Committee in exercise of the power conferred by s. 9(3), 22 and 29(3) of, and Sch. 5 to, that Act. Operative from 1 April 2009.

ARRANGEMENT OF REGULATIONS

REGULATION

Statutory Instruments

PART 4 – CORRECTING, SETTING ASIDE, REVIEWING AND APPEALING TRIBUNAL DECISIONS

PART 1 – INTRODUCTION

CITATION, COMMENCEMENT, APPLICATION AND INTERPRETATION

1(1)   These Rules may be cited as the Tribunal Procedure (First-tier Tribunal) (Tax Chamber) Rules 2009 and come into force on 1st April 2009.

1(2)   These Rules apply to proceedings before the Tax Chamber of the First-tier Tribunal.

1(3)   In these Rules–

"**the 2007 Act**" means the Tribunals, Courts and Enforcement Act 2007;

"**appellant**" means–

(a)   the person who starts proceedings (whether by bringing or notifying an appeal, by making an originating application, by a reference, or otherwise);

(b)   in proceedings started jointly by more than one person, such persons acting jointly or each such person, as the context requires;

(c)   a person substituted as an appellant under rule 9 (substitution and addition of parties);

"**Basic case**" means a case allocated to the Basic category under rule 23 (allocation of cases to categories);

"**CAA case**" means an application under section 563 of the Capital Allowances Act 2001;

"**Complex case**" means a case allocated to the Complex category under rule 23 (allocation of cases to categories);

"**Compliance Officer**" means the Compliance Officer for IPSA;

"**Default Paper case**" means a case allocated to the Default Paper category under rule 23 (allocation of cases to categories);

"**document**" means anything in which information is recorded in any form, and an obligation under these Rules to provide or allow access to a document or a copy of a document for any purpose means, unless the Tribunal directs otherwise, an obligation to provide or allow access to such document or copy in a legible form or in a form which can be readily made into a legible form;

"**financial restrictions civil penalty case**" means an appeal under paragraph 26(3) or 28(1) of Schedule 7 to the Counter-Terrorism Act 2008;

"**hearing**" means an oral hearing and includes a hearing conducted in whole or in part by video link, telephone or other means of instantaneous two-way electronic communication;

"**HMRC**" means Her Majesty's Revenue and Customs but also includes–

(a)   the Serious Organised Crime Agency when carrying out functions under section 317 of the Proceeds of Crime Act 2002; and

(b)   the Director of Border Revenue when carrying out functions under section 7 of the Borders, Citizenship and Immigration Act 2009;

"**IPSA**" means the Independent Parliamentary Standards Authority;

"**MP expenses case**" means an appeal under the Parliamentary Standards Act 2009;

"**party**" means a person who is (or was at the time that the Tribunal disposed of the proceedings) an appellant or respondent in proceedings before the Tribunal;

"**practice direction**" means a direction given under section 23 of the 2007 Act;

"respondent" means—

(a)   in a case other than an MP expenses case–

    (i)   HMRC, where HMRC is not an appellant;

    (ii)   in proceedings brought by HMRC alone, a person against whom the proceedings are brought or to whom the proceedings relate;

(b)   in a MP expenses case, the Compliance Officer; and

(c)   in any case, a person substituted or added as a respondent under rule 9 (substitution and addition of parties);

"Standard case" means a case allocated to the Standard category under rule 23 (allocation of cases to categories);

"Tribunal" means the First-tier Tribunal.

History – R. 1(2) substituted by SI 2010/2653, r. 6(2), with effect from 29 November 2010.
In r. 1(3), the definition of "CAA case" inserted by SI 2013/477, r. 34(a), with effect from 1 April 2013.
In r. 1(3), the definition of "Compliance Officer" inserted by SI 2010/2653, r. 6(3)(a), with effect from 29 November 2010.
In r. 1(3), the definition of "financial restrictions civil penalty case" inserted by SI 2013/477, r. 34(b), with effect from 1 April 2013.
In r. 1(3), the definition of "HMRC" substituted by SI 2010/2653, r. 6(3)(b), with effect from 29 November 2010.
In r. 1(3), the definition of "IPSA" inserted by SI 2010/2653, r. 6(3)(c), with effect from 29 November 2010.
In r. 1(3), the definition of "MP expenses case" inserted by SI 2010/2653, r. 6(3)(c), with effect from 29 November 2010.
In r. 1(3), the definition of "respondent" substituted by SI 2010/2653, r. 6(3)(d), with effect from 29 November 2010.
In r. 1(3), the definition of "Tax Chamber" omitted by SI 2011/651, r. 5(2), with effect from 1 April 2011.

OVERRIDING OBJECTIVE AND PARTIES' OBLIGATION TO CO-OPERATE WITH THE TRIBUNAL

2(1)   The overriding objective of these Rules is to enable the Tribunal to deal with cases fairly and justly.

2(2)   Dealing with a case fairly and justly includes–

(a)   dealing with the case in ways which are proportionate to the importance of the case, the complexity of the issues, the anticipated costs and the resources of the parties;

(b)   avoiding unnecessary formality and seeking flexibility in the proceedings;

(c)   ensuring, so far as practicable, that the parties are able to participate fully in the proceedings;

(d)   using any special expertise of the Tribunal effectively; and

(e)   avoiding delay, so far as compatible with proper consideration of the issues.

2(3)   The Tribunal must seek to give effect to the overriding objective when it–

(a)   exercises any power under these Rules; or

(b)   interprets any rule or practice direction.

2(4)   Parties must–

(a)   help the Tribunal to further the overriding objective; and

(b)   co-operate with the Tribunal generally.

ALTERNATIVE DISPUTE RESOLUTION AND ARBITRATION

3(1)   The Tribunal should seek, where appropriate–

(a)   to bring to the attention of the parties the availability of any appropriate alternative procedure for the resolution of the dispute; and

(b)   if the parties wish and provided that it is compatible with the overriding objective, to facilitate the use of the procedure.

3(2)   Part 1 of the Arbitration Act 1996 does not apply to proceedings before the Tribunal.

PART 2 – GENERAL POWERS AND PROVISIONS

DELEGATION TO STAFF

4(1)   Staff appointed under section 40(1) of the 2007 Act (tribunal staff and services) may, with the approval of the Senior President of Tribunals, carry out functions of a judicial nature permitted or required to be done by the Tribunal.

4(2)   The approval referred to at paragraph (1) may apply generally to the carrying out of specified functions by members of staff of a specified description in specified circumstances.

Statutory Instruments

4(3) Within 14 days after the date that the Tribunal sends notice of a decision made by a member of staff pursuant to an approval under paragraph (1) to a party, that party may make a written application to the Tribunal requiring that decision to be considered afresh by a judge.

CASE MANAGEMENT POWERS

5(1) Subject to the provisions of the 2007 Act and any other enactment, the Tribunal may regulate its own procedure.

5(2) The Tribunal may give a direction in relation to the conduct or disposal of proceedings at any time, including a direction amending, suspending or setting aside an earlier direction.

5(3) In particular, and without restricting the general powers in paragraphs (1) and (2), the Tribunal may by direction–

(a) extend or shorten the time for complying with any rule, practice direction or direction, unless such extension or shortening would conflict with a provision of another enactment setting down a time limit;

(b) consolidate or hear together two or more sets of proceedings or parts of proceedings raising common issues, or treat a case as a lead case (whether in accordance with rule 18 (lead cases) or otherwise);

(c) permit or require a party to amend a document;

(d) permit or require a party or another person to provide documents, information or submissions to the Tribunal or a party;

(e) deal with an issue in the proceedings as a preliminary issue;

(f) hold a hearing to consider any matter, including a case management hearing;

(g) decide the form of any hearing;

(h) adjourn or postpone a hearing;

(i) require a party to produce a bundle for a hearing;

(j) stay (or, in Scotland, sist) proceedings;

(k) transfer proceedings to another tribunal if that other tribunal has jurisdiction in relation to the proceedings and, because of a change of circumstances since the proceedings were started–

(i) the Tribunal no longer has jurisdiction in relation to the proceedings; or

(ii) the Tribunal considers that the other tribunal is a more appropriate forum for the determination of the case;

(l) suspend the effect of its own decision pending the determination by the Tribunal or the Upper Tribunal, as the case may be, of an application for permission to appeal, a review or an appeal.

PROCEDURE FOR APPLYING FOR AND GIVING DIRECTIONS

6(1) The Tribunal may give a direction on the application of one or more of the parties or on its own initiative.

6(2) An application for a direction may be made–

(a) by sending or delivering a written application to the Tribunal; or

(b) orally during the course of a hearing.

6(3) An application for a direction must include the reasons for making that application.

6(4) Unless the Tribunal considers that there is good reason not to do so, the Tribunal must send written notice of any direction to every party and to any other person affected by the direction.

6(5) If a party or other person sent notice of the direction under paragraph (4) wishes to challenge a direction which the Tribunal has given, they may do so by applying for another direction which amends, suspends or sets aside the first direction.

FAILURE TO COMPLY WITH RULES ETC.

7(1) An irregularity resulting from a failure to comply with any requirement in these Rules, a practice direction or a direction does not of itself render void the proceedings or any step taken in the proceedings.

7(2) If a party has failed to comply with a requirement in these Rules, a practice direction or a direction, the Tribunal may take such action as it considers just, which may include–

(a) waiving the requirement;

(b)   requiring the failure to be remedied;

(c)   exercising its power under rule 8 (striking out a party's case);

(d)   restricting a party's participation in proceedings; or

(e)   exercising its power under paragraph (3).

7(3)   The Tribunal may refer to the Upper Tribunal, and ask the Upper Tribunal to exercise its power under section 25 of the 2007 Act (Upper Tribunal to have powers of High Court or Court of Session) in relation to, any failure by a person to comply with a requirement imposed by the Tribunal—

(a)   to attend at any place for the purpose of giving evidence;

(b)   otherwise to make themselves available to give evidence;

(c)   to swear an oath in connection with the giving of evidence;

(d)   to give evidence as a witness;

(e)   to produce a document; or

(f)   to facilitate the inspection of a document or any other thing (including any premises).

STRIKING OUT A PARTY'S CASE

8(1)   The proceedings, or the appropriate part of them, will automatically be struck out if the appellant has failed to comply with a direction that stated that failure by a party to comply with the direction would lead to the striking out of the proceedings or that part of them.

8(2)   The Tribunal must strike out the whole or a part of the proceedings if the Tribunal—

(a)   does not have jurisdiction in relation to the proceedings or that part of them; and

(b)   does not exercise its power under rule 5(3)(k)(i) (transfer to another court or tribunal) in relation to the proceedings or that part of them.

8(3)   The Tribunal may strike out the whole or a part of the proceedings if—

(a)   the appellant has failed to comply with a direction which stated that failure by the appellant to comply with the direction could lead to the striking out of the proceedings or part of them;

(b)   the appellant has failed to co-operate with the Tribunal to such an extent that the Tribunal cannot deal with the proceedings fairly and justly; or

(c)   the Tribunal considers there is no reasonable prospect of the appellant's case, or part of it, succeeding.

8(4)   The Tribunal may not strike out the whole or a part of the proceedings under paragraphs (2) or (3)(b) or (c) without first giving the appellant an opportunity to make representations in relation to the proposed striking out.

8(5)   If the proceedings, or part of them, have been struck out under paragraphs (1) or (3)(a), the appellant may apply for the proceedings, or part of them, to be reinstated.

8(6)   An application under paragraph (5) must be made in writing and received by the Tribunal within 28 days after the date that the Tribunal sent notification of the striking out to the appellant.

8(7)   This rule applies to a respondent as it applies to an appellant except that—

(a)   a reference to the striking out of the proceedings must be read as a reference to the barring of the respondent from taking further part in the proceedings; and

(b)   a reference to an application for the reinstatement of proceedings which have been struck out must be read as a reference to an application for the lifting of the bar on the respondent taking further part in the proceedings.

8(8)   If a respondent has been barred from taking further part in proceedings under this rule and that bar has not been lifted, the Tribunal need not consider any response or other submissions made by that respondent, and may summarily determine any or all issues against that respondent.

SUBSTITUTION AND ADDITION OF PARTIES

9(1)   The Tribunal may give a direction substituting a party if—

(a)   the wrong person has been named as a party; or

(b)   the substitution has become necessary because of a change in circumstances since the start of proceedings.

9(2)   The Tribunal may give a direction adding a person to the proceedings as a respondent.

9(3)   A person who is not a party to proceedings may make an application to be added as a party under this rule.

Statutory Instruments

9(4) If the Tribunal refuses an application under paragraph (3) it must consider whether to permit the person who made the application to provide submissions or evidence to the Tribunal.

9(5) If the Tribunal gives a direction under paragraph (1) or (2) it may give such consequential directions as it considers appropriate.

ORDERS FOR COSTS

10(1) The Tribunal may only make an order in respect of costs (or, in Scotland, expenses)–

(a) under section 29(4) of the 2007 Act (wasted costs) and costs incurred in applying for such costs;

(b) if the Tribunal considers that a party or their representative has acted unreasonably in bringing, defending or conducting the proceedings;

(c) if–

    (i) the proceedings have been allocated as a Complex case under rule 23 (allocation of cases to categories); and

    (ii) the taxpayer (or, where more than one party is a taxpayer, one of them) has not sent or delivered a written request to the Tribunal, within 28 days of receiving notice that the case had been allocated as a Complex case, that the proceedings be excluded from potential liability for costs or expenses under this sub-paragraph; or

(d) in a MP expenses case, if–

    (i) the case has been allocated as a Complex case under rule 23 (allocation of cases to categories); and

    (ii) the appellant has not sent or delivered a written request to the Tribunal, within 28 days of receiving notice that the case had been allocated as a Complex case, that the proceedings be excluded from potential liability for costs or expenses under this sub-paragraph.

10(2) The Tribunal may make an order under paragraph (1) on an application or of its own initiative.

10(3) A person making an application for an order under paragraph (1) must–

(a) send or deliver a written application to the Tribunal and to the person against whom it is proposed that the order be made; and

(b) send or deliver with the application a schedule of the costs or expenses claimed in sufficient detail to allow the Tribunal to undertake a summary assessment of such costs or expenses if it decides to do so.

10(4) An application for an order under paragraph (1) may be made at any time during the proceedings but may not be made later than 28 days after the date on which the Tribunal sends–

(a) a decision notice recording the decision which finally disposes of all issues in the proceedings; or

(b) notice under rule 17(2) of its receipt of a withdrawal which ends the proceedings.

10(5) The Tribunal may not make an order under paragraph (1) against a person (the **"paying person"**) without first–

(a) giving that person an opportunity to make representations; and

(b) if the paying person is an individual, considering that person's financial means.

10(6) The amount of costs (or, in Scotland, expenses) to be paid under an order under paragraph (1) may be ascertained by–

(a) summary assessment by the Tribunal;

(b) agreement of a specified sum by the paying person and the person entitled to receive the costs or expenses (the **"receiving person"**); or

(c) assessment of the whole or a specified part of the costs or expenses, including the costs of the assessment incurred by the receiving person, if not agreed.

10(7) Following an order for assessment under paragraph (6)(c) the paying person or the receiving person may apply–

(a) in England and Wales, to a county court, the High Court or the Costs Office of the Supreme Court (as specified in the order) for a detailed assessment of the costs on the standard basis or, if specified in the order, on the indemnity basis; and the Civil Procedure Rules 1998 shall apply, with necessary modifications, to that application and assessment as if the proceedings in the tribunal had been proceedings in a court to which the Civil Procedure Rules 1998 apply;

(b) in Scotland, to the Auditor of the Sheriff Court or the Court of Session (as specified in the order) for the taxation of the expenses according to the fees payable in that court; or

(c)   in Northern Ireland, to the Taxing Office of the High Court of Northern Ireland for taxation on the standard basis or, if specified in the order, on the indemnity basis.

10(7A)   Upon making an order for the assessment of costs, the Tribunal may order an amount to be paid on account before the costs or expenses are assessed.

10(8)   In this rule **"taxpayer"** means a party who is liable to pay, or has paid, the tax, duty, levy or penalty to which the proceedings relate or part of such tax, duty, levy or penalty, or whose liability to do so is in issue in the proceedings.

History – In r. 10(1)(a), the words "and costs incurred in applying for such costs" inserted by SI 2013/477, r. 35, with effect from 1 April 2013.
R. 10(1)(d) inserted (and the "or" and the end of r. 10(1)(b) omitted, and the "or" at the end of r. 10(1)(c) inserted) by SI 2010/2653, r. 6(4), with effect from 29 November 2010.
In r. 10(4)(b), the words "under rule 17(2) of its receipt of a withdrawal" substituted for the words "of a withdrawal under rule 17 (withdrawal)" by SI 2013/477, r. 36, with effect from 1 April 2013.
In r. 10(6)(c), the words ", including the costs or expenses of the assessment" inserted by SI 2013/477, r. 37, with effect from 1 April 2013.
R. 10(7A) inserted by SI 2013/477, r. 38, with effect from 1 April 2013.

Notes – The officially published version of R. 10(8) ended with a semicolon. CCH have assumed that this was a drafting error and have replaced the semicolon with a full stop in the text above.

REPRESENTATIVES

11(1)   A party may appoint a representative (whether a legal representative or not) to represent that party in the proceedings.

11(2)   If a party appoints a representative, that party (or the representative if the representative is a legal representative) must send or deliver to the Tribunal and to each other party to the proceedings written notice of the representative's name and address.

11(3)   Anything permitted or required to be done by a party under these Rules, a practice direction or a direction may be done by the representative of that party, except signing a witness statement.

11(4)   A person who receives due notice of the appointment of a representative–

(a)   must provide to the representative any document which is required to be provided to the represented party, and need not provide that document to the represented party; and

(b)   may assume that the representative is and remains authorised as such until they receive written notification that this is not so from the representative or the represented party.

11(5)   At a hearing a party may be accompanied by another person who, with the permission of the Tribunal, may act as a representative or otherwise assist in presenting the party's case at the hearing.

11(6)   Paragraphs (2) to (4) do not apply to a person (other than an appointed representative) who accompanies a party in accordance with paragraph (5).

11(7)   In this rule **"legal representative"** means a person who, for the purposes of the Legal Services Act 2007, is an authorised person in relation to an activity which constitutes the exercise of a right of audience or the conduct of litigation within the meaning of that Act, an advocate or solicitor in Scotland, or a barrister or solicitor in Northern Ireland.

History – In r. 11(7), the words "a person who, for the purposes of the Legal Services Act 2007, is an authorised person in relation to an activity which constitutes the exercise of a right of audience or the conduct of litigation within the meaning of that Act" substituted for the words "an authorised advocate or authorised litigator as defined by section 119(1) of the Courts and Legal Services Act 1990" by SI 2010/43, r. 16, with effect from 18 January 2010.

CALCULATING TIME

12(1)   An act required by these Rules, a practice direction or a direction to be done on or by a particular day must be done before 5pm on that day.

12(2)   If the time specified by these Rules, a practice direction or a direction for doing any act ends on a day other than a working day, the act is done in time if it is done on the next working day.

12(3)   In this rule **"working day"** means any day except a Saturday or Sunday, Christmas Day, Good Friday or a bank holiday under section 1 of the Banking and Financial Dealings Act 1971.

SENDING AND DELIVERY OF DOCUMENTS

13(1)   Any document to be provided to the Tribunal under these Rules, a practice direction or a direction must be–

(a)   sent by pre-paid post or document exchange, or delivered by hand, to the address specified for the proceedings; or

(b)   sent or delivered by such other method as the Tribunal may permit or direct.

13(2) Subject to paragraph (3), if a party or representative provides a fax number, email address or other details for the electronic transmission of documents to them, that party or representative must accept delivery of documents by that method.

13(3) If a party informs the Tribunal and all other parties that a particular form of communication (other than pre-paid post or delivery by hand) should not be used to provide documents to that party, that form of communication must not be so used.

13(4) If the Tribunal or a party sends a document to a party or the Tribunal by email or any other electronic means of communication, the recipient may request that the sender provide a hard copy of the document to the recipient. The recipient must make such a request as soon as reasonably practicable after receiving the document electronically.

13(5) The Tribunal and each party may assume that the address provided by a party or its representative is and remains the address to which documents should be sent or delivered until receiving written notification to the contrary.

USE OF DOCUMENTS AND INFORMATION

14 The Tribunal may make an order prohibiting the disclosure or publication of–

(a)   specified documents or information relating to the proceedings; or

(b)   any matter likely to lead members of the public to identify any person whom the Tribunal considers should not be identified.

EVIDENCE AND SUBMISSIONS

15(1) Without restriction on the general powers in rule 5(1) and (2) (case management powers), the Tribunal may give directions as to–

(a)   issues on which it requires evidence or submissions;

(b)   the nature of the evidence or submissions it requires;

(c)   whether the parties are permitted or required to provide expert evidence, and if so whether the parties must jointly appoint a single expert to provide such evidence;

(d)   any limit on the number of witnesses whose evidence a party may put forward, whether in relation to a particular issue or generally;

(e)   the manner in which any evidence or submissions are to be provided, which may include a direction for them to be given–

   (i)   orally at a hearing; or

   (ii)   by written submissions or witness statement; and

(f)   the time at which any evidence or submissions are to be provided.

15(2) The Tribunal may–

(a)   admit evidence whether or not the evidence would be admissible in a civil trial in the United Kingdom; or

(b)   exclude evidence that would otherwise be admissible where–

   (i)   the evidence was not provided within the time allowed by a direction or a practice direction;

   (ii)   the evidence was otherwise provided in a manner that did not comply with a direction or a practice direction; or

   (iii)   it would otherwise be unfair to admit the evidence.

15(3) The Tribunal may consent to a witness giving, or require any witness to give, evidence on oath, and may administer an oath for that purpose.

SUMMONING OR CITATION OF WITNESSES AND ORDERS TO ANSWER QUESTIONS OR PRODUCE DOCUMENTS

16(1) On the application of a party or on its own initiative, the Tribunal may–

(a)   by summons (or, in Scotland, citation) require any person to attend as a witness at a hearing at the time and place specified in the summons or citation;

(b)   order any person to answer any questions or produce any documents in that person's possession or control which relate to any issue in the proceedings.

16(2) A summons or citation under paragraph (1)(a) must–

(a)   give the person required to attend at least 14 days' notice of the hearing, or such shorter period as the Tribunal may direct; and

(b)   where the person is not a party, make provision for the person's necessary expenses of attendance to be paid, and state who is to pay them.

16(3)   No person may be compelled to give any evidence or produce any document that the person could not be compelled to give or produce on a trial of an action in a court of law in the part of the United Kingdom where the proceedings are due to be determined.

16(4)   A person who receives a summons, citation or order may apply to the Tribunal for it to be varied or set aside if they did not have an opportunity to object to it before it was made or issued.

16(5)   A person making an application under paragraph (4) must do so as soon as reasonably practicable after receiving notice of the summons, citation or order.

16(6)   A summons, citation or order under this rule must—

(a)   state that the person on whom the requirement is imposed may apply to the Tribunal to vary or set aside the summons, citation or order, if they did not have an opportunity to object to it before it was made or issued; and

(b)   state the consequences of failure to comply with the summons, citation or order.

WITHDRAWAL

17(1)   Subject to any provision in an enactment relating to withdrawal or settlement of particular proceedings, a party may give notice to the Tribunal of the withdrawal of the case made by it in the Tribunal proceedings, or any part of that case—

(a)   by sending or delivering to the Tribunal a written notice of withdrawal; or

(b)   orally at a hearing.

17(2)   The Tribunal must notify each party in writing of its receipt of a withdrawal under this rule.

17(3)   A party who has withdrawn their case may apply to the Tribunal for the case to be reinstated.

17(4)   An application under paragraph (3) must be made in writing and be received by the Tribunal within 28 days after—

(a)   the date that the Tribunal received the notice under paragraph (1)(a); or

(b)   the date of the hearing at which the case was withdrawn orally under paragraph (1)(b).

History – In r. 17(1)(a), the words "at any time before a hearing to consider the disposal of the proceedings (or, if the Tribunal disposes of the proceedings without a hearing, before that disposal)," at the beginning omitted by SI 2013/477, r. 39(a), with effect from 1 April 2013.
In r. 17(2), the word "other" before the word "party" omitted and the words "its receipt of" inserted by SI 2013/477, r. 39(b), with effect from 1 April 2013.

LEAD CASES

18(1)   This rule applies if—

(a)   two or more cases have been started before the Tribunal;

(b)   in each such case the Tribunal has not made a decision disposing of the proceedings; and

(c)   the cases give rise to common or related issues of fact or law.

18(2)   The Tribunal may give a direction—

(a)   specifying one or more cases falling under paragraph (1) as a lead case or lead cases; and

(b)   staying (or, in Scotland, sisting) the other cases falling under paragraph (1) (**"the related cases"**).

18(3)   When the Tribunal makes a decision in respect of the common or related issues—

(a)   the Tribunal must send a copy of that decision to each party in each of the related cases; and

(b)   subject to paragraph (4), that decision shall be binding on each of those parties.

18(4)   Within 28 days after the date that the Tribunal sent a copy of the decision to a party under paragraph (3)(a), that party may apply in writing for a direction that the decision does not apply to, and is not binding on the parties to, that case.

18(5)   The Tribunal must give directions in respect of cases which are stayed or sisted under paragraph (2)(b), providing for the disposal of or further steps in those cases.

18(6)   If the lead case or cases are withdrawn or disposed of before the Tribunal makes a decision in respect of the common or related issues, the Tribunal must give directions as to—

(a)   whether another case or other cases are to be heard as a lead case or lead cases; and

(b)   whether any direction affecting the related cases should be set aside or amended.

PART 3 – PROCEDURE BEFORE THE TRIBUNAL

Chapter 1 – Starting Proceedings and Allocation of Cases to Categories

PROCEEDINGS WITHOUT NOTICE TO A RESPONDENT

19 If a case or matter is to be determined without notice to or the involvement of a respondent–

(a)   any provision in these Rules requiring a document to be provided by or to a respondent; and

(b)   any other provision in these Rules permitting a respondent to participate in the proceedings does not apply to that case or matter.

STARTING APPEAL PROCEEDINGS

20(1)   A person making or notifying an appeal to the Tribunal under any enactment must start proceedings by sending or delivering a notice of appeal to the Tribunal.

20(2)   The notice of appeal must include–

(a)   the name and address of the appellant;

(b)   the name and address of the appellant's representative (if any);

(c)   an address where documents for the appellant may be sent or delivered;

(d)   details of the decision appealed against;

(e)   the result the appellant is seeking; and

(f)   the grounds for making the appeal.

20(3)   The appellant must provide with the notice of appeal a copy of any written record of any decision appealed against, and any statement of reasons for that decision, that the appellant has or can reasonably obtain.

20(4)   If the notice of appeal is provided after the end of any period specified in an enactment referred to in paragraph (1) but the enactment provides that an appeal may be made or notified after that period with the permission of the Tribunal–

(a)   the notice of appeal must include a request for such permission and the reason why the notice of appeal was not provided in time; and

(b)   unless the Tribunal gives such permission, the Tribunal must not admit the appeal.

20(5)   When the Tribunal receives the notice of appeal it must give notice of the proceedings to the respondent.

History – R. 20(1) substituted by SI 2010/2653, r. 6(5)(a), with effect from 29 November 2010. Former r. 20(1) read as follows:

"**20(1)**   Where an enactment provides for a person to make or notify an appeal to the Tribunal, the appellant must start proceedings by sending or delivering a notice of appeal to the Tribunal within any time limit imposed by that enactment.".
R. 20(4) substituted by SI 2010/2653, r. 6(5)(b), with effect from 29 November 2010. Former r. 20(4) read as follows:

"**20(4)**   If the appellant provides the notice of appeal to the Tribunal later than the time required by paragraph (1) or by an extension of time allowed under rule 5(3)(a) (power to extend time)–

(a)   the notice of appeal must include a request for an extension of time and the reason why the notice of appeal was not provided in time; and

(b)   unless the Tribunal extends time for the notice of appeal under rule 5(3)(a) (power to extend time) the Tribunal must not admit the notice of appeal.".

STARTING PROCEEDINGS BY ORIGINATING APPLICATION OR REFERENCE

21(1)   Where an enactment provides for a person or persons to make an originating application or reference to the Tribunal, the appellant must start proceedings by providing an application notice or notice of reference to the Tribunal within any time limit imposed by that enactment.

21(2)   The application notice or notice of reference must state–

(a)   the name and address of the appellant;

(b)   the name and address of the appellant's representative (if any);

(c)   an address where documents for the appellant may be sent or delivered;

(d)   the name and address of each respondent (if any);

(e)   the facts relevant to the originating application or reference;

(f)   the result the appellant is seeking (if any); and

(g)   the grounds for making the originating application or reference.

21(3)   If the appellant provides the application notice or notice of reference to the Tribunal later than the time required by paragraph (1) or by any extension of time under rule 5(3)(a) (power to extend time)—

(a)   the application notice or notice of reference must include a request for an extension of time and the reason why the application notice or notice of reference was not provided in time; and

(b)   unless the Tribunal extends time for the application notice or notice of reference under rule 5(3)(a) (power to extend time) the Tribunal must not admit the application notice or notice of reference.

21(3A)   The power of the Tribunal under these Rules to extend time for starting proceedings shall not apply in a CAA case.

21(4)   When the Tribunal receives an application notice or a notice of reference it must send a copy of the notice and any accompanying document to any respondent.

History – R. 21(3A) inserted by SI 2013/477, r. 40, with effect from 1 April 2013.

HARDSHIP APPLICATIONS

22(1)   This rule applies where an enactment provides, in any terms, that an appeal may not proceed if the liability to pay the amount in dispute is outstanding unless HMRC or the Tribunal consent to the appeal proceeding.

22(2)   When starting proceedings, the appellant must include or provide the following in or with the notice of appeal—

(a)   a statement as to whether the appellant has paid the amount in dispute;

(b)   if the appellant has not paid the amount in dispute, a statement as to the status or outcome of any application to HMRC for consent to the appeal proceeding; and

(c)   if HMRC have refused such an application, an application to the Tribunal for consent to the appeal proceeding.

22(3)   An application under paragraph (2)(c) must include the reasons for the application and a list of any documents the appellant intends to produce or rely upon in support of that application.

22(4)   If the appellant requires the consent of HMRC or the Tribunal before the appeal may proceed, the Tribunal must stay the proceedings until any applications to HMRC or the Tribunal in that respect have been determined.

ALLOCATION OF CASES TO CATEGORIES

23(1)   When the Tribunal receives a notice of appeal, application notice or notice of reference, the Tribunal must give a direction—

(a)   in an MP expenses case, a financial restrictions civil penalty case or a CAA case, allocating the case to one of the categories set out in paragraph (2)(c) or (d); and

(b)   in any other case, allocating the case to one of the categories set out in paragraph (2).

23(2)   The categories referred to in paragraph (1) are—

(a)   Default Paper cases, which will usually be disposed of without a hearing;

(b)   Basic cases, which will usually be disposed of after a hearing, with minimal exchange of documents before the hearing;

(c)   Standard cases, which will usually be subject to more detailed case management and be disposed of after a hearing; and

(d)   Complex cases, in respect of which see paragraphs (4) and (5) below.

23(3)   The Tribunal may give a further direction re-allocating a case to a different category at any time, either on the application of a party or on its own initiative.

23(4)   The Tribunal may allocate a case as a Complex case under paragraph (1) or (3) only if the Tribunal considers that the case—

(a)   will require lengthy or complex evidence or a lengthy hearing;

(b)   involves a complex or important principle or issue; or

(c)   involves a large financial sum.

23(5)   If a case is allocated as a Complex case—

(a)   rule 10(1)(c) (costs in Complex cases) applies to the case; and

(b)   rule 28 (transfer of Complex cases to the Upper Tribunal) applies to the case.

Statutory Instruments

History – In r. 23(1)(a), the words ", a financial restrictions civil penalty case or a CAA case" inserted by SI 2013/477, r. 41, with effect from 1 April 2013.

R. 23(1) substituted by SI 2010/2653, r. 6(6), with effect from 29 November 2010. Former r. 23(1) read as follows:

"**23(1)**   When the Tribunal receives a notice of appeal, application notice or notice of reference, the Tribunal must give a direction allocating the case to one of the categories set out in paragraph (2).".

Chapter 2 – Procedure after Allocation of Cases to Categories

BASIC CASES

24(1)   This rule applies to Basic cases.

24(2)   Rule 25 (respondent's statement of case) does not apply and, subject to paragraph (3) and any direction given by the Tribunal, the case will proceed directly to a hearing.

24(3)   If the respondent intends to raise grounds for contesting the proceedings at the hearing which have not previously been communicated to the appellant, the respondent must notify the appellant of such grounds.

24(4)   If the respondent is required to notify the appellant of any grounds under paragraph (3), the respondent must do so–

(a)   as soon as reasonably practicable after becoming aware that such is the case; and

(b)   in sufficient detail to enable the appellant to respond to such grounds at the hearing.

RESPONDENT'S STATEMENT OF CASE

25(1)   A respondent must send or deliver a statement of case to the Tribunal, the appellant and any other respondent so that it is received–

(a)   in a Default Paper case, within 42 days after the Tribunal sent the notice of appeal or a copy of the application notice or notice of reference;

(b)   in an MP expenses case, within 28 days after the Tribunal sent the notice of appeal; or

(c)   in a Standard or Complex case other than an MP expenses case, within 60 days after the Tribunal sent the notice of appeal or a copy of the application notice or notice of reference.

25(2)   A statement of case must–

(a)   in an appeal, state the legislative provision under which the decision under appeal was made; and

(b)   set out the respondent's position in relation to the case.

25(3)   A statement of case may also contain a request that the case be dealt with at a hearing or without a hearing.

25(4)   If a respondent provides a statement of case to the Tribunal later than the time required by paragraph (1) or by any extension allowed under rule 5(3)(a) (power to extend time), the statement of case must include a request for an extension of time and the reason why the statement of case was not provided in time.

History – R. 25(1) substituted by SI 2010/2653, r. 6(7), with effect from 29 November 2010. Former r. 25(1) read as follows:

"**25(1)**   A respondent must send or deliver a statement of case to the Tribunal, the appellant and any other respondent so that it is received–

(a)   in a Default Paper case, within 42 days after the tribunal sent the notice of the appeal or a copy of the application notice or notice of reference; or

(b)   in a Standard or Complex case, within 60 days after the tribunal sent the notice of the appeal or a copy of the application notice or notice of reference.".

FURTHER STEPS IN A DEFAULT PAPER CASE

26(1)   This rule applies to Default Paper cases.

26(2)   The appellant may send or deliver a written reply to the Tribunal so that it is received within 30 days after the date on which the respondent sent to the appellant the statement of case to which the reply relates.

26(3)   The appellant's reply may–

(a)   set out the appellant's response to the respondent's statement of case;

(b)   provide any further information (including, where appropriate, copies of the documents containing such information) which has not yet been provided to the Tribunal and is relevant to the case; and

(c)   contain a request that the case be dealt with at a hearing.

26(4)   The appellant must send or deliver a copy of any reply provided under paragraph (2) to each respondent at the same time as it is provided to the Tribunal.

26(5)   If the appellant provides a reply to the Tribunal later than the time required by paragraph (2) or by any extension allowed under rule 5(3)(a) (power to extend time), the reply must include a request for an extension of time and the reason why the reply was not provided in time.

26(6)   Following receipt of the appellant's reply, or the expiry of the time for the receipt of the appellant's reply then, unless it directs otherwise and subject in any event to paragraph (7), the Tribunal must proceed to determine the case without a hearing.

26(7)   If any party has made a written request to the Tribunal for a hearing, the Tribunal must hold a hearing before determining the case.

FURTHER STEPS IN A STANDARD OR COMPLEX CASE

27(1)   This rule applies to Standard and Complex cases.

27(2)   Subject to any direction to the contrary, within 42 days after the date the respondent sent the statement of case (or, where there is more than one respondent, the date of the final statement of case) each party must send or deliver to the Tribunal and to each other party a list of documents–

(a)   of which the party providing the list has possession, the right to possession, or the right to take copies; and

(b)   which the party providing the list intends to rely upon or produce in the proceedings.

27(3)   A party which has provided a list of documents under paragraph (2) must allow each other party to inspect or take copies of the documents on the list (except any documents which are privileged).

TRANSFER OF COMPLEX CASES TO THE UPPER TRIBUNAL

28(1)   If a case has been allocated as a Complex case the Tribunal may, with the consent of the parties, refer a case or a preliminary issue to the President of the Tax Chamber of the First-tier Tribunal with a request that the case or issue be considered for transfer to the Upper Tribunal.

28(2)   If a case or issue has been referred by the Tribunal under paragraph (1), the President of the Tax Chamber may, with the concurrence of the President of the Tax and Chancery Chamber of the Upper Tribunal, direct that the case or issue be transferred to and determined by the Upper Tribunal.

History – In r. 28(1), the words "of the First-tier Tribunal" inserted by SI 2011/651, r. 5(3), with effect from 1 April 2011.
In r. 28(1), the words "or a preliminary issue" and "or issue" inserted by SI 2010/2653, r. 6(8)(a), with effect from 29 November 2010.
R. 28(2) substituted by SI 2010/2653, r. 6(8)(b), with effect from 29 November 2010. Former r. 28(2) read as follows:

> "**28(2)**   If a case has been referred by the Tribunal under paragraph (1), the President of the Tax Chamber may, with the concurrence of the President of the Finance and Tax Chamber of the Upper Tribunal (if that is a different person) direct that the case be transferred to and determined by the Upper Tribunal.".

Chapter 3 – Hearings

DETERMINATION WITH OR WITHOUT A HEARING

29(1)   Subject to rule 26(6) (determination of a Default Paper case without a hearing) and the following paragraphs in this rule, the Tribunal must hold a hearing before making a decision which disposes of proceedings, or a part of proceedings, unless–

(a)   each party has consented to the matter being decided without a hearing; and

(b)   the Tribunal considers that it is able to decide the matter without a hearing.

29(2)   This rule does not apply to decisions under Part 4 (correcting, setting aside, reviewing and appealing Tribunal decisions).

29(3)   The Tribunal may dispose of proceedings, or a part of proceedings, without a hearing under rule 8 (striking out a party's case).

ENTITLEMENT TO ATTEND A HEARING

30   Subject to rules 19 (proceedings without notice to a respondent) and 32(4) (exclusion from a hearing), each party to proceedings is entitled to attend a hearing.

NOTICE OF HEARINGS

31(1) The Tribunal must give each party entitled to attend a hearing reasonable notice of the time and place of any hearing (including any adjourned or postponed hearing) and any changes to the time and place of any hearing.

31(2) In relation to a hearing to consider the disposal of proceedings, the period of notice under paragraph (1) must be at least 14 days except that the Tribunal may give less than 14 days' notice–

(a)   with the parties' consent; or

(b)   in urgent or exceptional circumstances.

PUBLIC AND PRIVATE HEARINGS

32(1) Subject to the following paragraphs, all hearings must be held in public.

32(2) The Tribunal may give a direction that a hearing, or part of it, is to be held in private if the Tribunal considers that restricting access to the hearing is justified–

(a)   in the interests of public order or national security;

(b)   in order to protect a person's right to respect for their private and family life;

(c)   in order to maintain the confidentiality of sensitive information;

(d)   in order to avoid serious harm to the public interest; or

(e)   because not to do so would prejudice the interests of justice.

32(3) Where a hearing, or part of it, is to be held in private, the Tribunal may determine who is permitted to attend the hearing or part of it.

32(4) The Tribunal may give a direction excluding from any hearing, or part of it–

(a)   any person whose conduct the Tribunal considers is disrupting or is likely to disrupt the hearing;

(b)   any person whose presence the Tribunal considers is likely to prevent another person from giving evidence or making submissions freely;

(c)   any person where the purpose of the hearing would be defeated by the attendance of that person; or

(d)   a person under the age of eighteen years.

32(5) The Tribunal may give a direction excluding a witness from a hearing until that witness gives evidence.

32(6) If the Tribunal publishes a report of a decision resulting from a hearing which was held wholly or partly in private, the Tribunal must, so far as practicable, ensure that the report does not disclose information which was referred to only in a part of the hearing that was held in private (including such information which enables the identification of any person whose affairs were dealt with in the part of the hearing that was held in private) if to do so would undermine the purpose of holding the hearing in private.

HEARINGS IN A PARTY'S ABSENCE

33 If a party fails to attend a hearing the Tribunal may proceed with the hearing if the Tribunal–

(a)   is satisfied that the party has been notified of the hearing or that reasonable steps have been taken to notify the party of the hearing; and

(b)   considers that it is in the interests of justice to proceed with the hearing.

Chapter 4 – Decisions

CONSENT ORDERS

34(1) The Tribunal may, at the request of the parties but only if it considers it appropriate, make a consent order disposing of the proceedings and making such other appropriate provision as the parties have agreed.

34(2) Notwithstanding any other provision of these Rules, the Tribunal need not hold a hearing before making an order under paragraph (1), or provide reasons for the order.

NOTICE OF DECISIONS AND REASONS

35(1) The Tribunal may give a decision orally at a hearing.

35(2) The Tribunal must provide to each party within 28 days after making a decision (other than a decision under Part 4) which finally disposes of all issues in proceedings or of a preliminary issue dealt with following a direction under rule 5(3)(e) or as soon as practicable thereafter, a decision notice which—

(a)   states the Tribunal's decision; and

(b)   notifies the party of any right of appeal against the decision and the time within which, and the manner in which, the right of appeal may be exercised.

35(3) Unless each party agrees that it is unnecessary, the decision notice must—

(a)   include a summary of the findings of fact and reasons for the decision; or

(b)   be accompanied by full written findings of fact and reasons for the decision.

35(4) If the Tribunal provides no findings and reasons, or summary findings and reasons only, in or with the decision notice, a party to the proceedings may apply for full written findings and reasons, and must do so before making an application for permission to appeal under rule 39 (application for permission to appeal).

35(5) An application under paragraph (4) must be made in writing and be sent or delivered to the Tribunal so that it is received within 28 days after the date that the Tribunal sent or otherwise provided the decision notice under paragraph (2) to the party making the application.

35(6) The Tribunal must send a full written statement of findings and reasons to each party within 28 days after receiving an application for full written reasons made in accordance with paragraphs (4) and (5), or as soon as practicable thereafter.

History – In r. 35(2), the words "a decision (other than a decision under Part 4) which finally disposes of all issues in proceedings or of a preliminary issue dealt with following a direction under rule 5(3)(e)" substituted for the words "a decision which finally disposes of all issues in proceedings (except a decision under Part 4), " by SI 2013/477, r. 42, with effect from 1 April 2013.

PART 4 – CORRECTING, SETTING ASIDE, REVIEWING AND APPEALING TRIBUNAL DECISIONS

INTERPRETATION

36 In this Part—

    "appeal" means the exercise of a right of appeal against a decision of the Tribunal; and

    "review" means the review of a decision by the Tribunal under section 9 of the 2007 Act.

CLERICAL MISTAKES AND ACCIDENTAL SLIPS OR OMISSIONS

37 The Tribunal may at any time correct any clerical mistake or other accidental slip or omission in a decision, direction or any document produced by it, by—

(a)   sending notification of the amended decision or direction, or a copy of the amended document, to all parties; and

(b)   making any necessary amendment to any information published in relation to the decision, direction or document.

SETTING ASIDE A DECISION WHICH DISPOSES OF PROCEEDINGS

38(1) The Tribunal may set aside a decision which disposes of proceedings, or part of such a decision, and re-make the decision, or the relevant part of it, if—

(a)   the Tribunal considers that it is in the interests of justice to do so; and

(b)   one or more of the conditions in paragraph (2) is satisfied.

38(2) The conditions are—

(a)   a document relating to the proceedings was not sent to, or was not received at an appropriate time by, a party or a party's representative;

(b)   a document relating to the proceedings was not sent to the Tribunal at an appropriate time;

(c)   there has been some other procedural irregularity in the proceedings; or

(d)   a party, or a party's representative, was not present at a hearing related to the proceedings.

38(3) A party applying for a decision, or part of a decision, to be set aside under paragraph (1) must make a written application to the Tribunal so that it is received no later than 28 days after the date on which the Tribunal sent notice of the decision to the party.

38(4)   If the Tribunal sets aside a decision or part of a decision under this rule, the Tribunal must notify the parties in writing as soon as practicable.

APPLICATION FOR PERMISSION TO APPEAL

39(1)   A person seeking permission to appeal must make a written application to the Tribunal for permission to appeal.

39(2)   An application under paragraph (1) must be sent or delivered to the Tribunal so that it is received no later than 56 days after the latest of the dates that the Tribunal sends to the person making the application–

(za)   the relevant decision notice;

(a)   where–

   (i)   the decision disposes of all issues in the proceedings; or

   (ii)   subject to paragraph (2A), the decision disposes of a preliminary issue dealt with following a direction under rule 5(3)(e),

   full written reasons for the decision;

(b)   notification of amended reasons for, or correction of, the decision following a review; or

(c)   notification that an application for the decision to be set aside has been unsuccessful.

39(2A)   The Tribunal may direct that the 56 days within which a party may send or deliver an application for permission to appeal against a decision that disposes of a preliminary issue shall run from the date of the decision that disposes of all issues in the proceedings.

39(3)   The date in paragraph (2)(c) applies only if the application for the decision to be set aside was made within the time stipulated in rule 38 (setting aside a decision which disposes of proceedings), or any extension of that time granted by the Tribunal.

39(4)   If the person seeking permission to appeal sends or delivers the application to the Tribunal later than the time required by paragraph (2) or by any extension of time under rule 5(3)(a) (power to extend time)–

(a)   the application must include a request for an extension of time and the reason why the application notice was not provided in time; and

(b)   unless the Tribunal extends time for the application under rule 5(3)(a) (power to extend time) the Tribunal must not admit the application.

39(5)   An application under paragraph (1) must–

(a)   identify the decision of the Tribunal to which it relates;

(b)   identify the alleged error or errors in the decision; and

(c)   state the result the party making the application is seeking.

History – R. 39(2)(za) inserted by SI 2013/477, r. 43(a), with effect from 1 April 2013.
R. 39(2)(a) substituted by SI 2013/477, r. 43(b), with effect from 1 April 2013. Former r. 39(2)(a) read as follows:
   "(a)   full written reasons for the decision;"
R. 39(2A) inserted by SI 2013/477, r. 43(c), with effect from 1 April 2013.

TRIBUNAL'S CONSIDERATION OF APPLICATION FOR PERMISSION TO APPEAL

40(1)   On receiving an application for permission to appeal the Tribunal must first consider, taking into account the overriding objective in rule 2, whether to review the decision in accordance with rule 41 (review of a decision).

40(2)   If the Tribunal decides not to review the decision, or reviews the decision and decides to take no action in relation to the decision, or a part of it, the Tribunal must consider whether to give permission to appeal in relation to the decision or that part of it.

40(3)   The Tribunal must send a record of its decision to the parties as soon as practicable.

40(4)   If the Tribunal refuses permission to appeal it must send with the record of its decision–

(a)   a statement of its reasons for such refusal; and

(b)   notification of the right to make an application to the Upper Tribunal for permission to appeal and the time within which, and the method by which, such application must be made.

40(5)   The Tribunal may give permission to appeal against part only of the decision or on limited grounds, but must comply with paragraph (4) in relation to any part of the decision or grounds on which it has refused permission.

REVIEW OF A DECISION

41(1) The Tribunal may only undertake a review of a decision–

(a) pursuant to rule 40(1) (review on an application for permission to appeal); and

(b) if it is satisfied that there was an error of law in the decision.

41(2) The Tribunal must notify the parties in writing of the outcome of any review, unless the Tribunal decides to take no action following the review.

41(3) The Tribunal may not take any action in relation to a decision following a review without first giving every party an opportunity to make representations in relation to the proposed action.

POWER TO TREAT AN APPLICATION AS A DIFFERENT TYPE OF APPLICATION

42 The Tribunal may treat an application for a decision to be corrected, set aside or reviewed, or for permission to appeal against a decision, as an application for any other one of those things.

APPEALS (EXCLUDED DECISIONS) ORDER 2009

(SI 2009/275, as amended by SI 2010/41)

Made on 5 February 2009 by the Lord Chancellor in exercise of the power conferred by s. 11(5)(f) and 13(8)(f) of the Tribunals, Courts and Enforcement Act 2007. Operative from 1 April 2009.

CITATION AND COMMENCEMENT

1 This Order may be cited as the Appeals (Excluded Decisions) Order 2009 and comes into force on 1st April 2009.

EXCLUDED DECISIONS

2 For the purposes of section 11(1) of the Tribunals, Courts and Enforcement Act 2007, the following decisions of the First-tier Tribunal are excluded decisions—

(a) a decision under section 103 of the Immigration and Asylum Act 1999 (appeals); and

(b) a decision under paragraphs 22, 23, 24, 29, 30, 31, 32 and 33 of Schedule 2 to the Immigration Act 1971.

History – Art. 2 substituted by SI 2010/41, art. 3, with effect from 15 February 2010.

3 For the purposes of sections 11(1) and 13(1) of the Tribunals, Courts and Enforcement Act 2007, the following decisions of the First-tier Tribunal or the Upper Tribunal are excluded decisions—

(a) any decision under section 20(7), (8B) or (8G)(b) (power to call for documents of taxpayer and others), 20B(1B) or (6) (restrictions on powers under sections 20 and 20A) or 20BB(2)(a) (falsification etc. of documents) of the Taxes Management Act 1970;

(b) any decision under section 35A(2) (variation of undertakings), 79A(2) (variation of undertakings) or 219(1A) (power to require information) of the Inheritance Tax Act 1984;

(c) any decision under section 152(5) (notification of taxable amount of certain benefits) or 215(7) (advance clearance by Board of distributions and payments) of the Income and Corporation Taxes Act 1988;

(d) any decision under section 138(4) of the Taxation of Chargeable Gains Act 1992 (procedure for clearance in advance);

(e) any decision under section 187(5) or (6) (returns and information) of, or paragraph 3(2) or 6(2) of Schedule 21 (restrictions on powers under section 187) to, the Finance Act 1993;

(f) any decision under paragraph 91(5) of Schedule 15 to the Finance Act 2000 (corporate venturing scheme: advance clearance);

(g) any decision under paragraph 88(5) of Schedule 29 to the Finance Act 2002 (gains and losses from intangible fixed assets: transfer of business or trade);

(h) any decision under paragraph 2, 4, 7, 9, 10, 11 or 24 of Schedule 13 to the Finance Act 2003 (stamp duty land tax: information powers);

(i) any decision under section 306A (doubt as to notifiability), 308A (supplemental information), 313B (reasons for non-disclosure: supporting information) or 314A (order to disclose) of the Finance Act 2004;

(j) any decision under section 697(4) of the Income Tax Act 2007 (opposed notifications: determinations by tribunal);

(k) any decision under regulation 10(3) of the Venture Capital Trust (Winding up and Mergers) (Tax) Regulations 2004 (procedure for Board's approval);

(l) any decision under regulation 5A (doubt as to notifiability), 7A (supplemental information), 12B (reasons for non-disclosure: supporting information) or 12C (order to disclose) of the National Insurance Contributions (Application of Part 7 of the Finance Act 2004) Regulations 2007.

(m) any procedural, ancillary or preliminary decision made in relation to an appeal against a decision under section 40A of the British Nationality Act 1981, section 82, 83 or 83A of the Nationality, Immigration and Asylum Act 2002, or regulation 26 of the Immigration (European Economic Area) Regulations 2006.

History – Art. 3(m) inserted by SI 2010/41, art. 4, with effect from 15 February 2010.

REVOCATIONS

4 The Appeals (Excluded Decisions) Order 2008 and the Appeals (Excluded Decisions) (Amendment) Order 2008 are revoked.

BANKING ACT 2009 (PARTS 2 AND 3 CONSEQUENTIAL AMENDMENTS) ORDER 2009

(SI 2009/317)

Made on 19 February 2009 by the Treasury, in exercise of the powers conferred by s. 135 and 168 of the Banking Act 2009. Operative from 21 February 2009.

PART 1 – INTRODUCTION

CITATION AND COMMENCEMENT

1 This Order may be cited as the Banking Act 2009 (Parts 2 and 3 Consequential Amendments) Order 2009 and comes into force on 21st February 2009.

INTERPRETATION

2 In this Order—

"**the 2009 Act**" means the Banking Act 2009.

PART 2 – GENERAL MODIFICATIONS TO LEGISLATION

3(1) So far as the enactments set out in the Schedule ("the listed enactments") apply in relation to liquidation and administration, they apply with the modifications set out in paragraphs (2) to (4).

3(2) The modifications relating to bank insolvency under Part 2 of the 2009 Act are that references to—

(a)   "**liquidator**" include a reference to a bank liquidator under Part 2 of the 2009 Act;

(b)   "**provisional liquidator**" include a reference to a provisional bank liquidator under Part 2 of the 2009 Act;

(c)   "**liquidation**" or "**insolvent liquidation**" include a reference to bank insolvency under Part 2 of the 2009 Act;

(d)   "**winding up**" or "**winding up by the court**" include a reference to bank insolvency under Part 2 of the 2009 Act (and a reference to the "**commencement of winding up**" in this context is to the commencement of bank insolvency);

(e)   "**winding up order**" include a reference to a bank insolvency order under Part 2 of the 2009 Act;

(f)   "**wound up**" include a reference to a bank having been put into bank insolvency under Part 2 of the 2009 Act; and

(g)   "**winding up petition**" or "**petition to wind up**" include an application for bank insolvency under Part 2 of the 2009 Act.

3(3) The modifications relating to bank administration under Part 3 of the 2009 Act are that references to—

(a)   "**administrator**" include a reference to a bank administrator under Part 3 of the 2009 Act;

(b)   "**administration**" or "**insolvent administration**" include a reference to a bank administration under Part 3 of the 2009 Act;

(c)   "**administration order**" include a reference to a bank administration order under Part 3 of the 2009 Act; and

(d)   "**provisional liquidator**" include a reference to a provisional bank administrator under Part 3 of the 2009 Act.

3(4) The modifications relating to bank insolvency or bank administration under Parts 2 and 3 of the 2009 Act are that references to—

(a)   "**insolvency legislation**" or "**the law of insolvency**" include Parts 2 and 3 of the 2009 Act and the provisions of the Insolvency Act 1986 and the Insolvency (Northern Ireland) Order 1989 as applied by those Parts;

(b)   a person acting as an **"insolvency practitioner"** (as defined in section 388 of the Insolvency Act 1986) include a person acting as a bank liquidator or bank administrator under Parts 2 and 3 of the 2009 Act;

(c)   the provisions of the Insolvency Act 1986 and the Insolvency (Northern Ireland) Order 1989, in the context of bank insolvency or bank administration, shall be read to include those provisions as applied and modified by sections 103 and 145 of the 2009 Act; and

(d)   the provisions of the Insolvency Rules 1986, the Insolvency Rules (Northern Ireland) 1991 and the Insolvency (Scotland) Rules 1986, in the context of bank insolvency or bank administration, shall be read to include those provisions as applied and modified by rules made under section 411(1A) of the Insolvency Act 1986 in relation to bank insolvency, and under section 411(1B) of the Insolvency Act 1986 in relation to bank administration.

PART 3 – SPECIFIC MODIFICATIONS AND AMENDMENTS TO LEGISLATION

FINANCE (NO 2) ACT 1992

4(1)   The following provision of the Finance (No 2) Act 1992 applies with the modification set out in this article.

4(2)   Paragraph 2 of Schedule 12 (Banks etc. in Compulsory Liquidation) is to be read as if it included the following–

"**3A**   Where the company is a bank (as defined in section 91 of the Banking Act 2009), bank insolvency proceedings shall be taken to have commenced against the bank when the application for a bank insolvency order is made to the court under section 95 of the Banking Act 2009.".

FINANCIAL SERVICES AND MARKETS ACT 2000

5   [Not relevant.]

COMPANIES ACT 2006

6   [Not relevant.]

DORMANT BANK AND BUILDING SOCIETY ACCOUNTS ACT 2008

7   [Not relevant.]

PENSION PROTECTION FUND (ENTRY RULES) REGULATIONS 2005

8   [Not relevant.]

PENSION PROTECTION FUND (ENTRY RULES) REGULATIONS (NORTHERN IRELAND) 2005

9   [Not relevant.]

SCHEDULE – LEGISLATION SUBJECT TO THE GENERAL MODIFICATIONS IN PART 2

Article 3(1)

PRIMARY LEGISLATION

Notes – Only relevant items have been reproduced.

Taxes Management Act 1970

Income and Corporation Taxes Act 1988

Taxation of Chargeable Gains Act 1992

Finance (No 2) Act 1992

Pensions Act 1995

Finance Act 1996

Terrorism Act 2000
Finance Act 2000
Finance Act 2002
Proceeds of Crime Act 2002
Finance Act 2003
Pensions Act 2004
Companies Act 2006
Finance Act 2008

SECONDARY LEGISLATION

Notes – Only relevant items have been reproduced.

Individual Savings Account Regulations 1998
Corporation Tax (Simplified Arrangements for Group Relief) Regulations 1999

FINANCE ACT 2008, SCHEDULE 39 (APPOINTED DAY, TRANSITIONAL PROVISION AND SAVINGS) ORDER 2009

(SI 2009/403)

Made on 26 February 2009 by the Treasury in exercise of the powers conferred by s. 118(2) and (3) of the Finance Act 2008.

CITATION AND INTERPRETATION

1(1) This Order may be cited as the Finance Act 2008, Schedule 39 (Appointed Day, Transitional Provision and Savings) Order 2009.

1(2) In this Order a reference to a paragraph (without more) is a reference to that paragraph of Schedule 39 to the Finance Act 2008.

1(3) In this Order–

> **"the Taxes Acts"** has the meaning given in section 118(1) of the Taxes Management Act 1970;
>
> **"TMA 1970"** means the Taxes Management Act 1970;
>
> **"VATA 1994"** means the Value Added Tax Act 1994.

APPOINTED DAYS

2(1) The day appointed for the coming into force of paragraphs 32 to 36 is 1st April 2009.

2(2) Subject to article 10(2), the day appointed for the coming into force of paragraphs 1 to 31 and 37 to 66 is 1st April 2010.

TRANSITIONAL PROVISIONS AND SAVINGS

3 Paragraph 33 is disregarded where, for the purposes of section 33A of VATA 1994 (refunds of VAT to museums and galleries), the day on which the supply was made or the acquisition or importation took place was on or before 31st March 2006.

4 Paragraph 34 is disregarded–

(a)   where, for the purposes of section 77 of VATA 1994 (assessments: time limits and supplementary assessments), the end of the prescribed accounting period or the importation, acquisition or event giving rise to the penalty, as appropriate, occurred on or before 31st March 2006, and

(b)   where, after a person's death, a sum is assessed as due by reason of some conduct (however described) of the deceased, including a sum due by way of penalty, interest or surcharge, and the date of the death is on or before 31st March 2006.

5 Paragraph 35 is disregarded where, for the purposes of a claim under section 78 of VATA 1994 (interest in certain cases of official error), the end of the applicable period to which the claim relates was on or before 31st March 2006.

6 Paragraph 36 is disregarded where, for the purposes of section 80 of VATA 1994 (credit for, or repayment of, overstated or overpaid VAT), the relevant date is on or before 31st March 2006.

7 Section 36(1A)(b) and (c) of TMA 1970 (fraudulent and negligent conduct) shall not apply where the year of assessment is 2008-09 or earlier, except where the assessment on the person ("P") is for the purposes of making good to the Crown a loss of tax attributable to P's negligent conduct or the negligent conduct of a person acting on P's behalf.

8 Paragraph 46(2A)(b) and (c) of Schedule 18 to the Finance Act 1998 (general time limits for assessments) shall not apply where the end of the accounting period to which the assessment relates is on or before 31st March 2010, except in a case involving negligence on the part of–

(a)   the company, or

(b)   a person acting on behalf of the company, or

(c)   a person who was a partner of the company at the relevant time.

9 Section 77(4A)(c) and (d) of VATA 1994 (value added tax: assessments: time limits and supplementary assessments) shall not apply where the end of the prescribed accounting period or the importation, acquisition or event giving rise to the penalty, as appropriate, occurred on or before

31 March 2010, except where VAT has been lost in circumstances giving rise to a penalty under section 67 of VATA 1994 (failure to notify and unauthorised issue of invoices).

10(1)   This article applies where an event specified in paragraph 4 below relates to a year of assessment in respect of which a person ("P") has not been given notice under–

(a)   section 8 of TMA 1970 (personal return),

(b)   section 8A of TMA 1970 (trustee's return), or

(c)   section 12AA of TMA 1970 (partnership return),

within one year of the end of the year of assessment.

10(2)   Where this article applies, the day appointed for the coming into force of paragraphs 1 to 31 and 37 to 65 is 1st April 2012.

10(3)   But this article does not apply if, as regards P and a year of assessment, any income which ought to have been assessed to income tax or chargeable gains which ought to have been assessed to capital gains tax, have not been assessed, or an assessment to tax has become insufficient, or any relief which has been given has become excessive.

10(4)   The events referred to in paragraph (1) above are–

(a)   an assessment on P to income tax or capital gains tax,

(b)   a claim by or on behalf of P, provided for by any provision of the Taxes Acts, and

(c)   a notice given by P under section 711 of the Income Tax (Earnings and Pensions Act) 2003 (right to make a return).

10(5)   Nothing in this article has any application where P is a company.

FINANCE ACT 2008, SCHEDULE 36 (APPOINTED DAY AND SAVINGS) ORDER 2009

(SI 2009/404)

Made on 26 February 2009 by the Treasury in exercise of the powers conferred by s. 113(2) and (3) of the Finance Act 2008.

CITATION AND INTERPRETATION

1(1) This Order may be cited as the Finance Act 2008, Schedule 36 (Appointed Day and Savings) Order 2009.

1(2) In this Order a reference to a paragraph (without more) is a reference to that paragraph of Schedule 36 to the Finance Act 2008.

APPOINTED DAY

2 The day appointed for the coming into force of Schedule 36 to the Finance Act 2008 is 1st April 2009.

SAVINGS

3 Where a notice is given under section 19A of the Taxes Management Act 1970 ("TMA 1970") (power to call for documents for purposes of enquiries) on or before 31st March 2009, for the purposes of that notice–

(a) the provisions contained in that section and in section 97AA of TMA 1970 (penalties for failure to produce documents under section 19A) shall continue to have effect on and after 1st April 2009;

(b) the amendments made by paragraphs 71 and 75 (consequential amendments) shall be disregarded.

4 Where a notice is given under section 20 of TMA 1970 (power to call for documents of taxpayer and others) on or before 31st March 2009, for the purposes of that notice–

(a) the provisions contained in that section and in section 20BB of TMA 1970 (offence of falsification etc. of documents) shall continue to have effect on and after 1st April 2009;

(b) the amendments made by paragraphs 68, 70 and 76 (consequential amendments) shall be disregarded.

5 Where a notice is given under paragraph 6 of Schedule 1A to TMA 1970 (power to call for documents for the purposes of enquiries) on or before 31st March 2009, for the purposes of that notice–

(a) the provisions contained in paragraphs 6 and 6A (power to appeal against notice to produce documents) of that Schedule shall continue to have effect on and after 1st April 2009;

(b) the amendments made by paragraphs 72 and 75 (consequential amendments) shall be disregarded.

6 Where a notice is given under section 767C of the Income and Corporation Taxes Act (change in company ownership: information) on or before 31st March 2009, for the purposes of that notice–

(a) the provisions contained in that section shall continue to have effect on and after 1st April 2009;

(b) the amendments made by paragraph 73(a), 80, 81 and 82 (consequential amendments) shall be disregarded.

7 Where a notice is given under paragraph 27 of Schedule 18 to the Finance Act 1998 (company tax returns) on or before 31st March 2009, the provisions contained in paragraphs 27, 28 and 29 of that Schedule (notice to produce documents etc. for purposes of enquiry into company tax return, power to appeal against such notices and penalty for failure to produce such documents etc.) shall continue to have effect on and after 1st April 2009 for the purposes of that notice.

8 Where a notice is given for the purposes of regulation 5 (amendment of syndicate determinations and HMRC enquiries) of the Lloyd's Underwriters (Tax) Regulations 2005 on or before 31st March 2009, the provisions of paragraphs 27 to 29 of Schedule 18 to the Finance Act 1998 shall continue to have effect on and after 1st April 2009, with appropriate modification, for the purposes of that regulation.

9 In relation to a notice given on or before 31st March 2009, for the purposes of the application of section 20 of TMA 1970 (with sections 20B(i) and 20BB of that Act) to–

(a)   section 110ZA of the Social Security Administration Act 1992 (Class 1, 1A, 1B or 2 contributions: powers to call for documents etc),

(b)   section 104ZA of the Social Security Administration (Northern Ireland) Act 1992 (Class 1, 1A, 1B or 2 contributions: powers to call for documents etc), and

(c)   section 25 of the Tax Credits Act 2002 (payments of working tax credit by employers),

the amendments made respectively by paragraphs 84, 85 and 90 shall be disregarded.

10   In relation to a notice given on or before 31st March 2009, for the purposes of the application of–

(a)   subsections (1) to (8) and 8(C) to 9 of section 20 of TMA 1970 (powers to call for information relevant to liability to income tax, corporation tax or capital gains tax), and

(b)   sections 20B, 20BB and 20D of that Act so far as relating to those subsections,

to section 174 of the Finance Act 2006 (international tax enforcement arrangements: information powers), the amendments made by paragraph 91 shall be disregarded.

11   Where a notice is given on or before 31st March 2009, the amendments made by paragraph 78 (amendment to section 12(3) (secrecy) of the National Savings Bank Act 1971) shall be disregarded so far as they affect the notice.

12   In consequence of the preceding provisions of this Order, the amendments made by paragraph 92 shall be disregarded so far as they affect any notice referred to in those provisions, given on or before 31st March 2009.

Statutory Instruments

FINANCE ACT 2008, SCHEDULE 41 (APPOINTED DAY AND TRANSITIONAL PROVISIONS) ORDER 2009

(SI 2009/511)

Made on 5 March 2009 by the Treasury in exercise of the powers conferred by s. 122 and 123 of the Finance Act 2008.

CITATION AND INTERPRETATION

1(1) This Order may be cited as the Finance Act 2008, Schedule 41 (Appointed Day and Transitional Provisions) Order 2009.

1(2) In this Order a reference to a paragraph (without more) is a reference to that paragraph of Schedule 41 to the Finance Act 2008.

1(3) In this Order–

"**relevant excise provision**" has the meaning given in paragraph 3(1);

"**relevant obligation**" means an obligation specified in the Table in paragraph 1;

"**unauthorised issue of an invoice**" has the meaning given in paragraph 2(2).

APPOINTED DAY

2 The day appointed for the coming into force of Schedule 41 to the Finance Act 2008 is 1st April 2010.

3 That Schedule has effect–

(a) in relation to any relevant obligation arising on or after that date;

(b) in relation to any unauthorised issue of an invoice taking place on or after that date;

(c) in relation to any act which enables HMRC to assess an amount as duty under a relevant excise provision and which is done on or after that date; and

(d) in relation to any act giving rise to a penalty under paragraph 4 (handling goods subject to unpaid excise duty) which is done on or after that date.

TRANSITIONAL PROVISIONS

4 Paragraph 25 (consequential repeals), paragraph 29 of Schedule 24 to the Finance Act 2007 and paragraph 21 of Schedule 40 to the Finance Act 2008 repeal the following provisions only in so far as those provisions relate to conduct involving dishonesty which gives rise to a penalty under Schedule 41 to the Finance Act 2008–

(a) in the Value Added Tax Act 1994–

    (i) sections 60 and 61 (VAT evasion), and

    (ii) section 67(1)(b) (failure to notify);

(b) in the Finance Act 1994–

    (i) section 8 (penalty for evasion of excise duty), and

    (ii) paragraphs 12 and 13 of Schedule 7 (insurance premium tax: civil penalties);

(c) paragraphs 18 and 19 of Schedule 5 to the Finance Act 1996 (landfill tax: civil penalties: evasion and misdeclaration or neglect);

(d) paragraphs 98 and 99 of Schedule 6 to the Finance Act 2000 (climate change levy: civil penalties: evasion, liability of directors and misdeclaration or neglect);

(e) in Schedule 6 to the Finance Act 2001–

    (i) paragraphs 7 and 8 (aggregates levy: civil penalties: evasion, liability of directors and misdeclaration or neglect); and

    (ii) paragraph 9A(5)(b) (penalty under paragraph 7 above); and

(f) section 133(2) to (4) of the Finance Act 2002 (aggregates levy: amendments to provisions about civil penalties).

FINANCE ACT 2008, SCHEDULE 40 (APPOINTED DAY, TRANSITIONAL PROVISIONS AND CONSEQUENTIAL AMENDMENTS) ORDER 2009

(SI 2009/571)

Made on 9 March 2009 by the Treasury in exercise of the powers conferred by s. 122 of the Finance Act 2008. Operative from 1 April 2009.

CITATION AND INTERPRETATION

1(1) This Order may be cited as the Finance Act 2008, Schedule 40 (Appointed Day, Transitional Provisions and Consequential Amendments) Order 2009 and comes into force on 1st April 2009.

1(2) In this Order a reference to a paragraph (without more) is a reference to that paragraph of Schedule 40 to the Finance Act 2008.

1(3) In this Order–

> **"filing date"**, in relation to a relevant document, means–
>
> > (i) where the document is required to be given to HMRC, the date by which it is required to be given, and
> >
> > (ii) where the document is not required to be given to HMRC, the date on which it is given;
>
> **"HMRC"** means Her Majesty's Revenue and Customs;
>
> **"relevant documents"** means documents given to HMRC of a kind inserted in the Table in paragraph 1 of Schedule 24 by paragraph 2(4) or (5);
>
> **"relevant tax"** means any tax inserted in the Table in paragraph 1 of Schedule 24 by paragraph 2(4) or (5);
>
> **"tax period"** has the meaning given in paragraph 28(g) of Schedule 24.

APPOINTED DAY

2 The day appointed for the coming into force of Schedule 40 to the Finance Act 2008 is 1st April 2009.

3 In their application in relation to penalties payable under paragraph 1 of Schedule 24 (error in taxpayer's document), the entries inserted by paragraph 2(4) and (5) shall have effect in relation to–

(a) relevant documents–

> > (i) which relate to tax periods commencing on or after 1st April 2009, and
> >
> > (ii) for which the filing date is on or after 1st April 2010;

(b) relevant documents relating to all claims for repayments of relevant tax made on or after 1st April 2010 which are not related to a tax period;

(c) relevant documents produced under regulations under section 256 of the Inheritance Tax Act 1984 ("IHTA 1984") (regulations about accounts, etc), where the date of death is on or after 1st April 2009; and

(d) in any other case, relevant documents given where a person's liability to pay relevant tax arises on or after 1st April 2010.

4 In their application in relation to penalties payable under paragraph 1A of Schedule 24 (error in taxpayer's document attributable to another person), the entries inserted by paragraph 2(4) and (5) shall have effect in relation to–

(a) relevant documents–

> > (i) which relate to tax periods commencing on or after 1st April 2009, and
> >
> > (ii) for which the filing date is on or after 1st April 2010;

(b) relevant documents relating to all claims for repayments of relevant tax made on or after 1st April 2010 which are not related to a tax period;

(c) relevant documents produced under regulations under section 256 of IHTA 1984 (regulations about accounts, etc) where the date of death is on or after 1st April 2009; and

(d) in any other case, relevant documents given where a person's liability to pay relevant tax arises on or after 1st April 2010.

5 In their application in relation to assessments falling within paragraph 2 of Schedule 24 (under-assessment by HMRC), the entries inserted by paragraph 2(4) and (5) shall have effect in relation to tax periods commencing on or after 1st April 2009, where the filing date for the relevant document is on or after 1st April 2010.

Statutory Instruments

TRANSITIONAL PROVISIONS

6(1) Paragraph 21 (consequential repeals) repeals the provisions listed in paragraph (2) only in so far as those provisions relate to conduct involving dishonesty which relates to–

(a)   an inaccuracy in a document, or

(b)   a failure to notify HMRC of an under-assessment by HMRC.

6(2) The provisions referred to in paragraph (1) are–

(a)   in the Finance Act 1994–

    (i)   section 8 (penalty for evasion of excise duty), and

    (ii)   paragraphs 12 and 13 of Schedule 7 (insurance premium tax: civil penalties),

(b)   paragraphs 18 and 19 of Schedule 5 to the Finance Act 1996 (landfill tax: civil penalties: evasion and misdeclaration or neglect),

(c)   paragraphs 98 and 99 of Schedule 6 to the Finance Act 2000 (climate change levy: civil penalties: evasion, liability of directors and misdeclaration or neglect),

(d)   in Schedule 6 to the Finance Act 2001–

    (i)   paragraphs 7 and 8 (aggregates levy: civil penalties: evasion, liability of directors and misdeclaration or neglect), and

    (ii)   paragraph 9A(5)(b) (penalty under paragraph 7 above),

(e)   section 133(2) to (4) of the Finance Act 2002 (aggregates levy: amendments to provisions about civil penalties).

7 Notwithstanding paragraph 29(d) of Schedule 24 (consequential amendments), sections 60 and 61 of the Value Added Tax Act 1994 (VAT evasion) shall continue to have effect with respect to conduct involving dishonesty which does not relate to an inaccuracy in a document or a failure to notify HMRC of an under-assessment by HMRC.

CONSEQUENTIAL AMENDMENTS TO ENACTMENTS

8 Schedule 1 contains amendments of enactments in consequence of the provisions omitted by paragraph 21 and by paragraph 29 of Schedule 24.

9 Schedule 2 contains consequential amendments to secondary legislation.

SCHEDULES

SCHEDULE 1 – CONSEQUENTIAL AMENDMENTS – PRIMARY LEGISLATION

Article 8

TAXES MANAGEMENT ACT 1970

10–16 [Amends TMA 1970, s. 59C, 100B and 107A.]

FINANCE ACT 1982

17–18 [Not relevant to income tax, capital gains tax or corporation tax.]

INCOME AND CORPORATION TAXES ACT 1988

19–20 [Amends ICTA 1988, s. 827.]

FINANCE ACT 1994

21 [Not relevant to income tax, capital gains tax or corporation tax.]

VALUE ADDED TAX ACT 1994

22–27 [Not relevant to income tax, capital gains tax or corporation tax.]

FINANCE ACT 1996

28–29 [Not relevant to income tax, capital gains tax or corporation tax.]

FINANCE ACT 2000

30 [Not relevant to income tax, capital gains tax or corporation tax.]

FINANCE ACT 2001

31–35 [Not relevant to income tax, capital gains tax or corporation tax.]

FINANCE ACT 2004

36 [Amends FA 2004, s. 313.]

INCOME TAX (TRADING AND OTHER INCOME) ACT 2005

37–39 [Amends ITTOIA 2005, s. 54(2) and 869(4).]

SCHEDULE 2 – CONSEQUENTIAL AMENDMENTS – SECONDARY LEGISLATION

Article 9

REGISTERED PENSION SCHEMES (RELIEF AT SOURCE) REGULATIONS 2005

40 [Omits SI 2005/3448, reg. 14(4).]

41 Omit paragraph (4) of regulation 14.

DUTY STAMPS REGULATIONS 2006

42–43 Not relevant to income tax, capital gains tax or corporation tax.

REGISTERED PENSION SCHEMES (AUTHORISED PAYMENTS) REGULATIONS 2009

(SI 2009/1171, as amended by SI 2011/1751, SI 2012/522, SI 2012/1881, SI 2013/1818 and FA 2014)

Made on 6 May 2009 by the Commissioners for Her Majesty's Revenue and Customs in exercise of the powers conferred by s. 164(1)(f) and (2) of the Finance Act 2004, and now exercisable by them. Operative in accordance with reg. 1

PART 1 – INTRODUCTION

CITATION, COMMENCEMENT AND EFFECT

1(1) These Regulations may be cited as the Registered Pension Schemes (Authorised Payments) Regulations 2009 and shall come into force on 1st June 2009.

1(2) These Regulations shall have effect–

(a) for payments of a description within Part 2, in relation to payments made on or after 1st December 2009;

(b) for payments of a description within Part 3 or Part 4, in relation to payments made on or after 6th April 2006; and

(c) for payments of a description within Part 5, in relation to payments made on or after 8th August 2012.

History – Reg. 1(2)(c) (and the "; and" before it) inserted (and the "and" after (a) omitted) by SI 2012/1881, reg. 3, with effect from 8 August 2012.

INTERPRETATION

2(1) Any reference in these Regulations to a numbered section or a paragraph of a Schedule, without more, is a reference to the section or paragraph of the Finance Act 2004 bearing that number.

2(2) Any reference in these Regulations to a person's being entitled to a payment–

(a) if it is a payment of pension (or intended to be such a payment), shall be construed in accordance with section 165(3) (pension rules), and related expressions shall be construed accordingly;

(b) if it is a payment of a lump sum (or intended to be such a payment), shall be construed in accordance with section 166(2) (lump sum rule), and related expressions shall be construed accordingly.

2(3) For the purpose of these Regulations, whether a person is connected with another person is determined in accordance with section 993 of the ITA 2007 (meaning of "connected" persons).

2(4) For the purpose of these Regulations,

(a) a pension scheme is related to another pension scheme if each of them is–

    (i) a registered pension scheme that is an occupational pension scheme or a public service pension scheme, and

    (ii) a pension scheme relating to the same employment; but

(b) if the context is whether a person is or is not a controlling director of a sponsoring employer of a pension scheme, only registered pension schemes that are occupational pension schemes are related to other such pension schemes.

2(5) In these Regulations–

"controlling director" has the meaning given by section 273(9) (members liable as scheme administrator);

"excluded transfer" means–

(a) a recognised transfer; or

(b) any other transfer to the pension scheme of any sums or assets held for the purposes of, or representing accrued rights under, another pension scheme.

PRESCRIBED PAYMENTS AND TAXATION

3 A payment by a registered pension scheme to or in respect of a member that is described in Part 2 of these Regulations–

(a)   is a payment of a prescribed description for the purposes of section 164(1)(f) (authorised member payments);

(b)   if paid to the member, shall be treated as a trivial commutation lump sum paid to the member for the purposes of Part 9 of ITEPA 2003 (pension income); and

(c)   if not paid to the member, shall be treated as a trivial commutation lump sum death benefit paid to the recipient for the purposes of Part 9 of ITEPA 2003.

3A(1) This regulation applies to a lump sum if–

(a)   the sum ("the earlier sum") is paid under a registered pension scheme to a member of the scheme,

(b)   the earlier sum is paid to the member in connection with a pension under a registered pension scheme to which it is expected that the member will become entitled ("the expected pension"),

(c)   the earlier sum is paid before the member becomes entitled to the expected pension,

(d)   either–

       (i)   the earlier sum is paid on or after 19 September 2013 but before 27 March 2014, or

       (ii)   the earlier sum is paid before 19 September 2013, a contract for a lifetime annuity is entered into to provide the expected pension, and on or after 19 March 2014 the contract is cancelled,

(e)   all of the sums and assets for the time being representing the sums and assets that when the earlier sum was paid were held for the purpose of providing the expected pension are, before the member becomes entitled to the expected pension, used in paying a further lump sum to the member ("the further sum"),

(f)   the further sum is paid on or after 6 July 2014 but before 6 April 2015, and

(g)   either–

       (i)   the payment of the further sum is a payment described in regulation 11, 11A or 12, or

       (ii)   the further sum is a trivial commutation lump sum within paragraph 7A of Schedule 29 and the earlier sum is the pension commencement lump sum in connection with which the further sum is paid.

3A(2) If this regulation applies to the earlier sum, and the payment of the further sum is a payment described in regulation 11, 11A or 12–

(a)   the payment of the earlier sum is a payment of a prescribed description for the purposes of section 164(1)(f), and

(b)   section 636A of ITEPA 2003 (exemption from income tax for certain lump sums) applies in relation to the earlier sum as if the earlier sum were a pension commencement lump sum.

3A(3) When deciding for the purposes of this regulation whether the further sum is a trivial commutation lump sum within paragraph 7A of Schedule 29, sub-paragraph (2)(c) of that paragraph is to be omitted.

3A(4) If this regulation applies to the earlier sum, and only the sums and assets mentioned in paragraph (1)(e) are used in paying the further sum, section 636B of ITEPA 2003 applies in relation to the further sum with the omission of its subsection (3).

3A(5) If this regulation applies to the earlier sum, and the sums and assets mentioned in paragraph (1)(e) are used together with other sums and assets in paying the further sum–

(a)   section 636B of ITEPA 2003 applies in relation to the further sum as if instead of the further sum there were two separate trivial commutation lump sums as follows–

       (i)   one ("the first part of the further sum") consisting of so much of the further sum as is attributable to the sums and assets mentioned in paragraph (1)(e), and

       (ii)   another consisting of the remainder of the further sum,

(b)   the first part of the further sum is to be treated for the purposes of section 636B of ITEPA 2003 as having been paid immediately before the remainder of the further sum,

(c) section 636B of ITEPA 2003 applies in relation to the first part of the further sum with the omission of its subsection (3), and

(d) for the purposes of applying section 636B(3) of ITEPA 2003 in relation to the remainder of the further sum, the rights to which the first part of the further sum relates are to be treated as rights that are not uncrystallised rights immediately before the remainder of the further sum is paid.

3A(6) For the purposes of paragraph (1), if the circumstances are as described in paragraph (1)(d)(ii), the member is treated as not having become entitled to the expected pension as a result of the cancelled contract having been entered into."

History – Reg. 3A inserted by FA 2014, s. 43 and Sch. 5, para. 6(1), with effect from 19 March 2014.

4 A payment by a registered pension scheme that is described in Part 3 of these Regulations, to the extent specified in the regulation concerned–

(a) is a payment of a prescribed description for the purposes of section 164(1)(f) of the Finance Act 2004;

(b) shall be treated as pension paid to the recipient under a registered pension scheme for the purposes of Part 9 of ITEPA 2003; and

(c) shall be treated for those purposes as pension accruing in the tax year in which it is paid.

5 A payment by a registered pension scheme that is described in Part 4 of these Regulations–

(a) is a payment of a prescribed description for the purposes of section 164(1)(f) of the Finance Act 2004; and

(b) shall be treated as a pension commencement lump sum paid under a registered pension scheme for the purposes of Part 9 of ITEPA 2003.

5A A payment by a registered pension scheme that is described in Part 5 of these Regulations–

(a) is a payment of a prescribed description for the purposes of section 164(1)(f) of the Finance Act 2004; and

(b) shall be treated as a short service refund lump sum for the purposes of Part 9 of ITEPA 2003.

History – Reg. 5A inserted by SI 2012/1881, reg. 4, with effect from 8 August 2012.

PART 2 – COMMUTATION PAYMENTS

PAYMENT AFTER RELEVANT ACCRETION

6(1) A payment made after there has been a relevant accretion in respect of the member if–

(a) the payment extinguishes the member's entitlement to benefits under the pension scheme;

(b) it does not exceed £10,000;

(c) it does not exceed the value of the accretion; and

(d) it is made no later than the relevant date.

6(2) Regulation 7 defines **"relevant accretion"**.

6(3) In a case where the accretion is a relevant accretion by virtue of having occurred after the event described in regulation 7(2)(b), the scheme pension or annuity concerned shall be ignored in determining whether the member's entitlement to benefits under the scheme has been extinguished.

6(4) For the purposes of paragraph (1)(d) the relevant date is–

(a) if the accretion has occurred before 1st December 2009, 1st June 2010, otherwise

(b) six months after the date the accretion occurs.

History – In reg. 6(1)(b), "£10,000" substituted for "£2,000" by FA 2014, s. 42(6), with effect for payments made on or after 27 March 2014.

MEANING OF "RELEVANT ACCRETION"

7(1) The following are relevant accretions for the purposes of regulation 6 if they occur after either of the events mentioned in paragraph (2)–

(a) a payment ("the payment in") is received by the scheme in respect of the member, other than a contribution into the pension scheme or an excluded transfer into the pension scheme;

(b) there is an allocation to the arrangement in the amount by which the value of the sums and assets held for the purposes of the arrangement exceeds the value the scheme administrator had believed they had; and

(c) the scheme administrator becomes aware that the member is entitled to a benefit under the pension scheme, provided–

(i)   the scheme administrator had not been aware of the entitlement before the event in paragraph (2), and

(ii)   the scheme administrator [sic] could not reasonably have been expected to be aware of it before that event.

7(2)   The events are–

(a)   there is a recognised transfer to another registered pension scheme or to a qualifying recognised overseas pension scheme in respect of the member; and

(b)   a scheme pension or annuity is purchased for the member by the pension scheme from an insurance company.

7(3)   In order for the purchase of a scheme pension or annuity on or after 6th April 2006 to be an event within paragraph (2)(b), all or a part of the member's lifetime allowance must be available at the time of the purchase.

7(3A)   For the purposes of determining whether all or part of the member's lifetime allowance is available under paragraph (3)–

(a)   the fact that benefit crystallisation event 5 or benefit crystallisation event 5B has occurred in relation to the member is to be disregarded, and

(b)   anything which, but for paragraph 2 or 15A of Schedule 32, would have been such a benefit crystallisation event is to be treated as if it were such an event.

7(4)   The value of a relevant accretion is–

(a)   in the case of a payment in within paragraph (1)(a), the amount of the payment; or

(b)   in the case of an allocation within paragraph (1)(b), the amount by which the value of the sums and assets exceeds the value they had been believed to have;

(c)   in the case described in paragraph (1)(c), the value of the benefit to which the member is entitled.

7(5)   In paragraph (1)(a), **"contribution"** does not include any amount mentioned in section 188(3)(c) (rebates and minimum contributions paid by the Board of Inland Revenue).

Prospective amendments – Reg. 7(5) omitted by SI 2013/1818, reg. 2(3), with effect from 6 April 2015.

History – Reg. 7(3A) inserted by SI 2011/1751, reg. 8(2), which came into force on 11 August 2011, with effect for the tax year 2011–12 and subsequent tax years.

PAYMENTS UNDER THE FINANCIAL SERVICES COMPENSATION SCHEME

8(1)   A payment made by way of compensation under the Financial Services Compensation Scheme if–

(a)   the payment does not exceed £10,000; and

(b)   it extinguishes the member's entitlement to benefits under the pension scheme.

8(2)   The reference in paragraph (1) to the Financial Services Compensation Scheme is to the scheme established by Part 15 of the Financial Services and Markets Act 2000.

History – In reg. 8(1)(a), "£10,000" substituted for "£2,000" by FA 2014, s. 42(6), with effect for payments made on or after 27 March 2014.

PAYMENTS TO OR IN RESPECT OF MEMBERS WHO WERE UNTRACEABLE

9   [Omitted by SI 2011/1751, reg. 8(3), which came into force on 11 August 2011, with effect for the tax year 2011–12 and subsequent tax years.]

PAYMENTS TO MEMBERS RECEIVING ANNUITIES

10(1)   A payment to a member which would be a trivial commutation lump sum(c) but for the continuance after the payment of an annuity if–

(a)   the condition in paragraph (2) is satisfied; or

(b)   if the member is not a member of any other registered pension scheme, the conditions in paragraph (3) are satisfied.

10(2)   The condition mentioned in paragraph (1)(a) is that the payment is made before the end of the commutation period, as determined in accordance with paragraph 7(2) of Schedule 29.

10(3)   The conditions mentioned in paragraph (1)(b) are that–

(a)   the member had not previously received either a trivial commutation lump sum or a payment that was an authorised payment by virtue of this regulation; and

(b)   the value of the member's pension rights immediately before the payment, calculated in accordance with paragraph 7(5) of Schedule 29, does not exceed £30,000.

History – In reg. 10(3)(b), "£30,000" substituted for "£18,000" by FA 2014, s. 42(6), with effect for payments made on or after 27 March 2014.

In reg. 10(3)(b), "£18,000" substituted for the words "1% of the standard lifetime allowance" by SI 2011/1751, reg. 8(4), with effect in relation to payments made on or after 6 April 2012.

DE MINIMIS RULE FOR PENSION SCHEMES

11(1)   A payment by a public service pension scheme or an occupational pension scheme if—

(a)   the member has reached the age of 60;

(b)   the member—

      (i)   is not a controlling director of a sponsoring employer of this or of any related scheme, and

      (ii)   is not a person connected to such a person;

(c)   the payment does not exceed £10,000;

(d)   the commutation value of the benefits to which the member is entitled under this and any related scheme does not exceed £10,000 in total;

(e)   the payment extinguishes the member's entitlement to benefits under this scheme; and

(f)   no recognised transfer was made out of this or any related scheme in respect of the member during the 3 years preceding the date of the payment.

11(2)   For the purposes of paragraph (1)(d), the commutation value is equal to the amount of the lump sum that, if paid, would extinguish the member's entitlement to benefits under the scheme concerned.

History – In reg. 11(1)(a) the words ", but has not reached the age of 75", which appeared after the words "the age of 60", omitted by SI 2011/1751, reg. 8(5), which came into force on 11 August 2011, with effect for the tax year 2011–12 and subsequent tax years. In reg. 11(1)(c), "£10,000" substituted for "£2,000" by FA 2014, s. 42(6), with effect for payments made on or after 27 March 2014. In reg. 11(1)(d), "£10,000" substituted for "£2,000" by FA 2014, s. 42(6), with effect for payments made on or after 27 March 2014.

11A(1)   A payment to a member by a pension scheme which is not a public service pension scheme or an occupational pension scheme in respect of an arrangement under that scheme if—

(a)   the member has reached the age of 60;

(b)   the payment does not exceed £10,000;

(c)   the payment extinguishes the member's entitlement to benefits under the arrangement; and

(d)   the condition in paragraph (2) is satisfied.

11A(2)   The condition is that the member has not previously received more than two payments under this regulation.

History – In reg. 11A(1)(b), "£10,000" substituted for "£2,000" by FA 2014, s. 42(6), with effect for payments made on or after 27 March 2014.
In reg. 11A(2), "two payments" substituted for "one payment" by FA 2014, s. 42(6), with effect for payments made on or after 27 March 2014.
Reg. 11A inserted by SI 2012/522, reg. 2(2), with effect in relation to payments made on or after 6 April 2012.

PAYMENTS BY LARGER PENSION SCHEMES

12(1)   A payment by a public service pension scheme or an occupational pension scheme if—

(a)   there are at least 50 members;

(b)   any of conditions A, B or C is satisfied;

(c)   the member has reached the age of 60;

(d)   the member—

      (i)   is not a controlling director of a sponsoring employer of this or any related scheme, and

      (ii)   is not a person connected to such a person;

(e)   the payment does not exceed £10,000;

(f)   the payment extinguishes the member's entitlement to benefits under this scheme;

(g)   ignoring any transfer within paragraph (5), no excluded transfer was made into this scheme in relation to the member during the 5 years preceding the date of the payment; and

(h)   no recognised transfer was made out of this scheme in respect of the member during the 3 years preceding the date of the payment.

12(2)   Condition A is that the scheme was in existence on 1st July 2008.

12(3)   Condition B is that—

(a)   the payment is in respect of a defined benefits arrangement; and

(b)   the aggregate amount of the sums and assets held for the purposes of defined benefits arrangements is more than half of the aggregate amount of all the sums and assets held for the purposes of this scheme.

12(4)   Condition C is that in respect of at least 20 members the aggregate amount of the sums and assets held for the purpose of the arrangement exceed £10,000.

12(5)   A transfer is within this paragraph if it is a transfer of sums and assets described in paragraph 12(8)(b), (c) or (d) of Schedule 36 (enhanced protection – permitted transfers).

12(6) In paragraphs (3) and (4), the **"aggregate amount"** is an amount equal to the aggregate of the amount of the sums and the market value of the assets concerned.

History – In reg. 12(1)(c) the words ", but has not reached the age of 75", which appeared after the words "the age of 60", omitted by SI 2011/1751, reg. 8(5), which came into force on 11 August 2011, with effect for the tax year 2011–12 and subsequent tax years. In reg. 12(1)(e), "£10,000" substituted for "£2,000" by FA 2014, s. 42(6), with effect for payments made on or after 27 March 2014. In reg. 12(4), "£10,000" substituted for "£2,000" by FA 2014, s. 42(6), with effect for payments made on or after 27 March 2014.

PART 3 – PENSION ERRORS

PENSIONS PAID IN ERROR

13(1) A payment made in error which is intended to represent a payment permitted by the pension rules or the pension death benefit rules to or in respect of a member, if the scheme administrator or insurance company making the payment (in either case, "the payer") believed that–

(a) the recipient was entitled to the payment, and

(b) the recipient was entitled to it in that amount.

13(2) A payment is not within paragraph (1) if the error is that the recipient is no longer alive (as to which see regulation 15).

13(3) Regulation 4 applies to–

(a) the whole of the payment; or

(b) if the recipient was entitled to an authorised payment apart from under this regulation, the amount by which the payment exceeds the amount of the authorised payment.

PENSIONS PAID AFTER DISCOVERY OF ERROR

14(1) A payment made after the discovery of an error if either–

(a) it is made after there is a payment within regulation 13 to the same person and (apart from the discovery of the error) is of a similar nature to that payment; or

(b) if the error had not been discovered until after the payment, it would have been a payment within regulation 13.

14(2) A payment is not within paragraph (1) unless it falls within paragraph (3), (4) or (5).

14(3) A payment is within this paragraph if it is made even though the payer took reasonable steps to prevent its being made or its being made in that amount.

14(4) A payment is within this paragraph if it is made while the scheme administrator is considering whether the rules of the scheme should be amended so that such payments or payments in such amounts will be permitted by the pension rules or the pension death benefit rules (as the case may be), provided the scheme administrator has not taken an unreasonable amount of time to decide.

14(5) A payment is within this paragraph if it is made while the scheme administrator is in the process of amending the rules of the scheme so that such payments or payments in such amounts will be permitted by the pension rules or the pension death benefit rules (as the case may be), provided the scheme administrator has not taken an unreasonable amount of time to amend the rules.

14(6) Regulation 4 applies to–

(a) the whole of the payment; or

(b) if the recipient was entitled to an authorised payment apart from under this regulation, the amount by which the payment exceeds the amount of the authorised payment.

PENSIONS CONTINUING TO BE PAID AFTER DEATH

15(1) A payment which is intended to represent the payment of a pension permitted by the pension rules or the pension death benefit rules to or in respect of a member if–

(a) the member or dependant concerned ("the person") has died;

(b) the payment is made no later than six months after the date of the person's death;

(c) the payment would not have been an unauthorised payment if it had been made on the day before the person died; and

(d) either of the conditions in paragraph (2) is satisfied.

15(2) The conditions mentioned in paragraph (1)(d) are–

(a) the scheme administrator or insurance company making the payment (in either case, "the payer") did not know, and could not reasonably have been expected to know, that the person had died before the payment was made;

(b)   where the payer knew of the person's death before the payment was made, the payer took reasonable steps to prevent the payment's being made or its being made in that amount.

15(3)   Regulation 4 applies to the whole of the payment.

PAYMENTS OF ARREARS OF PENSION AFTER DEATH

16(1)   A payment of pension under the pension scheme to or in respect of a member who has died if–

(a)   the payment is in respect of a defined benefits arrangement;

(b)   [omitted by SI 2011/1751, reg. 8(6);]

(c)   the member–

    (i)   was not a controlling director of a sponsoring employer of this or any related scheme, and

    (ii)   was not a person connected to such a person; and

(d)   either–

    (i)   the conditions in paragraph (2) are satisfied, or

    (ii)   where the member died on or after 6th April 2006, the conditions in paragraph (3) are satisfied.

16(2)   The conditions where the member died before 6th April 2006 are that–

(a)   the payment represents accrued arrears of pension;

(b)   the payment was allowed or required by the rules of this scheme as they stood immediately before the member died; and

(c)   the existence of the rule or rules concerned would not have prejudiced approval of the scheme by the Inland Revenue or Her Majesty's Revenue and Customs.

16(3)   The conditions where the member died on or after 6th April 2006 are that–

(a)   the payment represents accrued arrears of scheme pension the member's entitlement to which the scheme administrator had not established until after the member's death;

(b)   the payment would not have been an unauthorised payment if the payment had been made immediately before the member's death and the member had been entitled to it; and

(c)   the scheme administrator could not reasonably have been expected to make the payment before the member's death.

16(4)   Regulation 4 applies to so much of the payment as does not exceed the amount accrued during the period–

(a)   beginning with the earliest date from which the member could have required the scheme administrator to make the payment if the member had been entitled to it; and

(b)   ending with the member's death.

16(5)   If the member died on or after 6th April 2006, the making of the payment shall be treated as a benefit crystallisation event for the purposes of the lifetime allowance charge, namely benefit crystallisation event 9.

16(6)   The amount crystallised for the purposes of benefit crystallisation event 9 is the amount of the payment to which regulation 4 applies.

16(7)   For the purpose of paragraph (2)(c), whether something would have prejudiced the approval of a scheme by the Inland Revenue or by Her Majesty's Revenue and Customs is to be determined in accordance with the publication IR 12(2001) (known as the Occupational Pension Schemes Practice Notes) published by the former Inland Revenue Pension Schemes Office on 23rd March 2001, as that publication stood–

(a)   if the member died before 23rd March 2001, on that date,

(b)   otherwise, on the date of the member's death.

History – Reg. 16(1)(b) omitted by SI 2011/1751, reg. 8(6), with effect in relation to any payment of pension made in respect of a member who died on or after 6 April 2011. Former reg. 16(1)(b) read as follows:

    "(b)   the member had not reached the age of 75;".

PART 4 – LUMP SUM ERRORS

COMMENCEMENT LUMP SUMS BASED ON PENSION ERRORS

17(1) A payment of a lump sum the whole of which is intended to represent a pension commencement lump sum, but which exceeds the permitted maximum, if–

(a)   the lump sum exceeds the permitted maximum only because it has been calculated by reference to the amount of a relevant pension; and

(b)   either–

       (i)   the payment of the pension is a payment within regulation 13 or 14 (1)(b), or

       (ii)   paragraph (3) applies.

17(2) The discovery that the lump sum exceeds the permitted maximum before the payment is made does not prevent the payment's being within paragraph (1) if the payer took reasonable steps to prevent its being made or its being made in that amount.

17(3) This paragraph applies where–

(a)   the lump sum is paid before the pension by reference to which its amount was calculated;

(b)   the pension is not in the event paid, or paid in the amount originally intended, because an error is discovered; and

(c)   if the error had not been discovered and the pension had been paid as intended, its payment would have been a payment within regulation 13.

17(4) The member's becoming entitled to the pension commencement lump sum that forms part of the payment within paragraph (1) shall be treated as a benefit crystallisation event for the purposes of the lifetime allowance charge, namely benefit crystallisation event 9 (and this does not prevent the member's becoming so entitled from also having effect for the purposes of benefit crystallisation event 6).

17(5) The amount crystallised for the purposes of benefit crystallisation event 9 is the amount by which the lump sum exceeds the permitted maximum.

COMMENCEMENT LUMP SUMS PAID IN ERROR – MONEY PURCHASE ARRANGEMENTS

18(1) A payment of a lump sum the whole of which is intended to represent a pension commencement lump sum, but which exceeds the permitted maximum, if–

(a)   the lump sum exceeds the permitted maximum only because it has been calculated by reference to the annuity purchase price or the scheme pension purchase price;

(b)   an error in that calculation means that the amount concerned is greater than it would have been; and

(c)   paragraph (3) applies.

18(2) The discovery that the lump sum exceeds the permitted maximum before the payment is made does not prevent the payment's being within paragraph (1) if the payer took reasonable steps to prevent its being made or its being made in that amount.

18(3) This paragraph applies where–

(a)   the lump sum is paid before the lifetime annuity or scheme pension is purchased; and

(b)   the lifetime annuity or scheme pension is not in the event purchased, or purchased for the amount originally intended, because the error is discovered.

18(4) The member's becoming entitled to the pension commencement lump sum that forms part of the payment within paragraph (1) shall be treated as a benefit crystallisation event for the purposes of the lifetime allowance charge, namely benefit crystallisation event 9 (and this does not prevent the member's becoming so entitled from also having effect for the purposes of benefit crystallisation event 6).

18(5) The amount crystallised for the purposes of benefit crystallisation event 9 is the amount by which the lump sum exceeds the permitted maximum.

COMMENCEMENT LUMP SUMS PAID AFTER DEATH

19(1) A payment of a lump sum under the pension scheme to or in respect of a member who has died if–

Statutory Instruments

(a)   the payment is in respect of a defined benefits arrangement;

(b)   the scheme administrator had not established the member's entitlement to the payment until after the member's death;

(c)   the scheme administrator could not reasonably have been expected to make the payment before the member died;

(d)   the payment would have been a pension commencement lump sum if it had been made immediately before the member's death and the member had been entitled to it;

(e)   it is made no later than the end of the period of one year beginning with the earlier of–

     (i)   the day on which the scheme administrator first knew of the member's death, and

     (ii) the day on which the scheme administrator could first reasonably be expected to have known of it; and

(f)   the member was neither–

     (i)   a controlling director of a sponsoring employer of this or any related scheme, nor

     (ii) a person connected to such a person.

19(2)   The making of the payment shall be treated as a benefit crystallisation event for the purposes of the lifetime allowance charge, namely benefit crystallisation event 9.

19(3)   The amount crystallised for the purposes of benefit crystallisation event 9 is the amount of the payment.

PART 5 – MISCELLANEOUS LUMP SUMS

PART REFUND PAYMENTS RELATING TO SHORT SERVICE

20(1)   A payment of a lump sum by an occupational pension scheme if–

(a)   the member's pensionable service was terminated before normal pension age but the member is not entitled to short service benefit by virtue of section 71 of the Pension Schemes Act 1993 (basic principle as to short service benefit);

(b)   there has been no previous benefit crystallisation event in relation to the member and the pension scheme;

(c)   it is paid when the member has not reached the age of 75;

(d)   it does not exceed an amount equal to the aggregate of the member's contributions under the pension scheme;

(e)   the payment extinguishes the member's entitlement to benefits under the scheme except to the extent that the entitlement is prohibited from being extinguished by rules of the pension scheme described in paragraph (2)(a); and

(f)   at the time that the lump sum is paid the condition in paragraph (2) is satisfied.

20(2)   The condition in this paragraph is satisfied if–

(a)   rules of the pension scheme ("the prohibition rules") have the effect of prohibiting a member's entitlement to benefits under the scheme from being extinguished by the payment of a lump sum;

(b)   at the time that the prohibition rules took effect a provision ("the relevant provision") made by or under any enactment–

     (i)   was in force; and

     (ii) had the effect of prohibiting a member's entitlement to benefits under the scheme from being extinguished by the payment of a lump sum; and

(c)   the relevant provision has been repealed or revoked or has otherwise ceased to apply.

20(3)   A payment mentioned in paragraph (1) shall be subject to the charge specified in section 205 of the Finance Act 2004 (short service refund lump sum charge) and shall accordingly be treated as a short service refund lump sum for the purposes of the application of that section.

20(4)   In this regulation **"pensionable service"**, **"normal pension age"** and **"short service benefit"** have the same meaning as in the Pension Schemes Act 1993 (see section 181(1) of that Act).

20(5)   In paragraph (1)(d) the reference to the member's contributions includes–

(a)   any amount paid under section 7 of the Social Security Act 1986 (incentive payments to schemes becoming contracted-out between 1986 and 1993),

(b)   any amount paid by the Commissioners for Her Majesty's Revenue and Customs under section 42A(3) of the Pension Schemes Act 1993 or section 38A(3) of the Pension Schemes (Northern Ireland) Act 1993 (rebates), and

(c)   any amount recovered by the member's employer under regulations falling within paragraph (6) in respect of minimum payments made to the scheme in relation to any period before 6th April 2012.

20(6)   Those regulations are regulations which were made under–

(a)   section 8(3) of the Pension Schemes Act 1993 (recovery of minimum payments), or

(b)   section 4(3) of the Pension Schemes (Northern Ireland) Act 1993 (corresponding provisions for Northern Ireland).

History – Reg. 20(5) and (6) inserted by SI 2013/1818, reg. 2(2), with effect from 6 April 2013.
Reg. 20 inserted by SI 2012/1881, reg. 5, with effect from 8 August 2012.

Other material – HMRC guidance on payments made under reg. 20 and short service refund lump sums is available at http://tinyurl.com/cdmzvb6.

TRANSFER OF TRIBUNAL FUNCTIONS (LANDS TRIBUNAL AND MISCELLANEOUS AMENDMENTS) ORDER 2009

(SI 2009/1307, as amended by SI 2013/2042)

Made on 21 May 2009 by the Lord Chancellor in exercise of the powers conferred by s. 30(1) and (4), 31(1), (2), (7) and (9), 38, 51(1) and 145 of the Tribunals, Courts and Enforcement Act 2007. Operative from 1 June 2009.

CITATION AND COMMENCEMENT

1 This Order may be cited as the Transfer of Tribunal Functions (Lands Tribunal and Miscellaneous Amendments) Order 2009 and comes into force on 1st June 2009.

TRANSFER OF FUNCTIONS AND ABOLITION OF THE LANDS TRIBUNAL

2(1) The functions of the Lands Tribunal are transferred to the Upper Tribunal.

2(2) The Lands Tribunal is abolished.

SCHEDULES

SCHEDULE 1 – CONSEQUENTIAL AMENDMENTS TO PRIMARY LEGISLATION

Article 5(1) and (2)

TAXES MANAGEMENT ACT 1970

95 The Taxes Management Act 1970 is amended as follows.

96 [Amends TMA 1970, s. 46D.]

97 [Amends TMA 1970, s. 47B.]

INHERITANCE TAX ACT 1984

167 [Amends IHTA 1984, s. 222.]

FINANCE ACT 2003

270 [Amends FA 2003, Sch. 10, para. 45.]

SCHEDULE 2 – CONSEQUENTIAL AMENDMENTS TO SECONDARY LEGISLATION

Article 5(1) and (3)

STAMP DUTY RESERVE TAX REGULATIONS 1986

25 [Amends SI 1986/1711, reg. 8.]

ADMINISTRATIVE JUSTICE AND TRIBUNALS COUNCIL (LISTED TRIBUNALS) ORDER 2007

121 [Omitted by SI 2013/2042, art. 75.]

History – Para. 121 omitted by SI 2013/2042, art. 75, with effect from 19 August 2013. Former para. 121 amended SI 2007/2951, art. 2.

SCHEDULE 5 – TRANSITIONAL AND SAVING PROVISIONS

Article 5(6)

TRANSITIONAL AND SAVING PROVISIONS

1 Any proceedings before the Lands Tribunal which are pending immediately before 1st June 2009 shall continue on and after 1st June 2009 as proceedings before the Upper Tribunal.

2(1) The following sub-paragraphs apply where proceedings are continued in the Upper Tribunal by virtue of paragraph 1.

2(2) Where a hearing began before 1st June 2009 but was not completed by that date, the Upper Tribunal must be comprised for the continuation of that hearing of the person or persons who began it.

2(3) The Upper Tribunal may give any direction to ensure that proceedings are dealt with fairly and, in particular, may–

(a) apply any provision in procedural rules which applied to the proceedings before 1st June 2009; or

(b) disapply provisions of Tribunal Procedure Rules.

2(4) In sub-paragraph (3) **"procedural rules"** means provision (whether called rules or not) regulating practice or procedure before a tribunal.

2(5) Any direction or order given or made in proceedings which is in force immediately before 1st June 2009 remains in force on and after that date as if it were a direction or order of the Upper Tribunal.

2(6) A time period which has started to run before 1st June 2009 and which has not expired shall continue to apply.

2(7) An order for costs may only be made if, and to the extent that, an order could have been made before 1st June 2009.

3 Where an appeal lies to a court from any decision made by the Lands Tribunal before 1st June 2009, that right of appeal has not been exercised, and the time to exercise that right of appeal has not expired prior to 1st June 2009, section 13 of the Tribunals, Courts and Enforcement Act 2007 (right to appeal to Court of Appeal etc.) shall apply as if the decision were a decision made on or after 1st June 2009 by the Upper Tribunal, and any reference to the Lands Tribunal in legislation relating to such an appeal, express or otherwise, is to be taken as a reference to the Upper Tribunal.

4 Any case to be remitted by a court on or after 1st June 2009 and which, if it had been remitted before 1st June 2009 would have been remitted to the Lands Tribunal, shall be remitted to the Upper Tribunal.

5 Staff appointed to the Lands Tribunal before 1st June 2009 are to be treated on and after that date, for the purpose of any enactment, as if they had been appointed by the Lord Chancellor under section 40(1) of the Tribunals, Courts and Enforcement Act 2007 (tribunal staff and services).

6 A decision made by the Lands Tribunal before 1st June 2009 is to be treated as a decision of the Upper Tribunal on or after 1st June 2009.

INFORMATION NOTICE: RESOLUTION OF DISPUTES AS TO PRIVILEGED COMMUNICATIONS REGULATIONS 2009

(SI 2009/1916)

Made by the Commissioners for Her Majesty's Revenue and Customs in exercise of the powers conferred on them by para. 23(3) and (4) of Sch. 36 to the Finance Act 2008. Operative from 7 August 2009.

CITATION AND COMMENCEMENT

1 These Regulations may be cited as the Information Notice: Resolution of Disputes as to Privileged Communications Regulations 2009 and come into force on 7th August 2009.

INTERPRETATION

2 In these Regulations—

"**document**" means information, a document or part of a document;

a "**document in dispute**" is a document over which there is a dispute between HMRC and a person who has been given an information notice as to whether the document is privileged;

"**officer**" means an officer of Revenue and Customs;

a "**person acting on behalf of**" a taxpayer or a third party means any person who is acting on behalf of a taxpayer or third party in relation to an information notice;

"**Schedule 36**" means Schedule 36 to the Finance Act 2008;

"**taxpayer**" means a person who is given a notice under paragraph 1 of Schedule 36;

"**third party**" means a person who is given a notice under paragraph 2 or paragraph 5 of Schedule 36;

"**working day**" means any day except a Saturday, Sunday, Christmas Day, Good Friday or a bank holiday under section 1 of the Banking and Financial Dealings Act 1971.

APPLICATION OF THESE REGULATIONS

3 These Regulations apply where there is a dispute between HMRC and a person to whom an information notice has been given either—

(a)   during the course of correspondence, or

(b)   during the course of an inspection of premises under Schedule 36,

as to whether a document is privileged.

REQUIREMENT TO PROVIDE INFORMATION AND PRODUCE DOCUMENTS NOT IN DISPUTE

4 Nothing in these Regulations shall affect—

(a)   the requirement under an information notice to provide information or produce a document, which is not in dispute; or

(b)   the power under Schedule 36 to inspect premises.

PROCEDURE WHERE INFORMATION NOTICE GIVEN IN CORRESPONDENCE IS IN DISPUTE

5(1) The following procedure applies where there is a dispute falling within regulation 3(a).

5(2) On receipt of the information notice, the taxpayer, third party or person acting on their behalf shall—

(a)   by the date given in the notice for providing information or producing documents, specify in a list each document, required under the information notice, which is in dispute, with a description of the nature and contents of that document;

(b)   serve that list on HMRC.

5(3) But no description of a document or type of document is required where such description would itself give rise to a dispute over privilege.

5(4) Within twenty working days of receiving the list referred to in sub-paragraph (2), HMRC must notify the person who served the list of any documents on the list that it requires to be produced and which it considers are not privileged.

5(5) On receipt of notification under paragraph (4), the taxpayer, third party or person acting on their behalf must make an application to the First-tier Tribunal to consider and resolve the dispute and must include copies of the documents which remain in dispute with that application.

5(6) The taxpayer, third party or person acting on their behalf shall provide HMRC with proof of service under paragraph (2)(b).

5(7) Service for the purposes of paragraph (2)(b) must take place within a reasonable time to be agreed between the taxpayer, third party or person acting on their behalf and HMRC but in any event no later than twenty working days after the date given in the notice for providing information or producing documents.

5(8) An application under paragraph (5) must be made within a reasonable time to be agreed between the taxpayer, third party or person acting on their behalf and HMRC but in any event no later than twenty working days of the date of the notification required under paragraph (4).

PROCEDURE WHERE INFORMATION NOTICE GIVEN DURING INSPECTION OF PREMISES IS IN DISPUTE

6(1) The following procedure applies where there is a dispute falling within regulation 3(b).

6(2) On receipt of the information notice, the taxpayer, third party or person acting on their behalf shall indicate to the officer carrying out the inspection each document, required under the information notice, which is in dispute.

6(3) The taxpayer, third party or person acting on their behalf must place the document or documents in dispute, or a copy of such document or documents, in an appropriate container which prevents the contents being visible.

6(4) The container shall be—

(a) sealed, labelled and signed by that person;

(b) countersigned by the officer; and

(c) given into the custody of the officer.

6(5) The officer shall deliver the container to the First-tier Tribunal with the seal intact within forty-two working days of having taken custody of it together with an application to that Tribunal to consider and resolve the dispute.

COMPLIANCE WITH INFORMATION NOTICE

7 Where a taxpayer or third party who has received an information notice, or a person acting on their behalf, complies with the procedure set out in regulation 5 or, as the case may be, regulation 6, those persons shall be treated as having complied with the information notice in relation to the documents in dispute until the First-tier Tribunal decides the status of the document or until an agreement has been reached under regulation 10.

FINDING OF THE FIRST-TIER TRIBUNAL

8 When an application is made under regulation 5(5) or 6(5), the First-tier Tribunal shall—

(a) resolve the dispute by confirming whether and to what extent the document, is or is not privileged;

(b) direct which part or parts of a document (if any) shall be disclosed.

9 The First-tier Tribunal must ensure that any document in dispute, or any copy of such document, is not inappropriately disclosed to any person pending the Tribunal's consideration of the status of the document.

RESOLUTION OF DISPUTES BY AGREEMENT

10 A dispute falling within regulation 3 may be resolved at any time by HMRC and the person to whom an information notice has been given reaching an agreement, whether in writing or otherwise.

GENERAL INSURERS' TECHNICAL PROVISIONS (APPROPRIATE AMOUNT) (TAX) REGULATIONS 2009

(SI 2009/1926)

Made on 17 July 2009 by the Commissioners for Her Majesty's Revenue and Customs in exercise of the powers conferred by para. 1(4), 3(7) and (15) of Sch. 11 to the Finance Act 2007. Operative from 1 September 2009.

PART 1 – INTRODUCTORY PROVISIONS

CITATION, COMMENCEMENT AND EFFECT

1(1)   These Regulations may be cited as the General Insurers' Technical Provisions (Appropriate Amount) (Tax) Regulations 2009 and come into force on 1st September 2009.

1(2)   In relation to a general insurer, other than a member of a Lloyd's syndicate, these Regulations shall have effect in relation to periods of account ending on or after 31st December 2009.

1(3)   In relation to a member of a Lloyd's syndicate, these Regulations shall have effect in relation to a syndicate return made in respect of profits or losses declared after 31st December 2009.

INTERPRETATION

2(1)   In these Regulations a reference to Schedule 11 is a reference to Schedule 11 to the Finance Act 2007.

2(2)   In these Regulations–

"Schedule 3 to the Accounts and Reports Regulations" means Schedule 3 to the Large and Medium-sized Companies and Groups (Accounts and Reports) Regulations 2008; and

"syndicate return" means a return of a syndicate's profit or loss for an underwriting year made under regulation 4 of the Lloyd's Underwriters (Tax) Regulations 2005.

PART 2 – GENERAL INSURERS (OTHER THAN MEMBERS OF LLOYD'S SYNDICATES)

APPROPRIATE AMOUNT OF TECHNICAL PROVISIONS: GENERAL INSURERS (OTHER THAN A MEMBER OF A LLOYD'S SYNDICATE)

3   This Part applies to a general insurer other than a member of a Lloyd's syndicate.

4   For a period of account, the appropriate amount of the technical provisions for the purposes of paragraph 1 of Schedule 11 is the aggregate of–

(a)   the amount of the provision for unearned premiums determined in accordance with paragraph 50 of Schedule 3 to the Accounts and Reports Regulations;

(b)   the amount of the provision for unexpired risks determined in accordance with paragraph 51 of that Schedule; and

(c)   the estimated amount of the liabilities in respect of claims outstanding arising from the general insurer's general business determined in accordance with regulations 5 to 8.

ESTIMATED AMOUNT OF CLAIMS OUTSTANDING: CONFIRMATION BY GENERAL INSURER

5(1)   For the purposes of regulation 4, the amount of the liabilities in respect of claims outstanding arising from the general insurer's general business is the amount of those liabilities stated in the general insurer's accounts for the period if conditions A to C are satisfied.

5(2)   Condition A is–

(a)   that the general insurer gives confirmation in writing that the amount of the liabilities stated in the accounts is not an excessive estimate of the amount of the liabilities, and

(b)   the confirmation is founded on or supported by an opinion in writing given to the general insurer by an actuary or other suitably skilled person (which may include a director or employee of the general insurer) stating that the amount is not an excessive estimate of the amount of the liabilities.

Regulation 6 contains provisions supplementing condition A.

5(3) Condition B is that the opinion referred to in condition A must reflect the circumstances prevailing at the time at which the technical provisions are adopted by the general insurer.

5(4) Condition C is that the amount of the liabilities stated in the accounts is determined in accordance with regulation 8 (provisions supplementing regulations 5 and 7).

PROVISIONS SUPPLEMENTING CONDITION A

6(1) In the case of a controlled foreign company which is a general insurer within the meaning of paragraph 3(1)(b) of Schedule 11—

(a)   references to **"general insurer"** in regulation 5(2)(a) and in this regulation (other than in sub-paragraph (b) of this paragraph) are to be construed as references to the company referred to in paragraph 3(2)(b) of Schedule 11, and

(b)   the reference to **"general insurer"** in regulation 5(2)(b) is to be construed as a reference to the controlled foreign company.

6(2) For the purposes of condition A in regulation 5, an estimate of the amount of the liabilities is an excessive estimate unless the estimate includes no more than a reasonable margin to take into account the nature or type of risks to which the liabilities relate and the uncertainty associated with those risks.

6(3) If the opinion referred to in condition A is given to the general insurer by a director, or by an employee who is not a director of the general insurer, the confirmation must include a statement identifying the status of the person who gave the opinion to the general insurer.

6(4) Subject to paragraph (5), the confirmation referred to in condition A must accompany the general insurer's company tax return which relates to the period of account (and if more than one company tax return relates to the period of account the confirmation need only be given with the return which relates to the earliest period in the period of account).

6(5) If, at the time the company tax return is made, the general insurer has a reasonable excuse for not providing the confirmation with the company tax return, the confirmation may be provided to an officer of Revenue and Customs separately from the return but must be provided as soon as reasonably possible after the return is made.

6(6) In this regulation **"company tax return"** means a return under paragraph 3 of Schedule 18 to the Finance Act 1998.

ESTIMATED AMOUNT OF CLAIMS OUTSTANDING WHERE CONDITIONS IN REGULATION 5 ARE NOT SATISFIED

7(1) This regulation applies in a case where any of conditions A to C in regulation 5 is not satisfied.

7(2) For the purposes of regulation 4, the amount of the liabilities in respect of claims outstanding arising from the general insurer's general business is the general insurer's undiscounted best estimate of the future cash flows in respect of claims outstanding.

7(3) For the purposes of paragraph (2)—

(a)   the reference to **"best estimate"** shall be construed as a reference to the mean of the distribution of the potential outcomes of the claims to which the estimate relates, and

(b)   the best estimate of the future cash flows must be the best estimate available at the time at which the technical provisions are adopted by the general insurer.

PROVISIONS SUPPLEMENTING REGULATIONS 5 AND 7

8(1) This regulation supplements regulations 5 and 7.

8(2) Any calculation, computation or estimate required to determine the amount of the liabilities in respect of claims outstanding must be made in accordance the standards specified in paragraph (3) in force at the time at which the technical provisions are adopted by the general insurer.

8(3) The specified standards are—

(a)   all generic technical actuarial standards and relevant specific technical actuarial standards published by the Board for Actuarial Standards in relation to the performance of actuarial functions, or

(b)   where the general insurer is not resident in the United Kingdom, such other standards or provisions of the law of the territory in which the general insurer is domiciled as may reasonably be regarded as equivalent in effect to the standards referred to in subparagraph (a).

In this paragraph, **"the Board for Actuarial Standards"** means the operating body of that name of the Financial Reporting Council.

8(4)   Any calculation, computation or estimate required to determine the amount of the liabilities in respect of claims outstanding must take into account–

(a)   the nature or type of risks to which the liabilities in respect of claims outstanding relate, and

(b)   the volatility and uncertainty associated with those risks.

8(5)   Without prejudice to the generality of paragraph (4), the reference in that paragraph to taking into account includes, in particular, taking into account liabilities–

(a)   on the basis of general insurance business reporting categories described in Annex 11.3 to Chapter 11 of Volume 1 of IPRU(INS), or

(b)   on the basis of grouping of risks in accordance with the descriptions of accounting classes for general insurance business set out in Appendix 9.16 to Volume 2 of IPRU(INS).

8(6)   In paragraph (5), **"IPRU(INS)"** means the Interim Prudential Sourcebook for Insurers made by the Financial Services Authority under the Financial Services and Markets Act 2000.

8(7)   Any estimate of the amount of the liabilities in respect of claims outstanding shall be determined–

(a)   net of reinsurance ceded, and

(b)   in accordance with paragraph 53 of Schedule 3 to the Accounts and Reports Regulations.

8(8)   A reference to claims outstanding includes–

(a)   the expense of handling a future claim (whether allocated or unallocated), and

(b)   a future claim which has been incurred as a liability of the general insurer but which is–

(i)   not reported to the general insurer at the time at which the technical provisions are adopted, or

(ii)   reported, but not fully reported, to the general insurer at that time.

8(9)   A reference in this Part to the time at which technical provisions are adopted is a reference–

(a)   to the time at which the directors of the general insurer approve the general insurers' annual accounts for the purposes of section 414 of the Companies Act 2006;

(b)   in the case of a general insurer to which that section does not apply, to such similar time as may apply under equivalent provisions of the law of the territory in which the general insurer is domiciled; or

(c)   in the case of general business carried on by a permanent establishment in the United Kingdom of a general insurer which is not resident in the United Kingdom and for which accounts of the permanent establishment are prepared for the period of account, the time at which the general insurer approves those accounts.

PART 3 – MEMBERS OF LLOYD'S SYNDICATES

APPROPRIATE AMOUNT OF TECHNICAL PROVISIONS: MEMBERS OF CLOSED LLOYD'S SYNDICATES

9(1)   This regulation applies to a general insurer which is a member of a closed Lloyd's syndicate.

In this regulation, a closed Lloyd's syndicate is a Lloyd's syndicate that is not an open Lloyd's syndicate.

9(2)   For a period of account, the appropriate amount of the technical provisions for the purposes of paragraph 1 of Schedule 11 is the member's allowable reinsurance to close amount in respect of the syndicate.

9(3)   For the purposes of paragraph (2), the allowable reinsurance to close amount for the period of account is the lesser of–

(a)   the reinsurance to close amount for the period of account which is treated as a technical provision in accordance with regulation 11 (reinsurance to close amounts); and

(b)   subject to paragraphs (4), the aggregate of the member's share of–

(i)   the amount of the provision for unearned premiums determined in accordance with paragraph 50 of Schedule 3 to the Accounts and Reports Regulations;

(ii)   the amount of the provision for unexpired risks determined in accordance with paragraph 51 of that Schedule; and

(iii)   the amount of the liabilities in respect of claims outstanding arising from the general business of the syndicate.

9(4)   For the purposes of paragraph (3)(b), amounts are to be determined on the assumption that–

(a)   the syndicate is an open Lloyd's syndicate, and

(b)   no reinsurance to close amounts have been paid in respect of the syndicate by any member of the syndicate.

APPROPRIATE AMOUNT OF TECHNICAL PROVISIONS: MEMBERS OF OPEN LLOYD'S SYNDICATES

10(1)   This regulation applies to any general insurer which is a member of an open Lloyd's syndicate.

10(2)   For a period of account, the appropriate amount of the technical provisions for the purposes of paragraph 1 of Schedule 11 is the aggregate of the member's share of–

(a)   the amount of the provision for unearned premiums determined in accordance with paragraph 50 of Schedule 3 to the Accounts and Reports Regulations;

(b)   the amount of the provision for unexpired risks determined in accordance with paragraph 51 of that Schedule 3; and

(c)   the amount of the liabilities in respect of claims outstanding arising from the general business of the syndicate.

REINSURANCE TO CLOSE AMOUNTS

11(1)   The reinsurance to close amount to be treated as a technical provision in the case of a member of a Lloyd's syndicate for a period of account is whichever is the lesser of–

(a)   the total of the reinsurance to close amounts which the member pays or gives, or is treated as paying or giving, in respect of the underwriting year for which profits or losses are declared; and

(b)   the total of the reinsurance to close amounts which the member receives, or is treated as receiving, in respect of the underwriting year for which profits or losses are declared.

This paragraph is subject to paragraph (2).

11(2)   If a company–

(a)   pays or gives, or is treated as paying or giving, a reinsurance to close amount to a member in respect of an underwriting year for which profits or losses are declared, and

(b)   the company is connected to the member,

the amount which the member receives, or is treated as receiving, shall also be treated as a reinsurance to close amount paid by the member in respect of that underwriting year.

11(3)   For the purposes of paragraph (2), section 839(5) to (8) of the Income and Corporation Taxes Act 1988 (connected persons) applies for the purpose of determining whether a company is connected to a member.

PROVISIONS SUPPLEMENTING REGULATIONS 9 AND 10: DETERMINATION OF MEMBER'S SHARE OF PROVISIONS

12(1)   For the purposes of regulations 9(3)(b) and 10(2), a member's share of the amounts referred to in those regulations shall be determined by reference to the member's proportionate entitlement to participate in the underwriting business of the syndicate.

12(2)   For the purposes of regulations 9(3)(b)(iii) and 10(2)(c), in determining the amount referred to in those provisions, regulations 5 to 8 shall apply with the following modifications–

(a)   a reference to **"the general insurer's general business"** shall be treated as a reference to the general business of the syndicate;

(b)   the reference in regulation 5(1) to **"the general insurer's accounts"** shall be treated as a reference to the syndicate's accounts;

(c)   references in regulations 5(3), 7(3) and 8(8) to **"the general insurer"** shall be treated as a reference to the syndicate;

(d)   regulation 6(1) shall be treated as omitted;

(e)   the reference in regulation 6(4) and (5) to the **"general insurer's company tax return"** shall be treated as a reference to the syndicate return which relates to the period of account;

(f)   the reference in regulation 6(5) to **"general insurer"** shall be treated as a reference to the syndicate's managing agent;

(g)   regulation 6(6) shall be treated as omitted;

(h)   the reference in regulation 7(2) to **"the general insurer's undiscounted best estimate"** shall be treated as a reference to the best estimate of the syndicate's managing agent;

(i)   regulation 8(3)(b) shall be treated as omitted; and

(j)   for regulation 8(9) there shall be treated as substituted–

"**8(9)**   A reference in this Part to the time at which technical provisions are adopted is a reference to the time at which the syndicate's managing agent approves the syndicate's profit or loss accounts for the period of account by signing them.".

SPECIAL ANNUAL ALLOWANCE CHARGE (APPLICATION TO MEMBERS OF CURRENTLY-RELIEVED NON-UK PENSION SCHEMES) ORDER 2009

(SI 2009/2031 as amended by SI 2010/429)

Made on 21 July 2009 by the Treasury in exercise of the powers conferred on them by para. 20(1) and (2) of Sch. 35 to the Finance Act 2009. Operative from 12 August 2009.

History – Correction slip of 22 November 2010 amends the numbering of articles in this Order.

CITATION, COMMENCEMENT AND INTERPRETATION

1(1) This Order may be cited as the Special Annual Allowance Charge (Application to Members of Currently-Relieved Non-UK Pension Schemes) Order 2009 and shall come into force on 12th August 2009.

1(2) This Order shall have effect for the tax year 2009–10 and subsequent tax years.

1(3) In this Order a reference to Schedule 35 is a reference to Schedule 35 to the Finance Act 2009.

APPLICATION OF THE SPECIAL ANNUAL ALLOWANCE CHARGE

2(1) The provisions in Schedule 35 shall apply to individuals who are members of currently relieved non-UK pension schemes as if those schemes were registered pension schemes.

2(2) Paragraph (1) shall have effect subject to the modifications of Schedule 35 specified in this Order.

MODIFICATIONS OF SCHEDULE 35

3 For the words "scheme administrator", in each place where they occur, substitute the words "scheme manager".

4(1) In paragraph 3 of Schedule 35 the calculation of the total adjusted pension input amount for members of currently-relieved non-UK pension schemes shall be arrived at with the following modifications.

4(2) Section 230(1) and 234(1) of FA 2004 (cash balance and defined benefits arrangements) shall apply as if the increase in the value of the individual's rights under an arrangement under the pension scheme relating to the individual during the tax year were the greater of–

(a)   the appropriate fraction of what it otherwise would be (see paragraph (3)); and

(b)   the amount of any contributions paid under the arrangement during the tax year by or on behalf of the individual (otherwise than by an employer) in respect of which relief is given by virtue of–

  (i)   Schedule 33 to FA 2004 (overseas pensions schemes: migrant member relief),

  (ii)   paragraph 51 of Schedule 36 to FA 2004 (individuals with pre-commencement entitlement to corresponding relief), or

  (iii) double tax arrangements,

  and section 237 of FA 2004 (hybrid arrangements) shall apply accordingly.

4(3) The appropriate fraction referred to in paragraph (2)(a) is–

$$\frac{TE}{EI}$$

where–

  EI is the total amount of employment income of the individual from any relevant employment or employments for the tax year, excluding any such income which is exempt income (within the meaning of section 8 of ITEPA 2003), and

  TE is so much of EI as constitutes taxable earnings from any such employment (within the meaning of section 10(2) of ITEPA 2003).

4(4) For the purposes of paragraph (3) an employment is a relevant employment if it is an employment with an employer who is a sponsoring employer in relation to the currently-relieved non-UK pension scheme.

4(5) Section 233(1) of FA 2004 (other money purchase arrangements) shall apply as if–

(a) the reference in section 233(1)(a) of FA 2004 to relievable pension contributions paid by or on behalf of the individual under an arrangement under the pension scheme relating to the individual were to those in respect of which relief from tax is given by virtue of–

    (i) Schedule 33 to FA 2004 (overseas pensions schemes: migrant member relief),

    (ii) paragraph 51 of Schedule 36 to FA 2004 (individuals with pre-commencement entitlement to corresponding relief), or

    (iii) double tax arrangements; and

(b) the reference in section 233(1)(b) of FA 2004 to contributions paid in respect of the individual under such an arrangement by an employer of the individual were to the appropriate fraction of the contributions so paid (as to which see paragraph (6)),

and section 237 of FA 2004 shall apply accordingly.

4(6) The appropriate fraction referred to in paragraph (5)(b) is–

$$\frac{TE}{EI}$$

where–

    EI is the total amount of employment income of the individual from any employment or employments with the employer for the tax year, excluding any such income which is exempt income (within the meaning of section 8 of ITEPA 2003), and

    TE is so much of EI as constitutes taxable earnings from any such employment (within the meaning of section 10(2) of ITEPA 2003).

5(1) Paragraph 6 of Schedule 35 shall be modified as follows.

5(2) In sub-paragraph (2)–

(a) after the words "under sub-paragraph (3)" insert "as modified by article 5 of the Special Annual Allowance Charge (Application to Members of Currently-Relieved Non-UK Pension Schemes) Order 2009 ("the 2009 Order")"; and

(b) after the words "in accordance with paragraph 3(2)" insert "as modified by article 4 of the 2009 Order".

5(3) Sub-paragraph (3) shall apply as if the amount arrived at were the appropriate fraction of what it otherwise would be (see paragraph (4)).

5(4) The appropriate fraction referred to in paragraph (4) is–

$$\frac{TE}{EI}$$

where–

    EI is the total amount of employment income of the individual from any relevant employment or employments for the tax year, excluding any such income which is exempt income (within the meaning of section 8 of ITEPA 2003), and

    TE is so much of EI as constitutes taxable earnings from any such employment (within the meaning of section 10(2) of ITEPA 2003).

5(5) For the purposes of paragraph (4) an employment is a relevant employment if it is an employment with an employer who is a sponsoring employer in relation to the currently-relieved non-UK pension scheme.

5(6) In sub-paragraph (6) after the words "(but as if references to the pension input period were to the tax year and whether or not the arrangement is a defined benefits arrangement)." insert "This sub-paragraph is subject to sub-paragraph (7)".

5(7) After sub-paragraph (6) insert–

    "**6(7)** The references to "amount" in subsections (2), (3) and (5) of section 236 shall be read as references to an amount referable to a member's UK tax-relieved fund only.".

6(1) Paragraph 13 of Schedule 35 shall be modified as follows.

6(2) In sub-paragraphs (2)(a) and (6) the references to **"employer"** and **"employment"** shall be read as including **"former employer"** and **"former employment"** where the individual was–

(a)   an employee of that former employer;

(b)   resident outside the UK, and either–

(i)   a member of an occupational pension scheme or a group personal pension scheme relating to that former employment or,

(ii)   a member of a public service pension scheme.

6(3) In sub-paragraph (2)(b) the reference to **"persons mentioned in sub-paragraph (1)(d)"** shall be read as including persons who are employees of the former employer referred to in paragraph (2).

7(1) Paragraph 15 of Schedule 35 shall be modified as follows.

7(2) For sub-paragraph (4) substitute–

"**15(4)** **"Relevant relievable pension contributions"** are contributions which–

(a)   are relievable pension contributions in relation to the individual, and are paid to the pension scheme under the arrangement in the tax year;

(b)   are contributions in respect of which the individual is given relief from tax under double tax arrangements and which are paid under the arrangement in the tax year; or

(c)   are contributions paid under the arrangement by the individual for which a deduction is given under Chapter 2 of Part 5 of ITEPA 2003 for the tax year in accordance with paragraph 51 of Schedule 36 to FA 2004,

but this is subject as follows.".

8 For sub-paragraph (3) of paragraph 16 of Schedule 35 substitute–

"**16(3)** In relation to a money purchase arrangement that is not a cash balance arrangement, a pre-22 April 2009 pension input amount is so much of the amount arrived at under paragraph 3(2) as is attributable to contributions–

(a)   which are paid in the period beginning with 6 April 2009 and ending with 22 April 2009, other than any contributions paid pursuant to an agreement for the payment of contributions on a quarterly or more frequent basis; and–

(b)   in respect of which relief is given by virtue of–

(i)   Schedule 33 to FA 2004 (overseas pensions schemes: migrant member relief),

(ii)   paragraph 51 of Schedule 36 to FA 2004 (individuals with precommencement entitlement to corresponding relief), or

(iii)   double tax arrangements.".

History – In art. 8 (formerly numbered art. 9), in the substituted para. 16(3)(a), "22" substituted for "21" by SI 2010/429, art. 11, with effect for the tax year 2009–10 and subsequent tax years.

9(1) Paragraph 17 of Schedule 35 shall be modified as follows.

9(2) In sub-paragraph (4) the definition of "infrequent money purchase contributions amount" shall be read as including any relevant contributions under overseas pension schemes paid in a tax year in which the individual was not resident in the UK.

9(3) For sub-paragraph (6) substitute–

"**17(6)** **"Relevant contributions"** for a tax year in which an individual is resident in the UK means contributions made to money purchase arrangements (other than cash balance arrangements) which–

(a)   are relievable pension contributions in relation to the individual, and are paid to the pension scheme under the arrangement in the tax year;

(b)   are contributions in respect of which the individual is given relief from tax under double tax arrangements and which are paid under the arrangement in the tax year;

(c)   are contributions paid under the arrangement by the individual for which a deduction is given under Chapter 2 of Part 5 of ITEPA 2003 for the tax year in accordance with paragraph 51 of Schedule 36 to FA 2004; or

(d)   are contributions paid by an employer of the individual in respect of the individual.".

9(4) After sub-paragraph (6) insert–

"**17(7)** **"Relevant contributions"** for a tax year in which an individual was not resident in the UK means contributions made to money purchase arrangements (other than cash balance arrangements) under an overseas pension scheme which–

(a)   are paid by or behalf of an individual; or

(b) are paid by an employer of the individual in respect of the individual.".

10 For paragraph 18 of Schedule 35 substitute–

"**18(1)** Part 4 of FA 2004 applies in relation to a contributions refund lump sum as if it were a short service refund lump sum in excess of the limit specified in section 205(4) of that Act (so that it is not an unauthorised payment and is liable to tax at the rate chargeable on a short service refund lump sum).

This sub-paragraph is subject to sub-paragraph (2).

18(2) Section 205 of FA 2004 shall apply with respect to a contributions refund lump sum paid to or in respect of an individual who is a member of a currently-relieved non-UK pension scheme so as to make the person to whom the sum is paid (rather than the scheme administrator) liable to any charge imposed by section 205 FA 2004.".

Statutory Instruments

TAX AVOIDANCE SCHEMES (PRESCRIBED DESCRIPTIONS OF ARRANGEMENTS) (AMENDMENT) REGULATIONS 2009

(SI 2009/2033, as revoked by SI 2013/2595)

Made on 21 July 2009 by the Treasury, in accordance with the powers conferred by s. 306(1)(a) and (b) and s. 317(2) of the Finance Act 2004. Operative from 1 September 2009.

History – SI 2009/2033 revoked by SI 2013/2595, reg. 11, with effect from 4 November 2013 (but the amendments do not have effect for the purposes of FA 2004, s. 308(1), if the relevant date falls before 4 November 2013 or for the purposes of FA 2004, s. 308(3), if the date on which the promoter first becomes aware of any transaction forming part of notifiable arrangements falls before 4 November 2013. Former SI 2009/2033 read as follows:

"CITATION AND COMMENCEMENT

1   These Regulations may be cited as the Tax Avoidance Schemes (Prescribed Descriptions of Arrangements) (Amendment) Regulations 2009 and shall come into force on 1st September 2009.

AMENDMENT TO THE TAX AVOIDANCE SCHEMES (PRESCRIBED DESCRIPTIONS OF ARRANGEMENTS) REGULATIONS 2006

2(1)   The Tax Avoidance Schemes (Prescribed Descriptions of Arrangements) Regulations 2006 are amended as follows.

2(2)   [Amends SI 2006/1543, reg. 5(2).]

2(3)   [Inserts SI 2006/1543, reg. 17A.]

TIME FOR PROVIDING INFORMATION: TRANSITIONAL PROVISIONS

3(1)   Where paragraph (2) applies, the prescribed period or time (as the case may be) to be found in accordance with regulation 4 of the Tax Avoidance Schemes (Information) Regulations 2004 (time for providing information under section 308, 308A, 309 or 310) shall end on 31st October 2009 instead of the day on which it would end by virtue of that regulation.

3(2)   This paragraph applies in respect of proposals or arrangements (as the case may be) that are notifiable by virtue of regulation 17A of the Tax Avoidance Schemes (Prescribed Descriptions of Arrangements) Regulations 2009.

(a)   for the purposes of section 308(1) of the Finance Act 2004 if the relevant date in relation to a proposal falls within the period beginning with 23rd April 2009 and ending with 31st August 2009;

(b)   for the purposes of section 308(3) of the Finance Act 2004 if the date on which the promoter first becomes aware of any transaction forming part of the arrangements falls within the period beginning with 23rd April 2009 and ending with 31st August 2009;

(c)   for the purposes of sections 309 and 310 of the Finance Act 2004 if the date on which any transaction forming part of the arrangements is entered into falls within the period beginning with 23rd April 2009 and ending with 31st August 2009.

3(3)   In paragraph (2)(a) **"the relevant date"** has the meaning given by section 308(2) of the Finance Act 2004.".

INVESTMENT TRUSTS (DIVIDENDS) (OPTIONAL TREATMENT AS INTEREST DISTRIBUTIONS) REGULATIONS 2009

(SI 2009/2034, as amended by SI 2011/2951 and SI 2013/605)

Made on 21 July 2009 by the Treasury in exercise of the powers conferred by s. 45 of the Finance Act 2009. Operative from 1 September 2009.

PART 1 – PRELIMINARY PROVISIONS

CITATION, COMMENCEMENT AND EFFECT

1(1) These Regulations may be cited as the Investment Trusts (Dividends) (Optional Treatment as Interest Distributions) Regulations 2009 and shall come into force on 1st September 2009.

1(2) These Regulations have effect in relation to amounts distributed on or after 1st September 2009.

STRUCTURE OF THESE REGULATIONS

2 The structure of these Regulations is as follows–

this Part contains preliminary provisions;

Part 2 deals with the optional treatment of dividends as interest distributions;

Part 3 deals with the duty to deduct tax from interest distributions; and

Part 4 deals with information and record keeping relating to distributions.

INTERPRETATION

3(1) In these Regulations–

the **"Commissioners"** means the Commissioners for Her Majesty's Revenue and Customs;

"ICTA" means the Income and Corporation Taxes Act 1988;

"interest distribution" has the meaning given in regulation 5(2);

"period of account" has the meaning given in section 832(1) of ICTA; and

"qualifying interest income" means the amount determined in accordance with regulation 8.

3(2) In these Regulations **"recipient"**, in relation to an interest distribution of an investment trust or prospective investment trust, means the beneficial owner of the interest distribution, except where the distribution is held on trust (other than under a bare trust) or forms part of the estate of a deceased person; and, in such a case, the recipient means the trustees of the trust on which the interest distribution is held or, as the case may be, the deceased person's personal representatives.

PART 2 – OPTIONAL TREATMENT OF DIVIDENDS AS INTEREST DISTRIBUTIONS

CIRCUMSTANCES IN WHICH DIVIDENDS MAY BE TREATED AS INTEREST DISTRIBUTIONS

4(1) Subject to paragraph (2), regulation 5 applies if–

(a) a company is an investment trust or a prospective investment trust as respects an accounting period;

(b) an amount is distributed by the company as a dividend in respect of a period of account which includes that accounting period; and

(c) the amount distributed in relation to the period of account is distributed on or before the first anniversary of the day on which that period of account ends.

4(2) In a case where an amount is distributed by the company as a dividend in respect of a period of account which includes two or more accounting periods of the company, the company must be an investment trust or prospective investment trust as respects all of those accounting periods.

TREATMENT OF DIVIDENDS AS INTEREST DISTRIBUTIONS

5(1) If this regulation applies, the company may designate as an interest distribution all or part of the amount distributed as a dividend or dividends in respect of the period of account which includes the accounting period.

5(2) A dividend, or part of a dividend, in respect of which a designation under this regulation has been made is referred to in these Regulations as an "interest distribution".

5(3) A designation under paragraph (1) becomes irrevocable at the time the interest distribution is made.

5(4) The aggregate of the amounts distributed as interest distributions in relation to an accounting period may not exceed the amount of the company's qualifying interest income for the accounting period.

Regulation 8 explains how a company's qualifying interest income for an accounting period is calculated.

5(5) For the purposes of paragraph (4), where an interest distribution is made in respect of a period of account which includes more than one accounting period the amount distributed as the interest distributions in relation to each accounting period is—

$$\frac{A \times I}{T}$$

where—

"**A**" is the amount of qualifying interest income for the accounting period;

"**I**" is the total of the amounts distributed as interest distributions in respect of the period of account; and

"**T**" is the total amount of the qualifying interest income in respect of all the accounting periods in the period of account.

NOTIFICATION OF DESIGNATION OF DIVIDENDS AS INTEREST DISTRIBUTIONS

6 [Omitted by SI 2011/2951.]

History – Reg. 6 omitted by SI 2011/2951, reg. 3, with effect in relation to amounts distributed in respect of accounting periods beginning on or after 1 January 2012. Former reg. 6 read as follows:

"**6** If a company makes a designation under regulation 5, the application by the company for approval as an investment trust under section 842 of ICTA (investment trusts) as respects the accounting period to which the designation relates must include details of the total amount distributed, or to be distributed, as interest distributions in respect of the accounting period.".

INTEREST DISTRIBUTIONS NOT TO BE TREATED AS DISTRIBUTIONS FOR PURPOSES OF THE TAX ACTS

7 An amount distributed as an interest distribution by an investment trust or prospective investment trust shall be treated for the purposes of the Tax Acts as if the amount distributed is not a distribution.

QUALIFYING INTEREST INCOME

8(1) The company's amount of qualifying interest income for an accounting period is the amount by which the aggregate of the company's relevant credits exceeds the aggregate of the company's relevant debits given for that period.

8(2) Subject to paragraph (3) and regulation 9, the company's relevant credits and relevant debits are—

(a) credits and debits given for the accounting period for the purposes of Part 5 of the Corporation Tax Act 2009 (loan relationships); and

(b) credits and debits given for the accounting period for the purposes of Part 7of that Act (derivative contracts) in relation to—

    (i) derivative contracts the underlying subject matter of which consists wholly of assets representing loan relationships or currency or both, and

    (ii) contracts for differences the underlying subject matter of which consists wholly of any one or more of interest rates, creditworthiness and currency.

8(3) The company's relevant debits for an accounting period do not include debits arising under regulation 10 in respect of interest distributions made in respect of the accounting period.

8(4) If, in relation to an accounting period, the aggregate of the company's relevant debits exceeds the aggregate of the company's relevant credits the amount of the qualifying interest income for that period shall be treated as nil.

8(5) In this regulation expressions used in Parts 5 and 7 of the Corporation Tax Act 2009 have the same meaning as they have in those Parts.

QUALIFYING INTEREST INCOME: FURTHER PROVISIONS

9(1) In the circumstances specified in paragraph (2), the underlying subject matter of a derivative contract is treated for the purposes of regulation 8 as consisting wholly of assets representing loan relationships or currency or both (as the case may be).

9(2) The circumstances specified are where the underlying subject matter consists only of–

(a) assets representing loan relationships or currency or both, and

(b) other underlying subject matter which is–

    (i) subordinate in relation to those assets, or

    (ii) of small value in comparison with the value of the underlying subject matter.

9(3) In the circumstances specified in paragraph (4), the underlying subject matter of a contract for differences is treated for the purposes of regulation 8 as consisting wholly of one or more of interest rates, creditworthiness and currency (the "principal subject matter").

9(4) The circumstances specified are where the underlying subject matter consists only of–

(a) the principal subject matter, and

(b) other underlying subject matter which is–

    (i) subordinate in relation to the principal subject matter, or

    (ii) of small value in comparison with the value of the underlying subject matter.

9(5) For the purposes of paragraphs (2) and (4), whether part of the underlying subject matter of a contract of a company is subordinate or of small value is to be determined by reference to the time when the company enters into or acquires the contract.

INTEREST DISTRIBUTIONS: EFFECT FOR INVESTMENT TRUST OR PROSPECTIVE INVESTMENT TRUST

10(1) This regulation applies in respect of an accounting period if a company–

(a) is an investment trust or prospective investment trust in respect of the accounting period, and

(b) makes an interest distribution in relation to the accounting period.

10(2) Subject to paragraph (3), the Corporation Tax Acts have effect in relation to the company as if the interest distribution made by the company in relation to the accounting period were interest under a debtor relationship of the company (and, accordingly is an amount recognised in determining the company's profit or loss for the period).

10(3) Paragraph (2) does not apply to the extent that the aggregate of the amount distributed as interest distributions in relation to the accounting period exceeds the amount of the company's qualifying interest income for that period.

10(4) In paragraph (2) **"debtor relationship"** has the same meaning as in section 302(6) of the Corporation Tax Act 2009 (loan relationships).

INTEREST DISTRIBUTIONS: EFFECT FOR RECIPIENTS

11(1) In relation to a recipient of an interest distribution within the charge to corporation tax, the Corporation Tax Acts have effect as if the interest distribution were interest under a creditor relationship of that person.

11(2) In paragraph (1) **"creditor relationship"** has the same meaning as in section 302(5) of the Corporation Tax Act 2009 (loan relationships).

11(3) In relation to a recipient of an interest distribution within the charge to income tax, the Income Tax Acts have effect as if the interest distribution were a payment of yearly interest on the date the interest distribution is made.

11(4) If a recipient of an amount distributed by a company–

(a) is informed (whether directly by the company or by a person who receives the amount on behalf of the recipient) that the amount is distributed to the recipient as an interest distribution, and

(b) is so informed at, or as soon as reasonably possible after, the time the amount is distributed,

the recipient shall treat that amount as an interest distribution (whether or not the amount distributed is an interest distribution for the purposes of the Corporation Tax Acts in relation to the company).

FAILURE TO OBTAIN APPROVAL AS AN INVESTMENT TRUST

12 No amount may be distributed as an interest distribution by a company in relation to an accounting period for which the company is not approved, or is treated as not having been approved, in accordance with regulations made under section 1159 of the Corporation Tax Act 2010.

History – Reg. 12 substituted by SI 2011/2951, reg. 4, with effect in relation to amounts distributed in respect of accounting periods beginning on or after 1 January 2012. Former reg. 12 read as follows:
"**12** No amount may be distributed as an interest distribution by a company in relation to an accounting period after the time the company is informed by the Commissioners that approval for the purposes of section 842 of ICTA is not given by them as respects that accounting period.".

PART 3 – DUTY TO DEDUCT TAX FROM INTEREST DISTRIBUTIONS

DUTY TO DEDUCT TAX INTEREST DISTRIBUTIONS

Duty to deduct tax from interest distributions: general

13(1) Any obligation to deduct a sum under section 874(2) of the Income Tax Act 2007 is subject to the provisions of this regulation.

13(2) n this Part the **"deduction obligation"** means the obligation specified in paragraph (1).

13(3) The deduction obligation does not apply to the interest distribution if–

(a) the recipient is a company (whether or not the company is resident in the United Kingdom for tax purposes);

(b) the recipient consists of the trustees of a unit trust scheme;

(c) the reputable intermediary condition in regulation 14 is met with respect to the recipient on the date the interest distribution is made; or

(d) the residence condition in regulation 17 is met with respect to the recipient on the date the interest distribution is made.

13(4) But if the recipient is a company acting in the capacity of a trustee of a trust, the deduction obligation is not excluded by virtue of paragraph (3)(a).

13(5) In this regulation, **"unit trust scheme"** has the meaning given by section 237 of the Financial Services and Markets Act 2000.

THE REPUTABLE INTERMEDIARY CONDITION

The reputable intermediary condition

14(1) The reputable intermediary condition is met with respect to a recipient on the date the interest distribution is made if conditions A to C are met.

14(2) Condition A is that the interest distribution is made on behalf of the recipient to a company.

14(3) Condition B is that the investment trust or prospective investment trust making the interest distribution has reasonable grounds for believing that the recipient is not resident in the United Kingdom.

14(4) Condition C is that the company mentioned in paragraph (2)–

(a) is subject to the EC Money Laundering Directive,

(b) is subject to equivalent non-EC provisions, or

(c) is a company which–

(i) is resident in a regulated country or territory, and

(ii) is an associated company of a company which is subject to sub-paragraph (a) or (b).

History – In reg. 14(3), the word "ordinarily", which appeared before the word "resident", omitted by SI 2013/605, reg. 6(2), with effect in relation to interest distributions made on or after 6 April 2014.

The reputable intermediary condition: further provisions

15(1) This regulation applies for the purposes of Condition C in regulation 14.

15(2) A company is subject to the EC Money Laundering Directive if it is a credit institution or financial institution as defined by Article 1 of Directive 91/308/EEC, as amended by Directive 2001/97/EC.

15(3) A company is subject to equivalent non-EC provisions if it is required by the law of any country or territory which is not a member State to comply with requirements similar to those which, under Article 3 of Directive 91/308/EEC (as so amended), member States must ensure are complied with by credit institutions and financial institutions.

15(4) A country or territory is a regulated country or territory if it either is a member State or imposes requirements similar to those, which, under Article 3 of that Directive (as so amended), member States must ensure are complied with by credit institutions and financial institutions.

15(5) A company is to be treated as another's associated company if it would be so treated for the purposes of Part 11 of ICTA (see section 416 of that Act).

The reputable intermediary condition: consequences of reasonable but incorrect belief

16(1) This regulation applies if conditions A to D are met.

16(2) Condition A is that an interest distribution is made by an investment trust or prospective investment trust.

16(3) Condition B is that the investment trust or prospective investment trust, in reliance on the reputable intermediary condition being met with respect to the recipient of the interest distribution, does not comply with the deduction obligation in relation to the interest distribution.

16(4) Condition C is that the deduction obligation would apply but for the reputable intermediary condition being met.

16(5) Condition D is that (contrary to the belief of the investment trust or prospective investment trust) the recipient is in fact resident in the United Kingdom.

16(6) The following provisions of the Income Tax Act 2007 have effect as if the deduction obligation applied–

(a)   section 874 (duty to deduct from certain payments of yearly interest), and

(b)   Chapter 15 of Part 15 (collection: deposit-takers, building societies and certain companies).

History – In reg. 16(5), the word "ordinarily", which appeared before the word "resident", omitted by SI 2013/605, reg. 6(3), with effect in relation to interest distributions made on or after 6 April 2014.

THE RESIDENCE CONDITION
The residence condition

17(1) The residence condition is met with respect to a recipient on the date the interest distribution is made if any of conditions A to E is met.

17(2) Condition A is that, in relation to an interest distribution which is not made to or received under a trust, there is a valid declaration, made by the recipient, that the recipient is not resident in the United Kingdom.

17(3) Condition B is–

(a)   that the recipient receives the interest distribution as the personal representative of a deceased person, and

(b)   that the deceased person had made a declaration, which was valid at the time of the deceased person's death, that the deceased person was not resident in the United Kingdom.

17(4) Condition C is–

(a)   that the recipient receives the interest distribution as a personal representative of a deceased person, and

(b)   that the personal representative has made a declaration that the deceased, immediately before the time at which the deceased died, was not resident in the United Kingdom.

17(5) Condition D is that, in the case of an interest distribution made to or received under a trust where the whole of the income is, or falls to be treated as, or under any provision of the Tax Acts is deemed to be, the income of a person other than the trustees of that trust, there is a valid declaration, made by the person in question that the person is not resident in the United Kingdom.

17(6) Condition E is that, in circumstances in which condition D does not apply and with respect to a recipient in the case of an interest distribution made to or received under a trust, there is a valid declaration, made by the trustees of that trust, that–

(a)   the trustees are not resident in the United Kingdom, and

(b)   each beneficiary of the trust is not resident in the United Kingdom.

History – In reg. 17(2), (3)(b) and (4)(b), the word "ordinarily", which appeared before the word "resident", omitted by SI 2013/605, reg. 6(4)(a), with effect in relation to the making of declarations on or after 6 April 2014 (and any declaration made before that date continues to have effect in respect of interest distributions made on or after that date as if those amendments had not been made).

In reg. 17(5), the words "either not ordinarily resident or, in the case of a company,", which appeared after the words "the person is", omitted by SI 2013/605, reg. 6(4)(b), with effect in relation to the making of declarations on or after 6 April 2014 (and any declaration made before that date continues to have effect in respect of interest distributions made on or after that date as if those amendments had not been made).

In reg. 17(6)(b), the words "either not ordinarily resident or, in the case of a beneficiary which is a company,", which appeared after the words "the trust is", omitted by SI 2013/605, reg. 6(4)(c), with effect in relation to the making of declarations on or after 6 April 2014 (and any declaration made before that date continues to have effect in respect of interest distributions made on or after that date as if those amendments had not been made).

The residence condition: declarations

18(1)   A declaration for the purposes of regulation 17 must–

(a)   be in such form as may be required or authorised by the Commissioners;

(b)   be made in writing to the investment trust or prospective investment trust making the interest distribution in question; and

(c)   contain any details or undertakings required by paragraphs (2) to (4).

18(2)   A declaration made for the purposes of condition A or B in regulation 17 must contain–

(a)   the name and principal residential address of the person making it; and

(b)   an undertaking that the investment trust or prospective investment trust will be notified by that person if the person becomes resident in the United Kingdom.

18(3)   A declaration made for the purposes of condition C in regulation 17 must contain the name of the deceased and the principal residential address of the deceased immediately before the time at which the deceased died.

18(4)   A declaration made for the purposes of condition D or E in regulation 17 must contain–

(a)   the names and principal residential addresses of the trustees of the trust or, in the case of a trustee which is a company, the name of the company and the address of its registered or principal office;

(b)   the names and principal residential addresses of the beneficiaries of the trust or, in the case of a beneficiary which is a company, the name of the company and the address of its registered or principal office; and

(c)   an undertaking that the trustees of the trust will notify the investment trust or prospective investment trust if–

    (i)   they become resident in the United Kingdom,

    (ii)   any beneficiary of the trust named in the declaration becomes resident in the United Kingdom, or

    (iii)   any person who becomes a beneficiary of the trust after making the declaration either is at the time of becoming a beneficiary, or subsequently becomes resident in the United Kingdom.

History – In reg. 18(2)(b), the word "ordinarily", which appeared before the word "resident", omitted by SI 2013/605, reg. 6(5)(a), with effect in relation to the making of declarations on or after 6 April 2014 (and any declarations made before that date continue to have effect in respect of interest distributions made on or after that date as if those amendments had not been made).

In reg. 18(4)(c)(ii) and (iii), the words "ordinarily resident or, in the case of a company,", which appeared after the word "becomes", omitted by SI 2013/605, reg. 6(5)(b), with effect in relation to the making of declarations on or after 6 April 2014 (and any declarations made before that date continue to have effect in respect of interest distributions made on or after that date as if those amendments had not been made).

References to beneficiaries in regulations 17 and 18

19   In regulations 17 and 18 references to a beneficiary are references to any person who is known to the trustees of the trust to be either–

(a)   a person who is, or will, or may become, entitled to any income of the trust, whether in the form of income or not, or

(b)   a person to whom any such income may be paid, or for whose benefit any such income may be applied, whether in the form of income or not, in the exercise of a discretion by the trustees.

Interest distributions: declarations and position of investment trust or prospective investment trust

20(1) For the purposes of determining whether an interest distribution should be made with or without any deduction required by the deduction obligation, an investment trust or prospective investment trust is entitled to treat a declaration made for the purposes of regulation 17 as valid.

20(2) But the investment trust or prospective investment trust may not treat the declaration as valid if condition A or B is met.

20(3) Condition A is that the investment trust or prospective investment trust receives a notification in compliance with an undertaking under regulation 18 that a person to whom the undertaking relates has become resident in the United Kingdom.

20(4) Condition B is that the investment trust or prospective investment trust comes into possession of information by some other means which indicates that such a person is or may be resident in the United Kingdom.

History – In reg. 20(3) and (4), the words "or ordinarily resident", which appeared after the word "resident", omitted by SI 2013/605, reg. 6(6), with effect in relation to the making of declarations on or after 6 April 2014 (and any declarations made before that date continue to have effect in respect of interest distributions made on or after that date as if those amendments had not been made).

PART 4 – INFORMATION AND RECORD KEEPING RELATING TO DISTRIBUTIONS

INFORMATION RELATING TO DISTRIBUTIONS

21(1) If an amount is distributed as an interest distribution, section 234A of ICTA (information relating to distributions: further provisions) shall apply to the company making the interest distribution as if the amount distributed were a payment of interest.

21(2) In the case of an investment trust or prospective investment trust, an appropriate statement for the purposes of section 234A of ICTA includes a written statement–

(a)   showing–
       (i)   the gross amount of the distribution made to the recipient,
       (ii)   the number and class of shares held by the recipient in respect of which the distribution is made,
       (iii)   the net amount of the distribution per share,
       (iv)   whether any tax has been deducted from the distribution,
       (v)   the date the distribution was made,
       (vi)   the percentage of the gross distribution attributable to the amount treated as an interest distribution and the percentage attributable to dividend;

(b)   providing details to allow the recipient to access an electronic means of calculating the amounts that would be shown in a written statement that would apart, from this paragraph, be provided in accordance with subsection (6) or (7) of section 234A; and

(c)   providing the recipient with an alternative method of obtaining the details of those amounts without recourse to electronic means.

NOTIFICATION OF INTEREST DISTRIBUTIONS MADE WITHOUT DEDUCTION OF TAX

22(1) If, during a tax year, a company has made interest distributions without deduction of tax, the company must give notice of that fact to the Commissioners within 14 days of the end of that tax year.

22(2) Notice given under paragraph (1)–

(a)   must be given in writing, and

(b)   has effect for the tax year in which the distribution was made and for subsequent tax years until the notice is withdrawn.

22(3) A company that fails to comply with paragraph (1) is liable to a penalty not exceeding £3,000 determined in accordance with section 100 of the Taxes Management Act 1970.

22(4) Sections 100A, 100B, 102, 103(4) and 118(2) of the Taxes Management Act 1970 apply to a penalty determined in accordance with paragraph (3).

DUTY TO KEEP AND PRESERVE RECORDS

23(1) A company must–

(a) keep such books, records and other documents as may be needed to enable the company to demonstrate that the information supplied in any written statement for the purposes of section 234A of ICTA is correct and complete,

(b) keep copies of all declarations made under Part 3 of these Regulations received by the company,

(c) keep such books, records and other documents as may be needed in relation to amounts distributed as interest distributions (whether or not the interest distributions were made without deduction of tax) for the purposes of demonstrating when and to whom those amounts were distributed, and

(d) preserve those books, records, other documents and declarations in accordance with this regulation.

In this regulation the books, records, other documents and declarations a company is required to keep and preserve are referred to as the "relevant records".

23(2) The relevant records must be preserved until the end of the day that is the sixth anniversary of the end of the tax year in which the distribution is made to which the relevant records relate.

23(3) Subject to paragraph (4), the duty under paragraphs (1) and (2) to preserve relevant records may be discharged–

(a) by preserving them in any form and by any means, or

(b) by preserving the information contained in them in any form and by any means.

23(4) Paragraph (3) does not apply in the case of any kind of record or document to which paragraph 22(3) of Schedule 18 to the Finance Act 1998 (preservation of information etc) applies.

Statutory Instruments

CORPORATION TAX
(LAND REMEDIATION RELIEF) ORDER 2009
(SI 2009/2037)

Made on 21 July 2009 by the Treasury in exercise of the powers conferred by s. 1145(2), 1145(3), 1146(3A) and (3B), 1146A(3) and (4), 1147(3), (3A) and (3B) and 1149(3), (3A) and (3B) of the Corporation Tax Act 2009 and paragraph 27 of Schedule 7 to the Finance Act 2009. Operative from 13 August 2009.

CITATION, COMMENCEMENT AND EFFECT

1(1) This Order may be cited as the Corporation Tax (Land Remediation Relief) Order 2009.

1(2) This Order shall come into force on 13th August 2009 and shall have effect in relation to expenditure incurred on or after 1st April 2009.

INTERPRETATION

2 In this Order–

"**the Act**" means the Corporation Tax Act 2009;

"**arsenic**" means the element whose chemical symbol is As and whose atomic number is 33;

"**arsenical compounds**" mean any compound one of whose constituent elements is arsenic;

"**Japanese Knotweed**" is the plant matter also known as Fallopia japonica, Reynoutria japonica or Polygonum cuspidatum;

"**radon**" means the element whose chemical symbol is Rn and whose atomic number is 86.

LAND IN A CONTAMINATED STATE

3(1) Section 1145(2) of the Act (land "in a contaminated state") shall not apply where the following are present in, on or under the land–

(a) arsenic,

(b) arsenical compounds,

(c) Japanese Knotweed, or

(d) radon.

3(2) This article is limited so that it has effect only in relation to–

(a) that part of the land where the items listed in paragraph (1) are present, and

(b) expenditure incurred for the purpose of remedying or mitigating the effects of relevant harm caused by the presence of one or more of the listed items.

RELEVANT CONTAMINATED LAND REMEDIATION: SPECIFIED ACTIVITY

4(1) For the purposes of Condition C in section 1146 of the Act ("relevant contaminated land remediation"), a specified activity is the removal of relevant material from the land in question to a licensed landfill site.

4(2) For the purposes of this article–

(a) "**relevant material**" means material which contains or may contain Japanese Knotweed;

(b) "**licensed landfill site**" means a site in respect of which a permit has been granted under the following–

(i) the Environmental Permitting (England and Wales) Regulations 2007,

(ii) the Pollution Prevention and Control (Scotland) Regulations 2000,

(iii) the Pollution Prevention and Control (Northern Ireland) Regulations 2003, or

(iv) Council Directive 1999/31/EC of 26th April 1999 on the landfill of waste.

RELEVANT CONTAMINATED LAND REMEDIATION: SPECIFIED ENACTMENTS

5 For the purposes of Condition C in section 1146 of the Act the following are specified enactments–

Statute	Section	Explanatory note
Building Act 1984	section 77	dangerous buildings
	section 79	ruinous and dilapidated buildings and neglected sites
Environmental Protection Act 1990	section 78E	duty of enforcing authority to require remediation of contaminated land
	section 79	statutory nuisances and inspections therefore
	section 80	summary proceedings for statutory nuisances
	section 81	supplementary provisions
	section 82	summary proceedings by persons aggrieved by statutory nuisances
Town and Country Planning Act 1990	section 215	power to require proper maintenance of land
Planning (Listed Buildings and Conversation Areas) Act 1990	section 48	repair notices preliminary to acquisitions under section 47
Town and Country Planning (Scotland) Act 1997	section 179	notice requiring proper maintenance of land
Planning (Listed Buildings and Conservation Areas) (Scotland) Act 1997	section 43	repair notices preliminary to acquisition under section 42
Building (Scotland) Act 2003	section 28	defective buildings
Pollution Control and Local Government (Northern Ireland) Order 1978	article 65	defective buildings
	article 66	ruinous and dilapidated buildings
Planning (Northern Ireland) Order 1991	article 39	orders requiring discontinuance of use or alteration or removal of buildings or works
	article 109	compulsory acquisition of listed buildings

RELEVANT DERELICT LAND REMEDIATION: SPECIFIED PURPOSES

6(1) For the purposes of Condition B in section 1146A of the Act ("relevant derelict land remediation"), the specified purposes are the removal of–

(a)   post-tensioned concrete heavyweight construction,

(b)   building foundations and machinery bases,

(c)   reinforced concrete pilecaps,

(d)   reinforced concrete basements, or

(e)   redundant services which are located below the ground.

6(2) For the purposes of this article, **"services"** means any pipes, wiring, cables, tunnels or other similar equipment or infrastructure used in relation to the following–

(a)   gas supply,

(b)   water supply, drainage or sewerage,

(c)   electricity supply, or

(d)   telecommunications.

EXCEPTION FROM CONDITION THAT LAND BE IN A CONTAMINATED STATE AT TIME OF ACQUISITION

7 Where land is in a contaminated state by virtue of the presence in, on or under it of Japanese Knotweed the following conditions need not be met—

(a) Condition B as specified by section 1147(3)(a) (deduction for capital expenditure), and

(b) Condition B as specified by section 1149(3)(a) (additional deduction for qualifying land remediation expenditure).

LLOYD'S UNDERWRITERS (EQUALISATION RESERVES) (TAX) REGULATIONS 2009

(SI 2009/2039)

Made on 21 July 2009 by the Treasury in exercise of the powers conferred by s. 47 of the Finance Act 2009. Operative from 1 September 2009.

CITATION, COMMENCEMENT AND EFFECT

1(1)   These Regulations may be cited as the Lloyd's Underwriters (Equalisation Reserves) (Tax) Regulations 2009 and shall come into force on 1st September 2009.

1(2)   These Regulations have effect in relation to accounting periods ending on or after 31st December 2008.

INTERPRETATION

2   In these Regulations–

(a)   **"underwriting business"** means, in relation to a corporate member or a partnership member, its underwriting business as a member of Lloyd's; and

(b)   references to section 444BA are references to section 444BA of the Income and Corporation Taxes Act 1988 (equalisation reserves for general business).

RESERVES MAINTAINED BY LLOYD'S MEMBERS WHICH ARE EQUIVALENT TO EQUALISATION RESERVES

3(1)   This regulation applies in a case where an equivalent Lloyd's reserve is maintained by a corporate member or a partnership member.

3(2)   For the purposes of this regulation a corporate member or a partnership member maintains an equivalent Lloyd's reserve if, and only if, the reserve is maintained by the member as if the equalisation reserves rules referred to in subsection (11) of section 444BA apply to the member notwithstanding that those rules do not otherwise apply to the member.

3(3)   Where this regulation applies, section 444BA shall apply with the modifications specified in regulation 4.

MODIFICATIONS OF SECTION 444BA INCOME AND CORPORATION TAXES ACT 1988 AND EQUALISATION RESERVES RULES

4(1)   The modifications to section 444BA referred to in regulation 3 are as follows–

(a)   in subsection (1), the words "and to sections 444BB to 444BD" shall be treated as omitted;

(b)   subject to paragraph (2), the equalisation reserves rules shall be treated as applying to the corporate member or partnership member (as the case may be);

(c)   references to **"an insurance company"** and **"the insurance company"** shall be treated as references to the corporate member or the partnership member (as the case may be);

(d)   references to **"business"** shall be treated as references to the underwriting business of the corporate member or the partnership member (as the case may be);

(e)   references to an **"equalisation reserve"** shall be treated as references to an "equivalent Lloyd's reserve"; and

(f)   subsection (10) shall be treated as omitted.

4(2)   For the purposes of the equalisation reserves rules treated as applied by paragraph (1), any calculation of the average of the amount of the annualised net written premiums shall be made without reference to any period prior to 1st January 2005.

4(3)   In paragraph (3), the reference to **"annualised net written premiums"** has the meaning given by the equalisation reserves rules.

FURTHER MODIFICATION FOR PURPOSES OF COMPUTING PROFITS OR LOSSES ARISING IN THE FIRST ACCOUNTING PERIOD TO WHICH THESE REGULATIONS APPLY

5(1)   This regulation applies for the purposes of computing the profits or losses of a corporate member or a partnership member arising in the first accounting period of the member in relation to which these Regulations have effect.

5(2)   In computing the profits or losses arising in the accounting period in accordance with section 444BA (as applied by and with the modifications made by these Regulations) any amount–

(a)   which is transferred into the equivalent Lloyd's reserve before or after the date these Regulations come into force,

(b)   which is an amount to which subsection (2)(a) of section 444BA applies by virtue of these Regulations, and

(c)   which is transferred into the reserve in respect of underwriting business written on or after 1st January 2005 and before 1st January 2006,

shall be deductible for the purposes of computing the profits or losses for that accounting period.

INTERNATIONAL MOVEMENT OF CAPITAL (REQUIRED INFORMATION) REGULATIONS 2009

(SI 2009/2192)

Made on 10 August 2009 by the Commissioners for Her Majesty's Revenue and Customs in exercise of the powers conferred by s. 37 of, and para. 4(2), 6(4), 8(4), 9(1)(e) and 14(2) of Sch. 17 to the Finance Act 2009. Operative from 1 September 2009.

CITATION, COMMENCEMENT AND EFFECT

1(1) These Regulations may be cited as the International Movement of Capital (Required Information) Regulations 2009 and shall come into force on 1st September 2009.

1(2) These Regulations shall have effect in relation to events taking place and transactions carried out on or after 1st July 2009.

INTERPRETATION

2(1) In these Regulations–

"group company" means any company which is resident in the United Kingdom and which would be deemed to be a member of the group of companies which includes the reporting body for the purposes of Chapter IV of Part X of the Income and Corporation Taxes Act 1988 if in section 413(3) of that Act the words "51 per cent" were substituted for the words "75 per cent";

"ICTA" means the Income and Corporation Taxes Act 1988;

"redeemable", in relation to shares, means that the shares satisfy one or both of the following conditions–

(a)   that, by virtue of the terms of their issue or the exercise of a right by any person or the existence of any arrangements, they are liable to be redeemed, cancelled or repaid, in whole or in part;

(b)   that, by virtue of any material arrangements, the holder has a right to require another person to acquire the shares or is obliged in any circumstances to dispose of them or another person has a right or is in any circumstances obliged to acquire them;

and arrangements are material arrangements if the company which issued the shares or a company connected with that company is a party to the arrangements;

"Schedule 17" means Schedule 17 (international movement of capital) to the Finance Act 2009.

2(2) For the purposes of these Regulations, whether a person is connected with another shall be determined as it would in accordance with the provisions of subsections (2) to (8) of section 839 (connected persons) of ICTA if the words "paragraph 12 of Schedule 17 to the Finance Act 2009" were substituted for the words "section 416" in the definition of "control" in subsection (8).

2(3) In these Regulations, references to a reporting body include a body corporate which would be a reporting body if it had not entered into an arrangement under paragraph 6 of Schedule 17.

INFORMATION

3(1) Paragraphs (2) and (3) specify the information (in this regulation referred to as "the required information") to be contained in the report which is required to be made to an officer of Revenue and Customs under paragraph 4(1) of Schedule 17.

3(2) The required information as it relates to a foreign subsidiary connected with the event or transaction is–

(a)   its name, and

(b)   the territory from the laws of which it derives its status as a body corporate.

3(3) The required information as it relates to an event or transaction is a full description of the event or transaction (and, in the case of a transaction, a full description of all the steps taken in the course of the transaction) and includes in particular–

(a)   the date on which the event took place or the transaction was carried out,

(b)   for a transaction, the name of each party to it,

(c)   the reason for the event or transaction, and

Statutory Instruments

(d)   an estimate of the effect of the event or transaction on the liability to tax in the United Kingdom of the reporting body and of any group company.

VALUE OF THE EVENT OR TRANSACTION

4(1)   The value of an event or transaction is to be determined for the purposes of paragraph 8 of Schedule 17 in accordance with this regulation.

4(2)   The value of an issue or transfer of shares or debentures is the market value of the shares or debentures.

4(3)   The value of an event or transaction which results in a foreign subsidiary becoming, or ceasing to be, a controlling partner in a partnership is the market value of the share of the subsidiary in the assets of the partnership immediately after it becomes a controlling partner or, as the case may be, immediately before it ceases to be a controlling partner.

4(4)   For the purposes of paragraphs (2) and (3), the value of an event or transaction that is one of a series is the aggregate of the value of all the events and transactions in the series.

EXCLUDED TRANSACTIONS

5(1)   A transaction is excluded for the purposes of Schedule 17 if—

(a)   it is a transaction within paragraph 8(2)(a) to (c) of Schedule 17 that is entered into pursuant to cash pooling arrangements in respect of which the conditions specified in paragraph (2) have been met; or

(b)   it is described in one of the paragraphs in the Schedule (excluded transactions) to these Regulations and meets such conditions (if any) as are specified there.

5(2)   The conditions mentioned in paragraph (1)(a) are that before the transaction takes place—

(a)   the parties to the cash pooling arrangements notify an officer of Revenue and Customs in writing of the terms of the arrangements;

(b)   an officer of Revenue and Customs gives notice in writing to the parties that transactions entered into pursuant to the cash pooling arrangements after the date of the notice will be excluded transactions for the purposes of Schedule 17.

5(3)   The Schedule (excluded transactions) to these Regulations has effect.

NOMINATION ARRANGEMENTS

6(1)   This regulation contains provision about an arrangement under paragraph 6 of Schedule 17.

6(2)   The parties to an arrangement must give notice to an officer of Revenue and Customs within 28 days of entering into it.

6(3)   The notice must be in writing and signed by all the parties to the arrangement.

6(4)   The notice must state—

(a)   the name of each party,

(b)   the tax reference of each party, and

(c)   which party is the nominated reporting body.

6(5)   The parties to an arrangement are treated as having withdrawn from it if they fail to give notice in accordance with paragraphs (2) to (4).

6(6)   A party to an arrangement is treated as having withdrawn from it if that party ceases to be controlled by the foreign parent.

6(7)   A party which withdraws from or is treated as having withdrawn from an arrangement must give notice in writing of that fact to an officer of Revenue and Customs and to any other party to the arrangement within 28 days of the date of withdrawal or, as the case may be, the date on which it ceases to be controlled by the foreign parent.

SCHEDULE – EXCLUDED TRANSACTIONS

Regulation 5(1)(b) and (3)

1   The following transactions are excluded transactions mentioned in regulation 5(1)(b).

2(1)   The first transaction is the issue of shares by the foreign subsidiary to the reporting body or to a group company.

2(2)   The conditions are that the issue—

(a)   is of shares that are not redeemable; and

(b)   is either–

    (i)   at market value and for consideration paid in cash to the foreign subsidiary, or

    (ii)   in or towards payment for any business undertaking or property acquired by the foreign subsidiary at market value.

3(1)   The second transaction is the issue of shares by the foreign subsidiary to a person not connected with the reporting body.

3(2)   The conditions are–

(a)   that the issue–

    (i)   is at market value and for consideration paid to the foreign subsidiary, and

    (ii)   is not to a nominee or trustee for a person who is connected with the reporting body;

(b)   that no arrangements exist as a consequence of which the reporting body or a person connected with the reporting body, or a nominee or trustee for that person or the reporting body, is or may become entitled to the shares so issued or to any of them or to any interest in them or in any of them.

4(1)   The third transaction is the issue of shares by the foreign subsidiary to all persons who are its shareholders at the time of the issue.

4(2)   The conditions are that the issue–

(a)   is in respect of and in proportion to the shares held by the shareholders in the foreign subsidiary at the time of the issue; and

(b)   either–

    (i)   is of shares that are not redeemable, or

    (ii)   where no shares are issued to a company which is resident in the United Kingdom or to a nominee or trustee for such a company, is at market value for consideration paid in cash to the foreign subsidiary.

5(1)   The fourth transaction is the issue of debentures by the foreign subsidiary to the reporting body or to a group company.

5(2)   The condition is that the circumstances specified in sub-paragraph (3) are not associated with or present in connection with the issue of the debentures.

5(3)   The circumstances are that a loan, whether or not of the same amount as that secured by the debentures, is made by a company which is not resident in the United Kingdom to a company which is resident in the United Kingdom.

6(1)   The fifth transaction is the issue of debentures by the foreign subsidiary to persons not connected with the reporting body.

6(2)   The conditions are–

(a)   that the issue–

    (i)   is at market value and for consideration paid to the foreign subsidiary, and

    (ii)   is not to a nominee or trustee for a person who is connected with the reporting body;

(b)   that no arrangements exist as a consequence of which the reporting body or a person connected with the reporting body, or a nominee or trustee for that person or the reporting body, is or may become entitled to the debentures so issued or to any of them or to any interest in them or in any of them.

7(1)   The sixth transaction is the transfer by the reporting body or a company (whether or not it is resident in the United Kingdom) of shares or debentures of the foreign subsidiary to a person not connected with the reporting body.

7(2)   The conditions are–

(a)   that the transfer–

    (i)   is at market value for consideration paid to the transferor company, and

    (ii)   is not to a nominee or trustee for a person who is connected with the reporting body;

(b)   that no arrangements exist as a consequence of which–

    (i)   the reporting body, or

    (ii)   a nominee or trustee for the reporting body, or

    (iii)   a person connected with the reporting body, or

    (iv)   a nominee or trustee for a person connected with the reporting body,

is or may become entitled to the shares or debentures transferred or to any of them or to any interest in them or in any of them.

8 The seventh transaction is a transfer by the reporting body of shares or debentures of the foreign subsidiary to a group company.

9(1) The eighth transaction is a transfer within sub-paragraph (2) to the reporting body or a group company.

9(2) A transfer is within this sub-paragraph if it–

(a) is not by the reporting body,

(b) is of shares or debentures of a foreign subsidiary in which the reporting body has an interest, and

(c) is permitted or caused by the reporting body.

10 The ninth transaction consists in the reporting body or a group company giving security over the shares of a foreign subsidiary in connection with borrowing money from a lender who is unconnected to the reporting body or the group company.

Statutory Instruments

MUTUAL SOCIETIES (TRANSFERS OF BUSINESS) (TAX) REGULATIONS 2009

(SI 2009/2971, as amended by SI 2011/37)

Made on 9 November 2009 by the Treasury in exercise of the powers conferred by s. 124 of the Finance Act 2009. Operative from 1 December 2009.

ARRANGEMENT OF REGULATIONS

REGULATION

30.   INTANGIBLE FIXED ASSETS TRANSFERRED AS IF AT NO GAIN OR NO LOSS
31.   EXEMPTION FROM STAMP DUTY LAND TAX
32.   EXEMPTION FROM STAMP DUTY

PART 4 – FURTHER PROVISIONS RELATING TO RELEVANT TRANSFERS

33.   STAMP DUTY LAND TAX – GROUP RELIEF
34.   TRANSITIONAL PROVISION
35.   ARRANGEMENTS THE PURPOSE OF WHICH IS TO SECURE A TAX ADVANTAGE

PART 1 – PRELIMINARY PROVISIONS AND INTERPRETATION

CITATION, COMMENCEMENT AND EFFECT

1(1) These Regulations may be cited as the Mutual Societies (Transfers of Business) (Tax) Regulations 2009 and shall come into force on 1st December 2009.

1(2) Regulations 2 to 11, 15 to 25, and 31 to 34 shall have effect–

(a)   in relation to any relevant transfer which takes place on or after 22 April 2009; and

(b)   in relation to any land transaction which forms part of a relevant transfer to which these Regulations apply where the effective date of that land transaction is on or after 22 April 2009.

1(3) Regulations 12 to 14, 26 to 30, and 35 shall have effect in relation to any relevant transfer which takes place on or after 1st December 2009.

INTERPRETATION

2(1) In these Regulations–

"**CTA**" means the Corporation Tax Act 2009;

"**FA, followed by a year**" means the Finance Act of that year;

"**ICTA**" means the Income and Corporation Taxes Act 1988;

"**TCGA**" means the Taxation of Chargeable Gains Act 1992;

"**75% subsidiary**" has the meaning given by section 838 of ICTA;

"**business**" includes engagements;

"**chargeable intangible asset**" has the meaning given by section 741 of CTA (meaning of "chargeable intangible asset");

"**commercial company**" means a company formed and registered under the Companies Act 2006 (or treated as formed and registered under that Act) which is a public company limited by shares;

"**creditor relationship**" has the meaning given by section 302(5) of CTA ("loan relationship", "creditor relationship", "debtor relationship");

"**debtor relationship**" has the meaning given by section 302(6) of CTA ("loan relationship", "creditor relationship", "debtor relationship");

"**effective date**" has the meaning given by section 119 of FA 2003 (meaning of "effective date" of a transaction);

"**fair value accounting**" has the meaning given by section 313 of CTA (basis of accounting);

"**land transaction**" has the meaning given by section 43(1) of FA 2003 (land transactions);

"**loan relationship**" includes matters treated as a loan relationship by Part 6 of CTA (relationships treated as loan relationships);

"**relevant transfer**" has the meaning given by regulation 3;

"**subsidiary of a mutual society**" means a company within the meaning of the Companies Act 2006–

(a)   in which a building society, an industrial and provident society or a friendly society, as the case may be, holds a majority of the voting rights or of which that society is a member and alone controls, pursuant to an agreement with other shareholders or members, a majority of the voting rights; and

(b)   in relation to which that society has the right to appoint or remove a majority of the company's board of directors;

"**tax-neutral**" has the meaning given by section 776 of CTA (meaning of tax neutral transfer).

2(2)   In regulations 5 to 7 and 16 to 18 "**asset**" has the meaning given by section 21 of TCGA (assets and disposals).

2(3)   In regulations 6, 7, 9, 17, 18 and 25 references to a company being a member of a group of companies are to be read in accordance with section 170 of TCGA (interpretation of sections 171 to 181).

2(4)   In regulations 13 and 29 "**group**" has the meaning given by Chapter 8 of Part 8 of CTA (intangible fixed assets).

2(5)   In these Regulations references to a person being connected with another are to be read in accordance with section 839 of ICTA (connected persons).

MEANING OF RELEVANT TRANSFER

3(1)   A "**relevant transfer**" by a building society is—

(a)   an amalgamation of two or more building societies ("the transferor") by the establishment of a successor building society ("the transferee") in accordance with section 93 of the Building Societies Act 1986 (amalgamations);

(b)   a transfer by a building society ("the transferor") of the whole of its business to another building society ("the transferee") in accordance with section 94 of the Building Societies Act 1986 (transfers of engagements);

(c)   a transfer by a building society ("the transferor") of part of its business to another building society ("the transferee") in accordance with section 94 (transfers of engagements) of the Building Societies Act 1986;

(d)   a transfer by a building society ("the transferor") of the whole of its business to a commercial company ("the transferee") in accordance with section 97 of the Building Societies Act 1986 (transfers of business to commercial company); or

(e)   a transfer by a building society ("the transferor") of the whole of its business to a subsidiary of a mutual society ("the transferee") in accordance with section 97 of the Building Societies Act 1986 (transfers of business to commercial company).

3(2)   A "**relevant transfer**" by an industrial and provident society is—

(a)   an amalgamation of two or more industrial and provident societies ("the transferor") into one industrial and provident society ("the transferee") in accordance with section 50 of the Industrial and Provident Societies Act 1965 (amalgamation of societies);

(b)   a transfer by an industrial and provident society ("the transferor") of the whole of its business to another industrial and provident society ("the transferee") in accordance with section 51 of the Industrial and Provident Societies Act 1965 (transfer of engagements between societies);

(c)   a transfer by an industrial and provident society ("the transferor") of part of its business to one or more industrial and provident societies ("the transferee") in accordance with section 51 of the Industrial and Provident Societies Act 1965 (transfer of engagements between societies);

(d)   a conversion of an industrial and provident society ("the transferor") into a company ("the transferee") in accordance with section 52 of the Industrial and Provident Societies Act 1965 (conversion into, amalgamation with, or transfer of engagements to company);

(e)   an amalgamation of an industrial and provident society ("the transferor") with a company ("the transferee") in accordance with section 52 of the Industrial and Provident Societies Act 1965 (conversion into, amalgamation with, or transfer of engagements to company); or

(f)   a transfer by an industrial and provident society ("the transferor") of the whole of its business to a company ("the transferee") in accordance with section 52 of the Industrial and Provident Societies Act 1965 (conversion into, amalgamation with, or transfer of engagements to company).

3(3)   A "**relevant transfer**" by a friendly society is—

(a)   an amalgamation of two or more friendly societies ("the transferor") by the establishment of a successor society ("the transferee") in accordance with section 85 of the Friendly Societies Act 1992 (amalgamation of friendly societies);

(b)   a transfer by a friendly society ("the transferor") of the whole of its business to a person ("the transferee") referred to in section 86 of the Friendly Societies Act 1992 (transfer of engagements by or to friendly society);

(c)   a transfer by a friendly society ("the transferor") of part of its business to a person ("the transferee") referred to in section 86 of the Friendly Societies Act 1992 (transfer of engagements by or to friendly society);

(d)   a transfer by a friendly society ("the transferor") of the whole of its business to a person ("the transferee") specified by the Financial Services Authority in accordance with section 90 of the Friendly Societies Act 1992 (power of authority to effect transfer of engagements); or

(e)   a conversion of a friendly society ("the transferor") into a company ("the transferee") in accordance with section 91 of the Friendly Societies Act 1992 (conversion of friendly society into company).

PART 2 – BUILDING SOCIETIES

RELEVANT TRANSFER BY A BUILDING SOCIETY

4(1)   This regulation applies if there is a relevant transfer by a building society.

4(2)   The Corporation Tax Acts shall have effect in relation to the relevant transfer subject to paragraphs (3) to (18).

4(3)   For the purposes of the allowances and charges provided for by the Capital Allowances Act 2001 a trade which is transferred or amalgamated as a result of the relevant transfer shall not be treated as permanently discontinued nor shall a new trade be treated as set up and commenced, and–

(a)   there shall be made to or on the transferee in accordance with that Act all such allowances and charges as would, if the transferor had continued to carry on the trade, have fallen to be made to or on the transferor; and

(b)   the amount of any such allowance or charge shall be computed as if–

    (i)   the transferee had been carrying on the trade since the transferor began to do so, and

    (ii)   everything done to or by the transferor had been done to or by the transferee (but so that no sale or transfer which, on the transfer of the trade, is made to the transferee by the transferor of any assets in use for the purpose of the trade shall be treated as giving rise to any such allowance or charge).

4(4)   The transferee shall be entitled to such relief under section 393(1) of ICTA (losses other than terminal losses), as for a loss sustained by the transferee in carrying on the trade, for any amount for which the transferor would have been entitled to relief if it had continued to carry on the trade.

This paragraph is subject to paragraph (5) and to any claim made by the transferor under section 393A(1) of ICTA (losses: set off against profits of the same, or an earlier, accounting period).

4(5)   If the amount of relevant liabilities exceeds the value of relevant assets, the transferee shall be entitled to relief by virtue of paragraph (4) only if, and only to the extent that, the amount of that excess is less than the amount mentioned in that paragraph.

4(6)   For the purposes of paragraph (5)–

(a)   the value of assets (other than money) shall be taken to be the price which they might reasonably be expected to have fetched on a sale in the open market immediately before the predecessor ceased to carry on the trade; and

(b)   the amount of liabilities shall be taken to be their amount at that time.

4(7)   Subsection (2A) of section 393A of ICTA (losses: set off against profits of the same, or an earlier, accounting period) shall not apply to any loss which (but for this paragraph) would fall within subsection (2B) of that section by virtue of the transferor ceasing to carry on the trade, and subsection (7) of that section shall not apply for the computation of any such loss.

4(8)   If, on the transferor ceasing to carry on the trade, the transferee begins to carry on the activities of the trade as part of its trade, then that part of the trade carried on by the transferee shall be treated for the purposes of this regulation as a separate trade, if the effect of so treating it is that paragraph (2) has effect on that event in relation to that separate trade.

4(9)   If, on the transferor ceasing to carry on part of a trade, the transferee begins to carry on the activities of that part as its trade or part of its trade, the transferor shall for the purposes of this regulation be treated as having carried on that part of its trade as a separate trade if the effect of so treating it is that paragraph (2) has effect on that event in relation to that separate trade.

4(10) If, under paragraphs (8) or (9), any activities of the transferor fall, on that transferor ceasing or beginning to carry them on, to be treated as a separate trade, such apportionments of receipts, expenses, assets or liabilities shall be made as may be just and reasonable.

4(11) If, by virtue of paragraph (10), any item falls to be apportioned and, at the time of the apportionment, it appears that it is material as respects the liability to tax (for whatever period) of two or more building societies or a commercial company or a subsidiary of a mutual society, any question which arises as to the manner in which the item shall be apportioned shall be determined, for the purposes of the tax of those building societies, commercial company or subsidiary of a mutual in like manner as an appeal, and all those companies shall be entitled to be a party to those proceedings.

4(12) If the amount of relevant liabilities does not exceed the value of relevant assets–

(a)   paragraph (10) shall have effect as if for the words following "separate trade," to the end of the paragraph there were substituted "any necessary apportionment shall be made of receipts or expenses."; and

(b)   paragraph (11) shall have effect as if for "item" there were substituted "sum".

4(13) In this regulation–

"**relevant assets**" means–

(a)   assets vested in the transferor immediately before it ceased to carry on the trade, which were not transferred to the transferee; and

(b)   consideration given to the transferor by the transferee in respect of the relevant transfer or change of the entity carrying on the business as a consequence of the relevant transfer; and for the purposes of sub-paragraph (b) the assumption by the transferee of any liabilities of the transferor shall not be treated as the giving of consideration to the transferor by the transferee;

"**relevant liabilities**" means liabilities outstanding and vested in the transferor immediately before it ceased to carry on the trade which were not transferred to the transferee; but a liability representing the transferor's share capital, share premium account, reserves or relevant loan stock is not a relevant liability.

4(14) Where the transferor transferred a liability to the transferee but the creditor concerned agreed to accept settlement of part of the liability as settlement of the whole, the liability shall be treated for the purposes of paragraph (13) as not having been transferred to the transferee except as to that part.

4(15) For the purposes of paragraph (13), a liability representing the transferor's share capital, share premium account, reserves or relevant loan stock shall be treated as not doing so, if, in the period of one year ending with the day on which the transferor ceased to carry on the trade, the liability arose on a conversion of a liability not representing its share capital, share premium account, reserves or relevant loan stock.

4(16) Where a liability of the transferor representing its relevant loan stock is not a relevant liability for the purposes of paragraph (5) but is secured on an asset of the transferor not yet transferred to the transferee, the value of the asset shall, for the purposes of paragraph (5), be reduced by an amount equal to the amount of the liability.

4(17) In this regulation "**relevant loan stock**" means any loan stock or similar security (whether secured or unsecured) except any in the case of which paragraph (18) applies.

4(18) This paragraph applies where, at the time the liability giving rise to the loan stock or other security was incurred, the person who was the creditor was carrying on a trade of lending money.

TRANSFER OF AN ASSET – TAXATION OF CHARGEABLE GAINS

5 If–

(a)   there is a relevant transfer within regulation 3(1)(e); and

(b)   there is a disposal of an asset by the transferor to the transferee,

the transferor and the transferee shall be treated for the purposes of corporation tax in respect of chargeable gains as if the asset were acquired from the transferor for a consideration of such amount as would secure that on the disposal neither a gain nor a loss would accrue to the transferor.

TRANSFER OF AN ASSET – TAXATION OF CHARGEABLE GAINS – COMPANY CEASING TO BE MEMBER OF GROUP

6 If–

(a)   there is a relevant transfer within regulation 3(1)(a), (b) or (e);

(b)   the transferor and the transferee are not members of the same group at the time of the relevant transfer; and

(c)   as a result of the relevant transfer, a company ceases to be a member of the same group as the transferor,

section 179 of TCGA (company ceasing to be a member of group: post-appointed day cases) shall not apply in respect of any asset acquired by the company referred to in paragraph (c) from the transferor or from any other member of the same group as the transferor.

TRANSFER OF AN ASSET – COMPANY CEASING TO BE A MEMBER OF A GROUP – FURTHER PROVISIONS

7(1)   This regulation applies if there is a relevant transfer within regulation 3(1)(a), (b) or (e).

7(2)   If this regulation applies and the transferor and the transferee–

(a)   as a result of the relevant transfer become members of the same group; but

(b)   subsequently cease to be members of the same group,

paragraph (3) applies.

7(3)   If paragraph (2) is satisfied, section 179 of TCGA (company ceasing to be a member of group: post-appointed day cases) shall not have effect as respects–

(a)   any asset acquired by the transferee as a consequence of the relevant transfer from the transferor or any other member of the same group; or

(b)   any asset acquired as a consequence of the relevant transfer from the transferor, or any other member of the same group, by any company which is a member of the same group as the transferor at the time of the relevant transfer.

7(4)   If this regulation applies and, as a result of the relevant transfer, a company which was a member of the same group as the transferor at the time of the relevant transfer–

(a)   ceases to be a member of that group;

(b)   becomes a member of the same group as the transferee; and

(c)   subsequently ceases to be a member of that group,

section 179 of TCGA shall have effect when the company ceases to be a member of the same group as the transferee as respects any relevant asset acquired by that company otherwise than from the transferee as if that asset had been acquired from the transferee.

This paragraph is subject to paragraph (6).

7(5)   In paragraph (4) **"relevant asset"** means any asset acquired by the company referred to in that paragraph from–

(a)   the transferor; or

(b)   any other company which is a member of the same group as the transferor at the time of the relevant transfer,

when the company referred to in that paragraph and the transferor, or the company referred to in that paragraph, the transferor and the other company, were members of the same group.

7(6)   Paragraph (4) shall not apply if the company referred to in that paragraph which acquired that asset and the company from which that asset was acquired (one being a 75 per cent subsidiary of the other) cease simultaneously to be members of the same group as the transferee but continue to be members of the same group as one another.

TRANSFER OF LOAN RELATIONSHIP OR DERIVATIVE CONTRACT

8(1)   This regulation applies if–

(a)   there is a relevant transfer by a building society;

(b)   the transferor has consistently applied appropriate accounting treatment in accordance with generally accepted accounting practice up to and including the date of the relevant transfer in respect of all loan relationships and derivative contracts shown in its balance sheet; and

(c)   as a result of the relevant transfer the transferee directly or indirectly replaces the transferor as a party to–

    (i)   the loan relationships; or

    (ii)   the derivative contracts.

8(2)   The transferee shall bring into account, in accordance with paragraphs (3) to (15), amounts in respect of the transfer adjustment.

8(3)   The **"transfer adjustment"** is the difference, if any, that arises on a comparison of the closing accounting balance sheet figure, adjusted for tax as appropriate, in respect of the loan relationships or the derivative contracts in the transferor's accounts and the opening accounting balance sheet figure, adjusted for tax as appropriate, in respect of the loan relationships or derivative contracts in the transferee's accounts.

8(4)   If the transferor carries out simultaneous relevant transfers of its business, within regulation 3(1)(c) of part of its business the **"transfer adjustment"** in respect of each transferee is to be computed by reference to the difference between the opening accounting balance sheet figure, adjusted for tax as appropriate, for the transferred loan relationships and derivative contracts in each transferee's accounts and the closing accounting balance sheet figure, adjusted for tax as appropriate, for those same loan relationships and derivative contracts in the transferor's accounts.

8(5)   For the purposes of paragraphs (3) and (4), where, in the Tax Acts, an accounting balance sheet figure is adjusted for tax, it is that adjusted figure that is to be used when calculating the transfer adjustment.

8(6)   The credits and debits to be brought into account as profits or deficits or losses for the purposes of Part 3, 5, 6 or 7 of CTA in respect of the transferee's transfer adjustment shall be determined in accordance with this regulation.

8(7)   The transferee shall bring one-sixth of the transfer adjustment ("the applicable amount") into account for each year of a six year period ("the prescribed period") beginning with the day on which the relevant transfer takes place. This is subject to paragraphs (8), (10) and (16).

8(8)   If there are two or more accounting periods falling in a year, the applicable amount for the year shall be apportioned between the accounting periods.

8(9)   An apportionment between accounting periods of an applicable amount in accordance with paragraph (8) shall be made according to the proportion of the year which is included in each accounting period.

8(10)   If the transferee ceases to be within the charge to corporation tax before the end of the prescribed period, the whole of the applicable amounts, so far as they have not been brought into account in an earlier accounting period, shall be brought into account as a credit or debit for the period ending when the transferee ceases to be within that charge. This paragraph is subject to paragraph (11).

8(11)   If before the end of the prescribed period–

(a)   the transferee transfers the business by way of a relevant transfer within regulation 3(1)(a) or (b) to a successor building society ("A") ; and,

(b)   as a result of the transfer, the transferee ceases to be within the charge to corporation tax,

8(11)   that relevant transfer will not cause the whole of the applicable amounts, so far as they have not been brought into account in an earlier period, to be brought into account for the period in which that relevant transfer takes place.

8(12)   Where there is a relevant transfer to which paragraph (11) applies, paragraph (7) will apply to the applicable amounts which have not been brought into account by the transferee as if references to "the transferee" were references to "A".

8(13)   If this regulation applies and the transferor has been bringing debits and credits into account in accordance with regulation 3A of the Loan Relationships and Derivative Contracts (Change of Accounting Practice) Regulations 2004, the relevant transfer shall be treated for the purposes of regulation 3A(6) of those Regulations as though it were a qualifying transfer.

8(14)   In paragraph (1)(c) the reference to "the transferee directly or indirectly replaces the transferor as a party" has the same meaning given by–

(a)   regulation 10 in the case of a loan relationship; and

(b)   regulation 11 in the case of a derivative contract.

8(15)   Paragraph (7) does not apply if the transferee has made an election under paragraph (16).

8(16) If the amount of the transfer adjustment does not exceed £1.5 million, the transferee may elect to bring into account the full amount of the transfer adjustment in the accounting period in which the relevant transfer takes place.

8(17) An election under paragraph (16)–

(a)   must be made–

   (i)   by notice in writing to an officer of Revenue and Customs; and

   (ii)   no later than 12 months after the end of the accounting period in which the relevant transfer took place;

(b)   must specify the amount of the transfer adjustment; and

(c)   is irrevocable.

8(18) In this regulation–

"**generally accepted accounting practice**" has the meaning given by section 50(1) of FA 2004 (generally accepted accounting practice);

"**officer of Revenue and Customs**" has the meaning given by section 2 of the Commissioners for Revenue and Customs Act 2005 (officers of revenue and customs).

TRANSFER OF LOAN RELATIONSHIP OR DERIVATIVE CONTRACT – FURTHER PROVISIONS

9(1) This regulation applies if–

(a)   there is a relevant transfer within regulation 3(1)(a), (b), (d) or (e); and

(b)   before the date of the relevant transfer there had been a transfer to a company of–

   (i)   a loan relationship to which section 336 of CTA (transfers of loans on group transactions) applied; or

   (ii)   a derivative contract to which section 625 of CTA (group member replacing another as party to a derivative contract) applied;

but this is subject to paragraph (6).

9(2) Paragraph (3) applies if, as a result of the relevant transfer, the company referred to in paragraph (1) ceases to be a member of the same group as the transferor–

(a)   before the end of the relevant six year period referred to in–

   (i)   section 344(4) of CTA (transferee leaving group after replacing transferor as party to loan relationship); or

   (ii)   section 630(4) of CTA (introduction to sections 631 and 632); and

(b)   whilst still a party to the relevant loan relationship or derivative contract.

9(3) If paragraph (2) is satisfied–

(a)   the company referred to in paragraph (1)(b) shall be treated as not having ceased to be a member of the same group as the transferor;

(b)   in the case of a loan relationship, section 345 of CTA (transferee leaving group otherwise than because of an exempt distribution) shall not apply to the loan relationship as a result of the relevant transfer; and

(c)   in the case of a derivative contract, section 631 of CTA (transferee leaving group otherwise than because of exempt distribution) shall not apply to the derivative contract as a result of the relevant transfer.

9(4) Paragraph (5) applies if the company referred to in paragraph (1)(b) ceases to be a member of the same group as the transferee–

(a)   before the end of the relevant six year period referred to in–

   (i)   section 344(4) of CTA (transferee leaving group after replacing transferor as party to loan relationship); or

   (ii)   section 630(4) of CTA (introduction to sections 631 and 632); and

(b)   whilst still a party to the relevant loan relationship or derivative contract.

9(5) If paragraph (4) is satisfied–

(a)   in the case of a loan relationship, section 345 of CTA (transferee leaving group otherwise than because of an exempt distribution) shall apply to the loan relationship as a result of the relevant transfer; and

(b)   in the case of a derivative contract, section 631 of CTA (transferee leaving group otherwise than because of exempt distribution) shall apply to the derivative contract as a result of the relevant transfer.

9(6)   This regulation does not apply where a transferor of a loan relationship is regarded as using fair value accounting in respect of that loan relationship.

9(7)   A transferor shall be regarded for the purposes of this regulation as using fair value accounting in respect of a loan relationship only if the credits and debits to be brought into account for the purposes of these Regulations as respects that loan relationship are determined on that basis.

9(8)   It does not matter for the purposes of paragraph (7) if the transferor does not otherwise use fair value accounting in respect of the loan relationship.

MEANING OF TRANSFEREE REPLACING BUILDING SOCIETY AS PARTY TO A LOAN RELATIONSHIP

10(1)   References in regulation 8 to a transferee replacing a transferor as a party to a loan relationship include references to a transferee becoming party to a loan relationship which–

(a)   confers rights within paragraph (2);

(b)   imposes obligations within paragraph (2); or

(c)   both confers such rights and imposes such obligations.

10(2)   Rights or obligations are within this paragraph if they are equivalent to those of the transferor under a loan relationship to which that transferor has ceased to be a party as a result of the relevant transfer.

10(3)   For the purposes of paragraph (2), a transferor's rights under a creditor relationship are equivalent to rights under another creditor relationship if each set of rights gives the holder of an asset representing the relationship in question–

(a)   the same rights against the same persons as to capital, interest and dividends; and

(b)   the same remedies to enforce those rights.

10(4)   For the purposes of paragraph (3), any difference in–

(a)   the total nominal amounts of the assets representing each loan relationship;

(b)   the form in which they are held; or

(c)   the way in which they can be transferred,

is ignored.

10(5)   For the purposes of paragraph (2), a transferee's obligations under a debtor relationship are equivalent to obligations under another debtor loan relationship if under each set of obligations the holder of the liability representing the loan relationship in question has–

(a)   the same obligations to the same persons as to capital, interest and dividends; and

(b)   the same remedies to enforce those obligations.

10(6)   For the purposes of paragraph (5), any difference in–

(a)   the total nominal amounts of the assets representing the creditor loan relationship corresponding to each relationship;

(b)   the form in which they are held; or

(c)   the way in which they can be transferred,

is ignored.

MEANING OF TRANSFEREE REPLACING BUILDING SOCIETY AS A PARTY TO A DERIVATIVE CONTRACT

11(1)   References in regulation 8 to a transferee replacing a transferor as a party to a derivative contract include references to the transferee becoming party to a derivative contract which–

(a)   confers rights within paragraph (2);

(b)   imposes obligations within paragraph (2); or

(c)   both confers such rights and imposes such obligations.

11(2)   Rights or obligations are within this paragraph if they are equivalent to those of the transferor under a derivative contract to which that transferor has ceased to be a party as a result of the relevant transfer.

TRANSFER OF INTANGIBLE FIXED ASSETS

12(1)   This regulation applies if–

(a)   there is a relevant transfer within regulation 3(1)(e) which includes intangible fixed assets;

(b)   those assets are chargeable intangible assets in relation to the transferor immediately before the relevant transfer; and

(c)   those assets are chargeable intangible assets in relation to the transferee immediately after the relevant transfer.

12(2)   The transfer of those assets is tax-neutral for the purposes of–

(a)   these Regulations; and

(b)   Part 8 of CTA (intangible fixed assets).

12(3)   For the application of sections 780 (deemed realisation and reacquisition at market value) and 785 (principal company becoming member of another group) of CTA where this regulation applies, see regulation 13.

12(4)   This regulation and regulations 13 and 14 apply to goodwill as they apply to intangible fixed assets.

TRANSFER OF INTANGIBLE FIXED ASSETS – FURTHER PROVISIONS

13(1)   This regulation applies if–

(a)   there is a relevant transfer within regulation 3(1)(a), (b) or (e) which includes intangible fixed assets;

(b)   those assets are–

     (i)   chargeable intangible assets in relation to the transferor immediately before the relevant transfer; and

     (ii)   chargeable intangible assets in relation to the transferee immediately after the relevant transfer; and

(c)   the transfer of those assets is tax-neutral for the purposes of these Regulations or Part 8 of CTA (intangible fixed assets).

13(2)   If because of the relevant transfer a company ceases to be a member of the same group as the transferor, that event does not cause–

(a)   section 780 of CTA (deemed realisation and reacquisition at market value); or

(b)   section 785 of that Act (principal company becoming member of another group),

to apply as respects any assets acquired by the company from the transferor or any other member of the same group as the transferor.

13(3)   If the transferor and transferee are members of the same group at the time of the relevant transfer but later cease to be, that later event does not cause section 780 or 785 of CTA to apply in relation to any asset to which this regulation applies.

13(4)   Paragraph (3) applies to–

(a)   any asset acquired by the transferee on or before the relevant transfer from the transferor, or from any other member of the same group; or

(b)   any asset acquired from the transferor or from any other member of the same group by a company (other than the transferee) that is a member of that group at the time of the relevant transfer.

13(5)   Paragraph (6) applies if a company which is a member of the same group as the transferor at the time of the relevant transfer–

(a)   ceases to be a member of that group and becomes a member of the same group as the transferee, and

(b)   later ceases to be a member of that group.

13(6)   Section 780 of CTA (deemed realisation and reacquisition at market value) applies on that later event as if any asset to which this paragraph applies that has not been acquired from the transferee had been so acquired.

13(7)   Paragraph (6) applies to–

(a)   any asset acquired by the company referred to in paragraph (5) from the transferor when that company and the transferor were members of the same group, or

(b)   any asset acquired by the company referred to in paragraph (5) from another company which is a member of the same group at the time of the relevant transfer when the company referred to in paragraph (5), the transferor and the other company were members of the same group.

13(8)   Paragraph (6) does not apply if–

(a)   the company which acquired the asset is a 75% subsidiary of the company from which it was acquired or vice versa;

(b)   those companies cease simultaneously to be members of the same group as the transferee; and

(c)   those companies continue to be members of the same group as one another.

INTANGIBLE FIXED ASSETS TRANSFERRED AS IF AT NO GAIN OR NO LOSS

14(1)   This regulation applies if–

(a)   there is a relevant transfer by a building society; and

(b)   the transferor is treated–

　　(i)   for the purposes of these Regulations; or

　　(ii)   by virtue of the provisions referred to in paragraph (2),

as disposing of any assets for a consideration of such amount as would secure that neither a gain nor a loss would accrue to the transferor on that disposal.

14(2)   The provisions referred to in this paragraph are–

(a)   section 215 of TCGA (disposal of assets on amalgamation of building societies); and

(b)   section 216 of that Act (assets transferred from society to company).

14(3)   The assets, in the hands of the transferee, shall be treated as not satisfying the general rule set out in section 882(1) of CTA (application of Part 8 to assets created or acquired on or after 1 April 2002).

PART 3 – INDUSTRIAL AND PROVIDENT SOCIETIES

INTERPRETATION

15   In this Part–

"carrying value" has the meaning given by section 317 of CTA (carrying value);

"discount" has the meaning given by section 480(5) of CTA (relevant non-lending relationships involving discounts);

"notional carrying value" in relation to an asset or liability has the same meaning as it has for section 340(6) of CTA (group transfers and transfers of insurance business: transfer at notional carrying value).

TRANSFER OF AN ASSET – TAXATION OF CHARGEABLE GAINS

16   If–

(a)   there is a relevant transfer within regulation 3(2)(d), (e) or (f); and

(b)   there is a disposal of an asset by the transferor to the transferee,

the transferor and the transferee shall be treated for the purposes of corporation tax in respect of chargeable gains as if the asset were acquired from the transferor for a consideration of such amount as would secure that on the disposal neither a gain nor a loss would accrue to the transferor.

TRANSFER OF AN ASSET – TAXATION OF CHARGEABLE GAINS – COMPANY CEASING TO BE A MEMBER OF GROUP

17   If–

(a)   there is a relevant transfer within regulation 3(2)(a), (b), (d), (e) or (f);

(b)   the transferor and the transferee are not members of the same group at the time of the relevant transfer; and

(c)   as a result of the relevant transfer, a company ceases to be a member of the same group as the transferor, section 179 of TCGA (company ceasing to be a member of group: post-appointed day cases) shall not apply in respect of any asset acquired by the company referred to in paragraph (c) from the transferor or from any other member of the same group as the transferor.

History – In reg. 17, the words "as a consequence of the relevant transfer", which appeared after the words "the company referred to in paragraph (c)", omitted by SI 2011/37, reg. 3(2), with effect in relation to any relevant transfer which takes place on or after 2 February 2011.

TRANSFER OF AN ASSET – COMPANY CEASING TO BE A MEMBER OF A GROUP – FURTHER PROVISIONS

18(1)   This regulation applies if there is a relevant transfer within regulation 3(2)(a), (b), (d), (e) or (f).

18(2)   If there is a relevant transfer to which this regulation applies, and the transferor and the transferee–

(a)   are members of the same group at the time of the relevant transfer; but

(b)   subsequently cease to be members of the same group,

paragraph (3) applies.

18(3)   If paragraph (2) is satisfied, section 179 of TCGA (company ceasing to be a member of group: post-appointed day cases) shall not have effect as respects–

(a)   any asset acquired by the transferee as a consequence of the relevant transfer from the transferor or any other member of the same group; or

(b)   any asset acquired as a consequence of the transfer from the transferor, or any other member of the same group, by any company which is a member of the same group as the transferor at the time of the relevant transfer.

18(4)   If this regulation applies and, as a result of the relevant transfer, a company which was a member of the same group as the transferor at the time of the relevant transfer–

(a)   ceases to be a member of that group;

(b)   becomes a member of the same group as the transferee; and

(c)   subsequently ceases to be a member of that group,

section 179 of TCGA shall have effect when the company ceases to be a member of the same group as the transferee as respects any relevant asset acquired by that company otherwise than from the transferee as if that asset had been acquired from the transferee.

This paragraph is subject to paragraph (6).

18(5)   In paragraph (4) **"relevant asset"** means any asset acquired by the company referred to in that paragraph from–

(a)   the transferor; or

(b)   any other company which is a member of the same group as the transferor at the time of the relevant transfer,

when the company referred to in that paragraph and the transferor, or the company referred to in that paragraph, the transferor and the other company, were members of the same group.

18(6)   Paragraph (4) shall not apply if the company referred to in that paragraph which acquired that asset and the company from which that asset was acquired (one being a 75 per cent subsidiary of the other) cease simultaneously to be members of the same group as the transferee but continue to be members of the same group as one another.

TRANSFER OF LOAN RELATIONSHIP

19(1)   Subject to paragraph (7), this regulation applies if–

(a)   there is a relevant transfer by an industrial and provident society; and

(b)   as a result of that transfer, the transferee directly or indirectly replaces the transferor as a party to a loan relationship (as to which see regulation 20).

19(2)   The credits and debits to be brought into account for the purposes of Parts 3, 5 and 6 of CTA as a result of the relevant transfer shall be determined in accordance with paragraphs (3) to (10).

19(3)   Subject to paragraph (5), for the accounting period in which the relevant transfer takes place, the transferor shall be treated as having entered into the relevant transfer for consideration of an amount equal to the notional carrying value of the asset or liability representing the loan relationship at the time of the relevant transfer.

19(4) For any accounting period in which the transferee is a party to the loan relationship, the transferee shall be treated as if it had acquired the asset or liability representing the loan relationship for consideration of an amount equal to the notional carrying value of the asset or liability in the accounts of the transferor at the time of the relevant transfer.

19(5) If a discount arises in respect of the relevant transfer, the consideration referred to in paragraph (3) shall be treated as increased by the amount of that discount.

19(6) Schedule 28AA to ICTA (provision not at arm's length) does not apply in relation to the amounts in respect of which credits or debits are to be brought into account under this regulation.

19(7) This regulation does not apply where the transferor is regarded as using fair value accounting in respect of the loan relationship (as to which see regulation 21).

19(8) The transferor shall be regarded for the purposes of this Part as using fair value accounting in respect of a loan relationship only if the credits and debits to be brought into account for the purposes of these Regulations as respects the relationship are determined on that basis.

19(9) It does not matter for the purposes of paragraph (8) if the transferor does not otherwise use fair value accounting in respect of the loan relationship.

19(10) For the purposes of this regulation, subsection (5) of section 480 of CTA (relevant nonlending relationships involving discounts) applies as it applies for the purposes of that section.

19(11) This regulation is subject to—

(a)   section 332 of CTA (repo, stock lending and other transactions); and

(b)   regulation 26.

MEANING OF TRANSFEREE REPLACING TRANSFEROR AS A PARTY TO A LOAN RELATIONSHIP

20(1) References in regulation 19 to a transferee replacing a transferor as a party to a loan relationship include references to a transferee becoming party to a relationship which—

(a)   confers rights within paragraph (2);

(b)   imposes obligations within paragraph (2); or

(c)   both confers such rights and imposes such obligations.

20(2) Rights or obligations are within this paragraph if they are equivalent to those of the transferor under a loan relationship to which that transferor ceased to be a party as a result of the relevant transfer.

20(3) For the purposes of paragraph (2), a transferor's rights under a creditor relationship are equivalent to rights under another creditor relationship if each set of rights gives the holder of an asset representing the relationship in question—

(a)   the same rights against the same persons as to capital, interest and dividends; and

(b)   the same remedies to enforce those rights.

20(4) For the purposes of paragraph (3), any difference in—

(a)   the total nominal amounts of the assets representing each relationship;

(b)   the form in which they are held; or

(c)   the way in which they can be transferred,

is ignored.

20(5) For the purposes of paragraph (2), a transferee's obligations under a debtor relationship are equivalent to obligations under another debtor relationship if under each set of obligations the holder of the liability representing the relationship in question has—

(a)   the same obligations to the same persons as to capital, interest and dividends; and

(b)   the same remedies to enforce those obligations.

20(6) For the purposes of paragraph (5), any difference in—

(a)   the total nominal amounts of the assets representing the creditor relationship corresponding to each relationship;

(b)   the form in which they are held; or

(c)   the way in which they can be transferred,

is ignored.

TRANSFER OF LOAN RELATIONSHIP WHERE FAIR VALUE ACCOUNTING IS USED

21(1) This regulation applies if regulation 19 would apply but for the fact that the transferor is regarded as using fair value accounting in respect of the loan relationship.

21(2) The credits and debits to be brought into account for the purposes of Parts 3, 5 and 6 of CTA as a result of the relevant transfer shall be determined in accordance with paragraphs (3) to (5).

21(3) The amount which is to be brought into account by the transferor in respect of the relevant transfer ("the transferor's amount") is–

(a) if the amount relates to an asset, either–

  (i) the fair value of the asset as at the date when the transferee becomes party to the loan relationship; or

  (ii) the fair value of the rights under or interest in the loan relationship as at that date; and

(b) if the amount relates to a liability, the fair value of the liability as at that date.

21(4) Subject to paragraph (5), for any accounting period in which the transferee is a party to the loan relationship, for the purpose of determining the credits and debits to be brought into account in respect of the relationship for the purposes of these Regulations, the transferee shall be treated as if it had acquired the asset or liability representing the relationship for consideration of an amount equal to the transferor's amount.

21(5) If a discount arises in respect of the transfer, the transferor's amount shall be treated as increased by the amount of the discount.

21(6) This regulation is subject to–

(a) section 332 of CTA (repo, stock lending and other transactions); and

(b) regulation 26.

REPLACEMENT OF INDUSTRIAL AND PROVIDENT SOCIETY AS PARTY TO A DERIVATIVE CONTRACT

22(1) Subject to paragraph (7), this regulation applies if–

(a) there is a relevant transfer by an industrial and provident society; and

(b) as a result of that transfer the transferee directly or indirectly replaces the transferor as a party to a derivative contract (as to which see regulation 23).

22(2) The credits and debits to be brought into account for the purposes of Part 3 or 7 of CTA as a result of the relevant transfer shall be determined in accordance with paragraphs (3) to (6).

22(3) Subject to paragraph (5), for the accounting period in which the relevant transfer takes place, the transferor shall be treated as having entered into the derivative contract for consideration of an amount equal to the notional carrying value of that contract (as to which see paragraph (8)).

22(4) For any accounting period in which the transferee is a party to the derivative contract, the transferee shall be treated as if it had acquired that derivative contract for consideration of an amount equal to the notional carrying value of that contract in the accounts of the transferor (as to which see paragraph (8)).

22(5) If a discount arises in respect of the relevant transfer, the consideration referred to in paragraph (3) shall be treated for the purposes of that paragraph as increased by the amount of the discount.

22(6) Schedule 28AA to ICTA (provision not at arm's length) does not apply in relation to the amounts in respect of which credits or debits are to be brought into account under this regulation.

22(7) This regulation does not apply where the transferor is regarded as using fair value accounting in respect of the derivative contract (as to which see regulation 24).

22(8) For the purposes of this regulation the notional carrying value of a derivative contract is the amount which would have been its carrying value in the accounts of the transferor if a period of account had ended immediately before the date on which the transferor had ceased to be a party to that derivative contract.

22(9) For the purposes of this regulation, subsection (5) of section 480 of CTA (relevant nonlending relationships involving discounts) applies as it applies for the purposes of that section.

22(10) This regulation is subject to regulation 27.

MEANING OF TRANSFEREE REPLACING TRANSFEROR AS PARTY TO A DERIVATIVE CONTRACT

23(1) References in regulation 22 to a transferee replacing a transferor as a party to a derivative contract include references to the transferee becoming party to a derivative contract which–

(a)   confers rights within paragraph (2),

(b)   imposes liabilities within paragraph (2), or

(c)   both confers such rights and imposes such liabilities.

23(2) Rights or liabilities are within this paragraph if they are equivalent to those of the transferor under a derivative contract to which the transferor has ceased to be a party as a result of the relevant transfer.

TRANSFER OF DERIVATIVE CONTRACT WHERE FAIR VALUE ACCOUNTING IS USED

24(1) This regulation applies in a case where regulation 22 would apply but for the fact that the transferor is regarded as using fair value accounting as respects the derivative contract.

24(2) Subject to paragraph (4), the amount which is to be brought into account by the transferor in respect of a relevant transfer is the fair value of the derivative contract as at the date of that transfer.

24(3) For any accounting period in which the transferee is a party to the derivative contract, for the purpose of determining the credits and debits to be brought into account in respect of the contract for the purposes of these Regulations, the transferee shall be treated as if it had acquired the contract for consideration of an amount equal to the fair value of the contract as at the date of the transfer.

24(4) If a discount arises in respect of the relevant transfer, the amount to be brought into account under paragraph (2) shall be treated as increased by the amount of the discount.

24(5) For the purposes of this regulation, subsection (5) of section 480 of CTA (relevant nonlending relationships involving discounts) applies as it applies for the purposes of that section.

24(6) This regulation is subject to regulation 27.

TRANSFER OF LOAN RELATIONSHIP OR DERIVATIVE CONTRACT – FURTHER PROVISIONS

25(1) This regulation applies if–

(a)   there is a relevant transfer within regulation 3(2)(a), (b), (d), (e) or (f); and

(b)   before the date of the relevant transfer there had been a transfer to a company of–

    (i)   a loan relationship to which section 336 of CTA (transfers of loans on group transactions) applied; or

    (ii)   a derivative contract to which section 625 of CTA (group member replacing another as party to derivative contract) applied,

but this is subject to paragraph (6).

25(2) Paragraph (3) applies if as a result of the relevant transfer the company referred to in paragraph (1)(b) ceases to be a member of the same group as the transferor–

(a)   before the end of the relevant six year period referred to in–

    (i)   section 344(4) of CTA (transferee leaving group after replacing transferor as party to loan relationship); or

    (ii)   section 630(4) of CTA (introduction to sections 631 and 632); and

(b)   whilst still a party to the relevant loan relationship or derivative contract.

25(3) If paragraph (2) is satisfied–

(a)   the company referred to in paragraph (1)(b) shall be treated as not having ceased to be a member of the same group as the transferor;

(b)   in the case of a loan relationship, section 345 of CTA (transferee leaving group otherwise than because of exempt distribution) shall not apply to the loan relationship as a result of the relevant transfer; and

(c)   in the case of a derivative contract, section 631 of CTA (transferee leaving group otherwise than because of exempt distribution) shall not apply to the derivative contract as a result of the relevant transfer.

25(4)   Paragraph (5) applies if the company referred to in paragraph (1)(b) ceases to be a member of the same group as the transferee–

(a)   before the end of the relevant six year period referred to in–

  (i)   section 344(4) of CTA (transferee leaving group after replacing transferor as party to loan relationship); or

  (ii)   section 630(4) of CTA (introduction to sections 631 and 632); and

(b)   whilst still a party to the relevant loan relationship or derivative contract.

25(5)   If paragraph (4) is satisfied–

(a)   in the case of a loan relationship, section 345 of CTA (transferee leaving group otherwise than because of exempt distribution) shall apply to the loan relationship as a result of the relevant transfer; and

(b)   in the case of a derivative contract, section 631 of CTA (transferee leaving group otherwise than because of exempt distribution) shall apply to the derivative contract as a result of the relevant transfer.

25(6)   This regulation does not apply where the transferor of a loan relationship is regarded as using fair value accounting in respect of that loan relationship.

25(7)   The transferor shall be regarded for the purposes of this Part as using fair value accounting in respect of a loan relationship only if the credits and debits to be brought into account for the purposes of these Regulations as respects that loan relationship are determined on that basis.

25(8)   It does not matter for the purposes of paragraph (7) if the transferor does not otherwise use fair value accounting in respect of the loan relationship.

25(9)   This regulation is subject to–

(a)   regulation 26 if there has been a transfer of a loan relationship to which section 336 of CTA (transfers of loans on group transactions) applied; or

(b)   regulation 27 if there has been a transfer of a derivative contract to which section 625 of CTA (group member replacing another as party to a derivative contract) applied.

TRANSFEROR OF LOAN RELATIONSHIP IS PARTY TO AVOIDANCE

26(1)   Regulations 19, 21 and 25 do not apply if conditions A and B are met.

26(2)   Condition A is that the transferor is a party to arrangements under which there is likely to be a transfer of rights or liabilities under the loan relationship by the transferee to another person in circumstances in which–

(a)   sections 336 and 340 of CTA; or

(b)   regulation 19, 21 or 25,

would not apply.

26(3)   Condition B is that the purpose, or one of the main purposes, of the arrangements is to obtain a tax advantage for the transferor or a person connected with the transferor.

26(4)   In this regulation **"transfer"** includes any arrangement which equates in substance to a transfer.

TRANSFEROR OF DERIVATIVE CONTRACT IS PARTY TO AVOIDANCE

27(1)   Regulations 22, 24 and 25 do not apply if conditions A and B are met.

27(2)   Condition A is that the transferor is a party to arrangements under which there is likely to be a transfer of rights or liabilities under the derivative contract by the transferee to another person in circumstances in which–

(a)   section 625 of CTA; or

(b)   regulation 22, 24 or 25,

would not apply.

27(3)   Condition B is that the purpose, or one of the main purposes, of the arrangements is to obtain a tax advantage for the transferor or a person connected with the transferor.

27(4)   In this regulation **"transfer"** includes any arrangement which equates in substance to a transfer.

TRANSFER OF INTANGIBLE FIXED ASSETS

28(1)   This regulation applies if–

(a)   there is a relevant transfer within regulation 3(2)(a), (b), (d), (e) or (f) which includes intangible fixed assets;

(b)   those assets are chargeable intangible assets in relation to the transferor immediately before the relevant transfer; and

(c)   those assets are chargeable intangible assets in relation to the transferee immediately after the relevant transfer.

28(2)   The transfer of those assets is tax-neutral for the purposes of—

(a)   these Regulations; and

(b)   Part 8 of CTA (intangible fixed assets).

28(3)   For the application of sections 780 (deemed realisation and reacquisition at market value) and 785 (principal company becoming member of another group) of CTA where this regulation applies, see regulation 29.

28(4)   This regulation and regulations 29 and 30 apply to goodwill as they apply to intangible fixed assets.

TRANSFER OF INTANGIBLE FIXED ASSETS – FURTHER PROVISIONS

29(1)   This regulation applies if—

(a)   there is a relevant transfer within regulation 3(2)(a), (b), (d), (e) or (f) which includes intangible fixed assets;

(b)   those assets are—

    (i)   chargeable intangible assets in relation to the transferor immediately before the relevant transfer; and

    (ii)   chargeable intangible assets in relation to the transferee immediately after the relevant transfer; and

(c)   the transfer is tax-neutral for the purposes of these Regulations or Part 8 of CTA (intangible fixed assets).

29(2)   If because of the relevant transfer a company ceases to be a member of the same group as the transferor, that event does not cause—

(a)   section 780 of CTA (deemed realisation and reacquisition at market value); or

(b)   section 785 of that Act (principal company becoming member of another group),

to apply as respects any assets acquired by the company from the transferor or any other member of the same group as the transferor.

29(3)   If the transferor and transferee are members of the same group at the time of the relevant transfer but later cease to be, that later event does not cause section 780 or 785 of CTA to apply in relation to any asset to which this regulation applies.

29(4)   Paragraph (3) applies to—

(a)   any asset acquired by the transferee on or before the relevant transfer from the transferor, or from any other member of the same group; or

(b)   any asset acquired from the transferor or from any other member of the same group by a company (other than the transferee) that is a member of that group at the time of the relevant transfer.

29(5)   Paragraph (6) applies if a company which is a member of the same group as the transferor at the time of the relevant transfer—

(a)   ceases to be a member of that group and becomes a member of the same group as the transferee, and

(b)   later ceases to be a member of that group.

29(6)   Section 780 of CTA (deemed realisation and reacquisition at market value) applies on that later event as if any asset to which this paragraph applies that has not been acquired from the transferee had been so acquired.

29(7)   Paragraph (6) applies to—

(a)   any asset acquired by the company referred to in paragraph (5) from the transferor when that company and the transferor were members of the same group; or

(b)   any asset acquired by the company referred to in paragraph (5) from another company which is a member of the same group at the time of the relevant transfer when the company referred to in paragraph (5), the transferor and the other company were members of the same group.

29(8)   Paragraph (6) does not apply if–

(a)   the company which acquired the asset is a 75% subsidiary of the company from which it was acquired or vice versa;

(b)   those companies cease simultaneously to be members of the same group as the transferee; and

(c)   those companies continue to be members of the same group as one another.

INTANGIBLE FIXED ASSETS TRANSFERRED AS IF AT NO GAIN OR NO LOSS

30(1)   This regulation applies if–

(a)   there is a relevant transfer by an industrial and provident society; and

(b)   the transferor is treated–

(i)   for the purposes of these Regulations; or

(ii)   by virtue of section 486 of ICTA (industrial and provident societies and co-operative associations),

as disposing of any assets for a consideration of such amount as would secure that neither a gain nor a loss would accrue to the transferor on that disposal.

30(2)   The assets, in the hands of the transferee, shall be treated as not satisfying the general rule set out in section 882(1) of CTA (application of Part 8 to assets created or acquired on or after 1 April 2002).

EXEMPTION FROM STAMP DUTY LAND TAX

31   [Not relevant to income tax, corporation tax or capital gains tax.]

EXEMPTION FROM STAMP DUTY

32   [Not relevant to income tax, corporation tax or capital gains tax.]

PART 4 – FURTHER PROVISIONS RELATING TO RELEVANT TRANSFERS

STAMP DUTY LAND TAX – GROUP RELIEF

33   [Not relevant to income tax, corporation tax or capital gains tax.]

TRANSITIONAL PROVISION

34(1)   This regulation applies if a relevant transfer takes place on or after 22 April 2009 but before the date on which these Regulations come into force.

34(2)   Subject to paragraph (4) nothing in these Regulations shall have effect so as to–

(a)   impose a charge to tax (or increase a charge to tax) on a party to the relevant transfer;

(b)   reduce a relief from tax, including a tax credit, available to a party to the relevant transfer; or

(c)   reduce losses available to a party to the relevant transfer;

where that charge or reduction arises only as a result of the application of these Regulations.

34(3)   If paragraph (2) applies–

(a)   any charge to tax (or increase in a charge to tax) on a party to the relevant transfer;

(b)   any reduction in relief from tax available to a party to the relevant transfer; or

(c)   any reduction in losses available to a party to the relevant transfer;

shall be disregarded.

34(4)   Paragraphs (2) and (3) do not apply in relation to–

(a)   any charge to tax (or increase in a charge to tax);

(b)   any reduction in relief from tax; or

(c)   any reduction in losses;

which may arise as a result of anything done or occurring on or after the date on which these Regulations come into force.

ARRANGEMENTS THE PURPOSE OF WHICH IS TO SECURE A TAX ADVANTAGE

35(1)   This regulation applies if a relevant transfer forms part of an unallowable arrangement.

35(2)   If paragraph (1) is satisfied the following Cases shall apply.

Case 1

Case 1 is where as a result of the arrangement any party to the relevant transfer obtains a relief from tax (including a tax credit) or an increased relief from tax.

Where Case 1 applies, the relief from tax, or increased relief from tax, shall not be allowed.

Case 2

Case 2 is where as a result of the arrangement any party to the relevant transfer obtains a repayment of tax or an increased repayment of tax.

Where Case 2 applies, the repayment of tax, or the increased repayment, shall not be allowed.

Case 3

Case 3 is where as a result of the arrangement any party to the relevant transfer avoids, reduces or delays a charge or assessment to tax.

Where Case 3 applies, a charge or an assessment to tax may be made upon that party.

Case 4

Case 4 is where as a result of the arrangement any party to the relevant transfer avoids a possible assessment to tax.

Where Case 4 applies, an assessment to tax may be made upon that party.

35(3)   For the purposes of this regulation an arrangement is an unallowable arrangement where the purpose, or one of the main purposes, of a person in being a party to the relevant transfer is to obtain a tax advantage as a result of that transfer for that person or any other person.

Statutory Instruments

SAVING GATEWAY ACCOUNTS REGULATIONS 2009
(SI 2009/2997)

Made on 11 November 2009 by the Treasury in exercise of the powers conferred by s. 2(2) and (3), 3(1)(b), (5) and (6), 4 to 7, 8(1) and (4), 9 to 12, 16, 17, 24(4) and 28(1) and (2) of the Saving Gateway Accounts Act 2009. Operative in accordance with reg. 1.

ARRANGEMENT OF REGULATIONS
REGULATION

PART 1 – INTRODUCTORY AND ELIGIBILITY

CITATION AND COMMENCEMENT

1 These Regulations may be cited as the Saving Gateway Accounts Regulations 2009 and shall come into force on the appointed day.

INTERPRETATION

2(1) In these Regulations–

(a)   the following expressions have the meanings given in the Saving Gateway Accounts Act 2009 ("the Act")–

"approved account provider" (see section 4(1));

"the Commissioners" (see section 1(2));

a "death payment" (see section 4(2)(b));

"eligible person" (see section 3(1) as supplemented by regulations 3 and 4);

the "first month of the account's operation" (see section 4(5)), and references to the sixth or any other month of the account's operation, and cognate expressions, have corresponding meanings;

"maturity payment" (see section 4(2)(a));

"maturity period" (see section 4(2)(a));

"month" (see section 4(5)), except in the expression "the first month of the account's operation;

(b)   "notice of eligibility" (see section 2);

(c)   the "qualifying balance" of a Saving Gateway account (see section 8(2));

(d)   the "relevant date" (see section 1(3));

(e)   "relevant person" (see section 17(2));

(f)   "Saving Gateway account" (see section 1(1));

(g)   "tax appeal" (see section 24(3));

(h)   except where the context otherwise requires–

"accepting deposits", in regulation 14, has the meaning in section 22 of FISMA 2000, taken with Schedule 2 of that Act and any order made under section 22;

"account", except in regulations 8, 10(2)(k), 20(1) and (2) and 21, means a Saving Gateway account;

"appointed day" means the day appointed under section 31 of the Act for the purposes of section 8 of the Act;

"credit union" means a society registered as a credit union under the Industrial and Provident Societies Act 1965, or the Credit Unions (Northern Ireland) Order 1985;

"EEA State" means a State, other than the United Kingdom, which is a Contracting Party to the EEA agreement;

"electronic communications" includes any communications by an electronic communications network (within the meaning in the Communications Act 2003);

"electronic signature" has the meaning given by section 7(2) of the Electronic Communications Act 2000;

"FISMA 2000" means the Financial Services and Markets Act 2000;

"full name" includes shortened details sufficient to identify the individual;

"ITA 2007" means the Income Tax Act 2007;

"ITTOIA 2005" means the Income Tax (Trading and Other Income) Act 2005;

"insolvency event" means the procedures listed in the definition of "insolvency event" in regulation 19(15) of the Payment Services Regulations 2009;

"the Management Act" means the Taxes Management Act 1970;

"notice" means notice in writing; and **"notify"** shall be construed accordingly;

"reference number", except in regulation 5(1), means an eligible person's reference number as stated on his or her notice of eligibility;

"tax year" means a period beginning with 6th April in one year and ending with 5th April in the next, and **"the tax year 2009–10"** means the tax year beginning with 6th April 2009;

"UK institution" means an institution which is incorporated in, or formed under the law of any part of, the United Kingdom.

2(2)   The table below indexes other definitions in these Regulations:

Term defined	Regulation
(a) "account holder"	10(1)(a)
(b) "agreed terms"	10(1)(h)
(c) "the disqualifying circumstances"	16
(d) "the eligibility window"	3(3)
(e) "qualifying circumstances"	14(1)

ELIGIBLE PERSONS – ENTITLEMENT TO WORKING TAX CREDIT OR CHILD TAX CREDIT

3(1)   A person is an eligible person by reason of entitlement (alone or with another person) to working tax credit or child tax credit, within the meaning in section 3(5) of the Act, only if he or she satisfies the following conditions.

3(2)   Those conditions are–

Condition 1

There is a decision under sections 18 to 21 of the 2002 Act, other than on the basis of estimated income (a "final award"), that the person was entitled (alone or with another person) to working tax credit or child tax credit (not being at a nil rate) for the tax year 2009–10, or a subsequent tax year.

Condition 2

(a)   The relevant income for that tax year ("the relevant tax year") did not exceed £16,040, or

(b)   the person's entitlement to working tax credit or child tax credit for the relevant tax year arose by virtue of section 7(2) of the 2002 Act (automatic entitlement where the claimant or one of the claimants is entitled to a prescribed social security benefit).

Where a higher amount is determined for the purposes of section 7(1)(a) of the 2002 Act in relation to child tax credit (income threshold for child tax credit) in relation to the relevant tax year, that higher amount shall be substituted for the figure of £16,040 in paragraph (a).

Condition 3

The final award for the relevant tax year (and calculation of the relevant income on which it is based) has not been overturned.

Condition 4

If–

(c)   the Commissioners have given the person a final notice under section 17 of the 2002 Act, relating to the relevant tax year, and

(d)   the notice contained a requirement to make a declaration or statement under section 17(2)(a), (4)(a) or (6)(a) of the 2002 Act (annual declaration form),

the person has made the declarations or statements required by the time at which eligibility is being determined.

Condition 5

The eligibility window for that final award has not ended.

3(3)   In this regulation–

the **"eligibility window"**, in relation to a final award, means the period–

(a)   beginning when that final award was made, and

(b)   ending 12 months after the date of that final award;

"estimated income" means estimated current year income, declared or stated as mentioned in section 17(8)(a) or (b) of the 2002 Act, unless the estimate has been treated as confirmed in the amount estimated, in accordance with section 17(8) of the 2002 Act;

"relevant income", in relation to a person or persons and a tax year, means the relevant income determined in accordance with section 7 of the 2002 Act, and with regulations made under that section, in relation to a claim by the person or persons for working tax credit or child tax credit for the tax year;

"the 2002 Act" means the Tax Credits Act 2002.

ELIGIBLE PERSONS – CONNECTION WITH THE U.K.

4(1)   The connection with the United Kingdom mentioned in section 3(1)(b) of the Act is that the person is ordinarily resident in the United Kingdom.

4(2)   A Crown servant posted overseas or his or her partner shall be treated as ordinarily resident in the United Kingdom.

4(3)   A person shall be treated as ordinarily resident in the United Kingdom if he or she is exercising in the United Kingdom his or her rights as a worker pursuant to Council Regulation (EEC) No. 1612/68.

4(4) A person who is in the United Kingdom as a result of his or her deportation, expulsion or other removal by compulsion of law from another country to the United Kingdom shall be treated as being ordinarily resident in the United Kingdom.

4(5) In paragraph (2)–

"**Crown servant posted overseas**" has the meaning in regulation 5(2) of the Tax Credits (Residence) Regulations 2003;

the "**partner**" of a Crown servant posted overseas means a person falling within the description in regulation 6(1) (read with regulation 2(1)) of those Regulations.

NOTICES OF ELIGIBILITY

5(1) The notice of eligibility to be issued under section 2(1) of the Act shall contain (in addition to the expiry date) the following particulars–

(a)   the full name of the eligible person; and

(b)   his or her Saving Gateway reference number.

5(2) The notice shall be issued by being sent to the eligible person by post, except in a case where there is a person acting under regulation 13(8), in which case it may be sent to that person.

5(3) A further notice of eligibility may be issued to an eligible person at the discretion of the Commissioners, where the expiry date of a previous notice has passed, and the person has not opened a Saving Gateway account.

OPENING OF ACCOUNT BY A PERSON WHO HAS RECEIVED A NOTICE OF ELIGIBILITY

6(1) For the purposes of these Regulations, an account is opened with an approved account provider on the date when all the following conditions are satisfied (but no later than the expiry date specified in the notice of eligibility):

Condition 1

6(2) The applicant produces his or her notice of eligibility to the approved account provider or, where the approved account provider's business systems provide for the opening of accounts without production of the relevant notice of eligibility, the applicant makes a true declaration to the approved account provider of the following information:

(a)   the expiry date of the notice, and

(b)   the applicant's reference number (as stated on the notice).

Condition 2

The applicant enters into agreed terms with the approved account provider (see regulation 10(1)(h)) which include the application and declaration required by regulation 13.

Condition 3

Where that application is not in writing the applicant has agreed, or is treated as having agreed, the contents of the copy of the declaration required by regulation 13(2).

6(3) Where–

(a)   an account is opened in accordance with paragraph (1), and

(b)   there is a right to cancel (or automatic cancellation of) the agreed terms, and the period during which it may be exercised or occur has not expired,

the account shall not be treated as open for the purposes of regulation 22 (monthly return and financial claim) and regulation 5(3) until the period during which that right may be exercised or cancellation occur has expired without the right being exercised or cancellation occurring.

MATURITY PERIOD (AND PAYMENT OF MATURITY PAYMENTS OR DEATH PAYMENTS)

7(1) Subject to paragraph (3), the maturity period for an account is the period–

(a)   beginning simultaneously with the first month of the account's operation (see section 4(5) of the Act), and

(b)   ending with the last day of the twenty fourth month of the account's operation.

7(2) The approved account provider must credit the account with the amount of the maturity payment, or otherwise pay the maturity payment to the account holder, within 21 days from the end of the maturity period for the account.

7(3) If the account holder of an account dies before the end of the account's maturity period calculated under paragraph (1), paragraph (2) shall not apply and the account provider shall pay to the account holder's personal representatives an amount (a "death payment") equal to the amount of the maturity payment to which the account holder would have become entitled if the maturity period for the account had ended immediately before the death.

7(4) A death payment shall be made within 21 days of the end of the month in which the account provider receives sufficient evidence of the death of the account holder and of the status of the personal representatives.

ACCOUNT CEASING TO BE A SAVING GATEWAY ACCOUNT (AND ROLLOVER CERTIFICATES)

8(1) An account ceases to be a Saving Gateway account–

(a)   on the death of the account holder;

(b)   for the purposes of section 8(4) of the Act, when the account provider has credited the account with the amount of the maturity payment, or otherwise paid the maturity payment to the account holder; or

(c)   for all other purposes, at the end of the maturity period for the account.

8(2) Where an account ceases to be a Saving Gateway account under paragraph (1)(c) for the purposes there mentioned ("on maturity"), if the account holder so requires by notice to the account provider, given within 6 months of that date, the account provider shall give to the account holder a certificate containing the information mentioned in paragraph (3) and the declaration mentioned in paragraph (4).

8(3) The information mentioned in this paragraph is–

(a)   the account holder's full name;

(b)   his or her permanent address including postcode;

(c)   the name of the account provider with which the account was held on maturity;

(d)   the number allocated to it by that account provider;

(e)   the date on which it matured; and

(f)   the credit balance of the account (if any) on maturity, and the amount of the maturity payment made or to be made.

8(4) The declaration mentioned in this paragraph is a declaration by the account provider that the account was a Saving Gateway account throughout its maturity period and that the information given in the certificate is correct.

GOVERNMENT CONTRIBUTION RATE

9 In the calculation of A × B to determine the maturity payment in relation to a Saving Gateway account in section 8(1) of the Act, the multiplier B is 50 pence.

PART 2 – OTHER REQUIREMENTS TO BE SATISFIED IN RELATION TO ACCOUNTS

GENERAL REQUIREMENTS FOR ACCOUNTS

10(1) A Saving Gateway account must satisfy the requirements that–

(a)   it is the account of a single person ("the account holder") who is "the applicant" in regulations 6(1) and 13;

(b)   the account holder is or has been an eligible person;

(c)   no person may open more than one Saving Gateway account in their lifetime;

(d)   it is a cash deposit account (including a share account held with a building society within the meaning of the Building Societies Act 1986, and a deposit by way of subscription for shares in a credit union);

(e)   the account is denominated in sterling;

(f)   the account is covered by the Financial Services Compensation Scheme, or another deposit-guarantee scheme introduced and officially recognised in a Member State or EEA State, in accordance with Article 3(1) of Council Directive 94/19/EEC;

(g)   the account must be in the beneficial ownership of the account holder, and not be held on behalf of any other person; and

(h)   the account must at all times be managed in accordance with the Act and these Regulations by an approved account provider and under terms agreed and recorded in an agreement (the "agreed terms") made between the account provider and the account holder.

10(2)   Apart from other requirements of the Act and these Regulations, the agreed terms shall include (or comply with, as the case may be) the conditions that—

(a)   if the account is held by the account holder until the end of the account's maturity period, the account provider shall pay the account holder a maturity payment (see section 8 of the Act);

(b)   if the account holder dies, while still holding the account, before the end of the account's maturity period, the account provider shall pay a death payment in accordance with regulation 7(3) and (4);

(c)   there is no restriction on the maximum or minimum amount or on timing (subject to the account provider's normal business hours) of withdrawals of the credit balance of the account;

(d)   there is no requirement that a minimum credit balance must be maintained in the account (with the result that an account with a nil balance is not automatically closed);

(e)   the account provider shall permit payment of sums into the account by cheque, direct debit, standing order, direct credit (other than standing order) or cash (unless, in the case of cash, the provider offers both internet and non-internet accounts, and the non-internet accounts accept cash);

(f)   no deductions or withdrawals from the account (by way of charges or otherwise) shall be made by the account provider;

(g)   the account provider shall have no right of charge, lien, set-off, mortgage or other security against the money in the account;

(h)   the account provider shall satisfy himself that any person to whom he delegates any of his functions or responsibilities under the agreed terms is competent to carry out those functions or responsibilities;

(i)   where there is a right to transfer the account under regulation 19(1), the whole of the account shall be transferred free of expense to the other approved account provider subject to and in accordance with regulation 19;

(j)   where the account is transferred to the account provider by a transfer under regulation 19, that no charges or expenses are due in respect of that transfer;

(k)   the account provider shall notify the account holder if by reason of any failure to satisfy the provisions of these Regulations an account is or will become no longer exempt from tax by virtue of regulation 3 of the Saving Gateway Accounts (No. 2) Regulations 2009.

10(3)   In applying paragraph (1)(c), any account opened and cancelled as mentioned in regulation 6(2) shall be ignored.

LIMIT ON SUMS PAID INTO THE ACCOUNT

11(1)   The total of the sums paid into an account in a month (excluding any interest or other sums paid by the approved account provider under the agreed terms) shall not exceed £25.

11(2)   In calculating the limit in paragraph (1) for the purpose of any payment into the account, previous withdrawals from the account shall be ignored.

STATEMENTS FOR AN ACCOUNT

12(1)   Except where a passbook is provided in accordance with paragraph (5), the account provider must issue a statement for the account—

(a)   at least six monthly, and

(b)   where an account is transferred to another account provider under regulation 19, as at the transfer date.

12(2)   The statement date in the case of a six monthly statement must be the end of the sixth, twelfth, eighteenth or twenty fourth month of the account's operation, as the case may be.

12(3)   The statement shall be sent to the account holder within 30 days of the statement date.

12(4)   Statements shall include the following information—

(a)   the full name of the account holder;

(b)   his or her address, including postcode;

(c)   the statement date;

(d)   the balance of the account at the previous statement date (if any), and otherwise at the opening of the account;

(e)   all payments into and withdrawals from the account during the statement period ending on the statement date;

(f)   a provisional calculation of the maturity payment (based on the qualifying balance achieved between the opening of the account and the statement date); and

(g)   the closing balance of the account at the statement date.

12(5)   An account provider may comply with its obligations under this regulation (other than under paragraph (4)(f), if paragraph (6) applies) by issuing the account holder with a passbook for the account which, on presentation at a branch of the account provider, is up-dated to include the same information as a statement, omitting references in paragraph (4) to a statement date or statement period.

12(6)   The information in paragraph (4)(f) may, at the option of the account provider, be provided in a notice to the account holder which is separate from the statement or passbook.

CONDITIONS FOR APPLICATION TO OPEN AN ACCOUNT

13(1)   An application by a person who has received a notice of eligibility ("the applicant") to open an account with an approved account provider must be made to the approved account provider, and satisfy the conditions in paragraphs (2) to (4).

13(2)   An application must incorporate a true declaration by the applicant that he or she–

(a)   has not previously opened a Saving Gateway account (excepting any account opened and closed as mentioned in regulation 6(2)); and

(b)   is ordinarily resident in the United Kingdom, or is so treated as ordinarily resident under regulation 4(2) to (5);

and where the application is not in writing, must authorise the approved account provider to record the terms of the declaration in a written declaration made on behalf of the applicant.

13(3)   An application must contain–

(a)   the applicant's full name and date of birth;

(b)   his or her address, including postcode,

(c)   the reference number, as stated on his or her notice of eligibility; and

(d)   an authorisation to the approved account provider to make on the account holder's behalf any claims to relief from tax in respect of the account.

13(4)   Where the application is not in writing, the approved account provider shall make the written declaration mentioned in paragraph (2), and notify the applicant of its contents, and such declaration shall take effect from the date on which the applicant agrees the contents (subject to any corrections), and if he or she neither agrees nor disagrees with the contents within 14 days, he or she shall be treated as having agreed them.

13(5)   An account provider shall decline to accept an application if he has reason to believe that–

(a)   the notice of eligibility has expired, or is not or might not be genuine,

(b)   the applicant's declaration (see Condition 1 in regulation 6(1) if applicable, and paragraph (2) of this regulation) or application is or might be untrue, or contains matters which are or might be untrue, or

(c)   opening an account would be a breach of, or failure to comply with, any requirement in or a direction made under the Money Laundering Regulations 2007.

13(6)   An application made under this regulation shall be regarded as in writing if it is made–

(a)   by telephonic facsimile transmission containing the signature of the individual, or

(b)   by electronic communication containing an electronic signature of the individual.

13(7)   Declarations made by the account provider under paragraph (4) shall be regarded as made in writing if they are produced by electronic means, and the copy of the declaration to be sent to the applicant in accordance with paragraph (4) may be sent by telephonic facsimile transmission or by electronic communication

13(8)   Where a person is or may be entitled to a benefit or tax credit specified in section 3(2) of the Act but is unable for the time being to act, the following persons may act for that person–

(a)   a deputy or receiver appointed by the Court of Protection with power to make a claim for a benefit or tax credit on behalf of that person;

(b)   in Scotland, a tutor, curator or guardian acting or appointed in terms of law who is administering the estate of that person;

(c)   in Northern Ireland, a controller appointed by the High Court, with power to make a claim for a benefit or tax credit on behalf of that person;

(d)   where there is no person mentioned in sub-paragraphs (a) to (c), a person appointed on behalf of the person under–

    (i)   regulation 33(1) of the Social Security (Claims and Payments) Regulations 1987,

    (ii)   regulation 33(1) of the Social Security (Claims and Payments) Regulations (Northern Ireland) 1987, or

    (iii)   regulation 18(3) of the Tax Credits (Claims and Notifications) Regulations 2002.

ACCOUNT PROVIDER – QUALIFICATIONS AND COMMISSIONERS' APPROVAL

14(1)   This regulation specifies the circumstances ("qualifying circumstances") in which a person may be approved by the Commissioners as an account provider.

14(2)   The qualifying circumstances are the following–

(a)   the person must make an application to the Commissioners for approval in a form specified by the Commissioners;

(b)   the person must undertake with the Commissioners (subject to regulation 13(5))–

    (i)   to accept properly completed applications from any person who has received a notice of eligibility and, where there is a right to transfer the account under regulation 19(1)(a), to accept transfers of an account in accordance with that regulation; or

    (ii)   in the case of a credit union, to accept properly completed applications from any person who has received a notice of eligibility and, where there is a right to transfer the account under regulation 19(1)(a), to accept transfers of an account in accordance with that regulation, if the applicant or account holder is a member, or fulfils or is treated as fulfilling a qualification for admission to membership, of the credit union;

(c)   the person must demonstrate to the satisfaction of the Commissioners that the person can correctly operate the procedures in regulation 22, and receive electronic communications for the purposes of these Regulations from H.M. Revenue and Customs;

(d)   an approved account provider must be–

    (i)   a UK institution which has permission under Part 4 of FISMA 2000 to carry on the regulated activity of accepting deposits;

    (ii)   an EEA firm mentioned in paragraph 5(b) of Schedule 3 to FISMA 2000 (credit institution) which has permission under paragraph 15 of that Schedule to carry on the activity of accepting deposits, as a result of qualifying for authorisation under paragraph 12(1) or (2) of that Schedule (exercise of passport rights by EEA firms); or

    (iii)   a credit institution (within the same meaning) incorporated outside the EEA which has permission under Part 4 of FISMA 2000 to carry on the regulated activity of accepting deposits through a branch in the United Kingdom;

(e)   an approved account provider must not be prevented from acting as such by any limitation or requirement imposed under section 42 or 43 of FISMA 2000, or by any prohibition or prohibition order in or made under that Act;

(f)   an account provider which is a credit institution within sub-paragraph (d)(ii) or (iii), and which does not intend to carry out all its functions as an account provider in the United Kingdom, must fulfil one of the requirements mentioned in regulation 15.

14(3)   The terms of the Commissioners' approval may include conditions designed to ensure that the provisions of these Regulations are satisfied.

APPROVED ACCOUNT PROVIDER – APPOINTMENT OF TAX REPRESENTATIVE

15(1)   This regulation specifies the requirements mentioned in regulation 14(2)(f).

15(2)   The first requirement is that–

(a) a person who falls within section 698(2) of ITTOIA 2005 is for the time being appointed by the account provider to be responsible for securing the discharge of the duties mentioned in paragraph (5) which fall to be discharged by the account provider, and

(b) his or her identity and the fact of the appointment have been notified to the Commissioners by the account provider.

15(3) The second requirement is that there are for the time being other arrangements with the Commissioners for a person other than the account provider to secure the discharge of such duties.

15(4) The third requirement is that there are for the time being other arrangements with the Commissioners designed to secure the discharge of such duties.

15(5) The duties mentioned in this paragraph are those that fall to be discharged by an account provider under the Act and these Regulations.

15(6) The appointment of a person in pursuance of the first requirement shall be treated as terminated in circumstances where—

(a) the Commissioners have reason to believe that the person concerned—

    (i) has failed to secure the discharge of any of the duties mentioned in paragraph (5), or

    (ii) does not have adequate resources to discharge those duties, and

(b) the Commissioners have notified the account provider and that person that they propose to treat his or her appointment as having terminated from the date specified in the notice.

15(7) Where, in accordance with the first requirement, a person is at any time responsible for securing the discharge of duties, the person concerned—

(a) shall be entitled to act on the account provider's behalf for any of the purposes of the provisions relating to the duties;

(b) shall secure (where appropriate by acting on the account provider's behalf) the account provider's compliance with and discharge of the duties; and

(c) shall be personally liable in respect of any failure of the account provider to comply with or discharge any such duty as if the duties imposed on the account provider were imposed jointly and severally on the account provider and the person concerned.

ACCOUNT PROVIDER – WITHDRAWAL BY COMMISSIONERS OF APPROVAL

16(1) This regulation specifies the circumstances ("the disqualifying circumstances") in which the Commissioners may by notice withdraw their approval of a person as an account provider.

16(2) The disqualifying circumstances are that the Commissioners have reason to believe—

(a) that any provision of the Act or these Regulations, or any term of an undertaking given in accordance with regulation 14(2)(b) or condition under regulation 14(3), is not or at any time has not been satisfied, either in respect of an account managed by the account provider or otherwise; or

(b) that a person to whom they have given approval to act as an account provider is not qualified so to act.

16(3) The notice to which paragraph (1) refers shall specify—

(a) the date from which the Commissioners' approval is withdrawn; and

(b) the disqualifying circumstances.

16(4) On receiving the notice referred to in paragraph (1), subject to any appeal under section 23(1)(b) of the Act, the account provider shall notify the account holder of the right to transfer the account under regulation 19(1)(a), and the notice shall inform the account holder of the rights under regulation 18(3).

APPROVED ACCOUNT PROVIDER CEASING TO ACT

17(1) A person shall give notice to the Commissioners and to the account holder of an account which it manages of its intention to cease to act as the approved account provider not less than 30 days before it so ceases so that its obligations to the Commissioners under the account can be conveniently discharged at or about the time it ceases so to act.

17(2) The notice to the account holder shall inform him or her of the right to transfer the account under regulation 19(1)(a), and of the rights under regulation 18(3).

ACCOUNT PROVIDER CEASING TO QUALIFY

18(1) A person shall cease to qualify as an approved account provider and shall notify the Commissioners within 30 days of the relevant event in sub-paragraphs (a) to (d), of that relevant event, where–

(a)   the person no longer fulfils the conditions of regulation 14;

(b)   there is an insolvency event in relation to the account provider;

(c)   an application has been made for a bank insolvency order or a bank administration order; or

(d)   in the case of a credit institution within regulation 14(2)(d)(ii) or (iii), action corresponding to that described in sub-paragraph (b) or (c) has been taken by or in relation to the institution under the law of an EEA State or other State.

18(2)   On giving the notice referred to in paragraph (1), the person shall also notify the account holder of the right to transfer the account under regulation 19(1)(a), and the notice shall inform the account holder of the rights under paragraph (3).

18(3)   Where an account holder–

(a)   receives a notice under paragraph (2), or regulation 16(4) or 17, and

(b)   gives instructions to the account provider in accordance with regulation 19(1)(a), with the consequence that the account is transferred pursuant to regulation 19 to another approved account provider ("the transferee") within 30 days of the sending of the notice,

the period between the account provider ceasing to be approved, or act or qualify as an approved account provider, and the transfer to the transferee, shall be ignored in determining whether the account has at all times been managed by an approved account provider.

TRANSFER OF ACCOUNTS TO OTHER ACCOUNT PROVIDERS

19(1)   Where–

(a)   in a case falling within regulation 16, 17 or 18, the account holder, within 14 days of the sending to him or her of the notice under regulation 16(4), 17(2) or 18(2), instructs the account provider to transfer the account to another named approved account provider,

(b)   in a case where both account providers have agreed to the transfer of the account, the account holder instructs the account provider to transfer the account to another named approved account provider, or

(c)   arrangements are made by an account provider (subject to complying with regulation 16, 17 or 18, as the case may be) to transfer all its accounts to another approved account provider,

the transfer shall have effect and be treated as a transfer of the account.

19(2)   Any transfer relating to an account shall be made directly between one account provider ("the transferor") and another approved account provider ("the transferee"), and the account shall not be affected for the purposes of these Regulations by reason of the transfer

19(3)   The account holder shall make a fresh application under regulation 13 (with any necessary modifications to reflect the fact that it is made on a transfer) to the transferee.

19(4)   The transferor shall on the date of the transfer give the transferee a notice containing the information mentioned in paragraph (5) and the declaration mentioned in paragraph (6).

19(5)   The information mentioned in this paragraph is–

(a)   the date of the transfer,

(b)   the account holder's full name and reference number,

(c)   the date of the opening of the account, and the expected end of the maturity period under regulation 7(1)(b),

(d)   the qualifying balance of the account achieved up to the date of the transfer, and

(e)   the total of the sums paid into the account (calculated in accordance with regulation 11(1) and (2)) in the month in which the transfer is made.

19(6)   The declaration mentioned in this paragraph is a declaration by the transferor that–

(a)   it has fulfilled all its obligations to the account holder, the Commissioners or otherwise, which are imposed by these Regulations;

(b)   it has transferred to the transferee or its nominee all the funds in the account;

(c)   it will forward any further payment received in respect of the account to the transferee, on receipt of the payment; and

(d)   the information contained in the notice is correct.

Statutory Instruments

RECOUPMENT OF MATURITY PAYMENTS AND DEATH PAYMENTS ETC.

20(1) Where–

(a) the account holder was not an eligible person at the relevant date;

(b) there is a breach of section 6(2)(a) or (b) of the Act in relation to an account;

(c) there is a breach of Condition 1 in regulation 6(1) in relation to an account; or

(d) there is a breach of regulation 10(1)(c) or 13(2) in relation to an account;

the account is void and the persons mentioned in paragraph (3) shall account to the Commissioners for any maturity payment or death payment wrongly made in respect of the account.

20(2) Where–

(a) a person was entitled to a benefit under the terms of section 3(1)(a) of the Act, or was an eligible person by reason of entitlement to working tax credit or child tax credit under the terms of regulation 3, but such entitlement has been overturned, or it has subsequently been determined that payment of the relevant benefit or tax credit should not have been made, or should have been made at a different rate; or

(b) an amount is paid by the Commissioners to an account provider in pursuance of the Act, due to a mis-statement in a monthly return or financial claim, or a mistake by an officer of Revenue and Customs;

the persons mentioned in paragraph (3) shall account to the Commissioners for any maturity payment, death payment or overpayment wrongly made in respect of the account.

20(3) The persons mentioned in paragraphs (1) and (2) are–

(a) the account provider (to the extent that it has assets relating to the account, or directly or indirectly representing any of the payments, in its possession or control);

(b) the account holder, or former account holder (to the extent that the payments have been made or credited to the account holder);

(c) any person in whom the maturity payments, death payments or overpayments, or any property directly or indirectly representing any of them, is vested (whether beneficially or otherwise);

and they shall be jointly and severally liable.

20(4) Sections 49 (late notice of appeal) and 54 (settling of appeals by agreement) of the Management Act apply in relation to appeals under section 23 of the Act, other than tax appeals.

20(5) Where a person accountable under this regulation is notified by the Commissioners that an amount is due from him or her under it, that amount shall be treated for the purposes of Part 6 of the Management Act (collection and recovery) as if it were tax charged in an assessment and due and payable.

20(6) The time limits in sections 34 to 36 of the Management Act shall apply to amounts payable under this regulation as they apply to assessments.

"REPAIR" OF INVALID ACCOUNTS

21(1) Except in the case of a breach of regulation 10(1)(b) or (c) or 13(2), or the case mentioned in regulation 20(2)(a), (where no repair of an account is possible), it is an overriding requirement to be satisfied in relation to an account that the account provider and account holder, as the case may be, take any steps necessary to remedy any breach of these Regulations.

21(2) Where a breach is remedied as mentioned in paragraph (1), the account shall, to the extent of that breach, be treated as having been a valid account at all times, except for the purposes of sections 19 to 21 of the Act (penalties).

PART 3 – REQUIREMENTS RELATING TO ADMINISTRATION OF ACCOUNTS

MONTHLY RETURN AND FINANCIAL CLAIM

22(1) In this regulation–

"initial return period", in relation to an account provider, means the period–

(a) beginning on the date on which the approval of the provider takes effect, or the appointed day (whichever is the later), and

(b)   ending simultaneously with the end of the then current month.

22(2)   The following provisions of this regulation apply to an account provider in relation to—

(a)   that provider's initial return period, and

(b)   each succeeding month,

during which, or any part of which, it acted as an account provider.

22(3)   Within 14 days of the end of—

(a)   a provider's initial return period, and

(b)   any succeeding period mentioned in paragraph (2),

the account provider shall deliver by means of electronic communications to the Commissioners, a return for that period, in a form specified by the Commissioners.

22(4)   The return shall include a declaration of the information in paragraph (5), and a claim as mentioned in paragraph (6).

22(5)   The information (to be given in relation to the return period) is—

(a)   for each account opened by the account provider in accordance with regulation 6, or transferred to the account provider in accordance with regulation 19—

    (i)   the account holder's full name and date of birth,

    (ii)   the account holder's reference number, and

    (iii)   the date of opening or transfer of the account;

(b)   for each account whose twelfth month of operation ends simultaneously with the end of the return period—

    (i)   the account holder's full name and date of birth,

    (ii)   the account holder's reference number,

    (iii)   a provisional calculation of the maturity payment, based on the qualifying balance achieved between the account's opening and the end of the return period, and

    (iv)   the balance of the account at the end of the return period (disregarding any interest or sums mentioned in section 8(3)(a) or (b) of the Act);

(c)   for each account closed before the end of the account's maturity period other than due to the death of the account holder, the account holder's full name, date of birth and reference number, and the date of closure of the account;

(d)   for each account so closed due to the death of the account holder—

    (i)   the account holder's full name and date of birth,

    (ii)   the account holder's reference number,

    (iii)   the date of death, and

    (iv)   the amount of the death payment made or due to be made;

(e)   for each account whose maturity period ended at the end of the return period—

    (i)   the account holder's full name and date of birth,

    (ii)   the account holder's reference number,

    (iii)   the amount of the maturity payment credited or due to be credited to the account, and

    (iv)   the balance of the account at the end of the maturity period (disregarding any interest or sums mentioned in section 8(3)(a) or (b) of the Act);

or a statement, in each relevant case, that there were no items falling within the relevant category.

22(6)   The claim (where there is an item falling with paragraph (5)(d) or (e)) is a claim for payment of an amount equal to the aggregate of those maturity payments and death payments, as the case may be.

22(7)   Paragraph (5)(a) shall apply notwithstanding any transfer of the account to another provider under regulation 19, before the end of the return period in question.

22(8)   The Commissioners (subject to checking and if necessary correcting the amount of the claim) shall pay the account provider—

(a)   where the return is made by the due date in paragraph (3), within 7 days of the due date, and

(b)   where the return is made later than the due date, within 7 days of receipt of the return.

22(9)   Where the Commissioners require further information to verify a claim, the 7 days shall be calculated from the date on which the information is received.

RECORDS TO BE KEPT BY ACCOUNT PROVIDER

23(1) An account provider shall during the period mentioned in paragraph (2) keep sufficient records to enable it to show that the requirements of the Act and of these Regulations have been satisfied.

23(2) In particular, an account provider shall produce (when required to do so by an officer of Revenue and Customs)–

(a) any application made under regulation 13 (where an account has been opened);

(b) copies of account statements for an account, or notices given under regulation 12(6);

(c) working papers supporting the calculation of each amount returned under regulation 22(5)(d)(iv) or (e)(iii); and

(d) evidence of the date on which a maturity payment or death payment was made;

or electronic copies, within the period of 3 years from when the record was made, issued or given, or the account ceased to be a Saving Gateway account (whichever is later), notwithstanding any transfer of the account pursuant to regulation 19.

INFORMATION TO BE PROVIDED TO THE COMMISSIONERS

24 The Commissioners may by notice require any relevant person to furnish them, within such time (not being less than 14 days) as may be provided in the notice, such information about any account (including copies of or extracts from any books or other records) as they may reasonably require for the purposes of the Act or these Regulations.

INSPECTION OF RECORDS BY OFFICER OF REVENUE AND CUSTOMS

25 The Commissioners may by notice require any relevant person, within such time (not being less than 14 days) as may be provided in the notice, to make available for inspection at a place within the United Kingdom by an officer of Revenue and Customs authorised for that purpose all documents (including books and other records) in his possession or under his control relating to Saving Gateway accounts.

SAVING GATEWAY ACCOUNTS (NO. 2) REGULATIONS 2009

(SI 2009/2998)

Made on 11 November 2009 by the Treasury in exercise of the powers conferred by s. 14, 24(4) and 28(1) and (2) of the Saving Gateway Accounts Act 2009. Operative in accordance with reg. 1.

CITATION AND COMMENCEMENT

1 These Regulations may be cited as the Saving Gateway Accounts (No. 2) Regulations 2009 and shall come into force on the appointed day.

INTERPRETATION

2 In these Regulations—

"**account**", except in regulations 5(1)(d) and (e) and 6, means a Saving Gateway account;

"**the Act**" means the Saving Gateway Accounts Act 2009;

"**the appointed day**" means the day appointed under section 31 of the Act, for the purposes of section 8 of the Act;

"**building society bonus**" excludes any bonus, distribution of funds or the conferring of rights in relation to shares—

   (i) in connection with an amalgamation, transfer of engagements or transfer of business of a building society, and

   (ii) mentioned in section 96 or 100 of the Building Societies Act 1986,

and "**payment under a building society bonus scheme**" shall be construed accordingly;

"**interest**" in regulation 3, where paid by a building society or credit union, includes a dividend paid by, and in respect of a share account held with, the society or credit union (and "**dividend**" includes any distribution, whether or not described as a dividend);

"**the principal Regulations**" means the Saving Gateway Accounts Regulations 2009;

other expressions defined in the principal Regulations have the same meanings as they have in those definitions.

EXEMPTION FROM TAX OF ACCOUNT INCOME, MATURITY PAYMENTS AND DEATH PAYMENTS

3 Subject to compliance with the principal Regulations (and in particular with regulation 11 of those Regulations)—

(a) no tax shall be chargeable on the account provider or his nominee, or on the account holder, in respect of—

   (i) interest paid or credited in respect of an account;

   (ii) profit share return from arrangements falling within section 49 of the Finance Act 2005, paid or credited by a financial institution (within the meanings in Chapter 5 of Part 2 of that Act), in respect of an account;

   (iii) a payment under a building society bonus scheme, so far as the bonus is calculated by reference to an account (and if paid directly by the society into the account, the payment shall not count towards the payment limits in regulation 11 of the principal Regulations);

(b) any gain or loss accruing on and attributable to a maturity payment or death payment shall not be a chargeable gain or allowable loss for capital gains tax purposes; and

(c) income arising from an account shall not be regarded as income for any income tax purposes (including section 629 of ITTOIA 2005).

TAX LIABILITIES AND RELIEFS – ACCOUNT PROVIDER TO ACT ON BEHALF OF ACCOUNT HOLDER

4 An account provider may under these Regulations make tax claims, conduct appeals and agree on behalf of the account holder liabilities for and reliefs from tax in respect of an account.

Statutory Instruments

TAX LIABILITIES AND RELIEFS – SUPPLEMENTARY PROVISIONS

5(1) Where—

(a) any relief or exemption from tax given in respect of income or gains under an account is found not to be due or to be excessive;

(b) the account holder was not an eligible person at the relevant date;

(c) a person was—

    (i) entitled to a benefit under the terms of section 3(1)(a) of the Act, or

    (ii) an eligible person by reason of entitlement to working tax credit or child tax credit under the terms of regulation 3 of the principal Regulations,

but such entitlement has been overturned, or it has subsequently been determined that payment of the relevant benefit or tax credit should not have been made, or should have been made at a different rate;

(d) an account does not comply with the requirements imposed by section 4(2)(a) and (b) of the Act, or by regulations 10 to 21 of the principal Regulations; or

(e) there is a breach of section 6(2)(a) or (b) of the Act in relation to an account;

the persons mentioned in paragraph (2) shall account to the Commissioners for any tax from which relief has been incorrectly given under regulation 3 in respect of an account.

5(2) The persons mentioned in paragraph (1) are—

(a) the account provider (to the extent that it has assets relating to the account, or directly or indirectly representing the tax, in its possession or control);

(b) the account holder, or former account holder;

(c) any person in whom the money in the account, or any property directly or indirectly representing it, is vested (whether beneficially or otherwise);

and they shall be jointly and severally liable.

5(3) The relevant provisions of Part 5 of the Management Act (within the meaning in section 48(3) of that Act) other than section 50 of that Act shall apply to tax appeals, with the necessary modifications mentioned in section 48(2)(b)(ii) of that Act.

ASSESSMENTS FOR WITHDRAWING RELIEF AND RECOVERING TAX

6(1) Where–

(a) any relief or exemption from tax given in respect of income or gains under an account is found not to be due or to be excessive, or

(b) the full amount of tax in respect of the income or gains under an account has not otherwise been fully accounted for and paid to the Commissioners on behalf of the account holder,

an assessment to tax may be made by the Commissioners in the amount or further amount which in their opinion ought to be charged.

6(2) An assessment to which paragraph (1) refers may be made on the account provider or on the account holder.

6(3) If the assessment is made to recover tax in respect of income under an account it shall be made under section 369 of ITTOIA 2005.

OFFSHORE FUNDS (TAX) REGULATIONS 2009

(SI 2009/3001, as amended by SI 2009/3139, SI 2010/294, SI 2011/244, SI 2011/1211, SI 2011/2192, SI 2011/2999, SI 2013/605, SI 2013/661, SI 2013/1400, SI 2013/1411, SI 2013/1770, SI 2013/1773, SI 2013/1810, SI 2013/2819 and SI 2014/685)

Made on 12 November 2009 by the Treasury in exercise of the powers conferred by s. 41(1) and 42 of the Finance Act 2008. Operative 1 December 2009.

PART 1 – INTRODUCTION

PRELIMINARY PROVISIONS

Citation, commencement and effect

1(1)   These Regulations may be cited as the Offshore Funds (Tax) Regulations 2009 and shall come into force on 1st December 2009.

1(2)   These Regulations have effect–

(a)   for the purposes of income tax–

    (i)   for the tax year 2009–10 and subsequent tax years, and

    (ii)   for distributions made on or after 1st December 2009;

(b)   for the purposes of corporation tax–

    (i)   on income, for accounting periods ending on or after 1st December 2009 and for distributions made on or after that date, and

    (ii)   on chargeable gains, in relation to disposals made on or after 1st December 2009; and

(c)   for the purposes of capital gains tax, in relation to disposals made on or after 1st December 2009.

1(3)   Paragraph (2) is subject to Schedule 1 to these Regulations (transitional provisions and savings).

Structure of these Regulations

2   The structure of these Regulations is as follows–

this Part contains introductory provisions;

Part 2 deals with the treatment of participants in non-reporting funds;

Part 3 deals with reporting funds and the treatment of participants in reporting funds;

Part 3A deals with annual payments to non-resident participants;

Part 4 makes consequential amendments to primary legislation.

History – In reg. 2, the words "Part 3A deals with annual payments to non-resident participants;" inserted by SI 2013/1770, reg. 2(2), with effect for the purposes of income tax for the tax year 2013–14 and subsequent tax years.

GENERAL PROVISIONS

Definition of "offshore fund"

3(1)   In these Regulations **"offshore fund"** has the meaning given by section 40A(2) of FA 2008 (read with the provisions of the relevant group of sections).

3(2)   Paragraph (1) does not apply to the use of the words "offshore fund" in the expression "material interest in an offshore fund".

Classification of offshore funds

4(1)   Offshore funds consist of–

(a)   non-reporting funds (see Part 2 of these Regulations), and

(b)   reporting funds (see Part 3 of these Regulations).

4(2)   In a period of account an offshore fund is a non-reporting fund unless it is a fund to which Part 3 of these Regulations applies.

History – In reg. 4(2), the words "In a period of account" inserted by SI 2011/1211, reg. 28(a), with effect: for the purposes of income tax or corporation tax, for distributions made, or treated as made, on or after 27 May 2011; and for the purposes of capital gains tax or corporation tax on chargeable gains, in relation to disposals made on or after 27 May 2011.
In reg. 4(2), the words "for a period of account", which appeared after "applies", omitted by SI 2011/1211, reg. 28(b), with effect: for the purposes of income tax or corporation tax, for distributions made, or treated as made, on or after 27 May 2011; and for the purposes of capital gains tax or corporation tax on chargeable gains, in relation to disposals made on or after 27 May 2011.

TREATMENT OF UMBRELLA ARRANGEMENTS AND OF FUNDS COMPRISING MORE THAN ONE CLASS OF INTEREST

Treatment of umbrella arrangements

5 In these Regulations, in relation to an offshore fund constituted by a part of umbrella arrangements (within the meaning of section 40C of FA 2008)–

(a)   a reference to the assets of an offshore fund is to such of the assets of the umbrella arrangements as under the arrangements form part of the separate pool to which that part of the umbrella arrangements relates;

(b)   a reference to the income of an offshore fund is to the income arising from those assets; and

(c)   a reference to a participant in an offshore fund is to a person for the time being owning an interest in that separate pool.

Treatment of funds comprising more than one class of interest

6 In these Regulations, in relation to an offshore fund constituted by a class of interest in the main arrangements (within the meaning of section 40D of FA 2008)–

(a)   a reference to the assets of an offshore fund is to the assets of the main arrangements;

(b)   a reference to the income of an offshore fund is to such of the income of the main fund as is attributable to interests of that class under the arrangements constituting the main arrangements; and

(c)   a reference to a participant in an offshore fund is to a person for the time being owning an interest of that class.

INTERPRETATION

Meaning of "participant"

7 In these Regulations references to a participant in a fund are to be read in accordance with section 40A(5) of FA 2008.

Meaning of "interest" (of a participant in an offshore fund)

8(1) For the purposes of these Regulations the interest of a participant in an offshore fund is the investment held by a participant taking part in arrangements (or arrangements constituting a fund) to which the relevant group of sections applies.

8(2) Paragraph (1) does not apply to the use of the word "interest" in the expression "material interest in an offshore fund".

Meaning of "guaranteed return fund"

9(1) For the purposes of these Regulations an offshore fund is a guaranteed return fund if conditions A to C are met.

9(2) Condition A is that the return on the shares or other interests in the fund is defined by reference to an index.

9(3) Condition B is that the assets of the fund which are held to produce the return on the shares or other interests concerned cannot give rise to a return which, if it arose directly to an individual resident in the United Kingdom, would be chargeable to income tax.

9(4) Condition C is that it is reasonable to assume that the main purpose, or one of the main purposes, of the arrangements constituting the offshore fund is or was the production for participants of a return that equates, in substance, to the return on an investment of money at interest.

Meaning of "market value"

10(1) For the purposes of these Regulations the market value of any asset is to be determined in like manner as it would be determined for the purposes of TCGA 1992.

10(2) But, in the case of an interest in an offshore fund for which there are separate published buying and selling prices, section 272(5) of that Act (meaning of "market value" in relation to rights of unit holders in a unit trust scheme) shall apply with any necessary modifications for determining the market value of the interest for the purposes of these Regulations.

Meaning of "transparent fund"

11 For the purposes of these Regulations a fund is a **"transparent fund"** if, in the case of holders of interests in the fund who are individuals resident in the United Kingdom, any sums which form part of the income of the fund are of such a nature that those holders–

(a)   are chargeable to tax under a provision specified in section 830(2) of ITTOIA 2005 in respect of such of those sums as are referable to their interests, or

(b)   if any of that income is derived from assets within the United Kingdom, would be so chargeable had the assets been outside the United Kingdom.

General interpretation

12   In these Regulations–

"**HMRC**" means Her Majesty's Revenue and Customs;

"**period of account**", in relation to an offshore fund, means any period for which accounts of the offshore fund are drawn up;

"**proposed prospectus**" includes–

(a)   any document supplementing or amending the proposed prospectus, and

(b)   any document fulfilling the same function as a proposed prospectus;

"**prospectus**" includes–

(a)   any document supplementing or amending the prospectus, and

(b)   any document fulfilling the same function as a prospectus;

"**regulated market**" has the same meaning as in Directive 2004/39/EC of the European Parliament and the Council on markets in financial instruments (see article 4.1(14));

the "**relevant group of sections**" means sections 40A to 42A of FA 2008;

"**tax year**"

(a)   in relation to income tax, has the meaning given by section 4(2) of ITA 2007, and

(b)   in relation to capital gains tax, has the meaning given by section 288(1ZA) of TCGA 1992;

"**tribunal**" means the First-tier Tribunal or, where determined by or under Tribunal Procedure Rules, the Upper Tribunal;

"**UCITS fund**" means a fund which is an undertaking for collective investments in transferable securities that is authorised by a European Union Member State in accordance with Article 4 of Council Directive 85/611/EEC.

History – In reg. 12, the definition of "regulated market" inserted by SI 2011/1211, reg. 29, with effect: for the purposes of income tax or corporation tax, for distributions made, or treated as made, on or after 27 May 2011; and for the purposes of capital gains tax or corporation tax on chargeable gains, in relation to disposals made on or after 27 May 2011.

TRANSITIONAL PROVISIONS ETC.

Transitional provisions and savings, repeals, abbreviations and general index

13(1)   Schedule 1 to these Regulations (which contains transitional provisions and savings) has effect.

13(2)   Schedule 2 to these Regulations (which contains repeals) has effect.

13(3)   The repeals contained in Schedule 2 have effect subject to the saving contained in paragraph 3(4) of Schedule 1.

13(4)   Schedule 3 to these Regulations (which contains abbreviations and defined expressions that apply for the purposes of these Regulations) has effect.

13(5)   Part 1 of Schedule 3 gives the meaning of the abbreviated references to Acts used in these Regulations.

13(6)   Part 2 of Schedule 3 lists the places where expressions used in these Regulations are defined or otherwise explained–

(a)   in these Regulations for the purposes of these Regulations, or

(b)   in these Regulations for the purposes of a Part or Chapter of these Regulations.

PART 2 – THE TREATMENT OF PARTICIPANTS IN NON-REPORTING FUNDS

Chapter 1 – Preliminary Provisions

Structure of this Part

14   The structure of this Part is as follows–

(a)   this Chapter contains preliminary provisions;

(b)   Chapter 2 deals with charges to tax on participants in non-reporting funds;

(c)   Chapter 3 deals with exceptions from the charge to tax;

(d)   Chapter 4 deals with disposals of interests in non-reporting funds;

(e)   Chapter 5 deals with offshore income gains and the computation of offshore income gains;

(f)   Chapter 6 deals with the deduction of offshore income gains in computing chargeable gains;

(g)   Chapter 7 deals with the conversion of a non-reporting fund into a reporting fund.

Meaning of "material disposal"

15   In these Regulations a **"material disposal"** means a disposal to which this Part applies.

Chapter 2 – Charges to Tax on Participants in Non-Reporting Funds

CHARGE TO TAX ON CERTAIN AMOUNTS TREATED AS DISTRIBUTIONS

Treatment of certain amounts as distributions

16(1)   This regulation applies if a non-reporting fund which is a transparent fund has an interest in a reporting fund.

16(2)   In the case of any excess specified in regulation 94(1) or (2) which is treated, under that regulation, as made to the non-reporting fund, the Tax Acts have effect as if the excess were additional income of the participants in the non-reporting fund in proportion to their rights.

16(3)   The additional income is treated as arising on the same date as the excess is treated as made to the non-reporting fund.

16(4)   If a participant in the non-reporting fund is chargeable to income tax, the additional income is charged as relevant foreign income within the meaning given by section 830 of ITTOIA 2005.

16(5)   If a participant in the non-reporting fund is chargeable to corporation tax, the additional income is charged under Chapter 8 of Part 10 of CTA 2009 (miscellaneous income: income not otherwise charged).

History – In reg. 16(2), "94(1) or (2)" substituted for "94(2)" by SI 2011/1211, reg. 30, with effect: for the purposes of income tax or corporation tax, for distributions made, or treated as made, on or after 27 May 2011; and for the purposes of capital gains tax or corporation tax on chargeable gains, in relation to disposals made on or after 27 May 2011.

CHARGE TO TAX ON DISPOSAL OF ASSET

The charge to tax

17(1)   There is a charge to tax if–

(a)   a person disposes of an asset,

(b)   either condition A or condition B is met, and

(c)   as a result of the disposal, an offshore income gain arises to the person making the disposal.

17(2)   Condition A is that the asset is an interest in a non-reporting fund at the time of the disposal.

17(3)   Condition B is that–

(a)   the asset is an interest in a reporting fund at the time of the disposal,

(b)   the reporting fund was previously a non-reporting fund (becoming a reporting fund as the result of an application under regulation 52),

(c)   the interest was an interest in a non-reporting fund during some or all of the material period,

(d)   an election under regulation 48 was not prevented by paragraph (5) of that regulation, and

(e)   no election has been made under regulation 48(2).

17(3A)   Where the asset is an interest in a reporting fund acquired in consequence of an arrangement to which section 135 (exchange of securities for those in another company treated as not involving a disposal) or section 136 (scheme of reconstruction involving issue of securities treated as exchange not involving a disposal) of TCGA 1992 applied, the reporting fund referred to in sub-paragraph (b) of condition B is the fund that was company A for the purposes of either of those sections and the interest referred to in sub-paragraph (c) of condition B is the interest in that fund.

17(4)   For the purposes of paragraph (3)(c) the **"material period"** means a period beginning with the day on which consideration was given for the acquisition of the asset or on 1st January 1984 (whichever is the later) and ending with the day on which the fund became a reporting fund.

17(5)   Chapter 5 of this Part deals with offshore income gains and the computation of offshore income gains.

History – Reg. 17(3A) inserted by SI 2013/661, reg. 2(2), with effect in relation to disposals made on or after 3 p.m on 20 March 2013.

The charge to tax: further provisions

18(1)   The offshore income gain arising is treated for all the purposes of the Tax Acts as income which arises at the time of the disposal to the person making the disposal (or treated as making the disposal).

18(2)   The tax is charged on the person making the disposal (or treated as making the disposal).

18(3)   In the case of a person chargeable to income tax, tax is charged under Chapter 8 of Part 5 of ITTOIA 2005 (miscellaneous income: income not otherwise charged) for the year of assessment in which the disposal is made, but sections 688(1) and 689 of ITTOIA 2005 (income charged and person liable) do not apply.

18(4)   In the case of a person chargeable to corporation tax, tax is charged under Chapter 8 of Part 10 of CTA 2009 (miscellaneous income: income not otherwise charged) for the accounting period in which the disposal is made.

18(5)   Paragraph (1) is subject to–

(a)   regulation 19 (income treated as arising under regulation 17: remittance basis);

(b)   regulation 20(1) (offshore income gain arising to non-resident trustees not treated as income of settlor);

(c)   regulation 20(5) (application to gains of non-resident settlements);

(d)   regulation 24(6) (application of section 13 of TCGA 1992).

18(6)   Nothing in regulation 17 of these Regulations applies to–

(a)   an authorised investment fund to which regulation 14ZB, 14ZD(1) or Part 6A of the Authorised Investment Fund (Tax) Regulations 2006 applies,

(b)   an investment trust company to which regulation 43 or 45 of the investment Trust (Approved Company) (Tax) Regulations 2011 apply, or

(c)   the trustees of an exempt unauthorised unit trust to which regulations 22 or 23 of the Unauthorised Unit Trusts (Tax) Regulations 2013 applies.

History – Reg. 18(6)(c) (and the ", or" before it) inserted (and the "or" at the end of (a) omitted) by SI 2013/2819, reg. 43, with effect from 6 April 2014.
In reg. 18(6), ", 14ZD(1)" inserted by SI 2011/2192, reg. 7, with effect: for the purposes of corporation tax on income, for accounting periods starting on or after 1 October 2011; and, for the purposes of corporation tax on chargeable gains or capital gains tax, in relation to disposals made on or after 1 October 2011.
Reg. 18(6) substituted by SI 2011/2999, reg. 46, with effect in relation to disposals made on or after 1 January 2012.
Reg. 18(6) substituted by SI 2011/244, reg. 9(2), with effect (subject to transitional provisions in SI 2011/244, reg. 8): for the purposes of corporation tax on income, for accounting periods ending on or after 6 March 2011; and for the purposes of corporation tax on chargeable gains and of capital gains tax, in relation to disposals made on or after 6 March 2011. Former reg. 18(6) read as follows:

> "**18(6)**   Nothing in regulation 17 or 18 of these Regulations applies to a fund to which Part 6A of the Authorised Investment Funds (Tax) Regulations 2006 applies.".

Reg. 18(6) inserted by SI 2010/294, reg. 27, with effect from 6 March 2010.

Income treated as arising under regulation 17: remittance basis

19(1)   This regulation applies to income treated as arising under regulation 17 to an individual in a tax year if–

(a)   section 809B, 809D or 809E of ITA 2007 (remittance basis) applies to the individual for that year, and

(b)   the individual is not domiciled in the United Kingdom in that year.

19(2)   The income is treated as relevant foreign income of the individual.

19(3)   For the purposes of Chapter A1 of Part 14 of ITA 2007 (remittance basis)–

(a)   any consideration obtained on the disposal of the asset is treated as deriving from the income, and

(b)   unless the consideration so obtained is of an amount equal to or exceeding the market value of the asset, the asset is treated as deriving from the income.

19(4)   In paragraph (3)–

(a)   **"the asset"** means the asset the disposal of which causes the income to be treated as arising, and

(b)   **"the disposal"** means the disposal mentioned in sub-paragraph (a) of that paragraph.

19(5)   This regulation does not apply for the purposes of regulation 20.

OFFSHORE FUNDS AND GAINS OF NON-RESIDENT SETTLEMENTS

Application to gains of non-resident settlements

20(1) If an offshore income gain arises to a settlement in a tax year and the trustees of the settlement are not resident in the United Kingdom in the tax year, the gain is not regarded as income for the purposes of Chapter 5 of Part 5 of ITTOIA 2005 (settlements: amounts treated as income of settlor).

20(2) If—

(a) offshore income gains arise to the trustees of a settlement in a tax year, and

(b) section 87 of TCGA 1992 (gains of non-resident settlements) applies to the settlement for that year,

the OIG amount for the settlement for that year is the amount of the offshore income gains.

20(3) Sections 12, 87 to 90A and 96 to 98 of, and Schedule 4C to, TCGA 1992 apply in relation to OIG amounts as if—

(a) references to section 2(2) amounts (except those in paragraph 7B(2)(b) and (4) of Schedule 4C) were to OIG amounts,

(b) references to chargeable gains (except the one in paragraph 1(5) of Schedule 4C) were to offshore income gains,

(c) references to anything accruing were to it arising (and similar references, except the one in paragraph 1(5) of Schedule 4C, were read accordingly),

(d) sections 87(4), 88(2) to (5) and 97(6) and paragraphs 1(3A), 3 to 7 and 12 of Schedule 4C were omitted, and

(e) regulation 21 did not apply.

20(4) Section 87A of TCGA 1992 applies for a tax year by virtue of paragraph (3) before it applies for that year otherwise than by virtue of that paragraph.

20(5) If this regulation applies, the person to whom the offshore income gain arises is treated as the person making the disposal.

History – In reg. 20(1), the word "not" substituted for the words "neither resident nor ordinarily" by SI 2013/605, reg. 7(2), with effect for the purposes of a person's liability to income tax for the tax year 2013–14 and any subsequent tax years.

OFFSHORE FUNDS AND THE TRANSFER OF ASSETS ABROAD

Application of transfer of assets abroad provisions

21(1) Chapter 2 of Part 13 of ITA 2007 (transfer of assets abroad) applies in relation to an offshore income gain arising to a person resident or domiciled outside the United Kingdom as if the offshore income gain were income becoming payable to the person.

21(2) Income treated as arising under that Chapter by virtue of paragraph (1) is regarded as **"foreign"** for the purposes of section 726, 730 or 735 of that Act.

21(3) Paragraph (1) does not apply in relation to an offshore income gain if (and to the extent that) it is treated, by virtue of regulation 24, as arising to a person resident in the United Kingdom.

21(4) The following provisions apply if regulation 20 applies in relation to an offshore income gain (the "relevant offshore income gain").

21(5) If—

(a) by virtue of regulation 20 an offshore income gain is treated as arising in a tax year to a person resident in the United Kingdom, and

(b) it is so treated by reason of the relevant offshore income gain (or part of it),

for that and subsequent tax years paragraph (1) does not apply in relation to the relevant offshore income gain (or that part).

21(6) If, by virtue of paragraph (1) as it applies in relation to the relevant offshore income gain, income is treated under Chapter 2 of Part 13 of ITA 2007 as arising in a tax year, the OIG amount in question must be reduced (with effect from the following tax year) by the amount of the income.

History – In reg. 21(3) and (5)(a), the words "or ordinarily resident" omitted by SI 2013/605, reg. 7(3), with effect for the purposes of a person's liability to income tax for the tax year 2013–14 or any subsequent tax years.

APPLICATION OF TCGA 1992

Application of certain provisions of TCGA 1992

22(1) The following enactments have effect in relation to income tax or corporation tax in respect of offshore income gains as they have effect in relation to capital gains tax or corporation tax in respect of chargeable gains–

(a)   section 2(1) of TCGA 1992 (persons chargeable to capital gains tax);

(b)   section 10 of TCGA 1992 (non-resident with a United Kingdom branch or agency);

(c)   section 10B of TCGA 1992 (non-resident company with United Kingdom permanent establishment).

22(2)   Paragraph (1) is subject to paragraphs (3) and (4).

22(3)   In the application of section 10 of TCGA 1992 in accordance with paragraph (1), paragraphs (a) and (b) of subsection (1) (assets on the disposal of which chargeable gains are taxable) have effect with the omission of the words "situated in the United Kingdom and".

22(4)   In the application of section 10B of TCGA 1992 in accordance with paragraph (1), paragraphs (a) and (b) of subsection (1) (assets on the disposal of which chargeable profits arise for the purposes of corporation tax) have effect with the omission of the words "situated in the United Kingdom and".

Temporary Non-residents

23(1)   This regulation applies where an individual ("the taxpayer") is temporarily non-resident.

23(2)   The taxpayer is chargeable to income tax as if offshore income gains within paragraph (3) were offshore income gains arising to the taxpayer in the period of return.

23(3)   The offshore income gains within this paragraph are those that–

(a)   arise to the taxpayer in the temporary period of non-residence, and

(b)   would be treated under section 13 of TCGA 1992 (attribution of gains to members of non-resident companies) as it applies to offshore income gains by virtue of regulation 24 as having arisen to the taxpayer in that period if the residence assumption were made.

23(4)   The residence assumption is–

(a)   that the taxpayer had been resident in the United Kingdom for the tax year in which the offshore income gain arose to the company, or

(b)   if that tax year was a split year as respects the taxpayer, that offshore income gain had arisen to the company in the UK part of it.

23(5)   But a gain is not within paragraph (3) if, ignoring this regulation, the taxpayer is chargeable to income tax in respect of it (and could not cease to be so chargeable by making a claim under section 6 of the Taxation (International and Other Provisions) Act 2010).

23(6)   Paragraph (2) is subject to regulation 23A.

23(7)   If section 809B, 809D or 809E of ITA 2007 (remittance basis) applies to the taxpayer for the year of return, any offshore income gains to which regulation 19(2) applies falling within paragraph (3) of this regulation by virtue of sub-paragraph (a) of that paragraph that were remitted to the United Kingdom at any time in the temporary period of non-residence are to be treated as remitted to the United Kingdom in the period of return.

23(8)   In this regulation–

(a)   **"remitted to the United Kingdom"** has the same meaning as in Chapter A1 of Part 14 of ITA 2007,

(b)   **"split year"** has the meaning given in paragraph 43 of Schedule 45 to the Finance Act 2013,

(c)   **"temporarily non-resident"** has the meaning given in paragraph 110 of that Schedule,

(d)   **"the UK part"** of a split year has the meaning given in paragraph 56 of that Schedule.

23(9)   In this regulation and regulation 23A–

(a)   **"period of return"** has the meaning given in paragraph 115 of Schedule 45 to the Finance Act 2013,

(b)   **"temporary period of non-residence"** has the meaning given in paragraph 113 of that Schedule, and

(c)   **"the year of return"** has the meaning given in section 10A(11) of TCGA 1992.

History – Reg. 23 (and the heading before it) substituted by SI 2013/1810, reg. 4(2), with effect for the purposes of income tax for the tax year 2013–14 and any subsequent tax year. Former reg. 23 read as follows:

"**Application of section 10A of TCGA 1992**

23(1)   Section 10A of TCGA 1992 (temporary non-residents) applies for the purposes of this Part with the following modifications.

23(2)   The section applies as if, in subsection (2)—

(a)   the reference to section 86A were omitted;

(b)   for the reference to capital gains tax there were substituted a reference to income tax;

(c)   in paragraph (a), for the reference to chargeable gains and losses there were substituted a reference to offshore income gains;

(d)   in paragraph (b)—

     (i)   for the reference to chargeable gains there were substituted a reference to offshore income gains;

     (ii)   for the reference to section 13 or 86 there were substituted a reference to regulation 24;

(e)   paragraph (c) were omitted; and

(f)   for the reference to gains or, as the case may be, losses there were substituted a reference to offshore income gains.

23(3)   The section applies as if, in subsection (3)—

(a)   for the reference to gains and losses there were substituted a reference to offshore income gains; and

(b)   for the reference to any gain or loss there were substituted a reference to any offshore income gains.

23(4)   The section applies as if subsection (4) were omitted.

23(5)   The section applies as if, in subsection (5)—

(a)   for the reference to gains and losses there were substituted a reference to offshore income gains;

(b)   for the reference to any chargeable gain or allowable loss there were substituted a reference to an offshore income gain; and

(c)   for the reference to section 10 or 16(3) there were substituted a reference to regulation 22(1)(b).

23(6)   The section applies as if subsection (6) were omitted.

23(7)   The section applies as if, in subsection (7), for the reference to capital gains tax there were substituted a reference to income tax.

23(8)   The section applies as if, in subsection (9ZA)—

(a)   for the reference to foreign chargeable gains there were substituted a reference to offshore income gains to which regulation 19 applied; and

(b)   the second sentence of that subsection were omitted.

23(9)   The section applies as if, in subsection (9B)—

(a)   in paragraph (a)—

     (i)   for the reference to section 87 or 89(2) there were substituted a reference to regulation 20;

     (ii)   for the reference to chargeable gains there were substituted a reference to offshore income gains; and

(b)   in paragraph (b) the references to subsections (2)(c) and (6) were omitted.

23(10)   The section applies as if, in subsection (9C)—

(a)   for the reference to capital gains tax there were substituted a reference to income tax; and

(b)   for the reference to chargeable gains there were substituted a reference to offshore income gains.".

Regulation 23: supplementary

23A(1)   Regulation 23(2) does not apply to an offshore income gain accruing on the disposal by the taxpayer of an asset if—

(a)   the asset was acquired by the taxpayer in the temporary period of non-residence,

(b)   it was so acquired otherwise than by means of a relevant disposal that by virtue of section 58, 73 or 258(4) TCGA 1992 is treated as having been a disposal on which neither a gain nor a loss accrued, and

(c)   the asset is not an interest created by or arising under a settlement.

23A(2)   Nothing in any double taxation relief arrangements is to be read as preventing the taxpayer from being chargeable to income tax in respect of any offshore income gains treated under regulation 23 as accruing to the taxpayer in the period of return (or as preventing a charge to that tax from arising as a result).

23A(3)   Nothing in any enactment imposing any limit on the time within which an assessment to income tax may be made prevents any assessment for the year of departure from being made in the taxpayer's case at any time before the end of the second anniversary of the 31 January next following the year of return.

23A(4)   In this regulation—

(a)   "**relevant disposal**" has the meaning given in section 10AA(2) of TCGA 1992, and

(b)   "**the year of departure**" has the meaning given in paragraph 114 of Schedule 45 to the Finance Act 2013.

History – Reg. 23A inserted by SI 2013/1810, reg. 4(2), with effect for the purposes of income tax for the tax year 2013–14 and any subsequent tax year.

Application of section 13 of TCGA 1992

24(1)   Section 13 of TCGA 1992 (chargeable gains accruing to certain non-resident companies) applies for the purposes of this Part with the following modifications.

24(2)   The section applies as if—

(a)   for any reference to a chargeable gain there were substituted a reference to an offshore income gain; and

(b)   for any reference to anything accruing there were substituted a reference to it arising (with similar references being read accordingly).

24(3)   The section applies as if, in subsection (5), paragraphs (b) and (c) were omitted.

24(4)   The section applies as if, in subsection (7), for the reference to capital gains tax there were substituted a reference to income tax or corporation tax.

24(5)   The section applies as if subsection (8) were omitted.

24(6)   If this regulation applies, the person to whom the offshore income gain arises is treated as the person making the disposal.

24(7)   To the extent that an offshore income gain is treated, by virtue of this regulation, as having accrued to any person resident in the United Kingdom, that gain shall not be deemed to be the income of any individual for the purposes of Chapter 2 of Part 13 of ITA 2007 (transfer of assets abroad).

History – In reg. 24(7), the words "or ordinarily resident" omitted by SI 2013/605, reg. 7(4), with effect for the purposes of a person's liability to income tax for the tax year 2013–14 or any subsequent tax years.

Chapter 3 – Exceptions etc. from the Charge to Tax

Exceptions from the charge

25(1)   No liability to tax arises under regulation 17 if any of conditions A to E is met.

25(2)   Condition A is that the participant is required to treat the interest in the fund as a loan relationship under Chapter 3 of Part 6 of CTA 2009.

25(3)   Condition B is that the participant is required to treat the interest in the fund as a derivative contract to which the provisions of Part 7 of CTA 2009 apply.

25(4)   Condition C is that the asset is an intangible fixed asset to which the provisions of Part 8 of CTA 2009 apply.

25(5)   Condition D is that the asset consists of excluded indexed securities as defined in section 433 of ITTOIA 2005.

25(6)   Condition E is that the asset is a right arising under a policy of insurance.

Trading stock etc.

26(1)   No liability to tax arises under regulation 17 if condition A or B is met.

26(2)   Condition A is that the interest in the fund is held as trading stock.

26(3)   Condition B is that the disposal of the interest is taken into account in computing the profits of a trade.

Long-term insurance funds of insurance companies

27(1)   No liability to tax arises under regulation 17 in respect of disposals of assets of an insurance company's long-term insurance fund.

27(2)   In paragraph (1) **"insurance company"** and **"long-term insurance fund"** have the same meaning as in section 431(2) of ICTA.

Loans other than participating loans

28(1)   No liability to tax arises under regulation 17 if the asset is a loan which is not a participating loan.

28(2)   For the purposes of paragraph (1) a **"participating loan"** means a loan where the amount payable on redemption exceeds the issue price by an amount which is determined in whole or in part by reference to the income of the non-reporting fund.

Interests in transparent funds

29(1)   No liability to tax arises under regulation 17 if–

(a)   the disposal is the disposal of an interest in an offshore fund falling within paragraph (b) or (c) of section 40A(2) of FA 2008, and

(b)   the fund is a transparent fund.

This is subject to paragraphs (2) and (3).

29(2)   But there is a charge to tax under regulation 17 if–

(a)   there is a disposal of an interest in a transparent fund, and

(b)   during a period beginning with the date the interest (or any part of it) was acquired and ending with the date of the disposal, the offshore fund has at any time held interests in other non-reporting funds which amounted in total to more than 5% by value of the offshore fund's assets.

29(3) And there is a charge to tax under regulation 17 if–

(a)   there is a disposal of an interest in a transparent fund,

(b)   the fund is a non-reporting fund, and

(c)   the fund fails to make sufficient information available to participants in the fund to enable those participants to meet their tax obligations in the United Kingdom with respect to their shares of the income of the fund.

29(4) If, on the disposal by an offshore fund of an interest in another non-reporting fund, no liability would arise under regulation 17 by virtue of this regulation, that interest is not taken into account for the purposes of paragraph (2)(b).

Rights in certain existing holdings

30(1) No liability to tax arises under regulation 17 in respect of any rights in an offshore fund to which this regulation applies if the rights are acquired by a person–

(a)   before 1st December 2009, or

(b)   in accordance with paragraph (2).

30(2) Rights are acquired in accordance with this paragraph if–

(a)   the rights are acquired by the participant in accordance with a legally enforceable agreement in writing that was entered into by the participant before 30th April 2009,

(b)   in the case of an agreement which was conditional, the conditions are met before that date, and

(c)   the agreement is not varied on or after that date.

30(3) Rights of a person in a fund are rights in an offshore fund to which this regulation applies if, on the date on which the person acquired the rights, those rights did not constitute a material interest in an offshore fund within the meaning of that expression given by section 759 of ICTA.

Charitable companies and charitable trusts

31(1) A charitable company shall be exempt from corporation tax in respect of an offshore income gain if the gain is applicable and applied for charitable purposes.

31(2) See section 535 of ITA 2007 for an exemption for income tax purposes for offshore income gains accruing to a charitable trust.

31(3) Paragraphs (4) and (5) apply if–

(a)   property held on charitable trusts ceases to be subject to charitable trusts, and

(b)   that property represents directly or indirectly an offshore income gain.

31(4) The trustees are treated as if they had disposed of and immediately reacquired that property for a consideration equal to its market value.

31(5) An offshore income gain accruing on the disposal arising under paragraph (4) is treated as an offshore income gain not accruing to a charity.

31(6) In this regulation **"charity"** and **"charitable company"** have the same meaning as in section 506 of ICTA.

Unlisted trading company exception

31A(1) No liability to tax arises under regulation 17 if conditions A to D are met.

31A(2) Condition A is that the disposal is a disposal of an interest in an offshore fund.

31A(3) Condition B is that the sole or main purpose of the fund is to invest in qualifying companies.

31A(4) Condition C is that throughout the period starting with the date on which the interest was acquired and ending 12 months before the date of the disposal the fund met the investment condition. This is subject to paragraph (6).

31A(5) Condition D is that participants in the fund have access to, and are able to obtain copies of, sufficient information to demonstrate that the fund intends to dispose of any holdings of shares or securities within regulation 31B(1)(b) or (d).

31A(6) Condition C is treated as met in relation to the period–

(a)   starting at the beginning of the first period of account of the fund, and

(b)   ending on the earlier of–

     (i)   the expiry of 3 months, and

     (ii)   the date the fund meets the investment condition,

if the only asset of the fund during that period is cash.

31A(7)   For the purposes of this regulation and regulation 31B–

> **"cash"** means cash deposited in a bank account or similar account, but not cash acquired wholly or partly for the purpose of realising a gain on its disposal;
>
> **"qualifying company"** means a trading company or the holding company of a trading group or a trading subgroup, where–
>
> > (a)   the shares of the company are not listed on a recognised stock exchange or admitted to trading on a regulated market, and
> >
> > (b)   the activities of the trading company or, in the case of a holding company, the activities of the members of the group or subgroup taken together, do not include to a substantial extent the carrying out of investment transactions undertaken in the course of a trade.

31A(8)   In paragraph (7) in the definition of **"qualifying company"**, **"holding company"**, **"trading company"**, **"trading group"** and **"trading subgroup"** have the same meanings as in Schedule 7AC to TCGA 1992 (see paragraphs 20 to 24 and 26 and 27 of that Schedule).

History – Reg. 31A inserted by SI 2011/1211, reg. 19, with effect: for the purposes of income tax or corporation tax, for distributions made, or treated as made, on or after 27 May 2011; and for the purposes of capital gains tax or corporation tax on chargeable gains, in relation to disposals made on or after 27 May 2011.

Unlisted trading company exception: the investment condition

31B(1)   The investment condition is that at least 90% of the value of the assets of the fund consists of–

(a)   direct or indirect holdings in qualifying companies,

(b)   holdings of shares or securities listed on a recognised stock exchange or admitted to trading on a regulated market which the fund intends to dispose of as soon as reasonably practicable, taking into account market conditions and commercial and contractual constraints, and which–

> (i)   were acquired by the fund in exchange for shares or securities in a qualifying company, or
>
> (ii)   were shares in a qualifying company at the time of their acquisition by the fund,

(c)   holdings of shares or securities listed on a recognised stock exchange or admitted to trading on a regulated market, which are holdings in a company that would be a qualifying company if it were not so listed or admitted, where it is reasonable to believe that the shares or securities will cease to be so listed or admitted within 12 months,

(d)   shares or securities which have ceased to be within sub-paragraph (c) because it is no longer reasonable to believe that they will cease to be listed or admitted, which the fund intends to dispose of as soon as reasonably practicable taking into account market conditions and commercial and contractual constraints.

31B(2)   For the purposes of the investment condition–

(a)   any holding of cash shall be disregarded, and

(b)   a holding in a qualifying company is held indirectly if it is held by a corporate body which is a 51% subsidiary of the fund.

31B(3)   For the purposes of paragraph (2) section 1154 of CTA 2010 applies to determine whether a corporate body is a 51% subsidiary of a fund.

History – Reg. 31B inserted by SI 2011/1211, reg. 19, with effect: for the purposes of income tax or corporation tax, for distributions made, or treated as made, on or after 27 May 2011; and for the purposes of capital gains tax or corporation tax on chargeable gains, in relation to disposals made on or after 27 May 2011.

Unlisted trading company exception: further provision

31C   No liability to tax arises under regulation 17 if–

(a)   the disposal is of an interest in an offshore fund whose business consists solely of holding an interest in another offshore fund ("X"), and

(b)   conditions B to D of regulation 31A apply in relation to X.

History – Reg. 31C inserted by SI 2011/1211, reg. 19, with effect: for the purposes of income tax or corporation tax, for distributions made, or treated as made, on or after 27 May 2011; and for the purposes of capital gains tax or corporation tax on chargeable gains, in relation to disposals made on or after 27 May 2011.

Chapter 4 – Disposals of Interests in Non-Reporting Funds

BASIC PROVISIONS

Application of this Chapter

32 This Chapter applies if a participant disposes of an asset and at the time of the disposal–

(a) the asset is an interest in a non-reporting fund, or

(b) the asset is an interest in a reporting fund and the requirements specified in paragraph (3) of regulation 17 (read, as appropriate, with paragraphs (4) and (5) of that regulation) are met.

Disposal of an asset: the basic rule

33(1) There is a disposal of an asset for the purposes of these Regulations if there would be a disposal of an asset for the purposes of TCGA 1992.

33(2) Paragraph (1) is subject to the following provisions of this Chapter.

FURTHER PROVISIONS

Provisions applicable on death

34(1) Notwithstanding anything in paragraph (b) of subsection (1) of section 62 of TCGA 1992 (general provisions applicable on death: no deemed disposal by the deceased), where a person dies and the assets of which the deceased was competent to dispose at the time of death include an interest in a non-reporting fund, then, for the purposes of these Regulations–

(a) immediately before the acquisition referred to in paragraph (a) of that subsection, that interest shall be deemed to be disposed of by the deceased for such a consideration as is mentioned in that subsection; but

(b) nothing in this regulation affects the determination, in accordance with regulation 32, of the question whether that deemed disposal is one to which this Chapter applies.

34(2) Subject to paragraph (1), section 62 of TCGA 1992 applies for the purposes of these Regulations as it applies for the purposes of that Act, and the reference in that paragraph to the assets of which a deceased person was competent to dispose are to be construed in accordance with subsection (10) of that section.

Application of section 135 of TCGA 1992

35 [Omitted (by substitution of reg. 36A) by SI 2013/1400, reg. 15(a).]

History – Reg. 35 omitted (by substitution of reg. 36A) by SI 2013/1400, reg. 15(a), with effect in relation to disposals on or after 8 June 2013. Former reg. 35 read as follows:

"**35(1)** Section 135 of TCGA 1992 (exchange of securities for those in another company treated as not involving a disposal) does not apply for the purposes of this Part to the extent that–

(a) the interest in the entity that is company A for the purposes of that section that is exchanged is an interest in a non-reporting fund, and

(b) the interest in the entity that is company B for those purposes that is exchanged is not an interest in such a fund.

35(2) In a case where section 135 of TCGA 1992 would apply apart from paragraph (1), the exchange in question shall for the purposes of this Part constitute a disposal of interests in the non-reporting fund for a consideration equal to their market value at the time of the exchange.".

Application of section 136 of TCGA 1992

36 [Omitted (by substitution of reg. 36A) by SI 2013/1400, reg. 15(a).]

History – Reg. 36 omitted (by substitution of reg. 36A) by SI 2013/1400, reg. 15(a), with effect in relation to disposals on or after 8 June 2013. Former reg. 36 read as follows:

"**36(1)** Section 136 of TCGA 1992 (scheme of reconstruction involving issue of securities treated as exchange not involving disposal) does not apply for the purposes of this Part to the extent that–

(a) the interest in the entity that is company A for the purposes of that section that is exchanged is an interest in a non-reporting fund, and

(b) the interest in the entity that is company B for those purposes that is exchanged is not an interest in such a fund.

36(2) In a case where section 136 of TCGA 1992 would apply apart from paragraph (1), the deemed exchange in question shall for the purposes of this Part constitute a disposal of interests in the non-reporting fund for a consideration equal to their market value at the time of the deemed exchange.".

EXCHANGES AND SCHEMES OF RECONSTRUCTION

36A(1) The following sections of TCGA 1992 do not apply to the extent that an interest in a non-reporting fund is exchanged or treated as exchanged for an asset which is not an interest in a non-reporting fund.

36A(2) The sections are–

(a) section 103G (exchange of units for those in another collective investment scheme),

(b) section 103H (scheme of reconstruction involving issue of units), (c)　　　section 135 (exchange of securities for those in another company), and

(d)　　　section 136 (scheme of reconstruction involving issue of securities).

36A(3)　In a case where one of those sections would apply apart from paragraph (1), the exchange or deemed exchange shall for the purposes of this Part constitute a disposal of interests in the non-reporting fund for a consideration equal to their market value at the time of the exchange or deemed exchange.

History – Reg. 36A substituted for reg. 35 and 36 by SI 2013/1400, reg. 15(a), with effect in relation to disposals on or after 8 June 2013.

Exchange of interests of different classes

37(1)　If conditions A to D are met, section 127 of TCGA 1992 (equation of original shares and new holding) does not prevent an exchange from constituting a disposal for the purposes of these Regulations.

37(2)　Condition A is that an offshore fund is constituted by a class of interest ("class A") in main arrangements.

37(3)　Condition B is that a participant exchanges an interest of class A for an interest in another offshore fund constituted by a different class of interest ("class B") in those main arrangements.

37(4)　Condition C is that the interest of class A is at the time of the exchange an interest in a non-reporting fund.

37(5)　Condition D is that the interest of class B is at the time of the exchange an interest which is not an interest in a non-reporting fund.

37(6)　Any disposal to which this regulation applies is to be treated as a disposal for a consideration equal to the market value of the rights at the time of the exchange.

Chapter 5 – Offshore Income Gains and the Computation of Offshore Income Gains

General provisions

38(1)　An offshore income gain arises to a person on the disposal of an asset if a basic gain arises on the disposal.

38(2)　The disposal gives rise to an offshore income gain of an amount equal to the basic gain on the disposal.

38(3)　The following provisions of this Chapter explain how the basic gain is computed.

The basic gain and its computation

39(1)　In the case of a participant chargeable to income tax, the basic gain is a gain of the amount which would be the gain on that disposal for the purposes of TCGA 1992 if the gain were computed without regard to any charge to income tax arising under this Part.

39(2)　In the case of a participant chargeable to corporation tax, the basic gain is a gain of the amount which would be the gain on that disposal for the purposes of TCGA 1992 if the gain were computed–

(a)　　　without regard to any charge to corporation tax arising under this Part, and

(b)　　　without regard to any indexation allowance on the disposal under TCGA 1992.

39(3)　The computation of the basic gain is subject to–

(a)　　　regulation 34 (provisions applicable on death);

(aa)　　regulation 36A (exchanges and schemes of reconstruction);

(b)　　　[omitted by SI 2013/1400, reg. 15(b),]

(c)　　　[omitted by SI 2013/1400, reg. 15(b),]

(d)　　　regulation 37 (exchange of interests of different classes;

(e)　　　regulation 40 (earlier disposal to which the no gain/no loss basis applies);

(f)　　　regulation 41 (modifications of TCGA 1992);

(g)　　　regulation 42 (losses);

(h)　　　regulation 43 (special rules for certain existing holdings).

History – Reg. 39(3)(aa) substituted for (b) and (c) by SI 2013/1400, reg. 15(b), with effect in relation to disposals on or after 8 June 2013. Former reg. 39(3)(b) and (c) read as follows:
　　　"(b)　　regulation 35 (application of section 135 of TCGA 1992);
　　　　(c)　　regulation 36 (application of section 136 of TCGA 1992);".

Earlier disposal to which the no gain/no loss basis applies

40(1) This regulation applies if–

(a) a participant is chargeable to corporation tax, and

(b) the amount of any chargeable gain or allowable loss which would arise on the disposal would fall to be computed in a way which, in whole or in part, would take account of the indexation allowance on an earlier disposal to which section 56(2) of TCGA 1992 (disposals on a no gain/no loss basis) applies.

40(2) The basic gain on the disposal is computed as if–

(a) no indexation allowance had been available on any such earlier disposal, and

(b) subject to that, neither a gain nor a loss had arisen to the person making such an earlier disposal.

Modifications of TCGA 1992

41(1) If the disposal forms part of a transfer to which section 162 of TCGA 1992 (roll-over relief on transfer of business) applies, the basic gain arising on the disposal is computed without regard to any deduction which falls to be made under that section in computing a chargeable gain.

41(2) If the disposal is made otherwise than under a bargain at arm's length and a claim for relief is made in respect of that disposal under section 165 or 260 of TCGA 1992 (relief for gifts), the claim does not affect the computation of the basic gain arising on the disposal.

Losses

42(1) If the effect of any computation under regulations 39 to 41 would be to produce a loss, the basic gain on the disposal is nil.

42(2) Paragraph (1) applies notwithstanding section 16 of TCGA 1992 (losses determined in like manner as gains).

42(3) Accordingly, for the purposes of these Regulations, no loss is to be treated as arising on the disposal.

Special rules for certain existing holdings

43(1) This regulation applies if–

(a) a person acquired rights (the "protected rights") in an offshore fund–

    (i) before 1st December 2009, or

    (ii) in accordance with paragraph (2),

(b) immediately before 1st December 2009 those rights did not constitute a material interest in an offshore fund within the meaning of that expression given by section 759 of ICTA, and

(c) on or after 1st December 2009 the person acquires additional rights in the offshore fund (the "non-protected rights").

43(2) Rights are acquired in accordance with this paragraph if–

(a) the rights are acquired by the participant in accordance with a legally enforceable agreement in writing that was entered into by the participant before 30th April 2009,

(b) in the case of an agreement which was conditional, the conditions are met before that date, and

(c) the agreement is not varied on or after that date.

43(3) For the purposes of tax in respect of chargeable gains–

(a) section 104 of TCGA 1992 (share pooling: general interpretative provisions) applies as if the protected rights were assets of a different class from the non-protected rights, and

(b) all the protected rights must be treated as disposed of before any of the non-protected rights may be so treated.

Chapter 6 – Deduction of Offshore Income Gains in Computing Chargeable Gains

Ambit of this Chapter

44(1) This Chapter applies if–

(a) a material disposal gives rise to an offshore income gain, and

(b) that disposal also constitutes the disposal of the interest concerned for the purposes of TCGA 1992.

44(2) In this Chapter the disposal specified in paragraph (1)(b) is called the "TCGA disposal".

Treatment of the TCGA disposal: general rules

45(1) This regulation applies for the purposes of the computation of the chargeable gain arising on the TCGA disposal.

45(2) The provisions of this regulation have effect in relation to the TCGA disposal in substitution for section 37(1) of TCGA 1992 (deduction of consideration chargeable to tax on income).

45(3) In the computation of the gain arising on the TCGA disposal, a sum equal to the offshore income gain shall be deducted from the sum which would otherwise constitute the amount or value of the consideration for the disposal.

45(4) Paragraph (3) is subject to the following provisions of this Chapter.

45(5) Paragraph (6) applies if the TCGA disposal is of such a nature that, by virtue of section 42 of TCGA 1992 (part disposals), an apportionment falls to be made of certain expenditure.

45(6) No deduction is to be made by virtue of paragraph (3) in determining the amount or value of the consideration for the purposes of the fraction in section 42(2) of TCGA 1992.

Modification of section 162 of TCGA 1992

46(1) This regulation applies if the TCGA disposal forms part of a transfer to which section 162 of TCGA 1992 applies (roll-over relief on transfer of business in exchange wholly or partly for shares).

46(2) For the purposes of subsection (4) of section 162 of TCGA 1992 (determination of the amount of the deduction from the gain on the old assets) "B" in the fraction in that subsection (the value of the whole of the consideration received by the transferor in exchange for the business) is to be taken to be what it would be if the value of the consideration other than shares so received by the transferor were reduced by an amount equal to the offshore income gain.

Application of section 128 of TCGA 1992

47(1) This regulation applies if there is a disposal to which this Part applies by virtue of–

(aa) regulation 36A (exchanges and schemes of reconstruction), or

(a) [omitted by SI 2013/1400, reg. 15(c),]

(b) [omitted by SI 2013/1400, reg. 15(c),]

(c) regulation 37 (exchange of interests of different classes).

47(2) TCGA 1992 has effect as if an amount equal to the offshore income gain to which that disposal gives rise were given (by the person making the exchange) as consideration for the new holding (within the meaning of section 128 of that Act (consideration given or received for new holding on a reorganisation)).

History – Reg. 47(1)(aa) substituted for (a) and (b) by SI 2013/1400, reg. 15(c), with effect in relation to disposals on or after 8 June 2013. Former reg. 47(1)(a) and (b) read as follows:
    "(a)   regulation 35 (application of section 135 of TCGA 1992),
    (b)   regulation 36 (application of section 136 of TCGA 1992), or".

Chapter 7 – The Conversion of a Non-Reporting Fund into a Reporting Fund

Consequences of conversion for participants

48(1) This regulation applies if an offshore fund ceases to be a non-reporting fund and becomes a reporting fund.

48(2) A participant in the fund may make an election to be treated–

(a) as disposing of the interest owned by the participant in the non-reporting fund at its market value on the disposal date, and

(b) as acquiring a holding in the reporting fund at the beginning of the reporting fund's first period of account.

This is subject to paragraph (5).

48(3) Chapter 5 of this Part applies to determine the offshore income gain arising on the deemed disposal referred to in paragraph (2)(a).

48(4) The deemed acquisition referred to in paragraph (2)(b) is treated as made for the same amount as the deemed disposal referred to in paragraph (2)(a).

Statutory Instruments

48(5) An election may not be made under paragraph (2) unless the offshore income gain arising on the deemed disposal referred to in paragraph (2)(a) (determined in accordance with paragraph (3)) is greater than zero.

48(6) If the participant is chargeable to income tax, the election mentioned in paragraph (2) must be made by being included in a return made for the tax year which includes the disposal date.

48(7) If the participant is chargeable to corporation tax, the election mentioned in paragraph (2) must be made by being included in the participant's company tax return for the accounting period which includes the disposal date.

48(8) In this regulation–

"company tax return" has the same meaning as in Schedule 18 to the Finance Act 1998;

the **"disposal date"** means the final day of the last period of account before the fund becomes a reporting fund.

PART 3 – REPORTING FUNDS AND THE TREATMENT OF PARTICIPANTS IN REPORTING FUNDS
Chapter 1 – Preliminary Provisions

Structure and application of this Part

History – In the heading before reg. 49, the words "and application" inserted by SI 2011/1211, reg. 22(2), with effect: for the purposes of income tax or corporation tax, for distributions made, or treated as made, on or after 27 May 2011; and for the purposes of capital gains tax or corporation tax on chargeable gains, in relation to disposals made on or after 27 May 2011.

49(1) The structure of this Part is as follows–

(a) this Chapter contains preliminary provisions;

(b) Chapter 2 deals with entry into the reporting fund regime;

(c) Chapter 3 deals with the general duties of reporting funds;

(d) Chapter 4 deals with the preparation of accounts;

(e) Chapter 5 deals with the computation of reportable income;

(f) Chapter 6 deals with transactions by certain reporting funds which are not treated as trading;

(fa) Chapter 6A deals with transparent reporting funds;

(g) Chapter 7 deals with reports to participants;

(h) Chapter 8 deals with the tax treatment of participants in reporting funds;

(i) Chapter 9 deals with the provision of information to HMRC;

(j) Chapter 10 deals with breaches of reporting fund requirements;

(k) Chapter 11 deals with leaving the reporting fund regime;

(l) Chapter 12 deals with constant NAV funds.

49(2) This Part contains provisions applying to–

(a) funds that are not constant NAV funds (see Chapters 2 to 11),

(aa) transparent reporting funds (see Chapter 6A), and

(b) constant NAV funds (see Chapter 12).

49(3) Chapters 4 to 6 do not apply to transparent reporting funds.

History – Reg. 49(1)(fa) inserted by SI 2011/1211, reg. 22(3), with effect: for the purposes of income tax or corporation tax, for distributions made, or treated as made, on or after 27 May 2011; and for the purposes of capital gains tax or corporation tax on chargeable gains, in relation to disposals made on or after 27 May 2011.
Reg. 49(2)(aa) inserted (and the "and" at the end of reg. 49(2)(a) omitted) by SI 2011/1211, reg. 22(4), with effect: for the purposes of income tax or corporation tax, for distributions made, or treated as made, on or after 27 May 2011; and for the purposes of capital gains tax or corporation tax on chargeable gains, in relation to disposals made on or after 27 May 2011.
Reg. 49(3) inserted by SI 2011/1211, reg. 22(5), with effect: for the purposes of income tax or corporation tax, for distributions made, or treated as made, on or after 27 May 2011; and for the purposes of capital gains tax or corporation tax on chargeable gains, in relation to disposals made on or after 27 May 2011.

Meaning of "reporting fund"

50 In these Regulations a **"reporting fund"** means an offshore fund to which this Part applies for a period of account.

Meaning of "equalisation arrangements", "full equalisation arrangements" and "equalisation amount"

50A   For the purposes of this Part–

(a)   a reporting fund operates equalisation arrangements if it has given a statement under regulation 53(1)(h) that it intends to operate such arrangements;

(b)   a reporting fund operates full equalisation arrangements if in relation to any interest acquired by way of initial purchase in the reporting period–

     (i)   the equalisation amount included in the consideration for the purchase is specified by the fund in a statement in writing to the participant making the acquisition, or

     (ii)   the equalisation amount per unit of interest in the fund is included in the report made available in accordance with regulation 90;

(c)   **"equalisation amount"** has the meaning given in regulation 72(2).

History – Reg. 50A inserted by SI 2011/1211, reg. 5, with effect, subject to transitional rules in SI 2011/1211, reg. 14–17: for the purposes of income tax or corporation tax, for distributions made, or treated as made, on or after 27 May 2011; and for the purposes of capital gains tax or corporation tax on chargeable gains, in relation to disposals made on or after 27 May 2011.

Chapter 2 – Entry into the Reporting Fund Regime

APPLICATIONS FOR THIS PART TO APPLY

Who may make an application

51(1)   The manager of an eligible offshore fund may make an application for this Part to apply to the fund.

51(2)   If it is proposed to establish an offshore fund which, on its establishment, is to be an eligible offshore fund, the person expected to become the manager of the fund on its establishment (the "applicant") may make an application for this Part to apply to the fund on its establishment.

51(3)   In this Part–

the **"applicant"** means the person referred to in paragraph (2);

an **"application"** means an existing fund application or a future fund application;

an **"eligible offshore fund"** means an offshore fund which is not a guaranteed return fund;

an **"existing fund application"** means an application made under paragraph (1);

a **"future fund application"** means an application made under paragraph (2);

the **"manager"**, in relation to an offshore fund, includes the manager or other person who has or is expected to have day to day control of the property of the fund.

Conversion of non-reporting fund into reporting fund

52(1)   The manager of a non-reporting fund may make an application for this Part to apply to a fund if the fund is an eligible offshore fund, and–

(a)   has never been a reporting fund, or

(b)   has been a reporting fund, but ceased to be such a fund because it gave notice under regulation 116.

52(2)   The provisions of this Part that apply to an existing fund application also apply to an application made under paragraph (1).

Contents of an application

53(1)   An application must include the following–

(a)   a statement of the first period of account for which it is proposed that this Part should apply to the fund;

(b)   an undertaking that no period of account will exceed 18 months;

(c)   a statement whether or not the fund intends to prepare its accounts in accordance with international accounting standards, and, if it does not, a statement of which generally accepted accounting practice it intends to use;

(d)   in a case in which the fund does not intend to prepare its accounts in accordance with international accounting standards, a statement specifying the entries in the fund's accounts that are considered to equate to "total comprehensive income for the period" as that expression is used in international accounting standards;

(e)   in a case in which the fund does not intend to prepare its accounts in accordance with international accounting standards, a statement specifying how the fund intends–

     (i)   to comply with regulation 66(1)(b), or

     (ii)   to calculate the adjustment required by regulation 66(2);

(f)   an undertaking to meet the requirements relating to reports to participants in the fund (see Chapter 7);

(g)   an undertaking to meet the requirements relating to the provision of information to HMRC (see Chapter 9);

(h)   a statement whether or not the fund intends to operate equalisation arrangements;

(i)   in a case in which the fund does intend to operate equalisation arrangements, a statement whether or not the fund intends to operate full equalisation arrangements;

(j)   in a case in which the fund does not intend to operate equalisation arrangements, a statement specifying whether or not the fund intends to make income adjustments in a reporting period;

(k)   in a case in which the fund intends to make income adjustments in a reporting period, a statement specifying–

     (i)   whether the fund intends to make those adjustments on the basis of reportable income (see regulation 72A) or on the basis of accounting income (see regulation 72B), and

     (ii)   the length of the computation period (see regulation 72C);

(l)   in a case in which the fund intends to make income adjustments in a reporting period on the basis of accounting income–

     (i)   a statement by the fund manager specifying how the accounting income is to be determined,

     (ii)   a statement by the fund manager that, on the basis of this determination, it is reasonable to expect that the difference between the amount of reportable income per unit calculated using this method and the amount of reportable income per unit calculated on the basis of reportable income will be 10% or less of the latter of those amounts, and

     (iii)   an undertaking by the manager to meet the requirements relating to alternative income adjustments and notice to HMRC (see regulation 72B(6)).

53(2)   An existing fund application must be accompanied by the prospectus.

53(3)   A future fund application must be accompanied by the proposed prospectus.

53(4)   The application must be in English.

53(5)   If the prospectus or the proposed prospectus (as the case may be) is not in English, it must be accompanied by an English translation.

53(6)   In the case of an offshore fund constituted in the manner described in regulation 5 or 6, the requirements of this regulation may be met by providing material which is–

(a)   applicable to an entity which includes the fund, and

(b)   relevant for the application for this Part to apply to the fund.

History – Reg. 53(1)(h), (i), (j), (k) and (l) inserted by SI 2011/1211, reg. 6, with effect, subject to transitional rules in SI 2011/1211, reg. 14–17: for the purposes of income tax or corporation tax, for distributions made, or treated as made, on or after 27 May 2011; and for the purposes of capital gains tax or corporation tax on chargeable gains, in relation to disposals made on or after 27 May 2011.

In reg. 53(1)(k)(i) and (l)(ii), the words "reportable income" substituted for the words "reported income" by SI 2013/1411, reg. 3(a), with effect from 28 June 2013 but subject to savings provision at SI 2013/1411, reg. 1; amendments do not apply in relation to a reporting period (as defined in reg. 91) which ended before 28 June 2013 if–

(a)   no report has previously been made available under reg. 90 for that reporting period, and

(b)   the manager of the fund elects by notice in writing within 10 months of the end of that reporting period that the amendments should not apply.

In reg. 53(1)(k)(i), the words "regulation 72A" substituted for the words "regulation 92A" and the words "regulation 72B" substituted for the words "regulation 92B" by SI 2013/1411, reg. 3(b) and (c), with effect from 28 June 2013 but subject to savings provision at SI 2013/1411, reg. 1; amendments do not apply in relation to a reporting period (as defined in reg. 91) which ended before 28 June 2013 if–

(a)   no report has previously been made available under reg. 90 for that reporting period, and

(b)   the manager of the fund elects by notice in writing within 10 months of the end of that reporting period that the amendments should not apply.

In reg. 53(1)(l)(ii), the words "regulation 72C" substituted for the words "regulation 92C" by SI 2013/1411, reg. 3(d), with effect from 28 June 2013 but subject to savings provision at SI 2013/1411, reg. 1; amendments do not apply in relation to a reporting period (as defined in reg. 91) which ended before 28 June 2013 if–

(a)   no report has previously been made available under reg. 90 for that reporting period, and

(b)   the manager of the fund elects by notice in writing within 10 months of the end of that reporting period that the amendments should not apply.

In reg. 53(1)(l)(iii), the words "regulation 72B(6)" substituted for the words "regulation 92B(5)" by SI 2013/1411, reg. 3(e), with effect from 28 June 2013 but subject to savings provision at SI 2013/1411, reg. 1; amendments do not apply in relation to a reporting period (as defined in reg. 91) which ended before 28 June 2013 if–

(a)   no report has previously been made available under reg. 90 for that reporting period, and

(b)   the manager of the fund elects by notice in writing within 10 months of the end of that reporting period that the amendments should not apply.

HMRC Manuals – OFM13550: list of acceptable GAAPs for Reporting Funds.

Form, timing and withdrawal of application

54(1)   An application must be made in writing to HMRC.

54(2)   The application must be received by HMRC before the later of–

(a)   the end of the first period of account for which it is proposed that this Part should apply to the fund, and

(b)   the expiry of a period of 3 months beginning with the first day on which interests in the fund are made available to investors resident in the United Kingdom.

54(3)   The application may be withdrawn–

(a)   at any time during a period beginning with the day the application is made and ending on the expiry of a period of 28 days beginning on the day on which HMRC give notice under regulation 55(1) or (5), or

(b)   at any later time, but before the end of the first reporting period, if HMRC are satisfied that the fund is not in breach of the requirements imposed by Part 3.

54(4)   The application must be withdrawn–

(a)   by the manager (in the case of an existing fund application), or

(b)   by the applicant (in the case of a future fund application).

History – Reg. 54(2) and (3) substituted by SI 2011/1211, reg. 31, with effect: for the purposes of income tax or corporation tax, for distributions made, or treated as made, on or after 27 May 2011; and for the purposes of capital gains tax or corporation tax on chargeable gains, in relation to disposals made on or after 27 May 2011. Former reg. 54(2) and (3) read as follows:

"**54(2)**   The application must be received by HMRC before the expiry of a period of three months beginning the last of–

(a)   the first day of the first period of account for which it is proposed that this Part should apply to the fund,

(b)   the day on which the first interests in the fund are issued to participants, and

(c)   in the case of an existing fund (as defined in Schedule 1), the first day on which interests in the fund are made available to investors resident in the United Kingdom.

54(3)   The application may be withdrawn at any time during a period beginning with the day the application is made and ending on the expiry of a period of 28 days beginning with the day on which HMRC give notice under regulation 55(1)."

In former reg. 54(2) the words from "the last of" to the end substituted for the words "with the first day of the first period of account for which it is proposed that this Part should apply to the fund." by SI 2009/3139, reg. 3, with effect: (for the purposes of income tax) for the tax year 2009–10 and subsequent tax years and for distributions made on or after 1 December 2009; (for the purposes of corporation tax on income) for accounting periods ending on or after 1 December 2009 and for distributions made on or after that date; and (for the purposes of capital gains tax or corporation tax on chargeable gains) in relation to disposals made on or after 1 December 2009.

PROCEDURE ON APPLICATIONS

Response by HMRC to application

55(1)   Within 28 days beginning with the day on which HMRC receive the application, HMRC must give notice to the person who made the application–

(a)   accepting the application,

(b)   rejecting the application, or

(c)   asking for further information in order to consider the application.

55(2)   HMRC must not accept an application if any item mentioned in regulation 53 is not supplied.

55(3)   HMRC must not accept an application if they consider that there will be a significant difference, in computing reportable income (see Chapter 5 or 6A), between–

(a)   the result given by the use of international accounting standards, and

(b)   the result given by the use of the accounting practice specified in the application and by the use of the entries in the fund's accounts, specified in the application, that are considered to equate to "total comprehensive income for the period" as that expression is used in international accounting standards (see regulation 63).

55(3A)   Where the fund intends to make income adjustments on the basis of accounting income (see regulation 53(1)(l)), HMRC must not accept an application if they do not consider that it is reasonable to expect that the difference between the amount of reportable income per unit calculated using this method and the amount of reportable income per unit calculated on the basis of reportable income will be 10% or less of the latter of those amounts.

55(4)   Paragraph (5) applies if–

(a)   HMRC have given notice under paragraph (1)(c), and

Statutory Instruments

(b)   the person who made the application provides further information within a period of 28 days beginning with the day on which HMRC ask for further information, or within such longer period as is agreed by HMRC.

55(5)   Within 28 days beginning with the day on which HMRC receive the further information, HMRC must give notice to the person who made the application–

(a)   accepting the application, or

(b)   rejecting the application.

History – In reg. 55(3), "or 6A" inserted by SI 2011/1211, reg. 7(2), with effect, subject to transitional rules in SI 2011/1211, reg. 14–17: for the purposes of income tax or corporation tax, for distributions made, or treated as made, on or after 27 May 2011; and for the purposes of capital gains tax or corporation tax on chargeable gains, in relation to disposals made on or after 27 May 2011.

In reg. 55(3A), the words "reportable income" substituted for the words "reported income" by SI 2013/1411, reg. 4, with effect from 28 June 2013 but subject to savings provision at SI 2013/1411, reg. 1; amendments do not apply in relation to a reporting period (as defined in reg. 91) which ended before 28 June 2013 if–
   (a)   no report has previously been made available under reg. 90 for that reporting period, and
   (b)   the manager of the fund elects by notice in writing within 10 months of the end of that reporting period that the amendments should not apply.

Reg. 55(3A) inserted by SI 2011/1211, reg. 7(3), with effect, subject to transitional rules in SI 2011/1211, reg. 14–17: for the purposes of income tax or corporation tax, for distributions made, or treated as made, on or after 27 May 2011; and for the purposes of capital gains tax or corporation tax on chargeable gains, in relation to disposals made on or after 27 May 2011.

Appeal against rejection of application

56(1)   If HMRC reject an application, the person who made the application may appeal.

56(2)   The notice of appeal must be given to HMRC within a period of 42 days beginning with the day on which the notice rejecting the application is given.

56(3)   On an appeal, the tribunal may uphold or quash the rejection of the application.

56(4)   If the tribunal quashes the rejection of the application, this Part applies as if HMRC had accepted the application in the form in which it was considered by the tribunal.

Chapter 2A – Amendment to Application for this Part to Apply

History – Ch. 2A inserted by SI 2011/1211, reg. 8 with effect, subject to transitional rules in SI 2011/1211, reg. 14–17: for the purposes of income tax or corporation tax, for distributions made, or treated as made, on or after 27 May 2011; and for the purposes of capital gains tax or corporation tax on chargeable gains, in relation to disposals made on or after 27 May 2011.

AMENDING A STATEMENT RELATING TO EQUALISATION

56A(1)   The manager of a reporting fund may apply to amend any statement under regulation 53(1)(h) to (l) in relation to a reporting period and subsequent reporting periods by application in writing to HMRC before the end of the first reporting period in relation to which the amendment is to have effect.

56A(2)   Paragraphs (4) to (8) do not apply in relation to an application to amend a statement under regulation 53(1)(h) and (i) or under regulation 53(1)(i) if the amendment sought is that the fund intends to operate full equalisation arrangements.

56A(3)   An application to which paragraph (2) applies must be accepted by HMRC within 28 days beginning with the day on which HMRC receive the application.

56A(4)   An application under paragraph (1) must specify–

(a)   the reason for the application,

(b)   the amendment sought to the statement, and

(c)   the first reporting period in which the amendment is to apply.

56A(5)   Within 28 days beginning with the day on which HMRC receive the application, HMRC must give notice to the manager–

(a)   accepting the application,

(b)   rejecting the application, or

(c)   asking for further information in order to consider the application.

56A(6)   HMRC must not accept an application if–

(a)   they consider the application is made for reasons other than commercial or administrative reasons, or

(b)   an application was accepted under this regulation in relation to either of the previous two reporting periods.

56A(7)   Paragraph (8) applies if–

(a)   HMRC have given notice under paragraph (5)(c), and

(b)   the manager provides further information within a period of 28 days beginning with the day on which HMRC ask for further information or within such longer period as is agreed by HMRC.

56A(8) Within 28 days beginning with the day on which HMRC receive the further information, HMRC must give notice to the manager–

(a)   accepting the application, or

(b)   rejecting the application.

History – Reg. 56A inserted by SI 2011/1211, reg. 8 with effect, subject to transitional rules in SI 2011/1211, reg. 14–17: for the purposes of income tax or corporation tax, for distributions made, or treated as made, on or after 27 May 2011; and for the purposes of capital gains tax or corporation tax on chargeable gains, in relation to disposals made on or after 27 May 2011.

APPEAL AGAINST REFUSAL OF APPLICATION TO AMEND A STATEMENT

56B(1) If HMRC reject an application the manager may appeal.

56B(2) The notice of appeal must be given to HMRC within a period of 42 days beginning with the day on which the notice rejecting the application is given.

56B(3) On an appeal, the tribunal may uphold or quash the rejection of the application.

56B(4) If the tribunal quashes the rejection of the application, this Part applies as if HMRC had accepted the application.

History – Reg. 56B inserted by SI 2011/1211, reg. 8 with effect, subject to transitional rules in SI 2011/1211, reg. 14–17: for the purposes of income tax or corporation tax, for distributions made, or treated as made, on or after 27 May 2011; and for the purposes of capital gains tax or corporation tax on chargeable gains, in relation to disposals made on or after 27 May 2011.

Chapter 3 – The General Duties of Reporting Funds

Effects of entry into the reporting fund regime

57(1) If HMRC accept an application, the offshore fund becomes a reporting fund on whichever is the later of–

(a)   the first day of the first period of account mentioned in regulation 53(1)(a), or

(b)   the day on which the fund is established.

This paragraph and paragraphs (2) and (3) are subject to paragraph (4).

57(2) This Part applies to the fund and to its participants on and after the date specified in paragraph (1).

57(3) Once this Part has begun to apply to a fund, it shall continue to apply unless and until it ceases to apply in accordance with Chapter 11 of this Part.

57(4) Where an application has been withdrawn under regulation 54(3)(b), the fund and its participants shall be treated as if the fund had never been a reporting fund.

History – In reg. 57(1), the words "This paragraph and paragraphs (2) and (3) are subject to paragraph (4)." inserted by SI 2011/1211, reg. 32(2), with effect: for the purposes of income tax or corporation tax, for distributions made, or treated as made, on or after 27 May 2011; and for the purposes of capital gains tax or corporation tax on chargeable gains, in relation to disposals made on or after 27 May 2011.
Reg. 57(4) inserted by SI 2011/1211, reg. 32(3), with effect: for the purposes of income tax or corporation tax, for distributions made, or treated as made, on or after 27 May 2011; and for the purposes of capital gains tax or corporation tax on chargeable gains, in relation to disposals made on or after 27 May 2011.

General duties of reporting funds

58 A reporting fund must–

(a)   prepare accounts in accordance with the requirements of Chapter 4 (except in the case of transparent reporting funds);

(b)   provide a computation of its reportable income in accordance with the requirements of Chapter 5 or 6A, as the case may be;

(c)   provide reports to participants in accordance with the requirements of Chapter 7; and

(d)   provide information to HMRC in accordance with the requirements of Chapter 9.

History – In reg. 58(a), the words "(except in the case of transparent reporting funds)" inserted by SI 2011/1211, reg. 23(2), with effect: for the purposes of income tax or corporation tax, for distributions made, or treated as made, on or after 27 May 2011; and for the purposes of capital gains tax or corporation tax on chargeable gains, in relation to disposals made on or after 27 May 2011.
In reg. 58(b), the words "or 6A, as the case may be" inserted by SI 2011/1211, reg. 23(3), with effect: for the purposes of income tax or corporation tax, for distributions made, or treated as made, on or after 27 May 2011; and for the purposes of capital gains tax or corporation tax on chargeable gains, in relation to disposals made on or after 27 May 2011.

Chapter 4 – The Preparation of Accounts

Accounts to be prepared in accordance with acceptable accounting policy

59 A reporting fund must prepare accounts–

(a) in accordance with international accounting standards, or

(b) in accordance with the generally accepted accounting practice specified in the application.

HMRC Manuals – OFM13550: list of acceptable GAAPs for Reporting Funds.

Change in accounting policy

60(1) This regulation applies if–

(a) there is a change of accounting policy in drawing up a reporting fund's accounts from one period of account (in this Chapter called the "earlier period") to the next (in this Chapter called the "later period"), and

(b) the approach in each of those periods accords with the law and practice applicable in relation to that period.

60(2) If there is a difference between–

(a) the accounting value of an asset or liability of the offshore fund at the end of the earlier period, and

(b) the accounting value of that asset or liability at the beginning of the later period,

a corresponding debit or credit (as the case may be) must be brought into account for the purposes of these Regulations in the later period.

60(3) In paragraph (2) **"accounting value"** means the carrying value of the asset or liability recognised for accounting purposes.

Change in accounting practice to a generally accepted accounting practice

61(1) This regulation applies if–

(a) there is a change of accounting practice in drawing up a reporting fund's accounts from the earlier period to the later period, and

(b) the fund prepares accounts for the later period in accordance with a generally accepted accounting practice.

61(2) If the accounts for the later period are not prepared in accordance with international accounting standards, the offshore fund must give notice to HMRC–

(a) applying for approval of the generally accepted accounting practice, and

(b) providing the statement mentioned in regulation 53(1)(d).

61(3) If the accounts for the later period are prepared in accordance with international accounting standards, the offshore fund must give notice to HMRC.

61(4) Within 28 days beginning with the day on which HMRC receive an application under paragraph (2), HMRC must give notice to the offshore fund–

(a) accepting the application, or

(b) rejecting the application.

61(5) If HMRC reject an application, the offshore fund may appeal.

61(6) The notice of appeal must be given to HMRC within a period of 42 days beginning with the day on which the notice rejecting the application is given.

61(7) On an appeal, the tribunal may uphold or quash the rejection of the application.

Chapter 5 – The Computation of Reportable Income

GENERAL

Duty to provide computation

62(1) This Chapter explains how reportable income is computed.

62(2) A reporting fund must provide a computation of its reportable income for a period of account.

Computation of reportable income: general

63(1) The starting point for computing the reportable income of a reporting fund for a period of account is—

(a) in a case in which the fund prepares its accounts in accordance with international accounting standards, the "total comprehensive income for the period" as that expression is used in international accounting standards, or

(b) in any other case, the entries in the fund's accounts that are considered to equate to "total comprehensive income for the period" as that expression is used in international accounting standards.

63(2) The starting point specified in paragraph (1) must be adjusted having regard to—

(a) capital items (see regulations 64 and 65),

(b) special classes of income (see regulations 66 to 71), and

(c) any arrangements to adjust income based on the number of units in issue (see regulations 72 to 72B).

63(3) In the case of any one item, an adjustment under paragraph (2) may be made only once (even if more than one of the regulations mentioned in that paragraph apply to that item).

63(4) The reportable income of the reporting fund for the period of account is the amount computed in accordance with the provisions of this Chapter and of Chapter 6.

63(5) But if the computation gives rise to a negative amount, the reportable income is nil.

History – Reg. 63(2)(c) substituted by SI 2013/1411, reg. 5, with effect from 28 June 2013 but subject to savings provision at SI 2013/1411, reg. 1; amendments do not apply in relation to a reporting period (as defined in reg. 91) which ended before 28 June 2013 if—

(a) no report has previously been made available under reg. 90 for that reporting period, and

(b) the manager of the fund elects by notice in writing within 10 months of the end of that reporting period that the amendments should not apply.

Former reg. 63(2)(c) read as follows:

"(c) equalisation arrangements (see regulation 72).".

HMRC Manuals – OFM13550: list of acceptable GAAPs for Reporting Funds.

ADJUSTMENTS FOR CAPITAL ITEMS

Treatment of capital items following IMA SORP

64(1) The capital items for which an adjustment is required are such profits, gains or losses as would fall to be dealt with under the heading "net capital gains/losses" in the statement of total return for the period of account if the accounts for that period were to be prepared in accordance with the IMA SORP.

64(2) The amount specified in regulation 63(1) must be adjusted by—

(a) deducting gains that fall within the heading specified in paragraph (1), and

(b) adding losses that fall within that heading.

64(3) A profit or loss from a trade may not be treated as a capital item for the purposes of this regulation.

This paragraph is subject to regulation 80.

64(4) For the purposes of paragraph (1) the IMA SORP applies to determine the "net capital gains/losses" of an offshore fund for a period of account in the same way that it applies to determine the "net capital gains/losses" of an authorised investment fund for an accounting period.

64(5) In this regulation—

"authorised investment fund" has the meaning given in the Authorised Investment Funds (Tax) Regulations 2006;

"the IMA SORP" means, in relation to any period of account for which it is required or permitted to be used, the Statement of Recognised Practice relating to authorised investment funds issued by the Investment Management Association in November 2008, as from time to time modified, amended or revised.

Treatment of other capital items

65(1) The amount specified in regulation 63(1) must also be adjusted by adding the amounts specified in paragraph (2).

65(2) Those amounts are—

(a) expenses directly related to acquisition or disposal of investments (other than those taken into account in arriving at the amounts specified in sub-paragraph (a) or (b) of regulation 64(2)), and

(b) costs relating to the setting up, merger or dissolution of the fund.

ADJUSTMENTS FOR SPECIAL CLASSES OF INCOME

Effective interest income or comparable amounts

66(1) This regulation applies if the accounting practice used does not include–

(a) the effective interest method for computing interest income (as described in international accounting standard 39 and equivalent United Kingdom financial reporting standards), or

(b) another method of accounting for interest in such a way that the difference between the purchase price of an asset and the expected redemption price of the asset is taken into account as part of the interest income over the expected life of the asset.

66(2) The amount specified in regulation 63(1) must be adjusted by the addition of the net income computed by taking into account the expected redemption price of any interest bearing assets over the expected life of the asset.

66(3) The sum mentioned in paragraph (2) may be computed by any reasonable method which–

(a) takes into account the full expected gain or loss on the asset, and

(b) gives a reasonably comparable result to the effective interest method.

Income from wholly-owned subsidiaries

67(1) This regulation applies if a reporting fund has a wholly-owned subsidiary.

67(2) For the purposes of this regulation, a company is a wholly-owned subsidiary of an offshore fund if and so long as the whole of the issued share capital of the company is–

(a) in the case of an offshore fund falling within paragraph (a) of the definition of "offshore fund" in section 40A(2) of FA 2008, directly or indirectly owned by the fund;

(b) in the case of an offshore fund falling within paragraph (b) of the definition of "offshore fund" in that enactment, directly or indirectly owned by the trustees of the fund for the benefit of the fund;

(c) in the case of an offshore fund falling within paragraph (c) of the definition of "offshore fund" in that enactment, owned in a manner which, as near as may be, corresponds either to paragraph (a) or paragraph (b) above.

67(3) But in the case of a company which has only one class of issued share capital, the reference in paragraph (2) to the whole of the issued share capital shall be construed as a reference to at least 95% of that share capital.

67(4) That percentage of the receipts, expenditure, assets and liabilities of the subsidiary which is equal to the percentage of the issued share capital of the company concerned which is owned as mentioned in paragraph (2) shall be regarded as the receipts, expenditure, assets and liabilities of the fund.

67(5) There shall be left out of account–

(a) the interest of the fund in the subsidiary, and

(b) any distributions or other payments made by the subsidiary to the fund or by the fund to the subsidiary.

67(6) The adjustments required under regulations 64 and 65 must be made to the amount determined under paragraph (4).

History – In reg. 67(2)(a), the words "or indirectly" substituted for the words "and beneficially" by SI 2011/1211, reg. 33(a), with effect: for the purposes of income tax or corporation tax, for distributions made, or treated as made, on or after 27 May 2011; and for the purposes of capital gains tax or corporation tax on chargeable gains, in relation to disposals made on or after 27 May 2011. In reg. 67(2)(b), the words "or indirectly" inserted by SI 2011/1211, reg. 33(b), with effect: for the purposes of income tax or corporation tax, for distributions made, or treated as made, on or after 27 May 2011; and for the purposes of capital gains tax or corporation tax on chargeable gains, in relation to disposals made on or after 27 May 2011.

Income from other reporting funds

68(1) This regulation applies if a reporting fund ("RF1") has an interest in another reporting fund ("RF2").

68(2) The excess (if any) of the income reported by RF2 in respect of RF1's interest in RF2 over the amount distributed by RF2 to RF1 must be added by RF1 to the amount specified in regulation 63(1) after making the adjustments specified in regulations 64 and 65.

68(3) The adjustment specified in paragraph (2) must be made in the computation of the reportable income of RF1 for the period of account in which the fund distribution date of RF2 falls or, if earlier, in which the date on which the reported income from RF2 in respect of that reporting period is recognised in the accounts of RF1.

68(4) [Omitted by SI 2011/1211, reg. 34(3).]

68(5)　If RF2 does not make a report available in accordance with regulation 90(5), RF1 must–

(a)　include its best estimate of reported income from RF2 as an adjustment to the computation of its reportable income for the period of account in which the latest possible fund distribution date for RF2 falls (to the extent that any such amount has not already been recognised in the computation of RF1's reportable income for that or any earlier period of account), and

(b)　make any necessary corrections to its best estimate in its computation of reportable income for the first later period of account in which it has sufficient information to make those corrections.

History – In reg. 68(3), the words "in which the fund distribution date of RF2 falls or, if earlier, in which the date on which the reported income from RF2 in respect of that reporting period is recognised in the accounts of RF1" substituted for the words "specified in paragraphs (4) and (5)" by SI 2011/1211, reg. 34(2), with effect: for the purposes of income tax or corporation tax, for distributions made, or treated as made, on or after 27 May 2011; and for the purposes of capital gains tax or corporation tax on chargeable gains, in relation to disposals made on or after 27 May 2011.
Reg. 68(4) omitted by SI 2011/1211, reg. 34(3), with effect: for the purposes of income tax or corporation tax, for distributions made, or treated as made, on or after 27 May 2011; and for the purposes of capital gains tax or corporation tax on chargeable gains, in relation to disposals made on or after 27 May 2011. Former reg. 68(4) read as follows:

"**68(4)**　The basic rule is that the period of account specified for the purposes of this regulation is the period of account in which the fund distribution date of RF2 falls.

The basic rule is subject to paragraph (5).".

In reg. 68(5), the words "RF2 does not make a report available in accordance with regulation 90(5)" substituted for the words "the fund distribution date of RF2 is determined in accordance with regulation 94(4)(b)" by SI 2011/1211, reg. 34(4), with effect: for the purposes of income tax or corporation tax, for distributions made, or treated as made, on or after 27 May 2011; and for the purposes of capital gains tax or corporation tax on chargeable gains, in relation to disposals made on or after 27 May 2011.

Index tracking funds

68A(1)　This regulation applies if–

(a)　a reporting fund has an interest in a non-reporting fund, and

(b)　the conditions in paragraph (2) are met for a period of account.

68A(2)　The conditions are that–

(a)　in accordance with the reporting fund's rule or the instrument constituting the reporting fund, the aim of the fund's investment policy is to replicate the performance of a qualifying index,

(b)　the main purpose of the investment in the non-reporting fund is to represent the composition of the qualifying index, and

(c)　the capital and income returns of the reporting fund replicate as closely as practicable the returns of the investments comprised in the qualifying index

68A(3)　For the purposes of paragraph (2) an index is a **"qualifying index"** if–

(a)　it is based solely on the value of securities listed on a recognised stock exchange or admitted to trading on a regulated market,

(b)　an authority responsible for regulating offshore funds recognises the index on the basis that–

(i)　its composition is sufficiently diverse,

(ii)　it represents an adequate benchmark for the market to which it refers, and

(iii)　it is published in such a way that it is widely available, and

(c)　it is calculated and published by a body which is managed independently from the management of the reporting fund.

68A(4)　Regulations 69 to 71 do not apply in respect of the interest in the non-reporting fund.

History – Reg. 68A inserted by SI 2011/1211, reg. 35, with effect: for the purposes of income tax or corporation tax, for distributions made, or treated as made, on or after 27 May 2011; and for the purposes of capital gains tax or corporation tax on chargeable gains, in relation to disposals made on or after 27 May 2011.

Income from non-reporting funds: first case

69(1)　This regulation applies if–

(a)　a reporting fund has an interest in a non-reporting fund, and

(b)　the conditions in paragraph (2) are met for a period of account.

69(2)　The conditions are that–

(a)　[omitted by SI 2011/1211, reg. 36(2);]

(b)　the reporting fund has access to the accounts of the non-reporting fund;

(c)　the reporting fund has sufficient information about the non-reporting fund to enable it to prepare a computation of reportable income for the non-reporting fund; and

(d)　the reporting fund can reasonably expect to be able to rely on continued access to that information for the period in which it will hold the investment in the non-reporting fund.

69(3) Regulation 68(1) to (3) applies as if the reporting fund were RF1 and the non-reporting fund were RF2.

69(4) For the purposes of the computation mentioned in paragraph (2)(c), regulation 80 applies if (and only if) the non-reporting fund is a UCITS fund.

69(5) For the purposes of applying regulation 68, **"fund distribution date"** means the date six months after the end of the period of account in which the income arose.

69(6) If the period of account referred to in paragraph (5) is more than 12 months, there shall be two periods of account and two fund distribution dates for the purposes of applying regulation 68.

The first fund distribution date is the date six months after the end of the first 12 months in the period of account.

The second fund distribution date is the date six months after the end of the period of account in which the income arose.

History – Reg. 69(2)(a) omitted by SI 2011/1211, reg. 36(2), with effect: for the purposes of income tax or corporation tax, for distributions made, or treated as made, on or after 27 May 2011; and for the purposes of capital gains tax or corporation tax on chargeable gains, in relation to disposals made on or after 27 May 2011. Former reg. 69(2)(a) read as follows:

"(a)   the main purpose or one of the main purposes of the investment in the non-reporting fund is not the deferral or avoidance of United Kingdom tax;".

In reg. 69(3), "68(1) to (3)" substituted for "68" by SI 2011/1211, reg. 36(3), with effect: for the purposes of income tax or corporation tax, for distributions made, or treated as made, on or after 27 May 2011; and for the purposes of capital gains tax or corporation tax on chargeable gains, in relation to disposals made on or after 27 May 2011.

Reg. 69(5) and (6) inserted by SI 2011/1211, reg. 36(4), with effect: for the purposes of income tax or corporation tax, for distributions made, or treated as made, on or after 27 May 2011; and for the purposes of capital gains tax or corporation tax on chargeable gains, in relation to disposals made on or after 27 May 2011.

Income from non-reporting funds: second case

70(1) This regulation applies if a reporting fund has an interest in a non-reporting fund, but the conditions in regulation 69(2) are not met for a period of account.

70(2) No adjustments may be made under regulations 64 and 65 in respect of the interest in the non-reporting fund.

70(3) But if the condition specified in paragraph (4) is met, losses made by a reporting fund in earlier periods of account on an investment in a non-reporting fund may be set against gains made on the investment in the non-reporting fund to reduce the reportable income of the reporting fund, but only to the extent that the losses–

(a)   have not previously had the effect of reducing income for the period of account in which they were incurred, or

(b)   have not been used previously to reduce gains arising to the non-reporting fund.

70(4) The condition specified is that the losses in earlier periods of account were all made during periods in which this Part applied continuously to the reporting fund.

Income from non-reporting funds if first case ceases to apply

71(1) This regulation applies if–

(a)   a reporting fund has an interest in a non-reporting fund, and

(b)   the conditions in regulation 69(2) have been met for an earlier period of account but are no longer met for a later period of account.

71(2) Regulation 70 applies for the later period of account and for all subsequent periods of account.

ADJUSTMENTS FOR EQUALISATION ARRANGEMENTS

Treatment of reporting funds operating equalisation arrangements

72(1) This regulation applies if a reporting fund operates equalisation arrangements.

72(2) If a person acquires an interest in the fund by way of initial purchase, the reportable income must be increased by an amount equal to that part of the acquisition price which is attributable to the undistributed income which has accrued to the fund in the period of account up to the time of the acquisition and which is taken into account in determining the acquisition price ("the equalisation amount").

72(3) If a participant disposes of an interest in the fund by way of redemption, the reportable income must be reduced by an amount equal to that part of the redemption price which is attributable to the undistributed income which has accrued to the fund in the period of account up to the time of the redemption and which is taken into account in determining the redemption price.

72(4) For the purposes of these Regulations a person acquires an interest in an offshore fund by way of initial purchase if the acquisition is by way of subscription for or allotment of new shares, units or other interests issued or created by the fund or by way of direct purchase from the managers of the fund acting in their capacity as managers of the fund.

72(5) For the purposes of this regulation a person disposes of an interest in a fund by way of redemption if the disposal is by way of cancellation of the units, shares or other interest or by way of direct sale to the managers of the fund acting in their capacity as managers of the fund.

History – Reg. 72 substituted by SI 2011/1211, reg. 9 with effect, subject to transitional rules in SI 2011/1211, reg. 14–17: for the purposes of income tax or corporation tax, for distributions made, or treated as made, on or after 27 May 2011; and for the purposes of capital gains tax or corporation tax on chargeable gains, in relation to disposals made on or after 27 May 2011. Former reg. 72 read as follows:

"**72(1)** This regulation applies if, in a period of account–
(a) a reporting fund operates equalisation arrangements, and
(b) a participant disposes of an interest in the fund.
72(2) For the purposes of this regulation, an offshore fund operates equalisation arrangements if, and at a time when, arrangements are in existence which have the result that where–
(a) a person ("X") acquires by way of initial purchase an interest in the fund at some time during a period relevant to the arrangements, and
(b) the fund makes a distribution for a period which begins before the date of X's acquisition of that interest, the amount of that distribution which is paid to X (assuming X still to retain that interest) will include a payment of capital which is debited to an account maintained under the arrangements (the "equalisation account") and which is determined by reference to the income which had accrued to the fund at the date of X's acquisition.
72(3) For the purposes of this regulation, a person ("X") acquires an interest in an offshore fund by way of initial purchase if–
(a) X's acquisition is by way of subscription for or allotment of new shares, units or other interests issued or created by the fund, or
(b) X's acquisition is by way of direct purchase from the managers of the fund and their sale to X is made in their capacity as managers of the fund.
72(4) For the purposes of calculating reportable income, there must be a deduction of an amount equal to so much of the consideration for the disposal as represents the amount which would be credited to the equalisation account of the offshore fund if, on the same date, a holding of the same size were to be acquired by another person by way of initial purchase.
72(5) But if the disposal mentioned in paragraph (4) is of a holding of units or shares which were issued within the same period of account as that in which the disposal takes place, the deduction must be limited to the income accrued or arising to those units or shares since issue.".

ADJUSTMENTS WHERE FUNDS DO NOT OPERATE EQUALISATION ARRANGEMENTS

Reporting Funds not operating equalisation: income adjustments based on reportable income for computation periods

72A(1) This regulation applies if a reporting fund does not operate equalisation arrangements and–
(a) the fund has given a statement under regulation 53(1)(k) that it intends to make income adjustments in a reporting period on the basis of reportable income, or
(b) regulation 72B(7) applies.

72A(2) The reportable income of the fund for a reporting period is the sum of the reportable income per unit for all the computation periods in the reporting period multiplied by the number of units in the fund in issue at the end of the reporting period.

72A(3) But if the sum results in a negative amount, the reportable income for that period is nil.

72A(4) Where a period of account consists of two reporting periods, the reportable income for the period of account is the sum of the reportable income for both those reporting periods.

72A(5) The reportable income per unit for a computation period is calculated by dividing the reportable income of the fund for the computation period by the average number of units in the fund in issue during the computation period.

72A(6) For the purposes of paragraph (5), the reportable income of the fund for a computation period means the reportable income of the fund for that period computed in accordance with this Chapter (ignoring regulation 63(5) and this regulation) and Chapter 6 of this Part.

72A(7) In the computation referred to in paragraph (6), this Chapter and Chapter 6 of this Part apply as if references to a period of account of the fund were references to a computation period.

History – Reg. 72A inserted by SI 2013/1411, reg. 6, with effect from 28 June 2013 but subject to savings provision at SI 2013/1411, reg. 1; amendments do not apply in relation to a reporting period which ended before that date if–
(a) no report has previously been made available under reg. 90 for that reporting period (as defined in reg. 91), and
(b) the manager of the fund elects by notice in writing within 10 months of the end of that reporting period that the amendments should not apply.

Reporting Funds not operating equalisation: income adjustments based on accounting income for computation periods

72B(1) This regulation applies if a reporting fund does not operate equalisation arrangements and the fund has given a statement under regulation 53(1)(k) that it intends to make income adjustments in a reporting period on the basis of accounting income.

72B(2) The reportable income of the fund for a reporting period is calculated as follows–

$$(AIU \times RI/AI) \times U$$

where–

AIU is the sum of the accounting income per unit for all the computation periods in the reporting period,

RI is the reportable income of the fund for the reporting period computed in accordance with this Chapter (ignoring this regulation), Chapter 6 of this Part and regulation 93,

AI is the sum of accounting income for all the computation periods in the reporting period, and

U is the number of units in the fund in issue at the end of the reporting period.

This is subject to paragraphs (6) and (7).

72B(3) Where a period of account consists of two reporting periods, the reportable income for the period of account is the sum of the reportable income for both those reporting periods.

72B(4) But if the sum results in a negative amount, the reportable income for that period is nil.

72B(5) The accounting income per unit for a computation period is calculated by dividing accounting income for the computation period by the average number of units in the fund in issue during the computation period.

72B(6) Where RI is zero the reportable income per unit of the fund for a reporting period is zero.

72B(7) Where the difference in the amount of reportable income per unit for any reporting period in a period of account calculated using this method and the amount of reportable income per unit for that reporting period calculated on the basis of reportable income is or is likely to be more than 10% of the latter of those amounts–

(a)   the fund must make income adjustments in that and future periods of account on the basis of reportable income, and

(b)   the manager must give notice to HMRC of the change in the method of income adjustment with the information provided to HMRC in relation to that period under regulation 106 (reporting requirements).

72B(8) In this Part **"accounting income"** means an amount proportionally related to the reportable income of the fund determined from the interim or management accounts of the fund, but this amount must not be less than zero.

History – Reg. 72B inserted by SI 2013/1411, reg. 6, with effect from 28 June 2013 but subject to savings provision at SI 2013/1411, reg. 1; amendments do not apply in relation to a reporting period which ended before that date if–
(a)   no report has previously been made available under reg. 90 for that reporting period (as defined in reg. 91), and
(b)   the manager of the fund elects by notice in writing within 10 months of the end of that reporting period that the amendments should not apply.

Supplementary provisions: average number of units and computation period

72C(1) For the purposes of regulations 72A(5) and 72B(5), the average number of units in the fund in issue during the computation period is the sum of the units in the fund in issue during the period after each unit has been multiplied by the fraction of the period for which it is held.

72C(2) In this Part a **"computation period"** means a period determined by a fund in accordance with the following rules.

Rule 1

A new computation period must start–

(a)   at the beginning of a reporting period, and

(b)   immediately after the end of a previous computation period.

Rule 2

A computation period must end–

(a)   at the end of a reporting period, and

(b)   at the end of a period in relation to which income is allocated to participants for distribution or accumulation.

Rule 3

If a reporting period consists of more than one computation period those periods must be of approximately equal length.

History – Reg. 72C inserted by SI 2013/1411, reg. 6, with effect from 28 June 2013 but subject to savings provision at SI 2013/1411, reg. 1; amendments do not apply in relation to a reporting period which ended before that date if–

   (a)   no report has previously been made available under reg. 90 for that reporting period (as defined in reg. 91), and

   (b)   the manager of the fund elects by notice in writing within 10 months of the end of that reporting period that the amendments should not apply.

Chapter 6 – Transactions by Certain Reporting Funds Which are not Treated as Trading

CONDITIONS TO BE MET BY REPORTING FUNDS FOR THIS CHAPTER TO APPLY

Introductory

Other material – M04/2010: HMRC confirmation that Ch. 6 has no relevance to matters relating to the taxation of funds potentially trading in the UK though a permanent establishment or agent

73(1)   A reporting fund meets the conditions for this Chapter to apply in respect of a period of account if it meets–

(a)   the equivalence condition (see regulation 74), and

(b)   the genuine diversity of ownership condition (see regulations 75 and 76).

73(2)   In this Part a **"diversely owned fund"** means a reporting fund in respect of which the conditions mentioned in paragraph (1) are met for a period of account.

The equivalence condition

74(1)   The equivalence condition is met if the fund meets condition A, B or C throughout the period of account.

74(2)   Condition A is that the fund is recognised by the Financial Services Authority within the meaning of section 264 or 272 of FISMA 2000.

74(3)   Condition B is that the fund is a UCITS fund.

74(4)   Condition C is that the fund–

(a)   is constituted in another EEA state and authorised by the competent authority in that state to market to retail or professional investors, and

(b)   is required either by the competent authority in that state or by other binding arrangements to limit its borrowing and its exposure under derivative contracts and forward transactions to 100% of its net asset value.

74(5)   In paragraph (4), the competent authority in an EEA state is the authority designated in accordance with Article 97 of Council Directive 2009/65/EC in relation to that fund.

History – In reg. 74(1), ", B or C" substituted for "or B" by SI 2011/1211, reg. 37(2), with effect: for the purposes of income tax or corporation tax, for distributions made, or treated as made, on or after 27 May 2011; and for the purposes of capital gains tax or corporation tax on chargeable gains, in relation to disposals made on or after 27 May 2011.
In reg. 74(2), ", 270" omitted by SI 2013/1773, reg. 81 and Sch. 2, para. 20, with effect from 22 July 2013.
Reg. 74(4) and (5) inserted by SI 2011/1211, reg. 37(3), with effect: for the purposes of income tax or corporation tax, for distributions made, or treated as made, on or after 27 May 2011; and for the purposes of capital gains tax or corporation tax on chargeable gains, in relation to disposals made on or after 27 May 2011.

The genuine diversity of ownership condition

75(1)   The genuine diversity of ownership condition is met if the fund meets, or, in relation to a fund constituted by a class of interests in the main arrangements, the main arrangements meet, conditions A to C throughout the period of account.

75(2)   Condition A is that the fund produces documents, available to investors and to HMRC, which contain–

(a)   a statement specifying the intended categories of investor,

(b)   an undertaking that interests in the fund will be widely available, and

(c)   an undertaking that interests in the fund will be marketed and made available in accordance with the requirements of paragraph (4)(a).

75(3)   Condition B is–

(a)   that the specification of the intended categories of investor do not have a limiting or deterrent effect, and

(b)   that any other terms or conditions governing participation in the fund do not have a limiting or deterrent effect.

75(4)   Condition C is–

(a)   that interests in the fund must be marketed and made available–

    (i)   sufficiently widely to reach the intended categories of investors, and

    (ii)   in a manner appropriate to attract those categories of investors, and

(b)   that a person who falls within one of the intended categories of investors can, upon request to the manager of this fund, obtain information about the fund and acquire units in it.

75(5)   A fund also meets the genuine diversity of ownership condition if–

(a)   an investor in the fund is an offshore fund, an open-ended investment company or an authorised unit trust scheme ("the feeder fund"),

(b)   conditions A to C are met in relation to the fund after taking into account–

    (i)   the fund documents relating to the feeder fund, and

    (ii)   the intended investors in the feeder fund, and

(c)   the fund and the feeder fund have the same manager (or proposed manager).

History – In reg. 75(1), the words ", or, in relation to a fund constituted by a class of interests in the main arrangements, the main arrangements meet," inserted by SI 2011/1211, reg. 38(2), with effect: for the purposes of income tax or corporation tax, for distributions made, or treated as made, on or after 27 May 2011; and for the purposes of capital gains tax or corporation tax on chargeable gains, in relation to disposals made on or after 27 May 2011.

Reg. 75(5) inserted by SI 2011/1211, reg. 37(3), with effect: for the purposes of income tax or corporation tax, for distributions made, or treated as made, on or after 27 May 2011; and for the purposes of capital gains tax or corporation tax on chargeable gains, in relation to disposals made on or after 27 May 2011.

The genuine diversity of ownership condition: further provisions

76(1)   For the purposes of regulation 75(3) a limiting or deterring effect means an effect which–

(a)   limits investors to a limited number of specific persons or specific groups of connected persons, or

(b)   deters a reasonable investor falling within one of the intended categories of investor from investing in the fund.

76(2)   Condition C (see regulation 75(4)) shall be treated as being met even if at the relevant time the fund has no capacity to receive additional investments, unless–

(a)   the capacity of the fund to receive investments in it is fixed by the fund documents (or otherwise), and

(b)   a pre-determined number of specific persons or specific groups of connected persons make investments in the fund which collectively exhausts all, or substantially all, of that capacity.

76(3)   For the purposes of this regulation–

(a)   sections 993 and 994 of ITA 2007 (connected persons) apply in the case of a person chargeable to income tax, and

(b)   section 839 of ICTA (connected persons) applies in the case of a person chargeable to corporation tax.

CLEARANCES IN RELATION TO THE EQUIVALENCE AND GENUINE DIVERSITY OF OWNERSHIP CONDITIONS

Who may apply for clearance

77(1)   The following may apply for clearance that the fund meets the equivalence condition and the genuine diversity of ownership condition–

(a)   the manager of an eligible offshore fund;

(b)   the manager of a non-reporting fund who makes an application under regulation 52.

77(2)   If it is proposed to establish an offshore fund which, on its establishment, is to be an eligible offshore fund, the applicant may apply for clearance that the fund will meet the equivalence condition and the genuine diversity of ownership condition on its establishment.

Procedure for obtaining clearance

78(1)   The relevant person specified in regulation 77 (the "relevant person") must apply in writing to HMRC for clearance that the fund meets the equivalence condition and the genuine diversity of ownership condition.

78(2) A document submitted in accordance with paragraph (1) must be accompanied by the documents specified in regulation 75(2).

78(3) HMRC may require the relevant person to provide further particulars if HMRC believe that full particulars of the fund have not been provided.

78(4) HMRC must notify the relevant person within 28 days beginning with the day on which HMRC receive the documents mentioned in paragraphs (1) and (2) (or, as the case may be, the further particulars mentioned in paragraph (3))–

(a)   giving clearance that the fund meets the equivalence condition and the genuine diversity of ownership condition,

(b)   giving that clearance subject to conditions, or

(c)   refusing to give that clearance.

Circumstances in which clearance may not be relied upon

79(1) An offshore fund (and investors in that fund) may not rely on a clearance given under regulation 78 if any of conditions A to D is met.

79(2) Condition A is that at the beginning of the first period of account of the fund to which the clearance relates (and at the beginning of each subsequent period of account), a relevant statement in the instrument constituting the fund or in its prospectus in issue for the time being is not in accordance with a relevant statement in the documents considered by HMRC before giving clearance.

79(3) Condition B is that the fund is operated otherwise than in accordance with condition C of the genuine diversity of ownership condition (see regulations 75 and 76).

79(4) Condition C is that the fund acts or is operated in contravention of a relevant statement in the instrument constituting the fund or in its prospectus.

79(5) Condition D is that the documents specified in regulation 75(2) are materially amended.

79(6) Condition D does not apply if the relevant person specified in regulation 77 has obtained a clearance given under regulation 78 which applies to the documents in their amended form.

79(7) For the purposes of condition D, a material amendment is one that may reasonably be construed as causing, or likely to cause, the fund to fail to meet the equivalence condition or the genuine diversity of ownership condition in relation to any period of account.

INVESTMENT TRANSACTIONS CARRIED OUT BY DIVERSELY OWNED FUNDS

Treatment of investment transactions carried out by diversely owned funds

80(1) This regulation applies if a diversely owned fund carries out an investment transaction in an accounting period.

80(2) The investment transaction is treated as a non-trading transaction.

80(3) For the purposes of these Regulations an **"investment transaction"** is an investment transaction specified by regulation 2 of the Investment Transactions (Tax) Regulations 2014.

History – Reg. 80(3) inserted by SI 2014/685, reg. 8(2), with effect from transactions entered into on or after 8 April 2014.

Other material – M04/2010: HMRC confirmation that Ch. 6 has no relevance to matters relating to the taxation of funds potentially trading in the UK though a permanent establishment or agent; reg. 80(2) applies only for the purposes of Ch. 5.

Meaning of "investment transaction"

81 [Omitted by SI 2014/685, reg. 8(3).]

History – Reg. 81 omitted by SI 2014/685, reg. 8(3), with effect from transactions entered into on or after 8 April 2014. Former reg. 81 read as follows:

"Meaning of "investment transaction"

81 For the purposes of these Regulations an **"investment transaction"** means–

(a)   any transaction in stocks and shares;

(b)   any transaction in a relevant contract (and see regulations 82 to 86);

(c)   any transaction which results in a diversely owned fund becoming a party to a loan relationship or a related transaction in respect of a loan relationship (and see regulation 87);

(d)   any transaction in units in a collective investment scheme (and see regulation 88);

(e)   any transaction in securities of any description not falling within paragraphs (a) to (d);

(f)   any transaction consisting in the buying or selling of any foreign currency;

(g)   any transaction in a carbon emission trading product (and see regulation 89).

History – In reg. 81, the words "these Regulations" substituted for the words "this Part" by SI 2011/1211, reg. 20, with effect: for the purposes of income tax or corporation tax, for distributions made, or treated as made, on or after 27 May 2011; and for the purposes of capital gains tax or corporation tax on chargeable gains, in relation to disposals made on or after 27 May 2011."

Meaning of "relevant contract": general

82 [Omitted by SI 2014/685, reg. 8(3).]

History – Reg. 82 omitted by SI 2014/685, reg. 8(3), with effect from transactions entered into on or after 8 April 2014. Former reg. 82 read as follows:

"Meaning of "relevant contract": general

82(1)   For the purposes of regulation 81(b) a relevant contract is–
(a)   an option,
(b)   a future, or
(c)   a contract for differences.

82(2)   For the purposes of this regulation an option, a future or a contract for differences which relates to land will only be a relevant contract where the option, the future or the contract for differences uses an index referred to in regulation 86(1)(b) and the index is–
(a)   publicly accessible,
(b)   comprised of a significant number of properties, and
(c)   not maintained by–
    (i)   the diversely owned fund,
    (ii)   the manager of the diversely owned fund, or
    (iii)   a person connected with the diversely owned fund or the manager of the diversely owned fund.

82(3)   For the purposes of this regulation–
(a)   sections 993 and 994 of ITA 2007 (connected persons) apply where the manager is a person other than a company, and
(b)   section 839 of ICTA (connected persons) applies in the case of a diversely owned fund or where the manager is a person who is a company."

Meaning of "relevant contract": options

83   [Omitted by SI 2014/685, reg. 8(3).]

History – Reg. 83 omitted by SI 2014/685, reg. 8(3), with effect from transactions entered into on or after 8 April 2014. Former reg. 83 read as follows:

"Meaning of "relevant contract": options

83(1)   For the purposes of regulation 82(1)(a) an "option" includes an instrument which entitles the holder to subscribe for shares in a company or assets representing a loan relationship of a company, and for these purposes it is immaterial whether the shares or assets to which the instrument relates exist or are identifiable.

83(2)   For the purposes of paragraph (1) the reference to a loan relationship of a company is to be construed in accordance with regulation 87 but with references in that regulation to "diversely owned fund" treated as references to "company"."

Meaning of "relevant contract": futures

84   [Omitted by SI 2014/685, reg. 8(3).]

History – Reg. 84 omitted by SI 2014/685, reg. 8(3), with effect from transactions entered into on or after 8 April 2014. Former reg. 84 read as follows:

"Meaning of "relevant contract": futures

84(1)   For the purposes of regulation 82(1)(b) a "future" is a contract for the sale of property under which delivery is to be made–
(a)   at a future date agreed when the contract is made, and
(b)   at a price so agreed.

84(2)   For the purposes of paragraph (1)(b) a price is taken to be agreed when the contract is made–
(a)   notwithstanding that the price is left to be determined by reference to the price at which a contract is to be entered into on a market or exchange or could be entered into at a time and place specified in the contract, or
(b)   in a case where the contract is expressed to be by reference to a standard lot and quality, notwithstanding that provision is made for a variation in the price to take account of any variation in quantity or quality on delivery."

Options and futures: further provisions

85   [Omitted by SI 2014/685, reg. 8(3).]

History – Reg. 85 omitted by SI 2014/685, reg. 8(3), with effect from transactions entered into on or after 8 April 2014. Former reg. 85 read as follows:

"Options and futures: further provisions

85(1)   For the purposes of regulations 83 and 84 references to an option or a future do not include references to a contract whose terms provide–
(a)   that, after setting off their obligations to each other under the contract, a cash payment is to be made by one party to the other in respect of the excess, if any, and do not provide for the delivery of any property, or
(b)   that each party is liable to make to the other party a cash payment in respect of all that party's obligations to the other under the contract and do not provide for the delivery of any property, or
(c)   for the delivery of any property other than property a transaction in which would fall within any of regulations 80 to 89 where the property is delivered.

85(2)   Nothing in paragraph (1) has effect to exclude, from references to an option or future, an option or future whose underlying subject matter is currency.

85(3)   In paragraph (1) "underlying subject matter" means–
(a)   in relation to an option, the property which would fall to be delivered if the option were exercised, and
(b)   in relation to a future, the property which, if the future were to run to delivery, would fall to be delivered at the date and price agreed when the contract is made."

Meaning of "relevant contract": contracts for differences

86   [Omitted by SI 2014/685, reg. 8(3).]

History – Reg. 86 omitted by SI 2014/685, reg. 8(3), with effect from transactions entered into on or after 8 April 2014. Former reg. 86 read as follows:

"Meaning of "relevant contract": contracts for differences

86(1) For the purposes of regulation 82(1)(c) a **"contract for differences"** is a contract the purpose or pretended purpose of which is to make a profit or avoid a loss by reference to fluctuations in–
(a)   the value or price of property described in the contract, or
(b)   an index or other factor designated in the contract.

86(2) But none of the following is a contract for differences–
(a)   a future;
(b)   an option;
(c)   a contract of insurance;
(d)   a contract effected in the course of capital redemption business;
(e)   a contract of indemnity;
(f)   a guarantee;
(g)   a warranty;
(h)   a loan relationship.

86(3) For the purposes of paragraph (2)–
"capital redemption business" means any business of a company carrying on insurance business in so far as it consists of the effecting on the basis of actuarial calculations, and the carrying out, of contracts under which, in return for one or more fixed payments, a sum or series of sums of a specified amount become payable at a future time or over a period;
"loan relationship" is to be construed in accordance with regulation 87, but with references to **"diversely owned fund"** in that regulation treated as references to "company".

86(4) For the purposes of paragraph (1)(b) an index or factor may be determined by reference to any matter and, for these purposes, a numerical value may be attributed to any variation in a matter."

Interpretation of regulation 81(c)

87 [Omitted by SI 2014/685, reg. 8(3).]

History – Reg. 87 omitted by SI 2014/685, reg. 8(3), with effect from transactions entered into on or after 8 April 2014. Former reg. 87 read as follows:

"Interpretation of regulation 81(c)

87(1) For the purposes of regulation 81(c) a diversely owned fund has a **"loan relationship"** where the fund stands (whether by reference to a security or otherwise) in the position of a creditor or debtor as respects any money debt and either–
(a)   that debt is one arising from a transaction for the lending of money, or
(b)   that debt is not one which arose from a transaction for the lending of money but is one–
     (i)   on which interest is payable to or by the diversely owned fund, or
     (ii)   in relation to which exchange gains or losses arise to the diversely owned fund, or
     (iii)   as respects which the conditions in paragraph (2) below are satisfied.

87(2) The conditions referred to in paragraph (1)(b)(iii) are that–
(a)   the diversely owned fund stands in the position of creditor in relation to the money debt, and
(b)   the money debt is one from which a discount (whether of an income or capital nature) arises to the diversely owned fund.

87(3) In this regulation **"exchange gains or losses"** means profits or gains or losses which arise as a result of comparing at different times the expression in one currency of the whole or some part of the valuation put by the diversely owned fund in another currency on an asset or liability of the diversely owned fund.

87(4) For the purposes of this regulation a **"money debt"** is a debt which is, or has at any time been, one that falls, or that may at the choice of the debtor or of the creditor, fall to be settled–
(a)   by the payment of money,
(b)   by the transfer of a right to settlement under a debt which is itself a money debt, or
(c)   by the issue or transfer of shares in any company,
disregarding any other alternative exercisable by either party.

87(5) Subject to paragraph (6), where an instrument is issued by any person for the purpose of representing security for, or the rights of a creditor in respect of, any money debt, then (whatever the circumstances of the issue of the instrument) that debt shall be taken for the purposes of this regulation to be a debt arising from a transaction for the lending of money.

87(6) For the purposes of this regulation a debt does not arise from a transaction for the lending of money to the extent that it is a debt arising from rights conferred by shares in a company.

87(7) For the purposes of this regulation so far as relating to exchange gains and losses, any currency held by the diversely owned fund shall be treated as a money debt.

87(8) For the purposes of this regulation **"money"** includes money expressed in a currency other than sterling.

87(9) For the purposes of regulation 81(c) a **"related transaction"** in relation to a loan relationship means any disposal or acquisition (in whole or in part) of rights or liabilities under that relationship."

Meaning of "units in a collective investment scheme"

88 [Omitted by SI 2014/685, reg. 8(3).]

History – Reg. 88 omitted by SI 2014/685, reg. 8(3), with effect from transactions entered into on or after 8 April 2014. Former reg. 88 read as follows:

"Meaning of "units in a collective investment scheme"

88(1) For the purposes of regulation 81(d)–
"collective investment scheme" has the meaning given by section 235 of FISMA 2000,
"units" means the rights or interests (however described) of the investors in the collective investment scheme.

88(2) In paragraph (1) a **"investor"**, in relation to a collective investment scheme, means a beneficial owner of units in the scheme, except where the units are held on trust (other than a bare trust) or are comprised in the estate of a deceased person, and in such a case the investor, in relation to the scheme, means the trustees of the trust, or, as the case may be, the deceased's personal representatives."

Meaning of "transaction in a carbon emission trading product"

89   [Omitted by SI 2014/685, reg. 8(3).]

History – Reg. 89 omitted by SI 2014/685, reg. 8(3), with effect from transactions entered into on or after 8 April 2014. Former reg. 89 read as follows:

> ### "Meaning of "transaction in a carbon emission trading product"
>
> **89(1)**   For the purposes of regulation 81(g) a **"transaction in a carbon emission trading product"** means a transaction–
>
> (a)   in Community tradable emissions allowances, or
>
> (b)   in transferable units issued pursuant to the Kyoto Protocol,
>
> where the transaction does not otherwise fall within any other paragraph of that regulation.
>
> **89(2)**   For the purposes of this regulation–
>
> **"Community tradable emissions allowances"** means transferable allowances which relate to the making of emissions of greenhouse gases, and are allocated as part of a system made for the purpose of implementing any community obligation of the United Kingdom relating to such emissions;
>
> **"the Kyoto Protocol"** means the Kyoto Protocol to the United Nations Framework Convention on Climate Change signed at Kyoto on 11th December 1997;
>
> **"units"** includes assigned amount units, certified emission reductions, emission reduction units and removal units."

Chapter 6A – Transparent Reporting Funds

History – Ch. 6A inserted by SI 2011/1211, reg. 24, with effect: for the purposes of income tax or corporation tax, for distributions made, or treated as made, on or after 27 May 2011; and for the purposes of capital gains tax or corporation tax on chargeable gains, in relation to disposals made on or after 27 May 2011.

TRANSPARENT REPORTING FUNDS

89A(1)   This Chapter explains how reportable income is computed in the case of a transparent reporting fund.

89A(2)   For the purposes of these Regulations a **"transparent reporting fund"** is a reporting fund which is a transparent fund.

History – Reg. 89A inserted by SI 2011/1211, reg. 24, with effect: for the purposes of income tax or corporation tax, for distributions made, or treated as made, on or after 27 May 2011; and for the purposes of capital gains tax or corporation tax on chargeable gains, in relation to disposals made on or after 27 May 2011.

REPORTABLE INCOME: GENERAL

89B(1)   A transparent reporting fund must provide a computation of its reportable income for a period of account.

89B(3)   The reportable income of a transparent reporting fund for a period of account is comprised of–

(a)   each of the separate sums of income for the period which fall within paragraph (a) or (b) of regulation 11 (meaning of transparent funds), and

(b)   the adjustments made to those sums in accordance with regulations 89C to 89E.

89B(4)   For the purposes of this Part the adjustments referred to in paragraph (3)(b) are excesses of reported income of the fund over the sums which form part of the income of the fund within paragraph (3)(a).

History – Reg. 89B inserted by SI 2011/1211, reg. 24, with effect: for the purposes of income tax or corporation tax, for distributions made, or treated as made, on or after 27 May 2011; and for the purposes of capital gains tax or corporation tax on chargeable gains, in relation to disposals made on or after 27 May 2011.

Notes – Reg. 89B appears here as it appears in the official publication of SI 2011/1211, without a para. (2). This is assumed to be a simple numbering error in the drafting of the regulation.

ADJUSTMENT IN RELATION TO INCOME FROM OTHER REPORTING FUNDS

89C(1)   This regulation applies if a transparent reporting fund ("TRF") has an interest in another reporting fund ("RF").

89C(2)   The reportable income of TRF in relation to that interest shall include the excess (if any) of the income reported by RF in respect of TRF's interest in RF over the amount distributed by RF in relation to that interest.

89C(3)   The excess is treated as reportable income of TRF for the period of account in which the fund distribution date of RF falls.

89C(4)   If RF does not make a report available in accordance with regulation 90(5), TRF must–

(a)   include its best estimate of reported income from RF as an adjustment to the computation of its reportable income in relation to that interest for the period of account in which the latest possible fund distribution date for RF falls (to the extent that any such amount has not already been recognised in the computation of TRF's reportable income for that or any earlier period of account), and

(b)   make any necessary corrections to its best estimate in its computation of reportable income for the first later period of account in which it has sufficient information to make those corrections.

History – Reg. 89C inserted by SI 2011/1211, reg. 24, with effect: for the purposes of income tax or corporation tax, for distributions made, or treated as made, on or after 27 May 2011; and for the purposes of capital gains tax or corporation tax on chargeable gains, in relation to disposals made on or after 27 May 2011.

ADJUSTMENT IN RELATION TO INCOME FROM NON-REPORTING FUNDS: FIRST CASE

89D(1)   This regulation applies if–

(a)   a transparent reporting fund has an interest in a non-reporting fund, and

(b)   the conditions in paragraph (2) are met for a period of account.

89D(2)   The conditions are that–

(a)   the transparent reporting fund has access to the accounts of the non-reporting fund;

(b)   the transparent reporting fund has sufficient information about the non-reporting fund to enable it to prepare a computation of reportable income for the non-reporting fund; and

(c)   the transparent reporting fund can reasonably expect to rely on continued access to that information for the period in which it will hold the investment in the non-reporting fund.

89D(3)   Regulation 89C applies as if the transparent reporting fund were TRF and the non-reporting fund were RF.

89D(4)   For the purposes of the computation mentioned in paragraph (2)(b), regulation 80 applies if (and only if) the non-reporting fund is a UCITS fund.

History – Reg. 89D inserted by SI 2011/1211, reg. 24, with effect: for the purposes of income tax or corporation tax, for distributions made, or treated as made, on or after 27 May 2011; and for the purposes of capital gains tax or corporation tax on chargeable gains, in relation to disposals made on or after 27 May 2011.

ADJUSTMENT IN RELATION TO INCOME FROM NON-REPORTING FUNDS: SECOND CASE

89E(1)   This regulation applies if a transparent reporting fund has an interest in a non-reporting fund, but the conditions in regulation 89D(2) are not met for a period of account.

89E(2)   The reportable income of the transparent reporting fund for a period of account in relation to that interest shall include an amount equal to the increase in the fair value of the interest in the non-reporting fund in that period.

89E(3)   But if the condition specified in paragraph (4) is met, decreases in the fair value of that interest in earlier periods of account may be set against the increase referred to in paragraph (2) to reduce the amount of the increase, but–

(a)   not to below zero, and

(b)   only to the extent that the decreases in fair value have not previously had the effect of reducing the amount of a fair value increase.

89E(4)   The condition specified is that the decrease in fair value in earlier periods of account all occurred during periods in which this Part applied continuously to the transparent reporting fund.

89E(5)   In this regulation **"fair value"** in relation to an interest in a non-reporting fund means the amount which, at the time the value is to be determined, is the amount for which the interest could be exchanged between knowledgeable and willing parties dealing at arm's length.

History – Reg. 89E inserted by SI 2011/1211, reg. 24, with effect: for the purposes of income tax or corporation tax, for distributions made, or treated as made, on or after 27 May 2011; and for the purposes of capital gains tax or corporation tax on chargeable gains, in relation to disposals made on or after 27 May 2011.

Chapter 7 – Reports to Participants

Report to participants for a reporting period

90(1)   A reporting fund must make a report available to each relevant participant for each reporting period.

90(2)   For the purposes of these Regulations a report is made available if the fund–

(a)   sends the report to a relevant participant by post,

(b)   sends the report to a relevant participant by means of an electronic communications service,

(c)   makes the report available on a website accessible to relevant participants and to HMRC, or

(d)   publishes the report in a newspaper which is published in English in the United Kingdom and readily available in all parts of the United Kingdom.

90(3)   In this regulation **"relevant participants"** means participants who–

(a)   are resident in the United Kingdom, or

(b)   are reporting funds,

during any part of the reporting period.

90(4)   If the fund does not provide the report to a relevant participant by sending it to the participant by post, the fund must, if so required by the participant, make the report available to the participant in some further manner (whether or not that further manner is also specified in regulation 90(2)) as the fund and the participant may agree.

90(5)   The reporting fund must make the report available within a period of six months beginning with the day immediately following the final day of the reporting period.

90(6)   The report must be in English.

History – In reg. 90(1), the word "relevant" inserted by SI 2011/1211, reg. 39(2)(a), with effect: for the purposes of income tax or corporation tax, for distributions made, or treated as made, on or after 27 May 2011; and for the purposes of capital gains tax or corporation tax on chargeable gains, in relation to disposals made on or after 27 May 2011.
In reg. 90(2)(a) and (b), the word "relevant" inserted by SI 2011/1211, reg. 39(2)(b), with effect: for the purposes of income tax or corporation tax, for distributions made, or treated as made, on or after 27 May 2011; and for the purposes of capital gains tax or corporation tax on chargeable gains, in relation to disposals made on or after 27 May 2011.
In reg. 90(4), the word "relevant" inserted by SI 2011/1211, reg. 39(2)(c), with effect: for the purposes of income tax or corporation tax, for distributions made, or treated as made, on or after 27 May 2011; and for the purposes of capital gains tax or corporation tax on chargeable gains, in relation to disposals made on or after 27 May 2011.
In reg. 90(3), the words "this regulation" substituted for "paragraph (2)(c)" by SI 2011/1211, reg. 39(3), with effect: for the purposes of income tax or corporation tax, for distributions made, or treated as made, on or after 27 May 2011; and for the purposes of capital gains tax or corporation tax on chargeable gains, in relation to disposals made on or after 27 May 2011.

Meaning of "reporting period"

91   In these Regulations a **"reporting period"** of a reporting fund means a period determined in accordance with the following rules–

First rule

If the reporting fund's period of account is twelve months or less, the reporting period is the same as the period of account.

Second rule

If the reporting fund's period of account is more than twelve months, there are two reporting periods.

The first reporting period is a period consisting of the first twelve months of the period of account. The second reporting period is a period consisting of the remainder of the period of account.

Contents of report to participants: non-transparent funds

History – In the heading before reg. 92, the words ": non-transparent funds" inserted by SI 2011/1211, reg. 25(2), with effect: for the purposes of income tax or corporation tax, for distributions made, or treated as made, on or after 27 May 2011; and for the purposes of capital gains tax or corporation tax on chargeable gains, in relation to disposals made on or after 27 May 2011.

92(1)   In the case of reporting funds which are not transparent funds, the report to participants for a reporting period must include the following information–

(a)   the amount actually distributed to participants per unit of interest in the fund in respect of the reporting period;

(b)   the amount per unit of any excess treated as additional distributions made to participants in the fund in respect of the reporting period;

(c)   the dates on which distributions were made;

(d)   the fund distribution date (see regulation 94(4));

(e)   a statement whether or not the fund remains a reporting fund at the date the fund makes the report available;

(f)   if the fund operates full equalisation arrangements and has not given a statement under regulation 50A(b)(i), the equalisation amount per unit of interest in the fund in relation to any interest acquired by way of initial purchase in the reporting period.

92(2)   In these Regulations the **"reported income"** of a reporting fund for a reporting period means the reportable income of the fund for the reporting period, computed by or on behalf of the fund, and provided, in the report for the reporting period, to the participants in the fund.

92(3)   For the purposes of paragraph (1)–

(a)   the amount in paragraph (b) is the amount of any excess specified in regulation 94(1) divided by the number of units in the fund in issue at the end of the reporting period,

(b)   the amount actually distributed to participants per unit of interest in the fund in respect of the reporting period must be computed at the time the distribution is made,

(ba)   subject to paragraphs (3A) and (3B), the fund may chose to calculate the equalisation amount per unit of interest in the fund either on the basis of–

      (i)   the sum of all the equalisation amounts in relation to all acquisitions by way of initial purchase in the reporting period divided by the total number of units acquired by way of initial purchase in the period, or

      (ii)   the equalisation amount in relation to the acquisition by the participant to whom the report is made available divided by the number of units acquired on that acquisition, and

(c)   the amount per unit of interest in the fund must be expressed to at least four decimal places of a pound (or other currency unit) of value per unit.

92(3A)   A fund cannot change the basis for calculating the equalisation amount per unit of interest in the fund more than once in three successive reporting periods.

92(3B)   In any reporting period all reports to participants must use the same basis for calculating the equalisation amount per unit of interest in the fund.

92(4)   If the amount of the reported income per unit of interest in the fund for the reporting period is equal to, or less than, the amount actually distributed to participants per unit of interest in the fund in respect of the reporting period, the amount to be stated for the purposes of paragraph (1)(b) is nil.

92(5)   This regulation is subject to regulation 93.

History – In reg. 92(1), the words "In the case of reporting funds which are not transparent funds," inserted by SI 2011/1211, reg. 25(3), with effect: for the purposes of income tax or corporation tax, for distributions made, or treated as made, on or after 27 May 2011; and for the purposes of capital gains tax or corporation tax on chargeable gains, in relation to disposals made on or after 27 May 2011.
Reg. 92(1)(b) substituted by SI 2013/1411, reg. 7(a), with effect from 28 June 2013 but subject to savings provision at SI 2013/1411, reg. 1; amendments do not apply in relation to a reporting period which ended before that date if–
(a)   no report has previously been made available under reg. 90 for that reporting period (as defined in reg. 91), and
(b)   the manager of the fund elects by notice in writing within 10 months of the end of that reporting period that those amendments should not apply.
Former reg. 92(1)(b) read as follows:
"(b)   the excess of the amount of the reported income per unit of interest in the fund for the reporting period over the amount actually distributed to participants per unit of interest in the fund in respect of the reporting period;".
Reg. 92(1)(f) inserted by SI 2011/1211, reg. 10(2), with effect, subject to transitional rules in SI 2011/1211, reg. 14–17: for the purposes of income tax or corporation tax, for distributions made, or treated as made, on or after 27 May 2011; and for the purposes of capital gains tax or corporation tax on chargeable gains, in relation to disposals made on or after 27 May 2011.
Reg. 92(3)(a) substituted by SI 2013/1411, reg. 7(b), with effect from 28 June 2013 but subject to savings provision at SI 2013/1411, reg. 1; amendments do not apply in relation to a reporting period which ended before that date if–
(a)   no report has previously been made available under reg. 90 for that reporting period (as defined in reg. 91), and
(b)   the manager of the fund elects by notice in writing within 10 months of the end of that reporting period that those amendments should not apply.
Former reg. 92(3)(a) read as follows:
"(a)   the reported income per unit of a reporting fund for a reporting period is–
      (i)   in the case of a reporting fund which operates equalisation arrangements, computed by dividing the reported income of the fund for the reporting period by the number of units in the fund in issue at the end of the reporting period,
      (ii)   in the case of a reporting fund which does not operate equalisation arrangements and does not make income adjustments, computed by dividing the reported income of the fund for the reporting period by the number of units in the fund in issue at the end of the reporting period,
      (iii)   in the case of a reporting fund which does not operate equalisation arrangements and which makes income adjustments in a reporting period on the basis of reported income, the amount determined in accordance with regulation 92A(2),
      (iv)   in the case of a reporting fund which does not operate equalisation arrangements and which makes income adjustments in a reporting period on the basis of accounting income, the amount determined in accordance with regulation 92B(2),".
Reg. 92(3)(a), (b) and (ba) substituted for former reg. 92(3)(a) and (b) by SI 2011/1211, reg. 10(3), with effect, subject to transitional rules in SI 2011/1211, reg. 14–17: for the purposes of income tax or corporation tax, for distributions made, or treated as made, on or after 27 May 2011; and for the purposes of capital gains tax or corporation tax on chargeable gains, in relation to disposals made on or after 27 May 2011. Former reg. 92(3)(a) and (b) read as follows:
"(a)   the reported income per unit of a reporting fund for a report is computed by dividing the reported income of the fund for the reporting period by the number of units in the fund in issue at the end of the reporting period,
(b)   the amount actually distributed to participants per unit of interest in the fund in respect of the reporting period must be computed at the time the distribution is made, and".
Reg. 92(3A) and (3B) inserted by SI 2011/1211, reg. 10(4), with effect, subject to transitional rules in SI 2011/1211, reg. 14–17: for the purposes of income tax or corporation tax, for distributions made, or treated as made, on or after 27 May 2011; and for the purposes of capital gains tax or corporation tax on chargeable gains, in relation to disposals made on or after 27 May 2011.

Funds which do not operate equalisation arrangements: income adjustments on the basis of reported income

92A   [Omitted by SI 2013/1411, reg. 8.]

History – Reg. 92A omitted by SI 2013/1411, reg. 8, with effect from 28 June 2013 but subject to savings provision at SI 2013/1411, reg. 1; amendments do not apply in relation to a reporting period which ended before that date if–
- (a)   no report has previously been made available under reg. 90 for that reporting period (as defined in reg. 91), and
- (b)   the manager of the fund elects by notice in writing within 10 months of the end of that reporting period that those amendments should not apply.

Former reg. 92A read as follows:
"**92A(1)**   This regulation applies if a reporting fund does not operate equalisation arrangements and–
- (a)   the fund has given a statement under regulation 53(1)(k)that it intends to make income adjustments in a reporting period on the basis of reported income, or
- (b)   regulation 92B(5) applies.

92A(2)   The reported income per unit of the fund for a reporting period is the sum of the reported income per unit for all the computation periods in the reporting period.

92A(3)   The reported income per unit for a computation period is calculated by dividing the reported income of the fund for the computation period by the average number of units in the fund in issue during the computation period.

92A(4)   For the purposes of paragraph (3) the reported income of the fund for a computation period means the reportable income of the fund for that period computed in accordance with Chapters 5 and 6 of this Part.

92A(5)   In the computation referred to in paragraph (4) Chapters 5 and 6 of this Part apply as if references to a period of account of the fund were references to a computation period.

92A(6)   For the purposes of paragraph (3) and regulation 92B(3) the average number of units in issue during a computation period is the sum of the units in the fund in issue during the period after each unit has been multiplied by the fraction of the period for which it is held.".

Former reg. 92A inserted by SI 2011/1211, reg. 11, with effect, subject to transitional rules in SI 2011/1211, reg. 14–17: for the purposes of income tax or corporation tax, for distributions made, or treated as made, on or after 27 May 2011; and for the purposes of capital gains tax or corporation tax on chargeable gains, in relation to disposals made on or after 27 May 2011.

Funds which do not operate equalisation arrangements: income adjustments on the basis of accounting income

92B   [Omitted by SI 2013/1411, reg. 8.]

History – Reg. 92B omitted by SI 2013/1411, reg. 8, with effect from 28 June 2013 but subject to savings provision at SI 2013/1411, reg. 1; amendments do not apply in relation to a reporting period which ended before that date if–
- (a)   no report has previously been made available under reg. 90 for that reporting period (as defined in reg. 91), and
- (b)   the manager of the fund elects by notice in writing within 10 months of the end of that reporting period that those amendments should not apply.

Former reg. 92B read as follows:
"**92B(1)**   This regulation applies if a reporting fund does not operate equalisation arrangements and the fund has given a statement under regulation 53(1)(k) that it intends to make income adjustments in a reporting period on the basis of accounting income.

92B(2)   The reported income per unit of the fund for a reporting period is calculated as follows–

$$AIU \times \frac{RI}{AI}$$

where–
AIU is the sum of the accounting income per unit for all the computation periods in the reporting period,
RI is the reported income of the fund for the reporting period, and
AI is the sum of accounting income per unit for all the computation periods in the reporting period.
This is subject to paragraphs (4) and (5).

92B(3)   The accounting income per unit for a computation period is calculated by dividing accounting income for the computation period by the average number of units in the fund in issue during the computation period.

92B(4)   Where RI is zero the reported income per unit of the fund for a reporting period is zero.

92B(5)   Where the difference in the amount of reported income per unit calculated using this method and the amount of reported income per unit calculated on the basis of reported income is or is likely to be more than 10% of the latter of those amounts–
- (a)   the fund must make income adjustments in that and future reporting periods on the basis of reported income, and
- (b)   the manager must give notice to HMRC of the change in the method of income adjustment with the information provided to HMRC in relation to that period under regulation 106 (reporting requirements).

92B(6)   In this Part **"accounting income"** means an amount proportionally related to the reportable income of the fund determined from the interim or management accounts of the fund, but this amount must not be less than zero.".

Former reg. 92B inserted by SI 2011/1211, reg. 11, with effect, subject to transitional rules in SI 2011/1211, reg. 14–17: for the purposes of income tax or corporation tax, for distributions made, or treated as made, on or after 27 May 2011; and for the purposes of capital gains tax or corporation tax on chargeable gains, in relation to disposals made on or after 27 May 2011.

Funds which do not operate equalisation arrangements: computation period

92C   [Omitted by SI 2013/1411, reg. 8.]

History – Reg. 92C omitted by SI 2013/1411, reg. 8, with effect from 28 June 2013 but subject to savings provision at SI 2013/1411, reg. 1; amendments do not apply in relation to a reporting period which ended before that date if–
- (a)   no report has previously been made available under reg. 90 for that reporting period (as defined in reg. 91), and
- (b)   the manager of the fund elects by notice in writing within 10 months of the end of that reporting period that those amendments should not apply.

Former reg. 92C read as follows:
"**92C**   In this Part a **"computation period"** means a period determined by a fund in accordance with the following rules.
Rule 1
A new computation period must start–
- (a)   at the beginning of a reporting period, and
- (b)   immediately after the end of a previous computation period.

Rule 2
A new computation period must end—
(a)　　at the end of a reporting period, and
(b)　　on any date on which income is allocated to participants for distribution or accumulation.
Rule 3
Subject to rules 1 and 2, if a reporting period consists of more than one computation period those periods must be of approximately equal length.".

Former reg. 92C inserted by SI 2011/1211, reg. 11, with effect, subject to transitional rules in SI 2011/1211, reg. 14–17: for the purposes of income tax or corporation tax, for distributions made, or treated as made, on or after 27 May 2011; and for the purposes of capital gains tax or corporation tax on chargeable gains, in relation to disposals made on or after 27 May 2011.

Contents of reports to participants: transparent reporting funds

92D　　In the case of transparent reporting funds, the report to participants for a reporting period must—

(a)　　contain sufficient information to enable those participants to meet their tax obligations in the United Kingdom with respect to their interests in the fund, and

(b)　　include a statement whether or not the fund remains a reporting fund at the date the fund makes the report available.

History – Reg. 92D inserted by SI 2011/1211, reg. 26, with effect: for the purposes of income tax or corporation tax, for distributions made, or treated as made, on or after 27 May 2011; and for the purposes of capital gains tax or corporation tax on chargeable gains, in relation to disposals made on or after 27 May 2011.

Lengthy periods of account where full information not available

93(1)　　This regulation applies if a reporting fund—

(a)　　has a period of account which is longer than twelve months, and

(b)　　has difficulty in computing its reportable income for the reporting period constituting the first twelve months of that period of account (the "relevant reporting period").

93(2)　　For the purpose of preparing its report to participants for the relevant reporting period, the fund may elect—

(a)　　to compute its reportable income based on such information as is reasonably available, or

(b)　　to make a just and reasonable apportionment of the income of the period of account.

93(3)　　The computation of reportable income for the reporting period following the relevant reporting period must include all amounts not accounted for in the relevant reporting period.

Chapter 8 – The Tax Treatment of Participants nn Reporting Funds

TAX TREATMENT OF THE REPORTED INCOME OF THE FUND IN THE HANDS OF PARTICIPANTS

Reported income: general provisions

94(1)　　In the case of a reporting fund which is not a transparent fund, the Tax Acts have effect as if the excess (if any) of the reported income of the fund in respect of a reporting period over the distributions made by the fund in respect of the reporting period were additional distributions made to the participants in the fund in proportion to their rights.

94(2)　　In the case of a reporting fund which is a transparent fund, the Tax Acts have effect as if the excess (if any) of the reported income of the fund in respect of a reporting period over the income of the fund for the reporting period were additional income of the participants in the fund in proportion to their rights.

94(2A)　　But to the extent that the participant's rights in the fund are rights to which regulation 30 (rights in certain existing holdings) applies, the excess specified in paragraphs (1) and (2) shall be reduced proportionately.

94(3)　　The excess specified in paragraphs (1) and (2) is treated as made, on the fund distribution date, or on such earlier date as the reported income in respect of that reporting period is recognised in the participant's accounts, to participants holding an interest in the fund at the end of the reporting period.

94(3A)　　If—

(a)　　a participant disposes of an interest in a reporting fund in a reporting period ("the earlier period"), and

(b)　　section 106A of TCGA 1992 (identification of securities: capital gains tax) applies to identify the whole or any part of that interest with an interest acquired in the next reporting period, then, for the purposes of paragraph (3), the disposal of the interest so identified shall be ignored and the participant shall be treated as holding that interest at the end of the earlier period.

94(4) In these Regulations the **"fund distribution date"** for a reporting period of a reporting fund means the date six months following the last day of the reporting period.

History – In reg. 94(2A), "paragraphs (1) and" substituted for "paragraph" by SI 2011/1211, reg. 40(2), with effect: for the purposes of income tax or corporation tax, for distributions made, or treated as made, on or after 27 May 2011; and for the purposes of capital gains tax or corporation tax on chargeable gains, in relation to disposals made on or after 27 May 2011.
Reg. 94(2A) inserted by SI 2009/3139, reg. 4, with effect: (for the purposes of income tax) for the tax year 2009–10 and subsequent tax years and for distributions made on or after 1 December 2009; (for the purposes of corporation tax on income) for accounting periods ending on or after 1 December 2009 and for distributions made on or after that date; and (for the purposes of capital gains tax or corporation tax on chargeable gains) in relation to disposals made on or after 1 December 2009.
In reg. 94(3), the words "or on such earlier date as the reported income in respect of that reporting period is recognised in the participant's accounts," inserted by SI 2011/1211, reg. 40(3), with effect: for the purposes of income tax or corporation tax, for distributions made, or treated as made, on or after 27 May 2011; and for the purposes of capital gains tax or corporation tax on chargeable gains, in relation to disposals made on or after 27 May 2011.
Reg. 94(3A) inserted by SI 2011/1211, reg. 40(4), with effect: for the purposes of income tax or corporation tax, for distributions made, or treated as made, on or after 27 May 2011; and for the purposes of capital gains tax or corporation tax on chargeable gains, in relation to disposals made on or after 27 May 2011.
In reg. 94(4), the words "means the date six months following the last day of the reporting period" substituted for the former wording by SI 2011/1211, reg. 40(5), with effect: for the purposes of income tax or corporation tax, for distributions made, or treated as made, on or after 27 May 2011; and for the purposes of capital gains tax or corporation tax on chargeable gains, in relation to disposals made on or after 27 May 2011. The former wording was as follows:
"means–
(a)   in a case where the reporting fund issues its report to participants within a period of six months beginning with the day immediately following the last day of the reporting period, the date on which the report is issued, and
(b)   in any other case, the last day of the reporting period.".

Equalisation amounts not treated as distributions

94A(1) This regulation applies if–

(a)   a participant has acquired by way of initial purchase an interest in a reporting fund, and

(b)   the reporting fund operates full equalisation arrangements.

94A(2) Where this regulation applies, distributions are reduced in accordance with either option 1 or option 2.

Option 1

Under this option–

(a)   the amount of any actual distributions to the participant in respect of the reporting period is reduced by the equalisation amount, and

(b)   the amount of any excess treated as additional distributions made to the participant is reduced by the amount, if any, by which the equalisation amount exceeds the amount of any actual distributions to the participant in respect of the reporting period.

Option 2

Under this option–

(a)   the amount of any excess treated as additional distributions made to the participant is reduced by the equalisation amount, and

(b)   the amount of any actual distributions to the participant in respect of the reporting period is reduced by the amount, if any, by which the equalisation amount exceeds the excess.

94A(3) But the amount of any excess treated as additional distributions or any actual distributions shall not be reduced to below nil.

94A(4) For the purposes of paragraph (2) the excess is the amount treated as additional distributions made to the participant in accordance with regulation 94(1) and (2).

History – Reg. 94A(2) substituted by SI 2013/1411, reg. 9, with effect from 28 June 2013 but subject to savings provision at SI 2013/1411, reg. 1; the amendments do not apply in relation to interests in offshore funds acquired in a reporting period (as defined in reg. 91) which began before 28 June 2013. Former reg. 94A(2) read as follows:
"**94A(2)** Where this regulation applies–
(a)   the amount of any excess treated as additional distributions made to the participant is reduced by the equalisation amount, and
(b)   the amount of any actual distributions to the participant in respect of the reporting period shall be treated as reduced by the amount, if any, by which the equalisation amount exceeds the excess.".
Reg. 94A inserted by SI 2011/1211, reg. 12, with effect, subject to transitional rules in SI 2011/1211, reg. 14–17: for the purposes of income tax or corporation tax, for distributions made, or treated as made, on or after 27 May 2011; and for the purposes of capital gains tax or corporation tax on chargeable gains, in relation to disposals made on or after 27 May 2011.

Participants chargeable to income tax: corporate funds

95(1) This regulation applies if–

(a)   a reporting fund makes a distribution to a participant chargeable to income tax in respect of a reporting period, and

(b)   the fund falls within section 40A(2)(a) of FA 2008.

95(2)   This regulation also applies if some or all of the excess specified in regulation 94(1) is treated as made by such a fund to such a participant.

95(3)   If section 378A of ITTOIA 2005 (offshore fund distributions) applies to any amount falling within paragraph (1) or (2), the amount is charged to income tax in accordance with that section.

95(4)   If paragraph (3) does not apply to any amount falling within paragraph (1) or (2), but the participant is entitled to a tax credit on receiving a distribution falling within paragraph (1), section 397A of ITTOIA 2005 (savings and investment income: dividends from non-UK resident companies) also applies to the excess falling within paragraph (2).

Participants chargeable to income tax: other non-transparent funds

96(1)   This regulation applies if–

(a)   a reporting fund makes a distribution to a participant chargeable to income tax in respect of a reporting period,

(b)   the fund falls within paragraph (b) or (c) of section 40A(2) of FA 2008, and

(c)   the fund is not a transparent fund.

96(2)   This regulation also applies if some or all of the excess specified in regulation 94(1) is treated as made by such a fund to such a participant.

96(3)   Any amount to which paragraph (1) or (2) applies is charged to income tax–

(a)   under section 378A of ITTOIA 2005 (offshore fund distributions), or

(b)   (if that section does not apply) under Chapter 8 of Part 5 of ITTOIA 2005 (miscellaneous income: income not otherwise charged) for the year of assessment in which the distribution is made, but sections 688(1) and 689 of ITTOIA 2005 (income charged and person liable) do not apply.

Participants chargeable to income tax: transparent funds

97(1)   This regulation applies if–

(a)   a reporting fund is a transparent fund, and

(b)   some or all of the excess specified in regulation 94(2) is treated as income of a participant by virtue of that provision.

97(2)   Any amount to which paragraph (1) applies is charged to income tax under Chapter 8 of Part 5 of ITTOIA 2005 as relevant foreign income within the meaning given by section 830 of ITTOIA 2005 for the year of assessment in which the distribution is made, but sections 688(1) and 689 of ITTOIA 2005 do not apply.

Participants chargeable to corporation tax

98(1)   This regulation applies if some or all of the excess specified in regulation 94 is treated as made to a participant chargeable to corporation tax.

98(2)   The amount is exempt if it would be exempt if it were an actual distribution made by the fund.

DISPOSALS AND DEEMED DISPOSALS OF INTERESTS

Disposals of interests

99(1)   If a participant has an interest in a reporting fund and disposes of the interest, the participant disposes of an asset for the purposes of tax in respect of chargeable gains.

99(2)   For the purposes of the disposal referred to in paragraph (1), an amount equal to the accumulated undistributed income is treated as expenditure–

(a)   given for the acquisition of the asset, and

(b)   falling within section 38(1)(a) of TCGA 1992 (acquisition and disposal costs).

99(2A)   But where regulation 94A has applied, the expenditure given for the acquisition of the asset shall be treated as reduced by an amount equal to the amount of any reduction in the actual distribution under regulation 94A(2).

99(3)   In paragraph (2) the **"accumulated undistributed income"** means the aggregate of amounts specified in regulation 94 on which the participant has been charged to tax under any of regulations 95 to 98.

99(4)   The expenditure mentioned in paragraph (2) is treated as incurred, in the case of each amount referred to in paragraph (3), on the fund distribution date for the reporting period in respect of which the amount is treated as distributed.

99(5)   But if the participant receives an amount in respect of the interest in the reporting fund which is chargeable to income tax, and that amount is received (or treated as received) after the date of the disposal referred to in paragraph (1), the amount is treated as received immediately before that disposal for the purposes of tax in respect of chargeable gains.

99(6)   This regulation is subject to regulation 17.

History – In reg. 99(2A), the words "in the actual distribution under regulation 94A(2)" substituted for the words "under regulation 94A(2)(b)" by SI 2013/1411, reg. 10, with effect from 28 June 2013 but subject to savings provision at SI 2013/1411, reg. 1; the amendments do not apply in relation to interests in offshore funds acquired in a reporting period (as defined in reg. 91) which began before 28 June 2013.

Reg. 99(2A) inserted by SI 2011/1211, reg. 13, with effect, subject to transitional rules in SI 2011/1211, reg. 14–17: for the purposes of income tax or corporation tax, for distributions made, or treated as made, on or after 27 May 2011; and for the purposes of capital gains tax or corporation tax on chargeable gains, in relation to disposals made on or after 27 May 2011.

Deemed disposals of interests

100(1)   This regulation applies if an offshore fund ceases to be a reporting fund and becomes a non-reporting fund.

100(2)   A participant in the fund may make an election to be treated for the purposes of TCGA 1992–

(a)   as disposing of an interest in the reporting fund at the end of that fund's final period of account, and

(b)   as acquiring an interest in the non-reporting fund at the beginning of that fund's first period of account.

This is subject to paragraph (3).

100(3)   The election mentioned in paragraph (2) may only be made if a report has been made available to the participant under regulation 90 for the reporting fund's final period of account.

100(4)   The disposal referred to in paragraph (2)(a) is treated as made for a consideration equal to the net asset value of the participant's interest in the fund at the end of the period of account for which the final reported income is reported to the participant.

100(5)   The acquisition referred to in paragraph (2)(b) is treated as made for the same amount as the disposal referred to in paragraph (2)(a).

100(6)   If the participant is chargeable to income tax, the election mentioned in paragraph (2) must be made by being included in a return made for the tax year which includes the disposal date.

100(7)   If the participant is chargeable to corporation tax, the election mentioned in paragraph (2) must be made by being included in the participant's company tax return for the accounting period which includes the disposal date.

100(8)   In this regulation–

"**company tax return**" has the same meaning as in Schedule 18 to the Finance Act 1998;

"**disposal date**" means the final day of the reporting fund's final period of account.

CHARITABLE COMPANIES AND CHARITABLE TRUSTS

Special provisions applying to charitable companies and charitable trusts

101(1)   This regulation applies if–

(a)   a charitable company is a participant in a reporting fund, or

(b)   the trustees of a charitable trust are participants in a reporting fund.

101(2)   No liability to tax arises in respect of any amount which, under regulation 94(1), is treated as distributed to a charitable company or the trustees of a charitable trust.

101(3)   Paragraph (2) of regulation 99 (read with paragraphs (3) and (4) of that regulation) does not apply to the disposal of an interest in a reporting fund by a charitable company or the trustees of a charitable trust.

101(4)   In this regulation "**charity**" and "**charitable company**" have the same meaning as in section 506 of ICTA.

ANTI-AVOIDANCE PROVISIONS

Treatment of financial traders if conditions specified in regulation 73 are met

102(1)   This group of regulations applies if a financial trader holds, or has held, an interest in a diversely owned fund.

102(2)   In this Chapter–

"**this group of regulations**" means this regulation and regulations 103 to 105;

"**financial trader**" has the meaning given by regulation 105.

102(3) In computing the trading profits or losses of the financial trader for the relevant period, the following amounts must be brought into account–

(a) all distributions received by or credited to the financial trader in respect of the interest for the relevant period, and

(b) any amount required to be brought into account under regulation 103.

102(4) In this group of regulations **"relevant period"** means–

(a) in the case of a financial trader within the charge to income tax, a period of account, and

(b) in the case of a financial trader within the charge to corporation tax, an accounting period.

102(5) In this group of regulations references to distributions are subject to section 130 of CTA 2009 (insurers receiving distributions etc).

Amounts brought into account in computing trading profits or losses of financial traders

103(1) The only amounts that may be brought into account in computing the trading profits or losses of the financial trader in respect of the interest in the reporting fund for the relevant period are–

(a) amounts within regulation 102(3)(a), and

(b) amounts brought into account in accordance with Cases A to D.

103(2) Paragraph (1) is subject to section 130 of CTA 2009 and to regulation 104.

103(3) Case A applies if the financial trader holds the interest at the beginning of the relevant period and continues to hold the interest throughout the relevant period.

If Case A applies, the amount to be brought into account is the difference between the market value of the interest at the end of the relevant period and the market value of the interest at the end of the period immediately preceding the relevant period.

103(4) Case B applies if the financial trader acquires the interest during the relevant period and continues to hold the interest throughout the remainder of the relevant period.

If Case B applies, the amount to be brought into account is the difference between the market value of the interest at the end of the relevant period and the acquisition cost of the interest.

103(5) Case C applies if the financial trader holds the interest at the beginning of the relevant period and disposes of the interest during the period.

If Case C applies the amount to be brought into account is the difference between the disposal value of the interest and the market value of the interest at the end of the period immediately preceding the relevant period.

103(6) Case D applies if the financial trader acquires and disposes of the interest during the relevant period.

If Case D applies the amount to be brought into account is the difference between the disposal value of the interest and its acquisition cost.

Interests not within regulation 103

104(1) Regulation 103 does not apply in respect of an interest in a reporting fund if–

(a) conditions A and B are met, or

(b) condition C is met.

104(2) Condition A is that the interest forms part of the financial trader's stock in trade and all the profits and losses, including distributions, arising in respect of the interest are included in the computation of the financial trader's trading profits for the relevant period.

104(3) Condition B is that the interest is accounted for under generally accepted accounting practice on the basis of fair value accounting.

104(4) Condition C is that the interest is a relevant holding in respect of which the provisions of section 490 of CTA 2009 (holdings in OEICs, unit trusts and offshore funds treated as creditor relationship rights) apply in relation to the financial trader.

104(5) In paragraph (4) a **"relevant holding"** means–

(a) any rights under a unit trust scheme,

(b) an interest in an offshore fund, or

(c) any shares in an open-ended investment company.

History – In reg. 104(5)(b), the words "an interest" substituted for the words "a material interest" by SI 2013/1411, reg. 14(b), with effect from 28 June 2013.

Meaning of "financial trader"

105(1) In this Chapter **"financial trader"** means a person who is carrying on a business which is–

(a)   a banking business,

(b)   an insurance business, or

(c)   a business consisting wholly or in part of dealing in trading assets such that any profit on such assets would form part of the trading profits of that business.

This is subject to paragraphs (2) and (3).

105(2) For the purposes of paragraph (1)(b) an insurance business does not include life assurance business carried on by an insurance company and if such a company carries on both life assurance business and any other insurance business the company must not be treated as a financial trader in respect of the life assurance business.

105(3) If–

(a)   a financial trader ("A") directly or indirectly transfers trading assets to a diversely owned fund under, or as part of, an arrangement which has an unallowable purpose, and

(b)   a connected person ("B")–

     (i)   holds an interest in the diversely owned fund at the time of the transfer, or

     (ii)   directly or indirectly acquires an interest in the diversely owned fund at a later time,

B is treated as being a financial trader in relation to that interest.

105(4) In this regulation **"trading assets"** means–

(a)   stocks or shares;

(b)   a relevant contract (construed in accordance with regulations 82 to 86);

(c)   a loan relationship (construed in accordance with regulation 87);

(d)   units in a collective investment scheme (construed in accordance with regulation 88);

(e)   securities of any description not falling within any of sub-paragraphs (a) to (d);

(f)   foreign currency; or

(g)   a carbon emission trading product (construed in accordance with regulation 89);

a profit on the sale of which would form part of the trading profits of the financial trader.

105(5) An arrangement includes any scheme, understanding or transaction of any kind, whether or not legally enforceable and whether involving a single transaction or two or more transactions.

105(6) An arrangement has an unallowable purpose if the main purpose or one of the main purposes for either A or B being party to the arrangement is to obtain a tax advantage or an income tax advantage for any person.

105(7) In paragraph (6)–

"**tax advantage**" has the meaning given by section 840ZA of ICTA;

"**income tax advantage**" has the meaning given by section 683 of ITA 2007.

Chapter 9 – The Provision of Information to HMRC

Reporting requirements

106(1) A reporting fund must provide the following information to HMRC in relation to each period of account–

(a)   subject to paragraph (3), its audited accounts;

(b)   its computation of its reportable income for the period of account based on its audited accounts (see Chapter 5 or 6A, as the case may be);

(c)   a copy of the report made available to participants for each reporting period falling within the period of account (including, for each reporting period, the information specified in regulation 92(1) or 92D, as the case may be);

(d)   the reported income of the fund for each reporting period falling within the period of account;

(e)   the amount actually distributed to participants in respect of each reporting period falling within the period of account;

(f)   the number of units in the fund in issue at the end of each reporting period falling within the period of account;

(g)   the amount of the reported income per unit of interest in the fund in respect of each reporting period falling within the period of account;

(h)   a declaration confirming that the fund has complied with the obligations specified in regulations 53 and 58.

106(2)   The information specified in paragraph (1) must be provided within six months of the end of the period of account.

106(3)   A reporting fund may provide unaudited accounts for a period of account if HMRC are satisfied, in relation to that period, that–

(a)   it would be impossible to provide audited accounts or unreasonable to expect them to be provided, and

(b)   there is no reason to believe that the unaudited accounts cannot be relied upon for the purposes of calculating reportable income.

History – In reg. 106(1)(a), the words "subject to paragraph (3)," inserted by SI 2011/1211, reg. 41(2), with effect: for the purposes of income tax or corporation tax, for distributions made, or treated as made, on or after 27 May 2011; and for the purposes of capital gains tax or corporation tax on chargeable gains, in relation to disposals made on or after 27 May 2011.
In reg. 106(1)(a), the words "(see Chapter 4)", which appeared after "audited accounts", omitted by SI 2011/1211, reg. 27(a), with effect: for the purposes of income tax or corporation tax, for distributions made, or treated as made, on or after 27 May 2011; and for the purposes of capital gains tax or corporation tax on chargeable gains, in relation to disposals made on or after 27 May 2011.
In reg. 106(1)(b), the words "or 6A, as the case may be" inserted by SI 2011/1211, reg. 27(b), with effect: for the purposes of income tax or corporation tax, for distributions made, or treated as made, on or after 27 May 2011; and for the purposes of capital gains tax or corporation tax on chargeable gains, in relation to disposals made on or after 27 May 2011.
In reg. 106(1)(c), the words "or 92D, as the case may be" inserted by SI 2011/1211, reg. 27(c), with effect: for the purposes of income tax or corporation tax, for distributions made, or treated as made, on or after 27 May 2011; and for the purposes of capital gains tax or corporation tax on chargeable gains, in relation to disposals made on or after 27 May 2011.
In reg. 106(3)(a), the words "to provide audited accounts or unreasonable to expect them to be provided, and" substituted for the words "or unreasonable to provide audited accounts, and" by SI 2013/1411, reg. 11, with effect from 28 June 2013.
Reg. 106(3) inserted by SI 2011/1211, reg. 41(3), with effect: for the purposes of income tax or corporation tax, for distributions made, or treated as made, on or after 27 May 2011; and for the purposes of capital gains tax or corporation tax on chargeable gains, in relation to disposals made on or after 27 May 2011.

Information obligations of reporting funds

107(1)   HMRC may give notice requiring a reporting fund or its managers, within such time, not being less than 42 days, as is specified in the notice, to provide any information, particulars or documents, in the possession or power of the reporting fund or its managers, as HMRC may reasonably require for the purposes of determining whether the fund has met, or continues to meet, its obligations under Chapter 3 of this Part.

107(2)   Before a notice is given to a reporting fund by HMRC under paragraph (1), the fund must have been given a reasonable opportunity to deliver the information, particulars or documents, or to make them available (the "initial request"); and HMRC must not give notice under paragraph (1) until the initial request has been given to the fund.

107(3)   HMRC must give the initial request to the reporting fund or its manager within a period of one year beginning with the day that the fund provides the information specified in regulation 106(1).

107(4)   HMRC may extend the time specified in paragraph (1) if they consider it reasonable to do so.

107(5)   A person to whom a notice under paragraph (1) is given may appeal.

107(6)   The notice of appeal must be given to HMRC within a period of 42 days beginning with the day on which the notice under paragraph (1) is given.

107(7)   On an appeal, the tribunal may uphold, vary or quash the notice.

Chapter 10 – Breaches of Reporting Fund Requirements

Types of breaches

108(1)   This Chapter applies if a reporting fund is in breach of a requirement imposed in this Part.

108(2)   A breach of a requirement imposed in this Part is–

(a)   a minor breach, or

(b)   a serious breach.

108(3)   For the purposes of these Regulations, a breach of a requirement imposed in this Part is a "**serious breach**" if it is–

(a)   a breach specified as a serious breach in a provision of this Chapter, or

(b)   a breach which is not a minor breach.

108(4) For the purposes of these Regulations, a breach of a requirement imposed in this Part is a **"minor breach"** if it is a breach (other than a breach specified as a serious breach in a provision of this Chapter)–

(a)   for which there is a reasonable excuse, or

(b)   which is inadvertent and remedied as soon as reasonably possible.

This paragraph is subject to the following provisions of this regulation.

108(5) For the purposes of this Part a minor breach is not regarded as a breach if the reporting fund corrects the breach without any HMRC intervention.

108(6) For the purposes of these Regulations there is an **"HMRC intervention"** in relation to a reporting fund if HMRC request the fund to provide them with information relating to a requirement imposed in this Part.

This is subject to paragraph (7).

108(7) There is no HMRC intervention in relation to a reporting fund if–

(a)   the fund takes the initiative to correct a minor breach, and

(b)   HMRC request the fund to provide them with information so that they may deal with the initiative taken.

108(8) Regulation 109 deals with the consequences of minor breaches.

108(9) Regulation 114 deals with the consequences of serious breaches.

Consequences of minor breaches

109(1) If a reporting fund is in breach of a requirement imposed in this Part and the breach is a minor breach, the fund continues to be treated as a reporting fund.

109(2) Paragraph (1) is subject to the following provisions of this Chapter.

109(3) If paragraph (1) applies on four separate occasions in a period of ten years beginning with the first day of the period of account in which the first breach occurs, the fourth breach is a serious breach.

109(4) If a single event results in more than one minor breach within a single period of account, there is only one minor breach in that period of account for the purposes of this Chapter.

Differences between reported income and reportable income

110(1) This regulation applies if there is a difference between–

(a)   the reportable income of a reporting fund for a period of account, and

(b)   the reported income of the fund for all reporting periods comprised in the period of account.

110(2) The following amounts must be determined for each reporting period comprised in the period of account–

(a)   the amount of the reported income for the reporting period, and

(b)   the amount of the reportable income for the period of account that is referable to that reporting period.

110(3) If the difference between the two amounts specified in paragraph (2) is 10% or less of the reportable income, there is no breach of a requirement imposed in this Part.

110(4) If the difference between the two amounts specified in paragraph (2) is more than 10% but not more than 15% of the reportable income–

(a)   an amount equal to the difference must be added to the reported income–

   (i)   for the reporting period in which the error is established, or

   (ii)   for the following reporting period; or

(b)   the reporting fund must make a supplementary report for the period of account in which the difference occurs before the end of a period of three months beginning immediately after the period of account in which the error is established.

110(5) If the difference between the two amounts specified in paragraph (2) is more than 15% of the reportable income, the reporting fund must make a supplementary report to participants for the period of account in which the difference occurs before the end of a period of three months beginning immediately after the period of account in which the error is established.

110(6) The supplementary report mentioned in paragraphs (4) and (5) must be made to those persons who were participants in the fund at the end of the period of account in which the difference occurs.

110(7) If paragraph (4) or (5) applies and the action specified in the applicable paragraph is taken as soon as reasonably possible, there is a minor breach.

110(8)   If paragraph (4) or (5) applies but the action specified in the applicable paragraph is not taken as soon as reasonably possible, there is a serious breach.

110(9)   For the purposes of paragraph (4) an error is established for a reporting period if, during that reporting period–

(a)   HMRC conclude–

    (i)   that an error has been made in respect of an earlier reporting period, and

    (ii)   that, as a result of the error, the difference between the reported income for the reporting period and the reportable income for the period of account in which the reporting period is comprised is more than 10% but not more than 15%; and

(b)   HMRC give notice to the reporting fund of the matters specified in sub-paragraph (a).

110(10)   For the purposes of paragraph (5) an error is established for a period of account if, during that period of account–

(a)   HMRC conclude–

    (i)   that an error has been made in respect of an earlier period of account, and

    (ii)   that, as a result of the error, the difference between the reported income and the reportable income for the period of account is more than 15%; and

(b)   HMRC give notice to the reporting fund of the matters specified in sub-paragraph (a).

Provision of report that is incorrect or incomplete

111(1)   This regulation applies if–

(a)   a reporting fund provides a report specified in paragraph (2) that is incorrect or incomplete, and

(b)   regulation 110 does not apply.

111(2)   The reports specified are–

(a)   the report to participants in accordance with the requirements of Chapter 7 of this Part, and

(b)   the report to HMRC in accordance with the requirements of Chapter 9 of this Part.

111(3)   If the reporting fund provides a correct report as soon as reasonably possible, there is a minor breach.

111(4)   If the reporting fund does not provide a correct report as soon as reasonably possible, there is a serious breach.

Cases where information is not provided

112(1)   This regulation applies if, on the relevant date, a reporting fund has not provided–

(a)   the information specified in regulation 106(1) to HMRC in relation to a period of account (the "requisite period of account"), and

(b)   a report to each participant for each reporting period comprised in the requisite period of account.

112(2)   In paragraph (1) the **"relevant date"** means the day immediately following the expiry of the period of six months beginning immediately after the end of the requisite period of account.

112(3)   If the reporting fund provides the information mentioned in paragraph (1)(a) and the reports mentioned in paragraph (1)(b) within a period of four months beginning with the relevant date, the breach is not regarded as a breach for the purposes of this Part.

112(4)   If the reporting fund does not provide the information mentioned in paragraph (1)(a) and the reports mentioned in paragraph (1)(b) within a period of four months beginning with the relevant date but does provide that information and those reports within a period of twelve months beginning with the relevant date, there is a minor breach.

112(5)   If the reporting fund does not provide the information mentioned in paragraph (1)(a) and the reports mentioned in paragraph (1)(b) within a period of twelve months beginning with the relevant date, there is a serious breach.

Serious breaches

113(1)   There is a serious breach if condition A, B, C or D is met.

113(2)   Condition A is that a period of account of a reporting fund exceeds 18 months.

113(3)   Condition B is that a reporting fund has used an accounting practice which–

(a)   is not in accordance with international accounting standards, and

(b)   has not been approved by HMRC (see regulations 53, 55 and 61).

113(4)   Condition C is that–

(a)   a reporting fund fails, or its managers fail, to provide the information, particulars or documents within the time specified in a notice given under regulation 107(1), and

(b)   there is no appeal against the notice within the time specified in regulation 107(6).

113(5)   Condition D is that–

(a)   on an appeal against a notice given under regulation 107(1), the tribunal varies the notice,

(b)   a reporting fund fails, or its managers fail, to provide the information, particulars or documents within the time specified in the notice (as so varied), and

(c)   there is no appeal against the decision of the tribunal.

Consequences of serious breaches

114(1)   This regulation applies if conditions A and B are met.

114(2)   Condition A is that–

(a)   a reporting fund is in breach of a requirement imposed in this Part, and

(b)   the breach is a serious breach.

114(3)   Condition B is that HMRC give notice to the fund–

(a)   stating that the fund is in breach of a requirement imposed in this Part and that the breach is a serious breach, and

(b)   specifying the serious breach.

114(4)   The fund is treated as a non-reporting fund for the reporting period in which HMRC give the notice and for all subsequent periods.

This is subject to paragraphs (5) and (6).

114(5)   If regulation 113(4) applies, the fund is treated as a non-reporting fund for the reporting period in which the notice is given and for all subsequent periods.

114(6)   If regulation 113(5) applies, the fund is treated as a non-reporting fund for the reporting period in which the notice as varied is given and for all subsequent periods.

Appeal against exclusion from the reporting fund regime

115(1)   If HMRC give notice to a fund under regulation 114(3) (an "exclusion notice"), the fund may appeal.

115(2)   The notice of appeal must be given to HMRC within a period of 42 days beginning with the day on which the exclusion notice is given.

115(3)   On an appeal, the tribunal may uphold or quash the exclusion notice.

Chapter 11 – Leaving the Reporting Fund Regime

Termination by notice given by reporting fund

116(1)   If a reporting fund gives a notice under this regulation specifying a day (the "specified day") at the end of which this Part is to cease to apply to the fund, this Part shall cease to apply to the fund at the end of that day.

116(2)   The specified day must be the last day of a period of account of the reporting fund.

116(3)   A notice under paragraph (1) must be given in writing to HMRC before the specified day.

116(4)   If the fund gives a notice under paragraph (1), the fund must also make the notice available to each participant before the specified day.

116(5)   Paragraphs (2) to (4) of regulation 90 apply to determine whether the notice is made available to a participant in the same way as they apply to determine whether a report for a reporting period is made available to a participant.

116(6)   This regulation is subject to regulation 117.

Reporting fund not complying with requirements

117(1)   This regulation applies if–

(a)   a reporting fund gives a notice under regulation 116, and

(b)   the fund has not complied with all requirements imposed in this Part for all periods during which it was a reporting fund.

117(2)   For the purposes of these Regulations the fund is treated as a fund to which regulation 114 has applied and not as a fund to which regulation 116 has applied.

Chapter 12 – Constant NAV Funds

INTERPRETATION

Meaning of "constant NAV fund"

118(1)　In these Regulations a **"constant NAV fund"** means an offshore fund that meets conditions A and B.

118(2)　Condition A is that the net asset value of the fund (expressed in the currency in which units are issued) will not fluctuate by more than an insignificant amount throughout the fund's existence.

118(3)　Condition B is that condition A is met as a result of–

(a)　the nature of the fund's assets, and

(b)　the frequency with which the fund distributes its income.

MODIFIED APPLICATION OF THIS PART

General

119　In the case of a constant NAV fund, Chapters 2 to 11 of this Part apply with the following modifications.

Modified application of Chapter 2

120(1)　Chapter 2 applies with the following modifications.

120(2)　In regulation 53 for paragraph (1) substitute–

"**53(1)**　An application must include the following–

(a)　a statement of the first period of account for which it is proposed that the fund should be treated as a constant NAV fund for the purposes of these Regulations,

(b)　a statement that the fund is, or will be, a constant NAV fund at the beginning of that first period of account, and

(c)　an undertaking to notify HMRC if the offshore fund ceases to be a constant NAV fund.".

120(3)　Regulations 55 and 56 do not apply.

Modified application of Chapter 3

121(1)　Chapter 3 applies with the following modifications.

121(2)　For regulation 57 substitute–

"Effects of Entry into the Reporting Fund Regime

57A(1)　Unless HMRC reject an application because an item specified in regulation 53(1) has not been supplied, the offshore fund becomes a constant NAV fund on whichever is the later of–

(a)　the first day of the first period of account mentioned in regulation 53(1)(a), or

(b)　the day on which the fund is established.

57A(2)　This Part applies to the constant NAV fund and to its participants on and after the date specified in paragraph (1).

57A(3)　Once this Part has begun to apply to a constant NAV fund, it shall continue to apply unless and until the fund notifies HMRC that it has ceased to be a constant NAV fund.

57A(4)　See regulation 108A for the consequences where the net asset value of the fund has risen by more than an insignificant amount and the fund has not notified HMRC that it has ceased to be a constant NAV fund.".

121(3)　Regulation 58 does not apply.

Disapplication of Chapters 4 to 9

122　Chapters 4 to 9 do not apply.

Modified application of Chapter 10

123　For regulations 108 to 115 substitute–

"Consequences of Rise in Net Asset Value of Fund

108A(1)　This regulation applies if–

(a)　this Part applies to a constant NAV fund,

(b)　the net asset value of the fund (expressed in the currency in which units are issued) has risen by more than an insignificant amount, and

(c)   the fund has not notified HMRC that it has ceased to be a constant NAV fund.

108A(2)   But this regulation does not apply if the net asset value of a constant NAV fund (expressed in the currency in which units are issued) has fallen by more than an insignificant amount.

108A(3)   A participant who disposes of an interest in the fund and who makes a chargeable gain on the disposal is treated as making an offshore income gain.".

Disapplication of Chapter 11

124   Chapter 11 does not apply.

PART 3A – ANNUAL PAYMENTS TO NON-RESIDENTS

History – Pt. 3A inserted by SI 2013/1770, reg. 2(3), with effect for the purposes of income tax for the tax year 2013–14 and subsequent tax years.

ANNUAL PAYMENTS – DUTY TO DEDUCT INCOME TAX

124A(1)   An annual payment made to a participant which meets the conditions in paragraphs (2) to (6) is not a qualifying annual payment for the purposes of Chapter 6 of Part 15 of ITA 2007 (deduction from annual payments and royalties).

124A(2)   The payment must be charged to income tax under Chapter 7 of Part 5 of ITTOIA 2005 (annual payments not otherwise charged).

124A(3)   The payment must be made in respect of the participant's interest in an offshore fund.

124A(4)   The payment and the amount of the payment must be directly or indirectly referable to, and must not be more than, any management fees paid to the manager of the offshore fund in respect of the participant's interest in the fund.

124A(5)   Any management fee must not exceed an amount representing a reasonable commercial amount in all the circumstances.

124A(6)   At the time the payment is made, the person making the payment must have reasonable grounds for believing that the participant is not resident in the United Kingdom.

CONSEQUENCES OF REASONABLE BUT INCORRECT BELIEF

124B(1)   This regulation applies if–

(a)   an annual payment is made to a participant without a sum representing income tax on the payment being deducted from it,

(b)   at the time the payment is made, the condition in regulation 124A(6) is met,

(c)   the payment would be a qualifying annual payment but for that condition being met, and

(d)   at the time the payment is made, the participant is resident in the United Kingdom.

124B(2)   Section 900 (deduction from commercial payments made by individuals) and section 901 (deduction from annual payments made by other persons) of ITA 2007 apply as if the payment were a qualifying annual payment.

PART 4 – CONSEQUENTIAL AMENDMENTS

Amendment of the Inheritance Tax Act 1984

125   [Amends IHTA 1984, s. 174(1)(a).]

Amendment of ICTA

126(1)   ICTA is amended as follows.

126(2)   [Amends ICTA 1988, s. 396(2).]

126(3)   [Amends ICTA 1988, s. 505(3)(b)(iii).]

126(4)   [Amends ICTA 1988, s. 587B(9).]

126(5)   [Amends ICTA 1988, s. 834A.]

126(6)   Amends ICTA 1988, s. 842(3A).

Amendment of TCGA 1992

127(1)   TCGA 1992 is amended as follows.

127(2) [Amends TCGA 1992, s. 108(1)(c).]

127(3) [Amends TCGA 1992, s. 212.]

127(4) [Amends TCGA 1992, Sch. 7AD, para. 7]

Amendment of ITTOIA 2005

128(1) ITTOIA 2005 is amended as follows.

128(2) [Amends ITTOIA 2005, s. 378A(7).]

128(3) [Amends ITTOIA 2005, s. 632.]

128(4) [Amends ITTOIA 2005, s. 830(4) .]

Amendment of ITA 2007

129(1) ITA 2007 is amended as follows.

129(2) [Amends ITA 2007, s. 152(8).]

129(3) [Amends ITA 2007, s. 482.]

129(4) [Amends ITA 2007, s. 535.]

129(5) [Amends ITA 2007, s. 734(5) .]

129(6) [Amends ITA 2007, s. 1016(2).]

Amendment of FA 2008

130(1) Schedule 7 to FA 2008 (remittance basis) is amended as follows.

130(2) [Amends FA 2008, Sch. 7, para. 100(1)(a).]

130(3) [Amends FA 2008, Sch. 7, para. 101(1)(b).]

130(4) [Amends FA 2008, Sch. 7, para. 102(1)(d).]

Amendment of CTA 2009

131(1) CTA 2009 is amended as follows.

131(2) [Amends CTA 2009, s. 489.]

131(3) [Amends CTA 2009, s. 490(1)(a)(iii).]

SCHEDULE 1 – TRANSITIONAL PROVISIONS AND SAVINGS

Regulation 1(3) and 13(1)

1 In this Schedule–

"**distributing fund**" means a fund which, immediately before 1st December 2009, was a distributing fund for the purposes of Chapter 5 of Part 17 of ICTA or a fund treated as a distributing fund in accordance with paragraph 3(3A);

"**existing fund**" means a fund to which, immediately before 1st December 2009, section 756A of ICTA applied;

"**non-qualifying fund**" means a fund which, immediately before 1st December 2009, was a non-qualifying fund for the purposes of Chapter 5 of Part 17 of ICTA;

the "**overlap period**" means the period of account of an existing fund which has begun, but not ended, on the day these Regulations come into force;

the "**succeeding period**" means the period of account of the fund immediately following the overlap period.

History – In para. 1, in the definition of "distributing fund", the words "or a fund treated as a distributing fund in accordance with paragraph 3(3A)" inserted by SI 2009/3139, reg. 5(2), with effect: (for the purposes of income tax) for the tax year 2009–10 and subsequent tax years and for distributions made on or after 1 December 2009; (for the purposes of corporation tax on income) for accounting periods ending on or after 1 December 2009 and for distributions made on or after that date; and (for the purposes of capital gains tax or corporation tax on chargeable gains) in relation to disposals made on or after 1 December 2009.

2(1) This paragraph applies in the case of an existing fund which, on 1st December 2009, becomes a non-reporting fund.

2(2) A participant begins to have an interest in the non-reporting fund at the beginning of the accounting period of the non-reporting fund current on 1st December 2009.

2(3) An offshore income gain arising to a person on the disposal of an asset must be computed in accordance with Part 2, but is to have regard to the entirety of the period of the person's ownership of the asset.

3(1) This paragraph applies in the case of an existing fund and umbrella arrangements but is subject to paragraph (3B).

3(2) The fund or any person within paragraph 18(1) of Schedule 27 to ICTA may apply in writing to HMRC for the fund to be treated as a distributing fund in respect of the overlap period or any earlier period of account.

3(3) If the fund or any person within paragraph 18(1) of Schedule 27 to ICTA has made a successful application under sub-paragraph (2), the fund or that person may apply in writing to HMRC for the fund to be continued to be treated as a distributing fund in respect of the succeeding period.

3(3ZA) But no application may be made under paragraph (3) if HMRC have accepted an application for Part 3 to apply to the fund.

3(3A) Where an existing fund is part of umbrella arrangements (within the meaning of section 40C of FA 2008) or is part of arrangements comprising more than one class of interest (within the meaning of section 40D of FA 2008), separate arrangements under the umbrella arrangements, and each class of interest under the main arrangements, established on or after 1st December 2009, may apply in writing to HMRC to be treated as a distributing fund in respect of a period of account if–

(a)   that period has the same accounting reference date as the overlap period or succeeding period of the existing fund, and

(b)   the existing fund is treated as a distributing fund in respect of the contemporaneous overlap period or succeeding period.

3(3B) This paragraph does not apply in respect of any period of account which ends after 31st May 2012.

3(4) The repeal by these Regulations of the enactments specified in Schedule 2 does not affect the continued operation of those provisions for the purposes of this paragraph.

History – In para. 3(1), the words "and umbrella arrangements but is subject to paragraph (3B)" inserted by SI 2009/3139, reg. 5(3)(a), with effect: (for the purposes of income tax) for the tax year 2009–10 and subsequent tax years and for distributions made on or after 1 December 2009; (for the purposes of corporation tax on income) for accounting periods ending on or after 1 December 2009 and for distributions made on or after that date; and (for the purposes of capital gains tax or corporation tax on chargeable gains) in relation to disposals made on or after 1 December 2009.
Para. 3(2), (3) and (3ZA) substituted for former para. 3(2) and (3) by SI 2011/1211, reg. 42(2), with effect: for the purposes of income tax or corporation tax, for distributions made, or treated as made, on or after 27 May 2011; and for the purposes of capital gains tax or corporation tax on chargeable gains, in relation to disposals made on or after 27 May 2011. Former para. 3(2) and (3) read as follows:
     "3(2) The fund may apply in writing to HMRC to be treated as a distributing fund in respect of the overlap period.
     3(3) If the fund has made a successful application under sub-paragraph (2), the fund may apply in writing to HMRC to continue to be treated as a distributing fund in respect of the succeeding period.".
Para. 3(3A) inserted by SI 2009/3139, reg. 5(3)(b), with effect: (for the purposes of income tax) for the tax year 2009–10 and subsequent tax years and for distributions made on or after 1 December 2009; (for the purposes of corporation tax on income) for accounting periods ending on or after 1 December 2009 and for distributions made on or after that date; and (for the purposes of capital gains tax or corporation tax on chargeable gains) in relation to disposals made on or after 1 December 2009.
In para. 3(3B), "2012" substituted for "2011" by SI 2011/1211, reg. 42(3), with effect: for the purposes of income tax or corporation tax, for distributions made, or treated as made, on or after 27 May 2011; and for the purposes of capital gains tax or corporation tax on chargeable gains, in relation to disposals made on or after 27 May 2011.
Para. 3(3B) inserted by SI 2009/3139, reg. 5(3)(b), with effect: (for the purposes of income tax) for the tax year 2009–10 and subsequent tax years and for distributions made on or after 1 December 2009; (for the purposes of corporation tax on income) for accounting periods ending on or after 1 December 2009 and for distributions made on or after that date; and (for the purposes of capital gains tax or corporation tax on chargeable gains) in relation to disposals made on or after 1 December 2009.

3A In the case of a reporting fund which has an interest in a distributing fund, income from the distributing fund is treated as income from a reporting fund but no adjustment shall be made to that income under regulation 68 (income from other reporting funds).

History – Para. 3A inserted by SI 2009/3139, reg. 5(3)(a), with effect: (for the purposes of income tax) for the tax year 2009–10 and subsequent tax years and for distributions made on or after 1 December 2009; (for the purposes of corporation tax on income) for accounting periods ending on or after 1 December 2009 and for distributions made on or after that date; and (for the purposes of capital gains tax or corporation tax on chargeable gains) in relation to disposals made on or after 1 December 2009.

3B(1) This paragraph applies in the case of a distributing fund which has an interest in a reporting fund.

3B(2) The reporting fund is treated as a qualifying fund for the purposes of Part 2 of Schedule 27 of ICTA (modifications of conditions for certification in certain cases).

3B(3) The amount of the adjustment required by paragraph 8(1) of Schedule 27 in respect of the excess income of the qualifying fund for any account period is the amount of the excess of the income reported by the reporting fund in respect of the distributing fund's interest in the reporting fund over the amount distributed by the reporting fund to the distributing fund.

History – Para. 3B inserted by SI 2009/3139, reg. 5(4), with effect: (for the purposes of income tax) for the tax year 2009–10 and subsequent tax years and for distributions made on or after 1 December 2009; (for the purposes of corporation tax on income) for accounting periods ending on or after 1 December 2009 and for distributions made on or after that date; and (for the purposes of capital gains tax or corporation tax on chargeable gains) in relation to disposals made on or after 1 December 2009.

3C   In the case of an exchange of an interest in a distributing fund for an interest in a reporting fund, regulation 37 (exchange of interests of different classes) shall not apply.

History – Para. 3C inserted by SI 2009/3139, reg. 5(4), with effect: (for the purposes of income tax) for the tax year 2009–10 and subsequent tax years and for distributions made on or after 1 December 2009; (for the purposes of corporation tax on income) for accounting periods ending on or after 1 December 2009 and for distributions made on or after that date; and (for the purposes of capital gains tax or corporation tax on chargeable gains) in relation to disposals made on or after 1 December 2009.

4(1)   This paragraph applies in the case of an existing fund which does not become a reporting fund immediately following its last account period as a distributing fund.

4(2)   A participant in the fund may make an election to be treated for the purposes of TCGA 1992–

(a)   as disposing of an interest in the distributing fund at the end of that fund's last account period, and

(b)   as acquiring an interest in the non-reporting fund immediately following the disposal treated as made by paragraph (a).

4(3)   The disposal referred to in paragraph (a) of sub-paragraph (2) is treated as made for a consideration equal to the net asset value of the participant's interest in the fund at the end of the final accounting period.

4(4)   The acquisition referred to in paragraph (b) of sub-paragraph (2) is treated as made for the same amount as the disposal referred to in paragraph (a) of that sub-paragraph.

4(5)   If the participant is chargeable to income tax, the election mentioned in sub-paragraph (2) must be made by being included in a return made for the tax year which includes the disposal date.

4(6)   If the participant is chargeable to corporation tax, the election mentioned in sub-paragraph (2) must be made by being included in the participant's company tax return for the accounting period which includes the disposal date.

4(7)   In this paragraph–

"**company tax return**" has the same meaning as in Schedule 18 to the Finance Act 1998;

"**disposal date**" means the final day of the distributing fund's final accounting period.

5(1)   This paragraph applies in the case of an existing fund which–

(a)   immediately before 1st December 2009 was a non-qualifying fund, and

(b)   on 1st December 2009 becomes a reporting fund.

5(2)   Regulation 48 applies as if, for references to the non-reporting fund, there were substituted references to the existing fund.

5(3)   Chapter 5 of Part 17 of ICTA applies to determine the offshore income gain arising by virtue of the application of regulation 48.

6(1)   This paragraph applies in the case of an existing fund which–

(a)   makes a successful application under paragraph 3 to continue to be treated as a distributing fund after 1st December 2009, and

(b)   becomes a reporting fund immediately following the end of the overlap period or the succeeding period.

6(2)   For the purposes of regulations 17 and 99 the fund is treated as a reporting fund for the entirety of a continuous period–

(a)   beginning with the day the fund becomes a distributing fund, and

(b)   ending on the last day of the overlap period or the succeeding period (as the case may be).

6(3)   If for any part of the period specified in sub-paragraph (2) the fund is not a distributing fund, the period is not continuous for the purposes of that sub-paragraph.

7(1)   This paragraph applies in the case of an arrangement ("Fund X") which, immediately before 1st December 2009, did not fall to be classified as an offshore fund, but which, on 1st December 2009, falls to be classified as an offshore fund.

7(2)   Fund X may make an application, in accordance with Part 3, in relation to the period of account that is current on 1st December 2009.

7(3)   The application must be received by HMRC on or before 31st May 2010.

SCHEDULE 2 – REPEALS

Regulation 13(2)

Short title and chapter	Extent of repeal
Income and Corporation Taxes Act 1988 (c. 1)	Chapter 5 of Part 17.
	In section 834A, in Part 1 of the Table, the entry relating to section 761(1)(b)(i).
	Schedules 27 and 28.
Finance Act 1988 (c. 39)	In Schedule 13, paragraph 12.
Finance Act 1990 (c. 29)	In Schedule 14, paragraphs 10 and 11.
Taxation of Chargeable Gains Act 1992 (c. 12)	In section 108(1)(c), the words ", or have at anytime been,".
	In section 212, subsections (5) to (7).
	In Schedule 10, paragraph 14(43) to (49) and (63).
Finance Act 1995 (c. 4)	Section 134.
Finance Act 1996 (c. 8)	In Schedule 28, in paragraph 6, the words "and in paragraph 5(5) of Schedule 27 to that Act".
Finance Act 2002 (c. 23)	In Schedule 9, paragraph 4(5) and (6).
Finance Act 2004 (c. 12)	In Schedule 26, paragraphs 1(1), 2(1), 4 to 9 and 13 to 16.
Income Tax (Trading and Other Income) Act 2005 (c. 5)	In Schedule 1, paragraphs 308, 309 and 350.
Finance (No. 2) Act 2005 (c. 22)	Section 23.
Finance Act 2006 (c. 25)	In Schedule 12, paragraph 47.
Income Tax Act 2007 (c. 3)	In section 1016(2), in Part 3 of the Table, the entry relating to section 761(1)(b)(i) of ICTA.
	In Schedule 1, paragraphs 179 to 181.
Finance Act 2008 (c. 9)	In Schedule 7, paragraphs 92 to 96.
	In Schedule 17, paragraph 30.

SCHEDULE 3 – ABBREVIATIONS AND DEFINED EXPRESSIONS

Regulation 13(4)

Part 1 – Abbreviations of Acts

TMA 1970	The Taxes Management Act 1970 (c. 9)
ICTA	The Income and Corporation Taxes Act 1988 (c.1)
TCGA 1992	The Taxation of Chargeable Gains Act 1992 (c. 12)
FA 1996	The Finance Act 1996 (c. 8)
FISMA 2000	The Financial Services and Markets Act 2000 (c. 8)
ITTOIA 2005	The Income Tax (Trading and Other Income) Act 2005 (c. 5)
ITA 2007	The Income Tax Act 2007 (c. 3)
FA 2008	The Finance Act 2008 (c. 9)
CTA 2009	The Corporation Tax Act 2009 (c. 4)
CTA 2010	The Corporation Tax Act 2010 (c. 4)

History – In Pt. 1, the entry for CTA 2010 inserted by SI 2011/1211, reg. 43(2), with effect: for the purposes of income tax or corporation tax, for distributions made, or treated as made, on or after 27 May 2011; and for the purposes of capital gains tax or corporation tax on chargeable gains, in relation to disposals made on or after 27 May 2011.

Part 2 – Index of Expressions Defined or Otherwise Explained in these Regulations

TCGA disposal (in Chapter 6 of Part 2)	Regulation 44(2)
This group of regulations (in Chapter 8 of Part 3)	Regulation 102(2)
Transparent fund	Regulation 11
Transparent reporting fund	Regulation 89A(2)
Tribunal	Regulation 12
UCITS fund	Regulation 12
Umbrella arrangements	Regulation 5

History – In Pt. 2, the entry relating to "investment transaction" omitted by SI 2014/685, reg. 8(4), with effect from transactions entered into on or after 8 April 2014.

In Pt. 2, entry for "accounting income (in Part 3)" substituted by SI 2013/1411, reg. 12, with effect from 28 June 2013 but subject to savings provision at SI 2013/1411, reg. 1; amendments do not apply in relation to a reporting period (as defined by reg. 91) which ended before that date if–

(a)   no report has previously been made available under reg. 90 for that reporting period, and

(b)   the manager of the fund elects by notice in writing within 10 months of the end of that reporting period that those amendments should not apply.

In Pt. 2, the entry for "accounting income (in Part 4)" inserted by SI 2011/1211, reg. 43(3)(b), with effect: for the purposes of income tax or corporation tax, for distributions made, or treated as made, on or after 27 May 2011; and for the purposes of capital gains tax or corporation tax on chargeable gains, in relation to disposals made on or after 27 May 2011.

In Pt. 2, the entry for "acquisition by way of initial purchase (in Part 4)" inserted by SI 2011/1211, reg. 43(3)(b), with effect: for the purposes of income tax or corporation tax, for distributions made, or treated as made, on or after 27 May 2011; and for the purposes of capital gains tax or corporation tax on chargeable gains, in relation to disposals made on or after 27 May 2011.

In Pt. 2, the entry for "computation period (in Part 4)" inserted by SI 2011/1211, reg. 43(3)(b), with effect: for the purposes of income tax or corporation tax, for distributions made, or treated as made, on or after 27 May 2011; and for the purposes of capital gains tax or corporation tax on chargeable gains, in relation to disposals made on or after 27 May 2011.

In Pt. 2, the entry for "equalisation amount per unit of interest (in Part 4)" inserted by SI 2011/1211, reg. 43(3)(b), with effect: for the purposes of income tax or corporation tax, for distributions made, or treated as made, on or after 27 May 2011; and for the purposes of capital gains tax or corporation tax on chargeable gains, in relation to disposals made on or after 27 May 2011.

In Pt. 2, the entry for "equalisation amount (in Part 4)" inserted by SI 2011/1211, reg. 43(3)(b), with effect: for the purposes of income tax or corporation tax, for distributions made, or treated as made, on or after 27 May 2011; and for the purposes of capital gains tax or corporation tax on chargeable gains, in relation to disposals made on or after 27 May 2011.

In Pt. 2, the entry for "fund operating equalisation arrangements (in Part 4)" inserted by SI 2011/1211, reg. 43(3)(b), with effect: for the purposes of income tax or corporation tax, for distributions made, or treated as made, on or after 27 May 2011; and for the purposes of capital gains tax or corporation tax on chargeable gains, in relation to disposals made on or after 27 May 2011.

In Pt. 2, the entry for "fund operating full equalisation arrangements (in Part 4)" inserted by SI 2011/1211, reg. 43(3)(b), with effect: for the purposes of income tax or corporation tax, for distributions made, or treated as made, on or after 27 May 2011; and for the purposes of capital gains tax or corporation tax on chargeable gains, in relation to disposals made on or after 27 May 2011.

In Pt. 2, in the entry for "investment transaction", the words "(in Part 3)" omitted by SI 2011/1211, reg. 43(3)(a), with effect: for the purposes of income tax or corporation tax, for distributions made, or treated as made, on or after 27 May 2011; and for the purposes of capital gains tax or corporation tax on chargeable gains, in relation to disposals made on or after 27 May 2011.

In Pt. 2, the entry for "regulated market" inserted by SI 2011/1211, reg. 43(3)(b), with effect: for the purposes of income tax or corporation tax, for distributions made, or treated as made, on or after 27 May 2011; and for the purposes of capital gains tax or corporation tax on chargeable gains, in relation to disposals made on or after 27 May 2011.

In Pt. 2, the entry for "transparent reporting fund" inserted by SI 2011/1211, reg. 43(3)(b), with effect: for the purposes of income tax or corporation tax, for distributions made, or treated as made, on or after 27 May 2011; and for the purposes of capital gains tax or corporation tax on chargeable gains, in relation to disposals made on or after 27 May 2011.

FINANCE ACT 2008, SECTION 128 AND PART 2 OF SCHEDULE 43 (APPOINTED DAY, TRANSITIONAL PROVISION AND SAVINGS) ORDER 2009

(SI 2009/3024)

Made on 9 November 2009 by the Commissioners for Her Majesty's Revenue and Customs, in exercise of the powers conferred by s. 129(4) and (5) of the Finance Act 2008.

CITATION AND INTERPRETATION

1(1) This Order may be cited as The Finance Act 2008, Section 128 and Part 2 of Schedule 43 (Appointed Day, Transitional Provision and Savings) Order 2009.

2 In this Order **"FA 2008"** means the Finance Act 2008.

APPOINTED DAY

3 The day appointed for the coming into force of Section 128 of, and Part 2 of Schedule 43 to, FA 2008 is 23rd November 2009.

TRANSITIONAL PROVISION AND SAVINGS

4(1) If, before the commencement date, a warrant has been granted under–

(a)   section 63 of the Taxes Management Act 1970 (recovery of tax in Scotland);

(b)   [not relevant to income tax, corporation tax or capital gains tax;]

(c)   [not relevant to income tax, corporation tax or capital gains tax;]

(d)   [not relevant to income tax, corporation tax or capital gains tax.]

that warrant shall continue to have effect according to the provisions under which it was granted.

5 [Not relevant to income tax, corporation tax or capital gains tax.]

REGISTERED PENSION SCHEMES (MODIFICATION OF THE RULES OF EXISTING SCHEMES) REGULATIONS 2009

(SI 2009/3055)

Made on 19 November 2009 by the Commissioners for Her Majesty's Revenue and Customs in exercise of the powers conferred by para. 3 of Sch. 36 to, and, s. 282(A1) of, the Finance Act 2004. Operative from 11 December 2009.

CITATION, COMMENCEMENT AND EFFECT

1(1) These Regulations may be cited as the Registered Pension Schemes (Modification of the Rules of Existing Schemes) Regulations 2009 and shall come into force on 11th December 2009.

1(2) Regulation 2 shall have effect in relation to any time on or after 6th April 2006.

SCHEME RULE AMENDMENTS NOT TO REQUIRE THE APPROVAL OF H M REVENUE AND CUSTOMS

2(1) Any provision (however framed) in the rules of an existing scheme, as they stood immediately before 6th April 2006, to make an amendment to a rule of a scheme which would require the agreement, consent, approval of, or confirmation of continued approval of the scheme by–

(a) the Inland Revenue, the Board of Inland Revenue, the Commissioners of Inland Revenue, or any officer of any of them (whether referred to as such or by reference to another title), or

(b) Her Majesty's Revenue and Customs, the Commissioners for Her Majesty's Revenue and Customs or an officer of Revenue and Customs,

shall be disregarded during the transitional period, to the extent that the provision requires such agreement, consent, approval or confirmation of continued approval of the scheme.

2(2) In this regulation–

"existing scheme" means a pension scheme to which paragraph 1(1) of Schedule 36 to the Finance Act 2004 applies,

"rules", in relation to an existing scheme, means the rules (whether contained in the governing instruments or otherwise) of an existing scheme,

"the transitional period", in relation to an existing scheme, means the period beginning with the 6th April 2006 and ending with the date on which, by virtue of paragraph 3(2) of Schedule 36 to the Finance Act 2004, the modifications in these Regulations cease to have effect.

CORPORATION TAX (FINANCING COSTS AND INCOME) REGULATIONS 2009

(SI 2009/3173)

Made on 2 December 2009 by the Commissioners for Her Majesty's Revenue and Customs in exercise of the powers conferred by para. 17(3), 24, 25(4) and (5), 26, 29(3), 36 and 38 of Sch. 15 to the Finance Act 2009. Operative in accordance with reg. 1.

PART 1 – PRELIMINARY PROVISIONS AND INTERPRETATION

CITATION, COMMENCEMENT AND EFFECT

1(1) These Regulations may be cited as the Corporation Tax (Financing Costs and Income) Regulations 2009 and, subject to paragraph (2), shall come into force on 1st January 2010.

1(2) Circumstance 4 in regulations 13(2) and 28(2) come into force on 1st April 2010.

1(3) These Regulations have effect in relation to periods of account beginning on or after 1st January 2010.

INTRODUCTION AND STRUCTURE OF REGULATIONS

2(1) These Regulations make provision about the treatment for the purposes of corporation tax of certain financing costs and certain financing income of companies that are members of a group.

2(2) The structure of these Regulations is as follows–

    Part 1 makes provision in relation to general and preliminary matters;

    Part 2 makes provision in relation to the disallowance of deductions;

    Part 3 makes provision in relation to the exemption of financing income.

INTERPRETATION

3(1) For the purposes of these Regulations–

(a) **"Schedule 15"** means Schedule 15 of the Finance Act 2009 (tax treatment of financing costs and income);

(b) a company is an **"immediate parent"** of another company if it directly owns more than 50% of the ordinary share capital of that other company;

(c) a company is an **"ultimate UK parent"** in relation to a group if it–

    (i) is a member of the group,

    (ii) is a corporate entity,

    (iii) is not a subsidiary (whether direct or indirect) of a corporate entity resident in the United Kingdom,

    (iv) is not a collective investment scheme, and

    (v) is a company to which Part 3 and Part 4 of Schedule 15 apply.

3(2) In this regulation, **"collective investment scheme"** has the meaning given by paragraph 80(2) of Schedule 15.

PART 2 – DISALLOWANCE OF DEDUCTIONS

Chapter 1 – Appointment of Authorised Company

APPOINTMENT OF AUTHORISED COMPANY

4(1) An appointment under paragraph 17 of Schedule 15 must be made in accordance with this regulation.

4(2) The company seeking to be appointed ("the applicant company") must make an application in writing to an officer of Revenue and Customs at least 3 months before the time specified in paragraph 19(2) of Schedule 15 (submission of statement of allocated disallowances).

4(3) The application must be sent to the tax office that deals with the corporation tax affairs of the applicant company.

4(4) The application must specify–

(a) the name and the tax office reference of the applicant company,

(b) the names and the tax office references of the other companies to which Part 3 of Schedule 15 applies,

(c) the first period of account of the worldwide group in relation to which the appointment is to apply, and

(d) except in relation to the ultimate parent, the name of the immediate parent of the applicant company and each of the other companies to which Part 3 of Schedule 15 applies.

4(5) The application must contain a statement by the applicant company and by each of the other companies to which Part 3 of Schedule 15 applies–

(a) that the appointment is made under paragraph 17 of Schedule 15,

(b) that the applicant company will act on behalf of all the companies to which Part 3 of Schedule 15 applies for all relevant periods of account for which the appointment has effect,

(c) that no application will be made by a company to amend its company tax return in relation to a financing expense amount specified under paragraph 21(4)(b) of Schedule 15 other than through a revised statement submitted by the applicant company in accordance with paragraph 20 of Schedule 15, and

(d) agreeing to be bound by any statement of allocated disallowances or revised statement delivered by the applicant company.

4(6) The application must be accompanied by a specimen copy of a statement of allocated disallowances that the applicant company proposes to submit in relation to the relevant period of account.

SUPPLEMENTAL PROVISIONS: TIMING AND EFFECT

5(1) An appointment under paragraph 17 of Schedule 15 has effect on the date ("the three month date") that is three months after the application is delivered to the tax office in accordance with regulation 4(3).

This is subject to paragraphs (2) to (4).

5(2) An officer of Revenue and Customs may accept the application before the three month date.

5(3) Where paragraph (2) applies, the officer of Revenue and Customs may amend the list of companies to which Part 3 of Schedule 15 applies specified under regulation 4(4)(b) to exclude any company that is not a company to which Part 3 of Schedule 15 applies for the relevant period of account.

5(4) An appointment under paragraph 17 of Schedule 15 is of no effect if before the three month date an officer of Revenue and Customs refuses the application on the grounds that–

(a) the specimen statement of allocated disallowances provided in accordance with regulation 4(6) is not adequate for the purposes of Part 3 of Schedule 15, or

(b) a company to which Part 3 of Schedule 15 applies has been omitted from the list of companies specified under regulation 4(4)(b).

DURATION OF APPOINTMENT

6 Once an appointment under paragraph 17 of Schedule 15 has effect, it continues to have effect until it ceases to have effect in accordance with regulations 7, 8 or 9.

REVOCATION OF APPOINTMENT BY NOTICE

7(1) An appointment under paragraph 17 of Schedule 15 ceases to have effect if revoked by the company appointed under that paragraph by notice in writing to an officer of Revenue and Customs at the tax office that deals with the corporation tax affairs of that company.

7(2) The appointment ceases to have effect in relation to the relevant period of account in which the notice is given or such subsequent relevant period of account as may be specified in the notice.

REVOCATION OF APPOINTMENT ON AUTHORISED COMPANY CEASING TO BE A RELEVANT GROUP COMPANY

8(1)   An appointment under paragraph 17 of Schedule 15 ceases to have effect if the company appointed under that paragraph ceases to be a company to which Part 3 of Schedule 15 applies.

8(2)   The appointment ceases to have effect in relation to the relevant period of account in which the company ceased to be a company to which Part 3 of Schedule 15 applies and subsequent periods of account.

REVOCATION OF APPOINTMENT ON A COMPANY BECOMING OR CEASING TO BE A COMPANY TO WHICH PART 3 OF SCHEDULE 15 APPLIES

9(1)   An appointment under paragraph 17 of Schedule 15 ceases to have effect if a company becomes or ceases to be a company to which Part 3 of Schedule 15 applies.

9(2)   The appointment ceases to have effect in relation to the relevant period of account in which the company becomes or ceases to be a company to which Part 3 of Schedule 15 applies and subsequent periods of account.

9(3)   But paragraph (1) does not apply if within three months of a company becoming or ceasing to be a company to which Part 3 of Schedule 15 applies, the reporting body notifies an officer of Revenue and Customs at the tax office that deals with its corporation tax affairs of the change.

9(4)   A notification under paragraph (3) must–

(a)   be in writing, and

(b)   specify the name and the tax office reference of the company that has become or ceased to be a company to which Part 3 of Schedule 15 applies.

9(5)   Where a new company has become a company to which Part 3 of Schedule 15 applies the notification must be accompanied by a statement by that company–

(a)   that the company appointed under paragraph 17 of Schedule 15 will act on its behalf for all relevant periods of account for which the appointment has effect;

(b)   that no application will be made to amend a financing expense amount specified under paragraph 21(4)(b) of Schedule 15 other than through a revised statement submitted by the reporting body in accordance with paragraph 20 of Schedule 15;

(c)   agreeing to be bound by a statement of allocated disallowances or a revised statement delivered by the reporting body.

Chapter 2 – Statement of Allocated Disallowances

SUBMISSION OF STATEMENT OF ALLOCATED DISALLOWANCES

10(1)   A statement of allocated disallowances must be submitted to the tax office dealing with the corporation tax affairs of–

(a)   in a case in which an appointment under paragraph 17 of Schedule 15 has effect in relation to the relevant period of account, the company appointed under that paragraph, or

(b)   in a case in which such an appointment does not have effect in relation to the relevant period of account–

    (i)   the ultimate parent where that entity is resident in the United Kingdom, or

    (ii)   in any other case, the UK ultimate parent.

10(2)   In a case within paragraph (1)(b)(ii), if there is more than one UK ultimate parent the statement of allocated disallowances must be submitted to the tax office dealing with the corporation tax affairs of each.

INFORMATION TO BE GIVEN IN CONNECTION WITH A STATEMENT OF ALLOCATED DISALLOWANCES

11   A statement of allocated disallowances must be accompanied by the following information–

(a)   the full name and the unique taxpayer number in relation to each company listed in the statement in accordance with paragraph 21(4)(a) of Schedule 15,

(b)   where a company has delivered a tax return for a relevant accounting period and as a result of submitting a statement or revised statement–

(i)   there is a change in the amount of profits on which corporation tax is chargeable for the period, or

(ii)   any other information contained in the return is incorrect,

details of the change mentioned in paragraph (i) or the information mentioned in paragraph (ii).

STATEMENT OF ALLOCATED DISALLOWANCES TREATED AS RECEIVED WITHIN SPECIFIED TIME

12(1)   A statement of allocated disallowances which is not received by HMRC by the time specified ("the specified time") in paragraph 19(2) of Schedule 15, shall be treated as if it were so received in one of the circumstances specified in paragraph (2).

12(2)   The specified circumstances are–

(a)   the statement was submitted without unreasonable delay and this regulation has not applied in relation to any previous statement of allocated disallowances, or

(b)   the statement was submitted as soon as possible but was not received by the specified time for exceptional reasons beyond the control of the reporting body.

REVISED STATEMENT OF ALLOCATED DISALLOWANCES TREATED AS RECEIVED WITHIN SPECIFIED TIME

13(1)   A revised statement of allocated disallowances which is not received by HMRC by the time specified ("the specified time") in paragraph 20(2) of Schedule 15, shall be treated as if it were so received if conditions A and B are met.

13(2)   Condition A is that the statement is received in one of the following circumstances.

Circumstance 1

A notice of enquiry is given before the specified time in relation to the company tax return of a company to which Part 3 of Schedule 15 applies, the enquiry is not completed until after the specified time and the revised statement is received by HMRC by the last of the following dates–

(a)   30 days after the enquiry is completed;

(b)   if the return is amended by notice under paragraph 34(2) of Schedule 18 to the Finance Act 1998, 30 days after the notice is given;

(c)   if an appeal is brought against such an amendment, 30 days after the date on which the appeal is finally determined.

Circumstance 2

A determination under paragraph 36 of Schedule 18 to the Finance Act 1998 is made in relation to a company to which Part 3 of Schedule 15 applies which is superseded by a self-assessment in accordance with paragraph 40 of that Schedule and the revised statement is received by HMRC within 30 days of delivery of the company tax return.

Circumstance 3

A discovery assessment or discovery determination is made under paragraph 41 of Schedule 18 to the Finance Act 1998 in relation to a company to which Part 3 of Schedule 15 applies and the revised statement is received by HMRC by the last of the following dates–

(d)   30 days after the discovery assessment or discovery determination is made;

(e)   if an appeal is brought against the discovery assessment or discovery determination, 30 days after the date on which the appeal is finally determined.

Circumstance 4

An amendment is made under paragraph 34(2A) of Schedule 18 to the Finance Act 1998 in relation to a company to which Part 3 of Schedule 15 applies and the revised statement is received by HMRC by the last of the following dates–

(f)   30 days after the notice of the amendment is given;

(g)   if an appeal is brought against such an amendment, 30 days after the date on which the appeal is finally determined.

13(3)   Condition B is that the amount of the difference between–

(a)   the financing expense amounts specified in accordance with paragraph 21(4)(b) of Schedule 15 in the statement of allocated disallowances, and

(b)   the amounts so specified in the revised statement,

does not exceed the change made to the amount of profit on which corporation tax is chargeable as a result of the enquiry, determination, assessment or amendment referred to in paragraph (2).

STATEMENT OF ALLOCATED DISALLOWANCES TREATED AS COMPLYING WITH PARAGRAPH 21 OF SCHEDULE 15

14 A statement of allocated disallowances which does not comply with paragraph 21 of Schedule 15 because of an obvious error or omission in the statement (whether an error of principle, an arithmetical mistake or otherwise) shall be treated as if it did so comply if the error or omission is corrected by the reporting body as soon as it becomes apparent.

Chapter 3 – Failure of Reporting Body to Submit a Statement of Allocated Disallowances

REDUCTION OF FINANCING EXPENSE AMOUNTS

15(1) The financing expense amounts of a company that must be reduced under paragraph 25(2) of Schedule 15 must be reduced in the following order until the amount of the reduction is equal to the amount determined under paragraph 25(3) of that Schedule.

First, reduce any amounts that meet condition A in paragraph 54(2) of Schedule 15 and would be brought into account in respect of a loan relationship under Part 5 of the Corporation Tax Act 2009 (other loan relationships).

Second, reduce any other amounts that meet condition A in paragraph 54(2) of Schedule 15.

Third, reduce any amounts that meet condition B in paragraph 54(4) of Schedule 15.

Fourth, reduce any amounts that meet condition C in paragraph 54(5) of Schedule 15.

15(2) But a company required to make reductions under paragraph 25 of Schedule 15 may elect to make such reductions differently.

15(3) An election under paragraph (2)–

(a)   must be made in the company's tax return,

(b)   must specify the particular reductions made, and

(c)   may be withdrawn, with or without making a new election, at any time that the company may amend its company tax return under paragraph 15(4) of Schedule 18 to the Finance Act 1998.

15(4) A company required to make reductions under paragraph 25 of Schedule 15 must notify its ultimate UK parent of the particular reductions made.

15(5) A notice under paragraph (4) must be made no later than the date on which the company delivers its company tax return and must be accompanied by–

(a)   any election made under paragraph (2), and

(b)   details of any error made by the company in calculating its net financing deduction for the relevant period together with the correct amount.

INFORMATION TO BE PROVIDED IN RELATION TO A COMPANY REQUIRED TO MAKE DEFAULT REDUCTIONS

16(1) An ultimate UK parent must send a company required to make default reductions details of the amounts of–

(a)   the tested expense amount, and

(b)   the total disallowed amount,

for the worldwide group for the relevant period of account.

16(2) The information in paragraph (1) must be supplied to the company required to make default reductions before the filing date for the company's tax return (see paragraph 14 of Schedule 18 to the Finance Act 1998).

NON-COMPLIANCE

17(1) If an ultimate UK parent does not provide the information specified by regulation 16 within the requisite time period, HMRC must determine to the best of their information and belief the amounts of the tested expense amount and the total disallowed amount for the worldwide group for the relevant period of account.

17(2) A notice of determination under this regulation must be sent to the company required to make the default reduction and to the ultimate UK parent stating the date on which the determination is issued.

17(3) No determination under this regulation may be made more than 3 years after the day on which the power becomes exercisable.

17(4) If after a determination has been made under this regulation, the ultimate UK parent provides the information specified by regulation 16, that information shall supersede the determination.

17(5) But paragraph (4) does not apply if the information is supplied more than 3 years after the determination is made.

AMENDMENT OF TAX RETURN BY COMPANY

18(1) A company required to make default reductions may amend its company tax return so as to reflect a reduction under paragraph 25 of Schedule 15 within 3 years of the end of the relevant period of account.

18(2) But where one of the following circumstances applies the company may amend its tax return at any time before the specified date.

Circumstance 1

Where there is an enquiry into the company tax return of the company, the specified date is the last of the following dates—

(a)   30 days after the enquiry is completed;

(b)   if after the enquiry HMRC amend the return under paragraph 34(2) of Schedule 18 to the Finance Act 1998, 30 days after notice of the amendment is issued;

(c)   if an appeal is brought against such an amendment, 30 days after the date on which the appeal is finally determined.

Circumstance 2

Where a determination under paragraph 36 of Schedule 18 to the Finance Act 1998 is made in relation to the company which is superseded by a self-assessment in accordance with paragraph 40 of that Schedule, the specified date is 30 days after delivery of the company tax return.

Circumstance 3

Where a discovery assessment or discovery determination is made under paragraph 41 of Schedule 18 to the Finance Act 1998 in relation to the company, the specified date is the last of the following dates–

(d)   30 days after the discovery assessment or discovery determination is made;

(e)   if an appeal is brought against such the discovery assessment or discovery determination, 30 days after the date on which the appeal is finally determined.

Circumstance 4

Where a determination under regulation 17 is made in relation to the company which is superseded by the provision of information under paragraph (4) of that regulation, the specified date is 30 days after the provision of that information.

PART 3 – EXEMPTION OF FINANCING INCOME
Chapter 1 – Appointment of Authorised Company

APPOINTMENT OF AUTHORISED COMPANY

19(1) An appointment under paragraph 29 of Schedule 15 must be made in accordance with this regulation.

19(2) The company seeking to be appointed ("the applicant company") must make an application in writing to an officer of Revenue and Customs at least 3 months before the time specified in paragraph 31(2) of Schedule 15 (submission of statement of allocated exemptions).

19(3) The application must be sent to the tax office that deals with the corporation tax affairs of the applicant company.

19(4) The application must specify–

(a)   the name and the tax office reference of the applicant company,

(b) the names and the tax office references of the other companies to which Part 4 of Schedule 15 applies,

(c) the first period of account of the worldwide group in relation to which the appointment is to apply, and

(d) except in relation to the ultimate parent, the name of the immediate parent of the applicant company and each of the other companies to which Part 3 of Schedule 15 applies.

19(5) The application must contain a statement by the applicant company and by each of the other companies to which Part 4 of Schedule 15 applies–

(a) that the appointment is made under paragraph 17 of Schedule 15,

(b) that the applicant company will act on behalf of all the companies to which Part 4 of Schedule 15 applies for all relevant periods of account for which the appointment has effect,

(c) that no application will be made by a company to amend its company tax return in relation to a financing income amount specified under paragraph 33(4)(b) of Schedule 15 other than through a revised statement submitted by the applicant company in accordance with paragraph 32 of Schedule 15, and

(d) agreeing to be bound by any statement of allocated exemptions or revised statement delivered by the applicant company.

19(6) The application must be accompanied by a specimen copy of a statement of allocated exemptions that the applicant company proposes to submit in relation to the relevant period of account.

SUPPLEMENTAL PROVISIONS: TIMING AND EFFECT

20(1) An appointment under paragraph 29 of Schedule 15 has effect on the date ("the three month date") that is three months after the application is delivered to the tax office in accordance with regulation 19(3).

This is subject to paragraphs (2) to (4).

20(2) An officer of Revenue and Customs may accept the application before the three month date.

20(3) Where paragraph (2) applies, the officer of Revenue and Customs may amend the list of companies to which Part 4 of Schedule 15 applies specified under regulation 19(4)(b) to exclude any company that is not a company to which Part 4 of Schedule 15 applies for the relevant period of account.

20(4) An appointment under paragraph 29 of Schedule 15 is of no effect if before the three month date an officer of Revenue and Customs refuses the application on the grounds that–

(a) the specimen statement of allocated exemptions provided in accordance with regulation 19(6) is not adequate for the purposes of Part 4 of Schedule 15, or

(b) a company to which Part 4 of Schedule 15 applies has been omitted from the list of companies specified under regulation 19(4)(b).

DURATION OF APPOINTMENT

21 Once an appointment under paragraph 29 of Schedule 15 has effect, it continues to have effect until it ceases to have effect in accordance with regulations 22, 23 or 24.

REVOCATION OF APPOINTMENT BY NOTICE

22(1) An appointment under paragraph 29 of Schedule 15 ceases to have effect if revoked by the company appointed under that paragraph by notice in writing to an officer of Revenue and Customs at the tax office that deals with the corporation tax affairs of that company.

22(2) The appointment ceases to have effect in relation to the relevant period of account in which the notice is given or such subsequent relevant period of account as may be specified in the notice.

REVOCATION OF APPOINTMENT ON AUTHORISED COMPANY CEASING TO BE A UK GROUP COMPANY

23(1) An appointment under paragraph 29 of Schedule 15 ceases to have effect if the company appointed under that paragraph ceases to be a company to which Part 4 of Schedule 15 applies.

23(2) The appointment ceases to have effect in relation to the relevant period of account in which the company ceased to be a company to which Part 4 of Schedule 15 applies and subsequent periods of account.

REVOCATION OF APPOINTMENT ON A COMPANY BECOMING OR CEASING TO BE A COMPANY TO WHICH PART 4 OF SCHEDULE 15 APPLIES

24(1)   An appointment under paragraph 29 of Schedule 15 ceases to have effect if a company becomes or ceases to be a company to which Part 4 of Schedule 15 applies.

24(2)   The appointment ceases to have effect in relation to the relevant period of account in which the company becomes or ceases to be a company to which Part 4 of Schedule 15 applies and subsequent periods of account.

24(3)   But paragraph (1) does not apply if within three months of a company becoming or ceasing to be a company to which Part 4 of Schedule 15 applies, the reporting body notifies an officer of Revenue and Customs at the tax office that deals with its corporation tax affairs of the change.

24(4)   A notification under paragraph (3) must—

(a)   be in writing, and

(b)   specify the name and the tax office reference of the company that has become or ceased to be a company to which Part 4 of Schedule 15 applies.

24(5)   Where a new company has become a company to which Part 4 of Schedule 15 applies the notification must be accompanied by a statement by that company—

(a)   that the company appointed under paragraph 29 of Schedule 15 will act on its behalf for all relevant periods of account for which the appointment has effect;

(b)   that no application will be made to amend a financing income amount specified under paragraph 33(4)(b) of Schedule 15 other than through a revised statement submitted by the reporting body in accordance with paragraph 20 of Schedule 15;

(c)   agreeing to be bound by a statement of allocated exemptions or a revised statement delivered by the reporting body.

Chapter 2 – Statement of Allocated Exemptions

SUBMISSION OF STATEMENT OF ALLOCATED EXEMPTIONS

25(1)   A statement of allocated exemptions must be submitted to the tax office dealing with the corporation tax affairs of—

(a)   in a case in which an appointment under paragraph 29 of Schedule 15 has effect in relation to the relevant period of account, the company appointed under that paragraph, or

(b)   in a case in which such an appointment does not have effect in relation to the relevant period of account—

    (i)   the ultimate parent where that entity is resident in the United Kingdom, or

    (ii)   in any other case, the UK ultimate parent.

25(2)   In a case within paragraph (1)(b)(ii), if there is more than one UK ultimate parent the statement of allocated exemptions must be submitted to the tax office dealing with the corporation tax affairs of each.

INFORMATION TO BE GIVEN IN CONNECTION WITH A STATEMENT OF ALLOCATED EXEMPTIONS

26   A statement of allocated exemptions must be accompanied by the following information—

(a)   the full name and the unique taxpayer number in relation to each company listed in the statement in accordance with paragraph 33(4)(a) of Schedule 15;

(b)   where a company has delivered a tax return for a relevant accounting period and as a result of submitting a statement or revised statement—

    (i)   there is a change in the amount of profits on which corporation tax is chargeable for the period, or

    (ii)   any other information contained in the return is incorrect,

details of the change mentioned in paragraph (i) or the information mentioned in paragraph (ii).

STATEMENT OF ALLOCATED EXEMPTIONS TREATED AS RECEIVED WITHIN SPECIFIED TIME

27(1) A statement of allocated exemptions which is not received by HMRC by the time specified ("the specified time") in paragraph 31(2) of Schedule 15, shall be treated as if it were so received in one of the circumstances specified in paragraph (2).

27(2) The specified circumstances are—

(a) the statement was submitted without unreasonable delay and this regulation has not applied in relation to any previous statement of allocated exemptions, or

(b) the statement was submitted as soon as possible but was not received by the specified time for exceptional reasons beyond the control of the reporting body.

REVISED STATEMENT OF ALLOCATED EXEMPTIONS TREATED AS RECEIVED WITHIN SPECIFIED TIME

28(1) A revised statement of allocated exemptions which is not received by HMRC by the time specified ("the specified time") in paragraph 32(2) of Schedule 15, shall be treated as if it were so received if conditions A and B are met.

28(2) Condition A is that the statement is received in one of the following circumstances.

Circumstance 1

A notice of enquiry is given before the specified time in relation to the company tax return of a company to which Part 4 of Schedule 15 applies, the enquiry is not completed until after the specified time and the revised statement is received by HMRC by the last of the following dates—

(a) 30 days after the enquiry is completed;

(b) if the return is amended by notice under paragraph 34(2) of Schedule 18 to the Finance Act 1998, 30 days after the notice is given;

(c) if an appeal is brought against such an amendment, 30 days after the date on which the appeal is finally determined.

Circumstance 2

A determination under paragraph 36 of Schedule 18 to the Finance Act 1998 is made in relation to a company to which Part 4 of Schedule 15 applies which is superseded by an a self-assessment in accordance with paragraph 40 of that Schedule and the revised statement is received by HMRC within 30 days of delivery of the company tax return.

Circumstance 3

A discovery assessment or discovery determination is made under paragraph 41 of Schedule 18 to the Finance Act 1998 in relation to a company to which Part 4 of Schedule 15 applies and the revised statement is received by HMRC by the last of the following dates—

(d) 30 days after the discovery assessment or discovery determination is made;

(e) if an appeal is brought against the discovery assessment or discovery determination, 30 days after the date on which the appeal is finally determined.

Circumstance 4

An amendment is made under paragraph 34(2A) of Schedule 18 to the Finance Act 1998 in relation to a company to which Part 3 of Schedule 15 applies and the revised statement is received by HMRC by the last of the following dates—

(f) 30 days after the notice of the amendment is given;

(g) if an appeal is brought against such an amendment, 30 days after the date on which the appeal is finally determined.

28(3) Condition B is that the amount of the difference between—

(a) the financing income amounts specified in accordance with paragraph 33(4)(b) of Schedule 15 in the statement of allocated exemptions, and

(b) the amounts so specified in the revised statement,

does not exceed the change made to the amount of profit on which corporation tax is chargeable as a result of the enquiry, assessment or determination referred to in paragraph (2).

STATEMENT OF ALLOCATED EXEMPTIONS TREATED AS COMPLYING WITH PARAGRAPH 26 OF SCHEDULE 15

29 A statement of allocated exemptions which does not comply with paragraph 33 of Schedule 15 because of an obvious error or omission in the statement (whether an error of principle, an arithmetical mistake or otherwise) shall be treated as if it did so comply if the error or omission is corrected by the reporting body as soon as it becomes apparent.

Chapter 3 – Failure of Reporting Body to Submit a Statement of Allocated Exemptions

INFORMATION TO BE PROVIDED IN RELATION TO A COMPANY REQUIRED TO MAKE DEFAULT REDUCTIONS

30(1) An ultimate UK parent must send a company required to make default reductions details of the amounts of–

(a)   the total of the unrestricted reductions,

(b)   the total disallowed amount, and

(c)   the tested income amount,

for the worldwide group for the relevant period of account.

30(2) The information in paragraph (1) must be supplied to the company required to make default reductions before the filing date for the company's tax return (see paragraph 14 of Schedule 18 to the Finance Act 1998).

NON-COMPLIANCE

31(1) If an ultimate UK parent does not provide the information specified by regulation 30 within the requisite time period, HMRC must determine to the best of their information and belief the amounts of the total of the unrestricted reductions, the total disallowed amount and the tested income amount for the worldwide group for the relevant period of account.

31(2) A notice of determination under this regulation must be sent to the company required to make the default reduction and to the ultimate UK parent stating the date on which the determination is issued.

31(3) No determination under this regulation may be made more than 3 years after the day on which the power becomes exercisable.

31(4) If after a determination has been made under this regulation, the ultimate UK parent provides the information specified by regulation 30, that information shall supersede the determination.

31(5) But paragraph (4) does not apply if the information is supplied more than 3 years after the determination is made.

AMENDMENT OF TAX RETURN BY COMPANY

32(1) A company required to make default reductions may amend its company tax return so as to reflect a reduction under paragraph 25 of Schedule 15 within 3 years of the end of the relevant period of account.

32(2) But where one of the following circumstances applies the company may amend its tax return at any time before the specified date.

Circumstance 1

Where there is an enquiry into the company tax return of the company, the specified date is the last of the following dates–

(a)   30 days after the enquiry is completed;

(b)   if after the enquiry HMRC amend the return under paragraph 34(2) of Schedule 18 to the Finance Act 1998, 30 days after notice of the amendment is issued;

(c)   if an appeal is brought against such an amendment, 30 days after the date on which the appeal is finally determined.

Circumstance 2

Where a determination under paragraph 36 of Schedule 18 to the Finance Act 1998 is made in relation to the company which is superseded by a self-assessment in accordance with paragraph 40 of that Schedule, the specified date is 30 days of delivery of the company tax return.

Circumstance 3

Where a discovery assessment or discovery determination is made under paragraph 41 of Schedule 18 to the Finance Act 1998 in relation to the company, the specified date is the last of the following dates–

(d)   30 days after the discovery assessment or discovery determination is made,

(e)   if an appeal is brought against such the discovery assessment or discovery determination, 30 days after the date on which the appeal is finally determined.

Circumstance 4

Where a determination under regulation 31 is made in relation to the company which is superseded by the provision of information under paragraph (4) of that regulation, the specified date is 30 days after the provision of that information.

CORPORATION TAX (TAX TREATMENT OF FINANCING COSTS AND INCOME) (ACCEPTABLE FINANCIAL STATEMENTS) REGULATIONS 2009

(SI 2009/3217)

Made on 3 December 2009 by the Commissioners for Her Majesty's Revenue and Customs in exercise of the powers conferred by para. 88(3)(b) of Sch. 15 to the Finance Act 2009. Operative from 1 January 2010.

CITATION, COMMENCEMENT AND EFFECT

1(1) These Regulations may be cited as the Corporation Tax (Tax Treatment of Financing Costs and Income) (Acceptable Financial Statements) Regulations 2009.

1(2) These Regulations shall come into force on 1st January 2010.

1(3) Subject to paragraph (4), these Regulations shall have effect in relation to periods of account beginning on or after 1st January 2010.

1(4) Paragraph (5) of regulation 2 shall have effect only in relation to periods of account beginning on or after 1st April 2011.

ACCEPTABLE FINANCIAL STATEMENTS

2(1) Financial statements are acceptable for the purposes of paragraph 88 of Schedule 15 to the Finance Act 2009 (non-compliant financial statements of worldwide group) if they meet one of conditions A to D.

2(2) Condition A is that the financial statements are drawn up in accordance with international accounting standards adopted with modifications by the European Commission in accordance with Regulation (EC) No 1606/2002 of the European Parliament and of the Council of 19th July 2002 on the application of international accounting standards.

2(3) Condition B is that the financial statements are drawn up in accordance with UK generally accepted accounting practice.

2(4) Condition C is that the financial statements are drawn up in accordance with generally accepted accounting principles or practice of one of the following territories–

(a)   Canada

(b)   China,

(c)   Japan,

(d)   South Korea,

(e)   the United States of America.

2(5) Condition D is that the financial statements are drawn up in accordance with generally accepted accounting principles or practice of India.

NORTHERN ROCK PLC (TAX CONSEQUENCES) REGULATIONS 2009

(SI 2009/3227)

Made on 8 December 2009 by the Treasury in exercise of the powers conferred by s. 10 of the Banking (Special Provisions) Act 2008. Operative from 1 January 2010.

CITATION AND COMMENCEMENT

1   These Regulations may be cited as the Northern Rock plc (Tax Consequences) Regulations 2009 and shall come into force on 1st January 2010.

INTERPRETATION

2   In these Regulations–

"**ACo**" means Northern Rock plc, company registered number 03273685, or, except in relation to regulation 7, any wholly owned subsidiary of that company;

"**BCo**" means Gosforth Subsidiary No.1 plc, company registered number 06952311, or any wholly owned subsidiary of that company;

"**CTA 2009**" means the Corporation Tax Act 2009;

"**relevant time**" means any time when both ACo and BCo are wholly owned by the Treasury;

"**relevant transfer**" means–

(a)   a transfer or novation of any securities, or of any property, rights or liabilities, between ACo and BCo, or

(b)   the grant of a lease, sublease, licence or sub-licence by ACo to BCo or by BCo to ACo, in relation to, in connection with, or by or under, the Northern Rock plc Transfer Order 2009 at a relevant time.

CHARGEABLE GAINS: NO GAIN OR LOSS DISPOSAL

3(1)   For the purposes of the Taxation of Chargeable Gains Act 1992, a disposal constituted by a relevant transfer is to be treated in relation to ACo and BCo as being for a consideration such that neither a gain nor a loss accrues to the transferor.

3(2)   For the purposes of any tax provision, paragraph (1) is to be treated as one of the no gain/no loss provisions in section 288(3A) of the Taxation of Chargeable Gains Act 1992 (meaning of "the no gain/no loss provisions").

CORPORATION TAX: TRADING ASSETS AND TRADING LIABILITIES

4(1)   For the purposes of Part 3 of CTA 2009 (trading income) ("Part 3"), a relevant transfer of a trading asset or a trading liability is to be treated in relation to ACo and BCo as being for a consideration such that neither a profit nor a loss accrues to the transferor.

4(2)   For the purposes of this regulation–

"**trading asset**" means an asset the proceeds of disposal of which would, but for this regulation, be brought into account as a receipt under Part 3 otherwise than in accordance with section 297 (trading credits and debits to be brought into account under Part 3), section 573 (trading credits and debits to be brought into account under Part 3) or section 747 (assets held for purposes of trade) of CTA 2009;

"**trading liability**" means a liability the payment for the assumption of which would, but for this regulation, be brought into account as an expense under Part 3 otherwise than in accordance with section 297 or section 573 of CTA 2009.

4(3)   Schedule 28AA to the Income and Corporation Taxes Act 1988 (provisions not at arm's length) does not apply in relation to a relevant transfer to which paragraph (1) applies.

CORPORATION TAX: LOAN RELATIONSHIPS

5(1)   For the purposes of Chapter 4 of Part 5 of CTA 2009 (continuity of treatment on transfers within groups or on reorganisations), in relation to a relevant transfer, ACo and BCo are to be treated as if, for the purposes of the transfer, they were members of the same group.

5(2) But a relevant transfer within paragraph (1) is not to be treated as a case within section 336 of CTA 2009 (transfers of loans on group transactions) for the purposes of section 344 of the Act (introduction).

CORPORATION TAX: INTANGIBLE ASSETS

6(1) For the purposes of Part 8 of CTA 2009 (intangible fixed assets), a relevant transfer of a chargeable intangible asset is to be treated as tax-neutral.

6(2) Schedule 28AA to the Income and Corporation Taxes Act 1988 (provisions not at arm's length) does not apply in relation to a relevant transfer to which paragraph (1) applies.

6(3) For the purposes of section 882 of CTA 2009 (application of Part 8 to assets created or acquired on or after 1st April 2002), assets acquired by ACo or BCo on a relevant transfer are to be treated as if they were acquired from a person who at the time of the acquisition is a related party.

6(4) Expressions used in this regulation and Part 8 of CTA 2009 have the same meaning in this regulation as they have in that Part.

INCOME TAX: INTEREST PAID BY BANKS

7(1) For the purposes of section 878 of the Income Tax Act 2007 (interest paid by banks), ACo is to be treated as a bank in relation to payments of interest made by ACo after 31st December 2009 on any securities or liabilities to which this regulation applies.

7(2) This regulation applies to–

(a) securities issued by ACo on or before 31st December 2009, and

(b) liabilities incurred under an agreement entered into by ACo on or before that date,

which are not transferred by a relevant transfer and in relation to which section 878 of the Income Tax Act 2007 applied to payments of interest made on or before 31st December 2009, or would have applied if a payment of interest had been made on or before that date.

STAMP DUTY

8 [Not relevant to income tax, corporation tax or capital gains tax.]

STAMP DUTY RESERVE TAX

9 [Not relevant to income tax, corporation tax or capital gains tax.]

CORPORATION TAX (EXCLUSION FROM SHORT-TERM LOAN RELATIONSHIPS) REGULATIONS 2009

(SI 2009/3313)

Made on 15 December 2009 by the Treasury, in exercise of the powers conferred by para. 62(4) of Sch. 15 to the Finance Act 2009. Operative from 1 January 2010.

CITATION, COMMENCEMENT AND INTERPRETATION

1(1) These Regulations may be cited as the Corporation Tax (Exclusion from Short-Term Loan Relationships) Regulations 2009.

1(2) These Regulations shall come into force on 1st January 2010.

1(3) In these Regulations **"FA 2009"** means the Finance Act 2009.

EXCLUSION FROM SHORT-TERM LOAN RELATIONSHIP

2 For the purposes of paragraph 60 of Schedule 15 to FA 2009 (intra-group short-term finance: financing expense), a finance arrangement is not to be taken as a short-term loan relationship for the relevant period or any parts of the relevant period where–

(a) any part or all of the finance arrangement is made for a long-term funding purpose; or

(b) the finance arrangement is a long-term aggregated loan relationship.

MEANING OF LONG-TERM FUNDING PURPOSE

3(1) A finance arrangement is made for a long-term funding purpose where at the date the finance arrangement is made–

(a) to the extent that the finance arrangement provides for the creation of money debt, it is reasonable to expect that all the money debt created under it will not be settled within 12 months of the money debt first being created under it, and

(b) to the extent that the finance arrangement is otherwise a loan relationship, it is reasonable to expect that it will not terminate within 12 months of its coming into force; or

(c) the conditions in regulation 4 are met.

3(2) For the purposes of this regulation circumstances where it is reasonable to expect that the finance arrangement will not be settled or terminated within 12 months include circumstances where–

(a) the finance arrangement may be settled or terminated by use of borrowing; or

(b) the finance arrangement may be settled or terminated temporarily by funds available for a limited period of time.

ANTI-AVOIDANCE

4(1) A sequence of finance arrangements is considered to be a single finance arrangement made for a long-term funding purpose if the following conditions are met.

4(2) The first condition is that the sequence of finance arrangements when taken together will not be settled or terminated within 12 months.

4(3) The second condition is that the sequence of finance arrangements is part of a scheme or arrangement the main purpose, or one of the main purposes, of which is to characterise a loan relationship as a short-term loan relationship for the purposes of paragraph 60 of Schedule 15 to FA 2009.

LONG-TERM AGGREGATED LOAN RELATIONSHIP

5(1) A number of finance arrangements are long-term aggregated loan relationships if the following conditions are met.

5(2) The first condition is that the finance arrangements exist between the same two companies.

5(3) The second condition is that there are no repayment terms relating specifically to each separate finance arrangement.

5(4) The third condition is that accounts show the finance arrangements as a single net balance between the companies at all times.

5(5) The fourth condition is that the finance arrangements when taken together do not meet the conditions mentioned in paragraph 62(1) of Schedule 15 to FA 2009.

DISTRIBUTIONS (EXCLUDED COMPANIES) REGULATIONS 2009

(SI 2009/3314)

Made on 15 December 2009 by the Treasury, in exercise of the powers conferred by s. 931C(2)(b) and (6) of the Corporation Tax Act 2009. Operative from 15 December 2009.

CITATION, COMMENCEMENT AND EFFECT

1(1) These Regulations may be cited as the Distributions (Excluded Companies) Regulations 2009 and shall come into force on the day on which they are made.

1(2) These Regulations shall have effect for accounting periods which are current on the day on which these Regulations are made and for accounting periods which begin after that day.

EXCLUDED COMPANIES

2(1) A territory which satisfies section 931C(1)(a) and (b) is nevertheless not a qualifying territory for the purpose of section 931B in respect of the payer of the distribution if the payer is an excluded company.

2(2) For the purposes of this regulation, an excluded company is one which is excluded from one or more of the benefits of any double taxation relief arrangements for the time being in force in relation to that territory.

Statutory Instruments

REAL ESTATE INVESTMENT TRUSTS (PRESCRIBED ARRANGEMENTS) REGULATIONS 2009

(SI 2009/3315)

Made on 15 December 2009 by the Treasury, in exercise of the powers conferred by s. 136A of the Finance Act 2006 and para. 8(2) of Sch. 34 to the Finance Act 2009. Operative from 15 December 2009.

CITATION, COMMENCEMENT AND EFFECT

1(1) These Regulations may be cited as the Real Estate Investment Trusts (Prescribed Arrangements) Regulations 2009 and shall come into force forthwith.

1(2) These Regulations shall have effect in relation to prescribed arrangements made on or after 7th May 2009 and during an accounting period which ends on or after 15th December 2009.

INTERPRETATION

2(1) In these Regulations—

(a) a reference to Part 4 is a reference to Part 4 of the Finance Act 2006 (real estate investment trusts), and

(b) a reference to a section (without more) is a reference to that section of the Finance Act 2006.

2(2) For the purposes of these Regulations, **"person"** includes, but is not limited to—

(a) a legal person,

(b) a natural person,

(c) a partnership,

(d) a limited partnership,

(e) a limited liability partnership,

(f) a trust, and

(g) any other body of persons.

2(3) For the purposes of these Regulations—

"arrangements" include any agreement, understanding, scheme, share reorganisation, transaction or series of transactions (whether or not legally enforceable), and

"prescribed arrangements" are arrangements (whether or not part of other arrangements) which have the purpose, or one of the main purposes, of allowing a REIT company to meet one or more of the conditions set out in sections 107 (conditions for tax exempt business) and 108 (conditions for balance of business) where, but for the arrangements, those conditions would not be satisfied.

SITUATIONS IN WHICH THESE REGULATIONS APPLY

3(1) These Regulations apply if conditions A and B are satisfied.

3(2) Condition A is that an amount ("the specified amount")—

(a) falls to be taken into account as part of a REIT company's tax exempt or residual business, or

(b) ceases to be taken into account as part of such business.

3(3) For the purposes of condition A, the specified amount may be taken into account (or may cease to be taken into account) as a liability, an expense, an asset or income.

3(4) Condition B is that the specified amount arises directly or indirectly from, or in consequence of, or otherwise in connection with, prescribed arrangements.

EXCLUDED ARRANGEMENTS

4(1) For the purposes of these Regulations, arrangements are not prescribed arrangements if at least one of the following conditions is satisfied.

4(2) Condition 1 is that the arrangements have been effected solely for genuine commercial purposes.

4(3) Condition 2 is that the arrangements are made between persons dealing at arm's length.

PERSONS TO BE TREATED AS MEMBER OF REIT GROUP IN CERTAIN SITUATIONS

5(1) Where a REIT company enters into prescribed arrangements with a person ("the person in question"), subject to paragraph (3), the entities listed in paragraph (2) shall be treated as members of the same REIT group for the purposes of the application of Part 4, from the beginning of the accounting period in which the arrangements are made.

5(2) The entities are—

(a) the REIT company,

(b) the person in question, and

(c) any person in which either the person in question, or the REIT company, have a direct or indirect interest.

5(3) But a person within paragraph (2)(c) shall not be treated as a member of the REIT group where it can be shown that the person falls outside the scope of the prescribed arrangements.

EFFECT OF REGULATIONS FOR CORPORATION TAX PURPOSES

6(1) This regulation applies if—

(a) a company enters into prescribed arrangements which take effect during the accounting period specified in a notice given under section 109 (notice), and

(b) that Part ceases to apply to it by reason of section 129 (termination notice: Commissioners).

6(2) Any corporation tax paid by the company pursuant to section 112 (entry charge) shall be fully taken into account for the purposes of assessing its liability to corporation tax.

TAX CREDITS (EXCLUDED COMPANIES) REGULATIONS 2009

(SI 2009/3333)

Made on 15 December 2009 by the Treasury, in exercise of the powers conferred by s. 397BA(3)(b) and (7)(1) of the Income Tax (Trading and Other Income) Act 2005. Operative from 22 April 2009.

CITATION, COMMENCEMENT AND EFFECT

1   These Regulations may be cited as the Tax Credits (Excluded Companies) Regulations 2009 and shall have effect from 22nd April 2009 for the tax year 2009–2010 and subsequent tax years.

EXCLUDED COMPANIES

2(1)   A territory which satisfies section 397BA(2)(a) and (b) of the Income Tax (Trading and Other Income) Act 2005 is nevertheless not a qualifying territory for the purposes of section 397AA of that Act in relation to the company which makes the relevant distribution if that company is an excluded company.

2(2)   For the purposes of this regulation, an excluded company is one which is excluded from one or more of the benefits of any double taxation relief arrangements for the time being in force in relation to that territory.

TRANSFER OF TRIBUNAL FUNCTIONS ORDER 2010

(SI 2010/22, as amended by SI 2013/2042)

*Made on 6 January 2010 by the Lord Chancellor in exercise of the powers conferred by s. 30(1) and (4)
, 31(1), (2) and (9) and 38 of, and para. of Sch. 5 to, the Tribunals, Courts and Enforcement Act 2007.
Operative in accordance with art. 1.*

CITATION, COMMENCEMENT AND EXTENT

1(1) This Order may be cited as the Transfer of Tribunal Functions Order 2010 and, subject to paragraph (2), comes into force on 18th January 2010.

1(2) The following provisions of this Order come into force on 6th April 2010–

(a) paragraph (5);

(b) article 2(2), (3)(b) and (4);

(c) article 3 in respect of the Financial Services and Markets Tribunal;

(d) Schedule 1 in respect of the Financial Services and Markets Tribunal and the Pensions Regulator Tribunal;

(e) in Schedule 2, paragraphs 3(c)(i), 4(c), 5 to 9, 12 to 14, 15(c), 17(b), 18(b), 20 to 23, 43 to 49, 74 to 89, 92(h) to (k) and 141 to 151;

(f) in Schedule 3, paragraphs 16 to 38, 90 to 94, 140 to 142, 143(d), 144 to 146, 148 to 158, 176 to 189 and 191 to 200; and

(g) Part 2 of Schedule 4.

1(3) Subject as follows, this Order extends to England and Wales, Scotland and Northern Ireland.

1(4) Except as provided by paragraph (5), an amendment, repeal or revocation of any enactment by any provision of Schedule 2, 3 or 4 extends to the part or parts of the United Kingdom to which the enactment extends.

1(5) The amendments, repeals and revocations made by the following provisions do not extend to Northern Ireland–

(a) in Schedule 2, paragraphs 5(b), 9(b), 77 to 79, 83 to 85, 88, 142(b) and 143(b);

(b) in Schedule 3, paragraphs 90 to 94;

(c) in Part 2 of Schedule 4, the entries relating to–

   (i) the Tribunals, Courts and Enforcement Act 2007 in so far as it relates to paragraph 40 of Schedule 10;

   (ii) the Pensions Act 2008;

   (iii) the Pensions Regulator Tribunal Rules 2005; and

   (iv) the Lord Chancellor (Transfer of Functions and Supplementary Provisions) (No. 2) Order 2006.

TRANSFER OF FUNCTIONS OF CERTAIN TRIBUNALS

2(1) The functions of the following tribunals are transferred to the First-tier Tribunal–

(a) tribunals drawn from the Adjudication Panel for England;

(b) the Claims Management Services Tribunal;

(c) the Gambling Appeals Tribunal;

(d) the Immigration Services Tribunal; and

(e) the Family Health Services Appeal Authority.

2(2) The functions of the Financial Services and Markets Tribunal are transferred to the Upper Tribunal.

2(3) The functions of the following tribunals are transferred to the First-tier Tribunal and the Upper Tribunal with the question as to which one of them is to exercise the functions in a particular case being determined by, or under, Tribunal Procedure Rules–

(a) the Information Tribunal; and

(b) subject to paragraph (4), the Pensions Regulator Tribunal.

2(4)   The functions of the Pensions Regulator Tribunal exercisable in relation to Northern Ireland are not transferred.

CONSEQUENTIAL, TRANSITIONAL AND SAVING PROVISIONS

5(1)   Schedule 2 contains amendments to primary legislation as a consequence of the transfers effected by this Order.

5(2)   Schedule 3 contains amendments to secondary legislation as a consequence of the transfers effected by this Order.

5(3)   Schedule 4 contains repeals and revocations as a consequence of the amendments in Schedules 2 and 3.

5(4)   Schedule 5 contains transitional and saving provisions.

SCHEDULES

SCHEDULE 2 – CONSEQUENTIAL AMENDMENTS TO PRIMARY LEGISLATION

Article 5(1)

PENSIONS ACT 2004

87   [Amends PA 2004, Sch. 3.]

SCHEDULE 3 – CONSEQUENTIAL AMENDMENTS TO SECONDARY LEGISLATION

Article 5(2)

MONEY LAUNDERING REGULATIONS 2007

140   The Money Laundering Regulations 2007 are amended as follows.

141   [Amends SI 2007/2157, reg. 44(2)(b) and (4).]

142   In Schedule 5 (modifications in relation to appeals)–

(a)   [amends SI 2007/2157, Sch. 5, para. 2;]

(b)   [omits SI 2007/2157, Sch. 5, Pt. 2.]

ADMINISTRATIVE JUSTICE AND TRIBUNALS COUNCIL (LISTED TRIBUNALS) ORDER 2007

143   [Omitted by SI 2013/2042, art. 81.]

History – Para. 143 omitted by SI 2013/2042, art. 81, with effect from 19 August 2013. Former para. 143 amended SI 2007/2951, art. 2.

SCHEDULE 5 – TRANSITIONAL AND SAVING PROVISIONS

Article 5(4)

INTERPRETATION OF SCHEDULE 5

1   In this Schedule–

"**old tribunal**" means a tribunal, the functions of which are transferred by article 2, but does not include the Pensions Regulator Tribunal in respect of its functions exercisable in Northern Ireland;

"**new tribunal**" means–

(a)   the Upper Tribunal, in respect of–

(i)   the functions of the Financial Services and Markets Tribunal and the Pensions Regulator Tribunal;

(ii) the functions of the Information Tribunal of deciding appeals under section 28 of the Data Protection Act 1998 or section 60 of the Freedom of Information Act 2000 (including that section as applied and modified by regulation 18 of the Environmental Information Regulations 2004(c)) (appeals in relation to national security certificates);

(b) the First-tier Tribunal, in respect of—

(i) the tribunal functions mentioned in article 2(1);

(ii) the functions of the Information Tribunal other than those mentioned in paragraph (a)(ii);

"**transfer date**" means the date on which the functions of an old tribunal are transferred to a new tribunal by article 2.

TRANSITIONAL AND SAVING PROVISIONS

2 Any proceedings before an old tribunal which are pending immediately before the transfer date shall continue on and after the transfer date as proceedings before the new tribunal.

3(1) The following sub-paragraphs apply where proceedings are continued in a new tribunal by virtue of paragraph 2.

3(2) Where a hearing began before the transfer date but was not completed by that date, the new tribunal must be comprised for the continuation of that hearing of the person or persons who began it.

3(3) The new tribunal may give any direction to ensure that proceedings are dealt with fairly and, in particular, may—

(a) apply any provision in procedural rules which applied to the proceedings before the transfer date; or

(b) disapply provisions of Tribunal Procedure Rules.

3(4) In sub-paragraph (3) "**procedural rules**" means provision (whether called rules or not) regulating practice or procedure before a tribunal.

3(5) Any direction or order given or made in proceedings which is in force immediately before the transfer date remains in force on and after that date as if it were a direction or order of the new tribunal.

3(6) A time period which has started to run before the transfer date and which has not expired shall continue to apply.

3(7) An order for costs may only be made if, and to the extent that, an order for costs could have been made by the old tribunal before the transfer date.

4 Paragraph 5 applies where—

(a) an appeal lies to a court from any decision made by an old tribunal before the transfer date;

(b) that right of appeal has not been exercised; and

(c) the time to exercise that right of appeal has not expired prior to the transfer date.

5 In the circumstances set out at paragraph 4, such of the following provisions as is appropriate shall apply as if the decision were a decision made on or after the transfer date by the new tribunal—

(a) section 11 of the Tribunals, Courts and Enforcement Act 2007 (right to appeal to Upper Tribunal);

(b) section 13 of the Tribunals, Courts and Enforcement Act 2007 (right to appeal to Court of Appeal);

(c) section 78(9A) to (9D) or section 78B(4) to (7) of the Local Government Act 2000 (as inserted or amended by Schedule 2 to this Order).

6 Any case to be remitted by a court on or after the transfer date and which, if it had been remitted before the transfer date, would have been remitted to an old tribunal, shall be remitted to the new tribunal.

7 Staff appointed to an old tribunal before the transfer date are to be treated on and after that date, for the purpose of any enactment, as if they had been appointed by the Lord Chancellor under section 40(1) of the Tribunals, Courts and Enforcement Act 2007 (tribunal staff and services).

8 A decision made by an old tribunal before the transfer date is to be treated on or after the transfer date as a decision of the new tribunal.

AUTHORISED INVESTMENT FUNDS (TAX) (AMENDMENT) REGULATIONS 2010

(SI 2010/294)

Made on 10 February 2010 by the Treasury in exercise of the powers conferred by s. 17(3) and 18 of the Finance (No. 2) Act 2005 and s. 41(1) and 42 of the Finance Act 2008. Operative from 6 March 2010.

PRELIMINARY

Citation, commencement and effect

1(1) These Regulations may be cited as the Authorised Investment Funds (Tax) (Amendment) Regulations 2010 and come into force on 6th March 2010.

This is subject to paragraph (3) and regulations 24 to 26.

1(2) These Regulations have effect from 6th March 2010.

1(3) Regulations 10 (amendment of regulation 20 of the principal Regulations) and 11 (amendment of regulation 21 of the principal Regulations) have effect for accounting periods beginning on or after 6 March 2010.

AMENDMENT OF THE PRINCIPAL REGULATIONS

Amendment of the Authorised Investment Funds (Tax) Regulations 2006

2 The Authorised Investment Funds (Tax) Regulations 2006 ("the principal Regulations") are amended as follows.

Amendment of regulation 2

3 [Amends SI 2006/964, reg. 2.]

Amendment of regulation 8

4 [Amends SI 2006/964, reg. 8.]

Amendment of regulation 12

5 [Omits SI 2006/964, reg. 12(3).]

Amendment of regulation 14B

6 [Amends SI 2006/964, reg. 14B(3).]

Amendment of regulation 15

7 [Substitutes SI 2006/964, reg. 15(1) and amends SI 2006/964, reg. 15(2) and omits SI 2006/964, reg. 15(3).]

Amendment of regulation 17

8 [Substitutes SI 2006/964, reg. 17(1) and (2) and amends the heading to SI 2006/964, reg. 17.]

Amendment of regulation 18

9 [Amends SI 2006/964, reg. 18(1).]

Amendment of regulation 20

10 [Amends SI 2006/964, reg. 20.]

Amendment of regulation 21

11 [Inserts SI 2006/964, reg. 21(5A)–(5C).]

Amendment of regulation 22

12 [Amends SI 2006/964, reg. 22(1).]

Amendment of regulation 23

13 [Amends SI 2006/964, reg. 23(3) and (7).]

Amendment of regulation 48

14 [Amends SI 2006/964, reg. 48(2A).]

Substitution of regulation 50

15 [Substitutes SI 2006/964, reg. 50.]

Amendment of regulation 69Z14

16 [Amends SI 2006/964, reg. 69Z14.]

Amendment of regulation 69Z25

17 [Amends SI 2006/964, reg. 69Z25(3)(b).]

Amendment of regulation 69Z59

18 [Amends SI 2006/964, reg. 69Z59.]

Amendment of regulation 69Z62

19 [Amends SI 2006/964, reg. 69Z62.]

Amendment of regulation 77

20 [Substitutes SI 2006/964, reg. 77(1).]

Insertion of Part 6A

21 [Inserts SI 2006/964, Pt. 6A.]

AMENDMENT OF THE SCHEDULE

22 [Amends SI 2006/964, Schedule, Pt. 2.]

CONSEQUENTIAL AMENDMENTS

23(1) [Amends SI 2006/964, reg. 7(4) and (8) and 77(4)(a).]

23(2) [Amends SI 2006/964, reg. 9A(9)(b) and 69E(2).]

23(3) [Omits SI 2006/964, reg. 69E(4).]

23(4) [Amends SI 2006/964, reg. 69Q(5)(b)(ii) and 69Z51(5)(b)(ii).]

TRANSITIONAL PROVISIONS

Transitional provisions relating to distribution dates for earlier accounting periods

24(1) Regulations 6 to 9, 12, 13 and 15 to 20 of these Regulations do not apply in relation to a distribution if conditions A to C are met.

24(2) Condition A is that the distribution date in relation to a distribution relates to an accounting period ending on or before 5th March 2010.

24(3) Condition B is that the distribution date in relation to a distribution falls on or after 6th March 2010 but on or before 5th July 2010.

24(4) Condition C is that that authorised investment fund has elected, in accordance with the transitional provisions in the Collective Investment Schemes Sourcebook (Accounting Amendments) Instrument 2010 made by the Financial Services Authority on 28th January 2010, to comply with the rules in the Authority's Collective Investment Schemes Sourcebook as they were in force on 5th March 2010.

24(5) For the purposes of this regulation–

(a) **"distribution"** has the meaning given in regulation 15(1)(b) of the principal Regulations (interpretation); and

(b) **"distribution date"** has the meaning given in regulation 15(4) of the principal Regulations.

Transitional provisions relating to entry into the FINROF regime: the first case

25(1) This regulation applies to an authorised investment fund which, on 6th March 2010, is investing more than 20% of its gross asset value in non-reporting funds.

25(2) Part 6A of the principal Regulations (inserted by these Regulations) applies to such an authorised investment fund from 6th July 2010.

25(3) But if the authorised investment fund satisfies the requirements of paragraph (1) on 6th July 2010 that date shall, for the purposes of regulation 85G(a) (entry into FINROF regime: the basic rule) of the principal Regulations (inserted by these Regulations), be treated as the date from which the authorised investment fund first met the investment condition in regulation 85D of the principal Regulations (inserted by these Regulations)

25(4) In this regulation **"gross asset value"** and **"non-reporting fund"** have the meanings given in regulation 85C of the principal Regulations (inserted by these Regulations).

Transitional provisions relating to entry into the FINROF regime: the second case

26(1)   This regulation applies to an authorised investment fund which holds investments in an offshore fund that is reasonably expected by the manager of the authorised investment fund to gain distributing fund status under the transitional rules in paragraph 3 of Schedule 1 to the Offshore Fund (Tax) Regulations 2009.

26(2)   Investments in the offshore fund mentioned in paragraph (1) shall be treated as investments in a reporting fund for the purposes of Part 6A of the principal Regulations (inserted by these Regulations).

26(3)   In this regulation **"offshore fund"** and **"reporting fund"** have the meanings given in regulation 85C of the principal Regulations (inserted by these Regulations).

AMENDMENT OF THE OFFSHORE FUNDS (TAX) REGULATIONS 2009

Consequential amendment of the Offshore Funds (Tax) Regulations 2009

27   [Inserts SI 2009/3001, reg. 18(6).]

FIELD ALLOWANCE FOR NEW OIL FIELDS ORDER 2010

(SI 2010/610)

Made on 4 March 2010 by the Commissioners for Her Majesty's Revenue and Customs in exercise of the powers conferred on them by para. 17(1) to (3) of Sch. 44 to the Finance Act 2009. Operative in accordance with art. 1(1).

History – SI 2010/610 revoked by SI 2012/3153, art. 7, with effect from 21 December 2012 in relation to oil fields whose authorisation day is on or after: 21 March 2012 in the case of small oil fields and large deep water oil fields; 25 July 2012 in the case of shallow water gas fields; and 21 December 2012 in the case of deep water gas fields. Former SI 2010/610 read as follows:

"CITATION, COMMENCEMENT AND INTERPRETATION

1(1) This Order may be cited as The Field Allowance for New Oil Fields Order 2010 and shall come into force on the day after the day on which it is made.

1(2) In this Order–

"pipe-line" means a pipe-line as defined by section 65 of the Pipe-lines Act 1962 (meaning of pipe-line),

"Schedule 44" means Schedule 44 to the Finance Act 2009 (supplementary charge: reduction for certain new oil fields).

1(3) In this Order, where any term is given a definition taken from legislation which is excluded from extension to Northern Ireland, that exclusion shall not be taken into account.

QUALIFYING OIL FIELD

2 A deep water gas field is a qualifying oil field for the purposes of Schedule 44 and paragraph 20 of Schedule 44 (qualifying oil fields) shall be treated as modified accordingly.

DEEP WATER GAS FIELD

3(1) An oil field is a **"deep water gas field"** if all of the following conditions are met.

3(2) The first condition is that–

(a)   the material submitted in support of the authorisation of the oil field identifies the planned route for the primary pipe-line (or pipe-lines) for transporting gas from the oil field to the relevant infrastructure, and

(b)   the distance gas is to be transported along the planned route is more than 60 kilometres.

3(3) The second condition is that the natural seabed above the oil field must lie below the water surface at a depth of more than 300 metres.

3(4) The third condition is that on the authorisation day of the oil field more than 75 per cent of the reserves of the oil field comprise gas.

RELEVANT INFRASTRUCTURE

4(1) In this Order "relevant infrastructure" means any–

(a)   pipe-line, or

(b)   gas processing facility,

which is being used by, or is planned for use by, another oil field whose development has been authorised before the authorisation day for the deep water gas field.

4(2) In this article "gas processing facility" has the same meaning as provided by section 12 of the Gas Act 1995 (acquisition of rights to use gas processing facilities).

WATER DEPTH

5 For the purpose of article 3(3), the depth is to be measured at the lowest astronomical tide from the water surface to the lowest point of the natural seabed at the location of the primary subsea manifold or first development well whichever is the deeper.

RESERVES

6 For the purpose of article 3(4), 1,100 cubic metres of gas at a temperature of 15 degrees Celsius and pressure of one atmosphere is to be counted as equivalent to one tonne of oil.

FIELD ALLOWANCE FOR DEEP WATER GAS FIELD

7 For the purpose of Schedule 44, the total field allowance ("TFA") for a new oil field in the case of a deep water gas field is, subject to article 8, calculated as follows–

$$TFA = Y \left(\frac{D - 60}{60} \right)$$

where

(a)   "Y" is–

     (i)   £800,000,000; or

     (ii)   where there are more than two deep water gas fields authorised on the same day, £1,600,000,000 divided by the number of deep water gas fields authorised on that day; and

(b)   "D" is–

     (i)   the length in kilometres of the distance covered by article 3(2) where that is more than 60 but less than 120; or

     (ii)   120 where that length is 120 kilometres or more.

OVERLAPPING CATEGORIES OF QUALIFYING OIL FIELD

8 Where a new oil field falls into two or more of the following categories–

(a)   a small oil field,

(b)   an ultra heavy oil field,

(c)   an ultra high pressure/high temperature oil field,

(d)   a deep water gas field;

it is to be treated as being in the category of qualifying oil field that yields the highest total field allowance and paragraph 24 of Schedule 44 (total field allowance for new oil field) is to be treated as modified accordingly.".

REGISTERED PENSION SCHEMES ETC (INFORMATION) (PRESCRIBED DESCRIPTIONS OF PERSONS) REGULATIONS 2010

(SI 2010/650, as amended by SI 2013/2259)

Made on 8 March 2010 by the Commissioners for Her Majesty's Revenue and Customs, in exercise of the powers conferred by para. 34B(8) of Sch. 36 to the Finance Act 2008. Operative from 1 April 2010.

CITATION, COMMENCEMENT AND INTERPRETATION

1(1) These Regulations may be cited as the Registered Pension Schemes etc (Information) (Prescribed Descriptions of Persons) Regulations 2010 and shall come into force on 1st April 2010.

1(2) In these Regulations, **"the description"** means the prescribed description of person for the purposes of sub-paragraph (8) of paragraph 34B of Schedule 36 to the Finance Act 2008 (information and inspection powers: registered pension schemes etc).

PRESCRIBED DESCRIPTIONS OF PERSONS: REGISTERED PENSION SCHEMES

2(1) In relation to a registered pension scheme, the descriptions are–

(a)   any person who is, or at any time during the relevant period has been, the scheme administrator;

(b)   any person who is, or at any time during the relevant period has been, a trustee of the scheme;

(c)   any person who is, or at any time during the relevant period has been, a sponsoring employer in relation to the scheme; and

(d)   any person who receives a notice under paragraph 5 of Schedule 36 to the Finance Act 2008 which requires information or the production of a document for the purposes of identifying the scheme administrator.

2(2) The relevant period is the period which–

(a)   begins with the time the event in relation to which information is required by the third party notice or notice under paragraph 5 of Schedule 36 to the Finance Act 2008 occurred; and

(b)   ends with the end of the sixth tax year following the one in which that event occurred.

2(3) **"Sponsoring employer"** has the meaning given by subsection (6) of section 150 of the Finance Act 2004.

PRESCRIBED DESCRIPTIONS OF PERSONS: QROPS AND FORMER QROPS

2A(1) In relation to a QROPS or former QROPS the description is any person who is, or at any time during the relevant period has been, the scheme manager.

2A(2) For the purposes of paragraph (1) the relevant period has the meaning given in regulation 2(2), subject to the substitution of "tenth" for "sixth" in regulation 2(2)(b).

History – Reg. 2A (and the heading before it) inserted by SI 2013/2259, reg. 25, with effect from 14 October 2013.

PRESCRIBED DESCRIPTION OF PERSONS: ANNUITIES PURCHASED WITH PENSION SCHEME ASSETS

3(1) In relation to an annuity purchased with sums or assets held for the purposes of a registered pension scheme, a pre-2006 pension scheme, a QROPS or a former QROPS the description is the insurance company or other person from whom the annuity has been purchased.

3(2) **"Insurance company"** has the meaning given by section 275 of the Finance Act 2004.

History – In reg. 3(1), the words ", a pre-2006 pension scheme, a QROPS or a former QROPS" substituted for the words "or a pre-2006 pension scheme" by SI 2013/2259, reg. 26, with effect from 14 October 2013.

PRESCRIBED DESCRIPTIONS OF PERSONS: EMPLOYER-FINANCED RETIREMENT BENEFIT SCHEMES

4(1) In relation to the coming into operation of an employer-financed retirement benefits scheme, the description is the responsible person at the time the scheme comes into operation.

4(2) In relation to the provision of relevant benefits under an employer-financed retirement benefits scheme, the description is the responsible person at the time the third party notice or notice under paragraph 5 of Schedule 36 to the Finance Act 2008 is issued.

Statutory Instruments

4(3) In relation to either the coming into operation of or the provision of relevant benefits under an employer-financed retirement benefits scheme, the description is also any person who receives a notice under paragraph 5 of Schedule 36 to the Finance Act 2008 which requires information or the production of a document for the purposes of identifying the responsible person.

4(4) A scheme comes into operation on the earlier of–

(a)　　the first date on or after the coming into force of these Regulations on which an employer makes a contribution to the scheme; and

(b)　　the first date on or after the coming into force of these Regulations on which relevant benefits are provided.

4(5) **"Relevant benefits"** has the meaning given by section 393B of the Income Tax (Earnings and Pensions) Act 2003.

CORPORATION TAX ACT 2010 (TRANSITIONAL PROVISION) ORDER 2010

(SI 2010/665)

Made on 9 March 2010 by the Treasury in exercise of the power conferred by s. 1180(2) of the Corporation Tax Act 2010. Operative from 1 April 2010.

CITATION, COMMENCEMENT AND EFFECT

1   This Order may be cited as the Corporation Tax Act 2010 (Transitional Provision) Order 2010 and shall come into force on 1st April 2010 and have effect for accounting periods ending on or after that date.

INTEREST ETC PAID IN RESPECT OF CERTAIN SECURITIES

2   In relation to any interest or other distribution paid before 1 July 2009 section 1032(2) of the Corporation Tax Act 2010 has effect as if after "any enactment" there were inserted ", other than section 1285 of CTA 2009 (exemption for UK company distributions),".

MFET LIMITED (APPLICATION OF SECTIONS 731, 733 AND 734 OF THE INCOME TAX (TRADING AND OTHER INCOME) ACT 2005) ORDER 2010

(SI 2010/673)

Made on 9 March 2010 by the Treasury in exercise of the power conferred by s. 732(2) of the Income Tax (Trading and Other Income) Act 2005. Operative from 1 April 2010.

CITATION, COMMENCEMENT AND INTERPRETATION

1(1) This Order may be cited as the MFET Limited (Application of Sections 731, 733 and 734 of the Income Tax (Trading and Other Income) Act 2005) Order 2010 and shall come into force on 1st April 2010.

1(2) In this Order **"MFET Limited"** and **"Eligible Person"** have the meanings given in respectively section 731(7) and (8) of the Income Tax (Trading and Other Income) Act 2005 (treated as inserted by article 2(2)(b)).

APPLICATION OF SECTIONS 731, 733 AND 734 OF THE INCOME TAX (TRADING AND OTHER INCOME) ACT 2005

2(1) Sections 731, 733 and 734 of the Income Tax (Trading and Other Income) Act 2005 (periodical payments of personal injury damages etc.) shall have effect with the following modifications in relation to payments made pursuant to a scheme or arrangement administered by MFET Limited to an Eligible Person.

2(2) In section 731 (periodical payments of personal injury damages)–

(a)   in subsection (2), the "or" at the end of paragraph (d) is treated as omitted and after paragraph (e) there is treated as inserted–

", or

     (f)   a scheme or arrangement administered by MFET Limited, so far as it relates to payments to an Eligible Person.";

(b)   after subsection (6) there is treated as inserted–

"731(7) In this section **"MFET Limited"** means the company limited by guarantee of that name (company number 7121661).

731(8) In this section and sections 733 and 734 **"Eligible Person"** has the meaning given in the Articles of Association of MFET Limited which were adopted by special resolution passed on 5th March 2010.".

2(3) In section 733(a) (persons entitled to exemptions for personal injury payments etc.)–

(a)   after "the person" there is treated as inserted "("A") who is an Eligible Person or who is";

(b)   "("A")" is treated as omitted.

2(4) In section 734(1)(a) (payments from trusts for injured persons) after "who is" there is treated as inserted "an Eligible Person or who is".

EXCHANGE GAINS AND LOSSES (BRINGING INTO ACCOUNT GAINS OR LOSSES) (AMENDMENT) REGULATIONS 2010

(SI 2010/809)

Made on 15 March 2010 by the Treasury in exercise of the powers conferred by s. 151E of the Taxation of Chargeable Gains Act 1992, para. 26(5) of Sch. 23 to the Finance Act 2002 and s. 328(5)–(7) and 606(5)–(7) of the Corporation Tax Act 2009. Operative from 6 April 2010.

CITATION, COMMENCEMENT AND EFFECT

1(1)   These Regulations may be cited as the Exchange Gains and Losses (Bringing into Account Gains or Losses) (Amendment) Regulations 2010 and shall come into force on 6th April 2010.

1(2)   Subject to regulations 13 and 14(4), these Regulations shall have effect in relation to a disposal of an asset made on or after 6th April 2010.

1(3)   In these Regulations, **"the principal Regulations"** means the Exchange Gains and Losses (Bringing into Account Gains or Losses) Regulations 2002.

AMENDMENTS TO THE EXCHANGE GAINS AND LOSSES (BRINGING INTO ACCOUNT GAINS OR LOSSES) REGULATIONS 2002

2   The principal Regulations are amended in accordance with regulations 3 to 12.

AMENDMENT OF REGULATION 2

3(1)   Regulation 2 (interpretation) is amended as follows.

3(2)   [Amends SI 2002/1970, reg. 2(1).]

3(3)   [Inserts SI 2002/1970, reg. 2(1A).]

3(4)   [Inserts SI 2002/1970, reg. 2(2A).]

SUBSTITUTION OF REGULATION 4

4   [Substitutes SI 2002/1970, reg. 4.]

AMENDMENT OF REGULATION 5

5(1)   Regulation 5 (calculation of the amount of any net gain or net loss for the purposes of regulation 4) is amended as follows.

5(2)   [Amends SI 2002/1970, reg. 5(2).]

5(3)   [Omits SI 2002/1970, reg. 5(4).]

AMENDMENT OF REGULATION 6

6   [Substitutes SI 2002/1970, reg. 6(2).]

AMENDMENT OF REGULATION 7

7   [Amends SI 2002/1970, reg. 7(3).]

AMENDMENT OF REGULATION 8

8(1)   Regulation 8 (no gain/no loss disposals) is amended as follows.

8(2)   [Substitutes SI 2002/1970, reg. 8(2).]

8(3)   [Amends SI 2002/1970, reg. 8(3).]

OMISSION OF REGULATION 9

9   [Omits SI 2002/1970, reg. 9.]

OMISSION OF REGULATION 10

10   [Omits SI 2002/1970, reg. 10.]

Statutory Instruments

OMISSION OF REGULATION 11

11 [Omits SI 2002/1970, reg. 11.]

OMISSION OF REGULATION 12

12 [Omits SI 2002/1970, reg. 12.]

FURTHER PROVISIONS – CASES WITHIN REGULATION 3(3)(A) OR (B) OF THE PRINCIPAL REGULATIONS

13 These Regulations shall not have effect in relation to a disposal of an asset where the circumstances prescribed by regulation 3(3)(a) or (b) of the principal Regulations are satisfied.

FURTHER PROVISIONS – NO GAIN/NO LOSS DISPOSALS

14(1) This regulation applies in relation to an asset as regards which regulation 8(2)(a) of the principal Regulations has had effect in respect of a no gain/no loss disposal before 6th April 2010 but the net gain or net loss accruing at the time of that disposal has not been brought into account as a chargeable gain or allowable loss in accordance with regulation 8(2)(b), 10(3) or 12(3).

This is subject to paragraph (4).

14(2) On the first disposal of the asset which is not a no gain/no loss disposal, the net gain or net loss referred to in paragraph (1) shall be brought into account in accordance with regulation 4 of the principal Regulations (as substituted by regulation 4 of these Regulations).

14(3) In paragraph (2) **"a no gain/no loss disposal"** has the meaning given in regulation 2(1) of the principal Regulations (as substituted by regulation 3(2) of these Regulations).

14(4) In a case to which this regulation applies, the company making the disposal of the asset may elect that these Regulations shall not apply.

14(5) An election under paragraph (4) must–

(a)   be made in writing to HMRC within 12 months of the date of the disposal referred to in paragraph (2),

(b)   identify the asset which is the subject of the disposal,

(c)   include a computation of the net gain or net loss, and

14(6) An election under paragraph 4 above is irrevocable.

REGISTERED PENSION SCHEMES (STANDARD LIFETIME AND ANNUAL ALLOWANCES) ORDER 2010

(SI 2010/922, as amended by FA 2011)

Made on 24 March 2010 by the Treasury in exercise of the powers conferred by s. 218(3) and 228(2) of the Finance Act 2004. Operative from 15 April 2010.

CITATION AND COMMENCEMENT

1 This Order may be cited as the Registered Pension Schemes (Standard Lifetime and Annual Allowances) Order 2010 and shall come into force on 15th April 2010.

STANDARD LIFETIME ALLOWANCE

2 [Omitted by FA 2011, s. 67 and Sch. 18, para. 12.]

History – Art. 2 omitted by FA 2011, s. 67 and Sch. 18, para. 12, with effect for the tax year 2012–13 and subsequent tax years, subject to transitional rules in FA 2011, Sch. 18, para. 14. Former art. 2 read as follows:
   "**2** The standard lifetime allowance for the tax years 2011–12, 2012–13, 2013–14, 2014–15 and 2015–16 is £1,800,000."

ANNUAL ALLOWANCE

3 [Omitted by FA 2011, s. 66 and Sch. 17, para. 26(2).]

History – Art. 3 omitted by FA 2011, s. 66 and Sch. 17, para. 26(2), with effect for the tax year 2011–12 and subsequent tax years, subject to transitional rules in FA 2011, Sch. 17, para. 28–34. Former art. 3 read as follows:
   "**3** The annual allowance for the tax years 2011–12, 2012–13, 2013–14, 2014–15 and 2015–16 is £255,000.".

FINANCIAL ASSISTANCE SCHEME (TAX) REGULATIONS 2010
(SI 2010/1187)

Made on 6 April 2010 by the Treasury, in exercise of the powers conferred by s. 73 of the Finance Act 2009. Operative from 1 May 2010.

PART 1 – PRELIMINARY

CITATION, COMMENCEMENT AND INTERPRETATION

1(1) These Regulations may be cited as the Financial Assistance Scheme (Tax) Regulations 2010 and shall come into force on 1st May 2010.

1(2) In these Regulations, unless otherwise stated, any reference to a numbered regulation is a reference to that regulation of the FAS Regulations.

1(3) In these Regulations–

"**assistance**" means–

interim assistance,

non-lump sum assistance,

a lump sum payment under regulation 17D (lump sum payments), and

a payment under regulation 18A (death benefit guarantees) in cases where that payment is in the form of a lump sum;

"**the FA 2004**" means the Finance Act 2004;

"**the FAS**" means the financial assistance scheme;

"**the FAS Regulations**" means the Financial Assistance Scheme Regulations 2005;

"**the FAS scheme manager**" means the person appointed by the Secretary of State by regulations under section 286 of the Pensions Act 2004 to manage the FAS;

"**interim assistance**" means–

an interim ill health payment from the FAS, and

an initial payment from the FAS;

"**non-lump sum assistance**" means–

an annual payment from the FAS under regulation 17 (annual payments),

an ill health payment from the FAS, and

an annual payment from the FAS under regulation 17C (annual payments for certain applications in cases of severe ill health);

"**qualifying member**" has the meaning given by regulation 15(1); and

"**qualifying pension scheme**" has the meaning given in regulation 9.

PART 2 – TAX RELIEFS, ETC

TRANSFER OF REGISTERED PENSION SCHEME ASSETS, ETC, TO THE SECRETARY OF STATE

2 A transfer of the property, rights and liabilities of a registered pension scheme to the Secretary of State is to be treated as if it were a payment authorised by section 164(1) of the FA 2004 (authorised member payments).

PAYMENTS TO THE SECRETARY OF STATE

3(1) This regulation applies where as a result of the transfer of the property, rights and liabilities of a registered pension scheme to the Secretary of State an employer is required to pay a sum to the Secretary of State.

3(2) Where section 199 of the FA 2004 (deemed contributions) would have applied if the payment had been made to the trustees or managers of the scheme, that section applies in relation to the payment in the same way as it applies in relation to a sum paid to the trustees or managers of a registered pension scheme.

3(3) Where the payment does not fall within paragraph (2), section 200 of the FA 2004 (no other relief for employers in connection with contributions) applies in relation to it in the same way that section applies in relation to a sum other than a contribution paid in connection with the cost of providing benefits under a registered pension scheme.

LUMP SUM PAYMENTS BY THE FINANCIAL ASSISTANCE SCHEME

4 Subsections (1) and (2) of section 636A of the Income Tax (Earnings and Pensions) Act 2003 (exemption for certain lump sums under registered pension schemes) apply to a lump sum payment under regulation 17D and a payment made under regulation 18A in the form of a lump sum as they apply to the lump sums listed in subsection (1).

PART 3 – LIFETIME ALLOWANCE

APPLICATION OF RELEVANT LIFETIME ALLOWANCE PROVISIONS

5(1) The relevant lifetime allowance provisions apply in relation to assistance from the FAS as they apply in relation to benefits that are provided under a registered pension scheme.

5(2) For the purposes of the relevant lifetime allowance provisions, unless the context requires otherwise–

(a) a qualifying member is to be treated as if that qualifying member were a member of a registered pension scheme; and

(b) the FAS is to be treated as if it were a registered pension scheme and the FAS scheme manager is to be treated as its scheme administrator.

5(3) Subject to regulations 6 to 11 of these Regulations, the relevant lifetime allowance provisions are–

(a) sections 214 to 226 and 263 of the FA 2004 (lifetime allowance charge and penalty in relation to relevant benefit accrual);

(b) Part 2 of Schedule 36 to the FA 2004 (lifetime allowance charge transitional provisions);

(c) orders made under section 218(3) of the FA 2004 (individual's lifetime allowance and standard lifetime allowance); and

(d) enhanced lifetime allowance regulations.

5(4) **"Enhanced lifetime allowance regulations"** has the meaning given by section 256(2) of the FA 2004 (enhanced lifetime allowance regulations).

AMOUNT OF CHARGE

6 For the purposes of section 215 of the FA 2004 (amount of charge) a payment under regulation 18A in the form of a lump sum is to be treated as if it was a lump sum death benefit.

BENEFIT CRYSTALLISATION EVENTS AND AMOUNTS CRYSTALLISED

7(1) In relation to assistance from the FAS, this table sets out–

(a) the events which are benefit crystallisation events in relation to the individual; and

(b) the amount which is crystallised by each of those events

in place of section 216 of the FA 2004 (lifetime allowance charge – benefit crystallisation events and amounts crystallised)

Benefit crystallisation events	Amount crystallised
1. Subject to paragraph (3), the individual becoming entitled for the first time to interim assistance in respect of membership of a qualifying pension scheme.	$(20 \times P)$ – RPSBCE

Benefit crystallisation events	Amount crystallised
2. Subject to paragraphs (3) and (4), the individual becoming entitled for the first time to one of the forms of non-lump sum assistance in respect of membership of a qualifying pension scheme in a case where the individual has not previously become entitled to one of the forms of interim assistance in respect of that scheme.	$(20 \times P) - RPSBCE$
3. The individual becoming entitled for the first time to an annual payment under regulation 17 in respect of membership of a qualifying pension scheme having previously become entitled to an initial payment in respect of that scheme.	Where paragraph (5) applies– $(20 \times P17) - BCE1$ Where paragraph (5) does not apply, nil.
4. The individual becoming entitled for the first time to an ill health payment from the FAS in respect of membership of a qualifying pension scheme having previously become entitled to an interim ill health payment in respect of that scheme.	Where paragraph (6) applies– $(20 \times P17A) - BCE1$ Where paragraph (6) does not apply, nil.
5. The individual becoming entitled to a lump sum payment under regulation 17D in respect of membership of a qualifying pension scheme in a case where the individual has not previously become entitled to interim assistance in respect of that scheme.	The amount of the lump sum paid to the individual.
6. A person becoming entitled to a lump sum in respect of the individual under regulation 18A in respect of the individual's membership of a qualifying pension scheme.	The amount of the lump sum.

7(2)   For the purposes of these Regulations, an individual becomes entitled to–

(a)   assistance from the FAS when that individual first acquires an actual (rather than a prospective) right to receive that assistance and the amount of that assistance has been determined by the FAS scheme manager; and

(b)   a lump sum under regulation 17D immediately before the individual becomes entitled to the non-lump sum assistance to which the lump sum relates.

7(3)   The individual becoming entitled to interim assistance, an annual payment under regulation 17 or an ill health payment from the FAS in respect of membership of a qualifying pension scheme does not result in a benefit crystallisation event where that entitlement is solely as a result of the transfer to the Secretary of State of property, rights and liabilities which represent the rights to which the individual had, prior to the transfer, become entitled in respect of a scheme pension under that scheme.

7(4)   The individual becoming entitled to an annual payment under regulation 17 or an ill health payment from the FAS does not result in a benefit crystallisation event where the individual had previously become entitled to–

(a)   an initial payment or an interim ill health payment, as the case may be, from the FAS prior to the coming into force of these Regulations; or

(b)   a payment under regulation 17H (payments to qualifying members receiving a pension from the qualifying pension scheme before entitlement to an annual payment or ill health payment).

7(5)   This paragraph applies where the value of $(20 \times P17)$ is more than the value of BCE1.

7(6)   This paragraph applies where the value of $(20 \times P17A)$ is more than the value of BCE1.

7(7)   In this regulation–

"**BCE 1**" is the amount crystallised at the first benefit crystallisation event in the table in paragraph (1) following the individual becoming entitled to the relevant interim assistance;

"**P**" is the value of the assistance which will be payable to the individual in the period of 12 months beginning with the day on which the individual becomes entitled to assistance (assuming assistance remains payable throughout that period at the rate at which it is payable on that day);

"**P17**" is the value of the assistance which would have been payable to the individual in the period of 12 months beginning with the day on which the individual became entitled to an initial payment if–

> the individual had become entitled to assistance in the form of an annual payment under regulation 17 on that day,

> that assistance had remained payable throughout that period at the rate at which it would have been payable on that day, and

> the individual had chosen not to commute any of that assistance for a lump sum;

"**P17A**" is the value of the assistance which would have been payable to the individual in the period of 12 months beginning with the day on which the individual became entitled to an interim ill health payment if–

> the individual had become entitled to assistance in the form of an ill health payment on that day,

> that assistance had remained payable throughout that period at the rate at which it would have been payable on that day, and

> the individual had chosen not to commute any of that assistance for a lump sum; and

"**RPSBCE**" is the amount, if any, crystallised by the second or fifth benefit crystallisation event, as the case may be, under section 216 of the FA 2004 in respect of rights under the registered pension scheme of which the individual was a member prior to the transfer of the property, rights and liabilities which represent those rights to the Secretary of State.

PERSONS LIABLE TO CHARGE

8   Section 217 of the FA 2004 (persons liable to charge) applies as if–

(a)   in subsection (1), the words after "individual" were omitted; and

(b)   in subsections (2), (3) and (4), the references to a "relevant lump sum death benefit" were references to a payment under regulation 18A in the form of a lump sum.

AVAILABILITY OF INDIVIDUAL'S LIFETIME ALLOWANCE

9(1)   Section 219(6) of the FA 2004 (availability of individual's lifetime allowance) applies as if after the words in brackets there appeared "and regulation 7(2)(b) of the Financial Assistance Scheme (Tax) Regulations 2010".

9(2)   A payment under regulation 18A in the form of a lump sum is to be treated as the payment of a lump sum death benefit for the purposes of section 219(7) of the FA 2004.

TRANSITIONAL PROVISIONS: PART 2 OF SCHEDULE 36 TO THE FA 2004

10   For the purposes of paragraph 12(2)(b) of Schedule 36 to the FA 2004 (enhanced protection), a transfer of the property, rights and liabilities of a registered pension scheme to the Secretary of State is to be treated as a permitted transfer.

INFORMATION AND PENALTIES

11(1)   Subject to regulation 12(2) of these Regulations, the Registered Pension Schemes (Provision of Information) Regulations 2006 do not apply in relation to the FAS.

11(2)   Sections 261 and 262 of the FA 2004 (enhanced lifetime allowance regulations: documents and information – penalties) apply to the reporting obligation in regulation 13 of these Regulations as if it was imposed by enhanced lifetime allowance regulations.

11(3)   Section 98 of the Taxes Management Act 1970 (special returns, etc: penalties) applies to the reporting obligations in regulations 14 to 18 of these Regulations as if they were listed in the second column of the Table in that section.

PERCENTAGE OF STANDARD LIFETIME ALLOWANCE EXPENDED ON THE HAPPENING OF A BENEFIT CRYSTALLISATION EVENT

12(1) The percentage of standard lifetime allowance expended on the happening of each benefit crystallisation event for the purposes of these Regulations is found by applying the formula–

$$\left(\frac{AC}{RSLA} \right) \times 100$$

where–

"AC" is the amount crystallised by the benefit crystallisation event; and

"RSLA" is the relevant standard lifetime allowance at the time of that event.

12(2) The total percentage of standard lifetime allowance expended in relation to a qualifying member is the sum of–

(a) the percentages found in accordance with this regulation in respect of that member; and

(b) the percentages found in accordance with regulation 7 of the Registered Pension Schemes (Provision of Information) Regulations 2006 (percentage of standard lifetime allowance expended on the happening of a registered pension scheme benefit crystallisation event) in respect of that member.

INFORMATION PROVIDED BY QUALIFYING MEMBERS TO THE FAS SCHEME MANAGER ABOUT ENHANCED LIFETIME ALLOWANCE

13 If a qualifying member intends to rely on entitlement to an enhanced lifetime allowance, or to enhanced protection, the qualifying member must notify the FAS scheme manager of the reference number issued by the Commissioners for Her Majesty's Revenue and Customs under the Registered Pension Schemes (Enhanced Lifetime Allowance) Regulations 2006 in respect of that entitlement.

INFORMATION PROVIDED BY THE FAS SCHEME MANAGER TO QUALIFYING MEMBERS ABOUT LIABILITY FOR A LIFETIME ALLOWANCE CHARGE

14 If assistance other than a payment under regulation 18A in the form of a lump sum results in a lifetime allowance charge, within three months of the benefit crystallisation event the FAS scheme manager must provide the qualifying member with a notice stating–

(a) the chargeable amount in respect of the benefit crystallisation event;

(b) how that chargeable amount has been calculated; and

(c) the amount of the resulting charge to tax.

INFORMATION PROVIDED BY THE FAS SCHEME MANAGER TO QUALIFYING MEMBERS ABOUT BENEFIT CRYSTALLISATION EVENTS

15(1) The FAS scheme manager must provide a statement containing the information in paragraph (2) to each qualifying member–

(a) who has become entitled to receive assistance, at least once in each tax year; or

(b) in respect of whom a benefit crystallisation event has occurred, within three months of that event,

or, if the member has died, the FAS scheme manager must provide the statement to the member's personal representatives.

15(2) The information is the percentage of standard lifetime allowance expended in relation to the member by–

(a) benefit crystallisation events in respect of the FAS; and

(b) benefit crystallisation events under section 216 of the FA 2004 prior to the transfer to the Secretary of State mentioned in regulation 2 of these Regulations except for a benefit crystallisation event which relates to a liability or pension obligation which is not discharged under section 161 of the Pensions Act 2004 as modified by paragraph 3D of Schedule 1 to the FAS Regulations 2005.

15(3) No obligation to provide a statement under paragraph (1)(b) arises if a statement is required to be provided under sub-paragraph (a) of that paragraph or under regulation 16(1)(a) of these Regulations.

15(4) For the purposes of paragraph (1)(a), a qualifying member becomes entitled to receive assistance in the circumstances set out in regulation 7(2) of these Regulations.

INFORMATION PROVIDED BY THE FAS SCHEME MANAGER TO PERSONAL REPRESENTATIVES

16(1) The FAS scheme manager must notify to the personal representatives of a deceased qualifying member–

(a)   the percentage of standard lifetime allowance expended by, and the amount and the date of payment of, a payment in the form of a lump sum under regulation 18A in relation to the member; and

(b)   the total percentage of standard lifetime allowance expended in relation to the member, at the date of the notification, by–

    (i)   benefit crystallisation events in respect of the FAS; and

    (ii)   benefit crystallisation events under section 216 of the FA 2004 prior to the transfer to the Secretary of State mentioned in regulation 2 of these Regulations except for a benefit crystallisation event which relates to a liability or pension obligation which is not discharged under section 161 of the Pensions Act 2004 as modified by paragraph 3D of Schedule 1 to the FAS Regulations 2005,

but excluding from that percentage any amount covered by paragraph (a).

16(2) The information required by paragraph (1)(a) must be provided no later than the last day of the period of three months beginning with the day on which the assistance payment is made.

16(3) The information required by paragraph (1)(b) must be provided no later than the last day of the period of two months beginning with the day on which a request for it is received from the member's personal representatives.

INFORMATION PROVIDED BY THE FAS SCHEME MANAGER TO HER MAJESTY'S REVENUE AND CUSTOMS

17(1) If assistance results in a lifetime allowance charge or would have done but for the qualifying member's entitlement to an enhanced lifetime allowance, or to enhanced protection, within three months of the benefit crystallisation event the FAS scheme manager must provide a report to Her Majesty's Revenue and Customs setting out–

(a)   the name, date of birth, address and national insurance number of the member;

(b)   the date of the relevant benefit crystallisation event;

(c)   the amount crystallised by the event;

(d)   if the member has benefited from an enhanced lifetime allowance or enhanced protection, the reference number issued under the Registered Pension Schemes (Enhanced Lifetime Allowance) Regulations 2006 in respect of that entitlement; and

(e)   in cases where the member is liable to a lifetime allowance charge, the amount of tax due in respect of each chargeable amount as constitutes a lump sum amount and each chargeable amount as constitutes a retained amount.

17(2) For the purposes of paragraph (1)(e), a chargeable amount that constitutes a retained amount includes cases where it is assumed under regulation 7 of these Regulations that the member has not chosen to commute any portion of non-lump sum assistance for a lump sum.

INFORMATION PROVIDED BY PERSONAL REPRESENTATIVES TO HER MAJESTY'S REVENUE AND CUSTOMS

18(1) Where–

(a)   a payment in the form of a lump sum is made in respect of a deceased qualifying member under regulation 18A; and

(b)   that payment, of itself or together with any other such payment or any relevant lump sum death benefit paid by a registered pension scheme in respect of the individual, results in a lifetime allowance charge, the personal representatives of the member shall provide to Her Majesty's Revenue and Customs the information specified in paragraph (2).

18(2) The information is—

(a) a statement that a payment in the form of a lump sum has been paid by the FAS under regulation 18A;

(b) the name of any registered pension scheme from which, and the name and address of the scheme administrator by whom, the benefits were paid;

(c) the name of the deceased member in respect of whom the benefits were paid;

(d) the amount and date of the payment by the FAS;

(e) the amount and date of the payment of any benefits by a registered pension scheme; and

(f) the chargeable amount in respect of which a lifetime allowance charge is payable by virtue of the payments.

18(3) The information required shall be provided on or before the later of—

(a) the end of the period of 13 months beginning with the death of the member; or

(b) representatives (or any of them) became aware that paragraph (1) applied to the deceased member.

18(4) Where a requirement to provide information under this regulation arises after the period specified in paragraph (3) has expired, the information shall be provided no later than the last day of the period of 30 months beginning with the death of the member.

18(5) If the personal representatives discover after the latest date for providing information under paragraph (4) any information required to be provided under paragraph (1), that information shall be provided no later than the last day of the period of 3 months beginning with the discovery of that information.

18(6) Where personal representatives are required to provide information under this regulation by virtue of a payment or payments in the form of a lump sum being made under regulation 18A in respect of the deceased member along with the payment of one or more relevant lump sum death benefits under Part 4 of the FA 2004 in respect of the deceased member, regulation 10 of the Registered Pension Schemes (Provision of Information) Regulations 2006 does not apply in relation to the payment or payments under Part 4 of the FA 2004.

PART 4 – MISCELLANEOUS

TRANSITIONAL PROVISIONS: LUMP SUMS

19 For the purposes of—

(a) paragraph 2 of Schedule 29 to the FA 2004 as modified by paragraph 28(3) of Schedule 36 to that Act; and

(b) regulation 25D of the Taxation of Pension Schemes (Transitional Provisions) Order 2006,

the reference to a pension commencement lump sum in the definition of "APCLS" in paragraph 2(6) of Schedule 29 shall be taken to include a lump sum under regulation 17D.

CHARITIES (DISCLOSURE OF REVENUE AND CUSTOMS INFORMATION TO THE CHARITY COMMISSION FOR NORTHERN IRELAND) REGULATIONS 2010

(SI 2010/1219)

Made on 7 April 2010 by the Minister for the Cabinet Office in exercise of the powers conferred by s. 72(2) and (3) and 74(2) of the Charities Act 2006. Operative from 8 April 2010.

CITATION, COMMENCEMENT AND INTERPRETATION

1(1) These Regulations may be cited as the Charities (Disclosure of Revenue and Customs Information to the Charity Commission for Northern Ireland) Regulations 2010 and shall come into force on the day after the day on which they are made.

1(2) In these Regulations **"charity"** has the meaning given by section 1 of the Charities Act (Northern Ireland) 2008 but does not include–

(a)   any ecclesiastical corporation (that is to say, any corporation in the Church of England, whether sole or aggregate, which is established for spiritual purposes) in respect of the corporate property of the corporation, except a corporation aggregate having some purposes which are not ecclesiastical in respect of its corporate property held for those purposes;

(b)   any Diocesan Board of Finance (or any subsidiary thereof) within the meaning of the Endowments and Glebe Measure 1976 for any diocese in respect of the diocesan glebe land of that diocese within the meaning of that Measure; or

(c)   any trust of property for purposes for which the property has been consecrated.

AUTHORISATION OF DISCLOSURE

2   Subject to regulation 3, the Commissioners of Her Majesty's Revenue and Customs are authorised to disclose Revenue and Customs information to the Charity Commission for Northern Ireland (which exercises functions similar in nature to those exercised in England and Wales by the Charity Commission), for the purposes of enabling or assisting it to discharge any of its functions.

LIMITATIONS ON DISCLOSURE

3(1)   Information may be disclosed under regulation 2 only if it relates to an institution, undertaking or body falling within one (or more) of the following sub-paragraphs–

(a)   a charity;

(b)   an institution which is established for charitable, benevolent or philanthropic purposes;

(c)   an institution by or in respect of which a claim for exemption has at any time been made under section 505(1) of the Income and Corporation Taxes Act 1988 or under Part 10 of the Income Tax Act 2007;

(d)   a subsidiary undertaking of a charity;

(e)   a body entered in the Scottish Charity Register or the Register of Charities for England and Wales which is managed or controlled wholly or mainly in or from Northern Ireland.

3(2)   In paragraph (1)(d), **"subsidiary undertaking of a charity"** means an undertaking (as defined by section 1161 of the Companies Act 2006) in relation to which–

(a)   a charity is (or is to be treated as) a parent undertaking in accordance with the provisions of section 1162 of, and Schedule 7 to, that Act, or

(b)   two or more charities would, if they were a single charity, be (or be treated as) a parent undertaking in accordance with those provisions.

3(3)   For the purposes of the references in this regulation to a parent undertaking, **"undertaking"** includes a charity which is not an undertaking as defined by section 1161(1) of the Companies Act 2006.

Statutory Instruments

REVENUE AND CUSTOMS (COMPLAINTS AND MISCONDUCT) REGULATIONS 2010

(SI 2010/1813, as amended by SI 2011/3061)

Made on 14 July 2010 by the Treasury in exercise of the powers conferred by s. 28(1), (2) and (6) and 29(3) of the Commissioners for Revenue and Customs Act 2005. Operative from 5 August 2010.

ARRANGEMENT OF REGULATIONS

REGULATION

REGULATION

PART 1 – GENERAL

CITATION AND COMMENCEMENT

1   These Regulations may be cited as the Revenue and Customs (Complaints and Misconduct) Regulations 2010 and shall come into force on 5th August 2010.

REVOCATION AND TRANSITIONAL PROVISION

2(1)   Subject to paragraph (2), the Revenue and Customs (Complaints and Misconduct) Regulations 2005 and the Revenue and Customs (Complaints and Misconduct) (Amendment) Regulations 2006 are revoked.

2(2)   Where an allegation in respect of the conduct by an officer came to the attention of the appropriate authority before the 5th August 2010, nothing in these Regulations shall apply and the Revenue and Customs (Complaints and Misconduct) Regulations 2005 shall continue to have effect.

INTERPRETATION

3(1)   In these Regulations–

"**2002 Act**" means the Police Reform Act 2002;

"**appropriate authority**"–

(a)   in relation to the Commissioners or an officer or in relation to any complaint, matter or investigation relating to the conduct of such a person, means–

(i)   if that person is the Chairman, the Chief Executive or the Permanent Secretary for Tax, the Head of the Home Civil Service,

(ii)   if that person is a Commissioner, the Chief Executive unless that Commissioner is the Chairman, the Permanent Secretary for Tax or the Chief Executive, or

(iii)   if that person is an officer, the Commissioners (other than the Chairman, the Chief Executive and the Permanent Secretary for Tax), and

(b)   in relation to a death or serious injury matter and the relevant officer, means the Commissioners (other than the Chairman, the Chief Executive and the Permanent Secretary for Tax);

"**the Chairman**" means the Chairman of the Board of HMRC;

"**the Chief Executive**" means the Chief Executive of HMRC;

"**chief officer**" means the chief officer of police of any police force;

"**the Commissioners**" unless a contrary intention appears, means the Commissioners for Her Majesty's Revenue and Customs and for the purposes of these Regulations includes the Chairman (and unless a contrary intention appears, "**Commissioner**" is to be construed accordingly);

"**complainant**" shall be construed in accordance with paragraph (4);

"**complaint**" has the meaning given by regulation 9 (complaints, matters and persons to which these Regulations apply);

"**conduct**" includes acts, omissions and statements (whether actual, alleged or inferred);

"**conduct matter**" has the meaning given by regulation 9;

"**death or serious injury matter**" and "**DSI matter**" have the meaning given by regulation 9;

"**disciplinary proceedings**" means any proceedings or management process during which the conduct of the Commissioners or an officer is considered in order to determine whether a sanction or punitive measure should be imposed against that person in relation to that conduct;

"**document**" means anything in which information of any description is recorded;

"**function**" in relation to the Commissioners or officers has the meaning given by section 51(2) of the Commissioners for Revenue and Customs Act 2005;

"**HMRC**" means Her Majesty's Revenue and Customs;

"**information**" includes estimates and projections, and statistical analyses;

"**IPCC**" means the Independent Police Complaints Commission and has the meaning given by section 9(1) of the 2002 Act;

"**officer**" means, unless the context otherwise requires, an officer of Revenue and Customs;

"**the Permanent Secretary for Tax**" means HMRC's Permanent Secretary for Tax;

"**the person complained against**", in relation to a complaint, means the person whose conduct is the subject-matter of the complaint;

"**the person investigating**", in relation to a complaint, recordable conduct matter or DSI matter, means the person appointed or designated to investigate that complaint or matter;

"**recordable conduct matter**" means—

(a)   a conduct matter that is required to be recorded by the appropriate authority under regulation 23 (conduct matters arising in civil proceedings) or 24 (recording etc. of conduct matters in other cases), or has been so recorded; or

(b)   except in paragraph (4) of regulation 19 (initial handling and recording of complaints), any matter brought to the attention of the appropriate authority under that paragraph;

"**relevant offence**" means—

(a)   an offence for which the sentence is fixed by law,

(b)   an offence for which a person of 18 years or over (not previously convicted) may be sentenced to imprisonment for a term of seven years or more (or might be so sentenced but for the restrictions imposed by section 33 of the Magistrates' Courts Act 1980);

"**serious injury**" means a fracture, a deep cut, a deep laceration or an injury causing damage to an internal organ or the impairment of any bodily function.

3(2)   In these Regulations "**the relevant officer**", in relation to a DSI matter, means the officer—

(a)   who arrested the person who has died or suffered serious injury,

(b)   in whose custody that person was at the time of the death or serious injury, or

(c)   with whom that person had the contact in question;

and where there is more than one such officer it means, subject to paragraph (3), the one who so dealt with that person last before the death or serious injury occurred.

3(3)   Where it cannot be determined which of two or more officers dealt with a person last before a death or serious injury occurred, the "**relevant officer**" is the most senior of them.

3(4)   References in these Regulations to the complainant, in relation to anything which is or purports to be a complaint, are references—

(a)   except in the case of anything which is or purports to be a complaint falling within regulation 9(1)(d) (complaints, matters and persons to which these Regulations apply), to the person by whom the complaint or purported complaint was made; and

(b)   in that case, to the person on whose behalf the complaint or purported complaint was made;

but where any person is acting on another's behalf for the purposes of any complaint or purported complaint, anything that is to be or may be done under these Regulations by or in relation to the complainant may be done, instead, by or in relation to the person acting on the complainant's behalf.

3(5)   Subject to paragraph (6), references in these Regulations, in relation to any conduct or anything purporting to be a complaint about any conduct, to a member of the public include references to any person who is a Commissioner or an officer (whether at the time of the conduct or any subsequent time).

3(6)   In these Regulations references, in relation to any conduct or to anything purporting to be a complaint about any conduct, to a member of the public do not include references to—

(a)   a person who, at the time when the conduct was supposed to have taken place in relation to that person, was a Commissioner or an officer (whether or not that person was on duty in that person's capacity as a Commissioner or officer at that time), or

(b)   a person who at the time when that person is supposed to have been adversely affected by it, or to have witnessed it, was on duty in that person's capacity as a Commissioner or officer.

Statutory Instruments

3(7) For the purposes of these Regulations, a person is adversely affected if that person suffers any form of loss or damage, distress or inconvenience, if that person is put in danger or if that person is otherwise unduly put at risk of being adversely affected.

3(8) References in these Regulations to the investigation of any complaint or matter by the appropriate authority on its own behalf, under the supervision of the IPCC, under the management of the IPCC or by the IPCC itself shall be construed as references to its investigation in accordance with–

(a)   regulation 44 (investigations by the appropriate authority on its own behalf),

(b)   regulation 45 (investigations supervised by the IPCC),

(c)   regulation 46 (investigations by a police force under the management or under the supervision of the IPCC),

(d)   regulation 47 (investigations managed by the IPCC), or

(e)   regulation 48 (investigations by the IPCC itself).

APPLICATION: GENERAL

4 These Regulations shall apply for the purpose of conferring functions on the IPCC in relation to the Commissioners and officers, in the exercise of their functions in or in relation to England and Wales.

APPLICATION OF THE 2002 ACT

5(1) Sections 9 (the Independent Police Complaints Commission), 19 (use of investigatory powers by or on behalf of the IPCC), 22 (power of the IPCC to issue guidance), 23 (regulations), 24 (consultation on regulations) and 27 (conduct of the IPCC's staff) of the 2002 Act shall apply to the Commissioners and officers with the following modifications.

5(2) In section 22 of the 2002 Act–

(a)   for subsection (1) substitute–

"**22(1)** The Commission may issue guidance to Her Majesty's Revenue and Customs and any person it sees fit concerning the exercise or performance by the persons to whom the guidance is issued, of any powers or duties specified in subsection (2).";

(b)   in subsection (2) for "persons serving with the police" substitute "persons serving with Her Majesty's Revenue and Customs";

(c)   for subsection (3) substitute–

"**22(3)** Before issuing any guidance under this section, the Commission shall consult Her Majesty's Revenue and Customs and any person it sees fit.";

(d)   in subsection (4) for "the Secretary of State" substitute "the Chancellor of the Exchequer";

(e)   omit subsection (5)(c).

5(3) In section 23 of the 2002 Act–

(a)   in subsection (2)(k), for "a person serving with the police" substitute "a person serving with Her Majesty's Revenue and Customs";

(b)   in subsection (2)(p), for "chief officers" substitute "the Commissioners for Her Majesty's Revenue and Customs".

5(4) In section 24 of the 2002 Act–

(a)   at the end of paragraph (a) insert "and Her Majesty's Revenue and Customs";

(b)   omit paragraphs (b) and (c).

TEMPORARY SERVICE AND COPIES OF ACCOUNTS

6(1) The IPCC may make arrangements with the Commissioners under which officers are engaged on temporary service with the IPCC.

6(2) Copies of the statement referred to in paragraph 17(1)(c) of Schedule 2 to the 2002 Act (accounts) shall also be sent to the Treasury.

GENERAL FUNCTIONS OF THE IPCC IN RELATION TO THE COMMISSIONERS AND OFFICERS

7(1) The functions of the IPCC in relation to the Commissioners and officers shall be–

(a)   to secure the maintenance by the IPCC itself, and by the Commissioners, of suitable arrangements with respect to the matters mentioned in paragraph (2);

(b)   to keep under review all arrangements maintained with respect to those matters;

(c)   to secure that arrangements maintained with respect to those matters comply with the requirements of the following provisions of this Part, are efficient and effective and contain and manifest an appropriate degree of independence;

(d)   to secure that public confidence is established and maintained in the existence of suitable arrangements with respect to those matters and with the operation of the arrangements that are in fact maintained with respect to those matters;

(e)   to make such recommendations, and to give such advice, for the modification of the arrangements maintained with respect to those matters, as appear, from the carrying out by the IPCC of its other functions, to be necessary or desirable.

7(2)   Those matters are–

(a)   the handling of complaints made about the conduct of the Commissioners or officers which the appropriate authority–

     (i)   has a duty to refer to the IPCC under regulation 28(1) (reference of complaints to the IPCC), or

     (ii)   may refer to the IPCC under regulation 28(5) or (6);

(b)   the recording of matters from which it appears that–

     (i)   there may have been conduct by such persons which constitutes or involves the commission of a criminal offence or behaviour justifying disciplinary proceedings, and

     (ii)   that conduct or behaviour is conduct or behaviour which the appropriate authority has a duty to refer to the IPCC under regulation 30(1) (reference of conduct matters to the IPCC) or may refer to the IPCC under regulation 30(5) or (6) of these Regulations;

(c)   the recording of matters from which it appears that a person has died or suffered serious injury during, or following, contact with an officer;

(d)   the manner in which any such complaints or any such matters as are mentioned in sub-paragraph (b) or (c) are investigated or otherwise handled and dealt with.

7(3)   It shall be the duty of the IPCC–

(a)   to exercise the powers and perform the duties conferred on it by the following provisions of these Regulations in the manner that it considers best calculated for the purpose of securing the proper carrying out of its functions under paragraph (1), and

(b)   to secure that arrangements exist which are conducive to, and facilitate, the reporting of misconduct by persons in relation to whose conduct the IPCC has functions.

7(4)   It shall also be the duty of the IPCC–

(a)   to enter into arrangements with the chief inspector of constabulary for the purpose of securing co-operation, in the carrying out of their respective functions in relation to the Commissioners and officers, between the IPCC and the inspectors of constabulary, and

(b)   to provide those inspectors with all such assistance and co-operation as may be required by those arrangements, or as otherwise appears to the IPCC to be appropriate, for facilitating the carrying out by those inspectors of their functions.

7(5)   Subject to the other provisions of these Regulations, the IPCC may do anything which appears to it to be calculated to facilitate, or is incidental or conducive to, the carrying out of its functions.

7(6)   The IPCC may, in connection with the making of any recommendation or the giving of any advice to any person for the purpose of carrying out its function under paragraph (1)(e), impose any such charge on that person for anything done by the IPCC for the purposes of, or in connection with, the carrying out of that function as it thinks fit.

7(7)   Nothing in these Regulations shall confer any function on the IPCC in relation to so much of any complaint or conduct matter as relates to the direction and control of HMRC by the Commissioners.

REPORTS TO THE CHANCELLOR OF THE EXCHEQUER

8(1)   As soon as practicable after the end of each of its financial years, the IPCC shall also make a report to the Chancellor of the Exchequer ("the Chancellor") on the carrying out of its functions during that year.

8(2)   The IPCC shall also make such reports to the Chancellor about matters relating generally to the carrying out of its functions as the Chancellor may, from time to time, require.

8(3) The IPCC may, from time to time, make such other reports to the Chancellor as it considers appropriate for drawing the Chancellor's attention to matters which–

(a)   have come to the IPCC's notice, and

(b)   are matters that it considers should be drawn to the Chancellor's attention by reason of their gravity or of other exceptional circumstances.

8(4) The IPCC shall prepare such reports containing advice and recommendations as it thinks appropriate for the purpose of carrying out its function under regulation 7(1)(e) (general functions of the IPCC in relation to Commissioners and officers).

8(5) Where the Chancellor receives any report under this regulation, the Chancellor shall–

(a)   in the case of every annual report under paragraph (1), and

(b)   in the case of any other report, if and to the extent that the Chancellor considers it appropriate to do so,

lay a copy of the report before Parliament and cause the report to be published.

8(6) The IPCC shall send a copy of every annual report under paragraph (1) to the Commissioners.

8(7) The IPCC shall send a copy of every report under paragraph (3) to the Commissioners.

8(8) The IPCC shall send a copy of every report under paragraph (4) to–

(a)   the Chancellor of the Exchequer, and

(b)   the Commissioners.

8(9) The IPCC shall send a copy of every report made or prepared by it under paragraphs (3) or (4) to such of the persons (in addition to those specified in the preceding paragraphs) who–

(a)   are referred to in the report, or

(b)   appear to the IPCC otherwise to have a particular interest in its contents,

as the IPCC thinks fit.

COMPLAINTS, MATTERS AND PERSONS TO WHICH THESE REGULATIONS APPLY

9(1) In these Regulations references to a complaint are references (subject to the following provisions of this regulation) to any complaint about the conduct of a Commissioner or an officer which is made (whether in writing or otherwise) by–

(a)   a member of the public who claims to be the person in relation to whom the conduct took place;

(b)   a member of the public not falling within sub-paragraph (a) who claims to have been adversely affected by the conduct;

(c)   a member of the public who claims to have witnessed the conduct;

(d)   a person acting on behalf of a person falling within any of sub-paragraphs (a) to (c).

9(2) In these Regulations **"conduct matter"** means (subject to the following provisions of this regulation, and regulation 19(4)) any matter which is not and has not been the subject of a complaint but in the case of which there is an indication (whether from the circumstances or otherwise) that a Commissioner or an officer may have–

(a)   committed a criminal offence, or

(b)   behaved in a manner which would justify the bringing of disciplinary proceedings.

9(3) In these Regulations **"death or serious injury matter"** ("DSI matter") means any circumstance (other than those which are or have been the subject of a complaint or which amount to a conduct matter)–

(a)   in or in consequence of which a person has died or has sustained serious injury, and

(b)   in relation to which the requirements of either paragraph (4) or (5) are satisfied.

9(4) The requirements of this paragraph are that at the time of the death or serious injury the person–

(a)   had been arrested by an officer and had not been released from that arrest, or

(b)   was otherwise detained in the custody of an officer.

9(5) The requirements of this paragraph are that–

(a)   at or before the time of the death or serious injury the person had contact (of whatever kind, and whether direct or indirect) with an officer who was acting in the execution of duties, and

(b)   there is an indication that the contact may have caused (whether directly or indirectly) or contributed to the death or serious injury.

9(6)   In paragraph (3) the reference to a person includes an officer, but in relation to such a person "contact" in paragraph (5) does not include contact that the officer has whilst acting in the execution of duties.

9(7)   The complaints that are complaints for the purposes of these Regulations by virtue of paragraph (1)(b) do not, except in a case falling within paragraph (8), include any made by or on behalf of a person who claims to have been adversely affected as a consequence only of having seen or heard the conduct, or any of the alleged effects of the conduct.

9(8)   A case falls within this paragraph if—

(a)   it was only because the person in question was physically present, or sufficiently nearby, when the conduct took place or the effects occurred that the person was able to see or hear the conduct or its effects, or

(b)   the adverse effect is attributable to, or was aggravated by, the fact that the person in relation to whom the conduct took place was already known to the person claiming to have suffered the adverse effect.

9(9)   For the purposes of this regulation a person shall be taken to have witnessed conduct if, and only if—

(a)   that person acquired knowledge of that conduct in a manner which would make that person a competent witness capable of giving admissible evidence of that conduct in criminal proceedings, or

(b)   that person possesses or controls anything which would in any such proceedings constitute admissible evidence of that conduct.

9(10)   For the purposes of these Regulations a person falling within paragraph (1)(a) to (c) shall not be taken to have authorised another person to act on that person's behalf unless—

(a)   that other person is for the time being designated for the purposes of these Regulations by the IPCC as a person through whom complaints may be made, or is of a description of persons so designated, or

(b)   the other person has been given, and is able to produce, the written consent to such action, of the person on whose behalf that action is taken.

HANDLING OF COMPLAINTS, CONDUCT MATTERS AND DSI MATTERS ETC

10   These Regulations shall have effect subject to regulation 11 (direction and control matters).

DIRECTION AND CONTROL MATTERS

11   Nothing in these Regulations shall have effect with respect to so much of any complaint as relates to the direction and control of HMRC by the Commissioners.

PART 2 – COMPLAINTS AND MISCONDUCT

CO-OPERATION, ASSISTANCE AND INFORMATION

12(1)   It shall be the duty of the Commissioners to ensure that they are kept informed, in relation to HMRC, about all matters falling within paragraph (2).

12(2)   Those matters are—

(a)   matters with respect to which any provision of these Regulations has effect;

(b)   anything which is done under or for the purposes of any such provision; and

(c)   any obligations to act or refrain from acting that have arisen by or under these Regulations, but have not yet been complied with or have been contravened.

12(3)   Where the IPCC requires the chief officer of a police force to provide a member of that person's force for appointment under regulation 46 or 47, it shall be the duty of the chief officer to whom the requirement is addressed to comply with it.

12(4)   It shall be the duty of the Commissioners to provide the IPCC and every member of the IPCC's staff with all such assistance as the IPCC or that member of staff may reasonably require for the purposes of, or in connection with, the carrying out of any investigation by the IPCC under these Regulations.

Statutory Instruments

12(5) It shall be the duty of the Commissioners to ensure that a person appointed under regulation 42 to carry out an investigation is given all such assistance and co-operation in the carrying out of that investigation as that person may reasonably require.

12(6) It shall be the duty of the Head of the Home Civil Service and the Commissioners to ensure that a person appointed under regulation 44, 45, 46 or 47 to carry out an investigation is given all such assistance and co-operation in the carrying out of that investigation as that person may reasonably require.

DISCLOSURE OF INFORMATION

13 Where the IPCC, or any person acting on its behalf, obtains information in the course of performing a function under these Regulations, that information may not be disclosed except as permitted under these Regulations or as otherwise prescribed by law.

USE OF INFORMATION

14 Where the IPCC or any person acting on its behalf, obtains information in the course of performing a function under these Regulations, that information may not be used for any purpose other than in the performance of a function under these Regulations or as otherwise prescribed by law.

PAYMENTS

15(1) The Commissioners shall pay such amount to the Secretary of State in respect of functions performed by the IPCC under these Regulations as may be agreed between the Commissioners and the IPCC.

15(2) In the absence of an agreement, the Commissioners shall pay such amount in respect of those functions as the Treasury, after consultation with the Secretary of State, shall determine.

PAYMENT FOR ASSISTANCE WITH INVESTIGATIONS

16(1) This regulation applies where–

(a)   a police force is required to provide assistance in connection with an investigation under Part 6 of these Regulations (investigations);

(b)   a police force is required to provide assistance in such a connection to the IPCC; or

(c)   a police force provides assistance by agreement under regulation 46(2).

16(2) For the purposes of this regulation–

(a)   assistance is required to be provided by a police force in connection with an investigation under Part 6 of these Regulations if the chief officer of that force complies with a requirement under regulation 12(3) or (5) (co-operation, assistance and information) that is made in connection with–

(i)   an investigation relating to the conduct of a person who, at the time of the conduct, was a Commissioner or an officer, or

(ii)   an investigation of a DSI matter in relation to which the relevant officer was, at the time of the death or serious injury, an officer; and

(b)   assistance is required to be provided in such a connection by a police force to the IPCC if the chief officer of that force complies with a requirement under regulation 12(6) that is made in connection with–

(i)   an investigation relating to the conduct of a person who, at the time of the conduct, was a Commissioner or an officer, or

(ii)   an investigation of a DSI matter in relation to which the relevant officer was, at the time of the death or serious injury, an officer.

16(3) Where the assistance is required to be provided by a police force, the appropriate authority shall pay to the local policing body maintaining that force such contribution towards the costs of the assistance–

(a)   as may be agreed between them; or

(b)   in the absence of an agreement, as may be determined in accordance with any arrangements which–

(i)   have been agreed to by local policing bodies generally and the Commissioners, and

(ii)   are for the time being in force with respect to the making of contributions towards the costs of assistance provided, in connection with investigations under Part 6 of these Regulations; or

(c)   in the absence of any such arrangements, as may be determined by the Secretary of State.

16(4) Paragraph (3) shall have effect in relation to assistance which a police force provides by agreement under regulation 46(2) as if the reference in that paragraph to required to be provided were a reference to provided by agreement under regulation 46(2).

16(5) Where the assistance is required to be provided by a police force to the IPCC, the IPCC shall pay to the local policing body maintaining the assisting force such contribution (if any) towards the costs of the assistance—

(a)   as may be agreed between the IPCC and that authority; or

(b)   in the absence of an agreement, as may be determined in accordance with any arrangements which—

(i)   have been agreed to by local policing bodies generally and by the IPCC, and

(ii)   are for the time being in force with respect to the making of contributions towards the costs of assistance provided, in connection with investigations under this Part, to the IPCC; or

(c)   in the absence of any such arrangements, as may be determined by the Secretary of State.

History – In reg. 16(3), the words "local policing body" substituted for the words "police authority" by SI 2011/3061, reg. 2(2)(a), with effect from 16 January 2012.
In reg. 16(3)(b)(i), the words "local policing bodies" substituted for the words "police authorities" by SI 2011/3061, reg. 2(2)(b), with effect from 16 January 2012.
In reg. 16(5), the words "local policing body" substituted for the words "police authority" by SI 2011/3061, reg. 2(2)(a), with effect from 16 January 2012.
In reg. 16(5)(b)(i), the words "local policing bodies" substituted for the words "police authorities" by SI 2011/3061, reg. 2(2)(b), with effect from 16 January 2012.

PART 3 – HANDLING OF COMPLAINTS AND CONDUCT MATTERS ETC

DUTIES TO PRESERVE EVIDENCE RELATING TO COMPLAINTS

17(1) This regulation applies where condition A or B is met.

17(2) Condition A is that—

(a)   a complaint is made to an appropriate authority about the conduct of an individual, and

(b)   that authority is the appropriate authority in relation to that individual.

17(3) Condition B is that—

(a)   an appropriate authority becomes aware that a complaint has been made to the IPCC, and

(b)   that authority is the appropriate authority in relation to that individual.

17(4) The appropriate authority shall take all such steps as appear to that authority to be appropriate for the purposes of these Regulations for obtaining and preserving evidence relating to the conduct complained of.

17(5) The duty of the appropriate authority under paragraph (4) must be performed as soon as practicable after the complaint is made or after it becomes aware of the complaint.

17(6) After that, the appropriate authority shall be under a duty, until it is satisfied that it is no longer necessary to do so, to continue to take the steps from time to time appearing to that authority to be appropriate for the purposes of these Regulations for obtaining and preserving evidence relating to the conduct complained of.

17(7) It shall be the duty of the appropriate authority to take all such specific steps for obtaining or preserving evidence relating to any conduct that is the subject-matter of a complaint as it may be directed by the IPCC to take for the purposes of this regulation.

DELEGATION OF POWERS AND DUTIES

18(1) Subject to paragraph (3), the appropriate authority may delegate all or any of the powers or duties conferred or imposed on it by or under these Regulations to a person mentioned in paragraph (2).

18(2) Those powers or duties may be delegated—

(a)   in the case of the Head of the Home Civil Service, to a member of the Senior Civil Service;

(b)   in the case of the Chief Executive, to a member of the Senior Civil Service employed in the service of the Commissioners;

(c)   in the case of a Commissioner (other than the Chief Executive), to an officer.

18(3) The appropriate authority shall not, in any particular case, delegate any power or duty under paragraph (1) to a person who has acted as investigating officer in that case.

INITIAL HANDLING AND RECORDING OF COMPLAINTS

19(1) Where a complaint is made to the IPCC–

(a)   it shall ascertain whether the complainant is content for the appropriate authority to be notified of the complaint, and

(b)   it shall give notification of the complaint to the appropriate authority if, and only if, the complainant is so content.

19(2) Where a complaint is made to an appropriate authority, the authority shall–

(a)   determine whether or not it is the appropriate authority in relation to the complaint, and

(b)   if it determines that it is not, give notification of the complaint to the appropriate authority for the individual complained against.

19(3) Where the IPCC–

(a)   is prevented by paragraph (1)(b) from notifying any complaint to the appropriate authority, and

(b)   considers that it is in the public interest for the subject-matter of the complaint to be brought to the attention of the appropriate authority and recorded under regulation 24,

the IPCC may bring that matter to the appropriate authority's attention under that regulation as if it were a recordable conduct matter, and (if it does so) the following provisions of these Regulations shall have effect accordingly as if it were such a matter.

19(4) Where the IPCC or the appropriate authority gives notification of a complaint under paragraph (1) or (2) or the IPCC brings any matter to the appropriate authority's attention under paragraph (3), the person who gave the notification or, as the case may be, the IPCC shall notify the complainant–

(a)   that the notification has been given and of what it contained, or

(b)   that the matter has been brought to the appropriate authority's attention to be dealt with otherwise than as a complaint.

19(5) Where–

(a)   an appropriate authority, in the case of any complaint made to it, decides that it is the appropriate authority, or

(b)   a complaint is notified to the appropriate authority under this regulation,

the appropriate authority shall record the complaint.

19(6) Nothing in this regulation shall require the notification or recording by any person of any complaint about any conduct if–

(a)   that person is satisfied that the subject-matter of the complaint has been, or is already being, dealt with by means of criminal or disciplinary proceedings against the person whose conduct it was, or

(b)   the complaint has been withdrawn.

KEEPING OF RECORDS

20 The appropriate authority shall keep records, in such form as the IPCC shall determine, of–

(a)   every complaint and purported complaint that is made to it;

(b)   every conduct matter recorded by it under regulation 23(3) (conduct matters arising in civil proceedings);

(c)   every DSI matter recorded by it under regulation 32 (duty to record DSI matters);

(d)   every exercise of a power or performance of a duty under these Regulations.

FAILURES TO NOTIFY OR RECORD A COMPLAINT

21(1) This regulation applies where anything which is or purports to be a complaint in relation to which regulation 19 (initial handling and recording of complaints) has effect is received by the Head of the Home Civil Service, the Chief Executive or the Commissioners (other than the Chairman, the Chief

Executive and the Permanent Secretary) (whether in consequence of having been made directly or of a notification under that regulation).

21(2)   Where the Head of the Home Civil Service, the Chief Executive or the Commissioners (other than the Chairman, the Chief Executive and the Permanent Secretary) decides or decide not to take action under regulation 19 for notifying or recording the whole or any part of what has been received, the Head of the Home Civil Service, the Chief Executive or the Commissioners (other than the Chairman, the Chief Executive and the Permanent Secretary) shall notify the complainant of the following matters–

(a)   the decision to take no action, and, if that decision relates to only part of what was received, the part in question;

(b)   the grounds on which the decision was made; and

(c)   whether the complainant has a right to appeal against that decision under this regulation.

21(3)   The complainant shall have a right of appeal to the IPCC against any failure by the Head of the Home Civil Service, the Chief Executive or the Commissioners (other than the Chairman, the Chief Executive and the Permanent Secretary) to make a determination under regulation 19 or to notify or record anything under that regulation if, but only if, the failure is in respect of conduct which the Head of the Home Civil Service, the Chief Executive or the Commissioners (other than the Chairman, the Chief Executive and the Permanent Secretary) is required to refer to the IPCC under regulation 28(1)(a) or (b) (reference of complaints to the IPCC).

21(4)   On an appeal under this regulation, the IPCC shall–

(a)   determine whether any action under regulation 19 should have been taken in the case in question, and

(b)   if the IPCC finds in the complainant's favour, give to the Head of the Home Civil Service, the Chief Executive or the Commissioners (other than the Chairman, the Chief Executive and the Permanent Secretary) such directions as the IPCC considers appropriate, as to the action to be taken for making a determination, or for notifying or recording what was received,

and it shall be the duty of the Head of the Home Civil Service, the Chief Executive or the Commissioners (other than the Chairman, the Chief Executive and the Permanent Secretary) to comply with any directions given under sub-paragraph (b).

21(5)   Directions under paragraph (4)(b) may require action taken in pursuance of the directions to be treated as taken in accordance with any such provision of regulation 19 as may be specified in the direction.

21(6)   The IPCC–

(a)   shall give notification both to the Head of the Home Civil Service, the Chief Executive or the Commissioners (other than the Chairman, the Chief Executive and the Permanent Secretary), as the case may be, and to the complainant, of any determination made by it under this regulation, and

(b)   shall give notification to the complainant of any direction given by it to the Head of the Home Civil Service, the Chief Executive or the Commissioners (other than the Chairman, the Chief Executive and the Permanent Secretary) under this regulation.

HANDLING OF COMPLAINTS BY THE APPROPRIATE AUTHORITY

22(1)   This regulation applies where a complaint has been recorded by the appropriate authority unless the complaint–

(a)   is one which has been, or must be, referred to the IPCC under regulation 28 (reference of complaints to the IPCC), and

(b)   is not for the time being either referred back to the authority under regulation 29 (duties of the IPCC on references under regulation 28) or the subject of a determination under regulation 38 (power of the IPCC to determine the form of an investigation).

22(2)   The appropriate authority shall not be required by virtue of any provisions of these Regulations to take any action in relation to the complaint but may handle the complaint in whatever manner it thinks fit, or take no action in relation to the complaint.

CONDUCT MATTERS ARISING IN CIVIL PROCEEDINGS

23(1) This regulation applies where–

(a) the appropriate authority has received notification (whether or not under this regulation) that civil proceedings relating to any matter have been brought by a member of the public against it, or it otherwise appears to the appropriate authority that such proceedings are likely to be so brought, and

(b) it appears to the appropriate authority (whether at the time of the notification or at any time subsequently) that those proceedings involve or would involve a conduct matter.

23(2) The appropriate authority–

(a) shall consider whether it is the appropriate authority in relation to the conduct matter in question, and

(b) if it is not, shall notify the person who is the appropriate authority about the proceedings, or the proposal to bring them, and about the circumstances that make it appear as mentioned in paragraph (1)(b).

23(3) Where the appropriate authority determines for the purposes of this regulation that it is the appropriate authority in relation to any conduct matter, it shall record that matter.

23(4) Where the appropriate authority records any matter under this regulation it–

(a) shall first determine whether the matter is one which it is required to refer to the IPCC under regulation 30 (reference of conduct matters to the IPCC) or is one which it would be appropriate so to refer, and

(b) if it is not required so to refer the matter and does not do so, may deal with the matter in such other manner (if any) as it may determine.

23(5) Nothing in paragraph (3) shall require the appropriate authority to record any conduct matter if it is satisfied that the matter has been, or is already being, dealt with by means of criminal or disciplinary proceedings against the person to whose conduct the matter relates.

23(6) For the purposes of this regulation civil proceedings involve a conduct matter if–

(a) they relate to such a matter, or

(b) they are proceedings that relate to a matter in relation to which a conduct matter, or evidence of a conduct matter, is or may be relevant.

RECORDING ETC. OF CONDUCT MATTERS IN OTHER CASES

24(1) Where–

(a) a conduct matter comes (otherwise than as mentioned in regulation 23 (conduct matters arising in civil proceedings)) to the attention of the appropriate authority in relation to that matter, and

(b) it appears to the appropriate authority that the conduct involved in that matter falls within paragraph (2),

it shall be the duty of the appropriate authority to record that matter.

24(2) Conduct falls within this paragraph if (assuming it to have taken place)–

(a) it appears to have resulted in the death of any person or in serious injury to any person;

(b) a member of the public has been adversely affected by it; or

(c) it is of a description specified in paragraph (3).

24(3) The following descriptions of conduct are specified for the purposes of paragraph (2)–

(a) a serious assault, as defined in guidance issued by the IPCC;

(b) a serious sexual offence, as defined in guidance issued by the IPCC;

(c) serious corruption, as defined in guidance issued by the IPCC;

(d) a criminal offence or behaviour liable to result in disciplinary proceedings which was aggravated by discriminatory behaviour on the grounds of a person's race, sex, religion, or other status identified in guidance by the IPCC;

(e) a relevant offence;

(f) conduct whose gravity or other exceptional circumstances make it appropriate to record the matter in which the conduct is involved; or

(g) conduct which is alleged to have taken place in the same incident as one in which conduct within sub-paragraphs (a) to (e) is alleged.

24(4)   Where the appropriate authority records any matter under this regulation it–

(a)   shall first determine whether the matter is one which it is required to refer to the IPCC under regulation 30 (reference of conduct matters to the IPCC) or is one which it would be appropriate to so refer, and

(b)   if it is not required so to refer the matter and does not do so, may deal with the matter in such other manner (if any) as it may determine.

24(5)   Nothing in paragraph (1) shall require the appropriate authority to record any conduct matter if it is satisfied that the matter has been, or is already being, dealt with by means of criminal or disciplinary proceedings against the person to whose conduct the matter relates.

24(6)   If it appears to the IPCC–

(a)   that any matter that has come to its attention is a recordable conduct matter, but

(b)   that that matter has not been recorded by the appropriate authority,

the IPCC may direct the appropriate authority to record that matter; and it shall be the duty of that authority to comply with the direction.

DUTIES TO PRESERVE EVIDENCE RELATING TO CONDUCT MATTERS

25(1)   Where the appropriate authority becomes aware of any recordable matter relating to the conduct of an individual, it shall be the duty of that authority to take all such steps as appear to it to be appropriate for the purposes of these Regulations for obtaining and preserving the evidence relating to that matter.

25(2)   The duty of the appropriate authority under paragraph (1) must be performed as soon as practicable after it becomes aware of the matter in question.

25(3)   After that, the appropriate authority shall be under a duty until it is satisfied that it is no longer necessary to do so, to continue to take the steps from time to time appearing to it to be appropriate for the purposes of these Regulations for obtaining and preserving evidence relating to the matter.

25(4)   It shall be the duty of the appropriate authority to take all such specific steps for obtaining or preserving evidence relating to any recordable conduct matter, as it may be directed by the IPCC to take for the purposes of these Regulations.

COMPLAINTS AGAINST A PERSON WHO HAS SUBSEQUENTLY CEASED TO SERVE WITH HMRC

26   Where a complaint or conduct matter relates to the conduct of a person who has ceased to be a Commissioner or an officer since the time of the conduct, these Regulations shall apply in relation to such person as if they did not include any requirement for an appropriate authority to determine whether disciplinary proceedings should be brought against a person whose conduct is reported to the appropriate authority.

PART 4 – REFERRAL OF MATTERS TO THE IPCC

RECORDING AND REFERENCE OF CONDUCT AND DSI MATTERS

27(1)   Any conduct matter which is required to be referred to the IPCC shall be referred in such manner as the IPCC specifies and–

(a)   if the matter falls within paragraph (1)(a) or (b) of regulation 30, not later than the end of the day following the day on which it first becomes clear to the appropriate authority that the conduct matter is one to which that paragraph applies, and

(b)   if the matter falls within paragraph (1)(c) of that regulation, not later than the end of the day following the day on which the IPCC notifies the appropriate authority that the conduct matter is to be referred.

27(2)   Any DSI matter which is required to be referred to the IPCC shall be referred in such manner as the IPCC specifies and–

(a)   in a case where the IPCC directs that the matter be referred to it, within time limits defined in guidance issued by the IPCC, but no later than the end of the day following the day on which the IPCC so directs;

(b)   in any other case, within time limits defined in guidance issued by the IPCC, but no later than the end of the day following the day on which the matter first comes to the attention of the appropriate authority.

REFERENCE OF COMPLAINTS TO THE IPCC

28(1)   It shall be the duty of the appropriate authority to refer a complaint to the IPCC where the complaint is—

(a)   one alleging that the conduct complained of has resulted in death or serious injury;

(b)   any complaint not falling within paragraph (a) but alleging conduct which constitutes—

  (i)   a serious assault, as defined in guidance issued by the IPCC;

  (ii)   a serious sexual offence, as defined in guidance issued by the IPCC;

  (iii) serious corruption, as defined in guidance issued by the IPCC;

  (iv)   a criminal offence or behaviour which is liable to lead to a disciplinary sanction and which in either case was aggravated by discriminatory behaviour on the grounds of a person's race, sex, religion, or other status identified in guidance by the IPCC;

  (v)   a relevant offence;

(c)   a complaint which arises from the same incident as one in which any conduct falling within paragraph (a) or (b) is alleged; or

(d)   one in respect of which the IPCC notifies the appropriate authority that it requires the complaint in question to be referred to the IPCC for its consideration.

28(2)   The obligation on the Head of the Home Civil Service under paragraph (1)(a) or (b) to refer a complaint about the conduct of a person in respect of whom the Head of the Home Civil Service is the appropriate authority arises only if the Head of the Home Civil Service is satisfied that the complaint contains an indication that a criminal offence may have been committed by that person.

28(3)   The obligation on the Chief Executive or the Commissioners (other than the Chairman, the Chief Executive and the Permanent Secretary for Tax) under paragraph (1)(a) or (b) to refer a complaint about the conduct of a person in respect of whom the Chief Executive is or the Commissioners are the appropriate authority arises only if the Chief Executive is or the Commissioners are satisfied that the complaint contains an indication that the person may have—

(a)   committed a criminal offence, or

(b)   behaved in a manner which would justify the bringing of disciplinary proceedings and that such behaviour (if it had taken place) would be likely to lead to the termination of that person's office or employment.

28(4)   In a case where there is no obligation under paragraph (1) to make a reference, the appropriate authority may refer a complaint to the IPCC if that authority considers that it would be appropriate to do so by reason of—

(a)   the gravity of the subject-matter of the complaint; or

(b)   any exceptional circumstances.

28(5)   In a case in which a reference under paragraph (1) or (4) is neither made nor required to be made, the Head of the Home Civil Service may refer a complaint to the IPCC if—

(a)   it is one in relation to which the Chief Executive is the appropriate authority; and

(b)   the Head of the Home Civil Service considers that it would be appropriate to do so by reason of—

  (i)   the gravity of the subject-matter of the complaint, or

  (ii)   any exceptional circumstances.

28(6)   Where a complaint is required to be referred to the IPCC under paragraph (1)(a), (b) or (c), notification of the complaint shall be given to the IPCC—

(a)   not later than the end of the day following the day on which it first becomes clear to the appropriate authority that the complaint is one to which that sub-paragraph applies, and

(b)   in such manner as the IPCC specifies.

28(7)   Where a complaint is required to be referred to the IPCC under paragraph (1)(d), notification of the complaint shall be given to the IPCC—

(a)   not later than the end of the day following the day on which the IPCC notifies the appropriate authority that the complaint is to be referred, and

(b)   in such manner as the IPCC specifies.

28(8)   Subject to paragraph (10), the power–

(a)   of the IPCC by virtue of paragraph (1)(d) to require a complaint to be referred to it, and

(b)   of the appropriate authority to refer a complaint to the IPCC under paragraph (2) or (3),

shall each be exercisable at any time irrespective of whether the complaint is already being investigated by any person or has already been considered by the IPCC.

28(9)   Where the appropriate authority refers a complaint to the IPCC under this regulation it shall give a notification of the making of the reference–

(a)   to the complainant, and

(b)   except in a case where it appears to the appropriate authority that to do so might prejudice a possible future investigation of the complaint, to the person complained against.

28(10)   A complaint that has already been referred to the IPCC under this regulation on a previous occasion–

(a)   shall not be required to be referred again under this regulation unless the IPCC so directs, and

(b)   shall not be referred in exercise of any power conferred by this regulation unless the IPCC consents.

DUTIES OF THE IPCC ON REFERENCES UNDER REGULATION 28

29(1)   It shall be the duty of the IPCC, in the case of every complaint referred to it by the appropriate authority, to determine whether or not it is necessary for the complaint to be investigated.

29(2)   Where the IPCC determines under this regulation that it is not necessary for a complaint to be investigated, it may, if it thinks fit, refer the complaint back to the appropriate authority in accordance with paragraph (3).

29(3)   In a case to which paragraph (2) applies, the appropriate authority shall not be required by virtue of any provisions of these Regulations to take any action in relation to the complaint but may handle the complaint in whatever manner it thinks fit, or take no action in relation to the complaint.

29(4)   Where the IPCC refers a complaint back under paragraph (2), it shall give a notification of the making of the reference back–

(a)   to the complainant, and

(b)   to the person complained against.

REFERENCE OF CONDUCT MATTERS TO THE IPCC

30(1)   It shall be the duty of the appropriate authority to refer a recordable conduct matter to the IPCC (whether or not the case falls within regulation 23), if–

(a)   that matter relates to any incident or circumstances in or in consequence of which any person has died or suffered serious injury;

(b)   that matter is of a description specified in paragraph (2); or

(c)   the IPCC notifies the appropriate authority that it requires that matter to be referred to the IPCC for its consideration.

30(2)   Any matter which relates to conduct falling within the following descriptions is specified for the purposes of paragraph (1)(b)–

(a)   a serious assault, as defined in guidance issued by the IPCC;

(b)   a serious sexual offence, as defined in guidance issued by the IPCC;

(c)   serious corruption, as defined in guidance issued by the IPCC;

(d)   a criminal offence or behaviour which is liable to lead to a disciplinary sanction and which in either case was aggravated by discriminatory behaviour on the grounds of a person's race, sex, religion, or other status identified in guidance issued by the IPCC;

(e)   a relevant offence; or

(f)   conduct which is alleged to have taken place in the same incident as one in which conduct within sub-paragraphs (a) to (e) is alleged.

30(3)   The obligation on the Head of the Home Civil Service under paragraph (1)(a) or (b) to refer a recordable conduct matter in respect of a person for whom the Head of the Home Civil Service is the appropriate authority arises only if the Head of the Home Civil Service is satisfied that the matter is one in respect of which there is an indication that a criminal offence may have been committed by that person.

30(4)   The obligation on the appropriate authority under paragraph (1)(a) or (b) to refer a recordable conduct matter in respect of a person for whom it is the appropriate authority arises only if it is satisfied that the matter is one in respect of which there is an indication that the person may have—

(a)   committed a criminal offence, or

(b)   behaved in a manner which would justify the bringing of disciplinary proceedings and that such behaviour (if it had taken place) would be likely to lead to the termination of that person's office or employment.

30(5)   In any case where there is no obligation under paragraph (1) to make a reference, the appropriate authority may refer a recordable conduct matter to the IPCC if that authority considers that it would be appropriate to do so by reason of—

(a)   the gravity of the matter, or

(b)   any exceptional circumstances.

30(6)   In a case in which a reference under paragraph (1) or (5) is neither made nor required to be made, the Head of the Home Civil Service may refer any recordable conduct matter to the IPCC if—

(a)   it is one in relation to which the Chief Executive is the appropriate authority, and

(b)   the Head of the Home Civil Service considers that it would be appropriate to do so by reason of—

   (i)   the gravity of the matter, or

   (ii) any exceptional circumstances.

30(7)   Where there is an obligation under this regulation to refer any matter to the IPCC, it must be so referred within such period as may be provided for by regulation 27.

30(8)   Subject to paragraph (10), the power—

(a)   of the IPCC by virtue of paragraph (1)(c) to require a matter to be referred to it, and

(b)   of the appropriate authority to refer any matter to the IPCC under paragraph (5) or (6),

shall each be exercisable at any time irrespective of whether the matter is already being investigated by any person or has already been considered by the IPCC.

30(9)   Where—

(a)   the appropriate authority refers a matter to the IPCC under this regulation, and

(b)   it does not consider that to do so might prejudice a possible future investigation of that matter,

it shall give a notification of the making of the reference to the person to whose conduct that matter relates.

30(10)   A matter that has already been referred to the IPCC under this regulation on a previous occasion—

(a)   shall not be required to be referred again under this regulation unless the IPCC so directs, and

(b)   shall not be referred in exercise of any power conferred by this regulation unless the IPCC consents.

DUTIES OF THE IPCC ON REFERENCES UNDER REGULATION 30

31(1)   It shall be the duty of the IPCC, in the case of every recordable conduct matter referred to it by the appropriate authority under regulation 30, to determine whether or not it is necessary for the matter to be investigated.

31(2)   Where the IPCC determines under this regulation that it is not necessary for a recordable conduct matter referred by the appropriate authority to be investigated, it may if it thinks fit refer the matter back to the appropriate authority to be dealt with by it in such manner (if any) as the appropriate authority may determine.

31(3)   Where—

(a)   the IPCC refers a matter back to the appropriate authority under this regulation, and

(b)   the IPCC does not consider that to do so might prejudice a possible future investigation of that matter,

the IPCC shall give a notification of the making of the reference to the person to whose conduct that matter relates.

PART 5 – HANDLING DEATH AND SERIOUS INJURY (DSI)

DUTY TO RECORD DSI MATTERS

32(1) Where a DSI matter comes to the attention of the appropriate authority, it shall be the duty of the appropriate authority to record that matter.

32(2) If it appears to the IPCC–

(a) that any matter that has come to its attention is a DSI matter, but

(b) that that matter has not been recorded by the appropriate authority,

the IPCC may direct the appropriate authority to record that matter; and it shall be the duty of that authority to comply with the direction.

DUTY TO PRESERVE EVIDENCE RELATING TO DSI MATTERS

33(1) Where a DSI matter comes to the attention of the appropriate authority it shall be the duty of that authority to take all such steps as appear to it to be appropriate for the purposes of these Regulations for obtaining and preserving evidence relating to that matter.

33(2) The duty of the appropriate authority under paragraph (1) must be performed as soon as practicable after it becomes aware of the matter in question.

33(3) After that, the appropriate authority shall be under a duty to continue to take the steps from time to time appearing to it to be appropriate for the purposes of these Regulations for obtaining and preserving evidence relating to the matter, until it is satisfied that it is no longer necessary to do so.

33(4) It shall be the duty of the appropriate authority to take all such specific steps for obtaining or preserving evidence relating to any DSI matter as it may be directed to take for the purposes of this regulation by the IPCC.

REFERENCE OF DSI MATTERS TO THE IPCC

34(1) It shall be the duty of the appropriate authority to refer a DSI matter to the IPCC.

34(2) The appropriate authority must do so within the period specified in regulation 27(2) (recording and reference of conduct matters).

34(3) A matter that has already been referred to the IPCC under this regulation on a previous occasion shall not be required to be referred again under this regulation unless the IPCC so directs.

DUTIES OF IPCC ON REFERENCES UNDER REGULATION 34

35(1) It shall be the duty of the IPCC, in the case of every DSI matter referred to it by the appropriate authority, to determine whether or not it is necessary for the matter to be investigated.

35(2) Where the IPCC determines under this regulation that it is not necessary for a DSI matter to be investigated, it may if it thinks fit refer the matter back to the appropriate authority to be dealt with by it in such manner (if any) as the appropriate authority may determine.

PROCEDURE WHERE CONDUCT MATTER IS REVEALED DURING INVESTIGATION OF DSI MATTER

36(1) If during the course of an investigation of a DSI matter it appears to a person appointed under regulation 47 or 48 or appointed to undertake an investigation under the management of the IPCC under regulation 46, that there is an indication that the person whose conduct is in question may have–

(a) committed a criminal offence, or

(b) behaved in a manner which would justify the bringing of disciplinary proceedings,

the person so appointed shall make a submission to that effect to the IPCC.

36(2) If, after considering a submission under paragraph (1), the IPCC determines that there is such an indication, it shall–

(a) notify the appropriate authority in relation to the DSI matter and (if different) the appropriate authority in relation to the person whose conduct is in question of its determination, and

(b) send to it (or each of them) a copy of the submission under paragraph (1).

36(3) If during the course of an investigation of a DSI matter it appears to a person appointed under regulation 44 or 45 or appointed to undertake an investigation under the supervision of the IPCC under regulation 46, that there is an indication that the person whose conduct is in question may have—

(a)   committed a criminal offence, or

(b)   behaved in a manner which would justify the bringing of disciplinary proceedings,

the person so appointed shall make a submission to that effect to the appropriate authority in relation to the DSI matter.

36(4) If, after considering a submission under paragraph (3), the appropriate authority determines that there is such an indication, it shall—

(a)   if it is not the appropriate authority in relation to the person whose conduct is in question, notify that other authority of its determination and send to that authority a copy of the submission under paragraph (3), and

(b)   notify the IPCC of its determination and send to it a copy of the submission under paragraph (3).

36(5) Where the appropriate authority in relation to the person whose conduct is in question—

(a)   is notified of a determination by the IPCC under paragraph (2),

(b)   (in a case where it is also the appropriate authority in relation to the DSI matter) makes a determination under paragraph (4), or

(c)   (in a case where it is not the appropriate authority in relation to the DSI matter) is notified by that other authority of a determination by it under paragraph (4),

it shall record the matter under regulation 24 (recording etc of conduct matters in other cases) as a conduct matter (and the other provisions of these Regulations shall apply in relation to that matter accordingly).

36(6) Where a DSI matter is recorded under regulation 24 as a conduct matter by virtue of paragraph (5)—

(a)   the person investigating the DSI matter shall (subject to any determination made by the IPCC under regulation 38(6)) continue the investigation as if appointed or designated to investigate the conduct matter, and

(b)   the other provisions of these Regulations shall apply in relation to that matter accordingly.

PART 6 – INVESTIGATIONS

INSPECTIONS OF HMRC PREMISES ON BEHALF OF THE IPCC

37(1) Where—

(a)   the IPCC requires the Commissioners to allow a person nominated for the purpose by the IPCC to have access to any premises occupied for the purposes of HMRC and to documents and other things on those premises, and

(b)   the requirement is imposed for any of the purposes mentioned in paragraph (2),

it shall be the duty of the Commissioners to secure that the required access is allowed to the nominated person.

37(2) Those purposes are—

(a)   the purposes of any examination by the IPCC of the efficiency and effectiveness of the arrangements made by the Commissioners for handling complaints or dealing with recordable conduct matters or DSI matters;

(b)   the purposes of any investigation by the IPCC under this Part or of any investigation carried out under its supervision or management.

37(3) A requirement imposed under this regulation for the purposes mentioned in paragraph (2)(a) must be notified to the Commissioners at least 48 hours before the time at which access is required.

37(4) Where—

(a)   a requirement imposed under this regulation for the purposes mentioned in paragraph (2)(a) requires access to any premises, document or thing to be allowed to any person, but

(b)   there are reasonable grounds for not allowing that person to have the required access at the time at which that person seeks to have it, the obligation to secure that the required access is allowed shall have effect as an obligation to secure that the access is allowed to that person at the earliest practicable time after there cease to be any such grounds as that person may specify.

37(5)   The provisions of this regulation are in addition to, and without prejudice to—

(a)   the rights of entry, search and seizure that are or may be conferred on—

(i)   a person designated for the purposes of regulation 48 (investigations by the IPCC itself), or

(ii)   any person who otherwise acts on behalf of the IPCC,

in that person's capacity as a constable or as a person with the powers and privileges of a constable; or

(b)   the obligations of the Commissioners under regulations 12 (co-operation, assistance and information) and 53 (provision of information to the IPCC).

POWER OF THE IPCC TO DETERMINE THE FORM OF AN INVESTIGATION

38(1)   This regulation applies where—

(a)   a complaint or recordable conduct matter or DSI matter is referred to the IPCC; and

(b)   the IPCC determines that it is necessary for the complaint or matter to be investigated.

38(2)   It shall be the duty of the IPCC to determine the form which the investigation shall take.

38(3)   In making a determination under paragraph (2) the IPCC shall have regard to the seriousness of the case and the public interest.

38(4)   The only forms which the investigation may take in accordance with a determination made under this regulation are—

(a)   an investigation by the appropriate authority on its own behalf;

(b)   an investigation by the appropriate authority under the supervision of the IPCC;

(c)   an investigation by a police force under the supervision of the IPCC;

(d)   an investigation by the appropriate authority under the management of the IPCC;

(e)   an investigation by a police force under the management of the IPCC;

(f)   an investigation by the IPCC.

38(5)   An investigation under this regulation relating to any conduct of the Commissioners may only be carried out in the form specified in paragraph (4)(c), (4)(e) or (4)(f).

38(6)   The IPCC may at any time make a further determination under this regulation to replace an earlier one.

38(7)   Where a determination under this regulation replaces an earlier determination under this regulation, or relates to a complaint or matter in relation to which the appropriate authority has already begun an investigation on its own behalf, the IPCC may give—

(a)   the appropriate authority, and

(b)   any person previously appointed to carry out the investigation,

such directions as it considers appropriate for the purpose of giving effect to the new determination.

38(8)   It shall be the duty of a person to whom a direction is given under paragraph (7) to comply with it.

38(9)   The IPCC shall notify the appropriate authority of any determination that it makes under this regulation in relation to a particular complaint or recordable conduct matter or DSI matter.

APPOINTMENT OF PERSONS TO CARRY OUT INVESTIGATIONS

39   No person shall be appointed to carry out an investigation under regulation 44, 45, 46 or 47—

(a)   unless that person has an appropriate level of knowledge, skills and experience to plan and manage the investigation;

(b)   if that person's involvement could reasonably give rise to a concern as to whether that person could act impartially under these Regulations; or

(c)   if that person works, directly or indirectly, under the management of the person whose conduct is being investigated.

POWER OF THE IPCC TO IMPOSE REQUIREMENTS IN RELATION TO AN INVESTIGATION WHICH IT IS SUPERVISING

40(1) For the purposes of regulation 45(6) the requirements which may be imposed by the IPCC on a person appointed to investigate a complaint, recordable conduct matter or DSI matter are, subject to paragraphs (2) and (3), any reasonable requirements as to the conduct of the investigation as appear to the IPCC to be necessary.

40(2) Where at any stage of an investigation of a complaint, recordable conduct matter or DSI matter the possibility of criminal proceedings arises, the IPCC shall not, under paragraph (1), impose any requirement relating to the obtaining or preservation of evidence of a criminal offence without first obtaining the consent—

(a)   in the case of an investigation carried out by an appointed person who is an officer, of the Director of Revenue and Customs Prosecutions, or

(b)   in any other case, of the Director of Public Prosecutions,

to the imposition of any such requirement.

40(3) The IPCC shall not, under paragraph (1), impose any requirement relating to the resources to be made available by the appropriate authority, for the purposes of an investigation, without first consulting it and having regard to any representations it may make.

COMBINING AND SPLITTING INVESTIGATIONS

41(1) An appropriate authority which is carrying out an investigation on its own behalf may—

(a)   combine that investigation with another such investigation, or

(b)   split that investigation into two or more such separate investigations,

if it considers that it is more efficient and effective, or is otherwise in the public interest, to do so.

41(2) Subject to paragraph (3), where the IPCC is supervising, managing or carrying out an investigation, it may—

(a)   combine that investigation with another investigation, or

(b)   split that investigation into two or more separate investigations,

if it considers that it is more efficient and effective, or is otherwise in the public interest, to do so.

41(3) The IPCC shall not take any action under paragraph (2) in relation to a supervised or managed investigation except after consultation with the appropriate authority.

41(4) Nothing in this regulation shall prevent the IPCC from determining—

(a)   that where an investigation is split into two or more separate investigations, those investigations may take different forms, or

(b)   that two or more separate investigations which take different forms (including an investigation being carried out by the appropriate authority on its own behalf) may be combined into a single investigation.

POWER OF THE IPCC TO DISCONTINUE AN INVESTIGATION

42(1) If, following a determination under regulation 29 (duties of the IPCC on reference under regulation 28), 31 (duties of the IPCC on reference under regulation 30) or 35 (duties of the IPCC on reference under regulation 34), it appears at any time to the IPCC (whether on an application by the appropriate authority or otherwise) that a complaint or matter that is being investigated—

(a)   by the appropriate authority on its own behalf, or

(b)   under the supervision or management of the IPCC,

is of a description of complaint or matter specified in paragraph (5), the IPCC may by order require the discontinuance of the investigation.

42(2) Where the IPCC makes an order under this regulation or discontinues an investigation being carried out in accordance with regulation 48 (investigations by the IPCC itself), it shall give notification of the discontinuance—

(a)   to the appropriate authority;

(b)   to every person entitled to be kept properly informed in relation to the subject matter of the investigation under regulation 55 (duty to provide information for other persons); and

(c)   in a case where the investigation that is discontinued is an investigation of a complaint, to the complainant.

42(3) Where an investigation of a complaint or recordable conduct matter or DSI matter is discontinued in accordance with this regulation–

(a)   the IPCC may give the appropriate authority directions to do any such things as it is authorised to direct under paragraphs (11) and (12);

(b)   the IPCC may itself take any such steps of a description specified in regulations so made as it considers appropriate for purposes connected with the discontinuance of the investigation; and

(c)   subject to the preceding paragraphs, neither the appropriate authority nor the IPCC shall take any further action in accordance with the provisions of these Regulations in relation to that complaint or matter.

42(4) The appropriate authority shall comply with any directions given to it under paragraph (3).

42(5) The descriptions of complaint or matter are–

(a)   one in which the complainant refuses to co-operate to the extent that the IPCC considers that it is not reasonably practicable to continue the investigation;

(b)   one which the IPCC considers is vexatious, oppressive or otherwise an abuse of the procedures for dealing with complaints, conduct matters or DSI matters;

(c)   one which is repetitious, as defined in paragraph (6); and

(d)   one which the IPCC otherwise considers is such as to make it not reasonably practicable to proceed with the investigation.

42(6) A complaint is repetitious only if–

(a)   it is substantially the same as a previous complaint (whether made by or on behalf of the same or a different complainant), or it concerns substantially the same conduct as a previous conduct matter;

(b)   it contains no fresh allegations which significantly affect the account of the conduct complained of;

(c)   no fresh evidence, being evidence which was not reasonably available at the time the previous complaint was made, is tendered in support of it; and

(d)   as respects the previous complaint or conduct matter, either–

        (i)   the requirements of regulation 67(9) or 68(11) (determination by the appropriate authority of what action to take) were complied with;

        (ii)   the IPCC gave the appropriate authority a direction under paragraph (11)(b) (requirement to dispense with the requirements of these Regulations); or

        (iii)   the complainant gave such notification of the withdrawal of the complaint as is mentioned in regulation 43(1)(a) (complainant withdraws the complaint).

42(7) The cases in which the IPCC is authorised to discontinue an investigation that is being carried out in accordance with regulation 48 are any cases where the complaint, conduct matter or DSI matter under investigation falls within paragraph (5) of this regulation.

42(8) Any application by an appropriate authority to the IPCC for an order that it discontinue an investigation shall be in writing and shall be accompanied by–

(a)   a copy of the complaint, and

(b)   a memorandum from the appropriate authority containing a summary of the investigation undertaken so far and explaining the reasons for the application to discontinue the investigation.

42(9) The appropriate authority shall–

(a)   send the complainant a copy of any such application on the same day as the day on which the application is sent to the IPCC, and

(b)   supply any further information requested by the IPCC for the purpose of considering that application.

42(10) The IPCC shall not require the discontinuance of an investigation in a case where there has been no application to do so by the appropriate authority unless it has consulted with that authority.

42(11) A direction given to an appropriate authority by the IPCC under paragraph (3) may–

(a)   require the appropriate authority to produce an investigation report on the discontinued investigation under regulation 66 and to take any subsequent steps under these Regulations;

(b)   where the investigation concerned a complaint, require the appropriate authority to dispense with the requirements of these Regulations as respects that complaint;

(c)   direct the appropriate authority to handle the matter in whatever manner (if any) that authority thinks fit.

42(12) For the purposes of this regulation the steps that may be taken by the IPCC where an investigation is discontinued are—

(a)   to produce an investigation report on the discontinued investigation and take any subsequent steps required under these Regulations;

(b)   where the investigation concerned a complaint, to dispense with the requirements of these Regulations as respects that complaint;

(c)   to handle the matter in whatever manner it thinks fit.

WITHDRAWN AND DISCONTINUED COMPLAINTS

43(1) If an appropriate authority receives from a complainant notification in writing signed by the complainant or by a solicitor or other authorised agent on the complainant's behalf to the effect either—

(a)   that the complainant withdraws the complaint, or

(b)   that the complainant does not wish any further steps to be taken in consequence of the complaint,

the appropriate authority shall forthwith record the withdrawal or the fact that the complainant does not wish any further steps to be taken, as the case may be, and subject to the following provisions of this regulation, the provisions of these Regulations shall cease to apply in respect of that complaint.

43(2) Where a complainant gives such notification as is mentioned in paragraph (1) to the IPCC but, so far as is apparent to the IPCC, has not sent that notification to the appropriate authority, then—

(a)   the IPCC shall send a copy of the notification to the appropriate authority;

(b)   that appropriate authority shall record the withdrawal or the fact that the complainant does not wish any further steps to be taken, as the case may be; and

(c)   subject to the following provisions of this regulation, the provisions of these Regulations shall cease to apply in respect of that complaint.

43(3) Where a complainant gives such notification as is mentioned in paragraph (1) to an appropriate authority, or where the appropriate authority receives a copy of a notification under paragraph (2), and it relates to a complaint—

(a)   which was referred to the IPCC under regulation 28(1) (reference of complaints to the IPCC) and which has not been referred back to the appropriate authority under regulation 29(2);

(b)   which the appropriate authority knows is currently the subject of an appeal to the IPCC under regulation 21 (failures to notify or record a complaint), or 74 (appeals to the IPCC with respect to an investigation; or

(c)   which was notified to the appropriate authority by the IPCC under regulation 19(1) (initial handling and recording of complaints),

the appropriate authority shall notify the IPCC that it has recorded the withdrawal of the complaint or the fact that the complainant does not wish any further steps to be taken, as the case may be.

43(4) In a case falling within paragraph (3)(a), the IPCC shall determine whether it is in the public interest for the complaint to be treated as a recordable conduct matter, and shall notify the appropriate authority of its decision.

43(5) In a case falling within sub-paragraphs (b) or (c) of paragraph (3), the appropriate authority shall also—

(a)   determine whether it is in the public interest for the complaint to be treated as a recordable conduct matter, and

(b)   notify the IPCC of its determination and the reasons for the determination.

43(6) Where a determination is made that a complaint is to be treated as a recordable conduct matter, the provisions of these Regulations shall apply to that matter.

43(7) Where a complainant gives such notification as is mentioned in paragraph (1) to an appropriate authority, or where an appropriate authority receives a copy of a notification under paragraph (2), and that notification relates to a complaint which does not fall within any of sub-paragraphs (a) to (c) of paragraph (3)—

(a)   the appropriate authority shall determine whether it is in the public interest for the complaint to be treated as a recordable conduct matter;

(b)   if the complaint is to be treated as a recordable conduct matter, the provisions of these Regulations shall apply to that matter;

(c)   if the complaint is not to be treated as a recordable conduct matter, the provisions of these Regulations shall cease to apply in respect of that complaint.

43(8)   In a case where—

(a)   a complaint has been subjected to an investigation by the appropriate authority on its own behalf;

(b)   the complaint is currently subject to an appeal to the IPCC under regulation 74; and

(c)   the appropriate authority has notified the IPCC under paragraph (5)(b) that it has determined that the complaint is not to be treated as a recordable conduct matter,

the IPCC shall consider whether it is in the public interest for that determination to be reversed, and if so it shall instruct the appropriate authority to reverse the decision.

43(9)   Where a complainant indicates the wish to withdraw the complaint or the wish that no further steps are to be taken in consequence of the complaint, but the complainant fails to provide a notification to that effect in writing signed by or on behalf of the complainant—

(a)   in the case of an indication received by the appropriate authority, the authority shall take the steps set out in paragraph (10);

(b)   in the case of an indication received by the IPCC, the IPCC shall refer the matter to the appropriate authority which shall take the steps set out in paragraph (10).

43(10)   Those steps are—

(a)   the appropriate authority shall write to the complainant to ascertain whether the complainant wishes to withdraw the complaint or does not wish any further steps to be taken in consequence of the complaint;

(b)   if the complainant indicates the wish to withdraw the complaint or does not wish any further steps to be taken in consequence of the complaint, or if the complainant fails to reply within 21 days from the date of the communication under sub-paragraph (a), the appropriate authority shall treat the indication as though it had been received in writing signed by the complainant;

(c)   if the complainant indicates the wish not to withdraw the complaint, or the wish that further steps be taken in consequence of the complaint, the appropriate authority shall start or resume the investigation as the case may be.

43(11)   The appropriate authority shall notify the person complained against if—

(a)   it records the withdrawal of a complaint or the fact that the complainant does not wish any further steps to be taken;

(b)   it determines that a complaint shall be treated as a recordable conduct matter;

(c)   the IPCC determines that a complaint shall be treated as a recordable conduct matter;

(d)   the IPCC instructs it to reverse a decision not to treat a complaint as a recordable conduct matter; or

(e)   the provisions of these Regulations cease to apply in respect of a complaint.

43(12)   But nothing in paragraph (11) shall require the appropriate authority to make a notification if it has previously decided under regulation 61(3) (copies of complaints etc) not to notify the person complained against of the complaint because it is of the opinion that that—

(a)   might prejudice any criminal investigation or pending proceedings, or

(b)   would be contrary to the public interest.

INVESTIGATIONS BY THE APPROPRIATE AUTHORITY ON ITS OWN BEHALF

44(1)   This regulation applies where the appropriate authority is required by virtue of any determination made by the IPCC under regulation 38 (power of the IPCC to determine the form of an investigation) to make arrangements for a complaint or recordable conduct matter or DSI matter to be investigated by the appropriate authority on its own behalf.

44(2)   It shall be the duty of the appropriate authority to appoint an officer to investigate the complaint or matter.

44(3)   The person to be appointed under this regulation to investigate any DSI matter in relation to which the relevant officer is the Chairman, the Chief Executive or the Permanent Secretary for Tax is the Head of the Home Civil Service.

INVESTIGATIONS SUPERVISED BY THE IPCC

45(1) This regulation applies where the IPCC has determined that it should supervise the investigation by the appropriate authority of any complaint or recordable conduct matter or DSI matter.

45(2) On being given notice of that determination, the appropriate authority shall, if it has not already done so, appoint an officer to investigate the complaint or matter.

45(3) The IPCC may require that no appointment is made under paragraph (2) unless it has given notice to the appropriate authority that it approves the person whom that authority proposes to appoint.

45(4) Where a person has already been appointed to investigate the complaint or matter, or is selected under this regulation for appointment, and the IPCC is not satisfied with that person, the IPCC may require the appropriate authority, as soon as reasonably practicable after being required to do so–

(a)   to select another person falling within paragraph (2) to investigate the complaint or matter, and

(b)   to notify the IPCC of the person selected.

45(5) Where a selection made in pursuance of a requirement under paragraph (4) has been notified to the IPCC, the appropriate authority shall appoint that person to investigate the complaint or matter if, but only if, the IPCC notifies the authority that it approves the appointment of that person.

45(6) The person appointed to investigate the complaint or matter shall comply with all the requirements of regulation 40.

INVESTIGATION BY A POLICE FORCE UNDER THE MANAGEMENT OR UNDER THE SUPERVISION OF THE IPCC

46(1) This regulation applies where the IPCC determines that there should be an investigation by a police force under the management or supervision of the IPCC.

46(2) The IPCC shall–

(a)   identify the police force whose force area includes the geographical area to which the subject matter of the complaint, recordable conduct matter or DSI matter most closely relates, and

(b)   take steps to obtain the agreement of–

(i)   the chief officer of police of that force, and

(ii)   the appropriate authority,

to the appointment by the IPCC of that force to carry out the investigation.

46(3) In the event that no agreement is reached under paragraph (2) the IPCC may require the chief officer of police of any police force it considers appropriate to carry out the investigation.

46(4) A chief officer of police of a police force who agrees to or is required to carry out an investigation shall, if that person has not already done so, appoint a person serving with the police who is a member of that force to investigate that complaint or matter.

46(5) Paragraphs (3) to (6) of regulation 45 (investigations supervised by the IPCC) shall apply as they apply to an investigation by the appropriate authority which the IPCC has determined is one that it should supervise; and the references to the appropriate authority in those paragraphs shall be treated as references to the chief officer of police concerned.

46(6) An appointment of a person under paragraph (4) or (5) shall be notified by the chief of police concerned to the appropriate authority.

46(7) The person appointed to investigate the complaint or matter shall, in relation to an investigation under the management of the IPCC, be under the direction and control of the IPCC.

46(8) The person appointed to investigate the complaint or matter shall comply with all such requirements in relation to the carrying out of that investigation as may be imposed by these Regulations.

INVESTIGATIONS MANAGED BY THE IPCC

47(1) This regulation applies where the IPCC has determined that it should manage the investigation by the appropriate authority of any complaint or recordable conduct matter or DSI matter.

47(2) Paragraphs (2) to (5) of regulation 45 shall apply as they apply in the case of an investigation which the IPCC has determined is one that it should supervise.

47(3) The person appointed to investigate the complaint or matter shall, in relation to that investigation, be under the direction and control of the IPCC.

INVESTIGATIONS BY THE IPCC ITSELF

48(1) This regulation applies where the IPCC has determined that it should itself carry out the investigation of a complaint or recordable conduct matter or DSI matter.

48(2) The IPCC shall designate both–

(a)   a member of the IPCC's staff to take charge of the investigation on behalf of the IPCC, and

(b)   all such other members of the IPCC's staff as are required by the IPCC to assist that member.

48(3) A member of the IPCC's staff who–

(a)   is designated under paragraph (2) in relation to any investigation, but

(b)   does not already, by virtue of section 97(8) of the Police Act 1996, have all the powers and privileges of a constable throughout England and Wales and the adjacent United Kingdom waters,

shall, for the purposes of the carrying out of the investigation and all purposes connected with it, have all those powers and privileges throughout England and Wales and those waters.

48(4) A member of the IPCC's staff who is not a constable shall not, as a result of paragraph (3), be treated as being in police service for the purposes of–

(a)   section 280 of the Trade Union and Labour Relations (Consolidation) Act 1992 (person in police service excluded from definitions of "worker" and "employee"); or

(b)   section 200 of the Employment Rights Act 1996 (certain provisions of that Act not to apply to persons in police service).

48(5) References in this regulation to the powers and privileges of a constable–

(a)   are references to any power or privilege conferred by or under any enactment (including one passed after the making of these Regulations) on a constable; and

(b)   shall have effect as if every such power were exercisable, and every such privilege existed, throughout England and Wales and the adjacent United Kingdom waters (whether or not that is the case apart from this paragraph).

48(6) In this regulation **"United Kingdom waters"** means the sea and other waters within the seaward limits of the United Kingdom's territorial sea.

RELINQUISHING THE IPCC'S SUPERVISION OR MANAGEMENT OF AN INVESTIGATION

49(1) This regulation applies where the IPCC–

(a)   relinquishes the management of an investigation in favour of a supervised investigation or an investigation by the appropriate authority on its own behalf, or

(b)   relinquishes the supervision of an investigation in favour of an investigation by the appropriate authority on its own behalf.

49(2) The IPCC–

(a)   shall notify the appropriate authority, the complainant, any interested person within the meaning of regulation 55 (duty to provide information for other persons) and the person complained against of its decision, and the reasons for that decision; and

(b)   shall send to the appropriate authority any documentation and evidence gathered during its investigations as will assist the appropriate authority to carry out its functions under these Regulations.

49(3) But nothing in paragraph (2)(a) shall require the IPCC to make a notification to the person complained against if it is of the opinion that that might prejudice any criminal investigation or pending proceedings or would be contrary to the public interest.

CIRCUMSTANCES IN WHICH AN INVESTIGATION OR OTHER PROCEDURE MAY BE SUSPENDED

50(1) Subject to the provisions of this regulation, proceedings under these Regulations shall proceed without delay.

50(2) In a case investigated by the IPCC or under the management of the IPCC, the IPCC may suspend any investigation or other procedure under these Regulations which would, if it were to continue, prejudice any criminal proceedings. Before referring a case to misconduct proceedings, the IPCC shall decide whether misconduct proceedings may prejudice any criminal proceedings.

50(3) For any period during which the IPCC considers misconduct proceedings would prejudice any criminal proceedings, no such misconduct proceedings shall take place.

50(4) Where a witness who is or may be a witness in any criminal proceedings is to be or may be asked to provide evidence in misconduct proceedings, the IPCC shall consult the relevant prosecutor (and when doing so must inform the prosecutor of the names and addresses of all such witnesses) before making a decision under paragraph (2).

50(5) For the purposes of this regulation, **"relevant prosecutor"** means the Director of Public Prosecutions or any other person who has or is likely to have responsibility for criminal proceedings.

50(6) In a case under the supervision of the IPCC or undertaken by the appropriate authority on its own behalf, the appropriate authority may, subject to paragraph (7), suspend any investigation or other procedure under these Regulations which would, if it were to continue, prejudice any criminal investigation or proceedings.

50(7) The IPCC may direct that any investigation or other procedure under these Regulations which is liable to be suspended under paragraph (6) shall continue if it is of the view that it is in the public interest to make such a direction.

50(8) The IPCC shall consult the appropriate authority before making such a direction.

RESUMPTION OF INVESTIGATION AFTER CRIMINAL PROCEEDINGS

51(1) Where the whole or part of the investigation of a complaint has been suspended until the conclusion of criminal proceedings, and after the conclusion of those proceedings the complainant has failed to express the wish for the investigation to start or to be resumed, the IPCC or, as the case may be, the appropriate authority, shall take the steps set out in paragraph (2).

51(2) The IPCC or the appropriate authority shall take all reasonable steps to contact the complainant to ascertain whether the complainant wants the investigation to start or to be resumed as the case may be.

51(3) If the complainant expresses the wish for the investigation to start or be resumed, the IPCC or the appropriate authority shall start or resume the investigation as the case may be.

51(4) If the complainant indicates that the complainant does not want the investigation to start or to be resumed, or if the complainant fails to reply within 21 days of the date of the letter to the complainant by the IPCC or the appropriate authority, the IPCC or the appropriate authority, as the case may be, shall determine whether it is in the public interest for the complaint to be treated as a recordable conduct matter.

51(5) If the IPCC or the appropriate authority determines that it is not in the public interest for the complaint to be treated as a recordable conduct matter, the provisions of these Regulations shall cease to apply to the complaint.

51(6) If the IPCC or the appropriate authority determines that it is in the public interest for the complaint to be treated as a recordable conduct matter, it shall be treated as such under these Regulations.

51(7) The IPCC or the appropriate authority shall notify the person complained against if paragraph (5) or (6) applies.

51(8) But nothing in paragraph (7) shall require the IPCC or the appropriate authority to make a notification if it is of the opinion that that might prejudice any criminal investigation or pending proceedings or would be contrary to the public interest.

RESTRICTIONS ON PROCEEDINGS PENDING THE CONCLUSION OF AN INVESTIGATION

52(1) No criminal or disciplinary proceedings shall be brought in relation to any matter which falls to be determined under these Regulations until a report on that investigation has been submitted to the IPCC or to the appropriate authority under regulation 66 (final reports on investigations: complaints, conduct matters and certain DSI matters) or 69 (final reports on investigations: other DSI matters).

52(2) Nothing in this regulation shall prevent the bringing of criminal or disciplinary proceedings in respect of any conduct at any time after the discontinuance of the investigation in accordance with the provisions of these Regulations which relate to that conduct.

52(3) The restrictions imposed by this regulation in relation to the bringing of criminal proceedings shall not apply to the bringing of criminal proceedings by the Director of Public Prosecutions or, as the case may be, the Director of Revenue and Customs Prosecutions in any case in which it appears to that person that there are exceptional circumstances which make it undesirable to delay the bringing of such proceedings.

PART 7 – PROVISION OF INFORMATION

PROVISION OF INFORMATION TO THE IPCC

53(1) It shall be the duty of the Commissioners at such times, in such circumstances and in accordance with such other requirements as may be set out in these Regulations, to provide the IPCC with all such information and documents as may be specified or described in these Regulations.

53(2) It shall also be the duty of the Commissioners–

(a) to provide the IPCC with all such other information and documents specified or described in a notification given by the IPCC to the Commissioners, and

(b) to produce or deliver up to the IPCC all such evidence and other things so specified or described,

as appear to the IPCC to be required by it for the purposes of the carrying out of any of its functions.

53(3) Anything falling to be provided, produced or delivered up by any person in pursuance of a requirement imposed under paragraph (2) must be provided, produced or delivered up in such form, in such manner and within such period as may be specified in–

(a) the notification imposing the requirement; or

(b) in any subsequent notification given by the IPCC to that person for the purposes of this paragraph.

53(4) Nothing in this regulation shall require the Commissioners–

(a) to provide the IPCC with any information or document, or to produce or deliver up any other thing, before the earliest time at which it is practicable for the Commissioners to do so; or

(b) to provide, produce or deliver up anything at all in a case in which it never becomes practicable for the Commissioners to do so.

53(5) A requirement imposed under this regulation may authorise or require information or documents to which it relates to be provided to the IPCC electronically.

DUTY TO KEEP THE COMPLAINANT INFORMED

54(1) Subject to regulation 60, in any case in which there is an investigation of a complaint in accordance with the provisions of these Regulations–

(a) by the IPCC, or

(b) under its management,

it shall be the duty of the IPCC to provide the complainant with all such information as will keep the complainant properly informed of all the matters specified in paragraph (4) while the investigation is being carried out and subsequently.

54(2) Subject to regulation 60, in any case in which there is an investigation of a complaint in accordance with the provisions of these Regulations–

(a) by the appropriate authority on its own behalf, or

(b) under the supervision of the IPCC,

it shall be the duty of the appropriate authority to provide the complainant with all such information as will keep the complainant properly informed, while the investigation is being carried out and subsequently, of all the matters specified in paragraph (4).

54(3) Where paragraph (2) applies, it shall be the duty of the IPCC to give the appropriate authority all such directions as it considers appropriate for securing that that authority complies with its duty under that paragraph; and it shall be the duty of the appropriate authority to comply with any direction so given.

54(4) The matters of which the complainant must be kept properly informed are–

(a) the progress of the investigation;

(b) any provisional findings of the person carrying out the investigation;

(c) whether any report has been submitted under regulation 69 (final reports on investigations: other DSI matters);

(d) the action (if any) that is taken in respect of the matters dealt with in any such report; and

(e) the outcome of any such action.

54(5)   It shall be the duty of a person appointed to carry out an investigation under these Regulations to provide the IPCC or, as the case may be, the appropriate authority, with all such information as the IPCC or that authority may reasonably require for the purpose of performing its duty under this regulation.

DUTY TO PROVIDE INFORMATION FOR OTHER PERSONS

55(1)   A person has an interest in being kept properly informed about the handling of a complaint or recordable conduct matter or DSI matter which is the subject of an investigation in accordance with the provisions of these Regulations if–

(a)   it appears to the IPCC or to an appropriate authority that that person is a person falling within paragraph (2) or (3); and

(b)   that person has indicated consent to the provision of information in accordance with this regulation and that consent has not been withdrawn.

55(2)   A person falls within this paragraph if, in the case of a complaint or recordable conduct matter, that person–

(a)   is a relative of a person whose death is the alleged result from the conduct complained of or to which the recordable conduct matter relates;

(b)   is a relative of a person whose serious injury is the alleged result from that conduct and that person is incapable of making a complaint;

(c)   has suffered serious injury as the alleged result of that conduct.

55(3)   A person falls within this paragraph if, in the case of a DSI matter, that person–

(a)   is a relative of the person who has died;

(b)   is a relative of the person who has suffered serious injury and that person is incapable of making a complaint;

(c)   is the person who has suffered serious injury.

55(4)   A person who does not fall within paragraph (2) or (3) has an interest in being kept properly informed about the handling of a complaint, recordable conduct matter or DSI matter if–

(a)   the IPCC or an appropriate authority considers that that person has an interest in the handling of the complaint, conduct matter or DSI matter which is sufficient to make it appropriate for information to be provided to that person in accordance with this regulation; and

(b)   that person has indicated consent to the provision of information in accordance with this regulation.

55(5)   In relation to a complaint, this section confers no rights on the complainant.

55(6)   A person who has an interest in being kept properly informed about the handling of a complaint, conduct matter or DSI matter is referred to in this regulation as an "interested person".

55(7)   In any case in which there is an investigation of the complaint, recordable conduct matter or DSI matter in accordance with the provisions of these Regulations–

(a)   by the IPCC, or

(b)   under its management,

it shall be the duty of the IPCC to provide the interested person with all such information as will keep the interested person properly informed of all the matters specified in paragraph (10) while the investigation is being carried out and subsequently.

55(8)   In any case in which there is an investigation of the complaint, recordable conduct matter or DSI matter in accordance with the provisions of these Regulations–

(a)   by the appropriate authority on its own behalf, or

(b)   under the supervision of the IPCC,

it shall be the duty of the appropriate authority to provide the interested person with all such information as will keep the interested person properly informed of all the matters specified in paragraph (10) while the investigation is being carried out and subsequently.

55(9)   Where paragraph (8) applies, it shall be the duty of the IPCC to give the appropriate authority all such directions as it considers appropriate for securing that that authority complies with its duty under that paragraph; and it shall be the duty of the appropriate authority to comply with any direction given to it under this paragraph.

55(10)   The matters of which the interested person must be kept properly informed are–

(a)   the progress of the investigation;

(b) any provisional findings of the person carrying out the investigation;

(c) whether the IPCC or the appropriate authority has made a determination under regulation 36 (procedure where conduct matter is revealed during investigation of a DSI matter);

(d) whether any report has been submitted under regulation 66 or 69;

(e) the action (if any) that is taken in respect of the matters dealt with in any such report; and

(f) the outcome of any such action.

55(11) The duties imposed by this regulation on the IPCC and the appropriate authority in relation to any complaint, recordable conduct matter or DSI matter shall be performed in such manner, and shall have effect subject to such exceptions, as may be provided for by regulation 60.

55(12) Paragraph (5) of regulation 54 (duty to keep the complainant informed) applies for the purposes of this regulation as it applies for the purposes of that regulation.

55(13) In this regulation **"relative"** means any spouse, partner, parent or adult child.

WRITTEN NOTICES

56(1) If during the course of an investigation of a complaint or matter which falls to be determined under these Regulations it appears to the person investigating that there is an indication that the person whose conduct is in question may have—

(a) committed a criminal offence, or

(b) behaved in a manner which would justify the bringing of disciplinary proceedings,

the person investigating the complaint or matter must give a notification to the person whose conduct is in question that complies with paragraph (2).

56(2) The notification must—

(a) provide sufficient details of the complaint or matter in question so that the person whose conduct is in question may make representations to the person investigating the complaint or matter;

(b) give the information about the effect of regulation 57 (duty to consider submissions from the person whose conduct is in question);

(c) set out the time limits for providing the person investigating the complaint or matter with relevant statements and relevant documents for the purposes of regulation 57(2);

(d) give such information that may be set out in guidance.

56(3) Paragraphs (1) and (2) do not apply for so long as the person investigating the complaint or the matter considers that giving the notification might prejudice—

(a) the investigation, or

(b) any other investigation (including, in particular, a criminal investigation).

56(4) In this regulation and regulations 57 and 58, the person whose conduct is in question—

(a) in relation to an investigation of a complaint, means the person in respect of whom it appears to the person investigating that there is the indication mentioned in paragraph (1);

(b) in relation to an investigation of a recordable conduct matter, means the person to whose conduct the investigation relates.

56(5) In this regulation—

(a) **"relevant document"** means—

(i) a document relating to any complaint or matter under investigation, and

(ii) includes such a document containing suggestions as to lines of inquiry to be pursued or witness to be interviewed;

(b) **"relevant statement"** means an oral or written statement relating to any complaint or matter under investigation.

DUTY TO CONSIDER SUBMISSIONS FROM THE PERSON WHOSE CONDUCT IS IN QUESTION

57(1) This regulation applies where a notification under regulation 56 (written notices) has been issued to the person whose conduct is in question.

57(2) If before the expiry of the appropriate time limit notified in pursuance of regulation 56(2)—

(a) the person whose conduct is in question provides the person investigating the complaint or matter with a relevant statement or a relevant document, or

(b)   any person provides the person investigating the complaint or matter with a relevant document, the person investigating must consider the statement or document.

DUTY TO PROVIDE CERTAIN INFORMATION TO THE APPROPRIATE AUTHORITY

58(1)   This regulation applies during the course of an investigation under these Regulations.

58(2)   The person investigating the complaint or matter must supply the appropriate authority with such information in that person's possession as the appropriate authority may reasonably request for the purpose mentioned in paragraph (3).

58(3)   That purpose is determining whether the person whose conduct is in question should be, or should remain, suspended from duty.

MANNER IN WHICH DUTIES TO PROVIDE INFORMATION TO THE COMPLAINANT ARE TO BE PERFORMED

59(1)   For the purposes of regulations 54(4) (duty to keep the complainant informed) and 55(10) (duty to provide information for other persons), the manner in which the IPCC or, as the case may be, an appropriate authority, shall perform the duties imposed by those regulations is as follows.

59(2)   The IPCC, in a case falling within regulation 54(1) or 55(7) (investigation of a complaint, conduct matter or DSI matter by or under the management of the IPCC), shall inform the complainant or, as the case may be, the interested person—

(a)   of the progress of the investigation promptly, and in any event—

     (i)   if there has been no previous notification, within four weeks of the start of the investigation; and

     (ii)   in any other case, within four weeks of the previous notification; and

(b)   of any provisional findings of the person carrying out the investigation as frequently as the IPCC determines to be appropriate in order for the complainant to be kept properly informed.

59(3)   An appropriate authority, in a case falling within regulation 54(2) (duty to keep the complainant informed or 55(8) (duty to provide information for other persons), shall inform the complainant or the interested person (as the case may be)—

(a)   of the progress of the investigation promptly and in any event—

     (i)   if there has been no previous notification, within four weeks of the start of the investigation; and

     (ii)   in any other case, within four weeks of the previous notification; and

(b)   of any provisional findings of the person carrying out the investigation as frequently as the appropriate authority determines to be appropriate in order for the complainant to be kept properly informed.

59(4)   When an investigation has been completed, each complainant and interested person shall be notified—

(a)   of the date on which the final report under regulation 66 (final reports on investigations: complaints, conduct matters and certain DSI matters) is likely to be submitted; and

(b)   of the date on which the notification under regulation 67(11) (action by the IPCC in response to an investigation report under regulation 66) or 68(12) (action by the appropriate authority in response to an investigation report under regulation 66) is likely to be given.

59(5)   In performing the duties imposed by regulations 54(1) and (2), 55(7) and (8), 67(11) and 68(12) , the IPCC or, as the case may be, the appropriate authority, shall determine whether it is appropriate to offer, or to accede to a request for, a meeting with a complainant or, as the case may be, an interested person.

59(6)   As soon as practicable after any such meeting, the IPCC or, as the case may be, the appropriate authority, shall send to the complainant or interested person a written record of the meeting and an account of how any concerns of that person will be addressed.

59(7)   As soon as practicable after any misconduct hearing or other action that is taken in respect of the matters dealt with in any report submitted under regulation 66, the IPCC or, as the case may be, the appropriate authority, shall notify any complainant and interested person of the outcome of that hearing or action, including the fact and outcome of any appeal against the findings of or sanctions imposed by such a hearing.

59(8) Subject to paragraphs (5) and (9), any notification under this regulation shall be given in writing.

59(9) If the IPCC or, as the case may be, the appropriate authority, considers that an investigation has made minimal or no progress since the previous notification, then the next notification may be made by any means that in the opinion of the IPCC or, as the case may be, the appropriate authority, is suitable.

EXCEPTIONS TO THE DUTY TO KEEP THE COMPLAINANT INFORMED AND TO PROVIDE INFORMATION FOR OTHER PERSONS

60(1) Subject to paragraph (2), the duties mentioned in regulation 54(1) and (2) (duty to keep the complainant informed), regulation 55(7) and (8) (duty to provide information for other persons) and in regulations 67(11) and 68(12) shall not apply in circumstances where in the opinion of the IPCC, or, as the case may be, of the appropriate authority, the non-disclosure of information is necessary for the purpose of—

(a) preventing the premature or inappropriate disclosure of information that is relevant to, or may be used in, any actual or prospective criminal proceedings;

(b) preventing the disclosure of information in any circumstances in which its non-disclosure–

    (i) is in the interests of national security;

    (ii) is for the purposes of the prevention or detection of crime, or the apprehension or prosecution of offenders;

    (iii) is required on proportionality grounds; or

    (iv) is otherwise necessary in the public interest; or

(c) preventing the disclosure of any information held by HMRC in connection with its functions which–

    (i) is obtained from the Head of the Home Civil Service, the Chief Executive, the Commissioners or an officer, and

    (ii) relates to a person whose identity is specified in the disclosure or can be deduced from it.

60(2) Paragraph (1)(c) does not apply to any information relating to internal administrative arrangements of HMRC (whether relating to the Commissioners, officers or others).

60(3) The IPCC or, as the case may be, the appropriate authority, shall not conclude that the nondisclosure of information is necessary under paragraph (1) unless it is satisfied that–

(a) there is a real risk of the disclosure of that information causing an adverse effect; and

(b) that adverse effect would be significant.

60(4) The IPCC shall consult the appropriate authority in any case under paragraph (1)(c) before deciding whether or not it is satisfied under paragraph (3).

60(5) Without prejudice to the generality of paragraph (1), the IPCC, or, as the case may be, the appropriate authority, shall consider whether the non-disclosure of information is justified under that paragraph in circumstances where–

(a) that information is relevant to, or may be used in, any actual or prospective disciplinary proceedings;

(b) the disclosure of that information may lead to the contamination of the evidence of witnesses during such proceedings;

(c) the disclosure of that information may prejudice the welfare or safety of any third party;

(d) that information constitutes criminal intelligence.

COPIES OF COMPLAINTS ETC.

61(1) Where a complaint is recorded under regulation 19(6) (initial handling and recording of complaints), the appropriate authority shall–

(a) supply to the complainant a copy of the record made of that complaint; and

(b) subject to paragraphs (2) to (4), supply to the person complained against a copy of the complaint.

61(2) A copy of a complaint supplied under this regulation may be in a form which keeps anonymous the identity of the complainant or of any other person.

61(3) The appropriate authority may decide not to supply such a copy of a complaint if it is of the opinion that to do so—

(a)   might prejudice any criminal investigation or pending proceedings, or

(b)   would otherwise be contrary to the public interest.

61(4)   Where the appropriate authority decides not to supply such a copy, it shall keep that decision under regular review.

NOTIFICATION OF ACTIONS AND DECISIONS

62(1)   So far as not covered by regulation 67(11) and (12) and regulation 74(11) and (12) (appeals to the IPCC with respect to an investigation), where the IPCC takes any action or decisions in consequence of it having received a memorandum under regulation 67(9) or regulation 74(3), it shall notify such action or decisions, together with an explanation of its reasons for having taken them, to–

(a)   the appropriate authority;

(b)   the complainant and any other interested person within the meaning of regulation 55(2) and (3); and

(c)   subject to paragraph (2), the person complained against.

62(2)   The IPCC may decide not to give such a notification and explanation to the person complained against if it is of the opinion that that notification might prejudice any criminal investigation, pending proceedings, or review of the complaint.

INFORMATION FOR COMPLAINANT ABOUT DISCIPLINARY RECOMMENDATIONS

63(1)   Where–

(a)   the IPCC makes recommendations under regulation 71 (duties with respect to disciplinary proceedings) in the case of an investigation of a complaint, and

(b)   the appropriate authority notifies the IPCC that the recommendations have been accepted,

the IPCC shall notify the complainant and every person entitled to be kept properly informed in relation to the complaint under regulation 55 of that fact and of the steps that have been, or are to be taken, by the appropriate authority to give effect to it.

63(2)   Where in the case of an investigation of a complaint the appropriate authority–

(a)   notifies the IPCC that it does not (either in whole or in part) accept recommendations made by the IPCC under regulation 71, or

(b)   fails to take steps to give full effect to any such recommendations,

it shall be the duty of the IPCC to determine what further steps (if any) to take under that regulation.

63(3)   It shall be the duty of the IPCC to notify the complainant and every person entitled to be kept properly informed in relation to the complaint under regulation 55–

(a)   of any determination under paragraph (2) not to take further steps under regulation 71; and

(b)   where it determines under that paragraph to take further steps under that regulation, of the outcome of the taking of those steps.

REGISTER TO BE KEPT BY THE IPCC

64(1)   The IPCC shall establish and maintain a register of all information supplied to it by the appropriate authority under these Regulations.

64(2)   Subject to paragraph (3), the IPCC may publish or otherwise disclose to any person any information held on the register provided that the publication or disclosure is necessary for or conducive to the purpose of–

(a)   learning lessons from the handling of, or demonstrating the thoroughness and effectiveness of, investigations by the IPCC or of managed or supervised investigations;

(b)   raising public awareness of the complaints system; or

(c)   improving the complaints system.

64(3)   Information may not be published or disclosed in circumstances where in the opinion of the IPCC the non-disclosure of information is necessary for the purposes mentioned in regulation 60(1)(a) and (b) (exceptions to the duty to keep the complainant informed and to provide information for other persons).

MANNER AND TIME LIMITS OF NOTIFICATIONS

65(1)   Any notification to be given under these Regulations shall–

(a)   unless otherwise specified in these Regulations or determined in guidance issued by the IPCC, be given in writing; and

(b)   unless otherwise specified in these Regulations, be made within such period as the IPCC may determine in guidance.

65(2)   No time limit mentioned in these Regulations or determined by the IPCC shall apply in any case where exceptional circumstances prevent that time limit being complied with.

PART 8 – REPORTS AND RECOMMENDATIONS

FINAL REPORTS ON INVESTIGATIONS: COMPLAINTS, CONDUCT MATTERS AND CERTAIN DSI MATTERS

66(1)   This regulation applies on the completion of an investigation of—

(a)   a complaint, or

(b)   a conduct matter.

66(2)   A person appointed under regulation 44 (investigation by the appropriate authority on its own behalf) shall submit a report on that person's investigation to the appropriate authority.

66(3)   A person appointed under regulation 45 (investigations supervised by the IPCC), 46 (investigations by a police force under the management or under the supervision of the IPCC), or 47 (investigations managed by the IPCC) shall—

(a)   submit a report on that person's investigation to the IPCC; and

(b)   send a copy of that report to the appropriate authority.

66(4)   In relation to a matter that was formerly a DSI matter but has been recorded as a conduct matter in pursuance of regulation 36(5) (procedure where conduct matter is revealed during investigation of a DSI matter), the references in paragraphs (2) and (3) of this regulation to the appropriate authority are references to—

(a)   the appropriate authority in relation to the DSI matter; and

(b)   (where different) the appropriate authority in relation to the person whose conduct is in question.

66(5)   A person designated under regulation 48 (investigations by the IPCC itself) as the person in charge of an investigation by the IPCC itself shall submit a report on the investigation to the IPCC.

66(6)   A person submitting a report under this regulation shall not be prevented by any obligation of secrecy imposed by any rule of law or otherwise from including all such matters in the report as that person thinks fit.

66(7)   A person who has submitted a report on an investigation under this regulation on an investigation within regulation 57(1) (duty to consider submissions from the person whose conduct is in question) must supply the appropriate authority with such copies of further documents or other items in that person's possession as the authority may request.

66(8)   The appropriate authority may only make a request under paragraph (7) in respect of a copy of a document or other item if the authority—

(a)   considers that the document or item is of relevance to the investigation, and

(b)   requires a copy of the document or the item for either or both of the purposes mentioned in paragraph (9).

66(9)   Those purposes are—

(a)   complying with any obligation which the authority has under the disciplinary proceedings in relation to any person whose conduct is the subject-matter of the investigation;

(b)   ensuring that any such officer (a person whose conduct is in question) receives a fair hearing at any disciplinary proceedings in respect of any such conduct of that officer.

ACTION BY THE IPCC IN RESPONSE TO AN INVESTIGATION REPORT UNDER REGULATION 66

67(1)   This regulation applies where—

(a)   a report on an investigation carried out under the management of the IPCC is submitted to it under paragraph (3) of regulation 66 (final report on investigations: complaints, conduct matters and certain DSI matters); or

(b)   a report on an investigation carried out by a person designated by the IPCC is submitted to it under paragraph (5) of that regulation.

67(2)   On receipt of the report, the IPCC–

(a)   if it appears that the appropriate authority has not already been sent a copy of the report, shall send a copy of the report to that authority;

(b)   shall determine whether the conditions set out in paragraphs (3) and (4) are satisfied in respect of the report;

(c)   if it determines that those conditions are so satisfied, shall notify the Director of Public Prosecutions or the Director of Revenue and Customs Prosecutions of the determination and send the Director a copy of the report; and

(d)   shall notify the appropriate authority and the persons mentioned in paragraph (7) of its determination under sub-paragraph (b) and of any action taken by it under sub-paragraph (c).

67(3)   The first condition is that the report indicates that a criminal offence may have been committed by a person to whose conduct the investigation related.

67(4)   The second condition is that the circumstances are such that, in the opinion of the IPCC, it is appropriate for the matters dealt with in the report to be considered by the Director of Public Prosecutions or, as the case may be, the Director of Revenue and Customs Prosecutions.

67(5)   The Director of Public Prosecutions or, as the case may be, the Director of Revenue and Customs Prosecutions shall notify the IPCC of any decision of the Director to take, or not to take, action in respect of the matters dealt with in any report a copy of which has been sent to the Director under paragraph (2)(c).

67(6)   It shall be the duty of the IPCC to notify the persons mentioned in paragraph (7) if criminal proceedings are brought against any person by the Director of Public Prosecutions or, as the case may be, the Director of Revenue and Customs Prosecutions in respect of any matters dealt with in a report copied to the Director under paragraph (2)(c).

67(7)   Those persons are–

(a)   in the case of a complaint, the complainant and every person entitled to be kept properly informed in relation to the complaint under regulation 55 (duty to provide information for other persons); and

(b)   in the case of a recordable conduct matter, every person entitled to be kept properly informed in relation to that matter under that regulation.

67(8)   On receipt of the report, the IPCC shall also notify the appropriate authority that it must–

(a)   determine–

 (i)   whether any officer (person whose conduct is in question) has a case to answer in respect of their conduct or has no case to answer, and

 (ii)   what action (if any) the authority is required to, or will in its discretion, take in respect of the matters dealt with in the report; and

(b)   determine what other action (if any) the authority will in its discretion take in respect of those matters.

67(9)   On receipt of a notification under paragraph (8) the appropriate authority shall make those determinations and submit a memorandum to the IPCC which–

(a)   sets out the determinations the authority has made; and

(b)   if the appropriate authority has decided in relation to any person whose conduct is the subject-matter of the report that disciplinary proceedings should not be brought against that person, sets out its reasons for so deciding.

67(10)   On receipt of a memorandum under paragraph (9), the IPCC shall–

(a)   consider the memorandum and whether the appropriate authority has made the determinations under paragraph (8)(a) that the IPCC considers appropriate in respect of the matters dealt with in the report;

(b)   determine, in the light of its consideration of those matters, whether or not to make recommendations under regulation 71 (duties with respect to disciplinary proceedings); and

(c)   make such recommendations (if any) under that regulation as it thinks fit.

67(11)   On the making of a determination under paragraph (10)(b) the IPCC shall give a notification–

(a)   in the case of a complaint, to the complainant and to every person entitled to be kept properly informed in relation to the complaint under regulation 55; and

(b)   in the case of a recordable conduct matter, to every person entitled to be kept properly informed in relation to that matter under that regulation.

67(12)   The notification required by paragraph (11) is one setting out–

(a)   the findings of the report;

(b)   the IPCC's determination under paragraph (10)(b); and

(c)   the action which the appropriate authority is to be recommended to take as a consequence of the determination.

67(13)   Regulation 60 shall have effect in relation to the duties imposed on the IPCC by paragraph (11) of this regulation.

67(14)   Except so far as may be otherwise provided by these Regulations, the IPCC shall be entitled (notwithstanding any obligation of secrecy imposed by any rule of law or otherwise) to discharge the duty to give a person mentioned in paragraph (11) notification of the findings of the report by sending that person a copy of the report.

67(15)   In relation to a DSI matter in respect of which a determination has been made under regulation 36(2) or (4) (procedure where conduct matter is revealed during the investigation of a DSI matter), the references in this regulation to the appropriate authority are references to the appropriate authority in relation to the person whose conduct is in question.

ACTION BY THE APPROPRIATE AUTHORITY IN RESPONSE TO AN INVESTIGATION REPORT UNDER REGULATION 66

68(1)   This regulation applies where–

(a)   a report of an investigation is submitted to the appropriate authority in accordance with regulation 66(2); or

(b)   a copy of a report on an investigation carried out under the supervision of the IPCC is sent to the appropriate authority in accordance with regulation 66(3).

68(2)   On receipt of the report or (as the case may be) of the copy, the appropriate authority–

(a)   shall determine whether the conditions set out in paragraphs (3) and (4) are satisfied in respect of the report;

(b)   if it determines that those conditions are so satisfied, shall notify the Director of Public Prosecutions or, as the case may be, the Director of Revenue and Customs Prosecutions of the determination and send the Director a copy of the report; and

(c)   shall notify the persons mentioned in paragraph (7) of its determination under sub-paragraph (a) and of any action taken by it under sub-paragraph (b).

68(3)   The first condition is that the report indicates that a criminal offence may have been committed by a person to whose conduct the investigation related.

68(4)   The second condition is that the circumstances are such that, in the opinion of the appropriate authority, it is appropriate for the matters dealt with in the report to be considered by the Director of Public Prosecutions or, as the case may be, the Director of Revenue and Customs Prosecutions.

68(5)   The Director of Public Prosecutions or, as the case may be, the Director of Revenue and Customs Prosecutions shall notify the appropriate authority of any decision of the Director to take, or not to take, action in respect of the matters dealt with in any report a copy of which has been sent to the Director under paragraph (2).

68(6)   It shall be the duty of the appropriate authority to notify the persons mentioned in paragraph (7) if criminal proceedings are brought against any person by the Director of Public Prosecutions or, as the case may be, the Director of Revenue and Customs Prosecutions in respect of any matters dealt with in a report copied to the Director under paragraph (2)(b).

68(7)   Those persons are–

(a)   in the case of a complaint, the complainant and every person entitled to be kept properly informed in relation to the complaint under regulation 55 (duty to provide information for other persons); and

(b)   in the case of a recordable conduct matter, every person entitled to be kept properly informed in relation to that matter under that regulation.

68(8)   In the case of a report falling within paragraph (1)(b) which relates to a recordable conduct matter, the appropriate authority shall also notify the IPCC of its determination under paragraph (2)(a).

68(9)   On receipt of such a notification that the appropriate authority has determined that the conditions in paragraphs (3) and (4) are not satisfied in respect of the report, the IPCC–

(a)   shall make its own determination as to whether those conditions are so satisfied; and

(b)   if it determines that they are so satisfied, shall direct the appropriate authority to notify the Director of Public Prosecutions or, as the case may be, the Director of Revenue and Customs Prosecutions of the IPCC's determination and send the Director a copy of the report.

68(10)   It shall be the duty of the appropriate authority to comply with any direction given to it under paragraph (9)(b).

68(11)   On receipt of the report or (as the case may be) copy, the appropriate authority shall also—

(a)   determine—

    (i)   whether any person to whose conduct the investigation related has a case to answer in respect of their conduct or has no case to answer, and

    (ii)   what action (if any) the authority is required to, or will in its discretion, take in respect of the matters dealt with in the report; and

(b)   determine what other action (if any) the authority will in its discretion take in respect of those matters.

68(12)   On the making of the determinations under paragraph (11) the appropriate authority shall give a notification—

(a)   in the case of a complaint, to the complainant and to every person entitled to be kept properly informed in relation to the complaint under regulation 55; and

(b)   in the case of a recordable conduct matter, to every person entitled to be kept properly informed in relation to that matter under that regulation.

68(13)   The notification required by paragraph (12) is one setting out—

(a)   the findings of the report;

(b)   the determinations the authority has made under paragraph (11); and

(c)   the complainant's right of appeal under regulation 74 (appeals to the IPCC with respect to an investigation).

68(14)   Regulation 60 shall have effect in relation to the duties imposed on the appropriate authority by paragraph (12) of this regulation.

68(15)   Except so far as may be otherwise provided by these Regulations, the appropriate authority shall be entitled (notwithstanding any obligation of secrecy imposed by any rule of law or otherwise) to discharge the duty to give a person mentioned in paragraph (12) notification of the findings of the report by sending that person a copy of the report.

68(16)   In relation to a DSI matter in respect of which a determination has been made under regulation 36(2) or (4), the references in this regulation to the appropriate authority are references to the appropriate authority in relation to the person whose conduct is in question.

FINAL REPORTS ON INVESTIGATIONS: OTHER DSI MATTERS

69(1)   This regulation applies on the completion of an investigation of a DSI matter in respect of which neither the IPCC nor the appropriate authority has made a determination under regulation 36(2) or (4) (procedure where conduct matter is revealed during investigation of DSI matter).

69(2)   The person investigating shall—

(a)   submit a report on the investigation to the IPCC; and

(b)   send a copy of that report to the appropriate authority.

69(3)   A person submitting a report under this regulation shall not be prevented by any obligation of secrecy imposed by any rule of law or otherwise from including all such matters in that report as that person thinks fit.

ACTION BY THE IPCC IN RESPONSE TO AN INVESTIGATION REPORT UNDER REGULATION 69

70(1)   On receipt of the report referred to in regulation 69, the IPCC shall determine whether the report indicates that an officer may have—

(a)   committed a criminal offence; or

(b)   behaved in a manner which would justify the bringing of disciplinary proceedings.

70(2)   If the IPCC determines under paragraph (1) that there is no indication in the report that an officer may have—

(a)   committed a criminal offence; or

(b)   behaved in a manner which would justify the bringing of disciplinary proceedings,

it shall make such recommendations or give such advice (if any) under regulation 7 as it considers necessary or desirable.

70(3) Paragraph (2) does not affect any power of the IPCC to make recommendations or give advice under regulation 7 in other cases (whether arising under these Regulations or otherwise).

70(4) If the IPCC determines under paragraph (1) that the report indicates that an officer may have–

(a)   committed a criminal offence; or

(b)   behaved in a manner which would justify the bringing of disciplinary proceedings,

it shall notify the appropriate authority in relation to the person whose conduct is in question of its determination, and, if it appears that the appropriate authority has not already been sent a copy of the report, send a copy of the report to that authority.

70(5) Where the appropriate authority in relation to the person whose conduct is in question is notified of a determination by the IPCC under paragraph (4), it shall record the matter under regulation 24 (recording etc. of conduct matters in other cases) as a conduct matter (and the other provisions of these Regulations shall apply in relation to that matter accordingly).

70(6) Where a DSI matter is recorded under regulation 24 as a conduct matter by virtue of paragraph (5)–

(a)   the person investigating the DSI matter shall (subject to any determination made by the IPCC under regulation 38(6) (power of the IPCC to determine the form of an investigation – further determination)) investigate the conduct matter as if appointed or designated to do so, and

(b)   the other provisions of these Regulations shall apply in relation to that matter accordingly.

DUTIES WITH RESPECT TO DISCIPLINARY PROCEEDINGS

71(1) This regulation applies where, in the case of any investigation, the appropriate authority–

(a)   has given, or is required to give, a notification under regulation 68(12) (action by the appropriate authority in response to an investigation report under regulation 66) of the action it is proposing to take in relation to the matters dealt with in any report of the investigation; or

(b)   has submitted, or is required to submit, a memorandum to the IPCC under regulation 67 (action by the IPCC in response to an investigation report under regulation 66) or 74 (appeals to the IPCC with respect to an investigation) setting out the action that it is proposing to take in relation to those matters.

71(2) Subject to regulation 52 (restrictions on proceedings pending the conclusion of an investigation) and to any recommendations or directions under this regulation, it shall be the duty of the appropriate authority–

(a)   to take the action which has been or is required to be notified or, as the case may be, which is or is required to be set out in the memorandum; and

(b)   in a case where that action consists of or includes the bringing of disciplinary proceedings, to secure that those proceedings, once brought, are proceeded with to a proper conclusion.

71(3) Where this regulation applies by virtue of paragraph (1)(b), the IPCC may make a recommendation to the appropriate authority in respect of any person whose conduct is in question–

(a)   that the person has a case to answer in respect of their conduct or has no case to answer in relation to their conduct to which the investigation related;

(b)   that disciplinary proceedings of the form specified in the recommendation are brought against that person in respect of the conduct to which the investigation related; or

(c)   that any disciplinary proceedings brought against that person are modified so as to deal with such aspects of that conduct as may be so specified;

and it shall be the duty of the appropriate authority to notify the IPCC whether it accepts the recommendation and (if it does) to set out in the notification the steps that it is proposing to take to give effect to it.

71(4) If, after the IPCC has made a recommendation under this regulation, the appropriate authority does not take steps to secure that full effect is given to the recommendation–

(a)   the IPCC may direct the appropriate authority to take steps for that purpose; and

(b)   it shall be the duty of the appropriate authority to comply with the direction.

71(5) A direction under paragraph (4) may, to such extent as the IPCC thinks fit, set out the steps to be taken by the appropriate authority in order to give effect to the recommendation.

71(6) Where the IPCC gives the appropriate authority a direction under this regulation, it shall supply the appropriate authority with a statement of its reasons for doing so.

71(7) Where disciplinary proceedings have been brought in accordance with a recommendation or direction under this regulation, it shall be the duty of the authority to ensure that they are proceeded with to a proper conclusion.

71(8) The IPCC may at any time withdraw a direction given under this regulation; and paragraph (7) shall not impose any obligation in relation to any time after the withdrawal of the direction.

71(9) The appropriate authority shall keep the IPCC informed–

(a) in a case in which this regulation applies by virtue of paragraph (1)(b), of whatever action it takes in pursuance of its duty under paragraph (2); and

(b) in every case of a recommendation or direction under this regulation, of whatever action it takes in response to that recommendation or direction.

COMPLAINTS AGAINST A PERSON WHOSE IDENTITY IS UNASCERTAINED

72(1) Where a complaint or conduct matter relates to the conduct of a person whose identity is unascertained at the time at which the complaint is made or the conduct matter is recorded, or whose identity is not ascertained during or subsequent to, the investigation of the complaint or recordable conduct matter, these Regulations shall apply in relation to such a person as if it did not include–

(a) any requirement for the person complained against to be given a notification or an opportunity to make representations;

(b) any requirement for the IPCC or the appropriate authority to determine whether a criminal offence may have been committed by the person whose conduct has been the subject-matter of an investigation, or to take any action in relation to such a determination;

(c) any requirement for an appropriate authority to determine whether disciplinary proceedings should be brought against a person whose conduct is the subject-matter of a report.

72(2) Where the identity of such a person is subsequently ascertained, the IPCC and the appropriate authority shall take such action in accordance with these Regulations as they see fit, regardless of any previous action taken.

PART 9 – APPEALS

APPEALS TO THE IPCC: FAILURES TO NOTIFY OR RECORD A COMPLAINT

73(1) An appeal under regulation 21 (failures to notify or record a complaint) against any failure referred to in regulation 21(3) shall be made within 28 days of the date on which notification of that failure is made or sent to the complainant under regulation 21(2).

73(2) Any such appeal shall be made in writing and shall state–

(a) details of the complaint;

(b) the date on which the complaint was made;

(c) the name of the Head of the Home Civil Service, the Chief Executive or the Commissioner (other than the Chairman, the Chief Executive and the Permanent Secretary) who gave notification of the failure;

(d) the grounds for the appeal; and

(e) the date on which the complainant was notified of the determination or of the failure to record the complaint.

73(3) Where the IPCC receives such an appeal it shall–

(a) notify the Head of the Home Civil Service, the Chief Executive or the Commissioners (other than the Chairman, the Chief Executive and the Permanent Secretary) concerned of the appeal, and

(b) request any information from any person which it considers necessary to dispose of the appeal.

73(4) Where the IPCC receives an appeal which fails to comply with one or more of the requirements mentioned in paragraph (2), it may decide to proceed as if those requirements had been complied with.

73(5) The Head of the Home Civil Service, the Chief Executive or the Commissioners (other than the Chairman, the Chief Executive and the Permanent Secretary) shall supply to the IPCC any information requested under paragraph (3)(b).

73(6) The IPCC shall determine the outcome of the appeal as soon as practicable.

73(7) The IPCC shall notify the complainant and the Head of the Home Civil Service, the Chief Executive or the Commissioners (other than the Chairman, the Chief Executive and the Permanent Secretary) concerned of the reasons for its determination.

73(8) The IPCC may extend the time period mentioned in paragraph (1) in any case where it is satisfied that by reason of the special circumstances of the case it is just to do so.

APPEALS TO THE IPCC WITH RESPECT TO AN INVESTIGATION

74(1) This regulation applies where a complaint has been subjected to–

(a) an investigation by the appropriate authority on its own behalf; or

(b) an investigation under the supervision of the IPCC.

74(2) The complainant shall have the following rights of appeal to the IPCC–

(a) a right of appeal on the grounds that the complainant has not been provided with adequate information–

    (i) about the findings of the investigation; or

    (ii) about any determination of the appropriate authority relating to the taking (or not taking) of action in respect of any matters dealt with in the report on the investigation;

(b) a right of appeal against the findings of the investigation;

(c) a right of appeal against any determination by the appropriate authority that a person to whose conduct the investigation related has a case to answer in respect of that person's conduct or has no case to answer;

(d) a right of appeal against any determination by the appropriate authority relating to the taking (or not taking) of action in respect of any matters dealt with in the report; and

(e) a right of appeal against any determination by the appropriate authority under regulation 68(2)(a) (action by the appropriate authority in response to an investigation report under regulation 66), as a result of which it is not required to send the Director of Public Prosecutions or, as the case may be, the Director of Revenue and Customs Prosecutions a copy of the report.

74(3) On the bringing of an appeal under this regulation, the IPCC may require the appropriate authority to submit a memorandum to the IPCC which–

(a) sets out whether the appropriate authority has determined that a person to whose conduct the investigation related has a case to answer in respect of that person's conduct or has no case to answer;

(b) if the appropriate authority is proposing to take any action, sets out what action it is proposing to take;

(c) if the appropriate authority has decided in relation to a person to whose conduct the investigation related, that disciplinary proceedings should not be brought against that person, sets out its reasons for so deciding; and

(d) if the appropriate authority made a determination under regulation 68(2)(a) as a result of which it is not required to send the Director of Public Prosecutions or, as the case may be, the Director of Revenue and Customs Prosecutions, a copy of the report relating to the investigation, sets out the reasons for that determination;

and it shall be the duty of the appropriate authority to comply with any requirement under this paragraph.

74(4) Where the IPCC so requires on the bringing of any appeal under this regulation in the case of an investigation by the appropriate authority on its own behalf, the appropriate authority shall provide the IPCC with a copy of the report of the investigation.

74(5) On an appeal under this regulation, the IPCC shall determine such of the following as it considers appropriate in the circumstances–

(a) whether the complainant has been provided with adequate information about the matters mentioned in paragraph (2)(a);

(b) whether the findings of the investigation need to be reconsidered; and

(c) whether the appropriate authority–

    (i) has made such a determination as is mentioned in paragraph (3)(a) that the IPCC considers to be appropriate in respect of matters dealt with in the report, and

(ii)   has determined that it is required to or will, in its discretion, take the action (if any) that the IPCC considers to be so appropriate; and

(d)   whether the conditions set out in regulation 68(3) and (4) are satisfied in respect of the report on the investigation.

74(6)   Where, on an appeal under this regulation, the IPCC determines that the complainant has not been provided with adequate information about any matter, the IPCC shall give the appropriate authority all such directions as the IPCC considers appropriate for securing that the complainant is properly informed.

74(7)   Nothing in paragraph (6) shall authorise the IPCC to require the disclosure of any information the disclosure of which to the appellant has been or is capable of being withheld by virtue of regulation 60.

74(8)   Where, on an appeal under this regulation, the IPCC determines that the findings of the investigation need to be reconsidered, it shall either–

(a)   review those findings without an immediate further investigation; or

(b)   direct that the complaint be re-investigated.

74(9)   Where, on an appeal under this regulation, the IPCC determines that the appropriate authority has not made a determination as to whether there is a case for a person to whose conduct the investigation related to answer that the IPCC considers appropriate or has not determined that it is required to or will, in its discretion, take the action in respect of the matters dealt with in the report that the IPCC considers appropriate, the IPCC shall–

(a)   determine, in the light of that determination, whether or not to make recommendations under regulation 71 (duties with respect to disciplinary proceedings); and

(b)   make such recommendations (if any) under that regulation as it thinks fit.

74(10)   Where, on an appeal under this regulation, the IPCC determines that the conditions set out in regulation 68(3) and (4) are satisfied in respect of the report, it shall direct the appropriate authority–

(a)   to notify the Director of Public Prosecutions or, as the case may be, the Director of Revenue and Customs Prosecutions, of the IPCC's determination; and

(b)   to send the Director a copy of the report.

74(11)   The IPCC shall give notification of any determination under this regulation–

(a)   to the appropriate authority;

(b)   to the complainant;

(c)   to every person entitled to be kept properly informed in relation to the complaint under regulation 55 (duty to provide information for other persons); and

(d)   except in a case where it appears to the IPCC that to do so might prejudice any proposed review or re-investigation of the complaint, to the person complained against.

74(12)   The IPCC shall also give notification of any directions given to the appropriate authority under this regulation–

(a)   to the complainant;

(b)   to every person entitled to be kept properly informed in relation to the complaint under regulation 55; and

(c)   except in a case where it appears to the IPCC that to do so might prejudice any proposed review or re-investigation of the complaint, to the person complained against.

74(13)   It shall be the duty of the appropriate authority to comply with any directions given to it under this regulation.

74(14)   Any appeal made by a complainant under this regulation shall be made within 28 days of the date on which the appropriate authority sends a notification to the complainant of its determination under regulation 68(12) as to what action (if any) it will take in respect of the matters dealt with in the investigation report.

74(15)   Any such appeal shall be in writing and shall state–

(a)   details of the complaint;

(b)   the date on which the complaint was made;

(c)   the grounds for the appeal; and

(d)   the date on which the complainant received notification under regulation 68(12).

74(16)   Where the IPCC receives such an appeal, it shall request any information from any person which it considers necessary to dispose of the appeal.

74(17)   Where the IPCC receives an appeal which fails to comply with one or more of the requirements mentioned in paragraph (15), it may decide to proceed as if those requirements had been complied with.

74(18)   The appropriate authority shall supply to the IPCC any further information requested of it under paragraph (16).

74(19)   The IPCC shall determine the outcome of the appeal as soon as practicable.

74(20)   The IPCC shall notify the complainant and the appropriate authority of the reasons for its determination.

74(21)   The IPCC may extend the time period mentioned in paragraph (14) in any case where it is satisfied that by reason of the special circumstances of the case it is just to do so.

REVIEWS AND RE-INVESTIGATIONS FOLLOWING AN APPEAL

75(1)   On a review under regulation 74(8)(a) (appeals to the IPCC with respect to an investigation) of the findings of an investigation, the powers of the IPCC shall be, according to its determination on that review, to do one or more of the following–

(a)   to uphold the findings in whole or in part;

(b)   to give the appropriate authority such directions as the IPCC thinks fit–

(i)   as to the carrying out by the appropriate authority of its own review of the findings,

(ii)   as to the information to be provided to the complainant, and

(iii)   generally as to the handling of the matter in future;

(c)   to direct that the complaint be re-investigated.

75(2)   Where the IPCC directs under regulation 74 or paragraph (1) that a complaint be re-investigated, it shall make a determination of the form that the re-investigation should take.

75(3)   Paragraphs (3) to (8) of regulation 38 (power of the IPCC to determine the form of an investigation) shall apply in relation to a determination under paragraph (2) as they apply in the case of a determination under that regulation.

75(4)   The provisions of these Regulations shall apply in relation to any re-investigation in pursuance of a direction under regulation 74(9) or paragraph (1) as they apply in relation to any investigation in pursuance of a determination under regulation 38.

75(5)   The IPCC shall give notification of any determination made by it under this regulation–

(a)   to the appropriate authority;

(b)   to the complainant;

(c)   to every person entitled to be kept properly informed in relation to the complaint under regulation 55 (duty to provide information for other persons); and

(d)   except in a case where it appears to the IPCC that to do so might prejudice any proposed re-investigation of the complaint, to the person complained against.

75(6)   The IPCC shall also give notification of any directions given to the appropriate authority under this regulation–

(a)   to the complainant;

(b)   to every person entitled to be kept properly informed in relation to the complaint under regulation 55; and

(c)   except in a case where it appears to the IPCC that to do so might prejudice any proposed review or re-investigation of the complaint, to the person complained against.

FINANCE ACT 2009, SECTIONS 101 TO 103 (APPOINTED DAY AND SUPPLEMENTAL PROVISION) ORDER 2010

(SI 2010/1878)

Made on 21 July 2010 by the Treasury in exercise of the powers conferred by s. 104(3) to (5) of the Finance Act 2009.

CITATION

1 This Order may be cited as the Finance Act 2009, Sections 101 to 103 (Appointed Day and Supplemental Provision) Order 2010.

APPOINTED DAY

2 The day appointed as the day on which sections 101 to 103 of the Finance Act 2009 come into force for the purposes of bank payroll tax (including any penalties assessed in relation to that tax) is 31st August 2010.

SUPPLEMENTAL PROVISION

3 Interest charged under section 101 of the Finance Act 2009 (late payment interest on sums due to HMRC) on an amount enforceable as if it were bank payroll tax may be enforced as if it were an amount of bank payroll tax.

TAXES (DEFINITION OF CHARITY) (RELEVANT TERRITORIES) REGULATIONS 2010

(SI 2010/1904)

Made on 23 July 2010 by the Commissioners for Her Majesty's Revenue and Customs in exercise of the powers conferred by para. 2 of Sch. 6 to the Finance Act 2010. Operative from 20 August 2010.

1   These Regulations may be cited as the Taxes (Definition of Charity) (Relevant Territories) Regulations 2010 and come into force on 20th August 2010.

2   The territories specified in the Schedule to these Regulations are relevant territories for the purposes of the meaning of a relevant territory in paragraph 2(3) of Schedule 6 to the Finance Act 2010 (the jurisdiction condition of the definition of "charity" in paragraph 1 of Schedule 6 to the Finance Act 2010).

SCHEDULE

Regulation 2

The Republic of Iceland
The Principality of Liechtenstein
The Kingdom of Norway

History – The words "The Principality of Liechtenstein" inserted by SI 2014/1807, reg. 2, with effect from 31 July 2014.

FIRST-TIER TRIBUNAL AND UPPER TRIBUNAL (CHAMBERS) ORDER 2010

(SI 2010/2655, as amended by SI 2012/1673, SI 2013/1187 and SI 2013/2068)

Made on 28 October 2010 by the Lord Chancellor, with the concurrence of the Senior President of Tribunals, in exercise of the power conferred by s. 7(1) and (9) of the Tribunals, Courts and Enforcement Act 2007.

Cross references – The Tribunals (Scotland) Act 2014 prospectively creates a new structure for tribunals dealing with devolved matters under the judicial leadership of the Lord President of the Court of Session as head of the Scottish Tribunals including the creation of a first-tier tribunal and an upper tribunal.

CITATION, COMMENCEMENT AND REVOCATIONS

1(1) This Order may be cited as the First-tier Tribunal and Upper Tribunal (Chambers) Order 2010 and comes into force on 29th November 2010.

1(2) The Orders listed in the first column of the Schedule to this Order are revoked to the extent specified in the second column.

FIRST-TIER TRIBUNAL CHAMBERS

2 The First-tier Tribunal shall be organised into the following chambers–

(a)   the General Regulatory Chamber;

(b)   the Health, Education and Social Care Chamber;

(c)   the Immigration and Asylum Chamber;

(cc)   the Property Chamber;

(d)   the Social Entitlement Chamber;

(e)   the Tax Chamber;

(f)   the War Pensions and Armed Forces Compensation Chamber.

History – Art. 2(cc) inserted by SI 2013/1187, art. 3, with effect from 1 July 2013.

FUNCTIONS OF THE GENERAL REGULATORY CHAMBER

3 To the General Regulatory Chamber are allocated all functions related to–

(a)   proceedings in respect of the decisions and actions of regulatory bodies which are not allocated to the Health, Education and Social Care Chamber by article 4 or to the Tax Chamber by article 7;

(b)   matters referred to the First-tier Tribunal under Schedule 1D to the Charities Act 1993 (references to Tribunal);

(c)   the determination of remuneration for carrying mail-bags in a ship or aircraft.

FUNCTIONS OF THE HEALTH, EDUCATION AND SOCIAL CARE CHAMBER

4 To the Health, Education and Social Care Chamber are allocated all functions related to–

(a)   an appeal against a decision related to children with special educational needs;

(b)   a claim of disability discrimination in the education of a child;

(c)   an application or an appeal against a decision or determination related to work with children or vulnerable adults;

(d)   an appeal against a decision related to registration in respect of the provision of health or social care;

(e)   an application in respect of, or an appeal against a decision related to, the provision of health care or health services;

(f)   an appeal against a decision related to registration in respect of social workers and social care workers;

(g)   an appeal against a decision related to the provision of childcare;

(h)   an appeal against a decision related to an independent school or other independent educational institution;

(i)   applications and references by and in respect of patients under the provisions of the Mental Health Act 1983 or paragraph 5(2) of the Schedule to the Repatriation of Prisoners Act 1984.

FUNCTIONS OF THE IMMIGRATION AND ASYLUM CHAMBER OF THE FIRST-TIER TRIBUNAL

5 To the Immigration and Asylum Chamber of the First-tier Tribunal are allocated all functions related to immigration and asylum matters, with the exception of matters allocated to–

(a)   the Social Entitlement Chamber by article 6(a);

(b)   the General Regulatory Chamber by article 3(a).

FUNCTIONS OF THE PROPERTY CHAMBER

5A To the Property Chamber are allocated all functions conferred on the First-tier Tribunal relating to–

(a)   a reference by the Chief Land Registrar and any other application, matter or appeal under the Land Registration Act 2002;

(b)   proceedings under any of the enactments referred to in section 6A(2) of the Agriculture (Miscellaneous Provisions) Act 1954 or the Hill Farming Act 1946;

(c)   housing etc, under the Housing Act 2004;

(d)   leasehold property;

(e)   residential property;

(f)   rents;

(g)   the right to buy;

(h)   applications and appeals under the Mobile Homes Act 1983.

History – Art. 5A inserted by SI 2013/1187, art. 4, with effect from 1 July 2013.

FUNCTIONS OF THE SOCIAL ENTITLEMENT CHAMBER

6 To the Social Entitlement Chamber are allocated all functions related to appeals–

(a)   in cases regarding support for asylum seekers, failed asylum seekers, persons designated under section 130 of the Criminal Justice and Immigration Act 2008, or the dependants of any such persons;

(b)   in criminal injuries compensation cases;

(c)   regarding entitlement to, payments of, or recovery or recoupment of payments of, social security benefits, child support, vaccine damage payments, health in pregnancy grant and tax credits, with the exception of–

    (i)   appeals under section 11 of the Social Security Contributions (Transfer of Functions, etc.) Act 1999(d) (appeals against decisions of Her Majesty's Revenue and Customs);

    (ii)   appeals in respect of employer penalties or employer information penalties (as defined in section 63(11) and (12) of the Tax Credits Act 2002);

    (iii)   appeals under regulation 28(3) of the Child Trust Funds Regulations 2004;

(d)   regarding saving gateway accounts with the exception of appeals against requirements to account for an amount under regulations made under section 14 of the Saving Gateway Accounts Act 2009;

(e)   regarding child trust funds with the exception of appeals against requirements to account for an amount under regulations made under section 22(4) of the Child Trust Funds Act 2004 in relation to section 13 of that Act;

(f)   regarding payments in consequence of diffuse mesothelioma;

(g)   regarding a certificate or waiver decision in relation to NHS charges;

(h)   regarding entitlement to be credited with earnings or contributions;

(i)   against a decision as to whether an accident was an industrial accident.

FUNCTIONS OF THE TAX CHAMBER

7 To the Tax Chamber are allocated all functions, except those functions allocated to the Social Entitlement Chamber by article 6 or to the Tax and Chancery Chamber of the Upper Tribunal by article 13, related to an appeal, application, reference or other proceeding in respect of–

(a)　　a function of the Commissioners for Her Majesty's Revenue and Customs or an officer of Revenue and Customs;

(b)　　the exercise by the Serious Organised Crime Agency of general Revenue functions or Revenue inheritance tax functions (as defined in section 323 of the Proceeds of Crime Act 2002);

(c)　　the exercise by the Director of Border Revenue of functions under section 7 of the Borders, Citizenship and Revenue Act 2009;

(d)　　a function of the Compliance Officer for the Independent Parliamentary Standards Authority.

FUNCTIONS OF THE WAR PENSIONS AND ARMED FORCES COMPENSATION CHAMBER

8　To the War Pensions and Armed Forces Compensation Chamber are allocated all functions related to appeals under the War Pensions (Administrative Provisions) Act 1919 and the Pensions Appeal Tribunals Act 1943.

UPPER TRIBUNAL CHAMBERS

9　The Upper Tribunal shall be organised into the following chambers–

(a)　　the Administrative Appeals Chamber;

(b)　　the Immigration and Asylum Chamber of the Upper Tribunal;

(c)　　the Lands Chamber;

(d)　　the Tax and Chancery Chamber.

FUNCTIONS OF THE ADMINISTRATIVE APPEALS CHAMBER

10　To the Administrative Appeals Chamber are allocated all functions related to–

(a)　　an appeal–

　　(i)　　against a decision made by the First-tier Tribunal, except an appeal allocated to the Tax and Chancery Chamber by article 13(1)(a) or the Immigration and Asylum Chamber of the Upper Tribunal by article 11(a);

　　(ii)　　under section 5 of the Pensions Appeal Tribunals Act 1943 (appeals against assessment of extent of disablement) against a decision of the Pensions Appeal Tribunal in Northern Ireland established under paragraph 1(3) of the Schedule to the Pensions Appeal Tribunals Act 1943 (constitution, jurisdiction and procedure of Pensions Appeal Tribunals);

　　(iii)　　against a decision of the Pensions Appeal Tribunal in Scotland established under paragraph 1(2) of the Schedule to the Pensions Appeal Tribunals Act 1943;

　　(iv)　　against a decision of the Mental Health Review Tribunal for Wales established under section 65 of the Mental Health Act 1983 (Mental Health Review Tribunals);

　　(v)　　against a decision of the Special Educational Needs Tribunal for Wales;

　　(vi)　　under section 4 of the Safeguarding Vulnerable Groups Act 2006 (appeals);

　　(vii)　　transferred to the Upper Tribunal from the First-tier Tribunal under Tribunal Procedure Rules, except an appeal allocated to the Tax and Chancery Chamber by article 13(1)(e);

　　(viii)　　against a decision in a road transport case;

(b)　　an application, except an application allocated to another chamber by article 11(c), (d) or (e), 12(c) or 13(1)(g), for the Upper Tribunal–

　　(i)　　to grant the relief mentioned in section 15(1) of the Tribunals, Courts and Enforcement Act 2007 (Upper Tribunal's "judicial review" jurisdiction);

　　(ii)　　to exercise the powers of review under section 21(2) of that Act (Upper Tribunal's "judicial review" jurisdiction: Scotland);

(c)　　a matter referred to the Upper Tribunal by the First-tier Tribunal–

　　(i)　　under section 9(5)(b) of the Tribunals, Courts and Enforcement Act 2007 (review of decision of First-tier Tribunal), or

　　(ii)　　under Tribunal Procedure Rules relating to non-compliance with a requirement of the First-tier Tribunal,

　　except where the reference is allocated to another chamber by article 11(b)or 13(1)(f);

(d)　　a determination or decision under section 4 of the Forfeiture Act 1982;

(e)   proceedings, or a preliminary issue, transferred under Tribunal Procedure Rules to the Upper Tribunal from the First-tier Tribunal, except those allocated to the Lands Chamber by article 12(cc) or to the Tax and Chancery Chamber by article 13(1)(e).

History – Art. 10(a)(viii) substituted by SI 2012/1673, art. 3, with effect from 20 July 2012.
In art. 10(b), the words ", (d) or (e)" substituted for the words "or (d)" by SI 2013/2068, art. 3, with effect from 1 November 2013.
In art. 10(b), the words "or (d)" inserted after "11(c)" by SI 2011/2342, art. 3, with effect from 17 October 2011.
In art. 10(e), the words "the Lands Chamber by article 12(cc) or to" inserted by SI 2013/1187, art. 5, with effect from 1 July 2013.

FUNCTIONS OF THE IMMIGRATION AND ASYLUM CHAMBER OF THE UPPER TRIBUNAL

11   To the Immigration and Asylum Chamber of the Upper Tribunal are allocated all functions related to–

(a)   an appeal against a decision of the First-tier Tribunal made in the Immigration and Asylum Chamber of the First-tier Tribunal;

(b)   a matter referred to the Upper Tribunal under section 9(5)(b) of the Tribunals, Courts and Enforcement Act 2007 or under Tribunal Procedure Rules by the Immigration and Asylum Chamber of the First-tier Tribunal;

(c)   an application for the Upper Tribunal to grant relief mentioned in section 15(1) of the Tribunals, Courts and Enforcement Act 2007 (Upper Tribunal's "judicial review" jurisdiction), or to exercise the power of review under section 21(2) of that Act (Upper Tribunal's "judicial review" jurisdiction: Scotland), which is made by a person who claims to be a minor from outside the United Kingdom challenging a defendant's assessment of that person's age;

(d)   an application for the Upper Tribunal to exercise the powers of review under section 21(2) of the Tribunals, Court and Enforcement Act (Upper Tribunal's "judicial review" jurisdictions: Scotland), which relates to a decision of the First-tier Tribunal mentioned in paragraph (a);

(e)   an application for the Upper Tribunal to grant relief mentioned in section 15(1) of the Tribunals, Courts and Enforcement Act 2007 (Upper Tribunal's "judicial review" jurisdiction), which is designated as an immigration matter–

     (i)   in a direction made in accordance with Part 1 of Schedule 2 to the Constitutional Reform Act 2005 specifying a class of case for the purposes of section 18(6) of the Tribunals, Courts and Enforcement Act 2007; or

     (ii)   in an order of the High Court in England and Wales made under section 31A(3) of the Senior Courts Act 1981, transferring to the Upper Tribunal an application of a kind described in section 31A(1) of that Act.

History – Art. 11(c)–(e) substituted for (c) and (d) by SI 2013/2068, art. 4, with effect from 1 November 2013. Former art. 11(c) and (d) read as follows:

> "(c)   an application for the Upper Tribunal to grant the relief mentioned in section 15(1) of the Tribunals, Courts and Enforcement Act 2007 (Upper Tribunal's "judicial review" jurisdiction), or to exercise the powers of review under section 21(2) of that Act (Upper Tribunal's "judicial review" jurisdiction: Scotland), which–
>   (i)   relates to a decision of the First-tier Tribunal mentioned in paragraph (a); or
>   (ii)   is made by a person who claims to be a minor from outside the United Kingdom challenging a defendant's assessment of that person's age.
> (d)   an application meeting the condition specified in section 31A(8) of the Senior Courts Act 1981 made to the Upper Tribunal or transferred to it by the High Court in England and Wales, to grant the relief mentioned in section 15(1) (Upper Tribunal's "judicial review" jurisdiction) of the Tribunals, Courts and Enforcement Act 2007.".

Art. 11(d) inserted by SI 2011/2342, art. 4, with effect from 17 October 2011.

FUNCTIONS OF THE LANDS CHAMBER

12   To the Lands Chamber are allocated–

(a)   all functions related to–

     (i)   compensation and other remedies for measures taken which affect the ownership, value, enjoyment or use of land or water, or of rights over or property in land or water;

     (ii)   appeals from decisions of–

(aa)   the First-tier Tribunal made in the Property Chamber other than appeals allocated to the Tax and Chancery Chamber by article 13(h);

(ab)   leasehold valuation tribunals in Wales, residential property tribunals in Wales, rent assessment committees in Wales, the Agricultural Land Tribunal in Wales or the Valuation Tribunal for Wales;

(ac)   the Valuation Tribunal for England;

(iii)   the determination of questions of the value of land or an interest in land arising in tax proceedings;

(iv)   proceedings in respect of restrictive covenants, blight notices or the obstruction of light;

(b)   the Upper Tribunal's function as arbitrator under section 1(5) of the Lands Tribunal Act 1949;

(c)   an application for the Upper Tribunal to grant the relief mentioned in section 15(1) of the Tribunals, Courts and Enforcement Act 2007 (Upper Tribunal's "judicial review" jurisdiction) which relates to a decision of a tribunal mentioned in sub-paragraph (a)(ii);

(cc)   any case which may be transferred under Tribunal Procedure Rules to the Upper Tribunal from the Property Chamber of the First-tier Tribunal in relation to functions listed in article 5A(c) to (h);

(d)   any other functions transferred to the Upper Tribunal by the Transfer of Tribunal Functions (Lands Tribunal and Miscellaneous Amendments) Order 2009.

History – Art. 12(a)(ii) substituted by SI 2013/1187, art. 6(a), with effect from 1 July 2013. Former art. 12(a)(ii) read as follows:
"(ii)   appeals from decisions of leasehold valuation tribunals, residential property tribunals, the Valuation Tribunal for England or the Valuation Tribunal in Wales;".
In former art. 12(a)(ii), the words "the Valuation Tribunal in Wales" substituted for the words "a valuation tribunal in Wales" by SI 2011/2342, art. 5, with effect from 17 October 2011.
Art. 12(cc) inserted by SI 2013/1187, art. 6(b), with effect from 1 July 2013.

FUNCTIONS OF THE TAX AND CHANCERY CHAMBER

13(1)   To the Tax and Chancery Chamber are allocated all functions related to–

(a)   an appeal against a decision of the First-tier Tribunal made–

(i)   in the Tax Chamber;

(ii)   in the General Regulatory Chamber in a charities case;

(b)   a reference or appeal in respect of–

(i)   a decision of the Financial Services Authority;

(ii)   a decision of the Bank of England;

(iii)   a decision of a person related to the assessment of any compensation or consideration under the Banking (Special Provisions) Act 2008;

(iv)   a determination or dispute within the meaning of regulation 14(5) or 15 of the Financial Services and Management Act 2000 (Contribution to Costs of Special Resolution Regime) Regulations 2010;

(c)   a reference in respect of a decision of the Pensions Regulator;

(d)   an application under paragraph 50(1)(d) of Schedule 36 to the Finance Act 2008;

(e)   proceedings, or a preliminary issue, transferred to the Upper Tribunal under Tribunal Procedure Rules–

(i)   from the Tax Chamber of the First-tier Tribunal;

(ii)   from the General Regulatory Chamber of the First-tier Tribunal in a charities case;

(f)   a matter referred to the Upper Tribunal under section 9(5)(b) of the Tribunals, Courts and Enforcement Act 2007 or under Tribunal Procedure Rules relating to non-compliance with a requirement of the First-tier Tribunal–

(i)   by the Tax Chamber of the First-tier Tribunal;

(ii)   by the General Regulatory Chamber of the First-tier Tribunal in a charities case;

(g)   an application for the Upper Tribunal to grant the relief mentioned in section 15(1)of the Tribunals, Courts and Enforcement Act 2007 (Upper Tribunal's "judicial review" jurisdiction), or to exercise the powers of review under section 21(2) of that Act (Upper Tribunal's "judicial review" jurisdiction: Scotland), which relates to–

(i)   a decision of the First-tier Tribunal mentioned in paragraph (1)(a)(i) or (ii);

(ii)   a function of the Commissioners for Her Majesty's Revenue and Customs or an officer of Revenue and Customs, with the exception of any function in respect of which an appeal would be allocated to the Social Entitlement Chamber by article 6;

(iii)   the exercise by the Serious Organised Crime Agency of general Revenue functions or Revenue inheritance tax functions (as defined in section 323 of the Proceeds of Crime Act 2002), with the exception of any function in relation to which an appeal would be allocated to the Social Entitlement Chamber by article 6;

    (iv)   a function of the Charity Commission, or one of the bodies mentioned in subparagraph (b) or (c);

(h)   an appeal against a decision of the First-tier Tribunal made in the Property Chamber in a case mentioned in article 5A(a).

13(2)   In this article **"a charities case"** means an appeal or application in respect of a decision, order or direction of the Charity Commission, or a reference under Schedule 1D to the Charities Act 1993.

History – Art. 13(1)(h) inserted by SI 2013/1187, art. 7, with effect from 1 July 2013.

RESOLUTION OF DOUBT OR DISPUTE AS TO CHAMBER

14   If there is any doubt or dispute as to the chamber in which a particular matter is to be dealt with, the Senior President of Tribunals may allocate that matter to the chamber which appears to the Senior President of Tribunals to be most appropriate.

RE-ALLOCATION OF A CASE TO ANOTHER CHAMBER

15   At any point in the proceedings, the Chamber President of the chamber to which a case or any issue in that case has been allocated by or under this Order may, with the consent of the corresponding Chamber President, allocate that case or that issue to another chamber within the same tribunal, by giving a direction to that effect.

SCHEDULE – REVOCATIONS

article 1(2)

Orders revoked	Extent to which revoked
The First-tier Tribunal and Upper Tribunal (Chambers) Order 2008, SI 2008/2684.	The whole Order.
The First-tier Tribunal and Upper Tribunal (Chambers) (Amendment) Order 2009, SI 2009/196.	The whole Order, except for the purposes of article 9 (transitional provision).
The First-tier Tribunal and Upper Tribunal (Chambers) (Amendment No. 2) Order 2009, SI 2009/1021.	The whole Order.
The First-tier Tribunal and Upper Tribunal (Chambers) (Amendment No. 3) Order 2009, SI 2009/1590.	The whole Order.
The First-tier Tribunal and Upper Tribunal (Chambers) (Amendment) Order 2010, SI 2010/40.	The whole Order.

Statutory Instruments

TAX TREATMENT OF FINANCING COSTS AND INCOME (AVAILABLE AMOUNT) REGULATIONS 2010

(SI 2010/2929)

Made on 8 December 2010 by the Commissioners for Her Majesty's Revenue and Customs, in exercise of the powers conferred by s. 332(1)(g) of the Taxation (International and Other Provisions) Act 2010. Operative from 1 January 2011.

CITATION AND COMMENCEMENT

1(1)   These Regulations may be cited as the Tax Treatment of Financing Costs and Income (Available Amount) Regulations 2010 and come into force on 1st January 2011.

1(2)   These Regulations have effect in relation to periods of account of the worldwide group beginning on or after 1st January 2011.

INTERPRETATION

2   For the purposes of these Regulations–

"**CTA 2009**" means the Corporation Tax Act 2009;

"**alternative finance arrangements**" has the meaning given in section 501(2) of CTA 2009 (introduction to chapter: definitions etc);

"**alternative finance return**" has the meaning given in sections 511 to 513 of CTA 2009 (purchase and resale arrangements, diminishing shared ownership arrangements and other arrangements);

"**loan relationship**" has the meaning given in section 302 of CTA 2009 (definitions of loan relationship, creditor relationship and debtor relationship);

"**manufactured interest**" has the meaning given in section 539(5) of CTA 2009 (introduction to chapter: definitions etc);

"**relevant non-lending relationship**" has the meaning given in sections 479 (relevant nonlending relationships not involving discounts) and 480 (relevant non-lending relationships involving discounts) of CTA 2009.

SPECIFIED MATTERS

3   The following matters are specified for the purposes of section 332(1) of the Taxation (International and Other Provisions) Act 2010 to the extent that they are not included in the available amount by virtue of any of paragraphs (a) to (f) of that subsection–

(a)   interest payable in respect of a relevant non-lending relationship;

(b)   alternative finance return under alternative finance arrangements;

(c)   manufactured interest;

(d)   a finance charge treated in accordance with section 551(4) of CTA 2009 (relief for borrower for finance charges in respect of the advance) as interest payable under a debt;

(e)   a finance charge treated in accordance with any of the following provisions of the Corporation Tax Act 2010 as interest payable under a transaction or a loan relationship–

(i)   section 761(3) (deemed loan relationship if borrower is a company),

(ii)   section 762(3) (deemed loan relationship if borrower is a partnership with a corporate member),

(iii)   section 766(3) (deemed loan relationship), or

(iv)   section 769(3) (deemed loan relationship).

FINANCE ACT 2009, SCHEDULE 35 (SPECIAL ANNUAL ALLOWANCE CHARGE) (CESSATION OF EFFECT) ORDER 2010

(SI 2010/2939)

Made on 9 December 2010 by the Treasury, in exercise of the power conferred by para. 21(2) of Sch. 35 to the Finance Act 2009. Operative from 10 December 2010.

CITATION AND COMMENCEMENT

1   This Order may be cited as the Finance Act 2009, Schedule 35 (Special Annual Allowance Charge) (Cessation of Effect) Order 2010 and comes into force on the day after the day on which it is made.

CESSATION OF EFFECT

2(1)   Schedule 35 to the Finance Act 2009 (special annual allowance charge) ceases to have effect after the tax year 2010–11 subject to paragraph (2).

2(2)   Paragraph 18 of Schedule 35 (taxation of contributions refund lump sums) continues to have effect for the tax year 2011–12 only and the provisions of Schedule 35 continue to have effect for the purposes of that paragraph for that tax year.

TAX TREATMENT OF FINANCING COSTS AND INCOME (CORRECTION OF MISMATCHES) REGULATIONS 2010

(SI 2010/3025, as amended by SI 2012/3111)

Made on 21 December 2010 by the Commissioners for Her Majesty's Revenue and Customs in exercise of the powers conferred by s. 336A(1), (4) and (5) and 353B of the Taxation (International and Other Provisions) Act 2010. Operative from 13 January 2011.

PART 1 – PRELIMINARY MATTERS AND INTERPRETATION

CITATION AND COMMENCEMENT

1(1) These Regulations may be cited as the Tax Treatment of Financing Costs and Income (Correction of Mismatches) Regulations 2010 and come into force on 13th January 2011.

1(2) These Regulations have effect in relation to periods of account beginning on or after 1st January 2010.

1(3) But paragraph (2) is subject to regulations 17 (election that specified regulations are not to apply to the worldwide group) and 18 (election that these Regulations are not to apply to periods of account beginning before they are made).

INTERPRETATION

2(1) In these Regulations–

"**CTA 2009**" means the Corporation Tax Act 2009;

"**TIOPA 2010**" means the Taxation (International and Other Provisions) Act 2010;

"**Part 7**" means Part 7 of TIOPA 2010 (tax treatment of financing costs and income);

"**accounting period**" is to be read in accordance with Chapter 2 of Part 2 of CTA 2009 (accounting periods);

"**debtor relationship**" has the meaning given in section 302 of CTA 2009 ("loan relationship" and other definitions);

"**deeply discounted security**" has the meaning given in Chapter 8 of Part 4 of the Income Tax (Trading and Other Income) Act 2005 (profits from deeply discounted securities);

"**fair value accounting**" means a basis of accounting under which assets or liabilities are shown in the company's balance sheet at their fair value;

"**fair value adjustment**" means–

(a) an adjustment which brings into account a profit or loss in relation to an asset or liability representing a loan relationship where for the accounting period in question fair value accounting is used, or

(b) where fair value accounting is used in relation to only part of an asset or a liability, an adjustment which brings into account a profit or loss in relation to that part,

and in either case includes an adjustment to bring into account a profit or loss recognised as a result of applying hedge accounting to a fair value hedge;

"**fair value hedge**" has the meaning for the time being given by international accounting standards;

"**financing expense amount**" in relation to a company means a financing expense amount of the company other than a financing expense amount that is treated by any provision within Chapter 7 of Part 7 ("financing expense amount" and "financing income amount") as not being a financing expense amount;

"**hedge accounting**" has the meaning for the time being given by international accounting standards;

"**loan relationship**" has the meaning given in section 302 of CTA 2009;

"**period of account**" means a period of account of the worldwide group;

"**relevant financial relationship**" has the meaning given in paragraph (2).

2(2)   In these Regulations, **"relevant financial relationship"**, in relation to a company, means–

(a)   a loan relationship of the company where the company stands in the position of a debtor as respects the debt in question;

(b)   a relationship treated as a loan relationship by virtue of any provision of Part 6 of CTA 2009 (relationships treated as loan relationships, etc), where the company stands in the position of a debtor as respects the debt in question;

(c)   an arrangement treated by section 761(2) of the Corporation Tax Act 2010 (deemed loan relationship if borrower is a company) or section 762(2) of that Act (deemed loan relationship if borrower is partnership with corporate member) as if it were a loan relationship of the company or partnership, as the case may be, where the company stands in the position of a debtor as respects the debt in question, but excluding a money debt owed by or to a firm in relation to which the company is required to bring credits and debits into account in accordance with section 380(3) of CTA 2009 (partnerships involving companies).

2(3)   In regulations 14 and 16, the expressions **"amortised cost"** and **"effective interest rate method"** have the meaning for the time being given by international accounting standards;

2(4)   In these Regulations, in any case in which either of sections 347 and 348 of TIOPA 2010 (non-compliant and non-existent financial statements of the worldwide group) applies, references to **"financial statements"** are to those financial statements of the group by reference to which Part 7 is applied.

PART 2 – CORRECTION OF MISMATCHES BETWEEN TAX TREATMENT AND ACCOUNTING TREATMENT

FAIR VALUE ADJUSTMENTS

3(1)   This regulation applies if the conditions given in regulation 4 are satisfied for a period of account.

3(2)   In any case in which Amount A exceeds Amount B in relation to the same relevant financial relationship, there shall be excluded from the available amount the lower of–

(a)   the amount of the fair value adjustment made in relation to the relevant financial relationship, and

(b)   the amount of the excess.

3(3)   In any case in which Amount B exceeds Amount A in relation to the same relevant financial relationship, there shall be included in the available amount the lower of–

(a)   the amount of the fair value adjustment made in relation to the relevant financial relationship, and

(b)   the amount of the excess.

3(4)   In this regulation–

(a)   Amount A in relation to a relevant financial relationship of a relevant group company in an accounting period is the amount in respect of the relevant financial relationship which is disclosed in the financial statements of the worldwide group for a period of account and included in the available amount for that period of account, and

(b)   Amount B in relation to a relevant financial relationship of a relevant group company in an accounting period is the amount which would be brought into account for the purposes of Part 5 of CTA 2009 (loan relationships) in respect of the relevant financial relationship if that amount were calculated by deducting the total financing income amounts relating to the relevant financial relationship from the total financing expense amounts relating to the relevant financial relationship.

3(5)   In any case in which the accounting period of the relevant group company does not coincide with the period of account, it is assumed for the purposes of paragraph (4)(b) that the accounting period of the relevant group company is–

(a)   the same as the period of account, if the relevant group company is a member of the worldwide group throughout that period of account;

(b)   in any other case, that part of the period of account during which the relevant group company is a member of the worldwide group.

3(6)   In any case in which, but for this paragraph, Amount B would be a negative amount, Amount B is taken to be zero.

CONDITIONS FOR THE APPLICATION OF REGULATION 3

4(1)   The first condition is that a relevant group company is a party to a relevant financial relationship in a relevant accounting period.

4(2)   The second condition is that a debit in respect of the relevant financial relationship is a financing expense amount of the company.

4(3)   The third condition is that an amount in respect of the relevant financial relationship is included in the available amount otherwise than by virtue of regulation 3.

4(4)   The fourth condition is that a fair value adjustment is made in relation to the relevant financial relationship by the relevant group company in the relevant accounting period.

LATE INTEREST TREATED AS NOT ACCRUING UNTIL PAID

5(1)   This regulation applies in relation to a debit in respect of interest payable under a debtor relationship of a relevant group company if the conditions given in regulation 6 are satisfied.

5(2)   In the period of account in which the interest to which the debit relates is paid, the amount of the debit shall be included in the available amount to the extent that it is not included in the available amount for that period by virtue of any other enactment.

CONDITIONS FOR THE APPLICATION OF REGULATION 5

6(1)   The first condition is that the debit is to be brought into account in a relevant accounting period for the purposes of Part 5 of CTA 2009 by virtue of section 373 of that Act (late interest treated as not accruing until paid in some cases).

6(2)   The second condition is that the debit is a financing expense amount of the company in the period of account in which the interest to which the debit relates is paid.

6(3)   The third condition is that the debit would be brought into account for the purposes of Part 5 of CTA 2009 in an accounting period beginning on or after 1st January 2010 if section 373 of CTA 2009 did not apply.

ADJUSTMENT FOR PERIOD OF ACCOUNT IN WHICH LATE INTEREST WOULD BE A FINANCING EXPENSE AMOUNT BUT FOR SECTION 373 OF CTA 2009

7(1)   This regulation applies in relation to a debit in respect of interest which has accrued under a debtor relationship of a relevant group company if the conditions given in regulation 8 are satisfied.

7(2)   In the period of account in which the debit would be a financing expense amount of a company but for section 373 of CTA 2009, any amount in respect of the debit that would be included in the available amount but for this paragraph shall be excluded from the available amount.

CONDITIONS FOR THE APPLICATION OF REGULATION 7

8(1)   The first condition is that but for section 373 of CTA 2009 the debit would be a financing expense amount of the company in a period of account.

8(2)   The second condition is that the debit would be brought into account for the purposes of Part 5 of CTA 2009 in an accounting period beginning on or after 1st January 2010 if section 373 of CTA 2009 did not apply.

POSTPONED DEBITS IN RELATION TO DEEPLY DISCOUNTED SECURITIES

9(1)   This regulation applies in relation to a debit in respect of a debtor relationship of a relevant group company if the conditions given in regulation 10 are satisfied.

9(2)   In the period of account in which the deeply discounted security to which the debit relates is redeemed, the amount of the debit shall be included in the available amount to the extent that it is not included in the available amount for that period by virtue of any other enactment.

CONDITIONS FOR THE APPLICATION OF REGULATION 9

10(1)   The first condition is that either of sections 407 and 409(6) of CTA 2009 (postponement until redemption of debits for deeply discounted securities of connected companies and of close companies) requires the debit to be brought into account for the purposes of Part 5 of CTA 2009 in a relevant accounting period.

10(2)   The second condition is that the debit is a financing expense amount of the company in the period of account in which the deeply discounted security is redeemed.

10(3)   The third condition is that a debit in respect of the deeply discounted security would be brought into account for the purposes of Part 5 of CTA 2009 in an accounting period beginning on or after 1st January 2010 if neither of sections 407 and 409 of CTA 2009 applied.

ADJUSTMENT WHERE DEBITS IN RESPECT OF DEEPLY DISCOUNTED SECURITIES WOULD BE BROUGHT INTO ACCOUNT BUT FOR EITHER OF SECTIONS 407 AND 409 OF CTA 2009

11(1)   This regulation applies in relation to a debit in respect of a debtor relationship of a relevant group company if the conditions given in regulation 12 are satisfied.

11(2)   In the period of account in which the debit would be a financing expense amount of a company but for either of sections 407 and 409 of CTA 2009, any amount in respect of the debit that would be included in the available amount but for this paragraph shall be excluded from the available amount.

CONDITIONS FOR THE APPLICATION OF REGULATION 11

12(1)   The first condition is that but for either of sections 407 and 409 of CTA 2009 the debit would be a financing expense amount of the company for a period of account.

12(2)   The second condition is that the debit would be brought into account for the purposes of Part 5 of CTA 2009 in an accounting period beginning on or after 1st January 2010 if neither of sections 407 and 409 of CTA 2009 applied.

LOAN RELATIONSHIPS WITH EMBEDDED DERIVATIVES

13(1)   This regulation applies in relation to a debit if the conditions given in regulation 14 are satisfied.

13(2)   In the period of account in which the debit is brought into account by the relevant group company, the amount referred to in paragraph (3) shall be included in the available amount to the extent that it is not included in the available amount for that period of account by virtue of any other enactment.

13(3)   The amount is such part of the debit as is directly attributable to the requirement referred to in regulation 14(4).

CONDITIONS FOR THE APPLICATION OF REGULATION 13

14(1)   The first condition is that a debit is brought into account under Part 5 of CTA 2009 in respect of a loan relationship to which section 415 of CTA 2009 (loan relationships with embedded derivatives) applies.

14(2)   The second condition is that the debit is a financing expense amount of the company.

14(3)   The third condition is that an amount in respect of the loan relationship is included in the available amount otherwise than by virtue of regulation 13.

14(4)   The fourth condition is that the debit is required by international accounting standards to be measured at amortised cost using the effective interest rate method.

DEBT RESTRUCTURING

15(1)   This regulation applies in relation to a debit if the conditions given in regulation 16 are satisfied.

15(2)   In the period of account in which the debit is brought into account by the relevant group company, the amount referred to in paragraph (3) shall be included in the available amount to the extent that it is not included in the available amount for that period of account by virtue of any other enactment.

15(3)   The amount is such part of the debit as is directly attributable to the requirement referred to in regulation 16(5).

CONDITIONS FOR THE APPLICATION OF REGULATION 15

16(1)   The first condition is that a relevant group company is a party to a relevant financial relationship in a relevant accounting period.

16(2)   The second condition is that a debit in respect of the relevant financial relationship is a financing expense amount of the relevant group company.

16(3)   The third condition is that an amount in respect of the relevant financial relationship is included in the available amount otherwise than by virtue of regulation 15.

16(4)   The fourth condition is that under international accounting standards the relevant financial relationship has been recognised using fair value accounting in the accounts of the relevant group company, in the relevant accounting period or in a previous accounting period, as a new financial liability upon the occurrence of one of the following events–

(a)   an exchange of the relevant financial relationship for an existing financial liability in substantially different terms, or

(b)   a substantial modification of the terms of an existing financial liability or part of it,

where in either case the event is accounted for, in relation to the existing financial liability, as an extinguishment of that liability.

16(5)   The fifth condition is that after the initial recognition of the relevant financial relationship using fair value accounting, the debit is required by international accounting standards to be measured at amortised cost using the effective interest rate method.

EMPLOYER ASSET-BACKED PENSION CONTRIBUTION MISMATCHES

16A(1)   This regulation applies in relation to a finance charge if the conditions in regulation 16B are satisfied.

16A(2)   In the period of account in which the finance charge is brought into account by the relevant group company, an amount equal to that finance charge shall be included in the available amount to the extent that it is not included in the available amount for that period of account by virtue of any other enactment.

History – Reg. 16A inserted by SI 2012/3111, reg. 3(2), with effect in relation to periods of account of the worldwide group beginning on or after 1 January 2012 but subject to SI 2012/3111, reg. 4 (see cross reference note below).

Cross references – SI 2012/3111, reg. 4: election to disapply reg. 16A in relation to periods of account of the worldwide group beginning before 14 December 2012.

CONDITIONS FOR THE APPLICATION OF REGULATION 16A

16B(1)   The first condition is that the finance charge is treated as interest payable under a transaction or a loan relationship under any of the following provisions of the Corporation Tax Act 2010–

(a)   section 761(3) (deemed loan relationship if borrower is a company),

(b)   section 762(3) (deemed loan relationship if borrower is a partnership with corporate member),

(c)   section 766(3) (deemed loan relationship), or

(d)   section 769(3) (deemed loan relationship).

16B(2)   The second condition is that the finance charge is a financing expense of the company.

16B(3)   The third condition is that the finance charge must arise in relation to—

(a)   an acceptable structured finance arrangement in connection with a contribution paid by an employer under a registered pension scheme in respect of which the employer is entitled to relief under Chapter 4 of Part 4 of the Finance Act 2004 (registered pension schemes: tax reliefs and exemptions), or

(b)   a finance arrangement which would be an acceptable structured finance arrangement in connection with a contribution paid by an employer under a registered pension scheme if the contribution was paid on or after 22 February 2012 and in respect of which the employer is entitled to relief under Chapter 4 of Part 4 of the Finance Act 2004.

16B(4)   In paragraph (3), **"acceptable structured finance arrangement"** has the meaning given in section 196C (employer asset-backed contributions: "acceptable structured finance arrangement" (1)), section 196E (employer asset-backed contributions: "acceptable structured finance arrangement" (2)) or section 196G (employer asset-backed contributions: "acceptable structured finance arrangement" (3)) of the Finance Act 2004, as the case may be.

History – Reg. 16B inserted by SI 2012/3111, reg. 3(2), with effect in relation to periods of account of the worldwide group beginning on or after 1 January 2012 but subject to SI 2012/3111, reg. 4 (see cross reference note below).

Cross references – SI 2012/3111, reg. 4: election to disapply reg. 16B in relation to periods of account of the worldwide group beginning before 14 December 2012.

PART 3 – ELECTIONS

ELECTION THAT SPECIFIED REGULATIONS ARE NOT TO APPLY TO THE WORLDWIDE GROUP

17(1)   A worldwide group may elect that one or more of the following regulations and pairs of regulations will not apply to it–

(a)   3;

(b)   5 and 7;

(c)   9 and 11;

(d)   13;

(e)   15.

17(2)   The election must specify to which regulations or pairs of regulations it relates.

17(3)   The election must comply with the requirements imposed by regulation 19.

17(4)   The election is irrevocable.

ELECTION THAT THESE REGULATIONS ARE NOT TO APPLY TO PERIODS OF ACCOUNT BEGINNING BEFORE THEY ARE MADE

18(1)   A worldwide group may elect that these Regulations are not to apply in relation to periods of account beginning before the date on which these Regulations are made.

18(2)   The election must comply with the requirements imposed by regulation 19.

18(3)   The election is irrevocable.

ELECTION REQUIREMENTS

19(1)   The election must be made by the later of–

(a)   31st March 2011;

(b)   12 months from the end of the first period of account that begins on or after 1st January 2010.

19(2)   The election must be made by the reporting body.

19(3)   The election must be signed by the appropriate person in relation to the reporting body.

19(4)   In this regulation the **"appropriate person"**, in relation to a company, means–

(a)   the proper officer of the company, or

(b)   such other person as may have the express, implied or apparent authority of the company to act on its behalf for the purposes of these Regulations.

19(5)   Subsections (3) and (4) of section 108 of the Taxes Management Act 1970 (responsibility of company officers: meaning of "proper officer") apply for the purposes of this regulation as they apply for the purposes of that section.

19(6)   An election which does not comply with the conditions set out in this regulation is of no effect.

19(7)   In this regulation, **"the reporting body"** has the meaning given by section 277 of TIOPA 2010 (meaning of "the reporting body").

DORMANT BANK AND BUILDING SOCIETY ACCOUNTS (TAX) REGULATIONS 2011

(SI 2011/22, as amended by SI 2012/756)

Made on 10 January 2011 by the Treasury in exercise of the powers conferred by s. 694 to 696, 699 and 701 of the Income Tax (Trading and Other Income) Act 2005 and the powers exercised by the Commissioners for Her Majesty's Revenue and Customs conferred by s. 17(5) and (6) of the Taxes Management Act 1970, s. 852 and 871 of the Income Tax Act 2007 and s. 39(1) of the Finance Act 2008. Operative from 1 February 2011.

CITATION, COMMENCEMENT AND EFFECT

1(1) These Regulations may be cited as the Dormant Bank and Building Society Accounts (Tax) Regulations 2011 and shall come into force on 1st February 2011.

1(2) Regulations 2 to 4 have effect in relation to notices under section 17(1) of the Taxes Management Act 1970 served on or after 1st February 2011.

1(3) Regulations 5 to 7 have effect in relation to interest paid or credited on or after 1st February 2011.

1(4) Regulation 8 has effect in relation to interest arising on or after 1st February 2011.

AMENDMENT OF THE INCOME TAX (INTEREST PAYMENTS) (INFORMATION POWERS) REGULATIONS 1992

2 The Income Tax (Interest Payments) (Information Powers) Regulations 1992 are amended as follows.

3 [Omitted by SI 2012/756, reg. 3(2).]

History – Reg. 3 revoked by SI 2012/756, reg. 3(2), with effect from 31 March 2012.

4 [Omitted by SI 2012/756, reg. 3(2).]

History – Reg. 4 revoked by SI 2012/756, reg. 3(2), with effect from 31 March 2012.

AMENDMENT OF THE INCOME TAX (DEPOSIT-TAKERS AND BUILDING SOCIETIES) (INTEREST PAYMENTS) REGULATIONS 2008

5 The Income Tax (Deposit-takers and Building Societies) (Interest Payments) Regulations 2008 are amended as follows.

6 [Amends SI 2008/2682, reg. 2.]

7 [Inserts SI 2008/2682, reg. 4A, 4B.]

DORMANT ACCOUNTS – POSTPONEMENT OF CHARGE TO TAX ON INTEREST

8(1) For the purposes of Chapter 2 of Part 4 of The Income Tax (Trading and Other Income) Act 2005 (Savings and investment income: interest), interest arising in respect of a relevant dormant account shall be treated as arising at the time (if any) at which the balance of the account is paid out following a repayment claim.

8(2) In paragraph (1), **"relevant dormant account"** has the meaning given in section 39(2) of the Finance Act 2008 and other terms used in that paragraph and in section 39 of that Act have the same meaning in that paragraph as in that section.

AMENDMENT OF THE INDIVIDUAL SAVINGS ACCOUNT REGULATIONS 1998

9(1) The Individual Savings Account Regulations 1998 are amended as follows.

9(2) [Amends SI 1998/1870, reg. 2(1)(a).]

9(3) [Inserts SI 1998/1870, reg. 5C.]

AUTHORISED INVESTMENT FUNDS (TAX) (AMENDMENT) REGULATIONS 2011

(SI 2011/244)

Made on 8 February 2011 by the Treasury in exercise of the powers conferred by s. 17(3) and 18 of the Finance (No. 2) Act 2005 and s. 354 of the Taxation (International and Other Provisions) Act 2010. Operative from 6 March 2011.

CITATION, COMMENCEMENT AND EFFECT

1(1) These Regulations may be cited as the Authorised Investment Funds (Tax) (Amendment) Regulations 2011 and come into force on 6th March 2011.

1(2) Subject to regulation 8, regulations 2 to 4 and 6, 7 and 9 of these Regulations have effect–

(a)   for the purposes of corporation tax–

(i)   on income, for accounting periods ending on or after 6th March 2011, and

(ii)   on chargeable gains, in relation to disposals made on or after 6th March 2011, and

(b)   for the purposes of capital gains tax, in relation to disposals made on or after 6th March 2011.

AMENDMENT OF THE PRINCIPAL REGULATIONS

2 The Authorised Investment Funds (Tax) Regulations 2006 ("the principal Regulations") are amended in accordance with these Regulations.

AMENDMENT OF REGULATION 8

3(1) Regulation 8 (general interpretation) is amended as follows.

3(2) [Amends SI 2006/964, reg. 8.]

3(3) [Amends SI 2006/964, reg. 8.]

3(4) [Amends SI 2006/964, reg. 8.]

INSERTION OF REGULATIONS 14ZA, 14ZB AND 14ZC

4 [Inserts SI 2006/964, reg. 14ZA, 14ZB, 14ZC.]

AMENDMENT OF REGULATION 85D

5 [Amends SI 2006/964, reg. 85D(1).]

AMENDMENT OF REGULATION 85E

6(1) Regulation 85E (interests in funds treated as not being interests in non-reporting funds) is amended in accordance with this regulation.

6(2) [Substitutes SI 2006/964, reg. 85E(2).]

AMENDMENT OF THE SCHEDULE

7(1) The Schedule (abbreviations and defined expressions) is amended as follows.

7(2) [Amends SI 2006/964, Schedule, Pt. 2.]

TRANSITIONAL PROVISION

8(1) This regulation applies to an authorised investment fund ("the fund") which, on 5th March 2011, met the requirement of paragraph (2).

8(2) The requirement is that the fund did not meet the investment condition in regulation 85D of the principal Regulations by virtue of holding an interest in an offshore fund that is treated as creditor relationship rights under section 490 of CTA 2009 (a "relevant interest").

8(3) A relevant interest shall continue to be treated as not being an interest in a non-reporting fund for the purposes of regulation 85E of the principal Regulations for the period beginning on 6th March 2011 and ending on 5th July 2011.

CONSEQUENTIAL AMENDMENTS

9(1) [Amends SI 2006/964, reg. 85C.]

9(2) [Substitutes SI 2009/3001, reg. 18(6).]

FINANCE ACT 2009, SECTIONS 101 TO 103 (INCOME TAX SELF ASSESSMENT) (APPOINTED DAYS AND TRANSITIONAL AND CONSEQUENTIAL PROVISIONS) ORDER 2011

(SI 2011/701)

Made on 10 March 2011 by the Treasury in exercise of the powers conferred by s. 104(3)–(7) of the Finance Act 2009. Operative from 1 April 2011.

CITATION, COMMENCEMENT AND EFFECT

1(1) This Order may be cited as the Finance Act 2009, Sections 101 to 103 (Income Tax Self Assessment) (Appointed Days and Transitional and Consequential Provisions) Order 2011 and comes into force on 1st April 2011.

1(2) The amendments made by articles 6 to 11 have effect on and after 31st October 2011.

INTERPRETATION

2 In this Order–

"**HMRC**" means Her Majesty's Revenue and Customs;

"**self-assessment amount**" means any tax or other amount in relation to which, for any tax year–

(a)   a return falls to be made under–

    (i)   section 8(1)(a) of the Taxes Management Act 1970 (personal return),

    (ii)   section 8A(1)(a) of that Act (trustee's return), or

    (iii)   section 12AA(2)(a) or (3)(a) of that Act (partnership return), or

(b)   an assessment is made under section 29 of that Act (assessment where loss of tax discovered),

and includes any penalties assessed in relation to that tax or amount.

APPOINTED DAYS

3(1) 31st October 2011 is the day appointed for the coming into force of sections 101 and 103 of the Finance Act 2009 (late payment interest on sums due to HMRC) for the purposes of any self-assessment amount payable by a person to HMRC.

3(2) 31st October 2011 is the day appointed for the coming into force of sections 102 and 103 of the Finance Act 2009 (repayment interest on sums to be paid by HMRC) for the purposes of any self-assessment amount payable or repayable by HMRC to any person.

Notes – SI 2011/2401, art. 2(1) (not reproduced) appoints 6 October 2011 as the day for the coming into force of FA 2009, s. 103 generally. SI 2011/2401, art. 2(2) states that references to s. 103 in art. 3 and 4 of SI 2011/701 are only affected by SI 2011/2401, art. 2(1) in relation to the making of regulations by the Treasury under s. 103.

TRANSITIONAL PROVISION

4(1) In relation to any self-assessment amount payable by a person to HMRC and outstanding immediately prior to 31st October 2011–

(a)   section 86 of the Taxes Management 1970 (interest on overdue income tax and capital gains tax) has effect up to and including 30th October 2011, and

(b)   sections 101 and 103 of the Finance Act 2009 have effect on and after 31st October 2011.

4(2) In relation to any self-assessment amount payable or repayable by HMRC to a person and outstanding immediately prior to 31st October 2011–

(a)   section 824 of the Income and Corporation Taxes Act 1988 (repayment supplements: individuals and others) and section 283 of the Taxation of Chargeable Gains Act 1992 (repayment supplements) have effect up to and including 30th October 2011, and

(b)   sections 102 and 103 of the Finance Act 2009 have effect on and after 31st October 2011.

Notes – SI 2011/2401, art. 2(1) (not reproduced) appoints 6 October 2011 as the day for the coming into force of FA 2009, s. 103 generally. SI 2011/2401, art. 2(2) states that references to s. 103 in art. 3 and 4 of SI 2011/701 are only affected by SI 2011/2401, art. 2(1) in relation to the making of regulations by the Treasury under s. 103.

5 For the avoidance of doubt, section 86 of the Taxes Management Act 1970, section 824 of the Income and Corporation Taxes Act 1988 and section 283 of the Taxation of Chargeable Gains Act 1992 do not have effect in relation to any self-assessment amount which becomes payable or repayable on or after 31st October 2011.

CONSEQUENTIAL PROVISION

6 The Taxes Management Act 1970 is amended as follows.

7 [Amends TMA 1970, s. 69(1).]

8(1) Section 107A (relevant trustees) is amended as follows.

8(2) In subsection (2)–

(a)   [amends TMA 1970, s. 107A(2)(a);]

(b)   [amends TMA 1970, s. 107A(2)(c);]

(c)   [amends TMA 1970, s. 107A(2)(d).]

8(3) In subsection (3)–

(a)   [substitutes TMA 1970, s. 107A(3)(a);]

(b)   [amends TMA 1970, s. 107A(3)(b);]

9 [Not relevant to income tax, corporation tax or capital gains tax.]

10 [Omits SI 1989/1297, reg. 3(1)(ab).]

11 [Not relevant to income tax, corporation tax or capital gains tax.]

TAXES, ETC. (FEES FOR PAYMENT BY INTERNET) REGULATIONS 2011

(SI 2011/711)

Made on 9 March 2011 by the Commissioners for Her Majesty's Revenue and Customs, in exercise of the powers conferred by s. 136(1)–(3) of the Finance Act 2008. Operative from 1 April 2011.

CITATION, COMMENCEMENT, EFFECT AND INTERPRETATION

1(1)   These Regulations may be cited as the Taxes, etc. (Fees for Payment by Internet) Regulations 2011.

1(2)   These Regulations come into force on 1st April 2011 and have effect in relation to any payment made by credit card on or after that date where internet authorisation is given to make that payment.

1(3)   In these Regulations **"internet authorisation"** means authorisation given by a credit card issuer via the internet.

FEE PAYABLE WHERE INTERNET AUTHORISATION IS GIVEN TO MAKE A PAYMENT BY CREDIT CARD

2(1)   Where–

(a)   internet authorisation is given for a person to make a payment by credit card, and

(b)   that person makes the payment to the Commissioners or a person authorised by the Commissioners,

the person must also pay a fee of 1.4 % of the amount of that payment.

2(2)   The fee must be paid by being added to the payment (so that, accordingly, the person must make a single overall payment, consisting of the payment and the fee).

2(3)   In these Regulations **"credit card"** means a card which–

(a)   is a credit-token within section 14(1)(b) of the Consumer Credit Act 1974, or

(b)   would be a credit-token falling within that enactment were the card to be given to an individual.

REVOCATION

3   The Taxes (Fees for Payment by Internet) Regulations 2008 are revoked.

QUALIFYING CARE RELIEF (SPECIFIED SOCIAL CARE SCHEMES) ORDER 2011

(SI 2011/712)

Made on 10 March 2011 by the Treasury, in exercise of powers conferred by s. 806A(4) and (5) of the Income Tax (Trading and other Income) Act 2005. Operative from 4 April 2011.

CITATION, COMMENCEMENT AND EFFECT

1(1) This Order may be cited as the Qualifying Care Relief (Specified Social Care Schemes) Order 2011.

1(2) This Order shall come into force on 4th April 2011.

1(3) This Order shall have effect for the tax year 2010–2011 and subsequent tax years.

INTERPRETATION

2 In this Order–

"**L**" is a local authority or a health service body within section 986 (meaning of "health service body") of the Corporation Tax Act 2010.

"**looked after child**" means a child–

(a)   in England and Wales, to whom section 22C (ways in which looked after children are to be accommodated and maintained) of the Children Act 1989 applies,

(b)   in Scotland, to whom section 26 (manner of provision of accommodation to child looked after by a local authority) of the Children (Scotland) Act 1995 applies, and

(c)   in Northern Ireland, to whom Article 27(2) (accommodation and maintenance for children) of the Children (Northern Ireland) Order 1995 applies.

"**section 806A**" means section 806A (meaning of providing shared lives care) of the Income Tax (Trading and Other Income) Act 2005,

"**X**" is a person who, by reason of age, illness, disability or other vulnerability, is in need of care, and

"**Y**" is the individual in section 806A(1).

SPECIFIED SOCIAL CARE SCHEMES: OVERVIEW

3(1) For the purposes of paragraph (c) of subsection (2) of section 806A, a specified social care scheme means a scheme, service or arrangement that provides–

(a)   adult placement care (article 4),

(b)   kinship care (article 5), or

(c)   staying put care (article 6).

SPECIFIED SOCIAL CARE SCHEMES FOR ADULT PLACEMENT CARE

4(1) A specified social care scheme in relation to adult placement care must meet Conditions A to C.

4(2) Condition A is that X is placed with Y.

4(3) Condition B is that Y is–

(a)   in England, an adult placement carer within the meaning of the Health and Social Care Act 2008 (Regulated Activities) Regulations 2010,

(b)   in Wales, an adult placement carer within the meaning of the Adult Placement Schemes (Wales) Regulations 2004,

(c)   in Scotland, a person with whom X has been accommodated by an adult placement service within the meaning of section 47(1)(j) of the Public Services Reform (Scotland) Act 2010, or

(d)   in Northern Ireland, an adult placement carer within the meaning of the Adult Placement Agencies Regulations (Northern Ireland) 2007.

4(4) Condition C is that Y receives payment from L for providing adult placement care to X.

4(5) Until the coming into force of section 47(1)(j) of the Public Services Reform (Scotland) Act 2010, the reference to that provision in sub-paragraph (c) of paragraph 3 is to section 2(16) of the Regulation of Care (Scotland) Act 2001.

SPECIFIED SOCIAL CARE SCHEMES FOR KINSHIP CARE

5(1) A specified social care scheme in relation to kinship care must meet Conditions A to F.

5(2) Condition A is that X has not yet attained 18 years of age.

5(3) Condition B is that X is a looked after child.

5(4) Condition C is that Y receives payment from L for providing kinship care to X.

5(5) Condition D is that Y is—

(a) related to X either by blood, marriage or civil partnership, but is not a parent or step-parent of X, or

(b) known to X and with whom X has a pre-existing relationship.

5(6) Condition E is that Y is regarded by L as a suitable person to care for X.

5(7) Condition F is that, in relation to X, Y is not a person in respect of whom a court has made—

(a) a residence order, or

(b) a special guardianship order.

SPECIFIED SOCIAL CARE SCHEMES FOR STAYING PUT CARE

6(1) A specified social care scheme in relation to staying put care must meet Conditions A to D.

6(2) Condition A is that X is—

(a) in full-time education,

(b) in full-time higher education, or

(c) pursuing full-time vocational training.

6(3) Condition B is that if X is aged 18 years or over, immediately prior to reaching 18 years X was—

(a) subject to a care order, or

(b) a looked after child.

6(4) Condition C is that Y receives payment from L for providing staying put care to X.

6(5) Condition D is that X has a pathway plan.

FINANCE ACT 2010, SCHEDULE 10 (APPOINTED DAYS AND TRANSITIONAL PROVISIONS) ORDER 2011

(SI 2011/975)

Made on 28 March 2011 by the Treasury in exercise of the power conferred by s. 35(2) and (3) of the Finance Act 2010.

CITATION AND INTERPRETATION

1(1) This Order may be cited as the Finance Act 2010, Schedule 10 (Appointed Days and Transitional Provisions) Order 2011.

1(2) In this Order–

"**HMRC**" means Her Majesty's Revenue and Customs; and

"**tax period**" has the same meaning as it has in paragraph 28(g) of Schedule 24 to the Finance Act 2007.

APPOINTED DAYS

2(1) 6th April 2011 is the day appointed for the coming into force of paragraphs 1 to 9 of Schedule 10 to the Finance Act 2010 (penalties: offshore income etc).

2(2) 6th April 2011 is the day appointed for the coming into force of paragraphs 10 to 14 of Schedule 10 to the Finance Act 2010 in relation to a return or other document which–

(a) is required to be made or delivered to HMRC in relation to the tax year 2011–12 or any subsequent tax year, and

(b) falls within item 1, 2 or 3 of the Table in paragraph 1 of Schedule 55 to the Finance Act 2009 (penalty for failure to make returns etc).

TRANSITIONAL PROVISIONS

3 Article 2 of this Order does not have effect in relation to Schedule 24 to the Finance Act 2007 in relation to–

(a) documents given to HMRC, and

(b) assessments issued by HMRC,

in relation to a tax period commencing on or before 5th April 2011.

4 Article 2 of this Order does not have effect in relation to Schedule 41 to the Finance Act 2008 in relation to–

(a) any relevant obligation arising under–

   (i) section 7 of the Taxes Management Act 1970 (notice of liability to income tax and capital gains tax),

   (ii) paragraph 2 of Schedule 18 to the Finance Act 1998 (duty to give notice of chargeability), and

   (iii) paragraphs 5, 6, and 14(2) and (3) of Schedule 1 (registration in respect of taxable supplies), paragraph 3 of Schedule 3 (registration in respect of acquisitions from other member states), and paragraphs 4 and 7(2) and (3) of Schedule 3A (registration in respect of disposals of assets for which a VAT repayment is claimed), to the Value Added Tax Act 1994,

in relation to a tax period commencing on or before 5th April 2011;

(b) all other relevant obligations arising on or before 5th April 2011;

(c) any unauthorised issue of an invoice taking place on or before 5th April 2011;

(d) any act which enables HMRC to assess an amount as duty under a relevant excise provision and which is done on or before 5th April 2011; and

(e) any act giving rise to a penalty under paragraph 4 of Schedule 41 to the Finance Act 2008 (handling goods subject to excise duty) which is done on or before 5th April 2011.

5 Article 2 of this Order does not have effect in relation to Schedule 55 to the Finance Act 2009 in relation to a return or other document which is required to be made or delivered to HMRC in relation to the tax year 2010–11 or any previous tax year.

PENALTIES, OFFSHORE INCOME ETC. (DESIGNATION OF TERRITORIES) ORDER 2011

(SI 2011/976, as amended by SI 2013/1618)

Made on 28 March 2011 by the Treasury in exercise of the powers conferred by para. 21A(1)–(4) of Sch. 24 to the Finance Act 2007. Operative from 6 April 2011.

CITATION AND COMMENCEMENT

1 This Order may be cited as the Penalties, Offshore Income etc. (Designation of Territories) Order 2011 and comes into force on 6th April 2011.

DESIGNATION OF TERRITORIES

2 The territories specified in the left hand column of the Table in the Schedule to this Order are designated as category 1 territories for the purposes of Schedule 24 to the Finance Act 2007 (penalties for errors).

3 The territories specified in the right hand column of the Table in the Schedule to this Order are designated as category 3 territories for the purposes of Schedule 24 to the Finance Act 2007.

SCHEDULE – DESIGNATED TERRITORIES

Articles 2 and 3

Category 1 territories	Category 3 territories
Anguilla	Albania
Aruba	Algeria
Australia	Andorra
Belgium	Bonaire, Sint Eustatius and Saba
Bulgaria	Brazil
Canada	Cameroon
Cayman Islands	Cape Verde
Cyprus	Colombia
Czech Republic	Congo, Republic of the
Denmark (not including, Faroe Islands and Greenland)	Cook Islands
Estonia	Costa Rica
Finland	Curacao
France	Cuba
Germany	Democratic People's Republish of Korea
Greece	Dominican Republic
Guernsey	Ecuador
Hungary	El Salvador
Ireland	Gabon
Isle of Man	Guatemala
Italy	Honduras
Japan	Iran
Korea, South	Iraq
Latvia	Jamaica
Liechtenstein	Kyrgyzstan
Lithuania	Lebanon
Malta	Macau

Category 1 territories

Montserrat

Netherlands (not including Bonaire, Sint Eustatius and Saba)

New Zealand (not including Tokelau)

Norway

Poland

Portugal

Romania

Slovakia

Slovenia

Spain

Sweden

Switzerland

United States of America (not including overseas territories and possessions)

Category 3 territories

Marshall Islands

Micronesia, Federated States of

Monaco

Nauru

Nicaragua

Niue

Palau

Panama

Paraguay

Peru

Seychelles

Sint Maarten

Suriname

Syria

Tokelau

Tonga

Trinidad and Tobago

United Arab Emirates

Uruguay

History – In Table, in "category 1 territories", entries "Liechtenstein" and "Switzerland" inserted by SI 2013/1618, art. 2(2)(a), with effect from 24 July 2013.

In Table, in "category 3 territories", entries "Antigua and Barbuda", "Armenia", "Bahrain", "Barbados", "Belize", "Dominica", "Grenada", "Mauritius", "San Marino", "Saint Kitts and Nevis", "Saint Lucia" and "Saint Vincent and the Grenadines" omitted by SI 2013/1618, art. 2(2)(b), with effect from 24 July 2013.

INTERNATIONAL MUTUAL ADMINISTRATIVE ASSISTANCE IN TAX MATTERS ORDER 2011

(SI 2011/1079)

Made on 7 April 2011 in exercise of the power conferred upon Her Majesty by s. 173(1)–(3) of the Finance Act 2006.

CITATION

1 This Order may be cited as the International Mutual Administrative Assistance in Tax Matters Order 2011.

MUTUAL ADMINISTRATIVE ASSISTANCE ARRANGEMENTS TO HAVE EFFECT

2 It is declared that–

(a) the arrangements relating to international tax enforcement set out in the joint Council of Europe/Organisation for Economic Co-operation and Development Convention on Mutual Administrative Assistance in Tax Matters, as varied by the arrangements specified in the Protocol set out in the Schedule to this Order, have been made with the other signatories, and

(b) it is expedient that the arrangements should have effect.

SKIPTON FUND LIMITED (APPLICATION OF SECTIONS 731, 733 AND 734 OF THE INCOME TAX (TRADING AND OTHER INCOME) ACT 2005) ORDER 2011

(SI 2011/1157, as amended by SI 2012/1188)

Made on 26 April 2011 by the Treasury in exercise of the powers conferred by s. 732(2) of the Income Tax (Trading and Other Income) Act 2005. Operative from 18 May 2011.

CITATION, COMMENCEMENT AND INTERPRETATION

1(1) This Order may be cited as the Skipton Fund Limited (Application of Sections 731, 733 and 734 of the Income Tax (Trading and Other Income) Act 2005) Order 2011 and shall come into force on 18th May 2011.

1(2) In this Order **"Skipton Fund Limited"** and **"Qualifying Person"** have the meanings given in respectively section 731(7) and (8) of the Income Tax (Trading and Other Income) Act 2005 (treated as inserted by article 2(2)(b)).

APPLICATION OF SECTIONS 731, 733 AND 734 OF THE INCOME TAX (TRADING AND OTHER INCOME) ACT 2005

2(1) Sections 731, 733 and 734 of the Income Tax (Trading and Other Income) Act 2005 shall have effect with the following modifications in relation to payments made pursuant to a scheme or arrangement administered by Skipton Fund Limited to a Qualifying Person.

2(2) In section 731 (periodical payments of personal injury damages etc.)–

(a) in subsection (2)–

    (i) the "or" at the end of the paragraph (d) is treated as omitted;

    (ii) after paragraph (e) there is treated as inserted–

", or

    (f) a scheme or arrangement administered by Skipton Fund Limited, so far as it relates to a Qualifying Person.";

(b) after subsection (6) there is treated as inserted–

    "731(7) In this section "Skipton Fund Limited" means the company limited by guarantee of that name (company number 5084964).

    731(8) In this section and sections 733 and 734 **"Qualifying person"** has the meaning given in the agreement entered into between the Secretary of State for Health and Skipton Fund Limited dated 24th March 2011, as amended on 30th April 2012.".

2(3) In section 733(a) (persons entitled to exemption for personal injury payments etc.)–

(a) after "the person" there is treated as inserted "("A") who is a Qualifying Person or who is";

(b) "("A")" is treated as omitted.

2(4) In section 734(1)(a) (payments from trusts for injured persons) after "who is" there is to be treated as inserted "a Qualifying Person or who is".

History – In art. 2(2), the words ", as amended on 30th April 2012" inserted by SI 2012/1188, art. 2, with effect from 23 May 2012.

OFFSHORE FUNDS (TAX) (AMENDMENT) REGULATIONS 2011

(SI 2011/1211, as amended by SI 2013/1411)

Made on 4 May 2011 by the Treasury in exercise of the powers conferred by s. 354 of the Taxation (International and Other Provisions) Act 2010. Operative from 27 May 2011.

PART 1 – INTRODUCTION

CITATION, COMMENCEMENT AND EFFECT

1(1) These Regulations may be cited as the Offshore Funds (Tax) (Amendment) Regulations 2011 and shall come into force on 27th May 2011.

1(2) These Regulations have effect–

(a) for the purposes of income tax for distributions made, or treated as made, on or after 27th May 2011;

(b) for the purposes of corporation tax–

   (i) on chargeable gains, in relation to disposals made on or after that date, and

   (ii) for distributions made, or treated as made, on or after that date;

(c) for the purposes of capital gains tax, in relation to disposals made on or after that date.
This is subject to regulation 16(1).

AMENDMENT OF THE OFFSHORE FUNDS (TAX) REGULATIONS 2009

2 The Offshore Funds (Tax) Regulations 2009 ("the principal Regulations") are amended as follows.

STRUCTURE OF THESE REGULATIONS AND INTERPRETATION

3(1) The structure of these Regulations is as follows–

this Part contains introductory provisions;

Part 2 deals with equalisation arrangements;

Part 3 deals with an exception from the charge to tax in relation to funds investing in certain types of unlisted trading company;

Part 4 deals with transparent funds;

Part 5 makes other amendments to the principal Regulations;

Part 6 makes amendments to primary legislation.

3(2) In these Regulations–

"equalisation arrangements" has the meaning given by regulation 50A of the principal Regulations (inserted by regulation 5 of these Regulations);

"transparent fund" has the same meaning as in regulation 11 of the principal Regulations.

PART 2 – EQUALISATION ARRANGEMENTS

Chapter 1 – Introduction and Amendments to Principal Regulations

INTRODUCTION

4 This Part makes the following provisions in relation to equalisation arrangements–

(a) this Chapter makes amendments to the principal Regulations,

(b) Chapter 2 makes transitional provisions.

INSERTION OF NEW REGULATION 50A (MEANING OF "EQUALISATION ARRANGEMENTS", "FULL EQUALISATION ARRANGEMENTS" AND "EQUALISATION AMOUNT")

5 [Inserts SI 2009/3001, reg. 50A.]

AMENDMENT TO REGULATION 53 (CONTENTS OF AN APPLICATION)

6 [Inserts SI 2009/3001, reg. 53(1)(h)–(l).]

AMENDMENT TO REGULATION 55 (RESPONSE BY HMRC TO APPLICATION)

7(1) Amend regulation 55 (response by HMRC to application) as follows.

7(2) [Amends SI 2009/3001, reg. 55(3).]

7(3) [Inserts SI 2009/3001, reg. 55(3A).]

INSERTION OF CHAPTER 2A (AMENDMENT TO APPLICATION FOR THIS PART TO APPLY)

8 [Inserts SI 2009/3001, Pt. 3, Ch. 2A.]

SUBSTITUTION OF REGULATION 72 (TREATMENT OF REPORTING FUNDS OPERATING EQUALISATION ARRANGEMENTS)

9 [Substitutes SI 2009/3001, reg. 72.]

AMENDMENT TO REGULATION 92 (CONTENTS OF REPORT TO PARTICIPANTS)

10(1) Amend regulation 92 (contents of report to participants) as follows.

10(2) [Inserts SI 2009/3001, reg. 92(1)(f).]

10(3) [Substitutes SI 2009/3001, reg. 92(3)(a), (b) and (ba).]

10(4) [Inserts SI 2009/3001, reg. 92(3A) and (3B).]

INSERTION OF NEW REGULATIONS 92A, 92B AND 92C (FUNDS WHICH DO NOT OPERATE EQUALISATION ARRANGEMENTS)

11 [Inserts SI 2009/3001, reg. 92A, 92B and 92C.]

INSERTION OF REGULATION 94A

12 [Inserts SI 2009/3001, reg. 94A.]

AMENDMENT TO REGULATION 99 (DISPOSALS OF INTERESTS)

13 [Inserts SI 2009/3001, reg. 99(2A).]

Chapter 2 – Transitional Provisions

TRANSITIONAL PROVISIONS: INTRODUCTION

14(1) This Chapter applies to offshore funds which are reporting funds at the date these Regulations come into force.

14(2) In this Chapter a reference to regulation 53(1) or any sub-paragraph of that regulation is a reference to regulation 53(1) (contents of an application) of the principal Regulations as amended by regulation 6 of these Regulations.

14(3) In this Chapter–

"**HMRC**" means Her Majesty's Revenue and Customs;

"**transitional fund**" means a fund to which this Chapter applies.

TRANSITIONAL PROVISIONS: GENERAL PROVISIONS

15(1)   The manager of a transitional fund must give the statements required by sub-paragraphs (h) to (l) of regulation 53(1) by a notice in writing to HMRC within one year of the date these Regulations come into force.

15(2)   A transitional fund will be treated as having operated equalisation arrangements or full equalisation arrangements or as not operating equalisation arrangements in accordance with those statements from the time that the fund first became a reporting fund for the purposes of any report made to participants after the date these Regulations come into force.

This is subject to regulation 16.

History – In reg. 15(2), the words "or full" substituted for the words ", full" by SI 2013/1411, reg. 15, with effect from 28 June 2013.

TRANSITIONAL PROVISIONS: SPECIAL CASES

16(1)   The amendments made by this Part shall not apply in relation to a reporting period which ended before the date these Regulations come into force if the manager of a transitional fund so elects by notice in writing given with the notice under regulation 15(1).

16(2)   If no notice is given under regulation 15(1) or if paragraph (3) applies, a transitional fund shall be treated as having given a statement under regulation 53(1)(k)(i) and be treated from the time that the fund first became a reporting fund as not operating equalisation arrangements and as intending to make adjustments on the basis of reported income.

16(3)   This paragraph applies if–

(a)   a transitional fund has given a statement that it does not intend to operate equalisation arrangements and intends to make income adjustments on the basis of accounting income (see regulation 53(1)(l)), and

(b)   HMRC do not consider that it is reasonable to expect that the difference between the amount of reported income per unit calculated using this method and the amount of reported income per unit calculated on the basis of reported income will be 10% or less of the latter of those amounts.

16(4)   Where paragraph (3) applies HMRC must give notice to the manager of the transitional fund within 28 days of receiving the notice under regulation 15(1).

16(5)   The notice under paragraph (4) must state that paragraph (2) of this regulation applies to the fund.

APPEAL AGAINST A REFUSAL TO ACCEPT A STATEMENT

17(1)   If HMRC give notice under regulation 16(4), the manager of the transitional fund may appeal.

17(2)   The notice of appeal must be given to HMRC within a period of 42 days beginning with the day on which the notice under regulation 16(4) is given.

17(3)   On an appeal, the tribunal may uphold or quash the notice.

17(4)   If the tribunal quashes the notice, this Chapter applies as if regulation 16(3) had never applied.

PART 3 – UNLISTED TRADING COMPANY EXCEPTION

INTRODUCTION

18   This Part inserts a new exception to the charge to tax arising under regulation 17 of the principal Regulations.

INSERTION OF REGULATIONS 31A TO 31C (UNLISTED TRADING COMPANY EXCEPTION)

19   [Inserts SI 2009/3001, reg. 31A, 31B and 31C.]

AMENDMENT TO REGULATION 81 (MEANING OF INVESTMENT TRANSACTION)

20   [Amends SI 2009/3001, reg. 81.]

Statutory Instruments

PART 4 – TRANSPARENT FUNDS

INTRODUCTION

21 This Part makes amendments in relation to transparent funds.

AMENDMENT TO REGULATION 49 (STRUCTURE OF THIS PART)

22(1) Amend regulation 49 (structure of this Part) as follows.

22(2) [Amends heading to SI 2009/3001, reg. 49.]

22(3) [Inserts SI 2009/3001, reg. 49(1)(fa).]

22(4) In paragraph (2)–

(a) [amends SI 2009/3001, reg. 49(2)(a),]

(b) [inserts SI 2009/3001, reg. 49(2)(aa).]

22(5) [Inserts SI 2009/3001, reg. 49(3).]

AMENDMENT TO REGULATION 58 (GENERAL DUTIES OF REPORTING FUNDS)

23(1) Amend regulation 58 (general duties of reporting funds) as follows.

23(2) [Amends SI 2009/3001, reg. 58(a).]

23(3) [Amends SI 2009/3001, reg. 58(b).]

INSERTION OF NEW CHAPTER 6A IN PART 3

24 [Inserts SI 2009/3001, Pt. 3, Ch. 6A.]

AMENDMENT TO REGULATION 92 (CONTENTS OF REPORT TO PARTICIPANTS)

25(1) Amend regulation 92 (contents of report to participants) as follows.

25(2) [Amends heading to SI 2009/3001, reg. 92.]

25(3) [Amends SI 2009/3001, reg. 92(1).]

INSERTION OF REGULATION 92D (CONTENTS OF REPORTS TO PARTICIPANTS: TRANSPARENT REPORTING FUNDS)

26 [Inserts SI 2009/3001, reg. 92D.]

AMENDMENT TO REGULATION 106 (REPORTING REQUIREMENTS)

27 In regulation 106 (reporting requirements) in paragraph (1)–

(a) [amends SI 2009/3001, reg. 106(1)(a),]

(b) [amends SI 2009/3001, reg. 106(1)(b),]

(c) [amends SI 2009/3001, reg. 106(1)(c).]

PART 5 – MISCELLANEOUS AMENDMENTS

AMENDMENT TO REGULATION 4 (CLASSIFICATION OF OFFSHORE FUNDS)

28 In regulation 4 (classification of offshore funds) in paragraph (2)–

(a) [amends SI 2009/3001, reg. 4(2),]

(b) [amends SI 2009/3001, reg. 4(2).]

AMENDMENT TO REGULATION 12 (GENERAL INTERPRETATION)

29 [Amends SI 2009/3001, reg. 12.]

AMENDMENT TO REGULATION 16 (TREATMENT OF CERTAIN AMOUNTS AS DISTRIBUTIONS)

30 [Amends SI 2009/3001, reg. 16.]

AMENDMENT TO REGULATION 54 (FORM, TIMING AND WITHDRAWAL OF APPLICATION)

31 [Substitutes SI 2009/3001, reg. 54(2) and (3).]

AMENDMENT TO REGULATION 57 (EFFECTS OF ENTRY INTO THE REPORTING FUND REGIME)

32(1) Amend regulation 57 (effects of entry into the reporting fund regime) as follows.

32(2) [Amends SI 2009/3001, reg. 57(1).]

32(3) [Inserts SI 2009/3001, reg. 57(2).]

AMENDMENT TO REGULATION 67 (INCOME FROM WHOLLY-OWNED SUBSIDIARIES)

33 In regulation 67 (income from wholly-owned subsidiaries) in paragraph (2)–

(a)   [amends SI 2009/3001, reg. 67(2)(a),]

(b)   [amends SI 2009/3001, reg. 67(2)(b).]

AMENDMENT TO REGULATION 68 (INCOME FROM OTHER REPORTING FUNDS)

34(1) Amend regulation 68 (income from other reporting funds) as follows.

34(2) [Amends SI 2009/3001, reg. 68(3).]

34(3) [Omits SI 2009/3001, reg. 68(4).]

34(4) [Amends SI 2009/3001, reg. 68(5).]

INSERTION OF NEW REGULATION 68A (INDEX TRACKING FUNDS)

35 [Inserts SI 2009/3001, reg. 68A.]

AMENDMENT TO REGULATION 69 (INCOME FROM NON-REPORTING FUNDS: FIRST CASE)

36(1) Amend regulation 69 (income from non-reporting funds: first case) as follows.

36(2) [Omits SI 2009/3001, reg. 69(2)(a).]

36(3) [Amends SI 2009/3001, reg. 69(3).]

36(4) [Inserts SI 2009/3001, reg. 69(5) and (6).]

AMENDMENT TO REGULATION 74 (THE EQUIVALENCE CONDITION)

37(1) Amend regulation 74 (the equivalence condition) as follows.

37(2) [Amends SI 2009/3001, reg. 74(1).]

37(3) [Inserts SI 2009/3001, reg. 74(4) and (5).]

AMENDMENT TO REGULATION 75 (THE GENUINE DIVERSITY OF OWNERSHIP CONDITION)

38(1) Amend regulation 75 (the genuine diversity of ownership condition) as follows.

38(2) [Amends SI 2009/3001, reg. 75(1).]

38(3) [Inserts SI 2009/3001, reg. 74(5).]

AMENDMENT TO REGULATION 90 (REPORT TO PARTICIPANTS FOR A REPORTING PERIOD)

39(1) Amend regulation 90 (report to participants for a reporting period) as follows.

39(2) In the following places before "participant" insert "relevant"–

(a)   [amends SI 2009/3001, reg. 90(1);]

(b)   [amends SI 2009/3001, reg. 90(2)(a) and (b);]

(c)   [amends SI 2009/3001, reg. 90(4).]

39(3) [Amends SI 2009/3001, reg. 90(3).]

Statutory Instruments

AMENDMENT TO REGULATION 94 (REPORTED INCOME: GENERAL PROVISIONS)

40(1)   Amend regulation 94 (reported income: general provisions) as follows.

40(2)   [Amends SI 2009/3001, reg. 94(2A).]

40(3)   [Amends SI 2009/3001, reg. 94(3).]

40(4)   [Inserts SI 2009/3001, reg. 94(3A).]

40(5)   [Amends SI 2009/3001, reg. 94(4).]

AMENDMENT TO REGULATION 106 (REPORTING REQUIREMENTS)

41(1)   Amend regulation 106 (reporting requirements) as follows.

41(2)   [Amends SI 2009/3001, reg. 106(1)(a).]

41(3)   [Inserts SI 2009/3001, reg. 106(3).]

AMENDMENT TO SCHEDULE 1 (TRANSITIONAL PROVISIONS AND SAVINGS)

42(1)   In Schedule 1 (transitional provisions and savings) amend paragraph 3 as follows.

42(2)   [Substitutes SI 2009/3001, Sch. 1, para. 3(2), (3) and (3ZA).]

42(3)   [Amends SI 2009/3001, Sch. 1, para. 3(3B).]

AMENDMENT TO SCHEDULE 3 (ABBREVIATIONS AND DEFINED EXPRESSIONS)

43(1)   Amend Schedule 3 (abbreviations and defined expressions) as follows.

43(2)   [Amends SI 2009/3001, Sch. 3, Pt. 1.]

43(3)   In Part 2 (index of expressions defined or otherwise explained in these Regulations)–

(a)   [amends SI 2009/3001, Sch. 3, Pt. 2,]

(b)   [amends SI 2009/3001, Sch. 3, Pt. 2.]

PART 6 – AMENDMENTS TO PRIMARY LEGISLATION

AMENDMENT TO THE TAXATION OF CHARGEABLE GAINS ACT 1992

44(1)   Amend the Taxation of Chargeable Gains Act 1992 as follows.

44(2)   In section 103A (application of Act to certain offshore funds)–

(a)   [amends TCGA 1992, s. 103A(2)(a),]

(b)   [substitutes TCGA 1992, s. 103A(3),]

44(3)   [Inserts TCGA 1992, s. 103B.]

44(4)   [Amends TCGA 1992, s. 106A(10).]

AMENDMENT TO THE CORPORATION TAX ACT 2009

45   [Amends CTA 2009, s. 490(7).]

TAXATION OF EQUITABLE LIFE (PAYMENTS) ORDER 2011

(SI 2011/1502)

Made on 15 June 2011 by the Treasury in exercise of the powers conferred by s. 1(3) and (4) of the Equitable Life (Payments) Act 2010. Operative from 16 June 2011.

Other material – HMRC Brief 26/11: The Equitable Life Payment Scheme: tax and tax credit implications.

CITATION, COMMENCEMENT, EFFECT AND INTERPRETATION

1(1) This Order may be cited as the Taxation of Equitable Life (Payments) Order 2011 and shall come into force on the day after the day on which it is made.

1(2) This Order has effect in relation to authorised payments made after the day on which this Order is made.

1(3) In this Order **"authorised payment"** means a payment to which section 1 of the Equitable Life (Payments) Act 2010 applies.

CAPITAL GAINS TAX

2 An authorised payment shall be disregarded for the purposes of capital gains tax.

CORPORATION TAX

3 An authorised payment shall be disregarded for the purposes of the Corporation Tax Acts.

INCOME TAX

4 An authorised payment shall be disregarded for the purposes of the Income Tax Acts.

INHERITANCE TAX

5 [Not relevant to income tax, corporation tax or capital gains tax.]

TAX CREDITS

6 [Not relevant to income tax, corporation tax or capital gains tax.]

REGISTERED PENSION SCHEMES (LIFETIME ALLOWANCE TRANSITIONAL PROTECTION) REGULATIONS 2011

(SI 2011/1752, as amended by SI 2013/1740)

Made on 20 July 2011 by the Commissioners for Her Majesty's Revenue and Customs in exercise of the powers conferred by para. 14(2) and (15) of Sch. 18 to the Finance Act 2011 and s. 251(1) of the Finance Act 2004. Operative from 11 August 2011.

CITATION, COMMENCEMENT AND INTERPRETATION

1 These Regulations may be cited as the Registered Pension Schemes (Lifetime Allowance Transitional Protection) Regulations 2011 and shall come into force on 11th August 2011.

2 In these Regulations—

   "paragraph 14" means paragraph 14 of Schedule 18 to the Finance Act 2011;

   "paragraph 14(4) event" means an event described in sub-paragraph (4) of paragraph 14;

   "paragraph 14 notice" means a notice of an intention to rely on paragraph 14; and

   "tribunal" means the First-tier Tribunal or, where determined in accordance with the Tribunal Procedure (First-tier Tribunal) (Tax Chamber) Rules 2009, the Upper Tribunal.

RELIANCE ON PARAGRAPH 14

3(1) Subject to paragraph (2), an individual may rely on paragraph 14 if—

(a) the individual has given a paragraph 14 notice to Her Majesty's Revenue and Customs, and

(b) Her Majesty's Revenue and Customs have accepted that notice by issuing a certificate to the individual.

3(2) An individual may not rely on paragraph 14 if—

(a) Her Majesty's Revenue and Customs have refused to accept a paragraph 14 notice in accordance with regulation 6,

(b) Her Majesty's Revenue and Customs have revoked the certificate in accordance with regulation 11, or

(c) a paragraph 14(4) event has occurred.

THE PARAGRAPH 14 NOTICE

4(1) A paragraph 14 notice must include the following information—

(a) the title, full name, address (including post code, if applicable) and date of birth of the individual submitting the paragraph 14 notice,

(b) the national insurance number of the individual or, where the individual does not qualify for a national insurance number, the reasons for this,

(c) a declaration that paragraph 7 of Schedule 36 to the Finance Act 2004 (primary protection) does not make provision for a lifetime allowance enhancement factor in the case of the individual, and

(d) a declaration that paragraph 12 of that Schedule (enhanced protection) will not apply in relation to the individual on and after 6th April 2012.

4(2) A paragraph 14 notice must be—

(a) in a form prescribed by Her Majesty's Revenue and Customs, and

(b) received by Her Majesty's Revenue and Customs on or before the following dates—

   (i) if it relates to an individual described in sub-paragraph (1) of paragraph 14, 5 April 2012; or

   (ii) if it relates to an individual described in sub-paragraph (1A) of paragraph 14, 5 April 2014.

4(3) The individual must sign and date the paragraph 14 notice.

History – Reg. 4(2)(b) substituted by SI 2013/1740, reg. 3(2), with effect from 12 August 2013. Former reg. 4(2)(b) read as follows:

   "(b)   received by Her Majesty's Revenue and Customs on or before 5th April 2012.".

ISSUE OF CERTIFICATE BY HER MAJESTY'S REVENUE AND CUSTOMS

5(1) If Her Majesty's Revenue and Customs accept the paragraph 14 notice, they must issue a certificate to the individual.

5(2) The certificate must have a unique reference number.

REFUSAL BY HER MAJESTY'S REVENUE AND CUSTOMS TO ACCEPT NOTICE

6(1) Her Majesty's Revenue and Customs may refuse to accept the paragraph 14 notice if it does not satisfy the requirements in regulation 4.

6(2) If Her Majesty's Revenue and Customs refuse to accept the paragraph 14 notice the individual may require that Her Majesty's Revenue and Customs provide reasons for the refusal.

APPEAL AGAINST REFUSAL TO ACCEPT NOTICE

7(1) The individual may appeal against a refusal by Her Majesty's Revenue and Customs to accept the paragraph 14 notice.

7(2) The notice of appeal must be given to Her Majesty's Revenue and Customs before the end of the period of 30 days beginning with the day on which the refusal to accept the paragraph 14 notice was given.

7(3) Where an appeal under this regulation is notified to the tribunal, the tribunal must determine whether Her Majesty's Revenue and Customs were entitled to take the view that the notice did not satisfy the requirements in regulation 4.

7(4) If the tribunal allows the appeal, the tribunal may direct Her Majesty's Revenue and Customs to accept the paragraph 14 notice and issue a certificate to the individual.

INCORRECT INFORMATION GIVEN IN, OR IN CONNECTION WITH, THE PARAGRAPH 14 NOTICE

8 If the individual realises that any information given in the paragraph 14 notice or given to Her Majesty's Revenue and Customs in connection with that notice was incorrect or has become incorrect, the individual must provide Her Majesty's Revenue and Customs with the correct information without undue delay.

REQUIREMENT TO INFORM HER MAJESTY'S REVENUE AND CUSTOMS OF A PARAGRAPH 14(4) EVENT

9 Where Her Majesty's Revenue and Customs have issued a certificate the individual must–

(a) inform Her Majesty's Revenue and Customs when a paragraph 14(4) event occurs, and

(b) provide that information before the end of the period of 90 days beginning with the day on which the event occurred.

REPLACEMENT OF A CERTIFICATE BY HER MAJESTY'S REVENUE AND CUSTOMS

10(1) Her Majesty's Revenue and Customs may issue a certificate, replacing the previous certificate, if they have reason to believe that information given in, or in connection with, the paragraph 14 notice was incorrect or has become incorrect.

10(2) A certificate issued in accordance with regulation 10(1) must have a unique reference number.

REVOCATION OF A CERTIFICATE BY HER MAJESTY'S REVENUE AND CUSTOMS

11 Her Majesty's Revenue and Customs may revoke a certificate if they–

(a) have reason to believe that a paragraph 14(4) event has occurred,

(b) have reason to believe that any of the conditions in sub-paragraph (1) of paragraph 14 have not been met, or

(c) have given notice to the individual under paragraph 1 of Schedule 36 to the Finance Act 2008 in connection with paragraph 14 and the individual does not reply to that notice within the time specified in the notice.

APPEAL AGAINST REVOCATION OR REPLACEMENT OF A CERTIFICATE

12(1) The individual may require Her Majesty's Revenue and Customs to provide reasons for revoking or replacing the certificate.

12(2) Paragraphs (1) and (2) of regulation 7 apply to a decision to revoke or replace the certificate as they apply to the refusal to accept the paragraph 14 notice.

12(3) Where an appeal under this regulation is notified to the tribunal, the tribunal must determine whether Her Majesty's Revenue and Customs replaced or revoked the certificate in accordance with regulations 10(1) or 11.

12(4) If the tribunal allows the appeal, the tribunal may direct Her Majesty's Revenue and Customs to issue a certificate to the individual.

PRESERVATION OF DOCUMENTS

13(1) Where Her Majesty's Revenue and Customs have issued a certificate the individual must preserve the certificate until no further benefit crystallisation event can occur in relation to the individual.

13(2) The requirement to preserve the certificate ceases where the certificate has been revoked.

History – In reg. 13(1), the words "in relation to any sums or assets held for the purposes of a registered pension scheme" omitted by SI 2013/1740, reg. 3(3), with effect from 12 August 2013.

REGISTERED PENSION SCHEMES (RELEVANT INCOME) REGULATIONS 2011

(SI 2011/1783)

Made on 20 July 2011 by the Treasury, in exercise of the powers conferred by para. 14B(2)(b) and 24D(2)(b) of Sch. 28 to, and s. 282(A1) of, the Finance Act 2004. Operative from 11 August 2011.

CITATION, COMMENCEMENT AND EFFECT

1(1) These Regulations may be cited as the Registered Pension Schemes (Relevant Income) Regulations 2011 and come into force on 11th August 2011.

1(2) These Regulations have effect for the tax year beginning on 6th April 2011 and subsequent tax years.

PAYMENTS NOT TO BE REGARDED AS RELEVANT INCOME

2 The payments described in regulations 3 and 4 are not to be regarded as relevant income for the purpose of ascertaining whether a member or dependant satisfies the minimum income requirement in paragraphs 14A(1) or 24C(1) of Schedule 28 to the Finance Act 2004.

3(1) Payments of a scheme pension payable by the scheme administrator and made in respect of a defined benefits arrangement where the pension scheme under which that arrangement is made has fewer than 20 pensioner members unless the payments fall within paragraph (4) or (5).

3(2) Payments of a scheme pension made in respect of a money purchase arrangement and payable by the scheme administrator where fewer than 20 pensioner members of the pension scheme under which that arrangement is made are entitled to payment of such a scheme pension unless the payments fall within paragraph (4) or (6).

3(3) Payments under an overseas pension scheme which, if the scheme were a registered pension scheme would fall within paragraph (1) or (2).

3(4) Paragraphs (1) and (2) do not apply in the case of payments of a scheme pension payable under an annuity contract where that annuity contract is made with an insurance company or a non-EEA annuity provider and was purchased by the application of sums and assets held for the purposes of–

(a)   a registered pension scheme

(b)   an overseas pension scheme, or

(c)   if the purchase took place before 6th April 2006 a pension scheme which at the time of purchase fell within one of the categories set out in paragraph 1(1)(a) to (g) of Schedule 36.

3(5) Paragraph (1) does not apply in the case of payments of a scheme pension or dependants' scheme pension payable in respect of a defined benefits arrangement where–

(a)   the pension scheme under which that arrangement was made ("the relevant pension scheme") had 20 or more members in relation to whom a defined benefits arrangement was in existence on or before 5th April 2011, and

(b)   the defined benefits arrangement under the relevant pension scheme was in existence in relation to the member on or before 5th April 2011.

3(6) Paragraph (2) does not apply in the case of payments of a scheme pension payable under an annuity contract where that annuity contract is treated as having become a registered pension scheme under section 153(8A) of the Finance Act 2004.

3(7) For the purposes of this regulation a **"non-EEA annuity provider"** means a person resident in a country or territory outside the European Economic Area–

(a)   whose normal business includes the provision of annuities; and

(b)   who is regulated in the conduct of that business by–

     (i)   the government of that country or territory, or

     (ii)   a body established under the law of that country or territory for the purpose of regulating such business.

4(1) Excess payments of a lifetime annuity or dependants' annuity unless the payments fall within paragraph (4).

4(2) Excess payments are payments that exceed the amount of the minimum annuity guaranteed to be paid each year under the annuity contract for the annuity over its full term.

4(3) For the purposes of this regulation **"full term"** means the minimum period over which a lifetime annuity or a dependants' annuity must be payable in accordance with the applicable provision of paragraphs 3(1), 17(1)(d) or (e) of Schedule 28 to the Finance Act 2004.

4(4) Paragraph (1) does not apply to payments of a lifetime or dependants' annuity where the annual amount of the annuity—

(a)   cannot decrease, or

(b)   is determined in accordance with the manner prescribed in regulation 2(2)(a)(i) (variation in line with the RPI) of the Registered Pension Schemes (Prescribed Manner of Determining Amount of Annuities) Regulations 2006.

CORPORATION TAX ACT 2010 (FACTORS DETERMINING SUBSTANTIAL COMMERCIAL INTERDEPENDENCE) ORDER 2011

(SI 2011/1784)

Made on 20 July 2011 by the Treasury, in exercise of the powers conferred by s. 27(3) of the Corporation Tax Act 2010 and s. 55(5) of the Finance Act 2011. Operative from 11 August 2011.

CITATION, COMMENCEMENT AND EFFECT

1(1) This Order may be cited as the Corporation Tax Act 2010 (Factors Determining Substantial Commercial Interdependence) Order 2011.

1(2) This Order shall come into force on 11th August 2011.

1(3) This Order shall have effect for accounting periods ending on or after 1st April 2011.

FACTORS TAKEN INTO ACCOUNT IN DETERMINING SUBSTANTIAL COMMERCIAL INTERDEPENDENCE

2 In determining for the purposes of section 27 of the Corporation Tax Act 2010 (attribution to persons of rights and powers of their associates) whether a relationship between two companies amounts to **"substantial commercial interdependence"**, the following factors are to be taken into account–

(a)   the degree to which the companies are financially interdependent,

(b)   the degree to which the companies are economically interdependent, and

(c)   the degree to which the companies are organisationally interdependent.

"FINANCIALLY INTERDEPENDENT"

3 Two companies are **"financially interdependent"** for the purposes of article 2 if (in particular)–

(a)   one gives financial support (directly or indirectly) to the other, or

(b)   each has a financial interest in the affairs of the same business.

"ECONOMICALLY INTERDEPENDENT"

4 Two companies are **"economically interdependent"** for the purposes of article 2 if (in particular)–

(a)   the companies seek to realise the same economic objective,

(b)   the activities of one benefit the other, or

(c)   the companies have common customers.

"ORGANISATIONALLY INTERDEPENDENT"

5 Two companies are **"organisationally interdependent"** for the purposes of article 2 if (in particular) the businesses of the companies have or use–

(a)   common management,

(b)   common employees,

(c)   common premises, or

(d)   common equipment.

REGISTERED PENSION SCHEMES (MODIFICATION OF SCHEME RULES) REGULATIONS 2011

(SI 2011/1791)

Made on 20 July 2011 by the Commissioners for Her Majesty's Revenue and Customs, in exercise of the power conferred by s. 237F of the Finance Act 2004. Operative from 11 August 2011.

CITATION AND COMMENCEMENT

1 These Regulations may be cited as the Registered Pension Schemes (Modification of Scheme Rules) Regulations 2011 and come into force on 11th August 2011.

MODIFICATION OF SCHEME RULES

2(1) This regulation applies where a scheme administrator of a registered pension scheme ("the scheme") satisfies all or part of a member's liability to the annual allowance charge, either on a voluntary basis or pursuant to a liability under section 237B of the Finance Act 2004.

2(2) The rules of the scheme shall be modified so as to allow for a consequential adjustment to be made to the entitlement of the member to benefits under the scheme on a basis that is just and reasonable having regard to normal actuarial practice. This paragraph is subject to paragraph (3).

2(3) Any modification to the scheme's rules made by virtue of paragraph (2) is subject to section 159 of the Pension Schemes Act 1993 or section 155 of the Pension Schemes (Northern Ireland) Act 1993 (inalienability of guaranteed minimum pension etc).

REGISTERED PENSION SCHEMES (PRESCRIBED REQUIREMENTS OF FLEXIBLE DRAWDOWN DECLARATION) REGULATIONS 2011

(SI 2011/1792)

Made on 20 July 2011 by the Commissioners for Her Majesty's Revenue and Customs, in exercise of the powers conferred by s. 251(1)(a), (4)(b), (5) and 282(A1) of, and para. 14E(1) and 24G(1) of Sch. 28 to, the Finance Act 2004 and now exercisable by them. Operative from 11 August 2011.

CITATION, COMMENCEMENT AND EFFECT

1(1) These Regulations may be cited as the Registered Pensions Schemes (Prescribed Requirements of Flexible Drawdown Declaration) Regulations 2011 and come into force on 11th August 2011.

1(2) These Regulations have effect for the tax year 2011–12 and subsequent years.

PRESCRIBED REQUIREMENTS OF VALID DECLARATION

2(1) Paragraphs (2) and (3) of this regulation provide for the prescribed requirements of a valid declaration made under sections 165(3A)(b) or 167(2A)(b) of the Finance Act 2004.

2(2) The declaration must be signed and dated by the member or dependant ("the member") and contain–

(a)   the information specified in paragraph (3);

(b)   a statement confirming that the flexible drawdown conditions are met;

(c)   a statement confirming that the contents of the declaration are correct and complete to the best of the member's knowledge and belief, and

(d)   (where sections 165(3A) or 167(2A) have previously applied to an arrangement relating to the member), a statement confirming that the declaration referred to in either of those subsections, was accepted by the scheme administrator of the registered pension scheme under which the arrangement was made.

2(3) The specified information is–

(a)   the member's full name;

(b)   the member's sole or main address;

(c)   the member's national insurance number (unless regulation 3 applies);

(d)   details of each source of relevant income payable to the member for the tax year in respect of which the minimum income requirement is satisfied ("the declaration year"), including the name and address of the person responsible for making the payments of the relevant income; and

(e)   the total amount of relevant pension income payable in respect of the source referred to in paragraph (d) for the declaration year.

PROCEDURE WHERE THE MEMBER DOES NOT QUALIFY FOR A NATIONAL INSURANCE NUMBER

3(1) This paragraph applies where a member does not qualify for a national insurance number and wishes to make a valid declaration under sections 165(3A)(b) or 167(2A)(b) of the Finance Act 2004.

3(2) The member must provide written confirmation to the scheme administrator that the member does not qualify for a national insurance number together with details of any unique tax references relating to the member (if available).

3(3) The scheme administrator must then provide Her Majesty's Revenue and Customs with the information referred to in paragraph (2) which has been received from the member together with the member's date of birth and address.

REGISTERED PENSION SCHEMES (NOTICE OF JOINT LIABILITY FOR THE ANNUAL ALLOWANCE CHARGE) REGULATIONS 2011

(SI 2011/1793)

Made on 20 July 2011 by the Commissioners for Her Majesty's Revenue and Customs, in exercise of the powers conferred by s. 237B(5)(b) and (c) and 251(4)(a) of the Finance Act 2004 and now exercisable by them. Operative from 11 August 2011.

Statutory Instruments

CITATION, COMMENCEMENT AND INTERPRETATION

1(1) These Regulations may be cited as the Registered Pension Schemes (Notice of Joint Liability for the Annual Allowance Charge) Regulations 2011 and shall come into force on 11th August 2011.

1(2) In these Regulations–

"**the further notice**" means a notice given by an individual to a scheme administrator in accordance with regulation 4;

"**the notice**" means a notice given by an individual to a scheme administrator in accordance with section 237B(3) of the Finance Act 2004; and

"**relevant tax year**" means the tax year to which the notice relates.

PARTICULARS TO BE INCLUDED IN THE NOTICE

2(1) An individual must include the following particulars in the notice–

(a)   the individual's title, full name and address (including post code, if applicable),

(b)   the individual's national insurance number, subject to paragraph (4),

(c)   the amount of the annual allowance charge for which the individual and the scheme administrator will be jointly and severally liable, and

(d)   the tax year in which the annual allowance charge arises.

2(2) Where the amount specified in the notice is £2,000 or less, the individual must confirm in the notice that the amount of the individual's liability to the annual allowance charge for the relevant tax year exceeds £2,000.

2(3) Where the notice is given to the scheme administrator in the relevant tax year and it is anticipated that in the relevant tax year–

(a)   the individual will become entitled to all of the benefits under the pension scheme to which the notice relates ("the relevant scheme"), or

(b)   benefit crystallisation events 5, 5A or 5B will occur in relation to the individual under the relevant scheme,

the individual must state in the notice the date on which it is anticipated that the event specified in sub-paragraph (a) or (b) will occur.

2(4) Where the individual does not qualify for a national insurance number the individual must set out in the notice the reasons for this in place of the national insurance number.

2(5) The notice must be in writing, signed and dated by the individual.

2(6) Where the notice is in an electronic format, the requirement in paragraph (5) that the notice must be signed will be satisfied if the notice includes a statement that the individual has personally submitted the notice.

DECLARATION TO BE INCLUDED IN THE NOTICE

3(1) The individual must declare in the notice that the individual understands that–

(a)   the notice cannot be revoked, and

(b)   future benefits to be paid to the individual from the pension scheme will be adjusted to take account of the payment of the annual allowance charge made by the scheme administrator.

3(2) The individual must declare that the amount specified in the notice has been calculated at the correct relevant rate as described in section 237B(4) of the Finance Act 2004.

AMENDMENT TO THE NOTICE

4(1)   Where the individual's liability to the annual allowance charge in relation to the relevant tax year changes after the submission of the notice to the scheme administrator, the individual may amend the notice by sending a further notice to the scheme administrator.

4(2)   The further notice must comply with regulations 2 and 3.

4(3)   The further notice must be given to the scheme administrator no later than 31st July following the end of the period of 4 years beginning with the last day of the relevant tax year.

ACKNOWLEDGEMENT OF RECEIPT OF THE NOTICE AND FURTHER NOTICE

5   A scheme administrator must send an acknowledgement to the individual upon receipt of the notice or further notice.

EMPLOYER SUPPORTED CHILDCARE (RELEVANT EARNINGS AND EXCLUDED AMOUNTS) REGULATIONS 2011

(SI 2011/1798)

Made on 20 July 2011 by the Treasury, in exercise of the powers conferred by s. 270B(3)(b) and (4) of the Income Tax (Earnings and Pensions) Act 2003 and para. 9 of Sch. 8 to the Finance Act 2011. Operative from 11 August 2011.

CITATION, COMMENCEMENT AND EFFECT

1 These Regulations may be cited as the Employer Supported Childcare (Relevant Earnings and Excluded Amounts) Regulations 2011 and come into force on 11th August 2011 with effect from 6th April 2011.

INTERPRETATION

2 In these Regulations—

"**ITEPA**" means the Income Tax (Earnings and Pensions) Act 2003;

"**PAYE Regulations**" means the Income Tax (Pay As You Earn) Regulations 2003.

RELEVANT EARNINGS

3 For the purposes of section 270B(1)(a) of ITEPA "**relevant earnings**" (in addition to salary, wages or fees as in section 270B(3)(a)) means—

(a) guaranteed contractual bonuses;

(b) contractual commission;

(c) guaranteed overtime payments;

(d) location or cost of living allowances;

(e) shift allowances;

(f) skills allowances;

(g) retention and recruitment allowances; and

(h) market rate supplements.

EXCLUDED AMOUNTS

4(1) For the purposes of section 270B(1)(b) of ITEPA "**excluded amounts**" means—

(a) contributions under a pension scheme if the employee has authorised the employer to make the deductions from relevant payments (as defined by regulation 4 of the PAYE Regulations) for which relief at source is given under section 192(1) of the Finance Act 2004;

(b) contributions under a pension scheme allowed under section 193(2) of the Finance Act 2004 (relief under net pay arrangements) to be deducted by the employer from the employee's employment income for the tax year in accordance with the PAYE Regulations;

(c) donations for which a deduction is made under section 713 of ITEPA (payroll giving) in calculating the employee's net taxable earnings from employment by the employer for the tax year in accordance with the PAYE Regulations;

(d) expenses within Chapter 3 of Part 3 of ITEPA (expenses payments) which the employer is authorised to exclude from the employee's taxable earnings for the tax year in accordance with the PAYE Regulations;

(e) payments in respect of removal expenses to which section 271 of ITEPA applies (as defined in section 272 of ITEPA) and which are taxable earnings of the employee from employment by the employer for the tax year;

(f) amounts equivalent to the amount of the personal allowance under section 35(1) of the Income Tax Act 2007, and in addition if applicable, the amount of the blind person's allowance under section 38 of the Income Tax Act 2007.

4(2) Paragraph (1)(f) does not apply if after taking into account any relevant earnings and excluded amounts in paragraph (1)(a) to (e) the relevant earnings amount is £150,000 or more.

TAXES AND DUTIES, ETC (INTEREST RATE) REGULATIONS 2011

(SI 2011/2446)

Made on 10 October 2011 by the Treasury in exercise of the powers conferred by s. 103 of the Finance Act 2009. Operative from 31 October 2011.

CITATION AND COMMENCEMENT

1 These Regulations may be cited as the Taxes and Duties, etc (Interest Rate) Regulations 2011 and come into force on 31st October 2011.

INTERPRETATION

2 In these Regulations–

"**Bank of England**" rate means the official bank rate as announced at the relevant meeting;

"**operative date**" means the 13th working day following the relevant meeting;

"**relevant meeting**" means the most recent meeting of the Bank of England Monetary Policy Committee;

"**working day**" means any day other than a non-business day within the meaning of section 92 of the Bills of Exchange Act 1882.

LATE PAYMENT INTEREST RATE

3(1) Except where regulation 5 applies, the late payment interest rate for the purposes of section 101 of the Finance Act 2009 (late payment interest on sums due to HMRC), is the percentage per annum found by applying the following formula–

Bank of England rate + 2.5.

3(2) The interest rate found under paragraph (1) applies on and after the operative date.

REPAYMENT INTEREST RATE

4(1) Except where regulation 5 applies, the repayment interest rate for the purposes of section 102 of the Finance Act 2009 (repayment interest on sums to be paid by HMRC), is the higher of–

(a)   0.5% per annum; and

(b)   the percentage per annum found by applying the following formula–

Bank of England rate − 1.

4(2) The interest rate found under paragraph (1) applies on and after the operative date.

INITIAL RATES OF INTEREST

5(1) This regulation applies immediately on the coming into force of these Regulations until the first operative date after the coming into force of these Regulations.

5(2) The late payment interest rate and repayment interest rate shall be the respective percentages per annum found by applying regulation 3(1) and regulation 4(1) as if the references in those regulations to the Bank of England rate were references to the official bank rate announced at the meeting of the Bank of England Monetary Policy Committee on, or most recently before, the 13th working day before the coming into force of these Regulations.

EFFECT OF CHANGE IN RATES OF INTEREST

6 Where the late payment interest rate or repayment interest rate changes in accordance with these Regulations with effect from an operative date, the change has effect in respect of interest running from before that date as well as interest running from or after that date.

EARLIER INSTRUMENT REVOKED

7 The Taxes and Duties (Interest Rate) Regulations 2010 are revoked.

EMPLOYMENT INCOME PROVIDED THROUGH THIRD PARTIES (EXCLUDED RELEVANT STEPS) REGULATIONS 2011

(SI 2011/2696)

Made on 9 November 2011 by the Commissioners for Her Majesty's Revenue and Customs, in exercise of the powers conferred by s. 554Y of the Income Tax (Earnings and Pensions) Act 2003. Operative from 6 December 2011.

CITATION, COMMENCEMENT AND APPLICATION

1(1) These Regulations may be cited as the Employment Income Provided Through Third Parties (Excluded Relevant Steps) Regulations 2011 and come into force on 6th December 2011.

1(2) The Regulations have effect in relation to relevant steps taken on and after 9th December 2010.

INTERPRETATION

2 In these Regulations–

"**Part 7A**" means Part 7A of the Income Tax (Earnings and Pensions) Act 2003 (employment income provided through third parties); and

"**relevant non-UK scheme**" means a scheme within paragraph 1(5) of Schedule 34 to FA 2004.

DISAPPLICATION OF CHAPTER 2 OF PART 7A: RELEVANT STEPS ARISING OR DERIVING FROM UK TAX-RELIEVED FUNDS AND RELEVANT TRANSFER FUNDS

3(1) Chapter 2 of Part 7A (treatment of relevant steps for income tax purposes) does not apply by reason of a relevant step if the subject of the relevant step is a sum of money or asset which represents or which has (wholly or partly) arisen or derived (directly or indirectly) from a sum of money or assets which represents or has represented–

(a) a UK tax-relieved fund under a relevant non-UK scheme, or

(b) a relevant transfer fund under a relevant non-UK scheme.

3(2) Paragraph (3) applies if the sum of money or asset which is the subject of the relevant step only partly–

(a) represents, or

(b) arises or derives from a sum of money or assets which represents or has represented,

a fund mentioned in paragraph (1).

3(3) The relevant step is to be treated for the purposes of this Part as being two separate relevant steps–

(a) one in relation to the sum of money or asset so far as it represents or arises or derives from a sum of money or assets which represents or has represented a fund mentioned in paragraph (1), and

(b) one in relation to the sum of money or asset so far as it does not represent or arise or derive from a sum of money or assets which represents or has represented a fund mentioned in paragraph (1),

and paragraph (1) applies only in relation to the separate relevant step mentioned in sub-paragraph (a).

3(4) In order to give effect to paragraph (3), the sum of money or asset which is the subject of the relevant step is to be apportioned between the two separate relevant steps on a just and reasonable basis.

3(5) In paragraph (1)–

"**relevant transfer fund**" has the meaning given in paragraph 4(2) of Schedule 34 to FA 2004;

"**UK tax-relieved fund**" has the meaning given in paragraph 3(2) of Schedule 34 to FA 2004.

DISAPPLICATION OF CHAPTER 2 OF PART 7A: RELEVANT STEPS ARISING OR DERIVING FROM A PAYMENT FROM A REGISTERED PENSION SCHEME THAT HAS BEEN SUBJECT TO THE UNAUTHORISED PAYMENTS CHARGE

4(1) Chapter 2 of Part 7A does not apply by reason of a relevant step if the subject of the relevant step is a sum of money or asset which has (wholly or partly) arisen or derived (directly or indirectly) from a payment—

(a)   made by a registered pension scheme,

(b)   that was subject to the unauthorised payments charge.

4(2) Paragraph (3) applies if the sum of money or asset which is the subject of the relevant step only partly arises or derives from a payment mentioned in paragraph (1).

4(3) The relevant step is to be treated for the purposes of Part 7A as being two separate relevant steps—

(a)   one in relation to the sum of money or asset so far as it arises or derives from a payment mentioned in paragraph (1), and

(b)   one in relation to the sum of money or asset so far as it does not arise or derive from a payment mentioned in paragraph (1),

and paragraph (1) applies only in relation to the separate relevant step mentioned in sub-paragraph (a).

4(4) In order to give effect to paragraph (3), the sum of money or asset which is the subject of the relevant step is to be apportioned between the two separate relevant steps on a just and reasonable basis.

4(5) In this regulation, **"the unauthorised payments charge"** means the charge under section 208 of FA 2004.

MODIFICATION OF SECTION 554S IN PART 7A

5 For the purposes of applying these Regulations, section 554S(2) in Part 7A applies as if after the reference to section 554W (and before the reference to section 554X) there were a reference to these Regulations.

MARD REGULATIONS 2011

(SI 2011/2931)

Regulations 1–7 and 9–18 made on 8 December 2011 by the Treasury in exercise of the powers conferred by para. 10 of Sch. 25 to the Finance Act 2011. Regulations 1(1) and 8 made on the same date by the Commissioners for Her Majesty's Revenue and Customs in exercise of the powers conferred by para. 9 of Sch. 25 to the Finance Act 2011. Operative from 1 January 2012.

CITATION, COMMENCEMENT AND INTERPRETATION

1(1) These Regulations may be cited as the MARD Regulations 2011 and come into force on 1 January 2012.

1(2) The Articles mentioned in these Regulations are those of MARD.

1(3) Regulations 2(1), 4(1), 5(1), 6, 7(2), 7(4) and 13(2) each applies to any Article it mentions only where the relevant UK authority is the requested authority in that Article.

1(4) Regulations 9, 10(1), 11, 12 and 13(3) each applies to any Article it mentions only where an applicant authority of the United Kingdom is the applicant authority in that Article.

CLAIMS, ETC TO THE UNITED KINGDOM (I.E. RELEVANT UK AUTHORITY IS THE REQUESTED AUTHORITY IN MARD)

Exchange of information

2(1) The relevant UK authority must comply with the provision made by Article 5 in relation to the requested authority.

2(2) This is subject to Articles 5(2) and 5(3).

3 A United Kingdom public authority that is to make a refund in Article 6 may follow that Article.

4(1) The relevant UK authority must make and carry out the agreement and arrangements for which Article 7(1) makes provision in relation to the requested authority, to the extent that this will promote the mutual assistance provided for in MARD.

4(2) This is subject to Articles 7(3) and 21(2).

Enforcement of foreign claims in the UK

5(1) The relevant UK authority must comply with the provision made by Articles 8, 9(1), 13(2), 13(3), 13(5), 14(1), 16, 18(4) and 19(3) in relation to the requested authority.

5(2) For Article 8: this is subject to Article 8(2).

5(3) For Article 16: paragraph (1) and regulation 7 apply in a way that gives effect to Article 17.

6(1) The relevant UK authority may follow Article 13(4), first sentence.

6(2) Where it does so, that authority must follow Article 13(4), second sentence.

7(1) Articles 12, 14(1), 14(2), 15(2) second and third sub-paragraphs, and 18 apply to a foreign claim.

7(2) The relevant UK authority must follow Article 15(2), first sub-paragraph, second sentence.

7(3) The provision in paragraph (1) for Articles 12 and 14 also apply where the foreign claim is based on a revised instrument in Article 15(2), third sub-paragraph.

7(4) The relevant UK authority may follow Articles 18(1) and 18(2).

7(5) The relevant UK authority may follow Article 18(3) where the United Kingdom is the Member State in that Article.

8 In the application of the Finance Act 2009, Schedule 49 to any kind of foreign claim for which the relevant UK authority is the Commissioners, the sum payable in paragraph 1(1) of that Schedule includes a foreign claim.

CLAIMS, ETC FROM THE UNITED KINGDOM (I.E. A UK AUTHORITY IS THE APPLICANT AUTHORITY IN MARD)

Request for notification of certain documents relating to claims

9 Any applicant authority of the United Kingdom must ensure compliance or comply with the provision made by Articles 8(1) and 8(2) in relation to the applicant authority.

Requests for recovery, and conditions governing them

10(1) Any applicant authority of the United Kingdom must comply with the provision made by Articles 10(2) and 11 in relation to the applicant authority.

10(2) A request in either Article by an applicant authority of the United Kingdom must comply with Article 12(1) (except for the obligations that Article places on the requested Member State).

The request may be accompanied by the other documents as mentioned in Article 12(2).

Disputes

11 Any applicant authority of the United Kingdom must comply with the provision made by Articles 14(3) and 14(4), third sub-paragraph, third sentence in relation to the applicant authority.

Amendment or withdrawal of UK request for recovery assistance

12 Any applicant authority of the United Kingdom must comply with the provision made by Article 15 in relation to the applicant authority.

CLAIMS WITHIN MARD: GENERAL

Questions on limitation

13(1) Article 19 applies to a foreign claim and to a claim for which the applicant Member State is the United Kingdom, as appropriate.

13(2) The relevant UK authority must comply with the provision made by Article 19(3) in relation to the requested authority.

13(3) Any applicant authority of the United Kingdom must comply with the provision made by Article 19(3) in relation to the applicant authority.

Costs

14(1) The relevant UK authority and an applicant authority of the United Kingdom may follow respectively Article 20(2), second sub-paragraph in relation to the requested and applicant authorities, as appropriate to the circumstances.

14(2) United Kingdom public authorities must seek to ensure compliance with Article 20(2), first sub-paragraph and with Article 20(3).

Standard forms and means of communication

15(1) Article 21(1) applies where the United Kingdom is the requested Member State or the applicant Member State in that Article, as appropriate.

15(2) This is subject to Article 21(3).

Use of languages

16(1) The documents mentioned in Article 22(1) sent from the United Kingdom must comply with that Article.

16(2) Where those documents are sent to the United Kingdom, the second sentence of that Article applies provided that the United Kingdom public authority concerned has agreed with the sending Member State as mentioned in that sentence.

16(3) This paragraph applies in relation to documents covered by Article 22(3) where the relevant UK authority is the requested authority or an applicant authority of the United Kingdom is the applicant authority in that Article.

The former authority may impose, and the latter authority must obey, the requirement in that Article. Either authority may enter the bilateral agreement in that Article.

16(4) English is the only official language in cases where the United Kingdom is the requested Member State in Articles 22(1) and 22(3), or is the applicant Member State in Article 22(2).

Disclosure of information and documents

17(1) Articles 23(1) and 23(6) apply where the United Kingdom is the Member State receiving the information within those Articles.

17(2) Any United Kingdom public authority in question must seek to ensure that the United Kingdom complies with Articles 23(3) and 23(5) where the United Kingdom is the Member State providing the information, or is the Member State from which it originates, within those Articles.

17(3) The relevant UK authority may follow Article 23(4), first sentence where it is the requested authority in that Article.

17(4) An applicant authority of the United Kingdom may follow Article 23(4), first sentence where it is the applicant authority in that Article.

17(5) Paragraphs (3) and (4) are subject to the second and third sentences of Article 23(4), and to Article 23(5), being satisfied.

STATUTORY INSTRUMENTS REVOKED

Statutory instruments revoked

18 The Regulations in the table in the Schedule are revoked.

SCHEDULES

SCHEDULE – TABLE OF STATUTORY INSTRUMENTS REVOKED

Regulation 18

(1) Regulations revoked	(2) References
The Recovery of Duties and Taxes Etc. Due in Other Member States (Corresponding UK Claims, Procedure and Supplementary) Regulations 2004	S.I. 2004/674
The Recovery of Agricultural Levies Due in Other Member States Regulations 2004	S.I. 2004/800
The Recovery of Duties and Taxes Etc. Due in Other Member States (Corresponding UK Claims, Procedure and Supplementary) (Amendment) Regulations 2005	S.I. 2005/1709
The Recovery of Duties and Taxes Etc. Due in Other Member States (Corresponding UK Claims, Procedure and Supplementary) (Amendment) Regulations 2007	S.I. 2007/3508
The Schedule 39 to the Finance Act 2002 and Recovery of Taxes etc Due in Other Member States (Amendment) Regulations 2010	S.I. 2010/792

INVESTMENT TRUST (APPROVED COMPANY) (TAX) REGULATIONS 2011

(SI 2011/2999, as amended by SI 2013/1406 and SI 2014/685)

Made on 14 December 2011 by the Treasury in exercise of the powers conferred by s. 622A, 1158(6) and 1159 of the Corporation Tax Act 2010 and s. 354 of the Taxation (International and Other Provisions) Act 2010. Operative from 1 January 2012.

ARRANGEMENT OF REGULATIONS

REGULATION

PART 1 – INTRODUCTORY AND GENERAL PROVISIONS

CITATION, COMMENCEMENT AND EFFECT

1(1) These Regulations may be cited as the Investment Trust (Approved Company) (Tax) Regulations 2011 and come into force on 1 January 2012.

1(2) Subject to paragraph (3), these Regulations have effect in relation to accounting periods beginning on or after 1 January 2012.

1(3) Regulations 43, 45 and 46 have effect in relation to disposals made on or after 1 January 2012.

STRUCTURE OF THESE REGULATIONS

2 The structure of these Regulations is as follows–

This Part contains introductory and general provisions;

Part 2 contains the following provisions about investment trusts–

Chapter 1 deals with applications for approval as an investment trust,

Chapter 2 deals with cases where the eligibility conditions are treated as being met,

Chapter 3 deals with the requirements to be met by investment trusts whilst approved,

Chapter 4 deals with breaches of the requirements to be met by investment trusts and subsequent withdrawal of approval,

Chapter 5 deals with an approved company treating itself as not being an investment trust;

Part 3 contains provisions about transactions by investment trusts which are treated as entered into otherwise than in the course of a trade; and

Part 4 contains provisions about investment trusts having interests in offshore non-reporting funds and index tracking funds, and makes consequential provision.

INTERPRETATION

3(1) In these Regulations–

"**company tax return**" has the same meaning as in paragraph 3(1) of Schedule 18 to the Finance Act 1998,

"**CTA 2009**" means the Corporation Tax Act 2009,

"**CTA 2010**" means the Corporation Tax Act 2010,

"**the Offshore Funds Regulations**" means the Offshore Funds (Tax) Regulations 2009, "**tribunal**" means the First-tier Tribunal or, where determined by or under Tribunal Procedure Rules, the Upper Tribunal.

3(2) For the purposes of these Regulations the market value of any asset is to be determined in a like manner as it would be determined for the purposes of the Taxation of Chargeable Gains Act 1992.

PART 2 – INVESTMENT TRUSTS
Chapter 1 – Application Procedure

INTERPRETATION

4 In this Part–

"**the eligibility conditions**" mean conditions A to C in section 1158 of CTA 2010,

"**the income distribution requirement**" has the meaning given in regulation 21(9).

APPLICATION FOR APPROVAL AS AN INVESTMENT TRUST

5(1) A company may apply to the Commissioners for approval as an investment trust in accordance with this Chapter.

5(2) A company which makes such an application is referred to in this Chapter as "**the applicant**".

CONTENTS OF APPLICATION

6(1) An application under regulation 5 must include the particulars specified in this regulation.

6(2) The application must–

(a) specify the date of the first day of an accounting period in respect of which the applicant seeks approval as an investment trust ("the specified date"),

(b) contain a statement that the applicant meets, or is expected to meet, in respect of the accounting period referred to in sub-paragraph (a)–

    (i) the eligibility conditions, and

    (ii) the requirements of Chapter 3 of this Part,

(c) contain an undertaking given in relation to the accounting period referred to in sub-paragraph (a) and each subsequent accounting period in respect of which it is or expects to be an investment trust, that the applicant will meet–

    (i) the eligibility conditions, and

    (ii) the requirements of Chapter 3 of this Part,

(d) include a copy of the applicant's current published investment policy, and

(e) provide evidence to show that the shares making up the applicant's ordinary share capital (or, if there are such shares of more than one class, those of each class) are admitted to trading on a regulated market.

This regulation is subject to regulations 7, 8, 9 and 13.

CONTENTS OF APPLICATION: ACCOUNTING PERIOD NOT COMMENCED AT TIME OF APPLICATION

7(1) This regulation applies if at the time the application is made the applicant has not commenced an accounting period.

7(2) If this regulation applies the applicant must–

(a) specify a provisional date for the purposes of regulation 6(2)(a), and

(b) where a provisional date is specified, as soon as reasonably practicable, confirm in writing to the Commissioners the date of the first day of the accounting period in respect of which the applicant seeks approval as an investment trust.

CONTENTS OF APPLICATION: SHARES NOT ADMITTED TO TRADING AT TIME OF APPLICATION

8(1) This regulation applies if at the time the application is made the shares making up the applicant's ordinary share capital (or, if there are such shares of more than one class, those of each class) are not admitted to trading on a regulated market.

8(2)   If this regulation applies, the application—

(a)   for the purposes of regulation 6(2)(d), may include a copy of the applicant's prospectus instead of the current published investment policy, and

(b)   must explain how the applicant will be in a position to comply with condition B in section 1158(3) of CTA 2010 by the specified date.

8(3)   The applicant must provide evidence to the Commissioners that the shares making up the applicant's ordinary share capital (or, if there are such shares of more than one class, those of each class) are admitted to trading on a regulated market—

(a)   before the end of a period of 60 days beginning with the date on which the shares were so admitted, or

(b)   by such other date as the Commissioners may agree.

FORM, TIMING AND WITHDRAWAL OF APPLICATION

9(1)   An application must be made in writing to the Commissioners.

9(2)   The application must be made to the Commissioners before the end of the period of 90 days beginning with the last day of the first accounting period for which approval is sought.

9(3)   The applicant may withdraw the application at any time during the period beginning with the day on which the application is made and ending 28 days after the day on which the Commissioners give notice under regulation 10 accepting the application.

RESPONSE BY COMMISSIONERS TO APPLICATION

10(1)   Within 28 days beginning with the date on which the application is made, the Commissioners must give notice in writing to the applicant—

(a)   accepting the application,

(b)   rejecting the application, or

(c)   asking for further information in order to consider the application.

10(2)   The Commissioners must not accept an application if any particular or information mentioned in regulation 6, 7 or 8 is not supplied.

10(3)   Paragraph (4) applies if—

(a)   the Commissioners have given a notice under paragraph (1)(c), and

(b)   the applicant provides the further information within the period of 28 days beginning with the day on which the Commissioners ask for the further information, or within such longer period as may be agreed by the Commissioners.

10(4)   Within 28 days beginning with the day on which they receive the further information, the Commissioners must give notice to the applicant—

(a)   accepting the application, or

(b)   rejecting the application.

10(5)   If the Commissioners reject the application, the notice given to the applicant under paragraph (1)(b) or (4)(b) must contain a statement of the reason for which the application was rejected.

APPEAL AGAINST REJECTION OF THE APPLICATION

11(1)   If the Commissioners reject an application, the applicant may appeal.

11(2)   The notice of appeal must be given to the Commissioners within a period of 42 days beginning with the day on which the notice rejecting the application is given.

11(3)   On an appeal, the tribunal may uphold or quash the rejection of the application.

11(4)   If the tribunal quashes the rejection of the application, these Regulations apply as if the Commissioners had accepted the application in the form in which it was considered by the tribunal.

EFFECT OF ACCEPTANCE OF APPLICATION

12   If the Commissioners accept (or are treated as accepting) an application, the applicant is approved as an investment trust—

(a)   for the accounting period commencing on the specified date (or commencing on such later date as may be confirmed in accordance with regulation 7(2)(b)), and

(b)   for each subsequent accounting period,

but this is subject to regulations 13 and 25 to 31.

ACCEPTANCE OF APPLICATION CONDITIONAL ON RECEIPT OF SPECIFIED INFORMATION

13(1)   An acceptance by the Commissioners of an application is conditional on the provision of any information or particulars required by regulations 7(2)(b) and 8(3).

13(2)   If the applicant does not provide any such information or particulars, the application shall be treated as if it had not been made and the company treated as if it had not been an investment trust for any of the period to which the application mentioned in paragraph (1) related.

Chapter 2 – Cases Where Eligibility Conditions Treated as Being Met

DELAY IN ADMISSION OF COMPANY'S ORDINARY SHARE CAPITAL TO TRADING ON A REGULATED MARKET

14(1)   Paragraph (3) applies if at the date on which the application under regulation 5 is made the applicant–

(a)   has commenced procedures to obtain admission of the shares making up its ordinary share capital (or, if there are such shares of more than one class, those of each class) to trading on a regulated market but has not obtained admission, or

(b)   has given a commitment in its prospectus to commence such procedures but has not started those procedures.

14(2)   Paragraph (3) also applies if a company which has been approved as an investment trust issues shares of a class ("the new shares") which is different from any of those which make up its ordinary share capital.

14(3)   Condition B in section 1158(3) of CTA 2010 is to be treated as met for the period of 60 days beginning with–

(a)   in the case of paragraph (1), the date of the application, or

(b)   in the case of paragraph (2), the date on which the new shares were issued.

WINDING UP OF COMPANY APPROVED AS INVESTMENT TRUST

15(1)   Paragraph (2) applies if–

(a)   a company is being wound up,

(b)   the company was approved as an investment trust in respect of the accounting period which ended immediately before the winding up started (see section 12 of CTA 2009),

(c)   the company satisfied the eligibility conditions in respect of the accounting period referred to in sub-paragraph (b), and

(d)   subject to paragraph (4), the company makes no new investments during the realisation period.

15(2)   Conditions A and B in section 1158 of CTA 2010 are to be treated as met in respect of the realisation period.

This paragraph is subject to regulation 16.

15(3)   In paragraphs (1) and (2) the **"realisation period"** is the period beginning with the date on which the winding up started and ending with the date on which the winding up is completed.

15(4)   For the purposes of paragraph (1)(d)–

(a)   the placing on deposit of the proceeds of the disposal of assets of the company, or

(b)   the purchase of gilts with the proceeds of the disposal of assets of the company,

shall not be treated as the making of a new investment by the company.

15(5)   In this regulation and regulation 16, references to **"a company being wound up"** and **"winding up"** are to be construed in accordance with section 12 of CTA 2009.

WINDING UP OF COMPANY APPROVED AS INVESTMENT TRUST – FURTHER CONDITIONS

16(1)   Paragraph (2) of regulation 15 shall only apply if paragraphs (2) to (4) of this regulation are met.

16(2)   The Commissioners must be notified in writing that the company is being wound up.

16(3) The notice under paragraph (2) must be given within one year beginning with the date on which the winding up started.

16(4) The Commissioners must be satisfied that the realisation period referred to in regulation 15 has not been unreasonably prolonged.

Chapter 3 – Investment Trust: Requirements to be Met Whilst Approved

INVESTMENT TRUST TO COMPLY WITH REQUIREMENTS OF THIS CHAPTER

17 A company must comply with the provisions of this Chapter in relation to each accounting period in respect of which it is approved as an investment trust.

INVESTMENT TRUST MUST NOT BE A CLOSE COMPANY

18(1) An investment trust must not be a close company at any time in an accounting period.

18(2) See section 439 of CTA 2010 for the definition of **"close company"**.

THE INCOME DISTRIBUTION REQUIREMENT

19(1) The maximum amount an investment trust is permitted to retain in respect of an accounting period is the highest of the following amounts–

(a) 15% of its income for the accounting period,

(b) where paragraph (1A) applies, the accumulated revenue losses brought forward from previous accounting periods, and

(c) any amount of income that the investment trust is required to retain in respect of the accounting period by virtue of a restriction imposed by law.

19(1A) This paragraph applies if in the accounting period the amount of income the investment trust is permitted to retain under this regulation and regulation 21 (taken together and ignoring this paragraph and paragraph (1)(b)) does not exceed the amount of any accumulated revenue losses brought forward from previous accounting periods.

19(2) The investment trust must distribute as a dividend the amount required to comply with paragraph (1) before the filing date for the investment trust's company tax return for the accounting period.

19(3) Where the investment trust company's tax return has been amended as a result of a notice served under paragraph 15 or 34 of Schedule 18 to the Finance Act 1998, any further distribution that is required by virtue of the amendment must be made before the end of the period of 180 days beginning with the date of the amendment.

19(4) In this regulation and regulation 23, **"filing date"** has the meaning given in paragraph 14 of Schedule 18 to the Finance Act 1998.

19(5) This regulation is subject to regulations 21 and 22.

History – Reg. 19(1) substituted by SI 2013/1406, reg. 2(2)(a), with effect in relation to accounting periods beginning on or after 28 June 2013. Former reg. 19(1) read as follows:

"**19(1)** An investment trust must not retain in respect of an accounting period an amount which is greater than 15% of its income for the accounting period.".

Reg. 19(1A) inserted by SI 2013/1406, reg. 2(2)(b), with effect in relation to accounting periods beginning on or after 28 June 2013.

CALCULATION OF INCOME

20(1) Paragraphs (2) and (3) apply for the purposes of regulation 19(1)(a) in determining the income of the investment trust for an accounting period.

20(2) The amounts to be brought into account under Part 5 of CTA 2009 in respect of the investment trust's loan relationships are to be determined without reference to any debtor relationships of the investment trust.

20(3) Income treated as arising under regulation 18(1) (the charge to tax: further provisions) of the Offshore Funds Regulations is to be ignored.

History – In reg. 20(1), the words "regulation 19(1)(a)" substituted for the words "regulation 19(1)" by SI 2013/1406, reg. 2(3), with effect in relation to accounting periods beginning on or after 28 June 2013.

THE INCOME DISTRIBUTION REQUIREMENT: REDUCTION IN AMOUNT OF INCOME PERMITTED TO BE RETAINED

21(1)   This regulation applies where conditions A to C are met.

21(2)   Condition A is that the investment trust is a participant in an offshore reporting fund within the meaning of regulation 50 (meaning of "reporting fund") of the Offshore Funds Regulations.

21(3)   Condition B is that there is an amount which falls to be reported to the investment trust in accordance with regulation 92(1)(b) (contents of a report to participants: non-transparent funds) of the Offshore Funds Regulations.

21(4)   Condition C is that the amount referred to in condition B is accounted for by the investment trust through the capital column of the income statement in accordance with the AIC Statement of Recommended Practice, or would have been so accounted for if that Statement had been applied correctly.

21(5)   Where this regulation applies the amount which the investment trust may retain in accordance with regulation 19(1) is reduced by an amount equal to 85% of the amount referred to in condition B.

21(6)   If the application of paragraph (5) has the effect that the sum which an investment trust is permitted to retain ("the retainable amount") is calculated to be less than zero, the investment trust must distribute as a dividend a further sum which is equal to the difference between the retainable amount and zero.

21(7)   The further distribution mentioned in paragraph (6) must be made in relation to the accounting period in which the fund distribution date for the offshore reporting fund in question falls.

21(8)   In this regulation–

(a)   **"fund distribution date"** has the meaning given in regulation 94 (reported income: general provisions) of the Offshore Funds Regulations, and

(b)   **"AIC Statement of Recommended Practice"** means the Statement of Recommended Practice relating to Investment Trust Companies, issued by the Association of Investment Trust Companies in January 2009.

21(9)   The distribution required under this regulation together with the distribution required under regulation 19 comprise **"the income distribution requirement"**.

21(10)   This regulation is subject to regulation 22.

THE INCOME DISTRIBUTION REQUIREMENT: EXCEPTIONS

22(1)   Regulations 19 and 21 do not apply in relation to an accounting period if the amount that the investment trust would be required to distribute in accordance with those regulations, taken together, would be less than £30,000.

22(2)   [Omitted by SI 2013/1406, reg. 2(4)(a).]

22(3)   If the accounting period mentioned in paragraph (1) is shorter than 12 months, the amount of £30,000 mentioned in that paragraph is proportionately reduced.

History – Reg. 22(2) omitted by SI 2013/1406, reg. 2(4)(a), with effect in relation to accounting periods beginning on or after 28 June 2013. Former reg. 22(2) read as follows:

> "**22(2)**   Regulations 19 and 21 do not apply in relation to an accounting period if–
> (a)   by virtue of a restriction imposed by law, the investment trust is required to retain in respect of the accounting period an amount of income that exceeds 15% of its income, and
> (b)   either–
> > (i)   the amount of income that the investment trust retains in respect of the accounting period does not exceed the amount of income that it is required to retain in respect of the period by virtue of a restriction imposed by law, or
> > (ii)   if there is such an excess, the amount of the excess plus the amount of any income that the investment trust distributes in respect of the period is less than £30,000.".

In reg. 22(3), the words "paragraph (1)" substituted for the words "paragraphs (1) and (2)" and the words "that paragraph" substituted for the words "paragraphs (1) and (2)(b)(ii)" by SI 2013/1406, reg. 2(4)(b), with effect in relation to accounting periods beginning on or after 28 June 2013.

REQUIREMENT TO NOTIFY COMMISSIONERS OF REVISED INVESTMENT POLICY

23(1)   An investment trust must notify the Commissioners if it revises its published investment policy.

23(2)   The investment trust must provide the Commissioners with a copy of any revised investment policy before the filing date for its company tax return for the accounting period in which the investment policy was revised.

REQUIREMENT TO NOTIFY COMMISSIONERS OF BREACH

24(1)   An investment trust must give notice in accordance with paragraph (2) if it has breached–

(a)   any of the eligibility conditions (see regulation 4), or

(b)   any other requirement of these Regulations (apart from this regulation).

24(2)   The notice must–

(a)   be given in writing to the Commissioners as soon as reasonably practicable after the investment trust becomes aware of any breach referred to in paragraph (1), and

(b)   specify the steps, if any, that have been taken, or are to be taken, to correct the breach.

Chapter 4 – Breach of the Regulations and Withdrawal of Approval

TYPES OF BREACH

25(1)   This Chapter applies if an investment trust is in breach of a requirement imposed by these Regulations.

25(2)   A breach is–

(a)   a minor breach, or

(b)   a serious breach.

25(3)   For the purposes of these Regulations, a breach is a **"serious breach"** if it is–

(a)   a breach specified as a serious breach in this Chapter, or

(b)   a breach which is not a minor breach.

25(4)   For the purposes of these Regulations, a breach is a **"minor breach"** if it is a breach (other than a breach specified as a serious breach in this Chapter)–

(a)   for which there is a reasonable excuse, and

(b)   which is inadvertent and corrected as soon as reasonably practicable.

25(5)   For the purposes of this Chapter a minor breach is not regarded as a breach if the investment trust–

(a)   notifies the Commissioners of the breach in accordance with regulation 24, and

(b)   corrects the breach as soon as reasonably practicable without any intervention by the Commissioners.

25(6)   For the purposes of this regulation there is an **"intervention by the Commissioners"** in relation to an investment trust if the Commissioners ask it to provide them with information relating to a requirement imposed by Chapter 3.

This paragraph is subject to paragraph (7).

25(7)   There is no intervention by the Commissioners in relation to an investment trust if–

(a)   the investment trust notifies the Commissioners of the breach in accordance with regulation 24,

(b)   the investment trust complies with regulation 25(5), and

(c)   the Commissioners request the investment trust to provide them with information so that they may determine whether the breach has been corrected.

SERIOUS BREACH

26   For the purposes of this Chapter a breach of regulation 18 (investment trust must not be a close company) is a serious breach.

MULTIPLE BREACHES

27(1)   Subject to the following provisions of this Chapter, if an investment trust is in breach of a requirement imposed by these Regulations, and the breach is a minor breach, it continues to be treated as approved as an investment trust.

27(2)   If paragraph (1) applies–

(a)   on three separate occasions in a period of ten years beginning with the first day of the accounting period in which the first breach occurs, and

(b)   in relation to the same requirement,

the third breach is a serious breach.

27(3) If paragraph (1) applies—

(a)   on four separate occasions in a period of ten years beginning with the first day of the accounting period in which the first breach occurs, and

(b)   in relation to more than one of the requirements,

the fourth breach is a serious breach.

27(4) If a single event results in more than one minor breach within a single accounting period there is only one minor breach in that period in relation to that event for the purposes of this Chapter.

BREACH OF THE INCOME DISTRIBUTION REQUIREMENT

28(1) Subject to paragraph (4), there is a breach of the income distribution requirement if—

(a)   there is a difference between—

> (i)   the amount that the investment trust is required to distribute in relation to an accounting period in accordance with regulations 19 and 21, and

> (ii)   the amount which the investment trust distributed in relation to that accounting period, and

(b)   the amount referred to in paragraph (ii) is less than the amount referred to in paragraph (i).

28(2) If the difference between the two amounts specified in paragraph (1) is greater than 1% but less than or equal to 5% of the income of the investment trust for the accounting period then, subject to paragraph (5), the breach is a minor breach.

28(3) If the difference between the two amounts specified in paragraph (1) is greater than 5% of the income of the investment trust for the accounting period, the breach is a serious breach.

28(4) If the difference between the two amounts specified in paragraph (1) is less than or equal to 1% of the income of the investment trust for the accounting period then, subject to paragraph (5), the investment trust is to be treated as not having breached the income distribution requirement.

28(5) Paragraph (4) only applies if the failure to comply with the income distribution requirement was inadvertent.

28(6) For the purpose of this regulation, the income of the investment trust includes income that falls to be reported to it in accordance with regulation 92(1)(b) (contents of report to participants: non-transparent funds) of the Offshore Funds Regulations.

CONSEQUENCES OF SERIOUS BREACHES

29(1) This regulation applies if conditions A and B are met.

29(2) Condition A is that—

(a)   the investment trust is in breach of a requirement imposed by these Regulations, and

(b)   the breach is a serious breach.

29(3) Condition B is that the Commissioners give notice in writing to the investment trust—

(a)   stating that the investment trust is in breach of a requirement imposed by these Regulations and that the breach is a serious breach, and

(b)   specifying the serious breach.

29(4) The investment trust is to be treated as a company which has not been approved as an investment trust for the accounting period in which the serious breach occurred (or, if there is more than one serious breach, the first of them) and, subject to paragraph (5), for all subsequent accounting periods.

29(5) A company to which this regulation applies may make an application under regulation 5 in respect of any accounting period subsequent to the accounting period in which the serious breach occurred.

BREACH OF THE ELIGIBILITY CONDITIONS

30(1) This regulation applies if an investment trust is in breach of any of the eligibility conditions.

30(2) The investment trust is to be treated as a company which has not been approved as an investment trust for the accounting period in which the breach of the eligibility condition occurred (or, if there is more than one breach, the first of them) and, subject to paragraph (3), for all subsequent accounting periods.

30(3) A company to which this regulation applies may make an application under regulation 5 in respect of any accounting period subsequent to the accounting period in which the breach of an eligibility condition occurred.

Chapter 5 – Approved Company Treating Itself as not Being an Investment Trust

COMPANY TAX RETURN SUBMITTED ON BASIS THAT COMPANY IS NOT AN INVESTMENT TRUST

31(1) This regulation applies if–

(a) a company (apart from this regulation) is approved as an investment trust in respect of an accounting period,

(b) the company makes a company tax return for that period, and

(c) the self-assessment of the amount of tax which is payable by it included in the return is made on the basis that the company is not an investment trust with respect to that period.

31(2) If this regulation applies the company is treated as not having been approved as an investment trust for the accounting period referred to in paragraph (1) with effect from the first day of that period and, subject to paragraph (3), for all subsequent accounting periods.

31(3) A company to which this regulation applies may make an application under regulation 5 in respect of any accounting period subsequent to the accounting period to which the company tax return relates.

PART 3 – TRANSACTIONS TO BE TREATED AS ENTERED INTO OTHERWISE THAN IN THE COURSE OF A TRADE

TREATMENT OF TRANSACTIONS CARRIED OUT BY INVESTMENT TRUSTS

32(1) This regulation applies if an investment trust carries out an investment transaction in an accounting period.

32(2) The investment transaction is treated as a transaction entered into otherwise than in the course of a trade for the purposes of the Corporation Tax Acts.

32(3) For the purposes of this Part an **"investment transaction"** is an investment transaction specified by regulation 2 of the Investment Transactions (Tax) Regulations 2014.

History – Reg. 32(3) inserted by SI 2014/685, reg. 9(2), with effect from transactions entered into on or after 8 April 2014.

MEANING OF "INVESTMENT TRANSACTION"

33 [Omitted by SI 2014/685, reg. 9(3).]

History – Reg. 33 omitted by SI 2014/685, reg. 9(3), with effect from transactions entered into on or after 8 April 2014. Former reg. 33 read as follows:

> "MEANING OF "INVESTMENT TRANSACTION"
>
> **33** For the purposes of this Part an investment transaction means–
> (a) any transaction in stocks and shares,
> (b) any transaction in a relevant contract (see regulations 34 to 40),
> (c) any transaction which results in an investment trust becoming a party to a loan relationship or a related transaction in respect of a loan relationship (see regulation 39),
> (d) any transaction in units in a collective investment scheme (see regulation 40),
> (e) any transaction in securities of any description not falling within paragraphs (a) to (d),
> (f) any transaction consisting in the buying or selling of any foreign currency, or
> (g) any transaction in a carbon emission trading product (see regulation 41)."

MEANING OF "RELEVANT CONTRACT"

34 [Omitted by SI 2014/685, reg. 9(3).]

History – Reg. 34 omitted by SI 2014/685, reg. 9(3), with effect from transactions entered into on or after 8 April 2014. Former reg. 34 read as follows:

> "MEANING OF "RELEVANT CONTRACT"
>
> **34(1)** For the purposes of regulation 33(b) a relevant contract is–
> (a) an option,
> (b) a future, or
> (c) a contract for differences.
> **34(2)** For the purposes of this regulation an option, a future or a contract for differences which relates to land will only be a relevant contract if the option, future or contract for differences uses an index referred to in regulation 38(1)(b) and the index is–

(a)   publicly accessible,
(b)   comprised of a significant number of properties, and
(c)   not maintained by–
       (i)   the investment trust,
       (ii)   the manager of the investment trust, or
       (iii)   a person connected with the investment trust or the manager of the investment trust.
34(3) For the purposes of this regulation–
(a)   sections 993 and 994 of the Income Tax Act 2007 (connected persons) apply where the manager is a person other than a company, and
(b)   sections 1122 and 1123 of CTA 2010 (connected persons) apply in the case of an investment trust or where the manager is a person which is a company.

MEANING OF "RELEVANT CONTRACT": OPTIONS

35   [Omitted by SI 2014/685, reg. 9(3).]

History – Reg. 35 omitted by SI 2014/685, reg. 9(3), with effect from transactions entered into on or after 8 April 2014. Former reg. 35 read as follows:

"MEANING OF "RELEVANT CONTRACT": OPTIONS

35(1) For the purposes of regulation 34(1)(a) an **"option"** includes an instrument which entitles the holder to subscribe for shares in a company or assets representing a loan relationship of a company, and for these purposes it is immaterial whether the shares or assets to which the instrument relates exist or are identifiable.
35(2) For the purposes of paragraph (1) the reference to a loan relationship of a company is to be construed in accordance with regulation 39 but with references in that regulation to **"investment trust"** treated as references to **"company".**"

MEANING OF "RELEVANT CONTRACT": FUTURES

36   [Omitted by SI 2014/685, reg. 9(3).]

History – Reg. 36 omitted by SI 2014/685, reg. 9(3), with effect from transactions entered into on or after 8 April 2014. Former reg. 36 read as follows:

"MEANING OF "RELEVANT CONTRACT": FUTURES

36(1) For the purposes of regulation 34(1)(b) a **"future"** is a contract for the sale of property under which delivery is to be made–
(a)   at a future date agreed when the contract is made, and
(b)   at a price so agreed.
36(2) For the purposes of paragraph (1)(b) a price is taken to be agreed when the contract is made–
(a)   notwithstanding that the price is left to be determined by reference to the price at which a contract is to be entered into on a market or exchange or could be entered into at a time and place specified in the contract, or
(b)   in a case where the contract is expressed to be by reference to a standard lot and quality, notwithstanding that provision is made for a variation in the price to take account of any variation in quantity or quality on delivery."

OPTIONS AND FUTURES: FURTHER PROVISIONS

37   [Omitted by SI 2014/685, reg. 9(3).]

History – Reg. 37 omitted by SI 2014/685, reg. 9(3), with effect from transactions entered into on or after 8 April 2014. Former reg. 37 read as follows:

"OPTIONS AND FUTURES: FURTHER PROVISIONS

37(1) For the purposes of regulations 35 and 36 references to an option or a future do not include reference to a contract the terms of which provide–
(a)   that, after setting off their obligations to each other under the contract, a cash payment is to be made by one party to the other in respect of the excess, if any, and do not provide for the delivery of any property,
(b)   that each party is liable to make to the other party a cash payment in respect of all that party's obligations to the other under the contract and do not provide for the delivery of any property, or
(c)   for the delivery of any property other than property a transaction in which would fall within any of the regulations in this Part where the property is delivered.
37(2) Nothing in paragraph (1) has effect to exclude, from references to an option or a future, an option or future whose underlying subject matter is currency.
37(3) In paragraph (2) **"underlying subject matter"** means–
(a)   in relation to an option, the property which would fall to be delivered if the option were exercised, and
(b)   in relation to a future, the property which, if the future were to run to delivery, would fall to be delivered at the date and price agreed when the contract is made."

MEANING OF "RELEVANT CONTRACT": CONTRACTS FOR DIFFERENCE

38   [Omitted by SI 2014/685, reg. 9(3).]

History – Reg. 38 omitted by SI 2014/685, reg. 9(3), with effect from transactions entered into on or after 8 April 2014. Former reg. 38 read as follows:

"MEANING OF "RELEVANT CONTRACT": CONTRACTS FOR DIFFERENCE

38(1) For the purposes of regulation 34(1)(c) a **"contract for differences"** is a contract the purpose or pretended purpose of which is to make a profit or avoid a loss by reference to fluctuations in–
(a)   the value or price of property described in the contract, or
(b)   an index or other factor designated in the contract.
38(2) But none of the following is a contract for differences–
(a)   a future,
(b)   an option,
(c)   a contract of insurance,

(d)   a contract effected in the course of capital redemption business,

(e)   a contract of indemnity,

(f)   a guarantee,

(g)   a warranty,

(h)   a loan relationship.

38(3) For the purposes of paragraph (2)–

"**capital redemption business**" means any business of a company carrying on insurance business in so far as it consists of the effecting on the basis of actuarial calculations, and the carrying out, of contracts under which, in return for one or more fixed payments, a sum or series of sums of a specified amount become payable at a future time or over a period,

"**loan relationship**" is to be construed in accordance with regulation 39 but with references to "**investment trust**" in that regulation being construed as references to "**company**".

38(4) For the purposes of paragraph (1)(b) an index or factor may be determined by reference to any matter and, for these purposes, a numerical value may be attributed to any variation in a matter."

INTERPRETATION OF REGULATION 33(C)

39 [Omitted by SI 2014/685, reg. 9(3).]

History – Reg. 39 omitted by SI 2014/685, reg. 9(3), with effect from transactions entered into on or after 8 April 2014. Former reg. 39 read as follows:

"INTERPRETATION OF REGULATION 33(C)

39(1) For the purposes of regulation 33(c) an investment trust has a loan relationship where the investment trust stands (whether by reference to a security or otherwise) in the position of a creditor or debtor as respects any money debt and either–

(a)   that debt is one arising from a transaction for the lending of money, or

(b)   that debt is not one which arose from a transaction for the lending of money but is one–

     (i)   on which interest is payable to or by the investment trust,

     (ii)   in relation to which the exchange gains or losses arise to the investment trust, or

     (iii)   as respects which the conditions in paragraph (2) are satisfied.

39(2) The conditions mentioned in paragraph (1)(b)(iii) are that–

(a)   the investment trust stands in the position of creditor in relation to the money debt, and

(b)   the money debt is one from which a discount (whether of an income or capital nature) arises to the investment trust.

39(3) In this regulation "**exchange gains or losses**" means profits or gains or losses which arise as a result of comparing at different times the expression in one currency of the whole or some part of the valuation put by the investment trust in another currency on an asset or liability of the investment trust.

39(4) For the purposes of this regulation a "**money debt**" is a debt which is, or has at any time been, one that falls, or that may at the choice of the creditor or of the debtor, fall to be settled–

(a)   by the payment of money,

(b)   by the transfer of a right to settlement under a debt which is itself a money debt, or

(c)   by the issue or transfer of shares in any company,

disregarding any other alternative exercisable by either party.

39(5) Subject to paragraph (6), if an instrument is issued by any person for the purpose of representing security for, or the rights of a creditor in respect of, any money debt, then (whatever the circumstances of the issue of the instrument) that debt shall be taken for the purposes of this regulation to be a debt arising from a transaction for the lending of money.

39(6) For the purposes of this regulation a debt does not arise from a transaction for the lending of money to the extent that it is a debt arising from rights conferred by shares in a company.

39(7) For the purposes of this regulation, so far as relating to exchange gains and losses, any currency held by the investment trust shall be treated as a money debt.

39(8) For the purpose of this regulation "**money**" includes money expressed in a currency other than sterling.

39(9) For the purposes of regulation 33(c) a "**related transaction**" in relation to a loan relationship means any disposal or acquisition (in whole or in part) of rights or liabilities under that relationship."

MEANING OF "UNITS IN A COLLECTIVE INVESTMENT SCHEME"

40 [Omitted by SI 2014/685, reg. 9(3).]

History – Reg. 40 omitted by SI 2014/685, reg. 9(3), with effect from transactions entered into on or after 8 April 2014. Former reg. 40 read as follows:

"MEANING OF "UNITS IN A COLLECTIVE INVESTMENT SCHEME"

40(1) For the purposes of regulation 33(d)–

"**collective investment scheme**" has the meaning given by section 235 of the Financial Services and Markets Act 2000,

"**units**" means the rights or interests (however described) of the investors in a collective investment scheme.

40(2) In paragraph (1) an "**investor**", in relation to a collective investment scheme, means a beneficial owner of units in the scheme, except where the units are held on trust (other than a bare trust) or are comprised in the estate of a deceased person, and in such a case the investor, in relation to the scheme, means the trustees of the trust or, as the case may be, the deceased's personal representatives."

MEANING OF "TRANSACTION IN A CARBON EMISSION TRADING PRODUCT"

41 [Omitted by SI 2014/685, reg. 9(3).]

History – Reg. 41 omitted by SI 2014/685, reg. 9(3), with effect from transactions entered into on or after 8 April 2014. Former reg. 41 read as follows:

"MEANING OF "TRANSACTION IN A CARBON EMISSION TRADING PRODUCT"

41(1) For the purposes of regulation 33(g) a "**transaction in a carbon emission trading product**" means a transaction–

(a)   in Community tradable emissions allowances, or

(b)   in transferable units issued pursuant to the Kyoto Protocol,

which does not otherwise fall within any other paragraph of regulation 33.

41(2) For the purposes of this regulation–

"**Community tradable emissions allowances**" means transferable allowances which relate to the making of emissions of greenhouse gases, and are allocated as part of a system made for the purpose of implementing any Community obligation of the United Kingdom relating to such emissions,

"**the Kyoto Protocol**" means the Kyoto Protocol to the United Nations Framework Convention on Climate Change signed at Kyoto on 11th December 1997,

"**units**" includes assigned amount units, certified emission reductions, emission reduction units and removal units."

PART 4 – INVESTMENT TRUST HAVING AN INTEREST IN OFFSHORE NON-REPORTING FUNDS AND INDEX TRACKING FUNDS

INTERESTS IN OFFSHORE NON-REPORTING FUNDS: GENERAL

42(1)   Regulation 43 applies if—

(a)   an investment trust disposes of an asset which is an interest in a non-reporting fund ("the asset"), and

(b)   the conditions in paragraph (2) are satisfied for the period starting with the date on which the investment trust acquired the asset and ending with the day of the disposal.

42(2)   The conditions are that—

(a)   the investment trust has access to the accounts of the non-reporting fund,

(b)   the investment trust had sufficient information about the non-reporting fund referred to in paragraph (1)(a) to enable it to prepare computations of reportable income for the non-reporting fund for every accounting period which, if the non-reporting fund were a reporting fund, would be a reporting period ending within the period mentioned in paragraph (1)(b),

(c)   the investment trust has prepared such computations, and

(d)   any excess of the investment trust's share of the reportable income of the non-reporting fund over the investment trust's share of the distributions made by the non-reporting fund is included in the amount available for distribution by the investment trust for each accounting period of the investment trust which falls within the period mentioned in paragraph (1)(b).

42(3)   An investment trust has an interest in a non-reporting fund if and to the extent that it has an interest in such a fund for the purposes of the Offshore Funds Regulations.

42(4)   For the purposes of the computations mentioned in paragraph (2)(b), regulation 80 (treatment of investment transactions carried out by diversely owned funds) of the Offshore Funds Regulations applies if (and only if) the non-reporting fund is a UCITS fund.

42(5)   In this regulation, "**UCITS fund**" has the same meaning as in regulation 12 (general interpretation) of the Offshore Funds Regulations and "**reporting period**" has the same meaning as in regulation 91 (meaning of "reporting period") of those Regulations.

TREATMENT OF DISPOSAL OF INTEREST IN NON-REPORTING FUND

43   No tax shall be charged on the investment trust under regulation 17 (the charge to tax) of the Offshore Funds Regulations on the disposal by the investment trust of an asset which is an interest in a non-reporting fund at the time of the disposal.

TREATMENT OF INTEREST IN NON-REPORTING FUND: CASES WHERE CONDITIONS IN REGULATION 42(2) WOULD NOT BE SATISFIED

44(1)   This regulation applies in relation to an asset of an investment trust ("the asset")—

(a)   which is an interest in a non-reporting fund, but

(b)   in relation to which the conditions in regulation 42(2) would not (apart from this regulation) be satisfied for the whole of the period specified in regulation 42(1)(b) in relation to the asset.

44(2)   Paragraph (4) applies if the investment trust, in relation to the asset, reasonably expects to satisfy the conditions in regulation 42(2) for the period beginning with a date to be determined in accordance with paragraph (3) ("the deemed start date") and ending with the date of the disposal of the asset.

44(3)   The deemed start date is a date to be determined by the investment trust which must not be earlier than 1st January 2012.

44(4)   The investment trust is treated for all purposes (including for the purposes of determining the beginning of the period mentioned in regulation 42(1)(b)) as if it had, on the deemed start date, disposed of the asset (and not satisfied the conditions in regulation 42(2)) and immediately reacquired the asset for a consideration equal to its market value on the deemed start date.

44(5)   The investment trust must notify the Commissioners of the deemed start date by making an appropriate entry in its company tax return for the accounting period in which the deemed start date falls.

INDEX TRACKING FUNDS

45(1)   This regulation applies if–

(a)   an investment trust has an interest in a non-reporting fund,

(b)   the conditions in paragraph (2) are met throughout the relevant period.

45(2)   The conditions are that–

(a)   in accordance with the instrument constituting the investment trust, the aim of the investment trust's policy is to replicate the performance of a qualifying index,

(b)   the main purpose of the investment in the non-reporting fund is to represent the composition of the qualifying index, and

(c)   the capital and income returns of the investment trust replicate as closely as practicable the returns of the investment comprised in the qualifying index.

45(3)   For the purposes of paragraph (2) an index is a **"qualifying index"** if–

(a)   it is based solely on the value of securities listed on a recognised stock exchange or admitted to trading on a regulated market,

(b)   either a competent authority for the United Kingdom or an authority responsible for regulating offshore funds recognises the index on the basis that–

     (i)   its composition is sufficiently diverse,

     (ii)   it represents an adequate benchmark for the market to which it refers, and

     (iii)   it is published in such a way that it is widely available, and

(c)   it is calculated and published by a body which is managed independently from the management of the investment trust.

45(4)   Regulation 17 of the Offshore Funds Regulations does not apply in respect of a disposal by the investment trust of the interest in the non-reporting fund.

45(5)   In this regulation the **"relevant period"** means the period–

(a)   starting with the day on which the investment trust acquires the interest in the non-reporting fund (or any part of it), and

(b)   ending with the day of the disposal of the interest.

45(6)   In this regulation–

(a)   a **"competent authority for the United Kingdom"** means the authority which is a competent authority for the United Kingdom for the purposes of Directive 2009/65/EC of the European Parliament and of the Council on the coordination of laws, regulations and administrative provisions relating to undertakings for collective investment in transferable securities (UCITS), and

(b)   **"regulated market"** has the same meaning as in Directive 2004/39/EC of the European Parliament and of the Council on markets in financial instruments (see article 4.1(14)).

CONSEQUENTIAL AMENDMENT

46   [Amending provision not reproduced.]

RESEARCH AND DEVELOPMENT (QUALIFYING BODIES) (TAX) ORDER 2012

(SI 2012/286)

Made on 6 February 2012 by the Treasury, in exercise of the powers conferred by s. 1142(1)(e), (3) and (4) of the Corporation Tax Act 2009. Operative from 28 February 2012.

CITATION, COMMENCEMENT AND EFFECT

1(1) This Order may be cited as the Research and Development (Qualifying Bodies) (Tax) Order 2012 and shall come into force on 28th February 2012.

1(2) In relation to a body specified in column (1) of the Schedule to this Order, this Order has effect in relation to expenditure incurred on or after the date set out in column (3) opposite the entry in column (1) for that body.

BODIES PRESCRIBED FOR THE PURPOSES OF PART 13 OF THE CORPORATION TAX ACT 2009

2 Each of the bodies specified in column (1) of the Schedule to this Order is a body prescribed for the purposes of Part 13 of the Corporation Tax Act 2009 (additional relief for expenditure on research and development).

3 The Research and Development (Qualifying Bodies) (Tax) Order 2009 is revoked.

SCHEDULE – PRESCRIBED BODIES

(1)	(2)	(3)
Name of prescribed body	**Address**	**Date**
Aristotle University of Thessaloniki	Thessaloniki, Greece	1 April 2002
Azienda Ospendaliera Universitaria Pisana	Messina, Italy	12 October 2010
British University in Egypt	El Sherouk City, Misr, Egypt	1 April 2002
Colorado School of Mines	Golden, Colorado, USA	1 April 2002
Colorado State University	Fort Collins, Colorado, USA	1 April 2002
Cornell University	Ithaca, New York, USA	1 April 2002
Delft University of Technology	Delft, Netherlands	1 April 2002
Ecole Polytechnique Federal de Lausanne	Lausanne, Switzerland	1 April 2002
Faculty Hospital Motol Prague	Prague, Czech Republic	12 October 2010
Fakultni Nemocnice Brno	Brno, Czech Republic	12 October 2010
Fakultni Nemocnice Ostrava	Ostrava, Czech Republic	12 October 2010
Freie University Berlin	Berlin, Germany	1 April 2002
Hospitais Da Universidade De Coimbra	Coimbra, Portugal	1 April 2002
Indian Institute of Technology Bombay	Maharashtra, India	1 April 2002
Indian Institute of Technology Kanpur	Kanpur, India	1 April 2002
Indiana University	Bloomington, Indiana, USA	22 March 2010
Institute of Computer Science	Crete, Greece	1 April 2002
Interuniversitair Micro-Elektronica Centrum	Leuven, Belgium	1 April 2002
Iowa State University	Ames, Iowa, USA	1 April 2002
Kansas State University	Manhattan, Kansas, USA	1 April 2002
Karlsruhe Institute of Technology	Karlsruhe, Germany	26 July 2011
Karolinska University Hospital	Stockohlm, Sweden	22 March 2010
Kazakh-British Technical University	Almaty, Kazakhstan	1 April 2002

(1) Name of prescribed body	(2) Address	(3) Date
King Abdulaziz University	Jeddah, Saudi Arabia	7 November 2011
Klinikum der Universität München	Munich, Germany	12 October 2010
Lawrence Berkeley National Laboratory	Berkeley, California, USA	1 April 2002
Martin-Luther University	Halle-Wittenburg, Germany	1 April 2002
Louisiana State University	Louisiana, USA	1 April 2002
Massachusetts Institute of Technology	Massachusetts, USA	1 April 2002
Massey University	Auckland, New Zealand	1 April 2002
McMaster University	Hamilton, Ontario, Canada	22 March 2010
Medical University of Lodz	Lodz, Poland	12 October 2010
Medizinische Universität Wien	Vienna, Austria	12 October 2010
Michigan State University	Michigan, USA	01 April 2002
Nanyang Technological University	Singapore	26 July 2011
National Medical University Vinnitsa	Vinnitsa, Ukraine	12 October 2010
National Technical University of Athens	Athens, Greece	22 February 2011
Norwegian University of Science & Technology	Trondheim, Norway	26 May 2010
Ohio State University	Columbus, Ohio, USA	1 April 2002
Otto-von-Guericke-Universität Magdeburg	Magdeburg, Germany	1 April 2002
OTRI- Universidad de Cordoba	Cordoba, Spain	22 March 2010
Politecnico Di Milano	Milan, Italy	1 April 2002
Pusan National University	Pusan, South Korea	26 July 2011
Ruhr Universität	Bochum, Germany	1 April 2002
RWTH Aachen University	Aachen, Germany	1 April 2002
St. James's Hospital	Dublin, Ireland	1 April 2002
Southern Illinois University	Illinois, USA	1 April 2002
Stanford University	Stanford, California, USA	1 April 2002
Swedish University of Agriculture Sciences	Uppsala, Sweden	1 April 2002
Swiss Federal Institute of Technology (ETH) Zurich	Zurich, Switzerland	1 April 2002
Technische Universität Clausthal	Clausthal-Zellerfeld, Germany	1 April 2002
Technische Universität Dresden	Dresden, Germany	1 April 2002
Technische Universität Munchen	Munich, Germany	1 April 2002
Texas A&M University	Texas, USA	1 April 2002
The Pennsylvania State University	Pennsylvania, USA	1 April 2002
The University of Antwerp	Antwerp, Belgium	22 March 2010
The University of Oklahoma	Norman, Oklahoma, USA	22 February 2011
The University of the West Indies	Kingston, Jamaica	1 April 2002
Tufts University	Massachusetts, USA	1 April 2002
UMC St Radbound	Nijmegen, Netherlands	12 October 2010
UMC Utrecht	Utrecht, Netherlands	1 April 2002
Umhat Alexandrovska Sofia	Sofia, Bulgaria	12 October 2010
Universidad de Las Palmas de Gran Canaria	Gran Canaria, Spain	1 April 2002
Universidad De Valladolid	Valladolid, Spain	1 April 2002
Universidade Do Minho	Braga, Portugal	22 February 2011
Universitair Ziekenhuis Gent	Gent, Belgium	1 April 2002

(1) Name of prescribed body	(2) Address	(3) Date
Universitat Politècnica de Catalonia of Jordi Girona	Barcelona, Spain	1 April 2002
Universite de Lausanne (UNIL)	Lausanne, Switzerland	1 April 2002
University Hospitals of Cleveland	Cleveland, USA	1 April 2002
University of Alberta	Edmonton, Alberta, Canada,	1 April 2002
University of Applied Sciences Braunschweig/ Wolfenbüttel	Wolfenbuttel, Germany	1 April 2002
University of Bergen	Bergen, Norway	1 April 2002
University of Berlin	Berlin, Germany	1 April 2002
University of British Columbia	British Columbia, Canada	1 April 2002
University of California at Davis	Davis, California, USA	1 April 2002
University of California, Berkeley	California, USA	1 April 2002
University of Dusseldorf	Dusseldorf, Germany	1 April 2002
University of Florida	Gainesville, Florida, USA	1 April 2002
University of Guelph	Ontario, Canada	1 April 2002
University of Hacettepe	Ankara, Turkey	1 April 2002
University of Hanover	Hanover, Germany	15 February 2011
University of Heidelberg	Heidelberg, Germany	22 March 2010
University of Houston	Houston, Texas, USA	1 April 2002
University of Limerick	Limerick, Ireland	17 May 2011
University of Manitoba	Winnipeg, Canada	1 April 2002
University of Massachusetts Medical School	Massachusetts, USA	1 April 2002
University of Memphis	Memphis, Tennessee, USA	22 March 2010
University of Michigan	Ann Arbor, Michigan, USA	1 April 2002
University of Minnesota	Minneapolis, USA	1 April 2002
University of Missouri-Columbia	Columbia, USA	1 April 2002
University of Munich	Munich, Germany	1 April 2002
University of Munster	Munster, Germany	1 April 2002
University of New England	Armidale, Australia	1 April 2002
University of New South Wales	Sydney, Australia	1 April 2002
University of Oslo	Oslo, Norway	22 March 2010
University of Pennsylvania	Pennsylvania, USA	1 April 2002
University of Pisa	Pisa, Italy	5 April 2011
University of Potsdam	Potsdam, Germany	1 April 2002
University of Queensland	Brisbane, Australia	1 April 2002
University of Santiago de Compostela	Santiago de Compostella, Spain	1 April 2002
University of Seville	Seville, Spain	1 April 2002
University of Sydney	New South Wales, Australia	1 April 2002
Universite of Stuttgart	Stuttgart, Germany	22 February 2011
University of Technology, Sydney	Broadway, Australia	1 April 2002
University of Tennessee	Knoxville, Tennessee, USA	1 April 2002
University of Texas	Austin, Texas	1 April 2002
University of Trento	Trento, Italy	5 April 2011
University of Tulsa	Tulsa, Oklahoma, USA	1 April 2002

(1) Name of prescribed body	(2) Address	(3) Date
University of Turku	Turku, Finland	15 February 2011
University of Utah	Salt Lake City, Utah, USA	1 April 2002
University of Utah School of Medicine	Salt Lake City, Utah, USA	1 April 2002
University of Utrecht	Utrecht, Netherlands	1 April 2002
University of Veterinary Medicine, Hannover	Hannover, Germany	1 April 2002
University of Wisconsin	Madison, Wisconsin, USA	1 April 2002
Uppasala University	Uppsala, Sweden	22 March 2010
Virginia Polytechnic Institute and State University	Blacksburg, Virginia, USA	1 April 2002
Washington University	St Louis, Missouri, USA	22 March 2010
Waterford Institute of Technology	Waterford, Ireland	17 May 2011
Westfaelische Wilhelms- Universität	Munster, Germany	1 April 2002
Wichita State University	Wichita, Kansas, USA	17 May 2011
Yale University School of Medicine	New Haven, Connecticut, USA	22 March 2010

BANK LEVY (DOUBLE TAXATION RELIEF) REGULATIONS 2012

(SI 2012/458)

Made on 21 February 2012 by the Treasury, in exercise of the powers conferred by para. 67 of Sch. 19 to the Finance Act 2011. Operative from 14 March 2012.

INTRODUCTION

Citation, commencement and effect

1(1) These Regulations may be cited as the Bank Levy (Double Taxation Relief) Regulations 2012 and come into force on 14th March 2012.

1(2) These Regulations have effect in relation to periods of account ending on or after 1st January 2011.

Application of these Regulations

2 These Regulations apply where–

(a)   the bank levy is charged in relation to–

     (i)   the relevant group which is a foreign banking group or a relevant non-banking group, or

     (ii)   the relevant entity which is a relevant foreign bank,

(b)   an equivalent foreign levy is imposed on that relevant group or relevant entity by the law of a foreign territory, and

(c)   the equivalent foreign levy is specified in regulation 3.

Specified equivalent foreign levy

3 The equivalent foreign levy in respect of which these Regulations are made is Art. 235 ter ZE du code gènèral des impôts imposed by the law of France.

DOUBLE TAXATION RELIEF BY WAY OF CREDIT

Double taxation relief

4(1) Where these Regulations apply, an amount of the equivalent foreign levy paid is allowed as a credit against the bank levy for a chargeable period (see regulation 5).

4(2) Subject to the provisions of these Regulations, the amount of the bank levy for the chargeable period is reduced by the amount of the credit.

4(3) But the amount of the bank levy shall not be reduced to below nil.

4(4) The credit under paragraph (2) requires a claim.

Calculation of the credit

5 Take steps 1 to 4 to determine how much of the equivalent foreign levy is available as a credit against the bank levy.

Step 1

Determine the amount ("A") of assets of the relevant group or the relevant entity as at the end of the chargeable period by reference to which the equivalent foreign levy is calculated.

Step 2

Determine the amount ("B") of UK assets as at the end of the chargeable period by reference to which the equivalent foreign levy is calculated.

Step 3

Determine the amount of the equivalent foreign levy paid ("C") in relation to the chargeable period.

If a proportion (Z%) of the period in relation to which the equivalent foreign levy is calculated falls in any other chargeable period, Z% of the equivalent foreign levy shall be attributable to that other period.

Step 4

The amount of the equivalent foreign levy available as a credit against the bank levy is $B/A \times C$.

Determining assets and UK assets

6(1) This regulation applies to determine the assets and the UK assets of the relevant group or relevant entity.

6(2) In the case of the relevant group, the amount of the assets and the UK assets are determined by reference to—

(a) the amounts recognised in the group's consolidated financial statements for the chargeable period as prepared under international accounting standards or UK GAAP, or

(b) if no such financial statements are prepared, the amounts which would have been so recognised had consolidated financial statements for the group been prepared for the chargeable period under international accounting standards.

6(3) In the case of the relevant entity, assets and UK assets are determined by reference to—

(a) the amounts recognised in the entity's financial statements for the chargeable period as prepared under international accounting standards or UK GAAP, or

(b) if no such financial statements are prepared, the amounts which would have been so recognised had such financial statements been prepared for the chargeable period under international accounting standards or under UK GAAP if that is what the entity prepares its financial statements under.

6(4) For the purposes of these Regulations, **"UK assets"** means—

(a) in relation to the relevant group—

　(i) the assets of any relevant UK sub-group which is a member of the relevant group,

　(ii) the assets of any UK resident entity which is a member of the relevant group but is not a member of a relevant UK sub-group,

　(iii) the assets of a non-UK resident entity which is a member of the relevant group and is a member of a UK sub-group but is not a member of a relevant UK sub-group, and

　(iv) the assets of any permanent establishment through which any member of the relevant group carries on a trade in the UK; and

(b) in relation to the relevant entity, the assets of any permanent establishment through which the entity carries on a trade in the UK.

6(5) Paragraph 26 (including sub-paragraph (4)) of Schedule 19 to the Finance Act 2011 applies for the purposes of determining the assets of a permanent establishment.

Exchange rates

7 Where the equivalent foreign levy is imposed in a currency other than sterling, for the purposes of regulation 5 the amount of equivalent foreign currency is to be translated into its sterling equivalent by reference to the spot rate of exchange for the last day of the chargeable period in relation to which the credit is claimed.

CLAIM FOR DOUBLE TAXATION RELIEF

General time limit for making a claim

8(1) A claim for credit under regulation 4(1) must be made not more than—

(a) four years after the end of the accounting period in relation to which the bank levy is treated as an amount of corporation tax chargeable on the responsible member (see paragraph 50 of Schedule 19 to the Finance Act 2011) or the relevant entity (see paragraph 51 of that Schedule), or

(b) if later, one year after the end of the accounting period in which the equivalent foreign levy is paid.

8(2) If the chargeable period in relation to which the bank levy is charged falls in more than one accounting period, the accounting period referred to in paragraph (1)(a) shall be the latest of those periods.

Relevant groups: responsible member to make claim

9 Where the bank levy is charged as provided for by paragraph 4 of Schedule 19 to the Finance Act 2011 (bank levy to be charged in relation to certain groups of entities) any claim for credit under regulation 4(1) must be made by the responsible member.

LIMITS ON CREDIT

Restriction of credit

10(1) Where the bank levy is charged in relation to the relevant group, if the parent entity is not resident in the foreign territory ("territory A") the law of which imposes the equivalent foreign levy, the credit under regulation 4(1) is only available to reduce the amount of the bank levy charged in relation to relevant chargeable equity and liabilities of the relevant group.

10(2) In paragraph (1), **"relevant chargeable equity and liabilities"** means chargeable equity and liabilities that would be recognised in relevant accounts for the chargeable period had such accounts been prepared for the member or members of the group ("the relevant member or members") resident in territory A.

10(3) In paragraph (2), **"relevant accounts"** mean a consolidated financial statement or financial statement–

(a)   prepared under international accounting standards or under UK GAAP if that is what the relevant member or members prepare financial statements under, and

(b)   in which the UK assets subject to the equivalent foreign levy in respect of which the credit is given would be recognised.

Reduction in credit: payment by reference to equivalent foreign levy

11(1) Paragraph (2) applies if–

(a)   credit for an equivalent foreign levy is to be allowed to an entity under these Regulations, and

(b)   a payment is made by a tax authority to that entity, or to any other person, by reference to the equivalent foreign levy.

11(2) The amount of the credit must be recalculated by repeating steps 3 and 4 in regulation 5, reducing the amount of the equivalent foreign levy by reference to the payment referred to in paragraph (1)(b).

Priority of credits

12(1) Where credits are allowed in relation to equivalent foreign levies imposed by the law of two or more foreign territories under these Regulations or under these Regulations and any Regulations made under paragraph 66 (arrangements affording double taxation relief) or paragraph 67 (power to provide for double taxation relief) of Schedule 19 to the Finance Act 2011, the credits apply to reduce the bank levy in the order specified in paragraph (2), subject to paragraphs (3) and (4).

12(2) The order is–

First, any credit allowed in relation to the equivalent foreign levy imposed by the law of the foreign territory in which the parent entity is resident.

Second, any credit allowed in relation to the equivalent foreign levy imposed by the law of the foreign territory in which a direct subsidiary ("the first subsidiary") is resident or a permanent establishment of the parent entity is located.

Third, any credit allowed in relation to an equivalent foreign levy imposed by the law of the foreign territory in which a direct subsidiary ("the second subsidiary") is resident or a permanent establishment of the first subsidiary is located.

Fourth, any credit allowed in relation to an equivalent foreign levy imposed by the law of the foreign territory in which a direct subsidiary of the second subsidiary is resident or a permanent establishment of the second subsidiary is located, and so on in relation to any fourth and further subsidiaries.

12(3) If an entity has direct subsidiaries ("the elected subsidiaries") in more than one foreign territory which imposes an equivalent foreign levy, the responsible member shall elect as to the order ("the elected order") in which the credits allowed in relation to the equivalent foreign levies shall be applied.

12(4) If any of the elected subsidiaries themselves have direct subsidiaries in more than one foreign territory which imposes an equivalent foreign levy, paragraphs (2) and (3) shall apply to those direct subsidiaries in the elected order and paragraph (2) shall apply as if each elected subsidiary were a parent entity.

12(5) For the purposes of this regulation, where an equivalent foreign levy is not imposed by the law of the foreign territory in which an entity ("E") is resident, any direct subsidiary of E shall be treated as the direct subsidiary of the entity which is the parent entity of E.

ACTION AFTER ADJUSTMENT OF AMOUNT PAYABLE BY WAY OF BANK LEVY OR EQUIVALENT FOREIGN LEVY

Consequences of adjustment of the bank levy or equivalent foreign levy

13(1)   Paragraph (2) applies to a claim or assessment if–

(a)   the amount of credit given under regulation 4(1) is reduced under regulation 11, or becomes excessive or insufficient by reason of any adjustment of the amount of any bank levy or equivalent foreign levy,

(b)   the reduction or adjustment gives rise to the claim or assessment, and

(c)   the claim or assessment is made not later than 6 years from the date on which all material determinations have been made, whether in the UK or elsewhere.

13(2)   Nothing in the Tax Acts limiting the time for the making of assessments, or limiting the time for the making of claims for relief, applies to the assessment or claim.

13(3)   In paragraph (1)(c) **"material determination"** means an assessment, reduction, adjustment or other determination that is material in determining whether any, and (if so) what, credit is to be given.

Duty to give notice that adjustment has rendered credit excessive

14(1)   This regulation applies if–

(a)   any credit has been allowed under regulation 4(1), and

(b)   later, the amount of that credit is reduced under regulation 11, or becomes excessive as a result of an adjustment of the amount of the equivalent foreign levy.

14(2)   The relevant entity or, in the case of the relevant group, the responsible member must give notice that a reduction has been made or that the amount of the credit has become excessive as a result of the making of an adjustment.

14(3)   Notice under paragraph (2) is to be given–

(a)   to an officer of Revenue and Customs, and

(b)   within one year from when the reduction or adjustment is made.

BANK LEVY (DOUBLE TAXATION ARRANGEMENTS) (FEDERAL REPUBLIC OF GERMANY) REGULATIONS 2012

(SI 2012/459)

Made on 21 February 2012 by the Treasury, in exercise of the powers conferred by para. 66(8) and (9) of Sch. 19 to the Finance Act 2011. Operative from 14 March 2012.

INTRODUCTION

Citation, commencement and effect

1(1) These Regulations may be cited as the Bank Levy (Double Taxation Arrangements) (Federal Republic of Germany) Regulations 2012 and come into force on 14th March 2012.

1(2) These Regulations have effect in relation to periods of account ending on or after 1st January 2011.

1(3) But regulation 10 has effect in relation to periods of account beginning on or after 14th March 2012.

Interpretation

2 In these Regulations–

"**double taxation arrangements**" means the Convention and the Protocol;

"**Convention**" means the Convention between the Federal Republic of Germany and the United Kingdom of Great Britain and Northern Ireland for the avoidance of double charging of bank levies signed on 7th December 2011 in London;

"**German bank levy**" means the equivalent foreign levy imposed by the Federal Republic of Germany;

"**Protocol**" means the Protocol attached to the Convention;

"**UK permanent establishment**" means a permanent establishment through which a trade is carried on in the United Kingdom by a relevant foreign bank which is a relevant entity or a member of a relevant group.

Application of these Regulations

3 These Regulations apply in relation to the provision of relief from the bank levy provided by the Convention where the bank levy and the German bank levy are charged in relation to a UK permanent establishment.

DOUBLE TAXATION RELIEF BY WAY OF CREDIT

Double taxation relief

4(1) Where these Regulations apply, the amount of the German bank levy paid which is attributable to the UK permanent establishment in relation to a chargeable period is allowed as a credit against the bank levy for that chargeable period.

4(2) Subject to the provisions of these Regulations, the amount of the bank levy for the chargeable period is reduced by the amount of the credit.

4(3) But the amount of the bank levy shall not be reduced to below nil.

4(4) The amount of the German bank levy attributable to the UK permanent establishment is the amount determined in accordance with paragraph 1 of the Protocol in relation to the chargeable period.

4(5) If a proportion (Z%) of the period in relation to which the German bank levy is calculated falls in any other chargeable period, Z% of the German bank levy shall be attributable to that other period.

Exchange rates

5 For the purposes of regulation 4, the amount of German bank levy is to be translated into its sterling equivalent by reference to the spot rate of exchange for the last day of the chargeable period in relation to which the credit is claimed.

CLAIM FOR DOUBLE TAXATION RELIEF

General time limit for making a claim

6(1) A claim for credit under regulation 4(1) must be made not more than–

(a) four years after the end of the accounting period in relation to which the bank levy is treated as an amount of corporation tax chargeable on the responsible member (see paragraph 50 of Schedule 19 to the Finance Act 2011) or the relevant entity (see paragraph 51 of that Schedule), or

(b) if later, one year after the end of the accounting period in which the German bank levy is paid.

6(2) If the chargeable period in relation to which the bank levy is charged falls in more than one accounting period, the accounting period referred to in paragraph (1)(a) shall be the latest of those periods.

Relevant groups: responsible member to make claim

7 Where the bank levy is charged as provided for by paragraph 4 of Schedule 19 to the Finance Act 2011 (bank levy to be charged in relation to certain groups of entities) any claim for credit under regulation 4(1) must be made by the responsible member.

LIMITS ON CREDIT

Restriction of credit

8(1) The credit under regulation 4(1) is only available to reduce the amount of the bank levy so far as it is attributable to chargeable equity and liabilities of the UK permanent establishment.

8(2) Bank levy is to be attributed for the purposes of paragraph (1) on a just and reasonable basis.

Reduction in credit: payment by reference to German bank levy

9(1) Paragraph (2) applies if–

(a) credit for the German bank levy is to be allowed to an entity under these Regulations, and

(b) a payment is made by a tax authority to that entity, or to any other person, by reference to the German bank levy.

9(2) The amount of the credit must be recalculated under regulation 4 reducing the amount of the German bank levy by reference to the payment referred to in paragraph (1)(b).

Priority of credits

10(1) Where credits are allowed in relation to equivalent foreign levies (including the German bank levy) under these Regulations and under any Regulations made under paragraph 66 (arrangements affording double taxation relief) or paragraph 67 (power to provide for double taxation relief) of Schedule 19 to the Finance Act 2011, the credits apply to reduce the bank levy in the order specified in paragraph (2), subject to paragraphs (3) and (4).

10(2) The order is–

First, any credit allowed in relation to the equivalent foreign levy imposed by the law of the foreign territory in which the parent entity is resident.

Second, any credit allowed in relation to the equivalent foreign levy imposed by the law of the foreign territory in which a direct subsidiary ("the first subsidiary") is resident or a permanent establishment of the parent entity is located.

Third, any credit allowed in relation to an equivalent foreign levy imposed by the law of the foreign territory in which a direct subsidiary ("the second subsidiary") is resident or a permanent establishment of the first subsidiary is located.

Fourth, any credit allowed in relation to an equivalent foreign levy imposed by the law of the foreign territory in which a direct subsidiary of the second subsidiary is resident or a permanent establishment of the second subsidiary is located, and so on in relation to any fourth and further subsidiaries.

10(3) If an entity has direct subsidiaries ("the elected subsidiaries") in more than one foreign territory which imposes an equivalent foreign levy, the responsible member shall elect as to the order ("the elected order") in which the credits allowed in relation to the equivalent foreign levies shall be applied.

10(4) If any of the elected subsidiaries themselves have direct subsidiaries in more than one foreign territory which imposes an equivalent foreign levy, paragraphs (2) and (3) shall apply to those direct subsidiaries in the elected order and paragraph (1) shall apply as if each elected subsidiary were a parent entity.

10(5)   For the purposes of this regulation, where an equivalent foreign levy is not imposed by the law of the foreign territory in which an entity ("E") is resident, any direct subsidiary of E shall be treated as the direct subsidiary of the entity which is the parent entity of E.

ACTION AFTER ADJUSTMENT OF AMOUNT PAYABLE BY WAY OF BANK LEVY OR GERMAN BANK LEVY

Consequences of adjustment of the bank levy or German bank levy

11(1)   Paragraph (2) applies to a claim or assessment if–

(a)   the amount of credit given under regulation 4 is reduced under regulation 9, or becomes excessive or insufficient by reason of any adjustment of the amount of any bank levy or German bank levy,

(b)   the reduction or adjustment gives rise to the claim or assessment, and

(c)   the claim or assessment is made not later than 6 years from the time when all material determinations have been made, whether in the UK or elsewhere.

11(2)   Nothing in the Tax Acts limiting the time for the making of assessments, or limiting the time for the making of claims for relief, applies to the assessment or claim.

11(3)   In paragraph (1)(c) " **material determination**" means an assessment, reduction, adjustment or other determination that is material in determining whether any, and (if so) what, credit is to be given.

Duty to give notice that adjustment has rendered credit excessive

12(1)   This regulation applies if–

(a)   any credit has been allowed under regulation 4, and

(b)   later, the amount of that credit is reduced under regulation 9, or becomes excessive as a result of an adjustment of the amount of the German bank levy.

12(2)   The relevant entity or, in the case of a relevant group, the responsible member must give notice that a reduction has been made or that the amount of the credit has become excessive as a result of the making of an adjustment.

12(3)   Notice under paragraph (2) is to be given–

(a)   to an officer of Revenue and Customs, and

(b)   within one year from when the reduction or adjustment is made.

CASES ABOUT BEING TAXED OTHERWISE THAN IN ACCORDANCE WITH THE CONVENTION

Giving effect to solutions to cases and mutual agreements resolving cases

13(1)   Paragraphs (2) and (4) apply if under, and for the purposes of, the double taxation arrangements–

(a)   an entity presents, to the Commissioners for Her Majesty's Revenue and Customs or to a competent authority in the Federal Republic of Germany, a case concerning the entity's being taxed (whether in the United Kingdom or the Federal Republic of Germany) otherwise than in accordance with the double taxation arrangements, and

(b)   the Commissioners arrive at a solution to the case or make a mutual agreement with a competent authority in the Federal Republic of Germany for the resolution of the case.

13(2)   The Commissioners are to give effect to the solution or mutual agreement despite anything in any enactment, and any such adjustment as is appropriate in consequence may be made.

13(3)   An adjustment under paragraph (2) may be made by way of discharge or repayment of tax, the allowance of credit against tax payable in the United Kingdom, the making of an assessment or otherwise.

13(4)   A claim for relief under any provision of the Tax Acts or the enactments relating to capital gains tax may be made in pursuance of the solution or mutual agreement at any time before the end of the period of 12 months following the notification of the solution or mutual agreement to the entity affected, even if that involves making the claim after a deadline imposed by another enactment.

13(5) In this regulation " **competent authority in the Federal Republic of Germany**" means the Federal Ministry of Finance or the agency to which it has delegated its powers.

Effect of, and deadline for, presenting a case

14(1) This regulation applies to the presentation of a case concerning an entity's being taxed (whether in the United Kingdom or the Federal Republic of Germany) otherwise than in accordance with the double taxation arrangements.

14(2) The presentation of any such case under and in accordance with the double taxation arrangements–

(a) does not constitute a claim for relief under the Tax Acts or the enactments relating to capital gains tax, and

(b) is accordingly not subject to section 42 of the Taxes Management Act 1970 or any other enactment relating to the making of such claims.

14(3) Any such claim must be presented before the end of the later of–

(a) the period of 3 years following the first notification of the action resulting in the entity being charged otherwise than in accordance with the double taxation arrangements, and

(b) the period of 6 years following the end of the chargeable period to which the case relates.

TAXES, ETC. (FEES FOR PAYMENT BY TELEPHONE) REGULATIONS 2012

(SI 2012/689)

Made on 5 March 2012 by the Commissioners for Her Majesty's Revenue and Customs, in exercise of the powers conferred by s. 136 of the Finance Act 2008. Operative from 2 April 2012.

CITATION AND COMMENCEMENT

1   These Regulations may be cited as the Taxes, etc. (Fees for Payment by Telephone) Regulations 2012 and come into force on 2nd April 2012.

FEE PAYABLE FOR TELEPHONE PAYMENTS MADE BY CREDIT CARD

2(1)   A person who—

(a)   gives telephone authorisation to make a payment by credit card, and

(b)   makes a payment to the Commissioners or the person authorised by the Commissioners,

must also pay a fee of 1.5% of the amount of that payment.

2(2)   The fee must be paid by being added to the payment (so that, accordingly, the person must make a single overall payment, consisting of the payment and the fee).

2(3)   In these Regulations **"credit card"** means a card which—

(a)   is a credit-token within section 14(1)(b) of the Consumer Credit Act 1974, or

(b)   would be a credit-token falling within that enactment were the card to be given to an individual.

REVOCATION

3   The Taxes, etc. (Fees for Payment by Telephone) Regulations 2009 are revoked.

LONDON LEGACY DEVELOPMENT CORPORATION (TAX CONSEQUENCES) REGULATIONS 2012
(SI 2012/701)

Made on 6 March 2012 by the Treasury, in exercise of the powers conferred by Pt. 3 of Sch. 24 to the Localism Act 2011. Operative from 31 March 2012.

CITATION AND COMMENCEMENT

1 These Regulations may be cited as the London Legacy Development Corporation (Tax Consequences) Regulations 2012 and come into force on 31st March 2012.

INTERPRETATION

2 In these Regulations–

"**CTA 2009**" means the Corporation Tax Act 2009;

"**CTA 2010**" means the Corporation Tax Act 2010;

"**LLDC**" means the London Legacy Development Corporation;

"**LTGDC**" means the London Thames Gateway Development Corporation;

"**LTGDC relevant transfer**" means a transfer of LTGDC's trading stock from LTGDC to LLDC in relation to, in connection with, or by or under, the London Legacy Development Corporation and the London Thames Gateway Development Corporation (No. 1) Transfer Scheme 2012;

"**OPLC**" means the Olympic Park Legacy Company Limited, company registered number 06900359;

"**OPLC relevant transfer**" means a transfer of property, rights and liabilities from OPLC to LLDC, in relation to, in connection with, or by or under, the London Legacy Development Corporation and the Olympic Park Legacy Company Transfer Scheme 2012;

"**trading stock**" has the same meaning as in section 163 of CTA 2009.

TRANSFERS FROM OPLC TO LLDC

3(1) This regulation applies to an OPLC relevant transfer.

3(2) For the purposes of any enactment about income tax or corporation tax–

(a)   OPLC and LLDC are to be treated as the same person, and

(b)   a relevant transfer is to be disregarded for those purposes.

3(3) A relevant transfer is not to be regarded for the purposes of Part 8 of CTA 2009 (intangible fixed assets) as involving any realisation of an asset by OPLC or acquisition of an asset by LLDC.

3(4) A relevant transfer is not to be regarded for the purposes of Part 14 of CTA 2010 (change in company ownership) as resulting in a change of ownership of a company.

3(5) A relevant transfer does not give rise to any liability to stamp duty land tax.

TRANSFERS FROM LTGDC TO LLDC

4(1) This regulation applies to a LTGDC relevant transfer.

4(2) Paragraphs (3) and (4) have effect in computing for any corporation tax purpose both–

(a)   the profits of LTGDC's trade in relation to which the stock transferred is trading stock immediately before the relevant transfer takes effect, and

(b)   the consideration given by LLDC, or the expenditure incurred by it, for the acquisition of the stock.

4(3) The stock must be taken to have been–

(a)   disposed of by LTGDC in the course of its trade, and

(b)   disposed of and acquired when the relevant transfer takes effect.

4(4) The stock must be valued as if the disposal and acquisition were for a consideration which in relation to LTGDC would have resulted in neither a profit nor a loss being brought into account in respect of the disposal in the accounting period of LTGDC which ends with, or is current at, the time when the relevant transfer takes effect.

FINANCE ACT 2010, SCHEDULE 6, PART 1 (FURTHER CONSEQUENTIAL AND INCIDENTAL PROVISION ETC) ORDER 2012

(SI 2012/735)

Made on 8 March 2012 by the Commissioners for Her Majesty's Revenue and Customs, in exercise of the powers conferred by para. 29(1) and (2) of Sch. 6 to the Finance Act 2010. Operative from 1 April 2012.

CITATION, COMMENCEMENT AND EFFECT

1   This Order may be cited as the Finance Act 2010, Schedule 6, Part 1 (Further Consequential and Incidental Provision etc) Order 2012 and comes into force on 1st April 2012.

2   [Not relevant to Income, Corporation or Capital Gains Taxes.]

3   Article 6 has effect–

(a)   for corporation tax purposes, for accounting periods beginning on or after 1st April 2012, and

(b)   for capital gains tax purposes, for the tax year 2012–13 and subsequent tax years.

4   Article 7 has effect–

(a)   for corporation tax purposes, for accounting periods beginning on or after 1st April 2012, and

(b)   for income tax purposes, for the tax year 2012–13 and subsequent tax years.

DEFINITION OF "CHARITY" FOR THE PURPOSES OF VALUE ADDED TAX

5   [Not relevant to Income, Corporation or Capital Gains Taxes.]

DEFINITION OF "CHARITY" FOR THE PURPOSES OF CAPITAL GAINS TAX

6(1)   The definition of "charity" in section 1(1) of the Charities Act 2011 ceases to apply for the purposes of the enactments relating to capital gains tax to which it would otherwise apply.

6(2)   Accordingly, by virtue of paragraph 33(2) of Schedule 6 to the Finance Act 2010, the definition of "charity" in Part 1 of that Schedule applies for the purposes of those enactments.

AMENDMENT OF CTA 2009

7   In Schedule 4 to CTA 2009 (index of defined expressions), in the entry for "charity", for "section 1119 of CTA 2010" substitute "paragraph 1 of Schedule 6 to FA 2010".

POSTAL SERVICES ACT 2011 (TAXATION) REGULATIONS 2012

(SI 2012/764)

Made on 8 March 2012 by the Treasury, in exercise of the power conferred by s. 23 and 89(2) of the Postal Services Act 2011. Operative in accordance with reg. 1(1).

ARRANGEMENT OF REGULATIONS

REGULATION

24.   FURTHER PROTECTION IN RELATION TO CHANGES TO TAX TREATMENT OF ACCRUED RIGHTS AS A RESULT OF THE TRANSFER

PART 4 – STAMP DUTY, STAMP DUTY LAND TAX AND STAMP DUTY RESERVE TAX

PART 1 – PRELIMINARY

CITATION, COMMENCEMENT AND EFFECT

1(1)   These Regulations may be cited as the Postal Services Act 2011 (Taxation) Regulations 2012 and come into force immediately after the coming into force of both–

(a)   the first order made under section 17(2) (transfer of qualifying accrued rights to new public scheme) of the Act by virtue of an order made under section 25(4) and (5) of the Act ("the specified day order"); and

(b)   the first order made under section 21(1) (transfer of assets of the RMPP) of the Act by virtue of the specified day order.

1(2)   Regulation 3 has effect in relation to the accounting period which begins on or before and ends on or after the date on which the first order made under section 17(2) of the Act comes into force by virtue of the specified day order, and subsequent accounting periods.

1(3)   Regulations 4 and 5 have effect in relation to accounting periods beginning on or after the date on which the first order made under section 17(2) of the Act comes into force by virtue of the specified day order.

INTERPRETATION

2(1)   In these Regulations–

"**accounting period**" is to be read in accordance with Chapter 2 of Part 2 of the Corporation Tax Act 2009 (accounting periods);

"**Accrued Rights**" means the rights transferred from the RMPP to the new public scheme pursuant to an order made under section 17(2) of the Act;

"**the Accrued Rights Transfer**" means the transfer of Accrued Rights from the RMPP to the new public scheme;

"**the Act**" means the Postal Services Act 2011;

"**the Assets Transfer**" means the transfer of assets of the RMPP pursuant to an order made under section 21(1) of the Act;

"**excluded contributions**" means contributions paid to the RMPP in advance of 31st March 2012 in respect of amounts falling due after that date under the existing Schedule of Contributions of the RMPP;

"**the final accounting period**" means the accounting period which ended immediately before the first qualifying accounting period;

"**the first qualifying accounting period**" means the first accounting period which begins on or after the date on which the first order made under section 17(2) of the Act comes into force by virtue of an order made under section 25(4) and (5) of the Act;

"**the new public scheme**" means the new public scheme established pursuant to an order made under section 17(1) of the Act;

"**Part 4**" means Part 4 (pension schemes etc) of the Finance Act 2004;

"**POL**" means the Post Office Limited (registered number 02154540);

"**RMGL**" means the Royal Mail Group Limited (registered number 04138203);

"**the Transfer**" means the Accrued Rights Transfer and the Assets Transfer;

"**the Transitional Provisions Order**" means the Taxation of Pension Schemes (Transitional Provisions) Order 2006;

a reference to a numbered section or Schedule (without more) is a reference to the section or Schedule bearing that number in the Finance Act 2004; and

expressions which are defined, or are otherwise explained, in section 280 (abbreviations and general index) have the same meaning in these Regulations as they have in Part 4.

Statutory Instruments

2(2) For the purposes of paragraph (1) **"Schedule of Contributions"** has the same meaning as in section 227(2) of the Pension Act 2004.

PART 2 – CORPORATION TAX

DE-RECOGNITION OF THE OBLIGATIONS AND ASSETS OF THE RMPP

3(1) Paragraph (2) applies where–

(a) RMGL or POL recognises a debit or credit in its accounts, in accordance with generally accepted accounting practice; and

(b) the debit or credit is recognised in that company's accounts as a consequence of–

   (i) the Accrued Rights Transfer;

   (ii) the division of the RMPP in accordance with an order made under section 18 of the Act (division of the RMPP into different sections);

   (iii) an amendment of the RMPP in accordance with an order made under section 19 of the Act (amendments of the RMPP) in connection with an order under section 17 or section 18 of the Act; or

   (iv) the Assets Transfer.

3(2) In computing the profits, gains or losses of that company for the purposes of corporation tax, no amount is to be brought into account in respect of the debit or credit.

3(3) In this regulation–

(a) **"accounts"** has the meaning given by section 17(1) of the Corporation Tax Act 2010 (interpretation); and

(b) **"generally accepted accounting practice"** has the same meaning as in section 1127 of the Corporation Tax Act 2010 (generally accepted accounting practice and related expressions).

EXTINGUISHMENT OF RELEVANT LOSSES OF RMGL

4(1) With effect from the first day of the first qualifying accounting period, the relevant losses of RMGL are to be treated for the purposes of corporation tax as extinguished.

4(2) The amount of the relevant losses that are to be treated as extinguished in accordance with paragraph (1) is the sum of the relevant loss incurred in each accounting period prior to the final accounting period.

4(3) In this regulation a loss is a relevant loss for an accounting period ("the relevant accounting period") if–

(a) the loss was incurred in the trade carried on by RMGL in the relevant accounting period; and

(b) the loss is included in the losses carried forward to the first qualifying accounting period as an unrelieved loss in accordance with section 45 of the Corporation Tax Act 2010 (carry forward of trade loss against subsequent trade profits),

but this paragraph is subject to paragraph (4).

4(4) A loss is not a relevant loss for the purposes of paragraph (3) to the extent that it is attributable to deductions in the computation of the loss for an accounting period for contributions that are excluded contributions.

4(5) For the purposes of this regulation–

(a) losses incurred by RMGL are the losses computed in accordance with section 47 of the Corporation Tax Act 2009 (losses calculated on the same basis as profits); and

(b) a loss is an unrelieved loss for an accounting period if no relief has been given in respect of the loss under section 37 (relief for trade losses against total profits) or Part 5 of the Corporation Tax Act 2010 (group relief).

EXTINGUISHMENT OF TRADING LOSSES OF POL

5(1) With effect from the first day of the first qualifying accounting period, the relevant losses of POL are to be treated for the purposes of corporation tax as extinguished.

5(2) In this regulation **"relevant losses"** means the aggregate of the losses incurred in each accounting period prior to the final accounting period calculated in accordance with paragraph (3). This paragraph is subject to paragraph (4).

5(3) The amount of the loss for each accounting period ("the relevant accounting period") is found by–

(a) calculating–

    (i) the amount of the loss incurred in the trade carried on by POL in the relevant accounting period which is carried forward to the first qualifying accounting period as an unrelieved loss in accordance with section 45 of the Corporation Tax Act 2010 ("L"); and

    (ii) the amount of deductions in the computation of the loss for that relevant accounting period for, or in connection with, contributions in respect of qualifying members of the RMPP ("P"); and

(b) comparing the figures given by L and P for each accounting period and where–

    (i) L is greater than P, the relevant loss for that period is the amount equal to P;

    (ii) L is less than P, the relevant loss for that period is the amount equal to L; and

    (iii) L and P are the same, the relevant loss for that period is the amount equal to P.

5(4) A loss is not a relevant loss for the purposes of this regulation to the extent that it is attributable to deductions in the computation of the loss for an accounting period for payments in relation to contributions that are excluded contributions.

5(5) For the purposes of this regulation–

(a) losses incurred by POL are the losses computed in accordance with section 47 of the Corporation Tax Act 2009; and

(b) a loss is an unrelieved loss for an accounting period if no relief has been given in respect of the loss under section 37 or Part 5 of the Corporation Tax Act 2010.

EXEMPTION FROM CORPORATION TAX

6(1) BCL is exempt from corporation tax for any accounting period that begins and ends before 1st April 2015.

6(2) For the purposes of this regulation **"BCL"** means the private company limited by shares incorporated on 8th February 2012 with the registered number 07941521 and with the name BIS (Postal Services Act 2011) Company Limited.

PART 3 – INCOME TAX

Chapter 1 – Transfer of Accrued Rights from the RMPP to the New Public Scheme

NEW PUBLIC SCHEME TO BE TREATED AS A REGISTERED PENSION SCHEME

7 The new public scheme is to be treated as a registered pension scheme for the purposes of Part 4.

TRANSFER TO BE TREATED AS A RECOGNISED TRANSFER

8(1) For the purposes of Part 4, the Transfer is to be treated as a recognised transfer of sums or assets held for the purposes of, or representing accrued rights under, the RMPP in connection with a member of that scheme within the meaning of section 169(1).

8(2) Paragraph (3) applies where the Accrued Rights Transfer has resulted in the transfer to the new public scheme of Accrued Rights in respect of a scheme pension to which a member of the RMPP has become entitled ("the original scheme pension").

8(3) The sums and assets which represented rights in respect of the original scheme pension are to be treated, after the Accrued Rights Transfer, as being applied towards the provision of a scheme pension for the purposes of regulations 3 and 5 of the Registered Pension Schemes (Transfer of Sums and Assets) Regulations 2006 (the "Transfer of Sums and Assets Regulations").

8(4) Paragraph (5) applies where the Accrued Rights Transfer has resulted in the transfer to the new public scheme of Accrued Rights in respect of a dependants' scheme pension to which a dependant of a member of the RMPP has become entitled in respect of the member ("the original dependants' scheme pension").

8(5) The sums and assets which represented rights in respect of the original dependants' scheme pension are to be treated, after the Accrued Rights Transfer, as being applied towards the provision of a dependants' scheme pension for the purposes of regulation 8 of the Transfer of Sums and Assets Regulations.

Chapter 2 – Continued Application of "A day" Transitional Provisions After the Accrued Rights Transfer

"ENHANCED PROTECTION" TO CONTINUE AFTER THE ACCRUED RIGHTS TRANSFER

9 Where the Accrued Rights Transfer has taken place–

(a) the Transfer is to be treated as a permitted transfer within the meaning of paragraph 12(7) of Schedule 36 for the purposes of paragraphs 12, 13 and 15 ("enhanced protection") of that Schedule; and

(b) that permitted transfer is to be treated as falling within paragraph 12(8)(c).

RIGHTS TO TAKE BENEFIT BEFORE NORMAL MINIMUM PENSION AGE TO CONTINUE AFTER THE ACCRUED RIGHTS TRANSFER

10(1) Paragraphs (2) and (3) apply where–

(a) the RMPP was a protected pension scheme under paragraph 22(2) of Schedule 36 in relation to a member; and

(b) the Accrued Rights Transfer has taken place.

10(2) The Transfer is to be treated as a block transfer within the meaning of paragraph 22(6) of Schedule 36 for the purposes of paragraphs 21 and 22 (rights to take benefit before normal minimum pension age) of that Schedule.

10(3) In relation to the retirement condition in paragraph 22(7) of Schedule 36–

(a) the requirement in paragraph (a) is to be treated as met if the member becomes entitled to all the benefits payable to the member under arrangements under both the RMPP and the new public scheme (to which the member did not have an actual entitlement on or before 5th April 2006) on the same date; and

(b) in respect of the requirement in paragraph (b), direct or indirect references to a sponsoring employer in Condition 1, 2 or 3 in sub-paragraphs (7A), (7B), (7C) or (7E) (as the case may be), are to be read as references to a sponsoring employer of the RMPP.

ENTITLEMENT TO LUMP SUMS EXCEEDING 25% OF UNCRYSTALLISED RIGHTS TO CONTINUE AFTER THE ACCRUED RIGHTS TRANSFER

11(1) Paragraph (2) applies where–

(a) the RMPP was a protected pension scheme under paragraph 31(4) of Schedule 36 in relation to a member; and

(b) the Accrued Rights Transfer has taken place.

11(2) The Transfer is to be treated as a block transfer within the meaning of paragraph 22(6) of Schedule 36 for the purposes of paragraphs 31 to 34 (entitlement to lump sums exceeding 25% of uncrystallised rights) of that Schedule.

TRANSITIONAL PROTECTION FOR STAND-ALONE LUMP SUMS TO CONTINUE AFTER THE ACCRUED RIGHTS TRANSFER

12(1) Paragraph (2) applies where–

(a) the RMPP was entitled to pay a stand-alone lump sum under article 25(3) (stand-alone lump sums: definition) of the Transitional Provisions Order to an individual which, if it had been paid, would have been a stand-alone lump sum paid in circumstances where article 25B(4) (circumstance C) applied; and

(b) the Accrued Rights Transfer has taken place.

12(2) The Transfer is to be treated as a block transfer within the meaning of paragraph 22(6) of Schedule 36 for the purposes of article 25D(4)(c) of the Transitional Provisions Order.

TRANSITIONAL PROTECTION FOR CONTINUED LIFE COVER (75+) TO CONTINUE AFTER THE ACCRUED RIGHTS TRANSFER

13(1) Paragraph (2) applies where–

(a) the conditions A to C and E in article 6 of the Transitional Provisions Order were satisfied in relation to a member of the RMPP; and

(b) the Accrued Rights Transfer has taken place.

13(2) Conditions A to C and E in article 6 of the Transitional Provisions Order are to be treated as satisfied in respect of the new public scheme and the RMPP.

13(3) Condition D in article 6 of the Transitional Provisions Order is to be treated as satisfied in respect of the new public scheme where the rules of that scheme in relation to life cover lump sums are the same as the equivalent rules of the RMPP relating to those sums on 10th December 2003.

TRANSITIONAL PROTECTION IN RELATION TO DEPENDANTS' SCHEME PENSION LIMIT TO CONTINUE AFTER THE ACCRUED RIGHTS TRANSFER

14(1) Paragraph (2) applies where–

(a) a member of the RMPP in respect of whom a dependants' scheme pension is payable was actually entitled to one or more relevant existing pensions, as defined in paragraph 10(2) of Schedule 36, under that scheme on 5th April 2006; and

(b) the Accrued Rights Transfer has taken place.

14(2) The transitional protection afforded by article 24 (disapplication of dependants' scheme pension limit) of the Transitional Provisions Order applies to a dependants' scheme pension payable under the new public scheme in respect of that member.

TRANSITIONAL PROVISION IN RELATION TO SERIOUS ILL-HEALTH LUMP SUMS AND PENSION PROTECTION LUMP SUM DEATH BENEFITS TO CONTINUE AFTER THE ACCRUED RIGHTS TRANSFER

15(1) Paragraphs (3) and (5) apply where–

(a) the Accrued Rights Transfer has taken place; and

(b) the requirements in paragraph (2) are met.

15(2) The requirements are that, in relation to article 33(2) (serious ill-health lump sums, pension protection lump sum death benefits and annuity protection lump sum death benefits) of the Transitional Provisions Order–

(a) condition A was met in respect of an individual in relation to the RMPP immediately before the Accrued Rights Transfer; and

(b) condition B had been met in respect of that individual in relation to the RMPP.

15(3) Article 33(3) (modification of paragraph 4(2) of Schedule 29 (serious ill-health lump sum)) of the Transitional Provisions Order is to be treated as applying to the new public scheme subject to the modification in paragraph (4).

15(4) A pension paid by the new public scheme is to be treated as a relevant existing pension, as defined by paragraph 10(2) of Schedule 36, if it would have been a relevant existing pension had it been paid by the RMPP.

15(5) Article 33(4) (modification of paragraph 14(3) of Schedule 29 (pension protection lump sum death benefit)) of the Transitional Provisions Order is to be treated as applying to the new public scheme as if it provided as follows–

"**33(4)** In paragraph 14(3) of Schedule 29 (pension protection lump sum death benefit)–

(a) for the definition of "AC" substitute–

"AC is the value of the individual's pre-commencement pension rights under the RMPP as defined in paragraph 20(3) and (5) of Schedule 36",

(b) for the definition of "AP" substitute–

"AP is the aggregate of the amounts of pension paid–

(a) under the RMPP in respect of the period before the Accrued Rights Transfer, and

(b) under the new public scheme in respect of the period on and after the day on which the Accrued Rights Transfer takes place,

between 6th April 2006 and the member's death.", and

(c)　　for the definition of TPLS substitute–

"TPLS is the total amount of pension protection lump sum death benefit previously paid in respect of the pension paid under–

(a)　　the RMPP in respect of the period before the Accrued Rights Transfer, and

(b)　　the new public scheme in respect of the period on and after the day on which the Accrued Rights Transfer takes place.''".

TRANSITIONAL PROTECTION IN RELATION TO PAYMENTS TO CHILDREN AGED 23 OR OVER TO CONTINUE AFTER THE ACCRUED RIGHTS TRANSFER

16(1)　Paragraph (2) applies where the Accrued Rights Transfer has resulted in the transfer from the RMPP to the new public scheme of Accrued Rights in respect of which article 34 (payments to children aged 23 or over) of the Transitional Provisions Order applied.

16(2)　The Transfer is to be treated as a block transfer within the meaning of article 34B(4) for the purposes of article 34(6).

17(1)　Paragraph (2) applies where the Accrued Rights Transfer has resulted in the transfer from the RMPP to the new public scheme of Accrued Rights in respect of which article 34A (payments to financially dependent children aged 23 or over) of the Transitional Provisions Order applied.

17(2)　The Transfer is to be treated as a block transfer within the meaning of article 34B(4) for the purposes of article 34A(5).

18(1)　Paragraph (2) applies where–

(a)　　Condition D in article 34A(3) of the Transitional Provisions Order was met in relation to a pension death benefit payable in respect of a member of the RMPP so that article 34A was capable of applying to the payment of a pension death benefit; and

(b)　　the Accrued Rights Transfer has taken place.

18(2)　The Transfer is to be treated as a block transfer within the meaning of article 34B(4) for the purpose of article 34A(5).

TRANSITIONAL PROTECTION IN RELATION TO LUMP SUM DEATH BENEFITS TO CONTINUE AFTER THE ACCRUED RIGHTS TRANSFER

19(1)　Paragraph (2) applies where–

(a)　　the Accrued Rights Transfer has resulted in the transfer from the RMPP to the new public scheme of Accrued Rights in respect of a member; and

(b)　　after the Accrued Rights Transfer a lump sum is paid under the new public scheme in respect of the death of that member which–

(i)　　meets the condition in sub-paragraph (b) of article 40(1) (lump sum death benefits – death of member) in respect of the administrator of the RMPP for the period before the Accrued Rights Transfer and in respect of the administrator of the new public scheme for the period on and after the day on which the Accrued Rights Transfer takes place; and

(ii)　　had the Transfer not taken place, would have met the conditions in sub-paragraphs (a) and (c) to (e) of article 40(1) of the Transitional Provisions Order.

19(2)　Article 40(2) is to be treated as applying to the payment of the lump sum under the new public scheme.

Chapter 3 – Miscellaneous Provisions

LIABILITY OF SCHEME ADMINISTRATOR OF THE NEW PUBLIC SCHEME IN RESPECT OF AN INDIVIDUAL'S ANNUAL ALLOWANCE CHARGE FOR THE TAX YEAR IN WHICH THE ACCRUED RIGHTS TRANSFER TAKES PLACE

20(1)　Paragraph (2) applies where–

(a)　　the Accrued Rights Transfer has taken place; and

(b)　　the requirements in section 237B(1) (liability of scheme administrator) are met in respect of an individual in relation to the RMPP for the tax year in which the Accrued Rights Transfer took place.

20(2) The Transfer is to be treated as a transfer of all the sums or assets held for the purposes of, or representing accrued rights under, the RMPP so as to become held for the purposes of, or to represent rights under, the new public scheme within the meaning of section 237B(9).

TRANSITIONAL PROTECTION UNDER PARAGRAPH 14 OF SCHEDULE 18 TO THE FINANCE ACT 2011 ("FIXED PROTECTION") TO CONTINUE AFTER THE ACCRUED RIGHTS TRANSFER

21(1) Paragraphs (2) and (3) apply where–

(a) the Accrued Rights Transfer has resulted in the transfer from the RMPP to the new public scheme of Accrued Rights in respect of an individual–

    (i) who was an active member of the RMPP immediately before the Accrued Rights Transfer; and

    (ii) to whom paragraph 14 (lifetime allowance charge: transitional provision) of Schedule 18 to the Finance Act 2011 applies.

21(2) In paragraph 14(13)–

(a) paragraph (a) is disapplied; and

(b) for paragraph (b) substitute–

    "(b) the percentage by which the retail prices index for the month of September in the previous tax year is higher than it was for the same month in the period of 12 months (or nil per cent if it is not higher)."

21(3) The **"retail prices index"** means–

(a) the general index of retail prices (for all items) published by the Statistics Board; or

(b) if that index is not published for the relevant month, any substituted index or index figures published by the Statistics Board.

CALCULATION OF PENSION INPUT AMOUNT WHERE THERE IS AN ADJUSTMENT TO BENEFIT ENTITLEMENT AFTER THE ACCRUED RIGHTS TRANSFER

22(1) Paragraph (2) applies where–

(a) the Accrued Rights Transfer has resulted in the transfer from the RMPP to the new public scheme of Accrued Rights; and

(b) as a result of the Transfer there is an adjustment to reduce the entitlement of an individual to benefits under the new public scheme and a corresponding adjustment to increase the entitlement of that individual to benefits under the RMPP.

22(2) The adjustment and corresponding adjustment referred to in subsection (1)(b) are to be disregarded when arriving at the pension input amount for the RMPP and the new public scheme under sections 234 to 236A (pension input amount: defined benefits arrangements).

PROVISION IN RELATION TO DOUBLE TAXATION RELIEF ARRANGEMENTS

23(1) Paragraph (2) applies where–

(a) immediately prior to the Accrued Rights Transfer a member of the RMPP had pensionable service in respect of the period prior to 1st October 1969;

(b) at any time after the Accrued Rights Transfer the recipient of a pension in respect of that member is resident outside the United Kingdom in a country which has entered into a double taxation relief arrangement with the United Kingdom; and

(c) as a result of the Transfer, there has been a change to the tax treatment of the pension payable in respect of that member in the new scheme under that double taxation relief arrangement.

23(2) The tax charged under Chapter 5A (pensions under registered pension schemes) of Part 9 of the Income Tax (Earnings and Pensions) Act 2003 in respect of the member's pension under the new public scheme must not exceed the tax which would have been charged in respect of that pension under that section had the pension been paid by the RMPP.

23(3) For the purposes of this regulation, a **"double taxation relief arrangement"** means an arrangement that has effect under section 2(1) of the Taxation (International and Other Provisions) Act 2010.

FURTHER PROTECTION IN RELATION TO CHANGES TO TAX TREATMENT OF ACCRUED RIGHTS AS A RESULT OF THE TRANSFER

24(1)   Paragraph 2 applies where—

(a)   the Accrued Rights Transfer has resulted in the transfer from the RMPP to the new public scheme of Accrued Rights in respect of a member;

(b)   as a result of the Transfer, there has been a change to the tax treatment of one or both of the following–

     (i)   those Accrued Rights under the new public scheme;

     (ii)   the member's rights under the RMPP; and

(c)   no other provision in these Regulations applies to that change.

24(2)   The tax charged under the provisions in paragraph (3) in respect of the member's Accrued Rights under the new public scheme and the member's rights under the RMPP must not exceed the tax which would have been charged under those provisions in respect of those rights had the Transfer not taken place.

24(3)   The provisions are–

(a)   section 208 (unauthorised payments charge);

(b)   section 209 (unauthorised payments surcharge) in relation to surchargeable unauthorised member payments within the meaning of section 210;

(c)   section 214 (lifetime allowance charge);

(d)   section 227 (annual allowance charge); and

(e)   Chapter 5A of Part 9 of the Income Tax (Earnings and Pensions) Act 2003.

PART 4 – STAMP DUTY, STAMP DUTY LAND TAX AND STAMP DUTY RESERVE TAX

[Not relevant to Income, Corporation and Capital Gains Taxes]

INCOME TAX (PAY AS YOU EARN) (AMENDMENT) REGULATIONS 2012

(SI 2012/822, as amended by SI 2013/521)

Made on 14 March 2012 by Commissioners for Her Majesty's Revenue and Customs, in exercise of the powers conferred by s. 59A(10), 59B(8), 98A and 113(1) of the Taxes Management Act 1970, s. 133 of the Finance Act 1999, s. 136 of the Finance Act 2002 and s. 684, 706, 707 and 710 of the Income Tax (Earnings and Pensions) Act 2003. Operative from 6 April 2012.

PART 1 – GENERAL

CITATION, COMMENCEMENT AND INTERPRETATION

1(1) These Regulations may be cited as the Income Tax (Pay As You Earn) (Amendment) Regulations 2012 and come into force on 6th April 2012.

1(2) In these Regulations, **"the 2003 Regulations"** means the Income Tax (Pay As You Earn) Regulations 2003.

AMENDMENT OF THE 2003 REGULATIONS

2 The 2003 Regulations are amended as provided for in regulations 3 to 52 and 58 to 68.

PART 2 – REAL TIME INFORMATION

Chapter 1 – Amendments to the 2003 Regulations

[Amending provisions not reproduced.]

Chapter 2 – Transitional Provisions

INFORMATION ABOUT EMPLOYEES

53 Subject to regulation 55, on becoming a Real Time Information employer, an employer must provide to HMRC the following information–

(a) the information specified in paragraphs 2 to 4 of Schedule A1 to the 2003 Regulations, as inserted by these Regulations,

(b) the income tax year in which the employer became a Real Time Information employer,

(c) the following information about each of the employer's employees during the tax year in which the employer became a Real Time Information employer–

  (i)   the employee's name,

  (ii)   the employee's date of birth,

  (iii) the employee's current gender,

  (iv)   if known, the employee's national insurance number,

  (v)   the employee's address,

  (vi)   the number used by the employer to identify the employee, if any,

  (vii) the date on which the employee's employment commenced, if that date is in the tax year in which the employer became a Real Time Information employer,

  (viii) if applicable, the date on which the employee's employment ceased,

  (ix)   if applicable, an indication that an occupational pension is being paid to the employee and that the employer is the pension payer,

  (x)   if applicable, an indication that the employee is a seconded expatriate,

  (xi)   if applicable, an indication that relevant payments are made in respect of the employee to a person other than the employee,

Statutory Instruments

(xia)   if applicable, an indication that payments are made to a person listed in paragraph 14A of Schedule A1 to the 2003 Regulations,

(xii)   if applicable, an indication that relevant payments are made to the employee on an irregular basis,

(xiii) the tax code operated on relevant payments made to the employee, and

(xiv)   if applicable, an indication that the tax code operated on relevant payments made to the employee is operated on the non-cumulative basis.

History – Reg. 53(c)(xia) inserted by SI 2013/521, reg. 39, with effect for the tax year 2013–14 and subsequent tax years.

INFORMATION ABOUT PAYMENTS TO EMPLOYEES

54(1)   Within one month of making the first return under regulation 67B or 67D of the 2003 Regulations a Real Time Information employer must provide to HMRC the information specified in paragraph (2) in respect of–

(a)   each employee who has been employed in the tax year the return was made in but whose employment had ceased before the date on which the return was made, and

(b)   each employee to whom relevant payments are made on an irregular basis and–

(i)   in respect of whom information was not included on that return, and

(ii) to whom the employer does not expect to make a relevant payment within one month of making the return.

54(2)   The information specified in this paragraph is the information specified in paragraphs 2 to 4, 8 to 13, 14A, 15 to 17 and 45 of Schedule A1 to the 2003 Regulations.

History – In reg. 54(1), the words ", as inserted by these Regulations," omitted by SI 2013/521, reg. 40(a), with effect for the tax year 2013–14 and subsequent tax years.
In reg. 54(2), "14A," inserted by SI 2013/521, reg. 40(b)(i), with effect for the tax year 2013–14 and subsequent tax years.
In reg. 54(2), the words ", as inserted by these Regulations" omitted by SI 2013/521, reg. 40(b)(ii), with effect for the tax year 2013–14 and subsequent tax years.

PROVISION OF INFORMATION UNDER REGULATIONS 53 AND 54

55(1)   If an employer is one to whom paragraph (3) applies, the information required by regulation 53 must be provided before the employer makes any returns under regulation 67B or 67D of the 2003 Regulations, as inserted by these Regulations.

55(2)   Any other employer may provide the information required by regulation 53 as part of the first return the employer makes under regulation 67B or 67D of the 2003 Regulations, as inserted by these Regulations.

55(3)   This paragraph applies to an employer who, on the day the employer becomes a Real Time Information employer, employs 250 or more employees.

55(4)   The information required by regulations 53 and 54 must be provided using an approved method of electronic communications unless the employer is one to whom regulation 67D of the 2003 Regulations, as inserted by these Regulations, applies in which case the information must be provided in the form specified by HMRC.

POSTPONEMENT OF FIRST RETURN UNDER REGULATION 67B OR 67D OF THE 2003 REGULATIONS

56(1)   This regulation applies if a return due under regulation 67B or 67D of the 2003 Regulations, as inserted by these Regulations, is the first return made under either of those provisions by an employer.

56(2)   HMRC may notify the employer that the return must not be sent until such a date as HMRC notifies.

56(3)   If a second or subsequent return falls to be made by the employer under either of those provisions before the date notified by HMRC, it is also to be made on that date.

REGULATIONS 53 TO 56: INTERPRETATION

57   Terms used in regulations 53 to 56 have the same meaning as they have in the 2003 Regulations, as amended by these Regulations.

PART 3 – SECURITY FOR PAYMENT OF PAYE

58-59 [Amending provisions not reproduced.]

PART 4 – OTHER AMENDMENTS

60-68 [Amending provisions not reproduced.]

SCHEDULE

Regulation 52

[Amending provisions not reproduced.]

Statutory Instruments

DATA-GATHERING POWERS (RELEVANT DATA) REGULATIONS 2012

(SI 2012/847, as amended by SI 2013/1811)

Made on 14 March 2012 by the Treasury, in exercise of the power conferred by para. 1(3) of Sch. 23 to the Finance Act 2011. Operative from 1 April 2012.

Other material – HMRC guidance on reporting under FA 2011, Sch. 23 and SI 2012/847, returns to be made in 2013 (for which data is collected from 6 April 2012) is available at www.hmrc.gov.uk/esd-guidance/s17-s18-si-reporting.htm#1.
HMRC Brief 12/13: EU savings directive: accession of Croatia.
HMRC Brief 34/13: Reporting of interest payments.
HMRC Brief 16/14: Reporting of interest payments.

ARRANGEMENT OF REGULATIONS

CITATION, COMMENCEMENT AND INTERPRETATION

1 These Regulations may be cited as the Data-gathering Powers (Relevant Data) Regulations 2012 and come into force on 1st April 2012.

2 In these Regulations "**Schedule 23**" means Schedule 23 to the Finance Act 2011.

SALARIES, FEES, COMMISSION ETC

3(1) The relevant data for a data-holder of the type described in paragraph 9(1)(a) of Schedule 23 are information relating to all payments made by the employer that relate to the employment (referred to in this regulation as "employment related payments").

3(2) The relevant data for a data-holder of the type described in paragraph 9(1)(b) are information relating to payments by any other person who has made employment related payments to the employer's employees or to the employees of another person.

3(3) Information relating to apportioned expenses incurred partly in respect of employment related payments and partly in, or in connection with, other matters are relevant data for the purposes of paragraph 9(1)(a) and 9(1)(b).

3(4) The relevant data for a data-holder of the type described in paragraph 9(1)(c) are information and documents relating to the donations made under Part 12 of the Income Tax (Earnings and Pensions) Act 2003 (payroll giving).

3(5) For the purposes of paragraph 9(1)(d) and, where relevant, paragraph 9(4)–

(a)   the relevant data are information relating to relevant payments made in connection with a business, or a part of a business;

(b)   particulars of the following payments are not relevant data–

     (i)   payments from which income tax is deductible; and

     (ii)   payments made to any one person where the total of those payments, particulars of which would otherwise fall to be provided, does not exceed £500.

4 The relevant data for a data-holder of the type described in paragraph 11 of Schedule 23 are the data described in paragraph 11(2)(b).

INTEREST ETC

5(1) The relevant data for a data-holder of the type described in paragraph 12 of Schedule 23 are information and documents relating to accounts or sums on which relevant interest is payable, including but not limited to the data in regulations 8, 9 and 10.

5(2) "**Relevant interest**" means interest paid or credited–

(a)   on money received or retained in the United Kingdom; and

(b)   either without deduction of income tax or after deduction of income tax.

6 Information relating to the following payments is not relevant data for the purposes of a data-holder of the type described in paragraph 12–

(a)   a payment in respect of a certificate of deposit within the meaning given by section 1019 of the Income Tax Act 2007;

(b)   a payment in respect of an investment or a deposit held by a branch of a person to whom a data-holder notice is issued, where the branch is situated in a territory other than the United Kingdom;

(c)   [omitted by SI 2013/1811, reg. 3;]

(d)   a payment in respect of an investment under a plan provided for by regulations made under Chapter 3 of Part 6 of the Income Tax (Trading and Other Income) Act 2005;

(e)   a payment to or a receipt for a person other than an individual (in whatever capacity the individual is acting), except where the case falls within regulation 9(c) or 10(d) or where the relevant data-holder is carrying on a trade or business and, in the ordinary course of the operations thereof, receives or retains money in such circumstances that interest becomes payable thereon;

(f)   any other payment not falling within any of paragraphs (a) to (e) which is specified in the data-holder notice as being a payment in respect of which information is not required.

History – Reg. 6(c) omitted by SI 2013/1811, reg. 3, with effect from 1 September 2013. Former reg. 6(c) read as follows:
"(c)   a payment falling within regulation 9(c) or 10(d) if the name and address of the person to whom the interest was paid or credited is not the person beneficially entitled to the interest;".
In reg. 6(e), the words "or where the relevant data-holder is carrying on a trade or business and, in the ordinary course of the operations thereof, receives or retains money in such circumstances that interest becomes payable thereon" inserted by SI 2013/1811, reg. 4, with effect from 1 September 2013.

7(1) Information is not relevant data for the purposes of a data-holder of the type described in paragraph 12 if it is in respect of a relevant dormant account before the balance of the account is paid out to the account-holder following a repayment claim (such payment being referred to in this regulation as the repayment claim being "settled").

7(2) Where a repayment claim to the balance of a dormant account is settled, all interest paid, credited or included in the balance of the account, during and at the end of the relevant dormant period, is relevant data for the purposes of paragraph 12 and shall be treated–

(a)   as paid at the time the repayment claim is settled; and

(b)   as if the bank or building society in question had retained the balance of the account, in the ordinary course of the operations of its trade or business.

7(3) If the data-holder notice specifies the year of assessment in which the relevant dormant period for any account ends, the notice shall (unless it states otherwise) be deemed to require as relevant data the inclusion of information for all relevant dormant accounts, in respect of which repayment claims were settled in that year.

7(4) Information in respect of a relevant dormant account which, at the time it first became a relevant dormant account, was a plan provided for by regulations made under Chapter 3 of Part 6 of the Income Tax (Trading and Other Income) Act 2005 (individual investment plans) is not relevant data for the purpose of paragraph 12.

7(5) In this regulation–

"**relevant dormant account**" has the meaning in section 39(2) of the Finance Act 2008;

"**relevant dormant period**" means the period between the time when a dormant account becomes a relevant dormant account and the time at which a repayment claim is settled; and

"**repayment claim**" means a repayment claim mentioned in section 5(6) of the Dormant Bank and Building Society Accounts Act 2008 ("the Dormant Accounts Act").

Other terms used have the same meaning as in the Dormant Accounts Act.

8 If a payment is made in circumstances in which a certificate has been supplied under regulation 4 of the Income Tax (Deposit-takers and Building Societies) (Interest Payments) Regulations 2008, that the person beneficially entitled to the payment is unlikely to be liable to pay any amount by way of income tax for the tax year in which the payment was made, the relevant data are–

(a) the name and address of the person or persons by or on behalf of whom a certificate has been given in connection with the payment ("the beneficiary") if other than the person or persons to whom the payment was made;

(b) the date of birth of the beneficiary;

(c) the national insurance number or tax identification number of the beneficiary (or confirmation that a national insurance number or tax identification number is not held) for any account in respect of which the payment was made opened on or after 6th April 2013, and for any account opened earlier if such number is provided to the deposit-taker or building society;

(d) notification of the fact that the account in respect of which the payment was made is or was one in connection with which a certificate or certificates had been given which had not ceased to be valid at the 5th April in the year in which the payment was made or at the date of closure of the account, if earlier in that year;

(e) the reference number of the account referred to in paragraph (d) and, where necessary for identifying the account, the branch of the payer where the account is held;

(f) where the payment was made to two or more account-holders each of whom was beneficially entitled to the payment, notification of that fact and, if known, the number of such persons;

(g) the national insurance numbers or tax identification numbers of persons referred to in paragraph (f) other than the beneficiary referred to in paragraphs (b) and (c) (or confirmation that a national insurance number or tax identification number is not held) for any account opened on or after 6th April 2013, and for any account opened earlier if such number is provided to the deposit-taker or building society;

(h) where a certificate was given by or on behalf of one, or more, but not all, of the persons referred to in paragraph (f) and had not ceased to be valid at the 5th April in the year in which the payment was made or at the date of closure of the account, if earlier in that year, notification of those facts;

(i) where the payment was the first payment made in respect of an account, notification of that fact;

(j) where the payment was in a currency other than sterling and the amount of the payment is recorded in that currency in the data provided under a data-holder notice notification of the fact that the amount is so recorded and the specification of the currency concerned.

9 In cases to which regulation 8 does not apply, the relevant data relating to payments in respect of deposits are–

(a) the reference number of the account in respect of which a payment was made and, where necessary for identifying the account, the branch of the payer where the account is held;

(b) where a payment was made to two or more account holders, notification of that fact and, if known, the number of such persons;

(c) where the payment was made without deduction of tax by virtue of a declaration made after 5th April 2001 under section 858, 859, 860 or 861 of the Income Tax Act 2007–

(i) the name and principal residential address of the individual beneficially entitled to the payment or, if more than one, of each individual entitled to the payment; or

(ii) where the person beneficially entitled to the payment is a Scottish partnership, all the partners in which are individuals, the name and principal residential address of each of the partners;

(d) in a case falling within paragraph (c) notification of the fact that the account in respect of which the payment was made was one in respect of which a declaration had been made as mentioned in that paragraph;

(e) the national insurance number or tax identification number (or confirmation that a national insurance number or tax identification number is not held) of the person or, where paragraph (b) applies, each person to whom a payment was made for any account opened on or after 6th April 2013, and for any account opened earlier if such number is provided to the deposit-taker or building society;

(f) where a payment made in the course of the year was the first payment in respect of an account, notification of that fact;

(g) where a payment was in a currency other than sterling and the amount of the payment is recorded in that currency in the data provided under a data-holder notice notification of the fact that the amount is so recorded and the specification of the currency concerned.

10 In cases to which regulation 8 does not apply, the relevant data relating to payments and receipts of interest other than payments in respect of deposits are–

(a) identification of the security or investment in respect of which the payment was made or received;

(b) where a payment or receipt was in a currency other than sterling and the amount of the payment is recorded in that currency in the data provided under a data-holder notice notification of the fact that the amount is so recorded and the specification of the currency concerned;

(c) where a payment was made to, or the receipt was for, two or more persons, notification of that fact and, if known, the number of such persons;

(d) where a payment was made without deduction of tax by virtue of a declaration made under regulation 31 of the Authorised Investment Funds (Tax) Regulations 2006, the name and principal residential address of the person beneficially entitled to the payment, or if more than one, of each person beneficially entitled to the payment;

(e) in a case falling within paragraph (d), notification of the fact that the account in respect of which the payment was made was one in respect of which the declaration had been made.

INCOME, ASSETS ETC BELONGING TO OTHERS

11 The relevant data for a data-holder of the type described in paragraph 13 of Schedule 23 are–

(a) information relating to the money or value received; and

(b) the name and address of the beneficial owner of the money or value.

MERCHANT ACQUIRERS ETC

11A(1) The relevant data for a data-holder of the type described in paragraph 13A of Schedule 23 are–

(a) in relation to a retailer, information relating to payment card transactions recorded against a merchant account, including the currency these payment card transactions were made in;

(b) the reference number of the account into which payments are made by the relevant data-holder to the retailer and, where necessary for identifying the account, the branch where the account is held;

(c) any unique identifier which has been allocated to a retailer, for the purposes of identifying the retailer, as part of the business arrangement between the relevant data-holder and the retailer;

(d) any identifier which has been allocated to a retailer, for the purposes of classifying the trade of the retailer, as part of the business arrangement between the relevant data-holder and the retailer;

(e) any unique identifier which has been allocated to a retailer's merchant account, for the purposes of identifying this merchant account, as part of the business arrangement between the relevant data-holder and the retailer;

(f) the name, address, telephone number, e-mail address, website address and VAT number ("relevant details") of a retailer and, if different, the relevant details associated with a merchant account.

Statutory Instruments

11A(2) In this regulation—

"merchant account" means an account held by a retailer with the relevant data-holder, by reference to which the amount due to be paid by the relevant data-holder to the retailer in settlement of payment card transactions is calculated; and

"VAT number" means "registration number" for the purposes of paragraph (1) of regulation 2 of the Value Added Tax Regulations 1995.

History – Reg. 11A inserted by SI 2013/1811, reg. 5, with effect from 1 September 2013.

PAYMENTS DERIVED FROM SECURITIES

12 The relevant data for a data-holder of the type described in paragraph 14 of Schedule 23 are—

(a) whether the relevant data-holder is the beneficial owner (or sole beneficial owner) of the securities or payment in question;

(b) if not—

(i) details of the beneficial owner (or other beneficial owners); and

(ii) if those details are not known or if different, details of the person for whom the securities are held or to whom the payment is or may be paid on; and

(c) if there is more than one beneficial owner or more than one person of the kind mentioned in paragraph (b)(ii), their respective interests in the securities or payment.

13 The relevant data for a data-holder of the type described in paragraph 15 of Schedule 23 are details of the amounts paid that were received from or paid on behalf of another person including the name and address of each such person.

GRANTS AND SUBSIDIES OUT OF PUBLIC FUNDS

14 The relevant data for a data-holder of the type described in paragraph 16 of Schedule 23 are—

(a) the name and address of the person to whom the payment has been made or on whose behalf the payment has been received;

(b) the amount of the payment so made or received; and

(c) the address of any property in respect of which the payment has been made.

LICENCES, APPROVALS ETC

15 The relevant data for a data-holder of the type described in paragraph 17 of Schedule 23 are—

(a) the name and address of anyone who is or has been the holder of a licence or approval or to whom an entry in the register relates or related;

(b) particulars of the licence, approval or entry;

(c) information relating to any application for such a licence or approval or for entry on that register.

RENT AND OTHER PAYMENTS ARISING FROM LAND

16(1) The relevant data for a data-holder of the type described in paragraph 18 of Schedule 23 are—

(a) information relating to the terms applying to the lease, occupation or use of land;

(b) information relating to any consideration given for the grant or assignment of the tenancy;

(c) information relating to any person on whose behalf the land is managed or the payments received, including particulars of payments arising from the land.

16(2) In this regulation—

(a) **"lease"** includes an agreement for a lease, and any tenancy, but does not include a mortgage or heritable security;

(b) **"lessee"** includes a successor in title of a lease; and

(c) in relation to Scotland, **"assignment"** means an assignation.

DEALING ETC IN SECURITIES

17(1) The relevant data for a data-holder of the type described in paragraph 19 of Schedule 23 are—

(a) information and documents relating to securities transactions in respect of which that person is a relevant data-holder; and

(b)   in relation to a person who carries on a business of effecting public issues or placings or otherwise effects public issues or placings, information relating to the issue, allotment or placing of the public issues or placings.

17(2)   In this regulation–

(a)   **"placing"** means a placing of shares or securities in a company; and

(b)   **"public issue"** means a public issue of shares or securities in a company.

DEALING IN OTHER PROPERTY

18   The relevant data for a data-holder of the type described in paragraph 20 of Schedule 23 are–

(a)   particulars of any transactions effected through a clearing house;

(b)   particulars of any transaction which meets the following conditions–

      (i)   the transaction is effected by or through that person;

      (ii)   in the transaction, an asset which is tangible moveable property is disposed of; and

      (iii) the amount or value of the consideration for the disposal exceeds, in the hands of the recipient, £6,000.

LLOYD'S

19   The relevant data for a data-holder of the type described in paragraph 21 of Schedule 23 are information and documents relating to, and to the activities of, the syndicate of underwriting members of Lloyd's.

INVESTMENT PLANS ETC

20   The relevant data for a data-holder of the type described in paragraph 22 of Schedule 23 are–

(a)   information and documents relating to the plan, including investments which are or have been held under the plan;

(b)   information and documents relating to the child trust fund including investments which are or have been held under the fund.

PETROLEUM ACTIVITIES

21   The relevant data for a data-holder of the type described in paragraph 23 of Schedule 23 are–

(a)   particulars of transactions in connection with any activities authorised by a petroleum licence as a result of which any person is or might be liable to tax by virtue of section 276 of the Taxation of Chargeable Gains Act 1992, section 1313 of the Corporation Tax Act 2009 or section 874 of the Income Tax (Trading and Other Income) Act 2005;

(b)   particulars of earnings or money treated as earnings, which constitute employment income (see section 7(2)(a) or (b) of the Income Tax (Earnings and Pensions) Act 2003) or other payments paid or payable in respect of duties or services performed in an area in which those activities may be carried on under the petroleum licence;

(c)   particulars of the persons to whom such earnings, money or other payments were paid and are payable;

(d)   information and documents relating to the oil field.

INSURANCE ACTIVITIES

22   The relevant data for a data-holder of the type described in paragraph 24 of Schedule 23 are–

(a)   information and documents relating to contracts of insurance entered into in the course of an insurance business;

(b)   if paragraph 24(b) or (c) applies, information and documents relating to the contracts of insurance.

ENVIRONMENTAL ACTIVITIES

23   The relevant data for a data-holder of the type described in paragraph 25 of Schedule 23 are–

(a)   information and documents relating to aggregates levy matters in which the person is or has been involved;

(b)   information and documents relating to climate change levy matters in which the person is or has been involved;

(c)   information and documents relating to any landfill disposal.

SETTLEMENTS

24 The relevant data for a data-holder of the type described in paragraph 26 of Schedule 23 are information and documents relating to the settlement in question and to income or gains arising to the settlement.

CHARITIES

25 The relevant data for a data-holder of the type described in paragraph 27 of Schedule 23 are information relating to donations to the charity that are eligible for tax relief under any of the following provisions–

(a)   section 257 of the Taxation of Chargeable Gains Act 1992 (gifts to charities etc);

(b)   section 63(2)(a) or (aa) of the Capital Allowances Act 2001 (cases in which disposal value is nil);

(c)   Part 12 of the Income Tax (Earnings and Pensions) Act 2003 (payroll giving);

(d)   section 108 of the Income Tax (Trading and Other Income) Act 2005 (gifts of trading stock to charities etc);

(e)   Chapter 2 or 3 of Part 8 of the Income Tax Act 2007 (gift aid, gifts of shares, securities and real property to charities etc);

(f)   section 105 of the Corporation Tax Act 2009 (gifts of trading stock to charities etc); and

(g)   Part 6 of the Corporation Tax Act 2010 (charitable donations relief).

FINANCE ACT 2004, SECTION 180(5) (MODIFICATION) REGULATIONS 2012

(SI 2012/1258)

Made on 10 May 2012 by the Treasury, in exercise of the power conferred by s. 70 of the Finance Act 2011. Operative from 1 June 2012.

CITATION, COMMENCEMENT AND EFFECT

1(1) These Regulations may be cited as the Finance Act 2004, Section 180(5) (Modification) Regulations 2012 and come into force on 1st June 2012.

1(2) Regulation 2 has effect in relation to any payments made on or after 6th April 2012.

DISREGARD OF SECTION 180(5)(B) OF THE FINANCE ACT 2004

2 In its application to a pension scheme established under section 67 of the Pensions Act 2008 (duty on Secretary of State to establish a pension scheme), section 180 of the Finance Act 2004 (scheme administration employer payments) has effect as if subsection (5)(b) were omitted.

BRITISH WATERWAYS BOARD (TAX CONSEQUENCES) ORDER 2012

(SI 2012/1709)

Made on 2 July 2012 by the Treasury, in exercise of the powers conferred by s. 25 of the Public Bodies Act 2011. Operative from 2 July 2012.

CITATION AND COMMENCEMENT

1 This Order may be cited as the British Waterways Board (Tax Consequences) Order 2012 and comes into force at 3.30 p.m. on 2nd July 2012.

INTERPRETATION

2 In this Order—

"TCGA 1992" means the Taxation of Chargeable Gains Act 1992;

"CAA 2001" means the Capital Allowances Act 2001;

"CTA 2009" means the Corporation Tax Act 2009;

"BWB" means the British Waterways Board;

"CRT" means the Canal & River Trust, company registration number 07807276;

"CRT CIC" means the Canal & River Trading CIC, company registration number 08069602;

"relevant transfer" means—

(a) a transfer of property, rights and liabilities from BWB to CRT, or

(b) a transfer of property, rights and liabilities from BWB to CRT CIC,

by, or under, the British Waterways Board Transfer Scheme 2012.

CAPITAL ALLOWANCES: TRANSFER OF A TRADE

3(1) This article applies where BWB is carrying on a trade and, as a result of a relevant transfer—

(a) BWB ceases to carry on that trade, and

(b) CRT or CRT CIC begins to carry on that trade.

3(2) For the purposes of the allowances and charges provided for by CAA 2001, the trade is not to be treated as permanently discontinued, nor a new trade as set up; but paragraphs (3) and (4) are to apply.

3(3) There are to be made to or on CRT, or CRT CIC, in accordance with CAA 2001, all such allowances and charges as would, if BWB had continued to carry on the trade, have fallen to be made to or on BWB.

3(4) The amounts of those allowances and charges are to be computed as if—

(a) CRT or CRT CIC had been carrying on the trade since BWB began to do so, and

(b) everything done to or by BWB had been done to or by CRT or CRT CIC,

but so that a relevant transfer, so far it relates to assets in use for the purposes of the trade, is not treated as giving rise to an allowance or charge.

CAPITAL ALLOWANCES: TRANSFER INVOLVING PART OF A TRADE

4(1) Where BWB is carrying on a trade and, as a result of a relevant transfer—

(a) BWB ceases to carry on that trade, and

(b) CRT or CRT CIC begins to carry on activities of that trade as part of a trade carried on by it,

then that part of the trade carried on by CRT, or CRT CIC, is treated for the purposes of article 3 as a separate trade.

4(2) Where BWB is carrying on a trade and, as a result of a relevant transfer—

(a) BWB ceases to carry on a part of that trade, and

(b) CRT or CRT CIC begins to carry on activities of that part of that trade,

then BWB is treated for the purposes of article 3 and paragraph (1) as having carried on that part of its trade as a separate trade.

4(3) Where activities fall to be treated under this article as a separate trade, such apportionments of receipts, expenses, assets and liabilities are to be made for the purposes of CAA 2001 as may be just and reasonable.

CHARGEABLE GAINS: NO GAIN OR LOSS ON DISPOSAL

5(1) For the purposes of TCGA 1992, a disposal constituted by a relevant transfer is to be treated in relation to BWB and CRT, or CRT CIC, as made for a consideration such that no gain or loss accrues to BWB.

5(2) For the purposes of any tax provision, paragraph (1) is to be treated as one of the no gain/no loss provisions in section 288(3A) of TCGA 1992 (meaning of "the no gain/no loss provisions").

CORPORATION TAX: COMPUTATION OF PROFITS AND LOSSES IN RESPECT OF TRANSFER OF TRADE

6(1) This article applies where BWB is carrying on a trade or part of a trade and, as a result of a relevant transfer–

(a)   BWB ceases to carry on that trade or part of a trade, and

(b)   CRT or CRT CIC begins to carry on that trade or part.

6(2) For the purposes of computing, in relation to the time when a relevant transfer takes effect and at subsequent times, the relevant trading profits or losses of BWB and CRT, or CRT CIC,–

(a)   the trade or part is to be treated as having been a separate trade at the time of its commencement and as having been carried on by CRT or CRT CIC at all times since its commencement as a separate trade, and

(b)   the trade carried on by CRT or CRT CIC after the time when a relevant transfer takes effect is to be treated as the same trade as that which CRT or CRT CIC is treated, by virtue of sub-paragraph (a), as having carried on as a separate trade before that time.

6(3) Where a trade or part of a trade falls to be treated under this article as a separate trade, such apportionments of receipts, expenses, assets, and liabilities are to be made for the purposes of computing relevant trading profits or losses as may be just and reasonable.

6(4) In this article **"relevant trading profits or losses"** means profits or losses under Part 3 of CTA 2009 in respect of the trade or part of a trade in question.

CORPORATION TAX: LOAN RELATIONSHIPS

7(1) For the purposes of Part 5 of CTA 2009 (loan relationships), in relation to a relevant transfer, BWB and CRT, or CRT CIC, are to be treated as if, for the purposes of the transfer, they were members of the same group.

7(2) In paragraph (1) the reference to being members of the same group is to be read in accordance with section 335(6) of that Act.

STAMP DUTY

8   [Not relevant to income tax.]

STAMP DUTY LAND TAX

9   [Not relevant to income tax.]

TAX AVOIDANCE SCHEMES (INFORMATION) REGULATIONS 2012

(SI 2012/1836, as amended by SI 2013/2592)

Made on 12 July 2012 by the Commissioners for Her Majesty's Revenue and Customs, in exercise of the powers conferred by s. 98C(2A), (2B) and (2C)(b) of the Taxes Management Act 1970, s. 132 of the Finance Act 1999, s. 135 of the Finance Act 2002 and s. 306A(6), 307(5), 308(1) and (3), 308A(5) and (6)(a), 309(1), 310, 312(2) and (5), 312A(2) and (5), 313(1) and (3), 313ZA(3) and (4), 313A(4)(a), 313B(2)(a), 313C(1) and (3)(a), 317(2) and 318(1) of the Finance Act 2004. Operative from 1 September 2012.

CITATION AND COMMENCEMENT

1 These Regulations may be cited as the Tax Avoidance Schemes (Information) Regulations 2012 and shall come into force on 1st September 2012.

INTERPRETATION

2(1) In these Regulations a reference to a numbered section (without more) is a reference to the section of the Finance Act 2004 which is so numbered.

2(2) In these Regulations–

"employment" has the same meaning as it has for the purposes of the employment income Parts of the Income Tax (Earnings and Pensions) Act 2003 (see section 4 of that Act) and includes offices to which the provisions of those Parts that are expressed to apply to employments apply equally (see section 5 of that Act); and **"employee"** and **"employer"** have corresponding meanings;

"the filing date" is–

(a) whichever date in regulation 12(4)(a) to (c) applies to the relevant return or in the case of inheritance tax the last day of the period mentioned in regulation 9(5)(b); or

(b) in the case of regulation 10(7) the date by which the relevant return is required to be delivered;

"the prescribed taxes" means capital gains tax, corporation tax, income tax, inheritance tax, stamp duty land tax and annual tax on enveloped dwellings.

2(3) In reckoning any period under regulation 5 (apart from paragraph (8)), or regulations 8A, 13A, 14, 15 and 16, any day which is a non-business day within the meaning of section 92 of the Bills of Exchange Act 1882 (computation of time) shall be disregarded.

2(4) In regulations 10(2) and (3), 11(4) and 12(2) expressions which are used in Part 4 of the Finance Act 2003 have the same meaning as in that Part.

History – In reg. 2(2), definition of "the prescribed taxes" substituted by SI 2013/2592, reg. 4, with effect from 4 November 2013. Former definition read as follows:

"**"the prescribed taxes"** means capital gains tax, corporation tax, income tax, inheritance tax and stamp duty land tax.". In reg. 2(3), the words "8A, 13A," inserted by SI 2013/2592, reg. 15, with effect from 4 November 2013.

REVOCATIONS

3(1) The Regulations described in the Schedule to these Regulations are revoked.

3(2) Anything begun under or for the purpose of any Regulations revoked by these Regulations shall be continued under or, as the case may be, for the purpose of the corresponding provision of these Regulations.

3(3) Where any document refers to a provision of a regulation revoked by these Regulations, such reference shall, unless the context otherwise requires, be construed as a reference to the corresponding provision of these Regulations.

History – In reg. 3(2), "continued" substituted for "construed" by correction slip dated 31 January 2013.

PRESCRIBED INFORMATION IN RESPECT OF NOTIFIABLE PROPOSALS AND ARRANGEMENTS

4(1) The information which must be provided to HMRC by a promoter under section 308(1) or (3) (duties of promoter) in respect of a notifiable proposal or notifiable arrangements is sufficient information as might reasonably be expected to enable an officer of HMRC to comprehend the manner in which the proposal or arrangements are intended to operate, including–

(a)   the promoter's name and address;

(b)   details of the provision of the Arrangements Regulations, the ATED Arrangements Regulations, the IHT Arrangements Regulations or the SDLT Arrangements Regulations by virtue of which the arrangements or the proposed arrangements are notifiable;

(c)   a summary of the arrangements or proposed arrangements and the name (if any) by which they are known;

(d)   information explaining each element of the arrangements or proposed arrangements (including the way in which they are structured) from which the tax advantage expected to be obtained under those arrangements arises; and

(e)   the statutory provisions, relating to any of the prescribed taxes, on which that tax advantage is based.

4(2)   The information which must be provided to HMRC by a client under section 309 (duty of person dealing with promoter outside the United Kingdom) in respect of notifiable arrangements is sufficient information as might reasonably be expected to enable an officer of HMRC to comprehend the manner in which the arrangements are intended to operate, including–

(a)   the client's name and address;

(b)   the name and address of the promoter;

(c)   details of the provision of the Arrangements Regulations, the ATED Arrangements Regulations, the IHT Arrangements Regulations or the SDLT Arrangements Regulations by virtue of which the arrangements are notifiable;

(d)   a summary of the arrangements, and the name (if any) by which they are known;

(e)   information explaining each element of the arrangements (including the way in which they are structured) from which the tax advantage expected to be obtained under the arrangements arises; and

(f)   the statutory provisions, relating to any of the prescribed taxes, on which that tax advantage is based.

4(3)   The information which must be provided to HMRC by a person obliged to do so by section 310 (duty of parties to notifiable arrangements not involving promoter) is sufficient information as might reasonably be expected to enable an officer of HMRC to comprehend the manner in which the arrangements of which that transaction forms part are intended to operate, including–

(a)   the name and address of the person entering into the transaction;

(b)   details of the provision of the Arrangements Regulations, the ATED Arrangements Regulations, the IHT Arrangements Regulations or the SDLT Arrangements Regulations by virtue of which the arrangements are notifiable;

(c)   a summary of the arrangements and the name (if any) by which they are known;

(d)   information explaining each element of the arrangements (including the way in which they are structured) from which the tax advantage expected to be obtained under the arrangements arises; and

(e)   the statutory provisions, relating to any of the prescribed taxes, on which that tax advantage is based.

4(4)   If, but for this paragraph–

(a)   a person would be obliged to provide information in relation to two or more notifiable arrangements,

(b)   those arrangements are substantially the same (whether they relate to the same parties or different parties), and

(c)   the person has already provided information under paragraph (2) or (3) in relation to any of the other arrangements,

the person need not provide further information under paragraph (2) or (3).

4(5)   In this regulation–

"**the Arrangements Regulations**" means the Tax Avoidance Schemes (Prescribed Descriptions of Arrangements) Regulations 2006;

"**the ATED Arrangements Regulations**" means the Annual Tax on Enveloped Dwellings Avoidance Schemes (Prescribed Descriptions of Arrangements) Regulations 2013;

Statutory Instruments

"the IHT Arrangements Regulations" means the Inheritance Tax Avoidance Schemes (Prescribed Descriptions of Arrangements) Regulations 2011;

"the SDLT Arrangements Regulations" means the Stamp Duty Land Tax Avoidance Schemes (Prescribed Descriptions of Arrangements) Regulations 2005.

History – In reg. 4(1)(b), the words "the ATED Arrangements Regulations," inserted by SI 2013/2592, reg. 5, with effect from 4 November 2013.

In reg. 4(2)(c), the words "the ATED Arrangements Regulations," inserted by SI 2013/2592, reg. 6, with effect from 4 November 2013.

In reg. 4(3)(b), the words "the ATED Arrangements Regulations," inserted by SI 2013/2592, reg. 7, with effect from 4 November 2013.

In reg. 4(5), definition of "the ATED Arrangements Regulations" inserted by SI 2013/2592, reg. 8, with effect from 4 November 2013.

TIME FOR PROVIDING INFORMATION UNDER SECTION 308, 308A, 309 OR 310

5(1) The period or time (as the case may be) within which–

(a) the prescribed information under section 308, 309 or 310, and

(b) the information or documents which will support or explain the prescribed information under section 308A (supplemental information),

must be provided to HMRC is found in accordance with the following paragraphs of this regulation.

5(2) Where a proposal or arrangements (not being otherwise notifiable) is or are treated as notifiable by virtue of an order under section 306A(1) (doubt as to notifiability) the prescribed period is the period of 10 days beginning on the day after that on which the order is made.

5(3) In the case of a requirement to provide specified information about, or documents relating to, the notifiable proposal or arrangements which arises by virtue of an order under section 308A(2), the prescribed period is the period of 10 days beginning on the day after that on which the order is made.

5(4) In any other case of a notification under section 308(1), the prescribed period is the period of 5 days beginning on the day after the relevant date.

5(5) In any other case of a notification under section 308(3), the prescribed period is the period of 5 days beginning on the day after that on which the promoter first becomes aware of any transaction forming part of arrangements to which that subsection applies.

5(6) In the case of a notification under section 309(1), the prescribed period is the period of 5 days beginning on the day after that on which the client enters into the first transaction forming part of notifiable arrangements to which that subsection applies.

5(7) In the case of a notification under section 310 which arises by virtue of the application of regulation 6 of the Tax Avoidance Schemes (Promoters and Prescribed Circumstances) Regulations 2004 (persons not to be treated as promoters: legal professional privilege), the prescribed time is any time during the period of 5 days beginning on the day after that on which the person enters into the first transaction forming part of the notifiable arrangements.

5(8) In any other case of a notification under section 310 the prescribed time is any time during the period of 30 days beginning on the day after that on which the person enters into the first transaction forming part of the notifiable arrangements.

Cross references – SI 2013/2592: transitional provisions in relation to the period of time to be found in accordance with reg. 5 in respect of proposals or arrangements that are notifiable by virtue of SI 2013/2571, reg. 4 in relation to annual tax on enveloped dwellings.

PRESCRIBED INFORMATION UNDER SECTIONS 312 AND 312A

6 For the purposes of sections 312(2) and (5) (duty of promoter to notify client of number) and 312A(2) (duty of client to notify parties of number) the prescribed information is–

(a) the name and address of the promoter;

(b) the name, or a brief description of the notifiable arrangements or proposal;

(c) the reference number (or if more than one, any one reference number) allocated by HMRC under section 311 (arrangements to be given reference number) to the notifiable arrangements or proposed notifiable arrangements;

(d) the date that the reference number was–

    (i) sent by the promoter to the client; or (as the case may be)

    (ii) sent to any other person by the client under section 312A(2).

TIME FOR PROVIDING INFORMATION UNDER SECTION 312A

7   In the case of a notification under section 312A(2) the prescribed period is the period of 30 days beginning on—

(a)   the day on which the client first becomes aware of any transaction forming part of notifiable arrangements or proposed notifiable arrangements; or, if later,

(b)   the day on which the prescribed information is notified to the client by the promoter under section 312.

EXEMPTION FROM DUTY UNDER SECTION 312A

8   The duty of a client to notify other persons under section 312A(2) does not apply to an employer of an employee where the employee by reason of employment receives or expects to receive a tax advantage in respect of income tax or capital gains tax as a result of notifiable arrangements or proposed notifiable arrangements.

PRESCRIBED INFORMATION UNDER SECTION 312B: INFORMATION AND TIMING

8A(1)   For the purposes of section 312B (duty of client to provide information to promoter)—

(a)   the prescribed period is 10 days from the later of the date that the client receives the reference number allocated by HMRC under section 311 to the notifiable arrangements, and the date the client first enters into a transaction which forms part of the notifiable arrangements; and

(b)   the prescribed information is—

(i)   any identification number allocated to the client by HMRC ("unique taxpayer number") and the client's national insurance number; or

(ii)   confirmation that the client does not have a unique taxpayer number or a national insurance number or has neither number.

History – Reg. 8A inserted by SI 2013/2592, reg. 16, with effect from 4 November 2013.

PRESCRIBED CASES UNDER SECTION 313(3)(A)

9(1)   The prescribed cases for the purposes of section 313(3)(a) (cases in which the information is to be included in returns) are as follows.

9(2)   Subject to regulation 10(4), (7) and (8), in the case of a person who—

(a)   expects an advantage to arise in respect of that person's liability to pay, entitlement to a repayment of, or to a deferment of the liability to pay, income tax or capital gains tax as a result of notifiable arrangements; and

(b)   is required to make a return to HMRC by a notice under section 8 or 8A of the Taxes Management Act 1970 (income tax and capital gains tax: personal return and trustee's return), in respect of income tax or capital gains tax,

the prescribed information shall be included in the return (under the section which applies) which relates to the year of assessment in which the person first enters into a transaction forming part of the notifiable arrangements and in the return for each subsequent year of assessment until the advantage ceases to apply to that person.

9(3)   Subject to regulation 10(4), (7) and (8) in the case of a company which—

(a)   expects a tax advantage to arise in respect of its liability to pay, entitlement to a repayment of, or to a deferment of its liability to pay, corporation tax as a result of notifiable arrangements; and

(b)   is required to make a return to HMRC by a notice under paragraph 3 of Schedule 18 to the Finance Act 1998 (company tax return), in respect of corporation tax,

the prescribed information shall be included in the return under that paragraph covering the period in which the company first enters into a transaction forming part of the notifiable arrangements and in the return covering each subsequent period until the tax advantage ceases to apply to the company.

9(4)   Subject to regulation 10(4), (7), and (8) in the case of a partnership—

(a)   which expects an advantage to arise in respect of a partner's liability to pay, entitlement to a repayment of, or to a deferment of the liability to pay income tax, capital gains tax or corporation tax in respect of partnership profits or gains as a result of notifiable arrangements; and

(b)   in respect of which a return is required to be made to HMRC by virtue of a notice under section 12AA of the Taxes Management Act 1970(c) (partnership return) in respect of income tax, capital gains tax or corporation tax,

in addition to any duty under paragraph (2) or (3) the prescribed information shall be included in the return under that section covering the period in which the partnership first enters into a transaction forming part of the notifiable arrangements and in the returns covering each subsequent period until the tax advantage ceases to apply to the partner in question.

9(5)   Subject to regulation 10(7) and (8) in the case of a person who–

(a)   expects an advantage to arise in respect of that person's liability to pay, entitlement to a repayment of, or to a deferment of the liability to pay inheritance tax as a result of notifiable arrangements; and

(b)   is required to make a return to HMRC under section 216 of the Inheritance Tax Act 1984 (accounts and information) in respect of a transaction forming part of the notifiable arrangements within a period of 12 months from the end of the month in which the first transaction forming part of the arrangements is entered into,

the prescribed information shall be included in the return under that section.

9(6)   Subject to regulation 10(7) and (8) in the case of a person who–

(a)   expects an advantage to arise in respect of that person's liability to pay, entitlement to a repayment of, or deferment of the liability to pay, annual tax on enveloped dwellings as a result of notifiable arrangements; and

(b)   is required to make a return to HMRC under section 159 of the Finance Act 2013 in respect of annual tax on enveloped dwellings;

the prescribed information shall be included in the return under that section.

History – Reg. 9(6) inserted by SI 2013/2592, reg. 9, with effect from 4 November 2013.

PRESCRIBED CASES UNDER SECTION 313(3)(B)

10(1)   The prescribed cases for the purposes of section 313(3)(b) (cases in which the information is to be provided separately) are as follows.

10(2)   In a case where a purchaser expects an advantage to arise in respect of that person's liability to pay, entitlement to a repayment of, or to a deferment of the liability to pay stamp duty land tax as a result of notifiable arrangements the prescribed information shall be provided separately to HMRC in such form and manner as they may specify.

10(3)   If paragraph (2) applies in relation to a land transaction entered into as purchaser by or on behalf of a partnership notification of the prescribed information by or in relation to the responsible partners may instead be done by or in relation to a representative partner or partners.

10(4)   In the case of a person who is the employer of an employee, by reason of whose employment a tax advantage is expected to arise to any person in respect of income tax, corporation tax or capital gains tax as a result of notifiable arrangements, the prescribed information shall be provided separately to HMRC in such form and manner as they may specify.

10(5)   In the case of a person who would be obliged to comply with a duty under regulation 9(2) to (4), but is not required, in respect of a year of assessment, accounting period or tax year–

(a)   in the case of notifiable arrangements to which regulation 9(2) applies, to make a return under either of the provisions referred to in regulation 9(2)(b);

(b)   in the case of notifiable arrangements to which regulation 9(3) applies, to make a return under the provision referred to in regulation 9(3)(b); or

(c)   in the case of notifiable arrangements to which regulation 9(4) applies, to make a return under the provision referred to in regulation 9(4)(b);

the prescribed information shall be provided separately to HMRC in such form and manner as they may specify.

10(6)   In the case of a person who–

(a)   expects an advantage to arise in respect of that person's liability to pay, entitlement to a repayment of, or to a deferment of the liability to pay inheritance tax as a result of notifiable arrangements; and

(b)   is not required to make a return to HMRC under section 216 of the Inheritance Tax Act 1984 in respect of a transaction forming part of the notifiable arrangements within a period of 12 months from the end of the month in which the first transaction forming part of the arrangements is entered into, the prescribed information shall be provided separately to HMRC in such form and manner as they may specify.

10(6A)   In the case of a person who–

(a)   expects an advantage to arise in respect of that person's liability to pay, entitlement to a repayment of, or deferment of the liability to pay, annual tax on enveloped dwellings as a result of notifiable arrangements; and

(b)   is not required to make a return to HMRC under section 159 of the Finance Act 2013 in respect of a transaction forming part of the notifiable arrangements within a period of 30 days beginning with the later of–

    (i)   the effective date of the first transaction which forms part of the arrangements; or

    (ii)   the date of the receipt of the reference number allocated under the provisions of section 311;

the prescribed information shall be provided separately to HMRC.

10(7)   In a case of a person who would, but for this paragraph, be obliged to comply with a duty under regulation 9 and–

(a)   the relevant return is not delivered by the filing date; or

(b)   the relevant return is delivered by the filing date but does not include the prescribed information;

the prescribed information shall be provided separately to HMRC in such form and manner as they may specify.

10(8)   In a case where–

(a)   a person is required to provide information relating to more than one reference number;

(b)   the information is included in a return under regulation 9; and

(c)   the number of reference numbers in relation to which information is required exceeds the number of spaces allocated to the information on the return form;

the information relating to so many of the reference numbers as exceeds the number of allocated spaces shall be provided separately to HMRC in such form and manner as they may specify.

10(9)   In addition to the duty under any other paragraph above, or regulation 9, in a case where the arrangements give rise to a claim submitted separately from the return under–

(a)   section 261B of the Taxation of Chargeable Gains Act 1992 (treating trade loss etc as CGT loss); or

(b)   Part 4 of the Income Tax Act 2007 (loss relief);

the prescribed information shall be provided separately to HMRC in such form and manner as they may specify.

History – Reg. 10(6A) inserted by SI 2013/2592, reg. 10, with effect from 4 November 2013.

PRESCRIBED INFORMATION UNDER SECTION 313(1)

11(1)   For the purposes of section 313(1) (duty of parties to notifiable arrangements to notify Board of number, etc) the prescribed information is that specified in whichever of paragraph (2), (3) or (4) is applicable.

11(2)   In cases prescribed in regulation 9 the prescribed information is–

(a)   the reference number (or if more than one, any one reference number) allocated by HMRC under section 311 to the notifiable arrangements or proposed notifiable arrangements; and

(b)   the year of assessment, tax year or accounting period (as the case may be) in which, or the date on which, the person providing the information expects a tax advantage to be obtained.

11(3)   In the cases prescribed in regulation 10 (apart from paragraph (2) and any case relating to annual tax on enveloped dwellings) the prescribed information is–

(a)   the name and address of the person providing it;

(b)   any National Insurance number, tax reference number, PAYE reference number or other personal identifier allocated by HMRC to the person to whom the information relates;

(c)   the reference number (or if more than one, any one reference number) allocated by HMRC under section 311 to the notifiable arrangements or proposed notifiable arrangements;

(d)   the year of assessment, tax year or accounting period (as the case may be) in which, or the date on which, the person providing the information or, in the case of regulation 10(4), an employee of that person, expects to obtain a tax advantage by virtue of the notifiable arrangements;

Statutory Instruments

(e)   the name of the person providing the declaration as to the accuracy and completeness of the notification; and

(f)   the capacity in which the person mentioned in sub-paragraph (e) is acting.

11(4)   In the case prescribed at regulation 10(2) the prescribed information is–

(a)   the name and address of the purchaser;

(b)   the reference number (or if more than one, any one reference number) allocated by HMRC under section 311 to the notifiable arrangements or proposed notifiable arrangements;

(c)   the address of the property forming the subject of the arrangements ("the property");

(d)   the title number of the property (if any is allocated);

(e)   the unique transaction reference number (if a land transaction return has been submitted to HMRC at the time the prescribed information is provided);

(f)   the market value of the property, taking into account all chargeable interests in the property held by the same person or connected persons;

(g)   the effective date of the first land transaction which forms part of the arrangements;

(h)   the name of the person providing the declaration as to the accuracy and completeness of the notification; and

(i)   the capacity in which that person is acting.

11(5)   In the cases prescribed in regulation 10(6A), (7) and (8), where they relate to annual tax on enveloped dwellings, the prescribed information is–

(a)   the name and address of the person providing the information;

(b)   any tax reference number or other personal identifier allocated by HMRC or a foreign tax authority to the person to whom the information relates;

(c)   where a foreign tax authority has allocated a personal identifier, the name of the country on behalf of which that foreign tax authority acts;

(d)   the reference number (or if more than one, any one reference number) allocated by HMRC under section 311 to the notifiable arrangements or proposed notifiable arrangements;

(e)   the address of the property forming the subject of the arrangements ("the property");

(f)   the title number of the property (if any is allocated);

(g)   the first chargeable period (within the meaning of section 94(8) of the Finance Act 2013) in which the person providing the information expects to obtain a tax advantage by virtue of the notifiable arrangements;

(h)   the name of the person providing the declaration as to the accuracy and completeness of the notification, where different from information provided under sub-paragraph (a); and

(i)   the capacity in which the person mentioned in sub-paragraph (h) is acting.

History – In reg. 11(3), the words "and any case relating to annual tax on enveloped dwellings" inserted by SI 2013/2592, reg. 11, with effect from 4 November 2013.
Reg. 11(5) inserted by SI 2013/2592, reg. 12, with effect from 4 November 2013.

TIME FOR PROVIDING INFORMATION UNDER SECTION 313(3)(B)

12(1)   The prescribed times for providing information in the cases prescribed in regulation 10 are as follows.

12(2)   In the case of regulation 10(2) any time during the period of 30 days beginning with the later of–

(a)   the effective date of the first land transaction which forms part of the arrangements; or

(b)   the date of the receipt of the reference number allocated under the provisions of section 311.

12(3)   In the case of regulation 10(4) whichever of (a) or (b) below applies in respect of the tax year in which the employer first enters into a transaction forming part of the notifiable arrangements and whichever applies in respect of each subsequent year until an advantage ceases to apply to any person–

(a)   for a non-Real Time Information employer, any time during the period ending on the date on which the return under regulation 73 of the Income Tax (Pay As You Earn) Regulations 2003 (annual return of relevant payments liable to deduction of tax (Forms P35 and P14)) is or would be due; or

(b)   for a Real Time Information employer, 14 days after the end of the final tax period of the tax year.

In this paragraph, **"non-Real Time Information employer"** and **"Real Time Information employer"** have the meanings given in regulation 2(1) (interpretation) of the Income Tax (Pay As You Earn) Regulations 2003.

12(4)   In the case of regulation 10(5)–

(a)   for regulation 10(5)(a), any time during the period ending on 31st January next following the end of the year of assessment in question;

(b)   for regulation 10(5)(b), any time during the period ending on the date defined as the filing date for the purposes of paragraph 14 of Schedule 18 to the Finance Act 1998 in respect of the period of account in question;

(c)   for regulation 10(5)(c), any time during the period ending on the earliest date by which the person in question could be required to file a return under section 12AA of the Taxes Management Act 1970, determined in accordance with whichever of subsections (4) and (5) of that section is applicable.

12(5)   In the case of regulation 10(6) any time during the period of 12 months from the end of the month in which the first transaction forming part of the arrangements is entered into.

12(5A)   In the cases of regulation 10(6A), (7) and (8), where it relates to annual tax on enveloped dwellings, any time during the period of 30 days beginning with the later of–

(a)   the effective date of the first transaction which forms part of the arrangements; or

(b)   the date of the receipt of the reference number allocated under the provisions of section 311.

12(6)   In the case of regulation 10(7) and (8), except where they relate to annual tax on enveloped dwellings, any time during the period ending on the filing date for the relevant return.

12(7)   In the case of regulation 10(9) the time that the claim is made.

History – Reg. 12(5) inserted by SI 2013/2592, reg. 13, with effect from 4 November 2013.
In reg. 12(6), the words ", except where they relate to annual tax on enveloped dwellings," inserted by SI 2013/2592, reg. 14, with effect from 4 November 2013.

PRESCRIBED INFORMATION UNDER SECTION 313ZA: INFORMATION AND TIMING

13(1)   For the purposes of section 313ZA(3) (duty of promoter to provide client lists)–

(a)   the prescribed period is–

    (i)   30 days; or

    (ii)   where the circumstances in sub-paragraph (d)(iii) apply, 60 days in respect of the information prescribed under sub-paragraph (b)(iii) only.

(b)   the prescribed information is–

    (i)   any reference number allocated by HMRC under section 311 to the arrangements (or to a proposal for them) to which the information provided relates;

    (ii)   the name and address of each client in relation to whom the relevant date (within the meaning of section 312(3)) occurs in the relevant period in relation to which the information is being provided;

    (iii)   any identification number allocated by HMRC ("unique taxpayer number") and national insurance number for each client in relation to whom the relevant date (within the meaning of section 312(3)) occurs in the relevant period in relation to which the information is being provided;

    (iv)   the promoter's name and address; and

    (v)   the end date of the relevant period in relation to which the information is being provided.

(c)   in sub-paragraph (b)(ii) the address of the client is the address to which the promoter has sent or would have sent the prescribed information under section 312.

(d)   at the end of the prescribed period under sub-paragraph (a)(i), where the promoter is unable to provide any unique taxpayer number or national insurance number, the prescribed information under sub-paragraph (b) must include confirmation that one of the following applies–

    (i)   the client has complied with section 312B and does not have a unique taxpayer number or national insurance number or has neither number;

    (ii)   the client has not complied with section 312B;

    (iii)   on the sixteenth day after the end of the relevant period, the prescribed period under regulation 8A(1)(a) had not yet expired;

(e)   at the end of the prescribed period under sub-paragraph (a)(ii), where the promoter is unable to provide any unique taxpayer number or national insurance number, the prescribed information under sub-paragraph (b) must include confirmation that either sub-paragraph (d)(i) or sub-paragraph (d)(ii) applies.

13(2)   For the purposes of section 313ZA(4) the relevant period is each calendar quarter.

History – Reg. 13(1)(a) substituted by SI 2013/2592, reg. 17, with effect from 4 November 2013. Former reg. 13(1)(a) read as follows:

     "(a)   the prescribed period is 30 days;".

Reg. 13(1)(b)(iii)–(v) substituted for (iii) and (iv) by SI 2013/2592, reg. 18, with effect from 4 November 2013. Former reg. 13(1)(b)(iii) and (iv) read as follows:

     "(iii)   the promoter's name and address; and

     (iv)   the end date of the relevant period in relation to which the information is being provided.".

Reg. 13(1)(d) and (e) inserted by SI 2013/2592, reg. 19, with effect from 4 November 2013.

PRESCRIBED INFORMATION UNDER SECTION 313ZB: INFORMATION AND TIMING

13A(1)   For the purposes of section 313ZB (further information from promoters)–

(a)   the prescribed period is 10 days from the date that the promoter receives the written notice under section 313ZB; and

(b)   the prescribed information is–

     (i)   the name and address of any person described in section 313ZB(2) (but only those who will, or are likely to, either sell the arrangements to another person, or achieve a tax advantage by implementing the arrangements);

     (ii)   any identification number allocated by HMRC to any person mentioned at sub-paragraph (b)(i); and

     (iii)   sufficient information as might reasonably be expected to enable an officer of HMRC to comprehend the manner in which any person mentioned at subparagraph (b)(i) is involved in the arrangements.

13A(2)   Paragraph (1)(b) only extends to information held by the promoter at the time of receipt of a written notice under section 313ZB(2).

History – Reg. 13A inserted by SI 2013/2592, reg. 20, with effect from 4 November 2013.

TIME FOR PROVIDING INFORMATION UNDER SECTION 313A AND 313B

14(1)   In the case of a requirement under or by virtue of section 313A(1) (pre-disclosure enquiry), the prescribed period is the period of 10 days beginning on the day after that on which the notice is issued.

14(2)   In the case of a requirement under or by virtue of section 313B(1) (reasons for nondisclosure: supporting information), the prescribed period is the period of 14 days beginning on the day after that on which the order is made.

PRESCRIBED INFORMATION UNDER SECTION 313C: INFORMATION AND TIMING

15(1)   For the purposes of section 313C(1) (information provided to introducers) the prescribed information is–

(a)   P's name and address; and

(b)   the name and address of each person who has provided P with any information relating to the proposal.

15(2)   For the purposes of section 313C(3)(a) the prescribed period is 10 days.

HIGHER RATE OF PENALTY FOLLOWING A FAILURE TO COMPLY WITH AN ORDER UNDER SECTION 306A OR 314A

16(1)   For the purposes of section 98C(2A) of the Taxes Management Act 1970 (higher rate of penalty after the making of an order under section 306A) the prescribed period is the period of 10 days beginning on the date on which the order is made.

16(2)   For the purposes of section 98C(2B) of the Taxes Management Act 1970 (higher rate of penalty after the making of an order under section 314A) the prescribed period is the period of 10 days beginning on the date on which the order is made.

ELECTRONIC DELIVERY OF INFORMATION

17(1)   Information required to be delivered to HMRC or to any other person by virtue of these Regulations may be delivered in such form and by such means of electronic communications as are for the time being authorised for that purpose.

17(2)   The use of a particular means of electronic communications is authorised for the purposes of paragraph (1) only if–

(a)   it is authorised by directions given by HMRC under section 132(5) of the Finance Act 1999 (voluntary filing by electronic means of returns and other documents); and

(b)   the user complies with any conditions imposed by HMRC under that section.

17(3)   Nothing in this regulation prevents the delivery of information by electronic communications if the information is contained in a return which is–

(a)   authorised to be delivered electronically by virtue of regulations under section 132 of the Finance Act 1999; or

(b)   required to be so delivered by virtue of regulations under section 135 of the Finance Act 2002 (mandatory e-filing).

AMENDMENT OF THE TAX AVOIDANCE SCHEMES (PROMOTERS AND PRESCRIBED CIRCUMSTANCES) REGULATIONS 2004

18   [Amends SI 2004/1865, reg. 6.]

SCHEDULE – REVOCATIONS

Regulation 3

[Revokes SI 2004/1864.]

BUSINESS INVESTMENT RELIEF REGULATIONS 2012

(SI 2012/1898)

Made on 18 July 2012 by the Commissioners for Her Majesty's Revenue and Customs, in exercise of the powers conferred by s. 809VJ(4) and (5) of the Income Tax Act 2007. Operative from 10 August 2012.

CITATION, COMMENCEMENT AND EFFECT

1(1) These Regulations may be cited as the Business Investment Relief Regulations 2012 and shall come into force on 10th August 2012.

1(2) These Regulations have effect in relation to qualifying investments made on or after 6 April 2012.

CIRCUMSTANCES IN WHICH GRACE PERIOD MAY BE EXTENDED

2 The grace period allowed for an appropriate mitigation step by section 809VJ of the Income Tax Act 2007 may be extended by an officer of Revenue and Customs if regulation 3 or 4 applies.

LOCK-UP AGREEMENTS

3(1) This regulation applies if conditions 1 and 2 are met.

3(2) Condition 1 is that–

(a) the target company has ceased to be a private limited company by virtue of having some or all of its shares listed on a recognised stock exchange; or

(b)

    (i) the target company has become a subsidiary of another company ("the new company"); and

    (ii) the new company is a body corporate some or all of whose shares are listed on a recognised stock exchange (or are to be so listed).

3(3) Condition 2 is that P is unable to comply with an appropriate mitigation step without breaching the terms of a lock-up agreement.

3(4) For the purposes of this regulation **"lock-up agreement"** means a contract–

(a) entered into by P with one or more relevant parties which is directly related to the listing of shares in the target company or, as the case may be, the new company, on a recognised stock exchange; and

(b) that imposes restrictions on the time or manner in which P may–

    (i) dispose of some or all of P's holding in the target company; or

    (ii) dispose of some or all of any shares in the new company received by P in return for P's holding in the target company.

3(5) For the purposes of this regulation **"relevant party"** means–

(a) the target company;

(b) the new company;

(c) professional advisors retained by the target company or the new company in relation to the listing of the shares of the target company (or, as the case may be, the shares of the new company) on a recognised stock exchange.

STATUTORY AND LEGAL BARS

4 This regulation applies if–

(a) P is prevented from taking an appropriate mitigation step by a prohibition imposed by or under any enactment; or

(b) the taking of an appropriate mitigation step by P would breach the terms of an order imposed by any court.

MONEY LAUNDERING (AMENDMENT) REGULATIONS 2012

(SI 2012/2298)

Made on 6 September 2012 by the Treasury, in exercise of the powers conferred on them by s. 2(2) of the European Communities Act 1972. Operative from 1 October 2012.

CITATION AND COMMENCEMENT

1   These Regulations may be cited as the Money Laundering (Amendment) Regulations 2012 and come into force on 1st October 2012.

AMENDMENT OF THE MONEY LAUNDERING REGULATIONS 2007

2-17   [Amends SI 2007/2157.]

REVIEW

18(1)   The Treasury must from time to time–

(a)   carry out a review of the Money Laundering Regulations 2007 as amended by regulations 2 to 17,

(b)   set out the conclusions of the review in a report, and

(c)   publish the report.

18(2)   In carrying out the review the Treasury must, so far as is reasonable, have regard to how Directive 2005/60/EC of the European Parliament and of the Council on the protection of the use of the financial system for the purpose of money laundering and terrorist financing (which is implemented in part by the Money Laundering Regulations 2007) is implemented in other member States.

18(3)   The report must in particular–

(a)   set out the objectives intended to be achieved by the regulatory system established by the Money Laundering Regulations 2007 as amended by regulations 2 to 17,

(b)   assess the extent to which those objectives are achieved, and

(c)   assess whether those objectives remain appropriate and, if so, the extent to which they could be achieved with a system that imposes less regulation.

18(4)   The first report under this regulation must be published before the end of the period of five years beginning with the day on which these Regulations come into force.

18(5)   Reports under this regulation are afterwards to be published at intervals not exceeding five years.

SCHEDULE

Regulation 17

[Amends SI 2007/2157.]

TERRORISM ACT 2000 AND PROCEEDS OF CRIME ACT 2002 (BUSINESS IN THE REGULATED SECTOR) (NO. 2) ORDER 2012

(SI 2012/2299)

Made on 6 September 2012 by the Treasury, in exercise of the powers conferred on them by para. 5 of Sch. 3A to the Terrorism Act 2000 and para. 5 of Sch. 9 to the Proceeds of Crime Act 2002. Operative from 1 October 2012.

CITATION AND COMMENCEMENT

1 This Order may be cited as the Terrorism Act 2000 and Proceeds of Crime Act 2002 (Business in the Regulated Sector) (No. 2) Order 2012 and comes into force on 1st October 2012.

AMENDMENT OF SCHEDULE 3A TO THE TERRORISM ACT 2000

2 [Amends TERA 2000, Sch. 3A, para. 1.]

AMENDMENT OF SCHEDULE 9 TO THE PROCEEDS OF CRIME ACT 2002

3 [Amends PCA 2002, Sch. 9, para. 1.]

REVIEW

4(1) The Treasury must from time to time–

(a)   carry out a review of Schedule 3A to the Terrorism Act 2000 and Schedule 9 to the Proceeds of Crime Act 2002 as amended respectively by articles 2 and 3,

(b)   set out the conclusions of the review in a report, and

(c)   publish the report.

4(2) In carrying out the review the Treasury must, so far as is reasonable, have regard to how Directive 2005/60/EC of the European Parliament and of the Council on the protection of the use of the financial system for the purpose of money laundering and terrorist financing (which is implemented in part by Part 3 of the Terrorism Act 2000 and Part 7 of the Proceeds of Crime Act 2002) is implemented in other member States.

4(3) The report must in particular–

(a)   set out the objectives intended to be achieved by Schedule 3A to the Terrorism Act 2000 and Schedule 9 to the Proceeds of Crime Act as amended by articles 2 and 3,

(b)   assess the extent to which those objectives are achieved, and

(c)   assess whether those objectives remain appropriate and, if so, the extent to which they could be achieved with a system that imposes less regulation.

4(4) The first report under this article must be published before the end of the period of five years beginning with the day on which this Order comes into force.

4(5) Reports under this article are afterwards to be published at intervals not exceeding five years.

FRIENDLY SOCIETIES (MODIFICATIONS OF THE TAX ACTS) REGULATIONS 2012

(SI 2012/3008)

Made on 3 December 2012 by the Treasury in exercise of the powers conferred by s. 151(3), (4) and (6), 158(5) and (7), 166(6) and (8) and 167(4) and (6) of the Finance Act 2012. Operative from 31 December 2012.

CITATION, COMMENCEMENT, EFFECT AND INTERPRETATION

1(1) These Regulations may be cited as the Friendly Societies (Modifications of the Tax Acts) Regulations 2012 and shall come into force on 31st December 2012.

1(2) These Regulations have effect in relation to accounting periods beginning on or after 1st January 2013.

1(3) In these Regulations **"FA 2012"** means "the Finance Act 2012".

FRIENDLY SOCIETIES SUBJECT TO THE SAME BASIC RULES AS MUTUAL INSURERS

2 The Corporation Tax Acts, in so far as they apply to—

(a) the life assurance business and other long-term business carried on by friendly societies,

(b) any part of the business of an insurance company which is exempt from corporation tax as a result of section 158 or section 166 (transfers from friendly societies to insurance companies etc) of FA 2012, or

(c) any part of the business of a friendly society which is exempt from corporation tax as a result of section 167 of FA 2012 (transfers between friendly societies),

have effect with the modifications specified in regulations 3 to 15.

3 In Schedule 7 to the Finance Act 1991, paragraph 16 (transitional relief for old general annuity contracts) applies as if in sub-paragraph (7)—

(a) in the definition of "general annuity contract" after "referable to" there were inserted "taxable", and

(b) at the appropriate place there were inserted—

""**taxable general annuity business**" means general annuity business the profits arising from which do not fall to be exempted from tax by virtue of section 153 (exemption for certain BLAGAB or eligible PHI business) or section 158 (transfers from friendly societies to insurance companies etc) of the Finance Act 2012, and for the purposes of this definition it shall be assumed that the friendly society has made a claim for exemption from tax under section 153 of that Act.".

4 Section 255 of CAA 2001 (apportionment of allowances and charges) applies as if for subsection (1) there were substituted—

"**255(1)** This section applies if the long-term business of the company consists of two or more of—

(a) basic life assurance and general annuity business,

(b) non-BLAGAB long-term business, or

(c) tax exempt business.

255(1A) In subsection (1)(c) **"tax exempt business"** has the same meaning as in section 57A of FA 2012 (section 57: meaning of "tax exempt business").".

5 Section 57 of FA 2012 (meaning of basic life assurance and general annuity business) applies as if in subsection (2)—

(a) the "or" at the end of paragraph (f) were omitted, and

(b) at the end of paragraph (g) there were inserted—

", or

(h) tax exempt business".

6 After section 57 of FA 2012 (meaning of basic life assurance and general annuity business) there is treated as inserted—

Statutory Instruments

"**57A   Section 57: meaning of "tax exempt business"**

57A   In this Part **"tax exempt business"** means business in respect of which an insurance company or a friendly society is exempt from corporation tax on its profits by virtue of–

(a)   section 153 (exemption for certain BLAGAB or eligible PHI business),

(b)   section 158 (transfers from friendly societies to insurance companies etc),

(c)   section 164 (societies registered before 1 June 1973, etc),

(d)   section 165 (incorporated friendly societies),

(e)   section 166 (transfers from friendly societies etc),

(f)   section 167 (transfers between friendly societies).".

7   Section 63 of FA 2012 (meaning of "long-term business" and "PHI business") applies as if after subsection (2) there were inserted–

"**63(3)**   But **"PHI business"** does not include tax exempt business.".

8   Section 66 of FA 2012 (separate businesses for BLAGAB and other long-term business) applies as if–

(a)   for subsections (1) to (3) there were substituted–

"**66(1)**   If an insurance company carries on two or more of–

(a)   basic life assurance and general annuity business,

(b)   tax exempt business, or

(c)   other long-term business

the general rule is that each business within paragraphs (a), (b) and (c) carried on by that company is to be treated for corporation tax purposes as a separate business carried on by that company.

66(2)   The business within subsection (1)(a) is to consist of the basic life assurance and general annuity business.

66(3)   The business within subsection (1)(b) is to consist of the tax exempt business.

66(3A)   The business within subsection (1)(c) is to consist of the other long-term business.", and

(b)   in subsection (5)(a) for "(3)" there were substituted "(3A)".

9   Section 67 (exemption where BLAGAB small part of long-term business) applies as if–

(a)   for subsection (3) there were substituted–

"**67(3)**   There are instead to be two businesses that are to be regarded for corporation tax purposes as consisting of–

(a)   that basic life assurance and general annuity business and the other long-term business, and

(b)   tax exempt business.", and

(b)   in subsection (4) for "that single trade" there were substituted "the trade in subsection (3)(a)".

10   Section 97 of FA 2012 (application of Chapter) applies as if for subsection (1) there were substituted–

"**97(1)**   This Chapter applies in the case of an insurance company that carries on basic life assurance and general annuity business and one or both of–

(a)   tax exempt business, or

(b)   other long-term business.".

11   Section 98 of FA 2012 (commercial allocation) applies as if after subsection (2) there were inserted–

"**98(2A)**   But in determining those items, the credits or other income, the debits or other losses and the expenses in relation to tax exempt business are not to be taken into account.".

12   Section 114 of FA 2012 (application of Chapter) applies as if–

(a)   in subsection (1)–

(i)   for ", has", there were substituted "carries on two or more of",

(ii)   the "and" at the end of paragraph (a) were omitted, and

(iii)   after paragraph (a) there were inserted–

"(aa) a tax exempt business, and",

(b)   in subsection (2)–

     (i)   in paragraph (a) "two" were omitted, and

     (ii)   in paragraph (b) "(a) and (b)" were omitted, and

(c)   in subsection (5)–

     (i)   the "and" at the end of paragraph (a) were omitted, and

     (ii)   after paragraph (a) there were inserted–

         "(aa)   calculating the profits of the tax exempt business, and".

13   In section 115 of FA 2012 (commercial allocation of accounting profit or loss and tax adjustments) subsections (1) and (2) apply as if "two" were omitted.

14   Section 172 of FA 2012 (minor definitions) applies as if in subsection (2) after "that Part", there were inserted–

     "except where the context otherwise requires".

15   Section 174 of FA 2012 (index of defined terms) applies as if in the table in the second column ("where explained") in relation to the expression "basic life and general annuity business (abbreviated to "BLAGAB")" after "section 57" there were inserted "(a) to (g)".

REVOCATION

16   The Regulations specified in the Schedule are revoked.

SCHEDULE

Regulation 16

Regulations	References
The Friendly Societies (Modification of the Corporation Tax Acts) Regulations 2005	SI 2005/2014
The Friendly Societies (Modification of the Corporation Tax Acts) (Amendment) Regulations 2007	SI 2007/2134
The Insurance Companies (Tax Exempt Business) Regulations 2007	SI 2007/2145
The Friendly Societies (Modification of the Corporation Tax Acts) (Amendment) Regulations 2008	SI 2008/1937
The Friendly Societies (Transfers of Other Business) (Modification of the Corporation Tax Acts) Regulations 2008	SI 2008/1942

INSURANCE COMPANIES (TRANSITIONAL PROVISIONS) REGULATIONS 2012

(SI 2012/3009)

Made on 3 December 2012 by the Treasury in exercise of the powers conferred by para. 6(3), 7(2)(e), 8(2) and 37 of Sch. 17 to the Finance Act 2012. Operative from 31 December 2012.

CITATION, COMMENCEMENT AND INTERPRETATION

1(1) These Regulations may be cited as the Insurance Companies (Transitional Provisions) Regulations 2012 and come into force on 31st December 2012

1(2) In these Regulations–

"**category**" means a category in the Table;

"**Schedule 17**" means Schedule 17 to the Finance Act 2012;

"**specified businesses**" means the businesses described in paragraph 8(1)(a) to (c) of Schedule 17;

"**the Table**" means the Table set out in regulation 4.

OVERVIEW

2 In these Regulations–

(a) regulations 3 to 6 make provision in relation to determining the amount of the particular items that when taken together result in the total transitional difference;

(b) regulation 7 specifies particular items that are excluded items;

(c) subject to regulation 15, regulations 8 to 14 make provision to apportion particular items that are relevant computational items between the specified businesses;

(d) regulation 15 makes provision in relation to items apportioned to basic life assurance and general annuity business where section 67 of the Finance Act 2012 (exception where BLAGAB small part of long-term business) applies;

(e) regulation 16 amends paragraph 20 of Schedule 17.

COMPARISON OF ITEMS IN THE 2012 PERIODICAL RETURN AND THE 2012 BALANCE SHEET

3(1) To determine the particular items that when taken together result in the total transitional difference, the insurance company must compare–

(a) the amounts included in the 2012 periodical return for the entry for each category specified in column 1 of the Table, with

(b) the amounts included in the 2012 balance sheet for the entry for that category specified in column 2 of the Table.

3(2) The difference between those amounts is the particular item in relation to each category.

This is subject to regulation 5(6).

3(3) The comparison must be made separately in relation to with-profits funds and non-profit funds and separately in relation to each with-profits fund.

3(4) Where no entry is specified as a comparator in relation to any category, the amount is treated as nil.

3(5) In determining the total amount for an entry, assets are given a positive figure and liabilities are given a negative figure.

3(6) For the purposes of paragraph (5), amounts in line 51 of Form 14 are treated as liabilities.

3(7) If the amount for the entry for a particular category in column 2 exceeds the amount shown in column 1 the particular item is a positive figure.

3(8) If the amount for the entry for a particular category in column 1 exceeds the amount shown in column 2, the particular item is a negative figure.

COMPARISON TABLE

4 The Table for the purposes of the comparison referred to in regulation 3 is as follows–

Category	Column 1 **Amounts shown in the 2012 periodical return**	Column 2 **Amounts shown in the 2012 balance sheet attributable to long-term business**
1	None	Deferred acquisition costs (however described in the balance sheet) and other tax deductible amounts, which represent costs relieved for tax in an accounting period ending on or before 31 December 2012 but which are debited in accounts for an accounting period beginning after that date
2	None	Amount included as an asset in respect of the value of future profits arising from a business (or part of a business) transferred to the company (but excluding an asset so far as it is regarded for accounting purposes as internally-generated)
3	None	Loan liability where receipt of the loan was brought into account in line 15 of Form 40 of any periodical return which is, or which represents, an outstanding contingent loan
4	None	Liability under a financial re-insurance arrangement which represents an outstanding re-insurance amount
5	None	Amount in respect of intangible assets to which Part 8 of CTA 2009 (intangible fixed assets) would apply but for section 902 of that Act
6	Amount in respect of the admissible value of structural assets held in a non-profit fund, reduced by any increase and increased by any decrease reflected in that value to the extent that subsection (1) of section 83XA of the Finance Act 1989 (structural assets) has not applied to that increase or decrease	Amount in respect of structural assets
7	None	Deferred income reserves and other amounts which represent income taxed in an accounting period ending on or before 31 December 2012 but which are credited in accounts for an accounting period beginning after that date
8	Amounts included in line 21 of Form 14 to the extent they relate to deferred policyholder tax	The closing deferred policyholder tax balance for the period of account where it is a net liability (subject to regulation 5(2) and (3))
9	Amounts – (a) that are not taxable or not deductible under Part 3 of CTA 2009 (Trading Income) as that Part applies to insurance companies, or (b) that are unrecognised capital amounts included in line 51 of Form 14, (subject to regulation 5(2), (4) and (5))	Amounts – (c) that are not taxable or not deductible under Part 3 of CTA 2009 as that Part applies to insurance companies, or (d) that relate to a non-profit fund included in the fund for future appropriations or the unallocated divisible surplus, (subject to regulation 5(2) and (5))

Category	Column 1 Amounts shown in the 2012 periodical return	Column 2 Amounts shown in the 2012 balance sheet attributable to long-term business
10	Amounts in relation to which the taxability or deductibility (or the timing of taxability or deductibility) in computing the company's life assurance trade profits is determined in accordance with a specific provision of the Corporation Tax Acts applying to such an amount where the same provision applies before and after the commencement of Part 2 of the Finance Act 2012	Equivalent amounts in relation to which the taxability or deductibility (or the timing of taxability or deductibility) in computing the company's life assurance trade profits is determined in accordance with a specific provision of the Corporation Tax Acts applying to such an amount where the same provision applies before and after the commencement of Part 2 of the Finance Act 2012
11	Amount in respect of linked assets (or part asset)	Amount in respect of linked assets (or part asset)
12	Mathematical reserves net of reinsured liabilities (subject to regulation 5(2))	Technical provisions net of reinsured liabilities (subject to regulation 5(2))
13	Amount included in line 51 of Form 14 relating to with-profits funds	Fund for future appropriations or the unallocated divisible surplus except in so far as it includes amounts arising in a non-profit fund
14	Amount included in line 51 of Form 14 relating to non-profit funds except in so far as this includes– (a) amounts brought into account by section 83YA of the Finance Act 1989 (changes in value of assets brought into account: non-profit companies), or (b) unrecognised capital amounts, reduced by the amount of any increase, and increased by the amount of any decrease, reflected in the admissible value of structural assets held in a non-profit fund to the extent that subsection (1) of section 83XA of the Finance Act 1989 (structural assets) has not applied to that increase or decrease (see also regulation 5(1))	None
15	None (subject to regulation 5(2) and (4))	The closing deferred policyholder tax balance for the period of account where it is a net asset (subject to regulation 5(2) and (3))
16	Amounts reflected in the cumulative taxed surplus which are not taken into account in determining any particular item in relation to categories 1 to 15 and which are referable to particular policies	Amounts reflected in the amount attributed to shareholders as at 31 December 2012 which are not taken into account in determining any particular item in relation to categories 1 to 15 and which are referable to particular policies
17	Amounts reflected in the cumulative taxed surplus which are not taken into account in determining any particular item in relation to any other category	Amounts reflected in the amount attributed to shareholders as at 31 December 2012 which are not taken into account in determining any particular item in relation to any other category

ADJUSTMENTS TO TABLE AMOUNTS

5(1) The amount in column 1 of category 14 cannot be reduced except as expressly provided in category 14.

5(2) Where the calculation of the mathematical reserves or the technical provisions referred to in category 12 includes amounts in respect of deferred tax, paragraphs (3) to (5) apply.

5(3) Amounts in column 2 of category 12 which relate to deferred policyholder tax are excluded from category 12 and are included in the determination of the particular item in category 8 or category 15 as the case may be.

5(4)   If the aggregate of amounts in column 1 of category 12 which relate to deferred policyholder tax is a positive figure, that aggregate amount is excluded from category 12 and is included–

(a)   in column 1 of category 15 to the extent that it does not exceed the amount in column 2 of category 15 (as adjusted under paragraph (3)), and

(b)   in column 1 of category 9 in so far as it exceeds the amount in column 2 of category 15.

5(5)   Amounts in respect of deferred tax not within paragraphs (3) or (4) are excluded from the amount in category 12 and are included as an amount in category 9.

5(6)   If the total of all the particular items in relation to category 15 determined by the comparisons made under regulation 3 (adjusted under paragraphs (2) to (4) of this regulation) exceeds the deferred policyholder tax–

(a)   the particular items in relation to category 15 are reduced by the amount of the excess (but not below nil), and

(b)   the particular items in relation to category 8 are increased by the same amount.

Where this paragraph applies and there is more than one particular item in relation to category 15, the extent to which each item is adjusted under subparagraphs (a) and (b) is determined on a just and reasonable basis.

5(7)   For the purposes of paragraph (6), **"deferred policyholder tax"** means–

(a)   the amount included in the accounts of the company for the accounting period ending on 31 December 2012 in respect of deferred tax so far as it is wholly attributable to policyholder tax, and

(b)   amounts in column 2 to which paragraph (3) applies.

TABLE DEFINITIONS

6   In the Table and regulation 5–

"admissible value" has the meaning given in section 83XA(9) of the Finance Act 1989;

"the closing deferred policyholder tax balance for the period of account" shall be interpreted in accordance with section 108 of the Finance Act 2012;

"deferred income reserves" means the fee, commission or other income received in respect of contracts with policyholders which for accounting purposes is deferred and recognised as income over more than one period of account;

"deferred policyholder tax" means the amount included in the 2012 periodical return or in the accounts of the company for the accounting period ending on 31 December 2012 in respect of deferred tax so far as it is wholly attributable to policyholder tax (except in regulation 5(6) in which case see regulation 5(7));

"life assurance trade profits" means profits arising from life assurance business calculated in accordance with the provisions applicable for the purposes of the taxation of such profits under section 35 of CTA (charge on trade profits);

"linked assets" means assets of an insurance company which are identified in its records as assets by reference to the value of which benefits provided for under a policy or contract are to be determined and in cases where only part of an asset is so identified, references to a linked asset are references to that part;

"mathematical reserves" are those reserves which are determined in accordance with section 1.2 of the Insurance Prudential Sourcebook;

"outstanding contingent loan" has the meaning given in paragraph 7(3) of Schedule 17;

"outstanding re-insurance amount" has the meaning given in paragraph 7(4) of Schedule 17;

"structural assets" has the meaning given in section 83XA(3) of the Finance Act 1989;

"unrecognised capital amounts" shall be interpreted in accordance with section 83YB(3) and (4) of the Finance Act 1989;

"wholly attributable to policyholder tax" shall be interpreted in accordance with section 108(2) of the Finance Act 2012.

EXCLUDED ITEMS

7(1)   A particular item is an excluded item for the purposes of paragraph 7 of Schedule 17 if it relates to an item in any of categories 1 to 10.

7(2)   Paragraph 7(6) of Schedule 17 applies to such items.

APPORTIONMENT IN RELATION TO A WITH-PROFIT FUND (1): CATEGORY 13

8(1) This regulation applies to a relevant computational item which relates to category 13 to the extent that–

(a)   the amount of the entries for that category are attributable to the component amounts in categories 1, 2, 5, 7 and 8, and

(b)   those component amounts in categories 1, 2, 5, 7 and 8 are referable to particular policies.

8(2) The relevant computational item (or part of the item) must be apportioned between the specified businesses by reference to the policies referable to each specified business to which the entries in column 1 and column 2 in the Table relate.

APPORTIONMENT IN RELATION TO A WITH-PROFIT FUND (2): CATEGORY 15

9(1) This regulation applies to a relevant computational item which relates to a with-profit fund and is an item within category 15.

9(2) The relevant computational item must be apportioned to the business described in paragraph 8(1)(a) of Schedule 17 (basic life assurance and general annuity business).

APPORTIONMENT IN RELATION TO A WITH-PROFIT FUND (3)

10(1) This regulation applies to a relevant computational item which relates to a with-profit fund where neither regulation 8 or 9 applies.

10(2) Each relevant computational item must be apportioned between the specified businesses in the same proportion as the bonuses declared for that with-profit fund are referable to each of the specified businesses in respect of the accounting period ending on 31 December 2012.

10(3) But if the bonuses declared in respect of the accounting period ending on 31 December 2012–

(a)   are nil,

(b)   are of a negligible amount by reference to the liabilities to the policyholders of the fund at that date, or

(c)   would otherwise give a result which is not representative of the respective contribution of the specified businesses to the fund,

the company must apportion each relevant computational item between the specified businesses in a way which fairly reflects the proportion of the fund that each of the specified businesses represents as at 31 December 2012.

10(4) Where a company is one to which paragraph 3 or paragraph 4 of Schedule 17 applies, paragraphs (2) and (3) of this regulation apply as if the references to the accounting period ending on 31 December 2012 were references to the last accounting period which ended before 31 December 2012.

APPORTIONMENT IN RELATION TO A NON-PROFIT FUND: CATEGORIES 11, 12, 15 AND 16

11(1) This regulation applies to a relevant computational item which relates to a non-profit fund and is an item within–

(a)   category 11,

(b)   category 12,

(c)   category 15, or

(d)   category 16.

11(2) Each relevant computational item must be apportioned between the specified businesses by reference to the policies referable to each specified business to which the entries in column 1 and column 2 in the Table relate.

APPORTIONMENT IN RELATION TO UNRELIEVED FAFTS CHARGE

12(1) This regulation applies to an amount treated as a relevant computational item under paragraph 16 of Schedule 17.

12(2) The relevant computational item must be apportioned between the businesses described in paragraphs 8(1)(a) and (b) of Schedule 17 in the same proportion as if it was an amount to which the

Financing-Arrangement-Funded Transfers to Shareholders Regulations 2008 applied and the relevant computational item was a section 83YC(3) amount within the meaning of those Regulations.

APPORTIONMENT IN RELATION TO A NON-PROFIT FUND: CATEGORY 14

13(1)   This regulation applies to a relevant computational item which relates to category 14.

13(2)   Each relevant computational item must be apportioned between the specified businesses as follows—

(a)   a fraction equal to the applicable relevant fraction must be apportioned to the business described in paragraph 8(1)(b) of Schedule 17 (gross roll up business);

(b)   a fraction equal to—

$$1 - AAF$$

must be apportioned to the business described in paragraph 8(1)(c) of Schedule 17 (PHI business), where AAF is the applicable appropriate fraction; and

(c)   the remainder must be apportioned to the business described in paragraph 8(1)(a) of Schedule 17 (basic life assurance and general annuity business).

13(3)   The applicable relevant fraction is, on the assumptions in paragraph (5), the total of—

(a)   the relevant fractions in relation to appropriate periods of account beginning on or after 9 December 2009, and

(b)   the relevant fraction in relation to the last period of account beginning before 9 December 2009 where section 47(4) of the Finance Act 2010 (apportionment of asset value increases) would apply,

weighted in accordance with the amount of the relevant computational item to which each of those fractions applies as a proportion of the total of those amounts.

13(4)   The applicable appropriate fraction is, on the assumptions in paragraph (5), the total of—

(a)   the appropriate fractions in relation to appropriate periods of account beginning on or after 9 December 2009, and

(b)   the appropriate fraction in relation to the last period of account beginning before 9 December 2009 where section 47(4) of the Finance Act 2010 (apportionment of asset value increases) would apply,

weighted in accordance with the amount of the relevant computational item to which each of those fractions applies as a proportion of the total of those amounts.

13(5)   The assumptions are that—

(a)   section 432CA of ICTA (apportionment of asset value increase where line 51 amount decreases) applies in relation to the period of account ending on 31 December 2012,

(b)   the period of account ending on 31 December 2012 is an **"appropriate period of account"** for the purposes of that section, and

(c)   **"the affected amount"** for the purposes of that section is equal to the relevant computational item to which this regulation applies.

13(6)   In this regulation—

"appropriate period of account" has the same meaning as in section 432CA(5) of ICTA (apportionment of asset value increase where line 51 amount decreases);

"the appropriate fraction" has the meaning given in section 432C(5) of ICTA (section 432B apportionment non-participating funds);

"the relevant fraction" has the meaning given in section 432C(9) of ICTA (section 432B apportionment non-participating funds).

APPORTIONMENT IN RELATION TO A NON-PROFIT FUND: OTHER CATEGORIES

14(1)   This regulation applies to a relevant computational item to which regulations 8 to 13 do not apply.

14(2)   Each relevant computational item must be apportioned between the specified businesses as follows—

(a)   a fraction equal to the relevant fraction calculated for the accounting period ending on 31 December 2012 in accordance with section 432C(9) of ICTA, is to be apportioned to the business described in paragraph 8(1)(b) of Schedule 17 (gross roll up business);

Statutory Instruments

(b)   a fraction equal to–

$$1 - AF$$

is to be apportioned to the business described in paragraph 8(1)(c) of Schedule 17 (PHI business), where AF is the appropriate fraction calculated for the accounting period ending on 31 December 2012 in accordance with 432C(5) of ICTA; and

(c)   the remainder is to be apportioned to the business described in paragraph 8(1)(a) of Schedule 17 (basic life assurance and general annuity business).

APPORTIONMENT TO BLAGAB WHERE SECTION 67 OF FINANCE ACT 2012 APPLIES

15(1)   If section 67 of the Finance Act 2012 (exception where BLAGAB small part of long-term business) ("section 67") applies to an insurance company for the accounting period beginning on 1 January 2013, any amount that would apart from this regulation be apportioned to basic life assurance and general annuity business under these Regulations must instead be apportioned to gross roll-up business.

15(2)   If section 67 applies to an insurance company in a subsequent accounting period when the full amount of the receipts or expenses within paragraph 9 of Schedule 17 of the business has not been treated as arising to the company, the receipts or expenses are to continue to be dealt with in accordance with the provisions of Schedule 17 but are treated as arising for that accounting period and the remainder of the 10 year period in question as receipts or expenses within paragraph 10 of Schedule 17.

15(3)   But paragraph (2) does not apply if paragraph 14 of Schedule 17 applies.

AMENDMENT TO PARAGRAPH 20 OF SCHEDULE 17

16   [Amends FA 2012, Sch. 17, para. 20(a) and (b).]

CONTROLLED FOREIGN COMPANIES (EXCLUDED TERRITORIES) REGULATIONS 2012

(SI 2012/3024)

Made on 3 December 2012 by the Commissioners for Her Majesty's Revenue and Customs in exercise of the powers conferred by s. 371KB(2) and (3) of the Taxation (International and Other Provisions) Act 2010. Operative from 1 January 2013.

CITATION, COMMENCEMENT AND EFFECT

1(1) These Regulations may be cited as the Controlled Foreign Companies (Excluded Territories) Regulations 2012 and come into force on 1st January 2013.

1(2) These Regulations have effect for accounting periods of CFCs beginning on or after 1st January 2013.

INTERPRETATION

2 In these Regulations–

"**TIOPA 2010**" means the Taxation (International and Other Provisions) Act 2010;

"**the Schedule**" means the Schedule to these Regulations.

EXCLUDED TERRITORIES

3 A territory listed in Part 1 of the Schedule is an excluded territory for the purposes of Chapter 11 of Part 9A of TIOPA 2010 (the excluded territories exemption).

MODIFIED EXCLUDED TERRITORIES EXEMPTION TO APPLY IN SPECIFIED CASES

4(1) For the purposes of Chapter 11 of Part 9A of TIOPA 2010, the requirements of section 371KB(1)(b) and (c) of that Act do not have to be met in order for the excluded territories exemption to apply for a CFC's accounting period if–

(a)　　for the purposes of that Chapter, the CFC is for the accounting period resident in–

    (i)　　Australia,

    (ii)　　Canada,

    (iii)　　France,

    (iv)　　Germany,

    (v)　　Japan, or

    (vi)　　the United States of America;

(b)　　requirement A is met (if applicable); and

(c)　　requirement B is met.

4(2) Requirement A is applicable only if the CFC is resident as mentioned in paragraph (1)(a) by virtue of section 371TA(1)(b) of TIOPA 2010.

4(3) Requirement A is that the CFC would still be resident as mentioned in paragraph (1)(a) were the following subsections to be substituted for section 371KC(3) of TIOPA 2010–

"**371KC(3)** But section 371TA(1)(b) is to be applied only if the CFC or persons with interests in the CFC are subject to taxation under the law of the territory in question on all of the CFC's income arising during the accounting period.

371KC(3A) For the purposes of subsection (3), the CFC's income does not include any dividend or other distribution received, other than one for which the company paying the dividend or other distribution is entitled to a deduction against its profits for tax purposes under the law of the territory in which it is resident.".

4(4) Requirement B is that at no time during the accounting period is the CFC's business carried on, to any extent, through a permanent establishment which the CFC has in a territory outside the territory in which it is resident for the accounting period for the purposes of Chapter 11 of Part 9A of TIOPA 2010.

Statutory Instruments

FURTHER REQUIREMENT TO BE MET FOR EXCLUDED TERRITORIES EXEMPTION TO APPLY

5 For the purposes of Chapter 11 of Part 9A of TIOPA 2010, Part 2 of the Schedule specifies a further requirement which must be met in order for the excluded territories exemption to apply for a CFC's accounting period.

SCHEDULE

Regulations 3 and 5

PART 1 – EXCLUDED TERRITORIES

Afghanistan	Fiji	Panama
Algeria	Finland	Papua New Guinea
Angola	France	Peru
Argentina	Gabon	Philippines
Armenia	Gambia	Poland
Aruba	Germany	Portugal
Australia	Ghana	Puerto Rico
Austria	Greece	Republic of Korea
Azerbaijan	Guyana	Russia
Bangladesh	Honduras	Saudi Arabia
Barbados	Iceland	Senegal
Belarus	India	Sierra Leone
Belgium	Indonesia	Slovakia
Belize	Iran	Slovenia
Benin	Israel	Solomon Islands
Bolivia	Italy	South Africa
Botswana	Ivory Coast	Spain
Brazil	Jamaica	Sri Lanka
Brunei	Japan	Swaziland
Burundi	Kenya	Sweden
Cameroon	Lesotho	Tanzania
Canada	Libya	Thailand
China	Luxembourg	Trinidad and Tobago
Colombia	Malawi	Tunisia
Croatia	Malaysia	Turkey
Cuba	Malta	Uganda
Czech Republic	Mexico	Ukraine
Democratic Republic of the Congo	Monaco	United States of America
Denmark	Morocco	Uruguay
Dominican Republic	Namibia	Venezuela
Ecuador	Netherlands	Vietnam
Egypt	New Zealand	Zambia
El Salvador	Nigeria	Zimbabwe
Falkland Islands	Norway	
Faroe Islands	Pakistan	

PART 2 – SPECIFIED FURTHER REQUIREMENT

If at any time during the accounting period the CFC carries on insurance business in relation to which the CFC is regulated in any territory, none of that business is carried on in Luxembourg at that time.

CONTROLLED FOREIGN COMPANIES (EXCLUDED BANKING BUSINESS PROFITS) REGULATIONS 2012

(SI 2012/3041)

Made on 5 December 2012 by the Commissioners for Her Majesty's Revenue and Customs in exercise of the powers conferred by s. 371FD of the Taxation (International and Other Provisions) Act 2010. Operative from 1 January 2013.

CITATION, COMMENCEMENT AND EFFECT

1(1) These Regulations may be cited as the Controlled Foreign Companies (Excluded Banking Business Profits) Regulations 2012.

1(2) These Regulations come into force on 1st January 2013 and have effect for accounting periods of CFCs beginning on or after 1st January 2013.

INTERPRETATION

2(1) In these Regulations–

"BIPRU 11" means the rules of that name set out in the FSA Handbook;

"the FSA Handbook" means the Handbook made by the Financial Services Authority under the Financial Services and Markets Act 2000 (as that Handbook has effect from time to time);

"GENPRU 2 Annex 2" means the rules of that name set out in the FSA Handbook;

"group consolidated accounts" means group accounts prepared in accordance with the requirements of Chapter 4 of Part 15 of the Companies Act 2006;

"group regulatory return" means consolidated financial information disclosed by a bank in accordance with BIPRU 11;

"regulatory return period" means the period to which a group regulatory return relates;

"total risk weighted assets" means the amount shown as such in the group regulatory return for a regulatory return period;

"total tier one capital" means the amount shown as such (or as **"total tier 1 capital"**) in the group regulatory return for a regulatory return period;

"UK banking group" means a group for which consolidated financial information is required to be compiled under BIPRU 11.

2(2) In these Regulations, the following expressions have the meaning given by the FSA Handbook–

(a) **"bank"**,

(b) **"exposure"**,

(c) **"group"**,

(d) **"risk weighted exposure amount"**.

2(3) In these Regulations, **"net total tier one capital"** so far as it is used in relation to a CFC means the CFC's total tier one capital after deductions, as calculated in accordance with the capital resources table shown in GENPRU 2 Annex 2.

DISAPPLICATION OF STEP 3 IN SECTION 371FA(1)

3(1) Paragraph (2) applies to an accounting period of a CFC if the CFC meets the conditions specified in regulation 4, as supplemented by regulation 5.

3(2) Step 3 in section 371FA(1) is not to apply in relation to the CFC's trading finance profits in that accounting period so far as they arise from banking business carried on by the CFC in relation to which the CFC is regulated in the territory in which it is resident.

REGULATORY CAPITAL REQUIREMENTS TEST

4(1) The first condition is that throughout the accounting period ("the relevant accounting period") the CFC is a member of a UK banking group ("the CFC's UK banking group").

4(2) The second condition is that the CFC's tier one capital ratio at the end of the relevant accounting period does not exceed the capital ratio limit.

Statutory Instruments

4(3) The third condition is that it is reasonable to suppose that the average tier one capital ratio of the CFC during the relevant accounting period did not exceed the capital ratio limit.

SUPPLEMENTARY PROVISIONS

5 For the purposes of regulation 4–

5(1) The capital ratio limit is 125% of the group tier one capital ratio of the CFC's UK banking group for its last regulatory return period ending before the beginning of the relevant accounting period.

5(2) The group tier one capital ratio of a UK banking group for a regulatory return period is to be calculated using the following formula–

$$100\% \times \frac{A}{B}$$

where–

(a) A is the total tier one capital of the group for the regulatory return period or, if different, the amount calculated in the same way but using amounts (calculated in accordance with BIPRU 11) shown in the group consolidated accounts (if any) for the same period, and

(b) B is the total risk weighted assets of the group for the regulatory return period or, if different, the amount calculated in the same way but using amounts (calculated in accordance with BIPRU 11) shown in the group consolidated accounts (if any) for the same period.

5(3) A CFC's tier one capital ratio at a time is to be calculated using the following formula–

$$100\% \times \frac{C}{D}$$

where–

(a) C is the net total tier one capital of the CFC at that time, and

(b) D is the aggregate of the risk weighted exposure amounts of the CFC for all its exposures at that time.

5(4) In the formula in paragraph (3), C and D are to be determined on the assumptions that BIPRU 11 applies to the CFC and that the CFC is required by those rules to make a disclosure of financial information other than as part of a group regulatory return.

INSURANCE COMPANIES AND CFCs (AVOIDANCE OF DOUBLE CHARGE) REGULATIONS 2012

(SI 2012/3044)

Made on 6 December 2012 by the Treasury in exercise of the powers conferred by s. 213A of the Taxation of Chargeable Gains Act 1992. Operative from 31 December 2012.

Other material – HMRC guidance "Insurance Companies and CFCs: Avoidance of Double Charge Regulations 2012" (M01/2013): guidance on SI 2012/3044; the new regime for the taxation of life insurance companies and interaction with the CFC legislation.

CITATION, COMMENCEMENT AND EFFECT

1(1)   These Regulations may be cited as the Insurance Companies and CFCs (Avoidance of Double Charge) Regulations 2012 and come into force on 31st December 2012.

1(2)   These Regulations have effect in relation to accounting periods beginning on or after 1st January 2013.

INTRODUCTION

2(1)   These Regulations apply in any case where–

(a)   an insurance company to which the I-E rules apply is deemed to make a disposal under section 212 of the Taxation of Chargeable Gains Act 1992 (annual deemed disposal of holdings of unit trusts etc) of an interest in an offshore fund,

(b)   the offshore fund is a CFC, and

(c)   there is (or, but for these Regulations, would be) a CFC charge on the company referable to its relevant interest in the CFC for the accounting period in which the disposal is deemed to have been made.

2(2)   These Regulations modify the operation of–

(a)   the CFC rules (see regulations 3 to 5), and

(b)   section 212 of the Taxation of Chargeable Gains Act 1992 (see regulation 6).

2(3)   In these Regulations–

"**principal CFC**" means the CFC referred to in paragraph (1);

"**associated CFC**" means an offshore fund which is a CFC in which the insurance company has an indirect interest by virtue of having an interest in the principal CFC.

CFC CONTROL TEST

3   The CFC rules apply to the insurance company by reference to its interest in the principal CFC or any associated CFC only if the insurance company controls the principal CFC by virtue of section 371RE of TIOPA 2010 (control determined by reference to accounting standards).

CFCS WHICH ARE EQUITY FUNDS

4(1)   The CFC rules do not apply to the insurance company by reference to its interest in the principal CFC or any associated CFC if–

(a)   at least 95% of the total assets of the CFC consists of shares, and

(b)   no more than 5% of the sum of the CFC's assumed taxable total profits and exempt distribution income consists of interest or returns which are economically equivalent to interest.

4(2)   But this regulation does not apply if the insurance company enters into any arrangements the main purpose or one of the main purposes of which is–

(a)   to secure a tax advantage for itself or any other company in relation to the operation of the CFC rules, or

(b)   to avoid bringing an amount into account under Part 5 or 6 of CTA 2009 (loan relationships and relationships treated as loan relationships etc).

4(3)   In this regulation–

"**arrangement**" includes any agreement, scheme, transaction or understanding (whether or not legally enforceable);

"**assumed taxable total profits**" has the same meaning as in Part 9A of TIOPA 2010 (see section 371VA);

"**economically equivalent to interest**" has the same meaning as in section 486B(2) of CTA 2009;

"**exempt distribution income**" has the same meaning as in section 371CC(9) of TIOPA 2010;

"**share**" has the same meaning as in section 476(1) of CTA 2009;

"**tax advantage**" has the meaning given by section 1139 of CTA 2010.

MODIFICATION RELATING TO I-E CALCULATION

5 Section 371BH of TIOPA 2010 (companies carrying on BLAGAB) applies as if in subsection (6) after "step 1" there were inserted "or 2".

MODIFICATION OF SECTION 212 OF THE TAXATION OF CHARGEABLE GAINS ACT 1992

6(1) For the purposes of section 212 of the Taxation of Chargeable Gains Act 1992 the market value at the time of the deemed disposal under that section is adjusted as follows.

6(2) The market value is treated as reduced by the total chargeable profits of the principal CFC and any associated CFC in any qualifying accounting period in so far as those profits are apportioned to the insurance company under the CFC rules and give rise to a CFC charge.

6(3) But if the insurance company has received a distribution from the principal CFC or any associated CFC in any accounting period in which the disposal is deemed to have been made, the market value at the time of the deemed disposal is adjusted on a just and reasonable basis having regard to all the circumstances.

6(4) For the purposes of paragraph (2), a "**qualifying accounting period**" is an accounting period of the principal CFC and any associated CFC which ends in an accounting period of the company in which a disposal of the company's interest in the principal CFC is deemed to have been made under section 212.

6(5) In this regulation, "**accounting period**" and "**chargeable profits**", in relation to a CFC, have the same meanings as in Part 9A of TIOPA 2010 (see section 371VA of that Act).

EUROPEAN ADMINISTRATIVE CO-OPERATION (TAXATION) REGULATIONS 2012

(SI 2012/3062)

Made on 10 December 2012 by the Treasury in exercise of the powers conferred by s. 2(2) of, and para. 1A of Sch. 2 to, the European Communities Act 1972. Operative from 1 January 2013.

CITATION, COMMENCEMENT, AND INTERPRETATION

1(1) These Regulations may be cited as the European Administrative Co-Operation (Taxation) Regulations 2012 and shall come into force on 1st January 2013.

1(2) In these Regulations **"the Directive"** means Council Directive 2011/16/EU of 15 February 2011 on administrative cooperation in the field of taxation (as amended from time to time).

HMRC FUNCTIONS

2(1) The Commissioners for Her Majesty's Revenue and Customs ("the Commissioners") are designated as the competent authority in the United Kingdom for the purposes of all matters under the Directive.

2(2) HM Revenue and Customs ("HMRC") is designated as the central liaison office in the United Kingdom for the purposes of all matters under the Directive.

EXCHANGE OF INFORMATION

3(1) No obligation of secrecy imposed by statute or otherwise precludes a public authority (or anyone acting on its behalf) from disclosing information if the disclosure is made for the purpose of giving effect, or enabling effect to be given, to the Directive.

3(2) Paragraph (1) applies, in particular, to any disclosure (to persons in the United Kingdom or elsewhere) in connection with a request or proposed request by or on behalf of an applicant authority of any member State for assistance in accordance with the Directive.

3(3) Paragraph (2) is not to be taken to limit paragraph (1).

ONWARD DISCLOSURE OF INFORMATION RECEIVED FROM HMRC

4(1) A public authority commits an offence if–

(a)   it discloses relevant information, and

(b)   the disclosure is not permitted by paragraph (3) below.

4(2) **"Relevant information"** is information that–

(a)   the public authority has received from HMRC by virtue of regulation 3, and

(b)   relates to a person whose identity is specified in the disclosure or can be deduced from it.

4(3) A disclosure is permitted by this paragraph if it is made–

(a)   in accordance with regulation 3,

(b)   in accordance with another enactment permitting the disclosure,

(c)   to comply with an order of a court,

(d)   for the purposes of civil proceedings (whether or not within the United Kingdom),

(e)   for the purposes of a criminal investigation or criminal proceedings (whether or not within the United Kingdom),

(f)   with the consent of each person to whom the information relates, or

(g)   with the consent of the Commissioners.

4(4) Paragraph (1) applies to each of the following as it applies to a public authority–

(a)   an employee or agent of the public authority,

(b)   anyone providing services or exercising functions on behalf of the public authority,

(c)   anyone authorised by the public authority to receive information on its behalf.

5(1) It is a defence for a person charged with an offence under regulation 4 to prove that the person reasonably believed–

(a)   that the disclosure was lawful, or

(b)   that the information had already and lawfully been made available to the public.

5(2) A person guilty of an offence under regulation 4 is liable—

(a) on conviction on indictment, to imprisonment for a term not exceeding 2 years or a fine, or both;

(b) on summary conviction, to imprisonment for a term not exceeding 3 months or a fine not exceeding level 5 on the standard scale, or both.

5(3) A prosecution for an offence under regulation 4 may be instituted in England and Wales only with the consent of the Director of Public Prosecutions.

5(4) A prosecution for an offence under regulation 4 may be instituted in Northern Ireland only—

(a) by the Commissioners, or

(b) with the consent of the Director of Public Prosecutions for Northern Ireland.

CONSEQUENTIAL PROVISIONS

6(1) [Amends FA 2008, Sch. 36, para. 63(4).]

6(2) [Amends FA 2011, Sch. 23, para. 45(4).]

REPEALS

7 The enactments mentioned in the Schedule to these Regulations (being enactments that are superseded or to be superseded by reason of EU obligations and of the provision made by these Regulations in relation thereto or are not compatible with EU obligations) are repealed, to the extent specified in the third column of the Schedule.

SCHEDULE 1

Regulation 7

REPEALS

[Repeals FA 2003, s. 197 and F(No. 2)A 2005, s. 68.]

Statutory Instruments

VISITING FORCES AND INTERNATIONAL MILITARY HEADQUARTERS (EU SOFA) (TAX DESIGNATION) ORDER 2012

(SI 2012/3070)

Made on 12 December 2012 at the Court at Buckingham Palace, in exercise of the powers conferred upon Her Majesty by s. 303 of the Income Tax (Earnings and Pensions) Act 2003, s. 833 of the Income Tax Act 2007, s. 155 of the Inheritance Tax Act 1984. Operative in accordance with art. 1(2).

CITATION AND COMMENCEMENT

1(1) This Order may be cited as the Visiting Forces and International Military Headquarters (EU SOFA) (Tax Designation) Order 2012.

1(2) This Order shall come into force immediately after the coming into force of the EU SOFA in respect of the United Kingdom.

INTERPRETATION

2 In this Order—

"**the EU SOFA**" means the Agreement between the member states of the European Union concerning the status of military and civilian staff seconded to the institutions of the European Union, of the headquarters and forces which may be made available to the European Union in the context of the preparation and execution of the tasks referred to in Article 17(2) of the Treaty on European Union, including exercises, and of the military and civilian staff of the member states put at the disposal of the European Union to act in this context;

"**the Treaty on European Union**" means the Treaty on European Union signed at Maastricht on 7 February 1992 (as amended by the Treaty of Lisbon).

DESIGNATION

3 For the purpose of giving effect to Article 16 of the EU SOFA, each of the countries specified in the First Schedule to this Order, and the international military headquarters specified in the Second Schedule to this Order, are hereby designated for the purposes of—

(a) section 303 of the Income Tax (Earnings and Pensions) Act 2003;

(b) section 833 of the Income Tax Act 2007; and

(c) section 155 of the Inheritance Tax Act 1984.

SCHEDULE 1 – DESIGNATED COUNTRIES

Article 3

Austria, Belgium, Bulgaria, Cyprus, Czech Republic, Denmark, Estonia, Finland, France, Germany, Greece, Hungary, Ireland, Italy, Latvia, Lithuania, Luxembourg, Malta, Netherlands, Poland, Portugal, Romania, Slovakia, Slovenia, Spain, Sweden.

SCHEDULE 2 – DESIGNATED INTERNATIONAL MILITARY HEADQUARTERS

Article 3

The European Union Operational Headquarters at Northwood.

VISITING FORCES AND INTERNATIONAL MILITARY HEADQUARTERS (NATO AND PFP) (TAX DESIGNATION) ORDER 2012

(SI 2012/3071)

Made on 12 December 2012 at the Court at Buckingham Palace, in exercise of the powers conferred upon Her Majesty by s. 74A of the Finance Act 1960, s. 155 of the Inheritance Tax Act 1984, s. 303 of the Income Tax (Earnings and Pensions) Act 2003 and s. 833 of the Income Tax Act 2007. Operative in accordance with art. 1(2).

CITATION AND COMMENCEMENT

1(1) This Order may be cited as the Visiting Forces and International Military Headquarters (NATO and PfP) (Tax Designation) Order 2012.

1(2) This Order shall come into force on the day after the date on which it is made.

REVOCATIONS

2 The Orders in Schedule 1 are revoked.

INTERPRETATION

3 In this Order—

"NATO" means the North Atlantic Treaty Organisation based on the North Atlantic Treaty dated 4th April 1949;

"the NATO SOFA" means the Agreement regarding the Status of Forces of Parties to the North Atlantic Treaty dated 19th June 1951;

"the Paris Protocol" means the Protocol on the Status of International Military Headquarters set up pursuant to the North Atlantic Treaty dated 28th August 1952;

"PfP" means the Partnership for Peace programme of practical bilateral cooperation between individual Partner countries and NATO;

"the PfP SOFA" means the Agreement among the State Parties to the North Atlantic Treaty and the Other States Participating in the Partnership for Peace regarding the Status of their Forces dated 19th June 1995.

NATO DESIGNATION

4 For the purpose of giving effect to Article X of the NATO SOFA and Article VII of the Paris Protocol each of the countries specified in the Second Schedule to this Order, and each of the headquarters specified in the Fourth Schedule to this Order, is hereby designated for the purposes of section 74A of the Finance Act 1960, section 155 of the Inheritance Tax Act 1984, section 303 of the Income Tax (Earnings and Pensions) Act 2003 and section 833 of the Income Tax Act 2007.

PFP DESIGNATION

5 For the purpose of giving effect to Article I of the PfP SOFA each of the countries specified in the Third Schedule to this Order is hereby designated for the purposes of section 74A of the Finance Act 1960, section 155 of the Inheritance Tax Act 1984, section 303 of the Income Tax (Earnings and Pensions) Act 2003 and section 833 of the Income Tax Act 2007.

SCHEDULE 1 – DESIGNATION ORDERS REVOKED

Article 2

Orders revoked	References
The Visiting Forces and Allied Headquarters (Income Tax and Death Duties) (Designation) Order 1961	S.I. 1961/580
The Visiting Forces and Allied Headquarters (Stamp Duties) (Designation) Order 1961	S.I. 1960/581
The Visiting Forces and Allied Headquarters (Income Tax and Capital Gains Tax) (Designation) Order 1998	S.I. 1998/1513
The Visiting Forces (Income Tax and Capital Gains Tax) (Designation) Order 1998	S.I. 1998/1514
The Visiting Forces and Allied Headquarters (Inheritance Tax) (Designation) Order 1998	S.I. 1998/1515
The Visiting Forces (Inheritance Tax) (Designation) Order 1998	S.I 1998/1516
The Visiting Forces and Allied Headquarters (Stamp Duties) (Designation) Order 1998	S.I. 1998/1517
The Visiting Forces (Stamp Duties) (Designation) Order 1998	S.I. 1998/1518

SCHEDULE 2 – DESIGNATED NATO COUNTRIES

Article 4

Albania, Belgium, Bulgaria, Canada, Croatia, Czech Republic, Denmark, Estonia, France, Germany, Greece, Hungary, Iceland, Italy, Latvia, Lithuania, Luxembourg, Netherlands, Norway, Poland, Portugal, Romania, Slovakia, Slovenia, Spain, Turkey, United States of America.

SCHEDULE 3 – DESIGNATED PFP COUNTRIES

Article 5

Armenia, Austria, Azerbaijan, Belarus, Bosnia and Herzegovina, Finland, Georgia, Ireland, Kazakhstan, Kyrgyz Republic, Malta, Moldova, Montenegro, Russia, Serbia, Sweden, Switzerland, Tajikistan, the former Yugoslav Republic of Macedonia, Turkmenistan, Ukraine, Uzbekistan.

SCHEDULE 4 – DESIGNATED HEADQUARTERS

Article 4

Headquarters of the Supreme Allied Commander Transformation (HQ SACT)
Supreme Headquarters Allied Powers Europe (SHAPE)
Maritime Component Command Headquarters Northwood (CC-MAR HQ Northwood)
Commander Submarines Allied Naval Forces North (COMSUBNORTH)
NATO Airborne Early Warning and Control Force (NAEW&CF)
NATO Joint Electronic Warfare Core Staff (NATO JEWCS)
Headquarters United Kingdom–Netherlands Amphibious Force (UKNLAF)
Headquarters United Kingdom–Netherlands Landing Force (UKNLLF)
The European Air Group (EAG)
The Intelligence Fusion Centre (IFC)
Headquarters Allied Rapid Reaction Corps (HQ ARRC)

TAX TREATMENT OF FINANCING COSTS AND INCOME (CORRECTION OF MISMATCHES: PARTNERSHIPS AND PENSIONS) REGULATIONS 2012
(SI 2012/3111)

Made on 14 December 2012 by the Commissioners for Her Majesty's Revenue and Customs in exercise of the powers conferred by s. 336A of the Taxation (International and Other Provisions) Act 2010. Operative from 7 January 2013.

CITATION, COMMENCEMENT, EFFECT AND INTERPRETATION

1(1) These Regulations may be cited as the Tax Treatment of Financing Costs and Income (Correction of Mismatches: Partnerships and Pensions) Regulations 2012 and come into force on 7th January 2013.

1(2) These Regulations have effect in relation to periods of account of the worldwide group beginning on or after 1 January 2012.

This is subject to regulation 4.

AMENDMENT TO PART 7 OF THE TAXATION (INTERNATIONAL AND OTHER PROVISIONS) ACT 2010

2(1) The Taxation (International and Other Provisions) Act 2010 is amended as follows.

2(2) [Inserts TIOPA 2010, s. 332D and 332E.]

AMENDMENT TO THE TAX TREATMENT OF FINANCING COSTS AND INCOME (CORRECTION OF MISMATCHES) REGULATIONS 2010

3(1) The Tax Treatment of Financing Costs and Income (Correction of Mismatches) Regulations 2010 are amended as follows.

3(2) [Inserts SI 2010/3025, reg. 16A and 16B.]

ELECTION THAT THESE REGULATIONS DO NOT APPLY

4(1) A worldwide group may elect that either or both of regulations 2 and 3 do not apply in relation to periods of account of the worldwide group beginning before 14th December 2012.

4(2) The election—

(a) is irrevocable,

(b) must be made in writing to HMRC by the reporting body within 12 months from the end of the first period of account of the worldwide group that begins on or after 14th December 2012,

(c) must be signed by the proper officer of the reporting body or such other person as may have the express, implied or apparent authority of the reporting body to make an election under this regulation.

4(3) In paragraph (2), **"the reporting body"** has the meaning given by section 289 of the Taxation (International and Other Provisions) Act 2010.

4(4) Subsections (3) and (4) of section 108 of the Taxes Management Act 1970 (responsibility of company officers: meaning of "proper officer") apply for the purposes of this regulation as they apply for the purposes of that section.

PROFITS FROM PATENTS (EEA RIGHTS) ORDER 2013

(SI 2013/420)

Made on 26 February 2013 by the Treasury, in exercise of the powers conferred by s. 357BB(1)(c) and (7) of the Corporation Tax Act 2010. Operative from 1 April 2013.

CITATION AND COMMENCEMENT

1(1) This Order may be cited as the Profits from Patents (EEA Rights) Order 2013.

1(2) This Order comes into force on 1st April 2013.

RIGHTS TO WHICH PART 8A OF CTA 2010 APPLIES

2(1) A right corresponding to a right within section 357BB(1)(a) or (b) of the Corporation Tax Act 2010 which is granted under the law of a qualifying EEA state under the standard process applicable in the state is a right to which Part 8A of that Act applies.

2(2) The following are qualifying EEA states—

Austria

Bulgaria

Czech Republic

Denmark

Estonia

Finland

Germany

Hungary

Poland

Portugal

Romania

Slovakia

Sweden.

2(3) A right is taken to be granted under the standard process applicable in a state in any case unless—

(a) there is more than one process for determining applications for the right under the law of the state, and

(b) the right in question is granted under a process which is less rigorous than another process.

2(4) A process is less rigorous than another if it requires—

(a) a less rigorous examination of the application than the other, or

(b) fewer conditions to be met than the other.

COLLECTIVE INVESTMENT IN TRANSFERABLE SECURITIES (CONTRACTUAL SCHEME) REGULATIONS 2013

(SI 2013/1388)

Made on 5 June 2013 by the Treasury in exercise of the powers conferred upon them by s. 2(2) of the European Communities Act 1972. Operative from 6 June 2013.

PART 1 – CITATION, COMMENCEMENT AND INTERPRETATION

CITATION AND COMMENCEMENT

1　These Regulations may be cited as the Collective Investment in Transferable Securities (Contractual Scheme) Regulations 2013, and come into force on the day after the day on which they are made.

INTERPRETATION

2　In these Regulations–

"**the 1986 Act**" means the Insolvency Act 1986;

"**the 1989 Order**" means the Insolvency (Northern Ireland) Order 1989;

"**authorised contract**" has the meaning given in section 261M(1) of FSMA;

"**authorised contractual scheme**" has the meaning given in section 237(3) of FSMA;

"**depositary**" has the meaning given in section 237(2) of FSMA;

"**the FCA**" means the Financial Conduct Authority;

"**FSMA**" means the Financial Services and Markets Act 2000;

"**operator**" has the meaning given in section 237(2) of FSMA;

"**participant**" has the meaning given in section 235(2) of FSMA;

"**partnership scheme**" has the meaning given in section 235A(5) of FSMA;

"**stand-alone co-ownership scheme**" has the meaning given in section 237(8) of FSMA;

"**sub-scheme**" has the meaning given in section 237(7) of FSMA;

"**umbrella co-ownership scheme**" has the meaning given in section 237(5) of FSMA; and

"**units**" has the meaning given in section 237(2) of FSMA.

PART 2 – AMENDMENTS TO PRIMARY LEGISLATION

AMENDMENT TO THE CORPORATION TAX ACT 2010

5　[Amends CTA 2010, s. 1121(1).]

PART 4 – MODIFICATION OF THE LIMITED PARTNERSHIPS ACT 1907

PARTNERSHIP SCHEMES

16(1)　The Limited Partnerships Act 1907 has effect with the following modifications in its application to a partnership scheme in respect of which an authorisation order is made.

16(2)　In this regulation "**authorisation order**" means an order made under section 261D(1) of FSMA.

16(3)　Section 4 (definition and constitution of limited partnership) is to be read as if–

(a)　in subsection (2)–

(i)   after the words "general partners, who" there were inserted ", subject to regulations 18 and 19 of the Collective Investment in Transferable Securities (Contractual Scheme) Regulations 2013,";

(ii)   for the words "who shall not be liable for the debts or obligations of the firm beyond the amount so contributed" there were substituted "whose liability for the debts or obligations of the firm is as set out in subsections (2A) and (2B).";

(b)   after subsection (2) there were inserted–

"**4(2A)**   The limited partners are not liable for the debts or obligations of the firm beyond the amount of the partnership property which is available to the general partner to meet such debts or obligations.

4(2B)   A person ("P") who ceases to be a limited partner ceases to have any liability for the debts or obligations of the firm.

4(2C)   Subsection (2B) does not prevent the debts and obligations of the firm from being taken into account, after P has ceased to be a limited partner, in determining the value of P's share in the partnership."; and

(c)   subsection (3) were omitted.

16(4)   In section 6 (modifications of general law in case of limited partnerships)–

(a)   subsection (1) is to be read as if at the end there were inserted–
"For the purposes of this subsection, the exercise of rights conferred on limited partners by rules made under section 261I of the Financial Services and Markets Act 2000 does not constitute taking part in the management of the partnership business.".

(b)   in subsection (3), the reference to the general partners is to be read as a reference to the general partner and the depositary of the partnership scheme; and

(c)   subsection (5) is to be read as if–

(i)   the words "Subject to any agreement expressed or implied between the partners" were omitted; and

(ii)   in paragraph (b), at the beginning there were inserted "Subject to any express agreement between the partners,".

16(5)   Section 7 (law as to private partnerships to apply where not excluded by this Act) is to be read as if after the words "Subject to the provisions of this Act" there were inserted "as modified by regulation 16 of the Collective Investment in Transferable Securities (Contractual Scheme) Regulations 2013".

16(6)   In section 9 (registration of changes in partnerships), subsection (1) is to be read as if–

(a)   paragraphs (d) and (f) were omitted; and

(b)   the changes giving rise to a duty to send a statement to the registrar included–

(i)   the making and the revocation of an authorisation order in respect of a limited partnership; and

(ii)   any change in the general partner or the name of the general partner of the limited partnership.

16(7)   Section 10 (advertisement in Gazette of statement of general partner becoming a limited partner and of assignment of share of limited partner) does not apply.

SCHEDULES

SCHEDULE 1 – FORM FOR REGISTERING CHANGES TO LIMITED PARTNERSHIPS

Regulation 13

Limited Partnerships Act 1907

LP6

Statutory Instruments

Statement specifying the nature of a change in the limited partnership and statement of increase in the amount contributed (in cash or otherwise) by limited partners.

Pursuant to section 9 of the Limited Partnerships Act 1907 (see Note 1)

Registration No.

Name of firm

The changes specified below have been made or have occurred in this limited partnership (see notes overleaf):

a. **Firm name**	Previous name	New name
b. **General nature of the business**	Business previously carried on	Business now carried on
c. **Principal place of business**	Previous place of business	New place of business

d. **Change in the partners or the name of any partner** (see note 2)
In the case of an authorised partnership state any change in the general partner or in the name of the general partner

e. **Term or character of the partnership** (see note 3) Where the change in character is authorisation as an authorised partnership or the revocation of such authorisation, give the date and the number of the authorisation order	Change in character	Previous term	New term

f. **Sum contributed by any limited partner** (see note 4)
Particulars of any increase in capital contributions must be provided in section h.
Not applicable to an authorised partnership

g. Liability of any partner by reason of partner becoming a limited instead of a general partner or a general instead of a limited partner

h. Statement of increase in capital contributions (*see note 4*)

Name of limited partner	Increase of additional sum now contributed (if otherwise than in cash, that fact, with particulars, must be stated)	Total amount contributed (if otherwise than in cash, that fact, with particulars, must be stated)

Signature of firm

Presented by: Presenter's reference:

NOTES

1.   This form is also to be used to notify changes in a limited partnership which is a partnership scheme (within the meaning given by section 235A(5) of the Financial Services and Markets Act 2000) for which an authorisation order has been made under section 261D of that Act ("an authorised partnership"). The requirement to notify changes in partnerships under section 9 of the Limited Partnerships Act 1907 has been modified for authorised partnerships by regulation 16(6) of the Collective Investment in Transferable Securities (Contractual Scheme) Regulations 2013.

2.   Changes brought about by death, transfer of interests, increase in the number of partners or change of name of any partner must be notified here. In the case of an authorised partnership, any change in the general partner or in the name of the general partner must be notified here (no change in the limited partners or in the name of a limited partner is required to be notified).

3.   If there is, or was, no definite term, state under 'previous term' the conditions under which the partnership was constituted and under 'new term' the conditions under which it is now constituted. In the case of an authorised partnership, notify here the making or revocation of the authorisation order by the Financial Conduct Authority (include the authorisation number).

4.   Any variation in the sum contributed by a limited partner must be stated in section f. A statement of any increase in the amount of the partnership capital, whether arising from an increase of contributions or the introduction of fresh partners, must also be stated in section h. In the case of an authorised partnership, no change in the sum contributed by a limited partner is required to be notified.

6.   Each change must be entered in the proper section (a, b, c, d, e, f, g or h, as the case may be). Provision is made in this form for notifying all the changes required by the Act to be notified, but it will frequently happen that only one change has to be notified. In any such case, the word 'Nil' should be inserted in the other sections.

7.   The statement must be signed at the end by the firm, and must be sent by post or delivered to the registrar for registration within seven days of the changes taking place.

REGISTERED PENSION SCHEMES AND RELIEVED NON-UK PENSION SCHEMES (LIFETIME ALLOWANCE TRANSITIONAL PROTECTION) (NOTIFICATION) REGULATIONS 2013

(SI 2013/1741)

Made on 19 July 2013 by the Commissioners for Her Majesty's Revenue and Customs in exercise of the powers conferred upon them by s. 251(1) of the Finance Act 2004 and now exercisable by them, and para. 3 and 4(1) of Sch. 22 to the Finance Act 2013. Operative from 12 August 2013.

CITATION, COMMENCEMENT AND INTERPRETATION

1   These Regulations may be cited as the Registered Pension Schemes and Relieved Non-UK Pension Schemes (Lifetime Allowance Transitional Protection) (Notification) Regulations 2013 and come into force on 12th August 2013.

2   In these Regulations–

     "HMRC" means Her Majesty's Revenue and Customs;

     "paragraph 1" means paragraph 1 of Schedule 22 to the Finance Act 2013;

     "paragraph 1(3) event" means an event described in sub-paragraph (3) of paragraph 1 (fixed protection 2014);

     "paragraph 1 notice" means a notice of intention to rely upon paragraph 1; and

     "tribunal" means the First-tier Tribunal or, where determined in accordance with the Tribunal Procedure (First-tier Tribunal) (Tax Chamber) Rules 2009, the Upper Tribunal.

RELIANCE ON PARAGRAPH 1

3(1)   Subject to paragraph (2), an individual may rely on paragraph 1 if–

(a)   the individual has given a paragraph 1 notice to HMRC, and

(b)   HMRC have accepted that notice by issuing a certificate to the individual.

3(2)   An individual may not rely on paragraph 1 if–

(a)   HMRC have refused to accept a paragraph 1 notice in accordance with regulation 6,

(b)   HMRC have revoked the certificate in accordance with regulation 11, or

(c)   a paragraph 1(3) event has occurred.

THE PARAGRAPH 1 NOTICE

4(1)   A paragraph 1 notice must include the following information–

(a)   the title, full name, address (including post code, if applicable) and date of birth of the individual submitting the paragraph 1 notice,

(b)   the national insurance number of the individual or, where the individual does not qualify for a national insurance number, the reasons for this,

(c)   a declaration that paragraph 7 of Schedule 36 to the Finance Act 2004 (primary protection) does not make provision for a lifetime allowance enhancement factor in the case of the individual,

(d)   a declaration that paragraph 12 of that Schedule (enhanced protection) will not apply in relation to the individual on and after 6th April 2014, and

(e)   a declaration that paragraph 14 of Schedule 18 to the Finance Act 2011 (transitional provision relating to new standard lifetime allowance for the tax year 2012–13) will not apply in relation to the individual on and after 6th April 2014.

4(2)   A paragraph 1 notice must–

(a)   be in a form prescribed by HMRC,

(b)   contain a declaration that the information provided in the notice is true and complete to the best of the knowledge and belief of the person completing the form, and

(c)   be received by HMRC on or before 5th April 2014.

ISSUE OF CERTIFICATE BY HMRC

5(1) If HMRC accept the paragraph 1 notice, they must issue a certificate to the individual.

5(2) The certificate must have a unique reference number.

REFUSAL BY HMRC TO ACCEPT NOTICE

6(1) HMRC may refuse to accept the paragraph 1 notice if it does not satisfy the requirements in regulation 4.

6(2) If HMRC refuse to accept the paragraph 1 notice the individual may require that HMRC provide reasons for the refusal.

APPEAL AGAINST REFUSAL TO ACCEPT NOTICE

7(1) The individual may appeal against a refusal by HMRC to accept the paragraph 1 notice.

7(2) The notice of appeal must be given to HMRC before the end of the period of 30 days beginning with the day on which the refusal to accept the paragraph 1 notice was given.

7(3) Where an appeal under this regulation is notified to the tribunal, the tribunal must determine whether HMRC were entitled to take the view that the notice did not satisfy the requirements in regulation 4.

7(4) If the tribunal allows the appeal, the tribunal may direct HMRC to accept the paragraph 1 notice and issue a certificate to the individual.

INCORRECT INFORMATION GIVEN IN, OR IN CONNECTION WITH, THE PARAGRAPH 1 NOTICE

8 If the individual realises that any information given in the paragraph 1 notice or given to HMRC in connection with that notice was incorrect or has become incorrect, the individual must provide HMRC with the correct information without undue delay.

REQUIREMENT TO INFORM HMRC OF A PARAGRAPH 1(3) EVENT

9 Where HMRC have issued a certificate the individual must—

(a) inform HMRC when a paragraph 1(3) event occurs, and

(b) provide that information before the end of the period of 90 days beginning with the day on which the individual could first reasonably be expected to have known that a paragraph 1(3) event had occurred.

REPLACEMENT OF A CERTIFICATE BY HMRC

10(1) HMRC may issue a certificate, replacing the previous certificate, if they have reason to believe that information given in, or in connection with, the paragraph 1 notice was incorrect or has become incorrect.

10(2) A certificate issued in accordance with regulation 10(1) must have a unique reference number.

REVOCATION OF A CERTIFICATE BY HMRC

11 HMRC may revoke a certificate if they—

(a) have reason to believe that a paragraph 1(3) event has occurred,

(b) have reason to believe that any of the conditions in paragraph 1(1) of Schedule 22 to the Finance Act 2013 have not been met, or

(c) have given a taxpayer notice to the individual under Part 1 of Schedule 36 to the Finance Act 2008 (power to obtain information and documents from taxpayer) in connection with paragraph 1 and the individual does not reply to that notice within the time specified in the notice.

APPEAL AGAINST REPLACEMENT OR REVOCATION OF A CERTIFICATE

12(1) The individual may require HMRC to provide reasons for replacing or revoking the certificate.

12(2) Paragraphs (1) and (2) of regulation 7 apply to a decision to replace or revoke the certificate as they apply to a refusal to accept the paragraph 1 notice.

12(3) Where an appeal under this regulation is notified to the tribunal, the tribunal must determine whether HMRC replaced or revoked the certificate in accordance with regulations 10(1) or 11.

12(4) If the tribunal allows the appeal, the tribunal may direct HMRC to issue a certificate to the individual.

PRESERVATION OF DOCUMENTS

13(1) Where HMRC have issued a certificate the individual must preserve the certificate until no further benefit crystallisation event can occur in relation to the individual.

13(2) The requirement to preserve the certificate ceases where the certificate has been revoked.

LIFE INSURANCE QUALIFYING POLICIES (STATEMENT AND REPORTING REQUIREMENTS) REGULATIONS 2013

(SI 2013/1820)

Made on 19 July 2013 by the Commissioners for Her Majesty's Revenue and Customs in exercise of the powers conferred upon them by s. 552ZB(1) of, and para. B3(2), (7) and (9)(c) of Sch. 15 to, the Income and Corporation Taxes Act 1988. Operative from 12 August 2013.

CITATION AND COMMENCEMENT AND INTERPRETATION

1(1) These Regulations may be cited as the Life Insurance Qualifying Policies (Statement and Reporting Requirements) Regulations 2013 and come into force on 12 August 2013.

1(2) In these Regulations, **"Schedule 15"** means Schedule 15 to the Income and Corporation Taxes Act 1988.

STATEMENT BY BENEFICIARY

2(1) In relation to a statement made under paragraph B3(2) of Schedule 15, the prescribed matters are set out in paragraphs (2) to (6).

2(2) The following information must be given in the statement in all cases–

(a) the beneficiary's full name;

(b) the beneficiary's date of birth;

(c) the beneficiary's address including postcode;

(d) the beneficiary's National Insurance number (if any);

(e) whether the beneficiary is a beneficiary under any other qualifying policy–

 (i) issued on or after 6 April 2013, or

 (ii) issued before that date but in relation to which a premium limit event has occurred;

(f) a statement that the beneficiary is–

 (i) not in breach of the premium limit for qualifying policies at the date the statement is made; or

 (ii) in breach of the premium limit for qualifying policies at the date the statement is made but the policy in respect of which the statement is made is a restricted relief qualifying policy;

(g) whether the event giving rise to the statement is an event within paragraph B3(1)(d) of Schedule 15 (protected policies within paragraph A2(12) of Schedule 15 – endowment policies);

(h) the date the statement is made; and

(i) confirmation that the statement is correct and complete to the best of the beneficiary's knowledge and belief.

2(3) Where the beneficiary is not the sole beneficiary under the policy in respect of which the statement is made, the statement must include details of the beneficiary's proportionate share of the rights under the policy.

2(4) Where there has been a variation of a policy within paragraph B3(1)(b) or (c) of Schedule 15, the statement must also include the following information–

(a) the date of the variation; and

(b) details of any variation in relation to the period over which premiums are payable under the policy.

2(5) Where there has been an assignment within paragraph B3(1)(e) of Schedule 15, the statement must also include the following information–

(a) the date of the assignment; and

(b) if the policy was issued on or after 6 April 2013, the name and address of the previous beneficiary.

2(6) For the purpose of paragraph (2)(f), whether a beneficiary is in breach of the premium limit for qualifying policies is determined in accordance with paragraph A3(1) of Schedule 15.

EXCEPTIONS TO THE REQUIREMENT TO MAKE A STATEMENT

3 A beneficiary is not required to make a statement under paragraph B3(2) of Schedule 15 in the following circumstances–

(a)   on the issue of a policy, if–

    (i)   the information that must be included in a statement has been provided to the issuer in connection with the application for the issue of that policy, and

    (ii)   that information has not changed since making the application;

(b)   on an assignment of a share in any rights under a policy, if–

    (i)   the beneficiary has previously made a statement under paragraph B3(2) of Schedule 15 in respect of that policy, and

    (ii)   that information has not changed since making that statement;

(c)   on a deceased beneficiary event, if before the event the beneficiary is a beneficiary under the policy in relation to which the event occurs.

APPLICATIONS AND STATEMENTS NOT IN WRITING

4 Where an application for the issue of a qualifying policy or a statement made under paragraph B3(2) of Schedule 15 is not in writing–

(a)   the relevant person must, within 3 business days of receiving the application or statement, make a written record of the information given in the application or statement;

(b)   the relevant person must send a copy of the written record to the applicant or beneficiary within 20 business days of making it; and

(c)   the applicant or beneficiary must notify the relevant person of any errors in the written record within 30 days of receiving it and the relevant person must amend the application or statement accordingly.

REPORTING REQUIREMENTS OF RELEVANT PERSON

5(1) A relevant person must provide the following information to an officer of Revenue and Customs within 3 months of the end of a tax year–

(a)   where in relation to a policy a statement has been made under paragraph B3(2) of Schedule 15 in that year, the information given in the statement;

(b)   where a policy has been issued in that year and regulation 3(a) applied in relation to the issue of that policy, the information given on the application for the issue of the policy;

(c)   in relation to any policy within sub-paragraphs (a) or (b) and any policy which ceased, terminated, matured or in relation to which the premiums payable have reduced in that year–

    (i)   the date the policy was issued;

    (ii)   the policy identification reference;

    (iii)   the premiums payable under the policy.

5(2) This regulation does not apply to qualifying policies issued before 6 April 2013 or to pure protection policies.

AMENDMENT TO THE LIFE ASSURANCE AND OTHER POLICIES (KEEPING OF INFORMATION AND DUTIES OF INSURERS) REGULATIONS 1997

6(1) The Life Assurance and Other Policies (Keeping of Information and Duties of Insurers) Regulations 1997 are amended as follows.

6(2) [Amends SI 1997/265, reg. 2.]

6(3) [Amends SI 1997/265, reg. 3.]

6(4) [Amends SI 1997/265, reg. 9.]

CULTURAL TEST (TELEVISION PROGRAMMES) REGULATIONS 2013

(SI 2013/1831)

Made on 18 July 2013 by the Secretary of State, in exercise of the powers conferred by s. 1216CB and 1216CC(7) of the Corporation Tax Act 2009. Operative from 13 August 2013.

PART 1 – INTRODUCTORY

CITATION AND COMMENCEMENT

1(1)   These Regulations may be cited as the Cultural Test (Television Programmes) Regulations 2013.

1(2)   These Regulations come into force on 13th August 2013.

INTERPRETATION

2(1)   In these Regulations–

"the Act" means the Corporation Tax Act 2009;

"cast" means the actors and performers in a drama or animation, but not any extras;

"heads of department" has the meaning given by paragraph (2);

"participant" means a presenter, narrator, subject, or any other person who both participates and appears in a documentary;

"production crew" means all the persons directly involved in the production of a programme who do not appear in the programme;

"programme" means a drama, a documentary or an animation which is a relevant programme;

"qualifying person" means a national of, or a person ordinarily resident in, an EEA state;

"recognised regional or minority language" means Welsh, Scottish-Gaelic, Irish, Scots, Ulster Scots, Cornish or British Sign Language;

"special effects" means artificial techniques or processes, which are not visual effects, used to create an illusion in a programme; and

"visual effects" means digital alterations to a programme's images.

2(2)   "Heads of department" means–

(a)   in relation to a drama, lead cinematographer, lead production designer, lead costume designer, lead editor, lead sound designer, lead visual effects supervisor and lead hair and makeup supervisor;

(b)   in relation to a documentary, lead camera operator, lead sound recordist, lead editor and lead researcher;

(c)   in relation to an animation, lead layout supervisor, lead production designer, lead character designer, lead editor, lead sound designer, lead visual effects supervisor and lead modelling supervisor.

PART 2 – THE CULTURAL TESTS

CULTURAL TEST: DRAMAS AND DOCUMENTARIES

3(1)   A drama or documentary will be certified by the Secretary of State as a British programme under section 1216CB(1) of the Act only if it passes the following cultural test.

3(2)   A drama or documentary passes the cultural test if it meets either of the following conditions–

(a)   subject to paragraph (3), it is awarded at least 16 points in total under paragraphs (4) to (7); or

(b)   it is a qualifying co-production made in accordance with an international agreement specified in Schedule 1.

3(3)   A drama or documentary that is awarded all the points available under paragraphs (4)(d) (language), (6) (where work carried out) and (7) (personnel) will not pass the cultural test unless it is awarded–

(a)   at least 2 points under paragraph (4)(a) (setting);

(b)   at least 2 points under paragraph (4)(b) (characters); or

(c)   4 points under paragraph (4)(c) (story).

3(4)   Up to 16 points will be awarded in respect of the content of the drama or documentary as follows—

(a)   up to 4 points depending on the percentage of the drama or documentary that is set in the United Kingdom or another EEA state as follows—

    (i)   4 points for at least 75%;

    (ii)   3 points for at least 66%;

    (iii)   2 points for at least 50%;

    (iv)   1 point for at least 25%;

(b)   up to 4 points depending on the number of the characters depicted in the drama or documentary that are from the United Kingdom or another EEA state as follows—

    (i)   if there are more than three characters depicted in the drama or documentary—

        (aa)   if two or three of the three lead characters are from the United Kingdom or another EEA state, 4 points;

        (bb)   if only one of the three lead characters is from the United Kingdom or another EEA state, 2 points if that character is the first or second lead, or 1 point if that character is the third lead;

    (ii)   if there are only three characters depicted in the drama or documentary—

        (aa)   if two or three of the characters are from the United Kingdom or another EEA state, 4 points;

        (bb)   if only one of the characters is from the United Kingdom or another EEA state, 2 points if that character is the first or second lead, or 1 point if that character is the third lead;

    (iii)   if there are only two characters depicted in the drama or documentary—

        (aa)   if both of the characters are from the United Kingdom or another EEA state, 4 points;

        (bb)   if one of the characters is from the United Kingdom or another EEA state, 2 points;

    (iv)   if there is only one character depicted in the drama or documentary, 4 points if that character is from the United Kingdom or another EEA state;

(c)   4 points if the drama or documentary depicts a British story or a story which relates to another EEA state;

(d)   up to 4 points depending on the percentage of the original dialogue that is recorded in the English language or a recognised regional or minority language as follows—

    (i)   4 points for at least 75%;

    (ii)   3 points for at least 66%;

    (iii)   2 points for at least 50%;

    (iv)   1 point for at least 25%.

3(5)   Up to 4 points will be awarded in respect of the contribution of the drama or documentary to the promotion, development and enhancement of British culture.

3(6)   Up to 3 points will be awarded in respect of work carried out in the making of the drama or documentary as follows—

(a)   2 points if at least 50% of the work carried out on any of the following is carried out in the United Kingdom—

    (i)   in relation to a drama—

        (aa)   principal photography;

        (bb)   visual effects;

        (cc)   special effects;

    (ii)   in relation to a documentary—

        (aa)   shooting;

        (bb)   visual effects;

        (cc)   research and development;

        (dd)   special effects;

(b)   1 point if at least 50% of the work carried out on any of the following is carried out in the United Kingdom—

        (i)   performing and recording the music score created for the drama or documentary;

        (ii)   audio post production;

        (iii)   picture post production.

3(7)   Up to 8 points will be awarded in respect of the personnel involved in the making of the drama or documentary as follows—

(a)   1 point if a director (or, if there are more than three, one of the three lead directors) is a qualifying person;

(b)   1 point if at least one of the scriptwriters (or, if there are more than three, one of the three lead scriptwriters) is a qualifying person;

(c)   1 point if at least one of the producers (or, if there are more than three, one of the three lead producers) is a qualifying person;

(d)   1 point if a composer (or, if there are more than three, one of the three lead composers) is a qualifying person;

(e)   1 point if at least one of the actors or participants (as the case may be) (or, if there are more than three, one of the three lead actors or participants) is a qualifying person;

(f)   1 point if at least 50% of the cast or participants (as the case may be) are qualifying persons;

(g)   1 point if at least one of the heads of department is a qualifying person;

(h)   1 point if at least 50% of the production crew are qualifying persons.

CULTURAL TEST: ANIMATION

4(1)   An animation will be certified by the Secretary of State as a British programme under section 1216CB(1) of the Act only if it passes the following cultural test.

4(2)   An animation passes the cultural test if it meets either of the following conditions—

(a)   subject to paragraph (3), it is awarded at least 16 points in total under paragraphs (4) to (7); or

(b)   it is a qualifying co-production made in accordance with an international agreement specified in Schedule 1.

4(3)   An animation that is awarded all the points available under paragraphs (4)(d) (language), (6) (where work carried out) and (7) (personnel) will not pass the cultural test unless it is awarded—

(a)   at least 2 points under paragraph (4)(a) (setting);

(b)   at least 2 points under paragraph (4)(b) (characters); or

(c)   4 points under paragraph (4)(c) (story).

4(4)   Up to 16 points will be awarded in respect of the content of the animation as follows—

(a)   up to 4 points depending on the percentage of the animation that is set in the United Kingdom or another EEA state as follows—

        (i)   4 points for at least 75%;

        (ii)   3 points for at least 66%;

        (iii)   2 points for at least 50%;

        (iv)   1 point for at least 25%;

(b)   up to 4 points depending on the number of the characters depicted in the animation that are from the United Kingdom or another EEA state as follows—

        (i)   if there are more than three characters depicted in the animation—

            (aa)   if two or three of the three lead characters are from the United Kingdom or another EEA state, 4 points;

            (bb)   if only one of the three lead characters is from the United Kingdom or another EEA state, 2 points if that character is the first or second lead, or 1 point if that character is the third lead;

        (ii)   if there are only three characters depicted in the animation—

            (aa)   if two or three of the characters are from the United Kingdom or another EEA state, 4 points;

        (bb)   if only one of the characters is from the United Kingdom or another EEA state, 2 points if that character is the first or second lead, or 1 point if that character is the third lead;

  (iii)   if there are only two characters depicted in the animation–

        (aa)   if both of the characters are from the United Kingdom or another EEA state, 4 points;

        (bb)   if one of the characters is from the United Kingdom or another EEA state, 2 points;

  (iv)   if there is only one character depicted in the animation, 4 points if that character is from the United Kingdom or another EEA state;

(c)   4 points if the animation depicts a British story or a story which relates to another EEA state;

(d)   up to 4 points depending on the percentage of the original dialogue that is recorded in the English language or a recognised regional or minority language as follows–

  (i)   4 points for at least 75%;

  (ii)   3 points for at least 66%;

  (iii)   2 points for at least 50%;

  (iv)   1 point for at least 25%.

4(5)   Up to 4 points will be awarded in respect of the contribution of the animation to the promotion, development and enhancement of British culture.

4(6)   Up to 3 points will be awarded in respect of work carried out in the making of the animation as follows–

(a)   2 points if at least 50% of the work carried out on any of the following is carried out in the United Kingdom–

  (i)   shooting;

  (ii)   visual design;

  (iii)   layout and storyboarding;

  (iv)   visual effects;

  (v)   special effects;

(b)   1 point if at least 50% of the work carried out on any of the following is carried out in the United Kingdom–

  (i)   performing and recording the music score created for the animation;

  (ii)   voice recording;

  (iii)   audio post production;

  (iv)   picture post production.

4(7)   Up to 8 points will be awarded in respect of the personnel involved in the making of the animation as follows–

(a)   1 point if a director (or, if there are more than three, one of the three lead directors) is a qualifying person;

(b)   1 point if at least one of the scriptwriters (or, if there are more than three, one of the three lead scriptwriters) is a qualifying person;

(c)   1 point if at least one of the producers (or, if there are more than three, one of the three lead producers) is a qualifying person;

(d)   1 point if a composer (or, if there are more than three, one of the three lead composers) is a qualifying person;

(e)   1 point if at least one of the actors (or, if there are more than three, one of the three lead actors) is a qualifying person;

(f)   1 point if at least 50% of the cast are qualifying persons;

(g)   1 point if at least one of the heads of department is a qualifying person;

(h)   1 point if at least 50% of the production crew are qualifying persons.

4(8)   An animation which is set in, or in which any character is from, an undetermined location is eligible to be awarded points under paragraphs (4)(a)(ii)–(iv) (setting) and (4)(b) (characters) as if that location were in the UK or another EEA state, provided it complies with the following condition.

4(9) The condition is that that animation is awarded at least one point under any of–

(a)   paragraph (4)(c) (story);

(b)   paragraph (4)(d) (language); or

(c)   paragraph (5) (culture).

EXCLUDED PROGRAMMES

5(1) A programme must not be certified as a British programme under these Regulations if parts of the programme whose playing time exceeds 10% of the total playing time are derived from a previous programme, unless–

(a)   the two programmes have the same television production company or producer; and

(b)   the previous programme has not been certified under these Regulations.

5(2) The Secretary of State may direct that paragraph (1) does not apply in relation to a programme if in the opinion of the Secretary of State–

(a)   it is a documentary within the meaning of section 1216AB(3)(b) of the Act; and

(b)   its subject matter makes it appropriate for paragraph (1) not to be applied.

5(3) For the purposes of this regulation–

(a)   no account may be taken of the programme soundtrack;

(b)   **"producer"** means the person by whom the arrangements necessary for the making of a programme are undertaken.

PART 3 – APPLICATIONS FOR CERTIFICATION

APPLICATIONS

6(1) An application under section 1216CC(1) for the certification of a relevant programme (other than a co-production) as a British programme must be made in writing to the Secretary of State.

6(2) For the purposes of this regulation–

(a)   **"in writing"** includes text which is–

(i)   transmitted by electronic means;

(ii) received in legible form; and

(iii) capable of being used for subsequent reference;

(b)   **"co-production"** means a programme which passes the cultural test by satisfying the condition in regulation 3(2)(b) or 4(2)(b).

PARTICULARS

7 An application in relation to a programme must set out the particulars (where applicable) described in Schedule 2 for that programme.

EVIDENCE

8(1) An application must be accompanied by a statutory declaration made by the applicant as to the truth of the particulars given in the application.

8(2) A statutory declaration will be deemed to be properly made by the applicant if it has been made on behalf of the company by the secretary or one of the directors of the company or by any person duly authorised by the company to make the declaration on its behalf.

9(1) Where an application for final certification seeks to rely on any point that may be awarded under regulation 3(6) or (7), or 4(6) or (7), the application must be accompanied by a report prepared by a person referred to in paragraph (2) verifying (where applicable) the particulars in paragraphs 17 to 19 of Schedule 2.

9(2) The person referred to in this paragraph is a person who is eligible for appointment as a statutory auditor under section 1212 of the Companies Act 2006 and is not and was not at any time while the programme was being made–

(a)   in partnership with the applicant or any officer or servant of the applicant;

(b)   in the employment of the applicant or any officer or servant of the applicant; or

(c) an officer or servant of the applicant or, if the applicant is a member of a group of companies, of any other company in that group.

9(3) In this regulation, **"group of companies"** means a company and all other companies which are its subsidiaries within the meaning of section 1159 of the Companies Act 2006.

PART 4 – GENERAL

10 For the purposes of these Regulations–

(a) a programme is set in the United Kingdom or another EEA state to the extent that it is set in a country which is now part of the United Kingdom or another EEA state;

(b) a programme depicts a British story or a story which relates to another EEA state if the subject matter of the programme or the underlying material on which the programme is based is British or relates to another EEA state;

(c) a person or a character in a programme is from the United Kingdom or another EEA state if the person or character is a national or resident of the United Kingdom or another EEA state (or was a national or resident of a country which is now part of the United Kingdom or another EEA state).

11 The amount of work that is carried out in the United Kingdom or elsewhere is determined–

(a) for the purposes of regulation 3(6)(a)(i)(aa) (principal photography), by reference to the number of days spent on the work;

(b) for the purposes of the rest of regulation 3(6) and regulation 4(6) (where work carried out), by reference to the amount of expenditure on the work.

12 No points will be awarded under any provision of regulation 3(6) or 4(6) (where work carried out) in respect of work the expenditure on which is, in the opinion of the Secretary of State, insignificant in relation to the expenditure on all the work carried out in the making of the programme.

SCHEDULES

SCHEDULE 1 – INTERNATIONAL AGREEMENTS

Regulation 3(2)(b), 4(2)(b)

The international agreements specified in this Schedule for the purposes of regulations 3(2)(b) and 4(2)(b) are the agreements made between the UK Government and the Governments of the countries, or the international organisations or authorities, referred to in the first column of the Table on the dates in the second column of the Table and as referred to by the Command Paper numbers in the third column.

Country/International Organisation/Authority	Date of Agreement	Command Paper
Australia	12th June 1990	Cm 1758
Canada	12th September 1975	Cmnd 6380
	9th July 1985	Cmnd 9887
	5th July 1991	Cm 1807
Israel	3rd November 2010	Cm 7994
New Zealand	14th April 1993	Cm 2638
Palestine Liberation Organisation for the benefit of the Palestinian Authority	3rd November 2010	Cm 7995

SCHEDULE 2 – PARTICULARS

Regulation 7

1 Title of the programme.

2 Whether the application relates to a drama, a documentary, or an animation.

3 Total playing time in minutes and seconds of the programme, including credits and titles.

4 Whether the application is for interim or final certification.

5 Whether the programme is intended for broadcast or supply to the general public (as the case may be).

6 Name of the applicant.

7 Address of the applicant's principal place of business.

8 Address of the applicant's registered office.

9 Registered number of the applicant.

10 Date of registration of the applicant.

11 In relation to a drama, the date of the first day of principal photography.

12 Date on which the programme was completed for the purposes of section 1216AA(5) of the Act.

13 A copy of the commissioning agreement.

14 The reasons why it should be considered to be a drama, documentary or animation (as the case may be).

15 The reasons why any point should be awarded under regulation 3(4) (drama or documentary) or 4(4) (animation) (as the case may be).

16 The reasons why any point should be awarded under regulation 3(5) (drama or documentary) or 4(5) (animation) (as the case may be).

17 If the applicant seeks to rely on regulation 3(6)(a)(i)(aa), the total number of days of principal photography and the number of days of principal photography carried out in the United Kingdom.

18 If the applicant seeks to rely on any other part of regulation 3(6) or 4(6), the total expenditure on such other work and the expenditure on such work as was carried out in the United Kingdom.

19 The nationality or ordinary residence of all the persons mentioned in regulation 3(7) or 4(7) in relation to whom the applicant is applying for a point to be awarded.

20 Total core expenditure.

21 Total UK expenditure.

22 Total non-UK expenditure by each country the expenditure is carried out in.

23 Other expenditure, meaning all the expenditure on the work carried out in the making of the programme which is not core expenditure.

24 Shooting script in the English language.

25 A complete synopsis or treatment of the screenplay in the English language.

26 Shooting schedule.

27 Production budget.

28 Copy of the chain of title in the programme.

29 The following particulars—

(a)   if any part of the programme that is the subject of the application is derived from any previous programme, the playing time in minutes and seconds of that part (the "derived part") and the combined playing time in minutes and seconds of all derived parts;

(b)   the particulars in paragraph (a) are only required in relation to any derived parts which—

   (i)   do not have the same television production company or producer as the programme that is the subject of the application; or

   (ii)   are derived from a previous programme that has been certified under these Regulations;

(c)   if the applicant seeks to rely on regulation 5(2), the reasons why the subject matter of the documentary makes it appropriate for the Secretary of State to direct that regulation 5(1) does not apply;

(d)   for the purposes of sub-paragraph (b)(i), **"producer"** has the same meaning as in regulation 5(3)(b).

ANNUAL TAX ON ENVELOPED DWELLINGS (RETURNS) REGULATIONS 2013

(SI 2013/1844)

Made on 22 July 2013 by the Commissioners for Her Majesty's Revenue and Customs, in exercise of the powers conferred by para. 1(1) and 1(2) of Sch. 33 to the Finance Act 2013 and s. 133 of the Finance Act 1999. Operative from 12 August 2013.

CITATION AND COMMENCEMENT

1   These Regulations may be cited as the Annual Tax on Enveloped Dwellings (Returns) Regulations 2013 and come into force on 12th August 2013.

INTERPRETATION

2   In these Regulations–

"ATED" means the annual tax on enveloped dwellings;

"the Commissioners" means the Commissioners for Her Majesty's Revenue and Customs;

"prescribed" means prescribed by the Commissioners in a published Notice as revised or replaced from time to time.

ATED RETURNS

3(1)   A return must be made in the manner prescribed.

3(2)   The return may require the chargeable person to provide the information (or any part of the information) listed in the Schedule.

3(3)   The Commissioners may modify or dispense with any particular requirement under this regulation where it appears to them to be reasonable to do so in an individual case.

DELIVERY OF RETURNS

4(1)   A return must be delivered in the prescribed manner.

4(2)   The Commissioners may in particular prescribe the form in which a return or related communication in relation to that return may be delivered electronically (an "electronic communication").

4(3)   Where provision is made for an electronic communication, the Commissioners may prescribe the method of delivery (a "prescribed electronic method").

4(4)   If a chargeable person has communicated with the Commissioners by means of a prescribed electronic method in respect of a return, the Commissioners must issue an electronic acknowledgement of the communication.

4(5)   If a person has communicated with the Commissioners by a prescribed electronic method, the Commissioners may communicate electronically with the chargeable person in respect of a return, unless they are notified by a prescribed method that the person is not, or is no longer willing to receive such communications electronically.

4(6)   The Commissioners may treat any information within a return as not having been provided unless it is provided in accordance with this regulation.

VALIDATION OF ELECTRONIC COMMUNICATION

5(1)   A prescribed electronic method must incorporate an electronic validation process.

5(2)   Unless the contrary is proved–

(a)   the use of a prescribed electronic method will be presumed to have resulted in the making of an electronic communication to the Commissioners only if this has been successfully recorded as such by the relevant electronic validation process; and

(b)   the time of making an electronic communication to the Commissioners using a prescribed electronic method will be presumed to be the time recorded as such by the relevant electronic validation process.

SCHEDULE – INFORMATION TO BE CONTAINED IN AN ATED RETURN

Regulation 3(3)

Information which the Commissioners may require a chargeable person to include in a return–

(a)   the name and correspondence address of the chargeable person;

(b)   the contact telephone number of the chargeable person;

(c)   an email address;

(d)   the business unique identifier (if any);

NOTES:

(a) where the chargeable person is a company, the business unique identifier is HMRC's Corporation Tax Unique Taxpayer Reference number. If such a reference is not held then one of the following may be used: Company Registration Number – allocated by the Registrar of Companies where the company is incorporated; VAT Registration Number; Employer PAYE Reference.

(b) where the chargeable person is not a company, for example a partnership, a UK tax reference number should be entered as the business unique identifier. For example: VAT Registration Number; Employer PAYE Reference; Self Assessment Unique Taxpayer Reference.

(e)   the origin and type of business unique identifier (if any);

NOTE:

The origin and type of business unique identifier is the name and country of the organisation that allocated the reference, plus the type of tax reference quoted, for example HMRC UK VAT Registration Number.

(f)   the scheme reference number (if any);

NOTE:

If using an avoidance scheme which is intended to produce an ATED advantage and the scheme promoter has disclosed it to the Commissioners as required by law, this is the Scheme Reference Number (SRN) that the promoter has been given by HMRC.

(g)   confirmation if this is the first time the chargeable person will be required to make an ATED payment to HMRC for this property;

(h)   to confirm whether this is an amended return;

NOTE:

An amended return changes the information on a return that has already been sent to HMRC.

(i)   to confirm whether this is a further return;

NOTE:

A further return may be required by law in certain circumstances, in particular where a claim to relief is no longer available, or an acquisition of a further interest in the single dwelling interest has increased its value, so that it is now chargeable in a different band.

(j)   the period start date for the return;

NOTE:

This is the period start date the return relates to. The ATED period commences on 1 April annually.

(k)   the period end date for the return;

NOTE:

The ATED period ends on 31 March annually, however, if the taxpayer is making a return where the period of ownership is for a part year, then the period end date would be the last day of ownership.

(l)   whether this return must be filed within 90 days;

NOTE:

The filing date is normally 30 days after the taxpayer first comes within the charge to ATED. So, for example, if the taxpayer has newly purchased a dwelling the return must be filed within 30 days of acquisition. However, there are two exceptions to the 30 day rule and these are:

(i) where a dwelling comes within the charge as a result of being newly built (section 124 of the Finance Act 2013) or

(ii) it is a new dwelling produced from other dwellings (section 125 of the Finance Act 2013) In either of these two circumstances the return must be made within 90 days of the defined "completion date" or occupation if earlier.

(m)   the ATED liability in pounds sterling (if there is an amount to pay);

(n)   the ATED relief code;

NOTE:

The list of ATED relief codes is:

1. Property rental businesses (to include the special conditions: sale, demolition, and, conversion)
2. Dwellings opened to the public
3. Property developers (including qualifying exchange of dwellings interests)
4. Property traders carrying on a property trading business
5. Financial institutions acquiring dwellings in the course of lending
6. Dwellings used for trade purposes (occupation by qualifying employees and partners)
7. Farmhouses (occupation for the purposes of carrying on a trade of farming)
8. Charitable companies (property held for qualifying charitable purposes)
9. Registered providers of Social Housing

if submitting an amended return under paragraph 3 of Schedule 33 to the Finance Act 2013

(o)   which results in a repayment, the charge reference number and reason for the repayment;

NOTE:

The charge reference number is the reference number from the original ATED payment.

(p)   the property title number;

(q)   the property address, postcode and date of acquisition;

(r)   the actual value of the dwelling in pounds sterling and date of valuation;

(s)   whether there has been a professional valuation in the period covered by the return;

(t)   whether a pre-return banding check has been requested and if so, the reference number;

NOTE:

(1) A request may be made to an officer of HMRC for a Pre-Return Banding Check (PRBC) where the valuation was within a ten per cent variance of a banding threshold.

(2) If a PRBC was requested, a PRBC reference number is given by HMRC as part of that check.

additional address information must be provided where relief is being claimed for more than

(u)   one dwelling;

(v)   total amount to be repaid;

(w)   agent details (if form is being completed by an agent of behalf of a client);

declaration – signed and dated and stating the capacity in which the person signing the

(x)   declaration is completing the form.

TAKING CONTROL OF GOODS REGULATIONS 2013

(SI 2013/1894)

Made on 26 July 2013 by the Lord Chancellor, in exercise of the powers conferred upon them by s. 73(8), 77(4), 81(5) and (6) and 90 of and paragraphs 3(1), 7(2) and (4), 8, 13(3), 14(3), 15(3), 19A(2) and (4), 22(1), 24(1), 25(1) and (2), 28(2) and (3), 31(2) and (4), 32(1) and (2), 33(2), 34(4), 35(2), 36, 39(2), 40(2) and (3), 41(3) and (5), 42, 43(1), (2) and (3), 48(1), (3) and (4), 49(3) and (4), 54(2) and 60(4) and (5) of Sch. 12 to the Tribunals, Courts and Enforcement Act 2007. Operative from 6 April 2014.

PART 1 – INTRODUCTORY

CITATION, COMMENCEMENT AND EXTENT

1(1) These Regulations may be cited as the Taking Control of Goods Regulations 2013 and come into force on 6th April 2014.

1(2) These Regulations extend to England and Wales only.

Interpretation

GENERAL INTERPRETATION

2 In these Regulations–

"**the Act**" means the Tribunals, Courts and Enforcement Act 2007;

"**child**" means a person under the age of 16;

"**clear days**" means that in computing the number of days–

(a)   the day on which the period begins; and

(b)   if the end of the period is defined by reference to an event, the day on which that event occurs,

are not included;

"**controlled goods**" has the meaning given in paragraph 3(1) of Schedule 12 (general interpretation);

"**co-owner**" has the meaning given in paragraph 3(1) of Schedule 12 (general interpretation);

"**CRAR**" has the meaning given in section 72 of the Act (commercial rent arrears recovery (CRAR));

"**creditor**" has the meaning given in paragraph 1(6) of Schedule 12 (the procedure);

"**debtor**" has the meaning given in paragraph 1(5) of Schedule 12 (the procedure);

"**disabled person**" means a person–

(a)   whose sight, hearing or speech is substantially impaired;

(b)   who has a mental disorder; or

(c)   who is physically substantially disabled by any illness, any impairment present since birth, or otherwise;

"**enforcement agent**" has the meaning given in paragraph 2(1) of Schedule 12 (enforcement agents);

"**net unpaid rent**" has the meaning given in section 77(5) of the Act (the rent recoverable);

"**notice of enforcement**" means the notice of enforcement required by paragraph 7(1) of Schedule 12;

"**notice of the enforcement agent's intention to re-enter premises**" means the notice of the enforcement agent's intention to re-enter premises required by paragraph 19A(1)(d) of Schedule 12;

"**older person**" means a person aged 65 or over;

"**premises**" has the meaning given in paragraph 3(1) of Schedule 12 (general interpretation);

"reference number" means a reference number assigned to the debt by the enforcement agent or the enforcement agent's office;

"relevant premises" has the meaning given by paragraph 14(4) and (6) of Schedule 12(entry without warrant);

"Schedule 12" means Schedule 12 to the Act;

"securities" has the meaning given in paragraph 3(1) of Schedule 12 (general interpretation);

"specified premises" means premises specified in a warrant issued under paragraph 15(1) of Schedule 12 (entry under warrant);

"the sum outstanding" means the outstanding debt together with any interest and any costs of enforcement to date;

"taking control of goods" has the meaning given by paragraph 13(1) of Schedule 12 (ways of taking control).

Application

APPLICATION OF THESE REGULATIONS

3(1)   These Regulations apply in relation to taking control of goods and selling them in the exercise of a power to use the procedure in Schedule 12.

3(2)   These Regulations apply to all such cases except to the extent that they provide otherwise.

Exempt Goods

EXEMPT GOODS

4(1)   Subject to paragraph (2) and to regulation 5, the following goods of the debtor are exempt goods—

(a)   items or equipment (for example, tools, books, telephones, computer equipment and vehicles) which are necessary for use personally by the debtor in the debtor's employment, business, trade, profession, study or education, except that in any case the aggregate value of the items or equipment to which this exemption is applied shall not exceed £1,350;

(b)   such clothing, bedding, furniture, household equipment, items and provisions as are reasonably required to satisfy the basic domestic needs of the debtor and every member of the debtor's household, including (but not restricted to)—

    (i)   a cooker or microwave;

    (ii)   a refrigerator;

    (iii)   a washing machine;

    (iv)   a dining table large enough, and sufficient dining chairs, to seat the debtor and every member of the debtor's household;

    (v)   beds and bedding sufficient for the debtor and every member of the debtor's household;

    (vi)   one landline telephone, or if there is no landline telephone at the premises, a mobile or internet telephone which may be used by the debtor or a member of the debtor's household;

    (vii)   any item or equipment reasonably required for—

        (aa)   the medical care of the debtor or any member of the debtor's household;

        (bb)   safety in the dwelling-house; or

        (cc)   the security of the dwelling-house (for example, an alarm system) or security in the dwelling-house;

    (viii)   sufficient lamps or stoves, or other appliance designed to provide lighting or heating facilities, to satisfy the basic heating and lighting needs of the debtor's household; and

    (ix)   any item or equipment reasonably required for the care of—

        (aa)   a person under the age of 18;

        (bb)   a disabled person; or

        (cc)   an older person;

Statutory Instruments

(c)   assistance dogs (including guide dogs, hearing dogs and dogs for disabled persons), sheep dogs, guard dogs or domestic pets;

(d)   a vehicle on which a valid disabled person's badge is displayed because it is used for, or in relation to which there are reasonable grounds for believing that it is used for, the carriage of a disabled person;

(e)   a vehicle (whether in public ownership or not) which is being used for, or in relation to which there are reasonable grounds for believing that it is used for, police, fire or ambulance purposes; and

(f)   a vehicle displaying a valid British Medical Association badge or other health emergency badge because it is being used for, or in relation to which there are reasonable grounds for believing that it is used for, health emergency purposes.

4(2)   Paragraph (1)(a) does not apply where the debt is being enforced under–

(i)   section 62A of the Local Government Finance Act 1988;

(ii)   section 54 of the Land Drainage Act 1991;

(iii)   paragraph 12 of Schedule 15 to the Water Resources Act 1991; or

(iv)   section 127 of the Finance Act 2008.

EXEMPT GOODS: GOODS WHICH ARE ALSO PREMISES AND ARE OCCUPIED AS ONLY OR PRINCIPAL HOME

5   Where any goods of the debtor are also premises and are occupied by the debtor or another person as the debtor's or that person's only or principal home, those goods are exempt goods.

PART 2 – PROCEDURE FOR TAKING CONTROL OF GOODS

Notice of Enforcement Prior to Taking Control of Goods

MINIMUM PERIOD OF NOTICE

6(1)   Subject to paragraph (3), notice of enforcement must be given to the debtor not less than 7 clear days before the enforcement agent takes control of the debtor's goods.

6(2)   Where the period referred to in paragraph (1) includes a Sunday, bank holiday, Good Friday or Christmas Day that day does not count in calculating the period.

6(3)   The court may order that a specified shorter period of notice may be given to the debtor.

6(4)   The court may only make an order under paragraph (3) where it is satisfied that, if the order is not made, it is likely that goods of the debtor will be moved to premises other than relevant premises, or otherwise disposed of, in order to avoid the goods being taken control of by the enforcement agent.

FORM AND CONTENTS OF NOTICE

7   Notice of enforcement must be given in writing, and must contain the following information–

(a)   the name and address of the debtor;

(b)   the reference number or numbers;

(c)   the date of notice;

(d)   details of the court judgment or order or enforcement power by virtue of which the debt is enforceable against the debtor;

(e)   the following information about the debt–

  (i)   sufficient details of the debt to enable the debtor to identify the debt correctly;

  (ii)   the amount of the debt including any interest due as at the date of the notice;

  (iii)   the amount of any enforcement costs incurred up to the date of notice; and

  (iv)   the possible additional costs of enforcement if the sum outstanding should remain unpaid as at the date mentioned in paragraph (h);

(f)   how and between which hours and on which days payment of the sum outstanding may be made;

(g)　　a contact telephone number and address at which, and the days on which and the hours between which, the enforcement agent or the enforcement agent's office may be contacted; and

(h)　　the date and time by which the sum outstanding must be paid to prevent goods of the debtor being taken control of and sold and the debtor incurring additional costs.

METHOD OF GIVING NOTICE AND WHO MUST GIVE IT

8(1)　Notice of enforcement must be given–

(a)　　by post addressed to the debtor at the place, or one of the places, where the debtor usually lives or carries on a trade or business;

(b)　　by fax or other means of electronic communication;

(c)　　by delivery by hand through the letter box of the place, or one of the places, where the debtor usually lives or carries on a trade or business;

(d)　　where there is no letterbox, by affixing the notice at or in a place where it is likely to come to the attention of the debtor;

(e)　　where the debtor is an individual, to the debtor personally; or

(f)　　where the debtor is not an individual (but is, for example, a company, corporation or partnership), by delivering the notice to–

　　(i)　　the place, or one of the places, where the debtor carries on a trade or business; or

　　(ii)　　the registered office of the company or partnership.

8(2)　Notice must be given by the enforcement agent or the enforcement agent's office.

Taking Control of Goods

TIME LIMIT FOR TAKING CONTROL OF GOODS

9(1)　Subject to paragraphs (2) and (3), the enforcement agent may not take control of goods of the debtor after the expiry of a period of 12 months beginning with the date of notice of enforcement.

9(2)　Where–

(a)　　after giving notice of enforcement the enforcement agent enters into an arrangement with the debtor for the repayment, by the debtor, of the sum outstanding by instalments (a repayment arrangement); and

(b)　　the debtor breaches the terms of the repayment arrangement,

the period in paragraph (1) begins with the date of the debtor's breach of the repayment arrangement.

9(3)　The court may order that the period in paragraph (1) be extended by 12 months.

9(4)　The court may make an order under paragraph (3) only–

(a)　　on application by the enforcement agent or the creditor;

(b)　　on one occasion; and

(c)　　if the court is satisfied that the applicant has reasonable grounds for not taking control of goods of the debtor during the period referred to under paragraph (1).

CIRCUMSTANCES IN WHICH THE ENFORCEMENT AGENT MAY NOT TAKE CONTROL OF GOODS

10(1)　The enforcement agent may not take control of goods of the debtor where–

(a)　　the debtor is a child;

(b)　　a child or vulnerable person (whether more than one or a combination of both) is the only person present in the relevant or specified premises in which the goods are located; or

(c)　　the goods are also premises in which a child or vulnerable person (whether more than one or a combination of both) is the only person present.

10(2)　Where an item which belongs to the debtor is in use by any person at the time at which the enforcement agent seeks to take control of it, the enforcement agent may not do so if such action is in all the circumstances likely to result in a breach of the peace.

10(3)　In paragraph (2), **"in use"** means that the item is in the hands of, or being operated by, the person.

CIRCUMSTANCES IN WHICH THE ENFORCEMENT AGENT MAY NOT TAKE CONTROL OF GOODS: HIGHWAYS

11(1)   This regulation applies in relation to relevant goods which the enforcement officer finds on a highway (see paragraph 13(1)(b) of Schedule 12).

11(2)   In this regulation–

(a)   **"relevant goods"** means–

    (i)   animals or livestock; or

    (ii)   any goods which the enforcement agent believes to be or to include–

        (aa)   hazardous goods or materials; or

        (bb)   perishable goods or materials;

(b)   **"hazardous goods or materials"** includes–

    (i)   nuclear matter;

    (ii)   radioactive waste; and

    (iii)   any other article or substance that has been and remains contaminated (whether radioactively or chemically); and

(c)   **"livestock"** includes cattle, sheep, pigs, horses and poultry.

11(3)   The enforcement agent may not take control of any relevant goods if–

(a)   to do so would pose a risk to public health; and

(b)   the enforcement agent is or ought to be aware of that risk.

11(4)   Where paragraph (1) applies the enforcement agent may not take control of a debtor's vehicle in which such goods are contained.

DAYS FOR TAKING CONTROL OF GOODS

12   The enforcement agent may take control of goods of the debtor on any day of the week.

PROHIBITED HOURS FOR TAKING CONTROL

13(1)   Subject to paragraph (2), the enforcement agent may not take control of goods of the debtor before 6 a.m. or after 9 p.m. on any day.

13(2)   Paragraph (1) does not apply where–

(a)   the court, on application by the enforcement agent, orders otherwise;

(b)   goods are located on the debtor's or another person's premises which are used (whether wholly or partly) to carry on a trade or business and the premises (or part of the premises) are open for the conduct of that trade or business during hours that are prohibited under paragraph (1); or

(c)   the enforcement agent has begun to take control of goods during hours that are not prohibited under paragraph (1), or during hours to which paragraph (1) does not apply by virtue of sub-paragraph (a) or (b), and to complete taking control of goods it is reasonably necessary for the enforcement agent to continue to do so during prohibited hours, provided the duration of time spent in taking control of goods is reasonable.

WHO MAY ENTER INTO A CONTROLLED GOODS AGREEMENT

14(1)   Subject to paragraph (2), a controlled goods agreement, as defined by paragraph 13(4) of Schedule 12, may only be entered into by an enforcement agent and–

(a)   a debtor who is not a child;

(b)   a person, aged 18 or over, authorised by the debtor to enter into a controlled goods agreement on the debtor's behalf; or

(c)   a person in apparent authority who is on the premises, where those premises are used (whether wholly or partly) to carry on a trade or business.

14(2)   The enforcement agent may not enter into a controlled goods agreement with the debtor or another person who it appears (or ought to appear) to the enforcement agent does not understand the effect of, and would therefore not be capable of entering into, such an agreement.

CONTROLLED GOODS AGREEMENTS

15(1)   This regulation applies where a controlled goods agreement is entered into under paragraph 13(1)(d) of Schedule 12.

15(2) The agreement must be in writing and signed by the enforcement agent and—

(a)   the debtor;

(b)   the person authorised by the debtor in accordance with regulation 14(1)(b); or

(c)   the person in apparent authority in accordance with regulation 14(1)(c).

15(3) The agreement must contain the following information—

(a)   the name and address of the debtor;

(b)   the reference number or numbers and the date of the agreement;

(c)   the names of the persons entering into the agreement;

(d)   a contact telephone number and address at which, and the days on which and the hours between which the enforcement agent or the enforcement agent's office may be contacted;

(e)   a list of the goods of which control has been taken with a description to enable the debtor to identify the goods correctly, including, where applicable—

     (i)   the manufacturer, model and serial number of the goods;

     (ii)   in the case of a vehicle, the manufacturer, model, colour and registration mark of the vehicle; and

     (iii)   the material, colour and usage, and (where appropriate) any other identifying characteristic of the goods; and

(f)   the terms of the arrangement entered into between the enforcement agent and the debtor for the repayment, by the debtor, of the sum outstanding.

15(4) At the time of entering into the agreement, the enforcement agent must give a copy of the signed agreement to the person who signed it under paragraph (2).

15(5) Where the enforcement agent enters into the agreement with a person authorised by the debtor in accordance with regulation 14(1)(b) or with a person in apparent authority in accordance with regulation 14(1)(c), the enforcement agent must also provide the debtor with a copy of the signed agreement by—

(a)   leaving it in a conspicuous place on the relevant or specified premises, where the enforcement agent has taken control of the goods on such premises; or

(b)   delivering it to any relevant premises, in a sealed envelope addressed to the debtor, where the enforcement agent has taken control of the goods on a highway.

15(6) Where the enforcement agent leaves a copy of the agreement in a conspicuous place on the relevant or specified premises under paragraph (5)(a) and the enforcement agent knows that a person other than the debtor is on the premises or that there are other occupiers, the copy must be left in a sealed envelope addressed to the debtor.

15(7) Paragraph (3)(e) is complied with if—

(a)   the enforcement agent provides the debtor with a list of goods of which control has been taken under regulation 30(2)(f)(i) or regulation 33(1)(e) at the same time as entering into the controlled goods agreement; and

(b)   the goods of which control has been taken are the same as those referred to in the list mentioned in sub-paragraph (a).

Ways of Securing Goods

SECURING GOODS OF THE DEBTOR ON PREMISES WHERE FOUND

16(1) Subject to paragraphs (2) and (3), an enforcement agent who is securing goods of the debtor on the premises on which they are found (under paragraph 13(1)(a) of Schedule 12) may secure the goods—

(a)   in a cupboard, room, garage or outbuilding;

(b)   in the case of goods on premises (or on a part of the premises) which are not occupied for residential purposes, by the enforcement agent remaining on the premises to guard the goods of the debtor of which the enforcement agent has taken control;

(c)   by fitting an immobilisation device (which must be provided by the enforcement agent); or

(d)   by securing—

     (i)   the whole of the premises, where the premises are occupied solely for the purpose of a trade or business; or

     (ii)   such part of the premises, where the premises are occupied for residential and trade or business purposes, that is occupied solely for the purpose of a trade or business.

16(2)   The enforcement agent may not secure goods in any of the ways listed under paragraph (1)(a) to (c) where any person (whether or not the debtor) in occupation of the premises, or any part of the premises, would, as a result, be deprived of adequate access to essential facilities, including exempt goods, or adequate means of entering and leaving the premises, including means of emergency entry and escape.

16(3)   Where the goods are secured by fitting an immobilisation device under paragraph (1)(c), the enforcement agent must, at the time of immobilising the goods, provide a written warning to the debtor, signed by the enforcement agent, to be affixed in a prominent position on the immobilised goods, which must contain the following information—

(a)   that the enforcement agent has immobilised the goods;

(b)   the date and time of immobilisation;

(c)   that the goods have been immobilised because the debtor has failed to pay the sum outstanding;

(d)   a telephone number, which is available 24 hours every day, for enquiries; and

(e)   the reference number or numbers.

16(4)   Premises may only be secured under paragraph (1)(d) if it is not practicable either—

(a)   to secure the goods in any of the other ways listed under paragraph (1); or

(b)   to take control of the goods under paragraph 13(1)(c) of Schedule 12.

SECURING GOODS OF THE DEBTOR ON A HIGHWAY OR ELSEWHERE

17(1)   Subject to paragraph (3), where the enforcement agent is proceeding under paragraph 13(1)(b) or (c) of Schedule 12 the enforcement agent may secure goods of the debtor by fitting an immobilisation device.

17(2)   Where the goods are secured by fitting an immobilisation device, the enforcement agent must—

(a)   provide the immobilisation device; and

(b)   provide a written warning to the debtor in accordance with regulation 16(3).

17(3)   This regulation does not apply where the goods to be secured on a highway under paragraph 13(1)(b) of Schedule 12 are a vehicle.

SECURING GOODS OF THE DEBTOR ON A HIGHWAY AND REMOVAL: VEHICLES

18(1)   Where the enforcement agent is proceeding under paragraph 13(1)(b) of Schedule 12 and the goods to be secured are a vehicle, those goods must be secured in accordance with this regulation.

18(2)   The vehicle must be secured by an immobilisation device, unless the debtor voluntarily surrenders the keys to the vehicle to the enforcement agent.

18(3)   The immobilisation device must be provided by the enforcement agent.

18(4)   At the time of immobilising the goods, the enforcement agent must provide a written warning to the debtor in accordance with regulation 16(3).

18(5)   A vehicle must remain immobilised where it is positioned for a period of not less than 2 hours from the time of immobilisation unless the sum outstanding is paid or an agreement to release the vehicle, on part payment of the sum outstanding, is made between the enforcement agent and the debtor.

18(6)   On expiry of the period of time referred to under paragraph (5), the enforcement agent may remove the vehicle to storage.

18(7)   Where a vehicle is removed to storage, the enforcement agent must comply with the requirements of regulation 34 (care of controlled goods).

REMOVAL AND SECURING GOODS OF THE DEBTOR: LOCATION

19   Subject to regulation 34 (care of controlled goods), where the enforcement agent takes control of the goods of the debtor under paragraph 13(1)(c) of Schedule 12 the enforcement agent must, save in exceptional circumstances, remove the goods and secure them in or at a place which is within a reasonable distance from the place where control was taken of the goods.

Entry

MODE OF ENTRY OR RE-ENTRY TO PREMISES

20 The enforcement agent may enter relevant or specified premises under paragraph 14 or 15 of Schedule 12 respectively, or re-enter premises under paragraph 16 of Schedule 12, only by—

(a)   any door, or any usual means by which entry is gained to the premises (for example, a loading bay to premises where a trade or business is carried on); or

(b)   any usual means of entry, where the premises are a vehicle, vessel, aircraft, hovercraft, a tent or other moveable structure.

DAYS OF ENTRY

21(1)   This regulation applies where the enforcement agent is—

(a)   entering or remaining on relevant or specified premises under paragraph 14 or 15 of Schedule 12 to search for and take control of goods; or

(b)   re-entering or remaining on premises under paragraph 16 of Schedule 12 to inspect controlled goods or to remove them for storage or sale.

21(2)   The enforcement agent may enter, re-enter or remain on the premises on any day of the week.

HOURS OF ENTRY

22(1)   This regulation applies where the enforcement agent is entering, re-entering or remaining on premises in the circumstances mentioned in regulation 21(1).

22(2)   Subject to paragraphs (3) to (5), the enforcement agent may only enter, re-enter or remain on the premises after 6 a.m. and before 9 p.m. on any day.

22(3)   Where premises are used (whether wholly or partly) for a trade or business, the enforcement agent may enter, re-enter or remain on the premises (or part of the premises so used) during any hours when the premises (or part of the premises) are open for the conduct of that trade or business.

22(4)   Where the enforcement agent has, during hours permitted under paragraph (2), (3) or (5), already entered or re-entered premises, the enforcement agent may, outside such permitted hours, remain on the premises, if it is reasonably necessary for him to continue to search for and take control of goods, inspect controlled goods or remove controlled goods for storage or sale, provided the duration of time spent is reasonable.

22(5)   The court may authorise the enforcement agent to enter, re-enter or remain on premises during times other than those permitted by paragraph (2), (3) or (4) if (and only if) an application for authorisation is made to the court by the enforcement agent.

RESTRICTIONS ON ENTRY AND RE-ENTRY TO, AND REMAINING ON, PREMISES

23(1)   This regulation applies where the enforcement agent is entering, re-entering or remaining on premises in the circumstances mentioned in regulation 21(1).

23(2)   The enforcement agent may enter, re-enter or remain on the premises only if—

(a)   the debtor is not a child; or

(b)   a child or vulnerable person (whether more than one or a combination of both) is not the only person present in the premises which the enforcement agent proposes to enter or re-enter.

RESTRICTIONS ON REPEATED ENTRY (WITH OR WITHOUT WARRANT) TO PREMISES

24(1)   This regulation applies where the enforcement agent, having entered relevant or specified premises under paragraph 14 or 15 of Schedule 12 respectively, has determined that there are no or insufficient goods of the debtor on the premises of which control may be taken that will pay the sum outstanding.

24(2)   The enforcement agent may enter the premises on a second or subsequent occasion only—

(a)   if the enforcement agent has reason to believe that, since the occasion of the enforcement agent's last entry, there have been brought on to the premises further goods of the debtor of which control has not yet been, but may be, taken; or

(b) where the enforcement agent was prohibited from taking control of particular goods at the time of the original entry by virtue of regulation 10(2) (control not to be taken of goods if those goods are in use and the enforcement agent considers that a breach of the peace would be likely if an attempt were made to take control of them).

24(3) Paragraph (2)(b) does not authorise the enforcement agent to enter to take control of any goods other than those to which that paragraph applies, except to the extent that paragraph (2)(a) also applies.

MINIMUM PERIOD OF NOTICE OF INTENTION TO RE-ENTER PREMISES

25(1) Subject to paragraph (3), notice of the enforcement agent's intention to re-enter premises must be given to the debtor not less than 2 clear days before the enforcement agent re-enters the premises.

25(2) Where the period referred to in paragraph (1) includes a Sunday, bank holiday, Good Friday or Christmas Day that day does not count in calculating the period.

25(3) The court may order that a specified shorter period of notice may be given to the debtor.

25(4) The court may only make an order under paragraph (3) where it is satisfied that, if the order is not made, it is likely that goods of the debtor will be moved to premises other than relevant premises, or otherwise disposed of, in order to avoid the goods being inspected or removed for storage or sale.

FORM AND CONTENTS OF NOTICE OF RE-ENTRY

26 Notice of the enforcement agent's intention to re-enter premises must be in writing, be signed by the enforcement agent and contain the following information–

(a) the name and address of the debtor;

(b) the reference number or numbers;

(c) the date of the notice;

(d) sufficient details of the controlled goods agreement, the repayment terms of which the debtor has failed to comply with, to enable the debtor to identify the agreement correctly;

(e) how the debtor has failed to comply with the repayment terms of the controlled goods agreement;

(f) the amount of the sum outstanding as at the date of the notice;

(g) how and between which hours and on which days payment of the sum outstanding may be made;

(h) a contact telephone number and address at which, and the days on which and hours between which, the enforcement agent or the enforcement agent's office may be contacted;

(i) the date and time by which the sum outstanding must be paid to prevent the controlled goods being inspected or removed for storage or sale; and

(j) that the enforcement agent may if necessary use reasonable force to re-enter the premises to inspect the goods or remove them for storage or sale.

METHOD OF GIVING NOTICE OF RE-ENTRY AND WHO MUST GIVE IT

27(1) Notice of the enforcement agent's intention to re-enter premises must be given–

(a) by fax or other means of electronic communication;

(b) by delivery by hand through the letter box of the place, or one of the places, where the debtor usually lives or carries on a trade or business;

(c) where there is no letterbox, by affixing the notice at or in a place that it is likely to come to the attention of the debtor;

(d) where the debtor is an individual, to the debtor personally; or

(e) where the debtor is not an individual (but is, for example, a company, corporation or partnership), by delivering the notice to–

(i) the place, or one of the places, where the debtor carries on a trade or business; or

(ii) the registered office of the company or partnership.

27(2) The notice must be given by the enforcement agent.

ISSUE OF WARRANT AUTHORISING ENFORCEMENT AGENT TO USE REASONABLE FORCE TO ENTER PREMISES

28(1) This regulation applies where the enforcement agent has power to enter premises under paragraph 14 or 15 of Schedule 12.

28(2) The conditions of which the court must be satisfied before it issues a warrant under paragraph 20(2) of Schedule 12, or includes provision in a warrant under paragraph 21(2) of that Schedule, are–

(a) either–

    (i) the enforcement agent is attempting to recover a debt enforceable under section 127 of the Finance Act 2008; or

    (ii) the premises are premises to which the goods have been deliberately removed in order to avoid control being taken of them;

(b) there are, or are likely to be, goods of the debtor on the premises of which control can be taken;

(c) the enforcement agent has explained to the court–

    (i) the likely means of entry, and the type and amount of force that will be required to make the entry;

    (ii) how, after entry, the enforcement agent proposes to leave the premises in a secure state; and

(d) in all the circumstances it is appropriate for the court to give an authorisation, having regard (among other matters) to–

    (i) the sum outstanding;

    (ii) the nature of the debt.

ISSUE OF WARRANT AUTHORISING ENFORCEMENT AGENT TO USE REASONABLE FORCE IN RELATION TO GOODS ON A HIGHWAY

29(1) This regulation applies where an enforcement agent is taking control of goods on a highway.

29(2) The conditions of which the court must be satisfied before it issues a warrant under paragraph 31(1) of Schedule 12 are–

(a) the enforcement agent is attempting to recover a debt enforceable by virtue of a writ or warrant referred to in paragraph (3) or under section 127 of the Finance Act 2008;

(b) the enforcement agent has explained to the court the type and amount of force that will be required to take control of the goods; and

(c) in all the circumstances an authorisation ought to be given, having regard to (among other matters)–

    (i) the sum outstanding; and

    (ii) the nature of the debt.

29(3) The writs and warrants (as the case may be) mentioned in paragraph (2)(a) are–

(a) a High Court writ of control which confers a power to recover a sum of money;

(b) a High Court writ of delivery which confers a power to take control of goods and sell them to recover a sum of money;

(c) a High Court writ of possession which confers a power to take control of goods and sell them to recover a sum of money;

(d) a county court warrant of control pursuant to section 85 of the County Courts Act 1984 except such a warrant which is issued to recover a traffic contravention debt as defined by section 82 of the Traffic Management Act 2004;

(e) a county court warrant of delivery which confers a power to take control of goods and sell them to recover a sum of money;

(f) a county court warrant of possession which confers a power to take control of goods and sell them to recover a sum of money;

(g) a magistrates' court warrant of control pursuant to section 76 of the Magistrates' Courts Act 1980.

Notice After Entry and Taking Control of Goods

FORM AND CONTENTS OF NOTICE AFTER ENTRY, AND/OR TAKING CONTROL OF GOODS ON A HIGHWAY

30(1) This regulation applies to the notices required by paragraph 28(1) and paragraph 33(1) of Schedule 12.

30(2) Subject to regulations 31 and 32, the notice must be in writing, be signed by the enforcement agent and contain the following information—

(a)   the name and address of the debtor;

(b)   the enforcement agent's name, the reference number or numbers and the date of the notice;

(c)   that the enforcement agent has done one or more of the following—

    (i)   entered the premises;

    (ii)   taken control of goods on a highway;

    (iii)   entered a vehicle on a highway with the intention of taking control of goods;

(d)   the address of the premises which the enforcement agent has entered or the location on the highway where the enforcement agent has taken control of goods or entered a vehicle;

(e)   where a vehicle on a highway has been entered with the intention of taking control of goods, the manufacturer, model, colour and registration mark of that vehicle; and

(f)   whether or not the enforcement agent has taken control of goods of the debtor and, if so, the location where and the time when control has been taken of the goods and—

    (i)   a list of the goods of which control has been taken with a description to enable the debtor to identify the goods correctly, including, where applicable—

        (aa)   the manufacturer, model and serial number of the goods;

        (bb)   in the case of a vehicle, the manufacturer, model, colour and registration mark of the vehicle; and

        (cc)   the material, colour and usage, and (where appropriate) any other identifying characteristic, of the goods;

    (ii)   the amount of the sum outstanding as at the date of the notice;

    (iii)   the date and time by which the sum outstanding must be paid to prevent the controlled goods being sold;

    (iv)   how and between which hours and on which days payment of the sum outstanding may be made; and

    (v)   that the controlled goods will be released on payment in full (or may be released on part payment) of the sum outstanding.

30(3) Where the enforcement agent is—

(a)   re-entering premises under paragraph 16 of Schedule 12 to inspect goods of which control has previously been taken; and

(b)   not using force to effect the re-entry,

the requirement to provide notice under paragraph 28(1) of Schedule 12 does not apply.

30(4) Paragraph (2)(f)(i) is complied with if—

(a)   the enforcement agent provides the debtor with a list of goods of which control has been taken under regulation 15(3)(e) or regulation 33(1)(e) at the same time as the notice; and

(b)   the goods of which control has been taken are the same as those referred to in the list mentioned in sub-paragraph (a).

ADDITIONAL NOTICE REQUIREMENTS WHERE GOODS ARE IMMOBILISED

31(1) Subject to paragraph (2), where control is taken of goods of the debtor in any of the ways listed under paragraph 13(1) of Schedule 12 and the goods have been immobilised, the notice mentioned in regulation 30(1) must also contain the information mentioned in regulation 16(3) (written warning on immobilisation).

31(2) Where control is taken of goods under paragraph 13(1)(b) of Schedule 12 (goods found on a highway and secured on a highway) and the goods are a vehicle which are immobilised, the notice

Statutory Instruments

mentioned in regulation 30(1) must also contain the information mentioned in regulation 18(4) (written warning on immobilisation).

ADDITIONAL NOTICE REQUIREMENTS WHERE GOODS ARE REMOVED FOR STORAGE OR SALE

32(1)   Where control is taken of goods of the debtor under paragraph 13(1)(c) of Schedule 12 or controlled goods are removed to storage or for sale, the notice under regulation 30(1) must also contain the following information—

(a)   that the enforcement agent has removed controlled goods to secure storage or for sale;

(b)   a list of the goods so removed (where the goods are different to those included in a list provided by virtue of regulation 30(2)(f)(i);

(c)   the date of removal of the goods to storage or for sale;

(d)   the daily or weekly storage charge payable, where the goods are removed to storage; and

(e)   the procedure for collection by or on behalf of the debtor of goods of which control has been taken on payment of the sum outstanding or on part payment of the sum outstanding where an agreement is made between the enforcement agent and the debtor.

32(2)   Where any of the information required by paragraph (1) is not known to the enforcement agent at the time of providing the notice to the debtor under regulation 30(1) the enforcement agent must provide such information, in writing, to the debtor, as soon as reasonably practicable.

32(3)   Paragraph (1)(b) is complied with if the enforcement agent provides the debtor with a copy of the inventory required by paragraph 34 of Schedule 12 at the same time as the notice, which describes all goods removed to storage or for sale.

Inventory

INVENTORY OF GOODS OF WHICH CONTROL HAS BEEN TAKEN: FORM AND CONTENTS

33(1)   The inventory required by paragraph 34 of Schedule 12 must be in writing, be signed by the enforcement agent and contain the following information—

(a)   the name and address of the debtor;

(b)   the enforcement agent's name, the reference number or numbers and the date of the inventory;

(c)   the name and address of the co-owner, if any;

(d)   that the enforcement agent has taken control of the goods of the debtor or of the debtor and the co-owner as specified in the inventory; and

(e)   a list of the goods of which control has been taken with a description to enable the debtor or the co-owner to identify the goods correctly, including, where applicable—

   (i)   the manufacturer, model and serial number of the goods;

   (ii)   in the case of a vehicle, the manufacturer, model, colour and registration mark of the vehicle; and

   (iii)   the material, colour and usage, and (where appropriate) any other identifying characteristic, of the goods.

33(2)   The inventory may be combined with a controlled goods agreement under regulation 15(1) or the notice required by paragraph 28(1) or 33(1) of Schedule 12 if—

(a)   the enforcement agent provides the debtor with the inventory at the same time as the controlled goods agreement or the notice; and

(b)   the goods of which control has been taken are the same as those listed in the list of goods of which control has been taken required by regulation 15(3)(e) or regulation 30(2)(f)(i).

Dealing with Controlled Goods

CARE OF CONTROLLED GOODS

34(1)   Where the enforcement agent removes controlled goods, other than securities, from premises or a highway where the enforcement agent has found them—

(a)   the enforcement agent must keep the controlled goods, so long as they remain in the enforcement agent's control, in a similar condition to that in which the enforcement agent found them immediately prior to taking control of them;

(b)   the goods must be removed to storage, unless the goods are removed for sale; and

(c)   the storage must be secure and the conditions of that storage such as to prevent damage to or deterioration of the goods for so long as they remain in the enforcement agent's control.

34(2)   The enforcement agent must not remove controlled goods to a place where there would be at any time a contravention of any prohibition or restriction imposed by or under any enactment.

Valuation

VALUATION OF CONTROLLED GOODS

35(1)   This regulation applies where an enforcement agent makes (paragraph (2)) or obtains (paragraph (3)) a valuation of controlled goods as required by paragraph 36(1) of Schedule 12.

35(2)   Where the enforcement agent makes the valuation–

(a)   the valuation must be in writing, signed by the enforcement agent and set out–

    (i)   the enforcement agent's name, the reference number or numbers and the date of the valuation; and

    (ii)   where appropriate, a separate value for each item of goods of which control has been taken; and

(b)   the enforcement agent must provide a copy of the written valuation, once made, to the debtor and any co-owner.

35(3)   Where the enforcement agent obtains the valuation the enforcement agent must–

(a)   only instruct a qualified, independent valuer;

(b)   instruct the valuer to make a written valuation and, where appropriate, to value each item of goods separately; and

(c)   provide a copy of the written valuation, once made by the valuer, to the debtor and any co-owner.

PART 3 – SALE OF CONTROLLED GOODS

PART 3 NOT TO APPLY TO SECURITIES

36   This Part does not apply to controlled goods which are securities.

Notice of Sale

MINIMUM PERIOD BEFORE SALE

37(1)   Subject to paragraph (2), the minimum period before sale required by paragraph 39 of Schedule 12 is 7 clear days from removing controlled goods for sale.

37(2)   Sale may take place on the day after removing controlled goods for sale where, if the sale were to take place after the expiry of the period of time referred to in paragraph (1), the goods would become unsaleable, or their sale value would be extinguished or substantially reduced due to the nature or any characteristic of those goods.

MINIMUM PERIOD OF NOTICE OF SALE

38(1)   Subject to paragraph (2), the minimum period of notice of the date, time and place of sale required by paragraph 40 of Schedule 12 is 7 clear days before the sale of the goods.

38(2)   Notice may be given on the day before the sale of the goods where, if the sale were to take place after the expiry of the period of time referred to in paragraph (1), the goods would become unsaleable, or their sale value would be extinguished or substantially reduced due to the nature or any characteristic of those goods.

FORM AND CONTENTS OF NOTICE OF SALE

39(1) Notice of the date, time and place of the sale required by paragraph 40 of Schedule 12 must be in writing, be signed by the enforcement agent and contain the following information–

(a) the name and address of the debtor;

(b) the enforcement agent's name, the reference number or numbers and the date of the notice;

(c) the name and address of the co-owner, if any;

(d) that the controlled goods may be sold as the debtor has failed to pay the sum outstanding;

(e) a list of the controlled goods that may be sold with a description to enable the debtor or the co-owner to identify the goods correctly, including, where applicable–

   (i) the manufacturer, model and serial number of the goods;

   (ii) in the case of a vehicle, the manufacturer, model, colour and registration mark of the vehicle; and

   (iii) the material, colour and usage and (where appropriate) any other identifying characteristic, of the goods;

(f) that the sale of the controlled goods is conditional on–

   (i) an offer to purchase the goods being made; and

   (ii) the reserve price, if any, on the controlled goods being met;

(g) that if the conditions in paragraph (f) are not met the date, time and place of sale will be set out in a further notice;

(h) the amount of the sum outstanding as at the date of the notice;

(i) the date and time by which the sum outstanding must be paid to prevent the controlled goods being sold;

(j) how and between which hours and on which days payment of the sum outstanding may be made; and

(k) the procedure for collection by or on behalf of the debtor or co-owner of goods of which control has been taken on payment of the sum outstanding or on part payment of the sum outstanding where an agreement is made between the enforcement agent and the debtor.

39(2) Where the conditions in paragraph (1)(f) are not met and a further notice is given to the debtor and any co-owner by virtue of paragraph (1)(g), the notice must–

(a) comply with the requirements of regulation 38;

(b) provide the information required by paragraph (1); and

(c) state that it is a further notice.

39(3) The enforcement agent may replace the notice with a new notice, in accordance with paragraph 40(3) of Schedule 12, only if–

(a) the date, time or location of the sale has had to be re-arranged;

(b) the minimum period of notice of the date, time and place of sale in the new notice is of the same period as in the notice which is to be replaced; and

(c) the new notice sets out–

   (i) the information required by paragraph (1);

   (ii) that it is a new notice;

   (iii) that it replaces the last notice given to the debtor or co-owner; and

   (iv) the date of the notice which it replaces.

METHOD OF GIVING NOTICE OF SALE

40(1) The method of giving the notice of the date, time and place of sale required by paragraph 40 of Schedule 12 is the method required under regulation 8(1) (method of giving notice).

40(2) For the purposes of this regulation, references in regulation 8(1) to a debtor include a co-owner.

Sale

METHODS OF SALE

41(1) Where an enforcement agent applies to the court under paragraph 41(2) of Schedule 12 for an order that the sale be by a method other than public auction, the types of sale the court may order include sale by–

(a)   private contract;

(b)   sealed bids;

(c)   advertisement; and

(d)   such other method as the court considers appropriate.

41(2) Where the enforcement agent has stated to the court (as required by paragraph 41(4) of Schedule 12) that the enforcement agent has reason to believe that an enforcement power has become exercisable by another creditor against the debtor or a co-owner, the notice of application required by paragraph 41(5) of that Schedule must–

(a)   be in writing, signed by the enforcement agent and set out–

      (i)   the name and address of the debtor; and

      (ii)   the enforcement agent's name, the reference number or numbers and the date of the notice;

(b)   attach a copy of the enforcement agent's application to the court; and

(c)   be given to that other creditor–

      (i)   by the enforcement agent; and

      (ii)   by a method required under regulation 8(1) (method of giving notice).

41(3) For the purposes of paragraph (2)(c)(ii), references in regulation 8(1) to a debtor are to be read as a reference to the other creditor.

PLACE OF SALE

42(1) Subject to paragraph (2), a sale of controlled goods by public auction may only be held in a public auction house or on an online or internet auction site.

42(2) The sale may be held on premises where goods were found by the enforcement agent where those premises are occupied solely for the purposes of a trade or business.

CONDUCT OF SALE

43 Where controlled goods are sold by public auction, the auction must be conducted by–

(a)   a qualified auctioneer; or

(b)   where the auction takes place online or on an internet auction site, an auction provider independent of the enforcement agent.

PART 4 – SECURITIES OF THE DEBTOR

PART 4 ONLY TO APPLY TO SECURITIES

44 This Part only applies to controlled goods which are securities.

HOLDING OF SECURITIES

45(1) The enforcement agent may hold securities until they mature.

45(2) While holding securities, the enforcement agent must ensure each security has the benefit of the same protection in every respect (for example, from damage, destruction, theft or unauthorised or fraudulent interference) as that security had immediately before the enforcement agent took control of it.

DISPOSAL OF SECURITIES

46(1) The minimum period of notice required by paragraph 49(1) of Schedule 12 (which requires the enforcement agent to give notice to the debtor, etc. of the disposal of securities) is 7 clear days.

46(2) Subject to paragraph (3), the notice must be in writing, be signed by the enforcement agent and contain the following information–

(a)   the name and address of the debtor;

(b)   the enforcement agent's name, the reference number or numbers and the date of the notice;

(c)   the name and address of the co-owner, if any;

(d)   for each security, sufficient details of the security to enable the debtor or any co-owner to identify the security correctly;

(e)   that the securities may be disposed of by–

   (i)   realising the sums secured or made payable by them;

   (ii)   the creditor issuing proceedings in the name of the debtor (or in the name of any person in whose name the debtor might have sued) for the recovery of any sum secured or made payable by securities, when the time of payment arrives; or

   (iii)   the creditor assigning the right to sue for the recovery of such sums to another person;

(f)   the date and time when the sums will be realised, where sub-paragraph (e)(i) applies;

(g)   the amount of the sum outstanding as at the date of the notice;

(h)   the date and time by which the sum outstanding must be paid to prevent the securities being disposed of;

(i)   how and between which hours and on which days payment of the sum outstanding may be made; and

(j)   the procedure for release to the debtor or co-owner of the securities of which control has been taken on payment of the sum outstanding or on part payment of the sum outstanding where an agreement is made between the enforcement agent and the debtor.

46(3) Where paragraph (2)(e)(ii) or (iii) applies, the notice must also provide the following information–

(a)   the name and address of the applicant to the proceedings;

(b)   the names and addresses of the defendants to the proceedings; and

(c)   the amount of the claim–

   (i)   in respect of each security; and

   (ii)   in total.

46(4) The enforcement agent may replace the notice with a new notice, in accordance with paragraph 49(4) of Schedule 12, only if–

(a)   the method of disposal under paragraph (2)(e) has changed; or

(b)   the date or time of the disposal under paragraph (2)(f) has had to be re-arranged,

and the new notice complies with the requirements of paragraph (5).

46(5) Where the notice is replaced with a new notice under paragraph (4)–

(a)   the minimum period of notice given in the new notice must be the same period as in the notice which is to be replaced; and

(b)   the new notice must provide the following information–

   (i)   the information required by paragraph (2);

   (ii)   the information required by paragraph (3), where paragraph (2)(e)(ii) or (iii) applies;

   (iii)   that it is a new notice;

   (iv)   that it replaces the last notice given to the debtor or co-owner; and

   (v)   the date of the notice which it replaces.

46(6) The method of giving the notice is the method required under regulation 8(1) (method of giving notice) and for the purposes of this regulation, references in that regulation to a debtor include a co-owner.

PART 5 – ABANDONMENT OF GOODS

ABANDONMENT OF GOODS OTHER THAN SECURITIES

47(1) This regulation applies where, pursuant to paragraph 54(1)(b) of Schedule 12, the enforcement agent makes controlled goods, which are abandoned, available for collection by the debtor.

47(2)   Where the goods are immobilised, the enforcement agent must on (but not before) collection by the debtor, remove all immobilisation devices from the goods.

47(3)   Where the enforcement agent removed the goods from where they were found the enforcement agent must as soon as reasonably practicable give the debtor a written notice, signed by the enforcement agent, which must contain the following information–

(a)   the name and address of the debtor;

(b)   the enforcement agent's name, the reference number or numbers and the date of the notice;

(c)   that the controlled goods are abandoned and the reason why they are abandoned;

(d)   a list of the abandoned goods with a description to enable the debtor to identify the goods correctly, including, where applicable–

    (i)   the manufacturer, model and serial number of the goods;

    (ii)   in the case of a vehicle, the manufacturer, model, colour and registration mark of the vehicle; and

    (iii)   the material, colour and usage, and (where appropriate) any other identifying characteristic of the goods;

(e)   that the goods are available for collection by the debtor;

(f)   the procedure for collection of the goods by the debtor; and

(g)   that if the debtor fails to collect the goods within 28 days from when the goods were made available for collection, the enforcement agent will make an application to the court for determination of how the uncollected goods are to be disposed of.

47(4)   The method of giving the notice is the method required under regulation 8(1) (method of giving notice).

47(5)   Where the debtor fails to collect the controlled goods within 28 days from when the goods were made available for collection, the enforcement agent must apply to the court to determine how the uncollected goods are to be disposed of.

47(6)   On application by the enforcement agent under paragraph (5), the court may make one of the following orders–

(a)   that the goods are to be made available for collection by the debtor during a further period of time (to be determined by the court);

(b)   that the goods are to be–

    (i)   given to a charitable organisation nominated by the court; or

    (ii)   destroyed; or

(c)   that the goods are to be made available for collection by the debtor during a further period of time (to be determined by the court) and, if not collected during that period, are to be–

    (i)   given to a charitable organisation nominated by the court; or

    (ii)   destroyed.

PART 6 – THIRD PARTY CLAIMING CONTROLLED GOODS

APPLICATION OF PART 6

48   This Part applies where a person ("the applicant") makes an application to the court claiming that goods of which control has been taken are that person's and not the debtor's.

PAYMENTS INTO COURT BY THIRD PARTY: UNDERPAYMENTS

49(1)   Any underpayment to be determined by reference to an independent valuation under paragraph 60(5) of Schedule 12 must be undertaken by a qualified independent valuer.

49(2)   Any underpayment determined by the qualified independent valuer must be paid within 14 clear days after provision of a copy of the valuation to the applicant.

PART 7 – COMMERCIAL RENT ARREARS RECOVERY (CRAR)

General

PART 7 TO APPLY ONLY TO CRAR

50-55   [Not relevant to income tax, corporation tax or capital gains tax.]

PUBLIC BODIES (ABOLITION OF ADMINISTRATIVE JUSTICE AND TRIBUNALS COUNCIL) ORDER 2013

(SI 2013/2042)

Made on 18 August 2013 by the Secretary of State, in exercise of the powers conferred by s. 1(1), 6(1) and (5) and 35(2) of the Public Bodies Act 2011. Operative in accordance with art. 1.

CITATION, COMMENCEMENT AND EXTENT

1(1) This Order may be cited as the Public Bodies (Abolition of Administrative Justice and Tribunals Council) Order 2013.

1(2) Subject to paragraph (3), this Order comes into force on the day after the date on which it is made.

1(3) Paragraph 41(a) of the Schedule comes into force on the day after that on which the other provisions of this Order come into force.

1(4) Amendments, repeals and revocations in this Order have the same extent as the provisions amended, repealed or revoked.

ABOLITION OF THE ADMINISTRATIVE JUSTICE AND TRIBUNALS COUNCIL

2(1) The Administrative Justice and Tribunals Council is abolished.

2(2) The Schedule (which makes consequential provision etc) has effect.

SCHEDULE – CONSEQUENTIAL PROVISION ETC

Article 2(2)

CHRONICALLY SICK AND DISABLED PERSONS ACT 1970

1 [Not relevant to income tax, corporation tax or capital gains tax.]

HEALTH AND SAFETY AT WORK ETC ACT 1974

2 [Not relevant to income tax, corporation tax or capital gains tax.]

HOUSE OF COMMONS DISQUALIFICATION ACT 1975

3-4 [Not relevant to income tax, corporation tax or capital gains tax.]

TOWN AND COUNTRY PLANNING ACT 1990

5 [Not relevant to income tax, corporation tax or capital gains tax.]

SOCIAL SECURITY ADMINISTRATION ACT 1992

6-8 [Not relevant to income tax, corporation tax or capital gains tax.]

TRANSPORT AND WORKS ACT 1992

9 [Not relevant to income tax, corporation tax or capital gains tax.]

TRIBUNALS AND INQUIRIES ACT 1992

10-14 [Not relevant to income tax, corporation tax or capital gains tax.]

PENSION SCHEMES ACT 1993

15 [Not relevant to income tax, corporation tax or capital gains tax.]

LAW OF PROPERTY (MISCELLANEOUS PROVISIONS) ACT 1994

16 [Not relevant to income tax, corporation tax or capital gains tax.]

TOWN AND COUNTRY PLANNING (SCOTLAND) ACT 1997

17 [Not relevant to income tax, corporation tax or capital gains tax.]

SCHOOL STANDARDS AND FRAMEWORK ACT 1998

18   [Not relevant to income tax, corporation tax or capital gains tax.]

GREATER LONDON AUTHORITY ACT 1999

19   [Not relevant to income tax, corporation tax or capital gains tax.]

WELFARE REFORM AND PENSIONS ACT 1999

20   [Not relevant to income tax, corporation tax or capital gains tax.]

FREEDOM OF INFORMATION ACT 2000

21-22   [Amending provisions not reproduced.]

EDUCATION ACT 2002

23   [Not relevant to income tax, corporation tax or capital gains tax.]

TITLE CONDITIONS (SCOTLAND) ACT 2003

24-26   [Not relevant to income tax, corporation tax or capital gains tax.]

GENDER RECOGNITION ACT 2004

27-28   [Not relevant to income tax, corporation tax or capital gains tax.]

CIVIL CONTINGENCIES ACT 2004

29   [Not relevant to income tax, corporation tax or capital gains tax.]

SERIOUS ORGANISED CRIME AND POLICE ACT 2005

30   [Amending provision not reproduced.]

TRIBUNALS, COURTS AND ENFORCEMENT ACT 2007

31-37   [Amending provisions not reproduced.]

LEGAL SERVICES ACT 2007

38-39   [Not relevant to income tax, corporation tax or capital gains tax.]

PLANNING ACT 2008

40   [Not relevant to income tax, corporation tax or capital gains tax.]

PUBLIC BODIES ACT 2011

41   [Not relevant to income tax, corporation tax or capital gains tax.]

CHILDREN'S HEARINGS (SCOTLAND) ACT 2011

42   [Not relevant to income tax, corporation tax or capital gains tax.]

THE NATIONAL HEALTH SERVICE (SERVICE COMMITTEES AND TRIBUNAL) REGULATIONS 1992

43-46   [Not relevant to income tax, corporation tax or capital gains tax.]

THE DEREGULATION (MODEL APPEAL PROVISIONS) ORDER 1996

47   [Not relevant to income tax, corporation tax or capital gains tax.]

THE SCOTLAND ACT 1998 (CROSS-BORDER PUBLIC AUTHORITIES) (SPECIFICATION) ORDER 1999

48-49   [Not relevant to income tax, corporation tax or capital gains tax.]

THE SCOTLAND ACT 1998 (CROSS-BORDER PUBLIC AUTHORITIES) (ADAPTATION OF FUNCTIONS ETC.) ORDER 1999

50-51 [Not relevant to income tax, corporation tax or capital gains tax.]

THE SEEDS (NATIONAL LISTS OF VARIETIES) REGULATIONS 2001

52 [Not relevant to income tax, corporation tax or capital gains tax.]

THE PAROLE BOARD (SCOTLAND) RULES 2001

53 [Not relevant to income tax, corporation tax or capital gains tax.]

THE LEASEHOLD VALUATION TRIBUNALS (PROCEDURE) (ENGLAND) REGULATIONS 2003

54 [Not relevant to income tax, corporation tax or capital gains tax.]

THE ADJUDICATOR TO HER MAJESTY'S LAND REGISTRY (PRACTICE AND PROCEDURE) RULES 2003

55 [Not relevant to income tax, corporation tax or capital gains tax.]

THE EMPLOYMENT TRIBUNALS (CONSTITUTION AND RULES OF PROCEDURE) REGULATIONS 2004

56 [Not relevant to income tax, corporation tax or capital gains tax.]

THE NATIONAL HEALTH SERVICE (TRIBUNAL) (SCOTLAND) REGULATIONS 2004

57 [Not relevant to income tax, corporation tax or capital gains tax.]

THE PENSION PROTECTION FUND (REVIEW AND RECONSIDERATION OF REVIEWABLE MATTERS) REGULATIONS 2005

58 [Not relevant to income tax, corporation tax or capital gains tax.]

THE PENSION PROTECTION FUND (PPF OMBUDSMAN) ORDER 2005

59 [Not relevant to income tax, corporation tax or capital gains tax.]

THE PENSION PROTECTION FUND (REFERENCE OF REVIEWABLE MATTERS TO THE PPF OMBUDSMAN) REGULATIONS 2005

60 [Not relevant to income tax, corporation tax or capital gains tax.]

THE FINANCIAL ASSISTANCE SCHEME (APPEALS) REGULATIONS 2005

61 [Not relevant to income tax, corporation tax or capital gains tax.]

THE MENTAL HEALTH TRIBUNAL FOR SCOTLAND (PRACTICE AND PROCEDURE) (NO. 2) RULES 2005

62 [Not relevant to income tax, corporation tax or capital gains tax.]

THE RAILWAYS AND OTHER GUIDED TRANSPORT SYSTEMS (SAFETY) REGULATIONS 2006

63 [Not relevant to income tax, corporation tax or capital gains tax.]

THE ADDITIONAL SUPPORT NEEDS TRIBUNALS FOR SCOTLAND (PRACTICE AND PROCEDURE) RULES 2006

64 [Not relevant to income tax, corporation tax or capital gains tax.]

THE NATIONAL HEALTH SERVICE (DISCIPLINE COMMITTEES) (SCOTLAND) REGULATIONS 2006

65 [Not relevant to income tax, corporation tax or capital gains tax.]

THE ADMINISTRATIVE JUSTICE AND TRIBUNALS COUNCIL (LISTED TRIBUNALS) (WALES) ORDER 2007

66 [Not relevant to income tax, corporation tax or capital gains tax.]

THE ADMINISTRATIVE JUSTICE AND TRIBUNALS COUNCIL (LISTED TRIBUNALS) ORDER 2007

67 [Amending provision not reproduced.]

THE ADMINISTRATIVE JUSTICE AND TRIBUNALS COUNCIL (LISTED TRIBUNALS) (SCOTLAND) ORDER 2007

68 [Not relevant to income tax, corporation tax or capital gains tax.]

THE ADJUDICATOR TO HER MAJESTY'S LAND REGISTRY (PRACTICE AND PROCEDURE) (AMENDMENT) RULES 2008

69 [Not relevant to income tax, corporation tax or capital gains tax.]

THE COMPANY NAMES ADJUDICATOR RULES 2008

70 [Not relevant to income tax, corporation tax or capital gains tax.]

THE TRIBUNALS, COURTS AND ENFORCEMENT ACT 2007 (TRANSITIONAL AND CONSEQUENTIAL PROVISIONS) ORDER 2008

71 [Not relevant to income tax, corporation tax or capital gains tax.]

THE TRANSFER OF TRIBUNAL FUNCTIONS ORDER 2008

72 [Not relevant to income tax, corporation tax or capital gains tax.]

THE MENTAL HEALTH TRIBUNAL FOR SCOTLAND (PRACTICE AND PROCEDURE) (NO. 2) AMENDMENT RULES 2008

73 [Not relevant to income tax, corporation tax or capital gains tax.]

THE TRANSFER OF TRIBUNAL FUNCTIONS AND REVENUE AND CUSTOMS APPEALS ORDER 2009

74 [Not relevant to income tax, corporation tax or capital gains tax.]

THE TRANSFER OF TRIBUNAL FUNCTIONS (LANDS TRIBUNAL AND MISCELLANEOUS AMENDMENTS) ORDER 2009

75 [Amending provision not reproduced.]

THE TRANSFER OF FUNCTIONS OF THE CHARITY TRIBUNAL ORDER 2009

76 [Not relevant to income tax, corporation tax or capital gains tax.]

THE TRANSFER OF FUNCTIONS OF THE CONSUMER CREDIT APPEALS TRIBUNAL ORDER 2009

77 [Not relevant to income tax, corporation tax or capital gains tax.]

THE ADMINISTRATIVE JUSTICE AND TRIBUNALS COUNCIL (LISTED TRIBUNALS) (AMENDMENT) ORDER 2009

78 [Not relevant to income tax, corporation tax or capital gains tax.]

THE NATIONAL HEALTH SERVICE (PHARMACEUTICAL SERVICES) (SCOTLAND) REGULATIONS 2009

79   [Not relevant to income tax, corporation tax or capital gains tax.]

THE TRANSFER OF FUNCTIONS OF THE ASYLUM AND IMMIGRATION TRIBUNAL ORDER 2010

80   [Not relevant to income tax, corporation tax or capital gains tax.]

THE TRANSFER OF TRIBUNAL FUNCTIONS ORDER 2010

81   [Amending provision not reproduced.]

THE ROAD TRAFFIC (PARKING ADJUDICATORS) (RENFREWSHIRE COUNCIL) REGULATIONS 2010

82   [Not relevant to income tax, corporation tax or capital gains tax.]

THE TRAIN DRIVING LICENCES AND CERTIFICATES REGULATIONS 2010

83   [Not relevant to income tax, corporation tax or capital gains tax.]

THE ADDITIONAL SUPPORT NEEDS TRIBUNALS FOR SCOTLAND (PRACTICE AND PROCEDURE) AMENDMENT RULES 2010

84   [Not relevant to income tax, corporation tax or capital gains tax.]

THE PAROLE BOARD (SCOTLAND) AMENDMENT RULES 2010

85   [Not relevant to income tax, corporation tax or capital gains tax.]

THE NATIONAL HEALTH SERVICE (DISCIPLINE COMMITTEES) (SCOTLAND) AMENDMENT REGULATIONS 2010

86   [Not relevant to income tax, corporation tax or capital gains tax.]

THE NATIONAL HEALTH SERVICE (TRIBUNAL) (SCOTLAND) AMENDMENT REGULATIONS 2010

87   [Not relevant to income tax, corporation tax or capital gains tax.]

THE RESIDENTIAL PROPERTY TRIBUNAL PROCEDURES AND FEES (ENGLAND) REGULATIONS 2011

88-90   [Not relevant to income tax, corporation tax or capital gains tax.]

THE RAILWAYS AND OTHER GUIDED TRANSPORT SYSTEMS (SAFETY) (AMENDMENT) REGULATIONS 2011

91   [Not relevant to income tax, corporation tax or capital gains tax.]

THE RAILWAYS (INTEROPERABILITY) REGULATIONS 2011

92   [Not relevant to income tax, corporation tax or capital gains tax.]

THE ADDITIONAL SUPPORT NEEDS TRIBUNALS FOR SCOTLAND (DISABILITY CLAIMS PROCEDURE) RULES 2011

93   [Not relevant to income tax, corporation tax or capital gains tax.]

THE ADMINISTRATIVE JUSTICE AND TRIBUNALS COUNCIL (LISTED TRIBUNALS) (SCOTLAND) AMENDMENT ORDER 2011

94   [Not relevant to income tax, corporation tax or capital gains tax.]

THE BUS LANE CONTRAVENTIONS (CHARGES, ADJUDICATION AND ENFORCEMENT) (SCOTLAND) REGULATIONS 2011

95 [Not relevant to income tax, corporation tax or capital gains tax.]

THE ROAD TRAFFIC (PARKING ADJUDICATORS) (EAST AYRSHIRE COUNCIL) REGULATIONS 2012

96 [Not relevant to income tax, corporation tax or capital gains tax.]

THE ROAD TRAFFIC (PARKING ADJUDICATORS) (SOUTH AYRSHIRE COUNCIL) REGULATIONS 2012

97 [Not relevant to income tax, corporation tax or capital gains tax.]

THE RESIDENTIAL PROPERTY TRIBUNAL PROCEDURES AND FEES (WALES) REGULATIONS 2012

98 [Not relevant to income tax, corporation tax or capital gains tax.]

BRB (RESIDUARY) LIMITED (TAX CONSEQUENCES) ORDER 2013

(SI 2013/2242)

Made on 5 September 2013 by the Treasury in exercise of the powers conferred upon them by s. 25 of the Public Bodies Act 2011. Operative from 30 September 2013.

CITATION AND COMMENCEMENT

1 This Order may be cited as the BRB (Residuary) Limited (Tax Consequences) Order 2013 and comes into force on 30th September 2013.

INTERPRETATION

2 In this Order–

"BRB Residuary" means BRB (Residuary) Limited (company registration number 4146505),

"LCR" means London & Continental Railways Limited (company registration number 2966054),

"Network Rail" means Network Rail Infrastructure Limited (company registration number 2904587),

"relevant transfer" means a transfer under a transfer scheme made by the Secretary of State for Transport under section 23 of the Public Bodies Act 2011 transferring property, rights or liabilities from BRB Residuary to the Secretary of State for Transport, LCR, Network Rail or the Rail Safety and Standards Board Limited (company registration number 04655675).

CHARGEABLE GAINS: NO GAIN OR LOSS ON DISPOSAL

3 For the purposes of the Taxation of Chargeable Gains Act 1992–

(a) in relation to a disposal constituted by a relevant transfer to LCR or the Secretary of State for Transport–

(i) the disposal is to be treated in relation to BRB Residuary and LCR as made for a consideration such that no gain or loss accrues to BRB Residuary, and

(ii) for the purposes of any tax provision, sub-paragraph (i) is to be treated as one of the no gain/no loss provisions in section 288(3A) of that Act (meaning of "no gain/no loss provisions"), and

(b) in relation to a disposal constituted by a relevant transfer to Network Rail, section 17 of that Act (disposals and acquisitions treated as made at market value) is not to have effect and the disposal is to be treated as made–

(i) in a case where consideration in money or money's worth is given by Network Rail or on its behalf, for a consideration equal to the amount or value of that consideration, or

(ii) in a case where no such consideration is given, for a consideration of nil.

CAPITAL ALLOWANCES

4(1) For the purposes of allowances and charges provided for by the Capital Allowances Act 2001, where as a result of a relevant transfer part of a property business ("the transferred part") ceases to be carried on by BRB Residuary and is begun to be carried on by LCR–

(a) any allowances that could have been claimed by, or charges that would have been made on, BRB Residuary in relation to the transferred part if BRB Residuary had continued to carry on that part of the business may be claimed by, or will be made on, LCR in relation to the transferred part, and

(b) the amount of any such allowance or charge is to be calculated as if everything done to or by BRB Residuary had been done to or by LCR,

but the relevant transfer to LCR is not to be treated as giving rise to any such allowance or charge.

4(2) For the purposes of paragraph (1)–

(a) the transferred part of the property business is to be treated as a separate property business carried on by LCR and any apportionments of receipts, expenses, assets and liabilities between that business and any other property business of LCR are to be made as may be just and reasonable, and

(b) the proportion of any allowances or charges of BRB Residuary's property business which relate to the transferred part of the property business is to be determined on a just and reasonable basis.

CORPORATION TAX: LOSSES

5(1) For the purposes of computing the profits of a property business under Part 4 of the Corporation Tax Act 2009 (property income), where as a result of a relevant transfer part of a property business ("the transferred part") ceases to be carried on by BRB Residuary and is begun to be carried on by LCR–

(a) any unrelieved loss relating to the transferred part of BRB Residuary's property business is treated as a loss ("the transferred loss") made by LCR in the first accounting period in which it carries on that business, and

(b) the transferred loss is not a "UK property loss" for the purposes of Part 5 of the Corporation Tax Act 2010 (group relief).

5(2) For the purposes of paragraph (1)–

(a) an unrelieved loss is the amount of any loss which–

  (i) cannot be deducted from the total profits of BRB Residuary for the last accounting period in which it carries on the transferred part of the business, and

  (ii) would be available for carry forward to the next accounting period of BRBR under section 62 of the Corporation Tax Act 2010 if BRB Residuary continued to carry on the business, and

(b) the proportion of any loss of BRB Residuary's property business which relates to the transferred part of the property business is to be determined on a just and reasonable basis.

CORPORATION TAX: PROVISIONS

6 For the purposes of corporation tax, where in accordance with generally accepted accounting practice a provision has been recognised in the accounts of BRB Residuary in relation to property, rights or liabilities transferred by a relevant transfer to LCR or the Secretary of State for Transport–

(a) in computing the profits of BRB Residuary, no amount is brought into account in respect of the removal or adjustment of that provision in the accounts as a consequence of the relevant transfer, and

(b) in computing the profits of LCR, no amount is brought into account in respect of a provision recognised in the accounts of LCR in accordance with generally accepted accounting practice in relation to the property, rights or liabilities transferred by the relevant transfer to the extent that an amount has been brought into account as a debit in computing the profits of BRB Residuary in any accounting period in respect of a liability or charge transferred by the relevant transfer.

CORPORATION TAX: LOAN RELATIONSHIPS

7 For the purposes of Part 5 of the Corporation Tax Act 2009 (loan relationships), in relation to a relevant transfer to LCR, BRB Residuary and LCR are to be treated as if they were members of the same group.

STAMP DUTY

8 Stamp duty is not chargeable on an instrument making or executing a relevant transfer to LCR.

REGISTERED PENSION SCHEMES AND OVERSEAS PENSION SCHEMES (MISCELLANEOUS AMENDMENTS) REGULATIONS 2013

(SI 2013/2259)

Made on 6 September 2013 by the Commissioners for Her Majesty's Revenue and Customs in exercise of the powers conferred upon them by s. 132 and 133 of the Finance Act 1999 and s. 150(8) and 251 of the Finance Act 2004 and now exercisable by them, s. 169(4), (4A) and (4B) and 282(A1) of that Act, and para. 34B(8) of Sch. 36 to the Finance Act 2008. Operative from 14 October 2013.

CITATION, COMMENCEMENT AND EFFECT

1 These Regulations may be cited as the Registered Pension Schemes and Overseas Pension Schemes (Miscellaneous Amendments) Regulations 2013 and come into force on 14th October 2013.

2 In relation to qualifying recognised overseas pension schemes (QROPS) in existence immediately before 6th April 2012, regulations 7 and 8 have effect from that date.

3 The obligations imposed by regulation 3(1A) of the Pension Schemes (Information Requirements for Qualifying Overseas Pension Schemes, Qualifying Recognised Overseas Pension Schemes and Corresponding Relief) Regulations 2006, substituted by regulation 11 of these Regulations, have effect in relation to five year periods ending on or after 1st April 2015.

4 Regulation 12—

(a) has effect in respect of information relating to payments that are made, or treated as made, on or after 14th October 2013; but

(b) in the case of a payment made by a former QROPS, does not have effect unless the former QROPS ceased to be a QROPS on or after 14th October 2013.

5 Regulations 16 and 20, so far as relating to former QROPS, have effect only in relation a scheme that ceased to be a QROPS on or after 14th October 2013.

TRANSITIONAL PROVISIONS

6(1) Notwithstanding regulation 3(7) of the Registered Pension Schemes (Provision of Information) Regulations 2006 ("the Information Regulations"), the period within which the event report referred to in that regulation must be delivered ends on 12th December 2013 in any case where—

(a) the event occurred on or after 6th April 2012 and before 14th October 2013; and

(b) the requirement to deliver the event report arose only by virtue of the coming into force of regulations 7 and 8 of these Regulations.

6(2) Notwithstanding regulation 11BA(3) of the Information Regulations, the period within which the information specified in regulation 11BA(2) must be provided ends on 12th December 2013 in any case where—

(a) the transfer request was made on or after 6th April 2012 and before 14th October 2013; and

(b) the requirement to provide the information arose only by virtue of the coming into force of regulations 7 and 8 of these Regulations.

6(3) Notwithstanding regulation 11BA(4) of the Information Regulations, the period within which the scheme administrator must send the member notification of the requirements specified in regulation 11BA ends on 12th November 2013 in any case where—

(a) the transfer request was made on or after 6th April 2012 and before 14th October 2013; and

(b) the requirement to provide the information arose only by virtue of the coming into force of regulations 7 and 8 of these Regulations.

6(4) In this regulation **"transfer request"** has the meaning given in regulation 11BA(1) of the Information Regulations.

AMENDMENT OF THE PENSION SCHEMES (CATEGORIES OF COUNTRY AND REQUIREMENTS FOR OVERSEAS PENSION SCHEMES AND RECOGNISED OVERSEAS PENSION SCHEMES) REGULATIONS 2006

7-8 [Amending provisions not reproduced.]

Statutory Instruments

AMENDMENT OF THE PENSION SCHEMES (INFORMATION REQUIREMENTS FOR QUALIFYING OVERSEAS PENSION SCHEMES, QUALIFYING RECOGNISED OVERSEAS PENSION SCHEMES AND CORRESPONDING RELIEF) REGULATIONS 2006

9-21 [Amending provisions not reproduced.]

AMENDMENT OF THE REGISTERED PENSION SCHEMES AND OVERSEAS PENSION SCHEMES (ELECTRONIC COMMUNICATION OF RETURNS AND INFORMATION) REGULATIONS 2006

22-23 [Amending provisions not reproduced.]

AMENDMENT OF THE REGISTERED PENSION SCHEMES ETC (INFORMATION) (PRESCRIBED DESCRIPTIONS OF PERSONS) REGULATIONS 2010

24-26 [Amending provisions not reproduced.]

ANNUAL TAX ON ENVELOPED DWELLINGS AVOIDANCE SCHEMES (PRESCRIBED DESCRIPTIONS OF ARRANGEMENTS) REGULATIONS 2013

(SI 2013/2571)

Made on 9 October 2013 by the Treasury in exercise of the powers conferred upon them by s. 306(1)(a) and 317(2) of the Finance Act 2004. Operative from 4 November 2013.

CITATION, COMMENCEMENT AND INTERPRETATION

1 These Regulations may be cited as the Annual Tax on Enveloped Dwellings Avoidance Schemes (Prescribed Descriptions of Arrangements) Regulations 2013 and come into force on 4th November 2013.

2 In these Regulations–

"**chargeable interest**" has the meaning given by section 107 of the Finance Act 2013;

"**company**" has the meaning given by section 166(1) of the Finance Act 2013;

"**collective investment scheme**" refers to a scheme as described by section 235(1) of the Financial Services and Markets Act 2000; and

"**partnership**" has the meaning given by section 167(1) of the Finance Act 2013.

3 In regulation 4(2)(a) and the Schedule reference to meeting the "**ownership condition**" is to be read in accordance with section 94(4) to (7) of the Finance Act 2013.

PRESCRIBED DESCRIPTION OF ARRANGEMENTS IN RELATION TO ANNUAL TAX ON ENVELOPED DWELLINGS

4(1) For the purposes of Part 7 of the Finance Act 2004 (disclosure of tax avoidance schemes) the arrangements specified in paragraph (2) are prescribed in relation to annual tax on enveloped dwellings.

4(2) Arrangements are prescribed if they are not excluded arrangements under the Schedule and as a result of any element of the arrangements–

(a) a company, partnership or collective investment scheme ceases to meet the ownership condition in respect of the chargeable interest;

(b) the taxable value of the chargeable interest is reduced to £2 million or less; or

(c) the taxable value of the chargeable interest is reduced with the consequence that a lower annual chargeable amount applies than that which otherwise would have applied.

4(3) In this regulation–

(a) reference to a lower annual chargeable amount applying is to be read in accordance with the table at section 99(4) of the Finance Act 2013; and

(b) reference to "**taxable value**" is to be read in accordance with section 102 of the Finance Act 2013.

Cross references – SI 2013/2592: relevant date for the purposes of FA 2004, s. 308(1) and date for the purposes of FA 2004, s. 308(3) in relation to proposals or arrangements that are notifiable by virtue of reg. 4.

SCHEDULE – EXCLUDED ARRANGEMENTS

Regulation 4(2)

Arrangements are excluded arrangements if they comprise a transfer of the chargeable interest from a company, partnership or collective investment scheme (a "transferor") to a transferee where one or more of the following applies.

(1) The transfer is on such terms as would reasonably be expected to be agreed between unconnected persons.

(2) The transferor and the transferee are members of the same group of companies and the transferee meets the ownership condition.

(3) The transfer constitutes a distribution out of the assets of the transferor, and the transferee is an individual, a corporation sole, a trustee or a person who meets the ownership condition.

(4) The transfer constitutes a settlement.

In paragraph 1 reference to being **"unconnected persons"** is to be read in accordance with section 1122 of the Corporation Tax Act 2010.

In paragraph 2 reference to companies being **"members of the same group of companies"** is to be read in accordance with section 152 of the Corporation Tax Act 2010.

In paragraph 4 **"settlement"** has the meaning given by section 43 of the Inheritance Tax Act 1984.

TAX AVOIDANCE SCHEMES (INFORMATION) (AMENDMENT, ETC) REGULATIONS 2013

(SI 2013/2592)

Made on 9 October 2013 by the Commissioners for Her Majesty's Revenue and Customs in exercise of the powers conferred upon them by s. 132 of the Finance Act 1999 and s. 308(1) and (3), 312B(2), 313(1), (3)(a) and (3)(b), 313ZA(3), 313ZB(2), 313ZB(3)(a), 317(2) and s. 318(1) of the Finance Act 2004. Operative from 4 November 2013.

CITATION AND COMMENCEMENT

1 These Regulations may be cited as the Tax Avoidance Schemes (Information) (Amendment, etc) Regulations 2013 and come into force on 4th November 2013.

TIME FOR PROVIDING INFORMATION: TRANSITIONAL PROVISIONS

2(1) Where paragraph (2) applies, the period or time (as the case may be) to be found in accordance with regulation 5 of the Tax Avoidance Schemes (Information) Regulations 2012 shall end on 17th January 2014 instead of the day on which it would otherwise end by virtue of that regulation.

2(2) This paragraph applies in respect of proposals or arrangements (as the case may be) that are notifiable by virtue of regulation 4 of the Annual Tax on Enveloped Dwellings Avoidance Schemes (Prescribed Descriptions of Arrangements) Regulations 2013 where–

(a)   for the purposes of section 308(1) of the Finance Act 2004, the relevant date in relation to a proposal falls within the period beginning with 31st January 2013 and ending on 3rd November 2013; or

(b)   for the purposes of section 308(3) of the Finance Act 2004, the date on which the promoter first becomes aware of any transaction forming part of the arrangements falls within the period beginning with 31st January 2013 and ending on 3rd November 2013.

AMENDMENTS TO THE TAX AVOIDANCE SCHEMES (INFORMATION) REGULATIONS 2012

3 The Tax Avoidance Schemes (Information) Regulations 2012 are amended as follows.

ANNUAL TAX ON ENVELOPED DWELLINGS

4-14 [Amending provisions not reproduced.]

SECTIONS 312B AND 313ZB

15-20 [Amending provisions not reproduced.]

UNAUTHORISED UNIT TRUSTS (TAX) REGULATIONS 2013

(SI 2013/2819 as amended by SI 2014/585 and SI 2014/685)

Made on 31 October 2013 by the Treasury, in exercise of the powers conferred by s. 217 of the Finance Act 2013. Operative in accordance with reg. 1(2) and (3).

PART 1 – INTRODUCTORY AND GENERAL PROVISIONS

CITATION, COMMENCEMENT AND EFFECT

Other material – HMRC Technical note: changes to the tax rules for unauthorised unit trusts and their investors.

1(1) These Regulations may be cited as the Unauthorised Unit Trusts (Tax) Regulations 2013.

1(2) Chapters 1 and 2 of Part 2 and Chapter 1 of Part 4 (and this Part so far as applying to those Chapters) come into force on the day after the day on which these Regulations are made.

1(3) Apart from that, these Regulations come into force on 6th April 2014.

INTERPRETATION

2 In these Regulations–

"**the AIF Regulations**" means the Authorised Investment Funds (Tax) Regulations 2006,

"**the Commissioners**" means the Commissioners for Her Majesty's Revenue and Customs,

"**eligible investor**" has the meaning given by regulation 3(2),

"**exempt unauthorised unit trust**" has the meaning given by regulation 3(1),

"**friendly society**" has the same meaning it has for the purposes of Part 3 of FA 2012 (friendly societies carrying on long-term business),

"**insurance company**" has the same meaning as it has for the purposes of Part 2 of FA 2012 (insurance companies carrying on long-term business),

"**non-reporting fund**" has the same meaning as it has for the purposes of the Offshore Funds Regulations,

"**notice**" means notice in writing,

"**the Offshore Funds Regulations**" means the Offshore Funds (Tax) Regulations 2009,

"**prospectus**" means a prospectus or similar document made available to investors,

"**UK resident**" means resident in the United Kingdom (and references to a UK resident company are to a company which is resident there).

PART 2 – EXEMPT UNAUTHORISED UNIT TRUSTS

Chapter 1 – Meaning of "Exempt Unauthorised Unit Trust"

MEANING OF "EXEMPT UNAUTHORISED UNIT TRUST"

3(1) For the purposes of these Regulations an unauthorised unit trust is an "**exempt unauthorised unit trust**" with respect to a period of account if–

(a)   its trustees are UK resident for the period,

(b)   throughout the period all of its unit holders are eligible investors,

(c)   it is approved under these Regulations for the period, and

(d)   it is not treated by regulations made in exercise of the powers conferred by section 1007(2) of ITA 2007 as not being a unit trust scheme for the purposes of the definition of "unauthorised unit trust" in section 989 of that Act.

3(2) For the purposes of these Regulations a unit holder is an "**eligible investor**" if–

(a)   any gain accruing in the event of a disposal of its units would be wholly exempt from capital gains tax or corporation tax (otherwise than by reason of residence), or

(b)   it holds all of its units pending disposal in the capacity of manager of the unauthorised unit trust.

3(3)   In determining whether paragraph (2)(a) applies no account is to be taken of the possibility of a charge to corporation tax on income in respect of a gain accruing on a disposal by an insurance company or a friendly society.

3(4)   An unauthorised unit trust is not to be regarded as failing to meet the condition in paragraph (1)(b) in relation to any unit holder if–

(a)   the managers or trustees of the unit trust become aware at any time that the unit holder is not an eligible investor,

(b)   they could not reasonably have been expected to have become aware of that fact before that time, and

(c)   the unit holder disposes of its units before the end of the period of 28 days beginning with that time.

3(5)   Paragraph (4) may not be relied on more than twice in any period of ten years.

History – In reg. 3(1), the word "and" at the end of para. (b) omitted by SI 2014/585, reg. 3(a), with effect from 6 April 2014. Reg. 3(1)(d) inserted by SI 2014/585, reg. 3(b), with effect from 6 April 2014.

Chapter 2 – Approval as an Exempt Unauthorised Unit Trust

APPLICATION FOR APPROVAL AS AN EXEMPT UNAUTHORISED UNIT TRUST

4(1)   The managers or trustees of an unauthorised unit trust may make an application in writing to the Commissioners for the trust ("the applicant") to be approved.

4(2)   An application must be made on or before the last day of the first period of account for which approval is sought (or such later date as the Commissioners may allow).

4(3)   If accepted, an approval has effect for the period of account the first day of which is specified in the application and all subsequent periods (unless withdrawn under regulation 8).

4(4)   The Commissioners may not approve an unauthorised unit trust unless they are satisfied that the unit trust has, or will have, in place appropriate arrangements for the purpose of securing that the condition in regulation 3(1)(b) is met.

CONTENTS OF APPLICATION

5(1)   An application under this Chapter must contain the following–

(a)   a statement specifying the first day of the first period of account for which approval is sought (such period ending no earlier than 6 April 2014),

(b)   a copy of the applicant's current trust deed,

(c)   a copy of the applicant's most recent prospectus,

(d)   a statement specifying the appropriate arrangements which are or will be in place for the purpose of securing that the condition in regulation 3(1)(b) is and will be met for the first period for which approval is sought and all subsequent periods,

(e)   a statement whether or not the applicant is or will be operating equalisation arrangements.

5(2)   A day specified in the application in paragraph (1)(a) may be provisional.

5(3)   If a provisional day is specified in the application, any approval by the Commissioners of the application has no effect unless the managers or trustees of the applicant give notice to the Commissioners either–

(a)   confirming that day is the first day of the first period of account for which approval is sought, or

(b)   specifying a different day as the first day of the first period of account for which approval is sought.

5(4)   The notice must be given no later than the date on or before which a return made under section 8A of TMA 1970 relating to the first period must be delivered.

5(5)   If a different day is specified under paragraph (3)(b), the application is to be treated for the purposes of regulation 4(3) as if that day had always been specified in the application.

RESPONSE BY THE COMMISSIONERS TO APPLICATION

6(1)   The Commissioners may by notice require the managers or trustees of the applicant to provide further particulars in order to enable them to determine an application.

6(2) A requirement may be imposed under paragraph (1) within 28 days of the receipt of the application or of any further particulars required under that paragraph.

6(3) If a notice under paragraph (1) is not complied with within 28 days or such longer period as the Commissioners may allow, they need not proceed further on the application.

6(4) The Commissioners must give notice to the applicant of their decision to accept or reject an application—

(a)   within 28 days of receiving the application, or

(b)   if they give a notice under paragraph (2), within 28 days of that notice being complied with.

6(5) A notice of a decision to reject an application must give reasons for that decision.

CONTINUING REQUIREMENTS FOR APPROVAL

7(1) Approval under this Chapter is conditional on the requirements in this regulation being met by the unauthorised unit trust with respect to a period of account.

7(2) Appropriate arrangements must be in place for the purpose of securing that the condition in regulation 3(1)(b) is met for the period.

7(3) The period of account of the unauthorised unit trust must not exceed 18 months.

7(4) The accounts for the period—

(a)   must be prepared in accordance with the IMA SORP or its principles so far as relating to determining revenue and capital, and

(b)   must be audited by a qualified independent auditor as being so prepared.

7(5) In the following provisions of this Part references to accounts of an exempt unauthorised unit trust are to accounts meeting the conditions in paragraph (4).

7(6) The managers or trustees of the trust must deliver with a return made under section 8A of TMA 1970—

(a)   a statement from the managers or the trustees that the condition in regulation 3(1)(b) has been met throughout the period, and

(b)   a copy of the trust's accounts.

7(7) In this regulation—

(a)   **"the IMA SORP"** means the Investment Management Association's Statement of Recommended Practice for the Financial Statements of Authorised Funds published in October 2010 as amended from time to time (or any successor statement of recommended practice), and

(b)   **"qualified independent auditor"** means a person who—

    (i)   is eligible for appointment as a statutory auditor under Part 42 of the Companies Act 2006, and

    (ii)   if the appointment were an appointment as a statutory auditor, would not be prohibited from acting by section 1214 of that Act (independence requirement).

WITHDRAWAL OF APPROVAL

8(1) The Commissioners may withdraw approval of an exempt unauthorised unit trust if they are satisfied that the requirements in regulation 7 are not met.

8(2) The Commissioners may withdraw approval of an exempt unauthorised unit trust if the managers or trustees of an exempt unauthorised unit trust request them to do so.

8(3) Withdrawal of an approval of an unauthorised unit trust is to be given by the Commissioners by notice to the managers or trustees of the trust.

8(4) Withdrawal of approval has effect as from the date specified in the notice withdrawing the approval.

APPEAL AGAINST REJECTION OF APPLICATION OR WITHDRAWAL OF APPROVAL

9(1) An unauthorised unit trust may appeal if an application is rejected or the Commissioners withdraw approval.

9(2) The notice of appeal must be given to the Commissioners within a period of 42 days beginning with the day on which the notice of rejection or withdrawal is given.

9(3) On an appeal, the tribunal may make a decision to uphold or quash the rejection or withdrawal.

9(4) If the tribunal decides to quash a rejection of an application, these Regulations apply as if the Commissioners had accepted the application in the form in which it was considered by the tribunal.

9(5) If the tribunal decides to quash the withdrawal of approval, these Regulations apply as if the Commissioners had not withdrawn their approval.

Chapter 3 – Gains Accruing to an Exempt Unauthorised Unit Trust

EXEMPTION FOR GAINS ACCRUING TO AN EXEMPT UNAUTHORISED UNIT TRUST

10 Gains accruing to an exempt unauthorised unit trust are not chargeable gains for the purposes of TCGA 1992.

Chapter 4 – Taxation of Income of Exempt Unauthorised Unit Trusts

BASIS PERIODS

11(1) The income of an exempt unauthorised unit trust for a tax year is taken to be the income of the exempt unauthorised unit trust arising in a basis period for the tax year.

11(2) The general rule is that the basis period for a tax year for an exempt unauthorised unit trust is the period of 12 months ending with the accounting date in that year.

11(3) The accounting date, in relation to a tax year, means–

(a)   the date in the tax year to which accounts are drawn up, or

(b)   if there are two or more such dates, the latest of them.

11(4) If there is no accounting date in the first tax year that the trust is an exempt unauthorised unit trust but there is an accounting date in the following tax year–

(a)   there is no basis period for the first tax year (so that the trust has no income for that year), but

(b)   the basis period for the following year is the period of account ending with the accounting date in that year.

11(5) If there is no accounting date in the first two tax years that the trust is an exempt unauthorised unit trust–

(a)   there is no basis period for the first tax year (so that the trust has no income for that year), but

(b)   the basis period for the second tax year is the period beginning on the first date of the period of account and ending on the 5 April in that year.

11(6) Otherwise, if there is no accounting date in the tax year, the basis period is the period of 12 months beginning immediately after the end of the basis period for the previous tax year.

11(7) If the basis period for a tax year does not coincide with a period of account of an exempt unauthorised unit trust, either of the steps in paragraph (8) must be taken if necessary in order to arrive at the amount of the income of the trust treated under regulation 14 as if it were accrued income profits arising in a basis period.

11(8) The steps are–

(a)   apportioning the income of a period of account to the parts of that period falling in different basis periods, and

(b)   adding the income of a period of account (or part of a period) to the income of other periods of account (or parts),

and the steps must be taken by reference to the number of days in the periods concerned.

TREATMENT OF INCOME OF AN EXEMPT UNAUTHORISED UNIT TRUST

12(1) If income arises to the trustees of an exempt unauthorised unit trust, the income is treated as the income of the trustees and not of the unit holders.

12(2) If income tax on any part of the income arising to the trustees of an exempt unauthorised unit trust would apart from this paragraph be charged at the dividend ordinary rate, income tax on that part of the income is instead charged at the basic rate.

12(3) None of the following applies in relation to the income–

(a) sections 397(1) and 397A(1) of ITTOIA 2005 (tax credits for qualifying distributions),

(b) section 399(2) and (6) of ITTOIA 2005 (person not entitled to tax credits treated as having paid income tax),

(c) section 400(2) and (3) of ITTOIA 2005 (person whose income includes non-qualifying distribution treated as having paid income tax), and

(d) section 479 of ITA 2007 (trustees' accumulated or discretionary income to be charged at special rates).

12(4) Sections 494, 495 and 496B of ITA 2007 (discretionary payments) do not apply in relation to payments made by the trustees.

TREATMENT OF CAPITAL EXPENDITURE OF AN EXEMPT UNAUTHORISED UNIT TRUST

13 The trustees (and not the unit holders) of an exempt unauthorised unit trust are treated as the persons to or on whom an allowance or charge is to be made under any provision relating to relief for capital expenditure.

SPECIAL PROVISION FOR ACCRUED INCOME PROFITS

14(1) This regulation applies to income of an exempt unauthorised unit trust which–

(a) arises from its investments in securities within the meaning of Chapter 2 of Part 12 of ITA 2007 (accrued income profits), and

(b) is shown in its accounts.

14(2) The income is charged to tax under Chapter 2 of Part 12 of ITA 2007–

(a) as if it were accrued income profits, and

(b) as if those profits were treated as made in the tax year in which the last day of the period of account in which the income is accounted for falls.

14(3) None of the income is charged to income tax under Chapter 2 of Part 4 of ITTOIA 2005 (interest).

Chapter 5 – Charge to Tax on Unit Holders of Exempt Unauthorised Unit Trusts

CHARGE TO TAX ON UNIT HOLDERS

15(1) Tax is charged on income treated as received by a unit holder from an exempt unauthorised unit trust in the tax year.

15(2) For the purposes of this regulation, unit holders are treated as receiving income if an amount is shown in the trust's accounts for a period of account as income available for payment to them or for investment.

15(3) The income is treated as received by a unit holder for a distribution period.

15(4) To calculate the amount of the income treated as received by a unit holder for a distribution period, calculate the unit holder's share of the trust's available income by applying the formula–

$$\text{TAI} \times \frac{R}{TR}$$

where–

TAI is the total amount shown in the trust's accounts as income available for payment to unit holders or for investment,

R is the unit holder's rights, and

TR is all the unit holders' rights.

15(5) The income for a distribution period is treated as received on the date or latest date provided by the terms of the trust for any distribution for the period, unless that date is more than 12 months after it ends.

15(6) If–

(a) that date is more than 12 months after the distribution period ends; or

(b) no date is so provided,

the income for the period is treated as received on the last day of the period.

15(7) If the terms of the trust provide for a period over which income from the investments subject to the trust is aggregated to ascertain the amount available for distribution to unit holders, the **"distribution period"** means–

(a) if the period is 12 months or less, that period, or

(b) if the period is more than 12 months, each successive period of 12 months within that period and any remaining period of less than 12 months.

15(8) In any other case, the **"distribution period"** means successive periods of 12 months, the first of which begins with the day on which the trust was established.

PERSON LIABLE

16 The person liable for any tax charged under this Chapter is the unit holder treated as receiving the income.

PRIORITY RULES

17(1) Any income, so far as it falls within–

(a) regulation 15, and

(b) Chapter 2 of Part 2 of ITTOIA 2005 or Chapter 2 of Part 3 of CTA 2009 (income taxed as trade profits),

is dealt with under Part 2 of ITTOIA 2005 or Part 3 of CTA 2009.

17(2) Any income, so far as it falls within–

(a) regulation 15, and

(b) Chapter 3 of Part 3 of ITTOIA 2005, or Chapter 3 of Part 4 of CTA 2009, so far as relating to a UK property business,

is dealt with under Part 3 of ITTOIA 2005 or Part 4 of CTA 2009.

Chapter 6 – Relief for Trustees of an Exempt Unauthorised Unit Trust

RELIEF FOR DEEMED PAYMENTS BY TRUSTEES OF AN EXEMPT UNAUTHORISED UNIT TRUST

18(1) If the unit holders of an exempt unauthorised unit trust are treated as receiving income under regulation 15(2), the trustees are treated as making a deemed payment of the same amount on the final day of the period of account referred to in regulation 15(2).

18(2) The trustees are entitled to relief for a tax year equal to the amount of the deemed payments treated as made in that year.

18(3) The relief is given by deducting that amount in calculating the trustees' net income for the tax year (see Step 2 of the calculation in section 23 of ITA 2007 (calculation of income tax liability)).

18(4) The total amount of the relief for a tax year must not exceed the amount of the trustees' modified net income for the tax year.

18(5) If there is an excess, that excess is to be treated as if it were a deemed payment in the basis period for the following tax year.

18(6) In this regulation **"modified net income"** has the meaning given by section 1025 of ITA 2007 but as if for subsection (2)(c) there were substituted–

"(c) any relief to which the person may be entitled under regulation 18 of the Unauthorised Unit Trusts (Tax) Regulations 2013,".

Statutory Instruments

AMOUNTS INELIGIBLE FOR RELIEF UNDER REGULATION 18

19(1) Relief is not to be given under regulation 18 for any part of a deemed payment so far as it is ineligible for relief.

19(2) In determining the extent (if any) to which the payment is ineligible for relief section 450 of ITA 2007 (payments ineligible for relief) applies in relation to the payment as that section applies in relation to a payment to which section 449 of that Act applies.

AMOUNTS INELIGIBLE FOR RELIEF UNDER REGULATION 18: PAYMENTS TO CERTAIN UNIT HOLDERS WHERE REGULATION 3(4) APPLIES

20 Relief is not to be given under regulation 18 for any part of a deemed payment so far as it is attributable to income treated as received by a unit holder under regulation 15 where the unit holder–

(a)   disposed of its units in the circumstances described in regulation 3(4)(c), and

(b)   was not UK resident at the time the income is treated as received.

EFFECT OF EQUALISATION ARRANGEMENTS ON RELIEF FOR TRUSTEES

21(1) This regulation applies to an exempt unauthorised unit trust which operates equalisation arrangements in the case of a disposal of units by way of either cancellation or acquisition by the managers of the trust.

21(2) The amount of the deemed payment for which the trustees are entitled to relief for a tax year under regulation 18 includes any amount paid to unit holders (in the basis period for the year) on a disposal of some or all of their units so far as attributable to the income of the trust which has accrued up to the date of the disposal (but has not otherwise been received, or treated as received, by unit holders).

Chapter 7 – Miscellaneous Provisions

NO TAX CHARGE FOR DISPOSAL OF INTERESTS IN OFFSHORE NON-REPORTING FUNDS: REPORTING CONDITION

22(1) No tax is charged on the trustees of an exempt unauthorised unit trust under regulation 17 of the Offshore Funds Regulations on the disposal of an interest in a non-reporting fund if the reporting condition is met.

22(2) The reporting condition is met if–

(a)   the trustees prepare computations of reportable income for the fund for all accounting periods which, if the fund were a reporting fund, would be reporting periods ending on or before the day of disposal, and

(b)   any excess of the trustees' share of the reportable income of the non-reporting fund over their share of the distributions made by the non-reporting fund is included in the amount mentioned in regulation 15(2) for each period of account ending on or before that day.

22(3) Nothing in paragraph (2) applies in relation to any time before the date on which the trustees acquire or re-acquire the interest.

22(4) The trustees are treated for all purposes as if they had disposed of and immediately reacquired an interest in a non-reporting fund on a date they specify if in the event of a subsequent disposal of the interest–

(a)   the reporting condition would not be met in relation to times before the date, but

(b)   the trustees reasonably expect the reporting condition will be met in relation to times on and after the date.

22(5) The date the trustees specify must be included in an appropriate entry in their return made under section 8A of TMA 1970 for the period of account in which the date falls but the date must not be earlier than 6 April 2014.

22(6) The deemed disposal and reacquisition of the interest is taken to be for a consideration equal to its market value on the specified date.

22(7) In this regulation–

"**market value**" has the meaning given by regulation 10 of the Offshore Funds Regulations,

"**reporting fund**" has the meaning given by regulation 50 of those Regulations, and

"**reporting period**" has the meaning given by regulation 91 of those Regulations.

22(8) If a non-reporting fund is a UCITS fund for the purposes of regulation 12 of the Offshore Funds Regulations, regulation 80 of those regulations (treatment of investment transactions carried out by diversely owned funds) applies for the purposes of the computations mentioned in paragraph (2)(a).

NO TAX CHARGE FOR DISPOSAL OF INTERESTS IN OFFSHORE NON-REPORTING FUNDS: QUALIFYING INDEX

23(1) No tax is charged on the trustees of an exempt unauthorised unit trust under regulation 17 of the Offshore Funds Regulations on the disposal of an interest in a non-reporting fund if–

(a) in accordance with the trust's investment strategy contained in its prospectus, the aim of the trust throughout the period during which the trustees held the interest has been to replicate the performance of a qualifying index,

(b) the main purpose of the investment in the non-reporting fund throughout that period is to represent the composition of the qualifying index, and

(c) the capital and income returns of the trust throughout that period replicated as closely as practicable the returns of the investment comprised in the qualifying index.

23(2) For the purposes of this regulation an index is a **"qualifying index"** if–

(a) it is based solely on the value of securities listed on a recognised stock exchange or admitted to trading on a regulated market,

(b) an authority (whether in the United Kingdom or elsewhere) recognises the index on the basis that–

    (i) its composition is sufficiently diverse,

    (ii) it represents an adequate benchmark for the market to which it refers, and

    (iii) it is published in such a way that it is widely available, and

(c) it is calculated and published by a body which is managed independently from the management of the exempt unauthorised unit trust.

23(3) In this regulation **"regulated market"** has the same meaning as in Directive 2004/39/EC of the European Parliament and of the Council on markets in financial instruments.

TREATMENT OF INVESTMENT TRANSACTIONS CARRIED OUT BY EXEMPT UNAUTHORISED UNIT TRUSTS

24(1) An investment transaction entered into by the trustees of an exempt unauthorised unit trust is treated for the purposes of the Income Tax Acts as entered into otherwise than in the course of a trade.

24(2) For the purposes of paragraph (1) an **"investment transaction"** is an investment transaction specified by regulation 2 of the Investment Transactions (Tax) Regulations 2014.

History – Reg. 24(2) substituted by SI 2014/685, reg. 10, with effect from transactions entered into on or after 8 April 2014. Former reg. 24(2) read as follows:

"**24(2)** **"Investment transaction"** has the same meaning as it has in Part 3 of the Investment Trust (Approved Company) (Tax) Regulations 2011, but as if–
(a) references to an investment trust were to an exempt unauthorised unit trust, and
(b) references to the manager of the investment trust were to the managers or trustees of the exempt unauthorised unit trust."

AUTHORISED INVESTMENT FUNDS INVESTING IN EXEMPT UNAUTHORISED UNIT TRUSTS

25 If an authorised investment fund (within the meaning given by the AIF Regulations) is at any time in a period of account a unit holder of an exempt unauthorised unit trust, the following provisions of CTA 2010 do not apply in relation to the fund for any financial year in which that period (or any part of it) falls–

(a) Part 3 (relief for companies with small profits), and

(b) sections 614 and 618 (applicable corporation tax rate),

(and, accordingly, the rate of corporation tax which applies in relation to the fund is the main rate within the meaning of section 3 of CTA 2010).

STATEMENTS ABOUT INCOME TREATED AS RECEIVED BY UNIT HOLDERS

26 A unit holder of an exempt unauthorised unit trust is entitled by notice to require the trustees of the trust to provide the unit holder with a statement in writing showing the amount of income treated as received by the unit holder for a distribution period under regulation 15.

PART 3 – NON-EXEMPT UNAUTHORISED UNIT TRUSTS

Chapter 1 – Definition of Non-Exempt Unauthorised Unit Trust

DEFINITION OF NON-EXEMPT UNAUTHORISED UNIT TRUST

27 An unauthorised unit trust is a **"non-exempt unauthorised unit trust"** if it is not–

(a)   an exempt unauthorised unit trust, or

(b)   treated by regulations made in exercise of the powers conferred by section 1007(2) of ITA 2007 as not being a unit trust scheme for the purposes of the definition of "unauthorised unit trust" in section 989 of that Act.

History – In reg. 27, the words from "not" (to the end) substituted and para. (a) and (b) inserted by SI 2014/585, reg. 4, with effect from 6 April 2014.

Chapter 2 – Tax Treatment of Non-Exempt Unauthorised Unit Trusts

NON-EXEMPT UNAUTHORISED UNIT TRUST TREATED AS UK RESIDENT COMPANY

28(1) In respect of income arising and chargeable gains accruing to UK resident trustees of a non-exempt unauthorised unit trust, and for the purposes of the provisions relating to relief for capital expenditure, the Tax Acts have effect as if–

(a)   the trustees were a UK resident company, and

(b)   the rights of the unit holders were shares in the company.

28(2) References in the Corporation Tax Acts to a body corporate are to be read in accordance with paragraph (1); and sections 1104 and 1107 of CTA 2010 (companies and nominees required to provide tax certificates) apply with any necessary modifications.

PART 3 OF CTA 2010 NOT TO APPLY TO NON-EXEMPT UNAUTHORISED UNIT TRUSTS

29 Part 3 of CTA 2010 (relief for companies with small profits) does not apply in relation to a non-exempt unauthorised unit trust.

APPLICATION OF SECTION 490 OF CTA 2009 TO NON-EXEMPT UNAUTHORISED UNIT TRUSTS

29A Section 490 of CTA 2009 does not apply to any rights held by a company under a non-exempt unauthorised unit trust scheme.

History – Reg. 29A and the heading immediately preceding it inserted by SI 2014/585, reg. 5, with effect from 6 April 2014.

PART 4 – TRANSITIONAL PROVISIONS

Chapter 1 – Transitional Provisions for Exempt Unauthorised Unit Trusts

TRANSITIONAL YEAR FOR EXEMPT UNAUTHORISED UNIT TRUSTS

30(1) This regulation applies in the case of a trust–

(a)   which was an unauthorised unit trust immediately before 6 April 2014, and

(b)   which is approved as an exempt unauthorised unit trust for a period including 6 April 2014.

30(2) For the purposes of this regulation a trust's **"transitional year"** is–

(a) the tax year 2013–14, where the trust has an accounting date in the tax year 2013–14 on or after the day after these Regulations are made, or

(b) the tax year 2014–15, where the trust either has an accounting date in the tax year 2013–14 before the day after these Regulations are made or has no accounting date in the tax year 2013–14.

30(3) In a tax year which is a trust's transitional year, the income of the trust for that tax year is taken to be the income arising in the period beginning with 6 April and ending with the accounting date in that year.

30(4) If a trust's transitional year is the tax year 2014–15, regulation 7(4), Chapters 3 to 7 of Part 2 and Parts 3 and 5 do not apply in relation to the trust for that year.

30(5) A transitional year does not count for the purposes of determining the first or second tax year that a trust is an exempt unauthorised unit trust under regulation 11(4) or (5).

30(6) Any deemed payment or deemed deduction which would (but for this regulation) have been treated as made by the trustees under section 941 of ITA 2007 after the accounting date of the transitional year of the trust is treated as made on that accounting date.

30(7) Any income of the trust which–

(a) is shown in the trust's accounts for its transitional year as available for payment to unit holders or for investment, and

(b) would (but for this regulation) arise to the trustees in a tax year later than the transitional year,

is treated as arising to the trustees in the trust's transitional year.

30(8) For the purposes of this regulation, the accounting date, in relation to a tax year, means–

(a) the date in the tax year to which accounts are drawn up, or

(b) if there are two or more such dates, the latest of them.

Chapter 2 – Transitional Provisions for Non-Exempt Unauthorised Unit Trusts

UNAUTHORISED UNIT TRUSTS COMING WITHIN CHARGE TO CORPORATION TAX: FINAL DEEMED PAYMENTS AND ACCRUED INCOME PROFITS

31(1) In the case of an unauthorised unit trust which comes within the charge to corporation tax on 6 April 2014 or a later date, any amount of income which would (but for this regulation) have been treated under–

(a) Chapter 10 of Part 4 of ITTOIA 2005, or

(b) Chapter 5 of Part 10 of CTA 2009,

as received by its unit holders on or after 6 April 2014 or that later date is treated as received on 5 April 2014 or, as the case may be, the day before that later date (and, accordingly, the trustees are treated as making a deemed payment under section 941 of ITA 2007 in respect of that income on the same day).

31(2) Any income of the trust which would (but for this regulation) be included in the amount of accrued income profits treated under Part 12 of ITA 2007 as made on or after 6 April 2014 or a later date, is included in the amount of accrued income profits treated under that Part as made on 5 April 2014 or, as the case may be, the day before that later date.

PART 5 NOT TO APPLY TO MIXED UNAUTHORISED UNIT TRUSTS

32(1) An unauthorised unit trust is not a non-exempt unauthorised unit trust, and Part 5 does not apply in relation to the trust, if at all times in the period beginning with 24 May 2012 and ending with 5 April 2014 it had at least one unit holder which was, and at least one unit holder which was not, an eligible investor.

32(2) But paragraph (1) ceases to apply in relation to the trust if subsequently it no longer has any unit holders which are eligible investors.

Statutory Instruments

PART 5 – REPEALS AND CONSEQUENTIAL AMENDMENTS

CHEVENING ESTATE ACT 1959

33 [Not relevant to income tax, corporation tax or capital gains tax.]

TCGA 1992

34 [Amending provisions not reproduced.]

FINANCE ACT 2000

35 [Amending provisions not reproduced.]

ITTOIA 2005

36 [Amending provisions not reproduced.]

ITA 2007

37 [Amending provisions not reproduced.]

CTA 2009

38 [Amending provisions not reproduced.]

CTA 2010

39 [Amending provisions not reproduced.]

FA 2012

40 [Amending provisions not reproduced.]

CONSEQUENTIAL REPEALS OF OTHER ENACTMENTS

41 [Amending provisions not reproduced.]

AIF REGULATIONS

42 [Amending provisions not reproduced.]

OFFSHORE FUNDS REGULATIONS

43 [Amending provisions not reproduced.]

TAX TREATMENT OF FINANCING COSTS AND INCOME (EXCLUDED SCHEMES) REGULATIONS 2013

(SI 2013/2892)

Made on 11 November 2013 by the Commissioners for Her Majesty's Revenue and Customs, in exercise of the powers conferred by s. 312(2) and (3) of the Taxation (International and Other Provisions) Act 2010. Operative from 4 December 2013.

INTRODUCTORY PROVISIONS

Citation, commencement, effect and interpretation

1(1) These Regulations may be cited as the Tax Treatment of Financing Costs and Income (Excluded Schemes) Regulations 2013 and come into force on 4th December 2013.

1(2) These Regulations have effect in relation to schemes entered into on or after that date.

1(3) In these Regulations–

"**finance arrangement**" has the meaning given by section 328 of TIOPA;

"**group treasury company**" has the same meaning as in section 316(2) of TIOPA;

"**relevant liability**" shall be construed in accordance with section 263(3) of TIOPA;

"**TIOPA**" means the Taxation (International and Other Provisions) Act 2010.

EXCLUDED SCHEMES IN RELATION TO A LARGE GROUP

Excluded schemes for the purposes of the application of Part 7 of TIOPA to a large group

2(1) A scheme is an excluded scheme for the purposes of section 305A of TIOPA (schemes preventing Part 7 applying to a large group) if it is a relevant event as a result of which subsection (2) of section 348A (financial statements: business combinations to which the worldwide group is a party) of TIOPA applies.

But this is subject to regulation 12.

2(2) In paragraph (1), "**relevant event**" has the same meaning as in section 348A of TIOPA.

EXCLUDED SCHEMES FOR THE PURPOSES OF THE GATEWAY TEST

Excluded schemes for the purposes of the application Chapter 2 of Part 7 of TIOPA

3 A scheme of a description within any of regulations 4 to 5 is an excluded scheme for the purposes of section 306 of TIOPA (schemes involving the manipulation of rules in Chapter 2).

But this is subject to regulation 12.

Repayment of relevant liability

4 A scheme is within this regulation if it is a transaction for the repayment of a relevant liability by a relevant group company or group securitisation company using–

(a)   funds derived directly from the company's trading or investment activity,

(b)   proceeds from the repayment of a relevant asset of the company within section 263(4)(b) or (d) of TIOPA,

(c)   proceeds from the issue of ordinary shares or preference shares in the company, or

(d)   where the relevant liability is owed to a subsidiary of the company (or a subsidiary of that subsidiary), dividend income received from that subsidiary.

Release of relevant liability

5 A scheme is within this regulation if it is a transaction for the release of a relevant group company or group securitisation company from a relevant liability on terms which would have been entered into between knowledgeable and willing parties dealing at arm's length.

EXCLUDED SCHEMES FOR THE PURPOSES OF THE MAIN RULES

Excluded schemes for the purposes of the application Chapters 3 and 4 of Part 7 of TIOPA

6   A scheme of a description within any of regulations 7 to 11 is an excluded scheme for the purposes of section 307 of TIOPA (schemes involving the manipulation of rules in Chapters 3 and 4).

But this is subject to regulation 12.

Repayment of finance arrangement

7   A scheme is within this regulation if it is a transaction–

(a)   for the repayment of a finance arrangement by a relevant group company using–

   (i)   funds derived directly from the company's trading or investment activity,

   (ii)   proceeds from the repayment of a finance arrangement which gives rise to a financing income amount,

   (iii)   proceeds from the issue of ordinary shares or preference shares in the company, or

   (iv)   where the relevant liability is owed to a subsidiary of the company (or a subsidiary of that subsidiary), dividend income received from that subsidiary, and

(b)   which gives rise to a financing expense amount.

Release from finance arrangement

8   A scheme is within this regulation if it is a transaction–

(a)   for the release of a relevant group company from a finance arrangement on terms which would have been entered into between knowledgeable and willing parties dealing at arm's length, and

(b)   which gives rise to a financing expense amount.

Transfer to group treasury company

9   A scheme is within this regulation if it is a transaction–

(a)   for the transfer of a finance arrangement from a relevant group company to a group treasury company which is a relevant group company, and

(b)   which gives rise to a financing expense amount.

Liability owed to UK group treasury company

10   A scheme is within this regulation if it comprises–

(a)   a transaction for the repayment of a finance arrangement by a relevant group company, and

(b)   a transaction for the replacement of that arrangement by an equivalent finance arrangement owed to a group treasury company which is a relevant group company.

Transfer to companies with net financing deduction or net financing income that is small

11(1)   A scheme is within this regulation if–

(a)   under or in relation to the scheme, a finance arrangement is transferred to a relevant group company or a UK group company, and

(b)   before the transfer the net financing deduction of the relevant group company, or the net financing income of the UK group company, is small and as a result of the transfer the net financing deduction or net financing income is not small.

11(2)   In paragraph (1)(b), **"small"** has the same meaning as in section 331(1) of TIOPA

TAX AVOIDANCE

Tax avoidance schemes

12(1)   A scheme is not an excluded scheme if the scheme is, or forms part of, a notifiable arrangement, or involves a notifiable proposal, in relation to which a member of the worldwide group is under a duty to provide HMRC with information under Part 7 of the Finance Act 2004 (disclosure of tax avoidance schemes).

12(2)   In paragraph (1), **"notifiable arrangement"** and **"notifiable proposal"** have the meanings given by section 306 of the Finance Act 2004;

ADDITIONALLY-DEVELOPED OIL FIELDS ORDER 2013

(SI 2013/2910)

Made on 15 November 2013 by the Commissioners for Her Majesty's Revenue and Customs, in exercise of the powers conferred by s. 349 and 349A of the Corporation Tax Act 2010 and para 22 of Sch. 22 to the Finance Act 2012. Operative from 1 April 2013.

CITATION, COMMENCEMENT AND INTERPRETATION

1(1) This Order may be cited as the Additionally-developed Oil Fields Order 2013 and is treated as having come into force on 1st April 2013.

1(2) In this Order **"CTA 2010"** means the Corporation Tax Act 2010.

ADDITIONALLY-DEVELOPED OIL FIELD

2(1) The conditions which a project that is described in a consent for development of an oil field must meet for the purposes of section 349A(1)(b) of CTA 2010 are as follows.

2(2) Condition A is that the project was authorised as mentioned in section 349A(1)(a) of CTA 2010 on or after 7th September 2012.

2(3) Condition B is that the cost per tonne of the project is more than £60.

2(4) Condition C is that the additional reserves of oil which the field has as a result of the project have not been taken into account in calculating the cost per tonne of any qualifying project that has previously been authorised in relation to the field.

2(5) A project authorised in relation to an oil field is a "qualifying project" for the purposes of paragraph (4) if a field allowance has at any time been held for the field as a result of the project.

2(6) Condition D is that, as at the authorisation day, the whole of the oil field lies on the seaward side of the baselines from which the territorial sea is measured.

2(7) Condition E is that the project does not involve enhanced oil recovery using carbon dioxide.

2(8) For the purposes of this article the "cost per tonne" of a project authorised in relation to an oil field means the amount given by—

$$\frac{E}{R}$$

where—

E is the expected capital expenditure of the project (see paragraph (9)), and

R is the sum of the amounts of additional reserves of oil (in tonnes) which the field and any other oil fields have as a result of the project.

2(9) The expected capital expenditure of a project is to be determined as follows—

Step 1

Calculate the amount of capital expenditure which it is reasonably expected, as at the authorisation day, will be incurred in carrying out the project.

In calculating that amount, ignore any expenditure incurred before the authorisation day which, if the project had not been authorised, would have been wasted expenditure.

Step 2

Calculate the amount of any capital expenditure which it is reasonably expected, as at the authorisation day, would have been incurred on or after that day if the project had not been authorised.

In calculating that amount, ignore any expenditure which—

(a) would have been incurred under an agreement entered into before the authorisation day, and

(b) would not have been wasted expenditure.

Step 3

Deduct the amount given by step 2 from the amount given by step 1.

But if the amount given by step 2 is greater than the amount given by step 1, the expected capital expenditure of the project is nil.

2(10)   In determining the expected capital expenditure of a project–

(a)   where an amount attributed to an item of expenditure includes an amount for contingencies, the amount so included may not exceed 20% of the amount that would be attributed to that item of expenditure in the absence of any amount for contingencies,

(b)   expenditure is not to be treated as wasted expenditure to the extent that it is recoverable, and

(c)   the following are to be disregarded–

     (i)   any decommissioning expenditure (within the meaning of section 330C of CTA 2010), and

     (ii)   any payments of interest.

2(11)   For the purposes of this article–

(a)   the amount of additional reserves of oil which a field has is to be determined on the authorisation day,

(b)   1,100 cubic metres of gas at a temperature of 15 degrees celsius and pressure of one atmosphere is to be counted as equivalent to one tonne,

(c)   **"authorisation day"**, in relation to a project, means the day when the project is authorised as mentioned in section 349A(1)(a) of CTA 2010, and

(d)   **"territorial sea"** means the territorial sea of the United Kingdom.

AMENDMENTS OF CTA 2010

3-12   [Amending provisions not reproduced.]

TAXATION OF REGULATORY CAPITAL SECURITIES REGULATIONS 2013

(SI 2013/3209)

Made on 18 December 2013 by the Treasury in exercise of the powers conferred upon them by s. 221 of the Finance Act 2012. Operative from 1 January 2014.

Other material – HMRC technical note: "Regulatory Capital Securities" is available at www.hmrc.gov.uk/drafts/reg-cap-technote.pdf.

CITATION, COMMENCEMENT AND EFFECT

1(1) These Regulations may be cited as the Taxation of Regulatory Capital Securities Regulations 2013 and shall come into force on 1st January 2014.

1(2) These Regulations have effect–

(a)   for the purposes of income tax, for payments made on or after 1st January 2014;

(b)   for the purposes of corporation tax, for accounting periods beginning on or after that date (this is subject to paragraph (3) and regulation 11);

(c)   for the purposes of capital gains tax, in relation to disposals made on or after that date;

(d)   for the purposes of stamp duty, in relation to instruments executed on or after that date;

(e)   for the purposes of stamp duty reserve tax–

    (i)   in the case of agreements to transfer securities which are not conditional, in relation to agreements made on or after that date, and

    (ii)   in the case of agreements to transfer securities which are conditional, in relation to agreements where the condition is satisfied on or after that date.

1(3) For the purposes of paragraph (2)(b), an accounting period beginning before and ending on or after 1st January 2014 is to be treated for the purposes of these Regulations as if so much of the period as falls before that date, and so much of the period as falls on or after that date, were separate accounting periods.

REGULATORY CAPITAL SECURITIES

2(1) For the purposes of these Regulations, **"regulatory capital security"** means a security which qualifies, or has qualified, as–

(a)   an Additional Tier 1 instrument and forms, or formed, a component of Additional Tier 1 capital for the purposes of CRR, or

(b)   a Tier 2 instrument and forms, or formed, a component of Tier 2 capital for the purposes of CRR.

2(2) In paragraph (1), **"security"** does not include shares other than deferred shares issued by a building society within paragraph (1)(a).

2(3) For the purposes of this regulation–

"Additional Tier 1 instrument" means a security which qualifies as an Additional Tier 1 instrument under Article 52 of CRR,

"building society" and **"deferred shares"** have the same meanings as in the Building Societies Act 1986,

"Tier 2 instrument" means a security which qualifies as a Tier 2 instrument under Article 63 of CRR.

2(4) In these Regulations, **"CRR"** means the Commission Regulation (EU) No 575/2013(b) (as amended from time to time).

REGULATORY CAPITAL SECURITIES TREATED AS LOAN RELATIONSHIPS

3(1) For the purposes of the Corporation Tax Acts, a regulatory capital security represents a loan relationship.

3(2) But in relation to the issuer of a regulatory capital security and any connected creditor–

(a)   sections 415, 416 and 585 of CTA 2009 (loan relationships with embedded derivatives) do not apply in relation to the security,

(b)   the credits and debits to be brought into account in respect of the security are determined as if fair value accounting were not generally accepted accounting practice in relation to the security or part of the security (including a hedged component), and

(c)   no credit or debit is to be brought into account under Part 5 of CTA 2009–

    (i)   in respect of the principal amount of the security being written down on a permanent or temporary basis or the security being converted to a Common Equity Tier 1 instrument in accordance with any regulatory requirements or the provisions governing the security, or

    (ii)   in respect of the principal amount of the security being written up, following a write down of the principal amount on a temporary basis, in accordance with any regulatory requirements or the provisions governing the security.

3(3)   Paragraph (2) applies for the purposes of determining the profits and losses to be recognised in determining the carrying value of a regulatory capital security for the purposes of section 317 of CTA 2009 as it applies for the purposes of determining the credits and debits to be brought into account under Part 5 of CTA 2009.

3(4)   In this regulation–

    "Common Equity Tier 1 instrument" means a capital instrument which qualifies as a Common Equity Tier 1 instrument under Article 28 or 29 of CRR,

    "connected creditor" means a company standing in the position of creditor as respects a regulatory capital security where the creditor relationship is a connected companies relationship for the purposes of Part 5 of CTA 2009,

    "fair value accounting" have the same meanings as in Part 5 of CTA 2009.

REGULATORY CAPITAL SECURITIES TREATED AS NORMAL COMMERCIAL LOANS

4   For the purposes of sections 158(1)(b) and 159(4)(b) of CTA 2010 and section 117(1)(a) of TCGA 1992, a regulatory capital security represents a normal commercial loan.

TREATMENT OF PAYMENTS

5(1)   A payment in respect of a regulatory capital security is–

(a)   not a distribution for the purposes of the Tax Acts, but

(b)   is income chargeable under Chapter 2 of Part 4 of ITTOIA 2005 (interest) for the purposes of income tax.

5(2)   In paragraph (1), **"payment"** does not include a repayment of the principal amount of the security.

EXCEPTION FROM DUTY TO DEDUCT INCOME TAX

6   The duty to deduct a sum representing income tax under section 874 (duty to deduct from certain payments of yearly interest) or section 889 (payments in respect of building society securities) of ITA 2007 does not apply to a payment in respect of a regulatory capital security.

EXEMPTION FROM STAMP DUTIES

7   A transfer of a regulatory capital security is exempt from all stamp duties.

ANTI-AVOIDANCE

8(1)   Regulations 3 to 7 do not apply in the case of a regulatory capital security if there are arrangements the main purpose, or one of the main purposes, of which is to obtain a tax advantage for any person as a result of the application of these Regulations in respect of that security.

8(2)   In paragraph (1), **"tax advantage"** has the meaning given in section 1139 of CTA 2010.

DUTY TO DEDUCT FROM PAYMENTS IN RESPECT OF REGULATORY CAPITAL SECURITY

9   The following sections of ITA 2007 do not apply to a payment in respect of a regulatory capital security–

(a)   section 878 (interest paid by banks), and

(b)   section 885 (authorised persons dealing in financial instruments).

AMENDMENT OF THE LOAN RELATIONSHIP AND DERIVATIVE CONTRACTS (DISREGARD AND BRINGING INTO ACCOUNT OF PROFITS AND LOSSES) REGULATIONS 2004

10(1) The Loan Relationship and Derivative Contracts (Disregard and Bringing into Account of Profits and Losses) Regulations 2004 are amended as follows.

10(2) In regulation 2(1)–

(a) omit the definition of "Additional Tier 1 instrument", and

(b) in the appropriate place insert–

""**regulatory capital security**" has the meaning given in regulation 2 of the Taxation of Regulatory Capital Securities Regulations 2013;".

10(3) In regulations 3(5)(c) and 4(4A)(c) for "an Additional Tier 1 instrument" substitute "a regulatory capital security".

10(4) In regulation 6, in paragraphs (5A) and (5C)–

(a) at the end of sub-paragraph (a), in both cases, omit "or", and

  at the end of both paragraphs insert–
  ", or

(c) where the hedged item is a regulatory capital security in relation to which the company uses fair value accounting.".

TRANSITIONAL PROVISIONS

11(1) This regulation applies for the purposes of corporation tax in relation to the first accounting period beginning, or treated as beginning, on or after 1st January 2014 in respect of a security–

(a) issued before that date,

(b) to which Part 5 of CTA 2009 applied in the accounting period ending, or treated as ending, on 31st December 2013, and

(c) which is a regulatory capital security for the purposes of these Regulations.

11(2) In this regulation–

(a) an accounting period ending, or treated as ending, on 31st December 2013 is referred to as "the earlier period", and

(b) an accounting period beginning, or treated as beginning, on 1st January 2014 is referred to as "the later period".

11(3) If there is an increase in the carrying value of a security which is an asset of the company between–

(a) the end of the earlier period, and

(b) the beginning of the later period,

a credit equal to the increase must be brought into account for the purposes of Part 5 of CTA 2009 in the later period.

11(4) If there is a decrease in the carrying value of such a security between–

(a) the end of earlier period, and

(b) the beginning of the later period,

a debit equal to the decrease must be brought into account for the purposes of Part 5 of CTA 2009 in the later period.

11(5) If there is an increase in the carrying value of a security which is a liability of the company between–

(a) the end of the earlier period, and

(b) the beginning of the later period,

a debit equal to the increase must be brought into account for the purposes of Part 5 of CTA 2009 in the later period.

11(6) If there is a decrease in the carrying value of such a security between–

(a) the end of earlier period, and

(b) the beginning of the later period,

a credit equal to the decrease must be brought into account for the purposes of Part 5 of CTA 2009 in the later period.

11(7)   But this regulation does not apply so far as any debit or credit as is mentioned in this regulation falls to be brought into account apart from this regulation.

11(8)   For the purposes of this regulation, where in the earlier period, in accordance with generally accepted accounting practice, the rights and liabilities under a security have been treated as divided between a loan relationship and one or more derivative financial instruments or equity instruments, the reference to the carrying value of the security means the sum of the carrying values for each of those component instruments.

11(9)   For the purposes of this regulation, "carrying value" must be construed in accordance with section 317 (subject to regulation 3(3) in the later period) and section 702 of CTA 2009.

REPEALS

12   [Repeals CTA 2010, s. 162(1A), 164A, 1029(1)(ca) and 1032A and FA 2013, s. 43.]

TAKING CONTROL OF GOODS (FEES) REGULATIONS 2014

(SI 2014/1)

Made on 4 January 2014 by the Lord Chancellor in exercise of the powers conferred upon them by s. 90 of and para. 13(3), 42, 50(4) and (7), and 62 of Sch. 12 to the Tribunals, Courts and Enforcement Act 2007. Operative from 6 April 2014.

CITATION, COMMENCEMENT AND EXTENT

1(1) These Regulations may be cited as the Taking Control of Goods (Fees) Regulations 2014 and come into force on 6th April 2014.

1(2) These Regulations extend to England and Wales only.

INTERPRETATION

2(1) In these Regulations–

"**the Act**" means the Tribunals, Courts and Enforcement Act 2007;

"**amount outstanding**" has the meaning given by paragraph 50(3) of Schedule 12;

"**controlled goods agreement**" has the meaning given by paragraph 13(4) of Schedule 12;

"**creditor**" has the meaning given by paragraph 1(6) of Schedule 12;

"**debtor**" has the meaning given by paragraph 1(5) of Schedule 12;

"**enforcement agent**" means an individual entitled to act as an enforcement agent by virtue of section 63(2) of the Act, but it does not include an individual who may so act by virtue of section 63(2)(c);

"**enforcement power**" has the meaning given by paragraph 1(2) of Schedule 12;

"**enforcement-related services**" has the meaning given by paragraph 62(5) of Schedule 12;

"**percentage fee**" means a fee calculated in accordance with regulation 7;

"**premises**" has the meaning given by paragraph 3 of Schedule 12;

"**proceeds**" has the meaning given by paragraph 50(2) of Schedule 12;

"**Schedule 12**" means Schedule 12 to the Act, and references to "the Schedule 12 procedure" are to be read accordingly;

"**sum to be recovered**" means the amount of the debt which remains unpaid, or an amount that the creditor agrees to accept in full satisfaction of the debt.

2(2) In these Regulations, references to "**the compliance stage**", "**the first enforcement stage**", "**the second enforcement stage**" and to "**the sale or disposal stage**" are to be construed in accordance with–

(a)   regulation 5 where the reference relates to enforcement other than under an enforcement power conferred by a High Court writ; and

(b)   regulation 6 where the reference relates to enforcement under an enforcement power conferred by a High Court writ.

APPLICATION OF THESE REGULATIONS

3   These Regulations apply when an enforcement agent uses the Schedule 12 procedure.

RECOVERY OF FEES FOR ENFORCEMENT-RELATED SERVICES FROM THE DEBTOR

4(1) The enforcement agent may recover from the debtor the fees indicated in the Schedule in accordance with this regulation and regulations regulations 11, 12, 13, 16 and 17, by reference to the stage, or stages, of enforcement for which enforcement-related services have been supplied.

4(2) The fees referred to in paragraph (1) may be recovered out of proceeds.

4(3) The enforcement agent may recover under this regulation the whole fee provided in the Schedule for a stage where the amount outstanding is paid after the commencement, but before the completion, of that stage.

4(4)   For the purposes of this regulation, the relevant stage of enforcement is determined according to regulation 5 or 6 as appropriate.

4(5)   Where the enforcement agent is acting under an enforcement power conferred by a High Court writ—

(a)   where the enforcement agent and the debtor enter into a controlled goods agreement which the debtor does not breach, only the first enforcement stage fee may be recovered from the debtor; and

(b)   where—

    (i)   the enforcement agent and the debtor enter into a controlled goods agreement which the debtor breaches; or

    (ii)   the enforcement agent and the debtor do not enter into a controlled goods agreement,

both the first enforcement stage and second enforcement stage fees may be recovered from the debtor, and the first enforcement stage fee is recoverable where sub-paragraph (ii) applies notwithstanding that the first enforcement stage did not apply.

STAGES OF ENFORCEMENT FOR WHICH FEES MAY BE RECOVERED – ENFORCEMENT OTHER THAN UNDER HIGH COURT WRITS

5(1)   The relevant stages of enforcement under an enforcement power which is not conferred by a High Court writ are as follows—

(a)   the compliance stage, which comprises all activities relating to enforcement from the receipt by the enforcement agent of instructions to use that procedure in relation to a sum to be recovered up to but not including the commencement of the enforcement stage;

(b)   the enforcement stage, which comprises all activities relating to enforcement from the first attendance at the premises in relation to the instructions up to but not including the commencement of the sale or disposal stage;

(c)   the sale or disposal stage, which comprises all activities relating to enforcement from the first attendance at the property for the purpose of transporting goods to the place of sale, or from commencing preparation for sale if the sale is to be held on the premises, until the completion of the sale or disposal (including application of the proceeds and provision of the information required by regulation 14).

5(2)   Where the goods against which enforcement is sought are securities, the sale or disposal stage commences with the provision of a notice of disposal in accordance with paragraph 49(2) of Schedule 12.

STAGES OF ENFORCEMENT FOR WHICH FEES MAY BE RECOVERED – ENFORCEMENT OF HIGH COURT WRITS

6(1)   The relevant stages of enforcement under an enforcement power conferred by a High Court writ are as follows—

(a)   the compliance stage, which comprises all activities relating to enforcement from the receipt by the enforcement agent of instructions to use that procedure in relation to a sum to be recovered up to but not including the commencement of the first enforcement stage, or, where sub-paragraph (c)(i) applies, the commencement of the second enforcement stage;

(b)   where the enforcement agent and the debtor enter into a controlled goods agreement, the first enforcement stage, which comprises all activities relating to enforcement from the first attendance at the premises in relation to the instructions until the agreement is completed or breached;

(c)   the second enforcement stage, which comprises—

    (i)   where the enforcement agent and the debtor do not enter into a controlled goods agreement, all activities relating to enforcement from the first attendance at the premises in relation to the instructions up to but not including the commencement of the sale or disposal stage;

    (ii)   where the enforcement agent and the debtor enter into a controlled goods agreement but the debtor breaches that agreement, all activities relating to enforcement from the time at which the debtor breaches the agreement up to but not including the commencement of the sale or disposal stage;

(d)   the sale or disposal stage, which comprises all activities relating to enforcement from the first attendance at the property for the purpose of transporting goods to the place of sale, or from commencing preparation for sale if the sale is to be held on the premises, until the completion of the sale or disposal (including application of the proceeds and provision of the information required by regulation 14).

6(2)   Where the goods against which enforcement is sought are securities, the sale or disposal stage commences with the provision of a notice of disposal in accordance with paragraph 49(2) of Schedule 12.

CALCULATION OF FEES BY REFERENCE TO VALUE OF SUM SOUGHT TO BE RECOVERED

7   The percentage fee or fees are to be calculated–

(a)   where enforcement takes place other than under a High Court writ, by multiplying the amount of the sum to be recovered which exceeds £1500 by the percentage indicated in the relevant column of table 1 in the Schedule;

(b)   where enforcement takes place under a High Court writ, by multiplying the amount of the sum to be recovered which exceeds £1000 by the percentage indicated in the relevant column of table 2 in the Schedule;

(c)   in either case, in the total amount of the fee so calculated, any fraction of £1 is to be reckoned as £1, but any fraction of a penny is to be disregarded.

DISBURSEMENTS RECOVERABLE FROM THE DEBTOR

8(1)   The enforcement agent may recover disbursements from the debtor only in accordance with this regulation and regulations 9, 10 and 11.

8(2)   The following disbursements are recoverable provided that they are reasonably and actually incurred–

(a)   the cost of storing goods which have been taken into control and removed from the premises or highway;

(b)   the cost of hiring a locksmith to gain access to premises when using reasonable force to enter them in accordance with Schedule 12, and to secure them thereafter;

(c)   court fees in relation to any applications made by the enforcement agent in relation to the enforcement power which are granted.

8(3)   The disbursements referred to in this regulation and regulations 9 and 10 may be recovered out of proceeds.

DISBURSEMENTS RECOVERABLE FROM THE DEBTOR IN RELATION TO SALE OF GOODS BY AUCTION OR BY PRIVATE SALE

9(1)   The enforcement agent may recover disbursements related to the sale of the goods from the debtor in accordance with this regulation and regulations 10 and 11.

9(2)   Where the sale is held on premises provided by the auctioneer conducting the sale, the enforcement agent may recover from the debtor–

(a)   a sum in respect of the auctioneer's commission not exceeding 15% of the sum realised by the sale of the goods;

(b)   the auctioneer's out of pocket expenses; and

(c)   reasonable disbursements incurred in respect of advertising the sale.

9(3)   Where the sale is held on other premises in accordance with regulations made under paragraph 43 of Schedule 12, the enforcement agent may recover from the debtor the sums and disbursements referred to in paragraph (2), except that the sum referred to in paragraph (2)(a) may not exceed 7.5% of the sum realised by the sale of the goods.

9(4)   Where the goods are–

(a)   auctioned by way of an internet auction site; or

(b)   sold other than by auction,

the enforcement agent may recover from the debtor 7.5% of the sum realised by the sale of the goods.

EXCEPTIONAL DISBURSEMENTS

10(1) Upon application by the enforcement agent with the consent of the creditor in accordance with rules of court, the court may order that the enforcement agent may recover from the debtor exceptional disbursements associated with the use of the Schedule 12 procedure which are not otherwise recoverable under these Regulations.

10(2) The court may not make an order under paragraph (1) unless satisfied that the disbursements to which it relates are necessary for effective enforcement of the sum to be recovered, having regard to all the circumstances including–

(a)   the amount of that sum; and

(b)   the nature and value of the goods which have been taken into control, or which it is sought to take into control.

MORE THAN ONE ENFORCEMENT POWER AVAILABLE AGAINST THE SAME DEBTOR

11(1) This regulation applies for the purpose of calculating the fees and disbursements payable to the enforcement agent in accordance with regulations 4, 8, 9 and 10 in a case where–

(a)   the enforcement agent receives instructions to use the procedure under Schedule 12 in relation to the same debtor but in respect of more than one enforcement power; and

(b)   those enforcement powers can reasonably be exercised at the same time.

11(2) In paragraph (1)(b), **"can reasonably be exercised at the same time"** means in particular–

(a)   taking control of goods in relation to all such enforcement powers on the same occasion; and

(b)   selling or disposing of all goods so taken into control on the same occasion,

except where it is impracticable to do so.

11(3) The enforcement agent may recover the compliance stage fee in respect of each enforcement power to which the instructions relate.

11(4) Where paragraph (1) applies, the fee recoverable in respect of the enforcement stage (or stages) and the sale or disposal stage respectively is to be calculated as follows–

(a)   the fixed fee for each stage may be recovered only once regardless of the number of enforcement powers to which the instructions relate;

(b)   the amount in relation to which the percentage fee for each stage, if any, is to be calculated is the total amount of the sums to be recovered under all enforcement powers to which paragraph (1) applies.

11(5) Where this regulation applies, the enforcement agent must, as far as practicable, minimise the disbursements recoverable from the debtor under these Regulations by dealing with the goods taken into control pursuant to the instructions together and on as few occasions as possible.

RECOVERY OF FEES FROM VULNERABLE DEBTORS

12 Where the debtor is a vulnerable person, the fee or fees due for the enforcement stage (or, where regulation 6 applies, the first, or first and second, enforcement stages as appropriate) and any disbursements related to that stage (or stages) are not recoverable unless the enforcement agent has, before proceeding to remove goods which have been taken into control, given the debtor an adequate opportunity to get assistance and advice in relation to the exercise of the enforcement power.

APPLICATION OF PROCEEDS WHERE LESS THAN THE AMOUNT OUTSTANDING

13(1) Subject to paragraph 50(6) of Schedule 12, when the proceeds from the exercise of an enforcement power are less than the amount outstanding, they must be applied in accordance with this regulation.

13(2) Where the goods are sold or disposed of at public auction (other than by internet auction), the proceeds must be applied first in payment of the auctioneer's fees calculated in accordance with regulation 9(2) or (3) as appropriate.

13(3) Following the payment at paragraph (2), the enforcement agent may then recover the compliance fee.

13(4) Subject to paragraph (5), following any payment due by virtue of paragraphs (2) and (3), the proceeds must be applied *pro rata* in payment of–

(a)   the sum to be recovered, and

(b)   any remaining amounts recoverable in respect of fees and disbursements payable to the enforcement agent in accordance with these Regulations.

13(5)   Where the same legal person is both the creditor and the enforcement agent, paragraph (4) does not apply and the proceeds must be applied in payment of the amount referred to in paragraph (4)(b) before payment of the amount at paragraph (4)(a).

13(6)   In paragraphs (4) and (5), references to the proceeds are to the proceeds after deduction of the sums, if any, to which paragraphs (2) and (3) relate.

PROVISION OF INFORMATION TO DEBTOR AND CO-OWNER BY ENFORCEMENT AGENT

14(1)   As soon as possible after sale or disposal of the goods, the enforcement agent must provide the debtor and any co-owner of goods of whom the enforcement agent is aware with—

(a)   an itemised list of the goods sold or otherwise disposed of;

(b)   a statement of—

    (i)   the sum received in relation to each item;

    (ii)   the proceeds;

    (iii)   the application of the proceeds;

    (iv)   the disbursements recoverable under these Regulations and incurred in relation to the goods.

14(2)   The enforcement agent must provide the debtor and any co-owner with a copy of all receipts for the disbursements referred to at paragraph (1)(b)(iv), except in relation to disbursements to which regulation 9(4) applies.

14(3)   Where the debtor pays, or seeks to pay, the amount outstanding at any time after the enforcement agent has incurred disbursements in relation to the enforcement power but before sale or disposal of the goods, the enforcement agent must provide the debtor with—

(a)   a statement of disbursements recoverable in accordance with paragraph (1)(b)(iv);

(b)   any receipts in accordance with paragraph (2);

(c)   a statement of the fixed and percentage fees (if any) charged.

DISPUTE REGARDING CO-OWNER'S SHARE OF PROCEEDS

15   Upon application in accordance with rules of court by the enforcement agent, the creditor, the debtor or a co-owner of goods, any dispute about the amount of the proceeds payable to that co-owner under paragraph 50(6)(a) of Schedule 12 is to be determined by the court.

DISPUTES ABOUT THE AMOUNT OF FEES AND DISBURSEMENTS RECOVERABLE UNDER REGULATIONS

16   Upon application in accordance with rules of court, any dispute regarding the amount recoverable under these Regulations is to be determined by the court.

FEES AND DISBURSEMENTS NOT RECOVERABLE WHERE ENFORCEMENT PROCESS CEASES

17(1)   The enforcement agent may not recover fees or disbursements from the debtor in relation to any stage of enforcement undertaken at a time when the relevant enforcement power has ceased to be exercisable.

17(2)   Paragraph (1) does not apply where the enforcement power ceases to be exercisable because the debtor has paid the amount outstanding or that amount has been recovered from proceeds or otherwise.

17(3)   In a case in which the enforcement agent is instructed by a landlord to exercise CRAR and the court makes an order under section 78(1) of the Act—

(a)   the enforcement agent may not recover fees or disbursements from the debtor where the order is made under section 78(1)(a);

(b)   where the order is made under section 78(1)(b), the enforcement agent may recover fees and disbursements from the debtor in accordance with these Regulations only if the court has made a further order permitting further steps to be taken under CRAR.

17(4)   In paragraph (3), **"CRAR"** has the meaning given by section 72(2) of the Act.

SCHEDULE

Regulation 4

FEES RECOVERABLE UNDER REGULATION 4

Table 1 – Enforcement other than under a High Court Writ

Fee Stage	Fixed Fee	Percentage fee (regulation 7): percentage of sum to be recovered exceeding £1500
Compliance stage	£75.00	0%
Enforcement stage	£235.00	7.5%
Sale or disposal stage	£110.00	7.5%

Table 2 – Enforcement under a High Court Writ

Fee Stage	Fixed Fee	Percentage fee (regulation 7): percentage of sum to be recovered exceeding £1000
Compliance stage	£75.00	0%
First enforcement stage	£190.00	7.5%
Second enforcement stage	£495.00	0%
Sale or disposal stage	£525.00	7.5%

INTERNATIONAL TAX COMPLIANCE (CROWN DEPENDENCIES AND GIBRALTAR) REGULATIONS 2014

(SI 2014/520)

Made on 6 March 2014 by the Treasury in exercise of the powers conferred upon them by s. 222(1)(c), (2) and (3) of the Finance Act 2013. Operative from 31 March 2014.

INTRODUCTORY

Citation and commencement

1(1) These Regulations may be cited as the International Tax Compliance (Crown Dependencies and Gibraltar) Regulations 2014.

1(2) These Regulations come into force on 31st March 2014.

Implementation of the agreements etc

2(1) These Regulations have effect for and in connection with the implementation of obligations arising under each of the Isle of Man agreement, the Guernsey agreement, the Jersey agreement and the Gibraltar agreement and apply separately in relation to each of those agreements.

2(2) In these Regulations–

(a) **"the Isle of Man agreement"** means the agreement between the Government of the United Kingdom of Great Britain and Northern Ireland and the Government of the Isle of Man to improve international tax compliance, signed on 10th October 2013,

(b) **"the Guernsey agreement"** means the agreement between the Government of the United Kingdom of Great Britain and Northern Ireland and the States of Guernsey to improve international tax compliance, signed on 22nd October 2013,

(c) **"the Jersey agreement"** means the agreement between the Government of the United Kingdom of Great Britain and Northern Ireland and the Government of Jersey to improve international tax compliance, signed on 22nd October 2013, and

(d) **"the Gibraltar agreement"** means the agreement between the Government of the United Kingdom of Great Britain and Northern Ireland and the Government of Gibraltar to improve international tax compliance, signed on 21st November 2013,

as each of those agreements has effect from time to time.

2(3) In these Regulations, **"the relevant agreement"** means–

(a) the Isle of Man agreement,

(b) the Guernsey agreement,

(c) the Jersey agreement, or

(d) the Gibraltar agreement,

as the context may require.

2(4) Any expression which is not defined in section 222 or 235 of FA 2013 or in these Regulations has the same meaning in these Regulations as it has in the relevant agreement.

SCOPE

Scope: Definition of "reporting financial institution"

3(1) In these Regulations **"reporting financial institution"** means a person who carries on business in the United Kingdom as–

(a) a depository institution,

(b) an investment entity,

(c) a custodial institution, or

(d) a specified insurance company.

3(2) But a person is not a reporting financial institution for the purposes of these Regulations if that person is a non-reporting financial institution.

3(3) For the purposes of these Regulations **"depository institution"** means–

(a)   a person carrying on a regulated activity for the purposes of the Financial Services and Markets Act 2000 by virtue of article 5 of the Financial Services and Markets Act 2000 (Regulated Activities) Order 2001, or

(b)   a person who is within paragraphs (a) to (e) or (h) to (j) of the definition of **"electronic money issuer"** in regulation 2(1) of the Electronic Money Regulations 2011.

3(4) For the purposes of these Regulations a person (person A) carries on business in the United Kingdom as an investment entity if–

(a)   person A undertakes any of the activities referred to in sub-paragraph 1.j(1) to (3) of Article 1 of the relevant agreement in the course of carrying on business in the United Kingdom, and the gross amount of person A's income of that business for the applicable period wholly or mainly derives from those activities, or

(b)   on behalf of person A, a financial institution (person B) undertakes any of the activities referred to in sub-paragraph 1.j(1) to (3) of Article 1 of the relevant agreement in the course of carrying on business in the United Kingdom, and the gross amount of person A's income from the activities undertaken on behalf of person A by person B for the applicable period wholly or mainly derives from investing or dealing in financial assets.

3(5) For the purposes of these Regulations–

(a)   if a collective investment scheme is constituted by a person (other than a trustee), who carries on business in the United Kingdom, that person (and no-one else) is a reporting financial institution in the case of the scheme and is to be regarded as the investment entity, and

(b)   if a collective investment scheme is constituted otherwise than as described in subparagraph (a) and the manager, operator or trustee of the scheme is a person who carries on business in the United Kingdom, the manager, operator or trustee of the scheme (and no-one else) is a reporting financial institution in the case of the scheme and is to be regarded as the investment entity.

3(6) In paragraph (5) **"collective investment scheme"** means–

(a)   an investment trust within the meaning of the Corporation Tax Acts,

(b)   a venture capital trust within the meaning of Part 6 of ITA 2007, or

(c)   any arrangements that are a **"collective investment scheme"** within the meaning of Part 17 of the Financial Services and Markets Act 2000.

3(7) For the purposes of these Regulations a person carries on a business in the United Kingdom as a custodial institution if–

(a)   more than 20% of the gross amount of the income of that business as is carried on in the United Kingdom for the applicable period derives from any of–

(i)   holding financial assets for the account of another person, and

(ii)   performing related financial services, or

(b)   the person holds assets in the United Kingdom as a nominee for another person who is a connected person within the meaning of section 1122 of CTA 2010.

3(8) In paragraph (7)(a)(ii) **"related financial services"** means financial services provided by the person that directly relate to that person holding financial assets on behalf of the other person.

3(9) In paragraphs (7)(a)(i) and (8) **"financial assets"** means–

(a)   assets capable of being the subject-matter of a transaction that is an **"investment transaction"** within the meaning of regulation 14F of Part 2B of the Authorised Investment Funds (Tax) Regulations 2006,

(b)   insurance or annuity contracts,

(c)   commodities, or

(d)   derivative contracts within the meaning of Part 7 of CTA 2009.

3(10) In paragraph (4) and sub-paragraph (7)(a) the **"applicable period"** is the shorter of–

(a)   the three year period–

(i)   ending with the person's most recent accounting date if that date is no more than twelve months earlier than the next reporting date, or

(ii)   in any other case, the 31st December immediately before the next reporting date, and

(b) the period—

    (i) starting on the later of the first day of the period determined under sub-paragraph (a) and the date that the person commenced the business, and

    (ii) ending on the earlier of the last day of the period determined under sub-paragraph (a) and the last day that the person carried on the business,

and **"accounting date"** here has the same meaning as is given to it by section 1119 CTA 2010.

Scope: Definition of "reportable account"

4(1) In these Regulations a **"reportable account"** means—

(a) an account which is a reportable account for the relevant agreement maintained in the United Kingdom by a reporting financial institution for the purposes of its business as described in regulation 3(1), and

(b) an account that is—

    (i) a preexisting individual account meeting the description at paragraph II.A of Annex I,

    (ii) a new individual account meeting the description at paragraph III.A of that Annex,

    (iii) a preexisting entity account meeting the description at paragraph IV.A of that Annex, or

    (iv) a new entity account meeting the description at paragraph V.A of that Annex.

4(2) But an account in any of paragraphs (i) to (iv) of paragraph (1)(b) is not a reportable account for a calendar year if—

(a) there is an election by the reporting financial institution in force for that year to treat such accounts as not being a reportable account, and

(b) the account meets any further description specified by the institution in its election.

4(3) An election under paragraph (2)—

(a) is to be made by being given to the Commissioners,

(b) must specify the description of accounts in relation to which the election is to have effect, and

(c) must be made in the return required by regulation 8.

4(4) For the purposes of these Regulations—

(a) any reference to an entity account is to a financial account which is not an account the account holder of which (or, if more than one, each account holder of which) is an individual holding the account otherwise than as a partner of a partnership, and

(b) any reference to an individual account is to a financial account held in the name of an individual (whether solely or jointly with another) but not as a partner or a partnership.

4(5) For the purposes of determining—

(a) whether or not a financial account maintained by an institution meets any of the descriptions in paragraph (1)(b), and

(b) which case in regulation 6(4) applies to an account,

the institution must apply the account balance aggregation and currency translation rules at paragraph VI.C of Annex I.

But, in determining the balance or value of an account denominated in a currency other than US dollars, instead of applying the currency translation rule in sub-paragraph VI.C.4 of Annex I, the institution may translate the relevant dollar threshold amounts referred to in Annex 1 and regulation 6(4) into the other currency by reference to the spot rate of exchange on the date for which the institution is determining the threshold amounts.

Scope: Non-Resident reporting financial institution's UK representative

5(1) If a reporting financial institution is not resident in the United Kingdom, the obligations of the institution under these Regulations are to be treated as if they were also the obligations of any UK representative of the institution.

5(2) **"UK representative"** has the same meaning as it has in—

(a) Chapter 6 of Part 22 of CTA 2010, in relation to a reporting financial institution that is within the charge to corporation tax, and

(b) Chapter 2C of Part 14 of ITA 2007, in relation to any other reporting financial institution.

5(3) For the purposes of this regulation–

(a) a reporting financial institution which is a partnership is resident in the United Kingdom if the control and management of the business of the partnership as a reporting financial institution takes place there, and

(b) a reporting financial institution which is not a partnership is resident in the United Kingdom if it is resident in the United Kingdom for corporation tax or income tax purposes.

OBLIGATIONS IN RELATION TO FINANCIAL ACCOUNTS

Identification obligations

6(1) A reporting financial institution must establish and maintain arrangements that are designed to identify reportable accounts.

6(2) Such arrangements must identify the territory in which either of the following persons is resident for income tax or corporation tax purposes or for the purposes of any tax imposed by the law of that territory that is of a similar character to either of those taxes–

(a) the account holder, and

(b) any controlling person of the account holder, unless the account holder is either

    (i) a financial institution, or

    (ii) an active NFFE.

6(3) The institution is taken to comply with the obligation to establish and maintain arrangements within paragraph (1) only if–

(a) the arrangements meet the applicable due diligence requirements as set out in this regulation (as modified by regulation 7 where an election under that regulation is in force), and

(b) the arrangements secure that the evidence used in accordance with this regulation or regulation 7, or a record of the steps taken in accordance with this regulation or regulation 7, is kept for a period of six years beginning with the end of the year in which the arrangements applied to the financial accounts.

6(4) The due diligence requirements for a calendar year are set out in the following cases.

Preexisting individual accounts

Case 1

In the case of preexisting individual accounts with a balance or value that does not exceed $1,000,000 as of 30 June 2014, the procedures described at paragraphs II.B and II.C of Annex I.

But this does not apply in relation to any preexisting individual account meeting the description at paragraph II.A of Annex I in relation to which an election under regulation 4(2) is in place.

Case 2

In the case of preexisting individual accounts with a balance or value that exceeds $1,000,000 as of 30 June 2014, or 31 December 2015 or 31 December in any subsequent year, the procedures described at paragraphs II.D and II.E of Annex I.

New individual accounts

Case 3

In the case of new individual accounts, the procedures described at paragraphs III.B to III.D of Annex I.

But this does not apply in relation to any new individual account meeting the description at paragraph III.A of Annex I in relation to which an election under regulation 4(2) is in place.

Preexisting entity accounts

Case 4

In the case of preexisting entity accounts, the procedures described at paragraphs IV.D and IV.E (1) and (3) of Annex I.

But this does not apply in relation to any preexisting entity account meeting the description at paragraph IV.A of Annex I in relation to which an election under regulation 4(2) is in place.

Case 5

In the case of preexisting entity accounts with a balance or value that does not exceed $250,000 as of 30 June 2014, but with a balance or value that exceeds $1,000,000 as of 31 December 2015 or 31 December in any subsequent year, the procedures at paragraphs IV.D and IV.E (2) and (3) of Annex I.

New entity accounts

Case 6

In the case of new entity accounts, the procedures described at paragraphs V.B to V.D of Annex I.

But this does not apply in relation to any new entity account meeting the description at paragraph V.A of Annex I in relation to which an election under regulation 4(2) is in place.

6(5) If in the case of an account within Case 1–

(a)   an institution has established the account holder's relevant tax status from documentary evidence mentioned in paragraph VI.D (4) of Annex I, and

(b)   it has done so in order to meet its obligations under a Qualifying Intermediary agreement as mentioned in that paragraph,

the due diligence requirements in the case of that account do not include the requirement to carry out the electronic search described in paragraph II.B (1) of Annex I.

6(6) If in the case of an account within Case 2–

(a)   an institution has established the account holder's relevant tax status from documentary evidence mentioned in paragraph VI.D (4) of Annex I, and

(b)   it has done so in order to meet its obligations under a Qualifying Intermediary agreement as mentioned in that paragraph,

the due diligence requirements in the case of that account do not include the requirement to carry out the electronic searches described in paragraph II.B (1) or II.D (1) of Annex I or the requirement to carry out the paper record search described in paragraph II.D (2) of that Annex.

6(7) If, as a result of this regulation, a person's relevant tax status is required to be certified, a reporting financial institution may require the person to supply to the institution such documentary evidence mentioned in paragraph VI.D of Annex I as the institution considers appropriate in support of the certification.

6(8) The due diligence requirements in this regulation must be applied in relation to each category of reportable account by reference to the special rules and definitions at paragraph I.D (1) to (3) and section VI of Annex I.

6(9) For the purposes of this regulation references to the documentary evidence set out in paragraph VI.D of Annex I are to be treated as if the words "other than a Form W-8 or W-9" were omitted.

Modification of due diligence requirements

7(1) This regulation modifies the due diligence requirements set out in regulation 6 in the case of a reporting financial institution but only if it makes an election applying those modifications.

7(2) If the institution obtains, or is in the process of obtaining, evidence of a person's relevant tax status in relation to any preexisting account, it is entitled to rely on the evidence in relation to any account opened after 30 June 2014 unless it has reasonable cause to believe that the person's relevant tax status has subsequently changed.

7(3) Paragraph (2) has effect in the case of preexisting individual accounts maintained by the institution for an account holder only if, for the purpose of establishing which of the cases in regulation 6(4) are applicable to those accounts, the institution treats all those accounts as a single preexisting individual account.

7(4) If the institution or a related entity obtains, or is in the process of obtaining, evidence of a person's relevant tax status in relation to a financial account, the institution is entitled to rely on the evidence in relation to all financial accounts maintained by the institution for the account holder unless the institution has reasonable cause to believe that the person's relevant tax status has subsequently changed.

7(5) The due diligence requirements set out in regulation 6 do not need to be met in relation to a financial account if–

(a)   the institution maintains the account as a result of a merger with, or acquisition of, a qualifying financial institution which had established the relevant tax status of the account holder and any controlling person, and

(b)   the institution has no reasonable cause to believe that the relevant tax status of the account holder or any controlling person has changed.

7(6)   For this purpose **"qualifying financial institution"**, in relation to a financial institution, means another financial institution—

(a)   which has not previously been a related entity of the institution, and

(b)   which immediately before the merger or acquisition was either a reporting financial institution for the purposes of these Regulations or a financial institution described under sub-paragraph 1(p) of Article 1 of the relevant agreement.

7(7)   An election under this regulation—

(a)   is to be made by being given to the Commissioners,

(b)   must be made in the return required under regulation 8, and

(c)   has effect in relation to the calendar year in respect of which the return is made and all later calendar years (unless subsequently withdrawn).

Reporting obligations

8(1)   A reporting financial institution must, in respect of 2014 and every following calendar year, prepare a return setting out—

(a)   the required information in relation to every reportable account of that category that is maintained by the institution at any time during the calendar year in question, and

(b)   the institution's Global Intermediary Identification Number (or, if it has not been allocated such a number, the Unique Taxpayer Reference number allocated to the institution by HMRC).

8(2)   If during the calendar year in question the reporting financial institution maintains no reportable accounts, the return must state that fact.

8(3)   The institution must send a return under this regulation to an officer of Revenue and Customs on or before 31st May of the year following the calendar year to which the return relates ("the reporting date").

8(4)   The required information is—

(a)   the name and address of the account holder,

(b)   the account holder's social security number,

(c)   if an account is identifiable by an account number, that number or, if not, any functional equivalents,

(d)   the balance or value of the account (including, in the case of a cash value insurance contract or annuity contract, the cash value or surrender value) as of the end of the calendar year or, if the account was closed during the year, the balance or value on the date that the reporting financial institution closed the account,

(e)   the relevant total gross credits, or if there are none, a statement of that fact,

(f)   if the account holder is an individual, that person's date of birth, and

(g)   if the account holder is a passive NFFE that has a controlling person who is a specified person, the name and address of that specified person, and, if that person is an individual, that person's—

    (i)   social security number, and

    (ii)   date of birth.

8(5)   The **"relevant total gross credits"** means—

(a)   in the case of a custodial account—

    (i)   the total gross amount of interest, the total gross amount of dividends and the total gross amount of other income generated with respect to assets held in the account which is paid into, or with respect to, the account during the calendar year, and

    (ii)   the total gross proceeds from the sale or redemption of property paid into the account during the calendar year if the institution acted as a custodian, broker, nominee or otherwise as an agent for the account holder,

(b)   in the case of a depository account, the total gross amount of interest paid to the account during the calendar year, and

(c)   in the case of any other account, the total gross amount of sums paid by the institution under a legal obligation to the account holder with respect to the account during the calendar year,

and **"interest"** here includes any amount that is chargeable as interest under Part 4 of ITTOIA 2005.

8(6) For the purposes of this regulation–

(a) references to the balance or value of an account include a nil balance or value,

(b) references to paying an amount include crediting an amount,

(c) "**social security number**" means–

(i) in relation to the Isle of Man agreement, either the number allocated to a person for the social security purposes or a person's United Kingdom National insurance number,

(ii) in relation to any other relevant agreement, the number allocated to a person for the social security purposes of Guernsey, Jersey or Gibraltar as the case may be.

8(7) If a reporting financial institution has an established practice for the periodic valuation of accounts of a particular description otherwise than at the end of a calendar year, the institution may report under paragraph (5)(a) or (c) by reference to a period of 12 months ending with the date (or, if more than one, the latest date) in the calendar year on which the institution values accounts of that description (instead of by reference to the calendar year).

8(8) If a reporting financial institution does not hold the information that it is required to report under paragraph (4)(b), (f) and (g), the institution must obtain that information from the account holder.

Modifications for calendar years 2014 to 2016

9(1) In relation to any reportable account–

(a) there is no requirement to include in the return for the calendar year 2014 information about relevant total gross credits, and

(b) there is no requirement to include in the return for the calendar year 2015 any information set out in regulation 8(5)(a)(ii).

9(2) In the case of preexisting accounts there is no requirement to include in the return for calendar years before 2017 any information set out in regulation 8(4)(b), (f) and (g) if the reporting financial institution does not hold that information.

9(3) In the case of the calendar year 2014 the reporting date is 31st May 2016.s

PENALTIES FOR BREACH OF OBLIGATIONS

Penalties for failure to comply

10 A person is liable to a penalty of £300 if the person fails to comply with any obligation under these Regulations.

Penalties for inaccurate information

11(1) A person is liable to a penalty not exceeding £3,000 if–

(a) in complying with an obligation under regulation 8 the person provides inaccurate information, and

(b) condition A, B or C is met.

11(2) Condition A is that the inaccuracy is–

(a) due to a failure to comply with regulation 6, or

(b) deliberate on the part of the person.

11(3) Condition B is that the person knows of the inaccuracy at the time the information is provided but does not inform HMRC at that time.

11(4) Condition C is that the person–

(a) discovers the inaccuracy some time later, and

(b) fails to take reasonable steps to inform HMRC.

Matters to be disregarded in relation to liability to penalties

12(1) Liability to a penalty under regulation 10 or 11 does not arise if the person satisfies HMRC or (on an appeal notified to the tribunal) the tribunal that there is a reasonable excuse for the failure.

12(2) For the purposes of this regulation neither of the following is a reasonable excuse–

(a) that there is an insufficiency of funds to do something, or

Statutory Instruments

(b)   that a person relies upon another person to do something.

12(3) If a person had a reasonable excuse for a failure but the excuse has ceased, the person is to be treated as having continued to have the excuse if the failure is remedied without unreasonable delay after the excuse ceased.

Assessment of penalties

13(1) If the reporting financial institution becomes liable to a penalty under regulation 10 or 11, an officer of Revenue and Customs may assess the penalty.

13(2) If an officer does so, the officer must notify the institution.

13(3) An assessment of a penalty under regulation 10 must be made within the period of 12 months beginning with the date on which the person became liable to the penalty.

13(4) An assessment of a penalty under regulation 11 must be made—

(a)   within the period of 12 months beginning with the date on which the inaccuracy first came to the attention of an officer of Revenue and Customs, and

(b)   within the period of 6 years beginning with the date on which the person became liable to the penalty.

Right to appeal against penalty

14 A person may appeal against a decision by an officer of Revenue and Customs—

(a)   that a penalty is payable under regulation 10 or 11, or

(b)   as to the amount of such a penalty.

Procedure on appeal against penalty

15(1) Notice of an appeal under regulation 14 must be given—

(a)   in writing,

(b)   before the end of the period of 30 days beginning with the date on which notification under regulation 13 was given, and

(c)   to HMRC.

15(2) It must state the grounds of appeal.

15(3) On an appeal under regulation 14(a) that is notified to the tribunal, the tribunal may confirm or cancel the decision.

15(4) On an appeal under regulation 14(b) that is notified to the tribunal, the tribunal may—

(a)   confirm the decision, or

(b)   substitute for the decision another decision that the officer of Revenue and Customs had power to make.

15(5) Subject to this regulation and regulation 16, the provisions of Part 5 of TMA 1970 relating to appeals have effect in relation to appeals under regulation 14 as they have effect in relation to an appeal against an assessment to income tax.

Enforcement of penalties

16(1) A penalty under these Regulations must be paid before the end of the period of 30 days beginning with the date mentioned in paragraph (2).

16(2) That date is—

(a)   the date on which notification under regulation 13 is given in respect of the penalty, or

(b)   if a notice of appeal under regulation 14 is given, the date on which the appeal is finally determined or withdrawn.

16(3) A penalty under these Regulations may be enforced as if it were income tax charged in an assessment and due and payable.

MISCELLANEOUS

Accounts with a negative value

17 For the purpose of applying paragraph VI.C of Annex I as required by these Regulations, an account balance that has a negative value is treated as having a nil value.

Anti-Avoidance

18 If a person does things wholly or mainly for the purpose of avoiding any obligation under these Regulations, these Regulations are to have effect as if those things had not been done.

SUPPLEMENTARY

Definitions

19(1) In these Regulations–

"**Annex 1**" means Annex 1 of the relevant agreement,

"**the Commissioners**" means the Commissioners for her Majesty's Revenue and Customs,

"**Global Intermediary Identification Number**" means a number allocated to a Financial Institution by the Internal Revenue Service in the United States of America for the purposes of the part of the law of that territory commonly known as the Foreign Account Tax Compliance Act, and

"**the tribunal**" means the first tier Tribunal or, where determined by or under Tribunal Procedure Rules, the Upper Tribunal.

19(2) In these Regulations references to a person's relevant tax status are to whether or not that person is–

(a)   in relation to the Isle of Man agreement, a specified Isle of Man person,

(b)   in relation to the Guernsey agreement, a specified Guernsey person,

(c)   in relation to the Jersey agreement, a specified Jersey person, and

(d)   in relation to the Gibraltar agreement, a specified Gibraltar person.

19(3) In these Regulations references to a value in dollars are references to a value in the currency of the United States of America.

19(4) The following table lists the places where expressions that apply for the purposes of these Regulations are defined or otherwise explained–

Expression	Reference
account holder	regulation 2(4) and sub-paragraph 1(dd) of Article 1 of the relevant agreement
Active NFFE	regulation 2(4) and paragraph VI.B (6) of Annex 1
Annex 1	regulation 19(1)
annuity contract	regulation 2(4) and sub-paragraph 1(w) of Article 1 of the relevant agreement
the Commissioners	regulation 19(1)
cash value insurance contract	regulation 2(4) and sub-paragraph 1(x) of Article 1 of the relevant agreement
controlling person	regulation 2(4) and sub-paragraph 1(ll) of Article 1 of the relevant agreement
custodial account	regulation 2(4) and sub-paragraph 1(t) of Article 1 of the relevant agreement
custodial institution	regulation 3(7)
depository account	regulation 2(4) and sub-paragraph 1(s) of Article 1 of the relevant agreement
depository institution	regulation 3(3)
entity account	regulation 4(4)(a)
financial account	regulation 2(4) and sub-paragraph 1(r) of Article 1 of the relevant agreement
financial institution	regulation 2(4) and sub-paragraph 1(g) of Article 1 of the relevant agreement
the Gibraltar agreement	regulation 2(2)
Global Intermediary Identification Number	regulation 19(1)
the Guernsey agreement	regulation 2(2)
HMRC	section 222(4) FA 2013

Statutory Instruments

Expression	Reference
individual account	regulation 4(4)(b)
insurance contract	regulation 2(4) and sub-paragraph 1(v) of Article 1 of the relevant agreement
investment entity	regulation 3(4)
the Isle of Man agreement	regulation 2(2)
the Jersey agreement	regulation 2(2)
new entity account	regulation 2(4) and paragraph V of Annex 1
new individual account	regulation 2(4) and paragraph III of Annex 1
non-reporting financial institution	regulation 2(4) and sub-paragraph 1(q) of Article 1 of the relevant agreement
passive NFFE	regulation 2(4) and sub-paragraph VI.B.5 of Annex 1 of the relevant agreement
preexisting account	regulation 2(4) and sub-paragraph 1(z) of Article 1 of the relevant agreement
preexisting entity account	regulation 2(4) and paragraph IV of Annex 1
preexisting individual account	regulation 2(4) and paragraph II of Annex 1
related entity	regulation 2(4) and sub-paragraph 1(kk) of Article 1 of the relevant agreement
the relevant agreement	regulation 2(3)
relevant tax status	regulation 19(2)
relevant total gross credits	regulation 8(5)
reportable account	regulation 4
reporting date	regulations 8(3) and 9(3)
reporting financial institution	regulation 3
specified Gibraltar person	regulation 2(4) and sub-paragraph 1(gg) of Article 1 of the Gibraltar agreement
specified Guernsey person	regulation 2(4) and sub-paragraph 1(gg) of Article 1 of the Guernsey agreement
specified insurance company	regulation 2(4) and sub-paragraph 1(k) of Article 1 of the relevant agreement
specified Isle of Man person	regulation 2(4) and sub-paragraph 1(gg) of Article 1 of the Isle of Man agreement
specified Jersey person	regulation 2(4) and sub-paragraph 1(gg) of Article 1 of the Jersey agreement
specified person	regulation 2(4) and sub-paragraph 1(ee) of Article 1 of the relevant agreement
the tribunal	regulation 19(1)
United Kingdom financial institution	regulation 2(4) and sub-paragraph 1(l) of Article 1 of the relevant agreement

TRIBUNALS, COURTS AND ENFORCEMENT ACT 2007 (CONSEQUENTIAL, TRANSITIONAL AND SAVING PROVISION) ORDER 2014

(SI 2014/600)

Made on 12 March 2014 by the Lord Chancellor in exercise of the powers conferred upon them by s. 145 of the Tribunals, Courts and Enforcement Act 2007 and s. 8 of the Law of Distress Amendment Act 1888. Operative in accordance with reg. 2.

CITATION AND INTERPRETATION

1(1)   This Order may be cited as the Tribunals, Courts and Enforcement Act 2007 (Consequential, Transitional and Saving Provision) Order 2014.

1(2)   In this Order–

(a)   **"the 2007 Act"** means the Tribunals, Courts and Enforcement Act 2007;

(b)   **"relevant subordinate legislation"** means an instrument made under an Act in or before the Session of Parliament in which the 2007 Act was passed;

(c)   **"the Schedule 12 procedure"** means the procedure under Schedule 12 of the 2007 Act.

COMMENCEMENT

2(1)   Subject to paragraph (2), this Order comes into force on 6th April 2014.

2(2)   The revocations of the Distress for Rent (Amendment) Rules 2009 and the Distress for Rent (Amendment) Rules 2011 in Part 2 of the Schedule come into force immediately before the repeal of section 8 of the Law of Distress Amendment Act 1888.

GENERAL CONSEQUENTIAL, TRANSITIONAL AND SAVING PROVISION

3(1)   Subject to any specific amendments or revocations made by this Order–

(a)   any reference (however expressed) in relevant subordinate legislation that is or is deemed to be to the use of a power to distrain or to levy distress is to be read, so far as necessary for continuing its effect, as a reference to the use of a power to use the Schedule 12 procedure;

(b)   any reference (however expressed) in relevant subordinate legislation to–

 (i)   a writ of fieri facias (other than a writ of fieri facias de bonis ecclesiasticis);

 (ii)   a warrant of execution; or

 (iii)   a warrant of distress (other than one which confers a power exercisable only against specific goods),

 is to be read, so far as necessary for continuing its effect, as a reference to a writ or warrant of control;

(c)   any form of writ or warrant which describes the writ or warrant as—

 (i)   a writ of fieri facias (other than a writ of fieri facias de bonis ecclesiasticis);

 (ii)   a warrant of execution; or

 (iii)   a warrant of distress (other than one which confers a power exercisable only against specific goods),

 is to be read, so far as necessary for its validity, as describing the writ or warrant as a writ or warrant of control; and

(d)   any reference (however expressed) in any form or notice (whether or not prescribed by virtue of any enactment) or other document–

 (i)   to a bailiff, is to be read as a reference to an enforcement agent; or

 (ii)   to the use of a power to distrain or to levy distress, is to be read as a reference to the use of a power to use the Schedule 12 procedure,

 so far as necessary for the validity of the form, notice or other document or any action pursuant to it.

3(2)   Where, by virtue of section 66 of the 2007 Act, Part 3 of the 2007 Act does not affect the continuing exercise of a power in relation to goods, the amendments and revocations made by this Order do not apply for the purposes of the continuing exercise of that power in relation to those goods.

TRANSITIONAL PROVISION WHERE CERTAIN PRE-COMMENCEMENT ENFORCEMENT ACTION TAKEN

4(1)   Paragraph (2) applies where, before 6th April 2014–

(a)   a writ of fieri facias has been issued;

(b)   a High Court Enforcement Officer has made at least one journey to seize goods pursuant to the writ; and

(c)   no goods have been seized and no walking possession agreement has been entered into, but the debtor–

     (i)   has entered into an agreement to pay the amount for which the writ was issued; and

     (ii)   has been making payments in accordance with the agreement through the duration of the writ.

4(2)   Where this paragraph applies, the action taken is to be regarded as constituting the compliance stage and the first enforcement stage within the meaning of regulation 6 of the Taking Control of Goods (Fees) Regulations 2014, but the fees for the compliance stage and the first enforcement stage will not be payable and instead, there may be recovered, as appropriate–

(a)   the mileage fee (fee 2 in Part A of Schedule 3 to the High Court Enforcement Officers Regulations 2004) in relation to the journey;

(b)   the percentage fee (fee 1 in Part A of Schedule 3 to the High Court Enforcement Officers Regulations 2004) in relation to any amounts paid under the agreement; and

(c)   if the agreement provided for the payment of such a fee, a miscellaneous fee (fee 12 in Part C of Schedule 3 to the High Court Enforcement Officers Regulations 2004).

4(3)   Paragraph (4) applies where, before 6th April 2014–

(a)   a liability order has been made or (as the case may be) the authority has issued a warrant for the enforcement of a specified debt, under–

     (i)   the Non-Domestic Rating (Collection and Enforcement) (Local Lists) Regulations 1989;

     (ii)   the Council Tax (Administration and Enforcement) Regulations 1992;

     (iii)   the Child Support (Collection and Enforcement) Regulations 1992; or

     (iv)   the Enforcement of Road Traffic Debts Order 1993;

(b)   a visit has (or visits have) been made to premises, or premises have been attended, to levy distress or with a view to levying distress; but

(c)   no goods have been seized and possession (whether close or walking possession) has not been taken of any goods.

4(4)   Where this paragraph applies, the action taken is to be regarded as constituting the compliance stage within the meaning of regulation 5 of the Taking Control of Goods (Fees) Regulations 2014, but the fee for the compliance stage will not be payable and instead, there may be recovered, as appropriate–

(a)   the fees for the matters under heads A(i) and A(ii) in paragraph 1 of Schedule 3 to the Non-Domestic Rating (Collection and Enforcement) (Local Lists) Regulations 1989 in relation to the visit or visits;

(b)   the fees for the matters under heads A(i) and A(ii) in paragraph 1 of Schedule 3 to the Council Tax (Administration and Enforcement) Regulations 1992 in relation to the visit or visits;

(c)   the fees for the matters under heads A and BB in paragraph 1 of Schedule 2 to the Child Support (Collection and Enforcement) Regulations 1992 in relation to the visit or visits and any associated letter; or

(d)   the fees for the matters under heads 1 and 3 in Schedule 1 to the Enforcement of Road Traffic Debts (Certificated Bailiffs) Regulations 1993 in relation to the visit or visits and any associated letter.

4(5)   Paragraph (6) applies where, before 6th April 2014, a bailiff has attended premises to levy distress for rent but the levy has not been made, and possession has not been taken of any goods.

4(6)   Where this paragraph applies, the action taken is to be regarded as constituting the compliance stage within the meaning of regulation 5 of the Taking Control of Goods (Fees) Regulations 2014, but the fee for the compliance stage will not be payable and instead the fee in paragraph 2 of Appendix 1 to the Distress for Rent Rules 1988 may be recovered.

4(7) Paragraph (8) applies where, before 6th April 2014–

(a) a warrant of distress has been issued under section 76(1) of the Magistrates' Courts Act 1980; and

(b) a bailiff has–

    (i) issued to the debtor a letter or notice requiring payment of the sum within a period specified in the letter or notice and giving notice of the intention to levy the sum if it is not paid within that period; or

    (ii) has, or has in addition, attended premises to levy the sum, but the levy has not been made, and possession has not been taken of any goods.

4(8) Where this paragraph applies, the action taken is to be regarded as constituting the compliance stage within the meaning of regulation 5 of the Taking Control of Goods (Fees) Regulations 2014, but the fee for the compliance stage will not be payable and instead there may be recovered the appropriate fee for the action taken provided for at the time the action was taken in any contractual or other binding arrangement in force between the creditor and the bailiff at that time.

4(9) In this article, references to any fees in any subordinate legislation other than the Taking Control of Goods (Fees) Regulations 2014 are references to the fees in that subordinate legislation as it was in force immediately before 6th April 2014.

SAVING FOR REGULATIONS TREATED AS IF MADE UNDER
SECTION 83 TRAFFIC MANAGEMENT ACT 2004

5 The repeal, by paragraph 156 of Schedule 13 to the 2007 Act, of section 83 of the Traffic Management Act 2004 does not have the effect of revoking any subordinate legislation having effect by virtue of subsection (4) of section 83 as if made under that section.

SAVING FOR CERTIFICATES UNDER SECTION 7 OF THE LAW OF
DISTRESS AMENDMENT ACT 1888

6 The–

(a) repeal, by paragraph 19 of Schedule 14 to the 2007 Act, of section 7 of the Law of Distress Amendment Act 1888; and

(b) revocation, by Part 2 of the Schedule to these Regulations, of the Distress for Rent Rules 1988,

do not have the effect of cancelling any certificate granted under section 7 of the Law of Distress Amendment Act 1888 which is in force at the time when the repeal and revocation come into force.

SPECIFIC CONSEQUENTIAL AMENDMENTS AND REVOCATIONS

7 The rules, regulations and orders listed in the Schedule are amended or revoked as set out in the Schedule.

SCHEDULE – CONSEQUENTIAL AMENDMENTS AND REVOCATIONS

Article 7

Part 1: Amendments

AMENDMENT OF MAGISTRATES' COURTS RULES

1 [Amends Magistrates' Courts Rules 1981.]

AMENDMENT OF NON-DOMESTIC RATING (COLLECTION AND
ENFORCEMENT) REGULATIONS

2 [Amends SI 1989/1058.]

AMENDMENT OF COUNCIL TAX (ADMINISTRATION AND ENFORCEMENT)
REGULATIONS

3 [Amends SI 1992/613.]

AMENDMENT OF CHILD SUPPORT (COLLECTION AND ENFORCEMENT) REGULATIONS

4 [Amends Child Support (Collection and Enforcement) Regulations 1992.]

AMENDMENT OF ENFORCEMENT OF ROAD TRAFFIC DEBTS ORDER

5 [Amends SI 1993/2073.]

AMENDMENT OF LOCAL AUTHORITIES (CONTRACTING OUT OF BILLING, COLLECTION AND ENFORCEMENT FUNCTIONS) ORDERS

6 [Amends Local Authorities (Contracting Out of Tax Billing, Collection and Enforcement Functions) Order 1996.]

AMENDMENT OF STAMP DUTY LAND TAX (ADMINISTRATION) REGULATIONS

7 [Revokes SI 2003/2837, reg. 29–32 and Sch. 3.]

AMENDMENT OF HIGH COURT ENFORCEMENT OFFICERS REGULATIONS

8 [Amends SI 2004/400.]

AMENDMENT OF BUSINESS IMPROVEMENT DISTRICTS REGULATIONS

9 [Amends Business Improvement Districts (England) Regulations 2004.]

10 [Amends Business Improvement Districts (Wales) Regulations 2005.]

Part 2: Revocations

Instrument revoked	Reference	Extent of revocation
The Distress for Rent Rules 1988	S.I. 1988/2050	The whole Rules
The Non-Domestic Rating (Collection and Enforcement) (Local Lists) Regulations 1989	S.I. 1989/1058	Schedule 3
The Council Tax (Administration and Enforcement) Regulations 1992	S.I. 1992/613	Regulations 45A and 46; Schedule 5
The Enforcement of Road Traffic Debts (Certificated Bailiffs) Regulations 1993	S.I. 1993/2072	The whole Regulations
The Enforcement of Road Traffic Debts Order 1993	S.I. 1993/2073	Articles 9 to 17
The Distraint by Collectors (Fees, Costs and Charges) Regulations 1994	S.I. 1994/236	The whole Regulations, to the extent that they apply to England and Wales only
The Distraint by Collectors (Fees, Costs and Charges) (Amendment) Regulations 1995	S.I. 1995/2151	The whole Regulations, to the extent that they apply to England and Wales only
The Distress for Customs and Excise Duties and Other Indirect Taxes Regulations 1997	S.I. 1997/1431	The whole Regulations, to the extent that they apply to England and Wales only
The Enforcement of Road Traffic Debts (Certificated Bailiffs) (Amendment) Regulations 1998	S.I. 1998/1351	The whole Regulations
The Distraint by Authorised Officers (Fees, Costs and Charges) Regulations 1999	S.I. 1999/980	The whole Regulations, to the extent that they apply to England and Wales only

Instrument revoked	Reference	Extent of revocation
The Distress for Rent (Amendment) Rules 1999	S.I. 1999/2360	The whole Rules
The Distress for Rent (Amendment No. 2) Rules 1999	S.I. 1999/2564	The whole Rules
The Distress for Rent (Amendment No. 3) Rules 1999	S.I. 1999/3186	The whole Rules
The Distraint by Collectors (Fees, Costs and Charges) (Stamp Duty Penalties) Regulations 1999	S.I. 1999/3263	The whole Regulations, to the extent that they apply to England and Wales only
The Distress for Rent (Amendment) Rules 2000	S.I. 2000/1481	The whole Rules
The Distress for Rent (Amendment No. 2) Rules 2000	S.I. 2000/2737	The whole Rules
The Distress for Rent (Amendment) Rules 2001	S.I. 2001/4026	The whole Rules
The Enforcement of Road Traffic Debts (Certificated Bailiffs) (Amendment) Regulations 2003	S.I. 2003/1857	The whole Regulations
The Distress for Rent (Amendment) Rules 2003	S.I. 2003/1858	The whole Rules
The Distress for Rent (Amendment No. 2) Rules 2003	S.I. 2003/2141	The whole Rules
The Stamp Duty Land Tax (Administration) Regulations 2003	S.I. 2003/2837	Regulations 29 to 32; Schedule 3
The High Court Enforcement Officers Regulations 2004	S.I. 2004/400	Regulations 15; Schedule 3 Part A; Schedule 4
The Distress for Rent (Amendment) Rules 2009	S.I. 2009/873	The whole Rules
The Distress for Rent (Amendment) Rules 2011	S.I. 2011/1542	The whole Rules

INVESTMENT TRANSACTIONS (TAX) REGULATIONS 2014

(SI 2014/685)

Made on 17 March 2014 by the Treasury in exercise of the powers conferred upon them by s. 17(3) and 18 of the Finance (No. 2) Act 2005, s. 622A of the Corporation Tax Act 2010, s. 354 of the Taxation (International and Other Provisions) Act 2010 and s. 217 of the Finance Act 2013. Operative from 8 April 2014.

CITATION, COMMENCEMENT AND EFFECT

1(1) These Regulations may be cited as the Investment Transactions (Tax) Regulations 2014 and come into force on 8th April 2014.

1(2) The Regulations have effect in relation to transactions entered into on or after that date.

INVESTMENT TRANSACTIONS

2(1) These Regulations specify certain kinds of transactions as investment transactions for the purposes of–

(a)   the Authorised Investment Funds (Tax) Regulations 2006,

(b)   the Offshore Funds (Tax) Regulations 2009,

(c)   the Investment Trust (Approved Company) (Tax) Regulations 2011, and

(d)   the Unauthorised Unit Trusts (Tax) Regulations 2013,

2(2) An investment transaction means–

(a)   any transaction in stocks and shares,

(b)   any transaction in a relevant contract,

(c)   any transaction which results in a fund becoming a party to a loan relationship or a related transaction in respect of a loan relationship,

(d)   any transaction in units in a collective investment scheme,

(e)   any transaction in securities of any description not falling within paragraphs (a) to (d),

(f)   any transaction consisting in the buying or selling of any foreign currency,

(g)   any transaction in a carbon emission trading product,

(h)   any transaction in rights under a life insurance policy.

2(3) For the purposes of these Regulations, **"fund"** means an authorised investment fund, an offshore fund, an investment trust or an exempt unauthorised unit trust, as the case may be.

"RELEVANT CONTRACT"

3(1) For the purposes of regulation 2(2)(b), **"relevant contract"** has the same meaning as in Part 7 of the Corporation Tax Act 2009.

This is subject to paragraphs (2) to (4).

3(2) A transaction which relates to land can only be a relevant contract if it uses an index which is–

(a)   publicly accessible,

(b)   comprised of a significant number of properties, and

(c)   not maintained by–

    (i)   the fund,

    (ii)   the manager of the fund, or

    (iii)   a person connected with the fund or the manager of the fund.

3(3) A contract the terms of which provide for the delivery of any property other than property a transaction in which would fall within regulation 2(2) where the property is delivered is not a relevant contract.

3(4) The reference to a loan relationship in the definition of **"warrant"** in section 710 of the Corporation Tax Act 2009 is to be construed in accordance with regulation 4 but with references to **"fund"** in that regulation being treated as references to **"company"**.

3(5) For the purposes of this regulation–

(a)   sections 993 and 994 of the Income Tax Act 2007 (connected persons) apply where the manager is a person other than a company, and

(b)   sections 1122 and 1123 of CTA 2010 (connected persons) apply in the case of a fund or where the manager is a person which is a company.

3(6) For the purposes of the Unauthorised Unit Trusts (Tax) Regulations 2013, references in this regulation to the manager of the fund are to treated as references to the manager or trustee of the fund.

LOAN RELATIONSHIPS AND RELATED TRANSACTIONS

4(1) For the purposes of regulation 2(2)(c), a fund has a loan relationship where the fund stands (whether by reference to a security or otherwise) in the position of a creditor or debtor as respects any money debt and either–

(a)   that debt is one arising from a transaction for the lending of money, or

(b)   that debt is not one which arose from a transaction for the lending of money but is one–

    (i)   on which interest is payable to or by the fund,

    (ii)   in relation to which the exchange gains or losses arise to the fund, or

    (iii) as respects which the conditions in paragraph (2) are satisfied.

4(2) The conditions mentioned in paragraph (1)(b)(iii) are that–

(a)   the fund stands in the position of creditor in relation to the money debt, and

(b)   the money debt is one from which a discount (whether of an income or capital nature) arises to the fund.

4(3) For the purposes of this regulation–

"exchange gains or losses" means profits or gains or losses which arise as a result of comparing at different times the expression in one currency of the whole or some part of the valuation put by the fund in another currency on an asset or liability of the fund,

"money debt" has the same meaning as it has for the purposes of Part 5 of the Corporation Tax Act 2009.

4(4) For the purposes of regulation 2(2)(c), a **"related transaction"** in relation to a loan relationship means any disposal or acquisition (in whole or in part) of rights or liabilities under that relationship.

"UNITS IN A COLLECTIVE INVESTMENT SCHEME"

5(1) For the purposes of regulation 2(2)(d)–

"collective investment scheme" has the meaning given by section 235 of the Financial Services and Markets Act 2000,

"units" means the rights or interests (however described) of the investors in a collective investment scheme.

5(2) In paragraph (1) an **"investor"**, in relation to a collective investment scheme, means a beneficial owner of units in the scheme, except where the units are held on trust (other than a bare trust) or are comprised in the estate of a deceased person, and in such a case the investor, in relation to the scheme, means the trustees of the trust or, as the case may be, the deceased's personal representatives.

"TRANSACTION IN A CARBON EMISSION TRADING PRODUCT"

6(1) For the purposes of regulation 2(2)(g), a **"transaction in a carbon emission trading product"** means a transaction–

(a)   in transferable units issued pursuant to the Kyoto Protocol, or

(b)   in any similar transferable units relating to emissions of greenhouse gases,

where the transaction does not otherwise fall within any other sub-paragraph of regulation 2(2).

6(2) For the purposes of this regulation–

"the Kyoto Protocol" means the Kyoto Protocol to the United Nations Framework Convention on Climate Change signed at Kyoto on 11th December 1997,

"units" includes assigned amount units, certified emission reductions, emission reduction units and removal units.

CONSEQUENTIAL AMENDMENTS

7   [Amends SI 2006/964.]

8   [Amends SI 2009/3001.]

9   [Amends SI 2011/2999.]

10   [Amends SI 2013/2819.]

ANNUAL TAX ON ENVELOPED DWELLINGS (INDEXATION OF ANNUAL CHARGEABLE AMOUNTS) ORDER 2014

(SI 2014/854)

Made on 26 March 2014 by the Treasury in exercise of the powers conferred upon them by s. 101(5) of the Finance Act 2013.

CITATION

1 This Order may be cited as the Annual Tax on Enveloped Dwellings (Indexation of Annual Chargeable Amounts) Order 2014.

CHARGEABLE AMOUNTS

2 The amounts that by virtue of section 101 (indexation of annual chargeable amounts) of the Finance Act 2013 are to be the annual chargeable amounts for the chargeable period beginning on 1st April 2014 are determined in accordance with the following table, by reference to the taxable value of the interest on the relevant day.

Annual chargeable amount	Taxable value of the interest on the relevant day
£15,400	More than £2 million but not more than £5 million.
£35,900	More than £5 million but not more than £10 million.
£71,850	More than £10 million but not more than £20 million.
£143,750	More than £20 million.

INTERNATIONAL TAX COMPLIANCE (UNITED STATES OF AMERICA) REGULATIONS 2014

(SI 2014/1506)

Made on 9 June 2014 by the Treasury in exercise of the powers conferred upon them by s. 222(1)–(3) of the Finance Act 2013. Operative from 30 June 2014.

INTRODUCTORY

Citation and commencement

1(1) These Regulations may be cited as the International Tax Compliance (United States of America) Regulations 2014.

1(2) These Regulations come into force on 30th June 2014.

Implementation of the treaty etc

2(1) These Regulations have effect for and in connection with the implementation of obligations arising under the treaty.

2(2) In these Regulations **"the treaty"** means the agreement reached between the Government of the United Kingdom of Great Britain and Northern Ireland and the Government of the United States of America to improve international tax compliance and to implement FATCA, signed on 12 September 2012, as that agreement has effect from time to time.

2(3) Any expression which is defined in the treaty but not in section 222 or 235 of FA 2013 or in these Regulations has the same meaning in these Regulations as in the treaty.

SCOPE

Meaning of "reporting financial institution"

3(1) In these Regulations **"reporting financial institution"** means a person who carries on business in the United Kingdom as–

(a)   a depository institution,

(b)   an investment entity,

(c)   a custodial institution,

(d)   a specified insurance company,

(e)   a relevant holding company, or

(f)   a treasury company.

3(2) But a person who is a non-reporting United Kingdom financial institution may only qualify as a reporting financial institution for the purposes of these Regulations if that person is a registered deemed-compliant financial institution.

Meaning of "depository institution"

4 For the purposes of these Regulations **"depository institution"** means–

(a)   a person carrying on a regulated activity for the purposes of the Financial Services and Markets Act 2000 by virtue of article 5 of the Financial Services and Markets Act 2000 (Regulated Activities) Order 2001, or

(b)   a person who is within paragraphs (a) to (e) or (h) to (j) of the definition of "electronic money issuer" in regulation 2(1) of the Electronic Money Regulations 2011.

Meaning of "investment entity"

5(1) For the purposes of these Regulations a person (person A) carries on business in the United Kingdom as an investment entity if–

(a)   person A undertakes any of the activities referred to in sub-paragraph 1(j)(1) to (3) of Article 1 of the treaty in the course of carrying on business in the United Kingdom, and A's gross income from that business for the applicable period wholly or mainly derives from those activities, or

(b)   on behalf of person A, a financial institution (person B) undertakes any of the activities referred to in sub-paragraph 1(j)(1) to (3) of Article 1 of the treaty in the course of carrying on business in the United Kingdom, and person A's gross income from the activities undertaken on behalf of person A by person B for the applicable period wholly or mainly derives from investing or dealing in financial assets.

5(2)   For these purposes—

(a)   if a collective investment scheme is constituted by a person (other than a trustee), who carries on business in the United Kingdom, that person (and no-one else) is a reporting financial institution in the case of the scheme and is to be regarded as the investment entity, and

(b)   if a collective investment scheme is constituted otherwise than as described in sub-paragraph (a) and the manager, operator or trustee of the scheme is a person who carries on business in the United Kingdom, the manager, operator or trustee of the scheme (and no-one else) is a reporting financial institution in the case of the scheme and is to be regarded as the investment entity.

5(3)   In paragraph (1) the **"applicable period"** is the shorter of—

(a)   the three year period—

     (i)   ending with the person's most recent accounting date if that date is no more than twelve months earlier than the next reporting date, or

     (ii)   in any other case, ending on the 31 December immediately before the next reporting date, and

(b)   the period—

     (i)   starting on the later of the first day of the period determined under sub-paragraph (a) and the date that the person commenced the business, and

     (ii)   ending on the earlier of the last day of the period determined under sub-paragraph (a) and the last day that the person carried on the business,

and **"accounting date"** here means the date to which a company makes up its accounts.

5(4)   In this regulation—

     "collective investment scheme" means—

     (a)   an investment trust within the meaning of the Corporation Tax Acts,

     (b)   a venture capital trust within the meaning of Part 6 of ITA 2007, or

     (c)   any arrangements that are a "collective investment scheme" within the meaning of Part 17 of the Financial Services and Markets Act 2000;

     "financial assets" means—

     (a)   assets capable of being the subject-matter of a transaction that is an "investment transaction" within the meaning of the Investment Transactions (Tax) Regulations 2014,

     (b)   insurance or annuity contracts,

     (c)   commodities, or

     (d)   derivative contracts within the meaning of Part 7 of CTA 2009;

Meaning of "custodial institution"

6(1)   For the purposes of these Regulations a person carries on a business in the United Kingdom as a custodial institution if—

(a)   20% or more of the gross income of that business as is carried on in the United Kingdom for the applicable period derives from any of—

     (i)   holding financial assets for the account of another person, and

     (ii)   performing related financial services, or

(b)   the person holds assets in the United Kingdom as a nominee for another person who is a connected person within the meaning of section 1122 of CTA 2010.

6(2)   In this regulation—

     "applicable period" and **"financial assets"** have the same meanings as in regulation 5;

     "related financial services" means financial services provided by the person that directly relate to that person holding financial assets on behalf of the other person.

Meaning of "relevant holding company"

7   For the purposes of these Regulations a **"relevant holding company"** means—

(a)   a person whose business consists wholly or mainly of holding (directly or indirectly) any shares or securities issued by a related entity which is within any of regulation 3(1)(a) to (d), or

(b)   a person whose business consists wholly or mainly of holding shares or securities, and who has a qualifying relationship with a qualifying entity.

7(2)   For the purposes of this regulation, a person has a **"qualifying relationship"** with a qualifying entity if—

(a)   the person is connected (within the meaning in section 1122 of CTA 2010) with the entity, or

7(3)   the person provides services or holds investments on behalf of the entity.

Meaning of "treasury company"

8(1)   For the purposes of these Regulations a **"treasury company"** means a company whose business consists wholly or mainly in carrying on for a financial group of which it is a member, or for a qualifying entity with whom it has a qualifying relationship, any of the activities within section 316(9) of TIOPA 2010, and for this purpose—

(a)   the reference in paragraph (d) of that subsection to a UK group company and a group treasury company is to a related entity which is within any of paragraph (1)(a) to (d) of regulation 3, and

(b)   **"financial group"** means a group of entities consisting of the company and its related entities where at least one of those entities falls within any of paragraph (1)(a) to (d) of regulation 3.

8(2)   In this regulation—

"applicable period" and **"financial assets"** have the same meanings as in regulation 5;

"qualifying entity" means an entity that is managed by a financial institution whose income from business in the United Kingdom for the applicable period derives wholly or mainly from investing or dealing in financial assets;

"qualifying relationship" has the same meaning as in regulation 7.

Meaning of "reportable account"

9(1)   In these Regulations a **"reportable account"**, in relation to a reporting financial institution, means—

(a)   subject to paragraph (2), a U.S. reportable account maintained by that institution in the United Kingdom for the purposes of its business as described in regulation 3(1), or

(b)   subject to paragraph (3), an account that is—

    (i)   a pre-existing individual account meeting the description at paragraph II.A of Annex I of the treaty,

    (ii)   a new individual account meeting the description at paragraph III.A of Annex I of the treaty, and

    (iii)   a pre-existing entity account meeting the description at paragraph IV.A of Annex I of the treaty.

9(2)   A U.S. reportable account is not a reportable account if—

(a)   the account holder is deceased or is a personal representative (within the meaning of section 989 of ITA 2007),

(b)   the account is held to comply with an order or judgment made or given in legal proceedings, or

(c)   the funds held in the account are held solely as security for the performance of a party's obligation under a contract for the disposal of an estate or interest in land or of tangible moveable property.

9(3)   An account within any of paragraphs (i) to (iii) of paragraph (1)(b) is not a reportable account for a calendar year if there is an election by the reporting financial institution in force for that year to treat any such account as not being a reportable account.

9(4)   An election under paragraph (3) must be made for each calendar year in which the election is to have effect in the return required by regulation 12 for that year.

9(5)   The institution must apply the account balance aggregation and currency translation rules at paragraph VI.C of Annex I of the treaty for the purposes of determining—

(a)   whether or not a financial account maintained by an institution meets any of the descriptions in paragraph (1)(b), and

(b)   which case in the table in regulation 11(3) applies to an account.

But, in determining the balance or value of an account denominated in a currency other than US dollars, instead of applying the currency translation rule in sub-paragraph VI.C.4 of Annex I, the institution may translate the relevant dollar threshold amounts referred to in Annex 1 and regulation 11(3) into the other currency by reference to the spot rate of exchange on the date for which the institution is determining the threshold amounts.

9(6) For the purposes of these Regulations–

(a)   any reference to an entity account is to a financial account which is not an account the account holder of which (or, if more than one, each account holder of which) is an individual holding the account otherwise than as a partner of a partnership, and

(b)   any reference to an individual account is to a financial account held in the name of an individual (whether solely or jointly with another) but not as a partner of a partnership.

Non-resident reporting financial institution's UK representative

10(1) If a reporting financial institution is not resident in the United Kingdom, the obligations of the institution under these Regulations are to be treated as if they were also the obligations of any UK representative of the institution.

10(2) "UK representative" has the same meaning as it has in–

(a)   Chapter 6 of Part 22 of CTA 2010, in relation to a reporting financial institution that is within the charge to corporation tax, and

(b)   Chapter 2C of Part 14 of ITA 2007, in relation to any other reporting financial institution.

10(3) For the purposes of this regulation–

(a)   a reporting financial institution which is a partnership is resident in the United Kingdom if the control and management of the business of the partnership as a reporting financial institution takes place there, and

(b)   a reporting financial institution which is not a partnership is resident in the United Kingdom if it is resident in the United Kingdom for corporation tax or income tax purposes.

OBLIGATIONS IN RELATION TO FINANCIAL ACCOUNTS

Identification obligation

11(1) A reporting financial institution must establish and maintain arrangements that are designed to identify reportable accounts.

11(2) Such arrangements must–

(a)   identify the territory in which an account holder or a controlling person, as the case may be, is resident for income tax or corporation tax purposes or for the purposes of any tax imposed by the law of that territory that is of a similar character to either of those taxes,

(b)   meet the due diligence procedures set out in this regulation,

(c)   secure that the evidence obtained in accordance with this regulation, or a record of the steps taken to comply with this regulation, in relation to any financial account is kept for a period of six years beginning with the end of the year in which the arrangements applied to the financial accounts.

11(3) The due diligence procedures for a calendar year are set out in the following table.

Case	Type of account	Balance or value	Procedure in Annex 1 of the treaty to be applied	Exceptions: accounts to which due diligence procedures do not apply
Case 1	Preexisting individual account	Not exceed $1,000,000 as of 30 June 2014	Paragraphs II.B and II.C, subject to paragraph (4) of this regulation	Accounts within paragraph II.A of Annex I in relation to which an election under regulation 9(3) is in place
Case 2	Preexisting individual account	Exceeds $1,000,000 as of 30 June 2014, or 31 December 2015 or 31 December in any subsequent year	Paragraphs II.D and II.E, subject to paragraph (5) of this regulation	None
Case 3	New individual account	Any	Paragraphs III.B, III.C and III.D	Accounts within paragraph III.A of Annex I in relation to which an election under regulation 9(3) is in place
Case 4	Preexisting entity account not within Case 5	Any	Paragraphs IV.D and IV.E (1) and (3)	Accounts within paragraph IV.A of Annex I in relation to which an election under regulation 9(3) is in place
Case 5	Preexisting entity account	Not exceed $250,000 as of 30 June 2014, but exceeds $1,000,000 as of 31 December 2015 or 31 December in any subsequent year	Paragraphs IV.D and IV.E (2) and (3)	None
Case 6	New entity account	Any	Paragraphs V.A, V.B and V.C	None

11(4) In the case of an account within Case 1, the due diligence requirements do not include the requirement to carry out the electronic search described in paragraph II.B (1) of Annex I of the treaty if–

(a) an institution has established the account holder's U.S. status from documentary evidence mentioned in paragraph VI.D of Annex I of the treaty, and

(b) it has done so in order to meet its obligations under a Qualifying Intermediary agreement as mentioned in that paragraph.

11(5) In the case of an account within Case 2, the due diligence requirements do not include the requirement to carry out the electronic searches described in paragraph II.B (1) or II.D (1) of Annex I of the treaty or the requirement to carry out the paper record search described in paragraph II.D (2) of that Annex if–

(a) an institution has established the account holder's U.S. status from documentary evidence mentioned in paragraph VI.D of Annex I of the treaty, and

(b) it has done so in order to meet its obligations under a Qualifying Intermediary agreement as mentioned in that paragraph.

11(6) If, as a result of this regulation, a person's U.S. status must be certified, a reporting financial institution may require the person to supply to the institution such documentary evidence mentioned in paragraph VI.D of Annex I of the treaty as the institution considers appropriate in support of the certification.

11(7) The due diligence procedures set out in this regulation must be applied by reference to the special rules and definitions at paragraph I.B (1) to (3) and section VI of Annex I of the treaty.

11(8) In applying the relevant due diligence procedures, a reporting financial institution may rely on evidence of a person's U.S. status obtained in relation to another financial account if the due diligence procedures in the relevant U.S. Treasury Regulations would allow such reliance.

11(9) For the purposes of this regulation references to the documentary evidence set out in paragraph VI.D of Annex I of the treaty are to be treated as if the words "other than a Form W-8 or W-9" were omitted.

Reporting obligation

12(1) A reporting financial institution must, in respect of 2014 and every following calendar year, prepare a return setting out–

(a)   the required information in relation to every reportable account that is maintained by the institution at any time during the calendar year in question (but this is subject to regulation 13),

(b)   the institution's Global Intermediary Identification Number, and

(c)   a statement of whether paragraph 5 of Article 4 of the treaty applies to the institution and, if it does, whether the requirements in sub-paragraphs (a) to (c) of that paragraph have been met.

12(2) If during the calendar year in question the reporting financial institution maintains no reportable accounts the return must state that fact.

12(3) The institution must send a return under this regulation to an officer of Revenue and Customs on or before 31 May of the year following the calendar year to which the return relates ("the reporting date").

12(4) The required information is–

(a)   the name and address of the account holder,

(b)   the account holder's U.S. federal taxpayer identifying number,

(c)   if an account is identifiable by an account number, that number or, if not, its functional equivalent,

(d)   the balance or value of the account (including, in the case of a cash value insurance contract or annuity contract, the cash value or surrender value) as of the end of the calendar year or, if the account was closed during the year, the balance or value on the date that the reporting financial institution closed the account,

(e)   the relevant total gross credits, or if there are none, a statement of that fact, and

(f)   if the account holder is a Non-US entity that has a controlling person who is a specified US person, that person's name, address and US federal taxpayer identification number.

12(5) The **"relevant total gross credits"** means–

(a)   in the case of a custodial account–

     (i)   the total gross amount of interest, the total gross amount of dividends and the total gross amount of other income generated with respect to assets held in the account which is paid into, or with respect to, the account during the calendar year, and

     (ii)   the total gross proceeds from the sale or redemption of property paid into the account during the calendar year if the institution acted as a custodian, broker, nominee or otherwise as an agent for the account holder,

(b)   in the case of a depository account, the total gross amount of interest paid into the account during the calendar year, and

(c)   in the case of any other account, the total gross amount of sums paid by the institution under a legal obligation to the account holder with respect to the account during the calendar year,

and **"interest"** here includes any amount that is chargeable as interest under Part 4 of ITTOIA 2005.

12(6) For the purposes of this regulation–

(a)   references to the balance or value of an account include a nil balance or value, and

(b)   references to paying an amount include crediting an amount.

12(7) If a reporting financial institution has an established practice for the periodic valuation of accounts of a particular description otherwise than at the end of a calendar year, the institution may report amounts referred to in paragraph (5)(a) or (c) by reference to a period of 12 months ending with the date (or, if more than one, the latest date) in the calendar year on which the institution values accounts of that description (instead of by reference to the calendar year).

12(8) For pre-existing accounts, in relation to returns for the calendar year 2017 and subsequent years, if a reporting financial institution does not hold a U.S. federal taxpayer identifying number that it is required to report under paragraph (4)(b) or (f) the institution must obtain that number from the account holder.

Modifications for calendar years 2014 to 2016

13(1) In the case of custodial accounts–

(a) there is no requirement to include in the return for the calendar year 2014 information about relevant total gross credits, and

(b) there is no requirement to include in the return for the calendar year 2015 any information set out in regulation 12(5)(a)(ii).

13(2) In the case of pre-existing accounts–

(a) there is no requirement to include in the return for calendar years before 2017 a U.S. federal taxpayer identifying number if the reporting financial institution does not hold that number, but

(b) if the account holder is an individual whose date of birth the institution does hold, the institution must include the account holder's date of birth instead.

OBLIGATIONS IN RELATION TO PAYMENTS TO A NON-PARTICIPATING FINANCIAL INSTITUTION

Identification and disclosure obligations

14(1) A reporting financial institution must establish and maintain arrangements that are designed to identify payments made by the institution to a non-participating financial institution in the calendar year 2015 or 2016,

14(2) **"Payment"** here includes amounts credited to a non-participating financial institution but does not include consideration given by the reporting financial institution for the provision of goods or services to it.

14(3) A reporting financial institution is entitled to regard a payment made by it to a financial institution as made to someone who is not a non-participating financial institution only if it has, in respect of the payment, taken the steps referred to at paragraph IV.D (3) of Annex I of the treaty.

14(4) For the purposes of this regulation a **"non-participating financial institution"** includes anyone who is required to be treated as a non-participating financial institution as a result of sub-paragraph 5(a) of Article 4 of the treaty.

14(5) In respect of any case in the calendar years 2015 and 2016 when a reporting financial institution is within the terms of sub-paragraph 1(e) of Article 4 of the treaty, the institution must make a disclosure of information in accordance with the requirements of that sub-paragraph.

Reporting obligation: Payments to non-participating financial institutions

15(1) A reporting financial institution must in respect of each of the calendar years 2015 and 2016 prepare a return setting out–

(a) the names of the non-participating financial institutions to whom payments identified in accordance with regulation 14(1) have been made in the year in question, and

(b) the total amount of those payments made to each of the non-participating financial institutions in question.

15(2) In determining the total amount of those payments the special rules and definitions at paragraph I.B (1) and paragraph VI.C of Annex I of the treaty must be applied.

15(3) If for a calendar year no payments are identified as referred to in paragraph (1), the reporting financial institution must prepare a return for the calendar year stating that fact.

15(4) The financial institution must send a return under this regulation to an officer of Revenue and Customs on or before 31 May of the year following the calendar year to which the return relates.

PENALTIES FOR BREACH OF OBLIGATIONS

Penalties for failure to comply with regulations

16 A person is liable to a penalty of £300 if the person fails to comply with any obligation under these Regulations otherwise than regulation 15.

Daily default penalty

17 If–

(a)   a penalty under regulation 16 is assessed, and

(b)   the failure in question continues after the person has been notified of the assessment,

the person is liable to a further penalty, for each subsequent day on which the failure continues, of an amount not exceeding £60 for each such day.

Penalties for inaccurate information: Reportable accounts

18(1)   A person is liable to a penalty not exceeding £3,000 if–

(a)   in complying with an obligation under regulation 12 the person provides inaccurate information, and

(b)   condition A, B or C is met.

18(2)   Condition A is that the inaccuracy is–

(a)   due to a failure to comply with regulation 11, or

(b)   deliberate on the part of the person.

18(3)   Condition B is that the person knows of the inaccuracy at the time the information is provided but does not inform HMRC at that time.

18(4)   Condition C is that the person–

(a)   discovers the inaccuracy some time later, and

(b)   fails to take reasonable steps to inform HMRC.

Penalties for failure to report or accurately report payments to non-participating financial institutions

19(1)   In relation to payments that are required to be identified under regulation 14(1), a person is liable to–

(a)   a penalty of £300 for each failure to report a payment, and

(b)   a penalty of £300 for each failure to set out a payment accurately in a report made under regulation 15.

19(2)   But in relation to a calendar year, a person's liability for penalties under this regulation is subject to a limit of £3000.

Matters to be disregarded in relation to liability to penalties

20(1)   Liability to a penalty under any of regulations 16, 17 or 19 does not arise if the person satisfies HMRC or (on an appeal notified to the tribunal) the tribunal that there is a reasonable excuse for the failure.

20(2)   For the purposes of this regulation neither of the following is a reasonable excuse–

(a)   that there is an insufficiency of funds to do something, or

(b)   that a person relies upon another person to do something.

20(3)   If a person had a reasonable excuse for a failure but the excuse has ceased, the person is to be treated as having continued to have the excuse if the failure is remedied without unreasonable delay after the excuse ceased.

Assessment of penalties

21(1)   If the reporting financial institution becomes liable to a penalty under any of regulations 16 to 19, an officer of Revenue and Customs may assess the penalty.

21(2)   If an officer does so, the officer must notify the institution.

21(3)   An assessment of a penalty under regulation 16, 17 or 19(1)(a) must be made within the period of 12 months beginning with the date on which the person became liable to the penalty.

21(4)   An assessment of a penalty under regulation 18 or 19(1)(b) must be made–

(a)   within the period of 12 months beginning with the date on which the inaccuracy first came to the attention of an officer of Revenue and Customs, and

(b)   within the period of 6 years beginning with the date on which the person became liable to the penalty.

Right to appeal against penalty

22 A person may appeal against a penalty assessment–

(a) on the grounds that liability to a penalty under any of regulations 16 to 19 does not arise, or

(b) as to the amount of such a penalty.

Procedure on appeal against penalty

23(1) Notice of an appeal under regulation 22 must be given–

(a) in writing,

(b) before the end of the period of 30 days beginning with the date on which notification under regulation 16 was given, and

(c) to HMRC.

23(2) It must state the grounds of appeal.

23(3) On an appeal under regulation 22(a) that is notified to the tribunal, the tribunal may confirm or cancel the assessment.

23(4) On an appeal under regulation 22(b) that is notified to the tribunal, the tribunal may–

(a) confirm the assessment, or

(b) substitute another assessment that the officer of Revenue and Customs had power to make.

23(5) Subject to this regulation and regulation 25, the provisions of Part 5 of TMA 1970 relating to appeals have effect in relation to appeals under regulation 22 as they have effect in relation to an appeal against an assessment to income tax.

Increased daily default penalty

24(1) This paragraph applies if–

(a) a penalty under regulation 17 is assessed under regulation 21,

(b) the failure in respect of which that assessment is made continues for more than 30 days beginning with the date on which notification of that assessment is given, and

(c) the person has been told that an application may be made under this paragraph for an increased daily penalty to be imposed.

24(2) If this regulation applies, an officer of Revenue and Customs may make an application to the tribunal for an increased daily penalty to be imposed on the person.

24(3) If the tribunal decides that an increased daily penalty should be imposed then for each applicable day on which the failure continues–

(a) the person is not liable to a penalty under regulation 17 in respect of the failure, and

(b) the person is liable instead to a penalty under this regulation of an amount determined by the tribunal.

24(4) The tribunal may not determine an amount exceeding £1000 for each applicable day.

24(5) If a person becomes liable to a penalty under this regulation, HMRC must notify the person.

24(6) The notification must specify the day from which the increased penalty is to apply.

24(7) That day and any subsequent day is an "applicable day" for the purposes of this regulation.

Enforcement of penalties

25(1) A penalty under these Regulations must be paid before the end of the period of 30 days beginning with the date mentioned in paragraph (2).

25(2) That date is–

(a) the date on which the assessment under regulations 21 or notification under 24(5) is given in respect of the penalty, or

(b) if a notice of appeal under regulation 22 is given, the date on which the appeal is finally determined or withdrawn.

25(3) A penalty under these Regulations may be enforced as if it were income tax charged in an assessment and due and payable.

MISCELLANEOUS

Accounts with a negative value

26 For the purpose of applying paragraph VI.C of Annex I of the treaty as required by these Regulations, an account balance that has a negative value is treated as having a nil value.

Anti-avoidance

27 If–

(a)   a person enters into any arrangements, and

(b)   the main purpose, or one of the main purposes, of the person in entering into the arrangements is to avoid any obligation under these Regulations,

these Regulations are to have effect as if the arrangements had not been entered into.

SUPPLEMENTARY

Definitions

28(1)   In these Regulations–

"**the Commissioners**" means the Commissioners for Her Majesty's Revenue and Customs,

"**Global Intermediary Identification Number**" means a number allocated to a financial institution by the Internal Revenue Service in the United States of America for FATCA purposes,

"**registered deemed-compliant financial institution**" means a non-reporting United Kingdom Financial Institution to which a Global Intermediary Identification Number has been properly allocated,

"**the tribunal**" means the First-tier Tribunal or, where determined by or under Tribunal Procedure Rules, the Upper Tribunal,

"**US Treasury Regulations**" mean the US Regulations Relating to Information Reporting by Foreign Financial Institutions and Other Foreign Entities.

28(2)   In these Regulations references to a person's U.S. status are to whether or not the person is a specified U.S. person.

28(3)   The following table lists the places where expressions that apply for the purposes of these Regulations are defined or otherwise explained–

Expression	Reference
account holder	regulation 2(3) with sub-paragraph 1(ee) of Article 1 of the treaty
annuity contract	regulation 2(3) with sub-paragraph 1(x) of Article 1 of the treaty
the Commissioners	regulation 28(1)
cash value insurance contract	regulation 2(3) with sub-paragraph 1(y) of Article 1 of the treaty
controlling person	regulation 2(3) with sub-paragraph 1(mm) of Article 1 of the treaty
custodial account	regulation 2(3) with sub-paragraph 1(u) of Article 1 of the treaty
custodial institution	regulation 6
depository account	regulation 2(3) with sub-paragraph 1(t) of Article 1 of the treaty
depository institution	regulation 4
entity	regulation 2(3) with sub-paragraph 1(hh) of Article 1 of the treaty
entity account	regulation 9(6)(a)
FATCA	section 222(4) FA 2013
financial account	regulation 2(3) with sub-paragraph 1(s) of Article 1 of the treaty
financial institution	regulation 2(3) with sub-paragraph 1(g) of Article 1 of the treaty
Global Intermediary Identification Number	regulation 28(1)
HMRC	section 222(4) FA 2013
individual account	regulation 9(6)(b)
insurance contract	regulation 2(3) with sub-paragraph 1(w) of Article 1 of the treaty
investment entity	regulation 5 and sub-paragraph 1(j) of Article 1 of the treaty
new entity account	regulation 2(3) and paragraph V of Annex 1 of the treaty

Expression	Reference
new individual account	regulation 2(3) and paragraph III of Annex 1 of the treaty
non-participating financial institution	regulation 2(3) with sub-paragraph 1(r) of Article 1 of the treaty
non-reporting United Kingdom financial institution	regulation 2(3) with sub-paragraph 1(q) Article 1 of the treaty
partner jurisdiction financial institution	regulation 2(3) with sub-paragraph 1(m) of Article 1 of the treaty
passive NFFE	regulation 2(3) and sub-paragraph VI.B.3 of Annex 1 of the treaty
preexisting account	regulation 2(3) and sub-paragraph 1(aa) of Article 1 of the treaty
preexisting entity account	regulation 2(3) and paragraph IV of Annex 1 of the treaty
preexisting individual account	regulation 2(3) and paragraph II of Annex 1 of the treaty
relevant total gross credits	regulation 12(5)
related entity	regulation 2(3) with sub-paragraph 1(kk) of Article 1 of the treaty
relevant holding company	regulation 7
registered deemed-compliant financial institution	regulation 28(1)
reportable account	regulation 9
reporting financial institution	regulation 3
specified insurance company	regulation 2(3) with sub-paragraph 1(k) of Article 1 of the treaty
specified U.S. person	regulation 2(3) with sub-paragraph 1(gg) of Article 1 of the treaty
the treaty	regulation 2(2)
treasury company	regulation 8
the tribunal	regulation 28(1)
United Kingdom financial institution	regulation 2(3) with sub-paragraph 1(l) of Article 1 of the treaty
U.S. reportable account	regulation 2(3) with sub-paragraph 1(dd) of Article 1 and paragraph I.B (4) of Annex I of the treaty
U.S. status	regulation 28(2)
U.S, Treasury Regulations	regulation 28(1)

Revocation

29 The International Tax Compliance (United States of America) Regulations 2013 are revoked.

Expression	Reference
new individual account	regulation 2(3) and paragraph III of Annex I of the treaty
non-participating financial institution	regulation 2(3) with sub-paragraph 1(r) of Article 1 of the treaty
non-reporting United Kingdom financial institution	regulation 2(3) with sub-paragraph 1(q) Article 1 of the treaty
partner jurisdiction financial institution	regulation 2(3) with sub-paragraph 1(m) of Article 1 of the treaty
passive NFFE	regulation 2(3) and sub-paragraph VI.B.3 of Annex I of the treaty
preexisting account	regulation 2(3) and sub-paragraph 1(aa) of Article 1 of the treaty
preexisting entity account	regulation 2(3) and paragraph IV of Annex I of the treaty
preexisting individual account	regulation 2(3) and paragraph II of Annex I of the treaty
relevant total gross credits	regulation 12(5)
related entity	regulation 2(3) with sub-paragraph 1(kk) of Article 1 of the treaty
relevant holding company	regulation 7
registered deemed-compliant financial institution	regulation 28(1)
reportable account	regulation 9
reporting financial institution	regulation 3
specified insurance company	regulation 2(3) with sub-paragraph 1(k) of Article 1 of the treaty
specified U.S. person	regulation 2(3) with sub-paragraph 1(gg) of Article 1 of the treaty
the treaty	regulation 2(2)
Treasury company	regulation 8
the tribunal	regulation 28(1)
United Kingdom financial institution	regulation 2(3) with sub-paragraph 1(l) of Article 1 of the treaty
U.S. reportable account	regulation 2(3) with sub-paragraph 1(dd) of Article 1 and paragraph I.B.(4) of Annex I of the treaty
U.S. status	regulation 28(2)
U.S. Treasury Regulations	regulation 28(1)

Revocation

19. The International Tax Compliance (United States of America) Regulations 2013 are revoked.